2013 Edition

V.I.P. ADDRESS BOOK

Edited by James M Wiggins, PhD

Associated Media Companies

Copyright ©1988, 1989, 1990, 1991, 1992, 1993, 1994, 1995, 1996, 1997, 1998, 1999, 2000, 2001, 2002, 2003, 2004, 2005, 2006, 2007, 2008, 2009, 2010, 2011, 2012, 2013 by

Associated Media Companies
PO Box 489
Gleneden Beach, OR 93788-0489
United States of America

Library of Congress Catalog Card Number 96-656029

(ISSN 1043-0261)

The V.I.P. Address Book/edited by James M. Wiggins, Ph.D.

Biography: p. Includes index.

1. Celebrities - Directories. 2. Celebrities - United States - Directories. 3. Social registers. 4. United States - Social registers.

I. Wiggins, James M., 1933- . II. Title: VIP Address Book. CT120.V15

1990i 920'.0025'73 - dci 96-656029 (ISBN 1043-0261)

International Standard Book Number 978-0-938731-58-0

Manufactured in the United States of America

TABLE OF CONTENTS

INTRODUCTION

The purpose of the **V.I.P. ADDRESS BOOK** is to provide readers with a means of reaching Very Important People — Celebrities, Government Officials, Business Leaders, Entertainers, Sports Stars, Scientists and Artists.

It is genuinely hoped that people will use this volume to write for information about an entrant's work or to express encouragement. Compliments and praise for one's efforts are always appreciated. Being at the top of one's chosen profession is no exception. And for those who are no longer active in a field, it is especially flattering to be contacted about one's past accomplishments.

Methodology

The determination of candidates for inclusion in this reference work is an on-going process. Committees of prominent and knowledgeable people review those included in the nine major areas (listed in **bold** below).

Public Service includes World Leaders, Government Officials (both U.S. and International), Law Enforcement Officials and Members of the Legal and Judicial Fields.

Adventure includes Military Leaders (both U.S. and International), Astronauts and Cosmonauts, Heroes and Explorers.

Business, Religion and Education includes Financial and Labor Leaders as well as Businesspeople and Nobel Prize Winners in Economics and Peace.

Life and Leisure includes Fashion Design, Modeling, Beauty and Health Care and Social Activists.

Communications includes Columnists, Commentators, Editors and Publishers, along with Editorial and Comic Book Cartoonists.

Fine Arts includes Architects, Artists, Opera, Ballet and Dance Performers, Conductors, Concert Artists, Composers (both classical and popular), Writers, Photographers and Nobel Literature Laureates.

Science covers Nobel Prize winners in Chemistry, Medicine and Physics, Engineers, Inventors, Earth, Space and Computer Scientists, Psychologists and Psychiatrists, Medical and Research Scientists.

Entertainment includes stars of Radio, Stage, Screen and Television, Musicians, Cinematographers, Producers and Directors.

Sports includes all major spectator and participatory sports.

The committees define the parameters of the people included and prepare a list of additions and deletions to the candidate list. The research staff checks and updates information daily.

Occupations and Titles

The category listed after an entrant's name is selected to best describe his/her most noteworthy accomplishment. No distinction is made as to whether the person still holds that position. It is felt that a person who made a name for herself or himself still retains that identity even if it was accomplished in the past.

How Addresses Are Obtained

The editors of the **V.I.P. ADDRESS BOOK** have made every effort possible to insure that the addresses listed are accurate and current. Once it is determined a person is eligible for inclusion in the book, that person is contacted to determine which address he or she prefers. If a person prefers a home address, it is included. If a person prefers a business address or one in care of an agent or representative, that address is included. If a person specifically asks that their name not be included, his/her name is omitted. Once an address is listed, we continue efforts to verify that the address has not changed. These efforts include random sampling of the entire database and follow-up on all returned mailings received including those received from users of the book.

Users of the book should realize that people's addresses are in a state of constant change. The U.S. Bureau of Statistics says that almost 20 percent of people move each year. Not only do people change places of residence, they may also change business affiliations. Businesses move their headquarters as well as downsizing, merging or selling portions of their companies. Athletes get traded or retire. Entertainers change agents or personal managers and television shows get canceled. Politicians leave office or run for new positions. In addition, there are deaths almost daily which affect the address listings.

National Change of Address Program

Our staff notes changes on a daily basis by watching television news shows and reading newspapers around the world. But we also take an extra step which few other directory or address book attempts. We match addresses of all U.S. listees with the U.S. Postal Service's National Change of Address program. The National Change of Address match is a process that compares mailing lists with more than 100 million address change cards filed by postal customers over the past three years. Address change information is provided for mailing list records that match with information from address change cards.

If a person/family/business moves, there are several factors which determine whether the National Change of Address program is effective. These include whether the mover filed an address change with the Postal Service, when the change was filed, whether the mover lived in an area covered by the automated address change systems (which includes more than 90 percent of the United States) and whether the name and address information in our files matches the information provided by the mover.

Bad Addresses/Corrections

We keep track of not only current addresses but outdated ones as well. Our files list more than 250,000 people and we have up to 40 addresses for some of the people in the book. We continually update our data base and you can help. While we no longer provide address corrections, we do welcome information about bad addresses from users of the book.

Envelope Markings

On your outgoing letters, you should always write "Address Correction Requested" beneath your return address in a clear and noticeable manner. If you do this, postal workers are supposed to send the forwarding address for a nominal fee.

V.I.P. Address Book Update

Realizing the ever-changing aspect of addresses, we also publish the **V.I.P. ADDRESS BOOK UPDATE** which is available in late August for an additional fee. The UPDATE lists several thousand address changes and new addresses as well as informing users of the names of celebrities who pass away.

Recommendations for the Book

If you are interested in people who are not listed in the book, send us a letter or email with their name, address and biographical information. If these people are deemed worthy for inclusion, they may be listed in a future edition.

Until people stop moving or changing jobs, there are going to be address changes. We want to provide the best service possible and we know we have the highest percentage of accuracy of any directory or address book.

If you have suggestions for improving accuracy beyond random follow-ups, following daily news events, checking on all bad address notifications and using the Postal Service's National Change of Address service, let us know your ideas.

Forms of Address

An important part of writing to people - regardless of their positions - is to properly address envelopes and to use the correct salutations in the letters. Although the titles and positions of people listed in this directory are too numerous to cover, there are a number of people whose forms of address are worth noting. The table below is a guide to enhance the likelihood your letter will be received in a favorable light.

POSITION	ENVELOPE/ADDRESS	SALUTATION
Presidents	The President of Countries	Dear Mr/Madam President - - -
Vice Presidents	The Vice President of Countries	Dear Mr/Madam Vice President - - -
Cabinet Officers	The Honorable John/Jane Doe Secretary of ---	Dear Mr/Madam Secretary of - - -
Senators	The Honorable John/Jane Doe US Senator from - - -	Dear Mr/Ms Senator - - -
Representatives	The Honorable John/Jane Doe US Representative from - - -	Dear Mr/Ms Representative - - -
Judges	The Honorable John/Jane Doe, Judge, US - - - Court	Dear Judge - - -
US Ambassadors	The Honorable John/Jane Doe US Ambassador to (Country)	Dear Mr/Ms Ambassador - - -

TABLE OF ABBREVIATIONS

A
AB	Alberta
ACT	Australian Capital Territory
AFB	Air Force Base
AK	Alaska
AL	Alabama
APO	Army Post Office
AR	Arkansas
Arc	Arcade
AS	American Samoa
Assn	Association
Assoc	Associates
Ave	Avenue
AZ	Arizona

B
BC	British Columbia
Bd	Board
Beds	Bedfordshire
Berks	Berkshire
Bldg	Building
Blvd	Boulevard
Br	Branch
Bros	Brothers
Bucks	Buckinghamshire
BWI	British West Indies
Byp	Bypass

C
CA	California
Cambs	Cambridgeshire
Cir	Circle
CM	Mariana Islands
CMH	Congressional Medal of Honor
CO	Colorado
Co	Company
Corp	Corporation
Cres	Crescent
Cswy	Causeway
CT	Connecticut
Ct	Court
Ctr	Center
Ctrl	Central
Cts	Courts
CZ	Canal Zone

D
DC	District of Columbia
DE	Delaware
Dept	Department
Dis	District
Div	Division
Dr	Drive
Drwy	Driveway

E
E	East
Edin	Edinburgh
Ent	Entertainment
Expy	Expressway
Ext	Extended, Extension

F
Fedn	Federation
FL	Florida
FPO	Fleet Post Office
Ft	Fort
Fwy	Freeway

G
GA	Georgia
Gdns	Gardens
Glos	Gloucestershire
Grp	Group
Grv	Grove
Gt	Great
GU	Guam

H
Hants	Hampshire
Herts	Hertfordshire
HI	Hawaii
HOF	Hall of Fame
Hq	Headquarters
Hts	Heights
Hwy	Highway

I
IA	Iowa
ID	Idaho
IL	Illinois
IN	Indiana
Inc	Incorporated
Inst	Institute
Int'l	International
Intercoll	Intercollegiate

J
Jr	Junior

K
KS	Kansas
KY	Kentucky

L
LA	Louisiana
Lab	Laboratory
Lancs	Lancashire
Lincs	Lincolnshire
Ln	Lane
Ltd	Limited

2013 Edition

V.I.P. ADDRESS BOOK

PUBLISHER AND EDITOR
James M Wiggins, PhD

PRESIDENT AND MANAGING EDITOR
Adele M Cooke

VICE PRESIDENT OF TECHNICAL AFFAIRS
Mike K Maloy

DESIGN DIRECTOR
LeeAnn Nelson

WEBSITE DESIGNER
Rawn Rhoades
Ernie Brown

PUBLISHER
Associated Media Companies
PO Box 489
Gleneden Beach, OR 97388-0489
United States of America
Phone/Fax - 1-541-764-4233
Email – info@vipaddress.com
Website - www.vipaddress.com

Abbreviations (Continued)

M

MA	Massachusetts
MB	Manitoba
MD	Maryland
Mddx	Middlesex
ME	Maine
Med	Medical
Mgmt	Management
MI	Michigan
MN	Minnesota
MO	Missouri
Mon	Monmouthshire
MS	Mississippi
MT	Montana
Mt	Mount

N

N	North
NB	New Brunswick
NC	North Carolina
ND	North Dakota
NE	Northeast, Nebraska
NH	New Hampshire
NJ	New Jersey
NL	Newfoundland
NM	New Mexico
Northants	Northamptonshire
Notts	Nottinghamshire
NS	Nova Scotia
NSW	New South Wales
NT	Northwest Territories, Northern Territory
NV	Nevada
NW	Northwest
NY	New York

O

OH	Ohio
OK	Oklahoma
ON	Ontario
OR	Oregon
Oxon	Oxfordshire

P

PA	Pennsylvania
PE	Prince Edward Island
Pkwy	Parkway
Pl	Place
Plz	Plaza
PO	Post Office
PR	Puerto Rico
Prof	Professional
Pt	Point

Q

QC	Quebec
QLD	Queensland

R

RD	Rural Delivery
Rd	Road
Rep	Republic
RI	Rhode Island
RR	Rural Route

S

S	South
SA	South Australia
SC	South Carolina
Sci	Science
SD	South Dakota
SE	Southeast
SK	Saskatchewan
Spdwy	Speedway
Sq	Square
St	Saint, Street
SW	Southwest

T

Tas	Tasmania
Ter	Territory
Terr	Terrace
TN	Tennessee
Tpke	Turnpike
Trl	Trail
TX	Texas

U

Univ	University
USA	United States of America
UT	Utah

V

VA	Virginia
VC	Victoria Cross
VI	Virgin Islands
VIC	Victoria
VT	Vermont

W

W	West
WA	Washington, Western Australia
WI	Wisconsin
Worcs	Worcestershire
WV	West Virginia
WY	Wyoming

X-Y-Z

YK	Yukon Territory
Yorks	Yorkshire

FORMS OF ADDRESS (Continued)

Foreign Ambassadors	His/Her Excellency John/Jane Doe	Dear Mr/MsAmbassador - - -
Kings/Queens	His/Her Royal Highness --- King/Queen of ---	Your Royal Highness ---
Military Leaders (Attention should be given to the actual rank)	General/Admiral John/Jane Doe	Dear General/Admiral - - -
Governors	The Honorable John/Jane Doe Governor of - - -	Dear Governor - - -
Mayors	The Honorable John/Jane Doe Mayor of - - -	Dear Mayor - - -

The Clergy

	Catholic		
	The Pope	His Eminence the Pope - - -	Your Holiness - - -
	Cardinals	His Eminence John Cardinal Doe	Dear Your Eminence Cardinal
	Episcopalian	The Rt Rev John Doe	Dear Bishop - - -
	Protestant	The Rev John Doe	Dear Mr/Mrs - - -
	Eastern Orthodox Patriarch	His Holiness, the Patriarch - - -	Your Holiness - - -
	Jewish	Rabbi John Doe	Dear Rabbi - - -

Forms of addresses can vary to almost impossible proportions. If you are a real stickler for proper protocol, you will need to obtain one of the many excellent reference books on etiquette or consult your local reference librarian for assistance.

Times are less formal so if you are polite and spell names correctly, your letter should be favorable received.

ACKNOWLEDGEMENTS

The Editors would like to thank the following people for their generous assistance in maintaining the accuracy of this publication:

Robert Allen, Jr., Florence Bagdasian, Ed Bielucke, III, Jake Bommer, John Gracen Brown, William Butts, Gloria & Len Bytnar, Thomas Burford, Bill Clogston, David Coston, James A. Cox, Charlie Dixon, Jimmy Dodson, Jr., Douglas Files, John T. Gillin, Brian Graybill, Tom Hall, Jack Hilton, Steve Koroknay, Dewey Linze, Helen Mangani, Wayne McDonald, Massee McKinley, Larry Miller, Pacer Center's Jan Flora, Mark J. Quilling, Ed Sammels, Ira Sabin, Juergen Schwarz, Eric Shuman, Jay F. Smith, Christopher Snowden, Darryl Spurlock, Kim Tangye, Jim Thomson, Anders Tvegard, Joe Wagner, Deanna Ward, Jim & Judy Watt, Marci Yates.

THE
DIRECTORY
OF
ADDRESS
LISTINGS

Although we have made every effort to provide
current addresses, we assume no responsibility for
address that become outdated.

Neither do we guarantee that people listed in the book
will personally answer their mail or that they will
respond to correspondence.

A$AP Rocky — Rap Artist
Polo Grounds Music, 243 W 30th St, #302, New York NY 10001, USA

Aaker, Lee W — Actor
PO Box 1386, Mammoth Lakes CA 93546, USA

Aalda, Marian — Actress
Rebecca Augustin Mgmt, 105 78 Avenue K, Brooklyn NY 11236, USA

Aalto, Antti — Ice Hockey Player
Esanpiha 2, 21220 Raisio, Finland

Aames, Willie — Actor
Jeff Ballard Public Relations, 4814 N Lemona Ave, Sherman Oaks CA 91403, USA

Aamodt, Kjetil Andre — Alpine Skier
8 Quai Jean Charles Rey, 98000 Monte Carlo, Monaco

Aardsma, David A — Baseball Player
6009 E Turquoise Ave, Paradise Valley AZ 85253, USA

Aaron, Caroline — Actress
Abrams Artists, 9200 W Sunset Blvd, #1125, West Hollywood CA 90069 USA

Aaron, Chester — Writer
PO Box 388, Occidental CA 95465, USA

Aaron, Henry J — Economist
1326 Hemlock St SW, Washington DC 20012, USA

Aaron, Henry L (Hank) — Baseball Player, Executive
1611 Adams Dr SW, Atlanta GA 30311, USA

Aaron, Jeffrey — Actor
Johnson & Laird Mgmt, PO Box 78340, Grey Lynn, Auckland 1245, New Zealand

Aaron, Lee — Singer, Songwriter
S L Feldman Mgmt, 1505 W 2nd Ave, #200, Vancouver BC V6H 3Y4, Canada

Aaron, Paul — Director
Suntaur/Elsboy Entertainment, 1581 N Crescent Heights Blvd, Los Angeles CA 90046, USA

Aaron, Thomas D (Tommy) — Golfer
440 E Lake Dr, Gainesville GA 30506, USA

Aarsleff, Hans — Linguist
Princeton University, English Dept, Princeton NJ 08544, USA

Aase, Donald W (Don) — Baseball Player
5055 Via Ricardo, Yorba Linda CA 92886, USA

Abad, F Andrus (Andy) — Baseball Player
1092 Chicksaw St, Jupiter FL 33458, USA

Abagnale, Frank W, Jr — Businessman
Abagnale Assoc, PO Box 701290, Tulsa OK 74170, USA

Abair, Mindi — Singer, Jazz Saxophonist
Chapman Company Mgmt, PO Box 55246, Sherman Oaks CA 91413, USA

Abakanowicz, Magdalena — Artist
Ul Bzowa 1, 02 708 Warsaw, Poland

Abalakin, Victor K — Astronomer
Main Observatory, Pulkovskoye Shosse 65, 196140 Saint Petersburg, Russia

Abalkin, Leonid I — Economist
38-8-89 Zelinskogo Str, 117334 Moscow, Russia

Abatantuono, Diego — Actor
Moviement, Via P Cavalini, 00193 Rome, Italy

Abbado, Claudio — Conductor
Askonas Holt, Lincoln House, 300 High Holborn, London WC1V 7JH, England

Abbado, Roberto — Conductor
Opus 3 Artists, 470 Park Ave S, #900N, New York NY 10016 USA

Abbas, Mahmoud — President, Palestine
President's Office, Gaza City, Gaza Strip, Palestine, Israel

Abbass, Hiam — Actress
Paradigm Agency, 360 N Crescent Dr, North Building, Beverly Hills CA 90210 USA

Abbate-Caldwell, Nancy — Actress
1855 Vista Way, Vista CA 92083, USA

Abbatiello, Carmine — Harness Racing Driver
7 Whirlaway Road, Manalapan NJ 07726, USA

Abbe, Elfriede M — Artist
Applewood, Manchester Center VT 05255, USA

Abbot, Charles S — Navy Admiral, Government Official
Military Officers Assn, 201 N Washington St, Alexandria VA 22314, USA

Abbott, Bruce — Actor
29500 Heathercliff Road, Malibu CA 90265, USA

Abbott, Christie — Actress
Kim Dawson Agency, 1645 Stemmons Freeway, #B, Dallas TX 75207, USA

Abbott, Diahnne — Actress
460 W Ave 46, Los Angeles CA 90065, USA

Abbott, Gregory — Singer
PO Box 68, Bergenfield NJ 07621, USA

Abbott, James A (Jim) — Baseball Player
Lilly Walters Schermerhorn, 740 W Purdue Dr, Claremont CA 91711, USA

Abbott, James W — Educator
University of South Dakota, President's Office, Vermillion SD 57069, USA

Abbott, Jeff — Writer
Hachette/Grand Central Publishing, 3 Center Plaza, Boston MA 02108, USA

Abbott, Jeffrey W (Jeff) — Baseball Player
119 Little John Lane, Murrayville GA 30564, USA

Abbott, Jeremy — Figure Skater
Care of the World Arena, 3185 Venetucci Blvd, Colorado Springs CO 80906, USA

Abbott, Joy — Singer
PO Box 403532, Miami Beach FL 33140, USA

Abbott, Jude — Singer (Chumbawamba)
Doug Smith Assoc, PO Box 1151, London W3 8ZJ, England

Abbott, Karen — Writer
Random House, 1745 Broadway, #1800, New York NY 10019 USA

Abbott, Kurt T — Baseball Player
1704 NW Spruce Ridge Dr, Stuart FL 34994, USA

Abbott, L Kyle — Baseball Player
332 Springfield Bend, Argyle TX 76226, USA

Abbott, Paul — Producer, Writer
The Agency, 24 Pottery Lane, Holland Park, London W11 4LZ, England

Abbott, Paul D — Baseball Player
1809 Yermo Place, Fullerton CA 92833, USA

Abbott, Preston S — Psychologist
6423 Wainfleet Court, Springfield VA 22152, USA
Abbott, Reg — Ice Hockey Player
5239 Hanover Place, Victoria BC V8Y 2C7, Canada
Abbott, Vinnie Paul — Drummer (Pantera, Damageplan)
Clubhouse, 2250 Manana Dr, Dallas TX 75220, USA
Abbott, W Glenn — Baseball Player
4413 Dawson Dr, North Little Rock AR 72116, USA
Abboud, A Robert — Businessman
209 Braeburn Road, Barrington Hills IL 60010, USA
Abboud, Francois M — Internist, Physician
24 Kennedy Parkway, Iowa City IA 52246, USA
Abboud, Joseph M — Fashion Designer
650 5th Ave, #2700, New York NY 10019, USA
Abdallah Mohamed Sambi, Ahmed — President, Comoros
President's Office, Palais de Beit Salam, BP 421, Moroni, Grand Comoro, Comoros
Abdel Aziz, Mohamed Ould — Head of State Council, Mauritania
President's Office, BP 184, Nouakchott, Mauritania
Abdrashitov, Vadim Y — Director
3D Frunzenskaya 8, #211, 119270 Moscow, Russia
Abdrazakov, Ildar — Opera Singer
Mariinsky Theater, Theater Square, 1 Pl Iskusstr, 190000 Saint Petersburg, Russia
Abdul Ahad Mohmand — Cosmonaut, Afghanistan
Cosmonaut Training Center, Star City, 141160 Zvezdny Gorodok, Moscow Oblast, Russia
Abdul, Paula J — Singer, Dancer
Marty Tudor, 2921 Cavendish Drive, Los Angeles CA 90064, USA
Abdul-Aziz, Zaid — Basketball Player
Sunlight Inc, PO Box 75184, Seattle WA 98175, USA
Abdul-Ghani, Abdul Aziz — Prime Minister, Yemen
Haddah St, San'a, Yemen
Abdul-Jabbar, Kareem — Basketball Player
Amsel Eisenstadt Frazier, 5055 Wilshire Blvd, #865, Los Angeles CA 90036 USA
Abdul-Jabbar, Karim — Football Player
17044 Downing St, Gaithersburg MD 20877, USA
Abdullah Ibn Abdul al-Aziz — King, Saudi Arabia
Council of Ministers, Murabba, Riyadh 11121, Saudi Arabia
Abdullah II — King, Jordan; Army General
Royal Palace, Royal Hashemite Court, Amman, Jordan
Abdullah, Rabih F — Football Player
12810 Wallingford Dr, Tampa FL 33624, USA
Abdul-Mahdi, Adel — Government Offical, Iraq
Al-Sijound Majalis, Karradat Mariam, Baghdad, Iraq
Abduraimov, Behzod — Concert Pianist
Harrison/Parrott, 5-6 Albion Court, London W6 0QT, England
Abdur-Rahim, Shareef — Basketball Player
9890 Wexford Circle, Granite Bay CA 95746, USA
Abe, Shana — Writer
303 S Broadway St, #200-124, Denver CO 80209, USA
Abegg, Martin G — Educator
4314 Travis St, #206, Dallas TX 75205, USA
Abel, Dana — Singer, Guitarist (Misty River)
1111B NW 131st Way, Vancouver WA 98685, USA
Abel, Gerald (Gerry) — Ice Hockey Player
23570 Samoset Trail, Southfield MI 48033, USA
Abel, Jake — Actor
I C M Partners, 10250 Constellation Blvd, #900, Los Angeles CA 90067 USA
Abel, Jessica — Cartoonist
Fantagraphics Books, 7563 Lake City Way NE, Seattle WA 98115, USA
Abel, Joy — Bowler
PO Box 296, Lansing IL 60438, USA
Abel, Yves — Conductor
Askonas Holt, Lincoln House, 300 High Holborn, London WC1V 7JH, England
Abela, George — President, Malta
President's Office, Palace, Valletta, Malta
Abelson, John N — Biologist
112 Laidley St, San Francisco CA 94131, USA
Abendroth, John — Golfer
1620 McDonald Way, Burlingame CA 94010, USA
Abercrombie, Jeff — Bassist (Fuel)
Media Five Entertainment, 3005 Broadhead Road, #170, Bethlehem PA 18020, USA
Abercrombie, John L — Jazz Guitarist
iGuitar Workshop, 290 Main St, Building #3, Cold Spring NY 10516, USA
Abercrombie, Walter A — Football Player
217 Westlane Circle, Woodway TX 76712, USA
Abernathy, Frederick H — Mechanical Engineer
43 Islington Road, Auburndale MA 02466, USA
Abernathy, M Brent — Baseball Player
5920 Buxton Dr, Columbus GA 31907, USA
Abernethy, Robert — Commentator
Public Broadcasting System, 1320 Braddock Place, Alexandria VA 22314, USA
Abernethy, Thomas C (Tom) — Basketball Player
5268 Woodfield Dr N, Carmel IN 46033, USA
Abeyta, Tony — Artist
1127 W Madison St, Chicago IL 60607, USA
Abgrall, Dennis — Ice Hockey Player
16607 S 12th Place, Phoenix AZ 85048, USA
Abidine, Dhafer — Actor
Associated International Mgmt, Fairfax House, Fulwood Place, London WC1V 6HU, England
Abil, Iolu Johnson — President, Vanuatu
President's Office, Port Vila, Vanuatu
Abiodun, Oyewole — Rap Artist (Last Poets)
Rykodisc, 3 Broadway, #E, Beverly MA 01915, USA
Abizaid, John P — Army General
United Services Automobile Assn, USAA Building, San Antonio TX 78288, USA
Abkarian, Simon — Actor
Voyez Mon Agent, 20 Ave Rapp, 75007 Paris, France

Able, Forest E — Basketball Player
11102 Mitchell Hill Road, Fairdale KY 40118, USA
Ableson, Andrew — Actor
Independent Group, 8721 W Sunset Blvd, #105, Los Angeles CA 90069, USA
Ablon, Ralph E — Businessman
Ogden Corp, PO Box 2615, Fairfield NJ 07004, USA
Ablow, Keith — Writer
Saint Martin's Press, 175 5th Ave, #400, New York NY 10010 USA
Abner, Shawn W — Baseball Player
1443 Olde Oak Court, Mechanicsburg PA 17050, USA
Aboud, John — Writer
Principato-Young, 9465 Wilshire Blvd, #880, Beverly Hills CA 90212 USA
Aboulela, Leila — Writer
Polygon Books, 22 George Square, Edinburgh EH8 9lF, Scotland
Abourezk, James G — Senator, SD
21 Dupont Circle NW, #400, Washington DC 20036, USA
Abragam, Anatole — Physicist
33 Rue Croulebarbe, 75013 Paris, France
Abraham, Arthur — Boxer
Boxsport Gmbh, Hanns-Braun-Str, 14053 Berlin, Germany
Abraham, E Spencer — Secretary of Energy; Senator, MI
Abraham Group, 600 14th St NW, #500, Washington DC 20005, USA
Abraham, F Murray — Actor
Innovative Artists, 1505 10th St, Santa Monica CA 90401 USA
Abraham, John A — Football Player
101 Irongate Dr, Columbia SC 29223, USA
Abraham, Marc — Producer
Strike Entertainment, 3000 W Olympic Blvd, Building 5, Santa Monica CA 90404, USA
Abraham, Phil — Director
Skouras Agency, 1149 3rd St, #300, Santa Monica CA 90403 USA
Abraham, Robert E — Football Player
831 Canal St, Myrtle Beach SC 29577, USA
Abrahamian, Emil — Cartoonist (Stumpy Stumbler)
147 Woodleaf Dr, Winter Springs FL 32708, USA
Abrahams, Elihu — Physicist
Rutgers University, Physics/Astronomy Dept, 136 Frelinghuysen Road, Piscataway NJ 08854, USA
Abrahams, Ivor — Sculptor
Royal Arts Academy, Burlington House, Piccadilly, London W1V 0DS, England
Abrahams, Jim S — Director
Ziffren Brittenham Branca, 1801 Century Park W, #700, Los Angeles CA 90067 USA
Abrahams, Michael T (Mick) — Guitarist (Jethro Tull)
Primary Talent Int'l, 2-12 Pentonville Road, London N1 9PL, England
Abrahamson, James A — Air Force General, Businessman
StratCom Int'l, 20112 Marble Quarry Road, Keedysville MD 21756, USA
Abramovic, Marina — Performance Artist, Photographer
Sean Kelly Gallery, 528 W 29th St, New York, NY 10001, USA
Abramowicz, Daniel S (Danny) — Football Player
143 Parkdale Road, Steubenville OH 43952, USA
Abrams, Bobby E — Football Player
1470 Pampas Dr, Montgomery AL 36117, USA
Abrams, Dan — Actor
MSNBC, 30 Rockefeller Plaza, New York NY 10112, USA
Abrams, Elliott — Government Official
10607 Dogwood Farm Lane, Great Falls VA 22066, USA
Abrams, Herbert L — Radiologist
620 Sand Hill Road, #109G, Palo Alto CA 94304, USA
Abrams, Jeffrey J (J J) — Director, Producer, Writer
Oasis Media Group, 8730 W Sunset Blvd, #700 , West Hollywood CA 90069, USA
Abrams, John N — Army General
Associated Press, 450 W 33rd St, #1500, New York NY 10001 USA
Abramson, Leslie — Attorney
4929 Wilshire Blvd, #490, Los Angeles CA 90010, USA
Abramson, Neil — Director, Writer
United Talent Agency, 9336 Civic Center Dr, Beverly Hills CA 90210 USA
Abreu, Bob K (Bobby) — Baseball Player
Los Angeles Dodgers, Stadium, 1000 Elysian Park Ave, Los Angeles CA 90090 USA
Abreu, Dilip J — Economist
Princeton University, Economics Dept, Princeton NJ 08544, USA
Abreu, Irina — Actress
Televisa, Blvd A Lopez Mateos 232, Colonia San Angel, DF CP 01060, Mexico
Abrigo, Megan — Model
Jet Set Models, 2160 Avenida de la Playa, La Jolla CA 92037, USA
Abrikosov, Alexei A — Nobel Physics Laureate
804 Houston St, Lemont IL 60439, USA
Abril Y Castello, Santos Cardinal — Religious Leader
Saint Mary Major Basilica, Via Liberiana 27, 00185 Rome, Italy
Abril, Victoria — Actress
Stephanie Zitzermann, Rue du Louvre 1, 75001 Paris, France
Abroms, Edward M — Director
E M A Enterprises, 1866 Marlowe St, Thousand Oaks CA 91360, USA
Abrosimova, Svetlana I — Basketball Player
Seattle Storm, Key Arena, 351 Elliott Ave W, #500, Seattle WA 98119 USA
Abruzzo, Ray — Actor
Bret Adams Agency, 448 W 44th St, New York NY 10036, USA
Absher, Richard A (Dick), Jr — Football Player
353 Tavistock Dr, Saint Augustine FL 32095, USA
Abshire, David M — Diplomat
4800 Fillmore Ave, #458, Alexandria VA 22311, USA
Abtahi, Omid — Actor
Greene Assoc, 1901 Ave of Stars, #130, Los Angeles CA 90067 USA
Abts, Tomma — Artist
Kunsthalle Basel, Steinenberg 7, 4051 Basel, Switzerland
Abu-Assad, Hany — Director
Creative Artists Agency, 2000 Ave of Stars, #100, Los Angeles CA 90067 USA
Abu-Jaber, Diana — Writer
W W Norton, 500 5th Ave, #600, New York NY 10110 USA

Acaba, Joseph M (Joe) — Astronaut
N A S A, Johnson Space Center, 2101 NASA Road, Houston TX 77058 USA
Accambray, William — Handball Player
Montpellier Agglomeration H B, 1000 Ave du val de Montferrand, 34090 Montpellier, France
Accardi, Vincent — Guitarist (Brand New)
Stunt Company Media, 20 Jay St, #208, Brooklyn NY 11201, USA
Accardo, Salvatore — Concert Violinist
Agenzia Resia Srl Rappresentanze, Via Manzoni 31, 20121 Milan, Italy
Accola, Candice — Actress
A P A Talent/Literary Agency, 405 S Beverly Dr, #300, Beverly Hills CA 90212 USA
Accola, Paul — Alpine Skier
Bolgenstr 17, 7270 Davos Platz, Switzerland
Acconci, Vito — Conceptual Artist
39 Pearl St, Brooklyn NY 11201, USA
Ace — Guitarist (Skunk Anansie)
13 Artists, 11-14 Kensington St, Brighton BN1 4AJ, England
Ace Hood — Rap Artist
Def Soul Records, 825 8th Ave, #2700, New York NY 10019 USA
Aceto, Raymond — Opera Singer
I M G Artists, Hogarth Business Park, Chiswick, London W4 2TH, England
Acevedo, Juan C — Baseball Player
143 Madera Circle, Mesa AZ 85204, USA
Acevedo, Kirk — Actor
Domain Talent, 9229 W Sunset Blvd, #710, West Hollywood CA 90069 USA
Achebe, Chinua — Writer
Bard College, Language & Literature Dept, PO Box 41, Annandale NY 12504, USA
Achen, Christopher H — Social Scientist
Princeton University, Politics Dept, Robertson Hall, Princeton NJ 08544, USA
Acheson, James — Costume Designer
I C M Partners, 10250 Constellation Blvd, #900, Los Angeles CA 90067 USA
Achica, George — Football Player
3165 Lone Bluff Way, San Jose CA 95111, USA
Achtymichuk, Gene — Ice Hockey Player
305-9985 93rd Ave, Fort Saskatchewan AB T8L 1N5, Canada
Acker, Amy — Actress
A P A Talent/Literary Agency, 405 S Beverly Dr, #300, Beverly Hills CA 90212 USA
Acker, James J (Jim) — Baseball Player
PO Box 214, Freer TX 78357, USA
Acker, Sharon — Actress
2530 Alister Ave, Tustin CA 92782, USA
Acker, William B (Bill), Jr — Football Player
1809 Walker Dr, Alice TX 78332, USA
Ackeren, Robert V — Director, Producer, Writer
Kurfurstendamm 132A, 10711 Berlin, Germany
Acker-Macosko, Anna — Golfer
304 Earl Dr, Kerrville TX 78028, USA
Ackerman, Bruce A — Attorney, Educator
Yale University, Law School, 127 Wall St, New Haven CT 06511, USA
Ackerman, Diane — Writer
W W Norton, 500 5th Ave, #600, New York NY 10110 USA
Ackerman, F Duane — Businessman
BellSouth Corp, 472 Ivy Park Lane NE, Atlanta GA 30342, USA
Ackerman, R Andrew (Andy) — Director
W M E Entertainment, 9601 Wilshire Blvd, #300, Beverly Hills CA 90210 USA
Ackerman, Richard C (Rick) — Football Player
995 N US Highway 30, Laramie WY 82072, USA
Ackerman, Robert Allan — Director
I C M Partners, 10250 Constellation Blvd, #900, Los Angeles CA 90067 USA
Ackerman, Thomas E — Cinematographer
1644 San Leandro Lane, Santa Barbara CA 93108, USA
Ackerman, Thomas M (Tom) — Football Player
17511 N Greenbluff Road, Colbert WA 99005, USA
Ackerman, William — Composer, Guitarist
Drake Assoc, 177 Woodland Ave, Westwood NJ 07675, USA
Ackermann, Rosemarie — Track Athlete
Yuri-Gagarin Str 14, 03046 Cottbus, Germany
Ackland, Joss — Actor
London Theatrical, 18 Leamore St, London W6 0JZ, England , USA
Ackles, Danneel — Actress
Gersh Agency, 9465 Wilshire Blvd, #600, Beverly Hills CA 90212 USA
Ackles, Jensen — Actor
W M E Entertainment, 9601 Wilshire Blvd, #300, Beverly Hills CA 90210 USA
Ackroyd, Barry — Cinematographer
United Agents, 12-26 Lexington St, London W1F 0LE, England
Ackroyd, David — Actor
PO Box 9041, Kalispell MT 59904, USA
Ackroyd, Norman — Artist
Royal Academy of Arts, Picadilly, London W1V 0DS, England
Ackroyd, Peter — Writer
Anthony Sheil Assoc, 43 Doughty St, London WC1N 2LF, England
Acks, Ronald W (Ron) — Football Player
563 Licklog Ridge, Hayesville NC 28904, USA
Acler, Rarika — Model
Ten Model Mgmt, Rua Iquatemi 448, CEP 01451 010 Sao Paulo SP, Brazil
Acogny, Germaine — Dancer, Choreographer
Jant-Bi, BP 22626, 15523 Dakar, Senegal
Acohido, Byron — Journalist
Seattle Times, Editorial Dept, 1120 John St, Seattle WA 98109 USA
Acord, Lance — Cinematographer
Creative Artists Agency, 2000 Ave of Stars, #100, Los Angeles CA 90067 USA
Acosta, Carlos — Ballet Dancer
Royal Opera House, Covent Garden, London WC2E 9DD, England
Acosta, George — Producer (Planet Soul)
Richard Walters, PO Box 2789, Toluca Lake CA 91610 USA
Acra, Reem — Fashion Designer
730 5th Ave, #205, New York NY 10019, USA

Acres, Mark R — Basketball Player
233 6th St, Manhattan Beach CA 90266, USA
Acrivos, Andreas — Chemical Engineer
788 Cedro Way, Stanford CA 94305, USA
Acta, Manuel E (Manny) — Baseball Manager
6427 Shoreline Dr, Saint Cloud FL 34771, USA
Acton, Charles R (Bud) — Basketball Player
PO Box 87, Empire MI 49630, USA
Acton, Keith — Ice Hockey Player
14 Cornell Place, Rye NY 10580, USA
Acton, Loren W — Astronaut
PO Box 1857, Bozeman MT 59771, USA
Acuff, Carl, Jr — Singer
PO Box 2367, Harrison AR 72602, USA
Aczel, Janos D — Mathematician
University of Waterloo, Pure Mathematics Dept, Waterloo ON N2L 3G1, Canada
Adair, Deborah — Actress
2530 J St, #330, Sacramento CA 95816, USA
Adair, Robert K — Physicist
Harvard University, Belfer Science Center, Cambridge MA 02138, USA
Adam, Ken — Designer
Film Designers Guild, 344 Finchley Road, #G, London NW3 7AJ, England
Adam, Mike — Curling Athlete
Curling Assn, 1660 Vimont Court, Cumberland ON K4A 4J4, Canada
Adam, Robert — Architect
Winchester Design, 9 Upper High St, Winchester, Hants SO23 8UT, England
Adam, Russ — Ice Hockey Player
69 Old Petty Harbour Road, Saint Johns NL A1G 1H5, Canada
Adam, Theo — Opera Singer
Schillerstr 14, 01326 Dresden, Germany
Adamek, Donna — Bowler
29834 Webster Place, Stevenson Ranch CA 91381, USA
Adamek, Tomasz — Boxer
Ul Viantykowka 6, 34-322 Gilowice, Poland
Adami, Franco — Sculptor
Via del Vicinato, Pontestrada, 55045 Piatrasanta, Italy
Adamle, Michael D (Mike) — Football Player, Sportscaster
826 Lincoln St, Evanston IL 60201, USA
Adams Beckham, Victoria — Singer (Spice Girls)
19 Entertainment, 32/33 Ransomes Dock, 35-37 Parkgate Road, London SW11 4NP, England
Adams, Alvan L — Basketball Player
5617 N Palo Cristi Road, Paradise Valley AZ 85253, USA
Adams, Amy — Actress
Brillstein Entertainment Partners, 9150 Wilshire Blvd, #350, Beverly Hills CA 90212 USA
Adams, Anthony L (Tony) — Football Player
14012 Juniper St, Overland Park KS 66224, USA
Adams, Brooke — Actress
Cunningham-Escott-Dipene, 261 S Robertson Blvd, Beverly Hills CA 90211, USA
Adams, Bryan — Singer, Guitarist, Songwriter
I C M Partners, Marlborough House, 10 Earlham St, #300, London WC2H 9LNP, England
Adams, Bryan — Singer (Color Me Badd)
J Bird Entertainment, 4905 S Atlantic Ave, Ponce Inlet FL 32127, USA
Adams, Christine — Actress
Innovative Artists, 1505 10th St, Santa Monica CA 90401 USA
Adams, Craig — Ice Hockey Player
8030 Sherwood Dr, Presto PA 15142, USA
Adams, Flozell J — Football Player
5201 Reflection Court, Flower Mound TX 75022, USA
Adams, Fred — Astrophysicist
University of Michigan, Astrophysics Dept, Ann Arbor MI 48109, USA
Adams, George — Basketball Player
508 Watergate Circle, Gastonia NC 28052, USA
Adams, George W — Football Player
2410 Damsel Katie Dr, Lewisville TX 75056, USA
Adams, Gerard (Gerry) — Political Leader, Northern Ireland
Sinn Fein/I R A, 51/55 Falls Road, Belfast BT12 4PD, Northern Ireland
Adams, Glenn C — Baseball Player
12333 E Tecumseh Road, Norman OK 73026, USA
Adams, Greg — Ice Hockey Player
Cowichan Valley Capitals, 2687 James St, Duncan BC V9L 2X5, Canada
Adams, Greg — Singer, Trumpeter (Tower of Power)
A L M Management Group, PO Box 16608, Encino CA 91416, USA
Adams, Hunter Patch — Physician
122 Franklin St, Urbana IL 61801, USA
Adams, Jane — Actress
Framework Entertainment, 9057 Nemo St, #C, West Hollywood CA 90069 USA
Adams, Joey Lauren — Actress
Paradigm Agency, 360 N Crescent Dr, North Building, Beverly Hills CA 90210 USA
Adams, John — Ice Hockey Player
109 Nottingham Crescent, Thunder Bay ON P7G 1B4, Canada
Adams, John C — Composer, Conductor
I M G Artists, 152 W 57th St, #500, New York NY 10019 USA
Adams, John G — Golfer
4610 County Road 42200, Paris TX 75462, USA
Adams, Julie — Actress
5915 Corbin Ave, Tarzana CA 91356, USA
Adams, Julius T — Football Player, Coach
2135 Jefferson Davis St, Macon GA 31201, USA
Adams, Katie — Actress
Hollander Talent Group, 14011 Ventura Blvd, #202, Sherman Oaks CA 91423, USA
Adams, Keith A — Football Player
9 N 9th St, #712, Philadelphia PA 19107, USA
Adams, Kenneth S (Bud) — Football Executive
3218 Del Monte Dr, Houston TX 77019, USA
Adams, Kevyn — Ice Hockey Player
Phoenix Coyotes, 6751 N Sunset Blvd, #200, Glendale AZ 85305 USA

Adams, Lindsey — Auto Racing Driver
819 W Arapho, #24B-188, Richardson TX 75080, USA
Adams, Lorraine — Journalist
Washington Post, Editorial Dept, 1150 15th St, Washington DC 20071, USA
Adams, Lynn — Golfer
2445 Bryant St, #207, San Diego CA 92101, USA
Adams, Mary Kay — Actress
Ingber Assoc, 1140 Broadway, #907, New York NY 10001, USA
Adams, Maud — Actress
PO Box 10838, Beverly Hills CA 90213, USA
Adams, Michael — Basketball Player
WWRC-Radio, Sports Dept, 8121 Georgia Ave, Silver Spring MD 20910, USA
Adams, Michael C (Mike) — Football Player
70 Graham Ave, Paterson NJ 07524, USA
Adams, Neal — Cartoonist
W M E Entertainment, 9601 Wilshire Blvd, #300, Beverly Hills CA 90210 USA
Adams, Noah — Commentator
National Public Radio, 635 Massachusetts Ave NW, #1, Washington DC 20001, USA
Adams, Norman — Artist
6 Gainsborough Road, London W4 1NJ, England
Adams, Oleta — Singer
Tom Estey Publicity, 144 E 22nd St, #1B, New York NY 10010, USA
Adams, Pat — Artist
370 Elm St, Bennington VT 05201, USA
Adams, Patrick J — Actor
Gersh Agency, 9465 Wilshire Blvd, #600, Beverly Hills CA 90212 USA
Adams, Paul L — WW II Army Air Corps Hero
6800 A St, #124, Lincoln NE 68510, USA
Adams, R Michael (Mike) — Baseball Player
13205 Jo Lane NE, Albuquerque NM 87111, USA
Adams, Ranald T, Jr — Air Force General
1002 Emerald Dr, Alexandria VA 22308, USA
Adams, Rhonda — Model
Playboy Promotions, 2706 Media Center Dr, Los Angeles CA 90065 USA
Adams, Richard G — Writer
Benwell's, 26 Church St, Whitechurch, Hants RG28 7AR, England
Adams, Robert B (Bob) — Football Player
16422 SE 17th St, Bellevue WA 98008, USA
Adams, Robert H — Photographer
306 Lincoln St, Longmont CO 80501, USA
Adams, Robert M, Jr — Anthropologist
PO Box ZZ, Basalt CO 81621, USA
Adams, Ryan — Singer, Songwriter
S A M, 722 Seward St, Los Angeles CA 90038, USA
Adams, Sam A — Football Player
218 Main St, #514, Kirkland WA 98033, USA
Adams, Sam E — Football Player
12010 Holly Stone Dr, Houston TX 77070, USA
Adams, Scott — Cartoonist (Dilbert)
Harper Business Publishers, 10 E 53rd St, New York NY 10022, USA
Adams, Seth — Actor
Mark Robert, PO Box 1549, Studio City CA 91614, USA
Adams, Stefon L — Football Player
937 Bingham Lane, Stone Mountain GA 30083, USA
Adams, Stephanie L — Model
PO Box 8202, New York NY 10116, USA
Adams, Terry — Pianist, Clarinet Player (NRBQ)
Skyline Music, 2270 Maiden Lane SW, Roanoke VA 24015, USA
Adams, Terry W — Baseball Player
PO Box 1035, Mobile AL 36633, USA
Adams, Tom — Actor
Langford, 17 Westfields Ave, London SW19 0AT, England
Adams, Tony (T-Bone) — Boxer
1209 56th Court, Northport AL 35473, USA
Adams, William J (Bill) — Football Player
12 Willowby Way, Lynnfield MA 01940, USA
Adams, Willis D — Football Player
7831 Quail Meadow Dr, Houston TX 77071, USA
Adams, Yolanda — Singer
Grand Gospel Bookings, 3933 Harrison St, #103, Oakland CA 94611, USA
Adams-Geller, Paige — Model, Fashion Designer
Paige Premium Denim, 10119 Jefferson Blvd, Culver City CA 90232, USA
Adamson, Andrew — Director, Producer
United Talent Agency, 9336 Civic Center Dr, Beverly Hills CA 90210 USA
Adamson, James C — Astronaut
25 Tradewind Circle, Fishersville VA 22939, USA
Adamson, Robert E, Jr — Navy Admiral
1709 Bohnhoff Court, Virginia Beach VA 23454, USA
Adams-Sassoon, Beverly — Model
1800 The Strand, Manhattan Beach CA 90266, USA
Addai, Joseph — Football Player
7521 Dubonnet Way, Indianapolis IN 46278, USA
Addario, Lisa — Writer
United Talent Agency, 9336 Civic Center Dr, Beverly Hills CA 90210 USA
Adderley, Herbert A (Herb) — Football Player
1058 Tristam Circle, Mantua NJ 08051, USA
Addington, Crandell — Poker Player
Phoenix Biotechnology, 8626 Tesoro Dr, #801, San Antonio TX 78217, USA
Addison, Adele — Concert Singer
98 Riverside Dr, New York NY 10024, USA
Addison, Chris — Actor, Comedian
Avalon Mgmt, 4A Exmoor St, London W10 6BD, England
Addison, Rafael — Basketball Player
6 Bernadette Court, East Hanover NH 07936, USA
Adduci, James D (Jim) — Baseball Player
16314 Crescent Lake Dr, Crest Hill IL 60403, USA

Adduono, Rick — Ice Hockey Player
153 Donald St W, Thunder Bay ON P7E 5X8, Canada

Addy, Mark — Actor
Independent Talent Group, Oxford House, 76 Oxford St, London W1D 1BS, England

Ade, King Sunny — Singer
Monterey International, 200 W Superior St, #202, Chicago IL 60654 USA

Adebimpe, Tunde — Singer (TV on the Radio)
D G C/Interscope Records, 2220 Colorado Ave, Santa Monica CA 90404, USA

Adel, Marwa — Photographer
Safar Khan Art Gallery, 6 Brazil St, Zamalek, Cairo 11211, Egypt

Adele — Singer, Songwriter
September Mgmt, 80/82 Chiswick High Road, London W4 1SY, England

Adelin, Jean-Claude — Actor
Artmedia, 20 Ave Rapp, 75007 Paris, France

Adell, Traci — Actress, Model
Playboy Promotions, 2706 Media Center Dr, Los Angeles CA 90065 USA

Adelman, Kenneth L — Government Official
George Washington University, English Dept, 2121 I St N, Washington DC 20052, USA

Adelman, Morris A — Economist
Massachusetts Institute of Technology, Economics Dept, Cambridge MA 02139, USA

Adelman, Richard L (Rick) — Basketball Player, Coach
5109 Tangle Lane, Houston TX 77056, USA

Adelson, Sheldon G — Businessman
Las Vegas Sands Corp, 3355 Las Vegas Blvd S, Las Vegas NV 89109, USA

Adelstein, Paul — Actor
Abrams Artists, 9200 W Sunset Blvd, #1125, West Hollywood CA 90069 USA

Ader, Tammy — Producer, Writer
Creative Artists Agency, 2000 Ave of Stars, #100, Los Angeles CA 90067 USA

Ades, Thomas J E — Composer, Pianist, Conductor
I M G Artists, Hogarth Business Park, Chiswick, London W4 2TH, England

Adey, Christopher — Conductor
Richard Haigh Performing Arts, 6 Windmill St, London W1P 1HF, England

Adey, William R — Physician
20 Sunrise Hill Road, Orinda CA 94563, USA

Adichie, Chimamanda N — Writer
Wylie Agency, 17 Bedford Square, London WC1B 3JA, England

Adickes, David P — Sculptor
2500 Summer St, Houston TX 77007, USA

Adickes, Mark S — Football Player
6146 Bordley Dr, Houston TX 77057, USA

Adiga, Aravind — Writer
Simon & Schuster, 1230 Ave of Americas, Concourse 1, New York NY 10020 USA

Adisa, Lawrence B — Actor
15105 Victory Blvd, #203, Van Nuys CA 91411, USA

Adjani, Isabelle — Actress
Orbis Media, 27 Rue Cardinet, 75017 Paris, France

Adkins, Derrick — Track Athlete
909 Derrick Adkins Lane, West Hempstead NY 11552, USA

Adkins, Jim — Singer, Guitarist (Jimmy Eat World)
S A M, 722 Seward St, Los Angeles CA 90038, USA

Adkins, Jonathan S (Jon) — Baseball Player
RR 3 Box 2306, Wayne WV 25570, USA

Adkins, Samuel A (Sam) — Football Player
15912 NE 160th St, Woodinville WA 98072, USA

Adkins, Scott — Actor
Zero Gravity Mgmt, 9255 Sunset Blvd, #1010, Los Angeles CA 90069 USA

Adkins, Seth — Actor
Paradigm Agency, 360 N Crescent Dr, North Building, Beverly Hills CA 90210 USA

Adkins, Trace — Singer
Creative Artists Agency, 2000 Ave of Stars, #100, Los Angeles CA 90067 USA

Adkisson, Perry L — Etomologist, Educator
9211 Lake Forest Court N, College Station TX 77845, USA

Adleman, Leonard M — Computer Scientist
University of Southern California, Computer Mathematics Dept, Los Angeles CA 90089, USA

Adler, Brian — Composer
Evolution Music Partners, 1680 Vine St, #500, Los Angeles CA 90028 USA

Adler, Charles — Actor
Innovative Artists, 1505 10th St, Santa Monica CA 90401 USA

Adler, Chris — Drummer (Lamb of God)
Entertainment Services, 1000 Main Street Plaza, #303, Voorhees NJ 08043, USA

Adler, Jerry — Actor
Paradigm Agency, 360 N Crescent Dr, North Building, Beverly Hills CA 90210 USA

Adler, Joanna — Actress
Innovative Artists, 235 Park Ave S, #1000, New York NY 10003 USA

Adler, Julius — Biologist, Biochemist
1234 Wellesley Road, Madison WI 53705, USA

Adler, Lee — Artist
Lime Kiln Farm, Climax NY 12042, USA

Adler, Lou — Director, Producer, Actor
Ode Sounds & Visuals, 3969 Villa Costera, Malibu CA 90265, USA

Adler, Max — Actor
Gersh Agency, 9465 Wilshire Blvd, #600, Beverly Hills CA 90212 USA

Adler, Renata — Writer, Journalist
198 Hattertown Road, Newtown CT 06470, USA

Adler, Stephen J — Editor
Business Week, Editor's Office, 1221 Ave of Americas, New York NY 10020, USA

Adler, Steven — Drummer (Guns N' Roses)
Artists Worldwide, 3921 Wilshire Blvd, #619, Los Angeles CA 90010, USA

Adler, Willie — Guitarist (Lamb of God)
Entertainment Services, 1000 Main Street Plaza, #303, Voorhees NJ 08043, USA

Adlington, Rebecca (Becky) — Swimmer
Nova Centurion S C, Beechdale Road, Bilborough, Nottingham NG8 3LL, England

Adlon, Pamela Segall — Actress
C E S D, 10635 Santa Monica Blvd, #130, Los Angeles CA 90025 USA

Adly-Guirgis, Stephen — Actor
W M E Entertainment, 9601 Wilshire Blvd, #300, Beverly Hills CA 90210 USA

Adonis — Writer
College de France, 11 Marchelin Berthelot, 75231 Paris Cedux O5, France
Adoor, Gopalakrishnan — Director
Darsanam, Trivandrum, 695017 Kerala, India
Adoti, Razaaq — Actor
Abrams Artists, 9200 W Sunset Blvd, #1125, West Hollywood CA 90069 USA
Adria, Ferran — Chef
El Bulli, Portaferrisa 7, Pral 2A, 08002 Barcelona, Spain
Adriana — Model
Luna Presse, Villa Grande Armee, 8 Rue des Acacias, 75017 Paris, France
Adsit, Scott — Actor
A P A Talent/Literary Agency, 405 S Beverly Dr, #300, Beverly Hills CA 90212 USA
Adu, Freddie — Soccer Player
Philadelphia Union, Union Field, Seaport Dr, Chester PA 19013 USA
Adubato, Richie — Basketball Coach
290 Chiswell Place, Lake Mary FL 32746, USA
Adway, Dwayne — Actor
House of Representatives, 1434 6th St, #1, Santa Monica CA 90401 USA
Adyrkhayeva, Svetlana D — Ballerina
1 Smolensky Pereulor 9, #74, 121099 Moscow, Russia
Aesop Rock — Rap Artist
Kork Agency, 1880 Century Park E, #711, Los Angeles CA 90067 USA
Afanasenkov, Dmitry — Ice Hockey Player
HC Moscow Dynamo, Leningradsky Prospect 36, 125167 Moscow, Russia
Afanasyev, Viktor M — Cosmonaut
Cosmonaut Training Center, Star City, 141160 Zvezdny Gorodok, Moscow Oblast, Russia
Aferiat, Paul — Interior Designer
Stamberg Aferiat Architect, 152 5th Ave, New York NY 10011, USA
Afewerki, Issaias — President, Eritrea
President's Office, PO Box 257, Gejeret, Asmara, Eritrea
Affeldt, Jeremy D — Baseball Player
6211 E Mandalay Lane, Spokane WA 99217, USA
Afflalo, Arron A — Basketball Player
Orlando Magic, 8701 Maitland Summit Blvd, Orlando FL 32810 USA
Affleck, Ben — Actor, Director, Writer
W M E Entertainment, 9601 Wilshire Blvd, #300, Beverly Hills CA 90210 USA
Affleck, Bruce — Ice Hockey Player
1847 Oxborough Court, Chesterfield MO 63017, USA
Affleck, Casey — Actor
I/D Public Relations, 7060 Hollywood Blvd, #800, Los Angeles CA 90028 USA
Affleck, James G — Businessman
American Cyanamid, 5 Giralda Farms, Madison NJ 07940, USA
Afinogenov, Maxim S — Ice Hockey Player
3700 S Ocean Blvd, #1502, Highland Beach FL 33487, USA
Afrika Bambaataa — Rap DJ Musician
K L B Productions, 302A W 12th St, PH A #26, New York NY 10014, USA
Afroman — Rap Artist
Crescent Moon Talent, 20 Music Square W, Nashville TN 37203, USA
Aga Khan IV, Prince Karim — Spiritual Leader
Aiglemont, 60270 Gouvieux, France
Agajanian, Benjamin J (Ben) — Football Player
27950 Avenida Terrazo, Cathedral City CA 92234, USA
Agam, Yaacov — Artist
26 Rue Boulard, 75014 Paris, France
Agassi, Andre — Tennis Player
9804 Caden Hills Ave, Las Vegas NV 89145, USA
Agatston, Arthur S — Cardiologist, Writer
1633 N View Dr, Miami Beach FL 33140, USA
Agbayani, Benny P, Jr — Baseball Player
66-948 Kolu Place, Waialua HI 96791, USA
Agee, Tommie L — Football Player
1505 Blackhawk Dr, Opelika AL 36801, USA
Agena, Keiko — Actress
C E S D, 10635 Santa Monica Blvd, #130, Los Angeles CA 90025 USA
Aghdashloo, Shohreh — Actress
Ken McReddie Assoc, 11 Connaught Place, London W2 2ET, England
Agler, Brian — Basketball Coach
Seattle Storm, Key Arena, 351 Elliott Ave W, #500, Seattle WA 98119 USA
Aglukark, Susan — Singer, Songwriter
Agency Group Ltd, 142 W 57th St, #600, New York NY 10019 USA
Agnelo, Geraldo Majella Cardinal — Religious Leader
Rua Martin Alfonso de Souza 270, 40100-050 Salvador BA, Brazil
Agnew, Chloe — Singer (Celtic Woman)
W M E Entertainment, 9601 Wilshire Blvd, #300, Beverly Hills CA 90210 USA
Agnew, Harold M — Physicist
322 Punta Baja Dr, Solana Beach CA 92075, USA
Agnew, Jim — Ice Hockey Player
10080 Equestrian Way, Missoula MT 59808, USA
Agnew, Paul — Conductor
Theatre de Caen, 135 Boulevard du Maréchal Leclerc, 14000 Caen, France
Agnew, Ray M, Jr — Football Player
2215 Cline St, Winston Salem NC 27107, USA
Agnew, Rudolph I J — Businessman
7 Eccleston St, London SW1X 9LX, England
Agoos, Jeff — Soccer Player, Executive
235 Pascack Road, Park Ridge NJ 07656, USA
Agosta, Meghan — Ice Hockey Player
Team Canada, 2424 University Dr NW, Calgary AB T2N 3Y9, Canada
Agosto Gonzalez, Juan R — Baseball Player
4748 Sweetmeadow Circle, Sarasota FL 34238, USA
Agosto, Benjamin A (Ben) — Ice Dancer
31284 Huntley Square E, #1124, Beverly Hills MI 48025, USA
Agranoff, Bernard W — Biochemist
University of Michigan, 1150 W Medical Center Dr, Ann Arbor MI 48109, USA
Agre, Bernard Cardinal — Religious Leader
Archeveche, Ave Jean-Paul II, 01 BP 1287, Abidjan, Ivory Coast

Name / Address	Profession
Agre, Peter 7033 Lenleigh Road, Baltimore MD 21212, USA	Nobel Chemistry Laureate
Agrelo, Marilyn Gersh Agency, 9465 Wilshire Blvd, #600, Beverly Hills CA 90212 USA	Director
Agresta, Maria I M G Artists, Hogarth Business Park, Chiswick, London W4 2TH, England	Opera Singer
Agron, Dianna W M E Entertainment, 9601 Wilshire Blvd, #300, Beverly Hills CA 90210 USA	Actress
Agt, Andries A M Van 6564 Heilig Landstichting AG, Netherlands	Prime Minister, Netherlands
Aguayo Muriel, Luis PO Box 1427, Vega Baja PR 00694, USA	Baseball Player
Aguayo, Albert J 648 Ave Belmont, Westmount QC H3Y 2W2, Canada	Neurophysiologist
Aguerre, Gustavo FÅ+, Drottninggatan 71A, 111 36 Stockholm, Sweden	Photographer, Artist
Aguilar, Louis R (Louie) 1411 Palmer Creek Dr, Columbia IL 62236, USA	Football Player
Aguilar, Pepe Agency Group Ltd, 142 W 57th St, #600, New York NY 10019 USA	Singer
Aguilera, Christina Creative Artists Agency, 2000 Ave of Stars, #100, Los Angeles CA 90067 USA	Singer, Songwriter, Actress
Aguilera, Richard W (Rick) PO Box 174, Rancho Santa Fe CA 92067, USA	Baseball Player
Aguirre, Mark A 10281 Highland Court, Frisco TX 75034, USA	Basketball Player, Executive
Agurcia, Ricardo Copan Assn, Casa Yax Na, Avenida Los Jaguares, Copan Runinas, Honduras	Archaeologist
Agustoni, Gilberto Cardinal Piazzi della Citta Leonina 9, 00193 Rome, Italy	Religious Leader
Agutter, Jenny Ken McReddie Assoc, 11 Connaught Place, London W2 2ET, England	Actress
Agyeman, Freema Independent Talent Group, Oxford House, 76 Oxford St, London W1D 1BS, England	Actress
Ahanotu, Chidi O 1000 S Harbour Island Blvd, #2611, Tampa FL 33602, USA	Football Player
Ahdout, Jonathan Paradigm Agency, 360 N Crescent Dr, North Building, Beverly Hills CA 90210 USA	Actor
Ahearn, Kevin J 174 Marlborough St, Boston MA 02116, USA	Ice Hockey Player
A'Hern, Basia Nickelodeon UK, PO Box 6425, London W1A 6UR, England	Actress
Ahern, Fred 21 Crescent St, Plympton MA 02367, USA	Ice Hockey Player
Ahern, Jim 130 E Glendale Ave, Phoenix AZ 85020, USA	Golfer
Ahern, Neal, Jr Paradigm Agency, 360 N Crescent Dr, North Building, Beverly Hills CA 90210 USA	Producer
Ahern, P Batholomew (Bertie) Saint Luke's, 161 Lower Drumcondra, Dublin 9, Ireland	Prime Minister, Ireland
Ahlberg, Dennis A Trinity University, President's Office, 1 Trinity Place, San Antonio TX 78212, USA	Educator
Ahlund, Joakim Paradigm Agency, 360 Park Ave, #1600, New York NY 10022 USA	Guitarist, Singer (Caesars)
Ahmadinejad, Mahmoud President's Office, Pastor Ave, Teheran, Iran	President, Iran
Ahmed, Akbar American University, International Relations Dept, Washington DC 20006, USA	Political Scientist
Ahmed, Fakhruddin Sere-e Bangla Nagar, Gono, Bhaban, Sher-e-Banglanagar, Dhakar 1207, Bangladesh	Prime Minister, Bangladesh
Ahmed, Iajuddin President's Office, Old Sangsad Bhaban, Bangabhaban, Dhaka 1207, Bangladesh	President, Bangladesh
Ahmed, Kazi Zafar National Parliament, Jatiya Sangsad, Dhaka 1801, Bangladesh	Prime Minister, Bangladesh
Ahmed, Rafi Emory University Medical Center, 954 Gatewood Road, Atlanta GA 30329, USA	Immunologist
Ahmed, Riz Gordon & French, 12-13 Poland St, London W1F 8QB, England	Actor
Ahn, Priscilla Blue Note Records, 6920 W Sunset Blvd, Los Angeles CA 90028 USA	Singer, Songwriter
Aho, Esko T Finnish Centre Party, Apollonkatu 11A, 00100 Helsinki, Finland	Prime Minister, Finland
Ahoussou-Kouadio, Jeannot Prime Minister's Office, Blvd Angoulvant Plateau, 01 BP 1533 Abidjan 01, Cote d'Ivoire	Prime Minister, Cote d'Ivoire
Ahrends, Peter 16 Rochester Road, London NW1 9JH, England	Architect
Ahrens, David I 5864 Manchester Court, Pittsboro IN 46167, USA	Football Player
Ahrens, Lynn W M E Entertainment, 1325 Ave of Americas, New York NY 10019 USA	Lyricist
Ahtisaari, Martti Erottajankatu 11A, #400, 00130 Helsinki, Finland	President, Finland; Nobel Peace Laureate
Aibel, Howard J 183 Steep Hill Road, Weston CT 06883, USA	Businessman
Aida, Takefumi 1-3-2 Okubo, Shinjukuku, Tokyo 169 0072, Japan	Architect
Aiello, Danny Jay D Schwartz & Associates, 6767 Forest Lawn Dr, #211, Los Angeles, CA 90068	Actor
Aigrain, Pierre R 56 Rue de Boulainvilliers, 75016 Paris, France	Physicist
Aiken, Clay Strategic Artist Mgmt, 1100 Glendon Ave, #1000, Los Angeles CA 90024, USA	Singer
Aiken, John (Johnny) 18 Pinetree Road, Billerica MA 01821, USA	Ice Hockey Player
Aiken, Liam Brillstein Entertainment Partners, 9150 Wilshire Blvd, #350, Beverly Hills CA 90212 USA	Actor

Agre - Aiken

Aiken, Linda H
2209 Lombard St, Philadelphia PA 19146, USA — Sociologist

Aiken, Sam
104 Winter Ridge Dr, Holly Springs NC 27540, USA — Football Player

Aikens, Curtis
PO Box 575, Conyers GA 30012, USA — Chef

Aikens, Willie M
10206 Locust St, Kansas City MO 64131, USA — Baseball Player

Aikin, Laura
Ingpen & Williams, 131 Putney Bridge Road, London SW15 2PA, England — Opera Singer

Aikman, Troy K
4425 Highland Dr, Dallas TX 75205, USA — Football Player, Sportscaster

Aiko
Imperial Palace, 1-1 Chiyoda, Chiyodaku, Tokyo 100 0001, Japan — Princess, Japan

Ailes, Roger E
218 Truman Dr, Cresskill NJ 07626, USA — Businessman

Aimard, Pierre-Laurent
Harrison/Parrott, 5-6 Albion Court, London W6 0QT, England — Concert Pianist

Aimee, Anouk
Artmedia, 20 Ave Rapp, 75007 Paris, France — Actress

Ainge, Daniel R (Danny)
140 Wellesley Ave, Wellesley Hills MA 02481, USA — Basketball Player, Coach

Ainsleigh, H Gordon
17119 Placer Hills Road, Meadow Vista CA 95722, USA — Ultra Marathon Athlete

Ainslie, C Benedict (Ben)
Royal Lymington Yacht Club, Bath Road, Lymington, Hamps S041 3SE, England — Yachtsman

Ainsworth, Kacey
United Agents, 12-26 Lexington St, London W1F 0LE, England — Actress

Ainsworth, Kurt
15220 Memorial Tower Dr, Baton Rouge LA 70810, USA — Baseball Player

Airiana
Ringling Bros Barnum & Bailey, 8607 Westwood Circle Dr, Vienna VA 22182 USA — Circus Aerialist

Airlie, Andrew
Noble/Caplan/Abrams, 1260 Yonge St, #200, Toronto ON MT4 1W6, Canada — Actor

Aitay, Victor
800 Deerfield Road, #203, Highland Park IL 60035, USA — Concert Violinist

Aitcheson, Joe, Jr
15404 Riding Stable Road, Laurel MD 20707, USA — Steeplechase Racing Jockey

Aitken, Brad
825 Royal Orchard Dr, Oshawa ON L1K 1Z8, Canada — Ice Hockey Player

Aitken, Doug
2437 Via Sonoma, Palos Verdes Estates CA 90274, USA — Artist

Aivazoff, Micah
6916 Hammond St, Powell River BC V8A 1R4, Canada — Ice Hockey Player

Aja, Alexandre
W M E Entertainment, 9601 Wilshire Blvd, #300, Beverly Hills CA 90210 USA — Director

Ajayan, Pulickel M
Rice University, Materials Science Dept, Houston TX 77005, USA — Materials Engineer

Ajodhia, Jules R
Prime Minister's Office, Paramaribo, Suriname — Prime Minister, Suriname

Akalaitis, JoAnne
Mabon Mimes, 150 1st Ave, New York NY 10009, USA — Director, Writer, Actress

Akbar, Taufik
Jalan Simp, Pahlawan III/24, Bandung 40124, Indonesia — Astronaut, Indonesia

Akebono
Azumazeki Stable, 4-6-4 Higashi Komagata, Ryogoku, Tokyo, Japan — Sumo Wrestler

Akel, Mike
United Talent Agency, 9336 Civic Center Dr, Beverly Hills CA 90210 USA — Director, Producer, Writer

Akens, Jewel
5228 Marburn Ave, Los Angeles CA 90043, USA — Singer, Producer

Aker, Jack D
5911 E Bloomfield Road, Scottsdale AZ 85254, USA — Baseball Player

Akerlof, George A
University of California, Economics Dept, Evans Hall, Berkeley CA 94720, USA — Nobel Economics Laureate

Akerlund, Jonas
I C M Partners, 10250 Constellation Blvd, #900, Los Angeles CA 90067 USA — Director

Akerman, Malin
Sanders Armstrong Caserta, 2120 Colorado Ave, #120, Santa Monica CA 90404, USA — Actress, Singer

Akers, Angie
Gaylord Sports Mgmt, 13845 N Northsight Blvd, #200, Scottsdale AZ 85260 USA — Volleyball Player

Akers, David R
16 Penhale Passage, Medford NJ 08055, USA — Football Player

Akers, John F
PO Box 194, Pebble Beach CA 93953, USA — Businessman

Akers, Michelle A
1690 Tallapoosa Dr, Geneva FL 32732, USA — Soccer Player

Akers, Thomas D (Tom)
HC 3 Box 35, Eminence MO 65466, USA — Astronaut

Akerson, Daniel F
General Motors Corp, Renaissance Center, Detroit MI 48243, USA — Businessman

Akey, Lisa
Metropolitan Talent Agency, 7020 La Presa Dr, Los Angeles CA 90068 USA — Actress

Akey, Robb
University of Idaho, Athletic Dept, Moscow ID 83844, USA — Football Coach

Akhmedov, Han A
Presidential Administration, Karl Marx 24, 744017 Ashgabat, Turkmenistan — Prime Minister, Turkmenistan

Akhurst, Lucy
Emptage Hallett, 14 Rathbone Place, London W1T 1HT, England — Actress

Akihito
Imperial Palace, 1-1 Chiyoda, Chiyodaku, Tokyo 100 0001, Japan — Emperor, Japan

Akil
Vision Entertainment Group, 1100 Glendon Ave, #1100, Los Angeles CA 90024, USA — Rap Artist (Jurassic 5)

Akilov, Akil G
Prime Minister's Office, Rudaki Prospect 42, 743051 Dushaube, Tajikistan — Prime Minister, Tajikistan

Akin, Fatih
Corazon International, Ditmar-Koel-Str 26, 20459 Hamburg, Germany — Director, Producer, Actor

Akin, Henry T — Basketball Player
18924 40th Place NE, Lake Forest Park WA 98155, USA
Akinnagbe, Gbenga — Actor
Stone Manners Salners, 9911 W Pico Blvd, #1400, Los Angeles CA 90035 USA
Akinnuoye-Agbaje, Adewale — Actor
A P A Talent/Literary Agency, 250 W 57th St, #1701, New York NY 10107 USA
Akins, Christopher D (Chris) — Football Player
60 Gold Mine Springs Road, Conway AR 72032, USA
Akins, Rhett — Singer
R P M Mgmt, 209 10th Ave S, #229, Nashville TN 37203, USA
Akishino — Prince, Japan
Imperial Palace, 1-1 Chiyoda, Chiyodaku, Tokyo 100, Japan
Akiyama, Kazuyoshi — Conductor
Columbia Artists Mgmt Inc, 1790 Broadway, #702, New York NY 10019 USA
Akiyoshi, Toshiko — Jazz Pianist, Composer
38 W 94th St, New York NY 10025, USA
Akon — Singer, Songwriter
H G X Marketing, 307 W 38th St, #807, New York NY 10018, USA
Akpan, Uwem — Writer
Little Brown, 3 Center Plaza, #100, Boston MA 02108 USA
Akre, Carrie — Singer
Good-Ink Records, 203 Underhill Ave, #3D, Brooklyn NY 11238, USA
Aksyonov, Vladimir V — Cosmonaut
Astrakhansky Per 5, Kv 100, 129010 Moscow, Russia
Al Hussein — Crown Prince, Jordan
Royal Palace, Royal Hashemite Court, Amman, Jordan
Aladag, Feo — Director, Writer, Actress
Gersh Agency, 9465 Wilshire Blvd, #600, Beverly Hills CA 90212 USA
Alagna, Roberto — Opera Singer
Askonas Holt, Lincoln House, 300 High Holborn, London WC1V 7JH, England
Alaia, Azzeddine — Fashion Designer
7 Rue de Moussy, 75002 Paris, France
Alaimo, Marc — Actor
1936 Seminole Dr, Agoura Hills CA 91301, USA
Alaimo, Simone — Opera Singer
Columbia Artists Mgmt Inc, 1790 Broadway, #702, New York NY 10019 USA
Alain, Marie-Claire — Concert Organist
4 Rue Victor Hugo, 78230 Le Pecq, France
Alan, Buddy — Singer
600 E Gilbert Dr, Tempe AZ 85281, USA
Alarcon, Arthur L — Judge
US Court of Appeals, 312 N Spring St, #G33, Los Angeles CA 90012, USA
Alarie, Mark S — Basketball Player, Coach
8514 Country Club Dr, Bethesda MD 20817, USA
Alas, Mert — Photographer
Art Partner, 155 6th Ave, #1500, New York NY 10013, USA
Alazzaqui, Carlos — Actor
Paradigm Agency, 360 N Crescent Dr, North Building, Beverly Hills CA 90210 USA
Alba, Jessica — Actress
W M E Entertainment, 9601 Wilshire Blvd, #300, Beverly Hills CA 90210 USA
Alban, Richard H (Dick) — Football Player
306 Belpaire Court, Newtown Square PA 19073, USA
Albanese, Alba — Actress
Loeb & Loeb, 10100 Santa Monica Blvd, #2200, Los Angeles CA 90067 USA
Albanese, Licia — Opera Singer
800 Park Ave, New York NY 10021, USA
Albarn, Damon — Singer (Blur, Gorillaz); Songwriter
C M O Mgmt, Shepherds East, Richmond Way, London W14 0DQ, England
Albeck, C Stanley (Stan) — Basketball Coach
130 Tall Oak Dr, San Antonio TX 78232, USA
Albee, Arden L — Space Scientist, Geologist
2040 Midlothian Dr, Altadena CA 91001, USA
Albee, Edward F — Writer
14 Harrison St, New York NY 10013, USA
Albelin, Tommy — Ice Hockey Player
23 Fellswood Dr, Verona NJ 07044, USA
Alberghetti, Anna Maria — Singer, Actress
10755 Massachusetts Ave, #204, Los Angeles CA 90024, USA
Albers, Kristi — Golfer
5872 Via Cuesta Dr, El Paso TX 79912, USA
Alberstein, Chava — Singer
Aviv Productions, 10418 E Meadowhill Dr, Scottsdale AZ 85255, USA
Albert II — Prince, Monaco
Palais de Monaco, BP 518, 98015 Monaco Cedex, Monaco
Albert II — King, Belgium
Koninklijk Palais, Rue de Brederode, 1000 Brussels, Belgium
Albert, Arthur — Cinematographer
707 Haverford Ave, Pacific Palisades CA 90272, USA
Albert, Calvin — Sculptor
6525 Brandywine Dr S, Margate FL 33063, USA
Albert, Jason — Singer (Heartland)
Country Thunder Records, 1016 17th Ave S, Nashville TN 37212, USA
Albert, Jodie — Actress, Singer
Susan Angel & Kevin Francis, 12 D'Arblay St, London W1F 8DU, England
Albert, John — Writer
Simon & Schuster, 1230 Ave of Americas, New York NY , USA
Albert, John G — Air Force General
Albert Farms, RR 2, Monroe VA 24574, USA
Albert, Kenny — Sportscaster
Fox-TV, Sports Dept, 205 W 67th St, New York NY 10065 USA
Albert, Marv — Sportscaster
TNT-TV, Sports Dept, 1050 Techwood Dr, Atlanta GA 30318 USA
Alberti, Maryse — Cinematographer
Dattner Dispoto, 10635 Santa Monica Blvd, #165, Los Angeles CA 90025, USA
Alberti, Micah — Actor
Innovative Artists, 1505 10th St, Santa Monica CA 90401 USA

Alberts, Andrew — Ice Hockey Player
205 Mill St, #302, Excelsior MN 55331, USA
Alberts, Bruce M — Foundation Executive, Biochemist
National Academy of Sciences, 500 5th St NW, #1, Washington DC 20001, USA
Alberts, Trev K — Football Player
University of Nebraska, Athletic Dept, Omaha, NE 68106, USA
Albertsen, Jordan — Director, Writer
Paradigm Agency, 360 N Crescent Dr, North Building, Beverly Hills CA 90210 USA
Alberty, Robert A — Chemist
1573 Cambridge St, #605, Cambridge MA 02138, USA
Albita — Singer, Songwriter
Albita Rodriguez Enterprises, 5825 SW 8th St, #200, Miami FL 33144, USA
Albom, Mitch — Writer
Hyperion Books, 114 5th Ave, New York NY 10011 USA
Alborn, Alan — Ski Jumper
PO Box 109, Willow AK 99688, USA
Albrecht, A Chim — Body Builder
Physique Promotions, 9668 Moss Glen Ave, Fountain Valley CA 92708, USA
Albrecht, Gerd — Conductor
Hamburg Opera, Grosse Theaterstr 34, 20354 Hamburg, Germany
Albrecht, Karl H — Businessman
Aldi Einkauf GmbH, Burgstr 37-39, 45476 Muelheim, Germany
Albrecht, Marc — Conductor
I M G Artists, Hogarth Business Park, Chiswick, London W4 2TH, England
Albrecht, Stan L — Educator
Utah State University, President's Office, Logan UT 84322, USA
Albrecht, Theodore C (Ted) — Football Player
1205 Cherry St, Winnetka IL 60093, USA
Albright, Christopher J (Chris) — Soccer Player
Philadelphia Union, Union Field, Seaport Dr, Chester PA 19013 USA
Albright, Gerald — Jazz Saxophonist, Singer
Chapman & Co Mgmt, PO Box 55246, Sherman Oaks CA 91413, USA
Albright, Jack L — Animal Scientist
839 E Village Dr, Carmel IN 46032, USA
Albright, L Ethan — Football Player
19181 Ferry Field Terrace, Leesburg VA 20176, USA
Albright, Madeleine K — Secretary, State
Albright Stonebridge Group, 1101 New York Ave NW, #900, Washington DC 20005, USA
Albright, Malvin Marr (Zsissly) — Artist
1500 N Lake Shore Dr, Chicago IL 60610, USA
Albright, Tenley E — Figure Skater
70 Suffolk Road, Chestnut Hill MA 02467, USA
Albuquerque, Lita — Artist
305 Boyd St, Los Angeles CA 90013, USA
Albus, Jim — Golfer
3972 Somerset Dr, #1, Sarasota FL 34242, USA
Alcaraz, Lalo — Editorial Cartoonist
PO Box 63052, Los Angeles CA 90063, USA
Alcock, Charles — Theoretical Physicist
Lawrence Livermore Laboratory, 7000 East St, Livermore CA 94550, USA
Alcott, Amy S — Golfer
323 Amalfi Dr, Santa Monica CA 90402, USA
Alda, Alan — Actor
I C M Partners, 10250 Constellation Blvd, #900, Los Angeles CA 90067 USA
Alda, Rutanya — Actress
Shallon Star Mgmt, 14320 Ventura Blvd, #624, Sherman Oaks CA 91423, USA
Aldaco, Marco — Architect
Paseo de la Canada 3872, Guadalajara 45129 Jalisco, Mexico
Aldean, Jason — Singer, Guitarist
Spalding Entertainment, 54 Music Square E, #200, Nashville TN 37203, USA
Alden, Ginger — Model, Actress, Singer
Ron Leyser, 25 Rolling Hill Court W, Sag Harbor NY 11963, USA
Alden, Howard — Jazz Guitarist
Hot Jazz Mgmt, 328 W 43rd St, New York NY 10036, USA
Alder, Berni J — Theoretical Physicist
1245 Contra Costa Dr, El Cerrito CA 94530, USA
Alderete, Loretta — Golfer
80194 Delphi Court, Indio CA 92201, USA
Alderfer-Benner, Gertrude — Baseball Player
2191 County Line Road, East Greenville PA 18041, USA
Alderman, Daniel — Drag Racing Driver
6730 Flemingsburg Road, Morehead KY 40351, USA
Alderman, Darrell — Auto Racing Driver
D A Construction, 8145 Flemingsburg Road, Morehead KY 40351, USA
Alderman, Grady C — Football Player
62 Elk Valley Way, Evergreen CO 80439, USA
Aldisert, Ruggero J — Judge
120 Cremona Dr, #D, Santa Barbara CA 93117, USA
Aldiss, Brian W — Writer
Hambledon, 39 Saint Andrews Road, Old Headington, Oxford OX3 9DL, England
Aldred, Scott W — Baseball Player
13435 Lakebrook Dr, Fenton MI 48430, USA
Aldred, Sophie — Actress
1 Duchess St, #1, London S1N 3EE, England
Aldrete, Michael P (Mike) — Baseball Player
22160 Toro Hills Dr, Salinas CA 93908, USA
Aldrich, Lance — Cartoonist (Real Life Adventures)
Universal Press Syndicate, 4520 Main St, #700, Kansas City MO 64111 USA
Aldridge, Allen R, Jr — Football Player
2111 Hammerwood Dr, Missouri City TX 77489, USA
Aldridge, Donald O — Air Force General
1004 Lincoln Road, #168, Bellevue NE 68005, USA
Aldridge, Edward C (Pete), Jr — Government Official, Businessman
4308 Lorcom Lane, Arlington VA 22207, USA
Aldridge, Keith — Ice Hockey
80 Joselyn Road, Lake Orion MI 48362, USA

Aldridge, LaMarcus — Basketball Player
23232 SW Stafford Hill Dr, West Linn OR 97068, USA
Aldrin, Edwin E (Buzz), Jr — Astronaut
10380 Wilshire Blvd, #703, Los Angeles CA 90024, USA
Aleandro, Norma — Actress
Blanco Encalada 1150, 1428 Buenos Aires, Argentina
Alechinsky, Pierre — Artist
2 Bis Rue Henri Barbusse, 78380 Bougival, France
Alejandro, Kevin — Actor
Gersh Agency, 9465 Wilshire Blvd, #600, Beverly Hills CA 90212 USA
Alekna, Virgilijus — Track Athlete
Prime Minister's Office, Tumo-Vaizganto 2, 01511 Vilnius, Lithuania
Aleksander, Grant — Actor
Abrams Artists, 9200 W Sunset Blvd, #1125, West Hollywood CA 90069 USA
Aleksandrov, Aleksandr P — Cosmonaut
Space Research Institute, 6 Moskovska St, BG1000 Sofia, Bulgaria
Aleksinas, Charles (Chuck) — Basketball Player
16 Litchfield Road, Morris CT 06763, USA
Aleksiy II — Religious Leader
Moscow Patriarchate, Chisty Per 5, 119034 Moscow, Russia
Alencherry, George Cardinal — Religious Leader
Archdiocese, Mount Saint Thomas, PO Box 2580, PO Kakkanad, Kochi 682031, Kerala, India
Alerlof, George — Nobel Economics Laureate
University of California, Economics Dept, Berkeley CA 94720, USA
Alesi, Jean — Auto Racing Driver
A F Corse Srl, Via Farnesiana 242/B, 29100 Piacenza, Italy
Alesi, Tommy — Percussionist (BeauSoleil)
Rosebud Agency, PO Box 170429, San Francisco CA 94117 USA
Alessi, Raquel — Actress
Vincent Cirrincione Assoc, 1516 N Fairfax Ave, Los Angeles CA 90046 USA
Alessio, Josephine — Actress
Giuseppino Alessio, Via Aquara 75, 84020 Bellosguardo, Italy
Alexakis, Art — Singer, Guitarist (Everclear)
Pinnacle Entertainment, 30 Glenn St, White Plains NY 10603, USA
Alexander — Crown Prince, Yugoslavia
Royal Palace, Dedinje, 11040 Belgrade, Serbia
Alexander, A J — Model, Actress
Playboy Promotions, 2706 Media Center Dr, Los Angeles CA 90065 USA
Alexander, Brooke — Actress, Model
Abrams Artists, 9200 W Sunset Blvd, #1125, West Hollywood CA 90069 USA
Alexander, Bruce E — Football Player
508 Englewood Dr, Lufkin TX 75901, USA
Alexander, Charles F, Jr — Football Player
3711 Heritage Colony Dr, Missouri City TX 77459, USA
Alexander, Christopher W J — Architect
2701 Shasta Road, Berkeley CA 94708, USA
Alexander, Claire — Ice Hockey Player
11 Tammy Circle, Saint Catherines ON L2N 1R2, Canada
Alexander, Claudia — Space Scientist
Jet Propulsion Laboratory, 4800 Oak Grove Dr, Pasadena CA 91109 USA
Alexander, Clifford L, Jr — Government Official
Alexander Assoc, 400 C St NE, Washington DC 20002, USA
Alexander, Dan L — Football Player
58520 Saint Clement Ave, Plaquemine LA 70764, USA
Alexander, Derrick S — Football Player
25381 W 149th Court, Olathe KS 66061, USA
Alexander, Doyle L — Baseball Player
5416 Hunter Park Court, Arlington TX 76017, USA
Alexander, Eliana — Actress
TalentWorks, 3500 W Olive Ave, #1400, Burbank CA 91505 USA
Alexander, Elizabeth — Writer
Yale University, English Dept, New Haven CT 06520, USA
Alexander, Emily — Model, Actress
Playboy Promotions, 2706 Media Center Dr, Los Angeles CA 90065 USA
Alexander, Eric — Jazz Saxophonist
Joel Chriss, 60 E 8th St, #34N, New York NY 10003 USA
Alexander, Erika — Actress
Untitled Entertainment, 350 S Beverly Dr, #200, Beverly Hills CA 90212 USA
Alexander, Flex — Actor
Global Artists Agency, 6253 Hollywood Blvd, #508, Los Angeles CA 90028 USA
Alexander, Gary W — Baseball Player
5420 Senford Ave, Los Angeles CA 90056, USA
Alexander, Jaimie — Actress
W M E Entertainment, 9601 Wilshire Blvd, #300, Beverly Hills CA 90210 USA
Alexander, James — Bassist (Bar-Kays)
Entertainment Artists, PO Box 120824, Nashville TN 37212 USA
Alexander, Jane — Actress, Government Official
W M E Entertainment, 9601 Wilshire Blvd, #300, Beverly Hills CA 90210 USA
Alexander, Jason — Actor, Comedian
Innovative Artists, 1505 10th St, Santa Monica CA 90401 USA
Alexander, Jesse — Producer, Writer
Creative Artists Agency, 2000 Ave of Stars, #100, Los Angeles CA 90067 USA
Alexander, Jessica (Jessi) — Singer, Songwriter
Columbia Records, 9830 Wilshire Blvd, Beverly Hills CA 90212 USA
Alexander, Jim — Actor
Associated International Mgmt, Fairfax House, Fulwood Place, London WC1V 6HU, England
Alexander, Joe A — Basketball Player
Chicago Bulls, United Center, 1901 W Madison St, Chicago IL 60612 USA
Alexander, John E — Artist
University of Houston, Art Dept, 4800 Calhoun, Houston TX 77004, USA
Alexander, Jules — Musician (Association)
Variety Artists, 793 Higuera St, #6, San Luis Obispo CA 93401 USA
Alexander, Kala — Actor, Surfer
Innovative Artists, 235 Park Ave S, #1000, New York NY 10003 USA
Alexander, Kermit J — Football Player
16651 Stallion Place, Riverside CA 92504, USA

Alexander, Manuel D (Manny) — Baseball Player
3660 N Lake Dr, #2664, Chicago IL 60613, USA
Alexander, Matthew (Matt) — Baseball Player
2419 Stonewall St, Shreveport LA 71103, USA
Alexander, Maximillian — Actor
Kritzer Levine Wilkins Griffin, 11872 La Grange Ave, #100, Los Angeles CA 90025 USA
Alexander, Monty — Jazz Pianist
Abby Hoffer, 223 1/2 E 48th St, New York NY 10017, USA
Alexander, Peter — Sculptor
1811 16th St, Santa Monica CA 90404, USA
Alexander, R Brent — Football Player
349 Remington Ave, Gallatin TN 37066, USA
Alexander, R Minter — Air Force General
824 Eden Court, Alexandria VA 22308, USA
Alexander, Sarah — Actress
Independent Talent Group, Oxford House, 76 Oxford St, London W1D 1BS, England
Alexander, Sasha — Actress
United Talent Agency, 9336 Civic Center Dr, Beverly Hills CA 90210 USA
Alexander, Shaun — Football Player
13655 NE 36th Place, Bellevue WA 98005, USA
Alexander, Stephen T — Football Player
4700 Flint Ridge Circle, Norman OK 73072, USA
Alexander, Tim (Herb) — Drummer (Perfect Circle, Primus)
Creative Artists Agency, 2000 Ave of Stars, #100, Los Angeles CA 90067 USA
Alexander, V Raymond (Ray) — Football Player
1631 Royal Palm Dr, Edgewater FL 32132, USA
Alexander, Willie — Bassist, Guitarist (Velvet Underground)
Toumaline Music Group, 894 Mayville Road, Bethel PA 19507, USA
Alexander, Willie J — Football Player
7219 Holder Forest Circle, Houston TX 77088, USA
Alexandre, Maxime — Cinematographer
Partos Co, 227 Broadway, #204, Santa Monica CA 90401, USA
Alexeev, Dmitri K — Concert Pianist
I M G Artists, Hogarth Business Park, Chiswick, London W4 2TH, England
Alexeev, Nikita — Ice Hockey Player
PO Box 3342, Riverview FL 33568, USA
Alexeev, Nikolai G — Conductor
Estonian National Symphony, Estonia Ave 4, 10148 Tallinn, Estonia
Alexie, Sherman — Writer
PO Box 376, Wellpinit WA 99040, USA
Alexi-Malle, Adam — Actor
Innovative Artists, 1505 10th St, Santa Monica CA 90401 USA
Alexis, Kim — Model
Axiom Sports & Entertainment, 28 W 44th St, #1600, New York NY 10036, USA
Alexrod, Albert — Fencer
798 Heritage Hills, #A, Somers NY 10589, USA
Alfaro, Andreu — Sculptor
Urbanizacion Sta Barbara 138R, 46111 Rocafort, Valencia, Spain
Alfaro, Victor — Fashion Designer
130 Barrow St, New York NY 10014, USA
Alferov, Zhores — Nobel Physics Laureate
Zhakia Duclo Str 8/3-82, 194223 Saint Petersburg, Russia
Alfieri, Janet — Cartoonist (Suburban Cowgirls)
15 Bumpus Road, Plymouth MA 02360, USA
Alfieri, Victor — Actor
Metropolitan Talent Agency, 7020 La Presa Dr, Los Angeles CA 90068 USA
Alfonseca, Antonio — Baseball Player
3020 SW 169th Terrace, Miramar FL 33029, USA
Alfonso, Kristian — Actress
I C M Partners, 10250 Constellation Blvd, #900, Los Angeles CA 90067 USA
Alfonzo, Edgardo A — Baseball Player
3745 Marietta Way, Saint Cloud FL 34772, USA
Alford, Steve — Basketball Player, Coach
11600 Zinfandel Ave NE, Albuquerque NM 87122, USA
Alford, William P — Attorney, Writer
Harvard University, International Legal Studies, Cambridge MA 02138, USA
Alfredson, Tomas — Director
Cinetic Mgmt, 555 W 25th St, #400, New York NY 10001, USA
Alfredsson, H Daniel — Ice Hockey Player
C A A Hockey, 822 11th Ave SW, #204, Calgary AB T2R 0E5, Canada
Alfredsson, Helen — Golfer
9034 Crichton Woods Dr, Orlando FL 32819, USA
Algabid, Hamid — Prime Minister, Niger
National Assembly, Vice President's Office, Niamey, Niger
Alger, Pat — Singer, Guitarist, Songwriter
A S C A P, 1 Lincoln Plaza, New York NY 10023, USA
Ali, Aires B B — Prime Minister, Mozambique
Prime Minister's Office, Avenida Julius Nyerere 1780, Maputo, Mozambique
Ali, Laila — Boxer
She Bee Stingin Inc, 20929 Ventura Blvd, #47-432, Woodland Hills CA 91364, USA
Ali, Monica — Writer
Charles Scribner's Sons, 866 3rd Ave, New York NY 10022 USA
Ali, Muhammad — Boxer
PO Box 160, Berrien Springs MI 49103, USA
Ali, Robin — Ophthalmologist
Moorfields Eye Hospital, 162 City Road, London EC1V 2PD, England
Ali, Tatyana — Singer, Actress
Innovative Artists, 1505 10th St, Santa Monica CA 90401 USA
Alicea de Jesus, Luis R — Baseball Player
2140 C Road, Loxahatchee FL 33470, USA
Alis, Robert — Cinematographer
13920 72nd Road, Flushing NY 11367, USA
Alisha — Singer, Songwriter
Brothers Mgmt, 141 Dunbar Ave, Fords NJ 08863 USA
Alison, Jane — Writer
Farrar Straus Giroux, 18 W 18th St, #700, New York NY 10011 USA

Alito, Samuel A, Jr — Judge
US Supreme Court, 1 1st St NE, Washington DC 20543 USA
Aliyev, Ilham — President, Azerbaijan
President's Office, Istiglaliyyat St 19, 371066 Baku, Azerbaijan
Allain, William A — Governor, MS
970 Morningside St, Jackson MS 39202, USA
Allan, Gabrielle — Producer, Writer
United Talent Agency, 9336 Civic Center Dr, Beverly Hills CA 90210 USA
Allan, Gary — Singer, Guitarist
W M E Entertainment, 1600 Division St, #300, Nashville TN 37203 USA
Allan, James — Singer, Guitarist (Glasvegas)
Sony Music, 9 Derry St, London W8 5HY, England
Allan, Jed — Actor
477 White Horse Trail, Palm Desert CA 92211, USA
Allan, Jennifer — Model
Playboy Promotions, 2706 Media Center Dr, Los Angeles CA 90065 USA
Allan, Rab — Singer, Guitarist (Glasvegas)
Sony Music, 9 Derry St, London W8 5HY, England
Allan, William G — Artist
73 Ranch Road, San Rafael CA 94903, USA
Allard, Beatrice (Bea) — Baseball Player
1040 Ridgewood Dr, Lillian AL 36549, USA
Allard, Linda M — Fashion Designer
Ellen Tracy Corp, 575 Fashion Ave, #300, New York NY 10018, USA
Allbaugh, Joseph — Government Official
Federal Emergency Management Agency, 500 C St SW, Washington DC 20472, USA
Allegre, Claude J — Geochemist
Institut de France, 23 Quai Conti, 75006 Paris, France
Allegre, Raul E — Football Player
6500 Rain Creek Parkway, Austin TX 78759, USA
Allem, Fulton P — Golfer
6786 Hidden Glade Place, Sanford FL 32771, USA
Allen, Aleisha — Actress
Jordan Gill Dornbaum Agency, 1133 Broadway, #623, New York NY 10010, USA
Allen, Amy — Actress
PO Box 8081, Calabasas CA 91372, USA
Allen, Andrew M — Astronaut
205 Highland Woods Dr, Safety Harbor FL 34695, USA
Allen, Anthony (Tony) — Basketball Player
70 Kodiak Way, #2638, Waltham MA 02451, USA
Allen, Anthony D — Football Player
956 20th Ave, Seattle WA 98122, USA
Allen, Ashley — Model
Playboy Promotions, 2706 Media Center Dr, Los Angeles CA 90065 USA
Allen, Bernard K (Bernie) — Baseball Player
3725 Coventry Way, Carmel IN 46033, USA
Allen, Bruce — Auto Racing Driver
Reher-Morrison Racing Engines, 1120 Enterprise Place, Arlington TX 76001, USA
Allen, Bryan — Ice Hockey Player
6635 NW 122nd Ave, Parkland FL 33076, USA
Allen, C Keith (Bingo) — Ice Hockey Coach, Executive
20011 Sanibel View Circle, #201, Fort Myers FL 33908, USA
Allen, Chad — Actor
Kazarian/Spencer/Ruskin, 11969 Ventura Blvd, #300, Studio City CA 91604 USA
Allen, Charles R (Chuck) — Football Player
192 Victoria Loop, Port Townsend WA 98368, USA
Allen, Dalva R — Football Player
337 Daingerfield St, Pittsburg TX 75686, USA
Allen, Davis — Interior Designer
Skidmore Owings Merrill, 14 Wall St, #2500, New York NY 10005, USA
Allen, Debbie — Dancer, Singer, Actress
Paradigm Agency, 360 N Crescent Dr, North Building, Beverly Hills CA 90210 USA
Allen, Deborah — Singer
Rolling Thunder Mgmt, PO Box 120717, Nashville TN 37212, USA
Allen, Dennis — Football Coach
Oakland Raiders, 1220 Harbor Bay Parkway, Alameda CA 94502 USA
Allen, Dion — Singer (Az Yet)
Richard Walters, PO Box 2789, Toluca Lake CA 91610 USA
Allen, Doug — Artist
Fantagraphics Books, 7563 Lake City Way NE, Seattle WA 98115, USA
Allen, Duane D — Singer (Oak Ridge Boys)
88 New Shackle Island Road, Hendersonville TN 37075, USA
Allen, Elizabeth Anne — Actress
Boutique, 3034 Havrone Way, Lawrence KS 66047, USA
Allen, Eric A — Football Player
484 San Elijo St, San Diego CA 92106, USA
Allen, George F — Senator, Governor, VA
4296 Neitzey Place, Alexandria VA 22309, USA
Allen, Geri — Jazz Pianist, Composer
Clayton Ross Productions, 508 Shoreline Highway, Mill Valley CA 94941, USA
Allen, Ginger Lynn — Actress
Schiowitz Connor, 1680 N Vine St, #1016, Los Angeles CA 90028 USA
Allen, Giselle — Opera Singer
Hazard Chase, 25 City Road, Cambridge CB1 1DP, England
Allen, Grady L — Football Player
317 Circleview Dr N, Hurst TX 76054, USA
Allen, Harold A (Hank) — Baseball Player
PO Box 4612, Upper Marlboro MD 20775, USA
Allen, Henry — Critic
Washington Post, Editorial Dept, 1150 15th St NW, Washington DC 20071 USA
Allen, India — Actress, Model
Playboy Promotions, 2706 Media Center Dr, Los Angeles CA 90065 USA
Allen, J Carl — Football Player
1614 Hornsby Ave, Saint Louis MO 63147, USA
Allen, J Randall (Randy) — Basketball Player
10185 Nichols Lake Road, Milton FL 32583, USA

Allen, Jackie — Singer
Dan Cleary Mgmt, 6399 Wilshire Blvd, #1019, Los Angeles CA 90048, USA

Allen, Jared S — Football Player
2303 Silver Breeze Court, San Jose CA 95138, USA

Allen, Jason J — Football Player
Cincinnati Bengals, 1 Paul Brown Stadium, Cincinnati OH 45202 USA

Allen, Jennifer — Sportscaster
N F L Network, 10950 Washington Blvd, #100, Culver City CA 90232 USA

Allen, Joan — Actress
I C M Partners, 10250 Constellation Blvd, #900, Los Angeles CA 90067 USA

Allen, John R — Marine Corps General
I S A Force/US Forces, N A T O Headquarters, Blvd Leopold III, Brussels 1110, Belgium

Allen, Joseph P, IV — Astronaut
N A S A, Johnson Space Center, 2101 NASA Road, Houston TX 77058 USA

Allen, Karen — Actress
Hyler Mgmt, 20 Ocean Park Blvd, #25, Santa Monica CA 90405 USA

Allen, Keith — Actor, Comedian
Independent Talent Group, Oxford House, 76 Oxford St, London W1D 1BS, England

Allen, Kevin — Director, Actor
United Talent Agency, 9336 Civic Center Dr, Beverly Hills CA 90210 USA

Allen, Kevin — Singer, Guitarist (And You Will Know Us)
Kork Agency, 1880 Century Park E, #711, Los Angeles CA 90067 USA

Allen, Kris — Singer
Sony Records, 550 Madison Ave, #600, New York NY 10022 USA

Allen, Krista — Actress, Model
Kazarian/Spencer/Ruskin, 11969 Ventura Blvd, #300, Studio City CA 91604 USA

Allen, L Patrick — Football Player
20801 32nd Lane S, #A, Seatac WA 98198, USA

Allen, Larry C — Football Player
7 Shelby Hill Lane, Danville CA 94526, USA

Allen, Laura — Actress
Gersh Agency, 9465 Wilshire Blvd, #600, Beverly Hills CA 90212 USA

Allen, Leopold R (Leo) — Actor, Comedian, Writer
Generate, 1545 26th St, #200, Santa Monica CA 90404, USA

Allen, Lily R B — Singer, Songwriter
E C I Music Agency, 1 Cowcross St, London EC1M 6DR, England

Allen, Lloyd C — Baseball Player
2340 Castlewood Dr, Toledo OH 43613, USA

Allen, Loy, Jr — Auto Racing Driver
323 Lochside Dr, Cary NC 27518, USA

Allen, Lucas G (Luke) — Baseball Player
282 Cooper Road, Social Circle GA 30025, USA

Allen, Lucius O — Basketball Player
1915 Buckingham Road, Los Angeles CA 90016, USA

Allen, Malik — Basketball Player
Orlando Magic, 8701 Maitland Summit Blvd, Orlando FL 32810 USA

Allen, Marcus L — Football Player, Sportscaster
9536 Wilshire Blvd, #300, Beverly Hills CA 90212, USA

Allen, Marty — Actor, Comedian
3847 Tropical Vine St, Las Vegas NV 89147, USA

Allen, Maryon P — Senator, AL
1551 Creekstone Circle, Birmingham AL 35243, USA

Allen, Michael L — Golfer
5827 E Anderson Dr, Scottsdale AZ 85254, USA

Allen, Nancy — Actress
Bauman Redanty Shaul Agency, 5757 Wilshire Blvd, #473, Los Angeles CA 90036 USA

Allen, Neil P — Baseball Player
3619 Torrey Pines Blvd, Sarasota FL 34238, USA

Allen, Patrick L — Governor General, Jamaica
Governor General's Office, King's House, Hope Road, Kingston 10, Jamaica

Allen, Paul G — Co-Developer (PC Language)
6451 W Mercer Way, Mercer Island WA 98040, USA

Allen, Rae — Actress
Kyle Fritz Mgmt, 6325 Heather Dr, Los Angeles CA 90068 USA

Allen, Rex, Jr — Singer
209 10th Ave, #527, Nashville TN 37203, USA

Allen, Richard — Actor
89 Saltergate, Chesterfield S40 IUS, England

Allen, Richard A (Richie) — Baseball Player
PO Box 254, Wampum PA 16157, USA

Allen, Richard J (Rick) — Drummer (Def Leppard)
Front Line Mgmt, 1100 Glendon Ave, #2000, Los Angeles CA 90024 USA

Allen, Richard V — Government Official
1615 L St NW, #900, Washington DC 20036, USA

Allen, Robert E — Businessman
11 Country Road W, Boynton Beach FL 33436, USA

Allen, Robert G (Bob) — Baseball Player
PO Box 667, Tatum TX 75691, USA

Allen, Robert J (Bob) — Basketball Player
117 Quarter Mile Way, Nicholasville KY 40356, USA

Allen, Rosalind — Actress
A K A Talent Agency, 6310 San Vicente Blvd, #200, Los Angeles CA 90048, USA

Allen, Scott — Figure Skater
511 Knickerbocker Road, Tenafly NJ 07670, USA

Allen, Sian Barbara — Actress
1411 NE 16th Ave, #219, Portland OR 97232, USA

Allen, Taje L — Football Player
1209 Valorie Court, Cedar Park TX 78613, USA

Allen, Ted — Entertainer
W M E Entertainment, 1325 Ave of Americas, New York NY 10019 USA

Allen, Teddy G — Army General
6900 Shackle Place, Burke VA 22015, USA

Allen, Terry — Singer (Stamps Quartet)
PO Box 1471, Brentwood TN 37024, USA

Allen, Terry — Artist, Songwriter
Route 10 Box 88N, Santa Fe NM 87501, USA

Allen, Terry T, Jr — Football Player
3176 Sable Ridge Dr, Buford GA 30519, USA
Allen, Tessa — Actress
Abrams Artists, 9200 W Sunset Blvd, #1125, West Hollywood CA 90069 USA
Allen, Thomas B — Opera Singer
Askonas Holt, Lincoln House, 300 High Holborn, London WC1V 7JH, England
Allen, Tim — Actor, Comedian
Boxing Cat Productions, 11500 Hart St, North Hollywood CA 91605, USA
Allen, W Ray — Basketball Player, Actor
10185 Nichols Lake Road, Milton FL 32583, USA
Allen, Will D — Football Player
2325 SW 105th Terrace, Davie FL 33324, USA
Allen, Woody — Actor, Comedian, Director
118 E 70th St, New York NY 10021, USA
Allenby, Robert — Golfer
4901 Pacifico Court, Palm Beach Gardens FL 33418, USA
Allende, Fernando — Actor, Singer
El Dorado Productions, PM Box 888, 425 Carr 693, Dorado PR 06646, USA
Allende, Isabel — Writer
92 Fernwood Dr, San Rafael CA 94901, USA
Allen-Dutton, Jordan — Writer
Gersh Agency, 9465 Wilshire Blvd, #600, Beverly Hills CA 90212 USA
Allen-Meares, Paula — Educator
University of Illinois, Chancellor's Office, 840 S Wood St, Chicago IL 60612, USA
Allenson, Gary M — Baseball Player
711 SE 34th St, Cape Coral FL 33904, USA
Allerman, Kurt D — Football Player
2511 Blue Heron Dr, Hudson OH 44236, USA
Allert, Ty H — Football Player
1504 County Road 308, Lexington TX 78947, USA
Alley, Kirstie — Actress
United Talent Agency, 9336 Civic Center Dr, Beverly Hills CA 90210 USA
Alley, L Eugene (Gene) — Baseball Player
10236 Steuben Dr, Glen Allen VA 23060, USA
Alley, Steve — Ice Hockey Player
545 College Road, Lake Forest IL 60045, USA
Allford, Simon — Architect
232 Bickenhall Mansions, Bickenhall St, London W1V 6BW, England
Allison, Brooke — Singer, Songwriter
2 K/E M I America Records, 6920 Sunset Blvd, Los Angeles CA 90028, USA
Allison, David B (Dave) — Ice Hockey Player, Coach
Iowa Stars, 833 5th Ave, Des Moines IA 50309, USA
Allison, Dorothy — Writer
E P Dutton/Penguin/GP Putnam/Signet, 375 Hudson St, New York NY 10014 USA
Allison, Dunkiny (Donnie) — Auto Racing Driver
355 Quail Dr, Salisbury NC 28147, USA
Allison, Glenn — Bowler
1844 S Haster St, #138, Anaheim CA 92802, USA
Allison, Graham T, Jr — Educator
69 Pinhurst Road, Belmont MA 02478, USA
Allison, Henry H (Hank) — Football Player
458 W Ellis Ave, Inglewood CA 90302, USA
Allison, Jerry — Drummer (Crickets), Songwriter
8455 New Bethal Road, Lyles TN 37098, USA
Allison, John A, IV — Financier
B B & T Corp, 200 W 2nd St, #260, Winston Salem NC 27101, USA
Allison, John V — Vietnam War Air Force Hero
6606 Britt St, Navarre FL 32566, USA
Allison, Margaret — Singer
I B A Productions, 3 Av Florimont, 1829 Montreux, Switzerland
Allison, Mike — Ice Hockey Player
7204 Birchmont Court NE, Bemidji MN 56601, USA
Allison, Mose J, Jr — Jazz Pianist, Composer, Singer
82 Ballad Court, Eastport NY 11941, USA
Allison, Odis — Basketball Player
3162 Majestic Shadows Ave, Henderson NV 89052, USA
Allison, Ray — Ice Hockey Player
106 N Valleybrook Road, Cherry Hill NJ 08034, USA
Allison, Richard C — Judge
224 Circle Dr, Manhasset NY 11030, USA
Allison, Robert A (Bobby) — Auto Racing Driver
PO Box 3696, Mooresville NC 28117, USA
Allison, Robert J, Jr — Businessman
Anadarko Petroleum Corp, 1201 Lake Robbins Dr, Spring TX 77380, USA
Allison, Stacy — Mountaineer
6633 SE 29th Ave, Portland OR 97202, USA
Allison, Verne — Singer (Dells)
Associated Booking Corp, 501 Madison Ave, #603, New York NY 10022 USA
Alliss, Peter — Sportscaster
Peter Alliss Golf Ltd, PO Box 224, Surrey GU26 6WQ, England
Allman, Gregory L (Gregg) — Singer, Musician, Songwriter
Allman Brothers Band Inc, 18 Tamworth Road, Waban MA 02468, USA
Allman, Jamie Anne — Actress
Greene Assoc, 1901 Ave of Stars, #130, Los Angeles CA 90067 USA
Allman, Marshall — Actor
Gersh Agency, 9465 Wilshire Blvd, #600, Beverly Hills CA 90212 USA
Allnutt, Robert — Space Scientist, Biochemist
5400 Edgemoor Lane, Bethesda MD 20814, USA
Allouache, Merzak — Director
Cite des Asphodeles, Bt D15, 183 Ben Aknoun, Algiers, Algeria
Allred, Corbin M — Actor
Aquarius Public Relations, 5320 Sylmar Ave, Sherman Oaks CA 91401, USA
Allred, Gloria R — Attorney
Allred Maroko Goldberg, 6300 Wilshire Blvd, #1500, Los Angeles CA 90048, USA
Allred, Jason — Golfer
10239 E Salt Bush Dr, Scottsdale AZ 85255, USA

A

Allen - Allred

A

Allred, John — Football Player
PO Box 748, Del Mar CA 92014, USA

Allyson, Karrin — Singer, Pianist
Stilleto Entertainment, 6295 S La Cienega Blvd, Inglewood CA 90301, USA

Almanza, Armando N — Baseball Player
1717 Villa Santos Circle, El Paso TX 79935, USA

Almers, Wolfhard — Biochemist
Oregon Health & Science University, Vollum Institute, Portland OR 97239, USA

Almirola, Aric — Auto Racing Driver
Aric Almirola Inc, 215 Overhill Dr, #A, Mooresville NC 28117, USA

Almodovar, Pedro — Director
El Deseo SA, Francisco Navacerrada 24, 28028 Madrid, Spain

Almon, William F (Billy) — Baseball Player
42 Channel View, #4, Warwick RI 02889, USA

Almond, Lincoln C — Governor, RI
82 Smith St, #222, Providence RI 02903, USA

Almond, Marc — Singer (Soft Cell), Songwriter
Take Out Productions, 630 9th Ave, #603, New York NY 10036, USA

Almond, Morris — Basketball Player
Red Star Belgrade, Obilicev Wreath 24, Belgrade, Serbia

Almquist, John O — Physiologist
300 Lions Hill Road, #W502, State College PA 16803, USA

Almunia Amann, Joaquin — Government Official, Spain
Carrera de San Jeronimo S/N 28014 Madrid, Spain

Alois — Prince, Liechtenstein
Schloss Vaduz, 9490 Vaduz, Liechtenstein

Alomar, Roberto V (Robbie) — Baseball Player
Urbana Monserrate B-56, PO Box 367, Salinas PR 00751, USA

Alomar, Santos C (Sandy), Jr — Baseball Player
1906 W Cortland St, Chicago IL 60622, USA

Alomar, Santos C (Sandy), Sr — Baseball Player
PO Box 367, Salinas PR 00751, USA

Alonso Bernardo, Jessica — Handball Player
R K Zajecar, Dositejeva 11, 19000 Zajecar, Serbia

Alonso, Adrian — Actor
Featured Artists Agency, 6210 Wilshire Blvd, #311, Los Angeles CA 90048, USA

Alonso, Alicia — Ballerina
Cuban National Ballet, Calzada 510 Entre D & E, El Vedado, Havana, Cuba

Alonso, Anabel — Actress
G R P C SL, Calles Fuencarral 17, 28004 Madrid, Spain

Alonso, Daniella — Actress, Model
Gersh Agency, 9465 Wilshire Blvd, #600, Beverly Hills CA 90212 USA

Alonso, Fernando — Auto Racing Driver
Carretera de Fuencarral, 14-16 Bloque C, 28108 Alcobendas, Madrid, Spain

Alonso, Laz — Actor
I C M Partners, 10250 Constellation Blvd, #900, Los Angeles CA 90067 USA

Alonso, Maria Conchita — Actress, Singer
Don Buchwald/Fortitude, 6500 Wilshire Blvd, #2200, Los Angeles CA 90048 USA

Alou, Felipe R — Baseball Player, Manager
6891 Cobia Circle, Boynton Beach FL 33437, USA

Alou, Jesus M R — Baseball Player
Apartado Postal 539/2 Lafaria, Santo Domingo, Dominican Republic

Alou, Moises R — Baseball Player
13095 NW 13th St, Pembroke Pines FL 33028, USA

Alpay, David — Actor
A P A Talent/Literary Agency, 405 S Beverly Dr, #300, Beverly Hills CA 90212 USA

Alpert, Herb — Musician
31930 Pacific Coast Highway, Malibu CA 90265, USA

Alpert, Joseph S — Physician
3440 E Cathedral Rock Circle, Tucson AZ 85718, USA

Alphand, Luc — Alpine Skier
Chalet Le Balme, Chantemerie, 05330 Sierre Chavalier, France

Alphin, W Kenneth (Big Kenny) — Singer, Songwriter
Morris Management Group, 818 19th Ave S, Nashville TN 37203, USA

Al-Sebesi, Al-Baji — Prime Minister, Tunisia
Prime Minister's Office, Place du Gouvernement, Tunis, Tunisia

Alsgaard, Thomas — Cross Country Skier
Cathinka Guldbergsveg 16, 2034 Holter, Norway

Alsop, Marin — Conductor
Baltimore Symphony Orchestra, 1212 Cathedral St, #1, Baltimore MD 21201, USA

Alsop, William A — Architect
72 Pembroke Road, London W8 6NX, England

Alston Reeves, Shirley — Singer (Shirelles)
G H R Entertainment, 6014 N Pointe Place, Woodland Hills CA 91367, USA

Alston, Barbara — Singer (Crystals)
Tingrassia Entertainment, PO Box 314, Holden MA 01520, USA

Alston, Gerald — Singer (Manhattans)
Rudolph & Beer, 432 Park Ave S, New York NY 10016, USA

Alston, Mack, Jr — Football Player
5421 Echols Ave, Alexandria VA 22311, USA

Alston, Rafer J — Basketball Player
9002 Legends Lane, Missouri City TX 77459, USA

Alstott, Michael J (Mike) — Football Player
7800 9th Ave S, Saint Petersburg FL 33707, USA

Alt, Carol — Model, Actress
Scott Hart Mgmt, 14622 Ventura Blvd, #746, Sherman Oaks CA 91403, USA

Alt, John M — Football Player
21 Crescent Lane, Saint Paul MN 55127, USA

Altbach, Philip G — Sociologist
Boston College, Campion Hall, Chestnut Hill MA 02467, USA

Altea, Rosemary — Writer, Medium
R A A H, PO Box 1151, Manchester VT 05254, USA

Alter, Harvey J — Hematologist
National Institutes of Health, Magnuson Center, 10 Center Dr, Bethesda MD 20892, USA

Alter, Hobie, Jr — Surfboard, Boat Designer
PO Box 1008, Oceanside CA 92051, USA

Allred - Alter

Alterman, Kent — Director
Creative Artists Agency, 2000 Ave of Stars, #100, Los Angeles CA 90067 USA
Alther, Lisa — Writer
1086 Silver St, Hinesburg VT 05461, USA
Altice, Summer — Model, Actress
Elite Model Mgmt, 404 Park Ave S, #900, New York NY 10016 USA
Altman, Bruce — Actor
Don Buchwald/Fortitude, 6500 Wilshire Blvd, #2200, Los Angeles CA 90048 USA
Altman, Chelsea — Actress
Liebman Entertainment, 25 E 21st St, #PH, New York NY 10010, USA
Altman, Jeff — Actor, Comedian
Agency S G H, 6525 Sunset Blvd, #PH9, Los Angeles CA 90028, USA
Altman, Scott — Opera Singer
Columbia Artists Mgmt Inc, 1790 Broadway, #702, New York NY 10019 USA
Altman, Scott D — Astronaut
1247 33rd St NW, Washington DC 20007, USA
Altman, Sidney — Nobel Chemistry Laureate
71 Blake Road, Hamden CT 06517, USA
Altman, Stuart H — Educator
11 Bakers Hill Road, Weston MA 02493, USA
Altmeyer, Jeannine T — Opera Singer
Im Muhlader, 8709 Herrliberg, Switzerland
Altobelli, Joseph (Joe) — Baseball Player, Manager
10 Stowell Dr, #3, Rochester NY 14616, USA
Alton, Kevin B — Chemist
Schering-Plough Research, 2000 Galloping Hill Road, Kenilworth NJ 07033, USA
Altschul, Serena — Commentator
MTV, News Dept, 1515 Broadway, New York NY 10036, USA
Altshuler, Alan A — Political Scientist
Harvard University, Kennedy Government School, Cambridge MA 02138, USA
Altwegg, Jeanette E — Figure Skater
British Olympic Assn, 60 Charlotte St, London W1T 2NU, England
Alusik, George J — Baseball Player
PO Box 454, Woodbridge NJ 07095, USA
Alvarado, Natividad (Naty) — Handball Player
Equitable of Iowa, 2700 N Main St, Santa Ana CA 92705, USA
Alvarez Martinez, Francisco Cardinal — Religious Leader
Arco de Palacio 3, 45002 Toledo, Spain
Alvarez, Al — Writer
Gillon Atkin, 18-21 Caraye Place, London SW10 9PT, England
Alvarez, Barry — Football Coach, Sportscaster
Fox-TV, Sports Dept, 205 W 67th St, New York NY 10065 USA
Alvarez, George — Actor
Michael Bruno Group, 13576 Cheltenham Dr, Sherman Oaks CA 91423, USA
Alvarez, Isabel — Baseball Player
2402 Monmouth Ave, Fort Wayne IN 46809, USA
Alvarez, Julia — Writer
Susan Bergholz Literary Agency, 17 W 10th St, #5N, New York NY 10011, USA
Alvarez, Kyle Patrick — Writer, Director
United Talent Agency, 9336 Civic Center Dr, Beverly Hills CA 90210 USA
Alvarez, Marcelo — Opera Singer
Zemsky/Greene Artists Mgmt, 104 W 73rd St, #1, New York NY 10023, USA
Alvarez, Rigoberto — Boxer
Golden Boy Promotions, 626 Wilshire Blvd, #350, Los Angeles CA 90017 USA
Alvarez, Saul (Canelo) — Boxer
Canelo Promotions, D Rodriguez 1667, Sec Libertad CP 44730, Guadalajara Jalisco, Mexico
Alvarez, Wilson E — Baseball Player
6927 Westchester Circle, Bradenton FL 34202, USA
Alvarez-Buylla, Arturo — Biologist
Rockefeller University Medical Center, 1230 York Ave, New York NY 10065 USA
Alvart, Christian — Director
Paradigm Agency, 360 N Crescent Dr, North Building, Beverly Hills CA 90210 USA
Alverson, Tommy — Singer, Songwriter
Two of a Kind, 5502 Silver Bow Trail, Arlington TX 76017, USA
Alves, Joe — Director
Gersh Agency, 9465 Wilshire Blvd, #600, Beverly Hills CA 90212 USA
Alves, Rick — Musician (Pirates of the Mississippi)
Third Coast Talent, PO Box 110225, Nashville TN 37222, USA
Alvin, Dave — Guitarist (Blasters); Songwriter
Mongrel Music, 743 Center Blvd, Fairfax CA 94930, USA
Alvis, R Maxwell (Max) — Baseball Player
806 Hunterwood Dr, Jasper TX 75951, USA
Alwaleed Bin Talal Bin Abdulaziz Alsaud — Prince, Saudi Arabia; Businessman
Kingdom Holdings, Kingdom Centre, Al-Urubah Road, Riyadh, Saudi Arabia
Alworth, Lance D — Football Player
Del Mar Corporate Center, 990 Highland Dr, #300, Solana Beach CA 92075, USA
Alyea, Garrabrant R (Brant) — Baseball Player
125 Dobbs Place, Goldsboro NC 27534, USA
Ama, Shola — Singer
Concorde International, 101 Shepherds Bush Road, London W6 7LP, England
Amadou, Hama — Prime Minister, Niger
Prime Minister's Office, State House, BP 353, Abuja, Niger
Amaechi, John E — Basketball Player
5747 E Aire Libre Ave, Scottsdale AZ 85254, USA
Amaker, Tommy — Basketball Player, Coach
Harvard University, Athletic Dept, Cambridge MA 02138, USA
Amalfitano, J Joseph (Joe) — Baseball Player, Manager
60 Sheath Dr, Sedona AZ 86336, USA
Amalric, Mathieu — Actor
Zelig Films, 57 Rue Reamur, 75002 Paris, France
Aman, Zeenat — Actress
Neelam Apts, Mount Mary Road, #300, Bandra, Mumbai MS 400050, India
Amandes, Tom — Actor
Paul Kohner, 9300 Wilshire Blvd, #555, Beverly Hills CA 90212 USA
Amanpour, Christiane — Commentator
Cable News Network, 2 Stephen St, #100, London W1P 1PL, England

Amante, Michael — Singer
PO Box 20275, Floral Park NY 11002, USA
Amara, Lucine — Opera Singer
260 W End Ave, #7A, New York NY 10023, USA
Amaral, Richard L (Rich) — Baseball Player
3122 Country Club Dr, Costa Mesa CA 92626, USA
Amaro, Ruben M, Sr — Baseball Player
4098 Cinnamon Way, Weston FL 33331, USA
Amato, Giuliano — Prime Minister, Italy
Carmera dei Deputati, Piazza di Montecitorio, 00186 Rome, Italy
Amato, Joe — Auto Racing Driver
PO Box 615, Wilkes Barre PA 18703, USA
Amato, Kenneth C (Ken) — Football Player
641 Old Hickory Blvd, #305, Brentwood TN 37027, USA
Amaury, Jean-Etienne — Businessman, Sports Executive
Amaury Sports, 2 Rue de Lisle, 92137 Issy-le-Mounlineaux, France
Amavia Lunkewitz, Daniela — Actress
Global Artists Agency, 6253 Hollywood Blvd, #508, Los Angeles CA 90028 USA
Amaya, Armando — Sculptor
Cuauh Temoc, 168 Col Deo Carmen, Coyoacan DF 04100, Mexico
Ambani, Anil — Businessman
Reliance Capital-Anil Ambani Group, Knowledge City, Mumbai 400 710, India
Ambani, Mukesh — Businessman
Reliance Industries, Makers Chambers IV, Nariman Point, 400021 Mumbai, India
Ambasz, Emilio — Architect
43 E 63rd St, New York NY 10065, USA
Amber — Singer, Songwriter
J M C A Entertainment, PO Box 375, 511 Ave of Americas, New York NY 10011, USA
Ambramovich, Roman A — Businessman
Chelsea F C, Stamford Bridge, Fulham Road, London SW6 1HS, England
Ambro, Thomas L — Judge
US Court of Appeals, Federal Building, 844 N King St, Wilmington DE 19801, USA
Ambros, Victor R — Geneticist
University of Massachusetts Medical School, 55 Lake Ave N, Worcester MA 01655, USA
Ambrose, Ashley A — Football Player
2726 Eudora Trail, Duluth GA 30097, USA
Ambrose, Lauren — Actress, Singer
United Talent Agency, 9336 Civic Center Dr, Beverly Hills CA 90210 USA
Ambrose, Marcus — Auto Racing Driver
Richard Petty Racing, 7065 Zephyr Place, Concord NC 28027, USA
Ambrose, Richard J (Dick) — Football Player
24049 Stonehedge Dr, Westlake OH 44145, USA
Ambrosio, Alessandra — Model
Elite Model Mgmt, 404 Park Ave S, #900, New York NY 10016 USA
Ambrosius, Marsha — Singer (Floetry), Songwriter
DreamWorks Records, 1000 Flower St, Glendale CA 91201 USA
Ambuehl, Cindy — Actress
28343 Ave Crocker, #1, Valencia CA 91355, USA
Amdahl, Gene M — Computer Engineer, Businessman
620 Sand Hill Road, #212G, Palo Alto CA 94304, USA
Amedori, John Patrick — Actor
Gersh Agency, 9465 Wilshire Blvd, #600, Beverly Hills CA 90212 USA
Ameling, Elly — Concert Singer
Hubstein Artist Services, 65 W 90th St, #13F, New York NY 10024, USA
Amelio, Gilbert F — Businessman
13416 Middle Fork Lane, Los Altos CA 94022, USA
Amelung, Edward V (Ed) — Baseball Player
16681 Cedar Circle, Fountain Valley CA 92708, USA
Amen, Irving — Artist
PO Box 812365, Boca Raton FL 33481, USA
Amend, Bill — Cartoonist (FoxTrot)
Universal Press Syndicate, 4520 Main St, #700, Kansas City MO 64111 USA
Amendola, Tony — Actor
Marc Bass Agency, 9255 W Sunset Blvd, #727, West Hollywood CA 90069, USA
Ament, Jeff — Bassist (Green River, Pearl Jam)
Curtis Mgmt, 1900 S Corgiat Dr, Seattle WA 98108, USA
Amentler, James (Jim) — Photographer
8117 Manchester Ave, #573, Playa del Rey CA 90293, USA
Amer, Nicholas — Actor
14 Great Russell St, London WC18 3NH, England
Amerie — Singer, Songwriter, Actress
Feenix Entertainment, 1360 Clifton Ave, #318, Clifton NJ 07012, USA
Ames, Bruce N — Biochemist
1324 Spruce St, Berkeley CA 94709, USA
Ames, Denise — Actress
Coralie Junior Theatrical Agency, 907 S Victory Blvd, Burbank CA 91502, USA
Ames, Ed — Singer, Actor
Paradise Artists, PO Box 1821, Ojai CA 93024 USA
Ames, Stephen M — Golfer
Professional Golfer's Assn, PO Box 109601, Palm Beach Gardens FL 33410 USA
Amick, Madchen — Actress
Gersh Agency, 9465 Wilshire Blvd, #600, Beverly Hills CA 90212 USA
Amiel, Jon — Director
Gersh Agency, 9465 Wilshire Blvd, #600, Beverly Hills CA 90212 USA
Amigo Vallejo, Carlos Cardinal — Religious Leader
Archdiocese, Plaza Virgen de los Reyes S/N, 41004 Seville, Spain
Amis, Martin L — Writer, Journalist
Wylie Agency, 17 Bedford Square, London WC1B 3JA, England
Amis, Suzy — Actress, Model
I C M Partners, 10250 Constellation Blvd, #900, Los Angeles CA 90067 USA
Amlee, Jessica — Actress
Real 2 Real Talent, 20475 Lougheed Highway, Maple Ridge BC V2X 9B6, Canada
Amlong, Joseph — Rowing Athlete
2445 4th Lane, Vero Beach FL 32962, USA
Amlong, Thomas — Rowing Athlete
166 Four Mile River Road, Old Lyme CT 06371, USA

Ammaccapane, Danielle — Golfer
13214 N 13th St, Phoenix AZ 85022, USA
Ammaccapane, Dina — Golfer
4407 E Blanche Dr, Phoenix AZ 85032, USA
Ammachi — Religious Leader
Amrita Institutions, Ettimadai, Coimbatore, Tamil Nadu 641105, India
Ammann, Simon — Ski Jumper
W W P Group, Lustenauerstra 64, 6850 Dornbirn, Austria
Amodeo, Mike — Ice Hockey Player
556 Fralicks Beach Road, RR 5, Port Perry ON L9L 1B6, Canada
Amoia, Charlene — Actress
House of Representatives, 1434 6th St, #1, Santa Monica CA 90401 USA
Amonte, Tony — Ice Hockey Player
PO Box 771, Humarock MA 02047, USA
Amorello, Matthew J — Government Administrator
Massachusettes Turnpike Authority, 10 Park Plaza, #4160, Boston MA 02116, USA
Amorosi, Vanessa — Singer, Songwriter
Harbour Agency, 135 Forbes Road, Woolloomooloo NSW 2011, Australia
Amory, Misha — Concert Violist
David Rowe Artists, 24 Bessom St, #2, Marblehead MA 01945, USA
Amos, Daniel P (Dan) — Businessman
A F L A C Inc, A F L A C Center, 1932 Wynnton Road, Columbus GA 31999, USA
Amos, James F — Marine Corps General
Commandant, HqUSMC, 2 Navy Annex, Washington DC 20380 USA
Amos, Tori — Singer, Pianist, Songwriter
Creative Artists Agency, 2000 Ave of Stars, #100, Los Angeles CA 90067 USA
Amos, Wally (Famous) — Businessman
Rosica Mulhern Assoc, 627 Grove St, Ridgewood NJ 07450, USA
Amoyal, Pierre A W — Concert Violinist
Jacques Thelen, 15 Ave Montaigne, 75008 Paris, France
Amram, David W, III — Jazz, Classical Composer, Conductor
Ed Keane Assoc, 573 Pleasant St, Winthrop MA 02152, USA
Amrapurkar, Sadashiv — Actor, Comedian
A/201 Panchdhara Off Yari Road, Versova Andheri, Mumbai MS 400058, India
Amritraj, Ashok — Actor, Producer, Writer
Hyde Park Entertainment, 16555 Sherman Way, #A1, Van Nuys CA 91406, USA
Amritraj, Vijay — Tennis Player
First Serve, 10/5A 13th Ave, Harrington Rd, Chennai 00031, India
Amsden, Ben C — WW II Navy Air Force Hero
514 C St, Farmington MO 63640, USA
Amsellem, Norah — Opera Singer
Columbia Artists Mgmt Inc, 1790 Broadway, #702, New York NY 10019 USA
Amsterdam, Anthony G — Attorney, Educator
68 Middle Lane Highway, Southampton NY 11968, USA
Amuka-Bird, Nikki — Actress
Greene Assoc, 1901 Ave of Stars, #130, Los Angeles CA 90067 USA
Amy, Susie — Actress
Curtis Brown Group, 28-29 Haymarket St, #500, London SW1Y 4SP, England
An Sang Mi — Speed Skater
Skating Union, 88 Bangyee-Dong, Songpaku, Seoul 138 749, South Korea
An Yulong — Speed Skater
Skating Assn, 56 Zhongguancun South St, Haidian, Beijing 100044, China
Ana Alicia — Actress
S D B Partners, 1801 Ave of Stars, #902, Los Angeles CA 90067 USA
Anagnostopoulos, Constantine E — Heart Surgeon
435 Dockside Dr, #902, Naples FL 34110, USA
Anahi — Actress, Singer, Model
E M I Music, Rio Tigris 33, Col Cuahtemoc CP 06500, Mexico
Anand, Vijay — Actor, Director
Ketnav 17 Union Park Pali Hill, Khar, Mumbai MS 400052, India
Anand, Viswanathan (Vishy) — Chess Player
F I D E, 9 Ave de Beaumont, 1012 Lausanne, Switzerland
Ananiashvili, Nina G — Ballerina
Frunzenskaya Nab 46, #79, 119270 Moscow, Russia
Anappau, Kristina — Actress
Untitled Entertainment, 350 S Beverly Dr, #200, Beverly Hills CA 90212 USA
Anastacia — Singer
Braude Mgmt, PO Box 7249, San Diego CA 92167, USA
Anastasio, Trey — Guitarist (Phish, Oysterhead)
Red Light Mgmt, 44 Wall St, #2200, New York NY 10005, USA
Anatsui, El — Sculptor
University of Nigeria, Art Dept, Nsukka, Nigeria
Anaya, Elena — Actress
Kuranda Mgmt, Santo Angel 84, 28043 Madrid, Spain
Anaya, Rudolfo — Writer
5324 Canada Vista NW, Albuquerque NM 87120, USA
Anaya, Toney — Governor, NM
711 E May Ave, Las Cruces NM 88001, USA
Anberlin — Rock Music Group
Arson Media Group, 23 N Summerlin Ave, #200, Orlando FL 32801, USA
Ancelotti, Carlo — Soccer Player, Coach
F C Milan, Via Filippo Turati 3, 20121 Milan, Italy
Anchultz Thoms, Daniela — Speed Skater
Eissportclub Erfurt, Arnstaedter Str 53, 99096 Erfurt, Germany
Ancona, Bill — Drag Racing Driver
260 Nelson Wyatt Road, Mansfield TX 76063, USA
Anconina, Richard — Actor
Artmedia, 20 Ave Rapp, 75007 Paris, France
Anden, Mini — Model, Actress
Medavoy Mgmt, 10203 Santa Monica Blvd, #400, Los Angeles CA 90067 USA
Anderegg, Robert H (Bob) — Basketball Player
11708 E Onyx Ave, Scottsdale AZ 85259, USA
Anders, Allison — Director, Writer
A P A Talent/Literary Agency, 405 S Beverly Dr, #300, Beverly Hills CA 90212 USA
Anders, Andrea — Actress
Abrams Artists, 9200 W Sunset Blvd, #1125, West Hollywood CA 90069 USA

A

Anders, David — Actor
Liberman/Zerman Mgmt, 252 N Larchmont Blvd, #200, Los Angeles CA 90004 USA
Anders, Kimble L — Football Player
Running Back Giving Back Foundation, 4435 Prospect Ave, Kansas City MO 64130, USA
Anders, Sean — Director, Producer, Writer, Actor
Mosiac Media Group, 9200 W Sunset Blvd, #1000, Los Angeles CA 90069 USA
Anders, William A — Astronaut, Air Force General
1 Aeroview Lane, Eastsound WA 98245, USA
Andersen, Anthony L — Businessman
H B Fuller Co, PO Box 64683, Saint Paul MN 55164, USA
Andersen, Christopher P — Writer
Hyperion Books, 114 5th Ave, New York NY 10011 USA
Andersen, Eric — Singer, Songwriter
Charles Rothschild Productions, 330 E 48th St, #2D, New York NY 10017, USA
Andersen, Greta — Swimmer
16222 Monterey Lane, #264, Huntington Beach CA 92649, USA
Andersen, Hjalmar (Hjallis) — Speed Skater
Velferden for Handelsflaten, Trondheimsvn 2, 0560 Oslo 5, Norway
Andersen, Kurt — Writer
Random House, 1745 Broadway, #1800, New York NY 10019 USA
Andersen, Ladell — Basketball Coach
41 W Cedar Dr, Hermiston OR 97838, USA
Andersen, Larry E — Baseball Player
2043 Sunray Circle, West Linn OR 97068, USA
Andersen, Linda — Yachtswoman
Aroysund, 3135 Torod, Norway
Andersen, Lisa — Surfer
Roxy Quik Silver, 15202 Graham St, Huntington Beach CA 92649, USA
Andersen, May — Model
2 P M Model Mgmt, Norregade 2, 1165 Copenhagen K, Denmark
Andersen, Mogens — Artist
Strandagervej 28, 2900 Hellerup, Copenhagen, Denmark
Andersen, Morten — Football Player
6501 Old Shadburn Ferry Road, Buford GA 30518, USA
Andersen, Susan — Writer
Jane Rotrosen Agency, 318 E 51st St, New York NY 10022, USA
Anderson, Al — Singer, Guitarist (NRBQ)
Skyline Music, 2270 Maiden Lane SW, Roanoke VA 24015, USA
Anderson, Alfa — Singer (Chic)
Lustig Talent, PO Box 770850, Orlando FL 32877 USA
Anderson, Alfred A — Football Player
2805 Chesterwood Court, Mansfield TX 76063, USA
Anderson, Anthony A — Actor, Comedian, Writer
United Talent Agency, 9336 Civic Center Dr, Beverly Hills CA 90210 USA
Anderson, Audrey Marie — Actress
I C M Partners, 10250 Constellation Blvd, #900, Los Angeles CA 90067 USA
Anderson, Bill — Singer, Guitarist, Songwriter
Bill Anderson Enterprises, PO Box 888, Hermitage TN 37076, USA
Anderson, Blake — Actor, Writer
United Talent Agency, 9336 Civic Center Dr, Beverly Hills CA 90210 USA
Anderson, Brad — Director
422 Santa Monica Court, Escondido CA 92029, USA
Anderson, Brad — Drag Racing Driver
Brad Anderson Enterprises, 1240 S Cucamonga Ave, Ontario CA 91761, USA
Anderson, Bradbury H — Businessman
Best Buy Co, 7601 Penn Ave S, Minneapolis MN 55423, USA
Anderson, Bradford — Actor
Michael Enfield Mgmt, 10630 Moorpark, #101, Toluca Lake CA 91602, USA
Anderson, Bradley J (Brad) — Cartoonist (Marmaduke)
13022 Wood Harbour Dr, Montgomery TX 77356, USA
Anderson, Brady K — Baseball Player
32800 Pacific Coast Highway, Malibu CA 90265, USA
Anderson, Brett — Singer (Suede)
Lookout Records, PO Box 40828, San Francisco CA 94140, USA
Anderson, Brett F — Baseball Player
Oakland Athletics, McAfee Coliseum, 7000 Coliseum Way, #3, Oakland CA 94621 USA
Anderson, Brian J — Baseball Player
3571 N Meyers Road, Geneva OH 44041, USA
Anderson, Bruce A — Football Player
910 NE Parkview Court, Roseburg OR 97470, USA
Anderson, C Neal — Football Player
10626 SW 41st Place, Gainesville FL 32608, USA
Anderson, Camille — Actress, Model
9461 Charleville Blvd, #605, Beverly Hills CA 90212, USA
Anderson, Christine — Singer, Pianist, Songwriter
Brian Lewis Presents, 781 Herman Ave, Medford OR 97501, USA
Anderson, Clarence E (Bud) — WW II Army Air Corps Hero
1060 Southridge Dr, Auburn CA 95603, USA
Anderson, Clayton C — Astronaut
N A S A, Johnson Space Center, 2101 NASA Road, Houston TX 77058 USA
Anderson, Craig — Guitarist (Heartland)
Country Thunder Records, 1016 17th Ave S, Nashville TN 37212, USA
Anderson, Dale — Ice Hockey Player
2217 Ave Haultain, Saskatoon SK S7J 1PT, Canada
Anderson, Daniel E (Dan) — Basketball Player
19000 NW Squirrel Tail Loop, Bend OR 97701, USA
Anderson, Daniel W (Dan) — Basketball Player
100 3rd Ave S, #2002, Minneapolis MN 55401, USA
Anderson, Darren H — Football Player
7328 Overland Park Court, West Chester OH 45069, USA
Anderson, Daryl — Actor
House of Representatives, 1434 6th St, #1, Santa Monica CA 90401 USA
Anderson, David C (Dave) — Baseball Player
421 Lockett St, Monticello KY 42633, USA
Anderson, David J — Biologist
California Institute of Technology, Biology Division, Pasadena CA 91125, USA

Anders - Anderson

Anderson, David P (Dave)   Sportswriter
8 Inness Road, Tenafly NJ 07670, USA
Anderson, Derek L   Basketball Player
Legendary Liquids, 500 Bishop St, Building B2, Atlanta GA 30318, USA
Anderson, Derek M   Football Player
Carolina Panthers, Ericsson Stadium, 800 S Mint St, Charlotte NC 28202 USA
Anderson, Dion   Actor
S D B Partners, 1801 Ave of Stars, #902, Los Angeles CA 90067 USA
Anderson, Don   Sculptor
3711 Cabrant Road, Everson WA 98247, USA
Anderson, Don L   Geophysicist
PO Box 1417, Cambria CA 93428, USA
Anderson, Duwayne M   Polar Scientist
6119 139th Place SE, Bellevue WA 98006, USA
Anderson, Earl   Ice Hockey Player
602 3rd Ave NE, Roseau MN 56751, USA
Anderson, Earl E   Marine Corps General
West Virginia University, Morgantown WV 26506 USA
Anderson, Eddie Lee, Jr   Football Player
PO Box 6363, Warner Robins GA 31095, USA
Anderson, Eric W   Basketball Player
12284 Whirlaway Dr, Noblesville IN 46060, USA
Anderson, Erich   Actor
Paradigm Agency, 360 N Crescent Dr, North Building, Beverly Hills CA 90210 USA
Anderson, Erika   Actress, Model
Click Model Mgmt, 9057 Nemo St, West Hollywood CA 90069, USA
Anderson, Ernestine I   Singer
Thomas Cassidy, 11761 E Speedway Blvd, Tucson AZ 85748 USA
Anderson, Fredell L (Fred)   Football Player
11810 NE 48th Place, Kirkland WA 98033, USA
Anderson, G Don (Donny)   Football Player
4516 Lovers Lane, #133, Dallas TX 75225, USA
Anderson, Garret J   Baseball Player
34 Vernal Spring, Irvine CA 92603, USA
Anderson, Gary A   Football Player
265 Miskow Close, Cannmore AB T1W 3G7, Canada
Anderson, Gary L   Marksman
National Rifle Assn, 11250 Waples Mill Road, Fairfax VA 22030, USA
Anderson, Gary W   Football Player
1 Ridgefield Court, Little Rock AR 72223, USA
Anderson, Gerry   Director, Puppeteer
Gerry Anderson Magazine, 332 Lytham Road, Blackpool FY4 1DW, England
Anderson, Gillian   Actress
Independent Talent Group, Oxford House, 76 Oxford St, London W1D 1BS, England
Anderson, Glenn   Ice Hockey Player
42 W 69th St, #2A, New York NY 10023, USA
Anderson, Harry L   Actor
Creative Artists Agency, 2000 Ave of Stars, #100, Los Angeles CA 90067 USA
Anderson, Howard A, Jr   Cinematographer
Howard A Anderson Co, 5161 Lankershim Blvd, North Hollywood CA 91601, USA
Anderson, Ian   Singer (Jethro Tull), Songwriter
Jethro Tull Productions, PO Box 2103, Malmesbury, Wilts SN16 9ZU, England
Anderson, J C   Golfer
232 Fairway Green Dr, O Fallon MO 63368, USA
Anderson, Jade   Singer
Evolution Entertainment, 901 N Highland Ave, Los Angeles CA 90038 USA
Anderson, Jamal S   Football Player
10540 Montclair Way, Duluth GA 30097, USA
Anderson, James L (Jim)   Baseball Player
2111 Bennington Court, Thousand Oaks CA 91360, USA
Anderson, James M (Jamie)   Cinematographer
19 Hanson St, Portland ME 04103, USA
Anderson, James W   Endocrinologist
University of Kentucky Medical Center, Endocrinology Dept, Lexington KY 40506, USA
Anderson, Jamie   Actress
Rage Talent Agency, 23501 Park Sorrento, Calabasas CA 91302, USA
Anderson, Janet   Golfer
4311 W Ardmore Road, Laveen AZ 85339, USA
Anderson, Janina   Actress
Ominiquest Entertainment, 1416 N La Brea Ave, Los Angeles CA 90028, USA
Anderson, Joel   Director, Writer
Bloom Hergott Diemer, 150 S Rodeo Dr, #300, Beverly Hills CA 90212 USA
Anderson, John B   Representative, Presidential Candidate
4120 48th St NW, Washington DC 20016, USA
Anderson, John D   Singer, Songwriter
Bobby Roberts, 3050 Business Park Circle, #303, Goodlettsville TN 37221 USA
Anderson, John M   Ice Hockey Player, Coach
260 Sunset Ave, Glen Ellyn IL 60137, USA
Anderson, John, Jr   Governor, KS
16609 W 133rd St, Olathe KS 66062, USA
Anderson, Jon   Singer (Yes)
Agency Group Ltd, 142 W 57th St, #600, New York NY 10019 USA
Anderson, Joseph (Joe)   Actor
United Agents, 12-26 Lexington St, London W1F 0LE, England
Anderson, June   Opera Singer
Hazard Chase, 25 City Road, Cambridge CB1 1DP, England
Anderson, Kenneth (Kenny)   Basketball Player
270 N Canon Dr, #1289, Beverly Hills CA 90210, USA
Anderson, Kenneth A (Ken)   Football Player, Coach
41 Sedge Fern Dr, Hilton Head SC 29926, USA
Anderson, Kerri   Businesswoman
P F Chang's, 7676 E Pinnacle Peak Road, Scottsdale AZ 85255, USA
Anderson, Kevin   Actor
Lighthouse Entertainment, 9220 W Sunset Blvd, #200, West Hollywood CA 90069 USA
Anderson, Kevin J   Writer
AnderZone, PO Box 767, Monument CO 80132, USA

A

Anderson - Anderson

Anderson, Kim S 6709 La Tijera Blvd, #222, Los Angeles CA 90045, USA	Football Player
Anderson, Lauren 5200 NW 43rd St, #102-304, Gainesville FL 32606, USA	Model
Anderson, Laurie Pomgranate Arts, 1140 Broadway, #305, New York NY 10001, USA	Performance Artist, Singer
Anderson, Lawrence A (Larry) 3170 Blanchard Road, Shreveport LA 71103, USA	Football Player
Anderson, Layke Ken McReddie Assoc, 11 Connaught Place, London W2 2ET, England	Actor
Anderson, Loni Innovative Artists, 1505 10th St, Santa Monica CA 90401 USA	Actress
Anderson, Louie A P A Talent/Literary Agency, 405 S Beverly Dr, #300, Beverly Hills CA 90212 USA	Actor, Comedian
Anderson, Lynn Spacek Co, 27 Drifting Wind Run, Austin TX 78738, USA	Singer
Anderson, Mary 1127 Norman Place, Los Angeles CA 90049, USA	Actress
Anderson, Melody PO Box 24483, Los Angeles CA 90024, USA	Actress
Anderson, Michael A&M Records, 70 Universal City Plaza, Universal City CA 91608 USA	Singer, Songwriter
Anderson, Michael A (Mike) 4112 Westbrook Dr, Florence SC 29501, USA	Baseball Player, Coach
Anderson, Michael H University of Colorado, Physics Dept, Boulder CO 80309, USA	Physicist
Anderson, Michael J C R Mgmt, 23852 Pacific Coast Highway, #627, Malibu CA 90265, USA	Actor
Anderson, Michael J Paul Burford, 52 Yorkminster Road, North York ON M2P 1M3, Canada	Director
Anderson, Michael M (Mike) PO Box 12753, Chandler AZ 85248, USA	Football Player
Anderson, Miles Gage Group, 14724 Ventura Blvd, #505, Sherman Oaks CA 91403 USA	Actor
Anderson, Murray 38 Head Ave, PO Box 38 Station Main, Pas MB R9A 1K3, Canada	Ice Hockey Player
Anderson, Nathan Geddes Agency, 8430 Santa Monica Blvd, #201, West Hollywood CA 90069 USA	Actor
Anderson, Nelison (Nick) 163 Harbor Isle Circle N, Memphis TN 38103, USA	Basketball Player
Anderson, Nick Courier-Journal, Editorial Dept, 525 W Broadway, Louisville KY 40202, USA	Editorial Cartoonist
Anderson, Nicole G PO Box 231624, Encinitas CA 92023, USA	Actress, Model
Anderson, Ottis J (O J) 9636 Guehring Dr, Saint Louis MO 63123, USA	Football Player
Anderson, Pamela I C M Partners, 10250 Constellation Blvd, #900, Los Angeles CA 90067 USA	Model, Actress
Anderson, Paul Thomas Creative Artists Agency, 2000 Ave of Stars, #100, Los Angeles CA 90067 USA	Director, Writer
Anderson, Paul W S Key Creatives, 1800 N Highland Ave, Los Angeles CA 90028, USA	Director
Anderson, Perry 3311 E Oregon Ave, Phoenix AZ 85018, USA	Ice Hockey Player
Anderson, Pete Little Dog Records, 2219 W Olive Ave, #150, Burbank CA 91506, USA	Guitarist
Anderson, Philip W Princeton University, Physics Dept, Princeton NJ 08544, USA	Nobel Physics Laureate
Anderson, R John 14739 Crestwood Court, Sewickley PA 15143, USA	Football Player
Anderson, R Lanier, III US Court of Appeals, PO Box 977, Macon GA 31202, USA	Judge
Anderson, Randy Anderson Racing, 1240 S Cucamonga Ave, Ontario CA 91761, USA	Auto Racing Driver
Anderson, Ray Ellicott Talent Group, 2503 Marilyn Circle, Petaluma CA 94954, USA	Jazz Trombonist, Trumpeter
Anderson, Rebecca Moesta Word Fire, PO Box 1840, Monument CO 80132, USA	Writer
Anderson, Reid B Stuttgart Ballet, Ober Schlossgarten 6, 70173, Stuttgart, Germany	Ballet Dancer, Artistic Director
Anderson, Richard Delta Air Lines, Hartsfield International Airport, Atlanta GA 30320, USA	Businessman
Anderson, Richard 10120 Cielo Dr, Beverly Hills CA 90210, USA	Actor
Anderson, Richard D (Richie) 6311 Meandering Woods Court, Frederick MD 21701, USA	Football Player
Anderson, Richard Dean I C M Partners, 10250 Constellation Blvd, #900, Los Angeles CA 90067 USA	Actor
Anderson, Richard P (Dick) 4603 Santa Maria St, Miami FL 33146, USA	Football Player
Anderson, Robert C (Bob) 3140 E 89th St, Tulsa OK 74137, USA	Baseball Player
Anderson, Robert C (Bobby) 79125 Big Horn Trail, La Quinta CA 92253, USA	Football Player
Anderson, Robert G W British Museum, Great Russell St, London WC1B 3DG, England	Museum Executive
Anderson, Robert P (Bob) 244 Carmel Dr, Melbourne FL 32940, USA	Football Player
Anderson, Ronald C (Ron) 72 Woodside Close, Airdrie AB T4B 2C7, Canada	Ice Hockey Player
Anderson, Ross Seattle Times, Editorial Dept, 1120 John St, Seattle WA 98109 USA	Journalist
Anderson, Russ 76 Fern Dr, Plantsville CT 06479, USA	Ice Hockey Player
Anderson, Ryan J New Orleans Hornets, 1250 Poydras St, #101, New Orleans LA 70113 USA	Basketball Player

Anderson, Samuel (Sam) — Actor
TalentWorks, 3500 W Olive Ave, #1400, Burbank CA 91505 USA
Anderson, Scott E — Director
I C M Partners, 10250 Constellation Blvd, #900, Los Angeles CA 90067 USA
Anderson, Shandon R — Basketball Player
63 Mangum St SW, #6, Atlanta GA 30313, USA
Anderson, Shawn — Ice Hockey Player
Hockey S T, 19 51st Ave, Notre Dame de L'ile Perrot QC J7V 7L8, Canada
Anderson, Shelly — Drag Racing Driver
Brad Anderson Racing, 1240 S Cucamonga Ave, Ontario CA 91761, USA
Anderson, Stephen H — Judge
US Court of Appeals, Federal Building, 125 S State St, Salt Lake City UT 84138, USA
Anderson, Sunshine — Singer
Music World Entertainment, 1505 Hadley St, Houston TX 77002, USA
Anderson, Tai — Bassist (Third Day)
Creative Trust, 5141 Virginia Way, #320, Brentwood TN 37027, USA
Anderson, Tazwell L (Taz), Jr — Football Player
Taz Anderson Realty, 2931 Paces Ferry Road SE, #150, Atlanta GA 30339, USA
Anderson, Terence (Terry) — Journalist, Iran Hostage
17 Sunlight Hill, Yonkers NY 10704, USA
Anderson, Thomas (Tom) — Businessman
MySpace, 1333 2nd St, Santa Monica CA 90401, USA
Anderson, Tim — Actor
Herb Tannen, 10801 National Blvd, #101, Los Angeles CA 90064 USA
Anderson, Todd — Drummer (Heartland)
Country Thunder Records, 1016 17th Ave S, Nashville TN 37212, USA
Anderson, Tom — Actor
Feast Mgmt, 34 Upper St, London N1 0PN, England
Anderson, Tyrone L (Bennie) — Football Player
6450 Virginia Ave, Saint Louis MO 63111, USA
Anderson, W French — Biochemist, Geneticist
University of Southern California Medical School, 1510 San Pablo St, Los Angeles CA 90033, USA
Anderson, W William (Bill) — Football Player
6924 Lark Lane, Knoxville TN 37919, USA
Anderson, Walter — Publisher
Parade Publications, Publisher's Office, 711 3rd Ave, New York NY 10017, USA
Anderson, Wendell — Ice Hockey Player
PO Box 49097, Minneapolis MN 55449, USA
Anderson, Wendell R — Governor, Senator, MN
Baker Building, 706 2nd Ave S, #720, Minneapolis MN 55402, USA
Anderson, Wes — Director, Writer
American Empirical Pictures, 405 W 13th St, #6R, New York NY 10014, USA
Anderson, Wessell — Jazz Saxophonist
Fat City Artists, 1906 Chet Atkins Place, #502, Nashville TN 37212 USA
Anderson, Wilford C — WW II Army Hero
3585 Round Barn Blvd, Santa Rosa CA 95403, USA
Anderson, Willie A — Football Player
1490 Meadowcreek Court, Atlanta GA 30338, USA
Anderson, Willie L — Basketball Player
Toronto Raptors, Air Canada Center, 20 Bay St, Toronto ON M5J 2N8, Canada
Anderson, Willie L (Flipper) — Football Player
190 Abbey Hill Road, Suwanee GA 30024, USA
Anderson, Winslow — Artist
PO Box 1700, Huntington WV 25717, USA
Anderson-Imbert, Enrique — Educator
909 Paramount Road, Oakland CA 94610, USA
Andersson, Benny — Singer (ABBA), Composer
Mono Music, Sodra Brobaeken 41A, 111 49 Stockholm, Sweden
Andersson, Bibi — Actress
Agents Associes, 201 Faubourg Saint Honore, 75008 Paris, France
Andersson, Harriet — Actress
Agentfirman Planthaber/Kildén, Drottninggatan 55, 111 21 Stockholm, Sweden
Andersson, Kim — Handball Player
T H W Kiel Handball, Ziegelteich 30, 24103 Kiel, Germany
Andersson, Mattias — Handball Player
S G Flensburg Handewitt, Schiffbrucke 66, 24939 Flensburg, Germany
Andersson, Susanna — Opera Singer
I M G Artists, Hogarth Business Park, Chiswick, London W4 2TH, England
Anderszewski, Piotr — Concert Pianist, Conductor
I M G Artists, Hogarth Business Park, Chiswick, London W4 2TH, England
Andes, Karen — Body Builder
G P Putnam's Sons, 375 Hudson St, New York NY 10014 USA
Andino, Robert L — Baseball Player
2250 NW 2nd St, Miami FL 33125, USA
Andion Gonzalez, Patxi — Singer, Songwriter, Actor
Calle Pavia N 2, 28013 Madrid, Spain
Ando, Kozue — Soccer Player
Football Assn, 3-10-15 Hongo, Bunkyoku, Tokyo 113 0033 Japan
Ando, Miki — Figure Skater
International Mgmt Group, 1 Erieview Plaza, 1360 E 9th St, Cleveland OH 44114 USA
Ando, Tadao — Pritzker Architectural Laureate
Tadao Ando Architect, 5-23-2 Toyosaki, Kitaku, Osaka 531, Japan
Andrade, William T (Billy) — Golfer
4429 E Brookhaven Dr NE, Atlanta GA 30319, USA
Andrascik, Steve — Ice Hockey Player
32 Early Lane, Annville PA 17003, USA
Andre 3000 — Rap Artist (Outkast), Actor
4016 Elizabeth Terrace, Rex GA 30273, USA
Andre, Annette — Actress
98 Fourwheel Dr, Willow NY 12495, USA
Andre, Carl — Sculptor
689 Crown St, Brooklyn NY 11213, USA
Andrea, Pat — Artist
18 Rue Henri Regnault, 75014 Paris, France
Andrea, Paul — Ice Hockey Player
136 Regent St, North Sydney NS B2A 2G5, Canada

A

Anderson - Andrea

A

Andreas - Andriessen

Andreas, G Allen Archer Daniels Midland Co, 4666 E Faries Parkway, Decatur IL 62526, USA	Businessman
Andreasen, Nancy C 200 Hawkings Dr, Iowa City IA 52242, USA	Psychiatrist
Andreason, Larry 10874 Kyle St, Los Alamitos CA 90720, USA	Diver
Andre-Deshays, Claudie Hopital Cochin, Rhumatologie Dept, 75000 Paris, France	Spatinaut, France
Andreeff, Starr C N A Assoc, 1875 Century Park East, #2250, Los Angeles CA 90067 USA	Actress
Andreessen, Marc Opsware, 19420 Homestead Road, Cupertino CA 95014, USA	Computer Software Designer
Andreoli, Severino Via Carolucci 19, 3706 Lugoguomo, Italy	Cyclist
Andreone, Leah Metropolitan Entertainment Group, 2 Penn Plaza, #1500, New York NY 10121, USA	Singer, Songwriter
Andres, Dominic Curling Assn, PO Box 606, 3000 Bern, Switzerland	Curling Athlete
Andresen, Frode Borgergt 3, 3514 Honefoss, Norway	Biathlete
Andress, Tuck T & P Productions, PO Box 1363, Menlo Park CA 94026, USA	Jazz Guitarist (Tuck & Patti)
Andress, Ursula Via Francesco Siacci 38, 00186 Rome, Italy	Actress
Andretti, John Andretti Autosport, 7615 Zionsville Road, Indianapolis IN 46268, USA	Auto Racing Driver
Andretti, Mario 457 Rose Inn Ave, Nazareth PA 18064, USA	Auto Racing Driver
Andretti, Michael M Andretti Autosport, 7615 Zionsville Road, Indianapolis IN 46268, USA	Auto Racing Driver, Executive
Andrew Buckingham Palace, London SW1A 1AA, England	Prince, England
Andrew, Philip Bohemia Entertainment, 8170 Beverly Blvd, #102, Los Angeles CA 90048, USA	Actor
Andrew, Samuel H (Sam), III Gen-X Entertainment, PO Box 128164, Nashville TN 37212, USA	Guitarist (Big Brother Holding Company)
Andrews, Amy Leigh Playboy Promotions, 2706 Media Center Dr, Los Angeles CA 90065 USA	Model
Andrews, Andy PO Box 17321, Nashville TN 37217, USA	Actor, Comedian
Andrews, Anthony Paradigm Agency, 360 N Crescent Dr, North Building, Beverly Hills CA 90210 USA	Actor
Andrews, Brittany Look North Promotions, 7-9 Clifford St, York, Yorkshire YO1 9RA, England	Exotic Dancer, Model, Actress
Andrews, D Shane 807 Dennis Way, Carlsbad NM 88220, USA	Baseball Player
Andrews, Donna 2301 Hawthorne Road, Lynchburg VA 24503, USA	Golfer
Andrews, Erin Fox-TV, Sports Dept, 205 W 67th St, New York NY 10065 USA	Sportscaster
Andrews, George E 119 Meadow Lane, Centre Hall PA 16828, USA	Mathematician
Andrews, George E, II 10195 Overhill Dr, Santa Ana CA 92705, USA	Football Player
Andrews, Giuseppe 1208 Strickland Dr, Austin TX 78748, USA	Actor, Director, Writer
Andrews, Jessica Creative Artists Agency, 2000 Ave of Stars, #100, Los Angeles CA 90067 USA	Singer
Andrews, John H Colleton, Cargo Road, Orange NSW 2800, Australia	Architect
Andrews, John R 9292 Gordon Ave, La Habra CA 90631, USA	Baseball Player
Andrews, Julie E PO Box 491668, Los Angeles CA 90049, USA	Actress, Singer
Andrews, Lee Mars Talent, 27 L'Ambiance Court, Nanuet NY 10954, USA	Singer
Andrews, Mark 3354 165th Ave SE, Mapleton ND 58059, USA	Senator, ND
Andrews, Michael J (Mike) Jimmy Fund, 10 Brookline Place W, #600, Brookline MA 02445, USA	Baseball Player
Andrews, Naveen Gersh Agency, 9465 Wilshire Blvd, #600, Beverly Hills CA 90212 USA	Actor
Andrews, Patricia (Patty) 9823 Aldea Ave, Northridge CA 91325, USA	Singer (Andrews Sisters)
Andrews, Real Abrams Artists, 275 7th Ave, #2600, New York NY 10001 USA	Actor
Andrews, Robert G P Putnam's Sons, 375 Hudson St, New York NY 10014 USA	Writer
Andrews, Robert F 5404 Sharon Trail, Lakeland FL 33810, USA	Religious Leader
Andrews, Robert P (Rob) 1280 Mountbatten Court, Concord CA 94518, USA	Baseball Player
Andrews, Theresa 2004 Homewood Road, Annapolis MD 21402, USA	Swimmer
Andrews, Tina Sharp Assoc, 1516 N Fairfax Ave, Los Angeles CA 90046, USA	Actress
Andrews, V C Pocket Books, 1230 Ave of Americas, New York NY 10020 USA	Writer
Andrews, William D (Billy), Jr PO Box 703, Clinton LA 70722, USA	Football Player
Andreychuck, Dave 18130 Longwater Run Dr, Tampa FL 33647, USA	Ice Hockey Player
Andrie, George J 26356 E Zeerip, Drummond Island MI 49726, USA	Football Player
Andriessen, Louis Nonesuch Records, 75 Rockefeller Plaza, #800, New York NY 10019 USA	Composer

26   V.I.P. Address Book

Androsky, Carol — Actress
Henderson/Hogan, 850 7th Ave, #1003, New York NY 10019 USA
Andruff, Ron — Ice Hockey Player
71 1/2 Irving Place, #1F, New York NY 10003, USA
Andrus, Cecil D — Secretary, Interior; Governor, ID
PO Box 852, Boise ID 83701, USA
Andrusak, Greg — Ice Hockey Player
5240 Highway 3A, Nelson BC V1L 6N6, Canada
Andruzzi, Joseph D (Joe) — Football Player
682 Bellmore Ave, East Meadow NY 11554, USA
Andsnes, Leif Ove — Concert Pianist
I M G Artists, Hogarth Business Park, Chiswick, London W4 2TH, England
Andujar, Joaquin — Baseball Player
Ave L Amiama Tio #47, San Pedro de Macoris, Dominican Republic
Andy, Horace — Singer, Songwriter
Agency Group Ltd, 1880 Century Park E, #711, Los Angeles CA 90067 USA
Ane, Charles T (Charlie), III — Football Player
Punahou School, 1601 Punahou St, Honolulu HI 96822, USA
Anemone — Actress
82 Rue Bonaparte, 75006 Paris, France
Angarano, Michael — Actor
United Talent Agency, 9336 Civic Center Dr, Beverly Hills CA 90210 USA
Angel Arango, Juan Pablo — Soccer Player
Chivas U S A, Home Depot Center, 18400 S Avalon Blvd, Carson CA 90746, USA
Angel, Alisha — Actress
Lisa Ann Talent, 17547 Ventura Blvd, #305, Encino CA 91316, USA
Angel, Ashley Parker — Singer (O-Town)
Mavrick Artists Agency, 6100 Wilshire Blvd, #550, Los Angeles CA 90048, USA
Angel, Criss — Illusionist
Renaissance Literary & Talent, PO Box 17379, Beverly Hills CA 90209, USA
Angel, Heather H — Photographer
Highways, 6 Vicarage Hill, Farnham, Surrey GU9 8HJ, England
Angel, J Roger P — Astronomer
University of Arizona, Stewart Observatory, 933 N Cherry Ave, Tucson AZ 85721, USA
Angel, Marie — Opera Singer
Allied Artists, 42 Montpelier Square, London SW7 1JZ, England
Angel, Vanessa — Actress, Model
Media Artists Group, 8255 Sunset Blvd, Los Angeles CA 90046, USA
Angela, Sharon — Actress
C E S D, 257 Park Ave S, #950, New York NY 10010 USA
Angelil, Rene — Actress, Writer
United Talent Agency, 9336 Civic Center Dr, Beverly Hills CA 90210 USA
Angelini, Fiorenzo Cardinal — Religious Leader
Via Anneo Lucano 47, 00136 Rome, Italy
Angell, Wayne D — Financier, Government Official
1600 N Oak St, Arlington VA 22209, USA
Angeloni, Umberto — Fashion Executive
Brioni's Srl, Via Barberini 79, 00187 Rome, Italy
Angelou, Maya — Writer
3240 Valley Road, #MB9, Winston-Salem NC 27106, USA
Angelyne — Actress, Artist, Model
Angelyne Mgmt, 5670 Wilshire Blvd, #2200, Los Angeles CA 90036, USA
Angerer, Paul — Composer
Esteplatz 3/26, 1030 Vienna, Austria
Angerer, Peter — Biathlete
Wagenau 2, 17326 Hammer, Germany
Angerer, Tobias — Cross Country Skier
Meet Success, Auf der Eierwiese 1, 82031 Gruenwald, Germany
Angier, Natalie M — Journalist
New York Times, Editorial Dept, 229 W 43rd St, New York NY 10036, USA
Anglade, Jean-Hughes — Actor
Intertalent, 48 Rue Gay Lussac, 75005 Paris, France
Angle, Kurt S — Freestyle Wrestler
227 Lakeview Dr, Coraopolis PA 15108, USA
Anglim, Philip — Actor
2404 Grand Canal, Venice CA 90291, USA
Anglin, Jennifer — Actress
Geddes Agency, 8430 Santa Monica Blvd, #201, West Hollywood CA 90069 USA
Angula, Nahas — Prime Minister, Namibia
Premier's Office, South Parliament Building, Windhoek 9000, Namibia
Angulo, Richard — Football Player
4801 W Libby St, Glendale AZ 85308, USA
Anholt, Darrell — Ice Hockey Player
4935 49th St, Hughenden, AL T0B 2E0, Canada
Anikulap-Kuti, Femi — Singer, Songwriter
M C A Records, 70 Universal City Plaza, Universal City CA 91608 USA
Anissina, Marina V — Figure Skater
Sports de Glace Federation, 35 Rue Felicien David, 75016 Paris, France
Aniston, Jennifer — Actress
Todd Shemarya Artists, 2550 Outpost Dr, Los Angeles CA 90068 USA
Aniston, John — Actor
Geddes Agency, 8430 Santa Monica Blvd, #201, West Hollywood CA 90069 USA
Anjou, Danielle — Sculptor
Voila Gallery, 518 N La Brea Ave, Los Angeles CA 90036, USA
Anka, Paul — Singer, Songwriter, Actor
2674 Stafford Road, Thousand Oaks CA 91361, USA
Ankiel, Richard A (Rick) — Baseball Player
126 Sandpiper Circle, Jupiter FL 33477, USA
Ankvab, Alexander Z — Prime Minister, Abkhazia
Prime Minister's Office, People's Assembly, Sukhumi, Abkhazia, Georgia
Anlyan, William G — Surgeon
Duke Medical Center, 100 Seeley Mudd Building, #109, Durham NC 27710, USA
Annable, Dave — Actor
Creative Artists Agency, 2000 Ave of Stars, #100, Los Angeles CA 90067 USA
Annan, Kofi A — Secretary-General, United Nations
799 United Nations Plaza, New York NY 10017, USA

Annaud, Jean-Jacques — Director
9 Rue Guenegard, 75006 Paris, France

Anne — Princess, England
Buckingham Palace, London SW1 1AA, England

Anne of Bourbon-Palma — Queen, Romania
Villa Serena, 77 Chemin Louis-Degallier, 1290 Versoix-Geneva, Switzerland

Annenberg, Wallis — Publisher
10273 Century Woods Dr, Los Angeles CA 90067, USA

Annett, Chloe — Actress
Spotlight, 7 Leicester Place, London WC2H 7RJ, England

Annis, Francesca — Actress
I C M Partners, Marlborough House, 10 Earlham St, #300, London WC2H 9LNP, England

Ann-Margret — Actress, Singer, Dancer
2707 Benedict Canyon Road, Beverly Hills CA 90210, USA

Anno, Sam S — Football Player
12934 Ferndale Ave, Los Angeles CA 90066, USA

Anosike, Nkolika N (Nicky) — Basketball Player
Los Angeles Sparks, 888 S Figueroa St, #2010, Los Angeles CA 90017 USA

Anouk — Singer
Artmedia, 20 Ave Rapp, 75007 Paris, France

Anozie, Nonso — Actor
Garricks-Megan Willis, Angel House, 76 Mallinson Road, London SW11 1BN, England

Ansa, Tina McElroy — Writer
Jonee Ansa, 422 Sea Breeze Dr, PO Box 20602, Saint Simons Island GA 31522, USA

Ansara, Michael — Actor
4624 Park Mirasol, Calabasas CA 91302, USA

Ansari, Anousheh — Tourist Cosmonaut
Prodea Systems, 6101 W Plano Parkway, #210, Plano TX 75093, USA

Ansari, Aziz — Actor, Comedian
3 Arts Entertainment, 9460 Wilshire Blvd, #700, Beverly Hills CA 90212 USA

Anschutz, Philip F — Businessman, Sports Executive
Qwest Communications, 1801 California St, #5200, Denver CO 80202, USA

Ansell, Jonathan — Singer
Agency Group Ltd, 142 W 57th St, #600, New York NY 10019 USA

Anselmo, Philip H — Singer (Pantera)
5869 Colbert St, New Orleans LA 70124, USA

Ansip, Andrus — Prime Minister, Estonia
Prime Minister's Office, Stenbocki Maja, Rahukohtu 3, 15161 Tallinn, Estonia

Anspach, Susan — Actress
11734 Wilshire Blvd, #207, Los Angeles CA 90025, USA

Anspaugh, David — Director
I C M Partners, 10250 Constellation Blvd, #900, Los Angeles CA 90067 USA

Ant — Actor, Comedian
Mavrick Artists Agency, 1680 N Vine St, #802, Hollywood CA 90028, USA

Ant, Adam — Singer, Guitarist
Tony Denton Promotions, PO Box 2839, London W1K 5LE, England

Antal, Nimrod — Director, Actor, Writer
Creative Artists Agency, 2000 Ave of Stars, #100, Los Angeles CA 90067 USA

Antes, Horst — Artist
Hohenbergstr 11, 76228 Karlsruhe (Wolfartsweier), Germany

Anthony, Carl — Environmentalist
Harvard University, Kennedy Government School, Cambridge MA 02138, USA

Anthony, Carmelo F — Basketball Player
New York Knicks, Madison Square Garden, 2 Penn Plaza, New York, NY 10121 USA

Anthony, Eric T — Baseball Player
42 Fosters Court, Sugar Land TX 77479, USA

Anthony, Gregory C (Greg) — Basketball Player
63 Corso Italia, Freehold NJ 07728, USA

Anthony, Lysette — Actress
Belfield & Ward, 80-81 Saint Martin's Lane, London WC2N 4AA, England

Anthony, Marc — Singer, Actor, Songwriter
Marc Anthony Productions, 146 W 57th St, #38C, New York NY 10019, USA

Anthony, Piers — Writer
PO Box 2289, Inverness FL 34451, USA

Anthony, Ray — Orchestra Leader, Trumpeter
9288 Kinglet Dr, Los Angeles CA 90069, USA

Anthony, Reidel C — Football Player
PO Box 23, South Bay FL 33493, USA

Anti, Michael (Mike) — Marksman
13383 Honey Run Way, Colorado Springs CO 80921, USA

Antin, Steve — Actor, Writer
United Talent Agency, 9336 Civic Center Dr, Beverly Hills CA 90210 USA

Antioco, John — Businessman
Blockbuster Inc, 3704 Stratford Ave, Dallas TX 75205, USA

Antoine, Lionel S — Football Player
1455 Glencliff Dr, Dallas TX 75217, USA

Antoine, Marc — Jazz Guitarist
Variety Artists, 793 Higuera St, #6, San Luis Obispo CA 93401 USA

Anton, Alan — Bassist (Cowboy Junkies)
S L Feldman Mgmt, 1505 W 2nd Ave, #200, Vancouver BC V6H 3Y4, Canada

Anton, Susan — Actress, Singer
10300 W Charleston Blvd, #13, Las Vegas NV 89135, USA

Antonakakis, Dimitris — Architect
Atelier 66, Emm Benaki 118, Athens 11473, Greece

Antonakakis, Suzana M — Architect
Atelier 66, Emm Benaki 118, Athens 11473, Greece

Antonelli, Dominic A (Tony) — Astronaut
4106 Oak Blossom Court, Houston TX 77059, USA

Antonelli, Ennio Cardinal — Religious Leader
Archdiocese, Piazza S Giovanni 3, 50129 Florence, Italy

Antonelli, Laura — Actress
Pietrovalle, Via B Buozzi 51, 00197 Rome, Italy

Antonetti, Lorenzo Cardinal — Religious Leader
Patrimony of the Holy See, Palazzo Apostolico, 00120 Vatican City

Antonicheva, Anna — Ballerina
Bolshoi Theater, Teatralnaya Pl 1, 103009 Moscow, Russia

Antonio — Spanish Dancer
Coslada 7, Madrid, Spain
Antonio, James D (Jim) — Actor
Epstein-Wyckoff, 280 S Beverly Dr, #400, Beverly Hills CA 90212 USA
Antonio, Lou — Actor
Actor's Studio, 8341 DeLongpre Ave, West Hollywood CA 90069, USA
Antonova, Lana — Actress
Creative Artists Agency, 2000 Ave of Stars, #100, Los Angeles CA 90067 USA
Antonovich, Mike — Ice Hockey Player
4701 Desmond Beach, Fort Gratiot MI 48059, USA
Antrim, Donald — Writer
Wylie Agency, 250 W 57th St, #2114, New York NY 10107 USA
Antunes, Arnaldo — Singer, Songwriter
Criacao Producao, Tra Santa Leocadia 40, Rio de Janiero 22061-050 Brazil
Antuofermo, Vito — Boxer, Actor
16019 81st St, Howard Beach NY 11414, USA
Anu, Christine — Singer
Robert Barnham Mgmt, 432 Tyagarah Road, Myocum NSW 2481, Australia
Anuszkiewicz, Richard J — Artist
76 Chestnut St, Englewood NJ 07631, USA
Anwar, Gabrielle — Actress
Innovative Artists, 1505 10th St, Santa Monica CA 90401 USA
Aoki, Chieko N — Businesswoman
Westin Hotels, Westin Building, 777 Westchester Ave, West Harrison NY 10604, USA
Aoki, Devon E — Actress, Model
Schiff Co, 8440 Warner Dr, #B1, Culver City CA 90232 USA
Aoki, Isao — Golfer
International Mgmt Group, 1 Erieview Plaza, 1360 E 9th St, Cleveland OH 44114 USA
Aoki, Jun — Architect, Interior Designer
Jun Aoki Assoc, 3-38-11 Jingumae, Shibuyaku, Tokyo 150-0001, Japan
Aoki, Satoshi — Businessman
Honda Motor Co, 2-1-1 Minami-Aoyama, Minatoku, Tokyo 107-8556, Japan
Aoki, Steve — DJ Musician
Ministry of Sound, 103 Gaunt St, London SE1 6DP, England
Aouita, Said — Track Athlete
Abdejil Bencheikh, 9 Rue Soivissi, Loubira, Rabat, Morocco
Aoun, Michel N — Prime Minister, Lebanon; Army General
Assemble Nationale, Place de L'Etoile, Beirut, Lebanon
Apache Indian — DJ Musician
Mission Control, City Business Center, Lower Road, London SE16 2XB, England
Apap, Gilles — Concert Violinist
Columbia Artists Mgmt Inc, 1790 Broadway, #702, New York NY 10019 USA
Aparicio, Luis E — Baseball Player
Calle 67, #26-82, Maracaibo, Venezuela
Apatow, Judd — Director, Producer, Writer
Apatow Productions, 11788 W Pico Blvd, Los Angeles CA 90064, USA
Apel, Katrin — Biathlete
Suedlung 9, 99330 Grafenroda, Germany
Apiata, Bill H (Willie) — Afghanistan War Army Hero (VC)
Victoria Cross Assn, Old Admiralty Building, London SW1A 2BL, England
Apicella, Lorenzo F — Architect
Pentagram, 11 Needham Road, London W11 2RP, England
Apking, Stephen A — Interior Designer
Skidmore Owings Merrill, 14 Wall St, #2500, New York NY 10005, USA
Apl.De.Ap — Rap Artist (Elephunk, Black Eyed Peas)
Paradigm Agency, 404 W Franklin St, Monterey CA 93940 USA
Apodaca, Raymond S (Jerry) — Governor, NM
6223 Utah Ave NW, Washington DC 20015, USA
Apodaca, Robert J (Bob) — Baseball Player
2999 SW Van Buren Terrace, Port Saint Lucie FL 34953, USA
Apollonia — Model, Actress, Singer
M G A Talent, 269 S Beverly Dr, #1088, Beverly Hills CA 90212, USA
Appadurai, Arjun — Anthropologist
New York University, Steinhardt School, New York, NY 10012, USA
Appel, Deena — Costume Designer
Montana Artists Agency, 7715 W Sunset Blvd, #300, Los Angeles CA 90046, USA
Appel, Jayne — Basketball Player
San Antonio Silver Stars, 1 AT&T Center, San Antonio TX 78219 USA
Appel, Peter — Actor
Hartig-Hilepo Agency, 54 W 21st St, #610, New York NY 10010 USA
Appel, Richard — Producer, Writer
W M E Entertainment, 9601 Wilshire Blvd, #300, Beverly Hills CA 90210 USA
Appelbaum, Ralph — Museum Designer
Ralph Appelbaum Assoc, 88 Pine St, #2900, New York NY 10005, USA
Appelfeld, Aharon — Writer
Wylie Agency, 17 Bedford Square, London WC1B 3JA, England
Appice, Carmine — Drummer (Vanilla Fudge, Cactus)
Enterprise, 1633 Ventura Blvd, #1450, Encino CA 91436, USA
Appier, R Kevin — Baseball Player
30743 Victory Road, Paola KS 66071, USA
Apple, Fiona — Singer, Songwriter
Paradigm Agency, 360 Park Ave, #1600, New York NY 10022 USA
Applebaum, Anne — Writer
Doubleday Press, 1745 Broadway, New York NY 10019 USA
Appleberry, James B — Educator
1400 Willow Ave, #1704, Louisville KY 40204, USA
Appleby, Malcolm A — Artist
Aultberg, Grandtully by Aberfeldy, Perthshire PH15 2QU, England
Appleby, Shiri — Actress
John Carrabino Mgmt, 5900 Wilshire Blvd, #406, Los Angeles CA 90036 USA
Appleby, Steven — Cartoonist, Writer
Bloomsbury Publishing, 36 Soho Square, London W1D 3Q4, England
Appleby, Stuart — Golfer
9724 Chestnut Ridge Dr, Windermere FL 34786, USA
Applegate, Christina — Actress
Management 360, 9111 Wilshire Blvd, Beverly Hills CA 90210 USA

A

Antonio - Applegate

Applegate, Debby — Writer
125 Lawrence St, New Haven CT 06511, USA

Applegate, Eddie — Actor
6711 Tampa Ave, Reseda CA 91335, USA

Applegate, Jodi — Commentator
News 12 Long Island, 1 Media Crossways, Woodbury NY 11797, USA

Applegate, K A — Writer
Scholastic Press, 555 Broadway, New York NY 10012 USA

Applegate, Kendall — Actress
Greene Assoc, 1901 Ave of Stars, #130, Los Angeles CA 90067 USA

Appleton, Marc — Architect
Appleton Assoc, 1556 17th St, Santa Monica CA 90404, USA

Appleton, Steve — Singer, Songwriter
Agency Group Ltd, 142 W 57th St, #600, New York NY 10019 USA

Apps, Gillian M — Ice Hockey Player
Team Canada, 2424 University Dr NW, Calgary AB T2N 3Y9, Canada

Apps, Sylvanus M (Syl), Jr — Ice Hockey Player
36 Pennock Crescent, Markham ON L3R 3M4, Canada

Aprea, John — Actor
Mavrick Artists Agency, 6100 Wilshire Blvd, #550, Los Angeles CA 90048, USA

April, Johnny — Bassist (Staind)
The Firm, 2049 Century Park E, #2550, Los Angeles CA 90067 USA

April, Renee — Costume Designer
Sandra Marsh Assoc, 9150 Wilshire Blvd, #220, Beverly Hills CA 90212 USA

Apt, Jerome (Jay) — Astronaut
4 Shadycourt Dr, Pittsburgh PA 15232, USA

Apted, Michael D — Director
1126 Indiana Ave, Venice CA 90291, USA

Aqualung — Singer, Songwrigter
First Column Mgmt, 60 Compton Road, Brighton BN1 5AN, England

Aqueduct — Singer, Keyboardist, Guitarist
Aero Booking, 8008 Greenwood Ave N, #3, Seattle WA 98103, USA

Aquilino, Thomas J, Jr — Judge
US Court of International Trade, 1 Federal Plaza, New York NY 10278, USA

Aquino Carmona, Javier I — Soccer Player
Federacion de Futbol, Colima 373 Colonia Roma, Delegacion Cuauhtemoc Mexico DF 06700, Mexico

Aquino, Amy — Actress
TalentWorks, 3500 W Olive Ave, #1400, Burbank CA 91505 USA

Aquino, Luis A C — Baseball Player
17201 Collins Ave, #606, Sunny Isles Beach FL 33160, USA

Arabo, Claude — Fencer
9 Rue Franquet, 75015 Paris, France

Arad, Michael — Architect
Handel Architects, 150 Varick St, #800, New York NY 10013, USA

Arad, Ron — Architect
Arad Assoc, 62 Chalk Farm Road, London NW1 8AN, England

Aragall Garriga, Giacomo — Opera Singer
Stafford Law Assoc, 6 Barham Close, Weybridge, Surrey KT1 9PR, England

Aragones, Sergio — Cartoonist (Mad Comics)
PO Box 696, Ojai CA 93024, USA

Araguz, Leo J — Football Player
3201 Araguz St, Harlingen TX 78552, USA

Araiza Herrera, Armando — Actor
Televisa, Blvd A Lopez Mateos 232, Colonia San Angel, DF CP 01060, Mexico

Araiza, Francisco — Opera Singer
Kuntsler Mgmt, M Kursidem, Tal 15, 80331 Munich, Germany

Arakawa, Shizuka — Figure Skater
International Skating Center, 1375 Hopemeadow St, Simsbury CT 06070, USA

Araki, Gregg — Director, Writer
KillerMoxie Management, 5890 W Jefferson Blvd, #J, Los Angeles CA 90016, USA

Arana, Tomas — Actor
Affirmative Entertainment, 425 N Robertson Blvd, Los Angeles CA 90048, USA

Aranauskas, Leonas S — Architect
Glavmozarchitectura, Mayakovsky Square 1, 103001 Moscow, Russia

Arango, Juan Carlos — Actor
Gabriel Blanco, Rio Balsas 35-32, Colonia Cuauhtemoc DF 6500, Mexico

Ararktsyan, Babken V — Supreme Council Chairman, Armenia
3 Tamanian St, #35, 375009 Yerevan, Armenia

Araskog, Rand V — Businessman
I T T Corp, 1330 Ave of Americas, New York NY 10019, USA

Arau, Alfonso — Director
Glick Agency, 1321 7th St, #203, Santa Monica CA 90401 USA

Araujo Razo, Nestor A — Soccer Player
Federacion de Futbol, Colima 373 Colonia Roma, Delegacion Cuauhtemoc Mexico DF 06700, Mexico

Araujo, Ana Paula — Model
Next Model Mgmt, 188 Rue de Rivoli, 75001 Paris, France

Araujo, Serafim Fernandes de Cardinal — Religious Leader
Curia Metropolitana, Av Brasil 2079, 30140-002 Belo Horizonte MG, Brazil

Arbanas, Frederick V (Fred) — Football Player
3350 SW Hook Road, Lees Summit MO 64082, USA

Arbatt, Alexandre — Actor
Artmedia, 20 Ave Rapp, 75007 Paris, France

Arber, Werner — Nobel Medicine Laureate
Klingelbergstr 70, 4056 Basel, Switzerland

Arbour, Alan (Al) — Ice Hockey Player, Coach, Executive
2071 Harbour Links Dr, Longboat Key FL 34228, USA

Arbour, Louise — Government Official, Canada; Judge
130 Queen St W, Toronto ON M5H 2N5, Canada

Arbulu Galliani, Guillermo — Prime Minister, Peru; Army General
Prime Minister's Office, Urb Corpac, Calle 1 Oeste S/N, Lima 27, Peru

Arbus, Alan — Actor
2208 N Beverly Glen, Los Angeles CA 90077, USA

Arcand, Denys — Director
Agence Goodwin, 839 E Sherbrooke St, #200, Montreal QC H2L 1K6, Canada

Arce, Jorge A — Boxer
Top Rank, 3908 Howard Hughes Highway, #580, Las Vegas NV 89169, USA

Arcgitzel, David — Navy Admiral
Commander, Naval Air Systems Command, Patuxent River MD 20670 USA
Archambault, Lee J — Astronaut
4318 Sweet Cicely Court, Houston TX 77059, USA
Archambeau, Lester M — Football Player
10520 Montclair Way, Duluth GA 30097, USA
Archer of Weston-Super-Mare, Jeffrey H — Government Official, England; Writer
Peninsula Heights, 93 Albert Embankment, London SE1 7TY, England
Archer, Anne — Actress
Kritzer Levine Wilkins Griffin, 11872 La Grange Ave, #100, Los Angeles CA 90025 USA
Archer, Dave — Artist
1541 Buckhorn Road, Roseburg OR 97470, USA
Archer, David — Football Player
3831 Upland Dr, Marietta GA 30066, USA
Archer, Glenn L, Jr — Judge
US Court of Appeals, 717 Madison Place NW, Washington DC 20439, USA
Archer, Jeffrey — Writer
Curtis Brown Group, Haymarket House, 28-29 Haymarket, #500, London SW1Y 4SP, England , USA
Archer, Robyn — Actress, Songwriter, Director
Rick Raftos Mgmt, Box 445, Paddington NSW 2021, Australia
Archibald, David (Dave) — Ice Hockey Player
PO Box 2108, Saint Sardis Main, Chilliwack BC V2R 1A6, Canada
Archibald, Jane — Opera Singer
I M G Artists, Hogarth Business Park, Chiswick, London W4 2TH, England
Archibald, Nathaniel (Nate) — Basketball Player
2720 Grand Concourse, #218, Bronx NY 10458, USA
Archibald, Nolan D — Businessman
Black & Decker Corp, 701 E Joppa Road, Towson MD 21286, USA
Archipowski, Ken — Singer (Randy & the Rainbows)
Brothers Mgmt, 141 Dunbar Ave, Fords NJ 08863 USA
Archuleta, Adam J — Football Player
1237 W Galveston St, Chandler AZ 85224, USA
Archuleta, David J — Singer, Keyboardist, Guitarist
Arch Consulting Group, 340 W Whitney Ave, Salt Lake City UT 84115, USA
Arcia Orta, Jose R — Baseball Player
7325 NW 3rd St, Miami FL 33126, USA
Arcieri, Leila — Actress
Luber Rocklin Entertainment, 8530 Wilshire Blvd, #555, Beverly Hills CA 90211 USA
Arciero, Frank — Auto Racing Executive
Arciero Racing, 1901 Nancita Circle, Placentia CA 92870, USA
Arcuri, Manuela — Actress, Model
Condominio L'Orologio, Via Isonzo Int 25, 04100 Latina, Italy
Arcuri, Robin — Model
17128 Colima Road, #411, Hacienda Heights CA 91745, USA
Ard, William D (Bill) — Football Player
41 Vail Lane, Watchung NJ 07069, USA
Ardant, Fanny — Actress
Les Visiteurs du Soir, 40 Rue de la Folie Regnault, 75011 Paris, France
Arden, Jann — Singer, Songwriter
Shore Fire Media, 32 Court St, #1600, Brooklyn NY 11201 USA
Arden, Toni — Singer
3434 75th St, Jackson Heights NY 11372, USA
Arditi, Pierre — Actor
Voyez Mon Agent, 20 Ave Rapp, 75007 Paris, France
Ardito Barletta Vallarino, Nicolas — President, Panama
PO Box 7737, Panama City 9, Panama
Arditti, Irvine — Concert Violinist
Lattidue Arts, 109 Boul Saint-Joseph Quest, Montreal PA H2T 2P7, Canada
Ardoin, Daniel W (Danny) — Baseball Player
1524 Lee St, Ville Platte LA 70586, USA
Arena, Bruce — Soccer Player, Coach
Los Angeles Galaxy, Home Depot Center, 18400 Avalon Blvd, Carson CA 90746 USA
Arena, Tina — Singer
Harbour Agency, 135 Forbes St, Wooloomooloo NSW 2011, Australia
Arenas, Gilbert J — Basketball Player
4550 Gable Dr, Encino CA 91316, USA
Arenas, L Joseph (Joe) — Football Player
780 W Bay Area Blvd, #1215, Webster TX 77598, USA
Arend, Geoffrey — Actor
United Talent Agency, 9336 Civic Center Dr, Beverly Hills CA 90210 USA
Arend, Jeff — Drag Racing Driver, Owner
Arend/Smith Racing, 2 Mallingham Court, Toronto ON M2N 6C4, Canada
Arens, Moshe — Government Official, Israel
49 Hagderot, Savyon, Israel
Areshenkoff, Ron — Ice Hockey Player
1701 1st St, Estevan SK S4A 0H5, Canada
Arestrup, Niels — Actor
Voyez Mon Agent, 20 Ave Rapp, 75007 Paris, France
Argent, Rod — Keyboardist (Zombies)
Gen-X Entertainment, PO Box 140, Cedar MN 55011, USA
Argento, Asia — Actress, Director
Cineart, 36 Rue de Ponthieu, 75008 Paris, France
Argento, Dario — Director
A D C, Via Balamonti 2, Rome, Italy
Argento, Dominick — Composer
University of Minnesota, Music Dept, Ferguson Hall, Minneapolis MN 55455, USA
Argerich, Martha — Concert Pianist
Jacques Thelen Agence, 15 Ave Montaigne, 75008 Paris, France
Argos, Eddie — Singer (Art Brut)
Coda Agency, 229 Shoreditch High St, London E1 6PJ, England
Argott, Don — Director, Producer, Cinematogapher
9.14 Pictures, 1804 Chestnut St, #2, Philadelphia PA 19104, USA
Ariail, Robert — Editorial Cartoonist
The State, Editorial Dept, PO Box 1333, Columbia SC 29202, USA
Arianda, Nina — Actress
I C M Partners, 10250 Constellation Blvd, #900, Los Angeles CA 90067 USA

Arias Sanchez - Armstead

Arias Sanchez, Oscar	Nobel Laureate; President, Costa Rica
Arias Foundation for Peace, Apdo 8-6410-1000, San Jose, Costa Rica	
Arias, Alejandro (Alex)	Baseball Player
37 Edmund Road, West Park FL 33023, USA	
Arias, Moises	Actor
Greene Assoc, 1901 Ave of Stars, #130, Los Angeles CA 90067 USA	
Arias, Yancey	Actor
Global Artists Agency, 6253 Hollywood Blvd, #508, Los Angeles CA 90028 USA	
Arienti, Luigi	Cyclist
Via Tardelle Frasche 80, 2003 Desio, Italy	
Arigoni, Dulio	Chemist
Im Glockenacker 42, 8053 Zurich, Switzerland	
Arii, Takendo	Architect
1117 W Arbor Dr, San Diego CA 92103, USA	
Arima, Akito	Physicist
Physical Research Institute, Hirosawa 2-1, Wakoshi, Saitama 351-01, Japan	
Arinze, Francis Cardinal	Religious Leader
Pontifical Council for Inter-Religious Dialogue, 00120 Vatican City	
Arison, M Micky	Businessman, Basketball Executive
Carnival Corp, 3655 NW 87th Ave, Doral FL 33178, USA	
Ariyoshi, George R	Governor, HI
745 Fort St, #500, Honolulu HI 96813, USA	
Ariza, Trevor A	Basketball Player
1111 S Grand Ave, #PH 2, Los Angeles CA 90015, USA	
Arizmendi, Yareli	Actress
C E S D, 10635 Santa Monica Blvd, #130, Los Angeles CA 90025 USA	
Arkhipov, Denis	Ice Hockey Player
716 Sweet Cherry Court, Nashville TN 37215, USA	
Arkin, Adam	Actor
3531 Coldwater Canyon Ave, Studio City CA 91604, USA	
Arkin, Adam	Physical Chemist
University of California, Physical Chemistry Dept, Berkeley CA 94720, USA	
Arkin, Alan W	Actor
Principal Entertainment, 1964 Westwood Blvd, #400, Los Angeles CA 90025 USA	
Arkin, Jordana	Producer
W M E Entertainment, 9601 Wilshire Blvd, #300, Beverly Hills CA 90210 USA	
Arkush, Allan	Director, Producer
Paradigm Agency, 360 N Crescent Dr, North Building, Beverly Hills CA 90210 USA	
Arlauckas, Joseph (Joe)	Basketball Player
917 Night Heron Dr, Mount Pleasant SC 29464, USA	
Arlen, Michael J	Writer
New Yorker, Editorial Dept, 4 Times Square, Basement C1B, New York NY 10036 USA	
Arlin, Stephen R (Steve)	Baseball Player
6819 Claremore Ave, San Diego CA 92120, USA	
Armacost, Michael H	Government Official, Diplomat
9425 Tarnberry Dr, Potomac MD 20854, USA	
Armadroff, Taft	Astronomer
W M Keck Observatory, 65-1120 Mamalahoa Highway, Kamuela HI 96743, USA	
Armani, Giorgio	Fashion Designer
Via Borgonuovo 21, 20121 Milan, Italy	
Armano, Mario	Bobsled Athlete
Olympic Committee, Foro Italico, Largo Lauro de Bosis 15, 00135 Rome, Italy	
Armant, Ivonne	Model, Actress
Tayrona Entertainment Group, 9663 Santa Monica Blvd, #623, Beverly Hills CA 90210, USA	
Armaou, Lindsay	Singer (B*Witched)
Clintons, 55 Drury Lane, Covent Garden, London WC2B 5SQ, England	
Armas, Antonio R (Tony)	Baseball Player
Calle Las Mercedes 37, Puerto Piritu, Venezuela	
Armas, Chris	Soccer Player
Chicago Fire, 700 S Harlem Ave, Bridgeview IL 60455 USA	
Armatrading, Joan	Singer, Songwriter
J A B A ,72 New Bond St, London W1Y 9DD, England	
Armbrister, Edison R (Ed)	Baseball Player
McQuay St, Box 2003, Nassau, Bahamas, West Indies	
Armedariz, Pedro, Jr	Actor
Diamond Artists, 9200 W Sunset Blvd, #701, West Hollywood CA 90069 USA	
Armenante, Jillian	Actress
Framework Entertainment, 9057 Nemo St, #C, West Hollywood CA 90069 USA	
Armerding, Hudson T	Educator
780 Schick Road, #29W, Bartlett IL 60103, USA	
Armesto, Sebastian	Actor
Curtis Brown Group, 28-29 Haymarket St, #500, London SW1Y 4SP, England	
Armey, Richard K	Representative, TX
Citizens for a Sound Economy, 1775 Pennsylvania Ave NW, Washington DC 20006, USA	
Armfield, Diana M	Artist
10 High Park, Kew, Richmond, Surrey TW9 4BH, England	
Armiliato, Marco	Conductor
I M G Artists, Hogarth Business Park, Chiswick, London W4 2TH, England	
Armisen, Fred	Actor, Comedian
W M E Entertainment, 9601 Wilshire Blvd, #300, Beverly Hills CA 90210 USA	
Armitage, Alison	Actress, Model
9220 W Sunset Blvd, #305, West Hollywood CA 90069, USA	
Armitage, George	Director, Producer, Writer
Gersh Agency, 9465 Wilshire Blvd, #600, Beverly Hills CA 90212 USA	
Armitage, Karole	Choreographer, Dancer
350 W 21st St, New York NY 10011, USA	
Armitage, Richard	Actor
United Agents, 12-26 Lexington St, London W1F 0LE, England	
Armitstead, Elizabeth M (Lizzie)	Cyclist
MTC (UK) Ltd, 71 Gloucester Place, London W1U 8JW, England	
Armour, Justin H	Football Player
8 Crystal Park Place, #B, Manitou Springs CO 80829, USA	
Armour, Thomas D (Tommy), III	Golfer
4211 Saint Andrews Blvd, Irving TX 75038, USA	
Armstead, Jessie W	Football Player
1316 Mill Stream Dr, Dallas TX 75232, USA	

Armstead, Ray — Track Athlete
7953 Bloom Dr, Saint Louis MO 63133, USA

Armstrong, A James — Religious Leader
Broadway Methodist Church, 1100 W 42nd St, #210, Indianapolis IN 46208, USA

Armstrong, Adger, Jr — Football Player
6403 Paddington St, Houston TX 77085, USA

Armstrong, Alex — Actor, Comedian
Rights House, 34-43 Russell St, London WC2B 5HA, England

Armstrong, Alun — Actor
Markham & Froggatt, Julian House, 4 Windmill St, London W1P 1HF, England

Armstrong, Ami — Producer, Director, Writer
United Talent Agency, 9336 Civic Center Dr, Beverly Hills CA 90210 USA

Armstrong, Anthony — Guitarist (Red)
Paradigm Agency, 404 W Franklin St, Monterey CA 93940 USA

Armstrong, Benjamin R (B J) — Basketball Player, Executive
1550 Hawthorne Lane, Highland Park IL 60035, USA

Armstrong, Bess — Actress
Vox Inc, 6420 Wilshire Blvd, #1080, Los Angeles CA 90048 USA

Armstrong, Billie Joe — Singer, Guitarist (Green Day)
5652 Florence Terrace, Oakland CA 94611, USA

Armstrong, Brandon S — Basketball Player
New Jersey Nets, 390 Murray Hill Parkway, East Rutherford NJ 07073 USA

Armstrong, Bruce C — Football Player
12543 Brookwood Court, Davie FL 33330, USA

Armstrong, Clay M — Physiologist
University of Pennsylvania Medical School, 3400 Spruce, Philadelphia PA 19104, USA

Armstrong, Craig — Composer
First Artists Mgmt, 4764 Park Granada, #210, Calabasas CA 91302 USA

Armstrong, Curtis — Actor
Marshak/Zachary Co, 8840 Wilshire Blvd, #100, Beverly Hills CA 90211 USA

Armstrong, Darrell E — Basketball Player
337 Broadmoor Way, McDonough GA 30253, USA

Armstrong, Deborah (Debbie) — Alpine Skier
PO Box 770925, Steamboat Springs CO 80477, USA

Armstrong, Derek — Ice Hockey Player
873 8th St, Manhattan Beach CA 90266, USA

Armstrong, George E — Ice Hockey Player
22 Saint Cuthbert's Road, East York ON M4G 1V1, Canada

Armstrong, Gillian — Director
Creative Artists Agency, 2000 Ave of Stars, #100, Los Angeles CA 90067 USA

Armstrong, Jack W — Baseball Player
272 E River Park Dr, Jupiter FL 33477, USA

Armstrong, Kerry — Actress
Barbara Leane Mgmt, 261 Miller St, North Sydney NSW 2060, Australia

Armstrong, Kit — Concert Pianist
I C M Artists, 40 W 57th St, #1800, New York NY 10019 USA

Armstrong, Kristin — Cyclist
455 E Cave Court, Boise ID 83702, USA

Armstrong, Lance — Cyclist
Capital Sports & Entertainment, 300 W 6th Street, #2150, Austin TX 78701, USA

Armstrong, Linda — Actress
Associated International Mgmt, Fairfax House, Fulwood Place, London WC1V 6HU, England

Armstrong, M Tate — Basketball Player
14704 Westbury Road, Rockville MD 20853, USA

Armstrong, Matthew John — Actor
Don Buchwald/Fortitude, 6500 Wilshire Blvd, #2200, Los Angeles CA 90048 USA

Armstrong, Michael D (Mike) — Baseball Player
525 Ashbrook Court, Athens GA 30605, USA

Armstrong, Neil — Ice Hockey Referee
1169 Sherwood Trail, Sarnia ON N7V 2H3, Canada

Armstrong, Neil F — Football Player, Coach
312 Lakewood Dr, Roanoke TX 76262, USA

Armstrong, Otis — Football Player
7183 S Newport St, Denver CO 80220, USA

Armstrong, Randy — Bassist (Red)
Paradigm Agency, 404 W Franklin St, Monterey CA 93940 USA

Armstrong, Raymond L (Trace) — Football Player
422 SW 88th Terrace, Gainesville FL 32607, USA

Armstrong, Rob — Singer, Cittern Player (Tarras)
Rounder Records, 1 Rounder Way, Burlington MA 01803 USA

Armstrong, Robb — Cartoonist (Jump Start)
United Feature Syndicate, PO Box 5610, Cincinnati OH 45201 USA

Armstrong, Robin L — Physicist
383 Ellis Park Road, #383-303, Toronto ON M6S 5B2, Canada

Armstrong, Rowland C O (Rolle) — Musician (Faithless)
Helter Skelter, 347-353 Chiswick High Road, London W4 4HS, England

Armstrong, Russell P — Vietnam War Marine Corps Hero
425 Bench Road, Fallon NV 89406, USA

Armstrong, Sheila A — Opera, Concert Singer
Harvesters, Tilford Road, Hindhead, Surrey GU26 6SQ, England

Armstrong, Spence M — Air Force General
9120 Belvoir Woods Parkway, #117, Fort Belvoir VA 22060, USA

Armstrong, T Robert (Bob) — Basketball Player
6802 Packer Dr NE, Belmont MI 49306, USA

Armstrong, Thomas — Auto Racing Driver
PacWest Racing Group, PO Box 1717, Bellevue WA 98009, USA

Armstrong, Thomas H W — Concert Organist
1 East St, Olney, Bucks MK46 4AP, England

Armstrong, Timothy L (Tim) — Guitarist (Rancid)
Leave Home Booking, 10 W Broadway, #608, Salt Lake City UT 84101, USA

Armstrong, Tom — Cartoonist (Marvin)
North American Syndicate, 235 E 45th St, New York NY 10017 USA

Armstrong, Ty — Golfer
11529 Kensington Dr, Eden Prairie MN 55347, USA

Armstrong, Valorie — Actress
Contemporary Artists, 610 Santa Monica Blvd, #202, Santa Monica CA 90401 USA

Armstrong, Vaughn — Actor
1903 Apex Ave, Los Angeles CA 90039, USA
Armstrong, Victor M (Vic) — Actor, Stuntman
Gersh Agency, 9465 Wilshire Blvd, #600, Beverly Hills CA 90212 USA
Armstrong, William — Writer
6 Roland St, Newton MA 02461, USA
Armstrong, William L — Senator, CO
Colorado Christian University, President's Office, Lakewood CO 80226, USA
Arnason, Chuck — Ice Hockey Player
39 Grimston Road, Winnipeg MB R3T 3T2, Canada
Arnaud, Jean-Loup — Government Official, France
55 Ave du Maine, 75014 Paris, France
Arnault, Bernard — Businessman
Moet Hennessy Louis Vuitton, 30 Ave Hoche, 75008 Paris, France
Arnaz, Desi, Jr — Actor
516 Avenue M, Boulder City NV 89005, USA
Arnaz, Lucie — Actress, Singer
PO Box 330, Georgetown CT 06829, USA
Arndt, Denis — Actor
Artist Group Int'l, 150 E 58th St, #1900, New York NY 10155, USA
Arndt, Judith — Cyclist
RC 90 Frankfurt, Kieler Str 9, 15234 Frankfurt/Oder, Germany
Arndt, Michael — Writer
Verve Talent, 9696 Culver Blvd, #301, Culver City CA 90232, USA
Arnelle, Jesse — Basketball Player
400 Urbano Dr, San Francisco CA 94127, USA
Arnesen, Liv — Polar Skier
16560 220th St N, Scandia MN 55073, USA
Arnett, Jon D — Football Player
200 Greenridge Dr, #715, Lake Oswego OR 97035, USA
Arnett, Peter — Commentator, Journalist
ForeignTV.com, 162 5th Ave, #105A, New York NY 10010, USA
Arnett, Will — Actor
W M E Entertainment, 9601 Wilshire Blvd, #300, Beverly Hills CA 90210 USA
Arnette, Jay H — Basketball Player
2 Hillside Court, Austin TX 78746, USA
Arnette, Jeannetta — Actress
Connor Ankrum Assoc, 1680 Vine St, #1016, Los Angeles CA 90028, USA
Arnez, J — Actor, Comedian
I C M Partners, 10250 Constellation Blvd, #900, Los Angeles CA 90067 USA
Arngrim, Alison — Actress
PO Box 98, Tujunga CA 91043, USA
Arnhold, Henry H — Financier
Arnhold & S Bleichroeder, 1345 Ave of Americas, #4300, New York NY 10105, USA
Arniel, Scott — Ice Hockey Player
6 Edmond Muys Place, Winnipeg MB R3P 2R1, Canada
Arning, Lisa — Actress
Chasen Agency, 8899 Beverly Blvd, #716, Los Angeles CA 90048 USA
Arnold, Andrea — Director
Sayle Screen, 11 Jubilee Place, London SW3 3TD, England
Arnold, Andrew — Geneticist
Massachusetts General Hospital, Genetics Dept, Boston MA 02114, USA
Arnold, Anna Bing — Philanthropist
Anna Bing Arnold Foundation, 9700 W Pico Blvd, Los Angeles CA 90035, USA
Arnold, Christopher P (Chris) — Baseball Player
2219 El Capitan Ave, Arcadia CA 91006, USA
Arnold, David — Composer
Coalition Mgmt, 12 Barley Mow Passage, London W4 4PH, England
Arnold, Gary H — Film Critic
5133 N 1st St, Arlington VA 22203, USA
Arnold, James E (Jim) — Football Player
223 Boxwood Dr, Franklin TN 37069, USA
Arnold, Kristine — Singer (Sweethearts of the Rodeo)
2803 Bransford Ave, Nashville TN 37204, USA
Arnold, Morris S — Judge
US Court of Appeals, 600 W Capitol Ave, #224, Little Rock AR 72201, USA
Arnold, Murray — Basketball Coach
Western Kentucky University, Athletic Dept, Bowling Green KY 42101, USA
Arnold, Richard R (Ricky), II — Astronaut
N A S A, Johnson Space Center, 2101 NASA Road, Houston TX 77058 USA
Arnold, Thomas D (Tom) — Actor, Comedian
9958 Kip Dr, Beverly Hills CA 90210, USA
Arnold, Tichina — Actress, Singer
A P A Talent/Literary Agency, 405 S Beverly Dr, #300, Beverly Hills CA 90212 USA
Arnold, Walt — Football Player
8503 La Sala Grande NE, Albuquerque NM 87111, USA
Arnold, Walter (Walt) — Rodeo Steer Roper
PO Box 713, Silverton TX 79257, USA
Arnoldi, Charles A — Artist
721 Hampton Dr, Venice CA 90291, USA
Arnott, Jason — Ice Hockey Player
155 Carondelet Plaza, #302, Saint Louis MO 63105, USA
Arnoul, Francoise — Actress
53 Rue Censier, 75005 Paris, France
Arns, Paulo E Cardinal — Religious Leader
Avenida Higienopolos 890, CP 6778, 01064 Sao Paulo, SP, Brazil
Arnsberg, Bradley J (Brad) — Baseball Player
706 Chaffee Court, Arlington TX 76006, USA
Arnsparger, Bill — Football Coach, Administrator
1574 Pine Needles Lane, Lexington KY 40513, USA
Arnstein, Holly — Singer (Dream)
Bad Boy Entertainment, 1540 Broadway, #3000, New York NY 10036, USA
Arnzen, Robert L (Bob) — Basketball Player
8 Grand Lake Dr, Fort Thomas KY 41075, USA
Aronofsky, Darren — Director
Creative Artists Agency, 2000 Ave of Stars, #100, Los Angeles CA 90067 USA

Arons, Arnold B — Physicist
10313 Lake Shore Blvd NE, Seattle WA 98125, USA
Aronsohn, Lee — Producer, Writer
Paradigm Agency, 360 N Crescent Dr, North Building, Beverly Hills CA 90210 USA
Aronson, David — Artist
137 Brimstone Lane, Sudbury MA 01776, USA
Aronson, Elliot — Psychologist
University of California, Psychology Dept, Santa Cruz CA 95064, USA
Aronson, Judie — Actress
A T M Mgmt, 292 5th Ave, #400, New York NY 10001, USA
Arp, Halton C — Astronomer
Max Planck Physics/Radiology Institute, 84518 Garching Munich, Germany
Arpaia, Donatella — Restaurateur
Anthos Restaurant, 36 W 52nd St, New York NY 10019, USA
Arpaio, Joseph M (Joe) — Law Enforcement Official
102 W Madison St, Phoenix AZ 85003, USA
Arpel, Adrien — Businesswoman
Adrien Arpel Cosmetics, 400 Hackensack Ave, Hackensack NJ 07601, USA
Arpey, Gerard J — Businessman
A M R Corp, 4333 Amon Carter Blvd, Fort Worth TX 76155, USA
Arquette, Alexis — Actress
Innovative Artists, 1505 10th St, Santa Monica CA 90401 USA
Arquette, David — Actor
United Talent Agency, 9336 Civic Center Dr, Beverly Hills CA 90210 USA
Arquette, Patricia — Actress
Gersh Agency, 9465 Wilshire Blvd, #600, Beverly Hills CA 90212 USA
Arquette, Rosanna — Actress
Lovett Mgmt, 1327 Brinkley Ave, Los Angeles CA 90049, USA
Arquez, Gaelle — Opera Singer
I M G Artists, Hogarth Business Park, Chiswick, London W4 2TH, England
Arraras, Maria Celeste — Commentator
Telemundo Network Group, News Dept, 2470 W 8th Ave, Hialeah FL 33010, USA
Arredondo, Rosa — Actress
TalentWorks, 3500 W Olive Ave, #1400, Burbank CA 91505 USA
Arriaga, Guillermo — Director, Writer
United Talent Agency, 9336 Civic Center Dr, Beverly Hills CA 90210 USA
Arrigo, Gerald W (Jerry) — Baseball Player
3740 Red Thorne Dr, Amelia OH 45102, USA
Arrington, Jill — Sportscaster
ESPN-TV, ESPN Plaza, 935 Middle St, Bristol CT 06010 USA
Arrington, LaVar R — Football Player
1514 Cedar Lane Farm Road, Annapolis MD 21409, USA
Arrow, Kenneth J — Nobel Economics Laureate
620 Sand Hill Road, #406C, Palo Alto CA 94304, USA
Arroyo, Bronson A — Baseball Player
23315 Frontier Way, Brooksville FL 34601, USA
Arroyo, Carlos — Basketball Player
1115 NW 126th Court, Miami FL 33182, USA
Arroyo, Fernando — Baseball Player
702 Hampton Woods Lane SW, Vero Beach FL 32962, USA
Arroyo, Harry — Boxer
726 S Salem Road, North Jackson OH 44451, USA
Arroyo, Luis E — Baseball Player
PO Box 354, Penuelas PR 00624, USA
Arroyo, Martina — Opera Singer
Berkshire Concert Artists, 20 Alfred Dr, Pittsfield MA 01201, USA
Artemas, Cole — Cartoonist
1050 Colonial St, Rutland VT 05701, USA
Arterton, Gemma — Actress
Creative Artists Agency, 2000 Ave of Stars, #100, Los Angeles CA 90067 USA
Artest, Ronald W (Ron) — Basketball Player
215 Ward Circle, #200, Brentwood TN 37027, USA
Arteta, Miguel — Director, Producer
W M E Entertainment, 9601 Wilshire Blvd, #300, Beverly Hills CA 90210 USA
Arthur, Darrell — Basketball Player
Memphis Grizzlies, 191 Beale St, Memphis TN 38103 USA
Arthur, Elizabeth — Writer
Bloomsbury LLC, 36 Soho Square, London W1D 3Q4, England
Arthur, Fred — Ice Hockey Player
203-1408 Ernest Ave, London ON N6E 3B2, Canada
Arthur, Michael S (Mike) — Football Player
11271 Terwilligers Vallet Lane, Cincinnati OH 45249, USA
Arthur, Perry — Golfer
7513 Zurich Dr, Plano TX 75025, USA
Arthur, Rebeca — Actress
Epstein-Wyckoff, 280 S Beverly Dr, #400, Beverly Hills CA 90212 USA
Arthur, Stacy Leigh — Model
Playboy Promotions, 2706 Media Center Dr, Los Angeles CA 90065 USA
Arthurs, John C — Basketball Player
1429 Henry Clay Ave, New Orleans LA 70118, USA
Arthurs, Paul (Bonehead) — Guitarist (Oasis)
Ignition Mgmt, 54 Linhope St, London NW1 6HL, England
Arthus-Bertrand, Yann M — Photographer
Altitude, 30 Rue des Favorites, 75015 Paris, France
Artschwager, Richard E — Artist
PO Box 23, Hudson NY 12534, USA
Artsebarsky, Anatoli P — Cosmonaut
Cosmonaut Training Center, Star City, 141160 Zvezdny Gorodok, Moscow Oblast, Russia
Artson, Bradley Shavit — Religious Leader, Rabbi, Educator
American Jewish University, 15600 Mulholland Dr, Los Angeles CA 90077, USA
Artur, Sophie — Actress
Agence Laurence Bagoe, 11 Rue Delambre, 75014 Paris, France
Artzt, Alice J — Concert Guitarist
51 Hawthorne Ave, Princeton NJ 08540, USA
Artzt, Edwin L — Businessman
3849 Hedgewood Dr, Lawrenceburg IN 47025, USA

A	

Arum, Robert (Bob) — Boxing Promoter
36 Gulf Stream Court, Las Vegas NV 89113, USA

Arutyunyan, Gagik G — Prime Minister, Armenia
Prime Minister's Office, Republic Square, Government House 1, 0010 Yerevan, Armenia

Arvesen, Nina — Actress
412 Culver Blvd, #9, Playa del Rey CA 90293, USA

Arvidsson, Margareta — Beauty Queen, Model
Miss Universe Organization, 1370 Ave of Americas, #1600, New York NY 10019 USA

Arvizu, Reginald (Fieldy) — Bassist (Korn)
The Firm, 2049 Century Park E, #2550, Los Angeles CA 90067 USA

Arwady, Meredith — Opera Singer
Columbia Artists Mgmt Inc, 1790 Broadway, #702, New York NY 10019 USA

Arzu Irigoyen, Álvaro E — President, Guatemala
Partida de Avanzada Nacional, 7A Avda 10-38, Guatemala City, Guatamala

Asada, Mao — Figure Skater
Kishi Kinen Taiikukan 1-1-1, Jinnan Shibuyahku, Tokyo 150-8050, Japan

Asano, Tadanobu — Actor
Anore, Ochiai Building, 6-17-15 Jingumae Shibuyuku, #9F, Tokyo 150-0001, Japan

Asante, Amma — Director, Writer
Judy Daish Assoc, 2 Saint Charles Place, London W10 6EG, England

Asawa, Brian — Opera Singer
Askonas Holt, Lincoln House, 300 High Holborn, London WC1V 7JH, England

Asay, Chuck — Cartoonist
Colorado Springs Gazette, 303 S Prospect St, Colorado Springs CO 80903, USA

Asbaek, Pilou — Actor
Lindberg Mgmt, Lavendelstraad 5-7, 1462 Copenhagen K, Denmark

Asbaty, Diandra — Bowler
Kaizen, 100 E 14th St, #1005, Chicago IL 60605, USA

Asbury, Kelly — Animator, Director, Writer
United Talent Agency, 9336 Civic Center Dr, Beverly Hills CA 90210 USA

Asbury, Martin — Cartoonist (Garth)
Stoneworld, Pitch Green, Princes Risborough, Buckinghamshire HP27 9QG, England

Asbury, Richard — WWII Army Air Corps Hero
1104 Kimberly Road, #907, Bettendorf IA 52722, USA

Ascaride, Ariane — Actress
Zelig, 57 Rue Reaumur, 75002 Paris, France

Asch, Peter — Water Polo Player
1946 Green St, San Francisco CA 94123, USA

Aselton, Kathryn — Actress, Director
I C M Partners, 10250 Constellation Blvd, #900, Los Angeles CA 90067 USA

Asencio, Henry — Artist
Crown Thorn Publishing, 2375 Northside Dr, #200, San Diego CA 92108, USA

Asfaw, Ingida — Physician, Social Activist
2278 W Philadelphia St, Detroit MI 48206, USA

Ash, Daniel — Guitarist (Bauhaus, Love & Rockets)
Agency Group Ltd, 142 W 57th St, #600, New York NY 10019 USA

Ash, Nadine — Golfer
Quantum Sports Mgmt, 5625 E Wethersfield Road, Scottsdale AZ 85254, USA

Ashanti — Singer, Songwriter, Actress
Momanger, 15 Remsen Ave, Roslyn NY 11576, USA

Ashbery, John L — Writer
326 Belmont Ave, Buffalo NY 14223, USA

Ashbrook, Dana — Actor
Gage Group, 14724 Ventura Blvd, #505, Sherman Oaks CA 91403 USA

Ashbrook, Daphne — Actress
Defining Artists, 10 Universal City Plaza, #2000, Universal City CA 91608, USA

Ashby, Alan D — Baseball Player
12011 Cypress Creek Lakes Dr, Cypress TX 77433, USA

Ashby, Andrew J (Andy) — Baseball Player
2 Osborne Dr, Pittston PA 18640, USA

Ashby, Jeffrey S — Astronaut
N A S A, Johnson Space Center, 2101 NASA Road, Houston TX 77058 USA

Ashby, Linden — Actor
639 N Larchmont Blvd, #207, Los Angeles CA 90004, USA

Ashcroft, John D — Attorney General; Senator, Governor, MO
5603 W Farm Road 54, Willard MO 65781, USA

Ashcroft, Richard — Singer (Verve), Songwriter
Paradigm Agency, 360 Park Ave, #1600, New York NY 10022 USA

Ashdown, J J D (Paddy) — Government Official, England
Vane Cottage, Norton Sub Hamdon, Somerset TA14 6SG, England

Ashenfelter, Horace, III — Track Athlete
100 Hawthorne Ave, Glen Ridge NJ 07028, USA

Asher, Barry — Bowler
Professional Bowlers Assn, 719 2nd Ave, #701, Seattle WA 98104 USA

Asher, Jane — Actress
Jane Asher Cakes & Sugarcraft, 22-24 Cole St, London SW3 3QU, England

Asher, Peter — Singer (Peter & Gordon), Businessman
Santuary Artist Mgmt, 45-53 Sinclair Road, London W14 0NS, England

Asher, Robert D (Bob) — Football Player
4800 S Chicago Beach Dr, #612, Chicago IL 60615, USA

Ashfield, Kate — Actress
Independent Talent Group, Oxford House, 76 Oxford St, London W1D 1BS, England

Ashford, Matthew — Actor
260 S Beverly Dr, #208, Beverly Hills CA 90212, USA

Ashford, Rob — Choreographer
Creative Artists Agency, 2000 Ave of Stars, #100, Los Angeles CA 90067 USA

Ashford, Roslyn — Singer (Martha & Vandellas)
Soundedge Personal Mgmt, 332 Southdown Road, Huntington NY 11743, USA

Ashford, Thomas S (Tucker) — Baseball Player
502 S Maple St, Covington TX 76636, USA

Ashida, Jun — Fashion Designer
1-3-3 Aobadai, Meguroku, Tokyo 153 8521, Japan

Ashihara, Yoshinobu — Architect
47-10 Nishihara 3, Shibuyaku, Tokyo 151 0066, Japan

Ashitey, Clare-Hope — Actress
United Agents, 12-26 Lexington St, London W1F 0LE, England

Arum - Ashitey

Ashkar, Saleem Abboud — Concert Pianist
I M G Artists, Hogarth Business Park, Chiswick, London W4 2TH, England

Ashkenasi, Shmuel — Concert Violinist
Caecilia, 5 Place de la Fustene, 1204 Geneva, Switzerland

Ashkenazy, Dimitri — Concert Clarinetist
Harrison/Parrott, 5-6 Albion Court, London W6 0QT, England

Ashkenazy, Vladimir D — Concert Pianist, Conductor
Savinka, Kappelistr 15, 6045 Meggen, Switzerland

Ashley, Adryenn — Actress, Writer, Filmmaker
925 Lakeville St, #304, Petaluma CA 94952, USA

Ashley, Billy M — Baseball Player
2787 Autumn Ridge Dr, Thousand Oaks CA 91362, USA

Ashley, Christopher — Director
I C M Partners, 730 5th Ave, New York NY 10019 USA

Ashley, David — Educator
University of Nevada Las Vegas, President's Office, Las Vegas NV 89154, USA

Ashley, Elizabeth — Actress
1223 N Ogden Dr, West Hollywood CA 90046, USA

Ashley, Jennifer — Actress
129 W Wilson, #202, Costa Mesa CA 92627, USA

Ashley, Merrill — Ballerina
New York City Ballet, Lincoln Center Plaza, New York NY 10023 USA

Ashley, Robert R — Composer
Brooklyn Academy of Music, 30 Lafayette Ave, New York NY 10007, USA

Ashman, Duane A — Football Player
2625 Antler Court, Silver Spring MD 20904, USA

Ashmore, Aaron — Actor
K G Talent, 55A Sumach St, Toronto ON M5A 3J6, Canada

Ashmore, Darryl A — Football Player
8695 Thornbrook Terrace Point, Boynton Beach FL 33473, USA

Ashmore, Edward B — Navy Admiral, England
Naval Secretary, Victory Building, H M Naval Base, Portsmouth, Hampshire, England

Ashmore, Shawn — Actor
Gersh Agency, 9465 Wilshire Blvd, #600, Beverly Hills CA 90212 USA

Ashrawi, Hanan — Political Leader, Palestine
Arab League, PO Box 11642, Tahrir Square, Cairo, Egypt

Ashton, Brent — Ice Hockey Player
311 Brabent Crescent, Saskatoon SK S7J 4Y9, Canada

Ashton, John — Actor
Stone Manners Salners, 9911 W Pico Blvd, #1400, Los Angeles CA 90035 USA

Ashton, Joseph — Actor
Don Buchwald/Fortitude, 6500 Wilshire Blvd, #2200, Los Angeles CA 90048 USA

Ashton, Susan — Singer
Sparrow Communications, 101 Winners Circle, Brentwood TN 37027, USA

Ashton-Griffiths, Roger — Actor
16 Chelmsford Road, London E11 1BS, England

Ashworth, Frank — Ice Hockey Player
5110 Hot Springs, Fairmont Hot Springs BC V0B 1L0, Canada

Ashworth, Gerald (Gerry) — Track Athlete
PO Box 2, Ogunquit ME 03907, USA

Ashworth, Jeanne C — Speed Skater
Whiteface Highway, Wilmington NY 12997, USA

Askew, Bobby D (B J), Jr — Football Player
4216 Lantana Dr, Lebanon OH 45036, USA

Askew, Desmond — Actor
Paul Kohner, 9300 Wilshire Blvd, #555, Beverly Hills CA 90212 USA

Askew, Reubin O — Governor, FL
PO Box 12487, Tallahassee FL 32317, USA

Askey, Tom — Ice Hockey Player
5732 S 6th St, Kalamazoo MI 49009, USA

Askson, Bert — Football Player
7713 Charlesmont St, Houston TX 77016, USA

Asman, David — Commentator
Fox-TV, News Dept, 205 E 67th St, New York NY 10065 USA

Asmussen, Cash — Thoroughbred Racing Jockey
111 Devonshire Court, Laredo TX 78041, USA

Asner, Edward — Actor
Greene Assoc, 1901 Ave of Stars, #130, Los Angeles CA 90067 USA

Asomugha, Nnamdi — Football Player, Actor
1050 Armitage St, Alameda CA 94502, USA

Asplin, Edward W — Businessman
601 Carlson Parkway, #1050, Hopkins MN 55305, USA

Aspromonte, Kenneth J (Ken) — Baseball Player, Manager
2 Derham Park St, Houston TX 77024, USA

Aspromonte, Robert T (Bob) — Baseball Player
1000 Uptown Park Blvd, #241, Houston TX 77056, USA

Assad, Badi — Singer, Guitarist, Pianist
Aviv Productions, 10418 E Meadowhill Dr, Scottsdale AZ 85255, USA

Assad, Bashar al- — President, Syria; Army General
Presidential Palace, Muharreem Abu Rumanch, Al-Rashid St, Damascus, Syria

Assad, Odair — Concert Guitarist
Opus 3 Artists, 470 Park Ave S, #900N, New York NY 10016 USA

Assad, Sergio — Concert Guitarist
Opus 3 Artists, 470 Park Ave S, #900N, New York NY 10016 USA

Assante, Armand — Actor
A P A Talent/Literary Agency, 405 S Beverly Dr, #300, Beverly Hills CA 90212 USA

Assayas, Olivier — Director, Writer
Creative Artists Agency, 2000 Ave of Stars, #100, Los Angeles CA 90067 USA

Asseltine, Brian H — Baseball Player
1488 Country Court, Santa Ynez CA 93460, USA

Assenmacher, Paul A — Baseball Player
500 Covington Cove, Alpharetta GA 30022, USA

Assim — Rap Artist
Bad Boy Entertainment, 1440 Broadway, #16, New York NY 10018 USA

Assinger, Armin — Skier
Kuhweg 23, 9620 Hermagor, Austria

A

Ashkar - Assinger

A

Astacio Pura, Pedro J 2695 E Long Lane, Littleton CO 80121, USA	Baseball Player
Astar, Shay Franchot Mgmt, PO Box 48890A, Los Angeles CA 90048, USA	Actress
Astbury, Ian R Tom Vitorino Mgmt, 11606 Viny Road, Granada Hills CA 91344, USA	Singer (Cult)
Astin, Allen V 5008 Battery Lane, Bethesda MD 20814, USA	Physicist
Astin, John 3801 Canterbury Road, #505, Baltimore MD 21218, USA	Actor, Director
Astin, Mackenzie Sovereign Talent Group, 8421 Wilshire Blvd, #200, Beverly Hills CA 90211, USA	Actor
Astin, Sean A P A Talent/Literary Agency, 405 S Beverly Dr, #300, Beverly Hills CA 90212 USA	Actor
Astley, Rick Unit 4 Plato St, 72-74 Saint Dionis Road, London SW6 4UT, England	Singer
Astrid Royal Palace, Rue Brederode, 1000 Brussels, Belgium	Queen, Belgium
Astroth, Joseph H (Joe) 6035 Verde Trail S, #J310, Boca Raton FL 33433, USA	Baseball Player
Asylmuratova, Altynai Mariinsky Ballet, Teatralnaya Square 1, 190000 Saint Petersburg, Russia	Ballerina
Atala, Anthony Wake Forest University, Regenerative Medical Institute, Winston-Salem NC 27109, USA	Surgeon
Atambayev, Almazbek S President's Office, Government House, 720003 Bishkek, Kyrgyzstan	Prime Minister, Kyrgyzstan
Ataneli, Lado I M G Artists, Hogarth Business Park, Chiswick, London W4 2TH, England	Opera Singer
Atchison, Doug United Talent Agency, 9336 Civic Center Dr, Beverly Hills CA 90210 USA	Director, Writer
Atchison, Michael Associated Press, 450 W 33rd St, #1500, New York NY 10001 USA	Editorial Cartoonist
Atchison, Scott B 1820 Barrington Dr, Keller TX 76262, USA	Baseball Player
Atelian, Taylor Abrams Artists, 9200 W Sunset Blvd, #1125, West Hollywood CA 90069 USA	Actress
Athas, Peter G (Pete) 1125 NW 130th St, Miami FL 33168, USA	Football Player
Atherton, David Askonas Holt, Lincoln House, 300 High Holborn, London WC1V 7JH, England	Conductor
Atherton, Keith R 1014 Cobbs Creek Lane, Cobbs Creek VA 23035, USA	Baseball Player
Atherton, Michael A Lancashire County Cricket Club, Old Trafford, Manchester M16 0PX, England	Cricketer
Atherton, William Stone Manners Salners, 9911 W Pico Blvd, #1400, Los Angeles CA 90035 USA	Actor
Atika, Aure Agence Artiste Adequet, 80 Rue d'Amsterdam, 75009 Paris, France	Actress
Atiyeh, Victor Victor Atiyeh Co, 519 SW Park Ave, #205, Portland OR 97205, USA	Governor, OR
Atkin, Harvey 527 S Curson St, Los Angeles CA 90036, USA	Actor
Atkins, Christopher 6934 Bevis Ave, Van Nuys CA 91405, USA	Actor
Atkins, Douglas L (Doug) 8005 Clapps Chapel Road, Knoxville TN 37902, USA	Football Player
Atkins, Eileen Independent Talent Group, Oxford House, 76 Oxford St, London W1D 1BS, England	Actress
Atkins, Erica Paradigm Agency, 404 W Franklin St, Monterey CA 93940 USA	Singer (Mary Mary), Songwriter
Atkins, Essence Don Buchwald/Fortitude, 6500 Wilshire Blvd, #2200, Los Angeles CA 90048 USA	Actress
Atkins, Garrett B Colorado Rockies Foundation, 2001 Blake St, #A, Denver CO 80205, USA	Baseball Player
Atkins, Gene R 3515 Sunnyside Dr, Tallahassee FL 32305, USA	Football Player
Atkins, Kenneth L (Chucky) 229 S Ortman Dr, Orlando FL 32811, USA	Basketball Player
Atkins, Pervis 8040 Ventura Canyon Ave, Springfield PA 19064, USA	Football Player
Atkins, Rodney Red Light Mgmt, PO Box 1467, Charlottesville VA 22902, USA	Singer
Atkins, Sharif Christopher Wright Mgmt, 3207 Winnie Dr, Los Angeles CA 90068, USA	Actor
Atkins, Tina Paradigm Agency, 404 W Franklin St, Monterey CA 93940 USA	Singer (Mary Mary), Songwriter
Atkins, Tom 106 Forestwood Dr, Venetia PA 15367, USA	Actor
Atkinson, Allen E (Al) 218 Wells Lane, Springfield PA 19064, USA	Football Player
Atkinson, Conrad 172 Erlanger Road, London SE14 5TJ, England	Artist
Atkinson, George H (Butch) 6331 Fairmount Ave, El Cerrito CA 94530, USA	Football Player
Atkinson, Jayne S M S Talent, 8383 Wilshire Blvd, #230, Beverly Hills CA 90211 USA	Actress
Atkinson, Kate Transworld Publishing, 61-63 Uxbridge Road, London W5 5SA, England	Writer
Atkinson, Rick Kansas City Times, Editorial Dept, 1729 Grand Ave, Kansas City MO 64108, USA	Journalist, Writer
Atkinson, Rowan S P B J Mgmt, 5 Soho Square, London W1D 3QA, England	Actor, Comedian
Atkov, Oleg Y Cosmonaut Training Center, Star City, 141160 Zvezdny Gorodok, Moscow Oblast, Russia	Cosmonaut
Atlantov, Vladimir A Vienna State Opera, Opernring 2, 1015 Vienna, Austria	Opera Singer

Astacio Pura - Atlantov

Atogwe, Oshiomogho I (O J) — Football Player
496 Speyer Place, Saint Charles MO 63303, USA
Attai, Kader — Artist
Saatachi Gallery, Duke of York's H Q, King's Road, London SW3 4RY, England
Attal, Yvan — Actor, Director
Voyez Mon Agent, 20 Ave Rapp, 75007 Paris, France
Attanasio, Paul — Writer
Creative Artists Agency, 2000 Ave of Stars, #100, Los Angeles CA 90067 USA
Attell, Dave — Actor, Comedian
Creative Artists Agency, 2000 Ave of Stars, #100, Los Angeles CA 90067 USA
Attenborough, David F — Entertainer, Writer, Naturist
5 Park Road, Richmond, Surrey TW10 6NS, England
Attenborough, Richard S — Actor, Director
Old Friars, Beaver Lodge, Richmond Green, Surrey TW9 1NQ, England
Attersee, Christian — Artist
Vienna University of Applied Arts, Oskar Kokoschka-Platz 2, #3, 1010 Vienna, Austria
Atterton, Edward — Actor
I C M Partners, 10250 Constellation Blvd, #900, Los Angeles CA 90067 USA
Attias, Daniel — Director, Producer
Principato-Young, 9465 Wilshire Blvd, #880, Beverly Hills CA 90212 USA
Attig, Rick — Journalist
Portland Oregonian, Editorial Dept, 1320 SW Broadway, Portland OR 97201, USA
Attkisson, Sharyl — Commentator
CNN-TV, 190 Marietta Ave SW, Atlanta GA 30303 USA
Attlee, Frank, III — Businessman
Monsanto Co, 800 N Lindbergh Blvd, Saint Louis MO 63167, USA
Attles, Alvin A (Al) — Basketball Player, Coach
195 Villanova Dr, Oakland CA 94611, USA
Atwal, Arjun — Golfer
International Mgmt Group, Burlington Lane, London W4 2TH, England
Atwater, H Brewster, Jr — Businessman
I D S Center, 80 S 8th St, Minneapolis MN 55402, USA
Atwater, Stephen D (Steve) — Football Player
2510 Sugarloaf Club Dr, Duluth GA 30097, USA
Atwell, Hayley — Actress
Hamilton Hodell, 66-68 Margaret St, #500, London, W1W 8SR, England
Atwood, Casey L — Auto Racing Driver
Day Enterprises, 107 Flat Ridge Road, Goodlettsville TN 37072, USA
Atwood, Colleen C — Costume Designer
232 Aderno Way, Pacific Palisades CA 90272, USA
Atwood, Harold L — Zoologist
602 Castlefield Ave, Toronto ON M5N 1L8, Canada
Atwood, Margaret E — Writer
Curtis Brown, Haymarket House, 28-29 Haymarket, London SW14 4SP, England
Atwood, Susie (Sue) — Swimmer
5624 E 2nd St, Long Beach CA 90803, USA
Atzmon, Moshe — Conductor
P M G, 59 Lansdowne Place, Hove, East Sussex BN3 1FL, England
Auber, Brigitte — Actress
Agence A Berthomme, 72 Rue Notre Dame des Champs, 75006 Paris, France
Auberjonois, Rene — Actor
448 S Arden Blvd, Los Angeles CA 90020, USA
Aubert, Brian — Singer, Guitarist (Silversun Pickups)
Ink Tank Public Relations, 1824 W Sunset Blvd, #102, Los Angeles CA 90026, USA
Aubert, Karen D (K D) — Actress
Sovereign Talent, 8421 Wilshire Blvd, #200, Beverly Hills CA 90211, USA
Aubin, Normand — Ice Hockey Player
1287 Rue des Berges, Sorel-Tracy QC J3P 7X5, Canada
Aubret, Isabelle — Singer
Gerard Mays Productions, 110 Rue Saint Martin, 75001 Paris, France
Aubrey, Juliet — Actress
Ken McReddie Assoc, 11 Connaught Place, London W2 2ET, England
Aubry, Eugene E — Architect
Morris/Aubry Architects, 3465 W Alabama St, Houston TX 77027, USA
Aubry, Pierre — Ice Hockey Player
110 Rue Buisson, Cap-de-la-Madelain, QC G8V 1K4, Canada
Auburn, David — Writer, Director
97 W Elmwood Ave, Clawson MI 48017, USA
Aucoin, Adrian M — Ice Hockey Player
421 N Grant St, Hinsdale IL 60521, USA
AuCoin, Les — Representative, OR
Bogle & Gates, 601 13th St NW, #370, Washington DC 20005, USA
Aucoin, Rich — Singer
Agency Group Ltd, 142 W 57th St, #600, New York NY 10019 USA
Audette, Donald (Don) — Ice Hockey Player
15 Rue de Chinon, Blainville QB J7B 1Y2, Canada
Audiard, Jacques — Director, Writer
Voyez Mon Agent, 20 Ave Rapp, 75007 Paris, France
Audick, Daniel J B (Dan) — Football Player
13253 Sparren Ave, San Diego CA 92129, USA
Audran, Stephane — Actress
Artmedia, 20 Ave Rapp, 75007 Paris, France
Auel, Jean M — Writer
PO Box 8278, Portland OR 97207, USA
Auer, Jonathon (Jon) — Musician, Songwriter (Posies)
Bright Touring Artists, 1 Irving Place, #V18C, New York NY 10003, USA
Auer, Joseph (Joe) — Football Player
1138 Washington Ave, Winter Park FL 32789, USA
Auer, Peter L — Plasma Physicist
220 Devon Road, Ithaca NY 14850, USA
Auer, Victor — Marksman
8 Dellbrook Ave, San Francisco CA 94131, USA
Auerbach, Daniel Q (Dan) — Singer, Guitarist (Black Keys)
Q-Prime South, 131 S 11th St, Nashville TN 37206 USA
Auerbach, Frank — Artist
Marlborough Fine Art Gallery, 6 Albermarle St, London W1X 4BY, England

Auerbach, Frederick S (Rick) — Baseball Player
2139 Stunt Road, Calabasas CA 91302, USA
Auerbach, Stanley I — Ecologist
3314 W End Ave, #202, Nashville TN 37203, USA
Auermann, Nadja — Model
Elite Model Mgmt, 8 Bis Rue Le Cuirot, 75014 Paris, France
Auger, Brian — Jazz Pianist
Earthtone, 8306 Wilshire Blvd, #981, Beverly Hills CA 90211, USA
Auger, Claudine — Actress
Steve Kenis Co, Royalty House, 72-74 Dean St, London WID 3SG, England
Auger, Pierre V — Physicist
12 Rue Emile Faguet, 75014 Paris, France
Augmon, Stacey — Basketball Player
2784 Botticelli Dr, Henderson NV 89052, USA
Auguin, Philippe — Conductor
I M G Artists, Hogarth Business Park, Chiswick, London W4 2TH, England
August, Bille — Director
Creative Artists Agency, 2000 Ave of Stars, #100, Los Angeles CA 90067 USA
August, John — Writer
United Talent Agency, 9336 Civic Center Dr, Beverly Hills CA 90210 USA
August, Pernilla — Actress, Director
Agentfirman Planthaber/Kilden, Drottninggatan 55, 111 21 Stockholm, Sweden
August, Steve P — Football Player
7704 E 86th St, Tulsa OK 74133, USA
Augusta, Kim — Golfer
16 Rachella Court, East Providence RI 02914, USA
Augusta, Patrik — Ice Hockey Player
HC Dukla Jihlava, Tolsteno 23, 58601 Jihlava, Czech Republic
Augustain, Ira — Actor
4715 Fauna St, Montclair CA 91763, USA
Augustin, Darrel J (D J), Jr — Basketball Player
Charlotte Bobcats, 333 E Trade St, #A, Charlotte NC 28202 USA
Augustine, Gerald L (Jerry) — Baseball Player
S74W13490 Courtland Lane, Muskego WI 53150, USA
Augustine, Norman R — Businessman
24131 Doreen Dr, Gaithersburg MD 20882, USA
Augustnyiak, Jerry — Drummer (10000 Maniacs)
Paradise Artists, PO Box 1821, Ojai CA 93024 USA
Augustus, Seimone — Basketball Player
Minnesota Lynx, Target Center, 600 1st Ave N, Minneapolis MN 55403 USA
Aulby, Michael (Mike) — Bowler
2331 Brothers Dr, Lafayette IN 47909, USA
Auld, Alexander (Alex) — Ice Hockey Player
2005 Swallow Crescent, Thunder Bay ON P7C 4T9, Canada
Ault, Chris — Football Coach
University of Nevada, Athletic Dept, Reno NV 89557, USA
Aumann, Robert J — Nobel Economics Laureate
Hebrew University, Economics Dept, Mount Scopus, 91904 Jerusalem, Israel
Aumont, Michel — Actor
8 Rue Herold, 75001 Paris, France
Aung San Suu Kyi — Nobel Peace Laureate
National League for Democracy, 97B W Shwegondine Road, Yangon, Myanmar
Auriemma, Geno — Basketball Coach
185 Garth Road, Manchester CT 06040, USA
Aurilla, Richard S (Rich) — Baseball Player
5448 E Mariposa St, Phoenix AZ 85018, USA
Ausbie, Hubert E (Geese) — Basketball Player
902 Arthur Dr, Little Rock AR 72204, USA
Ausmus, Bradley D (Brad) — Baseball Player
1644 Stratford Way, Del Mar CA 92014, USA
Auster, Paul — Writer, Director
I C M Partners, 10250 Constellation Blvd, #900, Los Angeles CA 90067 USA
Austin, A Woody — Golfer
10906 W Havenhurst St, Maize KS 67101, USA
Austin, Charles — Track Athlete
514 Duncan Dr, San Marcos TX 78666, USA
Austin, Cliff — Football Player
1278 Autumn Wood Trail, Sugar Hill GA 30518, USA
Austin, Dallas — Actor
J M G Mgmt, 18000 Coastline Dr, #8, Malibu CA 90265, USA
Austin, Debbie — Golfer
6733 Bittersweet Lane, Orlando FL 32819, USA
Austin, Denise — Physical Fitness Expert
PrimeCare Systems, 610 Thimble Shoals Blvd, #402A, Newport News VA 23606, USA
Austin, Issaac E (Ike) — Basketball Player
1221 S 800 E, Salt Lake City UT 84105, USA
Austin, Jake T — Actor
Paradigm Agency, 360 N Crescent Dr, North Building, Beverly Hills CA 90210 USA
Austin, John — Basketball Player
1330 Riggs St NW, Washington DC 20009, USA
Austin, Julie — Actress
Abrams Artists, 9200 W Sunset Blvd, #1125, West Hollywood CA 90069 USA
Austin, K Darrell — Football Player
268 Austin Road, Union SC 29379, USA
Austin, Karen — Actress
Gage Group, 14724 Ventura Blvd, #505, Sherman Oaks CA 91403 USA
Austin, Lynne — Model
Playboy Promotions, 2706 Media Center Dr, Los Angeles CA 90065 USA
Austin, Patti — Singer
Tom Estey Publicity, 144 E 22nd St, #1B, New York NY 10010, USA
Austin, Steve (Stone Cold) — Professional Wrestler
Caliber Media, 9229 W Sunset Blvd, #720, West Hollywood CA 90069, USA
Austin, Teri — Actress
4245 Laurel Grove, Studio City CA 91604, USA
Austin, Timothy (Tim) — Boxer
9261 Calista Dr, North Ridgeville OH 44039, USA

Austin, Tracy — Tennis Player
Octagon Worldwide, 1751 Pinnacle Dr, #1500, McLean VA 22102 USA
Austin, William L (Bill) — Football Player
9412 Shellfish Court, Las Vegas NV 89117, USA
Auteuil, Daniel — Actor
Artmedia, 20 Ave Rapp, 75007 Paris, France
Auth, W Anthony (Tony), Jr — Editorial Cartoonist
Philadelphia Inquirer, Editorial Dept, 1830 Town Center Dr, Langhorne PA 19047 USA
Autry, Alan — Actor
David Shapira Assoc, 193 N Robertson Blvd, Beverly Hills CA 90211 USA
Auzenne, Troy A — Football Player
1501 Bluff Court, Diamond Bar CA 91765, USA
Avalon, Frankie — Singer, Actor
4303 Spring Forest Lane, Westlake Village CA 91362, USA
Avant — Singer
Paradigm Agency, 360 N Crescent Dr, North Building, Beverly Hills CA 90210 USA
Avant, Jason — Football Player
112 Villas Court, Clementon NJ 08021, USA
Avari, Erick — Actor
Greene Assoc, 1901 Ave of Stars, #130, Los Angeles CA 90067 USA
Avary, Roger — Director, Writer
I C M Partners, 10250 Constellation Blvd, #900, Los Angeles CA 90067 USA
Avati, Pupi — Director
Via del Babuino 135, 00187 Rome, Italy
Avdeeva, Yulianna — Concert Pianist
Harrison/Parrott, 5-6 Albion Court, London W6 0QT, England
Avdeyev, Sergei V — Cosmonaut
Cosmonaut Training Center, Star City, 141160 Zvezdny Gorodok, Moscow Oblast, Russia
Avellini, Robert H (Bob) — Football Player
1085 Flamingo Dr, Roselle IL 60172, USA
Averbukh, Ilia — Ice Dancer
Skating Assn, Luchnesksia Nab 8, 119871 Moscow, Russia
Averill, Earl D — Baseball Player
1806 19th Dr NE, Auburn WA 98002, USA
Averitt, William R (Bird) — Basketball Player
Kim Averitt, 103 N O'Neal Ave, Hopkinsville KY 42240, USA
Averno, Sisto J — Football Player
4759 Bonnie Brae Road, Pikesville MD 21208, USA
Averre, Berton — Guitarist (Knack)
17510 Posetano Road, Pacific Palisades CA 90272, USA
Avery, Brad — Guitarist (Third Day)
Creative Trust, 5141 Virginia Way, #320, Brentwood TN 37027, USA
Avery, Bryan R — Architect
Avery Architects, 270 Vauxhall Bridge Road, London SW1V 1BB, England
Avery, Eric A — Bassist (Jane's Addiction)
DeMann Entertainment, 9465 Wilshire Blvd, #426, Beverly Hills CA 90212, USA
Avery, James — Actor
Abrams Artists, 9200 W Sunset Blvd, #1125, West Hollywood CA 90069 USA
Avery, John E, Jr — Football Player
12 Ballantree Circle, Asheville NC 28803, USA
Avery, Kenneth W (Ken) — Football Player
625 Indian Ridge Dr, Nashville TN 37221, USA
Avery, Margaret — Actress
TalentWorks, 3500 W Olive Ave, #1400, Burbank CA 91505 USA
Avery, Sean — Ice Hockey Player
I C M Partners, 10250 Constellation Blvd, #900, Los Angeles CA 90067 USA
Avery, Steven T (Steve) — Baseball Player
2 Glenagles Court, Dearborn MI 48120, USA
Avi — Writer
859 S York St, Denver CO 80209, USA
Avila, Jim — Commentator
ABC-TV, News Dept, 77 W 66th St, New York NY 10023 USA
Avildsen, John G — Director
2423 Briarcrest Road, Beverly Hills CA 90210, USA
Avise, John C — Geneticist
University of Georgia, Genetics Dept, Athens GA 30602, USA
Avital, Mili — Actress
Liebman Entertainment, 25 E 21st St, #PH, New York NY 10010, USA
Avnet, Jonathan M (Jon) — Director, Producer
Creative Artists Agency, 2000 Ave of Stars, #100, Los Angeles CA 90067 USA
Avni, Aki — Actor
Don Buchwald/Fortitude, 6500 Wilshire Blvd, #2200, Los Angeles CA 90048 USA
Avory, Mike — Drummer (Rolling Stones, Kinks)
Larry Page, 29 Rushton Mews, London W11 1RB, England
Avril, Clifford S (Cliff) — Football Player
Detroit Lions, 222 Republic Dr, Allen Park MI 48101 USA
Awalt, Robert M (Rob) — Football Player
5011 Highgrove Court, Granite Bay CA 95746, USA
Awrey, Donald W (Don) — Ice Hockey Player
1015 Alaska Ave, Lehigh Acres FL 33971, USA
Awtrey, Dennis W — Basketball Player
38245 James Road, Nehalem OR 97131, USA
Ax, Emmanuel — Concert Pianist
Opus 3 Artists, 470 Park Ave S, #900N, New York NY 10016, USA
Axel, Richard — Nobel Medicine Laureate
435 Riverside Dr, #62, New York NY 10025, USA
Axelrod, Jonathan H — Molecular Biologist
Goldyne Savad Institute of Gene Therapy, PO Box 12000, Jerusalem 91120, Israel
Axelsson, A Per Johan (P J) — Ice Hockey Player
50 Fleet St, #301, Boston MA 02109, USA
Axen, K Martin — Guitarist (The Ark)
Live Nation, Linnegatan 89, Box 21451, 10451 Stockholm, Sweden
Axley, Eric — Golfer
1700 Cottage Wood Way, Knoxville TN 37919, USA
Axwell — DJ Musician
Mission Control, City Business Center, Lower Road, London SE16 2XB, England

Ayadi, Naidra — Actress
Josiane Stoh, 3 Allee Marie Laurent, 75020 Paris, France

Ayala Gonzales, Robert J (Bobby) — Baseball Player
11011 W Cottonwood Lane, Avondale AZ 85392, USA

Ayala, Benigno (Benny) — Baseball Player
PO Box 222, Dorado PR 00646, USA

Ayala, Francisco J — Geneticist, Molecular Biologist
2 Locke Court, Irvine CA 92617, USA

Ayala, Luis I — Baseball Player
Baltimore Orioles, Oriole Park, 333 W Camden St, Baltimore MD 21201 USA

Ayala, Paulie — Boxer
3817 Southwest Blvd, Fort Worth TX 76116, USA

Ayanbadejo, Obafemi — Football Player
301 W G St, #134, San Diego CA 92101, USA

Ayanna, Charlotte — Actress
Bohemia Group, 8170 Beverly Blvd, #102, Los Angeles CA 90048, USA

Aybar, Erick J — Baseball Player
773 W Raven Dr, Chandler AZ 85286, USA

Ayckbourn, Alan — Writer, Director
Casorotto Ramsay, Waverley House, 7-12 Noel St, London W1F 8GQ, England

Aycock, Alice — Sculptor
62 Green St, #4, New York NY 10012, USA

Aycox, Nicki — Actress
Innovative Artists, 1505 10th St, Santa Monica CA 90401 USA

Ayer, David — Director, Writer
Creative Artists Agency, 2000 Ave of Stars, #100, Los Angeles CA 90067 USA

Ayer, William S (Bill) — Businessman
Alaska Airlines, 19300 International Blvd, Seattle WA 98188, USA

Ayers, Chuck — Cartoonist (Crankshaft)
Universal Press Syndicate, 4520 Main St, #700, Kansas City MO 64111 USA

Ayers, Dick — Cartoonist (Sgt Fury)
64 Beech St W, White Plains NY 10604, USA

Ayers, Sam — Actor
Bobby Ball Talent Agency, 4116 W Magnolia Blvd, #205, Burbank CA 91505, USA

Aykroyd, Dan — Actor, Comedian
Creative Artists Agency, 2000 Ave of Stars, #100, Los Angeles CA 90067 USA

Aylesworth, Reiko — Actress
Gersh Agency, 9465 Wilshire Blvd, #600, Beverly Hills CA 90212 USA

Ayling, Robert J — Businessman
Dwr Cymru Welsh Water, PO Box 690, Cardiff, CF3 5WL, Wales

Aylward, John J — Actor
Mitchell K Stubbs Assoc, 8695 Washington Blvd, #204, Culver City CA 90232, USA

Aylwin Azocar, Patricio — President, Chile
Teresa Salas 786, Providencia, Santiago, Chile

Ay-O — Artist
2-6-38 Matsuyama, Kiyoseshi, Tokyo, Japan

Ayoade, Richard — Director
W M E Entertainment, 9601 Wilshire Blvd, #300, Beverly Hills CA 90210 USA

Ayodele, Akinnola J (Akin) — Football Player
7105 David Lane, Colleyville TX 76034, USA

Ayrault, Jean-Marc — Prime Minister, France
Premier's Office, Hotel Matignon, 57 Rue de Varenne, 75700 Paris, France

Aytes, Rochelle — Actress
Innovative Artists, 1505 10th St, Santa Monica CA 90401 USA

Ayton, Sarah L — Yachtswoman
Lynx Sports Mgmt, Lymington Road, Lymington, Hampshire SO41 5S5, England

AZ — Rap Artist
Celebrity Talent Agency, 111 E 14th St, #249, New York NY 10003, USA

Azarenka, Victoria — Tennis Player
Best, 303 E Main St, #200, Louisville KY 40202 USA

Azaria, Hank — Actor, Singer
W M E Entertainment, 9601 Wilshire Blvd, #300, Beverly Hills CA 90210 USA

Azarov, Mykola Y — Prime Minister, Ukraine
Prime Minister's Office, Hrushevskoga 12/2, 252008 Kiev, Ukraine

Azinger, Paul W — Golfer
7847 Chick Evans Place, Sarasota FL 34240, USA

Aznavour, Charles — Singer, Actor, Songwriter
Agents Associes, 201 Faubourg Saint Honore, 75008 Paris, France

Azria, Max — Fashion Designer
B C B G/Max Azria, 1450 Broadway, #1700, New York NY 10018, USA

Azuma, Norio — Artist
4530 Broadway, #4F, New York NY 10040, USA

Azuma, Takamitsu — Architect
Azuma Architects, 3-6-1 Minami-Aoyama Minatoku, Tokyo 107 0016, Japan

Azumah, Jerry — Football Player
462 W Superior St, Chicago IL 60654, USA

Azzara, Candice — Actress
Maverick Entertainment, 6100 Wilshire Blvd, #550, Los Angeles CA 90048, USA

Azzi, Jennifer L — Basketball Player, Coach
Azzi Training, 8589 S Mardi Gras Lane, West Jordan UT 84088, USA

B o B — Rap Artist
Grand Hustle Entertainment, 541 10th St, #161, Atlanta GA 31318, USA

Baab, Michael J (Mike) — Football Player
PO Box 1808, Euless TX 76039, USA

Baas, David A — Football Player
7004 Lacantera Circle, Lakewood Ranch FL 34202, USA

Babando, Peter (Pete) — Ice Hockey Player
50 Sterling Ave W, Timmins ON P4N 3K3, Canada

Babashoff, Jack — Swimmer
17254 Santa Clara St, Fountain Valley CA 92708, USA

Babashoff, Shirley — Swimmer
17254 Santa Clara St, Fountain Valley CA 92708, USA

Babatunde, Obba — Actor
I C M Partners, 10250 Constellation Blvd, #900, Los Angeles CA 90067 USA

Babb, Albert L — Biomedical Engineer
PO Box 3429, Redmond WA 98073, USA

Babb, Charlie — Football Player
371 Heron Ave, Naples FL 34108, USA

Babb, Eugene W (Gene) — Football Player
5110 W 9th Ave, Stillwater OK 74074, USA

Babbidge, Homes D, Jr — Educator
3 Diving St, Stonington CT 06378, USA

Babbit, Jamie — Director
Innovative Artists, 1505 10th St, Santa Monica CA 90401 USA

Babbitt, Bruce E — Secretary, Interior; Governor, AZ
World Wildlife Fund,1250 24th St NW, Washington DC 20090, USA

Babbitt, Natalie — Writer
Farrar Straus Giroux, 18 W 18th St, #700, New York NY 10011 USA

Babb-Sprague, Kristen — Synchronized Swimmer
4677 Pine Valley Dr, Stockton CA 95219, USA

Babcock, Barbara — Actress
Paradigm Agency, 360 N Crescent Dr, North Building, Beverly Hills CA 90210 USA

Babcock, Michael (Mike), Jr — Ice Hockey Coach
17891 Stonebrook Circle, Northville MI 48168, USA

Babcock, Tim M — Governor, MT
Ox Bow Ranch, PO Box 877, Helena MT 59624, USA

Babe, Warren — Ice Hockey Player
15 Rocky Mountain Blvd W, Lethbridge AB T1K 6V7, Canada

Babenco, Hector E — Director
I C M Partners, 10250 Constellation Blvd, #900, Los Angeles CA 90067 USA

Babey, Pamela — Interior Designer
Babey Moulton Jue Booth, 510 3rd St, #110, San Francisco CA 94107, USA

Babic, Milos — Basketball Player
1500 Doris Dr, Cookeville TN 38501, USA

Babich, Robert (Bob) — Football Player
4994 Mount Ashmun Dr, San Diego CA 92111, USA

Babilonia, Tai R — Figure Skater
Diverse Talent Group, 1900 Ave of Stars, #2840, Los Angeles CA 90067, USA

Babin, Jason — Football Player
2735 Peninsulas Dr, Missouri City TX 77459, USA

Babin, Mitch — Ice Hockey Player
519 Pleasant St, Leominster MA 01453, USA

Babineaux, Jonathan J — Football Player
5659 Legends Club Circle, Braselton GA 30517, USA

Babineaux, Jordan J — Football Player
1015 N 29th St, Renton WA 98056, USA

Babiuk, Andy — Bassist (Chesterfield Kings)
Agency Group Ltd, 142 W 57th St, #600, New York NY 10019 USA

Babka, Richard (Rink) — Track Athlete
1080 Silver Hill Road, Redwood City CA 94061, USA

Babluani, Gela — Director, Writer
W M E Entertainment, 9601 Wilshire Blvd, #300, Beverly Hills CA 90210 USA

Baby Bash — Rap Artist
J L Entertainment, 18653 Ventura Blvd, #340, Tarzana CA 91356 USA

Baby Oje — Rap Artist (Arrested Development)
Agency Group Ltd, 142 W 57th St, #600, New York NY 10019 USA

Baby Peggy — Actress
7220 Durango Circle, Carlsbad CA 92011, USA

Baby, John — Ice Hockey Player
252 Brebeuf Ave, Sudbury ON P3C 5H1, Canada

Babych, Dave — Ice Hockey Player
1315 Wellington Crescent, Winnipeg MB R3N 0A9, Canada

Babych, Wayne — Ice Hockey Player
1315 Wellington Crescent, Winnipeg MB R3N 0A9, Canada

Baca, David — Drag Racing Driver
529 Garcia Ave, #C, Pittsburg CA 94565, USA

Baca, John P — Vietnam War Army Hero (CMH)
PO Box 154, Julian CA 92036, USA

Baca, Susana — Singer
Luaka Bop, 195 Chrystie St, #901, New York NY 10002, USA

Bacall, Lauren — Actress
Dakota Hotel, 1 W 72nd St, #43, New York NY 10023, USA

Bacall, Michael — Actor, Writer
W M E Entertainment, 9601 Wilshire Blvd, #300, Beverly Hills CA 90210 USA

Bacashihua, Jason — Ice Hockey Player
23411 Annapolis St, Dearborn Heights MI 48125, USA

Baccarin, Morena — Actress
United Talent Agency, 9336 Civic Center Dr, Beverly Hills CA 90210 USA

Bach Munez, Jaume — Architect
Avenida Diagonal 335, 08037 Barcelona, Spain

Bach, Barbara — Actress
2 Glynde Mews, London SW3 1SB, England

Bach, Catherine — Actress
Ziffren Brittenham Branca, 1801 Century Park W, #700, Los Angeles CA 90067 USA

Bach, David — Writer
W M E Entertainment, 9601 Wilshire Blvd, #300, Beverly Hills CA 90210 USA

Bach, Jillian — Actress
Abrams Artists, 9200 W Sunset Blvd, #1125, West Hollywood CA 90069 USA
Bach, John W (Johnny) — Basketball Player, Coach
2300 Clarendon Blvd, #306, Arlington VA 22201, USA
Bach, Pamela — Actress
International Talent Agency, 10 NBC Universal Studios Plaza, #2000, Universal City CA 91608, USA
Bach, Richard — Writer
Dell Publishing, 1540 Broadway, New York NY 10036, USA
Bach, Sebastian — Singer (Skid Row), Actor
Rick Sales Entertainment, 2850 Ocean Park Blvd, #300, Santa Monica CA 90405, USA
Bachar, Carmit — Singer (Pussycat Dolls), Dancer, Actress
R S S Mgmt, 137 N Larchmont Blvd, #213, Los Angeles CA 90004, USA
Bacharach, Burt — Composer, Musician
681 Amalfi Dr, Pacific Palisades CA 90272, USA
Bachardy, Don — Artist
145 Adelaide Dr, Santa Monica CA 90402, USA
Bachchan, Amitabh — Actor
Pratiksha, 10th Road, J V P D Scheme, Mumbai 400049, India
Bacher, Aron (Ali) — Cricketer, Administrator
17 Romajador Ave, Sandhurst #4, Sandton, South Africa
Bachfeld, Jochem — Boxer
Wandrumer Str 19, 19073 Wittenssorde, Germany
Bachleda, Alicja — Actress
Hofflund/Polone, 9465 Wilshire Blvd, #420, Beverly Hills CA 90212 USA
Bachman, Randy — Singer, Songwriter, Guitarist
Paquin Entertainment, 468 Stradbrooke Ave, Winnipeg MB R3L 0J9, Canada
Bachtadze, Michael — Opera Singer
I M G Artists, Hogarth Business Park, Chiswick, London W4 2TH, England
Baciocco, Albert J, Jr — Navy Admiral
747 Pitt St, Mount Pleasant SC 29464, USA
Back, Stephen A — Pediatric Neurologist
Oregon Health Science University, 3181 SW Jackson Park Dr, Portland OR 97239 USA
Backe, Brandon A — Baseball Player
103 E Viejo Dr, Friendswood TX 77546, USA
Backe, John D — Businessman
399 Park Ave, #1900, New York NY 10022, USA
Backhaus, Robin — Swimmer
PO Box 6271, Ocean View HI 96737, USA
Backis, Audrys Juozas Cardinal — Religious Leader
Sventaragio 4, 2001 Vilnius, Lithuania
Backley, Stephen (Steve) — Track Athlete
Cambridge Harriers, 56A-60 Glenhurst Ave, Bexley, Kent DA5 3QN, England
Backman, R Christian — Ice Hockey Player
784 Bellerive Manor Dr, Saint Louis MO 63141, USA
Backman, Walter W (Wally) — Baseball Player, Manager
241 SE Mercury Lane, Prineville OR 97754, USA
Backstrom, Niklas O — Ice Hockey Player
100 3rd Ave S, #3604, Minneapolis MN 55401, USA
Backstrom, Ralph G — Ice Hockey Player
1625 Pelican Lakes Point, Windsor CO 80550, USA
Backus, Christopher — Actor
Don Buchwald/Fortitude, 6500 Wilshire Blvd, #2200, Los Angeles CA 90048 USA
Backus, George E — Geophysicist
9362 La Jolla Farms Road, La Jolla CA 92037, USA
Backus, Gus — Singer (Del Vikings)
Lustig Talent, PO Box 770850, Orlando FL 32877 USA
Backus, Jeffrey C (Jeff) — Football Player
48075 Bellagio Court, Northville MI 48167, USA
Backus, Sharon — Softball Player, Coach
University of California, Athletic Dept, Los Angeles CA 90024, USA
Bacon, Henry — Basketball Player
10103 Grand Ave, #218, Louisville KY 40299, USA
Bacon, Kevin N — Actor
W M E Entertainment, 9601 Wilshire Blvd, #300, Beverly Hills CA 90210 USA
Bacon, Richard P — Entertainer
Rights House, 34-43 Russell St, London WC2B 5HA, England
Bacon, Roger F — Navy Admiral
24285 Johnson Road NW, Poulsbo WA 98370, USA
Bacquier, Gabriel — Opera Singer
141 Rue de Rome, 75017 Paris, France
Bacri, Jean-Pierre — Actor
Anne Alvares Correa, 34 Rue Jouffroy d'Abbans, 75017 Paris, France
Bacs, Ludovic — Conductor, Composer
31 D Golescu, Sc III, E7 V Ap 87, Bucharest 1, Romania
Bacsik, Michael Joseph (Mike) — Baseball Player
4014 Falcon Lake Dr, Arlington TX 76016, USA
Badalamenti, Angelo — Composer
11 Fidelian Way, Lincoln Park NJ 07035, USA
Badalucco, Michael — Actor
Stone Manners Salners, 9911 W Pico Blvd, #1400, Los Angeles CA 90035 USA
Badami, Anita Rau — Writer
Carlisle Co, 121 E 17th St, New York NY 10003, USA
Baddeley, Aaron — Golfer
8606 E Via del Sol Dr, Scottsdale AZ 85255, USA
Baddeley, Alan D — Psychologist
York University, Psychology Dept, Heslington, York YO10 5DD, England
Baddour, Raymond F — Chemical Engineer
6495 SW 122nd St, Miami FL 33156, USA
Bade, Lance — Marksman
9491 Berrey Lane, Colorado Springs CO 80925, USA
Bader, Beth — Golfer
713 S 7th St, Eldridge IA 52748, USA
Bader, Diedrich — Actor
Paradigm Agency, 360 N Crescent Dr, North Building, Beverly Hills CA 90210 USA
Bader, Larry — Ice Hockey Player
1413 Westwood Dr SW, Faribault MN 55021, USA

B

Badger, Brad — Football Player
3553 Milleford Court, Pleasanton CA 94588, USA
Badgley, Mark — Fashion Designer
Badgley Mischka, 215 W 40th St, New York NY 10018, USA
Badgley, Penn — Actor
Anonymous Content, 3532 Hayden Ave, Culver City CA 90232 USA
Badgley, William S — Financier
505 E Waters Edge Dr, Belleville IL 62221, USA
Badham, John M — Director, Producer
Badham Company, 16830 Ventura Blvd, #300, Encino CA 91436, USA
Badham, Mary — Actress
3720 Whitehall Road, Sandy Hook VA 23153, USA
Badian, Ernst — Historian
Harvard University, History Dept, Robinson Hall, Cambridge MA 02138, USA
Badler, Jane — Actress
PO Box 43, South Yarra VIC 3141, Australia
Badly Drawn Boy — Singer, Songwriter
Big Life Mgmt, 67-69 Charlton St, London NW11 1HY, England
Badrov, Sergei — Director
Arlook Group, 205 S Beverly Dr, #209, Beverly Hills CA 90212, USA
Badu, Erykah — Singer, Songwriter
Creative Artists Agency, 2000 Ave of Stars, #100, Los Angeles CA 90067 USA
Badura-Skoda, Paul — Concert Pianist, Composer
Hochschule Musik, Lothringerstr 18, 1037 Vienna, Austria
Baechtold, James E (Jim) — Basketball Player
225 W Irvine St, Richmond KY 40475, USA
Baek Sung-Dong — Soccer Player
Football Assn, 1-131 Sinmunno, 2-Ga Jongno-Gu, Seoul 110 062, South Korea
Baeling, Rebecca D (Becky) — Singer, Actress
Abrams Artists, 9200 W Sunset Blvd, #1125, West Hollywood CA 90069 USA
Baena, Marisa — Golfer
3605 Dandelion Dr, Plano TX 75093, USA
Baer, Gordy — Bowler
8577 Tullamore Dr, Tinley Park IL 60487, USA
Baer, Max, Jr — Producer, Director, Actor
2795 Tam O'Shanter Dr, El Dorado Hills CA 95762, USA
Baer, Olaf — Opera Singer
Olbersdorferstr 7, 01324 Dresden, Germany
Baer, Ralph H — Inventor (Video Game Console)
134 Mayflower Dr, Manchester NH 03104, USA
Baer, Robert — Writer
Crown Publishing Group, 1745 Broadway, New York NY 10019 USA
Baer, Robert J (Jacob) — Army General
6213 Militia Court, Fairfax Station VA 22039, USA
Baer, William — Attorney, Government Official
Arnold & Porter, 555 12th St NW, Washington DC 20004, USA
Baerga, Carlos O — Baseball Player
PO Box 1667, Bayamon PR 00960, USA
Baez Gonzalez, Danys — Baseball Player
6190 SW 114th St, Miami FL 33156, USA
Baez, Joan — Singer, Songwriter
Mark Spector Co, 100 5th Ave, #1100, New York NY 10011, USA
Baeza, Braulio — Thoroughbred Racing Jockey
1588 Rosalind Ave, Elmont NY 11003, USA
Baeza, Paloma — Actress
United Agents, 12-26 Lexington St, London W1F 0LE, England
Baffert, Robert A (Bob) — Thoroughbred Racing Trainer
705 Carriage House Dr, Arcadia CA 91006, USA
Bagayoko, Amadou — Singer, Guitarist (Amadou & Mariam)
Partisan Arts, PO Box 5085, Larkspur CA 94977, USA
Baggetta, Vincent — Actor
4812 Ranchito Ave, Sherman Oaks CA 91423, USA
Baggio, Roberto — Soccer Player
Brescia F C, Via Bazoli 10, 27127 Brescia, Italy
Baggott, Julianna — Writer
Pocket Books, 1230 Ave of Americas, New York NY 10020 USA
Bagian, James P — Astronaut
21537 Holmbury Road, Northville MI 48167, USA
Bagley, John E — Basketball Player
31W450 Circle Dr, Elgin IL 60120, USA
Bagley, Lorri — Actress
Cinetic Mgmt, 555 W 25th St, #400, New York NY 10001 USA
Bagnal, Charles W — Army General
Ratchford Assoc, 221 W Springs Road, Columbia SC 29223, USA
Bagnasco, Angelo Cardinal — Religious Leader
Arcivescovado, Piazza Matteotti 4, 16123 Genoa, Italy
Bagshawe, Tilly — Writer
Warner Books, 1271 Ave of Americas, New York NY 10020 USA
Bagwell, Jeffrey R (Jeff) — Baseball Player
405 Timberwilde Lane, Houston TX 77024, USA
Bahns, Maxine L — Actress, Model
Glick Agency, 1321 7th St, #203, Santa Monica CA 90401 USA
Bahnsen, Stanley R (Stan) — Baseball Player
3500 Blue Lake Dr, #402, Pompano Beach FL 33064, USA
Bahouth, Peter — Association Executive
Greenpeace, 702 H St NW, #300, Washington DC 20001, USA
Bahr, Chris — Football Player
122 Kaywood Dr, Boalsburg PA 16827, USA
Bahr, Iris — Actress
Abrams Artists, 9200 W Sunset Blvd, #1125, West Hollywood CA 90069 USA
Bahr, Matthew D (Matt) — Football Player
53 Parkridge Lane, Pittsburgh PA 15228, USA
Bahr, Walter A — Soccer Player
250 Elks Road, Boalsburg PA 16827, USA
Bahrani, Ramin — Director, Writer
Creative Artists Agency, 2000 Ave of Stars, #100, Los Angeles CA 90067 USA

Badger - Bahrani

Bahrke, Shannon — Freestyle Skier
Q Sports Marketing, 534 W Evergreen St, Wheaton IL 60187 USA

Bai Ling — Actress, Model
Global Artists Agency, 6253 Hollywood Blvd, #508, Los Angeles CA 90028 USA

Bailar, Benjamin F — Government Official, Educator
410 Walnut Road, Lake Forest IL 60045, USA

Bailes, Scott A — Baseball Player
5895 S Teters Court, Springfield MO 65804, USA

Bailey, Benjamin R (Ben) — Actor, Comedian
Gersh Agency, 9465 Wilshire Blvd, #600, Beverly Hills CA 90212 USA

Bailey, Christina (Chris) — Ice Hockey Player
3902 N Main St, Marion NY 14505, USA

Bailey, Christopher — Fashion Designer
Burberry Prorsum, 18-22 Haymarket St, London SW1Y 4DQ, England

Bailey, Damon — Basketball Player
723 Diamond Road, Heltonville IN 47436, USA

Bailey, David — Photographer
Robert Montgomery, 3 Junction Mews, Sale Place, London W2, England

Bailey, Donovan — Track Athlete
625 Hales Chapel Road, Johnson City TN 37615, USA

Bailey, Eion — Actor
Gersh Agency, 9465 Wilshire Blvd, #600, Beverly Hills CA 90212 USA

Bailey, F Lee — Attorney
38 Blueberry Cove, Yarmouth ME 04096, USA

Bailey, Fenton — Director, Producer
Creative Artists Agency, 2000 Ave of Stars, #100, Los Angeles CA 90067 USA

Bailey, G W — Actor
Essential Talent Management, 7958 Beverly Blvd, Los Angeles CA 90048, USA

Bailey, Harold — Football Player
22502 Prince George Lane, Katy TX 77449, USA

Bailey, J Mark — Baseball Player
32703 Waltham Crossing, Fulshear TX 77441, USA

Bailey, James R (Jim) — Football Player
5219 Stone Creek Court, Lawrence KS 66049, USA

Bailey, Jerry D — Thoroughbred Racing Jockey
105 Nurmi Dr, Fort Lauderdale FL 33301, USA

Bailey, Jim — Actor, Singer, Female Impersonator
Stephen Campbell Management, 350 N Crescent Dr, #105, Beverly Hills CA 90210, USA

Bailey, John I — Cinematographer
W M E Entertainment, 9601 Wilshire Blvd, #300, Beverly Hills CA 90210 USA

Bailey, Karsten M — Football Player
16 Salbide Ave, Newnan GA 30263, USA

Bailey, Keith E — Businessman
Williams Companies, 1 Williams Center, Tulsa OK 74172, USA

Bailey, Maxwell C — Air Force General
4704 W Pearl Ave, Tampa FL 33611, USA

Bailey, Mike — Actor
University of Teesside, Performing Arts Dept, Middlesbrough Tees Valley, TS1 3BA, England

Bailey, Norman S — Opera Singer
84 Warham Road, South Croydon, Surrey CR2 6LB, England

Bailey, Paul — Writer
79 Davisville Road, London W12 9SH, England

Bailey, Philip — Singer, Musician (Earth Wind & Fire)
Spirit Media, PO Box 43591, Phoenix AZ 85080, USA

Bailey, R Champ — Football Player
5744 Aspen Leaf Dr, Littleton CO 80125, USA

Bailey, Razzy — Singer, Songwriter
Doc Sedelmeier, PO Box 62, Geneva NE 68361, USA

Bailey, Robert M L — Football Player
15325 SW 99th Ave, Miami FL 33157, USA

Bailey, Robert S (Bob) — Baseball Player
3181 Lido Isle Court, Las Vegas NV 89117, USA

Bailey, Scott — Actor
Glick Agency, 1321 7th St, #203, Santa Monica CA 90401 USA

Bailey, Stacey D — Football Player
3400 Lakewind Way, Alpharetta GA 30005, USA

Bailey, T Wayne — Political Scientist, Social Activist
Stetson University, Political Science Dept, Deland FL 32720, USA

Bailey, Thurl L — Basketball Player
10265 N 6960 W, Highland UT 84003, USA

Bailey, W Donald (Don) — Football Player
14831 NW 7th Ave, North Miami FL 33168, USA

Baillie, Kathy — Singer (Baillie & the Boys)
1703 Old Hillsboro Road, Franklin TN 37063, USA

Baillie, Victoria — Singer, Songwriter
17 Coalville Road, Moe VIC 3825, Australia

Bailly, Sandrine — Biathlete
Residence Saint-Laurent, 10 Rue Jacques Cartier, 25300 Pontarlier, France

Bailon, Adrienne E — Singer (Cheetah Girls), Actress
Creative Artists Agency, 2000 Ave of Stars, #100, Los Angeles CA 90067 USA

Bailor, Robert M (Bob) — Baseball Player
1950 Swan Lane, Palm Harbor FL 34683, USA

Baily, Martin N — Government Official, Economist
McKinsey Global Institute, 1101 Pennsylvania Ave NW, Washington DC 20004, USA

Bailyn, Bernard — Historian
170 Clifton St, Belmont MA 02478, USA

Bain, Barbara — Actress
Jeffrey Leavitt Agency, 11500 West Olympic Blvd, #400, Los Angeles CA 90064, USA

Bain, Conrad — Actor
850 E Stanley Blvd, #36, Livermore CA 94550, USA

Bain, Michael — Actor
W M E Entertainment, 9601 Wilshire Blvd, #300, Beverly Hills CA 90210 USA

Bain, William E (Bill) — Football Player
27661 Paseo Barona, San Juan Capo CA 92675, USA

Baines, Harold D — Baseball Player
PO Box 10, Saint Michaels MD 21663, USA

Baines, Nicholas M (Peanut) — Keyboardist (Kaiser Chiefs)
Red Light Mgmt, 8439 Sunset Blvd, West Hollywood CA 90069, USA
Bainimarama, Josaia Voreqe (Frank) — Prime Minister, Fiji
Prime Minister's Office, New Government Buildings, 6 Berkeley Crescent, Suva, Viti Levu, Fiji
Baio, Scott — Actor
TalentWorks, 3500 W Olive Ave, #1400, Burbank CA 91505 USA
Baiocchi, Hugh — Golfer
142 Royal Saint Georges Way, Rancho Mirage CA 92270, USA
Bair, C Douglas (Doug) — Baseball Player
11545 Kemper Woods Dr, Cincinnati OH 45249, USA
Bair, Sheila C — Government Official
Federal Deposit Insurance Corp, 550 17th St NW, Washington DC 20429, USA
Baird, Briny — Golfer
3340 SW Rivers End Way, Palm City FL 34990, USA
Baird, Butch — Golfer
PO Box 2633, Carefree AZ 85377, USA
Baird, Diora — Model, Actress
Don Buchwald/Fortitude, 6500 Wilshire Blvd, #2200, Los Angeles CA 90048 USA
Baird, Janice — Opera Singer
Opera et Concert, 37 Rue de la Chaussee d'Antin, 75009 Paris, France
Baird, Jenni — Actress
Kritzer Levine Wilkins Griffin, 11872 La Grange Ave, #100, Los Angeles CA 90025 USA
Baird, Scott — Curling Athlete
5835 Tall Pines Road, Bemidji MN 56601, USA
Baird, Stuart — Director
Mirisch Agency, 8840 Wilshire Blvd, #100, Beverly Hills CA 90211 USA
Baird, William A (Bill) — Football Player
6050 E Heaton Ave, Fresno CA 93727, USA
Baird, Zoe — Attorney
Aetna Life & Casualty, 151 Farmington Ave, Hartford CT 06156, USA
Baitz, Jon Robin — Writer
Creative Artists Agency, 2000 Ave of Stars, #100, Los Angeles CA 90067 USA
Baiul, Oksana — Figure Skater
Bob Young, PO Box 988, Niantic CT 06357, USA
Bajcsy, Ruzena — Electrical Engineer
University of California, Electrical Engineering Dept, Berkeley CA 94720, USA
Bajema, Billy — Football Player
2605 SW 120th St, Oklahoma City OK 73170, USA
Bakatin, Vadim V — Government Official, Russia
Reforma, Kotelnicheskaya Nab 17, 103240 Moscow, Russia
Bakay, Nick — Actor, Producer
A P A Talent/Literary Agency, 405 S Beverly Dr, #300, Beverly Hills CA 90212 USA
Bakels, Kees — Conductor
I M G Artists, Hogarth Business Park, Chiswick, London W4 2TH, England
Baker, Alan — Mathematician
Mathematical Science Center, Wilberforce Road, Cambridge CB3 0WB, England
Baker, Anita — Singer
Tom Estey Publicity, 144 E 22nd St, #1B, New York NY 10010, USA
Baker, Betsy — Actress
C E S D, 10635 Santa Monica Blvd, #130, Los Angeles CA 90025 USA
Baker, Blanche — Actress
Abrams Artists, 9200 W Sunset Blvd, #1125, West Hollywood CA 90069 USA
Baker, Brian — Guitarist (Bad Religion)
Goldstar Public Relations, PO Box 130, Ross on Wye HR9 6WY, England
Baker, Carroll — Actress
Abrams Artists, 9200 W Sunset Blvd, #1125, West Hollywood CA 90069 USA
Baker, Charles E (Charlie) — Football Player
PO Box 112593, Carrollton TX 75011, USA
Baker, Colin — Actor
Evans & Reiss, 100 Fawe Park Road, London SW15 2EA, England
Baker, Dale — Drummer (Sixpence None the Richer)
Nettwerk Mgmt, 1201 Villa Place, #206, Nashville TN 37212 USA
Baker, Deanna — Model
Playboy Promotions, 2706 Media Center Dr, Los Angeles CA 90065 USA
Baker, Diane — Actress
Blake Agency, 23441 Malibu Colony Road, Malibu CA 90265 USA
Baker, Donald K — Cinematographer
11789 Lakeshore N, Auburn CA 95602, USA
Baker, Douglas L (Doug) — Baseball Player
116 Woodthrush Lane, Fallbrook CA 92028, USA
Baker, Dylan — Actor
Paradigm Agency, 360 N Crescent Dr, North Building, Beverly Hills CA 90210 USA
Baker, Earl P, Jr — WW II Navy Hero (CMH)
10100 Cypress Cove Dr, #320, Fort Myers FL 33908, USA
Baker, Ellen Shulman — Astronaut
2207 Garden Stream Court, Houston TX 77062, USA
Baker, Elzie W (Buddy), Jr — Auto Racing Driver
4860 Moonlite Bay Dr, Sherrills Ford NC 28673, USA
Baker, Ginger — Drummer (Cream/Masters of Reality)
Twist Mgmt, 4230 Del Rey Ave, #621, Marina del Rey CA 90292, USA
Baker, Graham — Director
United Agents, 12-26 Lexington St, London W1F 0LE, England
Baker, Homer — WW II Army Air Corps Hero
8112 S Los Feliz Dr, Tempe AZ 85284, USA
Baker, Howard H, Jr — Senator, TN; Diplomat
Baker Donelson Assoc, 920 Massachusetts Ave NW, Washington DC 20001, USA
Baker, J Albert L (Bubba) — Football Player
2784 Trinity Court, Avon OH 44011, USA
Baker, Jaime — Ice Hockey Player
210 Highland Oaks Dr, Los Gatos CA 95032, USA
Baker, James A, III — Secretary, State
Baker & Botts, 1299 Pennsylvania Ave NW, #1200, Washington DC 20004, USA
Baker, James P (Jamie) — Ice Hockey Player
18590 Farragut Lane, Los Gatos CA 95030, USA
Baker, Janet A — Opera, Concert Singer
Transart Ltd, 8 Bristol Gardens, London W9 2JG, England

Baker, Jason M — Football Player
435 S Tryon St, #906, Charlotte NC 28202, USA
Baker, Joe Don — Actor
23339 Hatteras St, Woodland Hills CA 91367, USA
Baker, John — Dog Sled Racer
General Delivery, Kotzebue AK 99752, USA
Baker, Johnnie B (Dusty), Jr — Baseball Player, Manager
40 Livingstone Terrace Dr, San Bruno CA 94066, USA
Baker, Jordan — Actress
Douglas Gorman Rothacker, 1501 Broadway, #703, New York NY 10036, USA
Baker, Kathy — Actress
Abrams Artists, 9200 W Sunset Blvd, #1125, West Hollywood CA 90069 USA
Baker, Kenneth (Kenny) — Actor
51 Mulgrave Ave, Aston upon Ribble, Preston, Lancashire PR2 1HJ, England
Baker, Kitana — Model, Actress
PO Box 452, 231 E Alessandro Blvd, #A, Riverside CA 92502, USA
Baker, Laurie — Ice Hockey Player
67 Prairie St, Concord MA 01742, USA
Baker, Leigh-Allyn — Actor
Stone Manners Salners, 9911 W Pico Blvd, #1400, Los Angeles CA 90035 USA
Baker, Leslie David — Actor
Sutton-Barth Vennari, 145 S Fairfax Ave, #310, Los Angeles CA 90036 USA
Baker, Lewis — Singer (Danny & the Juniors)
Joe Terry Mgmt, PO Box 279, Williamstown NJ 08094, USA
Baker, Mark — Bowler
665 Park Dr, #20, Costa Mesa CA 92627, USA
Baker, Mark-Linn — Actor
2625 6th St, #2, Santa Monica CA 90405, USA
Baker, Melissa — Model
Click Model Mgmt, 881 7th Ave, New York NY 10019 USA
Baker, Michael A (Mike) — Astronaut
N A S A, Johnson Space Center, 2101 NASA Road, Houston TX 77058 USA
Baker, Myron T — Football Player
297 Pearl Road, Alexandria LA 71302, USA
Baker, Paul T — Anthropologist
337 Upton Pyne Dr, Brentwood CA 94513, USA
Baker, Penny — Model, Actress
PO Box 1116, Orchard Park NY 14127, USA
Baker, Peter — Golfer
Int'l Mgmt Group, Hogarth Business Park, Chiswick, London W4 2TH, England
Baker, Phil — Producer, Writer
I C M Partners, 10250 Constellation Blvd, #900, Los Angeles CA 90067 USA
Baker, Ralph R — Football Player
36 Sunshine Circle, Lewistown PA 17044, USA
Baker, Raymond (Ray) — Actor
Abrams Artists, 9200 W Sunset Blvd, #1125, West Hollywood CA 90069 USA
Baker, Richard H — Representative, LA
Managed Funds Assn, 2025 M St NW, #610, Washington DC 20036, USA
Baker, Rick — Makeup Artist
Cinovation Studios, 6527 San Fernando Road, Glendale CA 91201, USA
Baker, Robby — Guitarist (Tragically Hip)
Bobby Breen Mgmt, 13 Blackburn St, #300, Toronto ON M4M 2B3, Canada
Baker, Robert — Actor
Paul Kohner, 9300 Wilshire Blvd, #555, Beverly Hills CA 90212 USA
Baker, Russell W — Columnist
New York Times, Editorial Dept, 229 W 43rd St, New York NY 10036, USA
Baker, Scott Thompson — Actor, Director
11661 San Vicente Blvd, #307, Los Angeles CA 90049, USA
Baker, Sean S — Director, Producer, Writer
Gersh Agency, 9465 Wilshire Blvd, #600, Beverly Hills CA 90212 USA
Baker, Simon — Actor
Untitled Entertainment, 350 S Beverly Dr, #200, Beverly Hills CA 90212 USA
Baker, Steve — Ice Hockey Player
2929 N 70th St, #3087, Scottsdale AZ 85251, USA
Baker, T Scott — Baseball Player
327 Lingering Lane, Henderson NV 89012, USA
Baker, Terry W — Football Player
3208 SW Fairmount Blvd, Portland OR 97239, USA
Baker, Tony F — Football Player
3847 Eagleston Court, High Point NC 27265, USA
Baker, Vincent L (Vin) — Basketball Player
PO Box 179, Old Saybrook CT 06475, USA
Baker, W Thane — Track Athlete
6704 Saint John Court, Granbury TX 76049, USA
Baker, William (Bill) — Ice Hockey Player
5638 Ojibwa Road, Brainerd MN 56401, USA
Baker-Finch, Ian M — Golfer
849 Harbour Island Place, West Palm Beach FL 33410, USA
Baker-Guadagnino, Kathy — Golfer
1535 SW 4th Circle, Boca Raton FL 33486, USA
Bakhit, Marouf al- — Prime Minister, Jordan
Prime Minister's Office, PO Box 80, 35216 Amman, Jordan
Bakhtair, Rudi — Commentator
CNN-TV, 190 Marietta Ave SW, Atlanta GA 30303 USA
Bakke, Brenda — Actress
10935 Pacific View Dr, Malibu CA 90265, USA
Bakkedahl, Dan — Actor
Paradigm Agency, 360 N Crescent Dr, North Building, Beverly Hills CA 90210 USA
Bakken, Earl — Heart Surgeon, Inventor
Medtronic Inc, PO Box 38460, Waikoloa HI 96738, USA
Bakken, James L (Jim) — Football Player
4801 Holiday Dr, Madison WI 53711, USA
Bakken, Jill — Bobsled Athlete
23701 3rd Place W, Bothell WA 98021, USA
Bakker, James O (Jim) — Religious Leader
180 Grace Chapel Road, #201, Blue Eye MO 65611, USA

Bako, Brigitte — Actress
Hartig-Hilepo Agency, 54 W 21st St, #610, New York NY 10010 USA

Bako, G Paul, II — Baseball Player
500 Princeton Woods Loop, Lafayette LA 70508, USA

Bakovic, Peter (Pete) — Ice Hockey Player
7991 S 47th St, Franklin WI 53132, USA

Bakshi, Ralph — Animator
PO Box 4322, Los Angeles CA 90076, USA

Bakula, Scott — Actor
Bakula Pictures, 16255 Ventura Blvd, #625, Encino CA 91436, USA

Bala, Chris — Ice Hockey Player
271 Beacon Dr, Phoenixville PA 19460, USA

Balaban, Bob — Actor, Director
Susan Smith, 1344 N Wetherly Dr, Los Angeles CA 90069 USA

Baladi, Patrick — Actor
United Agents, 12-26 Lexington St, London W1F 0LE, England

Baladmenti, Angelo — Composer
4146 Lankershim Blvd, #401, North Hollywood CA 91602, USA

Balandin, Aleksandr N — Cosmonaut
Cosmonaut Training Center, Star City, 141160 Zvezdny Gorodok, Moscow Oblast, Russia

Balaski, Belinda — Actress
PO Box 461011, Los Angeles CA 90046, USA

Balassa, Sandor — Composer
18 Sumegvar Str, 1118 Budapest, Hungary

Balasubramanyam, Rajeev — Writer
Bloomsbury Publishing, 36 Soho Square, London W1D 3Q4, England

Balaz, John L — Baseball Player
2916 Worden St, San Diego CA 92110, USA

Balbi, Raul H (Pepe) — Boxer
Edgardo Rosani Morresi, Cortina 2057, Buenos Aires 1408, Argentina

Balboa, Marcelo — Soccer Player
13139 Hedda Dr, Cerritos CA 90703, USA

Balboni, Stephen C (Steve) — Baseball Player
117 Burlington Road, New Providence NJ 07974, USA

Baldacci, David — Writer
Grand Central Publishing, 466 Lexington Ave, #1300L, New York NY 10017, USA

Baldacci, John E — Governor, ME; Government Official
Defense Department, Pentagon, Washington DC 20301 USA

Baldelli, Rocco D — Baseball Player
81 Windsong Road, Cumberland RI 02864, USA

Balderis-Sildedzis, Helmuts — Ice Hockey Player
Hockey Federation, Raunas Lela 23, 1039 Tiga, Latvia

Balderstone, James S — Businessman
115 Mont Albert Road, Canterbury VIC 3126, Australia

Baldes, Kevin — Bassist (Lit)
Sepetys Entertainment, 5543 Edmondson Park, #8A, Nashville TN 37211, USA

Baldeschwieler, John D — Chemist
PO Box 50065, Pasadena CA 91115, USA

Baldessari, John — Conceptual Artist, Photographer
702 6th Ave, Venice CA 90291, USA

Balding, Rebecca — Actress
2001 Winnetka Place, Woodland Hills CA 91364, USA

Baldinger, Brian D — Football Player, Sportscaster
21 S Elmwood Road, Marlton NJ 08053, USA

Baldinger, Gary T — Football Player
114 Adam Road, Massapequa NY 11758, USA

Baldinger, Richard L (Rich) — Football Player
5401 Phelps Road, Kansas City MO 64136, USA

Baldini, Ercole — Cyclist
Viale Bologna 103, 04710 Ferli, Italy

Baldischwiler, J Karl — Football Player
3033 N Willow Dr, Newcastle OK 73065, USA

Baldock, Bobby Ray — Judge
US Court of Appeals, PO Box 2388, Roswell NM 88202, USA

Baldoni, Justin — Actor
TalentWorks, 3500 W Olive Ave, #1400, Burbank CA 91505 USA

Baldschun, Jack E — Baseball Player
311 Erie Road, Green Bay WI 54311, USA

Balducci, Lorenzo — Actor
Carol Levi Mgmt, Via G Pisanelli 2, 00196 Rome, Italy

Baldwin, Adam — Actor
Innovative Artists, 1505 10th St, Santa Monica CA 90401 USA

Baldwin, Alec — Actor
N2N Entertainment, 1230 Montana Ave, #203, Santa Monica CA 90403, USA

Baldwin, Bobby — Poker Player
City Center Las Vegas, 3780 Las Vegas Boulevard S, Paradise NV 89109, USA

Baldwin, Daniel — Actor
Chaotik, 6446 Santa Monica Blvd, Los Angeles CA 90038 90038, USA

Baldwin, David G (Dave) — Baseball Player
PO Box 190, Yachats OR 97498, USA

Baldwin, Hunt — Producer, Writer
Creative Artists Agency, 2000 Ave of Stars, #100, Los Angeles CA 90067 USA

Baldwin, Jack — Auto Racing Driver
4748 Balmoral Way NE, Marietta GA 30068, USA

Baldwin, Jack E — Chemist
Oxford University, Dyson Perrins Laboratory, S Parks Road, Oxford OX1 3QY, England

Baldwin, John A (Jack), Jr — Navy Admiral
1371 Millersville Road, Millersville MD 21108, USA

Baldwin, John, Jr — Figure Skater
Lee Marshall Mgmt, 199 E Garfield Ave, Aurora OH 44202, USA

Baldwin, Judith — Actress
Grant Savic Kopaloff & Associates, 6399 Wilshire Blvd, #415, Los Angeles CA 90048, USA

Baldwin, Karen D — Beauty Queen, Actress
Miss Universe Organization, 1370 Ave of Americas, #1600, New York NY 10019 USA

Baldwin, Keith M — Football Player
124 Leonardville Road, Belford NJ 07718, USA

Baldwin, Kevin — Writer
Bloomsbury Publishing, 36 Soho Square, London W1D 3Q4, England

Baldwin, Margaret — Writer
PO Box 1106, Williams Bay WI 53191, USA

Baldwin, Randy C — Football Player
715 Peeples St SW, #10, Atlanta GA 30310, USA

Baldwin, Stephen — Actor
Chaotik, 6446 Santa Monica Blvd, Los Angeles CA 90038, USA

Baldwin, William — Editor
Forbes, Editorial Dept, 60 5th Ave, New York NY 10011, USA

Baldwin, William (Billy) — Actor
Brillstein Entertainment Partners, 9150 Wilshire Blvd, #350, Beverly Hills CA 90212 USA

Bale, Christian — Actor
W M E Entertainment, 9601 Wilshire Blvd, #300, Beverly Hills CA 90210 USA

Bale, John R — Baseball Player
9017 Roberts Road, Odessa FL 33556, USA

Bales, Michael (Mike) — Ice Hockey Player
470 Brunswick Ave, Toronto ON M5R 2Z5, Canada

Balestrini, Jose — Opera Singer
I M G Artists, Hogarth Business Park, Chiswick, London W4 2TH, England

Balfour, Earl — Ice Hockey Player
71 Beasley Crescent, Cambridge ON N1T 1P5, Canada

Balfour, Eric — Actor
United Talent Agency, 9336 Civic Center Dr, Beverly Hills CA 90210 USA

Balfour, Grant R — Baseball Player
2678 N McMullen Booth Road, Clearwater FL 33761, USA

Baliani, Marco — Actor
Carol Levi Mgmt, Via G Pisanelli 2, 00196 Rome, Italy

Baliga, Bantval Jayant — Electrical Engineer
2612 Bembridge Dr, Raleigh NC 27613, USA

Baliles, Gerald L — Governor, VA
University of Virginia, Miller Public Affairs School, Charlottesville VA 22903, USA

Balin, Marty — Singer, Songwriter
Joe Buchwald, 811 31st Ave, San Francisco CA 94121, USA

Balitran, Celine — Model
T F 6, 120 Ave Charles de Gaulle, 92522 Neuilly-sur-Seine Cedex, France

Bality, Oded — Photojournalist
Associated Press, 450 W 33rd St, #1500, New York NY 10001 USA

Balk, Fairuza — Actress
Don Buchwald/Fortitude, 6500 Wilshire Blvd, #2200, Los Angeles CA 90048 USA

Balkenhol, Klaus — Equestrian
Narzissenweg 11A, 40723 Hilden, Germany

Ball, Angeline — Actress
Marfarlane Chard, 7 Adelaide St, Dun Laoghaire, Dublin, Ireland

Ball, David — Singer (Soft Cell), Songwriter
Susan Collier Mgmt, 6204 Jocelyn Hollow Road, Nashville TN 37205, USA

Ball, David S (Dave) — Football Player
208 Tarrington Court, Brentwood TN 37027, USA

Ball, David W — Writer
7744 Valmont Road, Boulder CO 80301, USA

Ball, Eric C — Football Player
10614 Margate Terrace, Cincinnati OH 45241, USA

Ball, Jerry L — Football Player
3311 Meadowside Dr, Sugar Land TX 77478, USA

Ball, Larry L — Football Player
8830 SW 57th St, Cooper City FL 33328, USA

Ball, Marcia — Singer, Pianist, Songwriter
Rosebud Agency, PO Box 170429, San Francisco CA 94117 USA

Ball, Michael A — Singer, Actor
Works Public Relations, 11 Marshalsea Road, London SE1 1EN, England

Ball, Sam — Actor
Robert Stein Mgmt, 1180 S Beverly Drive, #304, Los Angeles CA 90035, USA

Ball, Taylor — Actor
W M E Entertainment, 9601 Wilshire Blvd, #300, Beverly Hills CA 90210 USA

Ball, Terry — Ice Hockey Player
4502 Torrington Ave, Parma OH 44134, USA

Balladur, Edouard — Prime Minister, France
5 Rue Jean Formige, 75015 Paris, France

Ballantine, Sara — Actress
Brady Brannon Rich, 5670 Wilshire Blvd, #820, Los Angeles CA 90036 USA

Ballantyne, Frederick — Governor General, St Vincent-Grenadines
Governor General's Office, Kingstown, Saint Vincent & Grenadines

Ballard, Alimi — Actor
Stone Manners Salners, 9911 W Pico Blvd, #1400, Los Angeles CA 90035 USA

Ballard, Carroll — Director
PO Box 556, Saint Helena CA 94574, USA

Ballard, Del, Jr — Bowler
Ebonite International, PO Box 746, Hopkinsville KY 42241, USA

Ballard, Donald E — Vietnam War Navy Hero (CMH)
PO Box 34593, Kansas City MO 64116, USA

Ballard, Glen — Songwriter
Gorfaine/Schwartz, 4111 W Alameda Ave, #509, Burbank CA 91505 USA

Ballard, Gregory (Greg) — Basketball Player
100 Arborcrest Court, Tyrone GA 30290, USA

Ballard, Howard L — Football Player
PO Box 584, Ashland AL 36251, USA

Ballard, Jeffrey S (Jeff) — Baseball Player
4828 Rimrock Road, Billings MT 59106, USA

Ballard, Kaye — Actress, Comedienne
C E S D, 10635 Santa Monica Blvd, #130, Los Angeles CA 90025 USA

Ballard, Keith — Ice Hockey Player
2336 River Pointe Circle, Minneapolis MN 55411, USA

Ballard, Robert D — Oceanographer (Titanic Discoverer)
Institute for Exploration, 55 Coogan Blvd, Mystic CT 06355, USA

Ballas, Mark A (Corky), Sr — Professional Dancer
Commercial Talent, 9255 Sunset Blvd, #505, West Hollywood CA 90069, USA

Ballas, Mark A, Jr — Professional Dancer
Nocturnal Entertainment, 11735 Dorothy St, #302, Los Angeles CA 90049, USA
Baller, Jay S — Baseball Player
303 Spring Valley Road, Reading PA 19605, USA
Ballerini, Edoardo — Actor
Markham & Froggatt, Julian House, 4 Windmill St, London W1P 1HF, England
Ballestrini, Veronica — Singer, Songwriter
11 Centre St, #6, Salem CT 06385, USA
Ballhaus, Michael — Cinematographer
11 Elm Place, Rye NY 10580, USA
Ballmer, Steven A (Steve) — Businessman
Microsoft Corp, 1 Microsoft Way, Redmond WA 98052, USA
Ballou, Mark — Actor
Total Talent Mgmt, 136 Centre St, Nutley NJ 07110, USA
Balloun, James S — Businessman
National Service Industry, 1420 Peachtree St NE, #200, Atlanta GA 30309, USA
Balmaseda, Liz — Journalist
Palm Beach Post, Editorial Dept, 2751 S Dixie Highway, West Palm Beach FL 33405, USA
Balmer, Dan — Jazz Guitarist
Sterling Talent, PO Box 231059, Tigard OR 97281, USA
Balmer, Jean-Francois — Actor
Artmedia, 20 Ave Rapp, 75007 Paris, France
Balmond, Cecil — Structural Engineer
University of Pennsylvania, School of Design, Philadelphia PA 19104, USA
Balsam, Talia — Actress
Gersh Agency, 9465 Wilshire Blvd, #600, Beverly Hills CA 90212 USA
Balsley, Philip E — Singer (Statler Brothers)
191 Abbington Road, Swoope VA 24479, USA
Balsom, Alison — Concert Trumpet Player
Harrison/Parrott, 5-6 Albion Court, London W6 0QT, England
Baltacha, Elena — Tennis Player
Octagon Worldwide, 1751 Pinnacle Dr, #1500, McLean VA 22102 USA
Baltimore, Bryon — Ice Hockey Player
McCauig Desrochers, 2401 10088th Ave NW, Edmonton AB T5J 2Z1, Canada
Baltimore, Charli — Rap Artist
The Inc Records, PO Box 40538, Glen Oaks NY 11004, USA
Baltimore, David L — Nobel Medicine Laureate, Educator
31460 Beach Park Road, Malibu CA 90265, USA
Baltsa, Agnes — Opera Singer
Schultz Mgmt, Rutistr 52, 8044 Zurich-Gockhausen, Switzerland
Baltz, Lewis — Photographer
23 Rue des Blancs Mantgaux, 75004 Paris, France
Balukas, Jean — Billiards Player
9818 4th Ave, Brooklyn NY 11209, USA
Balutin, Jacques — Actor
Artmedia, 20 Ave Rapp, 75007 Paris, France
Baluyut, James — Guitarist, Keyboardist (Versus)
Ground Control Touring, 20 Jay St, #838, Brooklyn NY 11201, USA
Baluyut, Richard — Singer, Guitarist (Versus)
Ground Control Touring, 20 Jay St, #838, Brooklyn NY 11201, USA
Bama, Jim — Artist
27 Dunn Creek Road, Cody WY 82414, USA
Bambaataa, Afrika — Rap Artist
K L B Productions, 70 Greenwich Ave, #441, New York NY 10011, USA
Bamber, David J — Actor
Ken McReddie Assoc, 11 Connaught Place, London W2 2ET, England
Bamert, Matthias — Conductor
Scottish National Orchestra, 3 La Belle Place, Glasgow G3 7LH, Scotland
Bamford, Maria — Actress, Comedienne
OmniPop Talent Group, 4605 Lankershim Blvd, #201, Toluca Lake CA 91602 USA
Ban Ki Moon — Government Official, South Korea
Secretary-General's Office, 1 United Nations Plaza, New York NY 10017, USA
Bana, Eric — Actor, Comedian
8-12 Sandilands St, #2, South Melbourne VIC 3205, Australia
Banach, Edward (Ed) — Freestyle Wrestler
2128 Country Club Blvd, Ames IA 50014, USA
Banach, Louis (Lou) — Freestyle Wrestler
1828 Tallgrass Circle, Waukesha WI 53188, USA
Banachowski, Andy — Volleyball Player, Coach
University of California, Athletic Dept, Los Angeles CA 90024, USA
Banas, Michaela — Actress
Channel 7 Sydney, Television Center, Mobbs Lane, Epping NSW 2121, Australia
Banaszak, John A — Football Player
420 Robinhood Lane, Canonsburg PA 15317, USA
Banaszak, Peter A (Pete) — Football Player
1021 Inverness Dr, Saint Augustine FL 32092, USA
Banaszek, Casimir J (Cas), II — Football Player
1018 Cohen Court, Petaluma CA 94952, USA
Banaszynski, Jacqui — Journalist
Saint Paul Pioneer Press, Editorial Dept, 345 Cedar St, Saint Paul MN 55101, USA
Bancroft, Ann — Explorer, Cross Country Skier
Yourexpedition, 1920 Oliver Place S, Minneapolis MN 55405, USA
Bancroft, Cameron — Actor
Characters Talent Mgmt, 8 Elm St, Toronto ON M5G 1G7, Canada
Bancroft, George M — Chemist
Western Ontario University, Chemistry Dept, London ON N6A 3K7, Canada
Band, Alexander M (Alex) — Singer (Calling), Songwriter
The Firm, 2049 Century Park E, #2550, Los Angeles CA 90067 USA
Band, Richard H — Composer
24053 Bessemer St, Woodland Hills CA 91367, USA
Banda, Joyce H — Government Official,
President's Office, BP 1463, Bamako, Mali
Banda, Rupiah — President, Zambia
Boston University, African President in Residence Program, Boston MA 02215, USA
Banderas, Antonio — Actor, Singer, Director
Media Art Mgmt, C/ Castelló 82, 2 Derecha, 28006 Madrid, Spain

Bandholz, Willy — Handball Player
Sonnholm 92, 24977 Westerholz, Germany

Bando, Christopher M (Chris) — Baseball Player
638 Walsall Road, El Cajon CA 92019, USA

Bando, Salvatore L (Sal) — Baseball Player
W308N6225 Shore Acres Road, Hartland WI 53029, USA

Bandy, Moe — Singer, Songwriter
Blackwood Mgmt, PO Box 5331, Sevierville TN 37864, USA

Bane, Edward N (Eddie) — Baseball Player
598 Paloma Court, Encinitas CA 92024, USA

Banes, Lisa — Actress
Don Buchwald/Fortitude, 6500 Wilshire Blvd, #2200, Los Angeles CA 90048 USA

Banfield, Ashleigh — Commentator
NBC-TV, News Dept, 30 Rockefeller Plaza, #270E, New York NY 10112 USA

Banfield, Bever-Leigh — Actress
Gersh Agency, 9465 Wilshire Blvd, #600, Beverly Hills CA 90212 USA

Banfield, J Anthony (Tony) — Football Player
1010 Myrtlewood Dr, Friendswood TX 77546, USA

Bang, Molly — Writer, Illustrator
43 Drumlin Road, Falmouth MA 02540, USA

Bangalter, Thomas — Musician (Daft Punk)
Primary Talent International, 10-11 Jockey's Fields, London WC1R 4BN, England

Bangemann, Martin — Government Official, West Germany
Telefonica, Gran Via 28, 28013 Madrid, Spain

Bangerter, Norman H — Governor, UT
603 E South Temple, Salt Lake City UT 84102, USA

Banham, Frank — Ice Hockey Player
139 W Grayling Lane, Suffield CT 06078, USA

Bank, Melissa — Writer
Rabineay Wachter Sanford, 1107 1/2 Glendon Ave, Los Angeles CA 90024, USA

Banker, Ted — Football Player
1862 Park Ave, East Meadow NY 11554, USA

Bankhead, M Scott — Baseball Player
1236 Idlewood Dr, Asheboro NC 27205, USA

Banks, Anthony L (Tony) — Football Player
2211 Vaquero Club Dr, Westlake TX 76262, USA

Banks, Azealia A — Rap Artist
Polydor Records, 364-366 Kensington High St, London W14 8NS, England

Banks, Barry — Opera Singer
I M G Artists, 152 W 57th St, #500, New York NY 10019 USA

Banks, Brian G — Baseball Player
2232 E 900 S, Salt Lake City UT 84108, USA

Banks, Carl E — Football Player
7 Glenview Dr, Warren NJ 07059, USA

Banks, Darren — Ice Hockey Player
11 Millington Road, Pleasant Ridge MI 48069, USA

Banks, Dennis — Indian Rights Activist
General Delivery, Oglala SD 57764, USA

Banks, Elizabeth — Actress, Model, Producer
United Talent Agency, 9336 Civic Center Dr, Beverly Hills CA 90210 USA

Banks, Ernest (Ernie) — Baseball Player
27 N Wacker Dr, #466, Chicago IL 60606, USA

Banks, Estes — Football Player
640 Gooseberry Dr, #703, Longmont CO 80503, USA

Banks, Eugene L (Gene) — Basketball Player
1210 Sloan St, Greensboro NC 27401, USA

Banks, Frederick R (Fred) — Football Player
5665 Orly Terrace, Atlanta GA 30349, USA

Banks, Gordon G — Football Player
2644 E Trinity Mills Road, Carrollton TX 75006, USA

Banks, Jonathan — Actor
Lovett Mgmt, 1327 Brinkley Ave, Los Angeles CA 90049, USA

Banks, Kelcie H — Boxer
Tocco's Ringside Gym, 9 W Charleston, Las Vegas NV 89102, USA

Banks, Leann — Bassist (Von Bondies)
Tsunami Entertainment, 2525 Hyperion Ave, Los Angeles CA 90027, USA

Banks, Lloyd — Rap Artist
Emmel Communications, 36 W 25th St, #1100, New York NY 10010, USA

Banks, Lynne Reid — Writer
Harper Collins Publishers, 10 E 53rd St, Cellar 1, New York NY 10022 USA

Banks, Morwenna — Actress, Comedienne
I C M Partners, 10250 Constellation Blvd, #900, Los Angeles CA 90067 USA

Banks, Russell — Writer
Trident Media Group, 41 Madison Ave, #3600, New York NY 10010, USA

Banks, Steven — Actor, Comedian, Writer
Creative Artists Agency, 2000 Ave of Stars, #100, Los Angeles CA 90067 USA

Banks, Thomas S (Tom), Jr — Football Player
358 Wisteria St, Fairhope AL 36532, USA

Banks, Tyra — Model, Actress
W M E Entertainment, 9601 Wilshire Blvd, #300, Beverly Hills CA 90210 USA

Banks, W Chip — Football Player
709 Albany Ave, Augusta GA 30901, USA

Banks, Walker B — Basketball Player
3207 Brentwood Dr, Champaign IL 61821, USA

Banks, William A (Willie), III — Track Athlete
250 Williams St NW, #6000, Atlanta GA 30303, USA

Banks, Willie A — Baseball Player
13 Michael St, Jamesburg NJ 08831, USA

Bankston, Michael — Football Player
182 N Burberry Park Circle, Spring TX 77382, USA

Bankston, Warren S — Football Player
4201 Bordeaux Dr, Kenner LA 70065, USA

Bannan, Justin L — Football Player
561 Mockingbird Dr, Belgrade MT 59714, USA

Banner, David — Rap Artist, Actor
Creative Artists Agency, 2000 Ave of Stars, #100, Los Angeles CA 90067 USA

Banner, Jon — Commentator
ABC-TV, News Dept, 77 W 66th St, New York NY 10023 USA
Bannerman, Isabella — Cartoonist (Six Chix)
41 South Drive, Hastings-on-Hudson NY 10706, USA
Bannerman, Murray — Ice Hockey Player
7222 Kiowa Road, Larkspur CO 80118, USA
Bannister, Alan — Baseball Player
6349 N 78th St, #129, Scottsdale AZ 85250, USA
Bannister, Brian P — Baseball Player
6701 E Caballo Dr, Paradise Valley AZ 85253, USA
Bannister, Floyd F — Baseball Player
6701 Caballo Dr, Paradise Valley AZ 85253, USA
Bannister, Kenneth (Ken) — Basketball Player
2322 Broadgreen Dr, Missouri City TX 77489, USA
Bannister, Roger G — Track Athlete, Neurologist
21 Bardwell Road, Oxford OX2 6SV, England
Bannon, Jack — Actor
6470 E Sunnyside Road, Coeur D'Alene ID 83814, USA
Bans, Jenna — Producer
I C M Partners, 10250 Constellation Blvd, #900, Los Angeles CA 90067 USA
Banse, Juliane — Opera Singer
Kunstler Sekretariat am Gasteig, Rosenheimer Str 52, 81669 Munich, Germany
Banta, D Bradford (Brad) — Football Player
1100 Smith Ave, Birmingham MI 48009, USA
Banta-Cain, Tully — Football Player
27 Apple Valley Dr, Sharon MA 2067, USA
Bantom, Michael A (Mike) — Basketball Player, Executive
418 Egret Lane, Secaucus NJ 07094, USA
Banton, Buju — Singer
Agency Group Ltd, 142 W 57th St, #600, New York NY 10019 USA
Banville, John — Writer
Gillon Aitken Assoc, 29 Fernshaw Road, London SW10 0TG, England
Bao, Joseph Y — Microsurgeon, Orthopedist
17436 Terry Lyn Lane, Cerritos CA 90703, USA
Baquero, Ivana — Actress
Eduardo Gonzalez Valdivia, Isaac Peral 48, #1B, 28040 Madrid, Spain
Bar, Olaf — Opera Singer
Opus 3 Artists, 470 Park Ave S, #900N, New York NY 10016 USA
Baraban, Yannis — Actor
Artmedia, 20 Ave Rapp, 75007 Paris, France
Barahona, Ralph — Ice Hockey Player
317 1/2 E Plymouth St, Long Beach CA 90805, USA
Barajas, Rodridgo R (Rod) — Baseball Player
8533 N 50th Place, Paradise Valley AZ 85253, USA
Barak, Ehud — Prime Minister, Israel; Army General
Defense Ministry, Kaplan St, Hakirya, Tel-Aviv 67659, Israel
Baraka, Imamu Amiri (LeRoi Jones) — Writer
State University of New York, Afro American Studies Dept, Stony Brook NY 11794, USA
Baranova, Anastasia — Actress
4 H M, 11340 Moorpark St, Studio City CA 91602, USA
Baranski, Christine — Actress
United Talent Agency, 9336 Civic Center Dr, Beverly Hills CA 90210 USA
Barasso, Tom — Ice Hockey Player
12820 Rosalie St, Raleigh NC 27614, USA
Barats, Luke — Actor, Comedian
Independent Artists, 9601 Wilshire Blvd, #750, Beverly Hills CA 90210, USA
Barbacid, Mariano — Onocologist
Spanish National Cancer Research Center, Melchor Fernandez Almagro 3, 28029 Madrid, Spain
Barbacini, Maurizio — Conductor
I M G Artists, Hogarth Business Park, Chiswick, London W4 2TH, England
Barbakow, Jeffrey C — Businessman
Tenet Healthcare Corp, 13737 Noel Road, #100, Dallas TX 75240, USA
Barbarin, Philippe X I Cardinal — Religious Leader
Archdiocese, 1 Place de Fourviere, 69321 Lyon Cedex 05, France
Barbaro, Gary W — Football Player
1000 Giuffrias Ave, Metairie LA 70001, USA
Barbato, Randy — Director, Producer
World of Wonder, 6650 Hollywood Blvd, #400, Los Angeles CA 90028, USA
Barbeau, Adrienne — Actress, Singer
Bauman Redanty Shaul Agency, 5757 Wilshire Blvd, #473, Los Angeles CA 90036 USA
Barber, Aaron — Golfer
2830 Fillmore St NE, Minneapolis MN 55418, USA
Barber, Atiim K (Tiki) — Football Player, Sportscaster
Greater Talent Network, 437 5th Ave, #700, New York NY 10016, USA
Barber, Bill — Ice Hockey Player, Coach
1112 Peppertree Court, #223, Sarasota FL 34242, USA
Barber, Christopher E (Chris) — Football Player
2621 Monaco Cove Circle, Orlando FL 32825, USA
Barber, Glynis — Actress
Waring & McKenna, Mayfair, 11-12 Dover St, London W1S 4LJ, England
Barber, J Oronde (Ronde) — Football Player
17119 Journeys End Dr, Odessa FL 33556, USA
Barber, John (Skip), III — Auto Racing Driver, Executive
497 Lime Rock Road, Lakeville CT 06039, USA
Barber, Lance — Actor
Paul Kohner, 9300 Wilshire Blvd, #555, Beverly Hills CA 90212 USA
Barber, Marion, III — Football Player
PO Box 191348, Dallas TX 75219, USA
Barber, Marion, Jr — Football Player
PO Box 46106, Minneapolis MN 55446, USA
Barber, Michael D (Mike) — Football Player
PO Box 2424, DeSoto TX 75123, USA
Barber, Michael L (Mike) — Football Player
43 Mill Creek Crossing, Hurricane WV 25526, USA
Barber, Miller — Golfer
8215 N 54th St, Paradise Valley AZ 85253, USA

B

Banner - Barber

Barber, Patricia — Jazz Singer, Pianist, Composer
Blue Note Records, 304 Park Ave S, New York NY 10010, USA

Barber, Paul — Actor, Writer, Producer
Diamond Mgmt, 31 Percy St, London W1T 2DD, England

Barber, Stewart C (Stew) — Football Player
2138 Country Manor Dr, Mount Pleasant SC 29466, USA

Barber, William — Cinematographer
2509 White Chapel Place, Thousand Oaks CA 91362, USA

Barberie, Bret E — Baseball Player
11607 Bos St, Cerritos CA 90703, USA

Barberie-Reynolds, Jillian — Sportscaster, Actress
KTTV Fox-TV, 1999 S Bundy Dr, Los Angeles CA 90025, USA

Barberos, Alessandro — Businessman
Fiat Spa, Corso G Marconi 10/20, 10125 Turin, Italy

Barbi, Shane — Model (Barbi Twins)
A T Y, 4725 N Lois Ave, Tampa FL 33614, USA

Barbi, Sia — Model (Barbi Twins)
A T Y, 4725 N Lois Ave, Tampa FL 33614, USA

Barbieri, Gato — Jazz Saxophonist
Andi Howard Entertainment, 100 N Crescent Ave, #275, Beverly Hills CA 90210, USA

Barbieri, Paula — Actress, Model
Warner Books, 1271 Ave of Americas, New York NY 10020 USA

Barbieri, Richard — Keyboardist (Japan, Porcupine Tree)
Agency Group Ltd, 361-373 City Road, London EC1V 2QA, England

Barbosa, Leandro M — Basketball Player
8046 E Vista Canyon St, Litchfield Park AZ 85340, USA

Barbour, Ian G — Nuclear Physicist, Templeton Laureate
Carleton College, Theology Dept, Northfield MN 55057, USA

Barbour, John — Actor, Comedian, Writer
10309 Denman St, Las Vegas NV 89178, USA

Barbuscia, Lisa — Actress, Singer
Independent Talent Group, Oxford House, 76 Oxford St, London W1D 1BS, England

Barbutti, Pete — Jazz Trumpeter
Thomas Cassidy, 11761 E Speedway Blvd, Tucson AZ 85748 USA

Barcelo, Rich — Golfer
5195 N Spring View Dr, Tucson AZ 85749, USA

Barch, Krystoger (Krys) — Ice Hockey Player
Dallas Stars, 2601 Ave of Stars, #100, Frisco TX 75034 USA

Barclay, Paris — Director, Producer
Paradigm Agency, 360 N Crescent Dr, North Building, Beverly Hills CA 90210 USA

Bard, Allen J — Chemist
6202 Mountainclimb Dr, Austin TX 78731, USA

Bard, Joshua D (Josh) — Baseball Player
2139 Beechnut Place, Castle Rock CO 80108, USA

Bard, Marjorie — Social Activist
Women Organized Against Homelessness, PO Box 911, Saint Michaels MD 21663, USA

Bardeen, William A — Physicist
Fermi National Accelerator Laboratory, PO Box 500, Batavia IL 60510, USA

Bardem, Javier E — Actor
Bloom Hergott Diemer, 150 S Rodeo Dr, #300, Beverly Hills CA 90212 USA

Barden, Brian D — Baseball Player
3935 E Rough Rider Road, #1173, Phoenix AZ 85050, USA

Barden, Jessica — Actress
W M E Entertainment, 9601 Wilshire Blvd, #300, Beverly Hills CA 90210 USA

Bardot, Brigitte — Actress
La Madrigue, 83990 Saint Tropez, Var, France

Bare, James — Air Force Hero
3618 NW 47th St, Oklahoma City OK 73112, USA

Bare, Richard L — Director
700 Harbor Island Dr, Newport Beach CA 92660, USA

Bare, Robert J (Bobby) — Singer, Guitarist, Songwriter
Bobby Bare Enterprises, 112 The Landing, Hendersonville TN 37075, USA

Barea, Jose J (J J) — Basketball Player
Minnesota Timberwolves, Target Center, 600 1st Ave N, Minneapolis MN 55403 USA

Bareikis, Arija — Actress
Gersh Agency, 41 Madison Ave, #3301, New York NY 10010 USA

Bareilles, Sara — Singer, Pianist, Songwriter
Career Artist Mgmt, 1100 Glendon Ave, #1100, Los Angeles CA 90024, USA

Barek, Djemel — Actor
Artmedia, 20 Ave Rapp, 75007 Paris, France

Baren, Justin — Bassist (Redwalls)
Pinnacle Entertainment, 30 Glenn St, White Plains NY 10603, USA

Baren, Logan — Singer, Guitarist (Redwalls)
Pinnacle Entertainment, 30 Glenn St, White Plains NY 10603, USA

Barenboim, Daniel — Conductor, Concert Pianist
29 Rue de la Coulouvreeniere, 1206 Geneva, Switzerland

Baretto, Ray — Percussionist
Creative Music Consultants, 181 Christie St, #300, New York NY 10002, USA

Barfield, Jesse L — Baseball Player
5814 Spanish Moss Court, Spring TX 77379, USA

Barfod, Hakon — Yachtsman
Jon Ostensensv 15, 1360 Nesbru, Norway

Barfoed, Kasper — Director
United Talent Agency, 9336 Civic Center Dr, Beverly Hills CA 90210 USA

Bargnani, Andrea — Basketball Player
Toronto Raptors, Air Canada Center, 20 Bay St, Toronto ON M5J 2N8, Canada

Barinholtz, Ike — Actor, Comedian
A P A Talent/Literary Agency, 405 S Beverly Dr, #300, Beverly Hills CA 90212 USA

Barisich, Carl J — Football Player
1744 N 134th Lane, Goodyear AZ 85395, USA

Barjatya, Sooraj — Director, Producer
1 Bhana, 422 Veer Sawarkar Road Prabhadevi Dadar, Mumbai MS 400025, India

Barkauskas, Antanas S — Chairman of Presidium, Lithuania
Akmenu Str 7A, Vilnus, Lithuania

Barker, Bryan C — Football Player
200 1st St, #203, Neptune Beach FL 32266, USA

Barker, Cameron (Cam) — Ice Hockey Player
Minnesota Wild, XCel Energy Arena, 1275 Saint Antoine W, Saint Paul MN 55104 USA
Barker, Clive — Writer, Director
Midnight Picture Show, PO Box 691821, West Hollywood CA 90069, USA
Barker, Clyde F — Surgeon
3 Coopertown Road, Haverford PA 19041, USA
Barker, David J P — Epidemiologist
Manor Farm, East Dean near Salisbury, Wiltshire SP5 1HB, England
Barker, James F — Educator
Clemson University, President's Office, Clemson SC 29634, USA
Barker, Kevin S — Baseball Player
PO Box 96, Mendota VA 24270, USA
Barker, Lee — Bass Guitar Designer
1842 SE 1st St, Redmond OR 97756, USA
Barker, Leo — Football Player
25 Via Lucena, San Clemente CA 92673, USA
Barker, Leonard H (Len) — Baseball Player
10690 Locust Grove Dr, Chardon OH 44024, USA
Barker, Lucius — Political Scientist
Stanford University, Political Science Dept, Stanford CA 94305, USA
Barker, Michael — Director
Sony Pictures Classics, 550 Madison Ave, New York NY 10022, USA
Barker, Mike — Producer, Writer, Actor
United Talent Agency, 9336 Civic Center Dr, Beverly Hills CA 90210 USA
Barker, Pamela — Boxer
1617 Mexican Poppy St, Las Vegas NV 89128, USA
Barker, Pat — Writer
Gillon Aitken, 29 Fernshaw Road, London SW10 0TG, England
Barker, Robert W (Bob) — Entertainer
Kazarian/Spencer/Ruskin, 11969 Ventura Blvd, #300, Studio City CA 91604 USA
Barker, Roy — Football Player
23 Saint Marks Circle, Islandia NY 11749, USA
Barker, Travis — Drummer (Blink-182, +44)
7325 Seafarer Place, Carlsbad CA 92011, USA
Barkett, Rosemary — Judge
US Court of Appeals, 99 NE 4th St, #1223, Miami FL 33132, USA
Barkin, Ellen — Actress
Creative Artists Agency, 2000 Ave of Stars, #100, Los Angeles CA 90067 USA
Barkley, Charles W — Basketball Player, Sportscaster
7615 E Vaquero Dr, Scottsdale AZ 85258, USA
Barkley, Douglas (Doug) — Ice Hockey Player, Coach
523-3131 63 Ave NE, Calgary AB T3E 6N4, Canada
Barkley, Iran — Boxer
John Henry Reetz, 222 E 27th St, #3, New York NY 10016, USA
Barkman Tyler, Jane (Janie) — Swimmer
Princeton University, Athletic Dept, Princeton NJ 08544, USA
Barkmin, Gun-Brit — Opera Singer
Columbia Artists Mgmt Inc, 1790 Broadway, #702, New York NY 10019 USA
Barks, Samantha — Actress, Singer
United Agents, 12-26 Lexington St, London W1F 0LE, England
Barksdale, Chuck — Singer (Dells)
Associated Booking Corp, 501 Madison Ave, #603, New York NY 10022 USA
Barksdale, James (Jim) — Businessman
Barksdale Group, 2730 Sand Hill Road, Menlo Park CA 94025, USA
Barksdale, Rhesa H — Judge
US Court of Appeals, 245 E Capitol St, Jackson MS 39201, USA
Barkum, Jerome P — Football Player
2720 Palmer Dr, #15, Gulfport MS 39507, USA
Barlett, Donald L — Journalist
Wylie Agency, 250 W 57th St, #2114, New York NY 10107 USA
Barletta, Joseph — Publisher
TV Guide, Publisher's Office, 100 Matsonford Road, Wayne PA 19080, USA
Barlow, Bob — Ice Hockey Player
4912 Wesley Road, Victoria BC V8Y 1Y5, Canada
Barlow, Craig — Golfer
644 Desert Passage St, Henderson NV 89002, USA
Barlow, Gary — Singer, Pianist, Songwriter
International Talent Booking, Ariel House, 74A Charlotte St, #100 London W1T 4QJ, England
Barlow, Kevan C — Football Player
82 Waterfront Dr, Pittsburgh PA 15222, USA
Barlow, Lou — Singer, Guitarist, Songwriter
Dog Day Press, 40 Bowling Green Lane, #35, London EC1R 0NE, England
Barlow, Michael R (Mike) — Baseball Player
Sheftic, 4524 Francis Road, Cazenovia NY 13035, USA
Barlow, Perry — Cartoonist
New Yorker, Editorial Dept, 4 Times Square, Basement C1B, New York NY 10036 USA
Barlow, Reggie D — Football Player
8311 Timber Trace Lane, Pike Road AL 36064, USA
Barmes, Clint H — Baseball Player
113 Mallard Court, Mead CO 80542, USA
Barnaby, Matthew — Ice Hockey Player
134 King Anthony Way, Getzville NY 14068, USA
Barnard, Aneurin — Actor
Ken McReddie Assoc, 11 Connaught Place, London W2 2ET, England
Barnathan, Michael — Producer
1492 Pictures, 4000 Warner Blvd, Building 3, Burbank CA 91522, USA
Barndt, Thomas A (Tom) — Football Player
11041 Romola St, Las Vegas NV 89141, USA
Barner, Bob — Writer
2100 Green St, #206, San Francisco CA 94123, USA
Barnes, Aaron — Cinematographer
Gersh Agency, 9465 Wilshire Blvd, #600, Beverly Hills CA 90212 USA
Barnes, Benny J — Football Player
5003 Fleming Ave, Richmond CA 94804, USA
Barnes, Brenda C — Businesswoman
Sara Lee Corp, 3500 Lacey Road, Downers Grove IL 60515, USA

B

Barnes, Brian — Golfer
International Golf Partners, 3300 PGA Blvd, #820, Palm Beach Gardens FL 33410, USA

Barnes, Brian K — Baseball Player
860 River Cove Dr, Dacula GA 30019, USA

Barnes, Chris — Bowler
Professional Bowlers Assn, 719 2nd Ave, #701, Seattle WA 98104 USA

Barnes, Christopher Daniel — Actor
Agency S G H, 6525 Sunset Blvd, #PH9, Hollywood CA 90028, USA

Barnes, Danny — Singer, Musician (Bad Livers)
East Central One, All Saints Road, Suffolk 1P6 8PR, England

Barnes, Darian D — Football Player
554 Clifton Ave, Toms River NJ 08753, USA

Barnes, David M (Dave) — Singer, Songwriter
Paradigm Agency, 360 N Crescent Dr, North Building, Beverly Hills CA 90210 USA

Barnes, David Wilson — Actor
Hartig-Hilepo Agency, 54 W 21st St, #610, New York NY 10010, USA

Barnes, Demore — Actor
S M S Talent, 8383 Wilshire Blvd, #230, Beverly Hills CA 90211 USA

Barnes, E Randolph (Randy) — Track Athlete
Randy Barnes Enterprises, PO Box 1373, Mechanicsburg PA 17055, USA

Barnes, Erich T — Football Player
712 Warburton Ave, Yonkers NY 10701, USA

Barnes, Frank — Baseball Player
1508 Brazil St, Greenville MS 38701, USA

Barnes, Frank S — Electronics Engineer
University of Colorado, Engineering Dept, Boulder CO 80309, USA

Barnes, Gary M — Football Player
849 Tiger Blvd, #406, Clemson SC 29631, USA

Barnes, Harrison B — Basketball Player
Golden State Warriors, 1011 Broadway, Oakland CA 94605 USA

Barnes, Jeff — Football Player
10738 Versailles Blvd, Clermont FL 34711, USA

Barnes, Jhane E — Fashion Designer
Jhane Barnes Inc, 140 W 57th St, #5B, New York NY 10019, USA

Barnes, Jimmy — Singer
Harbour Agency, 135 Forbes St, Woolloomooloo NSW 2011, Australia

Barnes, Joanna — Actress, Writer
PO Box 1103, Gualala CA 95445, USA

Barnes, Joey — Drummer (Daughtry)
19 Entertainment, 8560 W Sunset Blvd, #900, Los Angeles CA 90069, USA

Barnes, Jonathan — Philosopher
1 Place de la Taconnerie, 1204 Geneva, Switzerland

Barnes, Jonathan — Writer
William Morrow Publishers, 1350 Ave of Americas, New York NY 10019 USA

Barnes, Julian P — Writer
Gage Group, 14724 Ventura Blvd, #505, Sherman Oaks CA 91403 USA

Barnes, Khalif — Football Player
7967 Monterey Bay Dr, Jacksonville FL 32256, USA

Barnes, Luther — Singer
Universal Attractions, 135 W 26th St, #1200, New York NY 10001 USA

Barnes, Marvin J — Basketball Player
3420 Freemason Dr, Portsmouth VA 23703, USA

Barnes, Matt K — Basketball Player
Los Angeles Lakers, Staples Center, 1111 S Figueroa St, Los Angeles CA 90015 USA

Barnes, Michael — Singer (Red)
Paradigm Agency, 404 W Franklin St, Monterey CA 93940 USA

Barnes, Michael J (Mike) — Football Player
27474 Plank Road, Guys Mills PA 16327, USA

Barnes, Norm — Ice Hockey Player
17 Meadow Crossing, Simsbury CT 06070, USA

Barnes, Priscilla — Actress, Model
Glick Agency, 1321 7th St, #203, Santa Monica CA 90401 USA

Barnes, Rick — Basketball Coach
Texas University, Athletic Dept, Austin TX 78713, USA

Barnes, Robert H — Psychiatrist
Texas Tech University Medical School, Psychiatry Dept, PO Box 4349, Lubbock TX 79409, USA

Barnes, Stu — Ice Hockey Player
5069 Royal Creek Lane, Plano TX 75093, USA

Barnes, William H (Skeeter) — Baseball Player
11544 Winding Wood Dr, Indianapolis IN 46235, USA

Barnes, William R (Billy Ray) — Football Player
518 James C Lane, Dallas NC 28034, USA

Barnet, Will — Artist, Educator
National Arts Club, 15 Gramercy Park S, New York NY 10003, USA

Barnett of Heywood & Royton, Joel B — Government Official, England
7 Hillingdon Road, Whitefield, Manchester M25 7QQ, England

Barnett, Douglas S (Doug), Jr — Football Player
14105 Veracruz Dr, Bakersfield CA 93314, USA

Barnett, Fred L — Football Player
PO Box 604, Bala Cynwyd PA 19004, USA

Barnett, James F (Jim) — Basketball Player
7 Kittiwake Road, Orinda CA 94563, USA

Barnett, Jonathan — Architect
225 S Bonsall St, Philadelphia PA 19103, USA

Barnett, Mandy — Singer
Conway Entertainment Group, 1625 Broadway, #500, Nashville TN 37203, USA

Barnett, Nathaniel (Nate) — Basketball Player
710 N Jefferson St, Wilmington DE 19801, USA

Barnett, Nicholas A (Nick) — Football Player
3496 Country Winds Court, Green Bay WI 54311, USA

Barnett, Oliver W — Football Player
1133 Autumn Ridge Dr, Lexington KY 40509, USA

Barnett, Pamela (Pam) — Golfer
4908 E Rancho Tierra Dr, Cave Creek AZ 85331, USA

Barnett, Richard (Dick) — Basketball Player
1227 Pine Ridge, Bushkill PA 18324, USA

Barnett, Robby — Dance Artistic Director
Pilobolus Dance Theater, PO Box 388, Washington Depot CT 06794, USA
Barnett, Sabrina — Model
Next Model Mgmt, 23 Watts St, New York NY 10013 USA
Barnett, Samuel — Actor
I C M Partners, 10250 Constellation Blvd, #900, Los Angeles CA 90067 USA
Barnett, Tommy — Religious Leader
Phoenix First Assembly Church, 13613 N Cave Creek Road, Phoenix AZ 85022, USA
Barney, Lemuel J (Lem), Jr — Football Player
775 Kentbrook Dr, Commerce Township MI 48382, USA
Barno, David W — Army General
Center for a New American Security, 1301 Pennsylvania Ave NW, #403, Washington DC 20004, USA
Barnow, Alex — Producer, Writer
United Talent Agency, 9336 Civic Center Dr, Beverly Hills CA 90210 USA
Barnum, Harvey C, Jr — Vietnam War Marine Corps Hero (CMH)
12008 Walnut Branch Road, Reston VA 20194, USA
Barnwell, Malcolm — Football Player
4045 Gullah Ave, #103, North Charleston SC 29405, USA
Barocco, Rocco — Fashion Designer
Via Occhio Marion, 80773 Capri/Napoli, Italy
Baron Cohen, Sacha (Borat) — Actor, Comedian
W M E Entertainment, 9601 Wilshire Blvd, #300, Beverly Hills CA 90210 USA
Baron Crespo, Enrique — Government Official, Spain
European Parliament, Rue Wiertz 60, 1047 Brussels, Belgium
Baron, Lita — Actress
1508 S La Verne Way, Palm Springs CA 92264, USA
Baron, Martin D — Editor
Boston Globe, Editorial Dept, 135 William Morrissey Blvd, Dorchester MA 02125 USA
Baron, Murray — Ice Hockey Player
23623 N Scottsdale Road, #D3, Scottsdale AZ 85255, USA
Baron, Natalia — Actress
Evolution Entertainment, 901 N Highland Ave, Los Angeles CA 90038 USA
Barone, Anita — Actress
Paradigm Agency, 360 N Crescent Dr, North Building, Beverly Hills CA 90210 USA
Barone, Richard — Singer, Guitarist, Songwriter (Bongos)
Richard Barone Music, 240 Waverly Place, #23, New York NY 10014, USA
Baroux, Olivier — Actor
U B B A, 6 Rue de Braque, 75003 Paris, France
Barr, Dave — Ice Hockey Player
3100 Wilcrest Dr, #260, Houston TX 77042, USA
Barr, Douglas — Actor
Paradigm Agency, 360 N Crescent Dr, North Building, Beverly Hills CA 90210 USA
Barr, Jean-Marc — Actor
Zelig, 57 Rue Reaumur, 75002 Paris, France
Barr, Julia — Actress
Abrams Artists, 275 7th Ave, #2600, New York NY 10001 USA
Barr, Matt — Actor
Luber Rocklin Entertainment, 8530 Wilshire Blvd, #555, Beverly Hills CA 90211 USA
Barr, Michael J (Mike) — Basketball Player
350 38th St NW, Canton OH 44709, USA
Barr, Nathan (Nate) — Composer
First Artists Mgmt, 4764 Park Granada, #210, Calabasas CA 91302 USA
Barr, Nevada — Writer
85 Versailles Blvd, New Orleans LA 70125, USA
Barr, Tara Lynne — Actress
Bicoastal Talent, 210 N Pass Ave, #204, Burbank CA 91505, USA
Barr, William P — Attorney General
Time Warner, Board of Directors, 1 Time Warner Center, New York NY 10019, USA
Barraclough, Roy — Actor
Gavin Barker Assoc, 2D Wimpole St, London W1G 0EB, England
Barrasso, Thomas (Tom) — Ice Hockey Player
12820 Rosalie St, Raleigh NC 27614, USA
Barratier, Christophe — Director, Writer, Lyricist
Galatee Films, 19 Ave de Messine, 75008 Paris, France
Barratt, Michael R — Astronaut
2102 Pleasant Palm Circle, League City TX 77573, USA
Barrault, Doug — Ice Hockey Player
527 10th St S, Golden BC V0A 1H0, Canada
Barraza, Adriana — Actress
Innovative Artists, 1505 10th St, Santa Monica CA 90401 USA
Barrea, Juan J (J J) — Basketball Player
Dallas Mavericks, Pavilion, 2909 Taylor St, Dallas TX 75226 USA
Barrera, Marco Antonio — Boxer
Golden Boy Promotions, 626 Wilshire Blvd, #350, Los Angeles CA 90017, USA
Barrere, Paul — Singer, Guitarist, Songwriter
Skyline Music, 563 Willow High Dr NE, Atlanta GA 30328, USA
Barrese, Sasha — Actress
C E S D, 10635 Santa Monica Blvd, #130, Los Angeles CA 90025 USA
Barre-Sinoussi, Francois C — Nobel Medicine Laureate
Institut Pasteur, 25 Rue du Docteur Roux, 75724 Paris Cedex 15, France
Barreto, Bruno — Director
Creative Artists Agency, 2000 Ave of Stars, #100, Los Angeles CA 90067 USA
Barrett, Christina (Tina) — Golfer
Ladies Pro Golf Assn, 100 International Golf Dr, Daytona Beach FL 32124 USA
Barrett, Colleen — Businesswoman
Southwest Airlines, PO Box 36611, 2702 Love Field Dr, Dallas TX 75235, USA
Barrett, Craig R — Businessman
Intel Corp, 2200 Mission College Blvd, Santa Clara CA 95054, USA
Barrett, David — Football Player
3181 E Waterman Court, Gilbert AZ 85297, USA
Barrett, Edward G (Ted) — Baseball Umpire
855A Silverberry Circle SE, Albuquerque NM 87116, USA
Barrett, Fred W — Ice Hockey Player
3016 Leitrim Road, Gloucester ON K1T 3V9, Canada
Barrett, George S — Businessman
Cardinal Health, 7000 Cardinal Place, Dublin OH 43017, USA

B

Barnett - Barrett

B

Barrett, Jacinda I C M Partners, 10250 Constellation Blvd, #900, Los Angeles CA 90067 USA	Actress, Model
Barrett, James E US Court of Appeals, 2120 Capitol Ave, #2131, Cheyenne WY 82001, USA	Judge
Barrett, Jean M, Jr 7494 S Sleepy Hollow Dr, Tulsa OK 74136, USA	Football Player
Barrett, Malcolm Gersh Agency, 9465 Wilshire Blvd, #600, Beverly Hills CA 90212 USA	Actor
Barrett, Marcia International Artists, PO Box 100334, 47563 Goch, Germany	Singer (Boney M)
Barrett, Martin G (Marty) 3552 Ridge Meadow St, Las Vegas NV 89135, USA	Baseball Manager
Barrett, Michael P 126 Circle Dr, Port Saint Joe FL 32456, USA	Baseball Player
Barrett, Rona Rona Barrett Foundation, PO Box 1559, Santa Ynez CA 93460, USA	Columnist, Commentator
Barrett, Shirley H L A Mgmt, PO Box 1536, Strawberry Hills NSW 2012, Australia	Director
Barrett, Stephen PO Box 1747, Allentown PA 18105, USA	Psychiatrist, Social Activist
Barrichello, Rubens G Eng Luis Carlos Berrini 1140, 8 Andar, Sao Paulo Cep 04571 SP, Brazil	Auto Racing Driver
Barrick, Matt Mick Mgmt, 35 Washington St, Brooklyn NY 11201 USA	Singer, Guitarist (Walkmen)
Barrie, Amanda Associated International Mgmt, Fairfax House, Fulwood Place, London WC1V 6HU, England	Actress
Barrie, Barbara Innovative Artists, 1505 10th St, Santa Monica CA 90401 USA	Actress
Barrie, Douglas R (Doug) 12130 46th St NW, Edmonton AB T5W 2W4, Canada	Ice Hockey Player
Barrie, Len Bear Mountain, 208-2800 Bryn Maur Road, Victoria BC V9B 3T4, Canada	Ice Hockey Player
Barriere, Alain Discotheque Le Stirwen, Chemin Mane Brizil, 56340 Carmac, France	Singer, Songwriter
Barris, George Kustom City, 10811 Riverside Dr, North Hollywood CA 91602, USA	Custom Car Designer
Barro, Robert J Harvard University, Economics Dept, Cambridge MA 02138, USA	Economist
Barron, Alex B 630 Emerson Road, #206, Saint Louis MO 63141, USA	Football Player
Barron, Dana Epstein-Wyckoff, 280 S Beverly Dr, #400, Beverly Hills CA 90212 USA	Actress
Barron, Eric J Florida State University, Tallahassee FL 32306 USA	Educator
Barron, Kenneth (Kenny) Unlimited Myles, 6 Imaginary Place, Matawan NJ 07747, USA	Jazz Pianist, Composer
Barron, Mark Tampa Bay Buccaneers, 1 W Buccaneer Place, Tampa FL 33607 USA	Football Player
Barron, Steve M United Talent Agency, 9336 Civic Center Dr, Beverly Hills CA 90210 USA	Director
Barros, Ana Beatriz Elite Model Mgmt, 404 Park Ave S, #900, New York NY 10016 USA	Model
Barros, Dana B 67 Fairfield Circle, Norwood MA 02062, USA	Basketball Player
Barroso, Jose Manuel European Commission, Berlaymont, Rue la Loi 200, 1040 Brussels, Belgium	Prime Minister, Portugal
Barrow, Barbara 11427 Mayapple Way, San Diego CA 92131, USA	Golfer
Barrow, Dean O Prime Minister's Office, East Bloc, Belmopan, Belize	Prime Minister, Belize
Barrow, Geoffrey P (Geoff) High Road Touring, 751 Bridgeway, #200, Sausalito CA 94965 USA	Synthesizer Player (Portishead)
Barrow, John D Cambridge University, Math Sciences Center, Cambridge CB3 0WA, England	Mathematician, Templeton Prize Laureate
Barrow, Micheal C 1115 S Alhambra Circle, Coral Gables FL 33146, USA	Football Player
Barrowman, John 293 Villas Road, Plumstead, London SE18 7PR, England	Actor, Singer
Barrowman, Michael (Mike) 603 S Alp St, Bay City MI 48706, USA	Swimmer
Barrs, Jack L (Jay), Jr 646 E Kings Peak Cove, Draper UT 84020, USA	Archery Athlete
Barry, Allen (Al) 3760 Edgeview Dr, Pasadena CA 91107, USA	Football Player
Barry, Barbara Barbara Barry Inc, 9526 Pico Blvd, Los Angeles CA 90035, USA	Interior Designer
Barry, Brandon PO Box 1471, Brentwood TN 37024, USA	Singer (Stamps Quartet)
Barry, Brent R 712 The Strand, Hermosa Beach CA 90254, USA	Basketball Player
Barry, Daniel T (Dan) 46 Ashton Lane, South Hadley MA 01075, USA	Astronaut
Barry, Dave 6510 Granada Blvd, Coral Gables FL 33146, USA	Journalist, Writer
Barry, Ellen New York Times, Editorial Dept, 229 W 43rd St, New York NY 10036 USA	Journalist
Barry, Jeff B M I, 8730 W Sunset Blvd, #300, Los Angeles CA 90069 USA	Composer
Barry, Jon A 4555 Club Dr NE, Atlanta GA 30319, USA	Basketball Player
Barry, Jon B 1965 Magnolia Dr, Baton Rouge LA 70808, USA	Photographer
Barry, Kevin T 76 Amethyst Way, Franklin Park NJ 08823, USA	Baseball Player
Barry, Len Cape Entertainment, 8432 NW 31st Court, Sunrise FL 33351, USA	Singer (Dovells)

Barry, Lynda
PO Box 447, Footville WI 53537, USA
Cartoonist (Ernie Pook's Comeck)

Barry, Marion S, Jr
161 Raleigh St SE, Washington DC 20032, USA
Mayor, Washington DC

Barry, Mark
Spirit Media, PO Box 43591, Phoenix AZ 85080, USA
Singer, Flutist (BBMak)

Barry, Maryanne Trump
US Court of Appeals, US Courthouse, Federal Square, #333, Newark NJ 07101, USA
Judge

Barry, Patricia
6 South Dr, Toronto ON M4W 1P1, Canada
Actress

Barry, Paul F
409 Kingswood Dr, El Paso TX 79932, USA
Football Player

Barry, Raymond J
Metropolitan Talent Agency, 7020 La Presa Dr, Los Angeles CA 90068 USA
Actor

Barry, Richard F D (Rick), III
5240 Broadmoor Bluffs Dr, Colorado Springs CO 80906, USA
Basketball Player, Sportscaster

Barry, Seymour (Sy)
225 Fairfield Dr E, Holbrook NY 11741, USA
Cartoonist (Flash Gordon, Phantom)

Barry, Thom
Vox Inc, 6420 Wilshire Blvd, #1080, Los Angeles CA 90048 USA
Actor

Barry, Todd
3 Arts Entertainment, 9460 Wilshire Blvd, #700, Beverly Hills CA 90212 USA
Actor, Comedian

Barrymore, Drew
Creative Artists Agency, 2000 Ave of Stars, #100, Los Angeles CA 90067 USA
Actress, Model

Barsh, Gregory S
Stanford University Medical Center, Pediatrics Dept, Stanford CA 94305, USA
Pediatrician

Barshefsky, Charlene
Wilmer Cutler Pickering, 1875 Pennsylvania Ave NW, Washington DC 20006, USA
Government Official

Barson, Mike
I T F, Ariel House, 74A Charlotte St, London W1T 4QJ, England
Keyboardist (Madness)

Barsotti, Charles
419 E 55th St, Kansas City MO 64110, USA
Cartoonist

Barstow, David
New York Times, Editorial Dept, 229 W 43rd St, New York NY 10036 USA
Journalist

Barstow, Josephine C
Musichall Ltd, Vicarage Way, Ringmer BN8 5LA, England
Opera Singer

Bart, Peter B
Trident Media, 41 Madison Ave, #3600, New York NY 10010, USA
Editor

Bart, Roger
Innovative Artists, 1505 10th St, Santa Monica CA 90401 USA
Actor

Bartecko, Lubos
121 Windy Acres Estates Dr, Ballwin MO 63021, USA
Ice Hockey Player

Bartee, Kimera A
10808 N 57th Dr, Glendale AZ 85304, USA
Baseball Player

Bartee, William A
17 Talaquah Blvd, Ormond Beach FL 32174, USA
Football Player

Bartel, Robin
210 Forsyth Court, Saskatoon SK S7N 4H2, Canada
Ice Hockey Player

Barth, Francis
7105 Jackson St, North Bergen NJ 07047, USA
Artist

Barth, John M
Johnson Controls, 5757 N Green Bay Ave, PO Box 591, Milwaukee WI 53201, USA
Businessman

Barth, John S
Wylie Agency, 250 W 57th St, #2114, New York NY 10107 USA
Writer

Barth, T Fredrik W
Rodkleivfaret 16, 0788 Oslo, Norway
Anthropologist

Barth, Uta
Tanya Bonakdar Gallery, 521 W 21st St, Front 1, New York NY 10011, USA
Conceptual Artist, Photographer

Bartha, Justin
Creative Artists Agency, 2000 Ave of Stars, #100, Los Angeles CA 90067 USA
Actor

Bartholemew, Ian
Ken McReddie Assoc, 11 Connaught Place, London W2 2ET, England
Actor

Bartholomew I
Eastern Orthodox Church, Rum Ortoks Patrikhanesi, 34220 Istanbul, Turkey
Religious Leader

Bartholomew, Dave
Paramount Entertainment, 12 Kosakowski Dr, Morris Plains NJ 07590 USA
Jazz Trumpeter, Singer

Bartholomew, Logan
J L A Talent Agency, 9151 Sunset Blvd, West Hollywood CA 90069, USA
Actor

Bartilson, Lynsey
C E S D, 10635 Santa Monica Blvd, #130, Los Angeles CA 90025 USA
Actress

Bartiromo, Maria
CNBC-TV, 2200 Fletcher Ave, #600, Fort Lee NJ 07024, USA
Commentator

Bartkowiak, Andrzej
Paradigm Agency, 360 N Crescent Dr, North Building, Beverly Hills CA 90210 USA
Director

Bartkowski, Steven J (Steve)
10745 Bell Road, Duluth GA 30097, USA
Football Player

Bartlett, Bonnie
12805 Hortense St, Studio City CA 91604, USA
Actress, Singer

Bartlett, Don
Curling Assn, 1660 Vimont Court, Cumberland ON K4A 4J4, Canada
Curling Athlete

Bartlett, Erinn
Innovative Artists, 1505 10th St, Santa Monica CA 90401 USA
Actress

Bartlett, Jennifer L
134 Charles St, New York NY 10014, USA
Artist

Bartlett, Jim
8718 Chadwick Dr, Tampa FL 33635, USA
Ice Hockey Player

Bartlett, Robin
Gersh Agency, 9465 Wilshire Blvd, #600, Beverly Hills CA 90212 USA
Actress

Bartlett, Scott
Virgin Records, 338 N Foothill Road, Beverly Hills CA 90210 USA
Guitarist (Saving Abel)

Bartlett, Thomas A
1209 SW 6th St, #904, Portland OR 97204, USA
Educator

Bartletti, Don
Los Angeles Times, Editorial Dept, 202 W 1st St, Los Angeles CA 90012 USA
Photojournalist

Bartley, Adam
Gersh Agency, 9465 Wilshire Blvd, #600, Beverly Hills CA 90212 USA
Actor

Bartley, Geoff — Singer, Guitarist, Songwriter
Jean Schwartz Entertainment, 326 Grant St, Framingham MA 01702, USA

Bartoe, John-David F — Astronaut
2724 Lighthouse Dr, Houston TX 77058, USA

Bartoletti, Bruno — Conductor
Chicago Lyric Opera, 20 N Wacker Dr, #400, Chicago IL 60606, USA

Bartoletti, Louis — Golfer
1450 Longlea Terrace, Wellington FL 33414, USA

Bartoli, Cecilia — Opera Singer
Mastroianni Assoc, 161 W 61st St, #32B, New York NY 10023, USA

Bartolome, Victor (Vic) — Basketball Player
1025 Rinconada Road, #A, Santa Barbara CA 93101, USA

Bartolomew, Kenneth (Ken) — Speed Skater
4820 Bryant Ave S, Minneapolis MN 55419, USA

Barton, Austin — Sculptor
100 N Lake, Joseph OR 97846, USA

Barton, Daric W (D B) — Baseball Player
958 Naples Dr, Corona CA 92882, USA

Barton, Dorie — Actress
Abrams Artists, 9200 W Sunset Blvd, #1125, West Hollywood CA 90069 USA

Barton, Eric — Football Player
23 Hayes Hill Dr, Northport NY 11768, USA

Barton, Glenys — Artist
Angela Flowers Gallery, 199-205 Richmond Road, London E8 3NJ, England

Barton, Gregory (Greg) — Canoeing Athlete
6851 30th Ave NE, Seattle WA 98115, USA

Barton, Harris S — Football Player
334 Lincoln Ave, Palo Alto CA 94301, USA

Barton, Jacqueline K — Chemist
California Insitute of Techonolgy, Chemistry Dept, Pasadena CA 91125, USA

Barton, Lou Ann — Singer
Luther Wolf Agency, PO Box 162078, Austin TX 78716, USA

Barton, Mischa — Actress, Model
Domain Talent, 9229 W Sunset Blvd, #710, West Hollywood CA 90069 USA

Barton, Peter — Actor
2265 Westwood Blvd, #2619, Los Angeles CA 90064, USA

Barton, Rachel — Concert Violinist
I C M Artists, 40 W 57th St, #1800, New York NY 10019 USA

Barton, Robert W (Bob) — Baseball Player
37193 Stardust Way, Murrieta CA 92563, USA

Bartovic, Milan — Ice Hockey Player
141 Bennington Hills Court, West Henrietta NY 14586, USA

Bartrum, Mike W — Football Player
43375 Carlton Place, Pomeroy OH 45769, USA

Bartusiak, Skye McCole — Actress
C E S D, 10635 Santa Monica Blvd, #130, Los Angeles CA 90025 USA

Bartz, Gary L — Jazz Saxophonist, Composer
Joel Chriss, 60 E 8th St, #34N, New York NY 10003 USA

Bartz, Randall (Randy) — Speed Skater
3829 Baker Road, Hopkins MN 55305, USA

Baruch, Jordan J — Electrical Engineer
5630 Wisconsin Ave, #905, Chevy Chase MD 20815, USA

Baruchel, Jay — Actor
Thruline Entertainment, 9250 Wilshire Blvd, #100, Beverly Hills CA 90212 USA

Barwell, Eric — British WW II Air Force Hero
Toft, 5 Beldam's Close, Cambridge CB3 7RN, England

Baryshnikov, Mikhail — Ballet Dancer, Actor
Baryshnikov Productions, 1830 Rittenhouse Square, Philadelphia PA 19103, USA

Barzelay, Eef — Singer, Guitarist (Clem Snide)
Impact Artist Mgmt, 356 W 123rd St, New York NY 10027, USA

Barzilauskas, Carl J — Football Player
4444 Lower Schooner Road, Nashville IN 47448, USA

Barzini, Benedetta — Model
Donna Karan Co, 361 Newbury St, Boston MA 02115, USA

Basaraba, Gary — Actor
Stone Manners Salners, 9911 W Pico Blvd, #1400, Los Angeles CA 90035 USA

Basche, David Alan — Actor
New Wave Entertainment 2660 W Olive Ave, Burbank CA 91505, USA

Baschnagel, Brian D — Football Player
1824 Ridgewood Lane W, Glenview IL 60025, USA

Basco, Dante — Actor
Dayton-Milrad-Cho, 8899 Beverly Blvd, #918, Los Angeles CA 90048, USA

Basco, Dion — Actor
Schiowitz Connor, 1680 N Vine St, #1016, Los Angeles CA 90028 USA

Baselios Cleemis Cardinal Thottunkal — Religious Leader
Major Archbishop's House, Pattom, Thiruvananthapuram, Kerala 695004, India

Baselitz, Georg — Artist
Schloss Derneberg, 31188 Holle, Germany

Bashir, Idrees — Football Player
5579 Mountain View Pass, Stone Mountain GA 30087, USA

Bashir, Martin — Commentator
ABC-TV, News Dept, 77 W 66th St, New York NY 10023 USA

Bashkirov, Dmitri A — Concert Pianist
Studenceskaja 31, #74, Moscow, Russia

Bashmet, Yuri A — Concert Violist, Conductor
Briyusov 7, #16, 103009 Moscow, Russia

Bashoff, Blake — Actor
Abrams Artists, 9200 W Sunset Blvd, #1125, West Hollywood CA 90069 USA

Basia — Singer
Agency Group Ltd, 1880 Century Park E, #711, Los Angeles CA 90067 USA

Basilashuili, Oleg V — Actor
Borodinskaya Str 13, #58, 196180 Saint Petersburg, Russia

Basinger, Kim — Actress
Paradigm Agency, 360 N Crescent Dr, North Building, Beverly Hills CA 90210 USA

Basis, Austin — Actor
Don Buchwald/Fortitude, 6500 Wilshire Blvd, #2200, Los Angeles CA 90048 USA

Basler, Marianne — Actress
Agence Artiste Adequet, 80 Rue d'Amsterdam, 75009 Paris, France
Basri, Gibor — Astronomer
University of California, Astronomy Dept, Berkeley CA 94720, USA
Bass, Fontella — Singer, Keyboardist
3216 Mintleaf Dr, Charlotte NC 28269, USA
Bass, George F — Underwater Archaeologist
1600 Dominik Dr, College Station TX 77840, USA
Bass, Glenn A — Football Player
4185 Diplomacy Circle, Tallahassee FL 32308, USA
Bass, Hyman — Mathematician
435 Riverside Dr, New York NY 10025, USA
Bass, J Lance — Singer ('N Sync)
Owen Entertainment, 1708 21st Ave S, #274, Nashville TN 37212, USA
Bass, Kevin C — Baseball Player
3630 Maranatha Dr, Sugar Land TX 77479, USA
Bass, Michael T (Mike) — Football Player
4703 NW 36th St, Gainesville FL 32605, USA
Bass, Norman D (Norm), Jr — Baseball, Football Player
156 E 70th St, Los Angeles CA 90003, USA
Bass, Randy W — Baseball Player
2709 SW Coombs Road, Lawton OK 73505, USA
Bass, Ronald J (Ron) — Writer
I C M Partners, 10250 Constellation Blvd, #900, Los Angeles CA 90067 USA
Bassen, Robert P (Bob) — Ice Hockey Player
1742 Coldstone Dr, Frisco TX 75034, USA
Bassett, Angela — Actress
Lighthouse Entertainment, 9220 Sunset Blvd, #200, West Hollywood CA 90069, USA
Bassett, Brian — Editorial Cartoonist, Cartoonist (Adam)
Seattle Times, Editorial Dept, 1120 John St, Seattle WA 98109 USA
Bassett, E Timothy (Tim) — Basketball Player
1143 Dorsey Place, Plainfield NJ 07062, USA
Bassett, Leslie R — Composer
5433 Ashmore Lane, Flowery Branch GA 30542, USA
Bassett-Seguso, Carling — Tennis Player
1008 Vista del Mar Dr, Delray Beach FL 33483, USA
Bassey, Jennifer — Actress
12 E 86th St, #1728, New York NY 10028, USA
Bassey, Shirley — Singer
La Rocca Bella, 24 Ave Princess Grace, 1200 Monte Carlo, Monaco
Bassham, Lanny R — Marksman
2112 Bellanca Court, Flower Mound TX 75028, USA
Basso, Dennis — Fashion Designer
317 W 33rd St New York NY 10001, USA
Bastedo, Alexandra — Actress
Associated International Mgmt, Fairfax House, Fulwood Place, London WC1V 6HU, England
Bastel, Emily — Golfer
5377 County Highway 330, Uppper Sandusky OH 43351, USA
Basti, Juli — Actress
Krecsanyi Utca 6, 1025 Budapest, Hungary
Baston, Maceo — Basketball Player
PO Box 4846, Troy MI 48099, USA
Basu, Asish R — Geochemist
University of Rochester, Geochemistry Dept, Rochester NY 14627, USA
Batali, Dean — Writer
A P A Talent/Literary Agency, 405 S Beverly Dr, #300, Beverly Hills CA 90212 USA
Batali, Mario — Restauranteur, Chef
Babbo, 110 Waverly Place, Front A, New York NY 10011, USA
Batalli-Cosmovici, Cristiano — Astronaut
International Astronomical Union, Via Fosso del Cavaliere 100, 00133 Rome, Italy
Batbold, Sukhbaataryn — Prime Minister, Mongolia
Prime Minister's Office, Great Hural, Ulan Bator 12, Mongolia
Batch, Charles D (Charlie) — Football Player
1844 Willow Oak Dr, Wexford PA 15090, USA
Batchelder, Alice M — Judge
US Court of Appeals, 143 W Liberty St, Medina OH 44256, USA
Batchelder, Joseph L (Joe) — Yachtsman
11004 Hard Rock Road, Austin TX 78750, USA
Batchelor, Joy E — Animator
Educational Film Center, 5-7 Kean St, London WC2B 4AT, England
Bate, Jennifer L — Concert Organist
35 Collingwood Ave, Muswell Hill, London N10 3EH, England
Bateau, Laurent — Actor
Voyez Mon Agent, 20 Ave Rapp, 75007 Paris, France
Batelaan, Kelsey — Actor
C E S D, 10635 Santa Monica Blvd, #130, Los Angeles CA 90025 USA
Bateman, Brian — Golfer
100 Brunswick Ave, Saint Simons Island GA 31522, USA
Bateman, Jason — Actor
Creative Artists Agency, 2000 Ave of Stars, #100, Los Angeles CA 90067 USA
Bateman, Justine — Actress
8004 Woodrow Wilson Dr, Los Angeles CA 90046, USA
Bateman, Marvin F (Marv) — Football Player
1022 W Smithsonian Way, Apple Valley UT 84737, USA
Bateman, Robert M — Artist
PO Box 115 Fulford Harbour, Salt Spring Island BC V8K 2P2, Canada
Bates, Billy Ray — Basketball Player
8051 Gibbon St, Daniel Island SC 29492, USA
Bates, Charles C — Oceanographer
750 S La Posada Circle, #77, Green Valley AZ 85614, USA
Bates, David M — Artist
34 Horatio St, #4B, New York NY 10014, USA
Bates, Doug — Journalist
Portland Oregonian, Editorial Dept, 1320 SW Broadway, Portland OR 97201, USA
Bates, D'Wayne L — Football Player
1862 Sherman Ave, #1NE, Ponte Vedra Beach FL 32082, USA

Bates, Jared L (Jerry) — Army General
SyColeman Division, L-3 Communications Holdings, 600 3rd Ave, New York NY 10016, USA

Bates, Kathy — Actress
I C M Partners, 10250 Constellation Blvd, #900, Los Angeles CA 90067 USA

Bates, Mario D — Football Player
PO Box 5832, Scottsdale AZ 85261, USA

Bates, Michael D — Football Player, Track Athlete
1239 W Keuhne Court, Tucson AZ 85755, USA

Bates, Patrick (Pat) — Golfer
215 Ward Circle, #200, Brentwood TN 37027, USA

Bates, Quentin — Writer
Ampersand Agency, Ryman's Cottages, Little Tew, Oxfordshire OX7 4JJ, England

Bates, Richard (Dick) — Baseball Player
5858 W Cielo Grande, Glendale AZ 85310, USA

Bates, Shawn — Ice Hockey Player
35 Bradshaw St, Medford MA 02155, USA

Bates, Ted D — Football Player
4036 Paige St, Los Angeles CA 90031, USA

Bates, Tyler — Composer
Soundtrack Music, 2229 Cloverfield Blvd, Santa Monica CA 90405, USA

Bates, William F (Bill) — Football Player
1252 Neck Road, Ponte Vedra FL 32082, USA

Bathe, Frank — Ice Hockey Player
2 Meadowwood Dr, Scarborough ME 04074, USA

Bathgate, Andrew J (Andy) — Ice Hockey Player
43 Brentwood Dr, Brampton ON L6T 1R1, Canada

Bathgate, Frank — Ice Hockey Player
602-330 Mill St S, Brampton, ON L6Y 3V3, Canada

Bathurst, Otto — Director
Casorotto Ramsay, Waverley House, 7-12 Noel St, London W1F 8GQ, England

Batiashvili, Lisa — Concert Violinist
Harrison/Parrott, 5-6 Albion Court, London W6 0QT, England

Batinkoff, Randall — Actor
Glick Agency, 1321 7th St, #203, Santa Monica CA 90401 USA

Batiste, Kimothy E (Kim) — Baseball Player
16161 Aikens Road, Prairieville LA 70769, USA

Batiuk, Thomas M (Tom) — Cartoonist (Crankshaft)
Universal Press Syndicate, 4520 Main St, #700, Kansas City MO 64111 USA

Batiz Campbell, Enrique — Conductor
Cerrada Rancho los Colorines 11, Dele Tlalan, Mexico DF 14000, Mexico

Bator, Francis M — Economist
85 Grove St, #2, Wellesley MA 02482, USA

Batra, Pooja — Actress, Model
403H Gokul Vihar II, Thakar Complex Kandivli (E), Mumbai MS 400068, India

Batt, Michael P (Mike) — Singer, Songwriter
Dramatico Entertainment, PO Box 214, Farnham, Surrey GU10 5XZ, England

Battaglia, Jon (Bates) — Ice Hockey Player
832 Graham St, Raleigh NC 27605, USA

Battaglia, Marco — Football Player
15832 79th St, Howard Beach NY 11414, USA

Battaglia, Matt — Actor
Matt Battaglia Productions, 8033 Sunset Blvd, #3000, Los Angeles CA 90046, USA

Battelle, Ann — Moguls Skier
Mogul Logic, 4279 Monroe Dr, #D, Boulder CO 80303, USA

Batten, Kimberly (Kim) — Track Athlete
192 Sugar Plum Dr, Tallahassee FL 32312, USA

Battersby, Alan R — Chemist
20 Barrow Road, Cambridge CB2 2AS, England

Battie, D Antonio (Tony) — Basketball Player
11264 Bridge House Road, Windermere FL 34786, USA

Battier, Shane C — Basketball Player
490 Bruin Lake Road, Gregory MI 48137, USA

Battiste, P Francois — Actor
Innovative Artists, 1505 10th St, Santa Monica CA 90401 USA

Battistelli, Francesca — Singer, Songwriter
Proper Mgmt, PO Box 150867, Nashville TN 37215, USA

Battle, Arnaz J — Football Player
1091 Broadmoore Lane, Prosper TX 75078, USA

Battle, Hinton — Dancer, Actor
Borinstein Oreck Bogart, 3172 Dona Susana Dr, Studio City CA 91604 USA

Battle, John S — Basketball Player
125 Glen Beigh Run, Tyrone GA 30290, USA

Battle, Kathleen D — Opera Singer
Columbia Artists Mgmt Inc, 1790 Broadway, #702, New York NY 10019 USA

Battle, Texas — Actor
Innovative Artists, 1505 10th St, Santa Monica CA 90401 USA

Battles, Ainsley T — Football Player
1237 Misty Valley Court, Lawrenceville GA 30045, USA

Batton, Dave — Basketball Player
6506 Bayonne Dr, Spring TX 77389, USA

Batts, Lloyd — Basketball Player
500 S Dante Ave, Glenwood IL 60425, USA

Batts, Matthew D (Matt) — Baseball Player
17927 Silver Creek Court, Baton Rouge LA 70810, USA

Batum, Nicolas — Basketball Player
Portland Trail Blazers, Rose Garden, 1 N Center Court St, Portland OR 97227 USA

Baturin, Yuri M — Cosmonaut
Cosmonaut Training Center, Star City, 141160 Zvezdny Gorodok, Moscow Oblast, Russia

Baty, Gregory J (Greg) — Football Player
4 King St, Redwood City CA 94062, USA

Bauchau, Patrick — Actor
David Shapira Assoc, 193 N Robertson Blvd, Beverly Hills CA 90211 USA

Baudo, Serge — Conductor
Les Hautes du Ferra, Chemin Charre, 13600 Ceyreste, France

Baudry, Patrick — Spatinaut, France
305 Ave Mairie, 31600 Eaunas, France

B

Bauer, Chris Framework Entertainment, 9057 Nemo St, #C, West Hollywood CA 90069 USA	Actor
Bauer, Erwin A 8880 SE 19th Avenue Road, Ocala FL 34480, USA	Photographer
Bauer, Hans-Uwe Fitz & Skoglund Agnets, Liniestr 130, 10115 Berlin, Germany	Actor
Bauer, Henry J (Hank) 11150 Alejo Place, San Diego CA 92124, USA	Football Player
Bauer, Jaime Lyn Gar Lester Agency, 4130 Cahuenga Blvd, #108, Universal City CA 91602, USA	Actress
Bauer, Joy W M E Entertainment, 1325 Ave of Americas, New York NY 10019 USA	Writer
Bauer, Kristin Kritzer Levine Wilkins Griffin, 11872 La Grange Ave, #100, Los Angeles CA 90025 USA	Actress
Bauer, Lukas Muller Productions, Na Valech 45/32, 16000 Prague 6, Czech Republic	Cross Country Skier
Bauer, Michelle A I Productions, 6260 Laurel Canyon Blvd, #201, North Hollywood CA 91606, USA	Actress, Model
Bauer, Peggy 8880 SE 19th Avenue Road, Ocala FL 34480, USA	Photographer
Bauer, Peter Mick Mgmt, 35 Washington St, Brooklyn NY 11201 USA	Bassist, Organist (Walkmen)
Bauer, Richard E (Rick) 6805 Easthaven Way, Citrus Heights CA 95621, USA	Baseball Player
Bauer, Steven Global Artists Agency, 6253 Hollywood Blvd, #508, Los Angeles CA 90028 USA	Actor
Bauer, Viola Ski Verband, Hubertusstr 1, 82152 Planegg, Germany	Cross Country Skier
Bauer, William J 213 S Grace Ave, Elmhurst IL 60126, USA	Judge
Baugh, Laura 5225 Timberview Terrace, Orlando FL 32819, USA	Golfer
Baugh, Thomas A (Tom) 14716 S Bynum Road, Lone Jack MO 64070, USA	Football Player, Coach
Baughan, Maxie C, Jr 3355 Lawndale Road, Reisterstown MD 21136, USA	Football Player, Coach
Baughman, J Ross 31101 Harbour Vista Circle, Saint Augustine FL 32080, USA	Photojournalist
Baughman, Ray H 5428 Willow Road, Dallas TX 75252, USA	Nanotechnologist
Baulcombe, David C Cambridge University, Plant Institute, Cambridge CB2 1TN, England	Geneticist, Plant Scientist
Baulieu, Etienne-Emile Institut de France, 23 Quai de Conti, 75006 Paris, France	Biochemist, Inventor (Abortion Pill)
Baum, Bob 465 Bayle St W, Pickering ON L1W 3P6, Canada	Ice Hockey Player
Baum, John (Johnny) 8216 Fenton Road, Glenside PA 19038, USA	Basketball Player
Baum, William W Cardinal Via Rusticucci 13, 00193 Rome, Italy	Religious Leader
Bauman, Jon (Bowzer) David Belenzon Mgmt, PO Box 5000, PMB 67, Rancho Santa Fe CA 92067, USA	Singer, Pianist (Sha Na Na)
Baumann, Dieter Biesingerstr 18, 72070 Tubingen, Germany	Track Athlete
Baumann, Frank M 7712 Sunray Lane, Saint Louis MO 63123, USA	Baseball Player
Baumann, Herbert K W Franziskaserstr 16, #1419, 81669 Munich, Germany	Composer
Baumann, Kenny A K A Talent, 6310 San Vicente Blvd, #200, Los Angeles CA 90048 USA	Actor
Baumbach, Noah United Talent Agency, 9336 Civic Center Dr, Beverly Hills CA 90210 USA	Director, Writer
Baumbauer, Frank Deutsches Schauspielhaus, Kirchenallee 39, 20099 Hamburg, Germany	Director
Baumgarten, Ross 1020 Bluff Road, Glencoe IL 60022, USA	Baseball Player
Baumgartner, Brian 3-Bees Entertainment, 4217 Verdugo View Dr, Los Angeles CA 90065, USA	Actor
Baumgartner, Bruce 12765 Forrest Dr, Edinboro PA 16412, USA	Freestyle Wrestler
Baumgartner, Felix Red Bull Stratos Project, International Air Center, 1 Jerry Smith Circle, Roswell NM 88202, USA	Sky Diver
Baumgartner, Ken 39 Court St, #1, Newton MA 02458, USA	Ice Hockey Player
Baumgartner, Nolan Vancouver Canucks, 800 Griffiths Way, Vancouver BC V6B 6G1, Canada	Ice Hockey Player
Baumgartner, Steven J (Steve) 144 Brookside Dr, Mandeville LA 70471, USA	Football Player
Baumhower, Robert G (Bob) 21201 Ayrshire Lane, Fairhope AL 36532, USA	Football Player
Baumler, Hans-Jurgen Magt Rehling, Kirchenstr 17C, 82110 Germering, Germany	Figure Skater
Baumol, William J 455 N End Ave, #1204, New York NY 10282, USA	Economist
Baun, Robert N (Bob) 35 Pittman Crescent, Ajax ON L1S 3G4, Canada	Ice Hockey Player
Bauta, Eduardo G (Ed) 3786 Long Grove Lane, Port Orange FL 32129, USA	Baseball Player
Bautista, Daniel B (Danny) 901 E Van Buren St, #1063, Phoenix AZ 85006, USA	Baseball Player
Bautista, Jose A 100 Shockoe Slip, #400, Richmond VA 23219, USA	Baseball Player
Bautista, Jose J 15621 SW 16th Court, Pembroke Pines FL 33027, USA	Baseball Player
Bavaro, Mark 17 Long Hill, Boxford MA 01921, USA	Football Player

Bauer - Bavaro

Bavouzet, Jean-Efflam — Concert Pianist
Chandos Records, 1 Commerce Park, Commerce Way, Colchester, Essex CO2 8HX, England
Bawel, Edward R (Bibbles) — Football Player
1169 2nd Ave, Jasper IN 47546, USA
Bawoyeu, Jean Alingue — Prime Minister, Chad
Union for Democratic Republic, BP 1122, N'Djamena, Chad
Bax, Adriaan (Ad) — Biophysicist
National Institutes of Health, Biophysics Dept, 5 Memorial Dr, Building 5, Bethesda MD 20892, USA
Bax, Kylie — Model, Actress
Storm Model Agency, 5 Jubilee Place, Chelsea, London SW3 3TD, England
Baxendale, Helen — Actress
Yakety Yak, 8 Bloomsbury Square, London WC1A 2UA, England
Baxter, Frederick D (Fred) — Football Player
PO Box 14, Brundidge AL 36010, USA
Baxter, Gary W — Football Player
13749 Choctaw Dr, Tyler TX 75709, USA
Baxter, Glen — Artist, Cartoonist
Chris Beetle Gallery, 10 Ryder St, London SW1Y 6QB, England
Baxter, James — Animator
James Baxter Animation, 32 Mills Place, Pasadena CA 91105, USA
Baxter, Jeff (Skunk) — Guitarist (Doobie Brothers, Steely Dan)
Howard Rose, 9460 Wilshire Blvd, #310, Beverly Hills CA 90212, USA
Baxter, Jennifer — Actress
TalentWorks, 3500 W Olive Ave, #1400, Burbank CA 91505 USA
Baxter, Kirk — Editor
Motion Pictures Editors Guild, 7715 Sunset Blvd, #200, Los Angeles CA 90046, USA
Baxter, Meredith — Actress
TalentWorks, 3500 W Olive Ave, #1400, Burbank CA 91505 USA
Baxter, Paul — Ice Hockey Player
1610 Saint John St, Wichita Falls TX 76302, USA
Baxter, William E (Billy), Jr — Poker Player
CardPlayer Media, 6940 Obannon Drive, Las Vegas NV 89117, USA
Baxter-Johnson, Patricia — Golfer
111 Bryn Mawr Dr, Lake Worth FL 33460, USA
Bay, Jason R — Baseball Player
5811 106th Ave NE, Kirkland WA 98033, USA
Bay, Michael — Director
W M E Entertainment, 9601 Wilshire Blvd, #300, Beverly Hills CA 90210 USA
Bay, Susan — Actress
Gersh Agency, 9465 Wilshire Blvd, #600, Beverly Hills CA 90212 USA
Baye, Nathalie — Actress
Artmedia, 20 Ave Rapp, 75007 Paris, France
Bayh, Birch E, Jr — Senator, IN
PO Box 3353, Easton MD 21601, USA
Bayi, Filbert — Track Athlete
PO Box 60240, Morogoro Road, Dar es Salaam, Tanzania
Bayl, Benjamin — Conductor
Harrison/Parrott, 5-6 Albion Court, London W6 0QT, England
Bayldon, Geoffrey — Actor
Joy Jameson, 219 Plaza, 535 Kings Road, London SW10 0SZ, England
Bayle, Jean-Michel — Motorcycle Racing Rider
General Delivery, Manosque, France
Bayless, Jerryd — Basketball Player
New Orleans Hornets, 1250 Poydras St, #101, New Orleans LA 70113 USA
Bayless, Martin A — Football Player
834 Calle Lagasca, Chula Vista CA 91910, USA
Bayley, Clive — Opera Singer
I M G Artists, Hogarth Business Park, Chiswick, London W4 2TH, England
Baylor, Don E — Baseball Player, Manager
56325 Riviera, La Quinta CA 92253, USA
Baylor, Elgin G — Basketball Player, Executive
2480 Briarcrest Road, Beverly Hills CA 90210, USA
Baylor, Helen — Singer
Helen Baylor Ministries, 3267 Phantom Rock St, Las Vegas NV 89135, USA
Baylor, John M — Football Player
211 Oak St, Hattiesburg MS 39401, USA
Baynham, G Craig — Football Player
1 7th St, #1102, Augusta GA 30901, USA
Bayo, Maria — Opera Singer
Columbia Artists Mgmt Inc, 165 W 57th St, New York NY 10019, USA
Bayou, Bradley — Fashion Designer
Film Fashion, 8687 Melrose Center, #G684, Los Angeles CA 90069, USA
Bayrakdarian, Isabel — Opera Singer
I M G Artists, Hogarth Business Park, Chiswick, London W4 2TH, England
Bays, Carter — Producer, Writer
United Talent Agency, 9336 Civic Center Dr, Beverly Hills CA 90210 USA
Baz, Farouk El- — Geologist
213 Silver Hill Road, Concord MA 01742, USA
Baze, Russell A — Thoroughbred Racing Jockey
22 Somerset Place, Woodside CA 94062, USA
Bazell, Josh — Writer
United Talent Agency, 9336 Civic Center Dr, Beverly Hills CA 90210 USA
Bazell, Robert J — Commentator
NBC-TV, News Dept, 4001 Nebraska Ave NW, Washington DC 20016 USA
Bazelli, Bojan — Cinematographer
Dattner Dispoto, 10635 Santa Monica Blvd, #165, Los Angeles CA 90025, USA
Bazer, Fuller W — Animal Scientist
8600 Creekview Court, College Station TX 77845, USA
Bazzaz, Fakhri A — Plant Biologist
Harvard University, Organismic & Evolutionary Biology Dept, Cambridge MA 02138, USA
Beach, Adam — Actor
A P A Talent/Literary Agency, 405 S Beverly Dr, #300, Beverly Hills CA 90212 USA
Beach, Bill — Bowler
3715 Lee Run Road, Hermitage PA 16148, USA
Beach, Gary — Actor, Singer
122 Andalusia Way, Palm Beach Gardens FL 33418, USA

Beach, Michael — Actor
Medavoy Mgmt, 10203 Santa Monica Blvd, #400, Los Angeles CA 90067 USA

Beach, Patrick J (Pat) — Football Player
2523 NW Beach Road, Oak Harbor WA 98277, USA

Beach, Sanjay R — Football Player
2989 Riviera Lane, Westlake OH 44145, USA

Beacham, Stephanie — Actress
United Agents, 12-26 Lexington St, London W1F 0LE, England

Beachley, Layne — Surfer
Aim for Stars Foundation, PO Box H67, Sydney NSW 1213, Australia

Beadle, Michelle D — Sportscaster
NBC-TV, Sports Dept, 30 Rockefeller Plaza, #270E, New York NY 10112 USA

Beagle, Ronald G (Ron) — Football Player
3830 San Ysidro Way, Sacramento CA 95864, USA

Beahan, Kate — Actress
Management 360, 9111 Wilshire Blvd, Beverly Hills CA 90210 USA

Beal, Bradley — Basketball Player
Washington Wizards, M C I Centre, 601 F St NW, Washington DC 20004 USA

Beal, Jeff — Composer
B M I, 8730 W Sunset Blvd, #300, Los Angeles CA 90069 USA

Beale, Simon Russell — Actor
Richard Stone Partnership, 85 New Cavendish St, London W1W 6XD, England

Beals, Jennifer — Actress
Greenlight Mgmt, 13848 Valleyheart Dr, Sherman Oaks CA 91423, USA

Beam, C Arlen — Judge
US Court of Appeals, 100 Centennial Mall N, Lincoln NE 68508, USA

Beamer, Frank — Football Coach
Virginia Polytechnic Institute, Athletic Dept, Blacksburg VA 24061, USA

Beamer, Lisa — Writer
9 Cubberly Court, Cranbury NJ 08512, USA

Beamish, Lindsay — Actress, Dancer
Semler Entertainment, 13636 Ventura Blvd, #510, Sherman Oaks CA 91423, USA

Beamon, Autry, Jr — Football Player
2664 Lakeview Dr, Shakopee MN 55379, USA

Beamon, Robert (Bob) — Track Athlete
20533 Biscayne Blvd, #113, Miami FL 33180, USA

Bean, Alan L — Astronaut
9173 Briar Forest Dr, Houston TX 77024, USA

Bean, Andy — Golfer
2912 Grasslands Dr, Lakeland FL 33803, USA

Bean, Dawn Pawson — Synchronized Swimmer
11902 Red Hill Ave, Santa Ana CA 92705, USA

Bean, Henry — Director, Writer
Creative Artists Agency, 2000 Ave of Stars, #100, Los Angeles CA 90067 USA

Bean, Joe — Soccer Coach
Wheaton College, Athletic Dept, Wheaton IL 60187, USA

Bean, Noah — Actor
C E S D, 257 Park Ave S, #950, New York NY 10010 USA

Bean, Orson — Actor, Comedian
Stone Manners Salners, 9911 W Pico Blvd, #1400, Los Angeles CA 90035 USA

Bean, Sean — Actor
Independent Talent Group, Oxford House, 76 Oxford St, London W1D 1BS, England

Bean, William D (Billy) — Baseball Player, Writer
W M E Entertainment, 9601 Wilshire Blvd, #300, Beverly Hills CA 90210 USA

Beane, William L (Billy), Jr — Baseball Player
33 Brightwood Lane E, Danville CA 94506, USA

Bear, Gregory D (Greg) — Writer
506 Lakeview Road, Lynnwood WA 98087, USA

Bearak, Barry — Journalist
New York Times, Editorial Dept, 229 W 43rd St, New York NY 10036 USA

Beard, Alana M — Basketball Player
Washington Mystics, Verizon Center, 401 9th St NW, #750, Washington DC 20004 USA

Beard, Albert (Butch) — Basketball Player, Coach
3834 Berleigh Hill Court, Burtonsville MD 20866, USA

Beard, Amanda — Swimmer, Model
4609 W Saguaro Cliffs Dr, Tucson AZ 85745, USA

Beard, C David (Dave) — Baseball Player
5325 Derby Chase Court, Alpharetta GA 30005, USA

Beard, Edward L (Ed) — Football Player
4110 2nd St, Chesapeake VA 23324, USA

Beard, Frank — Golfer
73895 Shadow Mountain Dr, #4, Palm Desert CA 92260, USA

Beard, Frank — Drummer (ZZ Top)
Sanctuary Mgmt, 15301 Ventura Blvd, Building B, Sherman Oaks CA 91403, USA

Bearse, Amanda — Actress, Director, Producer
910 N 39th St, Seattle WA 98103, USA

Beart, Emmanuelle — Actress
Agence Artiste Adequet, 80 Rue d'Amsterdam, 75009 Paris, France

Beasley, Aaron B — Football Player
1635 Braid Hills Dr, Pasadena MD 21122, USA

Beasley, Allyce — Actress
Henderson/Hogan, 850 7th Ave, #1003, New York NY 10019 USA

Beasley, Bruce M — Sculptor
322 Lewis St, San Francisco CA 94607, USA

Beasley, Charles P (Charlie) — Basketball Player
6308 Winton St, Dallas TX 75214, USA

Beasley, Frederick J (Fred) — Football Player
PO Box 210931, Montgomery AL 36121, USA

Beasley, Jere L — Attorney; Governor, AL
Beasley Allen Crow, 218 Commerce St, Montgomery AL 36104, USA

Beasley, John — Actor
Bauman Redanty Shaul Agency, 5757 Wilshire Blvd, #473, Los Angeles CA 90036, USA

Beasley, John — Composer
24 Seven Artist Development, 6 Richmond St, Newark NJ 07103, USA

Beasley, John — Football Player
W3848 Turtle Patch Road, Pine River WI 54965, USA

Beasley, John M — Basketball Player
113 Oak Acres Dr W, Malakoff TX 75148, USA
Beasley, Michael P, Jr — Basketball Player
Phoenix Suns, 201 E Jefferson St, Phoenix AZ 85004 USA
Beasley, Terry P — Football Player
4052 Wellington Way, Moody AL 35004, USA
Beasley, Thomas L (Tom) — Football Player
RR 1 Box 185, Hiltons VA 24258, USA
Beasley, Walter — Jazz Saxophonist
Berklee College of Music, 1140 Boylston St, Boston MA 02215, USA
Beason, Jonathan (Jon) — Football Player
Carolina Panthers, Ericsson Stadium, 800 S Mint St, Charlotte NC 28202 USA
Beathard, Peter F (Pete) — Football Player
3770 Drake St, Houston TX 77005, USA
Beaton, Frank — Ice Hockey Player
3327 Chapel Hills Parkway, Fultondale AL 35068, USA
Beatrix — Queen, Netherlands
Soestdijk Palace, Amsterdamsestraatweg 1, 2513 AA Baarn, Netherlands
Beatriz Barros, Ana — Model
Elite Model Mgmt, 404 Park Ave S, #900, New York NY 10016 USA
Beattie, Ann — Writer
Janklow & Nesbit Assoc, 445 Park Ave, #1300, New York NY 10022 USA
Beattie, Bob — Alpine Skier
312 Aabc, #I, Aspen CO 81611, USA
Beattie, Bruce — Editorial Cartoonist
Daytona Beach News-Journal, Editorial Dept, 901 6th St, Daytona Beach FL 32117, USA
Beattie, James L (Jim) — Baseball Player
PO Box 231, Quechee VT 05059, USA
Beattie, Joseph — Actor
Ken McReddie Assoc, 11 Connaught Place, London W2 2ET, England
Beattie, Michael — Actor
W M E Entertainment, 9601 Wilshire Blvd, #300, Beverly Hills CA 90210 USA
Beatty, James T (Jim) — Track Athlete
6525 Morrison Blvd, Charlotte NC 28211, USA
Beatty, Linda — Model
Playboy Promotions, 2706 Media Center Dr, Los Angeles CA 90065 USA
Beatty, Ned — Actor
2706 N Beachwood Dr, Los Angeles CA 90068, USA
Beatty, Warren — Director, Producer, Actor
13671 Mulholland Dr, Beverly Hills CA 90210, USA
Beaty, Zelmo — Basketball Player
2808 120th Ave NE, Bellevue WA 98005, USA
Beaucham, Danny — Model
Select Model Mgmt, 17 Ferdinand St, London NW1 8EU, England
Beauchamp, Alfred (Al) — Football Player
533 Pinegate Road, Peachtree City GA 30269, USA
Beauchamp, Joseph S (Joe) — Football Player
8896 Highwood Dr, #A, San Diego CA 92119, USA
Beauchamp, Michelle — Actress
Amsel Eisenstadt Frazier, 5055 Wilshire Blvd, #865, Los Angeles CA 90036 USA
Beaudin, Norman J A (Norm) — Ice Hockey Player
11010 Longboat Key Lane, #106, Tampa FL 33626, USA
Beaudoin, Douglas L (Doug) — Football Player
15143 Springview St, Tampa FL 33624, USA
Beaufait, Mark — Ice Hockey Player
5454 Longwood Court SE, Ada MI 49301, USA
Beaufoy, Simon — Writer
Rod Hall Agency, 7 Mallow St, London EC1Y 8RQ, England
Beaumon, Sterling — Actor
Abrams Artists, 9200 W Sunset Blvd, #1125, West Hollywood CA 90069 USA
Beaumont, Jimmy — Singer (Skyliners)
Creative Entertainment Assoc, 1950 Old Cuthbert Road, #J, Cherry Hill NJ 08034 USA
Beaumont, Kathryn — Actress
Walt Disney Co, 500 S Buena Vista St, Burbank CA 91521, USA
Beaupre, Don — Ice Hockey Player
5020 Scriver Road, Minneapolis MN 55436, USA
Beauregard, Robin — Water Polo Player
467 Midvale Ave, Los Angeles CA 90024, USA
Beauregard, Stephane — Ice Hockey Player
175 Rue Des Plaines, Cowansville QC J2K 3T8, Canada
Beauvais, Garcelle — Model, Actress
S D B Partners, 1801 Ave of Stars, #902, Los Angeles CA 90067 USA
Beauvois, Xavier — Actor
Artmedia, 20 Ave Rapp, 75007 Paris, France
Beavan, Jenny — Costume Designer
United Talent Agency, 9336 Civic Center Dr, Beverly Hills CA 90210 USA
Beaver, James N (Jim) — Actor
House of Representatives, 1434 6th St, #1, Santa Monica CA 90401 USA
Beaver, Joe — Rodeo Rider
PO Box 1595, Huntsville TN 37756, USA
Beaver, Terry — Actor
Paradigm Agency, 360 N Crescent Dr, North Building, Beverly Hills CA 90210 USA
Beban, Gary J — Football Player
20 Timber Lane, Northbrook IL 60062, USA
Bebington, Anna — Rowing Athlete
Leander Club, Henly on Thames, Leander RG9 2LP, England
Bebout, Nick — Football Player
1606 Major Ave, Riverton WY 82501, USA
Becaert, Sylvie — Biathlete
F F S Biathlon, 50 Rue des Marquisats, 74011 Annecy, France
Bechara Boutros al-Rai, Mar — Religious Leader
Patriarchy of Maronite Catholic Church, Bkerke, Lebanon
Bechdel, Alison — Cartoonist, Writer
Houghton Mifflin Harcourt, 215 Park Ave S, #1200, New York NY 10003 USA
Becherer, Hans W — Businessman
432 Columbine St, Denver CO 80206, USA

Becht, Anthony Football Player
1122 Oxbridge Dr, Lutz FL 33549, USA
Bechtel, Riley P Businessman
Bechtel Group, 50 Beale St, San Francisco CA 94105, USA
Bechtel, Stephen D, Jr Businessman
Bechtel Group, 50 Beale St, San Francisco CA 94105, USA
Bechtol, T Bubba Actor, Comedian
The Consortium, 49 Music Square W, #210, Nashville TN 37203, USA
Beck Singer, Guitarist, Songwriter
Creative Artists Agency, 2000 Ave of Stars, #100, Los Angeles CA 90067 USA
Beck Hilton, Kimberly Actress
Sutton-Barth Vennari, 145 S Fairfax Ave, #310, Los Angeles CA 90036 USA
Beck, A Byron Basketball Player
1909 S Williams St, Kennewick WA 99338, USA
Beck, Aaron T Psychiatrist
3535 Market St, #200, Philadelphia PA 19104, USA
Beck, Barry Ice Hockey Player
Hong Kong Academy of Hockey, 183 Queens Rd E #64/F, Wanchai, Hong Kong, China
Beck, Charles (Charlie) Law Enforcement Official
Los Angeles Police Dept, 150 S Los Angeles St, Los Angeles CA 90012, USA
Beck, Charles H (Chip) Golfer
11 Pembroke Dr, Lake Forest IL 60045, USA
Beck, Ernest J (Ernie) Basketball Player
1523 Brierwood Road, Havertown PA 19083, USA
Beck, Glenn Commentator
2208 Vaquero Estates Blvd, Westlake TX 76262, USA
Beck, Jeff Singer, Guitarist (Yardbirds)
Creative Artists Agency, 2000 Ave of Stars, #100, Los Angeles CA 90067 USA
Beck, John C Geriatrics Physician
1562 Casale Road, Pacific Palisades CA 90272, USA
Beck, Maria Actress
C E S D, 257 Park Ave S, #950, New York NY 10010 USA
Beck, Marilyn M Columnist
2152 El Roble Lane, Beverly Hills CA 90210, USA
Beck, Martin Actor
Lichtman/Salners, 15865 Royal Haven Place, Sherman Oaks CA 91403 USA
Beck, Martina (Molly) Glagow Biathlete
Rehbergstr 40, 82481 Mittenwald, Germany
Beck, Noelle Actress
Gersh Agency, 41 Madison Ave, #3301, New York NY 10010 USA
Beck, Robin Singer
Cavaricci & White, 156 W 56th St, #1803, New York NY 10019, USA
Beckel, Graham Actor
Susan Smith, 1344 N Wetherly Dr, Los Angeles CA 90069 USA
Beckel, Robert D Air Force General
New Mexico Military Institute, Superintendent's Office, Roswell NM 88201, USA
Beckenbauer, Franz Soccer Player, Coach
Posrfach 700220, 81302 Munich, Germany
Becker, Arthur C (Art) Basketball Player
1879 E Bentrup Dr, Tempe AZ 85283, USA
Becker, Boris Tennis Player
Ruessenstr 6, 6341 Baar, Switzerland
Becker, Gary S Nobel Economics Laureate
1308 E 58th St, Chicago IL 60637, USA
Becker, Gerry Actor
Paradigm Agency, 360 Park Ave S, #1600, New York NY 10010 USA
Becker, Harold Director
I C M Partners, 10250 Constellation Blvd, #900, Los Angeles CA 90067 USA
Becker, Jo Journalist
Washington Post, Editorial Dept, 1150 15th St NW, Washington DC 20071 USA
Becker, Karl J Cardinal Religious Leader
Society of Jesus, Borgo S Spirito 4, CP6139, 00195 Rome-Prati, Italy
Becker, Kuno Actor
A P A Talent/Literary Agency, 405 S Beverly Dr, #300, Beverly Hills CA 90212 USA
Becker, Kurt F Football Player
49W412 Scott Road, Big Rock IL 60511, USA
Becker, Quinn H Army General, Surgeon
2111 Peninsula Dr, San Antonio TX 78239, USA
Becker, Richard G (Rich) Baseball Player
210 Mary Senica Court, LaSalle IL 61301, USA
Becker, Robert J Allergist
2200 S Ocean Lane, #1905, Fort Lauderdale FL 33316, USA
Becker, Walt W Director
Walt Becker Productions, 1680 Vine St, #1101, Los Angeles CA 90028, USA
Becker, Walter Bassist, Guitarist (Steely Dan)
Front Line Mgmt, 1100 Glendon Ave, #2000, Los Angeles CA 90024 USA
Beckert, Glenn A Baseball Player
1953 Arkansas Ave, Englewood FL 34224, USA
Beckett, Bob Ice Hockey Player
38 Fonthill Blvd, Markham ON L3R 1V7, Canada
Beckett, Joshua P (Josh) Baseball Player
1 Avery St, #20B, Boston MA 02111, USA
Beckett, Margaret M Government Official, England
Foreign Ministry, 11 Downing St, London SW1A 2AA, England
Beckett, Rogers Football Player
635 Gaelic Court, Apopka FL 32712, USA
Beckett, Sister Wendy Art Critic
BBC TV Center, Wood Lane, London W12 7R3, England
Beckett, William E, Jr Singer (Academy Is), Songwriter
Crush Music Media Mgmt, 60-62 E 11th St, #700, New York NY 10003, USA
Beckford, Roxanne Actress
Abrams Artists, 9200 W Sunset Blvd, #1125, West Hollywood CA 90069 USA
Beckford, Tyson Model, Actor
I C M Models, 2 Henrietta St, Covent Garden, London WC2E 8PS, England
Beckham, David R J Soccer Player
19 Entertainment, 32/33 Ransomes Dock, 35-37 Parkgate Road, London SW11 4NP, England , USA

Beckinsale, Kate — Actress
United Talent Agency, 9336 Civic Center Dr, Beverly Hills CA 90210 USA
Becklean, William — Rowing Athlete
30 Cambridgepark Dr, #445, Cambridge MA 02140, USA
Beckless, Ian H — Football Player
4915 Andros Dr, Tampa FL 33629, USA
Beckley, Gerald L (Gerry) — Singer, Guitarist (America), Songwriter
Morey Mgmt, 1100 Glendon Ave, #1100, Los Angeles CA 90024, USA
Beckman, Cameron — Golfer
23303 Wilderness Cove, San Antonio TX 78261, USA
Beckman, Edwin J (Ed) — Football Player
4295 18th St NE, Naples FL 34120, USA
Beckman, Julie — Architect
Kaseman Beckman Advanced Strategies, 408 Vine St, #2B, Philadelphia PA 19106, USA
Beckmann, M Patricia — Chemist
Homestead Clinical Corp, 235 E 42nd St, Seattle WA 98102, USA
Beckwith, T Joseph (Joe) — Baseball Player
859 Annabrook Dr, Auburn AL 36830, USA
Becquer, Julio V — Baseball Player
2461 Kyle Ave N, Minneapolis MN 55422, USA
Bedard, Eric — Speed Skater
Speed Skating Canada, 2781 Lancaster Road, #402, Ottawa ON K1B 1A7, Canada
Bedard, Irene — Actress
Don Buchwald/Fortitude, 6500 Wilshire Blvd, #2200, Los Angeles CA 90048 USA
Bedard, Myriam — Biathlete
3329 Pinecourt, Neufchatel QC G2B 2E4, Canada
Bedelia, Bonnie — Actress
Innovative Artists, 1505 10th St, Santa Monica CA 90401 USA
Bedell, Brad — Football Player
545 N Altura Road, Arcadia CA 91007, USA
Bedell, Robert G (Bob) — Basketball Player
3107 Kipling Way, Louisville KY 40205, USA
Bedford, Brian — Actor
Paradigm Agency, 360 N Crescent Dr, North Building, Beverly Hills CA 90210 USA
Bedford, Mark (Bedders) — Bassist (Madness)
I T F, Ariel House, 74A Charlotte St, London W1T 4QJ, England
Bedford, Martyn — Writer
Bloomsbury Publishing, 36 Soho Square, London W1D 3Q4, England
Bedford, Steuart J R — Conductor
76 Cromwell Ave, London N6 5HQ, England
Bedi, Bisban Singh — Cricketer
Ispat Bhawan, Lodhi Road, New Delhi 110 003, India
Bedi, Kabir — Actor
Beach House Park, Gandhigram, Juhu, Mumbai 400 049, India
Bedia, Jose — Artist, Sculptor
George Adams Gallery, 41 W 57th St, #700, New York NY 10019, USA
Bedingfield, Daniel — Singer, Songwriter
Primary Talent International, 10-11 Jockey's Fields, London WC1R 4BN, England
Bedingfield, Natasha — Singer, Songwriter
I/D Public Relations, 150 W 30th St, #1900, New York NY 10001, USA
Bednarik, Charles P (Chuck) — Football Player
6379 Winding Road, Coopersburg PA 18036, USA
Bednarski, John — Ice Hockey Player
1005 Windfaire Place, Roswell GA 30076, USA
Bednob, Gerry — Actor
Amsel Eisenstadt Frazier, 5055 Wilshire Blvd, #865, Los Angeles CA 90036 USA
Bednorz, J Georg — Nobel Physics Laureate
I B M Research Laboratory, Saumerstr 4, 8803 Ruschlikon, Switzerland
Bedows, Elliott — Oncologist
University of Nebraska Medical Center, Eppley Cancer Center, Omaha NE 68198, USA
Bedrosian, Stephen W (Steve) — Baseball Player
3335 Gordon Road, Senoia GA 30276, USA
Bee, Samantha — Actress
W M E Entertainment, 9601 Wilshire Blvd, #300, Beverly Hills CA 90210 USA
Beebe, Dion — Cinematographer
I C M Partners, 10250 Constellation Blvd, #900, Los Angeles CA 90067 USA
Beebe, Don L — Football Player
1246 Verona Ridge Dr, Aurora IL 60506, USA
Beebe, Reta — Astronomer
New Mexico State University, Astronomy Dept, Las Cruces NM 88003, USA
Beeby, Thomas H — Architect
Hammond Beeby Babka, 440 N Wells St, #630, Chicago IL 60654, USA
Beede, Frank, III — Football Player
1645 Somerset Place, Antioch CA 94509, USA
Beedle, Ashley — DJ Musician (X-Press 2)
International Talent Booking, Ariel House, 74A Charlotte St, #100 London W1T 4QJ, England
Beeli, Binia — Curling Athlete
Curling Assn, PO Box 606, 3000 Bern, Switzerland
Beem, Rich — Golfer
104 Bella Cima Dr, Austin TX 78734, USA
Been, Robert Levon — Bassist (Black Rebel Motorcycle Club)
Paradigm Agency, 360 Park Ave, #1600, New York NY 10022 USA
Beene, Frederick R (Fred) — Baseball Player
PO Box 143, Oakhurst TX 77359, USA
Beenie Man — Singer
Agency Group Ltd, 142 W 57th St, #600, New York NY 10019 USA
Beer, Donald — Rowing Athlete
2 Governors Lane, Princeton NJ 08540, USA
Beerbaum, Ludger — Equestrian
Altvaterweg 5, 86807 Buchloe, Germany
Beering, Steven C — Educator
10487 Windemere, Carmel IN 46032, USA
Beers, Betsy — Producer
ShondaLand, 4151 Prospect Ave, #400, Los Angeles CA 90027, USA
Beers, Bob — Ice Hockey Player
97 Blake Road, Lexington MA 02420, USA

Beers, Gary — Singer, Bassist (INXS)
8 Hayes St, #1, Neutral Bay 20891 NSW, Australia
Beers, Thom — Producer, Actor, Writer
Original Productions, 308 W Verdugo Ave, Burbank CA 91502 91502, USA
Beesley, Damon — Writer
Bwark Productions, 35-47 Bethnal Green Road, London E1 6LA, England
Beesley, Max — Actor
Untitled Entertainment, 350 S Beverly Dr, #200, Beverly Hills CA 90212 USA
Beeson, Terry E — Football Player
1302 Hibbard St, Coffeyville KS 67337, USA
Beeston, Paul M — Baseball Executive
Toronto Blue Jays, Skydome, 1 Blue Jay Way, Toronto ON M5V 1J1, Canada
Beetem, Chris — Actor
Abrams Artists, 9200 W Sunset Blvd, #1125, West Hollywood CA 90069 USA
Bega, Leslie — Actress
Sovereign Talent Group, 8421 Wilshire Blvd, #200, Beverly Hills CA 90211, USA
Bega, Lou — Singer
Unicade Music, Truderingestra 259, 8821 Munich, Germany
Begay, Notah — Golfer
3620 Vista del Sur St NW, Albuquerque NM 87120, USA
Beggs, Don — Educator
Wichita State University, President's Office, Wichita KS 67260, USA
Beggs, James M — Space Engineer, Government Official
1177 N Great Southwest Parkway, Grand Prairie TX 75050, USA
Begg-Smith, Dale — Freestyle Moguls Skier
Ski & Snowboard, 1 Cobden St, South Melbourne VIC 3205, Australia
Beghe, Jason — Actor
A P A Talent/Literary Agency, 405 S Beverly Dr, #300, Beverly Hills CA 90212 USA
Beghe, Renato — Judge
US Tax Court, 400 2nd St NW, Washington DC 20217, USA
Begler, Michael — Producer, Writer
W M E Entertainment, 9601 Wilshire Blvd, #300, Beverly Hills CA 90210 USA
Begley, Ed, Jr — Actor
Innovative Artists, 1505 10th St, Santa Monica CA 90401 USA
Beglin, Elizabeth (Beth) — Field Hockey Player
2070 Silver Maple Trail, North Liberty IA 52317, USA
Beguelin, Chad — Writer, Lyricist
Gersh Agency, 9465 Wilshire Blvd, #600, Beverly Hills CA 90212 USA
Behagen, Ronald M (Ron) — Basketball Player
1101 Juniper St NE, #401, Atlanta GA 30309, USA
Behar, Joy — Actress, Comedienne
I C M Partners, 10250 Constellation Blvd, #900, Los Angeles CA 90067 USA
Beharry, Johnson G — Iraq War British Army Hero (VC)
Victoria Cross Assn, Old Admiralty Building, London SW1A 2BL, England
Behe, Michael — Biochemist, Writer
Lehigh University, Biochemistry Dept, Bethlehem PA 18015, USA
Behle, Petra — Biathlete
Sonnenhof 1, 34508 Willingen, Germany
Behmen, Alija — Prime Minister
Prime Minister's Office, Alipasina 1, 71000 Sarajevo, Bosnia & Herzegovina
Behnisch, Stefan — Architect
Behnisch Behnisch Partners, 6 Christophstr, 70178 Stuttgart, Germany
Behnke, Elmer H — Basketball Player
3412 Ivy Chase Circle, Birmingham AL 35226, USA
Behnken, Lukas — Actor
Media Artists Group, 8222 Melrose Ave, #203, Los Angeles CA 90048 USA
Behnken, Robert L — Astronaut
N A S A, Johnson Space Center, 2101 NASA Road, Houston TX 77058 USA
Behr, Jason — Actor
Untitled Entertainment, 350 S Beverly Dr, #200, Beverly Hills CA 90212 USA
Behrend, Marc — Ice Hockey Player
1808 Savannah Way, Waunakee WI 53597, USA
Behrendt, Greg — Writer, Actor
Avalon Mgmt, 4A Exmoor St, London W10 6BD, England
Behrendt, Jan — Luge Athlete
Karl-Zink-Str 2, 96893 Ilmenau, Germany
Behrendt, Wolfgang — Boxer
Springbornstr 204, 12487 Berlin, Germany
Behrens, Sam — Actor
530 Bryant Dr, Canoga Park CA 91304, USA
Behrensmyer, Anna K — Paleobiologist
Amboseli National Park, PO Box 18, Namanga, Kenya
Behrman, David W (Dave) — Football Player
10187 25 1/2 Mile Road, Albion MI 49224, USA
Behrman, Richard E — Pediatrician
PO Box 4446, Santa Barbara CA 93140, USA
Behrs, Beth — Actress
Creative Artists Agency, 2000 Ave of Stars, #100, Los Angeles CA 90067 USA
Beickler, Ferdinand — Businessman
Adam Opel AG, Bahnhofsplatz 1, 65428 Russelsheim, Germany
Beikirch, Gary B — Vietnam War Army Hero (CMH)
468 Crosby Lane, Rochester NY 14612, USA
Beilein, John — Basketball Coach
University of Michigan, Athletic Dept, Ann Arbor MI 48109, USA
Beilina, Nina — Concert Violinist
400 W 43rd St, #7D, New York NY 10036, USA
Beimel, Joseph R (Joe) — Baseball Player
291 Fairview Road, Kersey PA 15846, USA
Beineix, Jean-Jacques — Director
Cargo Films, 9 Rue Ambroise Thomas, 75009 Paris, France
Beirne, James P (Jim) — Football Player
2 Cedar Chase Place, Spring TX 77381, USA
Beisel, Monty G — Football Player
608 Herkimer St, Oskaloosa KS 66066, USA
Beisler, Randall L (Randy) — Football Player
899 Northgate Dr, #500, San Rafael CA 94903, USA

Beisner, Michelle — Sportscaster
Maximum Talent Agency, 1873 S Bellaire St, #915, Denver CO 80222, USA

Beitz, Berthold — Businessman
Hugel 15, 45133 Essen, Germany

Bejo, Berenice — Actress
Agence Artiste Adequet, 80 Rue d'Amsterdam, 75009 Paris, France

Bekmambetov, Timur — Director
W M E Entertainment, 9601 Wilshire Blvd, #300, Beverly Hills CA 90210 USA

Bela, Magyari — Cosmonaut, Hungary
18885 P Alffy 7-11, Budapest, Hungary

Belafonte, David — Actor
12603 Walsh Ave, Los Angeles CA 90066, USA

Belafonte, Harry — Singer, Actor
W M E Entertainment, 1325 Ave of Americas, New York NY 10019, USA

Belafonte, Shari — Actress, Model
W M E Entertainment, 9601 Wilshire Blvd, #300, Beverly Hills CA 90210 USA

Belasco, Bert — Actor
TalentWorks, 3500 W Olive Ave, #1400, Burbank CA 91505 USA

Belbin, Tanith J L — Figure Skater
Detroit Skating Club, 888 Denison Court, Bloomfield Hills MI 48302, USA

Belcher, Daniel — Opera Singer
Columbia Artists Mgmt Inc, 1790 Broadway, #702, New York NY 10019 USA

Belcher, Timothy W (Tim) — Baseball Player
PO Box 153, Sparta OH 43350, USA

Belda, Alain J P — Businessman
Alcoa Inc, 201 Isabella St, Pittsburgh PA 15212, USA

Belen, Ana — Actress, Singer
Rompeolas Productions, Alabama St, #1761, San Gerardo, Rio Piedras PR 00926, USA

Belenky, Valery — Gymnast
Schillerstr 20, 73760 Ostfildern, Germany

Belfi, Jordan — Actor
Schumacher Mgmt, 10323 Santa Monica Blvd, #101, Los Angeles CA 90024, USA

Belford, Christine — Actress
C E S D, 10635 Santa Monica Blvd, #130, Los Angeles CA 90025 USA

Belfour, Edward J (Ed) — Ice Hockey Player
544 Studebaker Road, Whitewright TX 75491, USA

Belgrave, Elliott F — Governor General, Barbados
Governor General's Office, Bay St, Saint Michael, Bridgetown, Barbados

Belica, Marina — Singer, Keyboardist (October Project)
October Project, PO Box 539, Prince Street Station, New York NY 10012, USA

Belichik, William S (Bill) — Football Coach
116 Meadowbrook Road, Weston MA 02493, USA

Belin, Gaspard D — Attorney
4 Willard St, Cambridge MA 02138, USA

Belin, Nat — Cartoonist
Drawing Board, 820 W 7th St, #B, Winston Salem NC 27101, USA

Belinda, Stanley P (Stan) — Baseball Player
454 Sylvan Dr, State College PA 16803, USA

Belinelli, Marco A — Basketball Player
Chicago Bulls, United Center, 1901 W Madison St, Chicago IL 60612 USA

Belisle, Matthew T (Matt) — Baseball Player
4009 Sierra Dr, Austin TX 78731, USA

Beliveau, Jean A — Ice Hockey Player
155 Rue Victoria, Longuevil QC J4H 2J4, Canada

Belk, William A (Bill) — Football Player
12 Ricemill Ferry, Columbia SC 29229, USA

Belknap, Anna — Actress
S M S Talent, 8383 Wilshire Blvd, #230, Beverly Hills CA 90211 USA

Bell, Angellica — Entertainer
C B B C, PO Box 9989, London W12 6PA, England

Bell, Anthony D — Football Player
1564 Fitzgerald Dr, Pinole CA 94564, USA

Bell, Archie — Singer
Speer Entertainment Services, PO Box 2620, McDonough GA 30253, USA

Bell, Ashley — Actress
Paradigm Agency, 360 N Crescent Dr, North Building, Beverly Hills CA 90210 USA

Bell, Brad — Golfer
6255 Oakridge Way, Sacramento CA 95831, USA

Bell, Byron — Basketball Player
2546 Tech Dr, Bettendorf IA 52722, USA

Bell, C Gordon — Computer Scientist
Microsoft Corp, 1 Microsoft Way, Redmond WA 98052, USA

Bell, Carl — Guitarist (Fuel)
Media Five Entertainment, 3005 Brodhead Road, #170, Bethlehem PA 18020, USA

Bell, Catherine — Actress
Brillstein Entertainment Partners, 9150 Wilshire Blvd, #350, Beverly Hills CA 90212 USA

Bell, Clyde R (Bob) — Navy Admiral, Association Executive
1301 Harney St, Omaha NE 68102, USA

Bell, Darrin — Cartoonist
Washington Post Writers Group, 1150 15th St NW, Washington DC 20071 USA

Bell, Darryl M — Actor
Innovative Artists, 1505 10th St, Santa Monica CA 90401 USA

Bell, David G (Buddy) — Baseball Player, Manager
244 W Goldfinch Way, Chandler AZ 85286, USA

Bell, David M — Baseball Player
9710 E La Posada Circle, Scottsdale AZ 85255, USA

Bell, Dennis R — Basketball Player
111 Springfield Pike, Cincinnati OH 45215, USA

Bell, Derek N — Baseball Player
3404 Pine Top Dr, Valrico FL 33594, USA

Bell, Drake — Actor
Creative Artists Agency, 2000 Ave of Stars, #100, Los Angeles CA 90067 USA

Bell, Drew Tyler — Actor
Luber Rocklin Entertainment, 8530 Wilshire Blvd, #555, Beverly Hills CA 90211 USA

Bell, Edward A (Eddie) — Football Player
4529 Tacoma Terrace, Fort Worth TX 76123, USA

Bell, Eric A
1140 S 124th St, Chandler AZ 85286, USA — Baseball Player

Bell, Gary
2107 Oak Ranch, San Antonio TX 78259, USA — Baseball Player

Bell, Gerald A (Jerry)
1347 Deerbourne Dr, Wesley Chapel FL 33543, USA — Football Player

Bell, Gregory (Greg)
5983 E Division Road, Logansport IN 46947, USA — Track Athlete

Bell, Gregory L (Greg)
5849 Azalea Way, Goleta CA 93117, USA — Football Player

Bell, Heath J
7437 Los Brazos, San Diego CA 92127, USA — Baseball Player

Bell, Jacob
511 S Warson Road, Saint Louis MO 63124, USA — Football Player

Bell, James D
4512 San Marino Dr, Davis CA 95618, USA — Diplomat

Bell, Jamie
W M E Entertainment, 9601 Wilshire Blvd, #300, Beverly Hills CA 90210 USA — Actor

Bell, Jason D
3387 N Studebaker Road, Long Beach CA 90808, USA — Football Player

Bell, Jay S
PO Box 50249, Phoenix AZ 85076, USA — Baseball Player

Bell, John
Shore Fire Media, 32 Court St, #1600, Brooklyn NY 11201 USA — Singer (Widespread Panic)

Bell, John Anthony
Bell Shakespeare Co, 88 George St, Level 1, Rocks NSW 200, Australia — Director, Actor

Bell, Jorge A M (George)
Lamiama #14, Bell 2nd Planto, San Pedro de Macoris, Dominican Republic — Baseball Player

Bell, Joseph (Joe)
10522 11th Ave NE, Seattle WA 98125, USA — Ice Hockey Player

Bell, Joshua
Konzertdirektion Schmid, Konigstra 36, 30175 Hannover, Germany — Concert Violinist

Bell, Kendrell A
400 W Peachtree St NW, #1211, Atlanta GA 30308, USA — Football Player

Bell, Kevin R
621 Sue St, Little Chute WI 54140, USA — Baseball Player

Bell, Kristen
Brookside Artist Mgmt, 250 W 57th St, #2303, New York NY 10107, USA — Actress

Bell, Lake
United Talent Agency, 9336 Civic Center Dr, Beverly Hills CA 90210 USA — Actress

Bell, Larry S
PO Box 4101, Taos NM 87571, USA — Sculptor

Bell, Lauralee
Martin Bell Productions, 8033 Sunset Blvd, #799, West Hollywood CA 90046, USA — Actress

Bell, Leola
Playboy Promotions, 2706 Media Center Dr, Los Angeles CA 90065 USA — Model

Bell, Lynette
149 Henry St, Merewether NSW 2200, Australia — Swimmer

Bell, Madison Smartt
Random House, 1745 Broadway, #1800, New York NY 10019 USA — Writer

Bell, Mark E
2701 Wild Rose Ave, Wichita KS 67205, USA — Football Player

Bell, Michael P (Mike)
4906 Encino Ave, Encino CA 91316, USA — Actor

Bell, Michel
Kelly Productions, 824 Munras Ave, Monterey CA 93940, USA — Actor, Singer

Bell, Michelle
18895 Pond Cypress Court, Jupiter FL 33458, USA — Golfer

Bell, Mike
American Motorcycle Assn, 13515 Yarmouth Dr, Pickerington OH 43147 USA — Motorcycle Racing Rider

Bell, Mike J
7405 Lakewood Circle, Wichita KS 67205, USA — Football Player

Bell, Myron C
3027 Crawford Ave, Gastonia NC 28052, USA — Football Player

Bell, O'Neil
Warrior's Boxing Promotions, 5397 Orange Dr, #202, Davie FL 33314, USA — Boxer

Bell, Peter D
Care, 151 Ellis St NE, Atlanta GA 30303, USA — Association Executive

Bell, Raja
12962 Grand Oaks Dr, Davie FL 33330, USA — Basketball Player

Bell, Rini
Brady Brannon & Rich Talent, 5670 Wilshire Blvd, #820, Los Angeles CA 90036, USA — Actress

Bell, Robert A (Rob)
28 Blossom Hill Dr, Marlboro NY 12542, USA — Baseball Player

Bell, Robert E (Kool)
Spirit Media, PO Box 43591, Phoenix AZ 85080 USA — Bassist (Kool & the Gang)

Bell, Robert F (Bob)
7415 N 12th St, Elkins Park PA 19027, USA — Football Player

Bell, Robert H (Rob), Jr
Mars Hill Bible Church, 3501 Fairlanes Ave, Grandville MI 49418, USA — Religious Leader

Bell, Robert L (Bobby), Sr
208 NW Shagbark St, Lees Summit MO 64064, USA — Football Player

Bell, Ronald N
Spirit Media, PO Box 43591, Phoenix AZ 85080 USA — Saxophonist (Kool & the Gang)

Bell, Sam
2310 E Woodstock Place, Bloomington IN 47401, USA — Track Coach

Bell, Steve
Guardian, Editorial Dept, 1 Scott Place, Manchester M3 3GG, England — Editorial Cartoonist

Bell, Tatum A
18754 E Powers Dr, Aurora CO 80015, USA — Football Player

Bell, Thom
B M I, 8730 W Sunset Blvd, #300, Los Angeles CA 90069 USA — Songwriter

Bell, Tobin
C E S D, 10635 Santa Monica Blvd, #130, Los Angeles CA 90025 USA — Actor

Bell, Wallace R (Wally)
725 Purdue Ave, Youngstown OH 44515, USA — Baseball Umpire

Bell, William — Singer, Pianist, Songwriter
Gonzales Music, 1012 W Orice Roth Road, Gonzales LA 70737, USA
Bell, William Brent — Director
Creative Artists Agency, 2000 Ave of Stars, #100, Los Angeles CA 90067 USA
Bell, Yeremiah N — Football Player
1886 Sirius Lane, Weston FL 33327, USA
Bell, Zoe E — Actress, Stuntwoman
Runaway Films, 1338 Rhode Island St, San Francisco CA 94107, USA
Bella, Ivan — Cosmonaut
Cosmonaut Training Center, Star City, 141160 Zvezdny Gorodok, Moscow Oblast, Russia
Bella, Rachael — Actress
TalentWorks, 3500 W Olive Ave, #1400, Burbank CA 91505 USA
Bellamy, Bill — Actor, Comedian
A P A Talent/Literary Agency, 405 S Beverly Dr, #300, Beverly Hills CA 90212 USA
Bellamy, David — Singer (Bellamy Brothers), Songwriter
Bellamy Brothers Partners, 13917 Restless Lane, Dade City FL 33525, USA
Bellamy, David J — Botanist, Writer, Broadcaster
Mill House, Bedburn, Bishop Auckland, County Durham DL13 3NN, England
Bellamy, Howard — Singer (Bellamy Brothers), Songwriter
Bellamy Brothers Partners, 13917 Restless Lane, Dade City FL 33525, USA
Bellamy, Matthew — Singer, Guitarist (Muse)
Hall or Nothing P R, 35-37 Parkgate Road, London SW11 4NP, England
Bellamy, Ned — Actor
Evolution Entertainment, 901 N Highland Ave, Los Angeles CA 90038 USA
Bellamy, Walter J (Walt) — Basketball Player
PO Box 42751, Atlanta GA 30311, USA
Belland, Bruce — Singer (Four Preps)
4339 Ensenada Dr, Woodland Hills CA 91364, USA
Belland, Neil — Ice Hockey Player
868 Renaissance Dr, Oshawa ON L1J 8K9, Canada
Bellany, John — Artist
Clock House, Shortgrove Hall, Saffron Walden, Essex CO11 3TX, England
Bellar, Clara — Actress
Julian Belfrage Assoc, 9 Argyll St, #300, London W1F 7TG, England
Belle, Albert J — Baseball Player
9299 E Mariposa Grande Dr, Scottsdale AZ 85255, USA
Belle, Camilla — Actress
United Talent Agency, 9336 Civic Center Dr, Beverly Hills CA 90210 USA
Belle, Regina — Singer, Songwriter
Sony Records, 2100 Colorado Ave, Santa Monica CA 90404 USA
Bellefeuille, Blake — Ice Hockey Player
1 Angelica Lane, Southborough MA 1772, USA
Bellemer, John — Opera Singer
I M G Artists, Hogarth Business Park, Chiswick, London W4 2TH, England
Beller, Kathleen — Actress
PO Box 806, Half Moon Bay CA 94019, USA
Bellhorn, Mark C — Baseball Player
19550 N Grayhawk Dr, #1083, Scottsdale AZ 85255, USA
Belli, Gioconda — Writer
Carlisle Co, 121 E 17th St, New York NY 10003, USA
Belli, Paolo — Singer
Cicuta Produzioni, Via Barberini 29, 00187 Rome, Italy
Belliard, Rafael L — Baseball Player
10846 King Bay Dr, Boca Raton FL 33498, USA
Belliard, Ronald (Ronnie) — Baseball Player
2999 NW 96th St, Miami FL 33147, USA
Bellincampi, Giordano — Conductor
I M G Artists, Hogarth Business Park, Chiswick, London W4 2TH, England
Bellingham, Lynda — Actress
A R G, 4 Great Portland St, London W1W 8PA, England
Bellingham, Norman — Canoeing Athlete
1825 Cantwell Grove, Colorado Springs CO 80906, USA
Bellini, Mario — Architect
Architecture Center, 66 Portland Place, London W1, England
Bellino, Joseph M (Joe) — Football Player
45 Hayden Lane, Bedford MA 01730, USA
Bellisario, Donald P — Producer
Gelfand Rennert Feldman, 1880 Century Park E, #1600, Los Angeles CA 90067, USA
Bellisario, Troian — Actress
Innovative Artists, 1505 10th St, Santa Monica CA 90401 USA
Bell-Lundy, Sandra — Cartoonist (Between Friends)
255 Northwood Dr, Welland ON L3C 6V1, Canada
Bellman, Gina — Actress
Independent Talent Group, Oxford House, 76 Oxford St, London W1D 1BS, England
Bello, Frank — Bassist (Anthrax)
Zen Media Group, 272 Grand St, #B, Brooklyn NY 11211, USA
Bello, Maria — Actress
Creative Artists Agency, 2000 Ave of Stars, #100, Los Angeles CA 90067 USA
Bellocchio, Marco — Director, Writer
Bobbio Film Festival, Piazzetta Santa Chiara, 129022 Bobbio (PC), Italy
Bellotti, Mike — Football Coach, Executive, Sportscaster
ESPN-TV, ESPN Plaza, 935 Middle St, Bristol CT 06010 USA
Bellovin, Steven M — Computer Scientist
AT&T Research Laboratories, 180 Park Ave, PO Box 971, Florham Park NJ 07932, USA
Bellows, Brian — Ice Hockey Player
5205 Mirror Lakes Dr, Minneapolis MN 55436, USA
Bellows, Gil — Actor
Innovative Artists, 1505 10th St, Santa Monica CA 90401 USA
Bellucci, Monica — Model, Actress
Creative Artists Agency, 2000 Ave of Stars, #100, Los Angeles CA 90067 USA
Bellwood, Pamela — Actress
1696 San Leandro Lane, Santa Barbara CA 93108, USA
Bellynck, Lise — Actress
Agents Associes Chen, 201 Rue Faubourg Saint-Honore, 75008 Paris, France
Belmondo, Jean-Paul — Actor
6 Rue Gassendi, 75014 Paris, France

Belmondo, Olivier — Actor
Artmedia, 20 Ave Rapp, 75007 Paris, France
Belmont, Lara — Actress
Markham & Froggatt, Julian House, 4 Windmill St, London W1P 1HF, England
Belo, Carlos Filipe Ximenes — Nobel Peace Laureate, Religious Leader
Catholic Bishop, Caixa Postale 4, Dili-Leste, East Timor
Belote Hamlin, Melissa — Swimmer
7311 Exmore St, Springfield VA 22150, USA
Belousova, Ludmila Y — Figure Skater
Chalet Hubel, 3818 Grindelwald, Switzerland
Belser, Ceaser E — Football Player
317 Cooper Dr, Hurst TX 76053, USA
Belser, Jason D — Football Player
20474 Middlebury St, Ashburn VA 20147, USA
Beltrami, Marco — Composer
Agency Group, 9348 Civic Center Dr, #200, Beverly Hills CA 90210 USA
Beltran, Carlos I — Baseball Player
18 Paseo Alcala, Urb Hacienda Hermanos Mena, Manati PR 00674, USA
Beltran, Rigoberto (Rigo) — Baseball Player
3950 Laurelwood Lane, Delray Beach FL 33445, USA
Beltran, Robert A — Actor
Abrams Artists, 9200 W Sunset Blvd, #1125, West Hollywood CA 90069 USA
Beltre Perez, Adrian — Baseball Player
239 Walnut Ave, Arcadia CA 91007, USA
Belushi, James — Actor
Brillstein Entertainment Partners, 9150 Wilshire Blvd, #350, Beverly Hills CA 90212 USA
Belvaux, Lucas — Director
Voyez Mon Agent, 20 Ave Rapp, 75007 Paris, France
Belzer, Richard — Actor, Comedian
McBelz Enterprises, 1995 Broadway, #16, New York New York 10023, USA
Beman, Deane R — Golfer, Golf Executive
255 Deer Haven Dr, Ponte Vedra FL 32082, USA
Bement, Linda J — Beauty Queen
Miss Universe Organization, 1370 Ave of Americas, #1600, New York NY 10019 USA
Bemile, Paul Cardinal — Religious Leader
Diocese of Wa, PO Box 47, Wa, Upper West Region, Ghana
Bemiller, Al D — Football Player
5002 Armor-Duells Road, Orchard Park NY 14127, USA
Ben Tre, Howard B — Artist
Charles Cowles Gallery, 210 11th Ave, #500, New York NY 10001, USA
Benade, Leo Edward — Army General
417 Pine Ridge Road, #A, Carthage NC 28327, USA
Benanti, Laura — Actress, Singer
Brookside Artist Mgmt, 250 W 57th St, #2303, New York NY 10107, USA
Benard, Marvin L — Baseball Player
2806 S 38th Ave, West Richland WA 99353, USA
Benard, Maurice — Actor
Stone Manners Salners, 9911 W Pico Blvd, #1400, Los Angeles CA 90035 USA
Benassi, Benny — DJ Musician, Producer
Ultra DJ Mgmt, 42 City Business Center, Lower Road, London SE16 2XB, England
Benatar, Pat — Singer, Songwriter
W M E Entertainment, 9601 Wilshire Blvd, #300, Beverly Hills CA 90210 USA
Benavides, Fortunato P (Pete) — Judge
US Court of Appeals, 903 San Jacinto Blvd, #400, Austin TX 78701, USA
Benben, Brian — Actor
Paradigm Agency, 360 N Crescent Dr, North Building, Beverly Hills CA 90210 USA
Bench, John L (Johnny) — Baseball Player
Johnny Bench Enterprises, 3899 Ridgedale Dr, Cincinnati OH 45247, USA
Benchoff, Dennis L (Den) — Army General
380 Arbor Road, Lancaster PA 17601, USA
Bender, Gary N — Sportscaster
TNT-TV, Sports Dept, 1050 Techwood Dr, Atlanta GA 30318 USA
Bender, Jack — Cartoonist (Alley Oop)
RR 1 Box 540, Terlton OK 74081, USA
Bender, Jack — Director
United Talent Agency, 9336 Civic Center Dr, Beverly Hills CA 90210 USA
Bender, Jonathan R — Basketball Player
New York Knicks, Madison Square Garden, 2 Penn Plaza, New York, NY 10121 USA
Bender, Lawrence — Producer, Director
W M E Entertainment, 9601 Wilshire Blvd, #300, Beverly Hills CA 90210 USA
Bender, Lon — Sound Editor
Soundelux, 7080 Hollywood Blvd, #1100, Los Angeles CA 90028, USA
Bender, Thomas — Historian
54 Washington Mews, New York NY 10003, USA
Bendewald, Andrea — Actress
Metropolitan Talent Agency, 7020 La Presa Dr, Los Angeles CA 90068 USA
Bendinger, Jessica — Director, Writer
Creative Artists Agency, 2000 Ave of Stars, #100, Los Angeles CA 90067 USA
Bendix, Simone — Actress
Joy Jameson, 2/19 Plaza, 535 Kings Road, London SW10 0SZ, England
Bendlin, Kurt — Track Athlete
D L V, Asfelder Str 27, 64289 Leverkusen, Germany
Ben-Dor, Gisele — Conductor
I M G Artists, Hogarth Business Park, Chiswick, London W4 2TH, England
Bene, B Christopher — Architect
Chang Bene Design, 43-55 Wyndham St, Central, Hong Kong, China
Benedek, George B — Physicist
Massachusetts Institute of Technology, Physics Dept, Cambridge MA 02139, USA
Benedeti, Paulo — Actor
4201 N Ocean Blvd, #C505, Boca Raton FL 33431, USA
Benedetti, Nicola — Concert Violinist
I M G Artists, Hogarth Business Park, Chiswick, London W4 2TH, England
Benedict XVI, Pope — Religious Leader
Palazzo Apostolico Vaticano, 00120 Vatican City
Benedict, Bruce E — Baseball Player
335 Quiet Water Lane, Atlanta GA 30350, USA

Benedict, Dirk — Actor
Arsenal Productions & Management, 8200 Wilshire Blvd, #400, Beverly Hills CA 90211, USA

Benedict, Rob — Actor
S M S Talent, 8383 Wilshire Blvd, #230, Beverly Hills CA 90211 USA

Benedict-Jones, Linda — Photographer
256 Jefferson Dr, Pittsburgh PA 15228, USA

Benedicto, Lourdes — Actress
A P A Talent/Literary Agency, 405 S Beverly Dr, #300, Beverly Hills CA 90212 USA

Benepe, Jim — Golfer
602 Mountain Shadows Blvd, Sheridan WY 82801, USA

Benerito, Ruth R — Inventor
6417 Ruth St, Metairie LA 70003, USA

Benero, Edward Allen — Writer, Producer
Creative Artists Agency, 2000 Ave of Stars, #100, Los Angeles CA 90067 USA

Benes, Alan P — Baseball Player
754 Kraffel Lane, Chesterfield MO 63017, USA

Benes, Andrew C (Andy) — Baseball Player
1127 Highland Point Dr, Saint Louis MO 63131, USA

Benet, Eric — Singer, Songwriter
Avnet Mgmt, 4111 W Alameda Ave, #410, Burbank CA 91505, USA

Benetton, Carlo — Businessman
Benetton Group SpA, Via Minelli, 31050 Ponzano Treviso, Italy

Benetton, Gilberto — Businessman
Benetton Group SpA, Via Minelli, 31050 Ponzano Treviso, Italy

Benetton, Giuliana — Businesswoman
Benetton Group SpA, Via Minelli, 31050 Ponzano Treviso, Italy

Benetton, Luciano — Businessman
Benetton Group SpA, Via Minelli, 31050 Ponzano Treviso, Italy

Benga — Electronic Musician (Magnetic Man)
Columbia Records, 9 Derry St, London W8 5HY, England

Benglis, Lynda — Artist, Sculptor
917 Acequia Madre, Santa Fe NM 87505, USA

Bengston, Billy Al — Artist
110 Mildred Ave, Venice CA 90291, USA

Benguigui, Jean — Actor
U B B A, 6 Rue de Braque, 75003 Paris, France

Benhima, Mohamed — Prime Minister, Morocco
Km 5.5, Route des Zaers, Rabat, Morocco

Benichou, Maurice — Actor
Voyez Mon Agent, 20 Ave Rapp, 75007 Paris, France

Benigni, Roberto — Actor, Director
Melampo Cinematografica, Via Ludovisi 35, 00187 Rome, Italy

Bening, Annette — Actress
13671 Mulholland Dr, Beverly Hills CA 90210, USA

Benioff, David — Writer, Producer
Creative Artists Agency, 2000 Ave of Stars, #100, Los Angeles CA 90067 USA

Beniquez Torres, Juan J — Baseball Player
Villa Carolina 87-12, Calle 99A, Villa Carolina PR 00985, USA

Benirschke, Rolf J — Football Player
4326 Vista de la Tierra, San Diego CA 92130, USA

Benish, Daniel J (Dan) — Football Player
1158 Trailblazer Way NW, Lilburn GA 30047, USA

Benitez, Armando G — Baseball Player
520 N Parkway, Golden Beach FL 33160, USA

Benitez, Elsa — Model
Talent Entertainment Group, 9111 Wilshire Blvd, Beverly Hills CA 90210 USA

Benitez, Maria — Flamenco Dancer
Teatro Flamenco, Institute for Spanish Arts, PO Box 8418, Santa Fe NM 87504, USA

Benitez, Wilfredo — Boxer
Saint Just, 248 Calle 6, Trujilloo Alto, PR 00976, USA

Benjamin, Benoit — Basketball Player
28 Morning Green, San Antonio TX 78257, USA

Benjamin, George W J — Composer
Faber Music, 3 Queen Square, London WC1N 3AU, England

Benjamin, Guy E — Football Player
91-443 Ewa Beach Road, Ewa Beach HI 96706, USA

Benjamin, H Jon — Actor, Comedian
Creative Artists Agency, 2000 Ave of Stars, #100, Los Angeles CA 90067 USA

Benjamin, Jill — Actress
Principato-Young, 9465 Wilshire Blvd, #880, Beverly Hills CA 90212 USA

Benjamin, Julia — Actress
4054 Redwood Ave, #6, Los Angeles CA 90066, USA

Benjamin, Lloyd W, III — Educator
Indiana State University, President's Office, Terre Haute IN 47809, USA

Benjamin, Lucy — Actress
Iconic Publicity International, Wren House, #4, 334A Creek Road, London SE10 9SW, England

Benjamin, Michael P (Mike) — Baseball Player
25608 S 182nd Place, Queen Creek AZ 85142, USA

Benjamin, Regina M — Government Official, Physician
Surgeon General's Office, 5600 Fishers Lane, Rockville MD 20857, USA

Benjamin, Richard — Actor, Director
Gersh Agency, 9465 Wilshire Blvd, #600, Beverly Hills CA 90212 USA

Benjamin, Stephen (Steve) — Yachtsman
PO Box 399, Norwalk CT 06856, USA

Benkovic, Stephen J — Chemist
771 Teaberry Lane, State College PA 16803, USA

Benmosche, Robert H — Businessman
American International Group, 70 Pine St, New York NY 10270, USA

Benn, Anthony N W (Tony) — Government Official, England
12 Holland Park Ave, London W11 3QU, England

Benn, Nigel — Boxer
Matchroom Boxing, 10 Western Road, Romford Essex RM1 3JT, England

Bennack, Frank A, Jr — Publisher
Hearst Corp, 250 W 55th St, #4200, New York NY 10019, USA

Benneteau, Julian — Tennis Player
Association of Tennis Professionals, Palliser Road, London W14 9EB, England

Bennett Spector, Veronica (Ronnie) — Singer (Ronettes)
Absolute Artists, 8490 W Sunset Blvd, #403, West Hollywood CA 90069, USA
Bennett, Adam — Ice Hockey Player
7 Stockman Crescent, Georgetown ON L7G 1J5, Canada
Bennett, Alan — Writer, Actor
United Agents, 12-26 Lexington St, London W1F 0LE, England
Bennett, Albert F — Physiologist
University of California, Biological Sciences School, Irvine CA 92697, USA
Bennett, Andrew R (Drew) — Football Player
2335 Hyde St, #1, San Francisco CA 94109, USA
Bennett, Anthony G (Tony) — Basketball Player, Coach
3408 Cesford Grange, Keswick VA 22947, USA
Bennett, Barry M — Football Player
22047 Ginseng Road, Long Prairie MN 56347, USA
Bennett, Bob — Singer, Songwriter
Benjamin Artists Agency, PO Box 92348, Nashville TN 37209, USA
Bennett, Brandon — Football Player
308 Daybrook Court, Greenville SC 29605, USA
Bennett, Brooke — Swimmer
2585 Rowe Road, Milford MI 48380, USA
Bennett, Carl B — Basketball Executive
2834 Little River Run, Fort Wayne IN 46804, USA
Bennett, Charles L — Astrophysicist
Johns Hopkins University, Physics/Astronomy Dept, Baltimore MD 21218, USA
Bennett, Clay — Editorial Cartoonist
Christian Science Monitor, Editorial Dept, 1 Norway St, Boston MA 02136 USA
Bennett, Cornelius O — Football Player
818 S 7th Ave, Hollywood FL 33019, USA
Bennett, Curt A — Ice Hockey Player
260 Awapuhi Place, Wailuku HI 96793, USA
Bennett, Darren L — Football Player
3347 Corte del Cruce, Carlsbad CA 92009, USA
Bennett, Donnell — Football Player
8055 W Leitner Dr, Coral Springs FL 33067, USA
Bennett, Edgar, III — Football Player
1880 Horseshoe Lane, De Pere WI 54115, USA
Bennett, Eliza Hope — Actress
Independent Talent Group, Oxford House, 76 Oxford St, London W1D 1BS, England
Bennett, Elmer J — Basketball Player
2820 Ave of the Woods, Louisville KY 40241, USA
Bennett, Fleur A — Actress
25 Whitehall, London SW1A 2BS, England
Bennett, Fran — Actress
749 1/2 N Lafayette Park Place, Los Angeles CA 90026, USA
Bennett, Harvey, Jr — Ice Hockey Player
1096 Warwick Neck Ave, Warwick RI 02889, USA
Bennett, Hayley — Actress, Singer
Schiff Co, 9465 Wilshire Blvd, #480, Beverly Hills CA 90212, USA
Bennett, Hywel — Actor
116 Lots Road, Chelsea Creek, London SW10, England
Bennett, Jean — Molecular Geneticist, Physician
University of Pennsylvania, Medical School, 422 Curie Blvd, Philadelphia PA 19104, USA
Bennett, Jimmy — Actor
Brown Leader Management Group, 3000 Olympic Blvd, #1302, Santa Monica CA 90404, USA
Bennett, Joan — Model
Playboy Promotions, 2706 Media Center Dr, Los Angeles CA 90065 USA
Bennett, Joe C — Rheumatologist, Educator
4101 Altamont Road, Birmingham AL 35213, USA
Bennett, John — Track Athlete
US Olympic Committee, 1 Olympic Plaza, Building 6, Colorado Springs CO 80909 USA
Bennett, John O, III — Governor, NJ
Montclair State University, Political Science Dept, 1 Normal Ave, Upper Montclair NJ 07043, USA
Bennett, Jonathan — Actor
Evolution Entertainment, 901 N Highland Ave, Los Angeles CA 90038 USA
Bennett, Laurence — Production Designer
Innovative Artists, 1505 10th St, Santa Monica CA 90401 USA
Bennett, Matthew R — Actor
Edna Talent, 318 Dundas St W, Toronto ON M5T 1G5, Canada
Bennett, Michael A — Football Player
Minnesota Vikings, 9520 Viking Dr, Eden Prairie MN 55344 USA
Bennett, Michael V L — Neuroscientist
Albert Einstein College of Medicine, Neuroscience Dept, Bronx NY 10461, USA
Bennett, Monte L — Football Player
2075 Ave U, Sterling KS 67579, USA
Bennett, Nigel — Actor
Characters Talent, 8 Elm St, Toronto ON M5G 1G7, Canada
Bennett, Patricia — Singer (Chiffons)
Lustig Talent, PO Box 770850, Orlando FL 32877 USA
Bennett, Richard Rodney — Composer
Novello Co, 8-9 Firth St, London W1V 5TZ, England
Bennett, Rick — Ice Hockey Player
55 Evergreen Ave, Clifton Park NY 12065, USA
Bennett, Robert F (Rob) — Senator, UT
Arent Fox LLP, 1050 Connecticut Ave NW, Washington DC 20036, USA
Bennett, Robert R — Businessman
Home Shopping Network, 2501 118th Ave N, Saint Petersburg FL 33716, USA
Bennett, Ronan — Writer
Tavistock Wood, 45 Conduit St, London W1S 2YN, England
Bennett, Sarah — Actress
Willow Personal Mgmt, 151 Main St, Yaxley, Peterborough PE7 3LD, England
Bennett, Tom — Sculptor
Bennett Gallery, 6200 Pleasant Valley Road, El Dorado CA 95623, USA
Bennett, Tom — Actor, Writer
Susan Angel & Kevin Francis Ltd, 12 D'Arblay St, London W1F 8DU, England
Bennett, Tony — Singer
R P M Music Productions, 48 W 10th St, #B, New York NY 10011, USA

Bennett, Tony — Artist
48B W 10th St, New York NY 10011, USA
Bennett, Tony L — Football Player
7645 Ballinshire N, Indianapolis IN 46254, USA
Bennett, William (Bill) — Ice Hockey Player
75 Tucker Ave, Cranston RI 02905, USA
Bennett, William J — Secretary, Education
5716 3rd St NW, Washington DC 20011, USA
Bennett, Winston G, III — Basketball Player
54 Barrington Circle, Paducah KY 42003, USA
Bennett, Woodrow (Woody), Jr — Football Player
PO Box 25022, Fort Lauderdale FL 33320, USA
Bennetts, Leslie — Writer
Voice/Hyperion Books, 77 W 66th St, #1100, New York NY 10023, USA
Benning, Brian A — Ice Hockey Player
Interstate Batteries, 11216 156th St NW, Edmonton AB T5M 1Y3, Canada
Benning, James E (Jim) — Ice Hockey Player
20502 SW Kruger Road, Sherwood OR 97140, USA
Bennington, Chester — Singer (Linkin Park)
Special Artists Agency, 9465 Wilshire Blvd, #820, Beverly Hills CA 90212 USA
Bennis, Warren G — Educator, Writer
University of Southern California, Management School, Los Angeles CA 90089, USA
Benoit Samuelson, Joan — Track Athlete
95 Lower Flying Point Road, Freeport ME 04032, USA
Benoit, David — Jazz Pianist, Composer
Chapman & Co Mgmt, PO Box 55246, Sherman Oaks CA 91413, USA
Benrubi, Abraham — Actor
Stone Manners Salners, 9911 W Pico Blvd, #1400, Los Angeles CA 90035 USA
Benson, Amber N — Actress
Glick Agency, 1321 7th St, #203, Santa Monica CA 90401 USA
Benson, Andrew A — Marine Biologist, Plant Physiologist
6044 Folsom Dr, La Jolla CA 92037, USA
Benson, Anna — Model
6025 Sandy Springs Circle, #133, Atlanta GA 30328, USA
Benson, Ashley V — Actress
W K T Public Relations, 9350 Wilshire Blvd, #450, Beverly Hills CA 90212 USA
Benson, Bradley W (Brad) — Football Player
Brad Benson Mitsubishi, 3905 Route 1 S, Monmouth Junction NJ 08852, USA
Benson, Brendan — Singer, Guitarist, Songwriter
High Road Touring, 751 Bridgeway, #200, Sausalito CA 94965 USA
Benson, Bruce D — Educator
University of Colorado, President's Office, 1800 Grant St, #800, Denver CO 80203, USA
Benson, Cedric M — Football Player
20 Commerce Dr, #301, Cranford NJ 7016, USA
Benson, Charles — Football Player
1514 Hanover Lane, Van Alstyne TX 75495, USA
Benson, Clifford A (Cliff) — Football Player
PO Box 821957, Vancouver WA 98682, USA
Benson, Doug — Actor, Comedian
OmniPop Talent Group, 4605 Lankershim Blvd, #201, Toluca Lake CA 91602 USA
Benson, Duane D — Football Player
33053 Grit Road, Lanesboro MN 55949, USA
Benson, George — Jazz Guitarist, Singer
Apropos Management, 365 Avenida de los Arboles, #220, Thousand Oaks CA 91360, USA
Benson, Harry — Photographer
181 E 73rd St, #18A, New York NY 10021, USA
Benson, Herbert — Cardiologist
Mind/Body Medical Institute, Beth Israel Hospital, Brookline MA 02146, USA
Benson, Jodi — Actress, Singer
225 W Elm St, #D, Bishop CA 93514, USA
Benson, Jonathan (Johnny), Jr — Auto, Truck Racing Driver
19528 Mary Ardrey Circle, Cornelius NC 28031, USA
Benson, Kristen J (Kris) — Baseball Player
2140 Vicki Lane, Cumming GA 30041, USA
Benson, Linda — Surfer
SurfHer, PO Box 1, Solana Beach CA 92075, USA
Benson, M Kent — Basketball Player
4315 Weymouth Lane, Bloomington IN 47408, USA
Benson, Peter — Actor
Liebman Entertainment, 25 E 21st St, #PH, New York NY 10010 USA
Benson, Ray — Singer, Guitarist (Asleep at the Wheel)
Bismeaux Productions, PO Box 463, Austin TX 78767, USA
Benson, Raymond — Writer
Ian Fleming Foundation, PO Box 7312, Buffalo Grove IL 60089, USA
Benson, Robby — Actor
A K A Talent, 6310 San Vicente Blvd, #200, Los Angeles CA 90048 USA
Benson, Stephen R (Steve) — Editorial Cartoonist
Arizona Republic, Editorial Dept, 200 E Van Buren St, Phoenix AZ 85004, USA
Benson, Thomas C (Tom) — Football Player
PO Box 701341, Dallas TX 75370, USA
Benson, Vernon A (Vern) — Baseball Player, Manager
1040 De Lara Circle, Granite Quarry NC 28072, USA
Bent, Amel — Singer
19 Music & Mgmt, 35-37 Parkgate Road, London SW11 4NP, England
Bent, Lyriq — Actor
Stone Manners Salners, 9911 W Pico Blvd, #1400, Los Angeles CA 90035 USA
Bent, Margaret H — Musicologist
All Souls College, Oxford University, Music Dept, Oxford OX1 4AL, England
Bent, Ridley — Singer, Songwriter
Agency Group Ltd, 142 W 57th St, #600, New York NY 10019 USA
Bentas, Lily H — Businesswoman
Cumberland Farms, 100 Crossing Blvd, Framingham MA 01702, USA
Bentley, Albert T — Football Player
13631 Eagle Ridge Dr, #234, Fort Myers FL 33912, USA
Bentley, Ben — Sportswriter
6007 N Sheridan Road, #28G, Chicago IL 60660, USA

Bentley, Dierks — Singer, Guitarist, Songwriter
Erv Woosley Agency, 1000 18th Ave S, Nashville TN 37212, USA
Bentley, Jay D — Bassist (Bad Religion)
Goldstar Public Relations, PO Box 130, Ross on Wye HR9 6WY, England
Bentley, Kevin K — Football Player
3001 Murworth Dr, #904, Houston TX 77025, USA
Bentley, Ray — Football Player, Sportscaster
4050 Redbush Dr SW, Grandville MI 49418, USA
Bentley, Wes — Actor
W M E Entertainment, 9601 Wilshire Blvd, #300, Beverly Hills CA 90210 USA
Benton, Barbi — Model, Actress
40 N 4th St, Carbondale CO 81623, USA
Benton, Fletcher C — Sculptor
250 Dore St, San Francisco CA 94103, USA
Benton, Robert — Director
Creative Artists Agency, 2000 Ave of Stars, #100, Los Angeles CA 90067 USA
Benton, Susie — Actress
Associated International Mgmt, Fairfax House, Fulwood Place, London WC1V 6HU, England
Bentsen, William — Yachtsman
N1946 Birches Dr, Lake Geneva WI 53147, USA
Bentyne, Cheryl — Singer (Manhattan Transfer)
Bennett Morgan, 1022 RR 376, #3, Wappinger Falls NY 12590 USA
Benvenuti, Giovanni (Nino) — Boxer
V S Costanza 13, 00198 Rome, Italy
Ben-Victor, Paul — Actor
A P A Talent/Literary Agency, 405 S Beverly Dr, #300, Beverly Hills CA 90212 USA
Benymon, Chico — Actor
Don Buchwald/Fortitude, 6500 Wilshire Blvd, #2200, Los Angeles CA 90048 USA
Benyon, Margaret — Artist
Holography Studio, 40 Springdale, Broadstone, Dorset BH18 9EU, England
Benz, Amy — Golfer
80175 Avenue 52, #223, La Quinta CA 92253, USA
Benz, Edward J, Jr — Pediatrician, Pathologist
20 Beacon St, #4, Boston MA 02108, USA
Benz, Julie — Actress
I C M Partners, 10250 Constellation Blvd, #900, Los Angeles CA 90067 USA
Benza, Alfred Joseph (A J) — Actor, Writer
Media Artists Group, 8222 Melrose Ave, #203, Los Angeles CA 90048 USA
Benzali, Daniel — Actor
Vanguard Management Group, 8060 Melrose Ave, #400 Los Angeles CA 90046, USA
Benzi, Roberto — Conductor
12 Villa Sainte Foy, 92200 Neuilly-sur-Seine, France
Benzinger, Todd E — Baseball Player
1047 Shore Point Court, Loveland OH 45140, USA
Beranek, Josef — Ice Hockey Player
Pittsburgh Penguins, Consol Energy Center, 1001 5th Ave, Pittsburgh PA 15219 USA
Beranek, Leo — Acoustical Engineer
10 Longwood Dr, #265, Westwood MA 2090, USA
Berard, Bryan — Ice Hockey Player
9 Holly Lane, Cumberland RI 02864, USA
Berardi, Antonio — Fashion Designer
Saint Martin's House, 59 Saint Martin's Lane, London WC2N 4JS, England
Bercaw, John E — Chemist
California Institute of Technology, Chemistry Dept, Pasadena CA 91125, USA
Berce, Eugene D (Gene) — Basketball Player
1119 Hawthorne Place, #6, Pewaukee WI 53072, USA
Bercich, Peter J (Pete) — Football Player
17448 Honeysuckle Ave, Lakeville MN 55044, USA
Bercot, Emmanuelle — Director, Writer
U B B A, 6 Rue de Braque, 75003 Paris, France
Bercu, Michaela — Model, Actress
Elite Model Mgmt, 404 Park Ave S, #900, New York NY 10016 USA
Berdimuhammedow, Gurbanguly M — President, Turkmenistan
President's Office, Karl Marx Str 24, 744017 Ashkabat, Turkmenistan
Bere, Jason P — Baseball Player
40 Berrington Place, North Andover MA 01845, USA
Berehowsky, Drake — Ice Hockey Player
20455 N 95th St, Scottsdale AZ 85255, USA
Berendt, John L — Writer
W M E Entertainment, 9601 Wilshire Blvd, #300, Beverly Hills CA 90210 USA
Berendzen, Richard E — Educator
1300 Crystal Dr, Arlington VA 22202, USA
Berenger, Tom — Actor
Brillstein Entertainment Partners, 9150 Wilshire Blvd, #350, Beverly Hills CA 90212 USA
Berengo Gardin, Gianni — Photographer
Via S Michele del Carso 21, 20144 Milan, Italy
Berenguer, Juan B — Baseball Player
8616 Alisa Court, Chanhassen MN 55317, USA
Berenson, Gordon A (Red) — Ice Hockey Player, Coach
3555 Daleview Dr, Ann Arbor MI 48105, USA
Berenyi, Bruce M — Baseball Player
10 Pine Grove Road, Exeter NH 03833, USA
Berenzweig, Andrew — Ice Hockey Player
4603 Brookside Road, Ottawa Hills OH 43615, USA
Beresford, Bruce — Director
Steve Kenis Co, Royalty House, 72-74 Dean St, London WID 3SG, England
Beresford, Meg — Peace Activist
Wiston Lodge, Wiston, Biggar ML12 6HT, Scotland
Bereta, Joe — Actor, Comedian
Barats & Bereta Productions, 9601 Wilshire Blvd, #750, Beverly Hills CA 90210, USA
Berezan, Perry — Ice Hockey Player
Wellington West Capital, 1100-255 5th Ave SW, Calgary AB T2P 3G6, Canada
Berezhnaya, Elena V — Figure Skater
Figure Skating Federation, Luzhnetskaya Nab 8, 119871 Moscow, Russia
Berezin, Sergei — Ice Hockey Player
1645 SW 4th Ave, Boca Raton FL 33432, USA

B

Berezovsky - Berggren

Berezovsky, Boris V I M G Artists, Burlington Lane, Chiswick, London W4 2TH, England	Concert Pianist
Berezovy, Anatoli N Cosmonaut Training Center, Star City, 141160 Zvezdny Gorodok, Moscow Oblast, Russia	Cosmonaut
Berfield, Justin Virgin Produced, 315 S Beverly D, #506, Beverly Hills CA 90212 90212, USA	Actor
Berg, A Scott Creative Artists Agency, 2000 Ave of Stars, #100, Los Angeles CA 90067 USA	Writer
Berg, Aki-Petteri Toronto Maple Leafs, AirCanada Center, 40 Bay St, Toronto ON M5J 2K2, Canada	Ice Hockey Player
Berg, David S (Dave) 1917 Stonecastle Dr, Roanoke TX 76262, USA	Baseball Player
Berg, Elizabeth Random House, 1745 Broadway, #1800, New York NY 10019 USA	Writer
Berg, Laura USA Softball, 2801 NE 50th St, Oklahoma City OK 73111, USA	Softball Player
Berg, Matraca Universal Publishing Group, 1904 Adelicia St, Nashville TN 37212, USA	Singer, Songwriter
Berg, Paul 838 Santa Fe Ave, Stanford CA 94305, USA	Nobel Chemistry Laureate
Berg, Peter W M E Entertainment, 9601 Wilshire Blvd, #300, Beverly Hills CA 90210 USA	Actor, Director, Producer
Berg, William D (Bill) N H L Network, 9 Channel Nine Court, Toronto ON M1S 4B5, Canada	Ice Hockey Player
Berg, Yehuda Kabbalah Centre, 1054 S Robertson Blvd, Los Angeles CA 90035, USA	Religious Leader
Berganio, David, Jr 17811 Lahey St, Granada Hills CA 91344, USA	Golfer
Berganza, Teresa La Rossiniana, Archanda 5, 28200 San Lorenzo del Escorial, Madrid, Spain	Opera Singer
Berge, Francine Intertalent, 48 Rue Gay Lussac, 75005 Paris, France	Actress
Berge, Pierre V G Yves Saint Laurent SA, 5 Ave Marceau, 75116 Paris, France	Businessman
Bergen, Bob C E S D, 10635 Santa Monica Blvd, #130, Los Angeles CA 90025 USA	Actor
Bergen, Candice P 222 Central Park South, New York NY 10019, USA	Actress
Bergen, Gary D 1386 Graham Circle, Erie CO 80516, USA	Basketball Player
Bergen, Polly 1746 S Britain Road, Southbury CT 06488, USA	Actress
Berger Perdomo, Oscar J R President's Office, Palacio Nacional, 6 Avenida 419, Guatemala City, Guatemala	President, Guatemala
Berger, Christian Haus 7, 6072 Lans, Austria	Cinematographer
Berger, Gerhard Berger Motorsport, Postfach 1121, 9490 Vaduz, Austria	Auto Racing Driver
Berger, Glenn W M E Entertainment, 9601 Wilshire Blvd, #300, Beverly Hills CA 90210 USA	Writer
Berger, Helmut Viale Parioli 50, 00197 Rome, Italy	Actor
Berger, Howard K N B Effects Group, 7535 Woodman Place, Van Nuys CA 91405, USA	Makeup Artist
Berger, John Quincy, Mieussy, 74440 Taninges, France	Writer
Berger, Joseph D (Joe) Minnesota Vikings, 9520 Viking Dr, Eden Prairie MN 55344 USA	Football Player
Berger, Joseph S J S B Enterprises, 12605 W North Ave, #225, Brookfield WI 53005, USA	Inventor (Light Can Converter)
Berger, Lars Dombas/Byaasen I L, PB 9266, Stavset, 7424 Trondheim, Norway	Cross Country Skier
Berger, Mitchell S (Mitch) 9108 N 118th Place, Scottsdale AZ 85259, USA	Football Player
Berger, Peter I M G Artists, Hogarth Business Park, Chiswick, London W4 2TH, England	Opera Singer
Berger, Senta Sentana Films, Gebsattelstr 30, 81541 Munich, Germany	Actress
Berger, Thomas L PO Box 11, Palisades NY 10964, USA	Writer
Bergere, Jenica Innovative Artists, 1505 10th St, Santa Monica CA 90401 USA	Actress
Bergeron, Jean-Claude (J C) Reebok/C C M, 3400 Raymond-Lasnier St, Montreal QC H4R 3L3, Canada	Ice Hockey Player
Bergeron, Michel T Q S, 612 Rue Saint-Jacques, Montreal QC H3C 5R1, Canada	Ice Hockey Player, Coach
Bergeron, Patrice 234 Causeway St, #1109, Boston MA 02114, USA	Ice Hockey Player
Bergeron, Peter C 3495 Manatee Dr SE, Saint Petersburg FL 33705, USA	Baseball Player
Bergeron, Tom International Management Group, 2049 Century Park E, #2460, Los Angeles CA 90067, USA	Entertainer
Bergeron, Yves 1035 Clearwater Ave, Bathurst NB E2A 4H5, Canada	Ice Hockey Player
Bergevin, Marc 404 Canterbury Court, Hinsdale IL 60521, USA	Ice Hockey Player
Bergey, John 1807 Mayflower Circle, Lancaster PA 17603, USA	Inventor (Pulsar Watch)
Bergey, William E (Bill) 2 Hickory Lane, Chadds Ford PA 19317, USA	Football Player
Berggren, Jenny United Stage Mgmt, Asogatan 142, Box 11029, 100 61 Stockholm, Sweden	Singer (Ace of Base)
Berggren, Jonas United Stage Mgmt, Asogatan 142, Box 11029, 100 61 Stockholm, Sweden	Singer (Ace of Base)
Berggren, Linn United Stage Mgmt, Asogatan 142, Box 11029, 100 61 Stockholm, Sweden	Singer (Ace of Base)

Berggren, Thommy Swedish Film Institute, PO Box 27126, 102 52, Stockholm, Sweden	Actor
Bergh, Larry C 1849 Bent Pine Hill, Fogelsville PA 18051, USA	Basketball Player
Bergin, Joan Gersh Agency, 9465 Wilshire Blvd, #600, Beverly Hills CA 90212 USA	Costume Designer
Bergin, Michael Chasen Agency, 8899 Beverly Blvd, #716, Los Angeles CA 90048 USA	Model, Actor
Bergin, Patrick Sovereign Talent Group, 8421 Wilshire Blvd, #200, Beverly Hills CA 90211, USA	Actor
Bergkamp, Dennis Arsenal F C, Arsenal Stadium, Avenell Road, London N5 1BU, England	Soccer Player
Bergl, Emily Innovative Artists, 1505 10th St, Santa Monica CA 90401 USA	Actress
Bergland, Robert S (Bob) 1104 7th Ave SE, Roseau MN 56751, USA	Secretary, Agriculture
Bergland, Tim 721 Labree Ave N, Thief River Falls MN 56701, USA	Ice Hockey Player
Berglund, Art 1775 Bob Johnson Dr, Colorado Springs CO 80906, USA	Ice Hockey Executive
Berglund, Bo Buffalo Sabres, 1 Seymour Knox Plaza, #1, Buffalo NY 14203 USA	Ice Hockey Player
Bergman, Alan 714 N Maple Dr, Beverly Hills CA 90210, USA	Lyricist
Bergman, Andrew C Creative Artists Agency, 2000 Ave of Stars, #100, Los Angeles CA 90067 USA	Director, Writer
Bergman, David B (Dave) 728 Canterbury Road, Grosse Pointe Woods MI 48236, USA	Baseball Player
Bergman, John W Commander, Forces Reserve, HqUSMC, 2 Navy St, Washington DC 20380 USA	Marine Corps General
Bergman, Lowell New York Times, Editorial Dept, 229 W 43rd St, New York NY 10036 USA	Journalist
Bergman, Marilyn K 714 N Maple Dr, Beverly Hills CA 90210, USA	Lyricist
Bergman, Martin 641 Lexington Ave, New York NY 10022, USA	Producer
Bergman, Peter Abrams Artists, 9200 W Sunset Blvd, #1125, West Hollywood CA 90069 USA	Actor
Bergman, Robert G 501 Coventry Road, Kensington CA 94707, USA	Chemist
Bergman, Sean F 14421 Scott Road, Bryan OH 43506, USA	Baseball Player
Bergman, Thommie Tolvmansvagen 4, 18463 Akersberga, Sweden	Ice Hockey Player
Bergmann, Barbara R 5430 41st Place NW, Washington DC 20015, USA	Economist
Bergoglio, Jose Mario Cardinal Arzobispado, Rivadavia 415, 1002 Buenos Aires, Argentina	Religious Leader
Bergonzi, Carlo I Duc Foscari, Piazza Carl Rossi 15, 43011 Busseto (Parma), Italy	Opera Singer
Bergoust, Eric 2727 Mulberry Lane, Missoula MT 59804, USA	Freestyle Aerials Skier
Bergqvist, Kajsa M Box 5126, 200 77 Malmo, Sweden	Track Athlete
Bergsten, C Fred 4106 Sleepy Hollow Road, Annandale VA 22003, USA	Economist
Berheim, B Douglas Stanford University, Economics Dept, Stanford CA 94305, USA	Economist
Berisha, Sali Prime Minister's Office, Keshilli i Ministrave, Tirana, Albania	Prime Minister, Albania
Berke, Deborah Deborah Berke Partners Architects, 220 5th Ave, #700, New York NY 10001, USA	Architect
Berkeley, Michael F Oxford University Press, 70 Baker St, London W1U 7DN, England	Composer
Berkley, Elizabeth Kritzer Levine Wilkins Griffin, 11872 La Grange Ave, #100, Los Angeles CA 90025 USA	Actress, Model
Berkman, W Lance (Elvis) 5 Farnham Park Dr, Houston TX 77024, USA	Baseball Player
Berkoff, David Harvard University, Athletic Dept, Cambridge MA 02138, USA	Swimmer
Berkoff, Steven Rosica Colin Ltd, 1 Clareville Mews, London SW1 5AH, England	Actor, Writer
Berkowitz, Bob CNBC-TV, 1 CNBC Plaza, Englewood Cliffs NJ 07632, USA	Entertainer
Berkus, Nate Nate Berkus Assoc, 406 N Wood St, Chicago IL 60622, USA	Interior Designer
Berlant, Anthony (Tony) Los Angeles Louver Gallery, 55 N Venice Blvd, Venice CA 90291, USA	Artist
Berlanti, Greg W M E Entertainment, 9601 Wilshire Blvd, #300, Beverly Hills CA 90210 USA	Director, Producer, Writer
Berlekamp, Elwyn R 120 Hazel Lane, Piedmont CA 94611, USA	Mathematician
Berlin, Eddie 100 Market St, #421, Des Moines IA 50309, USA	Football Player
Berlin, Jeannie M C 2 Entertainment, 18541 Elkwood St, Reseda CA 91335, USA	Actress, Director
Berlin, Mike 12 Coventry Lane, Muscatine IA 52761, USA	Bowler
Berlin, Steve Gold Mountain, 3940 Laurel Canyon Blvd, #444, Studio City CA 91604 USA	Singer, Saxophonist (Los Lobos)
Berliner, Alain United Talent Agency, 9336 Civic Center Dr, Beverly Hills CA 90210 USA	Director
Berling, Charles Markham & Froggatt, Julian House, 4 Windmill St, London W1P 1HF, England	Actor
Berling, Clay 2935 Franciscan Way, Carmel CA 93923, USA	Soccer Executive, Publisher

B

Berling, Peter — Actor
12 V S Calisto, 00153 Rome, Italy

Berlinger, Warren — Actor
23291 Ventura Blvd, Woodland Hills CA 91364, USA

Berlinsky, Dmitri — Concert Violinist
35 W 64th St, #7F, New York NY 10023, USA

Berlusconi, Silvio — Prime Minister, Italy
Palazzo Grazioli, Via del Plebiscito 102, 00186 Rome, Italy

Berman, Andy — Actor
United Talent Agency, 9336 Civic Center Dr, Beverly Hills CA 90210 USA

Berman, Boris — Concert Pianist
Columbia Artists Mgmt Inc, 1790 Broadway, #702, New York NY 10019 USA

Berman, Christopher J (Chris) — Sportscaster
ESPN-TV, ESPN Plaza, 935 Middle St, Bristol CT 06010 USA

Berman, David — Actor
Optimism Entertainment, 303 N La Peer Dr, #205, Beverly Hills CA 90211, USA

Berman, Francine — Computer Scientist
San Diego Supercomputer Center, 9500 Gilman Dr, La Jolla CA 92093, USA

Berman, Jennifer — Physician
University of California, Women's Sexual Health Center, Los Angeles CA 90024, USA

Berman, Josh — Producer
Creative Artists Agency, 2000 Ave of Stars, #100, Los Angeles CA 90067 USA

Berman, Julia — Architect
Julia Berman Design, 947 Camino de Chelly, Santa Fe NM 87505, USA

Berman, Julius — Religious Leader, Attorney
Kaye Scholer Fierman, 425 Park Ave, #1200, New York NY 10022, USA

Berman, Kip — Singer (Pains of Being Pure at Heart)
Slumberland Records, PO Box 19029, Oakland CA 94619, USA

Berman, Laura — Psychotherapist
I C M Partners, 10250 Constellation Blvd, #900, Los Angeles CA 90067 USA

Berman, Saul J — Religious Leader, Rabbi, Writer
E D A H, 1501 Broadway, #501, New York NY 10036, USA

Berman, Shari Springer — Director, Producer, Writer
Anonymous Content, 3532 Hayden Ave, Culver City CA 90232 USA

Berman, Shelley — Actor, Comedian
268 Bell Canyon Road, Bell Canyon CA 91307, USA

Berman, Zev — Writer, Producer, Director
Gersh Agency, 9465 Wilshire Blvd, #600, Beverly Hills CA 90212 USA

Bern, Dan — Singer, Songwriter
Public Emily, 56 Main St, #206, Northampton MA 01060, USA

Bern, Howard A — Biologist
1010 Shattuck Ave, Berkeley CA 94707, USA

Bernal, Gael Garcia — Actor, Director
Canana Films, San Luis Potosi #211 Piso 8, Colonia Roma, Mexico City DF 06700, Mexico

Bernanke, Ben S — Government Official, Economist
Federal Reserve Board, 20th St & Constitution Ave NW, Washington DC 20557, USA

Bernard, Betsy — Businesswoman
American Telephone & Telegraph Corp, 32 Ave of Americas, New York NY 10013, USA

Bernard, Carlos — Actor
Innovative Artists, 1505 10th St, Santa Monica CA 90401 USA

Bernard, Crystal — Actress, Singer, Songwriter
8436 W 3rd St, #650, Los Angeles CA 90048, USA

Bernard, Robert (Rocky) — Football Player
16655 SE 69th Way, Bellevue WA 98006, USA

Bernard, Robyn — Actress
3227 Cardiff Ave, Los Angeles CA 90034, USA

Bernard, Rod — Singer
PO Box 90665, 2410 Eraste Landry, Lafayette LA 70509, USA

Bernardi, Mario — Conductor
Columbia Artists Mgmt Inc, 1790 Broadway, #702, New York NY 10019 USA

Bernath, Antonia — Actress
Creative Artists Agency, 2000 Ave of Stars, #100, Los Angeles CA 90067 USA

Bernauer, David W — Businessman
Walgreen Co, 200 Wilmot Road, Deerfield IL 60015, USA

Bernazard Garcia, Antonio (Tony) — Baseball Player
D25 Calle Santa Ana, Urb Santa Elvira, Caguas PR 00725, USA

Berne, Robert M — Physiologist
250 Pantops Mountain Road, #5134, Charlottesville VA 22911, USA

Bernero, Adam G — Baseball Player
11 Columbus Dr, Savannah GA 31405, USA

Bernero, Edward Allen — Producer, Writer
Creative Artists Agency, 2000 Ave of Stars, #100, Los Angeles CA 90067 USA

Berners-Lee, Timothy J — Computer Scientist
20 Powder Mill Road, Concord MA 1742, USA

Bernhard, Sandra — Actress, Comedienne, Singer
26500 Agoura Road, Calabasas CA 91302, USA

Bernhardt, Tim — Ice Hockey Player
RR 1, Schomberg ON L0G 1T0, Canada

Bernheimer, Martin — Music Critic
17350 Sunset Blvd, #702C, Pacific Palisades CA 90272, USA

Bernier, Serge J — Ice Hockey Player
534 Rue Elisabeth, Rimouski QC G5L 3M9, Canada

Berning, Susie Maxwell — Golfer
80413 Portobello Dr, Indio CA 92201, USA

Berninger, Matt — Singer (National), Songwriter
Brassland Records, PO Box 76, Prince Street Station, New York NY 10012, USA

Bernoldi, Enrique A L S — Auto Racing Driver
Bartels Motor & Sport, Kobbinghausen 2, 58840 Plettenberg, Germany

Berns, Richard R (Rick) — Football Player
127 Merry Trail, San Antonio TX 78232, USA

Bernsen, Corbin — Actor
Home Theater Films, 12041 Maxwellton Road, Studio City CA 91604, USA

Bernstein, Bonnie — Sportscaster
Monmouth County District Attorney, 71 Monmouth Park, Freehold NJ 07728, USA

Bernstein, Carl — Journalist
14 E 60th St, #705, New York NY 10022, USA

Bernstein, Charles — Composer
Soundtrack Music Assoc, 1460 4th St, #308, Santa Monica CA 90401 USA
Bernstein, Jake — Journalist
ProPublica, Editorial Dept, 1 Exchange Plaza, 55 Broadway, #2300, New York NY 10006, USA
Bernstein, Jamie — Concert Narrator
Opus 3 Artists, 470 Park Ave S, #900N, New York NY 10016 USA
Bernstein, Jared — Government Official, Economist
Budget and Policy Priorities Center, 820 1st St NW, #510, Washington DC 20002, USA
Bernstein, Kenny — Auto Racing Driver
Budweiser King Racing, 26231 Dimension Dr, Lake Forest CA 92630, USA
Bernstine, Rod E — Football Player
6675 S Robertsdale Way, Aurora CO 80016, USA
Bernthal, Jon — Actor
W M E Entertainment, 9601 Wilshire Blvd, #300, Beverly Hills CA 90210 USA
Berra, Dale A — Baseball Player
164 Eagle Rock Way, Montclair NJ 07042, USA
Berra, Lawrence P (Yogi) — Baseball Player, Manager
19 Highland Ave, Montclair NJ 07042, USA
Berrian, Bernard — Football Player
7209 Tokay Circle, Winton CA 95388, USA
Berridge, Elizabeth — Actress
Judy Schoen, 606 N Larchmont Blvd, #309, Los Angeles CA 90004 USA
Berridge, Michael J — Zoologist, Biologist
Babraham Institute, Babraham Hall, Cambridge CB2 4AT, England
Berrigan, Daniel — Clergyman, Social Activist
147 Thompson St, New York NY 10012, USA
Berroa, Geronimo E — Baseball Player
3681 Broadway, #23, New York NY 10031, USA
Berry, A Kenneth (Ken) — Baseball Player
1131 SW Camden Lane, Topeka KS 66604, USA
Berry, Ace — Rodeo Rider
12606 Victory Ave, Oakdale CA 95361, USA
Berry, Bertrand D (Bert) — Football Player
1402 E Coral Cove Dr, Gilbert AZ 85234, USA
Berry, Bill — Drummer (REM)
REM/Athens Ltd, 170 College Ave, Athens GA 30601, USA
Berry, Brad — Ice Hockey Player
PO Box 5182, Grand Forks ND 58206, USA
Berry, Brian J L — Geographer, Political Economist
2404 Forest Court, McKinney TX 75070, USA
Berry, Charles E (Chuck) — Singer, Songwriter
Berry Park, 691 Buckner Road, Wentzville MO 63385, USA
Berry, Cornelius J (Neil) — Baseball Player
407 Inkster Ave, Kalamazoo MI 49001, USA
Berry, David — Actor
9171 Orbiter Dr, Dallas TX 75243, USA
Berry, Halle — Actress, Model
Vincent Cirrincione Assoc, 1516 N Fairfax Ave, Los Angeles CA 90046 USA
Berry, Jim — Editorial Cartoonist
United Feature Syndicate, PO Box 5610, Cincinnati OH 45201 USA
Berry, John — Singer
Circle T Management, 44 Wiregrass Circle, Tifton GA 31794, USA
Berry, Kenneth R (Ken) — Actor
147 Sunny Lane, Branson West MO 65737, USA
Berry, Mark (Bez) — Percussionist (Happy Mondays)
145 S Fairfax, #310, Los Angeles CA 90036, USA
Berry, Michael J — Chemist
7801 Comfort Cove, Austin TX 78731, USA
Berry, R Stephen — Chemist
5317 S University Ave, Chicago IL 60615, USA
Berry, Raymond E — Football Player, Coach
1110 SE Broad St, Murfreesboro TN 37130, USA
Berry, Robert C (Bob) — Football Player
1351 Wilson Circle, Gardnerville NV 89410, USA
Berry, Robert V (Bob) — Ice Hockey Player, Coach, Executive
640 3rd St, Hermosa Beach CA 90254, USA
Berry, Royce E — Football Player
PO Box 909, Comfort TX 78013, USA
Berry, Sean R — Baseball Player
307 Susannah Lane, Paso Robles CA 93446, USA
Berry, Stephen J (Steve) — Journalist
6527 Ellenview Ave, West Hills CA 91307, USA
Berry, Walter — Basketball Player
5206 Village Court, Union City GA 30291, USA
Berry, Wendell E — Writer, Ecologist
PO Box 1, Port Royal KY 40058, USA
Berryhill, Damon S — Baseball Player
11 Springbrook Road, Laguna Niguel CA 92677, USA
Berryman, Guy R — Bassist (Coldplay)
Paradigm Agency, 360 N Crescent Dr, North Building, Beverly Hills CA 90210 USA
Berryman, Michael J — Actor
23150 Avenue San Luis, #320, Woodland Hills CA 91364, USA
Bersani, Leo — Educator
University of California, French Dept, Berkeley CA 94720, USA
Bersia, John — Journalist
Orlando Sentinel, Editorial Dept, 633 N Orange Ave, Orlando FL 32801, USA
Berson, Jerome A — Chemist
200 Leeder Hill Dr, #205, Hamden CT 06517, USA
Bertarelli, Ernesto — Businessman, Yachtsman
Serono SA, Chemin des Mines 15 Bis, 1211 Geneva 20, Switzerland
Bertello, Giuseppe Cardinal — Religious Leader
Governatorate of Vatican City State, Urbs Salvia, 00120 Vatican City
Bertelmann, Fred — Singer, Guitarist
Am Hohenberg 9, 82335 Berg, Germany
Bertelsen, James A (Jim) — Football Player
2001 Days End Road, Wimberley TX 78676, USA

B

Bernstein - Bertelsen

Berteotti, Missie — Golfer
300 Ocean Trail Way, #1304, Jupiter FL 33477, USA

Berthiaume, Daniel — Ice Hockey Player
PO Box 673, Hardy VA 24101, USA

Berti, Marco — Opera Singer
I M G Artists, Hogarth Business Park, Chiswick, London W4 2TH, England

Bertil — Crown Prince, Sweden
Hert Av Halland, Kungl Slottet, 111 30 Stockholm, Sweden

Bertinelli, Valerie — Actress
Innovative Artists, 1505 10th St, Santa Monica CA 90401 USA

Bertish, Suzanne — Actress
Jonathan Altaras Assoc, 11 Garrick St, London WC2E 9AR, England

Berto, Andre M — Boxer
Ray Rafoll, 1519 3rd St SE, Winterhaven FL 33880, USA

Bertolucci, Bernardo — Director
Via Della Lungara 3, 00165 Rome, Italy

Bertone, Tarcisco Cardinal — Religious Leader
Secretary of State's Office, Apostolic Palace, 00120 Vatican City

Bertotti, Michael D (Mike) — Baseball Player
14 Jupiter Road, Highland Mills NY 10930, USA

Bertsch, Jackie — Golfer
300 Ocean Trail Way, #1304, Jupiter FL 33477, USA

Bertsch, Shane — Golfer
11120 Night Heron Dr, Parker CO 80134, USA

Bertuzzi, Todd — Ice Hockey Player
900 Deer Ridge Court, Kitchener ON N2P 2L3, Canada

Berube, Craig — Ice Hockey Player
1314 Durham Road, New Hope PA 18938, USA

Berzins, Andris — President, Latvia
President's Office, Pils Laukums 3, Riga 22681 PDP, Latvia

Berzon, Marsha S — Judge
US Court of Appeals, Court Building, 95 7th St, San Francisco CA 94103, USA

Beshore, Delmer (Del) — Basketball Player
4724 N Crestmoor Ave, Clovis CA 93619, USA

Bess, Daniel — Actor
Coast to Coast Talent, 3350 Barham Blvd, Los Angeles CA 90068 USA

Bess, Rufus T, Jr — Football Player
10 Greenview Circle, Chico CA 95928, USA

Bessmertnykh, Aleksandr A — Government Official, Russia
International Foreign Policy Assn, Yakovo-Apostolski 10, 103064 Moscow, Russia

Besson, Luc — Director
Europa Corp, 137, Rue du Faubourg Saint-Honore, 75008 Paris, France

Best, Ahmed — Actor
PO Box 707, Renton WA 98057, USA

Best, Ben — Actor, Comedian, Producer
Creative Artists Agency, 2000 Ave of Stars, #100, Los Angeles CA 90067 USA

Best, Eve — Actress, Singer
Independent Talent Group, Oxford House, 76 Oxford St, London W1D 1BS, England

Best, Greg — Equestrian
39 Troon Terrace, Annandale NJ 08801, USA

Best, James — Actor
PO Box 5325, Hickory NC 28603, USA

Best, Karl J — Baseball Player
PO Box 1790, Snohomish WA 98291, USA

Best, R Peter (Pete) — Singer, Drummer (Beatles)
Splash Mgmt, 8 Hymans Green, West Derby, Liverpool L12 7JG, England

Best, Travis E — Basketball Player
703 Bradley Road, Springfield MA 01109, USA

Bester, Allan — Ice Hockey Player
12527 Crayford Ave, Orlando FL 32837, USA

Beswicke, Martine — Actress
4011 Primavera Road, #B, Santa Barbara CA 93110, USA

Betancourt Perez, Yuniesky — Baseball Player
1001 Brickell Bay Dr, #1710, Miami FL 33131, USA

Betancourt, Rafael J — Baseball Player
6857 Valhalla Way, Windermere FL 34786, USA

Betancur Cuartas, Belisario — President, Colombia
Fundacio Santilana, Calle 80, #3974, Santa Fe de Bogota, Colombia

Bethea, Elvin L — Football Player
16211 Leslie Lane, Missouri City TX 77489, USA

Bethell, Tabrett — Actress
W M E Entertainment, 9601 Wilshire Blvd, #300, Beverly Hills CA 90210 USA

Betker, Jan — Curling Athlete
Curling Assn, 1660 Vimont Court, Cumberland ON K4A 4J4, Canada

Betori, Giuseppe Cardinal — Religious Leader
Archdiocese, Piazza S Giovanni 3, 50129 Florence, Italy

Bets, Maxim — Ice Hockey Player
5566 Candlelight Dr, La Jolla CA 92037, USA

Bettany, Paul — Actor
Affirmative Entertainment, 425 N Robertson Blvd, Los Angeles CA 90048 USA

Bettencourt, Liliane — Businesswoman
L'Oreal Group, 41 Rue Matre, 92117 Clichy, France

Bettencourt, Nuno — Guitarist (Extreme)
Dreamscapers International, 1701 18th Ave S, Nashville TN 37212, USA

Bettenhausen, Gary — Auto Racing Driver
2410 W Wavelyn Circle S, Martinsville IN 46151, USA

Bettens, Gert — Guitarist, Keyboardist (K's Choice)
Sharpe Entertainment Services, 683 Palmera Ave, Pacific Palisades CA 90272, USA

Bettens-Wills, Sarah — Singer (K's Choice)
Sharpe Entertainment Services, 683 Palmera Ave, Pacific Palisades CA 90272, USA

Betters, Doug L — Football Player
77 Better Way, Whitefish MT 59937, USA

Bettinger, Walter — Financier
Charles Schwab Co, 101 Montgomery St, #200, San Francisco CA 94104, USA

Bettini, Paolo — Cyclist
Via Aurelia Sud 8, 77020 La California-Bibbona (LI), Italy

Bettis, Angela — Actress
BenderSpink, 5870 W Jefferson Blvd, #E, Los Angeles CA 90016 USA
Bettis, Jerome A — Football Player, Sportscaster
1651 Randall Mill Place NW, Atlanta GA 30327, USA
Bettis, W Thomas (Tom) — Football Player, Coach
24001 Cinco Village Center Blvd, #3116, Katy TX 77494, USA
Bettman, Gary B — Ice Hockey Executive
National Hockey League, 1251 Ave of Americas, #4601, New York NY 10020, USA
Betts, Daisy — Actress
I C M Partners, 10250 Constellation Blvd, #900, Los Angeles CA 90067 USA
Betts, F Richard (Dickie) — Singer, Guitarist (Allman Brothers Band)
David Spero Mgmt, 1679 S Belvoir Blvd, Cleveland OH 44121, USA
Betts, M Ladell — Football Player
42515 Regal Wood Dr, Ashburn VA 20148, USA
Beuerlein, Stephen T (Steve) — Football Player
15624 McCullers Court, Charlotte NC 28277, USA
Beukeboom, Jeff — Ice Hockey Player
464 Wagg Road, RR 4, Uxbridge ON L9P 1R4, Canada
Beuron, Yann — Opera Singer
I M G Artists, Hogarth Business Park, Chiswick, London W4 2TH, England
Beutler, Bruce — Nobel Medicine Laureate
Scripps Research Institute, 10550 N Torrey Pines Road, La Jolla CA 92037 USA
Bevan, Alonzo G — Bassist (Kula Shaker)
Little Big Man, 39A Grammercy Park N, #1C, New York NY 10010, USA
Bevan, Tim — Actor, Producer
Working Title Films, 9720 Wilshire Blvd, #400, Beverly Hills CA 90212, USA
Beverley, Nick — Ice Hockey Player, Coach, Executive
Nashville Predators, 501 Broadway, Nashville TN 37203 USA
Beverly, David E (Dave) — Football Player
15 Wood Cove Dr, Spring TX 77381, USA
Beverly, Eric R — Football Player
PO Box 492433, Lawrenceville GA 30049, USA
Beverly, Frankie — Singer (Maze)
115 Cherokee Rose Lane, Fayetteville GA 30214, USA
Beverly, Jo — Writer
Signet Books, 375 Hudson St, New York NY 10014, USA
Beverly, Randolph (Randy) — Football Player
PO Box 193, Monroe Township NJ 08831, USA
Bevill, Lisa — Singer
Jeff Roberts, 3050 Business Park Circle, #301, Goodlettsville TN 37072, USA
Bevington, Terry P — Baseball Manager
2600 Halle Parkway, Collierville TN 38017, USA
Bevis, Leslie — Actress
Epstein-Wyckoff, 280 S Beverly Dr, #400, Beverly Hills CA 90212 USA
Bewkes, Jeffrey L (Jeff) — Businessman
Time Warner, 10 Columbus Circle, New York NY 10019, USA
Bex, Shannon — Singer (Danity Kane)
Bad Boy Entertainment, 1440 Broadway, #16, New York NY 10018 USA
Bey, George — Anthropologist
Millsaps College, Anthropology Dept, 1701 State St, Jackson MS 39201, USA
Bey, Richard — Entertainer
445 Park Ave, #1000, New York NY 10022, USA
Bey, Yaslin — Rap Artist, Actor
Brookside Artists Mgmt, 250 W 57th St, #2303, New York NY 10107, USA
Beyer, Andy — Sportswriter
4237 Lenore Lane NW, Washington DC 20008, USA
Beyer, Brad — Actor
Abrams Artists, 9200 W Sunset Blvd, #1125, West Hollywood CA 90069 USA
Beyer, Frank M — Composer
Academie der Kunste, Hanseatenweg 10, 10557 Berlin, Germany
Beyer, Markus — Boxer
Daniela Haak, Niederende 1, 28865 Lilienthal, Germany
Beyer, Peter — Biochemist
Albert-Ludwigs-Universitat, Biochemistry Dept, 79104 Freiburg, Germany
Beyer, Tanya — Model
Playboy Promotions, 2706 Media Center Dr, Los Angeles CA 90065 USA
Beyer, Troy — Actress, Director
Independent Artists Agency, 9601 Wilshire Blvd, #750, Beverly Hills. CA 90210, USA
Beymer, Richard — Actor
147 N Ridgewood Place, Los Angeles CA 90004, USA
Bezos, Jeff — Businessman
Amazon Inc, 1200 12th Ave S, #1200, Seattle WA 98144, USA
Bezucha, Thomas G (Tom) — Director, Writer
Creative Artists Agency, 2000 Ave of Stars, #100, Los Angeles CA 90067 USA
BG — Rap Artist (Hot Boys)
Nene Musik Productions, 1460 SW Santiago Ave, Port Saint Lucie FL 34953 USA
Bhanupriya — Actress
4 1st Cross St, Vijayaraghava Road, Chennai TN 600017, India
Bhardwaj, Mohini — Gymnast
53 Juergens Ave, Cincinnati OH 45220, USA
Bhaskar, Sanjeev — Actor
United Agents, 12-26 Lexington St, London W1F 0LE, England
Bhattacharya, Sameer — Guitarist (Flyleaf)
W M E Entertainment, 9601 Wilshire Blvd, #300, Beverly Hills CA 90210 USA
Bhavsar, Natvar P — Artist
131 Greene St, New York NY 10012, USA
Bhraonain, Maire Ni — Singer, Harpist (Clannad); Songwriter
Soho Agency, 55 Fulham High St, London SW6 3JJ, England
Bhumibol Adulyadej (Rama IX) — King, Thailand
Royal Residence, Chitralada Villa, 9 Rama VI Road, Soi 30, Bangkok 10400, Thailand
Biafra, Jello — Singer (Dead Kennedys), Songwriter
Kork Agency, 1880 Century Park E, #711, Los Angeles CA 90067 USA
Biagiotti, Laura — Fashion Designer
Biagiotti Group, Via Palombarese Km 17 300, 00012 Guidonia, Italy
Biakabutuka, Tshimanga (Tim) — Football Player
110 Sonnys Way, Fort Mill SC 29708, USA

Biali, Laila — Singer, Songwriter
Agency Group Ltd, 142 W 57th St, #600, New York NY 10019 USA

Bialik, Mayim — Actress
TalentWorks, 3500 W Olive Ave, #1400, Burbank CA 91505 USA

Biancalana, Roland A (Buddy) — Baseball Player
1204 Lakeview Dr, Fairfield IA 52556, USA

Bianchi, Alfred A (Al) — Basketball Player, Coach
Miami Heat, American Airlines Arena, 601 Biscayne Blvd, Miami FL 33132 USA

Bianchin, Wayne — Ice Hockey Player
2091 Wellington Road E, Nanaimo BC V9S 5V2, Canada

Bianco, Esme — Actress
B/W/R, 9100 Wilshire Blvd, #500W, Beverly Hills CA 90212 USA

Bianco, Suzannah — Synchronized Swimmer
Cirque du Soleil, 8400 2nd Ave, Montreal QC H1Z 4M6, Canada

Biasucci, Dean — Football Player
3484 Sandy Beach Dr, Canandaigua NY 14424, USA

Bibb, Leslie — Actress
I C M Partners, 10250 Constellation Blvd, #900, Los Angeles CA 90067 USA

Bibby, C Henry — Basketball Player, Coach
191 Beale St, Memphis TN 38103, USA

Bibby, Michael (Mike) — Basketball Player
6439 E Gelding Dr, Scottsdale AZ 85254, USA

Bichette, A Dante — Baseball Player
2298 Robin Road, Orlando FL 32814, USA

Bichir, Demian — Actor
Creative Artists Agency, 2000 Ave of Stars, #100, Los Angeles CA 90067 USA

Bickerstaff, Bernard T (Bernie) — Basketball Coach, Executive
Portland Trail Blazers, Rose Garden, 1 N Center Court St, Portland OR 97227 USA

Bickett, Duane C — Football Player
508 Van Dyke Ave, Del Mar CA 92014, USA

Bickle, Richard (Rich), Jr — Truck, Auto Racing Driver
Billy Ballew Motorsports, 802A Performance Road, Mooresville NC 28115, USA

Bidart, Frank — Writer
Wellesley College, English Dept, 106 Central St, Wellesley MA 02481, USA

Bidaud, Laurence — Curling Athlete
Curling Assn, PO Box 606, 3000 Bern, Switzerland

Biddall, Jennifer — Actress
Associated International Mgmt, Fairfax House, Fulwood Place, London WC1V 6HU, England

Biddle, Lee F (Rocky) — Baseball Player
2031 E Rancho Culebra Dr, Covina CA 91724, USA

Biddle, Martin — Archaeologist
19 Hamilton Road, Oxford OX2 7OY, England

Biden, Joseph R (Joe), Jr — Vice President; Senator, DE
White House, 1600 Pennsylvania Ave NW, Washington DC 20502, USA

Bidner, Todd — Ice Hockey Player
434 Oozloffsky, Petrolia ON N0N 1R0, Canada

Bidstrup, Jane — Curling Athlete
Curling Assn, Idraettens Hus, 2605 Brondby, Denmark

Bidwell, Charles E — Sociologist
5835 S Kimbark Ave, Chicago IL 60637, USA

Bidwell, Joshua J (Josh) — Football Player
11924 Middlebury Dr, Tampa FL 33626, USA

Bidwell, William V — Football Executive
Arizona Cardinals, PO Box 888, Phoenix AZ 85001 USA

Bieber, Justin — Singer
Creative Artists Agency, 2000 Ave of Stars, #100, Los Angeles CA 90067 USA

Bieber, Nita — Actress
PO Box 1889, Avalon CA 90704, USA

Bieber, Owen F — Labor Leader
United Auto Workers Union, 8000 E Jefferson Ave, Detroit MI 48214, USA

Biebl-Prelevic, Heidi — Alpine Skier
Haus Olympia, 87534 Oberstaufen, Germany

Biedenbach, Edward (Ed) — Basketball Player
92 Kimberly Ave, Asheville NC 28804, USA

Biedermann, Jeanette — Singer, Actress
Postfach 121004, 10599 Berlin, Germany

Biegel, Kevin — Producer
I C M Partners, 10250 Constellation Blvd, #900, Los Angeles CA 90067 USA

Biehn, Michael — Actor
14358 Magnolia Blvd, #229, Sherman Oaks CA 91423, USA

Bieka, Silvestre Siale — Prime Minister, Equatorial Guinea
Prime Minister's Office, Malabo, Equatorial Guinea

Biekert, Greg — Football Player
2360 Fish Creek Place, Danville CA 94506, USA

Biel, Jessica — Actress
Management 360, 9111 Wilshire Blvd, Beverly Hills CA 90210 USA

Bielanko, Dave — Singer, Songwriter, Guitarist (Marah)
Yep Roc Records, 449A Trollingwood Road, Haw River NC 27258, USA

Bielanko, Serge — Singer, Songwriter, Guitarist (Marah)
Yep Roc Records, 449A Trollingwood Road, Haw River NC 27258, USA

Bielecki, J Krzysztof — Prime Minister, Poland
European Reconstruction Bank, 1 Exchange Square, London EC2A 2EA, England

Bielecki, Michael J (Mike) — Baseball Player
1505 Habersham Place, Crownsville MD 21032, USA

Bielke, Donald P (Don) — Basketball Player
126 Madelia Place, San Ramon CA 94583, USA

Biellmann, Denise — Figure Skater
Im Brachli 25, 8053 Zurich, Switzerland

Bielski, Richard (Dick) — Football Player
27 Malibu Court, Towson MD 21204, USA

Bieniemy, Eric — Football Player
5313 Westridge Dr, Boulder CO 80301, USA

Bier, Susanne — Director
Creative Artists Agency, 2000 Ave of Stars, #100, Los Angeles CA 90067 USA

Bierko, Craig — Actor, Singer
Impression Entertainment, 9229 W Sunset Blvd, #700 , Los Angeles CA 90069, USA

Bierman, Bernard (Bernie) — Songwriter
70 E 10th St, #17C, New York NY 10003, USA
Bierman, Bruce — Interior Designer
29 W 15th St, #A, New York NY 10011, USA
Bierman, Robert — Director
Independent Talent Group, Oxford House, 76 Oxford St, London W1D 1BS, England
Bies, Don — Golfer
1262 NW Blakely Court, Seattle WA 98177, USA
Bies, Don — Special Effects Artist
PO Box 522, Petaluma CA 94953, USA
Bieshu, Mariya L — Opera Singer
24 Pushkin Str, Chisinau 2012, Moldova
Biffi, Giacomo Cardinal — Religious Leader
Archdiocese of Bologna, Via Altabella 6, 40126 Bologna, Italy
Biffle, Gregory J (Greg) — Auto, Truck Racing Driver
8807 Heatherstone Court, Terrell NC 28682, USA
Big Boi — Rap Artist (OutKast), Songwriter
4016 Elizabeth Terrace, Rex GA 30273, USA
Big Daddy Kane — Rap Artist, Lyricist
Betty of Troy, 15 Meritoria Dr, East Willston NY 11596, USA
Big K R I T — Rap Artist
Agency Group Ltd, 142 W 57th St, #600, New York NY 10019 USA
Big Sean — Rap Artist
Agency Group Ltd, 142 W 57th St, #600, New York NY 10019 USA
Bigbie, Larry R — Baseball Player
102 Brooke Lane, Centreville MD 21617, USA
Bigelow, Kathryn A — Director
Creative Artists Agency, 2000 Ave of Stars, #100, Los Angeles CA 90067 USA
Biggio, Craig A — Baseball Player
6520 Belmont St, Houston TX 77005, USA
Biggs, Don — Ice Hockey Player
10050 Somerset Dr, Loveland OH 45140, USA
Biggs, Jason — Actor
Management 360, 9111 Wilshire Blvd, Beverly Hills CA 90210 USA
Biggs, John H — Businessman
240 E 47th St, #47D, New York NY 10017, USA
Biggs, Peter M — Veterinarian
Willows, London Road, Saint Ives PE27 5ES, England
Biggs, Tyrell (Burt) — Boxer
Scott Schiff, 330 S High St, Columbus OH 43215, USA
Bigham, John — Guitarist, Keyboardist (Fishbone)
Silverback Mgmt, 9469 Jefferson Blvd, #101, Culver City CA 90232, USA
Bigley, Thomas J — Navy Admiral
20530 Falcons Landing Circle, #3210, Sterling VA 20165, USA
Bignotti, George — Auto Racing Mechanic
9413 Steeplehill Dr, Las Vegas NV 89117, USA
Biittner, Lawrence D (Larry) — Baseball Player
915 3rd Ave NW, Pocahontas IA 50574, USA
Bikel, Theodore — Actor, Singer
167 Langley Road, Newton Center MA 02459, USA
Bilal — Singer, Songwriter
Creative Artists Agency, 2000 Ave of Stars, #100, Los Angeles CA 90067 USA
Bilardello, Dann J — Baseball Player
4600 2nd St, Vero Beach FL 32968, USA
Bilderback, Nicole — Actress
Rebel Entertainment Partners, 5700 Wilshire Blvd, #456, Los Angeles CA 90036, USA
Bildt, N D Carl — Prime Minister, Sweden
Kreab Group, Floragatan 13, 114 75, Stockholm, Sweden
Bileck, Pamela (Pam) — Gymnast
2475 Redbud Court, San Jose CA 95128, USA
Biletnikoff, Frederick (Fred) — Football Player, Coach
1736 Avondale Dr, Roseville CA 95747, USA
Bilk, Acker — Clarinetist, Composer
53 Cambridge Mansions, Cambridge Road, London SW11 4RX, England
Bill, Leo — Actor
Hamilton Hodell, 66-68 Margaret St, London W1W 8SR, England
Bill, Tony — Producer, Director, Actor
Barnstorm Films, 73 Market St, Venice CA 90291, USA
Billick, Brian H — Football Coach, Sportscaster
836 Stagwell Road, Queenstown MD 21658, USA
Billing, Roy — Actor
Sue Barnett Assoc, 1/96 Albion St, Surrey Hills, Sydney 2010, Australia
Billingham, John E (Jack) — Baseball Player
625 Faulkner St, New Smyrna FL 32168, USA
Billinglsey, Ronald S (Ron) — Football Player
PO Box 2455, Gadsden AL 35903, USA
Billings, Earl — Actor
Stone Manners Salners, 9911 W Pico Blvd, #1400, Los Angeles CA 90035 USA
Billings, Richard A (Dick) — Baseball Player
1917 Creek Wood Dr, Arlington TX 76006, USA
Billingslea, Beau — Actor
Abrams Artists, 9200 W Sunset Blvd, #1125, West Hollywood CA 90069 USA
Billingsley, Chad R — Baseball Player
25686 N Sandstone Way, Surprise AZ 85387, USA
Billingsley, Hobie — Diving Coach
746 E Pepperridge Dr, Bloomington IN 47401, USA
Billingsley, John A — Actor
Stone Manners Salners, 9911 W Pico Blvd, #1400, Los Angeles CA 90035 USA
Billingsley, Peter — Actor, Producer
Stone Meyer Genow, 9665 Wilshire Blvd, #510, Beverly Hills CA 90212 USA
Billingsley, Ray — Cartoonist (Curtis)
King Features Syndicate, 300 W 57th St, #1500, New York NY 10019 USA
Billington, Craig — Ice Hockey Player
Colorado Avalanche, Pepsi Center, 1000 Chopper Circle, Denver CO 80204 USA
Billington, David P — Civil Engineer
45 Hodge Road, Princeton NJ 08540, USA

Billington, Kevin — Director
Judy Daish Assoc, 2 Saint Charles Place, London W10 6EG, England

Billups, Chauncey R — Basketball Player
11 Sandy Lake Road, Englewood CO 80113, USA

Bilodeau, Jean-Luc — Actor
Kirk Talent, 134 Abbott St, #402, Vancouver BC V6B 2K4, Canada , USA

Bilson, Bruce — Director
Downwind Enterprises, 12505 Sarah St, Studio City CA 91604, USA

Bilson, Malcolm — Concert Pianist
132 N Sunset Dr, Ithaca NY 14850, USA

Bilson, Rachel — Actress
Creative Artists Agency, 2000 Ave of Stars, #100, Los Angeles CA 90067 USA

Binder, Mike — Actor, Director, Writer
Verve Talent/Literary Agency, 9696 Culver Blvd, #301, Culver City CA 90232 USA

Binder, Theodor — Physician
Taos Canyon, Taos NM 87571, USA

Bing, David (Dave) — Basketball Player; Mayor, Detroit
29555 Woodhaven Lane, Southfield MI 48076, USA

Bing, Jonathan — Writer
Trident Media Group, 41 Madison Ave, #3600, New York NY 10010, USA

Binger, Brittany — Model
Playboy Promotions, 2706 Media Center Dr, Los Angeles CA 90065 USA

Bingham, Gregory R (Greg) — Football Player
3710 W Valley Dr, Missouri City TX 77459, USA

Bingham, Guy R — Football Player
9214 Keegan Trail, Missoula MT 59808, USA

Bingham, Ryan — Singer, Songwriter
Creative Artists Agency, 2000 Ave of Stars, #100, Los Angeles CA 90067 USA

Bingham, Traci — Actress, Model
Vincent Cirrincione Assoc, 1516 N Fairfax Ave, Los Angeles CA 90046 USA

Binion, Jack B — Poker Player
Wynn Resorts, 3131 Las Vegas Blvd S, Las Vegas NV 89109, USA

Binkley, Gregg — Actor
Schachter Entertainment, 1157 S Beverly Dr, #200, Los Angeles CA 90035 USA

Binmore, Kenneth G — Economist
Newmills, Whitebrook, Monmouth, Gwent NP5 4TY, England

Binn, David A (Dave) — Football Player
2005 Loring St, San Diego CA 92109, USA

Binnie, Brian — Test Pilot
Scaled Composites, Mojave Airport, Hangar 78, Mojave CA 93501, USA

Binnig, Gerd K — Nobel Physics Laureate
I B M Research Laboratory, Saumerstr 4, 8803 Ruschlikon, Switzerland

Binns, Malcolm — Concert Pianist
Turner Mgmt, 223 Kingston Road, Leatherhead, Surrey KT22 7PE, England

Binoche, Juliette — Actress
Untitled Entertainment, 350 S Beverly Dr, #200, Beverly Hills CA 90212 USA

Bintley, David — Choreographer
Birmingham Ballet, Thorpe St, Birmingham B5 4AU, England

Biodrowski, Dennis J (Denny) — Football Player
1221 N Sylvania Ave, Fort Worth TX 76111, USA

Biondi, Frank J, Jr — Businessman
Biondi Reiss Capital Mgmt, 1114 Ave of Americas, New York NY 10036, USA

Biondi, Matthew N (Matt) — Swimmer
Parker School, 65-1224 Lindsey Road, Mathematics Dept, Kamuela HI 96743, USA

Birch, Diane — Singer, Songwriter
Special Artists Agency, 9465 Wilshire Blvd, #820, Beverly Hills CA 90212 USA

Birch, L Charles — Zoologist
5A/73 Yarranabbe Road, Darling Point NSW 2027, Australia

Birch, Stanley F, Jr — Judge
US Court of Appeals, 56 Forsyth St NW, Atlanta GA 30303, USA

Birch, Thora — Actress
Keep the Peace Productions, PO Box 691675, West Hollywood CA 90069, USA

Birck, Michael J — Businessman
Tellabs Inc, 1415 W Diehl Road, Naperville IL 60563, USA

Bird, Andrew — Singer, Guitarist, Songwriter
Ekonomisk Mgmt, PO Box 972, Stillwater MN 55062, USA

Bird, Antonia — Director
Independent Talent Group, Oxford House, 76 Oxford St, London W1D 1BS, England

Bird, Brad — Animator
Pixar Animation, 1200 Park Ave, Emeryville CA 94608, USA

Bird, Caroline — Social Activist, Writer
60 Grammercy Park, New York NY 10010, USA

Bird, Forrest M — Inventor (Medical Respirators)
Percussionaire Corp, PO Box 817, Sandpoint ID 83864, USA

Bird, J Douglas (Doug) — Baseball Player
11821 Lady Anne Circle, Cape Coral FL 33991, USA

Bird, Larry J — Basketball Player, Coach, Executive
4715 Ellery Lane, Indianapolis IN 46250, USA

Bird, R Byron — Chemical Engineer
University of Wisconsin, Chemical Engineering Dept, Madison WI 53706, USA

Bird, Simon — Actor
Avalon Mgmt, 4A Exmoore St, London W10 68D, England

Bird, Suzanne (Sue) — Basketball Player
Seattle Storm, Key Arena, 351 Elliott Ave W, #500, Seattle WA 98119 USA

Birden, LaJourdain J (J J) — Football Player
27743 N 70th St, Scottsdale AZ 85266, USA

Birdman — Rap Artist
J L Entertainment, 18653 Ventura Blvd, #340, Tarzana CA 91356 USA

Birdsong, Carl — Football Player
1807 Clubview Dr, Amarillo TX 79124, USA

Birdsong, Mary — Actress
United Talent Agency, 9336 Civic Center Dr, Beverly Hills CA 90210 USA

Birdsong, Otis L — Basketball Player
PO Box 316, Little Rock AR 72203, USA

Birdy — Singer, Pianist, Songwriter
Warner Bros Records, 75 Rockefeller Plaza, New York NY 10019, USA

Bires, Kelly — Auto Racing Driver
Black Cat Racing, 200 Swiggum Road, Westby WI 54667, USA
Birgeneau, Robert J — Physicist, Educator
University of California, Chancellor's Office, University Hall, Berkeley CA 94720, USA
Birgisson, Jon Thor — Singer (Sigur Ros)
Geffen Records, 10900 Wilshire Blvd, #1000, Los Angeles CA 90024 USA
Birk, Matthew R (Matt) — Football Player
5 Norfolk Court, Reisterstown MD 21136, USA
Birk, Roger E — Government Official, Financier
Federal National Mortgage Assn, 3900 Wisconsin Ave NW, Washington DC 20016, USA
Birkavs, Valdis — Prime Minister, Latvia
Justice Ministry, Brivbas Blvd 34, 1536 Riga, Latvia
Birkbeck, Michael L (Mike) — Baseball Player
1705 W Hill Dr, Orrville OH 44667, USA
Birkerts, Gunnar — Architect
Gunnar Birkerts Assoc, 65 Grove St, #241, Wellesley MA 02482, USA
Birkett, Zoe — Singer
Fremantle Media, 2700 Colorado Ave, #450, Santa Monica CA 90404 USA
Birkin, Jane — Actress
Agence Artiste Adequet, 80 Rue d'Amsterdam, 75009 Paris, France
Birmingham, Stephen — Writer
Brandt & Brandt, 1501 Broadway, #2310, New York NY 10036, USA
Birney, David — Actor
Bret Adams Agency, 448 W 44th St, New York NY 10036, USA
Birns, Jack — Photographer
2021 Castilian Dr, Los Angeles CA 90068, USA
Biron, Martin — Ice Hockey Player
93 Whippoorwill Road, Armonk NY 10504, USA
Biron, Mathieu — Ice Hockey Player
5723 NW 119th Dr, Coral Springs FL 33076, USA
Bironas, J Robert D (Rob) — Football Player
104 Loring Court, Nashville TN 37220, USA
Birren, James E — Gerontologist
University of California, Borun Gerontology Center, Los Angeles CA 90024, USA
Birthistle, Eva — Actress
Independent Talent Group, Oxford House, 76 Oxford St, London W1D 1BS, England
Birtsas, Timothy D (Tim) — Baseball Player
PO Box 96, Clarkston MI 48347, USA
Bisbal Ferre, David — Singer
Universal Music, 420 Lincoln Road, #200, Miami Beach FL 33139, USA
Bisby, Frank A — Biologist
Reading University, Plant Science Laboratories, Reading Berk RG6 6AS, England
Biscet Gonzalez, Oscar Elias — Human Rights Activist
Lawton Foundation for Human Rights, PO Box 430905, Miami FL 33243, USA
Bischof, Ole — Judo Athlete
Suelburgstr 237, 50937 Cologne, Germany
Bishe, Kerry — Actress
Brookside Artist Mgmt, 250 W 57th St, #2303, New York NY 10107 USA
Bishil, Summer — Actress
Paul Kohner, 9300 Wilshire Blvd, #555, Beverly Hills CA 90212 USA
Bishop, Blaine E — Football Player
PO Box 3082, Brentwood TN 37024, USA
Bishop, Elvin — Singer, Guitarist
Blue Mountain Artists, 810 Tyvola Road, #114, Charlotte NC 28217, USA
Bishop, Erwin W (Sonny) — Football Player
22843 Hale Road, Land O Lakes FL 34639, USA
Bishop, Gregory L (Greg) — Football Player
PO Box 2263, Lodi CA 95241, USA
Bishop, Harold L — Football Player
2709 20th Street Ensley, Birmingham AL 35208, USA
Bishop, J Michael — Nobel Medicine Laureate, Educator
University of California, Chancellor's Office, San Francisco CA 94143, USA
Bishop, Keith B — Football Player
PO Box 131048, Spring TX 77393, USA
Bishop, Kelly — Actress
Abrams Artists, 9200 W Sunset Blvd, #1125, West Hollywood CA 90069 USA
Bishop, Kevin — Actor
Independent Talent Group, Oxford House, 76 Oxford St, London W1D 1BS, England
Bishop, Michael L — Writer
PO Box 646, Pine Mountain GA 31822, USA
Bishop, Nicholas — Actor
United Talent Agency, 9336 Civic Center Dr, Beverly Hills CA 90210 USA
Bishop, Richard A — Football Player
1374 SW 142nd Terrace, Miami FL 33186, USA
Bishop, Stephen — Singer, Songwriter
2310 Apollo Dr, Los Angeles CA 90046, USA
Bishops, Thom — Actor
Brillstein Entertainment Partners, 9150 Wilshire Blvd, #350, Beverly Hills CA 90212 USA
Biss, Jonathan — Concert Pianist
Konzertdirektion Schmid, Konigstra 36, 30175 Hannover, Germany
Bissell, Charles O — Editorial Cartoonist
1006 Tower Place, Nashville TN 37204, USA
Bissell, Charles P (Phil) — Cartoonist
Cartoon Corner, 4 Cross Hill Circle, Forestdale MA 02644, USA
Bissell, Jean G — Judge
US Court of Appeals, 717 Madison Place NW, Washington DC 20439, USA
Bissell, Mina J — Physicist
Lawrence Berkeley Laboratory, 1 Cyclotron Road, Berkeley CA 94720, USA
Bisset, Jacqueline — Actress
1815 Benedict Canyon Dr, Beverly Hills CA 90210, USA
Bisson, Thomas N — Historian
21 Hammond St, Cambridge MA 02138, USA
Bisson, Yannick — Actor
Robert Stein Management, 1180 S Beverly Dr, #304, Los Angeles CA 90035, USA
Bista, Kirti Nidhi — Prime Minister, Nepal
Gyaneshwor, Kathmandu, Nepal

Biswas, Abdul Rahmana Residence Dhonmondi, Dhaka, Bangladesh	President, Bangladesh
Bitsch, Hans-Ullrich Kaiser-Wilhelm-Ring 23, RiveGauche, 40545 Dusseldorf-Oberkassel, Germany	Architect, Industrial Designer
Bittinger, Ned 1323 Escalante St, Santa Fe NM 87505, USA	Illustrator
Bittle, Ryan Hollander Talent, 3518 Cahuenga Blvd, #103, Los Angeles CA 90068, USA	Actor
Bittner, Armin Rauchbergstr 30, 83334 Izell, Germany	Alpine Skier
Bitton, Raquel I C M Partners, 10250 Constellation Blvd, #900, Los Angeles CA 90067 USA	Singer
Biya, Paul Palais de L'Unite, Rue de l'Exploratour, Yaounde, Cameroon	President, Cameroon Republic
Biyombo, Bismack Charlotte Bobcats, 333 E Trade St, #A, Charlotte NC 28202 USA	Basketball Player
Biz Markie Richard De La Font Agency, 4845 S Sheridan Road, #505, Tulsa OK 74145 USA	Rap Artist, Comedian
Bizarre Coast to Coast Talent, 3350 Barham Blvd, Los Angeles CA 90068 USA	Rap Artist (D-12)
Bizzy Bone Entertainment Artists, PO Box 120824, Nashville TN 37212 USA	Rap Artist (Bone Thugs-N-Harmony)
Bjedov-Gabrilo, Djurdjica Brace Santini 33, 5800 Split, Serbia	Swimmer
Bjoergen, Marit 7295 Rognes, Norway	Cross Country Skier
Bjoerndalen, Ole Einar Simostranda, Postboks 516, 3342 Amot, Norway	Biathlete
Bjork Addleshaw Goddard, 133 Aldersgate St, London EC1A 4EJ, England	Singer, Songwriter, Actress
Bjorken, James D Stanford Linear Accelerator Center, Stanford University, Stanford CA 94305, USA	Physicist
Bjorklund, Anders University of Lund, Neurology Dept, 221 00 Lund, Sweden	Neurologist
Bjorkman, Jonas Funke Promotions, Box 5126, 200 71 Malmo, Sweden	Tennis Player
Bjorkman, Olle E 3040 Greer Road, Palo Alto CA 94303, USA	Plant Biologist
Bjorkman, Rubin E 504 Lake St NW, Warroad MN 56763, USA	Ice Hockey Player, Coach
Bjorlin, Nadia Don Buchwald/Fortitude, 6500 Wilshire Blvd, #2200, Los Angeles CA 90048 USA	Actress
Bjornson, Eric 40 Orchard Road, Orinda CA 94563, USA	Football Player
Bjornson, Karen Ford Models Inc, 111 5th Ave, #900, New York NY 10003 USA	Model
Bjugstad, Scott 2874 Lisbon Ave N, Lake Elmo MN 55042, USA	Ice Hockey Player
Blab, Uwe K 5993 Mount Gainor, Wimberley TX 78676, USA	Basketball Player
Blacc, Aloe W M E Entertainment, 9601 Wilshire Blvd, #300, Beverly Hills CA 90210 USA	Rap Artist
Blachnik, Gabriele Blachnik Gabriele KG, Marstallstr 8, 80539 Munich, Germany	Fashion Designer
Black of Crossharbour, Conrad M 1 Canada Square, Canary Wharf, London E14 5DT, England	Publisher
Black Thought Universal Attractions, 135 W 26th St, #1200, New York NY 10019, USA	Rap Artist (Roots)
Black, Alexander (Alex) Howard Entertainment, 10850 Wilshire Blvd, #1260, Los Angeles CA 90024, USA	Actor
Black, B Jordan 4002 Tradewind Circle, Rowlett TX 75088, USA	Football Player
Black, Barbara A Columbia University, Law School, 435 W 116th St, New York NY 10027, USA	Attorney, Educator
Black, Bibi Columbia Artists Mgmt Inc, 1790 Broadway, #702, New York NY 10019 USA	Concert Trumpeter
Black, Cathleen P Hearst Corp, Magazine Division, 250 W 55th St, New York NY 10019, USA	Publisher
Black, Cilla Bobsons Productions, 10 Abbet Orchard St, London SW1P 2JP, England	Singer, Actress
Black, Claudia Farscape, Henson, 1416 N La Brea Ave, Los Angeles CA 90028, USA	Actress
Black, Clint Sussman Assoc, 1222 16th Ave S, #300, Nashville TN 37212, USA	Singer, Songwriter, Actor
Black, David Mark Holder Mgmt, 5225 Wilshire Blvd, #600, Los Angeles CA 90036 USA	Producer, Writer
Black, Dennis University of California Medical Center, 505 Parnassus, San Francisco CA 94122 USA	Epidemiologist
Black, Dustin Lance Creative Artists Agency, 2000 Ave of Stars, #100, Los Angeles CA 90067 USA	Writer
Black, Francis (Frank) X-Ray Touring, 77-79 Great Eastern St, #A, London EC2A 3HU, England	Singer, Guitarist, Songwriter
Black, Harry R (Bud) PO Box 2133, Rancho Santa Fe CA 92067, USA	Baseball Player, Manager
Black, Jack W M E Entertainment, 9601 Wilshire Blvd, #300, Beverly Hills CA 90210 USA	Actor, Singer, Comedian
Black, Jake Conservative Mgmt, 12700 Lake Ave, #2801, Lakewood OH 44107, USA	Singer (A3)
Black, James Mark Holder Mgmt, 5225 Wilshire Blvd, #600, Los Angeles CA 90036 USA	Actor
Black, James 235 Callingwood Place NW, Edmonton AB T5T 2C6, Canada	Ice Hockey Player
Black, Jay Charles Rapp Mgmt, 10775 Santa Laguna Dr, Boca Raton FL 33428, USA	Singer (Jay & the Americans)
Black, Jully Agency Group Ltd, 142 W 57th St, #600, New York NY 10019 USA	Singer, Songwriter

Black, Karen	Actress
Abrams Artists, 9200 W Sunset Blvd, #1125, West Hollywood CA 90069 USA	
Black, Lewis	Actor, Comedian
A P A Talent/Literary Agency, 405 S Beverly Dr, #300, Beverly Hills CA 90212 USA	
Black, Lucas	Actor
I C M Partners, 10250 Constellation Blvd, #900, Los Angeles CA 90067 USA	
Black, Mary	Singer
International Music Network, 278 Main St, #400, Gloucester MA 01930 USA	
Black, Michael Ian	Actor, Puppeteer, Producer
United Talent Agency, 9336 Civic Center Dr, Beverly Hills CA 90210 USA	
Black, P Michael (Mike)	Football Player
5690 Stonekirk Place NW, Acworth GA 30101, USA	
Black, Pippa	Actress
Aran Michael Mgmt, 118 Caroline St, South Yarra VIC 3141, Australia	
Black, Robert L	Pediatrician
976 Mesa Road, Monterey CA 93940, USA	
Black, Ron	Religious Leader
General Baptist Ministries, 100 Stinson Dr, Poplar Bluff MO 63901, USA	
Black, Ronnie	Golfer
5565 N Campbell Ave, Tucson AZ 85718, USA	
Black, Roy	Attorney
Black Strebnick Kornspan Stumpf, 201 S Biscayne Blvd, #1300, Miami FL 33131, USA	
Black, Shane	Director, Writer
W M E Entertainment, 9601 Wilshire Blvd, #300, Beverly Hills CA 90210 USA	
Black, Shirley Temple	Actress, Diplomat
Motion Picture Arts/Sciences, 8949 Wilshire Blvd, Beverly Hills CA 90211, USA	
Black, Susan H	Judge
US Court of Appeals, 311 W Monroe St, Jacksonville FL 32202, USA	
Black, Tim A	Football Player
10520 Kilo Road, Clarendon TX 79226, USA	
Blackburn, Ade	Singer, Guitarist (Clinic)
Windish Agency, 1658 N Milwaukee Ave, #211, Chicago IL 60647, USA	
Blackburn, Chase	Football Player
562 Wagonwheel Lane, Marysville OH 43040, USA	
Blackburn, Don	Ice Hockey Player
637 S Owl Dr, Sarasota FL 34236, USA	
Blackburn, Elizabeth H	Nobel Medicine Laureate
294 Yerba Buena Ave, San Francisco CA 94127, USA	
Blackburn, Greta	Actress, Model
PO Box 1168, Bridgehampton NY 11932, USA	
Blackburn, Tyler	Actor
Gersh Agency, 9465 Wilshire Blvd, #600, Beverly Hills CA 90212 USA	
Blackburn, Woody	Golfer
Frank W Brown Assoc, PO Box 215, Orange Park FL 32067, USA	
Blackiston, Caroline	Actress
Caroline Dawson, 125 Gloucester Road, London SW7 4TE, England	
Blackledge, Bob	Journalist
Birmingham News, Editorial Dept, 2701 4th Ave N, Birminhgam AL 35203, USA	
Blackledge, Todd A	Football Player, Sportscaster
2711 Glenmont Dr NW, Canton OH 44708, USA	
Blackman, Cindy	Jazz, Rock Drummer
BookArts Co, 6404 Wilshire Blvd, #1750, Los Angeles CA 90048, USA	
Blackman, Honor	Actress
N S M, Clapham North Arts Center, Voltaire Road, London SW4 6DH, England	
Blackman, Rolando A	Basketball Player, Sportscaster
14902 Preston Road, #404, Dallas TX 75254, USA	
Blackman, Steve	Professional Wrestler
Steve Blackman Fighting Systems, 2200 Paxton St, Harrisburg PA 17111, USA	
Blackmar, Phil	Golfer
4420 Janssen Dr, Corpus Christi TX 78411, USA	
Blackmon, Donald K (Don)	Football Player
4340 Lansfaire Terrace, Suwanee GA 30024, USA	
Blackmon, Douglas A	Writer
Wall Street Journal, 303 Peachtree St NE, #4200, Atlanta GA 30308, USA	
Blackmon, Justin	Football Player
Jacksonville Jaguars, 1 AllTel Stadium Place, Jacksonville FL 32202 USA	
Blackmon, Larry E	Singer (Cameo)
Red Entertainment, 481 8th Ave, #824, New York NY 10001, USA	
Blackmon, Robert J (Bob)	Football Player
70 Glenwood N, Van Vleck TX 77482, USA	
Blackmore, Richard H (Ritchie)	Singer, Guitarist (Deep Purple, Rainbow)
Performers of the World, 5657 Wilshire Blvd, #280, Los Angeles CA 90036 USA	
Blackmore, Stephanie	Actress
Chateau-Billings, 5667 Wilshire Blvd, #340, Los Angeles CA 90036, USA	
Blackshear, Jeffrey L (Jeff)	Football Player
9229 Christo Court, Owings Mill MD 21117, USA	
Blackwelder, Myra	Golfer
2009 Hill Gail Way, Versailles KY 40383, USA	
Blackwell, Alfonzo	Jazz Saxophonist
Celebrity Talent Agency, 111 E 14th St, #249, New York NY 10003, USA	
Blackwell, Nathaniel (Nate)	Basketball Player
1926 S 22nd St, Philadelphia PA 19145, USA	
Blackwell, Simon	Producer, Writer
P B J Mgmt, 5 Soho Square, London W1D 3QA, England	
Blackwell, Timothy P (Tim)	Baseball Player
8854 Whiteport Lane, San Diego CA 92119, USA	
Blackwell, William H (Will), Jr	Football Player
6168 Seneca Circle, Discovery Bay CA 94505, USA	
Blackwood, Ariel	Actress
Coast to Coast Talent, 3350 Barham Blvd, Los Angeles CA 90068 USA	
Blackwood, Glenn A	Football Player
3480 Ambassador Dr, Wellington FL 33414, USA	
Blackwood, Lyle V	Football Player
18020 Windtop Lane, Dallas TX 75287, USA	
Blackwood, Sarah	Singer (Dubstar)
Primary Talent International, 2-12 Petonville Road, London N1 9PL, England	

Blacque, Taurean — Actor
5049 Rock Springs Road, Lithonia GA 30038, USA

Bladd, Stephen Jo — Singer, Drummer (J Geils Band)
Nick Ben-Meir, 652 N Doheny Dr, West Hollywood CA 90069, USA

Blade, Brian — Jazz Drummer (Black Dub)
Ted Kurland, 173 Brighton Ave, Allston MA 02134 USA

Blade, Danielle — Artist
Gartner & Blade, 4-1354 Kuhio Highway, Kapaa HI 96746, USA

Blades, H Benedict (Bennie) — Football Player
1900 SW 70th Terrace, Plantation FL 33317, USA

Blades, Ruben — Singer, Songwriter, Actor
United Talent Agency, 9336 Civic Center Dr, Beverly Hills CA 90210 USA

Bladon, Tom — Ice Hockey Player
2595 Wilcox Terrace, Victoria, BC V8Z 7G5, Canada

Blagden, George — Actor
Paradigm Agency, 360 N Crescent Dr, North Building, Beverly Hills CA 90210 USA

Blaha, John E — Astronaut
346 Whitestone Dr, Spring Branch TX 78070, USA

Blahak, Joseph P (Joe) — Football Player
4040 N 21st St, Lincoln NE 68521, USA

Blahnik, Manolo — Fashion Designer
49-51 Old Church St, London SW3 5BS, England

Blahoski, Alana — Ice Hockey Player
60 E 9th St, #315, New York NY 10003, USA

Blaine, David — Illusionist
W M E Entertainment, 9601 Wilshire Blvd, #300, Beverly Hills CA 90210 USA

Blaine, Edward H (Ed) — Football Player
4 E Clarkson Road, Columbia MO 65203, USA

Blaine, Jason — Singer, Songwriter
Agency Group Ltd, 142 W 57th St, #600, New York NY 10019 USA

Blaine, Nell — Artist
210 Riverside Dr, #8A, New York NY 10025, USA

Blair, A Matthew (Matt) — Football Player
16725 43rd Ave N, Minneapolis MN 55446, USA

Blair, Anthony C L (Tony) — Prime Minister, England
PO Box 60519, London W2 7JU, England

Blair, Bonnie — Speed Skater
306 White Pine Road, Delafield WI 53018, USA

Blair, Charles (Chuck) — Ice Hockey Player
869 Niagara Parkway, Fort Erie ON L2A 5M4, Canada

Blair, DeJuan — Basketball Player
San Antonio Spurs, Alamodome, 1 AT&T Center Parkway, San Antonio TX 78219 USA

Blair, Dennis C — Navy Admiral
National Intelligence Dept, 725 17th St NW, Washington DC 20523 USA

Blair, George — Ice Hockey Player
61 Kingsnill St, Fort Erie ON L2A 4E5, Canada

Blair, Isla — Actress
Curtis Brown Group, 28-29 Haymarket St, #500, London SW1Y 4SP, England

Blair, M June — Model, Actress
Playboy Promotions, 2706 Media Center Dr, Los Angeles CA 90065 USA

Blair, Marie-Claire — Writer
4411 Rue Saint Denis, #401, Montreal QC H2J 2LN, Canada

Blair, Paul L D — Baseball Player
4177 Lotus Circle, Ellicott City MD 21043, USA

Blair, Selma — Actress
Gersh Agency, 9465 Wilshire Blvd, #600, Beverly Hills CA 90212 USA

Blair, William (Bill) — Astronomer, Space Scientist
Johns Hopkins University, Astronomy Dept, Baltimore MD 21218, USA

Blair, William (Bill) — Baseball Player
1411 E Red Bird Lane, Dallas TX 75241, USA

Blair, William E (Willie) — Baseball Player
62 Elder Lane, Pikeville KY 41501, USA

Blair, William M, Jr — Attorney, Diplomat
435 E 52nd St, #6B, New York NY 10022, USA

Blais, Richard — Chef
Home Restaurant, 111 W Paces Ferry Road NE, Atlanta GA 30305, USA

Blaise, Kerlin — Football Player
37026 Aspen Dr, Farmington Hills MI 48335, USA

Blake Nelson, Tim — Actor, Director, Writer
Gateway Mgmt, 860 Via de la Paz, #F10, Pacific Palisades CA 90272, USA

Blake, Francis (Frank) — Businessman
Home Depot Inc, 2455 Paces Ferry Road NW, Atlanta GA 30339, USA

Blake, Geoffrey — Actor
TalentWorks, 3500 W Olive Ave, #1400, Burbank CA 91505 USA

Blake, James — Tennis Player
35 Prospect Road, Westport CT 6880, USA

Blake, Jason — Ice Hockey Player
10 Meadow Lane, Glen Head NY 11545, USA

Blake, Jay Don — Golfer
2859 Calle del Sol, Saint George UT 84790, USA

Blake, Jeffrey B C (Jeff) — Football Player
5821 Sunset Ridge, Austin TX 78735, USA

Blake, John C — Artist
Oz Voorburgwal 131, 1012 ER Amsterdam, Netherlands

Blake, Johnathan — Drummer (Donny McCaslin Trio)
Greenleaf Records, PO Box 477364, Chicago IL 60647 USA

Blake, Josh — Actor
C E S D, 10635 Santa Monica Blvd, #130, Los Angeles CA 90025 USA

Blake, Norman — Guitarist, Mandolin Player
Scott O'Malley Assoc, PO Box 9188, Colorado Springs CO 80932, USA

Blake, Norman — Singer, Guitarist (Teenage Fanclub)
High Road Touring, 751 Bridgeway, #200, Sausalito CA 94965 USA

Blake, Peter T — Artist
Waddington Galleries, 11 Cork St, London W1X 1PD, England

Blake, Robert — Actor
Thomas Mesereau, 3055 Wilshire Blvd, #600, Los Angeles CA 90010, USA

Blake, Robert B (Rob)
75 Dwyer St, Buffalo NY 14224, USA — Ice Hockey Player

Blake, Stephanie
15101 Magnolia Blvd, #E12, Sherman Oaks CA 91403, USA — Actress

Blake, Steven H (Steve)
3479 Cascade Terrace, West Linn OR 97068, USA — Basketball Player

Blake, Susie
Gavin Barker Assoc, 2D Wimpole St, London W1G 0EB, England — Actress

Blake, W Casey
1801 Country Club Road, Indianola IA 50125, USA — Baseball Player

Blakely, Susan
Jaffe Co, 9663 Santa Monica Blvd, #214, Beverly Hills CA 90210, USA — Actress, Model

Blakemore, Colin B
University Laboratory of Physiology, Parks Road, Oxford OX1 3PT, England — Neurophysiologist, Physiologist

Blakemore, Michael H
18 Upper Park Road, London NW3 2UP, England — Director, Actor, Writer

Blakeney, Larry
Troy University, Athletic Dept, Troy AL 36082, USA — Football Coach

Blakenham, Michael J
House of Lords, Westminster, London SW1A 0PW, England — Businessman

Blaker, Clay
Texas Sounds Entertainment, 2317 Pecan St, Dickinson TX 77539, USA — Singer, Songwriter

Blakey, G Robert
947 Riverside Dr, South Bend IN 46616, USA — Attorney, Educator

Blakey, Marion
Aerospace Industries Assn, 1000 Wilson Blvd, #1700, Arlington VA 22209, USA — Government Official

Blakiston, Caroline
Coolwaters Productions, 10061 Riverside Dr, Box 531, Toluca Lake CA 91602 USA — Actress

Blakley, Ronee
1404 Fairview Ave, Caldwell ID 83605, USA — Actress, Singer

Blalack, Robert
12251 Huston St, Valley Village CA 91607, USA — Cinematographer

Blalock, Hank J
8797 Adobe Bluffs Dr, San Diego CA 92129, USA — Baseball Player

Blalock, Jane
197 8th St, #300, Charlestown MA 02129, USA — Golfer

Blalock, Jolene
W M E Entertainment, 9601 Wilshire Blvd, #300, Beverly Hills CA 90210 USA — Actress

Blanc, Dominique
Les Visiteurs du Soir, 40 Rue de la Folie Regnault, 75011 Paris, France — Actress

Blanc, Georges
Le Mere Blanc, 01540 Vonnas, Ain, France — Restauranteur

Blanc, Jennifer
Blancbiehn Productions, 10990 Wilshire Blvd, #800, Los Angeles CA 90024, USA — Actress

Blanc, Manuel
Cineart, 36 Rue de Ponthieu, 75008 Paris, France — Actor

Blanc, Michael
Artmedia, 20 Ave Rapp, 75007 Paris, France — Actor

Blanc, Raymond R A
Le Manoir, Church Road, Great Milton, Oxford OX44 7PD, England — Restauranteur

Blancas, Homero, Jr
6826 Queensclub Dr, Houston TX 77069, USA — Golfer

Blanchard, James J
426 4th St NE, Washington DC 20002, USA — Governor, MI; Diplomat

Blanchard, Kenneth
2048 Aldergrove, #B, Escondido CA 92029, USA — Writer, Business Consultant

Blanchard, Olivier J
Massachusetts Institute of Technology, Economics Dept, Cambridge MA 02139, USA — Economist

Blanchard, R Cary
7208 NW 131st St, Oklahoma City OK 73142, USA — Football Player

Blanchard, Rachel
Luber Rocklin Entertainment, 8530 Wilshire Blvd, #555, Beverly Hills CA 90211 USA — Actress

Blanchard, Tammy
I C M Partners, 10250 Constellation Blvd, #900, Los Angeles CA 90067 USA — Actress, Singer

Blanchard, Terence
Burgess Mgmt, 6110 Saint Charles Ave, New Orleans LA 70118, USA — Jazz Trumpeter, Composer

Blanchard, Thomas R (Tom)
217 Independence Dr, Grants Pass OR 97527, USA — Football Player

Blanchett, Cate
Robyn Gardiner Mgmt, PO Box 128, Surrey Hills NSW 2010, Australia — Actress

Blanckaert, Myriam
Agents Associes, 201 Rue du Faubourg Saint Honore, 75008 Paris, France — Actress

Blanco, Cuauhtemoc
Chicago Fire, 700 S Harlem Ave, Bridgeview IL 60455 USA — Soccer Player

Blanco, Henry R
5510 N 132nd St, Litchfield Park AZ 85340, USA — Baseball Player

Blanco, Roberto
Rotbuchenstr 25, 81547 Munich, Germany — Singer, Actor

Blanco-Cervantes, Raul
Apdo 918, San Jose, Costa Rica — President, Costa Rica

Bland, Bobby (Blue)
Entertainment Consultants, PO Box 21, Abingdon MD 21009, USA — Singer

Bland, Carl N
1985 Crossbridge Court, Saint Charles MO 63303, USA — Football Player

Bland, John
PO Box 451436, Westlake OH 44145, USA — Golfer

Blandford, Roger D
California Institute of Technology, Astrophysics Dept, Pasadena CA 91125, USA — Astronomer

Blaney, Dave
211 N Emily Court, High Point NC 27265, USA — Auto Racing Driver

Blaney, George R
1633 Main St, Glastonbury CT 06033, USA — Basketball Player

Blanford, Lawrence J (Larry)
210 5th Ave, Venice CA 90291, USA — Cinematographer

Blank, Arthur M
1080 W Paces Ferry Road NW, Atlanta GA 30327, USA — Businessman

B

Blake - Blank

Blank, Boris
Creative Artists Agency, 2000 Ave of Stars, #100, Los Angeles CA 90067 USA — Synthesizer Player (Yello)

Blank, Rebecca M
Commerce Department, 14th St & Constitution Ave NW, Washington DC 20230 USA — Secretary, Commerce

Blankenbuehler, Andy
W M E Entertainment, 9601 Wilshire Blvd, #300, Beverly Hills CA 90210 USA — Choreographer, Dancer

Blankenship, Lance R
340 Kimberwicke Court, Alamo CA 94507, USA — Baseball Player

Blankfein, Lloyd C
Goldman Sachs Co, 85 Broad St, Building 85, New York NY 10004, USA — Financier

Blankfield, Mark
K & K Entertainment, 1498 W Sunset Blvd, Los Angeles CA 90026 USA — Actor

Blanks, Billie, Jr
W M E Entertainment, 9601 Wilshire Blvd, #300, Beverly Hills CA 90210 USA — Actor

Blanks, Billy
Tae Bo, 7095 Hollywood Blvd, #500, Los Angeles CA 90028, USA — Physical Fitness Expert

Blanks, Larvell
PO Box 562, Del Rio TX 78841, USA — Baseball Player

Blanks, Sidney (Sid)
4402 Warm Springs Road, Houston TX 77035, USA — Football Player

Blanton, Arell
4191 Greenbush Ave, Sherman Oaks CA 91423, USA — Actor

Blanton, Dain
1615 Stoner Ave, #3, Los Angeles CA 90025, USA — Volleyball Player

Blanton, Gerald (Jerry)
1942 Calumet Ave, Toledo OH 43607, USA — Football Player

Blany, David (Dave)
Randy Humphrey Assoc, 18636 Starcreek Dr, Cornelius NC 28031, USA — Auto Racing Driver

Blasco, Chuck
Media Promotion Enterprises, 423 6th Ave, Huntington WV 25701, USA — Singer (Vogues)

Blashford-Snell, John N
Exploration Society, Motcome, Shaftesbury, Dorset SP7 9PB, England — Explorer

Blasi, Rosa
Untitled Entertainment, 350 S Beverly Dr, #200, Beverly Hills CA 90212 USA — Actress

Blasingame, Wade A
5207 Riverhill Road, Marietta GA 30068, USA — Baseball Player

Blass, Stephen R (Steve)
1756 Quigg Dr, Pittsburgh PA 15241, USA — Baseball Player

Blasucci, Richard (Dick)
A P A Talent/Literary Agency, 405 S Beverly Dr, #300, Beverly Hills CA 90212 USA — Actor, Producer

Blatche, Andray
15053 Doral Place, Haymarket VA 20169, USA — Basketball Player

Blatt, Melanie R
Concorde International, 101 Shepherds Bush Road, London W6 7LP, England — Singer

Blatter, Joseph S (Sepp)
Federation International Football Assn, Hitzigweg 11, 8030 Zurich, Switzerland — Soccer Executive

Blatty, William Peter
7018 Longwood Dr, Bethesda MD 20817, USA — Writer

Blatz, Kelly
Luber Rocklin Entertainment, 8530 Wilshire Blvd, #555, Beverly Hills CA 90211 USA — Actor

Blau, Daniel
Belgradstr 26, 80796 Munich, Germany — Artist

Blau, Peter M
7019 Old NC 86, Chapel Hill NC 27516, USA — Sociologist

Blauner, Peter
Warner Books, 1271 Ave of Americas, New York NY 10020 USA — Writer

Blauser, Jeffrey M (Jeff)
6080 Carlisle Lane, Alpharetta GA 30022, USA — Baseball Player

Blaustein, Barry W
Creative Artists Agency, 2000 Ave of Stars, #100, Los Angeles CA 90067 USA — Director

Blaylock, Anthony D
88 Brighton Dr, Garner NC 27529, USA — Football Player

Blaylock, Caroline
232 Hennon Dr NW, Rome GA 30165, USA — Golfer

Blaylock, Daron O (Mookie)
1017 Gresham Road, Zebulon GA 30295, USA — Basketball Player

Blaylock, Derrick D
1471 Edgewater Road, Crown Point IN 46307, USA — Football Player

Blaylock, Kenneth T
American Government Employees, 80 F St NW, #700, Washington DC 20001, USA — Labor Leader

Blayton, Anitra
Tarrant County College, Art Dept, 828 W Harwood Road, Hurst TX 76054, USA — Sculptor

Blazelowski, Carol A
126 Walnut St, Nutley NJ 07110, USA — Basketball Player, Executive

Blechacz, Rafal
Konzertdirektion Schmid, Konigstra 36, 30175 Hannover, Germany — Concert Pianist

Bledel, Alexis
New Wave Entertainment, 2660 W Olive Ave, Burbank CA 91505, USA — Actress, Model

Bledsoe, Drew
845 Delrey Road, Whitefish MT 59937, USA — Football Player

Bledsoe, Tempestt
House of Representatives, 1434 6th St, #1, Santa Monica CA 90401 USA — Actress

Bleeth, Yasmine
Gersh Agency, 9465 Wilshire Blvd, #600, Beverly Hills CA 90212 USA — Actress

Blegen, Judith
91 Central Park West, #1B, New York NY 10023, USA — Opera Singer

Blehm, Gary
PO Box 60607, Colorado Springs CO 80960, USA — Cartoonist (Penmen)

Bleibtreu, Moritz
Voyez Mon Agent, 20 Ave Rapp, 75007 Paris, France — Actor

Bleier, Robert P (Rocky)
929 Osage Road, Pittsburgh PA 15243, USA — Football Player

Bleifeld, Stanley
27 Spring Valley Road, Weston CT 06883, USA — Sculptor

Bleiler, Gretchen
PO Box 5774, Snowmass Village CO 81615, USA — Snowboard Athlete

Blessed, Brian
Associated International Mgmt, Fairfax House, Fulwood Place, London WC1V 6HU, England — Actor

Blessed, Rosalind
Associated International Mgmt, Fairfax House, Fulwood Place, London WC1V 6HU, England — Actress

Blessen, Karen A
Karen Blessen Illustration, 6327 Vickery Blvd, Dallas TX 75214, USA — Journalist, Illustrator

Blessing, Jack
Golan & Blumberg, 6528 W 6th St, Los Angeles CA 90048, USA — Actor

Blethen, Frank A
Seattle Times, Publisher's Office, 1120 John St, Seattle WA 98109, USA — Publisher

Blethyn, Brenda A
I C M Partners, 10250 Constellation Blvd, #900, Los Angeles CA 90067 USA — Actress

Bleu, Corbin
James/Levy Mgmt, 3500 W Olive Ave, #1470, Burbank CA 91505 USA — Actor, Singer

Bley, Carla B
Ted Kurland, 173 Brighton Ave, Allston MA 02134 USA — Composer, Jazz Pianist

Bley, Paul
Improvising Artists, PO Box 496, Cherry Valley NY 13320, USA — Jazz Pianist, Composer

Blieden, Michael
A K A Talent, 6310 San Vicente Blvd, #200, Los Angeles CA 90048 USA — Actor, Writer

Blier, Bertrand
11 Rue Margueritte, 75017 Paris, France — Director

Blige, Mary J
W M E Entertainment, 9601 Wilshire Blvd, #300, Beverly Hills CA 90210 USA — Rap Artist, Singer

Blilie, Hannah
Shotclock Mgmt, 20312 NE 259th St, Battle Ground WA 98604, USA — Drummer (Gossip)

Blim, Richard D
304 W 172nd St, Belton MO 64012, USA — Pediatrician

Blinder, Alan S
Princeton University, Economics Dept, Fischer Hall, Princeton NJ 08544, USA — Government Official, Financier

Blinka, Stanley J (Stan)
3304 Carriage Dr, Export PA 15632, USA — Football Player

Blinks, Susan
362 Vista del Rey Dr, Encinitas CA 92024, USA — Equestrian

Bliss, Boti
Stone Manners Salners, 9911 W Pico Blvd, #1400, Los Angeles CA 90035 USA — Actress

Bliss, Caroline
Rights House, 34-43 Russell St, London WC2B 5HA, England — Actress

Bliss, Julian
I M G Artists, Hogarth Business Park, Chiswick, London W4 2TH, England — Concert Clarinetist

Bliss, Michael (Mike)
156 Mariner Pointe Lane, Mooresville NC 28117, USA — Auto Racing Driver

Blitt, Ricky
Smart Entertainment, 9595 Wilshire Blvd, #900, Beverly Hills CA 90212, USA — Writer, Producer

Blitz, Jeffrey
Creative Artists Agency, 2000 Ave of Stars, #100, Los Angeles CA 90067 USA — Director, Writer

Blitzer, Wolf
8929 Holly Leaf Lane, Bethesda MD 20817, USA — Commentator

Blix, Hans M
Curtis Brown Group, 28-29 Haymarket, London SW1Y 4SP, England — Government Official

Blobel, Gunter K-J
1100 Park Ave, #10D, New York NY 10128, USA — Nobel Medicine Laureate

Bloch, Erich
National Science Foundation, 1800 C St NW, Washington DC 20002, USA — Electrical Engineer, Computer Scientist

Bloch, Phillip
Grand Central Publishing, 237 Park Ave, #1300, New York NY 10017, USA — Actor, Fashion Designer

Block, Gene D
University of California, Chancellor's Office, Los Angeles CA 90024, USA — Educator

Block, Hunt
Don Buchwald/Fortitude, 6500 Wilshire Blvd, #2200, Los Angeles CA 90048 USA — Actor

Block, John R
National Wholesale Grocers Assn, 201 Park Washington, Falls Church VA 22046, USA — Secretary, Agriculture

Block, John W
1069 Santa Barbara St, San Diego CA 92107, USA — Basketball Player

Block, Lawrence
299 W 12th St, #12D, New York NY 10014, USA — Writer

Block, Lawrence J (Larry)
Gage Group, 14724 Ventura Blvd, #505, Sherman Oaks CA 91403 USA — Actor

Block, Ned J
96 Ellery St, #2, Cambridge MA 02138, USA — Philosopher

Block, Ron
Rounder Records, 1 Rounder Way, Burlington MA 01803 USA — Singer, Banjo Player (Union Station)

Block, Susan
2725 Bentley Road, Highland Park IL 60035, USA — Artist

Blocker, Dirk
5063 La Ramada Dr, Santa Barbara CA 93111, USA — Actor

Bloemberg, Jeff
170 Diagonal Road, Wingham ON N0G 1W0, Canada — Ice Hockey Player

Bloembergen, Nicolaas
13835 E Langtree Lane, Tucson AZ 85747, USA — Nobel Physics Laureate

Blokhuijsen, Jan
K N S B, Postbus 1120, 3800 BC Arnesfoort, Netherlands — Speed Skater

Blomberg, Ronald M (Ron)
11660 Mountain Laurel Dr, Roswell GA 30075, USA — Baseball Player

Blomdahl, Benjamin E (Ben)
9 Emmy Lane, Ladera Ranch CA 92694, USA — Baseball Player

Blomkamp, Neill
W M E Entertainment, 9601 Wilshire Blvd, #300, Beverly Hills CA 90210 USA — Director, Writer

Blomqvist, Timo P
Helsinki Ligaforeningen H I F K Road, Mantytie 23, 00270 Helsinki, Finland — Ice Hockey Player

Blomstedt, Herbert T
Columbia Artists Mgmt Inc, 1790 Broadway, #702, New York NY 10019 USA — Conductor

Blomsten, Arto
Canal + TV, Teleluddsvagen 7, 11 584 Stockholm, Sweden — Ice Hockey Player

Blong, Jenni
Judy Schoen, 606 N Larchmont Blvd, #309, Los Angeles CA 90004 USA — Actress

Blonsky, Nikki
Innovative Artists, 1505 10th St, Santa Monica CA 90401 USA — Actress, Singer

Blood, Edward J
2 Beech Hill, Durham NH 03824, USA — Skier, Skiing Official

Bloodgood, Moon
United Talent Agency, 9336 Civic Center Dr, Beverly Hills CA 90210 USA — Actress, Model

Bloom, Amy
Gillon Aitken Assoc, 18-21 Cavaye Place, London SW10 9PT, England — Writer, Psychotherapist

Bloom, Brian
Osbrink Talent Agency, 4343 Lankershim Blvd, #100, North Hollywood CA 91602 USA — Actor

Bloom, Brooke
TalentWorks, 3500 W Olive Ave, #1400, Burbank CA 91505 USA — Actress

Bloom, Claire
Clive Conway, 32 Grove St, Oxford OX2 TJT, England — Actress

Bloom, Floyd E
628 Pacific View Dr, San Diego CA 92109, USA — Physician

Bloom, Harold
179 Linden St, New Haven CT 06511, USA — Educator, Writer

Bloom, Jane Ira
Joel Chriss, 60 E 8th St, #34N, New York NY 10003 USA — Jazz Saxophonist, Composer

Bloom, Jeremy
PO Box 770-311, Park City UT 84060, USA — Alpine Skier, Football Player

Bloom, John
Independent Talent Group, Oxford House, 76 Oxford St, London W1D 1BS, England — Editor

Bloom, Lindsay
3751 Recklaw, Studio City CA 91604, USA — Actress

Bloom, Luka
Howlin' Wuelf Media, 527 Barclay Ave, Morrisville PA 19067, USA — Singer, Guitarist, Songwriter

Bloom, Matthew J (Matt)
New Japan Dojo, PM Box 1245, 1223 Wilshire Blvd, Santa Monica CA 90403, USA — Professional Wrestler

Bloom, Mike
227 School Road, Delanson NY 12053, USA — Ice Hockey Player

Bloom, Orlando
Viddywell Productions, 1041 N Formosa Ave, Formosa Building, West Hollywood CA 90046, USA — Actor

Bloom, Scott
11 Croydon Court, Dix Hills NY 11746, USA — Actor

Bloom, Ursula
Newton House, Walls Dr, Ravenglass, Cumbria CA18 1SQ, England — Writer

Bloom, Vail
C E S D, 10635 Santa Monica Blvd, #130, Los Angeles CA 90025 USA — Actress

Bloom, Verna
327 E 82nd St, New York NY 10028, USA — Actress

Bloomberg, Michael R
Mayor's Office, Gracie Mansion, New York NY 10007, USA — Mayor, New York City; Publisher

Bloomfield, Michael J (Mike)
14302 Autumn Canyon Trace, Houston TX 77062, USA — Astronaut

Bloomfield, Sara
Holocaust Memorial Museum, 100 Wallenberg Place SW, Washington DC 20024, USA — Museum Director

Bloomquist, William P (Willie)
7026 E Blue Sky Dr, Scottsdale AZ 85266, USA — Baseball Player

Blotzer, Robert J (Bobby)
Paradise Artists, PO Box 1821, Ojai CA 93024 USA — Drummer (Ratt)

Blount, Corie K
5427 Kytes Lane, Liberty Township OH 45044, USA — Basketball Player

Blount, Mark D
5723 High Flyer Road S, Palm Beach Gardens FL 33418, USA — Basketball Player

Blount, Melvin C (Mel)
Mel Blount Youth Home, 6 Mel Blount Dr, Claysville PA 15323, USA — Football Player, Executive

Blount, Winton M, III
Blount Inc, 4909 SE International Way, Portland OR 97222, USA — Businessman

Blow, Kurtis
Green Light Talent Agency, PO Box 3172, Beverly Hills CA 90212 USA — Rap Artist

Blowers, Michael R (Mike)
22211 42nd Ave E, Spanaway WA 98387, USA — Baseball Player

Blowfly
Pandisc Music, 15982 NW 48th Ave, Hialeah FL 33014, USA — Singer, Rap Artist

Blubaugh, Douglas M (Doug)
6640 N Utt Dr, Bloomington IN 47408, USA — Freestyle Wrestler

Blucas, Marcus (Marc)
Anonymous Content, 3532 Hayden Ave, Culver City CA 90232 USA — Actor

Blue, Angel
I M G Artists, Hogarth Business Park, Chiswick, London W4 2TH, England — Opera Singer

Blue, Callum
Ken McReddie Assoc, 11 Connaught Place, London W2 2ET, England — Actor

Blue, John
2301 Half Moon Lane, Costa Mesa CA 92627, USA — Ice Hockey Player, Coach

Blue, Vida R
PO Box 1449, Pleasanton CA 94566, USA — Baseball Player

Blueprint
Kork Agency, 1880 Century Park E, #711, Los Angeles CA 90067, USA — DJ Musician

Bluford, Guion S (Guy), Jr
PO Box 549, North Olmsted OH 44070, USA — Astronaut

Blum, Arlene
University of California, Biochemistry Dept, Berkeley CA 94720, USA — Mountaineer

Blum, Don
Tsunami Entertainment, 2525 Hyperion Ave, Los Angeles CA 90027, USA — Singer, Drummer (VonBondies)

Blum, Geoffrey E (Geoff)
7 Calle Angelitos, San Clemente CA 92673, USA — Baseball Player

Blum, H Steven
Chief, National Guard Bureau, HqUSA, Pentagon, Washington DC 20310, USA — Army General

Blum, John
27420 Palomino Dr, Warren MI 48093, USA — Ice Hockey Player

Blum, Manuel
700 Euclid Ave, Berkeley CA 94708, USA — Computer Scientist, Turing Laureate

Blum, Stephanie
Don Buchwald/Fortitude, 6500 Wilshire Blvd, #2200, Los Angeles CA 90048 USA — Actress, Comedienne

Blum, Steve — Actor
Arlene Thornton Assoc, 12711 Ventura Blvd, #490, Studio City CA 91604, USA

Blum, Walter (Mousey) — Thoroughbred Racing Jockey
5710 NW 65th Way, Tamarac FL 33321, USA

Blumberg, Stuart — Actor, Writer, Producer
Class 5 Films, 200 Park Ave S, #800, New York NY 10003, USA

Blume, B Ray — Basketball Player
29248 SE Powell Valley Road, Gresham OR 97080, USA

Blume, Judy S — Writer
W M E Entertainment, 9601 Wilshire Blvd, #300, Beverly Hills CA 90210 USA

Blume, Martin — Physicist
Brookhaven National Laboratory, 2 Center St, Upton NY 11973 USA

Blumenfeld, Alan — Actor
Stone Manners Salners, 9911 W Pico Blvd, #1400, Los Angeles CA 90035 USA

Blumenthal, George R — Educator
University of California, Chancellor's Office, 1156 High St, Santa Cruz CA 95064, USA

Blumenthal, W Michael — Secretary, Treasury; Financier
227 Ridgeview Road, Princeton NJ 08540, USA

Blundell, Graeme — Actor
Shanahan Mgmt, 91 Campbell St, #300, Surry Hills NSW 2010, Australia

Blundell, Mark — Auto Racing Driver
4001 Methanol Lane, Indianapolis IN 46268, USA

Blundell, Pamela — Fashion Designer
Copperwheat Blundell, 14 Cheshire St, London E2 6EH, England

Blunstone, Colin — Singer (Zombies)
Rhino Mgmt, 60 Babbercombe Road, Bromley, Kent BR1 3CW, England

Blunt, Emily — Actress
Ken McReddie Assoc, 11 Connaught Place, London W2 2ET, England

Blunt, James — Singer, Guitarist, Songwriter
21 Artists Ltd, 1 Blythe Road, London W14 0HG, England

Blunt, Matthew R (Matt) — Governor, MO
Cassidy & Assoc, 700 13th St NW, #400, Washington DC 20005, USA

Bluteau, Lothaire — Actor
Don Buchwald/Fortitude, 6500 Wilshire Blvd, #2200, Los Angeles CA 90048 USA

Bluth, Ray — Bowler
569 Beauford Dr, Saint Louis MO 63122, USA

Bluth, Tony — Animator
C A A T Studios, 10630 Moorpark St, #303, North Hollywood CA 91602, USA

Bly, Donald A (Dre') — Football Player
4312 Topsail Landing, Chesapeake VA 23321, USA

Bly, Robert E — Writer, Psychologist
1904 Girard Ave S, Minneapolis MN 55403, USA

Blyleven, R Bert — Baseball Player
1501 McGregor Reserve Dr, Fort Myers FL 33901, USA

Blyth, Ann — Actress, Singer
PO Box 9754, Rancho Santa Fe CA 92067, USA

Blyth, Chay — Yachtsman, Explorer
Inmans House, 12 London Road, Sheet, Petersfield, Hamps GU31 4BE, England

Blythe, Arthur M — Jazz Saxophonist
Joel Chriss, 60 E 8th St, #34N, New York NY 10003 USA

Blythe, D Randall (Randy) — Singer (Lamb of God)
Entertainment Unlimited, 1000 Main Street Plaza, #303, Voorhees NJ 08043, USA

Blythe, Stephanie — Singer
Opus 3 Artists, 470 Park Ave S, #900N, New York NY 10016 USA

Bo Bae Song — Golfer
Ladies Pro Golf Assn, 100 International Golf Dr, Daytona Beach FL 32124 USA

Boal, Mark — Writer
Creative Artists Agency, 2000 Ave of Stars, #100, Los Angeles CA 90067 USA

Board, Dwaine P — Football Player
651 Arlington Road, Redwood City CA 94062, USA

Boardman, Christopher M (Chris) — Cyclist
Lindfield House, Station Approach Meols, Wirral L47 8XA, England

Boardman, Eric — Actor, Director
I C M Partners, 10250 Constellation Blvd, #900, Los Angeles CA 90067 USA

Boardman, Lee — Actor
Ken McReddie Assoc, 11 Connaught Place, London W2 2ET, England

Boat, William L (Billy) — Auto Racing Driver
Boat Indy Racing, 23045 N 15th Ave, Phoenix AZ 85027, USA

Boatman, Michael — Actor
1432 Sunnycrest Dr, Fullerton CA 92835, USA

Bob, Tim — Bassist (Rage Against the Machine)
ArtistDirect, 10900 Wilshire Blvd, #1400, Los Angeles CA 90024 USA

Bobbie, Walter — Director, Actor, Lyricist
Gage Group, 14724 Ventura Blvd, #505, Sherman Oaks CA 91403 USA

Bobby G — Singer (Bucks Fizz)
Barry Collings Entertainment, PO 2112, Hockley, Essex SS5 4WD, England

Bobek, Nicole — Figure Skater
19220 Seaview Road, #100, Jupiter FL 33469, USA

Bober, Chris — Football Player
605 N 264th St, Waterloo NE 68069, USA

Bobko, Karol J — Astronaut
91 Turnberry Road, Half Moon Bay CA 94019, USA

Bobo, Jonah — Actor
Abrams Artists, 9200 W Sunset Blvd, #1125, West Hollywood CA 90069 USA

Bocachica, Hiram — Baseball Player
2340 Carr 2, 2 Urb Rexville, Bayamon PR 00961, USA

Bocca, Julio — Ballet Dancer
F P S International, 150 Broadway, New York NY 10038, USA

Boccabella, John D — Baseball Player
1035 Lea Dr, San Rafael CA 94903, USA

Bocchi, Nicole — Actress
Carson Adler Agency, 250 W 57th St, #2030, New York NY 10107, USA

Bocelli, Andrea — Concert Singer
Vittoria Apauna, 55042 Forte dei Marmi, Italy

Bochco, Steven — Producer, Writer
22035 Saddle Peak Road, Topanga CA 90290, USA

Bochenski, Brandon — Ice Hockey Player
12962 Radisson Road NE, Minneapolis MN 55449, USA
Bochenski, Jacek — Writer
Ul Sonaty 6M 801, 02 744 Warsaw, Poland
Bochner, Hart — Actor
Don Buchwald/Fortitude, 6500 Wilshire Blvd, #2200, Los Angeles CA 90048 USA
Bochner, Salomon — Mathematician
4100 Greenbriar Ave, #239, Houston TX 77098, USA
Bochte, Bruce A — Baseball Player
80 Century Lane, Petaluma CA 94952, USA
Bochtler, Douglas E (Doug) — Baseball Player
154 Narrow Gate Road, Maryville TN 37801, USA
Bochy, Bruce D — Baseball Player, Manager
16144 Brittany Park Lane, Poway CA 92064, USA
Bock, Charles, Jr — Test Pilot
PO Box 4197, Incline Village NV 89450, USA
Bock, Dennis — Writer
Carlisle Co, 121 E 17th St, New York NY 10003, USA
Bock, John M — Football Player
627 Cambridge Terrace, Weston FL 33326, USA
Bockhorn, Arlen (Bucky) — Basketball Player
3540 Big Tree Road, Bellbrook OH 45305, USA
Bockrath, Tina — Actress, Model
755 S San Rafael Ave, Pasadena CA 91105, USA
Bockwinkel, Nick W F — Professional Wrestler
Cauliflower Alley Club, 383 Highway 00, Rolla MO 65401, USA
Bocuse, Paul — Restauranteur
40 Rue de la Plage, 69660 Collonges au Mont d'Or, France
Bodden, Alonzo — Actor, Comedian
Levity Entertainment Group, 6701 Center Drive W, #1111, Los Angeles CA 90045, USA
Bodden, Leigh E — Football Player
400 Foxboro Blvd, Foxborough MA 02035, USA
Boddicker, Michael J (Mike) — Baseball Player
11324 W 121st Terrace, Overland Park KS 66213, USA
Boddy, Gregg — Ice Hockey Player
2271 Sorrento Dr, Coquitlam BC V3K 6P4, Canada
Bode, Hendrick W — Research Engineer
Harvard University, Pierce Hall, Cambridge MA 02138, USA
Bode, John R — Vietnam War Air Force Hero
1100 Warm Sands Dr SE, Albuquerque NM 87123, USA
Bode, Ken — Commentator, Educator
Northwestern University, Journalism School, Evanston IL 60206, USA
Boden, Lynn R — Football Player
7103 N 146th St, Bennington NE 68007, USA
Boden, Margaret A — Philosopher, Psychologist
Brighton University, Cognitive Science School, Brighton BN1 9QH, England
Bodenheimer, George — Businessman, TV Executive
ABC-TV, Sports Dept, 77 W 66th St, New York NY 10023 USA
Bodett, Tom — Writer, Entertainer
PO Box 268, Putney VT 05346, USA
Bodger, Doug — Ice Hockey Player
Eddy's Hockey Shop, 2728 James St, Duncan BC V9L 2X9, Canada
Bodill, Colin — Aviator
Polar First, Onslow Gardens, #2, London SW7 3LX, England
Bodine, Brett — Auto Racing Driver
304 Performance Road, Mooresville NC 28115, USA
Bodine, Geoffrey E (Geoff) — Auto Racing Driver
18695 Northline Dr, #C2, Cornelius NC 28031, USA
Bodine, Todd — Auto Racing Driver
120 Harris Farm Dr, Mooresville NC 28115, USA
Bodmer, Walter F — Geneticist
Oxford University, Hertford College, Oxford OX1 3BW, England
Bodrov, Sergei V, Sr — Director
Arlook Group, 205 S Beverly Dr, #209, Beverly Hills CA 90212, USA
Boe, Alfie — Singer
Agency Group Ltd, 361-373 City Road, London EC1V 2QA, England
Boe, Eric A — Astronaut
N A S A, Johnson Space Center, 2101 NASA Road, Houston TX 77058 USA
Boecher, Katherine — Actress
Innovative Artists, 1505 10th St, Santa Monica CA 90401 USA
Boedeker, William H (Bill) — Football Player
1632 Thistle Lane, Fort Wayne IN 46825, USA
Boeheim, James A (Jim), Jr — Basketball Coach
701 Eagle Woods Trail, Kissimmee FL 34747, USA
Boehm, Gottfried K — Pritzker Architectural Laureate
Kunstgeschichtliches Seminar, Saint Alban-Graben 16, 4051 Basel, Switzerland
Boehner, John A — Speaker; Representative, OH
US House of Representatives, Longworth Office Building, Washington DC 20515 USA
Boehringer, Brian E — Baseball Player
10 Sunset Dr, Fenton MO 63026, USA
Boeke, James F (Jim) — Football Player
18914 San Blas St, Fountain Valley CA 92708, USA
Boerner, Jacqueline — Speed Skater
Bernhard-Bastlein-Str 55, 10367 Berlin, Germany
Boerwinkle, Thomas F (Tom) — Basketball Player
8524 Walredon Ave, Burr Ridge IL 60527, USA
Boesak, Allan — Religious Leader, Social Activist
16 Villa Bellini, Constantia St, Strand 7140, South Africa
Boeschenstein, William W — Businessman
10617 Cardiff Road, Perrysburg OH 43551, USA
Boesel, Raul D — Auto Racing Driver
150 SE 25th Road, #4E, Miami FL 33129, USA
Boesen, Dennis L (Denny) — Astronaut
6613 Sandra Ave NE, Albuquerque NM 87109, USA
Boever, Joseph M (Joe) — Baseball Player
416 Savannah Way, Franklin TN 37067, USA

Boeving, Christian — Actor
Diverse Talent Group, 9911 W Pico Blvd, #350W, Los Angeles CA 90035, USA

Boff — Guitarist (Chumbawamba)
Doug Smith Assoc, PO Box 1151, London W3 8ZJ, England

Boff, Leonardo G D — Theologian
Pr M Leao 12/204, Alto Vale Encantado, 20531-350 Rio de Janeiro, Brazil

Bofill, Angela — Singer
1385 York Ave, #6B, New York NY 10021, USA

Bofill, Ricardo — Architect
Taller de Arquitectura, 14 Ave de la Industria, 08960 Barcelona, Spain

Bofinger, Helge — Architect
Biebricher Allee 49, 65187 Wiesbaden, Germany

Bogaliy-Titovets, Anna — Biathlete
Biathlon Union, Luzhnetskaya Nab 8, 119992 Moscow, Russia

Boganyi, Tibor — Conductor
Konzertdirektion Hortnagel, Oranienburgen Str 50D, 10117 Berlin, Germany

Bogar, Timothy P (Tim) — Baseball Player
194 Gray St, North Andover MA 01845, USA

Bogardus, Stephen — Actor
TalentWorks, 3500 W Olive Ave, #1400, Burbank CA 91505 USA

Bogdanich, Walt — Journalist
New York Times, Editorial Dept, 229 W 43rd St, New York NY 10036 USA

Bogdanovich, Peter — Director
Abrams Artists, 9200 W Sunset Blvd, #1125, West Hollywood CA 90069 USA

Bogeberg, J B — Bassist (A-Ha)
Bandana Mgmt, 11 Elvaston Place, #300, London SW7 5QC, England

Boggs, Bill — Journalist
240 Central Park S, New York NY 10019, USA

Boggs, Danny J — Judge
US Court of Appeals, US Courthouse, 601 W Broadway, Louisville KY 40202, USA

Boggs, Haskell — Cinematographer
3710 Goodland Ave, Studio City CA 91604, USA

Boggs, Thomas W (Tommy) — Baseball Player
1450 Long Meadow, Salado TX 76571, USA

Boggs, Wade A — Baseball Player
6006 Windham Place, Tampa FL 33647, USA

Bogguss, Suzy — Singer, Guitarist, Songwriter
Creative Artists Agency, 2000 Ave of Stars, #100, Los Angeles CA 90067 USA

Bogle, Eric — Singer, Songwriter
Laing Entertainment, 35 Montague St, Goulburn NSW 2580, Australia

Bogle, John C — Financier
320 Fishers Road, Bryn Mawr PA 19010, USA

Boglioli, Wendy — Swimmer
2014 210th Circle, Sammamish WA 98074, USA

Bogner, Willy — Producer, Fashion Designer
Firma Willy Bogner GmbH, Saint-Veit-Str 4, 81673 Munich, Germany

Bogosian, Eric — Performance Artist, Actor, Writer
Brookside Artist Mgmt, 250 W 57th St, #2303, New York NY 10107 USA

Bogues, Tyrone (Muggsy) — Basketball Player, Coach
527 E 83rd St, #2W, New York NY 10028, USA

Boguniecki, Eric — Ice Hockey Player
129 Buttonball Road, Orange CT 06477, USA

Bogush, Elizabeth — Actress
Innovative Artists, 1505 10th St, Santa Monica CA 90401 USA

Bogut, Andrew — Basketball Player
1660 N Prospect Ave, #2607, Milwaukee WI 53202, USA

Bohan, Marc — Fashion Designer
35 Rue du Bourg a Mont, 21400 Chatillon sur Seine, France

Bohanon, Brian E — Baseball Player
243 W Thorn Way, Houston TX 77015, USA

Bohay, Heidi — Actress
Brogan Agency, 1517 Park Row Dr, Venice CA 90291, USA

Bohem, Leslie (Les) — Writer
United Talent Agency, 9336 Civic Center Dr, Beverly Hills CA 90210 USA

Bohigas Guardiola, Oriol — Architect
M B M Arquitectes, Placa Reial 18, 08002 Barcelona 21, Spain

Bohlin, Peter Q — Architect
Bohlin Cywinski Jackson, 49 Geary St, #300, San Francisco CA 94108, USA

Bohn, Jason — Golfer
757 Carl Sanders Dr, Acworth GA 30101, USA

Bohn, Laura — Interior Designer
Laura Bohn Design, 30 W 26th St, #1100, New York NY 10010, USA

Bohn, Parker, III — Bowler
25 Pitney Lane, Jackson NJ 08527, USA

Bohne, Bruce — Actor
Beacon Talent Agency, 170 Apple Ridge Road, Woodcliff Lake NJ 07677, USA

Bohner, Otto A — WW II German Luftwaffe Test Pilot
Barbarossastr 28, 78855 Annweller am Trifels, Germany

Bohon, Justin — Actor
Innovative Artists, 1505 10th St, Santa Monica CA 90401 USA

Bohorquez, Claudio — Concert Cellist
Conciertos Augusto, Calle Viento 15, 2B Majadahonda, 28220 Madrid, Spain

Bohrer, Corinne — Actress
Abrams Artists, 9200 W Sunset Blvd, #1125, West Hollywood CA 90069 USA

Bohrer, Thomas — Rowing Athlete
77 Crest St, Concord MA 01742, USA

Bohringer, Romane — Actress
Agence Artiste Adequet, 80 Rue d'Amsterdam, 75009 Paris, France

Boies, David — Attorney
Cravath Swaine Moore, 1 Chase Manhattan Plaza, New York NY 10005, USA

Boikov, Alexandre — Ice Hockey Player
2138 Charleys Creek Road, Culloden WV 25510, USA

Boileau, Linda — Editorial Cartoonist
Frankfort State Journal, Editorial Dept, 321 W Main St, Frankfort KY 40601, USA

Boiman, Rocky M — Football Player
9583 Dick Road, Harrison OH 45030, USA

Boisclair, Bruce A — Baseball Player
5423 Spanish Oak Lane, #D, Oak Park CA 91377, USA
Boise, Mike — Drummer (Chesterfield Kings)
Agency Group Ltd, 142 W 57th St, #600, New York NY 10019 USA
Boisset, Yves — Director
61 Blvd Inkerman, 92200 Neuilly-sur-Seine, France
Boisson, Christine — Actress
Artmedia, 20 Ave Rapp, 75007 Paris, France
Boisvert, Gilles — Ice Hockey Player
10213 Greenside Dr, Cockeysville MD 21030, USA
Boitano, Brian — Figure Skater
1072 Inverness Way, Sunnyvale CA 94087, USA
Boitano, Danny J — Baseball Player
15400 Winchester Blvd, #43, Los Gatos CA 95030, USA
Boivin, Leo J — Ice Hockey Player
PO Box 406, Prescott ON K0E 1T0, Canada
Bok, Bart J — Astronomer
200 N Sierra Vista Dr, Tucson AZ 85719, USA
Bok, Chip — Editorial Cartoonist
709 Castle Blvd, Akron OH 44313, USA
Bok, Derek C — Educator
Harvard University, Kennedy Government School, Cambridge MA 02138, USA
Bok, Sissela — Philosopher
75 Cambridge Parkway, #E610, Cambridge MA 02142, USA
Bokamper, Kim — Football Player
301 NW 127th Ave, Plantation FL 33325, USA
Bolam, James — Actor
Independent Talent Group, Oxford House, 76 Oxford St, London W1D 1BS, England
Bolcom, William E — Composer, Pianist
3080 Whitmore Lake Road, Ann Arbor MI 48105, USA
Bolden, Charles F, Jr — Astronaut, Marine Corps General
National Aviation & Space Administration, 300 C St SW, Washington DC 20024, USA
Bolden, Jeanette — Track Athlete
University of California, Athletic Dept, Los Angeles CA 90024, USA
Bolden, Juran T — Football Player
4618 Barkley Dr NW, Acworth GA 30101, USA
Bolden, Rickey A — Football Player
301 High Pointe Dr, LaGrange GA 30240, USA
Boldin, Anquan — Football Player
471 E Crescent Place, Chandler AZ 85249, USA
Boldirev, Ivan — Ice Hockey Player
2003 Woodmere Dr E, Valparaiso IN 46383, USA
Boldon, Ato — Track Athlete
PO Box 3703, Santa Cruz, Trinidad, Trinidad & Tobago
Bolduc, Danny — Ice Hockey Player
27 Daisy Lane, Sidney ME 04330, USA
Bole, Cliff — Director
374 Links Dr, Palm Desert CA 92211, USA
Boles, John E, Jr — Baseball Manager, Executive
7901 Timberlake Dr, Melbourne FL 32904, USA
Bolger, Dermot — Writer
A P Watt, 20 John St, London WC1N 2DR, England
Bolger, James B (Jim) — Prime Minister, New Zealand
New Zealand Embassy, 37 Observatory Circle NW, Washington DC 20008, USA
Bolger, James C (Jim) — Baseball Player
5524 Sidney Road, Cincinnati OH 45238, USA
Bolger, Sarah L — Actress
Hamilton Hodell, 66-68 Margaret St, London W1W 8SR, England
Bolick, Frank C — Baseball Player
381 Virginia Lane, Kulpmont PA 17834, USA
Bolin, Bobby D — Baseball Player
100 Medinah Dr, Easley SC 29642, USA
Boling, David — Writer
Bloomsbury Publishing, 36 Soho Square, London W1D 3Q4, England
Boll, Timo — Table Tennis Player
B Schmittenbecher-Sportsmarketing, Erlenring 16, 61118 Bad Vilbel, Germany
Boll, Uwe — Director
Bolu Filmproduktion, Holmanstr 8-10, 97421 Schweinfurt, Germany
Bollen, Roger — Cartoonist (Animal Crackers, Catfish)
8964 Little St, Mentor OH 44060, USA
Boller, Kyle B — Football Player
14945 Via La Senda, Del Mar CA 92014, USA
Bolles, Richard N — Writer
10 Stirling Dr, Danville CA 94526, USA
Bollettieri, Nick — Tennis Coach
Nick Bollettieri Tennis Academy, 5500 34th St W, Bradenton FL 34210, USA
Bolli, Justin — Golfer
136 Ramsford Lane, Simpsonville SC 29681, USA
Bolling, Claude — Jazz Pianist, Composer
20 Ave de Lorraine, 92380 Garches, France
Bolling, Dave — Writer
Bloomsbury Publishing, 36 Soho Square, London W1D 3Q4, England
Bolling, Frank E — Baseball Player
171 Fenwick Road, Mobile AL 36608, USA
Bolling, Milton J (Milt) — Baseball Player
4009 Old Shell Road, #E12, Mobile AL 36608, USA
Bolling, Tiffany — Actress
Tyler Kjar, 10153 1/2 Riverside Dr, #255, Toluca Lake CA 91602 USA
Bollinger, Brooks — Football Player
3549 Birchpond Road, Saint Paul MN 55122, USA
Bollinger, Lee C — Educator
Columbia University, President's Office, New York NY 10027, USA
Bollinger, R Randal — Surgeon
1120 Infinity Road, Durham NC 27712, USA
Bolocco Fonck, Cecilia C — Beauty Queen, Actress
Miss Universe Organization, 1370 Ave of Americas, #1600, New York NY 10019 USA

Bologna, Joseph — Actor
S M S Talent, 8383 Wilshire Blvd, #230, Beverly Hills CA 90211 USA

Bolonchuk, Larry — Ice Hockey Player
385 Woodlawn St, Winnipeg MB R3J 2J2, Canada

Bolstorff, Douglas — Basketball Player
1553 Skyline Court, Saint Paul MN 55121, USA

Bolt, Mae — Bowler
1516 Robinhood Lane, La Grange Park IL 60526, USA

Bolt, Usain — Track Athlete
Pace Sports Mgmt, 6 Causeway, Teddington, Middx TW11 0HE, England

Boltanski, Christian — Artist, Photographer
146 Blvd Carmelina, 92240 Malakoff, France

Bolten, Michael — Actor
C E S D, 10635 Santa Monica Blvd, #130, Los Angeles CA 90025 USA

Bolton, James R — Photochemist
Calgon Carbon Corp, 130 Royal Crest Court, Markham ON L6G 1A8, Canada

Bolton, Michael — Singer, Songwriter
Works Public Relations, 11 Marshalsea Road, London SE1 1EN, England

Bolton, Ronald C (Ron) — Football Player
408 Maiden Lane, Chesapeake VA 23325, USA

Bolton, Thomas E (Tom) — Baseball Player
2288 Rolling Hills Dr, Nolensville TN 37135, USA

Bolton-Holifield, Ruthie — Basketball Player
Sacramento Monarchs, Arco Arena, 1 Sports Parkway, Sacramento CA 95834 USA

Bolyard, Bob — Basketball Player
10607 Wild Flower Place, Fort Wayne IN 46845, USA

Bomar, Mary — Government Official
National Park Service, Interior Department, PO Box 37127, Washington DC 20013, USA

Bombardie, Brad — Ice Hockey Player
8959 Baywatch Trail NW, Walker MN 56484, USA

Bomer, Matthew (Matt) — Actor
Anonymous Content, 3532 Hayden Ave, Culver City CA 90232 USA

Bon Jovi, Jon — Singer (Bon Jovi), Songwriter, Actor
Bon Jovi Mgmt, 809 Elder Circle, Austin TX 78733, USA

Bona, Richard — Bassist, Singer
International Music Network, 278 Main St, Gloucester MA 01930, USA

Bonadio, Jeffrey — Physician
Pacific Rim Pathology, 5325 Metro St, San Diego CA 92110, USA

Bonaduce, Danny — Actor, Singer
Rebel Entertainment Partners, 5700 Wilshire Blvd, #456, Los Angeles CA 90036, USA

Bonaly, Surya — Figure Skater
35 Rue Felicien David, 75016 Paris, France

Bonamassa, Joe — Guitarist, Singer, Songwriter
Premier Artists Services, 10025 Vestal Place, Coral Springs FL 33071, USA

Bonar, Dan — Ice Hockey Player
361 Mandeville St, Winnipeg MB R3J 2J2, Canada

Bond, Alan — Yachtsman, Businessman
89 Watkins Road, Dalkeith WA 6069, Australia

Bond, Edward — Writer
Casorotto Ramsay, Waverley House, 7-12 Noel St, London W1F 8GQ, England

Bond, H Julian — Civil Rights Activist
5435 41st Place NW, Washington DC 20015, USA

Bond, Phillip (Phil) — Basketball Player
208 Northwestern Parkway, Louisville KY 40212, USA

Bond, Samantha — Actress
Innovative Artists, 1505 10th St, Santa Monica CA 90401 USA

Bond, Victoria A — Conductor, Composer
Roanoke Symphony, 541 Luck Ave SW, #200, Roanoke VA 24016, USA

Bond, Walter — Basketball Player
PO Box 87, Hamel MN 55340, USA

Bondar, Roberta L — Astronaut, Canada
Space Agency, Rockcliffe Base, Ottawa ON K1A 1A1, Canada

Bondarenko, Vtaly M — Architect
Communal Institute, Kalitnikovskaya Str 30, 109807 Moscow, Russia

Bonderman, Jeremy A — Baseball Player
10 Ridgeview Dr, Pasco WA 99301, USA

Bondevik, Kjell Magne — Prime Minister, Norway
Oslo Peace & Human Rights Center, Box 2753 Solli, 0204 Oslo, Norway

Bondi, Viggo — Bassist (A-Ha)
Bandana Mgmt, 11 Elvaston Place, London SW7 5QC, England

Bondra, Peter — Ice Hockey Player
372 Carriage Park Way, Annapolis MD 21401, USA

Bonds, Barry L — Baseball Player
44 Beverly Park Circle, Beverly Hills CA 90210, USA

Bonds, Gary U S — Singer
Entity Communications, 157 Broad St, #309, Red Bank NJ 07701, USA

Bondurant, Robert (Bob) — Auto Driving Instructor
Firebird International Speedway, PO Box 51980, Phoenix AZ 85076, USA

Bone Crusher — Rap Artist
Richard De La Font Agency, 4845 S Sheridan Road, #505, Tulsa OK 74145 USA

Bone, Ken — Basketball Coach
Washington State University, Athletic Dept, Pullman WA 99164, USA

Bonebreak, Donald J (D J) — Drummer (X)
A P A Talent/Literary Agency, 405 S Beverly Dr, #300, Beverly Hills CA 90212 USA

Bonehill, Richard — Actor
Bosun's Nest, Carthew Way, Saint Ives, Cornwall TR26 1RJ, England

Bonell, Carlos A — Concert Guitarist, Composer
Bravo Music International, PO Box 19060, London N7 0ZD, England

Bonerz, Peter — Actor, Comedian, Director
Shapiro/West Assoc, 141 El Camino Dr, #205, Beverly Hills CA 90212, USA

Bones, Ricardo (Ricky) — Baseball Player
908 NW 100th Ave, Pembroke Pines FL 33024, USA

Bonet, Lisa — Actress
Untitled Entertainment, 350 S Beverly Dr, #200, Beverly Hills CA 90212 USA

Bonet, Pep — Architect
C/Pujades 62, 08005 Barcelona, Spain

Boneta, Diego — Actor, Singer
Gersh Agency, 9465 Wilshire Blvd, #600, Beverly Hills CA 90212 USA
Bonetti, Mattia — Designer, Interior Decorator, Artist
10 Rue Rocjebrune, 75011 Paris, France
Bong Joon Ho — Director, Writer
Creative Artists Agency, 2000 Ave of Stars, #100, Los Angeles CA 90067 USA
Bong Jung Keun — Baseball Player
2917 Asteria Pointe, Duluth GA 30097, USA
Bonham Carter, Helena — Actress
7 W Heath Ave, London NW11 7QS, England
Bonham, Jason — Drummer
Agency Group Ltd, 142 W 57th St, #600, New York NY 10019 USA
Bonham, Ronald D (Ron) — Basketball Player
8020 S Country Road 700E, Selma IN 47383, USA
Bonham, S Shane — Football Player
321 Clover Hill Road, Maryville TN 37801, USA
Bonham, Tracy — Singer, Musician, Songwriter
Large Public Relations, 13 Bunning Way, London N7 9UN, England
Bonhomme, Brian — Guitarist (Roman Holliday)
Youngstown State University, History Dept, Youngstown OH 44555, USA
Bonhomme, Tessa — Ice Hockey Player
Team Canada, 2424 University Dr NW, Calgary AB T2N 3Y9, Canada
Boni, T Yayi — President, Benin
President's Office, Palais Presidentiel, BP 2028, Cotonou, Benin
Boniface, Bruce — Singer, Songwriter
Virgin Records, 338 N Foothill Road, Beverly Hills CA 90210 USA
Bonilla, Henry — Representative, TX
2 Lake Shore Dr, Corpus Christi TX 78413, USA
Bonilla, Juan G — Baseball Player
2902 Orchidcrest Dr, Crestview FL 32539, USA
Bonilla, Michelle C — Actress
Imperium 7 Artists, 5455 Wilshire Blvd, #1706, Los Angeles CA 90036 USA
Bonilla, Roberto M A (Bobby) — Baseball Player
1403 Kenilworth St, Sarasota FL 34231, USA
Bonin, Gordie — Auto Racing Driver
12471 Sanford St, Los Angeles CA 90066, USA
Bonin, Marcel — Ice Hockey Player
408 Rue Precieux-Sang, Joliette QC J6E 2M5, Canada
Bonington, Christian J S — Mountaineer
Badger Hill, Hesket Newmarket, Wigton, Cumbria, CA7 8LA, England
Boniol, Christopher D (Chris) — Football Player
PO Box 271396, Flower Mound TX 75027, USA
Bonior, David E — Representative, MI
38875 Harper Ave, Clinton Township MI 48036, USA
Bonjour, Daniel — Actor
Tinoco Mgmt, 8033 Sunset Blvd, #573, West Hollywood CA 90046, USA
Bonk, Radek — Ice Hockey Player
137 Allenhurst Circle, Franklin TN 37067, USA
Bonnaire, Sandrine — Actress
Artmedia, 20 Ave Rapp, 75007 Paris, France
Bonnefous, Jean-Pierre — Ballet Dancer, Choreographer
Indiana University, Ballet Dept, Music School, Bloomington IN 47405, USA
Bonnefoy, Yves J — Writer
College de France, Poetry Study Dept, 11 Place Marcelin Berthelot, 75005 Paris, France
Bonnell, R Barry — Baseball Player
2102 179th Court NE, Redmond WA 98052, USA
Bonner, Anthony — Basketball Player
5854 Elmbank Ave, Saint Louis MO 63120, USA
Bonner, DeWanna — Basketball Player
Phoenix Mercury, American West Arena, 201 E Jefferson St, Phoenix AZ 85004 USA
Bonner, Elayna G — Human Rights Activist
A D Sajharova Museum, Zemlyanoy Val 57, Building 6, 107120 Moscow, Russia
Bonner, Matthew R (Matt) — Basketball Player
San Antonio Spurs, Alamodome, 1 AT&T Center Parkway, San Antonio TX 78219 USA
Bonner, Robert C — Attorney, Judge
Gibson Dunn Crutcher, 333 S Grand Ave, #4400, Los Angeles CA 90071, USA
Bonner, Tony — Actor
Agents Associes, 201 Rue du Faubourg Saint Honore, 75008 Paris, France
Bonness, Richard K (Rik) — Football Player
18914 Boyle Circle, Elkhorn NE 68022, USA
Bonneville, Hugh — Actor
United Talent Agency, 9336 Civic Center Dr, Beverly Hills CA 90210 USA
Bonney, Barbara — Opera Singer
Universitat Mozarteum Salzburg, Mirabellplatz 1, 5020 Salzburg, Austria
Bono — Singer, Songwriter (U-2)
Regine Moylett, 9 Ivebury Court, 325 Latimer Rd, London W10 6RA, England
Bono, Chaz — Entertainer
Haber Entertainment, 434 S Canon Dr, #204, Beverly Hills CA 90212, USA
Bono, Steven C (Steve) — Football Player
1100 Hamilton Ave, Palo Alto CA 94301, USA
Bonoff, Karla — Singer, Pianist, Songwriter
2122 E Valley Road, Santa Barbara CA 93108, USA
Bonsall, Joseph S (Joe), Jr — Singer (Oak Ridge Boys)
88 New Shackle Island Road, Hendersonville TN 37075, USA
Bonser, John P (Boof) — Baseball Player
12060 Lucca St, #202, Fort Myers FL 33966, USA
Bonsey, Don — Photographer
257 Canyon Acres, Laguna Beach CA 92651, USA
Bonsignore, Jason — Ice Hockey Player
2152 Edgemere Dr, Rochester NY 14612, USA
Bontemps, Ronald (Ron) — Basketball Player
133 S Illinois Ave, Morton IL 61550, USA
Bonvie, Dennis — Ice Hockey Player
670 N River St, #210, Wilkes Barre PA 18705, USA
Bonvoisin, Berangere — Actress
Voyez Mon Agent, 20 Ave Rapp, 75007 Paris, France

Bonvoisin, Bernie — Actor
U B B A, 6 Rue de Braque, 75003 Paris, France
Bonynge, Richard A — Conductor
Chalet Monet, Route de Sonloup, 1833 Les Avants, Switzerland
Boo, Katherine — Journalist
Washington Post, Editorial Dept, 1150 15th St NW, Washington DC 20071 USA
Book, Asher M — Actor
Paradigm Agency, 360 N Crescent Dr, North Building, Beverly Hills CA 90210 USA
Booker, Gregory S (Greg) — Baseball Player
1535 Charleigh Court, Elon College NC 27244, USA
Booker, Marty M — Football Player
15982 SW 11th St, Pembroke Pines FL 33027, USA
Booker, Vaughn J — Football Player
11 Page St, Hurst TX 76053, USA
Bookwalter, J R — Director
PO Box 6573, Akron OH 44312, USA
Boomer, Linwood — Actor, Producer, Writer
Greenberg Taurig, 1840 Century Park E, #1900, Los Angeles CA 90067 USA
Boomer, Walter E — Marine Corps General
4 Pinckney Landing Dr, Sheldon SC 29941, USA
Boon, Dany — Actor
W M E Entertainment, 9601 Wilshire Blvd, #300, Beverly Hills CA 90210 USA
Boon, David C — Cricketer
Durham Cricket Club, Chester-le-Street, County Durham DH3 3QR, England
Boone, Aaron J — Baseball Player
10111 E Phantom Way, Scottsdale AZ 85255, USA
Boone, Alfonso — Football Player
14290 W Lyle Court, Libertyville IL 60048, USA
Boone, Brendon — Actor
9157 W Sunset Blvd, #206, West Hollywood CA 90069, USA
Boone, Bret R — Baseball Player
6383 Calle Ponte Bella, Rancho Santa Fe CA 92091, USA
Boone, Daneen — Actress
Sherrida Personal Mgmt, 110 Scollard St, Toronto ON M5R 1G2, Canada
Boone, Debby — Singer, Actress
I C M Talent, 825 Eighth Ave, New York NY 10019, USA
Boone, Pat — Actor, Singer
904 N Beverly Dr, Beverly Hills CA 90210, USA
Boone, Robert R (Bob) — Baseball Player, Manager
1432 Misty Sea Way, San Marcos CA 92078, USA
Boone, Ronald B (Ron) — Basketball Player
3877 Pheasant Ridge Road, Salt Lake City UT 84109, USA
Boone, Steve — Bassist, Singer (Lovin' Spoonful)
Lustig Talent, PO Box 770850, Orlando FL 32877 USA
Boorem, Mika — Actor
Untitled Entertainment, 350 S Beverly Dr, #200, Beverly Hills CA 90212 USA
Boorman, John — Director
Merlin Films, 16 Upper Pembroke St, Dublin 2, Ireland
Booros, James — Golfer
2615 W Pennsylvania St, Allentown PA 18104, USA
Boosler, Elayne — Actress, Comedienne, Writer
Levity Entertainment, 6701 Center Drive W, #1111, Los Angeles CA 90045, USA
Bootcheck, Christopher B (Chris) — Baseball Player
1204 Suncast Lane, #2, El Dorado Hills CA 95762, USA
Booth, Calvin L — Basketball Player
6001 E Horseshoe Road, Paradise Valley AZ 85253, USA
Booth, Connie — Actress
Lip Service Casting, 60-66 Wardour St, London W1F 0TA, England
Booth, Douglas — Actor
United Talent Agency, 9336 Civic Center Dr, Beverly Hills CA 90210 USA
Booth, Emma — Actress
Robyn Gardiner Mgmt, PO Box 128, Surry Hills NSW 2010, Australia
Booth, George — Cartoonist
PO Box 1539, Stony Brook NY 11790, USA
Booth, Kellee — Golfer
4804 Goldeneyes Lane, McKinney TX 75070, USA
Booth, Kristin — Actress
Edna Talent, 318 Dundas St W, Toronto ON M5T 1G5, Canada
Booth, Lindy — Actress
Innovative Artists, 1505 10th St, Santa Monica CA 90401 USA
Booth, Melanie L — Soccer Player
Canadian Soccer, Place Soccer Canada, 237 Metcalfe St, Ottawa ON K2P 1R2, Canada
Booth, Michael — Interior Designer
Babey Mountol Jue & Booth, 510 3rd St, #110, San Francisco CA 94107, USA
Boothe, Kevin — Football Player
12100 NW 18th St, Plantation FL 33313, USA
Boothe, Powers — Actor
23629 Long Valley Road, Hidden Hills CA 91302, USA
Booty, John F — Football Player
16401 Governor Bridge Road, #407, Bowie MD 20716, USA
Booty, Joshua G (Josh) — Football, Baseball Player
6248 N Windermere Dr, Shreveport LA 71129, USA
Boozer, Carlos A, Jr — Basketball Player
4550 S 700 E, Salt Lake City UT 84107, USA
Boozer, Emerson — Football Player
25 Windham Dr, Huntington Station NY 11746, USA
Borbon, Pedro F, Jr — Baseball Player
60 Enoch Crosby Road, Brewster NY 10509, USA
Borcherds, Richard E — Mathematician
University of California, Mathematics Dept, Berkeley CA 94720, USA
Borcherdt, Brian — Singer, Songwriter
Agency Group Ltd, 142 W 57th St, #600, New York NY 10019 USA
Bordeleau, Jean-Pierre (J P) — Ice Hockey Player
94 Lakemist Court, Dartmouth NS B3A 4Z1, Canada
Bordelon, Kenneth P (Ken) — Football Player
1224 Octavia St, New Orleans LA 70115, USA

Borden, Amanda — Gymnast
Cincinnati Gymnastics Academy, 3536 Woodridge Blvd, Fairfield OH 45014, USA
Borden, Robert — Producer, Writer
United Talent Agency, 9336 Civic Center Dr, Beverly Hills CA 90210 USA
Border, Allan R — Cricketer
Cricket Board, 90 Jolimont St, Jolimont VIC 3002, Australia
Borders, Patrick L (Pat) — Baseball Player
1135 S Lakeshore Blvd, Lake Wales FL 33853, USA
Bordi, Richard A (Rich) — Baseball Player
1133 Hailey Court, Rohnert Park CA 94928, USA
Bordick, Michael T (Mike) — Baseball Player
1302 Locust Ave, Towson MD 21204, USA
Boreanaz, David — Actor
Creative Artists Agency, 2000 Ave of Stars, #100, Los Angeles CA 90067 USA
Boren, David L — Educator; Governor, Senator, OK
University of Oklahoma, President's Office, 660 Parrington, Norman OK 73019, USA
Borg, Bjorn R — Tennis Player
Gotgatan 78, #28TR, 118 30 Stockholm, Sweden
Borg, Marcus J — Theologian
Oregon State University, School of Religion, Corvallis OR 97331, USA
Borges, Jacobo — Artist
Museo Jacobo Borges, Catia, Caracas, Venezuela
Borghi, Frank — Soccer Player
4123 Poepping St, Saint Louis MO 63123, USA
Borgman, James M (Jim) — Editorial Cartoonist
Cincinnati Enquirer, Editorial Dept, 617 Vine St, #500, Cincinnati OH 45202, USA
Boris, Robert (Bob) — Director, Writer
Marshak/Zachary Co, 8840 Wilshire Blvd, #100, Beverly Hills CA 90211 USA
Borisenko, Andrey I — Cosmonaut Engineer
Cosmonaut Training Center, Star City, 141160 Zvezdny Gorodok, Moscow Oblast, Russia
Boriso-Glebsky, Nikita — Concert Violinist
I M G Artists, The Light Box, 111 Power Road, London W4 5PY , England
Bork, Erik — Producer, Writer
Creative Artists Agency, 2000 Ave of Stars, #100, Los Angeles CA 90067 USA
Bork, Robert H — Government Official, Judge
6520 Ridge St, McLean VA 22101, USA
Borkar, Nitin — Computer Engineer
Intel Corp, 5200 NE Elam Young Parkway, Hillsboro OR 97124, USA
Borkh, Inge — Opera Singer
Florentinerstr 20, #2018, D 7000 Stuttgart 75, Germany
Borkowski, Robert V (Bob) — Baseball Player
1031 Gerhard St, Dayton OH 45404, USA
Borland, Toby S — Baseball Player
8642 Quitman Highway, Quitman LA 71268, USA
Borland, Wesley L (Wes) — Guitarist (Limp Bizkit), Songwriter
Flip/Interscope Records, 8733 Sunset Blvd, #205, West Hollywood CA 90069, USA
Borle, Christian — Actor
Management 360, 9111 Wilshire Blvd, Beverly Hills CA 90210 USA
Borman, Frank F, II — Astronaut, Businessman
PO Box 64, Bighorn MT 59010, USA
Born, Ruth — Baseball Player
4205 Meridian Woods Dr, Valpariso IN 46385, USA
Bornedal, Ole — Director, Writer
Principal Entertainment, 1964 Westwood Blvd, #400, Los Angeles CA 90025 USA
Borodina, Olga V — Opera Singer
Mariinsky Theater, Theater Square, 1 Pl Iskusstr, 190000 Saint Petersburg, Russia
Borofsky, Jonathan (Jon) — Artist
11301 W Olympic Blvd, #514, Los Angeles CA 90064, USA
Boros, Guy D — Golfer
2900 NE 40th St, Fort Lauderdale FL 33308, USA
Boross, Csilla — Opera Singer
I M G Artists, Hogarth Business Park, Chiswick, London W4 2TH, England
Boross, Peter — Prime Minister, Hungary
Kossouth Lajos Ter 1-3, 1055 Budapest, Hungary
Borowiak, Tony — Singer (All-4-One)
Universal Attractions, 135 W 26th St, #1200, New York NY 10001 USA
Borowitz, Anthony (Andy) — Writer
Creative Artists Agency, 2000 Ave of Stars, #100, Los Angeles CA 90067 USA
Borrego, Jesse — Actor
PO Box 1386, Pacifica CA 94044, USA
Borrell, Jonathan E (Johnny) — Singer, Guitarist (Razorlight)
Agency Group Ltd, 361-373 City Road, London EC1V 2QA, England
Borroff, Marie E — Writer
88 Notch Hill Road, #101, North Branford CT 6471, USA
Borsato, Luciano — Ice Hockey Player
200-4 Tortoise Crescent, Brampton ON L6P 0A1, Canada
Borschevsky, Nikolai — Ice Hockey Player
3 Geranium Court, Richmond Hill ON L4C 7M7, Canada
Borstein, Alex — Actress, Comedienne
W M E Entertainment, 1325 Ave of Americas, New York NY 10019 USA
Bortz, Mark S — Football Player
PO Box 3504, Quincy IL 62305, USA
Boruch, Robert F — Statistician
University of Pennsylvania, Wharton Business School, Philadelphia PA 19104, USA
Boryla, Vincent J (Vince) — Basketball Player, Executive
5577 S Emporia Circle, Greenwood Village CO 80111, USA
Borzov, Valeri F — Track Athlete
National Olympic Committee, Esplanadnaya 42, 252023 Kiev, Ukraine
Boschini, Victor J, Jr — Educator
Texas Christian University, Chancellor's Office, 2800 S University Dr, Fort Worth TX 76129, USA
Boschman, Laurie — Ice Hockey Player
27 Delamere Dr, Stittsville ON K2S 1G7, Canada
Bosco, Philip — Actor
Don Buchwald/Fortitude, 10 E 44th St, New York NY 10017 USA
Bose, Amar G — Inventor (Audio Waveguide)
Bose Corp, The Mountain, Framington MA 01701, USA

Bose, Bimal K — Electrical Engineer
215 Ski Mountain Road, Gatlinburg TN 37738, USA
Bose, Eleanora — Model
I M G Models, 304 Park Ave S, #PH-North, New York NY 10010 USA
Bose, Lucia — Actress
Anne Alvares Correa, 34 Rue Jouffroy d'Abbans, 75017 Paris, France
Bose, Miguel — Singer, Songwriter, Actor
R L M Producciones, Puerto Santa Maria 65, 28043 Madrid, Spain
Boselli, D Anthony (Tony), Jr — Football Player
12400 W Highway 71, #350-170, Bee Cave TX 78738, USA
Boseman, Chadwick — Actor
Greene Assoc, 1901 Ave of Stars, #130, Los Angeles CA 90067 USA
Bosetti, Richard A (Rick) — Baseball Player
1471 Arroyo Manor Dr, Redding CA 96003, USA
Bosh, Christopher W (Chris) — Basketball Player
20 W Kinzie St, #1000, Chicago IL 60654, USA
Bosio, Christopher L (Chris) — Baseball Player
417 Hidden Ridges Way, Combined Locks WI 54113, USA
Boskie, Shawn K — Baseball Player
10220 N 55th St, Paradise Valley AZ 85253, USA
Boskin, Michael J — Government Official, Economist
Stanford University, Hoover Institution, Stanford CA 94305, USA
Bosley, Thaddis (Thad), Jr — Baseball Player
19440 Amhurst Court, Cerritos CA 90703, USA
Bosman, Richard A (Dick) — Baseball Player
3511 Landmark Trail, Palm Harbor FL 34684, USA
Bosnak, Karyn — Writer
Harper Collins Publishers, 10 E 53rd St, Cellar 1, New York NY 10022 USA
Boso, Casper N (Cap) — Football Player
8811 Calumet Dr, Indianapolis IN 46236, USA
Bossard, Andre — Law Enforcement Official
228 Rue de la Convention, 75015 Paris, France
Bosson, Barbara — Actress
C E S D, 10635 Santa Monica Blvd, #130, Los Angeles CA 90025 USA
Bossy, Michael (Mike) — Ice Hockey Player
136 Place Ducharme, Rosemere QC J7A 4H8, Canada
Bostelle, Tom — Artist, Sculptor
Aeolian Palace Gallery, 267 Spring Run Lane, Downingtown PA 19335, USA
Bostic, Jeffrey L (Jeff) — Football Player
8250 Royal Saint Georges Lane, Duluth GA 30097, USA
Bostic, Joe E, Jr — Football Player
3507 Bromley Wood Lane, Greensboro NC 27410, USA
Bostick, Devon — Actor
Noble Caplan Abrams, 1260 Yonge St, #200, Toronto ON M4T 1W6, Canada
Bostock, Roy J — Businessman
Yahoo Inc, 701 1st Ave, Sunnyvale CA 94089, USA
Boston, Daryl L — Baseball Player
1016 Valley Lane, Cincinnati OH 45229, USA
Boston, David — Football Player
18502 Skippers Helm, Humble TX 77346, USA
Boston, Rachel — Actress
Gersh Agency, 9465 Wilshire Blvd, #600, Beverly Hills CA 90212 USA
Boston, Ralph H — Track Athlete
3301 Woodbine Ave, Knoxville TN 37914, USA
Bostridge, Ian — Opera Singer
Opus 3 Artists, 470 Park Ave S, #900N, New York NY 10016 USA
Bostwick, Barry — Actor
Vanguard Management Group, 8060 Melrose Ave, #400, Los Angeles CA 90046, USA
Boswell, Barbie — Model
2235 Arrowgrass Dr, #103, Wesley Chapel FL 33544, USA
Boswell, Bobby — Soccer Player
Houston Dynamo, 1415 Louisiana, #3400, Houston TX 77002 USA
Boswell, Kenneth G (Ken) — Baseball Player
1103 Live Oak Dr, Marble Falls TX 78654, USA
Boswell, Thomas M — Sportswriter
Washington Post, Sports Dept, 1150 15th St NW, Washington DC 20071, USA
Boswell, Tommy G (Tom) — Basketball Player
341 N Anton Dr, Montgomery AL 36105, USA
Bosworth, Brian — Football Player, Actor
4400 Arlen Court, Plano TX 75093, USA
Bosworth, Kate — Actress, Model
Creative Artists Agency, 2000 Ave of Stars, #100, Los Angeles CA 90067 USA
Bosworth, Libby — Singer, Songwriter
3011 Fort Worth Trail, Austin TX 78748, USA
Boteach, Shmuley — Religious Leader, Rabbi, Writer
Shalom in the Home, 7700 Wisconsin Ave, Bethesda MD 20814, USA
Botehho, Joao — Director
Assicuacai de Realizadores, Rua de Palmeira 7, R/C, 1200 Lisbon, Portugal
Botelho, Luciano — Opera Singer
I M G Artists, Hogarth Business Park, Chiswick, London W4 2TH, England
Botero, Fernando — Artist
Nohra Haime Gallery, 41 E 57th St, #600, New York NY 10022, USA
Botha, Francois (Frans) — Boxer
White Buffalo, PO Box 3982, Clearwater FL 33767, USA
Botha, Roelof F — Government Official, South Africa
PO Box 16176, Pretoria North 0116, South Africa
Botham, Ian T — Cricketer, Sportscaster
Mission Logistics, 158 Hurlington Road, Fulham, London SE6 3NGF, England
Bothmer, Bernard V — Museum Official, Egyptologist
Brooklyn Museum, 188 Eastern Parkway, Brooklyn NY 11238, USA
Bothwell, Tim — Ice Hockey Player, Coach
14 Billings Court, Burlington VT 05408, USA
Botone, Talia — Actress
C E S D, 10635 Santa Monica Blvd, #130, Los Angeles CA 90025 USA
Botsford, Beth — Swimmer
2210 River Bend Court, White Hall MD 21161, USA

Botsford, Sara — Actress
Kordek Agency, 8490 W Sunset Blvd, #403, West Hollywood CA 90069, USA
Botstein, David — Geneticist
Lewis-Sigler Institute, Princeton University Medical Center, Princeton NJ 08544, USA
Botstein, Leon — Educator
Bard College, President's Office, Annandale on Hudson NY 12504, USA
Botstein, Leon — Conductor
Columbia Artists Mgmt Inc, 1790 Broadway, #702, New York NY 10019 USA
Botta, Mario — Architect
Via Ciani 16, 6904 Lugano, Switzerland
Bottalico, Richard P (Ricky) — Baseball Player
10 Rocamora Road, Rocky Hill CT 06067, USA
Bottenfield, Kent D — Baseball Player
12168 142nd Court N, West Palm Beach FL 33418, USA
Botterill, Jason — Ice Hockey Player
Pittsburgh Penguins, Consol Energy Center, 1001 5th Ave, Pittsburgh PA 15219 USA
Botti, Chris — Trumpeter
Right Side Mgmt, 1624 Broadway, #4C, New York NY 10019, USA
Bottin, Rob — Director
Gersh Agency, 9465 Wilshire Blvd, #600, Beverly Hills CA 90212 USA
Botto, Juan Diego — Actor
Torres & Prieto, Calle Princesa 3, 28008 Madrid, Spain
Bottom, Joe — Swimmer
374 Spanish Garden Dr, Chico CA 95928, USA
Bottoms, Joseph — Actor
Bottoms Art Galleries, 1260 Channel Dr, Santa Barbara CA 93108, USA
Bottoms, Timothy — Actor
PO Box 15559, San Luis Obispo CA 93406, USA
Bottum, Roddy — Keyboardist (Faith No More)
Creative Artists Agency, 2000 Ave of Stars, #100, Los Angeles CA 90067 USA
Bouasone Bouphavanh — Prime Minister, Laos
Premier's Office, National Assembly, Vientiane Capital, Vientiane, Laos
Boublil, Alain A — Lyricist
Cameron Mackintosh Ltd, 1 Bedford Square, London WC1B 3RA, England
Boucha, Henry C — Ice Hockey Player
7200 Biglerville Circle, Anchorage AK 99507, USA
Bouchard, Daniel (Dan) — Ice Hockey Player
3111 Hillsdale Court SE, Marietta GA 30067, USA
Bouchard, Lucien — Government Official, Canada
Parti Quebecois, 1200 Ave Papineau, Montreal QC H2K 4R5, Canada
Bouchard, Pierre — Ice Hockey Player
1216-1705 Ave Victoria, Saint-Lambert QC, J4R 2T7, Canada
Bouchard, Ron — Auto Racing Driver
300 Lunenburg St, Fitchburg MA 01420, USA
Bouchareb, Rachid — Director, Writer
Casorotto Ramsay, Waverley House, 7-12 Noel St, London W1F 8GQ, England
Bouchaud, Jean — Actor
Artmedia, 20 Ave Rapp, 75007 Paris, France
Bouchee, Edward F (Ed) — Baseball Player
1621 E Tremaine Ave, Gilbert AZ 85234, USA
Boucher, Brian — Ice Hockey Player
30 Center St, Haddonfield NJ 8033, USA
Boucher, Candice — Model
Outlaws Models, 11 Wessels Road, Greenpoint 8011 Capetown, South Africa
Boucher, Gaetan — Speed Skater
Center Sportif, 3850 Edgar, Saint Hubert QC J4T 368, Canada
Boucher, Lawrence — Businessman
Adaptec Inc, 691 S Milpitas Blvd, Milpitas CA 95035, USA
Boucher, Philippe — Ice Hockey Player
Dallas Stars, 2601 Ave of Stars, #100, Frisco TX 75034 USA
Bouchez, Elodie — Actress
Evolution Entertainment, 901 N Highland Ave, Los Angeles CA 90038 USA
Bouchitey, Patrick — Actor
Voyez Mon Agent, 20 Ave Rapp, 75007 Paris, France
Boudart, Michel — Chemical Engineer
9636 El Venado Dr, Whittier CA 90603, USA
Boudia, David A — Diver
Premier Management Group, 1100 Crescent Green, #104, Cary, NC 27518 USA
Boudin, Michael — Judge
US Court of Appeals, 1 Courthouse Way, Boston MA 02210, USA
Boudreau, Bruce — Ice Hockey Player, Coach
PO Box 59727, Potomac MD 20859, USA
Boudrias, Andre — Ice Hockey Player
1008-4300 Place des Cageux, Laval QC H7W 4Z3, Canada
Boudrias, Christine-Isabel — Speed Skater
Speed Skating Canada, 2781 Lancaster Road, #402, Ottawa ON K1B 1A7, Canada
Boughner, Robert (Bob) — Ice Hockey Player
5541 La Puerta del Sol Blvd S, #414, Saint Petersburg FL 33715, USA
Bouillon, Jean-Christophe — Auto Racing Driver
Wildbacher 9, 8340 Hinwil, Switzerland
Bouix, Evelyne — Actress
Artmedia, 20 Ave Rapp, 75007 Paris, France
Boujenah, Michel — Actor
Voyez Mon Agent, 20 Ave Rapp, 75007 Paris, France
Boulanger, Veronique — Actress
Artmedia, 20 Ave Rapp, 75007 Paris, France
Boulerice, Jesse — Ice Hockey Player
152 McClellan Ave, West Berlin NJ 08091, USA
Boulez, Pierre — Conductor, Composer
Postfach 100022, 76481 Baden-Baden, Germany
Boulmetis, Samuel A (Sam), Sr — Thoroughbred Racing Jockey
711 Academy Road, Cantonsville MD 21228, USA
Boulos, Frenchy — Soccer Player
20 Elvin St, Staten Island NY 10314, USA
Boulton, Eric — Ice Hockey Player
37 Independence Trail, Totowa NJ 7512, USA

Boulud, David — Chef
Daniel Restaurant, 60 E 65th St, New York NY 10065, USA

Boulware, Peter — Football Player
3791 E Millers Bridge Road, Tallahassee FL 32312, USA

Bouman, Todd — Football Player
2080 140th Ave, Holland MN 56139, USA

Bouquet, Carole — Actress, Model
Agence Interlatent, 5 Rue Clement Marot, 75008 Paris, France

Bourboulon, Jacques — Photographer
24 Rue Rennequin, 75017 Paris, France

Bource, Ludovic — Film Composer
B M I, 8730 W Sunset Blvd, #300, Los Angeles CA 90069 USA

Bourdain, Anthony — Restauranteur, Chef, Writer
Brasserie Les Halles Park Avenue, 411 Park Ave S, New York NY 10016, USA

Bourdais, Sebastian — Auto Racing Driver
Newman-Haas Racing, 500 Tower Parkway, Lincolnshire IL 60069, USA

Bourdeaux, Michael — Templeton Religion Laureate
Keston College, Heathfield Road, Keston, Kent BR2 6BA, England

Bourdette, Christine — Sculptor, Artist
Elizabeth Leach Gallery, 417 NW 9th Ave, Portland OR 97209, USA

Bourdon, Rob — Drummer (Linkin Park)
The Firm, 2049 Century Park E, #2550, Los Angeles CA 90067 USA

Bourgeois, Benjamin C (Ben) — Surfer
Pro Surfing Mgmt, 320 High Tide Dr, #101, Saint Augustine FL 32080 USA

Bourgeois, Charles (Charlie) — Ice Hockey Player
PO Box 1481, Station Main, Moncton NB E1C 8T6, Canada

Bourgeois, Derek D — Composer
Portland House, Burton Road, Wool, Dorset BH20 6EY, England

Bourgoin, Louise — Actress
W M E Entertainment, 9601 Wilshire Blvd, #300, Beverly Hills CA 90210 USA

Bourn, Michael R — Baseball Player
24604 Belvon Valley Lane, Mulberry FL 33860, USA

Bourne, Bob — Ice Hockey Player
Bob Bourne Realty, 1-1890 Cooper Road, Kelowna BC V1Y 8B7, Canada

Bourne, Shae-Lynn — Figure Skater
Connecticut Skating Center, 300 Alumni Road, Newington CT 06111, USA

Bournigal, Rafael A — Baseball Player
230 Canterwood Lane, Mulberry FL 33860, USA

Bournissen, Chantal — Alpine Skier
1983 Evolene, Switzerland

Bourque, Phil — Ice Hockey Player
5117 Yale Dr, Aliquippa PA 15001, USA

Bourque, Pierre — Horticulturist; Mayor, Montreal
Hotel de Ville, 275 Rue Notre Dame E, Montreal QC H2Y 1C6, Canada

Bourque, Raymond J (Ray) — Ice Hockey Player
Tresca Restaurant, 233 Hanover St, Boston MA 02113, USA

Bourque, Rene G W — Ice Hockey Player
9110 93rd Ave, Lac La Biche AB T0A 2C0, Canada

Bourret, Caprice — Model, Actress
PO Box 509, Walton-on-Thames KT12 5XJ, England

Boushka, Richard (Dick) — Basketball Player
5414 W 145th St, Overland Park KS 66224, USA

Bousman, Darren Lynn — Director
Verve Talent, 9696 Culver Blvd, #301, Culver City CA 90232, USA

Bouteflika, Abdul Aziz — President, Algeria
138 Chemin Bachir Brahimi, El Biar, Algiers, Algeria

Boutette, Pat — Ice Hockey Player
Doctors House Restaurant, 21 Nashville Road, Kleinburg ON L0J 1C0, Canada

Boutilier, Paul — Ice Hockey Player
35 Elgin Lane, Bedford NS B4A 2K2, Canada

Bouton, Daniel — Financier
Societe Generale, 29 Blvd Hausman, 75009 Paris, France

Bouton, James A (Jim) — Baseball Player, Writer
PO Box 188, North Edgemont MA 01252, USA

Boutros-Ghali, Boutros — Secretary-General, United Nations
2 Ave Epnipgiza, Cairo, Egypt

Bouvet, Didier — Alpine Skier
Bouvet-Sports, 74360 Abondance, France

Bouvia, Gloria — Bowler
2072 NE Hogan Dr, Gresham OR 97030, USA

Bouvier, Jean-Pierre — Actor
Artmedia, 20 Ave Rapp, 75007 Paris, France

Bouwmeester, Jay — Ice Hockey Player
7824 NW 123rd Ave, Parkland FL 33076, USA

Bouza, Matthew K (Matt) — Football Player
1042 Via Nueva, Lafayette CA 94549, USA

Bova, Raoul — Actor
Cristiano Cucchini Mgmt, Lungoterre dei Mellini 10, 00193 Rome, Italy

Bow Wow — Rap Artist, Actor
United Talent Agency, 9336 Civic Center Dr, Beverly Hills CA 90210 USA

Bowa, Lawrence R (Larry) — Baseball Player, Manager
129 Upper Gulph Road, Radnor PA 19087, USA

Bowden, Craig — Golfer
4651 S Amber Dr, Bloomington IN 47401, USA

Bowden, Katrina — Actress
Management 360, 9111 Wilshire Blvd, Beverly Hills CA 90210 USA

Bowden, Mark — Writer
I C M Partners, 10250 Constellation Blvd, #900, Los Angeles CA 90067 USA

Bowden, Robert (Bobby) — Football Coach
2813 Shamrock St N, Tallahassee FL 32309, USA

Bowden, Terry — Football Coach, Sportscaster
University of North Alabama, Athletic Dept, Florence AL 35632, USA

Bowe, David — Actor
Karg/Weissenbach, 329 N Wetherly Dr, #101, Beverly Hills CA 90211 USA

Bowe, Riddick L — Boxer
714 Ahmer Dr, Fort Washington MD 20744, USA

Bowe, Rosemarie — Actress
321 Saint Pierre Road, Los Angeles CA 90077, USA

Bowen, Andrea — Actress
Domain Talent, 9229 W Sunset Blvd, #710, West Hollywood CA 90069 USA

Bowen, Andrew — Actor
Principato-Young, 9465 Wilshire Blvd, #880, Beverly Hills CA 90212 USA

Bowen, Anne — Fashion Designer
589 8th Ave, #200, New York NY 10018, USA

Bowen, Bruce — Basketball Player
1810 Settler Court, San Antonio TX 78258, USA

Bowen, Cameron — Actor
Stone Manners Salners, 9911 W Pico Blvd, #1400, Los Angeles CA 90035 USA

Bowen, Jason — Ice Hockey Player
4900 W 14th Ave, Kennewick WA 99338, USA

Bowen, Julie — Actress, Model
Liberman/Zerman Mgmt, 252 N Larchmont Blvd, #200, Los Angeles CA 90004, USA

Bowen, Michael — Actor
Martin Berneman Mgmt, 5820 Wilshire Blvd, #200, Los Angeles CA 90036 USA

Bowen, Nanci — Golfer
201 Carolina Point Parkway, #1119, Greenville SC 29607, USA

Bowen, Otis R — Secretary, Health & Human Services
2791 2B Road, Bremen IN 46506, USA

Bowen, Robert M (Rob) — Baseball Player
56 Spring Dr, Ellijay GA 30536, USA

Bowen, Ryan E — Baseball Player
2806 Maryland Ave, Fort Worth TX 76162, USA

Bowen, Stephen G — Astronaut
N A S A, Johnson Space Center, 2101 NASA Road, Houston TX 77058 USA

Bowen, Wade — Singer
W M E Entertainment, 1600 Division St, #300, Nashville TN 37203 USA

Bowen, William G — Foundation Executive, Educator
Andrew Mellon Foundation, 140 E 62nd St, New York NY 10065, USA

Bowens, David W — Football Player
15140 SW 16th St, Weston FL 33326, USA

Bowens, Malick — Actor
Don Buchwald/Fortitude, 6500 Wilshire Blvd, #2200, Los Angeles CA 90048 USA

Bowens, Timothy L (Tim) — Football Player
PO Box 93, Okolona MS 38860, USA

Bower, Antoinette — Actress
1529 N Beverly Glen Blvd, Los Angeles CA 90077, USA

Bower, Gary E — Bowler
256 Green Lane Dr, Camp Hill PA 17011, USA

Bower, Gordon H — Psychologist
Stanford University, Psychology Dept, Stanford CA 94305, USA

Bower, Jamie Campbell — Actor
Dalzell & Beresford, 26 Astwood Mews, London SW7 4DE, England

Bower, Jeff — Basketball Coach
New Orleans Hornets, 1250 Poydras St, #101, New Orleans LA 70113 USA

Bower, John W (Johnny) — Ice Hockey Player
Bower Enterprises, 3937 Parkgate Dr, Mississauga ON L5N 7B4, Canada

Bower, Robert W — Inventor (Semiconductor Insulated Gate)
University of California, Microelectronics Dept, Davis CA 95616, USA

Bower, Tom — Actor
United Talent Agency, 9336 Civic Center Dr, Beverly Hills CA 90210 USA

Bowering, Jodie — Softball Player
Boondall, Redcliffe QLD 4020, Australia

Bowers, Bryan — Singer, Autoharp Player
Scott O'Malley Assoc, PO Box 9188, Colorado Springs CO 80932, USA

Bowers, Chris — Actor
Gersh Agency, 9465 Wilshire Blvd, #600, Beverly Hills CA 90212 USA

Bowers, Dane — Singer, Songwriter
79 Byrbe Blood, Mill House, Millers Way, London W6 7NH, England

Bowers, David — Director
Independent Talent Group, Oxford House, 76 Oxford St, London W1D 1BS, England

Bowers, Glenn — WW II Marine Air Corps Hero
225 Mountain Road, Dillsburg PA 17019, USA

Bowers, Mary Helen — Ballerina
Rubenstein Public Relations, 1345 Ave of Americas, #30, New York NY 10105, USA

Bowers-Broadbent, Christopher J — Concert Organist, Composer
94 Colney Hatch, Muswell Hill, London N10 1EA, England

Bowersox, Crystal L — Singer, Songwriter
Orrigami Entertainment, 604 Santa Monica Blvd, Santa Monica CA 90401, USA

Bowersox, Kenneth D — Astronaut
16907 Soaring Forest Dr, Houston TX 77059, USA

Bowes, Bill — Financier
US Venture Partners, 2735 San Hill Road, Menlo Park CA 94025, USA

Bowie, David — Singer, Actor
Outside, 180-182 Tottenham Court Road, London W1P 9LE, England

Bowie, Heather — Golfer
3017 Elm River Dr, Fort Worth TX 76116, USA

Bowie, Larry G — Football Player
739 Echo Shores Court, Saint Paul MN 55115, USA

Bowie, Micah A — Baseball Player
2039 Small Town Dr, New Braunfels TX 78130, USA

Bowie, Samuel P (Sam) — Basketball Player
901 The Curtilage, Lexington KY 40502, USA

Bowker, Judi — Actress
Howes & Prior, 66 Berkeley House, Hay Hill, London W1X 7LH, England

Bowlby, April — Model, Actress
W M E Entertainment, 9601 Wilshire Blvd, #300, Beverly Hills CA 90210 USA

Bowler, Grant — Actor
Don Buchwald/Fortitude, 6500 Wilshire Blvd, #2200, Los Angeles CA 90048 USA

Bowles, Erskine B — Government Official
Forstman Little Co, 767 5th Ave, #4500, New York NY 10153, USA

Bowles, Lauren — Actress
Main Title Entertainment, 8383 Wilshire Blvd, #408, Beverly Hills CA 90211, USA

Bowlin, Michael R
Atlantic Richfield Co, 333 S Hope St, Los Angeles CA 90071, USA — Businessman

Bowling, Orbie L
10179 Frank Road, Collierville TN 38017, USA — Basketball Player

Bowman, Elizabeth
82 Davidson St, Chula Vista CA 91910, USA — Golfer

Bowman, Harry W
Outboard Marine, 1325 Remington Road, #H, Schaumburg IL 60173, USA — Businessman

Bowman, James E (Jim)
12 Stony Field Road, Norton MA 02766, USA — Football Player

Bowman, Kenneth B (Ken)
13664 N Placita Montansas de Oro, Tucson AZ 85755, USA — Football Player

Bowman, Kirk
740 Pointe Pelee Dr, RR 1, Leamington ON N8H 3V4, Canada — Ice Hockey Player

Bowman, Pasco M, II
US Court of Appeals, US Courthouse, 811 Grand Ave, Kansas City MO 64106, USA — Judge

Bowman, Rob
W M E Entertainment, 9601 Wilshire Blvd, #300, Beverly Hills CA 90210 USA — Director, Producer

Bowman, Simon
Associated International Mgmt, Fairfax House, Fulwood Place, London WC1V 6HU, England — Actor

Bowman, W Scott (Scotty)
56 Halston Parkway, East Amherst NY 14051, USA — Ice Hockey Coach, Executive

Bown, Jane H
Old Mill House, 50 Broad St, Alresford, Hants SO24 9AN, England — Photographer

Bown, R Charles (Chuck), Jr
Stock Car Racing Career Development, 5082 Old NC Highway 49, Asheboro NC 27203, USA — Auto Racing Driver

Bowness, Richard G (Rick)
10 Shadowstone Lane, Lawrence Township NJ 08648, USA — Ice Hockey Player, Coach

Bowsfield, Edward O (Ted)
980 Briar Rose Lane, Nipomo CA 93444, USA — Baseball Player

Bowyer, C Stuart
34 Seascape Dr, Muir Beach CA 94965, USA — Astronaut, Astronomer

Bowyer, Clint
Clint Bowyer Enterprises, 6221 Ramada Dr, Clemmons NC 27012, USA — Auto, Truck Racing Driver

Bowyer, William
12 Cleveland Ave, Chiswick, London W4 1SN, England — Artist

Box, C J
Penguin Books, 375 Hudson St, Basement 1, New York NY 10014 USA — Writer

Boxberger, Loa
PO Box 708, Russell KS 67665, USA — Bowler

Boxx, Gillian
15111 Chelsea Dr, San Jose CA 95124, USA — Softball Player

Boxx, Shannon
1454 Monterey Blvd, #102, Hermosa Beach CA 90254, USA — Soccer Player

Boyadjiev, Latchezar
48 Mark Dr, San Rafael CA 94903, USA — Sculptor

Boyarsky, Gerald M J (Jerry)
229 Boyarsky Road, Scott Township PA 18447, USA — Football Player

Boyarsky, Konstantin
Grant Rogers Mgmt, 8 Wren Crescent, Bushey Heath, Hertfordshire WD23 1AN, England — Concert Violinist, Composer

Boyce, Kim
200 Nathan Dr, Hollister MO 65672, USA — Singer

Boyd, Alan S
116 Fairview Ave N, #735, Seattle WA 98109, USA — Secretary, Transportation

Boyd, Brandon C
Creative Artists Agency, 2000 Ave of Stars, #100, Los Angeles CA 90067 USA — Singer, Percussionist (Incubus)

Boyd, Brent V
948 N Coast Highway 101, #185, Encinitas CA 92024, USA — Football Player

Boyd, Cayden
Gersh Agency, 9465 Wilshire Blvd, #600, Beverly Hills CA 90212 USA — Actor

Boyd, Darren
Independent Talent Group, Oxford House, 76 Oxford St, London W1D 1BS, England — Actor

Boyd, David
Montana Artists Agency, 625 Montana Ave, Santa Monica CA 90403 USA — Cinematographer

Boyd, Dennis R (Oil Can)
45 Swan St, East Providence RI 02914, USA — Baseball Player

Boyd, Douglas
Ingpen & Williams, 131 Putney Bridge Road, London SW15 2PA, England — Conductor

Boyd, Fred L
10915 Open Trail Road, Bakersfield CA 93311, USA — Basketball Player

Boyd, Guy
Stone Manners Salners, 9911 W Pico Blvd, #1400, Los Angeles CA 90035 USA — Actor

Boyd, Jenna
Gersh Agency, 9465 Wilshire Blvd, #600, Beverly Hills CA 90212 USA — Actress

Boyd, John
Dontanville/Frattaroli, 315 S Beverly Dr, #201, Beverly Hills CA 90212, USA — Actor

Boyd, Liona M C
B C Fiedler Mgmt, 53 Seton Park Road, Montreal ON M3C 3Z8, Canada — Concert Guitarist

Boyd, Lynda
Greene Assoc, 1901 Ave of Stars, #130, Los Angeles CA 90067 USA — Actress

Boyd, Malcolm
Saint Augustine by Sea Episcopal Church, 1227 4th St, Santa Monica CA 90401, USA — Writer, Religious Leader

Boyd, Randy
1769 Blackwillow Dr, Marietta GA 30066, USA — Ice Hockey Player

Boyd, Robert
828 Robert E Lee Dr, Wilmington NC 28412, USA — Golfer

Boyd, Robert D (Bobby)
2105 Lansdown Dr, Garland TX 75040, USA — Football Player

Boyd, Russell S
52 Sutherland St, Cremorne NSW 2090, Australia — Cinematographer

Boyd, Stephen G
1268 Marginal Road, Atlantic Beach NY 11509, USA — Football Player

Boyd, Tanya
Vincent Cirrincione Assoc, 1516 N Fairfax Ave, Los Angeles CA 90046 USA — Actress

Boyd, Willard L
3800 N Lake Shore Dr, #3A, Chicago IL 60613, USA — Educator, Museum Executive

B

Boyd - Brabham

Boyd, William A M	Writer
The Agency, 24 Pottery Lane, Holland Park, London W11 4LZ, England	
Boyden, Frank D	Artist
1914 N Three Rocks Road, Otis OR 97368, USA	
Boyega, John	Actor
Identity Agency Group, 11-15 Betterton St, Covent Garden, London WC2H 9BP, England	
Boyens, Philippa	Actress
I C M Partners, 10250 Constellation Blvd, #900, Los Angeles CA 90067 USA	
Boyer, Blaine T	Baseball Player
4825 Bellingham Dr, Marietta GA 30062, USA	
Boyer, Brant T	Football Player
1683 Old Lake Lane, Kaysville UT 84037, USA	
Boyer, Cloyd	Baseball Player
14528 County Road 210, Jasper MO 64755, USA	
Boyer, Herbert W	Biochemist, Inventor
PO Box 7318, Rancho Santa Fe CA 92067, USA	
Boyer, Mark	Football Player
21942 Kaneohe Lane, Huntington Beach CA 92646, USA	
Boyer, Paul D	Nobel Chemistry Laureate
1033 Somera Road, Los Angeles CA 90077, USA	
Boyer, Wally	Ice Hockey Player
400 Manly St, Midland ON L4R 3E3, Canada	
Boyes, Brad	Ice Hockey Player
11711 Fawnridge Dr, Saint Louis MO 63131, USA	
Boyette, Garland D	Football Player
4003 E Valley Dr, Missouri City TX 77459, USA	
Boykins, Earl A	Basketball Player
7572 Sanctuary Circle, Brecksville OH 44141, USA	
Boyko, Darren	Ice Hockey Player
1341 Wolseley Ave, Winnipeg MB R3G 1H8, Canada	
Boylan, Eileen April	Actress
S M S Talent, 8383 Wilshire Blvd, #230, Beverly Hills CA 90211 USA	
Boylan, Jeanne M	Forensics Artist
W M E Entertainment, 9601 Wilshire Blvd, #300, Beverly Hills CA 90210 USA	
Boylan, Jennifer Finney	Writer
Colby College, English Dept, 4000 Mayflower Hill, Waterville ME 04901, USA	
Boylan, John	Actor
Noble Caplan Abrams, 1260 Younge St, #200, Toronto ON M4T 1WG, Canada	
Boylan, Orla	Opera Singer
Harrison/Parrott, 5-6 Albion Court, London W6 0QT, England	
Boyle, Barbara D	Businesswoman
Boyle-Taylor Productions, 5200 Lankershim Blvd, #700, North Hollywood CA 91601, USA	
Boyle, Consolata	Costume Designer
Independent Talent Group, Oxford House, 76 Oxford St, London W1D 1BS, England	
Boyle, Daniel (Dan)	Ice Hockey Player
18232 Daves Ave, Monte Sereno CA 95030, USA	
Boyle, Danny	Director
Independent Talent Group, Oxford House, 76 Oxford St, London W1D 1BS, England	
Boyle, Jerry	Sculptor
Jerry Boyle Studio, 926 3rd Ave, Longmont CO 80501, USA	
Boyle, Lara Flynn	Actress
Don Buchwald/Fortitude, 6500 Wilshire Blvd, #2200, Los Angeles CA 90048 USA	
Boyle, Lisa D	Model, Actress
7336 Santa Monica Blvd, #776, West Hollywood CA 90046, USA	
Boyle, Susan	Singer
Syco Music, Bedford, House, 69-79 Fulham St, London SW6 3JW, England	
Boyle, T Coraghessan	Writer
Creative Artists Agency, 2000 Ave of Stars, #100, Los Angeles CA 90067 USA	
Boylen, Jim	Basketball Coach
University of Utah, Athletic Dept, Salt Lake City UT 84112, USA	
Boyne, Walter	Museum Executive, Writer
10833 Margate Road, Silver Spring MD 20901, USA	
Boynes, Winford G	Basketball Player
8979 Haflinger Way, Elk Grove CA 95757, USA	
Boynton, Nicholas (Nick)	Ice Hockey Player
3326 N Valencia Lane, Phoenix AZ 85018, USA	
Boynton, Robert M	Psychologist
6632 Grulla St, Carlsbad CA 92009, USA	
Boynton, Sandra	Graphic Artist
Recycled Paper Products, 111 N Canal St, #700, Chicago IL 60606, USA	
Boysen, Sarah	Psychologist
Ohio State University, Psychology Dept, Columbus OH 43210, USA	
Boyum, Steve	Director, Producer
Creative Artists Agency, 2000 Ave of Stars, #100, Los Angeles CA 90067 USA	
Bozanic, Josip Cardinal	Religious Leader
Zagreb Archdiocese, Kaptol 31, PP 553, 10001 Zagreb Hrvatska, Croatia	
Bozek, Steve	Ice Hockey Player
8410 E Whispering Wind Dr, Scottsdale AZ 85255, USA	
Bozeman, Todd	Basketball Coach
Morgan State University, Athletic Dept, Baltimore MD 21251, USA	
Bozize Yangouvonda, Francois	President, Central African Republic
Palais de la Renaissance, Bangui, Central African Republic	
Bozzio, Dale	Singer, Model
11935 Laurel Hills, Studio City CA 91604, USA	
Bozzo, Laura C	Entertainer
Televisa, Blvd A Lopez Mateos 232, Colonia San Angel, DF CP 01060, Mexico	
Braase, Ordell	Football Player
204 3rd St W, #201, Bradenton FL 34205, USA	
Braaten, Josh	Actor
A P A Talent/Literary Agency, 250 W 57th St, #1701, New York NY 10107 USA	
Brabants, Tim	Canoeing Athlete
Nottingham Canoe Club, Trentside North, Nottingham NG2 5FA, England	
Brabham, Geoff	Auto Racing Driver
B M W Group Australia, 783 Springvale Road, Mulgrave VIC 3170, Australia	
Brabham, John A (Jack)	Auto Racing Driver
Bag 1, #404, Robins Towne Centre QLD 4230, Australia	

Bracco, Lorraine — Actress
Innovative Artists, 1505 10th St, Santa Monica CA 90401 USA
Bracegirdle, Nick (Chicane) — Musician
Concorde International, 101 Shepherds Bush Road, London W6 7LP, England
Bracelin, Gregory L (Greg) — Football Player
5465 Calumet Ave, La Jolla CA 92037, USA
Bracey, Luke — Actor
Creative Artists Agency, 2000 Ave of Stars, #100, Los Angeles CA 90067 USA
Bracey, Stephen H (Steve) — Basketball Player
560 Lincoln Ave, Brooklyn NY 11208, USA
Bracher, Karl D — Political Scientist, Historian
Universitat Bonn, Stationsweg 17, 53127 Bonn, Germany
Bracht, Stephanie — Golfer
2004 Delancey Dr, Norman OK 73071, USA
Brack, Kenny — Auto Racing Driver
Allen Farst Mgmt, PO Box 90383, Dayton OH 45490, USA
Bracken, Donald C (Don) — Football Player
15950 W Diamond St, Goodyear AZ 85338, USA
Brackenbury, Curt — Ice Hockey Player
W378N5861 Valley Road, Oconomowoc WI 53066, USA
Brackens, Tony L, Jr — Football Player
193 Private Road 407, Fairfield TX 75840, USA
Brackett, Gary — Football Player
3591 Hintocks Circle, Carmel IN 46032, USA
Bradburn, James H — Architect
Fentress Bradburn Assoc, 421 Broadway, Denver CO 80203, USA
Bradbury, Janette Lane — Actress
10817 Kling St, North Hollywood CA 91602, USA
Braddock, Paige — Graphic Designer (Snoopy Stamp)
Creative Associates, 1 Snoopy Place, Santa Rosa CA 95403, USA
Braddy, Johanna E — Actress
Innovative Artists, 1505 10th St, Santa Monica CA 90401 USA
Brademas, John — Educator; Representative, NY
New York University, President's Emeritus Office, New York NY 10012, USA
Braden, Dallas L — Baseball Player
1459 W Walnut St, Stockton CA 95203, USA
Braden, Vic — Tennis Coach
22000 Trabuco Canyon Road, Trabuco Canyon CA 92678, USA
Bradford, Barbara Taylor — Writer
Bradford Enterprises, 450 Park Ave, #2303, New York NY 10022, USA
Bradford, Chadwick L (Chad) — Baseball Player
3867 Bill Downing Road, Raymond MS 39154, USA
Bradford, Charles W (Buddy) — Baseball Player
6440 Springpark Ave, Los Angeles CA 90056, USA
Bradford, Corey L — Football Player
13002 Highway 955 E, Ethel LA 70730, USA
Bradford, Richard — Actor
2511 Canyon Dr, Los Angeles CA 90068, USA
Bradford, Ronnie — Football Player, Coach
965 Allen Lake Lane, Suwanee GA 30024, USA
Bradford, Samuel J (Sam) — Football Player
Saint Louis Rams, 901 N Broadway, Saint Louis MO 63101 USA
Bradford, Sarah — Writer
Penguin Books, 375 Hudson St, Basement 1, New York NY 10014 USA
Bradlee, Benjamin C — Editor
3014 N St NW, Washington DC 20007, USA
Bradley, Alonzo — Basketball Player
1713 Briaroaks Dr, Flower Mound TX 75028, USA
Bradley, Bob — Soccer Player, Coach
Club Deportivo Chivas, 18400 Avalon Blvd, #500, Carson CA 90746 USA
Bradley, Brian — Ice Hockey Player
6417 MacLaurin Dr, Tampa FL 33647, USA
Bradley, Bruce — Water Polo Player
262 Saint Joseph Ave, Long Beach CA 90803, USA
Bradley, Carlos H — Football Player
1316 E Cliveden St, Philadelphia PA 19119, USA
Bradley, Charles W — Basketball Player
10810 Mountshire Circle, Highlands Ranch CO 80126, USA
Bradley, Christopher — Actor
Ford/Robert Black Agency, 4032 N Miller Road, #104, Scottsdale AZ 85251, USA
Bradley, David — Actor
United Agents, 12-26 Lexington St, London W1F 0LE, England
Bradley, Dick — Sports Cartoonist
10176 Corporate Square Dr, #200, Saint Louis MO 63132, USA
Bradley, Dudley L — Basketball Player
9830 Clanford Road, Randallstown MD 21133, USA
Bradley, Edward W (Ed), Jr — Football Player
187 Fryes Creek Lane, Clemmons NC 27012, USA
Bradley, Everett — Singer, Songwriter
Fretland Productions Mgmt, 70A Greenwich Ave, PMB 212, New York NY 10011, USA
Bradley, James — Actor
Spotlight, 7 Leicester Place, London WC2H 7RJ, England
Bradley, James — Writer
PO Box 367, Rye NY 10580, USA
Bradley, Kathleen — Actress
8412 S Denker Ave, Los Angeles CA 90047, USA
Bradley, Keegan H — Golfer
Altus Marketing & Managing, 177 Huntington Ave, Boston MA 02115, USA
Bradley, Lonnie — Boxer
405 Edgecombe Ave, New York NY 10032, USA
Bradley, Michael (Mike) — Golfer
5501 Branch Oak Place, Lithia FL 33547, USA
Bradley, Michael T — Basketball Player
6150 Blackjack Court N, Punta Gorda FL 33982, USA
Bradley, Milton O, Jr — Baseball Player
5359 Oak Park Ave, Encino CA 91316, USA

B

Bracco - Bradley

Bradley, Patricia E (Pat) — Golfer
PO Box 248, West Hyannisport MA 02672, USA
Bradley, Philip P (Phil) — Baseball Player
6950 Seminole Court, Columbia MO 65203, USA
Bradley, Rebecca — Golfer
7501 Alderwood Dr, Garland TX 75044, USA
Bradley, Robert A — Physician
2465 S Downing St, Denver CO 80210, USA
Bradley, Ryan — Figure Skater
Colorado Springs World Arena & Ice Hall, 3185 Venetucci Blvd, Colorado Springs, CO 80906, USA
Bradley, Sam — Singer, Songwriter
Agency Group Ltd, 142 W 57th St, #600, New York NY 10019 USA
Bradley, Scott W — Baseball Player
43 Chicory Lane, Pennington NJ 08534, USA
Bradley, Shawn P — Basketball Player
606 Sunny Flowers Lane, Salt Lake City UT 84107, USA
Bradley, Thomas W (Tom) — Baseball Player
4104 Woodberry St, University Park MD 20782, USA
Bradley, Timothy — Boxer
Top Rank Inc, 3908 Howard Hughes Parkway, #580, Las Vegas NV 89169 USA
Bradley, William C (Bill) — Football Player
1505 Whispering Water, Spring Branch TX 78070, USA
Bradley, William W (Bill) — Senator, NJ; Basketball Player
7 Kips Ridge, Verona NJ 07044, USA
Bradshaw, Ahmad — Football Player
New York Giants, Meadowlands Stadium, 102 Route 120, East Rutherford NJ 07073 USA
Bradshaw, Alan — Actor
Associated International Mgmt, Fairfax House, Fulwood Place, London WC1V 6HU, England
Bradshaw, James A — Football Player
5653 Eagle Harbor Dr, Westerville OH 43081, USA
Bradshaw, John E — Writer, Theologian
Becsey/Wisdom/Kalajian, 849 S Wooster St, #7, Los Angeles CA 90035, USA
Bradshaw, Morris, Jr — Football Player
82 Steuben Bay, Alameda CA 94502, USA
Bradshaw, Sufe — Actress
Affinity Artists Agency, 5724 W 3rd St, #511, Los Angeles CA 90036, USA
Bradshaw, Terry P — Football Player, Sportscaster
12221 Merit Dr, #750, Dallas TX 75251, USA
Brady, Ed J — Football Player
5755 White Path Lane, Liberty Township OH 45011, USA
Brady, James S (Jim) — Government Official, Journalist
Handgun Control, 1225 I St NW, #1100, Washington DC 20005, USA
Brady, Jeffrey T (Jeff) — Football Player
1506 NW 37th Place, Cape Coral FL 33993, USA
Brady, Kyle J — Football Player
2221 Alicia Lane, Atlantic Beach FL 32233, USA
Brady, Nicholas F — Secretary, Treasury; Senator, NJ
Darby Overseas Investments, 1133 Connecticut NW, #400, Washington DC 20036, USA
Brady, Orla — Actress
Independent Talent Group, Oxford House, 76 Oxford St, London W1D 1BS, England
Brady, Pat — Cartoonist (Rose Is Rose)
United Feature Syndicate, PO Box 5610, Cincinnati OH 45201 USA
Brady, Patrick H — Vietnam War Army Hero (CMH), General
10419 Felsblock Lane, New Braunfels TX 78132, USA
Brady, Paul J — Singer, Songwriter
International Music Network, 278 Main St, Gloucester MA 01930, USA
Brady, Ray — Commentator
CBS-TV, News Dept, 524 W 57th St, New York NY 10019, USA
Brady, Roscoe O — Neurogeneticist
6026 Valerian Lane, Rockville MD 20852, USA
Brady, Sarah — Social Activist
Handgun Control, 1225 I St NW, #1100, Washington DC 20005, USA
Brady, Sean B Cardinal — Religious Leader
Archbishop's House, Ara Coeli, Cathedral Road, Armagh BT6 7QY, Ireland
Brady, Thomas (Tom) — Football Player
310 Beacon St, #4, Boston MA 02116, USA
Brady, Wayne — Actor, Comedian, Singer
W M E Entertainment, 9601 Wilshire Blvd, #300, Beverly Hills CA 90210 USA
Braeden, Eric — Actor
Diverse Talent Group, 9911 Pico Blvd, #350W, Los Angeles CA 90035 USA
Braff, Zach — Actor, Director
Creative Artists Agency, 2000 Ave of Stars, #100, Los Angeles CA 90067 USA
Braga, Alice — Actress
Roar Mgmt, 9701 Wilshire Blvd, #800, Beverly Hills CA 90212 USA
Braga, Brannon — Writer, Producer
W M E Entertainment, 9601 Wilshire Blvd, #300, Beverly Hills CA 90210 USA
Braga, Sonia — Actress
Framework Entertainment, 9057 Nemo St, #C, West Hollywood CA 90069 USA
Bragg of Wigton, Melvyn — Writer
12 Hampstead Hill Gardens, London NW3 2PL, England
Bragg, Billy — Singer, Guitarist, Songwriter
Sincere Mgmt, 35 Bravington Road, #6, London W9 3AB, England
Bragg, Darren W — Baseball Player
163 Patriot Road, Southbury CT 06488, USA
Bragg, Donald G (Don) — Track Athlete
965 Oak St, Clayton CA 94517, USA
Bragg, Michael E (Mike) — Football Player
PO Box 4842, Falls Church VA 22044, USA
Bragg, Todd — Drummer (Caedmon's Call)
Breen Agency, 25 Music Square W, Nashville TN 37203, USA
Braggs, Glenn E — Baseball Player
28369 Falcon Crest Dr, Canyon Country CA 91351, USA
Braggs, Stephen — Football Player
120 Power House Road, Lawndale NC 28090, USA
Bragnalo, Rick — Ice Hockey Player
515 Christina St E, Thunder Bay ON P7E 4P3, Canada

Braham, Rich — Football Player
19 Miramichi Trail, Morgantown WV 26508, USA
Brahaney, Thomas F (Tom) — Football Player
1602 W Cuthbert Ave, Midland TX 79701, USA
Brainerd, Clayton — Opera Singer
Columbia Artists Mgmt Inc, 1790 Broadway, #702, New York NY 10019 USA
Braly, Angela — Businesswoman
WellPoint Inc, 120 Monument Circle, #200, Indianapolis IN 46204, USA
Bramall of Busfield, Edwin N W — Army Field Marshal, England
House of Lords, Westminster, London SW1A 0PW, England
Brambilla, Marco — Director
Creative Artists Agency, 2000 Ave of Stars, #100, Los Angeles CA 90067 USA
Bramhill, Gina — Actress
United Agents, 12-26 Lexington St, London W1F 0LE, England
Bramlett, Bonnie — Singer, Actress
Mark Pucci Media, 5000 Oak Bluff Court, Atlanta GA 30350, USA
Bramlett, David A (Dave) — Army General
61-100 Iliohu Way, Haleiwa HI 96712, USA
Bramlett, John C — Football Player
159 Cotton Ridge Cove S, Cordova TN 38018, USA
Brammell, Abby — Actress
Paul Kohner, 9300 Wilshire Blvd, #555, Beverly Hills CA 90212 USA
Branagh, Kenneth — Director, Actor
Troika, 74 Clerkenwell Road, #300, London EC1M 5QA, England
Branca, John G — Attorney
Ziffren Brittenham Branca, 1801 Century Park West, #700, Los Angeles CA 90067, USA
Branca, Ralph T J — Baseball Player
Westchester Country Club, 99 Biltmore Ave, Rye NY 10580, USA
Brancato, John — Writer, Producer, Actor
United Talent Agency, 9336 Civic Center Dr, Beverly Hills CA 90210 USA
Branch, A Deion, Jr — Football Player
New England Patriots, 1 Patriot Place, Foxboro MA 02035 USA
Branch, Adrian F — Basketball Player
18008 Fence Post Court, Gaithersburg MD 20877, USA
Branch, Alan K — Football Player
3076 E Kesler Lane, Gilbert AZ 85295, USA
Branch, Anthony (Deion) — Football Player
13382 W Sherbern Dr, Carmel IN 46032, USA
Branch, Clifford (Cliff) — Football Player, Coach
2071 Stonefield Lane, Santa Rosa CA 95403, USA
Branch, Michelle — Singer, Songwriter
50 Indian Ruin Road, Sedona AZ 86351, USA
Branch, Reginald E (Reggie) — Football Player
515 San Lanta Circle, Sanford FL 32771, USA
Branch, Taylor — Historian
Larjansoff & Verrill, 179 Franklin St, New York NY 10013, USA
Branco, Joaquim Rafael — Prime Minister, Sao Tome & Principe
Prime Minister's Office, CP 38, Sao Tome, Sao Tome & Principe
Brand, Elton T — Basketball Player
1077 Sentry Lane, Gladwyne PA 19035, USA
Brand, Esther C — Track Athlete
PO Box 11115, 9321 Universitas, South Africa
Brand, Joshua — Producer, Director
United Talent Agency, 9336 Civic Center Dr, Beverly Hills CA 90210 USA
Brand, Oscar — Singer, Songwriter
Douglas A Yeager Productions, 300 W 55th St, New York NY 10019, USA
Brand, Ronald G (Ron) — Baseball Player
4421 Staten Island Dr, Plano TX 75024, USA
Brand, Russell — Actor, Comedian
W M E Entertainment, 9601 Wilshire Blvd, #300, Beverly Hills CA 90210 USA
Brand, Stewart — Editor, Writer
E Gate 5 Road, Sausalito CA 94965, USA
Brand, Vance D — Astronaut
21825 Hidden Canyon Dr, Tehachapi CA 93561, USA
Brandauer, Klaus Maria — Actor
Bartensteingasse 8/9, 1010 Vienna, Austria
Brandenstein, Daniel C — Astronaut
648 N Tailwind Dr, Blanco TX 78606, USA
Brandes, Christine — Opera Singer
I M G Artists, Hogarth Business Park, Chiswick, London W4 2TH, England
Brandes, John W — Football Player
905 Ashland Court, Mansfield TX 76063, USA
Brandi — Model
Next Model Mgmt, 23 Watts St, New York NY 10013 USA
Brandmeier, Jonathon — Entertainer
C E S D, 10635 Santa Monica Blvd, #130, Los Angeles CA 90025 USA
Brandon, Barbara — Cartoonist (Where I'm Coming From)
Universal Press Syndicate, 4520 Main St, #700, Kansas City MO 64111 USA
Brandon, Christopher — Actor
Ken McReddie Assoc, 11 Connaught Place, London W2 2ET, England
Brandon, Clark — Actor
9000 W Sunset Blvd, #801, West Hollywood CA 90069, USA
Brandon, Darrell G — Baseball Player
590 White Cliff Dr, Plymouth MA 02360, USA
Brandon, Michael — Actor
TalentWorks, 3500 W Olive Ave, #1400, Burbank CA 91505 USA
Brandon, T Terrell — Basketball Player
3310 NE Shaver St, Portland OR 97212, USA
Brands, Terry — Freestyle Wrestler
3744 Lacina Dr SW, Iowa City IA 52240, USA
Brands, Tom — Freestyle Wrestler, Coach
4494 Taft Ave SE, Iowa City IA 52240, USA
Brandt, Betsy — Actress
TalentWorks, 3500 W Olive Ave, #1400, Burbank CA 91505 USA
Brandt, Brandi — Model, Actress
Esterman Entertainment, 220 Park Road, Riva MD 21140, USA

Brandt, Carlo — Actor
Artmedia, 20 Ave Rapp, 75007 Paris, France
Brandt, John G (Jackie), Jr — Baseball Player
5 Rabbit Trail, Wildwood FL 34785, USA
Brandt, Kyle — Actor
Sweeney Mgmt, 8755 Lookout Mountain Ave, Los Angeles CA 90046, USA
Brandt, Lesley-Ann — Actress
Karen Jay Mgmt, 2/25 State St, Aukland 1010, New Zealand
Brandt, Paul R — Singer, Songwriter
Warner Bros Records, 3300 Warner Blvd, Burbank CA 91505 USA
Brandt, Thordis — Actress
8171 Mannix Dr, Los Angeles CA 90046, USA
Brandt, Victor — Actor
H David Moss, 733 Seward St, #PH, Los Angeles CA 90038 USA
Branduardi, Angelo — Singer, Songwriter
Studio Legale Costa, Via Azzo Guardino 54, 40122 Bologna, Italy
Brandy — Singer, Actress
Norwood & Norwood, 22187 Ventura Blvd, #432, Woodland Hills CA 91364, USA
Brandywine, Marcia — Commentator
1428 Rising Glen, Los Angeles CA 90069, USA
Brannagh, Brigid — Actress
Innovative Artists, 1505 10th St, Santa Monica CA 90401 USA
Brannan, Charles F — Secretary, Agriculture
3131 E Alameda Ave, Denver CO 80209, USA
Branscomb, Lewis M — Physicist, Computer Scientist
Harvard University, Kennedy School of Government, Cambridge MA 02138, USA
Branshaw, David — Golfer
16220 Sierra de Avila, Tampa FL 33613, USA
Branson, Bradley A (Brad) — Basketball Player
7419 Cortes Dr, Houston TX 77083, USA
Branson, H Jesse — Basketball Player
309 Forest Dr, Graham NC 27253, USA
Branson, Jeffrey G (Jeff) — Baseball Player
10749 Spokane Court, Union KY 41091, USA
Branson, Richard — Businessman, Balloonist
Virgin Group, 120 Campden Hill Road, London W8 7AR, England
Branstad, Terry E — Governor, IA
Regency West 5, #201, 4500 Westown Parkway, West Des Moines IA 50266, USA
Brant, Tim — Sportscaster
12416 Ansin Circle Dr, Potomac MD 20854, USA
Brantley, Jeffrey H (Jeff) — Baseball Player
104 Cherry Laurel Cove, Ridgeland MS 39157, USA
Brantley, Larry — Actor
Home Agency, 4420 W Lovers Lane, Dallas TX 75209, USA
Brantley, Scot E — Football Player
11309 Galleria Dr, Tampa FL 33618, USA
Branton, Daniel — Biophysicist
Harvard Medical School, Molecular & Cell Biology Dept, 25 Shattuck St, Boston MA 02115, USA
Branyan, Russell O (Russ) — Baseball Player
3301 Running Spring Court, Franklin TN 37064, USA
Brasar, Per-Olov — Ice Hockey Player
Brasar Trav A B, Heden 99, 793 29 Leksand, Sweden
Brasco, James J (Jim) — Basketball Player
225 W Neck Road, Huntington NY 11743, USA
Brashares, Ann — Writer
Delacorte Press, 1540 Broadway, New York NY 10036 USA
Braslow, Paul — Sculptor
567 Virginia Dr, Belvedere Tiburon CA 94920, USA
Brasseur, Alexandre — Actor
Artmedia, 20 Ave Rapp, 75007 Paris, France
Brasseur, Claude — Actor
Artmedia, 20 Ave Rapp, 75007 Paris, France
Braswell, Joseph — Interior Designer
Joseph Braswell Assoc, 1148 E Jordan St, Pensacola FL 32503, USA
Brathwaite, Edward — Writer
University of West Indies, History Dept, Mona, Kingston 7, Jamaica
Brathwaite, Nicholas A — Prime Minister, Grenada
House of Representatives, Grenada Trade Center, Grand Anse, Saint George's, Grenada
Bratkowski, Edmund R (Zeke) — Football Player, Coach
224 Anchors Lake Dr N, Santa Rosa Beach FL 32459, USA
Bratt, Benjamin — Actor
D/F Mgmt, 270 Lafayette St, #402, New York NY 10012 USA
Bratt, Peter — Actor
Five Sick Films, 1438 N Gower St, Building 38, Los Angeles CA 90028, USA
Bratton, Creed — Actor, Guitarist (Grass Roots)
Artistry Mgmt, 340 N Camden Dr, #302, Beverly Hills CA 90210, USA
Bratton, Joseph K — Army General
5902 Blakeford Dr, Windermere FL 34786, USA
Bratton, William J — Law Enforcement Official
Altergrity Corp, 7799 Leesburg Pike, #1100 North, Falls Church VA 22043, USA
Bratz, Michael L (Mike) — Basketball Player
7503 Tillman Hill Road, Colleyville TX 76034, USA
Bratzke, Chad A — Football Player
1478 Landings Circle, Sarasota FL 34231, USA
Brauckmann, Linda — Figure Skating Coach
Center of Excellence, 6501 Sprott St, #2, Burnaby BC V5B 3B8, Canada
Braude, Peter R — Obstetrician, Gynecologist
King's College, Women's Health Dept, Strand, London WC2R 2LS, England
Brauer, Arik — Artist
Academy of Fine Arts, Schillerplatz 3, 1010 Vienna, Austria
Brauer, William (Bill) — Artist
Bill Brauer Studios, 4368 E Warren Road, Warren VT 05674, USA
Braugher, Andre — Actor
Principato-Young, 9465 Wilshire Blvd, #880, Beverly Hills CA 90212 USA
Brauman, John I — Chemist
849 Tolman Dr, Stanford CA 94305, USA

Braun, Allen — Neuroscientist
National Institute on Deafness, 9000 Rockville Pike, Bethesda MD 20892, USA

Braun, Colin — Truck Racing Driver
4502 Raceway Drive, Concord NC 28027, USA

Braun, Nicholas — Actor
Levine Okwu/Ericson Talent, 6363 Wilshire Blvd, #300, Los Angeles CA 90048, USA

Braun, Rick — Jazz Trumpeter
Chapman & Co Mgmt, PO Box 55246, Sherman Oaks CA 91413, USA

Braun, Russell — Opera, Concert Singer
Columbia Artists Mgmt Inc, 1790 Broadway, #702, New York NY 10019 USA

Braun, Ryan J — Baseball Player
8926 38th Ave, #8W, Kenosha WI 53142, USA

Braun, Steve — Actor
TalentWorks, 3500 W Olive Ave, #1400, Burbank CA 91505 USA

Braun, Tamara — Actress
John Carrabino Mgmt, 5900 Wilshire Blvd, #406, Los Angeles CA 90036 USA

Braun, Wendy — Actress
C E S D, 10635 Santa Monica Blvd, #130, Los Angeles CA 90025 USA

Braun, Zev — Producer
Zev Braun Pictures, 1438 N Gower St, #26, Los Angeles CA 90028, USA

Braunfels, Michael — Composer, Concert Pianist
Dransdorferstr 40, 50968 Cologne, Germany

Braunwald, Eugene — Physician
Partners Healthcare, 800 Boylston St, Boston MA 02199, USA

Braver, Rita — Commentator
CBS-TV, News Dept, 2020 M St NW, Washington DC 20036 USA

Braverman, Bart — Actor
House of Representatives, 1434 6th St, #1, Santa Monica CA 90401 USA

Braverman, Nachum — Religious Leader, Rabbi
Aish Hatorah, 9106 W Pico Blvd, Los Angeles CA 90035, USA

Bravman, John C — Educator
Bucknell University, President's Office, Marts Hall, Lewisburg PA 17837, USA

Braxton, Anthony — Jazz Saxophonist, Composer
Berkeley Agency, 2608 9th St, #301, Berkeley CA 94710 USA

Braxton, David H — Football Player
6406 Donnegal Farm Road, Charlotte NC 28270, USA

Braxton, Kara — Basketball Player
Phoenix Mercury, American West Arena, 201 E Jefferson St, Phoenix AZ 85004 USA

Braxton, Toni — Singer, Songwriter
A P A Talent/Literary Agency, 250 W 57th St, #1701, New York NY 10107 USA

Braxton, Tyrone S — Football Player
455 Kearney St, Denver CO 80220, USA

Bray, Robert — Interior Designer
Bray-Schaible Design, 80 W 40th St, #800, New York NY 10018, USA

Bray, Thomas E (Thom) — Actor
7006 SE 29th Ave, Portland OR 97202, USA

Brayton, Tyler — Football Player
412 Hunter Lane, Charlotte NC 28211, USA

Brazelton, Dewon C — Baseball Player
107 Scenic Dr, Tullahoma TN 37388, USA

Brazelton, T Berry — Pediatrician
23 Hawthorn St, Cambridge MA 02138, USA

Braziel, Larry — Football Player
7616 Carriage Lane, Fort Worth TX 76112, USA

Brazile, Robert L, Jr — Football Player
813 Felder Ave, Fort Worth TX 76112, USA

Brazile, Trevor — Rodeo Rider
715 County Road 3051, Decatur TX 76234, USA

Brazoban, Yhency J — Baseball Player
13609 N 20th St, Tampa FL 33613, USA

B-Real — Rap Artist (Cypress Hill)
W M E Entertainment, 9601 Wilshire Blvd, #300, Beverly Hills CA 90210 USA

Bream, Julian A — Concert Guitarist
Hazard Chase, 25 City Road, Cambridge CB1 1DP, England

Bream, Sidney E (Sid) — Baseball Player
115 Sable Run, Zelienople PA 16063, USA

Breathed, Berkeley — Cartoonist (Bloom County, Outland)
Washington Post Writers Group, 1150 15th St NW, Washington DC 20071, USA

Breathnach, Paddy — Director
I C M Partners, 10250 Constellation Blvd, #900, Los Angeles CA 90067 USA

Breaux, Jimmey — Accordian Player (BeauSoleil)
Rosebud Agency, PO Box 170429, San Francisco CA 94117, USA

Breaux, John B — Senator, LA
Lousiana State University, Mass Communications School, Baton Rouge LA 70803, USA

Breaux, Timothy (Tim) — Basketball Player
845 Augusta Dr, #E75, Houston TX 77057, USA

Brebner, Morwyn — Producer, Writer, Actress
Gary Goddard Agency, 10 Sainte Mary St, #305, Toronto ON M4Y 1P9, Canada

Brecher, John — Writer
I C M Partners, 10250 Constellation Blvd, #900, Los Angeles CA 90067 USA

Brechignac, Catherine — Physicist
Scientifique Recherche Centre, 3 Rue Michel Ange, 75794 Paris, France

Breckenridge, Alexandra — Actress
Paul Kohner, 9300 Wilshire Blvd, #555, Beverly Hills CA 90212 USA

Brecker, Randy — Jazz Trumpeter
Michael Bloom Media Relations, PO Box 41380, Los Angeles CA 90041, USA

Bredahl, Charlotte — Equestrian
PO Box 318, Solvang CA 93464, USA

Bredesen, Espen — Ski Jumper
Hellerud Gardsvei 18, 0671 Oslo, Norway

Bredow, Reinhard — Luge Athlete
Bert-Heller Str 12, 38855 Wernigerode, Germany

Breech, James T (Jim) — Football Player
5461 Union Centre Dr, West Chester OH 45069, USA

Breeden, Harold N (Hal) — Baseball Player
665 Middle Road S, Leesburg GA 31763, USA

Breeden, Louis E — Football Player
PO Box 62135, Cincinnati OH 45262, USA
Breeden, Richard C — Government Official
Coopers & Lybrand, 1800 M St NW, Washington DC 20036, USA
Breedlove, N Craig — Auto Racing Driver
World Speedway Team, 200 N Front St, Rio Vista CA 94571, USA
Breedlove, Rodney W (Rod) — Football Player
264 New Valley Road, Conowingo MD 21918, USA
Breen, Bobby — Singer, Actor
10550 NW 71st Place, Tamarac FL 33321, USA
Breen, Edward D, Jr — Businessman
Tyco International, 273 Corporate Dr, #100, Portsmouth NH 03801, USA
Breen, George — Swimmer
425 Pepper Mill Court, Sewell NJ 08080, USA
Breen, J Eugene (Gene) — Football Player
1018 Henley Downs Place, Lake Mary FL 32746, USA
Breen, Mike — Sportscaster
ABC-TV, Sports Dept, 77 W 66th St, New York NY 10023 USA
Breen, Patrick — Actor
Gersh Agency, 9465 Wilshire Blvd, #600, Beverly Hills CA 90212 USA
Breen, Shelley L P — Singer (Point of Grace)
Blanton Harrell Cooke Corzine, 1014 Cross Bow Court, Hendersonville TN 37075 USA
Breen, Stephen P (Steve) — Editorial Cartoonist
San Diego Union-Tribune, Editorial Dept, 350 Camino Reina, San Diego CA 92108 USA
Breer, Murle — Golfer
7008 Sand Road, Savannah GA 31410, USA
Brees, Drew C — Football Player
5500 Prytania St, New Orleans LA 70115, USA
Bregman Recht, Tracey E — Actress
Bell-Bregman Productions, 7800 Beverly Blvd, #3371, Los Angeles CA 90036, USA
Bregman, Anthony — Producer, Actor
Likely Story, 150 W 22nd St, #900, New York NY 10011, USA
Bregman, Buddy — Director, Producer, Composer
Paul Lane Entertainment, 468 N Camden Dr, Beverly Hills CA 90210, USA
Bregman, Martin — Producer
Martin Bregman Productions, 100 Universal City Plaza, Universal City CA 91608, USA
Bregvadze, Nani G — Singer
Irakly Abashidze Str 18A, #10, 380079 Tbilisi, Georgia
Brehaut, Jeff — Golfer
1085 Leonello Ave, Los Altos CA 94024, USA
Breidenbach, Warren — Surgeon
Jewish Hospital, Surgery Dept, 217 E Chestnut, Louisville KY 40202, USA
Breiman, Valerie — Director, Actress
Creative Artists Agency, 2000 Ave of Stars, #100, Los Angeles CA 90067 USA
Breining, Fred L — Baseball Player
2120 Ticonderoga Dr, San Mateo CA 94402, USA
Breitenbach, Ken — Ice Hockey Player
8 Greenvale Court, SS 1, Fonthill ON L0S 1E1, Canada
Breitenstein, Robert C (Bob) — Football Player
4215 E 95th St, Tulsa OK 74137, USA
Breitman, Zabou — Director
Zelig, 57 Rue Reaumur, 75002 Paris, France
Breitner, Paul — Soccer Player
Kuckucksweg 4, 85649 Brunnthal, Germany
Breitschwerdt, Werner — Businessman
Daimler-Benz AG, Mercedesstr 136, 70322 Stuttgart, Germany
Breland, Mark — Boxer, Trainer
20514 Heritage Highway, Denmark SC 29042, USA
Bremers, Peter — Artist
PO Box 27, 6120 AA Born, Netherlands
Bremner, Ewen — Actor
Independent Talent Group, Oxford House, 76 Oxford St, London W1D 1BS, England
Brenciu, Marius — Opera Singer
I M G Artists, Hogarth Business Park, Chiswick, London W4 2TH, England
Brendel, Alfred — Concert Pianist
Ingpen & Williams, 131 Putney Bridge Road, London SW15 2PA, England
Brendel, Wolfgang — Opera Singer
Manuela Kursidem, Wasagasse 12/1/3, 1090 Vienna, Austria
Brendlinger, Kai — Model
Playboy Promotions, 2706 Media Center Dr, Los Angeles CA 90065 USA
Brendon, Nicholas — Actor
Gage Group, 14724 Ventura Blvd, #505, Sherman Oaks CA 91403 USA
Breneman, Curtis E — Chemist
47 Farrell Road, Troy NY 12180, USA
Brener, Shirly — Actress, Model
Jackoway Tyerman Wertheimer, 1925 Century Park E, #2200, Los Angeles CA 90067 USA
Brengarth, Didier — Actor
Angy Co, 85 Rue Saint Honore, 75001 Paris, France
Brenly, Robert E (Bob) — Baseball Player, Manager
9726 E Laurel Lane, Scottsdale AZ 85260, USA
Brennan, Bernard F — Businessman
Montgomery Ward, 822 Montgomery Ave, #204, Narberth PA 19072, USA
Brennan, Bernard F — Businessman
B V-Cornerstone Ventures, 11001 W 120th St, #300, Broomfield CO 80021, USA
Brennan, Brian M — Football Player
2961 Edgewood Road, Cleveland OH 44124, USA
Brennan, Christine — Sportswriter
Washington Post, Sports Dept, 1150 15th Ave NW, Washington DC 20071, USA
Brennan, Dan — Ice Hockey Player
1912 108th Ave, Dawson Creek BC V1G 2T8, Canada
Brennan, Eileen — Actress
Unified Talent Mgmt, 4231 W National Ave, Burbank CA 91505, USA
Brennan, Gabriele — Actress
C E S D, 10635 Santa Monica Blvd, #130, Los Angeles CA 90025 USA
Brennan, George — Harness Racing Driver
2 Millpond Road, Millstone Township NJ 08535, USA

Brennan, Joseph E — Governor, ME
104 Frances St, Portland ME 04102, USA
Brennan, Melissa — Actress
6520 Platt Ave, #634, West Hills CA 91307, USA
Brennan, Richard (Rich) — Ice Hockey Player
14 Reflection Way, South Yarmouth MA 02664, USA
Brennan, Shane — Producer, Writer
Paradigm Agency, 360 N Crescent Dr, North Building, Beverly Hills CA 90210 USA
Brennan, Terrance — Restauranteur, Chef
Pichoine Restaurant, 35 W 64th St, New York NY 10023, USA
Brennan, Terrance P (Terry) — Football Player, Coach
1731 Wildberry Dr, #C, Glenview IL 60025, USA
Brennan, Thomas M (Tom) — Baseball Player
8204 Millbank Dr, Orland Park IL 60462, USA
Brenneman, Amy — Actress
Creative Artists Agency, 2000 Ave of Stars, #100, Los Angeles CA 90067 USA
Brenneman, Gregory D — Businessman
Quiznos, 1475 Lawrence St, #400, Denver CO 80202, USA
Brenneman, John — Ice Hockey Player
247 Radley Road, Mississauga ON L5G 2R6, Canada
Brenner, Carol — Actress
Jean-François Pignard de Mart, 11 Rrue Chanez, 75781 Paris Cedex 16, France
Brenner, David — Actor, Comedian
Street Corner Enterprises, 2027 Cape Cod Landing Dr, Las Vegas NV 89135, USA
Brenner, Hoby F J — Football Player
40 Calle Ameno, San Clemente CA 92672, USA
Brenner, Sydney — Nobel Medicine Laureate
Molecular Sciences Institute, 2168 Shattuck Ave, #200, Berkeley CA 94704, USA
Brenner, Teddy — Boxing Promoter
24 W 55th St, #9C, New York NY 10019, USA
Bresee, Bobbie — Actress
PO Box 1222, Los Angeles CA 90078, USA
Breslik, Pavel — Opera Singer
I M G Artists, Hogarth Business Park, Chiswick, London W4 2TH, England
Breslin, Abigail K — Actress
I C M Partners, 10250 Constellation Blvd, #900, Los Angeles CA 90067 USA
Breslin, Jimmy — Journalist
Newsday, Editorial Dept, 235 Pinelawn Road, Melville NY 11747, USA
Breslin, Spencer — Actor
B/W/R, 9100 Wilshire Blvd, #500W, Beverly Hills CA 90212 USA
Breslow, Craig A — Baseball Player
26 Finchwood Dr, Trumbull CT 06611, USA
Breslow, Ronald C — Chemist
295 Three Mile Harbor Road, East Hampton NY 11937, USA
Bresnik, Randolph J (Randy) — Astronaut
N A S A, Johnson Space Center, 2101 NASA Road, Houston TX 77058 USA
Bressoud, Edward F (Eddie) — Baseball Player
515 Marble Canyon Lane, San Ramon CA 94582, USA
Brest, Martin — Director, Producer
I C M Partners, 10250 Constellation Blvd, #900, Los Angeles CA 90067 USA
Bretos, Conchy — Social Activist
M I A Consulting, 5208 Aston Road, Miami Beach Fl 33140, USA
Brett, George H — Baseball Player, Executive
6528 Seneca Road, Mission Hills KS 66208, USA
Brett, Jan — Writer
132 Pleasant St, Norwell MA 02061, USA
Brettschneider, Carl — Football Player
4649 Bird View Court, Las Vegas NV 89129, USA
Bretz, Gabor — Opera Singer
I M G Artists, Hogarth Business Park, Chiswick, London W4 2TH, England
Breuer, Randall W (Randy) — Basketball Player
10481 Misty Morning Lane, Eden Prairie MN 55347, USA
Breunig, Robert P (Bob) — Football Player
9215 Westview Circle, Dallas TX 75231, USA
Brewer, Albert P — Governor, AL
2520 Ashford Place, Birmingham AL 35243, USA
Brewer, Christine — Opera Singer
I M G Artists, Hogarth Business Park, Chiswick, London W4 2TH, England
Brewer, Craig — Director, Writer
W M E Entertainment, 9601 Wilshire Blvd, #300, Beverly Hills CA 90210 USA
Brewer, David L — Navy Admiral
Commander, Military Sealift Command, Washington DC 20398 USA
Brewer, Donald — Drummer (Grand Funk Railroad)
Lustig Talent, PO Box 770850, Orlando FL 32877 USA
Brewer, Eric C — Ice Hockey Player
634 Riviera Dr, Tampa FL 33606, USA
Brewer, James T (Jim) — Basketball Player, Coach
1814 S 23rd Ave, Maywood IL 60153, USA
Brewer, Ronnie — Basketball Player
New York Knicks, Madison Square Garden, 2 Penn Plaza, New York, NY 10121 USA
Brewer, Thomas A (Tom) — Baseball Player
409 State Road, Cheraw SC 29520, USA
Brewer, William R (Billy) — Baseball Player
7405 Woodway Dr, Woodway TX 76712, USA
Brewster, Darrel B (Pete) — Football Player
PO Box 183, Peculiar MO 64078, USA
Brewster, Jordana — Actress
Creative Artists Agency, 2000 Ave of Stars, #100, Los Angeles CA 90067 USA
Brewster, Lamon T — Boxer
Don King Productions, 501 Fairway Dr, Deerfield Beach FL 33441 USA
Brewster, Lincoln — Singer, Guitarist, Songwriter
G O A Inc, 1710 General George Patten Dr, #104, Brentwood TN 37027, USA
Brewster, Paget — Actress
Burstein Co, 15304 W Sunset Blvd, #208, Pacific Palisades CA 90272, USA
Brewster, Patience — Artist, Writer
World Media Communications, PO Box 689, Skaneateles NY 13152, USA

Brey, Mike — Basketball Coach
Notre Dame University, Athletic Dept, Notre Dame IN 46556, USA

Breyer, Stephen G — Supreme Court Justice
US Supreme Court, 1 1st St NE, Washington DC 20543 USA

Breytenbach, Breyten — Writer, Political Activist
Houghton Mifflin Harcourt, 215 Park Ave S, #1200, New York NY 10003 USA

Brezec, Primoz — Basketball Player
10030 Hazelview Dr, Charlotte NC 28277, USA

Brezina, Gregory (Greg) — Football Player
155 Tillinghurst Trace, Newnan GA 30265, USA

Brezina, Robert P (Bobby) — Football Player
1204 Pine Hollow Dr, Friendswood TX 77546, USA

Breziner, Salome — Director, Writer
Rosen Law Group, 15 Brooks Ave, Venice CA 0291, USA

Brezis, Haim — Mathematician
18 Rue de la Glaciere, 75640 Paris Cedex 13, France

Brezner, Larry — Producer
M B S T Entertainment, 345 N Maple Dr, #200, Beverly Hills CA 90210, USA

Brian, Frank S (Frankie) — Basketball Player
4425 40th St, Zachary LA 70791, USA

Brice, Lee — Singer, Songwriter
377 Mgmt, 209 10th Ave, #332, Nashville TN 37203, USA

Brice, Pierre — Actor
8 Rue Orleans, Domaine des Moinets, 60800 Sezy-Magnefall, France

Brickel, James R — Air Force General, Hero
4798 Hanging Moss Lane, Sarasota FL 34238, USA

Brickell, Beth — Director, Actress
9630 Arby Dr, Beverly Hills CA 90210, USA

Brickell, Edie — Singer (New Bohemians), Songwriter
88 Central Park West, New York NY 10023, USA

Brickell, James — Wildlife Filmmaker
Caroline Rose Mgmt, Peter House, Oxford St, Manchester M1 5AN, England

Brickley, Andy — Ice Hockey Player
5 Mill River Lane, Hingham MA 02043, USA

Bricklin, Daniel S — Computer Software Designer (VisiCalc)
Trellix Corp, 300 Bahr Ave, Concord MA 01742, USA

Brickman, Jim — Pianist, Composer
Brickman Music, 28001 Chagrin Blvd, #307, Beachwood OH 44122, USA

Brickman, Marshall — Writer
I C M Partners, 10250 Constellation Blvd, #900, Los Angeles CA 90067 USA

Brickman, Paul M — Director, Producer, Writer
Creative Artists Agency, 2000 Ave of Stars, #100, Los Angeles CA 90067 USA

Brickowski, Frank A — Basketball Player
589 7th St, Lake Oswego OR 97034, USA

Bricusse, Leslie — Composer, Lyricist
8730 W Sunset Blvd, #300W, West Hollywood CA 90069, USA

Bridgeman, Ulysses L (Junior) — Basketball Player
1604 Cherokee Road, Louisville KY 40205, USA

Bridges, Alan J S — Director
28 High St, Shepperton, Middlesex TW7 9AW, England

Bridges, Alicia — Singer, Songwriter
Richard Walters, PO Box 2789, Toluca Lake CA 91610 USA

Bridges, Angelica — Actress, Model
C E S D, 10635 Santa Monica Blvd, #130, Los Angeles CA 90025 USA

Bridges, Beau — Actor
Creative Artists Agency, 2000 Ave of Stars, #100, Los Angeles CA 90067 USA

Bridges, Elisa — Model, Actress
Playboy Promotions, 2706 Media Center Dr, Los Angeles CA 90065 USA

Bridges, Everett L (Rocky) — Baseball Player
1128 W Shane Dr, Coeur D'Alene ID 83815, USA

Bridges, Jeff — Actor, Singer
Creative Artists Agency, 2000 Ave of Stars, #100, Los Angeles CA 90067 USA

Bridges, Jeremy — Football Player
15833 S 35th Way, Phoenix AZ 85048, USA

Bridges, Jordan — Actor
Don Buchwald/Fortitude, 6500 Wilshire Blvd, #2200, Los Angeles CA 90048 USA

Bridges, Krista — Actress
TalentWorks, 3500 W Olive Ave, #1400, Burbank CA 91505 USA

Bridges, Mark — Costume Designer
United Talent Agency, 9336 Civic Center Dr, Beverly Hills CA 90210 USA

Bridges, Roy D, Jr — Astronaut, Air Force General
113 William Barksdale, Williamsburg VA 23185, USA

Bridges, Ruby — Civil Rights Activist, Writer
Ruby Bridges Foundation, PO Box 870248, New Orleans LA 70187, USA

Bridges, Todd A — Actor
16002 Nordhoff St, North Hills CA 91343, USA

Bridges, William C (Bill) — Basketball Player
2322 33rd St, Santa Monica CA 90405, USA

Bridgewater, Brad M — Swimmer
3843 Echo Brook Lane, Dallas TX 75229, USA

Bridgewater, Dee Dee — Singer
Ted Kurland, 173 Brighton Ave, Allston MA 02134 USA

Bridgman, Mel — Ice Hockey Player
221 Concord St, El Segundo CA 90245, USA

Bridwell, Norman — Writer
PO Box 869, Edgartown MA 02539, USA

Briem, Anita — Actress
B/W/R, 9100 Wilshire Blvd, #500W, Beverly Hills CA 90212 USA

Brien, Douglas R Z (Doug) — Football Player
55 Cambrian Ave, Piedmont CA 94611, USA

Briere, Daniel — Ice Hockey Player
17 S Hinchman Ave, Haddonfield NJ 08033, USA

Briers, Richard — Actor, Comedian
Hamilton Hodell, 66-68 Margaret St, London W1W 8SR, England

Briesewitz, Uta — Cinematographer
W M E Entertainment, 9601 Wilshire Blvd, #300, Beverly Hills CA 90210 USA

Brigati, Eddie
Dassinger Creative, 172 2nd Ave, Little Falls NJ 07424, USA — Singer, Percussionist (Rascals)

Briggs of Lewes, Asa
Caprons, Keere Saint Lewes, Sussex BN7 1TX, England — Historian

Briggs, Daniel L (Dan)
8270 Rookery Way, Westerville OH 43082, USA — Baseball Player

Briggs, Edward S
3648 Lago Sereno, Escondido CA 92029, USA — Navy Admiral

Briggs, John E (Johnny)
238 Wall Ave, Paterson NJ 07504, USA — Baseball Player

Briggs, John T
216 Tom Bell Road, #133, Murphys CA 95247, USA — Baseball Player

Briggs, Johnny
Associated International Mgmt, Fairfax House, Fulwood Place, London WC1V 6HU, England — Actor

Briggs, Lance M
225 NE Mizner Blvd, #685, Boca Raton FL 33432, USA — Football Player

Briggs, Raymond R
Weston, Underhill Lane, Westmeston near Hassocks, Sussex, England — Writer, Illustrator, Cartoonist

Briggs, Shannon
22114 N Flamingo Road, Pembroke Pines FL 33028, USA — Boxer

Briggs, William R
480 Hale St, Palo Alto CA 94301, USA — Biologist

Briggs, Wilma
111 Summit Ave, Wakefield RI 02879, USA — Baseball Player

Bright, Leon, Jr
1183 Dutton Ave, Deland FL 32720, USA — Football Player

Bright, Myron H
655 1st Ave N, #340, Fargo ND 58102, USA — Judge

Brightman, Sarah
The Mill, Mill Lane, Cockham SL6 9QT, England — Singer

Brighton, Connie
Playboy Promotions, 2706 Media Center Dr, Los Angeles CA 90065 USA — Model, Actress

Brigman, D J
8304 Calle Soquelle NE, Albuquerque NM 87113, USA — Golfer

Briles, Arthur R (Art)
Baylor University, Athletic Dept, Waco TX 76798, USA — Football Coach

Briley, Gregory (Greg)
2170 Sunnybrook Road, Greenville NC 27834, USA — Baseball Player

Brill, Charlie
3635 Wrightwood Dr, Studio City CA 91604, USA — Actor

Brill, Francesca
Kate Feast, Primrose Hill Studios, Fitzroy Road, London NW1 8TR, England — Actress

Brill, Steven
American Lawyer, Editorial Dept, 600 3rd Ave, New York NY 10016, USA — Editor, Publisher

Brill, Steven (Steve)
United Talent Agency, 9336 Civic Center Dr, Beverly Hills CA 90210 USA — Director, Writer

Brill, Winston J
12529 237th Way NE, Redmond WA 98053, USA — Bacteriologist

Brillinger, Alysha
Agency Group Ltd, 142 W 57th St, #600, New York NY 10019 USA — Singer, Songwriter

Brilmayer, Roberta L
Yale University, Law School, 127 Wall St, New Haven CT 06511, USA — Attorney, Educator

Brimanis, Aris
12909 Badger Lane, Anchorage AK 99516, USA — Ice Hockey Player

Brimble, Nick
Curtis Brown Group, 28-29 Haymarket St, #500, London SW1Y 4SP, England — Actor

Brimblecombe, Richard
Associated International Mgmt, Fairfax House, Fulwood Place, London WC1V 6HU, England — Actor

Brimhall, Cynthia
Playboy Promotions, 2706 Media Center Dr, Los Angeles CA 90065 USA — Actress, Model

Brimley, Wilford
Wilford Brimley Enterprises, 240 Greybull Ave, Greybull WY 82426, USA — Actor

Brin, Sergey
Google Inc, 1600 Amphitheatre Parkway, #41, Mountain View CA 94043, USA — Businessman, Computer Engineer

Brind'Amour, Rod
1153 Four Wheel Dr, Wake Forest NC 27587, USA — Ice Hockey Player

Brink, Andre P
University of Cape Town, English Dept, Rondebosch 7700, South Africa — Writer

Brink, Elisabeth
Houghton Mifflin Harcourt, 215 Park Ave S, #1200, New York NY 10003 USA — Writer

Brink, Evelien
Sikelalodge, PO Box 2277, Hazyview 1242, South Africa — Balloonist

Brink, Frank, Jr
Pine Run, #E1, Ferry & Iron Hill Roads, Doylestown PA 18901, USA — Biophysicist

Brink, Henk
Sikelalodge, PO Box 2277, Hazyview 1242, South Africa — Balloonist

Brink, Lawrence (Larry)
13310 Tierra Heights Road, Redding CA 96003, USA — Football Player

Brink, R Alexander
8301 Old Sauk Road, #326, Middleton WI 53562, USA — Geneticist

Brinker, Nancy Goodman
Komen Breast Cancer Foundation, 5005 LBJ Freeway, #250, Dallas TX 75244, USA — Foundation Executive

Brinkley, Christine (Christie)
Ford Models, 9200 Sunset Blvd, #805, West Hollywood CA 90069, USA — Model, Actress

Brinkley, Douglas
Harper Collins Publishers, 10 E 53rd St, Cellar 1, New York NY 10022 USA — Historian

Brinkman, Charles E (Chuck)
126 Country Club Road, Bryan OH 43506, USA — Baseball Player

Brinkman, John A
1321 E 56th St, #4, Chicago IL 60637, USA — Historian

Brinkman, Joseph N (Joe)
10351 NW 70th St, Chiefland FL 32626, USA — Baseball Umpire

Brinkman, William F
1177 22nd St NW, #2C, Washington DC 20037, USA — Physicist

Brinkmann, Robert S
Mirisch Agency, 8840 Wilshire Blvd, #100, Beverly Hills CA 90211 USA — Cinematographer

Brinson, Gary — Financier
Brinson Partners, 1 N Wacker Dr, #3000, Chicago IL 60606, USA
Brion, Francoise — Actress
11 Rue de Seine, 75006 Paris, France
Brion, John — Composer
Kraft-Engel Mgmt, 15233 Ventura Blvd, #200, Sherman Oaks CA 91403 USA
Brisby, Vincent C — Football Player
1926 Norfolk St, #19, Houston TX 77098, USA
Brisco, Valerie A — Track Athlete
USA Track & Field, 4341 Starlight Dr, Indianapolis IN 46239 USA
Briscoe, Brent — Actor, Writer
Red Baron Mgmt, 600 Rosecrans Ave, Building 7, Manhattan Beach CA 90266, USA
Briscoe, Conie — Writer
Random House, 1745 Broadway, #1800, New York NY 10019 USA
Briscoe, John E — Baseball Player
8581 Southwestern Blvd, #2112, Dallas TX 75206, USA
Briscoe, Marlin — Football Player
675 Coronado Ave, Long Beach CA 90814, USA
Briscoe, Mary Beck — Judge
US Appeals Court, 4839 Billings Parkway, Lawrence KS 66049, USA
Briscoe, Ryan — Auto Racing Driver
Penske Racing, Penske Plaza, 366 Riverfront, Reading PA 19602, USA
Brisebois, Danielle — Actress, Singer
1311 Broadway, Santa Monica CA 90404, USA
Brisebois, Patrice — Ice Hockey Player
4723 Castle Circle, Broomfield CO 80023, USA
Briski, Zana — Photographer, Cinematographer
Kids with Cameras, 341 Lafayette St, #4407, New York NY 10012, USA
Brissie, Leland V (Lou) — Baseball Player
1908 White Pine Dr, North Augusta SC 29841, USA
Brister, Walter A (Bubby), III — Football Player
139 Fontainbleau Dr, Mandeville LA 70471, USA
Bristol, J David (Dave) — Baseball Player, Manager
1748 Fairview Road, Andrews NC 28901, USA
Bristow, Allan M — Basketball Player, Coach, Executive
510 Sand Hill Court, Marco Island FL 34145, USA
Britt, Chris — Editorial Cartoonist
State Journal-Register, Editorial Dept, 1 Copley Plaza, Springfield IL 62701, USA
Britt, James E — Football Player
PO Box 371202, Decatur GA 30037, USA
Britt, May — Actress
5059 Enfield Ave, Encino CA 91316, USA
Britt, Michael — Guitarist (Lonestar)
Borman Entertainment, 4322 Harding Pike, #429, Nashville TN 37205, USA
Britt, Thomas — Interior Designer
136 E 57th St, #700, New York NY 10022, USA
Brittan of Spennithorne, Leon — Government Official, England
1 Finsbury Ave, London EC2M 2PP, England
Brittany, Morgan — Actress, Model
Scott Stander Assoc, 4533 Van Nuys Blvd, #401, Sherman Oaks CA 91403 USA
Brittenham, Harry — Attorney
Ziffren Brittenham Branca, 1801 Century Park West, #700, Los Angeles CA 90067, USA
Brittingham, Eric — Singer, Bassist (Cinderella)
Union Entertainment Group, 1323 Newbury Road, #104, Thousand Oaks CA 91320, USA
Britton, Benjamin — Inventor (Lascaux Virtual Reality Cave)
University of Cincinnati, Fine Arts Dept, Cincinnati OH 45221, USA
Britton, Connie — Actress
W M E Entertainment, 9601 Wilshire Blvd, #300, Beverly Hills CA 90210 USA
Britton, Tony — Actor
Shepherd Mgmt, 45 Maddox St, #400, London W1S 2PE, England
Britz, Jerilyn — Golfer
415 E Lincoln St, #7, Luverne MN 56156, USA
Brixius, Liz — Producer, Writer
W M E Entertainment, 9601 Wilshire Blvd, #300, Beverly Hills CA 90210 USA
Broad, Eli — Businessman
SunAmerica Inc, 10900 Wilshire Blvd, #1200, Los Angeles CA 90024, USA
Broad, Molly Corbett — Educator
American Council on Education, 1 Dupont Circle, #800, Washington DC 20036, USA
Broadbent, Harry — Keyboardist (Kula Shakur)
Little Big Man, 39A Grammercy Park N, #1C, New York NY 10010, USA
Broadbent, Jim — Actor
Independent Talent Group, Oxford House, 76 Oxford St, London W1D 1BS, England
Broadbent, John Edward — Government Official, Canada
1386 Nicola, #30, Vancouver BC V6G 2G2, Canada
Broadhead, James L — Businessman
F P L Group, 700 Universe Blvd, North Palm Beach FL 33408, USA
Broadie, Sarah W — Philosopher
Saint Andrews University, Philosophy Dept, Fife KY16 9AJ, Scotland
Brobeck, John R — Physiologist
224 Vassar Ave, Swarthmore PA 19081, USA
Broberg, Peter S (Pete) — Baseball Player
220 Monterey Road, Palm Beach FL 33480, USA
Brocail, Douglas K (Doug) — Baseball Player
8011 Meadow Vista Dr, Missouri City TX 77459, USA
Brochet, Anne — Actress
Artmedia, 20 Ave Rapp, 75007 Paris, France
Brochtrup, William (Bill) — Actor
S D B Partners, 1801 Ave of Stars, #902, Los Angeles CA 90067 USA
Brochu, Devin — Actor
Greene Assoc, 1901 Ave of Stars, #130, Los Angeles CA 90067 USA
Brochu, Doug — Actor
A P A Talent/Literary Agency, 405 S Beverly Dr, #300, Beverly Hills CA 90212 USA
Brochu, Jim — Actor
Schiowitz Clay, 1680 N Vine St, #1016, Los Angeles CA 90028, USA
Brochu, Stephane — Ice Hockey Player
6029 Evergreen Lane, Grand Blanc MI 48439, USA

Brock, Chad — Singer
Buddy Lee Attractions, 38 Music Square E, #300, Nashville TN 37203 USA
Brock, Gregory A (Greg) — Baseball Player
3727 Valley Oak Dr, Loveland CO 80538, USA
Brock, Louis C (Lou) — Baseball Player
61 Barkley Place, Saint Charles MO 63301, USA
Brock, Matthew L (Matt) — Football Player
3105 SW 98th Ave, Portland OR 97225, USA
Brock, Peter A (Pete) — Football Player
111 Main St, Topsfield MA 01983, USA
Brock, Raheem F — Football Player
1017 Serpentine Lane, Wyncote PA 19095, USA
Brock, Stanley J (Stan) — Football Player, Coach
2555 SW 81st Ave, Portland OR 97225, USA
Brock, T Christopher (Chris) — Baseball Player
7684 Markham Bend Place, Sanford FL 32771, USA
Brock, Tarrik — Baseball Player
8111 Fairchild Ave, Winnetka CA 91306, USA
Brock, Tricia — Director
I C M Partners, 10250 Constellation Blvd, #900, Los Angeles CA 90067 USA
Brock, William E (Bill), III — Secretary of Labor; Senator, TN
16 Revell St, Annapolis MD 21401, USA
Brockermeyer, Blake W — Football Player
PO Box 789, Wilson WY 83014, USA
Brockers, Michael S — Football Player
Saint Louis Rams, 901 N Broadway, Saint Louis MO 63101 USA
Brockert, Richard C — Labor Leader
United Telegraph Workers, 701 E Gude Dr, Rockville MD 20850, USA
Brockington, John S — Football Player
1835 Fort Stockton Dr, San Diego CA 92103, USA
Brockington, Ryan — Actor
C E S D, 10635 Santa Monica Blvd, #130, Los Angeles CA 90025 USA
Brockovich-Ellis, Erin — Legal Activist, Writer
Masry & Vititoe, 5707 Corsa Ave, #200, Westlake Village CA 91362, USA
Brodbin, Kevin — Writer
Creative Artists Agency, 2000 Ave of Stars, #100, Los Angeles CA 90067 USA
Broden, Connie — Ice Hockey Player
88 Valecrest Dr, Etobicoke ON M9A 4P6, Canada
Broder, Samuel — Medical Administrator
I V A X Corp, 4400 Biscayne Blvd, Miami FL 33137, USA
Broderick, Beth — Actress
Vox Inc, 6420 Wilshire Blvd, #1080, Los Angeles CA 90048 USA
Broderick, J M — Artist
8825 SE 32nd Ave, Portland OR 97222, USA
Broderick, Kenneth L (Ken) — Ice Hockey Player
5142 Citation Road, Niagara Falls ON L2H 3H7, Canada
Broderick, Matthew — Actor
246 W 44th St, New York NY 10036, USA
Brodeur, Martin (Marty) — Ice Hockey Player
100 Mountain Ave, West Orange NJ 07052, USA
Brodeur, Richard — Ice Hockey Player
5007 Angus Dr, Vancouver BC V6M 3M6, Canada
Brodhead, Richard H — Educator
Duke University, President's Office, Durham NC 27708, USA
Brodie, H Keith H — Psychiatrist
63 Beverly Dr, Durham NC 27707, USA
Brodie, John R — Football Player, Sportscaster, Golfer
49350 Avenida Fernando, La Quinta CA 92253, USA
Brodie, Kevin — Actor
3925 Big Oak Dr, #5, Studio City CA 91604, USA
Brodowski, Richard S (Dick) — Baseball Player
120 Pine St, Manchester MA 01944, USA
Brody, Adam — Actor
Artist & Brand Management, 8687 Melrose Ave, #900, Los Angeles CA 90069, USA
Brody, Adrien — Actor
Paradigm Agency, 360 N Crescent Dr, North Building, Beverly Hills CA 90210 USA
Brody, Jane E — Journalist
4508 Cedros Ave, Sherman Oaks CA 91403, USA
Brody, Kenneth D — Financier
Export-Import Bank, 811 Vermont Ave NW, Washington DC 20571, USA
Brody, Lane — Singer, Songwriter
Center Stage Attractions, 20 Music Square W, #208, Nashville TN 37203, USA
Brody, William R — Educator
Biological Studies Institute, 10100 N Torrey Pines Road, La Jolla CA 92037, USA
Broecker, Wallace S — Geologist, Geochemist
Lamont-Doherty Earth Observatory, PO Box 1000, Palisades NY 10964, USA
Broelsch, Christopher E — Surgeon
University of Chicago Medical Center, Surgery Dept, Chicago IL 60690, USA
Brogdon, Cinderella J (Cindy) — Basketball Player
4162 Anson Trail, Suwanee GA 30024, USA
Broglio, Ernest G (Ernie) — Baseball Player
2838 Via Carmen, San Jose CA 95124, USA
Brogna, Rico J — Baseball Player
2 Gate Post Lane, Woodbury CT 06798, USA
Brohamer, John A (Jack), Jr — Baseball Player
39017 Narcissus Dr, Palm Desert CA 92211, USA
Brohawn, M Troy — Baseball Player
1619 Taylors Island Road, Woolford MD 21677, USA
Brokaw, Gary G — Basketball Player, Coach, Executive
6614 Augustine Way, Charlotte NC 28270, USA
Brokaw, Thomas J (Tom) — Commentator
941 Park Ave, #14C, New York NY 10028, USA
Brokop, Lisa — Singer, Songwriter
Libre Entertainment, 313-2906 W Broadway, Vancouver BC V6K 2GB, Canada
Brolin, James — Actor
Singer Burke, 6345 Balboa Blvd, #375, Encino CA 91316, USA

B

Brock - Brolin

Brolin, Josh — Actor
I/D Public Relations, 7060 Hollywood Blvd, #800, Los Angeles CA 90028 USA

Brolly, Shane — Actor
Luber Rocklin Entertainment, 8530 Wilshire Blvd, #555, Beverly Hills CA 90211 USA

Bromberg, David — Guitarist, Songwriter
Apex Artists, 818 N Market St, Wilmington DE 19801, USA

Bromell, Lorenzo A — Football Player
5020 Eisenhower Ave, #408, Alexandria VA 22304, USA

Bromley, Gary — Ice Hockey Player
1130 Munro St, Victoria BC V9A 5P1, Canada

Bromley, R Scott — Interior Designer
Bromley Caldari Architects, 242 W 27th St, #200, New York NY 10001, USA

Bromstad, David — Actor, Interior Designer
W M E Entertainment, 9601 Wilshire Blvd, #300, Beverly Hills CA 90210 USA

Bron, Eleanor — Actress
Rebecca Blond, 69A King's Road, London SW3 4NX, England

Bronars, Edward J — Marine Corps General
3354 Rose Lane, Falls Church VA 22042, USA

Bronfman, Charles R — Businessman, Baseball Executive
Koor Industries, 14 Hamelacha St, Rosh Ha'ayin 48091, Israel

Bronfman, Edgar M, Jr — Businessman
Warner Music Group, 75 Rockefeller Plaza, Basement 1, New York NY 10019, USA

Bronfman, Edgar M, Sr — Businessman
31122 Broad Beach Road, Malibu CA 90265, USA

Bronfman, Yefin — Concert Pianist
Opus 3 Artists, 470 Park Ave S, #900N, New York NY 10016 USA

Bronkey, J Jeffrey (Jeff) — Baseball Player
622 Sunny Brook Dr, Edmond OK 73034, USA

Bronleewe, Matt — Guitarist (Jars of Clay)
Creative Artists Agency, 2000 Ave of Stars, #100, Los Angeles CA 90067 USA

Bronner, Till — Jazz Singer, Trumpeter, Composer
Bam Bam Music, Alte Schonhauser Str 44, 10119 Berlin, Germany

Bronson, Po — Writer
Random House, 1745 Broadway, #1800, New York NY 10019 USA

Bronson, R Zack — Football Player
5735 Jackie Lane, Beaumont TX 77713, USA

Bronstein, Elizabeth — Producer
Creative Artists Agency, 2000 Ave of Stars, #100, Los Angeles CA 90067 USA

Brook, Jayne — Actress
Gersh Agency, 9465 Wilshire Blvd, #600, Beverly Hills CA 90212 USA

Brook, Kelly — Model, Actress
Curtis Brown Group, 28-29 Haymarket St, #500, London SW1Y 4SP, England

Brook, Michael — Composer
First Artists, 1631 N Bristol St, #B20, Santa Ana CA 92706 USA

Brook, Peter S P — Director
C I C T, 37 Bis Blvd de la Chapelle, 75010 Paris, France

Brook, Robert H — Physician
1474 Bienvenida Ave, Pacific Palisades CA 90272, USA

Brooke, Bob — Ice Hockey Player
15496 Stanbury Curve, Eden Prairie MN 55347, USA

Brooke, Edward W, III — Senator, MA
808 Brickell Key Dr, #3204, Miami FL 33131, USA

Brooke, Jonatha — Singer (Story), Songwriter
Patrick Rains Assoc, 1255 5th Ave, #7J, New York NY 10029, USA

Brooke, Paul — Actor
Caroline Dawson, 125 Gloucester Road, London SW7 4TE, England

Brookens, Thomas D (Tom) — Baseball Player
488 Black Gap Road, Fayetteville PA 17222, USA

Brooker, Gary — Singer (Procol Harum), Songwriter
195 Sandycombe Road, Kew TW9 2EW, England

Brooker, W Thomas (Tommy) — Football Player
306 Woodridge Dr, Tuscaloosa AL 35406, USA

Brookes, Harvey — Physicist
Harvard University, Aiken Computation Laboratory, Cambridge MA 02138, USA

Brookes, Jacqueline — Actress
Hartig-Hilepo Agency, 54 W 21st St, #610, New York NY 10010, USA

Brookes, Peter — Editorial Cartoonist
London Times, Editorial Dept, 1 Pennington St, London E98 1S5, England

Brooke-Taylor, Tim — Actor, Comedian
Jill Foster Ltd, 3 Lonsdale Road, London SW13 9ED, England

Brookhart, Maurice S — Chemist
University of North Carolina, Chemistry Dept, Chapel Hill NC 27514, USA

Brooking, Keith H — Football Player
883 Lennox Court NE, Atlanta GA 30324, USA

Brookins, Clarence — Basketball Player
8266 Fayette St, Philadelphia PA 19150, USA

Brookins, Gary — Editorial Cartoonist
Richmond Newspapers, Editorial Dept, PO Box 85333, Richmond VA 23293, USA

Brookner, Anita — Writer
68 Elm Park Gardens, #6, London SW10 9PB, England

Brooks, Aaron J — Basketball Player
Houston Rockets, 1730 Jefferson St, Houston TX 77003 USA

Brooks, Aaron L — Football Player
1005 Middle Quarter Court, Henrico VA 23238, USA

Brooks, Albert — Director, Writer, Actor
W M E Entertainment, 9601 Wilshire Blvd, #300, Beverly Hills CA 90210 USA

Brooks, Amanda — Actress
United Agents, 12-26 Lexington St, London W1F 0LE, England

Brooks, Avery — Actor
Lynn Coles Productions, PO Box 1918, El Cerrito CA 94530, USA

Brooks, Barrett — Football Player
11 Berkshire Dr, #25, Voorhees NJ 08043, USA

Brooks, Cindy — Model
Playboy Promotions, 2706 Media Center Dr, Los Angeles CA 90065 USA

Brooks, Clifford (Cliff), Jr — Football Player
12023 Briar Forest Dr, Houston TX 77077, USA

Brooks, Conrad — Actor
PO Box 264, Inwood WV 25428, USA
Brooks, Danny — Singer (Dovells)
Lustig Talent, PO Box 770850, Orlando FL 32877 USA
Brooks, Darin L — Actor
United Talent Agency, 9336 Civic Center Dr, Beverly Hills CA 90210 USA
Brooks, Deanna — Model, Actress
Playboy Promotions, 2706 Media Center Dr, Los Angeles CA 90065 USA
Brooks, Derrick D — Football Player
12815 Pacifica Place, Tampa FL 33625, USA
Brooks, Diana D — Businesswoman
Sotheby's Holdings, 1334 York Ave, New York NY 10021, USA
Brooks, Dolores (Lala) — Singer (Crystals)
Superstars Unlimited, PO Box 371371, Las Vegas NV 89137, USA
Brooks, Ed — Golfer
6604 Augusta Road, Fort Worth TX 76132, USA
Brooks, Ethan B — Football Player
8 Gatewood, Avon CT 06001, USA
Brooks, Frederick P, Jr — Mathematician, Computer Scientist
413 Granville Road, Chapel Hill NC 27514, USA
Brooks, Garth — Singer, Songwriter
Red Strokes Entertainment, 9465 Wilshire Blvd, #319, Beverly Hills CA 90212, USA
Brooks, Geraldine — Writer
PO Box 5056, Vineyard Haven MA 02568, USA
Brooks, Golden — Actress
Vincent Cirrincione Assoc, 1516 N Fairfax Ave, Los Angeles CA 90046 USA
Brooks, Hubert (Hubie) — Baseball Player
15001 Olive St, Hesperia CA 92345, USA
Brooks, James L — Director, Producer, Writer
I C M Partners, 10250 Constellation Blvd, #900, Los Angeles CA 90067 USA
Brooks, James R — Football Player
2876 Sycamore Creek Dr, Independence KY 41051, USA
Brooks, Jason — Actor
289 S Robertson Blvd, #424, Beverly Hills CA 90211, USA
Brooks, Jessica — Actress
United Agents, 12-26 Lexington St, London W1F 0LE, England
Brooks, Kevin C — Football Player
8201 Lighthouse Dr, Rowlett TX 75089, USA
Brooks, Kimberly A — Actress
Metropolitan Talent Agency, 7020 La Presa Dr, Los Angeles CA 90068 USA
Brooks, Kix — Singer (Brooks & Dunn), Songwriter
Team 2 Entertainment, 6345 Balboa Blvd, Building 4, #375, Encino CA 91316 91316, USA
Brooks, Lawrence L (Larry), Sr — Football Player, Coach
11200 NE 53rd St, Kirkland WA 98033, USA
Brooks, Lonnie — Singer, Guitarist
Alligator Records & Mgmt, PO Box 60234, Chicago IL 60660, USA
Brooks, Mark — Golfer
1712 S Adams St, Fort Worth TX 76110, USA
Brooks, Max — Writer
Creative Artists Agency, 2000 Ave of Stars, #100, Los Angeles CA 90067 USA
Brooks, Mehcad — Actor
Mosiac Media Group, 9200 W Sunset Blvd, #1000, Los Angeles CA 90069 USA
Brooks, Mel — Director, Actor, Composer
Brooksfilms, 9336 W Washington Blvd, Culver City CA 90232, USA
Brooks, Meredith — Singer, Songwriter, Guitarist
Creative Artists Agency, 2000 Ave of Stars, #100, Los Angeles CA 90067 USA
Brooks, Michael (Mike) — Football Player
716 2nd Ave, Ruston LA 71270, USA
Brooks, Michael A — Basketball Player
495 Bethany St, San Diego CA 92114, USA
Brooks, Nathan — Boxer
21274 Ellacott Parkway, #M208, Warrensville Heights OH 44128, USA
Brooks, Randi — Actress, Model
3205 Evergreen Point Road, Medina WA 98039, USA
Brooks, Ray — Actor
Ken McReddie Assoc, 11 Connaught Place, London W2 2ET, England
Brooks, Rich — Football Coach
88725 Sky High Dr, Springfield OR 97478, USA
Brooks, Richard — Actor
Greene Assoc, 1901 Ave of Stars, #130, Los Angeles CA 90067 USA
Brooks, Robert D — Football Player
8611 N 17th Place, Phoenix AZ 85020, USA
Brooks, Rodney — Computer Scientist
Massachusetts Institute of Technology, Computer Science Dept, Cambridge MA 02139, USA
Brooks, Ross — Ice Hockey Player
196 Old River Road, #215, Lincoln RI 02865, USA
Brooks, Scott W (Scottie) — Basketball Player, Coach
Oklahoma City Thunder, 211 N Robinson Ave, #300, Oklahoma City OK 73102 USA
Brooks, Terry — Writer
PO Box 244, 1150 Vienna, Austria
Brooks, William (Bill), Jr — Football Player
1088 Laurelwood, Carmel IN 46032, USA
Brooks, William M (Billy) — Football Player
313 E Garrett Run, Austin TX 78753, USA
Broome, David M — Equestrian
Mount Ballan Manor, Crick, Caldicot, Monmouthshire NP26 XP, Wales
Brophy, Kevin — Actor
15010 Hamlin St, Van Nuys CA 91411, USA
Brorby, Wade — Judge
US Court of Appeals, 2120 Capitol Ave, #2131, Cheyenne WY 82001, USA
Bros, Jose — Opera Singer
Opera et Concert, 37 Rue de la Chaussee d'Antin, 75009 Paris, France
Broshears, Robert — Sculptor
Robert Broshears Studio, 8020 NW Holly Road, Bremerton WA 98312, USA
Brosius, Scott D — Baseball Player
1780 NW Troon Court, McMinnville OR 97128, USA

Broski, David C
University of Illinois, President's Office, Chicago IL 60607, USA
Educator

Brosnan, James P (Jim)
7742 Churchill St, Morton Grove IL 60053, USA
Baseball Player

Brosnan, Pierce
31118 Broad Beach Road, Malibu CA 90265, USA
Actor

Brosnan, Sean
Sages Entertainment Group, 9107 Wilshire Blvd, #450, Beverly Hills CA 90210, USA
Actor

Brossart, Willy
9318 Susquehanna Trail, Ashland VA 23005, USA
Ice Hockey Player

Brostek, Bern
PO Box 44552, Kamuela HI 96743, USA
Football Player

Broten, Aaron
307 Delmore Dr, Roseau MN 56751, USA
Ice Hockey Player

Broten, Neal
N8216 690th St, River Falls WI 54022, USA
Ice Hockey Player

Broten, Paul
6972 Ashwood Road, #305, Saint Paul MN 55125, USA
Ice Hockey Player

Broth, Ed
Trident Media Group, 41 Madison Ave, #3600, New York NY 10010, USA
Writer

Brother Ali
Agency Group Ltd, 142 W 57th St, #600, New York NY 10019 USA
Rap Artist

Brothers, Joyce D
W M E Entertainment, 9601 Wilshire Blvd, #300, Beverly Hills CA 90210 USA
Psychologist

Brotman, Jeffrey
Costco Wholesale Corp, 999 Lake Dr, #200, Issaquah WA 98027, USA
Businessman

Brough Clapp, A Louise
1808 Voluntary Road, Vista CA 92084, USA
Tennis Player

Broughton, Willie L
1724 Lacy Lane, Mesquite TX 75181, USA
Football Player

Brouhard, Mark S
6289 Jackie Ave, Woodland Hills CA 91367, USA
Baseball Player

Brouse, Sharon
I K A R, 5870 W Olympic Blvd, Los Angeles CA 90036, USA
Religious Leader, Rabbi

Broussard, Benjamin I (Ben)
8917 Old Lampasas Trail, #14, Austin TX 78750, USA
Baseball Player

Broussard, Israel
Paradigm Agency, 360 N Crescent Dr, North Building, Beverly Hills CA 90210 USA
Actor

Broussard, Marc
Monterey Peninsula Artists, 404 W Franklin St, Monterey CA 93940 USA
Singer, Songwriter

Broussard, Rebecca
9911 W Pico Blvd, #PH A, Los Angeles CA 90035, USA
Actress

Browder, Ben
Gersh Agency, 9465 Wilshire Blvd, #600, Beverly Hills CA 90212 USA
Actor

Browder, Felix E
4 Foulet Dr, Princeton NJ 08540, USA
Mathematician

Brower, James R (Jim)
4947 Green Valley Road, Minnetonka MN 55345, USA
Baseball Player

Brown Heritage, Doris
Seattle Pacific College, Athletic Dept, Seattle WA 98119, USA
Track Athlete

Brown, Aaron C
3922 W Robson St, Tampa FL 33614, USA
Football Player

Brown, Alex J
Coyote Logistics, 2545 W Diversey Ave, Chicago IL 60647, USA
Football Player

Brown, Alison
S R O Artists, 6629 University Ave, #206, Middleton WI 53562, USA
Singer, Songwriter, Banjo Player

Brown, Alton
42 West, 220 W 42nd St, #1200, New York NY 10036 USA
Chef

Brown, Amanda
E P Dutton, 375 Hudson St, New York NY 10014 USA
Writer

Brown, Andre L
11245 S Emerald Ave, Chicago IL 60628, USA
Football Player

Brown, Andy
6243 S 125th W, Trafalgar IN 46181, USA
Ice Hockey Player

Brown, Angela
Columbia Artists Mgmt Inc, 1790 Broadway, #702, New York NY 10019 USA
Opera Singer

Brown, Anthony
42561 Cavalier Court, Canton MI 48187, USA
Football Player

Brown, Antron
Antron Brown Racing, 1681 E Northfield Drive, #A, Brownsburg IN 46112, USA
Drag Racing Driver, Motorcycle Rider

Brown, Arnie
General Delivery, Woodview ON K0L 3E0, Canada
Ice Hockey Player

Brown, Arthur E, Jr
35 Fairway Winds Place, Hilton Head Island SC 29928, USA
Army General

Brown, Ashley Nicole
Hervey/Grimes Talent, 10561 Missouri Ave, #2, Los Angeles CA 90025 USA
Actress

Brown, Billy
TalentWorks, 3500 W Olive Ave, #1400, Burbank CA 91505 USA
Actor

Brown, Billy Aaron
Stone Manners Salners, 9911 W Pico Blvd, #1400, Los Angeles CA 90035 USA
Actor

Brown, Billy Ray
7502 Whitman Lane, Sugar Land TX 77479, USA
Golfer

Brown, Blair
Innovative Artists, 1505 10th St, Santa Monica CA 90401 USA
Actress

Brown, Bobby
Universal Attractions, 135 W 26th St, #1200, New York NY 10001 USA
Singer, Dancer, Songwriter

Brown, Brant M
40756 Balch Park Road, Springville CA 93265, USA
Baseball Player

Brown, Bruce
3858 W Carson St, Torrance CA 90503, USA
Photographer, Surfer

Brown, Bryan
New Town Films, 12/37 Nicholson St, East Balmain NSW 2041, Australia
Actor

Brown, Bryan D (Doug)
Aurora Flight Services, 9950 Wakeman Dr, Manassas VA 20110, USA
Army General

Brown, Carlinhos
Tempest Entertainment, 245 W 25th St, #BD, New York NY 10001, USA
Percussionist, Composer

Brown, Cedric W — Football Player
9005 Salsbury Lane, #11, Oklahoma City OK 73132, USA

Brown, Chadwick — Actor
SirenSong Entertainment, PO Box 2919, New York NY 10163, USA

Brown, Chadwick E (Chad) — Football Player
10287 Dowling Way, Littleton CO 80126, USA

Brown, Charles (Charlie) — Football Player
3113 Cherry Valley Circle, Fairfield CA 94534, USA

Brown, Charles E — Ice Hockey Player
4677 Parkridge Dr, Saint Paul MN 55123, USA

Brown, Charles E (Charlie) — Football Player
7317 S Merrill Ave, Chicago IL 60649, USA

Brown, Christopher M (Chris) — Singer, Rap Artist, Actor
Tina Davis Co, 96 Linwood Plaza, #454, Fort Lee NJ 07024, USA

Brown, Christopher R (Chris) — Football Player
251 Riverbend Dr, Franklin TN 37064, USA

Brown, Clancy — Actor
I C M Partners, 10250 Constellation Blvd, #900, Los Angeles CA 90067 USA

Brown, Clare — Writer
A M Heath Co, 79 Saint Martin's Lane, London WC2N 4RE, England

Brown, Clarence (Chucky) — Basketball Player
102 Balsamwood Court, Cary NC 27513, USA

Brown, Cleophus — Baseball Player
3912 Sharon Church Road, Pinson AL 35126, USA

Brown, Clifton — Dancer
Alvin Ailey American Dance Theater, 405 W 55th St, New York NY 10019, USA

Brown, Collier (P J) — Basketball Player
2142 Hampshire Dr, Slidell LA 70461, USA

Brown, Cornell D — Football Player
1600 Sangloe Place, Lynchburg VA 24502, USA

Brown, Corwin A — Football Player
1124 E 90th St, Chicago IL 60619, USA

Brown, Courtney L — Football Player
1133 Schurlknight Road, Saint Stephen SC 29479, USA

Brown, Curtis — Ice Hockey Player
467 Carroll St, Sunnyvale CA 94086, USA

Brown, Curtis J — Football Player
1035 Lindenwood Ave, Saint Charles MO 63301, USA

Brown, Curtis L, Jr — Astronaut
204 Starrwood, Hudson WI 54016, USA

Brown, Cynthia G (Cindy) — Model
Playboy Promotions, 2706 Media Center Dr, Los Angeles CA 90065 USA

Brown, Dale — Writer
Renaissance Literary & Talent, PO Box 17379, Beverly Hills CA 90209, USA

Brown, Damone L — Basketball Player
83 Greenfield St, Buffalo NY 14214, USA

Brown, Dan — Writer
Atria/Washington Square Press, 1230 Ave of Americas, New York NY 10020, USA

Brown, Daniel (Dee) — Basketball Player
575 Birnamwood Dr, Suwanee GA 30024, USA

Brown, Dave — Ice Hockey Player
Philadelphia Flyers, 1st Union Center, 3601 S Broad St, Philadelphia PA 19148 USA

Brown, David M (Dave) — Football Player
216 Watchung Fork, Westfield NJ 07090, USA

Brown, David T — Businessman
Owings Corning, 1 Owens Corning Parkway, Toledo OH 43659, USA

Brown, Denise Scott — Architect
Venturi Scott Brown Assoc, 4236 Main St, Philadelphia PA 19127, USA

Brown, Derek V — Football Player
13 Four Leaf Manor, Rexford NY 12148, USA

Brown, Dermal B (Dee) — Baseball Player
2626 Balmoral Court, Kissimmee FL 34744, USA

Brown, Donald David — Biologist
6511 Abbey View Way, Baltimore MD 21212, USA

Brown, Doug — Ice Hockey Player
3188 Bradway Blvd, Bloomfield Hills MI 48301, USA

Brown, Dustin J — Ice Hockey Player
1717 8th St, Manhattan Beach CA 90266, USA

Brown, Eddie L — Football Player
628 Cedar Park Dr, Daytona Beach FL 32114, USA

Brown, Edward R — Cinematographer
3925 S Jones Blvd, #1011, Las Vegas NV 89103, USA

Brown, Emil Q — Baseball Player
18361 Olde Farm Road, Lansing IL 60438, USA

Brown, Eric G — Football Player
2226 Drake Falls Dr, Pearland TX 77584, USA

Brown, Ewart F, Jr — Prime Minister, Bermuda
Premier's Office, Cabinet Building, 105 Front St, Hamilton HM 12, Bermuda

Brown, Faith — Actress
Million Dollar Music Co, 12 Praed Mews, London W2 1QY, England

Brown, Foxy — Rap Artist
J L Entertainment, 18653 Ventura Blvd, #340, Tarzana CA 91356 USA

Brown, Fred — Basketball Player, Coach
3696 72nd Place SE, Mercer Island WA 98040, USA

Brown, Fred R — Football Player
4128 Rigel Ave, Lompoc CA 93436, USA

Brown, G Hanks (Hank) — Senator, CO; Educator
Daniels Fund, 101 Monroe St, Denver CO 80206, USA

Brown, Gary L — Football Player
35401 Saddle Creek, Avon OH 44011, USA

Brown, Georg Stanford — Actor
2565 Greenvalley Road, Los Angeles CA 90046, USA

Brown, George R — Basketball Player
24652 Santa Barbara St, Southfield MI 48075, USA

Brown, Greg — Ice Hockey Player
43 Trysting Road, Scituate MA 02066, USA

Brown, Greg — Businessman
Motorola Inc, 1303 E Algonquin Blvd, Schaumburg IL 60196, USA
Brown, Gregory (Greg) — Football Player
1016 Hartley Court, Sicklerville NJ 08081, USA
Brown, Guy, III — Football Player
2233 Forest Hollow Park, Dallas TX 75228, USA
Brown, H Harold (Hal) — Baseball Player
4216 Henderson Road, Greensboro NC 27410, USA
Brown, Harold — Secretary, Defense
Strategic/International Studies Center, 1800 K St NW, #400, Washington DC 20006, USA
Brown, Henry — Actor
1101 E Pike St, #300, Seattle WA 98122, USA
Brown, Henry Lee — Baseball Player
4075 N 61st St, Milwaukee WI 53216, USA
Brown, Henry W — WW II Army Air Force Hero
2825 Carter Road, #117, Sumter SC 29150, USA
Brown, Hubie — Basketball Coach
120 Foxridge Road NW, Atlanta GA 30327, USA
Brown, Hyman — Civil Engineer
Colorado State University, Civil Engineering Dept, Fort Collins CO 80523, USA
Brown, Ian A — Singer, Bassist (Stone Roses)
Magnum Public Relations, 32 E 31st St, #900, New York NY 10016, USA
Brown, Ivory L — Football Player
9811 Dale Crest Dr, #126, Dallas TX 75220, USA
Brown, J Gordon — Prime Minister, England
Prime Minister's Office, 10 Downing St, London SW1A 2AA, England
Brown, J Kevin — Baseball Player
105 Browns Ridge, Macon GA 31210, USA
Brown, James (J B) — Sportscaster
CBS-TV, Sports Dept, 51 W 52nd St, New York NY 10019 USA
Brown, James H (J B) — Football Player
12520 Woodsong Lane, Bowie MD 20721, USA
Brown, James N (Jim) — Football Player, Actor
100 Alfred Lerner Way, Cleveland OH 44114, USA
Brown, James R — Air Force General
18286 Buccaneer Terrace, Leesburg VA 20176, USA
Brown, Jamie S — Football Player
25023 Riding Center Dr, Chantilly VA 20152, USA
Brown, Jammal F — Football Player
2223 NE 36th St, Lawton OK 73507, USA
Brown, Janice Rogers — Judge
US Court of Appeals, 717 Madison Place NW, Washington DC 20439, USA
Brown, Jarvis A — Baseball Player
4201 S Decatur Blvd, #1161, Las Vegas NV 89103, USA
Brown, Jason W — Football Player
8810 Gilly Way, Randallstown MD 21133, USA
Brown, Jeff — Ice Hockey Player
800 Tara Oaks Dr, Chesterfield MO 63005, USA
Brown, Jenn — Actress, Sportscaster
2032 Armacost Ave, Los Angeles CA 90025, USA
Brown, Jim Ed — Singer
Joe Taylor Artist Agency, PO Box 279, Williamstown NJ 37068 USA
Brown, John C — Football Player
101 Gadshill Place, Pittsburgh PA 15237, USA
Brown, John Y — Basketball Player
1523 Oak Forest Dr, Rolla MO 65401, USA
Brown, John Y, Jr — Governor, KY
1990 Fort Harrods Dr, Lexington KY 40503, USA
Brown, Jonathan Daniel — Actor
Creative Artists Agency, 2000 Ave of Stars, #100, Los Angeles CA 90067 USA
Brown, Julie — Actress, Comedienne, Singer
11288 Ventura Blvd, #728, Studio City CA 91604, USA
Brown, Julie (Downtown) — Actress, Producer
Independent Management Group, 8444 Wilshire Blvd, #500, Beverly Hills CA 90211, USA
Brown, Julie Caitlin — Actress, Singer
2109 S Wilbur Ave, Walla Walla WA 99362, USA
Brown, June — Actress
Associated International Mgmt, Fairfax House, Fulwood Place, London WC1V 6HU, England
Brown, Junior — Singer, Guitarist
Curb Records, 48 Music Square E, Nashville TN 37203 USA
Brown, Keith — Ice Hockey Player
8515 Woodland Brooke Trail, Cumming GA 30028, USA
Brown, Kenneth J — Labor Leader
Graphic Communications International Union, 1900 L St NW, #800, Washington DC 20036, USA
Brown, Kevin L — Baseball Player
9201 Ryan Court, Evansville IN 47712, USA
Brown, Kimberly J — Actress
Global Artists Agency, 6253 Hollywood Blvd, #508, Los Angeles CA 90028 USA
Brown, Kristopher C (Kris) — Football Player
712 Holly St, Bellaire TX 77401, USA
Brown, Kwame — Basketball Player
7685 Veragua Dr, Playa del Rey CA 90293, USA
Brown, Larry — Football Player
1377 Glencoe Ave, Pittsburgh PA 15205, USA
Brown, Larry L — Baseball Player
13158 La Mirada Circle, Wellington FL 33414, USA
Brown, Larry, Jr — Football Player
5603 Sycamore Dr, Colleyville TX 76034, USA
Brown, Lawrence (Larry), Jr — Football Player
4390 Parliament Place, #A, Lanham MD 20706, USA
Brown, Lawrence H (Larry) — Basketball Player, Coach, Executive
1030 Green Valley Road, Bryn Mawr PA 19010, USA
Brown, Lester R — Ecologist
Worldwatch Institute, 1776 Massachusetts Ave NW, #800, Washington DC 20036, USA
Brown, Lomas, Jr — Football Player
5049 Elizabeth Lake Road, Waterford MI 48327, USA

Brown, Marc — Artist, Writer
Little Brown, 3 Center Plaza, #100, Boston MA 02108 USA
Brown, Marcia Joan — Writer
165 Avenida Majorca, #B, Laguna Hills CA 92637, USA
Brown, Mark A — Football Player
2761 SW 81st Way, Davie FL 33328, USA
Brown, Mark N — Astronaut
80 Earlsgate Road, Dayton OH 45440, USA
Brown, Marty — Singer, Guitarist
PO Box 190515, Nashville TN 37219, USA
Brown, Matthew B (Matt) — Baseball Player
11259 N Cutlass St, Hayden ID 83835, USA
Brown, Max — Actor
United Agents, 12-26 Lexington St, London W1F 0LE, England
Brown, Melanie J — Singer (Spice Girls)
I C M Partners, 10250 Constellation Blvd, #900, Los Angeles CA 90067 USA
Brown, Michael (Mike) — Basketball Player
304 Rays Mill Road, Aberdeen NC 28315, USA
Brown, Michael A — Astronomer
California Institute of Technology, Astronomy Dept, Pasadena CA 91125, USA
Brown, Michael C (Mike) — Baseball Player
2904 E Minton St, Mesa AZ 85213, USA
Brown, Michael D — Government Official
OnScreen Technologies, 600 NW 14th Ave, Portland OR 97209, USA
Brown, Michael E (Mike) — Astronomer
California Institute of Technology, Geological & Planetary Sciences Division, Pasadena CA 91125, USA
Brown, Michael G (Mike) — Baseball Player
710 95th Ave N, Naples FL 34108, USA
Brown, Michael S — Nobel Medicine Laureate
5719 Redwood Lane, Dallas TX 75209, USA
Brown, Miguel — Singer
International Artists, PO Box 32, Grave 5369 AA, Netherlands
Brown, Mike — Football Executive
Cincinnati Bengals, 1 Paul Brown Stadium, Cincinnati OH 45202 USA
Brown, Nancy E — Navy Admiral
Director, Communications/Computers, Joint Staff, Pentagon, Washington DC 20310 USA
Brown, Norman — Singer, Guitarist
Warner Bros Records, 3300 Warner Blvd, Burbank CA 91505 USA
Brown, Olivia — Actress
David Shapira Assoc, 193 N Robertson Blvd, Beverly Hills CA 90211 USA
Brown, Ollie L — Baseball Player
8462 Country Club Dr, Buena Park CA 90621, USA
Brown, Orlando — Actor
Abrams Artists, 9200 W Sunset Blvd, #1125, West Hollywood CA 90069 USA
Brown, Oscar L — Baseball Player
19113 Gunlock Ave, Carson CA 90746, USA
Brown, Patricia — Baseball Player
821 Solar Lane, Glenview IL 60025, USA
Brown, Patrick — Biochemist
Stanford University Medical School, Biochemistry Dept, Stanford CA 94305, USA
Brown, Patrick (Sleepy) — Singer, Songwriter
J Erving Group, 555 Whitehall St SW, #N, Atlanta GA 30303, USA
Brown, Paul — Jazz Guitarist
Chapman & Co Mgmt, PO Box 55246, Sherman Oaks CA 91413, USA
Brown, Peter — Actor
Special Artists Agency, 9465 Wilshire Blvd, #820, Beverly Hills CA 90212 USA
Brown, Peter R L — Historian
Princeton University, History Dept, Princeton NJ 08544, USA
Brown, Philip — Actor
8721 W Sunset Blvd, #200, West Hollywood CA 90069 USA
Brown, Pieta — Singer, Guitarist, Songwriter
Blind Ambition Mgmt, 6 Courthouse Way, Jonesboro GA 30236, USA
Brown, Preston M — Football Player
6804 Jones Valley Dr SE, Huntsville AL 35802, USA
Brown, R Anthony B (Tony), Jr — Football Player
PO Box 7122, Branson MO 65615, USA
Brown, R Hanbury — Astronomer
White Cottage, Penton Mewsey, Andover, Hants SP11 0RQ, England
Brown, Ralph, III — Football Player
9395 Old Post Dr, Rancho Cucamonga CA 91730, USA
Brown, Randy — Basketball Player
Chicago Bulls, United Center, 1901 W Madison St, Chicago IL 60612 USA
Brown, Raymond M — Football Player
4936 Lake Fjord Pass, Marietta GA 30068, USA
Brown, Reggie V — Football Player
1325 Oxford Lane, Union NJ 07083, USA
Brown, Rhyon Nicole — Actress
HeyGurl, 335 E Albertoni St, Carson CA 90746, USA
Brown, Richard S — Football Player
5652 Alfred Ave, Westminster CA 92683, USA
Brown, Rita Mae — Writer, Social Activist
Wendy Weill Agency, 232 Madison Ave, New York NY 10016, USA
Brown, Rob — Ice Hockey Player
5204 84th St, Edmonton AB T6E 5N8, Canada
Brown, Robert (Rob) — Actor
W M E Entertainment, 9601 Wilshire Blvd, #300, Beverly Hills CA 90210 USA
Brown, Robert A — Chemical Engineer, Educator
Boston University, President's Office, 1 Sherborn St, Boston MA 02215, USA
Brown, Robert D — Businessman
Milacron Inc, 2090 Florence Ave, Cincinnati OH 45206, USA
Brown, Robert E (Bob) — Football Player
PO Box 211081, Saint Louis MO 63121, USA
Brown, Robert S (Bob) — Football Player
1628 Fairmont Dr, San Leandro CA 94578, USA
Brown, Robert W (Bobby) — Baseball Player, Executive
4100 Clark Ave, Fort Worth TX 76107, USA

Brown, Roger Aaron — Actor
Innovative Artists, 1505 10th St, Santa Monica CA 90401 USA

Brown, Roger L — Football Player
9 N Point Dr, Portsmouth VA 23703, USA

Brown, Rogers L (Bobby) — Baseball Player
700 Pleasant Ridge Court, Chesapeake VA 23322, USA

Brown, Ron J — Football Player, Track Athlete
2212 Radcourt Dr, Hacienda Heights CA 91745, USA

Brown, Ronald K — Choreographer, Dance Executive
Evidence, 80 Hanson Place, #605, Brooklyn NY 11217, USA

Brown, Ronnie G, Jr — Football Player
3445 Stratford Road NE, #3707, Atlanta GA 30326, USA

Brown, Ruben — Football Player
170 Fox Meadow Lane, Orchard Park NY 14127, USA

Brown, Rupert A — Educator
Boston University, President's Office, 1 Silber Way, Boston MA 02215, USA

Brown, Ryan — Actor
Side by Side Literary Productions, 15 W 26th St, #200, New York NY 10010, USA

Brown, Sandra — Writer
1306 W Abram St, Arlington TX 76013, USA

Brown, Sara Suzanne — Actress
Media Artists Group, 8222 Melrose Ave, #203, Los Angeles CA 90048 USA

Brown, Shannon — Basketball Player
Phoenix Suns, 201 E Jefferson St, Phoenix AZ 85004 USA

Brown, Sheldon D — Football Player
6 Tuxedo Court, Marlton NJ 08053, USA

Brown, Shirley — Singer
Rodgers Redding, PO Box 4603, Macon GA 31208 USA

Brown, Sophina — Actress
Peter Strain, 5455 Wilshire Blvd, #1812, Los Angeles CA 90036 USA

Brown, Sterling K — Actor
Innovative Artists, 1505 10th St, Santa Monica CA 90401 USA

Brown, Steve — Football Player
2207 Osage St, Saint Louis MO 63118, USA

Brown, Susan — Actress
Hamilton Hodell, 66-68 Margaret St, London W1W 8SR, England

Brown, T Edward (Ted) — Football Player
7320 130th St W, Saint Paul MN 55124, USA

Brown, T Graham — Singer
Richard De La Font Agency, 4845 S Sheridan Road, #505, Tulsa OK 74145 USA

Brown, Terry L — Football Player
401 N 6th St, Marlow OK 73055, USA

Brown, Theotis, II — Football Player
9604 W 121st Terrace, Overland Park KS 66213, USA

Brown, Thomas A (Timmy) — Football Player
505 S Farrell Dr, #E28, Palm Springs CA 92264, USA

Brown, Thomas M (Tommy) — Baseball Player
8119 Shady Place, Brentwood TN 37027, USA

Brown, Thomas W (Tom) — Football, Baseball Player
27981 Nanticoke Road, Salisbury MD 21801, USA

Brown, Timothy D (Tim) — Football Player
1107 W Pleasant Run Road, DeSoto TX 75115, USA

Brown, Tom — Football Player
679 Aldford Ave, Delta BC V3M 5P5, Canada

Brown, Tracy — Ballerina
Royal Ballet, Covent Garden, Bow St, London WC2E 9DD, England

Brown, Trisha — Choreographer, Dancer
Trisha Brown Dance Co, 465 Greenwich St, Front 1, New York NY 10013, USA

Brown, Troy F — Football Player
PO Box 452, Foxboro MA 02035, USA

Brown, Vincent B — Football Player
PO Box 71268, Henrico VA 23255, USA

Brown, W Earl — Actor
Greene Assoc, 1901 Ave of Stars, #130, Los Angeles CA 90067 USA

Brown, W Mack — Football Coach
University of Texas, Athletic Dept, Austin TX 78712, USA

Brown, Wayne — Ice Hockey Player
50 Montgomery Blvd, Belleville ON K8N 1H9, Canada

Brown, William D (Bill) — Football Player
9365 Libby Lane, Eden Prairie MN 55347, USA

Brown, William F (Willie) — Football Player, Coach
27138 Lillegard Court, Tracy CA 95304, USA

Brown, William J (Gates) — Baseball Player
17206 Santa Barbara Dr, Detroit MI 48221, USA

Brown, Yvette Nicole — Actress
Abrams Artists, 9200 W Sunset Blvd, #1125, West Hollywood CA 90069 USA

Brown, Zac — Singer, Guitarist
Roar Mgmt, 9701 Wilshire Blvd, #800, Beverly Hills CA 90212, USA

Browne, Byron E — Baseball Player
2831 S 83rd Dr, Tolleson AZ 85353, USA

Browne, Chris — Cartoonist (Hagar the Horrible)
King Features Syndicate, 300 W 57th St, #1500, New York NY 10019 USA

Browne, Gerald — Writer
Warner Books, 1271 6th Ave, New York NY 10020, USA

Browne, Gordon W (Gordie) — Football Player
1001 Lakeridge Court, Colleyville TX 76034, USA

Browne, Herbert A, Jr — Navy Admiral
A F C E A International, 4400 Fair Lakes Court, #104, Fairfax VA 22033, USA

Browne, Jackson — Singer, Songwriter
Donald Miller Mgmt, 12746 Kling St, Studio City CA 91604, USA

Browne, Jann — Singer
Tracy Gershon Mgmt, PO Box 158400, Nashville TN 37215, USA

Browne, Jerome A (Jerry) — Baseball Player
2102 Company St, #1, Christiansted VI 00820, USA

Browne, Leslie — Ballerina, Actress
2025 Broadway, #6F, New York NY 10023, USA

Browne, Olin
9562 SE Sandpine Lane, Hobe Sound FL 33455, USA — Golfer

Browner, Carol M
White House, 1600 Pennsylvania Ave NW, Washington DC 20500, USA — Government Official

Browner, Jimmie L (Jim)
3369 Peachtree Corners Circle, Norcross GA 30092, USA — Football Player

Browner, Joey M
PO Box 22721, Saint Paul MN 55122, USA — Football Player

Browner, Keith T
5017 Chesley Ave, Los Angeles CA 90043, USA — Football Player

Browner, Ross
7900 Indian Springs Dr, Nashville TN 37221, USA — Football Player

Brown-Findlay, Jessica
Troika, 74 Clerkenwell Road, #300, London EC1M 5QA, England — Actress

Browning, David (Dave)
10117 S Lambs Lane, Mica WA 99023, USA — Football Player

Browning, Edmond L
5164 Imai Road, Hood River OR 97031, USA — Religious Leader

Browning, Emily
Signpost Mgmt, 250 S Beverly Dr, #201, Beverly Hills CA 90212, USA — Actress

Browning, Kurt
International Management Group, 175 Bloor St E, #400S, Toronto ON M4W 3R8, Canada — Figure Skater

Browning, Logan
Kazarian/Spencer/Ruskin, 11969 Ventura Blvd, #300, Studio City CA 91604 USA — Actress, Singer

Browning, Ricou
5221 SW 196th Lane, Southwest Ranches FL 33332, USA — Actor

Browning, Thomas L (Tom)
1110 Grindstone Court, Union KY 41091, USA — Baseball Player

Brownlee, Alistair E
Leeds Metropolitan University, Carnegie High Performance Center, Leeds LS1 3HE, England — Triathlete

Brownlee, Don
University of Washington, Astronomy Dept, PO Box 351580, Seattle WA 98195, USA — Astronomer

Brownlee, Jonathan
Leeds Metropolitan University, Carnegie High Performance Center, Leeds LS1 3HE, England — Triathlete

Brownlee, Lawrence
I M G Artists, Hogarth Business Park, Chiswick, London W4 2TH, England — Opera Singer

Brownlee, Shannon
New America Foundation, 1899 L St NW, #400, Washington DC 20036 20036, USA — Writer

Brownlow, Kevin
Photoplay Productions, 21 Princess Road, London NW1, England — Producer

Brown-Miller, Lisa
US Olympic Committee, 1 Olympic Plaza, Building 6, Colorado Springs CO 80909 USA — Ice Hockey Player

Brownmiller, Susan
61 Jane St, New York NY 10014, USA — Social Activist

Brownschidle, Jack
35 Hidden Pines Court, East Amherst NY 14051, USA — Ice Hockey Player

Brownstein, Carrie
High Road Touring, 751 Bridgeway, #200, Sausalito CA 94965 USA — Singer, Guitarist (Sleater-Kinney)

Broza, David
Aviv Productions, 10418 E Meadowhill Dr, Scottsdale AZ 85255, USA — Singer, Songwriter

Brozer, Kim
2700 N 16th St, Beaumont TX 77703, USA — Golfer

Brubaker, Charles W
82 Essex Road, Winnetka IL 60093, USA — Architect

Brubaker, Ed
United Talent Agency, 9336 Civic Center Dr, Beverly Hills CA 90210 USA — Cartoonist, Writer

Brubaker, Jeff
1827 Oak Ridge Road, #A, Oak Ridge NC 27310, USA — Ice Hockey Player

Brubeck, David W (Dave)
221 Millstone Road, Wilton CT 06897, USA — Jazz Pianist

Bruce Bruce
I C M Partners, 10250 Constellation Blvd, #900, Los Angeles CA 90067 USA — Actor, Comedian

Bruce, Aundray
1730 Wentworth Dr, Montgomery AL 36106, USA — Football Player

Bruce, Christopher
Rambert Dance Co, 94 Chiswick High Road, London W4 1SH, England — Choreographer

Bruce, David
975 Grand Blvd, Bellingham WA 98229, USA — Ice Hockey Player

Bruce, Ed
1022 16th Ave S, Nashville TN 37212, USA — Singer

Bruce, Isaac I
PO Box 550141, Fort Lauderdale FL 33355, USA — Football Player

Bruce, Jack
Agency Group Ltd, 142 W 57th St, #600, New York NY 10019 USA — Singer, Bassist (Cream), Songwriter

Bruce, Robert J (Bob)
800 E 15th St, #207, Plano TX 75074, USA — Baseball Player

Bruce, Thomas (Tom)
122 Sea Terrace Way, Aptos CA 95003, USA — Swimmer

Bruckheimer, Jerry
Jerry Bruckheimer Films, 1631 10th St, Santa Monica CA 90404, USA — Producer

Bruckner, Agnes
A P A Talent/Literary Agency, 405 S Beverly Dr, #300, Beverly Hills CA 90212 USA — Actress

Bruckner, Greg
3906 E Potter Dr, Phoenix AZ 85050, USA — Golfer

Bruckner, Leslie C (Les)
1325 Valley View Road, #307, Glendale CA 91202, USA — Football Player

Brudzinski, Robert L (Bob)
4607 Gleneagles Dr, Boynton Beach FL 33436, USA — Football Player

Brue, Bob
5699 N Centerpark Way, #422, Milwaukee WI 53217, USA — Golfer

Brueckner, Keith A
7723 Ludington Place, La Jolla CA 92037, USA — Physicist

Brueggemann, Walter
701 S Columbia Dr, Decatur GA 30030, USA — Theologian

Brueggergosman, Measha
I M G Artists, Hogarth Business Park, Chiswick, London W4 2TH, England — Opera Singer

Bruel, Patrick — Singer, Actor
Voyez Mon Agent, 20 Ave Rapp, 75007 Paris, France

Brueland, Lowell K — WW II Army Air Corps Hero
420 La Z Acres Road, Westminster SC 29693, USA

Bruen, John D — Army General, Businessman
6104 Greenlawn Court, Springfield VA 22152, USA

Bruener, Mark F — Football Player
19860 NE 133rd St, Woodinville WA 98077, USA

Bruening, Justin — Actor
Innovative Artists, 1505 10th St, Santa Monica CA 90401 USA

Bruer, Robert A (Bob) — Football Player
2406 Oakridge Road, Stillwater OK 55082, USA

Bruetti, Dana — Producer
Creative Artists Agency, 2000 Ave of Stars, #100, Los Angeles CA 90067 USA

Bruford, Bill — Drummer (U K, Yes)
Ted Kurland, 173 Brighton Ave, Allston MA 02134 USA

Brugge, Joan S — Cell Biologist
Harvard Medical School, Cell Biology Dept, 240 Longwood Ave, Boston MA 02115, USA

Brugge, Pieter Jan — Director
Innovative Artists, 1505 10th St, Santa Monica CA 90401 USA

Bruggen, Frans — Concert Recorder Player, Flutist
Askonas Holt, Lincoln House, 300 High Holborn, London WC1V 7JH, England

Bruggink, Eric G — Judge
US Claims Court, 717 Madison Place NW, Washington DC 20439, USA

Bruguera, Sergi — Tennis Player
C'Escipion 42, 08023 Barcelona, Spain

Bruhl, Daniel — Actress
Players Agentur Mgmt, Sophienstr 21, 10178 Berlin, Germany

Bruininks, Robert H — Educator
University of Minnesota, Humphries Institute, Saint Paul MN 55104, USA

Brukner, Caslav — Physicist
Quantum Foundations Theory, Boltzmanngasse 5, 1090 Vienna, Austria

Brumfield, Jacob D — Baseball Player
208 Wrights Mill Circle NE, Atlanta GA 30324, USA

Brumfield, Scott — Football Player
1150 E 900 S, Spanish Fork UT 84660, USA

Brumfield-White, Dolores (Dolly) — Baseball Player
1604 Millcreek Dr, Arkadelphia AR 71923, USA

Brumley, A Michael (Mike) — Baseball Player
112 Corral Dr, Keller TX 76244, USA

Brumm, Donald D (Don) — Football Player
511 County Road 442, New Franklin MO 65274, USA

Brummer, Glenn E — Baseball Player
1830 Dalton Dr, Belleville IL 62226, USA

Brummer, Renate L — Astronaut, Germany
Global Systems Division, 325 Broadway, Boulder CO 80305, USA

Brumwell, Murray — Ice Hockey Player
727 Tabriz Dr, Billings MT 59105, USA

Brunansky, Thomas A (Tom) — Baseball Player
15444 Harrow Lane, Poway CA 92064, USA

Brunckhorst, Natja — Actress
Carola Studlar, Agnesstr 47, 80798 Munich, Germany

Brundage, Howard D — Publisher
RR 2 Box 332-47, Old Lyme CT 06371, USA

Brundage, Jackson — Actor
Kazarian/Spencer/Ruskin, 11969 Ventura Blvd, #300, Studio City CA 91604 USA

Brundage, Jennifer — Softball Player
4487 Augusta Court, Ann Arbor MI 48108, USA

Brundige, William G (Bill) — Football Player
40 Corbett St, Salem VA 24153, USA

Brundy, Stanley D (Stan) — Basketball Player
4644 Stephen Girard Ave, New Orleans LA 70126, USA

Brunell, Mark A — Football Player
15 Manor Dr, Morristown NJ 07960, USA

Brunelli, Samuel A (Sam) — Football Player
1080 Wisconsin Ave NW, #104W, Washington DC 20007, USA

Bruner, Jack C (Teel) — Football Player
518 Oak, Kamiah ID 83536, USA

Bruner, Michael L (Mike) — Swimmer
339 Garcia Ave, Half Moon Bay CA 94019, USA

Brunet, Robert P (Bob) — Football Player
149 Aspen Square, Denham Springs LA 70726, USA

Brunet, Yasmine — Model
One Model Mgmt, 424 W Broadway, #200, New York NY 10012 USA

Brunette, Andrew — Ice Hockey Player
2392 Morgan Ave N, Stillwater MN 55082, USA

Brunetti, Dana — Producer
Creative Artists Agency, 2000 Ave of Stars, #100, Los Angeles CA 90067 USA

Bruney, Brian A — Baseball Player
1471 SW Pine Dr, Warrenton OR 97146, USA

Bruney, Fred — Football Player, Coach
800 Mountain Creek Trace NW, Atlanta GA 30328, USA

Brungardt, Kurt — Physical Fitness Trainer, Writer
Trident Media Group, 41 Madison Ave, #3600, New York NY 10010, USA

Bruni Tedeschi, Valeria — Actress
Carol Levi Mgmt, Via G Pisanelli 2, 00196 Rome, Italy

Bruni, Emily — Actress
Markham & Froggatt, Julian House, 4 Windmill St, London W1P 1HF, England

Bruni-Sarkozy, Carla — Model, Singer, Songwriter
Palais de l'Elysee, 55 Rue Faubourg Saint Honore, 75008 Paris, France

Brunkhorst, Brian J — Basketball Player
6182 Brumder Dr, Hartland WI 53029, USA

Brunner, Jerome S — Psychologist
200 Mercer St, New York NY 10012, USA

Bruno, Chris — Actor, Producer, Director
S D B Partners, 1801 Ave of Stars, #902, Los Angeles CA 90067 USA

Bruno, Dylan — Actor
Gersh Agency, 41 Madison Ave, #3301, New York NY 10010 USA
Bruno, Gioia — Singer (Expose), Songwriter
Groove Entertainment, 1005 N Alfred St, #2, West Hollywood CA 90069, USA
Bruns, George W — Basketball Player
16 E Poplar St, Floral Park NY 11001, USA
Brunson, Larry R — Football Player
6104 E Peakview Place, Centennial CO 80111, USA
Bruntlett, Eric K — Baseball Player
4445 Montecito Ave, Santa Rosa CA 95404, USA
Brupbacher, Ross A — Football Player
200 Pembroke Lane, Lafayette LA 70508, USA
Bruschi, Tedy L — Football Player
31 Jeffrey Dr, North Attleboro MA 02760, USA
Bruske, James S (Jim) — Baseball Player
5242 N Quail Run Place, Paradise Valley AZ 85253, USA
Bruskin, Grisha — Artist, Sculptor
236 W 26th St, #705, New York NY 10001, USA
Bruson, Renato — Opera Singer
Columbia Artists Mgmt Inc, 1790 Broadway, #702, New York NY 10019 USA
Brusstar, Warren S — Baseball Player
3320 Redwood Road, Napa CA 94558, USA
Brustein, Robert S — Educator, Producer, Critic
Harvard University, Loeb Drama Center, 64 Brattle St, Cambridge MA 02138, USA
Bruton, John G — Prime Minister, Ireland
Dail Eireann, Leinster House, Dublin 2, Ireland
Bry, Ellen — Actress
Media Artists Group, 8222 Melrose Ave, #203, Los Angeles CA 90048 USA
Bryan, Alan — Archaeologist
University of Alberta, Archaeology Dept, Edmonton AB T6G 2J8, Canada
Bryan, David — Keyboardist (Bon Jovi)
Bon Jovi Mgmt, 809 Elder Circle, Austin TX 78733, USA
Bryan, Donald S — WW II Army Air Force Hero
702 Melba St, Adel GA 31620, USA
Bryan, James — Fiddler
Chris Smith Mgmt, 21 Camden St, #500, Toronto ON M5V 1V2, Canada
Bryan, Luke — Singer, Guitarist, Songwriter
W M E Entertainment, 1600 Division St, #300, Nashville TN 37203 USA
Bryan, Mark — Guitarist (Hootie & the Blowfish)
FishCo Mgmt, 2519 Devine Street Columbia SC 29205, USA
Bryan, Michael C (Mike) — Tennis Player
1774 Ramona Dr, Camarillo CA 93010, USA
Bryan, Richard H — Governor, Senator, NV
Lionel Sawyer Collins, Bank America Plaza, 300 S 4th St, Las Vegas NV 89101, USA
Bryan, Robert C (Bob) — Tennis Player
1774 Ramona Dr, Camarillo CA 93010, USA
Bryan, Sabrina — Actress, Singer (Cheetah Girls)
Puravida Enterprises, 2480 Corinth Ave, #3, Los Angeles CA 90064, USA
Bryan, William K (Billy) — Football Player
3408 Creekwood Dr, Tuscaloosa AL 35453, USA
Bryan, William R (Billy) — Baseball Player
3001 Hickory Lane, Opelika AL 36801, USA
Bryan, Wright — Journalist
3747 Peachtree Road NE, #516, Atlanta GA 30319, USA
Bryan, Zachary Ty — Actor
Evolution Entertainment, 901 N Highland Ave, Los Angeles CA 90038 USA
Bryant Clark, Rosalyn — Track Athlete
3901 Somerset Dr, Los Angeles CA 90008, USA
Bryant, Anita — Social Activist, Singer
Blackwood Mgmt, PO Box 5331, Sevierville TN 37864, USA
Bryant, Bart H — Golfer
Professional Golfer's Assn, PO Box 109601, Palm Beach Gardens FL 33410, USA
Bryant, Bobby L — Football Player
13437 Lochrin Lane, Sylmar CA 91342, USA
Bryant, Bradley D (Brad) — Golfer
900 Mulberry Bush Court, Orlando FL 32828, USA
Bryant, Clara — Actress
Paradigm Agency, 360 N Crescent Dr, North Building, Beverly Hills CA 90210 USA
Bryant, Edward E (Junior), Jr — Football Player
2906 S 102nd St, Omaha NE 68124, USA
Bryant, Emmette (Em) — Basketball Player
PO Box 6229, Chicago IL 60680, USA
Bryant, Fernando A — Football Player
2336 Emerald Dr, Jonesboro GA 30236, USA
Bryant, Jeffrey D (Jeff) — Football Player
2665 Tilson Road, Decatur GA 30032, USA
Bryant, Joseph A (Red) — Football Player
Seattle Seahawks, 12 Seahawks Way, Renton WA 98056 USA
Bryant, Joseph W (Joe) — Basketball Player, Coach
1835 N 72nd St, Philadelphia PA 19151, USA
Bryant, Joy — Actress, Model
KillerMoxie Mgmt, 5890 W Jefferson Blvd, #J, Los Angeles CA 90016, USA
Bryant, Karyn — Actress, Producer, Commentator
Serendipity Entertainment, 9107 Wilshire Blvd, #400, Beverly Hills CA 90210, USA
Bryant, Kelvin L — Football Player
701 E Church St, Tarboro NC 27886, USA
Bryant, Kobe B — Basketball Player
Los Angeles Lakers, Staples Center, 1111 S Figueroa St, Los Angeles CA 90015 USA
Bryant, Mark C — Basketball Player
3300 Everett Dr, Edmond OK 73013, USA
Bryant, Robert L — Mathematician
Duke University, Math-Science Research Institute, Box 90220, Durham NC 27708, USA
Bryant, S Matt — Football Player
5689 Legends Club Circle, Braselton GA 30517, USA
Bryant, Sharon — Singer (Atlantic Starr)
Betty of Troy, 15 Meritoria Dr, East Williston NY 11596, USA

Bryant, Stephen (Steve) — Football Player
3602 George Washington Lane, Missouri City TX 77459, USA
Bryant, Tony — Football Player
2351 Sombrero Blvd, Marathon FL 33050, USA
Bryant, Trent B — Football Player
4801 S Tierney Dr, Independence MO 64055, USA
Bryars, R Gavin — Composer
Schott Co, 48 Great Marlborough St, London W1V 2BN, England
Bryce, Scott — Actor
Don Buchwald/Fortitude, 6500 Wilshire Blvd, #2200, Los Angeles CA 90048 USA
Brye, Stephen R (Steve) — Baseball Player
621 S Spring St, #603, Los Angeles CA 90014, USA
Bryers, Paul — Writer
Bloomsbury Publishing, 36 Soho Square, London W1D 3Q4, England
Brylin, Sergei — Ice Hockey Player
32 Robert Dr, Short Hills NJ 07078, USA
Bryson, A Shawn — Football Player
418 Heatherstone Dr, Franklin NC 28734, USA
Bryson, David — Singer, Guitarist (Counting Crowes)
Geffen Records, 10900 Wilshire Blvd, #1000, Los Angeles CA 90024 USA
Bryson, Jim — Singer, Songwriter
Agency Group Ltd, 142 W 57th St, #600, New York NY 10019 USA
Bryson, Peabo — Singer, Songwriter
Pyramid Entertainment, 377 Rector Place, #21A, New York NY 10280 USA
Bryson, William Curtis — Judge
US Appeals Court, 717 Madison Place NW, Washington DC 20439, USA
Bryzgalov, Ilya N — Ice Hockey Player
4092 Santa Anita Lane, Yorba Linda CA 92886, USA
Brzeska, Magdalena — Rhythmic Gymnast
Vitesse Karcher GmbH, Porscestr 6, 70736 Fellbach, Germany
Brzezinski, Douglas G (Doug) — Football Player
329 Greenhill Way, Silver Spring MD 20904, USA
Brzezinski, Zbigniew — Government Official, Educator
Strategic/International Studies Center, 1800 K NW, #400, Washington DC 20006, USA
BT — Musician
Big Machine Media, 575 Lexington Ave, #400, New York NY 10022, USA
Buanne, Patrizio — Singer
Agency Group Ltd, 142 W 57th St, #600, New York NY 10019 USA
Buatta, Mario — Interior Designer
120 E 80th St, New York NY 10075, USA
Bubka, Sergei N — Track Athlete
Physical Culture/Sport Committee, 42 Esplanadnaya, 252023 Kiev, Ukraine
Bubla, Jiri — Ice Hockey Player
405-1050 Bowron Crescent, North Vancouver BC V7H 2X7, Canada
Buble, Michael — Singer, Songwriter
Creative Artists Agency, 2000 Ave of Stars, #100, Los Angeles CA 90067 USA
Bucatinsky, Dan — Actor
Creative Artists Agency, 2000 Ave of Stars, #100, Los Angeles CA 90067 USA
Buccellato, Benedetta — Actress
Carol Levi Mgmt, Via G Pisanelli 2, 00196 Rome, Italy
Bucchieri, Stephen — Architect
Bucchieri Architects, 2026 Murray Hill, Cleveland,OH 44106, USA
Bucha, Paul W — Vietnam War Army Hero (CMH)
822 N Salem Road, Ridgefield CT 06877, USA
Buchan, William Carl — Yachtsman
826 Evergreen Point Road, Medina WA 98039, USA
Buchan, William Eastman — Yachtsman
7100 NE 42nd St, Bellevue WA 98004, USA
Buchanan, Brian J — Baseball Player
8600 El Mirasol Court, Fort Myers FL 33967, USA
Buchanan, Edna — Journalist
PO Box 403556, Miami Beach FL 33140, USA
Buchanan, Ian — Actor, Model
TalentWorks, 3500 W Olive Ave, #1400, Burbank CA 91505 USA
Buchanan, Isobel — Opera Singer
Marks Mgmt, 14 New Burlington St, London W1X 1FF, England
Buchanan, J Robert — Physician
19 Shipway Place, Charlestown MA 02129, USA
Buchanan, James M — Nobel Economics Laureate
George Mason University, Study of Public Choice Center, Fairfax VA 22030, USA
Buchanan, Jeff — Ice Hockey Player
220 Cedar Ave, Hershey PA 17033, USA
Buchanan, Jensen — Actress
Paradigm Agency, 360 N Crescent Dr, North Building, Beverly Hills CA 90210 USA
Buchanan, John M — Biochemist
56 Meriam St, Lexington MA 02420, USA
Buchanan, Ken — Boxer
45 Marmion Road, Greenfaulds, Cumbernaul G67 4AN, Scotland
Buchanan, Patrick J (Pat) — Commentator, Government Official
8233 Old Courthouse Road, #200, Vienna VA 22182, USA
Buchanan, Raymond L (Ray) — Football Player
2423 Strand Ave, Lawrenceville GA 30043, USA
Buchanan, Ron — Ice Hockey Player
156 Sierra Blanca Trail, Ruidoso NM 88345, USA
Buchanan, Simone — Actress
McMahon Mgmt, 2/24 Brereton St, South Brisbane QED 4101, Australia
Buchanan, Thomas (Tom) — Educator
University of Wyoming, President's Office, 1000 E University Ave, Laramie WY 82071, USA
Buchanon, Phillip D — Football Player
6425 Emerald Pines Circle, Fort Myers FL 33966, USA
Buchanon, Willie J — Football Player
2742 Mesa Dr, Oceanside CA 92054, USA
Buchberger, Kelly — Ice Hockey Player
Edmonton Oilers, 11230 110th St, Edmonton AB T5G 3H7, Canada
Buchek, Gerald P (Jerry) — Baseball Player
123 Royal Vista Dr, #502, Branson MO 65616, USA

Buchel, Marco — Alpine Skier
Ramschwagweg 55, 9496 Balzers, Switzerland
Buchholz, Clay D — Baseball Player
630 King Oaks St, Lumberton TX 77657, USA
Buchholz, Taylor — Baseball Player
194 Powell Road, Springfield PA 19064, USA
Buchli, James F (Jim) — Astronaut
14761A Innerarity Point Road, Pensacola FL 32507, USA
Buchmann, Rainer — Auto Racing Executive
Project Indy, 434 E Main St, Brownsburg IN 46112, USA
Buchwald, Ephraim — Religious Leader, Rabbi
National Jewish Outreach, 989 Ave of Americas, #1000, New York NY 10018, USA
Buchwald, Stephen L — Chemist
Massachusetts Institute of Technology, Chemistry Dept, Cambridge MA 02139, USA
Buck 65 — Rap Artist
Agency Group Ltd, 142 W 57th St, #600, New York NY 10019 USA
Buck, Craig — Volleyball Player
2272 Holyoke Lane, Superior CO 80027, USA
Buck, Jason O — Football Player
4759 Canyon View Dr, Highland UT 84003, USA
Buck, Joe — Sportscaster
18 Upper Warson Road, Saint Louis MO 63124, USA
Buck, John E — Sculptor
11229 Cottonwood Road, Bozeman MT 59718, USA
Buck, Jonathan R (John) — Baseball Player
15068 Desert Eagle Circle, Riverton UT 84065, USA
Buck, Linda B — Nobel Medicine Laureate
14295 Sherwood Road NW, Seattle WA 98177, USA
Buck, Mike E — Football Player
269 Matthews Road, Oakdale NY 11769, USA
Buck, Peter — Businessman
Subway Restaurants, 325 Bic Dr, Milford CT 06461, USA
Buck, Peter L — Guitarist (REM)
REM/Athens Ltd, 170 College Ave, Athens GA 30601, USA
Buck, Scott — Producer
Mosiac Media Group, 9200 W Sunset Blvd, #1000, Los Angeles CA 90069 USA
Buck, Tara — Actress
C E S D, 10635 Santa Monica Blvd, #130, Los Angeles CA 90025 USA
Buck, Travis G — Baseball Player
1443 W Roadrunner Dr, Chandler AZ 85286, USA
Buck, Vincent L (Vince) — Football Player
1005 Vintage Dr, Kenner LA 70065, USA
Buckens, Celine — Actress
Creative Artists Agency, 2000 Ave of Stars, #100, Los Angeles CA 90067 USA
Buckey, Jay C, Jr — Astronaut
1 Sargent St, Hanover NH 03755, USA
Buckfield, Clare — Actress
Associated International Mgmt, Fairfax House, Fulwood Place, London WC1V 6HU, England
Buckhalter, Correll — Football Player
408 Clariden Ranch Road, Southlake TX 76092, USA
Buckhalter, Joseph (Joe) — Basketball Player
3900 Rose Hill Ave, #201A, Hanover NH 03755, USA
Buckingham, Amyand D — Chemist
Crossways, 23 The Ave, Newmarket CB8 9AA, England
Buckingham, Gregory (Greg) — Swimmer
338 Ridge Road, San Carlos CA 94070, USA
Buckingham, Lindsey — Guitarist, Singer (Fleetwood Mac)
Front Line Mgmt, 1100 Glendon Ave, #2000, Los Angeles CA 90024 USA
Buckinghams — Pop, Rock Music Group
PO Box 220082, Great Neck NY 11022, USA
Buckland, Jonathan M (Jonny) — Guitarist (Coldplay)
Paradigm Agency, 360 N Crescent Dr, North Building, Beverly Hills CA 90210 USA
Buckley, A J — Actor
TalentWorks, 3500 W Olive Ave, #1400, Burbank CA 91505 USA
Buckley, Andy — Actor
Coronel Group, 1100 Glendon Ave, #1700, Los Angeles CA 90046, USA
Buckley, Betty L — Actress, Singer, Director
Parseghian/Planco, 388 2nd Ave, #506, New York, NY 10010 USA
Buckley, Carol — Elephant Conservationist
Elephant Sanctuary, PO Box 393, Hohenwald TN 38462, USA
Buckley, Curtis L — Football Player
2208 Cantura Dr, Mesquite TX 75181, USA
Buckley, D Terrell — Football Player
19106 S Gardenia Ave, Weston FL 33332, USA
Buckley, Dan — Publisher
Marvel Comics, Publisher's Office, 417 5th Ave, New York NY 10016, USA
Buckley, Dick — Director
I C M Partners, 10250 Constellation Blvd, #900, Los Angeles CA 90067 USA
Buckley, George — Businessman
Minnesota Mining & Manufacturing Co, 3-M Center, Saint Paul MN 55144, USA
Buckley, James L — Senator, NY; Judge
PO Box 597, Sharon CT 06069, USA
Buckley, Jean — Baseball Player
143 Monarch Dr, Fortuna CA 95540, USA
Buckley, Jerome H — Educator
52 Waverley St, Belmont MA 02478, USA
Buckley, Marcus W — Football Player
240 Yukon Court, Weatherford TX 76087, USA
Buckley, Richard E — Conductor
310 W 55th St, #1K, New York NY 10019, USA
Buckley, Robert E — Actor
W M E Entertainment, 9601 Wilshire Blvd, #300, Beverly Hills CA 90210 USA
Buckley, Roy — Bowler
6900 Lee Road, Westerville OH 43081, USA
Buckman, Phil — Actor
S M S Talent, 8383 Wilshire Blvd, #230, Beverly Hills CA 90211 USA

Buckner, Cleveland — Basketball Player
19227 S Grandee Ave, Carson CA 90746, USA
Buckner, Gregory D (Greg) — Basketball Player
4129 Catawba Ave, Carrollton TX 75010, USA
Buckner, Pam — Bowler
645 Utah St, Reno NV 89506, USA
Buckner, Paul E — Sculptor
2322 Rockwood Ave, Eugene OR 97405, USA
Buckner, Shelley — Actress
B/W/R, 9100 Wilshire Blvd, #500W, Beverly Hills CA 90212 USA
Buckner, W Quinn — Basketball Player, Coach
857 Valencia Blvd, Irving TX 75039, USA
Buckner, William J (Bill) — Baseball Player
4405 E Wild Horse Lane, Boise ID 83712, USA
Bucknor, C B — Baseball Umpire
46 Midwood St, Brooklyn NY 11225, USA
Buckson, David P — Governor, DE
60 Exchange Dr, Camden Wyoming DE 19934, USA
Buckwheat Zydeco — Singer, Accordionist
Ted Fox, PO Box 561, Rhinebeck NY 12572, USA
Bucyk, John P (Chief) — Ice Hockey Player
17 Boren Lane, Boxford MA 01921, USA
Budaj, Peter — Ice Hockey Player
1271 Buffalo Ridge Road, Castle Pines CO 80108, USA
Budarin, Nikolai M — Cosmonaut
Cosmonaut Training Center, Star City, 141160 Zvezdny Gorodok, Moscow Oblast, Russia
Budd Pieterse, Zola — Track Athlete
Coastal Carolina University, Athletic Dept, Myrtle Beach CA 29578, USA
Budd, David L (Dave) — Basketball Player
40 N Woodland Ave, Woodbury NJ 08096, USA
Budd, Frank — Track, Football Player
138 Dorchester Road, Mount Laurel NJ 08054, USA
Budd, Harold — Composer, Writer
Opal/Warner Bros Records, 6834 Camrose Dr, Los Angeles CA 90068, USA
Budd, Jersey — Singer, Songwriter
Agency Group Ltd, 361-373 City Road, London EC1V 2QA, England
Budd, Julie — Actress, Singer
Herb Bernstein Mgmt, 180 W End Ave, #2A, New York NY 10023, USA
Budde, Brad E — Football Player
5121 W 159th Terrace, Stilwell KS 66085, USA
Budde, Edward L (Ed) — Football Player
5121 W 159th Terrace, Stilwell KS 66085, USA
Budden, Joseph A (Joe), II — Rap Artist, Songwriter
I C M Partners, 10250 Constellation Blvd, #900, Los Angeles CA 90067 USA
Buddie, Michael J (Mike) — Baseball Player
157 Scottsdale Dr, Advance NC 27006, USA
Buddon, Joseph A (Joe), II — Rap Artist
I C M Partners, 10250 Constellation Blvd, #900, Los Angeles CA 90067 USA
Budig, Eugene A (Gene) — Baseball Executive, Educator
5 Sandwedge Lane, Isle of Palms SC 29451, USA
Budig, Rebecca — Actress
A P A Talent/Literary Agency, 405 S Beverly Dr, #300, Beverly Hills CA 90212 USA
Budimir, Zivko — President, Bosnia-Herzegovina
President's Office, Marsala Titz 7, 71000 Sarajevo, Bosnia & Herzegovina
Budko, Walter (Walt) — Basketball Player, Coach
2525 Pot Spring Road, #L703, Lutherville Timon MD 21093, USA
Budness, William W (Bill) — Football Player
401 Huckle Hill Road, Bernardston MA 01337, USA
Buechele, Steven B (Steve) — Baseball Player
1104 Arlena Dr, Arlington TX 76012, USA
Buechler, John Carl — Director
12031 Vose, #19-21, North Hollywood CA 91605, USA
Buehler, George S — Football Player
201 E Grant Line Road, #16, Tracy CA 95376, USA
Buehler, Judson D (Jud) — Basketball Player
1515 West Lane, Del Mar CA 92014, USA
Buehler, Rachel — Soccer Player
Atlanta Beat, 1955 Vaughn Road, #209, Kennesaw GA 30144, USA
Buehrle, Mark A — Baseball Player
51 Long Cove Dr, Lemont IL 60439, USA
Buell, Bebe — Model, Singer, Actress
International Management Group, 767 5th Ave, New York NY 10153, USA
Buell, Garett — Percussionist (Caedmon's Call)
Breen Agency, 25 Music Square W, Nashville TN 37203, USA
Bueno, Maria E — Tennis Player
Rua Consolagao 3414, #10, 1001 Edificio Augustus, Sao Paulo, Brazil
Buffa, Dudley W — Writer
William Morrow Publishers, 1350 Ave of Americas, New York NY 10019 USA
Buffenbarger, R Thomas — Labor Leader
International Machinists Assn, 9000 Machinists Place, Upper Marlboro MD 20772, USA
Buffer, Michael — Boxing Commentator
Buffer Enterprises, 131 Fleet St, Marina del Rey CA 90292, USA
Buffett, Jimmy — Singer, Songwriter
Margaritaville, 424 Flemming St, #A, Key West FL 33040, USA
Buffett, Warren E — Businessman
Berkshire Hathaway, 1440 Kiewit Plaza, 3555 Farnam St, Omaha NE 68131, USA
Buffkins, Archie Lee — Performing Arts Administrator
Kennedy Center, Executive Suite, 2700 F St NW, Washington DC 20566, USA
Buffone, Douglas J (Doug) — Football Player
1272 W Lexington St, Chicago IL 60607, USA
Bufman, Zev — Producer
520 Brickell Key Dr, #612, Miami FL 33131, USA
Buford, Damon J — Baseball Player
5055 W Ray Road, #2, Chandler AZ 85226, USA
Buford, Donald A (Don) — Baseball Player
15412 Valley Vista Blvd, Sherman Oaks CA 91403, USA

Buford, Jason (Brooks)   Rap Artist
50 Murray St, #415, New York NY 10007, USA
Buford, Maury A   Football Player
2901 Sweet Briar St, Grapevine TX 76051, USA
Buggs, Daniel (Danny)   Football Player
3186 Evans Mill Road, Lithonia GA 30038, USA
Buggy, Regina   Field Hockey Player
550 Limekiln Road, Oley PA 19547, USA
Bugliosi, Vincent T   Attorney, Writer
663 Arbor St, Pasadena CA 91105, USA
Bugner, Joe   Boxer
22 Buckingham St, Surrey Hills NSW 2010, Australia
Bugnon, Alex   Jazz Pianist, Composer
Talent & Literary Agency, 250 W 57th St, #1701, New York NY 10107, USA
Buhari, Muhammadu   President, Nigeria; Army General
G R A, PO Box 2010, Daura, Katsina State, Nigeria
Buhler, Urs   Singer (Il Divo)
Octagon, 81-83 Fulham High St, London SW6 3JW, England
Buhner, Jay C   Baseball Player
3219 300th Ave SE, Fall City WA 98024, USA
Bujnoch, Glenn   Football Player
7598 Fairway Glen Dr, Cincinnati OH 45248, USA
Bujold, Genevieve   Actress
C C A Mgmt, Garden Level, 32 Charlwood St, London SW1V 2DY, England
Bukich, Rudolph A (Rudy)   Football Player
7910 Ivanhoe Ave, #333, La Jolla CA 92037, USA
Bukin, Andrei A   Ice Dancer
Skating Federation, Lucjneskraia Nab 8, 119871 Moscow, Russia
Buktenica, Raymond   Actor
Special Artists Agency, 9465 Wilshire Blvd, #820, Beverly Hills CA 90212 USA
Bukvich, Ryan A   Baseball Player
200 Apple Blossom Circle, Brandon MS 39047, USA
Bulaich, Norman B (Norm)   Football Player
421 Lynndale Court, Hurst TX 76054, USA
Bulbrook, Anna   Violist (Airborne Toxic Event)
Island Def Jam Records, 8920 W Sunset Blvd, #200, West Hollywood CA 90069 USA
Bulger, Jason   Baseball Player
1898 Harbour Oaks Dr, Snellville GA 30078, USA
Bulger, Marc R   Football Player
2701 S Lindbergh Blvd, Saint Louis MO 63131, USA
Bulifant, Joyce   Actress
Glick Agency, 1321 7th St, #203, Santa Monica CA 90401 USA
Bulis, Jan   Ice Hockey Player
Vancouver Canucks, 800 Griffiths Way, Vancouver BC V6B 6G1, Canada
Buljung, Erich   Marksman
7570 Stampede Dr, Colorado Springs CO 80920, USA
Bull, Richard   Actor
750 N Rush St, #3404, Chicago IL 60611, USA
Bull, Ronald D (Ronnie)   Football Player
15 Redspire Court, Bolingbrook IL 60490, USA
Bullard, Matthew G (Matt)   Basketball Player
10 Balmoral Place, Spring TX 77382, USA
Bullard, Mike   Ice Hockey Player
1170 Shillington Ave, Ottawa ON K1Z 7Z4, Canada
Bullet, Scott D   Baseball Player
218 Vicky Bullett St, Martinsburg WV 25404, USA
Bullinger, James E (Jim)   Baseball Player
2504 Elise Ave, Metairie LA 70003, USA
Bullinger, Kirk M   Baseball Player
3608 David Dr, Metairie LA 70003, USA
Bullington, Bryan P   Baseball Player
20116 Oakwood Dr, Mokena IL 60448, USA
Bullins, Ed   Writer
Northeastern University, English Dept, Boston MA 02115, USA
Bulloch, Jeremy   Actor
Fett Photos, 10 Birchwood Road, London SW17 9BQ, England
Bullock, Bruce J   Ice Hockey Player
5226 W Redbird Road, Phoenix AZ 85083, USA
Bullock, Eric J   Baseball Player
17503 Harwick Court, Carson CA 90746, USA
Bullock, Jim J   Actor
1015 N Kings Road, #215, West Hollywood CA 90069, USA
Bullock, Sandra   Actress
Creative Artists Agency, 2000 Ave of Stars, #100, Los Angeles CA 90067 USA
Bullock, Susan   Opera Singer
Harrison/Parrott, 5-6 Albion Court, London W6 0QT, England
Bulluck, Keith J   Football Player
874 Nialta Lane, Brentwood TN 37027, USA
Bumbeck, David A   Artist
435 Farmers Dell Lane, Deltaville VA 23043, USA
Bumbry, Alonzo B (Al)   Baseball Player
28 Tremblant Court, Lutherville MO 21093, USA
Bumbry, Grace   Opera Singer
I M G Artists, 152 W 57th St, #500, New York NY 10019 USA
Bump, Dennis   Mathematician
Stanford University, Mathematics Dept, Stanford CA 94305, USA
Bump, J D   Sculptor
Onda Gallery, 220 A Ave, 104, Lake Oswego OR 97034, USA
Bumpass, Rodger   Actor
W M E Entertainment, 9601 Wilshire Blvd, #300, Beverly Hills CA 90210 USA
Bumpers, Dale L   Governor, Senator, AR
12723 Hunters Field Road, Little Rock AR 72211, USA
Bunch, Melvin L   Baseball Player
12 Tyler Lane, Hooks TX 75561, USA
Bund, Karlheinz   Businessman
Huyssenallee 82-84, 45128 Essen Ruhr, Germany

B

Buford - Bund

Bundchen, Gisele — Model, Actress
I M G Models, 304 Park Ave S, #PH-North, New York NY 10010 USA

Bundy, Brooke — Actress
1801 Ave of Stars, #1250, Los Angeles CA 90067, USA

Bundy, Laura Bell — Actress, Singer
Sanctuary Mgmt, 15301 Ventura Blvd, Building B, Sherman Oaks CA 91403, USA

Bunetta, Bill — Bowler
1176 E San Bruno Ave, Fresno CA 93710, USA

Bunin, Michael — Actor
Circle Talent, 433 N Camden Dr, #400, Beverly Hills CA 90210 USA

Bunker, Wallace E (Wally) — Baseball Player
66 Falmouth Way, Bluffton SC 29909, USA

Bunkley, Brodrick — Football Player
New Orleans Saints, 5800 Airline Highway, Metairie LA 70003 USA

Bunkowsky-Scherbak, Barb — Golfer
8725 Marlamoor Lane, West Palm Beach FL 33412, USA

Bunnell, Dewey — Singer, Guitarist (America)
Morey Mgmt, 1100 Glendon Ave, #1100, Los Angeles CA 90024, USA

Bunnett, Joseph F — Chemist
608 Arroyo Seca, Santa Cruz CA 95060, USA

Bunning, James P D (Jim) — Senator, KY; Baseball Player
4 Fairway Dr, Southgate KY 41071, USA

Bunting, Eve — Writer
1512 Rose Villa St, Pasadena CA 91106, USA

Bunting, John S — Football Player, Coach
134 Soundview Dr, Hampstead NC 28443, USA

Bunting, William C (Bill) — Basketball Player
11000 Pacer Court, Raleigh NC 27614, USA

Bunton, Emma L — Singer (Spice Girls)
Hall of Nothing, Poplar Mews, Uxbridge Road, London W12 7JS, England

Bunz, Dan — Football Player
4230 Rocklin Road, #2, Rocklin CA 95677, USA

Bunzow, John — Singer, Songwriter
T K O Artist Mgmt, 2303 21st Ave S, #300, Nashville TN 37212, USA

Buoniconti, Nicholas A (Nick) — Football Player, Businessman
445 Grand Bay Dr, #803, Key Biscayne FL 33149, USA

Buono, Cara — Actress
C E S D, 257 Park Ave S, #950, New York NY 10010 USA

Burba, David A (Dave) — Baseball Player
378 N Shore Lane, Gilbert AZ 85233, USA

Burba, Edwin H, Jr — Army General
256 Montrose Dr, McDonough GA 30253, USA

Burbank, Daniel C (Dan) — Astronaut
364 Route 6A, Yarmouth Port MA 02675, USA

Burbidge, E Margaret P — Astronomer
423 Washington St, #600, San Francisco CA 94111, USA

Burbules, Peter G — Army General
8287 Chestnut Point Lane, Hayes VA 23072, USA

Burch, Paul — Singer
Silverleaf Booking, 589 W 1st St, Boiling Springs PA 17007, USA

Burch, Rick — Bassist (Jimmy Eat World)
S A M, 722 Seward St, Los Angeles CA 90038, USA

Burch, Tory — Fashion Designer
11 W 19th St, #400, New York, NY 10011, USA

Burcham, David W — Educator
Loyola Marymount University, President's Office, L1 L M U Dr, Los Angeles CA 90045, USA

Burchfiel, Burrell C — Geologist
9 Robinson Park, Winchester MA 01890, USA

Burchuladze, Paata — Opera Singer
Askonas Holt, Lincoln House, 300 High Holborn, London WC1V 7JH, England

Burckhalter, Joseph H — Inventor (Florescent Dyes)
734 Green Valley Lane, Melbourne FL 32940, USA

Burckle, Caroline — Swimmer
Premier Management Group, 1100 Crescent Green, #104, Cary, NC 27518 USA

Burd, Steven A — Businessman
Safeway Inc, 5918 Stoneridge Mall Road, Pleasanton CA 94588, USA

Burden, Luther D (Ticky) — Basketball Player
4332 Grove Ave, #C, Winston Salem NC 27105, USA

Burden, William — Singer
Opus 3 Artists, 470 Park Ave S, #900N, New York NY 10016 USA

Burdick, Clinton D — WW II Army Air Corps Hero
1134 26th St, #4, Santa Monica CA 90403, USA

Burditt, Joyce — Writer
Jeff Ross Entertainment, 14560 Benefit St, #206, Sherman Oaks CA 91403, USA

Burdon, Eric — Singer (Animals); Songwriter
Lustig Talent, PO Box 770850, Orlando FL 32877 USA

Bure, Pavel V — Ice Hockey Player
11091 Redhawk St, Plantation FL 33324, USA

Bure, Valeri V — Ice Hockey Player
237 Monte Grigio Dr, Pacific Palisades CA 90272, USA

Burfeindt, Betty — Golfer
70 Sam Simeon Place, Rancho Mirage CA 92270, USA

Burford, Christopher W (Chris) — Football Player
1215 Broken Feather Court, Reno NV 89511, USA

Burg, Mark — Producer
Evolution Entertainment, 901 N Highland Ave, Los Angeles CA 90038 USA

Burgee, John H — Architect
Perelanda Farm, Skunks Misery Road, Millerton NY 12546, USA

Burger, Leslie — Association Executive, Librarian
Princeton Public Library, 65 Witherspoon St, Princeton NJ 08542, USA

Burger, Neil — Director, Writer
Creative Artists Agency, 2000 Ave of Stars, #100, Los Angeles CA 90067 USA

Burgess, Adrian — Mountaineer
324 G St, Anderson SC 29625, USA

Burgess, Albert A (Sonny) — Singer, Guitarist, Songwriter
AristoMedia, PO Box 22765, Nashville TN 37202, USA

Burgess, Christian — Actor
33 Gastein Road, London W6 8LT, England

Burgess, Derrick L — Football Player
New England Patriots, 1 Patriot Place, Foxboro MA 02035 USA

Burgess, Don — Cinematographer
Gersh Agency, 9465 Wilshire Blvd, #600, Beverly Hills CA 90212 USA

Burgess, Mitchell — Writer, Producer
Broder Webb Chervin Silbermann, 9242 Beverly Blvd, Beverly Hills CA 90210 USA

Burgess, Neil — Electrical Engineer
201 E 5th St, #2200, Cincinnati OH 45202, USA

Burgess, Ronald L, Jr — Army General
Director, Defense Intelligence Agency, Pentagon, Washington DC 20340 USA

Burgess, Timothy A (Tim) — Singer (Charlatans)
Solo Agency, 53-55 Fulham High St, #200, London SW6 3JJ, England

Burghard, Maria — Actress
Angentur Retzlaff, Kurfuerstenstra 34, 10785 Berlin, Germany

Burghoff, Gary — Actor
Scott Stander Assoc, 4533 Van Nuys Blvd, #401, Sherman Oaks CA 91403 USA

Burgi, Richard W — Actor
1019 Baja St, Laguna Beach CA 92651, USA

Burgmeier, Thomas H (Tom) — Baseball Player
13118 Walmer St, Leawood KS 66209, USA

Burhoe, Ralph Wendell — Templeton Religion Laureate
Montgomery Place, 5550 S South Shore Dr, #715, Chicago IL 60637, USA

Buribayev, Alan — Conductor
I M G Artists, Hogarth Business Park, Chiswick, London W4 2TH, England

Burka, Petra — Figure Skater
Skate Canada, 865 Shefford Road, Ottawa ON K1J 1H9, Canada

Burkart, Phil, Jr — Drag Racing Driver
Phil Burkart Racing, 114 Oriskany Blvd, Yorkville NY 13495, USA

Burke Charvet, Brooke — Actress, Model
Bx2 Mgmt, 1333 2nd St, #620, Santa Monica CA 90401, USA

Burke Hederman, Lynn — Swimmer
26 White Oak Tree Road, Syosset NY 11791, USA

Burke, Bernard F — Physicist, Astrophysicist
10 Bloomfield St, Lexington MA 02421, USA

Burke, Billy — Actor
Ellen Meyer Entertainment, 8899 Beverly Blvd, #616, Los Angeles CA 90048, USA

Burke, Cheryl B — Dancer
Cheryl Burke Dance, 1400 N Shoreline Blvd, #A1, Mountain View CA 94043, USA

Burke, Chris — Actor
Abrams Artists, 9200 W Sunset Blvd, #1125, West Hollywood CA 90069 USA

Burke, Christopher A (Chris) — Baseball Player
15415 Crystal Springs Way, Louisville KY 40245, USA

Burke, Clement (Clem) — Drummer (Blondie)
Agency Group Ltd, 142 W 57th St, #600, New York NY 10019 USA

Burke, David — Actor
Stone Manners Salners, 9911 W Pico Blvd, #1400, Los Angeles CA 90035 USA

Burke, Delta — Actress
Shelter Entertainment, 9454 Wilshire Blvd, #715, Beverly Hills CA 90212 USA

Burke, Doris — Sportscaster
ABC-TV, Sports Dept, 77 W 66th St, New York NY 10023 USA

Burke, James — Commentator
Henley House, Terrace Barnes, London SW13 0NP, England

Burke, James E (Jamie) — Baseball Player
374 W Lilburn Ave, Rosenburg OR 97470, USA

Burke, James Lee — Writer
Simon & Schuster, 1230 Ave of Americas, Concourse 1, New York NY 10020, USA

Burke, Jan — Writer
12437 Seal Beach Blvd, #101, Seal Beach CA 90740, USA

Burke, Jim — Producer, Actor
Ad Hominem Enterprises, 506 Santa Monica Blvd, #400 Santa Monica CA 90401, USA

Burke, John J (Jack), Jr — Golfer
5602 Glen Pines Dr, Houston TX 77069, USA

Burke, Kathy — Actress
Hatton McEwan, 3 Chocolate Studios, 7 Shepherdess Place, London N1 7LJ, England

Burke, Kelly — Model
Playboy Promotions, 2706 Media Center Dr, Los Angeles CA 90065 USA

Burke, Kelly H — Air Force General
803 Choctaw Lane, Shalimar FL 32579, USA

Burke, Kevin — Businessman
Consolidated Edison, 4 Irving Place, New York NY 10003, USA

Burke, Leo P — Baseball Player
3395 Torrey Pines Circle, Riner VA 24149, USA

Burke, Michael Reilly — Actor
Domain Talent, 9229 W Sunset Blvd, #710, West Hollywood CA 90069 USA

Burke, Robert John — Actor
Paradigm Agency, 360 N Crescent Dr, North Building, Beverly Hills CA 90210 USA

Burke, Sean — Ice Hockey Player
9016 N 60th St, Paradise Valley AZ 85253, USA

Burke, Simon — Actor
United Agents, 12-26 Lexington St, London W1F 0LE, England

Burke, Tim — Visual Effects Designer
Rocket Science Talent, 5023 N Parkway Calabasas, Calabasas CA 91302, USA

Burke, Timothy P (Tim) — Baseball Player
12108 W Ida Lane, Littleton CO 80127, USA

Burke, Will — Writer, Director, Actor
United Talent Agency, 9336 Civic Center Dr, Beverly Hills CA 90210 USA

Burkett, Bunny — Drag Racing Driver
Bunny Burkett Racing Team, 8314 Robert E Lee Dr, Spotsylvania VA 22551, USA

Burkett, Chris — Football Player
296 Dover Lane, Madison MS 39110, USA

Burkett, John D — Baseball Player
1404 Laurel Lane, Southlake TX 76092, USA

Burkett, W Jackson (Jackie) — Football Player
929 Lighthouse Road, Fort Walton Beach FL 32547, USA

Burkhalter, Edward A, Jr — Navy Admiral
4128 Fort Washington Place, Alexandria VA 22304, USA
Burkhard, Gedeon — Actor
Elisabeth von Molo, Nymphenburger Str 154, 80635 Munich, Germany
Burkhardt, Francois — Architect
3 Rue de Venise, 75004 Paris, France
Burkhart, Kathe — Artist
Moti Hasson Gallery, 230 Arabian Road, Palm Beach FL 33480, USA
Burkholder, JoAnn — Medical Activist, Physician
North Carolina State University, Botany Dept, Raleigh NC 27695, USA
Burkholder, Max Wolf — Actor
Osbrink Talent Agency, 4343 Lankershim Blvd, #100, North Hollywood CA 91602 USA
Burkley, Dennis — Actor
Tyler Kjar, 10153 1/2 Riverside Dr, #255, Toluca Lake CA 91602 USA
Burks, Audra — Golfer
1566 Woodmore Dr, Springfield IL 62711, USA
Burks, Ellis R — Baseball Player
115 South Lane, Chagrin Falls OH 44022, USA
Burleson, Nate — Football Player
15508 SE 79th Place, Newcastle WA 98059, USA
Burleson, Richard P (Rick) — Baseball Player
241 E Country Hills Dr, La Habra CA 90631, USA
Burleson, Tommy L (Tom) — Basketball Player
PO Box 596, Newland NC 28657, USA
Burley, Gary — Football Player
514 Bristol Lane, Birmingham AL 35226, USA
Burman, Alexandra — Model
Group Model Mmgt, Po de Gracia 67, Pral 1A, 08008 Barcelona, Spain
Burman, George R — Football Player
1646 James St, Syracuse NY 13203, USA
Burn, Malcolm — Singer
Anthem Entertainment, 189 Carlton St, Toronto ON M5A 2K7, Canada
Burnell, Jocelyn Bell — Astronomer
Bell Open University, Physics Dept, Milton Keynes MK7 6AA, England
Burner, David L — Businessman
B F Goodrich Co, 3 Coliseum Centre, 2550 W Tyvola Road, Charlotte NC 28205, USA
Burnes, Karen — Commentator
CBS-TV, News Dept, 51 W 52nd St, New York NY 10019 USA
Burnet, Guy — Actor
Collective, 8383 Wilshire Blvd, #1050, Beverly Hills CA 90211 USA
Burnett, Allan J (A J) — Baseball Player
15208 Jarrettsville Pike, Monkton MD 21111, USA
Burnett, Carol — Actress, Comedienne
I C M Partners, 10250 Constellation Blvd, #900, Los Angeles CA 90067 USA
Burnett, Kevin B — Football Player
2938 S Sunbeck Circle, Dallas TX 75234, USA
Burnett, Nancy — Actress
Pinnacle Commercial Talent, 5757 Wilshire Blvd, #510, Los Angeles CA 90036, USA
Burnett, Sean R — Baseball Player
14016 Aster Ave, Wellington FL 33414, USA
Burnett, T-Bone — Singer, Songwriter, Music Producer
Paradigm Agency, 360 Park Ave S, #1600, New York NY 10010 USA
Burnette, Olivia — Actress
A P A Talent/Literary Agency, 405 S Beverly Dr, #300, Beverly Hills CA 90212 USA
Burnette, Rocky — Singer
1900 Ave of Stars, #2530, Los Angeles CA 90067, USA
Burning Spear — Singer
13034 231st St, Springfield Gardens NY 11413, USA
Burningham, John — Writer
Conville & Walsh, 118-120 Wardour St, London W1V 3LA, England
Burnitz, Jeromy N — Baseball Player
PO Box 676032, Rancho Santa Fe CA 92067, USA
Burnley, James H, IV — Secretary, Transportation
Venable LLP, 575 7th St NW, #1, Washington DC 20004, USA
Burns, Annie — Singer (Burns Sisters), Songwriter
Burns Sisters Band, PO Box 845, Ithaca NY 14851, USA
Burns, Bob — Drummer (Lynyrd Skynyrd)
Vector Mgmt, PO Box 120479, Nashville TN 37212 USA
Burns, Bob — Golfer
12512 Fraser Ave, Granada Hills CA 91344, USA
Burns, Brooke — Actress
A P A Talent/Literary Agency, 405 S Beverly Dr, #300, Beverly Hills CA 90212 USA
Burns, Charles F (Charlie) — Ice Hockey Player, Coach
7 Fawn Dr, Wallingford CT 06492, USA
Burns, Christian — Singer, Guitarist (BBMak)
Spirit Media, 34 Salisbury St, London NW8 8QE, England
Burns, David D — Psychiatrist
Stanford University, Psychiatry/Behavioral Science Dept, Stanford CA 94305, USA
Burns, Edward — Director, Actor
Marlboro Road Gang Productions, 334 E 90th St, New York NY 10128, USA
Burns, Eric A — Entertainer
Fox News, 1211 Ave of Americas, Lower C3R, New York NY 10036, USA
Burns, Eric D (Ric) — Director
Steeplechase Films, 2095 Broadway, #503, New York NY 10023, USA
Burns, George — Golfer
403 S Sapodilla Ave, #516, West Palm Beach FL 33401, USA
Burns, Heather — Actress
I C M Partners, 10250 Constellation Blvd, #900, Los Angeles CA 90067 USA
Burns, James MacGregor — Political Scientist, Historian
High Mowing, Bee Hill Road, Williamstown MA 01267, USA
Burns, Jeannie — Singer (Burns Sisters), Songwriter
Burns Sisters Band, PO Box 845, Ithaca NY 14851, USA
Burns, Jere, II — Actor
Innovative Artists, 1505 10th St, Santa Monica CA 90401 USA
Burns, Jimmy — Writer
Bloomsbury Publishing, 36 Soho Square, London W1D 3Q4, England

Burns, Joey
Billions Corp, 3522 W Armitage Ave, Chicago IL 60647 USA — Singer, Guitarist (Calexico)

Burns, Keith B
13572 Heritage Farms Dr, Gainesville VA 20155, USA — Football Player

Burns, Kenneth L (Ken)
Florentine Films, 59 Maple Grove Road, Walpole NH 03608, USA — Documentary Director

Burns, M Anthony
Ryder System Inc, 11690 NW 105th St, Medley FL 33178, USA — Businessman

Burns, Marie
Burns Sisters Band, PO Box 845, Ithaca NY 14851, USA — Singer (Burns Sisters), Songwriter

Burns, Marilyn
Marilyn Burns Educational Assoc, 150 Gate 5 Road, #101, Sausalito CA 94965, USA — Writer

Burns, Marilyn
12951 Briar Forest Dr, Houston TX 77077, USA — Actress

Burns, Megan
Rights House, 34-43 Russell St, London WC2B 5HA, England — Actress

Burns, R Britt
1550 Katy Gap Road, #903, Katy TX 77494, USA — Baseball Player

Burns, Regan
OmniPop Talent Group, 4605 Lankershim Blvd, #201, Toluca Lake CA 91602 USA — Actor, Comedian

Burns, Robin
186 Sherwood Road, Beaconsfield QC H9W 2G8, Canada — Ice Hockey Player

Burns, Steve
Paradigm Agency, 360 N Crescent Dr, North Building, Beverly Hills CA 90210 USA — Actor

Burns, Todd E
PO Box 111, Princeton AL 35766, USA — Baseball Player

Burns, Ursula M
Xerox Corp, 800 Long Ridge Road, Stamford CT 06092, USA — Businesswoman

Burnside, Iain
Askonas Holt, Lincoln House, 300 High Holborn, London WC1V 7JH, England — Concert Pianist, Commentator

Burnside, Peter W (Pete)
1765 Washington Ave, Wilmette IL 60091, USA — Baseball Player

Burr, Bill
A P A Talent/Literary Agency, 405 S Beverly Dr, #300, Beverly Hills CA 90212 USA — Actor, Comedian

Burr, Matthew
Paradigm Agency, 404 W Franklin St, Monterey CA 93940 USA — Drummer (Grace Potter & the Nocturnals)

Burr, Shawn
1615 River Road, Saint Clair MI 48079, USA — Ice Hockey Player

Burrell Wiley, Kim
Universal Attractions, 135 W 26th St, #1200, New York NY 10001 USA — Singer, Pianist, Songwriter

Burrell, Garland L, Jr
US District Court, 501 I St, #3200, Sacramento CA 95814, USA — Judge

Burrell, Gary
Garmin International, 1200 E 151st St, Olathe KS 66062, USA — Businessman

Burrell, John B (Johnny)
376 Park Lake Dr, Mead OK 73449, USA — Football Player

Burrell, Kenneth E (Kenny)
Joel Chriss, 60 E 8th St, #34N, New York NY 10003 USA — Jazz Guitarist, Composer

Burrell, Leroy
University of Houston, Athletic Dept, Houston TX 77023, USA — Track Athlete

Burrell, Patrick B (Pat), III
PO Box 1770, Boulder Creek CA 95006, USA — Baseball Player

Burrell, Scott D
331 Evergreen Ave, Hamden CT 06518, USA — Basketball Player

Burrell, Ty
I C M Partners, 10250 Constellation Blvd, #900, Los Angeles CA 90067 USA — Actor

Burres, Brian
350 SE 2nd St, #1420, Fort Lauderdale FL 33301, USA — Baseball Player

Burress, Plaxico A
47 Huntington Terrace, Totowa NJ 07512, USA — Football Player

Burridge, Pam
Mark Rabbidge, 441B Bendalong Road, Bendalong NSW 2539, Australia — Surfer

Burridge, Randy
1911 Nuevo Road, Henderson NV 89014, USA — Ice Hockey Player

Burris, Jeffrey L (Jeff)
8074 Hopkins Lane, Indianapolis IN 46250, USA — Football Player

Burrough, Kenneth O (Ken)
5823 Tallow Lane, Indianapolis IN 46250, USA — Football Player

Burroughs, Augusten X
Picador/Saint Martin's Press, 175 5th Ave, New York NY 10010, USA — Writer

Burroughs, Jeffrey A (Jeff)
6155 Laguna Court, Long Beach CA 90803, USA — Baseball Player

Burroughs, Sean
6155 Laguna Court, Long Beach CA 90803, USA — Baseball Player

Burrow, Kenneth R (Ken)
5371 Dunwoody Club Creek, Atlanta GA 30360, USA — Football Player

Burrows, Darren E
Writers & Artists, 360 N Crescent Dr, Building North, Beverly Hills CA 90210, USA — Actor

Burrows, David J (Dave)
RR 1, Lake Harris ON P2A 2W7, Canada — Ice Hockey Player

Burrows, Edwin G
Oxford University Press, 198 Madison Ave, #800, New York NY 10016 USA — Writer

Burrows, Eva E
Domain Park, 193 Domain Road, #102, South Yarra VIC 3141, Australia — Religious Leader

Burrows, J Stuart
29 Blackwater Grove, Alderholt, Dorset SP6 3AD, England — Opera Singer

Burrows, James E (Jim)
I C M Partners, 10250 Constellation Blvd, #900, Los Angeles CA 90067 USA — Director

Burrows, Saffron
United Agents, 12-26 Lexington St, London W1F 0LE, England — Actress

Burrows, Stephen
10 W 57th St, New York NY 10019, USA — Fashion Designer

Burrs, Marcia Ann
Torque Entertainment, 3118 Wilshire Blvd, #160, Santa Monica CA 90403, USA — Actress

Burrus, William
American Postal Workers Union, 1300 L St NW, #200, Washington DC 20005, USA — Labor Leader

Burruss, Kandi — Singer (Xscape)
Richard Walters, PO Box 2789, Toluca Lake CA 91610 USA

Bursch, Daniel W — Astronaut
1305 Buena Vista Ave, Pacific Grove CA 93950, USA

Burshnick, Anthony J (Tony) — Air Force General
7715 Carrleigh Parkway, Springfield VA 22152, USA

Burson, Clare — Singer, Songwriter
Rounder Records, 1 Rounder Way, Burlington MA 01803 USA

Burson, Harold — Businessman
30 W 63rd St, #7H, New York NY 10023, USA

Burson, James O (Jimmy) — Football Player
351 Heath Road, Dawsonville GA 30534, USA

Burstyn, Ellen — Actress
Blue Flower Arts, PO Box 1361, Millbrook NY 12545, USA

Burt, Adam — Ice Hockey Player
34 Smull Ave, Caldwell NJ 07006, USA

Burt, Donald Graham — Art Director
Skouras Agency, 1149 3rd St, #300, Santa Monica CA 90403 USA

Burt, James P (Jim) — Football Player
10 River Farms Lane, Saddle River NJ 07458, USA

Burtnett, Wellington, Jr — Ice Hockey Player
1703 Pouliot Place, Wilmington MA 01887, USA

Burton, Brandie — Golfer
3480 Pleasant Hill Dr, Highland CA 92346, USA

Burton, Ellis N — Baseball Player
15621 Beach Blvd, #SP7, Westminster CA 92683, USA

Burton, F Shane — Football Player
PO Box 522, Hewitt Road, Catawba NC 28609, USA

Burton, Gary — Jazz Vibist
Berklee College of Music, 1140 Boylston St, Boston MA 02215, USA

Burton, Hilarie — Actress
I C M Partners, 10250 Constellation Blvd, #900, Los Angeles CA 90067 USA

Burton, Jake — Snowboard Skier
Burton Snowboards, 80 Industrial Parkway, Burlington VT 05401, USA

Burton, Jeffrey B (Jeff) — Auto Racing Driver
6000 Fairview Road, #635, Charlotte NC 28210, USA

Burton, Kate — Actress, Singer
Gersh Agency, 9465 Wilshire Blvd, #600, Beverly Hills CA 90212 USA

Burton, L Jared — Baseball Player
PO Box 506, Westminster SC 29693, USA

Burton, Lance — Illusionist
Monte Carlo Hotel, 3770 S Las Vegas Blvd, Las Vegas NV 89109, USA

Burton, Lawrence G (Larry), Jr — Football Player
41 San Gabriel, Rancho Santa Margarita CA 92688, USA

Burton, Leonard B (Len) — Football Player
3436 Beech Grove Road, Rancho Santa Margarita CA 92688, USA

Burton, LeVar — Actor
Dolores Robinson, 3815 Hughes Ave, #300, Culver City CA 90232 USA

Burton, Nelson, Jr — Bowler
9359 SW Eagles Landing, Stuart FL 34997, USA

Burton, Richard S V — Architect
1B Lady Margaret Road, London NW5 2NE, England

Burton, Steve — Actor
James/Levy Mgmt, 3500 W Olive Ave, #1470, Burbank CA 91505 USA

Burton, Thomas M — Journalist
Wall Street Journal, Editorial Dept, 1 World Financial Center, New York NY 10281, USA

Burton, Timothy W (Tim) — Director
Tim Burton Productions, 8033 W Sunset Blvd, #7500, West Hollywood CA 90046, USA

Burton, Ward — Auto Racing Driver
2046 Myers Road, Halifax VA 24550, USA

Burton, Willie R — Basketball Player
18900 Fleming St, Detroit MI 48234, USA

Burtt, Ben, Jr — Sound Editor
Anything Can Happen, 70 Park Dr, Amselmo CA 94960, USA

Burtt, Steven D (Steve) — Basketball Player
200 W 143rd Sr, #12D, New York NY 10030, USA

Burum, Stephen H — Cinematographer
Mirisch Agency, 8840 Wilshire Blvd, #100, Beverly Hills CA 90211 USA

Burwell, Carter — Composer
Body Studio, 105 Hudson St, New York NY 10013, USA

Burwitz, Nils — Artist, Sculptor
Calle Rosa 22, Valldemossa, Majorca, Spain

Bury, Pol — Sculptor
236 Blvd Raspail, 75014 Paris, France

Busby, Steven L (Steve) — Baseball Player
2701 Brittany Lane, Grapevine TX 76051, USA

Buscemi, Steve — Actor, Director
Gotham Group, 7250 Melrose Ave, Los Angeles CA 90046, USA

Busch, August A, III — Businessman, Baseball Executive
Anheuser-Busch Cos, 1 Busch Place, Saint Louis MO 63118, USA

Busch, Charles — Actor, Writer
Creative Artists Agency, 2000 Ave of Stars, #100, Los Angeles CA 90067 USA

Busch, Kurt T — Auto, Truck Racing Driver
199 Rustic Road, Mooresville NC 28115, USA

Busch, Kyle T — Auto, Truck Racing Driver
Kyle Busch Motorsports, 559 Pitts School Road, Concord NC 28027, USA

Buse, Donald R (Don) — Basketball Player
7300 W State Road 64, Huntingdon IN 47542, USA

Busemann, Frank — Track Athlete
Borkumstr 13A, 45665 Recklinghausen, Germany

Buser, Martin — Dog Sled Racer
PO Box 520997, Big Lake AK 99652, USA

Busey, Gary — Actor
Global Artists Agency, 6253 Hollywood Blvd, #508, Los Angeles CA 90028 USA

Busey, Jake — Actor
Kritzer Levine Wilkins Griffin, 11872 La Grange Ave, #100, Los Angeles CA 90025 USA

Busfield, Timothy	Actor, Producer, Director
Paradigm Agency, 360 N Crescent Dr, North Building, Beverly Hills CA 90210 USA	
Bush, Barbara P	Wife of US President
10000 Memorial Dr, #900, Houston TX 77024, USA	
Bush, Blair W	Football Player
16911 SE 32nd Place, Bellevue WA 98008, USA	
Bush, David T (Dave)	Baseball Player
8 Stevens Cove Road, Bridgton ME 04009, USA	
Bush, Devin M	Football Player
10278 Laurel Road, Davie FL 33328, USA	
Bush, George H W	President, USA
10000 Memorial Dr, #900, Houston TX 77024, USA	
Bush, George W	President, USA
Prairie Chapel Ranch, Crawford TX 76638, USA	
Bush, Guy L	Zoologist
Michigan State University, Zoology Dept, East Lansing MI 48824, USA	
Bush, Homer G	Baseball Player
1402 Exeter Court, Southlake TX 76092, USA	
Bush, Jim	Track Coach
5106 Bounty Lane, Culver City CA 90230, USA	
Bush, Johnny	Singer, Guitarist, Songwriter
Texas Sounds Entertainment, 633 Davis Road, League City TX 77573, USA	
Bush, Katherine (Kate)	Singer, Songwriter
Jukes Productions, PO Box 13995, London W9 2FL, England	
Bush, Kristian	Singer (Billy Pilgrim, Sugarland)
Gail Gellman Mgmt, 23852 Pacific Coast Highway, #920, Malibu CA 90265, USA	
Bush, Laura	Wife of US President
Prairie Chapel Ranch, Crawford TX 76638, USA	
Bush, Lesley L	Diver
65 Birch Ave, Princeton NJ 08542, USA	
Bush, Michael	Football Player
Chicago Bears, 1000 Football Dr, Lake Forest IL 60045 USA	
Bush, R Randall (Randy)	Baseball Player
37 Kings Canyon Dr, New Orleans LA 70131, USA	
Bush, Reggie	Football Player
2443 Poydras St, New Orleans LA 70119, USA	
Bush, Sam	Singer, Mandolinist (New Grass Revival)
Paradigm Agency, 360 N Crescent Dr, North Building, Beverly Hills CA 90210 USA	
Bush, Sophia	Actress
Joan Green Mgmt, 1836 Courtney Terrace, Los Angeles CA 90046 USA	
Bush, Walter L, Jr	Ice Hockey Executive
5200 Malibu Dr, Minneapolis MN 55436, USA	
Bush, William Green	Actor
TalentWorks, 3500 W Olive Ave, #1400, Burbank CA 91505 USA	
Bushinsky, Joseph M (Jay)	Commentator
Rehov Hatsafon 5, Savyon 56540, Israel	
Bushland, Raymond C	Entomologist
200 Concord Plaza Dr, San Antonio TX 78216, USA	
Bushnell, Bill	Director
2751 Pelham Place, Los Angeles CA 90068, USA	
Bushnell, Candace	Writer
Greater Talent Network, 437 5th Ave, #700, New York NY 10016, USA	
Bushnell, Nolan K	Businessman
UWink, 2100 N Main St, #A14, Los Angeles CA 90031, USA	
Bushwick Bill	Rap Artist (Geto Boys)
Richard Walters, PO Box 2789, Toluca Lake CA 91610 USA	
Bushy, Ronald (Ron)	Drummer (Iron Butterfly)
Lustig Talent, PO Box 770850, Orlando FL 32877 USA	
Busick, Steve R	Football Player
6246 W Long Dr, Littleton CO 80123, USA	
Busino, Orlando F	Cartoonist (Mugsy)
12 Shadblow Hill Road, Ridgefield CT 06877, USA	
Buskas, Rod	Ice Hockey Player
182 Wentworth Dr, Henderson NV 89074, USA	
Busniuk, Ron	Ice Hockey Player
540 Laurentian Dr, Thunder Bay ON P7C 5J8, Canada	
Buss, David M	Psychologist, Writer
University of Texas, Psychology Dept, Austin TX 78712, USA	
Buss, Jerry H	Basketball Executive
Los Angeles Lakers, Staples Center, 1111 S Figueroa St, Los Angeles CA 90015 USA	
Busse, Keith E	Businessman
Steel Dynamics, 7575 W Jefferson Blvd, Fort Wayne IN 46804, USA	
Bussell, Darcey A	Ballerina
155 New King's Road, London SW6 4SJ, England	
Bussey, Barney A	Football Player
5059 Park Ridge Court, West Chester OH 45069, USA	
Bussey, Dexter M	Football Player
American/S C I, 888 W Bauer Road, Troy MI 48084, USA	
Bustamante, Carlos	Molecular Scientist
University of California, Howard Hughes Medical Institute, Berkeley CA 94720, USA	
Bustamante, Hector Luis	Actor
Diverse Talent Group, 9911 Pico Blvd, #350W, Los Angeles CA 90035 USA	
Bustamante, Sergio	Artist, Sculptor
Independence 238, Col Centro, Tlaquepaque CP 45500 Jalisco, Mexico	
Butala, Tony	Singer (Lettermen)
PO Box 151, McKees Rocks PA 15136, USA	
Butcher, Adam	Actor
I C M Partners, 10250 Constellation Blvd, #900, Los Angeles CA 90067 USA	
Butcher, Garth	Ice Hockey Player
1524 Maple Lane, Bellingham WA 98229, USA	
Butcher, John D	Baseball Player
4245 Trillium Lane E, Mound MN 55364, USA	
Butcher, Page	Model
Next Model Mgmt, 23 Watts St, New York NY 10013 USA	
Butcher, Paul M	Football Player
31841 Seafield Dr, Malibu CA 90265, USA	

B

Busfield - Butcher

Butcher, Rodney — Golfer
7333 Hideaway Trail, New Port Richey FL 34655, USA
Butcher-Marsh, Mary — Baseball Player
1119 Cedar St, Carson City NV 89701, USA
Butera, Salvatore P (Sal) — Baseball Player
324 Tersas Court, Lake Mary FL 32746, USA
Buthelezi, Chief Mangosuthu G — Chief Minister, KwaZulu/Natal
Home Affairs Ministry, Private Bag X741, Pretoria 0001, South Africa
Butkus, Richard M (Dick) — Football Player, Actor
Butkus Foundation, 18920 NE 227th Ave, Brush Prairie WA 98606, USA
Butler of Brockwell, F E Robin — Government Official, England
Master's Residence, University College, Oxford OX1 4BH, England
Butler, Austin R — Actor
Anonymous Content, 3532 Hayden Ave, Culver City CA 90232 USA
Butler, Bernard — Guitarist (Suede)
Interceptor Enterprises, 98 White Lion St, London N1 9PF, England
Butler, Bill C — Cinematographer
1097 Aviation Blvd, Hermosa Beach CA 90254, USA
Butler, Brett — Actress, Comedienne
Maverick Artists, 6100 Wilshire Blvd, #550, Los Angeles CA 90048, USA
Butler, Brett M — Baseball Player
9512 E Canyon View Road, Scottsdale AZ 85255, USA
Butler, Caron — Basketball Player
3802 Millard Way, Fairfax VA 22033, USA
Butler, Chad M — Drummer, Percussionist (Switchfoot)
The Firm, 2049 Century Park E, #2550, Los Angeles CA 90067 USA
Butler, Cher — Model
Playboy Promotions, 2706 Media Center Dr, Los Angeles CA 90065 USA
Butler, Chris — Guitarist (Waitresses), Songwriter
C E S D, 10635 Santa Monica Blvd, #130, Los Angeles CA 90025 USA
Butler, Clay — Cartoonist
PO Box 245, Capitola CA 95010, USA
Butler, Dan — Actor
Innovative Artists, 1505 10th St, Santa Monica CA 90401 USA
Butler, Dean — Actor
1310 Westholme Ave, Los Angeles CA 90024, USA
Butler, Edwin F (Win), III — Singer (Arcade Fire), Songwriter
Billions Corp, 3522 W Armitage Ave, Chicago IL 60647 USA
Butler, Gayle Goodson — Editor
Better Homes & Gardens, Editor's Office, 1716 Locust St, Des Moines IA 50309, USA
Butler, George L (Lee) — Air Force General
Peter Kiewit & Sons, 11122 William Plaza, Omaha NE 68144, USA
Butler, Gerard — Actor, Singer
Creative Artists Agency, 2000 Ave of Stars, #100, Los Angeles CA 90067 USA
Butler, J Keith — Football Player
805 Cavan Dr, Cranberry Township PA 16066, USA
Butler, James (Cannonball) — Football Player
1261 Cahaba Dr SW, Atlanta GA 30311, USA
Butler, James W — Sculptor
Valley Farm Studios, Radway, Warwick CV35 0UJ, England
Butler, Jerry — Ice Hockey Player
3595 Eldridge Ave, Winnipeg MB R3R 0L5, Canada
Butler, Jerry (Iceman) — Singer, Songwriter
Jerry Butler Productions, 164 Woodstone Dr, Buffalo Grove IL 60089, USA
Butler, Jerry O — Football Player
17117 Shaker Blvd, Cleveland OH 44120, USA
Butler, John B (Jack) — Football Player
510 E 11th Ave, Homestead PA 15120, USA
Butler, Jonathan — Guitarist, Singer, Songwriter
Associated Talent Mgmt, 2800 Olympic Blvd, #100, Santa Monica CA 90404, USA
Butler, Joseph C (Joe) — Drummer, Singer (Lovin'Spoonful)
Lustig Talent, PO Box 770850, Orlando FL 32877 USA
Butler, Kevin G — Football Player
3256 Bagley Passage, Duluth GA 30097, USA
Butler, LeRoy — Football Player
4119 Westloop Lane, Jacksonville FL 32277, USA
Butler, Martin — Composer
University of Sussex, Music Dept, Brighton BN1 9RH, England
Butler, Michael A — Football Player
3107 Magdalene Forest Court, Tampa FL 33618, USA
Butler, Mitchell L — Basketball Player
3464 Meier St, Los Angeles CA 90066, USA
Butler, Raymond L (Ray) — Football Player
1300 Woodcrest Dr, Houston TX 77018, USA
Butler, Robert — Director
650 Club View Dr, Los Angeles CA 90024, USA
Butler, Robert C (Bobby) — Football Player
5567 Naylor Court, Norcross GA 30092, USA
Butler, Robert Olen — Writer
3909 Reserve Dr, #1611, Tallahassee FL 32311, USA
Butler, Samuel C — Attorney
Cravath Swain Moore, 825 8th Ave, New York NY 10019, USA
Butler, Terence M J (Geezer) — Bassist (Black Sabbath), Songwriter
Sharon Osborne Mgmt, 8899 Beverly Blvd, #905, West Hollywood CA 90048, USA
Butler, William F (Bill) — Baseball Player
141 Buckskin Lane, Berkeley Springs WV 25411, USA
Butler, William F (Skip) — Football Player
1311 Spyglass Dr, Mansfield TX 76063, USA
Butler, William R (Bill) — Football Player
200 E Liberty St, Berlin WI 54923, USA
Butler, Yancy — Actress
Framework Entertainment, 9057 Nemo St, #C, West Hollywood CA 90069 USA
Butor, Michel — Writer
A l'Ecart, 216 Place de L'Eglise, 74380 Lucinges, France
Butt, Yondani — Conductor
Gurtman & Murtha, 450 Fashion Ave, #603, New York NY 10123, USA

Butterfield, Alexander P
9237 Regents Road, #323, La Jolla CA 92037, USA — Government Official

Butterfield, Benjamin
I M G Artists, Hogarth Business Park, Chiswick, London W4 2TH, England — Opera Singer

Butterfield, Deborah K
11229 Cottonwood Road, Bozeman MT 59718, USA — Sculptor

Buttle, Gregory E (Greg)
5 Hollacher Dr, Northport NY 11768, USA — Football Player

Buttle, Jeffrey
International Management Group, 304 Park Ave, #PH N, New York NY 10010, USA — Figure Skater

Button, Jenson A L
Jenson Racing, 67 Valkenburgerweg, 6419 AP Heerlen, Netherlands — Auto Racing Driver

Button, Richard T (Dick)
Candio Productions, 765 Park Ave, #6B, New York NY 10021, USA — Figure Skater, Producer

Butts, James
16950 Belforest Dr, Carson CA 90746, USA — Track Athlete

Butz, David E (Dave)
746 E Adams St, Belleville IL 62220, USA — Football Player

Butz, Norbert Leo
Creative Artists Agency, 2000 Ave of Stars, #100, Los Angeles CA 90067 USA — Actor, Singer

Buxbaum, Richard M
University of California, Law School, Boalt Hall, Berkeley CA 94720, USA — Attorney, Educator

Buxton, Sarah
1416 N Hayvenhurst, North Hollywood CA 90046, USA — Actress, Singer

Buy, Margherita
Carol Levi Mgmt, Via G Pisanelli 2, 00196 Rome, Italy — Actress

Buyers, William
Atomic Energy of Canada, 2251 Speakman Dr, Mississauga ON L5K 1B2, Canada — Physicist

Buynak, Gordie
11512 Douglas Lake Road, Pellston MI 49769, USA — Ice Hockey Player

Buzzi, Ruth
PO Box 122416, Fort Worth TX 76121, USA — Actress, Comedienne

Byambasuren, Dashiin
C D S S R, Sergen Mandakh Gudamj 13, #4 Gin Hurd, Uuriin Javar, Mongolia — Prime Minister, Mongolia

Byars, Betsy C
401 Rudder Ridge, Seneca SC 29678, USA — Writer

Byars, Keith
3657 NW 5th Terrace, Boca Raton FL 33431, USA — Football Player

Byas, Richard R (Rick), Jr
19925 Greenwald Dr, Southfield MI 48075, USA — Football Player

Byatt, Antonia Susan (A S)
37 Rusholme Road, London SW15 3LF, England — Writer

Bybee, Jay
US Court of Appeals, Courthouse, 333 Las Vegas Blvd S, Las Vegas NV 89101, USA — Judge

Bychkov, Semyon
Buffalo Symphony Orchestra, 499 Franklin St, Buffalo NY 14202, USA — Conductor

Bye, Kermit E
US Court of Appeals, 657 2nd Ave N, Fargo ND 58102, USA — Judge

Bye-Dietz, Karyn
322 Gandy Dancer Circle, Hudson WI 54016, USA — Ice Hockey Player

Byer, Renee C
Sacramento Bee, Editorial Dept, 2100 Q St, Sacramento CA 95816 USA — Photojournalist

Byers, Lyndon
WAAF-FM Radio, 20 Guest St, #300, Brighton MA 02135, USA — Ice Hockey Player

Byers, Michael A (Mike)
28 Presidio Dr, Novato CA 94949, USA — Ice Hockey Player

Byers, Nina
University of California, Physics Dept, Los Angeles CA 90024, USA — Physicist

Byers, Steve
TalentWorks, 3500 W Olive Ave, #1400, Burbank CA 91505 USA — Actor

Byers, Walter
25707 Aiken Switch Road, Emmett KS 66422, USA — Athletic Association Executive

Bykovsky, Valeri F
Cosmonaut Training Center, Star City, 141160 Zvezdny Gorodok, Moscow Oblast, Russia — Cosmonaut

Bylsma, Dan
12637 Broadmoor Place, Grand Haven MI 49417, USA — Ice Hockey Player

Byman, Robert T (Bob)
9325 Eagle Ridge Dr, Las Vegas NV 89134, USA — Golfer

Byner, Earnest A
1016 Sattui Court, Franklin TN 37064, USA — Football Player

Byner, John
American Mgmt, 19948 Mayall St, Chatsworth CA 91311, USA — Actor, Comedian, Impressionist

Bynes, Amanda
B/W/R, 9100 Wilshire Blvd, #500W, Beverly Hills CA 90212 USA — Actress, Comedienne

Bynum, Andrew L
7412 Denrock Ave, Los Angeles CA 90045, USA — Basketball Player

Bynum, Caroline W
Institute for Advanced Study, Einstein Dr, Princeton NJ 08540 USA — Historian

Byrd, Chris
1181 Heatherwood Court, Flint MI 48532, USA — Boxer

Byrd, Dan
I C M Partners, 10250 Constellation Blvd, #900, Los Angeles CA 90067 USA — Actor

Byrd, Donald
Spectrum Dance Theater, 800 Lake Washington Blvd, Seattle WA 98122, USA — Choreographer

Byrd, Donaldson T L (Donald), II
Mosiac Media Group, 9200 W Sunset Blvd, #1000, Los Angeles CA 90069 USA — Jazz Trumpeter

Byrd, Eugene
Sanders/Armstrong/Caserta Mgmt, 2120 Colorado Ave, #120, Santa Monica CA 90404 USA — Actor

Byrd, George E (Butch)
23 Wayside Road, Westborough MA 01581, USA — Football Player

Byrd, Gill A
5347 Notting Hill Road, Gurnee IL 60031, USA — Football Player

Byrd, Harry F, Jr
Rockingham Publishing Co, 2 N Kent St, Winchester VA 22601, USA — Senator, VA

Byrd, Isaac, III
5712 Astra Ave, Saint Louis MO 63147, USA — Football Player

B

Byrd, Jonathan — Golfer
110 Meadow Brook, Saint Simons Island GA 31522, USA
Byrd, Marlon J — Baseball Player
3105 N Ashland Ave, Chicago IL 60657, USA
Byrd, Paul G — Baseball Player
910 Foxhollow Run, Alpharetta GA 30004, USA
Byrd, Richard — Football Player
2230 Haley Road, Terry MS 39170, USA
Byrd, Thomas J (Tom) — Actor
Stewart Talent, 318 W 53rd St, #201, New York NY 10019, USA
Byrd, Tracy — Singer
Star Keeper Public Relations, 4695 Monticello St, Beaumont TX 77706, USA
Byrdak, Timothy C (Tim) — Baseball Player
16721 W Seneca Dr, Lockport IL 60441, USA
Byrne, Alexandra — Costume Designer
Independent Talent Group, Oxford House, 76 Oxford St, London W1D 1BS, England
Byrne, Brendan T — Governor, NJ
6 Becker Farm Road, Roseland NJ 07068, USA
Byrne, David — Singer (Talking Heads), Songwriter
Primary Talent International, 10-11 Jockey's Fields, London WC1R 4BN, England
Byrne, Gabriel — Actor
Paradigm Agency, 360 N Crescent Dr, North Building, Beverly Hills CA 90210 USA
Byrne, Gerry — Publisher
Variety Inc, 360 Park Ave S, Basement B, New York NY 10010, USA
Byrne, Josh — Actor
Hervey/Grimes Talent, 10561 Missouri Ave, #2, Los Angeles CA 90025 USA
Byrne, Martha — Actress
Innovative Artists, 1505 10th St, Santa Monica CA 90401 USA
Byrne, Megan — Actress
Douglas Gorman Rothacker Wilhelm, 1501 Broadway, #703, New York NY 10036 USA
Byrne, Michael — Actor
Conway Van Gelder Grant, 8-12 Broadwick St, #300, London W1F 8HW, England
Byrne, Rose — Actress
Creative Artists Agency, 2000 Ave of Stars, #100, Los Angeles CA 90067 USA
Byrnes, Edd — Actor
PO Box 1623, Beverly Hills CA 90213, USA
Byrnes, Eric J — Baseball Player
17530 Ventura Blvd, #201, Encino CA 91316, USA
Byrnes, James T (Jim) — Actor, Singer
Characters Talent Agency, 8 Elm St, Toronto ON M5G 1G7, Canada
Byrnes, Martin W (Marty) — Basketball Player
8739 3rd Ave, Pleasant Prairie WI 53158, USA
Byrom, Monty — Singer (Big House), Songwriter
Gurley Co, PO Box 150657, Nashville TN 37215 USA
Byron, Don — Jazz Clarinetist
Hans Wendl Productions, 2220 California St, Berkeley CA 94703, USA
Byron, Jeffrey — Actor
Shapiro-Lichtman, 8827 Beverly Blvd, Los Angeles CA 90048 USA
Byrum, Curt A — Golfer
12441 N 86th St, Scottsdale AZ 85260, USA
Byrum, John W — Director
Creative Artists Agency, 2000 Ave of Stars, #100, Los Angeles CA 90067 USA
Byrum, Tom — Golfer
70 Sierra Oaks Dr, Sugar Land TX 77479, USA
Bystrom, Martin E (Marty) — Baseball Player
PO Box 89, Geigertown PA 19523, USA
Byun Chun Sa — Speed Skater
Skating Union, 88 Bangyee-Dong, Songpaku, Seoul 138 749, South Korea
Byzantine, Julian S — Concert Guitarist
42 Ennismore Gardens, #1, London SW7 1AQ, England
Bzdelik, Jeff — Basketball Coach
Wake Forest University, Athletic Dept, Winston-Salem NC 27109, USA

Byrd - Bzdelik

Caan, James
Rogers & Cowan, 8687 Melrose Ave, #G700, West Hollywood CA 90069 USA — Actor

Caan, Scott
Paradigm Agency, 360 N Crescent Dr, North Building, Beverly Hills CA 90210 USA — Actor

Caballe, Montserrat
Avenida Madronos 27, Madrid 28043, Spain — Opera Singer

Caballero, Eugenio
Sheldon Prosnit Agency, 800 S Robertson Blvd, #6, Los Angeles CA 90035, USA — Art Director

Caballero, Ralph J (Putsy)
6773 Milne Blvd, New Orleans LA 70124, USA — Baseball Player

Cabana, Robert D
10223 Live Oak Lane, Seabrook TX 77586, USA — Astronaut

Cabarga, Leslie
451 S Padre Juan Ave, Ojai CA 93023, USA — Cartoonist

Cabarkapa, Zarko
Golden State Warriors, 1011 Broadway, Oakland CA 94605 USA — Basketball Player

Cabas
J E P Entertainment, 16207 Ventura Blvd, #510, Encino CA 91436, USA — Singer, Musician

Cabell, Enos M
4103 Frost Lake Court, Missouri City TX 77459, USA — Baseball Player

Cabell, Nicole
Columbia Artists Mgmt Inc, 1790 Broadway, #702, New York NY 10019 USA — Opera Singer

Cable, Byrum W (Barney)
1134 S Main St, #69, Hampstead MD 21074, USA — Basketball Player

Cable, Tawnni
Playboy Promotions, 2706 Media Center Dr, Los Angeles CA 90065 USA — Actress, Model

Cable, Thomas L (Tom), Jr
Oakland Raiders, 1220 Harbor Bay Parkway, Alameda CA 94502 USA — Football Player, Coach

Cabral, Travis
Police Department, 1352 Johnson Blvd, South Lake Tahoe NV 96150, USA — Moguls Skier

Cabranes, Jose A
US Court of Appeals, 141 Church St, New Haven CT 06510, USA — Judge

Cabrera, Angel L
Professional Golfer's Assn, PO Box 109601, Palm Beach Gardens FL 33410 USA — Golfer

Cabrera, J Miguel T
3339 Virginia St, #PH2, Miami FL 33133, USA — Baseball Player

Cabrera, Melky A
806 Hudson Park, Edgewater NJ 07020, USA — Baseball Player

Cabrera, Orlando L
9248 Scarlette Oak Ave, Fort Myers FL 33967, USA — Baseball Player

Cabrera, Ryan
Luber Rocklin Entertainment, 8530 Wilshire Blvd, #555, Beverly Hills CA 90211 USA — Singer, Guitarist

Cabrera, Santiago
Conway Van Gelder Grant, 8-12 Broadwick St, #300, London W1F 8HW, England — Actor

Cabrinha, Pete
245A Kane Road, Haiku, Maui HI 96708, USA — Kiteboarding Athlete

Cabtaline, Anita
32455 Pinto Dr, Warren MI 48093, USA — Bowler

Cacciavillan, Agostino Cardinal
Patrimony of Holy See, Palazzo Apostolico, 00120 Vatican City — Religious Leader

Caceres, Kurt
Pakula/King, 9229 W Sunset Blvd, #315, West Hollywood CA 90069 USA — Actor

Cackowski, Liz
United Talent Agency, 9336 Civic Center Dr, Beverly Hills CA 90210 USA — Actress, Comedienne

Cadaret, Gregory J (Greg)
22636 Bridlewood Lane, Palo Cedro CA 96073, USA — Baseball Player

Caddell, Patrick H
Cambridge Research Inc, 1625 I St NW, Washington DC 20006, USA — Statistician

Cadell, Ava
Levin, 8484 Wilshire Blvd, #745, Beverly Hills CA 90211, USA — Actress, Model

Cadiff, Andy
United Talent Agency, 9336 Civic Center Dr, Beverly Hills CA 90210 USA — Director

Cadigan, Dave
14416 Katie Road, Phoenix MD 21131, USA — Football Player

Cadile, James D (Jim)
1738 Spring St, Medford OR 97504, USA — Football Player

Cadman, Sam
United Talent Agency, 9336 Civic Center Dr, Beverly Hills CA 90210 USA — Director, Producer, Actor

Cadogan, William J
A D C Telecommunications, PO Box 1101, Minneapolis MN 55440, USA — Businessman

Cadrez, Glenn E
1294 Mariposa Road, Carlsbad CA 92011, USA — Football Player

Caesar, Shirley
Shu-Bel Music, PO Box 3336, Durham NC 27702, USA — Singer

Caesar, Sid
1910 Loma Vista Dr, Beverly Hills CA 90210, USA — Actor, Comedian

Cafagna, Ashley
Tesoro Entertainment, 205 N Stephanie St, #D115, Henderson NV 89074, USA — Actress

Caffara, Carlo Cardinal
Archdiocese of Bologna, Via Altabella 6, 40126 Bologna, Italy — Religious Leader

Caffarelli, Luis A
University of Texas, Mathematics Dept, 1 University Station, Austin TX 78712, USA — Mathematician

Caffari, Denise (Dee)
Caroline Rose Mgmt, Peter House, Oxford St, Manchester M1 5AN, England — Yachtswoman

Cafferata, Hector A, Jr
1807 Plum Lane, Venice FL 34293, USA — Korean War Marine Corps Hero (CMH)

Caffey, Charlotte
Direct Management Group, 947 N La Cienega Blvd, #G, West Hollywood CA 90069, USA — Guitarist (Go-Go's)

Caffey, Jason A
PO Box 131, Roswell GA 30077, USA — Basketball Player

Caffie, Joseph C (Joe)
PO Box 1932, Warren OH 44482, USA — Baseball Player

Cafu
F C Milan, Via Filippo Turati 3, 20121 Milan, Italy — Soccer Player

Cagatay, Mustafa
60 Cumhuriyet Caddesi, 900 Kyrenia, Cyprus — Prime Minister, Cyprus Federated State

C

Cage — Rap Artist
Agency Group Ltd, 142 W 57th St, #600, New York NY 10019 USA

Cage, Byron — Singer
Universal Attractions, 135 W 26th St, #1200, New York NY 10001 USA

Cage, Michael J — Basketball Player
21163 Newport Coast Dr, Newport Coast CA 92657, USA

Cage, Nicolas — Actor
Creative Artists Agency, 2000 Ave of Stars, #100, Los Angeles CA 90067 USA

Cagle, Chris — Singer, Songwriter
McGhee Entertainment, 21 Music Square W, Nashville TN 37203, USA

Cagle, Myrtle K — Astronaut Candidate
RR 3, Lake Tobesofkee, Lizella GA 31052, USA

Cagle, Yvonne D — Astronaut
N A S A, Johnson Space Center, 2101 NASA Road, Houston TX 77058 USA

Cahill, Eddie — Actor
Management 360, 9111 Wilshire Blvd, Beverly Hills CA 90210 USA

Cahill, Laura — Writer
I C M Partners, 10250 Constellation Blvd, #900, Los Angeles CA 90067 USA

Cahill, Michael (Mike) — Director
W M E Entertainment, 9601 Wilshire Blvd, #300, Beverly Hills CA 90210 USA

Cahill, Teresa M — Opera, Concert Singer
65 Leyland Road, London SE12 8DW, England

Cahill, Thomas — Writer
Doubleday Press, 1540 Broadway, New York NY 10036, USA

Cahill, Trevor J — Baseball Player
Arizona Diamondbacks, Chase Field, 401 E Jefferson, Phoenix AZ 85003 USA

Cahn, John W — Metallurgist
2032 43rd Ave E, #18, Seattle WA 98112, USA

Cahouet, Frank V — Financier
Mellon Bank Corp, 1 Mellon Bank Center, 500 Grant St, #1, Pittsburgh PA 15219, USA

Cahow, Caitlin — Ice Hockey Player
USA Hockey, 1775 Bob Johnson Dr, Colorado Springs CO 80906 USA

Caillat, Colbie M — Singer, Songwriter
Fitzgerald Hartley, 34 N Palm St, #100, Ventura CA 93001, USA

Caillon, Anne — Actress
U B B A, 6 Rue de Braque, 75003 Paris, France

Cain, Carl — Basketball Player
3045 Sun Valley Dr, Pickerington OH 43147, USA

Cain, Chelsea — Writer
Saint Martin's Press, 175 5th Ave, #400, New York NY 10010 USA

Cain, Dean — Actor
W M E Entertainment, 9601 Wilshire Blvd, #300, Beverly Hills CA 90210 USA

Cain, Matthew T (Matt) — Baseball Player
1331 N 104th Place, Mesa AZ 85207, USA

Caine, Michael — Actor
Gwyn Foxx Talent Agency, 4401 Wilshire Blvd, Los Angeles CA 90010, USA

Cainero, Chiara — Markswoman
Comitato Olimpico Nazionale, Largo Lauro de Bocsis 15, 00194 Rome, Italy

Caio, Francesco — Businessman
Netscalibur, 9 Selsdon Way, Cityharbour, London E14 9GL, England

Caird, John — Director, Lyricist
Gersh Agency, 9465 Wilshire Blvd, #600, Beverly Hills CA 90212 USA

Cairns, Eric — Ice Hockey Player
1291 Treeland St, Burlington ON L7R 3T5, Canada

Cairns, Ian — Surfer
868 Wilson St, Laguna Beach CA 92651, USA

Cairo, Miguel J — Baseball Player
209 Highland Woods Dr, Safety Harbor FL 34695, USA

Caivano, Ernesto — Artist
Guild & Greyshkul, 131 Prince St, #4F, New York NY 10012, USA

Cajanek, Petr — Ice Hockey Player
Saint Louis Blues, Scott Trade Center, 1401 Clark Ave, Saint Louis MO 63103 USA

Cake, Jonathan — Actor
Independent Talent Group, Oxford House, 76 Oxford St, London W1D 1BS, England

Calabrese, Gerald A (Gerry) — Basketball Player
351 Esplanade Place, Cliffside Park NJ 07010, USA

Calabresi, Guido — Judge
US Court of Appeals, 157 Church St, #1800, New Haven CT 06510, USA

Calabro, Thomas — Actor
A K A Talent, 6310 San Vicente Blvd, #200, Los Angeles CA 90048 USA

Calame, Ingrid — Artist
Cohen Gallery, 533 W 26th St, New York NY 10001, USA

Calamos, John P, Sr — Financier
Calamos Asset Management, 1111 E Warrenville Road, Naperville IL 60563, USA

Calarco, Vincent A — Businessman
Crompton Corp, 199 Benson Road, Waterbury CT 06749, USA

Calatrava, Santiago — Architect, Engineer
Santiago Calatrava SA, Hoschgasse 5, 8008 Zurich, Switzerland

Calcagno, Domenico Cardinal — Religious Leader
Admin of Patrimony, Palazzo Apostolico, 00120 Vatican City

Calcevecchi, Mark — Golfer
2741 E Bighorn Ave, Phoenix AZ 85048, USA

Calder, Kyle — Ice Hockey Player
726 Monterey Blvd, Hermosa Beach CA 90254, USA

Calderon Fournier, Rafael A — President, Costa Rica
Partido Unidad Social Cristiana, San Jose, Costa Rica

Calderon, Mark — Singer (Color Me Badd)
J-Bird Entertainment, 4905 S Atlantic Ave, Ponce Inlet FL 32127 USA

Calderon, Paul — Actor
TalentWorks, 220 E 23rd St, #303, New York NY 10010, USA

Caldicott, Helen — Social Activist, Pediatrician
Physicians for Responsibility, 639 Massachusetts Ave, Cambridge MA 02139, USA

Caldwell Dyson, Tracy E — Astronaut
N A S A, Johnson Space Center, 2101 NASA Road, Houston TX 77058 USA

Caldwell, Adrian B — Basketball Player
10990 West Road, #311, Houston TX 77064, USA

Caldwell, Andrew — Actor
Management 101, 5527 1/2 Cahuenga Blvd, North Hollywood CA 91601 USA
Caldwell, Bobby — Singer, Musician, Songwriter
Universal Attractions, 135 W 26th St, #1200, New York NY 10001 USA
Caldwell, Gail — Journalist
Boston Globe, Editorial Dept, 135 William Morrissey Blvd, Dorchester MA 02125 USA
Caldwell, Isaiah (Mike), Jr — Football Player
646 Robertsville Road, Oak Ridge TN 37830, USA
Caldwell, James W (Jim) — Basketball Player
705 Freedom Lane, Roswell GA 30075, USA
Caldwell, Jim — Football Coach
Baltimore Ravens, Ravens Stadium, 1 Winning Dr, Baltimore MD 21230 USA
Caldwell, Joe L — Basketball Player
15 E Pebble Beach Dr, Tempe AZ 85282, USA
Caldwell, John — Cartoonist
King Features Syndicate, 300 W 57th St, #1500, New York NY 10019 USA
Caldwell, Kimberly — Singer, Actress
PO Box 8158, The Woodland TX 77387, USA
Caldwell, L Scott — Actor
Innovative Artists, 1505 10th St, Santa Monica CA 90401 USA
Caldwell, Nicholas — Singer (Whispers)
Pyramid Entertainment, 377 Rector Place, #21A, New York NY 10280 USA
Caldwell, R Michael (Mike) — Baseball Player
1645 Brook Run Dr, Raleigh NC 27614, USA
Caldwell, Ravin C, Jr — Football Player
4415 Johnson St, Fort Smith AR 72904, USA
Caldwell, Rex — Golfer
260 El Dorado Blvd, #3006, Webster TX 77598, USA
Caldwell, Stephen (Steve) — Singer (Orlons)
Lustig Talent, PO Box 770850, Orlando FL 32877 USA
Caldwell, Toy — Guitarist (Marshall Tucker Band)
Ron Rainey Mgmt, 315 S Beverly Dr, #407, Beverly Hills CA 90212, USA
Caldwell, Zoe — Actress
Whitehead-Stevens, 1501 Broadway, New York NY 10036, USA
Cale, J J — Singer, Guitarist, Songwriter
Rosebud Agency, PO Box 170429, San Francisco CA 94117 USA
Cale, Paula — Actress
Gersh Agency, 9465 Wilshire Blvd, #600, Beverly Hills CA 90212 USA
Calegari, Maria — Ballerina
404 Richardsville Road, Carmel NY 10512, USA
Caleo, Michael — Director, Writer
I C M Partners, 10250 Constellation Blvd, #900, Los Angeles CA 90067 USA
Calero, Enrique N (Kiko) — Baseball Player
1465 65th St, Emeryville CA 94608, USA
Caley, Don — Ice Hockey Player
7127 E Aloe Vera Dr, Scottsdale AZ 85266, USA
Calfa, Marian — President, Czechoslovakia
Calfa, Pravni Kancela Premyslovska 28, 130 00 Prague 3, Czech Republic
Calfan, Nicole — Actress
Agents Associes, 201 Rue du Faubourg Saint Honore, 75008 Paris, France
Calhoon, Jesse M — Labor Leader
Marine Engineers Union, 17 Battery Place, New York NY 10004, USA
Calhoun, David L (Corky) — Basketball Player
17912 Lafayette Dr, Olney MD 20832, USA
Calhoun, Donald C (Don) — Football Player
PO Box 49104, Wichita KS 67201, USA
Calhoun, James A (Jim) — Basketball Coach
PO Box 379, Pomfret Center CT 06259, USA
Calhoun, Jeffrey W (Jeff) — Baseball Player
10002 Springwood Forest Dr, Houston TX 77080, USA
Calhoun, Monica — Actress
Abrams Artists, 9200 W Sunset Blvd, #1125, West Hollywood CA 90069 USA
Calhoun, Troy — Football Coach
US Air Force Academy, Athletic Dept, Colorado Springs CO 80840, USA
Calhoun, Will — Drummer (Living Colour)
Entertainment Artists, PO Box 120824, Nashville TN 37212 USA
Calhoun, William C (Bill) — Basketball Player
3740 El Cerro View Circle, Reno NV 89509, USA
Cali, Joseph — Actor
25630 Edenwild Road, Calabasas CA 91302, USA
Caliendo, Frank — Actor, Comedian, Writer
Gersh Agency, 9465 Wilshire Blvd, #600, Beverly Hills CA 90212 USA
Califano, Joseph A, Jr — Secretary, Health Education & Welfare
Casa at Columbia, 633 3rd Ave, #1900, New York NY 10017, USA
Calipari, John — Basketball Coach
University of Kentucky, Athletic Dept, Lexington KY 40506, USA
Calis, Natasha — Actress
Creative Artists Agency, 2000 Ave of Stars, #100, Los Angeles CA 90067 USA
Call, Kevin B — Football Player
839 Carey Road, Carmel IN 46033, USA
Callahan, Daniel J — Educator
Hastings Center, 255 Elm Road, Briarcliff Manor NY 10510, USA
Callahan, John — Actor
Levin Representatives, 2402 4th St, #6, Santa Monica CA 90405, USA
Callahan, Ryan — Ice Hockey Player
New York Rangers, Madison Square Garden, 2 Penn Plaza, New York NY 10121 USA
Callahan, William E (Bill) — Football Coach
623 Lake Point Dr, Irving TX 75039, USA
Callan, K — Actress
Gage Group, 14724 Ventura Blvd, #505, Sherman Oaks CA 91403 USA
Callan, Michael — Actor
1651 Camden Ave, #3, Los Angeles CA 90025, USA
Calland, Albert M, III — Navy Admiral
Central Intelligence Agency, Deputy Director's Office, Washington DC 20505, USA
Calland, Lee — Football Player
6624 Windwood Circle, Douglasville GA 30135, USA

C

Callard, Rebecca — Actress
Curtis Brown Group, 28-29 Haymarket St, #500, London SW1Y 4SP, England
Callas, John L — Space Scientist, Physicist
Jet Propulsion Laboratory, 4800 Oak Grove Dr, Pasadena CA 91109 USA
Callaway, Ann Hampton — Jazz Singer, Pianist, Composer
Miller Wright Assoc, 1650 Broadway, #1210, New York NY 10019, USA
Callaway, Howard H (Bo) — Government Official; Representative, GA
Callaway Gardens, Pine Mountain GA 31822, USA
Callaway, Michael C (Mickey) — Baseball Player
8061 Stonewyck Road, Germantown TN 38138, USA
Callaway, Raymond — Air Force Hero
3421 Andree Dr, #A, Anchorage AK 99517, USA
Callaway, Thomas V — Actor
House of Representatives, 1434 6th St, #1, Santa Monica CA 90401 USA
Callen Jones, Gloria — Swimmer
1508 Chafton Road, Charleston WV 25314, USA
Callen, Bryan C — Actor, Comedian
Innovative Artists, 1505 10th St, Santa Monica CA 90401 USA
Callender, William D (Jock) — Ice Hockey Player
388 Lear Road, Avon Lake OH 44012, USA
Callery, Sean — Composer
Gorfaine/Schwartz, 4111 W Alameda Ave, #509, Burbank CA 91505 USA
Callie, Dayton — Actor
Abrams Artists, 9200 W Sunset Blvd, #1125, West Hollywood CA 90069 USA
Callighen, Brett — Ice Hockey Player
PO Box 249, Bala ON P0C 1A0, Canada
Callow, Simon — Actor
Paradigm Agency, 360 N Crescent Dr, North Building, Beverly Hills CA 90210 USA
Calloway, Christopher F (Chris) — Football Player
1213 Dawnview Dr, Locust Grove GA 30248, USA
Calloway, Jordan — Actor
Gold Levin, 8424A Santa Monica Blvd, #706, Los Angeles CA 90069, USA
Calloway, Vanessa Bell — Actress
Luber Rocklin Entertainment, 8530 Wilshire Blvd, #555, Beverly Hills CA 90211 USA
Calman, Robert F — Businessman
241 S 6th St, #2302, Philadelphia PA 19106, USA
Calmus, Rocky A — Football Player
4131 Trinity Road, Franklin TN 37067, USA
Calne, Roy Y — Surgeon
Douglas House Annexe, 18 Trumpington Road, Cambridge CB2 2AS, England
Caltabiano, Tom — Actor, Comedian, Producer, Writer
United Talent Agency, 9336 Civic Center Dr, Beverly Hills CA 90210 USA
Calvaer, Andre J — Electrical Engineer
Blvd Louis Mettewie 270, 1080 Molenbeek-Saint-Jean, Belgium
Calvert, Mark — Baseball Player
908 W Waco St, Broken Arrow OK 74011, USA
Calvet, Jacques — Businessman, Financier
Bazar de L'Hotel de Ville, 14 Rue du Temple, 75189 Paris, France
Calvin, John — Actor
445 Sudden Valley, Bellingham WA 98229, USA
Calvin, William H — Neurobiologist, Writer
University of Washington, Neurobiology Dept, Seattle WA 98195, USA
Calvo, Paul M — Governor, Guam
Calvo Enterprises, 138 Martyr St, Hagatna, GU 96910, USA
Calzaghe, Joseph W (Joe) — Boxer
Newbridge Boxing Gym, Bridge St, Newbridge, Caerphily South Wales NP11 5FR, Wales
Camacho, Carlos A — Actor
Telemundo Network Group, 2470 W 8th Ave, Hialeah FL 33010 USA
Camacho, Ernest C (Ernie) — Baseball Player
746 Saint Regis Way, Salinas CA 93905, USA
Camacho, Felix — Boxer
Lisa Terlizzi, 14 Fulton St, Weehawken NJ 07086, USA
Camacho, Felix P — Governor, Guam
Governor's Office, Executive Chamber, PO Box 2950, Hagatna GU 96932 USA
Camacho, Jesse — Actor
Rosenthal Mercer Hamou, 2101 Saint Laurent, Montreal QC H2X 2T5, Canada
Camacho, Jessie — Actress, Comedienne
L A Mgmt, 20501 Ventura Blvd, #380, Woodland Hills CA 91364, USA
Camarda, Charles J — Astronaut
2386 Sabal Park Lane, League City TX 77573, USA
Camargo, Christian — Actor
Innovative Artists, 1505 10th St, Santa Monica CA 90401 USA
Camarillo, Richard J (Rich) — Football Player
1941 E Clubhouse Dr, Phoenix AZ 85048, USA
Camastra, Danielle — Actress
Don Buchwald/Fortitude, 6500 Wilshire Blvd, #2200, Los Angeles CA 90048 USA
Cambage, Elizabeth (Liz) — Basketball Player
Tulsa Shock, B O K Center, 200 S Denver, Tulsa OK 74103 USA
Camberling, Sylvain — Conductor
S W R Orchestra, 76550 Baden-Baden, Germany
Cambor, Kathleen — Writer
Farrar Straus Giroux, 18 W 18th St, #700, New York NY 10011 USA
Cambor, Peter — Actor
Brillstein Entertainment Partners, 9150 Wilshire Blvd, #350, Beverly Hills CA 90212 USA
Cambre, Ronald C — Businessman
Newmont Mining, 1700 Lincoln St, Denver CO 80203, USA
Cambreling, Sylvain — Conductor
Van Walsum Mgmt, Tower Building, 11 York Road, London SE1 7NX, England
Cambria, John — Cinematogapher
9939 Topanga Canyon Blvd, #11, Chatsworth CA 91311, USA
Camby, Marcus D — Basketball Player
6725 Fite Road, Pearland TX 77584, USA
Camdessus, Michel J — Financier
27 Rue de Valois, 75001 Paris, France
Cameron Bure, Candace — Actress
10371 Golden Eagle Court, Plantation FL 33324, USA

Cameron, Al
1225 Ormsby Lane NW, Edmonton AB T5T 6R2, Canada — Ice Hockey Player

Cameron, Ann
Foster Books/Farrar Straus Giroux, 18 W 18th St, New York NY 10011, USA — Writer

Cameron, Cam
Miami Dolphins, 7500 SW 30th St, Davie FL 33314, USA — Football Coach

Cameron, Caressa
Miss America Organization, 1370 Ave of Americas, #1600, New York NY 10019 USA — Beauty Queen

Cameron, David
Schauspielschule Krauss, Weihburggasse 19, 1010 Vienna, Austria — Fashion Designer

Cameron, David
Prime Minister's Office, 10 Downing St, London SW1A 2AA, England — Prime Minister, England

Cameron, Dean
Maverick Artists, 6100 Wilshire Blvd, #550, Los Angeles CA 90048, USA — Actor

Cameron, Don R
National Education Association, 1201 16th St NW, Washington DC 20036, USA — Educator, Labor Leader

Cameron, Glenn S
250 S Australian Ave, West Palm Beach FL 33401, USA — Football Player

Cameron, James
Cameron/Pace Group, 2020 N Lincoln St, Burbank CA 91504, USA — Director, Producer

Cameron, Joanna
PO Box 198900-9MB 808, Hawi HI 96719, USA — Actress

Cameron, John
David Wilkinson Assoc, 115 Hazlebury Road, London SW6 2LX, England — Composer, Conductor

Cameron, Julia
Tarcher/Penguin Books, 375 Hudson St, Basement 1, New York NY 10014, USA — Writer

Cameron, Kenneth D
11333 Gulf Beach Highway, Pensacola FL 32507, USA — Astronaut

Cameron, Kirk
Mark Craig Productions, 1383 Callens, Ventura CA 93003, USA — Actor

Cameron, Michael T (Mike)
615 Champions Dr, McDonough GA 30253, USA — Baseball Player

Cameron, Michelle
Box 2 Site 1SS3, Calgary AB T3C 3N9, Canada — Synchronized Swimmer

Cameron, Nancy
Playboy Promotions, 2706 Media Center Dr, Los Angeles CA 90065 USA — Model

Cameron, Stephanie
Innovative Artists, 1505 10th St, Santa Monica CA 90401 USA — Actress

Cameron, Tassie
Creative Artists Agency, 2000 Ave of Stars, #100, Los Angeles CA 90067 USA — Producer

Camerota, Brett
Park City Nordic Ski Club, PO Box 682722, Park City UT 84081, USA — Nordic Combined Athlete

Camil, Jaime
Don Buchwald/Fortitude, 6500 Wilshire Blvd, #2200, Los Angeles CA 90048 USA — Singer, Actor

Camilleri, Andrea
Viking Press, 375 Hudson St, New York NY 10014, USA — Writer

Camilleri, Louis C
Kraft Foods Inc, 3 Lake Dr, Northfield IL 60093, USA — Businessman

Camilli, Douglas J (Doug)
4245 61st Ave, Vero Beach FL 32967, USA — Baseball Player

Camilo, Michel
Redondo Music & Mgmt, PO Box 216, Katonah NY 10536, USA — Jazz Pianist

Caminito, Jerry
Blue Thunder Racing, 480 Hyson Road, Jackson NJ 08527, USA — Auto Racing Driver

Cammalleri, Michael (Mike)
43 Stockdale Crescent, Richmond Hill ON L4C 3T1, Canada — Ice Hockey Player

Cammarata, Bernard
T J X Companies, 770 Cochituate Road, Framingham MA 01701, USA — Businessman

Cammuso, Frank
1725 James St, #1, Syracuse NY 13206, USA — Cartoonist

Camp, Anna
United Talent Agency, 9336 Civic Center Dr, Beverly Hills CA 90210 USA — Actress

Camp, Bill
Innovative Artists, 1505 10th St, Santa Monica CA 90401 USA — Actor

Camp, Colleen
8630 Pine Tree Place, Los Angeles CA 90069, USA — Actress

Camp, Greg
Creative Artists Agency, 2000 Ave of Stars, #100, Los Angeles CA 90067 USA — Guitarist (Smash Mouth)

Camp, Jeffrey B
Browse & Darby, 19 Cork St, London W1X 2LP, England — Artist

Camp, Jeremy T
Third Coast Artists Agency, 2021 21st Ave S, #220, Nashville TN 37212, USA — Singer

Camp, Rick L
638 Cass Pine Log Road, Rydal GA 30171, USA — Baseball Player

Camp, Shawn
Tamara Saviano Media, 1603 Horton Ave, Nashville TN 37212, USA — Singer, Guitarist, Songwriter

Camp, Shawn
9416 Deep Creek Lane, Fredericksburg VA 22407, USA — Baseball Player

Camp, Steve
Third Coast Artists Agency, 2021 21st Ave S, #220, Nashville TN 37212, USA — Singer

Campanella, Joseph
4196 Colfax Ave, Studio City CA 91604, USA — Actor

Campaneris, B Dagoberto (Bert)
9797 N 105th Place, Scottsdale AZ 85258, USA — Baseball Player

Campanis, James A (Jim)
17082 Cascades Ave, Yorba Linda CA 92886, USA — Baseball Player

Campau, Thomas E
2000 S Hammond Lake Dr, West Bloomfield MI 48324, USA — Cinematographer

Campbell, A P D Kim
Club de Madrid, C/Goya 5-7, Pasaje 2, 28001 Madrid, Spain — Prime Minister, Canada

Campbell, Alan
Douglas Gorman Rothacker Wilhelm, 1501 Broadway, #703, New York NY 10036 USA — Actor

Campbell, Allan McCulloch
947 Mears Court, Stanford CA 94305, USA — Biologist

Campbell, Andy
OmniPop Talent Group, 4605 Lankershim Blvd, #201, Toluca Lake CA 91602 USA — Actor, Comedian

Campbell, Brian W — Ice Hockey Player
Florida Panthers, 1 Panthers Parkway, Sunrise FL 33323 USA

Campbell, Bruce — Actor
A P A Talent/Literary Agency, 405 S Beverly Dr, #300, Beverly Hills CA 90212 USA

Campbell, Bruce A — Geophysicist
National Air/Space Museum, Smithsonian Institution, Earth/Planetary Studies, Washington DC 20560, USA

Campbell, Bryan A — Ice Hockey Player
10895 Tamoron Lane, Boca Raton FL 33498, USA

Campbell, Calais — Football Player
Arizona Cardinals, PO Box 888, Phoenix AZ 85001 USA

Campbell, Cassie — Ice Hockey Player
Team Canada, 2424 University Dr NW, Calgary AB T2N 3Y9, Canada

Campbell, Cheryl — Actress
Amanda Howard, 74 Clerkenwell Road, London EC1M 5QA, England

Campbell, Christa — Actress, Model
Sovereign Talent Group, 8421 Wilshire Blvd, #200, Beverly Hills CA 90211, USA

Campbell, Christian — Actor
Don Buchwald/Fortitude, 6500 Wilshire Blvd, #2200, Los Angeles CA 90048 USA

Campbell, Clifton — Producer
I C M Partners, 10250 Constellation Blvd, #900, Los Angeles CA 90067 USA

Campbell, Colin — Ice Hockey Player
National Hockey League, 50 Bay St, #1100, Toronto ON M5J 2X8, Canada

Campbell, Colin G — Foundation Executive
Colonial Williamsburg Foundation, PO Box 1776, Williamsburg VA 23187, USA

Campbell, Conchita — Actress
Paceiine Entertainment, 12444 Ventura Blvd, #103, Studio City CA 91604 USA

Campbell, D Chad — Golfer
200 Glade Road, Colleyville TX 76034, USA

Campbell, Daniel A (Dan) — Football Player
PO Box 977, County Road 2111, Meridian TX 76665, USA

Campbell, David — Actor, Singer
Caplice Mgmt, PO Box 381, Darlinghurst NSW 1300, Australia

Campbell, David W — Baseball Player
726 N Dundee Dr, Post Falls ID 83854, USA

Campbell, Derrick — Speed Skater
Skate Canada, 865 Shefford Road, Ottawa ON K1J 1H9, Canada

Campbell, Earl C — Football Player
8700 Brodie Lane, #816, Austin TX 78745, USA

Campbell, Elden J — Basketball Player
17252 Hawthorne Blvd, #493, Torrance CA 90504, USA

Campbell, Eugene E (Gene) — Ice Hockey Player
6149 Sugar Mill Lane, Mound MN 55364, USA

Campbell, Gary K — Football Player
PO Box 775353, Steamboat Springs CO 80477, USA

Campbell, Glen — Singer, Guitarist
W M E Entertainment, 1600 Division St, #300, Nashville TN 37203 USA

Campbell, Gregory — Ice Hockey Player
PO Box 342, Tilsonburg ON N4G 4H8, Canada

Campbell, Ian — Singer
Act 1 Entertainment, PO Box 1079, New Haven CT 06504, USA

Campbell, Isobel — Singer, Cellist (Belle & Sebastian)
Red Ryder Entertainment, 1532 N Milwaukee Ave, #207, Chicago IL 60622, USA

Campbell, Jason — Football Player
Chicago Bears, 1000 Football Dr, Lake Forest IL 60045 USA

Campbell, Jennifer L — Actress, Model
9200 W Sunset Blvd, #1130, West Hollywood CA 90069, USA

Campbell, Jim — Ice Hockey Player
32 Lemp Road, Saint Louis MO 63122, USA

Campbell, John — Harness Racing Driver
John D Campbell Stable, 823 Allison Dr, River Vale NJ 07675, USA

Campbell, John — Bassist (Lamb of God)
Entertainment Services, 1000 Main Street Plaza, #303, Voorhees NJ 08043, USA

Campbell, John W — Football Player
12908 Welcome Lane, Burnsville MN 55337, USA

Campbell, Jonny — Director
Independent Talent Group, Oxford House, 76 Oxford St, London W1D 1BS, England

Campbell, Julia — Actress
Innovative Artists, 1505 10th St, Santa Monica CA 90401 USA

Campbell, Kate — Singer, Songwriter
Large River Music, PO Box 121743, Nashville TN 37212, USA

Campbell, Kevin W — Baseball Player
207 Ridout Dr, Des Arc AR 72040, USA

Campbell, L Arthur — Molecular Genticist
Rockefeller University Medical Center, 1230 York Ave, New York NY 10065 USA

Campbell, LaMar — Football Player
2511 W 7th St, Chester PA 19013, USA

Campbell, Larry Joe — Actor
A P A Talent/Literary Agency, 405 S Beverly Dr, #300, Beverly Hills CA 90212 USA

Campbell, Levin H — Judge
US Court of Appeals, 1 Courthouse Way, #9400, Boston MA 02210, USA

Campbell, Lewis B — Businessman
Textron Inc, 40 Westminster St, #500, Providence RI 02903, USA

Campbell, Luther (Skywalker) — Rap Artist (2 Live Crew)
8000 Governors Square Blvd, #304, Hialeah FL 33016, USA

Campbell, Marion — Football Player, Coach
351 Marsh Point Circle, Saint Augustine FL 32080, USA

Campbell, Martin — Director
Independent Talent Group, Oxford House, 76 Oxford St, London W1D 1BS, England

Campbell, Mary Schmidt — Art Historian
New York University, Tisch Art School, 721 Broadway, New York NY 10003, USA

Campbell, Menzies — Government Official, England
House of Commons, Westminster, London SW1A 0AA, England

Campbell, Michael — Golfer
Master's International, Hurst Grove, Sandford Lane, Hurst Berkshire R10 0SQ, England

Campbell, Naomi — Model, Singer, Actress
I M G Models, 304 Park Ave S, #PH-North, New York NY 10010 USA

Campbell, Natalie
Playboy Promotions, 2706 Media Center Dr, Los Angeles CA 90065 USA — Model
Campbell, Nathaniel (Nate)
Don King Productions, 501 Fairway Dr, Deerfield Beach FL 33441 USA — Boxer
Campbell, Neve
United Talent Agency, 9336 Civic Center Dr, Beverly Hills CA 90210 USA — Actress
Campbell, Nicholas
Noble Caplan Abrams, 1260 Yonge St, #200, Toronto ON M4T 1W6, Canada — Actor
Campbell, Paul
Gersh Agency, 9465 Wilshire Blvd, #600, Beverly Hills CA 90212 USA — Actor
Campbell, Richard
National Hockey League, 50 Bay St, #1100, Toronto ON M5J 2X8, Canada — Ice Hockey Player, Coach
Campbell, Robert
54 Antrim St, Cambridge MA 02139, USA — Architectural Critic
Campbell, Tevin
Universal Attractions, 135 W 26th St, #1200, New York NY 10001 USA — Singer
Campbell, Tisha
Paul Kohner, 9300 Wilshire Blvd, #555, Beverly Hills CA 90212 USA — Actress, Singer
Campbell, Tracyanne
Ground Control Touring, 20 Jay St, #826, Brooklyn NY 11201 USA — Singer, Guitarist (Camera Obscura)
Campbell, Vivian
Front Line Mgmt, 1100 Glendon Ave, #2000, Los Angeles CA 90024 USA — Guitarist (Def Leppard/Whitesnake)
Campbell, William
Intuit Inc, PO Box 7850, Mountain View CA 94039, USA — Businessman
Campbell, William J
3267 Alex Findlay Place, Sarasota FL 34240, USA — Air Force General
Campbell, William R (Bill)
133 S Hale St, Palatine IL 60067, USA — Baseball Player
Campbell, Woodrow L (Woody)
9122 Weymouth Dr, Houston TX 77031, USA — Football Player
Campbell-Bower, Jamie
Dalzell & Beresford, 26 Astwood Mews, London SW7 4DE, England — Actor
Campbell-Hughes, Antonia
Independent Talent Group, Oxford House, 76 Oxford St, London W1D 1BS, England — Actress
Campbell-Martin, Tisha
Paul Kohner, 9300 Wilshire Blvd, #555, Beverly Hills CA 90212 USA — Actress, Singer
Campedelli, Dominic
732 Jerusalem Road, Cohasset MA 02025, USA — Ice Hockey Player
Campen, James F
2789 Ichabod Lane, Green Bay WI 54313, USA — Football Player
Campese, David I
D C Management Group, 870 Pacific Highway, #4, Gordon NSW 2072, Australia — Rugby Player
Campfield, William (Billy)
930 Glenmore Way, #K, Westerville OH 43082, USA — Football Player
Campi, Ray
2872 1/2 W Ave 35, Los Angeles CA 90065, USA — Singer, Guitarist
Campion, Cris
Artmedia, 20 Ave Rapp, 75007 Paris, France — Actor
Campion, Jane
H L A Mgmt, PO Box 1536, Strawberry Hills, Sydney NSW 2012, Australia — Director
Campisi, Amber
Playboy Promotions, 2706 Media Center Dr, Los Angeles CA 90065 USA — Model
Campo, David C (Dave)
Dallas Cowboys, 1 Cowboys Parkway, Irving TX 75063 USA — Football Coach
Campos, Alana
Ford Models Inc, 111 5th Ave, #900, New York NY 10003 USA — Model
Campos, Antonio
United Talent Agency, 9336 Civic Center Dr, Beverly Hills CA 90210 USA — Director, Producer
Campos, Jorge
Federacion de Futbol Assn, CP 06600, Col Juarez, Mexico City 6 DF, Mexico — Soccer Player
Campos, Tony
Warner Bros Records, 3300 Warner Blvd, Burbank CA 91505 USA — Bassist (Static-X, Soulfly, Asesino)
Campuzano Lopez, Felipe
Urbanizacion Cumbres de Marbella 47, Los Naguelos 29601 Marbella, Spain — Composer
Cam'ron
International Creative Mgmt, 10250 Constellation Blvd, Los Angeles CA 90067, USA — Rap Artist, Actor
Camus, Philippe
Alcatel-Lucent, 54 Rue Le Boetie, 75006 Paris, France — Businessman
Canada, Geoffrey
Harlem Children's Zone Project, 35 E 125th St, New York NY 10035, USA — Educator, Social Activist
Canada, Ron
C E S D, 10635 Santa Monica Blvd, #130, Los Angeles CA 90025, USA — Actor
Canadas, Esther
Wilhelmina Models, 300 Park Ave S, #200, New York NY 10010 USA — Model, Actress
Canady, Alexa I
6064 Forest Green Road, Pensacola FL 32505, USA — Pediatric Neurosurgeon
Canals-Barrera, Maria
A P A Talent/Literary Agency, 405 S Beverly Dr, #300, Beverly Hills CA 90212 USA — Actress
Canary, David
698 W End Ave, #1B, New York NY 10025, USA — Actor
Canby, William C, Jr
US Court of Appeals, US Courthouse, 401 W Washington St, #1, Phoenix AZ 85003, USA — Judge
Cancellara, Fabian
Team CSC, Riis Cycling, Firskovvej 36, 2800 Lyngby, Denmark — Cyclist
Candaele, Casey T
251 Broad St, San Luis Obispo CA 93405, USA — Baseball Player
Candelaria, John R
3122 Elroy Ave, Pittsburgh PA 15227, USA — Baseball Player
Candelaria, Richard G
3812 Conough Lane, Las Vegas NV 89129, USA — WW II Army Air Corps Hero
Candelo, Juan Carlos (J C)
T's K O Fight Club, 3730 Wheeling St, #10, Denver CO 80239, USA — Boxer
Candiotti, Thomas C (Tom)
6061 E Jenan Dr, Scottsdale AZ 85254, USA — Baseball Player
Candyman
Groove Entertainment, 1005 N Alfred St, #2, West Hollywood CA 90069, USA — Rap Artist

Cane, Louis P J — Artist
37 Rue D'Enghien, 75010 Paris, France

Cane, Mark A — Oceanographer, Climatologist
Lamont Doherty Earth Observatory, Route 9W, Palisades NY 10964, USA

Canella, Guido — Architect
Via Revere 7, 20123 Milan, Italy

Canepa, John C — Financier
Crowe Chizek, 400 Riverfront Plaza, Grand Rapids MI 49503, USA

Canestri, Giovanni Cardinal — Religious Leader
Archdiocese of Genoa-Bobbio, Piazza Matteotti 4, 16123 Genoa, Italy

Canet, Guillaume — Actor, Director
U B B A, 6 Rue de Braque, 75003 Paris, France

Canete, Ariel — Golfer
Advantage International, 1751 Pinnacle Dr, #1500, McLean VA 22102 USA

Canfield, Jack — Writer
PO Box 30880, Santa Barbara CA 93130, USA

Canfield, Mary Grace — Actress
434 Seaview Road, Santa Barbara CA 93108, USA

Canfield, Paul — Physicist
Iowa State University, Physics Dept, Ames IA 50011, USA

Canfield, William N (Bill) — Editorial Cartoonist
Star Ledger, Editorial Dept, 1 Star Ledger Plaza, Newark NJ 07102, USA

Cangelosi, John A — Baseball Player
10914 Caribou Lane, Orland Park IL 60467, USA

Cangemi, Joseph P — Psychologist
1409 Mount Ayr Circle, Bowling Green KY 42103, USA

Canibus — Rap Artist
J L Entertainment, 18653 Ventura Blvd, #340, Tarzana CA 91356 USA

Canin, Ethan — Writer
Rogers Coleridge White, 20 Powis Mews, London W11 1JN, England

Canin, Serena — Concert Violinist
David Rowe Artists, 24 Bessom St, #2, Marblehead MA 01945, USA

Canizales, Jose (Gaby) — Boxer
4215 Santa Marie Ave, Laredo TX 78041, USA

Canizales, Orlando — Boxer
17542 College Port Dr, Laredo TX 78045, USA

Canizares Llovera, Antonio Cardinal — Religious Leader
Archdiocese of Toledo, Arco de Palacio 3, 45001 Toledo, Spain

Cannavale, Bobby — Actor
I C M Partners, 730 5th Ave, New York NY 10019 USA

Cannavaro, Fabio — Soccer Player
F C Real Madrid, Avda Concha Espana 1, 28036 Madrid, Spain

Cannida, James T, II — Football Player
4504 Harmony Place, Rohnert Park CA 94928, USA

Cannizzaro, Christopher J (Chris) — Baseball Player
13597 Grain Lane, San Diego CA 92129, USA

Cannom, Greg — Makeup Artist
223 Alameda Ave, #1, Burbank CA 91502, USA

Cannon, Danny — Director
Steve Kenis Co, Royalty House, 72-74 Dean St, London WID 3SG, England

Cannon, Dyan — Actress
1100 Alta Loma Road, #808, West Hollywood CA 90069, USA

Cannon, Freddy (Boom Boom) — Singer, Songwriter
5119 Surfrider Way, Oxnard CA 93035, USA

Cannon, Joe — Soccer Player
Vancouver Whitecaps, 375 Water St, #550, Vancouver V6B 5C6, Canada

Cannon, John (Ace) — Saxophonist
J L Entertainment, 18653 Ventura Blvd, #340, Tarzana CA 91356 USA

Cannon, John R — Football Player
2911 W Bay Vista Ave, Tampa FL 33611, USA

Cannon, Katherine — Actress
1310 S Westholme Ave, Los Angeles CA 90024, USA

Cannon, Mark M — Football Player
2604 Riveroaks Dr, Arlington TX 76006, USA

Cannon, Nick — Actor, Comedian, Writer
I C M Partners, 10250 Constellation Blvd, #900, Los Angeles CA 90067 USA

Cannon, Robert H, Jr — Aerospace Engineer
Stanford University, Aeronautics/Astronautics Dept, Stanford CA 94305, USA

Cannon, William A (Billy) — Football Player
8851 Sage Hill Dr, Saint Francisville LA 70775, USA

Cano Mercedes, Robinson J — Baseball Player
New York Yankees, Yankee Stadium, E 161st St & River Ave, Bronx NY 10451 USA

Cano, Pablo D — Sculptor
501 SW 24th Ave, Miami FL 33135, USA

Canogar, Rafael — Artist
Calle de la Bolsa 14, 28012 Madrid, Spain

Canonero, Milena — Costume Designer
I C M Partners, 10250 Constellation Blvd, #900, Los Angeles CA 90067 USA

Canova, Diana — Actress
TalentWorks, 3500 W Olive Ave, #1400, Burbank CA 91505 USA

Canseco, Jose, Jr — Baseball Player
Canseco Inc, 112 Panlock Court, Irmo SC 29063, USA

Cantaline, Anita — Bowler
31455 Pinto Dr, Warren MI 48093, USA

Canterbury, Chandler — Actor
United Talent Agency, 9336 Civic Center Dr, Beverly Hills CA 90210 USA

Cantey, Charlsie — Sportscaster
ABC-TV, Sports Dept, 77 W 66th St, New York NY 10023 USA

Canton, Joanna — Actress
4381 Ventura Canyon Ave, #9, Sherman Oaks CA 91423, USA

Canton, Mark — Businessman, Producer
Atmosphere Entertainment, 4751 Wilshire Blvd, $300, Los Angeles CA 90010, USA

Cantona, Eric — Soccer Player
Mikado, 105 Ave Raymond Poincare, 75016 Paris, France

Cantone, Mario — Actor, Comedian
Gersh Agency, 9465 Wilshire Blvd, #600, Beverly Hills CA 90212 USA

Cantor, Charles R
Sequenom Inc, 3595 John Hopkins Court, San Diego CA 92121, USA — Molecular Biologist

Cantor, Geoffrey
Stone Manners Salners, 9911 W Pico Blvd, #1400, Los Angeles CA 90035 USA — Actor

Cantor, Nancy E
Syracuse University, Chancellor's Office, Syracuse NY 13244, USA — Educator

Cantor, Tim
527 4th Ave, San Diego CA 92101, USA — Artist

Cantrell, Blu
Universal Attractions, 135 W 26th St, #1200, New York NY 10001 USA — Singer

Cantrell, Cady
Playboy Promotions, 2706 Media Center Dr, Los Angeles CA 90065 USA — Model

Cantrell, Jerry F, Jr
Agency Group Ltd, 142 W 57th St, #600, New York NY 10019 USA — Singer, Guitarist (Alice in Chains)

Cantrell, Lana
300 E 71st St, #91A, New York NY 10021, USA — Singer

Cantu Guzman, Jorge L
5015 24th Ave S, Tampa Bay FL 33619, USA — Baseball Player

Canup, Robin
Southwest Research Institute, 1050 Walnut St, #300, Boulder CO 80302, USA — Astronomer

Caparulo, John
Parallel Entertainment, 9420 Wilshire Blvd, #250, Beverly Hills CA 90212, USA — Actor, Comedian

Capasso, Federico
Lucent Technologies, Bell Labs, 600 Mountain Ave, New Providence NJ 07974, USA — Physicist

Capecchi, Mario R
778 E 13800 S, Draper UT 84020, USA — Nobel Medicine Laureate

Capellas, Michael
M C I, 500 Clinton Center Dr, #2200, Clinton MS 39056, USA — Businessman

Capellino, Ally
N1R, Metropolitan Wharf, Wapping Wall, London E1 9SS, England — Fashion Designer

Capellmann, Nadine
Haller Str 46, 52325 Wurselen, Germany — Equestrian

Capello, Fabio
F C Real Madrid, Avda Concha Espana 1, 28036 Madrid, Spain — Soccer Player, Manager

Capers, Dom
814 Hilltop Dr, Walpole MA 02081, USA — Football Coach

Caperton, W Gaston, III
College Board, President's Office, 45 Columbus Ave, New York NY 10023, USA — Governor, WV; Foundation Executive

Capice, Philip C
1400 N Sweetzer Ave, #403, West Hollywood CA 90069, USA — Producer

Capilouto, Eli
University of Kentucky, President's Office, Lexington KY , USA — Educator

Caplan, Lizzy
Creative Artists Agency, 2000 Ave of Stars, #100, Los Angeles CA 90067 USA — Actress

Capleton
Agency Group Ltd, 142 W 57th St, #600, New York NY 10019 USA — Singer

Caplin, Mortimer M
5610 Wisconsin Ave NW, #18E, Chevy Chase MD 20815, USA — Government Official

Capobianco, Tito
Pittsburgh Opera Co, 711 Penn Ave, #800, Pittsburgh PA 15222, USA — Opera Director

Caponera, John
Messina Baker Entertainment, 955 Carillo Dr, #100, Los Angeles CA 90048, USA — Actor, Comedian

Caponi-Byrnes, Donna
2731 Silver River Trail, Orlando FL 32828, USA — Golfer

Cappelletti, Gino R M
19 Louis Dr, Wellesley MA 02481, USA — Football Player

Cappelletti, John R
23791 Brant Lane, Laguna Niguel CA 92677, USA — Football Player

Capps, Matthew D (Matt)
6348 S Summers Circle, Douglasville GA 30135, USA — Baseball Player

Capps, Ron
Copenhagen Racing, 1232 Distribution Way, Vista CA 92081, USA — Drag Racing Driver

Capps, Steve
Microsoft Corp, 1 Microsoft Way, Redmond WA 98052, USA — Computer Software Designer

Capra, Francis
Curtis Talent Mgmt, 9607 Arby Dr, Beverly Hills CA 90210, USA — Actor

Capra, Fritjof
PO Box 9066, Berkeley CA 94709, USA — Physicist, Systems Theorist

Capra, Lee W (Buzz)
15039 W Keswick Place, Lockport IL 60441, USA — Baseball Player

Capra, Nick L
PO Box 162, Medicine Park OK 73557, USA — Baseball Player

Capriati, Jennifer
5326 Foxhunt Dr, Wesley Chapel FL 33543, USA — Tennis Player

Caprice
Select Model Mgmt, 43 King St, London WC2E, England — Model, Singer, Songwriter

Caprioli, Anita
Carol Levi Mgmt, Via G Pisanelli 2, 00196 Rome, Italy — Actress

Capron, Robert
Generation TV, 20 W 20th St, #1008, New York NY 10011, USA — Actor

Capshaw, Jessica
Creative Artists Agency, 2000 Ave of Stars, #100, Los Angeles CA 90067 USA — Actress

Capshaw, Kate
PO Box 491356, Los Angeles CA 90049, USA — Actress

Capuano, Christopher F (Chris)
10953 E Tusayan Trail, Scottsdale AZ 85255, USA — Baseball Player

Capuano, Dave, Jr
145 Capuano Ave, Cranston RI 02920, USA — Ice Hockey Player

Capuano, Jack
New York Islanders, 1255 Hempstead Turnpike, Uniondale NY 11553 USA — Ice Hockey Player, Coach

Capucon, Gautier
Columbia Artists Mgmt Inc, 1790 Broadway, #702, New York NY 10019 USA — Concert Cellist

Capucon, Renaud
Columbia Artists Mgmt Inc, 1790 Broadway, #702, New York NY 10019 USA — Concert Violinist

Capurro, Scott
Coolwaters Productions, 10061 Riverside Dr, Box 531, Toluca Lake CA 91602 USA — Actor

Cara, Irene Countdown Entertainment, 110 W 26th St, #300, New York NY 10001, USA	Singer, Actress
Carafotes, Paul C E S D, 10635 Santa Monica Blvd, #130, Los Angeles CA 90025 USA	Actor
Caramanlis, Costas Prime Minister's Office, Maximos Mansion, 19 Irodou Attikou St, 10674 Athens, Greece	Prime Minister, Greece
Carano, Gina J Syndicate, 8265 Sunset Blvd, #205, Los Angeles CA 90046, USA	Actress
Carano, Glenn T 2551 Lakeridge Shores E, Reno NV 89519, USA	Football Player
Carapella, Alfred R (Al) 10 Woodlot Road, Eastchester NY 10709, USA	Football Player
Carasco, Joe (King) Texas Sounds, 2317 Pecan St, Dickinson TX 77539, USA	Singer
Carax, Leos Artmedia, 20 Ave Rapp, 75007 Paris, France	Director
Caray, Harry C (Chip), III 1302 Azalea Lane, Maitland FL 32751, USA	Sportscaster
Carbajal, Michael PO Box 510, Phoenix AZ 85001, USA	Boxer
Carberry, Deirdre American Ballet Theater, 890 Broadway, #300, New York NY 10003, USA	Ballerina
Carbo, Bernardo (Bernie) 6352 Woodside Dr S, Theodore AL 36582, USA	Baseball Player
Carbonara, David Creative Artists Agency, 2000 Ave of Stars, #100, Los Angeles CA 90067 USA	Composer
Carbonell, Nestor Paradigm Agency, 360 N Crescent Dr, North Building, Beverly Hills CA 90210 USA	Actor
Carcaterra, Lorenzo Pitt Group, 9465 Wilshire Blvd, #420, Beverly Hills CA 90212, USA	Writer
Card, Andrew H, Jr 1207 Buchana St, McLean VA 22101, USA	Secretary, Transportation
Card, Michael 1143 Dora Whitley Road, Franklin TN 37064, USA	Singer, Musician, Songwriter
Card, Orson Scott 401 Willoughby Blvd, Greensboro NC 27408, USA	Writer
Cardamone, Richard J US Court of Appeals, 10 Broad St, #322, Utica NY 13501, USA	Judge
Cardellini, Linda I/D Public Relations, 7060 Hollywood Blvd, #800, Los Angeles CA 90028 USA	Actress
Carden, Joan M Avere Artists Mgmt, 26 Oxley Dr, Bowral NSW 2576, Australia	Opera Singer
Carden, Michael (Mike) Crush Music Media Mgmt, 60-62 E 11th St, #700, New York NY 10003, USA	Guitarist (Academy Is), Songwriter
Cardenal, Jose D 118 Bridgewater Court, Bradenton FL 34212, USA	Baseball Player
Cardenas, Leonardo L (Chico) 5412 Ravenna St, Cincinnati OH 45227, USA	Baseball Player
Cardenas, Robert L Flight Test Historical Society, PO Box 57, Edwards CA 93523, USA	Test Pilot, Air Force General
Cardin, Claude 13 Rue Boucher, Sorel QC J3P 1E7, Canada	Ice Hockey Player
Cardin, Pierre 59 Rue du Faubourg-Saint-Honore, 75008 Paris, France	Fashion Designer
Cardinal, Brian L 1680 Lane 105 Lake James, Angola IN 46703, USA	Basketball Player
Cardinal, Douglas J 7011A Manchester Blvd, #315, Alexandria VA 22310, USA	Architect
Cardinale, Claudia Via Flamina del Mellini 10, 00192 Rome, Italy	Actress
Cardona, Manolo D2 Management, 9255 Sunset Blvd, #600, West Hollywood CA 90069, USA	Actor
Cardona, Manuel Max-Planck-Institut, Heisenbergstr 1, 70569 Stuttgart, Germany	Physicist
Cardona, Prudencio 4845 NW 7th St, #402, Miami FL 33126, USA	Boxer
Cardone, Vivian C E S D, 10635 Santa Monica Blvd, #130, Los Angeles CA 90025 USA	Actress
Cardow, Cameron (Cam) Ottawa Sentinental, 11 Baxter Road, Box 5020, Ottawa ON K2C 3M4, Canada	Editorial Cartoonist
Cardoza, Dennis A Manatt Phelps Phillips, 700 12th St NW, #1100, Washington DC 20005, USA	Representative, CA
Care, Peter Bob Industries, 1313 5th St, Santa Monica CA 90401, USA	Director, Producer, Writer
Carell, Steve W M E Entertainment, 9601 Wilshire Blvd, #300, Beverly Hills CA 90210 USA	Actor, Writer
Carelli, Rick PO Box 1000, Arvada CO 80001, USA	Truck Racing Driver
Caretto-Brown, Patty 16079 Mesquite Circle, Fountain Valley CA 92708, USA	Swimmer
Carew, Rodney C (Rod) 1171 Via Santiago, Corona CA 92882, USA	Baseball Player
Carey, Clare B/W/R, 9100 Wilshire Blvd, #500W, Beverly Hills CA 90212 USA	Actress
Carey, Danny Volcano Records, 3375 Cahuenga Blvd, #590, Los Angeles CA 90068, USA	Drummer (Tool)
Carey, Drew Gersh Agency, 9465 Wilshire Blvd, #600, Beverly Hills CA 90212 USA	Actor, Comedian
Carey, Duane G 5938 Instone Circle, Colorado Springs CO 80922, USA	Astronaut
Carey, Ezekiel 509 E Ridge Crest Blvd, #A, Ridge Crest CA 93555, USA	Singer (Flamingos)
Carey, George L Gloucestershire University, Chancellory, Cheltenham GL50 2RH, England	Religious Leader
Carey, Gerard Gavin Barker Assoc, 2D Wimpole St, London W1G 0EB, England	Actor

Carey, Harry, Jr	Actor, Writer, Producer
3113 S Beverly Dr, Los Angeles CA 90034, USA	
Carey, Jim	Ice Hockey Player
5351 Hunt Club Way, Sarasota FL 34238, USA	
Carey, Mariah	Singer, Songwriter
Creative Artists Agency, 2000 Ave of Stars, #100, Los Angeles CA 90067 USA	
Carey, Peter	Writer
I C M Partners, 730 5th Ave, New York NY 10019 USA	
Carey, Vernon A	Football Player
5321 Thoroughbred Lane, Southwest Ranches FL 33330, USA	
Cargo, David F	Governor, NM
6422 Concordia Road NE, Albuquerque NM 87111, USA	
Caria, Marco	Opera Singer
I M G Artists, Hogarth Business Park, Chiswick, London W4 2TH, England	
Carides, Gia	Actress
Innovative Artists, 1505 10th St, Santa Monica CA 90401 USA	
Caridis, Miltiades	Conductor
Himmelhofgasse 10, 1130 Vienna, Austria	
Carillo, Mary	Sportscaster
822 Boylston St, #203, Chestnut Hill PA 02467, USA	
Carillo, Tony	Cartoonist (F Minus)
United Feature Syndicate, PO Box 5610, Cincinnati OH 45201 USA	
Carion, Christian	Director, Writer
Fims Talents, 34 Rue du Louvre, 75001 Paris, France	
Carioti, Ricky	Photographer
Washington Post, Editorial Dept, 1150 15th St NW, Washington DC 20071 USA	
Cariou, Len	Actor
7004 Blvd E, #17D, West New York NJ 07093, USA	
Carithers, William C, Jr	Physicist
817 The Alameda, Berkeley CA 94707, USA	
Carkner, Terry	Ice Hockey Player
4 Remington Lane, Malvern PA 19355, USA	
Carl XVI Gustaf	King, Sweden
Kungliga Slottet, Slottsbacken, 111 30 Stockholm, Sweden	
Carle, Eric	Artist
PO Box 485, Northampton MA 01061, USA	
Carlei, Carlo	Director
Bloom Hergott Diemer, 150 S Rodeo Dr, #300, Beverly Hills CA 90212 USA	
Carles Gordo, Ricardo M Cardinal	Religious Leader
Carrer del Bisbe 5, 08002 Barcelona, Spain	
Carlesimo, Pete J (P J)	Basketball Coach, Sportscaster
1429 Willard Ave W, Seattle WA 98119, USA	
Carleson, Lennart A E	Abel Mathematics Laureate
Royal Institute, Kungl Tekniska Hogskloan SE 100 44, Stockholm, Sweden	
Carlestrom, John E	Astronomer
University of Chicago, Astronomy Dept, 5640 S Ellis Ave, Chicago IL 60637, USA	
Carleton, K Wayne	Ice Hockey Player
9846 Highway 26 E, RR 2 LCD Collingwood, Collingwood ON L9Y 3Z1, Canada	
Carley, Christopher	Actor
Untitled Entertainment, 350 S Beverly Dr, #200, Beverly Hills CA 90212 USA	
Carlile, Brandi	Singer, Guitarist, Songwriter
Paradigm Agency, 360 Park Ave, #1600, New York NY 10022 USA	
Carlile, Forbes	Swimming Coach
16 Cross St, Ryde NSW 2112, Australia	
Carlin, Amanda	Actress
Greene Assoc, 1901 Ave of Stars, #130, Los Angeles CA 90067 USA	
Carlin, Brian	Ice Hockey Player
103 Mount Norquay Park SE, Calgary AB T2Z 2R3, Canada	
Carlin, John W	Governor, KS
1208 Wyndham Heights Dr, Manhattan KS 66503, USA	
Carling, William D C	Rugby Player, Sportscaster
Mike Burton Mgmt, Brunswick Road, Gloucester GL1 1JJ, England	
Carlisle, Belinda	Singer, Songwriter, Model
Tony Denton Promotions, Charter House, 157/159 High St, London N14 7DY, England	
Carlisle, Bob	Singer, Songwriter
Ray Ware Artist Mgmt, 3708 Saint Stephens Way, Franklin TN 37064, USA	
Carlisle, Cooper M	Football Player
2032 Sorrelwood Court, San Ramon CA 94582, USA	
Carlisle, Jodi	Actress, Comedienne
I C M Partners, 10250 Constellation Blvd, #900, Los Angeles CA 90067 USA	
Carlisle, Mary	Actress
517 N Rodeo Dr, Beverly Hills CA 90210, USA	
Carlisle, Richard P (Rick)	Basketball Player, Coach
3925 Greenbrier Dr, Dallas TX 75225, USA	
Carll, Hayes	Singer, Guitarist, Songwriter
Crowley Artists Mgmt, 602 Wayside Dr, Wimberley TX 78676, USA	
Carlos Moco, Marcolino Jose	Prime Minister, Angola
Movimento Popular de Libertacao de Angola, Luanda, Angola	
Carlos, Bun E	Drummer (Cheap Trick)
Oakie Dokie Mgmt, 6090 Central Ave, Saint Petersburg FL 33707, USA	
Carlos, John	Track Athlete
68640 Tortuga Road, Cathedral City CA 92234, USA	
Carlos, Wendy	Composer
B M I, 8730 W Sunset Blvd, #300, Los Angeles CA 90069 USA	
Carlson, Amy	Actress
Principal Entertainment, 1964 Westwood Blvd, #400, Los Angeles CA 90025 USA	
Carlson, Arne H	Governor, MN
145 Holly Lane N, Minneapolis MN 55447, USA	
Carlson, Dudley L	Navy Admiral
Navy League, 2300 Wilson Blvd, #210, Arlington VA 22201, USA	
Carlson, Jack	Ice Hockey Player
22346 Metamora Dr, Beverly Hills MI 48025, USA	
Carlson, Jack W	Association Executive
American Assn of Retired Persons, 1901 K St NW, Washington DC 20006, USA	
Carlson, John A	Businessman
Cray Research, 655 Lone Oak Dr, #A, Saint Paul MN 55121, USA	

Carlson, John D, Jr — Football Player
Minnesota Vikings, 9520 Viking Dr, Eden Prairie MN 55344 USA
Carlson, K C — Cartoonist (Legion of Super Heroes)
D C Comics, 1700 Broadway, #400, New York NY 10019 USA
Carlson, Karen — Actress
3700 Ventura Canyon Ave, Sherman Oaks CA 91423, USA
Carlson, Kelly — Actress
Gersh Agency, 9465 Wilshire Blvd, #600, Beverly Hills CA 90212 USA
Carlson, Kent — Ice Hockey Player
58 Branch Turnpike, #103, Concord NH 03301, USA
Carlson, Lane — Model
Warning Models, 1590 S Lewis St, Anaheim CA 92805, USA
Carlson, M Cody — Football Player
3417 Foothill Terrace, Austin TX 78731, USA
Carlson, Mark C — Baseball Umpire
354 Tall Oak Trail, Tarpon Springs FL 34688, USA
Carlson, Monica — Model, Actress
Sports Unlimited, 1732 NW Quimby St, Portland OR 97209, USA
Carlson, Paulette — Singer
Fat City Artists, 1906 Chet Atkins Place, #502, Nashville TN 37212 USA
Carlson, Richard A — Interior Designer
Swanke Hayden Connell Architects, 295 Lafayette St, New York NY 10012, USA
Carlson, Shane — Model
Warning Models, 1590 S Lewis St, Anaheim CA 92805, USA
Carlson, Steve — Auto Racing Driver
539 Brickel Road, West Salem WI 54669, USA
Carlson, Steve E — Ice Hockey Player
PO Box 3476, Rancho Cordova CA 95741, USA
Carlson, Tucker — Commentator
Fox-TV, News Dept, 205 E 67th St, New York NY 10065 USA
Carlson, Veronica — Actress
7844 Kavanagh Court, Sarasota FL 34240, USA
Carlsson, Arvid — Nobel Medicine Laureate
Goteborg University, Sahlgrenska Academy, Box 100, 405 30 Sweden
Carlsson, Ingvar G — Prime Minister, Sweden
Riksdagen, 100 12 Stockholm, Sweden
Carlton, Carl — Singer
Randolph Enterprises, Oakland, Inkster MI 48141, USA
Carlton, Hope Marie — Actress, Model
Playboy Promotions, 2706 Media Center Dr, Los Angeles CA 90065 USA
Carlton, L Wray — Football Player
29 Pine Terrace, Orchard Park NY 14127, USA
Carlton, Larry — Jazz Guitarist, Composer
3981 Casparis Road, Columbia TN 38401, USA
Carlton, Paul K, Jr — Air Force General, Surgeon
ImmuneRegen BioSciences, 8777 Via de Ventura, #280, Scottsdale AZ 85258, USA
Carlton, Steven N (Steve) — Baseball Player
G W Sports, 555 S Camino del Rio, #B2, Durango CO 81303, USA
Carlton, Vanessa — Singer, Songwriter
Creative Artists Agency, 2000 Ave of Stars, #100, Los Angeles CA 90067 USA
Carlucci, Dave — Singer (Danny & the Juniors)
Joe Terry Mgmt, PO Box 279, Williamstown NJ 08094, USA
Carlucci, Frank C, III — Secretary, Defense; Businessman
Carlyle Group, 1001 Pennsylvania Ave NW, #220S, Washington DC 20004, USA
Carlyle, Earl L (Buddy) — Baseball Player
205 Ashmere Court, Tyrone GA 30290, USA
Carlyle, Joan H — Opera Singer
Laundry Cottage, Hammer, North Wales SY13 4QX, England
Carlyle, Liz — Writer
1939 High House Road, #185, Cary NC 27519, USA
Carlyle, Randy — Ice Hockey Player, Coach
180 S Lakeview Ave, Anaheim CA 92807, USA
Carlyle, Robert — Actor
Hamilton Hodell, 66-68 Margaret St, London W1W 8SR, England
Carmack, Chris — Actor
Luber Rocklin Entertainment, 8530 Wilshire Blvd, #555, Beverly Hills CA 90211 USA
Carman — Singer
Carman World Outreach, PO Box 470470, Tulsa OK 74147, USA
Carman, Brian — Singer, Guitarist (Chantays)
Bill Hollingshead Productions, 1010 Anderson Road, Davis CA 95616 USA
Carman, Donald W (Don) — Baseball Player
555 Murex Dr, Naples FL 34102, USA
Carman, Gregory W — Judge; Representative, NY
US Court of International Trade, 1 Federal Plaza, New York NY 10278, USA
Carmel, Leon J (Duke) — Baseball Player
116 Spring Lake Blvd, Waretown NJ 08758, USA
Carmen, Eric — Singer, Songwriter
David Spero Mgmt, 1679 S Belvoir Blvd, Cleveland OH 44121, USA
Carmen, Julie — Actress
Greene Assoc, 1901 Ave of Stars, #130, Los Angeles CA 90067 USA
Carmichael, Albert R (Hoagy) — Football Player
78641 Hampshire Ave, Palm Desert CA 92211, USA
Carmichael, Clint — Actor
Kazarian/Spencer/Ruskin, 11969 Ventura Blvd, #300, Studio City CA 91604 USA
Carmichael, Daniel A (Dan), Jr — WW II Navy Air Force Hero
2764 Elm Ave, Columbus OH 43209, USA
Carmichael, Jesse — Keyboardist (Maroon 5)
J Records, 745 5th Ave, #600, New York NY 10151 USA
Carmichael, Katy — Actress
Shining Mgmt, 12 D'Arblay St, London W1F 8DU, England
Carmichael, L Harold — Football Player
38 Birch Lane, Glassboro NJ 08028, USA
Carmichael, Ricky — Motorcycle Racing Rider
1219 Shady Rest Road, Havana FL 32333, USA
Carmine, Michael — Cinematographer
3615 West Dr, Little Neck NY 11363, USA

Carmody, Matt
Metropolitan Talent Agency, 7020 La Presa Dr, Los Angeles CA 90068 USA — Actor
Carmona, Richard H
Canyon Ranch Wellness Center, 8600 E Rockcliff Road, Tucson AZ 85750, USA — Physician, Government Official
Carmona, Wayne
W M E Entertainment, 9601 Wilshire Blvd, #300, Beverly Hills CA 90210 USA — Producer
Carnahan, Joe
Creative Artists Agency, 2000 Ave of Stars, #100, Los Angeles CA 90067 USA — Director, Producer, Writer
Carnahan, Matthew Michael
W M E Entertainment, 9601 Wilshire Blvd, #300, Beverly Hills CA 90210 USA — Writer
Carne, Jean
Walt Reeder Productions, 93 Old York Road, #1-604, Jenkintown PA 19046, USA — Singer
Carneiro, Joana
I M G Artists, Hogarth Business Park, Chiswick, London W4 2TH, England — Conductor
Carner, Charles Robert
4172 Sandy Hollow Court, Moorpark CA 93021, USA — Director, Producer, Writer
Carner, JoAnne Gunderson
3030 S Ocean Blvd, Palm Beach FL 33480, USA — Golfer
Carnes, Kim
1829 Tyne Blvd, Nashville TN 37215, USA — Singer, Songwriter
Carnes, Ryan
TalentWorks, 3500 W Olive Ave, #1400, Burbank CA 91505 USA — Actor
Carnesale, Albert
University of California, Chancellor's Office, Los Angeles CA 90024, USA — Educator
Carnesecca, Luigi (Lou)
18247 Midland Parkway, Jamaica NY 11432, USA — Basketball Coach
Carnevale, Mark
24 Loggerhead Lane, Ponte Vedra Beach FL 32082, USA — Golfer
Carney, Jay
White House, 1600 Pennsylvania Ave NW, Washington DC 20500 USA — Government Official, Journalist
Carney, John
Casorotto Ramsay, Waverley House, 7-12 Noel St, London W1F 8GQ, England — Director, Writer, Actor
Carney, John M
2950 Wishbone Way, Encinitas CA 92024, USA — Football Player
Carney, Keith E
8701 N 55th Place, Paradise Valley AZ 85253, USA — Ice Hockey Player
Carney, Patrick
Q-Prime South, 131 S 11th St, Nashville TN 37206 USA — Drummer (Black Keys)
Carney, Quinn
University of Maryland, Athletic Dept, College Park MD 20742, USA — Lacrosse Player
Carney, Rodney D
Memphis Grizzlies, 191 Beale St, Memphis TN 38103 USA — Basketball Player
Carney, Thomas P
Thomas P Carney Inc, PO Box 28, Langhorne PA 19047, USA — Army General
Carnoy, Martin
Stanford University, Economic Studies Center, Stanford CA 94305, USA — Economist
Carns, Michael P C (Mike)
966 Coral Dr, Pebble Beach CA 93953, USA — Air Force General
Caro, Anthony A
38C Georgiana St, London NW1 0EB, England — Sculptor
Caro, Niki
I C M Partners, 10250 Constellation Blvd, #900, Los Angeles CA 90067 USA — Director, Writer
Caro, Robert A
Robert A Caro Assoc, 250 W 57th St, #2215, New York NY 10107, USA — Writer
Caroit, Phillipe
Voyez Mon Agent, 20 Ave Rapp, 75007 Paris, France — Actor
Carol, Linda
William Kerwin Agency, 1605 N Cahuenga Blvd, #202, Los Angeles CA 90028, USA — Actress
Carolin, Heather M
Playboy Promotions, 2706 Media Center Dr, Los Angeles CA 90065 USA — Model
Caroline
Villa Le Clos Saint Pierre, Ave San-Martin, Monte Carlo, Monaco — Heir Presumptive, Monaco
Caroline, James C (J C)
2501 Stanford Dr, Champaign IL 61820, USA — Football Player
Carolla, Adam
Dixon Talent, 375 Greenwich St, #500, New York NY 10013, USA — Actor, Comedian
Carollo, Joseph P (Joe)
4634 Meyer Way, Carmichael CA 95608, USA — Football Player
Caron, Glenn Gordon
Picturemaker Productions, 1600 Rosecrans Ave, Building 2A, Manhattan Beach CA 90266, USA — Producer/Writer
Caron, Jacques
6426 Moorings Point Circle, #201, Lakewood Ranch FL 34202, USA — Ice Hockey Player
Caron, Jean-Claude
Artmedia, 20 Ave Rapp, 75007 Paris, France — Actor
Caron, Leslie
6 Rue De Bellechaisse, 75007 Paris, France — Actress, Dancer
Caron, Sandrine
Artmedia, 20 Ave Rapp, 75007 Paris, France — Actress
Carothers, Veronica
535 N Heatherstone Dr, Orange CA 92869, USA — Actress
Carp, Daniel A (Dan)
Delta Air Lines, Hartsfield International Airport, Atlanta GA 30320, USA — Businessman
Carpani, Rachael
Lisa Mann Agency, PO Box 1192, Bondi Junction NSW 1315, Australia — Actress
Carpenter, Andrew (Drew)
1894 SW Mistybrook Dr, Grants Pass OR 97527, USA — Baseball Player
Carpenter, Bobby
71 Chestnut St, North Reading MA 01864, USA — Ice Hockey Player
Carpenter, Carleton
RR 2, Chardavoyne Road, Warwick NY 10990, USA — Actor
Carpenter, Chad
Tundra Comics, PO Box 871354, Wasilla AK 99687, USA — Cartoonist
Carpenter, Charisma
John Carrabino Mgmt, 5900 Wilshire Blvd, #406, Los Angeles CA 90036 USA — Actress, Model
Carpenter, Christopher J (Chris)
809 S Warson Road, Saint Louis MO 63124, USA — Baseball Player

C

Carpenter, Cris H
1484 Heritage Place, Gainesville GA 30501, USA — Baseball Player

Carpenter, Ed
Vision Racing, 4760 Kingsway Dr, #B, Indianapolis IN 46205, USA — Auto Racing Driver

Carpenter, Jack
I C M Partners, 10250 Constellation Blvd, #900, Los Angeles CA 90067 USA — Actor

Carpenter, Jennifer
W M E Entertainment, 9601 Wilshire Blvd, #300, Beverly Hills CA 90210 USA — Actress

Carpenter, John H
Echo Lake Mgmt, 421 S Beverly Dr, #800, Beverly Hills CA 90212, USA — Director, Writer

Carpenter, Keion E
2009 Shin Court, Buford GA 30519, USA — Football Player

Carpenter, Kip
W375S10897 Prairie Lane, Eagle WI 53119, USA — Speed Skater

Carpenter, M Scott
PO Box 3161, Vail CO 81658, USA — Astronaut

Carpenter, Mary Chapin
Paradigm Agency, 360 N Crescent Dr, North Building, Beverly Hills CA 90210 USA — Singer, Guitarist, Songwriter

Carpenter, Richard L
960 Country Valley Road, Westlake Village CA 91362, USA — Pianist, Singer, Songwriter

Carpenter, Robert J (Bobby), III
103 Graeser Acres, Saint Louis MO 63146, USA — Football Player

Carpenter, Robert J (Rob), Jr
1601 Wheeling Road NE, Lancaster OH 43130, USA — Football Player

Carpenter, Russell P
Worldwide Production Agency, 5358 Melrose Ave, #209W, Los Angeles CA — Cinematographer

Carpenter, Stephen
Velvet Hammer Music, 9014 Melrose Ave, West Hollywood CA 90069, USA — Guitarist (Deftones)

Carpenter, William S (Bill), Jr
PO Box 4067, Whitefish MT 59937, USA — Army General, Hero, Football Player

Carpenter-Phinney, Connie
470 Juniper Ave, Boulder CO 80304, USA — Cyclist

Carpentier, Alain
Hospital Broussais, 96 Rue Didot, 75674 Bris Cedex 14, France — Heart Surgeon

Carpentier, Patrick
S A M A X Motorsports, 203 NW 16th St, Pompano Beach FL 33060, USA — Auto Racing Driver

Carpinello, James
A P A Talent/Literary Agency, 405 S Beverly Dr, #300, Beverly Hills CA 90212 USA — Actor, Singer

Carr, Antoine L
5724 Croyden Circle, Wichita KS 67220, USA — Basketball Player

Carr, Austin G
4547 Saint Germain Blvd, Cleveland OH 44128, USA — Basketball Player

Carr, Brandon C
Dallas Cowboys, 1 Cowboys Parkway, Irving TX 75063 USA — Football Player

Carr, Caleb
Grand Central Publishing, 237 Park Ave, #1300L, New York NY 10017, USA — Writer

Carr, Catherine (Cathy)
409 10th St, Davis CA 95616, USA — Swimmer

Carr, Charles L G (Chuck), Jr
5419 E Greenway St, Mesa AZ 85205, USA — Baseball Player

Carr, David
4771 Sweetwater Blvd, #226, Sugar Land TX 77479, USA — Football Player

Carr, Fred A
6274 S 17th Place, Phoenix AZ 85042, USA — Football Player

Carr, Gene
13529 Leadwell St, #1, Van Nuys CA 91405, USA — Ice Hockey Player

Carr, Gerald P (Jerry)
Camus Inc, 49 Maple St, #123, Manchester Center VT 05255, USA — Astronaut

Carr, Henry
4507 9th St W, #E2, Bradenton FL 34207, USA — Track Athlete, Football Player

Carr, Jane
Sovereign Talent Group, 8421 Wilshire Blvd, #200, Beverly Hills CA 90211 USA — Actress

Carr, Jimmy
P F D, Drury House, 34-43 Russell St, London WC2B 5HA, England — Actor

Carr, Katie
S M S Talent, 8383 Wilshire Blvd, #230, Beverly Hills CA 90211 USA — Actress

Carr, Kenneth A (Kenny)
24421 SW Valley View Dr, West Linn OR 97068, USA — Basketball Player

Carr, Kenneth M
16600 Warren Court, #302, Chagrin Falls OH 44023, USA — Navy Admiral

Carr, Michael Leon (M L)
168 Beaver Road, Weston MA 02493, USA — Basketball Player, Coach, Executive

Carr, Roger D
101 Green Forest Dr, Monroe LA 71203, USA — Football Player

Carr, Steve
Rumpus Entertainment, 9000 W Sunset Blvd, #650, Los Angeles CA 90048, USA — Director, Producer

Carr, Vikki
C E S D, 10635 Santa Monica Blvd, #130, Los Angeles CA 90025 USA — Singer

Carrabba, Christopher A (Chris)
Hard 8 Mgmt, 2118 Wilshire Blvd, #361, Santa Monica CA 90403, USA — Singer (Dashboard Confessional)

Carrack, Paul
Firstars Mgmt, 1830 N Sierra Bonita Ave, Los Angeles CA 90046 USA — Singer, Songwriter

Carradine, Ever
Management 360, 9111 Wilshire Blvd, Beverly Hills CA 90210 USA — Actress

Carradine, Keith
24342 Bridle Trail Road, Hidden Hills CA 91302, USA — Actor, Singer, Songwriter

Carradine, Robert
Triple Tap Productions, 5850 Canoga Ave, #200, Woodland Hills CA 91367, USA — Actor

Carrasco, Daniel J (D J)
508 Lonesome Trail, Haslet TX 76052, USA — Baseball Player

Carre, Isabelle
Agence Artiste Adequet, 80 Rue d'Amsterdam, 75009 Paris, France — Actress

Carreker, Alphonso
5599 Asheforde Lane, Marietta GA 30068, USA — Football Player

Carreon, Mark S
413 Ashland Creek, Victoria TX 77901, USA — Baseball Player

Carrera, Barbara
Alan David Mgmt, 8840 Wilshire Blvd, #200, Beverly Hills CA 90211, USA — Actress, Model

Carrera, Carlos
Creative Artists Agency, 2000 Ave of Stars, #100, Los Angeles CA 90067 USA — Director

Carrera, Christy
Michael Scott, PO Box 683, Lewis Center OH 43035, USA — Actress

Carreras, Jose
Fundacion Jose Carreras, Calle Muntaner 383, 08021 Barcelona, Spain — Opera Singer

Carrere, Emmanuel
Bloomsbury Publishing, 36 Soho Square, London W1D 3Q4, England — Writer

Carrere, Tia
Arlook Group, 205 S Beverly Dr, #209, Beverly Hills CA 90212, USA — Actress, Model

Carretto, Joseph A, Jr
Space Missile Systems Center, 483 N Aviation Blvd, El Segundo CA 90245, USA — Astronaut

Carrey, Jim
J C 23 Entertainment, 1925 Century Park E, #200, Los Angeles CA 90067, USA — Actor, Comedian

Carrick, Charlie
United Talent Agency, 9336 Civic Center Dr, Beverly Hills CA 90210 USA — Actor

Carrick, Ted
Carrick Graduate Studies Institute, 203-8941 Lake Dr, Cape Canaveral FL 32920, USA — Clinical Neurologist

Carrier, J Darel
4224 Glasgow Road, Oakland KY 42159, USA — Basketball Player

Carrier, J Mark
4115 Highland Park Circle, Lutz FL 33558, USA — Football Player

Carrier, Mark A
81 Southern Blvd, Chatham NJ 07928, USA — Football Player

Carriere, Jean P J
Le Devois, Super Camprieu, 30750 Treves, France — Writer

Carriere, Larry
94 Dawnbrook Lane, Buffalo NY 14221, USA — Ice Hockey Player

Carriere, Mathieu
Agence Elizabeth Simpson, 32 Blvd du Montparnasse, 75015 Paris, France — Actor

Carril, Pete
372 Carter Road, Princeton NJ 08540, USA — Basketball Coach

Carrillo, Elpidia
Bresler Kelly Assoc, 11500 W Olympic Blvd, #400, Los Angeles CA 90064 USA — Actress

Carrington, Alan
46 Lakewood Road, Chandler's Ford, Hampshire SO53 1EX, England — Chemist

Carrington, Darren R
14097 Montfort Court, San Diego CA 92128, USA — Football Player

Carrington, Debbie Lee
PO Box 9897, Marina del Rey CA 90295, USA — Actress

Carrington, Kelly
Playboy Promotions, 2706 Media Center Dr, Los Angeles CA 90065 USA — Model

Carrington, Paul D
Duke University, Law School, Durham NC 27708, USA — Attorney, Educator

Carrington, Peter A R
32A Ovinton Square, London SW3 1LR, England — Government Official, England

Carrington, Robert F (Bob)
PO Box 13191, Carlsbad CA 92013, USA — Basketball Player

Carrington, Rodney
P M G Entertainment Group, 1505 S Atlantic St, Melbourne Beach FL 32951, USA — Actor, Comedian

Carrington, Terri Lyne
Stax/Concord Records, 270 N Canon Dr, #1212, Beverly Hills CA 90210 USA — Jazz Drummer

Carroll, Charles C (Corky)
624 20th St, Huntington Beach CA 92648, USA — Surfer

Carroll, Clay P
3052 22nd St, Sarasota FL 34234, USA — Baseball Player

Carroll, Diahann
C E S D, 10635 Santa Monica Blvd, #130, Los Angeles CA 90025 USA — Singer, Actress

Carroll, Earl (Speedo)
P S #87, 180 W 78th St, New York NY 10024, USA — Singer (Cadillacs, Coasters)

Carroll, James S (Jim)
3101 N State Road 7, Hollywood FL 33021, USA — Football Player

Carroll, Jamey B
3492 Siderwheel Dr, Rockledge FL 32955, USA — Baseball Player

Carroll, Jason Michael
Paradigm Agency, 360 Park Ave, #1600, New York NY 10022 USA — Singer, Songwriter

Carroll, John
Rogers & Wells, 31 W 52nd St, #300, New York NY 10019, USA — Attorney

Carroll, John B
2158 Penrose Lane, Fairbanks AK 99709, USA — Psychologist

Carroll, Joseph B (Joe Barry)
5220 Cascade Road SW, Atlanta GA 30331, USA — Basketball Player

Carroll, Julian M
Carroll Assoc, PO Box 1491, Frankfort KY 40602, USA — Governor, KY

Carroll, Kent J
Country Club of North Carolina, 1600 Morganton Road, #30X, Pinehurst NC 28374, USA — Navy Admiral

Carroll, Lester (Les)
1715 Ivyhill Loop N, Columbus OH 43229, USA — Cartoonist (Our Boarding House)

Carroll, Liz
Mike Green Assoc, 339 E Liberty St, #220, Ann Arbor MI 48104, USA — Fiddler

Carroll, Madeline
Tri Star Sports & Entertainment, 215 Ward Circle, #200, Brentwood TN 37027, USA — Actress

Carroll, Peter C (Pete)
Seattle Seahawks, 12 Seahawks Way, Renton WA 98056 USA — Football Coach

Carroll, Philip J
10314 Crimston Canyon Dr, Houston TX 77098, USA — Businessman

Carroll, Roscoe (Rocky)
I C M Partners, 10250 Constellation Blvd, #900, Los Angeles CA 90067 USA — Actor

Carroll, Thomas (Tom)
Quiksilver, 363 George St, Sydney NSW 2000, Australia — Surfer

Carroll, Willard
Hyperion Pictures, 7510 Sunset Blvd, #228, Los Angeles CA 90046, USA — Director

Carrot Top
420 Sylvan Dr, Winter Park FL 32789, USA — Actor, Comedian

C

Carrera - Carrot Top

Carruthers, Alastair — Dermatologist
943 W Broadway, #820, Vancouver BC V5Z 4E1, Canada
Carruthers, Caitlin (Kitty) — Figure Skater
2106 White Eagle Lane, Katy TX 77450, USA
Carruthers, Dwight — Ice Hockey Player
9513 W Nelson Dr, Nine Mile Falls WA 99026, USA
Carruthers, Garrey E — Governor, NM
4405 Echo Canyon Road, Las Cruces NM 88011, USA
Carruthers, Jean — Opthamalogist
943 W Broadway, #820, Vancouver BC V5Z 4E1, Canada
Carruthers, Peter — Figure Skater
239 Via Monterey, Newbury Park CA 91320, USA
Carsey, Marcia L P — Producer
Carsey-Warner Productions, 4024 Radford Ave, Building 3, Studio City CA 91604, USA
Carson, Adam — Drummer, Singer (AFI)
S A M, 722 Seward St, Los Angeles CA 90038, USA
Carson, Benjamin S — Neurosurgeon
Johns Hopkins University Medical Center, Baltimore MD 21218 USA
Carson, Carlos A — Football Player
4747 W 150th Terrace, Overland Park KS 66224, USA
Carson, David — Director
Creative Artists Agency, 2000 Ave of Stars, #100, Los Angeles CA 90067 USA
Carson, Essence — Basketball Player
New York Liberty, Madison Square Garden, 2 Penn Plaza, New York NY 10121 USA
Carson, Harold D (Harry) — Football Player
PO Box 852, Westwood NJ 07675, USA
Carson, James (Jimmy) — Ice Hockey Player
1154 Ridgeway Dr, Rochester MI 48307, USA
Carson, Jeff — Singer
Buddy Lee Attractions, 38 Music Square E, #300, Nashville TN 37203 USA
Carson, Kendel — Singer, Songwriter
Train Wrecks Records, 218 Tallwood Dr, Hartsdale NY 10530, USA
Carson, Lisa Nicole — Actress
Beth Rosner Management, 4 Stuyvesant Oval, #10H, New York NY 10009, USA
Carson, William H (Willie) — Thoroughbred Racing Jockey
Minster House, Barnsley, Cirencester, Gloucestershire GL7 5DZ, England
Carswell, Dwyane — Football Player
PO Box 2488, Immokalee FL 34143, USA
Cartagena, Victoria — Actress
Gersh Agency, 9465 Wilshire Blvd, #600, Beverly Hills CA 90212 USA
Cartellone, Michael — Drummer (Lynyrd Skynyrd, Damn Yankees)
Vector Mgmt, PO Box 120479, Nashville TN 37212, USA
Carter, Aaron C — Singer, Actor
Roger Paul, 1650 Broadway, New York NY 10019, USA
Carter, Adrienne — Actress
Characters Talent Mgmt, 8 Elm St, Toronto ON M5G 1G7, Canada
Carter, Alex — Actor
Emmerdale Production Center, 27 Burley Lane, Leeds LS3 1JT, England
Carter, Anson — Ice Hockey Player
820 Haven Oaks Court NE, Atlanta GA 30342, USA
Carter, Anthony — Football Player
4314 Danielson Dr, Lake Worth FL 33467, USA
Carter, Anthony B — Basketball Player
15250 E Caley Ave, Centennial CO 80016, USA
Carter, Antonio M (Tony) — Football Player
7839 Maple Grove Dr, Lewis Center OH 43035, USA
Carter, Carlene — Singer, Songwriter
Gurley Co, PO Box 150657, Nashville TN 37215 USA
Carter, Cheryl — Actress
C E S D, 10635 Santa Monica Blvd, #130, Los Angeles CA 90025 USA
Carter, Christopher C (Chris) — Producer, Writer
Broder Webb Chervin Silbermann, 9242 Beverly Blvd, Beverly Hills CA 90210 USA
Carter, Christopher G (Chris) — Football Player
1500 Mill Creek Dr, DeSoto TX 75115, USA
Carter, Clarence — Singer
Rodgers Redding, PO Box 4603, Macon GA 31208 USA
Carter, Clarence E (Butch) — Basketball Player, Coach
900 Legacy Park Dr, Lawrenceville GA 30043, USA
Carter, Cristopher D (Cris) — Football Player, Sportscaster
2943 NW 46th St, Boca Raton FL 33431, USA
Carter, Cy — Actor
Archetype, 1608 Argyle Ave, Los Angeles CA 90028, USA
Carter, Dale L — Football Player
10416 Magnolia Heights Circle, Covington GA 30014, USA
Carter, Darren — Actor, Comedian
1633 S Crest Dr, Los Angeles CA 90035, USA
Carter, David — Football Player
2401 Long Reach Dr, Sugar Land TX 77478, USA
Carter, Deana — Singer, Songwriter
Peters Mgmt, PO Box 1710, Topanga CA 90290, USA
Carter, Dexter A — Football Player
7130 Nesters Dr, Tallahassee FL 32312, USA
Carter, Dixie — Professional Wrestler
T N A Wrestling, 209 10th Ave S, #302, Nashville TN 37203, USA
Carter, Duane (Pancho), Jr — Auto Racing Driver
32 Forest Dr, Brownsburg IN 46112, USA
Carter, E Graydon — Editor
Vanity Fair, Editorial Dept, 4 Times Square, Basement C1B, New York NY 10036, USA
Carter, Elan — Model, Actress
Playboy Promotions, 2706 Media Center Dr, Los Angeles CA 90065 USA
Carter, Finn — Actress
Front Line Entertainment, 867 S Muirfield Road, Los Angeles CA 90005, USA
Carter, Frederick J (Fred) — Basketball Player, Coach
2979 W School House Lane, #703K, Philadelphia PA 19144, USA
Carter, Gerald L — Football Player
3917 Cheshire Court, Bryan TX 77802, USA

Carter, Howard O 7572 Hanks Dr, Baton Rouge LA 70812, USA	Basketball Player
Carter, Jack 1023 Chevy Chase Dr, Beverly Hills CA 90210, USA	Actor, Comedian
Carter, James (Larry) American International Artists, 356 Pine Valley Road, Hoosick Falls NY 12090, USA	Jazz Saxophonist, Composer
Carter, James E (Jimmy), Jr Carter Center, 453 Freedom Parkway NE, Atlanta GA 30307, USA	President, USA; Nobel Peace Laureate
Carter, Jay PO Box 5357, Spring Hill FL 34611, USA	Singer (Crests)
Carter, Jeffrey A (Jeff) 4625 River Overlook Dr, Valrico FL 33596, USA	Baseball Player
Carter, Jim 12575 N 130th Way, Scottsdale AZ 85259, USA	Golfer
Carter, Jim Caroline Dawson, 125 Gloucester Road, London SW7 4TE, England	Actor
Carter, Joelle Innovative Artists, 1505 10th St, Santa Monica CA 90401 USA	Actress
Carter, John 27 Country Lane, Sharon MA 02067, USA	Ice Hockey Player
Carter, John Harden-Curtis Associates, 850 7th Ave, #903, New York NY 10019	Actor
Carter, John D (Jake) 5102 80th St, #132, Lubbock TX 79424, USA	Basketball Player
Carter, Joseph C (Joe) 3000 W 117th St, Leawood KS 66211, USA	Baseball Player
Carter, Joseph T (Jodie) 5921 Timberview Road, Little Rock AR 72204, USA	Football Player
Carter, Kevin L 17111 Journeys End Dr, Odessa FL 33556, USA	Football Player
Carter, Ki-Jana 1236 NW 121st Ave, Plantation Fl 33323, USA	Football Player
Carter, Lance D 306 74th Street Court NW, Bradenton FL 34209, USA	Baseball Player
Carter, Lynda Potomac Productions, PO Box 59110, Potomac MD 20859, USA	Actress, Singer
Carter, Mel Cape Entertainment, 8432 NW 31st Court, Fort Lauderdale FL 33351 USA	Actor, Singer
Carter, Michael D 901 Red Oak Creek Dr, Red Oak TX 75154, USA	Football Player, Track Athlete
Carter, Nicholas G (Nick) E M C Bowery, 8145 Santa Monica Blvd, #200, West Hollywood CA 90046, USA	Singer (Backstreet Boys), Songwriter
Carter, Powell F, Jr 699 Fillmore St, Harpers Ferry WV 25425, USA	Navy Admiral
Carter, Regina Depth of Field Mgmt, 1501 Broadway, #1304, New York NY 10036, USA	Jazz, Concert Violinist
Carter, Ronald L (Ron) Bridge Agency, 35 Clark St, #A5, Brooklyn NY 11201, USA	Jazz Bassist, Composer
Carter, Rosalynn S Carter Center, 453 Freedom Parkway NE, Atlanta GA 30307, USA	Wife of US President
Carter, Rubin 1793 Vineyard Way, Tallahassee FL 32317, USA	Football Player, Coach
Carter, Rubin (Hurricane) 498 20th Ave, Paterson NJ 07513, USA	Boxer
Carter, Sarah A P A Talent/Literary Agency, 405 S Beverly Dr, #300, Beverly Hills CA 90212 USA	Actress
Carter, Shawn C (Jay-Z) Roc Nation, 1411 Broadway, #3800, New York NY 10018, USA	Rap Artist, Songwriter, Record Producer
Carter, Stephen L Yale University, Law School, 127 Wall St, New Haven CT 06511, USA	Attorney, Educator, Writer
Carter, Terry 244 Madison Ave, #332, New York NY 10016, USA	Actor, Producer
Carter, Thomas Kazarian/Spencer/Ruskin, 11969 Ventura Blvd, #300, Studio City CA 91604 USA	Director
Carter, Thomas (Tom), III 4548 Bristol Lane, Cincinnati OH 45229, USA	Football Player
Carter, Timothy M (Tim) 4860 26th Court S, Saint Petersburg FL 33712, USA	Football Player
Carter, Tom 3787 County Lane Road, Quakertown PA 18951, USA	Golfer
Carter, Vincent L (Vince) 1978 Country Club Dr, Port Orange FL 32128, USA	Basketball Player
Carter, Virgil R (Virg) 2010 Whitebluff Dr, San Dimas CA 91773, USA	Football Player
Carter, W Hodding, III 214 N Columbus St, Alexandria VA 22314, USA	Government Official
Carter, W Patrick (Pat) 11321 Cambray Creek Loop, Riverview FL 33579, USA	Football Player
Carteri, Rosana Angel Records, 150 5th Ave, New York NY 10011 USA	Opera Singer
Carteris, Gabrielle 4019 Longridge Ave, Sherman Oaks CA 91423, USA	Actress
Carthon, Maurice 2040 E Indigo Dr, Chandler AZ 85286, USA	Football Player
Carthy, Eliza Glass Ceiling, 50 Stroud Green Road, London N4 3ES, England	Singer, Fiddler, Songwriter
Carthy, Martin Adastra-Moneypenny, 2 Star Row, Driffield, E Yorkshire YO25 9XA, England	Singer, Guitarist, Songwriter
Carthy-Deu, Deborah F Deborah Carthy-Deu Studio, 353 F Calder St, Urb Roosevelt, San Juan, PR 00918, USA	Beauty Queen, Actress
Cartwright, Angela Rubber Boots, 11333 Moorpark St, #433, North Hollywood CA 91602, USA	Actress
Cartwright, Catherine 4505 SE County Road 760, Arcadia FL 34266, USA	Golfer
Cartwright, J William (Bill) 1839 Wedgewood Court, Lake Forest IL 60045, USA	Basketball Player, Coach

Cartwright, Justin — Writer
P F D, Drury House, 34-43 Russell St, London WC2B 5HA, England

Cartwright, Nancy — Actress
Innovative Artists, 1505 10th St, Santa Monica CA 90401 USA

Cartwright, Nancy D — Philosopher
London School of Economics, Houghton St, London WC2A 2AE, England

Cartwright, Roderick R (Rock) — Football Player
231 Interstate 45 N, #21115, Conroe TX 77304, USA

Cartwright, Veronica — Actress
Mitch Clem Mgmt, 2600 W Olive Ave #500, Burbank CA 91505, USA

Carty, Donald J — Businessman
Dell Inc, 1 Dell Way, Round Rock TX 78682, USA

Carty, Jay J — Basketball Player
5425 Lower Honopaiilani Road, Lahaina HI 96761, USA

Carty, Ricardo A J (Rico) — Baseball Player
5 Ens Enriquillo, San Pedro de Macoris, Dominican Republic

Carty, Todd — Actor
Associated International Mgmt, Fairfax House, Fulwood Place, London WC1V 6HU, England

Caruana, Patrick P (Pat) — Air Force General
1922 Havemeyer Lane, Redondo Beach CA 90278, USA

Caruana, Peter R — Chief Minister, Gibraltar
Chief Minister's Office, 10/3 Irish Town, Gibraltar

Caruncho, Fernando — Landscape Architect
Paseo del Narcea 17, San Sebastian de los Reyes, 28707 Madrid, Spain

Caruso, D J — Director
Creative Artists Agency, 2000 Ave of Stars, #100, Los Angeles CA 90067 USA

Caruso, David — Actor
Untitled Entertainment, 350 S Beverly Dr, #200, Beverly Hills CA 90212 USA

Carver, Brent — Actor, Singer
Live Entertainment, 1500 Broadway, #902, New York NY 10036, USA

Carver, Johnny — Singer
Ace Productions, PO Box 428, Portland TN 37148, USA

Carver, Melvin (Mel) — Football Player
10840 Breaking Rocks Dr, Tampa FL 33647, USA

Carver, Randall — Actor
Kazarian/Spencer/Ruskin, 11969 Ventura Blvd, #300, Studio City CA 91604 USA

Carveth-Dunn, Betty — Baseball Player
11531 77th Ave, Edmonton AB T6G 0M2, Canada

Carvey, Dana — Actor, Comedian
B/W/R, 9100 Wilshire Blvd, #500W, Beverly Hills CA 90212 USA

Carville, C James, Jr — Political Consultant
424 S Washington St, Alexandria VA 22314, USA

Cary, Caitlin — Singer, Fiddler
Conqueroo, 11271 Ventura Blvd, #522, Studio City CA 91604, USA

Cary, Charles D (Chuck) — Baseball Player
1016 Stephen Dr, Niceville FL 32578, USA

Cary, W Sterling — Religious Leader
2344 Vardon Lane, Flossmoor IL 60422, USA

Cary-Williams, Robert — Fashion Designer
1A Wellington Row, London E2 7BB, England

Casablancas, John — Model Agency Executive
Elite Model Mgmt, 404 Park Ave S, #900, New York NY 10016 USA

Casablancas, Julian — Singer (Strokes), Songwriter
Creative Trust, 5141 Virginia Way, #320, Brentwood TN 37027, USA

Casadesus, Jean-Claude — Conductor
23 Blvd de la Liberte, 59800 Lille, France

Casady, Jack — Bassist (Jefferson Airplane, Hot Tuna)
Mission Control, 15030 Ventura Blvd, #541, Sherman Oaks CA 91403, USA

Casale, Francesco — Actor
Carol Levi Mgmt, Via G Pisanelli 2, 00196 Rome, Italy

Casale, Jerry J — Baseball Player
600 County Ave, #408, Secaucus NJ 07094, USA

Casali, Kim — Cartoonist (Love Is)
Times-Mirror Syndicate, Times-Mirror Square, Los Angeles CA 90053 USA

Casals, Rosemary (Rosie) — Tennis Player
Women's Tennis Assn, 1 Progress Plaza, #1500, Saint Petersburg FL 33701 USA

Casamayor Johnson, Joel — Boxer
Luis de Cubas, 19220 E Saint Andrews, Miami FL 33015, USA

Casanova, O Paulino (Paul) — Baseball Player
5370 NW 183rd St, Miami Gardens FL 33055, USA

Casanova, Raul — Baseball Player
1441 Ortiz Ave, Fort Myers FL 33905, USA

Casanova, Thomas H (Tommy) — Football Player
345 Casanova Road, Crowley LA 70526, USA

Casar, Amira — Actress
Conway Van Gelder Grant, 8-12 Broadwick St, #300, London W1F 8HW, England

Casares, Ricardo (Rick) — Football Player
4107 Starfish Lane, Tampa FL 33615, USA

Casbarian, John — Architect
Taft Architects, 2370 Rice Blvd, #112, Houston TX 77005, USA

Cascadden, Chad — Football Player
2611 Windsor Dr, Eau Claire WI 54703, USA

Casdin-Silver, Hariet — Artist
99 Pond Ave, #D403, Brookline MA 02445, USA

Case, Christopher — Producer, Writer
Evolution Entertainment, 901 N Highland Ave, Los Angeles CA 90038 USA

Case, J Scott — Football Player
4930 Price Dr, Suwanee GA 30024, USA

Case, John — Writer
Random House, 1745 Broadway, #1800, New York NY 10019 USA

Case, Neko — Singer (New Pornographers), Songwriter
Call Girl Public Relations, 4059 Patterson Ave, Chicago IL 60641, USA

Case, Peter — Singer, Guitarist
Yep Roc Records, 449A Trollingwood Road, Haw River NC 27258, USA

Case, Sharon — Actress
Innovative Artists, 1505 10th St, Santa Monica CA 90401 USA

Case, Stephen M (Steve)
8619 Westwood Center Dr, Vienna VA 22182, USA — Businessman
Case, Walter H, Jr
8795 Crow Dr, Macedonia OH 44056, USA — Harness Racing Driver
Casell, John W
3746 Willowcrest Ave, Studio City CA 91604, USA — Actor
Casey, Bernie
6145 Flight Ave, Los Angeles CA 90056, USA — Football Player, Actor
Casey, Brandon
Entertainment Artists, PO Box 120824, Nashville TN 37212 USA — Singer (Jagged Edge)
Casey, Brian
Entertainment Artists, PO Box 120824, Nashville TN 37212 USA — Singer (Jagged Edge)
Casey, Conor
Colorado Rapids, 1000 Chopper Circle, Denver CO 80204 USA — Soccer Player
Casey, Daniel
Curtis Brown Group, 28-29 Haymarket St, #500, London SW1Y 4SP, England — Actor
Casey, Dillon
A P A Talent/Literary Agency, 405 S Beverly Dr, #300, Beverly Hills CA 90212 USA — Actor
Casey, Dwane
Toronto Raptors, Air Canada Center, 20 Bay St, Toronto ON M5J 2N8, Canada — Basketball Player, Coach
Casey, Harry W (K C)
7530 Loch Ness Dr, Hialeah FL 33014, USA — Singer (K C & the Sunshine Band)
Casey, John D
University of Virginia, English Dept, Bryan Hall, Charlottesville VA 22903, USA — Writer
Casey, Jon
651 Bluffs View Court, Eureka MO 63025, USA — Ice Hockey Player
Casey, Patrick (Paddy)
Principal Mgmt, 30-32 John Robertson's Quay, Dublin 2, Ireland — Singer, Songwriter
Casey, Paul A
Paul Casey Foundation, 72 Salcott Road, London SW11 6DF, England — Golfer
Casey, Peter
Creative Artists Agency, 2000 Ave of Stars, #100, Los Angeles CA 90067 USA — Director
Casey, Sean T
271 Trotwood Dr, Pittsburgh PA 15241, USA — Baseball Player
Cash, Aya
Paradigm Agency, 360 N Crescent Dr, North Building, Beverly Hills CA 90210 USA — Actress
Cash, David (Dave), Jr
16308 Birkdale Dr, Odessa FL 33556, USA — Baseball Player
Cash, Keith L
9839 Heritage Farm Road, San Antonio TX 78245, USA — Football Player
Cash, Kerry L
9839 Heritage Farm Road, San Antonio TX 78245, USA — Football Player
Cash, Kevin F
14607 Mirabelle Vista Circle, Tampa FL 33626, USA — Baseball Player
Cash, Pat
Patrick Cash Assoc, PO Box 2238, Footscray 3011, Australia — Tennis Player
Cash, Richard F (Rick)
203 E Benton St, Savannah MO 64485, USA — Football Player
Cash, Rosanne
Concerted Efforts, PO Box 440326, Somerville MA 02144 USA — Singer, Songwriter
Cash, Swin M
Chicago Sky, 20 W Kinzie St, #1010, Chicago IL 60654 USA — Basketball Player
Cashell, Sophie
I M G Artists, Hogarth Business Park, Chiswick, London W4 2TH, England — Concert Pianist
Cashin, Patrick (Pat)
Kelly-Miller Circus, 2581 E 2070 Road, Hugo OK 74743, USA — Clown
Cashman, John
Boeing Commerical Airplane Group, PO Box 3707, Seattle WA 98124, USA — Test Pilot
Cashman, Terry
Metrostar Records, PO Box 5807, Englewood NJ 07631, USA — Singer (Buchanan Brothers)
Cashman, Wayne J
5150 NW 80th Avenue Road, Ocala FL 34482, USA — Ice Hockey Player
Casian, Lawrence P (Larry)
1939 Popcorn St NW, Salem OR 97304, USA — Baseball Player
Casida, John E
1570 La Vereda Road, Berkeley CA 94708, USA — Entomologist
Casile, Genevieve
Agents Associes, 201 Rue du Faubourg Saint Honore, 75008 Paris, France — Actress
Casillas, Tony S
6201 Bay Valley Court, Flower Mound TX 75022, USA — Football Player
Caslavska, Vera
S V S Sparta Prague, Korunovacni 29, Prague 7, Czech Republic — Gymnast
Casnoff, Philip
Don Buchwald/Fortitude, 6500 Wilshire Blvd, #2200, Los Angeles CA 90048 USA — Actor
Cason, Aveion M
5936 N 64th St, Milwaukee WI 53218, USA — Football Player
Cason, James A (Jim)
1802 E Washington Ave, Harlingen TX 78550, USA — Football Player
Cason, Rod
50623 Dossow St, Kenai AK 99611, USA — Football Player
Casorati, Francesco
C So Kossuth 19, Turin, Italy — Artist
Caspar, Donald L D
911 Gardenia Dr, Tallahassee FL 32312, USA — Biophysicist
Caspe, David
W M E Entertainment, 9601 Wilshire Blvd, #300, Beverly Hills CA 90210 USA — Producer, Writer
Casper, David J (Dave)
1525 Alamo Way, Alamo CA 94507, USA — Football Player
Casper, John H
4414 Village Corner Dr, Houston TX 77059, USA — Astronaut
Casper, William E (Billy)
2561 Stonebury Loop Road, Springville UT 84663, USA — Golfer
Cass, Christopher
Halpern Assoc, PO Box 5597, Santa Monica CA 90409 USA — Actor
Cassady, Howard (Hopalong)
Tails Sports Mgmt, PO Box 7828, Columbus OH 43207, USA — Football Player

Cassavetes, Nick — Actor, Director
I C M Partners, 10250 Constellation Blvd, #900, Los Angeles CA 90067 USA

Cassel, Matthew B (Matt) — Football Player
150 Street of Dreams, Village Loch Loyd MO 64012, USA

Cassel, Seymour — Actor
Abrams Artists, 9200 W Sunset Blvd, #1125, West Hollywood CA 90069 USA

Cassel, Vincent — Actor
Agence Artiste Adequet, 80 Rue d'Amsterdam, 75009 Paris, France

Cassell, Samuel J (Sam) — Basketball Player
5205 N Charles St, Baltimore MD 21210, USA

Cassels, Andrew — Ice Hockey Player
6550 Lockhart Lane, Dublin OH 43017, USA

Casserino, Frank J — Astronaut, Air Force General
Office of Under Secretary of Air Force, HqUSAF, Pentagon, Washington DC 20330, USA

Casserly, Charley — Football Executive, Sportscaster
N F L Network, 10950 Washington Blvd, #100, Culver City CA 90232 USA

Casseus, Gabriel — Actor
Don Buchwald/Fortitude, 6500 Wilshire Blvd, #2200, Los Angeles CA 90048 USA

Cassidy, Bruce — Ice Hockey Player
50 Park Row W, #911, Providence RI 2903, USA

Cassidy, Candice — Model
Playboy Promotions, 2706 Media Center Dr, Los Angeles CA 90065 USA

Cassidy, Christopher J (Chris) — Astronaut
N A S A, Johnson Space Center, 2101 NASA Road, Houston TX 77058 USA

Cassidy, David — Actor, Singer
D B C Inc, 1531 W 25th St, P M B 233, San Pedro CA 90732, USA

Cassidy, Edward I Cardinal — Religious Leader
Council for Christian Unity, Piazza del S Uffizio 11, 00193 Rome, Italy

Cassidy, Elaine — Actress
Rights House, 34-43 Russell St, London WC2B 5HA, England

Cassidy, Joanna — Actress
Stone Manners Salners, 9911 W Pico Blvd, #1400, Los Angeles CA 90035 USA

Cassidy, Katherine E (Katie) — Actress, Model, Singer
Anonymous Content, 3532 Hayden Ave, Culver City CA 90232 USA

Cassidy, Michael — Actor
Principal Entertainment, 1964 Westwood Blvd, #400, Los Angeles CA 90025 USA

Cassidy, Patrick — Actor
979 E 42nd St, Brooklyn NY 11210, USA

Cassidy, Ronald G (Ron) — Football Player
2214 W 171st St, Torrance CA 90504, USA

Cassidy, Shaun — Actor, Singer
Shaun Cassidy Productions, 8530 Wilshire Blvd, #200, Beverly Hills CA 90211, USA

Cassie — Rap Artist, Model
Bad Boy Entertainment, 1440 Broadway, #16, New York NY 10018 USA

Cassignard, Pierre — Actor
Artmedia, 20 Ave Rapp, 75007 Paris, France

Cassolato, Tony — Ice Hockey Player
576 Camino El Dorado, Encinitas CA 92024, USA

Casspi, Omri — Basketball Player
Cleveland Cavaliers, Gund Arena, 1 Center Court, Cleveland OH 44115 USA

Cast, Edward — Actor
4 Bankside Dr, Thames Ditton, Surrey KT7 0AQ, England

Cast, Tricia — Actress
20 Georgette Road, Rolling Hills Estates CA 90274, USA

Casta, Laetitia — Model, Actress
D Management Group, 13 Via Forcella, 20144 Milan, Italy

Castaneda, Cameron — Actor
Lewis & Beal Talent Agency, 15303 Ventura Blvd, #900, Sherman Oaks CA 91403, USA

Castaneda, Jorge A — Government Official, Mexico
Anillo Periferico Sur 3180, #1120, Jardines del Pedregal, 01900 Mexico

Castellaneta, Dan — Actor
Foster Entertainment, 12533 Woodgreen St, Building B, Los Angeles CA 90066, USA

Castellanos, Jonathan — Actor
Jaime Ferrar Agency, 4741 Laural Canyon Blvd, #110, Valley Village CA 91607, USA

Castellaw, John G — Marine Corps General
Deputy Commandant, Aviation, HqUSMC, 2 Navy St, Washington DC 20380 USA

Castelluccio, Federico — Actor
Barry Haft Brown Artists Agency, 165 W 46th St, #908, New York NY 10036, USA

Caster, Richard C (Rich) — Football Player
41 Lincoln Court, Rockville Centre NY 11570, USA

Castiglioni, Consuelo — Fashion Designer
Marni International, Palazzo Torre Delta, La Sguancia 23, 6902 Lugano, Switzerland

Castilla Soria, Vinicio S (Vinny) — Baseball Player
7680 Polo Ridge Dr, Littleton CO 80128, USA

Castille, Jeremiah — Football Player
2904 Kirkcaldy Lane, Birmingham AL 35242, USA

Castillo, Alberto T — Baseball Player
400 SW Lakota Ave, Port Saint Lucie FL 34953, USA

Castillo, Frank A — Baseball Player
9333 N 129th Place, Scottsdale AZ 85259, USA

Castillo, Jose Luis — Boxer
Top Rank Inc, 3908 Howard Hughes Parkway, #580, Las Vegas NV 89169 USA

Castillo, Luis A — Football Player
14165 Augusta Court, Poway CA 92064, USA

Castillo, Luis A D — Baseball Player
14149 N Forest Oak Circle, Davie FL 33325, USA

Castillo, M Carmelo (Carmen) — Baseball Player
344 Prospect Ave, #6A, Hackensack NJ 07601, USA

Castillo, Robert E (Bobby), Jr — Baseball Player
316 Calle Amraillo SW, Albuquerque NM 87121, USA

Castle, John — Actor
Larry Dalzell, 91 Regent St, London W1R 7TA, England

Castle, Michael N — Governor, Representative, DE
Castle Campaign Fund, PO Box 133, Wilmington DE 19899, USA

Castle, Nick C, Jr — Director
Jackoway Tyerman Wertheimer, 1925 Century Park E, #2200, Los Angeles CA 90067 USA

Castle-Hughes, Keisha
Gail Cowan Mgmt, 21 Village Fields Road, Waiau Pa, RD4, Pukekohe 2679, New Zealand — Actress

Castleman, Foster E
8250 Graves Road, Cincinnati OH 45243, USA — Baseball Player

Castrale, Nicole
Ladies Pro Golf Assn, 100 International Golf Dr, Daytona Beach FL 32124 USA — Golfer

Castrillon Hoyos, Dario Cardinal
Arzobispado, Calle 33, N 21-18, Bucaramanga, Santander, Colombia — Religious Leader

Castro Ruz, Fidel A
Palacio del Gobierno, Plaza de la Revolucion, Havana, Cuba — President, Cuba

Castro Ruz, Raul
Palacio de Gobierno, Cibsejo de la Revolucion, Havana, Cuba — President, Prime Minister, Cuba

Castro, Angelica
C E S D, 10635 Santa Monica Blvd, #130, Los Angeles CA 90025 USA — Actress

Castro, Cristian
Generamusica Mgmt, C Arcniegae 29A, Col Mixcoac, Naucalpan 03910, Mexico — Singer

Castro, Daniela
Televisa, Blvd A Lopez Mateos 232, Colonia San Angel, DF CP 01060, Mexico — Actress

Castro, Juan C
7324 W Artie Ave, Peoria AZ 85383, USA — Baseball Player

Castro, Ramon A
1230 Windway Circle, Kissimmee FL 34744, USA — Baseball Player

Castro, Raquel
Abrams Artists, 275 7th Ave, #2600, New York NY 10001 USA — Actress

Castro, Raul H
429 W Crawford St, Nogales AZ 85621, USA — Governor, AZ; Diplomat

Castro, Ruy
Bloomsbury Publishing, 36 Soho Square, London W1D 3Q4, England — Writer

Castro, Tommy
Under the Radar Mgmt, 1961 Rice St, Roseville MN 55113, USA — Singer, Guitarist, Band Leader

Castro, Williams R (Bill)
5217 W Harvard Dr, Franklin WI 53132, USA — Baseball Player

Castroneves, Helio
386 Isla Dorada Blvd, Coral Gables FL 33143, USA — Auto Racing Driver

Caswell, Ben
Progressive Artists Agency, 1041 N Formosa Ave, West Hollywood CA 90046, USA — Actor

Caswell, Dean
2309 Village Way Dr, Austin TX 78745, USA — WW II Marine Corps Air Force Hero

Cat Power
Ground Control Touring, 20 Jay St, #826, Brooklyn NY 11201 USA — Singer, Songwriter

Catalano, Laura
Noble Caplan Abrams, 1260 Yonge St, #200, Toronto ON M4T 1W6, Canada — Actress

Catalanotto, Frank J
4 Muffins Meadows, Saint James NY 11780, USA — Baseball Player

Catalifo, Patrick
Artmedia, 20 Ave Rapp, 75007 Paris, France — Actor

Catalino, Ken
Creators Syndicate, 737 3rd St, Hermosa Beach CA 90254 USA — Editorial Cartoonist

Catano, Mark
9036 Walton St, Indianapolis IN 46231, USA — Football Player

Catanzaro, Tony
8915 SW 207th St, Cutler Bay FL 33189, USA — Dancer

Catchings, Harvey L
17406 Edenwalk, Spring TX 77379, USA — Basketball Player

Catchings, Tamika D
Indiana Fever, Conseco Fieldhouse, 125 S Pennsylvania, Indianapolis IN 46204 USA — Basketball Player

Cate, Earl
1606 Cartwright Circle, Springdale AR 72762, USA — Singer, Songwriter (Cate Brothers)

Cate, Ernie
17464 Highway 90 W, Ravenden Springs AR 72460, USA — Singer, Pianist (Cate Brothers)

Cate, Field
J L A Talent Agency, 9151 Sunset Blvd, West Hollywood CA 90069, USA — Actor

Cater, Danny A
3268 Candlewood Trail, Plano TX 75023, USA — Baseball Player

Cater, Gregory W (Greg)
19 Warwick Way SE, Rome GA 30161, USA — Football Player

Cates, Darlene
13340 FM 740, Forney TX 75126, USA — Actress

Cates, Phoebe
Hofflund/Polone, 9465 Wilshire Blvd, #420, Beverly Hills CA 90212 USA — Actress

Cathcart, Patti
T & P Productions, PO Box 1363, Menlo Park CA 94026, USA — Singer (Tuck & Patti)

Catherine
Artery Foundation, 1412 S St, Sacramento CA 95811, USA — Singer

Catillon, Brigitte
Artmedia, 20 Ave Rapp, 75007 Paris, France — Actress

Catlett, Mary Jo
Robert Yacko, 4375 Farmdale Ave, Studio City CA 91604, USA — Actress

Catlett, Sidney L (Sid)
3110 Scottish Ave, Suitland MD 20746, USA — Basketball Player

Catley, Glenn
Bristol Gym, Trinity Road, Saint Phillips, Bristol BS2 0NW, England — Boxer

Cato, Kelvin T
13607 Winter Creek Court, Houston TX 77077, USA — Basketball Player

Caton-Jones, Michael
Gersh Agency, 9465 Wilshire Blvd, #600, Beverly Hills CA 90212 USA — Director

Catrow, David
Springfield News-Sun, Editorial Dept, 202 N Limestone St, Springfield OH 45503, USA — Editorial Cartoonist

Cattage, Robert L (Bobby)
4838 US Highway 29 S, Auburn AL 36830, USA — Basketball Player

Cattaneo, Peter
Independent Talent Group, Oxford House, 76 Oxford St, London W1D 1BS, England — Director

Cattell, Christine
Epstein-Wyckoff, 280 S Beverly Dr, #400, Beverly Hills CA 90212 USA — Actress

Cattrall, Kim
I C M Partners, 10250 Constellation Blvd, #900, Los Angeles CA 90067 USA — Actress, Model

C

Castle-Hughes - Cattrall

C

Catz, Caroline — Actress
Independent Talent Group, Oxford House, 76 Oxford St, London W1D 1BS, England

Caudill, William H (Bill) — Baseball Player
11605 NE 41st St, Kirkland WA 98033, USA

Cauduro, Eugenia — Actress, Model
Televisa, Blvd A Lopez Mateos 232, Colonia San Angel, DF CP 01060, Mexico

Cauffiel, Jessica — Actress
Greene Assoc, 1901 Ave of Stars, #130, Los Angeles CA 90067 USA

Caufield, Jay — Ice Hockey Player
106 Quail Hollow Lane, Wexford PA 15090, USA

Caughthran, Matt — Singer (Bronx)
Crush Music Mgmt, 60-62 E 11th St, #700, New York NY 10003, USA

Caulfield, Emma — Actress
TalentWorks, 3500 W Olive Ave, #1400, Burbank CA 91505 USA

Causey, J Wayne — Baseball Player
2905 Paynter Dr, Ruston LA 71270, USA

Causwell, Duane — Basketball Player
3 Pierce Dr, Stony Point NY 10980, USA

Caute, J David — Writer
41 Westcroft Square, London W6 0TA, England

Cauthen, Stephen M (Steve) — Thoroughbred Racing Jockey
15541 Porter Road, Verona KY 41092, USA

Cauthen, Terrance — Boxer
953 Beatty St, Trenton NJ 08611, USA

Cauty, James F (Jimmy) — Musician (KLF)
Nene Musik Productions, 1460 SW Santiago Ave, Port Saint Lucie FL 34953 USA

Cavaiani, Jon R — Vietnam War Army Hero (CMH)
10956 Green St, #230, Columbia CA 95310, USA

Cavalera, Max — Singer, Guitrist
Oasis Mgmt, 3010 E Bloomfield Road, Phoenix AZ 85032, USA

Cavaliere, Felix — Singer, Keyboardist, Composer (Rascals)
Brothers Mgmt, 141 Dunbar Ave, Fords NJ 08863 USA

Cavaliero, Rosie — Actress
Another Tongue, 10-11 D'Arblay St, London W1F 8DS, England

Cavallari, Kristin — Actress
W M E Entertainment, 9601 Wilshire Blvd, #300, Beverly Hills CA 90210 USA

Cavalli, Roberto — Fashion Designer
Via Senato 8, 20121 Milan, Italy

Cavallini, Gino — Ice Hockey Player
6614 Clayton Road, #315, Saint Louis MO 63117, USA

Cavallini, Paul — Ice Hockey Player
7201 Kingsbury Blvd, Saint Louis MO 63130, USA

Cavalli-Sforza, Luigi L — Geneticist
Stanford University, Human Population Genetics Laboratory, Stanford CA 94305, USA

Cavallo, Domingo F — Government Official, Argentina
Hipolito Yrigoyen 250, 1310 Buenos Aires, Argentina

Cavanagh, Thomas (Tom) — Actor
W M E Entertainment, 9601 Wilshire Blvd, #300, Beverly Hills CA 90210 USA

Cavanaugh, Kasie — Body Builder
PO Box 21882, El Cajon CA 92021, USA

Cavanaugh, Matthew A (Matt) — Football Player
8 Barstad Court, Lutherville Timon MD 21093, USA

Cavaney, Red — Association Executive
ConocoPhillips, 600 N Dairy Ashford Road, Houston TX 77079, USA

Cavazos, Lauro F — Secretary, Education
173 Annursnac Hill Road, Concord MA 01742, USA

Cavazos, Lumi — Actress
Talent on Road Mgmt, Av Revolucion 1716 Y\O Sagredo #155, Mexico City DF 03900, Mexico

Cavazos, Richard E — Army General
Texas Tech University, Board of Regents, Lubbock TX 79409, USA

Cave, Nick — Singer, Songwriter
429 Harrow Road, London W10 4RE, England

Caveness, Ronald G (Ronnie) — Football Player
684 N Cliffside Dr, Fayetteville AR 72701, USA

Caves, Richard E — Economist
Harvard University, Economics Dept, Cambridge MA 02138, USA

Cavett, Richard A (Dick) — Entertainer
1044 Northern Blvd, #304, Roslyn NY 11576, USA

Cavezza, Carmen J — Army General
Columbus State University, Leadership Development Center, Columbus GA 31907, USA

Caviezel, James — Actor
Tencer Assoc, 9777 Wilshire Blvd, #1005, Beverly Hills CA 90212, USA

Cavill, Henry — Actor
United Agents, 12-26 Lexington St, London W1F 0LE, England

Cawley, Tucker — Writer, Producer
Creative Artists Agency, 2000 Ave of Stars, #100, Los Angeles CA 90067 USA

Cawley, Warren (Rex) — Track Athlete
1655 San Rafael Dr, Corona CA 92882, USA

Caws, Matthew — Singer, Guitarist (Nada Surf)
M-Squared Mgmt, 201 W 72nd St, #12G, New York NY 10023, USA

Cayne, James E (Jimmy) — Financier
Bear Stearns Co, 383 Madison Ave, New York NY 10179, USA

Cazalot, Clarence P, Jr — Businessman
Marathon Oil, 5555 San Felipe Road, Basement B114, Houston TX 77056, USA

Ce, Marco Cardinal — Religious Leader
S Marco 318, 30124 Venice, Italy

Ceballos, Cedric Z — Basketball Player
2068 FM 1252 W, Kilgore TX 75662, USA

Ceberano, Kate — Singer, Songwriter
Ralph Carr Mgmt, 229 Lennox St, Richmond VIC 3121, Australia

Ceccarelli, Arthur E (Art) — Baseball Player
63 Hall Dr, Orange CT 06477, USA

Ceccato, Aldo — Conductor
Chaunt da Crusch, 7524 Zuoz, Switzerland

Cecchi, Carlo — Actor
Carol Levi Mgmt, Via G Pisanelli 2, 00196 Rome, Italy

Cech, Thomas R — Nobel Chemistry Laureate
Howard Hughes Medical Institute, 4000 Tones Bridge Road, Chevy Chase MD 20815, USA
Cechmanek, Roman — Ice Hockey Player
Los Angeles Kings, Staples Center, 1111 S Figueroa St, Los Angeles CA 90015 USA
Cechvala, Dean — Actor
Geddes Agency, 8430 Santa Monica Blvd, #201, West Hollywood CA 90069 USA
Cecil, Charles D (Chuck) — Football Player
2008 Waterstone Dr, Franklin TN 37069, USA
Cecil, Derek — Actor
One Entertainment, 12 W 57th St, #PH 1, New York NY 10019 USA
Cecil, Francesca — Actress
Cinematic Mgmt, 249 1/2 E 13th St, New York NY 10003, USA
Cecil, Henry R A — Thoroughbred Racing Trainer
Warren Place, Newmarket, Suffolk CB8 8QQ, England
Cedar, Joseph — Director
Kneller Artists Agency, Hayarkon 169, #420, Tel Aviv 63453, Israel
Cedarstrom, Gary L — Baseball Umpire
1610 18th St SE, Minot ND 58701, USA
Cedeno, Cesar E — Baseball Player
2112 Marisol Loop, Kissimmee FL 34743, USA
Cedeno, Matt — Actor, Model
Luber Rocklin Entertainment, 8530 Wilshire Blvd, #555, Beverly Hills CA 90211 USA
Cedeno, Roger L — Baseball Player
9325 Byron Ave, Surfside FL 33154, USA
Cederqvist, Jane — Swimmer
National Museum of Antiquities, PO Box 5428, 114 84 Stockholm, Sweden
Cedillo, Julio Cesar — Actor
Judy Fox Mgmt, 1525 1/2 S Beverly Dr, Los Angeles CA 90035, USA
Cedolins, Fiorenza — Opera Singer
Columbia Artists Mgmt Inc, 1790 Broadway, #702, New York NY 10019 USA
Cedric the Entertainer — Actor, Comedian
Creative Artists Agency, 2000 Ave of Stars, #100, Los Angeles CA 90067 USA
Cee-Lo — Singer, Rap Artist, Songwriter
Waxploitation Entertainment, 400 S Main St, #303, Los Angeles, CA 90013, USA
Cefalo, James C (Jimmy) — Football Player
6675 Roxbury Lane, Miami Beach FL 33141, USA
Ceglarski, Leonard (Len) — Ice Hockey Player, Coach
61 Lantern Lane, Duxbury MA 02332, USA
Cejka, Alexander — Golfer
11589 Caldicot Dr, Las Vegas NV 89138, USA
Cejudo, Henry — Freestyle Wrestler
USA Wrestling, 6155 Lehman Dr, Colorado Springs CO 80918, USA
Celestin, Oliver, Jr — Football Player
635 Hendee St, New Orleans LA 70114, USA
Cellier, Caroline — Actress
Artmedia, 20 Ave Rapp, 75007 Paris, France
Cellucci, A Paul — Governor, MA; Diplomat
State Department, 2201 C St NW, Washington DC 20520 USA
Celmins, Vija — Artist
49 Crosby St, New York NY 10012, USA
Celski, John R (J R) — Short Track Speed Skater
Agency Sports Mgmt, 230 Park Ave S, #851, New York NY 10169, USA
Cena, John — Actor, Professional Wrestler
I C M Partners, 10250 Constellation Blvd, #900, Los Angeles CA 90067 USA
Cenac, Wyatt — Actor, Comedian, Writer
United Talent Agency, 9336 Civic Center Dr, Beverly Hills CA 90210 USA
Cenker, Robert J — Astronaut
G O R C A Inc, 155 Hickory Corner Road, East Windsor NJ 08520, USA
Centers, Larry E — Football Player
5023 Stagecoach Way, Grand Prairie TX 75052, USA
Cenziper, Debbie — Journalist
Miami Herald, Editorial Dept, 1 Herald Plaza, Miami FL 33132 USA
Cepeda, Orlando M — Baseball Player
2305 Palmer Court, Fairfield CA 94534, USA
Cepero, Jaime — Actor
Hartig-Hilepo Agency, 54 W 21st St, #610, New York NY 10010 USA
Cepicky, Matthew W (Matt) — Baseball Player
7 Upper Bluffs View Court, Eureka MO 63025, USA
Cera, Michael — Actor
Thruline Entertainment, 9250 Wilshire Blvd, #100, Beverly Hills CA 90212 USA
Cerami, Anthony — Biochemist
Ram Island Dr, Shelter Island NY 11964, USA
Ceresino, Ray — Ice Hockey Player
13282 Ocean Vista Road, San Diego CA 92130, USA
Cerezo Arevalo, M Vinicio — President, Guatemala
Party of Christian Democracy, Avda Elena 20-66, Zone 3, Guatemala City, Guatemala
Cerf, Vinton G — Inventor (Internet)
3614 Camelot Dr, Annandale VA 22003, USA
Cerha, Friedrich — Composer, Conductor
Kupelwiesergasse 14, 1010 Vienna, Austria
Cermeno, Antonio — Boxer
San Antonio de los Altos Loma, U R B Residencial, Los Eucaliptos 1020, Venezuela
Cerne, Joseph (Joe) — Football Player
408 Prospect Ave, Minneapolis MN 55419, USA
Cerone, Laura — Actress
Don Buchwald/Fortitude, 6500 Wilshire Blvd, #2200, Los Angeles CA 90048 USA
Cerone, Richard A (Rick) — Baseball Player
34 Winding Way, West Paterson NJ 07424, USA
Cerra, Erica — Actress
Kritzer Levine Wilkins Griffin, 11872 La Grange Ave, #100, Los Angeles CA 90025 USA
Cerrudo, Ronald J (Ron) — Golfer
7 Fox Briar Court, Hilton Head Island SC 29926, USA
Cerruti, Nino — Fashion Designer
Via A Saffi 25, 20121 Milan, Italy
Cerry, Amanda — Model
Playboy Promotions, 2706 Media Center Dr, Los Angeles CA 90065 USA

C

Cech - Cerry

C

Certo, Tish — Golfer
151 Buffalo Ave, #211, Niagara Falls NY 14303, USA

Cerv, Robert H (Bob) — Baseball Player
805 N 22nd St, #1A, Blair NE 68008, USA

Cervantes, Hector — Guitarist (Casting Crowns)
Proper Mgmt, PO Box 150867, Nashville TN 37215, USA

Cervenka, Exene — Singer (X)
A P A Talent/Literary Agency, 405 S Beverly Dr, #300, Beverly Hills CA 90212 USA

Cerveris, Michael — Actor, Singer
Innovative Artists, 1505 10th St, Santa Monica CA 90401 USA

Cervi, Valentina — Actress
T N A, Via Parioli 41, 00197 Rome, Italy

Cesaire, Jacques E — Football Player
13388 Greenstone Court, San Diego CA 92131, USA

Cesarani, Sal — Fashion Designer
S J C Concepts, 40 E 80th St, New York NY 10075, USA

Cesare, William J (Billy) — Football Player
1655 Hendry Isles Blvd, Clewiston FL 33440, USA

Cesario, Jeff — Actor, Comedian
A P A Talent/Literary Agency, 405 S Beverly Dr, #300, Beverly Hills CA 90212 USA

Cetera, Peter — Singer, Bassist, Songwriter
M P I Talent, 9255 Sunset Blvd, #407, West Hollywood CA 90069, USA

Cetlinski, Matthew (Matt) — Swimmer
13121 SE 93rd Terrace Road, Summerfield FL 34491, USA

CeU — Singer, Songwriter
Six Degrees Records/A-Train Entertainment, PO Box 29242, Oakland CA 94604, USA

Cey, Ronald C (Ron) — Baseball Player
22714 Creole Road, Woodland Hills CA 91364, USA

Ceylan, Nuri Bilge — Actor, Director
N B C Film, Baskurt Sok 19/4, Urgup Palas Apt, 34433 Cihangir, Istanbul, Turkey

Chabat, Alain — Actor
Chez Wham, 18 Blvd Montmartre, 75009 Paris, France

Chaber, Madelyn J — Attorney
101 California St, San Francisco CA 94111, USA

Chabert, Lacey — Actress
Innovative Artists, 1505 10th St, Santa Monica CA 90401 USA

Chabon, Michael — Writer
United Talent Agency, 9336 Civic Center Dr, Beverly Hills CA 90210 USA

Chabraja, Nicholas D — Businessman
General Dynamics, 2941 Fairview Park Dr, #100, Falls Church VA 22042, USA

Chacon, Alex Pineda — Soccer Player
Los Angeles Galaxy, Home Depot Center, 18400 Avalon Blvd, Carson CA 90746 USA

Chacon, Bobby — Boxer
3010 Wilshire Blvd, #491, Los Angeles CA 90010, USA

Chacon, Shawn A — Baseball Player
162 50th Avenue Place, Greeley CO 80634, USA

Chacurian, Efrain (Chico) — Soccer Player
96 Stratford Road, Stratford CT 06615, USA

Chad — Singer, Guitarist (Chad & Jeremy)
Icon Performing Arts, 1557 Westwood Blvd, #242, Los Angeles CA 90024, USA

Chadbon, Tom — Actor
Caroline Dawson, 125 Gloucester Road, London SW7 4TE, England

Chadha, Gurinder — Director
I C M Partners, 10250 Constellation Blvd, #900, Los Angeles CA 90067 USA

Chadirji, Rifat Kamil — Architect
28 Troy Court, Kensington High St, London W8, England

Chadli, Bendjedid — President, Algeria; Army Officer
Palace Émir Abedelkader, Algiers, Algeria

Chadwick, Ed — Ice Hockey Player
12 Bowen Road, Fort Erie ON L2A 2Y4, Canada

Chadwick, J Leslie (Les) — Bassist (Gerry & the Pacemakers)
Barry Collins, 21A Cliftown Road, Southend on Sea, Essex SS1 1AB, England

Chadwick, Jeffrey A (Jeff) — Football Player
23062 Village Dr, #A, Lake Forest CA 92630, USA

Chadwick, June — Actress
Independent Artists, 9601 Wilshire Blvd, #750, Beverly Hills CA 90210, USA

Chadwick, Justin — Director, Actor
Independent Talent Group, Oxford House, 76 Oxford St, London W1D 1BS, England

Chadwick, Paul — Cartoonist (Concrete)
Dark Horse Publishing, 10956 SE Main St, Portland OR 97222 USA

Chae Ji Hoon — Speed Skater
Skating Union, 88 Bangyee-Dong, Songpaku, Seoul 138 749, South Korea

Chafee, Lincoln D — Senator, RI
Brown University, International Studies Institute, Providence RI 02912, USA

Chafer, Derek — Actor
Ugly Enterprises, Tigis House, 256 Edgware Road, London W2 1DS, England

Chafetz, Sidney — Artist
Ohio State University, Art Dept, Columbus OH 43210, USA

Chaffee, Don — Director
7020 La Presa Dr, Los Angeles CA 90068, USA

Chaffee, Susan (Suzy) — Alpine Skier
55 Roadrunner Road, Sedona AZ 86336, USA

Chagaev, Ruslan — Boxer
Universum Box-Promotion, Am Stadtrand 27, 22047 Hamburg, Germany

Chagoya, Enrique — Artist
59 Arroyo Way, San Francisco CA 94127, USA

Chaiken, Ilene — Producer, Writer
W M E Entertainment, 9601 Wilshire Blvd, #300, Beverly Hills CA 90210 USA

Chaikin, Carly — Actress
Paradigm Agency, 360 N Crescent Dr, North Building, Beverly Hills CA 90210 USA

Chailly, Riccardo — Conductor
Royal Concertgebrew, Jacob Obrechtstraat 51, 1071 KJ Amsterdam 41, Holland

Chakiris, George — Actor, Singer, Dancer
7266 Clinton St, Los Angeles CA 90036, USA

Chakvetadze, Anna D — Tennis Player
Best, 303 E Main St, #200, Louisville KY 40202, USA

Chalayan, Hussein
71 Endell Road, London WC2 9AJ, England — Fashion Designer
Chalenski, Michael (Mike)
225 S Michigan Ave, Kenilworth NJ 07033, USA — Football Player
Chalfant, Kathleen
Douglas Gorman Rothacker Wilhelm, 1501 Broadway, #703, New York NY 10036 USA — Actress
Chalfie, Martin
15 Claremont Ave, New York NY 10027, USA — Nobel Chemistry Laureate
Chalfont, A G (Arthur)
House of Lords, Westminster, London SW1A 0PW, England — Government Official, England
Chali 2na
Vision Entertainment Group, 1100 Glendon Ave, #1100, Los Angeles CA 90024, USA — Rap Artist
Chalk, David L (Dave)
137 Cross Timbers Trail, Coppell TX 75019, USA — Baseball Player
Chalke, Sarah
John Carrabino Mgmt, 5900 Wilshire Blvd, #406, Los Angeles CA 90036 USA — Actress
Challenger, James
Challenger Gray Christmas, 1200 Smith St, #1600, Houston TX 77002, USA — Businessman
Chalmers, Iain G
James Lind Initiative, Summertown Pavilion, Oxford OX2 7LG, England — Medical Research Executive
Chaloner, William G
20 Parke Road, London SW13 9NG, England — Botanist
Chalupny, Lori C
Octagon Worldwide, 1751 Pinnacle Dr, #1500, McLean VA 22102 USA — Soccer Player
Chamarande, Brigitte
Artmedia, 20 Ave Rapp, 75007 Paris, France — Actress
Chamberlain, Byron
PO Box 326, Montclair CA 91763, USA — Football Player
Chamberlain, Cliff
Brillstein Entertainment Partners, 9150 Wilshire Blvd, #350, Beverly Hills CA 90212 USA — Actor
Chamberlain, Dean
1795 Washington Way, Venice CA 90291, USA — Photographer, Artist
Chamberlain, Gary E
Harvard University, Littauer Center, Cambridge MA 02138, USA — Economist
Chamberlain, Jeffrey S
University of Michigan Medical Center, 301 E Liberty St, Ann Arbor MI 48104, USA — Geneticist
Chamberlain, Joba
1504 Kara Lane, Lincoln NE 68522, USA — Baseball Player
Chamberlain, Richard
Framework Entertainment, 9057 Nemo St, #C, West Hollywood CA 90069 USA — Actor
Chamberlain, Spencer
Red Light Mgmt, 44 Wall St, #2200, New York NY 10005, USA — Singer (Underoath)
Chamberlain, Wesley P (Wes)
PO Box 1358, Homewood IL 60430, USA — Baseball Player
Chamberlin, Beth
Paradigm Agency, 360 N Crescent Dr, North Building, Beverly Hills CA 90210 USA — Actress
Chamberlin, James J (Jimmy)
535 W Basil Road, Lake Bluff IL 60044, USA — Drummer (Smashing Pumpkins)
Chambers, Anne Cox
Cox Enterprises, 1400 Lake Hearn Dr NE, Atlanta GA 30319, USA — Businesswoman, Diplomat
Chambers, Christina
Don Buchwald/Fortitude, 6500 Wilshire Blvd, #2200, Los Angeles CA 90048 USA — Actress
Chambers, Jerome P (Jerry)
4135 Don Diablo Dr, Los Angeles CA 90008, USA — Basketball Player
Chambers, John T
Cisco Systems, 170 W Tasman Dr, San Jose CA 95134, USA — Businessman
Chambers, Justin
Gersh Agency, 41 Madison Ave, #3301, New York NY 10010 USA — Actor, Model
Chambers, Kasey
Essence Records, PO Box 200, Avoca Beach NSW 2251, Australia — Singer
Chambers, Kirk
1294 Lakeview Dr, Provo UT 84604, USA — Football Player
Chambers, Lester
Lustig Talent, PO Box 770850, Orlando FL 32877 USA — Singer (Chambers Brothers)
Chambers, Martin
Gailforce Mgmt, 91 Peterborough Road, London SW6 3BU, England — Drummer (Pretenders)
Chambers, Nancy
United Talent Agency, 9336 Civic Center Dr, Beverly Hills CA 90210 USA — Actress
Chambers, Raymond G
Malaria No More, 432 Park Ave S, #400, New York NY 10016, USA — Businessman, Social Activist
Chambers, Shawn R
9999 Wood Ridge, Pequot Lakes MN 56472, USA — Ice Hockey Player
Chambers, Thomas D (Tom)
7437 E Via Dona Road, Scottsdale AZ 85266, USA — Basketball Player
Chambers, Wallace H (Wally)
1838 Joslin St, Saginaw MI 48602, USA — Football Player
Chambers, Willie
Lustig Talent, PO Box 770850, Orlando FL 32877 USA — Singer, Guitarist (Chambers Brothers)
Chamblee, Brandel E
Golf Channel, 7580 Golf Channel Drive, Orlando FL 32819, USA — Golfer
Chambliss, C Christopher (Chris)
9100 Otter Creek Dr, #L, Charlotte NC 28277, USA — Baseball Player
Chambliss, Scott
Innovative Artists, 1505 10th St, Santa Monica CA 90401 USA — Art Director
Chambon, Pierre H
Institute of Genetics Molecular & Cellular Biology, 1 Rue Laurent Fries, 67404 Illkirch, France — Biochemist
Chamillionaire
Universal Records, 70 Universal City Plaza, Universal City CA 91608 USA — Rap Artist
Chamitoff, Gregory E
N A S A, Johnson Space Center, 2101 NASA Road, Houston TX 77058 USA — Astronaut
Chammah, Walid A
Morgan Stanley Co Inc, 1585 Broadway, New York NY 10036, USA — Financier
Champine, Robert
205 Tipton Road, Newport News VA 23606, USA — Test Pilot
Champion, B Billy
240 Triple H Farm Road, Inman SC 29349, USA — Baseball Player

Champion, Marge	Dancer, Actress
484 W 43rd St, New York NY 10036, USA	
Champion, William (Will)	Drummer (Coldplay)
Paradigm Agency, 360 N Crescent Dr, North Building, Beverly Hills CA 90210 USA	
Champlin, Charles D	Film Critic
2169 Linda Flora Dr, Los Angeles CA 90077, USA	
Champlin, James L	Vietnam War Air Force Hero
Distinguished Flying Cross Society, PO Box 530250, San Diego CA 92153, USA	
Champoux, Robert (Bob)	Ice Hockey Player
8861 Centuras Way, San Diego CA 92126, USA	
Chan, Ernie	Cartoonist (Conan the Barbarian)
4131 Vale Ave, Oakland CA 94619, USA	
Chan, Jackie	Actor
Jackie Chan Cinema, 70 Pak To Ave, Clearwater Bay Road, Kowloon, Hong Kong 852, China	
Chan, Julius	Prime Minister, Papua New Guinea
PO Box 6030, Boroto, Papua New Guinea	
Chan, Margaret F C	Government Official, China
World Health Organization, Ave Appia 20, 1211 Geneva 27, Switzerland	
Chan, Michael Paul	Actor
Tyler Kjar, 10153 1/2 Riverside Dr, #255, Toluca Lake CA 91602 USA	
Chance, Greyson	Singer
W M E Entertainment, 9601 Wilshire Blvd, #300, Beverly Hills CA 90210 USA	
Chance, Larry	Singer (Earls)
Brothers Mgmt, 141 Dunbar Ave, Fords NJ 08863 USA	
Chance, Robert (Bob)	Baseball Player
2258 Oakridge Dr, Charleston WV 25311, USA	
Chance, W Dean	Baseball Player
9505 W Smithville Western Road, Wooster OH 44691, USA	
Chancellor, Van	Basketball Coach
Lousiana State University, Athletic Dept, Baton Rouge LA 70803, USA	
Chancey, Robert D	Football Player
PO Box 212, Coosada AL 36020, USA	
Chanchez, Hosea	Actor
A P A Talent/Literary Agency, 405 S Beverly Dr, #300, Beverly Hills CA 90212 USA	
Chandler, Carrol H (Howie)	Air Force General
Vice Chief of Staff, HqUSAF, Pentagon, Washington DC 20330 USA	
Chandler, Christopher M (Chris)	Football Player
1625 Lugano Lane, Del Mar CA 92014, USA	
Chandler, Dianne	Model
110 River Oaks Dr, Woodstock GA 30188, USA	
Chandler, Gene	Singer
8829 S Bishop St, Chicago IL 60620, USA	
Chandler, Jeff	Boxer
6242 Horner St, Philadelphia PA 19144, USA	
Chandler, Karl V	Football Player
5 Plymouth Road, Newtown Square PA 19073, USA	
Chandler, Kyle	Actor
Gersh Agency, 9465 Wilshire Blvd, #600, Beverly Hills CA 90212 USA	
Chandler, Tyson C	Basketball Player
21731 Ventura Blvd, #300, Woodland Hills CA 91364, USA	
Chandler, Wesley S (Wes)	Football Player
207 Howard St, New Smyrna Beach FL 32168, USA	
Chandler, Wilson	Basketball Player
Denver Nuggets, Pepsi Center, 1000 Chopper Circle, Denver CO 80204 USA	
Chandola, Walter	Photographer
50 Spring Hill Road, Annandale NJ 08801, USA	
Chandor, J C	Director, Writer
W M E Entertainment, 9601 Wilshire Blvd, #300, Beverly Hills CA 90210 USA	
Chandrasekar	Actor
34 Senthil Nagar Main Road, Chinna Porur, Chennai TN 600116, India	
Chaney, Darrel L	Baseball Player
906 Woodbrier, Saute Nacoche GA 30571, USA	
Chaney, Donald R (Don)	Basketball Player, Coach
20711 Park Pine Dr, Katy TX 77450, USA	
Chaney, John	Basketball Coach
7840 Gilbert St, Philadelphia PA 19150, USA	
Chang, Christina	Actress
Myrna Jacoby Mgmt, 130 W 57th St, New York NY 10019, USA	
Chang, David	Chef, Restaurant
Momofuku Sam Bar, 207 2nd Ave, Front 1, New York NY 10003, USA	
Chang, Han-Na	Conductor, Concert Cellist
Harrison/Parrott, 5-6 Albion Court, London W6 0QT, England	
Chang, Jeannette	Publisher
Harper's Bazaar, Publisher's Office, 1700 Broadway, New York NY 10019, USA	
Chang, Michael	Tennis Player
Chang Foundation, 28562 Oso Parkway, #D343, Rancho Santa Margarita CA 92688, USA	
Chang, Sarah	Concert Violinist
Opus 3 Artists, 470 Park Ave S, #900N, New York NY 10016 USA	
Chang, Shirley	Architect
Chang Bene Design, 43-55 Wyndham St, Central, Hong Kong, China	
Chang-Diaz, Franklin R	Astronaut
Ad Astra Rocket Co, 141 W Bay Area Blvd, Webster TX 77598, USA	
Changeux, Jean-Pierre G	Molecular Biologist
47 Rue du Four, 75006 Paris, France	
Chanik, Evan M	Navy Admiral
Commander, 2nd Fleet, FPO AE 09506 USA	
Channing, Carol	Actress, Singer
C E S D, 10635 Santa Monica Blvd, #130, Los Angeles CA 90025 USA	
Channing, Stockard	Actress
Hofflund/Polone, 9465 Wilshire Blvd, #420, Beverly Hills CA 90212 USA	
Chante, Keshia	Singer, Songwriter
Agency Group Ltd, 142 W 57th St, #600, New York NY 10019 USA	
Chao, Charles	Businessman
Sina, 37F Jinmao Tower, 88 Century Blvd, Pudong, Shanghai 200121, China	
Chao, Manu	Singer, Guitarist
Cookman Mgmt, 10627 Burbank Blvd, North Hollywood CA 91601, USA	

Chao, Rosalind
Don Buchwald/Fortitude, 6500 Wilshire Blvd, #2200, Los Angeles CA 90048 USA — Actress

Chaovarat Chanweerakul
Prime Minister's Office, Thanon Nakhon Patnom, Bangkok 10300, Thailand — Prime Minister, Thailand

Chapdelaine, Rene
662 S Division Road, Petoskey MI 49770, USA — Ice Hockey Player

Chapin, Dwight L
San Francisco Examiner, 110 5th St, San Francisco CA 94103, USA — Publisher, Government Official

Chapin, Jen
Metropolitan Talent, 100 5th Ave, #1100, New York NY 10011, USA — Singer, Songwriter

Chapin, Lauren
726 63rd Ave, Vero Beach FL 32968, USA — Actress

Chapin, Miles
Abrams Artists, 275 7th Ave, #2600, New York NY 10001 USA — Actor

Chapin, Tom
Charles Rothschild, 330 E 48th St, #2D, New York NY 10017 USA — Singer, Songwriter

Chaplin, Ben
Independent Talent Group, Oxford House, 76 Oxford St, London W1D 1BS, England — Actor

Chaplin, Carmen
Talent Store, 8 # 10 Rue de Normandie, 7503 Paris, France , USA — Actress

Chaplin, Geraldine
Manoir de Bau, 1800 Vevey, Switzerland — Actress

Chaplin, Kiera
Limelight Films, 8913 1/2 W Sunset Blvd, West Hollywood CA 90069, USA — Actress, Model

Chapman, Beth Nielsen
PO Box 121551, Nashville TN 37212, USA — Singer, Songwriter

Chapman, Blair
2086 Redcoach Road, Allison Park PA 15101, USA — Ice Hockey Player

Chapman, Candace M M
Canadian Soccer, Place Soccer Canada, 237 Metcalfe St, Ottawa ON K2P 1R2, Canada — Soccer Player

Chapman, Clarence W
14820 Parkside St, Detroit MI 48238, USA — Football Player

Chapman, Dinos
Chapman Fine Arts, 49 Fashion St, London E1 6PX, England — Artist

Chapman, Gary W
PO Box 25330, Nashville TN 37202, USA — Singer, Songwriter, Entertainer

Chapman, Georgina
Marchesa, 60 W 26th St, #1425, New York NY 10001, USA — Fashion Designer (Marchesa), Actress

Chapman, Jake
Chapman Fine Arts, 49 Fashion St, London E1 6PX, England — Artist

Chapman, John
Elliott Agency, 94 Roundhill Crescent, Brighton BN2 3FR, England — Actor

Chapman, Judith
McCabe Group, 3211 Cahuenga Blvd W, #104, Los Angeles CA 90068, USA — Actress

Chapman, Kevin
TalentWorks, 3500 W Olive Ave, #1400, Burbank CA 91505 USA — Actor

Chapman, Lanei
Mitchell K Stubbs Assoc, 8695 W Washington Blvd, #204, Culver City CA 90232 USA — Actress

Chapman, Marshall
1906 South St, #704, Nashville TN 37212, USA — Singer, Guitarist, Songwriter

Chapman, Max C, Jr
Nomura Securities, 1 World Financial Center, #200, New York NY 10281, USA — Financier

Chapman, Michael G (Mike)
8731 Avator Circle, Boerne TX 78015, USA — Football Player

Chapman, Michael J
United Talent Agency, 9336 Civic Center Dr, Beverly Hills CA 90210 USA — Director, Cinematographer

Chapman, Nicki
19 Music & Mgmt, 35-37 Parkgate Road, London SW11 4NP, England — Actress, Entertainer

Chapman, Orville L
1213 Roscomare Road, Los Angeles CA 90077, USA — Chemist

Chapman, Philip K
11460 E Helm Dr, Scottsdale AZ 85255, USA — Astronaut

Chapman, Rex E
15215 N Kierland Blvd, #307, Scottsdale AZ 85254, USA — Basketball Player

Chapman, Robert F
PO Box 253, Linville NC 28646, USA — Judge

Chapman, Steven Curtis
Creative Trust, 5141 Virginia Way, #320, Brentwood TN 37027, USA — Singer, Guitarist, Songwriter

Chapman, Tracy
Elektra Records, 75 Rockefeller Plaza, 1700, New York NY 10019 USA — Singer, Songwriter

Chapman, Wayne G
3593 Salisbury Dr, Lexington KY 40510, USA — Basketball Player

Chapman, Wes
American Ballet Theater, 890 Broadway, #300, New York NY 10003, USA — Ballet Dancer

Chapot, Frank
1075 Opie Road, Branchburg NJ 08853, USA — Equestrian

Chappell, Crystal
247 Newport Ave, Grover Beach CA 93433, USA — Actress

Chappell, Lenonard R (Len)
7624 Chestnut Lane, Waterford WI 53185, USA — Basketball Player

Chappelle, David
Gersh Agency, 9465 Wilshire Blvd, #600, Beverly Hills CA 90212 USA — Actor, Comedian

Chapuisat, Stephane
Borussia Dortmund S C, Strobelallee, 44139 Dortmund, Germany — Soccer Player

Chaput, Charles J
Archdiocese, 222 N 17th St, Philadelphia PA 19103, USA — Religious Leader

Chaquico, Craig
I C M Partners, 10250 Constellation Blvd, #900, Los Angeles CA 90067 USA — Guitarist (Jefferson Starship)

Chara, Zdeno
343 Commercial St, #211-213, Boston MA 02109, USA — Ice Hockey Player

Charbonneau, Patricia
Mary Harden-Curtis Assoc, 850 7th Ave, #903, New York NY 10019, USA — Actress

Charbonneau, Stephane
1 Wilderness Dr, Voorhees NJ 08043, USA — Ice Hockey Player

Charest, Benoit
I C M Partners, 10250 Constellation Blvd, #900, Los Angeles CA 90067 USA — Composer

Charest, Isabelle — Speed Skater
Speed Skating Canada, 2781 Lancaster Road, #402, Ottawa ON K1B 1A7, Canada
Chargin, Don — Boxing Promoter
Don Chargin Productions, 1241 Knollwood Dr, #134, Cambria CA 93428, USA
Charhi, Liraz — Actress
Paradigm Agency, 360 N Crescent Dr, North Building, Beverly Hills CA 90210 USA
Charice — Actress, Singer
W M E Entertainment, 9601 Wilshire Blvd, #300, Beverly Hills CA 90210 USA
Charlap, William M (Bill) — Jazz Pianist
Ted Kurland, 173 Brighton Ave, Allston MA 02134 USA
Charlene — Princess Consort, Monaco
Palais de Monaco, BP 518, 98015 Monaco Cedex, Monaco
Charles — Prince of Wales, England
Saint James's Palace, London SW1A 1BS, England
Charles, Caroline — Fashion Designer
56/57 Beauchamp Place, London SW3, England
Charles, Craig — Actor
P F D, Drury House, 34-43 Russell St, London WC2B 5HA, England
Charles, Edwin D (Ed) — Baseball Player
57 Park Terrace E, #B58, New York NY 10034, USA
Charles, Fran — Sportscaster
N F L Network, 10950 Washington Blvd, #100, Culver City CA 90232 USA
Charles, Gaius — Actor
Gersh Agency, 9465 Wilshire Blvd, #600, Beverly Hills CA 90212 USA
Charles, John C (J C) — Football Player
5644 Westheimer Road, #164, Houston TX 77056, USA
Charles, Josh A — Actor
Kipperman Mgmt, 420 W End Ave, #1G, New York NY 10024 USA
Charles, Kenneth M (Ken) — Basketball Player
621 Putnam Ave, Brooklyn NY 11221, USA
Charles, Larry — Director
W M E Entertainment, 9601 Wilshire Blvd, #300, Beverly Hills CA 90210 USA
Charles, Robert J (Bob) — Golfer
5329 Sea Biscuit Road, Palm Beach Gardens FL 33418, USA
Charles, Tanika — Singer, Songwriter
Agency Group Ltd, 142 W 57th St, #600, New York NY 10019 USA
Charles, Tina — Pop, Disco Singer
74 Haveston Hill, Caterham, Surrey CR3 8DH, England
Charles, Tina — Basketball Player
Connecticut Sun, 1 Mohegan Sun Blvd, Uncasville CT 06382 USA
Charles-Furlow, Daedra — Basketball Player
19414 Spencer St, Detroit MI 48234, USA
Charleson, Leslie — Actress
4851 Cromwell Ave, Los Angeles CA 90027, USA
Charles-Roux, Edmonde — Writer
Editions Grasset, 61 Rue des Saints-Peres, 75006 Paris, France
Charlesworth, Brian — Evolutionary Biologist
Edinburgh University, Biology Institute, Edinburgh EH1 1HT, Scotland
Charlesworth, Sarah E — Photographer, Artist
Jay Gorney Modern Art, 534 W 26th St, New York NY 10001, USA
Charlesworth, Todd — Ice Hockey Player
2240 Pleasant Hill Dr, Muskegon MI 49441, USA
Charlone, Cesar — Cinematographer
I C M Partners, 10250 Constellation Blvd, #900, Los Angeles CA 90067 USA
Charlton, Norman W (Norm) — Baseball Player
312 Estes Dr, Rockport TX 78382, USA
Charlton, Robert (Bobby) — Soccer Player
Garthollerton, Cleford Road, Ollerton, Cheshire WA16 8RY, England
Charnin, Martin — Producer, Director, Lyricist
Richard Ticktin, 1345 Ave of Americas, New York NY 10105, USA
Charno, Stuart — Actor, Comedian
4147 Sunnyside Ave, Los Angeles CA 90066, USA
Charo — Singer, Guitarist
Charo Entertainment, 1801 Lexington Road, Beverly Hills CA 90210, USA
Charron, Paul R — Businessman
44 Contentment Island Road, Darien CT 06820, USA
Chartier, Dave — Ice Hockey Player
SW 13-19-28 W, Binscarth MB R0J 0G0, Canada
Chartoff, Melanie — Actress
Artists Agency, 1180 S Beverly Dr, #301, Los Angeles CA 90035 USA
Chartraw, Rick — Ice Hockey Player
600 Chaparral Road, Sierra Madre CA 91024, USA
Charvet, David — Actor
Chasen Agency, 8899 Beverly Blvd, #716, Los Angeles CA 90048 USA
Charyk, Joseph V — Businessman
790 Andrews Ave, #A302, Delray Beach FL 33483, USA
Charyn, Jerome — Writer
Bloomsbury Publishing, 36 Soho Square, London W1D 3Q4, England
Chase, Alison — Dance Artistic Director
Apogee Arts, PO Box 224, Brooksville ME 04617, USA
Chase, Alston — Writer
Bohrman Agency, 3141 Ellington Dr, Los Angeles CA 90068, USA
Chase, Bailey — Actor
Gersh Agency, 9465 Wilshire Blvd, #600, Beverly Hills CA 90212 USA
Chase, Barrie — Actress, Dancer
446 Carrol Canal, Venice CA 90291, USA
Chase, Brian — Drummer (Yeah Yeah Yeahs)
C E S D, 10635 Santa Monica Blvd, #130, Los Angeles CA 90025 USA
Chase, Chevy — Actor, Comedian
Kritzer Levine Wilkins Griffin, 11872 La Grange Ave, #100, Los Angeles CA 90025 USA
Chase, Daveigh — Actress
Brillstein Entertainment Partners, 9150 Wilshire Blvd, #350, Beverly Hills CA 90212 USA
Chase, David — Producer, Writer
United Talent Agency, 9336 Civic Center Dr, Beverly Hills CA 90210 USA
Chase, Debra Martin — Producer
Martin Chase Productions, 500 S Buena Vista St, Burbank CA 91521, USA

Chase, Jonathan — Actor
Main Title Mgmt, 8383 Wilshire Blvd, #408, Beverly Hills CA 90211 USA
Chase, Kelly W — Ice Hockey Player
16476 Horseshoe Ridge Road, Chesterfield MO 63005, USA
Chase, Lori — Actress, Comedienne
OmniPop Talent Group, 4605 Lankershim Blvd, #201, Toluca Lake CA 91602 USA
Chase, Lorraine — Actress
Burnett Granger Assoc, 3 Clifford St, London W1S 2LF, England
Chase, Qiana — Model
Playboy Promotions, 2706 Media Center Dr, Los Angeles CA 90065 USA
Chase, Steve — Interior Designer
Chase Design Assoc, 70005 Mirage Cove Dr, Rancho Mirage CA 92270, USA
Chasez, Joshua Scott (J C) — Singer ('N Sync)
Podwall Entertainment, 710 N Orlando Ave, #203, West Hollywood CA 90069, USA
Chass, Murray — Sportswriter
New York Times, Editorial Dept, 229 W 43rd St, New York NY 10036 USA
Chassagne, Regine — Musician (Arcade Fire), Actress
Billions Corp, 3522 W Armitage Ave, Chicago IL 60647 USA
Chast, Roz — Cartoonist
New Yorker, Editorial Dept, 4 Times Square, Basement C1B, New York NY 10036 USA
Chastain, Brandi — Soccer Player, Sportscaster
1661 University Way, San Jose CA 95126, USA
Chastain, Jessica — Actress
Mosiac Media Group, 9200 W Sunset Blvd, #1000, Los Angeles CA 90069 USA
Chastel, Andre — Writer
30 Rue de Lubeck, 75116 Paris, France
Chater, Eos — Violinist (Bond)
Mel Bush, Ranglewood, Arrowsmith Road, Wimborne, Dorset BH21 3B5, England
Chatham, Matthew (Matt) — Football Player
2502 Old Bridge Lane, Bellingham MA 02019, USA
Chatham, Russell — Artist
Clark City Press, PO Box 1358, Livingston MT 59047, USA
Chatham, Wes — Actor
Gersh Agency, 9465 Wilshire Blvd, #600, Beverly Hills CA 90212 USA
Chatroit, Francois — Auto Racing Driver
Artmedia, 20 Ave Rapp, 75007 Paris, France
Chattaway, Jay — Composer
May Artist Mgmt, 8491 W Sunset Blvd, #228, West Hollywood CA 90069, USA
Chatwin, Justin — Actor
Alchemy Entertainment, 7024 Melrose Ave, #420, Los Angeles CA 90038 USA
Chau, Francois — Actor
2335 Lake Shore Ave, Los Angeles CA 90039, USA
Chaudhry, Iftikhar Mohammed — Judge
Supreme Court, Constitution Ave, Islamabad, Pakistan
Chaudhry, Mahendra P — Prime Minister, Fiji
Fiji Labor Party, PO Box 2162, Suva, Fiji
Chaumette, Monique — Actress
Voyez Mon Agent, 20 Ave Rapp, 75007 Paris, France
Chauvin, Yves — Nobel Chemistry Laureate
10 Place Francois Sicard, 37000 Tours, France
Chauvire, Yvette — Ballerina
21 Place du Commerce, 75015 Paris, France
Chaves, Richard — Actor
Media Artists Group, 8222 Melrose Ave, #203, Los Angeles CA 90048 USA
Chavez Ramirez, Darvin F — Soccer Player
Federacion de Futbol, Colima 373 Colonia Roma, Delegacion Cuauhtemoc Mexico DF 06700, Mexico
Chavez, Endy D — Baseball Player
1406 Bonnie Lane, Bayside NY 11360, USA
Chavez, Hugo R — President, Venezuela
Palacio de Miraflores, Avenida Urdaneta, Caracas 1010, Venzuela
Chavez, Jorge F — Thoroughbred Racing Jockey
106 John St, Garden City NY 11530, USA
Chavez, Julio Cesar, Jr — Boxer
Team Chavez, 12620 Washington Blvd, Los Angeles CA 90066, USA
Chavira, Ricardo Antonio — Actor
Innovative Artists, 1505 10th St, Santa Monica CA 90401 USA
Chavous, Barney L — Football Player, Coach
601 Chavous Road, Aiken SC 29803, USA
Chavous, Corey L — Football Player
1218 S Main St, Saint Charles MO 63301, USA
Chawla, Juhi — Actress
153 Oxford Tower, Yamuna Nagar, Oshiwara Andheri (W), Mumbai 40058, India
Chayanne — Singer, Actress
Chaf Enterprises, 1717 N Bayshore Dr, #2146, Miami FL 33132, USA
Chbosky, Stephen — Writer, Producer
W M E Entertainment, 9601 Wilshire Blvd, #300, Beverly Hills CA 90210 USA
Cheadle, Don — Actor
United Talent Agency, 9336 Civic Center Dr, Beverly Hills CA 90210 USA
Cheaney, Calbert N — Basketball Player
110 Bow Lane, Indianapolis IN 46220, USA
Cheatham, Maree — Actress
Sutton-Barth Vennari, 145 S Fairfax Ave, #310, Los Angeles CA 90036 USA
Checker, Chubby — Singer, Songwriter
Twisted Entertainment, 320 Fayette St, #200, Conshohocken PA 19428, USA
Checkley, Laura — Actress
Gavin Barker Assoc, 2D Wimpole St, London W1G 0EB, England
Cheechoo, Jonathan — Ice Hockey Player
707 Iris Gardens Court, San Jose CA 95125, USA
Cheek, Jimmy G — Educator
University of Tennessee, Chancellor's Office, Andy Holt Tower, Knoxville TN 37996, USA
Cheek, Joey — Speed Skater
Q Sports Marketing, 534 W Evergreen St, Wheaton IL 60187 USA
Cheek, Louis R, Jr — Football Player
545 Woelke Road, Seguin TX 78155, USA
Cheek, Molly — Actress
Kazarian/Spencer/Ruskin, 11969 Ventura Blvd, #300, Studio City CA 91604 USA

C

Chase - Cheek

C

Cheeks, Maurice E (Mo) — Basketball Player, Coach
709 Broad Acres Road, Penn Valley PA 19072, USA
Cheena, Parvesh — Actor
Global Artists Agency, 6253 Hollywood Blvd, #508, Los Angeles CA 90028 USA
Cheeseborough, Chandra — Track Athlete
104 W Harbor, Hendersonville TN 37075, USA
Cheesman, Barry — Golfer
2901 Theresa Lane, Sarasota FL 34239, USA
Cheetham, Jay (Jay Kay) — Singer
Merlin Elite, Hammersmith Studios, 55 Yelman Road, London W6 8JF, England
Cheever, Eddie — Auto Racing Driver
8227 N West Blvd, #300, Indianapolis IN 46278, USA
Cheever, Susan — Writer
Simon & Schuster, 1230 Ave of Americas, Concourse 1, New York NY 10020 USA
Cheevers, Gerald M (Gerry) — Ice Hockey Player, Coach
106 Appleton St, North Andover MA 01845, USA
Chee-Yun — Concert Violinist
Opus 3 Artists, 470 Park Ave S, #900N, New York NY 10016 USA
Chef, Genia — Artist
Leibnizstr 61, 10629 Berlin, Germany
Chekamauskas, Vitautas — Architect
State Arts Academy, Maironio 6, 2600 Vilnius, Lithuania
Chelberg, Robert D — Army General
Cubic Applications, Patch Community, Unit 30400, Box R65, APO AE 09131, USA
Cheli, Giovanni Cardinal — Religious Leader
Pastoral Care of Migrants Council, Piazza Calisto 16, 00153 Rome, Italy
Cheli, Maurizio — Astronaut, Italy
European Space Center, Linder Hohe, Box 906096, 51127 Cologne, Germany
Cheli-Merchez, Marianne — Astronaut, Belgium
38 Via Ciro Santagata, Modena, Italy
Chelios, Christos K (Chris) — Ice Hockey Player
790 Falmouth Dr, Bloomfield Hills MI 48304, USA
Chellgren, Paul W — Businessman
Ashland Inc, PO Box 15391, Covington KY 41015, USA
Chelsom, Peter — Director
Principato-Young, 9465 Wilshire Blvd, #880, Beverly Hills CA 90212 USA
Chemetov, Paul — Architect
Chemetov-Huidobro, 4 Square Massena, 75013 Paris, France
Chen Kaige — Director
I C M Partners, 10250 Constellation Blvd, #900, Los Angeles CA 90067 USA
Chen Lu — Figure Skater
World Ice Arena, 1881th Bao'an Road, Luohu District, Shenzhen 518000 , China
Chen Xieyang — Conductor
Shanghai Symphony Orchestra, 105 Hunan Road, Shanghai 200031, China
Chen Yi — Composer
University of Missouri, Music Conservatory, Kansas City MO 64110, USA
Chen Yibing — Gymnast
Beijing Normal University, 19 Xin Jie Kou Wai St, Hai Dian District, Beijing 100875 PR, China
Chen Zuohuang — Conductor
Wichita Symphony Orchestra, Concert Hall, 225 W Douglas St, Wichita KS 67202, USA
Chen, Bruce K — Baseball Player
18372 W Ivy Lane, Surprise AZ 85388, USA
Chen, Daniel (Dan) — Sculptor, Artist
PO Box 41513, Eugene OR 97404, USA
Chen, Edison — Actor
Fulong Production, 8/F Baskerville House, 13 Duddell St, Central, Hong Kong, China
Chen, Irvin S Y — Geneticist
University of California Medical Center, Hematology Dept, Los Angeles CA 90024, USA
Chen, Joan — Actress, Director
2601 Filbert St, San Francisco CA 94123, USA
Chen, Joie — Commentator
CNN-TV, 190 Marietta Ave SW, Atlanta GA 30303 USA
Chen, Julie — Commentator
CBS-TV, News Dept, 51 W 52nd St, New York NY 10019 USA
Chen, Lincoln C — Nutritionist
302 Dean Road, Brookline MA 02445, USA
Chen, Steve — Businessman
YouTube, 1000 Cherry Ave, #200, San Bruno CA 94066, USA
Chen, Steve S — Computer Engineer
Chen Systems Corp, 1414 W Hamilton Ave, Eau Claire WI 54701, USA
Chen, Steven — Keyboardist (Airline Toxic Event)
Island Def Jam Records, 8920 W Sunset Blvd, #200, West Hollywood CA 90069 USA
Chenchikova, Olga — Ballerina
Kirov Ballet Theater, 1 Pl Iskusstr, 190000 Saint Petersburg, Russia
Chenery, Penny — Thoroughbred Racing Owner
20 Roberts Lane, Saratoga Springs NY 12866, USA
Cheney, Dorothy B (Dodo) — Tennis Player
442 Woodland Hills Dr, Escondido CA 92029, USA
Cheney, Lauren — Soccer Player
Boston Breakers, 400 Blue Hill Dr, #302, Westwood, MA 02090 USA
Cheney, Lynne V — Government Official
American Enterprise Institute, 1150 17th St NW, Washington DC 20036, USA
Cheney, Richard B — Vice President; Secretary, Defense
6613 Madison Dr, McLean VA 22101, USA
Cheng, Andy — Director
Paradigm Agency, 360 N Crescent Dr, North Building, Beverly Hills CA 90210 USA
Chenier, Philip (Phil) — Basketball Player
7807 Arbor Grove Dr, #407, Hanover MD 21076, USA
Chennault, Anna Chan — Businesswoman, Writer
T A C International, Chennault Building, 1049 30th St NW, Washington DC 20007, USA
Chenoweth, Kristin — Actress, Singer
Creative Artists Agency, 2000 Ave of Stars, #100, Los Angeles CA 90067 USA
Cheong Jin Suk, Nicholas Cardinal — Religious Leader
Seoul Archdiocese, Chunggu Myongdong 2-1, Seoul 100-022, South Korea
Chepik, Sergei — Artist
Galerie Guiter, 23 Rue Guenegaud, 75006 Paris, France

Cher
Schiff Co, 8440 Warner Dr, #B1, Culver City CA 90232 USA — Actress, Singer

Chereau, Patrice
Azor Films, 4 Rue de Braque, 75003 Paris, France — Director

Cherestal, Jean Marie
Villa d'Accueil, Delmas 60, Musseau, Port-au-Prince 6110, Haiti — Prime Minister, Haiti

Cherlin, Andrew J
Johns Hopkins University, Sociology Dept, Baltimore MD 21218, USA — Sociologist

Chermayeff, Peter
Chermayeff Sollogub Poolle, 51 Melcher St, #902, Boston MA 02210, USA — Architect

Chernicky, Laura
Jennifer's Talent, 740 N Plamkinton Ave, #300, Milwaukee WI 53203, USA — Actress

Chernin, Peter
Chernin Entertainment, 1733 Ocean Ave, Santa Monica CA 90401, USA — Businessman

Chernow, Ron
105 State St, Brooklyn NY 11201, USA — Writer

Cherrelle
Green Light Talent Agency, PO Box 3172, Beverly Hills CA 90212 USA — Singer

Cherry, Byron
Whitaker Entertainment, 4924 Vineland Ave, North Hollywood CA 91601, USA — Actor

Cherry, Deron L
13800 S Pebblebrook Lane, Greenwood MO 64034, USA — Football Player

Cherry, Dick
Box 346 RR 1, Bath ON K0H 1G0, Canada — Ice Hockey Player

Cherry, Don
928 Pinehurst Dr, Las Vegas NV 89109, USA — Singer, Golfer

Cherry, Don S
CBC-TV, PO Box 500, Station A, Toronto ON M5W 1E6, Canada — Ice Hockey Player, Coach, Sportscaster

Cherry, Eagle-Eye L
Umbrella Group, 1 West St, #3506, New York NY 10004, USA — Singer

Cherry, Fred V
720 Dale Dr, Silver Spring MD 20910, USA — Vietnam War Air Force Hero

Cherry, Jake
United Talent Agency, 9336 Civic Center Dr, Beverly Hills CA 90210 USA — Actor

Cherry, Je'rod L
993 Mimosa Dr, Macedonia OH 44056, USA — Football Player

Cherry, Jonathan
Roar, 2400 Broadway, #330, Santa Monica CA 90404, USA — Actor

Cherry, Marc
Paradigm Agency, 360 N Crescent Dr, North Building, Beverly Hills CA 90210 USA — Producer

Cherry, Neneh
Paradigm Agency, 360 Park Ave, #1600, New York NY 10022 USA — Singer

Chertoff, Michael
Covington & Burling, 1201 Pennsylvania Ave NW, Washington DC 20004, USA — Secretary, Homeland Security; Judge

Cherundolo, Charles J (Chuck), Jr
4230 Simms Road, Lakeland FL 33810, USA — Football Player

Cherundolo, Steve
Hanover 96, Arthur-Menge Ufer 5, 30169 Hannover, Germany — Soccer Player

Chervin, Stan
I C M Partners, 10250 Constellation Blvd, #900, Los Angeles CA 90067 USA — Writer

Chesnais, Patrick
Artmedia, 20 Ave Rapp, 75007 Paris, France — Actor

Chesnes, Shelby
Playboy Promotions, 2706 Media Center Dr, Los Angeles CA 90065 USA — Model

Chesney, Kenny
Morris Management Group, 818 19th Ave S, Nashville TN 37203, USA — Singer

Chesnutt, Mark N
Ladd Mgmt, 533 Hagan St, Nashville TN 37203, USA — Singer, Songwriter

Chester, Colby
Brady Brannon Rich, 5670 Wilshire Blvd, #820, Los Angeles CA 90036 USA — Actor

Chester, Larry T
14121 SW 33rd Court, Davie FL 33330, USA — Football Player

Chester, Raymond T
4722 Grass Valley Road, Oakland CA 94605, USA — Football Player

Chestnut, Cyrus
Avenue Management Group, 250 W 57th St, #2329, New York NY 10107, USA — Jazz Pianist, Songwriter

Chestnut, Mary Boykin
Sweet Briar College, President's Office, Sweet Briar VA 24595, USA — Educator

Chestnut, Morris
Gersh Agency, 9465 Wilshire Blvd, #600, Beverly Hills CA 90212 USA — Actor

Chet, Ilan
Weizmann Science Institute, President's Office, Rehovot 76100, Israel — Microbiologist

Chetry, Kiran
CNN-TV, 190 Marietta Ave SW, Atlanta GA 30303 USA — Commentator

Chetwynd, Lionel
Creative Artists Agency, 2000 Ave of Stars, #100, Los Angeles CA 90067 USA — Writer, Producer, Director

Cheung, Maggie
Schachter Entertainment, 1157 S Beverly Dr, Los Angeles CA 90035, USA — Actress

Cheveldae, Tim
Moose Jaw Warriors, 1251 Main St N, Moose Jaw SK S6H 6M3, Canada — Ice Hockey Player

Chevrier, Alain
5138 Greenwich Preserve Court, Boynton Beach FL 33436, USA — Ice Hockey Player

Chew, Geoffrey F
10 Maybeck Twin Dr, Berkeley CA 94708, USA — Physicist

Cheyunski, James M (Jim)
821 W Locust St, Seaford DE 19973, USA — Football Player

Chi Haotian
National Defense Ministry, Jingshanqia Jie, Beijing 100009, China — Army General, China

Chi, Chen
23 Washington Square N, New York NY 10011, USA — Artist

Chi, Tony
Tony Chi & Assoc, 121 Varick St, #500, New York NY 10013, USA — Interior Designer

Chia, Sandro
601 W 26th St, #12, New York NY 10001, USA — Artist

Chiacchia, Darren
PO Box 278, East Aurora NY 14052, USA — Equestrian

Chianese, Dominic — Actor
Liebman Entertainment, 25 E 21st St, #PH, New York NY 10010, USA
Chiao, Leroy — Astronaut
2108 Butler Dr, Friendswood TX 77546, USA
Chiara, Maria — Opera Singer
Narodni Divado, Ostrovni 1, 11230 Prague 1, Czech Republic
Chick, Austin — Director
Bloom Hergott Diemer, 150 S Rodeo Dr, #300, Beverly Hills CA 90212 USA
Chihara, Charles S — Philosopher
567 Cragmont Ave, Berkeley CA 94708, USA
Chihuly, Dale P — Artist, Sculptor
Chihuly Inc, 1111 NW 50th St, Seattle WA 98107, USA
Chikezie, Caroline — Actress
Paradigm Agency, 360 N Crescent Dr, North Building, Beverly Hills CA 90210 USA
Chiklis, Michael — Actor
W M E Entertainment, 9601 Wilshire Blvd, #300, Beverly Hills CA 90210 USA
Child, Desmond — Singer, Songwriter
D S W Entertainment, 3727 27th St, Long Island City NY 11101, USA
Child, Jane — Singer, Keyboardist, Songwriter
7095 Hollywood Blvd, #747, Los Angeles CA 90028, USA
Child, Lee — Writer
Delacorte Press, 1540 Broadway, New York NY 10036 USA
Childers, Ambyr — Actress
W M E Entertainment, 9601 Wilshire Blvd, #300, Beverly Hills CA 90210 USA
Childress, Joshua M (Josh) — Basketball Player
1433 Cherokee Trail, Lawrenceville GA 30043, USA
Childress, Kallie Flynn — Actress
Amsel Eisenstadt Frazier, 5055 Wilshire Blvd, #865, Los Angeles CA 90036 USA
Childress, Raymond C (Ray), Jr — Football Player
639 Shady Hill St, Houston TX 77056, USA
Childress, Richard (R C) — Auto Racing Executive
Childress Racing, 236 Industrial Dr, Welcome NC 27374, USA
Childs, Billy — Jazz Pianist
Integrity Talent, 1 Westcroft Court, Cockeysville MD 21030 USA
Childs, Chris — Basketball Player
10830 Willow Meadow Circle, Alpharetta GA 30022, USA
Childs, David M — Architect
Skidmore Owings Merrill, 14 Wall St, #2500, New York NY 10005, USA
Childs, Henry — Football Player
8304 Allman Road, Lenexa KS 66219, USA
Childs, Martin — Art Director
Independent Talent Group, Oxford House, 76 Oxford St, London W1D 1BS, England
Childs, Toni — Singer, Songwriter
Studio C Communications, 324 Sunset Ave, Venice CA 90291, USA
Chiles, Henry G (Hank), Jr — Navy Admiral
6436 Pima St, Alexandria VA 22312, USA
Chiles, Linden — Actor
2521 Topanga Skyline Dr, Topanga CA 90290, USA
Chiles, Lois — Actress, Model
Abrams Artists, 9200 W Sunset Blvd, #1125, West Hollywood CA 90069 USA
Chiles, Richard F (Rich) — Baseball Player
18147 Mallard St, Woodland CA 95695, USA
Chillar, Brandon O — Football Player
1030 Iris Court, Carlsbad CA 92011, USA
Chillemi, Connie — Golfer
2701 NE 10th St, #705, Ocala FL 34470, USA
Chilstom, Ken — Test Pilot
20 Selby Lane, Palm Beach Gardens FL 33418, USA
Chilton, Gene A — Football Player
45828 US Highway 69 N, Jacksonville TX 75766, USA
Chilton, Karen — Actress
Innovative Artists, 1505 10th St, Santa Monica CA 90401 USA
Chilton, Kevin P — Astronaut, Air Force General
2555 Talleson Court, Colorado Springs CO 80919, USA
Chilton, W Alexander (Alex) — Singer, Guitarist (Box Tops, Big Star)
High Road Touring, 751 Bridgeway, #200, Sausalito CA 94965 USA
Chiminazzo, Jeisa — Model
I M G Models, 304 Park Ave S, #PH-North, New York NY 10010 USA
Chiminello, Bianca — Actress
Matt Sherman Mgmt, 7510 W Sunset Blvd, #1413, Los Angeles CA 90046, USA
Chin, Lonny — Actress, Model
Playboy Promotions, 2706 Media Center Dr, Los Angeles CA 90065 USA
Chinchilla Miranda, Laura — President, Costa Rica
Casa Presidencial, Apdo 520-2010, San Jose 1000, Costa Rica
Ching, Brian — Soccer Player
Houston Dynamo, 1415 Louisiana, #3400, Houston TX 77002 USA
Chingy — Rap Artist
Titus Production & Mgmt, 16060 Ventura Blvd, #267, Encino CA 91436, USA
Chinlund, Nick — Actor
Innovative Artists, 1505 10th St, Santa Monica CA 90401 USA
Chinn, Simon — Documentary Producer
Independent Talent Group, Oxford House, 76 Oxford St, London W1D 1BS, England
Chipchura, Kyle D G — Ice Hockey Player
Phoenix Coyotes, 6751 N Sunset Blvd, #200, Glendale AZ 85305 USA
Chipperfield, David — Architect
Chipperfield Architects, Cobham Mews, Agar Grove, London NW1 9SB, England
Chipperfield, Ron — Ice Hockey Player
Optima World Sports, Box 248, Wilcox SK S0G 5E0, Canada
Chirac, Jacques R — President, France
110 Rue du Bac, 75007 Paris, France
Chirico, Emanuel — Businessman
Phillips-Van Heusen Corp, 200 Madison Ave, Basement 1, New York NY 10016, USA
Chisholm, Melanie J — Singer (Spice Girls)
Red Girl Records, PO Box 3532, Marlborough SN8 9AN, England
Chisholm, Sallie W (Penny) — Biological Oceanographer
Massachusetts Institute of Technology, Engineering Dept, Cambridge MA 02139, USA

Chislett, Michael Guy
Decaydance Records, 9229 Sunset Blvd, #900, West Hollywood CA 90069, USA — Guitarist (Academy Is)

Chissano, Joaquim A
Rua Pereira do Lago 10, Bairro de Sommerschield, Maputo, Mozambique — President, Mozambique

Chitalada, Sot
Home Express Co, 242/19 Moo 10, Sukhumvit Road, Cholburi 20210, Thailand — Boxer

Chittenden, Khan
Lisa Mann Creaqtive Mgmt, 99 Spring St, Bondi Junction NSW 2022, Australia — Actor

Chittister, Joan D
Saint Scholastica Priory, 335 E 9th St, Erie PA 16503, USA — Social Psychologist

Chitty, Dennis
1602-5775 Hampton Place, Vancouver BC V6T 2G6, Canada — Animal Ecologist

Chitwood, Joey, Jr
5324 Golden Isles Dr, Apollo Beach FL 33572, USA — Stunt Car Driver

Chiu, Raymond J
9075 Rue Omega, Brossard QC J4Y 3A9, Canada — Heart Surgeon

Chivian, Eric
Harvard University, Health & Global Environment Center, Cambridge MA 02138, USA — Psychiatrist, Social Activist

Chizevsky, Kim
PO Box 9101, Springfield MO 65801, USA — Body Builder

Chladek, Dana
5302 Flanders Ave, Kensington MD 20895, USA — Canoeing Athlete

Chlumsky, Anna
Innovative Artists, 235 Park Ave S, #1000, New York NY 10003 USA — Actress

Chmerkovskiy, Maksim
Rising Stars Dance Academy, 479 N Midland Ave, #H, Saddlebrook NJ 07663, USA — Dancer, Choreographer

Chmerkovskiy, Val
Lizzie Grubman Mgmt, 424 W 33 St, #110, New York NY 10001, USA — Dancer

Chmura, Mark W
S18W28948 Price Court, Waukesha WI 53188, USA — Football Player

Cho, Alfred Y
A T & T Bell Lucent Laboratory, 600 Mountain Ave, New Providence NJ 07974 USA — Electrical Engineer

Cho, Frank
Creators Syndicate, 737 3rd St, Hermosa Beach CA 90254 USA — Cartoonist (Liberty Meadows)

Cho, Fujio
Toyota Motor Corp, 1 Toyotacho, Toyota City, Aichi Pref 471 8701, Japan — Businessman

Cho, John
Gersh Agency, 9465 Wilshire Blvd, #600, Beverly Hills CA 90212 USA — Actor

Cho, Margaret
W M E Entertainment, 9601 Wilshire Blvd, #300, Beverly Hills CA 90210 USA — Actress, Comedienne

Cho, Paul Y
Full Gospel Central Church, 12 Yoido-dong, #1100, Youngdungpo-ku, Seoul 150869, Korea — Evangelist

Cho, Simon
US Speedskating, 5662 S Cougar Lane, Salt Lake City UT 84118 USA — Short Track Speed

Cho, Smith
Gersh Agency, 9465 Wilshire Blvd, #600, Beverly Hills CA 90212 USA — Actress

Choate, Jerry D
Allstate Insurance, Allstate Plaza, 2775 Sanders Road, Northbrook IL 60062, USA — Businessman

Choate, Randol (Randy)
22239 Yachtclub Terrace, Land O Lakes FL 34639, USA — Baseball Player

Chodron, Pemo
Gampo Abbey, Pleasant Bay, Cape Breton NS B0E 2P0, Canada — Religious Leader

Choi Eun-Kyung
Skating Union, 88 Bangyee-Dong, Songpaku, Seoul 138 749, South Korea — Speed Skater

Choi Min-Kyung
Skating Union, 88 Bangyee-Dong, Songpaku, Seoul 138 749, South Korea — Speed Skater

Choi, Kyung Ju (K J)
2205 Vaquero Estates Blvd, Westlake TX 76262, USA — Golfer

Chojnacka, Elisabeth
17 Rue Emile Dubois, 75014 Paris, France — Concert Harpsichordist

Chojnowska-Liskiewicz, Krystyna
Ul Norblina 29 m 50, 80 304 Gdansk-Oliwa, Poland — Yachtswoman

Chokachi, David
Pantheon Talent, 1801 Century Park East, #1910, Los Angeles CA 90067 90067, USA — Actor

Chomet, Sylvain
I C M Partners, 10250 Constellation Blvd, #900, Los Angeles CA 90067 USA — Animator, Lyricist

Chomski, Alejandro
Gersh Agency, 9465 Wilshire Blvd, #600, Beverly Hills CA 90212 USA — Director, Producer, Writer

Chomsky, A Noam
15 Suzanne Road, Lexington MA 02420, USA — Linguist

Chomsky, Marvin J
15200 W Sunset Blvd, #209, Pacific Palisades CA 90272, USA — Director

Chonacas, Katie
K Star Productions, 8491 Sunset Blvd, #549, Los Angeles CA 90069, USA — Actress, Model

Chones, James B (Jim)
26400 George Zeiger Dr, #405, Beachwood OH 44122, USA — Basketball Player

Chong, Rae Dawn
Metropolitan Talent Agency, 7020 La Presa Dr, Los Angeles CA 90068 USA — Actress

Chong, Thomas (Tommy)
1625 Casale Road, Pacific Palisades CA 90272, USA — Actor, Comedian (Cheech & Chong)

Chontosh, Brian R
1009 Harbour Dr, Stafford VA 22554, USA — Marine Corps Iraq War Hero

Choper, Jesse H
University of California, Law School, Boalt Hall, Berkeley CA 94720, USA — Attorney, Educator

Chopra, Daniel
9838 Laurel Valley Dr, Windermere FL 34786, USA — Golfer

Chopra, Deepak
Trident Media Group, 41 Madison Ave, #3600, New York NY 10010. USA — Writer

Chopra, Prem
144A Nibbana Pali Hill, Bandra, Mumbai MS 400050, India — Actor

Chopra, Priyanka
Creative Artists Agency, 2000 Ave of Stars, #100, Los Angeles CA 90067 USA — Beauty Queen, Actress

Chopra, Vidhu Vinod
B30 Kalpana Apts, Sheley Ranjan Road, Bandra, Mumbai MS 400050, India — Director, Producer

Chorley of Kendal, Roger R E
50 Kensington Place, London W8 7PW, England — Businessman

Chorske, Tom — Ice Hockey Player
23 Cooper Circle, Minneapolis MN 55436, USA
Chorvat, Scarlett — Actress
Innovative Artists, 1505 10th St, Santa Monica CA 90401 USA
Chorzempa, Daniel W — Concert Organist, Composer
Kunstleragentur Raab & Bohm, Plankengasse 7, 1010 Vienna, Austria
Choudhury, Sarita — Actress
Don Buchwald/Fortitude, 6500 Wilshire Blvd, #2200, Los Angeles CA 90048 USA
Chouinard, Guy — Ice Hockey Player
P E I Rocket, 46 Kensington Road, Charlottetown PE C1A 5H7, Canada
Chouinard, Marie — Dancer, Choreographer
Compagnie Chouinard, 3981 Boul Saint-Laurent, Montreal PQ H2W 1Y5, Canada
Chouinard, Robert W (Bobby) — Baseball Player
6024 S Paris Place, Englewood CO 80111, USA
Choummali Sayasone — President, Laos; Army General
Presidential House, Vientiane Capital, Vientiane, Laos
Chow Yun-Fat — Actor
2/F 192 Prince Edward Road W, Kowloon, Hong Kong, China
Chow, Amy Y Y — Gymnast
Lucille Packard Children's Hospital, Pediatrics Dept, Palo Alto CA 94304, USA
Chow, China — Actress, Model
Creative Artists Agency, 2000 Ave of Stars, #100, Los Angeles CA 90067 USA
Chow, Jeffrey — Fashion Designer
Jeffrey Chow Inc, 525 E 82nd St, New York NY 10028, USA
Chow, Kelsey — Actress
Coast to Coast Talent, 3350 Barham Blvd, Los Angeles CA 90068 USA
Chow, Raymond — Producer
Golden Harvest, 16/F Peninsula Office Tower, Tsim Sha Tsui, Kowloon, Hong Kong, China
Chow, Stephen — Actor, Director
Creative Artists Agency, 2000 Ave of Stars, #100, Los Angeles CA 90067 USA
Chowdhury, A Q M Badruddoza — President, Bangladesh
Residence Bari Dhara near Gulshan, Dhaka 1212, Bangladesh
Chrebet, Wayne — Football Player
147 Heulitt Road, Colts Neck NJ 07722, USA
Chretien, Jean J J — Prime Minister, Canada
541 Acacia Ave, Ottawa ON K1A 0A6, Canada
Chretien, Jean-Loup — Spatinaut, France; Air Force General
Astronautes Direction, 2 Place Maurice Quentin, 75029 Paris Cedex, France
Chriqui, Emmanuelle — Actress
Brookside Artist Mgmt, 250 W 57th St, #2303, New York NY 10107 USA
Chrisley, B O'Neil (Neil) — Baseball Player
280 Myrtle Green Dr, #8, Conway SC 29526, USA
Chrisman, Paul W (Woody Paul) — Singer, Fiddler (Riders in the Sky)
New Frontier Mgmt, 1921 Broadway, Nashville TN 37203, USA
Christakis, Nicholas A — Internist, Sociologist
Harvard University, Cambridge MA 02138 USA
Christensen, Calvin L (Cal) — Basketball Player
395 Canal Road, #419, Waterville OH 43566, USA
Christensen, Erika — Actress
Brillstein Entertainment Partners, 9150 Wilshire Blvd, #350, Beverly Hills CA 90212 USA
Christensen, Hayden — Actor
Forest Park Pictures, 11210 Briarcliff Lane, Studio City CA 91604, USA
Christensen, Helena — Model, Photographer
Panorama Agency, Ryesgade 103B, 2100 Copenhagen, Denmark
Christensen, Jesper — Actor
Conway Van Gelder Grant, 8-12 Broadwick St, #300, London W1F 8HW, England
Christensen, Kai — Architect
100 Vester Voldgade, 1552 Copenhagen V, Denmark
Christensen, Shawn — Singer, Guitarist (Stellarstarr*)
+1 Management/Public Relations, 242 Wythe Ave, #6, Brooklyn NY 11211, USA
Christensen, Todd J — Football Player, Sportscaster
991 Sunburst Lane, Alpine UT 84004, USA
Christensen, Tonja M — Model
Playboy Promotions, 2706 Media Center Dr, Los Angeles CA 90065 USA
Christenson, Ryan A — Baseball Player
100 Lismore Court, Tyrone GA 30290, USA
Christian, Claudia — Actress
Abrams Artists, 9200 W Sunset Blvd, #1125, West Hollywood CA 90069 USA
Christian, David W (Dave) — Ice Hockey Player
513 Queens Court, Moorhead MN 56560, USA
Christian, Gordon — Ice Hockey Player
604 Lake St NW, Warroad MN 56763, USA
Christian, Robert D (Bob) — Football Player
9450 Lincolnwood Dr, Evanston IL 60203, USA
Christian, Stephen T E — Singer (Anberlin)
Arson Media Group, 23 N Summerlin Ave, #200, Orlando FL 32801, USA
Christian, William (Bill) — Ice Hockey Player
502 Carrol St NW, Warroad MN 56763, USA
Christians, F Wilhelm — Financier
Konigsallee 51, 40212 Dusseldorf, Germany
Christiansen, Jason S — Baseball Player
3428 E Jasmine Circle, Mesa AZ 85213, USA
Christiansen, Keith R (Huffer) — Ice Hockey Player
1023 Timberline Lane, Duluth MN 55811, USA
Christianson, Claude V (Chris) — Army General
Director, National Defense University, Fort Lesley J McNair, Washington DC 20319, USA
Christie, Douglas D (Doug) — Basketball Player
13812 NE 40th St, Bellevue WA 98005, USA
Christie, G Stephen (Steve) — Football Player
PO Box 646, Buffalo NY 14231, USA
Christie, Gwendoline — Actress
United Agents, 12-26 Lexington St, London W1F 0LE, England
Christie, Julianne — Actress
252 N Larchmont Blvd, #200, Los Angeles CA 90004, USA
Christie, Julie — Actress, Model
Rene Missel Mgmt, 2376 Adrian St, #A, Newbury Park CA 91320, USA

Christie, Linford — Track Athlete
Nuff Respect, 107 Sherland Road, Twickenham, Middlesex TW9 4HB, England

Christie, Lou — Singer
Fox Entertainment, 1650 Broadway, #503, New York NY 10019, USA

Christie, Mike — Ice Hockey Player
6093 S Krameria St, Centennial CO 80111, USA

Christie, Perry G — Prime Minister, Bahamas
Prime Minister's Office, Rawson Square, PO Box N8301, Nassau NP, Bahamas

Christie, Tony — Singer
Amarillo Music, 31 Kensington Oval, Lichfield, Staffs WS13 6ND, England

Christie, Warren — Actor
I F A Talent Agency, 8730 W Sunset Blvd, #490, West Hollywood CA 90069 USA

Christie, William — Concert Harpsichordist
81 Ave Victor Hugo, 75116 Paris, France

Christin, Judith — Opera Singer
Columbia Artists Mgmt Inc, 1790 Broadway, #702, New York NY 10019 USA

Christine, Andrew (Andy) — Cartoonist (Man Called Horse)
King Features Syndicate, 300 W 57th St, #1500, New York NY 10019 USA

Christl, Lisy — Costume Designer
Claire Best Assoc, 736 Seward St, Los Angeles CA 90038, USA

Christlieb, Peter (Pete) — Jazz Saxophonist
J V C Music, 3800 Barham Blvd, #409, Los Angeles CA 90068, USA

Christman, Daniel W (Dan) — Army General, Educator
US Chamber of Commerce, 1615 H St NW, Washington DC 20062, USA

Christman, Kevin — Artist, Sculptor
714 S Pacific Highway, Talent OR 97540, USA

Christmas, G Ronald (Ron) — Marine Corps General
3809 Spicewood Springs Road, Stafford VA 22554, USA

Christo — Sculptor
48 Howard St, New York NY 10013, USA

Christoff, Steven (Steve) — Ice Hockey Player
542 Fairview Ave S, Saint Paul MN 55116, USA

Christon, Shameka D — Basketball Player
Chicago Sky, 20 W Kinzie St, #1010, Chicago IL 60654 USA

Christopher — Cartoonist (Ghouly Boys)
Colden McKuin Frankel, 141 El Camino Dr, #100, Beverly Hills CA 90212, USA

Christopher, Ann — Sculptor
Stable Block, Hay St, Marshfield near Chippenham SN14 8PF, England

Christopher, Dennis — Actor
B R & S, 5757 Wilshire Blvd, #473, Los Angeles CA 90036, USA

Christopher, Gretchen — Singer (Fleetwoods)
509 E Ridgecrest Blvd, #A, Ridgecrest CA 93555, USA

Christopher, Joseph O (Joe) — Baseball Player
PO Box 65240, Baltimore MD 21209, USA

Christopher, Tyler — Actor
Paradigm Agency, 360 N Crescent Dr, North Building, Beverly Hills CA 90210 USA

Christopher, William — Actor
Vox Inc, 6420 Wilshire Blvd, #1080, Los Angeles CA 90048 USA

Christopherson, James (Jim) — Football Player, Coach
526 Queens Court, Moorhead MN 56560, USA

Christy, James W — Astronomer
Hollinghead, 7285 Golden Eagle Dr, Flagstaff AZ 86004, USA

Christy, Jeffrey A (Jeff) — Football Player
138 Horseshoe Dr, Freeport PA 16229, USA

Chromy, Bronislaw — Sculptor
Ul Halki 5, 30 228 Cracow, Poland

Chryssa — Sculptor
565 Broadway, #5W, New York NY 10012, USA

Chu, Julie — Ice Hockey Player
USA Hockey, 1775 Bob Johnson Dr, Colorado Springs CO 80906 USA

Chu, Paul Ching-Wu — Physicist
University of Houston, Center for Superconductivity, Houston TX 77204, USA

Chu, Steven — Nobel Laureate; Secretary, Energy
Energy Department, 1000 Independence Ave SW, Washington DC 20585 USA

Chua, Amy L — Writer
Yale University, Law School, New Haven CT 06520, USA

Chua, Leon O — Electrical Engineer
University of California, Electrical Engineering Dept, Berkeley CA 94720, USA

Chuan Leekpai — Prime Minister, Thailand
Prachatipat, 67 Thanon Setsiri, Samsen Nai, Bangkok 10300, Thailand

Chubais, Anatoly B — Government Official, Russia
United Power Grids, Kitaigorodsky Proyezd 7, 103074 Moscow, Russia

Chuck D — Rap Artist (Public Enemy)
Richard Walters, PO Box 2789, Toluca Lake CA 91610 USA

Chuck, Wendy — Costume Designer
Paradigm Agency, 360 N Crescent Dr, North Building, Beverly Hills CA 90210 USA

Chudacoff, Katy — Interior Designer
Dovetail Design Works, 1005 Buckworth Ave, Franklin TN 37064, USA

Chukwurah, Patrick C — Football Player
6757 Camino Real, Irving TX 75039, USA

Chulack, Christopher — Producer, Director, Writer
Ken Gross Mgmt, 12135 Stanwood Drive, Los Angeles CA 90066, USA

Chulk, C Vincent (Vinnie) — Baseball Player
4607 Ballstonefield Lane, Katy TX 77494, USA

Chun Lee-Kyung — Speed Skater
Skating Union, 88 Bangyee-Dong, Songpaku, Seoul 138 749, South Korea

Chun, Tze — Writer
Gramercy Park Entertainment, 9701 Wilshire Blvd, #1000, Beverly Hills CA 90212, USA

Chung, Constance Y (Connie) — Commentator
Creative Artists Agency, 2000 Ave of Stars, #100, Los Angeles CA 90067 USA

Chung, Kyung-Wha — Concert Violinist
Harrison/Parrott, 5-6 Albion Court, London W6 0QT, England

Chung, Myung-Whun — Concert Pianist, Conductor
Askonas Holt, Lincoln House, 300 High Holborn, London WC1V 7JH, England

Chupack, Cindy — Writer, Producer
W M E Entertainment, 9601 Wilshire Blvd, #300, Beverly Hills CA 90210 USA

Church, Charlotte — Singer, Actress
Creative Artists Agency, 2000 Ave of Stars, #100, Los Angeles CA 90067 USA

Church, Eric — Singer, Songwriter
Q Prime South, 131 A 11th St, Nashville TN 37206, USA

Church, George — Molecular Geneticist
Harvard Medical School, Genetics Dept, 77 Ave Louis Pasteure, Boston MA 02115, USA

Church, Ryan M — Baseball Player
3500 Thurloe Dr, Rockledge FL 32955, USA

Church, Thomas Haden — Actor
Creative Artists Agency, 2000 Ave of Stars, #100, Los Angeles CA 90067 USA

Churchill, Caryl — Writer
Casorotto Ramsay, Waverley House, 7-12 Noel St, London W1F 8GQ, England

Churchill, Kim — Singer, Songwriter
Agency Group Ltd, 142 W 57th St, #600, New York NY 10019 USA

Churla, Shane — Ice Hockey Player
31826 Scotch Pine Lane, Bigfork MT 59911, USA

Chute, Robert M — Biologist, Writer
68 Schellinger Road, Poland ME 04274, USA

Chuy, Donald J (Don) — Football Player
11690 Oxnard St, North Hollywood CA 91606, USA

Chwast, Seymour — Artist, Illustrator
Push Pin Group, 38 W 26th St, #5A, New York NY 10010, USA

Chychrun, Jeff — Ice Hockey Player
6423 NW 32nd Way, Boca Raton FL 33496, USA

Chynoweth, Dean — Ice Hockey Player
131 Shawnee Rise SW, Calgary AB T2Y 2S3, Canada

Chyzowski, David B (Dave) — Ice Hockey Player
Kamloops Blazers, 300 Lorne St, Kamloops BC V2C 1W3, Canada

Cialini, Julie Lynn — Model, Actress
PO Box 55536, Valencia CA 91385, USA

Cianfrance, Derek — Director
Creative Artists Agency, 2000 Ave of Stars, #100, Los Angeles CA 90067 USA

Cianfrocco, Angelo D (Archi) — Baseball Player
12424 Addax Court, San Diego CA 92129, USA

Ciani, Suzanne — Composer
Musica International, 20 Sunnyside Ave, #A197, Mill Valley CA 94941, USA

Ciara — Singer, Songwriter
W M E Entertainment, 9601 Wilshire Blvd, #300, Beverly Hills CA 90210 USA

Ciaramello, Benjamin (Benny) — Actor
A P A Talent/Literary Agency, 405 S Beverly Dr, #300, Beverly Hills CA 90212 USA

Ciavaglia, Peter — Ice Hockey Player
1137 Carrie Court, Rochester Hills MI 48309, USA

Cibani, Tia — Fashion Designer
601 W 26th St, #875, New York NY 10001, USA

Cibrian, Eddie — Actor
I C M Partners, 10250 Constellation Blvd, #900, Los Angeles CA 90067 USA

Ciccarelli, Dino — Ice Hockey Player
37934 Lakeshore Dr, Harrison Township MI 48045, USA

Ciccolella, Jude — Actor
McKeon-Myrones Mgmt, 3500 Olive Ave, #770, Burbank CA 91505 USA

Ciccolini, Aldo — Concert Pianist
Gerhild Baron Mgmt, Dornbacher Str 41/III/3, 1170 Vienna, Austria

Ciccone, Enrico — Ice Hockey Player
Sports Prospects, 77 Rue de Bleury, Rosemere QC J7A 4L9, Canada

Cicerone, Ralph J — Environmental Scientist
University of California, Earth Science Dept, Rowland Hall, Irvine CA 92717, USA

Cichocki, Chris J — Ice Hockey Player
3955 Pine Lake Circle, Stockton CA 95219, USA

Cichy, Joseph J (Joe) — Football Player
1220 N Mandan St, Bismarck ND 58501, USA

Ciechanover, Aaron — Nobel Chemistry Laureate
Technion-Israel Institute, Box 9649, Bat Galim, Haifa 31096, Israel

Cienfuegos, Mauricio — Soccer Player
Los Angeles Galaxy, Home Depot Center, 18400 Avalon Blvd, Carson CA 90746 USA

Cierpinski, Waldemar — Track Athlete
Sport GmbH, Grosse Ulrichstr 60, 06108 Halle/Saale, Germany

Cigliuti, Natalia — Actress
Sager Mgmt, 260 S Beverly Dr, #205, Beverly Hills CA 90212, USA

Cimino, Michael — Director, Writer
9015 Alto Cedro, Beverly Hills CA 90210, USA

Cincotta, Anthony H — Biotechnologist
VeroScience, 1334 Main Road, Tiverton RI 02878, USA

Cincotti, Peter — Singer, Pianist, Songwriter
Vector Mgmt, 113 E 55th St, New York NY 10022, USA

Cink, Stewart — Golfer
2195 Lockett Court, Duluth GA 30097, USA

Cintron, Alexander (Alex) — Baseball Player
HC 2 Box 8575, Yabuccoa PR 00767, USA

Cintron, Kermit (Killer) — Boxer
DiBella Entertainment, 350 7th Ave, #800, New York NY 10001, USA

Cioffi, Charles — Actor
Paradigm Agency, 360 N Crescent Dr, North Building, Beverly Hills CA 90210 USA

Ciokey, Janna — Actress
J Michael Bloom, 9255 W Sunset Blvd, #710, West Hollywood CA 90069 USA

Ciorbea, Victor — Prime Minister, Romania
C D N P P, Bd Carol I34, 73231 Bucharest, Romania

Cipriani Thorne, Juan Luis Cardinal — Religious Leader
Arzobispado, Plaza de Armas S/N, Apartado 1512, Lima 100, Peru

Cirella, Joe — Ice Hockey Player
Teranet 600-1 Adelaide St E, Toronto ON M5C 2V9, Canada

Ciriani, Henri — Architect
61 Rue Pascal, 75013 Paris, France

Cirici, Cristian — Architect
Cirici Arquitecte, Carrer de Pujades 63 2-N, 08005 Barcelona, Spain

Cirillo, Jeffrey H (Jeff) — Baseball Player
604 Elmwood Lane, Celina OH 45822, USA

Cirio, Chuck — Composer, Director, Producer
B M I, 8730 W Sunset Blvd, #300, Los Angeles CA 90069 USA

Ciry, Michel — Artist
La Bergerie, 76119 Varengeville sur Mer, Seine-Maritime, France

Cisco, Galen B — Baseball Player
604 Elmwood Lane, Celina OH 45822, USA

Cisneros, Evelyn — Ballerina
San Francisco Ballet, 455 Franklin St, San Francisco CA 94102, USA

Cisneros, Henry G — Secretary, Housing & Urban Development
2002 W Houston St, San Antonio TX 78207, USA

Citerne, Philippe — Financier
Societe Generale, 29 Blvd Haussman, 75009 Paris, France

Citizen Cope — Singer, Songwriter
Agency Group Ltd, 142 W 57th St, #600, New York NY 10019 USA

Citro, Ralph — Boxing Historian
32 N Black Horse Pike, Blackwood NJ 08012, USA

Citron, Martin — Neurobiologist
Amgen Co, 152A 226 Amgen Center, Thousand Oaks CA 91320, USA

Citterio, Antonio — Architect, Interior Designer
Antonio Citterio Partners, Via Cerva 4, 20122 Milan, Italy

Citti, Christine — Actress
Artmedia, 20 Ave Rapp, 75007 Paris, France

Ciuha, Joze — Artist
Presernov 12, 61000 Ljubjana, Slovenia

Civiletti, Benjamin R — Attorney General
5900 Old Ocean Blvd, #B3, Boynton Beach FL 33435, USA

Cizik, Robert — Businessman
Cizik Interests, Chase Tower, 600 Travis St, #3628, Houston TX 77002, USA

Claassen, Yann — Actor
Artmedia, 20 Ave Rapp, 75007 Paris, France

Clackson, Kim — Ice Hockey Player
342 Thomas Road, Canonsburg PA 15317, USA

Claes, Willy — Government Official, Belgium
Berkenlaan 23, 3500 Hasselt, Belgium

Claflin, Bruce L — Businessman
Advanced Micro Devices, 1 A M D Plaza, Sunnyvale CA 94088, USA

Claflin, Sam — Actor
Creative Artists Agency, 2000 Ave of Stars, #100, Los Angeles CA 90067 USA

Claiborne, Chris — Football Player
Premier Sports Mgmt, 1000 N Green Valley Parkway, #440, Henderson NV 89074, USA

Claiborne, Morris L — Football Player
Dallas Cowboys, 1 Cowboys Parkway, Irving TX 75063 USA

Claire, Julie — Actress
I C M Partners, 10250 Constellation Blvd, #900, Los Angeles CA 90067 USA

Clamp, Shirley — Singer
Lionheart, PO Box 11108, Nytogstan 40A, 100 61 Stockholm, Sweden

Clampett, Robert D (Bobby), Jr — Golfer, Sportscaster
10600 Golf Link Dr, Raleigh NC 27617, USA

Clancy, Abigail R — Model
Money Mgmt, 42A Berwick St, London W1F 8RZ, England

Clancy, Aiofe — Singer
Producers Inc, 11806 N 56th St, Tampa FL 33617 USA

Clancy, Edward B Cardinal — Religious Leader
Sydney Archdiocese, Polding House, 276 Pitt St, Sydney NSW 2000, Australia

Clancy, James (Jim) — Baseball Player
177 Lance Dr, Twin Lakes WI 53181, USA

Clancy, Sam — Football Player
1308 Crest Lane, Oakdale PA 15071, USA

Clancy, Terry — Ice Hockey Player
65 Goldfale Road, Toronto ON M4N 2B5, Canada

Clancy, Thomas J (Tom) — Writer
2901 Boston St, #407, Baltimore MD 21224, USA

Clancy, William (Liam) — Singer (Clancy Brothers)
Charles Rothschild, 330 E 48th St, #2D, New York NY 10017 USA

Clanton, Jimmy — Singer
4425 Kingwood Dr, Kingwood TX 77339, USA

Clapp, Gordon — Actor
Cynthia Snyder Public Relations, 5739 Colfax Ave, North Hollywood CA 91601, USA

Clapp, Joss — Singer, Guitaist (Tarras)
Rounder Records, 1 Rounder Way, Burlington MA 01803 USA

Clapp, Nicholas R — Explorer (Ubar), Producer
PO Box 1019, Borrego Springs CA 92004, USA

Clapper, James R (Jim), Jr — Air Force General
National Intelligence Dept, 725 17th St NW, Washington DC 20523 USA

Clapton, Eric — Singer, Guitarist
Michael Eaton, 22 Blades Court, Deodar Road, London SW15 2NU, England

Clardy, Jon C — Chemist
Cornell University, Chemistry Dept, Ithaca NY 14853, USA

Clare, Jillian — Actress
Greene Assoc, 1901 Ave of Stars, #130, Los Angeles CA 90067 USA

Clarizio, Louis — Baseball Player
133 Lela Lane, Schaumburg IL 60193, USA

Clark, A Keon — Basketball Player
Phoenix Suns, 201 E Jefferson St, Phoenix AZ 85004 USA

Clark, Alan — Pianist (Dire Straits)
Damage Mgmt, 16 Lambton Place, London W11 2SH, England

Clark, Alan M (Allie) — Baseball Umpire
1185 SW 5th Ave, Boca Raotn FL 33432, USA

Clark, Anthony — Actor, Comedian
Innovative Artists, 1505 10th St, Santa Monica CA 90401 USA

Clark, Anthony C (Tony) — Baseball Player
14125 N 65th Ave, Glendale AZ 85306, USA

Clark, Archie L — Basketball Player
4268 10th St, Ecorse MI 48229, USA

Clark, Bob — Commentator
ABC-TV, News Dept, 5010 Creston St, Hyattsville MD 20781 USA

Cirio - Clark

Clark - Clark

Clark, Brady W
19275 Green Lakes Loop, Bend OR 97702, USA — Baseball Player

Clark, Brett
8745 Aberdeen Circle, Littleton CO 80130, USA — Ice Hockey Player

Clark, Brian M
811 Wonderland Forest Dr, Waxhaw NC 28173, USA — Football Player

Clark, Bryan D
508 E Clark St, Madera CA 93638, USA — Baseball Player

Clark, C Joseph (Joe)
Joe Clark Assoc, 237 4th Ave SW, #3000, Calgary AB T2P 4X7, Canada — Prime Minister, Canada

Clark, Candace J (Candy)
PO Box 3421, Memorial Station, Montclair NJ 07043, USA — Actress

Clark, Carol Higgins
524 E 72nd St, #28DE, New York NY 10021, USA — Writer

Clark, Chris
160 Pine Tree Lane, South Windsor CT 06074, USA — Ice Hockey Player

Clark, Colin W
9531 Finn Road, Richmond BC V7A 2L3, Canada — Mathematician

Clark, Dallas D
2995 Belle Maison Dr, Zionsville IN 46077, USA — Football Player

Clark, Daniel
Brightline Education, 3200 Port Royale Dr N, #906, Fort Lauderdale FL 33308, USA — Actor

Clark, Danny, IV
213 Seneca Trail, Bloomington IL 60108, USA — Football Player

Clark, David E (Dave)
4842 Mayfield Road W, Collierville TN 38017, USA — Baseball Player, Manager

Clark, Doran
Paul Kohner, 9300 Wilshire Blvd, #555, Beverly Hills CA 90212 USA — Actress

Clark, Dwight E
2511 Sedley Road, Charlotte NC 28211, USA — Football Player, Executive

Clark, Earl
Los Angeles Lakers, Staples Center, 1111 S Figueroa St, Los Angeles CA 90015 USA — Basketball Player

Clark, Elbernita (Twinkie)
Universal Attractions, 135 W 26th St, #1200, New York NY 10001 USA — Gospel Singer (Clark Sisters)

Clark, Gary C
PO Box 202, Dublin VA 24084, USA — Football Player

Clark, Gordie
985 Goose Pond Road, Shapleigh ME 4076, USA — Ice Hockey Player

Clark, Guy
Keith Case Assoc, 1025 17th Ave S, #200, Nashville TN 37212 USA — Singer, Songwriter

Clark, Hamish
Ken McReddie Assoc, 11 Connaught Place, London W2 2ET, England — Actor

Clark, Helen E
Labour Party, 160-62 Willis St, Wellington 6011, New Zealand — Prime Minister, New Zealand

Clark, Herbert H
Stanford University, Psychology Dept, Jordan Hall, Stanford CA 94305, USA — Pscycholinguist

Clark, Howard R (Howie)
14202 439th Ave SE, North Bend WA 98045, USA — Baseball Player

Clark, Jack A
6541 Scottsdale Way, Frisco TX 75034, USA — Baseball Player

Clark, James (Jim)
Neoteris, 940 Stewart Dr, Sunnyvale CA 94085, USA — Businessman

Clark, Jerald D
12325 Crisscross Lane, San Diego CA 92129, USA — Baseball Player

Clark, Jessie L
7611 S 9th Way, Phoenix AZ 85042, USA — Football Player

Clark, Jim
International Union of Electronic Workers, 401 3rd St NW, Washington DC 20001, USA — Labor Leader

Clark, Joe
1856 Clarence Dr, Hellertown PA 18055, USA — Educator

Clark, Kelly
PO Box 725, West Dover VT 05356, USA — Snowboarding Athlete

Clark, Kelvin
3812 Evesham Dr, Plano TX 75025, USA — Football Player

Clark, L Hill
Crane Co, 100 Stamford Place, #300, Stamford CT 06902, USA — Businessman

Clark, Larry
Untitled Entertainment, 350 S Beverly Dr, #200, Beverly Hills CA 90212 USA — Director

Clark, Louis S
6149 Kissengen Springs Court, Jacksonville FL 32258, USA — Football Player

Clark, Marcia R
A P A Talent/Literary Agency, 405 S Beverly Dr, #300, Beverly Hills CA 90212 USA — Attorney

Clark, Mario S
48100 Sandia Creek Dr, Temecula CA 92590, USA — Football Player

Clark, Martin
Knopf Publishers, 1745 Broadway, New York NY 10019 USA — Writer, Judge

Clark, Mary Ellen
117 Blue Hills Road, Amherst MA 01002, USA — Diver

Clark, Mary Higgins
15 Werimus Brook Road, Saddle River NJ 07458, USA — Writer

Clark, Mary Jane
Saint Martin's Press, 175 5th Ave, #400, New York NY 10010 USA — Writer

Clark, Matt
1199 Park Ave, #15D, New York NY 10128, USA — Actor

Clark, Melvin E (Mel)
18262 E Crescent, #520N, Kilbourne IL 62655, USA — Baseball Player

Clark, Michael, II
4007 Pintail Circle, Rocky Face GA 30740, USA — Golfer

Clark, Mystro
I C M Partners, 10250 Constellation Blvd, #900, Los Angeles CA 90067 USA — Actor

Clark, Oliver
House of Representatives, 1434 6th St, #1, Santa Monica CA 90401 USA — Actor

Clark, Perry
Miami University, Athletic Dept, Coral Gables FL 33124, USA — Basketball Coach

Clark, Peter B
7675 La Jolla Blvd, #203, La Jolla CA 92037, USA — Publisher

Clark, Petula — Singer, Actress
15 Chemin Rieu Coligny, 1208 Geneva, Switzerland
Clark, Philip E (Phil) — Football Player
208 George St, Barrington IL 60010, USA
Clark, Phillip B (Phil) — Baseball Player
PO Box 620612, Orlando FL 32862, USA
Clark, Ricardo — Soccer Player
Eintracht Frankfurt S C, Morfelder Landstr 362, 60528 Frankfurt, Germany
Clark, Richard C (Dick) — Senator, IA
4424 Edmunds St NW, #1070, Washington DC 20007, USA
Clark, Rickey C — Baseball Player
8953 Emerald Waters Court, Las Vegas NV 89147, USA
Clark, Robert A — Businessman
Munstead Wood, Godalming, Surrey GU7 1UN, England
Clark, Robert C — Artist
34 Monterey Court, Manhattan Beach CA 90266, USA
Clark, Robert C (Bobby) — Baseball Player
1030 Perrisito St, Perris CA 92570, USA
Clark, Ronald B (Ron) — Baseball Player
700 Starkey Road, #511, Largo FL 33771, USA
Clark, Roy — Singer, Guitarist
Ro-Bar, 3225 S Norwood Ave, #101, Tulsa OK 74135, USA
Clark, Ryan T — Football Player
1236 Camarta Dr, Pittsburgh PA 15227, USA
Clark, Sharon — Model, Actress
Playboy Promotions, 2706 Media Center Dr, Los Angeles CA 90065 USA
Clark, Spencer Trent — Actor
Untitled Entertainment, 350 S Beverly Dr, #200, Beverly Hills CA 90212 USA
Clark, Stephen E (Steve) — Swimmer
29 Martling Road, San Anselmo CA 94960, USA
Clark, Susan — Actress
13400 Riverside Dr, #308, Sherman Oaks CA 91423, USA
Clark, Terri — Singer, Songwriter
Spalding Entertainment, 54 Music Square E, #200, Nashville TN 37203, USA
Clark, Terry L — Baseball Player
1607 E Tam O'Shanter St, Ontario CA 91761, USA
Clark, Vernon E (Vern) — Navy Admiral
Raytheon Co, 870 Winter St, Waltham MA 02451, USA
Clark, Victoria — Actress, Singer
Untitled Entertainment, 350 S Beverly Dr, #200, Beverly Hills CA 90212 USA
Clark, W G — Architect
Clark & Menefee Architects, 4048 E Main St, Charlottesville VA 22902, USA
Clark, W Ramsey — Attorney General
37 W 12th St, #2B, New York NY 10011, USA
Clark, Wayne M — Football Player
14241 Lambeth Way, Tustin CA 92780, USA
Clark, Wendel L — Ice Hockey Player
Toronto Maple Leafs, AirCanada Center, 40 Bay St, Toronto ON M5J 2K2, Canada
Clark, Wesley Curley (W C) — Guitarist
Crossfire Productions, 304 Braeswood Road, Austin TX 78704, USA
Clark, Wesley K (Wes) — Army General
1 Crestmont Dr, Little Rock AR 72227, USA
Clark, William N (Will), Jr — Baseball Player
36170 Pleasant Hill Court, Prairieville LA 70769, USA
Clark, William P — Secretary, Interior
4424 Edmunds St NW, #1070, Washington DC 20007, USA
Clark-Chisholm, Jacky — Singer (Clark Sisters)
Universal Attractions, 135 W 26th St, #1200, New York NY 10001 USA
Clark-Cole, Dorinda — Singer (Clark Sisters)
Groove Entertainment, 1005 N Alfred St, #2, West Hollywood CA 90069, USA
Clarke, Allan — Singer, Musician (Hollies)
Hill Farm, Hackleton, Northamptonshire NN7 2DH, England
Clarke, Bob — Cartoonist
7480 Rivershore Dr, Seaford DE 19973, USA
Clarke, Brian — Artist
Tony Shafrazi Gallery, 544 W 26th St, #2, New York NY 10001, USA
Clarke, Brian Patrick — Actor
2102 Clubside Dr, Longwood FL 32779, USA
Clarke, Cam — Actor
Sutton-Barth Vennari, 145 S Fairfax Ave, #310, Los Angeles CA 90036 USA
Clarke, Darren C — Golfer
Darren Clarke Golf School, The Lodge, Greenmount Campus, Antrim BT41 4PU, England
Clarke, Emilia — Actress
Creative Artists Agency, 2000 Ave of Stars, #100, Los Angeles CA 90067 USA
Clarke, Emmy — Actress
Global Creative, 1051 N Cole Ave, #B, Los Angeles CA 90038, USA
Clarke, Frank D — Football Player
6016 Pine Ridge Blvd, McKinney TX 75070, USA
Clarke, Gary — Actor
1113 Heep Run, Buda TX 78610, USA
Clarke, Geoffrey — Artist, Sculptor
Stowe Hill, Hartest, Bury Saint Edmunds, Suffolk IP29 4EQ, England
Clarke, Gilby — Singer, Guitarist (Guns N' Roses)
Artists Worldwide, 3921 Wilshire Blvd, #619, Los Angeles CA 90010, USA
Clarke, Hagood, III — Football Player
2500 NE 37th Dr, Fort Lauderdale FL 33308, USA
Clarke, Horace M — Baseball Player
PO Box 891, Frederiksted VI 00841, USA
Clarke, Jacqueline (Jackie) — Actress
Paradigm Agency, 360 N Crescent Dr, North Building, Beverly Hills CA 90210 USA
Clarke, Jason — Actor, Producer
United Talent Agency, 9336 Civic Center Dr, Beverly Hills CA 90210 USA
Clarke, John — Actor
8350 Santa Monica Blvd, #206A, West Hollywood CA 90069, USA
Clarke, Judy — Attorney
Clarke & Rice, 1010 2nd Ave, #1800, San Diego CA 92101, USA

C

Clark - Clarke

Clarke, Justine — Actress
PO Box 125, Earlwood NSW 2206, Australia
Clarke, Kathy Kiera — Actress
Emptage Hallett, 14 Rathbone Place, London W1T 1HT, England
Clarke, Kenneth H — Government Official, England
House of Commons, Westminster, London SW1A 0AA, England
Clarke, Kenneth M (Ken) — Football Player
7610 Willoughby Court, Alpharetta GA 30005, USA
Clarke, Lenny — Actor
Paradigm Agency, 360 N Crescent Dr, North Building, Beverly Hills CA 90210 USA
Clarke, Martha — Dancer, Choreographer
Columbia Artists Mgmt Inc, 1790 Broadway, #702, New York NY 10019 USA
Clarke, Melinda — Actress
Innovative Artists, 1505 10th St, Santa Monica CA 90401 USA
Clarke, Noel A — Actor
Independent Talent Group, Oxford House, 76 Oxford St, London W1D 1BS, England
Clarke, Paul Charles — Singer
Welsh National Opera, Millennium Centre, Bute Place, Cardiff Bay, Cardiff CF10 5AL, Wales
Clarke, Richard A — Government Official
Simon & Schuster, 1230 Ave of Americas, Concourse 1, New York NY 10020 USA
Clarke, Robert E (Bobby) — Ice Hockey Player, Executive
420 Beechwood Ave, Haddonfield NJ 08033, USA
Clarke, Robert L — Government Official
Bracewell & Patterson, 711 Louisiana St, #2900, Houston TX 77002, USA
Clarke, Ronald (Ron) — Track Athlete
1 Bay St, Brighton VIC 3186, Australia
Clarke, Sarah — Actress
Levine Mgmt, 9028 W Sunset Blvd, #PH1, Los Angeles CA 90069, USA
Clarke, Stanley M — Jazz Bassist, Composer
4786 Topanga Canyon Blvd, Woodland Hills CA 91364, USA
Clarke, Stanley M (Stan) — Baseball Player
5533 Sanders Dr, Toledo OH 43615, USA
Clarke, Susanna — Writer
Curtis Brown Group, 28-29 Haymarket St, #500, London SW1Y 4SP, England
Clarke, Thomas E — Businessman
Nike Inc, 1 SW Bowerman Dr, Beaverton OR 97005, USA
Clark-Sheard, Karen — Singer (Clark Sisters)
Universal Attractions, 135 W 26th St, #1200, New York NY 10001 USA
Clarkson, Kelly — Singer
Creative Artists Agency, 2000 Ave of Stars, #100, Los Angeles CA 90067 USA
Clarkson, Patricia — Actress
Anonymous Content, 3532 Hayden Ave, Culver City CA 90232 USA
Claro, Manuel Alberto — Cinematographer
Sheldon Prosnit Agency, 800 S Robertson Blvd, #6, Los Angeles CA 90035, USA
Clary, Robert — Actor
10001 Sundial Lane, Beverly Hills CA 90210, USA
Clary, Tyler — Swimmer
Premier Management Group, 1100 Crescent Green, #104, Cary, NC 27518 USA
Clasby, Robert J (Bob) — Football Player
8180 E Shea Blvd, #1090, Scottsdale AZ 85260, USA
Clash, Kevin — Puppeteer
W M E Entertainment, 9601 Wilshire Blvd, #300, Beverly Hills CA 90210 USA
Clatterbuck, Tamara — Actress
House of Representatives, 1434 6th St, #1, Santa Monica CA 90401 USA
Clatworthy, Robert — Sculptor
Moelfre, Cynghordy, Landovery, Carmarthenshire SA20 OUW, Wales
Clauser, Francis H — Aeronautical Engineer, Educator
842 E Villa St, #161, Pasadena CA 91101, USA
Clauss, Jared — Football Player
215 S 82nd St, West Des Moines IA 50266, USA
Claver Arocas, Victor — Basketball Player
Portland Trail Blazers, Rose Garden, 1 N Center Court St, Portland OR 97227 USA
Clavier, Christian — Actor
Ouille, 7 Rue des Dames Agustines, 92200 Neuilly, France
Clawson, John R — Basketball Player
30 Eagle Lake Place, #31, San Ramon CA 94582, USA
Claxton, Craig (Speedy) — Basketball Player
11215 Fairhaven Dr, Riverside CA 92505, USA
Claxton, Paul — Golfer
PO Box 485, Claxton GA 30417, USA
Clay, Andrew — Actor, Comedian
Robert Bruce, 218 Richmond Road, Grey Lynn, Auckland 1021, New Zealand
Clay, Bryan E T — Track Athlete
Doyle Mgmt, 952 Chippendale Trail, Marietta GA 30064, USA
Clay, Eric L — Judge
US Court of Appeals, 231 W Lafayette Blvd, #564, Detroit MI 48226, USA
Clay, Kenneth E (Ken) — Baseball Player
4523 60th Street Court W, Bradenton FL 34210, USA
Clay, Otis — Singer
Universal Attractions, 135 W 26th St, #1200, New York NY 10001 USA
Clayborn, Raymond D (Ray) — Football Player
20610 Aspen Canyon Dr, Katy TX 77450, USA
Claycomb, Laura — Opera Singer
I M G Artists, Hogarth Business Park, Chiswick, London W4 2TH, England
Clayderman, Richard — Pianist
World Entertainment, 8815 County Windermeer Road, #407, Orlando FL 32835, USA
Clayman, Ralph V — Surgeon
Barnes Hospital, Surgery Dept, 416 S Kingshighway Blvd, Saint Louis MO 63110, USA
Claypool, James (Jim) — Ice Hockey Executive
302 Paine Farm Road, Duluth MN 55804, USA
Claypool, Leslie E (Les) — Singer, Bassist (Primus, Oysterhead)
Shore Fire Media, 32 Court St, #1600, Brooklyn NY 11201 USA
Claypool, Philip — Singer, Songwriter
B L T Mgmt, 2953 Sidco Dr, Nashville TN 37204, USA
Clayson, Jane — Commentator
CBS-TV, News Dept, 51 W 52nd St, New York NY 10019 USA

Clayton, Adam
Principle Mgmt, 30-32 Sir John Rogerson's Quay, Dublin 2, Ireland — Bassist (U-2)
Clayton, Beth
I M G Artists, Hogarth Business Park, Chiswick, London W4 2TH, England — Opera Singer
Clayton, Donald D
Clemson University, Physics/Astrophysics Dept, Clemson SC 29634, USA — Astrophysicist
Clayton, Harvey J
15303 SW 143rd St, Miami FL 33196, USA — Football Player
Clayton, Mark G
16426 Canyon Chase Dr, Houston TX 77095, USA — Football Player
Clayton, Mark J
9407 Manor Forge Way, Owings Mill MD 21117, USA — Football Player
Clayton, Michael R
10406 Oak Canopy Junction, Thonotosassa FL 33592, USA — Football Player
Clayton, Robert N
5201 S Cornell Ave, Chicago IL 60615, USA — Geochemist
Clayton, Royce S
6035 Murphy Way, Malibu CA 90265, USA — Baseball Player
Clayton, Willie
Universal Attractions, 135 W 26th St, #1200, New York NY 10001 USA — Singer, Songwriter
Clayton-Thomas, David
Live Tour Artists, 1451 White Oaks Blvd, Oakville ON L6H 4R9, Canada — Singer (Blood Sweat & Tears)
Claywell, Brett
Don Buchwald/Fortitude, 6500 Wilshire Blvd, #2200, Los Angeles CA 90048 USA — Actor
Cleamons, James M (Jim)
29 Sausalito Circle W, Manhattan Beach CA 90266, USA — Basketball Player, Coach
Clear, Mark A
15654 S Rene St, Olathe KS 66062, USA — Baseball Player
Clearwater, Keith A
4284 Stonecrossing, Provo UT 84604, USA — Golfer
Cleary, Beverly A
Harper Collins Publishers, 10 E 53rd St, Cellar 1, New York NY 10022 USA — Writer
Cleary, Jon
Madison House, 3565 19th St, Boulder CO 80304, USA — Pianist, Composer
Cleary, Robert B (Bob)
680 South Ave, #8, Weston MA 02493, USA — Ice Hockey Player
Cleary, Robert J
Proskauer Rose, 1585 Broadway, #2700, New York NY 10036, USA — Attorney
Cleary, William J (Bill), Jr
27 Kingswood Road, Auburndale MA 02466, USA — Ice Hockey Player, Coach
Cleave, Mary L
1901 E Belair Dr, Mount Vernon WA 98273, USA — Astronaut
Cleaver, Alan R
Byblos, Via Maggini 126, 60127 Ancona, Italy — Fashion Designer
Cleaves, Slaid
Keith Case Assoc, 1025 17th Ave S, #200, Nashville TN 37212 USA — Singer, Songwriter
Cleeland, Cameron S (Cam)
23160 Lanyard Lane, Mount Vernon WA 98274, USA — Football Player
Cleese, John
Anonymous Content, 3532 Hayden Ave, Culver City CA 90232 USA — Actor, Comedian, Writer
Clegg, Johnny
Monterey International, 200 W Superior St, #202, Chicago IL 60654 USA — Singer
Cleghorne, Ellen
Management 101, 468 N Camden Dr, #200, Beverly Hills CA 90210, USA — Actress, Comedienne
Cleland, J Maxwell (Max)
2460 Peachtree Road NW, #1406, Atlanta GA 30305, USA — Senator, GA
Clemens, Clarence (Big Man)
Vineberg Communications, 1695 Beach St, #303, San Francisco CA 94123, USA — Saxophonist (E Street Band)
Clemens, Donella
Mennonite Church, 722 N Main St, Newton KS 67114, USA — Religious Leader
Clemens, Douglas H (Doug)
4799 Lower Mountain Road, New Hope PA 18938, USA — Baseball Player
Clemens, J Barry
3111 Clinton Ave, Cleveland OH 44113, USA — Basketball Player
Clemens, W Roger
8572 Katy Freeway, #106, Houston TX 77024, USA — Baseball Player
Clemenson, Christian
Stone Manners Salners, 9911 W Pico Blvd, #1400, Los Angeles CA 90035 USA — Actor
Clement, Anthony
141 Navajo Lane, Opelousas LA 70570, USA — Football Player
Clement, Aurore
Artmedia, 20 Ave Rapp, 75007 Paris, France — Actress
Clement, Bill
6813 Upper York Road, New Hope PA 18938, USA — Ice Hockey Player
Clement, Edith Brown
US Court of Appeals, 600 Camp St, New Orleans LA 70130, USA — Judge
Clement, Jemaine
Creative Artists Agency, 2000 Ave of Stars, #100, Los Angeles CA 90067 USA — Singer (Flight of the Conchords), Actor
Clement, John
Tuddenham Hall, Tuddenham, Ipswich, Suffolk IP6 9DD, England — Businessman
Clement, Kerron
University of Florida, Athletic Dept, Gainesville FL 32611, USA — Track Athlete
Clement, Matthew P (Matt)
143 Milt Miller Road, Renfrew PA 16053, USA — Baseball Player
Clement, Paul D
Georgetown University, Law Center, Washington DC 20057, USA — Government Official, Attorney
Clemente, Carmine D
11737 Bellagio Road, Los Angeles CA 90049, USA — Anatomist
Clemente, Francesco
684 Broadway, New York NY 10012, USA — Artist
Clements, John A
University of California, Cardiovascular Institute, San Francisco CA 94143, USA — Physiologist
Clements, Kim
Creative Artists Agency, 2000 Ave of Stars, #100, Los Angeles CA 90067 USA — Writer
Clements, Lennie
PO Box 182197, Coronado CA 92178, USA — Golfer

Clements, Nathan D (Nate) — Football Player
Cincinnati Bengals, 1 Paul Brown Stadium, Cincinnati OH 45202 USA

Clements, Patrick B (Pat) — Baseball Player
166 Lazy S Lane, Chico CA 95928, USA

Clements, Ronald F (Ron) — Animator, Director
Creative Artists Agency, 2000 Ave of Stars, #100, Los Angeles CA 90067 USA

Clements, Suzanne — Fashion Designer
Clements Ribeiro Ltd, 48 S Molton St, London W1X 1HE, England

Clemmensen, Scott L — Ice Hockey Player
7 Woodbridge Court, Saratoga Springs NY 12886, USA

Clemons, Charlie F — Football Player
569 Inman Road, Fayetteville GA 30215, USA

Clemons, Craig L — Football Player
1517 D Ave NE, Cedar Rapids IA 52402, USA

Clemons, Duane — Football Player
7512 Dr Phillips Blvd, #50-908, Orlando FL 32819, USA

Clendenin, Robert T (Bob) — Actor
Stone Manners Salners, 9911 W Pico Blvd, #1400, Los Angeles CA 90035 USA

Clennon, David — Actor
Greene Assoc, 1901 Ave of Stars, #130, Los Angeles CA 90067 USA

Cleobury, Nicholas R — Conductor
Ben Rayfield, Southbank House, Black Prince Road, London SE1 7SJ, England

Cleobury, Stephen J — Conductor, Organist
King's College, Music Dept, Cambridge CB2 1ST, England

Clergue, Lucien — Photographer
Galerie Patrice Trigano, 229 C 4bis, Rue des Beaux-Arts, 75006 Paris, France

Clermont, Herve — Actor
Commercial Talent, 9255 Sunset Blvd, #505, Los Angeles CA 90069, USA

Clervoy, Jean-Francois — Spatinaut, France
European Space Center, Linder Hohe, Box 906096, 51127 Cologne, Germany

Clery, Corinne — Actress
C D A Studio di Nardo, 12 Cavour 171, 00184 Rome, Italy

Cleve, George W — Conductor
Columbia Artists Mgmt Inc, 1790 Broadway, #702, New York NY 10019 USA

Cleveland, Ashley — Singer, Songwriter
Street Level Artists, 107 E Center St, Warsaw IN 46580, USA

Cleveland, Charles G (Chick) — Air Force General, Hero
3603 Thomas Ave, Montgomery AL 36111, USA

Cleveland, Davis — Actor
Coast to Coast Talent, 3350 Barham Blvd, Los Angeles CA 90068 USA

Cleveland, Pat — Model
Ford Models Inc, 111 5th Ave, #900, New York NY 10003 USA

Cleveland, Patience — Actress
PO Box 490, Richland MO 65556, USA

Cleveland, Reginald L (Reggie) — Baseball Player
202 Creekview Dr, Anna TX 75409, USA

Cleven, Harry — Actor
U B B A, 6 Rue de Braque, 75003 Paris, France

Clevenger, Raymond C, III — Judge
US Court of Appeals, 717 Madison Place NW, Washington DC 20439, USA

Clevenger, Truman E (Tex) — Baseball Player
31727 Country Club Dr, Porterville CA 93257, USA

Clevlen, Brent A — Baseball Player
2405 La Rochelle Dr, Cedar Park TX 78613, USA

Clexton, Edward W, Jr — Navy Admiral
1000 Bobolink Dr, Virginia Beach VA 23451, USA

Cliburn, Van — Concert Pianist
Van Cliburn Foundation, 2525 Ridgmar Blvd, #307, Fort Worth TX 76116, USA

Cliff, Jimmy — Singer, Songwriter
51 Lady Musgrave Road, Kingston 10, Jamaica

Clifford, Keith — Actor
Jonathan Altaras Assoc, 11 Garrick St, London WC2E 9AR, England

Clifford, Linda — Singer
T-Best Talent Agency, 508 Honey Lake Court, Danville CA 94506 USA

Clifford, M Richard (Rich) — Astronaut
N A S A, Johnson Space Center, 2101 NASA Road, Houston TX 77058 USA

Clift, William B, III — Photographer
PO Box 6035, Santa Fe NM 87502, USA

Clifton, J Chad — Football Player
1641 Whispering Hills Dr, Franklin TN 37069, USA

Clifton, James — Actor
500 W 43rd St, #26J, New York NY 10036, USA

Clifton, Kyle — Football Player
777 South Point Court, Aledo TX 76008, USA

Clifton, Scott — Actor
Innovative Artists, 1505 10th St, Santa Monica CA 90401 USA

Clifton, Shaw — Religious Leader
Salvation Army International, 101 Queen Victoria St, London EC4 4EP, England

Clijsters, Kim A L — Tennis Player
Omselweg 37, 3960 Bree, Belgium

Cline, Richard — Cartoonist
New Yorker, Editorial Dept, 4 Times Square, Basement C1B, New York NY 10036 USA

Cline, Tyrone A (Ty) — Baseball Player
37 Wappoo Creek Place, Charleston SC 29412, USA

Clines, Eugene A (Gene) — Baseball Player
5303 9th Ave Dr W, Bradenton FL 34209, USA

Clinger, Debra — Actress
1206 Chickasaw Dr, Brentwood TN 37027, USA

Clinkscale, F Dextor — Football Player
206 Michaux Dr, Greenville SC 29605, USA

Clinton, George — Singer, Synthesizer Player, Songwriter
Agency Group, 9348 Civic Center Dr, #200, Beverly Hills CA 90210 USA

Clinton, George S — Composer
First Artists Mgmt, 4764 Park Granada, #210, Calabasas CA 91302 USA

Clinton, Hillary Rodham — Secretary, State; Senator, NY
State Department, 2201 C St NW, Washington DC 20520 USA

Clinton, Kate — Comedienne
I C M Partners, 10250 Constellation Blvd, #900, Los Angeles CA 90067 USA
Clinton, William J (Bill) — President, USA
15 Old House Lane, Chappaqua NY 10514, USA
Clippard, Tyler L — Baseball Player
13575 58th St N, #199, Clearwater FL 33760, USA
Clivilles, Robert M — Music Producer (C & C Music Factory)
Brothers Mgmt, 141 Dunbar Ave, Fords NJ 08863 USA
Clodagh — Interior Designer
Clodagh Design International, 670 Broadway, #400, New York NY 10012, USA
Cloepfil, Brad — Architect
4505 SW Bernard Dr, Portland OR 97239, USA
Clohessy, Robert — Actor
Don Buchwald/Fortitude, 6500 Wilshire Blvd, #2200, Los Angeles CA 90048 USA
Cloke, Kristen — Actress
Mitchell K Stubbs Assoc, 8695 W Washington Blvd, #204, Culver City CA 90232 USA
Cloninger, Tony L — Baseball Player
PO Box 1500, Denver NC 28037, USA
Clontz, J Bradley (Brad) — Baseball Player
General Delivery, Alpharetta GA 30009, USA
Clooney, George — Actor, Director, Writer
Stan Rosenfield Assoc, 2029 Century Park E, #1190, Los Angeles CA 90067 USA
Close, Charles T (Chuck) — Artist
20 Bond St, New York NY 10012, USA
Close, Eric — Actor
Untitled Entertainment, 350 S Beverly Dr, #200, Beverly Hills CA 90212 USA
Close, Glenn — Actress
Trillium Productions, PO Box 1560, #200, New Canaan CT 06840, USA
Close, Joshua — Actor
Gary Goddard Agency, 10 Sainte Mary St, #305, Toronto ON M4Y 1P9, Canada
Closs, William T (Bill) — Basketball Player
555 Byron St, #409, Palo Alto CA 94301, USA
Closton, Cory — Ice Hockey Coach
Ottawa Senators, Scotia Bank Place, Kanata ON K2V 1A5, Canada
Clotet, Lluis — Architect
Studio P E R, Caspe 151, 08013 Barcelona, Spain
Clottey, Joshua — Boxer
Top Rank Inc, 3908 Howard Hughes Parkway, #580, Las Vegas NV 89169 USA
Clotworthy, Robert — Actor
Amsel Eisenstadt Frazier, 5055 Wilshire Blvd, #865, Los Angeles CA 90036 USA
Clotworthy, Robert L (Bob) — Diver, Coach
2301 Moss Rose Lane, Fort Collins CO 80526, USA
Cloud, Michael A (Mike) — Football Player
5126 Miller Ave, Dallas TX 75206, USA
Clough, G Wayne — Educator, Administrator
Smithsonian Institution, 100 Jefferson Dr SW, Washington DC 20560, USA
Clough, Ray W, Jr — Structural Engineer
19800 SW Touchmark Way, #280, Bend OR 97702, USA
Cloutier, Jacques — Ice Hockey Player
12172 Triple Crown Dr, Parker CO 80134, USA
Clowes, Daniel — Cartoonist (Ghost World), Writer
United Talent Agency, 9336 Civic Center Dr, Beverly Hills CA 90210 USA
Clunes, Martin — Actor
Independent Talent Group, Oxford House, 76 Oxford St, London W1D 1BS, England
Clunie, Michelle — Actress
Abrams Artists, 9200 W Sunset Blvd, #1125, West Hollywood CA 90069 USA
Cluzet, Francois — Actor
Voyez Mon Agent, 20 Ave Rapp, 75007 Paris, France
Clyde, David E (Dave) — Baseball Player
7806 Pinehurst Shadows Dr, Humble TX 77346, USA
Clymer, Ben — Ice Hockey Player
2713 Plaza Verde, Lake Havasu City AZ 86406, USA
Clyne, Patricia — Fashion Designer
353 W 39th St, New York NY 10018, USA
Coachman Davis, Alice — Track Athlete
1317 Lee St, Albany GA 31701, USA
Coakley, W Dexter — Football Player
1304 Sunset Ridge Circle, Cedar Hill TX 75104, USA
Coan, E Bert, III — Football Player
14517 N US Highway 59, Nacogdoches TX 75965, USA
Coan, Gilbert F (Gil) — Baseball Player
70 Beach Lane, Brevard NC 28712, USA
Coase, Ronald H — Nobel Economics Laureate
University of Chicago, Law School, 1111 E 60th St, #1, Chicago IL 60637, USA
Coates, Anne V — Film Editor, Producer
United Talent Agency, 9336 Civic Center Dr, Beverly Hills CA 90210 USA
Coates, Ben T — Football Player, Coach
1740 Deer Creek Dr, #1, Xenia OH 45385, USA
Coates, James A (Jim) — Baseball Player
1098 Oak Hill Road, Lancaster VA 22503, USA
Coates, Kim — Actor
Oscars Abrams Zimel, 438 Queen St E, Toronto ON M5A 1T4, Canada
Coates, Phyllis — Actress
PO Box 1969, Boyes Hot Springs CA 95416, USA
Coates, Steve J — Ice Hockey Player, Sportscaster
102 Stoney Creek Dr, Egg Harbor Township NJ 08234, USA
Coats, Kristi — Golfer
185 Wildwood Place, Petal MS 39465, USA
Coats, Michael L — Astronaut
3203 Acorn Wood Way, Houston TX 77059, USA
Cobb, Garry W — Football Player
112 Society Hill Blvd, Cherry Hill NJ 08003, USA
Cobb, Geraldyn M (Jerrie) — Astronaut Candidate
1006 Beach Blvd, Sun City Center FL 33573, USA
Cobb, Henry N — Architect
Pei Cobb Freed Partners, 88 Pine St, Lobby 1, New York NY 10005, USA

Cobb, Jewel Plummer — Biologist
California State University, PO Box 3480, Fullerton CA 92834, USA
Cobb, John B, Jr — Social Activist
Claremont Graduate School, Center for Process Studies, Claremont CA 91711, USA
Cobb, Julie — Actress
C E S D, 10635 Santa Monica Blvd, #130, Los Angeles CA 90025 USA
Cobb, Keith Hamilton — Actor
Gage Group, 315 W 57th St, #4H, New York NY 10019 USA
Cobb, Marvin L — Football Player
655 S Flower St, #290, Los Angeles CA 90017, USA
Cobb, Reginald J (Reggie) — Football Player
PO Box 17416, Sugar Land TX 77496, USA
Cobbin, W Jim (James) — Baseball Player
121 E Rayen Ave, Youngstown OH 44503, USA
Cobbs, Bill — Actor
Stone Manners Salners, 9911 W Pico Blvd, #1400, Los Angeles CA 90035 USA
Coben, Harlan — Writer
E P Dutton, 375 Hudson St, New York NY 10014 USA
Cobert, Bob — Composer
B M I, 8730 W Sunset Blvd, #300, Los Angeles CA 90069 USA
Cobham, William C (Billy) — Jazz Drummer, Composer
Joel Chriss, 60 E 8th St, #34N, New York NY 10003 USA
Coble, G Drew — Baseball Umpire
205 80th Ave N, Myrtle Beach SC 29572, USA
Coblenz, Walter — Director, Producer
4310 Cahuenga Blvd, #401, Toluca Lake CA 91602, USA
Cobos, Alberto — Paleontologist
Teruel-Dinopolis Museum, Poligono de los Planos, 44002 Teruel, Spain
Cobos, Jesus Lopez — Conductor
Cincinnati Symphony, 1241 Elm St, Cincinnati OH 45202, USA
Coburn, Braydon — Ice Hockey Player
523 Chews Landing Road, Haddonfield NJ 8033, USA
Coburn, Doris — Bowler
130 Dalton Dr, Buffalo NY 14223, USA
Coburn, John G — Army General
7717 Island Creek Court, Alexandria VA 22315, USA
Coccopalmerio, Francesco Cardinal — Religious Leader
Pontifical Council for Legislative Texts, 00120 Vatican City
Cochinescu, Ioan Mihai — Photographer, Writer
CP 1-151, 2000 Ploiesti 1, Prahova, Romania
Cochran, Antonio D — Football Player
8433 Manchester Highway, Woodland GA 31836, USA
Cochran, Barbara Ann — Skier
Cochran's Ski Area, PO Box 789, Richmond VT 05477, USA
Cochran, John — Commentator
ABC-TV, News Dept, 5010 Creston St, Hyattsville MD 20781 USA
Cochran, Robert — Writer, Producer
A P A Talent/Literary Agency, 405 S Beverly Dr, #300, Beverly Hills CA 90212 USA
Cochran, Russ — Golfer
3 Circle Lake Dr, Paducah KY 42001, USA
Cochran, Shannon — Actress
Mitchell K Stubbs Assoc, 8695 W Washington Blvd, #204, Culver City CA 90232 USA
Cochran, Stacy — Director
I C M Partners, 10250 Constellation Blvd, #900, Los Angeles CA 90067 USA
Cochran, Tammy — Singer, Songwriter
Consortium, 49 Music Square W, #210, Nashville TN 37203, USA
Cochrane, David C (Dave) — Baseball Player
126 Silver Eagle Lane, Mooresville NC 28117, USA
Cochrane, Glen M — Ice Hockey Player
405 Collett Road, Kelowna BC V1W 1K6, Canada
Cochrane, Rory — Actor
Untitled Entertainment, 350 S Beverly Dr, #200, Beverly Hills CA 90212 USA
Cockburn, Bruce — Singer, Songwriter, Guitarist
Finkelstein Mgmt, 137 Berkeley St, Toronto ON M5V 1X2, Canada
Cocker, Jarvis — Singer (Pulp), Songwriter
Rough Trade Mgmt, 66 Golborne Road, London W10 5PS, England
Cocker, Joe — Singer
Mad Dog Ranch, 43401 Cottonwood Creek Road, Crawford CO 81415, USA
Cockerill, Franklin — Microbiologist
Mayo Clinic, Microbiology Dept, 200 1st St SW, Rochester MN 55905, USA
Cockerill, Kay — Golfer
131 Beulah St, San Francisco CA 94117, USA
Cockey, Tim — Writer
Hyperion Books, 114 5th Ave, New York NY 10011 USA
Cockrell, Kenneth D — Astronaut
2300 Richmond Ave, #350, Houston TX 77098, USA
Cockroft, Donald L (Don) — Football Player
2418 Dunkeith Dr NW, Canton OH 44708, USA
Coco, Lea — Actor, Writer
Gersh Agency, 9465 Wilshire Blvd, #600, Beverly Hills CA 90212 USA
Cocroft, Sherman — Football Player
2504 Christopher Lane, Costa Mesa CA 92626, USA
Codiroli, Christopher A (Chris) — Baseball Player
2700 Hillcrest Dr, Cameron Park CA 95682, USA
Codrescu, Andrei — Writer
Louisiana State University, English Dept, Baton Rouge LA 70803, USA
Coduri, Camille — Actress
Independent Talent Group, Oxford House, 76 Oxford St, London W1D 1BS, England
Cody, Diablo — Producer, Writer
W M E Entertainment, 9601 Wilshire Blvd, #300, Beverly Hills CA 90210 USA
Cody, William E (Bill) — Football Player
209 Orleans Dr, Fairhope AL 36532, USA
Coe of Ranmore, Sebastian N — Track Athlete
Starswood, High Barn Road, Effingham, Surrey KT24 5PW, England
Coe, David Allan — Singer, Guitarist, Songwriter
783 Rippling Creek, Nixa MO 65714, USA

Coe, George — Actor
Abrams Artists, 9200 W Sunset Blvd, #1125, West Hollywood CA 90069 USA
Coe, Sue — Artist
Galerie Saint Etienne, 24 W 57th St, New York NY 10019, USA
Coe-Jones, Dawn — Golfer
2945 SW 39th Ave, Gainesville FL 32608, USA
Coelho, Paulo — Writer
Caixa Postal 43003, Rio de Janiero 22052-970, Brazil
Coelho, Susie — Actress
1347 Rossmoyne Ave, Glendale CA 91207, USA
Coen, Ethan — Director, Writer
United Talent Agency, 9336 Civic Center Dr, Beverly Hills CA 90210 USA
Coen, Joel — Director, Writer
United Talent Agency, 9336 Civic Center Dr, Beverly Hills CA 90210 USA
Coetzee, Gergardus C (Gerrie) — Boxer
22 Sydney Road, Ravenswood, Boksburg 1460, South Africa
Coetzee, John M — Nobel Literature Laureate
PO Box 92, Rondebosch, Cape Province 7700, South Africa
Coetzer, Amanda — Tennis Player
PO Box 686, Florida Hills 1716, South Africa
Coeur De Pirate — Singer, Songwriter
Agency Group Ltd, 142 W 57th St, #600, New York NY 10019 USA
Cofer, J Michael (Mike) — Football Player, Truck Racing Driver
Racing West, 1772 Los Arboles, #J186, Thousand Oaks CA 91362, USA
Cofer, Michael L (Mike) — Football Player
110 Bridgestone Cove, Fayetteville GA 30215, USA
Coffey, J Todd — Baseball Player
109 Colonel Hampton Court, Rutherfordton NC 28139, USA
Coffey, Jeffrey (King) — Drummer (Butthole Surfers)
Kork Agency, 1880 Century Park E, #711, Los Angeles CA 90067, USA
Coffey, John L — Judge
US Court of Appeals, US Courthouse, 517 E Wisconsin Ave, Milwaukee WI 53202, USA
Coffey, Junior L — Football Player
17228 32nd Ave S, #E12, Seatac WA 98188, USA
Coffey, Kellie — Singer, Songwriter
W M E Entertainment, 1600 Division St, #300, Nashville TN 37203 USA
Coffey, Paul D — Ice Hockey Player
Bolton Toyota, 12050 Albion Vaughan Road, Bolton ON L7E 1S7, Canada
Coffin, Edmund (Tad) — Equestrian
1151 Dairy Road, Ruckersville VA 22968, USA
Coffin, Fredrick — Actor
Gage Group, 14724 Ventura Blvd, #505, Sherman Oaks CA 91403 USA
Coffman, Paul R — Football Player
14103 E 195th St, Peculiar MO 64078, USA
Cogan, Kevin — Auto Racing Driver
205 Rocky Point Road, Palos Verdes Estates CA 90274, USA
Cogdill, Gail R — Football Player
12922 E 36th Ave, Spokane Valley WA 99206, USA
Coggins, Richard A (Rich) — Baseball Player
4095 Fruit St, #219, La Verne CA 91750, USA
Coghill, Jonathan R (Jon) — Drummer (Powderfinger)
Secret Service, PO Box 401, Fortitude Valley QLD 4006, Australia
Coghlan, Eamon — Track Athlete
International Mgmt Group, 1 Erieview Plaza, 1360 E 9th St, Cleveland OH 44114 USA
Cogollo, Heriberto — Artist
54 Rue Faubourg du Courreau, 34000 Montpelier (Herault), France
Cohan, Lauren — Actress
A P A Talent/Literary Agency, 405 S Beverly Dr, #300, Beverly Hills CA 90212 USA
Cohan, Robert P — Choreographer
The Place, 17 Dukes Road, London WC1H 9AB, England
Coheleach, Guy J — Artist
Pandion Art, PO Box 96, Bernardsville NJ 07924, USA
Cohen, Adam — Singer, Guitarist, Songwriter
Gorfaine/Schwartz, 4111 W Alameda Ave, #509, Burbank CA 91505 USA
Cohen, Alexandra P (Sasha) — Figure Skater
International Mgmt Group, 1 Erieview Plaza, 1360 E 9th St, Cleveland OH 44114 USA
Cohen, Arnaldo — Concert Pianist
Arts Management Group, 1133 Broadway, #1025, New York NY 10010, USA
Cohen, Avishai — Jazz Bassist
Ron Moss Mgmt, 2635 Griffith Park Blvd, Los Angeles CA 90039, USA
Cohen, Bernard W — Artist
80 Camberwell Grove, London SE5 8RF, England
Cohen, Bruce — Producer
Bruce Cohen Productions, 4000 Warner Blvd, Building 138, Burbank CA 91522, USA
Cohen, David — Keyboardist (Country Joe & the Fish)
I C M Partners, 10250 Constellation Blvd, #900, Los Angeles CA 90067 USA
Cohen, David X — Producer, Writer
Creative Artists Agency, 2000 Ave of Stars, #100, Los Angeles CA 90067 USA
Cohen, Etan — Producer, Writer
Creative Artists Agency, 2000 Ave of Stars, #100, Los Angeles CA 90067 USA
Cohen, Jerome A — Attorney, Educator
New York University, Law School, 40 Washington Square, New York NY 10012, USA
Cohen, Joshua — Philosopher
Stanford University, Philosophy Dept, Stanford CA 94305, USA
Cohen, Larry — Labor Leader
Communications Workers of America, 501 3rd St NW, #C1, Washington DC 20001, USA
Cohen, Larry — Director, Writer
2111 Coldwater Canyon Dr, Beverly Hills CA 90210, USA
Cohen, Leonard N — Writer, Singer, Songwriter
R K Mgmt, 9300 Wilshire Blvd, #200, Beverly Hills CA 90212, USA
Cohen, Lynn — Actress
Paradigm Agency, 360 Park Ave S, #1600, New York NY 10010 USA
Cohen, Marshall H — Astronomer
California Institute of Technology, Astronomy Dept, Pasadena CA 91125, USA
Cohen, Marvin — Pharmacologist
Triumph Pharmaceuticals, 10403 Baur Blvd, #A, Saint Louis MO 63132, USA

Cohen, Marvin L — Physicist
10 Forest Lane, Berkeley CA 94708, USA

Cohen, Matt — Actor
Stone Manners Salners, 9911 W Pico Blvd, #1400, Los Angeles CA 90035 USA

Cohen, Peter M — Director, Producer, Writer
United Talent Agency, 9336 Civic Center Dr, Beverly Hills CA 90210 USA

Cohen, Rachel Leah — Actress
Avalon Artists Group, 143 W 29th St, #1103, New York NY 10001, USA

Cohen, Rob — Director
Nowita Pictures, 2900 Olympic Blvd, #345, Santa Monica CA 90404, USA

Cohen, Robert — Concert Cellist
15 Birchwood Ave, London N10 3BE, England

Cohen, Sacha Baron — Actor, Comedian
W M E Entertainment, 9601 Wilshire Blvd, #300, Beverly Hills CA 90210 USA

Cohen, Sarah — Journalist
Washington Post, Editorial Dept, 1150 15th St NW, Washington DC 20071 USA

Cohen, Scott — Actor
One Entertainment, 12 W 57th St, #PH 1, New York NY 10019 USA

Cohen, Sheldon S — Government Official
5518 Trent St, Chevy Chase MD 20815, USA

Cohen, Stanley — Nobel Medicine Laureate
4308 Lone Oak Road, Nashville TN 37215, USA

Cohen, Stanley N — Geneticist, Inventor
Stanford University Medical Center, Genetics Dept, Stanford CA 94305, USA

Cohen, William S — Secretary, Defense; Senator, ME
Cohen Group, 600 13th St NW, #640, Washington DC 20005, USA

Cohen-Tannoudji, Claude K — Nobel Physics Laureate
38 Rue des Cordelieres, 75013 Paris, France

Cohn, Alfred (Al) — Bowler
85 Odyssey Dr, Tinley Park IL 60477, USA

Cohn, Gary — Journalist
Baltimore Sun, Editorial Dept, 501 N Calvert St, Baltimore MD 21278, USA

Cohn, Gary — Financier
Goldman Sachs Co, 85 Broad St, Building 85, New York NY 10004, USA

Cohn, Marc — Singer, Songwriter
Michael Hausman Mgmt, 511 Ave of Americas, #197, New York NY 10011, USA

Cohn, Mindy — Actress
Arthouse Entertainment, 9350 Wilshire Blvd, #328, Beverly Hills CA 90212, USA

Coia, Angelo A — Football Player
11 McDermott Place, Brigantine NJ 08203, USA

Coia, Arthur A — Labor Leader
Laborers' International Union, 905 16th St NW, #600, Washington DC 20006, USA

Coifman, Ronald R — Computer Scientist
11 Hickory Road, North Haven CT 06473, USA

Cojocaru, Steven — Entertainer
Ballatine Books, 1745 Broadway, New York NY 10019 USA

Coker, Larry E — Football Coach, Sportscaster
University of Texas, Athletic Dept, San Antonio TX 78249, USA

Cokes, Curtis — Boxer
618 Calcutta Dr, Dallas TX 75241, USA

Colander-Richardson, LaTasha — Track Athlete
26 E Myrtle Dr, Angier NC 27501, USA

Colangelo, Jerry J — Basketball, Baseball Executive
70 E Country Club Dr, Phoenix AZ 85014, USA

Colantoni, Enrico — Actor
Innovative Artists, 1505 10th St, Santa Monica CA 90401 USA

Colao, Vittorio — Businessman
Vodaphone Group, Connection, Newbury, Berkshire RG14 2FN, England

Colbert, Jim — Golfer
118 Wanish Place, Palm Desert CA 92260, USA

Colbert, Nathan (Nate) — Baseball Player
2756 N Green Valley Parkway, Henderson NV 89014, USA

Colbert, Stephen — Actor, Comedian, Writer
Dixon Talent Agency, 375 Greenwich St, #500, New York NY 10013, USA

Colborn, James W (Jim) — Baseball Player
2932 Solimar Beach Dr, Ventura CA 93001, USA

Colbrunn, Gregory J (Greg) — Baseball Player
1544 Wellesley Circle, Mount Pleasant SC 29466, USA

Colburn, Richard — Drummer (Belle & Sebastian)
Ground Control Touring, 20 Jay St, #826, Brooklyn NY 11201 USA

Colchico, Daniel M (Dan) — Football Player
5160 Paul Scarlet Dr, Concord CA 94521, USA

Colclough, Henry — Singer
3040 Fontain St, Philadelphia PA 19121, USA

Cold 187um — Rap Artist (Above the Law)
Green Light Talent Agency, PO Box 3172, Beverly Hills CA 90212 USA

Cole, Alexander (Alex) — Baseball Player
6545 N Stevens Hollow Dr, Chesterfield VA 23832, USA

Cole, Anne — Fashion Designer
Cole of California, 6040 Bandini Blvd, Los Angeles CA 90040, USA

Cole, Artemas — Cartoonist
15 Regency Manor, #15-8, Rutland VT 05701, USA

Cole, Ashley — Soccer Player
Arsenal London, Avenell Road, Highbury, London N5 1BU, England

Cole, Bobby — Golfer
204 W 2nd Ave, Windermere FL 34786, USA

Cole, Bradley — Actor
Leading Artists, 145 W 45th St, #1000, New York NY 10036 10036, USA

Cole, Cheryl A (Tweedy) — Singer (Girls Aloud)
Concorde International, 101 Shepherds Bush Road, London W6 7LP, England

Cole, Christina — Actress
Conway Van Gelder Grant, 8-12 Broadwick St, #300, London W1F 8HW, England

Cole, Danton — Ice Hockey Player
7180 Wapiti Way, Saline MI 48176, USA

Cole, David D — Attorney
Georgetown University, Law School, Washington DC 20057, USA

Cole, Erik
1112 Stonekirk, Raleigh NC 27614, USA — Ice Hockey Player
Cole, Freddy
Producers Inc, 11806 N 56th St, Tampa FL 33617 USA — Singer
Cole, Gary
I C M Partners, 10250 Constellation Blvd, #900, Los Angeles CA 90067 USA — Actor
Cole, George
Joy Jameson, 21 Uxbridge St, Kensington, London W8 7TQ, England — Actor
Cole, Holly
Alert Music, 51 Hillsview Ave, Toronto ON M6P 1J4, Canada — Singer
Cole, Jasper
Newman-Thomas Mgmt, 8306 Wilshire Blvd, #996 Beverly Hills CA 90211, USA — Actor
Cole, Joanna
Scholastic Press, 555 Broadway, New York NY 10012, USA — Writer
Cole, John
Durham Herald-Sun, Editorial Dept, 2828 Pickett Road, Durham NC 27705, USA — Editorial Cartoonist
Cole, Johnnetta B
National African Art Museum, 950 Independence Ave SW, Washington DC 20560, USA — Museum Executive, Educator
Cole, Julie Dawn
Barry Burnett, 31 Coventry St, London W1V 8AS, England — Actress
Cole, Kenneth
Kenneth Cole Productions, 601 W 50th St, New York NY 10019, USA — Fashion Designer
Cole, Keyshia
The Firm, 2049 Century Park E, #2550, Los Angeles CA 90067 USA — Singer, Actress
Cole, Larry R
400 Country Place, Colleyville TX 76034, USA — Football Player
Cole, Lily
I M G Models, 304 Park Ave S, #PH-North, New York NY 10010 USA — Model, Actress
Cole, Marilyn
Playboy Promotions, 2706 Media Center Dr, Los Angeles CA 90065 USA — Model
Cole, Michael
University of California, Communications Dept, La Jolla CA 92093, USA — Psychologist
Cole, Michael
J K A Talent Agency, 12725 Ventura Blvd, #H, Studio City CA 91604, USA — Actor
Cole, Nadine E L
Concorde International, 101 Shepherds Bush Road, London W6 7LP, England — Singer (Girls Aloud)
Cole, Natalie
Moir/Borman, 1250 6th St, #401, Santa Monica CA 90401, USA — Singer, Actress
Cole, Nigel
Independent Talent Group, Oxford House, 76 Oxford St, London W1D 1BS, England — Director, Writer
Cole, Olivia
Century Artists, PO Box 59747, Santa Barbara CA 93150 USA — Actress
Cole, Paula
Monterey Peninsula Artists, 404 W Franklin St, Monterey CA 93940 USA — Singer, Songwriter
Cole, Richard (Richie)
Abby Hoffer, 223 1/2 E 48th St, New York NY 10017 USA — Jazz Saxophonist
Cole, Richard E
48 Blaschke Road, Comfort TX 78013, USA — WW II Army Air Corps Hero
Cole, Richard R (Dick)
3149 Madeira Ave, Costa Mesa CA 92626, USA — Baseball Player
Cole, Robert C (Bob)
CBC-TV, PO Box 500 Station A, Toronto ON M5W 1E6, Canada — Sportscaster
Cole, Robin
9 Brook Lane, Eighty Four PA 15330, USA — Football Player
Cole, Steve
Great Scott Productions, 4750 Lincoln Blvd, #229, Marina del Rey CA 90292, USA — Jazz Saxophonist
Cole, Steven
Columbia Artists Mgmt Inc, 1790 Broadway, #702, New York NY 10019 USA — Opera Singer
Cole, Susan A
Montclair State University, President's Office, Montclair NJ 07043, USA — Educator
Cole, Taylor
TalentWorks, 3500 W Olive Ave, #1400, Burbank CA 91505 USA — Actress
Cole, Tina
4603 Edison Ave, Sacramento CA 95821, USA — Actress, Singer
Cole, Trent
Philadelphia Eagles, 1 Novacare Way, Philadelphia PA 19145 USA — Football Player
Colella, Richard (Rick)
217 19th Place, Kirkland WA 98033, USA — Swimmer
Coleman, Andre C
2955 Megan Circle, Youngstown OH 44505, USA — Football Player
Coleman, Benjamin (Ben)
206 Mallard Dr, Shakopee MN 55379, USA — Basketball Player
Coleman, Bill
Coleman Lemieux Compagnie, 304 Paliament St, Toronto M5A 3A4, Canada — Dance Company Executive, Choreographer
Coleman, Bobby
Coast to Coast Talent, 3350 Barham Blvd, Los Angeles CA 90068 USA — Actor
Coleman, Brian
900 Old Evans Road, Watsonville CA 95076, USA — Artist
Coleman, Catherine G (Cady)
30 Frank Williams Road, Shelburne Falls MA 01370, USA — Astronaut
Coleman, Cosey C
11901 Northumberland Dr, Tampa FL 33626, USA — Football Player
Coleman, Dabney
Michael Black Mgmt, 9701 Wilshire Blvd, 1000, Beverly Hills CA 90212, USA — Actor
Coleman, David L (Dave)
4303 Delhi Dr, Dayton OH 45432, USA — Baseball Player
Coleman, Deborah
Piedmont Talent, PO Box 680006, Charlotte NC 28216, USA — Singer, Guitarist
Coleman, Don E
424 McPherson Ave, Lansing MI 48915, USA — Football Player
Coleman, E C, Jr
370 E Harmon Ave, Las Vegas NV 89169, USA — Basketball Player
Coleman, George E
63 E 9th St, New York NY 10003, USA — Jazz Saxophonist
Coleman, Gerald F (Jerry)
1004 Havenhurst Dr, La Jolla CA 92037, USA — Baseball Player, Manager; Sportscaster

C

Cole - Coleman

Coleman - Colletti

Coleman, Greg J	Football Player
2313 River Pointe Circle, Minneapolis MN 55411, USA	
Coleman, Jack	Actor
Domain Talent, 9229 W Sunset Blvd, #710, West Hollywood CA 90069 USA	
Coleman, Jeremy (Jaz)	Singer (Killing Joke), Songwriter
Agency Group, 9348 Civic Center Dr, #200, Beverly Hills CA 90210 USA	
Coleman, Joseph H (Joe)	Baseball Player
17851 Eagle View Lane, Cape Coral FL 33909, USA	
Coleman, Kari	Actress
C E S D, 10635 Santa Monica Blvd, #130, Los Angeles CA 90025 USA	
Coleman, Kelly	Basketball Player
PO Box 183, Higgins Lake MI 48627, USA	
Coleman, Kenyon O	Football Player
35723 Stock St, Murrieta CA 92562, USA	
Coleman, Marco D	Football Player
105 Monarch Court, Saint Augustine FL 32095, USA	
Coleman, Marcus	Football Player
1736 Mapleleaf Dr, Wylie TX 75098, USA	
Coleman, Marissa	Basketball Player
Los Angeles Sparks, 888 S Figueroa St, #2010, Los Angeles CA 90017 USA	
Coleman, Mary Sue	Educator
University of Michigan, President's Office, Ann Arbor MI 48109, USA	
Coleman, Monique	Actress
Magnolia Entertainment, 9595 Wilshire Blvd, #601, Beverly Hills CA 90212, USA	
Coleman, Norman B, Jr	Senator, MN
American Action Forum, 1455 Pennsylvania Ave NW, #350, Washington DC 20004, USA	
Coleman, Ornette	Jazz Saxophonist, Composer
Agency Group Ltd, 142 W 57th St, #600, New York NY 10019 USA	
Coleman, Phyllis	Model
Playboy Promotions, 2706 Media Center Dr, Los Angeles CA 90065 USA	
Coleman, Roderick D (Rod)	Football Player
6735 Great Water Dr, Flowery Branch GA 30542, USA	
Coleman, Ronnie L	Football Player
16039 Williwaw Dr, Houston TX 77083, USA	
Coleman, Rowan	Writer
Pocket Books, 1230 Ave of Americas, New York NY 10020 USA	
Coleman, Sidney	Football Player
15083 Highway 39 N, DeKalb MS 39328, USA	
Coleman, Signy	Actress
Abrams Artists, 9200 W Sunset Blvd, #1125, West Hollywood CA 90069 USA	
Coleman, Vincent M (Vince)	Baseball Player
7271 Primrose Lane, San Diego CA 92129, USA	
Coleman, William T, Jr	Secretary, Transportation
O'Melveny & Myers, 1625 I St NW, Washington DC 20006, USA	
Coleman, Zendaya	Actress
Monster Talent Mgmt, 6333 W 3rd St, #912, Los Angeles CA 90036, USA	
Coles, Darnell	Baseball Player
306 Signature Terrace, Safety Harbor FL 34695, USA	
Coles, Janet	Golfer
6083 Alumni Gym, Hanover NH 3755, USA	
Coles, Julie	Actress
6780 N Casa Real Place, Boise ID 83714, USA	
Coles, Kim	Actress, Comedienne
Abrams Artists, 9200 W Sunset Blvd, #1125, West Hollywood CA 90069 USA	
Coles, Laveranues L	Football Player
1 Sagamore Dr, Plainview NY 11803, USA	
Coles, Robert M	Psychiatrist
81 Carr Road, Concord MA 01742, USA	
Coles, Vernell E (Bimbo)	Basketball Player
203 E Washington St, Lewisburg WV 24901, USA	
Colescott, Warrington W	Artist
8788 County Road A, Hollandale WI 53544, USA	
Coley, Daryl	Clarinetist, Pianist
Daryl Coley Ministries, 417 E Regent St, Inglewood CA 90301, USA	
Coley, John Ford	Singer, Songwriter
Utopia Artists, PO Box 1821, Ojai CA 93024, USA	
Colfer, Chris	Actor
Coast to Coast Talent, 3350 Barham Blvd, Los Angeles CA 90068 USA	
Colgate, Stirling A	Physicist
422 Estante Way, Los Alamos NM 87544, USA	
Colicchio, Thomas P (Tom)	Chef, Restauranteur
Colicchio & Sons, 85 10th Ave, New York NY 10011, USA	
Colin, Charlie	Bassist (Train)
Jon Landau, 80 Main St, Greenwich CT 06830, USA	
Colin, Margaret	Actress
Innovative Artists, 1505 10th St, Santa Monica CA 90401 USA	
Colinet, Stalin	Football Player
3 Mohawk Dr, Framingham MA 01701, USA	
Coll, Ashley	Artist
1419 Chetwynd Ave, Plainfield NJ 07060, USA	
Coll, Ivonne	Actress
Don Buchwald/Fortitude, 6500 Wilshire Blvd, #2200, Los Angeles CA 90048 USA	
Coll, Stephen W	Journalist
New America Foundation, 1899 L St, NW, #400, Washington DC 20036, USA	
Collard, Jean-Philippe	Concert Pianist
Caroline Martin Musique, 126 Rue Vielle du Temple, 75003 Paris, France	
Collet-Serra, Jaume	Director
Ombra Films, 12444 Ventura Blvd, #103, Studio City CA 91604, USA	
Collett, C Elmer	Football Player
PO Box 522, 10 Avenida Farralone, Stinson Beach CA 94970, USA	
Collett, Jason	Singer, Songwriter
Agency Group Ltd, 142 W 57th St, #600, New York NY 10019 USA	
Collette, Toni	Actress
United Agents, 12-26 Lexington St, London W1F 0LE, England	
Colletti, Stephen	Actor
A P A Talent/Literary Agency, 405 S Beverly Dr, #300, Beverly Hills CA 90212 USA	

Colley, Dana
48 Laight St, New York NY 10013, USA — Saxophonist (Morphine)

Colley, Ed
11 Blaisdell Terrace, Ipswich MA 01938, USA — Cartoonist (Suburban Cowgirls)

Colley, Kenneth
Ken McReddie Assoc, 11 Connaught Place, London W2 2ET, England — Actor

Colley, Michael C
444 Magnolia Dr, Gulf Shores AL 36542, USA — Navy Admiral

Colley, Tom
71 Dillon Dr, Collingwood ON L9Y 4S4, Canada — Ice Hockey Player

Collie, Bruce S
9595 Ranch Road 12, #13, Wimberley TX 78676, USA — Football Player

Collie, Mark
Dreamcatcher Artist Mgmt, 2908 Poston Ave, Nashville TN 37203, USA — Singer, Songwriter, Actor

Collier, Charles (Charlie)
A M C Networks, 11 Penn Plaza, New York NY 10001, USA — Businessman

Collier, Don
9024 E 21st St, Tucson AZ 85710, USA — Actor

Collier, James Lincoln
71 Barrow St, New York NY 10014, USA — Writer

Collier, Lesley F
Royal Ballet, Covent Garden, Bow St, London WC2E 9DD, England — Ballerina

Collier, Louis K (Lou)
6409 S Kenwood Ave, Chicago IL 60637, USA — Baseball Player

Collier, Timothy (Tim)
3116 50th St, Dallas TX 75216, USA — Football Player

Colligan, Edward T
Equity Partners, 70 E 55th St, New York NY 10022, USA — Businessman

Colligan, John (Bud)
Macromedia Inc, 600 Townsend St, San Francisco CA 94103, USA — Businessman

Collingwood, Chris
Big Hassle, 157 Chambers St, #1200, New York NY 10007, USA — Singer (Fountains of Wayne), Songwriter

Collins, Anthony (Tony)
2712 Gulfstream Dr, Miramar FL 33023, USA — Football Player

Collins, Arthur W (Bud), Jr
822 Boylston St, #203, Chestnut Hill MA 02467, USA — Sportscaster

Collins, Bernard
Fast Lane International, 4856 Haygood Road, #200, Virginia Beach VA 23455, USA — Singer (Abyssinians)

Collins, Candace L
Playboy Promotions, 2706 Media Center Dr, Los Angeles CA 90065 USA — Model

Collins, Carla
Agency Group Ltd, 142 W 57th St, #600, New York NY 10019 USA — Comedienne, Actress

Collins, Clifton G, Jr
A P A Talent/Literary Agency, 405 S Beverly Dr, #300, Beverly Hills CA 90212 USA — Actor

Collins, David J
A2B Tracking Solutions, 207 Highpoint Ave, Portsmouth RI 02871, USA — Inventor (Bar Code)

Collins, David S (Dave)
206 N East St, #15, Mason OH 45040, USA — Baseball Player

Collins, Dean
Howard Entertainment, 10850 Wilshire Blvd, #1260, Los Angeles CA 90024, USA — Actor

Collins, Eileen M
2024 Pebble Beach Dr, League City TX 77573, USA — Astronaut

Collins, Francis S
National Institutes of Health, 9000 Rockville Pike, Bethesda MD 20892, USA — Geneticist

Collins, Gary
1908-1320 Islington Ave, Etobicoke M9A 5C6, Canada — Ice Hockey Player

Collins, Gary J
221 Lamp Post Lane, Hershey PA 17033, USA — Football Player

Collins, George F, III
2043 Northside Road, Perry GA 31069, USA — Football Player

Collins, Heidi
CNN-TV, News Dept, 820 1st St NE, #1000, Washington DC 20002 USA — Commentator

Collins, J Maxwell S (Max), III
Agency Group Ltd, 1880 Century Park E, #711, Los Angeles CA 90067 USA — Singer, Bassist (Eve 6)

Collins, Jackie
10624 Wellworth Ave, Los Angeles CA 90024, USA — Writer

Collins, James B (Jim)
2140 E Oceanfront, Newport Beach CA 92661, USA — Football Player

Collins, Jarron T
11173 Cashmere St, Los Angeles CA 90049, USA — Basketball Player

Collins, Jason P
13120 Constable Ave, Granada Hills CA 91344, USA — Basketball Player

Collins, Jeff
1429 Limestone Road, Redfield KS 66769, USA — Rodeo Rider

Collins, Jerry
United Talent Agency, 9336 Civic Center Dr, Beverly Hills CA 90210 USA — Actor, Writer, Producer

Collins, Jesse
Oscars Abrams Zimel, 438 Queen St E, Toronto ON M5A 1T4, Canada — Actor

Collins, Jessica
I C M Partners, 10250 Constellation Blvd, #900, Los Angeles CA 90067 USA — Actress

Collins, Jim
Harper Business Books, 10 E 53rd St, Cellar 1, New York NY 10022, USA — Writer, Management Consultant

Collins, Jo
Playboy Promotions, 2706 Media Center Dr, Los Angeles CA 90065 USA — Model, Actress

Collins, Joan
Paul Keylock, 16 Bulbecks Walk, S Woodham Ferrers, Essex CM3 5ZN, England — Actress

Collins, John
Secret Service, PO Box 401, Fortitude Valley QLD 4006, Australia — Bassist (Powderfinger)

Collins, John W
Clorox Co, 1221 Broadway, Oakland CA 94612, USA — Businessman

Collins, Judy
845 W End Ave, #10E, New York NY 10025, USA — Singer, Songwriter

Collins, K C
Glick Agency, 1321 7th St, #203, Santa Monica CA 90401 USA — Actor

Collins, Kate
1410 York Ave, #4D, New York NY 10021, USA — Actress

C

Colley - Collins

Collins, Kayla
Playboy Promotions, 2706 Media Center Dr, Los Angeles CA 90065 USA — Model

Collins, Kerry M
1090 Stockett Dr, Nashville TN 37221, USA — Football Player

Collins, Kevin M
9121 Point Charity Dr, Pigeon MI 48755, USA — Baseball Player

Collins, Lauren
A M I Artist Management, 464 King St E, Toronto ON M5A 1L7, Canada , USA — Actress

Collins, Lily J
Creative Artists Agency, 2000 Ave of Stars, #100, Los Angeles CA 90067 USA — Actress, Model

Collins, Lynn
3 Arts Entertainment, 9460 Wilshire Blvd, #700, Beverly Hills CA 90212 USA — Actress

Collins, Mark A
2568 Baseline St, #155, Highland CA 92346, USA — Football Player

Collins, Martha Layne
921 Taborlake Court, Lexington KY 40502, USA — Governor, KY; Educator

Collins, Marva
1507 E 53rd St, Chicago IL 60615, USA — Educator

Collins, Michael
272 Polynesia Court, Marco Island FL 34145, USA — Astronaut, Air Force General

Collins, Michael
Hazard Chase, 72 Charlotte St, London W1T 4QQ, England — Conductor, Concert Clarinetist

Collins, Michael
Viking Penguin Books, 375 Hudson St, Basement 1, New York NY 10014 USA — Writer

Collins, Misha
Framework Entertainment, 9057 Nemo St, #C, West Hollywood CA 90069 USA — Actor

Collins, Mo
Diverse Talent Group, 9911 Pico Blvd, #350W, Los Angeles CA 90035 USA — Actress, Comedienne

Collins, Nancy A
Harper Collins Publishers, 10 E 53rd St, Cellar 1, New York NY 10022 USA — Writer

Collins, P Douglas (Doug)
10040 E Happy Valley Road, #617, Scottsdale AZ 85255, USA — Basketball Player, Coach, Sportscaster

Collins, Patrick
Tisherman Agency, 6767 Forest Lawn Dr, #101, Los Angeles CA 90068 USA — Actor

Collins, Pauline
Independent Talent Group, Oxford House, 76 Oxford St, London W1D 1BS, England — Actress

Collins, Phil
Alfred House, 23-24 Cromwell Place, #300, London SW7 2LD, England — Singer, Songwriter, Drummer

Collins, Randall
University of Pennsylvania, Sociology Dept, Philedelphia PA 19104, USA — Sociologist

Collins, Shanna
A K A Talent, 6310 San Vicente Blvd, #200, Los Angeles CA 90048 USA — Actress

Collins, Shawn
PO Box 711933, San Diego CA 92171, USA — Football Player

Collins, Sherron M
Charlotte Bobcats, 333 E Trade St, #A, Charlotte NC 28202 USA — Basketball Player

Collins, Stephen
A P A Talent/Literary Agency, 405 S Beverly Dr, #300, Beverly Hills CA 90212 USA — Actor

Collins, Steve
Rock Solid Productions, PO Box 70642, Houston TX 77270, USA — Boxer

Collins, Terry L
40992 Hollydale, Novi MI 48375, USA — Baseball Manager

Collins, Thomas C Cardinal
Archdiocese, Chancery Office, 1155 Yonge St, Toronto ON M4T 1W2, Canada — Religious Leader

Collins, Todd S
26 Cambridge Circle, Victor NY 14564, USA — Football Player

Collins, William (Billy)
RR 202, Somers NY 10589, USA — Writer

Collins, William E (Bill)
5000 Town Center, #505, Southfield MI 48075, USA — Ice Hockey Player

Collins, William E (Bootsy)
Agency Group Ltd, 1880 Century Park E, #711, Los Angeles CA 90067 USA — Singer, Bassist

Collinson, Madeleine
Playboy Promotions, 2706 Media Center Dr, Los Angeles CA 90065 USA — Model, Actress

Collinson, Mary
Playboy Promotions, 2706 Media Center Dr, Los Angeles CA 90065 USA — Model, Actress

Collinsworth, A Cris
31 Crow Hill Road, Fort Thomas KY 41075, USA — Football Player, Sportscaster

Collison, Darren M
Dallas Mavericks, Pavilion, 2909 Taylor St, Dallas TX 75226 USA — Basketball Player

Collison, Frank
Amsel Eisenstadt Frazier, 5055 Wilshire Blvd, #865, Los Angeles CA 90036 USA — Actor

Collison, Nicholas J (Nick)
16 Comstock St, Seattle WA 98109, USA — Basketball Player

Collister, Christine
Running Media, 14 Victoria Road, Douglas, Isle of Man IM2 4ER, England — Singer

Collman, James P
794 Tolman Dr, Stanford CA 94305, USA — Chemist

Collomb, Bertrand P
4 Rue de Lota, 75116 Paris, France — Businessman

Collyer, Laurie
Gersh Agency, 9465 Wilshire Blvd, #600, Beverly Hills CA 90212 USA — Director, Writer, Actress

Colman, Booth
2160 Century Park E, #603, Los Angeles CA 90067, USA — Actor

Colman, Oliva
United Agents, 12-26 Lexington St, London W1F 0LE, England — Actress

Colman, Paul
W M E Entertainment, 9601 Wilshire Blvd, #300, Beverly Hills CA 90210 USA — Singer, Guitarist, Pianist, Composer

Colman, Wayne C
604 N Somerset Ave, Ventnor NJ 08406, USA — Football Player

Colmes, Alan
Fox-TV, News Dept, 1211 Ave of Americas, New York NY 10036, USA — Commentator

Colo, Donald R (Don)
7355 E Claremont St, Scottsdale AZ 85250, USA — Football Player

Coloma, Marcus
Don Buchwald/Fortitude, 6500 Wilshire Blvd, #2200, Los Angeles CA 90048 USA — Actor

Colombo, Marc E — Football Player
7219 Marigold Dr, Irving TX 75063, USA
Colomby, Scott — Actor
Borinstein Oreck Bogart, 3172 Dona Susana Dr, Studio City CA 91604 USA
Colon, Bartolo — Baseball Player
14 Federal St, #1, Passaic NJ 07055, USA
Colon, Willie — Football Player
Pittsburgh Steelers, 3400 S Water St, Pittsburgh PA 15203 USA
Colon, Willie A — Singer, Trombonist, Composer
El Malo Inc, 1333A North Ave, #153, New Rochelle NY 10804, USA
Colosimo, Vince — Actor
Robyn Gardiner Mgmt, 397 Riley St, Surry Hills NSW 2010, Australia
Colquitt, Dustin F — Football Player
1905 Pitts Field Lane, Knoxville TN 37922, USA
Colquitt, J Craig — Football Player
1905 Pitts Field Lane, Knoxville TN 37922, USA
Colson, Elizabeth F — Anthropologist
University of California, Anthropology Dept, Berkeley CA 94720, USA
Colston, Marques — Football Player
New Orleans Saints, 5800 Airline Highway, Metairie LA 70003 USA
Colter, Jessie — Singer
Dan Gillis Mgmt, 1305 Clinton St, #120, Nashville TN 37203, USA
Colter, Steve — Basketball Player
802 E Mountain Sage Dr, Phoenix AZ 85048, USA
Colton, Graham — Singer, Songwriter
Back Bay Mgmt, 397 Little Neck Road, #305, Virginia Beach VA 23452, USA
Coltrane, Chi — Singer, Pianist, Songwriter
5955 Tuxedo Terrace, Los Angeles CA 90068, USA
Coltrane, Ravi — Jazz Saxophonist
Joel Chriss, 60 E 8th St, #34N, New York NY 10003 USA
Coltrane, Robbie — Actor, Comedian
Caroline Dawson, 125 Gloucester Road, London SW7 4TE, England
Coluccio, Robert P (Bob) — Baseball Player
369 Flower St, Costa Mesa CA 92627, USA
Columbo, Marc E — Football Player
Miami Dolphins, 7500 SW 30th St, Davie FL 33314 USA
Columbu, Franco — Body Builder
2265 Westwood Blvd, #A, Los Angeles CA 90064, USA
Columbus, Christopher J (Chris) — Director, Writer
Leavensden Studios, PO Box 3000, Leavesden WD2 7LT, England
Colville, Alexander — Artist
PO Box 550, Wolfville NS B0P 1X0, Canada
Colvin, James R (Jim) — Football Player
1310 Rancho Vista Dr, McKinney TX 75070, USA
Colvin, John O — Judge
US Tax Court, 400 2nd St NW, Washington DC 20217, USA
Colvin, Roosevelt, III — Football Player
9340 Sargent Road, Indianapolis IN 46256, USA
Colvin, Shawn — Singer, Songwriter
Vector Mgmt, PO Box 120479, Nashville TN 37212 USA
Colvin, Shelly — Singer, Songwriter
Parallel Entertainment, 209 10th Ave S, #506, Nashville TN 37203, USA
Colwell, John A — Association Executive, Physician
American Diabetes Assn, 1701 N Beauregard St, #100, Alexandria VA 22311, USA
Colwell, Rita R — Microbiologist, Foundation Executive
5010 River Hill Road, Bethesda MD 20816, USA
Colwill, Les — Ice Hockey Player
714 20th St, North Lethbridge AB T1H 3N6, Canada
Comaneci, Nadia — Gymnast
4421 Hidden Hill Road, Norman OK 73072, USA
Comart, Jean-Paul — Actor
Artmedia, 20 Ave Rapp, 75007 Paris, France
Comastri, Angelo Cardinal — Religious Leader
Basilica di San Pietro, 00120 Vatican City
Combeau, Muriel — Actress
Voyez Mon Agent, 20 Ave Rapp, 75007 Paris, France
Combes, Willard W — Editorial Cartoonist
1266 Oakridge Dr, Cleveland OH 44121, USA
Combs, David — Actor
Special Artists Agency, 9465 Wilshire Blvd, #820, Beverly Hills CA 90212 USA
Combs, E Leroy — Basketball Player
1631 Glenn Bo Dr, Norman OK 73071, USA
Combs, Glenn — Basketball Player
3627 Dogwood Lane SW, Roanoke VA 24015, USA
Combs, Holly Marie — Actress
Gersh Agency, 9465 Wilshire Blvd, #600, Beverly Hills CA 90212 USA
Combs, Jeffrey — Actor
Bleu, 5225 Wilshire Blvd, #401, Los Angeles CA 90036, USA
Combs, Rodney — Auto Racing Driver
American Diecast, 16173 Edgemont Dr, Fort Myers FL 33908, USA
Combs, Sean, (Puff Daddy, P Diddy) — Rap Artist, Actor
Creative Artists Agency, 2000 Ave of Stars, #100, Los Angeles CA 90067, USA
Comeau, Andy — Actor
TalentWorks, 3500 W Olive Ave, #1400, Burbank CA 91505 USA
Comeau, Ray — Ice Hockey Player
4 Rue de Cernay, Lorraine QC J6Z 2Z1, Canada
Comeaux, Darren — Football Player
6313 Kristie Lane, Brusly LA 70719, USA
Comegys, Dallas A — Basketball Player
4330 Wayne Ave, Philadelphia PA 19140, USA
Comella, Greg — Football Player
90 Fairbanks Ave, Wellesley Hills MA 02481, USA
Comer, H Wayne — Baseball Player
145 Marcus St, Shenandoah VA 22849, USA
Comer, Steven M (Steve) — Baseball Player
525 Lake Dr, #377, Chanhassen MN 55317, USA

Comess, Aaron D A S Communications, 83 Riverside Dr, New York NY 10024 USA	Musician (Spin Doctors)
Comi, Paul 2395 Ridgeway Road, San Marino CA 91108, USA	Actor
Commander Cody Jacobson & Colfin, 60 Madison Ave, #1026, New York NY 10010, USA	Musician
Commissiong, Janelle Bowen Marine, Western Main Road, Chaguaramas, Trinidad	Beauty Queen
Commodore, Michael (Mike) 12017 Fern Dr, Detroit Lakes MN 56501, USA	Ice Hockey Player
Common 42 West, 220 W 42nd St, #1200, New York NY 10036 USA	Rap Artist, Actor
Compagnon, Antoine M T 875 W End Ave, #15D, New York NY 10025, USA	Educator, Writer
Compagnoni, Deborah Via Frodonfo 3, 2303 Santa Catarina Valfurna, Italy	Alpine Skier
Compaore, Blaise President's Office, 03 BP 7030, Ouagadougou 03, Burkina Faso	President, Burkina Faso
Compte, Maurice Don Buchwald/Fortitude, 6500 Wilshire Blvd, #2200, Los Angeles CA 90048 USA	Actor
Compton, Ann Woodruff ABC-TV, News Dept, 3361 75th Ave, #X, Hyattsville MD 20785, USA	Commentator
Compton, Richard A P A Talent/Literary Agency, 405 S Beverly Dr, #300, Beverly Hills CA 90212 USA	Actor
Compton, Richard L (Dick) 3408 S Briarcliff Court, Irving TX 75062, USA	Football Player
Comrie, Michael W (Mike) 10800 Wilshire Blvd, #1703, Los Angeles CA 90024, USA	Ice Hockey Player
Comstock, Harold 2809 Aberdeen Lane, El Dorado Hills CA 95762, USA	Air Force Hero
Comstock, Keith M 9615 E Desert Trail, Scottsdale AZ 85260, USA	Baseball Player
Cona, Louis New Yorker, Publisher's Office, 4 Times Square, New York NY 10036, USA	Publisher
Conacher, Brian 202-500 Avenue Road, Toronto ON M4V 2J6, Canada	Ice Hockey Player
Conacher, Jim 422-980 Lynn Valley Road, West Vancouver BC V7J 3V7, Canada	Ice Hockey Player
Conacher, Pat 18371 W Sweet Acacia Dr, Goodyear AZ 85338, USA	Ice Hockey Player
Conacher, Pete 3 Conifer Dr, Etobicoke ON M9C 1X3, Canada	Ice Hockey Player
Conant, Kenneth J 3 Carlton Village, #T105, Bedford MA 01730, USA	Archaeologist
Conatsor, Clinton A (Connie) 26701 Quail Creek, #191, Laguna Hills CA 92656, USA	Baseball Player
Conaty, William B (Billy), Jr 203 Country Club Dr, Moorestown NJ 08057, USA	Football Player
Conaway, Cristi 1759 Old Ranch Road, Los Angeles CA 90049, USA	Actress
Conaway, John B Spectrum Group, 11 Canal Center Plaza, #103, Alexandria VA 22314, USA	Air Force General
Conaway, Ronald C Stowers Medical Research Institute, 1000 E 50th St, Kansas City MO 64110, USA	Geneticist
Concepcion Benitez, David I (Davey) Urb el Castano Botalon 5D, Maracay 5, Venezuela	Baseball Player
Concepcion Cardona, Onix C 1486 Steeplechase Lane, Deltona FL 32725, USA	Baseball Player
Conde, Alpha President's Office, Palais Presidentiel, Cite des Nations, Conakry, Guinea	President, Guinea
Conde, Ninel H Apodaca Promotions, 717 E Tidwell Road, Houston TX 77022, USA	Actress, Singer
Condit, Gary A 2509 Acorn Lane, Ceres CA 95307, USA	Representative, CA
Condo, George 108 E 78th St, New York NY 10075, USA	Artist
Condon of Langton Green, Paul L I C C, Clock Tower, Lord's Cricket Ground, London NW8 8QN, England	Law Enforcement Official
Condon, Kerry I C M Partners, 10250 Constellation Blvd, #900, Los Angeles CA 90067 USA	Actress
Condon, Thomas J (Tom) 99 Oakleigh Lane, Saint Louis MO 63124, USA	Football Player
Condon, William (Bill) Anonymous Content, 3532 Hayden Ave, Culver City CA 90232 USA	Director, Writer
Condon, Zach Ba Da Bing Records, 181 Clermont Ave, #403, Brooklyn NY 11205, USA	Singer (Beirut), Songwriter
Condren, Glen P 8557 N 175th East Ave, Owasso OK 74055, USA	Football Player
Condrey, Clayton L (Clay) 412 N 8th St, Navasota TX 77868, USA	Baseball Player
Cone Vanderbush, Carin 47 Rose Dr, Highland Falls NY 10928, USA	Swimmer
Cone, David B 219 Dolphin Cove Quay, Stamford CT 6902, USA	Baseball Player
Cone, Fred PO Box 1819, Blairsville GA 30514, USA	Football Player
Confino, Edmond 676 N Saint Clair St, #1845, Chicago IL 60611, USA	Obstetrician, Gynecologist
Conforti, Gino Orange Grove Group, 12178 Ventura Blvd, #205, Studio City CA 91604 USA	Actor
Congdon, Jeffrey D (Jeff) 505 Highway View Court, Mesquite NV 89027, USA	Basketball Player
Conigliaro, William M (Billy) 501 Cabot St, #2, Beverly MA 01915, USA	Baseball Player
Conine, Jeffrey G (Jeff) 3166 Iverness, Weston FL 33332, USA	Baseball Player

Conkey, Margaret — Archaeologist
University of California, Archaeological Research Facility, Berkeley CA 94720, USA

Conklin, Harold C — Anthropologist
200 Leeder Hill Dr, #607, Hamden CT 06517, USA

Conklin, Ty — Ice Hockey Player
PO Box 10, East Winthrop ME 4343, USA

Conlan, Shane P — Football Player
521 East Dr, Sewickley PA 15143, USA

Conlee, Jenny — Organist, Accordianist (Decemberists)
Big Hassle, 44 Wall St, #2200, New York NY 10005, USA

Conlee, John — Singer
John Conlee Enterprises, 38 Music Square E, #117, Nashville TN 37203, USA

Conley, Clare D — Editor
Hemlock Farms, Hawley PA 18428, USA

Conley, D Eugene (Gene) — Baseball, Basketball Player
400 Foxboro Blvd, #3102, Foxboro MA 02035, USA

Conley, Earl Thomas — Singer, Songwriter
657 Baker Road, Smyrna TN 37167, USA

Conley, Joe — Actor
PO Box 6487, Westlake Village CA 91359, USA

Conley, Mike, Jr — Basketball Player
3496 Windgarden Cove, Memphis TN 38125, USA

Conley, Wayne — Writer
Paradigm Agency, 360 Park Ave S, #1600, New York NY 10010 USA

Conlin, Edward J (Ed) — Basketball Player
153 N Mountain Ave, Montclair NJ 07042, USA

Conlin, Michaela — Actress
Evolution Entertainment, 901 N Highland Ave, Los Angeles CA 90038 USA

Conlon, Edward W — Writer
Random House, 1745 Broadway, #1800, New York NY 10019 USA

Conlon, James J — Conductor
Opus 3 Artists, 470 Park Ave S, #900N, New York NY 10016 USA

Conlon, Martin M (Marty) — Basketball Player
204 Head of Pond Road, Water Mill NY 11976, USA

Conn, Didi — Actress, Singer
C E S D, 10635 Santa Monica Blvd, #130, Los Angeles CA 90025 USA

Conn, Richard R (Dick) — Football Player
144 Sugarmill Lane, Moore SC 29369, USA

Conn, Shelley — Actress
United Agents, 12-26 Lexington St, London W1F 0LE, England

Conneff, Kevin — Singer, Percussionist (Chieftains)
Macklam/Feldman Mgmt, 1505 W 2nd Ave, #200, Vancouver BC V6H 3Y4, Canada

Connell, Albert G A — Football Player
3522 Ruth St, Houston TX 77004, USA

Connell, Desmond Cardinal — Religious Leader
Archbishop's House, Drumcondra, Dublin 9, Ireland

Connell, Evan S, Jr — Writer
640 Alta Vista St, #124, Santa Fe NM 87505, USA

Connell, Jane — Singer, Actress
905 W End Ave, New York NY 10025, USA

Connelly, Jennifer — Actress
Creative Artists Agency, 2000 Ave of Stars, #100, Los Angeles CA 90067 USA

Connelly, Michael — Writer
Little Brown, 3 Center Plaza, #100, Boston MA 02108 USA

Connelly, Wayne F — Ice Hockey Player
RR 2 Site 2, Box 61, Swastika ON P0K 1T0, Canada

Conner, Bart — Gymnast
4421 Hidden Hill Road, Norman OK 73072, USA

Conner, Chris — Actor
A K A Talent, 6310 San Vicente Blvd, #200, Los Angeles CA 90048 USA

Conner, Clyde R — Football Player
510 Valencia Dr, Los Altos Hills CA 94022, USA

Conner, Darion — Football Player
9553 Prairie Point Road, Macon MS 39341, USA

Conner, Dennis W — Yachtsman
881 Golden Park Ave, San Diego CA 92106, USA

Conner, Lester A — Basketball Player
13836 Coldwater Dr, Carmel IN 46032, USA

Conner, Lois — Photographer
36 Gramercy Park E, #4E, New York NY 10003, USA

Conners, Daniel J (Dan) — Football Player
1032 Chorro St, San Luis Obispo CA 93401, USA

Conners, Sheralee — Model
Playboy Promotions, 2706 Media Center Dr, Los Angeles CA 90065 USA

Connery, Jason — Actor
David Shapira Assoc, 193 N Robertson Blvd, Beverly Hills CA 90211 USA

Connery, Sean — Actor
Lyford Cay, PO Box N7776, Nassau, Bahamas

Connery, Vincent L — Labor Leader
National Treasury Employees Union, 1730 K St NW, Washington DC 20006, USA

Connes, Alain — Mathematician
Leon Motchane l'H E S, 35 Route Chartres, 91440 Bures-sur-Yvette, France

Connick, Harry, Jr — Pianist, Singer, Actor
Wilkins Mgmt, 323 Broadway, Cambridge MA 02139, USA

Conniff, Cal — Skier
157 Pleasantview Ave, Longmeadow MA 01106, USA

Connolly, Billy — Actor
Tickety-Boo Ltd, 94 Charity St, Victoria VCT 105, Gozo, Malta

Connolly, John — Writer
Simon & Schuster, 1230 Ave of Americas, Concourse 1, New York NY 10020 USA

Connolly, Kevin — Actor
Creative Artists Agency, 2000 Ave of Stars, #100, Los Angeles CA 90067 USA

Connolly, Kristen — Actress
Untitled Entertainment, 350 S Beverly Dr, #200, Beverly Hills CA 90212 USA

Connolly, Nathan — Singer, Guitarist (Snow Patrol)
Big Life Mgmt, 67-69 Charlton St, London NW1 1HY, England

Conkey - Connolly

Connolly, Olga Fikotova — Track Athlete
307 Avocado St, #4, Costa Mesa CA 92627, USA
Connolly, Theodore W (Ted) — Football Player
1805 N Carson St, #86, Carson City NV 89701, USA
Connolly, Tom — Actor
Innovative Artists, 1505 10th St, Santa Monica CA 90401 USA
Connor, Cam — Ice Hockey Player
1331 Leeward Way, Qualicum Beach BC V9K 2M1, Canada
Connor, Daniel M (Dan) — Football Player
Dallas Cowboys, 1 Cowboys Parkway, Irving TX 75063 USA
Connor, Kate — Actress
Jay Schwartz Assoc, 3151 Cahuenga Blvd, W, #220, Los Angeles CA 90068, USA
Connor, Linda S — Photographer
87 Rutherford, San Anselmo CA 94960, USA
Connor, Paolo — Actor
Abrams Artists, 275 7th Ave, #2600, New York NY 10001 USA
Connor, Sarah — Singer, Songwriter
World Concerts, Hamburger Str 273A, 38114 Braunschweig, Germany
Connors, Carol — Songwriter
1709 Ferrari Dr, Beverly Hills CA 90210, USA
Connors, James S (Jimmy) — Tennis Player
1962 E Valley Road, Santa Barbara CA 93108, USA
Connors, Mike — Actor
4810 Louise Ave, Encino CA 91316, USA
Connors, Norman — Jazz Drummer
Universal Attractions, 135 W 26th St, #1200, New York NY 10001 USA
Connors, William A (Bill) — Jazz Guitarist
Michael Bloom Media Relations, PO Box 41380, Los Angeles CA 90041, USA
Conover, K Scott — Football Player
28 Windsor Terrace, #B, Freehold NJ 07728, USA
Conover, Lloyd H — Inventor (Tetracycline)
5200 Brittany Dr S, #304, Saint Petersburg FL 33715, USA
Conquest, G Robert A — Historian
52 Peter Coutts Circle, Stanford CA 94305, USA
Conrad, Brooks L — Baseball Player
9860 La Cresta Road, Spring Valley CA 91977, USA
Conrad, David — Actor
Gersh Agency, 9465 Wilshire Blvd, #600, Beverly Hills CA 90212 USA
Conrad, Fred — Photographer
New York Times, Editorial Dept, 229 W 43rd St, New York NY 10036, USA
Conrad, James A — Financier
Source One Mortgage, 100 Galleria Officentre, #300, Southfield MI 48034, USA
Conrad, Jimmy — Soccer Player
Sporting Kansas City, 210 W 19th Terrace, #200, Kansas City MO 64108 USA
Conrad, Lauren K — Actress, Model
United Talent Agency, 9336 Civic Center Dr, Beverly Hills CA 90210 USA
Conrad, Robert — Actor
3800 Weatherly Circle, Westlake Village CA 91361, USA
Conrad, Robert J (Bobby Joe) — Football Player
148 County Road 3270, Clifton TX 76634, USA
Conrad, Shane — Actor
Sutton-Barth Vennari, 145 S Fairfax Ave, #310, Los Angeles CA 90036 USA
Conrad, Steve — Director, Writer
Elephant Pictures, 1466 N Milwaukee Ave, #2, Chicago IL 60622, USA
Conradt, Jody — Basketball Coach
9614 Leaning Rock Circle, Austin TX 78730, USA
Conran, Jasper A T — Fashion Designer
1-7 Rostrevor Mews, Fulham, London SW6 5AZ, England
Conran, Kerry — Director, Writer
Paradigm Agency, 360 N Crescent Dr, North Building, Beverly Hills CA 90210 USA
Conran, Philip J — Vietnam War Air Force Hero
4706 Calle Reina, Santa Barbara CA 93110, USA
Conran, Terence O — Interior Designer
22 Shad Thames, London SE1 2YU, England
Conroy, Craig — Ice Hockey Player
PO Box 549, Henderson Harbor NY 13651, USA
Conroy, D Patrick (Pat) — Writer
247 Brighton Road NE, Atlanta GA 30309, USA
Conroy, Kevin — Actor
Imperium 7 Talent, 5455 Wilshire Blvd, #1706, Los Angeles CA 90036, USA
Conroy, Patricia — Singer, Songwriter
Live Tour Artists, 1451 White Oaks Blvd, Oakville ON L6H 4R9, Canada
Conroy, Timothy J (Tim) — Baseball Player
109 Moonlight Dr, Monroeville PA 15146, USA
Considine, Paddy — Actor, Director
Creative Artists Agency, 2000 Ave of Stars, #100, Los Angeles CA 90067 USA
Considine, Tim — Actor
3708 Mountain View Ave, Los Angeles CA 90066, USA
Constantine II — King, Greece
4 Linnell Dr, Hampstead Way, London NW11 7LN, England
Constantine, Kevin L — Ice Hockey Coach
5928 Jenny Lind Court, San Jose CA 95120, USA
Constantine, Michael — Actor
6861 Colbath Ave, Van Nuys CA 91405, USA
Constantine, Susannah — Actress
Paradigm Agency, 360 N Crescent Dr, North Building, Beverly Hills CA 90210 USA
Constantinescu, Roxana — Opera Singer
Harrison/Parrott, 5-6 Albion Court, London W6 0QT, England
Consuelos, Mark — Actor, Model
Milojo Productions, 270 Lafayette St, #702, New York NY 10012, USA
Contador Velasco, Alberto — Cyclist
Team Saxo Bank, Firskowej 38, 2800 KGS Lynby, Denmark
Conte, Paolo — Singer, Pianist, Composer
Partisan Arts, PO Box 5085, Larkspur CA 94977, USA
Conteh, John — Boxer
8 Cedar Dr, Hatch End, Pinner, Middlesex HA5 4DE, England

Conti, Bill
117 Fremont Place W, Los Angeles CA 90005, USA — Composer

Conti, Jason
740 N April Dr, Chandler AZ 85226, USA — Baseball Player

Conti, Tom
Gersh Agency, 9465 Wilshire Blvd, #600, Beverly Hills CA 90212 USA — Actor

Contino, Dick
3355 Nahatan Way, Las Vegas NV 89169, USA — Singer, Accordianist

Contner, James A
3020 Kensington Ave, Richmond VA 23221, USA — Cinematographer

Contreras Camejo, Jose A
1001 Brickell Bay Dr, #1710, Miami FL 33131, USA — Baseball Player

Contz, William (Bill)
106 Grace Dr, Cranberry Township PA 16066, USA — Football Player

Converse, Frank
I C M Partners, 10250 Constellation Blvd, #900, Los Angeles CA 90067 USA — Actor

Converse, James D (Jim)
11865 Cobble Brook Dr, Rancho Cordova CA 95742, USA — Baseball Player

Converse-Roberts, William
Don Buchwald/Fortitude, 6500 Wilshire Blvd, #2200, Los Angeles CA 90048 USA — Actor

Convertino, John
Billions Corp, 3522 W Armitage Ave, Chicago IL 60647 USA — Drummer, Percussionist (Calexico)

Convertino, Michael
Soundtrack Music Assoc, 1460 4th St, #308, Santa Monica CA 90401 USA — Composer

Conway Mitchell, Susan
70 Highbourne Road, Toronto ON M5R 3H8, Canada — Actress

Conway, Billy
Spivak Entertainment, 11845 W Olympic Blvd, Los Angeles CA 90064, USA — Drummer (Morphine)

Conway, Brett A
630 Virginia Ave NE, Atlanta GA 30306, USA — Football Player

Conway, Craig
Ken McReddie Assoc, 11 Connaught Place, London W2 2ET, England — Actor

Conway, Curtis L
446 E Phelps St, Gilbert AZ 85295, USA — Football Player

Conway, Gary
11240 Chimney Rock Road, Paso Robles CA 93446, USA — Actor

Conway, James L
Kaplan-Stahler Agency, 8383 Wilshire Blvd, #923, Beverly Hills CA 90211 USA — Director

Conway, James T
8164 Ambach Way, Hypoluxo FL 33462, USA — Marine Corps General

Conway, Jill K
65 Commonwealth Ave, #8B, Boston MA 02116, USA — Educator, Historian

Conway, Joe
Gersh Agency, 9465 Wilshire Blvd, #600, Beverly Hills CA 90212 USA — Writer

Conway, John Horton
120 Prospect Ave, #1A, Princeton NJ 08540, USA — Mathematician

Conway, Karla (Sachi)
PO Box 249, Honaunau HI 96726, USA — Model, Artist

Conway, Kevin
Innovative Artists, 1505 10th St, Santa Monica CA 90401 USA — Actor

Conway, Robert T, Jr
Commander, Installations Cmd, 2713 Mitscher Road SW, Anacostia Annex DC 20373, USA — Navy Admiral

Conway, Tim
Innovative Artists, 1505 10th St, Santa Monica CA 90401 USA — Actor, Comedian

Conwell, Ernest H (Ernie)
5301 McGavock Road, Brentwood TN 37027, USA — Football Player

Conwell, Esther M
800 Phillips Road, Webster NY 14580, USA — Physicist

Conwell, Tommy
Brothers Mgmt, 141 Dunbar Ave, Fords NJ 08863 USA — Guitarist

Coo Coo Cal
Celebrity Talent Agency, 111 E 14th ST, #249, New York NY 10003, USA — Rap Artist

Cooder, Ry
326 Entrada Dr, Santa Monica CA 90402, USA — Singer, Guitarist, Composer

Coody, B Charles
1555 Oldham Lane, Abilene TX 79602, USA — Golfer

Coogan, Keith
Media Artists Group, 8222 Melrose Ave, #203, Los Angeles CA 90048 USA — Actor

Coogan, Richard
5504 Allott Ave, Sherman Oaks CA 91401, USA — Actor

Coogan, Steve
Independent Talent Group, Oxford House, 76 Oxford St, London W1D 1BS, England — Actor, Comedian

Cook, Aaron L
6113 Liberty Fairfield Road, Liberty Township OH 45011, USA — Baseball Player

Cook, Andrea Joy (A J)
Paradigm Agency, 360 N Crescent Dr, North Building, Beverly Hills CA 90210 USA — Actress

Cook, Anthony A
PO Box 961404, Riverdale GA 30296, USA — Football Player

Cook, Barbara
Irvin Arthur Assoc, 320 W 38th St, #1803, New York NY 10018 USA — Singer, Actress

Cook, Brian J
24 Malaga Place E, Manhattan Beach CA 90266, USA — Basketball Player

Cook, Carole
8829 Ashcroft Ave, West Hollywood CA 90048, USA — Actress, Comedienne

Cook, Claire
Voice/Hyperion Books, 77 W 66th St, #1100, New York NY 10023, USA — Writer

Cook, Daequan
Houston Rockets, 1730 Jefferson St, Houston TX 77003 USA — Basketball Player

Cook, Dane J
United Talent Agency, 9336 Civic Center Dr, Beverly Hills CA 90210 USA — Actor, Comedian

Cook, Darwin L
1840 W Avenue J12, #103, Lancaster CA 93534, USA — Basketball Player

Cook, David R
19 Entertainment, 8560 W Sunset Blvd, #900, Los Angeles CA 90069 USA — Singer, Guitarist, Songwriter

Cook, Dennis B
3413 Serene Hills Court, Austin TX 78738, USA — Baseball Player

Cook, Doris — Baseball Player
1059 Airport Road, Muskegon MI 49441, USA

Cook, Elizabeth — Singer
Thirty Tigers Mgmt, 1604 8th Ave S, #200, Nashville TN 37203, USA

Cook, Frederick H (Fred), III — Football Player
4402 Market St, Pascagoula MS 39567, USA

Cook, Gareth — Journalist
Boston Globe, Editorial Dept, 135 William Morrissey Blvd, Dorchester MA 02125 USA

Cook, Jamie R — Guitarist (Arctic Monkeys)
Wildlife Entertainment, 21 Heathmans Road, London SW6 4TJ, England

Cook, Jeffrey A (Jeff) — Singer, Guitarist (Alabama)
Cook Sound Studio, PO Box 680067, Fort Payne AL 35968, USA

Cook, Jeffrey J (Jeff) — Basketball Player
4908 E Doubletree Ranch Road, Paradise Valley AZ 85253, USA

Cook, Jesse — Jazz, Latin Guitarist
Macklam/Feldman Mgmt, 1505 W 2nd Ave, #200, Vancouver BC V6H 3Y4, Canada

Cook, John N — Golfer
8815 Conroy Windermere Road, #40, Orlando FL 32835, USA

Cook, Kristy Lee — Singer
Arista/RCA Records, 1400 18th Ave S, Nashville TN 37212, USA

Cook, Marvin E (Marv) — Football Player
425 Butternut Lane, Iowa City IA 52246, USA

Cook, Michael H (Mike) — Baseball Player
216 Harlech Way, Charleston SC 29414, USA

Cook, Paul — Drummer (Sex Pistols)
Solo Agency, 53-55 Fulham High St, #200, London SW6 3JJ, England

Cook, Paul M — Businessman
S R I International, 333 Ravenswood Ave, Menlo Park CA 94025, USA

Cook, Peter F C — Architect
54 Compayne Gardens, London NW6 3RY, England

Cook, Rachel Leigh — Actress
James/Levy Mgmt, 3500 W Olive Ave, #1470, Burbank CA 91505 USA

Cook, Rebecca — Director, Actress
G Williams Agency, 525 S 4th St, #365, Philadelphia PA 19147, USA

Cook, Robert — Opera Singer
Quavers, 53 Friars Ave, Fiern Barnet, London N2O OXG, England

Cook, Robin — Writer
10 Louisburg Square, Boston MA 02108, USA

Cook, Ron — Actor
I C M Partners, Marlborough House, 10 Earlham St, #300, London WC2H 9LNP, England

Cook, Stanton R — Publisher
224 Raleigh Road, Kenilworth IL 60043, USA

Cook, Stephen A — Computer Scientist, Mathematician
6 Indian Valley Crescent, Toronto M6R 1Y6, Canada

Cook, Steve — Bowler
1209 Devonshire Court, Roseville CA 95661, USA

Cook, Terry — Auto, Truck Racing Driver
PO Box 86, Mount Mourne NC 28123, USA

Cook, Thomas A — Writer
Bantam Books, 1745 Broadway, New York NY 10019 USA

Cook, Timothy D (Tim) — Businessman
Apple Computer, 1 Infinite Loop, Cupertino CA 95014, USA

Cook, Toi F — Football Player
8430 Winnetka Ave, #20, Winnetka CA 91306, USA

Cook, Victor Trent — Singer, Actor
Gage Group, 315 W 57th St, #4H, New York NY 10019 USA

Cooke, Amelia — Actress
John Pierce Agency, 800 S Robertson Blvd, #5, Los Angeles CA 90035, USA

Cooke, Christian — Actor
United Agents, 12-26 Lexington St, London W1F 0LE, England

Cooke, Christopher (Chris) — Editor
2157 Ridgeview Ave, Los Angeles CA 90041, USA

Cooke, David D — Basketball Player
PO Box 270591, San Diego CA 92198, USA

Cooke, Edward G (Ed) — Football Player
2093 Wake Forest St, Virginia Beach VA 23451, USA

Cooke, Janis — Journalist
Washington Post, Editorial Dept, 1150 15th St NW, Washington DC 20071, USA

Cooke, John P — Rower
290 Old Branchville Road, Ridgefield CT 06877, USA

Cooke, Josh — Actor
Gersh Agency, 9465 Wilshire Blvd, #600, Beverly Hills CA 90212 USA

Cooke, Michael (Mick) — Trumpet Player (Belle & Sebastian)
Ground Control Touring, 20 Jay St, #826, Brooklyn NY 11201 USA

Cooke, Nicole D — Cyclist
PO Box 38, Cowbridge CF71 7XU, England

Cooke, Pamela D (Pam) — Animator
1809 San Jacinto St, Los Angeles CA 90026, USA

Cooke, Sasha — Opera Singer
I M G Artists, Hogarth Business Park, Chiswick, London W4 2TH, England

Cooke, Steven M (Steve) — Baseball Player
20709 SW Trails End Dr, Sherwood OR 97140, USA

Cooke, Victoria — Model, Actress
Playboy Promotions, 2706 Media Center Dr, Los Angeles CA 90065 USA

Cooke, William M (Bill) — Football Player
1851 Hillside Road, Fairfield CT 06824, USA

Cooks, Johnie E — Football Player
1305 Meadow Creek Dr, #111, Irving TX 75038, USA

Cool, Tre — Drummer (Green Day)
P M C, 5900 Wilshire Blvd, #1720, Los Angeles CA 90036, USA

Cooley, Chelsea — Beauty Queen
Miss Universe Organization, 1370 Ave of Americas, #1600, New York NY 10019 USA

Cooley, Cheryl — Guitarist (Klymaxx)
R D M J Entertainment Mgmt, 3619 Rose Ave, Long Beach CA 90807 USA

Cooley, Denton A — Surgeon
3014 Del Monte Dr, Houston TX 77019, USA

Coolidge, Charles H
1054 Balmoral Dr, Signal Mountain TN 37377, USA — WW II Army Hero (CMH)

Coolidge, Harold J
38 Standley St, Beverly MA 01915, USA — Conservationist

Coolidge, Jennifer
Mannic Productions, 1170 26th St, #600, New York NY 10001, USA — Actress, Comedienne

Coolidge, Martha
A P A Talent/Literary Agency, 405 S Beverly Dr, #300, Beverly Hills CA 90212 USA — Director

Coolidge, Rita
Axis Artist Mgmt, 9715 Belmar Ave, Northridge CA 91324, USA — Singer, Actress

Coolio
Intrigue Mgmt, 25 Spinney Way, Needingworth, Cambridgeshire PE27 4SR, England — Rap Artist, Actor

Coombs, Daniel B (Danny)
14130 Cleobrook Dr, Houston TX 77070, USA — Baseball Player

Coombs, Stephen
Wordplay, 35 Lisbon ST, Blackheath, London SE3 8SS, England — Concert Pianist

Coombs-Mueller, Carol
772 Tyrol Court, Crestline CA 92325, USA — Actress

Coomer, Ronald B (Ron)
7021 Howard Lane, Eden Prairie MN 55346, USA — Baseball Player

Coon, Charles (Chuck), Sr
9433 E Shady Grove Court, White Lake MI 48386, USA — Harness Racing Executive

Cooney, Gerry
PO Box 525, Fanwood NJ 07023, USA — Boxer

Cooney, Joan Ganz
Children's TV Workshop, 1 Lincoln Plaza, New York NY 10023, USA — Educator, Businesswoman

Cooney, Thomas M
854 Country Club Dr, Cincinnati OH 45245, USA — Businessman

Coonts, Stephen
40 Upland Road, Colorado Springs CO 80906, USA — Writer

Cooper, A Louis
200 Gregg Ave, Marion SC 29571, USA — Football Player

Cooper, A Wayne
5013 Millstone Way, Granite Bay CA 95746, USA — Basketball Player

Cooper, Abraham
Simon Wiesental Center, 1399 S Roxbury, #100, Los Angeles CA 90035, USA — Religious Leader, Rabbi

Cooper, Adam
Diamond Mgmt, 31 Percy St, London, England W1T 2DD, England — Actor, Singer

Cooper, Adrian
3120 Saint Paul St, Denver CO 80205, USA — Football Player

Cooper, Alice
Solid Rock Foundation, 4250 E Camelback Road, #K260, Phoenix, AZ 85018 85018, USA — Singer, Songwriter

Cooper, Amy Levin
60 Sutton Place S, #16C, New York NY 10022, USA — Editor

Cooper, Anderson
CNN-TV, 190 Marietta Ave SW, Atlanta GA 30303 USA — Commentator

Cooper, Bernadette
R D M J Entertainment Mgmt, 3619 Rose Ave, Long Beach CA 90807 USA — Musician (Klymaxx)

Cooper, Bradley
Creative Artists Agency, 2000 Ave of Stars, #100, Los Angeles CA 90067 USA — Actor, Comedian

Cooper, Brian J
346 W Ada Ave, Glendora CA 91741, USA — Baseball Player

Cooper, Camille
New York Liberty, Madison Square Garden, 2 Penn Plaza, New York NY 10121 USA — Basketball Player

Cooper, Cecil C
24802 Boulder Lakes Court, Katy TX 77494, USA — Baseball Player, Manager

Cooper, Charles G
3410 Barger Dr, Falls Church VA 22044, USA — Marine Corps General

Cooper, Chris
Paradigm Agency, 360 N Crescent Dr, North Building, Beverly Hills CA 90210 USA — Actor

Cooper, Christin
1001 E Hyman Ave, Aspen CO 81611, USA — Alpine Skier

Cooper, Daniel L
121 Leisure Court, Reading PA 19610, USA — Navy Admiral

Cooper, Dominic
Markham & Froggatt, Julian House, 4 Windmill St, London W1P 1HF, England — Actor

Cooper, Eric R
4330 NW 169th Court, Clive IA 50325, USA — Baseball Umpire

Cooper, Helene
New York Times, Editorial Dept, 229 W 43rd St, New York NY 10036 USA — Writer, Journalist

Cooper, Imogen
Askonas Holt, Lincoln House, 300 High Holborn, London WC1V 7JH, England — Concert Pianist

Cooper, James A (Jim)
12910 Low Meadow Court, Charlotte NC 28277, USA — Football Player

Cooper, Jeanne
8401 Edwin Dr, Los Angeles CA 90046, USA — Actress

Cooper, Jilly
Curtis Brown Group, 28-29 Haymarket St, #500, London SW1Y 4SP, England — Writer

Cooper, John
ESPN-TV, ESPN Plaza, 935 Middle St, Bristol CT 06010 USA — Football Coach

Cooper, John M
182 Western Way, Princeton NJ 08540, USA — Philosopher

Cooper, Leon N
49 Intervale Road, Providence RI 02906, USA — Nobel Physics Laureate

Cooper, Lester I
45 Morningside Dr S, Westport CT 06880, USA — Producer

Cooper, M Earl
2224 E Highway 21, Lincoln TX 78948, USA — Football Player

Cooper, Martin
Dyna Inc, 100 Via de la Valley, #200, Del Mar CA 92014, USA — Inventor (Cell Phone)

Cooper, Matthew T
9326 Fairfax St, Alexandria VA 22309, USA — Marine Corps General

Cooper, Pat
243 W 70th St, #8D, New York NY 10023, USA — Actor, Comedian

Cooper, Richard N
33 Washington Ave, Cambridge MA 02140, USA — Economist

Cooper, Roxanne — Singer
Freemantle Media, 2700 Colorado Ave, #450, Santa Monica CA 90404, USA
Cooper, Stuart — Director, Actor
Creative Artists Agency, 2000 Ave of Stars, #100, Los Angeles CA 90067 USA
Cooper, Susan M — Writer
Simon & Schuster, 1230 Ave of Americas, Concourse 1, New York NY 10020 USA
Cooper, Wayne — Artist, Sculptor
PO Box 106, Depew OK 74028, USA
Cooper, William A (Bill) — Football Player
16056 Greenwood Road, Monte Sereno CA 95030, USA
Cooper-Dyke, Cynthia — Basketball Player, Coach
University of North Carolina, Athletic Dept, Wilmington NC 28403, USA
Coor, Lattie F — Educator
Arizona State University, Public Affairs School, Tempe AZ 85287, USA
Coors, William K — Businessman
Adolph Coors Co, 311 10th St, Golden CO 80401, USA
Coote, Alice — Opera Singer
I M G Artists, Hogarth Business Park, Chiswick, London W4 2TH, England
Coover, Robert — Writer
Brown University, Linden Press, 49 George St, Providence RI 02912, USA
Cope, Derrike — Auto Racing Driver
103 Turnerlair Court, Mooresville NC 28117, USA
Cope, Jonathan — Ballet Dancer
Royal Ballet, Covent Garden, Bow St, London WC2E 9DD, England
Copeland, Horace C — Football Player
4195 Blakemore Place. Spring Hill FL 34609, USA
Copeland, Kenneth — Evangelist
Kenneth Copeland Ministries, PO Box 2908, Fort Worth TX 76113, USA
Copeland, Shemekia — Singer
Alligator Records, PO Box 60234, Chicago IL 60660, USA
Copeland, Stewart — Drummer (Police, Oysterhead), Composer
2420 Arbutus Dr, Los Angeles CA 90049, USA
Coples, Quinton — Football Player
New York Jets, 1 Jets Dr, Florham Park NJ 07932 USA
Copley, Teri — Actress, Model
13351 Riverside Dr, #D513, Sherman Oaks CA 91423, USA
Copley, William — Artist
1 Frisbie Road, Roxbury CT 06783, USA
Copon, Michael S — Actor, Model, Singer
Don Buchwald/Fortitude, 6500 Wilshire Blvd, #2200, Los Angeles CA 90048 USA
Copp, D Harold — Physiologist
4755 Belmont Ave, Vancouver BC V6T 1A8, Canada
Coppa, Giovanni — Religious Leader
Apostolic Nuncio, Vorsilska Ul 12, 11000 Prague 1, Czech Republic
Coppens, Yves — Paleoanthropologist
4 Rue du Pont-aux-Choux, 75003 Paris, France
Copperfield, David — Illusionist
Magic Arts Entertainment, 10145 Philipp Parkway, #A, Streetsboro OH 44241, USA
Copperwheat, Lee — Fashion Designer
Copperwheat Blundell, 14 Cheshire St, London E2 6EH, England
Coppinger, John T (Rocky) — Baseball Player
7280 Alto Rey Ave, El Paso TX 79912, USA
Coppo, Paul — Ice Hockey Player
3458 Solitude Road, De Pere WI 54115, USA
Coppola, Alicia — Actress
A P A Talent/Literary Agency, 405 S Beverly Dr, #300, Beverly Hills CA 90212 USA
Coppola, Francis Ford — Director
Niebaum-Coppola Estate, 1991 Saint Helena Highway, Rutherford CA 94573, USA
Coppola, Imani — Singer, Songwriter
International Talent Booking, Ariel House, 74A Charlotte St, #100 London W1T 4QJ, England
Coppola, Sofia — Actress, Director, Writer
Cinetic Mgmt, 555 W 25th St, #400, New York NY 10001, USA
Copps Michael J — Government Official
Federal Communications Commission, 1919 M St NW, Washington DC 20036, USA
Cora, Catherine (Cat) — Chef
W M E Entertainment, 9601 Wilshire Blvd, #300, Beverly Hills CA 90210 USA
Cora, J Alexander (Alex) — Baseball Player
150 Brookline Ave, Boston MA 02215, USA
Cora, Jose M (Joey) — Baseball Player
17734 SW 47th St, Miramar FL 33029, USA
Corabi, John — Singer, Guitarist (Motley Crue)
Union Entertainment Group, 1323 Newbury Road, #104, Newbury Park CA 91320, USA
Coraci, Frank — Director
I C M Partners, 10250 Constellation Blvd, #900, Los Angeles CA 90067 USA
Corbat, Michael L (Mike) — Financier
Citigroup Inc, 55 E 52nd St, New York NY 10055, USA
Corbato, Fernando J — Computer Scientist
88 Temple St, West Newton MA 02465, USA
Corbet, Brady — Actor, Director
W M E Entertainment, 9601 Wilshire Blvd, #300, Beverly Hills CA 90210 USA
Corbett, Douglas M (Doug) — Baseball Player
75083 Edwards Road, Yulee FL 32097, USA
Corbett, Gretchen — Actress
S D B Partners, 1801 Ave of Stars, #902, Los Angeles CA 90067 USA
Corbett, Michael — Actor
I C M Partners, 10250 Constellation Blvd, #900, Los Angeles CA 90067 USA
Corbett, Mike — Rock Climber
41828 Road 600, Ahwahnee CA 93601, USA
Corbett, Ronnie — Actor, Comedian
International Artists, 235 Regent St, London W1R 8AX, England
Corbijn, Anton — Photographer, Cinematographer
Independent Talent Group, Oxford House, 76 Oxford St, London W1D 1BS, England
Corbin, A Ray — Baseball Player
65 Moore St, Franklin NC 28734, USA
Corbin, Barry — Actor
Linda McAlister Talent, 530 S Lake Ave, #435, Pasadena CA 91101, USA

Corbin, Tom
201 Wyandotte St, #102, Kansas City MO 64105, USA — Sculptor
Corbin, Tyrone K
652 Edgewood Dr, North Salt Lake UT 84054, USA — Basketball Player, Coach
Corbitt, Jerry
First Rainbow, 1650 Barnes Mill Road, #1214, Marietta GA 30062, USA — Singer, Guitarist (Youngbloods)
Corchiani, Christopher (Chris)
1106 Harvey St, Raleigh NC 27608, USA — Basketball Player
Corcoran, Barbara
W M E Entertainment, 9601 Wilshire Blvd, #300, Beverly Hills CA 90210 USA — Writer
Corcoran, Kevin
8617 Balcom Ave, Northridge CA 91325, USA — Actor
Corcoran, Norm
20 Nickerson Ave, Saint Catherines ON L2N 3L4, Canada — Ice Hockey Player
Corcoran, Roy E
PO Box 173, Slaughter LA 70777, USA — Baseball Player
Corcoran, Timothy M (Tim)
4349 Friar Circle, La Verne CA 91750, USA — Baseball Player
Cord, Alex
Cord Equestrian, 7639 FM 2071, Gainesville TX 76240, USA — Actor
Corday, Barbara
317 N Van Ness Ave, Los Angeles CA 90004, USA — Businesswoman, Writer, Producer
Corday, Mara
29532 Mendoze Dr, Valencia CA 91355, USA — Actress, Model
Corddry, Nathan (Nate)
B/W/R, 9100 Wilshire Blvd, #500W, Beverly Hills CA 90212 USA — Actor
Corddry, Rob
Principato-Young, 9465 Wilshire Blvd, #880, Beverly Hills CA 90212 USA — Actor, Comedian
Corden, James
United Agents, 12-26 Lexington St, London W1F 0LE, England — Actor
Cordero Lanza di Montezemolo, Andrea
Nunciature to Italy, Via Po 27-29, 00198 Rome, Italy — Religious Leader
Cordero, Angel T, Jr
4 Osborne Lane, Greenvale NY 11548, USA — Thoroughbred Racing Jockey
Cordero, Chad P
13305 Noble Place, Chino CA 91710, USA — Baseball Player
Cordero, Francisco J
4125 Oak Tree Court, Loveland OH 45140, USA — Baseball Player
Cordero, Sebastian
Creative Artists Agency, 2000 Ave of Stars, #100, Los Angeles CA 90067 USA — Director, Writer
Cordero, Wilfredo N (Wil)
25844 Kensington Dr, Westlake OH 44145, USA — Baseball Player
Cordes, Paul J Cardinal
Pontifical Council Cor Unum, Piazza S Calisto 16, 00153 Rome, Italy — Religious Leader
Cordes-Elliott, Gloria
86 Malone Ave, Staten Island NY 10306, USA — Baseball Player
Cordingly, Beth
Hatton McEwan, 3 Chocolate Studios, 7 Shepherdess Place, London N1 7LJ, England — Actress
Cordova, France A
Purdue University, President's Office, West Lafayette IN 47907, USA — Educator
Cordova, Francisco J (CoCo)
Cincinnati Reds, Great American Ball Park, 100 Main St, Cincinnati OH 45202 USA — Baseball Player
Cordova, Martin K (Marty)
47 Club Vista Dr, Henderson NV 89052, USA — Baseball Player
Corduner, Allan
Conway Van Gelder Grant, 8-12 Broadwick St, #300, London W1F 8HW, England — Actor
Core, Ericson
Gersh Agency, 9465 Wilshire Blvd, #600, Beverly Hills CA 90212 USA — Director, Cinematographer
Corea, Armando A (Chick)
Chick Corea Productions, 10400 Samoa Ave, Tujunga CA 91042, USA — Jazz Pianist, Composer
Corey, Bryan S
7829 E Riverdale Circle, Mesa AZ 85207, USA — Baseball Player
Corey, Clint
30635 W Mission Road, Powell Butte OR 97753, USA — Rodeo Rider
Corey, Elias J
20 Avon Hill St, Cambridge MA 02140, USA — Nobel Chemistry Laureate
Corey, Irwin (Professor)
Worlds Foremost Mgmt, 165 W 21st St, New York NY 10011, USA — Actor, Comedian
Corey, Jill
64 Division Ave, Levittown NY 11756, USA — Singer
Corey, Walter M (Walt)
26007 Timber Meadow Dr, Lees Summit MO 64086, USA — Football Player
Corfield, Kenneth G
10 Chapel Place, Rivington St, London EC2A 3DQ, England — Businessman
Corgan, William P (Billy), Jr
Evolution Music Partners, 1680 N Vine St, #500, Los Angeles CA 90028, USA — Singer (Smashing Pumpkins), Songwriter
Corigliano, John P
365 W End Ave, New York NY 10024, USA — Composer
Corinealdi, Emayatzy
I C M Partners, 10250 Constellation Blvd, #900, Los Angeles CA 90067 USA — Actress
Corkins, Michael P (Mike)
3760 Chemehuevi Blvd, Lake Havasu City AZ 86406, USA — Baseball Player
Corley, Al
1177 Embury St, Pacific Palisades CA 90272, USA — Actor
Corley, W Gene
Construction Tech Laboratories, 5400 Old Orchard Road, Skokie IL 60077, USA — Structural Engineer
Cormack, Danielle
Johnson & Laird Mgmt, PO Box 78340, Grey Lynn, Auckland 1002, New Zealand — Actress
Corman, Roger W
Concorde New Horizons, 11600 San Vicente Blvd, Los Angeles CA 90049, USA — Director, Producer
Cormier, Lance R
3630 Windy Ridge, Tuscaloosa AL 35406, USA — Baseball Player
Cormier, Rheal P
2640 Cody Circle, Park City UT 84098, USA — Baseball Player
Corn, Alfred
350 W 14th St, #6A, New York NY 10014, USA — Writer

C

Corbin - Corn

Cornelison, Jerry G — Football Player
12713 Cedar St, Leawood KS 66209, USA

Cornelius — Singer, Guitarist
Magnum Public Relations, 32 E 31st St, #900, New York NY 10016, USA

Cornelius, Helen — Singer, Songwriter
PO Box 12089, Nashville TN 37212, USA

Cornelius, James M — Businessman
Bristol-Myers Squibb, 345 Park Ave, New York NY 10154, USA

Cornelius, Kathy — Golfer
5744 W Dek Rio St, Chandler AZ 85226, USA

Cornell, Chris — Singer, Drummer (Soundgarden)
W M E Entertainment, 9601 Wilshire Blvd, #300, Beverly Hills CA 90210 USA

Cornell, Eric A — Nobel Physics Laureate
University of Colorado, Physics Dept, PO Box 440, Boulder CO 80328, USA

Cornell, Harry M, Jr — Businessman
Leggett & Platt Inc, 1 Leggett Road, Carthage MO 64836, USA

Cornell, Lydia — Actress
Venus Flix, 269 S Beverly Dr, #698, Beverly Hills CA 90212, USA

Cornell, Robert P (Bo) — Football Player
2605 239th Ave SE, Sammamish WA 98075, USA

Cornette, Jim — Wrestler
PO Box 436963, Louisville KY 40253, USA

Cornforth, John W — Nobel Chemistry Laureate
Saxon Down, Cuilfail, Lewes, East Sussex BN7 2BE, England

Cornforth, Mark — Ice Hockey Player
11 Indian Spring Road, Milton MA 02186, USA

Cornish, Abbie — Actress
W M E Entertainment, 9601 Wilshire Blvd, #300, Beverly Hills CA 90210 USA

Cornish, Frank E, III — Football Player
1024 Inca Dr. #A, Harvey LA 70058, USA

Cornish, Nick — Actor
James Levy Jacobson Mgmt, 3500 W Olive Ave, #900, Burbank CA 91505, USA

Cornwell, Bernard — Writer
Harper Collins Publishers, 10 E 53rd St, Cellar 1, New York NY 10022 USA

Cornwell, Frederick K (Fred) — Football Player
2107 Windward Lane, Newport Beach CA 92660, USA

Cornwell, Hugh — Singer, Guitarist (Stranglers)
Concorde International, 101 Shepherds Bush Road, London W6 7LP, England

Cornwell, Patricia D — Writer
G P Putnam's Sons, 375 Hudson St, New York NY 10014 USA

Cornwell, Peter — Director, Producer, Writer
I C M Partners, 10250 Constellation Blvd, #900, Los Angeles CA 90067 USA

Corona, Jose de Jesus — Soccer Player
Federacion de Futbol, Colima 373 Colonia Roma, Delegacion Cuauhtemoc Mexico DF 06700, Mexico

Corr, Andrea — Singer, Tin Whistle Player (Corrs)
John Hughes, 6 Martello Terr, Sandycove, Dunlaoughaire, Dublin, Ireland

Corr, Caroline — Singer, Percussionist, Pianist (Corrs)
John Hughes, 6 Martello Terr, Sandycove, Dunlaoughaire, Dublin, Ireland

Corr, Jim — Singer, Keyboardist, Guitarist (Corrs)
John Hughes, 6 Martello Terr, Sandycove, Dunlaoughaire, Dublin, Ireland

Corr, Karen — Billiards Player
PO Box 1392, Goodlettsville TN 37070, USA

Corr, Sharon — Singer, Violinist (Corrs)
John Hughes, 6 Martello Terr, Sandycove, Dunlaoughaire, Dublin, Ireland

Corraface, Georges — Actor
Agents Associes, 201 Rue du Faubourg Saint Honore, 75008 Paris, France

Corrales, Patrick (Pat) — Baseball Player, Manager
2 W Wesley Road NW, #18, Atlanta GA 30305, USA

Correa Delgado, Rafael V — President, Ecuador
Palacio de Gobierno, Garcia Moreno 1043, Quito, Ecuador

Correa, Charles M — Architect
Sonmarg, Napean Sea Road, Mumbai 400006, India

Correia, Amy — Singer, Guitarist, Songwriter
Season of Mist Records, 111 Rt de la Valentinell, 13011 Marseille, France

Correia, Kevin J — Baseball Player
1200 Crestview Dr, Cardiff CA 92007, USA

Correll, Victor C (Vic) — Baseball Player
119 Kentucky Downs, Perry GA 31069, USA

Corretja, Alex — Tennis Player
Association of Tennis Professionals, 200 Tournament Road, Ponte Vedra Beach FL 32082 USA

Corri, Adrienne — Actress
Rolf & Rachel Kruger, 205 Chudleigh Road, London SE4 1EG, England

Corrie, Emily — Actress
United Agents, 12-26 Lexington St, London W1F 0LE, England

Corrigan, E Gerald — Government Official, Financier
Goldman Sachs Co, 85 Broad St, Building 85, New York NY 10004, USA

Corrigan, Kevin — Actor
Innovative Artists, 1505 10th St, Santa Monica CA 90401 USA

Corrigan, Michale D (Mike) — Ice Hockey Player
21 Birchwood Road, Enfield CT 06082, USA

Corrigan, Patrick — Editorial Cartoonist
Toronto Star, Editorial Dept, 1 Yonge St, Toronto ON M5E 1E5, Canada

Corrigan-Maguire, Mairead — Nobel Peace Laureate
Peace People, 224 Lisburn Road, Belfast BT9 6GE, Northern Ireland

Corriveau, Yvon — Ice Hockey Player
396 Willard Ave, #A2, Newington CT 06111, USA

Corsaro, Frank A — Director
33 Riverside Dr, New York NY 10023, USA

Corsi, James B (Jim) — Baseball Player
6 Edwards Circle, Bellingham MA 02019, USA

Corso, John A — Cinematographer
241 W 13th St, #21, New York NY 10011, USA

Corso, Leland (Lee) — Sportscaster
ESPN-TV, ESPN Plaza, 935 Middle St, Bristol CT 06010 USA

Corson, Shayne — Ice Hockey Player
Tappo Restaurant, 3-55 Mill St, Toronto ON M5A 3C4, Canada

Cort, Barry L
1812 E Okaloosa Ave, Tampa FL 33604, USA — Baseball Player

Cort, Bud
2609 Lake View Ave, Los Angeles CA 90039, USA — Actor

Cortazar, Esteban
111 NE 1st St, #900, Miami FL 33132, USA — Fashion Designer

Cortes Granados, Javier
Federacion de Futbol, Colima 373 Colonia Roma, Delegacion Cuauhtemoc Mexico DF 06700, Mexico — Soccer Player

Cortes, Joaquin
W M E Entertainment, 9601 Wilshire Blvd, #300, Beverly Hills CA 90210 USA — Flamenco Dancer, Choreographer

Cortes, Ron
Philadelphia Inquirer, Editorial Dept, 400 N Broad St, Philadelphia PA 19130, USA — Journalist

Cortese, Dan
3 Arts Entertainment, 9460 Wilshire Blvd, #700, Beverly Hills CA 90212 USA — Actor

Cortese, Federico
Boston Youth Symphony, 855 Commonwealth Ave, Boston MA 02215, USA — Conductor

Cortese, Genevieve
Innovative Artists, 1505 10th St, Santa Monica CA 90401 USA — Actress

Cortese, Joe
100 S Hayworth Ave, #201, Los Angeles CA 90048, USA — Actor

Cortese, Valentina
Pretta S Erasmo 6, 20121 Milan, Italy — Actress

Cortez, Alfonso
C E S D, 10635 Santa Monica Blvd, #130, Los Angeles CA 90025 USA — Actor

Cortright, Edgar M, Jr
9701 Calvin St, Northridge CA 91324, USA — Aerospace Engineer

Corvo, Joe
2004 Falls Forest Dr, Raleigh NC 27615, USA — Ice Hockey Player

Corwin, Jeff
Jeff Corwin Experience, PO Box 2904, Toluca Lake CA 91610, USA — Actor

Corwin, Morena
Playboy Promotions, 2706 Media Center Dr, Los Angeles CA 90065 USA — Model

Coryatt, Quentin J
611 Cannon Lane, Sugar Land TX 77479, USA — Football Player

Coryell, Larry
Ellicot Talent Group, 2503 Marilyn Circle, Petaluma CA 94954, USA — Guitarist

Corzine, David J (Dave)
1161 W Hunting Dr, Palatine IL 60067, USA — Basketball Player

Cosbie, Douglas D (Doug)
1503 Fordham Court, Mountain View CA 94040, USA — Football Player

Cosby, Bill
PO Box 808, Bardwell Ferry Road, Greenfield MA 01302, USA — Actor, Comedian

Coscina, Dennis
211 Main St, East Windsor CT 06088, USA — Golfer

Cosgrave, Liam
Beech Park, Templeogue County, Dublin 6W, Ireland — Prime Minister, Ireland

Cosgriff, Kevin J
Deputy Commander, Fleet Forces Command, Norfolk VA 23551, USA — Navy Admiral

Cosgrove, Daniel
James/Levy Mgmt, 3500 W Olive Ave, #1470, Burbank CA 91505 USA — Actor

Cosgrove, Miranda
Creative Artists Agency, 2000 Ave of Stars, #100, Los Angeles CA 90067 USA — Actress, Singer

Cosic, Dobrica
Sciences & Arts Academy, Knez Mihailova 35, 11000 Belgrade, Serbia — President, Yugoslavia

Coslet, Bruce N
1778 Ivy Pointe Court, Naples FL 34109, USA — Football Player, Coach

Cosmo, James
United Agents, 12-26 Lexington St, London W1F 0LE, England — Actor

Cosmos, Jean
57 Rue de Versailles, 92410 Ville d'Avray, France — Writer

Cosmovici, Cristiano B
Instituto Fisica Spazio Interplanetario, CP 27, 00044 Frascati, Italy — Astronaut, Italy

Cosper, Kina
Richard Walters, PO Box 2789, Toluca Lake CA 91610 USA — Singer (Brownstone), Songwriter

Cossack, Roger
ESPN-TV, ESPN Plaza, 935 Middle St, Bristol CT 06010 USA — Attorney, Commentator

Cosso, Pierre
Agents Associes, 201 Rue du Faubourg Saint Honore, 75008 Paris, France — Actor

Cossotto, Fiorenza
Via Ezio Biondi 1, 21 Milan, Italy — Opera Singer

Costa, David J (Dave)
40 Halili Lane, #4M, Kihei HI 96753, USA — Football Player

Costa, Manuel Rui
F C Milan, Via Filippo Turati 3, 20121 Milan, Italy — Soccer Player

Costa, Mary
California Artists Mgmt, 41 Sutter St, #420, San Francisco CA 94104, USA — Opera Singer

Costa, Nikka
Virgin Records, 338 N Foothill Road, Beverly Hills CA 90210 USA — Singer, Songwriter

Costa, S Paul
8017 Kristina Lane, North Richland Hills TX 76182, USA — Football Player

Costa-Gavras, Konstantinos
Artmedia, 20 Ave Rapp, 75007 Paris, France — Director

Costanzo, Paulo
Principato-Young, 9465 Wilshire Blvd, #880, Beverly Hills CA 90212 USA — Actor

Costanzo, Robert
Valeo Entertainment, 8265 Sunset Blvd, #103, Los Angeles CA 90046, USA — Actor

Costas, Robert Q (Bob)
W M E Entertainment, 9601 Wilshire Blvd, #300, Beverly Hills CA 90210 USA — Sportscaster

Costello, Barry M
A D S Ventures, 500 New Jersey Ave NW, #400, Washington DC 20001 20001, USA — Navy Admiral

Costello, Elvis
I C M Partners, 10250 Constellation Blvd, #900, Los Angeles CA 90067 USA — Singer, Guitarist, Songwriter

Costello, Mariclare
Borinstein Oreck Bogart, 3172 Dona Susana Dr, Studio City CA 91604 USA — Actress

Costello, Murray
105 Kenilworth St, Ottawa ON K1Y 3Y8, Canada — Ice Hockey Player, Executive

Costello, Vince — Football Player
12300 Perry Road, Overland Park KS 66213, USA

Costelloe, Paul — Fashion Designer
30 Westminster Palace Gardens, Artillery Row, London SW1P 1RR, England

Coster, Nicolas — Actor
Momentum Talent, 9401 Wilshire Blvd, 501, Beverly Hills CA 90212, USA

Coster, Ritchie — Actor
Gersh Agency, 9465 Wilshire Blvd, #600, Beverly Hills CA 90212 USA

Coster-Waldau, Nikolaj — Actor
Lindberg Mgmt, Lavendelstr 5-7, Baghuset, 4 Sal, 1462 Copenhagen K, Denmark

Costigan, C C — Actress
I C M Partners, 10250 Constellation Blvd, #900, Los Angeles CA 90067 USA

Costle, Douglas M — Government Official, Educator
Harvard University, Public Health School, Cambridge MA 02138, USA

Costner, Kevin — Actor, Director
Treehose Films, 4450 Lakeside Dr, #225, Burbank CA 91505, USA

Cota, Chad G — Football Player
216 Island Pointe Dr, Medford OR 97504, USA

Cotchery, Jerricho — Football Player
79 Carriage Lane, Plainview NY 11803, USA

Cote, Alain — Ice Hockey Player
1352 Rue Gabrielle Roy, Quebec QC G1Y 3K3, Canada

Cote, David M — Businessman
Honeywell International, 61 Columbia Road, Morristown NJ 07960, USA

Cote, Laurence — Actress
Agents Associes, 201 Rue du Faubourg Saint Honore, 75008 Paris, France

Cote, Sylvain — Ice Hockey Player
1432 Wild Cranberry Court, Crownsville MD 21032, USA

Cothran, Sherry — Singer (EvinRudes)
Turner Management Group, 9200 W Sunset Blvd, #600, West Hollywood CA 90069, USA

Cotillard, Marion — Actress
Agence Artiste Adequet, 80 Rue d'Amsterdam, 75009 Paris, France

Cotroneo, Vince — Sportscaster
4455 E Palmdale Lane, Gilbert AZ 85298, USA

Cotrubas, Ileana — Opera Singer
Royal Opera House, Covent Garden, Bow St, London WC2, England

Cotte, Pascal — Engineer
Lumiere Technology, 215 Bis Blvd Saint Germain, 75007 Paris, France

Cottee, Kay — Yachtswoman
Showboat Productions, 113 Willoughby Road, Crows Nest NSW 2065, Australia

Cottencon, Fanny — Actress
Artmedia, 20 Ave Rapp, 75007 Paris, France

Cotti, Flavio — President, Switzerland
Christian Democratic Party, Klaraweg 6, 3001 Bern, Switzerland

Cottier, Charles K (Chuck) — Baseball Player, Manager
7129 Lake Ballinger Way, Edmonds WA 98026, USA

Cottier, George Cardinal — Religious Leader
Convento Santa Sabina, Piazza Pierro d'Illiria, 00193 Rome, Italy

Cottingham, Robert — Artist
PO Box 604, Blackman Road, Newtown CT 06470, USA

Cottle, Tameka — Singer (Xscape)
Richard Walters, PO Box 2789, Toluca Lake CA 91610 USA

Cotto, Miguel — Boxer
Top Rank Inc, 3908 Howard Hughes Parkway, #580, Las Vegas NV 89169 USA

Cotton, Blaine — Actor
Jack Scagnetti Talent, 5118 Vineland Ave, #102, North Hollywood CA 91601, USA

Cotton, James — Singer, Harmonica Player
James Cotton Mgmt, 235 W Eugene St, #G10, Chicago IL 60614, USA

Cotton, John G — Navy Admiral
Commander, Naval Reserve Force, HqUSN, Pentagon, Washington DC 20350 USA

Cotton, John J (Jack) — Basketball Player
11426 Country Road 4 S, Alamosa CO 81101, USA

Cotton, Joseph F — Test Pilot
20 Linda Vista Ave, Atherton CA 94027, USA

Cotton, Maxwell Perry — Actor
Greene Assoc, 1901 Ave of Stars, #130, Los Angeles CA 90067 USA

Cotton, Shamika — Actress
Don Buchwald/Fortitude, 6500 Wilshire Blvd, #2200, Los Angeles CA 90048 USA

Cottrell, Erin — Actress
TalentWorks, 3500 W Olive Ave, #1400, Burbank CA 91505 USA

Cottrell, William H (Bill) — Football Player
39675 Patterson Lane, Solon OH 44139, USA

Couch, Chris — Golfer
307 Johns Creek Parkway, Saint Augustine FL 32092, USA

Couch, Timothy S (Tim) — Football Player
3041 Brookmonte Lane, Lexington KY 40515, USA

Couchepin, Pascal — President, Switzerland
Federal Chancellery, Bundeshaus-W, Bundesgasse, 3033 Berne, Switzerland

Couelle, Savin — Architect
Localita Abbiadori CP 4, 07020 Porto Cervo, Italy

Couffer, Jack — Cinematographer
Original Artists, 9465 Wilshire Blvd, #324, Beverly Hills CA 90212, USA

Coughlan, Marisa — Actress
Mosaic Media Group, 9200 W Sunset Blvd, #1000, Los Angles CA 90069, USA

Coughlin, Jeg (Jeggy), Jr — Auto Racing Driver
Jeg's High Performance Racing, 751 E 11th Ave, Columbus OH 43211, USA

Coughlin, Natalie — Swimmer
4139 Coralee Lane, Lafayette CA 94549, USA

Coughlin, Tom — Football Coach
New York Giants, Meadowlands Stadium, 102 Route 120, East Rutherford NJ 07073 USA

Coughran, John W — Basketball Player
5476 Morningside Dr, San Jose CA 95138, USA

Coulier, David — Actor
Brillstein Entertainment Partners, 9150 Wilshire Blvd, #350, Beverly Hills CA 90212 USA

Coulson, Catherine E — Actress
1115 Terra Ave, Ashland OR 97520, USA

Coulter, Ann H — Commentator, Writer
Crown Publishing Group, 1745 Broadway, New York NY 10019 USA
Coulter, Catherine — Writer
PO Box 17, Mill Valley CA 94942, USA
Coulter, Michael — Cinematographer
35 Carlton Mansions, Randolph Ave, London W9 1NP, England
Coulthard, David M — Auto Racing Driver
Red Bull, Am Brunnen 1, 5330 Puschi am See, Austria
Coulthard, Raymond — Actor
United Agents, 12-26 Lexington St, London W1F 0LE, England
Counsell, Craig J — Baseball Player
992 E Circle Dr, Milwaukee WI 53217, USA
Countryman, Michael — Actor
Paradigm Agency, 360 N Crescent Dr, North Building, Beverly Hills CA 90210 USA
Counts, Mel G — Basketball Player
1581 Matheny Road, Gervais OR 97026, USA
Coupe, Eliza — Actress
W M E Entertainment, 9601 Wilshire Blvd, #300, Beverly Hills CA 90210 USA
Coupland, Douglas — Writer, Producer, Actor
United Talent Agency, 9336 Civic Center Dr, Beverly Hills CA 90210 USA
Couples, Fredrederick S (Fred) — Golfer
Players Group, 1851 Alexander Bell Dr, #410, Reston VA 20191, USA
Courant, Ernest D — Physicist
40 W 72nd St, #4I, New York NY 10023, USA
Couric, Katherine (Katie) — Commentator
1155 Park Ave, #2SW, New York NY 10128, USA
Courier, James S (Jim), Jr — Tennis Player
9533 Blandford Road, Orlando FL 32827, USA
Cournoyer, Yvan S — Ice Hockey Player
104 Boul Des Chateaux, Blainville PQ J7B 1K6, Canada
Courreges, Andre — Fashion Designer
27 Rue Delabordere, 92 Neuilly-Sur-Seine, France
Court, Charles — Government Official, Australia
21 Lewanna Way, City Beach, Perth WA 9060, Australia
Courtenay, Ed — Ice Hockey Player
1422 Whispering Oaks Trail, Mount Pleasant SC 29466, USA
Courtenay, Tom — Actor
Jonathan Altaras Assoc, 11 Garrick St, London WC2E 9AR, England
Courtnall, Geoffrey L (Geoff) — Ice Hockey Player
2730 Queenswood Dr, Victoria BC V8N 1X5, Canada
Courtnall, Russ — Ice Hockey Player
398 W Stafford Road, Thousand Oaks CA 91361, USA
Courtney, Jai — Actor
United Talent Agency, 9336 Civic Center Dr, Beverly Hills CA 90210 USA
Courtney, Joel — Actor
Creative Artists Agency, 2000 Ave of Stars, #100, Los Angeles CA 90067 USA
Courtney, Stephanie — Actress
Greene Assoc, 1901 Ave of Stars, #130, Los Angeles CA 90067 USA
Courtney, Thomas W (Tom) — Track Athlete
336 Edgemere Way E, Naples FL 34105, USA
Coury, Fred — Singer, Drummer (Cinderella)
Union Entertainment Group, 1323 Newbury Road, #104, Thousand Oaks CA 91320, USA
Cousin, Philip R — Religious Leader
African Methodist Episcopal Church, 2625 Orange Picker Road, Jacksonville FL 32223, USA
Cousin, Terry S — Football Player
9213 Everwood Court, Tampa FL 33647, USA
Cousineau, Tom — Football Player
910 Eaton Ave, Akron OH 44303, USA
Cousino, Tishara — Model, Actress
T L C, 1602 Alton Road, Miami Beach FL 33139, USA
Cousins, Christopher — Actor
DiSante Frank, 10061 Riverside Dr, #377, Toluca Lake CA 91602, USA
Cousins, Derryl — Baseball Umpire
78136 Desert Mountain Circle, Bermuda Dunes CA 92203, USA
Cousins, Robin — Figure Skater
Billy Marsh, 174-8 N Gower St, London NW1 2NB, England
Cousins, Rose — Singer, Songwriter, Guitarist
Old Farm Pony Records, PO Box 36054, RPO Spring Garden Road, Halifax NS B3J 3S9, Canada
Cousins, Tina — Singer, Model
T-Best Talent Agency, 508 Honey Lake Court, Danville CA 94506 USA
Cousteau, Jean-Michel — Oceanographer
Ocean Futures Society, 325 Chapala St, Santa Barbara CA 93101, USA
Cousy, Robert J (Bob) — Basketball Player
427 Salisbury St, Worcester MA 01609, USA
Couture, Barbara — Educator
Association of Public & Land Grant Universities, 1307 New York Ave NW, #400, Washington DC 20005, USA
Couture, Randy D (Natural) — Martial Arts Fighter, Wrestler, Actor
Gersh Agency, 9465 Wilshire Blvd, #600, Beverly Hills CA 90212 USA
Covay, Don — Singer, Songwriter
Rawstock, PO Box 110002, Cambria Heights NY 11411, USA
Coventry, Kirsty — Swimmer
Octagon Worldwide, 1751 Pinnacle Dr, #1500, McLean VA 22102 USA
Coveny, John — Producer, Writer
Creative Artists Agency, 2000 Ave of Stars, #100, Los Angeles CA 90067 USA
Coverdale, David — Singer (Whitesnake, Deep Purple)
Agency Group Ltd, 142 W 57th St, #600, New York NY 10019 USA
Coverly, Dave — Editorial Cartoonist (Speed Bump)
Bloomington Herald-Times, Editorial Dept, 1900 S Walnut, Bloomington IN 47401, USA
Covert, Allen — Actor
B/W/R, 9100 Wilshire Blvd, #500W, Beverly Hills CA 90212 USA
Covert, James P (Jimbo) — Football Player
2647 Nelson Court, Weston FL 33332, USA
Covey, Richard O — Astronaut
1155 High Lake View, Colorado Springs CO 80906, USA
Covic, Nebojsa — Prime Minister, Serbia & Montenegro
Prime Minister's Office, Nemanjina 11, 11000 Belgrade, Serbia

Coville, Bruce — Writer
Oddly Enough, PO Box 6110, Syracuse NY 13217, USA

Covington, Bucky — Singer
30141 Deercroft Dr, Wagram NC 28396, USA

Covington, Warren — Orchestra Leader
1627 Open Field Loop, Brandon FL 33510, USA

Cowan, Billy R — Baseball Player
1539 Via Coronel, Palos Verdes Estates CA 90274, USA

Cowan, John — Singer, Bassist (John Cowan Band)
Squire Mgmt, 3960 Radio Road, #206, Naples FL 34104, USA

Cowan, Ralph Wolfe — Artist
243 29th St, West Palm Beach FL 33407, USA

Cowart, Sam, III — Football Player
11110 Fallgate Point Court, Jacksonville FL 32256, USA

Cowell, Simon P — Actor
J G M, 15 Lexham Mews, London W8 6JW, England

Cowen, Robert E — Judge
US Court of Appeals, Judicial Complex, 402 E State St, Trenton NJ 08608, USA

Cowen, Scott S — Educator
Tulane University, President's Office, New Orleans LA 70118, USA

Cowens, David W (Dave) — Basketball Player, Coach
132 Deep Cove, Raymond ME 04071, USA

Cowher, William L (Bill) — Football Player, Coach; Sportscaster
1225 Briar Patch Lane, Raleigh NC 27615, USA

Cowhill, William J — Navy Admiral
9428 Vernon Dr, Great Falls VA 22066, USA

Cowie, Lennox L — Astronomer
University of Hawaii, Astronomy Dept, 2600 Campus Road, Honolulu HI 96822, USA

Cowin, Dana — Editor
Food & Wine, Editor's Office, 1120 Ave of Americas, New York NY 10036, USA

Cowley, Anthony (Tony) — Art Director
Innovative Artists, 1505 10th St, Santa Monica CA 90401 USA

Cowley, John M — Physicist
Arizona State University, Physics & Astronomy Dept, Tempe AZ 85287, USA

Cowley, Joseph A (Joe) — Baseball Player
904 Andover Garden, Lexington KY 40509, USA

Cowlings, Allen G (A C) — Football Player
PO Box 1064, Pacific Palisades CA 90272, USA

Cowper, Nicola — Actress
Brunskill Mgmt, 169 Queens Gate, #A8, London SW7 5EH, England

Cowper, Stephen C (Steve) — Governor, AK
PO Box A, Juneau AK 99811, USA

Cox, Archibald, Jr — Financier
998 5th Ave, #6W, New York NY 10028, USA

Cox, Brian — Actor
I F A Talent Agency, 8730 W Sunset Blvd, #490, West Hollywood CA 90069 USA

Cox, Brian E — Physicist
Sue Rider Mgmt, PO Box 49175, London SW19 3WY, England

Cox, Bryan K — Football Player
1306 Preservation Way, Oldsmar FL 34677, USA

Cox, C Christopher — Government Official
4000 MacArthur Blvd, #430, Newport Beach CA 92660, USA

Cox, Christina — Actress
Brillstein Entertainment Partners, 9150 Wilshire Blvd, #350, Beverly Hills CA 90212 USA

Cox, Courteney — Actress
W M E Entertainment, 9601 Wilshire Blvd, #300, Beverly Hills CA 90210 USA

Cox, Craig — Writer, Producer
Kaplan/Perrone Entertainment, 9744 Wilshire Blvd, #300, Beverly Hills CA 90212, USA

Cox, Danny B — Baseball Player, Manager
306 Feagin Mill Road, Warner Robins GA 31088, USA

Cox, David R — Statistician
Nuffield College, Statistics Dept, Oxford OX1 1NF, England

Cox, David R — Geneticist
Stanford University, Human Genome Center, Stanford CA 94305, USA

Cox, DeAnna — Singer
McFadden Artists, 818 18th Ave S, Nashville TN 37203, USA

Cox, Deborah — Singer, Songwriter
J Records, 745 5th Ave, #600, New York NY 10151 USA

Cox, Don — Singer
Stellar Entertainment, 1019 17th Ave S, Nashville TN 37212, USA

Cox, Emmett R — Judge
US Court of Appeals, 113 Saint Joseph St, #433, Mobile AL 36602, USA

Cox, Fletcher — Football Player
Philadelphia Eagles, 1 Novacare Way, Philadelphia PA 19145 USA

Cox, Frederick W (Fred) — Football Player
401 E River St, Monticello MN 55362, USA

Cox, Gary W — Political Scientist
University of California, Political Science Dept, La Jolla CA 92093, USA

Cox, Gerald — Respirologist
McMasters University Medical School, Respirology Division, Hamilton ON L85 4L8, Canada

Cox, Harvey G, Jr — Educator, Theologian
Harvard University, Divinity School, Cambridge MA 02140, USA

Cox, J Casey — Baseball Player
2840 La Concha Dr, Clearwater FL 33762, USA

Cox, Jennifer Elise — Actress
Don Buchwald/Fortitude, 6500 Wilshire Blvd, #2200, Los Angeles CA 90048 USA

Cox, Johnny W — Basketball Player, Coach
849 N Main St, Hazard KY 41701, USA

Cox, Kris — Golfer
2009 Lunenburg Dr, Allen TX 75013, USA

Cox, Lynne — Distance Swimmer
Martha Kaplan Agency, 115 W 29th St, #3, New York NY 10001, USA

Cox, Paul — Director, Producer, Writer
Illumination Films, 1 Victoria Ave, Albert Park VIC 3208, Australia

Cox, Philip S — Architect
Cox Richardson Architects, 204 Clarence St, Sydney NSW 2000, Australia

Cox, Ralph — Ice Hockey Player
8R Rolfes Lane, Newbury MA 01951, USA
Cox, Robert J (Bobby) — Baseball Manager, Executive
2190 Heathermoor Hill Dr, Marietta GA 30062, USA
Cox, Ronny — Actor
A P A Talent/Literary Agency, 405 S Beverly Dr, #300, Beverly Hills CA 90212 USA
Cox, Stephanie R — Soccer Player
Atlanta Beat, 1955 Vaughn Road, #209, Kennesaw GA 30144, USA
Cox, Stephen J — Artist
154 Barnsbury Road, Islington, London N1 0ER, England
Cox, Steve — Football Player
1001 E Lakeshore Dr, Jonesboro AR 72401, USA
Cox, Tony — Actor
New Wave Entertainment, 2660 W Olive Ave, Burbank CA 91505, USA
Cox, Torrie T — Football Player
42 NW 92nd St, Miami Shores FL 33150, USA
Cox, W Ted — Baseball Player
109 W Pratt Dr, Oklahoma City OK 73110, USA
Cox, Warren J — Architect
3111 N St NW, Washington DC 20007, USA
Coxe, Craig — Ice Hockey Player
Teddy Griffin Arena, 3450M 119th, Harbor Springs MI 49740, USA
Coxon, Graham L — Singer, Guitarist (Blur)
C M O Mgmt, Shepherds East, Richmond Way, London W14 0DQ, England
Coyle, Brendan — Actor
Rights House, 34-43 Russell St, London WC2B 5HA, England
Coyle, Richard — Actor
Troika, 74 Clerkenwell Road, #300, London EC1M 5QA, England
Coyne, Colleen — Ice Hockey Player
79 Cedar St, Amesbury MA 01913, USA
Coyne, Jonny — Actor
Louisa Spring Mgmt, 404 Carroll Canal Court, Venice CA 90291, USA
Coyne, Wayne M — Singer, Guitarist (Flaming Lips)
World's Fair Mgmt, 1208 Chowning Ave, Edmond OK 73034, USA
Coyote, Peter — Actor
Untitled Entertainment, 350 S Beverly Dr, #200, Beverly Hills CA 90212 USA
Coz, Steve — Editor
National Enquirer, 1000 American Media Way, Boca Raton FL 33464, USA
Cozier, Jimmy — Singer, Songwriter
Padell Nadell Fine Wineberger, 59 Maiden Lane, #2700, New York NY 10038 USA
Crabbe, Claude C — Football Player
49581 Wayne St, Indio CA 92201, USA
Crable, Robert E (Bob) — Football Player
564 Miami Trace Court, Loveland OH 45140, USA
Crabtree, Colleen — Actress
A P A Talent/Literary Agency, 405 S Beverly Dr, #300, Beverly Hills CA 90212 USA
Crabtree, Eric L — Football Player
3101 Walnut St, Denver CO 80205, USA
Crabtree, Michael — Football Player
San Francisco 49ers, 4949 Centennial Blvd, Santa Clara CA 95054 USA
Crabtree, Timothy L (Tim) — Baseball Player
1503 Kingswood Lane, Colleyville TX 76034, USA
Cracknell, James — Rowing Athlete
Headway, 190 Bagnall Road, Old Basford, Nottingham Nottinghamshire NG6 8SF, England
Craddock, Bantz J — Army General
Military Professional Resources, 1320 Braddock Place, Alexandria VA 22314, USA
Craddock, Billy (Crash) — Singer, Songwriter
3007 Old Martinsville Road, Greensboro NC 27455, USA
Craft, Christine — Commentator
KRBK-TV, News Dept, 500 Media Place, Sacramento CA 95815, USA
Craft, Jason D A — Football Player
11688 Armistad Court, Jacksonville FL 32256, USA
Crafter, Jane — Golfer
317 W Almeria Road, Phoenix AZ 85003, USA
Cragg, Anthony D (Tony) — Sculptor
Lise-Meitner-Str 33, 42119 Wuppertal, Germany
Cragg, Stephen — Director
Thrive Entertainment, 1093 Broxton Ave, Ste 228, Los Angeles CA 90024, USA
Craggs, George — Soccer Player
6223 6th Ave NW, Seattle WA 98107, USA
Craig of Radley, David B — Air Force Marshal, England
House of Lords, Westminster, London SW1A 0PW, England
Craig, Adam Jamal — Actor
S M S Talent, 8383 Wilshire Blvd, #230, Beverly Hills CA 90211 USA
Craig, Cornelius (Neal), Jr — Football Player
2231 Crane Ave, Cincinnati OH 45207, USA
Craig, Daniel — Actor
Independent Talent Group, Oxford House, 76 Oxford St, London W1D 1BS, England
Craig, Eli — Director, Producer
Creative Artists Agency, 2000 Ave of Stars, #100, Los Angeles CA 90067 USA
Craig, Elijah — Actor
Gilbertson Entertainment, 1334 3rd Street Promenade, #201, Santa Monica CA 90401 USA
Craig, James D (Jim) — Ice Hockey Player
PO Box 1199, Mattapoisett MA 02739, USA
Craig, Jenny — Nutritionist
5770 Fleet St, Carlsbad CA 92008, USA
Craig, Jonny — Singer
Agency Group Ltd, 142 W 57th St, #600, New York NY 10019 USA
Craig, Judy — Singer (Chiffons)
Lustig Talent, PO Box 770850, Orlando FL 32877 USA
Craig, Keren — Fashion Designer (Marchesa), Model
Marquesa, 60 W 26th St, #1425, New York NY 10001, USA
Craig, Larry E — Senator, ID
PO Box 2271, Eagle ID 83616, USA
Craig, Michael — Actor
Chatto & Linnit, 123A King's Road, London SW3 4PL, England

C

Craig, Mike — Ice Hockey Player
29907 County Road 3, Merrifield MN 56465, USA

Craig, Richard — Inventor (Land-Mine Detector)
Pacific Northwest National Laboratory, 902 Battelle Blvd, Richland WA 99354, USA

Craig, Roger L — Baseball Player, Manager
16327 Bassett Court, Ramona CA 92065, USA

Craig, Roger T — Football Player
271 Vista Verde Way, Portola Valley CA 94028, USA

Craig, Ryan — Director, Writer
United Agents, 12-26 Lexington St, London W1F 0LE, England

Craig, Stuart — Production Designer
Skouras Agency, 1149 3rd St, #300, Santa Monica CA 90403 USA

Craig, William (Bill) — Swimmer
PO Box 629, Newport Beach CA 92661, USA

Craig, Yvonne — Actress
Y C/M C Ltd, PO Box 827, Pacific Palisades CA 90272, USA

Craighead, John J — Ecologist
5125 Orchard Ave, Missoula MT 59803, USA

Crain, Jesse A — Baseball Player
20702 Hartford Way, Lakeville MN 55044, USA

Crain, William — Director
Contemporary Artists, 610 Santa Monica Blvd, #202, Santa Monica CA 90401 USA

Crais, Robert — Writer
12829 Landale St, Studio City CA 91604, USA

Cramer, Darrell — Hero
708 E 150 N, Springville UT 84663, USA

Cramer, Grant — Actor
9911 W Pico Blvd, #1060, Los Angeles CA 90035, USA

Cramer, James J (Jim) — Entertainer
Street.com. 14 Wall St, #1500, New York NY 10005, USA

Cramer, Tom — Artist
Mark Wooley Gallery, 120 NW 9th, Portland OR 97209, USA

Crampton, Barbara — Actress
Amsel Eisenstadt Frazier, 5055 Wilshire Blvd, #865, Los Angeles CA 90036 USA

Crampton, Bruce — Golfer
225 Winter Crest Lane, Severna Park MD 21146, USA

Cramton, Roger C — Attorney, Educator
475 Savage Farm Dr, Ithaca NY 14850, USA

Crandall, Bruce P — Vietnam War Air Force Hero (CMH)
PO Box 736, Manchester WA

Crandall, Delmar W (Del) — Baseball Player
807 Azalea Lane, Vero Beach FL 32963, USA

Crandall, Stephen H — Mechanical Engineer
80 Deaconess Road, #348, Concord MA 01742, USA

Crane, Benjamin M (Ben) — Golfer
2223 Cedar Elm Terrace, Westlake TX 76262, USA

Crane, Brian — Cartoonist (Pickles)
PO Box 51771, Sparks NV 89435, USA

Crane, David — Writer, Director, Producer
W M E Entertainment, 9601 Wilshire Blvd, #300, Beverly Hills CA 90210 USA

Crane, Paul E — Football Player
12 N Monterey St, Mobile AL 36604, USA

Crane, Tony — Actor
Abrams Artists, 9200 W Sunset Blvd, #1125, West Hollywood CA 90069 USA

Cranham, Kenneth — Actor
Markham & Froggatt, Julian House, 4 Windmill St, London W1P 1HF, England

Cranston, Bryan — Actor
United Talent Agency, 9336 Civic Center Dr, Beverly Hills CA 90210 USA

Cranston, Toller — Figure Skater
International Management Group, 1 Saint Clair Ave E, Toronto ON M4T 2V7, Canada

Crary, Dan — Singer, Guitarist
Thunderation Music, PO Box 371, Carson City NV 89702, USA

Crashley, Bart — Ice Hockey Player
90 Goacher Road, Campbellford ON K0L 1L0, Canada

Craven, Matt — Actor
Paradigm Agency, 360 N Crescent Dr, North Building, Beverly Hills CA 90210 USA

Craven, Murray — Ice Hockey Player
2814 Rest Haven Dr, Whitefish MT 59937, USA

Craven, Richard A (Ricky) — Auto Racing Driver
3585 Boy Scout Camp Road, Kannapolis NC 28081, USA

Craven, Wesley E (Wes) — Director
2419 Solar Dr, Los Angeles CA 90046, USA

Craver, Aaron L — Football Player
821 W Maple St, Compton CA 90220, USA

Crawford Stanley, Marianne — Basketball Coach
Washington Mystics, Verizon Center, 401 9th St NW, #750, Washington DC 20004 USA

Crawford, Billy J — Singer
Concorde International, 101 Shepherds Bush Road, London W6 7LP, England

Crawford, Bob — Ice Hockey Player
6 Progress Dr, Cromwell CT 06416, USA

Crawford, Brad — Football Player
RR 2, Winamac IN 46996, USA

Crawford, Bryce L, Jr — Chemist
3220 Lake Johanna Blvd, #58, Saint Paul MN 55112, USA

Crawford, Carl D — Baseball Player
12515 Silverglen Estates Dr, Houston TX 77014, USA

Crawford, Chace — Actor
Podwall Entertainment, 710 N Orbach Ave, #203, West Hollywood CA 90069, USA

Crawford, Christina — Writer
Seven Springs Farm, Sanders Road, Tensed ID 83870, USA

Crawford, Chuck — Fiddler, Singer (Heartland)
Country Thunder Records, 1016 17th Ave S, Nashville TN 37212, USA

Crawford, Cindy — Model, Actress
Creative Artists Agency, 2000 Ave of Stars, #100, Los Angeles CA 90067 USA

Crawford, Clayne — Actor
Elevate Entertainment, 10100 Santa Monica Blvd, #300, Los Angeles CA 90067, USA

Crawford, Eve
Nobel Caplan Abrams, 1260 Younge St, #200, Toronto ON M4T 1W6, Canada — Actress

Crawford, Frederick R (Fred)
24 W Lawn Dr, Teaneck NJ 07666, USA — Basketball Player

Crawford, Gerald J (Gerry)
111 9th St E, Saint Petersburg FL 33715, USA — Baseball Umpire

Crawford, Jamal
Los Angeles Clippers, Staples Center, 1111 S Figueroa St, Los Angeles CA 90015 USA — Basketball Player

Crawford, Joan
4748 S Harvard Ave, #80, Tulsa OK 74135, USA — Basketball Player

Crawford, John E (Johnny)
PO Box 1851, Los Angeles CA 90078, USA — Actor, Singer

Crawford, Keith L
119 A N County Road 2203, Palestine TX 75803, USA — Football Player

Crawford, Kirsty
All Terrain Music Rights, 53 Chandos Place, London WC2N 4HS, England — Singer, Songwriter

Crawford, Lavell
Anonymous Content, 3532 Hayden Ave, Culver City CA 90232 USA — Actor, Comedian

Crawford, Mac
C V S/Caremark Corp, 1 C V S/Caremark Dr, Woonsocket RI 02895, USA — Businessman

Crawford, Michael
McLean Williams Mgmt, Gainsborough House, 81 Oxford St, London W1D 2EU, England — Actor, Singer

Crawford, Nancy
Playboy Promotions, 2706 Media Center Dr, Los Angeles CA 90065 USA — Model, Actress

Crawford, Rachel
Edna Talent Mgmt, 318 Dundas St W, Toronto ON M5T 1G5, Canada — Actress

Crawford, Randy
Performers of the World, 5657 Wilshire Blvd, #280, Los Angeles CA 90036 USA — Singer

Crawford, Steve
4011 Hillman Way, #100, Youngstown OH 44512, USA — Singer (Annointed), Songwriter

Crawford, Steven R (Steve)
6122 E 480, Salina OK 74365, USA — Baseball Player

Crawley, Sylvia
Ohio University, Athletic Dept, Athens OH 45701, USA — Basketball Player, Coach

Cray, Robert
Conquero Public Relations, 11271 Ventura Blvd, #522, Studio City CA 91604, USA — Singer, Guitarist

Crayton, Patrick J
2301 Silver Table Dr, Lewisville TX 75056, USA — Football Player

Crazy Mohan
5 Hokkalingam St, Mandavelli, Chennai TN 600028, India — Actor, Comedian

Crea, Vivien S
Vice Commandant, US Coast Guard, 2100 2nd St SW, Washington DC 20593 USA — Coast Guard Admiral

Creadon, Patrick
Paradigm Agency, 360 N Crescent Dr, North Building, Beverly Hills CA 90210 USA — Director

Creager, Melora
Ken-Ran Entertainment, 418 S Barton St, Grapevine TX 76051, USA — Singer, Cellist, Songwriter

Creamer, Paula
4705 Joanna Garden Court, Windermere FL 34786, USA — Golfer

Creamer, Roger W
180 E Hartsdale Ave, #2E, Hartsdale NY 10530, USA — Sportswriter

Creamer, Timothy J
5103 Carefree Dr, League City TX 77573, USA — Astronaut

Crean, Tom
University of Indiana, Athletic Dept, Bloomington IN 47405, USA — Basketball Coach

Crear, Mark
27023 McBean Parkway, Valencia CA 91355, USA — Track Athlete

Crebassa, Marianne
I M G Artists, Hogarth Business Park, Chiswick, London W4 2TH, England — Opera Singer

Crede, Joseph (Joe)
42 Dry Creek Trail, Linn MO 65051, USA — Baseball Player

Creech, Sharon
Harper Collins Publishers, 10 E 53rd St, Cellar 1, New York NY 10022 USA — Writer

Creeggan, Jim
Nettwerk Mgmt, 6525 W Sunset Blvd, #800, Los Angeles CA 90028 USA — Bassist (Barenaked Ladies)

Creek, P Douglas (Doug)
17500 White Water Court, Punta Gorda FL 33982, USA — Baseball Player

Creekmore, Nathaniel R (Nate)
Universal Press Syndicate, 4520 Main St, #700, Kansas City MO 64111 USA — Cartoonist (Maintaining)

Creel, Gavin
Bill Silva Mgmt, 8225 Santa Monica Blvd, West Hollywood CA 90046, USA — Actor, Singer

Creel, Monica
Amsel Eisenstadt Frazier, 5055 Wilshire Blvd, #865, Los Angeles CA 90036 USA — Actress

Cregeen, Peter
Associated International Mgmt, Fairfax House, Fulwood Place, London WC1V 6HU, England — Director, Producer

Cregger, Zach
B/W/R, 9100 Wilshire Blvd, #500W, Beverly Hills CA 90212 USA — Actor, Producer, Director, Writer

Creighton, Adam
5202 Spectacular Bid Dr, Wesley Chapel FL 33544, USA — Ice Hockey Player

Creighton, David T (Dave), Sr
5202 Spectacular Bid Dr, Wesley Chapel FL 33544, USA — Ice Hockey Player, Coach

Creighton, Jim
5297 S Geneva St, Englewood CO 80111, USA — Basketball Player

Creighton, Joanne V
Mount Holyoke College, President's Office, South Hadley MA 01075, USA — Educator

Creighton, John O
2111 SW 174th St, Burien WA 98166, USA — Astronaut

Crennel, Romeo
411 W 46th Terrace, #701, Kansas City MO 64112, USA — Football Coach

Crensha, George
22 Morning State Way, Sequim WA 98382, USA — Cartoonist (Belvedere)

Crenshaw, Ben D
2610 Kenmore Court, Austin TX 78703, USA — Golfer

Crenshaw, Lewis W, Jr
DCNO, Resource/Warfare Requirements, HqUSN, Pentagon, Washington DC 20350, USA — Navy Admiral

Crenshaw, Marshall
Razor & Tie Records, 214 Sullivan St, #4A, New York NY 10012, USA — Singer, Songwriter

Crenshaw, Willis C
21 Carly Dr, Woodstock NY 12498, USA — Football Player

Crescentini, Carolina
Stefano Chiappi Mgmt, Via Ippolito Nievo 6, Scala D, 00149 Rome, Italy — Actress

Creskoff, Rebecca
Innovative Artists, 1505 10th St, Santa Monica CA 90401 USA — Actress

Crespino, Robert (Bob)
109 Heatherdown Road, Decatur GA 30030, USA — Football Player

Crespo Claudio, Felipe J
PO Box 592363, Orlando FL 32859, USA — Baseball Player

Crespo, Elvis
A-P R Media, 8334 Lefferts Blvd, #3C, Kew Gardens NY 11415, USA — Singer

Crespo, Hernan
Chelsea F C, Stamford Bridge, Fulham Road, London SW6 1HS, England — Soccer Player

Cressend, Jack
11 Jacqueline Court, Mandeville LA 70471, USA — Baseball Player

Cressida, Kathryn
W M E Entertainment, 9601 Wilshire Blvd, #300, Beverly Hills CA 90210 USA — Actress

Cresson, Edith
Mairie, 86018 Chatellerault Cedex, France — Prime Minister, France

Cretier, Jean-Luc
153 Ave du Marechal Leclerc, BP 20, 73700 Bourq Saint Maurice, France — Alpine Skier

Crew, Amanda
United Talent Agency, 9336 Civic Center Dr, Beverly Hills CA 90210 USA — Actress

Crewdson, Gregory
247 16th St, Brooklyn NY 11215, USA — Photographer

Crewe, Candida
Bloomsbury Publishing, 36 Soho Square, London W1D 3Q4, England — Writer

Crews, David P
University of Texas, Biological Science Division, Zoology Dept, Austin TX 78712, USA — Psychobiologist

Crews, Frederick C
636 Vicente Ave, Berkeley CA 94707, USA — Educator, Writer

Crews, Phillip
University of California, Chemistry Dept, 1156 High St, Santa Cruz CA 99064, USA — Chemist

Crews, Terry A
3 Arts Entertainment, 9460 Wilshire Blvd, #700, Beverly Hills CA 90212 USA — Actor, Football Player

Crewson, Wendy
Oscars Abrams Zimel, 438 Queen St E, Toronto ON M5A 1T4, Canada — Actress

Crha, Jiri
16390 Braeburn Ridge Trail, Delray Beach FL 33446, USA — Ice Hockey Player

Cribbins, Bernard
Gavin Barker Assoc, 2D Wimpole St, London W1G 0EB, England — Actor

Cribbs, Joe S
5333 Creekside Loop, Birmingham AL 35244, USA — Football Player

Cribbs, Joshua
9333 W Hampton Dr, North Royalton OH 44133, USA — Football Player

Crichlow, Lenora
B W H Agency, 117 Shaftesbury Ave, London WC2H 8AD, England — Actress

Crickhowell of Pont Esgob, Nicholas E
4 Henning St, London SW11 3DR, England — Government Leader, England

Crider, Melissa (Missy)
Metropolitan Talent Agency, 7020 La Presa Dr, Los Angeles CA 90068 USA — Actress

Crier, Catherine
Crier Communications, PO Box 627, Katonaj NY 10536, USA — Commentator

Crile, Susan
168 W 86th St, New York NY 10024, USA — Artist

Crilley, Mark
PO Box 103, Walled Lake MI 48390, USA — Writer

Crim, Charles R (Chuck)
50039 Golden Horse Dr, Oakhurst CA 93644, USA — Baseball Player

Crippen, Robert L
781 Harbour Isle Place, West Palm Beach FL 33410, USA — Astronaut

Crisostomo, Manny
Pacific Daily News, PO Box DN, Hagatna GU 96932, USA — Photojournalist

Crisp, Covelli L (Coco)
5 Devonshire Road, Middleton MA 01949, USA — Baseball Player

Crisp, Terry A
805 Cherry Laurel Court, Nashville TN 37215, USA — Ice Hockey Player, Coach

Crispin, Anne C (A C)
Anne Arundel Community College, 101 College Parkway, Arnold MD 21012, USA — Writer

Criss, Charles W (Charlie)
4310 Melanie Lane, Atlanta GA 30349, USA — Basketball Player

Criss, Peter
2111 Friar Court, Wall Township NJ 07719, USA — Singer, Drummer (Kiss)

Crist, Charles T (Chuck)
PO Box 369, Greenhurst NY 14742, USA — Football Player

Crist, George B
406 East St, Beaufort SC 29902, USA — Marine Corps General

Crist, Myndy
Abrams Artists, 9200 W Sunset Blvd, #1125, West Hollywood CA 90069 USA — Actress

Crista, Heloise
Taliesin West, PO Box 4430, Scottsdale AZ 85261, USA — Sculptor

Cristal, Linda
9129 Hazen Dr, Beverly Hills CA 90210, USA — Actress

Cristofer, Michael
I C M Partners, 10250 Constellation Blvd, #900, Los Angeles CA 90067 USA — Writer, Director, Actor

Cristol, Stanley J
1638 W 3rd Ave, Durango CO 81301, USA — Chemist

Criswell, Jeffrey L (Jeff)
811 Walnut St, Kansas City MO 64106, USA — Football Player

Critelli, Michael
Pitney Bowes Inc, 1 Elmcroft Road, Stamford CT 06926, USA — Businessman

Criter, Kenneth W (Ken)
PO Box 441343, Aurora CO 80044, USA — Football Player

Crittenton, Javaris C
Washington Wizards, M C I Centre, 601 F St NW, Washington DC 20004 USA — Basketball Player

Croasdell, Adam
Ken McReddie Assoc, 11 Connaught Place, London W2 2ET, England — Actor

Croce, Adrian J (A J)
1027 Meade Ave, San Diego CA 92116, USA — Singer

Croce, Joseph
Wolfman Jack Entertainment, 105 Rivershore Dr, Hertford NC 27944 USA — Singer (Chimes)

Crocicchia, Olivia
United Talent Agency, 9336 Civic Center Dr, Beverly Hills CA 90210 USA — Actress

Crocker, Ian
8901 Ovalia Ave, Austin TX 78749, USA — Swimmer

Crocker, J Dillard
5601 Holiday Park Blvd, North Port FL 34287, USA — Basketball Player

Crocker, Mary Lou
1403 Sutton Dr, Carrollton TX 75006, USA — Golfer

Crocker, Ryan C
State Department, 2201 C St NW, Washington DC 20520 USA — Diplomat

Crockett, Affion
Lejan Entertainment, 11271 Ventura Blvd, #186, Studio City CA 91604, USA — Actor

Crockett, Affion
Creative Artists Agency, 2000 Ave of Stars, #100, Los Angeles CA 90067 USA — Actor

Crockett, Billy
Street Level Artists Agency, 106 N Buffalo St, #200, Warsaw IN 46580, USA — Singer, Songwriter

Crockett, D Ray
1526 Highland Lakes Dr, Keller TX 76248, USA — Football Player

Crockett, Robert P (Bobby)
PO Box 26, Harriet AR 72639, USA — Football Player

Crockett, Zack
3301 NE 183rd St, #604, Aventura FL 33160, USA — Football Player

Croel, Mike
8305 Lookout Mountain Ave, Los Angeles CA 90046, USA — Football Player

Croft, Dwayne
I M G Artists, 152 W 57th St, #500, New York NY 10019 USA — Opera Singer

Croft, Richard
I M G Artists, Hogarth Business Park, Chiswick, London W4 2TH, England — Opera Singer

Crofts, Dash
4Star Entertainment, 1675 York Ave, #32C, New York NY 10128, USA — Singer, Songwriter (Seals & Crofts)

Croker, Stephen B (Steve)
2 Byford Court, Chestertown MD 21620, USA — Air Force General

Cromartie, Antonio
New York Jets, 1 Jets Dr, Florham Park NJ 07932 USA — Football Player

Crombeen, Mike
817 Foxcroft Blvd, Newmarket ON L3X 1MB, Canada — Ice Hockey Player

Crombey, Bernard
Artmedia, 20 Ave Rapp, 75007 Paris, France — Actor

Crombie, Jonathan
Gage Group, 315 W 57th St, #4H, New York NY 10019 USA — Actor

Cromer, Roy B (Tripp), III
32 W Tombee Lane, Columbia SC 29209, USA — Baseball Player

Cromme, Gerhard
Siemens AG, Wittelsbacherplatz 2, 80333 Munich, Germany — Businessman

Crompton, Alfred W
Harvard University, Museum of Comparative Zoology, Cambridge MA 02138, USA — Archaeologist, Ethnologist, Biologist

Crompton, Steven S
PO Box 2018, Scottsdale AZ 85252, USA — Cartoonist (Demi the Demoness)

Cromwell, James
Koshari Films, 13251 Ventura Blvd, #1, Studio City CA 91604, USA — Actor

Cromwell, Nolan
29427 Hummingbird Circle, Westlake OH 44145, USA — Football Player, Coach

Cronan, Peter J (Pete)
13 Saddle Hill Road, Hopkinton MA 01748, USA — Football Player

Cronbach, Lee J
2614 Oregon St, Union City CA 94587, USA — Psychologist

Crone, Raymond H (Ray)
508 Panarama, Waxahachie TX 75165, USA — Baseball Player

Cronenberg, David
Sentient Entertainment, 1617 Broadway, Mezzanine Suite, Santa Monica CA 90404, USA — Director

Cronenweth, Jeffrey S (Jeff)
2241 Corinth Ave, Los Angeles CA 90064, USA — Cinematographer

Cronin, Anthony
30 Oakley Road, Dublin 6, Ireland — Writer

Cronin, Eugene E (Gene)
2445 37th Ave, Sacramento CA 95822, USA — Football Player

Cronin, James W
175 N Harbor Dr, #4902, Chicago IL 60601, USA — Nobel Physics Laureate

Cronin, Shawn
4163 SE Oakland St, Stuart FL 34997, USA — Ice Hockey Player

Cronk, William F (Rick), III
Boy Scouts of America, National Council, PO Box 152079, Irving TX 75015, USA — Businessman, Non-Profit Executive

Crook, Mackenzie
Karushi Mgmt, 7 Wenlock Road, #10, London N1 7SL, England — Actor, Comedian

Croom, Sylvester
3909 12th St NE, Tuscaloooosa AL 35404, USA — Football Player, Coach

Crosbie, Annette
Independent Talent Group, Oxford House, 76 Oxford St, London W1D 1BS, England — Actress

Crosbie, John C
Scotia Center, 235 Water St, Saint John's NF A1C 5L3, Canada — Political Leader, Canada

Crosby, Alfred W
2506 Bowman Ave, Austin TX 78703, USA — Historian

Crosby, B J
Gage Group, 14724 Ventura Blvd, #505, Sherman Oaks CA 91403 USA — Actress, Singer

Crosby, Caitlin
Paradigm Agency, 360 N Crescent Dr, North Building, Beverly Hills CA 90210 USA — Actress

Crosby, Cathy Lee
Epstein Wyckoff Corsa Ross, 11350 Ventura Blvd, #100, Studio City CA 91604, USA — Actress

Crosby, David
Creative Artists Agency, 2000 Ave of Stars, #100, Los Angeles CA 90067 USA — Singer (Byrds, Crosby Stills Nash)

C

Crosby - Crow

Crosby, Denise Rebel Entertainment Partners, 5700 Wilshire Blvd, #456, Los Angeles CA 90036, USA	Actress, Model
Crosby, Edward C (Ed) 6952 Brightwood Lane, #9, Garden Grove CA 92845, USA	Baseball Player
Crosby, Elaine 2580 Meadowbrook Lane, Jackson MI 49201, USA	Golfer
Crosby, Kathryn Grant 508 W 3rd St, Carson City NV 89703, USA	Actress
Crosby, Lucinda Coast to Coast Talent, 3350 Barham Blvd, Los Angeles CA 90068 USA	Actress
Crosby, Mary 2875 S Barrymore Dr, Malibu CA 90265, USA	Actress
Crosby, Robert E (Bobby) 11463 Anticost Way, Cypress CA 90630, USA	Baseball Player
Crosby, Sidney P Pittsburgh Penguins, Consol Energy Center, 1001 5th Ave, Pittsburgh PA 15219 USA	Ice Hockey Player
Croshere, Austin 11721 Sea Star Dr, Indianapolis IN 46256, USA	Basketball Player
Cross, Ben Shepherd & Ford, 13 Radnor Walk, London SW3 4BP, England	Actor
Cross, Christopher Hoffman Talent Agency, PO Box 26037, Minneapolis MN 55426, USA	Singer, Guitarist, Songwriter
Cross, Cory 2963 Bayshore Pointe Dr, Tampa FL 33611, USA	Ice Hockey Player
Cross, David Brillstein Entertainment Partners, 9150 Wilshire Blvd, #350, Beverly Hills CA 90212 USA	Actor, Comedian
Cross, Donna Woolfolk Onondaga Community College, English Dept, Syracuse NY 13202, USA	Writer
Cross, Helen Rogers Coleridge White, 20 Powis Mews, London W11 1JN, England	Writer
Cross, Howard E 79 Poplar Dr, Paramus NJ 07652, USA	Football Player
Cross, Irv A 2196 Marion Road, Roseville MN 55113, USA	Football Player, Sportscaster
Cross, Jeffrey A (Jeff) 8045 SW 100th St, Miami FL 33156, USA	Football Player
Cross, Joseph United Talent Agency, 9336 Civic Center Dr, Beverly Hills CA 90210 USA	Actor
Cross, Justin A 10 Longwood Dr, Hampton NH 03842, USA	Football Player
Cross, Marcia Gersh Agency, 9465 Wilshire Blvd, #600, Beverly Hills CA 90212 USA	Actress
Cross, Mike Blade Agency, PO Box 1556, Gainesville FL 32602, USA	Guitarist, Fiddler
Cross, Randall L (Randy) 155 Travertine Trail, Alpharetta GA 30022, USA	Football Player, Sportscaster
Cross, Shauna W K T Public Relations, 9350 Wilshire Blvd, #450, Beverly Hills CA 90212 USA	Writer
Crossan, David H (Dave) 3314 Emory Dr, Winston Salem NC 27103, USA	Football Player
Crosse, Clay Gordon Group, 833 Todd Preis Dr, Nashville TN 37221, USA	Singer
Crossett, Howard W US Bobsled/Skeleton Federation, 1631 Mesa Ave, #A, Colorado Springs CO 80906 USA	Bobsled Athlete
Crossley, Paul C R Connaught Artists, 2 Molasses Row, London SW11 3UX, England	Concert Pianist
Crossley-Mercer, Edwin I M G Artists, Hogarth Business Park, Chiswick, London W4 2TH, England	Opera Singer
Crossman, Doug 107 Franklin Road, Glassboro NJ 08028, USA	Ice Hockey Player
Croteau, Gary P 8380 E Hinsdale Ave, Centennial CO 80112, USA	Ice Hockey Player
Crotty, John K 370 NE Edgewater Dr, #404, Stuart FL 34996, USA	Basketball Player
Crouch, Andrae Universal Attractions, 135 W 26th St, #1200, New York NY 10001 USA	Singer, Pianist, Songwriter
Crouch, Eric E 19453 Walnut Circle, Omaha NE 68130, USA	Football Player
Crouch, Paul Trinity Broadcasting Network, PO Box A, Santa Ana CA 92711, USA	Evangelist
Crouch, Roger K 120 6th St NE, Washington DC 20002, USA	Astronaut
Crouch, Sandra Sparrow Communications Group, 101 Winners Circle, Brentwood TN 37027, USA	Drummer, Songwriter
Crouch, Stanley Georges Borchardt Agency, 136 E 57th St, #1400, New York NY 10022, USA	Writer, Columnist
Crouch, William W (Bill) Isilon Systems, 3101 Western Ave, Seattle WA 98121, USA	Army General
Croucier, Juan C 45 Cayuse Lane, Rancho Palos Verdes CA 90275, USA	Bassist (Dokken, Ratt)
Crouse, Lindsay 263 Monte Grigio Dr, Pacific Palisades CA 90272, USA	Actress
Crouther, Lance Circle of Confusion, 8548 Washington Blvd, Culver City CA 90232, USA	Actor
Crow, Ashley Don Buchwald/Fortitude, 6500 Wilshire Blvd, #2200, Los Angeles CA 90048 USA	Actress
Crow, Harlan R Trammell Crow Co, Trammell Crow Center, 2001 Ross Ave, #325, Dallas TX 75201, USA	Businessman
Crow, John David 5004 Augusta Circle, College Station TX 77845, USA	Football Player, Coach
Crow, Lindon 6800 S Strand Ave, #481, Yuma AZ 85364, USA	Football Player
Crow, Mark H 501 W Bay St, Jacksonville FL 32202, USA	Basketball Player
Crow, Michael M Arizona State University, President's Office, Tempe AZ 85287, USA	Educator

Crow, Sheryl
W M E Entertainment, 9601 Wilshire Blvd, #300, Beverly Hills CA 90210 USA — Singer, Songwriter, Actress

Crow, Thomas E
New York University, Art History Institute, New York NY 10012, USA — Art Historian

Crow, William R (Bill)
21300 River Road, #15, Perris CA 92570, USA — Basketball Player

Crowder, Bruce
7 Kyle Dr, Nashua NH 03062, USA — Ice Hockey Player

Crowder, David
E M I Records, 150 5th Ave, #700, New York NY 10011 USA — Singer, Guitarist, Pianist

Crowder, J Corey
725 Ballard Bridge Road, Carrollton GA 30117, USA — Basketball Player

Crowder, Keith
PO Box 95 Station Main, Essex ON N8M 2Y1, Canada — Ice Hockey Player

Crowder, R Channing, Jr
8921 Southern Orchard Road, Davie FL 33328, USA — Football Player

Crowder, Randolph C (Randy)
803 Strawberry Lane, Brandon FL 33511, USA — Football Player

Crowder, Troy
103 Panache North Shore Road, Whitefish ON P0M 3E0, Canada — Ice Hockey Player

Crowder, William D
Deputy CNO, Operations/Plans/Strategy, HqUSN, Pentagon, Washington DC 20350 USA — Navy Admiral

Crowe, Cameron
1016 Amalfi Dr, Pacific Palisades CA 90272, USA — Director, Writer

Crowe, Martin D
PO Box 109302, Newmarket, Auckland 1149, New Zealand — Cricketer

Crowe, Mia
C E S D, 10635 Santa Monica Blvd, #130, Los Angeles CA 90025 USA — Actress

Crowe, Phil
204 Duffield St, Willow Grove PA 19090, USA — Ice Hockey Player

Crowe, Russell
W M E Entertainment, 9601 Wilshire Blvd, #300, Beverly Hills CA 90210 USA — Actor

Crowe, Sara
Bronia Buchanan Assoc, 23 Tavistock St, London WC2E 7NV, England — Actress

Crowe, Tonya
13030 Mindanao Way, #4, Marina del Rey CA 90292, USA — Actress

Crowell, Angelo D
PO Box 38203, Tallahassee FL 32315, USA — Football Player

Crowell, Germane L
200 Luzelle Dr, Winston Salem NC 27103, USA — Football Player

Crowell, John C
300 Hot Springs Road, Santa Barbara CA 93108, USA — Geologist

Crowell, Rodney J
Maine Road Mgmt, 195 Chrystie St, #901F, New York NY 10002, USA — Singer, Songwriter

Crowley, Dermot
United Agents, 12-26 Lexington St, London W1F 0LE, England — Actor

Crowley, Mart
I C M Partners, 10250 Constellation Blvd, #900, Los Angeles CA 90067 USA — Writer

Crowley, Michael
Three Rivers Press, 1745 Broadway, New York NY 10019, USA — Columnist, Writer

Crowley, Patricia
T M C E, 270 N Canon Dr, #1064, Beverly Hills CA 90210, USA — Actress

Crowley, Ted
41 Westchester Dr, Westwood MA 02090, USA — Ice Hockey Player

Crowley, Terrence M (Terry)
18405 Ensor Farm Court, Parkton MD 21120, USA — Baseball Player

Crowson, Richard
Wichita Eagle-Beacon, Editorial Dept, 825 E Douglas Ave, Wichita KS 67202, USA — Editorial Cartoonist

Crowton, Gary
Brigham Young University, Athletic Dept, Provo UT 84602, USA — Football Coach

Croyle, J Brodie
105 Apple Blossom Dr, Brandon MS 39047, USA — Football Player

Croze, Marie-Josee
U B B A, 6 Rue de Braque, 75003 Paris, France — Actress

Crozier, Joseph R (Joe)
299 Randwood Dr, Buffalo NY 14221, USA — Ice Hockey Player, Coach

Crudup, Billy
Creative Artists Agency, 2000 Ave of Stars, #100, Los Angeles CA 90067 USA — Actor

Cruickshank, John A
Victoria Cross Assn, Old Admiralty Building, London SW1A 2BL, England — WW II Air Force Hero (VC)

Cruikshank, Thomas H
5949 Sherry Lane, #1035, Dallas TX 75225, USA — Businessman

Cruise, Tom
42 West, 220 W 42nd St, #1200, New York NY 10036 USA — Actor

Crum, E Denzel (Denny)
6901 Routt Road, Louisville KY 40299, USA — Basketball Coach

Crumb, George H
240 Kirk Lane, Media PA 19063, USA — Composer

Crumb, Robert (R)
20 Rue du Pont Vieux, 30610 Sauve, France — Cartoonist (Keep on Truckin')

Crump, Simon
A M Heath Co, 79 Saint Martin's Lane, London WC2N 4RE, England — Writer

Crumpler, Algernon D (Alge)
2155 Enclave Mill Dr, Dacula GA 30019, USA — Football Player

Crusan, Douglas G (Doug), Jr
6263 Hanover Court, Fishers IN 46038, USA — Football Player

Crutcher, Chris
3405 E Marion Court, Spokane WA 99223, USA — Writer

Crutzen, Paul J
Am Fort Gonsenheim 36, 55122 Mainz, Germany — Nobel Chemistry Laureate

Cruyff, Johan
Koninklijke Nederk Voetbalbod, Postbus 515, 3700 AM Zeist, Netherlands — Soccer Player, Coach

Cruz Dilan, Jose L, Sr
2309 Delta Bridge Dr, Pearland TX 77584, USA — Baseball Player

Cruz Garcia, Deivi
611 Woodward Ave, Detroit MI 48226, USA — Baseball Player

Cruz Martinez, Nelson R — Baseball Player
Texas Rangers, Ameriquest Field, 1000 Ballpark Way, #306, Arlington TX 76011 USA

Cruz Smith, Martin — Writer
Simon & Schuster, 1230 Ave of Americas, Concourse 1, New York NY 10020 USA

Cruz, Alexis — Actor
McGowan Mgmt, 8733 W Sunset Blvd, #103, West Hollywood CA 90069 USA

Cruz, Anthony — Singer
Latin Artist Group, 11271 Ventura Blvd, #151, Studio City CA 91604, USA

Cruz, Brandon — Actor, Musician
Taang Records & Retail, 706 Pismo Court, San Diego CA 92109, USA

Cruz, Hector L — Baseball Player
1646 N Monticello Ave, Chicago IL 60647, USA

Cruz, Jacob — Baseball Player
1582 W Commerce Ave, Gilbert AZ 85233, USA

Cruz, Jose L, Jr — Baseball Player
8475 SW 53rd Ave, Miami FL 33143, USA

Cruz, Julio L — Baseball Player
12012 98th Ave NE, #205, Kirkland WA 98034, USA

Cruz, Nilo — Writer
Paradigm Agency, 360 N Crescent Dr, North Building, Beverly Hills CA 90210 USA

Cruz, Penelope — Actress, Model
Kuranda Mgmt, Santo Angel 84, 28043 Madrid, Spain

Cruz, Raymond — Actor
Media Artists Group, 8222 Melrose Ave, #203, Los Angeles CA 90048 USA

Cruz, Taio — Singer, Songwriter
Energon Entertainment, 276 5th Ave, #712, New York NY 10001, USA

Cruz, Valerie — Actress
Innovative Artists, 1505 10th St, Santa Monica CA 90401 USA

Cruz, Victor — Football Player
New York Giants, Meadowlands Stadium, 102 Route 120, East Rutherford NJ 07073 USA

Cruzado, Waded — Educator
Montana State University, President's Office, Bozeman MT 59717, USA

Cruz-Diez, Carlos — Artist
23 Rue Pierre Semard, 75009 Paris, France

Crvenkovski, Branko — President, Macedonia
Bihacka 8, 1000 Skopje, Macedonia

Cryder, Robert J (Bob) — Football Player
17411 NE 129th St, Redmond WA 98052, USA

Cryer, Gretchen — Writer, Lyricist, Actress
885 W End Ave, New York NY 10025, USA

Cryer, Jon — Actor
Forward Entertainment, 9255 Sunset Blvd, #805, Los Angeles CA 90069, USA

Cryer, Suzanne — Actress
Essential Talent Mgmt, 3151 Cahuenga Blvd W, #220, Los Angeles CA 90068, USA

Crystal, Billy — Actor, Comedian
Creative Artists Agency, 2000 Ave of Stars, #100, Los Angeles CA 90067 USA

Crystal, Ronald G — Molecular Biologist
435 E 70th St, #34B, New York NY 10021, USA

Csikszentmihalyi, Mihaly — Psychologist
700 Alamosa Dr, Claremont CA 91711, USA

Csokas, Marton — Actor
Sue Barnett Assoc, 1/96 Albion St, Surry Hills NSW 2010, Australia

Csonka, Lawrence R (Larry) — Football Player
6940 Stella Place, Anchorage AK 99507, USA

Csupo, Gabor — Director
Grand Allure Entertainment, 12835 Mulholland Drive, Beverly Hills CA 90210, USA

Ctvrtlik, Robert (Bob) — Volleyball Player
22 Leon Way, Rancho Mirage CA 92270, USA

Cua, Rick — Singer, Pianist
Greg Menza, 1086 Rip Steele Road, Columbia TN 38401, USA

Cuaron Orozoco, Carlos J — Director, Producer, Writer
United Talent Agency, 9336 Civic Center Dr, Beverly Hills CA 90210 USA

Cuaron, Alfonso — Director, Producer
United Talent Agency, 9336 Civic Center Dr, Beverly Hills CA 90210 USA

Cuba, Alex — Singer, Songwriter
Agency Group Ltd, 1880 Century Park E, #711, Los Angeles CA 90067 USA

Cuban, Mark — Basketball Executive, Businessman
Dallas Mavericks, Pavilion, 2909 Taylor St, Dallas TX 75226 USA

Cubbage, Michael L (Mike) — Baseball Player, Manager
3349 Carroll Creek Road, Keswick VA 22947, USA

Cubitt, David — Actor
United Talent Agency, 9336 Civic Center Dr, Beverly Hills CA 90210 USA

Cuccarini, Lorella — Actress
Assoziazione Italia, CP 6323, 00100 Rome-Prati, Italy

Cuccurullo, Warren — Guitarist (Duran Duran)
D D Productions, 93A Westbourne Park Villas, London W2 5ED, England

Cuche, Didier — Alpine Skier
Les Bugnenets, 2058 Le Paquier, Switzerland

Cucinotta, Maria Grazia — Actress, Model
Class Mgmt, Pizza Cavour 66, 02100 Rieti, Italy

Cudahy, Richard D — Judge
US Court of Appeals, 219 S Dearborn St, #2302B, Chicago IL 60604, USA

Cuddy, Jim — Singer, Guitarist (Blue Rodeo)
Starfish Entertainment, 906A Logan Ave, Toronto ON M4K 3E4, Canada

Cuddyer, Michael B — Baseball Player
10240 Washington Palm Way, Malverne NY 11565, USA

Cudi, Kid — Rap Artist, Actor
I C M Partners, 10250 Constellation Blvd, #900, Los Angeles CA 90067 USA

Cudlitz, Michael — Actor
Gold Coast, 1023 1/2 Abbot Kinney Blvd, Venice CA 90291, USA

Cuesta, Michael — Director
W M E Entertainment, 9601 Wilshire Blvd, #300, Beverly Hills CA 90210 USA

Cuevas, Beto — Singer, Actor, Composer
Espada-Zimmatore, PO Box 6577, Burbank CA 91510, USA

Cuevas, Jose Luis — Artist
Galeana 109, San Angel Inn, Mexico City 20 DF, Mexico

Culbertson, Brian
Stiletto Entertainment, 8295 S La Cienega Blvd, Inglewood CA 90301, USA — Jazz Musician

Culbertson, Frank L, Jr
15500 Meherrin Dr, Centreville VA 20120, USA — Astronaut

Culbreath, Joshua (Josh)
Central State University, Athletic Dept, Wilberforce OH 45384, USA — Track Athlete

Culbreth, Fieldin H, III
224 Claiborne Court, Spartanburg SC 29301, USA — Baseball Umpire

Culea, Melinda
Blueline Productions, 212 26th St, #295, Santa Monica CA 90402, USA — Actress

Culhane, Jim
8547 Hathaway Road, Kalamazoo MI 49009, USA — Ice Hockey Player

Culkin, Courtney Rachel
Playboy Promotions, 2706 Media Center Dr, Los Angeles CA 90065 USA — Model

Culkin, Kieran
W K T Public Relations, 9350 Wilshire Blvd, #450, Beverly Hills CA 90212 USA — Actor

Culkin, Macaulay
Brookside Artist Mgmt, 250 W 57th St, #2303, New York NY 10107 USA — Actor

Culkin, Rory
Brookside Artists Mgmt, 450 N Roxbury Dr, #400, Beverly Hills CA 90210, USA — Actor

Cullen, Barry
Cullen Motors, 905 Woodlawn Road W, Guelph ON N1K 1B7, Canada — Ice Hockey Player

Cullen, Brett
Lovett Mgmt, 1327 Brinkley Ave, Los Angeles CA 90049, USA — Actor

Cullen, Brian
Brian Cullen Motors, 386 Ontario St, Saint Catherines ON L2R 6S8, Canada — Ice Hockey Player

Cullen, John
1002 Legacy Hills Dr, McDonough GA 30253, USA — Ice Hockey Player

Cullen, Matthew (Matt)
6008 Over Hadden Court, Raleigh NC 27614, USA — Ice Hockey Player

Cullen, Ray
20 Sydenham Dr, RR 2, Iderton ON N0M 2A0, Canada — Ice Hockey Player

Cullen, Sean M
Henderson Hogan Agency, 850 7th Ave, #1003, New York NY 10019, USA — Actor

Cullen, Timothy L (Tim)
159 W G St, Benicia CA 94510, USA — Baseball Player

Culler, Glen
Culler Scientific Systems Corp, 100 Burns Place, Goleta CA 93117, USA — Computer Scientist

Cullerton, William
3S220 Warren Ave, Warrenville IL 60555, USA — Air Force Hero

Culligan, Joe
Research Investigative Services, 650 NE 126th St, North Miami FL 33161, USA — Private Investigator, Writer

Cullimore, Jassen
5509 S Washington St, Hinsdale IL 60521, USA — Ice Hockey Player

Cullinan, Edward H
Wharf, 1 Baldwin Terrace, London N1 7RU, England — Architect

Cullum, Jamie
Marleah Leslie Assoc, 1645 N Vine St, #712, Los Angeles CA 90028, USA — Jazz Pianist, Singer, Songwriter

Cullum, John
Stone Manners Salners, 9911 W Pico Blvd, #1400, Los Angeles CA 90035 USA — Actor, Singer

Cullum, Mark E
5401 Forest Acres Dr, Nashville TN 37220, USA — Editorial Cartoonist

Culp, Curley
16811 Gravesend Road, Pflugerville TX 78660, USA — Football Player

Culp, Joseph
Gage Group, 14724 Ventura Blvd, #505, Sherman Oaks CA 91403 USA — Actor

Culp, Ray L
7400 Waterline Road, Austin TX 78731, USA — Baseball Player

Culp, Steven
Miriam Milgrom Entertainment, 3614 Lankershim Blvd, Los Angeles CA 90068, USA — Actor

Culpepper, Daunte
16730 Berkshire Court, Southwest Ranches FL 33331, USA — Football Player

Culpepper, J Broward (Brad)
136 W Davis Blvd, Tampa FL 33606, USA — Football Player

Culpepper, James
W M E Entertainment, 9601 Wilshire Blvd, #300, Beverly Hills CA 90210 USA — Drummer (Flyleaf)

Culpepper, R Edward (Ed)
811 Bluewater Dr, Sun City Center FL 33573, USA — Football Player

Culver, George R
5409 Rustic Canyon St, Bakersfield CA 93306, USA — Baseball Player

Culver, John C
5409 Spangler Ave, Bethesda MD 20816, USA — Senator, IA

Culver, Michael
Waring & McKenna, 22 Grafton St, London W1S 4EX, England — Actor

Culver, Molly
Jonas Public Relations, 240 26th St, #3, Santa Monica CA 90402, USA — Actress

Cumberbatch, Benedict
United Talent Agency, 9336 Civic Center Dr, Beverly Hills CA 90210 USA — Actor

Cumberland, John S
19417 Golden Slipper Place, Lutz FL 33558, USA — Baseball Player

Cumby, George E
12090 Cross Fence Trail, Tyler TX 75706, USA — Football Player

Cuming, Ry
Agency Group Ltd, 142 W 57th St, #600, New York NY 10019 USA — Singer, Songwriter

Cumming, Alan
Troika, 74 Clerkenwell Road, #300, London EC1M 5QA, England — Actor, Singer, Director

Cumming, Charles
Jankow & Nesbit, 33 Drayson Mews, London W8 4LY, England — Writer

Cumming, Ian M
Leucadia National Corp, 315 Park Ave S, New York NY 10010, USA — Businessman

Cummings, Burton
S L Feldman Mgmt, 1505 W 2nd Ave, #200, Vancouver BC V6H 3Y4, Canada — Singer (Guess Who), Songwriter

Cummings, Erin
Paradigm Agency, 360 N Crescent Dr, North Building, Beverly Hills CA 90210 USA — Actress

Cummings, James J (Jim)
Atlas Talent Agency, 15 E 32nd St, #600, New York NY 10016, USA — Actor

Cummings, John R — Baseball Player
21 Park Paseo, Laguna Beach CA 92677, USA

Cummings, Midre A — Baseball Player
19525 Morden Blush Dr, Lutz FL 33558, USA

Cummings, Quinn — Actress, Writer
HipHugger Inc, PO Box 93963, Pasadena CA 91109, USA

Cummings, Stephen P (Steve) — Cyclist
Barloworld, 1800 Katherine St, Sandton 2146, Scotland

Cummings, T Terrell (Terry) — Basketball Player
12820 W Golden Lane, San Antonio TX 78249, USA

Cummings, Whitney — Actress, Comedienne
Creative Artists Agency, 2000 Ave of Stars, #100, Los Angeles CA 90067 USA

Cummins, Barry — Ice Hockey Player
155 Marsden St, Kimberley BC V1A 1G8, Canada

Cummins, Corryn — Actress
Mitchell K Stubbs Assoc, 8695 W Washington Blvd, #204, Culver City CA 90232 USA

Cummins, Gregory Scott — Actor
Schiowitz Connor, 1680 N Vine St, #1016, Los Angeles CA 90028 USA

Cummins, Jim — Ice Hockey Player
15 W Quincy St, #B, Westmont IL 60559, USA

Cummins, Peggy — Actress
17 Brockley Road, Bexhill on Sea, Sussex TN39 4TT, England

Cumpsty, Michael — Actor
Innovative Artists, 1505 10th St, Santa Monica CA 90401 USA

Cundey, Dean R — Cinematographer
250 S De Lacey Ave, #207, Pasadena CA 91105, USA

Cundieff, Rusty — Actor
Paradigm Agency, 360 N Crescent Dr, North Building, Beverly Hills CA 90210 USA

Cunnane, William J (Will) — Baseball Player
123 Sleepy Hollow Lane, Congers NY 10920, USA

Cunneyworth, Randy W — Ice Hockey Player, Coach
141 Caversham Woods, Pittsford NY 14534, USA

Cunningham, Bennie L — Football Player
Quincy Road, Seneca SC 29672, USA

Cunningham, Bill — Singer, Bassist, Pianist (Box Tops)
Horizon Mgmt, PO Box 8770, Endwell NY 13762, USA

Cunningham, Carl M — Football Player
4471 Saddleworth Circle, Orlando FL 32826, USA

Cunningham, Danny — Actor
United Agents, 12-26 Lexington St, London W1F 0LE, England

Cunningham, David L — Director
United Talent Agency, 9336 Civic Center Dr, Beverly Hills CA 90210 USA

Cunningham, J Douglas (Doug) — Football Player
5060 Harling Place, Jackson MS 39211, USA

Cunningham, Jared — Basketball Player
Dallas Mavericks, Pavilion, 2909 Taylor St, Dallas TX 75226 USA

Cunningham, John — Actor
Gage Group, 14724 Ventura Blvd, #505, Sherman Oaks CA 91403 USA

Cunningham, Joseph R (Joe) — Baseball Player
RR 1 Box 80A, Koshkonong MO 65692, USA

Cunningham, Liam — Actor
Management 360, 9111 Wilshire Blvd, Beverly Hills CA 90210 USA

Cunningham, Michael — Writer
Columbia University, Creative Writing Center, Lewisohn Hall, New York NY 10014, USA

Cunningham, R Walter (Walt) — Astronaut
A V D, PO Box 604, Glenn Dale MD 20769, USA

Cunningham, Randall — Football Player
380 E Robindale Road, Las Vegas NV 89123, USA

Cunningham, Richard A (Richie) — Football Player
610 Cheyenne Dr, Houma LA 70360, USA

Cunningham, Richard K (Dick) — Football Player
100 Rosewood Court, Peachtree City GA 30269, USA

Cunningham, Samuel L (Sam), Jr — Football Player
9316 S 4th Ave, Inglewood CA 90305, USA

Cunningham, Sean S — Director, Producer
Crystal Lake Entertainment, 4420 Hayvenhurst Ave, Encino CA 91436, USA

Cunningham, Wallace E — Architect
PO Box 371493, San Diego CA 92137, USA

Cunningham, William J (Billy) — Basketball Player, Coach, Executive
Court Restaurant, 31 Front St, #33, Conshohocken PA 19428, USA

Cuoco, Kaley — Actress, Comedienne
S D B Partners, 1801 Ave of Stars, #902, Los Angeles CA 90067 USA

Cuomo, Andrew M — Governor, NY; Secretary, HUD
Governor's Office, State Capitol, Albany NY 12224 USA

Cuomo, Christopher — Commentator
ABC-TV, News Dept, 147 Columbus Ave, New York NY 10023, USA

Cuomo, Jerome J — Inventor (Read-Write Optical Storage)
I B M Watson Research Center, PO Box 218, Yorktown Heights NY 10598 USA

Cuomo, Mario M — Governor, NY
50 Sutton Place S, #11G, New York NY 10022, USA

Cuomo, Rivers — Singer, Guitarist (Weezer), Songwriter
W M E Entertainment, 1600 Division St, #300, Nashville TN 37203 USA

Cuozzo, Gary S — Football Player
4 Swimming River Road, #4, Lincroft NJ 07738, USA

Cura, Jose — Opera Singer
Columbia Artists Mgmt Inc, 1790 Broadway, #702, New York NY 10019 USA

Curatola, Vincent — Actor
Stone Manners Salners, 9911 W Pico Blvd, #1400, Los Angeles CA 90035 USA

Curb, Michael (Mike) — Composer, Businessman
3907 W Alameda Ave, #2, Burbank CA 91505, USA

Curbeam, Robert L, Jr — Astronaut
15806 Virginia Fern Way, Houston TX 77059, USA

Curci, Francis (Fran) — Football Player, Coach
14707 Croydon Place, Tampa FL 33618, USA

Cureton, Earl — Basketball Player
31190 Country Way, Farmington Hills MI 48331, USA

Curfman, Shannon — Singer, Guitarist
13431 Narcissus St NW, Andover MN 55304, USA
Curl, Carolyn — Speed Skier, Mountain Cyclist
Robert U Curl, 405 N Westridge Dr, Idaho Falls ID 83402, USA
Curl, Robert F, Jr — Nobel Chemistry Laureate
1824 Bolsover St, Houston TX 77005, USA
Curlander, Paul J — Businessman
Lexmark International, 740 W New Circle Road, Lexington KY 40550, USA
Curless, Ann — Singer (Expose), Songwriter
Richard Walters, PO Box 2789, Toluca Lake CA 91610 USA
Curley, Edwin M — Philosopher
2645 Pin Oak Dr, Ann Arbor MI 48103, USA
Curley, John — Bassist (Afghan Whigs)
Rascoff/Zysblat Organization, 250 W 57th St, New York NY 10107 USA
Curley, John J — Publisher
Gannett Co, 1100 Wilson Blvd, Arlington VA 22209, USA
Curley, William M (Bill) — Basketball Player
377 Autumn Ave, Duxbury MA 02332, USA
Curnen, Monique Gabriela — Actress
Kritzer Levine Wilkins, 8840 Wilshire Blvd, #100, Beverly Hills CA 90211, USA
Curran, Brian — Ice Hockey Player
Kalamazoo Wings, 3600 Vanrick Dr, Kalamazoo MI 49001, USA
Curran, Brittany — Actress
Medavoy Mgmt, 10203 Santa Monica Blvd, #400, Los Angeles CA 90067 USA
Curran, Charles E — Theologian
Southern Methodist University, Theology Dept, Dallas Hall, Dallas TX 75275, USA
Curran, John — Director
Protea Group International, 23975 Park Sorrento, #365, Calabasas CA 91302, USA
Curran, Kelly — Actress
J K A Talent, 12725 Ventura Blvd, #H, Studio City CA 91604 91604, USA
Curran, Michael V (Mike) — Ice Hockey Player
7615 Lanewood Lane N, Osseo MN 55311, USA
Curran, Patrick M (Pat) — Football Player
3195 Avenida Magoria, Escondido CA 92029, USA
Curran, Paul — Director
National Opera, Millenium Centre, Bute Place, Cardiff CF10 5AL, Wales
Curran, Sean — Dancer
Sean Curran Co, 21 1st Ave, #18, New York NY 10003, USA
Curran, Tony — Actor
Paradigm Agency, 360 N Crescent Dr, North Building, Beverly Hills CA 90210 USA
Curren, Thomas R (Tom) — Surfer
Troubadour Entertainment, 3732 Gregory Way, #4, Santa Barbara CA 93105, USA
Currentzis, Teodor — Conductor
I M G Artists, Hogarth Business Park, Chiswick, London W4 2TH, England
Curreri, Lee — Composer
Gorfaine/Schwartz, 4111 W Alameda Ave, #509, Burbank CA 91505 USA
Currey, Francis S — WW II Army Hero (CMH)
PO Box 515, Selkirk NY 12158, USA
Currie, Cherie — Singer, Actress
Times Productions, 520 Washington Blvd, #199, Marina del Rey CA 90292, USA
Currie, Daniel G (Dan) — Football Player
6650 W Flamingo Road, #152, Las Vegas NV 89103, USA
Currie, Gordon — Actor
Characters Talent Agency, 8 Elm St, Toronto ON M5G 1G7, Canada
Currie, Louise — Actress
1317 Delresto Dr, Beverly Hills CA 90210, USA
Currie, Monique — Basketball Player
Washington Mystics, Verizon Center, 401 9th St NW, #750, Washington DC 20004 USA
Currie, Nancy J — Astronaut
1023 Knoll Bridge Lane, Friendswood TX 77546, USA
Currie, Sondra — Actress
Geddes Agency, 8430 Santa Monica Blvd, #201, West Hollywood CA 90069 USA
Currier, William F (Bill) — Football Player
8661 Monticello Road, Columbia SC 29203, USA
Currington, William M (Billy) — Singer, Songwriter
Vector Mgmt, PO Box 120479, Nashville TN 37212 USA
Curry, Aaron — Football Player
Seattle Seahawks, 12 Seahawks Way, Renton WA 98056 USA
Curry, Adrianne — Model, Actress
Wilhelmina Models, 300 Park Ave S, #200, New York NY 10010 USA
Curry, Alana — Actress
Sovereign Talent Group, 8421 Wilshire Blvd, #200, Beverly Hills CA 90211, USA
Curry, Ann — Commentator
NBC-TV, News Dept, 30 Rockefeller Plaza, #270E, New York NY 10112 USA
Curry, Anne E — Actress
Edna Talent Mgmt, 318 Dundas St West, Toronto ON M5T 1G5, Canada
Curry, Christopher — Actor
Darlene Kaplan, 4450 Balboa Ave, Encino CA 91316, USA
Curry, Clifford — Singer
Fat City, 1906 Chet Atkins Place, #502, Nashville TN 37212, USA
Curry, Denise — Basketball Player, Coach
21 Maple Dr, Aliso Viejo CA 92656, USA
Curry, Don (DC) — Actor, Comedian
Rush Hour Productions, 6464 Sunset Blvd, #750, Los Angeles CA 90028, USA
Curry, Donald (Don) — Boxer
41 Woodland Ave, West Orange NJ 07052, USA
Curry, Eddy, Jr — Basketball Player
17 Magnolia Dr, Purchase NY 10577, USA
Curry, Eric F — Football Player
PO Box 17321, Jacksonville FL 32245, USA
Curry, George J (Buddy) — Football Player
4407 Trestle Way, Buford GA 30518, USA
Curry, John A H — Tennis Executive
All England Lawn Tennis Club, Wimbledon, England
Curry, Mark — Actor
Nine Yards Entertainment, 8530 Wilshire Blvd, #500, Beverly Hills CA 90211 USA

Curry, Michael E (Mike) — Basketball Player, Coach
2880 Wells Dr, Augusta GA 30906, USA
Curry, Stephen — Actor, Comedian
R G M Assoc, 64076 Kippax St, #202, Surry Hills NSW 2010, Australia
Curry, Tim — Singer, Actor
Innovative Artists, 1505 10th St, Santa Monica CA 90401 USA
Curry, Valorie — Actress
I C M Partners, 10250 Constellation Blvd, #900, Los Angeles CA 90067 USA
Curry, W Stephen — Basketball Player
Golden State Warriors, 1011 Broadway, Oakland CA 94605 USA
Curry, Wardell S (Dell) — Basketball Player
1615 Rutledge Ave, Charlotte NC 28211, USA
Curry, William A (Bill) — Football Player, Coach
2660 Peachtree Road NW, #27H, Atlanta GA 30305, USA
Curtin, David S — Journalist
Colorado Springs Gazette Telegraph, 30 S Prospect, Colorado Springs CO 80903, USA
Curtin, Jane T — Actress
I C M Partners, 10250 Constellation Blvd, #900, Los Angeles CA 90067 USA
Curtin, John J, Jr — Attorney
Bingham Dana Gould, 100 High St, #1500, Boston MA 02110, USA
Curtin, Phyllis — Opera Singer
Boston University, Fine Arts College, 855 Commonwealth Ave, Boston MA 02215, USA
Curtin, Valerie — Actress
15622 Meadowgate Road, Encino CA 91436, USA
Curtis, A Scott — Football Player
31661 Prairie Dunes Court, Evergreen CO 80439, USA
Curtis, Ben — Golfer
8959 Bevington Lane, Orlando FL 32827, USA
Curtis, Benjamin B (Ben) — Actor
Hatton McEwan, PO Box 37385, London N1 7XF, England
Curtis, Catie — Singer, Guitarist, Songwriter
Deep Blue Arts, 4440 Morse Ave, Studio City CA 91604, USA
Curtis, Chad D — Baseball Player
621 Eagle Point Road, Lake Odessa MI 48849, USA
Curtis, Christopher Paul — Writer
Random House, 1745 Broadway, #1800, New York NY 10019 USA
Curtis, Cliff — Actor
Abrams Artists, 9200 W Sunset Blvd, #1125, West Hollywood CA 90069 USA
Curtis, Isaac F — Football Player
711 Clinton Springs Ave, Cincinnati OH 45229, USA
Curtis, J Michael (Mike) — Football Player
5101 River Road, #1803, Bethesda MD 20816, USA
Curtis, Jamie Lee — Actress
Creative Artists Agency, 2000 Ave of Stars, #100, Los Angeles CA 90067 USA
Curtis, John D, II — Baseball Player
1800 Roundhill Road, #1207, Charleston WV 25314, USA
Curtis, Kenneth M — Governor, ME; Diplomat
1211 Southport Dr, Sarasota FL 34242, USA
Curtis, Kevin D — Football Player
Tennessee Titans, 460 Great Circle Road, Nashville TN 37228 USA
Curtis, Paul E — Ice Hockey Player
PO Box 6325, Abilene TX 79608, USA
Curtis, Richard — Director, Writer
United Agents, 12-26 Lexington St, London W1F 0LE, England
Curtis, Simon — Director
United Talent Agency, 9336 Civic Center Dr, Beverly Hills CA 90210 USA
Curtis, Thomas N (Tom) — Football Player
5433 NW 94th Doral Place, Doral FL 33178, USA
Curtis-Hall, Vondie — Actor, Director
Film Independent, 9911 W Pico Blvd, #1100, Los Angeles CA 90035, USA
Curtiss, Shelley Smith — Sculptor
PO Box 497, Joseph OR 97846, USA
Cusack, Ann — Actress
Innovative Artists, 1505 10th St, Santa Monica CA 90401 USA
Cusack, Joan — Actress, Comedienne
W M E Entertainment, 9601 Wilshire Blvd, #300, Beverly Hills CA 90210 USA
Cusack, John — Actor
New Crime Productions, 1041 N Formosa Ave, Formosa Building, West Hollywood CA 90046, USA
Cusack, Sinead M — Actress
Curtis Brown Group, 28-29 Haymarket St, #500, London SW1Y 4SP, England
Cuse, Carlton — Writer, Producer
W M E Entertainment, 9601 Wilshire Blvd, #300, Beverly Hills CA 90210 USA
Cushenan, Ian — Ice Hockey Player
4014 Dryden Dr, North Olmsted OH 44070, USA
Cushing, Matthew J (Matt) — Football Player
5752 Lyman Ave, Downers Grove IL 60516, USA
Cushman, Karen — Writer
17804 Thorsen Road SW, Vashon WA 98070, USA
Cusick, Henry Ian — Actor
Ken McReddie Assoc, 11 Connaught Place, London W2 2ET, England
Cussler, Clive E — Writer
13835 N Tatum Blvd, #9-421, Phoenix AZ 85032, USA
Cust, John J (Jack), III — Baseball Player
9 Club House Dr, Whitehouse Station NJ 08889, USA
Custom — Singer
ArtistDirect, 10900 Wilshire Blvd, #1400, Los Angeles CA 90024 USA
Cut Chemist — DJ, Rap Musician
Vision Entertainment Group, 1100 Glendon Ave, #1100, Los Angeles 90024, USA
Cutcliffe, David — Football Coach
Duke University, Athletic Dept, Durham NC 27708, USA
Cutell, Lou — Actor
Conan Carroll Assoc, 11350 Ventura Blvd, #200, Studio City CA 91604, USA
Cuthbert, Elisha — Actress
I C M Partners, 10250 Constellation Blvd, #900, Los Angeles CA 90067 USA
Cuthbeth, Elizabeth (Betty) — Track Athlete
4/7 Karara Close, Hall's Head, Mandurah WA 6210, Australia

Cutler, Eric — Opera Singer
I M G Artists, Hogarth Business Park, Chiswick, London W4 2TH, England

Cutler, James — Architect
Cutler Anderson Architects, 135 Parfitt Way, Bainbridge Island WA 98110, USA

Cutler, Jay C — Football Player
39 Bancroft Place, Nashville TN 37215, USA

Cutler, Laurel — Businesswoman
Foote Cone Belding, 767 5th Ave, New York NY 10153, USA

Cutler, Walter L — Diplomat
Meridian International Center, 1630 Crescent Place NW, Washington DC 20009, USA

Cutrone, Angela — Speed Skater
Speed Skating Canada, 2781 Lancaster Road, #402, Ottawa ON K1B 1A7, Canada

Cutrufello, Mary — Singer, Songwriter
Mercury Records, 11150 Santa Monica Blvd, #1000, Los Angeles CA 90025 USA

Cutsinger, Gary L — Football Player
600 Mountain Dew Road, Horseshoe Bay TX 78657, USA

Cutter, Lise — Actress
PO Box 2665, Sag Harbor NY 11963, USA

Cuyler, Milton (Milt), Jr — Baseball Player
962 Lamar Road, Macon GA 31210, USA

Cuzin, Francois — Cell Biologist
Instit Pasteur, 25 Rue du Docteur Roux, 75724 Paris Cedex 15, France

Cuzzi, Philip (Phil) — Baseball Umpire
32 Maples Ave, Nutley NJ 07110, USA

Cvijanovic, Adam — Artist
Bellwether Gallery, 134 10th St, Front A, New York NY 10011, USA

Cwiklinski, Stanley — Rowing Athlete
2840 Maple St, San Diego CA 92104, USA

Cymphonique — Singer, Songwriter, Actress
I C M Partners, 10250 Constellation Blvd, #900, Los Angeles CA 90067 USA

Cypher, Jon — Actor
PO Box 25040, Ventura CA 93002, USA

Cyphers, Charles — Actor
C R Mgmt, 23852 Pacific Coast Highway, #627, Malibu CA 90265, USA

Cyr, Denis — Ice Hockey Player
9816 N Townsend Dr, Peoria IL 61615, USA

Cyr, Myriam — Actress
John DeHority Mgmt, 125 Christopher St, #6C, New York NY 10014, USA

Cyrus, Billy Ray — Singer, Guitarist, Songwriter
Octagon Entertainment, 8687 Melrose Ave, #700, Los Angeles CA 90069, USA

Cyrus, Miley — Actress, Singer
Creative Artists Agency, 2000 Ave of Stars, #100, Los Angeles CA 90067 USA

Czapsky, Stefan — Cinematographer
RR 3 Box 278, Unadilla NY 13849, USA

Czerny, Henry — Actor
Oscars Abrams Zimel, 438 Queen St E, Toronto ON M5A 1T4, Canada

Czerwinska, Anna — Mountaineer
Anamax-Import-Export, Ul Lomianska 10 m 4, 01 685 Warsaw, Poland

Czisny, Alissa — Figure Skater
Detroit Skating Club, 888 Denison Court, Bloomfield Hills MI 48302, USA

Czuchry, Matt — Actor
Gersh Agency, 9465 Wilshire Blvd, #600, Beverly Hills CA 90212 USA

C

Cutler - Czuchry

Da Brat — Rap Artist
Mauldin Brand Agency, 1280 W Peachtree St NW, #300, Atlanta GA 30309, USA

Daal, Omar J — Baseball Player
3859 E Bellerive Dr, Queen Creek AZ 85142, USA

Daane, James D — Financier, Government Official
102 Westhampton Place, Nashville TN 37205, USA

D'Abaldo, Chris — Guitarist (Saliva)
Helter Skelter, 347-353 Chiswick High Road, London W4 4HS, England

Dabich, Mike — Basketball Player
PO Box 236, Hudson WY 82515, USA

D'Abo, Maryam — Actress
Protea Group International, 23975 Park Sorrento, #365, Calabasas CA 91302, USA

D'Abo, Olivia — Actress
Great Vision Artists Talent Agency, 8981 Sunset Blvd, #101, Los Angeles CA 90069, USA

Dabul, Brian — Tennis Player
Octagon Worldwide, 1751 Pinnacle Dr, #1500, McLean VA 22102 USA

D'Accone, Frank A — Music Educator
725 Fontana Way, Laguna Beach CA 92651, USA

Dacic, Ivica — Prime Minister, Serbia
Prime Minister's Office, Nemanjina 11, 11000 Belgrade, Serbia

DaCosta, Rebecca — Actress
Rogers & Cowan, 8687 Melrose Ave, #G700, West Hollywood CA 90069 USA

DaCosta, Yaya — Actress, Model
Gersh Agency, 41 Madison Ave, #3301, New York NY 10010 USA

D'Acquisto, John F — Baseball Player
32010 N 20th Lane, Phoenix AZ 85085, USA

Daddario, Alexandra — Actress
United Talent Agency, 9336 Civic Center Dr, Beverly Hills CA 90210 USA

Daddo, Cameron — Actor
Collective, 8383 Wilshire Blvd, #1050, Beverly Hills CA 90211 USA

Daddy Yankee — Reggaeton Singer
Nevarez Communications, 5362 NW 110th Ave, Miami FL 33178, USA

Dade, L Paul — Baseball Player
5212 66th Street Court W, University Place WA 98467, USA

Daehlie, Bjorn — Cross Country Skier
Cathinka Guldbergs Veg 64, 2034 Holter, Norway

Dafoe, Bryon — Ice Hockey Player
6620 Lakeshore Road, Kelowna BC V1W 4J5, Canada

Dafoe, Willem — Actor
I C M Partners, 10250 Constellation Blvd, #900, Los Angeles CA 90067 USA

Daggett, Timothy (Tim) — Gymnast
134 Country Club Dr, East Longmeadow MA 01028, USA

Daghe, Noelle — Golfer
1300 Tamarac St, Denver CO 80220, USA

D'Agostino, James S, Jr — Businessman
Encore Bank, 1220 Augusta Dr, Houston TX 77057, USA

D'Agosto, Nicholas (Nick) — Actor
Emerald Talent Group, 15260 Ventura Blvd, #1200, Sherman Oaks CA 91403, USA

D'Aguanno, Emanuele — Opera Singer
I M G Artists, Hogarth Business Park, Chiswick, London W4 2TH, England

Dagworthy Prew, Wendy A — Fashion Designer
Royal College of Art, Kensington Gore, London SW7 3EU, England

Dahal, Pushpa Kamal (Prachanda) — Prime Minister, Nepal
Premier's Office, Central Secretariat, Singha Durbar, Kathmandu, Nepal

Dahan, Olivier — Director, Writer
Agents Associes, 201 Rue du Faubourg Saint Honore, 75008 Paris, France

Dahl, Arlene — Actress
Dahlmark Productions, PO Box 116 Rockland Road, Sparkill NY 10976, USA

Dahl, John — Director, Writer
United Talent Agency, 9336 Civic Center Dr, Beverly Hills CA 90210 USA

Dahl, Kevin C — Ice Hockey Player
4000 Astoria Way, Avon OH 44011, USA

Dahl, Lawrence F — Chemist
4817 Woodburn Dr, Madison WI 53711, USA

Dahl, Robert A — Political Scientist
200 Leeder Hill Dr, Hamden CT 06517, USA

Dahl, Sophie — Model, Actress
Ed Victor, 6 Bayley St, London WC18 3HE, England

Dahlberg, James E — Biomolecular Chemist
University of Wisconsin, Biochemical Sciences Building, Madison WI 53706, USA

Daigle, Alain — Ice Hockey Player
3510 Rue Bordeaux, Trois-Rivieres-Ouest QC G8Y 3P7, Canada

Daigle, Alexandre — Ice Hockey Player
3510 Rue Bordeaux, Trois-Rivieres-Quest QC G8Y 3P7, Canada

Daigle, Sylvie — Speed Skater
Speed Skating Canada, 2781 Lancaster Road, #402, Ottawa ON K1B 1A7, Canada

Daigneault, Jean-Jacques (J J) — Ice Hockey Player
Hartford Wolf Pack, 196 Trumbull St, #300, Hartford CT 06103, USA

Dailey, Benjamin P — Chemist
440 Riverside Dr, New York NY 10027, USA

Dailey, Janet — Writer
HC 4 Box 2197, Branson MO 65616, USA

Dailey, John R — Marine Corps General
National Air & Space Museum, Director's Office, Independence Ave, Washington DC 20472, USA

Dailor, Brann — Drummer, Singer (Mastodon)
Pinnacle Entertainment, 30 Glenn St, White Plains NY 10603, USA

Daily, Bill — Actor
1331 Park Ave SW, #802, Albuquerque NM 87102, USA

Daily, Bob — Producer
Gersh Agency, 9465 Wilshire Blvd, #600, Beverly Hills CA 90212 USA

Daily, E G — Singer, Songwriter, Actress
369 Universal Artists, 468 N Camden Dr, #200, Beverly Hills CA 90210, USA

Daish, Charles — Actor
Gavin Barker Assoc, 2D Wimpole St, London W1G 0EB, England

Dajani, Nadia — Actress
Innovative Artists, 1505 10th St, Santa Monica CA 90401 USA

Dalai Lama — Religious Leader; Nobel Peace Laureate
Thekchen Choeling, McLeod Ganj 176219, Dharamsal, Himachal Pradesh, India

Daland, Peter — Swimming Coach
14 Chris Court, Riverhead NY 11901, USA

Dalberto, Michel — Concert Pianist
13 Blvd Henri Plumhof, 1800 Vevey, Switzerland

Daldry, Stephen — Director
Creative Artists Agency, 2000 Ave of Stars, #100, Los Angeles CA 90067 USA

Dale, Alan — Actor
Vox Inc, 6420 Wilshire Blvd, #1080, Los Angeles CA 90048 USA

Dale, Bruce — Photographer
National Geographic, Editorial Dept, 1145 17th St NW, Washington DC 20036 USA

Dale, Carroll W — Football Player
Clinch Valley College, Athletic Department, 1 College Ave, Wise VA 24293, USA

Dale, Dick — Singer, Guitarist, Songwriter
Dick Dale Mgmt, PO Box 1713, Twentynine Palms CA 92277, USA

Dale, Ian Anthony — Actor
Aquarius Public Relations, 5320 Sylar Ave, Sherman Oaks CA 91401, USA

Dale, James Badge — Actor
M J Mgmt, 130 W 57th St, New York NY 10019, USA

Dale, Jim — Actor, Comedian
C E S D, 10635 Santa Monica Blvd, #130, Los Angeles CA 90025 USA

Dalembert, Samuel D — Basketball Player
899 NE Orchid Bay Dr, Boca Raton FL 33487, USA

D'Alemberte, Talbot (Sandy) — Educator
Florida State University, Law College, 425 W Jefferson, Tallahassee FL 32301, USA

D'Aleo, Angelo — Singer (Dion & the Belmonts)
Paramount Entertainment, 12 Kosakowski Dr, Morris Plains NJ 07590 USA

Dalesandro, Mark A — Baseball Player
1908 Arbor Fields Dr, Plainfield IL 60586, USA

D'Alessio, Diana — Golfer
6955 Nunn Road, Lakeland FL 33813, USA

Daley, Joe — Ice Hockey Player
Joe Daley's Cards, 666 Saint James St, Winnipeg MB R3G 3J6, Canada

Daley, Joe — Golfer
10015 E Mountain View Road, #2126, Scottsdale AZ 85258, USA

Daley, John Francis — Actor
United Talent Agency, 9336 Civic Center Dr, Beverly Hills CA 90210 USA

Daley, Leavitt L (Buddy) — Baseball Player
922 Moose Dr, Riverton WY 82501, USA

Daley, Patrick — Ice Hockey Player
118 Mount Olive Dr, Toronto ON M9V 2E2, Canada

Daley, Peter H (Pete) — Baseball Player
4019 Calle Mira Monte, Newbury Park CA 91320, USA

Daley, Richard M — Mayor, Chicago
University of Chicago, Harris Public Policy School, Chicago IL 60637, USA

Daley, Rosie — Chef, Writer
Harpo Productions, 110 N Carpenter St, Chicago IL 60607, USA

DalFabbro, Corrado — Bobsled Athlete
Olympic Committee, Foro Italico, Largo Lauro de Bosis 15, 00135 Rome, Italy

Dalgarno, Alexander — Astronomer
27 Robinson St, Cambridge MA 02138, USA

Dalgarno, Brad — Ice Hockey Player
1146 Fairfield Place, Oakville ON L6M 2L9, Canada

Dalglish, Kenneth M (Kenny) — Soccer Player, Manager
Celtic FC, Celtic Park, Glasgow G4O 3RE, Scotland

Dalhausser, Philip — Volleyball Player
Premier Management Group, 1100 Crescent Green, #104, Cary, NC 27518 USA

Dalheimer, Patrick — Musician (Live)
Freedman & Smith, 350 W End Ave, #1, New York NY 10024, USA

Dali, Tracy — Actress, Model
PO Box 69541, West Hollywood CA 90069, USA

Dalis, Irene — Opera Singer, Executive
San Jose Opera, 2149 Paragon Dr, San Jose CA 95131, USA

Dalkas, Nicole — Golfer
288 Green Mountain Dr, Palm Desert CA 92211, USA

Dall, Bobby — Bassist (Poison)
Front Line Mgmt, 1100 Glendon Ave, #2000, Los Angeles CA 90024 USA

Dallafior, Kenneth R (Ken) — Football Player
188 Four Seasons Dr, Lake Orion MI 48360, USA

Dallara, Charles H — Government Official, Financier
International Finance Institute, 2000 Pennsylvania Ave NW, Washington DC 20006, USA

Dalle, Beatrice — Actress
Artmedia, 20 Ave Rapp, 75007 Paris, France

Dallek, Robert — Historian
2138 Cathedral Ave NW, Washington DC 20008, USA

Dallenbach, Wally — Auto Racing Executive
5315 Stowe Lane, Harrisburg NC 28075, USA

Dallesandro, Joe — Actor
Stephen J Cannell Productions, 7083 Hollywood Blvd, #600, Los Angeles CA 90028, USA

Dallman, Marty — Ice Hockey Player
3843 Main St, Niagara Falls ON L2G 6B4, Canada

Dalrymple, Clayton E (Clay) — Baseball Player
28248 Mateer Road, Gold Beach OR 97444, USA

Dalrymple, Gary B — Geologist
1847 NW Hillcrest Dr, Corvallis OR 97330, USA

Dalton, Abby — Actress
Artists Agency, 1180 S Beverly Dr, #301, Los Angeles CA 90035 USA

Dalton, Audrey — Actress
2241 Labrusca, Mission Viejo CA 92692, USA

Dalton, James E — Air Force General
61 Misty Acres Road, Rolling Hills Estates CA 90274, USA

Dalton, John H — Government Official
3710 University Ave NW, Washington DC 20016, USA

Dalton, Lacy J — Singer
Lustig Talent, PO Box 770850, Orlando FL 32877 USA

Dalton, Lional D — Football Player
9858 Clint Moore Road, #128, Boca Raton FL 33496, USA
Dalton, Nic — Bassist (Lemonheads)
Agency Group Ltd, 142 W 57th St, #600, New York NY 10019 USA
Dalton, Nicole — Actress
Domain Talent, 9229 W Sunset Blvd, #710, West Hollywood CA 90069 USA
Dalton, Suzy — Singer
Gold Dust Talent, Route 78, Exit 19, Strausstown PA 19559, USA
Dalton, Timothy — Actor
Independent Talent Group, Oxford House, 76 Oxford St, London W1D 1BS, England
Daltrey, Roger — Singer (Who), Actor
TalentWorks, 3500 W Olive Ave, #1400, Burbank CA 91505 USA
Daluiso, Bradley W (Brad) — Football Player
13258 Glencliff Way, San Diego CA 92130, USA
Daly, Andrew (Andy) — Actor, Comedian, Writer
Creative Artists Agency, 2000 Ave of Stars, #100, Los Angeles CA 90067 USA
Daly, Carson — Actor, Entertainer
Dixon Talent, 375 Greenwich St, #500, New York NY 10013, USA
Daly, Herman — Social Activist
6934 Pineway, University Park MD 20782, USA
Daly, John P — Golfer
1009 Par St, Dardanelle AR 72834, USA
Daly, Lance — Director, Writer
FastNet Films, 75-76 Camden St, Lower, Dublin 2, Ireland
Daly, Timothy (Tim) — Actor
Gateway Mgmt, 860 Via de la Paz, #F10, Pacific Palisades CA 90272 90272, USA
Daly, Tyne — Actress
405 E 54th St, #12D, New York NY 10022, USA
Daly-Donofrio, Heather — Golfer
414 Long Cove Court, Ormond Beach FL 32174, USA
Dalziel, Ryan — Auto Racing Driver
S A M A X Motorsports, 203 NW 16th St, Pompano Beach FL 33060, USA
Dam, Kenneth W — Government Official
University of Chicago, Law School, 1111 E 60th St, #1, Chicago IL 60637, USA
Damadian, Raymond V — Inventor (Cancer Tissue Detector-M R I)
F O N A R Corp, 110 Marcus Dr, Melville NY 11747, USA
Damas, Bertila — Actress
Craig Wyckoff Assoc, 11350 Ventura Blvd, #100, Studio City CA 91604, USA
D'Amato, Alfonse M — Senator, NY
Park Strategies, 101 Park Ave, #2506, New York NY 10178, USA
DaMatta, Cristiano M — Auto Racing Driver
Newman-Haas Racing, 50 Tower Parkway, Lincolnshire IL 60069, USA
D'Amboise, Charlotte — Actress, Dancer
Don Buchwald/Fortitude, 10 E 44th St, New York NY 10017 USA
D'Amboise, Jacques J — Dancer, Choreographer
National Dance Institute, 594 Broadway, #805, New York NY 10012, USA
Dame Edna — Actor, Comedian
P B J Mgmt, 5 Soho Square, London W1V 5DE, England
Dameshek, David — Actor, Writer
Creative Artists Agency, 2000 Ave of Stars, #100, Los Angeles CA 90067 USA
Damian, Michael — Actor, Singer
United Talent Agency, 9336 Civic Center Dr, Beverly Hills CA 90210 USA
Damiani, Damiano — Director
Via Delle Terme Deciane 2, 00153 Rome, Italy
Damiano, Jennifer — Actress
Innovative Artists, 1505 10th St, Santa Monica CA 90401 USA
Damiao, Leandro — Soccer Player
Confederacion de Futebol, Rua Victor Civita 66, #1, Rio de Janeiro 22775 044, Brazil
D'Amico, Jeffrey C (Jeff) — Baseball Player
2223 Muirfield Way, Oldsmar FL 34677, USA
D'Amico, Marcus — Actor
26 Astwood Mews, London SW7 4DE, England
D'Amico, Mike — Percussionist (Wondermints)
Paradise Artists, PO Box 1821, Ojai CA 93024 USA
Dam-Jensen, Inger — Opera Singer
Hollaendervej 4A, 1855 Frederiksberg C, Denmark
Damon, Grey — Actor
Paradigm Agency, 360 N Crescent Dr, North Building, Beverly Hills CA 90210 USA
Damon, Johnny D — Baseball Player
904 Main St, Windermere FL 34786, USA
Damon, Mark — Actor, Producer
2781 Benedict Canyon Dr, Beverly Hills CA 90210, USA
Damon, Matt — Actor
Pearl Street Productions, 517 N Robertson, #200, West Hollywood CA 90048, USA
Damon, Una — Actress, Director, Writer
DeWalt & Muzik Mgmt, 623 N Parish Place, Burbank CA 91506, USA
Damone, Vic — Singer, Actor
International Ventures, 25115 Ave Stanford, #102, Valencia CA 91355, USA
D'Amore, Caroline — Actress
Element Talent Agency, 120 S Vignes, #202, Los Angeles CA 90012, USA
Damphousse, Vincent — Ice Hockey Player
Le Scandinave Spa, 4280 Montee Ryan, Mont-Tremblant QC J8E 1S4, Canada
Dampier, Erick T — Basketball Player
18724 Wainsborough Lane, Dallas TX 75287, USA
Dampier, Louie (Lou) — Basketball Player
Dampier Distributing, 2808 New Moody Lane, La Grange KY 40031, USA
Damson, Barrie M — Businessman
1720 Post Road E, #215, Westport CT 06880, USA
Damus, Mike — Actor
Untitled Entertainment, 350 S Beverly Dr, #200, Beverly Hills CA 90212 USA
Dana, Bill — Actor, Comedian
Amsel Eisenstadt Frazier, 5055 Wilshire Blvd, #865, Los Angeles CA 90036 USA
Dana, William (Bill) — Test Pilot
15805 W Vale Dr, Goodyear AZ 85395, USA
Danby, Gordon T — Inventor (Magnetic Levitation Train)
PO Box 12, Wading River NY 11792, USA

Dance, Charles — Actor
Tavistock Wood Mgmt, 45 Conduit St, London W1S 2YN, England
Dancy, Hugh — Actor, Model
United Agents, 12-26 Lexington St, London W1F 0LE, England
Dancy, John — Commentator
Harvard University, Kennedy Government School, Cambridge MA 02138, USA
Dando, Carolyn — Actress
Red11 Mgmt, 441 Queen St, Auckland 1010, New Zealand
Dando, Evan — Singer (Lemonheads), Songwriter
Agency Group Ltd, 142 W 57th St, #600, New York NY 10019 USA
Dandridge, Robert L (Bob) — Basketball Player
1708 Saint Denis Ave, Norfolk VA 23509, USA
Dandry, Evelyne — Actress
Artmedia, 20 Ave Rapp, 75007 Paris, France
Dane, Eric — Actor
Management 360, 9111 Wilshire Blvd, Beverly Hills CA 90210 USA
Dane, Paul — Test Pilot
17105 Ambassador Dr, #515, Colorado Springs CO 80921, USA
Dane, Shelton — Actor
Innovative Artists, 235 Park Ave S, #1000, New York NY 10003 USA
Danelli, Dino — Drummer (Rascals)
Thomas Cassidy, 11761 E Speedway Blvd, Tucson AZ 85748 USA
Danelo, Joseph P (Joe) — Football Player
3601 Roxbury St, San Pedro CA 90731, USA
Danenhauer, Eldon V — Football Player
1030 SW Exmoor Lane, Topeka KS 66604, USA
Danes, Claire — Actress
W M E Entertainment, 9601 Wilshire Blvd, #300, Beverly Hills CA 90210 USA
Daneyko, Ken — Ice Hockey Player
11 Combs Hollow Road, Mendham NJ 07945, USA
Danforth, Douglas D — Businessman, Baseball Executive
8787 Bay Colony Dr, #1002, Naples FL 34108, USA
Danforth, Fred — Artist
PO Box 828, Middlebury VT 05753, USA
Danforth, John C (Jack) — Senator, MO
Bryan Cave LLP, 211 N Broadway, #3600, Saint Louis MO 63102, USA
D'Angelo — Singer, Songwriter
Cheeba Mgmt, 304 Park Ave S, New York NY 10010, USA
D'Angelo, Beverly — Actress
I C M Partners, 10250 Constellation Blvd, #900, Los Angeles CA 90067 USA
Danger Mouse — Rap Artist (Gnarls Barkley)
Hall or Nothing, Poplar Mews, Uxbridge Road, London W12 7JS, England
D'Angio, Giulio J — Radiation Therapist
201 S 18th St, #1818, Philadelphia PA 19103, USA
Daniel — Prince, Sweden
Royal Palace, Kundg Slottet, Stottsbacken, 111 30 Stockholm, Sweden
Daniel, Brittany — Actress
A P A Talent/Literary Agency, 405 S Beverly Dr, #300, Beverly Hills CA 90212 USA
Daniel, Elizabeth A (Beth) — Golfer
219 Palm Trail, Delray Beach FL 33483, USA
Daniel, Eugene, Jr — Football Player
PO Box 80345, Baton Rouge LA 70898, USA
Daniel, Jeffrey — Singer (Shalamar)
Green Light Talent Agency, PO Box 3172, Beverly Hills CA 90212 USA
Daniel, Paul W — Conductor
Ingpen & Williams, 131 Putney Bridge Road, London SW15 2PA, England
Daniel, William P (Willie) — Football Player
1711 Oktoc Road, Starkville MS 39759, USA
Daniele, Graciela — Director, Choreography
Abrams Artists, 9200 W Sunset Blvd, #1125, West Hollywood CA 90069 USA
Danielpour, Richard — Composer
Sony Classics Records, 2100 Colorado Ave, Santa Monica CA 90404, USA
Daniels, Anthony — Actor
Fifi Oscard Agency, 110 W 40th St, #1601, New York NY 10018 USA
Daniels, Antonio — Basketball Player
Philadelphia 76ers, 1st Union Center, 3601 S Broad St, Philadelphia PA 19148 USA
Daniels, Ben — Actor
Markham & Froggatt, Julian House, 4 Windmill St, London W1P 1HF, England
Daniels, Bennie, Jr — Baseball Player
938 W 156th St, Compton CA 90220, USA
Daniels, Charlie — Singer, Songwriter
C D B Mgmt, 14410 Central Pike, Mount Joliet TN 37122, USA
Daniels, Cheryl — Bowler
6574 Crest Top Dr, West Bloomfield MI 48322, USA
Daniels, Clemon (Bo) — Football Player
8683 Mountain Road, Oakland CA 94605, USA
Daniels, David — Opera Singer
Askonas Holt, Lincoln House, 300 High Holborn, London WC1V 7JH, England
Daniels, Erin — Actress
Framework Entertainment, 129 W 27th St, #1200, New York NY 10001, USA
Daniels, Faith — Commentator
CBS-TV, News Dept, 51 W 52nd St, New York NY 10019 USA
Daniels, Greg — Actor, Director, Producer, Writer
W M E Entertainment, 9601 Wilshire Blvd, #300, Beverly Hills CA 90210 USA
Daniels, Jeff — Ice Hockey Player
108 Delaplane Court, Morrisville NC 27560, USA
Daniels, Jeff — Actor
701 Glazier Road, Chelsea MI 48118, USA
Daniels, Kalvoski (Kal) — Baseball Player
PO Box 9632, Warner Robins GA 31095, USA
Daniels, Kevin — Actor
TalentWorks, 3500 W Olive Ave, #1400, Burbank CA 91505 USA
Daniels, Lee — Director, Producer
Cinetic Mgmt, 555 West 25th St, #440, New York NY 10001, USA
Daniels, Marquis A — Basketball Player
2501 Sutton Place Dr S, Carmel IN 46032, USA

Daniels, Melvin J (Mel) — Basketball Player
19789 Centennial Road, Sheridan IN 46069, USA

Daniels, Mitchell E (Mitch), Jr — Governor, IN
Purdue University, West Lafayette IN 47907 USA

Daniels, Owen — Football Player
5425 Inwood Dr, Houston TX 77056, USA

Daniels, Phillip B — Football Player
1703 N Pebble Beach Way, Vernon Hills NJ 60061, USA

Daniels, Quincey — Boxer
112 Sunny Meadows Dr, Blackshear GA 31516, USA

Daniels, Scott — Ice Hockey Player
36 Deer Run, Southwick MA 01077, USA

Daniels, Travis A — Football Player
4665SW 75th Way, #104, Davie FL 33314, USA

Daniels, William — Actor
Gage Group, 14724 Ventura Blvd, #505, Sherman Oaks CA 91403 USA

Daniels, William B — Physicist
1100 Lovering Ave, #1208, Wilmington DE 19806, USA

Danielsen, Egil — Track Athlete
Roreks Gate 9, 2300 Hamar, Norway

Danielson, Gary D — Football Player
10112 Magnolia Bend, Bonita Springs FL 34135, USA

Danielsson, Bengt F — Anthropologist
PO Box 558, Papette, Tahiti

Daniloff, Nicholas — Journalist
PO Box 892, Chester VT 05143, USA

Danko, William D — Writer
PO Box 9125, Niskayuna NY 12309, USA

Danks, John W — Baseball Player
702 Oaklands Dr, Round Rock TX 78681, USA

Danmeier, Richard C (Rick) — Football Player
4917 Ridge Road, Minneapolis MN 55436, USA

Danneels, Godfried Cardinal — Religious Leader
Aartsbisdom, Wollemarkt 15, 2800 Mechelen, Belgium

Dannelly, Brian — Director, Writer
Creative Artists Agency, 2000 Ave of Stars, #100, Los Angeles CA 90067 USA

Danner, Blythe — Actress
Anonymous Content, 3532 Hayden Ave, Culver City CA 90232 USA

Danning, Sybil — Actress, Model
8491 W Sunset Blvd, #361, West Hollywood CA 90069, USA

Dano, Linda — Actress
70 Riverside Lane, Riverside CT 06878, USA

Dano, Paul F — Actor
Anonymous Content, 3532 Hayden Ave, Culver City CA 90232 USA

Dansby, Karlos M — Football Player
16850 Stratford Court, Southwest Ranches FL 33331, USA

Danson, Ted — Actor
Creative Artists Agency, 2000 Ave of Stars, #100, Los Angeles CA 90067 USA

Dante, Joe — Director
Renfield Productions, 1041 N Formosa Ave, Writers Building, West Hollywood CA 90046, USA

Dantley, Adrian D — Basketball Player, Coach
9 Barn Ridge Court, Silver Spring MD 20906, USA

D'Antoni, Mike — Basketball Player, Coach
9 Hunter Lane, Rye NY 10580, USA

D'Antoni, Philip — Producer, Director
Saint Andrews, 10 Old Jackson Ave, Hastings on Hudson NY 10706, USA

Dantonio, Mark — Football Coach
Michigan State University, Athletic Dept, East Lansing MI 48824, USA

Dantzscher, Jamie A — Gymnast
Arizona State University, Athletic Dept, Tempe AZ 85287, USA

Danvers, Tasha — Track Athlete
Shaftesbury Barnet, Greenlands Lane, Herndon, London NW 1RL, England

Danz, Ingeborg — Opera Singer
Kunstler Sekretariat am Gasteig, Rosenheimer Str 52, 81669 Munich, Germany

Danz, Shirley — Baseball Player
330 Greystone Dr, Hendersonville NC 28792, USA

Danza, Tony — Actor
Paradigm Agency, 360 N Crescent Dr, North Building, Beverly Hills CA 90210 USA

Danzenie, Billy — Rap Artist (M O P)
Pyramid Entertainment, 377 Rector Place, #21A, New York NY 10280 USA

Danziger, Jeff — Editorial Cartoonist
RFD, Plainfield VT 05667, USA

Danziger, Sheldon H — Economist
University of Michigan, Public Policy School, Ann Arbor MI 48109, USA

Daoust, Dan — Ice Hockey Player
55 John Silver Crescent, Markham ON L3R 9B, Canada

Dapper, Marco — Actor, Model
Himber Entertainment, PO Box 950, South Orange NJ 07079 USA

D'Aquino, Carl — Interior Designer
D'Aquino Monaco Inc, 214 W 29th St, #1202, New York NY 10001, USA

D'Aquino, Rosca — Actress
Carol Levi Mgmt, Via G Pisanelli 2, 00196 Rome, Italy

Darabont, Frank — Director, Writer
Darkwoods Productions, 301 E Colorado Blvd, #705, Pasadena CA 91101, USA

D'Arbanville-Quinn, Patti — Actress
Hartig-Hilepo Agency, 54 W 21st St, #610, New York NY 10010 USA

Darbinyan, Armen R — Prime Minister, Armenia
19 Str Sayat Nova, 375001 Yerevan, Armenia

Darby, Chartric T — Football Player
14335 Simonds Road NE, Bothell WA 98011, USA

Darby, Craig — Ice Hockey Player
40 Vista Dr, Saratoga Springs NY 12866, USA

Darby, Kim — Actress
C R Mgmt, 22337 Pacific Coast Highway, #627, Malibu CA 90265, USA

Darby, Matthew L (Matt) — Football Player
501 Sagecreek Court, Winter Springs FL 32708, USA

Darby, Rhys — Actor
Creative Artists Agency, 2000 Ave of Stars, #100, Los Angeles CA 90067 USA
D'Arby, Terence Trent — Singer
Agency Group Ltd, 142 W 57th St, #600, New York NY 10019 USA
Darc, Mireille — Actress
Agents Associes, 201 Faubourg Saint Honore, 75008 Paris, France
D'Arcangelo, Ildebrando — Opera Singer
I M G Artists, Hogarth Business Park, Chiswick, London W4 2TH, England
D'Arcevia, Bruno — Artist, Sculptor
Via Luigi Angeloni 29, 00149 Rome, Italy
Darche, Jean-Philippe — Football Player
9507 W 160th Terrace, Stilwell KS 66085, USA
Darchinyan, Vic — Boxer
Billy Hussein, 49 The Avenue, Yagoona NSW 2199, Australia
Darcy, Dame — Cartoonist, Artist
22 W Bryan St, #185, Savannah GA 31401, USA
D'Arcy, James — Actor
Creative Artists Agency, 2000 Ave of Stars, #100, Los Angeles CA 90067 USA
Darden, Thomas V (Thom) — Football Player
637 20th Ave SW, Cedar Rapids IA 52404, USA
Darensbourg, Victor A (Vic) — Baseball Player
4151 Abernethy Forest Place, Las Vegas NV 89141, USA
Darin, Ricardo — Actor
Media Art Mgmt, C/ Castelló 82, 2 Derecha, 28006 Madrid, Spain
Darius, Donovin (Don) — Football Player
12051 Scarsdale Dr, Jacksonville FL 32246, USA
Dark, Alvin R (Al) — Baseball Player, Manager
103 Cranberry Way, Easley SC 29642, USA
Darlan, Eva — Actress
Agents Associes, 201 Rue du Faubourg Saint Honore, 75008 Paris, France
Darling, Alistair M — Government Official, England
Chancellory of Exchequer, 1 Horse Guards Road, London SW1A 2HQ, England
Darling, Charles (Chuck) — Basketball Player
8066 S Kramerie Way, Centennial CO 80112, USA
Darling, David — Astronomer, Writer
John Wiley & Sons, 111 River St, Hoboken NJ 07030 USA
Darling, Devard L — Football Player
4234 NE Park Springs Dr, Lees Summit MO 64064, USA
Darling, Gary R — Baseball Umpire
16609 S 32nd Lane, Phoenix AZ 85045, USA
Darling, Jean — Actress
294 S Circular Road, Dublin 8, Ireland
Darling, Jennifer — Actress
C E S D, 10635 Santa Monica Blvd, #130, Los Angeles CA 90025 USA
Darling, Katrina — Dancer, Model
Playboy Promotions, 2706 Media Center Dr, Los Angeles CA 90065 USA
Darling, Ronald M (Ron) — Baseball Player
10 Barclay St, #34C, New York NY 10007, USA
Darlington, Jonathan — Conductor
I M G Artists, Hogarth Business Park, Chiswick, London W4 2TH, England
Darmaatmadja, Julius Riyadi Cardinal — Religious Leader
Keuskupan Agung, J I Katedral 7, Jakarta 10710, Indonesia
Darnell, August — Singer (Kid Creole & the Coconuts)
Ron Rainey Mgmt, 315 S Beverly Dr, #407, Beverly Hills CA 90212, USA
Darnell, Bruce — Model
Fashion4Art, Ingendorfer Str 34, 50529 Pulheim, Germany
Darnell, Daniel J — Air Force General
Deputy Commander, Pacific Command, Camp H M Smith HI 96861, USA
Darnell, Erik — Truck Racing Driver
Darmer Motorsports, 3627 Washington St, Park City IL 60085, USA
Darnell, James E, Jr — Molecular Biologist
Rockefeller University Medical Center, 1230 York Ave, New York NY 10065 USA
Darnton, John — Journalist, Writer
New York Times, Editorial Dept, 229 W 43rd St, New York NY 10036 USA
Darnton, Robert C — Historian
985 Memorial Dr, #403, Cambridge MA 02138, USA
Darr, Lisa — Actress
Stone Manners Salners, 9911 W Pico Blvd, #1400, Los Angeles CA 90035 USA
Darrell, Katrina — Singer, Actress
Avo Talent, 8500 Melrose Ave, #212, West Hollywood CA 90069, USA
Darren, James — Singer, Actor
PO Box 1088, Beverly Hills CA 90213, USA
Darrow, Henry — Actor
Hervey/Grimes Talent, 10561 Missouri Ave, #2, Los Angeles CA 90025 USA
Darvill, Arthur — Actor
Independent Talent Group, Oxford House, 76 Oxford St, London W1D 1BS, England
Darvish, Yu — Baseball Player
Texas Rangers, Ameriquest Field, 1000 Ballpark Way, #306, Arlington TX 76011 USA
Darwin, Daniel W (Danny) — Baseball Player
6489 Stags Leap Road, Sanger TX 76266, USA
Darwin, Matthew W (Matt) — Football Player
414 Love Bird Lane, Murphy TX 75094, USA
Darwitz, Natalie — Ice Hockey Player
4655 Pine Cone Circle, Saint Paul MN 55123, USA
Dascascos, Mark — Actor
Three-X Vision, 18850 Vista del Canon, #A, Newhall CA 91321, USA
D'Ascoli, Bernard — Concert Pianist
C L B Mgmt, 28 Earlswood Road, London NW10 5QB, England
Dash, Damon — Actor, Director, Producer
Dash Films, 825 8th Ave, #2900, New York NY 10019, USA
Dash, Leon D, Jr — Journalist
Washington Post, Editorial Dept, 1150 15th St NW, Washington DC 20071, USA
Dash, Stacey — Actress, Model
Bleecker Street Entertainment, 853 Broadway, #1214, New York NY 10003
DaSilva, Danilo L — Soccer Player
Confederacion de Futebol, Rua Victor Civita 66, #1, Rio de Janeiro 22775 044, Brazil

DaSilva, Rafael Pereira — Soccer Player
Manchester United, Busby Way, Old Trafford, Manchester M16 0RA, England

Dassler, Uwe — Swimmer
Stolze-Schrey-Str 6, 15745 Wilday, Germany

Dater, Judy L — Photographer
2430 5th St, #J, Berkeley CA 94710, USA

Datsyuk, Pavel V — Ice Hockey Player
3166 Rosedale St, Ann Arbor MI 48108, USA

Daub, Matthew — Artist
A C A Galleries, 529 W 20th St, #500, New York NY 10011, USA

Daubach, Brian M — Baseball Player
2709 Timberline Dr, Belleville IL 62226, USA

Daubechies, Ingrid C — Computer Mathematician, Physicist
Princeton University, Mathematics Dept, Princeton NJ 08544, USA

Dauer, Richard F (Rich) — Baseball Player
2510 Brook Haven Lane, Hinckley OH 44233, USA

Daughaday, William H — Endocrinologist
1840 N Prospect Ave, #322, Milwaukee WI 53202, USA

Daugherty, Bradley L (Brad) — Basketball Player, Sportscaster
10 Inspiration Way, Swananoa NC 28778, USA

Daugherty, George — Conductor
I M G Artists, Hogarth Business Park, Chiswick, London W4 2TH, England

Daugherty, John M (Jack) — Baseball Player
20360 N 95th Place, Scottsdale AZ 85255, USA

Daugherty, Michael — Composer
Argo London Records, 810 7th Ave, New York NY 10019, USA

Daughtrey, Martha Craig — Judge
US Court of Appeals, 701 Broadway, #207, Nashville TN 37203, USA

Daughtry, Christopher (Chris) — Singer, Guitarist, Songwriter
19 Music & Mgmt, 35-37 Parkgate Road, London SW11 4NP, England

Daugman, John — Inventor (Scan Security System)
Cambridge University, Computer Laboratory, Cambridge CB3 0FD, England

Dauline, Marie — Singer (Zap Mama)
Todo Mundo, PO Box 319, New York NY 10012, USA

Daulton, Darren A — Baseball Player
643 Woodbridge Dr, Melbourne FL 32940, USA

Dauterive, Jim — Producer, Writer
United Talent Agency, 9336 Civic Center Dr, Beverly Hills CA 90210 USA

Davalillo Romero, Victor J (Vic) — Baseball Player
Calle Trujillo 7, Mriperez QV, Caracas, Venezuela

Davalos, Alexa — Actress
Brillstein Entertainment Partners, 9150 Wilshire Blvd, #350, Beverly Hills CA 90212 USA

Davalos, Richard — Actor
23388 Mulholland Dr, #28, Woodland Hills CA 91364, USA

Davanger, Flemming — Curling Athlete
Curling Assn, Sognsveien 75, Serviceboks 1, 0840 Oslo, Norway

Davanon, F Jeffrey (Jerry) — Baseball Player
350 Greypine W, Montgomery TX 77356, USA

Davanon, Jeffrey G (Jeff) — Baseball Player
731 E Buena Vista Dr, Chandler AZ 85249, USA

Davenport, Jack — Actor
Hamilton Hodell, 66-68 Margaret St, London W1W 8SR, England

Davenport, James H (Jim) — Baseball Player, Manager
1016 Hewitt Dr, San Carlos CA 94070, USA

Davenport, Jeremy — Trumpeter, Singer
Columbia Artists Mgmt Inc, 1790 Broadway, #702, New York NY 10019 USA

Davenport, Jessica — Basketball Player
Indiana Fever, Conseco Fieldhouse, 125 S Pennsylvania, Indianapolis IN 46204 USA

Davenport, Lindsay — Tennis Player
PO Box 10179, Newport Beach CA 92658, USA

Davenport, Madison — Actress
C E S D, 10635 Santa Monica Blvd, #130, Los Angeles CA 90025 USA

Davenport, N'Dea — Singer, Dancer
Sangfroid Music Group, 24 Caradoc St, Greenwich, London SE10 9AG, England

Davenport, N'Dea — Singer (Brand New Heavies), Songwriter
David Levin Business Mgmt, 200 W 57th St, #1101, New York NY 10019, USA

Davenport, Nigel — Actor
5 Ann's Close, Kinnerton St, London SW1X E8S, England

Davenport, Wilbur B, Jr — Electrical Engineer
1120 Skyline Dr, Medford OR 97504, USA

Daves, Michael — Singer
Paradigm Agency, 360 N Crescent Dr, North Building, Beverly Hills CA 90210 USA

Davey, Donald V (Don) — Football Player
1525 Beach Ave, Atlantic Beach FL 32233, USA

Davi, Robert — Actor
Chuck Binder Mgmt, 1465 Lindacrest Dr, Beverly Hills CA 90210 USA

Daviau, Allen — Cinematographer
2249 Bronson Hill Dr, Los Angeles CA 90068, USA

Davich, Marty — Composer
530 S Greenwood Lane, Pasadena CA 91107, USA

David Mohato — Crown Prince, Lesotho
Royal Palace, PO Box 524, Maseru, Lesotho

David, Anna — Columnist, Writer
8424 Santa Monica Blvd, #A754, West Hollywood CA 90069, USA

David, Craig A — Singer, Songwriter
Creative Artists Agency, 2000 Ave of Stars, #100, Los Angeles CA 90067 USA

David, Edward E, Jr — Underwater Sound, Electrical Engineer
E E D Inc, PO Box 435, Bedminster NJ 07921, USA

David, George A L — Businessman
United Technologies Corp, United Technologies Building, Hartford CT 06101, USA

David, John R — Internist
Harvard Public Health School, Tropical Health Dept, 665 Huntington Ave, Boston MA 02115, USA

David, Keith — Actor, Singer
Stone Manners Salners, 9911 W Pico Blvd, #1400, Los Angeles CA 90035 USA

David, Larry — Writer, Actor, Producer
L D Productions, 3000 Olympic Blvd, Santa Monica CA 90404, USA

D

Name & Address	Profession
David, Michael Stahl Management 360, 9111 Wilshire Blvd, Beverly Hills CA 90210 USA	Actor
David, Peter PO Box 239, Bayport NY 11705, USA	Actor
Davidoff, Dov United Talent Agency, 9336 Civic Center Dr, Beverly Hills CA 90210 USA	Actor, Comedian
Davidovich, Bella Agnes Bruneau Assoc, 155 W 68th St, #1010, New York NY 10023, USA	Concert Pianist
Davidovich, Lolita Sanders/Armstrong/Caserta Mgmt, 2120 Colorado Ave, #120, Santa Monica CA 90404 USA	Actress
Davidovsky, Mario 490 W End Ave, New York NY 10024, USA	Composer
Davids, Edgar F C Juventus, Corso Galilo Ferraris 32, 10128 Turin, Italy	Soccer Player
Davidson, Adam Creative Artists Agency, 2000 Ave of Stars, #100, Los Angeles CA 90067 USA	Director
Davidson, Amy Stone Manners Salners, 9911 W Pico Blvd, #1400, Los Angeles CA 90035 USA	Actress
Davidson, Andrew Doubleday Press, 1745 Broadway, New York NY 10019 USA	Writer
Davidson, Barbara Los Angeles Times, Editorial Dept, 202 W 1st St, Los Angeles CA 90012 USA	Photographer
Davidson, Bruce O RR 842, Unionville PA 19375, USA	Equestrian
Davidson, Diane Mott William Morrow Publishers, 1350 Ave of Americas, New York NY 10019 USA	Writer
Davidson, Eileen Media Artists Group, 8222 Melrose Ave, #203, Los Angeles CA 90048 USA	Actress
Davidson, Ernest R 5051 50th Ave NE, #22, Seattle WA 98105, USA	Chemist
Davidson, Francis M (Cotton) 435 Old Osage Road, Gatesville TX 76528, USA	Football Player
Davidson, Gordon 165 Mabery Rd, Santa Monica CA 90402, USA	Producer, Director
Davidson, J Mark 996 Old Mountain Road, Statesville NC 28677, USA	Baseball Player
Davidson, Jeff Breathing Space Institute, 3202 Ruffin St, Raleigh NC 27607, USA	Motivational Speaker
Davidson, Jeremy Insight Entertainment, 1134 S Cloverdale Ave, Los Angeles CA 90019, USA	Actor
Davidson, Jim International Artistes, 193-197 High Holborn, London WC1V 7BD, England	Actor
Davidson, John 8605 Santa Monica Blvd, West Hollywood CA 90069, USA	Singer, Actor
Davidson, John 6 Briarbrook Trail, Saint Louis MO 63131, USA	Ice Hockey Player, Executive
Davidson, Justin New York Newsday, Editorial Dept, 235 Pinelawn Road, Melville NY 11747 USA	Journalist
Davidson, Kenneth D (Kenny) 1922 Thompson Crossing Dr, Richmond TX 77406, USA	Football Player
Davidson, Owen 39 N Lakemist Harbour Place, Spring TX 77381, USA	Tennis Player
Davidson, Richard University of Wisconsin, Keck Brain Imaging & Behavior Laboratory, Madison WI 53706, USA	Neuroplastic Surgeon
Davidson, Tommy Glick Agency, 1321 7th St, #203, Santa Monica CA 90401 USA	Actor, Comedian
David-Weill, Michel Lazard, 121 Blvd Haussmann, 75008 Paris, France	Financier
Davie, J Alan Gamels Studio, Rush Green, Hertfordshire SG13 7SB, England	Artist
Davie, Robert (Bob) University of New Mexico, Athletic Dept, Albuquerque NM , USA	Football Coach, Sportscaster
Davies, Alan Rights House, 34-43 Russell St, London WC2B 5HA, England	Actor
Davies, Caryn Columbia University, Law School, New York NY 10027, USA	Rowing Athlete
Davies, Dave Talent Consultants International, 105 Shad Row, #B, Piermont NY 10968 USA	Singer, Guitarist (Kinks)
Davies, David R 4224 Franklin St, Kensington MD 20895, USA	Biophysicist
Davies, Dennis Russell Columbia Artists Mgmt Inc, 1790 Broadway, #702, New York NY 10019 USA	Conductor, Concert Pianist
Davies, Gail 246 Cherokee Road, Nashville TN 37205, USA	Singer, Guitarist, Songwriter
Davies, Geraint Wyn Oscars Abrams Zimel, 438 Queen St W, Toronto ON M5A 1T4, Canada	Actor
Davies, H Kyle 1495 E Lake Road, McDonough GA 30252, USA	Baseball Player
Davies, Jeremy Untitled Entertainment, 350 S Beverly Dr, #200, Beverly Hills CA 90212 USA	Actor
Davies, John G 520 Madeline Dr, Pasadena CA 91105, USA	Judge, Swimmer
Davies, Karle Curtis Brown Group, 28-29 Haymarket St, #500, London SW1Y 4SP, England	Actor
Davies, Lane PO Box 20531, Thousand Oaks CA 91358, USA	Actor
Davies, Laura Tytherington Club, Tytherington Macclesfield SK10 2JP, England	Golfer
Davies, Linda Calle Once 286, La Molona, Lima, Peru	Writer
Davies, Matt Journal News, Editorial Dept, 1 Gannett Dr, West Harrison NY 10604, USA	Editorial Cartoonist
Davies, Mike Rogers Partnership, Thames Wharf, Rainville Road, London N6 94A, England	Architect
Davies, Paul C W PO Box 389, Burnside SA 5066, Australia	Mathematical Physicist

David - Davies

Davies, Peter Maxwell — Composer
Judy Arnold, 50 Hogarth Road, London SW5 OPU, England
Davies, Raymond D (Ray) — Singer, Guitarist (Kinks)
High Road Touring, 751 Bridgeway, #200, Sausalito CA 94965 USA
Davies, Ryland — Opera Singer
71 Fairmile Lane, Cobham, Surrey KT11 2DG, England
Davies, S Howard — Director
Royal National Theater, South Bank, London SE 19PX, England
Davies, William — Writer
United Talent Agency, 9336 Civic Center Dr, Beverly Hills CA 90210 USA
Davila, Robert — Educator
Gallaudet University, President's Office, 800 Florida NW, Washington DC 20002, USA
Davis, A Willard (Bill) — Baseball Player
6638 Knox Ave S, Minneapolis MN 55423, USA
Davis, Alia — Singer (Allure)
Universal Attractions, 135 W 26th St, #1200, New York NY 10001 USA
Davis, Alvin G — Baseball Player
7983 Armagosa Dr, Riverside CA 92508, USA
Davis, Andra R — Football Player
6009 S Olathe St, Centennial CO 80016, USA
Davis, Andre' N — Football Player
11407 Jutland Road, Houston TX 77048, USA
Davis, Andrew — Director
Chicago Pacific Entertainment, 1475 Hillcrest Road, Santa Barbara CA 93103, USA
Davis, Andrew F — Conductor
Columbia Artists Mgmt Inc, 1790 Broadway, #702, New York NY 10019 USA
Davis, Angela Y — Political Activist, Educator
Speakout, PO Box 22748, Oakland CA 94609, USA
Davis, Ann B — Actress
23315 Eagle Gap Road, San Antonio TX 78255, USA
Davis, Anthony — Football Player
8011 Carter Ave, #2606, Overland Park KS 66204, USA
Davis, Anthony — Jazz Pianist, Composer
Andriolo Communications, 115 E 9th St, New York NY 10003, USA
Davis, Anthony, Jr — Basketball Player
New Orleans Hornets, 1250 Poydras St, #101, New Orleans LA 70113 USA
Davis, Antone — Football Player
2252 Red Bud Road, Sevierville TN 37876, USA
Davis, Antonio L — Basketball Player
21 Buford Village Walk, Buford GA 30518, USA
Davis, Baron W L — Basketball Player
PO Box 12109, Marina del Rey CA 90295, USA
Davis, Barry — Freestyle Wrestler
417 N High Point Road, Madison WI 53717, USA
Davis, Benjamin (Ben) — Opera Singer
Encompass Arts, 119 W 72nd St, 371, New York NY 10023, USA
Davis, Benjamin F (Ben) — Football Player
1144 Brandon Road, Cleveland OH 44112, USA
Davis, Benjamin Jay — Actor
Untitled Entertainment, 350 S Beverly Dr, #200, Beverly Hills CA 90212 USA
Davis, Bennie L — Air Force General
101 Golden Road, Georgetown TX 78633, USA
Davis, Bill — Auto Racing Executive
Bill Davis Racing, 810 Newport Road, Batesville AR 72501, USA
Davis, Billy, Jr — Singer (Fifth Dimension)
PO Box 7905, Beverly Hills CA 90212, USA
Davis, Bradley E (Brad) — Basketball Player
2703 Ridge Top Lane, Arlington TX 76006, USA
Davis, Brian W — Football Player
6442 W Park Ave, Chandler AZ 85226, USA
Davis, Brianne — Actress
Sager Mgmt, 260 S Beverly Dr, #205, Beverly Hills CA 90212, USA
Davis, Bryshear B (Brock) — Baseball Player
23759 Heliotrope Way, Moreno Valley CA 92557, USA
Davis, Charles A — Jazz Saxophonist
201 E 19th St, #9E, New York NY 10003, USA
Davis, Charles E (Charlie) — Basketball Player
615 Main St, Nashville TN 37206, USA
Davis, Charles F — Sportscaster
N F L Network, 10950 Washington Blvd, #100, Culver City CA 90232 USA
Davis, Charles M (Charlie) — Football Player
2400 Bowler Road, Waller TX 77484, USA
Davis, Charles T (Chili) — Baseball Player
4625 Lake Washington Blvd SE, Bellevue WA 98006, USA
Davis, Clarence E — Football Player
171 Longleaf St, Pickerington OH 43147, USA
Davis, Clifton — Actor
C E S D, 10635 Santa Monica Blvd, #130, Los Angeles CA 90025 USA
Davis, Clive J — Businessman
R C A Records, 8750 Wilshire Blvd, Beverly Hills CA 90211 USA
Davis, Colin R — Conductor
Columbia Artists Mgmt Inc, 1790 Broadway, #702, New York NY 10019 USA
Davis, Dana — Actress
Marshak/Zachary Co, 8840 Wilshire Blvd, #100, Beverly Hills CA 90211 USA
Davis, Daniel — Actor
Innovative Artists, 1505 10th St, Santa Monica CA 90401 USA
Davis, Daniel M — Immunologist
Imperial College, Biological Sciences Dept, London SW7 2AZ, England
Davis, David (Dave) — Bowler
DeStasio, 710 Shore Road, Spring Lake Heights NJ 07762, USA
Davis, David Brion — Writer, Historian
783 Lambert Road, Orange CT 06477, USA
Davis, Debbie — Model
Playboy Promotions, 2706 Media Center Dr, Los Angeles CA 90065 USA
Davis, DeRay — Actor
Principato-Young, 9465 Wilshire Blvd, #880, Beverly Hills CA 90212 USA

Davis, Destiny — Model
10624 S Eastern Ave, #A157, Henderson NV 89052, USA
Davis, Dexter W — Football Player
5054 Vermack Road, Atlanta GA 30338, USA
Davis, Diane — Actress
Paradigm Agency, 360 N Crescent Dr, North Building, Beverly Hills CA 90210 USA
Davis, Don — Golfer
15910 FM 529, #219, Houston TX 77095, USA
Davis, Douglas N (Doug) — Baseball Player
26125 N 116th St, Scottsdale AZ 85255, USA
Davis, E Lydell (Dale) — Basketball Player
2000 Westwood Circle SE, Smyrna GA 30080, USA
Davis, Edgar — Space Scientist
Jet Propulsion Laboratory, 4800 Oak Grove Dr, Pasadena CA 91109 USA
Davis, Elliot M — Cinematographer
1328 Arch St, Berkeley CA 94708, USA
Davis, Eric K — Baseball Player
6203 Variel Ave, #118, Woodland Hills CA 91367, USA
Davis, Eric W — Football Player
3737 Coyote Canyon, Soquel CA 95073, USA
Davis, Essie — Actress
United Agents, 12-26 Lexington St, London W1F 0LE, England
Davis, Gary C — Football Player
10750 San Marcus Road, Atascadero CA 93422, USA
Davis, Geena — Actress
Creative Artists Agency, 2000 Ave of Stars, #100, Los Angeles CA 90067 USA
Davis, George E (Storm) — Baseball Player
7931 Dawsons Creek Dr, Jacksonville FL 32222, USA
Davis, Glenn E — Baseball Player
27 Cascade Road, Columbus GA 31904, USA
Davis, Gregory B (Greg) — Football Player
793 Vernon Road NE, Rome GA 30165, USA
Davis, H Thomas (Tommy) — Baseball Player
9767 Whirlaway St, Rancho Cucamonga CA 91737, USA
Davis, Harry A — Basketball Player
1966 E 75th St, Cleveland OH 44103, USA
Davis, Harry R, Jr — Chemist
Schering-Plough Research, 2000 Galloping Hill Road, Kenilworth NJ 07033, USA
Davis, Hope — Actress
United Talent Agency, 9336 Civic Center Dr, Beverly Hills CA 90210 USA
Davis, Hubert I — Basketball Player
204 Lancaster Dr, Chapel Hill NC 27517, USA
Davis, J Graham (Gray), Jr — Governor, CA
Loeb & Loeb, 10100 Santa Monica Blvd, #2200, Los Angeles CA 90067, USA
Davis, James B — Air Force General
3600 Wimber Blvd, Palm Harbor FL 34685, USA
Davis, James O — Physician
612 Maplewood Dr, Columbia MO 65203, USA
Davis, James R (Jim) — Cartoonist (Garfield)
Paws Inc, 5440 E Country Road 450 N, Albany IN 47320, USA
Davis, James S — Football Player
5701 S Saint Andrews Place, Los Angeles CA 90062, USA
Davis, Jamie — Actress
Curtis Brown Group, 28-29 Haymarket St, #500, London SW1Y 4SP, England
Davis, Jason T — Baseball Player
474 Leatha Lane NW, Cleveland TN 37312, USA
Davis, Jay — Golfer
2152 S State St, Springfield IL 62704, USA
Davis, Jeff — Producer, Writer
Magnet Mgmt, 11704 Wilshire Blvd, #210, Los Angeles CA 90025, USA
Davis, Jeff (Stick) — Bassist (Amazing Rhythm Aces)
Gen-X Entertainment, PO Box 128164, Nashville TN 37212, USA
Davis, Jeff Bryan — Actor, Comedian, Director
Domain Talent, 9229 W Sunset Blvd, #710, West Hollywood CA 90069 USA
Davis, Jeffrey E (Jeff) — Football Player
106 Sycamore Dr, Clemson SC 29631, USA
Davis, Jesse — Jazz Saxophonist
Concord Records, 100 N Crescent Dr, #275, Beverly Hills CA 90210 USA
Davis, Jill A — Writer
Random House, 1745 Broadway, #1800, New York NY 10019 USA
Davis, Jody R — Baseball Player
5631 N 79th St, #4, Scottsdale AZ 85250, USA
Davis, John A — Actor, Director, Producer, Writer
W M E Entertainment, 9601 Wilshire Blvd, #300, Beverly Hills CA 90210 USA
Davis, John H — Football Player
901 Forest Pond Dr, Marietta GA 30068, USA
Davis, John K — Marine Corps General
303 Calle Empalome, San Clemente CA 92672, USA
Davis, Johnny L — Football Player
PO Box 550, Edgewater NJ 07020, USA
Davis, Johnny R — Basketball Player, Coach
135 W Market St, #2D, Indianapolis IN 46204, USA
Davis, Jonathan H — Singer (Korn), Bagpipe Player
The Firm, 2049 Century Park E, #2550, Los Angeles CA 90067 USA
Davis, Josie — Actress
Stone Manners Salners, 9911 W Pico Blvd, #1400, Los Angeles CA 90035 USA
Davis, Judy — Actress
Shanahan Mgmt, PO Box 1509, Darlinghurst NSW 1300, Australia
Davis, Julie — Director, Writer
Felker Toczak Gellman, 10880 Wilshire Blvd, #2070, Los Angeles CA 90024 USA
Davis, Kane — Baseball Player
1558 Noble Ridge, Reedy WV 25270, USA
Davis, Keith B — Football Player
1343 Marvin Gardens, Lancaster TX 75134, USA
Davis, Kenneth E — Football Player
1224 Brooklawn Dr, Arlington TX 76018, USA

Davis - Davis

Davis, Keno — Basketball Coach
Providence College, Athletic Dept, Providence RI 02918, USA

Davis, Kim — Ice Hockey Player
14 Shorecrest Dr, Winnipeg MB R3P 1N2, Canada

Davis, Kristin — Actress, Model
Mosiac Media Group, 9200 W Sunset Blvd, #1000, Los Angeles CA 90069 USA

Davis, Kyle — Actor
Global Artists Agency, 6253 Hollywood Blvd, #508, Los Angeles CA 90028, USA

Davis, Lance — Baseball Player
5845 Old Berkley Road, Auburdale FL 33823, USA

Davis, Lance E — Economist
9717 Thistle Court, Fort Smith AR 72908, USA

Davis, Lee C — Basketball Player
5024 Fieldgreen Crossing, #82, Stone Mountain GA 30088, USA

Davis, Linda K — Singer
5548 Shady Trail, Old Hickory TN 37138, USA

Davis, Louis (Chip), Jr — Musician
Sound Trak, 9120 Mormon Bridge Road, Omaha NE 68152, USA

Davis, Lowell — Artist, Sculptor
1070 3rd St, #E, Carthage MO 64836, USA

Davis, Lucy — Actress
Melanie Greene Mgmt, 425 N Robertson Blvd, West Hollywood CA 90048 USA

Davis, Mac — Singer, Songwriter, Actor
Abrams Artists, 9200 W Sunset Blvd, #1125, West Hollywood CA 90069 USA

Davis, Mark A — Basketball Player
108 Government Circle, #A, Thibodaux LA 70301, USA

Davis, Mark C (Ben) — Baseball Player
416 Homestead Dr, West Chester PA 19382, USA

Davis, Mark M — Microbiologist
Stanford University Medical Center, Microbiology Dept, Stanford CA 94305, USA

Davis, Mark W — Baseball Player
8867 E Sierra Pinta Dr, Scottsdale AZ 85255, USA

Davis, Martha — Singer (Motels)
Paradise Artists, PO Box 1821, Ojai CA 93024 USA

Davis, Matthew (Matt) — Actor
Brillstein Entertainment Partners, 9150 Wilshire Blvd, #350, Beverly Hills CA 90212 USA

Davis, Melvyn J (Mel) — Basketball Player
PO Box 29, Suffern NY 10901, USA

Davis, Meryl — Ice Dancer
Artic Edge Skating Club, 46615 Michigan Ave, Canton MI 48188, USA

Davis, Michael — Director, Writer
I C M Partners, 10250 Constellation Blvd, #900, Los Angeles CA 90067 USA

Davis, Michael D (Mike) — Baseball Player
2491 San Ramon Valley Blvd, #1407, San Ramon CA 94583, USA

Davis, Michael L (Mike) — Football Player
37039 N 109th St, Scottsdale AZ 85262, USA

Davis, N Jan — Astronaut
4105 Cumberland Pass, #814, Fort Worth TX 76116, USA

Davis, Oliver J — Football Player
1708 Fountain Court, #3702, Columbus GA 31904, USA

Davis, Paige — Actress, Entertainer
3 Arts Entertainment, 9460 Wilshire Blvd, #700, Beverly Hills CA 90212 USA

Davis, Phyllis — Actress
29330 SE Hillyard Dr, #D14, Boring OR 97009, USA

Davis, Preston — Actor
Vincent Cirrincione Assoc, 1516 N Fairfax Ave, Los Angeles CA 90046 USA

Davis, R Glen (Big Baby) — Basketball Player
Performance Sports Mgmt, PO Box 270715, Houston TX 77277, USA

Davis, Rajal L — Baseball Player
31 Pond Edge Dr, Waterford CT 06385, USA

Davis, Reuben C — Football Player
4424 Lystra Road, Chapel Hill NC 27517, USA

Davis, Richard — Jazz Bassist
S R O Artists, 6629 University Ave, #206, Middleton WI 53562, USA

Davis, Richard D (Rick) — Soccer Player
12501 Isis Ave, Hawthorne CA 90250, USA

Davis, Richard E (Dick) — Baseball Player
11091 Sultan St, Moreno Valley CA 92557, USA

Davis, Richard K (Ted) — Football Player
5401 Riverbend Dr, Knoxville TN 37919, USA

Davis, Robert E (Bob), Jr — Football Player
500 W 111th St, #4F, New York NY 10025, USA

Davis, Robert J E (Bob) — Baseball Player
PO Box 198, Locust Grove OK 74352, USA

Davis, Roger W — Football Player
17522 Harvard Ave, Cleveland OH 44128, USA

Davis, Ronald (Ron) — Artist
PO Box 293, Arroyo Hondo NM 87513, USA

Davis, Ronald G (Ron) — Baseball Player
11748 N 90th Place, Scottsdale AZ 85260, USA

Davis, Ronald H — Basketball Player
5668 W Evergreen Road, Glendale AZ 85302, USA

Davis, Russell M — Football Player
605 Jones Ferry Road, Carrboro NC 27510, USA

Davis, Russell S (Russ) — Baseball Player
3351 Crescent Dr, Bessemer AL 35023, USA

Davis, Sammy J, Jr — Football Player
4020 Murphy Canyon Road, San Diego CA 92123, USA

Davis, Sammy L — Vietnam War Army Hero (CMH)
3376 N 100th St, Flat Rock IL 62427, USA

Davis, Sampson — Physician
Three Doctors Foundation, 65 Hazelwood Ave, Newark NJ 07106, USA

Davis, Samuel R (Sam) — Football Player
423 Edgemont St, Mount Washington PA 15211, USA

Davis, Scott — Figure Skater, Coach
5308 Worthington Dr, Bethesda MD 20816, USA

Davis, Shani	Speed Skater
Team Davis, PO Box 60832, Chicago IL 60660, USA	
Davis, Sharen	Costume Designer
Sandra Marsh & Associates, 9150 Wilshire Blvd, #220, Beverly Hills CA 90212, USA	
Davis, Spencer	Singer, Guitarist
Geoffrey Blumenauer Artists, PO Box 343, Burbank CA 91503 USA	
Davis, Stephen H	Mathematician, Engineer
2735 Simpson St, Evanston IL 60201, USA	
Davis, Stephen L	Football Player
PO Box 31847, Saint Louis MO 63131, USA	
Davis, Steve	Snooker Player
Matchroom Snooker, 10 Western Road, Romford, Essex RM1 3JT, England	
Davis, Steven K (Steve)	Baseball Player
6717 Westbury Court, Benbrook TX 76132, USA	
Davis, Steven M	Baseball Player
6011 86th St, Lubbock TX 79424, USA	
Davis, Tamra	Director, Cinematographer
Paradigm Agency, 360 N Crescent Dr, North Building, Beverly Hills CA 90210 USA	
Davis, Tania	Violist (Bond)
Mel Bush, Tanglewood, Arrowsmith Road, Wimborne, Dorset BH21 3BG, England	
Davis, Terrell L	Football Player, Sportscaster
19750 E Geddes Place, Centennial CO 80016, USA	
Davis, Terry R	Basketball Player
2933 Kenmore Road, Richmond VA 23225, USA	
Davis, Thomas J (Tommy)	Baseball Player
4685 Cavalier Dr, Semmes AL 36575, USA	
Davis, Trench N	Baseball Player
306 40th Street Circle W, Palmetto FL 34221, USA	
Davis, Vernon	Football Player
San Francisco 49ers, 4949 Centennial Blvd, Santa Clara CA 95054 USA	
Davis, Viola	Actress
Principal Entertainment, 130 W 42nd St, #614, New York NY 10036, USA	
Davis, W Eugene	Judge
US Court of Appeals, 800 Lafayette St, #2100, Lafayette LA 70501, USA	
Davis, Wallace M (Butch)	Baseball Player
1108 Brucemont Dr, Garner NC 27529, USA	
Davis, Walter F (Buddy)	Track Athlete, Basketball Player
5200 E Donald Ave, #A, Denver CO 80222, USA	
Davis, Walter P	Basketball Player
5200 E Donald Ave, #A, Denver CO 80222, USA	
Davis, Warwick A	Actor
Independent Talent Group, Oxford House, 76 Oxford St, London W1D 1BS, England	
Davis, Wendy	Actress
Pakula/King, 9229 W Sunset Blvd, #315, West Hollywood CA 90069 USA	
Davis, William A (Billy), III	Football Player
5813 Tautoga Dr, El Paso TX 79924, USA	
Davis, William D (Willie)	Football Player
100 Corporate Pointe, #310, Culver City CA 90230, USA	
Davis, Willie C	Football Player
Kansas City Chiefs, 1 Arrowhead Dr, Kansas City KS 64129 USA	
Davison, Bruce	Actor
Innovative Artists, 1505 10th St, Santa Monica CA 90401 USA	
Davison, Fred C	Foundation Executive, Educator
National Science Foundation, 1 7th St, #502, Augusta GA 30901, USA	
Davison, Peter	Actor
Conway Van Gelder Grant, 8-12 Broadwick St, #300, London W1F 8HW, England	
Davis-Wrightsil, Clarissa	Basketball Player
Phoenix Mercury, American West Arena, 201 E Jefferson St, Phoenix AZ 85004 USA	
Davitian, Ken	Actor
Luber Rocklin Entertainment, 8530 Wilshire Blvd, #555, Beverly Hills CA 90211 USA	
Dawber, Pam	Actress
TalentWorks, 3500 W Olive Ave, #1400, Burbank CA 91505 USA	
Dawe, Jason	Ice Hockey Player
9077 Drayton Lane, Fort Mill SC 29707, USA	
Dawes, Dominque M	Gymnast
5484 Randolph Road, Rockville MD 20852, USA	
Dawes, Scott	Construction Engineer
Dawes Construction Co, 1122 W 156th St, #100, Glenpool OK 74033, USA	
Dawid, Igor B	Molecular Geneticist
Tufts Regenerative & Developmental Biology Center, 200 Boston Ave, #4600, Medford , MA 02155, USA	
Dawkins, Brian P	Football Player
9874 Red Sumac Place, Parker CO 80138, USA	
Dawkins, C Richard	Biologist, Ethologist, Writer
Oxford University, Museum, Parks Road, Oxford OX1 3PW, England	
Dawkins, Darryl	Basketball Player
1708 Glacier Court, Allentown PA 18104, USA	
Dawkins, Johnny E	Basketball Player, Coach
40 Sunkist Lane, Los Altos CA 94022, USA	
Dawkins, Peter M (Pete)	Football Player, Businessman
80 W River Road, Rumson NJ 07760, USA	
Dawkins, Sean R	Football Player
826 Weichert Dr, Morgan Hill CA 95037, USA	
Dawkins, Travis S (Gookie)	Baseball Player
106 Hunter Ridge Court, Boiling Springs SC 29316, USA	
Dawley, Joseph W (Joe)	Artist
13 Holly St, Cranford NJ 07016, USA	
Dawley, William C (Bill)	Baseball Player
8127 Landau Park Lane, Spring TX 77379, USA	
Dawsey, Lawrence	Football Player
4341 Cheval Blvd, Lutz FL 33558, USA	
Dawson, Andre N	Baseball Player
10601 SW 74th Ave, Miami FL 33156, USA	
Dawson, Carol	Writer
Simon & Schuster, 1230 Ave of Americas, Concourse 1, New York NY 10020 USA	
Dawson, Chad	Boxer
Gary Shaw Productions, 555 Preakness Ave, #9, Totowa NJ 07502, USA	

D

Davis - Dawson

Dawson, Dermontti F — Football Player
PO Box 712481, San Diego CA 92171, USA

Dawson, Douglas A (Doug) — Football Player
Dawson Financial Services, 1 Riverway, #900, Houston TX 77056, USA

Dawson, J Cutler, Jr — Navy Admiral
Navy Federal Credit Union, PO Box 3000, Merrifield VA 22119, USA

Dawson, James C (Jim) — Basketball Player
61 Glendale Road, Rye NY 10580, USA

Dawson, Leonard R (Lenny) — Football Player, Sportscaster
1030 W 59th Terrace, Kansas City MO 64113, USA

Dawson, Lynne — Opera Singer
I M G Artists, Hogarth Business Park, Chiswick, London W4 2TH, England

Dawson, Marco — Golfer
3053 Shoal Creek Village Dr, Lakeland FL 33803, USA

Dawson, Philip D (Phil) — Football Player
4000 Dunning Lane, Austin TX 78746, USA

Dawson, Rosario — Actress, Singer
Creative Artists Agency, 2000 Ave of Stars, #100, Los Angeles CA 90067 USA

Dawson, Roxann — Actress, Director
Andrea Simon Entertainment, 4230 Woodman Ave, Sherman Oaks CA 91423, USA

Dawson, Trent — Actor
Innovative Artists, 1505 10th St, Santa Monica CA 90401 USA

Day George, Lynda — Actress
10310 Riverside Dr, #104, Toluca Lake CA 91602, USA

Day, Bill — Editorial Cartoonist
Memphis Commercial-Appeal, Editorial Dept, 495 Union Ave, Memphis TN 38103, USA

Day, Charles F (Boots) — Baseball Player
1154 Vespasian Way, Chesterfield MO 63017, USA

Day, Charles P (Charlie) — Actor, Producer
3 Arts Entertainment, 9460 Wilshire Blvd, #700, Beverly Hills CA 90212 USA

Day, Doris — Singer, Actress
Doris Day Pet Foundation, PO Box 1008, Versailles KY 40383, USA

Day, Felicia — Actress
I C M Partners, 10250 Constellation Blvd, #900, Los Angeles CA 90067 USA

Day, George E (Bud) — Vietnam War Air Force Hero (CMH)
3187 Desert St, Pensacola FL 32514, USA

Day, Glen — Golfer
6 Hickory Hills Circle, Little Rock AR 72212, USA

Day, Joe — Ice Hockey Player
805 Shoreline Road, Lake Barrington IL 60010, USA

Day, Julian — Businessman
Kmart, 3000 W 14 Mile Road, Royal Oak MI 48073, USA

Day, Laura — Writer
Harper Collins Publishers, 10 E 53rd St, Cellar 1, New York NY 10022 USA

Day, Matt — Actor
United Agents, 12-26 Lexington St, London W1F 0LE, England

Day, Patrick (Pat) — Thoroughbred Racing Jockey
14703 Isleworth Court, Louisville KY 40245, USA

Day, Peter R — Agricultural Scientist
8200 Tarsier Ave, New Port Richey FL 34653, USA

Day, Robert — Director
8832 Ferncliff Ave NE, Bainbridge Island WA 98110, USA

Day, S Zachary (Zach) — Baseball Player
9663 Lupine Dr, Cincinnati OH 45241, USA

Day, Skyler — Actress
I C M Partners, 10250 Constellation Blvd, #900, Los Angeles CA 90067 USA

Daye, Darren K — Basektball Player
17 Elderberry, Irvine CA 92603, USA

Dayett, Brian K — Baseball Player
276 Phillips Dr, Winchester TN 37398, USA

Daykin, Anthony A (Tony) — Football Player
5204 Cross Ridge Circle, Woodstock GA 30188, USA

Day-Lewis, Daniel — Actor
Julian Belfrage Assoc, 9 Argyll St, #300, London W1F 7TG, England

Dayley, Kenneth G (Ken) — Baseball Player
1300 Wingate Way Court, Chesterfield MO 63005, USA

Dayne, Ron — Football Player
2135 Regent St, Madison WI 53726, USA

Dayne, Taylor — Singer, Songwriter, Actress
Almond Talent Agency, 8217 Beverly Blvd, #8, West Hollywood CA 90048, USA

Days, Drews S, III — Government Official
Yale University, Law School, New Haven CT 06520, USA

Dayton, Jonathan — Director
United Talent Agency, 9336 Civic Center Dr, Beverly Hills CA 90210 USA

Dea, Billy — Ice Hockey Player
2636 W Bartlett Way, Queen Creek AZ 85142, USA

Deacon, Max — Actor
Julian Belfrage Assoc, 9 Argyll St, #300, London W1F 7TG, England

Deacon, Richard — Sculptor
Lisson Gallery, 67 Lisson St, London NW1 5DA, England

Deadmarsh, Adam — Ice Hockey Player
PO Box 3346, Coeur D'Alene ID 83816, USA

Deadmarsh, Ernest C (Butch) — Ice Hockey Player
282 Diamond Dr SE, Calgary AB T2J 7E2, Canada

DeAgostini-Rossetti, Doris — Alpine Skier
Strada de Valle, 6780 Airolo, Switzerland

Deakin, Julia — Actress
Curtis Brown Group, 28-29 Haymarket St, #500, London SW1Y 4SP, England

Deakin, Paul — Drummer (Mavericks)
AristoMedia, 1620 16th Ave S, Nashville TN 37212, USA

Deakins, Roger A — Cinematographer
Independent Talent Group, Oxford House, 76 Oxford St, London W1D 1BS, England

Deal, Ellis F (Cot) — Baseball Player
9009 N May Ave, #164, Oklahoma City OK 73120, USA

Deal, Kimberly A (Kim) — Singer, Bassist (Pixies, Breeders)
X-Ray Touring, 77-79 Great Eastern St, London EC2A 3HU, England

Deal, Lance — Track Athlete
845 Park Ave, Eugene OR 97404, USA
DeAlmeida, Joaquim — Actor
A P A Talent/Literary Agency, 405 S Beverly Dr, #300, Beverly Hills CA 90212 USA
Dean, Barry — Ice Hockey Player
315 Marsh St, Maple Creek SK S0N 1N0, Canada
Dean, Billy — Singer, Songwriter
Bobby Roberts, 3050 Business Park Circle, #303, Goodlettsville TN 37221 USA
Dean, Christopher — Ice Dancer
4575 Governors Point, Colorado Springs CO 80906, USA
Dean, David — Football Coach
Valdosta State University, Athletic Dept, Valdosta GA 31698, USA
Dean, Frederick G (Fred) — Football Player, Coach
3911 Whitchurch Dr, Houston TX 77066, USA
Dean, Fredrick R (Fred) — Football Player
2411 Highway 3061, Ruston LA 71270, USA
Dean, Graham — Artist
Lacey Gallery, 1 Crawford Passage, Bay Street, London EC1R 3DP, England
Dean, Hazell — Singer, Songwriter
7 Kentish Town Road, London NW1 8N4, England
Dean, Ira — Singer (Trick Pony)
Warner Bros Records, 20 Music Square East, Nashville TN 37203 USA
Dean, John G — Diplomat
Chalet Crettaz, BP 1318, 1936 Verbier Valais, Switzerland
Dean, John W, III — Watergate Figure
9496 Rembert Lane, Beverly Hills CA 90210, USA
Dean, Kevin — Ice Hockey Player
1905 Wayzata Blvd, Wayzata MN 55391, USA
Dean, Kiley — Singer
Music World Entertainment, 1505 Hadley St, Houston TX 77002, USA
Dean, Laura — Choreographer, Composer
Dean Dance & Music Foundation, 552 Broadway, #400, New York NY 10012, USA
Dean, Stafford R — Opera Singer
I M G Artists, Burlington Lane, Chiswick, London W4 2TH, England
Dean, Theodore C (Ted) — Football Player
16474 W Lava Dr, Surprise AZ 85374, USA
Dean, Vernon D — Football Player
2345 Hemlock St, Beaumont TX 77701, USA
DeAnda, Paula — Singer
I C M Partners, 10250 Constellation Blvd, #900, Los Angeles CA 90067 USA
DeAndrea, John — Artist
2220 Suncrest Dr, Loveland CO 80537, USA
Deane, William Patrick — Governor General, Australia
PO Box 4168, Manu Ka 2603 ACT, Australia
DeAngelis, Beverly — Psychiatrist
505 S Beverly Dr, #1017, Beverly Hills CA 90212, USA
DeAngelis, William R (Billy) — Basketball Player
14 Pickering Dr, Trenton NJ 08691, USA
DeAragon, Maria — Actress
1159 10th Ave, San Diego CA 92101, USA
Dearborn, Matthew (Matt) — Producer, Writer
Caro Entertainment, 3221 Hutchison Ave, #H, Los Angeles CA 90034, USA
Deardurff-Schmidt, Deena — Swimmer
742 Murray Dr, El Cajon CA 92020, USA
Dearman, John — Guitarist (LAGQ)
California State University, Music Dept, 18111 Nordhoff St, Northridge CA 91330, USA
DeArmond, Frank M — Astronaut
3086 Ravencrest Circle, Prescott AZ 86303, USA
Deas, Justin — Actor
I C M Partners, 10250 Constellation Blvd, #900, Los Angeles CA 90067 USA
D'Eath, Tom — Boat Racing Driver
435 Bay Road, Mount Dora FL 32757, USA
Deaton, Brady J — Educator
University of Missouri, Chancellor's Office, Jesse Hall, Columbia MO 65211, USA
Deaver, Jeffrey — Writer
Simon & Schuster, 1230 Ave of Americas, Concourse 1, New York NY 10020 USA
deAviz, Joao B Cardinal — Religious Leader
Institutes of Consecrated Life, Piazza Pio XII 3, 00193 Rome, Italy
DeBankole, Isaach — Actor
Magrit Polak Mgmt, 1411 Carroll Ave, Los Angeles CA 90026, USA
DeBarge, Chico — Singer, Songwriter
Entertainment Artists, PO Box 120824, Nashville TN 37212 USA
DeBarge, Eldra P (El) — Singer, Pianist, Songwriter
Universal Attractions, 135 W 26th St, #1200, New York NY 10001 USA
DeBarge, Kristina — Singer, Songwriter
Soda Pop/Def Soul Records, 825 8th Ave, #2700, New York NY 10019, USA
Debarr, Dennis L (Denny) — Baseball Player
33843 Juliet Circle, Fremont CA 94555, USA
Debbie Deb — Singer
Harmony Artists, 6399 Wilshire Blvd, #914, Los Angeles CA 90048, USA
Debbouze, Jamel — Actor
Artmedia, 20 Ave Rapp, 75007 Paris, France
DeBeaufort, India — Actress, Singer
Safron Co, 2000 Ave of Stars, #600N, Los Angeles CA 90067, USA
DeBellevue, Charles B — Vietnam War Air Force Hero
916 Huntsman Road, Edmond OK 73003, USA
Debello, James — Actor
Full Circle Mgmt, 4932 Lankershim Blvd, #202, North Hollywood CA 91601, USA
Debenedet, Nelson — Ice Hockey Player
38142 N Vista Dr, Livonia MI 48152, USA
DeBenning, Burr — Actor
4235 Kingfisher Road, Calabasas CA 91302, USA
DeBerg, Steve — Football Player, Coach
17920 Simms Road, Odessa FL 33556, USA
Debie, Benoit — Cinematographer
Sheldon Prosnit Agency, 800 S Robertson Blvd, Los Angeles CA 90035, USA

Debison, Aselin (Azi) — Singer
S L Feldman Mgmt, 1505 W 2nd Ave, #200, Vancouver BC V6H 3Y4, Canada

DeBlois, Dean — Director, Writer
W M E Entertainment, 9601 Wilshire Blvd, #300, Beverly Hills CA 90210 USA

Deblois, Lucien — Ice Hockey Player
407-350 Boul Graham, Mont Royal QC H3P 2C8, Canada

Debney, John — Composer
First Artists Mgmt, 4764 Park Granada, #210, Calabasas CA 91302 USA

DeBoer, Nicole — Actress
Kritzer Levine Wilkins Griffin, 11872 La Grange Ave, #100, Los Angeles CA 90025 USA

DeBoer, Peter — Ice Hockey Coach
New Jersey Devils, Arena, 50 State Route 120, East Rutherford NJ 07073 USA

DeBont, Jan — Cinematographer, Director
Blue Tulip Productions, 2202 Main St, Santa Monica CA 90405, USA

DeBoor, Carl-Wilhelm R — Mathematician
University of Wisconsin, Mathematics Dept, Madison WI 53706, USA

Debre, Michel — Prime Minister, France
20 Rue Jacob, 75006 Paris, France

DeBruijn, Inge — Swimmer
Top Voor Talent, Van Ostadestraat 368-2, Amsterdamn 1074 XA, Netherlands

DeBrunhoff, Laurent — Writer, Illustrator (Babar)
Mary Ryan Gallery, 527 W 26th St, New York NY 10001, USA

Debrusk, Louie — Ice Hockey Player
27502 N 84th Dr, Peoria AZ 85383, USA

DeBurgh, Chris — Singer, Songwriter
Kenny Thomson Mgmt, 754 Fulham Road, London SW6 5SH, England

Deby Itno, Idriss — President, Chad; Army General
President's Office, Presidential Palace, BP 74, N'Djamena, Chad

DeCamilli, Pietro V — Biologist
Yale University Medical School, Cell Biology Dept, New Haven CT 06512, USA

DeCarlo, Arthur A (Art), Jr — Football Player
9030 Manordale Lane, Ellicott City MD 21042, USA

DeCarlo, Mark — Actor
3292 Carse Dr, Los Angeles CA 90068, USA

Decarnin, Christophe — Fashion Designer
Balmain, 44 Rue Francois, 75008 Paris, France

DeCaro, Frank — Actor, Comedian
Sirius, 1221 Ave of Americas, #1900, New York NY 10020, USA

DeCasabianca, Camille — Actress
Artmedia, 20 Ave Rapp, 75007 Paris, France

DeCastella, F Robert — Track Athlete
Smart Start, PO Box 3808, Weston ACT 2611, Australia

DeCastro, David — Football Player
Pittsburgh Steelers, 3400 S Water St, Pittsburgh PA 15203 USA

DeCastro, Manuel M Cardinal — Religious Leader
Apostolic Penitentiary, Palazzo della Cancelleria 1, 00186 Rome, Italy

DeCercio, Tom — Director
Farah Films Mgmt, 11640 Mayfield, #208, Brentwood CA 90049, USA

DeCinces, Douglas V (Doug) — Baseball Player
124 Riviera Way, Laguna Beach CA 92651, USA

Decker, Brooklyn — Model, Actress
Marilyn Model Agency, 32 Union Square E, #PH, New York NY 10003 USA

Decker, D Martin (Marty) — Baseball Player
1036 Bryn Mawr Dr, Yuba City CA 95993, USA

Decker, Steven M (Steve) — Baseball Player
1024 Laurelridge St NE, Keizer OR 97303, USA

Declan — Singer, Guitarist, Pianist
PO Box 161, Market Rasen LN8 6EX, England

Decoder — Drum, Bass Producer (Kosheen)
Moskaha Mgmt, PO Box 102, London E15 2HH, England

DeConcini, Dennis — Senator, AZ
6014 Chesterbrook Road, McLean VA 22101, USA

DeCosta, Sara — Ice Hockey Player
200 Cowesett Green Dr, Warwick RI 02886, USA

DeCoster, Roger — Motorcycle Racing Rider
M C Sports, 1919 Torrance Blvd, Torrance CA 90501, USA

DeCrane, Alfred C, Jr — Businessman
30 Wax Myrtle Way, Vero Beach FL 32963, USA

Decrem, Bart — Educator, Social Activist
Tapulous, 854 High St, Palo Alto CA 94301, USA

Decter, Midge — Writer, Journalist
120 E 81st St, New York NY 10028, USA

Dedes, Spero — Sportscaster
N F L Network, 10950 Washington Blvd, #100, Culver City CA 90232 USA

Dedkov, Anatoli I — Cosmonaut
Cosmonaut Training Center, Star City, 141160 Zvezdny Gorodok, Moscow Oblast, Russia

Dedmon, Jeffrey L (Jeff) — Baseball Player
21102 Broadwell Ave, Torrance CA 90502, USA

Dedrick, James M (Jim) — Baseball Player
2929 NW Kennedy Court, Portland WA 97229, USA

DeDuve, Christian R — Nobel Medicine Laureate
80 Central Park West, New York NY 10023, USA

Dee, Donald M (Don) — Basketball Player
7924 N Pennsylvania Ave, Kansas City MO 64118, USA

Dee, Joey — Singer
Universal Attractions, 135 W 26th St, #1200, New York NY 10001 USA

Dee, Kiki — Singer, Songwriter
Alan Cottam Agency, 8 Cabin End Row, Kruzden, Blackburn BB1 2DP, England

Dee, Ruby — Actress
44 Cortland Ave, New Rochelle NY 10801, USA

Dee, Sally — Golfer
3508 W Barcelona St, Tampa FL 33629, USA

Dee, Wanda — Singer, Songwriter
Universal Attractions, 135 W 26th St, #1200, New York NY 10001 USA

Deeb, Gary — TV Critic
Chicago Sun-Times, Editorial Dept, 401 N Wabash Ave, Chicago IL 60611 USA

Deeley, Catherine E (Cat) — Actress, DJ, Model
Collective, 8383 Wilshire Blvd, #1050, Beverly Hills CA 90211 USA

Deemer, Audrey — Baseball Player
4401 Country Club Dr, #30, Steubenville OH 43953, USA

Deen, Paula H — Chef, Restaurateur, Writer
102 W Congress St, Savannah GA 31401, USA

Deep Roy — Actor
C E S D, 10635 Santa Monica Blvd, #130, Los Angeles CA 90025 USA

Deer, Ada E — Government Official
2537 Mutchler Road, Fitchburg WI 53711, USA

Deer, Robert G (Rob) — Baseball Player
22217 N 78th St, Scottsdale AZ 85255, USA

Deering, John — Editorial Cartoonist
6701 Westover Dr, Little Rock AR 72207, USA

Deery, Tom — Football Player
49 Yale Square, Morton PA 19070, USA

Dees, Archie W — Basketball Player
4405 N Hillview Dr, Bloomington IN 47408, USA

Dees, Charles H (Charlie) — Baseball Player
1064 Allison Woods Court, Lawrenceville GA 30043, USA

Dees, Morris S, Jr — Attorney, Civil Rights Activist
Southern Poverty Law Center, PO Box 548, Montgomery AL 36101, USA

Dees, Rick — Entertainer, Singer
Dees Entertainment, 3601 W Olive St, #675, Burbank CA 91505, USA

Deese, Derrick — Football Player
PO Box 3356, Cerritos CA 90703, USA

Deezen, Eddie — Actor
Coolwaters Productions, 10061 Riverside Dr, Box 531, Toluca Lake CA 91602 USA

Deezer D — Actor, Rap Artist
Acme Talent Agency, 4727 Wilshire Blvd, #333, Los Angeles CA 90010, USA

Def Jef — Rap Artist
Turner Accountancy, 13245 Riverside Dr, #330, Sherman Oaks CA 91423, USA

DeFanti, Sylvia — Actress
Fox & Gould Mgmt, Via Arenula 29, 00186 Rome, Italy

DeFanti, Thomas A (Tom) — Inventor (Cave Electronic Visualization)
University of Illinois, Electronic Visualization Laboratory, 842 W Taylor St, Chicago IL 60607, USA

DeFelitta, Raymond — Director, Writer
Paradigm Agency, 360 N Crescent Dr, North Building, Beverly Hills CA 90210 USA

DeFer, Kaylee — Actress
Innovative Artists, 1505 10th St, Santa Monica CA 90401 USA

DeFerran, Gil — Auto Racing Driver
524 Royal Plaza Dr, Fort Lauderdale FL 33301, USA

DeFilippo, Jacy — Actress
C E S D, 10635 Santa Monica Blvd, #130, Los Angeles CA 90025 USA

Deford, Frank — Sportswriter
PO Box 1109, Greens Farms CT 06838, USA

DeFrance, Cecile — Actress
Margrit Polak Mgmt, 1920 Hillhurst, #405, Los Angeles CA 90027, USA

DeFranceschi, Alexandre — Editor
I C M Partners, 10250 Constellation Blvd, #900, Los Angeles CA 90067 USA

DeFrancisco, Joseph E (Joe) — Army General
1201 N Nash St, #203, Arlington VA 22209, USA

DeFranco, Buddy — Jazz Clarinetist
978 Colorado Ave, #A, Whitefish MT 59937, USA

DeFrank, Joe — Harness Racing Official
PO Box 655, Lake Pleasant NY 12108, USA

DeFreitas, Eric — Bowler
175 W 12th St, New York NY 10011, USA

DeGale, James — Boxer
Amateur Boxing Assn, National Sports Centre, London SE19 2B8, England

DeGarmo, Diana K — Singer, Actress, Songwriter
American Idol, PO Box 900, Beverly Hills CA 90213, USA

DeGarmo, Todd — Architect, Interior Designer
Studios Architecture, 1625 M St NW, Washington DC 20036, USA

DeGeneres, Ellen — Actress, Comedienne
I C M Partners, 10250 Constellation Blvd, #900, Los Angeles CA 90067 USA

Degerick, Michael A (Mike) — Baseball Player
2702 Lake Osborne Dr, Lake Worth FL 33461, USA

DeGiorgi, Salvatore Cardinal — Religious Leader
Curia Archivescovile, Corso Vittorio Emanuele 461, 90134 Palermo, Italy

DeGivenchy, Hubert T — Fashion Designer
3 Ave George V, 75008 Paris, France

Degler, Carl N — Historian
907 Mears Court, Stanford CA 94305, USA

Degout, Stephane — Opera Singer
I M G Artists, Hogarth Business Park, Chiswick, London W4 2TH, England

DeGraw, Gavin — Singer, Songwriter
C E S D, 257 Park Ave S, #950, New York NY 10010 USA

Degray, Dale — Ice Hockey Player
Owen Sound Attack, Box 1420 Station Main, Owen Sound ON N4K 6T5, Canada

DeHaan, Dane — Actor
Creative Artists Agency, 2000 Ave of Stars, #100, Los Angeles CA 90067 USA

Dehaan, Kory — Baseball Player
1212 W Kesler Lane, Chandler AZ 85224, USA

Dehaene, Jean-Luc J M — Prime Minister, Belgium
Berkendallaan 52, 1800 Vilvoorde, Belgium

Dehart, Richard A (Rick) — Baseball Player
811 NE Wabash Ave, Topeka KS 66616, USA

DeHaven, Gloria — Actress
2223 W San Miguel Ave, North Las Vegas NV 89032, USA

DeHavilland, Olivia — Actress
BP 156-16, 75764 Paris Cedex 16, France

Dehmelt, Hans G — Nobel Physics Laureate
1600 43rd Ave E, #211, Seattle WA 98112, USA

Dehner, Dorothy — Artist
33 5th Ave, New York NY 10003, USA

DeHomem Christo, Guy-Manuel — Musician (Daft Punk)
Primary Talent International, 10-11 Jockey's Fields, London WC1R 4BN, England
Deibert, Charles (Larry) — Vietnam War Army Hero
201 NE Saizman Road, Corbett OR 97019, USA
Deidel, James L (Jim) — Baseball Player
14312 Wright Way, Broomfield CO 80023, USA
Deighton, Leonard C (Len) — Writer
Fairymount, Blackrock, Dundalk, County Louth, Ireland
Deisenhofer, Johann — Nobel Chemistry Laureate
3860 Echo Brook Lane, Dallas TX 75229, USA
Deitch, Donna — Director
Paradigm Agency, 360 N Crescent Dr, North Building, Beverly Hills CA 90210 USA
Deja, Andreas — Animator
Disney Animation, PO Box 10200, Orlando FL 32830, USA
DeJager, Cornelis — Astronomer
Zonnenburg 1, 352 NL Utrecht, Netherlands
DeJesus, David C — Baseball Player
28 Muirfield Circle, Wheaton IL 60189, USA
DeJesus, Ivan — Baseball Player
14608 Velleux Dr, Orlando FL 32837, USA
DeJesus, Wanda — Actress
McGowan Mgmt, 8733 W Sunset Blvd, #3, West Hollywood CA 90069, USA
DeJohnette, Jack — Jazz Drummer, Composer
Silver Hollow Road, Willow NY 12495, USA
DeJong, Bob — Speed Skater
Cefvi-Praag Intershow, Lindelaan 101B, 1231 CK Loosdrecht, Netherlands
DeJong, Pierre — Geneticist
Lawrence Livermore Laboratory, 7000 East St, Livermore CA 94550, USA
DeJonge, Peter — Writer
Little Brown, 3 Center Plaza, #100, Boston MA 02108 USA
DeJongh, John P, Jr — Governor, Virgin Islands
Governor's Office, 21-2 Kongens Gade, Charlotte Amalie, Saint Thomas VI 00802 USA
DeJordy, Denis E — Ice Hockey Player
472 Chemin Des-Patriotes, Saint Charles QC J0L 2G0, Canada
DeJurnett, Charles R — Football Player
1355 Heritage Court, Escondido CA 92027, USA
DeKay, Tim — Actor
Paradigm Agency, 360 N Crescent Dr, North Building, Beverly Hills CA 90210 USA
Dekker, Thomas — Actor
Schiff Co, 8440 Warner Dr, #B1, Culver City CA 90232 USA
DeKlerk, Albert — Concert Organist, Composer
Crayenesterlaan 22, 2012 Haarlem DK, Netherlands
DeKlerk, Frederik W — Nobel Laureate; President, South Africa
DeKlerk Foundation, PO Box 15785, Panorama, Cape Town 7506, South Africa
Deklin, Mark — Actor
Michael Black Mgmt, 9701 Wilshire Blvd, #1000, Beverly Hills CA 90212, USA
DeKnight, Steven S — Producer, Writer
Creative Artists Agency, 2000 Ave of Stars, #100, Los Angeles CA 90067 USA
DeLaBilliere, Peter — Army General, England
Naval & Military Club, 4 Saint James's Square, London SW1Y 4JU, England
Delacote, Jacques — Conductor
Dr Hilbert Maximilianstr 22, 80539 Munich, Germany
DeLaCruz, Rosie — Model
Wilhelmina Models, 300 Park Ave S, #200, New York NY 10010 USA
DeLaFuente, Cristian — Actor
Abrams Artists, 9200 W Sunset Blvd, #1125, West Hollywood CA 90069 USA
DeLaFuente, Marian — Commentator
Latin World Entertainment, 2601 S Bayshore Dr, #235, Miami FL 33133, USA
DelaGarza, Alana — Actress
Brillstein Entertainment Partners, 9150 Wilshire Blvd, #350, Beverly Hills CA 90212 USA
Delahoussay, Edward (Eddie) — Thoroughbred Racing Jockey
1024 S 4th Ave, Arcadia CA 91006, USA
Delahoussaye, Ryan — Violinist (Blue October)
Rainmaker Artists, PO Box 551665, Dallas TX 75355, USA
DeLaHoya, Oscar — Boxer
Golden Boy Promotions, 626 Wilshire Blvd, #350, Los Angeles CA 90017, USA
DeLaHoz, Miguel A (Mike) — Baseball Player
PO Box 441233, Miami FL 33144, USA
DeLaHuerta, Paz — Actress
Don Buchwald/Fortitude, 6500 Wilshire Blvd, #2200, Los Angeles CA 90048 USA
Delahunt, William D (Bill) — Representative, MA
Prime Policy Group LLP, 1110 Vermont Ave NW, #1000, Washington DC 20005, USA
Delainey, Gary — Cartoonist (Bub Slug, Betty)
United Feature Syndicate, PO Box 5610, Cincinnati OH 45201 USA
Delaire, Suzy — Actress, Singer
46 Rue de Varenne, 75007 Paris, France
DeLaMaza, Roland — Baseball Player
28533 Silverking Trial, Santa Clarita CA 91390, USA
DeLamielleure, Joseph M (Joe) — Football Player
7818 Ridgeloch Place, Charlotte NC 28226, USA
DeLancey, William J, III — Businessman
200 Public Square, #1950, Cleveland OH 44114, USA
DeLancie, John — Actor
S D B Partners, 1801 Ave of Stars, #902, Los Angeles CA 90067 USA
Delaney, F James (Jim) — Track Athlete
3787 Skyfarm Dr, Santa Rosa CA 95403, USA
Delaney, Frank — Writer
Random House, 1745 Broadway, #1800, New York NY 10019 USA
Delaney, Jeffrey J (Jeff) — Football Player
215 Village Green Dr, Canonsburg PA 15317, USA
Delaney, Kim — Actress, Model
Gersh Agency, 9465 Wilshire Blvd, #600, Beverly Hills CA 90212 USA
Delaney, Simon — Actor, Writer
Lorraine Brennan Mgmt, Greenmount Industrial Estate, #22, Harold's Cross, Dublin 6, Ireland
Delano, Diane — Actress
Abrams Artists, 9200 W Sunset Blvd, #1125, West Hollywood CA 90069 USA

Delano, Robert B
American Farm Bureau, 1501 E Woodfield Road, #300W, Schaumburg IL 60173, USA — Association Executive

Delany, Dana
United Talent Agency, 9336 Civic Center Dr, Beverly Hills CA 90210 USA — Actress

Delany, Samuel R
Vintage Books, 1745 Broadway, New York NY 10019 USA — Writer

DeLap, Tony
225 Jasmine St, Corona del Mar CA 92625, USA — Artist, Sculptor

DeLaParra, Alondra
I M G Artists, Hogarth Business Park, Chiswick, London W4 2TH, England — Conductor

DelArco, Jonathan
S D B Partners, 1801 Ave of Stars, #902, Los Angeles CA 90067 USA — Actor

DeLaria, Lea
TalentWorks, 3500 W Olive Ave, #1400, Burbank CA 91505 USA — Actress

Delarme, Julie
Artmedia, 20 Ave Rapp, 75007 Paris, France — Actress

DeLaRocha, Zack
Creative Artists Agency, 2000 Ave of Stars, #100, Los Angeles CA 90067 USA — Singer (Rage Against the Machine)

DeLaRosa, Evelyn
Dorothy Cone Artists, 150 W 55th St, New York NY 10019, USA — Opera Singer

DeLaRosa, Pedro M
P D L R, Pedro de la Creu, 08017 Barcelona, Spain — Auto Racing Driver

DeLaSalle, Lise
Frank Salomon, 121 W 27th St, #703, New York NY 10001 USA — Concert Pianist

Delasin, Dorothy
20 Longview Dr, Daly City CA 94015, USA — Golfer

DeLaTour, Frances
Independent Talent Group, Oxford House, 76 Oxford St, London W1D 1BS, England — Actress

Delaughter, Tim
Gorfaine/Schwartz, 4111 W Alameda Ave, #509, Burbank CA 91505 USA — Singer, Musician (Polyphonic Spree)

DeLaurentiis, Giada
W M E Entertainment, 9601 Wilshire Blvd, #300, Beverly Hills CA 90210 USA — Chef, Writer

DeLautour, David
Karen Kay Mgmt, 2/25 Sale St, Freemans Bay, Auckland 1010, New Zealand — Actor, Writer, Producer

Delavan, Mark
Columbia Artists Mgmt Inc, 1790 Broadway, #702, New York NY 10019 USA — Opera Singer

Delbanco, Nicholas
Warner Books, 1271 Ave of Americas, New York NY 10020 USA — Writer

Delbonnel, Bruno
United Talent Agency, 9336 Civic Center Dr, Beverly Hills CA 90210 USA — Cinematographer

DelBuono, Brett
C E S D, 10635 Santa Monica Blvd, #130, Los Angeles CA 90025 USA — Actor

DelCarlo, John
Opus 3 Artists, 470 Park Ave S, #900N, New York NY 10016 USA — Singer

Delcarmen, Manny
68 Surrey Lane, East Bridgewater MA 02333, USA — Baseball Player

DelCastillo Galvez, Jorge A A
Premier's Office, Urb Corpac, Calle 1 Oeste, San Isidro, Lima 27, Peru — Prime Minister, Peru

DelCastillo, Kate
Creative Artists Agency, 2000 Ave of Stars, #100, Los Angeles CA 90067 USA — Actress

DeLean, Catherine
Agence Goodwin, 839 E Sherbrooke St, #200, Montreal QC H2L 1K6, Canada — Actress

DeLeeuw, Ton
Costeruslaan 4, 1217 Hilversum JT, Netherlands — Composer

Delehanty, Hugh
A A R P Publications, Editorial Dept, 601 E St NW, Washington DC 20049, USA — Editor

DeLeo, Dean
Q Prime, 729 7th Ave, #1600, New York NY 10019 USA — Guitarist (Stone Temple Pilots)

DeLeo, Robert
Q Prime, 729 7th Ave, #1600, New York NY 10019 USA — Bassist (Stone Temple Pilots), Composer

Deleon, Luis A
120 Calle San Antonio, Bda Clausells, Ponce PR 00730, USA — Baseball Player

DeLeone, Thomas D (Tom)
PO Box 681472, Park City UT 84068, USA — Football Player

Delerm, Graziella
Artmedia, 20 Ave Rapp, 75007 Paris, France — Actress

Delfino, Carlos F
Milwaukee Bucks, Bradley Center, 1001 N 4th St, #2, Milwaukee WI 53203 USA — Basketball Player

Delgado, Alvaro
Biarritz 5, Parque de las Avenidas, 28028 Madrid, Spain — Artist

Delgado, Carlos J
9 Repto Ramos Bo Borinquen, Aguadilla PR 00603, USA — Baseball Player

Delgado, Emilio
Sesame Street Workshop, 1 Lincoln Plaza, New York NY 10023, USA — Actor

Delgado, Issac
Ralph Mercado Mgmt, 568 Broadway, #806, New York NY 10012, USA — Singer, Orchestra Leader

DelGreco, Albert L (Al), Jr
1012 Little Turtle Circle, Birmingham AL 35242, USA — Football Player

DelGreco, Robert G (Bobby)
625 Southview Dr, Pittsburgh PA 15226, USA — Baseball Player

Delhomme, Jake C
1459 Mills Highway, Breaux Bridge LA 70517, USA — Football Player

D'Elia, Bill
W M E Entertainment, 9601 Wilshire Blvd, #300, Beverly Hills CA 90210 USA — Director, Producer, Writer

D'Elia, Chris
United Talent Agency, 9336 Civic Center Dr, Beverly Hills CA 90210 USA — Actor, Writer

Deligne, Pierre R
Institute for Advanced Study, Math School, Einstein Dr, Princeton NJ 08540, USA — Mathematician

DeLillo, Don
57 Rossmore Ave, Bronxville NY 10708, USA — Writer

DeLint, Derek
Features Creative Mgmt, Entrepotdok 76A, 101 AD Amsterdam, Netherlands — Actor

DeLisle, Paul
Interscope Records, 2220 Colorado Ave, Santa Monica CA 90404 USA — Bassist (Smash Mouth), Actor

Delk, Denny
Innovative Artists, 235 Park Ave S, #700, New York NY 10003, USA — Actor

D

Delano - Delk

D

Delk, Joan — Golfer
830 Forest Path Lane, Alpharetta GA 30022, USA

Delk, Tony L — Basketball Player
1843 Glenhill Dr, Lexington KY 40502, USA

Dell, Charlie — Actor
Scott Stander Assoc, 4533 Van Nuys Blvd, #401, Sherman Oaks CA 91403 USA

Dell, Donald L — Tennis Player, Attorney
Blue Entertainment, 333 E Main St, #200, Louisville KY 40202 USA

Dell, Michael S — Businessman
Dell Inc, 1 Dell Way, Round Rock TX 78682, USA

DellaCasa-Debeljevic, Lisa — Opera Singer
Schloss Gottlieben, 8274 Thurgau, Switzerland

Dellanos, Myrka — Actress
United Talent Agency, 9336 Civic Center Dr, Beverly Hills CA 90210 USA

DelleDonne, Elena — Basketball Player
University of Delaware, Athletic Dept, Newark DE 19716, USA

Dellenbach, Jeffrey A (Jeff) — Football Player
1002 Pine Branch Dr, Weston FL 33326, USA

Dellinger, Walter — Educator, Attorney
Duke University, Law School, Durham NC 27706, USA

Dellinger, William (Bill) — Track Athlete, Coach
1993 Fircrest Dr, Eugene OR 97403, USA

Dell'Orefice, Carmen — Model
Ford Models Inc, 111 5th Ave, #900, New York NY 10003 USA

Dellucci, David M — Baseball Player
5512 Summer Lake Dr, Baton Rouge LA 70817, USA

Dellums, Ronald V (Ron) — Representative, CA
658 Santa Ray Ave, Oakland,CA 94610, USA

Delly, Emmanuel III Cardinal — Religious Leader
Patriarat Chaldeen Catholique, PO Box 6112, Al-Mansouri, Baghdad, Iraq

DelNegro, Vincent J (Vinny) — Basketball Player, Coach
58 Bagnell Dr, Pembroke MA 02359, USA

DeLoach, Nikki — Singer (Innosense), Actress
R C A Records, 8750 Wilshire Blvd, Beverly Hills CA 90211 USA

Delock, Ivan M (Ike) — Baseball Player
433 Cypress Way E, Naples FL 34110, USA

Delon, Alain — Actor
Alain Delon Diffusion, 12 Rue Saint-Victor, 1206 Geneva, Switzerland

Delon, Anthony — Actor
Intertalent, 5 Rue Clement-Marot, 75008 Paris, France

Delong, Gregory A (Greg) — Football Player
4960 Shady Maple Lane, Winston-Salem NC 27106, USA

DeLong, Keith A — Football Player
1850 Greywell Road, Knoxville TN 37922, USA

DeLong, Michael P — Marine Corps General
Deputy Commander, US Central Command, MacDill Air Force Base, Tampa FL 33621, USA

Delong, Nathan J (Nate) — Basketball Player
PO Box 485, Hayward WI 54843, USA

DeLonge, Tom — Singer, Guitarist, Songwriter
1665 Neptune Ave, Encinitas CA 92024, USA

DeLongis, Anthony — Actor
PO Box 2445, Canyon Country CA 91386, USA

DeLorenzo, Michael — Actor
Geddes Agency, 8430 Santa Monica Blvd, #201, West Hollywood CA 90069 USA

Delorme, Daniele — Actress
Gueville Productions, 16 Rue de Marignan, 75008 Paris, France

Delorme, Ronald (Ron) — Ice Hockey Player
94 Ravine Dr, Port Moody BC V3H 4T8, Canada

Delors, Jacques L J — Government Official, France
Notre Europe Assn, 41 Blvd des Capucines, 75002 Paris, France

DeLosReyes, Kamar — Actor
TalentWorks, 3500 W Olive Ave, #1400, Burbank CA 91505 USA

DeLosSantos, Becky — Model
Playboy Promotions, 2706 Media Center Dr, Los Angeles CA 90065 USA

DeLosSantos, Marisa — Writer
Hudson Street Press, 375 Hudson St, Basement 3, New York NY 10014, USA

DeLosSantos, Valerio L — Baseball Player
9838 N 119th Place, Scottsdale AZ 85259, USA

Delpeyrat, Scali — Actor
U B B A, 6 Rue de Braque, 75003 Paris, France

DelPiero, Alessandro — Soccer Player
F C Juventus, Corso Galilo Ferraris 32, 10128 Turin, Italy

Delpino, Robert L — Football Player
9569 Calle Del Casa, Riverside CA 92503, USA

DelPonte, Carla — Attorney
War Crimes Tribunal, Churchilluplein 1, 2501 Hague, Netherlands

DelPorto, Juan Martin — Tennis Player
Association of Tennis Professionals, Palliser Road, London W14 9EB, England

Delpy, Julie — Actress, Director
Markham & Froggatt, Julian House, 4 Windmill St, London W1P 1HF, England

DelRio, David — Actor
Paradigm Agency, 360 N Crescent Dr, North Building, Beverly Hills CA 90210 USA

DelRío, Jack — Football Player, Coach
1605 Beach Ave, Atlantic Beach FL 32233, USA

Delsing, Jay — Golfer
14020 Woods Mill Cove Dr, Chesterfield MO 63017, USA

Delson, Brad — Guitarist (Linkin Park)
The Firm, 2049 Century Park E, #2550, Los Angeles CA 90067 USA

Delson, Rudolph — Writer
Houghton Mifflin Harcourt, 215 Park Ave S, #1200, New York NY 10003 USA

DelToro, Guillermo — Director, Writer
W M E Entertainment, 9601 Wilshire Blvd, #300, Beverly Hills CA 90210 USA

DelTredici, David — Composer
463 West St, #G121, New York NY 10014, USA

Deluc, Xavier — Actor
A A C Agence Artistique, 10 Ave George V, 75009 Paris, France

Delk - Deluc

DeLuca, Annette
7 Turtle Creek Dr, #D, Jupiter FL 33469, USA — Golfer

DeLuca, Fred
1924 Sunrise Key Blvd, Fort Lauderdale FL 33304, USA — Businessman

DeLuca, Rocco
Mick Mgmt, 35 Washington St, Brooklyn NY 11201 USA — Singer, Dobro Player

DeLucas, Lawrence J
909 19th St S, Birmingham AL 35205, USA — Astronaut

DeLucca, Gerald D (Jerry)
27 Pulaski St, Peabody MA 01960, USA — Football Player

DeLucchi, Michele
Via Cenisio 40, 20154 Milan, Italy — Architect

DeLucia, Paco
International Music Network, 278 Main St, #400, Gloucester MA 01930 USA — Jazz Guitarist

Delugg, Milton
2740 Claray Dr, Los Angeles CA 90077, USA — Accordionist, Band Leader, Composer

DeLuise, David
Domain Talent, 9229 W Sunset Blvd, #710, West Hollywood CA 90069 USA — Actor

DeLuise, Michael
Stone Manners Salners, 9911 W Pico Blvd, #1400, Los Angeles CA 90035 USA — Actor

DeLuise, Peter
Premiere Artists Agency, 1875 Century Park E, #2250, Los Angeles CA 90067 USA — Actor

DelVecchi, Mauro
Senato Della Repubblica, Piazza Madama, 00196 Rome, Italy — Army General, Italy

Delvecchio, Alexander P (Alex)
Pen Pro, 2602 Stoodleigh Dr, Rochester Hills MI 48309, USA — Ice Hockey Player

Demaestri, Joseph P (Joe)
50 Fairway Dr, Novato CA 94949, USA — Baseball Player

DeMaistre, Xavier
Konzertdirektion Schmid, Konigstra 36, 30175 Hannover, Germany — Concert Harpist

DeMaiziere, K E Thomas
Bundesministerium der Verteidigung, Hardthohe, 53125 Bonn, Germany — Government Official, Germany

DeMaiziere, Lothar
Buro Berlin Mitte, Chausseestr 128A, 10115 Berlin, Germany — Prime Minister, East Germany

Demarchelier, Patrick
162 W 21st St, New York NY 10011, USA — Photographer

DeMarco, Albert (Ab), Jr
211 Regal Road, North Bay ON P1B 8G4, Canada — Ice Hockey Player

DeMarco, Jean
Cervaro 03044, Prov-Frosinore, Italy — Sculptor

DeMarco, Robert A (Bob)
13055 Midfield Terrace, Saint Louis MO 63146, USA — Football Player

DeMarco, Tony
150 Staniford St, #709, Boston MA 02114, USA — Boxer

DeMarcus, Jay
Turner & Nichols, 49 Music Square W, #500, Nashville TN 37203, USA — Singer, Bassist (Rascal Flatts)

Demarest, Arthur A
Vanderbilt University, Anthropology Dept, Nashville TN 37235, USA — Archaeologist

Demarie, John E
416 Greenway St, Lake Charles LA 70605, USA — Football Player

Demars, Bruce
41 Manters Point Road, Plymouth MA 02360, USA — Navy Admiral

Demars, William L (Billy)
770 Island Way, #305, Clearwater Beach FL 33767, USA — Baseball Player

DeMartini, Warren J (Torch)
2666 Carmar Dr, Los Angeles CA 90046, USA — Guitarist (Ratt)

DeMartino, Jules
Paradigm Agency, 404 W Franklin St, Monterey CA 93940 USA — Drummer (Ting Tings)

DeMatteo, Drea
Gersh Agency, 9465 Wilshire Blvd, #600, Beverly Hills CA 90212 USA — Actress

Dembo, Fennis M
430 N Pine St, San Antonio TX 78202, USA — Basketball Player

DeMedeiros, Maria
Alsira Garcia-Maroto Talent Agency, Calle de Los Invencibles 8, Bajo, Madrid 28019, Spain — Actress

DeMenezes, Fradique B M
President's Office, Pargo do Povo, Sao Tome, Sao Tome & Principe — President, Sao Tome & Principe

DeMent, Iris
Nick Ben-Meir, 652 N Doheny Dr, West Hollywood CA 90069, USA — Singer, Songwriter

DeMent, Jack
Oregon Health Care Center, 11325 NE Weidler St, #44, Portland OR 97220, USA — Chemist

Dement, Kenneth
316 S Kingshighway St, Sikeston MO 63801, USA — Football Player

Dementieva, Elena V
Myasnitskaya Str, #6/7, 10100 Moscow, Russia — Tennis Player

DeMerit, Jay
Watford F C, Vicarage Stadium, Vicarage Road, Watford, Hertfordshire WD18 0ER, England — Soccer Player

DeMerit, John S
550 W Walters St, Port Washington WI 53074, USA — Baseball Player

Demery, Lawrence C (Larry)
10407 Pinnacle Ridge Ave, Bakersfield CA 93311, USA — Baseball Player

Demet-Barry, Dede
2607 Thornbird Place, Boulder CO 80304, USA — Cyclist

Demeter, Donald L (Don)
6240 S Country Club Dr, Oklahoma City OK 73159, USA — Baseball Player

Demetral, Christopher (Chris)
J M G Mgmt, 18000 Coastline Dr, #8, Malibu CA 90265, USA — Actor

Demetrios
Greek Orthodox Church, 89 E 79th St, #19, New York NY 10075, USA — Religious Leader

Demetrius, Duppy
Creative Artists Agency, 2000 Ave of Stars, #100, Los Angeles CA 90067 USA — Writer

Demetz, Peter
Rutgers State University, German Dept, 172 College Ave, New Brunswick NJ 08901, USA — Educator

Demeulemeester, Ann
6 Rue Milne Edwards, 75017 Paris, France — Fashion Designer

DeMeuron, Pierre
Herzog & DeMeuron Architekten, Rheinschanze 6, 4056 Basel, Switzerland — Pritzker Architectural Laureate

D

DeLuca - DeMeuron

Demic, Lawrence C (Larry) — Basketball Player
680 S Lassen Court, Anaheim CA 92804, USA

DeMille, Nelson — Writer
61 Hilton Ave, #23, Garden City NY 11530, USA

Demin, Lev S — Cosmonaut
Cosmonaut Training Center, Star City, 141160 Zvezdny Gorodok, Moscow Oblast, Russia

Deming, Peter — Cinematographer
Sandra Marsh Assoc, 9150 Wilshire Blvd, #220, Beverly Hills CA 90212 USA

DeMita, L Ciriaco — Prime Minister, Italy
Partito Democrazia Cristiana, Piazza de Gesu 46, 00186 Rome, Italy

Demme, Jonathan — Director
Clinico Estetico, 319 Lafayette St, #144, New York NY 10012, USA

DeMol, Johannes H H (John) — Producer, Director
Talpa, Zevenend 45-IV, Laren, Noord Holland 1250 AD, Netherlands

Demola, Donald J (Don) — Baseball Player
352 Village Dr, Hauppauge NY 11788, USA

DeMonaco, James — Writer, Producer, Director
United Talent Agency, 9336 Civic Center Dr, Beverly Hills CA 90210 USA

Demong, Bill — Nordic Combined Skier
N Y S E F, Route 86, PO Box 300, Wilmington NY 12997, USA

Demongeot, Mylene — Actress
Artmedia, 20 Ave Rapp, 75007 Paris, France

DeMont, Rick — Swimmer
84-596 Upena St, Waianae HI 96792, USA

DeMontebello, Philippe L — Museum Executive
40 E 94th St, #11G, New York NY 10128, USA

DeMontreuil, Ricardo — Director
3 Arts Entertainment, 9460 Wilshire Blvd, #700, Beverly Hills CA 90212 USA

DeMoraes, Ronaldo (Ron) — Producer
W M E Entertainment, 9601 Wilshire Blvd, #300, Beverly Hills CA 90210 USA

DeMornay, Rebecca — Actress
Binder & Assoc, 1465 Lindacrest Dr, Beverly Hills CA 90210, USA

DeMoss, Harold R, Jr — Judge
US Court of Appeals, 515 Rusk Ave, #12015, Houston TX 77002, USA

Demps, Jeff — Track Athlete, Football Player
New England Patriots, 1 Patriot Place, Foxboro MA 02035 USA

Dempsey, Clint — Soccer Player
Fulham F C, Craven Cottage, Stevenage Road, London SW6 6HH, England

Dempsey, George P — Basketball Player
6945 Cedar Ave, Pennsauken NJ 08109, USA

Dempsey, J Rikard (Rick) — Baseball Player
3081 Township Ave, Simi Valley CA 93063, USA

Dempsey, M Clinton (Clint) — Soccer Player
New England Revolution, 1 Patriot Place, Foxboro MA 02035 USA

Dempsey, Martin E — Army General
Chairman, Joint Chiefs of Staff, Pentagon, Washington DC 20318 USA

Dempsey, Michael — Bassist (Cure)
Primary Talent International, 10-11 Jockey's Fields, London WC1R 4BN, England

Dempsey, Patrick — Actor
Burstein Co, 15304 Sunset Blvd, #208, Pacific Palisades CA 90272, USA

Dempsey, Thomas (Tom) — Football Player
541 Julius Ave, New Orleans LA 70121, USA

Dempsie, Joseph — Actor
Troika, 74 Clerkenwell Road, #300, London EC1M 5QA, England

Dempster, Ryan S — Baseball Player
3537 N Greenview Ave, Chicago IL 60657, USA

Demsetz, Harold — Economist
University of California, Economics Dept, Los Angeles CA 90024, USA

Demsey, Todd — Golfer
Gaylord Sports Mgmt, 13845 N Northsight Blvd, #200, Scottsdale AZ 85260 USA

DeMulder, Kim — Cartoonist, Illustrator
76 Lafayette Ave, Coxsackie NY 12051, USA

DeMunn, Jeffrey (Jeff) — Actor
Davis Spylios Agency, 244 W 54th St, #707, New York NY 10019, USA

Demuro, Francesco — Opera Singer
I M G Artists, Hogarth Business Park, Chiswick, London W4 2TH, England

Demus, Chaka — Singer (Chaka Demus & Pliers)
Mission Control, City Business Center, Lower Road, London SE16 2XB, England

Demus, Jorg — Concert Pianist
Lyra Artists Mgmt, Doblinger Hauptstr 77A/10, 1190 Vienna, Austria

Demuth, Richard H — Attorney, Financier
7 Eliot Road, Lexington MA 02421, USA

Denault, Jim — Cinematographer
Gersh Agency, 9465 Wilshire Blvd, #600, Beverly Hills CA 90212 USA

Denberg, Susan — Model
Playboy Promotions, 2706 Media Center Dr, Los Angeles CA 90065 USA

Dench, Judi — Actress
Julian Belfrage, 9 Argyll St, London W1F 7TG, England

Denehy, William F (Bill) — Baseball Player
2528 Clarinet Dr, Orlando FL 32837, USA

Deneriaz, Antoine — Alpine Skier
775 Ave de la Republique, 74300 Cluses, France

Denes, Agnes C — Artist
595 Broadway, New York NY 10012, USA

Deneuve, Catherine — Actress
Artmedia, 20 Ave Rapp, 75007 Paris, France

Denevan, William M — Geographer, Ecologist
University of Wisconsin, Geography Dept, Madison, WI 53706, USA

Deneve, Stephane — Conductor
I C M Artists, 40 W 57th St, #1800, New York NY 10019 USA

Deng Yaping — Table Tennis Player
International Olympic Committee, Chateau de Vidy, 1007 Lausanne, Switzerland

Deng, Luol — Basketball Player
3280 Sunset Trail, Northbrook IL 60062, USA

Dengler, Carlos — Bassist (Interpol)
Flowerbooking, 1532 N Milwaukee Ave, #201, Chicago IL 60622, USA

Denham, Alice — Model
Playboy Promotions, 2706 Media Center Dr, Los Angeles CA 90065 USA
Denhardt, David T — Biologist
Rutgers University, Nelson Biological Laboratories, Piscataway NJ 08855, USA
DenHerder, Vern W — Football Player
2342 Riviera Road, Sioux Center IA 51250, USA
Denicourt, Marianne — Actress
Artmedia, 20 Ave Rapp, 75007 Paris, France
Denier, Lydie — Actress
C E S D, 10635 Santa Monica Blvd, #130, Los Angeles CA 90025 USA
DeNiese, Danielle — Opera Singer
I M G Artists, Hogarth Business Park, Chiswick, London W4 2TH, England
DeNiro, Robert — Actor
Stan Rosenfield Assoc, 2029 Century Park E, #1190, Los Angeles CA 90067, USA
Denisof, Alexis — Actor
Don Buchwald/Fortitude, 6500 Wilshire Blvd, #2200, Los Angeles CA 90048 USA
Denisov, Edison V — Composer
Studentcheskaia 44/28, #35, 121165 Moscow, Russia
Denisse, Francois-Jean — Astronomer
48 Rue Monsieur Le Prince, 75006 Paris, France
Denisyuk, Yuri N — Optical Engineer
Vavilov Optical Institute, 12 Burzhevaya, 199034 Saint Petersburg, Russia
Denk, Jeremy — Concert Pianist
Opus 3 Artists, 470 Park Ave S, #900N, New York NY 10016 USA
Denman, David — Actor
Hofflund/Polone, 9465 Wilshire Blvd, #420, Beverly Hills CA 90212 USA
Dennard, Mark W — Football Player
4990 Afton Oaks Dr, College Station TX 77845, USA
Dennard, Preston — Football Player
4545 Greene Ave NW, Albuquerque NM 87114, USA
Dennard, Robert H — Inventor (Random Access Memory Cell)
2054 Quaker Ridge Road, Croton-on-Hudson NY 10520, USA
Dennehy, Brian — Actor
I C M Partners, 10250 Constellation Blvd, #900, Los Angeles CA 90067 USA
Dennehy, Elizabeth — Actress
Mitchell K Stubbs Assoc, 8695 W Washington Blvd, #204, Culver City CA 90232 USA
Dennehy, Kathleen — Actress
Independent Artists, 9601 Wilshire Blvd, #750, Beverly Hills CA 90210 USA
Dennen, Brett — Singer
Mick Mgmt, 44 Wall St, #2300, New York NY 10005, USA
Dennerlein, Barbara — Jazz Organist
Tsingtauer Str 66, 81827 Munich, Germany
Dennett, Daniel C — Philosopher
20 Ironwood Road, North Andover MA 01845, USA
Denney, Kyle — Baseball Player
PO Box 300, Prague OK 74864, USA
Denney, Ryan C — Football Player
351 Silver Circle, Alpine UT 84004, USA
Denning, Blaine — Basketball Player
1283 NW Bentley Circle, #A, Port Saint Lucie FL 34986, USA
Dennings, Kat — Actress
Management 360, 9111 Wilshire Blvd, Beverly Hills CA 90210 USA
Dennis, Cathy — Singer
19 Mgmt, Ransomes Dock, 35-37 Parkgate Road, London SW11 4NP, England
Dennis, Clark — Golfer
4117 Sarita Dr, Fort Worth TX 76109, USA
Dennis, Donna F — Sculptor, Artist
131 Duane St, New York NY 10013, USA
Dennis, Gabrielle — Actress
Pantheon Talent Group, 1900 Ave of the Stars, #2840, Los Angeles CA 90064, USA
Dennis, Guy D — Football Player
PO Box 2500, Hawthorne FL 32640, USA
Dennis, James L — Judge
US Court of Appeals, 600 Camp St, New Orleans LA 70130, USA
Dennis, Jim — Harness Racing Driver, Trainer
1810 Little Masters Corner Road, Harrington DE 19952, USA
Dennis, Mark F — Football Player
52 Cambridge Lane, Lincolnshire IL 60069, USA
Dennis, Mike — Singer (Dovells)
American Promotions, 2011 Ferry Ave, #U19, Camden NJ 08104, USA
Dennis, Norm — Ice Hockey Player
1531 Highway 3B, Fruitvale BC V0G 1L0, Canada
Dennis, Pamela — Fashion Designer
10 McGuirk Lane, West Orange NJ 7052, USA
Dennis, Rowly — Actor
H R I Talent, 100 Universal City Plaza, #7152, Universal City CA 91608, USA
Dennis, Wesley — Singer, Guitarist
Mercury Records, 54 Music Square E, #300, Nashville TN 37203 USA
Dennison, George M — Educator
International Heart Institute Foundation, 500 W Broadway, #350, Missoula MT 59802, USA
Dennison, Rick S — Football Player
12322 Overcup Dr, Houston TX 77024, USA
Dennison, W Douglas (Doug) — Football Player
2309 Daybreak Trail, Plano TX 75093, USA
Denny, Floyd W, Jr — Pediatrician
1 Carolina Meadows, #308, Chapel Hill NC 27517, USA
Denny, John A — Baseball Player
13750 W Colonial Dr, #350, Winter Garden FL 34787, USA
Denny, Robyn — Artist
20/30 Wilds Rents, #4B, London SE1 4QG, England
Denorfia, Christopher A (Chris) — Baseball Player
3468 Longmeadow, Sarasota FL 34235, USA
Densmore, John — Drummer (Doors)
Doors Music, 8899 Beverly Blvd, #812, Los Angeles CA 90048, USA
Denson, Alfred F (Al) — Football Player
10838 Naples Court S, Jacksonville FL 32218, USA

Denson, Karl — Musician, Singer
Agency Group Ltd, 142 W 57th St, #600, New York NY 10019 USA

Dent, Burnell J — Football Player
2904 Essex Ave, La Place LA 70068, USA

Dent, Catherine — Actress
S D B Partners, 1801 Ave of Stars, #902, Los Angeles CA 90067 USA

Dent, Frederick B — Secretary, Commerce
221 Montgomery St, Spartanburg SC 29302, USA

Dent, Jim — Golfer
17817 Simms Road, Odessa FL 33556, USA

Dent, Kevin — Football Player
221 Brannan Ave, Byram MS 39272, USA

Dent, Richard L — Football Player, Coach
R L D Resources, 333 N Michigan Ave, #2800, Chicago IL 60601, USA

Dent, Russell E (Bucky) — Baseball Player, Manager
8895 Indian River Run, Boynton Beach FL 33472, USA

Denton, Derek A — Physiologist
816 Irring Road, Toorak VIC 3142, Australia

Denton, James — Actor
Paradigm Agency, 360 N Crescent Dr, North Building, Beverly Hills CA 90210 USA

Denton, Jeremiah A, Jr — Senator, AL; WW II Navy Hero
531 Thomas Bransby, Williamsburg VA 23185, USA

Denton, Randall D (Randy) — Basketball Player
515 Sunnybrook Road, Raleigh NC 27610, USA

Denton, Robert (Bob) — Football Player
6669 Embarcadero Dr, #7, Stockton CA 95219, USA

Denton, Sandi (Pepa) — Rap Artist (Salt'N'Pepa)
Richard Walters, PO Box 2789, Toluca Lake CA 91610 USA

Denton, Will — Actor
Gersh Agency, 9465 Wilshire Blvd, #600, Beverly Hills CA 90212 USA

Denzongapa, Danny — Actor
29 Dzongrilla 11th Road, J V P D Scheme, Juhu, Mumbai MB 400049, India

Deol, Sunny — Actor, Director
Plot 22 11th Road, J V P D Scheme Juhu, Mumbai MS 400049, India

DeOliveira, Manoel — Director
Rua H Lopes Mendoca, 4010 Porto, Portugal

DeOre, Bill — Editorial Cartoonist
Dallas News, Editorial Dept, Communications Center, Dallas TX 75265, USA

DeOssie, Steven L (Steve) — Football Player
835 Chestnut St, North Andover MA 01845, USA

DePaiva, James — Actor
PO Box 11152, Greenwich CT 06831, USA

DePaiva, Kassie — Actress, Singer
Cornerstone Talent Agency, 37 W 20th St, #1108, New York NY 10011, USA

DePalma, Brian R — Director
I C M Partners, 10250 Constellation Blvd, #900, Los Angeles CA 90067 USA

DePaolis, Luciano — Bobsled Athlete
Olympic Committee, Foro Italico, Largo Lauro de Bosis 15, 00135 Rome, Italy

Depardieu, Elisabeth — Actress
Artmedia, 20 Ave Rapp, 75007 Paris, France

Depardieu, Gerard X M — Actor
4 Place de la Chapelle, 78380 Bougival, France

Depardieu, Julie — Actress
Cineart, 36 Rue de Ponthieu, 75008 Paris, France

Depardon, Raymond — Photographer
18 Bis Rue Henri Barbusse, 75005 Paris, France

DePaul, Lynsey — Singer, Songwriter
21A Clifftown Road, Southend-on-Sea, Essex SS1 1AB, England

Depaula, Sean M — Baseball Player
2 Thomas St, Derry NH 03038, USA

DePaulo, Lisa — Golfer
Tournament Treasures, 2 Muirfield Greens Lane, Lakeway TX 78738, USA

Depenbusch, Anna — Singer
105 Music GmbH, Hopfensack 20, 20457 Hamburg, Germany

DePencier, Miranda — Producer
United Talent Agency, 9336 Civic Center Dr, Beverly Hills CA 90210 USA

DePeyer, Gervase — Concert Clarinetist, Conductor
42 Tower Bridge Wharf, Saint Katherine's Way, London E1 9UR, England

DePortzamparc, Christian — Pritzker Architectural Laureate
Architecte D P L G, 1 Rue de l'Aude, 75014 Paris, France

Depp, John C (Johnny) — Actor, Director
United Talent Agency, 9336 Civic Center Dr, Beverly Hills CA 90210 USA

Depre, Joe — Basketball Player
59 Oneida St, Rochester NY 14621, USA

DePreist, James A — Conductor
142 W End Ave, #3U, New York NY 10023, USA

Depres, Cyril — Motorcycle Racing Rider
Red Bull GmbH, Am Brunnen 1, 5330 Fuschl am See Austria

DePriest, Tommy Lee — Actor
Paceline Entertainment, 12444 Ventura Blvd, #103, Studio City CA 91604 USA

Deptula, David A — Air Force General
Deputy CofS, Intelligence & Survelliance, HqUSAF, Pentagon, Washington DC 20310, USA

DeQuadros, Ciro — Epidemiologist
Pan American Health Organization, 525 23rd St NW, Washington DC 20037, USA

Dequenne, Emilie — Actress
Cineart, 36 Rue de Ponthieu, 75008 Paris, France

Der, Lambert — Editorial Cartoonist
Houston Post, Editorial Dept, 4888 Loop Central Dr, #390, Houston TX 77081, USA

DeRakoff, Alex — Director, Writer
W M E Entertainment, 9601 Wilshire Blvd, #300, Beverly Hills CA 90210 USA

DeRavin, Emilie — Actress
Gersh Agency, 41 Madison Ave, #3301, New York NY 10010 USA

Derby, C Dean — Football Player
1682 Corkrum Road, Walla Walla WA 99362, USA

Derbyshire, Andrew G — Architect
4 Sunnyfield, Hatfield, Hertsforshire AL9 5DX, England

Dercho, Natalia I M G Artists, Hogarth Business Park, Chiswick, London W4 2TH, England	Opera Singer
Dercum, Max PO Box 189, Dillon CO 80435, USA	Skier
Derek, Bo Guttman Assoc, 118 S Beverly Dr, #201, Beverly Hills CA 90212 USA	Actress, Model
DeRist, Joseph University of California Medical Center, 505 Parnassus, San Francisco CA 94122 USA	Molecular Biologist
Dern, Bruce Pure Arts, 9925 Jefferson Blvd, Culver City CA 90232, USA	Actor
Dern, Laura Creative Artists Agency, 2000 Ave of Stars, #100, Los Angeles CA 90067 USA	Actress
Dernesch, Helga Salztogasse 8/11, 1013 Vienna, Austria	Opera Singer
Dernier, Robert E (Bob) 1242 SW Arbormill Terrace, Lees Summit MO 64082, USA	Baseball Player
Deromedi, Herbert 885 Hiawatha Dr, Mount Pleasant MI 48858, USA	Football Coach
DeRoo, David C (Dave) Novi Entertainment, PO Box 17077, Beverly Hills CA 90209, USA	Bassist (Adema)
Deroo, Romain Artmedia, 20 Ave Rapp, 75007 Paris, France	Actor
DeRosa, Mark T 58 Avalon Way, Waretown NJ 08758, USA	Baseball Player
DeRosario, Dwayne A D C United, R F K Stadium, 2400 E Capitol St SE, Washington DC 20003 USA	Soccer Player
DeRosier, David 27 Chesterfield Road, West Newton MA 02465, USA	Biophysicist
Derosier, Michael Borman Entertainment, 1250 6th St, #401, Santa Monica CA 90401, USA	Drummer (Heart)
DeRossi, Massimo Carol Levi Mgmt, Via G Pisanelli 2, 00196 Rome, Italy	Actor
DeRossi, Portia W M E Entertainment, 9601 Wilshire Blvd, #300, Beverly Hills CA 90210 USA	Actress, Model
Derow, Peter A PO Box 534, Bedford NY 10506, USA	Publisher
Deroyer, Jean I M G Artists, Hogarth Business Park, Chiswick, London W4 2TH, England	Conductor
DeRozan, DeMar D Toronto Raptors, Air Canada Center, 20 Bay St, Toronto ON M5J 2N8, Canada	Basketball Player
Derr, Kenneth T Chevron Corp, 6001 Bollinger Canyon Road, San Ramon CA 94583, USA	Businessman
Derricks, Cleavant 5D Unlimited, PO Box 4304, Thousand Oaks CA 91359, USA	Actor
Derrickson, Scott W M E Entertainment, 9601 Wilshire Blvd, #300, Beverly Hills CA 90210 USA	Director, Writer
D'Errico, Donna Michael Forman Agency, 409 N Camden Drive, #205, Beverly Hills CA 90210, USA	Model, Actress
Derringer, Rick Buddy Lee Attractions, 38 Music Square E, #300, Nashville TN 37203 USA	Singer, Guitarist
Derrington, C James (Jim) 107 Oliver St, West Columbia SC 29169, USA	Baseball Player
Derry, Kathy Co-Ed Trainers Club, PO Box 785, New York NY 10101, USA	Physical Fitness Instructor
Dersch, Hans 7217 E 55th Place, Tulsa OK 74145, USA	Swimmer
Dershowitz, Alan M 1563 Massachusetts Ave, Cambridge MA 02138, USA	Attorney, Educator
Dervan, Peter B California Institute of Technology, Chemistry Dept, Pasadena CA 91125, USA	Chemist
Derwin, Mark Innovative Artists, 1505 10th St, Santa Monica CA 90401 USA	Actor
Desai, Anita Deborah Rogers Ltd, 20 Powis Mews, London W11 1JN, England	Writer
Desailly, Marcel Chelsea F C, Stamford Bridge, Fulham Road, London SW6 1HS, England	Soccer Player
DeSalvo, Anne Don Buchwald/Fortitude, 6500 Wilshire Blvd, #2200, Los Angeles CA 90048 USA	Actress, Director
DeSalvo, Matthew T (Matt) 10 Village Gate Blvd, Delaware OH 43015, USA	Baseball Player
DeSanctis, Roman W 5 Thoreau Circle, Winchester MA 01890, USA	Cardiologist
DeSando, Anthony D2 Mgmt, 9255 Sunset Blvd, #600, West Hollywood CA 90069, USA	Actor
DeSantis, Jaclyn Paradigm Agency, 360 N Crescent Dr, North Building, Beverly Hills CA 90210 USA	Actress
DeSanto, Greg Big Apple Circus, 505 8th Ave, #1900, New York NY 10018 USA	Clown
DeSanto, Karen Big Apple Circus, 505 8th Ave, #1900, New York NY 10018 USA	Clown
Descas, Alex Artmedia, 20 Ave Rapp, 75007 Paris, France	Actor
Deschamps, Didier C Monaco Association Sportive, 7 Ave des Castelans, 98000 Monaco	Soccer Player
Deschanel, Caleb Optimism Entertainment, 303 N La Peer Dr, #205, Beverly Hills CA 90211, USA	Cinematographer
Deschanel, Emily Management 360, 9111 Wilshire Blvd, Beverly Hills CA 90210 USA	Actress
Deschanel, Mary Jo 844 Chautauqua Blvd, Pacific Palisades CA 90272, USA	Actress
Deschanel, Zooey Creative Artists Agency, 2000 Ave of Stars, #100, Los Angeles CA 90067 USA	Actress, Model, Singer
Deser, Stanley Brandeis University, Physics Dept, Waltham MA 02254, USA	Physicist
Desfor, Max 15115 Interlachen Dr, #1018, Silver Spring MD 20906, USA	Photojournalist

Desfosses, Erik — Actor
Artmedia, 20 Ave Rapp, 75007 Paris, France

Deshaies, James J (Jim) — Baseball Player
151 N Taylor Point Dr, Spring TX 77382, USA

DeShields, Delino L — Baseball Player
3399 Kiveton Court, Norcross GA 30092, USA

Deshorties, Alexandra — Singer
Opus 3 Artists, 470 Park Ave S, #900N, New York NY 10016 USA

Desiderio, Robert — Actor
1475 Sierra Vista Dr, Aspen CO 81611, USA

DeSilva, John R — Baseball Player
32750 Airport Road, Fort Bragg CA 95437, USA

Desjardins, Eric — Ice Hockey Player
9 Woodglen Lane, Voorhees NJ 08043, USA

Desjardins, Gerry — Ice Hockey Player
252 Suffolk Place, London ON N6G 3S4, Canada

DesLauriers, Kit — Free Skier
Teton Village, Jackson Hole WY 83001, USA

Deslongchamps, Pierre — Chemist
RR 1, 11 Church McFarland, North Hatley PQ J0B 2C0, Canada

Desormeaux, Kent — Thoroughbred Racing Jockey
292 W Carter Ave, Sierra Madre CA 91024, USA

DeSousa, Mauricio — Cartoonist (Monica)
Mauricio de Sousa Producoes, Rua do Curtume 745, Sao Paulo SP, Brazil

DeSousa, Melissa — Actress
Stone Manners Salners, 9911 W Pico Blvd, #1400, Los Angeles CA 90035 USA

Desplat, Alexandre — Composer
B M I, 8730 W Sunset Blvd, #300, Los Angeles CA 90069 USA

Des'ree — Singer
Solo Agency, 53-55 Fulham High St, #200, London SW6 3JJ, England

Desrosiers, David P — Bassist (Simple Plan)
Depot Sainte-Dorothee, PO Box 223, Lavel PQ H7X 2T4, Canada

Dess, Darrell C — Football Player
224 Summer Ave, New Castle PA 16105, USA

Desselle, Natalie — Actress
Innovative Artists, 1505 10th St, Santa Monica CA 90401 USA

Dessens Jusaino, Elmer — Baseball Player
5427 E Sheena Dr, Scottsdale AZ 85254, USA

Dessner, Bryce — Guitarist (National)
Brassland Records, PO Box 76, Prince Street Station, New York NY 10012, USA

Destrade, Orestes — Baseball Player
10653 Garda Dr, Trinity FL 34655, USA

Destri, James (Jimmy) — Keyboardist (Blondie)
Agency Group Ltd, 142 W 57th St, #600, New York NY 10019 USA

Desurvive, Emmanuel — Optical Fiber Engineer
Alcatel Submarine Networks, Villarceaux Centre, 91625 Nozay, France

DeTar, Dean E — Vietnam War Air Force Hero
7785 Portwood Road, Azle TX 76020, USA

DeThe, Guy Blaudin — Oncologist, Biologist
14 Rue Le Regrattier, 75004 Paris, France

Detmer, Amanda — Actress
John Carrabino Mgmt, 5900 Wilshire Blvd, #406, Los Angeles CA 90036 USA

Detmer, Koy D — Football Player
2906 Spring Bend St, San Antonio TX 78209, USA

Detmer, Ty H — Football Player
18449 Flagler Dr, Austin TX 78738, USA

Detmers, Maruschka — Actress
Agence Metropolitan Paris, 23 Blvd des Capucines, 75002 Paris, France

Detorie, Rick — Cartoonist (One Big Happy)
Creators Syndicate, 737 3rd St, Hermosa Beach CA 90254 USA

Detroit, Marcella — Singer, Songwriter
M C M Mgmt, 40 Langham St, #300, London W1N 5RG, England

Dettlaff, Bill — Golfer
133 Clearlake Dr, Ponte Vedra Beach FL 32082, USA

Dettmer, John F — Baseball Player
549 Hickory View Lane, Ballwin MO 63011, USA

Dettore, Thomas A (Tom) — Baseball Player
1120 McEven Ave, Canonsburg PA 15317, USA

DeTurck, Dennis — Mathematician
University of Pennsylvania, Arts & Sciences College, Philadelphia PA 19104, USA

Detweiler, David K — Physiologist
1055 Huntingdon Road, Abington PA 19001, USA

Detweiler, Robert S (Ducky) — Baseball Player
312 Holt St, Federalsburg MD 21632, USA

Detwiler, Ross — Baseball Player
359 Brown Swiss Circle, Duncansville PA 16635, USA

Deukmejian, C George — Governor, CA
Sidley & Austin, 555 W 5th St, #3900, Los Angeles CA 90013, USA

Deutch, Howard — Director, Producer, Writer
I C M Partners, 10250 Constellation Blvd, #900, Los Angeles CA 90067 USA

Deutch, John M — Government Official
51 Clifton St, Belmont MA 02478, USA

Deutch, Zoey — Actress
Innovative Artists, 1505 10th St, Santa Monica CA 90401 USA

Deutekom, Cristina — Opera Singer
Lancasterdreef 41, Dronten 8251 TG, Holland

Deutsch, David (Dave) — Basketball Player
315 Fairmont Road, Long Valley NJ 07853, USA

Dev — Singer, Rap Artist, Songwriter
Paradigm Agency, 360 N Crescent Dr, North Building, Beverly Hills CA 90210 USA

Dev, Mukul — Actor
Karan Apts, #500, Yari Road Versova, Mumbai MS 400061, India

Deva, Prabhu — Actor, Dancer, Director
68 T T K Road, Alwarpet, Chennai TN 600018, India

DeValeria, Dennis — Sportswriter
213 Hillendale Road, Pittsburgh PA 15237, USA

Devane, William
Innovative Artists, 1505 10th St, Santa Monica CA 90401 USA — Actor

Devarez, Cesar S
35 Arden St, #B, New York NY 10040, USA — Baseball Player

DeVarona, Donna
3 Avon Lane, Greenwich CT 06830, USA — Swimmer, Sportscaster

DeVasquez, Devin
9903 Santa Monica Blvd, #169, Beverly Hills CA 90212, USA — Model, Actress

Devault, Calvin
Amsel Eisenstadt Frazier, 5055 Wilshire Blvd, #865, Los Angeles CA 90036 USA — Actor

Devayani
51 Indira Gandhi St, Saligramam, Chennai TN 600093, India — Actress

Devendorf, Bryan
Brassland Records, PO Box 76, Prince Street Station, New York NY 10012, USA — Drummer (National)

Devendorf, Scott
Brassland Records, PO Box 76, Prince Street Station, New York NY 10012, USA — Guitarist (National)

DeVenzio, Dick
1116 Home Place, Matthews NC 28105, USA — Basketball Player

Dever, Barbara
Wolf Artists Mgmt, 13 E 69th St, #3R, New York NY 10021, USA — Opera Singer

Dever, Kaitlyn
United Talent Agency, 9336 Civic Center Dr, Beverly Hills CA 90210 USA — Actress

Dever, Seamus
A P A Talent/Literary Agency, 405 S Beverly Dr, #300, Beverly Hills CA 90212 USA — Actor

Deveraux, Jude
Atria/Simon & Schuster, 1230 Ave of Americas, Concourse 1, New York NY 10020, USA — Writer

Devereaux, Michael (Mike)
2236 W Doublegrove St, West Covina CA 91790, USA — Baseball Player

Devers, Gail
G B M Mgmt, 4207 Corrales Dr, #100, Florissant MO 63034, USA — Track Athlete

DeVevo, Juan
Proper Mgmt, PO Box 150867, Nashville TN 37215, USA — Guitarist (Casting Crowns)

DeVevo, Melodee
Proper Mgmt, PO Box 150867, Nashville TN 37215, USA — Violinist (Casting Crowns)

Devgan, Ajay
5/6 Sheetak Apts, Opp Chandand Cinema, Juhu, Mumbai MS 400049, India — Actor, Director, Producer

DeVicenzo, Roberto
Noni Lann, 5025 Veloz Ave, Tarzana CA 91356, USA — Golfer

DeVilla, Alfredo
Underground Films & Mgmt, 447 S Highland Ave, Los Angeles CA 90036, USA — Director

DeVille, Cecil (C C)
Front Line Mgmt, 1100 Glendon Ave, #2000, Los Angeles CA 90024 USA — Guitarist (Poison)

Deville, Michel
36 Rue Reinhardt, 92100 Boulogne, France — Director

Devin, Anna
I M G Artists, Hogarth Business Park, Chiswick, London W4 2TH, England — Opera Singer

DeVine, Adam
United Talent Agency, 9336 Civic Center Dr, Beverly Hills CA 90210 USA — Actor, Writer

Devine, Aidan
S M S Talent, 8383 Wilshire Blvd, #230, Beverly Hills CA 90211 USA — Actor

Devine, Elizabeth
Creative Artists Agency, 2000 Ave of Stars, #100, Los Angeles CA 90067 USA — Writer, Producer

Devine, Joseph N (Joey)
2616 Long Pointe, Roswell GA 30076, USA — Baseball Player

Devine, Loretta
Essential Talent Mgmt, 3151 Cahuenga Blvd W, #220, Los Angeles CA 90068, USA — Actress

Devine, P Adrian
271 Timber Laurel Lane, Lawrenceville GA 30043, USA — Baseball Player

DeVita, Vincent T, Jr
Yale Comprehensive Cancer Center, 333 Cedar St, New Haven CT 06510, USA — Oncologist

DeVito, Danny
1028 Ridgedale Dr, Beverly Hills CA 90210, USA — Actor, Comedian, Director

DeVito, Joe
OmniPop Talent Group, 4605 Lankershim Blvd, #201, Toluca Lake CA 91602 USA — Actor, Comedian

Devitt, John
46 Beacon Ave, Beacon Hill NSW 2100, Australia — Swimmer

Devlin, Bruce
3601 Foot Hills Dr, Weatherford TX 76087, USA — Golfer

Devlin, Christopher J (Chris)
100 Meadowlark Lane, Boalsburg PA 16827, USA — Football Player

Devlin, Dean
Electric Entertainment, 940 N Highland Ave, #A, Los Angeles CA 90038, USA — Director, Producer, Actor

Devlin, Joseph (Joe)
3815 Schintzius Road, Eden NY 14057, USA — Football Player

Devlin, Michael R (Mike)
48 Shore Road, Mount Sinai NY 11766, USA — Football Player

Devlin, Peter J
Doug Apatow Agency, 12049 Jefferson Blvd, #200, Culver City CA 90230, USA — Sound Mixer

Devlin, Ryan
Michelle Grant Mgmt, 1158 26th St, #414, Santa Monica CA 90403, USA — Actor

DeVoe, Ronald (Ronnie)
Pyramid Entertainment, 377 Rector Place, #21A, New York NY 10280 USA — Singer (New Edition, Bell Biv DeVoe)

Devoll, Hal
8928 Fox Ave, Allen Park MI 48101, USA — Basketball Player

Devor, Robinson
United Talent Agency, 9336 Civic Center Dr, Beverly Hills CA 90210 USA — Director, Writer

Devore, Doug
5247 Willow Grove Place S, Dublin OH 43017, USA — Baseball Player

DeVore, Irven
Harvard University, Peabody Archaeology Museum, Cambridge MA 02138, USA — Anthropologist, Evolutionary Biologist

DeVorzon, Barry
MasterWriter, 70 State St, Santa Barbara CA 93101, USA — Songwriter

Devos, Emmanuelle
Zelig, 57 Rue Reaumur, 75002 Paris, France — Actress

DeVos, Richard M
6565 Otis Lane, Harbor Springs MI 49740, USA — Businessman, Philanthropist

DeVries, Greg — Ice Hockey Player
25 Colonel Winstead Dr, Brentwood TN 37027, USA

Devries, Jared — Football Player
15342 Lambert Dr, Clear Lake IA 50428, USA

DeVries, Jill — Model
Playboy Promotions, 2706 Media Center Dr, Los Angeles CA 90065 USA

DeVries, Marius — Composer
Gorfaine/Schwartz, 4111 W Alameda Ave, #509, Burbank CA 91505 USA

DeVries, William C — Surgeon
Hardin Memorial Hospital, 913 N Dixie Ave, Elizabethtown KY 42701, USA

DeWaal, Frans — Primatologist
Emory University, Primate Behavior Dept, Atlanta GA 30322, USA

DeWaart, Edo — Conductor
Essenlaan 68, Rotterdam 3016, Netherlands

Dewan-Tatum, Jenna — Actress, Producer
Sanders/Armstrong/Caserta Mgmt, 2120 Colorado Ave, #120, Santa Monica CA 90404 USA

Dewar, Susan — Cartoonist (Us & Them)
Universal Press Syndicate, 4520 Main St, #700, Kansas City MO 64111 USA

DeWarren, Patrick — Photographer
153 Roebling St, #100, Brooklyn NY 11211, USA

Dewdney, Christopher — Writer
Bloomsbury Publishing, 36 Soho Square, London W1D 3Q4, England

DeWet, Shaun — Model
Elite Model Mgmt, 404 Park Ave S, #900, New York NY 10016 USA

Dewey, Duane E — Korean War Marine Corps Hero (CMH)
10550 N Forman Road, Irons MI 49644, USA

Dewey, Mark A — Baseball Player
28150 Rivermont Dr, Meadowview VA 24361, USA

DeWilde, Edy — Museum Executive
Stedelijk Museum, Oosterdokskade 5, 1011 AD Amsterdam, Netherlands

DeWillis, Jeffrey A (Jeff) — Baseball Player
8918 Wind Side Dr, Richmond Hill ON L4C 1T4, Canada

DeWinne, Frank — Cosmonaut
349th Squadron, Vliegbasis 10W T A C Kleine Brogel, 3990 Peer, Belgium

DeWit, Peter — Cartoonist
Galerie Lambiek, Kerkstaat 78, 1017 GP Amsterdam, Netherlands

DeWit, William T (Willie) — Boxer
Wolch Hursh DeWit, 1500-633 6th Ave SW, Calgary AB T2P 2Y5, Canada

DeWitt, Doug — Boxer
176 Garth Road, #TM, Scarsdale NY 10583, USA

DeWitt, Joyce — Actress, Model
PO Box 7309, Santa Monica CA 90406, USA

DeWitt, Rosemarie — Actress
I C M Partners, 10250 Constellation Blvd, #900, Los Angeles CA 90067 USA

Dewitt, Willie — Boxer
605 N Water St, Burnet TX 78611, USA

DeWitt-Morette, Cecile — Physicist
2411 Vista Lane, Austin TX 78703, USA

Dews, Peter B — Psychiatrist
99 Norumbega Road, #231, Weston MA 02493, USA

DeWulf, Noureen — Actress
Evolution Entertainment, 901 N Highland Ave, Los Angeles CA 90038 USA

DeWyze, Lee — Singer, Songwriter
Sony Records, 2100 Colorado Ave, Santa Monica CA 90404 USA

Dexter, Mary — Director
Hank Tani, 14542 Delaware Dr, Moorpark CA 93021, USA

Dexter, N Colin — Writer
456 Banbury Road, Oxford OX2 7RG, England

Dexter, Peter W — Writer, Columnist
Sacramento Bee, Editorial Dept, 21st & Q Sts, Sacramento CA 95852, USA

Dey, Charles — Association Executive
Start on Success, 910 16th Ave NW, Washington DC 20006, USA

Dey, Susan — Actress
I C M Partners, 10250 Constellation Blvd, #900, Los Angeles CA 90067 USA

Dey, Tom — Director
W M E Entertainment, 9601 Wilshire Blvd, #300, Beverly Hills CA 90210 USA

DeYoung, Cliff — Actor
481 Savona Way, Oak Park CA 91377, USA

DeYoung, Michelle — Singer
Opus 3 Artists, 470 Park Ave S, #900N, New York NY 10016 USA

DeZarn, Tim — Actor
C E S D, 10635 Santa Monica Blvd, #130, Los Angeles CA 90025 USA

Dezhurov, Vladimir N — Cosmonaut
Cosmonaut Training Center, Star City, 141160 Zvezdny Gorodok, Moscow Oblast, Russia

DeZordo, Nevio — Bobsled Athlete
Olympic Committee, Foro Italico, Largo Lauro de Bosis 15, 00135 Rome, Italy

Dhabhara, Firdaus S — Neuroscientist
Rockefeller University, Neurology Dept, 1230 York Ave, New York NY 10065, USA

Dhalia, Heitor — Director
W M E Entertainment, 9601 Wilshire Blvd, #300, Beverly Hills CA 90210 USA

Dhaliwal, Daljit — Commentator
Knight Ayton Mgmt, 114 Saint Martin's Lane, London WC2N 4BE, England

Dhanapala, Jayantha C P — Government Official, Sri Lanka
United Nations, Sri Lanka Delegation, United Nations Plaza, New York NY 10007, USA

Dhanoa, Guddu — Director
8A My Little Home, 10th Road J V P D Scheme, Mumbai MS 400049, India

Dharker, Ayesha — Actress
Independent Talent Group, Oxford House, 76 Oxford St, London W1D 1BS, England

Dharma Master Cheng Yen — Religious Leader
Tzu Chi Foundation, 701 Zhongyang Road, Hualien 97004, Taiwan

Dhavernas, Caroline — Actress
Gersh Agency, 41 Madison Ave, #3301, New York NY 10010 USA

Dhawan, Sacha — Actress
Hatton McEwan, 3 Chocolate Studios, 7 Shepherdess Place, London N1 7LJ, England

Dhoinine, Ikililou — President, Comores
President's Office, Palais de Beit Salam, BP 421, Moroni, Grand Comoro, Comoros

Dhoni, Mahendra Singh — Cricket Athlete
Chennai Super Kings, Gummidipundi, Tamil Nadu, 09865132400 India

Diadkova, Larissa — Opera Singer
I M G Artists, Hogarth Business Park, Chiswick, London W4 2TH, England

Diamandis, Peter G — Publisher
Diamandis Communications, 1515 Broadway, New York NY 10036, USA

Diamantopoulos, Chris — Actor
Untitled Entertainment, 350 S Beverly Dr, #200, Beverly Hills CA 90212 USA

Diamond of Gloucester, John — Government Official, England
Aynhoe, Doggetts Wood Lane, Chalfont Saint Giles, Bucks HP8 4TH, England

Diamond, Abel J — Architect
Diamond Schmitt Co, 2 Berkeley St, #600, Toronto ON M5A 2W3, Canada

Diamond, Jared M — Biologist
University of California Medical School, Physiology Dept, Los Angeles CA 90024, USA

Diamond, Marian C — Neuroanatomist
100 Bay Place, #804, Oakland CA 94610, USA

Diamond, Michael (Mike D) — Rap Artist (Beastie Boys)
Nasty Little Man, 110 Greene St, #605, New York NY 10012, USA

Diamond, Neil L — Singer, Songwriter
H K Mgmt, 1100 Glendon Ave, #1100, Los Angeles CA 90069, USA

Diamond, Peter A — Nobel Economics Laureate
Massachusetts Institute of Technology, Economics Dept, Cambridge MA 02139, USA

Diamond, Reed — Actor
Paradigm Agency, 360 N Crescent Dr, North Building, Beverly Hills CA 90210 USA

Diamond, Seymour — Physician
Diamond Headache Clinic, 467 W Deming Place, #500, Chicago IL 60614, USA

Diamond, William — Financier
28 Preakness Court, Owings Mills MD 21117, USA

Diamont, Anita — Writer
Charles Scribner's Sons, 866 3rd Ave, New York NY 10022 USA

Diamont, Don — Actor, Model
Craig Mgmt, 2240 Miramonte Circle E, #C, Palm Springs CA 92264 USA

Dias, Ivan Cardinal — Religious Leader
Archbishop's House, 21 Nathalal Parekh Marg, Mumbai 400001, India

DiasDosSantos, Fernando da Piedade — Prime Minister, Angola
Prime Minister's Office, Avda 4 de Fevereiro, Luanda CP 2723, Angola

Diaw, Boris — Basketball Player
10430 N 108th Place, Scottsdale AZ 85259, USA

Diaz, Alex — Photojournalist
Associated Press, 450 W 33rd St, #1500, New York NY 10001 USA

Diaz, Cameron — Actress, Model
Creative Artists Agency, 2000 Ave of Stars, #100, Los Angeles CA 90067, USA

Diaz, Carlos A — Baseball Player
45-236 Ka Hanahou Circle, Kaneohe HI 96744, USA

Diaz, David — Boxer
1524 N Avers Ave, Chicago IL 60651, USA

Diaz, Einar A — Baseball Player
4315 70th Ave E, Ellenton FL 34222, USA

Diaz, Gloria M A — Beauty Queen, Actress
Miss Universe Organization, 1370 Ave of Americas, #1600, New York NY 10019 USA

Diaz, Guillermo — Actor
Innovative Artists, 1505 10th St, Santa Monica CA 90401 USA

Diaz, Jorge A — Football Player
10801 Starkey Road, Seminole FL 33777, USA

Diaz, Juan — Boxer
13616 Monarch Road, Houston TX 77047, USA

Diaz, Julio — Boxer
PO Box 1812, Indio CA 92202, USA

Diaz, Junot — Writer
Riverhead/Penguin Books, 375 Hudson St, Basement 1, New York NY 10014, USA

Diaz, Laura — Golfer
Ladies Pro Golf Assn, 100 International Golf Dr, Daytona Beach FL 32124 USA

Diaz, Manuel A (Manny) — Mayor, Miami
Mayor's Office, 3500 Pan American Dr, Miami FL 33133, USA

Diaz, Mario R — Baseball Player
90 Calle Menta Ciudad Jardin, Gurabo PR 00778, USA

Diaz, Matthew E (Matt) — Baseball Player
1124 Afton St, Lakeland FL 33803, USA

Diaz, Melonie — Actress
Gersh Agency, 9465 Wilshire Blvd, #600, Beverly Hills CA 90212 USA

Diaz, Michael A (Mike) — Baseball Player
1113 Everglades Dr, Pacifica CA 94044, USA

Diaz-Balart, Jose — Commentator
Telmundo, 2470 W 8th Ave, Hialeah FL 33010, USA

Diaz-Infante, G David M — Football Player
24723 E Park Crescent Dr, Aurora CO 80016, USA

Diaz-Rahi, Yamila — Model
Next Model Mgmt, 9 Boul de la Madeleine, 75001 Paris, France

Dibaba, Tirunesh — Track Athlete
Global Athletics & Marketing, 437 Boylston St, #400, Boston MA 02116, USA

Dibb, Sam — Director
Casorotto Ramsay, Waverley House, 7-12 Noel St, London W1F 8GQ, England

Dibble, Dorne A — Football Player
18601 Jamestown Circle, Northville MI 48168, USA

Dibble, Robert K (Rob) — Baseball Player
30020 Trail Creek Dr, Agoura Hills CA 91301, USA

DiBeligiojoso, Lodovico B — Architect
8 Via Perugia, 20121 Milan, Italy

DiBenedetto, Kaitlyn — Instrumentalist (Just Kait)
Transfer Media Group, 5200 Lankershim Blvd, #400, North Hollywood CA 91601, USA

DiBlasio, Raul — Singer
Estefan Enterprises, 420 Jefferson Ave, Miami Beach FL 33139, USA

DiBona, Craig — Cinematographer
333 E 66th St, #7-O, New York NY 10065, USA

DiBonaventura, Lorenzo — Producer
Rogers & Cowan, 8687 Melrose Ave, #G700, West Hollywood CA 90069 USA

Dibos, Alicia — Golfer
1465 E Putnam Ave, #112E, Old Greenwich, T 06870, USA
Dibowski, Andreas — Equestrian
Waldwinkel 2, 21272 Egestorf, Germany
Dibra, Bash — Dog Trainer
3476 Bailey Ave, Bronx NY 10463, USA
DiCamillo, Gary T — Businessman
1001 Saint Georges Road, Baltimore MD 21210, USA
DiCamillo, Katrice E (Kate) — Writer
Candlewick Press, 99 Dover St, Somerville MA 02144, USA
DiCaprio, Leonardo — Actor
L B I Entertainment, 2000 Avenue of Stars, Century City CA 90067 90067, USA
DiCenta, Giorgio — Cross Country Skier
33020 Treppo Carnico (UD), Italy
Dichter, Misha — Concert Pianist
Columbia Artists Mgmt Inc, 1790 Broadway, #702, New York NY 10019 USA
Dick, Andrew R (Andy) — Actor, Comedian
Collective, 8383 Wilshire Blvd, #1050, Beverly Hills CA 90211 USA
Dick, Bryan — Actor
Markham & Froggatt, Julian House, 4 Windmill St, London W1P 1HF, England
Dick, Douglas — Actor
604 S Gretna Green Way, Los Angeles CA 90049, USA
Dickau, Daniel D (Dan) — Basketball Player
190 Marietta St SW, Atlanta GA 30303, USA
Dickel, Daniel L (Dan) — Football Player
970 Maplewood Dr, Coralville IA 52241, USA
Dicken, Paul — Baseball Player
4421 NW Blitchton Road, Ocala FL 34482, USA
Dickens, Chris — Editor
United Agents, 12-26 Lexington St, London W1F 0LE, England
Dickens, Kim — Actress
Gersh Agency, 41 Madison Ave, #3301, New York NY 10010 USA
Dickens, Little Jimmy — Singer
5010 W Concord Road, Brentwood TN 37027, USA
Dickenson, Gary — Bowler
501 Wade Martin Dr, Edmond OK 73034, USA
Dickenson, Herb — Ice Hockey Player
240 Jerseyville Road, RR 8 Station Main, Brantford ON N3T 5M1, Canada
Dickerson, Christopher C (Chris) — Baseball Player
Milwaukee Brewers, Miller Park, 1 Brewers Way, Milwaukee WI 53214 USA
Dickerson, Eric D — Football Player, Sportscaster
516 Dickerson St, Sealy TX 77474, USA
Dickerson, Ernest R — Director
Untitled Entertainment, 350 S Beverly Dr, #200, Beverly Hills CA 90212 USA
Dickerson, Marty — Golfer
4225 Luzon Way, Sarasota FL 34241, USA
Dickerson, Sandra — Actress
Howes & Prior, Berkeley House, Hay Hill, London W1X 7LH, England
Dickey, Boh A — Businessman
Safeco Corp, Safeco Plaza, 1001 4th Ave, #800, Seattle WA 98154, USA
Dickey, C Lynn — Football Player
9220 Pawnee Lane, Leawood KS 66206, USA
Dickey, Curtis R — Football Player
1817 Sheehan Court, Arlington TX 76012, USA
Dickey, Doug — Football Coach
11677 Thornapple Dr, Jacksonville FL 32223, USA
Dickey, Robert A (R A) — Baseball Player
1015 Lynnwood Blvd, Nashville TN 37215, USA
Dickinson, Amy — Columnist
Tribune Media Services, 435 N Michigan Ave, #1500, Chicago IL 60611 USA
Dickinson, Angie — Actress
1715 Carla Ridge, Beverly Hills CA 90210, USA
Dickinson, Bruce — Singer (Iron Maiden)
Chipster, 800 Village Square Crossing, Palm Beach Gardens FL 33410 USA
Dickinson, Gary — Bowler
501 Wade Martin Road, Edmond OK 73034, USA
Dickinson, Janice — Model, Actress, Photographer
W M E Entertainment, 9601 Wilshire Blvd, #300, Beverly Hills CA 90210 USA
Dickinson, Judy — Golfer
18277 SE Heritage Dr, Jupiter FL 33469, USA
Dickinson, Peter — Writer
Mysterious Press, Warner Books, 1271 Ave of Americas, New York NY 10020 USA
Dickinson, Richard L (Bo) — Football Player
PO Box 166, New Augusta MS 39462, USA
Dickinson, Rob — Singer, Guitarist (Catherine Wheel)
Paradigm Agency, 360 Park Ave, #1600, New York NY 10022 USA
Dickinson, Sandra — Actress
Associated International Mgmt, Fairfax House, Fulwood Place, London WC1V 6HU, England
Dickinson, Steve — Cartoonist (Tar Pit)
King Features Syndicate, 300 W 57th St, #1500, New York NY 10019 USA
Dickman, James B (Jay) — Photographer
3176 S Vine St, Englewood CO 80113, USA
Dickson, Billy — Director
Paradigm Agency, 360 N Crescent Dr, North Building, Beverly Hills CA 90210 USA
Dickson, Chris — Yachtsman
International Mgmt Group, 1 Erieview Plaza, 1360 E 9th St, Cleveland OH 44114 USA
Dickson, Jason R — Baseball Player
15 Edison St, Sainte Margarets NB E1N 5B4, Canada
Dickson, Jennifer — Artist, Photographer
20 Osborne St, Ottawa ON K1S 4Z9, Canada
Dickson, Neil — Actor
Clear Talent Group, 10950 Ventura Blvd, Studio City CA 91604, USA
Dickson, Ngila — Costume Designer
Weta Workshop, PO Box 15208, Miramar, Wellington, New Zealand
DiCorcia, Philip-Lorca — Photographer
55 Hudson St, #8D, New York NY 10013, USA

Dicus, Charles W (Chuck)
852 N Mansfield Ave, Los Angeles CA 90038, USA — Football Player

Dicus, John C
Capitol Federal Savings & Loan, 700 S Kansas Ave, #100, Topeka KS 66603, USA — Financier

Diczfalusy, Egon R
Ronninger 21, 144 61 Ronninge, Sweden — Endocrinologist

Didier, Clint
8770 N Glade Road, Pasco WA 99301, USA — Football Player

Didier, Robert D (Bob)
1819 N Lynch, Mesa AZ 85207, USA — Baseball Player

Didion, Joan
Creative Artists Agency, 2000 Ave of Stars, #100, Los Angeles CA 90067 USA — Writer

Didion, John L
48 Elk Ridge Lane, Naselle WA 98638, USA — Football Player

Dido
Paradigm Agency, 360 N Crescent Dr, North Building, Beverly Hills CA 90210 USA — Singer, Songwriter

Diduck, Gerald
3303 Drexel Dr, Dallas TX 75205, USA — Ice Hockey Player

Diebel, John C
Meade Instruments Corp, 27 Hubble, #100, Irvine CA 92618, USA — Businessman

Diebel, Nelson
401 Webb Road, Newark DE 19711, USA — Swimmer

Diegel, Adam
I M G Artists, Hogarth Business Park, Chiswick, London W4 2TH, England — Opera Singer

Diego Florez, Juan
Opera et Concert, 37 Rue de la Chaussee d'Antin, 75009 Paris, France — Opera Singer

Diehl, David M
116 Liberty Ridge Trail, Totowa NJ 07512, USA — Football Player

Diehl, Digby R
788 S Lake Ave, Pasadena CA 91106, USA — Journalist

Diehl, John
Don Buchwald/Fortitude, 6500 Wilshire Blvd, #2200, Los Angeles CA 90048 USA — Actor

Diehl, John A
900 S Henry St, Williamsburg VA 23185, USA — Football Player

Dieken, Doug H
29876 Lake Road, Bay Village OH 44140, USA — Football Player

Diemberger, Kurt
Via Amola 23/1, 40050 Calderino (BO), Italy — Mountaineer

Diemecke, Enrique Arturo
Herbert Barrett, 266 W 37th St, #2000, New York NY 10018 USA — Conductor

Diemer, Brian
Calvin College, Athletic Dept, Grand Rapids MI 49506, USA — Track Athlete

Diener, Theodor O
PO Box 272, 11711 Battersea Dr, Beltsville MD 20704, USA — Plant Virologist

Dierdorf, Daniel L (Dan)
13302 Buckland Hall Road, Saint Louis MO 63131, USA — Football Player, Sportscaster

Diering, Charles E A (Chuck)
1 Nob Hill Dr, Saint Louis MO 63138, USA — Baseball Player

Dierker, Lawrence E (Larry)
8318 N Tahoe Dr, Houston TX 77040, USA — Baseball Player, Manager

Dierking, Conrad W (Connie)
5730 Windridge View, Cincinnati OH 45243, USA — Basketball Player

Dierking, Scott E
1862 Wingate Lane, Wheaton IL 60189, USA — Football Player

Dierkop, Charles R
10 Town Plaza, #428, Durango CO 81301, USA — Actor

Diesel, Vin
One Race Productions, 9100 Wilshire Blvd, 535 East Tower, Beverly Hills CA 90212, USA — Director, Actor

Dieterich, Christian J (Chris)
804 Edisto River Road, Myrtle Beach SC 29588, USA — Football Player

Dietrich, Don
310 Finlay Avenue E, Deloraine MB R0M 0M0, Canada — Ice Hockey Player

Dietrich, William A (Bill)
Seattle Times, Editorial Dept, 1120 John St, Seattle WA 98109 USA — Journalist

Dietrick, Coby J
644 Patterson Ave, San Antonio TX 78209, USA — Basketball Player

Dietz, Michael
Michael Bruno Group, 13576 Cheltenham Dr, Sherman Oaks CA 91423, USA — Actor

Dietzel, Leroy L (Roy)
8421 Coulwood Oak Lane, Charlotte NC 28214, USA — Baseball Player

Difelice, Michael W (Mike)
3980 Mimosa Place, Palm Harbor FL 34685, USA — Baseball Player

Diffie, Joe
50 Music Square W, #300, Nashville TN 37203, USA — Singer, Songwriter

Diffie, Whitfield
Sun Microsystems, 4150 Network Circle, Santa Clara CA 95054, USA — Inventor (Public Key Cryptology)

Diffrient, Niels
General Delivery, Ridgefield CT 06877, USA — Industrial Designer

DiFiore, Vince
Umbrella Group, 1 West St, #3506, New York NY 10004, USA — Trumpeter, Keyboardist (Bush)

DiFranco, Ani
Scot Fisher, 121 W Tupper St, Buffalo NY 14201, USA — Singer, Songwriter, Musician

Digby, Marie
Hollywood Records, 1851 Ivar, #500, Los Angeles CA 90028, USA — Singer, Guitarist

DiGenova, Joseph E
DiGenova & Toensing, 1776 K St NW, #700, Washington DC 20006, USA — Attorney

Diggins, Skylar
University of Notre Dame, Athletic Dept, Notre Dame IN 46556, USA — Basketball Player

Diggle, Steve
Free Trade Place, Chapel Place, Rivington St, London EC2A 3DQ, England — Guitarist, Bassist (Buzzcocks)

Diggs, Na'il R
2006 Connonade Dr, Waxhaw NC 28173, USA — Football Player

Diggs, Taye
O'Taye Productions, 12001 Ventura Place, #340, Studio City CA 91604, USA — Actor, Singer

DiGiallonardo, Rick
Pacific Talent Agency, PO Box 19145, Portland OR 97280, USA — Keyboardist (Quarterflash)

DiGiovanni, Janine
David Godwin Assoc, 55 Monmouth St, London WC2H 9DG, England — Journalist, Writer

DiGregorio, Ernest (Ernie)
60 Chestnut Ave, Narragansett RI 02882, USA — Basketball Player

Dijkstra, Rineke
Marian Goodman Gallery, 24 W 57th St, New York NY 10019, USA — Photographer

DiLauro, Jack E
102 Sea Oats Dr, Panama City Beach FL 32413, USA — Baseball Player

Dilba
United Stage Production, PO Box 11029, 100 61 Stockholm, Sweden — Singer, Musician, Songwriter

Dildarian, Steve
W M E Entertainment, 9601 Wilshire Blvd, #300, Beverly Hills CA 90210 USA — Producer, Writer, Actor

Dileita, Dileita Mohamed
Prime Minister's Office, BP 2086, Djibouti City, Djibouti — Prime Minister, Djibouti

Dilfer, Trent F
15288 Quito Road, Saratoga CA 95070, USA — Football Player, Sportscaster

Dilger, Kennth R (Ken)
10403 Windemere, Carmel IN 46032, USA — Football Player

Dill, Craig H
10200 Thomas Woods Road, Saginaw MI 48609, USA — Basketball Player

Dill, Guy
13215 Innes Place, Venice CA 90291, USA — Artist, Sculptor

Dill, Laddie John
1625 Electric Ave, Venice CA 90291, USA — Artist

Dill, Terry
7003 Western Oaks Blvd, Austin TX 78749, USA — Golfer

Dillahunt, Garret
United Talent Agency, 9336 Civic Center Dr, Beverly Hills CA 90210 USA — Actor

Dillane, Stephen
W M E Entertainment, 9601 Wilshire Blvd, #300, Beverly Hills CA 90210 USA — Actor

Dillard, Alex
Dillard's Inc, 1600 Cantrell Road, Little Rock AR 72201, USA — Businessman

Dillard, Annie
Russell Volkering, 50 W 29th St, New York NY 10001, USA — Writer

Dillard, Stephen B (Steve)
154 Drive 841, Saltillo MS 38866, USA — Baseball Player

Dillard, Timothy C (Tim)
154 Drive 841, Saltillo MS 38866, USA — Baseball Player

Dillard, Victoria
Alliance Talent, 2734 E Oakland Park Blvd, #101, Fort Lauderdale FL 33306 USA — Actress

Dillard, W Harrison
3449 Glencairn Road, Shaker Heights OH 44122, USA — Track Athlete

Dillard, William T, Jr
Dillard's Inc, 1600 Cantrell Road, Little Rock AR 72201, USA — Businessman

Dillehay, Thomas (Tom)
University of Kentucky, Anthropology Dept, Lexington KY 40506, USA — Anthropologist

Diller, Barry
I A C/InterActive Corp, 152 W 57th St, #4200, New York NY 10019, USA — Businessman

Diller, Elizabeth
Diller Scofidio & Renfro, 601 W 26th St, #1815, New York NY 10001, USA — Architect, Designer

Dillman, Bradford
770 Hot Springs Road, Santa Barbara CA 93108, USA — Actor

Dillon, Bobby D
1289 Morgan Dr, Temple TX 76502, USA — Football Player

Dillon, Corey
31 Marlboro Road, Woburn MA 01801, USA — Football Player

Dillon, Joseph W (Joe)
2360 Water Way, Rockwall TX 75087, USA — Baseball Player

Dillon, Kevin
I C M Partners, 10250 Constellation Blvd, #900, Los Angeles CA 90067 USA — Actor

Dillon, Matt
Untitled Entertainment, 350 S Beverly Dr, #200, Beverly Hills CA 90212 USA — Actor, Director

Dillon, Melinda
Innovative Artists, 1505 10th St, Santa Monica CA 90401 USA — Actress

Dillon, Wayne
Hockey Development, 301-1185 Eglinton E, North York ON M3C 3C6, Canada — Ice Hockey Player

Dilly, Erin
Paradigm Agency, 360 N Crescent Dr, North Building, Beverly Hills CA 90210 USA — Actress, Singer

Dilone, Miguel A
Calle El Sol, #190; Santiago, Dominican Republic — Baseball Player

DiLoreto, Dante
Creative Artists Agency, 2000 Ave of Stars, #100, Los Angeles CA 90067 USA — Producer

Dils, Stephen W (Steve)
10285 Midway Ave, Alpharetta GA 30022, USA — Football Player

DiMaggio, John
Gersh Agency, 9465 Wilshire Blvd, #600, Beverly Hills CA 90212 USA — Actor

Dimaio, Robert (Rob)
Saint Louis Blues, Scott Trade Center, 1401 Clark Ave, Saint Louis MO 63103 USA — Ice Hockey Player

DiMarco, Chris
3545 Rice Lake Loop, Longwood FL 32779, USA — Golfer

Dimas, Trent
Gold Cup Gymnastics School, 6009 Carmel Ave NE, Albuquerque NM 87113, USA — Gymnast

Dimbleby, David
14 King St, Richmond, Surrey TW9 1NF, England — Journalist, Commentator

DiMeco, Allie
Untitled Entertainment, 350 S Beverly Dr, #200, Beverly Hills CA 90212 USA — Singer (Naked Brothers Band)

DiMeola, Al
Entourage Talent, 133 W 25th St, #500, New York NY 10001, USA — Jazz Guitarist

Dimitrakos, Niko
71 Pennsylvania Ave, Somerville MA 02145, USA — Ice Hockey Player

Dimmel, Michael W (Mike)
526 Country Lane, Coppell TX 75019, USA — Baseball Player

Dimon, James (Jamie)
J P Morgan Chase, 270 Park Ave, #1200, New York NY 10017, USA — Businessman

Dimry, Charles L, III
PO Box 461266, Escondido CA 92046, USA — Football Player

DiNardo, Daniel N Cardinal
Chancery Office, PO Box 907, 1700 San Jacinto St, Houston TX 77002, USA — Religious Leader

Dinardo, Lenny
10000 SW 52nd Ave, #164, Gainesville FL 32608, USA — Baseball Player

Dindal, Mark
I C M Partners, 10250 Constellation Blvd, #900, Los Angeles CA 90067 USA — Animator, Director

Dine, James
Pace Wildenstein Gallery, 32 E 57th St, #400, New York NY 10022, USA — Artist, Sculptor, Photographer

Dineen, Gord
51 Fitzgerald Road, Queensbury NY 12804, USA — Ice Hockey Player

Dineen, Kevin
149 Birdsall Road, Queensbury NY 12804, USA — Ice Hockey Player, Coach

Dineen, Peter
65 Birch Road, Lake George NY 12845, USA — Ice Hockey Player

Dineen, William P (Bill)
18 Fairwood Dr, Queensbury NY 12804, USA — Ice Hockey Player, Executive

Dinerstein, James
Salander-O'Reilly Gallery, 22 E 71st St, New York NY 10021, USA — Sculptor

Dingle, Adrian K
3228 W Canyon Ave, San Diego CA 92123, USA — Football Player

Dingman, Chris
9220 Pine Island Court, Tampa FL 33647, USA — Ice Hockey Player

Dingman, Craig
3573 W Del Sienno St, Wichita KS 67203, USA — Baseball Player

Dinicol, Joe
Anthem Entertainment, 5225 Wilshire Blvd, #615, Los Angeles CA 90036 USA — Actor

Dinkel, Thomas (Tom)
877 Squire Lake Court, Villa Hills KY 41017, USA — Football Player

Dinkeloo, John
Roche & Dinkeloo, 20 Davis St, Hamden CT 06517, USA — Architect

Dinkins, Byron
10326 Tallent Lane, Huntersville NC 28078, USA — Basketball Player

Dinkins, Darnell J
9006 Pembroke Court, Pittsburgh PA 15237, USA — Football Player

Dinklage, Peter
Arcieri Assoc, 305 Madison Ave, #2315, New York NY 10165 USA — Actor

Dinnel, Harry
1427 El Nido Dr, Fallbrook CA 92028, USA — Basketball Player

Dinner, Michael
Creative Artists Agency, 2000 Ave of Stars, #100, Los Angeles CA 90067 USA — Director

Dinnerstein, Simone
I M G Artists, Hogarth Business Park, Chiswick, London W4 2TH, England — Concert Pianist

Dinnigan, Collette
22-24 Hutchinson St, Surry Hills, Sydney NSW 2010, Australia — Fashion Designer

Diogu, Ikechukwa S (Ike)
2052 W Lagoon Road, Pleasanton CA 94566, USA — Basketball Player

DioGuardi, Kara
Arthouse Entertainment, PO Box 3900, Los Angeles CA 90078, USA — Songwriter, Producer, Entertainer

Dion
Lustig Talent, PO Box 770850, Orlando FL 32877 USA — Singer

Dion, Celine
Feelings, 2540 Blvd Daniel-Johnson, #755, Lavel QC H7T 2S3, Canada — Singer

Dion, Michel
33 Mulrain Way, Bluffton SC 29910, USA — Ice Hockey Player

Dionisi, Stefano
Media Art Mgmt, C/ Castelló 82, 2 Derecha, 28006 Madrid, Spain — Actor

Dionne, Marcel E
4424 Montrose Road, Niagara Falls ON L2H 1K2, Canada — Ice Hockey Player

Diop, Bineta
Femmes Africa Solidarite, 8 Rue du Vieux-Billard, Box 5037, 1211 Geneva 11, Switzerland — Human Rights Activist

Diop, DeSagana N
4300 Haddonfield Road, #309, Pennsauken NJ 8109, USA — Basketball Player

DiOrio, Nicholas (Nick)
273 Clark St, Lemoyne PA 17043, USA — Soccer Player

Diorio, Ronald M (Ron)
2 White Oak Lane, Waterbury CT 06705, USA — Baseball Player

DiPasquale, James
Gorfaine/Schwartz, 4111 W Alameda Ave, #509, Burbank CA 91505 USA — Composer

Dipino, Frank M
5479 Pebble Beach Dr, Camillus NY 13031, USA — Baseball Player

Dipoto, Gerald P (Jerry)
15130 E Camelview Dr, Fountain Hills AZ 85268, USA — Baseball Player

DiPrete, Edward D
555 Wilbur Ave, Cranston RI 02921, USA — Governor, RI

Dirda, Michael
Washington Post, Editorial Dept, 1150 15th St NW, Washington DC 20071 USA — Journalist

Dirie, Waris
London Mgmt, 2-4 Noel St, London W1V 3RB, England — Model, Human Rights Activist, Actress

Dirk, Robert
4441 Lee Ave, Groves TX 77619, USA — Ice Hockey Player

Dirnt, Mike
P M C, 5900 Wilshire Blvd, #1720, Los Angeles CA 90036, USA — Bassist (Green Day)

Disarcina, Gary T
141 Martingale Lane, Plymouth MA 2360, USA — Baseball Player

Dischinger, Terry G
1739 Oak Ave, Northbrook IL 60062, USA — Basketball Player

Dishman, Cris E
5019 Mariposa Circle, Fresno TX 77545, USA — Football Player

Dishman, Gleneig E (Glenn)
5400 Fairway Dr, San Jose CA 95127, USA — Baseball Player

Diskin, Ben
C E S D, 10635 Santa Monica Blvd, #130, Los Angeles CA 90025 USA — Actor

Disl, Ursula (Uschi)
Powerplay Mgmt, Seepromenade 53, 14467 Gross Glienicke, Germany — Biathlete, Cross Country Skier

Disney, Anthea
News America Corp, 1211 Ave of Americas, #700, New York NY 10036, USA — Editor

Disney, William		Speed Skater
1610 Kirk Dr, Lake Havasu City AZ 86404, USA		
DiSpirito, Rocco		Chef, Restauranteur
Linda Lisco Mgmt, 360 E Randolph St, #3203, Chicago IL 60601, USA		
DiStefano, Andrea		Actor
W M E Entertainment, 9601 Wilshire Blvd, #300, Beverly Hills CA 90210 USA		
DiStefano, Philip P		Educator
University of Colorado, Chancellor's Office, 914 Broadway St, Boulder CO 80309, USA		
Disterheft, Brandi		Bassist, Composer
Agency Group Ltd, 1880 Century Park E, #711, Los Angeles CA 90067 USA		
Distler, Natalie		Actress
A P A Talent/Literary Agency, 405 S Beverly Dr, #300, Beverly Hills CA 90212 USA		
DiSuvero, Mark		Sculptor
PO Box 2218, Astoria NY 11102, USA		
Ditka, Michael K (Mike)		Football Player, Coach, Sportscaster
161 E Chicago Ave, #39F, Chicago IL 60611, USA		
Ditmar, Arthur J (Art)		Baseball Player
6687 Wisteria Dr, Myrtle Beach SC 29588, USA		
Dittl, Ursula		Sculptor
216 Munsel Creek Road, Florence OR 97439, USA		
Dittmer, Andreas		Canoeing Athlete
Fischerbank 5, 17033 Neubrandenburg, Germany		
Dittmer, Edward C		Space Scientist
702 Old Mescalero Road, Tularosa NM 88352, USA		
Dittmer, John D (Jack)		Baseball Player
200 S Main St, Elkader IA 52043, USA		
Ditz, Nancy		Track Athlete
524 Moore Road, Woodside CA 94062, USA		
Divac, Vlade		Basketball Player
811 Haverford Ave, Pacific Palisades CA 90272, USA		
Divakaruni, Chitra Banerjee		Writer
Doubleday Press, 1745 Broadway, New York NY 10019 USA		
Divoff, Andrew		Actor
Marshak/Zachary Co, 8840 Wilshire Blvd, #100, Beverly Hills CA 90211 USA		
Dix, Drew D		Vietnam War Army Hero (CMH)
HC 68, Box 70, Mimbres NM 88049, USA		
Dixit, Avinash K		Economist
36 Gordon Way, Princeton NJ 08540, USA		
Dixit, Madhuri		Actress
Vijaydeep, #300, Iris Park, Juhu, Mumbai MS 400049, India		
Dixon, Alan J		Senator, IL
7606 Foley Dr, Belleville IL 62223, USA		
Dixon, Alesha		Singer (Mis-Teeq)
Independent Talent Group, Oxford House, 76 Oxford St, London W1D 1BS, England		
Dixon, Becky		Sportscaster
ABC-TV, Sports Dept, 77 W 66th St, New York NY 10023 USA		
Dixon, Blake		Drummer (Saving Abel)
Virgin Records, 338 N Foothill Road, Beverly Hills CA 90210 USA		
Dixon, Calvert R (Cal)		Football Player
179 Las Palmas, Merritt Island FL 32953, USA		
Dixon, Craig		Track Athlete
10630 Wellworth Ave, Los Angeles CA 90024, USA		
Dixon, D Jeremy		Architect
44 Gloucester Ave, #6C, London NW1 8JD, England		
Dixon, David T		Football Player
4795 W 131 1/2 St, Savage MN 55378, USA		
Dixon, Donna		Actress
Applied Action Research, 859 N Hollywood Way, #497, Burbank CA 91505, USA		
Dixon, Hanford		Football Player
2034 Acadia Trace, Westlake OH 44145, USA		
Dixon, Jack E		Biochemist
Howard Hughes Medical Institute, 4000 Jones Bridge Road, Chevy Chase MD 20815, USA		
Dixon, Jamie		Basketball Coach
University of Pittsburgh, Athletic Dept, Pittsburgh PA 15260, USA		
Dixon, Kenneth J (Ken)		Baseball Player
4317 Highview Ave, Baltimore MD 21229, USA		
Dixon, Larry		Drag Racing Driver
Willow Oak Court, Avon IN 46123, USA		
Dixon, Leslie		Writer, Producer, Director
Creative Artists Agency, 2000 Ave of Stars, #100, Los Angeles CA 90067 USA		
Dixon, Mark K		Football Player
4016 Ivy Lane, Kitty Hawk NC 27949, USA		
Dixon, Michael		Actor
Markham & Froggatt, Julian House, 4 Windmill St, London W1P 1HF, England		
Dixon, Randolph C (Randy)		Football Player
9910 Summerlakes Dr, Carmel IN 46032, USA		
Dixon, Rodney P (Rod)		Track Athlete
22 Entrican Ave, Remuera, Auckland 1050, New Zealand		
Dixon, Ronnie C		Football Player
1440 W Kemper Road, #510, Cincinnati OH 45240, USA		
Dixon, Scott R		Auto Racing Driver
7161 Zionville Road, Indianapolis IN 45250, USA		
Dixon, Steven R (Steve)		Baseball Player
6510 Hollow Tree Road, Louisville KY 40228, USA		
Dixon, Thomas E (Tom)		Baseball Player
2945 Delaney St, Orlando FL 32806, USA		
Dixon, Thomas F		Aerospace Engineer
1761 Cuba Island Lane, Hayes VA 23072, USA		
Dixon, Tony		Football Player
4588 Gibson Dr, Bessemer AL 35022, USA		
Dixon, Zachary		Football Player
19365 Hottinger Circle, Germantown MD 20874, USA		
Dizon, Jesse		Actor
PO Box 572105, Tarzana CA 91357, USA		
DJ Babu		Rap Artist (Dilated Peoples)
W M E Entertainment, 9601 Wilshire Blvd, #300, Beverly Hills CA 90210 USA		

DJ Champion
Agency Group Ltd, 142 W 57th St, #600, New York NY 10019 USA — DJ Musician

DJ Clue
Roc-A-Fella Records, 825 8th Ave, #2900, New York NY 10019, USA — DJ Musician

DJ Diesel
International Talent Booking, Ariel House, 74A Charlotte St, #100 London W1T 4QJ, England — DJ Musician (X-Press 2)

DJ Enuff
J L Entertainment, 18653 Ventura Blvd, #340, Tarzana CA 91356 USA — DJ Musician

DJ Green Lantern
Central Entertainment Group, 166 5th Ave, #400, New York NY 10010, USA — DJ Musician

DJ Jazzy Jeff
Coast to Coast Entertainment, 8671 Wilshire Blvd, Beverly Hills, CA 90211, USA — Rap Artist

DJ Kool
Big Bloc Entertainment, 93 Yorke Road, 1-619, Jenkintown PA 19046, USA — DJ Musician, Rap Artist

DJ Kool Herc
Kool Herc Productions, PO Box 20472, Huntington Station NY 11746, USA — Rap Artist

DJ Magic Mike
Entertainment Artists, PO Box 120824, Nashville TN 37212 USA — DJ Musician

DJ Muggs
Golath Mgmt, 151 Lafayette St, #600, New York NY 10013, USA — Rap Artist (Cypress Hill)

DJ Pam
Windish Agency, 1658 N Milwaukee Ave, #211, Chicago IL 60647, USA — DJ Musician (Coup)

DJ Premier
Richard Walters, PO Box 2789, Toluca Lake CA 91610 USA — Rap Artist (Gang Starr)

DJ Quik
Stampede Mgmt, 12530 Beatrice St, Los Angeles CA 90066, USA — Rap Artist, Record Producer

DJ Rocky
International Talent Booking, Ariel House, 74A Charlotte St, #100 London W1T 4QJ, England — DJ Musician (X-Press 2)

DJ Shadow
Universal/Island Records, 1755 Broadway, #600, New York NY 10019, USA — Rap Artist

DJ Spooky
Music & Art Mgmt, 9 W Walnut St, #2D, Asheville NC 28801, USA — Electronica Musician

DJ Total Eclipse
Agency Group Ltd, 142 W 57th St, #600, New York NY 10019 USA — Rap Artist (X-Ecutioners), DJ

DJ Total K-Oss
Green Light Talent Agency, PO Box 3172, Beverly Hills CA 90212 USA — Rap Artist (Above the Law)

DJ Virman
Stampede Mgmt, 12530 Beatrice St, Los Angeles CA 90066, USA — Singer (Far East Movement)

Djalili, Omid
Independent Talent Group, Oxford House, 76 Oxford St, London W1D 1BS, England — Actor

Djawadi, Ramin
Gorfaine/Schwartz, 4111 W Alameda Ave, #509, Burbank CA 91505 USA — Composer

Djebar, Assia
13 University Place, #621, New York, New York NY 1003, USA — Writer

Djerassi, Carl
2325 Bear Gulch Road, Redwood City CA 94062, USA — Inventor (Oral Contraceptive)

Djerassi, Isaac
2034 Delancey Place, Philadelphia PA 19103, USA — Physician

Djokovic, Novak
Association of Tennis Professionals, 200 Tournament Road, Ponte Vedra Beach FL 32082 USA — Tennis Player

Djou, Charles K
Majority Group LLP, 1701 Pennsylvania Ave NW, #300, Washington DC 20006, USA — Representative, HI

Dlamini, A Themba
Prime Minister's Office, PO Box 395, Mbabane, Swaziland — Prime Minister, Swaziland

D'Lyn, Shae
Talent House,3000 Olympic Blvd, #2226, Santa Monica CA 90404, USA — Actress

Dmitriev, Artur
Russian Skating Federation, Luchneksaia Nab 8, 119871 Moscow, Russia — Figure Skater

DMX
The Firm, 2049 Century Park E, #2550, Los Angeles CA 90067 USA — Rap Artist (Ruff Ryders), Actor

Do Amaral, Diogo F
Ave Fontes Pereira de Melo 35, #13A, 1050 Lisbon, Portugal — Government Official, Portugal

Do Carma Silveira, Maria
Prime Minister's Office, CP 38, Sao Tome, Sao Tome & Principe — Prime Minister, Sao Tome & Principe

Do Muoi
Communist Party, 1 Hoang Van Thu, Hanoi, Vietnam — Secretary General, Vietnam

Do Nascimento, Alexandre Cardinal
Arcebispado, CP 87, 1230C Luanda, Angola — Religious Leader

Doak, Gary W
47 Highland Ave, Lynnfield MA 1940, USA — Ice Hockey Player

Doan, Shane A
9820 E Thompson Peak Parkway, #725, Scottsdale AZ 85255, USA — Ice Hockey Player

Doane, Melanie
Live Tour Artists, 1451 White Oak Blvd, Oakville ON L6H 4R9, Canada — Singer, Songwriter

Dobbek, Daniel J (Dan)
4042 SE Yamhill St, Portland OR 97214, USA — Baseball Player

Dobbin, Brian
5075 Shiloh Line, Petrolia ON N0N 1R0, Canada — Ice Hockey Player

Dobbs, Greg S
2255 Richey Dr, La Canada Flintridge CA 91011, USA — Baseball Player

Dobbs, Louis C (Lou)
Fox-TV, News Dept, 205 E 67th St, New York NY 10065 USA — Commentator

Dobbs, Mattiwilda
1101 S Arlington Ridge Road, #301, Arlington VA 22202, USA — Opera Singer

Dobek, Michelle
292 Chicopee St, Chicopee MA 01013, USA — Golfer

Dobey, James K
Carmel Valley Manor, 8545 Carmel Valley Road, Carmel CA 93923, USA — Financier

Dobie, Alan
Pontus Molash, Kent CT4 8HW, England — Actor

Dobkins, Carl, Jr
5618 Harbourside Dr, Mason OH 45040, USA — Singer

Dobler, Conrad F
6227 W 126th Terrace, Leawood KS 66209, USA — Football Player

Dobo, Kata
Paradigm Agency, 360 N Crescent Dr, North Building, Beverly Hills CA 90210 USA — Actress

Dobrev, Nina — Actress
Noble Caplan Abrams, 1260 Yonge St, #200, Toronto ON M4T 1W6, Canada
Dobrin, Tory — Choreographer, Dance Executive
Les Ballets Trockadero de Monte Carlo, Box 46 Cathedral Station, New York City, NY 10025, USA
Dobslow, Bill — Singer (Rivieras)
945 Handlebar Road, Mishawaka IN 46544, USA
Dobson, Anita — Actress
I T G, 1 Stedham Place, London W1CA 1HU, England
Dobson, Charles T (Chuck) — Baseball Player
4208 Locust St, Kansas City MO 64110, USA
Dobson, Dominic — Auto Racing Executive
PacWest Racing Group, PO Box 1717, Bellevue WA 98009, USA
Dobson, FeFe — Singer, Songwriter
Island Records, 925 8th St, New York NY 10019 USA
Dobson, Helen — Golfer
7638 Eagle Creek Dr, Sarasota FL 34243, USA
Dobson, James C — Religious Leader
Focus on the Family, 8605 Explorer Dr, Colorado Springs CO 80920, USA
Dobson, Kevin — Actor
Rothman/Patino/Andrés Entertainment, 4370 Tujunga Ave, #120, Studio City CA 91604, USA
Dobson, Peter — Actor
Shelter Entertainment, 9454 Wilshire Blvd, #715, Beverly Hills CA 90212 USA
Dobtcheff, Vernon — Actor
U B B A, 1 Rue Elzevir, 75003 Paris, France
Dockery, Derrick D — Football Player
21522 Wild Timber Court, Broadlands VA 20148, USA
Dockery, John P — Football Player
360 Furman St, #1208, Brooklyn NY 11201, USA
Dockery, Michelle — Actress
Hamilton Hodell, 66-68 Margaret St, London W1W 8SR, England
Dockett, Darnell — Football Player
2197 E Teakwood Place, Chandler AZ 85249, USA
Dockser, Amy — Journalist
Wall Street Journal, Editorial Dept, 1 World Financial Center, New York NY 10281, USA
Dockson, Robert R — Financier
1301 Collingwood Place, Los Angeles CA 90069, USA
Dockstader, Frederick J — Museum Executive
165 W 66th St, New York NY 10023, USA
Doctorow, Edgar Lawrence (E L) — Writer
333 E 57th St, #118, New York NY 10022, USA
Doda, Carol — Exotic Dancer, Actress
PO Box 387, Fremont CA 94537, USA
Dodd, Christina — Writer
Pocket Books, 1230 Ave of Americas, New York NY 10020 USA
Dodd, Deryl — Singer, Songwriter
Hook Entertainment, 26033 Mulholland Highway, Calabasas CA 91302, USA
Dodd, Kenneth A — Actor, Comedian
Michael O'Mara Books, 9 Lion Yard, Tremadoc Road, London SW4 7NQ, England
Dodd, Lois — Artist
30 E 2nd St, New York NY 10003, USA
Dodd, Michael T (Mike) — Volleyball Player
1017 Manhattan Ave, Manhattan Beach CA 90266, USA
Dodd, Patty Orozco — Volleyball Player
1017 Manhattan Ave, Manhattan Beach CA 90266, USA
Dodd, Robert W — Baseball Player
3467 Overhill Dr, Frisco TX 75034, USA
Dodd, Thomas M (Tom) — Baseball Player
3735 NE Shaver St, Portland OR 97212, USA
Dodds, Megan — Actress
Independent Talent Group, Oxford House, 76 Oxford St, London W1D 1BS, England
Dodds, Trevor — Golfer
13103 Beaver Dam Road, Saint Louis MO 63131, USA
Dodge, Brooks — Skier
PO Box C, Jackson NH 03846, USA
Dodge, Charles M — Composer
Brooklyn College, Center for Computer Music, Brooklyn NY 11210, USA
Dodge, Dedrick A — Football Player
1109 Bowlin Dr, Locust Grove GA 30248, USA
Dodge, Geoffrey A — Publisher
Business Week, Publisher's Office, 1221 Ave of Americas, New York NY 10020, USA
Dodge, Marcia Milgrom — Director, Choreographer
Abrams Artists, 275 7th Ave, #2600, New York NY 10001, USA
Dodik, Milorad — Prime Minister, Serb Republic
Prime Minister's Office, Nemanjina 11, 11000 Belgrade, Serbia
Dodrill, Dale F — Football Player
2579 S Independence St, Lakewood CO 80227, USA
Dods, Walter A, Jr — Financier
Banc West Corp, PO Box 3200, Honolulu HI 96847, USA
Dodson, Patrick N (Pat) — Baseball Player
4104 Holly Hill Road, Mebane NC 27302, USA
Doe, John — Actor
TalentWorks, 3500 W Olive Ave, #1400, Burbank CA 91505 USA
Doelling, Fred F — Football Player
60 South St, Valparaiso IN 46383, USA
Doering, Christopher P (Chris) — Football Player
3723 SW 20th St, Gainesville FL 32608, USA
Doering-Powell, Mark — Cinematographer
Paradigm Agency, 360 N Crescent Dr, North Building, Beverly Hills CA 90210 USA
Doerr, Robert P (Bobby) — Baseball Player
94449 Territorial Highway, Junction City OR 97448, USA
Doherty, John H — Baseball Player
202 Alpine Place, Tuckahoe NY 10707, USA
Doherty, John M — Baseball Player
109 Wakefield St, Reading MA 01867, USA
Doherty, Matt — Basketball Player, Coach
Southern Methodist University, Athletic Dept, Dallas TX 75275, USA

Doherty, Pete — Singer (Libertines, Babyshambles)
Primary Talent International, 10-11 Jockey's Fields, London C1R 4BN, England , USA
Doherty, Peter C — Nobel Medicine Laureate
67 Madison Ave, #417, Memphis TN 38103, USA
Doherty, Shannen — Actress, Model
Collective, 8383 Wilshire Blvd, #1050, Beverly Hills CA 90211 USA
Dohle, Markus — Businessman, Publisher
Random House, 1745 Broadway, #1800, New York NY 10019 USA
Dohmann, Scott — Baseball Player
3222 W Paxton Ave, Tampa FL 33611, USA
Dohring, Jason — Actor
Innovative Artists, 1505 10th St, Santa Monica CA 90401 USA
Dohrmann, Angela — Actress
Innovative Artists, 235 Park Ave S, #1000, New York NY 10003 USA
Dohrmann, George — Journalist
Saint Paul Pioneer Press, Editorial Dept, 345 Cedar St, Saint Paul MN 55101, USA
Doi, Takako — Government Official, Japan
Socialist Democratic Party, 1-8-1 Nagatacho, Chiyodaku, Tokyo 100 8910, Japan
Doi, Takao — Astronaut, Japan
Japanese Aerospace Exploration Agency, 2-1-1 Sengen, Tsukuba-shi, Ibaraki 305 8505, Japan
Doig, Ivan — Writer
University of Washington, English Dept, Seattle WA 98195, USA
Doig, Jason — Ice Hockey Player
2153 Broderick Ave, Duarte CA 91010, USA
Doig, Lexa — Actress
TalentWorks, 3500 W Olive Ave, #1400, Burbank CA 91505 USA
Doig, Stephen G (Steve) — Football Player
PO Box 206, North Reading MA 01864, USA
Doillon, Lou — Actress, Model
Gersh Agency, 41 Madison Ave, #3301, New York NY 10010 USA
Dokic, Jelena — Tennis Player
Octagon Worldwide, 7100 Forest Ave, #201, Richmond VA 23226 USA
Dokish, Wanita — Baseball Player
2480 S Grande Blvd, Greensburg PA 15601, USA
Dokiwari, Duncan — Boxer
Thell Torrence Enterprises, 5449 S Eastern Ave, #3, Las Vegas NV 89119, USA
Dokovic, Novak (Nole) — Tennis Player
Studio Magnet, Milan Marijanac, Sime Solaje 55A, 21410 Futog, Serbia , USA
Dolan, Charles F — Businessman
Cablevision Systems Corp, 1111 Stewart Ave, Bethpage NY 11714, USA
Dolan, James — Businessman
Cablevision Systems Corp, 1111 Stewart Ave, Bethpage NY 11714, USA
Dolan, Julie — Actress
Laura Lichen Mgmt, PO Box 33051, Granada Hills CA 91394, USA
Dolan, Louise A — Physicist
University of North Carolina, Physics Dept, Chapel Hill NC 27599, USA
Dolan, Mary Anne — Editor
M A D Inc, 1033 Gayley Ave, #205, Los Angeles CA 90024, USA
Dolan, Michael P — Government Official
Internal Revenue Service, 1111 Constitution Ave NW, Washington DC 20224, USA
Dolan, Timothy M Cardinal — Religious Leader
Archdiocese of New York, 1011 First St, New York NY 10022, USA
Dolan, Tom — Swimmer
12 S Manchester St, Arlington VA 22204, USA
Dolan, Xavier — Actor
W M E Entertainment, 9601 Wilshire Blvd, #300, Beverly Hills CA 90210 USA
Dolbin, John T (Jack) — Football Player
1775 Howard Ave, Pottsville PA 17901, USA
Dolby, Raymond M (Ray) — Inventor, Sound Engineer
Dolby Laboratories, 100 Potrero Ave, San Francisco CA 94103, USA
Dolby, Thomas — Singer, Songwriter
International Talent Group, 729 7th Ave, #1600, New York NY 10019 USA
Dolce, Domenico — Fashion Designer
Dolce & Gabbana, Via Santa Cecilia 7, 20122 Milan, Italy
Dold, R Bruce — Journalist
501 N Park Road, #HSE, La Grange Park IL 60526, USA
Dole, Elizabeth H — Secretary, Transportation & Labor
Wings of Hope, 18370 Wings of Hope Blvd, Saint Louis MO 63005, USA
Dole, Kathryn — Landscape Architect
512 Brinkerhoff Ave, Santa Barbara CA 93101, USA
Dole, Robert J — Senator, KS
Verner Liipfert Berhard, 1200 19th St NW, Washington DC 20036, USA
Doleac, Michael S — Basketball Player
1155 Old Rail Lane, Park City UT 84098, USA
Doleman, Christopher J (Chris) — Football Player
1025 Leadenhall St, Alpharetta GA 30022, USA
Dolenz, Ami — Actress
K C Talent, 2408 W 8th Ave, Vancouver BC V6K 2B1, Canada
Dolenz, Micky — Actor, Singer, Drummer (Monkees)
Amsel Eisenstadt Frazier, 5055 Wilshire Blvd, #865, Los Angeles CA 90036 USA
Dolgen, Jonathan L — Businessman
Viacom Inc, 1515 Broadway, New York NY 10036, USA
D'Oliveira, Damon — Actor, Film Producer
LeFeaver Talent Agency, 2 College St, #202, Toronto ON M5G 1K5, Canada
Doll, W Richard S — Epidemiologist
12 Rawlinson Road, Oxford OX2 6UE, England
Dollar, Linda — Volleyball Coach
Southwest Missouri State University, Athletic Dept, Springfield MO 65804, USA
Dollard, Christopher Edward — Actor
TalentWorks, 3500 W Olive Ave, #1400, Burbank CA 91505 USA
Dolley, Jason S — Actor
Paradigm Agency, 360 N Crescent Dr, North Building, Beverly Hills CA 90210 USA
Dolman, Bob — Director, Writer, Actor
United Talent Agency, 9336 Civic Center Dr, Beverly Hills CA 90210 USA
Dolmayan, John — Drummer (System of a Down)
Velvet Hammer Music, 9014 Melrose Ave, West Hollywood CA 90069, USA

Domar, Evsey D — Economist
264 Heath's Bridge Road, Concord MA 01742, USA

Dombasle, Arielle — Actress
Agence Intertalent, 5 Rue Clement Marot, 75008 Paris, France

Dombroski, Paul M — Football Player
19122 Beckett Dr, Odessa FL 33556, USA

Dombrovskis, Vladis — Prime Minister, Latvia
Prime Minister's Office, Brivibus Bulv 36, Riga 226170 PDP, Latvia

Dombrowski, James M (Jim) — Football Player
220 Evangeline Dr, Mandeville LA 70471, USA

Domenichelli, Hnat A — Ice Hockey Player
H C Lugano, Casella Postale 4226, 6904 Lugano, Switzerland

Domi, Tie — Ice Hockey Player
1-7357 Woodbine Ave, #415, Markham ON L3R 6L3, Canada

Dominczyk, Dagmara — Actress
Paradigm Agency, 360 N Crescent Dr, North Building, Beverly Hills CA 90210 USA

Dominczyk, Marika — Actress
I C M Partners, 10250 Constellation Blvd, #900, Los Angeles CA 90067 USA

Domingo, Placido — Opera Singer
2728 Thomson Ave, #712, Long Island City NY 11101, USA

Dominguez, Adolfo — Fashion Designer
Polingono Industrial Calle 4, 32901 San Ciprian de Vinas, Ourense, Spain

Dominguez, Mario — Auto Racing Driver
Herdez Competition, 57 Gasoline Alley, #A, Indianapolis IN 46222, USA

Dominik, Andrew — Director
Creative Artists Agency, 2000 Ave of Stars, #100, Los Angeles CA 90067 USA

Dominis, John — Photographer
252 W 102nd St, #4, New York NY 10025, USA

Domino, Antoine (Fats) — Singer, Pianist
9 Wedgwood Court, Harvey LA 70058, USA

Dominy, Charles E (Chuck) — Army General
300 Fox Mill Road, Oakton VA 22124, USA

Domracheva, Darya — Biathlete
Biathlon Federation, Karl Marx Ul 10, 1220020 Minsk, Belarus

Domres, Martin F (Marty) — Football Player
Deutsche Bank, 1 South St, #2400, Baltimore MD 21202, USA

Donahoe, John — Businessman
eBay, 2125 Hamilton Ave, San Jose CA 95125, USA

Donahue, Ann M — Producer, Writer
W M E Entertainment, 9601 Wilshire Blvd, #300, Beverly Hills CA 90210 USA

Donahue, Elinor — Actress
Scott Stander Assoc, 4533 Van Nuys Blvd, #401, Sherman Oaks CA 91403 USA

Donahue, Heather — Actress
Screen Actors Guild, 5757 Wilshire Blvd, Los Angeles CA 90036, USA

Donahue, Kenneth — Museum Executive
245 S Westgate Ave, Los Angeles CA 90049, USA

Donahue, Phil — Entertainer
244 Madison Ave, #707, New York NY 10016, USA

Donahue, Terry — Football Coach, Sportscaster
707 N Bayfront, Newport Beach CA 92662, USA

Donahue, Thomas R — Labor Leader
2425 L St NW, #326, Washington DC 20037, USA

Donaire, Nonito — Boxer
Golden Boy Promotions, 626 Wilshire Blvd, #350, Los Angeles CA 90017 USA

Donald, Jason T — Baseball Player
Cleveland Indians, Jacobs Field, 2401 Ontario St, Cleveland OH 44115 USA

Donald, Kirkland H — Navy Admiral
Commander, Nuclear Propulsion, Washington Navy Yard, Washington DC 20374, USA

Donald, Luke — Golfer
8 Bristol Road, Northfield IL 60093, USA

Donald, Mike — Golfer
2400 NW 65th Way, Hollywood FL 33024, USA

Donaldson, James L, III — Basketball Player
2843 34th Ave W, Seattle WA 98199, USA

Donaldson, Jeffery M (Jeff) — Football Player
PO Box 270634, Fort Collins CO 80527, USA

Donaldson, Lily — Model
I M G Models, 304 Park Ave S, #PH-North, New York NY 10010 USA

Donaldson, Mark G — Afghanistan War Hero (VC)
Victoria Cross Assn, Old Admiralty Building, London SW1A 2BL, England

Donaldson, Roger — Director
Cameron Creswell, 61 Marlborough St, #700, Surry Hills NSW 2010, Australia

Donaldson, Samuel A (Sam) — Commentator
1125 Crest Lane, McLean VA 22101, USA

Donaldson, Simon K — Mathematician
Imperial College, 180 Queen's Gate, London SW7 2BZ, England

Donan, Holland R (Hollie) — Football Player
213 Southwinds, Tinton Falls NJ 7753, USA

Donat, Peter — Actor
Gersh Agency, 9465 Wilshire Blvd, #600, Beverly Hills CA 90212 USA

Donatelli, Clark — Ice Hockey Player
1101 Curtis Corner Road, Wakefield RI 02879, USA

Donath, Helen — Opera Singer
Hannagret Bueker Agentur, Fuhsestr 2, 30419 Hannover, Germany

Donato, Marc — Actor
C E S D, 10635 Santa Monica Blvd, #130, Los Angeles CA 90025 USA

Donato, Ted — Ice Hockey Player
34 Whitcomb Road, Scituate MA 02066, USA

Done, Kenneth S (Ken) — Graphic Artist
17 Thurlow St, Redfern NSW 2016, Australia

Donegan, Dan — Guitarist (Disturbed)
Agency Group Ltd, 142 W 57th St, #600, New York NY 10019 USA

Donella, Chad E — Actor
TalentWorks, 3500 W Olive Ave, #1400, Burbank CA 91505 USA

Donelly, Tanya — Singer, Songwriter
Helter Skelter, 347-353 Chiswick High Road, London W4 4HS, England

Donen, Stanley	Director
30 W 63rd St, #25, New York NY 10023, USA	
Doniger, Wendy	Theologian, Historian
1319 E 55th St, Chicago IL 60615, USA	
Donlan, Yolande	Actress
11 Mellina Place, Belgravia, London NW8 9SA, England	
Donleavy, James Patrick (J P)	Writer
Levington Park, Mullingar, County Westmeath, Ireland	
Donlon, Roger H C	Vietnam War Army Hero (CMH)
2101 Wilson Ave, Leavenworth KS 66048, USA	
Donnalley, Kevin E	Football Player
8910 Dove Stand Lane, Charlotte NC 28226, USA	
Donnalley, W Frederick (Rick)	Football Player
10408 Buck Brush Road, Cheyenne WY 82009, USA	
Donnan, Jim	Football Coach
ESPN-TV, ESPN Plaza, 935 Middle St, Bristol CT 06010 USA	
Donnellan, Declan	Director
Cheek by Jowl Theatre Co, Aveline St, London SW11 5DQ, England	
Donnelly, Brendan K	Baseball Player
2815 E Arrowhead Trail, Gilbert AZ 85297, USA	
Donnelly, Declan	Actor
B/W/R, 9100 Wilshire Blvd, #500W, Beverly Hills CA 90212 USA	
Donnelly, Gord	Ice Hockey Player
110 Ave Claude, Dorval QC H9S 3A7, Canada	
Donnelly, John J	Navy Admiral
Commander, Submarine Command Atlantic, 7958 Blandy Road, Norfolk VA 23511 USA	
Donnelly, Rick	Football Player
1796 Danforth Dr, Marietta GA 30062, USA	
Donnelly, Russell J	Physicist
2175 Olive St, Eugene OR 97405, USA	
Donnelly, Tanya	Singer, Guitarist
High Road Touring, 751 Bridgeway, #200, Sausalito CA 94965 USA	
Donnels, Chris B	Baseball Player
5 Stone Pine, Aliso Viejo CA 92656, USA	
Donner, Jorn J	Director
Pohjoisranta 12, 00170 Helsinki 17, Finland	
Donner, Richard D	Director
1444 Forest Knoll, Los Angeles CA 90069, USA	
D'Onofrio, Vincent	Actor
Collective, 8383 Wilshire Blvd, #1050, Beverly Hills CA 90211 USA	
Donoghue, Denis	Writer
Gaybrook, North Ave, Mount Merrion, County Dublin, Ireland	
Donoghue, Mary Agnes	Writer
Gersh Agency, 9465 Wilshire Blvd, #600, Beverly Hills CA 90212 USA	
Donoghue, Paul	Singer, Bassist (Glasvegas)
Sony Music, 9 Derry St, London W8 5HY, England	
Donohoe, Amanda	Actress
Artist Rights Group, 4 Great Portland Place, London W1W 8PA, England	
Donohoe, Michael P (Mike)	Football Player
1110 E Acacia Circle, Litchfield Park AZ 85340, USA	
Donohoe, Peter H	Concert Pianist
82 Hampton Lane, Solihull, West Midlands B91 2RS, England	
Donohue, James T (Jim)	Baseball Player
16 Huntleigh Downs, Saint Louis MO 63131, USA	
Donohue, Leon	Football Player
1904 Bechelli Lane, Redding CA 96002, USA	
Donohue, Peter M	Educator
Villanova University, President's Office, 800 Lancaster Ave, Villanova PA 19085, USA	
Donohue, Thomas J (Tom)	Baseball Player
249 Liberty Ave, Westbury NY 11590, USA	
Donohue, Timothy	Businessman
Nextel Communications, 2001 Edmund Halley Dr, Reston VA 20191, USA	
Donose, Ruxandra	Opera Singer
Columbia Artists Mgmt Inc, 1790 Broadway, #702, New York NY 10019 USA	
Donovan	Singer, Songwriter, Actor
PO Box 1119, London SW9 9JW, England	
Donovan, Anne	Basketball Player, Coach
138 Ridge Road, Nutley NJ 7110, USA	
Donovan, Arthur J (Art), Jr	Football Player
8300 Alston Road, Towson MD 21204, USA	
Donovan, Brian	Journalist
Newsday, Editorial Dept, 235 Pinelawn Road, Melville NY 11747, USA	
Donovan, Daisy	Actress
Independent Talent Group, Oxford House, 76 Oxford St, London W1D 1BS, England	
Donovan, Elisa	Actress
S M S Talent, 8383 Wilshire Blvd, #230, Beverly Hills CA 90211 USA	
Donovan, Francis R (Frank)	Navy Admiral
9216 Dellwood Dr, Vienna VA 22180, USA	
Donovan, H Harry	Basketball Player
8303 Bayonet Point Court, #C, Gainesville FL 32608, USA	
Donovan, Jason S	Singer, Actor
United Agents, 12-26 Lexington St, London W1F 0LE, England	
Donovan, Jeffrey	Actor
Paradigm Agency, 360 Park Ave S, #1600, New York NY 10010 USA	
Donovan, Landon	Soccer Player
Los Angeles Galaxy, Home Depot Center, 18400 Avalon Blvd, Carson CA 90746 USA	
Donovan, Martin	Actor
Parseghian/Planco, 388 2nd Ave, #506, New York, NY 10010 USA	
Donovan, Patrick E (Pat)	Football Player
113 S Prairiesmoke Circle, Whitefish MT 59937, USA	
Donovan, Raymond J	Secretary, Labor
1600 Paterson Park Road, Secaucus NJ 07094, USA	
Donovan, Shaun L S	Secretary, Housing & Urban Development
Housing & Urban Development Department, 451 7th SW, Washington DC 20410 USA	
Donovan, Tate	Actor
Gersh Agency, 9465 Wilshire Blvd, #600, Beverly Hills CA 90212 USA	

D

Donen - Donovan

Donovan, Trevor Michael Yanni Mgmt, 1642 N Fairfax Ave, Los Angeles CA 90046, USA	Actor
Donovan, William J (Billy) 8515 SW 31st Ave, Gainesville FL 32608, USA	Basketball Player, Coach
Donowho, Ryan Schiff Co, 8440 Warner Dr, #B1, Culver City CA 90232 USA	Actor, Producer
Donzelli, Valerie U B B A, 6 Rue de Braque, 75003 Paris, France	Director
Doo Ri Chung Doo Ri Fashions, 831 Madison Ave, New York NY 10021, USA	Fashion Designer
Doody, Alison Commercial Agency, 16 Harcourt Terrace, London SW1W 9JR, England	Actress
Doolan, Wendy 3353 Turnberry Dr, Lakeland FL 33803, USA	Golfer
Dooley, David M University of Rhode Island, President's Office, 6 Rhodney Ram Way, Kingston RI 02881, USA	Educator
Dooley, James M (Jim) Gorfaine/Schwartz, 4111 W Alameda Ave, #509, Burbank CA 91505 USA	Composer
Dooley, Paul Innovative Artists, 1505 10th St, Santa Monica CA 90401 USA	Actor
Dooley, Taylor M One Entertainment, 12 W 57th St, #PH 1, New York NY 10019 USA	Actress
Dooley, Thomas 20 Via Paquete, San Clemente CA 92673, USA	Soccer Player
Dooley, Vincent J (Vince) University of Georgia, Athletic Dept, PO Box 1472, Athens GA 30603, USA	Football Player, Coach, Administrator
Dooling, Keyon L 6001 N Ocean Dr, #302, Hollywood FL 33019, USA	Basketball Player
Doolittle, Eliza Insanity Artists, 5 Little Portland St, London W1W 7JD, England	Singer, Songwriter
Doolittle, Melinda 1524 Braden Circle, Franklin TN 37067, USA	Singer
Doorman, Dana David Binkley, 201 W Big Beaver Road, #500, Troy MI 48084, USA	Golfer
Doornink, Daniel E (Dan) 401 S 12th Ave, Yakima WA 98902, USA	Football Player
Dopson, John R 3337 Old Gambler Road, Finksburg MD 21048, USA	Baseball Player
Dor, Karin Nordliche Munchner Str 43, 82031 Grunwald, Germany	Actress
Doran, William P (Bill) 5720 Grand Legacy Dr, Maineville OH 45039, USA	Baseball Player
Dore, Andre 73 Betsys Lane, Kingston ON K7M 7B6, Canada	Ice Hockey Player
Dore, Jon Gersh Agency, 9465 Wilshire Blvd, #600, Beverly Hills CA 90212 USA	Actor, Comedian
Dore, Ronald Philip 157 Surrenden Road, Brighton, East Sussex BN1 6ZA, England	Sociologist
Dorensky, Sergey L Bryusov Per 8/10, #75, Moscow 103009, Russia	Concert Pianist
Dorey, Jim 105 Aaron Place, Amherstview ON K7N 2A1, Canada	Ice Hockey Player
Dorff, Stephen I C M Partners, 10250 Constellation Blvd, #900, Los Angeles CA 90067 USA	Actor
Dorfman, Ariel Duke University, International Studies Center, 2122 Campus Dr, Durham NC 27708, USA	Writer
Dorfman, David Abrams Artists, 9200 W Sunset Blvd, #1125, West Hollywood CA 90069 USA	Actor
Dorfmeister, Michaela Quellensteig 12, 2763 Neusiedl, Austria	Alpine Skier
Dorgan, Byron L Arent Fox LLP, 1050 Connecticut Ave NW, Washington DC 20036, USA	Senator, ND
Dorian, Antonia 3940 Laurel Canyon Blvd, PO Box 342, Studio City CA 91604, USA	Actress
Dorin, Marie Le Ruisseay, 38190 Laval, France	Biathlete
Dorin-Ballard, Carolyn Del Ballard, Ebonite International, PO Box 746, Hopkinsville KY 42241, USA	Bowler
Dorion, Dan 3910 28th St, Long Island City NY 11101, USA	Ice Hockey Player
Dority, Douglas H United Food/Commercial Workers Union, 1775 K St NW, Washington DC 20006, USA	Labor Leader
Dorman, Dave Rolling Thunder, 405 Windham Trail, Carpentersville IL 60110, USA	Illustrator
Dorman, Lee Entertainment Services International, 6400 Pleasant Park Dr, Chanhassen MN 55317, USA	Bassist (Captain Beyond, Iron Butterfly)
Dormann, Dana 4887 Arlene Place, Pleasanton CA 94566, USA	Golfer
Dormer, Natalie United Agents, 12-26 Lexington St, London W1F 0LE, England	Actress
Dorn, Michael Innovative Artists, 1505 10th St, Santa Monica CA 90401 USA	Actor
Dornan, Jamie Management 360, 9111 Wilshire Blvd, Beverly Hills CA 90210 USA	Actor, Model
Dorney, Keith R 2450 Blucher Valley Road, Sebastopol CA 95472, USA	Football Player
Dornhelm, Robert Paradigm Agency, 360 N Crescent Dr, North Building, Beverly Hills CA 90210 USA	Actor
Dornhoefer, Gary 267 Chestnut Neck Road, Port Republic NJ 08241, USA	Ice Hockey Player
Doronina, Tatyana V Gorky Arts Theater, 22 Tverskoi Blvd, 119146 Moscow, Russia	Actress
Dorough, Howie Mitch Schneider Organization, 14724 Ventura Blvd, #500, Sherman Oaks CA 91403 USA	Singer (Backstreet Boys)
Dorris, Andrew M (Andy) 12391 Ike White Road, Conroe TX 77303, USA	Football Player

Dorris, Derek R
4504 Adobe Dr, Fort Worth TX 76123, USA — Football Player

Dorroh, Jefferson D
10032 136th Ave NE, Kirkland WA 98033, USA — WW II Marine Corps Air Force Hero

Dorrough, Holley Ann
D G I Mgmt, 609 Greenwich St, #600, New York NY 10014, USA — Model

D'Orsay, Brooke
M B S T Entertainment, 345 N Maple Dr, #200, Beverly Hills CA 90210, USA — Actress

Dorsaz, Damien
Artmedia, 20 Ave Rapp, 75007 Paris, France — Actor

Dorsen, Norman
146 Central Park W, New York NY 10023, USA — Attorney

Dorsett, Anthony D (Tony)
Tony Dorsett Foods, 321 High St, Burlington NJ 08016, USA — Football Player

Dorsett, Anthony, Jr
3817 Bowser Ave, #C, Dallas TX 75219, USA — Football Player

Dorsett, Brian R
700 Dobbs Glen St, Terre Haute IN 47803, USA — Baseball Player

Dorsey, Eric H
5 London Court, Teaneck NJ 07666, USA — Football Player

Dorsey, Glenn
4242 NE Edmonson Court, Lees Summit MO 64064, USA — Football Player

Dorsey, Jack
Twitter Inc, 795 Folsom St, #600, San Francisco CA 94107, USA — Businessman

Dorsey, Jacky
1231 S Teal Estates Circle, Fresno TX 77545, USA — Basketball Player

Dorsey, James E (Jim)
335 Elm St, Seekonk MA 02771, USA — Baseball Player

Dorsey, John M
425 Arrowhead Dr, Green Bay WI 54301, USA — Football Player

Dorsey, Kenneth S (Ken)
7108 Presidio Glen, Lakewood Ranch FL 34202, USA — Football Player

Dorsey, Kerris Lilla
Lewis & Beal Talent Agency, 15303 Ventura Blvd, #900, Sherman Oaks CA 91403, USA — Actress

Dorsey, Richard E (Joey)
Houston Rockets, 1730 Jefferson St, Houston TX 77003 USA — Basketball Player

Dorta, Melvin
1351 Cambridge Court, Palmyra PA 17078, USA — Baseball Player

Doshi, Balkkrishna V
14 Shree Sadma Society, Navrangpura, Ahmedabad 380009, India — Architect

Dosoretz, Daniel E
1120 Lee Blvd, Lehigh Acres FL 33936, USA — Physician, Businessman

DosSantos Ramirez, Giovani
Federacion de Futbol, Colima 373 Colonia Roma, Delegacion Cuauhtemoc Mexico DF 06700, Mexico — Soccer Player

DosSantos, Alexandre J M Cardinal
Paco Arquiepiscopal, Avenida Eduardo Mondlane 1448, CP Maputo, Mozambique — Religious Leader

DosSantos, Jose Eduardo
President's Office, Palacio do Povo, Luanda, Angola — President, Angola

Doster, David E
4123 Sugarhill Run, New Haven IN 46774, USA — Baseball Player

Dotel, Octavio E
382 Oakland Road, Lawrenceville GA 30044, USA — Baseball Player

Dotrice, Roy
Lord, 6 Meadow Lane, Leasingham, Sleaford, Lincolnshire NG34 8LL, England — Actor

Dotson, Alphonse A (Al)
Coyues 24 Las Playas, Acapulco 39390, Mexico — Football Player

Dotson, Earl C
1112 Azalea Dr, Longview TX 75601, USA — Football Player

Dotson, Richard E (Rich)
7 Colonel Watson Dr, New Richmond OH 45157, USA — Baseball Player

Dotson, Santana N
PO Box 79134, Houston TX 77279, USA — Football Player

Dotter, Bobby
3630 N Pacific Ave, Chicago IL 60634, USA — Auto, Truck Racing Driver

Dotter, Gary R
7413 Ravenswood Road, Granbury TX 76049, USA — Baseball Player

Dottley, Jason
B/W/R, 9100 Wilshire Blvd, #500W, Beverly Hills CA 90212 USA — Actor

Doty, Mark
Rutgers State University, English Dept, New Brunswick NJ 08903, USA — Writer

Douaihy, Saliba
Vining Road, Windham NY 12496, USA — Artist

Doucet, David
Rosebud Agency, PO Box 170429, San Francisco CA 94117 USA — Singer, Guitarist (BeauSoleil)

Doucet, Michael
Rosebud Agency, PO Box 170429, San Francisco CA 94117 USA — Singer, Fiddler (BeauSoleil)

Doucett, Linda
Michael Slessinger, 8730 W Sunset Blvd, #220W, West Hollywood CA 90069 USA — Actress, Model

Doucette, Jeff
C E S D, 10635 Santa Monica Blvd, #130, Los Angeles CA 90025 USA — Actor

Doufexis, Stella
Kunstler Sekretariat am Gasteig, Rosenheimer Str 52, 81669 Munich, Germany — Opera Singer

Doug, Doug E
Brillstein Entertainment, 375 Greenwich St, New York NY 10013, USA — Actor, Comedian

Dougherty, Dennis A
1817 Bushnell Ave, South Pasadena CA 91030, USA — Chemist

Dougherty, Ed
448 SW Fairway Vista, Port Saint Lucie FL 34986, USA — Golfer

Dougherty, James E (Jim)
102 Pinnacle Court, Kitty Hawk NC 27949, USA — Baseball Player

Dougherty, Joseph
Katz Golden Sullivan Rosenman, 2001 Wilshire Blvd, #400, Santa Monica CA 90403, USA — Producer, Director, Writer

Dougherty, Mike
High Road Touring, 751 Bridgeway, #200, Sausalito CA 94965 USA — Guitarist, Songwriter

Dougherty, Tom
Ringling Bros Barnum & Bailey, 8607 Westwood Circle Dr, Vienna VA 22182 USA — Clown

Dougherty, William A, Jr — Navy Admiral
1505 Colonial Court, Arlington VA 22209, USA
Doughty, Glenn — Football Player
8808 Saint Charles Rock Road, Saint Louis MO 63114, USA
Doughty, Kenny — Actor
United Agents, 12-26 Lexington St, London W1F 0LE, England
Doughty, Neal — Keyboardist (REO Speedwagon)
Front Line Mgmt, 1100 Glendon Ave, #2000, Los Angeles CA 90024 USA
Doughty, Reed — Football Player
Washington Redskins, 21300 Redskin Park Dr, Ashburn VA 20147 USA
Douglas, Andrew — Director
W M E Entertainment, 9601 Wilshire Blvd, #300, Beverly Hills CA 90210 USA
Douglas, Anslem — Composer, Entertainer
J W Records, 2833 Church Ave, Brooklyn NY 11226, USA
Douglas, Barry — Concert Pianist
I M G Artists, Hogarth Business Park, Chiswick, London W4 2TH, England
Douglas, Bobby — Wrestler, Coach
Bobby Douglas Wrestling Camps, 5520 Hickory Hills Dr, Ames IA 50014, USA
Douglas, Brandon — Actor
1546 Caitlyn Circle, Westlake Village CA 91361, USA
Douglas, Cameron — Actor
Creative Management Group, 8522 National Blvd, #108, Culver City CA 90232 USA
Douglas, Charles W (Whammy) — Baseball Player
1711 Caterine Lake Road, Jacksonville NC 28540, USA
Douglas, Cullen — Actor
Greene Assoc, 1901 Ave of Stars, #130, Los Angeles CA 90067 USA
Douglas, David A (Dave) — Drummer (Relient K, Attack Cat)
Janlyn Public Relations, 106 Cabrini Blvd, #4-I, New York NY 10033, USA
Douglas, David G — Football Player
605 Snowshill Way, Maryville TN 37803, USA
Douglas, Denzil L — Prime Minister, Saint Kitts & Nevis
Prime Minister's Office, Government Building, Waterfront, Basseterre, Saint Kitts & Nevis
Douglas, Donna — Actress
B G A Music, PO Box 1038, Lincolnton NC 28093, USA
Douglas, Gabriel C V (Gabby) — Gymnast
Shade Global, 10 E 40th St, #4800, New York NY 10016, USA
Douglas, Illeana — Actress
Eleven Minutes Entertainment, 11812 San Vicente Blvd, Los Angeles CA 90049, USA
Douglas, James (Buster) — Boxer
545 Towne Court N, Gahanna OH 43230, USA
Douglas, Jerry — Actor
Stone Manners Salners, 9911 W Pico Blvd, #1400, Los Angeles CA 90035 USA
Douglas, Jordy — Ice Hockey Player
Courts Financial Group, 5-2727 Portage Ave, Winnipeg MB R3J 0R2, Canada
Douglas, Kirk — Actor
805 N Rexford Dr, Beverly Hills CA 90210, USA
Douglas, Kyan — Actor
Creative Artists Agency, 2000 Ave of Stars, #100, Los Angeles CA 90067 USA
Douglas, Leon — Basketball Player
6265 Sun Blvd, #402G, Saint Petersburg FL 33715, USA
Douglas, Marques L — Football Player
Miami Dolphins, 7500 SW 30th St, Davie FL 33314 USA
Douglas, Merrill G — Football Player
2185 E 3970 S, Salt Lake City UT 84124, USA
Douglas, Michael K — Actor, Director, Producer
Furthur Films, 825 8th Ave, #3000, New York NY 10019, USA
Douglas, Sarah — Actress
R D F Mgmt, 3-6 Kenrick Place, London W1U 6HD, England
Douglas, Sherman — Basketball Player
10401 Stapleford Hall Dr, Potomac MD 20854, USA
Douglas, Toney — Basketball Player
Houston Rockets, 1730 Jefferson St, Houston TX 77003 USA
Douglass, Dale — Golfer
6601 E San Miguel Ave, Paradise Valley AZ 85253, USA
Douglass, Maurice G — Football Player
1021 Sunset Dr, Englewood OH 45322, USA
Douglass, Robert G (Bobby) — Football Player
151 E Laurel Ave, #203, Lake Forest IL 60045, USA
Doumbia, Mariam — Singer (Amadou & Mariam)
Partisan Arts, PO Box 5085, Larkspur CA 94977, USA
Doumit, Ryan M — Baseball Player
5232 Ridgeview Dr Loop NE, Moses Lake WA 98837, USA
Doumit, Sam — Actress
B/W/R, 9100 Wilshire Blvd, #500W, Beverly Hills CA 90212 USA
Dourdan, Gary — Actor
TalentWorks, 3500 W Olive Ave, #1400, Burbank CA 91505 USA
Dourif, Bradford C (Brad) — Actor
Innovative Artists, 1505 10th St, Santa Monica CA 90401 USA
Dourif, Fiona — Actress
Innovative Artists, 1505 10th St, Santa Monica CA 90401 USA
Douris, Peter — Ice Hockey Player
PO Box 488, York Beach ME 03910, USA
Dove, Dennis — Baseball Player
144 Kirk Lane, Ocilla GA 31774, USA
Dove, Edward E (Eddie) — Football Player
1750 Poppy Ave, Menlo Park CA 94025, USA
Dove, Rita F — Writer
1757 Lambs Road, Charlottesville VA 22901, USA
Dove, Ronnie — Singer
Ken Keene Artists, PO Box 1875, Gretna LA 70054, USA
Dovolani, Driton (Tony) — Dancer
Abrams Artists, 9200 W Sunset Blvd, #1125, West Hollywood CA 90069 USA
Dow, Ellen Albertini — Actress
Greene Assoc, 1901 Ave of Stars, #130, Los Angeles CA 90067 USA
Dow, Peggy — Actress
2121 S Yorktown Ave, Tulsa OK 74114, USA

Dow, Tony
Imperium 7 Artists, 5455 Wilshire Blvd, #1706, Los Angeles CA 90036 USA — Actor

Dowd, Ann
Innovative Artists, 1505 10th St, Santa Monica CA 90401 USA — Actress

Dowd, Jim
708 New Jersey Ave, Point Pleasant Beach NJ 08742, USA — Ice Hockey Player

Dowd, Maureen
New York Times, Editorial Dept, 229 W 43rd St, New York NY 10036 USA — Columnist

Dowding, Leilani
A C Talent Agency, 9595 Wilshire Blvd, #900, Beverly Hills CA 90212, USA — Model, Actress

Dowell, Anthony J
Royal Ballet, Covent Garden, Bow St, London WC2E 9DD, England — Ballet Dancer

Dowell, Kenneth A (Ken)
5221 Helen Way, Sacramento CA 95822, USA — Baseball Player

Dower, John W
Massachusetts Institute of Technology, History Dept, Cambridge MA 02139, USA — Writer

Dowhower, Rod
5 Fairway Court, Dahlonega GA 30533, USA — Football Coach

Dowle, David
International Talent Booking, Ariel House, 74A Charlotte St, #100 London W1T 4QJ, England — Drummer (Whitesnake)

Dowler, Boyd H
5309 Creek Heights Dr, Midlothian VA 23112, USA — Football Player

Dowling, David B (Dave)
173 Whelan Way, Manteca CA 95336, USA — Baseball Player

Dowling, John E
135 Charles St, Boston MA 02114, USA — Biologist, Neurobiologist

Dowling, Timothy (Tim)
Mosiac Media Group, 9200 W Sunset Blvd, #1000, Los Angeles CA 90069 USA — Actor, Writer

Dowling, Vincent
322 East River Road, Huntington MA 01050, USA — Director, Writer

Down, Lesley-Anne
6252 Paseo Canyon Dr, Malibu CA 90265, USA — Actress

Down, Sarah
Playboy, Reader Services, 680 N Lake Shore Dr, Chicago IL 60611, USA — Cartoonist (Betsey's Buddies)

Downes, Lorraine E
Miss Universe NZ, PO Box 39624, Howick, Auckland 2145, New Zealand — Beauty Queen

Downes, Terry
Oaklea, 29 Meadowsbank, Watford WD19 4NP, England — Boxer

Downey, Chris
Creative Artists Agency, 2000 Ave of Stars, #100, Los Angeles CA 90067 USA — Producer, Writer

Downey, Raymond
Boxing Canada, 888 Belfast Road, Ottawa ON K1G 0Z6, Canada — Boxer

Downey, Robert J
I C M Partners, 10250 Constellation Blvd, #900, Los Angeles CA 90067 USA — Director

Downey, Robert, Jr
Creative Artists Agency, 2000 Ave of Stars, #100, Los Angeles CA 90067 USA — Actor, Singer, Songwriter

Downey, Roma
Abrams Artists, 9200 W Sunset Blvd, #1125, West Hollywood CA 90069 USA — Actress

Downey, William K (Bill)
1035 S Moorings Dr, Arlington Heights IL 60005, USA — Basketball Player

Downie, Gordon
Bobby Breen Mgmt, 13 Blackburn St, #300, Toronto ON M4M 2B3, Canada — Singer, Guitarist (Tragically Hip)

Downing, Alphonso E (Al)
25343 Silver Aspen Way, #735, Valencia CA 91381, USA — Baseball Player

Downing, Brian J
8095 County Road 135, Celina TX 75009, USA — Baseball Player

Downing, George
Get Wet!, 3021 Waialae Ave, Honolulu HI 96816, USA — Surfer, Surfing Executive

Downing, James (Jim)
5096 Peachtree Road, Atlanta GA 30341, USA — Auto Racing Driver

Downing, Kenneth K (K K), Jr
Trinifold Mgmt, 12 Oval Road, #300, Camden, London NW1 7D4, England — Guitarist (Judas Priest)

Downing, Sara
Amsel Eisenstadt Frazier, 5055 Wilshire Blvd, #865, Los Angeles CA 90036 USA — Actress

Downing, Vern
523 Napa St, Rodeo CA 94572, USA — Bowler

Downing, Walter T (Walt)
1141 Durham Circle NW, Massillon OH 44646, USA — Football Player

Downs, Anthony
Brookings Institute, 1775 Massachusetts Ave NW, Washington DC 20036 USA — Political Scientist

Downs, David R (Dave)
925 E 1050 N, Bountiful UT 84010, USA — Baseball Player

Downs, Gary M
3953 Balleycastle Dr, Duluth GA 30097, USA — Football Player

Downs, Hugh M
7993 N Ridgeview Dr, Paradise Valley AZ 85253, USA — Commentator

Downs, Kelly R
6459 Willow Creek Road, Morgan UT 84050, USA — Baseball Player

Downs, Michael (Mike)
1405 Knob Hill Dr, DeSoto TX 75115, USA — Football Player

Downs, Scott
6814 Barbrook Road, Louisville KY 40258, USA — Baseball Player

Dowson, Philip M
Royal Academy of Arts, Piccadilly, London W1V 0DS, England — Architect

Doyle, Allan
Fleming Assoc, 167 Little Lake Dr, Ann Arbor MI 48103, USA — Singer (Great Big Sea)

Doyle, Alien
512 Riverside Dr, LaGrange GA 30240, USA — Golfer

Doyle, Brian R
1310 Meadow Circle NE, Winter Haven FL 33881, USA — Baseball Player

Doyle, Christopher
I C M Partners, Marlborough House, 10 Earlham St, #300, London WC2H 9LNP, England — Cinematographer

Doyle, J Patrick
Domino's Pizza, PO Box 997, Ann Arbor MI 48106, USA — Businessman

Doyle, James H, Jr
6200 Oregon Ave NW, #420, Washington DC 20015, USA — Navy Admiral

Doyle, Jeffrey D (Jeff) — Baseball Player
830 SE Bayshore Circle, Corvallis OR 97333, USA

Doyle, Patrick — Composer
Air Edel, 8687 Melrose Ave, #900, Los Angeles CA 90069 USA

Doyle, R Dennis (Denny) — Baseball Player
PO Box 9156, Winter Haven FL 33883, USA

Doyle, Roddy — Writer
Random House, 1745 Broadway, #1800, New York NY 10019 USA

Doyle, Shawn — Actor
Paul Kohner, 9300 Wilshire Blvd, #555, Beverly Hills CA 90212 USA

Doyle-Murray, Brian — Actor, Comedian
Abrams Artists, 9200 Sunset Blvd, #625, Los Angeles CA 90069, USA

Doyne, Cory — Baseball Player
20229 County Line Road, Lutz FL 33558, USA

Dozier, James L — Army General
2150 Channel Way, North Fort Myers FL 33917, USA

Dozier, Lamont — Singer, Songwriter
320 E Charleston Blvd, #205-130, Las Vegas NV 89104, USA

Dozier, Terry — Basketball Player
1037 Congress Road, Arlington Heights IL 60005, USA

Dozier, Thomas D (Tom) — Baseball Player
1231 Willow Ave, #D7, Hercules CA 94547, USA

Dozier, William H (D J) — Football, Baseball Player
PO Box 2722, Norfolk VA 23501, USA

Dozy — Bassist (Dave Dee Dozy Beaky Mick Tich)
Gerd Kehren Mgmt, Postfach 1408, 41804 Erkelenz, Germany

Dr Demento — Entertainer
6102 Pimenta Ave, Lakewood CA 90712, USA

Dr Dre — Rap Artist, Record Producer, Actor
Aftermath Entertainment, 2220 Colorado Ave, Santa Monica CA 90404, USA

Dr John — Jazz Pianist, Singer, Songwriter
Impact Artists, 356 W 123rd St, New York NY 10027, USA

Drabble, Margaret — Writer
Penguin Books, 375 Hudson St, Basement 1, New York NY 10014 USA

Drabek, Douglas D (Doug) — Baseball Player
2 Peony Springs Court, Spring TX 77382, USA

Drabinsky, Garth H — Producer
Livent Inc, 165 Avenue Road, #600, Toronto ON M5R 3S4, Canada

Draffen, Willis — Singer (Bloodstone)
16103 Vista Del Mar Dr, Houston TX 77083, USA

Draft, Christopher M (Chris) — Football Player
970 E Oak St, Anaheim CA 92805, USA

Dragic, Goran — Basketball Player
Phoenix Suns, 201 E Jefferson St, Phoenix AZ 85004 USA

Draglia, Stacy — Track Athlete
PO Box 30931, Phoenix AZ 85046, USA

Drago, Billy — Actor
Deborah Miller, 9454 Wilshire Blvd, #715, Beverly Hills CA 90212, USA

Drago, Richard A (Dick) — Baseball Player
4703 Belle Chase Circle, Tampa FL 33634, USA

Dragon, Daryl — Musician (Captain & Tennille)
Greenlaw, 1251 S Cimarron Road, #22, Las Vegas NV 89117, USA

Dragoti, Stan — Director
1800 Ave of Stars, #430, Los Angeles CA 90067, USA

Drahman, Brian S — Baseball Player
46 Mariner Green Dr, Corte Madera CA 94925, USA

Drahos, Nicholas (Nick) — Football Player
3158 State Route 90, Aurora NY 13026, USA

Draiman, Dave — Singer (Disturbed)
Agency Group Ltd, 142 W 57th St, #600, New York NY 10019 USA

Drake — Singer, Rap Artist, Actor
Bryant Mgmt, 800 Brickell Ave, #550, Miami FL 33131, USA

Drake, Bebe — Actress
Ashby/Rojo Entertainment, 1485 S Beverly Dr, Los Angeles CA 90035, USA

Drake, Dallas — Ice Hockey Player
11472 E Cedar Bay Trail, Traverse City MI 49684, USA

Drake, Frank D — Astronomer
Search for ExtraTerrestrial Intelligence Institute, 515 N Whisman Road, Mountain View CA 94043, USA

Drake, Jamie — Interior Designer
Drake Design Assoc, 315 E 62nd St, #500, New York NY 10065, USA

Drake, Jeremy — Astronomer
Harvard University, Smithsonian Center for Astrophysics, Cambridge MA 02138, USA

Drake, Judith — Actress
Schiowitz Connor, 1680 N Vine St, #1016, Los Angeles CA 90028 USA

Drake, Julius — Concert Pianist
I M G Artists, Hogarth Business Park, Chiswick, London W4 2TH, England

Drake, Kenneth — Artist, Sculptor
Carrer D'es Port 2, #6, 07720 Es Castell, Minorca, Balearic Islands, Spain

Drake, Larry — Actor
Amsel Eisenstadt Frazier, 5055 Wilshire Blvd, #865, Los Angeles CA 90036 USA

Drake, Michael V — Educator
University of California, Chancellor's Office, Irvine CA 92697, USA

Drake, Solomon L (Solly) — Baseball Player
1732 S Corning St, Los Angeles CA 90035, USA

Drake, Thomas — Basketball Coach
Drake University, Athletic Dept, Des Moines IA 50311, USA

Drakeford, Tyronne J — Football Player
2311 Baron DeKalb Road, Camden SC 29020, USA

Drane, Dwight — Football Player
200 NW 107th Ave, Plantation FL 33324, USA

Draper, Courtnee — Actress
C E S D, 10635 Santa Monica Blvd, #130, Los Angeles CA 90025 USA

Draper, Dave — Body Builder
837 California St, Santa Cruz CA 95060, USA

Draper, Kris — Ice Hockey Player
3418 Westchester Road, Bloomfield Hills MI 48304, USA

Doyle - Draper

Draper, Michael H (Mike)
18317 Manor Church Road, Boonsboro MD 21713, USA — Baseball Player
Draper, Polly
Innovative Artists, 1505 10th St, Santa Monica CA 90401 USA — Actress
Draper, Timothy C
Draper Fisher Jurvetson, 2802 Sand Hill Road, Menlo Park CA 94025, USA — Financier
Draper, Tom
76 Blackstone Ave, Binghamton NY 13903, USA — Ice Hockey Player
Draper, William H, III
91 Tallwood Court, Atherton CA 94027, USA — Financier
Dratch, Rachel
Paradigm Agency, 360 N Crescent Dr, North Building, Beverly Hills CA 90210 USA — Actress, Comedienne
Dravecky, David F (Dave)
475 W 12th Ave, #8F, Denver CO 80204, USA — Baseball Player
Draxl, Tim
Management 360, 9111 Wilshire Blvd, Beverly Hills CA 90210 USA — Actor
Dray, Albert
Artmedia, 20 Ave Rapp, 75007 Paris, France — Actor
Drayton, Kia
Playboy Promotions, 2706 Media Center Dr, Los Angeles CA 90065 USA — Model
Drayton, T Anthony (Troy)
31 Oak St, #1, Patchogue NY 11772, USA — Football Player
Drechsler, Heike
Ans Sport GmbH, An der Eickesmuhle 31, 41238 Monohengladbach, Germany — Track Athlete
Drecker, Anneli M
Vox Mgmt, Tollbugata 28, Oslo 0156, Norway — Singer (Bel Canto)
Drees, Thomas K (Tom)
18638 Bearpath Trail, Eden Prairie MN 55347, USA — Baseball Player
Dreesen, Tom
14538 Benefit St, #301, Sherman Oaks CA 91403, USA — Actor, Comedian
Dreier, R Chad
Ryland Group, 6300 Canoga Ave, Woodland Hills CA 91367, USA — Businessman
Dreifort, Darren J
463 Wynola St, Pacific Palisades CA 90272, USA — Baseball Player
Dreiling, Gregory A (Greg)
5952 Willowross Way, Plano TX 75093, USA — Basketball Player
Drell, Persis
Stanford University, Linear Accelerator Center, Stanford CA 94305, USA — Physicist
Drell, Sidney D
620 Sand Hill Road, #420D, Palo Alto CA 94304, USA — Physicist
Drescher, Fran
Manatt Phelps Phillips, 11355 W Olympic Blvd, #20, Los Angeles CA 90064 USA — Actress
Drese, Ryan
2201 Bear Lake Dr, Euless TX 76039, USA — Baseball Player
Dressel, Chris
410 Whiskey Hill Road, Woodside CA 94062, USA — Football Player
Dresselhaus, Mildred S
Energy Department, 1000 Independence Ave SW, Washington DC 20585, USA — Physicist, Electrical Engineer
Dressendorfer, Kirk R
1004 Oaklands Dr, Round Rock TX 78681, USA — Baseball Player
Dressler, Alan M
Carnegie Observatories, 813 Santa Barbara St, Pasadena CA 91101, USA — Astronomer
Dressler, Douglas J (Doug)
118 Frostwood Dr, Westwood CA 96137, USA — Football Player
Dressler, Robert A (Rob)
2037 17th Ave, Forest Grove OR 97116, USA — Baseball Player
Dretske, Frederick I
212 Selkirk St, Durham NC 27707, USA — Philosopher
Drew, B Alvin, Jr
2814 Lighthouse Dr, Houston TX 77058, USA — Astronaut
Drew, Cameron S
31 Highbridge Road, Trenton NJ 08620, USA — Baseball Player
Drew, David J (J D)
5006 Old US Highway 41 N, Hahira GA 31632, USA — Baseball Player
Drew, Griffin
9066 Cambridge Circle, Vallejo CA 94591, USA — Actress, Model
Drew, Heather
76160 Desert Mountain Circle, Indio CA 92203, USA — Golfer
Drew, John E
2303 W Tidwell Road, #3404, Houston TX 77091, USA — Basketball Player
Drew, Larry D
4942 Densmore Ave, Encino CA 91436, USA — Basketball Player, Coach
Drew, Sarah
Innovative Artists, 1505 10th St, Santa Monica CA 90401 USA — Actress
Drew, Tim
5006 Old US Highway 41N, Hahira GA 31632, USA — Baseball Player
Drew, Urban
451 Neptune Ave, Encinitas CA 92024, USA — WW II Army Air Corps Hero
Drewrey, Willie J
2714 Cheryl Court, Missouri City TX 77459, USA — Football Player
Drexler Prada, Jorge A
Morgan Britos Mgmt, Princesa 3 Dpdo Of 1331, 28008 Madrid, Spain — Singer, Songwriter
Drexler, Clyde A
4045 Piping Rock Lane, Houston TX 77027, USA — Basketball Player, Coach
Drexler, Millard S (Mickey)
J Crew, 770 Broadway, #1200, New York NY 10003, USA — Businessman
Dreyer, Steven W (Steve)
6018 Greywood Circle, Johnston IA 50131, USA — Baseball Player
Dreyfus, George
3 Grace St, Camberwell VIC 3124, Australia — Composer
Dreyfus, Hubert L
University of California, Industrial Engineering Dept, Berkeley CA 94720, USA — Philosopher
Dreyfuss, Richard S
A P A Talent/Literary Agency, 405 S Beverly Dr, #300, Beverly Hills CA 90212 USA — Actor
Drickamer, Harry G
1174 Old Racebrook Road, Woodbridge CT 06525, USA — Chemical Engineer

V.I.P. Address Book

Draper - Drickamer

Driessen, Daniel (Dan) 208 Mitchellville Road, Hilton Head Island SC 29926, USA	Baseball Player
Drinfeld, Vladimir Steklov Mathematics Institute, 42 Vavilova, 117966 ESP-1 Moscow, Russia	Mathematician
Drinkwater, Carol Ken McReddie Assoc, 11 Connaught Place, London W2 2ET, England	Actress
Driscoll, Edward C (Terry) 101 Taylor Circle, Williamsburg VA 23185, USA	Basketball Player
Driscoll, James B (Jim) 18 Coyne Road, Waban MA 02468, USA	Baseball Player
Driscoll, Jean Pat Fettig, 8142 Traverse Court, Cincinnati OH 45242, USA	Track Athlete
Driskill, Travis 800 Blue Spring Circle, Round Rock TX 78681, USA	Baseball Player
Driver, Bruce 21A Crest Terrace, Montville NJ 07045, USA	Ice Hockey Player
Driver, Donald J 1942 Ledgeview Road, De Pere WI 54115, USA	Football Player
Driver, Minnie Untitled Entertainment, 350 S Beverly Dr, #200, Beverly Hills CA 90212 USA	Actress, Singer
D'Rivera, Paquito Charismic Productions, 2604 Mozart Place NW, Washington DC 20009, USA	Jazz, Concert Saxophonist
Drmanac, Radoje (Rade) Complete Genomics, 2071 Stierlin Court, Mountain View CA 94043, USA	Research Scientist
Droge, Pete 1423 34th Ave, Seattle WA 98122, USA	Singer, Songwriter
Drolet, Francois L Speed Skating Canada, 2781 Lancaster Road, #402, Ottawa ON K1B 1A7, Canada	Speed Skater
Drolet, Marie-Eve Skate Canada, 865 Shefford Road, Ottawa ON K1J 1H9, Canada	Speed Skater
Drollinger, Ralph K 22831 Market St, Newhall CA 91321, USA	Basketball Player
Drosdick, John G Sunoco Inc, 10 Penn Center, 1801 Market St, Philadelphia PA 19103, USA	Businessman
Drougas, Thomas C (Tom) PO Box 1596, Sun Valley ID 83353, USA	Football Player
Droughns, Reuben 5955 S Elkhart Court, Centennial CO 80016, USA	Football Player
Drouin, Jude 44479 Maltese Falcon Square, Ashburn VA 20147, USA	Ice Hockey Player
Drozd, Steven G World's Fair Mgmt, 1208 Chowning Ave, Edmond OK 73034, USA	Drummer, Guitarist (Flaming Lips)
Drozdova, Margarita S	Ballerina
Druce, John Freedom 55 Financial, 405-360 George St N, Peterborough ON K9H 7E7, Canada	Ice Hockey Player
Drucker, Eugene I M G Artists, Burlington Lane, Chiswick, London W4 2TH, England	Violinist (Emerson String Quartet)
Drukarova, Dinara Voyez Mon Agent, 20 Ave Rapp, 75007 Paris, France	Actress
Druken, Harold 16 Shaw Dr, Wayland MA 01778, USA	Ice Hockey Player
Druker, Brian J Oregon Health Science University, Cancer Research Center, Portland OR 97201, USA	Oncologist, Hematologist
Drulia, Stan 3939 Essex Place, Fort Gratiot MI 48059, USA	Ice Hockey Player
Drummond, Alice 351 E 50th St, New York NY 10022, USA	Actress
Drummond, Andre Detroit Pistons, Palace, 4 Championship Dr, Auburn Hills MI 48326 USA	Basketball Player
Drummond, Jonathan (Jon) PO Box 982, Arlington TX 76004, USA	Track Athlete
Drummond, Lauren Associated International Mgmt, Fairfax House, Fulwood Place, London WC1V 6HU, England	Actress
Drummond, Ryan Artists Management Agency, 835 5th Ave, #411, San Diego CA 92101, USA	Actor
Drummond, Timothy D (Tim) 102 Haldane Court, La Plata MD 20646, USA	Baseball Player
Drummond, Tom Uppercut Mgmt, 805 N Milwaukee Ave, #401, Chicago IL 60642, USA	Singer, Bassist (Better Than Ezra)
Drummond, William E (Bill) Nene Musik Productions, 1460 SW Santiago Ave, Port Saint Lucie FL 34953 USA	Guitarist (KLF), Record Producer
Drury, Chris 25 Central Park W, #27J, New York NY 10023, USA	Ice Hockey Player
Drury, James 100 Spring Lake Dr, Montgomery TX 77356, USA	Actor
Drury, Theodore E (Ted) 305 Hibbard Road, Wilmette IL 60091, USA	Ice Hockey Player
Drut, Guy J Mairie, 77120 Coulommiers, France	Track Athlete
Dryburgh, Stuart Gersh Agency, 9465 Wilshire Blvd, #600, Beverly Hills CA 90212 USA	Cinematographer
Dryden, Dave 2257 All Saints Crescent, Oakville ON L6J 5N1, Canada	Ice Hockey Player
Dryden, Kenneth W (Ken) 58 Poplar Plains Road, Toronto ON M4V 2M8, Canada	Ice Hockey Player
Dryer, J Frederick (Fred) Fred Dryer Productions, 2934 Beverly Glen Circle, #703, Los Angeles CA 90077, USA	Football Player, Actor
Dryke, Matthew (Matt) 292 Dryke Road, Sequim WA 98382, USA	Marksman
Drysdale, Cliff A T Y, 4725 N Lois Ave, Tampa FL 33614, USA	Tennis Player, Sportscaster
Duany, Andres Duany & Plater-Zyberk Architects, 1023 SW 25th Ave, Miami FL 33135, USA	Architect
Duato, Nacho Compania Nacional de Danza, Paseo de la Chopera 4, 28045 Madrid, Spain	Ballet Dancer, Choreographer

Dube, Desmond
Mahogany, PO Box 3085, Saxonwold, Johannesburg 2132, South Africa — Actor
Dubenion, Elbert (Duby)
610 E Walnut St, Westerville OH 43081, USA — Football Player
Duberman, Justin
4004 Avalon Pointe Dr, Boca Raton FL 33496, USA — Ice Hockey Player
Dubia, John A
10095 Cover Place, Fairfax VA 22030, USA — Army General
Dubinbaum, Gail
Metropolitan Opera Assn, Lincoln Center Plaza, New York NY 10023 USA — Opera Singer
Dubinin, Yuri V
Boslhoy Palashevsky Per 3, #34, 102104 Moscow, Russia — Government Official, Russia
Dubinsky, Steve
939 Central Ave, Highland Park IL 60035, USA — Ice Hockey Player
Dublinski, Thomas E (Tom), Jr
15918 El Lago Blvd, Fountain Hills AZ 85268, USA — Football Player
Dubner, Stephen J
William Morrow Publishers, 1350 Ave of Americas, New York NY 10019 USA — Economist, Writer
Dubois, Brian A
3 Spartan Place, Springfield IL 62703, USA — Baseball Player
DuBois, G Macy
175 Carlton St, Toronto ON M5A 2K3, Canada — Architect
DuBois, Ja'Net
C E S D, 10635 Santa Monica Blvd, #130, Los Angeles CA 90025 USA — Actress
Dubois, Jason
2204 Lord Seaton Circle, Virginia Beach VA 23454, USA — Baseball Player
Dubois, Marie
Artmedia, 20 Ave Rapp, 75007 Paris, France — Actress
DuBois, Marta
Orange Grove Group, 12178 Ventura Blvd, #205, Studio City CA 91604, USA — Actress
Dubose, Eric
326 County Road 8, Gilbertown AL 36908, USA — Baseball Player
Dubreuil, Maroussia
Agence Artistique Sophie Lemaitre, 9 Rue de Mubeuge, 75009 Paris, France — Actress
Dubus, Andre, III
Penguin Group, 375 Hudson St, Basement 1, New York NY 10014, USA — Writer
Ducasse, Alain
Groupe Alain Ducasse, 25 Ave Montaigne, 75008 Paris, France — Chef
Duce, Sharon
Jonathan Altaras Assoc, 11 Garrick St, London WC2E 9AR, England — Actress
Ducey, Caroline
Agents Associes, 201 Rue du Fauboug Saint Honore, 75008 Paris, France — Actress
Ducey, Robert T (Rob)
699 Richmond Close, Tarpon Springs FL 34688, USA — Baseball Player
Duchesnay, Isabelle
Im Steinach 30, 87561 Oberstdorf, Germany — Ice Dancer
Duchesnay, Paul
Bundesleistungszentrum, Rossbichstr 2-6, 87561 Oberstdorf, Germany — Ice Dancer
Duchesne, Steve
2104 Cedar Elm Terrace, Westlake TX 76262, USA — Ice Hockey Player
Duchin, Peter
Peter Duchin Orchestra, 60 E 42nd St, #1132, New York NY 10165, USA — Jazz Pianist, Orchestra Leader
Duchovny, David
Affirmative Entertainment, 425 N Robertson Blvd, Los Angeles CA 90048 USA — Actor, Director
DuCille, Michel
9571 Pine Meadow Lane, Burke VA 22015, USA — Photojournalist
Duckett, Todd J (T J)
Seattle Seahawks, 12 Seahawks Way, Renton WA 98056 USA — Football Player
Duckworth, Brandon J
34 Indian Birch Road, Blackwood NJ 8012, USA — Baseball Player
Duckworth, Charles
Landis-Simon Productions, 3625 E Thousand Oaks Blvd, #279, Thousand Oaks CA 91362, USA — Actor
Duckworth, James R (Jim)
3736 Ferrero Way, Redding CA 96001, USA — Baseball Player
Duckworth, Marilyn
41 Queen St, Mount Victoria, Wellington 6001, New Zealand — Writer
Ducornet, Rikki
University of Denver, English Dept, Denver CO 80208, USA — Writer
Ducsmal Jaroszewska, Agnieszka
Polish Radio Orchestra, Al Marchinkowskiego 3, 61 745 Pozna, Poland — Conductor
Dudek, Anne
Innovative Artists, 1505 10th St, Santa Monica CA 90401 USA — Actress
Dudek, Joseph A (Joe)
31 Ryan Road, Auburn NH 03032, USA — Football Player
Duden, H Richard (Dick), Jr
11 Old Station Road, Severna Park MD 21146, USA — Football Player
Duderstadt, James J
National Science Foundation, 1800 G St NW, Washington DC 20006, USA — Educator, Government Official
Dudikoff, Michael
4341 Birch St, #201, Newport Beach CA 92660, USA — Actor
Dudley, Charles
4032 42nd Ave S, Seattle WA 98118, USA — Basketball Player
Dudley, Christen G (Chris)
1150 Fairway Road, Lake Oswego OR 97034, USA — Basketball Player
Dudley, Jaquelin
University of Texas, Microbiology Dept, Austin TX 78712, USA — Microbiologist
Dudley, Jared
Phoenix Suns, 201 E Jefferson St, Phoenix AZ 85004 USA — Basketball Player
Dudley, Rick
5150 Oakhill Dr, Lewiston NY 14092, USA — Ice Hockey Player, Coach
Dudley, Rickey D
4529 Mahogany Lane, Lewisville TX 75077, USA — Football Player
Dudman, Nick
Pigs Might Fly, Gawithfield Barn, Arrad Foot, Ulverston, Cumbria LA12 7SL, England — Makeup Artist
Duenkel Fuldner, Virginia (Ginny)
2132 NE 17th Terrace, #500, Wilton Manors FL 33305, USA — Swimmer

Dube - Duenkel Fuldner

D

Duensing, Brian 524 S 198th St, Elkhorn NE 68022, USA	Baseball Player
Duerod, Terry 6542 Chirrewa St, Westland MI 48185, USA	Basketball Player
Duesenberry, James S 514 Harvard St, #3B, Brookline MA 02446, USA	Economist
Dufay, Rick H K Mgmt, 9200 W Sunset Blvd, #530, West Hollywood CA 90069 USA	Guitarist (Aerosmith)
Dufek, Donald P (don) 570 S Maple Road, Ann Arbor MI 48103, USA	Football Player
Duff, Anne-Marie Gordon & French, 12-13 Poland St, London W1F 8QB, England	Actress
Duff, Haylie Curtis Talent Mgmt, 9607 Arby Dr, Beverly Hills CA 90210, USA	Actress, Singer, Songwriter
Duff, Hilary Creative Artists Agency, 2000 Ave of Stars, #100, Los Angeles CA 90067 USA	Actress, Singer, Model
Duff, John E 5 Doyers St, New York NY 10013, USA	Sculptor
Duff, T Richard (Dick) 4-7 Elmwood Ave S, Mississauga ON L5G 3J6, Canada	Ice Hockey Player
Duffalo, James F (Jim) 1505 Savannah St, Mesquite TX 75149, USA	Baseball Player
Duffey, Joseph D 2891 New Mexico Ave NW, #311, Washington DC 20007, USA	Educator
Duffie, John B 177 Lakeside Circle, Douglas GA 31535, USA	Baseball Player
Duffield, Burkely United Talent Agency, 9336 Civic Center Dr, Beverly Hills CA 90210 USA	Actor
Duffner, Christof Am Sagebauer 1, 78141 Schonwald, Germany	Ski Jumper
Duffner, Mark University of Maryland, Athletic Dept, College Park MD 20740, USA	Football Coach
Duffus, Parris 8609 Timbermill Place, Fort Wayne IN 46804, USA	Ice Hockey Player
Duffy Rough Trade Records, 66 Golborne Road, London W10 5PS, England	Singer, Songwriter
Duffy, Brian Des Moines Register, Editorial Dept, PO Box 957, Des Moines IA 50306, USA	Editorial Cartoonist
Duffy, Brian 16410 Heather Bend Court, Houston TX 77059, USA	Astronaut
Duffy, Carol Ann Manchester Metropolitan University, English Dept, All Saints, Manchester M15 6BH, England	Writer
Duffy, Francis (Frank) Three Ways, Street, Walberswick near Southwold, Suffolk IP18 6UE, England	Architect
Duffy, Frank T 1740 E Silver St, Tucson AZ 85719, USA	Baseball Player
Duffy, J C Universal Press Syndicate, 4520 Main St, #700, Kansas City MO 64111 USA	Cartoonist (Fusco Brothers)
Duffy, John Meet the Composer, 2112 Broadway, New York NY 10023, USA	Composer
Duffy, Julia C E S D, 10635 Santa Monica Blvd, #130, Los Angeles CA 90025 USA	Actress
Duffy, Keith Carol/War Mgmt, Bushy Park Road, 57 Meadowgate, Dublin 6, Ireland	Singer (Boyzone)
Duffy, Maureen P 18 Fabian Road, London SW6 7TZ, England	Writer
Duffy, Patrick PO Box 749, Eagle Point OR 97524, USA	Actor
Duffy, Roger T 6509 Lutz Ave NW, Massillon OH 44646, USA	Football Player
Duffy, Troy Original Artists, 9465 Wilshire Blvd, #324, Beverly Hills CA 90212, USA	Actor, Director, Writer
Duffy, William H (Billy) Tom Vitorino Mgmt, 11606 Viny Road, Granada Hills CA 91344, USA	Guitarist (Cult)
Duflo, Esther Massachusetts Institute of Technology, Cambridge MA 02139 USA	Economist
Dufner, Jason 2002 Saint Patrick Court, Auburn AL 36830, USA	Golfer
Dufour, Luc 334 Rue des Champs-Elysees, Chicoutimi QC G7H 2V8, Canada	Ice Hockey Player
Dufresne, Donald Rimouski Oceanic Club, CP 816 Succ A, Rimouski QC G5L 7C9, Canada	Ice Hockey Player
Dufresne, John W W Norton, 500 5th Ave, #600, New York NY 10110 USA	Writer
Dufresne, Mark Bobby Roberts, 3050 Business Park Circle, #303, Goodlettsville TN 37221 USA	Drummer (Confederate Railroad)
Dugan, Dennis United Talent Agency, 9336 Civic Center Dr, Beverly Hills CA 90210 USA	Actor, Director
Dugan, J Fred 1827 Tamiami Trail N, Nokomia FL 34275, USA	Football Player
Dugan, Jeffrey S (Jeff) 13701 Ashcroft Road, Savage MN 55378, USA	Football Player
Dugan, Michael J 36 James Court, Dillon CO 80435, USA	Air Force General, Association Executive
Duggan, James S (Hacksaw Jim) 1328 Hornsby Circle, Lugoff SC 29078, USA	Professional Wrestler, Football Player
Dugger, John Scott 410 Evelyn Ave, #201, Albany CA 94706, USA	Artist
Dugoni, Robert Warner Books, 1271 Ave of Americas, New York NY 10020 USA	Writer
Duguay, Christian Gersh Agency, 9465 Wilshire Blvd, #600, Beverly Hills CA 90212 USA	Director
Duguay, Ron 982 Porte Vedra Blvd, Ponte Vedra Beach FL 32082, USA	Ice Hockey Player
Duhamel, Josh John Carrabino Mgmt, 5900 Wilshire Blvd, #406, Los Angeles CA 90036 USA	Actor

Duhe, Adam J (A J), Jr
379 Coconut Circle, Weston FL 33326, USA — Football Player

Duhe, John M, Jr
US Court of Appeals, 556 Jefferson St, Lafayette LA 70501, USA — Judge

Duigan, John
54A Tite St, London SW3 4JA, England — Director

Dujardin, Jean
W M E Entertainment, 9601 Wilshire Blvd, #300, Beverly Hills CA 90210 USA — Actor, Comedian

Duk Kim, Randall
Charles Bright, 135 Houpe Road, Great Meadows NJ 07838, USA — Actor

Duka, Dominik J Cardinal
Archdiocese, Hradcanske nam 16, 11902 Prague 1, Czech Republic — Religious Leader

Dukakis, Michael S
85 Perry St, Brookline MA 02446, USA — Governor, MA

Dukakis, Olympia
Innovative Artists, 235 Park Ave S, #1000, New York NY 10003 USA — Actress

Duke, Annie
Federated Sports & Gaming, Palms Casino & Resort, 4301 W Flamingo Road, Las Vegas NV 89103, USA — Poker Player

Duke, Bill
Duke Media, 7510 Sunset Blvd, #523, Los Angeles CA 90046, USA — Director

Duke, Charles M, Jr
Duke Ministry for Christ, PO Box 310345, New Braunfels TX 78131, USA — Astronaut, Air Force General

Duke, Clark
W M E Entertainment, 9601 Wilshire Blvd, #300, Beverly Hills CA 90210 USA — Actor, Director, Writer

Duke, Elizabeth
Federal Reserve System, 20th St & Constitution Ave NW, Washington DC 20551, USA — Government Official, Financier

Duke, George
Associated Booking Corp, 501 Madison Ave, #603, New York NY 10022 USA — Jazz Keyboardist, Songwriter

Duke, Kenneth W (Ken)
3612 SW Rivers End Way, Palm City FL 34990, USA — Golfer

Duke, Michael
Wal-Mart Stores, 702 SW 8th St, Bentonville AR 72716, USA — Businessman

Duke, Norm
719 2nd Ave, #701, Seattle WA 98104, USA — Bowler

Duke, Patty
Mitchell K Stubbs Assoc, 8695 W Washington Blvd, #204, Culver City CA 90232 USA — Actress

Duke, Robin Chandler
435 E 52nd St, New York NY 10022, USA — Association Executive, Diplomat

Duke, Zachary T (Zach)
2517 County Road 4240, Clifton TX 76634, USA — Baseball Player

Dukes, Elijah D, Jr
739 Straw Lake Dr, Brandon FL 33510, USA — Baseball Player

Dukes, Jamie D
2553 Northern Oak Dr, Braselton GA 30517, USA — Football Player, Sportscaster

Dukes, Jan N
959 Helena Dr, Sunnyvale CA 94087, USA — Baseball Player

Dukes, Thomas E (Tom)
325 Monte Vista Road, Arcadia CA 91007, USA — Baseball Player

Dukuchitz, Jonathan
Innovative Artists, 235 Park Ave S, #1000, New York NY 10003 USA — Actor

Dulany, Caitlin
TalentWorks, 3500 W Olive Ave, #1400, Burbank CA 91505 USA — Actress

Dulery, Antoine
Artmedia, 20 Ave Rapp, 75007 Paris, France — Actor

Duliba, Robert J (Bob)
327 Philadelphia Ave, West Pittston PA 18643, USA — Baseball Player

Dullea, Keir
310 W 72nd St, #9B, New York NY 10023, USA — Actor

Dulli, Gregory (Greg)
Rascoff/Zysblat Organization, 250 W 57th St, New York NY 10107 USA — Singer, Guitarist (Afghan Whigs)

Dumais, Troy M
2301 N Millbend Dr, Spring TX 77380, USA — Diver

Dumars, Joe, III
3499 Franklin Road, Bloomfield Hills MI 48302, USA — Basketball Player

Dumaux, Christophe
I M G Artists, Hogarth Business Park, Chiswick, London W4 2TH, England — Opera Singer

Dumervil, Elvis K
6115 Trailhead Road, Littleton CO 80130, USA — Football Player

Dumont, J P
1512 Kimberleigh Court, Franklin TN 37069, USA — Ice Hockey Player

DuMont, James
House of Representatives, 1434 6th St, #1, Santa Monica CA 90401 USA — Actor

Dumoulin, Daniel L (Dan)
202 Nancy Dr, Kokomo IN 46901, USA — Baseball Player

Dunaev, Andrej
I M G Artists, Hogarth Business Park, Chiswick, London W4 2TH, England — Opera Singer

Dunagin, Ralph
North American Syndicate, 235 E 45th St, New York NY 10017 USA — Cartoonist (Dunagin's People)

Dunaway, Faye
Don Buchwald/Fortitude, 6500 Wilshire Blvd, #2200, Los Angeles CA 90048 USA — Actress

Dunaway, James E (Jim)
170 Mount Carmel Church Road, Sandy Hook MS 39478, USA — Football Player

Dunbar, Bonnie J
2200 Todville Road, Seabrook TX 77586, USA — Astronaut

Dunbar, Dale
41 Nahant Ave, Winthrop MA 02152, USA — Ice Hockey Player

Dunbar, Gavin
Ground Control Touring, 20 Jay St, #826, Brooklyn NY 11201 USA — Bassist (Camera Obscura)

Dunbar, Jo-Lonn D
Saint Louis Rams, 901 N Broadway, Saint Louis MO 63101 USA — Football Player

Dunbar, Matt
6328 County Donegal Court, Charlotte NC 28277, USA — Baseball Player

Dunbar, Rockmond
Untitled Entertainment, 350 S Beverly Dr, #200, Beverly Hills CA 90212 USA — Actor

Duncan, Arne
Education Department, 400 Maryland Ave SW, Washington DC 20202 USA — Secretary, Education

	Secretary, Energy
Duncan, Charles W, Jr 9 Briarwood Court, Houston TX 77019, USA	Baseball Player
Duncan, Christopher E (Chris) 6421 N Foothills Dr, Tucson AZ 85718, USA	Baseball Player
Duncan, Courtney 121 Adalene Lane, Madison AL 35757, USA	Football Player
Duncan, Curtis E 4915 Glen Hollow St, Sugar Land TX 77479, USA	Photojournalist
Duncan, David Douglas Castellaras Mouans-Sartoux 06370, France	Writer
Duncan, Glen Knopf Publishers, 1745 Broadway, New York NY 10019 USA	Actor
Duncan, Ian Ken McReddie Assoc, 11 Connaught Place, London W2 2ET, England	Football Player
Duncan, Jamie R 217 Remi Dr, New Castle DE 19720, USA	Baseball Player
Duncan, Jeff 825 Lincoln Lane, Frankfort IL 60423, USA	Football Player
Duncan, Kenneth W (Ken) 4 Christina Ave, Camarillo CA 93012, USA	Football Player
Duncan, Leslie H (Speedy) 1607 Porter Way, Stockton CA 95207, USA	Actress
Duncan, Lindsay V Dalzell & Beresford, 26 Astwood Mews, London SW7 4DE, England	Baseball Player
Duncan, Mariano Ingenio Angelina #137, San Pedro de Macoris, Dominican Republic	Baseball Player
Duncan, Melvin (Mel) 470 Bedford St, PO Box 980407, Ypsilanti MI 48198, USA	Director
Duncan, Peter Cameron Creswell, 61 Marlborough St, #700, Surry Hills NSW 2010, Australia	Actor
Duncan, Robert Ken McReddie Assoc, 11 Connaught Place, London W2 2ET, England	Astrophysicist
Duncan, Robert C University of Texas, Astronomy Dept, Austin TX 78712, USA	WW II Navy Air Force Hero
Duncan, Robert W 1511 Ryder Cup Blvd, Marion IL 62959, USA	Actress, Comedienne
Duncan, Sandy Douglas Gorman Rothacker Wilhelm, 1501 Broadway, #703, New York NY 10036, USA	Baseball Player
Duncan, Shelley 6421 N Foothills Dr, Tucson AZ 85718, USA	Basketball Player
Duncan, Timothy T (Tim) 13215 Vista del Mundo, San Antonio TX 78216, USA	Singer, Songwriter
Duncan, Whitney W B R Nashville, 20 Music Square E, Nashville TN 37203, USA	Ice Hockey Player
Duncanson, Craig Laurentian University, Athletic Dept, Sudbury ON P3E 2C6, Canada	Actress
Dundas, Jennifer Paradigm Agency, 360 N Crescent Dr, North Building, Beverly Hills CA 90210 USA	Fashion Designer
Dundas, Peter H Palazzo Pucci, 6 Via de Pucci, 50122 Florence, Italy	Ice Hockey Player
Dundas, Rocky 14 Nantucket Dr, Richmond Hill ON L4E 3V1, Canada	Baseball Player
Dunegan, James W (Jim) 20246 180th St, New London IA 52645, USA	Marine Corps General
Dunford, Joseph F, Jr Assistant Commandant, HqUSMC, 2 Navy St, Washington DC 20380 USA	Actor
Dungey, Lon Auckland Actors, PO Box 56460, Auckland 1030, New Zealand	Actress
Dungey, Merrin Gersh Agency, 9465 Wilshire Blvd, #600, Beverly Hills CA 90212 USA	Football Coach
Dungy, Tony 16604 Villalonda de Avila, Tampa FL 33613, USA	Businessman
Dunham, Archie W ConocoPhillips Inc, 600 N Dairy Ashford, Houston TX 77079, USA	Cartoonist (Overboard)
Dunham, Chip Universal Press Syndicate, 4520 Main St, #700, Kansas City MO 64111 USA	Writer, Film Director, Actress
Dunham, Lena United Talent Agency, 9336 Civic Center Dr, Beverly Hills CA 90210 USA	Ice Hockey Player
Dunham, Michael (Mike) 39 Garfield Road, Concord MA 01742, USA	Actor
Dunigan, Tim Hervey/Grimes Talent, 10561 Missouri Ave, #2, Los Angeles CA 90025 USA	Chemist
Dunitz, Jack D Obere Heslibachstr 77, 8700 Kusnacht, Switzerland	Basketball Player
Dunkle, Nancy 1350 Lorawood St, La Habra CA 90631, USA	Astronaut
Dunlap, Alexander W N A S A, Johnson Space Center, 2101 NASA Road, Houston TX 77058 USA	Baseball Player
Dunlap, Grant L 1431 Alga Court, Vista CA 92081, USA	Basketball Coach
Dunlap, Michael (Mike) Charlotte Bobcats, 333 E Trade St, #A, Charlotte NC 28202 USA	Golfer
Dunlap, Page 8728 Misty Creek Dr, Sarasota FL 34241, USA	Golfer
Dunlap, Scott 104 Summerour Vale, Duluth GA 30097, USA	Opera Singer
Dunleavy, Mary Fletcher Artist Mgmt, 809 W 181st St, #274, New York NY 10033, USA	Basketball Player
Dunleavy, Michael J (Mike), Jr Indiana Pacers, Conseco Fieldhouse, 125 S Pennsylvania, Indianapolis IN 46204 USA	Basketball Player, Coach
Dunleavy, Michael J (Mike), Sr 127 S Carmelina Ave, Los Angeles CA 90049, USA	Guitarist (Travis)
Dunlop, Andy Wildlife Entertainment, 21 Heathmans Road, London SW6 4TJ, England	Ice Hockey Player
Dunlop, Blake 8112 Maryland Ave, Saint Louis, MO 63105, USA	

Dunmore, Laurence
Independent Talent Group, Oxford House, 76 Oxford St, London W1D 1BS, England — Director
Dunn, Adam T
533 Tusculum Ave, Cincinnati OH 45226, USA — Baseball Player
Dunn, Andrew W
525 Broadway, #250, Santa Monica CA 90401, USA — Cinematographer
Dunn, Colton
Paradigm Agency, 360 N Crescent Dr, North Building, Beverly Hills CA 90210 USA — Actor
Dunn, Dave
1433 Hamilton St, Regina SK S4H 7V4, Canada — Ice Hockey Player
Dunn, Gary E
243 Navajo St, Tavernier FL 33070, USA — Football Player
Dunn, Holly
303 Royal View Road, Salado TX 76571, USA — Singer, Songwriter
Dunn, John M
Western Michigan University, President's Office, Kalamazoo MI 49008, USA — Educator
Dunn, Jourdan
Storm Model Agency, 5 Jubilee Place, Chelsea, London SW3 3TD, England — Model
Dunn, Keldrick D (K D)
1640 Township Terrace, McDonough GA 30252, USA — Football Player
Dunn, Kevin
Gersh Agency, 9465 Wilshire Blvd, #600, Beverly Hills CA 90212 USA — Actor
Dunn, Larry
Spirit Media, PO Box 43591, Phoenix AZ 85080, USA — Pianist (Earth Wind & Fire), Songwriter
Dunn, Lin
Indiana Fever, Conseco Fieldhouse, 125 S Pennsylvania, Indianapolis IN 46204 USA — Basketball Coach
Dunn, Mignon
Bloch Artists Mgmt, 360 W 28th St, #6B, New York NY 10001, USA — Opera Singer
Dunn, Mike
PO Box 128, Wrightsville PA 17368, USA — Drag Racing Driver
Dunn, Moira
15803 Bridgewater Lane, Tampa FL 33624, USA — Golfer
Dunn, Nora
Stone Manners Salners, 9911 W Pico Blvd, #1400, Los Angeles CA 90035 USA — Actress, Comedienne
Dunn, Perry L
64 Glenway Place, Brandon MS 39042, USA — Football Player
Dunn, Richard (Richie)
12229 Clarence Center Road, Akron NY 14001, USA — Ice Hockey Player
Dunn, Robert F
Lexington Institute, 1600 Wilson Blvd, #900, Arlington VA 22209 USA — Navy Admiral
Dunn, Ronald R (Ron)
1161 Husted Ave, San Jose CA 95125, USA — Baseball Player
Dunn, Ronnie
Spalding Entertainment, 54 Music Square E, #200, Nashville TN 37203, USA — Singer (Brooks & Dunn), Songwriter
Dunn, Scott
1331 Arizona Ash St, San Antonio TX 78232, USA — Baseball Player
Dunn, Stephen
Stockton State College, Humanities & Fine Arts Dept, Pomona NJ 08240, USA — Writer
Dunn, Steven R (Steve)
484 Broadmoor Dr, Maryville TN 37803, USA — Baseball Player
Dunn, Susan
Herbert Breslin, 119 W 57th St, #1505, New York NY 10019, USA — Opera Singer
Dunn, Teala
Abrams Artists, 275 7th Ave, #2600, New York NY 10001 USA — Actress, Singer
Dunn, Theodore R (T R)
1014 19th St SW, Birmingham AL 35211, USA — Basketball Player
Dunn, Todd K
12030 London Lake Dr W, Jacksonville FL 32258, USA — Baseball Player
Dunn, Warrick D
6016 Beacon Shores St, Tampa FL 33616, USA — Football Player
Dunne, Colin
I M G Artists, Hogarth Business Park, Chiswick, London W4 2TH, England — Dancer
Dunne, Griffin
Arcieri Assoc, 305 Madison Ave, #2315, New York NY 10165 USA — Actor, Director
Dunne, Michael D (Mike)
5115 W Ancient Oak Dr, Peoria IL 61615, USA — Baseball Player
Dunne, Robin
Empera Southpaw Productions, #317 1275 W 6th Ave, Vancouver BC BC V6H 1A6, Canada — Actor, Writer, Producer
Dunning, Debbe
1373 Crest Road, Del Mar CA 92014, USA — Actress, Model
Dunning, Jeanne
2438 N Bernard St, Chicago IL 60647, USA — Artist, Photographer
Dunning, John
Pocket Books, 1230 Ave of Americas, New York NY 10020 USA — Writer
Dunning, Steven J (Steve)
35 Prairie, Irvine CA 92618, USA — Baseball Player
Dunn-Luoma, Tricia
4 Huson Ave, Derry NH 03038, USA — Ice Hockey Player
Duno, Milka
S A M A X Motorsports, 203 NW 16th St, Pompano Beach FL 33060, USA — Auto Racing Driver
Dunphy, Marv
33370 Decker School Road, Malibu CA 90265, USA — Volleyball Coach
Dunsky, Evan
Creative Artists Agency, 2000 Ave of Stars, #100, Los Angeles CA 90067 USA — Director
Dunsmore, Barrie
ABC-TV, News Dept, 5010 Creston St, Hyattsville MD 20781 USA — Commentator
Dunst, Kirsten
United Talent Agency, 9336 Civic Center Dr, Beverly Hills CA 90210 USA — Actress
Dunstan, A H Bernard
10 High Park Road, Kew, Richmond, Surrey TW9 4BH, England — Artist
Dunstan, William E (Bill)
PO Box 514, Rancho Mirage CA 92270, USA — Football Player
Dunston, Shawon D
957 Corte del Sol, Fremont CA 94539, USA — Baseball Player
Dunwoody, Ann E
Commanding General, Army Material Command, Alexandria VA 22333, USA — Army General

V.I.P. Address Book

Dunwoody, T Richard
Sports Marketing, Litten, Newtown Road, Newbury, Berkshire RG14 7BB, England

Baseball Player

Dunwoody, Todd F
1704 King Eider Dr, West Lafayette IN 47906, USA

Actress

DuPage, Julie
Artmedia, 20 Ave Rapp, 75007 Paris, France

Football Player

Dupard, J Reginald (Reggie)
1316 Green Hills Court, Duncanville TX 75137, USA

Football Player

Duper, Mark K
1905 Banks Road, Margate FL 33063, USA

Ice Hockey Player

Dupere, Denis
26 Lorraine Ave, Kitchener ON N2B 2M8, Canada

Actress

Duperey, Anny
Agents Associes, 201 Rue du Faubourg Saint Honore, 75008 Paris, France

Actress, Model

Duplaix, Daphnee Lynn
Greene Assoc, 1901 Ave of Stars, #130, Los Angeles CA 90067 USA

Writer, Director, Actor

Duplass, Jay
I C M Partners, 10250 Constellation Blvd, #900, Los Angeles CA 90067 USA

Actor, Director, Writer

Duplass, Mark
Brigade Marketing, 548 W 28th St, #670, New York NY 10001, USA

Ice Hockey Player

Dupont, Andre (Moose)
905 Rue Gilbert, Trois-Rivieres QC G8T 5V5, Canada

Ice Hockey Player

Dupont, Jerry
216 Rosemar Gardens, Richmond Hill ON L4C 3Z9, Canada

Governor, DE

DuPont, Pierre S, IV
Richards Layton Finger, 1 Rodney Square, PO Box 551, Wilmington DE 19899, USA

Actress

Dupont, Tiffany
Paradigm Agency, 360 N Crescent Dr, North Building, Beverly Hills CA 90210 USA

Philosopher

Dupre, John
University of Exeter, Genomics Center, Exeter, Devon EX4 4QJ, England

Football Player

DuPree, Billy Joe
3621 Llano River Trail, McKinney TX 75070, USA

Basketball Player

Dupree, Candice
Phoenix Mercury, American West Arena, 201 E Jefferson St, Phoenix AZ 85004 USA

Baseball Player

Dupree, Mike
2358 E Richmond Ave, Fresno CA 93720, USA

Composer

DuPrez, John
Air Edel, 18 Rodmarton St, London W1U 8BJ, England

Rap Artist, Singer

Dupri, Jermaine
Three Rings Projects, 111 Westwood Place, #101, Brentwood TN 37027, USA

Ice Hockey Player

Dupuis, Bob
446 Algonquin Ave, North Bay ON P1B 4W5, Canada

Actor

Dupuis, Roy
Agence Premier Role, 3451 Hotel de Ville, Montreal QC H2X 3B5, Canada

Astronaut, Spain

Duque, Pedro
European Space Center, Linder Hohe, Box 906096, 51127 Cologne, Germany

Physician

Durack, David T
815 W Knox St, Durham NC 27701, USA

Baseball Player

Duran, Daniel J (Dan)
493 Maxine Court, Sunnyvale CA 94086, USA

Producer, Director, Writer

Duran, Elise
Creative Artists Agency, 2000 Ave of Stars, #100, Los Angeles CA 90067 USA

Boxer

Duran, Roberto
Calle F El Cangrejo, Casa 33, Panama City, Panama

Actress

Durance, Erica
Gersh Agency, 9465 Wilshire Blvd, #600, Beverly Hills CA 90212 USA

Actor

Durand, Kevin
Alchemy Entertainment, 7024 Melrose Ave, #420, Los Angeles CA 90038 USA

Writer

Durang, Christopher
I C M Partners, 730 5th Ave, New York NY 10019 USA

Inventor (Antiulcer Compound)

Durant, Graham J
Cambridge NeuroScience, 333 Boston Providence Turnpike, Norwood MA 02062, USA

Golfer

Durant, Joseph S (Joe)
PO Box 910, Gulf Breeze FL 32562, USA

Basketball Player

Durant, Kevin
Oklahoma City Thunder, 211 N Robinson Ave, #300, Oklahoma City OK 73102 USA

Baseball Player

Durant, Michael J (Mike)
7520 Marston Lane, Dublin OH 43016, USA

Ballerina

Durante, Viviana P
20 Bristol Gardens, Little Venice, London W9, England

Baseball Player

Durazo Cardenas, Erubiel
3800 S Cantabria Circle, #1079, Chandler AZ 85248, USA

Baseball Player

Durbin, Chad G
17918 Jefferson Ridge Dr, Baton Rouge LA 70817, USA

Actress, Singer

Durbin, Deanna
BP 3315, 75123 Paris Cedex 03, France

Baseball Player

Durbin, Joseph A (J D)
1913 E Pinto Dr, Gilbert AZ 85296, USA

Bowler

Durbin, Mike
1042 Wilshire Dr, Roanoke TX 76262, USA

Football Player

Duren, Clarence E
201 W 54th St, Los Angeles CA 90037, USA

Basketball Player

Duren, John T
1107 1st St NW, Washington DC 20001, USA

Baseball Player

Durham, Donald G (Don)
2627 Pennington Bend Road, Nashville TN 37214, USA

Basketball Coach

Durham, Hugh
Jacksonville University, Athletic Dept, Jacksonville FL 32211, USA

Baseball Player

Durham, Joseph V (Joe)
9715 Mendoza Road, Randallstown MD 21133, USA

Baseball Player

Durham, Ray (Sugar Ray)
199 Lake Road, Stanley NC 28164, USA

Actor

Duris, Romain
Agents Associes, 201 Rue du Faubourg Saint Honore, 75008 Paris, France

Ice Hockey Player

Duris, Slava
1-92 Walmer Road, Toronto ON M5H 2X7, Canada

Duritz, Adam — Singer (Counting Crowes), Lyricist
Interscope/Geffen Records, 2220 Colorado Ave, #300, Santa Monica CA 90404, USA

Durjan'narc, Ogan — Conductor, Composer
Moscow Symphony Orchestra, Gorky Park, 9 Krymsky Val, 119049 Moscow, Russia

Durkin, Clare — Model
Ford Models Inc, 111 5th Ave, #900, New York NY 10003 USA

Durko, Sandy V — Football Player
2020 Paseo del Mar, Palos Verdes Estates CA 90274, USA

Durnbaugh, Robert E (Bobby) — Baseball Player
1638 N Central Dr, Dayton OH 45432, USA

Durning, Charles — Actor
Paradigm Agency, 360 N Crescent Dr, North Building, Beverly Hills CA 90210 USA

Durr Browning, Francoise — Tennis Player
195 Rue de Lourmel, 75015 Paris, France

Durr, Jason — Actor
Ken McReddie Assoc, 11 Connaught Place, London W2 2ET, England

Durrance, Samuel T — Astronaut, Astronomer
770 Kerry Downs Circle, Melbourne FL 32940, USA

Durrant, Devin G — Basketball Player
6239 Pineview Road, Dallas TX 75248, USA

Durrant, Jennifer A — Artist
9-10 Holly Grove, London SE15 5DF, England

Durrington, Trent J — Baseball Player
499 N Canon Dr, #400, Beverly Hills CA 90210, USA

Durst, W Frederick (Fred) — Musician (Limp Bizkit), Director
KillerMoxie Mgmt, 5890 W Jefferson Blvd, #J, Los Angeles CA 90016, USA

Durst, Will — Actor, Comedian
Entertainment Alliance, PO Box 1544, Mendocino CA 95460, USA

Dusard, Jay — Photogapher
5261 N Stewart Ranch Road, Douglas AZ 85607, USA

Dusay, Marj — Actress
1964 Westwood Blvd, #6F, New York NY 10025, USA

Dusek, J Bradley (Brad) — Football Player
4th Quarter Ranch, 8311 FM 2086, Temple TX 76501, USA

Dusenberg, Walter — Sculptor
Stone Mill Hall, 109 Cemetery Road, Fly Creek NY 13337, USA

Dusenberry, Ann — Actress
1615 San Leandro Lane, Santa Barbara CA 93108, USA

Duser, Carl R — Baseball Player
3021 Cornwall Road, Bethlehem PA 18017, USA

Dushku, Eliza — Actress, Producer, Director
United Talent Agency, 9336 Civic Center Dr, Beverly Hills CA 90210 USA

Dussault, Jean H — Endocrinologist
Laval Medical Center, 2705 Blvd Laurier, Sainte Foy PQ G1V 4G2, Canada

Dussault, Nancy — Actress, Singer
4406 Moorpark Way, Toluca Lake CA 91602, USA

Dussollier, Andre — Actor
Artmedia, 20 Ave Rapp, 75007 Paris, France

Dustal, Robert A (Bob) — Baseball Player
625 Marian Lane, Lakeland FL 33813, USA

Dutch, Deborah — Actress
William Carroll Agency, 12811 Garden Grove Blvd, #209, Garden Grove CA 92843 USA

Dutilleux, Henri — Composer
12 Rue Saint Louis-en-l'Isle, 75004 Paris, France

Dutoit, Charles E — Conductor
Montreal Symphony, 260 Blvd Maisonneuve W, Montreal PQ H2X 1Y9, Canada

DuToit, Élize — Actress
Special Artists Agency, 9465 Wilshire Blvd, #820, Beverly Hills CA 90212 USA

Dutronc, Jacques — Actor
Voyez Mon Agent, 20 Ave Rapp, 75007 Paris, France

Dutrow, Richard E (Rick), Jr — Thoroughbred Racing Trainer
2 The Howl W, East Norwich NY 11732, USA

Dutt, Hank — Concert Violist (Kronos Quartet)
Kronos Quartet, 1235 9th Ave, San Francisco CA 94122, USA

Dutt, Sanjay — Actor
58 Smt Nargis Dutt Road, Pali Hill Bandra (W), Mumbai MS 400050, India

Dutta Bhupathi, Lara — Beauty Queen, Actress, Model
401 Merry Ville, 25 Saint Andrews Road, Bandra (W), Mumbai 400050, India

Dutton, Charles S — Actor, Director
Marsh Entertainment, 12444 Ventura Blvd, #203, Studio City CA 91604, USA

Dutton, James P (Jim), Jr — Astronaut
1604 Mossy Stone Dr, Friendswood TX 77546, USA

Dutton, John O — Football Player
5706 Moss Creek Trail, Dallas TX 75252, USA

Dutton, Lawrence — Violist (Emerson String Quartet)
I M G Artists, Burlington Lane, Chiswick, London W4 2TH, England

Dutton, Simon — Actor
Marmont Mgmt, Langham House, 302/8 Regent St, London W1R 5AL, England

Duty, Kenton — Actor
Osbrink Talent Agency, 4343 Lankershim Blvd, #100, North Hollywood CA 91602 USA

Duva, Louis (Lou) — Boxing Promoter, Trainer, Manager
Main Events, 811 Totowa Road, #100, Totowa NJ 07512, USA

Duval, Daniel — Actor
U B B A, 6 Rue de Braque, 75003 Paris, France

Duval, David R — Golfer
1000 E Oxford Lane, Englewood CO 80113, USA

Duval, Dennis — Basketball Player
8105 Verbeck Dr, Manlius NY 13104, USA

Duval, Helen — Bowler
PO Box 2071, Oakland CA 94604, USA

Duval, James — Actor
Artistry Mgmt, 340 N Camden Dr, #302, Beverly Hills CA 90210, USA

Duval, Michael A (Mike) — Baseball Player
2743 Nature Pointe Loop, Fort Myers FL 33905, USA

DuVall, Clea — Actress
Framework Entertainment, 9057 Nemo St, #C, West Hollywood CA 90069 USA

Duvall, Jed — Commentator
ABC-TV, News Dept, 5010 Creston St, Hyattsville MD 20781 USA

Duvall, Robert — Actor
PO Box 520, The Plains VA 20198, USA

Duvall, Sammy — Water Skier
PO Box 871, Windermere FL 34786, USA

Duvauchelle, Nicolas — Actor
U B B A, 6 Rue de Braque, 75003 Paris, France

DuVernay, Ava — Director
Paradigm Agency, 360 N Crescent Dr, North Building, Beverly Hills CA 90210 USA

Duvert, Michael — Actor
Liebman Entertainment, 25 E 21st St, #PH, New York NY 10010, USA

Duvillard, Henri — Alpine Skier
Le Mont d'Arbois, 74120 Megere, France

Duwelius, Rich — Volleyball Player
266 Stoddards Wharf Road, Gales Ferry CT 06335, USA

Dvorak, Radek — Ice Hockey Player
10342 Lexington Estates Blvd, Boca Raton FL 33428, USA

Dvorak, Tomas — Track Athlete
Stadium Juliska, 160 00 Prague 6, Czech Republic

Dvorak, Wayne C — Actor
2204 Stanley Hills Dr, Los Angeles CA 90046, USA

Dvorsky, Peter — Opera Singer
J Hronca 1A, 84102 Bratislava, Slovakia

Dwight, Edward, Jr — Astronaut
4022 Montview Blvd, Denver CO 80207, USA

Dwight, Timothy J (Tim), Jr — Football Player
26164 Indigo Dr, Park Rapids MN 56470, USA

Dworaczyk, Hope — Model
Playboy Promotions, 2706 Media Center Dr, Los Angeles CA 90065 USA

Dwork, Melvin — Interior Designer
Melvin Dwork Inc, 50 Murray St, #1710, New York NY 10007, USA

Dworkin, Martin — Microbiologist
2123 Hoyt Ave W, Saint Paul MN 55108, USA

Dworkin, Ronald M — Attorney, Educator
13 Chester Row, London SW1W 9JF, England

Dworkins, Lenny — Cartoonist (Buck Rogers)
2906 Wilmette Ave, Wilmette IL 60091, USA

Dworsky, Daniel L (Dan) — Football Player, Architect
9225 Nightingale Dr, Los Angeles CA 90069, USA

Dwurnik, Edward — Artist
Ul Podgorska 5, 02 921 Warsaw, Poland

Dwyer, James E (Jim) — Baseball Player
826 Hancock Bridge Parkway, Cape Coral FL 33990, USA

Dwyer, Jim — Journalist
New York Times, Editorial Dept, 229 W 43rd St, New York NY 10036 USA

Dwyer, Karyn — Actress
Oscars Abrams Zimel, 438 Queen St E, Toronto ON M5A 1T4, Canada

Dyas, Guy Hendrix — Production Designer
United Talent Agency, 9336 Civic Center Dr, Beverly Hills CA 90210 USA

Dybzinski, Jerome M (Jerry) — Baseball Player
1626 Haywood Place, Fort Collins CO 80526, USA

Dychtwald, Ken — Psychologist
Age Wave Inc, 1900 Powell St, Emeryville CA 94608, USA

Dye, Ernest T — Football Player
580 Bienville Court, Alpharetta GA 30004, USA

Dye, Ian — Composer
Gorfaine/Schwartz, 4111 W Alameda Ave, #509, Burbank CA 91505, USA

Dye, Jermaine T — Baseball Player
6655 N 66th Place, Paradise Valley AZ 85253, USA

Dye, Lee — Golf Course Architect
Dye Designs, 5500 E Yale Ave, #300, Denver CO 80222, USA

Dye, Melissa Dori — Singer, Songwriter
Dye Productions, 5403 Everhart Road, #140, Corpus Christi TX 78411, USA

Dye, Paul B (Pete) — Golf Course Architect
3247 Polo Dr, Delray Beach FL 33483, USA

Dyer, Danny — Actor
Independent Talent Group, Oxford House, 76 Oxford St, London W1D 1BS, England

Dyer, Donald R (Duffy) — Baseball Player
742 W Las Palmaritas Dr, Phoenix AZ 85021, USA

Dyer, Michael L (Mike) — Baseball Player
22392 Manacor, Mission Viejo CA 92692, USA

Dyk, Timothy B — Judge
US Court of Appeals, 717 Madison Place NW, Washington DC 20439, USA

Dyka, Oksana — Opera Singer
I M G Artists, Hogarth Business Park, Chiswick, London W4 2TH, England

Dyke, Charles W — Army General, Association Executive
International Technical/Trade Assoc, 1330 Connecticut NW, Washington DC 20036, USA

Dykema, Craig — Basketball Player
10525 Destino St, Bellflower CA 90706, USA

Dykers, Craig — Architect
Snohetta, Skur 39, Vippetangen, 0150 Oslo, Norway

Dykes Bower, John — Concert Organist
4Z Artillery Mansions, Westminster, London SW1P 1RR, England

Dykinga, Jack — Photojournalist
1519 E Tascal Loop, Tucson AZ 85737, USA

Dykstra, John — Artist, Animator, Cinematographer
15060 Encanto Dr, Sherman Oaks CA 91403, USA

Dykstra, Leonard K (Lenny) — Baseball Player
10550 Wilshire Blvd, #1203, Los Angeles CA 90024, USA

Dylan, Bob — Singer, Songwriter
Creative Artists Agency, 2000 Ave of Stars, #100, Los Angeles CA 90067 USA

Dylan, Jakob — Singer, Guitarist (Wallflowers)
Paradigm Agency, 360 N Crescent Dr, North Building, Beverly Hills CA 90210 USA

Dylan, Jesse — Director
Creative Artists Agency, 2000 Ave of Stars, #100, Los Angeles CA 90067 USA

Dymott, Adiam   Singer
Agency Group Ltd, 361-373 City Road, London EC1V 2QA, England
Dynam, Jacques   Actor
Artmedia, 20 Ave Rapp, 75007 Paris, France
Dynarski, Eugene (Gene)   Actor
PO Box 17081, North Hollywood CA 91615, USA
Dyrdek, Robert D (Rob)   Skateboarder, Actor
I C M Partners, Marlborough House, 10 Earlham St, #300, London WC2H 9LNP, England
Dyroen-Lancer, Rebekah (Becky)   Sychronized Swimmer
31101 Via Madera, San Juan Capistrano CA 92675, USA
Dysart, Richard   Actor
654 Copeland Court, Santa Monica CA 90405, USA
Dyson, Andre   Football Player
3367 N Shoreline Circle, Layton UT 84040, USA
Dyson, Esther   Businesswoman, Writer
Edventure Holdings, 104 5th Ave, #2000, New York NY 10011, USA
Dyson, Freeman J   Physicist, Templeton Religion Laureate
105 Battle Road Circle, Princeton NJ 08540, USA
Dyson, James   Industrial Designer
Dyson Appliances, Tetbury Hill, Malmesbury Wiltshire SN16 0RP, England
Dyson, Kevin T   Football Player
3109 Chase Point Dr, Franklin TN 37067, USA
Dyson, Michael Eric   Writer
DePaul University, English Dept, Chicago IL 60604, USA
Dzau, Victor J   Molecular Biologist
Duke University Health System, Chancellor's Office, Durham NC 27708, USA
Dzhanibekov, Vladimir A   Cosmonaut, Air Force General
Cosmonaut Training Center, Star City, 141160 Zvezdny Gorodok, Moscow Oblast, Russia
Dziedzic, Joe   Ice Hockey Player
2195 Marion Road, Saint Paul MN 55113, USA
Dziedzic, Stanley   Freestyle Wrestler
835 Hedgegate Court, Roswell GA 30075, USA
Dziena, Alexis   Actress
Paradigm Agency, 360 N Crescent Dr, North Building, Beverly Hills CA 90210 USA
Dziewonski, Adam M   Seismologist, Geophysicist
Harvard University, Seismology Dept, Cambridge MA 02138, USA
Dziubinska, Anulka   Model, Actress
Playboy Promotions, 2706 Media Center Dr, Los Angeles CA 90065 USA
Dziwisz, Stanislaw Cardinal   Religious Leader
Archdiocese of Cracow, Ul Franciszkanska 3, 31 004 Cracow, Poland
Dzundza, George   Actor
PO Box 133, Netarts OR 97143, USA
Dzyaloshinskii, Igor E   Physicist
University of California, Physics Dept, Irvine CA 92697, USA

D

Dymott - Dzyaloshinskii

Eackles, Ledell — Basketball Player
9134 Elmgrove Garden Dr, Baton Rouge LA 70807, USA

Eade, George J — Air Force General
1131 Sunnyside Dr, Healdsburg CA 95448, USA

Eads, George — Actor
Innovative Artists, 1505 10th St, Santa Monica CA 90401 USA

Eagle, Ian — Sportscaster
CBS-TV, Sports Dept, 51 W 52nd St, New York NY 10019 USA

Eagles, Mike — Ice Hockey Player
59 Abbott Court, Fredericton NB E3B 5V8, Canada

Eagling, Wayne J — Ballet Dancer, Choreographer
Postbus 16486, 1001 RN Amsterdam, Netherlands

Eakes, Bobbie — Actress, Singer
Bauman Redanty Shaul Agency, 5757 Wilshire Blvd, #473, Los Angeles CA 90036 USA

Eakin, Thomas C — Businessman
245 Sandover Dr, Aurora OH 44202, USA

Eakins, Dallas — Ice Hockey Player
19705 N 84th Way, Scottsdale AZ 85255, USA

Eakins, James S (Jim) — Basketball Player
2575 Little Cottonwood Road, Sandy UT 84092, USA

Ealy, Michael — Actor
Epidemic Pictures, 1635 N Cahuenga Blvd, #500, Los Angeles CA 90028, USA

Eanes, Antonio dos Santos Ramalho — President, Portugal; Army General
Partido Renovador Democratico, Travessa do Falo 9, 1200 Lisbon, Portugal

Earl, Anthony S — Governor, WI
Quarles & Brady, 1st Wisconsin Plaza, 1 S Pinckney St, Madison WI 53703, USA

Earl, Robin D — Football Player
1457 E Evergreen Dr, #303, Palatine IL 60074, USA

Earl, Roger — Drummer (Foghat)
Lustig Talent, PO Box 770850, Orlando FL 32877 USA

Earle Mead, Sylvia A — Oceanographer
12812 Skyline Blvd, Oakland CA 94619, USA

Earle, Acie B — Basketball Player
2301 14th Ave, Moline IL 61265, USA

Earle, Steve — Singer, Guitarist, Songwriter
Dan Gillis Mgmt, 215 Bonifay Dr, Smyrna TN 37167, USA

Earles, Jason — Actor
C E S D, 10635 Santa Monica Blvd, #130, Los Angeles CA 90025 USA

Earley, Liz — Golfer
24 Morton Dr, Buffalo NY 14226, USA

Early, Gerald L — Writer, Educator
Washington University, English Dept, McMillan Hall, Saint Louis MO 63130, USA

Early, Quinn R — Football Player
PO Box 675752, Rancho Santa Fe CA 92067, USA

Earnhardt, R Dale, Jr — Auto Racing Driver
955 Shinnville Road, Mooresville NC 28115, USA

Earp, Mildred — Baseball Player
217 Dolly, West Fork AR 72774, USA

Easler, Michael A (Mike) — Baseball Player
2824 White Peaks Ave, North Las Vegas NV 89081, USA

Easley, Bill — Jazz Saxophonist, Clarinetist, Flutist
Hot Jazz Mgmt, 328 W 43rd St, #4FW, New York NY 10036, USA

Easley, J Damion — Baseball Player
6420 W Line Dr, Glendale AZ 85310, USA

Easley, Kenny M (Ken) — Football Player
3906 Kegagie Dr, Norfolk VA 23518, USA

Eason, Bo — Football Player, Actor, Writer
Creative Artists Agency, 2000 Ave of Stars, #100, Los Angeles CA 90067 USA

Eason, Charles C (Tony), IV — Football Player
PO Box 340, Walnut Grove CA 95690, USA

East, Clyde B — WW II Army Air Corps Hero
6643 Maplegrove St, Oak Park CA 91377, USA

East, Jeff — Actor
99 Spinfdrift Dr, Rancho Palos Verdes CA 90275, USA

East, Ronald A (Ron) — Football Player
PO Box 3442, Redmond WA 98073, USA

Easter, Robert A — Educator
University of Illinois, President's Office, 506 S Wright St, Urbana IL 61801, USA

Easterbrook, Frank H — Judge
US Court of Appeals, 219 S Dearborn St, #2302B, Chicago IL 60604, USA

Easterbrook, Leslie — Actress, Singer
Tufield Entertainment, 19521 Rosita St, Tarzana CA 91356, USA

Easterlin, Richard A — Economist
329 Patrician Way, Pasadena CA 91105, USA

Easterly, James M (Jamie) — Baseball Player
1306 Plantation Dr, Crockett TX 75835, USA

Eastin, Jeff — Producer, Writer
Creative Artists Agency, 2000 Ave of Stars, #100, Los Angeles CA 90067 USA

Eastman, Dean E — Physicist
336 Coonley Road, Riverside IL 60546, USA

Eastman, John — Attorney
Eastman & Eastman, 39 W 54th St, #200, New York NY 10019, USA

Eastman, Kevin — Cartoonist (Ninja Turtles)
1527 N Wickiup Road, Apache Junction AZ 85119, USA

Eastman, Marilyn — Actress
Greater Talent Network, 437 5th Ave, #700, New York NY 10016, USA

Easton, David Anthony — Interior Designer
72 Spring St, #700, New York NY 10012, USA

Easton, Earnest Lee — Educator
3040 E Charleston Blvd, #1046, Las Vegas NV 89104, USA

Easton, Michael — Actor
2810 Baseline Trail, Los Angeles CA 90068, USA

Easton, Sheena — Singer, Actress
Emmis Mgmt, 18136 Califa St, Tarzana CA 91356, USA

Eastwick, Rawlins J (Rawly) — Baseball Player
10 River Meadow Dr, West Newbury MA 01985, USA

Eastwood, Alison — Model, Actress, Director
Mosiac Media Group, 9200 W Sunset Blvd, #1000, Los Angeles CA 90069 USA

Eastwood, Bob — Golfer
PO Box 14769, Haltom City TX 76117, USA

Eastwood, Clint — Director, Actor
Hogs Breath Inn, Carlos St, PO Box 4366, Carmel by the Sea CA 93921, USA

Eastwood, Kyle — Actor
Chapman Co, PO Box 55246, Sherman Oaks CA 91413, USA

Eathorne, A J — Golfer
23023 N 25th Place, Phoenix AZ 85024, USA

Eaton, Adam T — Baseball Player
17404 NE 126th Place, Redmond WA 98052, USA

Eaton, Don (Babtunde) — Rap Artist, Drummer (Last Poets)
Agency Group Ltd, 361-373 City Road, London EC1V 2QA, England

Eaton, John C — Composer
4585 N Hartstrait Road, Bloomington IN 47404, USA

Eaton, Mark — Ice Hockey Player
3 Fieldstone Circle, Greenville RI 02828, USA

Eaton, Mark E — Basketball Player
2104 Dayton Ave NE, Renton WA 98056, USA

Eaton, Meredith — Actress
Bresler Kelly Assoc, 11500 W Olympic Blvd, #400, Los Angeles CA 90064 USA

Eaton, Shirley — Actress
Guild House, Upper Saint Martin's Lane, London WC2H PEG, England

Eaton, T Scott — Football Player
3950 W Lake Sammamish Parkway SE, Bellevue WA 98008, USA

Eaton, Tracey B — Football Player
PO Box 881, Preston WA 98050, USA

Eatough, Jeff — Ice Hockey Player
2050 Insley Road, Mississauga ON L4Y 1P9, Canada

Eaves, Jerry L — Basketball Player
10 Perch Place, Greensboro NC 27455, USA

Eaves, Michael G (Mike) — Ice Hockey Player, Coach
3615 Culver Trail, Faribault MN 55021, USA

Eaves, Murray J — Ice Hockey Player
Shattuck-Saint Mary's School, 1000 Shumway Ave, Faribault MN 55021, USA

Eaves, Patrick C — Ice Hockey Player
3693 Chappuis Trail, Faribault MN 55021, USA

Ebadi, Shirin — Nobel Peace Laureate
University of Tehran, Enghelab Ave & 16 Azar St, 14174 Tehran, Iran

Ebanks, Selita — Model
Women Model Mgmt, 199 Lafayette St, #700, New York NY 10012 USA

Ebashi, Setsuro — Biophysicist, Pharmacologist
17-503 Nagaizumi Myodaiji, Okazaki 444 0864, Japan

Ebel, David M — Judge
US Court of Appeals, US Courthouse, 1929 Stout St, Denver CO 80294, USA

Eberhart, Ralph E (Ed) — Air Force General
Armed Forces Benefit Assn, 909 N Washington St, #767, Alexandria VA 22314, USA

Eberharter, Stefan — Alpine Skier
Dorfstr 21, 6272 Stumm, Austria

Eberle, Markus — Alpine Skier
Unterwestweg 27, 87567 Riezlern, Germany

Ebersol, Dick — Businessman
174 West St, #54, Litchfield CT 06759, USA

Ebersole, Christine — Actress, Singer
PO Box 1291, Maplewood NJ 07040, USA

Ebersole, John J — Football Player
1470 Village Square, Mount Pleasant SC 29464, USA

Ebert, Peter — Opera Director
Col di Mura, 06010 Lippiano, Italy

Ebert, Roger J — Film Critic
PO Box 146366, Chicago IL 60614, USA

Ebnoether, Luzia — Curling Athlete
Curling Assn, PO Box 606, 3000 Bern, Switzerland

Ebron, Roy — Basketball Player
7100 Virgilian St, New Orleans LA 70126, USA

Ebsen, Bonnie — Actress
PO Box 356, Agoura CA 91376, USA

Eby, Betsy — Artist
Winston Wachter Fine Art, 39 E 78th St, New York NY 10075, USA

Eccles, Spencer F — Financier
Wells Fargo Bank, 299 S Main St, #400, Salt Lake City UT 84111, USA

Eccleston, Christopher — Actor
Independent Talent Group, Oxford House, 76 Oxford St, London W1D 1BS, England

Ecclestone, Bernie — Auto Racing Executive
Formula One Ltd, 6 Prince's Gate, London SW7 1QJ, England

Ecclestone, Timothy J (Tim) — Ice Hockey Player
10095 Fairway Village Dr, Roswell GA 30076, USA

Echevarria, Angel S — Baseball Player
23830 231st Place SE, Maple Valley WA 98038, USA

Echeverria Alvarez, Luis — President, Mexico
Magnolia 131, San Jeronimo Lidice, Magdalena Contreras CP 10200, Mexico

Echikunwoke, Megalyn — Actress
United Talent Agency, 9336 Civic Center Dr, Beverly Hills CA 90210 USA

Ecker, Haylie — Violinist
Mel Bush, Tanglewood, Arrowsmith Road, Wimborne, Dorset BH21 2BS, England

Eckersley, Dennis L — Baseball Player
6 Macy Lane, Ipswich MA 01938, USA

Eckert, Shari — Actress, Model
PO Box 5761, Sherman Oaks CA 91413, USA

Eckhart, Aaron — Actor
Creative Artists Agency, 2000 Ave of Stars, #100, Los Angeles CA 90067 USA

Eckholdt, Steven — Actor
Innovative Artists, 1505 10th St, Santa Monica CA 90401 USA

Eckstein, David M — Baseball Player
6969 Sylvan Woods Dr, Sanford FL 32771, USA

E

Eco - Edmondson

Eco, Umberto — Writer, Educator
Piazza Castello 13, 20121 Milan, Italy

Edberg, Rolf — Ice Hockey Player
Helmerdaisv 4, 12 352 Farst, Sweden

Edberg, Stefan — Tennis Player
Swedish Tennis Assn, Box 27915, 115 95 Stockholm, Sweden

Eddery, Patrick J — Thoroughbred Racing Jockey
Musk Hill Farm, Nether Winchendon, Aylesbury, Bucks HP18 0DT, England

Eddings, Douglas L (Doug) — Baseball Umpire
8072 Constitution Road, Las Cruces NM 88007, USA

Eddington, Roderick I (Rod) — Businessman
British Airways, Waterside, PO Box 365, Harmondsworth UB7 0GB, England

Eddy, Duane — Singer, Songwriter, Guitarist
1906 Chet Atkins Blvd, #502, Nashville TN 37212, USA

Edel, Uli — Director
Gersh Agency, 9465 Wilshire Blvd, #600, Beverly Hills CA 90212 USA

Edell, Marc Z — Attorney
Budd Larner Gross, 150 John F Kennedy Parkway, #301, Short Hills NJ 07078, USA

Edelman, Brad M — Football Player
828 Royal St, #410, New Orleans LA 70116, USA

Edelman, Elazer R — Cardiologist
Harvard-MIT Biomedical Center, 77 Massachusetts Ave, Cambridge MA 02139, USA

Edelman, Gerald M — Nobel Medicine Laureate
Scripps Research Institute, Neurobiology Dept, La Jolla CA 92037, USA

Edelman, Ian — Producer, Writer
I C M Partners, 10250 Constellation Blvd, #900, Los Angeles CA 90067 USA

Edelman, Marian Wright — Association Executive
Children's Defense Fund, 25 E St NW, Washington DC 20001, USA

Edelman, Pawel — Cinematographer
I C M Partners, 10250 Constellation Blvd, #900, Los Angeles CA 90067 USA

Edelman, Randy — Composer
Gorfaine/Schwartz, 4111 W Alameda Ave, #509, Burbank CA 91505 USA

Edelstein, Jean — Artist
48 Brooks Ave, Venice CA 90291, USA

Edelstein, Lisa — Actress
Anthem Entertainment, 5225 Wilshire Blvd, #615, Los Angeles CA 90036 USA

Edelstein, Victor A — Fashion Designer, Artist
3 Stanhope Mews West, London SW7 5RB, England

Eden, Barbara — Actress
9816 Denbigh Dr, Beverly Hills CA 90210, USA

Eden, Harry — Actor
Independent Talent Group, Oxford House, 76 Oxford St, London W1D 1BS, England

Eden, Richard — Actor
Abrams Artists, 9200 W Sunset Blvd, #1125, West Hollywood CA 90069 USA

Edens, Thomas P (Tom) — Baseball Player
2033 Quailridge Court, Clarkston WA 99403, USA

Eder, Linda — Singer, Actress
Hart Mgmt, 1900 Ave of Stars, #1800, Los Angeles CA 90067, USA

Eder, Richard G — Journalist
Los Angeles Times, Editorial Dept, 202 W 1st St, Los Angeles CA 90012 USA

Edestrand, Darryl — Ice Hockey Player
391 Beechwood Ave, London ON N6J 3J9, Canada

Edgar, David — Writer
Alan Brodie Representation, 211 Piccadilly, London W1V 9LD, England

Edgar, David (Dave) — Swimmer
2633 Middle River Dr, #3, Fort Lauderdale FL 33306, USA

Edgar, James (Jim) — Governor, IL
University of Illinois, Public Affairs Institute, Urbana IL 61801, USA

Edgar, Robert W (Bob) — Religious Leader; Representative, PA
National Council of Churches, 475 Riverside Dr, #817, New York NY 10115, USA

Edgar, Ross — Cyclist
Ashwood Laboratories, Brockhall Village, Blackburn, Lancashire BB6 8BB, England

Edge — Guitarist (U-2), Singer
Regine Moylet, 9 Ivebury Court, 325 Latimer Road, London W10 6RA, England

Edge, Graeme — Drummer (Moody Blues)
Insight Mgmt, 1222 16th Ave S, #300, Nashville TN 37212, USA

Edge, Mitzi — Golfer
118 Kings Chapel Road, Augusta GA 30907, USA

Edgerson, Booker T — Football Player
68 Union Common, Buffalo NY 14221, USA

Edgerton, Joel — Actor
Markham & Froggatt, Julian House, 4 Windmill St, London W1P 1HF, England

Edgley, Gigi — Actress, Singer
Soverign Talent Group, 8421 Wilshire Blvd, #200, Beverly Hills CA 90211, USA

Edinger, Paul E, IV — Football Player
2313 York Place, Lakeland FL 33810, USA

Edlund, Ben — Comic Book Artist, Animator
United Talent Agency, 9336 Civic Center Dr, Beverly Hills CA 90210 USA

Edlund, Richard P — Cinematographer
2710 Wilshire Blvd, Santa Monica CA 90403, USA

Edmonds, Albert J (Al) — Air Force General
Military Officers Assn, 201 N Washington St, Alexandria VA 22314, USA

Edmonds, Jacque — Actor
Paradigm Agency, 360 N Crescent Dr, North Building, Beverly Hills CA 90210 USA

Edmonds, James P (Jim) — Baseball Player
25 Boulder View, Irvine CA 92603, USA

Edmonds, Kenneth (Babyface) — Singer, Keyboardist, Songwriter
Creative Artists Agency, 2000 Ave of Stars, #100, Los Angeles CA 90067 USA

Edmonds, Tracey E — Actress, Producer
Our Stories Films, 1635 N Cahuenga Blvd, Los Angeles CA 90028, USA

Edmondson, Adrian — Actor
Jonathan Altaras Assoc, 11 Garrick St, London WC2E 9AR, England

Edmondson, Brian C — Baseball Player
304 Ridgeview Trace, Canton GA 30114, USA

Edmondson, Jaime Faith — Model
Playboy Promotions, 2706 Media Center Dr, Los Angeles CA 90065 USA

Edmondson, James L (J L)
US Court of Appeals, 56 Forsyth St NW, Atlanta GA 30303, USA — Judge

Edmondson, Sarah
Characters Talent, 200-1505 W 2nd Ave, Vancouver BC V6H 3Y4, Canada — Actress

Edmunds, Dave
Entertainment Services, Main Street Plaza 1000, #303, Voorhees NJ 08043, USA — Singer, Guitarist, Songwriter

Edmunds, Ferrell, Jr
PO Box 414, Blairs VA 24527, USA — Football Player

Edmundson, Gary
Silvercrest Western Homes, 299 N Smith Ave, Corona CA 92880, USA — Ice Hockey Player

Edner, Ashley
10061 Riverside Dr, #341, North Hollywood CA 91602, USA — Actress

Edney, Leon A (Bud)
1037 Encino Row, Coronado CA 92118, USA — Navy Admiral

Edney, Tyus D
1800 S Floyd Court, La Habra CA 90631, USA — Basketball Player

Edsall, Randy D
University of Maryland, Athletic Dept, College Park MD 20742 USA — Football Coach

Eduardo dos Santos, Jose
President's Office, Palacio do Povo, Luanda, Angola — President, Angola

Edur, Tom
Puhanzu 77, 10316 Talinn, Estonia — Ice Hockey Player

Edward
Bagshot, Bagshot Park, Surrey GU19 5PN, England — Prince, England

Edward, John
Berkley Publishing Group, 375 Hudson St, Basement 1, New York NY 10014 USA — Psychic

Edwards, Anthony
Creative Artists Agency, 2000 Ave of Stars, #100, Los Angeles CA 90067 USA — Actor

Edwards, Antonio
716 2nd St NW, Moultrie GA 31768, USA — Football Player

Edwards, Antuan M
8108 Connestee Dr, McKinney TX 75070, USA — Football Player

Edwards, Barbara
Hansen, 7767 Hollywood Blvd, #202, Los Angeles CA 90046, USA — Model, Actress

Edwards, Bradford W (Brad)
202 Southwood Dr, Columbia SC 29205, USA — Football Player

Edwards, Braylon J
32388 Legacy Pointe Parkway, Avon Lake OH 44012, USA — Football Player

Edwards, Carl M
3910 Trinity Church Road, Concord NC 28027, USA — Auto, Truck Racing Driver

Edwards, Chris
Independent Talent Group, Oxford House, 76 Oxford St, London W1D 1BS, England — Bassist (Kasabian)

Edwards, Cleophus (Cid)
5343 Adobe Fall Road, San Diego CA 92120, USA — Football Player

Edwards, David
5 Champion Place, Stillwater OK 74074, USA — Golfer

Edwards, David L (Dave)
5059 Quail Run Road, #75, Riverside CA 92507, USA — Baseball Player

Edwards, Dennis
Pyramid Entertainment, 377 Rector Place, #21A, New York NY 10280 USA — Singer (Temptations)

Edwards, Don
Scott O'Malley Assoc, 433 E Cuchamas St, Colorado Springs CO 80903, USA — Singer

Edwards, Don
530 Saint Andrews Road, #4, Saginaw MI 48638, USA — Ice Hockey Player

Edwards, Earl
1534 W Saint Thomas Dr, Gilbert AZ 85233, USA — Football Player

Edwards, Eddie
533 SW 61st Terrace, Margate FL 33068, USA — Football Player

Edwards, Eric
3404 SW Water Ave, Portland OR 97239, USA — Cinematographer

Edwards, Gareth
W M E Entertainment, 9601 Wilshire Blvd, #300, Beverly Hills CA 90210 USA — Writer

Edwards, Gareth O
Hamdden Ltd, Plas y Ffynnon, Cambrian Way, Brecon Powys LD3 7HP, Wales — Rugby Player

Edwards, Gary
6818 Pecan Ave, Moorpark CA 93021, USA — Ice Hockey Player

Edwards, Glen
4115 31st St S, Saint Petersbug FL 33712, USA — Football Player

Edwards, Harry
University of California, Sociology Dept, Berkeley CA 94720, USA — Educator, Social Activist

Edwards, Harry T
US Court of Appeals, 333 Constitution Ave NW, #4400, Washington DC 20001, USA — Judge

Edwards, Herman L (Herm)
433 Ward Parkway, #1, Kansas City MO 64112, USA — Football Player, Coach, Sportscaster

Edwards, Howard R (Doc)
3706 Driftwood Dr, San Angelo TX 76904, USA — Baseball Player, Manager

Edwards, James B
100 Venning St, Mount Pleasant SC 29464, USA — Secretary, Energy; Governor, SC

Edwards, Jay C
121 N Washington St, #506, Marion IN 46952, USA — Basketball Player

Edwards, Jennifer
I C M Partners, 10250 Constellation Blvd, #900, Los Angeles CA 90067 USA — Actress

Edwards, Joe F, Jr
National Sciences Center, 1 7th St, #502, Augusta GA 30901, USA — Astronaut

Edwards, Joel
5809 Shoreside Bend, Irving TX 75039, USA — Golfer

Edwards, John
Buddy Allen Mgmt, 3750 Hudson Manor Terrace, #3AE, Bronx NY 10463, USA — Singer (Spinners)

Edwards, John A (Johnny)
2511 E Blue Lake Dr, Magnolia TX 77354, USA — Baseball Player

Edwards, John R
North Carolina University, Work Poverty Center, Chapel Hill NC 27599, USA — Senator, NC

Edwards, Jonathan
Jonathan Marks, 20 York St, London W1U 6PU, England — Track Athlete

Edwards, Jonathan
Northern Lights, 437 Live Oak Loop NE, Albuquerque NM 87122, USA — Singer, Songwriter

Edwards, Kalimba 6140 Sibling Pine Dr, Durham NC 27705, USA	Football Player
Edwards, Kathleen Potty Mouth, 13 Blackburn St, #300, Toronto ON M4M 2B3, Canada	Singer, Songwriter
Edwards, Kevin 821 Reilly Lane, Lake Forest IL 60045, USA	Basketball Player
Edwards, Kim Penguin Books, 375 Hudson St, Basement 1, New York NY 10014 USA	Writer
Edwards, Luke Ensemble Entertainment, 10474 Santa Monica Blvd, #380, Los Angeles CA 90025, USA	Actor
Edwards, Mario L PO Box 216, Prosper TX 75078, USA	Football Player
Edwards, Mark J Deputy CNO, Communications Networks, HqUSN, Pentagon, Washington DC 20350, USA	Navy Admiral
Edwards, Marshall L 1061 Gamble Ave, Riverside CA 95208, USA	Baseball Player
Edwards, Marv 3277 1st Ave, #40, Mims FL 32754, USA	Ice Hockey Player
Edwards, Michael L (Mike) 11370 Moreno Beach Dr, Moreno Valley CA 92555, USA	Baseball Player
Edwards, Mike 502 Sharon Ave, Mechanicsburg PA 17055, USA	Baseball Player
Edwards, R LaVell Brigham Young University, Athletic Dept, Provo UT 84602, USA	Football Player, Coach
Edwards, Robert Creative Artists Agency, 2000 Ave of Stars, #100, Los Angeles CA 90067 USA	Director, Producer, Writer
Edwards, Robert A (Bob) Sirius XM Satellite Radio, 1500 Eckington Place NE, Washington DC 20002, USA	Commentator
Edwards, Robert G Duck End Farm, Dry Drayton, Cambridge CB3 8DB, England	Nobel Medicine Laureate
Edwards, Sandra Playboy Promotions, 2706 Media Center Dr, Los Angeles CA 90065 USA	Model, Actress
Edwards, Sian 70 Twisden Road, London NW5 1DN, England	Conductor
Edwards, Stacy TalentWorks, 3500 W Olive Ave, #1400, Burbank CA 91505 USA	Actress
Edwards, Stephen (Steve) 3980 Royal Oak Place, Encino CA 91436, USA	Composer
Edwards, Teresa 600 1st Ave N, #Sky, Minneapolis MN 55403, USA	Basketball Player, Coach
Edwards, Theodore (Blue) 11945 Maria Ester Court, Charlotte NC 28277, USA	Basketball Player
Edwards, Tommy Lee D C Comics, 1700 Broadway, #400, New York NY 10019 USA	Illustrator
Edwards, Trent Oakland Raiders, 1220 Harbor Bay Parkway, Alameda CA 94502 USA	Football Player
Edwards, Troy 6835 Foghorn Lane, Grand Prairie TX 75054, USA	Football Player
Edwards, Wayne PO Box 153, 2441Q Old Fort Parkway, Murfreesboro TN 37133, USA	Guitarist
Edwin, Colin Agency Group Ltd, 361-373 City Road, London EC1V 2QA, England	Bassist (Porcupine Tree)
Eenhoorn, Robert F Zermilieplaats 15, 3068J Rotterdam, Netherlands	Baseball Player
Efremova, Svetlana Greene Assoc, 1901 Ave of Stars, #130, Los Angeles CA 90067 USA	Actress
Efron, Zac Ninjas Runnin' Wild Productions, 7024 Melrose Ave, #420, Los Angeles CA 90038, USA	Actor
Egan, Christopher (Chris) Troika, 74 Clerkenwell Road, #300, London EC1M 5QA, England	Actor
Egan, Edward M Cardinal Archdiocese of New York, 1011 1st St, New York NY 10022, USA	Religious Leader
Egan, Jennifer Knopf Publishers, 1745 Broadway, New York NY 10019 USA	Writer
Egan, John F (Johnny) 2124 Nantucket Dr, #B, Houston TX 77057, USA	Basketball Player, Coach
Egan, John L Inchape PLC, 33 Cavendish Square, London W1M 9HF, England	Businessman
Egan, Melissa Claire Don Buchwald/Fortitude, 6500 Wilshire Blvd, #2200, Los Angeles CA 90048 USA	Actress
Egan, Peter I C M Partners, Marlborough House, 10 Earlham St, #300, London WC2H 9LNP, England	Actor
Egan, Richard W (Dick) 709 Carnoustie Court, Garland TX 75044, USA	Baseball Player
Egan, Susan 13801 Ventura Blvd, Sherman Oaks CA 91423, USA	Actress, Singer, Dancer
Egan, Thomas P (Tom) 184 E Myrna Lane, Tempe AZ 85284, USA	Baseball Player
Egdahl, Richard H 2400 Beacon St, #501, Chestnut Hill MA 02467, USA	Surgeon
Egers, Jack 24 Zinkann Crescent Gardens, Wellesley ON 0B 2T0, Canada	Ice Hockey Player
Egerszegi, Krisztina Budapest Spartacus, Koer Utca 1/A, 1103 Budapest, Hungary	Swimmer
Egerton, Tamsin Independent Talent Group, Oxford House, 76 Oxford St, London W1D 1BS, England	Actress
Eggar, Samantha 5005 Varna Ave, Sherman Oaks CA 91423, USA	Actress
Eggby, David 4344 Promenade Way, #209, Marina del Rey CA 90292, USA	Cinematographer
Eggeling, Dale 8918 Magnolia Chase Circle, Tampa FL 33647, USA	Golfer
Eggers, Dave Simon & Schuster 1230 Ave of Americas, New York NY 10020, USA	Writer
Eggers, Douglas B (Doug) 12803 Cedarbrook Lane, Laurel MD 20708, USA	Football Player

Eggert, Nicole — Actress
Global Artists Agency, 6253 Hollywood Blvd, #508, Los Angeles CA 90028, USA
Eggert, Robert J — Economist
Eggert Economic Enterprises, 1195 S Bates Road, Cottonwood AZ 86326, USA
Eggler, Markus — Curling Athlete
Bruckfeldstr 2, 4142 Munchenstein BL, Switzerland
Egglesfield, Colin — Actor
United Talent Agency, 9336 Civic Center Dr, Beverly Hills CA 90210 USA
Eggleston, William — Photographer, Artist
Robert Miller Gallery, 526 W 26th St, #10A, New York NY 10001, USA
Eggleton, Arthur C — Government Official, Canada
National Defense Ministry, 101 Colonel By Dr, Ottawa ON K1A 0K2, Canada
Eggold, Ryan J — Actor
Gersh Agency, 9465 Wilshire Blvd, #600, Beverly Hills CA 90212 USA
Egielski, Richard — Illustrator
525 B St, #1900, San Diego CA 92101, USA
Egington, Richard P — Rowing Athlete
Leander Club, Henley on Thames, Leander RG9 2LP, England
Egloff, Bruce E — Baseball Player
3136 S Emporia Court, Denver CO 80231, USA
Egon, Nicholas — Artist
Villa Aetos, Katakali, Corinthia 20100, Greece
Ehart, Phil — Drummer (Kansas)
Lustig Talent, PO Box 770850, Orlando FL 32877 USA
Eheart, Brenda Krause — Social Activist
Hope Meadows, 1530 Fairway Dr, Rantoul IL 61866, USA
Ehle, Jennifer — Actress
I C M Partners, 10250 Constellation Blvd, #900, Los Angeles CA 90067 USA
Ehlers, Beth — Actress
Stone Manners Salners, 9911 W Pico Blvd, #1400, Los Angeles CA 90035 USA
Ehlers, Edwin S (Eddie) — Basketball Player
PO Box 303, Notre Dame IN 46556, USA
Ehlers, Walter D — WW II Army Hero (CMH)
8382 Valley View, Buena Park CA 90620, USA
Ehlert, Lois — Writer
Scholastic Press, 555 Broadway, New York NY 10012 USA
Ehlo, J Craig — Basketball Player
3323 E 77th Ave, Spokane WA 99223, USA
Ehrenfeld, Rachel — Writer
American Center for Democracy, 330 W 56th St, #24E, New York NY 10019, USA
Ehrenkrantz, Dan — Religious Leader, Rabbi, Educator
Reconstructionist Rabbinical College, 1299 Church Road, Wyncote PA 19095, USA
Ehrenreich, Alden — Actor
Creative Artists Agency, 2000 Ave of Stars, #100, Los Angeles CA 90067 USA
Ehrenreich, Barbara — Women's Activist, Writer
I C M Partners, 10250 Constellation Blvd, #900, Los Angeles CA 90067 USA
Ehret, Gloria — Golfer
3335 Royal Lane, Dallas TX 75229, USA
Ehrhoff, Christian — Ice Hockey Player
4517 Carlyle Court, Santa Clara CA 95054, USA
Ehrlich, Paul R — Population Biologist
Stanford University, Biological Sciences Dept, Stanford CA 94305, USA
Ehrlich, Thomas — Educator
Carnegie Teaching Foundation, 51 Vista Lane, Stanford CA 94305, USA
Ehrmann, Joseph C (Joe) — Football Player
5 Elmhurst Road, Baltimore MD 21210, USA
Eichelberger, Charles B — Army General
California Microwave, 124 Sweetwater Oaks, Peachtree City GA 30269, USA
Eichelberger, David — Golfer
1947 Judd Hillside Road, Honolulu HI 96822, USA
Eichelberger, Juan T — Baseball Player
14674 Silverset St, Poway CA 92064, USA
Eichhorn, Lisa — Actress
1919 W 44th St, #1000, New York NY 10036, USA
Eichhorn, Mark A — Baseball Player
147 Norma Court, Aptos CA 95003, USA
Eichhorst, Richard A (Dick) — Basketball Player
2701 Sheridan Road, Saint Louis MO 63125, USA
Eigen, Manfred — Nobel Chemistry Laureate
Georg-Dehio-Weg 4, 37075 Gottingen, Germany
Eigenberg, David — Actor
Paul Kohner, 9300 Wilshire Blvd, #555, Beverly Hills CA 90212 USA
Eijk, Willem J (Wim) Cardinal — Religious Leader
Archdiocese, P B 14019, 3508 SB Utrecht, Netherlands
Eikenberry, Jill — Actress
PO Box 843, Santa Ynez CA 93460, USA
Eikenberry, Karl W — Army General
State Department, 2201 C St NW, Washington DC 20520 USA
Eiland, David W (Dave) — Baseball Player
2824 Blue Springs Place, Wesley Chapel FL 33544, USA
Eilbacher, Lisa — Actress
Metropolitan Talent Agency, 7020 La Presa Dr, Los Angeles CA 90068 USA
Eilber, Janet — Actress
Irv Schechter, 9460 Wilshire Blvd, #300, Beverly Hills CA 90212 USA
Eilers, David L (Dave) — Baseball Player
602 Perkins Lane, Brenham TX 77833, USA
Eilers, Patrick C (Pat) — Football Player
177 De Windt Road, Winnetka IL 60093, USA
Eine, Simon — Actor
Anne Alvares Correa, 34 Rue Jouffroy d'Abbans, 75017 Paris, France
Einertson, Darrell — Baseball Player
221 Hawthorne Dr, Norwalk IA 50211, USA
Einhorn, Lawrence — Oncologist
Indiana University Medical School, Oncology Dept, Bloomington IN 47405, USA
Einhorn, Richard — Composer
320 Riverside Dr, #15C, New York NY 10025, USA

Einstein, Bob (Super Dave Osbourne)
9842 Cardigan Place, Beverly Hills CA 90210, USA — Actor, Comedian

Einziger, Mike
Variety Artists, 793 Higuera St, #6, San Luis Obispo CA 93401 USA — Guitarist (Incubus), Songwriter

Eischeid, Michael D (Mike)
306 Auburn St, West Union IA 52175, USA — Football Player

Eischen, Joseph R (Joey)
3678 E Thornton Ave, Gilbert AZ 85297, USA — Baseball Player

Eisen, Herman N
75 Cambridge Parkway, #E806, Cambridge MA 02142, USA — Immunologist

Eisen, Rich
N F L Network, 10950 Washington Blvd, #100, Culver City CA 90232 USA — Sportscaster

Eisen, Tripp
United Talent Agency, 9336 Civic Center Dr, Beverly Hills CA 90210 USA — Guitarist (Static-X)

Eisenach, Kathleen
University of Arkansas Medical Sciences, 4301 W Markham, Little Rock AR 72205, USA — Pathologist

Eisenberg, David S
University of California, Chemisty & Biochemistry Dept, Los Angeles CA 90024, USA — Chemist

Eisenberg, Hallie Kate
Abrams Artists, 9200 W Sunset Blvd, #1125, West Hollywood CA 90069 USA — Actress

Eisenberg, Jesse A
I C M Partners, 10250 Constellation Blvd, #900, Los Angeles CA 90067 USA — Actor

Eisenberg, Lee
W M E Entertainment, 9601 Wilshire Blvd, #300, Beverly Hills CA 90210 USA — Actor, Comedian, Writer

Eisenberg, Melvin A
1197 Keeler Ave, Berkeley CA 94708, USA — Attorney, Educator

Eisenhauer, Lawrence C (Larry)
19 Hobart Lane, Cohasset MA 02025, USA — Football Player

Eisenhauer, Stephen S (Steve)
105 Abbey Road, Winchester VA 22602, USA — Football Player

Eisenman, Peter D
Eisenman Architects, 40 W 25th St, New York NY 10010, USA — Architect

Eisenreich, James M (Jim)
11 Emerald Shore Dr, Blue Springs MO 64015, USA — Baseball Player

Eisenstein, Michael
Little Big Man, 155 Ave of Americas, #700, New York NY 10013, USA — Guitarist (Letters to Cleo)

Eisinger, Jesse
ProPublica, Editorial Dept, 1 Exchange Plaza, 55 Broadway, #2300, New York NY 10006, USA — Journalist

Eisler, Barry
Penguin Group, 375 Hudson St, Basement 1, New York NY 10014, USA — Writer

Eisler, Lloyd E
Los Angeles Kings Valley Ice Center, 8750 Van Nuys Blvd, Panorama City CA 91402, USA — Figure Skater

Eisley, Howard J
20250 Rodeo Court, Southfield MI 48075, USA — Basketball Player

Eisley, India
I C M Partners, 10250 Constellation Blvd, #900, Los Angeles CA 90067 USA — Actress

Eisman, Hy
99 Boulevard, Glen Rock NJ 07452, USA — Cartoonist (Katzenjammer Kids)

Eisner, Breck
Creative Artists Agency, 2000 Ave of Stars, #100, Los Angeles CA 90067 USA — Director

Eisner, Michael D
Tornante Co, 233 S Beverly Dr, #200, Beverly Hills CA 90212, USA — Businessman

Eitner, Lorenz E A
684 Mirada Ave, Stanford CA 94305, USA — Art Historian

Eitzel, Mark
Legends of 21st Century, 7 Trinity Row, Florence MA 01062, USA — Singer, Songwriter

Eizenstat, Stuart E
5610 Wisconsin Ave, #603, Chevy Chase MD 20815, USA — Government Official, Diplomat

Ejiofor, Chiwetel
B/W/R, 9100 Wilshire Blvd, #500W, Beverly Hills CA 90212 USA — Actor

Ejogo, Carmen
I F A Talent Agency, 8730 W Sunset Blvd, #490, West Hollywood CA 90069 USA — Actress

Ek, Klara
Harrison/Parrott, 5-6 Albion Court, London W6 0QT, England — Opera Singer

Ekberg, Anita
Via Aspro N 1, 00045 Genzano di Rome, Italy — Actress, Model

Ekberg, Niclas
T H W Kiel Handball, Ziegelteich 30, 24103 Kiel, Germany — Handball Player

Ekberg, Ulf
United Stage Mgmt, Asogatan 142, Box 11029, 100 61 Stockholm, Sweden — Singer (Ace of Base)

Ekimov, Viatcheslav V
TeamRadio Shack, Capital Sports & Mgmt, 98 San Jacinto Blvd, #430, Austin, TX 78701, USA — Cyclist

Ekland, Britt
1888 N Crescent Heights Blvd, Los Angeles CA 90069, USA — Actress

Eklund, Greg
Pinnacle Entertainment, 30 Glenn St, White Plains NY 10603, USA — Drummer (Everclear)

Eklund, Per-Erik (Pelle)
Sunnanangyttervagen 67, 793 90 Leksand, Sweden — Ice Hockey Player

Ekman, Paul
University of California Medical Center, 505 Parnassus, San Francisco CA 94122 USA — Psychologist

Ekstrom, Michael
1616 SE 282nd Ave, Gresham OR 97080, USA — Baseball Player

Ekuban, Ebenezer, Jr
5391 Moonlight Way, Parker CO 80134, USA — Football Player

El DeBarge
205 Hill St, Santa Monica CA 90405, USA — Singer

El Fadil, Siddig
Paramount, 5555 Melose Ave, Los Angeles CA 90038, USA — Actor

El Fassi, Abbas
Prime Minister's Office, Palais Royal, Le Mechouar, Rabat, Morocco — Prime Minister, Morocco

Elam, Jason
PO Box 1425, Soldotna AK 99669, USA — Football Player

Elam, Katrina
PO Box 209, Marlow OK 73055, USA — Singer

Elarton, V Scott
52922 Raines Road, Limon CO 80828, USA — Baseball Player

Elba, Idris — Actor
United Talent Agency, 9336 Civic Center Dr, Beverly Hills CA 90210 USA
ElBaradei, Mohamed M — Nobel Peace Laureate
International Atomic Energy Agency, Wagramerstra 5, 1400 Vienna, Austria
Eldard, Ron — Actor
United Talent Agency, 9336 Civic Center Dr, Beverly Hills CA 90210 USA
Elder, Larry — Actor
C E S D, 10635 Santa Monica Blvd, #130, Los Angeles CA 90025 USA
Elder, Lee E — Golfer
PO Box 667200, Pompano Beach FL 33066, USA
Elder, Mark P — Conductor
Ingpen & Williams, 131 Putney Bridge Road, London SW15 2PA, England
Elders, M Jocelyn — Pediatrician, Government Official
810 Marcia Cove, Little Rock AR 72206, USA
Eldon, Kevin — Actor
R D F Mgmt, 3-6 Kendrick Place, London W1U 6HD, England
Eldred, Bradley R (Brad) — Baseball Player
4182 SW Saint Lucie Lane, Palm City FL 34990, USA
Eldred, Calvin J (Cal) — Baseball Player
1893 Horn Road, Mount Vernon IA 52314, USA
Eldredge, Todd — Figure Skater
2463 N Lake Angelus Road W, Auburn Hills MI 48326, USA
Electra, Carmen — Actress, Singer, Model
Hollywood/Sunset Pictures, 12408 La Pomelo Road, #2, La Mirada CA 90638, USA
Eleniak, Erika — Model, Actress
Kirk Talent Agencies, 70 E 2nd Ave, #301, Vancouver BC V5T 1B1, Canada
Elephant Man — Singer
Bad Boy Entertainment, 1440 Broadway, #16, New York NY 10018 USA
Elfman, Bodhi — Actor
Lewis & Beal Talent Agency, 15303 Ventura Blvd, #900, Sherman Oaks CA 91403, USA
Elfman, Danny — Singer, Composer
Musica de la Muerte, 1901 Ave of Stars, #1450, Los Angeles CA 90067, USA
Elfman, Jenna — Actress, Model
Brillstein Entertainment Partners, 9150 Wilshire Blvd, #350, Beverly Hills CA 90212 USA
Elg, Taina — Actress
789 W End Ave, New York NY 10025, USA
Elgart, Larry J — Orchestra Leader
2065 Gulf of Mexico Dr, Longboat Key FL 34228, USA
Elia, Lee C — Baseball Player, Manager
11613 Innfields Dr, Odessa FL 33556, USA
Elia, Nicolas — Actor
Paceline Entertainment, 12444 Ventura Blvd, #103, Studio City CA 91604 USA
Eliane, Elias — Singer, Pianist, Composer
RR 376 Box 1282, Wappingers FL 12590, USA
Elias, Antonio L — Space Scientist
Orbital Sciences Corp, 21839 Atlantic Blvd, Dulles VA 20166, USA
Elias, Eliane — Jazz Pianist, Singer, Composer
Impact Artist Mgmt, 356 W 123rd St, New York NY 10027, USA
Elias, Hector — Actor
C E S D, 10635 Santa Monica Blvd, #130, Los Angeles CA 90025 USA
Elias, Jonathan — Composer
Elias Arts, 2219 Main St, Santa Monica CA 90405, USA
Elias, Keith H — Football Player
4507 Norma Place, Toms River NJ 08755, USA
Elias, Patrik — Ice Hockey Player
1005 Smith Manor Blvd, #98, West Orange NJ 07052, USA
Elias, Rosalind — Opera Singer
Robert Lombardo Assoc, Harkness Plaza, 61 W 62nd St, #6F, New York NY 10023 USA
Elice, Rick — Writer
I C M Partners, 10250 Constellation Blvd, #900, Los Angeles CA 90067 USA
Elie, Mario A — Basketball Player
1 Mott Lane, Houston TX 77024, USA
Elinson, Jack — Sociomedical Scientist
655 Pomander Walk, #210, Teaneck NJ 07666, USA
Eliot, Darren J — Ice Hockey Player
1100 Grayton St, Grosse Pointe Park MI 48230, USA
Eliot, Jan — Cartoonist (Stone Soup)
PO Box 50032, Eugene OR 97405, USA
Elise, Christine — Actress
Luber Rocklin Entertainment, 8530 Wilshire Blvd, #555, Beverly Hills CA 90211 USA
Elise, Kimberly — Actress
Untitled Entertainment, 350 S Beverly Dr, #200, Beverly Hills CA 90212 USA
Eliuk, Dallas — Lacrosse Player
Portland LumberJax, Rose Garden Arena, 1 N Center Court, Portland OR 97227, USA
Elizabeth II — Queen, England
Buckingham Palace, London SW1A 1AA, England
Elizabeth, Sarah — Model
Playboy Promotions, 2706 Media Center Dr, Los Angeles CA 90065 USA
Elizabeth, Shannon — Actress, Model
Kritzer Levine Wilkins Griffin, 11872 La Grange Ave, #100, Los Angeles CA 90025 USA
Elizondo, Hector — Actor
Gersh Agency, 9465 Wilshire Blvd, #600, Beverly Hills CA 90212 USA
Elkaim, Jeremie — Actor
Artmedia, 20 Ave Rapp, 75007 Paris, France
Elkes, Joel — Psychiatrist
University of Louisville, Psychiatry & Behavioral Science Dept, Louisville KY 40292, USA
Elkind, Mortimer M — Biophysicist
10234 Rue Chamonix, San Diego CA 92131, USA
Elkington, Steve — Golfer
7010 Kelsey Rae Court, Houston TX 77069, USA
Elkins, Lawrence C (Larry) — Football Player
1 Keats Ave, Norden, Rochdale, Lancashire OL12 7PZ, England
Ellard, Henry A — Football Player
5800 Airline Dr, Metairie LA 70003, USA
Ellena, Jack D — Football Player
73164 Monterra Circle N, Palm Desert CA 92260, USA

Ellenshaw, Harrison — Special Effects Artist
2060 Avenida de los Arboles, #D317, Thousand Oaks CA 91362, USA
Ellenson, David — Religious Leader, Rabbi, Educator
Hebrew Union College, Jewish Religious Institute, 1 W 4th St, New York NY 10012, USA
Eller, Carl — Football Player, Executive
1035 Washburn Ave N, Minneapolis MN 55411, USA
Eller, Walter (Glenn), III — Marksman
US Army Marksmanship Unit, Fort Benning GA 31905, USA
Ellerbee, Linda — Commentator
Lucky Duck Productions, 96 Morton St, #400, New York NY 10014, USA
Ellerson, Rich — Football Coach
US Military Academy, Athletic Dept, West Point NY 10996, USA
Ellett, Dave — Ice Hockey Player
36611 N 51st St, Cave Creek AZ 85331, USA
Ellickson, Robert C — Attorney, Educator
Yale University, Law School, 127 Wall St, New Haven CT 06511, USA
Elliman, Yvonne — Singer
Talent Consultants International, 105 Shad Row, #B, Piermont NY 10968 USA
Ellin, Doug — Director, Producer
Leverage Mgmt, 3030 Pennsylvania Ave, Santa Monica CA 90404, USA
Elling, Kurt — Singer
Open Door Mgmt, 15327 Sunset Blvd, #365, Pacific Palisades CA 90272, USA
Ellingsen, H Bruce — Baseball Player
5873 Daneland St, Lakewood CA 90713, USA
Ellingson, Evan — Actor
Innovative Artists, 1505 10th St, Santa Monica CA 90401 USA
Elliot, Janet — Steeplechase Racing Trainer
Kirkwood Stables, 21 Mount Eden Road, Kirkwood PA 17536, USA
Elliot, Lawrence L (Larry) — Baseball Player
13010 Caminito Bracho, San Diego CA 92128, USA
Elliot, Ross — Actor
5702 Graves Ave, Encino CA 91316, USA
Elliott, Abby — Actress, Comedienne
Creative Artists Agency, 2000 Ave of Stars, #100, Los Angeles CA 90067 USA
Elliott, Alecia — Singer, Actress
Creative Artists Agency, 2000 Ave of Stars, #100, Los Angeles CA 90067 USA
Elliott, Alison — Actress
Innovative Artists, 1505 10th St, Santa Monica CA 90401 USA
Elliott, Andrea — Journalist
New York Times, Editorial Dept, 229 W 43rd St, New York NY 10036 USA
Elliott, Brennan — Actor
Stone Manners Salners, 9911 W Pico Blvd, #1400, Los Angeles CA 90035 USA
Elliott, Brooke — Actress, Singer
Innovative Artists, 1505 10th St, Santa Monica CA 90401 USA
Elliott, Chalmers (Bump) — Football Player, Coach
1 Oaknoll Court, Iowa City IA 52246, USA
Elliott, Chris — Actor, Comedian
Mosiac Media Group, 9200 W Sunset Blvd, #1000, Los Angeles CA 90069 USA
Elliott, David James — Actor
Paradigm Agency, 360 N Crescent Dr, North Building, Beverly Hills CA 90210 USA
Elliott, Dennis — Drummer (Foreigner)
Hard to Handle Mgmt, 16501 Ventura Blvd, #602, Encino CA 91436, USA
Elliott, Donald G (Donnie) — Baseball Player
1206 Bayou Vista Dr, Deer Park TX 77536, USA
Elliott, E Matthew (Matt) — Football Player
7453 Coventry Woods Dr, Dublin OH 43017, USA
Elliott, Gordon — Chef
Food Network, 1180 Ave of Americas, #1200, New York NY 10036 USA
Elliott, Harry L — Baseball Player
9608 Los Coches Road, Lakeside CA 92040, USA
Elliott, Herbert (Herb) — Track Athlete
Athletics Australia, 431 Saint Kilda Road, Melbourne VIC 3004, Australia
Elliott, Ira S — Drummer (Fuzztones, Nada Surf)
M-Squared Mgmt, 201 W 72nd St, #12G, New York NY 10023, USA
Elliott, Joe — Singer, Musician (Def Leppard)
Front Line Mgmt, 1100 Glendon Ave, #2000, Los Angeles CA 90024 USA
Elliott, John H — Historian
122 Church Way, Iffley, Oxford OX4 4EG, England
Elliott, John S (Jumbo) — Football Player
17 Fieldstone Lane, Oyster Bay NY 11771, USA
Elliott, Missy — Singer, Songwriter, Actress
Monami Entertainment, 100 Church St, #849, New York NY 10007, USA
Elliott, Paul H — Cinematographer
Sandra Marsh Assoc, 9150 Wilshire Blvd, #220, Beverly Hills CA 90212 USA
Elliott, Peter R (Pete) — Football Player, Coach
3003 Dunbarton Ave NW, Canton OH 44708, USA
Elliott, Ralph E — WW II Navy Air Force Hero
5150 Damascus Road S, Jacksonville FL 32207, USA
Elliott, Ramblin' Jack — Singer, Songwriter, Guitarist
Day, 300 W 55th St, New York NY 10019, USA
Elliott, Rand — Architect
Elliott Assoc, 35 Harrison Ave, Oklahoma City OK 73104, USA
Elliott, Randy L — Baseball Player
1002 Steuben St, Wausau WI 54403, USA
Elliott, Robert A (Bob) — Basketball Player
6760 E Fieldstone Lane, Tucson AZ 85750, USA
Elliott, Sam — Actor
33050 Pacific Coast Highway, Malibu CA 90265, USA
Elliott, Sean M — Basketball Player
1726 Greystone Ridge, San Antonio TX 78258, USA
Elliott, Steve — Harness Racing Driver, Trainer
36 Brookwood Road, Mount Laurel NJ 8054, USA
Elliott, Ted A — Writer, Producer
Creative Artists Agency, 2000 Ave of Stars, #100, Los Angeles CA 90067 USA
Elliott, William C (Bill) — Auto Racing Driver
Bill Elliott Racing, 200 Woodhaven Lane, Ball Ground GA 30107, USA

Ellis Bextor, Sophie
Primary Talent International, 10-11 Jockey's Fields, London WC1R 4BN, England — Singer

Ellis, Alex
10121 Lone Wolf Dr, Indianapolis IN 46235, USA — Basketball Player

Ellis, Allan D
7352 S Dante Ave, Chicago IL 60619, USA — Football Player

Ellis, Anita
130 E End Ave, New York NY 10028, USA — Jazz Singer

Ellis, Aunjanue
I C M Partners, 10250 Constellation Blvd, #900, Los Angeles CA 90067 USA — Actress

Ellis, Bret Easton
Vintage Books, 1745 Broadway, New York NY 10019 USA — Writer

Ellis, Caroline
8060 Saint Clair Ave, North Hollywood CA 91605, USA — Actress

Ellis, Chris
Bauman Redanty Shaul Agency, 5757 Wilshire Blvd, #473, Los Angeles CA 90036 USA — Actor

Ellis, Cliff
Auburn University, Athletic Dept, Auburn AL 36831, USA — Basketball Coach

Ellis, Dale
3564 W Hampton Dr NW, Marietta GA 30064, USA — Basketball Player

Ellis, Danny
1543 Cherry Lake Way, Lake Mary FL 32746, USA — Golfer

Ellis, David R
Principato-Young, 9465 Wilshire Blvd, #880, Beverly Hills CA 90212 USA — Director

Ellis, Don
34 Crestwood Circle, Sugar Land TX 77478, USA — Bowler

Ellis, Elmer
3300 New Haven Ave, #223, Columbia MO 65201, USA — Historian, Educator

Ellis, F (Cot)
9505 N Silver Lake Dr, Oklahoma City OK 73162, USA — Baseball Player

Ellis, George F R
3 Marlowe Road, Capetown 7700, South Africa — Mathematician, Templeton Laureate

Ellis, Gerry L
250 Cavil Way, De Pere WI 54115, USA — Football Player

Ellis, Greg
Kritzer Levine Wilkins Griffin, 11872 La Grange Ave, #100, Los Angeles CA 90025 USA — Actor

Ellis, Gregory L (Greg)
PO Box 96075, Southlake TX 76092, USA — Football Player

Ellis, Harold
9420 Parkwood Ave, Douglasville GA 30135, USA — Basketball Player

Ellis, Hunter
Ideal Mgmt, 5780 W Centennial Ave, #313, Los Angeles CA 90045, USA — Actor

Ellis, James R
4213 Swann Ave, Tampa FL 33609, USA — Army General

Ellis, James R (Jim)
13608 Ave 24, Tulare CA 93274, USA — Baseball Player

Ellis, Janet
Arlington Entertainments, 1/3 Charlotte St, London W1P 1HD, England — Actress

Ellis, Jimmy
5218 Saint Gabriel Lane, Louisville KY 40291, USA — Boxer

Ellis, John C
14 Marina Point Dr, Old Saybrook CT 06475, USA — Baseball Player

Ellis, Joseph J
Mount Holyoke College, History Dept, South Hadley MA 01075, USA — Writer

Ellis, K Ray
4666 E Olney Ave, Gilbert AZ 85234, USA — Football Player

Ellis, Kenneth A (Ken)
2700 Gulf Freeway, #2111, Texas City TX 77591, USA — Football Player

Ellis, LaPhonso
51215 Shannon Brook Court, Granger IN 46530, USA — Basketball Player

Ellis, Larry R
3425 SW 2nd Ave, Gainesville FL 32607, USA — Army General

Ellis, Mary Elizabeth
Flutie Entertainment, 9320 Wilshire Blvd, #202, Beverly Hills CA 90212 USA — Actress

Ellis, MeShaunda P (Shaun)
26 Green St, Newbury MA 01951, USA — Football Player

Ellis, Monta
Milwaukee Bucks, Bradley Center, 1001 N 4th St, #2, Milwaukee WI 53203 USA — Basketball Player

Ellis, Nelsan
I C M Partners, 10250 Constellation Blvd, #900, Los Angeles CA 90067 USA — Actor

Ellis, Osian G
90 Chandos Ave, London N20 9DZ, England — Concert Harpist

Ellis, Richard S
California Institute of Technology, Astronomy Dept, Pasadena CA 91125, USA — Astronomer

Ellis, Robin
Ken McReddie Assoc, 11 Connaught Place, London W2 2ET, England — Actor

Ellis, Romallis
2062 San Marco Dr, Ellenwood GA 30294, USA — Boxer

Ellis, Ronald J E (Ron)
B C E Place, 30 Yonge St, Toronto ON M5E 1X8, Canada — Ice Hockey Player

Ellis, Rosemary
Good Housekeeping, Editor's Office, 300 W 57th St, New York NY 10019, USA — Editor

Ellis, Samuel J (Sam)
12511 Forest Highlands Dr, Dade City FL 33525, USA — Baseball Player

Ellis, Scott
301 W 118th St, #10-I, New York NY 10026, USA — Director

Ellis, Sedrick
New Orleans Saints, 5800 Airline Highway, Metairie LA 70003 USA — Football Player

Ellis, Terry
East West Records, 75 Rockefeller Plaza, #1200, New York NY 10019, USA — Singer (En Vogue)

Ellison, Brooke
Hyperion Books, 114 5th Ave, New York NY 10011 USA — Writer

Ellison, Harlan J
Kilimanjaro Group, PO Box 55548, Sherman Oaks CA 91413, USA — Writer

Ellison, Jason J
3745 248th Ave SE, Issaquah WA 98029, USA — Baseball Player

Ellison, Jennifer — Actress
C A M, 55-59 Shaftsbury Ave, London W1D 6LD, England
Ellison, Keith — Football Player
Buffalo Bills, 1 Bills Dr, Orchard Park NY 14127 USA
Ellison, Lawrence J — Businessman, Yachtsman
Oracle Systems, 500 Oracle Parkway, Redwood Shores CA 94065, USA
Ellison, Pervis — Basketball Player
4602 Kettering Dr NE, Roswell GA 30075, USA
Ellison, William H (Willie) — Football Player
3503 Mosley Court, Houston TX 77004, USA
Elliss, Luther J — Football Player
118 E 3200 N, Kamas UT 84036, USA
Ellmann, Lucy — Writer
David Godwin Assoc, 55 Monmouth St, London WC2H 9DG, England
Ellroy, James — Writer
Sobel Weber Assoc, 146 E 19th St, New York NY 10003, USA
Ellsberg, Daniel — Political Activist
90 Norwood Ave, Kensington CA 94707, USA
Ellsbury, Jacoby M — Baseball Player
1204 Suncast Lane, #2, El Dorado Hills CA 95762, USA
Ellsworth, Frank L — Educator
2935 Sequoia Dr S, Palm Springs CA 92262, USA
Ellsworth, Kiko — Actor
Stone Manners Salners, 9911 W Pico Blvd, #1400, Los Angeles CA 90035 USA
Ellsworth, Percy D — Football Player
11261 Fortsville Road, Capron VA 23829, USA
Ellsworth, Richard C (Dick) — Baseball Player
1099 W Morris Ave, Fresno CA 93711, USA
Ellwood, Paul M, Jr — Physician
68 Dell Creek Road, Bondurant WY 82922, USA
Ellyson, Erica — Model
9850 S Maryland Parkway, #A5-446, Las Vegas NV 89183, USA
Elmaleh, Gad — Actor, Comedian
Thruline Entertainment, 9250 Wilshire Blvd, #100, Beverly Hills CA 90212 USA
Elmendorf, David C (Dave) — Football Player
17990 FM 1452 W, Normangee TX 77871, USA
Elmes, Fredrick — Cinematographer
Mirisch Agency, 8840 Wilshire Blvd, #100, Beverly Hills CA 90211 USA
Elmore, Leonard J (Len) — Basketball Player, Sportscaster
PO Box 22, Highland MD 20777, USA
Elrod, Jack — Cartoonist (Mark Trail)
7240 Hunter's Branch Dr NE, Atlanta GA 30328, USA
Elrod, Scott — Actor
Independent Group, 8444 Wilshire Blvd, #500, Beverly Hills CA 90211, USA
Els, T Ernest (Ernie) — Golfer
Ernie Els Design, PO Box 73, Virginia Water GU25 4ZS, England
Elshire, Neil J — Football Player
2441 NW Torsway St, Bend OR 97701, USA
Elsley, Bryan — Producer
The Agency, 24 Pottery Lane, London W11 4LZ, England , USA
Elsna, Hebe — Writer
Curtis Brown Group, 28-29 Haymarket St, #500, London SW1Y 4SP, England
Elsner, Christian — Opera Singer
Kunstler Sekretariat am Gasteig, Rosenheimer Str 52, 81669 Munich, Germany
Elson, Andrea — Actress
Flick East-West, 9057 Nemo St, #A, West Hollywood, CA 90069 USA
Elson, Francisco — Basketball Player
92 Foxton Dr, San Antonio TX 78258, USA
Elson, Karen — Model
Elite Model Mgmt, 404 Park Ave S, #900, New York NY 10016 USA
Elster, Jennifer — Director
P M K-B N C, 622 3rd Ave, #800, New York NY 10017 USA
Elswit, Richard (Rik) — Singer, Guitarist (Dr Hook)
Artists International Mgmt, 9850 Sandalwood Blvd, #458, Boca Raton FL 33428, USA
Elswit, Robert — Cinematographer
United Talent Agency, 9336 Civic Center Dr, Beverly Hills CA 90210 USA
Elton, Ben — Actor, Comedian
Phil McIntyre Mgmt, 35 Soho Square, London W1D 3QX, England
Elts, Olari — Conductor
Van Walsum Mgmt, Tower Building, 11 York Road, London SE1 7NX, England
Elvin, Violetta — Ballerina
Marina di Equa, 80066 Seiano, Bay of Naples, Italy
Elvin-Lewis, Memory — Ethnobotanist
7915 Park Dr, Saint Louis MO 63117, USA
Elvira, (Cassandra Peterson) — Actress
Queen B Productions, PO Box 38246, Los Angeles CA 90038, USA
Elway, John A — Football Player
13644 E Dole Valley, Englewood CO 80112, USA
Elwes, Cary — Actor
Kritzer Levine Wilkins Griffin, 11872 La Grange Ave, #100, Los Angeles CA 90025 USA
Elwood, Hugh M — WW II Marine Corps Air Force Hero
1 Fleet Landing Blvd, Atlantic Beach FL 32233, USA
Ely, Alexandre (Alex) — Soccer Player
5526 N 2nd St, Philadelphia PA 19120, USA
Ely, Jack — Singer, Guitarist
Rolling Highway Mgmt, PO Box 1176, Marfa TX 79843, USA
Ely, Joe — Singer, Guitarist, Songwriter
L C Media, PO Box 965, Antioch TN 37011, USA
Ely, Ron — Actor
4161 Mariposa Dr, Santa Barbara CA 93110, USA
Ely, Shyra — Basketball Player
Indiana Fever, Conseco Fieldhouse, 125 S Pennsylvania, Indianapolis IN 46204 USA
Elynuik, Patrick G (Pat) — Ice Hockey Player
143 Aspen Green, Calgary AB T3Z 3B9, Canada
Emanuel, Alphonsia — Actress
Marina Martin, 12/13 Poland St, London W1V 3DE, England

Emanuel, Bert T
15 Bees Creek Court, Missouri City TX 77459, USA — Football Player
Emanuel, David
David Emanuel Couture, Lanesborough Hotel, London SW1X 7TA, England — Fashion Designer
Emanuel, Elizabeth F
Sew Forth Productions, 26 Chiltern St, London W1M 1PF, England — Fashion Designer
Emanuel, Kerry A
Massachusetts Institute of Technology, Atmospheric Science Center, Cambridge MA 02139, USA — Meteorologist
Emanuel, Rahm
Mayor's Office, 121 N La Salle St, #507, Chicago IL 60602, USA — Mayor, Chicago; Government Official
Emanuel, T Frank
10211 Deercliff Dr, Tampa FL 33647, USA — Football Player
Embach, Carsten
B S R Rennsteig e V, Grafenrodaer Str 2, 98559 Oberhof, Germany — Bobsled Athlete
Emberg, Kelly
PO Box 675401, Rancho Santa Fe CA 92067, USA — Actress, Model
Embery, Joan
American Zoo Keepers Assn, 3601 SW 29th St, #133, Topeka KS 66614, USA — Animal Activist
Embree, Ainslie T
PO Box 433, Centerville MA 02632, USA — Historian
Embree, Alan D
61971 Kildonan Court, Bend OR 97702, USA — Baseball Player
Embry, Ethan
A P A Talent/Literary Agency, 405 S Beverly Dr, #300, Beverly Hills CA 90212 USA — Actor
Embry, Wayne R
1101-211 Queens Quay W, Toronto ON M5J 2M6, Canada — Basketball Player, Executive
Emburey, John E
Middlesex Cricket Club, Lord's Cricket Ground, London NW8 8QN, England — Cricketer
Emerick, Kate
Matt Sherman Mgmt, 9107 Wilshire Blvd, #225, Beverly Hills CA 90210, USA — Actress
Emerick, Scotty
Paradise Artists, PO Box 1821, Ojai CA 93024 USA — Singer, Songwriter
Emerson, Claudia
Mary Washington University, English Dept, 1301 College, Frederickburg VA 22401, USA — Writer
Emerson, David F
211 E 18th St, #5O, New York NY 10003, USA — Navy Admiral
Emerson, Keith
Asia, 9 Hillgate St, London W8 7SP, England — Keyboardist (Emerson Lake & Palmer)
Emerson, Michael
Innovative Artists, 1505 10th St, Santa Monica CA 90401 USA — Actor
Emerson, Nelson
717 33rd St, Manhattan Beach CA 90266, USA — Ice Hockey Player
Emerson, Roy
2221 Alta Vista Dr, Newport Beach CA 92660, USA — Tennis Player
Emery, Gideon
Greene Assoc, 1901 Ave of Stars, #130, Los Angeles CA 90067 USA — Actor
Emery, John
Bobsled Canada, 140 Canada Olympic Road SW, Calgary AB T3B 5R5, Canada — Bobsled Athlete
Emery, Julie Ann
Principal Entertainment, 1964 Westwood Blvd, #400, Los Angeles CA 90025 USA — Actress
Emery, Lin
7520 Dominican St, New Orleans LA 70118, USA — Artist, Sculptor
Emery, R Lee
Bill Rogin Mgmt, 427 N Canon Dr, #215, Beverly Hills CA 90210, USA — Actor
Emery, Ralph
RFD-TV, Rural Media Group, 1 Valmont Plaza, #400, Omaha NE 68154, USA — Entertainer
Emery, Ray
1723 Haldimand Road 20, Cayuga ON N0A 1E0, Canada — Ice Hockey Player
Emery, Victor (Vic)
Bobsled Canada, 140 Canada Olympic Road SW, Calgary AB T3B 5R5, Canada — Bobsled Athlete
Emick, Jarrod
Douglas Gorman Rothacker Wilhelm, 1501 Broadway, #703, New York NY 10036 USA — Actor
Emilio
Refugee Mgmt, 209 10th Ave S, #347 Cummins Station, Nashville TN 37203, USA — Singer
Eminem
Shady Records Mgmt, 151 Lafayette St, #600, New York NY 10013, USA — Rap Artist, Actor
Emma, David
193 Eugenia Dr, Naples FL 34108, USA — Ice Hockey Player
Emmanuel
Sendyk Leonard, 532 Colorado Ave, Santa Monica CA 90401, USA — Singer
Emmanuel, Tommy
Paradigm Agency, 360 N Crescent Dr, North Building, Beverly Hills CA 90210 USA — Guitarist
Emme
EmmeNation, PO Box 546, Closter NJ 07624, USA — Model
Emmerich, Noah J
Gersh Agency, 9465 Wilshire Blvd, #600, Beverly Hills CA 90212 USA — Actor
Emmerich, Roland
Creative Artists Agency, 2000 Ave of Stars, #100, Los Angeles CA 90067 USA — Director, Producer
Emmerich, Toby
New Line Cinema, 888 7th Ave, #1900, New York NY 10106, USA — Producer, Writer
Emmert, Mark A
National Collegiate Athletic Assn, President's Office, 700 W Washington St, Indianapolis IN 46204, USA — Association Executive, Educator
Emmett, John C
Oak House, Hatfield Broad Oak, Bishop's Stortford, Hertfordshire CM22 7HG, England — Inventor (Antiulcer Compound)
Emmett, Rik
Agency Group Ltd, 142 W 57th St, #600, New York NY 10019 USA — Singer, Guitar Player
Emory, Sonny
Great Scott Productions, 4750 Lincoln Blvd, #229, Marina del Rey CA 90292, USA — Drummer (Earth Wind & Fire)
Emtman, Steven C (Steve)
19601 S Cheney Spangle Road, Cheney WA 99004, USA — Football Player
Enberg, Dick
1275 Virginia Way, La Jolla CA 92037, USA — Sportscaster
Encarnacion, Juan D
Toronto Blue Jays, Skydome, 1 Blue Jay Way, Toronto ON M5V 1J1, Canada — Baseball Player
Endelman, Stephen
First Artists Mgmt, 4764 Park Granada, #210, Calabasas CA 91302 USA — Composer

Ender Grummt, Kornelia
D S V, Postfach 420140, 34070 Kassel, Germany — Swimmer

Enders, Anthony T
Brown Brothers Harriman, 59 Wall St, New York NY 10005, USA — Financier

Enders, Thomas
Airbus Industrie, Ronde Point Maurice Bellont 1, 31707 Blagnac, France — Businessman

Endicott, Lori
351 Dogwood Ridge, Rogersville MO 65742, USA — Volleyball Player

Endicott, Sam
+1 Mgmt, 242 Wythe Ave, #6, Brooklyn NY 11211, USA — Singer, Guitarist (Bravery)

Endicott, William F (Bill)
14219 Oak Knoll Road, Sonora CA 95370, USA — Baseball Player

Enevoldsen, Einar
103 City Limits Circle, Emeryville CA 94608, USA — Test Pilot

Enfeldt, Monique Gabrecht
Rosenthaler Str 40-41, Hackesche Hofe, 10178 Berlin, Germany — Speedskater

Engberg, Lotta
Gallviksvagen 20, 44163 Alingsas, Sweden — Singer

Engblom, Brian
824 Ridgemont Circle, Littleton CO 80126, USA — Ice Hockey Player

Engel, Albert J, Jr
5497 Forest Bend Dr SE, Ada MI 49301, USA — Judge

Engel, Georgia
C E S D, 10635 Santa Monica Blvd, #130, Los Angeles CA 90025 USA — Actress

Engelbart, Douglas C
89 Catalpa Dr, Atherton CA 94027, USA — Computer Scientist, Inventor (Mouse)

Engelberger, John A
8176 Cliffview Ave, Springfield VA 22153, USA — Football Player

Engelberger, Joseph F
HelpMate Robotics, Shelter Rock Lane, Danbury CT 06810, USA — Robotics Engineer

Engelhardt, Thomas A (Tom)
Saint Louis Post-Dispatch, Editorial Dept, 900 N Tucker, Saint Louis MO 63101, USA — Editorial Cartoonist

Engen, D Travis
I T T Industries, 4 W Red Oak Lane, #200, West Harrison NY 10604, USA — Businessman

Enger, Leif
Grove/Atlantic Monthly Press, 841 Broadway, New York NY 10003, USA — Writer

Engerman, Stanley L
181 Warrington Dr, Rochester NY 14618, USA — Economist, Historian

Engh, Michael E
Santa Clara University, President's Office, 500 El Camino Real, Santa Clara CA 95053, USA — Educator

Engibous, Thomas J
Texas Instruments, 8505 Forest Lane, PO Box 660199, Dallas TX 75266, USA — Businessman

England, Anthony W
7949 Ridgeway Court, Dexter MI 48130, USA — Astronaut, Geophysicist

England, Richard
The Gardens, 8 Oleander St, Saint Julians SJ 12, Malta — Architect

England, Tyler (Ty)
Buddy Lee Attractions, 38 Music Square E, #300, Nashville TN 37203 USA — Singer, Guitarist, Songwriter

Englander, Harold R
625 Baldwin Ave, Charlotte NC 28204, USA — Public Health Dentist

Engle, Joe H
PO Box 58386, Houston TX 77258, USA — Astronaut, Air Force General

Engle, Robert F
New York University, Stern Business School, 44 W 4th St, New York NY 10012, USA — Nobel Economics Laureate

Englehart, Robert W (Bob), Jr
Hartford Courant, Editorial Dept, 280 Broad St, Hartford CT 06105, USA — Editorial Cartoonist

Englehorn, Shirley
849 Shrine View, Colorado Springs CO 80906, USA — Golfer

Engler, Erich
80 Valley Way Circle SE, Huntsville AL 35802, USA — Space Scientist

Engler, Michael
W M E Entertainment, 9601 Wilshire Blvd, #300, Beverly Hills CA 90210 USA — Director

Englert, Alice
Creative Artists Agency, 2000 Ave of Stars, #100, Los Angeles CA 90067 USA — Actress

English, Alexander (Alex)
596 Rimer Pond Road, Blythewood SC 29016, USA — Basketball Player

English, Bill
Innovative Artists, 1505 10th St, Santa Monica CA 90401 USA — Actor

English, CariDee
Elite Model Mgmt, 404 Park Ave S, #900, New York NY 10016 USA — Model

English, Diane
Shukovsky-English Entertainment, 4024 Radford Ave, Studio City CA 91604, USA — Writer

English, James F, Jr
31 Potter St, Groton CT 06340, USA — Educator

English, Joseph T
Saint Vincent's Hospital, 203 W 12th St, New York NY 10011, USA — Psychiatrist

English, Kim
Universal Attractions, 135 W 26th St, #1200, New York NY 10001 USA — Singer

English, L Douglas (Doug)
Lone Star Paralysis, 1215 Red River St, Austin TX 78701, USA — Football Player

English, Larry
San Diego Chargers, 4020 Murphy Canyon Road, San Diego CA 92123 USA — Football Player

English, Michael
Trifecta Entertainment, 209 10th Ave S, #302, Nashville TN 37203, USA — Singer

English, Mitch
Abrams Artists, 9200 W Sunset Blvd, #1125, West Hollywood CA 90069 USA — Actor, Writer, Producer

English, Paul
Int'l Casting Service, 2/218 Crown St, Darlinghurst NSW 2010, Australia — Actor

Englund, Robert
1278 Glenneyre, #73, Laguna Beach CA 92651, USA — Actor

Engram, Simon J (Bobby), III
2009 High Pointe Court, Murrysville PA 15668, USA — Football Player

Engstrom, Erik
General Atlantic Partners, 3 Pickwick Plaza, #8, Greenwich CT 06830, USA — Businessman

Engstrom, Molly
7582 Southshore Dr, Siren WI 54872, USA — Ice Hockey Player

Engstrom, Royce C
University of Montana, President's Office, 32 Campus Dr, Missoula MT 59812, USA — Educator

Engvall, Bill
Paradigm Agency, 360 N Crescent Dr, North Building, Beverly Hills CA 90210 USA — Actor, Comedian

Enke, Frederick W (Fred), Jr
206 E McMurray Road, Casa Grande AZ 85122, USA — Football Player

Enkhsaikhan, Mendsaikhany
Pease Ave 11A, Ulan Bator 210648, Mongolia — Prime Minister, Mongolia

Ennis, Garth
Avatar Press, 515 N Century Blvd, Rantoul IL 61866, USA — Cartoonist, Writer

Ennis, Jessica
Sheffield Athletic Club, 54 Stradbroke Drive, Sheffield, S13 8SD, England — Track Athlete

Ennis, John
14255 Dearborn St, Panorama City CA 91402, USA — Baseball Player

Ennis, Ralph
2 Kirklake Bank, Formby, Liverpool L37 2Y5, England — Singer, Guitarist

Ennis, Raymond V (Ray)
2 Kirklake Bank, Formby, Liverpool L37 2Y5, England — Singer, Guitarist

Ennis, Victor Ray
Soundelux, 7080 Hollywood Blvd, #1100, Los Angeles CA 90028, USA — Sound Editor

Eno, Brian
Creative Artists Agency, 2000 Ave of Stars, #100, Los Angeles CA 90067 USA — Composer, Keyboardist

Enoch, Ed
PO Box 1471, Brentwood TN 37024, USA — Singer (Stamps Quartet)

Enos, Clay
96 5th Ave, #2, New York NY 10011, USA — Photographer

Enos, John, III
I C M Partners, 10250 Constellation Blvd, #900, Los Angeles CA 90067 USA — Actor

Enos, Mark
Enos Co, 705 N Alfred St, West Hollywood CA 90069, USA — Interior Designer

Enos, Mireille
Gartner / Green Entertainment, 5225 Wilshire Blvd, #1200, Los Angeles CA 90036, USA — Actress

Enos, Randall
402 N Park Ave, Easton CT 06612, USA — Cartoonist, Illustrator

Enrico, Roger A
PepsiCo Inc, 700 Anderson Hill Road, Purchase NY 10577, USA — Businessman

Enright, Agnes Leahy
W M E Entertainment, 9601 Wilshire Blvd, #300, Beverly Hills CA 90210 USA — Singer, Keyboardist (Leahy)

Enright, Anne
Jonathan Cape Ltd, 20 Vauxhall Bridge Road, London SW1V 2SA, England — Writer

Enright, Barbara
All American Speakers, 437 5th Ave, New York NY 10016, USA — Poker Player

Enright, George A
3075 Strawflower Way, Lake Worth FL 33467, USA — Baseball Player

Enriquez Garcia, Jorge
Federacion de Futbol, Colima 373 Colonia Roma, Delegacion Cuauhtemoc Mexico DF 06700, Mexico — Soccer Player

Enriquez, Jocelyn
Nene Musik Productions, 1460 SW Santiago Ave, Port Saint Lucie FL 34953 USA — Singer

Enriquez, Joy
W M E Entertainment, 9601 Wilshire Blvd, #300, Beverly Hills CA 90210 USA — Singer

Enroth-Cugell, Christina A E
Northwestern University, Engineering School, 2145 Sheridan, Evanston IL 60208, USA — Neurophysiologist

Ensberg, Morgan P
5535 Memorial Dr, #F114, Houston TX 77007, USA — Baseball Player

Ensher, Jason R
University of Colorado, Physics Dept, Boulder CO 80309, USA — Physicist

Ensign, Michael
Abrams Artists, 9200 W Sunset Blvd, #1125, West Hollywood CA 90069 USA — Actor

Ensler, Eve
Grand Central Publishing, 237 Park Ave, New York NY 10017, USA — Actress, Comedienne, Writer

Ensler, Jason
Pitt Group, 9465 Wilshire Blvd, #420, Beverly Hills CA 90212, USA — Director

Enthoven, Alain C
1 McCormick Lane, Atherton CA 94027, USA — Economist

Entner, Warren
Thomas Cassidy, 11761 E Speedway Blvd, Tucson AZ 85748 USA — Singer, Guitarist (Grass Roots)

Entremont, Philippe
Columbia Artists Mgmt Inc, 1790 Broadway, #702, New York NY 10019 USA — Conductor, Concert Pianist

Enya
Manderley, Victoria Road, Killiney, County Dublin, Ireland — Singer, Composer

Enyart, William (Bill)
61070 Parrell Road, Bend OR 97702, USA — Football Player

Enzensberger, Hans M
Lindenstr 29, 60325 Frankfurt am Maim, Germany — Writer

Eotvos, Peter
Naardeweg 56, 1261 BV Blaircum, Netherlands — Composer, Conductor

Ephron, Hallie
William Morrow Publishers, 1350 Ave of Americas, New York NY 10019 USA — Writer

Epic
Wyze Mgmt, 34 Maple St, London W1 5GD, England — Rap Artist (Crazy Town)

Epley, John M
Portland Otologic Clinic, 52657 NE 2nd St, Scappoose OR 97056, USA — Otologist, Inventor

Eppard, James G (Jim)
23115 153rd Ave, Rapid City SD 57703, USA — Baseball Player

Epperson-Doumani, Brenda
Kazarian/Spencer/Ruskin, 11969 Ventura Blvd, #300, Studio City CA 91604 USA — Actress

Eppinger, Dale L
4100 Colina Cove, Round Rock TX 78681, USA — Vietnam War Air Force Hero

Epple, Maria
Gunzesried 3, 87544 Blaicach, Germany — Alpine Skier

Epple-Beck, Irene
Aufmberg 235, 87637 Seeg, Germany — Alpine Skier

Epps, Mike
I C M Partners, 10250 Constellation Blvd, #900, Los Angeles CA 90067 USA — Actor, Comedian

Epps, Omar
Anonymous Content, 3532 Hayden Ave, Culver City CA 90232 USA — Actor

Epps, Phillip E (Phil)
212 Boulder Creek Dr, DeSoto TX 75115, USA — Football Player

Epps, Raymond E (Ray)
4030 Old Warwick Road, Richmond VA 23234, USA — Basketball Player

Epstein, Daniel M
843 W University Parkway, Baltimore MD 21210, USA — Writer

Epstein, Emmanuel
University of California, Land Air Water Resources Dept, Davis CA 95616, USA — Plant Nutritionist, Microbiologist

Epstein, Jason
PO Box 1143, Sag Harbor NY 11963, USA — Editor

Epstein, Joseph
522 Church St, #6B, Evanston IL 60201, USA — Writer, Educator

Epstein, Michael P (Mike)
6384 S Blackhawk Way, Aurora CO 80016, USA — Baseball Player

Erat, Martin
4 Crooked Stick Lane, Brentwood TN 37027, USA — Ice Hockey Player

Erautt, Edward L S (Eddie)
7252 Waite Dr, La Mesa CA 91941, USA — Baseball Player

Erb, Fred
I C M Partners, 10250 Constellation Blvd, #900, Los Angeles CA 90067 USA — Lyricist

Erb, Richard D
University of Montana, Business School, Missoula MT 59807, USA — Government Official

Erbe, Kathryn
Innovative Artists, 1505 10th St, Santa Monica CA 90401 USA — Actress

Ercegan, Milan
F I L A, Rue du Chateau 6, 1804 Corsier-sur-Vevey, Switzerland — Wrestling Executive

Erdman, Dennis
Creative Artists Agency, 2000 Ave of Stars, #100, Los Angeles CA 90067 USA — Actor, Director, Producer

Erdman, Richard
3188 S Brownell Road, Williston VT 05495, USA — Sculptor

Erdman, Richard
5655 Greenbush Ave, Van Nuys CA 91401, USA — Actor

Erdmann, Susi-Lisa
Karwendelstr 8A, 81369 Munich, Germany — Bobsled Athlete

Erdo, Peter Cardinal
Mindszenty Hercegprimas Ter 2, 2501 Esztergom Magyarirszay, Hungary — Religious Leader

Erdogan, Recep Tayyip
Premier's Office, Eski Basbakanlik Binasi, Bakanliklar, 06573 Ankara, Turkey — Prime Minister, Turkey

Erdos, Todd M
118 Windsor Court, Cranberry Township PA 16066, USA — Baseball Player

Erdrich, K Louise
Andrew Wylie Agency, 250 W 57th St, #2114, New York NY 10107, USA — Writer

Ergen, Charles W
EchoStar Communications Corp, 5701 S Santa Fe Dr, Littleton CO 80120, USA — Businessman

Eric B
Richard Walters, PO Box 2789, Toluca Lake CA 91610 USA — Rap Artist (Eric B & Rakim)

Ericks, John E
17000 Oketo Ave, Tinley Park IL 60477, USA — Baseball Player

Erickson, Bryan L
114 3rd St NW, #A, Roseau MN 56751, USA — Ice Hockey Player

Erickson, Craig N
420 N Country Club Dr, Lake Worth FL 33462, USA — Football Player

Erickson, Dennis
911 W Kidd Island Road, Coeur D'Alene ID 83814, USA — Football Coach

Erickson, Ethan
Greater Visions Artists Talent Agency, 8981 W Sunset Blvd, #101, West Hollywood CA 90069 USA — Actor

Erickson, Grant
222 Parks St, Whitewood SK S0G 5C0, Canada — Ice Hockey Player

Erickson, Keith R
333 23rd St, Santa Monica CA 90402, USA — Basketball, Volleyball Player

Erickson, Matt
1408 S Fidelis St, Appleton WI 54915, USA — Baseball Player

Erickson, Roger F
PO Box 235, Sautee Nacoochee GA 30571, USA — Baseball Player

Erickson, Roger K (Roky)
Ten Pin Mgmt, 176 Park Ave, Warwick RI 02889, USA — Singer, Guitarist, Songwriter

Erickson, Roky
Agency Group Ltd, 142 W 57th St, #600, New York NY 10019 USA — Singer, Songwriter

Erickson, Scott
I C M Partners, 10250 Constellation Blvd, #900, Los Angeles CA 90067 USA — Actor

Erickson, Scott G
1183 Corral Ave, Sunnyvale CA 94086, USA — Baseball Player

Ericson, John
7 Avenida Vista Grande, #310, Santa Fe NM 87508, USA — Actor

Erika Jo
Universal South Artists, 2303 21st Ave S, #400, Nashville TN 37212, USA — Singer

Eriksen, Stein
7700 Stein Way, Park City UT 84060, USA — Skier

Erikson, Duke
Borman Entertainment, 1250 6th St, #401, Santa Monica CA 90401, USA — Bassist, Keyboardist (Garbage)

Erikson, Raymond L
Harvard University Medical School, Biology Dept, 25 Shattuck St, Boston MA 02115, USA — Medical Researcher

Eriksson, Aleksandra
Elite Model Mgmt, 404 Park Ave S, #900, New York NY 10016 USA — Model

Eriksson, Anders
2259 Arlington Ave, Columbus OH 43221, USA — Ice Hockey Player

Eriksson, Per-Olaf
Hedasvagen 57, 81 161 Sandviken, Sweden — Businessman

Eriksson, Peter
Vastra Storgatan 10, 55 315 Jonokoping, Sweden — Ice Hockey Player

Erixon, Jan
Stenbackav 58, Skelleftea 93 142, Sweden — Ice Hockey Player

Erland, Jonathan
Composite Components Co, 134 N Ave 61, #102-103, Los Angeles CA 90042, USA — Visual Effects Artist

Erlandson, Eric
Artist Group International, 9560 Wilshire Blvd, #400, Beverly Hills CA 90212 USA — Guitarist (Hole), Songwriter

Erlandson, Thomas D (Tom), Sr
1045 E Possee Road, Castle Rock CO 80108, USA — Football Player

Erman, John
Creative Artists Agency, 2000 Ave of Stars, #100, Los Angeles CA 90067 USA — Director

Ermey, R Lee
Bill Rogin Mgmt, 427 N Canon Dr, #215, Beverly Hills CA 90210, USA — Actor

Erna, Salvatore P (Sully)
Front Line Mgmt, 1100 Glendon Ave, #2000, Los Angeles CA 90024 USA — Singer, Guitarist (Godsmack); Songwriter

Ernaga, Frank J
50 N Roop St, Susanville CA 96130, USA — Baseball Player

Ernst, Bret
United Talent Agency, 9336 Civic Center Dr, Beverly Hills CA 90210 USA — Actor, Comedian

Ernst, Richard R
Kurlistr 24, 8404 Winterthur, Switzerland — Nobel Chemistry Laureate

Ernst, Wallace Gary
Stanford University, Earth & Environment Sciences Dept, Stanford CA 94305, USA — Geologist

Eroglu, Dervis
National Unity Party, 9 Ataturk Meydani, Lefkosa, Turkish Northern Cyprus — Prime Minister, Turkish Northern Cyprus

Errazuriz Ossa, Francisco J Cardinal
Casilla 30D, Erasmo Escala 1894, Santiago, Chile — Religious Leader

Errey, Bob
156 Hickory Heights Dr, Bridgeville PA 15017, USA — Ice Hockey Player

Errico, Melissa
Paradigm Agency, 360 N Crescent Dr, North Building, Beverly Hills CA 90210 USA — Actress, Singer

Erskine, Carl D
4031 Fallbrook Lane, Anderson IN 46011, USA — Baseball Player

Erskine, Peter
1727 Hill St, Santa Monica CA 90405, USA — Jazz Drummer, Composer

Erstad, Darin C
6230 Doe Creek Circle, Lincoln NE 68516, USA — Baseball Player

Ertegun, Mica
M A C II, 125 E 81st St, New York NY 10028, USA — Interior Designer

Ertl, Gerhard L
Garystr 18, 14195 Berlin, Germany — Nobel Chemistry Laureate

Ertl, Martina
Ertlhofe 17, 83661 Lenggries, Germany — Alpine Skier

Ertl, Sue
4707 Sabal Key Dr, Bradenton FL 34203, USA — Golfer

Eruzione, Michael (Mike)
40 Floyd St, Winthrop MA 02152, USA — Ice Hockey Player

Erving, Julius W (Dr J)
108 Windrush Road, Winston-Salem NC 27106, USA — Basketball Player

Ervins, Ricky
20984 Nightshade Place, Ashburn VA 20147, USA — Football Player

Erwin, Mike
Leverage Mgmt, 3030 Pennsylvania Ave, Santa Monica CA 90404 USA — Actor

Erwitt, Elliott R
88 Central Park West, #1S, New York NY 10023, USA — Photographer

Erxleban, Russell A
PO Box 1731, Dripping Springs TX 78620, USA — Football Player

Esaki, Reona (Leo)
12-6 Sanbancho, Chiyodaku, Tokyo 102 0075, Japan — Nobel Physics Laureate

Esasky, Nicholas A (Nick)
1779 Starlight Dr, Marietta GA 30062, USA — Baseball Player

Escalera, Alfredo, Jr
Star Boxing, 991 Morris Park Ave, Bronx NY 10462, USA — Boxer

Escarpeta, Arlen
A P A Talent/Literary Agency, 405 S Beverly Dr, #300, Beverly Hills CA 90212 USA — Actor

Esche, Robert
6750 W Carter Road, Rome NY 13440, USA — Ice Hockey Player

Eschenbach, Christoph
National Symphony Orchestra, Kennedy Performing Arts Center, 2700 F St NW, Washington, DC 20566, USA — Conductor, Concert Pianist

Eschenmoser, Albert J
Bergstra 9, 8700 Kusnacht ZH, Switzerland — Chemist

Eschert, Jurgen
Tornowstr 8, 14473 Potsdam, Germany — Canoeing Athlete

Escobar, Kelvin J B
12296 Circula Panorama, Santa Ana CA 92705, USA — Baseball Player

Escobar, Yunel
15763 SW 43rd St, Miami FL 33185, USA — Baseball Player

Escovedo, Alejandro
Back Porch/Manhattan Records, 150 5th Ave, New York NY 10011, USA — Singer, Songwriter

Escovedo, Peter
Universal Attractions, 135 W 26th St, #1200, New York NY 10001 USA — Percussionist

Eselin, Caroline
United Talent Agency, 9336 Civic Center Dr, Beverly Hills CA 90210 USA — Costume Designer

Esfahani, Mahan
Borletti-Buitoni Trust, 20 Leythe Road, London W3 8AW, England — Concert Harpsichordist

Eshelman, Vaughn M
30106 Falher Dr, Spring TX 77386, USA — Baseball Player

Esiason, Norman J (Boomer)
25 Heights Road, Manhasset NY 11030, USA — Football Player, Sportscaster

Eskew, Michael L
United Parcel Service, 55 Glenlake Parkway NE, Atlanta GA 30328, USA — Businessman

Eskridge, William N, Jr
Yale University, Law School, 127 Wall St, New Haven CT 06511, USA — Attorney, Educator

Esler-Smith, Frank
PO Box 3367, Beverly Hills CA 90212, USA — Keyboardist (Air Supply)

Esparza, Raul
Elin Flack Mgmt, 435 W 57th St, #3M, New York NY 10019, USA — Actor, Singer

Esper, Michael
Gersh Agency, 9465 Wilshire Blvd, #600, Beverly Hills CA 90212 USA — Actor

Esperian, Kallen R
514 Lindseywood Cove, Memphis TN 38117, USA — Opera Singer

Espineli, Geno
1222 Park Lane, Katy TX 77450, USA — Baseball Player

E

Erlandson - Espineli

Espinosa, Daniel
United Talent Agency, 9336 Civic Center Dr, Beverly Hills CA 90210 USA — Director

Espinosa, Eden
Gersh Agency, 41 Madison Ave, #3301, New York NY 10010 USA — Actress, Singer

Espinoza, Alvaro A
1157 SW Dalton Ave, Port Saint Lucie FL 34953, USA — Baseball Player

Esposito, Anthony J (Tony)
418 55th Ave, Saint Pete Beach FL 33706, USA — Ice Hockey Player

Esposito, Frank
200 N State Route 17, Paramus NJ 07652, USA — Bowling Executive

Esposito, Jennifer
Don Buchwald/Fortitude, 6500 Wilshire Blvd, #2200, Los Angeles CA 90048 USA — Actress

Esposito, Laura
Stewart Talent, 318 W 53rd St, #201, New York NY 10019, USA — Actress

Esposito, Philip A (Phil)
4003 W Tacon St, Tampa FL 33629, USA — Ice Hockey Player, Coach

Esposito, Samuel (Sammy)
PO Box 1826, Banner Elk NC 28604, USA — Baseball Player

Espy, A Michael (Mike)
Commodity Credit Corp, PO Box 2415, Washington DC 20013, USA — Secretary, Agriculture

Espy, Cecil E
5480 Encina Dr, San Diego CA 92114, USA — Baseball Player

Esquivel, Manuel
United Democratic Party, 19 King St, PO Box 1143, Belize City, Belize — Prime Minister, Belize

Essandoh, Ato
S M S Talent, 8383 Wilshire Blvd, #230, Beverly Hills CA 90211 USA — Actor

Essegian, Charles A (Chuck)
15639 Bronco Dr, Canyon Country CA 91387, USA — Baseball Player

Essensa, Bob
1130 Iroquois Trail, Oxford MI 48371, USA — Ice Hockey Player

Esser, Mark G
717 S US Highway 1, #708, Jupiter FL 33477, USA — Baseball Player

Essex, David
Stratford Saye, 20 Wellington Road, Bournemouth, Dorset BG8 8JN, England — Singer, Actor, Composer

Essex, Myron E
Harvard School of Public Health, 665 Huntington Ave, Boston MA 02115, USA — Microbiologist

Essian, James S (Jim)
134 Eckford Dr, Troy MI 48085, USA — Baseball Player, Manager

Essick, Todd
PO Box 2376, West Palm Beach FL 33402, USA — Photographer

Essink, Ronald A
PO Box 265, Hamilton MI 49419, USA — Football Player

Esslinger, Hartmut
FrogDesign, 3460 Hillview Ave, Palo Alto CA 94304, USA — Industrial Designer

Essman, Susan (Susie)
Paradigm Agency, 360 N Crescent Dr, North Building, Beverly Hills CA 90210 USA — Actress, Comedienne

Esswood, Paul L V
Jasmine Cottage, 42 Ferring Lane, Ferring, West Sussex BN12 6QT, England — Opera Singer

Estabrook, Christine
Don Buchwald/Fortitude, 6500 Wilshire Blvd, #2200, Los Angeles CA 90048 USA — Actress

Estalella, Robert M (Bobby)
3612 Churchill Downs Dr, Davie FL 33328, USA — Baseball Player

Esteban, Manuel A
California State University, O'Connell Hall, Chico CA 95929, USA — Educator

Estefan, Emilio, Jr
Estefan Enterprises, 420 Jefferson Ave, Miami Beach FL 33139, USA — Musician, Producer

Estefan, Gloria
39 Star Island Dr, Miami Beach FL 33139, USA — Singer, Songwriter

Estelle
I C M Partners, 10250 Constellation Blvd, #900, Los Angeles CA 90067 USA — Singer

Estelle, Richard H (Dick)
2221 Taylor St, Point Pleasant NJ 08742, USA — Baseball Player

Esten, Charles (Chip)
Stone Manners Salners, 9911 W Pico Blvd, #1400, Los Angeles CA 90035 USA — Actor, Comedian

Estern, Neil
432 Cream Hill Road, West Cornwall CT 06796, USA — Sculptor

Estes, A Shawn
9694 E Legacy Lane, Scottsdale AZ 85255, USA — Baseball Player

Estes, Bob
4408 Long Champ Dr, #21, Austin TX 78746, USA — Golfer

Estes, Clarissa Pinkola
Knopf Publishers, 201 E 50th St, New York NY 10022, USA — Psychologist, Writer

Estes, Jacob Aaron
Management 360, 9111 Wilshire Blvd, Beverly Hills CA 90210 USA — Director, Writer

Estes, James
1103 Callahan St, Amarillo TX 79106, USA — Cartoonist

Estes, Lawrence G (Larry)
115 Alida St, Hammond LA 70403, USA — Football Player

Estes, Richard
PO Box 685, Northeast Harbour ME 04662, USA — Artist

Estes, Robert (Rob)
Thruline Entertainment, 9250 Wilshire Blvd, #100, Beverly Hills CA 90212 USA — Actor

Estes, Simon L
Hochstr 43, 8706 Feldmeilen, Switzerland — Opera Singer

Estes, Will
Paradigm Agency, 360 N Crescent Dr, North Building, Beverly Hills CA 90210 USA — Actor

Estes, William K
65 Gaston Road, Morristown NJ 07960, USA — Psychologist

Esteve-Coll, Elizabeth
27 Ursula St, London SW11 3DW, England — Museum Executive

Estevez, Emilio
Alchemy Entertainment, 7024 Melrose Ave, #420, Los Angeles CA 90038 USA — Actor, Director

Estevez, Luis
122 E 7th St, Los Angeles CA 90014, USA — Fashion Designer

Estevez, Ramon L
Special Artists Agency, 9465 Wilshire Blvd, #820, Beverly Hills CA 90212 USA — Actor

Estevez, Renee — Actress
House of Representatives, 1434 6th St, #1, Santa Monica CA 90401 USA

Esthero — Singer
ArtistDirect, 10900 Wilshire Blvd, #1400, Los Angeles CA 90024 USA

Estil, Frode — Cross Country Skier
7530 Meraker, Norway

Estill, Michelle — Golfer
2716 E Boston St, Gilbert AZ 85295, USA

Estleman, Loren Daniel — Writer
5552 Walsh Road, Whitmore Lake MI 48189, USA

Estrada, Charles L (Chuck) — Baseball Player
1289 Manzanita Way, San Luis Obispo CA 93401, USA

Estrada, Erik — Actor
Creative Talent Group, 1900 Ave of Stars, #2475, Los Angeles CA 90067, USA

Estrada, Erik-Michael — Singer (O-Town)
Trans Continental Records, 127 W Church St, #350, Orlando FL 32801, USA

Estrada, Johnny P — Baseball Player
20 Winged Foot Ridge, Newnan GA 30265, USA

Estrich, Susan R — Attorney
947 Berkeley St, Santa Monica CA 90403, USA

Estrin, Zack — Producer, Writer
W M E Entertainment, 9601 Wilshire Blvd, #300, Beverly Hills CA 90210 USA

Eswaran, Vijay — Businessman
Q I Group, Bank of China Tower, #5500, Hong Kong Central, China

E-Swift — Rap Artist
Likwit Entertainment, PO Box 360713, Los Angeles CA 90036, USA

Eszterhas, Joseph A — Writer
Baumgarten Mgmt, 406 Wilshire Blvd, Santa Monica CA 90401, USA

Etaix, Pierre — Director, Actor
Editions du Seuil, 27 Rue Jacob, 75261 Paris Cedex 06, France

Etchebarren, Andrew A (Andy) — Baseball Player
1488 Vermeer Dr, Nokomis FL 34275, USA

Etchegaray, Roger Cardinal — Religious Leader
Piazza San Calisto, 00120 Vatican City

Etcheverry, Marco — Soccer Player
D C United, R F K Stadium, 2400 E Capitol St SE, Washington DC 20003 USA

Etcoff, Nancy — Psychologist
Harvard Medical School, Mind Brain Behavior Initiative, 25 Shattuck St, Boston MA 02115, USA

Etebari, Eric — Actor
Mystic Warrior Productions, 12400 Ventura Blvd, #237, Studio City CA 91604, USA

Etel, Alex — Actor
Independent Talent Group, Oxford House, 76 Oxford St, London W1D 1BS, England

Etheridge, Bobby L — Baseball Player
118 Portland Road, Eudora AR 71640, USA

Etheridge, Melissa L — Singer, Songwriter, Guitarist
Creative Artists Agency, 2000 Ave of Stars, #100, Los Angeles CA 90067 USA

Etherton, Seth — Baseball Player
16 Saint John, Dana Point CA 92629, USA

Ethier, Andre E — Baseball Player
21423 S 147th St, Gilbert AZ 85298, USA

Ethier, Linda — Artist
2846 NE Glissan St, Portland OR 97232, USA

Ethridge, Mark F, III — Editor
5516 Gorham Dr, Charlotte NC 28226, USA

Etienne, Jean-Louis — Explorer
Musee Oceanographique de Monaco, Ave Saint-Martin, 98000 Monaco

Etienne, Pauline — Actress
A C T 1, 83 Rue Saint Honore, 75001 Paris, France

Etrog, Sorel — Artist
PO Box 67034, 2300 Yonge St, Toronto ON M4P 1E0, Canada

Etsel, Edward (Ed) — Marksman
University of Virginia, Athletic Dept, Charlottesville VA 22906, USA

Ettinger, Cynthia — Actress
Thruline Entertainment, 9250 Wilshire Blvd, #100, Beverly Hills CA 90212 USA

Ettinger, Dan — Conductor
Mannheim Opera House, Mozartstr 9, 68161 Mannheim, Germany

Ettles, Mark — Baseball Player
3-10 Rose Ave, Perth WA 6151, Australia

Ettlin, Lukas — Cinematographer
Mirisch Agency, 8840 Wilshire Blvd, #100, Beverly Hills CA 90211 USA

Etura, Marta — Actress
Kuranda Mgmt, Santo Angel 84, 28043 Madrid, Spain

Etzel, Gregory A M — Vietnam War Air Force Hero
7822 Wonder St, Citrus Heights CA 95610, USA

Etzioni, Amitai W — Sociologist
George Washington University, Sociology Dept, Washington DC 20052, USA

Etzwiler, Donnell D — Pediatrician
International Diabetes Center, 5000 W 39th St, Minneapolis MN 55416, USA

Eubank, Chris — Boxer
3 Vallensdean Cottages, Hangleton Lane, Portslade, Sussex BN41 2FQ, England

Eubanks, Kevin — Jazz Guitarist
Blue Note Records, 6920 W Sunset Blvd, Los Angeles CA 90028 USA

Eubanks, Robert L (Bob) — Actor, Producer
Cheryl Kagan Public Relations, 4422 E 103rd St, Tulsa OK 74137, USA

Eubesio, R Antonio (Tony) — Baseball Player
2078 Shannon Lakes Blvd, Kissimmee FL 34743, USA

Euge Groove — Jazz Saxophonist
Variety Artists, 793 Higuera St, #6, San Luis Obispo CA 93401 USA

Eugenides, Jeffrey — Writer
Janklow & Nesbit Assoc, 445 Park Ave, #1300, New York NY 10022 USA

Eustis, Joshua — Musician (Telefon Tel Aviv)
Aero Booking, 8008 Greenwood Ave N, #3, Seattle WA 98103, USA

Evancho, Jackie — Singer
W M E Entertainment, 9601 Wilshire Blvd, #300, Beverly Hills CA 90210 USA

Evangelista, Christine — Actress
M J Management, 130 W 57th St, #11A, New York NY 10019, USA

Evangelista, Linda — Model
D N A Model Mgmt, 520 Broadway, #1100, New York NY 10012, USA

Evanovich, Janet — Writer
PO Box 2889, Naples FL 34106, USA

Evans, Alice — Actress
Domain Talent, 9229 W Sunset Blvd, #710, West Hollywood CA 90069 USA

Evans, Andrea — Actress
A R L, 8075 W 3rd St, #303, Los Angeles CA 90048, USA

Evans, B Heath — Football Player
16752 Bollinger Dr, Pacific Palisades CA 90272, USA

Evans, Barry S — Baseball Player
128 Russell Dr, McDonough GA 30252, USA

Evans, Bart S — Baseball Player
3725 S Forest Ave, Springfield MO 65807, USA

Evans, Bill — Jazz Saxophonist, Keyboardist, Composer
Sony Records, 2100 Colorado Ave, Santa Monica CA 90404 USA

Evans, Byron N — Football Player
1763 E Carter Road, Phoenix AZ 85042, USA

Evans, Cadell — Cyclist
B M C Racing Team, Sportstr 49, 2540 Grenchen, Switzerland

Evans, Christine — Singer, Songwriter
Jane Harbury Publicity, 1290 Sundas St, #E, Toronto ON M4M 1S6, Canada

Evans, Christopher R (Chris) — Actor
3 Arts Entertainment, 9460 Wilshire Blvd, #700, Beverly Hills CA 90212 USA

Evans, Daniel — Actor, Singer
Hamilton Hodell, 66-68 Margaret St, London W1W 8SR, England

Evans, Daniel E — Businessman
Bob Evans Farms, 3776 S High St, Columbus OH 43207, USA

Evans, Daniel J — Governor, Senator, WA; Educator
Daniel J Evans Assoc, 1111 3rd Ave, #3400, Seattle WA 98101, USA

Evans, Danielle — Model
Click Model Mgmt, 881 7th Ave, New York NY 10019 USA

Evans, Darrell W — Baseball Player
1400 E Tahquitz Canyon Way, Palm Springs CA 92262, USA

Evans, Daryl — Ice Hockey Player
22403 Marjorie Ave, Torrance CA 90505, USA

Evans, David A — Chemist
Harvard University, Chemistry & Chemical Biology Dept, Cambridge MA 02138, USA

Evans, Demetric U — Football Player
PO Box 2256, Allen TX 75013, USA

Evans, Dick — Bowling Columnist
121 Morning Dove Court, Daytona Beach FL 32119, USA

Evans, Donald L — Secretary, Commerce
Financial Services Forum, 601 13th Street NW, #750 South, Washington DC 20005, USA

Evans, Donald L — Football Player
12407 Beauvoir St, Raleigh NC 27614, USA

Evans, Douglas E (Doug) — Football Player
8099 Highway 534, Haynesville LA 71038, USA

Evans, Dwight M — Baseball Player
123 Johnson Woods Dr, Reading MA 01867, USA

Evans, Evans — Actress
3114 Abington Dr, Beverly Hills CA 90210, USA

Evans, Faith — Singer, Songwriter
J L Entertainment, 18653 Ventura Blvd, #340, Tarzana CA 91356 USA

Evans, Frederick H (Fred) — Football Player
Minnesota Vikings, 9520 Viking Dr, Eden Prairie MN 55344 USA

Evans, Gareth — Director
Management 360, 9111 Wilshire Blvd, Beverly Hills CA 90210 USA

Evans, George — Cartoonist (Anna & Corrigan)
King Features Syndicate, 300 W 57th St, #1500, New York NY 10019 USA

Evans, Glen — Molecular Biologist
Salk Institute, 10100 N Torrey Pines Road, La Jolla CA 92037 USA

Evans, Greg — Cartoonist (Luann)
216 Country Garden Lane, San Marcos CA 92069, USA

Evans, Harold J — Plant Physiologist
17360 Holy Names Dr, #2037, Lake Oswego OR 97034, USA

Evans, J Thomas — Freestyle Wrestler
607 S Fir Court, Broken Arrow OK 74012, USA

Evans, Jahri — Football Player
New Orleans Saints, 5800 Airline Highway, Metairie LA 70003 USA

Evans, James B (Jim) — Baseball Umpire
1801 Rogge Lane, Austin TX 78723, USA

Evans, Janet — Swimmer
8 Barneburg, Trabuco Canyon CA 92679, USA

Evans, John R — Foundation Executive
Rockefeller Foundation, 1133 Ave of Americas, New York NY 10036, USA

Evans, John V — Governor, ID
D L Evans Bank, 397 N Overland, Burley ID 83318, USA

Evans, Lee — Actor
Off the Kerb Productions, Hammer House, 113-117 Wardour St, #300, London W1F 0UN, England

Evans, Lee E — Track Athlete
250 S Sage Ave, Mobile AL 36606, USA

Evans, Linda — Actress
PO Box 29, Rainier WA 98576, USA

Evans, Lindsey Gayle — Model
Playboy Promotions, 2706 Media Center Dr, Los Angeles CA 90065 USA

Evans, Luke — Actor
United Agents, 12-26 Lexington St, London W1F 0LE, England

Evans, Lynn — Singer (Chordettes)
Richard Paul Assoc, 16207 Mott Dr, Macomb Township MI 48044, USA

Evans, Marc — Director
Tessa Sayle Agency, 11 Jubilee Place, London SW3 3TE, England

Evans, Martin J — Nobel Medicine Laureate
Cardiff University Museum, PO Box 911, Cardiff CF10 3US, Wales

Evans, Martina — Writer
Sayle Literary Agency, 25-27 Bickerton Road, London N19 5JT, England

Evans, Mary Beth
Michael Bruno Group, 13576 Cheltenham Dr, Sherman Oaks CA 91423, USA — Actress

Evans, Maurice E
Washington Wizards, M C I Centre, 601 F St NW, Washington DC 20004 USA — Basketball Player

Evans, Michael L (Mike)
9931 Cottoncreek Dr, Littleton CO 80130, USA — Basketball Player

Evans, Mijoshki A (Josh)
PO Box 273309, Boca Raton FL 33427, USA — Football Player

Evans, Nicholas (Nick)
Signet Books, 375 Hudson St, New York NY 10014 USA — Writer

Evans, Nicky
Associated International Mgmt, Fairfax House, Fulwood Place, London WC1V 6HU, England — Actor

Evans, Norm E
360 NW Boulder Place, Issaquah WA 98027, USA — Football Player

Evans, Richard
Madison Square Garden, 4 Pennsylvania Plaza, New York NY 10001, USA — Sports Executive

Evans, Richard Paul
PO Box 712137, Salt Lake City UT 84171, USA — Writer

Evans, Robert J (Bob)
Robert Evans Productions, Paramount Pictures, 5555 Melrose, Los Angeles, CA 90038, USA — Producer

Evans, Robert S
Crane Co, 100 Stamford Plaza, Stamford CT 06902, USA — Businessman

Evans, Ronald M
Salk Institute, 10100 N Torrey Pines Road, La Jolla CA 92037 USA — Geneticist

Evans, Roy
15221 Lime St, Hesperia CA 92345, USA — WW II Army Air Corps Hero

Evans, Rupert
Curtis Brown Group, 28-29 Haymarket St, #500, London SW1Y 4SP, England — Actor

Evans, Sara E
Gersh Agency, 9465 Wilshire Blvd, #600, Beverly Hills CA 90212 USA — Singer, Songwriter

Evans, Shaun
Hamilton Hodell, 66-68 Margaret St, London W1W 8SR, England — Actor

Evans, Sian
Moksha Mgmt, PO Box 102, London E15 2HH, England — Singer, Songwriter (Kosheen)

Evans, Terence T
US Court of Appeals, 517 E Wisconsin Ave, Milwaukee WI 53202, USA — Judge

Evans, Terry
1049 Dunedin Trail, Woodstock GA 30188, USA — Baseball Player

Evans, Tiffany
Dupree & Raffill Mgmt, 377 Central Square, 199 New Road, Linwood NJ 08221, USA — Singer, Actress

Evans, Troy
Stone Manners Salners, 9911 W Pico Blvd, #1400, Los Angeles CA 90035 USA — Actor

Evans, Tyreke
Sacramento Kings, Arco Arena, 1 Sports Parkway, Sacramento CA 95834 USA — Basketball Player

Evans, Vincent T (Vince)
14084 Bronte Dr, Whittier CA 90602, USA — Football Player

Evans, Walker
Walker Evans Racing, PO Box 2469, Riverside CA 92516, USA — Truck, Off-Road Racing Driver

Evans, William (Billy)
24369 Sandpiper Isle Way, #105, Bonita Springs FL 34134, USA — Basketball Player

Evason, Dean C
Washington Capitals, 627 N Glebe Road, #850, Arlington VA 22203 USA — Ice Hockey Player

Evatt, Christopher
P O Box 294, 06101 Porvoo, Finland — Motivational Speaker

Eve
1438 N Gower St, #115, Los Angeles CA 90028, USA — Rap Artist (Ruff Ryders), Actress

Eve, Alice
Artist Rights Group, 4 Great Portland Place, London W1W 8PA, England — Actress

Eve, Trevor J
Insight Entertainment, 1134 S Cloverdale Ave, Los Angeles CA 90019, USA — Actor

Eveland, Dana J
37138 Liana Lane, Palmdale CA 93551, USA — Baseball Player

Evensen, Johan Remen
Molde og Omega I F, PB 2326, 6402 Molde, Norway — Ski Jumper

Everett, Adam
4374 Oglethorpe Loop NW, Acworth GA 30101, USA — Baseball Player

Everett, Carl E
19108 Harborbridge Lane, Lutz FL 33558, USA — Baseball Player

Everett, Danny
Santa Monica Track Club, 1801 Ocean Park Ave, #112, Santa Monica CA 90405, USA — Track Athlete

Everett, James S (Jim)
555 N El Camino Real, #A445, San Clemente CA 92672, USA — Football Player

Everett, Major D
PO Box 1441, Pine Lake GA 30072, USA — Football Player

Everett, Mark Oliver (E, Eels)
Monterey Peninsula Artists, 404 W Franklin St, Monterey CA 93940 USA — Singer, Guitarist, Songwriter

Everett, Rupert
Rights House, 34-43 Russell St, London WC2B 5HA, England — Actor

Everett, Thomas G
PO Box 795337, Dallas TX 75379, USA — Football Player

Everhard, Nancy
Talent Management Group, 339 E 3900 S, #200, Salt Lake City UT 84107, USA — Actress

Everhart, Angie
13562 Valleyheart Dr N, Sherman Oaks CA 91423, USA — Model, Actress

Everhart, Thomas E
705 Poinsettia Way, Santa Barbara CA 93111, USA — Educator

Everitt, Steven M (Steve)
17252 Snapper Lane, Summerland Key FL 33042, USA — Football Player

Everlast
A A Music Mgmt, 1100 Glendon Ave, #2000, Los Angeles CA 90024, USA — Rap Artist, Actor, Songwriter

Everly, Donald (Don)
401 W 9th St, Columbia TN 38401, USA — Singer (Everly Brothers)

Everly, Phil
401 W 9th St, Columbia TN 38401, USA — Singer (Everly Brothers)

Evers, Charles
1018 Pecan Park Dr, Jackson MS 39209, USA — Civil Rights Activist

E

Eversgerd, Bryan D — Baseball Player
9212 Huey Road, Centralia IL 62801, USA

Eversley, Frederick J — Sculptor
1110 W Abbot Kinney Blvd, Venice CA 90291, USA

Eversman, Nick — Actor
Medavoy Mgmt, 10203 Santa Monica Blvd, #400, Los Angeles CA 90067 USA

Everson, Corinna (Cory) — Body Builder
23705 Van Owen St, West Hills CA 91307, USA

Evers-Williams, Myrlie — Association Executive
15 SW Colorado Ave, #310, Bend OR 97702, USA

Evert, Christine M (Chris) — Tennis Player
8563 Horseshoe Lane, Boca Raton FL 33496, USA

Evert, Ray F — Botanist
810 Woodward Dr, Madison WI 53704, USA

Evidence — Rap Artist (Dilated Peoples)
W M E Entertainment, 9601 Wilshire Blvd, #300, Beverly Hills CA 90210 USA

Evigan, Briana — Actress
Gersh Agency, 9465 Wilshire Blvd, #600, Beverly Hills CA 90212 USA

Evigan, Greg — Actor, Singer
Stone Manners Salners, 9911 W Pico Blvd, #1400, Los Angeles CA 90035 USA

Evren, Kenan — President, Turkey; Army General
Beyaz Ev Sokak 21, Armutalan, 48700 Marmaris, Turkey

Ewald, Elwyn — Religious Leader
Free Lutheran Congregations, 12015 Manchester Road, Saint Louis MO 63131, USA

Ewald, Reinhold — Cosmonaut, Germany
D L R Astronauterburo WT/AN, Linder Hohe, 51140 Cologne, Germany

Ewell, Kayla — Actress
Innovative Artists, 1505 10th St, Santa Monica CA 90401 USA

Ewen, Harold I — Astronomer, Physicist
60 Hillcrest Dr, South Deerfield MA 01373, USA

Ewen, Paterson — Artist
1015 Wellington St, London ON N6A 3T5, Canada

Ewen, Todd — Ice Hockey Player
420 Thunderhead Canyon Dr, Ballwin MO 63011, USA

Ewing, Barbara — Actress
1 Candover St, #4, London W1W 7DG, England

Ewing, Donald Ralph (Skip) — Singer, Songwriter
Sussman Assoc, 1222 16th Ave S, #300, Nashville TN 37212, USA

Ewing, Maria L — Opera Singer
Mitchell-Godfrey Mgmt, 48 Gary's Inn Road, London WC1X 8LT, England

Ewing, Patrick A — Basketball Player
Orlando Magic, 8701 Maitland Summit Blvd, Orlando FL 32810 USA

Ewing, Reid — Actor
United Talent Agency, 9336 Civic Center Dr, Beverly Hills CA 90210 USA

Ewing, Samuel J (Sam) — Baseball Player
1048 Cedarview Lane, Franklin TN 37067, USA

Exelby, Garnet — Ice Hockey Player
1182 Saint Louis Place NE, Atlanta GA 30306, USA

Eyharts, Leopold — Spatinaut, France
49 Rue Desnouttes, 75015 Paris, France

Eyoghe Ndong, Jean — Prime Minister, Gabon
Prime Minister's Office, BP 91, Immeuble du 2 Decembre, Libreville, Gabon

Eyre, Chris — Actor, Director, Producer
Critical Mass Mgmt, 1158 26th St, #414, Santa Monica CA 90403, USA

Eyre, Ivan — Artist
1098 Des Trappistes St, Winnipeg MB R3V 1B8, Canada

Eyre, Richard — Director, Writer
Judy Daish Assoc, 2 Saint Charles Place, London W10 6EG, England

Eyre, Scott A — Baseball Player
7010 190th St E, Bradenton FL 34211, USA

Eyre, Willie — Baseball Player
PO Box 125, Parowan, UT 84761, USA

Eyring, Henry B — Religious Leader
Church of Latter Day Saints, 50 E North Temple, Salt Lake City UT 84150, USA

Eyskens, Mark M F — Prime Minister, Belgium
Graaf de Grunnelaan 17, 3001 Heverlee-Leuven, Belgium

Eytchison, Ronald M — Navy Admiral
11 Prentice Lane, Signal Mountain TN 37377, USA

Ezeli, I Festus — Basketball Player
Golden State Warriors, 1011 Broadway, Oakland CA 94605 USA

Ezersky, John J (Johnny) — Basketball Player
2564 Walnut Blvd, #103, Walnut Creek CA 94596, USA

Ezra, Derek — Government Official, Businessman
2 Salisbury Road, Wimbledon, London SW19 4EZ, England

Eversgerd - Ezra

Fabares, Shelley	Actress, Singer
Innovative Artists, 1505 10th St, Santa Monica CA 90401 USA	
Fabbricini, Tiziana	Opera Singer
Gianni Testa, Via Wrenteggio 31/6, 20146 Milan, Italy	
Fabel, Brad	Golfer
247 Windsor Terrace Dr, Nashville TN 37221, USA	
Faber, Michel	Writer
Canongate Books, 14 High St, Edinburgh EH1 1TE, Scotland	
Faber, Sandra M	Astronomer
16321 Ridgecrest Ave, Monte Sereno CA 95030, USA	
Faber, Steve	Writer, Producer
Collective, 8383 Wilshire Blvd, #1050, Beverly Hills CA 90211 USA	
Fabian	Singer
All Gold, 2228 Whitefield Road, Springfield IL 62704, USA	
Fabian DeLa Mora, Marco J	Soccer Player
Federacion de Futbol, Colima 373 Colonia Roma, Delegacion Cuauhtemoc Mexico DF 06700, Mexico	
Fabian, Ava	Actress, Model
Commercial Talent, 9255 W Sunset Blvd, #505, West Hollywood CA 90069, USA	
Fabian, John M	Astronaut
100 Shine Road, Port Ludlow WA 98365, USA	
Fabian, Lara	Singer, Songwriter
Productions Clandestines, 1 Place du Commerce, #400, Ile des Soeurs QC H3E 1A2, Canada	
Fabian, Patrick	Actor
Essential Talent Mgmt, 3151 Cahuenga Blvd W, #220, Los Angeles CA 90068, USA	
Fabini, Jason	Football Player
7106 Nighthawk Dr, Fort Wayne IN 46835, USA	
Fabio	Model, Actor
Thor Four, 3000 Olympic Blvd, #2378, Santa Monica CA 90404, USA	
Fabiola Mora y Aragon, Dona	Queen Mother, Belgium
Royal Palace of Laeken, Laeken-Brussels, Belgium	
Fabius, Laurent	Premier, France
National Assembly, Casier de la Poste, Paris Bourbon, 75355 Paris, France	
Fabolous	Rap Artist
Artist Representation Group, 9701 Wilshire Blvd, #1000, Beverly Hills CA 90212, USA	
Fabray, Nanette	Singer, Actress
13834 Magnolia Blvd, Sherman Oaks CA 91423, USA	
Fabre, Jan	Artist
Pastorihstaat 23, 2060 Antwerp, Belgium	
Fabregas, Jorge	Baseball Player
9504 SW 125th Terrace, Miami FL 33176, USA	
Face, Elroy L (Roy)	Baseball Player
608 Della Dr, #5F, North Versailles PA 15137, USA	
Fachinetti, Alessandra	Fashion Designer
Gucci Group, 1 Amstelplein, 10966 HA Amsterdam, Netherlands	
Facinelli, Peter	Actor
A P A Talent/Literary Agency, 405 S Beverly Dr, #300, Beverly Hills CA 90212 USA	
Fadden, Jimmie	Musician (Nitty Gritty Dirt Band)
W M E Entertainment, 9601 Wilshire Blvd, #300, Beverly Hills CA 90210 USA	
Faddeyev, Ludwig D	Mathematician, Physicist
Steklov Mathematics Institute, Gubkina Str 8, 119991 Moscow, Russia	
Faddis, Jonathan (Jon)	Jazz Trumpeter, Flugelhorn Player
Carolyn McClair, PO Box 55, Radio Station, New York NY 10101, USA	
Fadek, Timothy	Photographer
Polaris Images, 259 W 30th St, #1300, New York NY 10001, USA	
Fadeyechev, Alexei	Ballet Dancer
Karenty Ryad Str 5/10, #20, 103006 Moscow Russia	
Fadeyechev, Nicolai B	Ballet Dancer
Bolshoi Theater, Teatralnaya Pl 1, 103009 Moscow, Russia	
Fadiman, Anne	Editor, Writer
Farrar Straus Giroux, 18 W 18th St, #700, New York NY 10011 USA	
Faedo, Leonardo L (Lenny)	Baseball Player
2920 W Collins St, Tampa FL 33607, USA	
Faerch, Daeg	Actor
Stone Manners Salners, 9911 W Pico Blvd, #1400, Los Angeles CA 90035 USA	
Fagan, Garth	Choreographer
Garth Fagan Dance, 50 Chestnut Plaza, #1, Rochester NY 14604, USA	
Fagan, Giles	Actor
Ken McReddie Assoc, 11 Connaught Place, London W2 2ET, England	
Fagan, Kevin	Cartoonist (Drabble)
26771 Ashford, Mission Viejo CA 92692, USA	
Fagan, Kevin S	Football Player
1161 Conejo Way, Walnut Creek CA 94597, USA	
Fagen, Donald	Singer (Steely Dan); Songwriter
Front Line Mgmt, 1100 Glendon Ave, #2000, Los Angeles CA 90024 USA	
Fagenson, Anthony E (Tony)	Drummer (Eve 6)
Agency Group Ltd, 1880 Century Park E, #711, Los Angeles CA 90067 USA	
Fagerbakke, Bill	Actor
Main Title Mgmt, 8383 Wilshire Blvd, #408, Beverly Hills CA 90211 USA	
Fagg, George G	Judge
US Court of Appeals, US Courthouse, 110 E Court Ave, Des Moines IA 50309, USA	
Faggin, Federico	Co-Inventor (Microprocessor)
27910 Roble Blanco Dr, Los Altos Hills CA 94022, USA	
Faggins, DeMarcus	Football Player
3002 Southworth Lane, Manvel TX 77578, USA	
Fagin, Claire M	Educator
200 Central Park S, #12E, New York NY 10019, USA	
Fahey, Damien	Actor
Creative Artists Agency, 2000 Ave of Stars, #100, Los Angeles CA 90067 USA	
Fahey, Jeff	Actor
Jeff Goldberg Mgmt, 817 Monte Leon Dr, Beverly Hills CA 90210, USA	
Fahey, John M, Jr	Association Executive
National Geographic, President's Office, 1145 17th St NW, Washington DC 20036, USA	
Fahey, William R (Bill)	Baseball Player
5740 Mona Lane, Dallas TX 75236, USA	
Fahl, Mary	Singer
Sony Records, 550 Madison Ave, #600, New York NY 10022 USA	

F

Fabares - Fahl

Fahn, Stanley — Neurologist
155 Edgars Lane, Hastings on Hudson NY 10706, USA

Fahnhorst, James J (Jim) — Football Player
2365 Brockton Lane N, Minneapolis MN 55447, USA

Fahnhorst, Keith V — Football Player
12216 Chadwick Lane, Eden Prairie MN 55344, USA

Fainaru, Steve — Journalist
Washington Post, Editorial Dept, 1150 15th St NW, Washington DC 20071 USA

Fair, Lorrie — Soccer Player
300 3rd St, #1515, San Francisco CA 94107, USA

Fair, Terrtance D (Terry) — Football Player
12910 W Monte Vista Road, Avondale AZ 85392, USA

Fairbairn, Bruce — Actor
975 N Vendome St Apt 214, Los Angeles CA 90026, USA

Fairbank, Richard D — Financier
Capital One Financial, 1680 Capital One Dr, #1, McLean VA 22102, USA

Fairbanks, Charles L (Chuck) — Football Coach
25191 N 104th Way, Scottsdale AZ 85255, USA

Fairbrass, Craig — Actor
Zero Gravity Mgmt, 9255 Sunset Blvd, #1010, Los Angeles CA 90069 USA

Fairchild, John B — Publisher
Chalet Bianchina, Talstr GR, 7250 Klosters, Switzerland

Fairchild, Morgan — Actress
McGowan Mgmt, 8733 W Sunset Blvd, #103, West Hollywood CA 90069 USA

Fairchild, Paul J — Football Player
PO Box 25442, Overland Park KS 66225, USA

Fairchild, Shelly — Singer
Creative Artists Agency, 2000 Ave of Stars, #100, Los Angeles CA 90067 USA

Faircloth, D McLauchlin (Lauch) — Senator, NC
PO Box 496, Clinton NC 28329, USA

Fairley, Michelle — Actress
C A M, 111 Shoreditch High St, #400, London E1 6JN, England

Fairley, Nick — Football Player
Detroit Lions, 222 Republic Dr, Allen Park MI 48101 USA

Fairly, Ronald R (Ron) — Baseball Player, Sportscaster
75369 Spyglass Dr, Indian Wells CA 92210, USA

Fairs, Eric J — Football Player
32707 Wales Circle, Fulshear TX 77441, USA

Fairstein, Linda — Writer, Attorney
I C M Partners, 10250 Constellation Blvd, #900, Los Angeles CA 90067 USA

Faison, Donald — Actor
A P A Talent/Literary Agency, 405 S Beverly Dr, #300, Beverly Hills CA 90212 USA

Faison, Matthew — Actor
Snavely Assoc, 112 W Foster Ave, #401, State College PA 16801, USA

Faison, W Earl — Football Player
2279 N Sequoia Dr, Prescott AZ 86301, USA

Faithfull, Marianne — Singer, Songwriter, Actress
Republic Media, Westbourne Studios, 242 Acklam Road, #202, London W10 5JJ, England

Fakhri, Nargis — Actress
Ford Models Inc, 111 5th Ave, #900, New York NY 10003 USA

Fakir, Abdul (Duke) — Singer (Four Tops)
I C M Partners, 730 5th Ave, New York NY 10019 USA

Falana, Lola — Singer, Dancer
Capital Entertainment, 217 Seaton Place NE, Washington DC 20002, USA

Falcao, Jose Freire Cardinal — Religious Leader
QL 12-CJ12, Lote 1, Lago Sul, Brasilia DF 71660 325, Brazil

Falchi, Anna — Model, Actress
Class Mgmt, Piazza Cavour 66, 02100 Rieti, Italy , USA

Falchuk, Brad — Producer, Director, Writer
W M E Entertainment, 9601 Wilshire Blvd, #300, Beverly Hills CA 90210 USA

Falco, Ed — Writer
Virginia Polytechnic Institute, English Dept, Blacksburg VA 24060, USA

Falco, Edie — Actress
I C M Partners, 10250 Constellation Blvd, #900, Los Angeles CA 90067 USA

Falcon, Rose — Singer, Songwriter
Show Dog/Universal Records, 70 Universal City Plaza, Universal City CA 91608, USA

Falcone, Ben — Actor
Creative Artists Agency, 2000 Ave of Stars, #100, Los Angeles CA 90067 USA

Falcone, Peter F (Pete) — Baseball Player
2232 Thornton Court, Alexandria LA 71301, USA

Falconer, Eric — Producer, Writer, Actor
United Talent Agency, 9336 Civic Center Dr, Beverly Hills CA 90210 USA

Falconer, Ian W — Writer, Illustrator
Simon & Schuster, 1230 Ave of Americas, Concourse 1, New York NY 10020 USA

Faldo, Nicholas A (Nick) — Golfer, Sportscaster
Elizabeth House, 18-20 Sheet St, Windsor Berkshire SL4 1BG, England

Falk, Adam F — Educator
Williams College, President's Office, 880 Main St, Williamstown MA 01267, USA

Falk, David B — Sports Attorney
Falk Assoc, 5335 Wisconsin Ave NW, #850, Washington DC 20015, USA

Falk, Ingrid — Photographer, Artist
FA+, Drottninggatan 71A, 111 36 Stockholm, Sweden

Falk, Lisanne — Actress
9255 W Sunset Blvd, #515, West Hollywood CA 90069, USA

Falk, Paul — Figure Skater
Sybelstr 21, 40239 Dusseldorf, Germany

Falk, Thomas J — Businessman
Kimberly-Clark Corp, 351 Phelps Dr, Irving TX 75038, USA

Falkenborg, Brian T — Baseball Player
30223 N 125th Dr, Peoria AZ 85383, USA

Falkow, Stanley — Microbiologist
Stanford University Medical School, Microbiology Dept, Stanford CA 94305, USA

Fall, Timothy — Actor
Greenberg Glusker, 1900 Ave of Stars, #2100, Los Angeles CA 90067 USA

Falldin, N O Thorbjorn — Prime Minister, Sweden
As, 870 16 Ramvik, Sweden

Fallon, Brian — Singer, Guitarist (Gaslight Anthem)
Esther Creative Group, 27 W 24th St, #404, New York NY 10010, USA

Fallon, James T (Jimmy), Jr — Actor, Comedian
Creative Artists Agency, 2000 Ave of Stars, #100, Los Angeles CA 90067 USA

Fallon, Robert J (Bob) — Baseball Player
801 Somerset Circle, Hanover Park IL 60133, USA

Fallon, Tiffany — Model, Actress
Enter Talking Client Relations, 645 W 9th St, #110, Los Angeles CA 90010, USA

Falloon, Pat — Ice Hockey Player
112-155 10th St, Birtle MB R0M 0C0, Canada

Falls, Kevin — Producer, Writer
W M E Entertainment, 9601 Wilshire Blvd, #300, Beverly Hills CA 90210 USA

Falls, Robert A — Director
Creative Artists Agency, 2000 Ave of Stars, #100, Los Angeles CA 90067 USA

Faloona, Christopher J — Cinematographer
Paradigm Agency, 360 N Crescent Dr, North Building, Beverly Hills CA 90210 USA

Falsani, Cathleen — Columnist
Chicago Sun-Times, Editorial Dept, 401 N Wabash Ave, Chicago IL 60611 USA

Falteisek, Steven J (Steve) — Baseball Player
540 W Iris Dr, Chandler AZ 85248, USA

Faltings, Gerd — Mathematician
Princeton University, Mathematics Dept, Princeton NJ 08544, USA

Faltskog, Agnetha (Anna) — Singer (ABBA)
Postbus 3079, 4700 Roosendaal GB, Netherlands

Faludi, Susan C — Writer, Journalist
Sandra Dijkstra Literary Agency, 1155 Camino del Mar, #515, Del Mar CA 92014, USA

Fama, Eugene F — Economist
University of Chicago, Booth Business School, Chicago IL 60637, USA

Fambrough, Henry — Singer (Spinners)
Buddy Allen Mgmt, 3750 Hudson Manor Terrace, #3AG, Bronx NY 10463, USA

Famechon, Johnny — Boxer
9 Wandana Court, Frankston VIC 3199, Australia

Famie, Keith — Chef, Director, Producer
W M E Entertainment, 9601 Wilshire Blvd, #300, Beverly Hills CA 90210 USA

Famiglietti, Mark — Actor
Hofflund/Polone, 9465 Wilshire Blvd, #420, Beverly Hills CA 90212 USA

Fanaro, Barry — Writer, Producer
I C M Partners, 10250 Constellation Blvd, #900, Los Angeles CA 90067 USA

Fancher, Hampton — Director, Writer, Actor
Earthbourne Films, 1810 14th St, #214, Santa Monica CA 90404, USA

Fancy, Richard — Actor
Paul Kohner, 9300 Wilshire Blvd, #555, Beverly Hills CA 90212 USA

Faneca, Alan J, Jr — Football Player
3800 S Clubhouse Dr, #6, Chandler AZ 85248, USA

Fang Lijun — Artist
Max Protetch Gallery, 511 W 22nd St, New York NY 10011, USA

Fankhauser, Merrell — Guitarist, Composer
PO Box 1504, Arroyo Grande CA 93421, USA

Fankhouser, Scott — Ice Hockey Player
2043 Crippled Oak Trail, Jasper GA 30143, USA

Fann, Al — Actor
6051 Hollywood Blvd, #207, Los Angeles CA 90028, USA

Fanning, Bernard — Singer (Powderfinger)
Secret Service, PO Box 401, Fortitude Valley QLD 4006, Australia

Fanning, Dakota — Actress
One Talent Mgmt, 9220 Sunset Blvd, #306, Los Angeles CA 90069, USA

Fanning, Elle — Actress
W M E Entertainment, 9601 Wilshire Blvd, #300, Beverly Hills CA 90210 USA

Fanning, Michael L (Mike) — Football Player
28808 S 4190 Road, Inola OK 74036, USA

Fanning, W James (Jim) — Baseball Player, Manager
154 Tiner Ave, Dorchester ON N0L 1G2, Canada

Fano, Robert M — Computer Scientist, Electrical Engineer
51 Woodland Way, North Chatham MA 02650, USA

Fanok, Harry M — Baseball Player
12373 Old State Road, Chardon OH 44024, USA

Fantetti, Ken M — Football Player
1211 SE 175th Place, Portland OR 97233, USA

Fantoni, Sergio — Actor
Via del Cappellari 35, 00186 Rome, Italy

Fanzone, Carmen R — Baseball Player
5114 Ranchito Ave, Sherman Oaks CA 91423, USA

Faraci, John V, Jr — Businessman
International Paper Corp, 2 Manhattanville Road, Purchase NY 10577, USA

Faracy, Stephanie — Actress
Michael Slessinger, 8730 W Sunset Blvd, #220W, West Hollywood CA 90069 USA

Faragalli, Lindy — Bowler
113 N 5th Ave, Manville NJ 08835, USA

Farah — Queen, Iran
Hellen Medien Projekte, Kornweg 1G, 44805 Bochum, Germany

Farar, Hassan Abshir — Prime Minister, Somalia
Prime Minister's Office, People's Palace, Mogadishu, Somalia

Farenthold, Frances T — Women's Activist, Educator
2929 Buffalo Speedway, #18B, Houston TX 77098, USA

Farentino, Debrah — Actress
Innovative Artists, 1505 10th St, Santa Monica CA 90401 USA

Fares, Muhammad Ahmed Al — Cosmonaut, Syria
PO Box 1272, Aleppo, Syria

Fargis, Joseph H (Joe), IV — Equestrian
25 Hampton Road, Southampton NY 11968, USA

Fargo, Donna — Singer, Guitarist
PO Box 150527, Nashville TN 37215, USA

Fargo, Thomas B — Navy Admiral
Trex Enterprises, 10455 Pacific Center Court, San Diego CA 92121, USA

Farha, Ihsam (Sam) — Poker Player
14027 Memorial Dr, #234, Houston TX 77079, USA

Farhadi, Asghar — Director, Producer, Writer
United Talent Agency, 9336 Civic Center Dr, Beverly Hills CA 90210 USA

Farham, John — Singer
Gotham/B M G Records, 69-79 Fulham High St, London SW6 3JW, England

Farhi, Nicole — Fashion Designer
16 Foubert's Place, London W1F 7PJ, England

Farina, Dennis — Actor
Creative Artists Agency, 2000 Ave of Stars, #100, Los Angeles CA 90067 USA

Farina, Johnny — Guitarist (Santo & Johnny)
Bellrose Music, 308 E 6th St, #13, New York NY 10003, USA

Farina, Raffaele Cardinal — Religious Leader
Vatican Library, 00120 Vatican City

Farino, Julian — Director
Independent Talent Group, Oxford House, 76 Oxford St, London W1D 1BS, England

Faris, Al — Actor
Chaotik, 6446 Santa Monica Blvd, Los Angeles CA 90038, USA

Faris, Anna — Actress
Anonymous Content, 3532 Hayden Ave, Culver City CA 90232 USA

Faris, Sean H — Actor
Gersh Agency, 9465 Wilshire Blvd, #600, Beverly Hills CA 90212 USA

Faris, Valerie — Director
United Talent Agency, 9336 Civic Center Dr, Beverly Hills CA 90210 USA

Farish, William S — Diplomat
W S Farish Co, 1100 Louisiana St, #2200, Houston TX 77002, USA

Fariss, Monty T — Baseball Player
PO Box 249, Leedey OK 73654, USA

Farkas, Bertalan — Cosmonaut, Hungary
A Magyar Koztarsasag, Kutato Urhajosa, Pf 25, 1885 Budapest, Hungary

Farkas, Ferenc — Composer
Nagyatai Utca 12, 1026 Budapest, Hungary

Farkas, Jeff — Ice Hockey Player
284 Patrice Terrace, Buffalo NY 14221, USA

Farley, Carole — Opera, Concert Singer
270 Riverside Dr, New York NY 10025, USA

Farley, Kevin P — Actor
Brillstein Entertainment Partners, 9150 Wilshire Blvd, #350, Beverly Hills CA 90212 USA

Farley, Terrence M — Financier
Brown Brothers Harriman, 59 Wall St, New York NY 10005, USA

Farmar, Jordan R — Basketball Player
2625 Zinfandel Dr, Rancho Cordova CA 95670, USA

Farmer, Charles (Red) — Auto Racing Driver
Talladega Walk of Fame, PO Drawer 1179, Talladega AL 35161, USA

Farmer, D Michael (Mike) — Basketball Player, Coach
2520 Lakeview Dr, Santa Rosa CA 95405, USA

Farmer, Edward J (Ed) — Baseball Player
4581 Camino del Sol, Calabasas CA 91302, USA

Farmer, Gary — Actor
Gonzo Drive Records, PO Box 31096, Santa Fe NM 87594, USA

Farmer, George T — Football Player
332 Lorraine Blvd, Los Angeles CA 90020, USA

Farmer, George, III — Football Player
12422 S Denker Ave, Los Angeles CA 90047, USA

Farmer, Howard E — Baseball Player
316 Duke Dr, #A, Kenner LA 70065, USA

Farmer, James H (Jim) — Basketball Player
214 Ashborough Circle, Dothan AL 36301, USA

Farmer, John, Jr — Governor, NJ
Attorney General's Office, Hughes Justice Complex, Trenton NJ 08625, USA

Farmer, Paul — Physician, Anthropologist
Partners in Health, 641 Huntington Ave, #100, Boston MA 02115, USA

Farmiga, Vera A — Actress, Director
Creative Artists Agency, 2000 Ave of Stars, #100, Los Angeles CA 90067 USA

Farner, Mark — Singer, Guitarist
Bobby Roberts, 3050 Business Park Circle, #303, Goodlettsville TN 37221 USA

Farnham, John P — Singer, Actor
PO Box 6500, Saint Kilda Road, Melbourne VIC 3004, Australia

Farnon, Shannon — Actress
12743 Milbank St, Studio City CA 91604, USA

Farnsworth, Kyle L — Baseball Player
1163 Wilde Dr, Kissimmee FL 34747, USA

Farquhar, John W — Physician
Stanford University Medical School, Disease Prevention Center, Stanford CA 94305, USA

Farquhar, Kurt — Composer
First Artists Mgmt, 4764 Park Granada, #210, Calabasas CA 91302 USA

Farquhar, Marilyn G — Cell Biologist, Pathologist
12894 Via Latina, Del Mar CA 92014, USA

Farr, David N — Businessman
Emerson Electric, 800 S Florissant Ave, Saint Louis MO 63135, USA

Farr, Diane — Actress
United Talent Agency, 9336 Civic Center Dr, Beverly Hills CA 90210 USA

Farr, Felicia — Actress
1143 Tower Road, Beverly Hills CA 90210, USA

Farr, James A (Jimmy) — Baseball Player
3 Tyndal Court, Williamsburg VA 23188, USA

Farr, Jamie — Actor
51 Ranchero Road, Bell Canyon CA 91307, USA

Farr, Melvin (Mel), Sr — Football Player
5000 Town Center, #2803, Southfield MI 48075, USA

Farr, Miller, Jr — Football Player
11815 Rowood Dr, Houston TX 77070, USA

Farr, Norman (Rocky) — Ice Hockey Player
3850 Overton Park Dr W, Fort Worth TX 76109, USA

Farr, Shonda — Actress
Creative Artists Agency, 2000 Ave of Stars, #100, Los Angeles CA 90067 USA

Farr, Steven M (Steve) — Baseball Player
126 Chicahauk Trail, Kitty Hawk NC 27949, USA

Farrakhan, Louis — Religious Leader
Nation of Islam, 734 W 79th St, Chicago IL 60620, USA
Farrar, Frank L — Governor, SD
PO Box 936, Britton SD 57430, USA
Farrar, Jay — Singer (Uncle Tupelo, Son Volt)
Steel Toe Artist Mgmt, PO Box 3165, Jersey City NJ 07303, USA
Farrell, Colin — Actor
Creative Artists Agency, 2000 Ave of Stars, #100, Los Angeles CA 90067 USA
Farrell, John E — Baseball Player, Manager
PO Box 3519, Clearwater Beach FL 33767, USA
Farrell, Mike — Actor
Innovative Artists, 1505 10th St, Santa Monica CA 90401 USA
Farrell, Perry — Singer (Jane's Addiction)
Paradigm Agency, 360 N Crescent Dr, North Building, Beverly Hills CA 90210 USA
Farrell, Sean W — Football Player
PO Box 21426, Tampa FL 33622, USA
Farrell, Sharon — Actress
Wallis Agency, 210 Pass Ave, Burbank CA 91505, USA
Farrell, Suzanne — Ballet Dancer
Kennedy Center for Performing Arts, 2700 F St NW, Washington DC 20566, USA
Farrell, Terence (Terry) — Architect
Terry Farrell Partners, 7 Hatton St, London NW8 8PL, England
Farrell, Terry — Actress
Don Buchwald/Fortitude, 6500 Wilshire Blvd, #2200, Los Angeles CA 90048 USA
Farrelly, Bernard (Midget) — Surfer
Parkes Australia, PO Box 505, Byron Bay NSW 2481, Australia
Farrelly, Bobby — Director
Conundrum Entertainment, 325 Wilshire Blvd, #201, Santa Monica CA 90401, USA
Farrelly, Peter J — Director
Conundrum Entertainment, 325 Wilshire Blvd, #201, Santa Monica CA 90401, USA
Farrimond, Richard A — Astronaut, England
Metra Marconi Center, Gunnels Wood Road, Stevenage, Herts SG1 2AS, England
Farrington, Robert G (Bob) — Harness Racing Driver
105 Country Place, Sanford FL 32771, USA
Farrior, James A — Football Player
5925 Almeda Road, #11115, Houston TX 77004, USA
Farris, Dionne — Singer (Arrested Development)
Creative Artists Agency, 2000 Ave of Stars, #100, Los Angeles CA 90067 USA
Farris, Isaac Newton, Jr — Religious Leader
Southern Christian Leadership Conference, 320 Auburn Ave NE, Atlanta GA 30303, USA
Farris, J Jerome — Judge
US Court of Appeals, US Courthouse, 1010 5th Ave, Seattle WA 98104, USA
Farris, Joseph — Cartoonist
Long Meadow Lane, Bethel CT 06801, USA
Farris, Roy Wayne — Professional Wrestler
H T M Enterprises, 4655 E Harwell St, Gilbert AZ 85234, USA
Farriss, Andrew — Keyboardist (INXS)
8 Hayes St, #1, Neutral Bay 20891 NSW, Australia
Farriss, Jon — Drummer, Singer (INXS)
8 Hayes St, #1, Neutral Bay 20891 NSW, Australia
Farrow, Mallory — Actress
Hervey/Grimes Talent, 10561 Missouri Ave, #2, Los Angeles CA 90025 USA
Farrow, Mia V — Actress, Social Activist
Hofflund/Polone, 9465 Wilshire Blvd, #420, Beverly Hills CA 90212 USA
Faryniarz, Brett A — Football Player
1021 S Patrick Way, Anaheim CA 92808, USA
Fasano, Salvatore F (Sal) — Baseball Player
905 Catherine Glenn, Minooka IL 60447, USA
Fasman, Gerald D — Biochemist
180 Wells Ave, #106, Newton Center MA 02459, USA
Fassbaender, Brigitte — Opera Singer
Sekretariat, Haiming 2, 83119 Obing, Germany
Fassbender, Michael — Actor
Creative Artists Agency, 2000 Ave of Stars, #100, Los Angeles CA 90067 USA
Fassell, James E (Jim) — Football Player, Coach
56 Jacquelin Ave, Ho Ho Kus NJ 07423, USA
Fassero, Jeffrey J (Jeff) — Baseball Player
9841 N 56th St, Paradise Valley AZ 85253, USA
Fassio, Anne — Actress
U B B A, 6 Rue de Braque, 75003 Paris, France
Fast, Alexia — Actress
Sanders/Armstrong/Caserta Mgmt, 2120 Colorado Ave, #120, Santa Monica CA 90404 USA
Fat Joe — Rap Artist (Terror Squad), Actor
Media Artists Group, 333 E 43rd St, #115,New York NY 10017, USA
Fatmi, Mourir — Artist
Galerie Hussenot, 5 bis Rue des Haudriettes, 75003 Paris, France
Fatone, Joseph (Joey), Jr — Singer ('N Sync)
P M K-B N C, 8687 Melrose Ave, #800, Los Angeles CA 90069 USA
Fauci, Anthony S — Immunologist
3012 43rd St NW, Washington DC 20016, USA
Faucon, Bernard — Photographer
6 Rue Barbanegre, 75019 Paris, France
Faulk, Kevin T — Football Player
190 Summer St, South Wapole MA 02071, USA
Faulk, Marshall — Football Player, Sportscaster
6340 Clayton Road, #305, Saint Louis MO 63117, USA
Faulkner, Frank — Artist
Arden Gallery, 129 Newbury St, Mezzanine 2, Boston MA 02116, USA
Faulkner, Newton — Singer, Guitarist, Songwriter
Sony-BMG Records, 69-79 Fulham High St, London SW8 3JW, England
Faulkner, Shannon — Educational Activist
Woodmont High School, 2831 W Georgia Road, Piedmont SC 29673, USA
Faure, Maurice H — Government Official, France
28 Blvd Raspail, 75007 Paris, France
Fauria, Christian — Football Player
51 Jeffrey Dr, North Attleboro MA 02760, USA

F

Farrakhan - Fauria

Fauser, Mark
United Talent Agency, 9336 Civic Center Dr, Beverly Hills CA 90210 USA — Actor

Faussart, Helene
Evolution Talent Agency, 1501 Broadway, #1301, New York NY 10036, USA — Singer

Faust, Chad
Untitled Entertainment, 350 S Beverly Dr, #200, Beverly Hills CA 90212 USA — Actor

Faust, Chris
308 Prince St, Saint Paul MN 55101, USA — Photographer

Faust, Drew G
Harvard University, President's Office, 33 Elmwood Ave, Cambridge MA 02138, USA — Educator

Faustino, David
Stone Manners Salners, 9911 W Pico Blvd, #1400, Los Angeles CA 90035 USA — Actor

Fauza, Dario O
Harvard Medical School, Surgery Dept, 25 Shattuck St, Boston MA 02115, USA — Surgeon

Favier, Jean-Jacques
Technologies Avances, 17 Ave des Martys, 38054 Grenoble Cedex, France — Spatinaut, France

Favor, Mike
Robinsdale Cooper High School, 8230 47th Ave N, New Hope MN 55428, USA — Football Player

Favors, Derrick B
Utah Jazz, Energy Solutions Arena, 301 W South Temple, Salt Lake City UT 84101 USA — Basketball Player

Favors, Gregory B (Greg)
1990 Sandgate Circle, Atlanta GA 30349, USA — Football Player

Favre, Brett L
7698 US Highway 98W, Sumrall MS 39482, USA — Football Player

Favreau, Jon
Creative Artists Agency, 2000 Ave of Stars, #100, Los Angeles CA 90067 USA — Actor, Writer, Director

Fawcett, Don W
3710 American Way, #325, Missoula MT 59808, USA — Anatomist

Fawcett, Joy
11 Calle Marta, Rancho Santa Margarita CA 92688, USA — Soccer Player

Fawcett, Sherwood L
1800 Riverside Dr, #2314, Columbus OH 43212, USA — Physicist

Faxon, Brad
85 Nayatt Road, Barrington RI 02806, USA — Golfer

Faxon, Nat
Creative Artists Agency, 2000 Ave of Stars, #100, Los Angeles CA 90067 USA — Actor, Writer

Fay, Johnny
Bobby Breen Mgmt, 13 Blackburn St, #300, Toronto ON M4M 2B3, Canada — Drummer (Tragically Hip)

Fay, Martin
Macklam/Feldman Mgmt, 1505 W 2nd Ave, #200, Vancouver BC V6H 3Y4, Canada — Fiddler (Chieftains)

Fay, Meagen
Main Title Mgmt, 8383 Wilshire Blvd, #408, Beverly Hills CA 90211 USA — Actress

Fay, Peter T
US Court of Appeals, 36 NE 1st St, #300, Miami FL 33132, USA — Judge

Faydoedeelay
Q Prime, 729 7th Ave, #1600, New York NY 10019, USA — Rap Artist, Bassist (Crazy Town)

Fayed, Mohamed al-
Craven Cottage, Stevenage Road, Fulham, London SW6 6HH, England — Businessman

Fazio, Ernest J (Ernie)
2310 Royal Oaks Dr, Alamo CA 94507, USA — Baseball Player

Fazio, Tom
Fazio Golf Course Designers, 401 N Main St, #400, Hendersonville NV 28792, USA — Golf Course Architect

Fazzini, Enrico
New York University Medical Center, Neurology Dept, 353 Lexington Ave, #101, New York NY 10016, USA — Neurologist

Fazzino, Charles
32 Relyea Place, #2, New Rochelle NY 10801, USA — Artist

Feachem, Richard
Global Fund, Chemin de Blandonnet 8, 1214 Vernier, Switzerland — Foundation Executive

Feacher, I Ricky
1522 Ferman Ave, Cleveland OH 44109, USA — Football Player

Feagles, Jeffrey A (Jeff)
326 W End Ave, Ridgewood NJ 07450, USA — Football Player

Fearnley, James
Agency Group Ltd, 361-373 City Road, London EC1V 2QA, England — Accordianist (Pogues)

Fearnley-Whittingstall, Hugh
Bloomsbury Publishing, 36 Soho Square, London W1D 3Q4, England — Writer, Chef

Featherstone, Glen
8 Larrabee Ave, Danvers MA 01923, USA — Ice Hockey Player

Fedak, Chris
W M E Entertainment, 9601 Wilshire Blvd, #300, Beverly Hills CA 90210 USA — Producer, Writer

Federer, Michelle
Gotham Talent Agency, 570 7th Ave, New York NY 10018, USA — Actress, Singer

Federer, Roger
Lynette Federer, Postfach, 4103 Bottmingen, Switzerland — Tennis Player

Federighi, Christine M
1315 Obispo Ave, Coral Gables FL 33134, USA — Sculptor

Federko, Bernie
2219 Devonsbrook Dr, Chesterfield MO 63005, USA — Ice Hockey Player

Federspiel, Joseph M (Joe)
2016 Lakeside Dr, Lexington KY 40502, USA — Football Player

Fedewa, Tim
1737 Onondaga Road, Holt MI 48842, USA — Auto Racing Driver

Fedorov, Sergei V
Metallurg Magnitogorsk, Pr Lenin 105, 455000, Magnitogorsk, Chelysbinsk Oblast, Russia — Ice Hockey Player

Fedoruk, Todd
4578 Liam Dr, Frisco TX 75034, USA — Ice Hockey Player

Fedoseyev, Vladimir I
Recording/Broadcasting House, Malaya Nikitskaya 24, 121069 Moscow, Russia — Conductor

Fedotenko, Ruslan V
230 W 56th St, #54E, New York NY 10019, USA — Ice Hockey Player

Fedotov, Maxim V
Tolbukhin Str 8, Korp 1, #6, 121596 Moscow, Russia — Concert Violinist

Feehan, Christine
Penguin Books, 375 Hudson St, Basement 1, New York NY 10014 USA — Writer

Feehery, Gerald (Gerry)
5 Sharpless Lane, Media PA 19063, USA — Football Player

Feehily, Mark Solo Agency, 53-55 Fulham High St, #200, London SW6 3JJ, England	Singer (Westlife)
Feeley, Adam J (A J) 19062 Park Ridge St, Weston FL 33332, USA	Football Player
Feely, T James (Jay) 15923 Noting Hill Dr, Lutz FL 33548, USA	Football Player
Feeney, Mark Boston Globe, Editorial Dept, 135 William Morrissey Blvd, Dorchester MA 02125 USA	Journalist
Fegan, Roshon B W M E Entertainment, 9601 Wilshire Blvd, #300, Beverly Hills CA 90210 USA	Actor
Feher, George University of California, Physics Dept, 9500 Gilman Dr, La Jolla CA 92093, USA	Physicist
Feher, Raymond 62 Cool Springs Road, Signal Mountain TN 37377, USA	Basketball Player
Feherty, David 6422 Prestonshire Lane, Dallas TX 75225, USA	Golfer
Fehr, Brendan Roar Mgmt, 9701 Wilshire Blvd, #800, Beverly Hills CA 90212 USA	Actor
Fehr, Oded Abrams Artists, 9200 W Sunset Blvd, #1125, West Hollywood CA 90069 USA	Actor
Fehr, Richard E (Rick) 2869 W Haley Dr, Anthem AZ 85086, USA	Golfer
Fehr, Steve 1329 Castlebridge Court, Cincinnati OH 45233, USA	Bowler
Fei Junlong Japanese Aerospace Exploration Agency, 2-1-1 Sengen, Tsukuba-shi, Ibaraki 305 8505, Japan	Taikonaut
Feiffer, Halley Gersh Agency, 9465 Wilshire Blvd, #600, Beverly Hills CA 90212 USA	Actress
Feiffer, Jules PO Box 373, Southampton NY 11969, USA	Cartoonist
Feig, Paul S Creative Artists Agency, 2000 Ave of Stars, #100, Los Angeles CA 90067 USA	Actor, Director, Writer
Feigenbaum, Armand V General Systems, 23 South St, #250, Pittsfield MA 01201, USA	Businessman, Systems Engineer
Feigenbaum, Edward A 1017 Cathcart Way, Stanford CA 94305, USA	Computer Scientist
Feign, Larry Heineman Educational Books, GPO Box 6086, Tsim Sha Tsui Post Office, Kowloon, Hong Kong, China	Cartoonist (World of Lily Wong)
Feigum, Christopher I M G Artists, Hogarth Business Park, Chiswick, London W4 2TH, England	Opera Singer
Feild, J J Ken McReddie Assoc, 11 Connaught Place, London W2 2ET, England	Actor
Feilden, Richard J R Bradley Architects, Bath Brewery, Toll Bridge Road, Bath BA1 7DE, England	Architect
Feinberg, Alan C M Artists, 127 W 96th St, #13B, New York NY 10025 USA	Concert Pianist
Feinberg, Wilfred US Court of Appeals, Moynihan Courthouse, 500 Pearl St, New York NY 10007, USA	Judge
Feiner, Edward F General Services Administration, 1800 F St NW, #3341, Washington DC 20405, USA	Architect
Feinstein, A Richard 1760 2nd Ave, #32C, New York NY 10128, USA	Epidemiologist
Feinstein, Alan Schiowitz Connor, 1680 N Vine St, #1016, Los Angeles CA 90028 USA	Actor
Feinstein, John Little Brown, 1271 Ave of Americas, New York NY 10020, USA	Sportswriter, Commentator
Feinstein, Michael Paradigm Agency, 360 N Crescent Dr, North Building, Beverly Hills CA 90210 USA	Singer, Pianist
Feist, Leslie Interscope Records, 2220 Colorado Ave, Santa Monica CA 90404 USA	Singer, Songwriter
Feitl, Dave S 12255 Highway 62 E, Harrison AR 72601, USA	Basketball Player
Felber, Dean FishCo Mgmt, 2519 Devine Street Columbia SC 29205, USA	Bassist (Hootie & the Blowfish)
Felch, William C 8545 Carmel Valley Road, Carmel CA 93923, USA	Physician
Feld, Eliot Feld Ballet, 890 Broadway, #800, New York NY 10003, USA	Dancer, Choreographer
Feld, Steven New Mexico University, Anthropology Dept, Albuquerque NM 87131, USA	Ethnomusicologist, Anthropologist
Felder, Donald W (Don) Renaissance Literary & Talent, PO Box 17379, Beverly Hills CA 90209, USA	Singer, Guitarist (Eagles)
Felder, Michael Ó (Mike) 322 S 17th St, Richmond CA 94804, USA	Baseball Player
Felder, Raoul Lionel 437 Madison Ave, #3000, New York NY 10022, USA	Attorney
Feldman, Bella 12 Summit Lane, Berkeley CA 94708, USA	Artist
Feldman, Corey Scott Carlson Entertainment, 5739 Bucknell Ave, Valley Village CA 91607, USA	Actor
Feldman, Donna TalentWorks, 3500 W Olive Ave, #1400, Burbank CA 91505 USA	Actress, Model
Feldman, Ed Gersh Agency, 9465 Wilshire Blvd, #600, Beverly Hills CA 90212 USA	Actor
Feldman, Jerome M 2744 Sevier St, Durham NC 27705, USA	Physician
Feldman, Jon H Gersh Agency, 9465 Wilshire Blvd, #600, Beverly Hills CA 90212 USA	Producer, Writer
Feldman, Kurt Slumberland Records, PO Box 19029, Oakland CA 94619, USA	Drummer (Pains of Being Pure at Heart)
Feldman, Marcus W Stanford University, Biological Sciences Dept, Stanford CA 94305, USA	Biological Scientist
Feldman, Michael Inphenate, 9701 Wilshire Blvd, #1000, Beverly Hills CA 90212 USA	Producer, Writer
Feldman, Michelle Gary Feldman, PO Box 713, Skaneateles NY 13152, USA	Bowler

Feldman, Scott W — Baseball Player
30895 N 119th Lane, Peoria AZ 85383, USA

Feldman, Susie — Actress
Scott Carlso Entertainment, 5739 Bucknell Ave, Valley Village CA 91607, USA

Feldman, Tamara — Actress
A P A Talent/Literary Agency, 405 S Beverly Dr, #300, Beverly Hills CA 90212 USA

Feldmann, Marc — Rheumatologist
Charing Cross Hospital, Saint Dunstan's Road, London W6 8RP, England

Feldmann, Sabine — Publisher
Shape, Publisher's Office, 1 Park Ave, New York NY 10016, USA

Feldon, Barbara — Actress, Model
Creative Artists Agency, 2000 Ave of Stars, #100, Los Angeles CA 90067 USA

Feldshuh, Tovah S — Actress
Gage Group, 315 W 57th St, #4H, New York NY 10019 USA

Feldstein, Martin S — Government Official, Economist
147 Clifton St, Belmont MA 02478, USA

Felipe — Crown Prince, Spain
Palacio de la Zarzuela, Carretera del Pardo S/N, 28071 Madrid, Spain

Felix Sanchez, Junior F — Baseball Player
7545 Treadway Road, Gresham SC 29546, USA

Feliz, Pedro J — Baseball Player
Houston Astros, Minute Maid Park, 501 Crawford St, Houston TX 77002 USA

Felke, Petra — Track Athlete
S C Motor Jena, Wollnitzevstr 42, 07749 Jena, Germany

Fellag, Mohamed — Actor
Agence Artiste Adequet, 80 Rue d'Amsterdam, 75009 Paris, France

Feller, Anke — Track Athlete, Model
Heinrich-Claes Str 11, 51373 Leverkusen, Germany

Fellmeth, Catherine — Bowler
Professional Bowlers Assn, 719 2nd Ave, #701, Seattle WA 98104 USA

Fellner, Till — Concert Pianist
Ingpen & Williams, 131 Putney Bridge Road, London SW15 2PA, England

Fellowes, Julian — Director, Writer
Independent Talent Group, Oxford House, 76 Oxford St, London W1D 1BS, England

Fellows, Ron — Auto Racing Driver
PO Box 564, RPO Turtle Creek, Mississauga ON L5J 4S6, Canada

Fellows, Ronald L (Ron) — Football Player
202 Creekview Dr, Wylie TX 75098, USA

Fellows, Simon — Director
United Agents, 12-26 Lexington St, London W1F 0LE, England

Felmy, Hansjorg — Actor
Berghofen, 84174 Eching, Germany

Felsenfeld, Gary — Molecular Biologist
National Institutes of Health, Physical Chemistry Section, 5 Memorial Dr, Bethesda MD 20892, USA

Felsenstein, Lee — Inventor (Portable Computer)
1479 Regent St, Redwood City CA 94061, USA

Felske, John F — Baseball Player, Manager
3804 Ridge Road, Spring Grove IL 60081, USA

Felt, Richard G (Dick) — Football Player
3993 N 750 E, Provo UT 84604, USA

Felton, Dennis — Basketball Coach
University of Georgia, Athletic Dept, Athens GA 30602, USA

Felton, John — Singer (Diamonds)
G M S, PO Box 1031, Montrose CA 91021, USA

Felton, Lindsay — Actress
Geddes Agency, 8430 Santa Monica Blvd, #201, West Hollywood CA 90069 USA

Felton, Raymond B — Basketball Player
15814 Sullivan Ridge Road, Charlotte NC 28277, USA

Felton, Tom — Actor
Untitled Entertainment, 350 S Beverly Dr, #200, Beverly Hills CA 90212 USA

Felts, Narvel — Singer, Songwriter
2005 Narvel Felts Way, Malden MO 63863, USA

Feltus, Alan E — Artist
Porziano 68, 06081 Assisi, Italy

Fencik, J Gary — Football Player
1134 W Schubert Ave, Chicago IL 60614, USA

Fenech Adami, Edward (Eddie) — President, Malta
176 Main St, Birkikara, Malta

Fenech, Edwige — Actress
Anne Alvares Correa, 34 Rue Jouffroy d'Abbans, 75017 Paris, France

Fenech, Jeff — Boxer, Trainer
Team Fenech, PO Box 66, Millers Point NSW 2000, Australia

Feng Ying — Ballerina
Central Ballet of China, 3 Taiping St, Beijing 100050, China

Feng-Hsiung Hsu — Computer Engineer
I B M Watson Research Center, PO Box 218, Yorktown Heights NY 10598 USA

Fenical, William — Organic Chemist
Scripps Institution of Oceanography, Organic Chemistry Dept, La Jolla CA 92093, USA

Fenn, Sherilyn — Actress
Anthem Entertainment, 5225 Wilshire Blvd, #615, Los Angeles CA 90036 USA

Fenner, Derrick S — Football Player
7533 33rd Ave NW, Seattle. WA 98117, USA

Fenney, Richard D (Rick) — Football Player
1901 75th St SE, Everett WA 98203, USA

Fenson, Pete — Curling Athlete
3760 Crest Court NE, Bemidji MN 56601, USA

Fenton, George — Composer
Gorfaine/Schwartz, 4111 W Alameda Ave, #509, Burbank CA 91505 USA

Fenton, James — Writer
Farrar Straus Giroux, 18 W 18th St, #700, New York NY 10011 USA

Fenton, Paul — Ice Hockey Player
16 Bridle Path Road, Brewster MA 02631, USA

Fentress, Curtis W — Architect
Fentress Bradburn Assoc, 421 Broadway, Denver CO 80203, USA

Fenty, Adrian — Mayor, Washington DC
Mayor's Office, 1 Judiciary Square, 414 4th St NW, Washington DC 20001, USA

Fenwick, Robert R (Bobby) — Baseball Player
51201 Hutchinson Road, Three Rivers MI 49093, USA
Fenyves, Dave — Ice Hockey Player
940 Parish Place, Hummelstown PA 17036, USA
Feore, Colm — Actor
Coronel Group, 1100 Glendon Ave, #1700, Los Angeles CA 90046, USA
Feranec, Peter — Conductor
Bolshoi Theater, Teatralnaya Pl 1, 103009 Moscow, Russia
Feraud, Gianfranco — Fashion Designer
25 Rue Saint Honore, 75001 Paris, France
Ferdinand, Ron — Inventor (Portable Computer)
PO Box 1997, Monterey CA 93942, USA
Ferdinand-Harris, Marie — Basketball Player
Los Angeles Sparks, 888 S Figueroa St, #2010, Los Angeles CA 90017 USA
Ference, Andrew — Ice Hockey Player
220 Commercial St, Boston MA 02109, USA
Ferentz, Kirk J — Football Coach
University of Iowa, Athletic Dept, Iowa City IA 52242, USA
Fergie — Rap Artist
13701 Ventura Blvd, #800, Sherman Oaks CA 91423, USA
Fergon, Vicki — Golfer
44 Partridge Lane, Aliso Viejo CA 92656, USA
Fergus, Keith C — Golfer
11515 Noblewood Crest Lane, Houston TX 77082, USA
Fergus, Tom — Ice Hockey Player
Blue Leaf Ltd, 2134 Speers Road, Oakville ON L6L 2X8, Canada
Ferguson Cullum, Cathy — Swimmer
515 Amanda Dr, Bear DE 19701, USA
Ferguson, Alexander C (Alex) — Soccer Player, Manager
Manchester United, Busby Way, Old Trafford, Manchester M16 0RA, England
Ferguson, Charles A — Editor
123 Walnut St, #801, New Orleans LA 70118, USA
Ferguson, Charles E (Charley) — Football Player
81 Stonecroft Lane, Buffalo NY 14226, USA
Ferguson, Charles H — Director
Representational Pictures, 75 E 4th St, #83, New York NY 10003, USA
Ferguson, Christopher J — Astronaut
16111 Park Center Way, Houston TX 77059, USA
Ferguson, Colin — Actor, Comedian
United Talent Agency, 9336 Civic Center Dr, Beverly Hills CA 90210 USA
Ferguson, Craig — Actor, Comedian
Green Mountain Werst, 7800 Beverly Blvd, Los Angeles CA 90036, USA
Ferguson, D'Brickashaw M — Football Player
New York Jets, 1 Jets Dr, Florham Park NJ 07932 USA
Ferguson, Frederick E — Vietnam War Army Hero (CMH)
5420 E Lincoln Dr, Paradise Valley AZ 85253, USA
Ferguson, James (Jim) — Water Polo Player
2404 Stonybrook Road, Opelika AL 36804, USA
Ferguson, James L — Businessman
General Foods Corp, 800 Westchester Ave, Rye Brook NY 10573, USA
Ferguson, Jay R — Actor
Wishlab, 2225A Hyperion Ave, Los Angeles CA 90027, USA
Ferguson, Jesse Tyler — Actor
I C M Partners, 10250 Constellation Blvd, #900, Los Angeles CA 90067 USA
Ferguson, Joe C, Jr — Football Player, Coach
12 Mason Lane, Bella Vista AR 72715, USA
Ferguson, Joseph V (Joe) — Baseball Player
11322 River Run Lane, Berlin MO 21811, USA
Ferguson, Keith T — Football Player
PO Box 19006, Sugar Land TX 77496, USA
Ferguson, Kent — Diver, Model
199 Tiffany Ave, #407, San Francisco CA 94110, USA
Ferguson, Lynnda — Actress
606 N Larchmont Blvd, #309, Los Angeles CA 90004, USA
Ferguson, M Paul — Drummer (Killing Joke)
Agency Group, 9348 Civic Center Dr, #200, Beverly Hills CA 90210 USA
Ferguson, Mark E, III — Navy Admiral
Chief, Naval Personnel, 2 Navy St, Washington DC 20380 USA
Ferguson, Megan — Actress
Don Buchwald/Fortitude, 6500 Wilshire Blvd, #2200, Los Angeles CA 90048 USA
Ferguson, Nick — Football Player
114 Arlington Ave SW, Atlanta GA 30310, USA
Ferguson, Robert A — Educator, Attorney
Columbia University, Jerome Green Hall, New York NY 10027, USA
Ferguson, Robert C — Football Player
15102 Oldtown Bridge Court, Sugar Land TX 77498, USA
Ferguson, Sarah — Duchess of York, England
Birchhall, Windlesham, Surrey GU20 6BN, England
Ferguson, Stacy — Actress
Paradigm Agency, 360 N Crescent Dr, North Building, Beverly Hills CA 90210 USA
Ferguson, Thomas A, Jr — Businessman
Newell Rubbermaid Inc, Newell Center, 29 E Stephenson St, Freeport IL 61032, USA
Ferguson, Tom — Rodeo Rider
General Delivery, Miami OK 74354, USA
Fergus-Thompson, Gordon — Concert Pianist
12 Audley Road, Hendon, London NW4 3EY, England
Ferilli, Sabrina — Actress
Camelia Srl, Via Giorgio Vasari 4, 00196 Rome, Italy
Ferland, E James — Businessman
Public Service Enterprise, 80 Park Plaza, PO Box 1171, Newark NJ 07101, USA
Ferland, Guy V — Director
W M E Entertainment, 9601 Wilshire Blvd, #300, Beverly Hills CA 90210 USA
Ferland, Jodelle — Actress
Play Mgmt, 807 Powell St, #220, Vancouver BC V6A 1H7, Canada
Ferlinghetti, Lawrence — Writer, Publisher
City Lights Booksellers, 261 Columbus Ave, San Francisco CA 94133, USA

Ferlito, Vanessa — Actress
Alchemy Entertainment, 7024 Melrose Ave, #420, Los Angeles CA 90038 USA

Fermin, Felix J — Baseball Player
Akron Aeros, 300 S Main St, Akron OH 44308, USA

Fernandez de Kirchner, Cristina E — President, Argentina
Casa de Gobierno, Balcarce 50, Buenos Aires 1064, Argentina

Fernandez Krupij, Stefania — Beauty Queen
Miss Universe Organization, 1370 Ave of Americas, #1600, New York NY 10019 USA

Fernandez Molinos, Begona — Handball Player
Z R K Zajecar, Dositejeva 11, 19000 Zajecar, Serbia

Fernandez, Adrian — Auto Racing Driver
Fernandez Racing, PO Box 68828, Indianapolis IN 46268, USA

Fernandez, Alejandro — Singer, Actor
Creative Artists Agency, 2000 Ave of Stars, #100, Los Angeles CA 90067 USA

Fernandez, Alexander (Alex) — Baseball Player
12323 SW 55th St, #1007, Cooper City FL 33330, USA

Fernandez, C Sidney (Sid) — Baseball Player
25 Aulike St, #218, Kailua HI 96734, USA

Fernandez, Emmanuel (Manny) — Ice Hockey Player
Boston Bruins, 100 Legends Way, #250, Boston MA 02114 USA

Fernandez, Ferdinand F — Judge
US Court of Appeals, 125 S Grand Ave, Pasadena CA 91105, USA

Fernandez, Frank — Baseball Player
37 Couglan Ave, Staten Island NY 10310, USA

Fernandez, Gigi — Tennis Player
US Lawn Tennis Assn, 1212 Ave of Americas, New York NY 10036, USA

Fernandez, Humberto P (Chico) — Baseball Player
8401 NW 40th Court, Sunrise FL 33351, USA

Fernandez, Jared W — Baseball Player
4298 S 4625 West, Salt Lake City UT 84120, USA

Fernandez, Karina — Actress
United Agents, 12-26 Lexington St, London W1F 0LE, England

Fernandez, Lisa — Softball Player
1460 Homewood Road, #95B, Seal Beach CA 90740, USA

Fernandez, Lujan — Model, Actress
Fashion Model Mgmt, 40 Ang Via Monte Rosa, 20149 Milan, Italy

Fernandez, Manuel J (Manny) — Football Player
5805 SW 120th St, Cooper City FL 33330, USA

Fernandez, Mariestela — Costume Designer
Sandra Marsh Assoc, 9150 Wilshire Blvd, #220, Beverly Hills CA 90212 USA

Fernandez, Mary Joe — Tennis Player
1121 Crandon Blvd, #D606, Key Biscayne FL 33149, USA

Fernandez, Mervyn — Football Player
2477 Briarwood Dr, San Jose CA 95125, USA

Fernandez, O Antonio (Tony) — Baseball Player
Tony Fernandez Foundation, 19232 N Gardenia Ave, Weston FL 33332, USA

Fernandez, Pedro — Singer, Songwriter
Exclusive Artists Productions, PO Box 65948, Los Angeles CA 90065, USA

Fernandez, Shiloh — Actor
Creative Artists Agency, 2000 Ave of Stars, #100, Los Angeles CA 90067 USA

Fernandez, Vicente — Singer
Hauser Entertainment, 3703 San Gabriel River Parkway, Pico Rivera CA 90660, USA

Ferneyhough, Brian J P — Composer
848 Allardice Way, Stanford CA 94305, USA

Ferns, Alex — Actor
Ken McReddie Assoc, 11 Connaught Place, London W2 2ET, England

Fernsten, Eric R — Basketball Player
5634 Linden St, Dublin CA 94568, USA

Ferragamo, Vince A — Football Player
Touchdown Real Estate, 6200 E Canyon Rim Road, #204, Anaheim CA 92807, USA

Ferrara, Abel — Director
I C M Partners, 10250 Constellation Blvd, #900, Los Angeles CA 90067 USA

Ferrara, Adam — Actor, Comedian
Gersh Agency, 9465 Wilshire Blvd, #600, Beverly Hills CA 90212 USA

Ferrara, Alfred J (Al) — Baseball Player
4901 Whitsett Ave, #207, Valley Village CA 91607, USA

Ferrara, Jerry — Actor
W M E Entertainment, 9601 Wilshire Blvd, #300, Beverly Hills CA 90210 USA

Ferrara, Stephane — Actress
Artmedia, 20 Ave Rapp, 75007 Paris, France

Ferrare, Cristina — Model, Entertainer
10727 Wilshire Blvd, #1602, Los Angeles CA 90024, USA

Ferrarese, Donald H (Don) — Baseball Player
15290 Myalon Road, Apple Valley CA 92307, USA

Ferrari, Albert R (Al) — Basketball Player
5911 Bristlecone Court, Saint Louis MO 63129, USA

Ferrari, Gillian — Ice Hockey Player
Team Canada, 2424 University Dr NW, Calgary AB T2N 3Y9, Canada

Ferrari, Michael R, Jr — Educator
570 Greenway Dr, Lake Forest IL 60045, USA

Ferrari, Tina — Dancer, Wrestler
2901 S Las Vegas Blvd, Las Vegas NV 89109, USA

Ferraro, Dave — Bowler
672 E Chester St, Kingston NY 12401, USA

Ferraro, Michael D (Mike) — Baseball Player, Manager
5201 Rim View Lane, Las Vegas NV 89130, USA

Ferraro, Raymond (Ray) — Ice Hockey Player, Sportscaster
Team 1040 Sports Radio, 30-380 W 2nd Ave, Vancouver BC V5Y 1C8, Canada

Ferrarone, Jessica — Actress
Evolution Entertainment, 901 N Highland Ave, Los Angeles CA 90038 USA

Ferratti, Rebecca M — Model, Actress
10061 Riverside Dr, #721, Toluca Lake CA 91602, USA

Ferrazzi, Pierpaolo — Canoeing Athlete
EuroGrafica, Via del Progresso, 36035 Marano Vicenza, Italy

Ferree, Jim — Golfer
12 Kings Tree Road, Hilton Head Island SC 29928, USA

Ferreira, Anthony R (Tony) — Baseball Player
3006 Merrill Ave, Clearwater FL 33759, USA
Ferreira, Gabriel Vasconcellos — Soccer Player
Confederacion de Futebol, Rua Victor Civita 66, #1, Rio de Janeiro 22775 044, Brazil
Ferreira, Wayne — Tennis Player
International Mgmt Group, 1 Erieview Plaza, 1360 E 9th St, Cleveland OH 44114 USA
Ferrell Edmonson, Barbara A — Track Athlete
University of Nevada, Athletic Dept, Las Vegas NV 89154, USA
Ferrell, Conchata — Actress
Gage Group, 14724 Ventura Blvd, #505, Sherman Oaks CA 91403 USA
Ferrell, Earl T — Football Player
107 E Forest Trail, South Boston VA 24592, USA
Ferrell, Perry — Singer (Porno for Pyros)
DeMann Entertainment, 1017 N La Cienega Blvd, #103, West Hollywood CA 90069, USA
Ferrell, Rachelle — Singer
Vida Music Group, 19800 Cornerstone Square, #415, Ashburn VA 20147, USA
Ferrell, Robert S (Bobby) — Football Player
1090 N Shooting Star Dr, Beaumont CA 92223, USA
Ferrell, Tyra — Actress
Gersh Agency, 9465 Wilshire Blvd, #600, Beverly Hills CA 90212 USA
Ferrell, Will — Actor, Comedian
Mosiac Media Group, 9200 W Sunset Blvd, #1000, Los Angeles CA 90069 USA
Ferreol, Andrea — Actress
Artmedia, 20 Ave Rapp, 75007 Paris, France
Ferrer Ern, David — Tennis Player
Association of Tennis Professionals, 200 Tournament Road, Ponte Vedra Beach FL 32082 USA
Ferrer, Danay — Singer (Innosense)
R C A Records, 8750 Wilshire Blvd, Beverly Hills CA 90211 USA
Ferrer, Miguel — Actor
Danis Panaro Nist, 9201 W Olympic Blvd, Beverly Hills CA 90212, USA
Ferrera, America — Actress
I C M Partners, 10250 Constellation Blvd, #900, Los Angeles CA 90067 USA
Ferreras, Francisco (Pipin) — Free Diver
7548 W Treasure Dr, North Bay Village FL 33141, USA
Ferrero, Juan Carlos — Tennis Player
Echegaray 2, 468 70 Ontynent, Spain
Ferretti, Alberta — Fashion Designer
Via delle Querce 51, 47842 San Giovanni in Marignano, Italy
Ferretti, Dante — Art Director
Sandra Marsh & Associates, 9150 Wilshire Blvd, #220, Beverly Hills CA 90212, USA
Ferrick, Melissa — Singer, Songwriter
Agency Group Ltd, 142 W 57th St, #600, New York NY 10019 USA
Ferrigno, Lou — Actor, Body Builder
Lou Ferrigno Enterprises, PO Box 1671, Santa Monica CA 90406, USA
Ferrigno, Robert — Writer
Charles Scribner's Sons, 866 3rd Ave, New York NY 10022 USA
Ferrin, Arnold (Arnie) — Basketball Player
2104 S Barona Road, Palm Springs CA 92264, USA
Ferrin, Jennifer — Actress
Gersh Agency, 9465 Wilshire Blvd, #600, Beverly Hills CA 90212 USA
Ferris, Charles D — Government Official
Mintz Levin Ferris Assoc, 701 Pennsylvania Ave NW, Washington DC 20004, USA
Ferris, John — Swimmer
1961 Klamath River Dr, Rancho Cordova CA 95670, USA
Ferris, Michael (Mike) — Writer, Producer, Actor
United Talent Agency, 9336 Civic Center Dr, Beverly Hills CA 90210 USA
Ferriss, David M (Boo) — Baseball Player
510 Robinson Dr, Cleveland MS 38732, USA
Ferro, Cindy — Golfer
1901 Brookside Dr, Scotch Plains NJ 07076, USA
Ferron — Singer, Synthesizer Player, Songwriter
Cherrywood Station Records, 20112 Ridge Road SW, Vashon WA 98070, USA
Ferry, April — Costume Designer
United Talent Agency, 9336 Civic Center Dr, Beverly Hills CA 90210 USA
Ferry, Bjorn — Biathlete
Hojdvagen 24G, 923 31 Storuman, Sweden
Ferry, Bryan — Singer, Songwriter
Agency Group Ltd, 142 W 57th St, #600, New York NY 10019 USA
Ferry, Daniel J W (Danny) — Basketball Player, Executive
604 Castano Ave, San Antonio TX 78209, USA
Ferry, David R — Writer
Wellesley College, English Dept, Wellesley MA 02181, USA
Ferry, Robert D (Bob) — Basketball Player
2129 Beach Haven Road, Annapolis MD 21409, USA
Fersht, Alan R — Organic Chemist
2 Barrow Close, Cambridge CB2 2AT, England
Fert, Albert — Nobel Physics Laureate
C N R S/Thales, Domaine de Corbeville, 91404 Orsay Cedex, France
Fery, John B — Businessman
PO Box 15407, Boise ID 83715, USA
Ferzetti, Gabriele — Actor
NCE Italiana, Viale Bruno Buozzi 53, 00197 Rome, Italy
Fesler, James W — Political Scientist
Yale University, New Haven CT 06520 USA
Fessel, Craig — Cartoonist (Sandman)
40 Camino Alto, #2306, Mill Valley CA 94941, USA
Fessenden, Larry — Director, Writer
Glass Eye Pix, 18 Bridge St, #2G, Brooklyn NY 11201, USA
Fest, Howard A — Football Player
133 Forest Circle, Bandera TX 78003, USA
Feste, Shana — Writer, Director
Creative Artists Agency, 2000 Ave of Stars, #100, Los Angeles CA 90067 USA
Festinger, Leon — Psychologist
37 W 12th St, New York NY 10011, USA
Fetisov, Vyacheslav A (Slava) — Ice Hockey Player
196 Rensselaer Road, Essex Falls NJ 07021, USA

Fetter, Laurie — Model
Playboy Promotions, 2706 Media Center Dr, Los Angeles CA 90065 USA
Fetterman, John H (Jack), Jr — Navy Admiral
Naval Aviation Museum Foundation, 1750 Radford Blvd, Pensacola FL 32508, USA
Fetters, Michael L (Mike) — Baseball Player
2411 E Cedar Place, Chandler AZ 85249, USA
Fettig, Jeff M — Businessman
Whirlpool Corp, 2000 N State St, RR 63, Benton Harbor MI 49022, USA
Fetting, Katie — Actress, Writer
United Talent Agency, 9336 Civic Center Dr, Beverly Hills CA 90210 USA
Fetting, Rainer — Artist, Sculptor
Andino Fine Arts, 2450 Virginia Ave NW, Washington DC 20037, USA
Fettman, Martin J — Astronaut, Veterinarian
1572 N Saguaro Cliffs Court, Tucson AZ 85745, USA
Feuer, Debra — Actress
United Talent Agency, 9336 Civic Center Dr, Beverly Hills CA 90210 USA
Feuerman, Carole A — Sculptor
200 Mercer St, #1F, New York NY 10012, USA
Feuerstein, Mark — Actor
United Talent Agency, 9336 Civic Center Dr, Beverly Hills CA 90210 USA
Feuerwerker, Albert — Historian
827 Asa Gray Dr, #356, Ann Arbor MI 48105, USA
Feuerzeig, Jeff — Director, Writer
W M E Entertainment, 9601 Wilshire Blvd, #300, Beverly Hills CA 90210 USA
Feustel, Andrew J (Drew) — Astronaut
4003 Elm Crest Trail, Houston TX 77059, USA
Feuti, Norm — Cartoonist (Gil)
King Features Syndicate, 300 W 57th St, #1500, New York NY 10019 USA
Fewx, Gene — Sculptor
666 15th St NE, Salem OR 97301, USA
Fexler, Forrest O — Golfer
6270 Old Water Oak Road, Tallahassee FL 32312, USA
Fey — Singer
R A C, Paseo Palmas 1005, Chapultapec Lomas, Mexico City DF 11000, Mexico
Fey, Michael — Cartoonist (Committed)
United Feature Syndicate, PO Box 5610, Cincinnati OH 45201 USA
Fey, Tina — Actress, Comedienne, Producer
3 Arts Entertainment, 9460 Wilshire Blvd, #700, Beverly Hills CA 90212 USA
Fezler, Forrest — Golfer
6270 Old Water Oak Road, Tallahassee FL 32312, USA
Fforde, Jasper — Writer
Viking Press, 375 Hudson St, New York NY 10014, USA
Fiala, John C — Football Player
12113 268th Dr NE, Duvall WA 98019, USA
Fiala, Neil S — Baseball Player
4709 Woody Terrace Court, Saint Louis MO 63129, USA
Fialkowska, Janina — Concert Pianist
Ingpen & Williams, 131 Putney Bridge Road, London SW15 2PA, England
Fiasco, Lupe — Rap Artist, Songwriter
1st & 15th Records, 437 Brookwood Dr, Olympia Fields IL 60461, USA
Ficarra, Glenn — Writer, Director
W M E Entertainment, 9601 Wilshire Blvd, #300, Beverly Hills CA 90210 USA
Ficatier, Carol — Model, Actress
Playboy Promotions, 2706 Media Center Dr, Los Angeles CA 90065 USA
Ficca, Billy — Drummer (Television, Waitresses)
Primary Talent International, 10-11 Jockey's Fields, London WC1R 4BN, England
Ficca, Daniel R (Dan) — Football Player
151 Kansas Lane, Kulpmont PA 17834, USA
Fichaud, Eric — Ice Hockey Player
191 Rue Charron, Lemoyne QC J4R 2K6, Canada
Fichtel-Mauritz, Anja — Fencer
Stauffering 104, 97941 Taunerbischofsheim, Germany
Fichter, Michael (Mike) — Baseball Umpire
2942 192nd Place, Lansing IL 60438, USA
Fichter, Rick T — Cinematographer
3630 Cabrillo St, San Francisco CA 94121, USA
Fichtner, Hans J — Space Scientist
612 Cleermont Dr SE, Huntsville AL 35801, USA
Fichtner, Ross W — Football Player
46833 Danbridge St, Plymouth MI 48170, USA
Fichtner, William (Bill) — Actor
Paradigm Agency, 360 N Crescent Dr, North Building, Beverly Hills CA 90210 USA
Fick, Robert C — Baseball Player
164 Brodia Way, Walnut Creek CA 94598, USA
Fickman, Andy — Director
W M E Entertainment, 9601 Wilshire Blvd, #300, Beverly Hills CA 90210 USA
Fico, Robert — Prime Minister, Slovakia
Prime Minister's Office, Nam Slobody, 81370 Bratislava 1, Slovakia
Fiddler, Vernon (Vern) — Ice Hockey Player
3659 Hickory Grove Lane, Frisco TX 75033, USA
Fiedler, Jay B — Football Player
25 Russell Road, Garden City NY 11530, USA
Fieger, Geoffrey — Attorney
Fieger Fieger Schwartz, 19390 W Ten Mile Road, Southfield MI 48075, USA
Field, Arabella — Actress
S M S Talent, 8383 Wilshire Blvd, #230, Beverly Hills CA 90211 USA
Field, Ayda — Actress, Comedienne
Paradigm Agency, 360 N Crescent Dr, North Building, Beverly Hills CA 90210 USA
Field, Chelsea — Actress
J D Schwartz Assoc, 6767 Forest Lawn Dr, #211, Los Angeles CA 90068, USA
Field, George B — Theoretical Astrophysicist
Harvard University Observatory, 60 Garden St, Cambridge MA 02138, USA
Field, Helen — Opera Singer
Athole Still, Foresters Hall, 25-27 Weston St, London SE19 3RV, England
Field, John J (J J) — Actor
Ken McReddie Assoc, 11 Connaught Place, London W2 2ET, England

Field, Nathan P (Nate)
1040 W Ridge Road, Littleton CO 80120, USA — Baseball Player
Field, Sally
Hofflund/Polone, 9465 Wilshire Blvd, #420, Beverly Hills CA 90212 USA — Actress
Field, Shirley Ann
Roger Carey Assoc, Old House, Shepperton Film Studios, Shepperton, Middlesex TW17 0QD, England — Actress
Field, Todd
Smuggler, 38 W 21st St, #1200, New York NY 10010, USA — Actor, Director, Writer
Fielder, Cecil G
6907 Smokey Brook Lane, Katy TX 77494, USA — Baseball Player
Fielder, Harry
Guild House, Upper Saint Martins, London WC2H 9EG, England — Actor
Fielder, Prince S
Detroit Tigers, Comerica Park, 2100 Woodward Ave, Detroit MI 48201 USA — Baseball Player
Fielding, Fred F
Wiley Rein Fielding, 1776 K St NW, #300, Washington DC 20006, USA — Attorney, Government Official
Fielding, Helen
Creative Artists Agency, 2000 Ave of Stars, #100, Los Angeles CA 90067 USA — Writer
Fielding, Joy
Atria Books, 1230 Ave of Americas, New York NY 10020, USA — Writer
Fields, Alexis
Rookery, 8200 Wilshire Blvd, #100, Beverly Hills CA 90212, USA — Actress
Fields, Edgar E
435 Musket Entry, Roswell GA 30076, USA — Football Player
Fields, Harold T, Jr
126 Deer Run Strut, Enterprise AL 36330, USA — Army General
Fields, Johnny
Blind Ambition Mgmt, 6 Courthouse Way, Jonesboro GA 30236, USA — Singer (Blind Boys of Alabama)
Fields, Joseph C (Joe), Jr
Widener University, Alumni Association, 1 University Place, Chester PA 19013, USA — Football Player
Fields, Joshua D (Josh)
4819 61st Ave Dr W, Bradenton FL 34210, USA — Baseball Player
Fields, Kenny
1050 E Ramon Road, #81, Palm Springs CA 92264, USA — Basketball Player
Fields, Kim
Rookery, 8200 Wilshire Blvd, #100, Beverly Hills CA 90212, USA — Actress
Fields, Mark L
887 W Palo Brea Dr, Litchfield Park AZ 85340, USA — Football Player
Fields, Stanley
University of Washington Medical School, Microbiology Dept, Seattle WA 98195, USA — MIcrobiologist
Fiennes, Joseph
Ken McReddie Assoc, 11 Connaught Place, London W2 2ET, England — Actor
Fiennes, Ralph N
Dalzell & Beresford, 26 Astwood Mews, London SW7 4DE, England — Actor
Fiennes, Ranulph T-W
Greenlands, Exford, Minehead, West Sussex TA24 7NU, England — Transglobal Explorer
Fierek, Wolfgang
Scenario Agentur, S, 80799 Munich, Germany — Singer, Actor
Fierstein, Harvey F
10106 Empyrean Way, #101, Los Angeles CA 90067, USA — Actor, Singer, Writer
Fieser, Louis
58 Medford St, Arlington MA 02474, USA — Inventor (Napalm)
Fifty Cent
Shady Records, 151 Lafayette St, #6, New York NY 10013, USA — Rap Artist, Actor
Figaro, Cedric N
205 Staten St, Lafayette LA 70501, USA — Football Player
Figga, Mike
16434 Turnbury Oak Dr, Odessa FL 33556, USA — Baseball Player
Figg-Currier, Cindy
109 Blue Jay Dr, Lakeway TX 78734, USA — Golfer
Figgins, D DeChone (Chone)
16 San Sovino, Newport Coast CA 92657, USA — Baseball Player
Figgis, Michael (Mike)
Red Mullet, Waterside, 44-48 Wharf Road, #22, London N1 7UX, England — Director
Figo, Luis
F C Real Madrid, Avda Concha Espana 1, 28036 Madrid, Spain — Soccer Player
Figueroa, Eduardo (Ed)
Calle 41, #AN15, Santa Juanita PR 00619, USA — Baseball Player
Figueroa, Nelson
1950 E Woodsman Place, Chandler AZ 85286, USA — Baseball Player
Figures, Deon J
1520 S Visalia Ave, Compton CA 90220, USA — Football Player
Fike, Dan C, Jr
23479 Wingedfoot Dr, Westlake OH 44145, USA — Football Player
Fikrig, Erol
Yale University Medical Center, Infectious Disease Dept, New Haven CT 06510, USA — Immunologist
Filali, Yasmina
Agency GmbH, Under Krahnenbeumer 9, 50688 Cologne, Germany — Actress
Filat, Vladimir
Prime Minister's Office, Piata Marii Adunari Nacional, 227033 Chishinev, Moldova — Prime Minister, Moldova
Filer, Thomas C (Tom)
425 Fox Hollow Dr, Feasterville Terrace PA 19053, USA — Baseball Player
Filicia, Thom
Collective, 8383 Wilshire Blvd, #1050, Beverly Hills CA 90211 USA — Actor, Interior Designer
Filigno, Jonelle
Canadian Soccer, Place Soccer Canada, 237 Metcalfe St, Ottawa ON K2P 1R2, Canada — Soccer Player
Filion, Herve
18 Evans Ave, Albertson NY 11507, USA — Harness Racing Driver
Filipacchi, Daniel
Hachette Filipacchi, 149-151 Rue Anatole-France, 92534 Levallois, France — Publisher
Filipchenko, Anatoli N
Cosmonaut Training Center, Star City, 141160 Zvezdny Gorodok, Moscow Oblast, Russia — Cosmonaut; Air Force General
Filippini, Andre
Olympic Committee, Foro Italico, Largo Lauro de Bosis 15, 00135 Rome, Italy — Bobsled Athlete
Fillion, Nathan
United Talent Agency, 9336 Civic Center Dr, Beverly Hills CA 90210 USA — Actor

Fillmore, Charles J — Linguist
University of California, Linguistics Dept, Berkeley CA 94720, USA
Fillmore, Gregory P (Greg) — Basketball Player
12449 Blueberry Woods Circle E, #E, Jacksonville FL 32258, USA
Fillon, Francois-Charles A — Prime Minister, France
Premier's Office, Hotel Matignon, 57 Rue de Varenne, 75700 Paris, France
Filo, David — Businessman, Computer Scientist
Yahoo!, 701 1st Ave, Sunnyvale CA 94089, USA
Filson, W Peter (Pete) — Baseball Player
1034 10th Ave, Folsom PA 19033, USA
Fimbres, Andrea — Singer (Danity Kane)
Bad Boy Entertainment, 1440 Broadway, #16, New York NY 10018 USA
Fimmel, Travis — Model, Actor
Paradigm Agency, 360 N Crescent Dr, North Building, Beverly Hills CA 90210 USA
Fimple, John J (Jack) — Baseball Player
8012 Cliffrose St, Windsor CA 95492, USA
Fina, John J — Football Player
5180 E Fort Lowell Road, Tucson AZ 85712, USA
Finch, Jennie — Softball Player, Model
3265 W Bird Haven Place, Tucson AZ 85745, USA
Finch, Joel D — Baseball Player
68571 Oak Spring Road, Edwardsburg MI 49112, USA
Finch, Jon N — Actor
London Mgmt, 2-4 Noel St, London W1V 3RB, England
Finch, Linda — Aviatrix
World Flight, 211 Switch Oak, Shavano Park TX 78230, USA
Finchem, Timothy W — Golf Executive
Professional Golfer's Assn, Sawgrass, Ponte Vedra Beach FL 32082, USA
Finck, George C — Vietnam War Air Force Hero
143 Beaver Lane, Benton LA 71006, USA
Fincke, E Michael (Mike) — Astronaut
15819 El Dorado Oaks Dr, Houston TX 77059, USA
Finckel, David — Cellist (Emerson String Quartet)
I M G Artists, Burlington Lane, Chiswick, London W4 2TH, England
Finder, Joseph — Writer
United Talent Agency, 9336 Civic Center Dr, Beverly Hills CA 90210 USA
Findlay, Conn F — Rowing Athlete, Yachtsman
1920 Oak Knoll, Belmont CA 94002, USA
Findlay, Jessica Brown — Actress
Troika, 74 Clerkenwell Road, #300, London EC1M 5QA, England
Findley, Vern M (Rusty), II — Air Force General
Vice Commander, Air Mobility Command, Scott Air Force Base IL 62225 USA
Fine, Jud — Sculptor
1366 Appleton Way, Venice CA 90291, USA
Fine, Russell Lee — Cinematographer
Creative Artists Agency, 2000 Ave of Stars, #100, Los Angeles CA 90067 USA
Finer, Jeremy (Jem) — Banjoist (Pogues)
Agency Group Ltd, 361-373 City Road, London EC1V 2QA, England
Finer, Lawrence — Sociologist
Guttmacher Institute, 120 Wall St, #2100, New York NY 10005, USA
Fingaz, Sticky — Rap Artist, Actor
Major Independents, 22425 Ventura Blvd, #106, Woodland Hills CA 91364, USA
Fingers, Roland G (Rollie) — Baseball Player
PO Box 230729, Las Vegas NV 89105, USA
Fink, Kenneth — Director, Producer, Writer
United Talent Agency, 9336 Civic Center Dr, Beverly Hills CA 90210 USA
Fink, Michael — Visual Effects Editor
B U F, 7720 W Sunset Blvd, Los Angeles CA 90046, USA
Fink, Natascha — Golfer
Golfclub Murhof, Adriach 54, 8130 Irohnleiten, Austria
Finkel, David — Journalist
Washington Post, Editorial Dept, 1150 15th St NW, Washington DC 20071 USA
Finkel, Fyvush — Actor
C E S D, 10635 Santa Monica Blvd, #130, Los Angeles CA 90025 USA
Finkel, Henry J (Hank) — Basketball Player
2 Pocahontas Way, Lynnfield MA 01940, USA
Finkel, Sheldon (Shelly) — Boxing Promoter, Manager
Shelly Finkel Mgmt, 110 Greene St, #403, New York NY 10012, USA
Finlay, Frank — Actor
Ken McReddie Assoc, 11 Connaught Place, London W2 2ET, England
Finley, Charles E (Chuck) — Baseball Player
500 Mccormick Road, West Monroe LA 71291, USA
Finley, David — Astronaut, Astronomer
1642 Milvia St, #3S, Berkeley CA 94709, USA
Finley, Gerard H — Opera Singer
I M G Artists, Hogarth Business Park, Chiswick, London W4 2TH, England
Finley, Greg — Actor
Paul Kohner, 9300 Wilshire Blvd, #555, Beverly Hills CA 90212 USA
Finley, Karen — Conceptual Artist
Creative Time, 59 E 4th St, #6E, New York NY 10003, USA
Finley, Michael H — Basketball Player
11 Highgate Dr, San Antonio TX 78257, USA
Finley, Steven A (Steve) — Baseball Player
PO Box 2101, Rancho Santa Fe CA 92067, USA
Finn, Charlie — Actor
Brillstein Entertainment Partners, 9150 Wilshire Blvd, #350, Beverly Hills CA 90212 USA
Finn, James (Jim) — Football Player
12-14 Western Dr, Fair Lawn NJ 07410, USA
Finn, John — Actor
Domain Talent, 9229 W Sunset Blvd, #710, West Hollywood CA 90069 USA
Finn, Neil — Singer (Split Enz, Crowded House)
Ignition Mgmt, 54 Linhope St, London NW1 7JQ, England
Finn, Patrick — Actor
Brillstein Entertainment Partners, 9150 Wilshire Blvd, #350, Beverly Hills CA 90212 USA
Finn, Tim — Singer (Split Enz, Crowded House)
Grant Thomas Mgmt, 98 Surrey St, Darlinghurst NSW 2010, Australia

Finn, Veronica
R C A Records, 8750 Wilshire Blvd, Beverly Hills CA 90211 USA — Singer (Innosense)

Finn, William
New York University, Music Dept, New York NY 10012, USA — Composer, Lyricist

Finn-Burrell, Michelle
1801 Ocean Park Blvd, #112, Santa Monica CA 90405, USA — Track Athlete

Finnegan, Cortland T
9254 Wardley Park Lane, Brentwood TN 37027, USA — Football Player

Finneran, Brian
1905 Sugarloaf Club Dr, Duluth GA 30097, USA — Football Player

Finneran, John G
2904 N Leisure World Blvd, #404, Silver Spring MD 20906, USA — Navy Admiral

Finneran, Katie
Innovative Artists, 1505 10th St, Santa Monica CA 90401 USA — Actress

Finneran, Siobhan
Shane Collins Assoc, 11-15 Betterton St, Covent Garden, London WC2H 9BP, England — Actress

Finnerty, Dan
Gersh Agency, 9465 Wilshire Blvd, #600, Beverly Hills CA 90212 USA — Actor, Comedian, Musician

Finney, Albert
Simpkins Partnership, 45/51 Whitfield St, London W1P 4HB, England — Actor

Finney, Allison
78160 Desert Mountain Circle, Bermuda Dunes CA 92203, USA — Golfer

Finney, Tom
4 Newgate, Fulwood, Preston PR2 8LR, England — Soccer Player, Executive

Finnie, Linda A
16 Golf Course, Girvan, Ayrshire KA26 9HW, England — Concert Singer

Finnie, Roger L
937 NW 58th St, Miami FL 33127, USA — Football Player

Finnigan, Jennifer
I C M Partners, 10250 Constellation Blvd, #900, Los Angeles CA 90067 USA — Actress

Finnvold, A Gar
1204 NE 4th Ave, Boca Raton FL 33432, USA — Baseball Player

Finsterwald, Dow
2772 Fawn Grove Court, Colorado Springs CO 80906, USA — Golfer

Fiona, Melanie
Creative Artists Agency, 2000 Ave of Stars, #100, Los Angeles CA 90067 USA — Singer

Fionda, Andrew
Pearce Fionda, Loft, 27 Horsell Road, Highbury, London N5 1XL, England — Fashion Designer

Fiordaliso, Marina
Mithos Agency, Via Koristka 8, 20154 Milan, Italy — Singer

Fiore, David A (Dave)
868 Southampton Dr, Palo Alto CA 94303, USA — Football Player

Fiore, Kathryn
TalentWorks, 3500 W Olive Ave, #1400, Burbank CA 91505 USA — Actress

Fiore, Mark
265 Frisco St, San Francisco CA 94133, USA — Editorial Cartoonist

Fiore, Michael G J (Mike)
17 Silver St, Malverne NY 11565, USA — Baseball Player

Fiore, William J (Bill)
Access Talent Mgmt, 171 Madison Ave, #910, New York NY 10016, USA — Actor

Fiorentini, Jeffrey P (Jeff)
4200 Chardonnay Dr, Rockledge FL 32955, USA — Baseball Player

Fiori, Ed
50 Burwick St, Sugar Land TX 77479, USA — Golfer

Fiorillo, Elisabetta
I U M A Mgmt, Via E Filiberto 125, 00185 Rome, Italy — Opera Singer

Fire, Andrew Z
Stanford University Medical School, Pathology Dept, 3000 Pasteur Dr, Stanford CA 94305, USA — Nobel Medicine Laureate

Firek, Marc
United Talent Agency, 9336 Civic Center Dr, Beverly Hills CA 90210 USA — Producer, Writer

Fireman, Paul B
Reebok International, 1895 J W Foster Blvd, Canton MA 02021, USA — Businessman

Fireovid, Stephen J (Steve)
1408 Woodstream Dr, Bryan OH 43506, USA — Baseball Player

Fires, Earlie S
2603 Arlingdale Dr, Palatine IL 60067, USA — Thoroughbred Racing Jockey

Firestone, Andrew
Paradigm Agency, 360 N Crescent Dr, North Building, Beverly Hills CA 90210 USA — Actor

Firestone, Roy
Seizen/Wallach Productions, 257 S Rodeo Dr, Beverly Hills CA 90212, USA — Sportscaster, Actor

Firova, Daniel M (Dan)
5115 Coos Bay, Laredo TX 78041, USA — Baseball Player

First, Neal L
9437 W Garnette Dr, Sun City AZ 85373, USA — Geneticist

Firth, Colin
Independent Talent Group, Oxford House, 76 Oxford St, London W1D 1BS, England — Actor

Firth, Peter
Lou Coulson Assoc, 37 Berwick St, London W1V 8RS, England — Actor

Fisch, Asher
Opus 3 Artists, 470 Park Ave S, #900N, New York NY 10016 USA — Conductor

Fisch, Jonas
Joel Stevens Entertainment, 750 Fairmont Ave, #100, Glendale CA 91203, USA — Actor, Comedian

Fischbacher, Andrea
5531 Eben im Pongau, Salzburg, Austria — Alpine Skier

Fischer Schmidt, Birgit
Kuckuckswald 11, 14532 Kleinmachnow, Germany — Canoeing Athlete

Fischer, Adam
Askonas Holt, Lincoln House, 300 High Holborn, London WC1V 7JH, England — Conductor

Fischer, Edmond H
5540 N Windermere Road, Seattle WA 98105, USA — Nobel Medicine Laureate

Fischer, Fanny
Kanu Club Potsdam, Am Luftschiffhafen 2, 14471 Potsdam, Germany — Canoeing Athlete

Fischer, Gotthiff
Buro Gotthilf Fischer, Postfach 45, 71715 Berlin, Germany — Composer

Fischer, Heinz
Prasidentschaftskanzlei, Hofburg, Alderstiege, 1010 Vienna, Austria — President, Austria

Fischer, Henry W (Hank)
10367 Big Canoe, Big Canoe GA 30143, USA — Baseball Player

Fischer, Ivan
1 Andrassy Utca 27, 1061 Budapest, Hungary — Conductor

Fischer, Jeffrey T (Jeff)
215 Worth Court N, West Palm Beach FL 33405, USA — Baseball Player

Fischer, Jenna
Odenkirk Provissiero Entertainment, 650 N Bronson Ave, #B145, Los Angeles CA 90004 USA — Actress

Fischer, Joschka
Princeton University, Liechtenstein Institute, Princeton NJ 08544, USA — Government Official, Germany

Fischer, Julia
Kunstler Sekretariat am Gasteig, Rosenheimer Str 52, 81669 Munich, Germany — Concert Violinist

Fischer, Lisa
Alive Enterprises, 3264 S Kihei Road, Kihei HI 96753, USA — Singer

Fischer, Patrick (Pat)
PO Box 4289, Leesburg VA 20177, USA — Football Player

Fischer, Stanley
Bank of Israel, PO Box 780, 91007 Jerusalem, Israel — Economist

Fischer, Sven (Fritz)
Schillerhoehe 7, 98574 Schmalkalden, Germany — Biathlete

Fischer, Takayo
Avo Talent, 8500 Melrose Ave, #212, West Hollywood CA 90069, USA — Actress

Fischer, Tanya
Abrams Artists, 9200 W Sunset Blvd, #1125, West Hollywood CA 90069 USA — Actress

Fischer, Todd
7347 Linwood Court, Pleasanton CA 94588, USA — Golfer

Fischer, Todd R
12734 Newtown Road, Unionville TN 37180, USA — Baseball Player

Fischer, William A (Moose)
23191 Shady Oak Lane, Estero FL 33928, USA — Football Player

Fischer, William C (Bill)
139 Upland Dr, Council Bluffs IA 51503, USA — Baseball Player

Fischetti, Brad
Evolution Talent Agency, 1501 Broadway, #1301, New York NY 10036 USA — Singer, Rap Artist

Fischetti, Vincent A
Rockefeller University Medical Center, 1230 York Ave, New York NY 10065 USA — Microbiologist

Fischl, Eric
Mary Boone Gallery, 745 5th Ave, #405, New York NY 10151, USA — Artist

Fischlin, Michael T (Mike)
1010 Curtright Place, Greensboro GA 30642, USA — Baseball Player

Fish, Ginger
Interscope Records, 2220 Colorado Ave, Santa Monica CA 90404 USA — Drummer (Marilyn Manson)

Fish, Howard M
15797 Dockside Court, Tyler TX 75703, USA — Air Force General

Fish, Mardy
S F X Sports, 846 Lincoln Road, #500, Miami Beach Fl 33139 USA — Tennis Player

Fish, Matt
4138 E Waterman Court, Gilbert AZ 85297, USA — Basketball Player

Fishburne, Laurence
Paradigm Agency, 360 N Crescent Dr, North Building, Beverly Hills CA 90210 USA — Actor

Fishburne, Rodes
Delacorte Press, 1540 Broadway, New York NY 10036 USA — Writer

Fishel, Danielle
Innovative Artists, 1505 10th St, Santa Monica CA 90401 USA — Actress

Fisher Hartman, Sarah
Sarah Fisher Racing, 4701 Rockville Road, #A, Indianapolis IN 46222, USA — Auto Racing Driver

Fisher, Allison
Bailey's Sports Bar, 8500 Pineville-Mathew Road, Charlotte NC 28226, USA — Billiards Player

Fisher, Anna L
1912 Elmen St, Houston TX 77019, USA — Astronaut

Fisher, Bernard
5636 Aylesboro Ave, Pittsburgh PA 15217, USA — Surgeon

Fisher, Bernard F
4200 W King Road, Kuna ID 83634, USA — Vietnam War Air Force Hero (CMH)

Fisher, Brian K
3660 S Uravan St, Aurora CO 80013, USA — Baseball Player

Fisher, Carrie
1700 Coldwater Canyon Road, Beverly Hills CA 90210, USA — Actress, Writer

Fisher, Debra Mae
2150 NW Hill St, #2, Bend OR 97701, USA — Artist

Fisher, Derek L
25515 Prado de Azul, Calabasas CA 91302, USA — Basketball Player

Fisher, Eddie G
408 Cardinal Circle S, Altus OK 73521, USA — Baseball Player

Fisher, Edwin L (Ed)
4734 E Redfield Road, Phoenix AZ 85032, USA — Football Player

Fisher, Elder A (Bud)
7551 Brackenwood Circle N, Indianapolis IN 46260, USA — Bowling Executive

Fisher, Evan
G E M S, PO Box 1031, Montrose CA 91021, USA — Singer (Diamonds)

Fisher, Frances
Greene Assoc, 1901 Ave of Stars, #130, Los Angeles CA 90067 USA — Actress

Fisher, Frederick
Frederick Fisher Partners, 12248 Santa Monica Blvd, Los Angeles CA 90025, USA — Interior Designer, Architect

Fisher, Isla
Mosiac Media Group, 9200 W Sunset Blvd, #1000, Los Angeles CA 90069 USA — Actress

Fisher, Jeffrey M (Jeff)
Saint Louis Rams, 901 N Broadway, Saint Louis MO 63101 USA — Football Player, Coach

Fisher, Jeremy
Agency Group Ltd, 142 W 57th St, #600, New York NY 10019 USA — Singer, Songwriter

Fisher, Joel
PO Box 65, Palisades NY 10964, USA — Sculptor

Fisher, Joely
John Carrabino Mgmt, 5900 Wilshire Blvd, #406, Los Angeles CA 90036 USA — Actress

Fisher, John H (Jack)
4407 Nicholas St, Easton PA 18045, USA — Baseball Player

Fisher, John Norwood — Bassist (Fishbone)
Silverback Mgmt, 9469 Jefferson Blvd, #101, Culver City CA 90232, USA
Fisher, Kimberly — Model, Actress
PO Box 69330, #436, West Hollywood CA 90069, USA
Fisher, Mary — AIDS Activist
Charles Scribner's Sons, 866 3rd Ave, New York NY 10022 USA
Fisher, Matthew — Organist (Procol Harum), Songwriter
39 Croham Road, South Croydon CR2 7HD, England
Fisher, Maurice J (Maury) — Baseball Player
15920 Lucerne Road, Fredericktown OH 43019, USA
Fisher, Noel — Actor
United Talent Agency, 9336 Civic Center Dr, Beverly Hills CA 90210 USA
Fisher, Raymond C — Judge
US Court of Appeals, 125 S Grand Ave, Pasadena CA 91105, USA
Fisher, Red — Sportswriter
Montreal Gazette, 250 Saint Antoine W, Montreal QC H2Y 3R7, Canada
Fisher, Richard W — Financier, Government Official
Dallas Federal Reserve Bank, 2200 N Pearl St, Dallas TX 75201, USA
Fisher, Rob — Conductor
I M G Artists, 152 W 57th St, #500, New York NY 10019 USA
Fisher, Robert J — Businessman
Gap Inc, 2 Folsom St, San Francisco CA 94105, USA
Fisher, Roger — Guitarist (Heart)
PO Box 1162, Woodinville WA 98072, USA
Fisher, Scott — Astronomer
Gemini Observatory, Mauna Kea, Hilo HI 96720, USA
Fisher, Steve — Basketball Coach
San Diego State University, Athletic Dept, San Diego CA 92182, USA
Fisher, Thomas G (Tom) — Baseball Player
6515 Lake Suzzanne Circle, Panama City FL 32404, USA
Fisher, Todd — Producer
Paradigm Agency, 360 N Crescent Dr, North Building, Beverly Hills CA 90210 USA
Fisher, William F — Astronaut
1119 Woodbank Dr, Seabrook TX 77586, USA
Fishman, Alan F — Financier
Columbia Financial Partners, 195 Montague St, Brooklyn NY 11201, USA
Fishman, Bill — Director
Fallout Entertainment, 3100 Airport Ave, Santa Monica CA 90405, USA
Fishman, James H (Jim) — Publisher
A A R P Magazine, Publisher's Office, 601 E St NW, Washington DC 20049, USA
Fishman, Jay S — Businessman
Saint Paul Travelers, 388 Greenwich St, #3900, New York NY 10013, USA
Fishman, Jerald G — Businessman
Analog Devices Inc, 1 Technology Way, Norwood MA 02062, USA
Fishman, Jon — Drummer (Phish)
Dionysian Productions, 431 Pine St, Burlington VT 05401, USA
Fishman, Michael — Actor
4141 Ball Road, Cypress CA 90630, USA
Fisichella, Giancarlo — Auto Racing Driver
Movie & Sport Mgmt, Finsgate, 5-7 Cranwood St, London EC1V 9EE, England
Fisk, Carlton E — Baseball Player
18705 63rd Ave E, Bradenton FL 34211, USA
Fisk, Jason — Football Player
2619 Regatta Lane, Davis CA 95618, USA
Fisk, Sari K — Ice Hockey Player
Ice Hockey Assn, Makelankatu 91, 00610 Helsinki, Finland
Fisk, Schuyler — Actress
Innovative Artists, 1505 10th St, Santa Monica CA 90401 USA
Fiske, James (Jim) — Electrical Engineer
Launchpoint Technologies, 5735 Hollister Ave, #B, Goleta CA 93117, USA
Fiske, Robert B, Jr — Attorney
19 Juniper Road, Darien CT 06820, USA
Fister, Bruce L — Air Force General
400 Regatta Dr, Niceville FL 32578, USA
Fitch, Janet — Writer
Little Brown, 3 Center Plaza, #100, Boston MA 02108 USA
Fitch, Val L — Nobel Physics Laureate
292 Hartley Ave, Princeton NJ 08540, USA
Fitch, William C (Bill) — Basketball Coach
627 Nerita St, #A, Sanibel FL 33957, USA
Fites, Donald V — Businessman
Caterpillar Inc, 100 NE Adams St, Peoria IL 61629, USA
Fitial, Benigno R — Governor, Northern Mariana Islands
Governor's Office, Caller Box 10007, Saipan MP 96950 USA
Fittipaldi, Christian — Auto Racing Driver
282 Alphaville Barueri, Sao Paulo 0640 500, Brazil
Fittipaldi, Emerson — Auto Racing Driver
Ave Reboucas 3551, Jardim Paulistano, Sao Paulo 05401 400, Brazil
Fittipaldi, Lisa — Artist
Mind's Eye Foundation, 215 Beauregard, San Antonio TX 78204, USA
Fitts, Rick — Actor
Gage Group, 14724 Ventura Blvd, #505, Sherman Oaks CA 91403 USA
Fitzgerald, Annie — Actress
Stone Manners Salners, 9911 W Pico Blvd, #1400, Los Angeles CA 90035 USA
Fitzgerald, Brian — Baseball Player
7226 John Taylor Mews, Ruther Glen VA 22546, USA
Fitzgerald, Caitlin — Actress, Model
I C M Partners, 730 5th Ave, New York NY 10019 USA
Fitzgerald, Christopher — Actor
United Talent Agency, 9336 Civic Center Dr, Beverly Hills CA 90210 USA
FitzGerald, Edward R (Ed) — Baseball Player
431 Christopher St, Folsom CA 95630, USA
Fitzgerald, Fern — Actress
7409 Leescott Ave, Van Nuys CA 91406, USA
FitzGerald, Frances — Writer
Simon & Schuster, 1230 Ave of Americas, Concourse 1, New York NY 10020, USA

Fitzgerald, Frankie — Actor
Associated International Mgmt, Fairfax House, Fulwood Place, London WC1V 6HU, England

FitzGerald, Helen — Actress
Paul Kohner, 9300 Wilshire Blvd, #555, Beverly Hills CA 90212 USA

Fitzgerald, Jack — Actor
William Kerwin Agency, 1605 N Cahuenga, #202, Los Angeles CA 90028, USA

Fitzgerald, John R — Football Player
408 Arborcrest Dr, Richardson TX 75080, USA

Fitzgerald, Larry D, Jr — Football Player
15832 S 22nd St, Phoenix AZ 85048, USA

Fitzgerald, Mark P — Navy Admiral
Commander, Naval Forces Africa, PSC 809, Box 70, FPO AE 09626 USA

Fitzgerald, Michael P (Mike) — Baseball Player
415 Parkview Dr, Rochester IL 62563, USA

Fitzgerald, Michael R (Mike) — Baseball Player
502 Flint Ave, Long Beach CA 90814, USA

FitzGerald, Niall W A — Businessman
Hakluyt Co, 34 Upper Brook St, London W1K 7QS, England

Fitzgerald, Pat — Football Player, Coach
Northwestern University, Athletic Dept, Evanston IN 60208, USA

Fitzgerald, Patrick J — Attorney, Government Official
Justice Dept, Dirksen Building, 219 S Dearborn St, #500, Chicago IL 60604, USA

Fitzgerald, Tara — Actress
United Agents, 12-26 Lexington St, London W1F 0LE, England

FitzGerald, Thomas — Environmentalist
Kentucky Resources Council, 213 Saint Clair St, Frankfort KY 40601, USA

Fitzgerald, Tom — Ice Hockey Player
3 Samuel Phelps Way, North Reading MA 01864, USA

Fitzgerald-Brown, Benita — Track Athlete
Women in Cable/Telecommunications, 14555 Avion Parkway, Chantilly VA 20151, USA

Fitzmaurice, David J — Labor Leader
Electrical Radio & Machinists Union, 11256 156th St NW, Washington DC 20005, USA

Fitzmaurice, Deanne — Photojournalist
San Francisco Chronicle, Editorial Dept, 925 Mission, San Francisco CA 94103 USA

Fitzmaurice, Michael J — Vietnam War Army Hero (CMH)
PO Box 178, Hartford SD 57033, USA

Fitzmorris, Alan J (Al) — Baseball Player
17512 W 159th Terrace, Olathe KS 66062, USA

Fitzpatrick, Leo — Actor
Don Buchwald/Fortitude, 6500 Wilshire Blvd, #2200, Los Angeles CA 90048 USA

Fitzpatrick, Stephen — Guitarist (Veruca Salt, Ashtar Command)
S T C Entertainment, 5627 Sepulveda Blvd, #230, Van Nuys CA 91411, USA

FitzRandolph, Casey — Speed Skater
Janey Miller Mgmt, 1435 Cherryvale Dr, Boulder CO 80303, USA

Fitzsimmons, Greg — Actor, Comedian
United Talent Agency, 9336 Civic Center Dr, Beverly Hills CA 90210 USA

Fitzsimonds, Roger L — Financier
Firstar Corp, 777 E Wisconsin Ave, Milwaukee WI 53202, USA

FitzSimons, Dennis J — Publisher
Tribune Co, 435 N Michigan Ave, Chicago IL 60611, USA

Fitzwater, Marlin — Government Official
851 Cedar Dr, Deale MD 20751, USA

Fitzwilliam, Wendy M — Beauty Queen
Evolving TecKnologies, Don Miguel Road Extension, El Socorro, Trinidad

Fix, Oliver — Canoeing Athlete
Ringstr 6, 86391 Stadtbergen, Germany

Fixman, Marshall — Chemist
Colorado State University, Chemistry Dept, Fort Collins CO 80523, USA

Fjuioka, Sachio — Conductor
I M G Artists, Hogarth Business Park, Chiswick, London W4 2TH, England

Flacco, Joe V — Football Player
Baltimore Ravens, Ravens Stadium, 1 Winning Dr, Baltimore MD 21230 USA

Flach, Ken — Tennis Player, Coach
Vanderbilt University, Athletic Dept, Nashville TN 37240, USA

Flach, Thomas — Yachtsman
Johanna-Resch-Str 13, 12439 Berlin, Germany

Flack, Enya — Actress
C E S D, 10635 Santa Monica Blvd, #130, Los Angeles CA 90025 USA

Flack, Roberta — Singer, Songwriter
Universal Attractions, 135 W 26th St, #1200, New York NY 10001 USA

Flade, H Klaus-Dietrich — Cosmonaut, Germany
Airbus Industries, 1 Rond Point M Bellonte, 31707 Blagnac Cedex, France

Flagg, Fannie — Actress, Comedienne
Creative Artists Agency, 2000 Ave of Stars, #100, Los Angeles CA 90067 USA

Flaherty, Joe — Actor, Comedian
S M S Talent, 8383 Wilshire Blvd, #230, Beverly Hills CA 90211 USA

Flaherty, John T — Baseball Player
17 Joseph Bow Court, Pearl River NY 10965, USA

Flaherty, Stephen — Composer
W M E Entertainment, 9601 Wilshire Blvd, #300, Beverly Hills CA 90210 USA

Flaim, Eric J — Speed Skater
52 East St, Rutland VA 05701, USA

Flair, Ric — Professional Wrestler
5701 Providence Country Club Dr, Charlotte NC 28277, USA

Flamand, Didier — Actor
U B B A, 6 Rue de Braque, 75003 Paris, France

Flanagan, Crista — Actress
Liberman/Zerman Mgmt, 252 N Larchmont Blvd, #200, Los Angeles CA 90004 USA

Flanagan, Edward J (Ed) — Football Player
10981 Clayton St, Northglenn CO 80233, USA

Flanagan, Edward M, Jr — Army General
Parade Rest, 12 Oyster Catcher Road, Beaufort SC 29907, USA

Flanagan, Fionnula — Actress
Lisa Richards Agency, 108 Upper Leeson St, Dublin 4, Ireland

Flanagan, Helen — Actress
Granada Television, Quay St, Manchester M60 9EA, England

Flanagan, Michael C (Mike)	Football Player
5 Moss Springs Court, Henderson NV 89052, USA	
Flanagan, Tommy	Actor
Untitled Entertainment, 350 S Beverly Dr, #200, Beverly Hills CA 90212 USA	
Flanery, Sean Patrick	Actor
Don Buchwald/Fortitude, 6500 Wilshire Blvd, #2200, Los Angeles CA 90048 USA	
Flanigan, James M (Jim)	Football Player
3820 Sand Point Road, Sturgeon Bay WI 54235, USA	
Flanigan, James M (Jim), Jr	Football Player
4511 Wyandot Trail, Green Bay WI 54313, USA	
Flanigan, Joe	Actor, Writer
C E S D, 10635 Santa Monica Blvd, #130, Los Angeles CA 90025 USA	
Flanigan, Lauren	Opera Singer
Robert Lombardo Assoc, Harkness Plaza, 61 W 62nd St, #6F, New York NY 10023 USA	
Flanigan, Thomas A (Tom)	Baseball Player
114 E 40th St, Covington KY 41015, USA	
Flannery, John M	Baseball Player
9002 Scottish Pastures Dr, Austin TX 78750, USA	
Flannery, Susan	Actress
Bell-Phillip Television Productions, 7800 Beverly Blvd, #3371, Los Angeles CA 90036, USA	
Flannery, Thomas	Editorial Cartoonist
911 Dartmouth Glen Way, Baltimore MD 21212, USA	
Flannery, Timothy E (Tim)	Baseball Player
715 Hymettus Ave, Encinitas CA 92024, USA	
Flannigan, Maureen	Actress
Don Buchwald/Fortitude, 10 E 44th St, New York NY 10017 USA	
Flansburgh, John C	Singer, Guitarist (They Might Be Giants)
Hornblow Group, PO Box 176, Palisades NY 10964, USA	
Flathman, Richard E	Political Scientist
112 Rafael Dr, San Rafael CA 94901, USA	
Flatley, Michael	Dancer
Creative Artists Agency, 2000 Ave of Stars, #100, Los Angeles CA 90067 USA	
Flatley, Paul R	Football Player
795 Woods Road, Richmond IN 47374, USA	
Flaum, Joel M	Judge
US District Court, 219 S Dearborn St,, #2302B, Chicago IL 60604, USA	
Flavell, Richard A	Immunologist
Yale University Medical Center, Immunology Dept, New Haven CT 06520, USA	
Flavin, Jennifer	Model
30 Beverly Park, Beverly Hills CA 90210, USA	
Flavin, John T	Baseball Player
23060 16th St, Newhall CA 91321, USA	
Flavor Flav	Rap Artist, Actor, Comedian
Entertainment Artists, PO Box 120824, Nashville TN 37212, USA	
Flay, Bobby	Restauranteur, Chef
Bold Food, PO Box 1102, New York NY 10159, USA	
Flea	Bassist (Red Hot Chili Peppers)
Innovative Artists, 1505 10th St, Santa Monica CA 90401 USA	
Fleck, Bela	Guitarist, Banjoist, Composer
Shore Fire Media, 32 Court St, #1600, Brooklyn NY 11201 USA	
Fleck, Jack	Golfer
12006 Edgewater Road, Fort Smith AR 72903, USA	
Fleck, John	Performance Artist, Actor
Greater Vision Artists Talent, 8981 Sunset Blvd, #101, Los Angeles CA 90069, USA	
Fleck, Ryan	Director, Writer
Management 360, 9111 Wilshire Blvd, Beverly Hills CA 90210 USA	
Fleder, Gary R	Director
Mojo Films, Animation Building, 500 S Buena Vista St, Burbank CA 91521, USA	
Fleeshman, Richard	Actor
Independent Talent Group, Oxford House, 76 Oxford St, London W1D 1BS, England	
Fleetwood, Mick J K	Drummer (Fleetwood Mac)
Sabre Entertainment, 5737 Kanan Road, #237, Agoura Hills CA 91301, USA	
Fleigel, Bernie	Basketball Player
21 Granville Road, #3, Cambridge MA 02138, USA	
Fleischer, Ari	Government Official, Journalist
Harper Collins Publishers, 10 E 53rd St, Cellar 1, New York NY 10022 USA	
Fleischer, Ruben	Director, Writer
United Talent Agency, 9336 Civic Center Dr, Beverly Hills CA 90210 USA	
Fleischman, Paul	Writer
PO Box 646, Aromas CA 95004, USA	
Fleischmann, Peter	Director, Producer
Filmzentrum Babelsberg, August-Bebel-Str 26-53, 14482 Potsdam, Germany	
Fleisher, Bruce	Golfer
301 Grand Key Terrace, Palm Beach Gardens FL 33418, USA	
Fleisher, Leon	Concert Pianist, Conductor
20 Merrymount Road, Baltimore MD 21210, USA	
Fleiss, Michael	Producer, Writer
Creative Artists Agency, 2000 Ave of Stars, #100, Los Angeles CA 90067 USA	
Fleming Jenkins, Peggy	Figure Skater
16387 Aztec Ridge Dr, Los Gatos CA 95030, USA	
Fleming, Andrew M (Andy)	Director
I/D Public Relations, 7060 Hollywood Blvd, #800, Los Angeles CA 90028 USA	
Fleming, Anne Taylor	Journalist, Writer
Janklow & Nesbit Assoc, 445 Park Ave, #1300, New York NY 10022 USA	
Fleming, David A	Baseball Player
PO Box 692, Lincolndale NY 10540, USA	
Fleming, Eric	Actor
A P A Talent/Literary Agency, 405 S Beverly Dr, #300, Beverly Hills CA 90212 USA	
Fleming, Jacky	Writer
Bloomsbury Publishing, 36 Soho Square, London W1D 3Q4, England	
Fleming, James P	Vietnam War Air Force Hero (CMH)
PO Box 487, Manvel TX 77578, USA	
Fleming, Marvin (Marv)	Football Player
909 Howard St, Marina del Rey CA 90292, USA	
Fleming, Renee	Opera Singer
Paradigm Agency, 360 N Crescent Dr, North Building, Beverly Hills CA 90210 USA	

F

Fleming, Rhonda — Actress
10281 Century Woods Dr, Los Angeles CA 90067, USA
Fleming, Scott — Government Official
2425 Elendil Lane, Davis CA 95616, USA
Fleming, Valerie — Bobsled Athlete
Q Sports Marketing, 534 W Evergreen St, Wheaton IL 60187 USA
Fleming, Vern — Basketball Player
10713 Brixton Lane, Fishers IN 46037, USA
Flemings, Merton C — Materials Engineer
975 Memorial Dr, #608, Cambridge MA 02138, USA
Flemming, John — Artist
1409 Cambronne St, New Orleans LA 70118, USA
Flemyng, Jason — Actor
Conway Van Gelder Grant, 8-12 Broadwick St, #300, London W1F 8HW, England
Flender, Rodman — Director, Producer, Actor
Apostle Mgmt, 9696 Culver Blvd, #110, Culver City CA 90232, USA
Flener, Gregory A (Huck) — Baseball Player
2186 North Ave, Chico CA 95926, USA
Flesch, Steve — Golfer
PO Box 440, Union KY 41091, USA
Fletcher, Andrew J (Andy) — Synthesizer Musician (Depeche Mode)
Reach Media, 295 Greenwich St. #109, New York NY 10007, USA
Fletcher, Anne — Director, Choreographer
United Talent Agency, 9336 Civic Center Dr, Beverly Hills CA 90210 USA
Fletcher, Christopher C (Chris) — Football Player
4818 La Cruz Dr, La Mesa CA 91941, USA
Fletcher, Cliff — Ice Hockey Executive
19980 N 94th Way, Scottsdale AZ 85255, USA
Fletcher, Darrin G — Baseball Player
9146 E 2100 North Road, Oakwood IL 61858, USA
Fletcher, Dexter — Actor
Independent Talent Group, Oxford House, 76 Oxford St, London W1D 1BS, England
Fletcher, Diane — Actress
Ken McReddie Assoc, 11 Connaught Place, London W2 2ET, England
Fletcher, E Paul — Baseball Player
548 Mockingbird Way, Warrington PA 18976, USA
Fletcher, Guy — Keyboardist (Dire Straits)
Air Edel, 8687 Melrose Ave, #900, Los Angeles CA 90069 USA
Fletcher, Jamar M — Football Player
11063 Worchester Dr, Saint Louis MO 63136, USA
Fletcher, London L — Football Player
18898 Shropshire Court, Leesburg VA 20176, USA
Fletcher, Louise — Actress
1520 Camden Ave, #105, Los Angeles CA 90025, USA
Fletcher, Martin — Commentator
NBC-TV, News Dept, 4001 Nebraska Ave NW, Washington DC 20016 USA
Fletcher, Scott B — Baseball Player
300 Birkdale Dr, Fayetteville GA 30215, USA
Fletcher, Simon R — Football Player
1722 N Avenue U, Freeport TX 77541, USA
Fletcher, Terrell A — Football Player
13889 Etude Road, San Diego CA 92128, USA
Fletcher, Thomas W (Tom) — Baseball Player
9287 E 2085 North Road, Oakwood IL 61858, USA
Fletcher, William A — Judge
US Court of Appeals, Court Building, 95 7th St, San Francisco CA 94103, USA
Fleury, Marc-Andre — Ice Hockey Player
1123 Castletown Court, Sewickley PA 15143, USA
Fleury, Theoren W (Theo) — Ice Hockey Player
Concrete Coatings, 4519 Manhattan Road SE, Calgary AB T2G 4B3, Canada
Flick, Bob — Singer, Fiddle Player (Brothers Four)
Bob Flick Productions, 300 Vine St, #14, Seattle WA 98121, USA
Flicker, John — Association Executive
National Audubon Society, 225 Varick St, #700, New York NY 10014, USA
Flindt, George H — Football Player
PO Box 2486, Prescott AZ 86302, USA
Flinn, John R — Baseball Player
6221 Lake Providence Lane, Charlotte NC 28277, USA
Flint, Jill — Actress
Innovative Artists, 1505 10th St, Santa Monica CA 90401 USA
Flint, Keith — Dancer, Singer (Prodigy)
Maverick Records, 3300 Warner Blvd, Burbank CA 91505, USA
Flippin, Lucy Lee — Actress
713 Eagle Road, Fleetwood PA 19522, USA
Fliter, Ingrid — Concert Pianist
C M Artists, 127 W 96th St, #13B, New York NY 10025 USA
Flitter, Josh — Actor
Abrams Artists, 9200 W Sunset Blvd, #1125, West Hollywood CA 90069 USA
Float, Jeffrey (Jeff) — Swimmer
1906 University Park Dr, Sacramento CA 95825, USA
Flockhart, Calista — Actress
Industry Entertainment, 955 Carillo Dr, #300, Los Angeles CA 90048 USA
Flood, Debbie — Rowing Athlete
Leander Club, Henley on Thames, Leander RG9 2LP, England
Flor, Claus Peter — Conductor
I M G Artists, Hogarth Business Park, Chiswick, London W4 2TH, England
Florance, Sheila — Actress
Melbourne Artists, 643 Saint Kikla Road, Melbourne VIC 3004, Australia
Florek, Dann — Actor
Access Talent Mgmt, 171 Madison Ave, #910, New York NY 10016, USA
Flores, Gene — Artist
Portland Commnity College, Art Dept, 1200 SW 49th Ave, Portland OR 97219, USA
Flores, Randy A — Baseball Player
8230 E Hoverland Road, Scottsdale AZ 85255, USA
Flores, Rosie — Singer, Guitarist
Rounder Records, 1 Rounder Way, Burlington MA 01803 USA

Fleming - Flores

Flores, Thomas R (Tom)	Football Player, Coach, Executive
77741 Cove Point Circle, Indian Wells CA 92210, USA	
Floria, Holly	Actress
Epstein-Wyckoff, 280 S Beverly Dr, #400, Beverly Hills CA 90212 USA	
Florie, Bryce B	Baseball Player
1118 Lands End Dr, Hanahan SC 29410, USA	
Florin, Susan	Golfer
10342 Pontofino Circle, Trinity FL 34655, USA	
Florio, James J (Jim)	Governor, NJ
Mudge Rose Guthrie, Corporate Center 2, 1673 E 16th St, #16, Brooklyn NY 11229, USA	
Florio, Thomas A	Publisher
New Yorker, Publisher's Office, 4 Times Square, New York NY 10036, USA	
Florschuetz, Thomas	Photographer
Gary Tatintsian Gallery, 526 W 26th St, New York NY 10001, USA	
Flory, Med	Actor
6044 Ensign Ave, North Hollywood CA 91606, USA	
Flowers, Brandon	Singer, Pianist (Killers)
W M E Entertainment, 9601 Wilshire Blvd, #300, Beverly Hills CA 90210 USA	
Flowers, Bruce	Basketball Player
276 W Grantley Ave, Elmhurst IL 60126, USA	
Flowers, Charles (Charlie)	Football Player
6170 Mountain Brook Way NW, Atlanta GA 30328, USA	
Flowers, Frank E	Director, Writer
Brillstein Entertainment Partners, 9150 Wilshire Blvd, #350, Beverly Hills CA 90212 USA	
Flowers, Richmond M, Jr	Football Player
3434 Indian Lake Dr, Pelham AL 35124, USA	
Floyd, C Clifford (Cliff), Jr	Baseball Player
3283 Birch Terrace, Davie FL 33330, USA	
Floyd, Carlisle	Composer
3552 Trillium Court, Tallahassee FL 32312, USA	
Floyd, Eddie	Singer, Songwriter
Jason West, Gables House, Saddlebow Kings Lynn PE34 3AR, England	
Floyd, Elson S	Educator
Washington State University, President's Office, Pullman WA 99164, USA	
Floyd, Eric A (Sleepy)	Basketball Player
3191 Ivy Creek Road, Gastonia NC 28056, USA	
Floyd, Eric C	Football Player
18047 Sailfish Dr, Lutz FL 33558, USA	
Floyd, Gavin C	Baseball Player
9809 Milano Dr, Trinity FL 34655, USA	
Floyd, George, Jr	Football Player
8621 Heritage Dr, Florence KY 41042, USA	
Floyd, Heather	Singer (Point of Grace)
W M E Entertainment, 1600 Division St, #300, Nashville TN 37203 USA	
Floyd, Marlene	Golfer
Marlene Floyd Golf School, 5370 Club House Lane, Hope Mills NC 28348, USA	
Floyd, Michael	Football Player
Arizona Cardinals, PO Box 888, Phoenix AZ 85001 USA	
Floyd, Raymond (Ray)	Golfer
505 S Flagler Dr, #910, West Palm Beach FL 33401, USA	
Floyd, Robert	Actor
C E S D, 10635 Santa Monica Blvd, #130, Los Angeles CA 90025 USA	
Floyd, Robert N (Bobby)	Baseball Player
1757 SE Dominic Ave, Port Saint Lucie FL 34952, USA	
Floyd, Susan	Actress
Untitled Entertainment, 350 S Beverly Dr, #200, Beverly Hills CA 90212 USA	
Floyd, Tim	Basketball Coach
University of Texas, Athletic Dept, El Paso TX 79968, USA	
Floyd, William A	Football Player
7827 Glen Echo Road, Jacksonville FL 32211, USA	
Fluckey, Tim	Guitarist, Pianist (Adema)
Novi Entertainment, PO Box 17077, Beverly Hills CA 90209, USA	
Fluegel, Darlanne	Actress
Shelter Entertainment, 9454 Wilshire Blvd, #715, Beverly Hills CA 90212 USA	
Flueger, Patrick John	Actor
United Talent Agency, 9336 Civic Center Dr, Beverly Hills CA 90210 USA	
Flutie, Douglas R (Doug)	Football Player, Sportscaster
22 Chieftain Lane, Natick MA 01760, USA	
Flynn, Barbara	Actress
Yakety-Yak, 8 Bloomsbury Square, London WC1A 2UA, England	
Flynn, Colleen	Actress
Envision Entertainment, 8840 Wilshire Blvd, Beverly Hills CA 90211 USA	
Flynn, George W	Chemist
382 Summit Ave, Leonia NJ 07605, USA	
Flynn, Jackie	Actress, Comedienne
Don Buchwald/Fortitude, 6500 Wilshire Blvd, #2200, Los Angeles CA 90048 USA	
Flynn, Johnny	Singer, Musician
Agency Group Ltd, 1880 Century Park E, #711, Los Angeles CA 90067 USA	
Flynn, Jonny F	Basketball Player
Portland Trail Blazers, Rose Garden, 1 N Center Court St, Portland OR 97227 USA	
Flynn, Matt	Drummer (Maroon 5)
J Records, 745 5th Ave, #600, New York NY 10151 USA	
Flynn, Matthew C (Matt)	Football Player
Seattle Seahawks, 12 Seahawks Way, Renton WA 98056 USA	
Flynn, Michael D (Mike)	Basketball Player
3934 E Battala Ave, Gilbert AZ 85297, USA	
Flynn, Michael P (Mike)	Football Player
1922 Clifden Road, Catonsville MD 21228, USA	
Flynn, Neil	Actor
A P A Talent/Literary Agency, 405 S Beverly Dr, #300, Beverly Hills CA 90212 USA	
Flynn, R Douglas (Doug), Jr	Baseball Player
2465 Vale Dr, Lexington KY 40514, USA	
Flynn, Raymond L	Mayor, Boston; Diplomat
Catholic Alliance, Via Catholic City, PO Box 1872, Chesapeake VA 23327, USA	
Flynn, Sean	Actor
Innovative Artists, 1505 10th St, Santa Monica CA 90401 USA	

F

Flores - Flynn

Flynn, Thomas J (Tom) — Football Player
4008 Holiday Park Dr, Murrysville PA 15668, USA

Flynn, Vince — Writer
I C M Partners, 10250 Constellation Blvd, #900, Los Angeles CA 90067 USA

Flynt, Larry — Publisher
Larry Flynt Publications Inc, 8484 Wilshire Blvd, #900, Beverly Hills CA 90211, USA

Fo, Dario — Nobel Literature Laureate
C T F R, Corso di Porta Romana 132, 20122 Milan, Italy

Foale, C Michael (Mike) — Astronaut
2101 Todville Road, #11, Seabrook TX 77586, USA

Foale, Marion A — Fashion Designer
Foale Ltd, 133A Long St, Atherstone, Warwicks CV9 1AD, England

Fobbs, Brandon — Actor
Stone Manners Salners, 9911 W Pico Blvd, #1400, Los Angeles CA 90035 USA

Foege, William H — Public Health Executive
PO Box 450989, Atlanta GA 31145, USA

Foeger, Luggi — Skier
Christopher Foeger, 230 S Balsamina Way, Portola Valley CA 94028, USA

Foer, Jonathan Safran — Writer
Little Brown, 237 Park Ave, #1300, New York NY 10017, USA

Foerster, Paul — Yachtsman
126 Dunford Dr, Rockwall TX 75032, USA

Fofana, Mohamed Said — Prime Minister, Guinea
Prime Minister's Office, PO Box 5141, Cite des Nations, Conakry, Guinea

Fogarty, Thomas J — Inventor (Embolectomy Catheter)
Thomas Fogarty Winery, 3270 Alpine Road, Portola Valley CA 94028, USA

Fogel, Daniel M — Educator
University of Vermont, President's Office, Burlington VT 05405, USA

Fogel, Robert W — Nobel Economics Laureate
5321 S University Ave, Chicago IL 60615, USA

Fogerty, John — Singer, Guitarist, Songwriter
Paradigm Agency, 360 N Crescent Dr, North Building, Beverly Hills CA 90210 USA

Fogg, Joshua S (Josh) — Baseball Player
4910 S Quincy St, Tampa FL 33611, USA

Fogle, Larry — Basketball Player
72 Beechwood St, Rochester NY 14609, USA

Fogleman, Ronald R (Ron) — Air Force General
406 Snowshoe Lane, Durango CO 81301, USA

Fogler, Dan — Actor
W M E Entertainment, 9601 Wilshire Blvd, #300, Beverly Hills CA 90210 USA

Fogler, Eddie — Basketball Coach
University of South Carolina, Athletic Dept, Columbia SC 53233, USA

Foglesong, Robert H (Doc) — Air Force General, Educator
Council on Foreign Relations, 58 E 68th St, New York NY 10065, USA

Fohrer, Alan J — Businessman
Edison International, 2244 Walnut Grove Ave, Rosemead CA 91770, USA

Foiles, Henry L (Hank), Jr — Baseball Player
4333 Silverleaf Court, Virginia Beach VA 23462, USA

Fois, Marina — Actress
U B B A - Cecile Feisenberg, 6 Rue de Braque, 75003 Paris, France

Fok, Clarence — Director
Becsey Wisdom Kalajian, 849 S Wooster St, #7, Los Angeles CA 90035, USA

Fokin, Vitold P — Prime Minister, Ukraine
Vezkhovna Rada, M Hrushevskoho Rul 5, 252019 Kiev, Ukraine

Folau, Spencer S — Football Player
14003 Woodens Lane, Reisterstown MD 21136, USA

Folds, Ben — Singer, Pianist, Songwriter
I C M Partners, 10250 Constellation Blvd, #900, Los Angeles CA 90067 USA

Foley, Alina — Actress
Seven Summits Mgmt, 8906 W Olympic Blvd, Beverly Hills CA 90211 USA

Foley, Dave — Football Player
4500 Redmond Road, Springfield OH 45505, USA

Foley, David S (Dave) — Actor, Comedian
Brillstein Entertainment Partners, 9150 Wilshire Blvd, #350, Beverly Hills CA 90212 USA

Foley, Gerry — Ice Hockey Player
352 Skead Road, Garson ON P3L 1N4, Canada

Foley, James — Director
W M E Entertainment, 9601 Wilshire Blvd, #300, Beverly Hills CA 90210 USA

Foley, Kathleen — Neurologist
Memorial Sloan Kettering Cancer Center, 1275 York Ave, New York NY 10065, USA

Foley, Mark A — Representative, FL; Commentator
WSVU-FM, News Dept, 8895 N Military Trail, West Palm Beach FL 33410, USA

Foley, Marvis E (Marv) — Baseball Player
10166 Glenmore Ave, Bradenton FL 34202, USA

Foley, Maurice B — Judge
US Tax Court, 400 2nd St NW, Washington DC 20217, USA

Foley, Robert F — Vietnam War Army Hero (CMH), General
2121 Jamieson Ave, #606, Alexandria VA 22314, USA

Foley, Scott — Actor
I C M Partners, 10250 Constellation Blvd, #900, Los Angeles CA 90067 USA

Foley, Stephen J (Steve) — Football Player
6321 S Newport Circle, Centennial CO 80111, USA

Foley, Sue — Singer, Guitarist, Songwriter
Shanachie Records, 37 E Clinton St, #1, Newton NJ 07860 USA

Foley, Sylvester R, Jr — Navy Admiral
50 Apple Hill Dr, Tewksbury MA 01876, USA

Foley, Thomas D (Tim) — Football Player
3029 Isola Bella Blvd, Mount Dora FL 32757, USA

Foley, Thomas M (Tom) — Baseball Player
5237 Karlsburg Place, Palm Harbor FL 34685, USA

Foley, Thomas S — Representative, WA; Speaker; Diplomat
PO Box 1047, Medical Lake WA 99022, USA

Folger, Franklin — Cartoonist
King Features Syndicate, 300 W 57th St, #1500, New York NY 10019 USA

Folguera, Ruy — Composer
Gorfaine/Schwartz, 4111 W Alameda Ave, #509, Burbank CA 91505 USA

Foli, Timothy J (Tim) — Baseball Player
525 Timberline Dr, Lenoir City TN 37772, USA

Folk, Nicholas A (Nick) — Football Player
New York Jets, 1 Jets Dr, Florham Park NJ 07932 USA

Folk, Robert — Composer
A S C A P, 7920 Sunset Blvd, #300, Los Angeles CA 90046, USA

Folkenberg, Robert S — Religious Leader
Seventh-Day Adventists, 12501 Old Columbia Pike, Silver Spring MD 20904, USA

Folkers, Richard N (Rich) — Baseball Player
7100 3rd Ave N, Saint Petersburg FL 33710, USA

Folkins, L Leroy (Lee) — Football Player
8749 The Esplanade, #13, Orlando FL 32836, USA

Folkson, Sheree — Director
Casorotto Ramsay, Waverley House, 7-12 Noel St, London W1F 8GQ, England

Follesdal, Dagfinn K — Philosopher
Staverhagen 7, 1312 Slepemdem, Norway

Follett, Ken — Writer
Creative Artists Agency, 2000 Ave of Stars, #100, Los Angeles CA 90067 USA

Followill, Caleb — Singer (Kings of Leon)
Vector Mgmt, 1100 Glendon Ave, #2000, Los Angeles CA 90024, USA

Followill, Jared — Bassist (Kings of Leon)
Vector Mgmt, 1100 Glendon Ave, #2000, Los Angeles CA 90024, USA

Followill, Matthew — Guitarist (Kings of Leon)
Vector Mgmt, 1100 Glendon Ave, #2000, Los Angeles CA 90024, USA

Followill, Nathan — Drummer (Kings of Leon)
Vector Mgmt, 1100 Glendon Ave, #2000, Los Angeles CA 90024, USA

Follows, Megan — Actress
Greene Assoc, 1901 Ave of Stars, #130, Los Angeles CA 90067 USA

Folman, Ari — Director, Writer
Creative Artists Agency, 2000 Ave of Stars, #100, Los Angeles CA 90067 USA

Folsom, Allan R — Writer
Marion Rosenberg, PO Box 69826, Los Angeles CA 90069, USA

Folsom, James E (Jim), Jr — Governor, AL
1482 Orchard Dr NE, Cullman AL 35055, USA

Folsome, Claire — Microbiologist
University of Hawaii, Microbiology Dept, 2600 Campus Road, Honolulu HI 96822, USA

Folta, Danelle M — Model
537 S Highland Ave, Winter Garden FL 34787, USA

Fonda, Bridget — Actress
I F A Talent Agency, 8730 W Sunset Blvd, #490, West Hollywood CA 90069 USA

Fonda, Jane — Actress
Fonda Foundation, PO Box 5840, Atlanta GA 31107, USA

Fonda, Peter — Actor
Indian Hills Ranch, RR 38G, Box 2024, Livingston MT 59047, USA

Fondacaro, Phil — Actor
C E S D, 10635 Santa Monica Blvd, #130, Los Angeles CA 90025 USA

Foner, Eric — Historian
606 W 116th St, New York NY 10027, USA

Fong, Bobby — Educator
Ursinus College, President's Office, 601 E Main St, Collegeville PA 19426, USA

Fonseca, Caio — Artist
Charles Cowles, 210 11th Ave, #500, New York NY 10001, USA

Fonseca, Lyndsy — Actress
I C M Partners, 10250 Constellation Blvd, #900, Los Angeles CA 90067 USA

Fonsi, Luis — Singer, Songwriter
Azoff Music Mgmt, 1100 Glendon Ave, Los Angeles CA 90024, USA

Fontaine, Joan — Actress
PO Box 222600, Carmel CA 93922, USA

Fontaine, Levi — Basketball Player
25 11th Ave, San Mateo CA 94401, USA

Fontaine, Lucien — Thoroughbred Racing Jockey
1680 Riverwood Lane, Coral Springs FL 33071, USA

Fontaine, Maurice A — Physiologist
25 Rue Pierre Nicole, 75005 Paris, France

Fontamillas, Jerome E — Singer, Guitarist, Pianist (Switchfoot)
The Firm, 2049 Century Park E, #2550, Los Angeles CA 90067 USA

Fontana, Arianna — Speed Skater
23010 Berbenno di Valtellina (SO), Italy

Fontana, Isabeli — Model
Women Model Mgmt, 199 Lafayette St, #700, New York NY 10012 USA

Fontana, Wayne — Singer
Brian Gannon Mgmt, PO Box 106, Rochdale OL16 4HW, England

Fontas, Jon — Ice Hockey Player
38a Worthen Road, #1, Lexington MA 02421, USA

Fontenot, Albert P (Al) — Football Player
4919 Gammage St, Houston TX 77021, USA

Fontenot, Jerry P — Football Player
938 Bristol Dr, Deerfield IL 60015, USA

Fontenot, S Ray — Baseball Player
1674 N Crestview Dr, Lake Charles LA 70605, USA

Fontes, Wayne H — Football Player, Coach
2043 Harbour Watch Circle, Tarpon Springs FL 34689, USA

Fonteyne, Valere R (Val) — Ice Hockey Player
5403 52nd Ave, Wetaskiwin AB T9A 0X8, Canada

Fonville, Chad E — Baseball Player
2338 Piney Green Road, Midway Park NC 28544, USA

Fonville, Charles — Track Athlete
1845 Wintergreen Court, Ann Arbor MI 48103, USA

Foo, Sharin — Singer, Guitarist, Bassist (Raveonettes)
Orchard, 100 Park Ave, #200, New York NY 10017, USA

Foor, James E (Jim) — Baseball Player
2018 Bolsover St, Houston TX 77005, USA

Foote, Adam D V — Ice Hockey Player
4656 S Ogden St, Englewood CO 80113, USA

Foote, Barry C — Baseball Player
2588 High Hammock Road, Johns Island SC 29455, USA

F

Foli - Foote

Foote, Chris D — Football Player
1140 Harbin Ridge Lane, Knoxville TN 37909, USA

Foote, Dan — Editorial Cartoonist
Dallas Times Herald, Editorial Dept, Herald Square, Dallas TX 75202, USA

Foote, Lawrence E (Larry), Jr — Football Player
24605 Franklin Farms Dr, Franklin MI 48025, USA

Footman, Dan E — Football Player
PO Box 37024, Jacksonville FL 32236, USA

Foppert, Jesse — Baseball Player
PO Box 150682, San Rafael CA 94915, USA

Foray, June — Actress
22745 Erwin St, Woodland Hills CA 91367, USA

Forbert, Steve — Singer, Guitarist, Songwriter
W N S Group, 6 Rolyn Hills Dr, Orangeburg NY 10962, USA

Forbes, Bryan — Director, Writer
Andrew Manso Mgmt, 288 Munster Road, London SW6 6BQ, England

Forbes, James A, Jr — Religious Leader
Riverside Church, Senior Minister Office, 490 Riverside Dr, New York NY 10027, USA

Forbes, Malcolm S (Steve), Jr — Editor
Forbes, President's Office, 60 5th Ave, New York NY 10011, USA

Forbes, Maya — Producer, Writer
I C M Partners, 10250 Constellation Blvd, #900, Los Angeles CA 90067 USA

Forbes, Michelle R — Actress
Hofflund/Polone, 9465 Wilshire Blvd, #420, Beverly Hills CA 90212 USA

Forbes, Patrick J (P J) — Baseball Player
9017 W Chartwell Circle, Wichita KS 67205, USA

Forbes, West — Singer (Five Satins)
Paramount Entertainment, 12 Kosakowski Dr, Morris Plains NJ 07590 USA

Forbes-Robinson, Elliott — Auto Racing Driver
7118 Vinewood Road, Sherrills Ford NC 28673, USA

Forbis, Clifton — Opera Singer
Columbia Artists Mgmt Inc, 1790 Broadway, #702, New York NY 10019 USA

Force, John — Drag Racing Driver
John Force Racing, 22722 Old Canal Road, Yorba Linda CA 92887, USA

Ford, Alissa — Actress
Innovative Artists, 1505 10th St, Santa Monica CA 90401 USA

Ford, Atina — Curling Athlete
Curling Assn, 1660 Vimont Court, Cumberland ON K4A 4J4, Canada

Ford, Benjamin C (Ben) — Baseball Player
1717 Applewood Place NE, Cedar Rapids IA 52402, USA

Ford, Bette — Actress
Innovative Artists, 1505 10th St, Santa Monica CA 90401 USA

Ford, Bruce — Opera Singer
Athole Still, Foresters Hall, 25-27 Wistrow St, London SE19 3BY, England

Ford, Candy — Actress
C E S D, 10635 Santa Monica Blvd, #130, Los Angeles CA 90025 USA

Ford, Charles G (Charlie) — Football Player
2995 South St, Beaumont TX 77702, USA

Ford, Cheryl — Basketball Player
Tulsa Shock, B O K Center, 200 S Denver, Tulsa OK 74103 USA

Ford, Christopher J (Chris) — Basketball Player, Coach
424 N Vendome Ave, Margate City NJ 08402, USA

Ford, Colin — Actor
Management 360, 9111 Wilshire Blvd, Beverly Hills CA 90210 USA

Ford, Courtney — Actress
Main Title Mgmt, 8383 Wilshire Blvd, #408, Beverly Hills CA 90211 USA

Ford, Curtis G (Curt) — Baseball Player
6306 Sprig Oak Court, #B, Saint Louis MO 63128, USA

Ford, Darnell G (Dan) — Baseball Player
1271 Linton Road, Benton LA 71006, USA

Ford, Donald (Don) — Basketball Player
519 W Quinto St, #B, Santa Barbara CA 93105, USA

Ford, Douglas (Doug) — Golfer
3737 Gulfstream Road, Delray Beach FL 33483, USA

Ford, Edward C (Whitey) — Baseball Player
PO Box 160, Sea Cliff NY 11579, USA

Ford, Eileen O — Businesswoman
Ford Models Inc, 111 5th Ave, #900, New York NY 10003 USA

Ford, Faith — Actress
Hofflund/Polone, 9465 Wilshire Blvd, #420, Beverly Hills CA 90212 USA

Ford, Frankie — Singer, Songwriter
Ken Keane Artists, PO Box 1875, Gretna LA 70054, USA

Ford, Gilbert (Gib) — Basketball Player, Coach
264 Edgemere Way E, Naples FL 34105, USA

Ford, Harrison — Actor
3555 N Moose Wilson Road, Jackson Hole WY 83001, USA

Ford, Henry — Football Player
7222 Shannon Road, Verona PA 15147, USA

Ford, J Lewis (Lew) — Baseball Player
2201 Lady Cornwall Dr, Lewisville TX 75056, USA

Ford, Jack — Commentator
CBS-TV, News Dept, 51 W 52nd St, New York NY 10019 USA

Ford, Katie — Businesswoman
Ford Models Inc, 111 5th Ave, #900, New York NY 10003 USA

Ford, Kevin A — Astronaut
3526 E 200 N, Hartford City IN 47348, USA

Ford, Lita — Singer, Guitarist (Runaways)
Monterey International, 200 W Superior St, #202, Chicago IL 60654 USA

Ford, Luke — Actor
W K T Public Relations, 9350 Wilshire Blvd, #450, Beverly Hills CA 90212 USA

Ford, Maria — Actress
Momentum Talent, 9401 Wilshire Blvd, #501, Beverly Hills CA 90212, USA

Ford, Mark — Publisher
Time Inc Sports Group, Publisher's Office, Time-Life Building, New York NY 10020, USA

Ford, Melyssa — Model, Actress
Don Buchwald/Fortitude, 6500 Wilshire Blvd, #2200, Los Angeles CA 90048 USA

Ford, Phil J, Jr — Basketball Player
2928 Cone Manor Lane, Raleigh NC 27613, USA
Ford, Ray — Actor
Rectangle Entertainment, 357 S Fairfax Ave, #414, Los Angeles CA 90036, USA
Ford, Richard — Writer
Ecco/Harper Collins Publishers, 10 E 53rd St, Cellar 1, New York NY 10022, USA
Ford, Robben — Jazz Guitarist (Yellowjackets)
Axis Artist Mgmt, 9715 Belmar Ave, Northridge CA 91324, USA
Ford, Robert A (Bob) — Basketball Player
202 Pathway Lane, West Lafayette IN 47906, USA
Ford, Scott — Businessman
Alltel Corp, PO Box 94255, Palatine IL 60094, USA
Ford, Thomas Mikal — Actor
TalentWorks, 3500 W Olive Ave, #1400, Burbank CA 91505 USA
Ford, Tom — Fashion Designer, Director
Creative Artists Agency, 2000 Ave of Stars, #100, Los Angeles CA 90067 USA
Ford, Trent — Actor
TalentWorks, 3500 W Olive Ave, #1400, Burbank CA 91505 USA
Ford, Wendell H — Governor, Senator, KY
423 Frederica St, #314, Owensboro KY 42301, USA
Ford, Willa — Singer, Model, Actress
A P A Talent/Literary Agency, 405 S Beverly Dr, #300, Beverly Hills CA 90212 USA
Ford, William Clay, Jr — Businessman
Ford Motor Co, American Road, Dearborn MI 48121, USA
Fordham, Julia — Singer, Songwriter
Vanguard Records, 2700 Pennsylvania Ave, #1100, Santa Monica CA 90404 USA
Fordham, Thomas J (Tom) — Baseball Player
14559 Miguel Lane, El Cajon CA 92021, USA
Fordyce, Brook A — Baseball Player
5 River Crest, Stuart FL 34996, USA
Foreman, Amanda — Actress
Lloyd & Kass Entertainment, 10202 Washington Blvd, Culver City CA 90232, USA
Foreman, Carol L T — Government Official
5600 Wisconsin Ave, #502, Chevy Chase MD 20815, USA
Foreman, Chris (Chrissie Boy) — Guitarist (Madness)
I T F, Ariel House, 74A Charlotte St, London W1T 4QJ, England
Foreman, George — Boxer
PO Box 14267, Humble TX 77347, USA
Foreman, Michael J — Astronaut
N A S A, Johnson Space Center, 2101 NASA Road, Houston TX 77058 USA
Foreman, Timothy D (Tim) — Singer, Bassist (Switchfoot)
The Firm, 2049 Century Park E, #2550, Los Angeles CA 90067 USA
Foreman, Walter E (Chuck) — Football Player
9716 Mill Creek Dr, Eden Prairie MN 55347, USA
Foremsky, Fred (Skee) — Bowler
914 Manchester Dr, Conroe TX 77304, USA
Forest, Michael — Actor
1327 N Vista, #203, Los Angeles CA 90046, USA
Forester, Nicole — Actress
Paradigm Agency, 360 N Crescent Dr, North Building, Beverly Hills CA 90210 USA
Forestier, Sara — Actress
Hamilton Hodell, 66-68 Margaret St, London W1W 8SR, England
Foret, Mickey P — Businessman
7829 Brookhollow Blvd, Frisco TX 75034, USA
Foret, Sarah — Actress
B/W/R, 9100 Wilshire Blvd, #500W, Beverly Hills CA 90212 USA
Forgeard, Noel — Businessman
85 Ave de Wagram, 75017 Paris, France
Forget, Guy — Tennis Player
Rue des Pacs 2, 2000 Neuchatel, Switzerland
Forke, Farrah — Actress
Pop Art Mgmt, 9615 Brighton Way, #426, Beverly Hills CA 90210, USA
Forlani, Arnaldo — Prime Minister, Italy
Piazzale Schumann 15, Rome, Italy
Forlani, Claire — Actress
Independent Talent Group, Oxford House, 76 Oxford St, London W1D 1BS, England
Forman, Donald J (Donnie) — Basketball Player
1532 Gormican Lane, Naples FL 34110, USA
Forman, Milos — Director
Aspland Mgmt, 245 W 55th St, #1102, New York NY 10019, USA
Forman, Stanley — Photojournalist
17 Cherry Road, Beverly MA 01915, USA
Forman, Tom — Cartoonist (Motley's Crew)
10544 James Road, Celina TX 75009, USA
Formia, Osvaldo — Harness Racing Trainer
6501 Winfield Blvd, #A10, Margate FL 33063, USA
Forney, G David, Jr — Computer Scientist
6 Coolidge Hill Road, Cambridge MA 02138, USA
Forney, Kynan L — Football Player
2046 Skybrooke Lane, Hoschton GA 30548, USA
Fornos, Werner H — Association Executive
Population Institute, 107 2nd St NE, Washington DC 20002, USA
Foronjy, Richard — Actor
House of Representatives, 1434 6th St, #1, Santa Monica CA 90401 USA
Forrest, Bayard — Basketball Player
300A Squaw Valley Place, Pagosa Springs CO 81147, USA
Forrest, Emma — Writer
Lutyens & Rubinstein, 231 Westbourne Park Road, London W11 1EB, England
Forrest, Frederic — Actor
11300 W Olympic Blvd, #610, Los Angeles CA 90064, USA
Forrest, Sally — Actress
1125 Angelo Dr, Beverly Hills CA 90210, USA
Forrest, Steve — Actor
2208 Crespi Lane, Westlake Village CA 91361, USA
Forrest, Steve — Drummer (Placebo)
Riverman Records, George House, Brecon Road, London W6 8PY, England

Forrestal, Robert P — Government Official, Financier
1200 Brookhaven Park Place NE, Atlanta GA 30319, USA

Forrester, Jay W — Inventor (Digital Storage Device)
Massachusetts Institute of Technology, Management School, Cambridge MA 02139, USA

Forrester, Patrick G — Astronaut
3923 Park Circle Way, Houston TX 77059, USA

Forsberg, Fred C — Football Player
1727 223rd Ave SE, Sammamish WA 98075, USA

Forsberg, Peter M — Ice Hockey Player
1155 Sherman St, Denver CO 80203, USA

Forsch, Kenneth R (Ken) — Baseball Player
881 S Country Glen Way, Anaheim CA 92808, USA

Forsee, Gary D — Businessman, Educator
University of Missouri System, President's Office, University Hall, Columbia MO 65211, USA

Forslund, Constance — Actress
165 W 46th St, #1109, New York NY 10036, USA

Forsman, Dan — Golfer
88 W 4500 N, Provo UT 84604, USA

Forsse, Ken — Inventor (Teddy Ruxpin), Animator
Alchemy II, 9207 Eton Ave, Chatsworth CA 91311, USA

Forst, Bill — Cartoonist
2320 Byer Road, Santa Cruz CA 95062, USA

Forster, K Dieter — Religious Leader
First Church of Christ Scientist, 175 Huntington Ave, Boston MA 02115, USA

Forster, Marc — Director, Producer
Management 360, 9111 Wilshire Blvd, Beverly Hills CA 90210 USA

Forster, Robert — Actor
Don Buchwald/Fortitude, 6500 Wilshire Blvd, #2200, Los Angeles CA 90048 USA

Forster, Terry J — Baseball Player
PO Box 711658, Santee CA 92072, USA

Forster, William H — Army General
10245 Fairfax Dr, Fort Belvoir VA 22060, USA

Forsyth, Bill — Director
20 Winton Dr, Glasgow G12 0QA, Scotland

Forsyth, Bruce — Actor, Comedian
Straidarran, Wentworth Dr, Virginia Water, Surrey GU25 4NY, England

Forsyth, David — Actor
C E S D, 10635 Santa Monica Blvd, #130, Los Angeles CA 90025 USA

Forsyth, Frederick — Writer
Trans World Publishers, 61-63 Oxbridge Road, Ealing, London W5 5SA, England

Forsyth, Rosemary — Actress
1591 Benedict Canyon, Beverly Hills CA 90210, USA

Forsythe, Gerald (Gary) — Auto Racing Executive
Forsythe Racing, 7231 Georgetown Road, Indianapolis IN 46268, USA

Forsythe, William — Actor
Innovative Artists, 1505 10th St, Santa Monica CA 90401 USA

Forsythe, William — Choreographer
Frankfurt Ballet, Untermainanlage 11, 60311 Frankfurt, Germany

Fort-Brescia, Bernardo — Architect
Arquitectonica International, 801 Brickell Ave, #1100, Miami FL 33131, USA

Forte, Allen — Musicologist
Columbia University, Music Dept, New York NY 10027, USA

Forte, Donald R (Ike) — Football Player
5811 Winchester Dr, Texarkana TX 75503, USA

Forte, Marlene — Actress, Producer, Director
Greater Visions Artists Talent Agency, 8981 W Sunset Blvd, #101, West Hollywood CA 90069 USA

Forte, Matthew G (Matt) — Football Player
2067 N Laurel Valley Dr, Vernon Hills IL 60061, USA

Forte, Will — Actor, Comedian
Mosiac Media Group, 9200 W Sunset Blvd, #1000, Los Angeles CA 90069 USA

Fortier, David E (Dave) — Ice Hockey Player
150 Kingsmount Blvd, Sudbury ON P3E 1K9, Canada

Fortier, Laurie — Actress
Vincent Cirrincione Assoc, 1516 N Fairfax Ave, Los Angeles CA 90046 USA

Fortin, Roman B — Football Player
10741 Bell Road, Duluth GA 30097, USA

Fortner, Nell — Basketball Coach
Auburn University, Athletic Dept, Auburn AL 36849, USA

Fortson, Daniel A (Danny) — Basketball Player
3447 W Blaine St, Seattle WA 98199, USA

Fortunato, Joseph F (Joe) — Football Player
PO Box 934, Natchez MS 39121, USA

Fortunato, Ron — Cinematographer
1 Columbus Place, #N5G, New York NY 10019, USA

Fortune, Jimmy — Singer (Statler Brothers)
American Major Talent, 8747 Highway 304, Hernando MS 38632, USA

Fortuno Burset, Luis G — Governor, Representative, PR
Governor's Office, La Fortaleza, PO Box 9020082, San Juan PR 00902 USA

Fosbury, Richard D (Dick) — Track Athlete
708 Canyon Run Blvd, Ketchum ID 83340, USA

Foss, Anita — Baseball Player
452 S Highland Ave, Los Angeles CA 90036, USA

Foss, Eric — Businessman
Pepsi Bottling Group, 1 Pepsi Way, #1, Somers NY 10589, USA

Foss, John W, II — Army General
16 Hampton Key, Williamsburg VA 23185, USA

Fossas, E Anthony (Tony) — Baseball Player
11302 NW 9th St, Plantation FL 33325, USA

Fosse, Raymond E (Ray) — Baseball Player
PO Box 567, Diablo CA 94528, USA

Fossey, Brigitte — Actress
Anne Alvares Correa, 34 Rue Jouffroy d'Abbans, 75017 Paris, France

Fossum, Casey P — Baseball Player
1087 White Bluff Dr, Whitney TX 76692, USA

Fossum, Michael E — Astronaut
822 Rolling Run Court, Houston TX 77062, USA

Foster of Thames Bank, Norman R — Architect
Foster Assoc, Riverside 3, 22 Hester Road, London SW11 4AN, England
Foster, Alan B — Baseball Player
10330 Grandview Dr, La Mesa CA 91941, USA
Foster, Alan Dean — Writer
Thranx Inc, PO Box 12757, Prescott AZ 86304, USA
Foster, Barry — Football Player
PO Box 750, Colleyville TX 76034, USA
Foster, Ben — Actor
Ken Jacobson Mgmt, 11271 Ventura Blvd, #464, Studio City CA 91604, USA
Foster, Catherine — Artist
19689 7th Ave NE, #351, Poulsbo WA 98370, USA
Foster, Corey J — Ice Hockey Player
71 Pine Ridge Dr, Arnprior ON K7S 3G8, Canada
Foster, Coy — Balloonist
5486 Glen Lakes Dr, Dallas TX 75231, USA
Foster, David — Producer
Paradigm Agency, 360 N Crescent Dr, North Building, Beverly Hills CA 90210 USA
Foster, David — Songwriter, Musician
3903 Carbon Canyon Road, Malibu CA 90265, USA
Foster, DeShaun X — Football Player
2391 Apple Tree Dr, Tustin CA 92780, USA
Foster, George — Football Player
4057 Meadowbrook Dr, Macon GA 31204, USA
Foster, George A — Baseball Player
15 E Putnam Ave, #320, Greenwich CT 06830, USA
Foster, Hunter — Actor, Singer
Gersh Agency, 41 Madison Ave, #3301, New York NY 10010 USA
Foster, Jeffrey D (Jeff) — Basketball Player
333 Pickwick Court, Noblesville IN 46062, USA
Foster, Jodie — Actress, Director
Egg Pictures, 21515 Hawthorne Blvd, #1250, Torrance CA 90503, USA
Foster, Jon — Actor
Gersh Agency, 9465 Wilshire Blvd, #600, Beverly Hills CA 90212 USA
Foster, Karen — Model, Actress
Playboy Promotions, 2706 Media Center Dr, Los Angeles CA 90065 USA
Foster, Lawrence T — Conductor
Opus 3 Artists, 470 Park Ave S, #900N, New York NY 10016 USA
Foster, Leonard N (Leo) — Baseball Player
699 Glensprings Dr, Cincinnati OH 45246, USA
Foster, Meg — Actress
741 Fort Ebey Road, Coupeville WA 98239, USA
Foster, Radney (Randy) — Singer, Songwriter
Fitzgerald Hartley, 1964 Wedgewood Ave, Nashville TN 37212 USA
Foster, Robert W (Bob) — Boxer
913 Valencia Dr NE, Albuquerque NM 87108, USA
Foster, Roderick A (Rod) — Basketball Player
1246 Armacost Ave, #105, Los Angeles CA 90025, USA
Foster, Roy A — Football Player
12110 Salem Dr, Granada Hills CA 91344, USA
Foster, Ruthie — Singer, Songwriter
Rosebud Agency, PO Box 170429, San Francisco CA 94117 USA
Foster, Sara — Actress
Innovative Artists, 1505 10th St, Santa Monica CA 90401 USA
Foster, Scott Michael — Actor
United Talent Agency, 9336 Civic Center Dr, Beverly Hills CA 90210 USA
Foster, Stan — Actor, Writer, Producer, Director
I C M Partners, 10250 Constellation Blvd, #900, Los Angeles CA 90067 USA
Foster, Stephen E (Steve) — Baseball Player
1020 Heathrow Dr, Frisco TX 75034, USA
Foster, Sutton — Actress, Singer
Creative Artists Agency, 2000 Ave of Stars, #100, Los Angeles CA 90067 USA
Foster, Todd (Kid) — Boxer
303 13th St NW, Great Falls MT 59404, USA
Foster, William E (Bill) — Basketball Coach
152 Hollywood Dr, Coppell TX 75019, USA
Fotiu, Nicholas E (Nick) — Ice Hockey Player
16 Backus River Road, East Falmouth MA 02536, USA
Foucault, Steven R (Steve) — Baseball Player
24353 Rolling View Court, Lutz FL 33559, USA
Foudy Sawyers, Judy (Julie) — Soccer Player, Model, Sportscaster
6208 Colina Pacifica, San Clemente CA 92673, USA
Fought, John, III — Golfer
5010 E Shea Blvd, #A217, Scottsdale AZ 85254, USA
Foules, Elbert — Football Player
633 E Ohea St, Greenville MS 38701, USA
Foulke, Keith C — Baseball Player
4844 W Electra Lane, Glendale AZ 85310, USA
Foulkes, Arthur A — Governor General, Bahamas
Governor General's Office, Government House, PO Box N8301, Nassau NP, Bahamas
Foulkes, Llyn — Artist
6010 Eucalyptus Lane, Los Angeles CA 90042, USA
Fountain, Clarence — Singer (Blind Boys of Alabama)
Blind Ambition Mgmt, 6 Courthouse Way, Jonesboro GA 30236, USA
Fountain, Peter D (Pete), Jr — Jazz Clarinetist
Paradise Artists, PO Box 1821, Ojai CA 93024 USA
Fourcade, Martin — Biathlete
Ski Federation, 50 Rue des Marquisats, BP 2451, 74011 Annecy Cedex, France
Fournier, Evan — Basketball Player
Denver Nuggets, Pepsi Center, 1000 Chopper Circle, Denver CO 80204 USA
Foust, Nina — Golfer
901 East Dr, Morehead City NC 28557, USA
Fouts, Daniel F (Dan) — Football Player, Sportscaster
16820 Varco Road, Bend OR 97701, USA
Fowke, Philip F — Concert Pianist
Patrick Garvey, 59 Lansdowne Place, Hove, East Sussex BN3 1FL, England

Fowler, Beth — Actress, Singer
Gage Group, 315 W 57th St, #4H, New York NY 10019 USA

Fowler, Calvin B (Cal) — Basketball Player
10121 Godspeed Dr, Ocean City MD 21842, USA

Fowler, E Michael C — Architect
Branches, Giffords Road, RD 3, Blenheim, New Zealand

Fowler, Mark S — Government Official
Latham & Watkins, 555 11th St NW, #1000, Washington DC 20004, USA

Fowler, Rick Y (Rickie) — Golfer
Professional Golfer's Assn, PO Box 109601, Palm Beach Gardens FL 33410 USA

Fowler, Ryan O — Football Player
1713 Montclair Blvd, Brentwood TN 37027, USA

Fowler, W Wyche, Jr — Senator, GA; Diplomat
701 A St NE, Washington DC 20002, USA

Fowles, Sylvia — Basketball Player
Chicago Sky, 20 W Kinzie St, #1010, Chicago IL 60654 USA

Fowlkes, Alan K — Baseball Player
405 Emerald Lake Dr, Lumberton NC 28358, USA

Fowlkes, Curtis — Trombonist (Jazz Passengers)
Cross Road Mgmt, 45 W 11th St, #7B, New York NY 10011, USA

Fox Quesada, Vicente — President, Mexico
San Francisco del Rincon, San Cristobal, Guanajuato 36440 CP, Mexico

Fox, Andy — Baseball Player
9087 Tarmac Court, Fair Oaks CA 95628, USA

Fox, Bernard — Actor
6601 Burnet Ave, Van Nuys CA 91405, USA

Fox, Chad D — Baseball Player
6007 Windrose Hollow Lane, Spring TX 77379, USA

Fox, Charles I — Composer, Conductor
American International Artists, 356 Pine Valley Road, Hoosick Falls NY 12090, USA

Fox, Edward — Actor
25 Maida Ave, London W2 1ST, England

Fox, Emilia — Actress
Tavistock Wood Management, 45 Conduit St, London W1S 2YN, England , USA

Fox, George — Singer, Songwriter
Agency Group Ltd, 142 W 57th St, #600, New York NY 10019 USA

Fox, Greg — Ice Hockey Player
323 Resource Parkway # 6A, Winder GA 30680, USA

Fox, Harold — Basketball Player
6511 Wilburn D, Capitol Heights MD 20743, USA

Fox, J Carter — Businessman
1467 Floyd Ave, Richmond VA 23220, USA

Fox, Jack — Actor
I C M Partners, 10250 Constellation Blvd, #900, Los Angeles CA 90067 USA

Fox, James — Actor
Dalzell & Beresford, 26 Astwood Mews, London SW7 4DE, England

Fox, Jessica — Actress
Associated International Mgmt, Fairfax House, Fulwood Place, London WC1V 6HU, England

Fox, Jim — Basketball Player
4136 N 52nd St, Phoenix AZ 85018, USA

Fox, John — Football Coach
7512 Baltusrol Lane, Charlotte NC 28210, USA

Fox, Jorja — Actress
Framework Entertainment, 9057 Nemo St, #C, West Hollywood CA 90069 USA

Fox, Kerry — Actress
R G M Associates, 64-76 Kippax St, #202, Surry Hills NSW 2010, Australia

Fox, Marye Anne P — Educator, Organic Chemist
5926 Sagebrush Road, La Jolla CA 92037, USA

Fox, Matthew — Actor
Management 360, 9111 Wilshire Blvd, Beverly Hills CA 90210 USA

Fox, Megan — Actress
I C M Partners, 10250 Constellation Blvd, #900, Los Angeles CA 90067 USA

Fox, Michael J — Actor
B/W/R, 9100 Wilshire Blvd, #500W, Beverly Hills CA 90212 USA

Fox, Neil — Actor, Entertainer
Magic 105.4, Mappin House, 4 Winsley St, London W1W 8HF, England

Fox, Paula — Writer
Robert Lescher, 47 E 19th St, New York NY 10003, USA

Fox, Rachel G — Actress
Paradigm Agency, 360 N Crescent Dr, North Building, Beverly Hills CA 90210 USA

Fox, Samantha K — Singer, Model
Richard Walters, PO Box 2789, Toluca Lake NY 91610 USA

Fox, Terrence E (Terry) — Baseball Player
2312 Sugar Mill Road, New Iberia LA 70563, USA

Fox, Timothy R (Tim) — Football Player
11 Glover Ave, Hull MA 02045, USA

Fox, Tom — Opera Singer
Columbia Artists Mgmt Inc, 1790 Broadway, #702, New York NY 10019 USA

Fox, Ulrich A (Rick) — Basketball Player, Actor
17530 Ventura Blvd, #201, Encino CA 91316, USA

Fox, Vernon L, III — Football Player
6704 Willow Run Court, Las Vegas NV 89108, USA

Fox, Vivica A — Actress
Foxy Brown Productions, PO Box 6305, Woodland Hills CA 91365, USA

Fox, Wesley L — Vietnam War Marine Corps Hero (CMH)
855 Deercraft Dr, Blacksburg VA 24060, USA

Foxworth, Domonique — Football Player
3533 S Sherwood Road SE, Smyrna GA 30082, USA

Foxworth, Robert — Actor
C E S D, 10635 Santa Monica Blvd, #130, Los Angeles CA 90025 USA

Foxworthy, Jeff — Actor, Comedian
Parallel Entertainment, 9420 Wilshire Blvd, #250, Beverly Hills CA 90212 USA

Foxx, Jamie — Actor, Comedian, Singer
1355 W Potrero Road, Thousand Oaks CA 91361, USA

Foye, Randy — Basketball Player
Washington Wizards, M C I Centre, 601 F St NW, Washington DC 20004 USA

Foyle, Adonal D
174 Crestview Dr, Orinda CA 94563, USA — Basketball Player

Foyt, Anthony J (A J), Jr
Foyt Racing, 19480 Stokes Road, Waller TX 77484, USA — Auto Racing Driver

Foytack, Paul E
1910 Portview Dr, Spring Hill TX 37174, USA — Baseball Player

Frabotta, Don
PO Box 962, Douglas MA 01516, USA — Actor

Fraccaro, Walter
Opera et Concert, 37 Rue de la Chaussee d'Antin, 75009 Paris, France — Opera Singer

Fradon, Dana
2 Brushy Hill Road, Newtown CT 06470, USA — Cartoonist

Fradon, Ramona
Tribune Media Services, 435 N Michigan Ave, #1500, Chicago IL 60611 USA — Cartoonist (Brenda Starr)

Frailing, Kenneth D (Ken)
2150 Shadow Oaks Road, Sarasota FL 34240, USA — Baseball Player

Frain, James
A P A Talent/Literary Agency, 405 S Beverly Dr, #300, Beverly Hills CA 90212 USA — Actor

Fraisse, Robert
Paradigm Agency, 360 N Crescent Dr, North Building, Beverly Hills CA 90210 USA — Cinematographer

Fraiture, Nikolai
M V O Ltd, 370 7th Ave, #807, New York NY 10001, USA — Bassist (Strokes)

Frakes, Jonathan
Paradigm Agency, 360 N Crescent Dr, North Building, Beverly Hills CA 90210 USA — Actor, Director

Fraley, Mark
Northern Iowa University, Athletic Dept, Cedar Falls IA 50614, USA — Football Coach

Fralic, William (Bill)
280 Galsworthy Court, Roswell GA 30075, USA — Football Player

Frampton, Peter
C E S D, 10635 Santa Monica Blvd, #130, Los Angeles CA 90025 USA — Singer, Guitarist, Songwriter

France, Brian
1151 N Halifax Ave, Daytona Beach FL 32118, USA — Auto Racing Executive

France, F Douglas (Doug), Jr
6056 Great Falls Ave, Las Vegas NV 89110, USA — Football Player

Francella, Meaghan
16 Maywood Ave, Port Chester NY 10573, USA — Golfer

Franchitti, G Dario M
G P Sports Mgmt, 299 Milwaukee St, #329, Denver CO 80020, USA — Auto Racing Driver

Francis, Clarence (Bevo)
18340 Steubenville Pike Road, Salineville OH 43945, USA — Basketball Player

Francis, Connie
6413 NW 102nd, Pompano Beach FL 33076, USA — Singer, Actress

Francis, Emile P
7220 Crystal Lake Dr, West Palm Beach FL 33411, USA — Ice Hockey Player, Coach

Francis, Genie
10990 Wilshire Blvd, #1600, Los Angeles CA 90024, USA — Actress

Francis, Hubert
I M G Artists, Hogarth Business Park, Chiswick, London W4 2TH, England — Opera Singer

Francis, James
2727 Crossview Dr, Houston TX 77063, USA — Football Player

Francis, Jeffrey W (Jeff)
3191 Quitman St, Denver CO 80212, USA — Baseball Player

Francis, Norman C
Xavier University, President's Office, New Orleans LA 70125, USA — Educator

Francis, Robert
Aeronaut Records, PO Box 361432, Los Angeles CA 90036, USA — Singer

Francis, Robert E (Bob)
23725 N 75th Place, Scottsdale AZ 85255, USA — Ice Hockey Player, Coach

Francis, Ron
12312 Birchfalls Dr, Raleigh NC 27614, USA — Ice Hockey Player

Francis, Russell R (Russ)
800 Putney Road, Brattleboro VT 05301, USA — Football Player

Francis, Steve D
632 Pifer Road, Houston TX 77024, USA — Basketball Player

Francis, Wallace D (Wally)
2452 Wilshire Way, Douglasville GA 30135, USA — Football Player

Francis, William (Bill)
Artists International, 9850 Sandalwood Blvd, #458, Boca Raton FL 33428, USA — Keyboardist, Singer

Francisco, Aaron
5064 W Geronimo St, Chandler AZ 85226, USA — Football Player

Francisco, Don
Univision, 605 3rd Ave, #1200, New York NY 10158, USA — Entertainer

Francisco, Franklin (Frank)
Texas Rangers, Ameriquest Field, 1000 Ballpark Way, #306, Arlington TX 76011 USA — Baseball Player

Francks, Rainbow Sun
Characters Talent Mgmt, 8 Elm St, Toronto ON M5G 1G7, Canada — Actor

Franco Gomez, L Frederico
Palacio de Gobinerno, Ave Mariscal Lopez, 1807 Asuncion, Paraguay — President,

Franco, Carlos
10561 NW 51st St, Doral FL 33178, USA — Golfer

Franco, Dave
Paradigm Agency, 360 N Crescent Dr, North Building, Beverly Hills CA 90210 USA — Actor

Franco, David
Global Artists Agency, 6253 Hollywood Blvd, #508, Los Angeles CA 90028 USA — Cinematographer

Franco, James
Creative Artists Agency, 2000 Ave of Stars, #100, Los Angeles CA 90067 USA — Actor

Franco, John A
111 Helena Road, Staten Island NY 10309, USA — Baseball Player

Franco, Julio C
651 NE 23rd Court, Pompano Beach FL 33064, USA — Baseball Player

Franco, L Federico
Palacio de Gobinerno, Ave Mariscal Lopez, 1807 Asuncion, Paraguay — President, Paraguay

Franco, Matthew N (Matt)
1008 Clear Sky Place, Simi Valley CA 93065, USA — Baseball Player

Franco, Ramon
Greene Assoc, 1901 Ave of Stars, #130, Los Angeles CA 90067 USA — Actor

Francoeur, Jeffrey B (Jeff)   Baseball Player
3111 Willowstone Dr, Duluth GA 30096, USA

Francois, Jacques   Actor
Artmedia, 20 Ave Rapp, 75007 Paris, France

Francois, Mike   Body Builder
PO Box 3184, Westerville OH 43086, USA

Francona, John P (Tito)   Baseball Player
1109 Penn Ave, New Brighton PA 15066, USA

Francona, Terry J (Tito)   Baseball Player, Manager
750 Newton St, Chestnut Hill MA 02467, USA

Frandsen, Kevin V   Baseball Player
2521 Coffee Ave, San Jose CA 95125, USA

Frank Chang ting Hsieh   Prime Minister, Taiwan
Premier's Office, 1 Chunghsiao East Road, Section 1, Taipei, Taiwan

Frank, Anthony A   Educator
Colorado State University, President's Office, Fort Collins CO 80523, USA

Frank, Anthony M   Government Official, Financier
Independent Bancorp, 3800 N Central, Phoenix AZ 85012, USA

Frank, Charles   Actor
S D B Partners, 1801 Ave of Stars, #902, Los Angeles CA 90067 USA

Frank, Claude   Concert Pianist
Columbia Artists Mgmt Inc, 1790 Broadway, #702, New York NY 10019 USA

Frank, David Michael   Composer
Soundtrack Music, 229 Cloverfield Blvd, Santa Monica CA 90405, USA

Frank, Diana   Actress
The Agency, 3711 Ocean Front Walk, #1, Marina del Rey CA 90292 USA

Frank, Donald L   Football Player
2039 Weston Green Loop, Cary NC 27513, USA

Frank, Gary   Actor
861 S Bundy Dr, Los Angeles CA 90049, USA

Frank, Joanna   Actress
1274 Capri Dr, Pacific Palisades CA 90272, USA

Frank, Joe   Actor
I C M Partners, 10250 Constellation Blvd, #900, Los Angeles CA 90067 USA

Frank, John E   Football Player
Medical Hair Restoration, 150 Central Park S, #299, New York NY 10019, USA

Frank, Louis A   Astronomer
University of Iowa, Astronomy Dept, Iowa City IA 52242, USA

Frank, Pamela   Concert Violinist
Opus 3 Artists, 470 Park Ave S, #900N, New York NY 10016 USA

Frank, S Michael (Mike)   Baseball Player
1343 W 19th St, Upland CA 91784, USA

Frank, Scott   Director, Writer
Creative Artists Agency, 2000 Ave of Stars, #100, Los Angeles CA 90067 USA

Frank, Tellis S   Basketball Player
4936 Van Noord Ave, Sherman Oaks CA 91423, USA

Franke, William A (Bill)   Businessman
Spirit Airlines, 2800 Executive Way, Miramar FL 33025, USA

Frankee   Singer
Levine Communication Office, 10333 Ashton Ave, Los Angeles CA 90024, USA

Frankel, Bethenny   Chef, Entertainer, Writer
Creative Artists Agency, 2000 Ave of Stars, #100, Los Angeles CA 90067 USA

Frankel, Max   Editor
New York Times, Editorial Dept, 229 W 43rd St, New York NY 10036, USA

Frankel, Neil   Interior Designer
Frankel & Coleman, 727 S Dearborn St, #412, Chicago IL 60605, USA

Franken, Al   Senator, Actor, Comedian, Writer
US Senate, Hart Office Building, Washington DC 20510 USA

Frankfort, Lew   Businessman
Coach Inc, 516 W 34th St, Basement 5, New York NY 10001, USA

Frankie J   Singer, Songwriter
Esterman Entertainment, PO Box 214, Riva MD 21140, USA

Franklin, Anthony R (Tony)   Football Player
117 Shady Trail St, San Antonio TX 78232, USA

Franklin, Aretha   Singer
2948 Turtle Pond Court, Bloomfield Hills MI 48302, USA

Franklin, Aubrayo R   Football Player
1 Castleton Court, Johnson City TN 37615, USA

Franklin, Barbara Hackman   Secretary, Commerce
1875 Perkins St, Bristol CT 06010, USA

Franklin, Bobby R   Football Player
384 Country Club Dr, Senatobia MS 38668, USA

Franklin, Bonnie   Actress
C E S D, 10635 Santa Monica Blvd, #130, Los Angeles CA 90025 USA

Franklin, Byron P   Football Player
2613 Singapore Dr, Birmingham AL 35211, USA

Franklin, Carl M   Director, Writer
I C M Partners, 10250 Constellation Blvd, #900, Los Angeles CA 90067 USA

Franklin, Diane   Actress
Third Hill Entertainment, 195 S Beverly Dr, #400, Beverly Hills CA 90212, USA

Franklin, G Wayne   Baseball Player
PO Box 679, North East MD 21901, USA

Franklin, Howard   Director, Writer
W M E Entertainment, 9601 Wilshire Blvd, #300, Beverly Hills CA 90210 USA

Franklin, John   Actor
Gilla Roos, 9744 Wilshire Blvd, #203, Beverly Hills CA 90212 USA

Franklin, Jon D   Journalist
9650 Strickland Road, Raleigh NC 27615, USA

Franklin, Kirk   Singer, Songwriter
Paradigm Agency, 360 N Crescent Dr, North Building, Beverly Hills CA 90210 USA

Franklin, Marcus Carl   Actor, Singer
Don Buchwald/Fortitude, 10 E 44th St, New York NY 10017 USA

Franklin, Melissa   Physicist
Harvard University, Physics Dept, Cambridge MA 02138, USA

Franklin, Melissa J (Missy)   Swimmer
Colorado Stars Swim Club, 6400 S Lewiston Way, Aurora CO 80016, USA

Franklin, Micah I
3948 E Lafayette Ave, Gilbert AZ 85298, USA — Baseball Player

Franklin, Nelson
W M E Entertainment, 9601 Wilshire Blvd, #300, Beverly Hills CA 90210 USA — Actor

Franklin, Robert M, Jr
Morehouse College, President's Office, 830 Westview Dr SW, Atlanta GA 30314, USA — Educator

Franklin, Ronnie
Max Bauer's Cabinet Shop, 12811 Folly Quarter Road, Ellicott City MD 21042, USA — Thoroughbred Racing Jockey

Franklin, Roshawn
B/W/R, 9100 Wilshire Blvd, #500W, Beverly Hills CA 90212 USA — Actor

Franklin, Ryan R
1009 Muirfield Dr, Shawnee OK 74801, USA — Baseball Player

Franklin, Scott
Protozoa Films, 104 N 7th St, Brooklyn NY 11211, USA — Producer

Franklin, Shirley
Mayor's Office, City Hall, 55 Trinity Ave S, Atlanta GA 30303, USA — Mayor, Atlanta

Franklin, William
920 La Sombra Dr, San Marcos CA 92078, USA — Bowling Executive

Franklyn, Sabina
C C A Mgmt, 4 Court Lodge, 48 Sloane Square, London SW1W 8AT, England — Actress

Franks, Daniel L (Bubba)
108 Solomon Lane, Midland TX 79705, USA — Football Player

Franks, Elvis
2147 Rusk St, Beaumont TX 77701, USA — Football Player

Franks, Frederick M, Jr
5016 Kensington High St, Naples FL 34105, USA — Army General

Franks, Lucinda L
64 E 86th St, New York NY 10028, USA — Journalist

Franks, Michael
A P A Talent/Literary Agency, 405 S Beverly Dr, #300, Beverly Hills CA 90212 USA — Singer, Songwriter, Guitarist

Franks, Tommy R (Tom)
Franks Assoc, 15273 N 2280 Road, Roosevelt OK 73564, USA — Army General

Frankston, Robert M (Bob)
Software Arts Inc, 675 Massachusetts Ave, Boston MA 02118, USA — Computer Software Designer (VisiCalc)

Franquin, Andre
21 Ave Belelaere, 1170 Brussels, Belgium — Cartoonist

Fransioli, Thomas A
55 Dodges Row, Wenham MA 01984, USA — Artist

Frantí, Michael
Creative Artists Agency, 2000 Ave of Stars, #100, Los Angeles CA 90067 USA — Singer (Spearhead)

Frantz, Adrienne
Innovative Artists, 1505 10th St, Santa Monica CA 90401 USA — Actress

Frantz, Chris
Premier Talent, 3 E 54th St, #1100, New York NY 10022 USA — Drummer (Talking Heads, Tom Tom Club)

Frantz, Justus
Osterbekstr 90B, 22083 Hamburg, Germany — Concert Pianist

Franz, Dennis
PO Box 5370, Santa Barbara CA 93150, USA — Actor

Franz, Judy R
American Physical Society, 1 Physics Eclipse, College Park MD 20740, USA — Physicist

Franz, Ron
8590 Beaverwood Dr, Germantown TN 38138, USA — Basketball Player

Franz, S Todd
5629 N Classen Blvd, Oklahoma City OK 73118, USA — Football Player

Franzen, Johan
22726 Summer Lane, Novi MI 48374, USA — Ice Hockey Player

Franzen, Jonathan
Farrar Straus Giroux, 18 W 18th St, #700, New York NY 10011 USA — Writer

Frasca, Robert J
Zimmer Gunsul Frasca, 1223 SW Washington St, #200, Portland OR 97205, USA — Architect

Frascatore, John V
PO Box 1411, Brooksville FL 34605, USA — Baseball Player

Frasconi, Antonio
26 Dock Road, Norwalk CT 06854, USA — Artist

Frase, Paul M
124 Crossroad Lakes Dr, Ponte Vedra FL 32082, USA — Football Player

Fraser, Antonia
Curtis Brown Group, 28-29 Haymarket St, #500, London SW1Y 4SP, England — Writer

Fraser, Brad
Great North Artists Mgmt, 350 Dupont Ave, Toronto ON M5R 1V9, Canada — Writer

Fraser, Brendan
Brillstein Entertainment Partners, 9150 Wilshire Blvd, #350, Beverly Hills CA 90212 USA — Actor

Fraser, Curt
2205 Whitney Pointe Dr, Chesterfield MO 63005, USA — Ice Hockey Player, Coach

Fraser, Dawn
87 Birchgrove Road, Balmain NSW 2041, Australia — Swimmer

Fraser, Elisabeth
International Talent Booking, Ariel House, 74A Charlotte St, #100 London W1T 4QJ, England — Singer (Cocteau Twins)

Fraser, Honor
Select Model Mgmt, Archer House, 43 King St, London WC2E 8RJ, England — Model

Fraser, Hugh
3 Gate Apartments, 2 Chepstow Road, London W2 5BH, England — Actor

Fraser, J Malcolm
101 Collins St, Level 2, Melbourne VIC 3000, Australia — Prime Minister, Australia

Fraser, Laura
Emptage Hallett, 14 Rathbone Place, London W1T 1HT, England — Actress

Fraser, Liz
Peter Charlesworth, 68 Old Brompton Road, #200, London SW7 3LQ, England — Actress

Fraser, Neale A
21 Bolton Ave, Hampton VIC 3188, Australia — Tennis Player

Fraser, Toa
I C M Partners, 10250 Constellation Blvd, #900, Los Angeles CA 90067 USA — Director

Fraser, William M, III
Commander, Air Combat Command, Langley Air Force Base VA 23665 USA — Air Force General

Frasor, Jason A
15043 Landings Lane, Oak Forest IL 60452, USA — Baseball Player

Frassinelli, Adriano
Olympic Committee, Foro Italico, Largo Lauro de Bosis 15, 00135 Rome, Italy — Bobsled Athlete

Fratello, Michael R (Mike)
7642 Fisher Island Dr, Miami Beach FL 33109, USA — Basketball Coach, Sportscaster

Fratianne Maricich, Linda S
3352 Whispering Glen Court, Simi Valley CA 93065, USA — Figure Skater

Frayn, Michael
Greene & Heaton, 37A Goldhawk Road, London W12 8QQ, England — Writer

Frazar, Harrison
3208 Villanova St, Dallas TX 75225, USA — Golfer

Frazier, A Louis (Lou)
1371 N Concord Ave, Chandler AZ 85225, USA — Baseball Player

Frazier, Amy
Octagon Worldwide, 1751 Pinnacle Dr, #1500, McLean VA 22102 USA — Tennis Player

Frazier, Andre
9650 Fallshill Circle, Cincinnati OH 45231, USA — Football Player

Frazier, Charles
I C M Partners, 10250 Constellation Blvd, #900, Los Angeles CA 90067 USA — Writer

Frazier, Charles D (Charlie0
4018 Brookston St, Houston TX 77045, USA — Football Player

Frazier, Dallas
RR 5 Box 133, Longhollow Pike, Gallatin TN 37066, USA — Singer, Songwriter

Frazier, George A
6886 S Evanston Ave, Tulsa OK 74136, USA — Baseball Player

Frazier, Guy S
3944 Dickson Ave, Cincinnati OH 45229, USA — Football Player

Frazier, Herman
1024 E Frye Road, #1011, Phoenix AZ 85048, USA — Track Athlete

Frazier, Ian
Farrar Straus Giroux, 18 W 18th St, #700, New York NY 10011 USA — Writer

Frazier, Kevin
250 President St, #201, Baltimore MD 21202, USA — Actor

Frazier, Leslie A
17559 Bearpath Trail, Eden Prairie MN 55347, USA — Football Player, Coach

Frazier, Owsley B
Brown-Forman Corp, 850 Dixie Highway, Louisville KY 40210, USA — Businessman

Frazier, Sheila
J K A Talent Agency, 12725 Ventura Blvd, #H, Studio City CA 91604, USA — Actress

Frazier, Stan
Lava/Atlantic Records, 9229 W Sunset Blvd, #900, West Hollywood CA 90069, USA — Drummer (Sugar Ray)

Frazier, Walter (Clyde), II
200 E 82nd St, New York NY 10028, USA — Basketball Player

Frazier, Will
PO Box 389772, Duncanville TX 75138, USA — Basketball Player

Frazier, Willie
6203 Bankside Dr, Houston TX 77096, USA — Football Player

Frears, Stephen A
Casorotto Ramsay, Waverley House, 7-12 Noel St, London W1F 8GQ, England — Director

Freberg, Stanley V (Stan)
Radio Spirits, PO Box 3107, Wallingford CT 06494, USA — Actor, Comedian

Frechette, Sylvie
Cirque du Soleil, 8400 2nd Ave, Montreal QC H1Z 4M6, Canada — Synchronized Swimmer

Frederick, Andrew B (Andy)
7247 Alexander Dr, Dallas TX 75214, USA — Football Player

Frederick, Kevin
5701 Foxlake Dr, #A, North Fort Myers FL 33917, USA — Baseball Player

Frederick-Blanchette, Marcia
105 High St, Assonet MA 02702, USA — Gymnast

Fredericks, Frank (Frankie)
4497 Wimbledon Dr, Provo UT 84604, USA — Track Athlete

Fredericks, Fred
PO Box 475, Eastham MA 02642, USA — Cartoonist (Mandrake the Magician)

Frederickson, Ivan C (Tucker)
12414 Indian Road, North Palm Beach FL 33408, USA — Football Player

Frederickson, Scott E
20703 Turning Leaf Lake Court, Cypress TX 77433, USA — Baseball Player

Frederik
Amalienborg Palace, 1257 Copenhagen K, Denmark — Prince, Denmark

Fredette, James T (Jimmer)
Sacramento Kings, Arco Arena, 1 Sports Parkway, Sacramento CA 95834 USA — Basketball Player

Fredrickson, Robert J (Rob)
8312 N 50th St, Paradise Valley AZ 85253, USA — Football Player

Fredriksson, Marie
D & D Mgmt, Drottning Gatan 55, 111 21 Stockholm, Sweden — Singer, Songwriter (Roxette)

Free, Helen M
3752 E Jackson Blvd, Elkhart IN 46516, USA — Chemist, Inventor (Glucose Detector)

Free, Lloyd B (World)
1131 E County Lane Road, Lakewood NJ 08701, USA — Basketball Player, Coach, Executive

Freed, Jack H
108 Homestead Circle, Ithaca NY 14850, USA — Chemist

Freedman, Alix M
Wall Street Journal, Editorial Dept, 1 World Financial Center, New York NY 10281 USA — Journalist

Freedman, Eric
Detroit News, Editorial Dept, 615 W Lafayette Blvd, Detroit MI 48226, USA — Journalist

Freedman, Ronald
1200 Earhart Road, #228, Ann Arbor MI 48105, USA — Sociologist

Freeh, Louis J
Saint Martin's Press, 175 5th Ave, #400, New York NY 10010 USA — Law Enforcement Official

Freehan, William A (Bill)
6999 Indian Garden Road, Petoskey MI 49770, USA — Baseball Player

Freel, Ryan P
4409 Stone Meadow Dr, Orlando FL 32826, USA — Baseball Player

Freelon, Nnenna
Ed Keene Assoc, 573 Pleasant St, Winthrop MA 02152, USA — Singer

Freeman, Antonio M
PO Box 450718, Fort Lauderdale FL 33345, USA — Football Player

Freeman, Arturo C
PO Box 551612, Fort Lauderdale FL 33355, USA — Football Player

Freeman, Bobby
Lustig Talent, PO Box 770850, Orlando FL 32877 USA — Singer

Freeman, Cassidy
Paul Kohner, 9300 Wilshire Blvd, #555, Beverly Hills CA 90212 USA — Actress

Freeman, Catherine A (Cathy)
Jane Cowmeadow, Bron Madigan, PO Box 5138, Ringwood VIC 3134, Australia — Track Athlete

Freeman, Charles W, Jr
Project International, 1800 K St NW, #1010, Washington DC 20006, USA — Diplomat

Freeman, Gary C
PO Box 1399, Albany OR 97321, USA — Basketball Player

Freeman, Gregory A
PO Box 680922, Marietta GA 30068, USA — Writer

Freeman, Harold P
Lauren Cancer Prevention Center, 1919 Madison Ave, New York NY 10035, USA — Oncologist

Freeman, Isaac
Keith Case Assoc, 1025 17th Ave S, #200, Nashville TN 37212 USA — Singer

Freeman, J E
Opus Entertainment, 5225 Wilshire Blvd, #905, Los Angeles CA 90036, USA — Actor

Freeman, Jennifer
Pakula/King, 9229 W Sunset Blvd, #315, West Hollywood CA 90069 USA — Actress, Model

Freeman, Jimmy L
4716 E 106th St, Tulsa OK 74137, USA — Baseball Player

Freeman, Jonathan
Bauman Redanty Shaul Agency, 5757 Wilshire Blvd, #473, Los Angeles CA 90036 USA — Actor

Freeman, LaVel M
8941 Laguna Place Way, Elk Grove CA 95758, USA — Baseball Player

Freeman, Martin
United Talent Agency, 9336 Civic Center Dr, Beverly Hills CA 90210 USA — Actor

Freeman, Marvin
20135 Mohawk Trail, Olympia Fields IL 60461, USA — Baseball Player

Freeman, Morgan
Creative Artists Agency, 2000 Ave of Stars, #100, Los Angeles CA 90067 USA — Actor

Freeman, Paul
Ken McReddie Assoc, 11 Connaught Place, London W2 2ET, England — Actor

Freeman, R Matthew (Matt)
Leave Home Booking, 10 W Broadway, #608, Salt Lake City UT 84101, USA — Singer, Bassist (Rancid)

Freeman, Rich
Paramount Entertainment, 12 Kosakowski Dr, Morris Plains NJ 07590 USA — Singer (Five Satins)

Freeman, Richard
Economic Research Bureau, 1050 Massachusetts Ave, Cambridge MA 02138, USA — Economist

Freeman, Robin
1112 1st St, Coronado CA 92118, USA — Golfer

Freeman, Rod
6308 Murray Lane, Brentwood TN 37027, USA — Basketball Player

Freeman, Yvette
Stone Manners Salners, 9911 W Pico Blvd, #1400, Los Angeles CA 90035 USA — Actress, Singer

Freeney, Dwight J
11021 Hintocks Circle, Carmel IN 46032, USA — Football Player

Freese, David R
Saint Louis Cardinals, Busch Stadium, 250 Stadium Plaza, Saint Louis MO 63102 USA — Baseball Player

Freese, Eugene L (Gene)
6504 Glendale St, Metairie LA 70003, USA — Baseball Player

Freese, Josh
The Firm, 2049 Century Park E, #2550, Los Angeles CA 90067 USA — Drummer (9 Inch Nails, Perfect Circle)

Freeway
Agency Group Ltd, 142 W 57th St, #600, New York NY 10019 USA — Rap Artist

Freeze, Hugh
University of Mississippi, Athletic Dept, University MS 38677, USA — Football Coach

Fregosi, James L (Jim)
1092 Copeland Court, Tarpon Springs FL 34688, USA — Baseball Player, Manager

Frehley, Paul D (Ace)
Creative Artists Agency, 2000 Ave of Stars, #100, Los Angeles CA 90067 USA — Singer, Guitarist (Kiss)

Frei Ruiz-Tagle, Eduardo
Christian Democratic Party, O'Higgins 1460, #20, Santiago, Chile — President, Chile

Frei, Emil, III
Dana-Farber Cancer Institute, 44 Binney St, Boston MA 02115, USA — Oncologist

Frei, Tanya
Curling Assn, PO Box 606, 3000 Bern, Switzerland — Curling Athlete

Freiberger, Marcus
985 US Highway 64 W, Mocksville NC 27028, USA — Basketball Player

Freidheim, Cyrus
Chiquita Brands International, 250 E 5th St, #2600, Cincinnati OH 45202, USA — Businessman

Freilicher, Jane
51 5th Ave, New York NY 10003, USA — Artist

Freire, Nelson
Columbia Artists Mgmt Inc, 1790 Broadway, #702, New York NY 10019 USA — Concert Pianist

Freireich, Emil J
M D Anderson Medical Center, 1515 Holcombe Blvd, #207, Houston TX 77030 USA — Physician

Freisleben, David J (Dave)
1326 Diamante Dr, Pasadena TX 77504, USA — Baseball Player

Freitas, Acelino (Popo)
Banner Promotions, 1231 Bainbridge St, Philadelphia PA 19147, USA — Boxer

Freitas, Rockne C (Rocky)
2667 E Manoa Road, Honolulu HI 96822, USA — Football Player

Frelich, Phyllis
Artists Group, 3345 Wilshire Blvd, #915, Los Angeles CA 90010, USA — Actress

Fremaux, Louis J F
25 Edencroft, Wheeley's Road, Birmingham B15 2LW, England — Conductor

French, Dawn
United Agents, 12-26 Lexington St, London W1F 0LE, England — Actress, Comedienne

French, Heather R
567 Circle Dr, Maysville KY 41056, USA — Beauty Queen

French, Jay Jay
Rebellion Entertainment, 2440 Broadway, #111, New York NY 10024, USA — Singer, Guitarist (Twisted Sister)

French, Kate — Actress
Caliber Media, 9229 W Sunset Blvd, #705, West Hollywood CA 90069, USA

French, Leigh — Actress
1850 N Vista St, Los Angeles CA 90046, USA

French, Nicola S (Niki) — Singer
Energise Records, 347 Caspian Way, Purfleet, Essex RM19 1LB, England

French, Paige — Actress
Collier Talent Agency, 2313 Lake Austin Blvd, #103, Austin TX 78703, USA

French, R James (Jim) — Baseball Player
PO Box 6452, Chicago IL 60680, USA

French, Tara — Writer
Viking Press, 375 Hudson St, New York NY 10014 USA

Frenette, Matt — Drummer (Loverboy)
Loverboy Touring Offices, 425 Carrall St, Vancouver BC V6A 6E3, Canada

Freni, Mirella — Opera Singer
I M G Artists, Hogarth Business Park, Chiswick, London W4 2TH, England

Frenkel, Jacob A — Economist
J P MorganChase Co, 270 Park Ave, New York NY 10017, USA

Frenkiel, Richard H — Systems Engineer, Inventor
Rutgers University, WinLab, PO Box 909, Piscataway NJ 08855, USA

Frentzen, Heinz-Harald — Auto Racing Driver
Jordan Grand Prix, Silverstone Circuit, Towcester Northhamptonshire NN12 8TN, England

Frenzel, Eric — Nordic Combined Skier
Wiesenstr 11, 09468 Geyer, Germany

Frerotte, Gustave J (Gus) — Football Player
10040 Litzsinger Road, Saint Louis MO 63124, USA

Fresco, Michael — Director
I C M Partners, 10250 Constellation Blvd, #900, Los Angeles CA 90067 USA

Fresco, Paolo — Businessman
Fiat SpA, Corso Marconi 10/20, 10125 Turin, Italy

Fresco, Victor — Writer, Producer
I C M Partners, 10250 Constellation Blvd, #900, Los Angeles CA 90067 USA

Fresh, Doug E — Rap Artist
Pyramid Entertainment, 377 Rector Place, #21A, New York NY 10280 USA

Fresnadillo, Juan Carlos — Director
United Talent Agency, 9336 Civic Center Dr, Beverly Hills CA 90210 USA

Freston, Thomas E (Tom) — Businessman
MTV Networks, 1515 Broadway, Front 7, New York NY 10036, USA

Fretton, Anthony (Tony) — Architect
49-59 Old St, London EC1V 9XH, England

Freud, Bella L — Fashion Designer
21 Saint Charles Square, London W10 6EF, England

Freudenberger, Nell — Writer
Harper Collins Publishers, 10 E 53rd St, Cellar 1, New York NY 10022 USA

Freund, Lambert B — Mechanical Engineer
3 Palisade Lane, Barrington RI 02806, USA

Freundlich, Bart — Director
Creative Artists Agency, 2000 Ave of Stars, #100, Los Angeles CA 90067 USA

Frewer, Matt — Actor
Gilbertson Entertainment, 1334 3rd Street Promenade, #201, Santa Monica CA 90401 USA

Frey, Glenn — Singer (Eagles), Songwriter, Actor
I C M Partners, 10250 Constellation Blvd, #900, Los Angeles CA 90067 USA

Frey, James G (Jim) — Baseball Manager
12101 Tullamore Court, #406, Lutherville Timonium MD 21093, USA

Frey, Sami — Actor
Les Visiteurs du Soir, 40 Rue de la Folie Regnault, 75011 Paris, France

Frey, Steven F (Steve) — Baseball Player
1414 2nd Street Pike, Southampton PA 18966, USA

Freytag, Arny — Photographer
22735 MacFarlane Dr, Woodland Hills CA 91364, USA

Frias, Arturo — Boxer
12418 Penn St, Whittier CA 90602, USA

Frick, Stephen N — Astronaut
27998 Mercurio Road, Carmel CA 93923, USA

Fricke, Janie — Singer, Guitarist
Janie Fricke Concerts, PO Box 798, Lancaster TX 75146, USA

Fricker, Brenda — Actress
Aegis Entertainment Group, 7510 Sunset Blvd, #275, Los Angeles CA 90046, USA

Frickman, Andrew J (Andy) — Director, Producer
W M E Entertainment, 9601 Wilshire Blvd, #300, Beverly Hills CA 90210 USA

Friday, Gavin — Singer, Composer, Artist
Bloomsbury Publishing, 36 Soho Square, London W1D 3Q4, England

Friday, Nancy — Writer
Harper Collins Publishers, 10 E 53rd St, Cellar 1, New York NY 10022 USA

Fridell, Squire — Actor
Stars Agency, 23 Grant Ave, #400, San Francisco CA 94108, USA

Fridovich, David P — Army General
Special Operations Center, 7701 Tampa Point Blvd, McDill Air Force Base FL 33621, USA

Fried, Charles — Government Official, Judge, Educator
Harvard University, Law School, Cambridge MA 02138, USA

Fried, Miriam — Concert Violinist
Opus 3 Artists, 470 Park Ave S, #900N, New York NY 10016 USA

Friedberg, Rick — Director
A P A Talent/Literary Agency, 405 S Beverly Dr, #300, Beverly Hills CA 90212 USA

Friedberger, Eleanor — Singer (Fiery Furnaces)
High Road Touring, 751 Bridgeway, #200, Sausalito CA 94965 USA

Friedberger, Matthew — Singer, Drummer (Fiery Furnaces)
High Road Touring, 751 Bridgeway, #200, Sausalito CA 94965 USA

Frieden, Tanja — Snowboard Athlete
Kari Frieden, Freisestr 29A, 3604 Thun, Switzerland

Frieden, Thomas R — Government Official, Physician
Centers for Disease Control, 1600 Clifton Road NE, Atlanta GA 30329 USA

Friedericy, Bonita — Actress
Amsel Eisenstadt Frazier, 5055 Wilshire Blvd, #865, Los Angeles CA 90036 USA

Friedkin, William — Director
10741 Levico Way, Los Angeles CA 90077, USA

Friedlaender, Jonathan — Biological Anthropologist
3401 N Broad St, Philadelphia PA 19140, USA
Friedlander, Judah — Actor, Comedian
Cohen & Gardner, 345 N Maple Drive, #181, Beverly Hills CA 90210, USA
Friedlander, Lee — Artist, Photographer
Janet Borden, 560 Broadway, #601, New York NY 10012, USA
Friedlander, Liz — Director
Gersh Agency, 9465 Wilshire Blvd, #600, Beverly Hills CA 90212 USA
Friedlander, Saul — Writer
University of California, History Dept, Los Angeles CA 90024, USA
Friedle, Will — Actor
Innovative Artists, 1505 10th St, Santa Monica CA 90401 USA
Friedman, Bruce Jay — Writer
Biblioasis, PO Box 92, Emeryville ON N0R 1C0, Canada
Friedman, Caitlin — Writer
Y C Media, 145 W 28th St, #1200, New York NY 10001, USA
Friedman, Emanuel A — Obstetrician
Beth-Israel Hospital, 330 Brookline Ave, Boston MA 02215, USA
Friedman, Jeffrey M — Molecular Geneticist
Rockefeller University Hughes Medical Institute, Molecular Genetics Laboratory, New York NY 10021, USA
Friedman, Jeremiah — Writer
United Talent Agency, 9336 Civic Center Dr, Beverly Hills CA 90210 USA
Friedman, Jerome I — Nobel Physics Laureate
75 Greenough St, Brookline MA 02445, USA
Friedman, Kinky — Singer, Songwriter, Writer
1101 Crown Ridge Path, Austin TX 78753, USA
Friedman, Leonard L (Lennie) — Football Player
1000 Cross Clay Court, Raleigh NC 27614, USA
Friedman, Maggie — Producer
Ensemble Entertainment, 280 South Beverly Dr, #402, Beverly Hills CA 90212, USA
Friedman, Mal — Actor
J E Talent, 323 Geary St, #302, San Francisco CA 94102, USA
Friedman, Mark — Writer, Producer
United Talent Agency, 9336 Civic Center Dr, Beverly Hills CA 90210 USA
Friedman, Michael — Composer, Lyricist
I C M Partners, 10250 Constellation Blvd, #900, Los Angeles CA 90067 USA
Friedman, Peter — Actor, Singer
J Michael Bloom, 233 Park Ave S, #1000, New York NY 10003 USA
Friedman, Philip — Writer
Ivy Books/Random House, 1745 Broadway, #B1, New York NY 10019, USA
Friedman, Sonya — Psychologist, Entertainer
111 S Old Woodward Ave, #212B, Birmingham MI 48009, USA
Friedman, Thomas L — Journalist
New York Times, Editorial Dept, 229 W 43rd St, New York NY 10036 USA
Friedrich, Hans-Peter — Government Official, Germany
Bundestag, Platz der Republik 1, 10557 Berlin, Germany , USA
Friel, Anna — Actress
Ken McReddie Assoc, 11 Connaught Place, London W2 2ET, England
Friel, Brian — Writer
Drumaweir House, Greencastle, County Donegal, Ireland
Friels, Colin — Actor
129 Brooke St, Woollomooloo, Sydney NSW 2011, Australia
Friend, Robert B (Bob) — Baseball Player
4 Salem Circle, Pittsburgh PA 15238, USA
Friend, Rupert — Actor
Independent Talent Group, Oxford House, 76 Oxford St, London W1D 1BS, England
Friesinger-Postma, Anna (Anni) — Speed Skater
Am Bichl 4, 83334 Inzell, Germany
Friesz, John M — Football Player
1454 E W Pebblestone Court, Hayden ID 83835, USA
Frigo, Francesco — Model, Actress
Playboy Promotions, 2706 Media Center Dr, Los Angeles CA 90065 USA
Friis, Morten — Percussion Musician (Safri Duo)
P D H Music, Dag Hammarskjold Alle 42 G, 2100 Copenhagen 0, Denmark
Frimout, Dirk D — Astronaut, Belgium
Flanders Language Foundation, Merghelynckstraat 4, 8900 Iper, Belgium
Fripp, Robert — Guitarist (King Crimson), Songwriter
Agency Group Ltd, 361-373 City Road, London EC1V 2QA, England
Frischmann, Justine — Singer (Elastica)
C M O Mgmt, Ransomes Dock, 357 Parkgate Road, London SW11 4NP, England
Frisell, Sonja — Director
Columbia Artists Mgmt Inc, 1790 Broadway, #702, New York NY 10019 USA
Frisell, William R (Bill) — Jazz Guitarist
Rosebud Agency, PO Box 170429, San Francisco CA 94117 USA
Frishberg, David L — Jazz Singer, Pianist, Composer
Irvin Arthur Assoc, 320 W 38th St, #1803, New York NY 10018 USA
Frist, William H (Bill), Sr — Senator, TN
V O L P A C, PO Box 15852, Nashville TN 37215, USA
Fristsche, Jim — Basketball Player
470 Emerson Ave W, Saint Paul MN 55118, USA
Fritsch, Theodore E (Ted), Jr — Football Player
5014 Odins Way, Marietta GA 30068, USA
Fritsche, Dan — Ice Hockey Player
116 Olentangy Point, Columbus OH 43202, USA
Fritts, Debra — Artist
Chase Gallery, 129 Newbury St, Mezzanine, Boston MA 02116, USA
Fritz, Harold A — Vietnam War Army Hero (CMH)
1017 W Scottwood Dr, Peoria IL 61615, USA
Fritz, Laurence J (Larry) — Baseball Player
2632 Schrage Ave, Whiting IN 46394, USA
Fritz, Nikki — Actress
1158 28th St, #683, Santa Monica CA 90403, USA
Frizza, Riccardo — Conductor
I M G Artists, Hogarth Business Park, Chiswick, London W4 2TH, England
Frizzell, David — Singer
4694 E Robertson Road, Cross Plains TN 37049, USA

Frizzell, John — Composer
First Artists Mgmt, 4764 Park Granada, #210, Calabasas CA 91302 USA
Frizzelle, William J — Football Player
8001 Tylerton Dr, Raleigh NC 27613, USA
Frobel, Douglas S (Doug) — Baseball Player
169 Springwater Dr, Kanata ON K2K 1Z8, Canada
Froboess, Cornelia — Singer, Actress
Rinkhof Kleinholzhausen, 83064 Raubling, Germany
Froch, Carl — Boxer
Gedling Road, Carlton, Nottingham NG4 3FG, England
Froemming, Bruce N — Baseball Umpire
702 W Haddonstone Place, Thiensville WI 53092, USA
Froese, Bob — Ice Hockey Player
11701 Clarence Center Road, Akron NY 14001, USA
Froggatt, Joanne — Actress
Conway Van Gelder Grant, 8-12 Broadwick St, #300, London W1F 8HW, England
Frohnmayer, John E — Government Official
38511 Kelly Road, Jefferson OR 97352, USA
Frohwirth, Todd G — Baseball Player
S66W24360 Skyline Ave, Waukesha WI 53189, USA
Froines, John R — Social Activist, Educator
University of California Public Health School, Environmental Health Science Dept, Los Angeles CA 90024, USA
Frolov, Alexander — Ice Hockey Player
1467 3rd St, Manhattan Beach CA 90266, USA
Fromm, Fritz — Handball Player
An der Bismarckschule 64, 30173 Hannover, Germany
Frongillo, John R — Football Player
10230 Elmhurst Dr NW, Albuquerque NM 87114, USA
Fronius, Hans — Artist
Guggenberggasse 18, 2380 Perchtoldadorf bei Vienna, Austria
Frosch, Robert A — Government Official, Space Scientist
18 Heritage Hills Dr, Somers NY 10589, USA
Frost, Alex — Actor
Industry Entertainment, 955 Carillo Dr, #300, Los Angeles CA 90048 USA
Frost, C David (Dave) — Baseball Player
2206 Ocana Ave, Long Beach CA 90815, USA
Frost, David L — Golfer
5836 Royal Lane, Dallas TX 75230, USA
Frost, David P — Producer, Writer, Commentator
Noel Gay Artists, 19 Denmark St, London WC2H 8NA
Frost, Lindsay — Actress
Glick Agency, 1321 7th St, #203, Santa Monica CA 90401 USA
Frost, Mark — Writer
Mark Frost Productions, PO Box 1723, Studio City CA 91614, USA
Frost, Martin — Concert Clarinetist
Svenski Konsertdirekton, Danska Vagen 25B, 412 74 Goteborg, Sweden
Frost, Nick — Actor, Comedian, Writer
Hamilton Hodell, 66-68 Margaret St, London W1W 8SR, England
Frost, Sadie — Actress
Money Mgmt, 22 Noel St, London W1F 8GS, England
Frost, Scott A — Football Player
99 Thomas Lake, Ashland NE 68003, USA
Fruchtman, Lisa — Film Editor
United Talent Agency, 9336 Civic Center Dr, Beverly Hills CA 90210 USA
Fruhbeck de Burgos, Rafael — Conductor
Avenida del Mediterraneo 21, 28007 Madrid, Spain
Fruhwirth, Amy — Golfer
26431 N 44th Way, Phoenix AZ 85050, USA
Frusciante, John A — Guitarist (Red Hot Chili Peppers)
Q Prime, 729 7th Ave, #1600, New York NY 10019 USA
Fry Irvin, Shirley — Tennis Player
1970 Asylum Ave, West Hartford CT 06117, USA
Fry, Jerry R — Baseball Player
3300 Stanton St, Springfield IL 62703, USA
Fry, John A — Educator
Drexel University, President's Office, 3141 Chestnut St, #103, Philadelphia PA 19104, USA
Fry, Michael — Cartoonist (Committed, Over the Hedge)
United Feature Syndicate, PO Box 5610, Cincinnati OH 45201 USA
Fry, Robert N (Bob) — Football Player
1604 Bexley Dr, Wilmington NC 28412, USA
Fry, Stephen J — Actor, Comedian, Director
Hamilton Hodell, 66-68 Margaret St, London W1W 8SR, England
Fryar, Chris — Drummer (Zac Brown Band)
Roar, 9701 Wilshire Blvd, #800, Beverly Hills CA 90212, USA
Fryar, Irving D — Football Player, Sportscaster
51 Applegate Road, Jobstown NJ 08041, USA
Frye, Bernie — Basketball Player
PO Box 2052, Sequim WA 98382, USA
Frye, Channing T — Basketball Player
Phoenix Suns, 201 E Jefferson St, Phoenix AZ 85004 USA
Frye, Jeffrey A (Jeff) — Baseball Player
6833 Lahontan Dr, Fort Worth TX 76132, USA
Frye, Soliel Moon — Actress
Herb Tannen, 10801 National Blvd, #101, Los Angeles CA 90064 USA
Fryling, Victor J — Businessman
C M S Energy, Fairlane Plaza South, 330 Town Center Dr, Dearborn MI 48126, USA
Fryman, D Travis — Baseball Player
2600 Highway 196, Molino FL 32577, USA
Ftorek, Robert B (Robbie) — Ice Hockey Player, Coach
79 Sunset Point Road, Wolfeboro NH 03894, USA
Fu Mingxia — Diver
General Physical Culture Bureau, 9 Tiyuguan Road, Dongcheng District, Beijing 100061, China
Fu, Haijing — Opera Singer
I M G Artists, Hogarth Business Park, Chiswick, London W4 2TH, England
Fucarino, Frank A — Basketball Player
21 Heathcote Court, Shirley NY 11967, USA

Fuchs, Victor R 796 Cedro Way, Stanford CA 94305, USA	Economist
Fudenberg, Drew Harvard University, Economics Dept, Cambridge MA 02138, USA	Economist
Fuente, David I Office Depot Inc, 6600 N Military Trail, Boca Raton FL 33496, USA	Businessman
Fuentes, Brian C 1342 El Portal Dr, Merced CA 95340, USA	Baseball Player
Fuentes, Daisy Shelter Entertainment, 9454 Wilshire Blvd, #715, Beverly Hills CA 90212 USA	Actress, Model
Fuentes, Julio M US Court of Appeals, US Courthouse, 50 Walnut St, #5032, Newark NJ 07102, USA	Judge
Fuentes, Rigoberto B (Tito) 61 S Maddux Dr, Reno NV 89512, USA	Baseball Player
Fuentes, Val Tabletop Productions, PO Box 698, Carson City NV 89702, USA	Drummer (It's a Beautiful Day)
Fugard, Athol H PO Box 5090, Walmer, Port Elizabeth 6065, South Africa	Writer
Fugate, Katherine Stakevich-Gothman, 9777 Wilshire Blvd, #550, Beverly Hills CA 90212, USA	Producer, Writer
Fugelsang, John Brillstein Entertainment Partners, 9150 Wilshire Blvd, #350, Beverly Hills CA 90212 USA	Actor, Comedian
Fugere, Joseph (Joe) 415 Cinnamon Ridge, Rutherfordton NC 28139, USA	Baseball Umpire
Fugett, Jean S, Jr 4801 Westparkway, Baltimore MD 21229, USA	Football Player
Fugit, Patrick Levin/Brown Mgmt, M M Productions, 1351 4th St, #201, Santa Monica CA 90401, USA	Actor
Fuglesang, Christer PO Box 555, Bellaire TX 77402, USA	Astronaut
Fuhrman, Isabelle Trilogy Talent, 13425 Ventura Blvd, #200, Sherman Oaks CA 91423, USA	Actress
Fujita, Hiroyuki Fujita Laboratory, 4-6-1 Komaba, Meguroku, Tokyo 153 8505, Japan	Microbiotics Engineer
Fuksas, Massimiliano Piazzi del Monte di Pieta 30, 00186 Rome, Italy	Architect
Fukuda, Yasuo 4-20-7 Nazawa, Setagayaku, Tokyo 154 0003, Japan	Prime Minister, Japan
Fukui, Takeo Honda Motor Co, 2-1-1 Minami-Aoyama, Minatoku, Tokyo 107 8556, Japan	Businessman
Fukumoto, Miho Football Assn, 3-10-15 Hongo, Bunkyoku, Tokyo 113 0033 Japan	Soccer Player
Fukunaga, Cary J Anonymous Content, 3532 Hayden Ave, Culver City CA 90232 USA	Director
Fukuto, Maru Jim Preminger Agency, 10866 Wilshire Blvd, #1000, Los Angeles CA 90024 USA	Director
Fukuyama, Francis George Mason University, Public Policy Dept, Fairfax VA 22030, USA	Social Scientist
Fulcher, David D All Pro Sports, PO Box 378, Mason OH 45040, USA	Football Player
Fulcher, Rich United Talent Agency, 9336 Civic Center Dr, Beverly Hills CA 90210 USA	Actor
Fulchino, Jeffrey P (Jeff) 6 Beacon Square, Fairfield CT 06825, USA	Baseball Player
Fuld, Samuel B (Sam) 8 Meadow Road, Durham NH 03824, USA	Baseball Player
Fulghum, Robert Random House, 1745 Broadway, #1800, New York NY 10019 USA	Writer, Religious Leader
Fulgoni, Sara I M G Artists, Hogarth Business Park, Chiswick, London W4 2TH, England	Opera Singer
Fulhage, Scott A 2430 N Road, Beloit KS 67420, USA	Football Player
Fulks, Robbie Countrier Than Thou, PO Box 4, Wilmette IL 60091, USA	Singer, Songwriter
Fuller, Anthony I (Tony) 4222 Lost Springs Dr, Agoura Hills CA 91301, USA	Basketball Player
Fuller, Carl 8302 Kirkville Dr, Houston TX 77089, USA	Basketball Player
Fuller, Charles Creative Artists Agency, 2000 Ave of Stars, #100, Los Angeles CA 90067 USA	Writer
Fuller, Cindy Playboy Promotions, 2706 Media Center Dr, Los Angeles CA 90065 USA	Model
Fuller, Corey 626 Raspberry Way, Tallahassee FL 32312, USA	Football Player
Fuller, Delores 3628 Ottawa Circle, Las Vegas NV 89169, USA	Actress, Songwriter
Fuller, Drew Gersh Agency, 9465 Wilshire Blvd, #600, Beverly Hills CA 90212 USA	Actor
Fuller, James H (Jim) 5107 Bur Oak Dr, Pasadena TX 77505, USA	Baseball Player
Fuller, John C (Johnny) 1925 Highland Dr, Salado TX 76571, USA	Football Player
Fuller, John E 31912 Paseo Terraza, San Juan Capistrano CA 92675, USA	Baseball Player
Fuller, Kathryn S World Wildlife Fund, 1250 24th St NW, #600, Washington DC 20037, USA	Association Executive
Fuller, Linda Habitat for Humanity, 121 Habitat St, Americus GA 31709, USA	Association Executive, Social Activist
Fuller, Mark Wet Design, 90 Universal City Plaza, Universal City CA 91608, USA	Sculptor
Fuller, Marvin D 6799 Patton Dr, Fort Hood TX 76544, USA	Army General
Fuller, Michael D (Mike) 4241 Abingdon Trail, Birmingham AL 35243, USA	Football Player
Fuller, Penny Paradigm Agency, 360 N Crescent Dr, North Building, Beverly Hills CA 90210 USA	Actress

Fuller, Randy L — Football Player
2257 Patsy Lane, Columbus GA 31903, USA
Fuller, Robert (Bob) — Actor
5012 Auckland Ave, North Hollywood CA 91601, USA
Fuller, Rod — Drag Racing Driver
David Powers Motorsports, 10205 Westheimer Road, Houston TX 77042, USA
Fuller, Simon — Producer, Writer
Creative Artists Agency, 2000 Ave of Stars, #100, Los Angeles CA 90067 USA
Fuller, Stephen R (Steve) — Football Player
81 Oak Tree Lane, Bluffton SC 29910, USA
Fuller, Todd D — Basketball Player
Miami Heat, American Airlines Arena, 601 Biscayne Blvd, Miami FL 33132 USA
Fuller, Vernon G (Vern) — Baseball Player
155 Ironwood Circle, Aurora OH 44202, USA
Fuller, Victoria — Model, Actress
PO Box 6010-513, Sherman Oaks CA 91453, USA
Fuller, William H, Jr — Football Player
4025 Church Point Road, Virginia Beach VA 23455, USA
Fullerton, C Gordon — Astronaut, Test Pilot
44046 28th St W, Building 4800D, Lancaster CA 93536, USA
Fullerton, Larry — Inventor (Low Power Pulses for Messages)
Time Domain, 6700 Odyssey Dr NW, Huntsville AL 35806, USA
Fullington, Darrell — Football Player
1023 W Patrick Circle, Daytona Beach FL 32117, USA
Fullmer, Bradley R (Brad) — Baseball Player
400 S Barrington Ave, #202, Los Angeles CA 90049, USA
Fullmer, Gene — Boxer
9250 S 2200 St West, West Jordan UT 84088, USA
Fulmer, Phillip — Football Coach, Sportscaster
CBS-TV, Sports Dept, 51 W 52nd St, New York NY 10019 USA
Fulton, Christina — Actress
Innovative Artists, 1505 10th St, Santa Monica CA 90401 USA
Fulton, Eileen — Actress, Singer
60 E 42nd St, #305, New York NY 10165, USA
Fulton, Fitzhugh, Jr — Test Pilot
1023 E Ave J, #5, Lancaster CA 93535, USA
Fulton, Hamish — Artist
John Weber Gallery, 529 W 20th St, New York NY 10011, USA
Fulton, Keith — Director
Sloss Law Office, 555 W 25th St, #400, New York NY 10001, USA
Fulton, Robert D — Governor, IA
PO Box 2634, Waterloo IA 50704, USA
Fulton, Soren — Actor
Paradigm Agency, 360 N Crescent Dr, North Building, Beverly Hills CA 90210 USA
Fulton, William D (Bill) — Baseball Player
3001 Lexington Dr, Export PA 15632, USA
Fultz, Jeff — Auto Racing Driver
J C R 3 Racing, PO Box 561001, Charlotte NC 28256, USA
Fultz, Michael D (Mike) — Football Player
1900 W Foothills Road, Lincoln NE 68523, USA
Fultz, R Aaron — Baseball Player
2575 Beaver Road, Munford TN 38058, USA
Fumusa, Dominic — Actor
Gersh Agency, 9465 Wilshire Blvd, #600, Beverly Hills CA 90212 USA
Funaro, Frank — Drummer (Cracker)
Back Bay Mgmt, 397 Little Neck Road, #305, Virginia Beach VA 23452 USA
Funchess, Thomas (Tom) — Football Player
1015 Funchess St, Crystal Springs MS 39059, USA
Funderburk, Leonard J — Vietnam War Air Force Hero
2311 Lathan Road, Monroe NC 28112, USA
Funderburke, Lawrence — Basketball Player
1688 Meadoway Court, Blacklick OH 43004, USA
Funes Cartagena, C Mauricio — President, El Salvador
Casa Presidencial, Calle Dario Gonzales 806, San Salvador, El Salvador
Funicello, Annette J — Actress, Singer
I C M Partners, 10250 Constellation Blvd, #900, Los Angeles CA 90067 USA
Funk, Eric — Composer
PO Box 1073, Helena MT 59624, USA
Funk, Fred — Golfer
24729 Harbour View Dr, Ponte Vedra FL 32082, USA
Funk, Mary Wallace (Wally) — Astronaut Candidate
243 Oak Hill Dr, Roanoke TX 76262, USA
Funk, Thomas J (Tom) — Baseball Player
6952 N Olive St, Kansas City MO 64118, USA
Funke, Alex — Cinematographer
1176 Fiske St, Pacific Palisades CA 90272, USA
Fuqua, Antoine — Director
Steve Callas Assoc, 12424 Wilshire Blvd, Los Angeles CA 90025, USA
Fuqua, Johnny W Frenchy) — Football Player
13983 Glastonbury Ave, Detroit MI 48223, USA
Furay, Richie — Singer (Buffalo Springfield, Poco)
Agency Group, 9348 Civic Center Dr, #200, Beverly Hills CA 90210, USA
Furcal, Rafael A — Baseball Player
397 Sweet Bay Ave, Plantation FL 33324, USA
Furie, Sidney J — Director
I C M Partners, 10250 Constellation Blvd, #900, Los Angeles CA 90067 USA
Furlan, Mira — Actress
Imperium 7 Artists, 5455 Wilshire Blvd, #1706, Los Angeles CA 90036 USA
Furler, Sia — Singer
Dance Pool/Sony Records, 2100 Colorado Ave, Santa Monica CA 90404, USA
Furlong, Shirley — Golfer
6251 S Kimberele Way, Chandler AZ 85249, USA
Furman, Brad — Director, Producer, Writer
Atlas Entertainment, 9200 W Sunset Blvd, Los Angeles CA 90069, USA
Furmaniak, Jason J (J J) — Baseball Player
184 Nottingham Dr, Bolingbrook IL 60440, USA

Furmann, Benno
Gersh Agency, 41 Madison Ave, #3301, New York NY 10010 USA — Actor

Furnas, Barnaby
Marianne Boesky Gallery, 509 W 24th St, New York NY 10011, USA — Artist

Furness, Deborra-Lee
Lou Coulson Assoc, 37 Berwick St, London W1V 8RS, England — Actress

Furniss, Bruce M
1 Segada, Rancho Santa Margarita CA 92688, USA — Swimmer

Furniss, Steve
6478 Frampton Circle, Huntington Beach CA 92648, USA — Swimmer

Furno, Carlo Cardinal
Piazza Della Citta Leonina, 00193 Rome, Italy — Religious Leader

Furrey, Michael T (Mike)
12397 Steeplechase Lane, Strongsville OH 44149, USA — Football Player

Furshpan, Edwin J
27 Stonewall Lane, Falmouth MA 02540, USA — Neurobiologist

Furst, Alan
Random House, 1745 Broadway, #1800, New York NY 10019 USA — Writer

Furst, Stephen
Marshak/Zachary Co, 8840 Wilshire Blvd, #100, Beverly Hills CA 90211 USA — Actor, Comedian

Furstenberg, Frank F, Jr
University of Pennsylvania, Population Studies Center, Phildelphia PA 19104, USA — Sociologist

Furstenfeld, Jeremy
Rainmaker Artists, PO Box 551665, Dallas TX 75355, USA — Drummer (Blue October)

Furstenfeld, Justin
Rainmaker Artists, PO Box 551665, Dallas TX 75355, USA — Singer, Guitarist (Blue October)

Furtado, Nelly
Chris Smith, 21 Camden St, #500, Toronto ON M5V 1V2, Canada — Singer, Singwriter

Furtsch Ojeda, Evelyn
841 Clemenson Ave, Santa Ana CA 92705, USA — Track Athlete

Furuholmen, Magne
Agency Group Ltd, 361-373 City Road, London EC1V 2QA, England — Singer, Keyboardist (A-Ha)

Furukawa, Satoshi
Japanese Aerospace Exploration Agency, 2-1-1 Sengen, Tsukuba-shi, Ibaraki 305 8505, Japan — Astronaut

Furuseth, Ole Christian
John Colletts Alle 74, 0854 Oslo, Norway — Alpine Skier

Furyk, James M (Jim)
240 Deer Haven Dr, Ponte Vedra FL 32082, USA — Golfer

Fusco, Mark E
155 Grove St, Westwood MA 02090, USA — Ice Hockey Player

Fusco, Scott M
25083 Pioneer Way NW, Poulsbo WA 98370, USA — Ice Hockey Player

Fusco, Simona
Scott Stander Assoc, 4533 Van Nuys Blvd, #401, Sherman Oaks CA 91403 USA — Actress, Model

Fusco, Simona
B/W/R, 9100 Wilshire Blvd, #500W, Beverly Hills CA 90212 USA — Actress, Model

Fusina, Charles A (Chuck)
1548 King James St, Pittsburgh PA 15237, USA — Football Player

Fuss, Adam
151 Ave B, New York NY 10009, USA — Photographer

Futey, Bohdan A
US Claims Court, 717 Madison Place NW, Washington DC 20439, USA — Judge

Futia, Leo R
18 Interlaken Road, Greenwich CT 06830, USA — Businessman

Futral, Elizabeth
Neil Funkhouser Mgmt, 105 Arden St, #5G, New York NY 10040, USA — Opera Singer

Futterman, Daniel (Dan)
Principal Entertainment, 1964 Westwood Blvd, #400, Los Angeles CA 90025 USA — Actor, Writer

Fyfe, William S
1 Joanna Dr, Sainte Catherines ON L2N 1V1, Canada — Geochemist, Geologist

Fyhie, Michael E (Mike)
4 Wellesley Court, Trabuco Canyon CA 92679, USA — Baseball Player

Fylstra, Daniel
Frontline Systems, PO Box 4288, Incline Village CA 89450, USA — Computer Software Designer

Fywell, Tim
I C M Partners, 10250 Constellation Blvd, #900, Los Angeles CA 90067 USA — Director

F

Furmann - Fywell

G

Gaarder, Jostein
Gullkroken 22A, 0377 Oslo, Norway
Writer

Gabaldon, Diana
PO Box 584, Scottsdale AZ 85252, USA
Soccer Player, Coach

Gabarra, Carin L
305 Rosslare Dr, Arnold MD 21012, USA
Fashion Designer

Gabbana, Stefano
Dolce & Gabbana, Via Santa Cecilia 7, 20122 Milan, Italy
Baseball Player

Gabbard, Kason R
855 Dogtown Dr, Savannah TN 38372, USA
Football Player

Gabbert, Blaine
Jacksonville Jaguars, 1 AllTel Stadium Place, Jacksonville FL 32202 USA
Actor

Gabel, Seth
Management 360, 9111 Wilshire Blvd, Beverly Hills CA 90210 USA
Director

Gabel, Shainee
Creative Artists Agency, 2000 Ave of Stars, #100, Los Angeles CA 90067 USA
Financier

Gabelli, Mario J
Gabelli Asset Mgmt, 1 Corporate Center, Rye NY 10580, USA
Interior Designer

Gabellini, Michael
Gabellini-Sheppard Assoc, 665 Broadway, #706, New York NY 10012, USA
Concert Cellist

Gabetta, Sol
Harrison/Parrott, Lucile-Grahn-Str 37, 81675 Munich, Germany
Freestyle Wrestler, Coach

Gable, Daniel M (Danny)
4343 Treefarm Lane NE, Iowa City IA 52240, USA
Baseball Player

Gabler, William L (Gabe)
3227 Bayshore Parkway, Arnold MO 63010, USA
Basketball Player

Gabor, William A (Billy)
101 Ocean Bluffs Blvd, #501, Jupiter FL 33477, USA
Actress

Gabor, Zsa Zsa
1001 Bel Air Road, Los Angeles CA 90077, USA
Singer, Composer, Actress

Gabriel, Ana B
A G Musicales, Peten 117 Col Narvarte, Mexico City DF 03020, Mexico
Actress

Gabriel, Andrea
Global Artists Agency, 6253 Hollywood Blvd, #508, Los Angeles CA 90028 USA
Model

Gabriel, Jani
Premier Model Mgmt, 40-42 Parker St, London WC2B 5PQ, England
Actor

Gabriel, John
Access Talent Voice Overs, 171 Madison Ave, #910, New York NY 10016, USA
Singer, Songwriter

Gabriel, Juan
J E P Entertainment Group, 16027 Ventura Blvd, #510, Encino CA 91436, USA
Director, Animator

Gabriel, Mike
I C M Partners, 10250 Constellation Blvd, #900, Los Angeles CA 90067 USA
Singer, Keyboardist, Songwriter

Gabriel, Peter
Box Mill, Mill Lane, Corsham SN13 8PL, England
Football Player

Gabriel, Roman I, Jr
PO Box 4173, Calabash NC 28467, USA
Circus Trapeze Artist

Gabriela
Ringling Bros Barnum & Bailey, 8607 Westwood Circle Dr, Vienna VA 22182 USA
Model, Actress

Gabrielle, Monique
Purrfect Productions, 1231 NE 28th Ave, Pompano Beach FL 33062 USA
Baseball Player

Gabrielson, Leonard G (Len)
24230 Hillview Road, Los Altos Hills CA 94024, USA
Historian

Gaddis, John L
Ohio University, Contemporary History Institute, Brown House, Athens OH 45701, USA
Actress

Gade, Ariel
Paradigm Agency, 360 N Crescent Dr, North Building, Beverly Hills CA 90210 USA
DJ Musician

Gadjo
Mission Control, City Business Center, Lower Road, London SE16 2XB, England
Actress

Gadon, Sarah
Creative Drive Artists, 166 King St E, #400, Toronto ON M5A 1J3, Canada
Actress, Model

Gadot, Gal
I C M Partners, 10250 Constellation Blvd, #900, Los Angeles CA 90067 USA
Ice Hockey Player

Gadsby, William A (Bill)
28765 E Kalong Circle, Southfield MI 48034, USA
Football Player

Gadsden, Oronde B
11241 NW 15th St, Plantation FL 33323, USA
Basketball Player

Gadzuric, Dan
1312 Villa Barolo Ave, Henderson NV 89052, USA
Singer

Gaebel, Tom
Telemedia Music, Distlerstr 39, 70184 Stuttgart, Germany
Football Player

Gaechter, Michael T (Mike)
13 Horizon Point, Frisco TX 75034, USA
Optical Engineer

Gaeta, Alexander L
Cornell University, Applied & Engineering Physics Dept, Clark Hall, Ithaca NY 14853, USA
Special Effects Designer

Gaeta, John
Creative Artists Agency, 2000 Ave of Stars, #100, Los Angeles CA 90067 USA
Baseball Player

Gaetti, Gary J
2704 Barbara Lane, Houston TX 77005, USA
Conductor

Gaffigan, James
C M Artists, 127 W 96th St, #13B, New York NY 10025 USA
Actor, Comedian

Gaffigan, Jim
Creative Artists Agency, 2000 Ave of Stars, #100, Los Angeles CA 90067 USA
Football Player

Gaffney, D Jabar
11750 Cherry Bark Dr E, Jacksonville FL 32218, USA
Football Player

Gaffney, Derrick T
11750 Cherry Bark Dr E, Jacksonville FL 32218, USA
Astronaut

Gaffney, F Andrew (Drew)
2311 Pierce Ave, Nashville TN 37232, USA
Actor

Gaffney, Mo
Stone Manners Salners, 9911 W Pico Blvd, #1400, Los Angeles CA 90035 USA
Neurobiologist

Gage, Fred H
Salk Biological Study Institute, 10110 N Torrey Pines Road, La Jolla CA 92037, USA
Labor Leader

Gage, John
American Government Employees Federation, 80 F St NW, #700, Washington DC 20001, USA
Educator

Gage, Nathaniel L
6033 45th Ave NE, Seattle WA 98115, USA

Gage, Nicholas — Columnist, Writer
37 Nelson St, North Grafton MA 01536, USA
Gage, Paul — Computer Scientist
Crag Research, Highway 178 N, Chippewa Falls WI 55402, USA
Gaghan, Stephen — Director, Writer
Unsupervised, 10201 W Pico Blvd, #75, Los Angeles CA 90035, USA
Gagliano, Philip J (Phil) — Baseball Player
1095 Crescent Dr, Hollister MO 65672, USA
Gagliano, Robert F (Bob) — Football Player
1064 Dover Lane, Ventura CA 93001, USA
Gagliardi, John — Football Coach
Saint John's University, Athletic Dept, Collegeville MN 56321, USA
Gagne, Eric S — Baseball Player
Los Angeles Dodgers, Stadium, 1000 Elysian Park Ave, Los Angeles CA 90090 USA
Gagne, Greg C — Baseball Player
746 Whetstone Hill Road, Somerset MA 02726, USA
Gagne, Paul L — Ice Hockey Player
Gagne Hockey, 2100 Airport Road, RR 2, Timmons ON P4N 7C3, Canada
Gagne, Simon — Ice Hockey Player
1167 10th St, Manhattan Beach CA 90266, USA
Gagner, Larry J — Football Player
205 W Curtis St, Tampa FL 33603, USA
Gagnier, Holly — Actress
Commercial Talent, 9255 Sunset Blvd, #505, Los Angeles CA 90069, USA
Gagnon, Andre-Philippe — Actor, Comedian, Impressionist
89 Rue Alexandra, Ganby PQ J2C 2P4, Canada
Gagnon, Marc — Speed Skater
Speed Skating Canada, 2781 Lancaster Road, #402, Ottawa ON K1B 1A7, Canada
Gago, Jenny — Actress
Paul Kohner, 9300 Wilshire Blvd, #555, Beverly Hills CA 90212 USA
Gahan, David — Singer (Depeche Mode)
Mute Records, 429 Harrow Road, London W10 4RE, England
Gail, Max — Actor
28198 Rey de Copas Lane, Malibu CA 90265, USA
Gailes, Jason — Rowing Athlete
17 Mark Vincent Dr, Westford MA 01886, USA
Gailey, T Chandler (Chan) — Football Player, Coach
176 Rocky Branch Road, Clarkesville GA 30523, USA
Gaillard, Bob — Basketball Coach
Lewis & Clark University, Athletic Dept, Pamplin Sports Center, Portland OR 97219, USA
Gaillard, J Edward (Eddie) — Baseball Player
134 Sweet Bay Circle, Jupiter FL 33458, USA
Gaillard, Mary Katharine — Physicist
University of California, Physics Dept, Berkeley CA 94720, USA
Gaiman, Neil R — Cartoonist, Writer
Creative Artists Agency, 2000 Ave of Stars, #100, Los Angeles CA 90067 USA
Gain, Robert (Bob) — Football Player
11 Nokomis Dr, Eastlake OH 44095, USA
Gainer, Derrick — Boxer
3256 Tallship Lane, Pensacola FL 32526, USA
Gaines Miller, Chryste — Track Athlete
5408 E Saddleridge Lane, Lithonia GA 30038, USA
Gaines, A Joe — Baseball Player
77 Anair Way, Oakland CA 94605, USA
Gaines, Ambrose (Rowdy), IV — Swimmer
6800 Hawaii Kai Dr, Honolulu HI 96825, USA
Gaines, Boyd P — Actor, Singer
9220 Sunset Blvd, #625, West Hollywood CA 90069, USA
Gaines, C Reece — Basketball Player
Milwaukee Bucks, Bradley Center, 1001 N 4th St, #2, Milwaukee WI 53203 USA
Gaines, Clark — Football Player
21364 Scara Place, Broadlands VA 20148, USA
Gaines, Corey Y — Basketball Player
3968 Windansea St, Las Vegas NV 89147, USA
Gaines, Davis — Actor, Singer
315 W 57th St, #4H, New York NY 10019, USA
Gaines, Ernest J — Writer
PO Box 81, Oscar LA 70762, USA
Gaines, William C — Journalist
Chicago Tribune, Editorial Dept, 435 N Michigan Ave, #1, Chicago IL 60611, USA
Gainey, Kathleen — Army General
Director, Defense Logistics Agency, Joint Staff, Pentagon, Washington DC 20318 USA
Gainey, M C — Actor
Miriam Milgrom Mgmt, 3614 Lankershim Blvd, Los Angeles CA 90068, USA
Gainey, Robert M (Bob) — Ice Hockey Player, Coach
PO Box 829, Coppell TX 75019, USA
Gait, Gary — Lacrosse Player, Coach
Colorado Mammoth, Pepsi Center, 1000 Chopper Circle, Denver CO 80204, USA
Gaiter, Dorothy J — Writer
I C M Partners, 10250 Constellation Blvd, #900, Los Angeles CA 90067 USA
Gaither, Gloria S — Singer, Songwriter
Gaither Music Co, PO Box 737, Alexandria IN 46001, USA
Gaither, Israel L — Religious Leader
Salvation Army USA, 615 Slaters Lane, Alexandria VA 22314, USA
Gaither, Jared — Football Player
San Diego Chargers, 4020 Murphy Canyon Road, San Diego CA 92123 USA
Gaither, William J (Bill) — Singer, Songwriter
Gaither Music Co, PO Box 737, Alexandria IN 46001, USA
Gaitskill, Mary — Writer
Pantheon/Random House, 1745 Broadway, New York NY 10019, USA
Gajarsa, Arthur J — Judge
US Court of Appeals, 717 Madison Place NW, Washington DC 20439, USA
Galan, Nely — Actress, Writer
Galan Entertainment, 523 Victoria Ave, Venice CA 90291, USA
Galanos, James — Fashion Designer
1316 Sunset Plaza Dr, Los Angeles CA 90069, USA

Galanos, Mike CNN-TV, 190 Marietta Ave SW, Atlanta GA 30303 USA	Commentator
Galanter, Marc S University of Wisconsin, Law School, Madison WI 53706, USA	Attorney, Educator
Galarraga, Andres J P 1639 Enclave Circle, West Palm Beach FL 33411, USA	Baseball Player
Galasso, Robert J (Bob) 267 Adelaide Road, Connellsville PA 15425, USA	Baseball Player
Galbraith, A Scott 4440 Plato Court, Stockton CA 95207, USA	Football Player
Galbraith, Clint PO Box 902, Edwardsville IL 62025, USA	Harness Racing Driver
Galbreath, Anthony D (Tony) 411 W 9th St, Fulton MO 65251, USA	Football Player
Galdikas, Birute M F Orangutan Foundation International, 822 Wellesley Ave, Los Angeles CA 90049, USA	Anthropologist
Gale, M Robert (Bob) A P A Talent/Literary Agency, 405 S Beverly Dr, #300, Beverly Hills CA 90212 USA	Writer, Producer, Director
Gale, Michael E (Mike) 18003 4th Ave S, Burien WA 98148, USA	Basketball Player
Gale, Richard B (Rich) 869 Center Park St, Daniel Island SC 29492, USA	Baseball Player
Gale, Robert P 11808 Dorothy St, #304, Los Angeles CA 90049, USA	Physician, Medical Researcher
Gale, Tristan Ego Sports Mgmt, PO Box 680051, Park City UT 84068, USA	Skeleton Athlete
Galecki, John M (Johnny) Creative Artists Agency, 2000 Ave of Stars, #100, Los Angeles CA 90067 USA	Actor, Comedian
Galella, Ronald E (Ron) Ron Galella Ltd, 12 Nelson Lane, Montville NJ 07045, USA	Photographer
Galeotti, Bethany Joy Gersh Agency, 9465 Wilshire Blvd, #600, Beverly Hills CA 90212 USA	Actress
Galfione, Jean Athletes du Monde, 2 Passage de Melun, 75019 Paris, France	Track Athlete
Galiena, Anna Media Art Mgmt, C/ Castelló 82, 2 Derecha, 28006 Madrid, Spain	Actress
Galifianakis, Zach Brillstein Entertainment Partners, 9150 Wilshire Blvd, #350, Beverly Hills CA 90212 USA	Actor, Comedian
Galigher, Edward A (Ed) 1025 Prospect St, #150, La Jolla CA 92037, USA	Football Player
Galina, Stacy 11400 Cashmere St, Los Angeles CA 90049, USA	Actress
Galindo, Rudy 1115 E Haley St, Santa Barbara CA 93103, USA	Figure Skater
Gall, Hugues R Opera National de Paris, 120 Rue de Lyon, 75012 Paris, France	Opera Executive
Gall, John C 20 Corte del Sol, Millbrae CA 94030, USA	Baseball Player
Gall, Joseph G 5702 Ainsley Garth, Baltimore MD 21212, USA	Biologist
Gallacher, Kevin Blackburn Rovers, Ewood Park, Blackburn, Lancashire BB2 4JF, England	Soccer Player
Gallagher 14984 Roan Court, Wellington FL 33414, USA	Actor, Writer, Producer
Gallagher, Alan M E G P H (Al) 1810 N Parkwood Dr, Harlingen TX 78550, USA	Baseball Player
Gallagher, Brian United Way of America, 701 N Fairfax Ave, Lobby, Alexandria VA 22314, USA	Association Executive
Gallagher, Bronagh Hamilton Hodell, 66-68 Margaret St, London W1W 8SR, England	Actor
Gallagher, Chad A 482 Wynstone Way, Rockton IL 61072, USA	Basketball Player
Gallagher, David Innovative Artists, 1505 10th St, Santa Monica CA 90401 USA	Actor
Gallagher, David D (Dave) 6105 Horizon Dr, Columbus IN 47201, USA	Football Player
Gallagher, David T (Dave) 29 Carrs Tavern Road, Millstone Township NJ 08510, USA	Baseball Player
Gallagher, Ellen Mario Diacono Gallery, 207 South St, Boston MA 02111, USA	Artist
Gallagher, Frank J 6572 Enclave Dr, Clarkston MI 48348, USA	Football Player
Gallagher, Gus Ken McReddie Assoc, 11 Connaught Place, London W2 2ET, England	Actor
Gallagher, Helen 260 W End Ave, New York NY 10023, USA	Singer, Actress
Gallagher, Jim, Jr PO Box 507, Greenwood MS 38935, USA	Golfer
Gallagher, John, Jr Gersh Agency, 9465 Wilshire Blvd, #600, Beverly Hills CA 90212 USA	Actor, Singer
Gallagher, Kathleen Milwaukee Journal Sentinel, Editorial Dept, PO Box 371, Milwaukee WI 53201 USA	Journalist
Gallagher, Liam Beady Eye Records, PO Box 14877, London NW1 62X, England	Singer (Oasis)
Gallagher, Mary Don Buchwald/Fortitude, 6500 Wilshire Blvd, #2200, Los Angeles CA 90048 USA	Actress
Gallagher, Megan Shelter Entertainment, 9454 Wilshire Blvd, #715, Beverly Hills CA 90212, USA	Actress
Gallagher, Noel T D Ignition Mgmt, 54 Linhope St, London NW1 6HL, England	Singer, Guitarist (Oasis), Songwriter
Gallagher, Peter Gersh Agency, 9465 Wilshire Blvd, #600, Beverly Hills CA 90212 USA	Actor, Singer
Gallagher, Richard K US Representative, NATO Military Committee, PSC 80, Box 300, APO AE 09724 USA	Navy Admiral
Gallagher, Robert C (Bob) 315 Fair Ave, Santa Cruz CA 95060, USA	Baseball Player

Gallagher, Tim
Cornell University, Ornithology Laboratory, Ithaca NY 14853, USA — Ornithologist

Gallagher-Smith, Jackie
193 Paradise Circle, Jupiter FL 33458, USA — Golfer

Gallant, Mavis
14 Rue Jean Ferrandi, 75006 Paris, France — Writer

Gallardo, Yovani
Milwaukee Brewers, Miller Park, 1 Brewers Way, Milwaukee WI 53214 USA — Baseball Player

Gallatin, Harry J
2010 Madison Ave, Edwardsville IL 62025, USA — Basketball Player, Coach

Gallego, Gina
6550 Murietta Ave, Van Nuys CA 91401, USA — Actress

Gallego, Michael A (Mike)
20205 Chandler Dr, Yorba Linda CA 92887, USA — Baseball Player

Gallery, Robert J
3163 210th St, Masonville IA 50654, USA — Football Player

Galles, Rick
Galles Racing, PO Box 2507, Albuquerque NM 87165, USA — Auto Racing Executive

Galley, Garry M
CBC-TV, PO Box 500, Station A, Toronto ON M5W 1E6, Canada — Ice Hockey Player

Galli, Joseph, Jr
Newell Rubbermaid Co, Newell Center, 29 E Stephenson St, Freeport IL 61032, USA — Businessman

Gallico, Gregory, III
Massachusetts General Hospital, 275 Cambridge St, Boston MA 02114, USA — Surgeon, Inventor (Synthetic Skin)

Galligan, Zach
Innovative Artists, 1505 10th St, Santa Monica CA 90401 USA — Actor

Gallinari, Danilo
Denver Nuggets, Pepsi Center, 1000 Chopper Circle, Denver CO 80204 USA — Basketball Player

Gallion, Billy Ray
A K A Talent, 6310 San Vicente Blvd, #200, Los Angeles CA 90048 USA — Actor

Gallison, Joseph
PO Box 10187, Wilmington NC 28404, USA — Actor

Gallo, Frank
T R A Art Group, 1700 Stutz Dr, #15, Troy MI 48084, USA — Sculptor

Gallo, Richard L
University of California Medical Center, Dermatology Dept, 200 W Arbor Dr, San Diego CA 92103, USA — Dermatologist

Gallo, Robert C
University of Maryland, Study of Viruses Institute, Baltimore MD 21228, USA — Research Scientist

Gallo, Vincent
432 La Guardia Place, #600, New York NY 10012, USA — Actor, Director

Gallois, Louis
Airbus E A D S, Ronde Point Maurice Bellont 1, 31207 Blagnac, France — Businessman

Gallop, Tom
A P A Talent/Literary Agency, 405 S Beverly Dr, #300, Beverly Hills CA 90212 USA — Actor

Galloway, David L
5441 NW 184th St, Miami Gardens FL 33055, USA — Football Player

Galloway, George
Talk Sport Radio, 18 Hatfields, London SE1 8DJ, England — Government Official, England

Galloway, Joseph S (Joey)
1611 Cherokee Trail, Plano TX 75023, USA — Football Player

Gallucci, Robert L
MacArthur Foundation, 140 S Dearborn St, Chicago IL 60603, USA — Foundation Executive

Galvez, Balvino
3986 SW 190th St, Miramar FL 33029, USA — Baseball Player

Galvin, James
University of Iowa, Writers' Workshop, Iowa City IA 52242, USA — Writer

Galvin, John R
2714 Lake Jodeco Dr, Jonesboro GA 30236, USA — Army General

Galway, James
Benseholzstr 11, 6045 Meggan, Switzerland — Concert Flutist, Conductor

Galyon, Scott
4631 Horseshoe Trail, Morristown TN 37814, USA — Football Player

Gam, Rita
180 W 58th St, #8B, New York NY 10019, USA — Actress

Gamache, Joey
60 Pettingill St, #2, Lewiston ME 4240, USA — Boxer

Gamba, Rumon
NorrlandsOperan, Operaplan 5, 901 08 Umea, Sweden — Conductor

Gamba, Veronica
32230 Alvarado Blvd, #128, Union City CA 94587, USA — Actress, Model

Gambee, David P (Dave)
6175 SW Arrow Wood Lane, Portland OR 97223, USA — Basketball Player

Gambino, Richard J
State University of New York, Materials Science Dept, Stony Brook NY 11794, USA — Inventor (Read-Write Optical Storage)

Gamble, Chris L
13335 Pierre Reverdy Dr, Davidson NC 28036, USA — Football Player

Gamble, Ed
Florida Times-Union, Editorial Dept, 1 Riverside Ave, Jacksonville FL 32202, USA — Editorial Cartoonist

Gamble, John R
369 Caliente St, Reno NV 89509, USA — Baseball Player

Gamble, Kenneth (Kenny)
W M E Entertainment, 9601 Wilshire Blvd, #300, Beverly Hills CA 90210 USA — Songwriter

Gamble, Kenneth P (Kenny)
4 Algonquin Dr, Wilbraham MA 01095, USA — Football Player

Gamble, Kevin D
41 W Huckleberry Road, Lynnfield MA 01940, USA — Basketball Player

Gamble, Mason
Bresler Kelly Assoc, 11500 W Olympic Blvd, #400, Los Angeles CA 90064 USA — Actor

Gamble, Nathan
Paradigm Agency, 360 N Crescent Dr, North Building, Beverly Hills CA 90210 USA — Actor

Gamble, Oscar C
9705 Bent Brook Dr, Montgomery AL 36117, USA — Baseball Player

Gamble, Patrick K
PO Box 107500, Anchorage AK 99510, USA — Air Force General, Educator

Gamble, Richard F (Dick)
1 Vantage Dr, Pittsford NY 14534, USA — Ice Hockey Player

Gamblin, Jacques — Actor
Agence Artiste Adequet, 80 Rue d'Amsterdam, 75009 Paris, France

Gambon, Michael J — Actor
Independent Talent Group, Oxford House, 76 Oxford St, London W1D 1BS, England

Gambrell, David H — Senator, GA
3205 Arden Road NW, Atlanta GA 30305, USA

Gambrell, William E (Billy) — Football Player
341 Osceola Ave, Bogart GA 30622, USA

Gambril, Don — Swimming Coach
4409 Spring Row, Northport AL 35473, USA

Gambucci, Andre P (Andy) — Ice Hockey Player, Coach
9241 Yukon Ave S, Minneapolis MN 55438, USA

Gambucci, Gary A — Ice Hockey Player
9241 Yukon Ave S, Minneapolis MN 55438, USA

Gambucci, Sergio (Serge) — Ice Hockey Coach
4365 Carriage House View, Colorado Springs CO 80906, USA

Game — Rap Artist
I C M Partners, 10250 Constellation Blvd, #900, Los Angeles CA 90067 USA

Gamez, Robert — Golfer
Team Gamez Foundation, PO Box 690362, Orlando FL 32869, USA

Gammon, Kendall R — Football Player
14429 Maple St, Overland Park KS 66223, USA

Gammons, Peter — Sportswriter
Boston Globe, Editorial Dept, 135 William Morrissey Blvd, Dorchester MA 02125 USA

Ganassi, Floyd (Chip) — Auto Racing Driver, Executive
Chip Ganassi Racing, 8500 Westmoreland Dr, Concord NC 28027, USA

Ganassi, Sonia — Opera Singer
Columbia Artists Mgmt Inc, 1790 Broadway, #702, New York NY 10019 USA

Ganatra, Nitin C — Actor
United Agents, 12-26 Lexington St, London W1F 0LE, England

Ganchar, Perry — Ice Hockey Player
8043 Summerhouse Dr W, Dublin OH 43016, USA

Gand, Gayle — Chef
674 N Saint Clair St, Chicago IL 60611, USA

Gandee, Sherman H (Sonny) — Football Player
1525 Hinton St, Port Charlotte FL 33952, USA

Gandhi, Sonia — Government Official, India
All India Congress Party, 24 Akbar Road, New Delhi 110011, India

Gandolfini, James — Actor
Creative Artists Agency, 2000 Ave of Stars, #100, Los Angeles CA 90067 USA

Gandy, Mike J — Football Player
8508 E Sweetwater Ave, Scottsdale AZ 85260, USA

Gandy, Wayne L — Football Player
6 Pinecrest Road NE, Atlanta GA 30342, USA

Ganellin, C Robin — Inventor (Antiulcer Compound)
University College, Chemistry Dept, 20 Gordon, London WC1H 0AJ, England

Gangel, Geraldine (Gig) — Model, Actress
Playboy Promotions, 2706 Media Center Dr, Los Angeles CA 90065 USA

Gangloff, Mark — Swimmer
5318 Camden Dr, Stow OH 44224, USA

Gann, Jason W — Actor, Writer
W M E Entertainment, 9601 Wilshire Blvd, #300, Beverly Hills CA 90210 USA

Gann, Mike A — Football Player
1479 Ashford Place NE, Atlanta GA 30319, USA

Gann, Pamela B — Educator
Claremont McKenna College, President's Office, 500 E 9th, Claremont CA 91711, USA

Gannascoli, Joseph R — Actor, Writer
Acme Talent Agency, 4727 Wilshire Blvd, #333, Los Angeles CA 90010 USA

Gannaway, Preston — Photojournalist
Concord Monitor, Editorial Dept, 1 Monitor Dr, Concord NH 03301, USA

Gannon, Richard J (Rich) — Football Player, Sportscaster
6472 Smithtown Road, Atlanta GA 30319, USA

Ganso, Paulo Henrique — Soccer Player
Confederacion de Futebol, Rua Victor Civita 66, #1, Rio de Janeiro 22775 044, Brazil

Gant, Harry P — Auto Racing Driver
7531 Millersville Road, Taylorsville NC 28681, USA

Gant, Kenneth D (Kenny) — Football Player
1820 W 10th St, Lakeland FL 33805, USA

Gant, Reuben C — Football Player
PO Box 3051, Tulsa OK 74101, USA

Gant, Richard — Actor
Pakula/King, 9229 W Sunset Blvd, #315, West Hollywood CA 90069 USA

Gant, Robert — Actor
Mythgarden, 960 N Ridgewood Place, Los Angeles CA 90038, USA

Gant, Ronald E (Ron) — Baseball Player
1027 Wellesley Crest Dr, Woodstock GA 30189, USA

Gantz, Robert J — Cinematographer
20 Kettle Creek Road, Weston CT 06883, USA

Ganum, John — Actor
Geddes Agency, 8430 Santa Monica Blvd, #201, West Hollywood CA 90069 USA

Ganz, Bruno — Actor
Braumbauer Actors, Hanfelderstr 32, 82319 Starnberg, Germany

Ganzel, Teresa — Actress
I C M Partners, 10250 Constellation Blvd, #900, Los Angeles CA 90067 USA

Gao Min — Diver
Olympic Committee, 9 Tiyuguan Road, Chongwen District, Beijing 100763, China

Gao Xingjian — Nobel Literature Laureate
Editions l'Aube, Le Moulin de Chateau, 84240 Le Tour d'Aigues, France

Gao, Xiang — Concert Violinist
Columbia Artists Mgmt Inc, 1790 Broadway, #702, New York NY 10019 USA

Gaona, Tito — Circus Trapeze Artist
432 Spadora Dr, Venice FL 34285, USA

Gara, Jeremy — Musician (Arcade Fire)
Billions Corp, 3522 W Armitage Ave, Chicago IL 60647 USA

Garabaldi, Robert R (Bob) — Baseball Player
2143 Oregon Ave, Stockton CA 95204, USA

Garagiola, Joseph H (Joe) 4555 E Mayo Blvd, #3331, Phoenix AZ 85050, USA	Sportscaster, Baseball Player
Garagozzo, Keith J 16 Foxcroft Way, Mount Laurel NJ 08054, USA	Baseball Player
Garai, Romola Artist Rights Group, 4 Great Portland Place, London W1W 8PA, England	Actress
Garan, Ronald J, Jr 2002 Sea Cove Court, Houston TX 77058, USA	Astronaut
Garant, Robert Ben Creative Artists Agency, 2000 Ave of Stars, #100, Los Angeles CA 90067 USA	Actor
Garant, Sylvie Playboy Promotions, 2706 Media Center Dr, Los Angeles CA 90065 USA	Model, Actress
Garas, Kaz 400 W 43rd St, #42L, New York NY 10036, USA	Actor
Garavito, R Michael Michigan State University, Biochemistry Dept, East Lansing MI 48824, USA	Biochemist
Garbacz, Lori 777 Albany Post Road, Briarcliff Manor NY 10510, USA	Golfer
Garber, H Eugene (Gene) 771 Stonemill Dr, Elizabethtown PA 17022, USA	Baseball Player
Garber, Terri 38 E 1st St, #2B, New York NY 10003, USA	Actress
Garber, Victor Paradigm Agency, 360 N Crescent Dr, North Building, Beverly Hills CA 90210 USA	Actor
Garbey, Barbaro G 14094 Woodside Sr, Livonia MI 48154, USA	Baseball Player
Garces, Paula B/W/R, 9100 Wilshire Blvd, #500W, Beverly Hills CA 90212 USA	Actress
Garces, Richard A (Rich) 605 Swigert St, Kerrville TX 78028, USA	Baseball Player
Garci, Jose Luis Direccion General del Libro, Paseo de la Castellana 109, 20846 Madrid, Spain	Director, Producer, Writer
Garcia Bernal, Gael Canana Films, San Luis Potosi, #211 Piso 8, Colonia Roma, Mexico City DF 06700, Mexico	Actor, Director, Producer
Garcia Marquez, Gabriel Fuego 144, Pedregal de San Angel, Mexico City DF, Mexico	Nobel Literature Laureate
Garcia Swisher, Joanna John Carrabino Mgmt, 5900 Wilshire Blvd, #406, Los Angeles CA 90036 USA	Actress
Garcia, Adam G I C M Partners, 10250 Constellation Blvd, #900, Los Angeles CA 90067 USA	Actor
Garcia, Aimee Paradigm Agency, 360 N Crescent Dr, North Building, Beverly Hills CA 90210 USA	Actress
Garcia, Alfonso R (Kiko) 526 Trailview Circle, Martinez CA 94553, USA	Baseball Player
Garcia, Andy CineSon Entertainment, 4519 Varna Ave, Sherman Oaks CA 91423, USA	Actor
Garcia, Carlos J 5208 William St, Lancaster NY 14086, USA	Baseball Player
Garcia, Daniel R (Danny) 22 Silo Lane, Levittown NY 11756, USA	Baseball Player
Garcia, Danna Innovative Artists, 1505 10th St, Santa Monica CA 90401 USA	Actress, Singer, Model
Garcia, Danny (Swift) Golden Boy Promotions, 626 Wilshire Blvd, #350, Los Angeles CA 90017 USA	Boxer
Garcia, David (Dave) 17842 Avenida Cordillera, #28, San Diego CA 92128, USA	Baseball Manager
Garcia, Eric W M E Entertainment, 9601 Wilshire Blvd, #300, Beverly Hills CA 90210 USA	Writer
Garcia, Freddy A Quisquella Gta Etapa M22, #52, La Ramana, Dominican Republic	Baseball Player
Garcia, G Karim 38 Agnew Farm Road, Armonk NY 10504, USA	Baseball Player
Garcia, Gina Garcia Art Glass, 123 Losoya St, #5, San Antonio TX 78205, USA	Artist
Garcia, Gregory Thomas Creative Artists Agency, 2000 Ave of Stars, #100, Los Angeles CA 90067 USA	Producer, Writer
Garcia, Guillermo A 3806 Shoma Dr, West Palm Beach FL 33414, USA	Baseball Player
Garcia, Jeffrey J (Jeff) PO Box 8977, Rancho Santa Fe CA 92067, USA	Football Player
Garcia, Jesse TalentWorks, 3500 W Olive Ave, #1400, Burbank CA 91505 USA	Actor
Garcia, Jesus Columbia Artists Mgmt Inc, 1790 Broadway, #702, New York NY 10019 USA	Singer
Garcia, Jorge Kritzer Levine Wilkins Griffin, 11872 La Grange Ave, #100, Los Angeles CA 90025 USA	Actor
Garcia, Juan Carlos Gabriel Blanco, Rio Balsas 35-32, Colonia Cuauhtemoc DF 6500, Mexico	Actor
Garcia, Leonardo A (Leo) 5416 W Sunland Ave, Laveen AZ 85339, USA	Baseball Player
Garcia, Lucrezia I M G Artists, Hogarth Business Park, Chiswick, London W4 2TH, England	Opera Singer
Garcia, Mayte C E S D, 10635 Santa Monica Blvd, #130, Los Angeles CA 90025 USA	Actress
Garcia, Miguel A (Mike) 28428 Eagle St, Moreno Valley CA 92555, USA	Baseball Player
Garcia, Nicole Voyez Mon Agent, 20 Ave Rapp, 75007 Paris, France	Actress
Garcia, Pedro M Parque del Condado L4, Urb Bairoa Park, Caguas PR 00725, USA	Baseball Player
Garcia, Richard R (Rich) 769 Harbor Isle, Clearwater FL 33767, USA	Baseball Umpire
Garcia, Rodrigo Kuranda Mgmt, Santo Angel 84, 28043 Madrid, Spain	Director, Producer
Garcia, Rupert Aurobora Press, 370 Brannan St, #100, San Francisco CA 94107, USA	Artist

Garcia, Sergio — Golfer
International Mgmt Group, 1 Erieview Plaza, 1360 E 9th St, Cleveland OH 44114 USA

Garciaparra, A Nomar — Baseball Player
613 15th St, Manhattan Beach CA 90266, USA

Garcon, Pierre — Football Player
Washington Redskins, 21300 Redskin Park Dr, Ashburn VA 20147 USA

Gard, Robert G, Jr — Army General
Center for Arms Control, 322 4th St NE, Washington DC 20002, USA

Gard, Toby — Video Games Designer (Lara Croft)
SCi Entertainment Group, 1 Hartfield Road, London SW19 3RU, England

Gardell, Billy — Actor, Comedian
Creative Artists Agency, 2000 Ave of Stars, #100, Los Angeles CA 90067 USA

Gardener, Daryl R — Football Player
8925 Legacy Court, #106, Kissimmee FL 34747, USA

Gardener, Jason — Track Athlete
Athletics World Mgmt, 7097 Alvern St, #308, Los Angeles CA 90045 USA

Gardenhire, Ronald C (Ron) — Baseball Player, Manager
585 County Road B2 E, Saint Paul MN 55117, USA

Gardiner, Greg — Cinematographer
Paradigm Agency, 360 N Crescent Dr, North Building, Beverly Hills CA 90210 USA

Gardiner, John Eliot — Conductor
Gore Farm, Ashmore, Salisbury, Wilts SP5 5AR, England

Gardiner, Margaret — Beauty Queen
Andre Nel, 200 UCLA Medical Plaza, Los Angeles CA 90095, USA

Gardiner, Michael J (Mike) — Baseball Player
26 Read Dr, Hanover MA 02339, USA

Gardner, Ashley — Actress
S M S Talent, 8383 Wilshire Blvd, #230, Beverly Hills CA 90211 USA

Gardner, Barry A — Football Player
24964 S Willow Brook Trail, Crete IL 60417, USA

Gardner, Brett M — Baseball Player
117 Drake St, Charleston SC 29403, USA

Gardner, Carwell E — Football Player
9603 Galene Dr, Louisville KY 40299, USA

Gardner, Christopher J (Chris) — Baseball Player
2304 SW Abalon Circle, Port Saint Lucie FL 34953, USA

Gardner, Dale A — Astronaut
60 Blue Mesa Circle, Divide CO 80814, USA

Gardner, David P — Educator, Foundation Executive
2989 American Saddler Dr, Park City UT 84060, USA

Gardner, Emerson N, Jr — Marine Corps General
Deputy CofS, Programs/Resources, HqUSMC, 2 Navy St, Washington DC 20380 USA

Gardner, Guy S — Astronaut
N A S A, Johnson Space Center, 2101 NASA Road, Houston TX 77058 USA

Gardner, Howard E — Psychologist, Neurobiologist
Harvard University, Graduate Education School, Cambridge MA 02138, USA

Gardner, James — Director
Shapiro-Lichtman, 8827 Beverly Blvd, Los Angeles CA 90048 USA

Gardner, Jeffrey S (Jeff) — Baseball Player
1906 Port Weybridge Place, Newport Beach CA 92660, USA

Gardner, John — Ballet Dancer
American Ballet Theatre, 890 Broadway, #300, New York NY 10003 USA

Gardner, Lisa — Writer
Jane Rotrosen Agency, 318 E 51st St, New York NY 10022, USA

Gardner, Mark A — Baseball Player
15216 Mesa View Ave, Friant CA 93626, USA

Gardner, Randy — Figure Skater
4640 Glencoe Ave, #6, Marina del Rey CA 90292, USA

Gardner, Robert G — Educator
Harvard University, Visual & Environmental Studies Dept, Cambridge MA 02138, USA

Gardner, Roderick F (Rod) — Football Player
1883 Executive Dr, Duluth GA 30096, USA

Gardner, Rulon — Greco-Roman Wrestler
Elite Training Center, 981 S Main St, #130, Logan UT 84321, USA

Gardner, Tom — Editor
124 N Pitt St, Alexandria VA 22314, USA

Gardner, W Booth — Governor, WA
Norton Building, 801 2nd Ave, #1300, Seattle WA 98104, USA

Gardner, Wesley B (Wes) — Baseball Player
305 Ruth, Benton AR 72019, USA

Gardner, Wilford R — Physicist
University of California, Natural Resources College, Berkeley CA 94720, USA

Gardner, William F (Billy) — Baseball Player, Manager
35 Dayton Road, Waterford CT 06385, USA

Gardocki, Christopher A (Chris) — Football Player
63 Yorkshire Dr, Hilton Head Island SC 29928, USA

Gardot, Melody — Singer, Pianist, Guitarist
W M E Entertainment, 9601 Wilshire Blvd, #300, Beverly Hills CA 90210 USA

Gare, Danny — Ice Hockey Player
950 Hopkins Road, #F, Buffalo NY 14221, USA

Garelick, Jeremy — Producer, Writer
United Talent Agency, 9336 Civic Center Dr, Beverly Hills CA 90210 USA

Garfat, Jance — Bassist, Singer (Dr Hook)
Artists Int'l Mgmt, 9850 Sandalwood Blvd, #458, Boca Raton FL 33428, USA

Garfield, Allen — Actor
8271 Melrose Ave, #203, Los Angeles CA 90046, USA

Garfield, Andrew — Actor
Gordon & French, 12-13 Poland St, London W1F 8QB, England

Garfinkel, Jack (Dutch) — Basketball Player
300 Ocean Parkway, #2E, Brooklyn NY 11218, USA

Garfunkel, Art — Singer, Actor
120 E 87th St, #P28B, New York NY 10128, USA

Garibaldi, Bob R — Baseball Player
2143 Oregon Ave, Stockton CA 95204, USA

Garity, Troy — Actor
Untitled Entertainment, 350 S Beverly Dr, #200, Beverly Hills CA 90212 USA

Garland, Alex
Creative Artists Agency, 2000 Ave of Stars, #100, Los Angeles CA 90067 USA — Writer

Garland, George D
5 Mawhiney Court, Huntsville ON P0A 1K0, Canada — Geophysicist

Garland, Jon S
2924 Summerwood Dr, Springfield IL 62712, USA — Baseball Player

Garland, Nicholas
Daily Telegraph, 111 Buckingham Palace Road, London SW1W 0DT, England — Editorial Cartoonist

Garland, R Wayne
7556 Mossback St, Las Vegas NV 89123, USA — Baseball Player

Garland, Winston K
2304 Cleveland St, Gary IN 46404, USA — Basketball Player

Garlin, Jeff
I C M Partners, 10250 Constellation Blvd, #900, Los Angeles CA 90067 USA — Actor, Producer

Garlits, Donald G (Big Daddy)
Garlits Racing Museum, 13700 SW 16th Ave, Ocala FL 34473, USA — Drag Racing Driver

Garmaker, Richard E (Dick)
5824 E 111th St, Tulsa OK 74137, USA — Basketball Player

Garman, Michael D (Mike)
15144 Kings Row Road, Caldwell ID 83607, USA — Baseball Player

Garn, E Jacob (Jake)
1267 Chalder Circle, Salt Lake City UT 84103, USA — Senator, UT; Astronaut

Garn, Stanley M
1200 Earhart Road, #223, Ann Arbor MI 48105, USA — Anthropologist

Garneau, Marc
Space Agency, 6767 Route de Aeroport, Sainte-Hubert QC J3Y 8Y9, Canada — Astronaut, Canada

Garner, Charlie, III
12944 Royal George Ave, Odessa FL 33556, USA — Football Player

Garner, James
2515 Fountain Hill Loop, Lincoln CA 95648, USA — Actor

Garner, Jennifer
Vandalia Films, 9100 Wilshire Blvd, #1000W, Beverly Hills CA 90212, USA — Actress

Garner, Kelli
John Carrabino Mgmt, 5900 Wilshire Blvd, #406, Los Angeles CA 90036 USA — Actress

Garner, Philip M (Phil)
2 Sapling Place, Spring TX 77382, USA — Baseball Player, Manager

Garner, Wendell R
105 Northcreek Circle, Walnut Creek CA 94598, USA — Psychologist

Garner, William S
Memphis Commercial Appeal, Editorial Dept, 495 Union Ave, Memphis TN 38103, USA — Editorial Cartoonist

Garnes, Sam A
7322 S Valdai Circle, Aurora CO 80016, USA — Football Player

Garnett, Kevin M
75 Buttricks Hill Dr, Concord MA 01742, USA — Basketball Player

Garofalo, Janeane
I C M Partners, 10250 Constellation Blvd, #900, Los Angeles CA 90067 USA — Actress, Comedienne

Garouste, Gerard
La Mesangere, 27810 Marcilly-sur-Eure, France — Artist

Garr, Ralph A
22314 Auburn Canyon Lane, Richmond TX 77469, USA — Baseball Player

Garr, Teri
Paradigm Agency, 360 N Crescent Dr, North Building, Beverly Hills CA 90210 USA — Actress

Garrard, David D
2209 Alicia Lane, Atlantic Beach FL 32233, USA — Football Player

Garrard, Rose
105 Carpenters Road, #21, London E18, England — Artist, Sculptor

Garre, Gregory G
George Washington University, Law Center, Washington DC 20052, USA — Government Official, Attorney

Garrelts, Scott W
11070 Ashland Way, Shreveport LA 71106, USA — Baseball Player

Garrett, Brad
United Talent Agency, 9336 Civic Center Dr, Beverly Hills CA 90210 USA — Actor, Comedian

Garrett, Carl L
203 S Crawford St, Denton TX 76205, USA — Football Player

Garrett, David
Music & Media Partnership, 126-129 Power Road, London W4 5PY, England — Concert Violinist

Garrett, Dick
7100 N Park Manor Dr, Milwaukee WI 53224, USA — Basketball Player

Garrett, H Adrian (Ade)
PO Box 201, Manchaca TX 78652, USA — Baseball Player

Garrett, H Lawrence, III
RR 1 Box 136-18, Boyce VA 22620, USA — Government Official

Garrett, Jason C
3656 Maplewood Ave, Dallas TX 75205, USA — Football Player, Coach

Garrett, Jeremy
W M E Entertainment, 9601 Wilshire Blvd, #300, Beverly Hills CA 90210 USA — Actor

Garrett, John M
Rogers Sportsnet, 181 Keefer Place, #221, Vancouver BC V6B 6C1, Canada — Ice Hockey Player

Garrett, Kathleen
Don Buchwald/Fortitude, 10 E 44th St, New York NY 10017 USA — Actress

Garrett, Kenneth
National Geographic, Editorial Dept, 1145 17th St NW, Washington DC 20036 USA — Photographer

Garrett, Kenny
Von Productions, 1915 Cullen Ave, Austin TX 78757, USA — Jazz Saxophonist, Flutist

Garrett, LaMonica
Elevate Entertainment, 1925 Century Park E, #2320 Los Angeles CA 90067, USA — Actor

Garrett, Leif
Barbara Papageorge, 790 Amsterdam Ave, #4E, New York NY 10025, USA — Actor, Singer

Garrett, Leonard N (Len)
9413 W Tampa Dr, Baton Rouge LA 70815, USA — Football Player

Garrett, Lesley
Music Partnership, 41 Aldebert Terrace, London SW8 1BH, England — Opera Singer

Garrett, Maureen
Paradigm Agency, 360 N Crescent Dr, North Building, Beverly Hills CA 90210 USA — Actress

Garrett, Megan
Proper Mgmt, PO Box 150867, Nashville TN 37215, USA — Keyboardist (Casting Crowns)

	Profession
	Singer, Guitarist, Songwriter
Garrett, Pat Patrick Sickafus, PO Box 1, Strausstown PA 19559, USA	
	Singer (Midnight Oil)
Garrett, Peter PO Box 249, Marubra NSW 2035, Australia	
	Baseball Player
Garrett, R Wayne 4331 Linwood St, Sarasota FL 34232, USA	
	Singer (Brand New Heavies), Songwriter
Garrett, Siedah McClure & Associates Public Relations, 5225 Wilshire Blvd, #909, Los Angeles CA 90036, USA	
	Actor
Garrett, Spencer Stone Manners Salners, 9911 W Pico Blvd, #1400, Los Angeles CA 90035 USA	
	Editor
Garrett, Wilbur E (Bill) 209 Seneca Road, Great Falls VA 22066, USA	
	Actress
Garrick, Barbara Cornerstone Talent, 37 W 20th St, #1108, New York NY 10011, USA	
	Basketball Player
Garrick, Thomas S (Tom) 235 Providence St, West Warwick RI 02893, USA	
	Football Player
Garrido Davidds, Norberto, Jr 15633 Briarbank St, La Puente CA 91744, USA	
	Baseball Player
Garrido, Gil G 11311 SW 200th St, #110D, Miami FL 33157, USA	
	Marksman
Garrigus, Thomas PO Box 681, Plains MT 59859, USA	
	Astronaut
Garriott, Owen K 111 Lost Tree Dr SW, Huntsville AL 35824, USA	
	Tourist Cosmonaut
Garriott, Richard A NCsoft, 6801 N Capital of Texas Highway, #1-102, Austin TX 78731, USA	
	Director
Garris, Mick Paradigm Agency, 360 N Crescent Dr, North Building, Beverly Hills CA 90210 USA	
	Actor
Garrison, David S M S Talent, 8383 Wilshire Blvd, #230, Beverly Hills CA 90211 USA	
	Football Player
Garrison, Gary L 7757 Caminito Encanto Lane, #102, Carlsbad CA 92009, USA	
	Actor, Writer
Garrison, Lane Untitled Entertainment, 350 S Beverly Dr, #200, Beverly Hills CA 90212 USA	
	Football Player
Garrison, Walter B (Walt) 3475 E Hickory Hill Road, Argyle TX 76226, USA	
	Baseball Player
Garrison, Webster L 2038 Rue Racine, Marrero LA 70072, USA	
	Tennis Player
Garrison, Zina All Court Tennis Foundation, 12335 Kingsride, #106, Houston TX 77024, USA	
	Football Player
Garrity, Gregg D 86 Seldom Seen Road, Bradfordwoods PA 15015, USA	
	Ice Hockey Player
Garrity, John (Jack) 1530 Beacon St, #1201, Brookline MA 02446, USA	
	Basketball Player
Garrity, Patrick J (Pat) 6126 Ches Court, Orlando FL 32819, USA	
	Actress
Garro, Julia Innovative Artists, 1505 10th St, Santa Monica CA 90401 USA	
	Football Player
Garron, Lawrence (Larry), Jr 3 Debra Lane, Framingham MA 01701, USA	
	Director
Garrone, Matteo Archimede, Via Tiburtina 521, 00159 Rome, Italy	
	Actor
Garson, Willie John Carrabino Mgmt, 5900 Wilshire Blvd, #406, Los Angeles CA 90036 USA	
	Food Expert
Garten, Ina 46 Newton Ave, #3, East Hampton NY 11937, USA	
	Actress
Garth, Jennie W M E Entertainment, 9601 Wilshire Blvd, #300, Beverly Hills CA 90210 USA	
	Judge
Garth, Leonard I US Court of Appeals, US Courthouse, 50 Walnut St, #5040, Newark NJ 07102, USA	
	Actor
Gartner, Claus-Theo Postfach 230313, 45071 Essen, Germany	
	Director
Gartner, James I C M Partners, 10250 Constellation Blvd, #900, Los Angeles CA 90067 USA	
	Ice Hockey Player
Gartner, Michael A (Mike) N H L Players Assn, 1700-20 Bay St, Toronto ON M5J 2N8, Canada	
	Publisher, Editor, Businessman
Gartner, Michael G 100 Market St, #515, Des Moines IA 50309, USA	
	Artist
Gartner, Stephen Gartner & Blade, 4-1354 Kuhio Highway, Kapaa HI 96746, USA	
	Actress
Garver, Kathy PO Box 117345, Burlingame CA 94011, USA	
	Baseball Player
Garver, Ned F 1121 Town Line Road, #164, Bryan OH 43506, USA	
	Baseball Player
Garvey, Steven P (Steve) Athlete Promotions, 2247 Rickover Place, Winter Garden FL 34787, USA	
	Physicist
Garwin, Richard L 1 Christie Place, #402W, Scarsdale NY 10583, USA	
	Football Player
Gary, Keith J 450 Massachusetts Ave NW, #903, Washington DC 20001, USA	
	Actress
Gary, Lorraine 1158 Tower Dr, Beverly Hills CA 90210, USA	
	Singer
Garza, David Partisan Arts, PO Box 5085, Larkspur CA 94977, USA	
	Judge
Garza, Emilio M US Court of Appeals, US Courthouse, 8200 I-10 W, San Antonio TX 78230, USA	
	Guitarist (Los Lonely Boys)
Garza, Henry Loophole Entertainment, PO Box 162045, Austin TX 78716, USA	
	Bassist (Los Lonely Boys)
Garza, JoJo Loophole Entertainment, PO Box 162045, Austin TX 78716, USA	
	Boxer
Garza, Loreto 6 Napa Place, Woodland CA 95695, USA	
	Actress, Model
Garza, Nicole Kritzer Levine Wilkins Griffin, 11872 La Grange Ave, #100, Los Angeles CA 90025 USA	
	Drummer (Los Lonely Boys)
Garza, Ringo Loophole Entertainment, PO Box 162045, Austin TX 78716, USA	

Garzon, Baltasar
Audiencia Nacional, Garcia Gutierrez 1, 28004 Madrid, Spain — Judge

Gascoigne, Paul J
Robertson Craig Co, Clairmont Gardens, Glasgow G3 7LW, Scotland — Soccer Player

Gascoine, Jill
Marina Martin, 12/13 Poland St, London W1V 3DE, England — Actress

Gash, Samuel L (Sam)
18549 Steep Hollow Court, Northville MI 48168, USA — Football Player

Gaskell, Anna
Albright-Kerr Gallery, 1285 Elmwood Ave, Buffalo NY 14222, USA — Photographer

Gaskins, Reggie
I C M Partners, 10250 Constellation Blvd, #900, Los Angeles CA 90067 USA — Actor, Director, Writer

Gasol, Marc
Memphis Grizzlies, 191 Beale St, Memphis TN 38103 USA — Basketball Player

Gasol, Pau
Los Angeles Lakers, Staples Center, 1111 S Figueroa St, Los Angeles CA 90015 USA — Basketball Player

Gaspar, Rodney E (Rod)
28771 Peach Blossom, Mission Viejo CA 92692, USA — Baseball Player

Gasparovic, Ivan
President's Office, Hodzova Namestie 2978/1, 81006 Bratislava, Slovakia — President, Slovakia

Gasquet, Richard
Association of Tennis Professionals, 200 Tournament Road, Ponte Vedra Beach FL 32082 USA — Tennis Player

Gass, Kyle R
Greene Assoc, 1901 Ave of Stars, #130, Los Angeles CA 90067 USA — Actor, Singer, Guitarist

Gass, William H
6304 Westminster Place, Saint Louis MO 63130, USA — Philosopher, Writer

Gass-Donnelly, Ed
I C M Partners, 10250 Constellation Blvd, #900, Los Angeles CA 90067 USA — Director

Gassiyev, Nikolai T
Mariinsky Theater, Teatralnaya Square 1, 190000 Saint Petersburg, Russia — Opera Singer

Gassner, Dave
N1376 Woodland Dr, Greenville WI 54942, USA — Baseball Player

Gast, Alice P
Lehigh University, President's Office, 27 Memorial Dr W, Bethlehem PA 18015, USA — Educator

Gasteyer, Ana K
Gersh Agency, 9465 Wilshire Blvd, #600, Beverly Hills CA 90212 USA — Actress, Comedienne

Gastineau, Marcus D (Mark)
22202 N 48th St, Phoenix AZ 85054, USA — Football Player

Gaston, Clarence E (Cito)
1454 Woodstream Dr, Oldsmar FL 34677, USA — Baseball Player, Manager

Gaston, Marilyn H
Gaston-Porter Health Improvement Center, 8612 Timber Hill, Potomac MD 20854, USA — Physician, Administrator

Gaston, Michael
A P A Talent/Literary Agency, 405 S Beverly Dr, #300, Beverly Hills CA 90212 USA — Actor

Gates, Antonio M
PO Box 11369, Charlotte NC 28220, USA — Football Player

Gates, Brent R
4229 Haralson Court SE, Grand Rapids MI 49546, USA — Baseball Player

Gates, David
Paradise Artists, PO Box 1821, Ojai CA 93024 USA — Singer, Keyboardist (Bread), Songwriter

Gates, Gareth P
Syco Mgmt, 69-79 Fulham High St, London SW6 3JW, England — Singer

Gates, Henry Lewis, Jr
Harvard University, Afro-American Studies Dept, Cambridge MA 02138, USA — Educator

Gates, Marshall D, Jr
41 W Brook Road, Pittsford PA 14534, USA — Chemist

Gates, Tucker
United Talent Agency, 9336 Civic Center Dr, Beverly Hills CA 90210 USA — Director, Producer

Gates, William H (Bill), III
Microsoft Corp, 1 Microsoft Way, Redmond WA 98052, USA — Computer Software Designer, Businessman

Gatewood, Mark
Gatewood Studio, 211 SE Morrison St, Portland OR 97214, USA — Artist

Gathegi, Edi
Framework Entertainment, 9057 Nemo St, #C, West Hollywood CA 90069 USA — Actor

Gathright, Joey R
9100 Dr Martin Luther King Jr St N, #902, Saint Petersburg FL 33702, USA — Baseball Player

Gatien, Elise
Carrie Wheeler Mgmt, 101-1001 W Broadway, #338, Vancouver BC V6H 4E4, Canada — Actress

Gatlin, Larry W
R P R Media, 952 Harpeth Bend Drive, Nashville TN 37221, USA — Singer, Songwriter (Gatlin Brothers)

Gatling, Chris R
175 Canon Dr, Orinda CA 94563, USA — Basketball Player

Gatos, Harry C
20 Indian Hill Road, Weston MA 02493, USA — Electrical Engineer

Gatti, Daniele
Via Scaglia Est 134, 41100 Modena, Italy — Conductor

Gatti, Jennifer
S D B Partners, 1801 Ave of Stars, #902, Los Angeles CA 90067 USA — Actress

Gatting, Michael W
Middlesex Cricket Club, Saint John's Wood Road, London NW8 8QN, England — Cricketer

Gattison, Kenneth A (Kenny)
1115 I St NE, Washington DC 20002, USA — Basketball Player

Gaubatz, Dennis E
1250 County Road 943, West Columbia TX 77486, USA — Football Player

Gauci, Miriam
Kunstleragentur Raab & Bohm, Plankengasse 7, 1010 Vienna, Austria — Opera Singer

Gauck, Joachim
Bundeskanzlerant, Schlossplatz 1, 10178 Berlin, Germany — President, Germany; Political Activist

Gaudin, Chad E
108 Cirtus Road, New Orleans LA 70123, USA — Baseball Player

Gaudio, Robert J (Bob)
I C M Partners, 10250 Constellation Blvd, #900, Los Angeles CA 90067 USA — Singer, Organist (Four Seasons)

Gaughan, Brendan
Germain Racing, 218 Raceway Drive, Mooresville NC 28117, USA — Truck Racing Driver

Gault, William Campbell
481 Mountain Dr, Santa Barbara CA 93103, USA — Writer

Gault, Willie J	Football Player
15460 La Maida St, Sherman Oaks CA 91403, USA	
Gaultier, Jean-Paul	Fashion Designer
30 Rue Saint Martin, 75003 Paris, France	
Gauthier, Dan	Actor
Michael Einfeld Mgmt, 10630 Moorpark Ave, #101, Toluca Lake CA 91602, USA	
Gauthier, Daniel	Circus Executive
Cirque du Soleil, 8400 2nd Ave, Montreal QC H1Z 4M6, Canada	
Gauthier, Denis, Jr	Ice Hockey Player
1658 9th St, Manhattan Beach CA 90266, USA	
Gauthier, Jean P	Ice Hockey Player
415 Vinet Ave, Dorval QC H9S 2M7, Canada	
Gauthier, Mary	Singer, Songwriter
Mark Spector Company, 826 Broadway, 400, New York NY 10003, USA	
Gautier, Dick	Actor
11333 Moorpark St, #59, North Hollywood CA 91602, USA	
Gava, Cassandra	Actress
1745 Camino Palmero St, #210, Los Angeles CA 90046, USA	
Gavanelli, Paolo	Opera Singer
I M G Artists, Hogarth Business Park, Chiswick, London W4 2TH, England	
Gavankar, Janina	Actress
TalentWorks, 3500 W Olive Ave, #1400, Burbank CA 91505 USA	
Gavaskar, Sunil M	Cricketer
Nirlon Synthetics, Dr Annie Besant Road, #254B, Worli, Mumbai 18, India	
Gavey, Aaron	Ice Hockey Player
84 Park Place Dr, Saulte Sainte Mariee ON P6B 6L3, Canada	
Gavin, John	Actor, Diplomat
606 N Larchmont Blvd, #210, Los Angeles CA 90004, USA	
Gaviria Trujillo, Cesar	President, Colombia
Club de Madrid, C/Goya 5-7, Pasaje 2, 28001 Madrid, Spain	
Gavrilov, Andrei V	Concert Pianist
Konzertdirektion Schlote, Danreitergasse 4, 5020 Salzburg, Austria	
Gavron, Rafi	Actor
Affirmative Entertainment, 425 N Robertson Blvd, Los Angeles CA 90048 USA	
Gay, Don	Rodeo Rider
1818 Rodeo Dr, Mesquite TX 75149, USA	
Gay, Gerald H (Jerry)	Photojournalist
2121 Madison St, #C, Everett WA 98203, USA	
Gay, J Brian	Golfer
Professional Golfer's Assn, PO Box 109601, Palm Beach Gardens FL 33410 USA	
Gay, Peter J	Historian
270 Riverside Dr, #8C, New York NY 10025, USA	
Gay, Randall J, Jr	Football Player
6706 Joyce Dr, #3C, Addis LA 70710, USA	
Gay, Rudy C, Jr	Basketball Player
91 W Galloway Dr, Memphis TN 38111, USA	
Gay, Tyson	Track Athlete
Global Athletics & Marketing, 437 Boylston St, #400, Boston MA 02116, USA	
Gay, William H (Bill)	Football Player
8200 E Jefferson Ave, #804, Detroit MI 48214, USA	
Gaydukov, Sergei N	Cosmonaut
Cosmonaut Training Center, Star City, 141160 Zvezdny Gorodok, Moscow Oblast, Russia	
Gaye, Nona	Singer, Model, Actress
Kritzer Levine Wilkins Griffin, 11872 La Grange Ave, #100, Los Angeles CA 90025 USA	
Gayheart, Rebecca	Actress, Model
Gersh Agency, 9465 Wilshire Blvd, #600, Beverly Hills CA 90212 USA	
Gayl, Franz	Military Activist
5823 Crowfoot Dr, Burke VA 22015, USA	
Gayle, Crystal	Singer
Gayle Enterprises, 51 Music Square E, Nashville TN 37203, USA	
Gayle, Michelle P	Singer, Actress
Mission Control, City Business Center, Lower Road, London SE16 2XB, England	
Gayle, Shaun L	Football Player
1530 N Elk Grove Ave, #1, Chicago IL 60622, USA	
Gaylor, Christopher J (Chris)	Drummer (All-American Rejects)
Creative Artists Agency, 2000 Ave of Stars, #100, Los Angeles CA 90067 USA	
Gaylord, Frank	Sculptor
2844 Vermont Route 14, Williamstown VT 05679, USA	
Gaylord, Mitchell J (Mitch)	Gymnast, Actor
4824 Cargill Circle, Fort Worth TX 76244, USA	
Gaynes, George	Actor
Innovative Artists, 1505 10th St, Santa Monica CA 90401 USA	
Gaynor, Gloria	Singer
Brothers Mgmt, 141 Dunbar Ave, Fords NJ 08863 USA	
Gaynor, Mitzi	Actress, Dancer, Singer
610 N Arden Dr, Beverly Hills CA 90210, USA	
Gayoom, Maumoon Abdul	President, Maldives
Ma Ki'nbigasdhoshuge, Male 20229, Maldives	
Gayson, Eunice	Actress
Spotlight, 7 Leicester Place, London WC2H 7BP, England	
Gayton, Joe	Producer, Writer
A P A Talent/Literary Agency, 405 S Beverly Dr, #300, Beverly Hills CA 90212 USA	
Gayton, Tony	Producer, Writer
A P A Talent/Literary Agency, 405 S Beverly Dr, #300, Beverly Hills CA 90212 USA	
Gazarek, Sara	Singer, Guitarist
Stiletto Entertainment, 8259 La Cienega Blvd, Inglewood CA 90301, USA	
Gaze, Andrew	Basketball Player
Basketball Resources, PO Box 2222, Ivanhoe East 3029, Australia	
Gazit, Doron	Artist
Air Dimensional Inc, 14141 Covello St, Building 1, Van Nuys CA 91405, USA	
Gazzaniga, Michael S	Psychologist
University of California, Study of Mind Center, Santa Barbara CA 93106, USA	
Gbaja-Biamila, Akbar O	Football Player
1050 Armitage St, Alameda CA 94502, USA	
Gbowee, Leymah R	Nobel Peace Activist
Women's Peace & Security Network, 68 Onyankle St, Abelempke, Accra, Ghana	

Geale, Daniel	Boxer
Team Fenech, PO Box 66, Millers Point NSW 2000, Australia	
Gearhart, G David	Educator
University of Arkansas, Chancellor's Office, Administration Building, Fayetteville AR 72701, USA	
Gearhart, John P	Neurologist, Biologist
Johns Hopkins University Medical Center, Baltimore MD 21218 USA	
Gearing, Ashley	Singer
Violator Mainstar, 2805 Azalea Place, Nashville TN 37204, USA	
Geary, Anthony (Tony)	Actor
7010 Pacific View Dr, Los Angeles CA 90068, USA	
Geary, Cynthia	Actress
Baumgarten/Prophet, 1041 N Formosa Ave, #200, West Hollywood CA 90046, USA	
Geary, Geoffrey M (Geoff)	Baseball Player
175 Maple Ave, #2, Carlsbad CA 92008, USA	
Geary, Nancy	Writer
Nicholas Ellison, 55 5th Ave, #1500, New York NY 10003, USA	
Geathers, James A (Jumpy)	Football Player
200 Tony Dr, Cape Elizabeth ME 04107, USA	
Geathers, Robert L, Jr	Football Player
1 Dab Dr, Georgetown SC 29440, USA	
Gebhard, Robert H (Bob)	Baseball Player, Executive
5242 E Otero Place, Littleton CO 80122, USA	
Gebo, Daniel	Paleontologist
Northern Illinois University, Paleontology Dept, DeKalb IL 60115, USA	
Gebrselassie, Haile	Track Athlete
Waterdelweg 14, 5427 LS Boehel 98007, Monaco	
Gedda, Nicolai	Opera Singer
Valhavagen 128, 114 41 Stockholm, Sweden	
Geddes, Anne	Photographer
K Geddes Mgmt, 2 York St, Parnell 1001, Auckland, New Zealand	
Geddes, James L (Jim)	Baseball Player
6738 Harrisburg London Road, Orient OH 43146, USA	
Geddes, Jane	Golfer
60 Buckingham Dr, Stamford CT 6902, USA	
Geddes, Kenneth L (Ken)	Football Player
7702 147th Ave NE, Redmond WA 98052, USA	
Geddis, Peter	Actor
Brown & Simcocks, 109 Blackfriars Road, London SE1 8HW, England	
Gedeck, Martina	Actress
Postfach 307521, 14135 Berlin, Germany	
Gedman, Richard L (Rich)	Baseball Player
10 Parmenter Road, Framingham MA 01701, USA	
Gedney, Christopher J (Chris)	Football Player
4881 Excalibur Dr, Syracuse NY 13215, USA	
Gedrick, Jason	Actor
I F A Talent Agency, 8730 W Sunset Blvd, #490, West Hollywood CA 90069 USA	
Gee, E Gordon	Educator
Ohio State University, President's Office, Columbus OH 43210, USA	
Gee, Prunella	Actress
Michael Ladkin Mgmt, 1 Duchess St, #1, London W1N 3DE, England	
Geer, Charlotte	Rowing Athlete
PO Box 324, Hinesburg VT 05461, USA	
Geer, Ellen	Actress
Kyle Fritz Mgmt, 6325 Heather Dr, Los Angeles CA 90068 USA	
Geer, Josh	Baseball Player
10836 Peach Circle, Forney. TX 75126, USA	
Geesaman, Lynn	Photographer
Thomas Barry Fine Arts, 530 N 3rd St, #B10, Minneapolis MN 55401, USA	
Geesen, Masha	Writer
Bloomsbury Publishing, 36 Soho Square, London W1D 3Q4, England	
Geeson, Judy	Actress
Media Artists Group, 8222 Melrose Ave, #203, Los Angeles CA 90048 USA	
Geffen, David	Producer, Businessman
22108 Pacific Coast Highway, Malibu CA 90265, USA	
Gehring, Frederick W	Mathematician
1200 Earhart Road, Ann Arbor MI 48105, USA	
Gehring, Lana	Speed Skater
US Speedskating, 5662 S Cougar Lane, Salt Lake City UT 84118 USA	
Gehring, Walter J	Geneticist
Hochfeldstr 32, 4106 Therwil, Switzerland	
Gehry, Frank O	Pritzker Architectural Laureate
Gehry Partners, 12541 Beatrice St, Los Angeles CA 90066, USA	
Geiberger, Al	Golfer
80555 Tangelo Court, Indio CA 92201, USA	
Geiduschek, E Peter	Biologist
University of California, Biology Dept, 9500 Gilman Dr, La Jolla CA 92093, USA	
Geier, Philip H, Jr	Businessman
Geier Group, Heron Tower, 70 E 55th St, #1500, New York NY 10022, USA	
Geiger, Ken	Photojournalist
National Geographic Magazine, Editorial Dept, PO Box 98199, Washington DC 20090, USA	
Geiger, Matthew A (Matt)	Basketball Player
3385 Old Keystone Road, Tarpon Springs FL 34688, USA	
Geiger, Teddy	Singer, Songwriter, Actor
I C M Partners, 10250 Constellation Blvd, #900, Los Angeles CA 90067 USA	
Geisel, J David (Dave)	Baseball Player
4 Blacksmith Lane, Media PA 19063, USA	
Geisenberger, Natalie	Luge Athlete
On the Green 35, 83714 Miesbach, Germany	
Geismar, Thomas H	Architect
Chermayeff & Geismar, 15 E 26th St, #1200, New York NY 10010, USA	
Geiss, Johannes	Physicist
International Space Science Institute, Hallestr 6, 3012 Berne, Switzerland	
Geist, William (Willie)	Sports Commentator
NBC-TV, Sports Dept, 30 Rockefeller Plaza, #270E, New York NY 10112 USA	
Geithner, Timothy	Secretary, Treasury
Treasury Department, 1500 Pennsylvania Ave NW, Washington DC 20220 USA	

G

Gelb, Leslie H
Council on Foreign Relations, 58 E 68th St, New York NY 10065, USA — Educator

Gelb, Peter
Metropolitan Opera Assn, Lincoln Center Plaza, New York NY 10023 USA — Opera Executive

Gelbaugh, Stanley M (Stan)
10819 Hob Nail Court, Potomac MD 20854, USA — Football Player

Geldof, Bob
Bond Street House, 14 Clifford St, London W1X 2JD, England — Singer, Songwriter

Gellar, Sarah Michelle
I C M Partners, 10250 Constellation Blvd, #900, Los Angeles CA 90067 USA — Actress

Geller, Margaret J
Harvard University, Astronomy Dept, 60 Garden St, Cambridge MA 02138, USA — Astronomer

Geller, Uri
Celeb Agents, 77 Oxford St, London W1D 2ES, England — Psychic, Illusionist

Gellman, Marc
Temple Beth Torah, 35 Bagatelle Road, Melville NY 11747, USA — Religious Leader, Rabbi, Commentator

Gell-Mann, Murray
Santa Fe Institute, 1399 Hyde Park Road, Santa Fe NM 87501, USA — Nobel Physics Laureate

Gelman, Barton
Washington Post, Editorial Dept, 1150 15th St NW, Washington DC 20071 USA — Journalist

Gelman, Larry
5121 Greenbush Ave, Sherman Oaks CA 91423, USA — Actor

Gelman, Michael S
7 W 63rd St, #500, New York NY 10023, USA — Producer

Gelnar, John R
300 N Hitchcock St, Hobart OK 73651, USA — Baseball Player

Gemar, Charles D
7660 N 159th St Court E, Benton KS 67017, USA — Astronaut

Gemignani, Alexander
Innovative Artists, 1505 10th St, Santa Monica CA 90401 USA — Actor, Singer

Gemma
I M G Models, 304 Park Ave S, #PH-North, New York NY 10010 USA — Model

Gemmell, Ruth
Hamilton Hodell, 66-68 Margaret St, London W1W 8SR, England — Actress

Genachowski, Julius
Federal Communications Commission, 445 12th St SW, Washington DC 20554, USA — Government Official

Genaux, Vivica
K K N Enterprises, 277 W End Ave, #11A, New York NY 10023, USA — Opera Singer

Gendron, George M
Clark University, Graduate Management School, 950 Main St, Worcester MA 01610, USA — Editor, Educator

Genest, Veronique
Artmedia, 20 Ave Rapp, 75007 Paris, France — Actress

Genova, Lisa
Pocket Books, 1230 Ave of Americas, New York NY 10020 USA — Writer

Genovese, George M
11474 Erwin St, North Hollywood CA 91606, USA — Baseball Player

Genscher, Hans-Dietrich
Am Kottenforst 16, 53343 Wachtberg-Pech, Germany — Government Official, Germany

Genser, Eli Morgan
Innovative Artists, 1505 10th St, Santa Monica CA 90401 USA — Actor

Genshaft, Judy L
University of South Florida, President's Office, Tampa FL 33620, USA — Educator

Gensler, M Arthur, Jr
Gensler & Assoc Architects, 550 Kearny St, San Francisco CA 94108, USA — Architect

Genthe, Eva Z
C A 1 Photography, Scholdstr 1, 76227 Karlsruhe-Durlach, Germany — Photographer

Gentile, James E (Jim)
1016 W Neptune Road, Edmond OK 73003, USA — Baseball Player

Gentry, Alvin
Phoenix Suns, 201 E Jefferson St, Phoenix AZ 85004 USA — Basketball Coach, Executive

Gentry, Dennis L
916 Queen Elizabeth Dr, McGregor TX 76657, USA — Football Player

Gentry, Gary E
301 W Lawrence Lane, Phoenix AZ 85021, USA — Baseball Player

Gentry, Teddy W
Alabama Band Promotions, PO Box 680529, Fort Payne AL 35968, USA — Singer, Guitarist (Alabama)

Gentry, Troy
Parallel Entertainment, 209 10th Ave S, #506, Nashville TN 37203, USA — Singer (Montgomery Gentry)

Genzel, Carrie
Pakula/King, 9229 W Sunset Blvd, #315, West Hollywood CA 90069 USA — Actress

Genzel, Reinhard
Extraterrestrial Institute, Schwarzschild Str 1, 85741 Garching, Germany — Astrophysicist

Geoffroy, Gregory
Iowa State University, President's Office, Ames IA 50011, USA — Educator

George, Anton H (Tony)
Vision Racing, 6803 Coffman Road, Indianapolis IN 46268, USA — Auto Racing Executive

George, Christopher S (Chris)
7703 Goldengrove Dr, Spring TX 77379, USA — Baseball Player

George, Devean J
14001 53rd Ave N, Minneapolis MN 55446, USA — Basketball Player

George, Edward N (Eddie)
9538 Sanctuary Place, Brentwood TN 37027, USA — Football Player

George, Elizabeth
Byron's Mgmt, 76 Saint James Lane, London N10 3DF, England — Writer

George, Eric
Lasher McManus Robinson, 1964 Westwood Blvd, #400, Los Angeles CA 90025, USA — Actor

George, Francis E Cardinal
Chicago Pastoral Center, PO Box 1979, Chicago IL 60690, USA — Religious Leader

George, Helen
Associated International Mgmt, Fairfax House, Fulwood Place, London WC1V 6HU, England — Actress

George, Inara
Blue Note Records, 6920 W Sunset Blvd, Los Angeles CA 90028 USA — Singer, Guitarist (Bird & the Bee)

George, James (Jim)
4319 Regal Dr, Akron OH 44321, USA — Weightlifter

George, Jason Winston
Management 360, 9111 Wilshire Blvd, Beverly Hills CA 90210 USA — Actor

George, Jeffrey S (Jeff) — Football Player
1980 Schwier Court, Indianapolis IN 46229, USA
George, Maximillian A (Max) — Singer (Wanted)
Industry Music Group, 128 Regent Road, Hanley Stoke, Trent ST1 3AY, England
George, Melissa — Actress
I C M Partners, 10250 Constellation Blvd, #900, Los Angeles CA 90067 USA
George, Oorlagh — Producer
Northwood Productions, 2901 Ocean Park Blvd, #217, Santa Monica CA 90405, USA
George, Phyllis — Entertainer, Beauty Queen
C E S D, 10635 Santa Monica Blvd, #130, Los Angeles CA 90025 USA
George, Rocky — Guitarist (Fishbone)
Silverback Mgmt, 9469 Jefferson Blvd, #101, Culver City CA 90232, USA
George, Ronald L (Ron) — Football Player
13720 Piedmont Vista Dr, Haymarket VA 20169, USA
George, Susan — Actress
McKorkindale & Holton, 1-2 Langham Place, London W1A 3DD, England
George, Tami-Adrian — Actress
C E S D, 10635 Santa Monica Blvd, #130, Los Angeles CA 90025 USA
George, Tate — Basketball Player
55 Georgetown Road, Bristol CT 06010, USA
George, Terry — Director, Writer
Independent Talent Group, Oxford House, 76 Oxford St, London W1D 1BS, England
George, William W — Businessman, Educator
Harvard University, Business School, Cambridge MA 02138, USA
Georgel, Pierre — Museum Official
41 Blvd Saint-Germain, 75005 Paris, France
Georgi, Howard — Physicist
Harvard University, Physics Dept, Lyman Laboratory, Cambridge MA 02138, USA
Georgian, Theodore J — Religious Leader
Orthodox Presbyterian Church, PO Box P, Willow Grove PA 19090, USA
Georgije, Bishop — Religious Leader
Serbian Orthodox Church, Sava Monastery, PO Box 519, Libertyville IL 60048, USA
Georgis, William T — Architect
233 E 72nd St, New York NY 10021, USA
Geraci, Sonny — Singer (Outsiders, Climax)
Mars Talent, 27 L'Ambiance Court, Nanuet NY 10954 USA
Geraghty, Brian T — Actor
United Talent Agency, 9336 Civic Center Dr, Beverly Hills CA 90210 USA
Geragos, Mark J — Attorney
Geragos & Geragos, 2 California Plaza, 350 S Grand Ave, Los Angeles CA 90071, USA
Gerard, Cindy — Writer
Pocket/Star Books, 1230 Ave of Americas, New York NY 10020, USA
Gerard, Daniel J (Gus) — Basketball Player
614 Cypresswood Dr, Spring TX 77388, USA
Gerard, Gil — Actor
40 Villa Rosa Road, #A161, Temple GA 30179, USA
Gerard, Leo W — Labor Leader
United Steel Workers of America, 5 Gateway Center, Pittsburgh PA 15222, USA
Gerardo — Rap Artist
Tapestry Artists, 17337 Ventura Blvd, #208, Encino CA 91316, USA
Gerber, Craig S — Baseball Player
4297 N Pershing Ave, San Bernardino CA 92407, USA
Gerber, H Joseph — Businessman
Gerber Scientific Inc, 83 Gerber Road W, South Windsor CT 06074, USA
Gerber, Joel — Judge
US Tax Court, 400 2nd St NW, Washington DC 20217, USA
Gerberding, Julie L — Government Official, Physician
Emory University Medical School, Infectious Disease Dept, Atlanta GA 30322, USA
Gere, Richard — Actor
Hirsch Wallerstein, 10100 Santa Monica Blvd, #1700, Los Angeles CA 90067, USA
Gerela, Roy — Football Player
3933 Ramrod Forge, Las Cruces NM 88012, USA
Geren, Robert P (Bob) — Baseball Player, Manager
2710 Bay Canyon Court, San Diego CA 92117, USA
Gerety, Tom, Jr — Educator
Amherst College, President's Office, Amherst MA 01002, USA
Gerg, Hilde — Alpine Skier
Richard-Voss-Str 63, 83471 Schonau am Konigssee, Germany
Gergen, David R — Editor
31 Ash St, Cambridge MA 02138, USA
Gergiev, Valery A — Conductor
Kirov Ballet Theater, 1 Pl Iskusstr, 190000 Saint Petersburg, Russia
Gergov, Rossen — Conductor
Harrison/Parrott, 5-6 Albion Court, London W6 0QT, England
Gerhaher, Christian — Opera Singer
Kunstler Sekretariat am Gasteig, Rosenheimer Str 52, 81669 Munich, Germany
Gering, Jenna — Actress
Paradigm Agency, 360 N Crescent Dr, North Building, Beverly Hills CA 90210 USA
Germann, Greg — Actor
Innovative Artists, 1505 10th St, Santa Monica CA 90401 USA
Germano, Lisa — Singer, Violinist, Songwriter
Artists & Audience Entertainment, PO Box 35, Pawling NY 12564 USA
Germany, Willie — Foobtall Player
4401 Pratt St, Omaha NE 68111, USA
Germeshausen, Bernhard — Bobsled Athlete
Hinter Dem Salon 39, 99195 Schwansee, Germany
Gernert, Richard E (Dick) — Baseball Player
1801 Cambridge Ave, #C12, Reading PA 19610, USA
Gernhardt, Michael L — Astronaut
2705 Lighthouse Dr, Houston TX 77058, USA
Gero, Gary D — Cinematographer
2 McLaren, #A, Irvine CA 92618, USA
Gerring, Cathy — Golfer
3328 Tarrant Springs Trail, Fort Wayne IN 46804, USA
Gerrish, Brian A — Theologian
9142 Sycamore Hill Place, Mechanicsville VA 23116, USA

Gerritsen, Tess — Writer
11 Pleasant Ridge Dr, Camden ME 04843, USA

Gersbach, Carl R — Football Player
PO Box 433, Devon PA 19333, USA

Gershon, Gina — Actress
International Talent Agency, 10 NBC Universal Studios Plaza, #2000, Universal City CA 91608, USA

Gerson, Mark — Photographer
3 Regal Lane, Regent's Park, London NW1 7TH, England

Gerstein, Kirill — Concert Pianist
I M G Artists, Hogarth Business Park, Chiswick, London W4 2TH, England

Gerstell, A Frederick — Businessman
CalMat Co, 3200 San Fernando Road, Los Angeles CA 90065, USA

Gerth, Jeff — Journalist
New York Times, Editorial Dept, 229 W 43rd St, New York NY 10036 USA

Gertz, Jami — Actress
Innovative Artists, 1505 10th St, Santa Monica CA 90401 USA

Gerut, Joseph D (Jody) — Baseball Player
623 Rochdale Circle, Lombard IL 60148, USA

Gervais, Ricky — Actor, Comedian, Producer, Director
United Agents, 12-26 Lexington St, London W1F 0LE, England

Gervin, Derrick — Basketball Player
1110 Vista Valet, #1507, San Antonio TX 78216, USA

Gervin, George — Basketball Player, Coach
44 Gervin Pass, Spring Branch TX 78070, USA

Gerwick, Ben C, Jr — Construction Engineer
5727 Country Club Dr, Oakland CA 94618, USA

Gerwig, Greta — Actress
United Talent Agency, 9336 Civic Center Dr, Beverly Hills CA 90210 USA

Gerzmava, Hibla — Opera Singer
I M G Artists, Hogarth Business Park, Chiswick, London W4 2TH, England

Geschke, Charles — Businessman
Adobe Systems, 375 Park Ave, San Jose CA 95110, USA

Gesek, John C, Jr — Football Player
105 Sand Point Court, Coppell TX 75019, USA

Gesinger, Michael — Photographer
1136 Umatilla Ave, Port Townsend WA 98368, USA

Gesner, Zen — Actor
Jenny Delaney Mgmt, 3238 Fond Dr, Encino CA 91436, USA

Gessendorf, Mechthild — Opera Singer
Columbia Artists Mgmt Inc, 1790 Broadway, #702, New York NY 10019 USA

Gessle, Per — Singer, Guitarist (Roxette)
D & D Mgmt, Drottning Gatan 55, 111 28 Stockholm, Sweden

Gethard, Chris — Actor
Creative Artists Agency, 2000 Ave of Stars, #100, Los Angeles CA 90067 USA

Gets, Malcolm — Actor, Singer
One Entertainment, 12 W 57th St, #PH 1, New York NY 10019, USA

Gettelfinger, Ron — Labor Leader
United Auto Workers Union, 800 E Jefferson Ave, Detroit MI 48214, USA

Gettis, Byron — Baseball Player
6313 Whalen Ave, East Saint Louis IL 62207, USA

Getty, Charles M (Charlie) — Football Player
3736 W Morningside St, Springfield MO 65807, USA

Getz, John — Actor
Beddingfield Co, 13600 Ventura Blvd, #B, Sherman Oaks CA 91423, USA

Getzenberg, Robert — Urologist
Johns Hopkins University Medical Center, Urological Institute, Baltimore MD 21218, USA

Geyer, Hugh — Singer (Vogues)
2218 Ridge Road, McKeesport PA 15135, USA

Ghaffari, Matt — Greco-Roman Wrestler
32834 Fox Chappel Lane, Avon Lake OH 44012, USA

Ghai, Subhash — Director, Producer
Mount Saint Mary Church Road, #12, Bandra (W), Mumbai MS 400050, India

Ghalawanji, Omar Ibrahim — Prime Minister, Syria
Prime Minister's Office, Rue Chahbandar, Damascas, Syria

Ghauri, Yasmeen — Model
Next Model Mgmt, 23 Watts St, New York NY 10013 USA

Ghedi, Ali Muhammad — Prime Minister, Somalia
Prime Minister's Office, People's Palace, Mogadishu, Somalia

Ghelfi, Anthony P (Tony) — Baseball Player
3414 Geneva Lane, La Crosse WI 54601, USA

Gheorghiu, Angela — Opera Singer
Askonas Holt, Lincoln House, 300 High Holborn, London WC1V 7JH, England

Gheorghiu, Ion A — Artist
6 Aviator Petre Cretu St, 012151 Bucharest, Romania

Gheorghiu, Teo — Concert Pianist
Harrison/Parrott, 5-6 Albion Court, London W6 0QT, England

Ghesquiere, Nicolas — Fashion Designer
Angie Rubioni, 40 Rue du Cherche-Midi, 75006 Paris, France

Ghez, Andrea M — Physicist, Astronomer
University of California, Physics & Astronomy Dept, Los Angeles CA 90024, USA

Ghiardi, John F L — Government Official, Economist
12 Park Overlook Court, Bethesda MD 20817, USA

Ghiuselev, Nicola — Opera Singer
Villa della Pisana 370/B2, 00163 Rome, Italy

Ghomeshi, Jian — Broadcaster, Writer
Agency Group Ltd, 142 W 57th St, #600, New York NY 10019 USA

Ghormley, Antony — Sculptor
European Graduate School, Alter Kehr 20, 3953 Leuk-Stadt, Switzerland.

Ghosh, Amitrav — Writer
Farrar Straus Giroux, 18 W 18th St, #700, New York NY 10011 USA

Ghosh, Gautam — Director
28/1A Gariahat Road, Block 5, #50, Mumbai WB 700029, India

Ghosn, Carlos — Businessman
Nissan Motor Co, 1-1-1 Takashima, Nishi-ku, Yokohamashi, Kanagawa 220 8686, Japan

Ghostface Killa — Rap Artist (Wu-Tang Clan)
A&M Entertainment, 13280 NE Freeway, #F328, Houston TX 77040, USA

Ghuman, J B, Jr
The Firm, 2049 Century Park E, #2550, Los Angeles CA 90067 USA — Actor, Director
Giacchino, Michael
Gorfaine/Schwartz, 4111 W Alameda Ave, #509, Burbank CA 91505 USA — Composer
Giacconi, Riccardo
5630 Wisconsin Ave, #604, Chevy Chase MD 20815, USA — Nobel Physics Laureate
Giacomin, Edward (Ed)
6575 Red Maple Lane, Bloomfield MI 48301, USA — Ice Hockey Player
Giaever, Ivar
2080 Van Antwerp Road, Schenectady NY 12309, USA — Nobel Physics Laureate
Giallombardo, Robert P (Bob)
7903 Antique Circle, Waxhaw NC 28173, USA — Baseball Player
Giamatti, Marcus
Innovative Artists, 1505 10th St, Santa Monica CA 90401 USA — Actor
Giamatti, Paul
United Talent Agency, 9336 Civic Center Dr, Beverly Hills CA 90210 USA — Actor
Giambi, Jason G
34 Iselworth Dr, Henderson NV 89052, USA — Baseball Player
Giambi, Jeremy D
23360 S Power Road, Gilbert AZ 85298, USA — Baseball Player
Giambra, Joey
4673 Ashington St, Las Vegas NV 89147, USA — Boxer
Giammarese, Carl
Thomas Cassidy, 11761 E Speedway Blvd, Tucson AZ 85748 USA — Guitarist (Buckinghams)
Gianelli, John A
28241 Pine Ave, Pinecrest CA 95364, USA — Basketball Player
Giannelli, Raymond J (Ray)
56 E Saltaire Road, Lindenhurst NY 11757, USA — Baseball Player
Giannini, Adriano
Media Art Mgmt, C/ Castelló 82, 2 Derecha, 28006 Madrid, Spain — Actor
Giannini, Alfreda
Gucci Group, 1 Amstelplein, 1096 HA Amsterdam, Netherlands — Fashion Designer
Giannini, Giancarlo
Via Salaria 292, 00199 Rome, Italy — Actor
Giannoni, Giovani
Co-Regent's Office, Government Palace, 47031 San Marino — Co-Regent, San Marino
Giannulli, Mossimo
Mossimo Supply, 2450 White Road, #200, Irvine CA 92614, USA — Fashion Designer
Gianopulos, Mimi
I C M Partners, 10250 Constellation Blvd, #900, Los Angeles CA 90067 USA — Actress
Gianotti, Fabiola
C E R N, Large Hadron Collider, 1211 Geneva 23, Switzerland — Physicist
Gibara, Samir
Goodyear Tire & Rubber, 1144 E Market St, Akron OH 44316, USA — Businessman
Gibb, Barry
Rhino Entertainment, 3400 Olive Ave, #400, Burbank CA 91505, USA — Singer (Bee Gees), Songwriter
Gibb, Cynthia
Scott Hart Mgmt, 14622 Ventura Blvd, #746, Sherman Oaks CA 91403, USA — Actress
Gibb, Donald
Ashby/Rojo Entertainment, 1485 S Beverly Dr, Los Angeles CA 90035, USA — Actor
Gibbard, Allan F
University of Michigan, Philosophy Dept, Ann Arbor MI 48109, USA — Philosopher
Gibbard, Benjamin (Ben)
Zeitgeist Artist Mgmt, 660 York St, #216, San Francisco CA 94110, USA — Singer (Death Cab for Cutie)
Gibbon, Joseph C (Joe)
26 County Road 24142, Newton MS 39345, USA — Baseball Player
Gibbons, Beth
Fruit, 98 Keslak Road, London NW6 6DG, England — Singer (Portishead), Songwriter
Gibbons, Billy
Sanctuary Mgmt, 15301 Ventura Blvd, Building B, Sherman Oaks CA 91403, USA — Singer, Guitarist (ZZ Top)
Gibbons, Gail
1 Goose Green St, Corinth VT 05039, USA — Writer, Illustrator
Gibbons, James E (Jim)
9 Sagewood Court, Basalt CO 81621, USA — Football Player
Gibbons, James F
15 Red Berry Ridge, Portola Valley CA 94028, USA — Electrical Engineer
Gibbons, Jay J
758 Donnington Court, Simi Valley CA 93065, USA — Baseball Player
Gibbons, John D
Leeward, 5 Leeside Dr, Pembroke HM 05, Bermuda — Prime Minister, Bermuda
Gibbons, John M (Gibby)
3602 Hunters Quail, San Antonio TX 78230, USA — Baseball Player, Manager
Gibbons, Julia Smith
US Court of Appeals, 167 N Main St, #970, Memphis TN 38103, USA — Judge
Gibbons, Kaye
Houghton Mifflin Harcourt, 215 Park Ave S, #1200, New York NY 10003 USA — Writer
Gibbons, Leeza
9025 Ashcroft Ave, West Hollywood CA 90048, USA — Actress, Producer
Gibbs, Cory
New England Revolution, 1 Patriot Place, Foxboro MA 02035 USA — Soccer Player
Gibbs, Freddie
Agency Group Ltd, 1880 Century Park E, #711, Los Angeles CA 90067 USA — Rap Artist
Gibbs, Jerry D (Jake)
223 Saint Andres Circle, Oxford MS 38655, USA — Football, Baseball Player
Gibbs, Joe J
19133 Penisula Point Dr, Cornelius NC 28031, USA — Football Coach, Auto Racing Executive
Gibbs, L Richard (Lance)
276 Republic Park, Peter's Hall EBD, Guyana — Cricketer
Gibbs, Marla
Momentum Talent, 9401 Wilshire Blvd, #501, Beverly Hills CA 90212, USA — Actress, Singer
Gibbs, Martin
5 Arbor Court, Burlington MA 01803, USA — Biologist
Gibbs, Terri
1439 Clary Cut Road, Appling GA 30802, USA — Singer, Songwriter
Gibbs, Terry
Thomas Cassidy, 11761 E Speedway Blvd, Tucson AZ 85748 USA — Jazz Vibist, Drummer

Gibbs, Timothy B — Actor
Jefferson Rilke Cooper, 50 Lexington Ave, #23D, New York NY 10010, USA
Giblett, Eloise R — Hematologist
2518 3rd Ave W, Seattle WA 98119, USA
Giblin, Vincent J — Labor Leader
Internationall Union of Operating Engineers, 1125 17th St NW, Washington DC 20036, USA
Gibney, Alex — Director
I C M Partners, 10250 Constellation Blvd, #900, Los Angeles CA 90067 USA
Gibney, Rebecca — Actress
Robyn Gardiner Mgmt, PO Box 128, Surrey Hills NSW 2010, Australia
Gibney, Susan — Actress
Insight Mgmt, 11245 Cloverdale Ave, Los Angeles CA 90019, USA
Gibran, Kahlil G — Sculptor
160 W Canton St, Boston MA 02118, USA
Gibson, Aaron — Football Player
PO Box 637, Roanoke IN 46783, USA
Gibson, Antonio M — Football Player
2320 Jaguar Dr, #502, Bryan TX 77807, USA
Gibson, Beau — Opera Singer
I M G Artists, Hogarth Business Park, Chiswick, London W4 2TH, England
Gibson, Charles D — Commentator
ABC-TV, News Dept, 47 W 66th St, New York NY 10023, USA
Gibson, Claude — Football Player
47 Gladstone Road, Asheville NC 28805, USA
Gibson, Deborah — Singer, Actress, Model
David Shapira Assoc, 193 N Robertson Blvd, Beverly Hills CA 90211 USA
Gibson, Dennis M — Football Player
6900 NE 11th Court, Ankeny IA 50023, USA
Gibson, Derrick A — Baseball Player
303 Ave O NW, Winter Haven FL 33881, USA
Gibson, Ernest G — Football Player
6518 Paradise Point Road, Flowery Branch GA 30542, USA
Gibson, Fred — Golfer
2006 Avenel St, Orlando FL 32828, USA
Gibson, John R — Judge
US Court of Appeals, US Courthouse, 811 Grand Ave, Kansas City MO 64106, USA
Gibson, Kelly — Golfer
13 Wisteria Lane, Covington LA 70433, USA
Gibson, Kirk H — Baseball, Football Player
33 Sunset Lane, Grosse Pointe Farms MI 48236, USA
Gibson, Mel — Actor, Director
Icon Productions, 808 Wilshire Blvd, #400, Santa Monica CA 90401, USA
Gibson, Oliver D — Football Player
1448 E 52nd St, #406, Chicago IL 60615, USA
Gibson, Paul M — Baseball Player
23421 Water Circle, Boca Raton FL 33486, USA
Gibson, Quentin H — Biochemist
5 Carrot Hill Road, Woods Hole MA 02543, USA
Gibson, Ralph H — Photographer
331 W Broadway, #400, New York NY 10013, USA
Gibson, Raquel — Model
Playboy Promotions, 2706 Media Center Dr, Los Angeles CA 90065 USA
Gibson, Reginald W — Judge
US Claims Court, 717 Madison Place NW, Washington DC 20439, USA
Gibson, Richie — Actor
Associated International Mgmt, Fairfax House, Fulwood Place, London WC1V 6HU, England
Gibson, Robert (Bob) — Baseball Player
215 Bellevue Blvd S, Bellevue NE 68005, USA
Gibson, Robert L (Bob) — Baseball Player
751 W Rolling Road, Springfield PA 19064, USA
Gibson, Robert L (Hoot) — Astronaut
1709 Shagbark Trail, Murfreesboro TN 37130, USA
Gibson, Thomas — Actor
Paradigm Agency, 360 N Crescent Dr, North Building, Beverly Hills CA 90210 USA
Gibson, Thomas A (Tom) — Football Player
5940 E Sandra Terrace, Scottsdale AZ 85254, USA
Gibson, Tyrese — Singer, Songwriter, Actor
B/W/R, 9100 Wilshire Blvd, #500W, Beverly Hills CA 90212 USA
Gibson, William Ford — Writer, Photographer
G P Putnam's Sons, 375 Hudson St, New York NY 10014 USA
Giddins, Gary — Writer, Columnist
Oxford University Press, 198 Madison Ave, #800, New York NY 10016 USA
Giddish, Kelli — Actress
Paradigm Agency, 360 N Crescent Dr, North Building, Beverly Hills CA 90210 USA
Gideon, Raynold — Actor, Writer
3524 Multiview Dr, Los Angeles CA 90068, USA
Gidley, Pamela — Actress
32 Cliff Ave, Hampton NH 03842, USA
Gidzenko, Yuri P — Cosmonaut
Cosmonaut Training Center, Star City, 141160 Zvezdny Gorodok, Moscow Oblast, Russia
Gielen, Michael A — Conductor, Composer
Ingpen & Williams, 131 Putney Bridge Road, London SW15 2PA, England
Giella, Joseph — Cartoonist (Mary Worth)
191 Morris Dr, East Meadow NY 11554, USA
Gien, Pamela — Actress
I C M Partners, 10250 Constellation Blvd, #900, Los Angeles CA 90067 USA
Gierasch, Adam — Director, Writer
Gersh Agency, 9465 Wilshire Blvd, #600, Beverly Hills CA 90212 USA
Gierer, Vincent A, Jr — Businessman
U S T Inc, 100 W Putnam Ave, Greenwich CT 06830, USA
Gierowski, Stefan — Artist
Ul Gagarina 15 m 97, 00 753 Warsaw, Poland
Giesler, Jon W — Football Player
141 Via Isabela, Jupiter FL 33458, USA
Gietz, Gordon — Opera Singer
I M G Artists, Hogarth Business Park, Chiswick, London W4 2TH, England

Giff, Patricia Reilly
Bantam Books, 1745 Broadway, New York NY 10019 USA — Writer

Gifford, Barry
Creative Artists Agency, 2000 Ave of Stars, #100, Los Angeles CA 90067 USA — Writer

Gifford, Frank N
I C M Partners, 10250 Constellation Blvd, #900, Los Angeles CA 90067 USA — Football Player, Sportscaster

Gifford, Gloria
Gloria Gifford Theater, 6468 Santa Monica Blvd, Los Angeles CA 90038, USA — Actress

Gifford, Kathie Lee
Artist Brand Alliance, 11 E 86th St, #900, New York NY 10028, USA — Entertainer

Gift, Roland
Primary Talent International, 10-11 Jockey's Fields, London WC1R 4BN, England — Singer (Fine Young Cannibals), Actor

Gigandet, Cam
Luber Rocklin Entertainment, 8530 Wilshire Blvd, #555, Beverly Hills CA 90211 USA — Actor

Giggie, Robert T (Bob)
89 McAndrew Road, Braintree MA 02184, USA — Baseball Player

Gigli, Romeo
37 W 57th St, #900, New York NY 10019, USA — Fashion Designer

Gigon, Norman P (Norm)
2503 Rio Vista Dr, Mahwah NJ 07430, USA — Baseball Player

Gigot, Paul A
Wall Street Journal, Editorial Dept, 1 World Financial Center, New York NY 10281, USA — Journalist

Giguere, Jean-Sebastien
Colorado Avalanche, Pepsi Center, 1000 Chopper Circle, Denver CO 80204 USA — Ice Hockey Player

Giguere, Russ
Variety Artists, 793 Higuera St, #6, San Luis Obispo CA 93401 USA — Singer, Guitarist (Association)

Gil, Gilberto
M G Ltd, 15 W 26th St, New York NY 10010, USA — Singer, Songwriter

Gil, Maria Luisa
Playboy Promotions, 2706 Media Center Dr, Los Angeles CA 90065 USA — Model

Gil, R Benjamin (Benji)
1654 Paseo Aurora, San Diego CA 92154, USA — Baseball Player

Gilbert, Bradley (Brad)
ProServe, 1101 Woodrow Wilson Blvd, #1800, Arlington VA 22209 USA — Tennis Player

Gilbert, Chris
Greenbriar Mgmt, 4422 FM 1960 Road W, Houston TX 77068, USA — Football Player

Gilbert, David
King Features Syndicate, 300 W 57th St, #1500, New York NY 10019 USA — Cartoonist (Buckles)

Gilbert, Drew E (Buddy)
1913 Belcaro Dr, Knoxville TN 37918, USA — Baseball Player

Gilbert, Elizabeth
Penguin Books, 375 Hudson St, Basement 1, New York NY 10014 USA — Writer

Gilbert, Greg
Toronto Marlies, 100 Princess Blvd, Toronto ON M6K 3C3, Canada — Ice Hockey Player, Coach

Gilbert, J Freeman
780 Kalamath Dr, Del Mar CA 92014, USA — Geophysicist

Gilbert, Joe D
512 W Martin Luther King Blvd, Jasper TX 75951, USA — Baseball Player

Gilbert, Kenneth A
11 Rue Ernest-Psichari, 75007 Paris, France — Concert Harpsichordist

Gilbert, Lawrence I
857 Fearrington Post, Pittsboro NC 27312, USA — Biologist

Gilbert, Lewis
19 Blvd de Suisse, 98000 Monte Carlo, Monaco — Director, Producer

Gilbert, Mark D
2340 NW 45th St, Boca Raton FL 33431, USA — Baseball Player

Gilbert, Martin J
Merton College, History Dept, Oxford OX1 4JD, England — Historian

Gilbert, Melissa
Innovative Artists, 1505 10th St, Santa Monica CA 90401 USA — Actress, Labor Leader

Gilbert, Richard W
Des Moines Register & Tribune, 715 Locust St, Des Moines IA 50309, USA — Publisher

Gilbert, Rodrigue G (Rod)
52 E End Ave, #33A, New York NY 10028, USA — Ice Hockey Player

Gilbert, Ronnie
Donna Korones Mgmt, 1031 Merced St, Berkeley CA 94707, USA — Singer

Gilbert, S J, Sr
Baptist Convention of America, 6717 Centennial Blvd, Nashville TN 37209, USA — Religious Leader

Gilbert, Sara
Framework Entertainment, 9057 Nemo St, #C, West Hollywood CA 90069 USA — Actress

Gilbert, Sean
7912 N Baltusrol Lane, Charlotte NC 28210, USA — Football Player

Gilbert, Simon
Interceptor Enterprises, 98 White Lion St, London N1 9PF, England — Drummer (Suede)

Gilbert, Walter
15 Gray Gardens W, Cambridge MA 02138, USA — Nobel Chemistry Laureate

Gilberto, Astrud
Absolute Artists, 530 Howard Ave, #200, San Francisco CA 94105, USA — Singer

Gilberto, Bebel
W M E Entertainment, 1600 Division St, #300, Nashville TN 37203 USA — Singer

Gilbertson, Bob
Terminator Motorsports, 2250 Toomey Ave, Charlotte NC 28203, USA — Drag Racing Driver, Owner

Gilbreath, Rodney J (Rod)
1438 Ridgeland Way SW, Lilburn GA 30047, USA — Baseball Player

Gilbride, Kevin
New York Giants, Meadowlands Stadium, 102 Route 120, East Rutherford NJ 07073 USA — Football Player, Coach

Gilburg, Thomas D (Tom)
29 Valley Road, Warminster PA 18974, USA — Football Player

Gilchrist, Brent
Bank of Montreal, 200-3200 30th Ave, Vernon BC V1T 2C5, Canada — Ice Hockey Player

Gilchrist, Guy
20 Bristol Dr, Canton CT 06019, USA — Cartoonist (Nancy, Mudpie)

Gilchrist, Keir
I C M Partners, 10250 Constellation Blvd, #900, Los Angeles CA 90067 USA — Actor

Gilchrist, Lara
Lauren Levitt Assoc, 1525 W 8th Ave, #300, Vancouver BC V6J 1T5, Canada — Actress

Gilchrist, Paul R — Religious Leader
Presbyterian Church in America, 1862 Century Place, Atlanta GA 30345, USA

Gilder, Bob — Golfer
1977 NW Bonney Dr, Corvallis OR 97330, USA

Gilder, George F — Economist
Gilder Publishing, 291A Main St, Great Barrington MA 01230, USA

Gildon, Jason L — Football Player
1562 Barrington Dr, Wexford PA 15090, USA

Giles, Brian J — Baseball Player
136 Coronation Ave, Las Vegas NV 89123, USA

Giles, Brian S — Baseball Player
4130 Rancho Las Brisas Trail, San Diego CA 92130, USA

Giles, Curtis J (Curt) — Ice Hockey Player
5225 Grandview Square, #402, Minneapolis MN 55436, USA

Giles, Jimmie, Jr — Football Player
10429 Greenmont Dr, Tampa FL 33626, USA

Giles, Marcus W — Baseball Player
2285 Marquand Court, Alpine CA 91901, USA

Giles, Nancy — Actress
12047 178th St, Jamaica NY 11434, USA

Giletti, Alain — Figure Skater
103 Place de L'Eglise, 74400 Chamonix, France

Gilfillan, Jason — Baseball Player
153 Gilfillan Road, Blacksburg SC 29702, USA

Gilford, Zach — Actor
W M E Entertainment, 9601 Wilshire Blvd, #300, Beverly Hills CA 90210 USA

Gilfry, Rodney — Opera Singer
Askonas Holt, Lincoln House, 300 High Holborn, London WC1V 7JH, England

Gilhousen, Klein — Inventor
Qualcomm, 5775 Morehouse Dr, San Diego CA 92121, USA

Gilkey, O Bernard — Baseball Player
11463 Patty Ann Dr, Saint Louis MO 63146, USA

Gill, Harold P (Hal) — Ice Hockey Player
1 Fairfield Place, #4, Boston MA 02109, USA

Gill, Janis — Singer (Sweethearts of the Rodeo)
2803 Bransford Ave, Nashville TN 37204, USA

Gill, Johnny — Singer, Songwriter
Universal Attractions, 135 W 26th St, #1200, New York NY 10001 USA

Gill, Kendall C — Basketball Player
3133 S Calumet Ave, Chicago IL 60616, USA

Gill, Tim — Computer Software Designer (Quark)
Gill Foundation, 2215 Market St, Denver CO 80205, USA

Gill, Tonya — Golfer
3655 Habersham Road NE, #B229, Atlanta GA 30305, USA

Gill, Turner H — Football Player, Coach
University of Kansas, Athletic Dept, Lawrence KS 66045, USA

Gill, Vince — Singer, Songwriter, Guitarist
PO Box 128496, Nashville TN 37212, USA

Gill, William A, Jr — Labor Leader, Government Official
15975 Cove Lane, Dumfries VA 22025, USA

Gillan, Ian — Singer, Musician (Deep Purple)
Thames Talent, 1920 Post Road E, #101, Westport CT 06880, USA

Gillan, Karen S — Actress
United Talent Agency, 9336 Civic Center Dr, Beverly Hills CA 90210 USA

Gillanders, J David — Swimmer
1617 Briarwood Dr, Jonesboro AR 72401, USA

Gillani, Yousaf Raza — Prime Minister, Pakistan
Prime Minister's Office, Old State Bank Building, Islamabad, Pakistan

Gillard, Julia E — Prime Minister, Australia
Prime Minister's Office, Parliament House, Canberra ACT 2600, Australia

Gillen, Aidan — Actor
Independent Talent Group, Oxford House, 76 Oxford St, London W1D 1BS, England

Gilles, Frederic — Actor
Martinez Creative Mgmt, 6856 Saint-Laurent Blvd, #205, Montreal QC H2S 3C7, Canada

Gilles, Thomas B (Tom) — Baseball Player
14615 W Southern St, Princeville IL 61559, USA

Gillespie, Aaron — Singer, Drummer (Underoath)
Red Light Mgmt, 44 Wall St, #2200, New York NY 10005, USA

Gillespie, Jack A — Basketball Player
1104 37th Ave NE, Great Falls MT 59404, USA

Gillespie, Jim — Director
Creative Artists Agency, 2000 Ave of Stars, #100, Los Angeles CA 90067 USA

Gillespie, Rhondda M — Concert Pianist
2 Princess Road, Saint Leonards on Sea, East Sussex TN37 6EL, England

Gillespie, Robert W — Financier
KeyCorp, 127 Public Square, Cleveland OH 44114, USA

Gillespie, Ronald J — Chemist
150 Wilson St W, Ancaster ON L9G 4E7, Canada

Gillette, Anita — Actress
Judy Schoen, 606 N Larchmont Blvd, #309, Los Angeles CA 90004 USA

Gillette, Gabby — Actress
Amsel Eisenstadt Frazier, 5055 Wilshire Blvd, #865, Los Angeles CA 90036 USA

Gillette, James (Jim) — Singer (Tuff, Nitro)
Nene Musik Productions, 1460 SW Santiago Ave, Port Saint Lucie FL 34953 USA

Gillette, Walker A — Football Player
401 N College Dr, Franklin VA 23851, USA

Gilley, J Wade — Educator
University of Tennessee, President's Office, Knoxville TN 37996, USA

Gilley, Mickey L — Singer, Pianist, Songwriter
Gilley's Interests, PO Box 1242, Pasadena TX 77501, USA

Gilliam, Elijah — Baseball Player
1617 5th Ave N, Birmingham AL 35203, USA

Gilliam, John R — Football Player
4045 Moheb St SW, Atlanta GA 30331, USA

Gilliam, Jon R — Football Player
440 S Walnut Grove Road, Midlothian TX 76065, USA

Gilliam, Sam — Artist
Lou Stovall Workshop, 3145 Newark St NW, Washington DC 20008, USA
Gilliam, Terry V — Actor, Animator, Writer (Monty Python)
Old Hall, South Grove, Highgate, London N6 6BP, England
Gilliard, Lawrence (Larry), Jr — Actor
Innovative Artists, 1505 10th St, Santa Monica CA 90401 USA
Gillick, L Patrick D (Pat) — Baseball Executive
Philadelphia Phillies, 1 Citizens Bank Way, Philadelphia PA 19148 USA
Gillies, Ben — Drummer (Silverchair)
John Watson Mgmt, PO Box 281, Sunny Hills NSW 2010, Australia
Gillies, Clark (Jethro) — Ice Hockey Player
17 Pinta Court, Greenlawn NY 11740, USA
Gillies, Daniel — Actor
A P A Talent/Literary Agency, 405 S Beverly Dr, #300, Beverly Hills CA 90212 USA
Gillies, Isabel — Actress, Writer
Charles Scribner's Sons, 866 3rd Ave, New York NY 10022 USA
Gilliford, Paul G — Baseball Player
7 Woodland Dr, Malvern PA 19355, USA
Gilligan, Carol — Educator
Harvard University, Gender Studies Dept, Cambridge MA 02138, USA
Gilligan, Paul — Cartoonist
160 Baldwin St, #607, Toronto ON M5T 1L8, Canada
Gilligan, Vince — Producer
I C M Partners, 10250 Constellation Blvd, #900, Los Angeles CA 90067 USA
Gillilan, William J, III — Businessman
Centex Corp, PO Box 199000, Dallas TX 75219, USA
Gilliland, David — Auto Racing Driver
8556 Dog Leg Road, Sherrills Ford NC 28673, USA
Gilliland, Richard — Actor
9145 W Sunset Blvd, #228, West Hollywood CA 90069, USA
Gilliland, Robert J (Bob) — Test Pilot
PO Box 84, Palm Desert CA 92261, USA
Gillingham, Charles T (Charlie) — Musician (Counting Crowes)
Geffen Records, 10900 Wilshire Blvd, #1000, Los Angeles CA 90024 USA
Gillispie, Billy C — Basketball Coach
Texas Tech University, Athletic Dept, Lubbock TX 79409, USA
Gillom, Jennifer — Basketball Player
Washington Mystics, Verizon Center, 401 9th St NW, #750, Washington DC 20004 USA
Gilman, Alfred G — Nobel Medicine Laureate
10996 Crooked Creek Dr, Dallas TX 75229, USA
Gilman, Jared — Actor
D-mand Talent Agency, 85 S Broadway, #4, Nyack NY 10960, USA
Gilman, Richard C — Educator
131 Annandale Road, Pasadena CA 91105, USA
Gilman, Richard H — Publisher
Boston Globe, Publisher's Office, 135 Morrissey Blvd, Dorchester MA 02125, USA
Gilman, Ronald Lee — Judge
US Court of Appeals, 167 N Main St, #1176, Memphis TN 38103, USA
Gilman, Sid — Neurologist
3441 Geddes Road, Ann Arbor MI 48105, USA
Gilmartin, Paul — Actor, Comedian
Gersh Agency, 9465 Wilshire Blvd, #600, Beverly Hills CA 90212 USA
Gilmer, Harry V — Football Player
7467 Highway N, O'Fallon MO 63368, USA
Gilmore, Alexie — Actress
Paradigm Agency, 360 N Crescent Dr, North Building, Beverly Hills CA 90210 USA
Gilmore, Artis — Basketball Player
11043 Turnbridge Dr, Jacksonville FL 32256, USA
Gilmore, Bryan — Football Player
PO Box 815, Prosper TX 75078, USA
Gilmore, Jimmie Dale — Singer, Songwriter
Concerted Efforts, PO Box 440326, Somerville MA 02144 USA
Gilmore, Stephone — Football Player
Buffalo Bills, 1 Bills Dr, Orchard Park NY 14127 USA
Gilmore, Thea — Singer, Songwriter
Sara Austin, PO Box 2162, Stoke on Trent ST7 1XA, England
Gilmore, Walt — Basketball Player
257 Benjamin Blvd, Bear DE 19701, USA
Gilmour, Buddy — Harness Racing Driver
50 Merrick Ave, #410, East Meadow NY 11554, USA
Gilmour, David — Singer, Guitarist (Pink Floyd)
One Fifteen, Globe House, Middle Lane Mews, London N8 8PN, England
Gilmour, Doug — Ice Hockey Player
Octagon Worldwide, 1751 Pinnacle Dr, #1500, McLean VA 22102 USA
Gilmur, Charles E (Chuck) — Basketball Player
230 Farallone Ave, Fircrest WA 98466, USA
Gilpin, Peri — Actress
Burstein Co, 15304 W Sunset Blvd, #208, Pacific Palisades CA 90272 USA
Gilpin, Robert G, Jr — Political Scientist
133 Covington Lane, Shelburne VT 05482, USA
Gilroy, Frank D — Writer
8 Mangin Road, Monroe NY 10950, USA
Gilroy, Tom — Actor, Director, Producer, Writer
Sweet 180, 141 W 28th St, #300, New York NY 10001, USA
Gilroy, Tony — Writer, Director, Producer
Creative Artists Agency, 2000 Ave of Stars, #100, Los Angeles CA 90067 USA
Gilsean, Matthew — Singer (Celtic Tenors)
PO Box 32, Kells, County Meath, Ireland
Gilsig, Jessalyn — Actress
Paradigm Agency, 360 N Crescent Dr, North Building, Beverly Hills CA 90210 USA
Gilyard, Clarence, Jr — Actor, Director, Producer
Dick Delson Assoc, 4520 Bakman Ave, Studio City CA 91602, USA
Gimble, Johnny — Fiddle Player
Nancy Fly Agency, 6618 Wolfcreek Pall, Austin TX 78749, USA
Gimbrone, Michael A, Jr — Pathologist
Brigham & Women's Hospital, Vascular Pathology Dept, Boston MA 02115, USA

Gimeno, Andres — Tennis Player
Paseo de la Bonanova 38, Barcelona 6, Spain

Gimpel, Erica — Actress
Innovative Artists, 1505 10th St, Santa Monica CA 90401 USA

Gina G — Singer
What Mgmt, PO Box 1463, Culver City CA 90232, USA

Ginepri, Robby — Tennis Player
Olde Towne Athletic Club, 4950 Olde Towne Parkway, Marietta GA 30068, USA

Ging, Jack — Actor
48701 San Pedro St, La Quinta CA 92253, USA

Ginger Fish — Drummer (Marilyn Manson)
Coast II Coast Entertainment, 8671 Wilshire Blvd, Beverly Hills, CA 90211, USA

Gingrich, Newton L (Newt) — Representative, GA; Speaker
7410 Windy Hill Court, McLean VA 22102, USA

Ginibre, Jean-Louis — Editor
Hachette Filipacchi, Editorial Dept, 1633 Broadway, #4001, New York NY 10019, USA

Ginn, Chad — Golfer
Signature Sports Group, 4150 Olson Memorial Highway, #110, Minneapolis, MN 55422, USA

Ginn, Hubert (Hubie) — Football Player
16 Egrets Nest Dr, Savannah GA 31406, USA

Ginn, Theodore (Ted), Jr — Football Player
18289 SW 54th St, Savannah GA 31406, USA

Ginobili, Emmanuel (Manny) — Basketball Player
10 Queens Hill, San Antonio TX 78257, USA

Ginsburg, Ruth Bader — Supreme Court Justice
US Supreme Court, 1 1st St NE, Washington DC 20543 USA

Ginter, Keith — Baseball Player
2907 Maple Ave, Fullerton CA 92835, USA

Ginter, Matthew S (Matt) — Baseball Player
3320 Boonesboro Road, Winchester KY 40391, USA

Ginuwine — Singer
Universal Attractions, 135 W 26th St, #1200, New York NY 10001 USA

Giocante, Vahina — Actress
Artmedia, 20 Ave Rapp, 75007 Paris, France

Giola, Dana — Government Official, Writer
National Endowment for Arts, 1100 Pennsylvania Ave NW, Washington DC 20004, USA

Gionta, Brian — Ice Hockey Player
PO Box 16499, Rochester NY 14616, USA

Giordano, Thomas A (Tommy) — Baseball Player
176 Riverside Ave, Amityville NY 11701, USA

Giovanelli, Gordon — Rowing Athlete
332 Ouci de la Loma, Escondido CA 92029, USA

Giovanni, Joseph — Architect
Giovanni Assoc, 140 E 40th St, New York NY 10016, USA

Giovanni, Nikki E — Writer
Virginia Polytechnic Institute, English Dept, Blacksburg VA 24061, USA

Giovanola, Edward T (Ed) — Baseball Player
1741 Nomark Court, San Jose CA 95125, USA

Giovinazzo, Carmine — Actor
Paradigm Agency, 360 N Crescent Dr, North Building, Beverly Hills CA 90210 USA

Gipson, Charles W — Baseball Player
632 S Earlham St, Orange CA 92869, USA

Gipson, Dre — Singer, Keyboardist (Fishbone)
Silverback Mgmt, 9469 Jefferson Blvd, #101, Culver City CA 90232, USA

Giradelli, Marc — Alpine Skier
Marc Giradelli Sport AG, Wiesentalstr 6, 9445 Reibstein, Switzerland

Giraldo, Neil — Producer, Composer
Bel Chiasso Entertainment, 15541 Lapeyre Road, Moorpark CA 93021, USA

Girard, Ken — Ice Hockey Player
6-519 Riverside Dr, London ON N6H 5J3, Canada

Girardi, Joseph E (Joe) — Baseball Player, Manager
7320 Wisteria Ave, Parkland FL 33076, USA

Girardin, Ray — Actor
Academy of Performing Arts, PO Box 1843, Orleans MA 02653, USA

Girardot, Hippolyte — Actor
Artmedia, 20 Ave Rapp, 75007 Paris, France

Giraud, Joyce — Actress
C E S D, 10635 Santa Monica Blvd, #130, Los Angeles CA 90025 USA

Giri, Tulsi — Prime Minister, Nepal
Jawakpurdham, District Dhanuka, Nepal

Girone, Remo — Actor
Cristiano Cucchino Mgmt, Lungotevere dei Mellini 10, 00193 Rome, Italy

Giscard d'Estaing, Valery M R — President, France
11 Rue Benouville, 75116 Paris, France

Gisele — Model
I M G Models, 304 Park Ave S, #PH-North, New York NY 10010 USA

Gish, Annabeth — Actress
Innovative Artists, 1505 10th St, Santa Monica CA 90401 USA

Gisler, Michael (Mike) — Football Player
407 Tampa Dr, Victoria TX 77904, USA

Gisolo, Margaret — Baseball Player
4405 S Newberry Road, Tempe AZ 85282, USA

Gisondo, Skyler — Actor
Paradigm Agency, 360 N Crescent Dr, North Building, Beverly Hills CA 90210 USA

Gissell, Chris — Baseball Player
4310 NW 121st Circle, Vancouver WA 98685, USA

Gitlin, Todd — Historian
New York University, Culture & Communications Dept, New York NY 10012, USA

Gittins, Calum — Actor
Wing Nut Films, PO Box 15 208, Miramar, Wellington, New Zealand

Gittins, Jeremy — Actor
Associated International Mgmt, Fairfax House, Fulwood Place, London WC1V 6HU, England

Giuliani, Rudolph W — Mayor, New York City
Giuliani Partners, 5 Times Square, Converse Level 1, New York NY 10036, USA

Giuliano, Louis J — Businessman
I T T Industries, 4 W Red Oak Lane, #200, West Harrison NY 10604, USA

Giuliano, Tom — Singer (Happenings)
6929 N Hayden Road, Scottsdale AZ 85250, USA
Giuranna, Bruno — Concert Violist
Via Bembo 96, 31011 Asolo TV, Italy
Giurescu, Dino — Historian
3033 32nd St, Astoria NY 11102, USA
Giusti, David J (Dave) — Baseball Player
524 Clair Dr, Pittsburgh PA 15241, USA
Giusti, Katy — Foundation Executive
Multiple Myeloma Research Consortium, 383 Main Ave, #500, Norwalk CT 06851, USA
Givens, Adele — Actress, Comedienne
Artistry Mgmt, 340 N Camden Dr, #302, Beverly Hills CA 90210, USA
Givens, David L — Football Player
1117 Lochland Dr, Galllatin TN 37066, USA
Givens, Robin — Actress, Model
Marshak/Zachary Co, 8840 Wilshire Blvd, #100, Beverly Hills CA 90211 USA
Givhan, Robin — Journalist
Washington Post, Editorial Dept, 1150 15th St NW, Washington DC 20071 USA
Givins, Brian A — Baseball Player
719 Stonemont Court, Castle Rock CO 80108, USA
Givins, Ernest P, Jr — Football Player
3115 48th Ave S, Saint Petersburg FL 33712, USA
Gizenga, Antoine — Premier, Congo Democratic Republic
Palais de la Primature, BP 1354, Brazzaville, Congo Republic
Gizyn, Louie — Artist
1161 NW Taylor Ave, Corvallis OR 97330, USA
Gjertsen, Douglas (Doug) — Swimmer
7130 Havenridge Way, McDonough GA 30253, USA
Gjokaj, Enver — Actor
Suskin Mgmt, 2 Charlton St, #5K, New York NY 10014, USA
Gladden, C Daniel (Dan) — Baseball Player
6543 Pinnacle Dr, Eden Prairie MN 55346, USA
Gladding, Fred E — Baseball Player
436 Marsh Pointe Dr, Columbia SC 29229, USA
Gladis, Michael — Actor
Stone Manners Salners, 9911 W Pico Blvd, #1400, Los Angeles CA 90035 USA
Gladwell, Malcolm — Writer
Black Bay/Little Brown, 3 Center Plaza, Boston MA 02108, USA
Glaister, Lesley — Writer
A M Heath Co, 79 Saint Martin's Lane, London WC2N 4RE, England
Glance, Harvey — Track Athlete
2408 Old Creek Road, Montgomery AL 36117, USA
Glanfield, Joe — Yachtsman
W N W Design, 24A Upper Church St, Exmouth, Devon EX8 2TA, England
Glanville, Brian L — Writer
160 Holland Park Ave, London W11 4UH, England
Glanville, Douglas M (Doug) — Baseball Player
2043 W McLean Ave, Chicago IL 60647, USA
Glanville, Jerry — Football Coach, Auto Racing Driver
Jerry Glanville Motorsports, 550 Twinflower Court, Roswell GA 30075, USA
Glasbergen, Randy — Cartoonist (Better Half)
King Features Syndicate, 300 W 57th St, #1500, New York NY 10019 USA
Glaser, Daniel — Sociologist
63 Walk Hill St, Jamaica Plain MA 02130, USA
Glaser, Donald A — Nobel Physics Laureate
41 Hill Road, Berkeley,CA 94708, USA
Glaser, Jim — Singer
Joe Taylor Artist Agency, PO Box 279, Williamstown NJ 37068 USA
Glaser, Jon — Actor, Writer
Creative Artists Agency, 2000 Ave of Stars, #100, Los Angeles CA 90067 USA
Glaser, Milton — Graphic Artist
Milton Glaser Assoc, 207 E 32nd St, New York NY 10016, USA
Glaser, Paul Michael — Actor, Director
508 San Juan Ave, Venice CA 90291, USA
Glaser, Rob — Businessman, Inventor
Real Networks, 2601 Elliott Ave, Seattle WA 98121, USA
Glaser, Robert J — Foundation Executive
868 Boyce Ave, Palo Alto CA 94301, USA
Glaser, Rose Mary — Baseball Player
8929 Long Lane, Cincinnati OH 45231, USA
Glasgow, Nesby L — Football Player
8402 165th Ave NE, #106, Redmond WA 98052, USA
Glasgow, Walter — Yachtsman
781 Silver Spur Dr, Weatherford TX 76087, USA
Glashow, Sheldon Lee — Nobel Physics Laureate
30 Prescott St, Brookline MA 02446, USA
Glaspie, April — Diplomat
State Department, 2201 C St NW, Washington DC 20520 USA
Glass, Charles (Chip) — Football Player
7704 NE 140th St, Bothell WA 98011, USA
Glass, David D — Businessman
Wal-Mart Stores, 702 SW 8th St, Bentonville AK 72712, USA
Glass, Gerald — Basketball Player
1123 Tillman Road, Port Gibson MS 39150, USA
Glass, Glenn M — Football Player
301 Portsmouth Road, Knoxville TN 37909, USA
Glass, Leland S — Football Player
9 Bayou Court, Sacramento CA 95831, USA
Glass, Mona — Actress
Agentur Eberstein, Mullenhoffstr 2, 10967 Berlin, Germany
Glass, Philip — Composer
48 E 3rd St, #2, New York NY 10003, USA
Glass, Ron — Actor
Mitchell K Stubbs Assoc, 8695 W Washington Blvd, #204, Culver City CA 90232 USA
Glass, William S (Bill) — Football Player
Bill Glass Ministries, PO Box 761101, Dallas TX 75376, USA

G

Glasser, Ira S — Attorney
American Civil Liberties Union, 132 W 43rd St, New York NY 10036, USA
Glassic, Thomas J (Tom) — Football Player
1030 S Pine Dr, Bailey CO 80421, USA
Glassner, Barry — Educator, Sociologist
Lewis & Clark College, President's Office, 0615 SW Palatine Hill Road, Portland OR 97219, USA
Glasson, Bill — Golfer
5819 W Villas Court, Stillwater OK 74074, USA
Glasson, Stephanie — Model
Playboy Promotions, 2706 Media Center Dr, Los Angeles CA 90065 USA
Glatter, Lesli Linka — Director, Producer
Anonymous Content, 3532 Hayden Ave, Culver City CA 90232 USA
Glau, Summer L — Actress
Schiff Co, 8440 Warner Dr, #B1, Culver City CA 90232 USA
Glauber, Keith H — Baseball Player
20 Highland Court, Freehold NJ 07728, USA
Glauber, Robert R — Businessman
National Assn of Securities Dealers, 33 Whitehall St, New York NY 10004, USA
Glauber, Roy J — Nobel Physics Laureate
221 Pleasant St, Arlington MA 02476, USA
Glaudini, Lola — Actress
Paul Kohner, 9300 Wilshire Blvd, #555, Beverly Hills CA 90212 USA
Glaus, Troy E — Baseball Player
4300 Bibleway Court, Holly Springs NC 27540, USA
Glave, Matthew — Actor
Sanders/Armstrong/Caserta Mgmt, 2120 Colorado Ave, #120, Santa Monica CA 90404 USA
Glaviano, Marco — Photographer
150 W 56th St, New York NY 10019, USA
Glavine, Thomas M (Tom) — Baseball Player
920 Hurleston Lane, Alpharetta GA 30022, USA
Glazer, Eugene Robert — Actor
20058 Ventura Blvd, #61, Woodland Hills CA 91364, USA
Glazer, Jay — Sportscaster
Fox-TV, Sports Dept, 205 W 67th St, New York NY 10065 USA
Glazer, Jonathan — Director
Independent Talent Group, Oxford House, 76 Oxford St, London W1D 1BS, England
Glazer, Nathan — Sociologist
12 Scott St, Cambridge MA 02138, USA
Glazunov, Ilya S — Artist
Academy of Painting, Myasnitskaya Str 21, 101000 Moscow, Russia
Gleason, Joanna — Actress
Innovative Artists, 1505 10th St, Santa Monica CA 90401 USA
Gleason, Timothy (Tim) — Ice Hockey Player
2908 Spaldwick Court, Raleigh NC 27613, USA
Gleason, Vanessa — Model, Actress
4821 Lankershim Blvd, #F, North Hollywood CA 91601, USA
Gleaton, Jerry Don — Baseball Player
3008 Ave K, Brownwood TX 76801, USA
Glebova, Natalie — Beauty Queen
Miss Universe Organization, 1370 Ave of Americas, #1600, New York NY 10019 USA
Gleeson, Brendan — Actor
Agency Ltd, 9 Upper Fitzwilliam St, Dublin 2, Ireland
Gleeson, Domhnall — Actor
The Agency, 9 Upper Fitzwilliam St, Dubln 2, Ireland
Glemp, Jozef Cardinal — Religious Leader
Sekretariat Prymasa, Kolski, Ul Miodowa 17/19, 00 246 Warsaw, Poland
Glen, Iain — Actor
Independent Talent Group, Oxford House, 76 Oxford St, London W1D 1BS, England
Glen, John — Director
Skouras Agency, 1149 3rd St, #300, Santa Monica CA 90403 USA
Glen, Marla — Singer
Mom Productions, 20 Rue de la Providence, 75013 Paris, France
Glendon, Mary Ann — Attorney, Educator
Harvard University, Law School, Cambridge MA 02138, USA
Glenesk, Dean — Modern Pentathlete
1705 Ben Crenshaw Way, Austin TX 78746, USA
Glenister, Philip — Actor
Ken McReddie Assoc, 11 Connaught Place, London W2 2ET, England
Glenn, Aaron D — Football Player
30 Commanders Cove, Missouri City TX 77459, USA
Glenn, Devon — Drummer (Buckcherry)
10th Street Mgmt, 700 N San Vicente Blvd, #G410, West Hollywood CA 90069, USA
Glenn, Jason — Football Player
15530 Ella Blvd, #501, Houston TX 77090, USA
Glenn, John — Director, Writer
Brian Lutz Mgmt, 6565 Sunset Blvd, #416, Los Angeles CA 90028, USA
Glenn, John — Baseball Player
32 Edgewater Ave, Beverly NJ 08010, USA
Glenn, John H, Jr — Senator, OH; Astronaut
Ohio State University, Stillman Hall, 1810 S College Road, Columbus OH 43210, USA
Glenn, Mike T — Basketball Player
3571 Kilpatrick Lane, Snellville GA 30039, USA
Glenn, Scott — Actor
Innovative Artists, 1505 10th St, Santa Monica CA 90401 USA
Glenn, Tarik — Football Player
5216 N Delaware St, Indianapolis IN 46220, USA
Glenn, Terrance T (Terry) — Football Player
Dallas Cowboys, 1 Cowboys Parkway, Irving TX 75063 USA
Glenn, Wendy — Actress
Paradigm Agency, 360 N Crescent Dr, North Building, Beverly Hills CA 90210 USA
Glennie, Brian A — Ice Hockey Player
4 Curling Road, Bracebridge ON P1L 1M6, Canada
Glennie, Evelyn E A — Concert Percussionist
PO Box 6, Sawtry, Huntingdon, Cambs PE17 5WE, England
Glennie-Smith, Nick — Composer
First Artists Mgmt, 4764 Park Granada, #210, Calabasas CA 91302 USA

Glasser - Glennie-Smith

Gless, Sharon
Domain Talent, 9229 W Sunset Blvd, #710, West Hollywood CA 90069 USA — Actress
Glick, Frederick C (Freddy)
4226 Antlers Court, Fort Collins CO 80526, USA — Football Player
Glick, Gary G
2801 Middlesborough Court, Fort Collins CO 80525, USA — Football Player
Glicker, Daniel (Danny)
I C M Partners, 10250 Constellation Blvd, #900, Los Angeles CA 90067 USA — Costume Designer
Glickman, Andrew Z
4903 Newport Ave, Bethesda MD 20816, USA — Photographer
Glickman, Daniel R
Motion Picture Assn, 4635 Ashby St NW, Washington DC 20007, USA — Secretary, Agriculture
Glidden, Bob
Route 1, Box 236, Whiteland IN 46184, USA — Auto Racing Driver
Glidewell, Iain
Rough Heys Farm, Macclesfield, Cheshire SK11 9PF, England — Judge
Glier, Seth
Mpress Records, 200 E 10th St, #106, New York NY 10003, USA — Singer, Songwriter
Glimcher, Arnold O (Arne)
Paradigm Agency, 360 N Crescent Dr, North Building, Beverly Hills CA 90210 USA — Director, Producer, Composer
Glimm, James G
State University of New York, Applied Math Dept, Stony Brook NY 11794, USA — Mathematician
Glinatsis, George
13742 W 59th Ave, Arvada CO 80004, USA — Baseball Player
Glisson, Henry T (Tom)
V T Services, 40 E 52nd St, #1400, New York NY 10022, USA — Army General
Glitter, Gary
Jef Hanlon Mgmt, 1 York St, London W1H 1PZ, England — Singer, Songwriter
Glitter, Lesli Linka
Anonymous Content, 3532 Hayden Ave, Culver City CA 90232 USA — Director
Gload, Ross P
23 Harrison Ave, East Hampton NY 11937, USA — Baseball Player
Globus, Yoram
Pathe International, 8670 Wilshire Blvd, Beverly Hills CA 90211, USA — Producer
Glocer, Tom
Reuters Group PLC, Canary Wharf, South Colonnade, London E14 5EP, England — Businessman
Glockner, Michael
Kaiserslautener Str 54, 66123 Saarbrucken, Germany — Cyclist
Gloor, Olga
Professional Bowlers Assn, 719 2nd Ave, #701, Seattle WA 98104 USA — Bowler
Glouberman, Michael
Creative Artists Agency, 2000 Ave of Stars, #100, Los Angeles CA 90067 USA — Producer, Writer
Glover, Andrew L
33226 Magnolia Circle, Magnolia TX 77354, USA — Football Player
Glover, Bloc
American Motorcycle Assn, 13515 Yarmouth Dr, Pickerington OH 43147 USA — Motorcycle Racing Rider
Glover, Bruce
11449 Woodbine St, Los Angeles CA 90066, USA — Actor
Glover, Clarence
811 Lake Forest Parkway, Louisville KY 40245, USA — Basketball Player
Glover, Corey
Entertainment Artists, PO Box 120824, Nashville TN 37212 USA — Singer (Living Colour), Actor
Glover, Crispin
Don Buchwald/Fortitude, 6500 Wilshire Blvd, #2200, Los Angeles CA 90048 USA — Actor
Glover, Danny
Carrie Productions, 2625 Alcatraz Ave, #243, Berkeley CA 94705, USA — Actor
Glover, Dion
3691 Seton Hall Way, Decatur GA 30034, USA — Basketball Player
Glover, Donald
Creative Artists Agency, 2000 Ave of Stars, #100, Los Angeles CA 90067 USA — Actor
Glover, Jane A
Askonas Holt, Lincoln House, 300 High Holborn, London WC1V 7JH, England — Conductor
Glover, John
Innovative Artists, 1505 10th St, Santa Monica CA 90401 USA — Actor
Glover, Julian
Conway Van Gelder Grant, 8-12 Broadwick St, #300, London W1F 8HW, England — Actor
Glover, Kevin B
11553 Manorstone Lane, Columbia MD 21044, USA — Football Player
Glover, La'Roi D
PO Box 410589, Saint Louis MO 63141, USA — Football Player
Glover, Lucas
105 Annas Place, Simpsonville SC 29681, USA — Golfer
Glover, M Dionae (Dion)
2052 Channing Dr, Conyers GA 30094, USA — Basketball Player
Glover, Martin (Youth)
Agency Group, 9348 Civic Center Dr, #200, Beverly Hills CA 90210 USA — Bassist (Killing Joke)
Glover, Richard E (Rich)
215 Claremont Ave, Jersey City NJ 07305, USA — Football Player
Glover, Roger D
Thames Talent, 1720 Post Road E, #101, Westport CT 06880, USA — Bassist (Deep Purple)
Glover, Savion
Savion Glover Productions, 131 Brunswick St, Newark NJ 07114, USA — Dancer, Choreographer, Actor
Glover, Stephen (Steve-O)
I C M Partners, 10250 Constellation Blvd, #900, Los Angeles CA 90067 USA — Actor, Writer
Glowacki, Janusz
845 W End Ave, #4B, New York NY 10025, USA — Writer
Glowinski, Jacques
Unite INSERM College de France, 111 Pl M Berthelot, 75005 Paris, France — Neuropharmacologist
Gluck, Carol
440 Riverside Dr, New York NY 10027, USA — Historian
Gluck, Louise E
14 Ellsworth Park, Cambridge MA 02139, USA — Writer
Gluck, Will
United Talent Agency, 9336 Civic Center Dr, Beverly Hills CA 90210 USA — Director
Gluckman, Richard
Gluckman Mayer Architects, 250 Hudson Ave, New York NY 10013, USA — Architect

G

Gage - Gluckman

G

Glueck, Lawrence D (Larry) — Football Player
10 Cooper Road, East Falmouth MA 02536, USA
Glushchenko, Fedor I — Conductor
1st Pryadilnaya Str 11, #5, 105037 Moscow, Russia
Glushenko, Yevgenia K — Actress
1905 Goda Str 3, #91, 123100 Moscow, Russia
Glynn, Brian — Ice Hockey Player
Prince Albert Police Dept, 1084 Central, Prince Albert SK S6V 7P3, Canada
Glynn, Carlin — Actress
1165 5th Ave, New York NY 10029, USA
Glynn, Edward P (Ed) — Baseball Player
157 San Carlos St, Toms River NJ 08757, USA
Glynn, Ian M — Physiologist
Daylesford, Conduit Head Road, Cambridge CB3 0EY, England
Glynn, Ryan D — Baseball Player
1226 Melaleuca Lane, Fort Myers FL 33901, USA
Gminski, Michael T (Mike) — Basketball Player, Sportscaster
1309 Canterbury Hill Circle, Charlotte NC 28211, USA
Gnedovsky, Yuri P — Architect
Union of Architects, Granatny Per 22, 103001 Moscow, Russia
Goad, Jim — Journalist, Writer
Simon & Schuster Books, 1230 Ave of Americas, Concourse 1, New York NY 10020, USA
Goad, Timothy R (Tim) — Football Player
138 Birchwood Dr, Pittsboro NC 27312, USA
Goalby, Bob — Golfer
904 Briar Hill Road, Belleville IL 62223, USA
Goapele — Singer
Skyblaze Records, 360 Grand Ave, #295, Oakland CA 94610, USA
Gobble, B James (Jimmy) — Baseball Player
150 Lake View Estates Dr, Bristol TN 37620, USA
Goc, Marcel — Ice Hockey Player
12348 NW 69th Court, Parkland FL 33076, USA
Gocong, Christopher A (Chris) — Football Player
PO Box 93, Berea OH 44017, USA
Godal, Tore — Physician
World Health Organization, 20 Ave Appia, 1211 Geneva 27, Switzerland
Godard, Jean-Luc — Director
26 Ave Pierre 1er de Serbie, 75116 Paris, France
Godber, John — Writer
Alan Brodie, Fairgate House, 78 New Oxford St, London WC1A 1HB, England
Godby, Danny R — Baseball Player
RR 2 Box 17A, Chapmanville WV 25508, USA
Godchaux, Stephen — Producer
Paradigm Agency, 360 N Crescent Dr, North Building, Beverly Hills CA 90210 USA
Goddard, John — Explorer
4224 Beulah Dr, La Canada CA 91011, USA
Goddard, Joseph H (Joe) — Baseball Player
304 Ridgepark Dr, Beckley WV 25801, USA
Goddet, Michelle — Actress
Artmedia, 20 Ave Rapp, 75007 Paris, France
Godfread, Dan — Basketball Player
622 Michigan St, Eagle River WI 54521, USA
Godfrey — Actor, Comedian
Paradigm Agency, 360 N Crescent Dr, North Building, Beverly Hills CA 90210 USA
Godfrey, Christopher J (Chris) — Football Player
52383 Swanson Dr, South Bend IN 46635, USA
Godfrey, Paul V — Businessman
Postmedia Network, 1450 Don Mills Road, Don Mills ON M3B 3R5, Canada
Godfrey, Randall E — Football Player
4102 Mount Zion Church Road, South Bend IN 46635, USA
Godley, Georgina — Fashion Designer
42 Bassett Road, London W10 6UL, England
Godmanis, Ivars — Prime Minister, Latvia
Palasta St 1, 1954 Riga, Latvia
Godovsky, Yan — Ballet Dancer, Executive
Bolshoi Theater, Teatralnaya Pl 1, 103009 Moscow, Russia
Godwin, Gail K — Writer
PO Box 946, Woodstock NY 12498, USA
Godwin, Linda M — Astronaut, Physicist
3801 Eagle View Court, Columbia MO 65203, USA
Godynyuk, Alexander — Ice Hockey Player
217 Follen Road, Lexington MA 02421, USA
Goeas, Leo D — Football Player
95-104 Hiilei Place, Mililani HI 96789, USA
Goebel, Timothy — Figure Skater
Lee Marshall Mgmt, 199 E Garfield Road, Aurora OH 44202, USA
Goeddeke, George A — Football Player
1227 Pinecrest Dr, White Lake MI 48386, USA
Goeddel, David V N — Biochemist
Tularik Inc, 270 Grand Ave, San Francisco CA 94108, USA
Goedgedrag, Frits M D L S — Governor, Netherlands Antilles
Governor's Office, Fort Amsterdam 2, Willemstad, Netherlands Antilles
Goehr, P Alexander — Composer
University of Cambridge, Music Faculty, 11 West Road, Cambridge, England
Goellner, Marc-Kevin — Tennis Athlete
Blau-Weiss Neuss, Tennishall Jahnstra, 41464 Neuss, Germany
Goelz, Dave (Gonzo) — Puppeteer
Jim Henson Productions, 117 E 69th St, New York NY 10021, USA
Goen, Robert K (Bob) — Entertainer
Rebel Entertainment Partners, 5700 Wilshire Blvd, #456, Los Angeles CA 90036, USA
Goerke, Christine — Opera Singer
I M G Artists, Hogarth Business Park, Chiswick, London W4 2TH, England
Goerke, Glenn A — Educator
University of Houston, President's Office, Houston TX 77204, USA
Goerne, Matthias — Opera Singer
I M G Artists, Hogarth Business Park, Chiswick, London W4 2TH, England

Glueck - Goerne

Goertz, LeRoy
Refiner's Fire, PO Box 66612, Portland OR 97290, USA — Sculptor, Jewelry Designer, Composer

Goestschi, Renate
Schwarzenbach 3, 8742 Obdach, Austria — Alpine Skier

Goetz, Dick
4301 Fillbrook Lane, Tyler TX 75707, USA — Golfer

Goetz, Eric
Eric Goetz Marine & Technology, 15 Broad Common Road, Bristol RI 02809, USA — Yacht Builder

Goetz-Ackerman, Vicki
3621 Sally Parrish Trail, Valrico FL 33596, USA — Golfer

Goetzman, Gary M
Playtone Productions, PO Box 7340, Santa Monica CA 90406, USA — Producer

Goff, Michael J (Mike)
2225 5th St, Peru IL 61354, USA — Football Player

Goffin, Gerry
9171 Hazen Dr, Beverly Hills CA 90210, USA — Lyricist

Goffin, Louise L
DreamWorks Records, 1000 Flower St, Glendale CA 91201 USA — Singer, Songwriter

Gogan, Kevin P
4643 286th Ave E, Fall City MA 98024, USA — Football Player

Goganious, Keith L
4173 Cheswick Lane, Virginia Beach VA 23455, USA — Football Player

Gogel, Matt
3509 W 68th St, Mission Hills KS 66208, USA — Golfer

Goggin, Charles F (Chuck)
1224 Roundhouse Lane, Alexandria VA 22314, USA — Baseball Player

Goggins, Walton
A P A Talent/Literary Agency, 405 S Beverly Dr, #300, Beverly Hills CA 90212 USA — Actor

Gogo, David
Cordova Bay Entertainment, 2750 Quadra St, #209, Victoria BC V8T 4E8, Canada — Guitarist

Gogolak, Charles P (Charlie)
PO Box 361, Northeast Harbor ME 04662, USA — Football Player

Gogolak, Peter (Pete)
24 Arrowhead Way, Darien CT 06820, USA — Football Player

Gogolewski, William J (Bill)
1522 Graham Ave, Oshkosh WI 54902, USA — Baseball Player

Gogue, Jay
Auburn University, President's Office, Auburn AL 36849, USA — Educator

Goh Chok Tong
Senior Minister's Office, Istana Annexe, 238823 Singapore, Singapore — Prime Minister, Singapore

Goh, Rex
PO Box 3367, Beverly Hills CA 90212, USA — Guitarist (Air Supply)

Gohl, Matthias
I C M Artists, 40 W 57th St, #1800, New York NY 10019 USA — Composer

Gohlke, Frank
Howard Greenberg Gallery, 41 E 57th St, #1406, New York NY 10022, USA — Photographer

Gohr, Gregory J (Greg)
77 Scotland Road, Reading MA 01867, USA — Baseball Player

Goich, Daniel J (Dan)
PO Box 19068, Las Vegas NV 89132, USA — Football Player

Goicolea, Anthony
149-151 Grand St, #1, Brooklyn NY 11211, USA — Photographer

Goin, Suzanne
Lucques, 8484 Melrose Ave, West Hollywood CA 90069, USA — Restauranteur

Goines, Siena
Don Buchwald/Fortitude, 6500 Wilshire Blvd, #2200, Los Angeles CA 90048 USA — Actress

Going, Joanna
Vanguard Management Group, 8060 Melrose Ave, #400, Los Angeles CA 90046, USA — Actress

Goings, E V
Tupperware Corp, PO Box 2353, Orlando FL 32802, USA — Businessman

Goings, Nick A
9603 Sunset Grove Dr, Huntersville NC 28078, USA — Football Player

Goitschel-Beranger, Marielle
Val Thorens, 73440 Saint-Martin de Belleville, France — Alpine Skier

Gola, Thomas J (Tom)
15 Kings Oak Lane, Philadelphia PA 19115, USA — Basketball Player, Coach

Golay, Jeanne
PO Box 1697, Glenwood Springs CO 81602, USA — Cyclist

Gold, Christina A
Western Union, 12500 Belford Ave, Englewood CO 80112, USA — Businesswoman

Gold, Elon
Gersh Agency, 9465 Wilshire Blvd, #600, Beverly Hills CA 90212 USA — Actor, Comedian

Gold, Herbert
1051 Broadway, #A, San Francisco CA 94133, USA — Writer

Gold, Ian M
10275 Tradition Place, Lone Tree CO 80124, USA — Football Player

Gold, Jack
The Agency, 24 Pottery Lane, Holland Park,London W11 4LZ, England , USA — Director

Gold, Jonathan
L A Weekly, Editorial Dept, 6715 Sunset Blvd, Los Angeles CA 90028, USA — Journalist

Gold, Louise
Gavin Barker Assoc, 2D Wimpole St, London W1G 0EB, England — Actress

Gold, Tracey
TalentWorks, 3500 W Olive Ave, #1400, Burbank CA 91505 USA — Actress

Goldberg, Adam C
Luber Rocklin Entertainment, 8530 Wilshire Blvd, #555, Beverly Hills CA 90211 USA — Actor

Goldberg, Bernard R
CBS-TV, News Dept, 51 W 52nd St, New York NY 10019 USA — Commentator

Goldberg, Bill
Kritzer Levine Wilkins Griffin, 11872 La Grange Ave, #100, Los Angeles CA 90025 USA — Actor

Goldberg, Daryl
Pipeline Entertainment, 305 2nd Ave, #302, New York NY 10003, USA — Director, Producer

Goldberg, Eric
Walt Disney Studios, Animation Dept, 500 S Buena Vista St, Burbank CA 91521, USA — Animator

Goldberg, Evan
United Talent Agency, 9336 Civic Center Dr, Beverly Hills CA 90210 USA — Producer

G

Gage - Goldberg

Goldberg, Fred T, Jr — Government Official
Skadden Arps Slate, 1440 New York Ave NW, #600, Washington DC 20005, USA

Goldberg, Harris — Director, Writer
Key Creatives, 1800 N Highland Ave, Los Angeles CA 90028, USA

Goldberg, Iddo — Actor
Gordon & French, 12-13 Poland St, London W1F 8QB, England

Goldberg, Jim — Photographer
California College of Arts, Fine Arts Dept, San Francisco CA 94107, USA

Goldberg, Leonard — Producer
Spectradyne Inc, 1198 Commerce Dr, Richardson TX 75081, USA

Goldberg, Lucianne S — Publisher
4 Oak St, Weehawken NJ 7086, USA

Goldberg, Luella G — Educator
7019 Tupa Dr, Minneapolis MN 55439, USA

Goldberg, Myla — Writer
Doubleday Press, 1745 Broadway, New York NY 10019, USA

Goldberg, Richard W — Judge
US International Trade Court, 1 Federal Plaza, New York NY 10278, USA

Goldberg, Stan — Cartoonist (Archie)
8 White Birch Lane, Scarsdale NY 10583, USA

Goldberg, Whoopi — Actress, Comedienne
Indie Flix, 4111 E Madison St, #310, Seattle WA 98112, USA

Goldberg, William S (Bill) — Professional Wrestler, Football Player
Vox Inc, 6420 Wilshire Blvd, #1080, Los Angeles CA 90048 USA

Goldberger, Andreas — Ski Jumper
Bleckenwegen 4, 4924 Waldzell, Austria

Goldberger, Marvin L — Physicist, Educator
7867 La Jolla Vista Dr, La Jolla CA 92037, USA

Goldberger, Paul J — Journalist, Architectural Critic
New York Times, Editorial Dept, 229 W 43rd St, New York NY 10036, USA

Goldblatt, David — Photographer
South Picture Portal, Box 91776, Auckland Park, 2006 Gauteng, South Africa

Goldblatt, Stephen L — Cinematographer
Skouras Agency, 1149 3rd St, #300, Santa Monica CA 90403 USA

Goldblum, Jeff — Actor
Creative Artists Agency, 2000 Ave of Stars, #100, Los Angeles CA 90067 USA

Golden, Alfred J (Al) — Football Player, Coach
University of Miami, Athletic Dept, Coral Gables FL 33124, USA

Golden, Arthur — Writer
Vintage Books, 1745 Broadway, New York NY 10019 USA

Golden, Daniel — Journalist
Wall Street Journal, Editorial Dept, 1 World Financial Center, New York NY 10281, USA

Golden, Harry — Bowling Executive
Professional Bowlers Assn, 719 2nd Ave, #701, Seattle WA 98104 USA

Golden, James E (Jim) — Baseball Player
8630 SW 10th Ave, Topeka KS 66615, USA

Golden, Kate — Golfer
969 Hunterwood Dr, Jasper TX 75951, USA

Golden, William Lee — Singer (Oak Ridge Boys); Songwriter
329 Rockland Road, Hendersonville TN 37075, USA

Goldenhersh, Heather — Actress
Gersh Agency, 9465 Wilshire Blvd, #600, Beverly Hills CA 90212 USA

Goldenthal, Elliot — Composer
Gorfaine/Schwartz, 4111 W Alameda Ave, #509, Burbank CA 91505 USA

Goldfaden, Benjamin P (Ben) — Basketball Player
5819 Bounty Circle, Tavares FL 32778, USA

Goldfinger, June — Interior Designer
June Goldfinger Designs, 109 Katonah Ave, Katonah NY 10536, USA

Goldfinger, Myron — Architect
PO Box 53, Waccabuc NY 10597, USA

Goldfinger, Sarah — Actress, Producer
Creative Artists Agency, 2000 Ave of Stars, #100, Los Angeles CA 90067 USA

Goldhor, David — Director
Eagle Eye, 4013 Topanga Ave, Studio City CA 91604, USA

Goldin, Claudia D — Economist
Harvard University, Economics Dept, Cambridge MA 02138, USA

Goldin, Judah — Educator
3300 Darby Road, Haverford PA 19041, USA

Goldin, Nan — Photographer
334 Bowery, New York NY 10012, USA

Goldin, Ricky Paull — Actor
Stone Manners Salners, 9911 W Pico Blvd, #1400, Los Angeles CA 90035 USA

Golding, Meta — Actress
I F A Talent Agency, 8730 W Sunset Blvd, #490, West Hollywood CA 90069 USA

Golding, O Bruce — Prime Minister, Jamaica
Prime Minister's Office, 1 Devon Road, PO Box 272, Kingston 6, Jamaica

Goldman, Bo — Writer
Creative Artists Agency, 2000 Ave of Stars, #100, Los Angeles CA 90067 USA

Goldman, Dan — Writer
I C M Partners, 10250 Constellation Blvd, #900, Los Angeles CA 90067 USA

Goldman, Jean-Jacques — Singer, Guitarist, Songwriter
J S M Music, 73 Ave de la Republique, 92120 Montrouge, France

Goldman, Julie — Actress, Comedienne
427 Union St, #3, Brooklyn NY 11231, USA

Goldman, Matt — Entertainer (Blue Man Group)
Blue Man Group Productions, 411 Lafayette St, #300, New York NY 10003, USA

Goldman, William — Writer
Janklow & Nesbit Assoc, 445 Park Ave, #1300, New York NY 10022 USA

Goldreich, Peter M — Astronomer
471 S Catalina Ave, Pasadena CA 91106, USA

Goldsboro, Bobby — Singer, Songwriter
La Rana Productions, PO Box 5250, Ocala FL 34478, USA

Goldschmidt, Neil E — Secretary, Transportation; Governor, OR
1150 SW King Ave, Portland OR 97205, USA

Goldsman, Akiva — Director, Writer
Weed Road Pictures, 4000 Warner Blvd, Building 81, Burbank CA 91522, USA

Goldsmith, Barbara Writer
Janklow Nesbit Assocs, 445 Park Ave, #1300, New York NY 10022, USA
Goldsmith, Clio Actress
Elephant Family, 81 Gower St, London WC1E 6HJ, England
Goldsmith, Judy Social Activist
National Organization for Women, 425 13th St NW, Washington DC 20002, USA
Goldsmith, Myron Architect
Skidmore Owings Merrill, 224 S Michigan Ave, #1000, Chicago IL 60604, USA
Goldsmith, Paul Auto Racing Driver, Motorcycle Rider
1705 E Main St, Griffith IN 46319, USA
Goldsmith, Timothy H Biologist
Yale University, Biology Dept, New Haven CT 06520, USA
Goldson, Dashon H Football Player
San Francisco 49ers, 4949 Centennial Blvd, Santa Clara CA 95054 USA
Goldstein, Allan A Director
6488 Mary Ellen Ave, Van Nuys CA 91401, USA
Goldstein, Allan L Biochemist, Immunologist
800 25th St NW, #1005, Washington DC 20037, USA
Goldstein, Alon Concert Pianist
Frank Salomon, 121 W 27th St, #703, New York NY 10001 USA
Goldstein, Avram Pharmacologist
6466 Bluebird Ave, Longmont CO 80503, USA
Goldstein, Joseph L Nobel Medicine Laureate
3831 Turtle Creek Blvd, #22B, Dallas TX 75219, USA
Goldstein, Lisa Actress
Harrison Stokes, 8730 W Sunset Blvd, #270, West Hollywood CA 90069, USA
Goldstein, Murray Physician, Association Executive
United Cerebral Palsy Foundation, 1660 L St NW, #700, Washington DC 20036, USA
Goldstein, Rebecca Writer, Philosopher
2 Payamel Lane, Truro MA 02666, USA
Goldstone, Jeffrey Physicist
77 Massachusetts Ave, #6-313, Cambridge MA 02139, USA
Goldstone, Richard J Judge
Constitutional Court, Private Bag X32, Braamfontein 2017, South Africa
Goldsworthy, Andrew C (Andy) Artist, Photographer
Hue-Williams Fine Art, 21 Cork St, London W1X 1HB, England
Goldthwait, Bob (Bobcat) Actor, Comedian, Director
Gersh Agency, 9465 Wilshire Blvd, #600, Beverly Hills CA 90212 USA
Goldwyn, Samuel J, Jr Producer
Samuel Goldwyn Co, 9570 W Pico Blvd, #400, Los Angeles CA 90035, USA
Goldwyn, Tony Actor, Director
Creative Artists Agency, 2000 Ave of Stars, #100, Los Angeles CA 90067 USA
Golic, Mike Football Player
108 Westland Road, Avon CT 06001, USA
Golic, Robert P (Bob) Football Player, Sportscaster
6130 Loch Lomond Court, Solon OH 44139, USA
Golijov, Osvaldo Composer
Opus 3 Artists, 470 Park Ave S, #900N, New York NY 10016, USA
Golimowski, David A Astronomer
515 Holden Road, Towson MD 21286, USA
Golino, Valeria Actress
Cineart, 36 Rue de Ponthieu, 75008 Paris, France
Golisano, B Thomas Businessman
Paychex Inc, 911 Panorama Trail S, Rochester NY 14625, USA
Golonka, Arlene Actress
S M S Talent, 8383 Wilshire Blvd, #230, Beverly Hills CA 90211 USA
Golota, Andrzej Boxer
26852 W Apple Tree Lane, Barrington IL 60010, USA
Golovkin, Gennady G Boxer
Spotlight Boxing, Am Stadtrand 27, 22047 Hamburg, Germany
Golson, Benny Jazz Saxophonist, Composer
Abby Hoffer, 223 1/2 E 48th St, New York NY 10017 USA
Golsteyn, Jerry M Football Player
243 Tadcaster Court, Raeford NC 28376, USA
Goltz, David A (Dave) Baseball Player
1009 Stonybrook Manor, Fergus Falls MN 56537, USA
Golub, Jeff Jazz Guitarist
Narada/Blue Note Productions, 150 5th Ave, #600, New York NY 10011, USA
Golubeva, Yekatarina Actress
Artmedia, 20 Ave Rapp, 75007 Paris, France
Goluboff, Bryan Writer, Director
Paradigm Agency, 360 N Crescent Dr, North Building, Beverly Hills CA 90210 USA
Golzari, Sam Actor
Innovative Artists, 1505 10th St, Santa Monica CA 90401 USA
Gomes Junior, Carlos D Prime Minister, Guinea-Bissau
Premier's Office, Ave Unidad Africana, CP 137, Bissau, Guinea-Bissau
Gomes, Jessica Model
Vivien's Model Mgmt, 43 Bay St, Double Bay, Sydney NSW 2028, Australia
Gomes, Jonathan J (Jonny) Baseball Player
7901 Garden Dr N, Saint Petersburg FL 33710, USA
Gomes, Wayne M Baseball Player
5104 W Creek Court, Suffolk VA 23435, USA
Gomez, Andres Tennis Player
ProServe, 1101 Woodrow Wilson Blvd, #1800, Arlington VA 22209 USA
Gomez, Carlos Actor
Stone Manners Salners, 9911 W Pico Blvd, #1400, Los Angeles CA 90035 USA
Gomez, Chris C Baseball Player
8 Vernal Spring, Irvine CA 92603, USA
Gomez, Christian Soccer Player
D C United, R F K Stadium, 2400 E Capitol St SE, Washington DC 20003 USA
Gomez, Ian Actor
Innovative Artists, 1505 10th St, Santa Monica CA 90401 USA
Gomez, Jaime P Actor
Susan Nathe Assoc, 8281 Melrose Ave, #200, Los Angeles CA 90046, USA
Gomez, Jeff Cartoonist
Starlight Runner Entertainment, 5 Union Square, #400, New York NY 10003, USA

Gomez, Jesus R Salazar — Religious Leader
Arzobispado, Carrera 7A, #10-20, Bogota DC 1, Colombia

Gomez, Jill — Opera Singer
16 Milton Park, London N6 5QA, England

Gomez, Joshua E — Actor
Progressive Artists Agency, 1041 N Formosa Ave, West Hollywood CA 90046 USA

Gomez, Leonardo (Leo) — Baseball Player
273 Portofino Dr, North Venice FL 34275, USA

Gomez, Luis J — Baseball Player
676 Chesterfield Dr, Lawrenceville CA 30044, USA

Gomez, Mariette Himes — Interior Designer
504 E 74th St, #300, New York NY 10021, USA

Gomez, Randall S (Rocky) — Baseball Player
50 Oak St, San Martin CA 95046, USA

Gomez, Rick — Actor, Writer, Producer
A P A Talent/Literary Agency, 405 S Beverly Dr, #300, Beverly Hills CA 90212 USA

Gomez, Scott — Ice Hockey Player
14121 Thunder Road, Anchorage AK 99516, USA

Gomez, Selena M — Actress, Singer
July Moon Productions, 10100 Santa Monica Blvd, #1300, Los Angeles CA 90067, USA

Gomez, Wilfredo — Boxer
U E C A, Edificio 54 Apt 01, Trujillo Alto PR 00976, USA

Gomez-Preston, Reagan — Actress
Innovative Artists, 1505 10th St, Santa Monica CA 90401 USA

Gomory, Ralph E — Foundation Executive, Mathematician
Alfred P Sloan Foundation, President's Office, 630 5th Ave, New York NY 10111, USA

Gompf, Thomas (Tom) — Diver
2716 Barret Ave, Plant City FL 33566, USA

Gomyo, Karen — Concert Violinist
Seldy Cramer Artists, 3439 Springhill Road, Lafayette CA 94549, USA

Gonchar, Sergei V — Ice Hockey Player
7 Kevin Dr, Sewickley PA 15143, USA

Gonchor, Jess — Art Director
Murtha Agency, 4240 Promenade Way, #232, Marina del Rey CA 90292, USA

Gondoline, Michel — Actor
Alais Agence Artisqaue, 13 Rue Chevreul, 75011 Paris, France

Gondrezick, Grant — Basketball Player
5906 Etiwanda Ave, #19, Tarzana CA 91356, USA

Gondry, Michel — Director
Creative Artists Agency, 2000 Ave of Stars, #100, Los Angeles CA 90067 USA

Gonet, Stella — Actress
Markham & Froggatt, Julian House, 4 Windmill St, London W1P 1HF, England

Gong Li — Actress, Model
I C M Partners, 10250 Constellation Blvd, #900, Los Angeles CA 90067 USA

Gongora, Omar — Drummer (Kinky)
Marcella C Public Relations, 646 S Barrington Ave, #206, Brentwood CA 90049, USA

Gonick, Larry — Cartoonist (Prehistoric Animals)
247 Missouri St, San Francisco CA 94107, USA

Gonnenwein, Wolfgang — Conductor
Buro Beate Gienger, Im Boblinger 2, 71636 Ludwigsburg, Germany

Gonsalves, Ralph E — Premier, Saint Vincent & Grenadines
Prime Minister's Office, Administration Centre, Kingstown, Saint Vincent & Grenadines

Gonshaw, Francesca — Actress
Greg Mellard, 12 D'Arblay St, #200, London W1V 3FP, England

Gonsoulin, Austin W Goose) — Football Player
8062 Indian Blanket, Beaumont TX 77713, USA

Gonzales, Carlos — Cinematographer
3850 Tracy St, Los Angeles CA 90027, USA

Gonzales, Chilly — Singer, Songwriter
Agency Group Ltd, 1880 Century Park E, #711, Los Angeles CA 90067 USA

Gonzales, Rene A — Baseball Player
755 E Orangewood Dr, Covina CA 91723, USA

Gonzalez Echevarria, Roberto — Educator
Yale University, Hispanic/Comparative Literature Dept, New Haven CT 06520, USA

Gonzalez Gonzalez, Clifton — Actor
Paradigm Agency, 360 N Crescent Dr, North Building, Beverly Hills CA 90210 USA

Gonzalez Inarritu, Alejandro — Director
Creative Artists Agency, 2000 Ave of Stars, #100, Los Angeles CA 90067 USA

Gonzalez Marquez, Felipe — Prime Minister, Spain
Fundacion Socialismo XXI, Gobelas 31, 28023 Madrid, Spain

Gonzalez Zumarraga, Antonio J Cardinal — Religious Leader
Arzobispado, Apartado 17-01-00106, Called Chile 1140, Quito, Ecuador

Gonzalez, A Antonio (Tony) — Baseball Player
8011 SW 196th Terrace, Cutler Bay FL 33189, USA

Gonzalez, Adrian — Baseball Player
Los Angeles Dodgers, Stadium, 1000 Elysian Park Ave, Los Angeles CA 90090 USA

Gonzalez, Alex — Actor
Kuranda Mgmt, Santo Angel 84, 28043 Madrid, Spain

Gonzalez, Alexander S (Alex) — Baseball Player
7743 SW 119th Court, Miami FL 33183, USA

Gonzalez, Anthony D (Tony) — Football Player
18935 Evening Breeze Circle, Huntington Beach CA 92648, USA

Gonzalez, Arthur — Judge
US Bankruptcy Court, 1 Bowling Green, #534, New York NY 10004, USA

Gonzalez, Ashie — Bowler
Professional Bowlers Assn, 719 2nd Ave, #701, Seattle WA 98104 USA

Gonzalez, Carlos A — Baseball Player
Colorado Rockies, Coors Field, 2001 Blake St, #A, Denver CO 80205 USA

Gonzalez, Fredi J — Baseball Manager
2768 Pete Shaw Road, Marietta GA 30066, USA

Gonzalez, Giovanny A (Gio) — Baseball Player
Oakland Athletics, McAfee Coliseum, 7000 Coliseum Way, #3, Oakland CA 94621 USA

Gonzalez, Hector — Religious Leader
Baptist Churches USA, PO Box 851, Valley Forge PA 19482, USA

Gonzalez, Jaslene — Model
Elite Model Mgmt, 404 Park Ave S, #900, New York NY 10016 USA

Gonzalez, Juan A — Baseball Player
Ext Catoni A9, Vega Baja PR 00693, USA
Gonzalez, Lissette — Commentator, Model
CBS4-TV, 8900 NW 18th Terrace, Doral FL 33172, USA
Gonzalez, Luis E — Baseball Player
6026 E Jenan Dr, Scottsdale AZ 85254, USA
Gonzalez, Michael V (Mike) — Baseball Player
2414 Pine Brook Court, Deer Park TX 77536, USA
Gonzalez, Nicholas — Actor
Pakula/King, 9229 W Sunset Blvd, #315, West Hollywood CA 90069 USA
Gonzalez, Pedro O — Baseball Player
104 Gen Cabral, San Pedro de Macoris, Dominican Republic
Gonzalez, Raul — Soccer Player
F C Real Madrid, Avda Concha Espana 1, 28036 Madrid, Spain
Gonzalez, Rick — Actor
Framework Entertainment, 9057 Nemo St, #C, West Hollywood CA 90069 USA
Gonzalo, Julie — Actress
United Talent Agency, 9336 Civic Center Dr, Beverly Hills CA 90210 USA
Gonzi, Lawrence — Prime Minister, Malta
Prime Minister's Office, Auberge de Castille, 13 Saint Paul's St, Valletta VLT 1210, Malta
Gooch, Jeffrey L (Jeff) — Football Player
12709 Seronera Valley Court, Spring Hill FL 34610, USA
Gooch, Rich — Bassist (Quarterflash)
Pacific Talent Agency, PO Box 19145, Portland OR 97280, USA
Good, Andrew — Baseball Player
1433 S Belcher Road, #G4, Clearwater FL 33764, USA
Good, Hugh W — Religious Leader
Primitive Advent Christian Church, 6403 Frame Road, Elkview WV 25071, USA
Good, Meagan — Actress
Untitled Entertainment, 350 S Beverly Dr, #200, Beverly Hills CA 90212 USA
Good, Melanie — Actress
11288 Ventura Blvd, #175, Studio City CA 91604, USA
Good, Michael T — Astronaut
3874 Cherry Plum Dr, Colorado Springs CO 80920, USA
Goodacre Connick, Jill — Model
Harry Connick, Wilkins Mgmt, 323 Broadway, Cambridge MA 02139, USA
Goodacre, Glenna — Sculptor
1202 Ojo Verde, Santa Fe NM 87501, USA
Goodall, Caroline — Actress
United Agents, 12-26 Lexington St, London W1F 0LE, England
Goodall, V Jane — Ethologist, Primatologist
Jane Goodall Institute, 4245 Fairfax Dr, #600, Arlington VA 22203, USA
Goodburn, Kelly J — Football Player
3710 W 52nd Place, Mission KS 66205, USA
Goode, Chris K — Football Player
1428 Egret Lane, Birmingham AL 35214, USA
Goode, David R — Businessman
Norfolk Southern Corp, 3 Commercial Place, #100, Norfolk VA 23510, USA
Goode, Donald R (Don) — Football Player
30177 Tattersall Way, Menifee CA 92584, USA
Goode, Irvin L (Irv) — Football Player
1030 Schnucks Woodsmill Plaza, Chesterfield MO 63017, USA
Goode, Joe — Artist
PO Box 10372, Playa del Rey CA 90291, USA
Goode, Matthew — Actor
Dazwell & Beresford, 26 Astwood Mews, London SW7 4DE, England
Goode, Richard S — Concert Pianist
Frank Salomon, 121 W 27th St, #703, New York NY 10001 USA
Goode, W Wilson — Mayor, Philadelphia; Social Activist
Amachi, 2000 Market St, #600, Philadelphia PA 19103, USA
Goodell, Brian S — Swimmer
27040 S Ridge Dr, Mission Viejo CA 92692, USA
Goodell, Roger — Football Executive
National Football League, 280 Park Ave, #12W, New York NY 10017, USA
Gooden, Andrew M (Drew) — Basketball Player
Milwaukee Bucks, Bradley Center, 1001 N 4th St, #2, Milwaukee WI 53203 USA
Gooden, Dwight E — Baseball Player
20114 Nob Oak Ave, Tampa FL 33647, USA
Goodenough, Ward H — Anthropologist
3300 Darby Road, #5306, Haverford PA 19041, USA
Goodeve, Grant — Actor
21416 NE 68th Court, Redmond WA 98053, USA
Goodfellow, Peter N — Geneticist
Cancer Research Fund, Lincoln Inn Fields, London WC2A 3PX, England
Goodfriend, Lynda — Actress
338 S Beachwood Dr, Burbank CA 91506, USA
Gooding, Cuba, Sr — Singer (Main Ingredient)
Winston Collection, 630 9th Ave, #908, New York NY 10036, USA
Gooding, Omar — Actor
Innovative Artists, 1505 10th St, Santa Monica CA 90401 USA
Goodison, Paul — Yachtsman
Utley Sailing Club, Pleasley Road, Aughton, Sheffield S26 3XL, England
Goodkind, Terry — Writer
G P Putnam's Sons, 375 Hudson St, New York NY 10014 USA
Goodman, Alfred — Composer
Bodenstedtstr 31, 81241 Munich, Germany
Goodman, Allegra — Writer
Dial Press, 375 Hudson St, New York NY 10014, USA
Goodman, Brian — Actor
Nine Yards Entertainment, 8530 Wilshire Blvd, #500, Beverly Hills CA 90211 USA
Goodman, Corey S — Neurobiologist
Howard Hughes Medical Institute, Molecular/Cell Biology Dept, Berkeley CA 94720, USA
Goodman, Eli — Actor
Maverick Artists Agency, 1680 N Vine St, #802, Los Angeles CA 90028, USA
Goodman, Ellen H — Columnist
Boston Globe, Editorial Dept, 135 William Morrissey Blvd, Dorchester MA 02125 USA

Goodman, Hazelle — Actress
C E S D, 10635 Santa Monica Blvd, #130, Los Angeles CA 90025 USA

Goodman, John — Actor
Gersh Agency, 9465 Wilshire Blvd, #600, Beverly Hills CA 90212 USA

Goodman, John F — Marine Corps General
Commander, Marine Forces Pacific, Camp H M Smith HI 96861 USA

Goodman, John R — Football Player
800 E 9th St, Edmond OK 73034, USA

Goodman, Joseph W — Electrical Engineer
570 University Terrace, Los Altos CA 94022, USA

Goodman, Katy (La Sera) — Singer, Songwriter
Agency Group Ltd, 1880 Century Park E, #711, Los Angeles CA 90067 USA

Goodman, Len — Dance Judge
Strictly Come Dancing, BBC Television, Wood Lane, London W12 7RJ, England

Goodman, Oscar — Attorney
520 S 4th St, Las Vegas NV 89101, USA

Goodrem, Delta — Singer, Pianist
Harbour Agency, 135 Forbes St, Woolloomooloo NSW 2011, Australia

Goodrich, Gail C, Jr — Basketball Player
PO Box 4969, Greenwich CT 06831, USA

Goodridge, Robin J — Drummer (Bush)
Front Line Mgmt, 1100 Glendon Ave, #2000, Los Angeles CA 90024 USA

Goodrum, Charles L (Charlie) — Football Player
117 Pico Road, East Palatka FL 32131, USA

Goodson, J Edward (Ed) — Baseball Player
PO Box 1655, Palatka FL 32178, USA

Goodson, James A — WW II Army Air Corps Hero
37 Carolina Trail, Marshfield MA 02050, USA

Goodwin, Carly — Singer
3624 Westbrook Ave, Nashville TN 37205, USA

Goodwin, Curtis L — Baseball Player
14939 Western Ave, San Leandro CA 94578, USA

Goodwin, Danny K — Baseball Player
1555 Linksview Close, Stone Mountain GA 30088, USA

Goodwin, Doris Kearns — Historian, Commentator
1649 Monument Lane, Concord MA 01742, USA

Goodwin, Frederick Tutu — Queen's Representative, Cook Islands
Queen's Representative's Office, Avarua, Rarotonga, Cook Islands

Goodwin, Ginnifer — Actress
John Carrabino Mgmt, 5900 Wilshire Blvd, #406, Los Angeles CA 90036 USA

Goodwin, Gordon — Jazz Orchestra Leader
Peter Levinson Communications, 23854 Malibu Crest Dr, Malibu CA 90265, USA

Goodwin, Malcolm J — Actor
I F A Talent Agency, 8730 W Sunset Blvd, #490, West Hollywood CA 90069 USA

Goodwin, Michael — Actor
Dulcina Eisen Assoc, 154 E 61st St, New York NY 10065, USA

Goodwin, Michael — Labor Leader
Office & Professional Employees, 1660 L St NW, #801, Washington DC 20036, USA

Goodwin, R Hunter — Football Player
1011 Lyceum Court, College Station TX 77840, USA

Goodwin, Raven — Actress
C E S D, 10635 Santa Monica Blvd, #130, Los Angeles CA 90025 USA

Goodwin, Ronald R (Ronnie) — Football Player
3702 Sul Ross St, San Angelo TX 76904, USA

Goodwin, Thomas J (Tom) — Baseball Player
8 Maple St, Massapequa NY 11758, USA

Goodwin, Trudie — Actress
Bosun House, 1 Deer Park Road, Merton, London SW19 3TL, England

Goodwyn, Myles — Singer, Guitarist (April Wine)
S L Feldman Mgmt, 1505 W 2nd Ave, #200, Vancouver BC V6H 3Y4, Canada

Goody, Joan E — Architect
Goody Clancy Assoc, 334 Boylston St, Boston MA 02116, USA

Goodyear, Scott — Auto Racing Driver
Scott Goodyear Racing, PO Box 589, Carmel IN 46082, USA

Goodyear, Stewart — Concert Pianist
Columbia Artists Mgmt Inc, 1790 Broadway, #702, New York NY 10019 USA

Goolagong Cawley, Yvonne F — Tennis Player
PO Box 1347, Noosa Heads QLD 4567, Australia

Goolrick, Robert — Writer
Algonquin Books, PO Box 27515, Chapel Hill NC 27515 USA

Goolsby, Austan D — Government Official, Economist
White House, 1600 Pennsylvania Ave NW, Washington DC 20500 USA

Goorjian, Michael — Actor
Lyceum Entertainment, 4221 Hollis St, Emeryville CA 94608, USA

Goose, Claire — Actress
C A M, 55-59 Shaftesbury Ave, London W1D 6LD, England

Goosen, Don — Boxing Promoter, Manager
1315 N Riverview Ave, Reedley CA 93654, USA

Goosen, Retief — Golfer
9228 Sloane St, Orlando FL 32827, USA

Goossen, Jeanne — Actress
Characters Talent Agency, 8 Elm St, Toronto, ON M5G 1G7, Canada

Gopnik, Adam — Writer
New Yorker, Editorial Dept, 4 Times Square, Basement C1B, New York NY 10036 USA

Gora, Jo Ann M — Educator
Ball State University, President's Office, A D Building, Muncie IN 47306, USA

Goranson, Alicia — Actress
Paradigm Agency, 360 Park Ave S, #1600, New York NY 10010 USA

Gorbachev, Mikhail S — Nobel Peace Laureate; Gen Sec, USSR
Leningradsky Prospekt 39, 125167 Moscow, Russia

Gorbachev, Yuri — Artist
Adrienne Editions, 377 Geary St, San Francisco CA 94102, USA

Gorbatko, Viktor V — Cosmonaut; Air Force General
Cosmonaut Training Center, Star City, 141160 Zvezdny Gorodok, Moscow Oblast, Russia

Gorchakova, Galina — Opera Singer
Kirov Opera, Mariinsky Theater, Teatralnaya Pl 1, 190000 Saint Petersburg, Russia

Gordeeva, Ekaterina	Figure Skater, Model
1714 Ivar St, Los Angeles CA 90028, USA	
Gordeyev, Vyacheslav M	Ballet Dancer, Choreographer
Tverskaya Str 9, #78, 103009 Moscow, Russia	
Gordimer, Nadine	Nobel Literature Laureate
7 Frere Road, Parktown, Johannesburg 2193, South Africa	
Gordley, James R	Attorney, Educator
University of California, Law School, Boalt Hall, Berkeley CA 94720, USA	
Gordon, Barry	Actor, Singer
1912 Kaweah Dr, Pasadena CA 91105, USA	
Gordon, Benjamin (Ben)	Basketball Player
5174 Barrington Dr, Rochester MI 48306, USA	
Gordon, Bert I	Director
9640 Arby Dr, Beverly Hills CA 90210, USA	
Gordon, Bridgette	Basketball Player
Pattonville High School, 2497 Creve Coeur Mill Road, Maryland Heights MO 63043, USA	
Gordon, Bryan	Director, Producer, Writer
Creative Artists Agency, 2000 Ave of Stars, #100, Los Angeles CA 90067 USA	
Gordon, Christopher	Composer
I C M Partners, 10250 Constellation Blvd, #900, Los Angeles CA 90067 USA	
Gordon, Cornell K	Football Player
4029 Spring Meadow Crescent, Chesapeake VA 23321, USA	
Gordon, Dan	Director, Producer, Writer
I C M Partners, 10250 Constellation Blvd, #900, Los Angeles CA 90067 USA	
Gordon, Danso	Actor
Evolution Entertainment, 901 N Highland Ave, Los Angeles CA 90038 USA	
Gordon, Darrien X J	Football Player
1500 Pecos Dr, Southlake TX 76092, USA	
Gordon, David	Choreographer
47 Great Jones St, #2, New York NY 10012, USA	
Gordon, Dennie	Director, Producer, Actress
Creative Artists Agency, 2000 Ave of Stars, #100, Los Angeles CA 90067 USA	
Gordon, Don	Actor
10576 Rocca Way, Los Angeles CA 90077, USA	
Gordon, Donald T (Don)	Baseball Player
711 Sunset Mountain Dr, Chattanooga TN 37421, USA	
Gordon, Ed	Commentator
NBC-TV, News Dept, 30 Rockefeller Plaza, #270E, New York NY 10112 USA	
Gordon, Eric, Jr	Basketball Player
Los Angeles Clippers, Staples Center, 1111 S Figueroa St, Los Angeles CA 90015 USA	
Gordon, Eve	Actress
TalentWorks, 3500 W Olive Ave, #1400, Burbank CA 91505 USA	
Gordon, Hannah Taylor	Actress
Conway Van Gelder Grant, 8-12 Broadwick St, #300, London W1F 8HW, England	
Gordon, Harold P	Businessman
Hasbro Inc, 1027 Newport Ave, Pawtucket RI 02861, USA	
Gordon, Howard	Writer, Producer
W M E Entertainment, 9601 Wilshire Blvd, #300, Beverly Hills CA 90210 USA	
Gordon, Josh	Director, Producer, Writer
Creative Artists Agency, 2000 Ave of Stars, #100, Los Angeles CA 90067 USA	
Gordon, Keith	Director
Arlook Group, 205 S Beverly Dr, #209, Beverly Hills CA 90212, USA	
Gordon, Keith B	Baseball Player
4601 Thornhurst St, Olney MD 20832, USA	
Gordon, Kim	Singer, Bassist (Sonic Youth)
Silva Artist Mgmt, 722 Seward St, Los Angeles CA 90038, USA	
Gordon, Kiowa	Actor
A P A Talent/Literary Agency, 405 S Beverly Dr, #300, Beverly Hills CA 90212 USA	
Gordon, Lamar D	Football Player
5428 N 19th St, Milwaukee WI 53209, USA	
Gordon, Lancaster	Basketball Player
550 Robinhood Road, Jackson MS 39206, USA	
Gordon, Lawrence	Businessman
Largo Entertainment, 20th Century Fox, 10201 W Pico Blvd, Los Angeles CA 90064, USA	
Gordon, Mark	Producer
Mark Gordon Productions, 12200 W Olympic Blvd, #250, Los Angeles CA 90064, USA	
Gordon, Mary C	Writer
Viking Penguin Press, 375 Hudson St, New York NY 10014, USA	
Gordon, Matt	Actor
Edna Talent Mgmt, 318 Dundas St W, Toronto, ON M5T 1G5, Canada	
Gordon, Michael W (Mike)	Baseball Player
17 Highland Court, Needham MA 02492, USA	
Gordon, Mike	Bassist (Phish)
Dionysian Productions, 431 Pine St, Burlington VT 05401, USA	
Gordon, Milton A	Educator
California State University, President's Office, Fullerton CA 99264, USA	
Gordon, Nina	Singer, Guitarist, Songwriter
Q Prime, 729 7th Ave, #1600, New York NY 10019 USA	
Gordon, Pamela F	Prime Minister, Bermuda
United Bermuda Party, Chancery Lane, Box HM715, Hamilton HM CX, Bermuda	
Gordon, Phil	Actor
Alexandria Alvarez, 3145 Geary Blvd, #744, San Francisco CA 94118, USA	
Gordon, Richard	Writer, Anaesthetist
1 Craven Hill, London W2 3EN, England	
Gordon, Richard F (Dick)	Football Player
7119 Sandy Springs Road, Maumee OH 43537, USA	
Gordon, Richard F, Jr	Astronaut
65 Woodside Dr, Prescott AZ 86305, USA	
Gordon, Robert W (Robby)	Auto Racing Driver
19525 Mary Ardrey Circle, Cornelius NC 28031, USA	
Gordon, Seth	Director
W M E Entertainment, 9601 Wilshire Blvd, #300, Beverly Hills CA 90210 USA	
Gordon, Stuart	Director
Red Hen Productions, 3607 W Magnolia, #L, Burbank CA 91505, USA	
Gordon, Thomas (Tom)	Baseball Player
2006 Lake Lotela Dr, Avon Park FL 33825, USA	

G

Gage - Gordon

Gordon, Zachary — Actor
Industry Entertainment, 955 Carillo Dr, #300, Los Angeles CA 90048 USA
Gordon-Levitt, Joseph — Actor
W M E Entertainment, 9601 Wilshire Blvd, #300, Beverly Hills CA 90210 USA
Gordon-Reed, Annette — Writer, Educator
New York University, Law School, 57 Worth St, New York NY 10013, USA
Gordy, Berry, Jr — Businessman, Composer
878 Stradella Road, Los Angeles CA 90077, USA
Gordy, Walter — Physicist
2521 Perkins Road, Durham NC 27705, USA
Gore, Albert A, Jr — Nobel Peace Laureate, Vice President
312 Lynnwood Blvd, Nashville TN 37205, USA
Gore, Frank — Football Player
6641 SW 159th Place, Miami FL 33193, USA
Gore, Lesley — Singer, Songwriter, Actress
228 W 71st St, #1E, New York NY 10023, USA
Gore, Michael — Composer
Soundtrack Music Assoc, 1460 4th St, #308, Santa Monica CA 90401 USA
Gore, Robert W — Inventor (Gore-Tex)
W L Gore Assoc, 555 Paper Mill Road, Newark DE 19711, USA
Gorenstein, Mark B — Conductor
Rublevskoye Shosse 28, #25, 121609 Moscow, Russia
Gorfinkel, Jordan (Gorf) — Cartoonist
2427 White Road, Cleveland OH 44118, USA
Gorgal, Kenneth R (Ken) — Football Player
4 The Court of Harborside, Northbrook IL 60062, USA
Gorgl, Elisabeth — Alpine Skier
Helmut Zangerl, Innrain 15/4/32, 6020 Innsbruck, Austria
Gorham, Christopher — Actor
Creative Artists Agency, 2000 Ave of Stars, #100, Los Angeles CA 90067 USA
Gorham, Mel — Actress
Gage Group, 315 W 57th St, #4H, New York NY 10019 USA
Gorie, Dominic L — Astronaut
13656 Hidden Valley Lane, Salida CO 81201, USA
Gorilla Zoe — Rap Artist
Bad Boy Entertainment, 1440 Broadway, #16, New York NY 10018 USA
Gorin, Brandon M — Football Player
11031 Mirador Lane, Fishers IN 46037, USA
Goring, Robert T (Butch) — Ice Hockey Player, Coach
245 W 5th Ave, #108, Anchorage AK 99501, USA
Gorinski, Robert J (Bob) — Baseball Player
PO Box 133, Calumet PA 15621, USA
Goris, Eva — Actress
I C M Partners, 10250 Constellation Blvd, #900, Los Angeles CA 90067 USA
Gorka, John — Singer, Songwriter
Fleming/Tamulevich, 733 N Main St, #735, Ann Arbor MI 48104, USA
Gorlin, Alexander — Architect
Alexander Gorlin Architect, 137 Varick St, #500, New York NY 10013, USA
Gorman, Bryan — Golfer
Auld Course, 525 Hunte Parkway, Chula Vista CA 91914, USA
Gorman, E J — Writer
PO Box 669, Cedar Rapids IA 52406, USA
Gorman, John G — Pathologist
Mediware Information Systems, 11711 W 79th St, Lenexa KS 66214, USA
Gorman, Joseph T — Businessman
T R W Inc, 1900 Richmond Road, Cleveland OH 44124, USA
Gorman, Leigh — Bassist (Bow Wow Wow)
M O B Agency, 6404 Wilshire Blvd, #505, Los Angeles CA 90048 USA
Gorman, Patrick — Actor
Circle Talent Assoc, 520 Broadway, #350, Santa Monica CA 90401, USA
Gorman, Paul F, Jr — Army General
9175 Batesville Road, Afton VA 22920, USA
Gorman, Steve — Drummer (Black Crowes)
Angeles Entertainment, 16000 Ventura Blvd, #600, Encino CA 91436, USA
Gorman, Thomas P (Tom) — Baseball Player
1615 SW 5th Ave, Portland OR 97201, USA
Gorman, Tom — Tennis Player
ProServe, 1101 Woodrow Wilson Blvd, #1800, Arlington VA 22209 USA
Gorme, Eydie — Singer
944 Pinehurst Dr, Las Vegas NV 89109, USA
Gormley, Antony — Sculptor
13 South Villas, London NW1 9BS, England
Gorneault, Nick — Baseball Player
94 Seymour Ave, Springfield MA 01109, USA
Gorney, Karen Lynn — Actress, Model
Karen Company, PO Box 231060, New York NY 10023, USA
Gorouuch, Edward Lee — Educator
University of Alaska, President's Office, Anchorage AK 99508, USA
Gorrell, Bob — Editorial Cartoonist
Creators Syndicate, 737 3rd St, Hermosa Beach CA 90254 USA
Gorrell, Fred — Balloonist
501 E Port au Prince Lane, Phoenix AZ 85022, USA
Gorris, Marleen — Director
Gersh Agency, 9465 Wilshire Blvd, #600, Beverly Hills CA 90212 USA
Gorshkov, Aleksandr G — Ice Dancer
Skating Federation, Luchnesksaia Nab 8, 119871 Moscow, Russia
Gorsky, Alex — Businessman
Johnson & Johnson, 1 Johnson & Johnson Plaza, New Bruswick NJ 08993, USA
Gortat, Marcin — Basketball Player
Phoenix Suns, 201 E Jefferson St, Phoenix AZ 85004 USA
Goryl, John A — Baseball Player, Manager
528 Dry Run Road, Monongahela PA 15063, USA
Gorzelanny, Thomas A (Tom) — Baseball Player
208 Shadow Creek, Cranberry Township PA 16066, USA
Gosger, James C (Jim) — Baseball Player
1823 7th St, Port Huron MI 48060, USA

Gosling, James — Computer Software Designer (Java)
Sun Microsystems, 2550 Garcia Ave, Mountain View CA 94043, USA
Gosling, Ryan T — Actor
I F A Talent Agency, 8730 W Sunset Blvd, #490, West Hollywood CA 90069 USA
Gosnell, Raja — Director
Creative Artists Agency, 2000 Ave of Stars, #100, Los Angeles CA 90067 USA
Goss, Fred — Actor, Director
A P A Talent/Literary Agency, 405 S Beverly Dr, #300, Beverly Hills CA 90212 USA
Goss, Luke — Actor
Luber Rocklin Entertainment, 8530 Wilshire Blvd, #555, Beverly Hills CA 90211 USA
Gossage, John — Photographer
Light Work, 316 Waverly Ave, Syracuse NY 13210, USA
Gossage, Richard M (Goose) — Baseball Player
35 Marland Dr, Colorado Springs CO 80906, USA
Gossard, Stone — Guitarist (Green River, Pearl Jam)
Curtis Mgmt, 1900 S Corgiat Dr, Seattle WA 98108, USA
Gosselaar, Mark-Paul — Actor
Paradigm Agency, 360 N Crescent Dr, North Building, Beverly Hills CA 90210 USA
Gosselin, Jonathan K (Jon) — Actor
The Alexander, 201 W 72nd St, New York NY 10023, USA
Gosselin, Katie I (Kate) — Actress
The Alexander, 201 W 72nd St, New York NY 10023, USA
Gosselin, Mario — Ice Hockey Player
Energie Ecole, 70 Rue Favvettes, Saint Basile Grand QC J3N 1P4, Canada
Gossett, D Bruce — Football Player
6109 Puerto Dr, Rancho Murieta CA 95683, USA
Gossett, David — Golfer
4501 Spanish Oaks Club Blvd, #9, Austin TX 78738, USA
Gossett, Jeffery A (Jeff) — Football Player
6 Lake Forest Court, Roanoke TX 76262, USA
Gossett, Louis, Jr — Actor
Logo Entertainment, PO Box 6187, Malibu CA 90265, USA
Gossett, Robert — Actor
Stone Manners Salners, 9911 W Pico Blvd, #1400, Los Angeles CA 90035 USA
Gossick Crockatt, Sue — Diver
11738 Villageview Court, Moorpark CA 93021, USA
Gostowski, Stephen C (Steve) — Football Player
18 Rhodes Dr, Wrentham MA 02093, USA
Gotschlich, Emil C — Internist
1435 Lexington Ave, New York NY 10128, USA
Gotshalk, Leonard W (Len) — Football Player
1200 Butler Creek Road, Ashland OR 97520, USA
Gott, James W (Jim) — Baseball Player
860 La Vina Lane, Altadena CA 91001, USA
Gott, Karel — Singer
Goja Spol, Pod Prusekem 3, 102 00 Prague 10, Czech Republic
Gottfried, Brian — Tennis Player
10671 NW 51st St, Coral Springs FL 33076, USA
Gottfried, Gilbert — Actor, Comedian
W M E Entertainment, 1325 Ave of Americas, New York NY 10019 USA
Gotti, Yo — Rap Artist
J Records, 745 5th Ave, #600, New York NY 10151 USA
Gottlieb, Lisa — Director
Stone Manners Salners, 9911 W Pico Blvd, #1400, Los Angeles CA 90035 USA
Gottschalk, Thomas — Actor
Agenehme Unterhaultungs, Von-Simolin-Str 1, 82402 Seeshaupt, Germany
Gottwald, Felix — Nordic Combined Skier
Rosengasse 12, 5700 Zell am See, Austria
Gotye — Singer, Musician, Songwriter
Agency Group Ltd, 361-373 City Road, London EC1V 2QA, England
Gotz, George — Actor
Terrassenstr 32, 14129 Berlin, Germany
Gough, Alfred, III — Producer, Writer
Millar Gough Ink, 500 S Buena Vista St, Animations 1E17, Burbank CA 91521, USA
Gough, Darren — Cricketer
Octagon, 81-83 Fulham High St, London SW6 3JW, England
Goulart, Izabel — Model
One Model Mgmt, 424 W Broadway, New York NY 10012, USA
Goulart, Ron — Writer, Cartoonist (Star Hawks)
232 Georgetown Road, Weston CT 06883, USA
Gould, Alexander — Actor
Coast to Coast Talent, 3350 Barham Blvd, Los Angeles CA 90068 USA
Gould, Dana — Actor, Writer, Producer
United Talent Agency, 9336 Civic Center Dr, Beverly Hills CA 90210 USA
Gould, Elliott — Actor
A P A Talent/Literary Agency, 405 S Beverly Dr, #300, Beverly Hills CA 90212 USA
Gould, Jason E — Actor, Director, Writer
837 N West Knoll Dr, #214, West Hollywood CA 90069, USA
Gould, Nolan — Actor
Stone Manners Salners, 9911 W Pico Blvd, #1400, Los Angeles CA 90035 USA
Gould, Peter — Writer
Larchmont Literary Agency, 444 N Larchmont Blvd, #200, Los Angeles CA 90004, USA
Gould, Robert P (Robbie) — Football Player
544 Cliffwood Lane, Gurnee IL 60031, USA
Gould, Ronald M — Judge
US Court of Appeals, US Courthouse, 1010 5th Ave, Seattle WA 98104, USA
Gould, Tony — Writer
Rogers Coleridge White, 20 Powis Court, London W11 1JN, England
Goulding, Ellie — Singer, Songwriter
Polydor Records, 364-366 Kensington High St, London W14 8NS, England
Goulet, Michel — Ice Hockey Player
PO Box 656, Sedalia CO 80135, USA
Goulet-Nadon, Amelie — Speed Skater
Speed Skating Canada, 2781 Lancaster Road, #402, Ottawa ON K1B 1A7, Canada
Goulian, Mehran K — Physician, Biochemist
8433 Prestwick Dr, La Jolla CA 92037, USA

Goulston - Gracey

Goulston, Mark — Psychiatrist, Commentator
1150 Yale St, #3, Santa Monica CA 90403, USA
Gourley, Roark — Artist
Roark Gourley Art Gallery, 33151 Paso Dr, South Laguna Beach CA 92677, USA
Gourmet, Olivier — Actor
Artmedia, 20 Ave Rapp, 75007 Paris, France
Gouveia, Kurt K — Football Player
138 Seagrove Lane, Mooresville NC 28117, USA
Govan, Gerald — Basketball Player
30 Newport Parkway, #2112, Jersey City NJ 07310, USA
Gove, Jeff — Golfer
21323 31st Ave SE, Bothell WA 98021, USA
Govich, Danira — Actress
Arcadia Assoc, 188 Vicarage Gate, London W8 4AA, England
Govich, Milena — Actress
Gersh Agency, 9465 Wilshire Blvd, #600, Beverly Hills CA 90212 USA
Govinda — Actor
105 Jal Darshan, A Wing Ruia Park, Juhu, Mumbai MS 400049, India
Gowan, Caroline — Golfer
209 Crescent Ave, Greenville SC 29605, USA
Gowan, James — Architect
2 Linden Gardens, London W2 4ES, England
Gowariker, Ashutosh — Director
I C M Partners, 10250 Constellation Blvd, #900, Los Angeles CA 90067 USA
Gowda, H D Deve — Prime Minister, India
5 Safdarjung Lane, New Delhi 110011, India
Gower, David I — Cricketer
David Gower Promotions, 6 George St, Nottingham NG1 3BE, England
Gowers, W Timothy — Mathematician
Math Services Centre, Wilberforce Road, Cambridge CB3 0WB, England
Gowin, Toby — Football Player
1605 Oak Creek Circle, Tyler TX 75703, USA
Gowon, Yakub — President, Nigeria; Army General
National Oil & Chemical Marketing Co, 38-39 Marina, 2052 Lagos, Nigeria
Gowrie, Earl of — Government Official, England
Government Securities, Stag Place, London SW1E 5DS, England
Goycoechea, Sergio J — Soccer Player
Football Assn, Via Monte 1366-76, Buenos Aires 1053, Argentina
Goydos, Paul — Golfer
1864 Stearnlee Ave, Long Beach CA 90815, USA
Goyer, David S — Director, Writer
Holmes Defender of the Faith, PO Box 6873, Malibu CA 90265, USA
Goyette, Danielle — Ice Hockey Player
Team Canada, 2424 University Dr NW, Calgary AB T2N 3Y9, Canada
Goyette, Philippe J G (Phil) — Ice Hockey Player
815 38 E Ave, Lachine QC H8T 2C4, Canada
Gozlan, Yann — Writer, Director
Gersh Agency, 9465 Wilshire Blvd, #600, Beverly Hills CA 90212 USA
Gozney, Richard H T — Governor General, Bermuda
Governor General's Office, 11 Langton Hill, Pembroke HM 13, Bermuda
Gozzo, Mauro P — Baseball Player
156 Newton St, Berlin CT 06037, USA
Grabarkewitz, Billy C — Baseball Player
2162 Estes Park Road, Southlake TX 76092, USA
Grabe, Ronald J — Astronaut
3380 S Price Road, Chandler AZ 85248, USA
Grabeel, Lucas — Actor, Singer
Paradigm Agency, 360 N Crescent Dr, North Building, Beverly Hills CA 90210 USA
Graber, Rodney B (Rod) — Baseball Player
4674 Mount Armet Dr, San Diego CA 92117, USA
Graber, Susan P — Judge
US Court of Appeals, Pioneer Courthouse, 555 SW Yamhill St, Portland OR 97204, USA
Grabois, Neil R — Educator
Colgate University, President's Office, Hamilton NY 13346, USA
Grabow, John W — Baseball Player
6810 S Amethyst Dr, Chandler AZ 85249, USA
Grabowski, James S (Jim) — Football Player
1523 Withorn Lane, Inverness IL 60067, USA
Grace, Alana — Actress, Singer, Songwriter
Kaleidoscope Media, 1226 17th Ave S, Nashville TN 37212
Grace, April — Actress
Innovative Artists, 1505 10th St, Santa Monica CA 90401 USA
Grace, Bud — Cartoonist (Ernie, Piranha Club)
King Features Syndicate, 300 W 57th St, #1500, New York NY 10019 USA
Grace, Dick — Businessman, Social Activist
Grace Vineyards, 1210 Rockland Dr, Saint Helena CA 94574, USA
Grace, Emily — Actress
Bad Girl Productions, 14 Parkside Court, Brooklyn NY 11225, USA
Grace, Helen — Actress
Gavin Barker Assoc, 2D Wimpole St, London W1G 0EB, England
Grace, Jillian — Model, Actress
Playboy Promotions, 2706 Media Center Dr, Los Angeles CA 90065 USA
Grace, Maggie — Actress
United Talent Agency, 9336 Civic Center Dr, Beverly Hills CA 90210 USA
Grace, Mark E — Baseball Player
5624 E Via Buena Vista, Paradise Valley AZ 85253, USA
Grace, Michael J (Mike) — Baseball Player
1156 Buell Ave, Joliet IL 60435, USA
Grace, Nancy — Commentator
Breaking News Public Relations, 9601 Wilshire Blvd, #1106, Beverly Hills CA 90210, USA
Grace, Topher — Actor
I C M Partners, 10250 Constellation Blvd, #900, Los Angeles CA 90067 USA
Gracen, Elizabeth — Actress, Beauty Queen
James Levy Mgmt, 3500 W Olive Ave, #920, Burbank CA 91505, USA
Gracey, James S — Coast Guard Admiral, Businessman
1 Westin Center, 2445 M St NW, #260, Washington DC 20037, USA

Grach, Eduard D
1st Smolensky Per 9, #98, 121099 Moscow, Russia — Concert Violinist

Gracheva, Nadezhda A
1st Truzhennikov Per 17, #49, 119121 Moscow, Russia — Ballerina

Gracias, Oswald Cardinal
Archbishop's House, 1 Nathalal Parekh Marg, Mumbai 40001, India — Religious Leader

Gracie, Charlie
Joe Taylor Artist Agency, PO Box 279, Williamstown NJ 37068 USA — Singer, Guitarist

Gracin, Joshua M
W M E Entertainment, 1600 Division St, #300, Nashville TN 37203 USA — Singer

Grad, Harold
248 Overlook Road, New Rochelle NY 10804, USA — Mathematician

Graddy, Sam
4792 Brasac Dr, Stone Mountain GA 30083, USA — Football Player, Track Athlete

Gradishar, Randy C
7628 Pineridge Terrace, Castle Rock CO 80108, USA — Football Player

Grady, Michael
I C M Partners, 10250 Constellation Blvd, #900, Los Angeles CA 90067 USA — Actor

Grady, Michael P
1708 Walnut Ave, Manhattan Beach CA 90266, USA — Cinematographer

Grady, Wayne
PO Box 78, Coolum Beach QLD 4573, Australia — Golfer

Graebner, Clark
411 Harbor Road, Fairfield CT 06431, USA — Tennis Player

Graebner, Norman A
University of Virginia, History Dept, Charlottesville VA 22903, USA — Historian

Graef, Jed
PO Box 880, Shelburne VT 05482, USA — Swimmer

Graells, Francisco (Pancho)
Le Monde, Editorial Dept, 21 Bis Rue Claude Bernard, 75005 Paris, France — Editorial Cartoonist

Graf, David F (Dave)
1825 Bel Air Ave, Pompano Beach FL 33062, USA — Football Player

Graf, Hans
Konzertdirektion Schmid, Konigstra 36, 30175 Hannover, Germany — Conductor

Graf, Jim
Jet Propulsion Laboratory, 4800 Oak Grove Dr, Pasadena CA 91109 USA — Space Scientist

Graf, Richard G (Rick)
6609 Biscayne Blvd, Minneapolis MN 55436, USA — Football Player

Graf, Stefanie M (Steffi)
9804 Camden Hills Ave, Las Vegas NV 89145, USA — Tennis Player

Graff, Ilene
Sovereign Talent Group, 8421 Wilshire Blvd, #200, Beverly Hills CA 90211, USA — Actress

Graff, Randy
Peter Strawn Assoc, 1501 Broadway, #2900, New York NY 10036, USA — Actress

Graff, Todd
United Talent Agency, 9336 Civic Center Dr, Beverly Hills CA 90210 USA — Director, Writer, Actor

Graffanino, Anthony J (Tony)
16 Amberfield Lane, Hockessin DE 19707, USA — Baseball Player

Graffin, Gregory W (Greg)
Goldstar Public Relations, PO Box 130, Ross on Wye HR9 6WY, England — Singer (Bad Religion), Songwriter

Graffin, Guillaume
American Ballet Theatre, 890 Broadway, #300, New York NY 10003, USA — Ballet Dancer

Graffman, Gary
Curtis Institute of Music, 1726 Locust St, Philadelphia PA 19103, USA — Concert Pianist

Grafstein, Bernice
Weill Medical College, Physiology Dept, 1300 York Ave, New York NY 10065, USA — Neurologist, Physiologist

Grafton, Anthony T
Princeton University, History Dept, Dickinson Hall, Princeton NJ 08544, USA — Historian

Grafton, Sue
PO Box 41446, Santa Barbara CA 93140, USA — Writer

Gragg, Scott
583 Cash Nichols Road, Stevensville MT 59870, USA — Football Player

Graham, Alex
Tribune Media Services, 435 N Michigan Ave, #1500, Chicago IL 60611 USA — Cartoonist (Fred Basset)

Graham, Arthur W (Art), III
PO Box 785, South Orleans MA 02662, USA — Football Player

Graham, Charles P
134 Warbler Way, Georgetown TX 78633, USA — Army General

Graham, Currie
Paradigm Agency, 360 N Crescent Dr, North Building, Beverly Hills CA 90210 USA — Actor

Graham, Daniel J (Dan)
225 N Standage, #33, Mesa AZ 85201, USA — Baseball Player

Graham, David
99 Mountainside Dr, Whitefish MT 59937, USA — Golfer

Graham, Detrice A (Derrick)
203 Pine Hill Road, West End NC 27376, USA — Football Player

Graham, Dirk M
17001 S Blackfoot Dr, Lockport IL 60441, USA — Ice Hockey Player

Graham, Donald E
Washington Post Co, 1150 15th St NW, Washington DC 20071, USA — Publisher

Graham, Franklin
Samaritan's Purse, PO Box 3000, Boone NC 28607, USA — Religious Leader

Graham, Gary
Amsel Eisenstadt Frazier, 5055 Wilshire Blvd, #865, Los Angeles CA 90036 USA — Actor

Graham, Gerrit
S M S Talent, 8383 Wilshire Blvd, #230, Beverly Hills CA 90211 USA — Actor

Graham, Glen
Shapiro Co, 9229 W Sunset Blvd, #607, West Hollywood CA 90069 USA — Drummer (Blind Melon)

Graham, Heather
Gersh Agency, 9465 Wilshire Blvd, #600, Beverly Hills CA 90212 USA — Actress

Graham, Jack
Prestonwood Baptist Church, 6801 W Park Blvd, Plano TX 75093, USA — Religious Leader

Graham, Jeffrey T (Jeff)
1849 Infirmary Road, Dayton OH 45417, USA — Football Player

Graham, Joey J
Cleveland Cavaliers, Gund Arena, 1 Center Court, Cleveland OH 44115 USA — Basketball Player

Name / Address	Occupation
Graham, Jorie 12 Quincy St, Cambridge MA 02138, USA	Writer
Graham, Julie Troika, 74 Clerkenwell Road, #300, London EC1M 5QA, England	Actress
Graham, Kate Gavin Barker Assoc, 2D Wimpole St, London W1G 0EB, England	Actress
Graham, Katerina Simmon & Scott, 7942 Mulholland Dr, Los Angeles CA 90046, USA	Actress
Graham, Kenneth J (Kenny) PO Box 7402, Santa Monica CA 90406, USA	Football Player
Graham, Kent D 1001 N Washington St, Wheaton IL 60187, USA	Football Player
Graham, Larry Groove Entertainment, 1005 N Alfred St, #2, West Hollywood CA 90069, USA	Guitarist (Sly & Family Stone), Singer
Graham, Lauren John Carrabino Mgmt, 5900 Wilshire Blvd, #406, Los Angeles CA 90036 USA	Actress
Graham, Lee W 481 Richmond Road, Cleveland OH 44143, USA	Baseball Player
Graham, Linda 4147 E Seneca Ave, Des Moines IA 50317, USA	Bowler
Graham, Loren R 7 Francis Ave, Cambridge MA 02138, USA	Historian
Graham, Louis K (Lou) 85 Concord Park W, Nashville TN 37205, USA	Golfer
Graham, Marcus Shanahan Mgmt, 91 Campbell St, #300, Surry Hills NSW 2010, Australia	Actor
Graham, Mary Lou Professional Bowlers Assn, 719 2nd Ave, #701, Seattle WA 98104 USA	Bowler
Graham, Michael J Xavier University, President's Office, 3800 Victory Parkway, Cincinnati OH 45207, USA	Educator
Graham, Mikey J C Music, 84A Strand-on-the-Green, London W43 PU, England	Singer (Boyzone)
Graham, Nancy Perry A A R P Magazine, Editorial Dept, 601 E St NW, Washington DC 20049, USA	Editor
Graham, Norma V Columbia University, Psychology Dept, New York NY 10027, USA	Psychologist
Graham, Patricia A Harvard University, Graduate School of Education, Cambridge MA 02138, USA	Educator
Graham, Patrick Jack Rutberg Fine Arts, 357 N La Brea Ave, Los Angeles CA 90036, USA	Artist, Writer
Graham, Ronald L University of California, Computer & Information Science Dept, La Jolla CA 92093, USA	Mathematician
Graham, Stephen Independent Talent Group, Oxford House, 76 Oxford St, London W1D 1BS, England	Actor
Graham, Susan I M G Artists, Hogarth Business Park, Chiswick, London W4 2TH, England	Opera Singer
Graham, Susan L University of California, Computer Science Dept, Soda Hall, Berkeley CA 94720, USA	Computer Scientist
Graham, Thomas L (Tom) 4084 S Wisteria Way, Denver CO 80237, USA	Football Player
Graham, Wayne L 2017 Dryden Road, Houston TX 77030, USA	Baseball Player
Graham, William F (Billy) Billy Graham Evangelistic Assn, 1 Billy Graham Parkway, Charlotte NC 28201, USA	Evangelist
Graham, William R (Bill) 11013 Sierra Verde Trail, Austin TX 78759, USA	Football Player
Grahame, Ron 9000 E Jewell Circle, Denver CO 80231, USA	Ice Hockey Player
Grahe, Joseph M (Joe) 2317 N Wallen Dr, West Palm Beach FL 33410, USA	Baseball Player
Grahn, Nancy Lee Innovative Artists, 1505 10th St, Santa Monica CA 90401 USA	Actress
Grainger, Holliday Dimetos, Donmar Warehouse, 41 Earlham St, London WC2H 9LD, England	Actress
Grainger, Katherine Saint Andrews Boat Club, 48 The Pleasance, Edinburgh EH8 9TJ, Scotland	Rowing Athlete
Grainger, Sebastien A Biz 3 Publicity, 1321 N Milwaukee Ave, #452, Chicago IL 60622, USA	Singer, Drummer (Death from Above 1979)
Grais, Michael Metropolitan Talent Agency, 7020 La Presa Dr, Los Angeles CA 90068 USA	Writer
Gralish, Tom 203 E Cottage Ave, Haddonfield NJ 08033, USA	Photojournalist
Graman, Alex 450 E Sunset Dr, Huntingburg IN 47542, USA	Baseball Player
Gramatica, Martin 3912 Northampton Way, Tampa FL 33618, USA	Football Player
Gramly, B Thomas (Tommy) 16485 Red Wood Circle W, McKinney TX 75071, USA	Baseball Player
Gramm, Lou Hard to Handle Mgmt, 16501 Ventura Blvd, #602, Encino CA 91436, USA	Singer (Foreigner)
Gramm, W Philip (Phil) U B S Securities, 299 Park Ave, New York NY 10171, USA	Senator, TX
Gramm, Wendy L George Mason University, 3301 N Fairfax Dr, #450, Arlington VA 22201, USA	Government Official, Economist
Grammas, Alexander P (Alex) 4030 Vestview Dr, Vestavia AL 35242, USA	Baseball Player, Manager
Grammer, Kathy Artists Agency, 1180 S Beverly Dr, #301, Los Angeles CA 90035 USA	Actress
Grammer, Kelsey Grammnet Productions, 2461 Santa Monica Blvd, #521, Santa Monica CA 90404, USA	Actor
Grammer, Spencer United Talent Agency, 9336 Civic Center Dr, Beverly Hills CA 90210 USA	Actress
Granada, Julieta Ladies Pro Golf Assn, 100 International Golf Dr, Daytona Beach FL 32124 USA	Golfer
Granatelli, Anthony (Andy) 1469 Edgecliff Lane, Santa Barbara CA 93108, USA	Auto Racing Executive

V.I.P. Address Book

Granato, Anthony L (Tony)
1481 Hollow Tree Dr, Pittsburgh PA 15241, USA — Ice Hockey Player, Coach

Granby, John E, Jr
8905 Melwood Oak Dr, Arlington TN 38002, USA — Football Player

Grandage, Michael
Donmar Warehouse, 41 Earlham St, Seven Dials, London WC2H 9LX, England — Director

Grande, Ariana
Don Buchwald/Fortitude, 6500 Wilshire Blvd, #2200, Los Angeles CA 90048 USA — Actress

Granderson, Curtis
1450 S Emerald St, Chicago IL 60607, USA — Baseball Player

Grandholm, Jim
211 Spring Park Ave, Sawyer MI 49125, USA — Basketball Player

Grandin, Temple
2918 Silver Plume Dr, #C3, Fort Collins CO 80526, USA — Animal Scientist

Grandison, Ronnie
6151 Chappellfield Dr, West Chester OH 45069, USA — Basketball Player

Grandmaster Flash
Universal Attractions, 135 W 26th St, #1200, New York NY 10001 USA — Rap Artist

Grandmaster Roc Raida
Agency Group Ltd, 142 W 57th St, #600, New York NY 10019 USA — Rap Artist (X-Ecutioners)

Grandmont, Jean-Michel
55 Blvd de Charonne, Les Doukas 23, 75011 Paris, France — Economist

Grandpa Pike
PO Box 3008, Hillsborough NB E4H 4W5, Canada — Singer

GrandPre, Mary
Scholastic Press, 555 Broadway, New York NY 10012 USA — Illustrator

Grandy, Fred
9417 Spruce Tree Circle, Bethesda MD 20814, USA — Actor; Representative, IA

Granger, Danny
141 S Meridian St, #602, Indianapolis IN 46225, USA — Basketball Player

Granger, Hoyle J
10611 Cranbrook Road, Houston TX 77042, USA — Football Player

Granger, Jeffrey A (Jeff)
2905 Glasgow Dr, Arlington TX 76015, USA — Baseball Player

Granger, Stewart F
552 E 53rd St, Brooklyn NY 11203, USA — Basketball Player

Granger, Wayne A
133 Redtail Place, Winter Springs FL 32708, USA — Baseball Player

Granholm, Jennifer M
University of California, Public & Public Policy Dept, Berkeley CA 94720, USA — Governor, MI

Granier-Deferre, Celia
Artmedia, 20 Ave Rapp, 75007 Paris, France — Actress

Granik, Debra
Gersh Agency, 9465 Wilshire Blvd, #600, Beverly Hills CA 90212 USA — Director, Writer, Cinematographer

Grannis, Kina
Agency Group Ltd, 142 W 57th St, #600, New York NY 10019 USA — Singer, Songwriter

Grannis, Paul D
Fermi National Accelerator Laboratory, C D F Collaboration, PO Box 500, Batavia IL 60510, USA — Physicist

Grant Walsh, Margo
Gensler & Associates/Architects, 1 Rockefeller Plaza, #500, New York NY 10020, USA — Interior Designer

Grant, Alan
148 Cisco Road, Asheville NC 28805, USA — Football Player

Grant, Allie
Stein Entertainment Group, 8335 W Sunset Blvd, #302, West Hollywood CA 90069, USA — Actress

Grant, Amy
Branton Jarrell Cooke Corzine, 1014 Cross Bow Court, Hendersonvlle TN 37075, USA — Singer, Songwriter

Grant, B Rosemary
Princeton University, Ecology & Evolution Biology Dept, Princeton NJ 08544, USA — Evolutionary Biologist

Grant, Beth
Don Buchwald/Fortitude, 6500 Wilshire Blvd, #2200, Los Angeles CA 90048 USA — Actress

Grant, Boyd
Colorado State University, Athletic Dept, Fort Collins CO 80523, USA — Basketball Coach

Grant, Brea
B/W/R, 9100 Wilshire Blvd, #500W, Beverly Hills CA 90212 USA — Actress

Grant, Brian W, III
24152 SW Petes Mountain Road, West Linn OR 97068, USA — Basketball Player

Grant, Charles
Spotlight, 7 Leicester Place, London WC2H 7RJ, England — Actor

Grant, Daniel F (Danny)
1163 Route 101 Highway, Nasonworth NB E3C 2C3, Canada — Ice Hockey Player

Grant, Darryl
6931 Compton Lane, Centreville VA 20121, USA — Football Player

Grant, David Marshall
Creative Artists Agency, 2000 Ave of Stars, #100, Los Angeles CA 90067 USA — Actor, Writer

Grant, Deon D
4465 Cape Cod Dr, Evans GA 30809, USA — Football Player

Grant, Edmond (Eddy)
Paradigm Agency, 360 N Crescent Dr, North Building, Beverly Hills CA 90210 USA — Singer, Songwriter

Grant, Faye
S M S Talent, 8383 Wilshire Blvd, #230, Beverly Hills CA 90211 USA — Actress

Grant, Frank
2126 Glencourse Lane, Reston CA 20191, USA — Football Player

Grant, Gil
Principal Entertainment, 1964 Westwood Blvd, #400, Los Angeles CA 90025 USA — Producer, Writer

Grant, Gogi
10323 Alamo Ave, #202, Los Angeles CA 90064, USA — Singer

Grant, Harold P (Bud)
8134 Oakmere Road, Minneapolis MN 55438, USA — Football, Basketball Player, Coach

Grant, Harvey
15604 Marathon Circle, #401, Gaithersburg MD 20878, USA — Basketball Player

Grant, Horace J
195 Michael Lane, Arroyo Grande CA 93420, USA — Basketball Player

Grant, Hugh
42 West, 220 W 42nd St, #1200, New York NY 10036 USA — Actor

Grant, Hugh, Jr
35 E 84th St, #8B, New York NY 10028, USA — Harness Racing Executive

Grant, James T (Mudcat)
1020 S Dunsmuir Ave, Los Angeles CA 90019, USA — Baseball Player

Grant, Jennifer
Propaganda Films Mgmt, 1741 Ivar Ave, Los Angeles CA 90028 USA — Actress

Grant, John D
6365 S Harrison Court, Centennial CO 80121, USA — Football Player

Grant, Joshua D (Josh)
3191 S Davis Blvd, Bountiful UT 84010, USA — Basketball Player

Grant, Kate Jennings
Melanie Greene Mgmt, 425 N Robertson Blvd, West Hollywood CA 90048 USA — Actress

Grant, Lee
Fleury/Grant Entertainment, 610 W End Ave, #7B, New York NY 10024, USA — Actress, Director

Grant, Mark A
2837 Via Dieguenos, Alpine CA 91901, USA — Baseball Player

Grant, Mickie
250 W 94th St, #6G, New York NY 10025, USA — Actress

Grant, Natalie
Maximum Artist Mgmt, 1305 Clinton St, #200A, Nashville TN 37203, USA — Singer, Songwriter

Grant, Peter R
Princeton University, Ecology & Evolutionary Biology Dept, Princeton NJ 08544, USA — Evolutionary Biologist

Grant, Quiana
Traffic Models, Pasaje Sert, 2, 08010 Barcelona, Spain — Model

Grant, Richard E
Independent Talent Group, Oxford House, 76 Oxford St, London W1D 1BS, England — Actor, Director

Grant, Robert M
5807 S Dorchester Ave, #11E, Chicago IL 60637, USA — Educator

Grant, Rodney A
Omar, 526 N Larchmont Blvd, Los Angeles CA 90004, USA — Actor

Grant, Stephen M (Steve)
20134 SW 123rd Dr, Miami FL 33177, USA — Football Player

Grant, Susannah
Creative Artists Agency, 2000 Ave of Stars, #100, Los Angeles CA 90067 USA — Writer, Director

Grant, Thomas R (Tom)
36 Millville Road, Mendon MA 01756, USA — Baseball Player

Grant, Tom
Brad Simon Organization, 155 W 46th St, #500, New York NY 10036 USA — Jazz Musician

Grant, Toni
610 S Ardmore Ave, Los Angeles CA 90005, USA — Radio Psychologist

Grant, Travis
3314 Pointe Bleue Court, Decatur GA 30034, USA — Basketball Player

Grant, Wally
4853 Lone Oak Court, Ann Arbor MI 48108, USA — Ice Hockey Player

Grantham, George
Rick Alter Mgmt, 1018 17th Ave S, #12, Nashville TN 37212, USA — Singer, Drummer (Poco)

Grantham, J Larry
106 Harmony Road, Crystal Springs MS 39059, USA — Football Player

Grantham, Victoria
VGrantham, Via Morimondo 2/3, 20143 Milan, Italy — Fashion Designer

Granville, Joseph
Granville Market Letter, 2525 Market St, Kansas City MO 64108, USA — Financier, Writer

Grapenthin, Richard R (Dick)
5040 170th Ave, Linn Grove IA 51033, USA — Baseball Player

Grapey, Marc
TalentWorks, 3500 W Olive Ave, #1400, Burbank CA 91505 USA — Actor

Grasmanis, Paul R
1073 Watkins Creek Dr, Franklin TN 37067, USA — Football Player

Grasmick, Louis J (Lou)
6715 Quad Ave, Rosedale MD 21237, USA — Baseball Player

Grass, Gunter
Sekretariat, Glockengiesserstr 21, 23552 Lubeck, Germany — Nobel Literature Laureate

Grassle, Karen
Scott Stander Assoc, 4533 Van Nuys Blvd, #401, Sherman Oaks CA 91403 USA — Actress

Grata, Enrique
Univision, 605 3rd Ave, #1200, New York NY 10158, USA — Actor

Grate, Donald (Don)
1245 NW 203rd St, Miami FL 33169, USA — Baseball, Basketball Player

Grater, Mark A
1136 Indiana Ave, Monaca PA 15061, USA — Baseball Player

Grau, Shirley Ann
12 Nassau Dr, Metairie LA 70005, USA — Writer

Grauer, Ona
Performers Mgmt, 258 E 3rd St, #B, Vancouver BC V7W 1E7, Canada — Actress

Grausman, Phillip
21 Barnes Road, Washington CT 06793, USA — Sculptor

Gravel, Maurice R (Mike)
1600 N Oak St, #1412, Arlington VA 22209, USA — Senator, AK

Graveline, Duane E
PO Box 92, Underhill Center VT 05490, USA — Astronaut

Gravelle, Gordon C
2208 Cordoba Court, Antioch CA 94509, USA — Football Player

Graves, Adam
574 Lis Crescent, Windsor ON N9G 2M5, Canada — Ice Hockey Player

Graves, Alex
Creative Artists Agency, 2000 Ave of Stars, #100, Los Angeles CA 90067 USA — Director, Producer, Writer

Graves, Daniel P (Danny)
5041 Rishley Run Way, Mount Dora FL 32757, USA — Baseball Player

Graves, Denyce A
I M G Artists, 152 W 57th St, #500, New York NY 10019 USA — Opera Singer

Graves, Earl
123 Random Farms Dr, Chappaqua NY 10514, USA — Basketball Player

Graves, Earl G
Black-Enterprise Magazine, 130 5th Ave, #1000, New York NY 10011, USA — Publisher

Graves, Ernest, Jr
2328 S Nash St, Arlington VA 22202, USA — Army General

Graves, Harold N, Jr
PO Box 8390, Gaithersburg MD 20898, USA — Journalist, Government Official

Graves, Liza
The Kirby Organization, 9200 Sunset Blvd, #600, Los Angeles CA 90069, USA — Singer (Civet)

Graves, Michael
Michael Graves Assoc, 341 Nassau St, Princeton NJ 08540, USA — Architect

Graves, Ray
420 Bay Ave, #821, Clearwater FL 33756, USA — Football Coach

Graves, Richard G
12069 Sage Hollow Circle, Kamas UT 84036, USA — Army General

Graves, Rupert
A P A Talent/Literary Agency, 405 S Beverly Dr, #300, Beverly Hills CA 90212 USA — Actor

Graves, Thomas E (Tom)
1902 Montclair Ave, Norfolk VA 23523, USA — Football Player

Gravett, Michael G
University of Washington, Obstetrics Dept, PO Box 356460, Seattle WA 98195, USA — Obstetrician

Gravitte, Beau
Gage Group, 315 W 57th St, #4H, New York NY 10019 USA — Actor

Gray, Aaron M
Toronto Raptors, Air Canada Center, 20 Bay St, Toronto ON M5J 2N8, Canada — Basketball Player

Gray, Alasdair J
Rogers Coleridge White, 20 Powis Mews, London W11 1JN, England — Writer

Gray, Alfred M, Jr
6317 Chaucer View Circle, Alexandria VA 22304, USA — Marine Corps General

Gray, Billy
19612 Grandview Dr, Topanga Canyon CA 90290, USA — Actor

Gray, C Boyden
Wilmer Cutler Pickering, 1875 Pennsylvania Ave NW, Washington DC 20006, USA — Government Official

Gray, Carleton P
11981 Kenn Road, Cincinnati OH 45240, USA — Football Player

Gray, Chad (Kud)
Agency Group Ltd, 142 W 57th St, #600, New York NY 10019 USA — Singer (Mudvayne)

Gray, Cleve
102 Melius Road, Warren CT 06754, USA — Artist, Sculptor

Gray, Coleen
2841 Roscomare Road, Los Angeles CA 90077, USA — Actress

Gray, David
Helter Skelter, 347-353 Chiswick High Road, London W4 4HS, England — Singer, Songwriter

Gray, David A (Dave)
PO Box 13861, Ogden UT 84412, USA — Baseball Player

Gray, Del
Splash Public Relations, 1520 16th Ave S, #2, Nashville TN 37212, USA — Drummer (Little Texas)

Gray, Doug
Ron Rainey Mgmt, 315 S Beverly Dr, #407, Beverly Hills CA 90212, USA — Singer (Marshall Tucker Band)

Gray, D'Wayne
3423 Barger Dr, Falls Church VA 22044, USA — Marine Corps General

Gray, Earnest
6746 Kirby Oaks Lane, Memphis TN 38119, USA — Football Player

Gray, Edward (Ed)
Houston Rockets, 1730 Jefferson St, Houston TX 77003 USA — Basketball Player

Gray, Erin
10921 Alta View Dr, Studio City CA 91604, USA — Actress, Model

Gray, F Gary
United Talent Agency, 9336 Civic Center Dr, Beverly Hills CA 90210 USA — Director

Gray, Fred, Sr
1005 Lakeshore Dr, Tuskegee AL 36083, USA — Attorney

Gray, Gary G
PO Box 98, La Place LA 70069, USA — Baseball Player

Gray, George W
Juniper House, Furzehill, Wimborne, Dorset BH21 4HD, England — Organic Chemist

Gray, Harry B
1415 E California Blvd, Pasadena CA 91106, USA — Chemist

Gray, James
Creative Artists Agency, 2000 Ave of Stars, #100, Los Angeles CA 90067 USA — Director, Writer

Gray, Jeffrey E (Jeff)
3229 Stonebridge Trail, Valrico FL 33596, USA — Baseball Player

Gray, Jerry
27 Birdsong Parkway, Orchard Park NY 14127, USA — Football Player

Gray, John
Relationship Speakers Network, PO Box 12695, Scottsdale AZ 85267, USA — Director, Writer

Gray, John E
4115 Bloomdale Dr, #16, Charlotte NC 28211, USA — WW II, Korean & Vietnam Army Hero

Gray, John L (Johnny)
10645 Greenbriar Court, Boca Raton FL 33498, USA — Baseball Player

Gray, Johnnie L
220 Short St, Wrightstown WI 54180, USA — Football Player

Gray, Kenneth D (Ken)
356 Campa Pajama Lane, Kingsland TX 78639, USA — Football Player

Gray, Linda
PO Box 5064, Sherman Oaks CA 91413, USA — Actress

Gray, Lorenzo
2680 E 19th St, #1, Signal Hill CA 90755, USA — Baseball Player

Gray, Macy
Sunshine Sachs Assoc, 8409 Santa Monica Blvd, Los Angeles CA 90069, USA — Singer, Songwriter, Actress

Gray, Melvin D (Mel)
4507 Skyline Dr, Rockford IL 61107, USA — Football Player

Gray, Melvin J (Mel)
137 Winterset Pass, Williamsburg VA 23188, USA — Football Player

Gray, Richard B (Dick)
503 S Hampton St, Anaheim CA 92804, USA — Baseball Player

Gray, Shan R
The American, 3600 E 32nd St, Edmond OK 73013, USA — Sculptor

Gray, Stuart A
909 Andover Green, Lexington KY 40509, USA — Basketball Player

Gray, Sylvester
4929 Bilrae Circle S, Millington TN 38053, USA — Basketball Player

Gray, Tamyra M
19 Music & Mgmt, 35-37 Parkgate Road, London SW11 4NP, England — Singer, Actress

Gray, Timothy (Tim) — Football Player
6109 Crane St, Houston TX 77026, USA

Gray, Tom — Guitarist, Keyboardist (Gomez)
Red Light Mgmt, 44 Wall St, #2200, New York NY 10005, USA

Gray, William H, III — Association Leader; Representative, PA
2316 Cecil Moore Ave, Philadelphia PA 19121, USA

Graybiel, Ann M — Anatomist
Massachusetts Institute of Technology, Cognitive Science Dept, Cambridge MA 02139, USA

Gray-Cabey, Noah — Actor
Kritzer Levine Wilkins Griffin, 11872 La Grange Ave, #100, Los Angeles CA 90025 USA

Grayden, Sprague — Actress
Untitled Entertainment, 350 S Beverly Dr, #200, Beverly Hills CA 90212 USA

Graydon, Michael J — Air Force Marshal, England
Lloyds Bank, Cox & King's Branch, 7 Pall Mall, London SW1Y 5NA, England

Grayer, Jeffrey (Jeff) — Basketball Player
1617 Barbara Dr, Flint MI 48504, USA

Gray-Garcia, Lisa (Tiny) — Social Activist
City Lights Books, 261 Columbus Ave, San Francisco CA 94133, USA

Grayling, A C — Philosopher, Writer
Bloomsbury Publishing, 36 Soho Square, London W1D 3Q4, England

Graynor, Ari — Actress
United Talent Agency, 9336 Civic Center Dr, Beverly Hills CA 90210 USA

Graysmith, Robert — Editorial Cartoonist, Writer
Berkley Publishing Group, 375 Hudson St, Basement 1, New York NY 10014 USA

Grayson, C Jackson, Jr — Government Official, Educator
123 N Post Oak Lane, Houston TX 77024, USA

Grayson, David L (Dave), Jr — Football Player
5962 Rancho Mission Road, #218, San Diego CA 92108, USA

Grayson, David L (Dave), Sr — Football Player
PO Box 601292, San Diego CA 92160, USA

Gray-Stanford, Jason — Actor
Headline Talent Agency, 138 W 25th St, #1000, New York NY 10001, USA

Grazer, Brian — Producer
Imagine Entertainment, 9465 Wilshire Blvd, #700, Beverly Hills CA 90212, USA

Grazia, Eugene (Gene) — Ice Hockey Player
2344 NE 12th St, #10, Pompano Beach FL 33062, USA

Graziadei, Michael — Actor
Main Title Mgmt, 8383 Wilshire Blvd, #408, Beverly Hills CA 90211 USA

Grazzola, Kenneth E — Publisher
Aviation Week, Publisher's Office, 1221 Ave of Americas, New York NY 10020, USA

Grba, Eli — Baseball Player
106 Fox Run, Florence AL 35633, USA

Grbac, Elvis — Football Player
17361 Coldwater Trail, Chagrin Falls OH 44023, USA

Greason, Staci — Actress
8831 W Sunset Blvd, #304, West Hollywood CA 90069, USA

Greason, William H (Bill) — Baseball Player
4536 Hillman Dr NW, Birmingham AL 35221, USA

Grebeck, Craig A — Baseball Player
27856 Homestead Road, Laguna Nigel CA 92677, USA

Grebenshchikov, Boris — Singer, Guitarist (Akvarium)
2 Marata St, #3, 191025 Saint Petersburg, Russia

Greceanii, Zinaida — Prime Minister, Moldova
Prime Minister's Office, Piata Marii Adunari Nacional, 227033 Chishinev, Moldova

Grech, Prospero (Stanley) Cardinal — Religious Leader
Order of Saint Augustine, Via Paolo VI, 25, 00193 Rome, Italy

Grechko, Georgi M — Cosmonaut
Cosmonaut Training Center, Star City, 141160 Zvezdny Gorodok, Moscow Oblast, Russia

Greco, Buddy — Singer, Pianist
Fast Forward Communications, PO Box 1655, Troy NY 12181, USA

Greco, Emilio — Sculptor
Viale Cortina d'Ampezzo 132, 00135 Rome, Italy

Greco, Juliette — Actress, Singer
Productions Gerald Meys, 110 Rue Saint Florentin, 75001 Paris, France

Greco, Marco — Auto Racing Driver
11717 W Rockville Road, Indianapolis IN 46232, USA

Greco, Michael — Actor
BBC Centre, Clarendon Road, Borehamwood Herts WD6 1JF, England

Greczyn, Alice — Actress
A P A Talent/Literary Agency, 405 S Beverly Dr, #300, Beverly Hills CA 90212 USA

Greehey, William E — Businessman
Valero Energy Corp, 530 McCullough Ave, San Antonio TX 78215, USA

Greeley, Andrew M (Andy) — Writer, Sociologist
6030 S Ellis Ave, Chicago IL 60637, USA

Green, A C — Basketball Player
904 Silver Spur Road, Rolling Hills Estates CA 90274, USA

Green, Adam — Director, Writer
ArieScope Pictures, 10750 Cumpston St, North Hollywood CA 91601, USA

Green, Ahman R — Football Player
1750 Limestone Trail, De Pere WI 54115, USA

Green, Al — Singer, Songwriter
Al Green Music, PO Box 456, Millington TN 38083, USA

Green, Andy D — Land Speed Racing Driver
London Speaker Bureau, Elsinore House, 77 Fulham Palace Road, London W6 8JA, England

Green, Anthony W (Bubba) — Football Player
9611 Wesland Circle, Randallstown MD 21133, USA

Green, Art — Religious Leader, Rabbi, Educator
Hebrew College, Rabbinical School, 160 Herrick Road, Newton Centre MA 02459, USA

Green, B Eric — Football Player
13131 Luntz Point Lane, Windermere FL 34786, USA

Green, B Scarborough — Baseball Player
2020 Crimson Meadows Dr, O Fallon MO 63366, USA

Green, Barrett — Football Player
1004 Green Pine Blvd, #D1, West Palm Beach FL 33409, USA

Green, Barry — Auto Racing Executive
Team Green, 7615 Zionsville Road, Indianapolis IN 46268, USA

Green, Benny — Jazz Pianist
Jazz Tree, 211 Thompson St, #1D, New York NY 10012, USA
Green, Boyce K — Football Player
18812 Parting Oaks Lane, Davidson NC 28036, USA
Green, Brian Austin — Actor
I C M Partners, 10250 Constellation Blvd, #900, Los Angeles CA 90067 USA
Green, Brunson — Producer
Slate Public Relations, 9000 Sunset Blvd, #915, West Hollywood CA 90069 USA
Green, Charles H (Charlie) — Football Player
255 S Kyrene Road, #214, Chandler AZ 85226, USA
Green, Chris A — Football Player
331 Patio Village Terrace, Weston FL 33326, USA
Green, Christopher D (Chris) — Baseball Player
4054 Uppergate Lane, Charlotte NC 28215, USA
Green, Cornell D — Football Player
2106 Trinidad Dr, Dallas TX 75232, USA
Green, D Jacquez — Football Player
5102 Madison Lakes Circle W, Davie FL 33328, USA
Green, Dallas — Singer, Songwriter
Agency Group Ltd, 142 W 57th St, #600, New York NY 10019 USA
Green, Darrell R — Football Player
20998 Rostormel Court, Ashburn VA 20147, USA
Green, David — Director
Independent Talent Group, Oxford House, 76 Oxford St, London W1D 1BS, England
Green, David A — Baseball Player
Colinia Managua Grupo H407, Managua, Nicaragua
Green, David A — Auto Racing Driver
118 Reel Brook Lane, Mooresville NC 28117, USA
Green, David E — Chemist
5339 Brody Dr, Madison WI 53705, USA
Green, David E — Football Player
8311 Pat Blvd, Tampa FL 33615, USA
Green, David Gordon — Director, Writer
Rough House, 1722 Whitley Ave, Los Angeles CA 90028, USA
Green, David T — Inventor (Surgical Instruments)
401 Black Rock Turnpike, Easton CT 06612, USA
Green, Debbie — Volleyball Player
239 5th St, Seal Beach CA 90740, USA
Green, Dennis — Football Coach
3930 Torrey Hill Lane, San Diego CA 92130, USA
Green, Donnie G — Football Player
PO Box 685, Hagerstown MD 21741, USA
Green, Donte D — Basketball Player
Houston Rockets, 1730 Jefferson St, Houston TX 77003 USA
Green, Douglas B (Ranger Doug) — Singer (Riders in the Sky), Songwriter
New Frontier Mgmt, 1921 Broadway, Nashville TN 37203, USA
Green, Eric — Medical Administrator
National Institutes of Health, 50 South Dr, Bethesda MD 20892, USA
Green, Ernest (Ernie) — Football Player
424 Rue Marseille, Dayton OH 45429, USA
Green, Eva — Actress
8 Bis Blvd de Courcelles, 75017 Paris, France
Green, G Dallas — Baseball Player, Manager, Executive
846 Conowingo Road, Conowingo MD 21918, USA
Green, Gary A — Baseball Player
939 Kennebec St, Pittsburgh PA 15217, USA
Green, Gary F — Football Player
16330 Walnut Creek Dr, San Antonio TX 78247, USA
Green, Gaston A, III — Football Player
13524 Stanford Ave, Los Angeles CA 90059, USA
Green, Gerald, Jr — Basketball Player
Indiana Pacers, Conseco Fieldhouse, 125 S Pennsylvania, Indianapolis IN 46204 USA
Green, Hamilton — Prime Minister, Guyana
Plot D Lodge, Georgetown, Guyana
Green, Harold, Jr — Football Player
145 Folk Road, Blythewood SC 29016, USA
Green, Howard — Cellular Physiologist
Harvard Medical School, Physiology & Biophysics Dept, Boston MA 02115, USA
Green, Hubert (Hubie) — Golfer
Assured Management Co, 1901 W 47th Place, #200, Mission KS 66205, USA
Green, Hugh D — Football Player
4758 Highway 61, Fayette MS 39069, USA
Green, Jacob C — Football Player
4921 Whistling Straits Loop, College Station TX 77845, USA
Green, Janine — Actress
Don Buchwald/Fortitude, 6500 Wilshire Blvd, #2200, Los Angeles CA 90048 USA
Green, Jarvis P — Football Player
21717 Turkey Creek Dr, Baton Rouge LA 70817, USA
Green, Jeffrey (Jeff) — Auto Racing Driver
Haas C N C Racing, 6001 Haas Way, Kanapolis NC 28081, USA
Green, Jeffrey L (Jeff) — Basketball Player
Boston Celtics, 226 Causeway St, #4, Boston MA 02114 USA
Green, John M (Johnny) — Basketball Player
9 Susan Lane, Dix Hills NY 11746, USA
Green, John N (Jack), Jr — Cinematographer
516 Esplanade, #E, Redondo Beach CA 90277, USA
Green, Lamar — Basketball Player
PO Box 490208, Chicago IL 60649, USA
Green, Leonard C (Lenny) — Baseball Player
18693 Sunset St, Detroit MI 48234, USA
Green, Leonard I — Businessman
Rite Aid Corp, 30 Hunter Lane, Camp Hill PA 17011, USA
Green, Litterial — Basketball Player
1500 N Opdyke Road, Auburn Hills MI 48326, USA
Green, Mark J — Activist, Attorney, Writer
Democracy Project, 43 E 19th St, #300, New York NY 10003, USA

G

Gage - Green

Green, Michael — Cinematographer
11 Stevenson Lane, Upper Saddle River NJ 07458, USA
Green, Pat — Singer, Songwriter
Spaulding Entertainment, 1025 16th Ave S, #103, Nashville TN 37212, USA
Green, Richard D (Rick) — Ice Hockey Player
RR 1, Peterborough ON K9J 6X2, Canada
Green, Richard L (Dick) — Baseball Player
3924 Ridemoor Dr, Rapid City SD 57702, USA
Green, Rickey — Basketball Player
20584 Tyler Dr, Lynwood IL 60411, USA
Green, Robson — Actor
25B Broadchare, Quayside, Newcastle upon Tyne NE1 3DQ, England
Green, Seth — Actor, Comedian
United Talent Agency, 9336 Civic Center Dr, Beverly Hills CA 90210 USA
Green, Shawn D — Baseball Player
1430 Village Way, Santa Ana CA 92705, USA
Green, Tammie — Golfer
4990 Township Road 147 NE, Somerset OH 43783, USA
Green, Timothy J (Tim) — Football Player, Sportscaster, Writer
1194 Greenfield Lane, Skaneateles NY 13152, USA
Green, Tom — Actor, Comedian
From Out of Nowhere Productions, 6715 Hollywood Blvd, #103, Los Angeles CA 90028, USA
Green, Travis — Ice Hockey Player
2 Riverside, Irvine CA 92602, USA
Green, Trent J — Football Player
12109 Alhambra St, Leawood KS 66209, USA
Green, Tyler S — Baseball Player
15065 S 39th St, Phoenix AZ 85044, USA
Green, Victor B — Football Player
245 Woodscape Court, Alpharetta GA 30022, USA
Green, Vivian — Singer, Songwriter, Actress
I C M Partners, 10250 Constellation Blvd, #900, Los Angeles CA 90067 USA
Green, William D — Businessman
Accenture, 50 W San Fernando St, #1200, San Jose CA 95113, USA
Green, Willie A — Football Player
152 Farmington Road, Shelby NC 28150, USA
Green, Willie J — Basketball Player
Los Angeles Clippers, Staples Center, 1111 S Figueroa St, Los Angeles CA 90015 USA
Greenawalt, Kent — Attorney, Educator
Columbia University, Law School, 435 W 116th St, New York NY 10027, USA
Greenaway, Peter — Director
Allarts Ltd, 387B King St, London W6 9NH, England
Greenbaum, Michael — Religious Leader, Rabbi, Educator
Jewish Theological Seminary, 3080 Broadway, New York NY 10027, USA
Greenbaum, Norman — Singer, Songwriter
Greenbaum Music, 2513 Saddleback Court, Santa Rosa CA 95401, USA
Greenberg, Adam — Cinematographer
Gersh Agency, 9465 Wilshire Blvd, #600, Beverly Hills CA 90212 USA
Greenberg, Adam D — Baseball Player
79 Fernwood Dr, Guilford CT 06437, USA
Greenberg, Alan C — Financier
Bear Stearns Co, 383 Madison Ave, New York NY 10179, USA
Greenberg, Bernard — Biological Scientist, Entomologist
1463 E 55th Place, Chicago IL 60637, USA
Greenberg, Bryan — Actor
Gersh Agency, 9465 Wilshire Blvd, #600, Beverly Hills CA 90212 USA
Greenberg, Carl — Journalist
6001 Canterbury Dr, Culver City CA 90230, USA
Greenberg, Evan — Businessman
American International Group, 70 Pine St, New York NY 10270, USA
Greenberg, Jack — Attorney, Educator
118 Riverside Dr, New York NY 10024, USA
Greenberg, Jay — Composer
I M G Artists, 152 W 57th St, #500, New York NY 10019 USA
Greenberg, Kathy — Writer, Producer
Kaplan/Perrone Entertainment, 9744 Wilshire Blvd, #300, Beverly Hills CA 90212, USA
Greenberg, Morton I — Judge
US Court of Appeals, Judicial Complex, 402 E State St, Trenton NJ 08608, USA
Greenberg, Peter S — Travel Commentator, Producer, Actor
CBS-TV, News Dept, 51 W 52nd St, New York NY 10019 USA
Greenberg, Robbie S — Cinematographer
11 Reef St, Marina del Rey CA 90292, USA
Greenblatt, Stephen J — Writer
Harvard University, English Dept, Cambridge MA 02138, USA
Greenburg, Dan — Writer
323 E 50th St, New York NY 10022, USA
Greenburg, Paul — Journalist
5900 Scenic Dr, Little Rock AR 72207, USA
Greenbush, Rachel Lindsay — Actress
Inmotion Management, 5200 Kanan Road, Agoura Hills CA 91377, USA
Greenbush, Sidney Robin — Actress
Inmotion Management, 5200 Kanan Road, Agoura Hills CA 91377, USA
Greene, Anthony (Tony) — Football Player
1890 Briarcliff Circle NE, #D, Atlanta GA 30329, USA
Greene, Ashley — Actress
McKeon-Myrones Mgmt, 3500 Olive Ave, #770, Burbank CA 91505 USA
Greene, Bob — Exercise Physiologist, Writer
Simon & Schuster Books, 1230 Ave of Americas, Concourse 1, New York NY 10020, USA
Greene, Brian — Physicist, Mathematician
Columbia University, Physics Dept, New York NY 10027, USA
Greene, Charles E (Charlie) — Track Athlete
PO Box 6938, Lincoln NE 68506, USA
Greene, Charles P (Charlie) — Baseball Player
1449 Oldfield Dr, Tallahassee FL 32308, USA
Greene, Daniel — Actor
Michael Slessinger, 8730 W Sunset Blvd, #220W, West Hollywood CA 90069 USA

Greene, Ellen — Actress, Singer
Innovative Artists, 1505 10th St, Santa Monica CA 90401 USA
Greene, Graham — Actor
Greene Assoc, 1901 Ave of Stars, #130, Los Angeles CA 90067 USA
Greene, Herb — Photographer
PO Box 1141, Vineyard Haven MA 02568, USA
Greene, I Thomas (Tommy) — Baseball Player
PO Box 10, Warrington PA 18976, USA
Greene, Jack — Singer, Guitarist, Drummer
Ace Productions, PO Box 428, Portland TN 37148, USA
Greene, Jack P — Historian
1974 Division Road, East Greenwich RI 02818, USA
Greene, James — Actor
TalentWorks, 3500 W Olive Ave, #1400, Burbank CA 91505 USA
Greene, Joseph E (Mean Joe) — Football Player, Coach
PO Box 270953, Flower Mound TX 75027, USA
Greene, Kenneth E (Ken) — Football Player
5569 Nevil Point, Brentwood TN 37027, USA
Greene, Kevin D — Football Player
3448 Amber Lane, Green Bay WI 54311, USA
Greene, Khalil T — Baseball Player
10 Green Hill Dr, Simpsonville SC 29681, USA
Greene, Kim Morgan — Actress
Kazarian/Spencer/Ruskin, 11969 Ventura Blvd, #300, Studio City CA 91604 USA
Greene, Maurice — Track Athlete
H S I Sports Mgmt, 9871 Irvine Center Dr, Irvine CA 92618, USA
Greene, Michele — Actress, Singer, Writer
PO Box 382, Skyforest CA 92385, USA
Greene, Robert B (Bob), Jr — Columnist
Chicago Tribune, Editorial Dept, 435 N Michigan Ave, #1, Chicago IL 60611, USA
Greene, Shecky — Actor, Comedian
Bessie's Boy Products, PO Box 4362, Palm Springs CA 92263, USA
Greene, Todd A — Baseball Player
725 Pine Leaf Court, Alpharetta GA 30022, USA
Greene, William L (Willie) — Baseball Player
1044 Georgia Highway 22 E, Haddock GA 31033, USA
Green-Ellis, BenJarvus — Football Player
Cincinnati Bengals, 1 Paul Brown Stadium, Cincinnati OH 45202 USA
Greene-Mercier, Marie Z — Sculptor
1232 E 57th St, Chicago IL 60637, USA
Greenert, Jonathan W — Navy Admiral
Vice Chief of Naval Operations, HqUSN, Pentagon, Washington DC 20350 USA
Greenfield, James L — Journalist
470 Park Ave, #9A, New York NY 10022, USA
Greenfield, Jeff — Commentator
CNN-TV, News Dept, 820 1st St NE, #1000, Washington DC 20002 USA
Greenfield, Luke — Director
Creative Artists Agency, 2000 Ave of Stars, #100, Los Angeles CA 90067 USA
Greenfield, Max — Actor
W M E Entertainment, 9601 Wilshire Blvd, #300, Beverly Hills CA 90210 USA
Greengard, Paul — Nobel Medicine Laureate
450 E 63rd St, #11J, New York NY 10065, USA
Greengrass, James R (Jim) — Baseball Player
232 Rock Creek Road, Chatsworth CA 30705, USA
Greengrass, Paul — Director
Creative Artists Agency, 2000 Ave of Stars, #100, Los Angeles CA 90067 USA
Greenhouse, Linda — Journalist
New York Times, Editorial Dept, 229 W 43rd St, New York NY 10036, USA
Greenland, Seth — Writer
R W S H Agency, 1107 1/2 Glendon Ave, Los Angeles CA 90024, USA
Greenough, George — Filmmaker, Surfer
PO Box 611, Byron Bay NSW 2481, Australia
Greenquist, Brad — Actor
Gage Group, 14724 Ventura Blvd, #505, Sherman Oaks CA 91403 USA
Greenspan, Alan — Producer
International Arts Entertainment, 8899 Beverly Blvd, #800, Los Angeles CA 90048, USA
Greenspan, Alan — Government Official, Financier
Greenspan Assoc, 1133 Connecticut Ave NW, Washington DC 20036, USA
Greenspan, Gerald (Jerry) — Basketball Player
291 County Line Road, Riegelsville PA 18077, USA
Greenspoon, Jimmy — Organist (Three Dog Night)
McKenzie Accountancy, 5171 Caliente St, #134, Las Vegas NV 89119, USA
Greenstein, Barry — Poker Player, Writer
3303 Palos Verdes Dr, Rancho Palos Verdes CA 90272, USA
Greenstein, Jeff — Producer
I C M Partners, 10250 Constellation Blvd, #900, Los Angeles CA 90067 USA
Greenville, Georgina — Model
Next Model Mgmt, 188 Rue de Rivoli, 75001 Paris, France
Greenwald, Alex — Actor, Model, Singer (Phantom Planet)
C A M, 10635 Santa Monica Blvd W, #340, Los Angeles CA 90025, USA
Greenwald, Milton — Paleontologist
University of California, Museum of Paleontology, Berkeley CA 94720, USA
Greenwald, Robert — Director
Brave New Films, 10510 Culver Blvd, Culver City CA 90232, USA
Greenwald, Todd J — Producer, Writer
Creative Artists Agency, 2000 Ave of Stars, #100, Los Angeles CA 90067 USA
Greenwalt, T Jack — Medical Administrator
2444 Madison Road, #1501, Cincinnati OH 45208, USA
Greenway, Chad — Football Player
39448 250th St, Mount Vernon SD 57363, USA
Greenwell, Michael L (Mike) — Baseball Player, Auto Racing Driver
20150 S River Road, Alva FL 33920, USA
Greenwood, Bruce — Actor
Chuck Binder Mgmt, 1465 Lindacrest Dr, Beverly Hills CA 90210 USA
Greenwood, Colin C — Bassist (Radiohead)
Courtyard, 21 Nursery, Sutton Courtenay, Abingdon, Oxon OX14 4UA, England

Greenwood, David K
4991 Glenview St, Chino Hills CA 91709, USA — Basketball Player

Greenwood, James C (Jim)
Biotechnology Industry, 1201 Maryland Ave SW, Washington DC 20024, USA — Representative, PA

Greenwood, Jonathan R G (Jonny)
Courtyard, 21 Nursery, Sutton Courtenay, Abingdon, Oxon OX14 4UA, England — Guitarist (Radiohead)

Greenwood, L C Henderson (L C)
Badgeley Promotions, PO Box 3528, Parkersburg WV 26103, USA — Football Player

Greenwood, Lee
Lee Greenwood Inc, PO Box 22025, Huntsville AL 35814, USA — Singer, Songwriter

Greenwood, Morlon O
2772 Drummossie Dr, Henderson NV 89044, USA — Football Player

Greenwood, Norman
University of Leeds, Chemistry Dept, Leeds LS2 9JT, England — Chemist

Greer, Brian
307 Bagnall Ave, Placentia CA 92870, USA — Baseball Player

Greer, David S
Brown University, PO Box G, Providence RI 02901, USA — Internist

Greer, Donovan O
3423 Shadowside Court, Houston TX 77082, USA — Football Player

Greer, Germaine
Atkin & Stone, 29 Fernshaw Road, London SW10 0TG, England — Social Activist, Writer

Greer, Harold E (Hal)
7900 E Princess Dr, #1021, Scottsdale AZ 85255, USA — Basketball Player

Greer, Howard E
2845 Granada Blvd, #2A, Coral Gables FL 33134, USA — Navy Admiral

Greer, Judy
Creative Artists Agency, 2000 Ave of Stars, #100, Los Angeles CA 90067 USA — Actress

Greer, Kenneth W (Kenny)
17 Hill St, Cohasset MA 02025, USA — Baseball Player

Greer, Thurman C (Rusty), III
4793 Patterson Lane, Colleyville TX 76034, USA — Baseball Player

Gregg, A Forrest
926 Summer Spring View, Colorado Springs CO 80906, USA — Football Player, Coach, Administrator

Gregg, Clark
United Talent Agency, 9336 Civic Center Dr, Beverly Hills CA 90210 USA — Actor

Gregg, John
International Casting Service, 2/218 Crown St, Darlinghurst NSW 2010, Australia — Actor

Gregg, Kelly M
13800 Hollow Glen Road, Edmond OK 73013, USA — Football Player

Gregg, Kevin M
1907 SW Brooklane Dr, Corvallis OR 97333, USA — Baseball Player

Gregg, Ricky Lynn
E R Rimes Mgmt, 1103 Bell Grimes Lane, Nashville TN 37207, USA — Singer

Gregg, Stephen
Creative Artists Agency, 2000 Ave of Stars, #100, Los Angeles CA 90067 USA — Writer

Gregg, W Thomas (Tommy)
16 Cottage Dr, Newnan GA 30265, USA — Baseball Player

Gregga, Bruce
Gregga Jordan Smieszny, 1255 N State Parkway, Chicago IL 60610, USA — Interior Designer

Gregor, Gary W
444 Dove Ridge Road, Columbia SC 29223, USA — Basketball Player

Gregorian, Vartan
Carnegie Corp, President's Office, 437 Madison Ave, New York NY 10022, USA — Educator

Gregorio, Rose
Bauman Redanty Shaul Agency, 5757 Wilshire Blvd, #473, Los Angeles CA 90036 USA — Actress

Gregorio, Tom
66 McArthur Ave, Staten Island NY 10312, USA — Baseball Player

Gregorios, Metropolitan Paulos M
Orthodox Seminary, PO Box 98, Kottayam, Kerala 686001, India — Religious Leader

Gregory, Bettina L
ABC-TV, News Dept, 3361 75th Ave, #X, Hyattsville MD 20785, USA — Commentator

Gregory, Claude
14621 Blackburn Road, Burtonsville MD 20866, USA — Basketball Player

Gregory, Cynthia
American Ballet Theatre, 890 Broadway, #300, New York NY 10003 USA — Ballet Dancer

Gregory, David
NBC-TV, News Dept, 4001 Nebraska Ave NW, Washington DC 20016 USA — Commentator

Gregory, Dick
Dick Gregory Health Enterprises, PO Box 3270, Plymouth MA 02361, USA — Actor, Comedian, Social Activist

Gregory, E Jackson (Jack), Jr
108 Robertson St, Okolona MS 38860, USA — Football Player

Gregory, Frederick D
506 Tulip Road, Annapolis MD 21403, USA — Astronaut

Gregory, G Leroy (Lee)
6456 N Teilman Ave, Fresno CA 93711, USA — Baseball Player

Gregory, James M (Jim)
National Hockey League, 75 International Blvd, Rexdale ON M9W 6L9, Canada — Ice Hockey Executive

Gregory, Kathy
Playboy, Reader Services, 680 N Lake Shore Dr, Chicago IL 60611, USA — Cartoonist

Gregory, Richard
Independent Fundamental Churches, 2684 Meadow Ridge, Byron Center MI 49315, USA — Religious Leader

Gregory, Sebastian
Active Artists Mgmt, 43/38 Manchester Lane, Melbourne VIC 3000, Australia — Actor

Gregory, Stephen
Carey, 64 Thornton Ave, London W4 1QQ, England — Actor

Gregory, William G
2027 E Freeport Lane, Gilbert AZ 85234, USA — Astronaut

Gregory, William P (Bill), Jr
4317 Cityview Dr, Plano TX 75093, USA — Football Player

Gregory, Wilton D
Illinois Diocese, Chancery Office, 222 S 3rd St, Belleville IL 62220, USA — Religious Leader

Gregson Wagner, Natasha
1014 N Doheny Dr, #8, West Hollywood CA 90069, USA — Actress

Gregson, Wallace C
Commander, Marine Forces Pacific, Camp H M Smith HI 96861 USA — Marine Corps General

Gregson-Williams, Harry
Gorfaine/Schwartz, 4111 W Alameda Ave, #509, Burbank CA 91505 USA — Composer

Grehl, Michael
Memphis Commercial Appeal, Editorial Dept, 495 Union Ave, Memphis TN 38103, USA — Editor

Greider, Carolyn W (Carol)
Johns Hopkins University Medical Center, Greider Laboratory, 725 N Wolfe Ave, Baltimore MD 21205, USA — Nobel Medicine Laureate

Greif, Matthew
California State University Dominguez Hills, Music Dept, 1000 E Victoria St, Carson CA 90747, USA — Guitarist (LAGQ)

Greif, Michael
I C M Partners, 730 5th Ave, New York NY 10019 USA — Director

Greif, William B (Bill)
807 E 31st St, Austin TX 78705, USA — Baseball Player

Greifeld, Robert A
NASDAQ OMX Group, 1 Liberty Plaza, 165 Broadway, New York NY 10006, USA — Financier

Greig, John W
2031 218th Place NE, Sammamish WA 98074, USA — Basketball Player

Greilsammer, David
I M G Artists, The Light Box, 111 Power Road, London W4 5PY, England — Conductor, Concert Pianist

Greiner, William R
80 Aspenwood Dr, East Amherst NY 14051, USA — Educator

Greinke, D Zackary (Zack)
8629 Vista Pine Court, Orlando FL 32836, USA — Baseball Player

Greis, Michael
Von-Lingg-Str 22, 87484 Nesselwang, Germany — Biathlete

Greisen, Nick A
12865 Biggin Church Road S, Jacksonville FL 32224, USA — Football Player

Greisinger, Seth A
6460 Overbrook St, Falls Church VA 22043, USA — Baseball Player

Greist, Kim
Jeffrey Leavitt Agency, 11500 W Olympic Blvd, #400, Los Angeles CA 90064, USA — Actress

Grenier, Adrian
Leverage Mgmt, 3030 Pennsylvania Ave, Santa Monica CA 90404 USA — Actor

Grenier, Sylvain
World Wrestling Entertainment, Titan Towers, 1241 E Main St, Stamford CT 06902 USA — Professional Wrestler

Grenier, Zach
Hartig-Hilepo Agency, 54 W 21st St, #610, New York NY 10010 USA — Actor

Grentz, Theresa Shank
University of Illinois, Athletic Dept, Champaign IL 61820, USA — Basketball Coach

Greschner, Ron
PO Box 4513, Greenwich CT 6831, USA — Ice Hockey Player

Gresham, Robert C (Bob)
2428 Portstewart Lane, Charlotte NC 28270, USA — Football Player

Gretsch, Joel J
A P A Talent/Literary Agency, 405 S Beverly Dr, #300, Beverly Hills CA 90212 USA — Actor

Gretzky, Wayne D
6436 E Gainsborough Road, Scottsdale AZ 85251, USA — Ice Hockey Player, Coach

Greutert, Kevin
Paradigm Agency, 360 N Crescent Dr, North Building, Beverly Hills CA 90210 USA — Director, Editor

Grevelius, Anna
I M G Artists, Hogarth Business Park, Chiswick, London W4 2TH, England — Opera Singer

Grevey, Kevin M
528 River Bend Road, Great Falls VA 22066, USA — Basketball Player

Grevill, Laurent
Artmedia, 20 Ave Rapp, 75007 Paris, France — Actor

Grewal, Alexi
US Cycling Federation, 1750 E Boulder, Colorado Springs CO 80909, USA — Cyclist

Grey, Beryl E
Fernhill, Priory Road, Forest Row, East Sussex RH18 5JE, England — Ballerina

Grey, Brad
Paramount Pictures, 5555 Melrose Ave, Los Angeles CA 90038, USA — Businessman, Producer, Agent

Grey, Jennifer
United Talent Agency, 9336 Civic Center Dr, Beverly Hills CA 90210 USA — Actress

Grey, Joel
Chaplin Entertainment, 1650 Broadway, #303, New York NY 10019, USA — Actor

Grey, Skylar
W M E Entertainment, 9601 Wilshire Blvd, #300, Beverly Hills CA 90210 USA — Singer, Songwriter

Greyeyes, Michael
TalentWorks, 3500 W Olive Ave, #1400, Burbank CA 91505 USA — Actor

Gribble, David
Sheldon Prosnit Agency, 800 S Robertson Blvd, Los Angeles CA 90035, USA — Cinematographer

Grich, Robert A (Bobby)
31 Madison Lane, Trabuco Canyon CA 92679, USA — Baseball Player

Grichting, Damian
Curling Assn, PO Box 606, 3000 Bern, Switzerland — Curling Athlete

Grider, Robbin
R D M J Entertainment Mgmt, 3619 Rose Ave, Long Beach CA 90807 USA — Keyboardist (Klymaxx)

Grieco, Richard
Independent Artists, 9601 Wilshire Blvd, #750, Beverly Hills CA 90210 USA — Actor

Grieder, William
Simon & Schuster, 1230 Ave of Americas, Concourse 1, New York NY 10020, USA — Journalist

Grier, David Alan
Innovative Artists, 1505 10th St, Santa Monica CA 90401 USA — Actor, Comedian

Grier, Herbert E
9648 Blackgold Road, La Jolla CA 92037, USA — Electrical Engineer

Grier, J A D
Cincinnati Milacron Inc, 4701 Marbury Ave, Cincinnati OH 45209, USA — Businessman

Grier, Mike
72 Stonecrest Dr, Needham MA 2492, USA — Ice Hockey Player

Grier, Pam
TalentWorks, 3500 W Olive Ave, #1400, Burbank CA 91505 USA — Actress

Grier, Roosevelt (Rosey)
1250 4th St, #600, Santa Monica CA 90401, USA — Football Player, Actor

Griese, Brian D
17 Polo Club Dr, Denver CO 80209, USA — Football Player

Griese, Robert A (Bob)
3195 Ponce de Leon Blvd, #412, Coral Gables FL 33134, USA — Football Player, Sportscaster

Griesemer, John N
RR 2 Box 204B, Springfield MO 65802, USA — Government Official

Grieve, Benjamin (Ben)
6906 Fairway Road, La Jolla CA 92037, USA — Baseball Player

Grieve, Pierson M
Ecolab Inc, Ecolab Center, 370 Wabasha St N, Saint Paul MN 55102, USA — Businessman

Griffey, G Kenneth (Ken)
1102 Portmoor Way, Winter Garden FL 34787, USA — Baseball Player

Griffey, G Kenneth (Ken), Jr
8815 Conroy Windermere Road, Orlando FL 32835, USA — Baseball Player

Griffin, Adrian D
2909 Taylor St, Dallas TX 75226, USA — Basketball Player

Griffin, Alfredo C
9731 NW 41st St, Doral FL 33178, USA — Baseball Player

Griffin, Archie M
6845 Temperance Point Place, Westerville OH 43082, USA — Football Player

Griffin, Blake A
Los Angeles Clippers, Staples Center, 1111 S Figueroa St, Los Angeles CA 90015 USA — Basketball Player

Griffin, Cedric L
10567 Parker Dr, Eden Prairie MN 55347, USA — Football Player

Griffin, Cornelius
224 Countryside Dr, Troy AL 36079, USA — Football Player

Griffin, Douglas L (Doug)
15811 El Soneto Dr, Whittier CA 90603, USA — Baseball Player

Griffin, Eddie
Gersh Agency, 9465 Wilshire Blvd, #600, Beverly Hills CA 90212 USA — Actor, Comedian

Griffin, Greg
12051 Bayport St, #1-208, Garden Grove CA 92840, USA — Basketball Player

Griffin, John
Geddes Agency, 8430 Santa Monica Blvd, #201, West Hollywood CA 90069 USA — Actor, Writer, Producer

Griffin, John-Ford
PO Box 1359, Sarasota FL 34230, USA — Baseball Player

Griffin, Kathleeen (Kathy)
W M E Entertainment, 9601 Wilshire Blvd, #300, Beverly Hills CA 90210 USA — Actress, Comedienne

Griffin, Keith
4330 Canada Hills Court, Waldorf MD 20602, USA — Football Player

Griffin, Kevin
Uppercut Mgmt, 805 N Milwaukee Ave, #401, Chicago IL 60642, USA — Singer, Guitarist (Better Than Ezra)

Griffin, Khamani
Commercial Talent, 9255 Sunset Blvd, #505, West Hollywood CA 90069, USA — Actor

Griffin, Larry A
5617 Silchester Lane, Charlotte NC 28215, USA — Football Player

Griffin, Leonard J, Jr
PO Box 480, Calhoun, LA 71225, USA — Football Player

Griffin, Michael D (Mike)
University of Alabama, Mechanical & Aerospace Engineering Dept, Huntsville AL 35805, USA — Government Official

Griffin, Michael L (Mike)
1620 Grove Ave, Woodland CA 95695, USA — Baseball Player

Griffin, Nikki
Corsa Agency, 11704 Wilshire Blvd, #204, Los Angeles CA 90025, USA — Actress

Griffin, Patty
Monterey Peninsula Artists, 404 W Franklin St, Monterey CA 93940 USA — Singer, Songwriter, Guitarist

Griffin, Paul A
903 Great Tree Dr, San Antonio TX 78260, USA — Basketball Player

Griffin, Raymond (Ray)
5395 Anacala Court, Westerville OH 43082, USA — Football Player

Griffin, Robert L, III
Washington Redskins, 21300 Redskin Park Dr, Ashburn VA 20147 USA — Football Player

Griffin, Robert P
Michigan Supreme Court, PO Box 30052, Lansing MI 48909, USA — Senator, MI; Judge

Griffin, Thomas C
3935 School Section Road, #1, Cincinnati OH 45211, USA — WW II Army Air Corps Hero

Griffin, Thomas J (Tom)
13147 Avenida La Valencia, Poway CA 92064, USA — Baseball Player

Griffin, Thomas N, Jr
9749 S Park Circle, Fairfax Station VA 22039, USA — Army General

Griffin, Tim
Untitled Entertainment, 350 S Beverly Dr, #200, Beverly Hills CA 90212 USA — Actor

Griffin, W E B
Penguin Books, 375 Hudson St, Basement 1, New York NY 10014 USA — Writer

Griffin, Wade H, Jr
2937 Highway 72, Holly Springs MS 38635, USA — Football Player

Griffith, Anastasia
Paradigm Agency, 360 Park Ave S, #1600, New York NY 10010 USA — Actress

Griffith, Anthony
Spivak Sobol Entertainment, 11845 W Olympic Blvd, #1125, Los Angeles CA 90064, USA — Actor

Griffith, Bill
Pinhead Productions, PO Box 88, Hadlyme CT 06439, USA — Cartoonist (Zippy the Pinhead)

Griffith, Darrell S
PO Box 24841, Louisville KY 40224, USA — Basketball Player

Griffith, Emile A
20 Mount Vernon Place, Newark NJ 07106, USA — Boxer

Griffith, Howard T
9152 S Clyde Ave, Chicago IL 60617, USA — Football Player

Griffith, James
Timken Co, 1835 Dueber Ave SW, Canton OH 44706, USA — Businessman

Griffith, James
eBay, 2145 Hamilton Ave, San Jose CA 95125, USA — Businessman

Griffith, Melanie
Green Moon Productions, Paseo Maritimo, Cludad de Melilla 23, 29016 Malaga, Spain — Actress, Model

Griffith, Nanci
Gold Mountain, 2 Music Circle S, #212, Nashville TN 37203, USA — Singer, Songwriter

Griffith, R Derrell
201 E Central Blvd, Anadarko OK 73005, USA — Baseball Player

Griffith, Richard P (Rich)
9368 Stoneglen Dr, Colorado Springs CO 80920, USA — Football Player

Griffith, Robert O 3525 Del Mar Heights Road, #331, San Diego CA 92130, USA	Football Player
Griffith, Ronald H (Ron) Military Professional Resources, 1320 Braddock Place, Alexandria VA 22314, USA	Army General
Griffith, Thomas B US Court of Appeals, 333 Constitution Ave NW, #4400, Washington DC 20001, USA	Judge
Griffith, Thomas Ian Pitt Group, 9465 Wilshire Blvd, #420, Beverly Hills CA 90212, USA	Actor
Griffith, Tom W Rural Letter Carriers Assn, 1448 Duke St, #100, Alexandria VA 22314, USA	Labor Leader
Griffith, Tracy Rodriguez Mgmt, 223 S Beverly Dr, #207, Beverly Hills CA 90212, USA	Actress
Griffiths, Jeremy 120 Beachdale Dr, Avon Lake OH 44012, USA	Baseball Player
Griffiths, Phillip A Advanced Study Institute, Director's Office, Olden Lane, Princeton NJ 08540, USA	Mathematician, Educator
Griffiths, Rachel W M E Entertainment, 9601 Wilshire Blvd, #300, Beverly Hills CA 90210 USA	Actress
Griffiths, Richard Dalzell & Beresford, 26 Astwood Mews, London SW7 4DE, England	Actor
Griggs, Andy PO Box 120835, Nashville TN 37212, USA	Singer
Griggs, William E (Bill), III 18 Summerhill Lane, Medford NJ 08055, USA	Football Player
Grijalva, Lucy PO Box 1634, Benicia CA 94510, USA	Writer
Grijalva, Victor E Schlumberger Ltd, 277 Park Ave, New York NY 10172, USA	Businessman
Grilli, Jason 9037 Point Cypress Dr, Orlando FL 32836, USA	Baseball Player
Grillo, Frank Creative Artists Agency, 2000 Ave of Stars, #100, Los Angeles CA 90067 USA	Actor
Grim, Robert L (Bob) 18 NW Saginaw Ave, Bend OR 97701, USA	Football Player
Grimaldi, Dan Kingsborough Community College, Mathematics Dept, Brooklyn NY 11235, USA	Actor
Grimaldi, James V Washington Post, Editorial Dept, 1150 15th St NW, Washington DC 20071 USA	Journalist
Grimaud, Helene Harm's Way Mgmt, Fritschestr 27/28, Fabrik 2, Aufgang C, 10585 Berlin, Germany	Concert Pianist
Grimes, Brent Atlanta Falcons, 4400 Falcon Parkway, Flowery Branch GA 30542 USA	Football Player
Grimes, Kareem Coast to Coast Talent, 3350 Barham Blvd, Los Angeles CA 90068 USA	Actor
Grimes, Karolyn PO Box 432, Manchester WA 98353, USA	Actress
Grimes, Luke Global Creative, 1051 N Cole Ave, #B, Los Angeles CA 90038, USA	Actor
Grimes, Martha 115 D St SE, #G6, Washington DC 20003, USA	Writer
Grimes, Randall C (Randy) 13214 Halifax St, Houston TX 77015, USA	Football Player
Grimes, Scott Innovative Artists, 1505 10th St, Santa Monica CA 90401 USA	Actor
Grimes, Shenae Gersh Agency, 9465 Wilshire Blvd, #600, Beverly Hills CA 90212 USA	Actress
Grimes, Tammy Don Buchwald/Fortitude, 10 E 44th St, New York NY 10017 USA	Actress, Singer
Grimes, Tinsely Innovative Artists, 1505 10th St, Santa Monica CA 90401 USA	Actress
Grimm, Alexander Wallgauer Weg 7A, 86163 Augsburg, Germany	Canoeing Athlete
Grimm, Daniel J (Dan) 2514 Smith Harbour Dr, Denver NC 28037, USA	Football Player
Grimm, Russ 2654 E Mead Place, Chandler AZ 85249, USA	Football Player, Coach
Grimm, Tim Abrams Artists, 9200 W Sunset Blvd, #1125, West Hollywood CA 90069 USA	Actor
Grimmette, Mark 21 Snowberry Lane, Lake Placid NY 12946, USA	Luge Athlete
Grimshaw, Nicholas T Fitzroy Square, 1 Conway St, London W1P 5HA, England	Architect
Grimsley, Jason A 13315 Timberwild Court, Tomball TX 77375, USA	Baseball Player
Grimsley, Ross A 92 Conewago Court, Owings Mill MD 21117, USA	Baseball Player
Grimsmo, Anthon Curling Assn, Sognsveien 75, Serviceboks 1, 0840 Oslo, Norway	Curling Athlete
Grimson, A Stuart (Stu) 999 Jones Parkway, Brentwood TN 37027, USA	Ice Hockey Player
Grimsson, Olafur Ragnar President's Office, Stadastadur, Soleyjargata 1, 150 Reykjavik, Iceland	President, Iceland
Grinberg, Anouk Voyez Mon Agent, 20 Ave Rapp, 75007 Paris, France	Actress
Grindenko, Tatyana T Moscow State Philharmonic, Tverskaya Str 31, 103050 Moscow, Russia	Concert Violinist
Griner, Brittney Baylor University, Athletic Dept, Waco TX 76798, USA	Basketball Player
Griner, Paul Random House, 1745 Broadway, #1800, New York NY 10019 USA	Writer
Grinham Rawley, Judy 103 Green Lane, Northwood, Middx HA6 1AP, England	Swimmer
Grinnage, Jack Discover Mgmt, 11624 Moorpark St, Studio City CA 91602, USA	Actor
Grinnell, Alan D University of California Medical School, Lewis Center, Los Angeles CA 90024, USA	Physiologist

G

Gage - Grinnell

G

Grinnell, Todd A — Actor
Gersh Agency, 9465 Wilshire Blvd, #600, Beverly Hills CA 90212 USA

Grinney, Jay — Businessman
Healthsouth Corp, 3660 Grandview Parkway, #200, Birmingham AL 35243, USA

Grinstead, Irish — Singer (702)
Richard Walters, PO Box 2789, Toluca Lake CA 91610, USA

Grinstead, LeMisha — Singer (702)
Richard Walters, PO Box 2789, Toluca Lake CA 91610 USA

Grint, Rupert — Actor
Gersh Agency, 9465 Wilshire Blvd, #600, Beverly Hills CA 90212 USA

Grinville, Patrick — Writer
Academie Goncourt, 38 Rue du Faubourg Saint Jacques, 75014 Paris, France

Grione, Remo — Actor
Cristiano Cucchino Mgmt, Lungotevere dei Mellini 10, 00193 Rome, Italy

Grippe, Peter — Artist, Sculptor
1190 Boylston St, Newton Upper Falls MA 02464, USA

Grisanti, Eugene P — Businessman
International Flavors, 521 W 57th St, New York NY 10019, USA

Grisez, Germain — Theologian
Mount Saint Mary's College, Christian Ethics Dept, Emmitsburg MD 21727, USA

Grisham, John — Writer
Oakwood Books, 105 W Water St, Charlottesville VA 22902, USA

Grishin, Aleksei — Freestyle Aerials Skier
Olympic Committee, Ul Ya Kolas 2, 220005 Minsk, Belarus

Grishuk, Oksana (Pasha) — Ice Dancer, Actress
PO Box 420, Beverly Hills CA 90213, USA

Grisman, David — Singer, Mandolin Player, Composer
C M Mgmt, 5749 Larryan Dr, Woodland Hills CA 91367, USA

Grissom, Marquis D — Baseball Player
110 Fiddlers Ridge, Fayetteville GA 30214, USA

Grissom, Steve — Auto Racing Driver
5901 Orr Road, Charlotte NC 28211, USA

Groat, Richard M (Dick) — Baseball, Basketball Player
320 Beech St, Pittsburgh PA 15218, USA

Grob, Mike — Golfer
3611 Quimet Circle, Billings MT 59106, USA

Groban, Joshua W (Josh) — Singer, Actor, Songwriter
Avnet Mgmt, 3815 W Olive St, #202, Burbank CA 91505, USA

Grobe, Jim — Football Coach
Wake Forest University, Athletic Dept, Winston-Salem NC 27109, USA

Grobert, Xavier Perez — Cinematographer
Dattner Dispoto, 10635 Santa Monica Blvd, #165, Los Angeles CA 90025, USA

Groce, Clifton A (Clif) — Football Player
1632 Park Place, College Station TX 77840, USA

Grocholewski, Zenon Cardinal — Religious Leader
Palazzo della Congregazioni, Piazzo Pio XII, #3, 00193 Rome, Italy

Grodin, Charles — Actor
187 Chestnut Hill Road, Wilton CT 06897, USA

Grodnikaite, Liora — Opera Singer
I M G Artists, Hogarth Business Park, Chiswick, London W4 2TH, England

Groening, Matthew (Matt) — Cartoonist (Life in Hell, Simpsons)
1650 21st St, Santa Monica CA 90404, USA

Groetzinger, Jon, Jr — Businessman
American Greetings Corp, 1 American Road, Cleveland OH 44144, USA

Groff, Jonathan — Actor, Singer
W M E Entertainment, 9601 Wilshire Blvd, #300, Beverly Hills CA 90210 USA

Grogan, Clare — Actress
United Agents, 12-26 Lexington St, London W1F 0LE, England

Grogan, John — Writer
Harper Collins Publishers, 10 E 53rd St, Cellar 1, New York NY 10022 USA

Grogan, Steven J (Steve) — Football Player
PO Box 530, Foxboro MA 02035, USA

Groh, Gary — Golfer
331 Signe Court, Lake Bluff IL 60044, USA

Grohl, David E (Dave) — Singer, Songwriter, Drummer
S A M, 722 Seward St, Los Angeles CA 90038, USA

Gromada, John — Sound Designer, Composer
I C M Partners, 10250 Constellation Blvd, #900, Los Angeles CA 90067 USA

Groman, William F (Bill) — Football Player
7906 Scherzo Lane, Houston TX 77040, USA

Gromov, Mikhael L — Abel Mathematics Laureate
91 Rue de la Sante, 75013 Paris, France

Grondin, Marc-Andre — Actor
United Talent Agency, 9336 Civic Center Dr, Beverly Hills CA 90210 USA

Gronk — Artist
Daniel Saxon Gallery, 7000 Romaine St, #211, West Hollywood CA 90038, USA

Gronkowski, Rob — Football Player
New England Patriots, 1 Patriot Place, Foxboro MA 02035 USA

Gronman, Tuomas O — Ice Hockey Player
Pittsburgh Penguins, Consol Energy Center, 1001 5th Ave, Pittsburgh PA 15219 USA

Gronvole, Audun — Freestyle Cross Skier
Ski Federation, Ulleval Stadion, 0840 Oslo, Norway

Groom, Sam — Actor
8730 W Sunset Blvd, #440, West Hollywood CA 90069, USA

Groom, Wedsel G (Buddy) — Baseball Player
1991 Saint Andrews Dr, Red Oak TX 75154, USA

Grooms, Charles R (Red) — Artist
85 Walker St, New York NY 10013, USA

Groop, Monica — Opera Singer
I M G Artists, Hogarth Business Park, Chiswick, London W4 2TH, England

Groopman, Jerome — Hematologist
Beth Israel Deaconess Medical Center, 330 Brookline Ave, Boston MA 02215, USA

Gropper, Steven L (Steve) — Guitarist (Mar-Keys), Songwriter
Insomnia Studios, 119 17th Ave S, Nashville TN 37203, USA

Gros, Earl R — Football Player
17424 Airline Highway, #12, Prairieville LA 70769, USA

Grosek, Michal	Ice Hockey Player
5 Samba Circle, Sandwich MA 02563, USA	
Gross, Alfred E (Al), Jr	Football Player
8227 Grandstaff Dr, Sacramento CA 95823, USA	
Gross, Arye	Actor
S D B Partners, 1801 Ave of Stars, #902, Los Angeles CA 90067 USA	
Gross, Brian	Actor
Amsel Eisenstadt Frazier, 5055 Wilshire Blvd, #865, Los Angeles CA 90036 USA	
Gross, Charles G	Psychologist
18 E Shore Dr, Princeton NJ 08540, USA	
Gross, Clayton K	WW II Army Air Corps Hero
13303 SE McGillivray Blvd, #124, Vancouver WA 98683, USA	
Gross, David	Actor, Comedian, Writer
Creative Artists Agency, 2000 Ave of Stars, #100, Los Angeles CA 90067 USA	
Gross, David J	Nobel Physics Laureate
30 Pueblo Vista Road, Santa Barbara CA 93103, USA	
Gross, Gabriel J (Gabe)	Baseball Player
1756 Raymer Place, Auburn AL 36830, USA	
Gross, Gregory E (Greg)	Baseball Player
802 Hallowell Dr, West Chester PA 19382, USA	
Gross, Henry	Guitarist (Sha Na Na)
Zelda Mgmt, PO Box 150163, Nashville TN 37215, USA	
Gross, Jordan A	Football Player
12725 Ninebark Trail, Charlotte NC 28278, USA	
Gross, Kevin F	Baseball Player
117 Principia Court, Claremont CA 91711, USA	
Gross, Kip L	Baseball Player
2015 Ridgeview Court, Redlands CA 92373, USA	
Gross, Lance	Actor
Schiff Co, 8440 Warner Dr, #B1, Culver City CA 90232 USA	
Gross, Mary	Actress, Comedienne
Danis Panaro Nist Mgmt, 9201 W Olympic Blvd, Beverly Hills CA 90212, USA	
Gross, Michael	Actor
Stone Manners Salners, 9911 W Pico Blvd, #1400, Los Angeles CA 90035 USA	
Gross, Michael	Swimmer
Paul-Ehrlich-Str 6, 60596 Frankfurt/Main, Germany	
Gross, Paul	Actor
Bresler Kelly Assoc, 11500 W Olympic Blvd, #400, Los Angeles CA 90064 USA	
Gross, Ricco	Biathlete
Waldbahnstr 34A, 83324 Ruhpolding, Germany	
Gross, Robert A	Physicist
14 Sunnyside Way, New Rochelle NY 10804, USA	
Gross, Robert E (Bob)	Basketball Player
13466 SE Red Rose Lane, Happy Valley OR 97086, USA	
Gross, Sam	Cartoonist
New Yorker, Editorial Dept, 4 Times Square, Basement C1B, New York NY 10036 USA	
Gross, Terry R	Commentator
WHYY-Radio, News Dept, Independence Mall W, Philadelphia PA 19104, USA	
Gross, Wayne D	Baseball Player
45 Leonard Court, Danville CA 94526, USA	
Grossfeld, Stanley	Photojournalist
Boston Globe, Editorial Dept, 135 William Morrissey Blvd, Dorchester MA 02125 USA	
Grossheusch, Leroy (Lee)	WW II Army Air Corps Hero
1239 Kupau St, Kailua HI 96734, USA	
Grossman, Allen R	Writer
113 Richdale Ave, #25, Cambridge MA 02140, USA	
Grossman, Austin	Writer
Pantheon/Random House, 1745 Broadway, New York NY 10019, USA	
Grossman, Ben	Visual Effects Designer
Syndicate, 100 Universal City Plaza, #6148, Universal City CA 91608, USA	
Grossman, Burt	Football Player
1482 Antioch Ave, Chula Vista CA 91913, USA	
Grossman, C Randy	Football Player
204 Ridge Road, Pittsburgh PA 15238, USA	
Grossman, David	Director, Producer
United Talent Agency, 9336 Civic Center Dr, Beverly Hills CA 90210 USA	
Grossman, David	Writer
Bloomsbury Publishing, 36 Soho Square, London W1D 3Q4, England	
Grossman, Eric	Bassist (K's Choice)
Sharpe Entertainment Services, 683 Palmera Ave, Pacific Palisades CA 90272, USA	
Grossman, Gene M	Economist
Princeton University, Economics Dept, Princeton NJ 08544, USA	
Grossman, Judith	Writer
Warren Wilson College, English Dept, Swannanoa NC 28778, USA	
Grossman, Leslie	Actress
Marsh Entertainment, 12444 Ventura Blvd, #203, Sherman Oaks CA 91604, USA	
Grossman, Rex D	Football Player
17230 Crawley Road, Odessa FL 33556, USA	
Grossman, Robert	Illustrator
19 Crosby St, New York NY 10013, USA	
Grosvenor, Benjamin	Concert Pianist
Hazard Chase, 25 City Road, Cambridge CB1 1DP, England	
Grosvenor, Gilbert M	Foundation Executive, Publisher
National Geographic, Editorial Dept, 1145 17th St NW, Washington DC 20036 USA	
Grote, Gerald W (Jerry)	Baseball Player
2608 N Main St, #B, Belton TX 76513, USA	
Grotenfelt, Georg E J	Architect
Kapteeninkatu 20D, 00140 Helsinki, Finland	
Groth, Jeffrey E (Jeff)	Football Player
13824 Driftwood Dr, Carmel IN 46033, USA	
Groth, John T (Johnny)	Baseball Player
170 N Ocean Blvd, #307, Palm Beach FL 33480, USA	
Grott, Matthew A (Matt)	Baseball Player
19431 N Concho Circle, Sun City AZ 85373, USA	
Grouch, Roger K	Astronaut
Life/Microgravity Sciences Office, NASA Headquarters, Washington DC 20546, USA	

Grove, Andrew S — Businessman
Intel Corp, 2200 Mission College Blvd, Santa Clara CA 95054, USA

Grove, Jill — Opera Singer
I M G Artists, Hogarth Business Park, Chiswick, London W4 2TH, England

Groves, Kristina — Speed Skater
Agenda Sport Marketing, 119-9A St NE, Calgary AB T2E 9C5, Canada

Groves, Richard H — Army General
9110 Belvoir Woods Parkway, #216, Fort Belvoir VA 22060, USA

Groves, Robert M — Government Official, Statistician
Georgetown University, Provost's Office, Washington DC 20057, USA

Groves, S Russell — Architect
210 11th Ave, New York NY 10001, USA

Growney, Robert L — Businessman
Motorola Inc, 1303 E Algonquin Road, Schaumburg IL 60196, USA

Grubb, John M — Baseball Player
6618 Bel Lac Dr, Chester VA 23831, USA

Grubbs, Benjamin R (Ben) — Football Player
New Orleans Saints, 5800 Airline Highway, Metairie LA 70003 USA

Grubbs, Gary — Actor
TalentWorks, 3500 W Olive Ave, #1400, Burbank CA 91505 USA

Grubbs, Robert H — Nobel Chemist Laureate
1700 Spruce St, South Pasadena CA 91030, USA

Gruber, J Mackye — Director
New Wave Entertainment, 2660 W Olive Ave, Burbank CA 91505, USA

Gruber, Kelly W — Baseball Player
3306 Blue Jay Lane, Austin TX 78732, USA

Gruber, Michael — Writer
William Morrow Publishers, 1350 Ave of Americas, New York NY 10019 USA

Gruber, Paul B — Football Player
PO Box 4239, Edwards CO 81632, USA

Gruberova, Edita — Opera Singer
Theateragentur Hilbert, Maximilianstr 22, 80539 Munich, Germany

Grubinger, Martin — Concert Percussionist
Harrison/Parrott, 5-6 Albion Court, London W6 0QT, England

Grubman, Allen J — Attorney
Grubman Indursky Schindler Goldstein, 152 W 57th St, New York NY 10019, USA

Grubnic, Dave — Drag Racing Driver
Kalitta Motorsports, 1010 James L Hart Parkway, Ypsilanti MI 48197, USA

Gruden, Jon — Football Coach, Sportscaster
709 Guisando de Avila, Tampa FL 33613, USA

Grudt, Mona — Beauty Queen
Ditt Bryllup, Editor's Office, PO Box 24, 1485 Hakadal, Norway

Grudzielanek, Mark J — Baseball Player
833 Aspen Peak Loop, #1113, Henderson NV 89011, USA

Gruenberg, Erich — Concert Violinist
80 Northway, Hampstead Garden Suburb, London NW11 6PA, England

Gruenberg, Peter — Nobel Physics Laureate
Solid State Research Institute, Wilhelm-Johnen-Str, 52425 Juelich, Germany

Gruevski, Nikola — Prime Minister, Macedonia
Prime Minister's Office, Ilindenska BB, 1000 Skopje, Macedonia

Gruffudd, Ioan — Actor
Hamilton Hodell, 66-68 Margaret St, London W1W 8SR, England

Grum, Clifford J — Businessman
Temple-Inland Inc, 303 S Temple Dr, Diboll TX 75941, USA

Grumman, Cornelia — Journalist
Chicago Tribune, Editorial Dept, 350 N Orleans St, Chicago IL 60654 USA

Grummer, Elisabeth — Opera Singer
Am Schlachtensee 104, 14163 Berlin, Germany

Grunberg, Gregory P (Greg) — Actor
I C M Partners, 10250 Constellation Blvd, #900, Los Angeles CA 90067 USA

Grunberg-Manago, Marianne — Biochemist
80 Boulevard Pasteur, 75015 Paris, France

Grundfest, Joseph A — Government Official
Stanford University, Law School, Stanford CA 94305, USA

Grundhofer, Jerry A — Financier
US Bancorp, 601 2nd Ave S, Minneapolis MN 55402, USA

Grundhofer, John F — Financier
Donaldson Co, 1400 W 94th St, Minneapolis MN 55431, USA

Grundman, Bernie — Music Executive
Bernie Grundman Mastering, 1640 N Gower St, Los Angeles CA 90028, USA

Grundt, Kenneth A (Ken) — Baseball Player
4814 W Parker Ave, Chicago IL 60639, USA

Grundy, Hugh — Drummer (Zombies)
Lustig Talent, PO Box 770850, Orlando FL 32877 USA

Grune, George V — Publisher, Foundation Executive
PO Box 2348, Ponte Vedra Beach FL 32004, USA

Gruneisen, Samuel K (Sam) — Football Player
569 Finsbay Court, Ocoee FL 34761, USA

Grunfeld, Ernest (Ernie) — Basketball Player, Executive
10121 Counselman Road, Potomac MD 20854, USA

Grunhard, Timothy G (Tim) — Football Player
2005 Arno Road, Mission Hills KS 66208, USA

Grunsfeld, John M — Astronaut
PO Box 279, Highland MD 20777, USA

Grunstein, Michael — Biological Chemist
University of California, Biological Chemistry Dept, Los Angeles CA 90024, USA

Grunwald, Alfred H (Al) — Baseball Player
21001 Plummer St, Chatsworth CA 91311, USA

Grunwald, Ernie — Actor
Stone Manners Salners, 9911 W Pico Blvd, #1400, Los Angeles CA 90035, USA

Grupp, Robert W (Bob) — Football Player
305 Hill Ave, Langhorne PA 19047, USA

Grusin, Dave — Composer, Pianist
Gorfaine/Schwartz, 4111 W Alameda Ave, #509, Burbank CA 91505 USA

Grutman, N Roy — Attorney
Grutman Miller Greenspoon Hendler, 505 Park Ave, New York NY 10022, USA

Gruttadauria, Michael J (Mike) 4250 Swift Road, Sarasota FL 34231, USA	Football Player
Grybauskaite, Dalia President's Office, Gediminas 53, 232026 Vilnius, Lithuania	President, Lithuania
Gryboski, Kevin 127 Castlebrooke Dr, Venetia PA 15367, USA	Baseball Player
Grylls, Edward M (Bear) Second Assn, Gilwell Park, Chingford, London E4 7QW, England	Entertainer, Writer, Mountaineer
Grzanich, Michael E (Mike) 176 Holliday Trace, Raymond MS 39154, USA	Baseball Player
Guang Yang Columbia Artists Mgmt Inc, 1790 Broadway, #702, New York NY 10019 USA	Opera Singer
Guanlao, Christopher Ink Tank Public Relations, 1824 W Sunset Blvd, #102, Los Angeles CA 90026, USA	Drummer (Silversun Pickps)
Guard, Christopher 76 Oxford St, London W1N 0AX, England	Actor
Guardado, Edward A (Eddie) 11268 Overlook Point, Tustin CA 92782, USA	Baseball Player
Guare, John R Andrew Boose, 1 Dag Hammarskjold Plaza, New York NY 10017, USA	Writer
Guarini, Justin Kazarian/Spencer/Ruskin, 11969 Ventura Blvd, #300, Studio City CA 91604 USA	Singer
Guaty, Camille B/W/R, 9100 Wilshire Blvd, #500W, Beverly Hills CA 90212 USA	Actress
Guay, Paul F 34 Kirkbrae Dr, Lincoln RI 02865, USA	Ice Hockey Player
Gubaidulina, Sofia A 2D Pugachevskaya 8, Korp 5, #130, 107061 Moscow, Russia	Composer
Gubanich, Creighton W 10 Galicia Dr, Phoenixville PA 19460, USA	Baseball Player
Gubanova, Ekaterina Mariinsky Theater, Theater Square, 1 PI Iskusstr, 190000 Saint Petersburg, Russia	Opera Singer
Gubarev, Aleksei A Cosmonaut Training Center, Star City, 141160 Zvezdny Gorodok, Moscow Oblast, Russia	Cosmonaut; Air Force General
Guber, Peter Mandalay Entertainment, 10202 W Washington Blvd, #1070, Culver City CA 90232, USA	Producer
Gubicza, Mark S 11808 Macoda Lane, Chatsworth CA 91311, USA	Baseball Player
Gubler, Matthew Gray Creative Artists Agency, 2000 Ave of Stars, #100, Los Angeles CA 90067 USA	Actor
Guccione, Christopher (Chris) 15362 W Iliff Dr, Denver CO 80228, USA	Baseball Umpire
Guckel, Henry University of Wisconsin, Engineering Dept, Madison WI 53706, USA	Microbiotics Engineer
Gudereit, Marcia Curling Assn, 1660 Vimont Court, Cumberland ON K4A 4J4, Canada	Curling Athlete
Gudgeon, Simon Halcyon Gallery, 144-146 New Bond St, London W1S 2PF, England	Sculptor
Gudmundsson, Petur 2423 Vibrant Oak, San Antonio TX 78232, USA	Basketball Player
Guebuza, Armando President's Office, Avenida Julius Nyerere 1780, Maputo, Mozambique	President, Mozambique
Guelleh, Ismail Omar President's Office, 8-10 Ahmed Nessim St, BP 109, Djibouti City, Djibouti	President, Djibouti
Guennel, Joe 835 Front Range Road, Littleton CO 80120, USA	Soccer
Gueno, James A (Jim) 6939 General Haig St, New Orleans LA 70124, USA	Football Player
Guenther, Johnny 23826 115th Place W, Woodway WA 98020, USA	Bowler
Guerard, Michel E Les Pres d'Eugenie, 40320 Eugenie les Bains, France	Chef
Guerin, Richard V (Richie) 1355 Bear Island Dr, West Palm Beach FL 33409, USA	Basketball Player
Guerin, Wiliam R (Bill) 12 North Road, Oyster Bay NY 11771, USA	Ice Hockey Player
Guerra, Eddie Creative Artists Agency, 2000 Ave of Stars, #100, Los Angeles CA 90067 USA	Actor
Guerra, Juan Luis Joyce Agency Entertainment, 370 Harrison Ave, Harrison NY 10528, USA	Singer, Songwriter
Guerra, Vida It Girl Public Relations, 225 1/2 Howland Canal, Venice CA 90291, USA	Actress, Model, Singer
Guerrero Coles, Lisa Lorraine Berglund Mgmt, 11537 Hesby St, North Hollywood CA 91601, USA	Sportscaster, Actress, Model
Guerrero, Giancarlo Opus 3 Artists, 470 Park Ave S, #900N, New York NY 10016 USA	Conductor
Guerrero, Julen A C Bilbao, Alameda Mazarredo 23, 48009 Bilbao, Spain	Soccer Player
Guerrero, Mario M Calle Duarte 450, 10211 Santo Domingo, Dominican Republic	Baseball Player
Guerrero, Pedro 10720 NW 66th St, #408, Doral FL 33178, USA	Baseball Player
Guerrero, Robert J (Ghost) 14810 Delano St, Van Nuys CA 91411, USA	Boxer
Guerrero, Roberto J 31642 Via Cervantes, San Juan Capistrano CA 92675, USA	Auto Racing Driver
Guerrero, Vladimir A 5160 E Copa de Oro Dr, Anaheim CA 92807, USA	Baseball Player
Guerrier, Matthew O (Matt) 200 Highland View Dr, Birmingham AL 35242, USA	Baseball Player
Guers, Paul 40 Rue de Buci, 75006 Paris, France	Actor
Guesmi, Samir Artmedia, 20 Ave Rapp, 75007 Paris, France	Actor
Guest, Christopher H United Talent Agency, 9336 Civic Center Dr, Beverly Hills CA 90210 USA	Director, Actor, Comedian

G

Guest, Cornelia
Brillstein Entertainment Partners, 9150 Wilshire Blvd, #350, Beverly Hills CA 90212 USA
Actor

Guest, Lance
116 Pinehurst Ave, #G23, New York NY 10033, USA
Actor

Guetary, Francois
Paola Bonelli Consulenza Cinematografica, 50, Viale Parioli, 00197 Rome, Italy
DJ Musician, Songwriter

Guetta, David
Creative Artists Agency, 2000 Ave of Stars, #100, Los Angeles CA 90067 USA
Composer, Lyricist

Guettel, Adam
Gersh Agency, 9465 Wilshire Blvd, #600, Beverly Hills CA 90212 USA
Baseball Player

Guetterman, A Lee
108 1/2 E Broadway St, Lenoir City TN 37771, USA
Baseball Player

Guevara, Carlos
501 S Crisp St, Uvalde TX 78801, USA
Businessman

Guffey, John W, Jr
Coltec Industries, 2550 W Tyvola Road, Charlotte NC 28217, USA
Auto Racing Driver

Gugelmin, Mauricio
Ave 7 de Septembre 4476-60-62, Cuiriba PR 80250210, Brazil
Inventor (Hydrogen Energy Processor)

Guggenheim, Alan
Northwest Power Systems, PO Box 5339, Bend OR 97708, USA
Director

Guggenheim, Davis
Electric Kinney Films, 1661 Lincoln Blvd, #101, Santa Monica CA 90404, USA
Actress

Gugino, Carla
Untitled Entertainment, 350 S Beverly Dr, #200, Beverly Hills CA 90212 USA
Football Player

Guglielmi, Ralph V
159 Red Berry Dr, Wallace NC 28466, USA
Basketball Player

Gugliotta, Thomas J (Tom)
1267 Francis St NW, Atlanta GA 30318, USA
Cartoonist (Resurrection Man)

Guice, Jackson
D C Comics, 1700 Broadway, #400, New York NY 10019 USA
Actress

Guida, Gloria
C D A Studio di Nardo, Via Cavour 171, 00184 Rome, Italy
Harness Racing Driver, Trainer

Guida, Louis P (Lou)
173 San Remo Dr, Jupiter FL 33458, USA
Conductor

Guidarini, Marco
I M G Artists, Hogarth Business Park, Chiswick, London W4 2TH, England
Basketball Player

Guidinger, Jay P
N39W22702 Grandview Dr, Pewaukee WI 53072, USA
Ice Hockey Player

Guidolin, Aldo
34 Blair Dr, Guelph ON N1L 1N7, Canada
Astronaut

Guidoni, Umberto
European Space Center, Linder Hohe, Box 906096, 51127 Cologne, Germany
Thoroughbred Racing Jockey

Guidry, Mark
102 S William Dr, Lafayette LA 70506, USA
Aeronautical Engineer

Guidry, N T
23971 Coral Springs Lane, Tehachapi CA 93561, USA
Football Player

Guidry, Paul M
880 Noel Dr, Mount Juliet TN 37122, USA
Baseball Player

Guidry, Ronald A (Ron)
PO Box 278, Scott LA 70583, USA
Baseball Player

Guiel, Aaron
18944 69th Ave, Surrey BC V4N 5K1, Canada
Handball Player

Guigou, Michael
Montpellier Agglomeration H B, 1000 Ave du val de Montferrand, 34090 Montpellier, France
Actress

Guilbert, Ann
550 Erskine Dr, Pacific Palisades CA 90272, USA
Actor

Guilfoyle, Paul
S M S Talent, 8383 Wilshire Blvd, #230, Beverly Hills CA 90211 USA
Actress

Guill, Julianna
Luber Rocklin Entertainment, 8530 Wilshire Blvd, #555, Beverly Hills CA 90211 USA
Hereditary Grand Duke, Luxembourg

Guillaume
Palais Grand-Ducal, 17 Rue du Marche-aux-Herbes, 1728 Luxembourg-Ville, Luxembourg
Actor

Guillaume, Robert
Alan David Mgmt, 8840 Wilshire Blvd, #200, Beverly Hills CA 90211, USA
Ballerina

Guillem, Sylvie
Royal Ballet, Covent Garden, Bow St, London WC2E 9DD, England
Nobel Medicine Laureate

Guillemin, Roger C L
7316 Encelia Ave, La Jolla CA 92037, USA
Baseball Player, Manager

Guillen, Oswaldo J (Ozzie)
19462 38th Court, Golden Beach FL 33160, USA
Director

Guillerman, John
309 S Rockingham Ave, Los Angeles CA 90049, USA
Actor

Guillo, Dominique
Agence Artiste Adequet, 80 Rue d'Amsterdam, 75009 Paris, France
Actress

Guillory, Sienna
United Talent Agency, 9336 Civic Center Dr, Beverly Hills CA 90210 USA
Speed Skater

Guilmette, Jonathan
Speed Skating Canada, 2781 Lancaster Road, #402, Ottawa ON K1B 1A7, Canada
Cartoonist (Guindon)

Guindon, Richard G
321 W Lafayette Blvd, Detroit MI 48226, USA
Baseball Player

Guindon, Robert J (Bob)
437 Marsh Creek Road, Venice FL 34292, USA
Actor

Guinee, Tim
Innovative Artists, 1505 10th St, Santa Monica CA 90401 USA
Attorney, Educator

Guinier, Lani
University of Pennsylvania, Law School, 3400 Chestnut, Philadelphia PA 19104, USA
Baseball Player

Guinn, Drannon E (Skip)
PO Box 911, Stilwell OK 74960, USA
Actor, Comedian

Guirgis, Stephen Adly
Anonymous Content, 3532 Hayden Ave, Culver City CA 90232 USA
Actor

Guiry, Tom
Gersh Agency, 9465 Wilshire Blvd, #600, Beverly Hills CA 90212 USA
Cartoonist (Cathy)

Guisewite, Cathy L
4039 Camilla Ave, Studio City CA 91604, USA
Actress

Guiter, Sophie
Artmedia, 20 Ave Rapp, 75007 Paris, France

V.I.P. Address Book

Guest - Guiter

Gujral, Inder Kumar
5 Janpath, New Delhi 11011, India — Prime Minister, India

Gul, Abdullah
President's Office, Cumhurbaskanlgl Kosku, Cankaya, 06689 Ankara, Turkey — President, Turkey

Gulan, Michael W (Mike)
4409 Fairway Dr, Steubenville OH 43953, USA — Baseball Player

Gulbinowicx, Henryk Roman Cardinal
Metropolita Wroclawski, Ul Katedraina 11, 50 328 Wroclaw, Poland — Religious Leader

Gulbis, Natalie
7733 Glenn Ave, Citrus Heights CA 95610, USA — Golfer, Model

Gulden, Bradford L (Brad)
15820 Lundstead Road, Carver MN 55315, USA — Baseball Player

Guleghina, Maria
I M G Artists, 152 W 57th St, #500, New York NY 10019 USA — Opera Singer

Gullett, Donald E (Don)
194 Kingsway Dr, South Shore KY 41175, USA — Baseball Player

Gullickson, William L (Bill)
3 Banchory Court, Palm Beach Gardens FL 33418, USA — Baseball Player

Gulliver, Harold
Atlanta Constitution, 223 Perimeter Center Parkway NE, Atlanta GA 30346, USA — Editor

Gullotta, Leo
Carol Levi Mgmt, Via G Pisanelli 2, 00196 Rome, Italy — Actor

Gulutzan, Glen
Dallas Stars, 2601 Ave of Stars, #100, Frisco TX 75034 USA — Hockey Coach

Gulyas, Denes
Hungarian State Opera, Andrassy Utca 22, 1061 Budapest, Hungary — Opera Singer

Gulzar
Boskiyana Pali Hill, Bandra (W), Mumbai MS 400050, India — Director, Songwriter

Guman, Michael D (Mike)
3913 Pleasant Ave, Allentown PA 18103, USA — Football Player

Gumbel, Bryant C
Home Box Office, 1100 Ave of Americas, Front 300, New York NY 10036 USA — Commentator

Gumbel, Greg
10372 N Lake Vista Circle, Davie FL 33328, USA — Sportscaster

Gummer, Grace
Creative Artists Agency, 2000 Ave of Stars, #100, Los Angeles CA 90067 USA — Actress

Gummer, Mamie
Creative Artists Agency, 2000 Ave of Stars, #100, Los Angeles CA 90067 USA — Actress

Gummersall, Devon
A P A Talent/Literary Agency, 405 S Beverly Dr, #300, Beverly Hills CA 90212 USA — Actor

Gump, Scott
8013 Old Town Dr, Orlando FL 32819, USA — Golfer

Gumpert, David L (Dave)
68371 Fleetwood Dr, South Haven MI 49090, USA — Baseball Player

Gund, Agnes
Museum of Modern Art, 11 W 53rd St, New York NY 10019, USA — Museum Executive

Gund, Graham
47 Thorndike St, #1, Cambridge MA 02141, USA — Architect

Gunderson, Eric A
19809 SE 10th St, Camas WA 98607, USA — Baseball Player

Gundi
RR 1, Roseneath ON K0K 2X0, Canada — Artist

Gunesekera, Romesh
A M Heath Co, 79 Saint Martin's Lane, London WC2N 4RE, England — Writer

Gunn, Anna
United Talent Agency, 9336 Civic Center Dr, Beverly Hills CA 90210 USA — Actress

Gunn, Chanda L
74 Rockcroft Road, Weymouth MA 02188, USA — Ice Hockey Player

Gunn, James E
Princeton University, Astrophysics Dept, Princeton NJ 08544, USA — Astrophysicist

Gunn, Janet
David Shapira Assoc, 193 N Robertson Blvd, Beverly Hills CA 90211 USA — Actress

Gunn, Lee F
Public Research Institute, CNA Corp, 4825 Mark Center Dr, Alexandria VA 22311, USA — Navy Admiral

Gunn, Nathan
Opus 3 Artists, 470 Park Ave S, #900N, New York NY 10016 USA — Concert, Opera Singer

Gunn, Richard
Thruline Entertainment, 9250 Wilshire Blvd, #100, Beverly Hills CA 90212 USA — Actor

Gunn, Sean
Stone Manners Salners, 9911 W Pico Blvd, #1400, Los Angeles CA 90035 USA — Actor

Gunnarsson, Martin
3536 Saint Marys Road, #D24, Columbus GA 31906, USA — Marksman

Gunnell, Owen
Sony/BMI Records, 550 Madison Ave, #600, New York NY 10022, USA — Concert Percussionist (O Duo)

Gunnell, Sally
Old School Cottage, School Lane, Pycombe, West Sussex BN45 7FQ, England — Track Athlete

Gunnels, J Riley
606 Wesley Ave, Ocean City NJ 08226, USA — Football Player

Gunnestad, Stig-Arne
Curling Assn, Sognsveien 75, Serviceboks 1, 0840 Oslo, Norway — Curling Athlete

Gunther, Dan
Century Artists, PO Box 59747, Santa Barbara CA 93150 USA — Actor

Gunther, David C (Dave)
4510 Cherry St, Grand Forks ND 58201, USA — Basketball Player

Gunton, Bob
Abrams Artists, 275 7th Ave, #2600, New York NY 10001 USA — Actor

Guokas, Matthew G (Matt), Jr
2410 S 19th St, Philadelphia PA 19145, USA — Basketball Player, Coach, Executive

Guolla, Steve
733 Spartan Dr, Rochester Hills MI 48309, USA — Ice Hockey Player

Gupta, Amit
United Agents, 12-26 Lexington St, London W1F 0LE, England — Director

Gupta, Modadugu V
Jalan Batu Maung, Batu Maung 11960 Bayan Lepas, Penang, Malaysia — Fish Culture Scientist

Gupta, Raj
Rohm & Haas Co, 100 S Independence Mall W, #1A, Philadelphia PA 19106, USA — Businessman

G

Gage - Gupta

Gupta, Sudhir — Immunologist
University of California, Medicine Dept, Irvine CA 92717, USA

Gupton, Damon — Actor
Harden-Curtis Associates, 850 7th Ave, #903, New York NY 10019, USA

Gur, Mordechai — Army General, Israel
25 Mishmeret St, Afeka, Tel-Aviv 69694, Israel

Gura, Larry C — Baseball Player
PO Box 94, Litchfield Park AZ 85340, USA

Gurdon, John B — Nobel Medicine Laureate
Whittlesford Grove, Whittlesford, Cambridge CB2 4NZ, England

Guren, Peter — Cartoonist (Ask Shagg, Committed)
Creators Syndicate, 737 3rd St, Hermosa Beach CA 90254 USA

Gurewitz, Brett W — Guitarist (Bad Religion)
Goldstar Public Relations, PO Box 130, Ross on Wye HR9 6WY, England

Gurgenidze, Vladimer (Lado) — Prime Minister, Georgia
Premier's Office, Government House, Ingorkva 7, 380034 Tbilsi, Georgia

Gurian, Michael — Psychotherapist, Social Philosopher
417 W 32nd Ave, Spokane WA 99203, USA

Gurira, Danai Jekesai — Actress
Paradigm Agency, 360 N Crescent Dr, North Building, Beverly Hills CA 90210 USA

Gurnah, Abdulrazak — Writer
Roger Coleridge White, 20 Powis Mews, London W11 1KN, England

Gurnett, Jane — Actress
Hamilton Hodell, 66-68 Margaret St, London W1W 8SR, England

Gurney, Albert R (A R), Jr — Writer
Gersh Agency, 9465 Wilshire Blvd, #600, Beverly Hills CA 90212 USA

Gurney, Daniel S (Dan) — Auto Racing Driver, Executive
All-American Racers Inc, 2334 S Broadway, Santa Ana CA 92707, USA

Gurney, Hilda — Equestrian
8430 Waters Road, Moorpark CA 93021, USA

Gurney, James — Writer, Illustrator
PO Box 693, Rhinebeck NY 12572, USA

Gurraggchaa, Jugderdemidijn — Cosmonaut, Mongolia; Air Force General
Lyotchik Kosmonavt, MNR, Central Post Office Box 378, Ulan Bator, Mongolia

Gursky, Andreas — Photographer
Matthew Marks Gallery, 123 W 24th St, New York NY 10011, USA

Gurung, Prabal — Fashion Designer
209 W 38th St, #1211, New York NY 10018, USA

Gurwitch, Annabelle — Actress
TalentWorks, 3500 W Olive Ave, #1400, Burbank CA 91505 USA

Guryakova, Olga — Opera Singer
I M G Artists, Hogarth Business Park, Chiswick, London W4 2TH, England

Gusarov, Alexei — Ice Hockey Player
1168 Yankee Creek Road, Evergreen CO 80439, USA

Gusella, James — Biologist
Harvard Medical School, 25 Shattuck St, Boston MA 02115, USA

Gusenbauer, Alfred — Chancellor, Austria
Chancellor's Office, Ballhausplatz 2, 1014, Vienna, Austria

Gushue, Brad — Curling Athlete
Curling Assn, 1660 Vimont Court, Cumberland ON K4A 4J4, Canada

Gusmao, Jose Alexandre (Xanana) — Prime Minister, Timor-Leste
Prime Minister's Office, Government Palace, President Nicolau Lobato Ave, Dili, Timor-Leste

Gustafson, Elisabet — Curling Athlete
Curling Assn, Idrottshuser, Marbackagatan 19, 123 43 Farsta, Sweden

Gustafson, Kathryn — Landscape Architect
Gustafson Guthrie Nichol, Pier 55, #31101, Alaskan Way, Seattle WA 98101, USA

Gustafson, Steven — Bassist (10000 Maniacs)
Geffen Records, 10900 Wilshire Blvd, #1000, Los Angeles CA 90024 USA

Gustafsson, Per — Ice Hockey Player
5605 NE 3rd Ave, Fort Lauderdale FL 33334, USA

Gustin, Grant — Actor
C E S D, 10635 Santa Monica Blvd, #130, Los Angeles CA 90025 USA

Guterres, Antonio Manuel de Oliveira — Prime Minister, Portugal
U N High Commission for Refugees, CP 2500, 1211 Geneva 2, Switzerland

Guterson, David — Writer
Georges Borchardt, 136 E 57th St, #1400, New York NY 10022, USA

Guth, Alan H — Physicist
Massachusetts Institute of Technology, Physics Dept, Cambridge MA 02139, USA

Guthe, Manfred — Cinematographer
122 Collier St, Toronto ON M4W 1M3, Canada

Guthe, Nick — Writer, Director, Producer
Artist International Mgmt, 9107 Wilshire Blvd, #600, Beverly Hills CA 90210, USA

Guthrie, Arlo — Singer, Guitarist, Songwriter
Rising Son Records, 218 Beach Road, Washington MA 01223, USA

Guthrie, Janet — Auto Racing Driver
PO Box 505, Aspen CO 81612, USA

Guthrie, Jeremy S — Baseball Player
1004 Clay St, Ashland OR 97520, USA

Guthrie, Mark A — Baseball Player
3129 Donald Rosse Road E, Sarasota FL 34240, USA

Guthrie, Savannah C — Commentator
NBC-TV, News Dept, 30 Rockefeller Plaza, #270E, New York NY 10112 USA

Guthy, Jackson — Singer
Creative Artists Agency, 2000 Ave of Stars, #100, Los Angeles CA 90067 USA

Gutierrez, Brock — Football Player
1040 Pueblo Pass, Weidman MI 48893, USA

Gutierrez, Carlos M — Businessman
Woodrow Wilson Center, 1300 Pennsylvania Ave NW, #300, Washington DC 20004, USA

Gutierrez, Diego — Producer, Writer
Creative Artists Agency, 2000 Ave of Stars, #100, Los Angeles CA 90067 USA

Gutierrez, F Javier — Director
Paradigm Agency, 360 N Crescent Dr, North Building, Beverly Hills CA 90210 USA

Gutierrez, Franklin R — Baseball Player
5130 Preferred Place, Hilliard OH 43026, USA

Gutierrez, Gustavo — Theologian
Instituto Bartolome Las Casas-Rimac, Apartado 3090, Lima 100, Peru

Gutierrez, Horacio
C M Artists, 127 W 96th St, #13B, New York NY 10025 USA — Concert Pianist
Gutierrez, Joaquin F (Jackie)
10631 SW 126th Ave, Miami FL 33186, USA — Baseball Player
Gutierrez, Ricardo (Ricky)
13803 NW 10th Court, Pembroke Pines FL 33028, USA — Baseball Player
Gutierrez, Sidney M
324 Sarah Lane NW, Albuquerque NM 87114, USA — Astronaut
Gutman, Natalia G
Augstein & Hahn, Tal 28, 80331 Munich, Germany — Concert Cellist
Gutman, Roy W
1349 Windy Hill Road, McLean VA 22102, USA — Journalist
Gutmann, Amy
University of Pennsylvania, President's Office, 3451 Walnut St, Philadelphia PA 19104, USA — Educator
Gutsche, Torsten
Hans-Marchwitza-Ring 51, 14473 Potsdam, Germany — Canoeing Athlete
Guttenberg, Steve
Chuck Binder Mgmt, 1465 Lindacrest Dr, Beverly Hills CA 90210 USA — Actor
Guttman, Ronald
Don Buchwald/Fortitude, 6500 Wilshire Blvd, #2200, Los Angeles CA 90048 USA — Actor
Guy, Buddy
Buddy Guy's Legends, 754 S Wabash Ave, Chicago IL 60605, USA — Singer, Guitarist
Guy, Francois-Frederic
Van Walsum Mgmt, Tower Building, 11 York Road, London SE1 7NX, England — Concert Pianist
Guy, Jasmine
Kass & Stokes Mgmt, 9229 W Sunset Blvd, #504, Los Angeles CA 90069 USA — Actress
Guy, Ralph B, Jr
US Court of Appeals, PO Box 7910, Ann Arbor MI 48107, USA — Judge
Guy, W Ray
936 Central Road SW, Thomson GA 30824, USA — Football Player
Guy, William L
225 13th Ave W, #204, West Fargo ND 58078, USA — Governor, ND
Guyer, Cindy
2 Lincoln Square, New York NY 10023, USA — Model, Producer
Guyer, David B
Save the Children Foundation, 514 2nd St, Owyhee NV 89832, USA — Foundation Executive
Guyot, Paul
Gersh Agency, 9465 Wilshire Blvd, #600, Beverly Hills CA 90212 USA — Actor, Writer
Guyton, Myron M
PO Box 3481, Thomasville GA 31799, USA — Football Player
Guzman Pinal, Alejandra G
B M G, 1540 Broadway, #9E, New York NY 10036, USA — Singer, Actress
Guzman, Jose A
4401 Shadycreek Lane, Colleyville TX 76034, USA — Baseball Player
Guzman, Juan A
176 Dockside Circle, Weston FL 33327, USA — Baseball Player
Guzman, Luis
Gersh Agency, 9465 Wilshire Blvd, #600, Beverly Hills CA 90212 USA — Actor
Guzman, Ryan
Luber Rocklin Entertainment, 8530 Wilshire Blvd, #555, Beverly Hills CA 90211 USA — Actor
Guzman, Santiago D
1712 N Douty St, Hanford CA 93230, USA — Baseball Player
Guzy, Carol
2412 Fort Scott Dr, Arlington VA 22202, USA — Photojournalist
Gwinn, Mary Ann
Seattle Times, Editorial Dept, 1120 John St, Seattle WA 98109 USA — Journalist
Gwynn, Anthony K (Tony)
San Diego State University, Athletic Dept, San Diego CA 92182, USA — Baseball Player, Coach
Gwynn, Christopher K (Chris)
10975 Hillside Road, Rancho Cucamonga. CA 91737, USA — Baseball Player
Gwynn, Darrell
Darrell Gwynn Ventures, 4850 SW 52nd St, Davie FL 33314, USA — Drag Racing Driver
Gyanendra
Royal Palace, Narayanhiti, Durbag Marg, Kathmandu, Nepal — King, Nepal
Gyll, J Soren
Volvo AB, 405 08 Goteborg, Sweden — Businessman
Gyllenhaal, Jake
W M E Entertainment, 9601 Wilshire Blvd, #300, Beverly Hills CA 90210 USA — Actor
Gyllenhaal, Maggie
Schiff Co, 8440 Warner Dr, #B1, Culver City CA 90232 USA — Actress
Gyllenhaal, Stephen
Gersh Agency, 9465 Wilshire Blvd, #600, Beverly Hills CA 90212 USA — Director, Writer, Actor
Gyllenhammar, Pehr G
C G U, Saint Helen's, 1 Undershaft, London EC3P 3DQ, England — Businessman
Gyurcsany, Ferenc
Prime Minister's Office, Kossuth Lajos Ter 1-3, 1055 Budapest, Hungary — Prime Minister, Hungary
GZA
A&E Entertainment, 13280 NE Freeway, #F328, Houston TX 77040, USA — Rap Artist (Wu-Tang Clan)

Ha Jin — Writer
Emory University, English Dept, Atlanta GA 30332, USA
Haack, Susan — Philosopher
University of Miami, Philosophy Dept, Coral Gables FL 33124, USA
Haacke, Hans C — Artist
Paula Cooper, 534 W 21st St, New York NY 10011, USA
Haag, Anna M — Cross Country Skier
Swedish Ski Federation, Riksskidstadion, 791 19 Falun, Sweden
Haag, Rudolf — Theoretical Physicist
Waldschmidt Str 4B, 83727 Schliersee-Neuhaus, Germany
Haake, James — Actor
1256 N Flores, #1, West Hollywood CA 90069, USA
Haakon — Crown Prince, Norway
Royal Palace, Det Kongelige Slott, Drammensveien 1, 0010 Oslo, Norway
Haarhuis, Paul — Tennis Player
Octagon Worldwide, 1751 Pinnacle Dr, #1500, McLean VA 22102 USA
Haas, Bryan E (Moose) — Baseball Player
4351 E Lariat Lane, Phoenix AZ 85050, USA
Haas, Carl — Auto Racing Executive
Newman-Haas Racing, 500 Tower Parkway, Lincolnshire IL 60069, USA
Haas, Ed — Photographer
180 W End Ave, #11C, New York NY 10023, USA
Haas, G Edwin (Eddie) — Baseball Player, Manager
8314 Alpena Way, Louisville KY 40242, USA
Haas, Hunter J — Golfer
6424 Barkwood Lane, Dallas TX 75248, USA
Haas, Jay D — Golfer
4 Tuscany Court, Greer SC 29650, USA
Haas, Lukas — Actor
Innovative Artists, 1505 10th St, Santa Monica CA 90401 USA
Haas, R David (Dave) — Baseball Player
160 E 6th Place, Mesa AZ 85201, USA
Haas, Richard J — Artist
361 W 36th St, #5A, New York NY 10018, USA
Haas, Robert D — Businessman
Levi Strauss Assoc, 1155 Battery St, San Francisco CA 94111, USA
Haas, Thomas (Tommy) — Tennis Player
Thomas Haas Tennis Academy, Lindenstr 12, 83043 Bad Aibling, Germany
Haas, Victoria — Actress
Leudtke Agency, 1674 Broadway, #7A, New York NY 10019, USA
Haas, William H — Golfer
Professional Golfer's Assn, PO Box 109601, Palm Beach Gardens FL 33410 USA
Haataja, Samuli (J J) — Singer, Bassist (Crash)
Welldone Agency, Hameentie 15, 00500 Helsinki, Finland
Haavisto, Nina — Body Builder
Aleksanterinkatu 29 B 29, 15040 Lahti, Finland
Habek, Janine — Model
Playboy Promotions, 2706 Media Center Dr, Los Angeles CA 90065 USA
Habel, Karl — Medical Researcher
Reading Institute of Rehabilitation, RR 1 Box 252, Reading PA 19607, USA
Habeler, Peter — Mountaineer
Apinschule Mount Everest, Haupstra 458, 6290 Mayrhofen Zillertal, Austria
Haber, Karen — Writer
2270 N Beachwood Terrace, Los Angeles CA 90068, USA
Haber, Norman — Inventor (Electromolecular Propulsion)
Haber Inc, 470 Main Road, Towaco NJ 07082, USA
Habib, Brian R — Football Player
17235 Sangallo Lane, San Diego CA 92127, USA
Habib, Hasan — Poker Player
World Poker Tour Enterprises, 5700 Wilshire Blvd, #350, Los Angeles CA 90036 USA
Habib, Munir — Cosmonaut, Syria
Cosmonaut Training Center, Star City, 141160 Zvezdny Gorodok, Moscow Oblast, Russia
Habibie, Baharuddin Jusuf — President, Indonesia
Bina Craha, Istana Negana, Jarkata 10110, Indonesia
Habiger, Eugene E (Gene) — Air Force General
University of Georgia, International Trade & Security Center, Athens GA 30602, USA
Habumuremyi, Pierre Damien — Prime Minister, Rwanda
Prime Minister's Office, Kigali, Rwanda
Habyan, John G — Baseball Player
4 Dorfer Lane, Nesconset NY 11767, USA
Hachette, Jean-Louis — Publisher
Hachette Livre, 83 Ave Marceau, 75116 Paris, France
Hack, Shelley — Actress, Model
Deborah Miller, 9454 Wilshire Blvd, #715, Beverly Hills CA 90212, USA
Hackbart, Dale L — Football Player
2541 Cowley Dr, Lafayette CO 80026, USA
Hacke, Axel — Writer
Bloomsbury Publishing, 36 Soho Square, London W1D 3Q4, England
Hacker, Alan — Concert Clarinetist, Composer
Royal Academy of Music, Marylebone Road, London NW1 5HT, England
Hacker, Joseph — Actor
University of Southern California, Theater School, Los Angeles CA 90089, USA
Hackett, B Dean (Dino) — Football Player
1152 Kearns Hackett Road, Pleasant Garden NC 27313, USA
Hackett, Grant — Swimmer
Swimming Australia, PO Box 3286, Belconnen ACT 2617, Australia
Hackett, James T — Businessman
Anadarko Petroleum, 1201 Lake Robbins Dr, Spring TX 77380, USA
Hackett, Jeff — Ice Hockey Player
Colorado Avalanche, Pepsi Center, 1000 Chopper Circle, Denver CO 80204 USA
Hackett, Rudy — Basketball Player
10330 Downey Ave, #30, Downey CA 90241, USA
Hackett, Steve — Guitarist (Genesis)
Solo Agency, 53-55 Fulham High St, #200, London SW6 3JJ, England
Hackford, Taylor — Director, Producer
2003 La Brea Terrace, Los Angeles CA 90046, USA

Hackl, Georg
Caftehaus Soamatl, Ramsauerstr 100, 83471 Berchtesgaden-Engedey, Germany — Luge Athlete

Hackman, Gene
Guttman Assoc, 118 S Beverly Dr, #201, Beverly Hills CA 90212 USA — Actor

Hackman, Luther G
1406 12th Ave N, #16G, Columbus MS 39701, USA — Baseball Player

Hackney, F Sheldon
University of Pennsylvania, History Dept, Philadelphia PA 19104, USA — Educator

Hadas, Rachel C
838 W End Ave, #3A, New York NY 10025, USA — Writer, Educator

Haddix, Michael M
614 Fox Run Road, Sewell NJ 08080, USA — Football Player

Haddock, Marcus
Columbia Artists Mgmt Inc, 1790 Broadway, #702, New York NY 10019 USA — Opera Singer

Haddon, Dayle
Hyperion Books, 114 5th Ave, New York NY 10011 USA — Actress, Model

Haddon, Laurence
14950 Sutton St, Sherman Oaks CA 91403, USA — Actor

Hadek, Krystof
Markham & Froggatt, Julian House, 4 Windmill St, London W1P 1HF, England — Actor

Haden, Charles E (Charlie)
Michael Kline Artists, PO Box 312, Cape May Point NJ 08212, USA — Jazz Bassist, Composer

Haden, Patrick C (Pat)
1525 Wilson Ave, San Marino CA 91108, USA — Football Player, Sportscaster

Hader, Bill
Odenkirk Provissiero Entertainment, 650 N Bronson Ave, #B145, Los Angeles CA 90004 USA — Actor, Comedian

Hadfield, Chris A
N A S A, Johnson Space Center, 2101 NASA Road, Houston TX 77058 USA — Astronaut, Canada

Hadid, Zaha
Studio 9, 10 Bowling Green Lane, London WC1R 0BD, England — Pritzker Architectural Laureate

Hadjii
Paradigm Agency, 360 N Crescent Dr, North Building, Beverly Hills CA 90210 USA — Director, Writer

Hadl, John W
3700 Quail Creek Court, Lawrence KS 66047, USA — Football Player

Hadlee, Richard J
PO Box 29186, Fendalton, Christchurch 8540, New Zealand — Cricketer

Hadley, Stephen
White House, 1600 Pennsylvania Ave NW, Washington DC 20500, USA — Government Official

Hadley, Tony
Universal Records, 70 Universal City Plaza, Universal City CA 91608 USA — Singer (Spandau Ballet)

Hadnot, J Rex, Jr
2677 Center Court Dr, Weston FL 33332, USA — Football Player

Hadnott, Joy
M P G Mgmt, 1136 Roxbury Drive, Los Angeles CA 90035, USA — Actress

Haebler, Ingrid
5412 Saint Jakob am Thurn, Post Puch Bei Hallein, 5020 Land Salzburg, Austria — Concert Pianist

Haefliger, Andrea
Opus 3 Artists, 470 Park Ave S, #900N, New York NY 10016 USA — Concert Pianist

Haegele, Patricia
Good Housekeeping, Publisher's Office, 300 W 57th St, New York NY 10019, USA — Publisher

Haenchen, Hartmut
Van Walsum Mgmt, Tower Building, 11 York Road, London SE1 7NX, England — Conductor

Haensch, Theodor W
Ludwig-Maximilian University, Geschwister-Scholl, 80539 Munich, Germany — Nobel Physics Laureate

Hafer, Fred D
G P U Inc, 300 Madison Ave, Morristown NJ 07960, USA — Businessman

Haffner, Scott R
5062 Sweetwater Dr, Noblesville IN 46062, USA — Basketball Player

Hafner, Dudley H
140 Estrada Maya, Santa Fe NM 87506, USA — Foundation Executive

Hafner, Travis L
32696 Lake Road, Avon Lake OH 44012, USA — Baseball Player

Hagan, Clifford O (Cliff)
8839 Lakeside Circle, Vero Beach FL 32963, USA — Basketball Player, Coach

Hagan, Derek S, Jr
14611 SW 7th St, Pembroke Pines FL 33027, USA — Football Player

Hagan, Glenn
34 Roth St, Rochester NY 14621, USA — Basketball Player

Hagan, Molly
Paul Kohner, 9300 Wilshire Blvd, #555, Beverly Hills CA 90212 USA — Actress

Hagan, Victoria
Victoria Hagan Interiors, 654 Madison Ave, #2201, New York NY 10065, USA — Interior Designer

Hagar, Sammy
Rogers & Cowan, 8687 Melrose Ave, #G700, West Hollywood CA 90069 USA — Singer, Songwriter, Guitarist

Hagee, Michael W
Rackable Systems, 46600 Landing Parkway, Fremont CA 94538, USA — Marine Corps General

Hagegard, Hakan
Gunnarsbyn, 670 30 Edane, Sweden — Opera Singer

Hageman, Fred J
4608 Merion Court, Lawrence KS 66047, USA — Football Player

Hagemeister, Charles C
1908 Canterbury Court, Leavenworth KS 66048, USA — Vietnam War Army Hero (CMH)

Hagen, Halvor R
32 Algonquin Road, Canton MA 02021, USA — Football Player

Hagen, Kevin E
24826 164th Ave SE, Covington WA 98042, USA — Baseball Player

Hagen, Nina
Kork Agency, 1880 Century Park E, #711, Los Angeles CA 90067, USA — Singer

Hagen, Reinhard
I M G Artists, Hogarth Business Park, Chiswick, London W4 2TH, England — Opera Singer

Hagenbeck, Franklin L
Superintendent's Office, US Military Academy, West Point NY 10996 USA — Army General, Educator

Hager, Britt H
6200 Indian Canyon Dr, Austin TX 78746, USA — Football Player

Hager, Kristen
Magnolia Entertainment, 9595 Wilshire Blvd, #601, Beverly Hills CA 90212, USA — Actress

Hagerman, Jamie — Ice Hockey Player
USA Hockey, 1775 Bob Johnson Dr, Colorado Springs CO 80906 USA

Hagerty, Julie — Actress
The Firm, 2049 Century Park E, #2550, Los Angeles CA 90067 USA

Hagerty, Michael (Mike) — Actor
Mark Holder Mgmt, 5225 Wilshire Blvd, #600, Los Angeles CA 90036, USA

Haggard, Merle — Singer, Songwriter
Department 56, 22410 Collins St, Woodland Hills CA 91367, USA

Haggard, Piers — Director
Casorotto Ramsay, Waverley House, 7-12 Noel St, London W1F 8GQ, England

Hagge, Marlene Bauer — Golfer
PO Box 570, La Quinta CA 92247, USA

Haggerty, Dan — Actor
Collective, 8383 Wilshire Blvd, #1050, Beverly Hills CA 90211 USA

Haggerty, Dylan — Actor, Writer, Director
KillerMoxie Mgmt, 5890 W Jefferson Blvd, #J, Los Angeles CA 90016, USA

Haggerty, Tim — Cartoonist (Ground Zero)
PO Box 4203, New York NY 10163, USA

Haggis, Paul E — Director, Writer
Hwy61, 1660 Euclid, Santa Monica CA 90404, USA

Hagins, Isaac B (Ike) — Football Player
9008 Tudor Dr, #105, Tampa FL 33615, USA

Hagler, Marvin — Boxer
Valerie Sweet, 1 Design Center Place, #600, Boston MA 02210, USA

Haglund, Kirsten — Beauty Queen
Miss America Organization, 1370 Ave of Americas, #1600, New York NY 10019 USA

Hagman, Niklas O — Ice Hockey Player
48 Crimson Rose, Irvine CA 92603, USA

Hagn, Johanna — Judo Athlete
A S G Elsdorf, Behrgasse 6, 50198 Elsdorf, Germany

Hagner, Meredith — Actress
Abrams Artists, 9200 W Sunset Blvd, #1125, West Hollywood CA 90069, USA

Hagner, Viviane — Concert Violinist
Kirshbaum Demler, 711 W End Ave, #5KN, New York NY 10025, USA

Hagon, Garrick — Actor
Conway Van Gelder Grant, 8-12 Broadwick St, #300, London W1F 8HW, England

Hague, William J — Government Official, England
House of Commons, Westminster, London SW1A 0AA, England

Hahn, Beatrice H — Microbiologist
University of Alabama Medical School, Microbiology Dept, Birmingham AL 35294, USA

Hahn, Donald A (Don) — Baseball Player
1046 Boise Dr, Campbell CA 95008, USA

Hahn, Erwin L — Physicist
69 Stevenson Ave, Berkeley CA 94708, USA

Hahn, Frank H — Economist
16 Adams Road, Cambridge CB3 9AD, England

Hahn, Hilary — Concert Violinist
Lovell House, 616 Chiswick High Road, London W4 5RX, England

Hahn, Jessica — Model, Actress
6345 Balboa Blvd, #375, Encino CA 91316, USA

Hahn, Joseph — DJ Musician (Linkin Park)
United Talent Agency, 9336 Civic Center Dr, Beverly Hills CA 90210 USA

Hahn, Kathryn — Actress
Gersh Agency, 41 Madison Ave, #3301, New York NY 10010 USA

Haid, Charles — Actor, Director
4376 Forman Ave, Toluca Lake CA 91602, USA

Haiduk, Stacy — Actress
Stone Manners Salners, 9911 W Pico Blvd, #1400, Los Angeles CA 90035 USA

Haig, Matt — Writer
A P Watt, 20 John St, London WC1N 2DR, England , USA

Haig, Sid — Actor
Don Buchwald/Fortitude, 6500 Wilshire Blvd, #2200, Los Angeles CA 90048 USA

Haight, Michael (Mike) — Football Player
2401 Biltmore Lane, Coralville IA 52241, USA

Haignere, Jean-Pierre — Spatinaut, France
C N E S, 2 Place Maurice Quentin, 75039 Paris Cedeux, France

Hailemaria-Mariam Desalegn — Prime Minister, Ethiopia
Prime Minister's Office, PO Box 1031, Addis Ababa, Ethiopia

Hailey, Cedric (K-Ci) — Singer (Jodeci, Ki-C & JoJo)
Red Entertainment Agency, 16 Penn Plaza, #824, New York NY 10001, USA

Hailey, Joel L (JoJo) — Singer (Jodeci, K-Ci & JoJo)
Creative Artists Agency, 2000 Ave of Stars, #100, Los Angeles CA 90067 USA

Hailey, Leisha — Singer (Murmurs), Songwriter, Actress
Innovative Artists, 1505 10th St, Santa Monica CA 90401 USA

Hailston, Earl B — Marine Corps General
Commanding General, Marine Force Central Asia, HqUSMC, Washington DC 20380, USA

Haines, Randa — Director
1429 Avon Park Terrace, Los Angeles CA 90026, USA

Hairston, Carl B — Football Player, Coach
9009 Gleneagle Dr, Blaine WA 98230, USA

Hairston, Jerry W, Jr — Baseball Player
6 Austringer Court, Pikesville MD 21208, USA

Hairston, Jerry W, Sr — Baseball Player
7831 W Peace Pipe Road, Tucson AZ 85743, USA

Haise, Fred W, Jr — Astronaut, Test Pilot
PO Box 5765, Pasadena TX 77508, USA

Haislett, Nicole — Swimmer
275 N Poplar St, Massapequa NY 11758, USA

Haislip, Marcus L — Basketball Player
Milwaukee Bucks, Bradley Center, 1001 N 4th St, #2, Milwaukee WI 53203 USA

Haith, Frank — Basketball Coach
University of Missouri, Athletic Dept, Columbia MO 65211, USA

Haitink, Bernard J H — Conductor
Askonas Holt, Lincoln House, 300 High Holborn, London WC1V 7JH, England

Haje, Khrystyne — Actress
C E S D, 10635 Santa Monica Blvd, #130, Los Angeles CA 90025 USA

Hajek, Andreas — Rowing Athlete
Weissbundenweg 18, 06128 Halle/Saale, Germany
Haji — Actress
PO Box 2304, Malibu CA 90265, USA
Haji-Sheikh, Ali — Football Player
550 S Spinningwheel Lane, Bloomfield Township MI 48304, USA
Hakkinen, Henri — Marksman
Joensuun Ampujat Ry, Sepankatu 18A B15, 80110 Joensuu, Finland
Hakkinen, Mika P — Auto Racing Driver
Le Scguylkill, Blvd de Suisse 8, 98000 Monte Carlo, Monaco
Halama, John T — Baseball Player
7615 Fort Hamilton Parkway, Brooklyn NY 11228, USA
Halas, John — Animator
Educational Film Center, 5-7 Kean St, London WC2B 4AT, England
Halbert, Charles P (Chuck) — Basketball Player
100 E Whidbey Ave, #35, Oak Harbor WA 98277, USA
Haldeman, Charles (Ed), Jr — Financier, Government Official
McGraw-Hill, 1221 Avenue of Americas, #4700, New York NY 10020, USA
Haldorson, Burdette (Burdie) — Basketball Player
2868 Stonewall Heights, Colorado Springs CO 80909, USA
Hale, Alan — Astronomer
Southwest Space Research Institute, 15 E Spur Road, Cloudcraft NM 88317, USA
Hale, Barbara — Actress
PO Box 6061-261, Sherman Oaks CA 91413, USA
Hale, David — Ice Hockey Player
3470 Cortina Dr, Colorado Springs CO 80918, USA
Hale, David R (Dave) — Football Player
1204 S Maple St, #B, Ottawa KS 66067, USA
Hale, Georgina — Actress
74A Saint John's Wood, High St, London NW8, England
Hale, John S — Baseball Player
2200 Pine St, Bakersfield CA 93301, USA
Hale, Lucy K — Actress
W M E Entertainment, 9601 Wilshire Blvd, #300, Beverly Hills CA 90210 USA
Hale, Robert H (Bob) — Baseball Player
616 Overhill Ave, Park Ridge IL 60068, USA
Hale, Tony — Actor
I C M Partners, 10250 Constellation Blvd, #900, Los Angeles CA 90067 USA
Hale, Walter W (Chip) — Baseball Player
190 Driftwood Court, Aptos CA 95003, USA
Haley, Charles L — Football Player
3787 Royal Cove Dr, Dallas TX 75229, USA
Haley, G Richard (Dick), Jr — Football Player
5248 Shoreline Circle, Sanford FL 32771, USA
Haley, Jackie Earle — Actor
Leslie Allan-Rice Mgmt, 1007 Maybrooke Dr, Beverly Hills CA 90210, USA
Haley, Jermaine — Football Player
16806 Heather Knolls Place, Hamilton VA 20158, USA
Haley, Shay — Singer, Rap Artist (NERD)
Virgin Records, 338 N Foothill Road, Beverly Hills CA 90210 USA
Haley, Todd — Football Coach
Pittsburgh Steelers, 3400 S Water St, Pittsburgh PA 15203 USA
Halford, Robert J A (Rob) — Singer (Judas Priest)
Trinifold Mgmt, 12 Oval Road, Camden, London NW1 7DH, England
Halfpenny, Jill — Actress
Ken McReddie Assoc, 11 Connaught Place, London W2 2ET, England
Halfvarson, Eric F — Opera Singer
1264 Harwood Road, #100, Bedford, TX 76021, USA
Hali, Tamba B — Football Player
13227 Outlook Dr, Leawood KS 66209, USA
Halicki, Edward L (Ed) — Baseball Player
19605 Paddlewheel Lane, Reno NV 89521, USA
Halimon, Shaler — Basketball Player
9535 SW Millen Dr, Portland OR 97224, USA
Hall Greff, Kaye — Swimmer
906 3rd St, Mukilteo WA 98275, USA
Hall, Ahmad R — Football Player
4103 Creek Ridge Lane, Missouri City TX 77459, USA
Hall, Albert — Baseball Player
1628 Spaulding Ishkooda Road, Birmingham AL 35211, USA
Hall, Albert — Actor
Stone Manners Salners, 9911 W Pico Blvd, #1400, Los Angeles CA 90035 USA
Hall, Andrew C (Drew) — Baseball Player
4107 Spreading Oaks Court, Waxhaw NC 28173, USA
Hall, Anthony Michael — Actor, Comedian
I C M Partners, 10250 Constellation Blvd, #900, Los Angeles CA 90067 USA
Hall, Arsenio — Actor, Producer, Writer
Career Mgmt, 9229 Sunset Blvd, #720, West Hollywood CA 90069, USA
Hall, Brad, II — Actor, Comedian
W M E Entertainment, 9601 Wilshire Blvd, #300, Beverly Hills CA 90210 USA
Hall, Bridget — Model
I M G Models, 304 Park Ave S, #PH-North, New York NY 10010 USA
Hall, Bruce — Guitarist (REO Speedwagon)
Front Line Mgmt, 1100 Glendon Ave, #2000, Los Angeles CA 90024 USA
Hall, Bug — Actor
Don Buchwald/Fortitude, 6500 Wilshire Blvd, #2200, Los Angeles CA 90048 USA
Hall, Charles — Inventor (Waterbed)
Basic Designs, 5815 Bennett Valley Road, Santa Rosa CA 95404, USA
Hall, Charles L (Charlie) — Football Player
602 Lavaca St, Yaokum TX 77995, USA
Hall, Daryl — Singer (Hall & Oates), Songwriter
Doyle-Kos Entertainment, 1 Penn Plaza, 2107, New York, NY 10119, USA
Hall, DeAngelo E — Football Player
5553 Legends Dr, Braselton GA 30517, USA
Hall, Deidre — Actress
PO Box 715, 11041 Santa Monica Blvd, Los Angeles CA 90078, USA

Hall, Delton D 9 Mystic Court, Greensboro NC 27406, USA	Football Player
Hall, Donald Eagle Point Farm, Wilmot NH 03287, USA	Writer
Hall, Donald J Hallmark Cards, 2501 McGee St, Kansas City MO 64108, USA	Businessman
Hall, Donald R (Dino) 355 Chestnut Neck Road, Port Republic NJ 08241, USA	Football Player
Hall, Esther United Agents, 12-26 Lexington St, London W1F 0LE, England	Actress
Hall, Fawn 9008 Norma Place, West Hollywood CA 90069, USA	Government Secretary
Hall, Galen Pennsylvania State University, Athletic Dept, Greenberg Complex, University Park PA 16802, USA	Football Player, Coach
Hall, Gary 151 Kahiki Dr, Tavernier FL 33070, USA	Swimmer
Hall, Gary, Jr 2409 E Luke Ave, Phoenix AZ 85016, USA	Swimmer
Hall, Glenn H PO Box 2483, Main Station, Stony Plain AB T7Z 1X, Canada	Ice Hockey Player
Hall, Hanna Glick Agency, 1321 7th St, #203, Santa Monica CA 90401, USA	Actress
Hall, James E (Jim) Jim Hall Kart Racing School, 1555 Morse Ave, #G, Ventura CA 93003, USA	Auto Racing Driver, Executive
Hall, James S (Jim) Jazz Tree, 211 Thompson St, #LD, New York NY 10012, USA	Jazz Guitarist
Hall, Jerry Ford Models, 9200 Sunset Blvd, #805, West Hollywood CA 90069, USA	Model, Actress
Hall, Jimmie R 8622 Carter Grove Dr, Elm City NC 27822, USA	Baseball Player
Hall, Joe B Central Bank & Trust Co, 300 W Vine St, #3, Lexington KY 40507, USA	Basketball Coach
Hall, John L 3748 Davidson Place, Boulder CO 80305, USA	Nobel Physics Laureate
Hall, Joseph G (Joe) 961 Preachers Mill Road, Clarksville TN 37042, USA	Baseball Player
Hall, Kevan Kevan Hall Studio, 756 S Spring St, #11E, Los Angeles CA 90014, USA	Fashion Designer
Hall, Kristen Gail Gelman Mgmt, 23852 Pacific Coast Highway, #920, Malibu CA 90265, USA	Singer, Guitarist (Sugarland)
Hall, Lani 31930 Pacific Coast Highway, Malibu CA 90265, USA	Singer
Hall, Lawrence University of California, Physics Dept, Berkeley CA 94720, USA	Physicist
Hall, Lemanski S 2336 Wimbledon Circle, Franklin TN 37069, USA	Football Player
Hall, Leon 2343 Clydes Crossing, Cincinnati OH 45244, USA	Football Player
Hall, Lloyd M, Jr Congregation Christian Church Assn, PO Box 1620, Oak Creek MI 53154, USA	Religious Leader
Hall, M Darren 5008 Townsend Dr, Flower Mound TX 75028, USA	Baseball Player
Hall, Mark Proper Mgmt, PO Box 150867, Nashville TN 37215, USA	Singer (Casting Crowns)
Hall, Michael C Hamilton Hodell, 66-68 Margaret St, London W1W 8SR, England	Actor
Hall, Nigel J 11 Kensington Park Gardens, London W11 3HD, England	Artist
Hall, Peter R F 68 Lamont Road, London SW10 0HX, England	Director
Hall, Philip Baker Paradigm Agency, 360 N Crescent Dr, North Building, Beverly Hills CA 90210 USA	Actor
Hall, Reamy Amsel Eisenstadt Frazier, 5055 Wilshire Blvd, #865, Los Angeles CA 90036 USA	Actress
Hall, Rebecca Julian Belfrage Assoc, 9 Argyll St, #300, London W1F 7TG, England	Actress
Hall, Regina I C M Partners, 10250 Constellation Blvd, #900, Los Angeles CA 90067 USA	Actress
Hall, Richard W (Dick) 403 Plumbridge Court, #202, Lutherville Timonium MD 21093, USA	Baseball Player
Hall, Robert David Gage Group, 14724 Ventura Blvd, #505, Sherman Oaks CA 91403 USA	Actor
Hall, Robert E (Bob) Stanford University, Hoover Institution, Stanford CA 94305, USA	Economist
Hall, Robert N 325 Kings Road, #8, Schenectady NY 12304, USA	Inventor (Semiconductor Injection Laser)
Hall, Ronald G (Ronnie) 14008 NE 162nd St, Kearney MO 64060, USA	Football Player
Hall, Samuel (Sam) 5759 Wilcke Way, Dayton OH 45459, USA	Diver
Hall, Sonny AFL-CIO, 815 16th St, NW, Washington DC 20006, USA	Labor Leader
Hall, Thomas E (Tom) 3592 Lillian St, Riverside CA 92504, USA	Baseball Player
Hall, Thomas F (Tom) PO Box 60441, Longmeadow MA 01116, USA	Football Player
Hall, Toby J 3814 Evergreen Oaks Dr, Lutz FL 33558, USA	Baseball Player
Hall, Tom T Tom T Hall Enterprises, PO Box 1246, Franklin TN 37065, USA	Singer, Guitarist, Songwriter
Hall, Trevor Monterey International, 200 W Superior St, #202, Chicago IL 60654 USA	Singer, Guitarist, Songwriter
Hall, Willie C 717 S Hacienda St, Anaheim CA 92804, USA	Football Player
Hall, Windlan E 13609 Pleasant Lane, Burnsville MN 55337, USA	Football Player

Halla, Brian L — Businessman
National Semiconductor, 2900 Semiconductor Dr, Santa Clara CA 95051, USA
Halladay, H Leroy (Roy), III — Baseball Player
18509 Council Crest Dr, Odessa FL 33556, USA
Halldorson, Daniel A (Dan) — Golfer
209 South Road, Cambridge IL 61238, USA
Hallen, Robert J (Bob) — Football Player
7052 Rushmore Way, Painesville OH 44077, USA
Haller, Fritz — Furniture Designer, Architect
U S M Berlin, Franzosische Str 48, 10117 Berlin, Germany
Haller, Gordon — Triathlete
16 Thetford Dr, Bella Vista AR 72715, USA
Haller, Kevin — Ice Hockey Player
Hockey Ministries, 1100 Dela Gauchetiere W, Montreal QC H3B 2S2, Canada
Hallett, Bob — Singer (Great Big Sea)
Fleming Assoc, 167 Little Lake Dr, Ann Arbor MI 48103, USA
Hallinan, Joseph T (Joe) — Journalist, Writer
Random House, 1745 Broadway, #1800, New York NY 10019 USA
Halliwell, Geri — Singer (Spice Girls)
19 Entertainment, 35-37 Parkgate Road, #32/33, London SW11 4NP, England
Hallman, Tom, Jr — Journalist
Portland Oregonian, Editorial Dept, 1320 SW Broadway, Portland OR 97201, USA
Hallock, Bob — Auto Racing Driver
2185 Santa Ana Ave, Costa Mesa CA 92627, USA
Hallock, Ty E — Football Player
3676 Hunters Way Dr SE, Ada MI 49301, USA
Hallstrom, Lasse — Director
LaHa Films, 137 W 57th St, #700, New York NY 10019, USA
Hallstrom, Ronald D (Ron) — Football Player
Hallstrom's Marina, PO Box 379, Woodruff WI 54568, USA
Hallyday, Estelle — Model
I M G Models, 304 Park Ave S, #PH-North, New York NY 10010 USA
Hallyday, Johnny — Singer, Actor
Voyez Mon Agent, 20 Ave Rapp, 75007 Paris, France
Halmich, Regina — Boxer
Gunter Halmich, Inselstr 3, 76189 Karlsruhe, Germany
Halperin, Bertrand I — Physicist
Harvard University, Lyman Physics Laboratory, Cambridge MA 02138, USA
Halpern, Daniel — Writer
57 Mountain Ave, Princeton NJ 08540, USA
Halpern, Jack — Chemist
5801 S Dorchester Ave, #4A, Chicago IL 60637, USA
Halpern, James S — Judge
US Tax Court, 400 2nd St NW, Washington DC 20217, USA
Halpern, Jeff — Ice Hockey Player
9212 Sprinklewood Lane, Potomac MD 20854, USA
Halsell, James D, Jr — Astronaut
257 River Cove Road, Huntsville AL 35811, USA
Halsey, Darcy — Actress
Arts & Letters Mgmt, 7715 W Sunset Blvd, #208, Los Angeles CA 90046, USA
Halter, Shane D — Baseball Player
2701 W 140th St, Overland Park KS 66224, USA
Halton, Thomas L — Nutritionist
Harvard Public Health School, Nutrition Dept, 655 Huntington, Boston MA 02115, USA
Halver, John E — Biochemist, Nutritionist
16502 41st Ave NE, Lake Forest Park WA 98155, USA
Halverson, R Dean — Football Player
45971 State Highway 74, Palm Desert CA 92260, USA
Halvorsen, Gail — Berlin Airlift Air Force Hero
1525 W Dove Way, Amado AZ 85645, USA
Ham, Carter F — Army General
Commander, Army Europe & 7th Army, APO AE 09014 USA
Ham, Jack R — Football Player
Ham Enterprises, 540 Lindbergh Dr, Coraopolis PA 15108, USA
Ham, Kenneth T — Astronaut
1315 Falling Leaf Dr, Friendswood TX 77546, USA
Hamada, Hiroshi — Businessman
Ricoh Co, 1-15-5 Minami-Aoyama, Minatoku, Tokyo 107 8544, Japan
Hamari, Julia — Opera Singer
Max Brodweg 14, 70437 Stuttgart, Germany
Hambling, Maggi — Artist
Morley College, Westminster Bridge Road, London SE1 7HT, England
Hambright, Roger D — Baseball Player
8709 NE 37th Ave, Vancouver WA 98665, USA
Hambrock, John — Cartoonist
King Features Syndicate, 300 W 57th St, #1500, New York NY 10019 USA
Hambuchen, Fabian — Gymnast
Vitesse Karcher GmbH, Karolingerstra 41, 70736 Fellbach, Germany
Hamburg, John — Director
W M E Entertainment, 9601 Wilshire Blvd, #300, Beverly Hills CA 90210 USA
Hamburg, Margaret (Peggy) — Government Official
Food & Drug Administration, 10903 New Hampshire Ave, Silver Spring MD 20903, USA
Hamburger, Cao — Director
Anonymous Content, 3532 Hayden Ave, Culver City CA 90232 USA
Hamed, Naseem (Prince) — Boxer
Ciaralinn, Woodlands Road W, Virginia Water, Surrey GU25 4PL, England
Hamel, Dean — Football Player
1007 Hawthorne Dr NE, Lenoir NC 28645, USA
Hamel, Peter Michael — Composer
Bergsedter Markt 12, 22395 Hamburg, Germany
Hamel, Veronica — Actress, Model
12305 Fifth Helen Dr, Brentwood CA 94513, USA
Hamelin, Charles — Speed Skater
Club Montreal, 930 Av Roland-Beaudin, Quebec QC G1V 4H8, Canada
Hamelin, Francois — Speed Skater
Speed Skating Canada, 2781 Lancaster Road, #402, Ottawa ON K1B 1A7, Canada

Hamelin, Robert J (Bob)	Baseball Player
51 Patton Court SE, Concord NC 28025, USA	
Hamhuis, Dan	Ice Hockey Player
9553 Hampton Reserve Dr, Brentwood TN 37027, USA	
Hamill, Dorothy S	Figure Skater
10045 Red Run Blvd, #250, Owings Mills MD 21117, USA	
Hamill, Mark	Actor
Danis Panaro Nist Talent, 9201 W Olympic Blvd, Beverly Hills CA 90212, USA	
Hamill, W Pete	Writer, Editor
8 Whiskey Hill Road, Wallkill NY 12589, USA	
Hamilton	Guitarist (British Sea Power)
Agency Group Ltd, 361-373 City Road, London EC1V 2QA, England	
Hamilton, Allan G (Al)	Ice Hockey Player
2452 115th St, Edmonton AB T6J 3S1, Canada	
Hamilton, Ann	Sculptor
64 Smith Place, Columbus OH 43201, USA	
Hamilton, Anthony	Singer, Rap Artist
247 S Beverly Dr, #102, Beverly Hills CA 90212, USA	
Hamilton, Ashley G	Actor
A P A Talent/Literary Agency, 405 S Beverly Dr, #300, Beverly Hills CA 90212 USA	
Hamilton, Benjamin T (Ben)	Football Player
5240 Golden Ridge Court, Parker CO 80134, USA	
Hamilton, C Robert (Bobby), Jr	Auto Racing Driver
Motorsports Decisions, 1435 W Morehead St, #190, Charlotte NC 28208, USA	
Hamilton, Clyde H	Judge
US Appeals Court, Federal Courthouse, 1100 Laurel St, Columbia SC 29201, USA	
Hamilton, Conrad	Football Player
19619 N 35th Place, Phoenix AZ 85050, USA	
Hamilton, Darryl Q	Baseball Player
4721 Southwind Dr, Baton Rouge LA 70816, USA	
Hamilton, David	Photographer
41 Blvd du Montparnasse, 75006 Paris, France	
Hamilton, David E (Dave)	Baseball Player
9464 Cherry Hills Lane, San Ramon CA 94583, USA	
Hamilton, De'Marr	Drummer (Plain White T's), Songwriter
One Moment Mgmt, PO Box 55156, Sherman Oaks CA 91413 USA	
Hamilton, Forestorn (Chico)	Jazz Drummer
Chico Hamilton Productions, 321 E 45th St, #PH A, New York NY 10017, USA	
Hamilton, George	Actor
TalentWorks, 3500 W Olive Ave, #1400, Burbank CA 91505 USA	
Hamilton, George, IV	Singer, Songwriter, Guitarist
Blade Agency, 203 SW 3rd Ave, Gainesville FL 32601, USA	
Hamilton, Guy	Director
Palma de Mallorca, Apartado III, 01753 Andratz, Baleric Islands, Spain	
Hamilton, Harry E	Football Player
PO Box 986, Lemont PA 16851, USA	
Hamilton, Hugo	Writer
Harper Collins Publishers, 10 E 53rd St, Cellar 1, New York NY 10022 USA	
Hamilton, J Joseph (Joey)	Baseball Player
4035 Wellington Mist Point, Duluth GA 30097, USA	
Hamilton, Jane	Writer
Doubleday Press, 1540 Broadway, New York NY 10036, USA	
Hamilton, Jeffrey R (Jeff)	Baseball Player
2485 Golfview Circle, Fenton MI 48430, USA	
Hamilton, Josh	Actor
Paradigm Agency, 360 N Crescent Dr, North Building, Beverly Hills CA 90210 USA	
Hamilton, Joshua H (Josh)	Baseball Player
4317 Willowdale Court, Apex NC 27539, USA	
Hamilton, Keith L	Football Player
6 Bonnieview Lane, Towaco NJ 07082, USA	
Hamilton, Laird J	Surfer
Ziffren Brittenham Branca, 1801 Century Park W, #700, Los Angeles CA 90067 USA	
Hamilton, Laurell K	Writer
PO Box 190306, Saint Louis MO 63119, USA	
Hamilton, Leonard	Basketball Coach
Florida State University, Athletic Dept, Tallahassee FL 32306, USA	
Hamilton, Lewis C	Auto Racing Driver
Lewis Hamilton Motorsports, 32 Saint James's St, London SW1A 1HD, England	
Hamilton, Linda	Actress
Innovative Artists, 1505 10th St, Santa Monica CA 90401 USA	
Hamilton, Lisa Gay	Actress
Paradigm Agency, 360 N Crescent Dr, North Building, Beverly Hills CA 90210 USA	
Hamilton, Marcus	Cartoonist (Dennis the Menance)
12225 Ranburne Road, Charlotte NC 28227, USA	
Hamilton, Melinda Page	Actress
Don Buchwald/Fortitude, 6500 Wilshire Blvd, #2200, Los Angeles CA 90048 USA	
Hamilton, Michael	Artist
2012 N 19th St, Boise ID 83702, USA	
Hamilton, Milo	Sportscaster
2001 Holcombe Blvd, #901, Houston TX 77030, USA	
Hamilton, Page	Guitarist (Band of Susans, Helmet)
Maine Road Mgmt, 195 Chrystie St, #901F, New York NY 10002, USA	
Hamilton, Richard C	Basketball Player
2301 W Big Beaver Road, #535, Troy MI 48084, USA	
Hamilton, Roy Lee	Basketball Player
1644 Del Mar Road, Oceanside CA 92057, USA	
Hamilton, Ruffin, III	Football Player
236 Sumac Trail, Woodstock GA 30188, USA	
Hamilton, Scott S	Figure Skater
2451 Hidden River Lane, Franklin TN 37069, USA	
Hamilton, Suzanna	Actress
Julian Belfrage Assoc, 9 Argyll St, #300, London W1F 7TG, England	
Hamilton, Thomas W (Tom)	Bassist (Aerosmith)
Front Line Mgmt, 1100 Glendon Ave, #2000, Los Angeles CA 90024 USA	
Hamilton, Todd	Golfer
2004 Rock Dove Court, Westlake TX 76262, USA	

Hamelin - Hamilton

Hamilton, Tom	Sportscaster
31704 Sailors Cove, Avon Lake OH 44012, USA	
Hamilton, Tyler	Cyclist
32 Russell St, Marblehead MA 01945, USA	
Hamilton, Victoria	Actress
Paradigm Agency, 360 Park Ave S, #1600, New York NY 10010 USA	
Hamilton, Wendy	Model, Actress
Playboy Promotions, 2706 Media Center Dr, Los Angeles CA 90065 USA	
Hamilton, William	Cartoonist, Writer
17 E 95th St, #3F, New York NY 10128, USA	
Hamlett, Denis	Soccer Coach
Chicago Fire, 700 S Harlem Ave, Bridgeview IL 60455 USA	
Hamlin, Harry	Actor
Global Artists Agency, 6253 Hollywood Blvd, #508, Los Angeles CA 90028 USA	
Hamlin, J Dennis A (Denny)	Auto Racing Driver
19135 Pennsylvanis Point Dr, Cornelius NC 29031, USA	
Hamlin, Kenneth L (Ken)	Baseball Player
5242 County Road 413, McMillan MI 49853, USA	
Hamlin, Shelley	Golfer
4311 W Ardmore Road, Laveen AZ 85339, USA	
Hamm, Jon	Actor
I C M Partners, 10250 Constellation Blvd, #900, Los Angeles CA 90067 USA	
Hamm, Mia	Soccer Player, Model
613 15th St, Manhattan Beach CA 90266, USA	
Hamm, Morgan	Gymnast
Sandy Hamm, W230S3827 Milky Way Road, Waukesha WI 53189, USA	
Hamm, Nick	Director
I C M Partners, 10250 Constellation Blvd, #900, Los Angeles CA 90067 USA	
Hamm, Paul	Gymnast
Sandy Hamm, W230S3827 Milky Way Road, Waukesha WI 53189, USA	
Hammaker, C Atlee	Baseball Player
12740 Manning Lane, Knoxville TN 37932, USA	
Hammel, Eugene A	Anthropologist
2332 Piedmont Ave, Berkeley CA 94720, USA	
Hammell, Penny	Golfer
4786 Orchard Lane, Delray Beach FL 33445, USA	
Hammer	Rap Artist
Terrie Williams Agency, 1500 Broadway Front, #7, New York NY 10036, USA	
Hammer, A J	Commentator
CNN-TV, 190 Marietta Ave SW, Atlanta GA 30303 USA	
Hammer, Armie	Actor
W M E Entertainment, 9601 Wilshire Blvd, #300, Beverly Hills CA 90210 USA	
Hammer, Barbara	Director
55 Bethune St, #523H, New York NY 10014, USA	
Hammer, Jan, Jr	Jazz Keyboardist, Composer
2 W 45th St, #1102, New York NY 10036, USA	
Hammer, Victor S	Cinematographer
Gersh Agency, 9465 Wilshire Blvd, #600, Beverly Hills CA 90212 USA	
Hammergren, John H	Businessman
McKesson Inc, 1 Post St, #1800, San Francisco CA 94104, USA	
Hammes, Gordon G	Chemist
11 Staley Place, Durham NC 27705, USA	
Hammett, Kirk	Guitarist (Metallica)
2505 Divisadero St, San Francisco CA 94115, USA	
Hammock, Robert W (Robby)	Baseball Player
8644 S 21st Place, Phoenix AZ 85042, USA	
Hammon, Becky	Basketball Player
San Antonio Silver Stars, 1 AT&T Center, San Antonio TX 78219 USA	
Hammond, Albert, Jr	Guitarist (Strokes)
Provitent FM/2850, 2850 Ocean Park Blvd, #300, Santa Monica CA 90405, USA	
Hammond, Christopher A (Chris)	Baseball Player
116144 Palomino Valley Road, San Diego CA 92127, USA	
Hammond, Darrell	Actor, Comedian
W M E Entertainment, 1325 Ave of Americas, New York NY 10019 USA	
Hammond, Donnie	Golfer
1642 Bridgewater Dr, Lake Mary FL 32746, USA	
Hammond, Fred	Singer (Radical for Christ)
Face to Face, 21421 Hilltop St, #20, Southfield MI 48033, USA	
Hammond, Gary A	Football Player
5321 Seascape Lane, Plano TX 75093, USA	
Hammond, George S	Chemist
27 Timber Lane, Painted Post NY 14870, USA	
Hammond, Joan H	Opera Singer
Private Bag 101, Geelong Mail Center VIC 3221, Australia	
Hammond, John	Singer, Guitarist
Shore Fire Media, 32 Court St, #1600, Brooklyn NY 11201 USA	
Hammond, Josh	Actor
Hines & Hurt Entertainment, 1213 W Magnolia Blvd, Burbank CA 91506, USA	
Hammond, Julie	Basketball Player
2943 S Ulster St, Denver CO 80231, USA	
Hammond, L Blaine, Jr	Astronaut
Gulfstream Aircraft, 4150 E Donald Douglas Dr, #926, Long Beach CA 90808, USA	
Hammond, Richard	Actor
Independent Talent Group, Oxford House, 76 Oxford St, London W1D 1BS, England	
Hammond, Robert D	Army General
219 Del Mesa Carmel, Carmel CA 93923, USA	
Hammond, Robert L (Bobby)	Football Player
2535 Butler St, East Elmhurst NY 11369, USA	
Hammond, Steven B (Steve)	Baseball Player
11104 Lake Butler Road, Windermere FL 34786, USA	
Hammond, Tom	Sportscaster
NBC-TV, Sports Dept, 30 Rockefeller Plaza, #270E, New York NY 10112 USA	
Hammonds, Bruce	Businessman
M B N A Corp, 1100 N King St, Wilmington DE 19884, USA	
Hammonds, Jeffrey B (Jeff)	Baseball Player
2950 Meadow Lane, Weston FL 33331, USA	

Hamilton - Hammonds

Hammonds, Tom E
122 Windsor Dr, Crestview FL 32539, USA — Basketball Player

Hammons, David
Studio Museum in Harlem, 144 W 125th St, #200, New York NY 10027, USA — Sculptor

Hamner, Earl, Jr
11575 Amanda Dr, Studio City CA 91604, USA — Producer, Writer

Hamnett, Katharine
Aberdeen Studios, 22-24 Highbury Grove, #3D, London N5 2EA, England — Fashion Designer

Hamon, Gwendoline
Artmedia, 20 Ave Rapp, 75007 Paris, France — Actress

Hamon, Lucienne
Agents Associes, 201 Rue du Faubourg Saint Honore, 75008 Paris, France — Actress

Hampe, Michael
Tiergartenstr 36, 01219 Dresden, Germany — Director

Hampshire, Susan
Rob Groves Personal Management, 33 Glasshouse St, Soho London W1B 5DG, England — Actress

Hampson, Edward G (Ted)
4436 Claremore Dr, Minneapolis MN 55435, USA — Ice Hockey Player

Hampson, Justin M
7018 Richmond Dr, Glen Carbon IL 62034, USA — Baseball Player

Hampson, Thomas
Starkfriedgasse 53, 1180 Vienna, Austria — Opera Singer

Hampton, Brenda
Paradigm Agency, 360 N Crescent Dr, North Building, Beverly Hills CA 90210 USA — Producer

Hampton, Casey, Jr
105 Conover Road, Pittsburgh PA 15208, USA — Football Player

Hampton, Christopher J
Casorotto Ramsay, Waverley House, 7-12 Noel St, London W1F 8GQ, England — Writer

Hampton, Daniel O (Dan)
9191 Falling Waters Dr E, Burr Ridge IL 60527, USA — Football Player

Hampton, Isaac B (Ike)
4415 E Ridge Gate Road, Anaheim CA 92807, USA — Baseball Player

Hampton, James
102 Forest Hill Dr, Roanoke TX 76262, USA — Actor

Hampton, Locksley (Slide)
Charismic Productions, 2604 Mozart Place NW, Washington DC 20009, USA — Jazz Trombonist

Hampton, Lorenzo T
16231 NW 77th Place, Hialeah FL 33016, USA — Football Player

Hampton, Mark G
Mark Hampton Architect, 3900 Loquat Ave, Miami FL 33133, USA — Architect

Hampton, Michael W (Mike)
8601 N 59th Place, Paradise Valley AZ 85253, USA — Baseball Player

Hampton, Millard
201 W Mission St, San Jose CA 95110, USA — Track Athlete

Hampton, Ralph C, Jr
Free Will Baptist Bible College, 3606 W End Ave, Nashville TN 37205, USA — Religious Leader

Hampton, Rodney C
5603 Grand Floral Blvd, Houston TX 77041, USA — Football Player

Hamri, Sanaa
Creative Artists Agency, 2000 Ave of Stars, #100, Los Angeles CA 90067 USA — Director

Hamrlik, Roman
56 Alhambra Dr, Oceanside NY 11572, USA — Ice Hockey Player

Hamulack, Tim
530 Campbell Road, York PA 17402, USA — Baseball Player

Han Seung-Soo
Prime Minister's Office, 77 Sejong-no, Chongnogu, Seoul 110 760, South Korea — Prime Minister, South Korea

Han, Jefferson Y (Jeff)
New York University, Courant Math Sciences Institute, New York NY 10012, USA — Computer Scientist

Hanafusa, Hidesaburo
500 E 63rd St, New York NY 10065, USA — Microbiologist

Hanauer, Lee E (Chip)
Hanauer Enterprises, 2702 NE 88th St, Seattle WA 98115, USA — Boat Racing Driver

Hanburger, Christian (Chris), Jr
125 Wyandot St, Darlington SC 29532, USA — Football Player

Hancock, Anthony D
8233 Corteland Dr, Knoxville TN 37909, USA — Football Player

Hancock, Herbert J (Herbie)
Vector Mgmt, 1100 Glendon Ave, #2000, Los Angeles CA 90024, USA — Jazz Pianist, Composer

Hancock, John
Columbia Artists Mgmt Inc, 1790 Broadway, #702, New York NY 10019 USA — Opera Singer

Hancock, John D
7355 N Fail Road, La Porte IN 46350, USA — Director

Hancock, John Lee
Creative Artists Agency, 2000 Ave of Stars, #100, Los Angeles CA 90067 USA — Director

Hancock, Lee
8338 Brentwood Blvd, Brentwood CA 94513, USA — Baseball Player

Hancock, Phillip
3339 Handy Road, #728, Tampa FL 33618, USA — Golfer

Hancock, R Garry
2217 Greenhills Dr, Valrico FL 33596, USA — Baseball Player

Hancock, Sheila
Independent Talent Group, Oxford House, 76 Oxford St, London W1D 1BS, England — Actress, Writer

Hand, Elizabeth
Editions Denoel, 9 Rue du Cherche-Midi, 75278 Paris Cedex 06, France — Writer

Hand, Joey
Joey Hand Racing, 5877 Power Inn Road, Sacramento CA 95824, USA — Auto Racing Driver

Hand, Jon T
13013 Broad St, Carmel IN 46032, USA — Football Player

Hand, Richard A (Rich)
3824 Bay Court, Fort Worth TX 76179, USA — Baseball Player

Handelsman, Walt
Newsday, Editorial Dept, 235 Pinelawn Road, Melville NY 11747, USA — Editorial Cartoonist

Handford, Martin
Walker Books, 87 Vauxhall Walk, London SE11 5HU, England — Cartoonist (Where's Waldo)

Handke, Peter
Farrar Straus Giroux, 18 W 18th St, #700, New York NY 10011 USA — Writer

Handler, Chelsea
Borderline Amazing Productions, 12312 W Olympic Blvd, Los Angeles CA 90064, USA — Actress, Comedienne
Handler, Daniel
Harper Collins Publishers, 10 E 53rd St, Cellar 1, New York NY 10022 USA — Writer
Handler, Evan
C E S D, 10635 Santa Monica Blvd, #130, Los Angeles CA 90025 USA — Actor
Handley, Robert R (Ray)
PO Box 275, Glenbrook NV 89413, USA — Football Coach
Handley, Taylor
Paradigm Agency, 360 N Crescent Dr, North Building, Beverly Hills CA 90210 USA — Actor
Hands, Guy
Terra Firma Capital, 2 More London Riverside, London SE1 2AP, England — Businessman
Hands, Terence D
Clwyd Theater Cymru, Mold, Flintshire CH7 1YA, North Wales — Director
Hands, William A (Bill)
PO Box 334, Orient NY 11957, USA — Baseball Player
Handy, James
C E S D, 10635 Santa Monica Blvd, #130, Los Angeles CA 90025 USA — Actor
Handy, John
Integrity Talent, 1 Westcroft Court, Cockeysville MD 21030 USA — Jazz Saxophonist
Haneke, Michael
Filmakademie Vienna, Metternichgasse 12, 1030 Vienna, Austria — Director
Hanevold, Halvard
Barlindbakken 23, 1388 Borgen, Norway — Biathlete
Haney, Cecil D
Commander, Pacific Command, 250 Makalapa Dr, Pearl Harbor HI 96860 USA — Navy Admiral
Haney, Christopher D (Chris)
PO Box 135, Barboursville VA 22923, USA — Baseball Player
Haney, Lee
Lee Haney Enterprises, 105 Trail Point Circle, Fayetteville GA 30214, USA — Body Builder
Haney, Todd M
5404 Pointwood Circle, Waco TX 76710, USA — Baseball Player
Hanft, Ruth S
606 Rainier Road, Charlottesville VA 22903, USA — Medical Researcher
Hangartner, Geoffrey T (Geoff)
805 Park Slope Dr, Charlotte NC 28209, USA — Football Player
Hanggi, Kristin
Wonderfalls Entertainment, 1041 N Formosa Ave, Formosa Building, Los Angeles CA 90067, USA — Director
Hanifan, James M (Jim)
1217 Grey Fox Run, Weldon Spring MO 63304, USA — Football Coach
Hanigan, Ryan M
55 Bailey Road, Andover MA 01810, USA — Baseball Player
Hanin, Roger
9 Rue du Boccador, 75008 Paris, France — Actor
Hanisch, Cornelia
Rosemarie Hanisch, Via San Rocco 25, 18017 Linguegietta/Imperia, Italy — Fencer
Hankin, Larry
Amsel Eisenstadt Frazier, 5055 Wilshire Blvd, #865, Los Angeles CA 90036 USA — Actor
Hankinson, Tim
Columbus Crew, 1 Black & Gold Blvd, Columbus OH 43211 USA — Soccer Coach
Hankowsky, William
Liberty Property Trust, 7201 Wayne Ave, Philadelphia PA 19119, USA — Financier
Hanks, Colin
Creative Artists Agency, 2000 Ave of Stars, #100, Los Angeles CA 90067 USA — Actor
Hanks, Merton E
62 Oakland Ave, Bloomfield NJ 07003, USA — Football Player
Hanks, Tom
Playtone Productions, PO Box 7340, Santa Monica CA 90406, USA — Actor, Director, Producer
Hankton, Karl C
12532 Hennigan Place Lane, Charlotte NC 28214, USA — Football Player
Hanley, Charles
Associated Press, 450 W 33rd St, #1500, New York NY 10001 USA — Journalist
Hanley, Dan
I C M Partners, 10250 Constellation Blvd, #900, Los Angeles CA 90067 USA — Editor
Hanley, Frank
International Union of Operating Engineers, 1125 17th St NW, Washington DC 20036, USA — Labor Leader
Hanley, Jenny
M G A, Southbank House, Black Prince Road, London SE1 7SJ, England — Actress
Hanley, Kay
Little Big Man, 155 Ave of Americas, #700, New York NY 10013, USA — Singer (Letters to Cleo)
Hanley, Richard (Dick)
266 Lake Road, Hurley WI 54534, USA — Swimmer
Hanlon, Edward, Jr
US Representative NATO Military Committee, PSC 80, Box 300, APO AE 09724, USA — Marine Corps General
Hanlon, Glenn
8781 Piney Orchard Parkway, Odenton MD 21113, USA — Ice Hockey Player, Coach
Hanna, Preston L
5555 Mayfair Dr, Pensacola FL 32506, USA — Baseball Player
Hannah, Bob
University of Delaware, Athletic Dept, Newark DE 19716, USA — Baseball Coach
Hannah, Charles A (Charley)
PO Box 2671, Lutz FL 33548, USA — Football Player
Hannah, Daryl
Chuck Binder Mgmt, 1465 Lindacrest Dr, Beverly Hills CA 90210 USA — Actress, Model
Hannah, John
Clerkenwell Films, 82-84 Clerkenwell Road, #200, London EC1M 5RF, England — Actor
Hannah, John A
2407 Hideaway Place SE, Decatur AL 35603, USA — Football Player
Hannah, Kristin
Saint Martin's Press, 175 5th Ave, #400, New York NY 10010 USA — Writer
Hannah, Robert (Bob)
Bob Hannah Aviation, 22499 Channel Road, Caldwell ID 83607, USA — Motorcycle Racing Rider
Hannahan, John J (Jack), IV
1995 Bayard Ave, Saint Paul MN 55116, USA — Baseball Player
Hannan, David P (Dave)
408 Timberlake Dr, Venetia PA 15367, USA — Ice Hockey Player

H

Hannan, James J (Jim)
3907 Cherry Hill Way, Annandale VA 22003, USA — Baseball Player

Hannan, K Scott
35 S Bellaire St, Denver CO 80246, USA — Ice Hockey Player

Hannan, Mary Claire
Dattner Dispoto, 10635 Santa Monica Blvd, #165, Los Angeles CA 90025, USA — Costume Designer

Hannawald, Sven
W H Sport International GmbH, Im Sabel 4, 54294 Trier, Germany — Ski Jumper

Hanneman, Craig L
4350 Gibson Road NW, Salem OR 97304, USA — Football Player

Hannibal, Lars
Nordskraenten 3, 2980 Kokkedal, Denmark — Concert Guitarist

Hannigan, Alyson
A P A Talent/Literary Agency, 405 S Beverly Dr, #300, Beverly Hills CA 90212 USA — Actress

Hannigan, Barbara
Harrison/Parrott, 5-6 Albion Court, London W6 0QT, England — Opera Singer, Conductor

Hanning, Rob
Ziffren Brittenham Branca, 1801 Century Park W, #700, Los Angeles CA 90067 USA — Producer, Writer

Hannity, Sean
Hannity & Colmes, Fox-TV, News Dept, 1211 Ave of Americas, New York NY 10036, USA — Commentator

Hannon, Thomas E (Tom)
17398 Roxbury Ave, Southfield MI 48075, USA — Football Player

Hannula, Dick
1021 Westley Dr, Tacoma WA 98465, USA — Swimming Coach

Hannum, Taimie
7095 Hollywood Blvd, #762, Los Angeles CA 90028, USA — Actress, Model

Hano, Gregg R
Popular Science, Publisher's Office, 2 Park Ave, #900, New York NY 10016, USA — Publisher

Hanold, Marilyn
Playboy Promotions, 2706 Media Center Dr, Los Angeles CA 90065 USA — Model, Actress

Hanover, Donna
Helen Brezinsky, 1301 Ave of Americas, New York NY 10019, USA — Commentator

Hanrahan, Joel R
94156 River Marsh Dr, Fernandina FL 32034, USA — Baseball Player

Hanratty, Samantha (Sammi)
Schiff Co, 8440 Warner Dr, #B1, Culver City CA 90232 USA — Actress

Hanratty, Terrance R (Terry)
31 Gower Road, New Canaan CT 06840, USA — Football Player

Hans-Adam II
Prince's Residence, Schloss Vaduz, 9490 Vaduz, Liechtenstein — Prince, Liechtenstein

Hansard, Glen
Frames, PO Box 67 Gorey, County Wexford, Ireland — Actor, Singer, Songwriter

Hansbrough, A Tyler
Indiana Pacers, Conseco Fieldhouse, 125 S Pennsylvania, Indianapolis IN 46204 USA — Basketball Player

Hansch, Theodor W
Max Plack Institut, Hans-Kopermann-Str 1, 85748 Garching, Germany — Nobel Physics Laureate

Hansell, Gregory M (Greg)
1791 W Prescott Dr, Chandler AZ 85248, USA — Baseball Player

Hansen, Alfred G
Lockheed Aero Systems, 86 S Cobb Dr, Marietta GA 30063, USA — Air Force General, Businessman

Hansen, Barbara C
University of Maryland, Obesity/Diabetes Research Center, Baltimore MD 21201, USA — Neuroscientist

Hansen, Brendan J
8704 Framdale Cove, Austin TX 78749, USA — Swimmer

Hansen, Brian
US Speedskating, 5662 S Cougar Lane, Salt Lake City UT 84118 USA — Speed Skater

Hansen, Brian D
101 W Hazletine Lane, Sioux Falls SD 57108, USA — Football Player

Hansen, Chris
NBC-TV, News Dept, 30 Rockefeller Plaza, #270E, New York NY 10112 USA — Commentator

Hansen, Craig R
1180 Washington St, #508, Boston MA 02118, USA — Baseball Player

Hansen, David A (Dave)
9852 Orchard Lane, Villa Park CA 92861, USA — Baseball Player

Hansen, Donald R (Don)
3390 Spain Road, Snellville GA 30039, USA — Football Player

Hansen, Frederick M (Fred)
201 Vanderpool Lane, #12, Houston TX 77024, USA — Track Athlete

Hansen, Gale
Artists Agency, 1180 S Beverly Dr, #301, Los Angeles CA 90035 USA — Actress

Hansen, Gunnar
Amsel Eisenstadt Frazier, 5055 Wilshire Blvd, #865, Los Angeles CA 90036 USA — Actor

Hansen, J Stanley (Stan)
233 Fannin Dr, Hewitt TX 76643, USA — Professional Wrestler

Hansen, James E
Space Studies Institute, Columbia University, 2880 Broadway, Front 1, New York NY 10025, USA — Meteorologist, Physicist

Hansen, James Lee
28219 NE 63rd Ave, Battle Ground WA 98604, USA — Sculptor

Hansen, Joseph T
United Food/Commercial Workers Union, 1775 K St NW, Washington DC 20006, USA — Labor Leader

Hansen, Lars P
University of Chicago, Economics Dept, Chicago IL 60637, USA — Economist

Hansen, Mark Victor
PO Box 7665, Newport Beach CA 92658, USA — Motivational Speaker, Writer

Hansen, Monica
Playboy Promotions, 2706 Media Center Dr, Los Angeles CA 90065 USA — Model

Hansen, Patti
Redlands, West Wittering, Chichester, Sussex PO20 8QE, England — Model, Actress

Hansen, Peter
Stone Manners Salners, 9911 W Pico Blvd, #1400, Los Angeles CA 90035 USA — Actor

Hansen, Phillip A (Phil)
24921 N Melissa Dr, Detroit Lakes MN 56501, USA — Football Player

Hansen, Robert L (Bob)
710 36th St, West Des Moines IA 50265, USA — Basketball Player

Hansen, Ronald L (Ron)
13602 Alliston Dr, Baldwin MD 21013, USA — Baseball Player

V.I.P. Address Book

Hansen, Ryan — Actor
Gersh Agency, 9465 Wilshire Blvd, #600, Beverly Hills CA 90212 USA
Hanshaw, Anthony L — Boxer
Gary Shaw Productions, 555 Preakness Ave, #9, Totowa NJ 07502, USA
Hanson, Carl T — Navy Admiral
3377 E Arroyo Chico, Tucson AZ 85716, USA
Hanson, Curtis — Director, Writer
United Talent Agency, 9336 Civic Center Dr, Beverly Hills CA 90210 USA
Hanson, Erik B — Baseball Player
20333 N 83rd Place, Scottsdale AZ 85255, USA
Hanson, Hart — Producer, Writer
W M E Entertainment, 9601 Wilshire Blvd, #300, Beverly Hills CA 90210 USA
Hanson, Isaac — Singer, Guitarist (Hanson); Songwriter
10th Street Entertainment, 700 San Vicente Blvd, #G410, West Hollywood CA 90069, USA
Hanson, J Taylor — Singer, Keyboardist (Hanson); Songwriter
10th Street Entertainment, 700 San Vicente Blvd, #G410, West Hollywood CA 90069, USA
Hanson, Jason D — Football Player
27272 Ovid Court, Franklin MI 48025, USA
Hanson, Jennifer K — Singer
Capitol Records, 3322 West End Ave, #1100, Nashville TN 37203 USA
Hanson, Joselio B — Football Player
2531 Hudspeth St, Inglewood CA 90303, USA
Hanson, Marcy — Model, Actress
8721 W Sunset Blvd, #101, West Hollywood CA 90069, USA
Hanson, Scott — Sportscaster
N F L Network, 10950 Washington Blvd, #100, Culver City CA 90232 USA
Hanson, Zachary — Singer, Drummer (Hanson); Songwriter
10th Street Entertainment, 700 San Vicente Blvd, #G410, West Hollywood CA 90069, USA
Hanson-Sfingi, Beverly — Golfer
79915 Horseshoe Road, La Quinta CA 92253, USA
Hanus, Tomas — Conductor
I M G Artists, Hogarth Business Park, Chiswick, London W4 2TH, England
Hanway, H Edward — Businessman
C I G N A Corp, 1 Liberty Place, 1650 Market St, Philadelphia PA 19103, USA
Hanzlik, William H (Bill) — Basketball Player, Coach
5701 Green Oaks Dr, Greenwood Village CO 80121, USA
Hape, Patrick S — Football Player
105 Sutton Circle, Birmingham AL 35242, USA
Happ, J A — Baseball Player
902 14th St, Peru IL 61354, USA
Harad, George J — Businessman
Boise Cascade Corp, 1111 W Jefferson St, Boise ID 83728, USA
Harada, Ann — Actress
Davis Spylios Management, 244 W 54th St, #707, New York NY 10019, USA
Harald V — King, Norway
Royal Palace, Henrik Ibsens Gate 1, 0010 Oslo, Norway
Harang, Aaron M — Baseball Player
7828 Sendero Angelica, San Diego CA 92127, USA
Harangody, Luke C — Basketball Player
Cleveland Cavaliers, Gund Arena, 1 Center Court, Cleveland OH 44115 USA
Harareet, Haya — Actress
Herons Flight, Marlow, Buckinghamshire SL7 2LE, England
Harbaugh, Gregory J — Astronaut
1936 Thornwood Ave, Wilmette IL 60091, USA
Harbaugh, James J (Jim) — Football Player, Coach
San Francisco 49ers, 4949 Centennial Blvd, Santa Clara CA 95054 USA
Harbaugh, John — Football Coach
Baltimore Ravens, Ravens Stadium, 1 Winning Dr, Baltimore MD 21230 USA
Harbison, John H — Composer
479 Franklin St, Cambridge MA 02139, USA
Hard, Darlene R — Tennis Player
22924 Erwin St, Woodland Hills CA 91367, USA
Hardaway, Anfernee D (Penny) — Basketball Player
3217 Point Hill Cove, Memphis TN 38125, USA
Hardaway, Timothy D (Tim) — Basketball Player
10050 SW 62nd Ave, Miami FL 33156, USA
Hardeman, Donald R (Don) — Football Player
901 S Valley Mills Dr, #207B, Waco TX 76711, USA
Harden, J Richard (Rich) — Baseball Player
Texas Rangers, Ameriquest Field, 1000 Ballpark Way, #306, Arlington TX 76011 USA
Harden, James — Basketball Player
Houston Rockets, 1730 Jefferson St, Houston TX 77003 USA
Harden, Marcia Gay — Actress
Framework Entertainment, 9057 Nemo St, #C, West Hollywood CA 90069 USA
Harden, Michael (Mike) — Football Player
21512 E Portland Place, Aurora CO 80016, USA
Hardesty, Brandon A — Actor
Strong Mgmt, 9350 Wilshire Blvd, #224, Beverly Hills CA 90212, USA
Hardin, Melora — Actress, Singer, Director
Paul Kohner, 9300 Wilshire Blvd, #555, Beverly Hills CA 90212 USA
Harding, Daniel — Conductor
Columbia Artists Mgmt Inc, 1790 Broadway, #702, New York NY 10019 USA
Harding, Ian — Actor
Gersh Agency, 9465 Wilshire Blvd, #600, Beverly Hills CA 90212 USA
Harding, John Wesley — Singer, Guitarist, Songwriter, Writer
Sincere Mgmt, 6 Bravington Road, #6, London W9 3AH, England
Harding, Josh — Ice Hockey Player
1415 Brown St, Regina SK S4N 5C9, Canada
Harding, Lindsey — Basketball Player
Minnesota Lynx, Target Center, 600 1st Ave N, Minneapolis MN 55403 USA
Harding, Peter R — Air Force Marshal, England
Avalon House, Marnhull, Dorset DT10 1PT, England
Harding, Sarah N — Actress, Singer (Girls Aloud)
Concorde International, 101 Shepherds Bush Road, London W6 7LP, England
Harding, Tonya M — Figure Skater, Actress
11805 Bastrop St, Manor TX 78653, USA

Hardis, Stephen R — Businessman
Eaton Corp, Eaton Center, 1111 Superior Ave, #1900, Cleveland OH 44114, USA

Hardison, Bethann — Producer
Bethann Entertainment, 388 2nd Ave, #223, New York NY 10010, USA

Hardison, Kadeem — Actor
Peter Strain, 5455 Wilshire Blvd, #1812, Los Angeles CA 90036 USA

Hardison, W David (Dee) — Football Player
756 Belvin Maynard Road, Harrells NC 28444, USA

Hardman, Cedrick W — Football Player
364 Myrtle St, Laguna Beach CA 92651, USA

Hardnett, Charles (Charlie) — Basketball Player, Coach
1906 Swainsboro Dr, Louisville KY 40218, USA

Hardrict, Cory — Actor
A P A Talent/Literary Agency, 405 S Beverly Dr, #300, Beverly Hills CA 90212 USA

Hardt, Michael — Educator
Duke University, English Dept, Durham NC 27708, USA

Hardwick, Catherine — Director
Creative Artists Agency, 2000 Ave of Stars, #100, Los Angeles CA 90067 USA

Hardwick, Chris — Actor, Comedian (Hard n Phirm)
Brillstein Entertainment Partners, 9150 Wilshire Blvd, #350, Beverly Hills CA 90212 USA

Hardwick, Gary C — Director, Writer
Gersh Agency, 9465 Wilshire Blvd, #600, Beverly Hills CA 90212 USA

Hardwick, Johnny — Writer
Creative Artists Agency, 2000 Ave of Stars, #100, Los Angeles CA 90067 USA

Hardwick, Nicholas A (Nick) — Football Player
San Diego Chargers, 4020 Murphy Canyon Road, San Diego CA 92123 USA

Hardwick, Omari — Actor
3 Arts Entertainment, 9460 Wilshire Blvd, #700, Beverly Hills CA 90212 USA

Hardwick, William B (Billy) — Bowler
1576 S White Station Road, Memphis TN 38117, USA

Hardwicke, Catherine — Director, Writer
Creative Artists Agency, 2000 Ave of Stars, #100, Los Angeles CA 90067 USA

Hardy, Bruce A — Football Player
252 W 325 N, Ivins UT 84738, USA

Hardy, Carroll W — Football, Baseball Player
1514 Whitehall Dr, Longmont CO 80504, USA

Hardy, Francoise — Singer, Songwriter
Voyez Mon Agent, 20 Ave Rapp, 75007 Paris, France

Hardy, Hagood — Vibrist, Composer
S O C A N, 41 Valleybrook Dr, Don Mills ON M3B 2S6, Canada

Hardy, Hugh — Architect
Hardy Holzman Pfeiffer, 902 Broadway, #1900, New York NY 10010, USA

Hardy, James F (Jim) — Football Player
48490 San Vicente St, La Quinta CA 92253, USA

Hardy, James J (J J) — Baseball Player
5070 S Roosevelt St, Tempe AZ 85282, USA

Hardy, Jessica A — Swimmer
Premier Management Group, 1100 Crescent Green, #104, Cary, NC 27518 USA

Hardy, Kevin L — Football Player
1228 Windsor Harbor Dr, Jacksonville FL 32225, USA

Hardy, Kevin T — Football Player
298 Paraiso Dr, Danville CA 94526, USA

Hardy, Robert — Actor
Chatto & Linnit, 123A King's Road, London SW3 4PL, England

Hardy, Robert B (Bob) — Bassist (Franz Ferdinand)
M A M A Group, 57-65 Worship Ave, London EC2A 2DU, London, England

Hardy, Thomas A (Tom) — Sculptor
1530 SW Harrison, #203, Portland OR 97201, USA

Hardy, Tom — Actor
United Agents, 12-26 Lexington St, London W1F 0LE, England

Hare, David — Writer, Director
Casorotto Ramsay, Waverley House, 7-12 Noel St, London W1F 8GQ, England

Haren, Daniel J (Dan) — Baseball Player
7724 E Santa Catalina Dr, Scottsdale AZ 85255, USA

Harewood, Dorian — Actor
S M S Talent, 8383 Wilshire Blvd, #230, Beverly Hills CA 90211 USA

Hargan, Steven L (Steve) — Baseball Player
2502 E Morongo Trail, Palm Springs CA 92264, USA

Harge, Ira L — Basketball Player
328 Yucca Dr NW, Albuquerque NM 87105, USA

Hargett, Edward E (Edd) — Football Player
379 County Road 222, Nacogdoches TX 75965, USA

Hargis, V Burns — Educator
Oklahoma State University, President's Office, Stillwater OK 74078, USA

Hargitay, Mariska — Actress
Creative Artists Agency, 2000 Ave of Stars, #100, Los Angeles CA 90067 USA

Hargreaves, Brad — Drummer (Third Eye Blind)
Eric Godtland Mgmt, 1040 Mariposa St, #200, San Francisco CA 94107, USA

Hargrove, Brian — Director
Broder Webb Chervin Silbermann, 9242 Beverly Blvd, Beverly Hills CA 90210 USA

Hargrove, D Michael (Mike) — Baseball Player, Manager
3925 Ramblewood Dr, Richfield OH 44286, USA

Harikkala, Timothy A (Tim) — Baseball Player
W6132 Everglade Road, Greenville WI 54942, USA

Haring, Robert W — Editor
Tulsa World, Editorial Dept, 315 S Boulder Ave, Tulsa OK 74103, USA

Harington, Kit — Actor
Creative Artists Agency, 2000 Ave of Stars, #100, Los Angeles CA 90067 USA

Hariri, Gisue — Architect
Hariri & Hariri, 39 W 29th St, #1200, New York NY 10001, USA

Hariri, Mojgan — Architect
Hariri & Hariri, 39 W 29th St, #1200, New York NY 10001, USA

Harker, Patrick T — Educator
University of Delaware, President's Office, Newark DE 19716, USA

Harker, Susannah — Actress
55 Ashburnham Grove, Greenwich, London SW10 8UL, England

Harket, Morten
Agency Group Ltd, 361-373 City Road, London EC1V 2QA, England — Singer (A-Ha)
Harkey, Michael A (Mike)
2344 Eaglewood Dr, Chino Hills CA 91709, USA — Baseball Player
Harkleroad, Ashley
Women's Tennis Assn, 1 Progress Plaza, #1500, Saint Petersburg FL 33701 USA — Tennis Player, Model
Harkless, Maurice (Moe)
Orlando Magic, 8701 Maitland Summit Blvd, Orlando FL 32810 USA — Basketball Player
Harkness, Jerald B (Jerry)
8340 Misty Dr, Indianapolis IN 46236, USA — Basketball Player
Harlan, Jack R
University of Illinois, Agronomy Dept, Urbana IL 61801, USA — Plant Geneticist
Harlan, Kevin
CBS-TV, Sports Dept, 51 W 52nd St, New York NY 10019 USA — Sportscaster
Harley, Carol
1111B NW 131st Way, Vancouver WA 98685, USA — Singer, Guitarist (Misty River)
Harley, Steve
Work Hard, 19D Pinfold Road, London SW16 2SL, England — Singer (Steve Harley & Cockney Rebel)
Harlin, Renny
Midnight Sun Pictures, 10960 Wilshire Blvd, #700, Los Angeles CA 90024, USA — Director, Producer
Harlock, David A
4714 Oak Hollow Court, Dexter MI 48130, USA — Ice Hockey Player
Harlow, Bill
Charles Scribner's Sons, 866 3rd Ave, New York NY 10022 USA — Writer
Harlow, Larry D
26348 W Burnett Road, Buckeye AZ 85396, USA — Baseball Player
Harlow, Patrick C (Pat)
230 W Avenida San Antonio, San Clemente CA 92672, USA — Football Player
Harlow, Shalom
United Talent Agency, 9560 Wilshire Blvd, #500, Beverly Hills CA 90212, USA — Model, Actress
Harman, Denham
1337 S 101st St, #215, Omaha NE 68124, USA — Biochemist
Harman, Jennifer
Prince Marketing Group, 18 Carillon Circle, Livingston NJ 07039 USA — Poker Player
Harman, Katie
3631 NW 1st Court, Gresham OR 97030, USA — Beauty Queen, Singer
Harmel, Pierre C J M
8 Ave de l'Horizon, 1150 Brussels, Belgium — Prime Minister, Belgium
Harmer, Nicholas (Nick)
Zeitgeist Artist Mgmt, 660 York St, #216, San Francisco CA 94110, USA — Bassist (Death Cab for Cutie)
Harmer, Sarah
Rounder Records, 1 Rounder Way, Burlington MA 01803 USA — Singer, Songwriter
Harmon, Amy
New York Times, Editorial Dept, 229 W 43rd St, New York NY 10036 USA — Journalist
Harmon, Andrew P (Andy)
1258 Waters Edge Dr, Dayton OH 45458, USA — Football Player
Harmon, Angie
John Carrabino Mgmt, 5900 Wilshire Blvd, #406, Los Angeles CA 90036 USA — Actress, Model
Harmon, Charles B (Chuck)
6035 Ridgeacres Dr, #A, Cincinnati OH 45237, USA — Baseball Player
Harmon, Clarence, Jr
PO Box 571, Verona MS 38879, USA — Football Player
Harmon, Curtis
23309 Commerce Park Road, Cleveland OH 44122, USA — Drummer (Pieces of a Dream)
Harmon, Dan
United Talent Agency, 9336 Civic Center Dr, Beverly Hills CA 90210 USA — Producer, Writer, Actor
Harmon, Joy
9901 Poole Ave, Sunland CA 91040, USA — Actress
Harmon, Mark
Wings Inc, 2236 Encinitas Blvd, #A, Encinitas CA 92024, USA — Actor
Harmon, Noah
Island Def Jam Records, 8920 W Sunset Blvd, #200, West Hollywood CA 90069 USA — Bassist (Airborne Toxic Event)
Harmon, Robert
Paradigm Agency, 360 N Crescent Dr, North Building, Beverly Hills CA 90210 USA — Director
Harmon, Ronnie K
13022 218th St, Springfield Gardens NY 11413, USA — Football Player
Harmon, Winsor
Michael Bruno Mgmt, 13576 Cheltenhan Dr, Sherman Oaks CA 91423, USA — Actor
Harms, Alfred G, Jr
Commander, Education/Training Command, Naval Air Station, Pensacola FL 32508 USA — Navy Admiral
Harms, Joni
PO Box 272, Canby OR 97013, USA — Singer, Songwriter
Harner, Jason Butler
I C M Partners, 10250 Constellation Blvd, #900, Los Angeles CA 90067 USA — Actor
Harner, Levi
RR 1, Millville PA 17846, USA — Harness Racing Driver
Harney, Corinna
Playboy Promotions, 2706 Media Center Dr, Los Angeles CA 90065 USA — Model, Actress
Harnick, Sheldon M
Deutsch Deutsch & Blasband, 800 3rd Ave, New York NY 10022, USA — Writer, Lyricist
Harnisch, Peter T (Pete)
35 Brentwood Dr S, Colts Neck NJ 07722, USA — Baseball Player
Harnois, Elisabeth R
Schachter Entertainment, 1157 S Beverly Dr, #200, Los Angeles CA 90035 USA — Actress
Harnoncourt, Nikolaus
38 Piaristangasse, 1080 Vienna, Austria — Conductor
Harnoy, Ofra
437 Spadina Road, PO Box 23046, Toronto ON M5P 2W0, Canada — Concert Cellist
Haro, Melissa
Elite Model Mgmt, 119 Washington Ave, #501, Miami Beach FL 33139, USA — Model, Actress
Harold, Erika
212 W Washington St, #2011, Chicago IL 60606, USA — Beauty Queen
Harold, Gale
Gersh Agency, 9465 Wilshire Blvd, #600, Beverly Hills CA 90212 USA — Actor
Harouche, Serge
College de France, 11 Place Marcelin Berthelot, 75231 Paris Cedex 05, France — Nobel Physics Laureate

H

Harket - Harouche

Harout, Magda	Actress
13452 Vose St, Van Nuys CA 91405, USA	
Harper, Alvin C	Football Player
501 Harry S Truman Dr, #109, Upper Marlboro MD 20774, USA	
Harper, Ben	Singer, Guitarist, Songwriter
Partisan Arts, PO Box 5085, Larkspur CA 94977, USA	
Harper, Billy	Jazz Saxophonist
Joel Chriss, 60 E 8th St, #34N, New York NY 10003 USA	
Harper, Bob	Physical Fitness Instructor, Actor
Entertainment Fusion Group, 8899 Beverly Blvd, #412, West Hollywood CA 90046, USA	
Harper, Brian D	Baseball Player
8319 E Shetland Trail, Scottsdale AZ 85258, USA	
Harper, Bruce S	Football Player
311 Lindbergh Ave, Closter NJ 07624, USA	
Harper, Charles L (Charlie)	Football Player
2115 Augusta, McKinney TX 75070, USA	
Harper, Charles M	Businessman
6625 State St, Omaha NE 68152, USA	
Harper, Conrad K	Attorney, Government Official
US State Department, 2201 C St NW, Washington DC 20520, USA	
Harper, Derek R	Basketball Player
301 W 53rd St, #14F, New York NY 10019, USA	
Harper, Deveron A	Football Player
2749 Huntsville St, Kenner LA 70062, USA	
Harper, Donald D W (Don)	Diver
1765 Lynnhaven Dr, Columbus OH 43221, USA	
Harper, Dwayne A	Football Player
104 Cue St, Orangeburg SC 29115, USA	
Harper, Heather M	Opera Singer
Royal Academy of Music/Drama, 100 Renfrew St, Glasgow G2 3DB, England	
Harper, Helen	Actress
Gavin Barker Assoc, 2D Wimpole St, London W1G 0EB, England	
Harper, Hill	Actor
Innovative Artists, 1505 10th St, Santa Monica CA 90401 USA	
Harper, Jessica	Actress, Singer
2337 Roscomare Road, #2-244, Los Angeles CA 90077, USA	
Harper, Judson M	Chemical Engineer
1818 Westview Road, Fort Collins CO 80524, USA	
Harper, Mark	Football Player
2162 Albany Ave, Memphis TN 38108, USA	
Harper, Michael S	Writer
Brown University, English Dept, Providence RI 02912, USA	
Harper, Nicholas N (Nick)	Football Player
9549 Sanctuary Place, Brentwood TN 37027, USA	
Harper, Roland	Football Player
1391 Westbourne Parkway, Algonquin IL 60102, USA	
Harper, Ron	Actor
13317 Ventura Blvd, #1, Sherman Oaks CA 91423, USA	
Harper, Ronald (Ron)	Basketball Player
8934 Brecksville Road, #417, Brecksville OH 44141, USA	
Harper, Stephen J	Prime Minister, Canada
Prime Minister's Office, Langevin Block, Ottawa ON K1A 0A1, Canada	
Harper, Terry J	Baseball Player
4225 Jailette Road, Atlanta GA 30349, USA	
Harper, Tess	Actress
Bauman Redanty Shaul Agency, 5757 Wilshire Blvd, #473, Los Angeles CA 90036 USA	
Harper, Thomas (Tommy)	Baseball Player
5 Cow Hill Road, Sharon MA 02067, USA	
Harper, Tom	Actor
Ken McReddie Assoc, 11 Connaught Place, London W2 2ET, England	
Harper, Valerie	Actress
David Shapira Assoc, 193 N Robertson Blvd, Beverly Hills CA 90211 USA	
Harpring, Matthew H (Matt)	Basketball Player
4550 Stella Dr NW, Atlanta GA 30327, USA	
Harrah, Colbert D (Toby)	Baseball Player, Manager
316 Leewood Circle, Azle TX 76020, USA	
Harrah, Dennis W	Football Player
925 Rockin One Way, Paso Robles CA 93446, USA	
Harrell, James C, Jr	Football Player
17826 Crystal Preserve Dr, Lutz FL 33548, USA	
Harrell, Lynn M	Concert Cellist, Conductor
Opus 3 Artists, 470 Park Ave S, #900N, New York NY 10016 USA	
Harrell, Maestro	Actor
C E S D, 10635 Santa Monica Blvd, #130, Los Angeles CA 90025 USA	
Harrell, Willard R	Football Player
8 Scarlet Oak Court, Lake Saint Louis MO 63367, USA	
Harrell, William (Billy)	Baseball Player
253 Mount Hope Court, Albany NY 12202, USA	
Harrelson, Derrell M (Bud)	Baseball Player, Manager
357 Ridgefield Road, Hauppauge NY 11788, USA	
Harrelson, Kenneth S (Ken)	Baseball Player
90006 Shawn Park Place, Orlando FL 32819, USA	
Harrelson, Woody	Actor
Creative Artists Agency, 2000 Ave of Stars, #100, Los Angeles CA 90067 USA	
Harries, Kathryn	Opera Singer
Ingpen & Williams, 131 Putney Bridge Road, London SW15 2PA, England	
Harrigan, Lori	Softball Player
828 Rainbow Rock St, Las Vegas NV 89123, USA	
Harring, Laura E	Actress, Beauty Queen
Brillstein Entertainment Partners, 9150 Wilshire Blvd, #350, Beverly Hills CA 90212 USA	
Harrington, Albert F (Al)	Basketball Player
16124 Chancellors Ridge Way, Noblesville IN 46062, USA	
Harrington, C Michael (Mickey)	Baseball Player
135 Scenic Dr, Hattiesburg MS 39401, USA	
Harrington, Dan	Poker Player, Writer
Poker Gives, Nevada Community Foundation, 1635 Village Center Circle, #160, Las Vegas NV 89134, USA	

Harrington, Dennis
Stanford Roberts, 5668 S Rex Road, #101, Memphis TN 38119, USA — Golfer
Harrington, Desmond
Untitled Entertainment, 350 S Beverly Dr, #200, Beverly Hills CA 90212 USA — Actor
Harrington, Donald J
Saint John's University, President's Office, 8000 Utopia Parkway, Queens NY 11439, USA — Educator
Harrington, Jay
A Mgmt, 12001 Ventura Place, #340, Studio City CA 91604 USA — Actor
Harrington, John
8138 Golden Valley Road, Minneapolis MN 55427, USA — Ice Hockey Player, Coach
Harrington, Laura
Creative Artists Agency, 2000 Ave of Stars, #100, Los Angeles CA 90067 USA — Actress
Harrington, Othella F
1602 Rika Point, Houston TX 77077, USA — Basketball Player
Harrington, Padraig
International Mgmt Group, Pier House, Strand on the Green, London W4 3NN, England — Golfer
Harrington, Pat
730 Marzella Ave, Los Angeles CA 90049, USA — Actor
Harrington, Pat, Jr
C E S D, 10635 Santa Monica Blvd, #130, Los Angeles CA 90025 USA — Actor
Harrington, Perry D
1302 Roxbury Court, Jackson MS 39211, USA — Football Player
Harrington, William W (Bill)
7219 Cleveland School Road, Garner NC 27529, USA — Baseball Player
Harris, Alfred C (Al)
12 Stone Ridge Dr, South Barrington IL 60010, USA — Football Player
Harris, B Gail
14367 Clearview Ave, Gainesville VA 20155, USA — Baseball Player
Harris, Barbara C
Episcopal Diocese of Massachusetts, 138 Tremont St, Boston MA 02111, USA — Religious Leader, Social Activist
Harris, Barry
Brad Simon Organization, 155 W 46th St, #500, New York NY 10036 USA — Jazz Pianist
Harris, Bernard A, Jr
1330 Post Oak Blvd, #2550, Houston TX 77056, USA — Astronaut
Harris, Brendon M
30 Fox Hollow Lane, Queensbury NY 12804, USA — Baseball Player
Harris, Callard
United Talent Agency, 9336 Civic Center Dr, Beverly Hills CA 90210 USA — Actor
Harris, Carter
W M E Entertainment, 9601 Wilshire Blvd, #300, Beverly Hills CA 90210 USA — Producer, Director, Writer
Harris, Charlaine
PO Box 354, Magnolia AR 71754, USA — Writer
Harris, Clifford A (Cliff)
722 Kentwood Dr, Rockwall TX 75032, USA — Football Player
Harris, Clint L (Bo)
PO Box 52539, Shreveport LA 71135, USA — Football Player
Harris, Corey
Piedmont Talent, PO Box 680006, Santa Monica CA 90404, USA — Guitarist
Harris, Corey L
933 N Tremont St, Indianapolis IN 46222, USA — Football Player
Harris, Cristi Ellen
House of Representatives, 1434 6th St, #1, Santa Monica CA 90401 USA — Actress
Harris, Cynthia
Paradigm Agency, 360 N Crescent Dr, North Building, Beverly Hills CA 90210 USA — Actress
Harris, Damian
I C M Partners, 10250 Constellation Blvd, #900, Los Angeles CA 90067 USA — Director
Harris, Daniel P (Dan)
Chasen Agency, 8899 Beverly Blvd, #716, Los Angeles CA 90048 USA — Director, Writer
Harris, Danielle
Sager Mgmt, 260 S Beverly Dr, #205, Beverly Hills CA 90212, USA — Actress
Harris, Danneel
Untitled Entertainment, 350 S Beverly Dr, #200, Beverly Hills CA 90212 USA — Actress
Harris, Delmar (Del)
1229 Ducks Landing, Frisco TX 75034, USA — Basketball Coach
Harris, Devin
8 Green Park Dr, Dallas TX 75248, USA — Basketball Player
Harris, Duriel L, Jr
3875 San Pablo Road S, #1212, Jacksonville FL 32224, USA — Football Player
Harris, Ed
Special Artists Agency, 9465 Wilshire Blvd, #820, Beverly Hills CA 90212 USA — Actor
Harris, Emmylou
PO Box 158568, Nashville TN 37215, USA — Singer, Songwriter
Harris, Estelle
Danis Panaro Nist, 9201 W Olympic Blvd, Beverly Hills CA 90212, USA — Actress
Harris, Franco
200 Chaucer Court S, Sewickley PA 15143, USA — Football Player
Harris, Gail
Don Gerler, 3349 Cahuenga Blvd W, #1, Los Angeles CA 90068 USA — Actress
Harris, Greg A
PO Box 2665, Orleans MA 02653, USA — Baseball Player
Harris, Gregory W (Greg)
6708 Green Hollow Court, Wake Forest NC 27587, USA — Baseball Player
Harris, Henry
William Dunn Pathology School, South Parks Road, Oxford OX1 3RE, England — Cell Biologist
Harris, Hollis L
200 Horseshoe Cir, Fayetteville GA 30215, USA — Businessman
Harris, Hugh
150 Sycamore Dr, Carmel IN 46033, USA — Ice Hockey Player
Harris, Jackie B
7905 Haydenberry Court, Nashville TN 37221, USA — Football Player
Harris, James L
9838 Old Baymeadows Road, Jacksonville FL 32256, USA — Football Player
Harris, Jamie
Innovative Artists, 1505 10th St, Santa Monica CA 90401 USA — Actor
Harris, Jared
Paradigm Agency, 360 N Crescent Dr, North Building, Beverly Hills CA 90210 USA — Actor

V.I.P. Address Book

Harris, Jay
King Features Syndicate, 300 W 57th St, #1500, New York NY 10019 USA — Cartoonist (Better Half)

Harris, Joanne
Knopf Publishers, 1745 Broadway, New York NY 10019 USA — Writer

Harris, Joe Frank
712 West Ave, Cartersville GA 30120, USA — Governor, GA

Harris, John E
270 NW 120th St, Miami FL 33168, USA — Football Player

Harris, John R
24 Devonshire Place, London W1N 2BX, England — Architect

Harris, John R
4316 Fremont Ave S, Minneapolis MN 55409, USA — Golfer

Harris, Joseph A (Joe)
4747 River Road, Ellenwood GA 30294, USA — Football Player

Harris, Joshua
TalentWorks, 3500 W Olive Ave, #1400, Burbank CA 91505 USA — Actor

Harris, Julie
132 Barn Hill Road, #1267, West Chatham MA 02669, USA — Actress

Harris, Lara
Arlook Group, 205 S Beverly Dr, #209, Beverly Hills CA 90212, USA — Actress

Harris, Lee
Pilobolus Dance Theater, PO Box 388, Washington Depot CT 06794, USA — Dance Executive

Harris, Leon
CNN-TV, 190 Marietta Ave SW, Atlanta GA 30303 USA — Commentator

Harris, Leonard A (Lenny)
7435 N Augusta Dr, Hialeah FL 33015, USA — Baseball Player

Harris, Leroy
1919 Live Oak St, Savannah GA 31404, USA — Football Player

Harris, Leroy, Jr
890 Arlington Heights Dr, Brentwood TN 37027, USA — Football Player

Harris, Louis
200 E 66th St, #2004, New York NY 10065, USA — Statistician

Harris, Lucious H
1149 W 62nd St, Los Angeles CA 90044, USA — Basketball Player

Harris, Mark Yale
Artwork, 170 Lena St, #A, Santa Fe NM 87505, USA — Sculptor

Harris, Mel
Abrams Artists, 9200 W Sunset Blvd, #1125, West Hollywood CA 90069 USA — Actress

Harris, Melanie
Associated International Mgmt, Fairfax House, Fulwood Place, London WC1V 6HU, England — Actress

Harris, Michael L (M L)
M L Harris Outreach, 15589 Apple Valley Road, Apple Valley CA 92307, USA — Football Player

Harris, Mike
Curling Assn, 1660 Vimont Court, Cumberland ON K4A 4J4, Canada — Curling Athlete

Harris, Naomie M
United Talent Agency, 9336 Civic Center Dr, Beverly Hills CA 90210 USA — Actress

Harris, Napoleon B
Napoleon Harris Foundation, 15774 S LaGrange Road, #214, Orland Park IL 60462, USA — Football Player

Harris, Neil
5555 S Everett Ave, Chicago IL 60637, USA — Historian

Harris, Neil Patrick
Paradigm Agency, 360 N Crescent Dr, North Building, Beverly Hills CA 90210 USA — Actor

Harris, Nicholas J (Nick)
2035 Kingsway Dr, Troy MI 48098, USA — Football Player

Harris, Quentin H
3013 W Glass Lane, Phoenix AZ 85041, USA — Football Player

Harris, Rachael E
United Talent Agency, 9336 Civic Center Dr, Beverly Hills CA 90210 USA — Actress, Comedienne

Harris, Raymont L
1144 Aroya Court, New Albany OH 43054, USA — Football Player

Harris, Reginald A (Reggie)
133 Paige St, Waynesboro VA 22980, USA — Baseball Player

Harris, Richard
Paramount Entertainment, 12 Kosakowski Dr, Morris Plains NJ 07590 USA — Singer (Jive Five)

Harris, Rickie C
613 Q St NW, Washington DC 20001, USA — Football Player

Harris, Robert D
Inkwell Mgmt, 521 5th Ave, New York NY 10175, USA — Writer

Harris, Robert L
2711 13th St SW, Lehigh Acres FL 33976, USA — Football Player

Harris, Rolf
Billy Marsh, 76A Grove End, Saint John's Wood, London NW8 9ND, England — Entertainer

Harris, Rosemary
Independent Talent Group, Oxford House, 76 Oxford St, London W1D 1BS, England — Actress

Harris, Sam
Barry Krost Mgmt, 9229 Sunset Blvd, #303, Los Angeles CA 90069, USA — Singer, Actor

Harris, Samantha
E! Network, 5750 Wilshire Blvd, Los Angeles CA 90036, USA — Actress, Model

Harris, Sean
Troika, 74 Clerkenwell Road, #300, London EC1M 5QA, England — Actor

Harris, Sidney
302 W 86th St, #9A, New York NY 10024, USA — Cartoonist

Harris, Stefon
Unlimited Myles, 6 Imaginary Place, Matawan NJ 07747, USA — Jazz Vibraphone Player

Harris, Stephen E
Stanford University, Ginzton Laboratory, 450 Via Palou, Stanford CA 94305, USA — Electrical Engineer, Physicist

Harris, Steve
Brillstein Entertainment Partners, 9150 Wilshire Blvd, #350, Beverly Hills CA 90212 USA — Actor

Harris, Steve
Sanctuary Music Mgmt, 82 Bishop's Bridge Road, London W2 6BB, England — Bassist (Iron Maiden)

Harris, Steven D (Steve)
3005 W Fort Worth St, Broken Arrow OK 74012, USA — Basketball Player

Harris, T Eugene (Gene)
1267 NE 16th Ave, Okeechobee FL 34972, USA — Baseball Player

Harris, Ted
1 Stonegate Court, Blackwood NJ 08012, USA — Ice Hockey Player

Harris, Thomas
Creative Artists Agency, 2000 Ave of Stars, #100, Los Angeles CA 90067 USA — Writer

Harris, Timothy D (Tim)
843 N N St, Livermore CA 94551, USA — Football Player

Harris, Tommie, Jr
San Diego Chargers, 4020 Murphy Canyon Road, San Diego CA 92123 USA — Football Player

Harris, Victor L (Vic)
5420 S Garth Ave, Los Angeles CA 90056, USA — Baseball Player

Harris, Walt
Akron University, Athletic Dept, Akron OH 44325, USA — Football Coach

Harris, Walter F (Buddy)
2305 Carol Lane, Norristown PA 19401, USA — Baseball Player

Harris, Walter L (Walt)
4103 Shinault Lane, Olive Branch MS 38654, USA — Football Player

Harris, William C (Willie)
1176 Willie C Harris Dr, Cairo GA 39828, USA — Baseball Player

Harris, William E (Billy)
Muskoka Candle Co, PO Box 233, Rosseau ON P0C 1J0, Canada — Ice Hockey Player

Harris, William T (Bill)
322 S Reed St, Kennewick WA 99336, USA — Baseball Player

Harris, Wood
Gersh Agency, 9465 Wilshire Blvd, #600, Beverly Hills CA 90212 USA — Actor

Harrison Breetzke, Joan
16 Clevedon Road, East London 5201, South Africa — Swimmer

Harrison, Alvin
Octagon Worldwide, 7100 Forest Ave, #201, Richmond VA 23226 USA — Track Athlete

Harrison, Audley
Thell Torrence, 5449 S Eastern Ave, #3, Las Vegas NV 89119, USA — Boxer

Harrison, Bret
United Talent Agency, 9336 Civic Center Dr, Beverly Hills CA 90210 USA — Actor

Harrison, C Richard
Parametric Technology, 140 Kendrick St, #C120, Needham Heights MA 02494, USA — Businessman

Harrison, Charles (Tex)
Harlem Globetrotters, 400 E Van Buren St, #300, Phoenix AZ 85004, USA — Basketball Player, Coach

Harrison, Charles W (Chuck)
222 Buckskin Road, Abilene TX 79602, USA — Baseball Player

Harrison, Christopher (Chris)
Allure Model & Talent, 5556 S Centinela Ave, Los Angeles CA 90066, USA — Actor

Harrison, Colin
Farrar Straus Giroux, 18 W 18th St, #700, New York NY 10011 USA — Writer

Harrison, Dennis
1048 Hickory Hollow Road, Nashville TN 37221, USA — Football Player

Harrison, Donald (Duck)
Carolyn McClair, PO Box 55, Radio City Station, New York NY 10101, USA — Jazz Saxophonist

Harrison, Dwight W
2265 Buchanan St, Beaumont TX 77703, USA — Football Player

Harrison, Fiona
California Institute of Technology, Physics Dept, Pasadena CA 91125, USA — Physicist

Harrison, Gregory
Himber Entertainment, PO Box 950, South Orange NJ 07079 USA — Actor

Harrison, James D (Jim)
102-645 Barrera Road, Kelowna BC V1W 3C9, Canada — Ice Hockey Player

Harrison, James, Jr
2525 Matterhorn Dr, Wexford PA 15090, USA — Football Player

Harrison, Jenilee
J Lee Corp, 19528 Ventura Blvd, #365, Tarzana CA 91356, USA — Actress

Harrison, Jim
Grove Press, 841 Broadway, New York NY 10003 USA — Writer

Harrison, Kathryn
Random House, 1745 Broadway, #1800, New York NY 10019 USA — Writer

Harrison, Linda
10370 Ashton Ave, Los Angeles CA 90024, USA — Actress

Harrison, Marcus
New England Patriots, 1 Patriot Place, Foxboro MA 02035 USA — Football Player

Harrison, Marvin D
928 Morgan Road, Jenkintown PA 19046, USA — Football Player

Harrison, Matthew
Trisko Talent Management, 209 Carrall St, #240, Vancouver, BC V6B 2J2, Canada — Director

Harrison, Michael Allen
M A H Records, 828 NE Prescott St, Portland OR 97211, USA — Pianist, Composer

Harrison, Nolan
2121 N Westmoreland St, #543, Arlington VA 22213, USA — Football Player

Harrison, Paul D
5-215 Royale St, Timmins ON P4N 8S7, Canada — Ice Hockey Player

Harrison, Randy
Paradigm Agency, 360 N Crescent Dr, North Building, Beverly Hills CA 90210 USA — Actor

Harrison, Robert L (Bob)
1104 N Meridian St, Lebanon IN 46052, USA — Baseball Player

Harrison, Robert L (Bob), Jr
3 Westwind Circle, Stamford TX 79553, USA — Football Player

Harrison, Robert W (Bob)
Harbour Ridge, 13405 NW Wax Myrtle Trail, Palm City FL 34990, USA — Basketball Player

Harrison, Rodney
24 Country Club Dr, Olympia Fields IL 60461, USA — Football Player, Sportscaster

Harrison, Roric E
2932 Channing Way, Los Alamitos CA 90720, USA — Baseball Player

Harrison, Sabrina Ward
Chronicle Books, 680 2nd St, San Francisco CA 94107 USA — Writer

Harrison, Teri Marie
2973 Harbor Blvd, #350, Costa Mesa CA 92626, USA — Model, Actress

Harrison, Thomas J (Tom)
2932 Channing Way, Los Alamitos CA 90720, USA — Baseball Player

Harrison, Tony
Gordon Dickinson, 2 Crescent Grove, London SW4 7AH, England — Writer

Harrison, William B, Jr
J P Morgan Chase Corp, 270 Park Ave, #1200, New York NY 10017, USA — Financier

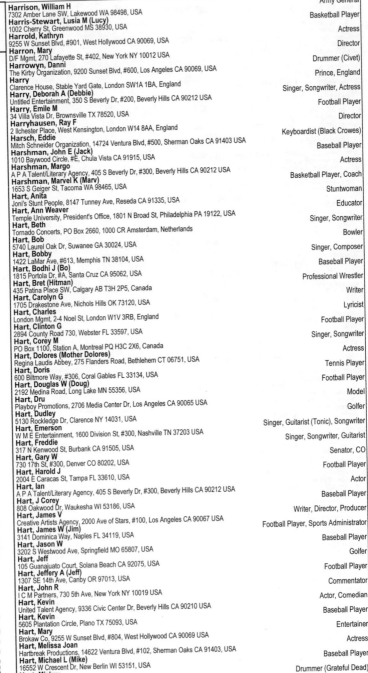

H

Harrison, William H
7302 Amber Lane SW, Lakewood WA 98498, USA — Army General

Harris-Stewart, Lusia M (Lucy)
1002 Cherry St, Greenwood MS 38930, USA — Basketball Player

Harrold, Kathryn
9255 W Sunset Blvd, #901, West Hollywood CA 90069, USA — Actress

Harron, Mary
D/F Mgmt, 270 Lafayette St, #402, New York NY 10012 USA — Director

Harrowyn, Danni
The Kirby Organization, 9200 Sunset Blvd, #600, Los Angeles CA 90069, USA — Drummer (Civet)

Harry
Clarence House, Stable Yard Gate, London SW1A 1BA, England — Prince, England

Harry, Deborah A (Debbie)
Untitled Entertainment, 350 S Beverly Dr, #200, Beverly Hills CA 90212 USA — Singer, Songwriter, Actress

Harry, Emile M
34 Villa Vista Dr, Brownsville TX 78520, USA — Football Player

Harryhausen, Ray F
2 Ilchester Place, West Kensington, London W14 8AA, England — Director

Harsch, Eddie
Mitch Schneider Organization, 14724 Ventura Blvd, #500, Sherman Oaks CA 91403 USA — Keyboardist (Black Crowes)

Harshman, John E (Jack)
1010 Baywood Circle, #E, Chula Vista CA 91915, USA — Baseball Player

Harshman, Margo
A P A Talent/Literary Agency, 405 S Beverly Dr, #300, Beverly Hills CA 90212 USA — Actress

Harshman, Marvel K (Marv)
1653 S Geiger St, Tacoma WA 98465, USA — Basketball Player, Coach

Hart, Anita
Joni's Stunt People, 8147 Tunney Ave, Reseda CA 91335, USA — Stuntwoman

Hart, Ann Weaver
Temple University, President's Office, 1801 N Broad St, Philadelphia PA 19122, USA — Educator

Hart, Beth
Tornado Concerts, PO Box 2660, 1000 CR Amsterdam, Netherlands — Singer, Songwriter

Hart, Bob
5740 Laurel Oak Dr, Suwanee GA 30024, USA — Bowler

Hart, Bobby
1422 LaMar Ave, #613, Memphis TN 38104, USA — Singer, Composer

Hart, Bodhi J (Bo)
1815 Portola Dr, #A, Santa Cruz CA 95062, USA — Baseball Player

Hart, Bret (Hitman)
435 Patina Place SW, Calgary AB T3H 2P5, Canada — Professional Wrestler

Hart, Carolyn G
1705 Drakestone Ave, Nichols Hills OK 73120, USA — Writer

Hart, Charles
London Mgmt, 2-4 Noel St, London W1V 3RB, England — Lyricist

Hart, Clinton G
2894 County Road 730, Webster FL 33597, USA — Football Player

Hart, Corey M
PO Box 1100, Station A, Montreal PQ H3C 2X6, Canada — Singer, Songwriter

Hart, Dolores (Mother Dolores)
Regina Laudis Abbey, 275 Flanders Road, Bethlehem CT 06751, USA — Actress

Hart, Doris
600 Biltmore Way, #306, Coral Gables FL 33134, USA — Tennis Player

Hart, Douglas W (Doug)
2192 Medina Road, Long Lake MN 55356, USA — Football Player

Hart, Dru
Playboy Promotions, 2706 Media Center Dr, Los Angeles CA 90065 USA — Model

Hart, Dudley
5130 Rockledge Dr, Clarence NY 14031, USA — Golfer

Hart, Emerson
W M E Entertainment, 1600 Division St, #300, Nashville TN 37203 USA — Singer, Guitarist (Tonic), Songwriter

Hart, Freddie
317 N Kenwood St, Burbank CA 91505, USA — Singer, Songwriter, Guitarist

Hart, Gary W
730 17th St, #300, Denver CO 80202, USA — Senator, CO

Hart, Harold J
2004 E Caracas St, Tampa FL 33610, USA — Football Player

Hart, Ian
A P A Talent/Literary Agency, 405 S Beverly Dr, #300, Beverly Hills CA 90212 USA — Actor

Hart, J Corey
808 Oakwood Dr, Waukesha WI 53186, USA — Baseball Player

Hart, James V
Creative Artists Agency, 2000 Ave of Stars, #100, Los Angeles CA 90067 USA — Writer, Director, Producer

Hart, James W (Jim)
3141 Dominica Way, Naples FL 34119, USA — Football Player, Sports Administrator

Hart, Jason W
3202 S Westwood Ave, Springfield MO 65807, USA — Baseball Player

Hart, Jeff
105 Guanajuato Court, Solana Beach CA 92075, USA — Golfer

Hart, Jeffery A (Jeff)
1307 SE 14th Ave, Canby OR 97013, USA — Football Player

Hart, John R
I C M Partners, 730 5th Ave, New York NY 10019 USA — Commentator

Hart, Kevin
United Talent Agency, 9336 Civic Center Dr, Beverly Hills CA 90210 USA — Actor, Comedian

Hart, Kevin
5605 Plantation Circle, Plano TX 75093, USA — Baseball Player

Hart, Mary
Brokaw Co, 9255 W Sunset Blvd, #804, West Hollywood CA 90069 USA — Entertainer

Hart, Melissa Joan
Hartbreak Productions, 14622 Ventura Blvd, #102, Sherman Oaks CA 91403, USA — Actress

Hart, Michael L (Mike)
16552 W Crescent Dr, New Berlin WI 53151, USA — Baseball Player

Hart, Mickey
Pinnacle Entertainment, 30 Glenn St, White Plains NY 10603, USA — Drummer (Grateful Dead)

Hart, Roxanne
Abrams Artists, 9200 W Sunset Blvd, #1125, West Hollywood CA 90069 USA — Actress

Hart, Stanley R
PO Box 625, Green Valley AZ 85622, USA — Geologist

Hart, Terry J
PO Box V, Hellertown PA 18055, USA — Astronaut

Hart, Tommy L
3503 Highland Ave, Redwood City CA 94062, USA — Football Player

Harte, Houston H
Harte-Hanks Communications, 200 Concord Plaza Dr, San Antonio TX 78216, USA — Publisher

Hartenstein, Charles O (Chuck)
10735 Cassia Dr, Austin TX 78759, USA — Baseball Player

Hartenstine, Michael A (Mike)
322 Winchester Court, Lake Bluff IL 60044, USA — Football Player

Hartings, Jeffrey A (Jeff)
171 Manchester Circle, Pittsburgh PA 15237, USA — Football Player

Hartley, Hal
True Fiction Pictures, 39 W 14th St, #406, New York NY 10011, USA — Director

Hartley, Harry J
University of Connecticut, President's Office, Storrs CT 06269, USA — Educator

Hartley, Justin
Innovative Artists, 1505 10th St, Santa Monica CA 90401 USA — Actor, Director, Writer

Hartley, Mariette
J Michael Bloom, 9255 W Sunset Blvd, #710, West Hollywood CA 90069 USA — Actress

Hartley, Michael E (Mike)
9845 Quail Canyon Road, El Cajon CA 92021, USA — Baseball Player

Hartley, Robert (Bob)
2713 Bonar Hall Path, Duluth GA 30097, USA — Ice Hockey Coach

Hartman Black, Lisa
Innovative Artists, 1505 10th St, Santa Monica CA 90401 USA — Actress

Hartman, Arthur A
A P C O Consulting Group, 1615 L St NW, Washington DC 20036, USA — Diplomat

Hartman, David
3215 Stoneybrook Dr, Durham NC 27705, USA — Actor, Commentator

Hartman, Elmer E (Butch), IV
Gotham Group, 9255 Sunset Blvd, #515, Los Angeles CA 90069, USA — Animator, Composer, Director

Hartman, Geoffrey H
200 Leeder Hill Dr, #2401, Hamden CT 6517, USA — Language Educator

Hartman, George E
1657 31st St, Washington DC 20007, USA — Architect

Hartman, J C
3425 Rosedale St, Houston TX 77004, USA — Baseball Player

Hartman, Kevin
Sporting Kansas City, 210 W 19th Terrace, #200, Kansas City MO 64108 USA — Soccer Player

Hartman, William K (Bill)
Planetary Science Institute, 1700 E Fort Lowell Road, #106, Tucson AZ 85719, USA — Astrophysicist

Hartmanis, Juris
43 Janivar Dr, Ithaca NY 14850, USA — Computer Scientist

Hartman-Smith, Rhonda
Hart Enterprises, 5611 Highway 81 N, Williamston SC 29697, USA — Auto Racing Driver

Hartner, Rona
Artmedia, 20 Ave Rapp, 75007 Paris, France — Actress

Hartnett, Josh
Management 360, 9111 Wilshire Blvd, Beverly Hills CA 90210 USA — Actor

Harto, Joshua
Madhouse Entertainment, 8484 Wilshire Blvd, #640, Beverly Hills CA 90211, USA — Actor

Harts, Gregory R (Greg)
829 Humphries St SW, Atlanta GA 30310, USA — Baseball Player

Hartsburg, Craig W
Columbus Blue Jackets, Arena, 200 W Nationwide Blvd, #1, Columbus OH 43215 USA — Ice Hockey Player, Coach

Hartsfield, Henry W (Hank), Jr
422 Willow Vista Dr, Seabrook TX 77586, USA — Astronaut

Hartsock, Jeffrey R (Jeff)
1720 Swannanoa Dr, Greensboro NC 27410, USA — Baseball Player

Hartung, James
6426 Tanglewood Lane, Lincoln NE 68516, USA — Gymnast

Hartwell, Edgerton (Ed), II
3830 Galendo Dr, N Las Vegas NV 89032, USA — Football Player

Hartwell, Leland H (Lee)
Hutchinson Cancer Research Center, PO Box 19024, Seattle WA 98109, USA — Nobel Medicine Laureate

Hartwig, Carter
5539 FM 762 Road, Richmond TX 77469, USA — Football Player

Hartwig, Justin J
2250 Mary St, #117, Pittsburgh PA 15203, USA — Football Player

Hartzell, Paul F
1 Hays Mews, London W1J 5PU, England — Baseball Player

Haruf, Kent
Southern Illinois University, English Dept, Carbondale IL 62901, USA — Writer

Harutyunyan, Arayik
Premier's Office, Nagorno-Karabakh, Stepanaret, Nagornyi, Azerbaijan — Prime Minister, Nagorno-Karabakh

Harvey, Adam Paul
Associated International Mgmt, Fairfax House, Fulwood Place, London WC1V 6HU, England — Actor

Harvey, Anthony
Arthur Greene, 101 Park Ave, #2607, New York NY 10178, USA — Director

Harvey, Antonio
5906 Yaupon Ave, Moss Point MS 39563, USA — Basketball Player

Harvey, Brian
National Geographic, Editorial Dept, 1145 17th St NW, Washington DC 20036 USA — Photographer, Explorer

Harvey, Bryan S
1224 Astoria Parkway, Catawba NC 28609, USA — Baseball Player

Harvey, Cynthia T
American Ballet Theater, 890 Broadway, #300, New York NY 10003, USA — Ballerina

Harvey, H Douglas (Doug)
32398 River Island Dr, Springville CA 93265, USA — Baseball Umpire

Harvey, Harry
34 Deep Hollow Lane N, Columbus NJ 08022, USA — Harness Racing Driver, Trainer

Harvey, James B (Jim), Jr
3685 Clarice Cove, Memphis TN 38133, USA — Football Player

H

Hart - Harvey

Harvey, James Michael — Religious Leader
Papal Household Prefecture, Roman Curia, 00120 Vatican City

Harvey, John C, Jr — Navy Admiral
Commander, Fleet Forces Command, 1562 Mitscher Ave, Norfolk VA 23551 USA

Harvey, Jonathan D — Composer
Faber Music, 3 Queen Square, London WC1N 3AU, England

Harvey, Kenneth E (Ken) — Baseball Player
5012 Grand Ave, #C, Kansas City MO 64112, USA

Harvey, Kenneth R (Ken) — Football Player
11600 Great Falls Way, Great Falls VA 22066, USA

Harvey, Maurice — Football Player
27 Clark St, #4, Pontiac MI 48342, USA

Harvey, Nancy — Golfer
7006 E Jensen St, #62, Mesa AZ 85207, USA

Harvey, Polly Jean (P J) — Singer, Guitarist, Songwriter
Creative Artists Agency, 2000 Ave of Stars, #100, Los Angeles CA 90067 USA

Harvey, Richard C — Football Player
3414 Baltimore Ave, Pascagoula MS 39581, USA

Harvey, Stephen P — Archaeologist
University of Chicago, Oriental Institute, 1155 E 58th St, Chicago IL 60637, USA

Harvey, Steve — Actor, Comedian
W M E Entertainment, 9601 Wilshire Blvd, #300, Beverly Hills CA 90210 USA

Harvick, Kerry — Singer
L G B Media, 861 High Point Ridge Road, Franklin TN 37069, USA

Harvick, Kevin M — Auto Racing Driver
703 Park Lawn Court, Kernersville NC 27284, USA

Harville, Chad A — Baseball Player
261 Farmington Road, Savannah TN 38372, USA

Harvin, W Percy, III — Football Player
Minnesota Vikings, 9520 Viking Dr, Eden Prairie MN 55344 USA

Harwell, Steve — Singer (Smash Mouth)
Creative Artists Agency, 2000 Ave of Stars, #100, Los Angeles CA 90067 USA

Harwood, Ronald — Writer
Judy Daish Assoc, 2 Saint Charles Place, London W10 6EG, England

Hase, Dagmar — Swimmer
Niederndodeleber Str 14, 29110 Magdeburg, Germany

Hasegawa, Hozumi — Boxer
Senrina Kobe Boxing Gym, 3-2-16 Shinonoedo, Cyuoku, Kobe City, Hyogooken, Japan

Hasegawa, Shigetoshi — Baseball Player
110 Newport Center Dr, #200, Newport Beach CA 92660, USA

Haselkorn, Robert — Virologist
5834 S Stony Island Ave, Chicago IL 60637, USA

Haselman, William J (Bill) — Baseball Player
14501 SE 85th St, Newcastle WA 98059, USA

Haselrig, Carlton L — Football Player, Wrestler
386 William Penn Ave, Johnstown PA 15901, USA

Haseltine, Daniel P (Dan) — Singer (Jars of Clay)
Nettwerk Mgmt, 1650 W 2nd Ave, Vancouver BC V6J 4R3, Canada

Haseltine, William A — Molecular Biologist
Human Genome Sciences, 14200 Shady Grove Road, Rockville MD 20850, USA

Hasen, Irvin H — Cartoonist (Goldbergs, Dondi)
68 E 79th St, #E, New York NY 10075, USA

Hasenmayer, Donald I (Don) — Baseball Player
721 Golf Dr, Warrington PA 18976, USA

Hashu, Nick — Basketball Player
2514 W Orangethorpe Ave, #27, Fullerton CA 92833, USA

Hasina Wajed, Sheikh — Prime Minister, Bangladesh
Sere-e Bangla Nagar, Gono, Bhaban, Sher-e-Banglanagar, Dhakar 1207, Bangladesh

Haskins, Clem S — Basketball Player, Coach
2632 Roberts Road, Campbellsville KY 42718, USA

Haskins, Dennis — Actor
Maverick Artists Agency, 1680 N Vine St, #802, Los Angeles CA 90028, USA

Haslem, Udonis J — Basketball Player
3489 Gulfstream Way, Davie FL 33328, USA

Haslett, James D (Jim) — Football Player, Coach
118 Crandon Dr, Saint Louis MO 63105, USA

Hass, Robert — Writer
University of California, English Dept, Berkeley CA 94720, USA

Hassan Ibn Talal — Crown Prince, Jordan
Deputy King's Office, Royal Palace, Amman, Jordan

Hassan, Fred — Businessman
Schering-Plough Corp, 2000 Galloping Hill Road, Kenilworth NJ 07033, USA

Hassan, Kamal — Actor, Director
63 Lutz Church Road, Chennai TN 600004, India

Hassan, Mohammed Waheed — President, Maldives
Presidential Palace, Orchid Magu, Male 20208, Maldives

Hassanal Bolkiah — Sultan, Brunei
Istana Darul Hana, Bandar Seri Begawan, BA 1000 Brunei

Hassel, Gerald L — Financier
Bank of New York, 1 Wall St, #200, New York NY 10286, USA

Hasselbeck, Donald W (Don) — Football Player
38 Noon Hill Ave, Norfolk VA 02056, USA

Hasselbeck, Matthew M (Matt) — Football Player
9027 NE 1st St, Bellevue WA 98004, USA

Hasselbeck, Timothy T (Tim) — Football Player, Sportscaster
38 Noon Hill Ave, Norfolk VA 02056, USA

Hasselhoff, David — Actor, Singer
Larry Thompson Organization, 9663 Santa Monica Blvd, #801, Beverly Hills CA 90210, USA

Hasselmo, Nils — Educator
Association of American Universities, 1200 New York Ave, #550, Washington DC 20005, USA

Hassenfeld, Alan G — Businessman
Hasbro Inc, 1027 Newport Ave, Pawtucket RI 02861, USA

Hassett, Joseph P (Joey) — Basketball Player
28 Marigold Circle, Providence RI 02904, USA

Hassett, Marilyn — Actress
8905 Rosewood Ave, West Hollywood CA 90048, USA

Hassey, Ronald W (Ron)
6330 N Calle Tregua Serena, Tucson AZ 85750, USA — Baseball Player

Hassler, Andrew E (Andy)
PO Box 15932, Phoenix AZ 85060, USA — Baseball Player

Hasson, Maddie
Coast to Coast Talent, 3350 Barham Blvd, Los Angeles CA 90068 USA — Actress

Hasson, Maurice
18 West Heath Court, North End Road, London NW11, England — Concert Violinist

Hastings, Andre O
700 N Dobson Road, #17, Chandler AZ 85224, USA — Football Player

Hastings, Barry G
Northern Trust Corp, 50 S La Salle St, #1, Chicago IL 60603, USA — Financier

Hastings, Don
524 W 57th St, #5330, New York NY 10019, USA — Actor

Hastings, Reed
Netflix Inc, 100 Winchester Circle, Los Gatos CA 95032, USA — Businessman

Hastings, Scott A
10210 Ridgegate Circle, Lone Tree CO 80124, USA — Basketball Player

Hasty, James E
8212 127th Ave SE, Newcastle WA 98056, USA — Football Player

Hatch, Annia P
1800 Sans Souci Blvd, #239, North Miami FL 33181, USA — Gymnast

Hatch, Harold A
8655 White Beach Way, Vienna VA 22182, USA — Marine Corps General

Hatch, Henry J
2715 Silkwood Court, Oakton VA 22124, USA — Army General

Hatch, Monroe W, Jr
8210 Thomas Ashleigh Lane, Clifton VA 20124, USA — Air Force General

Hatch, Richard
Omniquest Media, 1416 N La Brea Ave, Hollywood CA 90028, USA — Actor

Hatchell, Sylvia
University of North Carolina, Athletic Dept, Chapel Hill NC 27515, USA — Basketball Coach

Hatcher, Derian
567 Chews Landing Road, Haddonfield NJ 08033, USA — Ice Hockey Player

Hatcher, Kevin J
1225 S Water St, Marine City MI 48039, USA — Ice Hockey Player

Hatcher, Michael V (Mickey)
1179 N Williams Dr, Queen Valley AZ 85118, USA — Baseball Player

Hatcher, R Dale
906 White Plains Road, Gaffney SC 29340, USA — Football Player

Hatcher, Teri
United Talent Agency, 9336 Civic Center Dr, Beverly Hills CA 90210 USA — Actress

Hatcher, William A (Billy)
7079 Shawnee Run Road, Cincinnati OH 45243, USA — Baseball Player

Hatchett, Joseph W
9119 Shoal Creek Dr, Tallahassee FL 32312, USA — Judge

Hatchette, Matthew (Matt)
3222 Winding Pine Trail, Longwood FL 32779, USA — Football Player, Actor

Hatfield, Juliana
Ye Olde Records, PO Box 398110, Cambridge MA 02139, USA — Singer, Songwriter

Hathaway, Amy
Peter Strain, 5455 Wilshire Blvd, #1812, Los Angeles CA 90036 USA — Actress

Hathaway, Anne
Management 360, 9111 Wilshire Blvd, Beverly Hills CA 90210 USA — Actress

Hathaway, Lalah
Performers of the World, 5657 Wilshire Blvd, #280, Los Angeles CA 90036 USA — Singer

Hathaway, William D
Federal Maritime Commission, 800 N Capitol St NW, Washington DC 20002, USA — Senator, ME

Hatori, Miho
Billions Corp, 3522 W Armitage Ave, Chicago IL 60647, USA — Singer (Cibo Matto)

Hatosy, Shawn
Vox Inc, 6420 Wilshire Blvd, #1080, Los Angeles CA 90048 USA — Actor

Hatoum, Milton
Rogers Coleridge White, 20 Powis Mews, London W11 1JN, England — Writer

Hatsopoulos, George N
Thermo Electron Corp, 81 Wyman St, PO Box 9046, Waltham MA 02454, USA — Businessman, Mechanical Engineer

Hatteberg, Scott A
802 Berg Court NW, Gig Harbor WA 98335, USA — Baseball Player

Hatten, Tom
1759 Sunset Plaza Dr, Los Angeles CA 90069, USA — Actor

Hattersley, Roy S G
House of Lords, Westminster, London SW1A 0PW, England — Government Official, England

Hattestad, Stine Lise
Sundlia 1B, 1315 Nesoya, Norway — Moguls Skier

Hatton, Grady E
PO Box 97, Warren TX 77664, USA — Baseball Player, Manager

Hatton, Ricky
Heart Break Hotel, 47 Rock St, Hyde, Cheshire SK14 5JH, England — Boxer

Hatton, W Vernon (Vern)
PO Box 8405, Lexington KY 40533, USA — Basketball Player

Hatzigiannis, Mihalis
Universal Records, 70 Universal City Plaza, Universal City CA 91608 USA — Singer

Hau, Lene Vestergaard
Harvard University, Applied Physics Dept, Cambridge MA 02138, USA — Physicist

Hauck, Frederick H (Rick)
2 Redwood Lane, Falmouth ME 04105, USA — Astronaut

Hauck, Timothy C (Tim)
2410 42nd St, Missoula MT 59803, USA — Football Player

Hauer, Brett
2921 Branch St, Duluth MN 55812, USA — Ice Hockey Player

Hauer, Rutger
Glick Agency, 1260 6th St, #100, Santa Monica CA 90401, USA — Actor

Hauerwas, Stanley
Duke University, Divinity School, Durham NC 27706, USA — Theologian

Haug, Ian
Secret Service, PO Box 401, Fortitude Valley QLD 4006, Australia — Guitarist (Powderfinger)

H

Haug, Norbert F — Auto Racing Executive
Mercedes-Benz Motorsport, Brackley, Northantshire UNN 13 7BD, England

Haugedal, Majken — Model
Playboy Promotions, 2706 Media Center Dr, Los Angeles CA 90065 USA

Haugen, Greg — Boxer
PO Box 155, 1802 A St SE, Auburn WA 98002, USA

Haukohl, Guenter — Space Scientist
714 Watts Dr SE, Huntsville AL 35801, USA

Haun, Lindsey — Actress
TalentWorks, 3500 W Olive Ave, #1400, Burbank CA 91505 USA

Hauptman, Micah A — Actor
Chaiotek, 6446 Santa Monica Blvd, Los Angeles CA 90038, USA

Haus, Hermann A — Electrical Engineer, Computer Scientist
38 Jeffrey Terrace, Lexington MA 02420, USA

Hauser, Arthur A (Art) — Football Player
2816 Walsh Road, Cincinnati OH 45208, USA

Hauser, Cole — Actor
A P A Talent/Literary Agency, 405 S Beverly Dr, #300, Beverly Hills CA 90212 USA

Hauser, Erich — Sculptor
Saline 36, 78628 Rottweil, Germany

Hauser, Marc D — Ethnologist, Neurologist
Harvard University, Cognitive Evolution Laboratory, 33 Kirkland, Cambridge MA 02138, USA

Hauser, Tim — Singer (Manhattan Transfer)
Merlin Co, 16574 Bosque Dr, Encino CA 91436, USA

Hauser, Wings — Actor
David Shapira Assoc, 193 N Robertson Blvd, Beverly Hills CA 90211 USA

Hausman, Jerry A — Economist
Massachusetts Institute of Technology, Economics Dept, Cambridge MA 02139, USA

Hausman, Thomas M (Tom) — Baseball Player
3165 Westfield Circle, Las Vegas NV 89121, USA

Hauss, Lenard M (Len) — Football Player
110 Portmere Dr, Jesup GA 31546, USA

Hauswald, Simone H — Biathlete
Robert-Schumannstr 15, 78141 Schoenwald, Germany

Hauver, Charles D — Hero
6250 S Commerce Court, #1118, Tucson AZ 85746, USA

Havelid, A Niclas — Ice Hockey Player
PO Box 129, Point Roberts WA 98281, USA

Havens, Bradley D (Brad) — Baseball Player
3227 Eden Trail, Brighton MI 48114, USA

Havens, Frank B — Canoeing Athlete
PO Box 55, Harborton VA 23389, USA

Havens, Richie — Singer, Guitarist, Songwriter
Drake, 177 Woodland Ave, Westwood NJ 07675, USA

Havergal, Giles — Actor, Director
Gavin Barker Assoc, 2D Wimpole St, London W1G 0EB, England

Havig, Dennis E — Football Player
5964 Old Stilesboro Road NW, Acworth GA 30101, USA

Havlicek, John J — Basketball Player
Naismith Basketball Hall of Fame, 1150 W Columbus Ave, Springfield MA 01105 USA

Havlish, Jean — Bowler, Baseball Player
PO Box 122, Rockville MN 56369, USA

Havnevik, Kate — Singer, Songwriter
Continentica Records, 1/710 Fulham Road, London SW6 5SB, England

Havok, Davey — Singer (AFI)
S A M, 722 Seward St, Los Angeles CA 90038, USA

Havrilak, Samuel C (Sam) — Football Player
1 Trojan Horse Dr, Phoenix MD 21131, USA

Hawerchuk, Dale — Ice Hockey Player
Grande Farms, RR 5 LCD Main, Orangeville ON L9W 2Z2, Canada

Hawes, Keeley — Actress
Troika, 74 Clerkenwell Road, #300, London EC1M 5QA, England

Hawes, Roy L — Baseball Player
PO Box 854, Ringgold GA 30736, USA

Hawes, Spencer — Basketball Player
Philadelphia 76ers, 1st Union Center, 3601 S Broad St, Philadelphia PA 19148 USA

Hawes, Steven S (Steve) — Basketball Player
400 W Highland Dr, Seattle WA 98119, USA

Hawk, Aaron James (A J) — Football Player
460 B Olden Glen, De Pere WI 54115, USA

Hawk, John D — WW II Army Hero (CMH)
3243 Solie Ave, Bremerton WA 98310, USA

Hawk, Kali — Actress
Intellectual Artists Management, 10585 Santa Monica Blvd, #135, Los Angeles CA 90025

Hawk, Tony — Skateboarder, Actor
900 Films, 1203 Activity Dr, Vista CA 92081, USA

Hawke, Ethan — Actor, Writer
I/D Public Relations, 7060 Hollywood Blvd, #800, Los Angeles CA 90028 USA

Hawke, Robert J L (Bob) — Prime Minister, Australia
Westfield Towers, 100 William St, Level 13, Sydney NSW 2001, Australia

Hawkes, John — Actor
Innovative Artists, 1505 10th St, Santa Monica CA 90401 USA

Hawkes, Rechelle M — Field Hockey Player
I C M I, PO Box 2311, Praham VIC 3181, Australia

Hawking, Stephen W — Theoretical Physicist
University of Cambridge, Applied Math Dept, Cambridge CB3 9EW, England

Hawkins, Artrell — Football Player
12166 Peak Dr, Cincinnati OH 45246, USA

Hawkins, Barbara — Singer (Dixie Cups)
Superstars Unlimited, PO Box 371371, Las Vegas NV 89137, USA

Hawkins, Benjamin C (Ben) — Football Player
104 Deforest St, Roslindale MA 02131, USA

Hawkins, C Alexander (Alex) — Football Player
215 Bonanza Road, Denmark SC 29042, USA

Hawkins, Cornelius L (Connie) — Basketball Player, Executive
33 W Missouri Ave, #27, Phoenix AZ 85013, USA

Haug - Hawkins

Hawkins, Courtney T, Jr
8305 Gale Road, Goodrich MI 48438, USA — Football Player

Hawkins, Dan
Whitehouse Mgmt, PO Box 43829, London NW6 3PJ, England — Guitarist (Darkness)

Hawkins, Edwin
Sierra Mgmt, 1035 Bates Court, Hendersonville TN 37075, USA — Gospel Musician

Hawkins, Frank
2300 Alta Dr, Las Vegas NV 89107, USA — Football Player

Hawkins, Hersey R, Jr
2687 Beacon Hill Dr, West Linn OR 97068, USA — Basketball Player

Hawkins, Jennifer
22 Mgmt, 34 Darling St, #B, Balmain NSW 2041, Australia — Beauty Queen, Model, Actress

Hawkins, Justin
Whitehouse Mgmt, PO Box 43829, London NW6 3PJ, England — Singer (Darkness)

Hawkins, LaTroy (Roy)
3521 Amberwood Lane, Prosper TX 75078, USA — Baseball Player

Hawkins, M Andrew (Andy)
PO Box 1595, Bruceville TX 76630, USA — Baseball Player

Hawkins, Michael Daly
US Court of Appeals, 230 N 1st St, Phoenix AZ 85004, USA — Judge

Hawkins, Ronnie
Agency Group Ltd, 59 Berkeley St, Toronto ON M5A 2W5, Canada — Singer

Hawkins, Rosa
Superstars Unlimited, PO Box 371371, Las Vegas NV 89137, USA — Singer (Dixie Cups)

Hawkins, Ross C (Rip)
100 Tower Road, Devils Tower WY 82714, USA — Football Player

Hawkins, Sally
Conway Van Gelder Grant, 8-12 Broadwick St, #300, London W1F 8HW, England — Actress

Hawkins, Sophie B
Trumpet Swan Productions, 520 Washington Blvd, #337, Marina del Rey CA 90292, USA — Singer, Songwriter

Hawkins, Taylor
S A M, 722 Seward St, Los Angeles CA 90038, USA — Drummer (Foo Fighters)

Hawkins, Thomas J (Tommy)
1745 Manzanita Park Ave, Malibu CA 90265, USA — Basketball Player, Sportscaster

Hawkins, Wayne A
1 Dogwood Court, San Ramon CA 94583, USA — Football Player

Hawkins, Wynn F
5326 Cottage Dr, Cortland OH 44410, USA — Baseball Player

Hawkinson, Tim
Ace Gallery, 5514 Wilshire Blvd, #200, Los Angeles CA 90036, USA — Artist

Hawlata, Franz
Columbia Artists Mgmt Inc, 1790 Broadway, #702, New York NY 10019 USA — Opera Singer

Hawley, D Sanford (Sandy)
9625 Merrill Road, Silverwood MI 48760, USA — Thoroughbred Racing Jockey

Hawley, Frank
Frank Hawley Racing School, 3300 Hamilton Mill Road, #102, Buford, GA 30519, USA — Auto Racing Driver

Hawley, Noah
26 Keys Productions, 500 S Buena Vista St, Old Animation Building, Burbank CA 91521, USA — Producer, Writer

Hawley, Steven A
3303 Calvin Dr, Lawrence KS 66049, USA — Astronaut

Hawn, Goldie
Renaissance Literary & Talent, PO Box 17379, Beverly Hills CA 90209, USA — Actress

Haworth, Alan
845 112E Ave, Drummondville QC J2B 4K5, Canada — Ice Hockey Player

Hawpe, David V
507 Penwood Road, Louisville KY 40206, USA — Editor

Hawthorne, Chris
Hawthorne Gallery, 517 Jefferson St, Port Orford OR 97465, USA — Artist

Hawthorne, Gregory D (Greg)
1428 E Jefferson Ave, Fort Worth TX 76104, USA — Football Player

Hawthorne, Julie
Hawthorne Gallery, 517 Jefferson St, Port Orford OR 97465, USA — Artist

Hawthorne, Mayer
Creative Artists Agency, 2000 Ave of Stars, #100, Los Angeles CA 90067 USA — Singer, Songwriter

Hax, Carolyn
Washington Post, Editorial Dept, 1150 15th St NW, Washington DC 20071 USA — Columnist

Hay, Colin
T P A, PO Box 125, Round Corner NSW 2158, Australia — Singer (Men at Work)

Hay, Louise L
Hay House, PO Box 5100, Carlsbad CA 92018, USA — Writer

Haya Rashed Al Khalifa, Sheikha
General Assemby, United Nations, United Nations Plaza, New York NY 10017, USA — Government Official, Bahrain

Hayaishi, Osamu
1-29 Izumigawacho, Shimogamo Sakyoku, Kyoto 606 0807, Japan — Biochemist

Hayashi, Izuo
OptoElectrics Research Laboratory, 5-5 Tohkodai, Tsukuba, Ibaraki 300 26, Japan — Engineer

Hayashida, Erika
1470 NW 107th St, Doral FL 33172, USA — Golfer

Haydee, Marcia
Stuttgart Ballet, Oberer Schlossgarten 6, 70173 Stuttgart, Germany — Ballerina

Haydel, J Harold (Hal)
304 Lynwood Dr, Houma LA 70360, USA — Baseball Player

Hayden
Fat Possum Records, PO Box 1923, Oxford MS 38655, USA — Singer

Hayden, Eugene F (Gene)
424 W Locust St, Lodi CA 95240, USA — Baseball Player

Hayden, J Michael (Mike)
5809 Sagamore Court, Lawrence KS 66047, USA — Governor, KS

Hayden, Jim
Philadelphia Inquirer, 400 N Broad St, Philadelphia PA 19130, USA — Publisher

Hayden, Linda
Michael Ladkin Mgmt, 1 Duchess St, #1, London W1N 3DE, England — Actress

Hayden, Michael
H W A Talent, 3500 W Olive Ave, #1400, Burbank CA 91505 USA — Actor

Hayden, Neil Steven
1755 York Ave, #19A, New York NY 10128, USA — Publisher

Hayden, Pamela
W M E Entertainment, 9601 Wilshire Blvd, #300, Beverly Hills CA 90210 USA — Actress

Hayden, Tom
152 Wadsworth Ave, Santa Monica CA 90405, USA — Political Activist

Hayden, William George
GPO Box 7829, Waterfront Place, Brisbane QLD 4001, Australia — Governor General, Australia

Haydon Jones, Ann
85 Westerfield Road, Edge Aston, Birmingham West Midlands B15 3JF, England — Tennis Player

Haye, David D
Golden Boy Promotions, 626 Wilshire Blvd, #350, Los Angeles CA 90017 USA — Boxer

Hayek, Salma
Management 360, 9111 Wilshire Blvd, Beverly Hills CA 90210 USA — Actress, Model

Hayers, Sidney A
John Redway, 5 Denmark St, London WC2H 8LP, England — Director

Hayes, Amy
PO Box 717, Burgin KY 40310, USA — Model, Sportscaster

Hayes, Ben J
3501 10th St NE, Saint Petersburg FL 33704, USA — Baseball Player

Hayes, Bill
4528 Beck Ave, North Hollywood CA 91602, USA — Singer, Actor

Hayes, Cathy Lind
Talent Agency, 6310 San Vicente Blvd, #200, Los Angeles CA 90048, USA — Actress

Hayes, Charles D (Charlie)
22503 Holy Creek Trail, Tomball TX 77377, USA — Baseball Player

Hayes, Charles E (Chuck), Jr
Houston Rockets, 1730 Jefferson St, Houston TX 77003 USA — Basketball Player

Hayes, Darren
PO Box 193, Jimboomba QLD 4280, Australia — Singer (Savage Garden)

Hayes, Denis A
Bulitt Foundation, 1212 Minor Ave, Seattle WA 98101, USA — Environmentalist

Hayes, Dennis C
Hayes Microcomputer Products, 945 E Paces Ferry Road NE, Atlanta GA 30326, USA — Engineer, Co-Inventor (Modem)

Hayes, Elvin E
14 Canaveral Creek Lane, Sugar Land TX 77479, USA — Basketball Player

Hayes, Erinn
Innovative Artists, 1505 10th St, Santa Monica CA 90401 USA — Actress

Hayes, Gemma
Paradigm Agency, 360 N Crescent Dr, North Building, Beverly Hills CA 90210 USA — Singer, Songwriter

Hayes, Gerald B
3841 E Windsong Dr, Phoenix AZ 85048, USA — Football Player

Hayes, Jarvis J
4495 Greycliff Pointe, Douglasville GA 30135, USA — Basketball Player

Hayes, Joanna D
Brentwood School, 100 S Barrington Place, Los Angeles CA 90049, USA — Track Athlete

Hayes, John
Oceanographic Institution, 266 Woods Hole Road, Woods Hole MA 02543, USA — Geologist, Geophysicist

Hayes, John P (J P)
740 Camino Real Ave, El Paso TX 79922, USA — Golfer

Hayes, Jonathan M
9632 W 116th Place, Overland Park KS 66210, USA — Football Player

Hayes, Julia
Carolina Moon Enterprises, PO Box 2571, Columbia SC 29202, USA — Actress, Model

Hayes, Laura
Performance Artists Agency, 137 Goswell Road, London EC1V 7ET, England — Actress

Hayes, Louis S
AudioWorks, 245 W 25th St, New York NY 10001, USA — Jazz Drummer

Hayes, Mark S
1014 Saint Andrews Dr, Edmond OK 73025, USA — Golfer

Hayes, Patty
3436 Sipsey St, Villages FL 32162, USA — Golfer

Hayes, Peter
Paradigm Agency, 360 Park Ave, #1600, New York NY 10022 USA — Guitarist (Black Rebel Motorcycle Club)

Hayes, Reginald C (Reggie)
Amsel Eisenstadt Frazier, 5055 Wilshire Blvd, #865, Los Angeles CA 90036 USA — Actor

Hayes, Robert M
National Coalition for the Homeless, 105 E 22nd St, New York NY 10010, USA — Social Activist

Hayes, Sean P
Hazy Mills Productions, 4024 Radford Ave, Studio City CA 91604, USA — Actor

Hayes, Steven L (Steve)
1630 Mercoal Dr, Spring TX 77386, USA — Basketball Player

Hayes, Von F
1118 S Moody Ave, Tampa FL 33629, USA — Baseball Player

Hayes, Wade
Trey Turner Assoc, 40 Music Square W, Nashville TN 37203, USA — Singer

Hayes, Wendell
1935 E 30th St, #23, Oakland CA 94606, USA — Football Player

Hayhoe, William (Bill), II
5146 Santa Anita Dr, Sparks NV 89436, USA — Football Player

Hayhurst, Dirk V
570 Harvey St, Kent OH 44240, USA — Baseball Player

Hayhurst, John O
14741 SE Wanda Dr, Portland OR 97267, USA — Inventor (Bone Tissue Reattachment)

Hayman, Conway
6811 Stiller Dr, Missouri City TX 77489, USA — Football Player

Hayman, David T
Markham & Froggatt, Julian House, 4 Windmill St, London W1P 1HF, England — Actor, Director

Hayman, Fred
6946 Wildlife Road, Malibu CA 90265, USA — Fashion Designer

Hayman, Gordon I
54 Lakes Lane, Beaconsfield, Buckinghamshire HP9 2LB, England — Cinematographer

Hayman, James
Paradigm Agency, 360 N Crescent Dr, North Building, Beverly Hills CA 90210 USA — Producer, Director

Haymond, Alvin H (Juggie)
2857 Mantis Dr, San Jose CA 95148, USA — Football Player

Haynes, Abner
1950 FM 489, Oakwood TX 75855, USA — Football Player

Haynes, Al
4410 S 182nd St, Seatac WA 98188, USA — Airline Pilot Hero

Haynes, Betsy
5973 Sandhill Circle, The Colony TX 75056, USA — Writer

Haynes, Gibson J (Gibby)
Kork Agency, 1880 Century Park E, #711, Los Angeles CA 90067, USA — Singer, Guitarist (Butthole Surfers)

Haynes, Jimmy W
516 Riverside Dr, LaGrange GA 30240, USA — Baseball Player

Haynes, Mark
220 S Oneida St, Denver CO 80230, USA — Football Player

Haynes, Marques O
954 Taylor Dr, Winnsboro TX 75494, USA — Basketball Player, Coach

Haynes, Michael D
2375 Saddlesprings Dr, Alpharetta GA 30004, USA — Football Player

Haynes, Michael J (Mike)
7931 Entrada Lazanja, San Diego CA 92127, USA — Football Player

Haynes, Richard
2701 Fannin St, Houston TX 77002, USA — Attorney

Haynes, Roy O
Ted Kurland, 173 Brighton Ave, Allston MA 02134 USA — Jazz Drummer

Haynes, Todd
Creative Artists Agency, 2000 Ave of Stars, #100, Los Angeles CA 90067 USA — Director

Haynes, Verron U
2500 Northwinds Parkway, #275, Alpharetta GA 30009, USA — Football Player

Haynes, Warren
Writers & Artists Agency, 8383 Wilshire Blve, #550, Beverly Hills CA 90211 USA — Singer, Guitarist, Songwriter

Haynesworth, Albert (Al), III
5060 Abington Ridge Lane, Franklin TN 37067, USA — Football Player

Haynie, Jim
2721 Reynier Ave, Los Angeles CA 90034, USA — Actor

Haynie, Kristin
Sacramento Monarchs, Arco Arena, 1 Sports Parkway, Sacramento CA 95834 USA — Basketball Player

Haynie, Sandra J
2962 Beachtree Lane, Bedford TX 76021, USA — Golfer

Hays, Kathryn
Look Talent Agency, 166 Geary St, San Francisco CA 94108, USA — Actress

Hays, L Harold
10410 Ravenswood Road, Granbury TX 76049, USA — Football Player

Hays, Robert
Fran Saperstein Organization, 919 Victoria Ave, Venice CA 90291, USA — Actor

Hays, Ronald J
869 Kamoi Place, Honolulu HI 96825, USA — Navy Admiral

Hays, Todd
US Bobsled/Skeleton Federation, 1631 Mesa Ave, #A, Colorado Springs CO 80906 USA — Bobsled Athlete

Haysbert, Dennis
G S Mgmt, 861 S Windsor Blvd, #105, Los Angeles CA 90005, USA — Actor

Hayter, David
United Talent Agency, 9336 Civic Center Dr, Beverly Hills CA 90210 USA — Director, Writer, Actor

Haythe, Justin
Creative Artists Agency, 2000 Ave of Stars, #100, Los Angeles CA 90067 USA — Writer

Hayward, Jimmy
United Talent Agency, 9336 Civic Center Dr, Beverly Hills CA 90210 USA — Animator, Director, Actor

Hayward, Justin
Threshold Records, 54 High St, Cobham, Surrey KT11 3DP, England — Singer, Guitarist (Moody Blues)

Hayward, Kara
I C M Partners, 10250 Constellation Blvd, #900, Los Angeles CA 90067 USA — Actress

Hayward, Matt
Pias Entertainment Group, Trading Centre, 101 Farm Lane, #24, London SW6 1QJ, England — Drummer (Band of Skulls)

Hayward, Reginald J (Reggie), Jr
4651 Swilcan Bridge Lane S, Jacksonville FL 32224, USA — Football Player

Hayward, Thomas B
2200 Ross Ave, #3800, Dallas TX 75201, USA — Navy Admiral

Haywood, Brendan T
4514 Lawndale Dr, #E, Greensboro NC 27455, USA — Basketball Player

Haywood, Dave
Capitol Records, 3322 West End Ave, #1100, Nashville TN 37203 USA — Singer, Musician (Lady Antebellum)

Haywood, Hurley
1445 Ponte Vedra Blvd, Ponte Vedra Beach FL 32082, USA — Auto Racing Driver

Haywood, Spencer
49447 Plymouth Way, Plymouth MI 48170, USA — Basketball Player

Hayworth, Tracy K
528 Knights Church Road, Decherd TN 37324, USA — Football Player

Hazan, Marcella
1211 Gulf of Mexico Dr, #109, Longboat Key FL 34228, USA — Chef

Hazanavicius, Michel
Creative Artists Agency, 2000 Ave of Stars, #100, Los Angeles CA 90067 USA — Director, Editor, Writer

Hazard, Geoffrey C, Jr
200 W Willow Grove Ave, Philadelphia PA 19118, USA — Attorney, Educator

Hazell, Keeley R
98 De Beauvoir Road, London N1 4EN, England — Model, Singer

Hazelwood, Rebecca
Don Buchwald/Fortitude, 6500 Wilshire Blvd, #2200, Los Angeles CA 90048 USA — Actress

Hazen, Maya
Kritzer Levine Wilkins Griffin, 11872 La Grange Ave, #100, Los Angeles CA 90025 USA — Actress, Model

Haziza, Shlomi
H Studio, 8421 Lankershim Blvd, Sun Valley CA 91352, USA — Artist

Hazzard, Shirley
200 E 66th St, New York NY 10065, USA — Writer

He Kang
Agriculture Ministry, 11 Nongzhanguan Nanli, Beijing 10026, China — Government Official, China

Head, Anthony Stewart
Gordon & French, 12-13 Poland St, London W1F 8QB, England — Actor

Head, Dena
Central Connecticut State University, Athletic Dept, New Britain CT 06050, USA — Basketball Player

Head, Donald C (Don)
15240 NE Knott St, Portland OR 97230, USA — Ice Hockey Player

Head, Emily — Actress
United Talent Agency, 9336 Civic Center Dr, Beverly Hills CA 90210 USA
Head, Glenn O — Financier
First Investors Corp, 95 Wall St, #2200, New York NY 10005, USA
Head, Luther D — Basketball Player
3952 Feagan St, Houston TX 77007, USA
Head, Roy — Singer
Texas Sounds Entertainment, 2317 Pecan, Dickinson TX 77539, USA
Head, Tim D — Artist
271 Eversholt St, London NW1 1BA, England
Headden, Susan M — Journalist
US News & World Report, 2400 N St NW, Washington DC 20037, USA
Headen, Andrew R (Andy) — Football Player
PO Box 821, Liberty NC 27298, USA
Headey, Lena — Actress
Troika, 74 Clerkenwell Road, #300, London EC1M 5QA, England
Headley, Chase J — Baseball Player
5243 Avery Woods Lane, Knoxville TN 37921, USA
Headley, Heather — Singer, Actress
Creative Artists Agency, 2000 Ave of Stars, #100, Los Angeles CA 90067 USA
Headly, Glenne — Actress
I C M Partners, 10250 Constellation Blvd, #900, Los Angeles CA 90067 USA
Headon, Nicky (Topper) — Drummer (Clash)
Clash, 268 Camden Road, London NW1 9AB, England
Heald, Anthony — Actor
Abrams Artists, 9200 W Sunset Blvd, #1125, West Hollywood CA 90069 USA
Healey, Denis W — Government Official, England
Pingles Place, Alfriston, East Sussex BN26 5TT, England
Healey, Derek E — Composer
29 Stafford Road, Ruislip Gardens, Middlesex H4A 6PB, England
Healey, John G — Association Executive
Amnesty International USA, 322 8th Ave, New York NY 10001, USA
Healy, Cornelius T — Labor Leader
Plate Die Engravers Union, 228 S Swarthmore Ave, Ridley Park PA 19078, USA
Healy, Fran — Singer (Travis)
Wildlife Entertainment, 21 Heathmans Road, London SW6 4TJ, England
Healy, Francis X (Fran) — Baseball Player, Sportscaster
1 Primrose Lane, Holyoke MA 01040, USA
Healy, Jane E — Journalist
Orlando Sentinel, Editorial Dept, 633 N Orange Ave, Lobby, Orlando FL 32801, USA
Healy, Jeremiah — Writer
625 Oaks Dr, #703, Pompano Beach FL 33069, USA
Healy, M Donald (Don) — Football Player
3427 Boca Ciega Dr, Naples FL 34112, USA
Healy, Patricia — Actress
McCabe Group, 3211 Cahuenga Blvd W, #104, Los Angeles CA 90068, USA
Healy, Timothy M (Tim) — Actor
Ken McReddie Assoc, 11 Connaught Place, London W2 2ET, England
Heaney, Brian P — Basketball Player
153 Spinnaker Dr, Halifax NS B3N 3C3, Canada
Heaney, Seamus J — Nobel Literature Laureate
191 Strand Road, Dublin 4, Ireland
Heap, Imogen — Singer (Frou Frou)
Primary Talent International, 10-11 Jockey's Fields, London WC1R 4BN, England
Heap, Mark — Actor, Comedian
Curtis Brown Group, 28-29 Haymarket St, #500, London SW1Y 4SP, England
Heap, Todd B — Football Player
4320 N Essex Circle, Mesa AZ 85207, USA
Heard, Amber — Actress
I/D Public Relations, 7060 Hollywood Blvd, #800, Los Angeles CA 90028 USA
Heard, Garfield (Gar) — Basketball Player, Coach
185 Saddle Ridge Way, Fayetteville GA 30215, USA
Heard, Herman W, Jr — Football Player
PO Box 938, Broomfield CO 80038, USA
Heard, Jerry — Golfer
PO Box 429, Central Lake MI 49622, USA
Heard, John — Actor
Forster Entertainment, 12533 Woodgreen St, Building B, Los Angeles CA 90066, USA
Hearn, Edward J (Ed) — Baseball Player
5737 Theden St, Shawnee KS 66218, USA
Hearn, George — Actor, Singer
Paradigm Agency, 360 Park Ave S, #1600, New York NY 10010 USA
Hearn, Kevin — Musician (Barenaked Ladies)
Nettwerk Mgmt, 6525 W Sunset Blvd, #800, Los Angeles CA 90028 USA
Hearne, Bill — Singer, Guitarist
Class Act Entertainment, PO Box 160236, Nashville TN 37216, USA
Hearney, Richard D — Marine Corps General
Armed Forces Y M C A, PO Box 555028, Building 16144, Camp Pendleton CA 92055, USA
Hearns, Thomas (Tommy) — Boxer
20551 S Norwood St, Southfield MI 48075, USA
Hearron, Jeffrey V (Jeff) — Baseball Player
5820 Hill Road, Powder Springs GA 30127, USA
Hearst Shaw, Patricia C (Patty) — Writer
110 5th St, San Francisco CA 94103, USA
Hearst, G Garrison — Football Player
3753 Augusta Highway, Lincolnton GA 30817, USA
Hearst, Richard C (Rick) — Actor
Debbie O'Connor, PO Box 16212, Irvine CA 92623, USA
Heath, Albert (Tootie) — Jazz Drummer (Modern Jazz Quarter)
Ted Kurland, 173 Brighton Ave, Allston MA 02134 USA
Heath, James E (Jimmy) — Jazz Saxophonist, Composer
Ted Kurland, 173 Brighton Ave, Allston MA 02134 USA
Heath, Michael T (Mike) — Baseball Player
2107 Timothy Terrace, Valrico FL 33594, USA
Heath, Stanley (Stan), III — Basketball Player, Coach
University of South Florida, Athletic Dept, Tampa FL 33620, USA

Heath, Tobin P   Soccer Player
US Soccer Federation, 1801 S Prairie Ave, Chicago IL 60616 USA
Heath, William C (Bill)   Baseball Player
1626 Lake Charlotte Lane, Richmond TX 77406, USA
Heathcock, Clayton H   Chemist
5235 Alhambra Valley Road, Martinez CA 94553, USA
Heathcock, R Jeffrey (Jeff)   Baseball Player
24962 Calle Vecindad, Lake Forest CA 92630, USA
Heathcote, Alastair   Rowing Athlete
Amateur Rowing Assn, 6 Lower Mall, London W6 9DJ, England
Heathcote, Jud   Basketball Coach
5418 S Quail Ridge Circle, Spokane WA 99223, USA
Heatley, Daniel J (Dany)   Ice Hockey Player
686 Leguime Road, #306, Kelowna BC V1W 1A4, Canada
Heaton, Neal   Baseball Player
3 Nursery Court, East Patchogue NY 11772, USA
Heaton, Patricia   Actress
Creative Artists Agency, 2000 Ave of Stars, #100, Los Angeles CA 90067 USA
Heaverlo, David W (Dave)   Baseball Player
3720 W Lakeshore Dr, Moses Lake WA 98837, USA
Hebert, Bobby J, Jr   Football Player
855 Walker St, New Orleans LA 70124, USA
Hebert, Doug   Auto Racing Driver
1443 E Gastib St, Lincolnton NC 28092, USA
Hebert, Guy   Ice Hockey Player
8 Gleneagles Dr, Newport Beach CA 92660, USA
Hebert, Johnny   Auto Racing Driver
Team Lotus, Kettering Hamm Hall, Wymondham, Norfolk NR18 7HW, England
Hebner, Richard J (Richie)   Baseball Player
6 Tetreault Dr, Walpole MA 02081, USA
Hebron, Vaughn H   Football Player
800 Summit Trace Road, Langhorne PA 19047, USA
Hebson, Bryan   Baseball Player
1151 Fairmont Lane, Auburn AL 36830, USA
Heche, Anne   Actress
United Talent Agency, 9336 Civic Center Dr, Beverly Hills CA 90210 USA
Hecht, Duvall   Rower
2910 W Garry Ave, Santa Ana CA 92704, USA
Hecht, Gina   Actress
5930 Foothill Dr, Los Angeles CA 90068, USA
Hecht, Jessica   Actress
Innovative Artists, 1505 10th St, Santa Monica CA 90401 USA
Hecht, William F   Businessman
P P & L Resources, 2 N 9th St, Allentown PA 18101, USA
Heck, Andrew R (Andy)   Football Player
1 Bullrush Court, Stafford VA 22554, USA
Heck, Ralph A   Football Player
1906 Wicks Ridge Lane, Marietta GA 30062, USA
Hecker, Zvi   Architect
19 Elzar St, Tel Aviv 65157, Israel
Heckerling, Amy   Director, Producer
1330 Schuyler Road, Beverly Hills CA 90210, USA
Heckler, Margaret M   Secretary, Health & Human Services
1401 N Oak St, Arlington VA 22209, USA
Heckman, James J   Nobel Economics Laureate
4807 S Greenwood Ave, Chicago IL 60615, USA
Heckscher, August   Writer
333 E 68th St, New York NY 10065, USA
Hector, Jamie   Actor
T C A/Jed Root, 9220 Sunset Blvd, #315, Los Angeles CA 90069, USA
Hector, Johnny L   Football Player
525 Caroline St, New Iberia LA 70560, USA
Hedaya, Dan   Actor
Gersh Agency, 9465 Wilshire Blvd, #600, Beverly Hills CA 90212 USA
Hedberg, Johan   Ice Hockey Player
2967 Silvermere Lane, Duluth GA 30097, USA
Hedeman, Richard (Tuff)   Rodeo Bull Rider
PO Box 224, Morgan Mill TX 76465, USA
Heder, Jon   Actor
B/W/R, 9100 Wilshire Blvd, #500W, Beverly Hills CA 90212 USA
Hedford, Eric   Singer, Drummer (Dandy Warhols)
Monqui Mgmt, PO Box 5908, Portland OR 97228, USA
Hedgepeth, Whitney   Swimmer
9801 Westward Dr, Austin TX 78733, USA
Hedges, Peter   Director, Writer
Creative Artists Agency, 2000 Ave of Stars, #100, Los Angeles CA 90067 USA
Hedican, Bret   Ice Hockey Player
290 Las Quebradas Lane, Alamo CA 94507, USA
Hedison, David   Actor
Ambrosio/Mortimer, 165 W 46th St, New York NY 10036 USA
Hedlund, Garrett   Actor, Singer
Brillstein Entertainment Partners, 9150 Wilshire Blvd, #350, Beverly Hills CA 90212 USA
Hedlund, Michael D (Mike)   Baseball Player
2412 Klinger Road, Arlington TX 76016, USA
Hedren, Tippi   Actress
PO Box 189, Acton CA 93510, USA
Hedrick, Chad   Speed Skater
5504 Fellowship Lane, Spring TX 77379, USA
Hedrick, Joan D   Writer
Trinity College, Women's Studies Program, 300 Summit St, Hartford CT 06106, USA
Heeger, Alan J   Nobel Chemistry Laureate
1042 Las Alturas Road, Santa Barbara CA 93103, USA
Heep, Daniel W (Dan)   Baseball Player
18610 Crosstimber, San Antonio TX 78258, USA
Heeschen, David S   Radio Astronomer
702 Copa de Oro, Marathon FL 33050, USA

H

Heath - Heeschen

Heeter, Carrie — Inventor (Sign-Language Software)
Michigan State University, Communication Technology Laboratory, East Lansing MI 48824, USA
Heffernan, Bertram A (Bert) — Baseball Player
130 Eagle Court, Locust Grove VA 22508, USA
Heffernan, John — Actor
Ken McReddie Assoc, 11 Connaught Place, London W2 2ET, England
Heffernan, Kevin — Actor, Comedian
Broken Lizard Industries, PO Box 642809, Los Angeles CA 90064, USA
Heffner, Robert F (Bob) — Baseball Player
910 N 12th St, Allentown PA 18102, USA
Heffron, John — Actor, Comedian
Gersh Agency, 9465 Wilshire Blvd, #600, Beverly Hills CA 90212 USA
Heflin, Vincent G (Vince) — Football Player
5603 Regency Park Court, #3, Suitland MD 20746, USA
Hefner, Hugh M — Publisher, Editor
10236 Charing Cross Road, Los Angeles CA 90024, USA
Hegamin, George R — Football Player
1409 S Lamar St, #512, Dallas TX 75215, USA
Hegan, J Michael (Mike) — Baseball Player
7 Wild Turkey Run, Hilton Head Island SC 29926, USA
Hegarty, John F — Labor Leader
National Postal Mail Handlers Union, 1101 Connecticut Ave NW, #500, Washington DC 20036, USA
Hegman, Michael W (Mike) — Football Player
2958 Suesand Dr, Memphis TN 38128, USA
Hegman, Robert H (Bob) — Baseball Player
3529 NW Winding Woods Dr, Lees Summit MO 64064, USA
Hegre, Petter — Photographer
Ocinum, Rua das Hortas, 9050-024 Funchal Madeira, Portugal
Heidemann, Jack S — Baseball Player
1816 S Salida del Sol Circle, Mesa AZ 85202, USA
Heiden, Elizabeth L (Beth) — Speed Skater
915 Swarthmore Court, Madison WI 53705, USA
Heiden, Eric A — Speed Skater, Cyclist
1219 Cottonwood Lane, Park City UT 84098, USA
Heiden, Steve A — Football Player
12047 Tivoli Park Row, #3, San Diego CA 92128, USA
Heigl, Katherine — Actress, Model
Jason Heigl Foundation, 2046 Hillhurst Ave, #90, Los Angeles CA 90027, USA
Heil, Jennifer — Freestyle Moguls Skier
Newport Sports Mgmt, 201 City Centre Dr, #400, Mississauga ON L5B 2T4, Canada
Heilman, Aaron M — Baseball Player
39W814 Kellar Square, Geneva IL 60134, USA
Heilmeier, George H — Inventor (Liquid Crystal Display)
Telecordia Technologies, 1 Telecordia Dr, Piscataway NJ 08854, USA
Heimbold, Charles A, Jr — Businessman
Bristol-Myers Squibb, 345 Park Ave, Basement LC3, New York NY 10154, USA
Heimlich, Henry J — Physician
3939 Erie Ave, #4060, Cincinnati OH 45208, USA
Heimueller, Gorman J — Baseball Player
2148 Glen Ave, Riverton UT 84065, USA
Heine, Jutta — Track Athlete
Blaue Muhle, 57614 Burglahr, Germany
Heineman, Kenneth R (Ken) — Football Player
300 Innis Free Circle, #C4, Rogers AR 72758, USA
Heinen, Mike — Golfer
4518 E Meadow Lane, Lake Charles LA 70605, USA
Heinkel, Donald E (Don) — Baseball Player
508 Covington Ave, Birmingham AL 35206, USA
Heinle, Amelia — Actress
Don Buchwald/Fortitude, 6500 Wilshire Blvd, #2200, Los Angeles CA 90048 USA
Heinrich, Stephanie — Model
294 S Beverly Dr, Beverly Hills CA 90212, USA
Heinrichs, Albert M — Philologist
Harvard University, Classics Dept, Cambridge MA 02138, USA
Heinrichs, Rick — Art Director, Production Designer
Sandra Marsh & Associates, 9150 Wilshire Blvd, #220, Beverly Hills CA 90212, USA
Heins, Trevor — Actor
Abrams Artists, 275 7th Ave, #2600, New York NY 10001 USA
Heinsohn, Thomas W (Tom) — Basketball Player, Coach
15 Hunters Way, Needham Heights MA 02494, USA
Heintz, Christopher J (Chris) — Baseball Player
6002 Laketree Lane, #N, Tampa FL 33617, USA
Heinz, Andras — Writer
Luber Rocklin Entertainment, 8530 Wilshire Blvd, #555, Beverly Hills CA 90211 USA
Heinz, Robert K (Bob) — Football Player
516 Mansion Court, #502, Santa Clara CA 95054, USA
Heise, Robert L (Bob) — Baseball Player
537 Live Oak Dr, Angels Camp CA 95222, USA
Heiser, Rolland V — Army General
4721 Ocean Blvd, #W7, Sarasota FL 34242, USA
Heisler, Eileen — Producer
United Talent Agency, 9336 Civic Center Dr, Beverly Hills CA 90210 USA
Heisler, Todd — Photojournalist
Rocky Mountain News, Editorial Dept, 101 W Colfax Ave, Denver CO 80202, USA
Heiss Jenkins, Carol — Figure Skater
3183 Regency Place, Westlake OH 44145, USA
Heist, Ari — Singer, Songwriter
Agency Group Ltd, 142 W 57th St, #600, New York NY 10019 USA
Heitman, Dana C — Trumpeter (Cherry Poppin' Daddies)
Paradise Artists, PO Box 1821, Ojai CA 93024 USA
Hejda, Jan — Ice Hockey Player
9929 Sara Gulch Circle, Parker CO 80138, USA
Hejduk, Milan — Ice Hockey Player
7895 Forest Keep Circle, Parker CO 80134, USA
Hejlik, Dennis J — Marine Corps General
Commander, Marine Forces Command, 1468 Ingram St, Norfolk VA 23511 USA

Hekman, Peter M, Jr	Navy Admiral
5021 Via Papel, San Diego CA 92122, USA	
Helberg, Simon	Actor, Comedian
Brillstein Entertainment Partners, 9150 Wilshire Blvd, #350, Beverly Hills CA 90212 USA	
Held, Alan	Opera Singer
Opus3 Artists, 470 Park Ave S, #900, New York NY 10016, USA	
Held, Archie	Sculptor
A New Leaf Garden, 1286 Gilman St, Albany CA 94706, USA	
Held, Franklin (Bud)	Track Athlete
13367 Caminito Mar Villa, Del Mar CA 92014, USA	
Held, Ingrid	Actress
Agents Associes, 201 Rue du Faubourg Saint Honore, 75008 Paris, France	
Held, Melvin N (Mel)	Baseball Player
103 Hogan Lane, Cookson OK 74427, USA	
Held, Richard M	Psychologist
Massachusetts Institute of Technology, Psychology Dept, Cambridge MA 02139, USA	
Helders, Matthew (Matt)	Drummer (Arctic Monkeys)
Wildlife Entertainment, 21 Heathmans Road, London SW6 4TJ, England	
Helfand, Eric J	Baseball Player
7314 Jackson Dr, San Diego CA 92119, USA	
Helfer, Ricki Tigert	Government Official, Financier
Federal Deposit Insurance, 550 17th St NW, Washington DC 20429, USA	
Helfer, Tricia	Model, Actress
Gilbertson Entertainment, 1334 3rd Street Promenade, #201, Santa Monica CA 90401 USA	
Helfgott, David	Concert Pianist
PO Box 264, Vellengen NSW 2454, Australia	
Helford, Bruce	Producer, Writer
United Talent Agency, 9336 Civic Center Dr, Beverly Hills CA 90210 USA	
Helgeland, Brian	Director, Writer
Brillstein Entertainment Partners, 9150 Wilshire Blvd, #350, Beverly Hills CA 90212 USA	
Helgenberger, Marg	Actress
Sanders/Armstrong/Caserta Mgmt, 2120 Colorado Ave, #120, Santa Monica CA 90404 USA	
Heline, DeAnn	Producer, Writer
United Talent Agency, 9336 Civic Center Dr, Beverly Hills CA 90210 USA	
Helland, J Roy	Make-Up Artist
Crew Co, 3941 E Chandler Blvd, #106-259, Phoenix AZ 85048, USA	
Hellawell, Keith	Law Enforcment Official
Government Offices, Great George St, London SW1A 2AL, England	
Hellekant, Charlotte	Opera Singer
Harrison/Parrott, 5-6 Albion Court, London W6 0QT, England	
Heller, Andre	Actor, Entertainer
Singerstr 8, 1010 Vienna, Austria	
Heller, Bruno	Producer/Screenwriter
W M E Entertainment, 9601 Wilshire Blvd, #300, Beverly Hills CA 90210 USA	
Heller, Jane	Writer
1014 Ladera Lane, Santa Barbara CA 93108, USA	
Heller, Jeffrey M	Businessman
Electronic Data Systems, 5400 Legacy Dr, Plano TX 75024, USA	
Heller, Joe	Editorial Cartoonist
Green Bay Press-Gazette, Editorial Dept, 435 E Walnut St, Green Bay WI 54301, USA	
Heller, John H	Physician, Research Scientist
74 Horseshoe Road, Wilton CT 06897, USA	
Heller, Ronald J (Ron)	Football Player
3894 Nathan Road, Santa Barbara CA 93110, USA	
Heller, Ronald R (Ron)	Football Player
538 Stillwater River Road, Absarokee MT 59001, USA	
Hellerman, Fred	Singer (Weavers), Songwriter
83 Good Hill Road, Weston CT 06883, USA	
Hellestrae, Dale R	Football Player
4960 E Fellars Dr, Scottsdale AZ 85254, USA	
Hellickson, Russell (Russ)	Freestyle Wrestler
6893 Lauren Place, Columbus OH 43235, USA	
Helliker, Kevin	Journalist
Wall Street Journal, Editorial Dept, 1 World Financial Center, New York NY 10281, USA	
Helling, Ricky A (Rick)	Baseball Player
3672 Landings Dr, Excelsior MN 55331, USA	
Hellman, Bonnie	Actress
C E S D, 257 Park Ave S, #950, New York NY 10010 USA	
Hellman, Martin E	Inventor (Public Key Cryptology)
855 Serra St, Stanford CA 94305, USA	
Hellman, Monte	Director
8588 Appian Way, Los Angeles CA 90046, USA	
Hellmuth, Phil	Poker Player
World Poker Tour, 1041 N Formosa, Building 99, West Hollywood CA 90046, USA	
Hellner, Marcus	Cross Country Skier
Swedish Ski Federation, Riksskidstadion, 791 19 Falun, Sweden	
Hellstrand, Kristoffer	Microbiologist
Goteborg University, Virology Dept, 40 503 Goteborg, Sweden	
Helluin, F Jerome (Jerry)	Football Player
3930 Southdown Mandalay Road, Houma LA 70360, USA	
Hellyer, Paul T	Government Official, Canada
65 Harbour Square, #506, Toronto ON M5J 2L4, Canada	
Helm, Amy	Singer (Ollabelle)
Columbia Records, 9830 Wilshire Blvd, Beverly Hills CA 90212 USA	
Helm, Zach	Director, Writer
Gang of Two Productions, 8750 Wilshire Blvd, Beverly Hills CA 90211, USA	
Helmberger, Don V	Seismologist
California Institute of Technology, Seismology Dept, Pasadena CA 91125, USA	
Helmer, Thomas	Soccer Player
Rosenthaler Str 40-41, Hackesche Hofe, 10178 Berlin, Germany	
Helmerich, Hans C	Businessman
Helmerich & Payne Inc, 1437 S Boulder Ave, #1400, Tulsa OK 74119, USA	
Helmerich, Walter H, III	Businessman
Helmerich & Payne Inc, 1437 S Boulder Ave, #1400, Tulsa OK 74119, USA	
Helmick, Frank	Army General
Multi-National Security Transition Command, Bagdad Iraq, APO AE 09348, USA	

H

Hekman - Helmick

Helminen, Raimo I   Ice Hockey Player
269 N Regent St, Port Chester NY 10573, USA
Helmond, Katherine   Actress
14170 Montecito Place, Victorville CA 92395, USA
Helmreich, Ernst J M   Chemist
University of Wurzburg Biozentrum, Am Hubland, 97074 Wurzburg, Germany
Helms, Cory   Writer
Writers Guild of America, 700 W 3rd St, Los Angeles CA 90071, USA
Helms, Edward P (Ed)   Actor, Comedian
Creative Artists Agency, 2000 Ave of Stars, #100, Los Angeles CA 90067 USA
Helms, Susan J   Astronaut, Air Force General
Commander, 14th Air Force, Vandenberg Air Force Base CA 93437 USA
Helms, Tommy V   Baseball Player, Manager
5427 Blue Sky Dr, Cincinnati OH 45247, USA
Helms, Wesley R (Wes)   Baseball Player
9314 Bear Creek Road, Sterrett AL 35147, USA
Helnwein, Gottfried   Artist
Auf der Burg 2, 56659 Burgbrohl, Germany
Heloise, (Cruse Evans)   Columnist, Writer
PO Box 795000, San Antonio TX 78279, USA
Helpern, Joan G   Fashion Designer
Joan & David Helpern Inc, 46 W 55th St, #200, New York NY 10019, USA
Helseth, Tine Ting   Concert Trumpeter
I M G Artists, Hogarth Business Park, Chiswick, London W4 2TH, England
Helton, Michael (Mike)   Auto Racing Executive
National Assn of Stock Car Racing, 1801 Speedway Blvd, Daytona Beach FL 32114 USA
Helton, Todd L   Baseball Player
8720 E 127th Court, Brighton CO 80602, USA
Helvin, Marie   Model
I M G Models, 131-151 Great Titchfield St, London W1W 5BB, England
Helwig, David G   Writer
General Delivery, Belfast PE C0A 1A0, Canada
Hely, Steve   Actor
W M E Entertainment, 9601 Wilshire Blvd, #300, Beverly Hills CA 90210 USA
Heman, Russell F (Russ)   Baseball Player
5555 Canyon Crest Dr, #30, Riverside CA 92507, USA
Hemingway, Gerardine   Fashion Designer
Red or Dead Ltd, Courtney Road, Bldg 201, Wembley, Middlesex HA9 7PP, England
Hemingway, Mariel   Model, Actress
21300 Victory Blvd, Woodland Hills CA 91367, USA
Hemingway, Toby   Actor
United Talent Agency, 9336 Civic Center Dr, Beverly Hills CA 90210 USA
Hemingway, Wayne   Fashion Designer
15 Wembley Park Dr, Wembley, Middlesex HA9 8HD, England
Hemme, Christy (Sunni)   Wrestler, Model, Actress
Strachota Insurance Agency, 43500 Ridge Park Dr, #203, Temecula CA 92590, USA
Hemmens, Heather   Actress
Untitled Entertainment, 350 S Beverly Dr, #200, Beverly Hills CA 90212 USA
Hemmer, Bill   Commentator
Fox-TV, News Dept, 205 E 67th St, New York NY 10065 USA
Hemmi, Heini   Alpine Skier
Chalet Bel-Lia, 7077 Valbella, Switzerland
Hemming, Lindy   Costume Designer
Independent Talent Group, Oxford House, 76 Oxford St, London W1D 1BS, England
Hemmings, Fred, Jr   Surfer, Surfing Executive
45-075 Auloa Road, Kaneohe HI 96744, USA
Hemmis, Paige   Actress
Tuff Chix, 22817 Ventura Blvd, #317, Woodland Hills CA 91364, USA
Hemond, Scott M   Baseball Player
263 Florida Ave, Dunedin FL 34698, USA
Hempel, Amy   Writer
Charles Scribner's Sons, 866 3rd Ave, New York NY 10022 USA
Hemphill, Joel   Singer, Songwriter
PO Box 656, Joelton TN 37080, USA
Hemphill, Labreeska   Singer
PO Box 656, Joelton TN 37080, USA
Hemric, N Dixon (Dick)   Basketball Player
1220 7th St NE, North Canton OH 44720, USA
Hemse, Rebecka   Actress
A I S Agency, Bergmansgatan 20, 00150 Helsinfors, Finland
Hemsley, Stephen J   Businessman
United HealthCare Corp, Opus Center, 9900 Bren Road E, Hopkins MN 55343, USA
Hemsworth, Chris   Actor
Roar Mgmt, 9701 Wilshire Blvd, #800, Beverly Hills CA 90212 USA
Hemsworth, Liam   Actor
Roar Mgmt, 9701 Wilshire Blvd, #800, Beverly Hills CA 90212 USA
Hemsworth, Martin C   Mechanical Engineer
11200 Springfield Pike, Cincinnati OH 45246, USA
Hemus, Solomon J (Solly)   Baseball Player, Manager
5100 San Felipe St, #194E, Houston TX 77056, USA
Henao, Zulay   Actress
I C M Partners, 10250 Constellation Blvd, #900, Los Angeles CA 90067 USA
Henchy, Chris   Actor, Producer, Writer
Mosiac Media Group, 9200 W Sunset Blvd, #1000, Los Angeles CA 90069 USA
Hencken, John F   Swimmer
PO Box 2540, Weaverville NC 28787, USA
Henderson, Alan L   Basketball Player
Philadelphia 76ers, 1st Union Center, 3601 S Broad St, Philadelphia PA 19148 USA
Henderson, Bruce   Singer, Songwriter
Fitch Thomas Mgmt, 75 E End Ave, #4C, New York NY 10028, USA
Henderson, Cathy   Guitarist (Antigone Rising)
W Mgmt, 266 Elizabeth St, #1A, New York NY 10012, USA
Henderson, Cedric   Basketball Player
PO Box 148, Smyrna GA 30081, USA
Henderson, Craig   Actor
Associated International Mgmt, Fairfax House, Fulwood Place, London WC1V 6HU, England

Henderson, David L (Dave) — Baseball Player
6004 142nd Court SE, Bellevue WA 98006, USA
Henderson, David M (Dave) — Basketball Player
805 Sweet Hollow Court, Middletown DE 19709, USA
Henderson, Devery V, Jr — Football Player
835 E Bellevue St, Opelousas LA 70570, USA
Henderson, Donald A (D A) — Epidemologist, Educator
3802 Greenway, Baltimore MD 21218, USA
Henderson, Eric N (E J), Jr — Football Player
Minnesota Vikings, 9520 Viking Dr, Eden Prairie MN 55344 USA
Henderson, Felicia D — Producer, Director, Writer
Paradigm Agency, 360 N Crescent Dr, North Building, Beverly Hills CA 90210 USA
Henderson, Fergus — Chef, Writer
Lutyens & Rubinstein, 231 Westbourne Park Road, London W11 1EB, England
Henderson, Florence — Actress, Singer
F H B Productions, PO Box 11295, Marina del Rey CA 90295, USA
Henderson, Gordon — Fashion Designer
World Hong Kong, 80 W 40th St, New York NY 10018, USA
Henderson, James A — Businessman
Cummins Engine Co, PO Box 3005, 500 Jackson St, Columbus IN 47201, USA
Henderson, Jerome M (Gerald) — Basketball Player
185 Birkdale Dr, Blue Bell PA 19422, USA
Henderson, Jerome M (Gerald), Jr — Basketball Player
Charlotte Bobcats, 333 E Trade St, #A, Charlotte NC 28202 USA
Henderson, John W — Football Player
11667 Blackstone River Dr, Jacksonville FL 32256, USA
Henderson, Joseph L (Jose) — Baseball Player
525 Agua Clara St, El Paso TX 79928, USA
Henderson, Josh — Actor
Impression Entertainment, 9229 W Sunset Blvd, #700, Los Angeles CA 90069, USA
Henderson, Kara — Sportscaster
N F L Network, 10950 Washington Blvd, #100, Culver City CA 90232 USA
Henderson, Karen LeCraft — Judge
US Court of Appeals, 333 Constitution Ave NW, #4400, Washington DC 20001, USA
Henderson, Kenneth J (Ken) — Baseball Player
182 La Montagne Court, Los Gatos CA 95032, USA
Henderson, Kristen — Guitarist (Antigone Rising)
W Mgmt, 266 Elizabeth St, #1A, New York. NY 10012, USA
Henderson, Martin — Actor
Management 360, 9111 Wilshire Blvd, Beverly Hills CA 90210 USA
Henderson, Melissa — Soccer Player
Sky Blue F C, 80 Cottontail Lane, #400, Somerset NJ 08873 USA
Henderson, Michael (Mike) — Singer, Guitarist, Songwriter
Press Network, PO Box 176, Pleasant Shade TN 37145, USA
Henderson, Paul, III — Journalist
Seattle Times, Editorial Dept, 1120 John St, Seattle WA 98109 USA
Henderson, Pete — Comedian (Skiles & Henderson)
Jack Grenier Productions, 32630 Concord Dr, Madison Heights MI 48071 USA
Henderson, Rickey H — Baseball Player
10561 Englewood Dr, Oakland CA 94605, USA
Henderson, Shirley — Actress
Hamilton Hodell, 66-68 Margaret St, London W1W 8SR, England
Henderson, Stephen C (Steve) — Baseball Player
10509 Gretna Green Dr, Tampa FL 33626, USA
Henderson, Tareva — Singer
PO Box 17678, Nashville TN 37217, USA
Henderson, Thomas E (Hollywood) — Football Player
3106 E 13th St, Austin TX 78702, USA
Henderson, Thomas E (Tom) — Basketball Player
6822 Baron Gate Court, Spring TX 77379, USA
Henderson, Wayne (Trombone) — Jazz Trombonist
I C M Partners, 10250 Constellation Blvd, #900, Los Angeles CA 90067 USA
Henderson, Wymon — Football Player
634 Braidwood Dr NW, Acworth GA 30101, USA
Hendley, C Robert (Bob) — Baseball Player
645 Wimbish Road, Macon GA 31210, USA
Hendrick, George A, Jr — Baseball Player
72 Wildwing Court, Las Vegas NV 89135, USA
Hendricks, Barbara — Opera Singer
Ingpen & Williams, 131 Putney Bridge Road, London SW15 2PA, England
Hendricks, Barkley L — Artist
Connecticut College, Art Dept, 270 Mohegan Ave, New London CT 06320, USA
Hendricks, Christina — Actress
Kritzer Levine Wilkins Griffin, 11872 La Grange Ave, #100, Los Angeles CA 90025 USA
Hendricks, Jon — Singer
Universal Attractions, 135 W 26th St, #1200, New York NY 10001 USA
Hendricks, Theodore P (Ted) — Football Player
PO Box 7470, Buffalo Grove IL 60089, USA
Hendrickson, Darby J — Ice Hockey Player
3939 Huntingdon Dr, Hopkins MN 55305, USA
Hendrickson, Elizabeth — Actress
TalentWorks, 3500 W Olive Ave, #1400, Burbank CA 91505 USA
Hendrickson, Mark A — Baseball, Basketball Player
1585 Wyndham Dr, York PA 17403, USA
Hendrickson, Steven D (Steve) — Football Player
2558 Miller Ave, Escondido CA 92029, USA
Hendrie, Phil — Actor
I C M Partners, 10250 Constellation Blvd, #900, Los Angeles CA 90067 USA
Hendrix, Elaine — Actress
Innovative Artists, 1505 10th St, Santa Monica CA 90401 USA
Hendrix, John W — Army General
Military Officers Assn, 201 N Washington St, Alexandria VA 22314, USA
Hendry, Gloria — Actress
H David Moss, 733 Seward St, #PH, Los Angeles CA 90038 USA
Hendryx, Nona — Singer, Songwriter
Black Rock, 6201 W Sunset Blvd, #329, Los Angeles CA 90028, USA

Henderson - Hendryx

Henenlotter, Frank
81 Bedford St, #6E, New York NY 10014, USA — Director
Hengel, David L (Dave)
2642 Kingfisher Lane, Lincoln CA 95648, USA — Baseball Player
Henin, Justine
Blue Entertainment, 333 E Main St, #200, Louisville KY 40202 USA — Tennis Player
Henke, Brad William
B/W/R, 9100 Wilshire Blvd, #500W, Beverly Hills CA 90212 USA — Actor
Henke, Edgar E (Ed)
769 Lisa Lane, Ashland OR 97520, USA — Football Player
Henke, Nolan
1323 Florida Ave, Fort Myers FL 33901, USA — Golfer
Henke, Thomas A (Tom)
6200 Saint Francis Dr, Jefferson City MO 65101, USA — Baseball Player
Henkel, Andrea
Friedensstr 37, 98701 Grossbrietenbach, Germany — Biathlete
Henkel, Heike
Tannenbergstr 57, 51373 Leverkusen, Germany — Track Athlete
Henkel, Herbert L
Ingersoll-Rand Co, PO Box 6820, Piscataway NJ 08855, USA — Businessman
Henle, Gertrude
533 Ott Road, Bala Cynwyd PA 19004, USA — Virologist
Henley, Don
Azoff Music Mgmt, 1100 Glendon Ave, #2000, Los Angeles CA 90024, USA — Singer (Eagles), Songwriter
Henley, Drewe
1 Granary Cottages, Combpyne, Axminster, Devon EX13 8SX, England — Actor
Henley, Elizabeth B (Beth)
W M E Entertainment, 9601 Wilshire Blvd, #300, Beverly Hills CA 90210 USA — Writer
Henley, Gail C
7338 Alta Vista, La Verne CA 91750, USA — Baseball Player
Henley, Georgie
Hamilton Hodell, 66-68 Margaret St, London W1W 8SR, England — Actress
Henley, Jeff
Oracle Systems, 500 Oriole Parkway, Redwood Shores CA 94065, USA — Businessman
Henley, Larry
Creative Directions, PO Box 335, Brentwood TN 37024, USA — Composer
Henley, Patricia
803 N Chauncey Ave, West Lafayette IN 47906, USA — Writer
Henley, Robert C (Bob)
11050 Moreland Dr E, Grand Bay AL 36541, USA — Baseball Player
Henley, Virginia
Penguin Putnam Press, 375 Hudson St, New York NY 10014, USA — Writer
Henn, Mark
Walt Disney Animation, PO Box 10200, Orlando FL 32830, USA — Animator (Little Mermaid)
Henn, Sean M
3658 Snow Creek Dr, Aledo TX 76008, USA — Baseball Player
Hennagan, Monique
505 Winter View Way, Stockbridge GA 30281, USA — Track Athlete
Henne, Chad S
Jacksonville Jaguars, 1 AllTel Stadium Place, Jacksonville FL 32202 USA — Football Player
Henneman, Brian
Undertow, 2307 Milan Court, Champaign IL 61822, USA — Singer, Guitarist (Bottle Rockets)
Henneman, Michael A (Mike)
806 Lake Creek Dr, McKinney TX 75070, USA — Baseball Player
Hennen, Thomas J
16315 Cascade Caverns Lane, Houston TX 77044, USA — Astronaut
Henner, Marilu
Gutmann Assoc, 188 S Bevery Dr, Beverly Hills CA 90212, USA — Actress
Hennessey, Brad
6657 Brentridge Lane, Lambertville MI 48144, USA — Baseball Player
Hennessey, Debbie
Rustic Music, 10736 Jefferson Blvd, #777, Culver City CA 90230, USA — Singer, Songwriter
Hennessey, Walter (Wally)
4141 NW 9th Court, Coconut Creek FL 33066, USA — Harness Racing Driver
Hennessy, Angelique
7923 Reseda Blvd, #57, Reseda CA 91335, USA — Actress, Model
Hennessy, Jill
Paradigm Agency, 360 N Crescent Dr, North Building, Beverly Hills CA 90210 USA — Actress, Model
Hennessy, John L
Stanford University, President's Office, Stanford CA 94305, USA — Educator
Henney, Daniel
W M E Entertainment, 9601 Wilshire Blvd, #300, Beverly Hills CA 90210 USA — Actor
Hennig, Larry
7426 43rd Ave SE, Saint Cloud MN 56304, USA — Wrestler
Hennigan, Charles T (Charley)
3875 Line Ave, #108, Shreveport LA 71106, USA — Football Player
Hennigan, Phillip W (Phil)
PO Box 1212, Cookeville TN 38503, USA — Baseball Player
Hennigan, T Michael (Mike)
542 N Washington Ave, Cookeville TN 38501, USA — Football Player, Coach
Henning, Cameron
Swimming Canada, 2197 Riverside Dr, #700, Ottawa ON K1H 7X3, Canada — Swimmer
Henning, Dan
116 Meeting Way, Ponte Vedra Beach FL 32082, USA — Football Player, Coach
Henning, Linda
Trinkets & Treasures, 4342 Tujunga Ave, Studio City CA 91604, USA — Actress
Henning, Lorne E
18 Coldbrook, Irvine CA 92604, USA — Ice Hockey Player, Coach
Henning, Megan
Greene Assoc, 1901 Ave of Stars, #130, Los Angeles CA 90067 USA — Actress
Henninger, Brian
25481 SW Newland Road, Wilsonville OR 97070, USA — Golfer
Hennings, Chad W
6101 Bay Valley Court, Flower Mound TX 75022, USA — Football Player
Hennings, Sam
Thirdhill Entertainment, 195 S Beverly Dr, #400, Beverly Hills CA 90212, USA — Actor

Henning-Walker, Anne — Speed Skater
12359 E LaSalle Place, Aurora CO 80014, USA
Hennis, Randall P (Randy) — Baseball Player
1747 Sienna Dr, Melbourne FL 32934, USA
Henri — Grand Duke, Luxembourg
Palais Grand-Ducal, 17 Rue du Marche-aux-Herbes, 1728 Luxembourg-Ville, Luxembourg
Henrich, Robert E (Bobby) — Baseball Player
1531 Via Los Coyotes, La Habra CA 90631, USA
Henrichs, April — Soccer Player, Coach
US Olympic Committee, 1 Olympic Plaza, Building 6, Colorado Springs CO 80909 USA
Henricks, Jon N — Swimmer
254 Laurel Ave, Des Plaines IL 60016, USA
Henricks, Terence T (Tom) — Astronaut
Aviation Week, President's Office, 1200 G St NW, #922, Washington DC 20005, USA
Henrie, David — Actor
Untitled Entertainment, 350 S Beverly Dr, #200, Beverly Hills CA 90212 USA
Henrik — Prince Consort, Denmark
Amalienborg Palace, 1257 Copenhagen K, Denmark
Henriksen, Donald A (Don) — Basketball Player
18160 Cottonwood Road, Bend OR 97707, USA
Henriksen, Lance — Actor
9200 Old Stage Road, Santa Clarita CA 91390, USA
Henriquez, Ron — Actor
PO Box 38027, Los Angeles CA 90038, USA
Henry, Albert J (Al) — Basketball Player
2410 N 52nd St, Philadelphia PA 19131, USA
Henry, Alex — Ice Hockey Player
Montreal Canadiens, 1275 Saint Antoine St W, Montreal QC H3C 5L2, Canada
Henry, Anthony D — Football Player
2611 Ross Ave, #4024, Dallas TX 75201, USA
Henry, Boris — Track Athlete
Semperstr 18, 66123 Saarbrucken, Germany
Henry, Buck — Actor, Writer
117 E 57th St, New York NY 10022, USA
Henry, Clarence (Frogman) — Singer, Pianist, Songwriter
3309 Lawrence St, New Orleans LA 70114, USA
Henry, Dale (Hank) — Ice Hockey Player
8611 Datapoint Dr, #43, San Antonio TX 78229, USA
Henry, David — Actor
Rights House, Drury House, 34-43 Russell St, London WC2B 5HA, England
Henry, Dwayne A — Baseball Player
407 E Hampstead Court, Middletown DE 19709, USA
Henry, F Buford (Butch), III — Baseball Player
12072 Paseo de Amor Lane, El Paso TX 79936, USA
Henry, Gloria — Actress
849 N Harper Ave, Los Angeles CA 90046, USA
Henry, Gregg — Actor
Framework Entertainment, 9057 Nemo St, #C, West Hollywood CA 90069 USA
Henry, J J — Golfer
6901 Sanctuary Lane, Fort Worth TX 76132, USA
Henry, Joe — Singer, Guitarist, Songwriter
Maine Road Mgmt, 195 Chrystie St, #901F, New York NY 10002, USA
Henry, Joseph L — Dentist
60 Marinita Ave, San Rafael CA 94901, USA
Henry, Justin — Actor
Metropolitan Talent Agency, 7020 La Presa Dr, Los Angeles CA 90068 USA
Henry, Kevin L — Football Player
2408 Sardis Chase Court, Buford GA 30519, USA
Henry, Lenny — Actor, Comedian
P B J Management Ltd, 5 Soho St, London W1D 3QA, England
Henry, Michael (Mike) — Producer, Writer, Actor
United Talent Agency, 9336 Civic Center Dr, Beverly Hills CA 90210 USA
Henry, Michael D (Mike) — Football Player, Actor
10803 Blix St, #3, North Hollywood CA 91602, USA
Henry, Nicole — Singer
NikiSings, PO Box 192011, Miami Beach FL 33119, USA
Henry, R Douglas (Doug) — Baseball Player
1804 Burries Road, Hartland WI 53029, USA
Henry, Robert H — Judge
US Court of Appeals, PO Box 1767, Oklahoma City OK 73101, USA
Henry, Steve A — Football Player
1907 Darlene Way, Emporia KS 66801, USA
Henry, Thierry (Titi) — Soccer Player
Red Bulls New York, 600 Cape May St, Harrison, NJ 07029 USA
Henry, Travis D — Football Player
6698 S Shawnee Court, Aurora CO 80016, USA
Henry, Wallace (Wally) — Football Player
3444 Bernadette Court, #A, West Covina CA 91792, USA
Henry, William R (Bill) — Baseball Player
2313 Kilkenny Lane, Deer Park TX 77536, USA
Hensby, Mark — Golfer
7175 E Camelback Road, #501, Scottsdale AZ 85251, USA
Henshall, Douglas — Actor
Ken McReddie Assoc, 11 Connaught Place, London W2 2ET, England
Henshall, Ruthie — Singer, Dancer, Actress
Conway Van Gelder Grant, 8-12 Broadwick St, #300, London W1F 8HW, England
Hensilwood, Christopher — Anthropologist
Iziko Museum, 25 Queen Victoria St, Cape Town, South Africa
Henske, Judy — Singer
Fair Star Music, PO Box 326, Plaza Station, Pasadena CA 91102, USA
Hensley, Charles F (Chuck) — Baseball Player
259 Bonanza Dr, Erie CO 80516, USA
Hensley, Clayton A (Clay) — Baseball Player
3601 Dogwood Blossom Court, Pearland TX 77581, USA
Hensley, Jimmy — Auto, Truck Racing Driver
2570 Horsepasture Price Road, Ridgeway VA 24148, USA

Hensley, John C — Actor
A P A Talent/Literary Agency, 405 S Beverly Dr, #300, Beverly Hills CA 90212 USA

Hensley, Pamela — Actress
Overlook Press, 141 Wooster St, #4B, New York NY 10012, USA

Hensley, Shuler — Actor, Singer
Paradigm Agency, 360 N Crescent Dr, North Building, Beverly Hills CA 90210 USA

Henson, Darrin Dewitt — Actor, Choreographer
Darrin's Dance Group, PO Box 3383, Memorial Station, Montclair NJ 07042, USA

Henson, John — Actor, Comedian
6347 Ivarene Ave, Los Angeles CA 90068, USA

Henson, John — Basketball Player
Milwaukee Bucks, Bradley Center, 1001 N 4th St, #2, Milwaukee WI 53203 USA

Henson, Robby — Director, Writer
New Wave Entertainment, 2660 W Olive Ave, Burbank CA 91505, USA

Henson, Samuel (Sammy) — Freestyle Wrestler
U S Military Academy, Athletic Dept, West Point NY 10996, USA

Henson, Taraji P — Actress, Singer
Vincent Cirrincione Assoc, 1516 N Fairfax Ave, Los Angeles CA 90046 USA

Henstridge, Natasha — Actress, Model
Mosiac Media Group, 9200 W Sunset Blvd, #1000, Los Angeles CA 90069 USA

Hentgen, Patrick G (Pat) — Baseball Player
14451 Knightsbridge Dr, Shelby Township MI 48315, USA

Hentoff, Nathan I (Nat) — Jazz Critic
Village Voice, Editorial Dept, 36 Cooper Square, Front 1, New York NY 10003, USA

Hentrich, Craig A — Football Player
9130 Old Smyrna Road, Brentwood TN 37027, USA

Hephner, Jeff — Actor
W M E Entertainment, 9601 Wilshire Blvd, #300, Beverly Hills CA 90210 USA

Hepler, William L (Bill) — Baseball Player
12518 Fort King Road, Dade City FL 33525, USA

Heppel, Leon A — Biochemist
Cornell University, Biochemistry Dept, Ithaca NY 14850, USA

Heppner, Ben — Opera Singer
Columbia Artists Mgmt Inc, 1790 Broadway, #702, New York NY 10019 USA

Heras-Casado, Pablo — Conductor
21C Media Group, 162 W 56th Street, #506, New York NY 10019, USA

Herbers, Ian — Ice Hockey Player
1135 Ridgeway Road, Brookfield WI 53045, USA

Herbert of Hemingford, D Nicholas — Publisher
Old Rectory, Hemingford Abbots, Huntington Cambridgeshire PE18 9AN, England

Herbert, Bob — Columnist
New York Times, Editorial Dept, 229 W 43rd St, New York NY 10036 USA

Herbert, Doug — Drag Racing Driver
Herbert Performance Parts, 4030 Concord Parkway S, Concord NC 28027, USA

Herbert, Johnny — Auto Racing Driver
P P Sayber AG, Wildbachstr 9, 8340 Hinwil, Switzerland

Herbert, Michael K — Editor
990 Grove St, Evanston IL 60201, USA

Herbert, Raymond E (Ray) — Baseball Player
9360 Taylors Turn, Gadsden AL 35901, USA

Herbig, George H — Astronomer
University of Hawaii, Astronomy Institute, 2680 Woodlawn Dr, Honolulu HI 96822, USA

Herbig, Gunther — Conductor
Toronto Symphony, 60 Simcoe St, #C116, Toronto ON MJ5 2H5, Canada

Herbig, Michael (Bully) — Actor, Comedian, Director
HerbX, Suedliche Muenchner Str 35A, 82931 Gruenwald, Germany

Herbst, Jeffrey — Educator
Colgate University, President's Office, 13 Oak Dr, Hamilton NY 13346, USA

Herbst, Susan — Educator
University of Connecticut, President's Office, Storrs CT 06269, USA

Herbst, William — Astronomer
Wesleyan University, Astronomy Dept, Middletown CT 06459, USA

Herbstreit, Kirk — Sportscaster
ESPN-TV, ESPN Plaza, 935 Middle St, Bristol CT 06010, USA

Herczegh, Gezar G — Judge
International Justice Court, Carnegieplein 2, 2517 KJ Hague, Netherlands

Herd, Richard — Actor
PO Box 56297, Sherman Oaks CA 91413, USA

Herda, Frank A — Vietnam War Army Hero (CMH)
PO Box 30967, Cleveland OH 44130, USA

Heredia, Felix P — Baseball Player
PO Box 4842, Hialeah FL 33014, USA

Heredia, Gilbert (Gil) — Baseball Player
4233 E Pontatoc Dr, Tucson AZ 85718, USA

Heredia, Wilson Jermaine — Actor, Singer
Shadow, 10 Universal City Plaza, #2000, Universal City CA 91608, USA

Herek, Stephen R — Director
Hughes Capital Entertainment, 22817 Ventura Blvd, #471, Woodland Hills CA 91364, USA

Herges, Matthew T (Matt) — Baseball Player
21029 N 79th Place, Scottsdale AZ 85255, USA

Herincx, Raimund — Opera Singer
Monks' Vineyard, Larkbarrow, Shepton Mallet, Somerset BA4 4NR, England

Herkenhoff, Matthew B (Matt) — Football Player
16000 Baywood Lane, Eden Prairie MN 55346, USA

Herlihy, Tim — Writer, Actor
W M E Entertainment, 9601 Wilshire Blvd, #300, Beverly Hills CA 90210 USA

Herman, Bill — Basketball Player
200 Laurel Lake Dr, #305, Hudson OH 44236, USA

Herman, David — Actor
Gersh Agency, 9465 Wilshire Blvd, #600, Beverly Hills CA 90212 USA

Herman, David J (Dave) — Football Player
19 Stephens Lane, Valhalla NY 10595, USA

Herman, Jerry — Composer, Lyricist
1100 Alta Loma Road, #1508, West Hollywood CA 90069, USA

Herman, Mark — Director
United Agents, 12-26 Lexington St, London W1F 0LE, England

Herman, Pee Wee, (Paul Reubens) — Actor, Comedian
PO Box 29373, Los Angeles CA 90029, USA
Herman, Susan — Social Activist
American Civil Liberties Union, 125 Broad St, #1800, New York NY 10004, USA
Hermann, Allen M — Physicist
2704 Lookout View Dr, Golden CO 80401, USA
Hermann, Peter — Actor
Gersh Agency, 41 Madison Ave, #3301, New York NY 10010 USA
Hermansen, Chad B — Baseball Player
2104 Rhonda Terrace, Henderson NV 89074, USA
Hermanson, Dustin M — Baseball Player
9002 E Rimrock Dr, Scottsdale AZ 85255, USA
Herman-Wurmfeld, Charles — Director
A P A Talent/Literary Agency, 405 S Beverly Dr, #300, Beverly Hills CA 90212 USA
Hermaszewski, Miroslav — Cosmonaut, Poland; Air Force General
Ul Zwirki Wigury 105A, 00 912 Warsaw, Poland
Hermeling, Terry A — Football Player
PO Box 7321, Bend OR 97708, USA
Hermesh, Michael — Sculptor
104-800 Macleod Trail SE, Calgary AB T2G 5E6, Canada
Hermida, Jeremy R — Baseball Player
3728 Paces Park Circle SE, Smyrna GA 30080, USA
Hernandez Colon, Rafael — Governor, PR
Puerta de Tierra, PO Box 5788, San Juan PR 00906, USA
Hernandez, Aaron — Football Player
New England Patriots, 1 Patriot Place, Foxboro MA 02035 USA
Hernandez, Carlos — Boxer
2038 Milan, San Antonio TX 78258, USA
Hernandez, David — Singer
Jeff Ballard Public Relations, 4814 N Lemona Ave, Sherman Oaks CA 91403, USA
Hernandez, E Livan — Baseball Player
560 Gate Lane, Miami FL 33137, USA
Hernandez, F Xavier — Baseball Player
3002 E Autumn Run Circle, Sugar Land TX 77479, USA
Hernandez, Gerard — Actor
Artmedia, 20 Ave Rapp, 75007 Paris, France
Hernandez, Guillermo (Willie) — Baseball Player
Calle C Buzon, PO Box 125, Bo Espina, Aguada PR 00602, USA
Hernandez, Jay — Actor
Alchemy Entertainment, 7024 Melrose Ave, #420, Los Angeles CA 90038 USA
Hernandez, Jose A — Baseball Player
22 Calle Sur, Vega Alta PR 00692, USA
Hernandez, Jose M — Astronaut
N A S A, Johnson Space Center, 2101 NASA Road, Houston TX 77058 USA
Hernandez, Keith — Baseball Player
14 Woodland Court, Southampton NY 11968, USA
Hernandez, Lazaro — Fashion Designer
Proenza Schouler, 120 Walker St, #1600, New York NY 10013, USA
Hernandez, Orlando (El Duque) — Baseball Player
1001 Brickell Bay Dr, #1710, Miami FL 33131, USA
Hernandez, Robert J — Businessman
U S X Corp, 600 Grant St, #450, Pittsburgh PA 15219, USA
Hernandez, Roberto M — Baseball Player
5969 Bayview Circle S, Saint Petersburg FL 33707, USA
Hernandez, Rodolfo P — Korean War Army Hero (CMH)
5328 Bluewater Place, College Lakes, Fayetteville NC 28311, USA
Hernandez, Runelvys A — Baseball Player
18717 E 24th Street Court S, Independence MO 64057, USA
Herndon, Junior — Baseball Player
1477 Sequoia Ave, Craig CO 81625, USA
Herndon, Kelly E — Football Player
8932 Merryvale Dr, Twinsburg OH 44087, USA
Herndon, Larry D — Baseball Player
6149 Brunswick Road, Arlington TN 38002, USA
Herndon, Mark J — Singer, Drummer (Alabama)
Alabama Band Promotions, PO Box 680529, Fort Payne AL 35968, USA
Herndon, Ty — Singer
Aristo Media Group, PO Box 22765, Nashville TN 37202, USA
Herold, Catherine — Actress
Agence Peggy Fischer, 11 Rue Du Bouloi, 75001 Paris, France
Herr, Matt — Ice Hockey Player
1951 Holly Creek Place, Concord CA 94521, USA
Herr, Michael — Writer
I C M Partners, 730 5th Ave, New York NY 10019 USA
Herr, Thomas M (Tommy) — Baseball Player
1077 Olde Forge Crossing, Lancaster PA 17601, USA
Herranz Casado, Julian Cardinal — Religious Leader
Legislative Texts Curia, Piazza Pio XII, #10, 00193 Rome, Italy
Herremans, Todd — Football Player
Philadelphia Eagles, 1 Novacare Way, Philadelphia PA 19145 USA
Herrera Lopez, Hector M — Soccer Player
Federacion de Futbol, Colima 373 Colonia Roma, Delegacion Cuauhtemoc Mexico DF 06700, Mexico
Herrera, Carl V — Basketball Player
1201 Dulles Ave, #6305, Stafford TX 77477, USA
Herrera, Carolina — Fashion Designer
Carolina Herrera Ltd, 501 Fashion Ave, #1700, New York NY 10018, USA
Herrera, Efren — Football Player
861 Atlanta Court, Claremont CA 91711, USA
Herrera, Michael A (Mike) — Singer, Guitarist (MxPx)
W M E Entertainment, 9601 Wilshire Blvd, #300, Beverly Hills CA 90210 USA
Herrera, Paloma — Ballerina
American Ballet Theatre, 890 Broadway, #300, New York NY 10003, USA
Herriage, W Troy — Baseball Player
238 California Ave, Oakdale CA 95361, USA
Herring, Hayim — Religious Leader, Rabbi
S T A R, 1660 S Highway 100, #344, Saint Louis Park MO 55416, USA

Herring, Kimani M (Kim) — Football Player
6503 Cartmel Lane, Windermere FL 34786, USA

Herring, Lynn — Actress
Cynthia Snyder Public Relations, 5739 Colfax Ave, North Hollywood CA 91601, USA

Herring, W Conyers — Physicist
2668 Gerald Way, San Jose CA 95125, USA

Herrington, John B — Astronaut
University of Colorado, Space Studies Center, Colorado Springs CO 80918, USA

Herrmann, Donald B (Don) — Football Player
PO Box 318, Brookside NJ 07926, USA

Herrmann, Edward — Actor
Kass & Stokes Mgmt, 9229 W Sunset Blvd, #504, Los Angeles CA 90069 USA

Herrmann, Edward M (Ed) — Baseball Player
13153 Tobiasson Road, Poway CA 92064, USA

Herrmann, Mark D — Football Player
8525 Tidewater Dr W, Indianapolis IN 46236, USA

Herrmann, Walter — Basketball Player
Charlotte Bobcats, 333 E Trade St, #A, Charlotte NC 28202 USA

Herrnstein, John E — Baseball Player
603 Seminole Road, Chillicothe OH 45601, USA

Herrod, Jeff S — Football Player
7645 Ballinshire N, Indianapolis IN 46254, USA

Herron, Bruce W — Football Player
8504 S Calumet Ave, Chicago IL 60619, USA

Herron, Denis — Ice Hockey Player
12841 Marsh Pointe Way, West Palm Beach FL 33418, USA

Herron, Keith O — Basketball Player
5374 Chew Ave, #G2, Philadelphia PA 19138, USA

Herron, Robert J — Architect
Herron Assoc, 28-30 Rivington St, London EC2A 3DU, England

Herron, Tim (Lumpy) — Golfer
20440 Linden Road, Excelsior MN 55331, USA

Herron-Braggs, Cindy — Singer (En Vogue)
28396 Falcon Crest Dr, Canyon Country CA 91351, USA

Herrscher, Richard F (Rick) — Baseball Player
7714 Marquette St, Dallas TX 75225, USA

Hersch, Fred — Jazz Pianist
Bennett Morgan, 1022 RR 376, #3, Wappinger Falls NY 12590 USA

Hersch, Michael — Composer
21C Music Publishing, 30 W 63rd St, #15S, New York NY 10023, USA

Herschbach, Dudley R — Nobel Chemistry Laureate
116 Conanat Road, Lincoln MA 01773, USA

Herscher, Uri D — Religious Leader, Rabbi
Skirball Cultural Center, 2701 N Sepulveda Blvd, Los Angeles CA 90049, USA

Herschler, E David — Artist
New Horizon Gallery, PO Box 5859, Santa Barbara CA 93150, USA

Herschman, Adam — Actor
Kazarian/Spencer/Ruskin, 11969 Ventura Blvd, #300, Studio City CA 91604 USA

Hersh, Earl W — Baseball Player
682 Morning Glory Dr, Hanover PA 17331, USA

Hersh, Kristin — Singer, Guitarist (Throwing Muses)
Throwing Mgmt, PO Box 248, Batesville VA 22924, USA

Hersh, Seymour M — Writer, Journalist
1211 Connecticut Ave NW, #320, Washington DC 20036, USA

Hershey, Barbara — Actress
Independent Artists, 9601 Wilshire Blvd, #750, Beverly Hills CA 90210 USA

Hershiser, Orel L Q — Baseball Player, Sportscaster
2167 Orchard Mist St, Las Vegas NV 89135, USA

Hershko, Avram — Nobel Chemistry Laureate
Technion-Israel Institute, Medical Faculty, 1 Efron St, Haifa 31096, Israel

Herskovitz, Marshall — Director
Bedford Falls Co, 409 Santa Monica Blvd, #PH, Santa Monica CA 90401, USA

Herta, Bryan J — Auto Racing Driver
24803 Los Altos Dr, Santa Clarita CA 91355, USA

Hertford, Brighton — Actor
C E S D, 10635 Santa Monica Blvd, #130, Los Angeles CA 90025 USA

Herthum, Louis — Actor
Ransack Films, 10000 Celtic Drive, #504, Baton Rouge LA 70809, USA

Hertling, Mark P — Army General
Deputy Commanding General, Initial Military Training, TraDoc, Fort Monroe VA 23651, USA

Hertweck, Neal C — Baseball Player
111 Leesburg Lane, Troutman NC 28166, USA

Hertz, C Hellmuth — Physicist
Lund Institute of Technology, Physics School, 221 00 Lund, Sweden

Hertz, Stephen A (Steve) — Baseball Player
10211 SW 96th Terrace, Miami FL 33176, USA

Hertz, Tom — Producer, Writer
W M E Entertainment, 9601 Wilshire Blvd, #300, Beverly Hills CA 90210 USA

Hertzberg, Daniel — Journalist
Wall Street Journal, Editorial Dept, 1 World Financial Center, #900, New York NY 10281, USA

Hervey, Jason — Actor
Hervey/Grimes Talent, 10561 Missouri Ave, #2, Los Angeles CA 90025 USA

Herzfeld, John M — Director
New Redemption Pictures, 3000 W Olympic Blvd, Building 3, Santa Monica CA

Herzigova, Eva — Model
One Model Mgmt, 424 W Broadway, #200, New York NY 10012 USA

Herzog, Dorrel N E (Whitey) — Baseball Player, Manager, Executive
9426 Sappington Estates Dr, Saint Louis MO 63127, USA

Herzog, Jacques — Pritzker Architectural Laureate
Herzog & De Meuron Architekten, Rheinschanze 6, 4056 Basel, Switzerland

Herzog, Maurice — Mountaineer, Explorer
84 Chemin De La Tournette, 74400 Chamoinix-Mont-Blanc, France

Herzog, Roman — President, Germany
Schloss Bellevue, Spreeweg 1, 10557 Berlin, Germany

Herzog, Werner — Director
Werner Herzog Film, Spiegelgasse 9, 1010 Vienna, Austria

Hesburgh, Theodore M
University of Notre Dame, 1301 Hesburgh Library, Notre Dame IN 46556, USA — Educator
Heseltine, Michael R D
Thenford House, Banbury, Oxon OX17 2BX, England — Government Official, England
Hesketh, Joseph T (Joe)
202 Glenridge Road, East Aurora NY 14052, USA — Baseball Player
Heskett, Myles
John Watson Mgmt, PO Box 281, Surry Hills NSW 2010, Australia — Drummer (Wolfmother)
Heskin, Kam
Thruline Entertainment, 9250 Wilshire Blvd, #100, Beverly Hills CA 90212 USA — Actress
Heslov, Grant
Abrams Artists, 9200 W Sunset Blvd, #1125, West Hollywood CA 90069 USA — Actor, Producer, Writer
Hesme, Clotilde
Artmedia, 20 Ave Rapp, 75007 Paris, France — Actress
Hess, Erika
Aeschi, 6388 Gratenort, Switzerland — Alpine Skier
Hess, Jared
United Talent Agency, 9336 Civic Center Dr, Beverly Hills CA 90210 USA — Director, Writer, Actor
Hess, John B
Amerada Hess Corp, 1185 Ave of Americas, #3900, New York NY 10036, USA — Businessman
Hess, Robert
2661 Dorfs Ave NE, Salem OR 97301, USA — Sculptor
Hess, Robert G (Bob)
PO Box 598, Chesterfield MO 63006, USA — Ice Hockey Player
Hesse, Dan
Sprint Nextel Corp, 2001 Edmund Halley Dr, Reston VA 20191, USA — Businessman
Hesse, Jonathan A (Jon)
3401 S 30th St, Lincoln NE 68502, USA — Football Player
Hesseman, Howard
Kass Mgmt, 501 Santa Monica Blvd, #604, Santa Monica CA 90401, USA — Actor
Hessler, Gordon
8910 Holly Place, Los Angeles CA 90046, USA — Director
Hessler, Robert R
Scripps Institute of Oceanography, Biodiversity Dept, La Jolla CA 92037, USA — Oceanographer
Hester, Dan
13846 N Sunset Dr, Fountain Hills AZ 85268, USA — Basketball Player
Hester, Devin
2600 Lyndale Lane, Riverwoods IL 60015, USA — Football Player
Hester, Jessie L
12813 Pineacre Court, Wellington FL 33414, USA — Football Player
Hester, Phil
Advanced Micro Devices, 1 A M D Place, PO Box 3453, Sunnyvale CA 94088, USA — Businessman
Hetfield, James
Q Prime Inc, 729 7th Ave, #1400, New York NY 10019, USA — Singer, Guitarist (Metallica)
Hetki, John E (Johnny)
4004 Stary Dr, Cleveland OH 44134, USA — Baseball Player
Hetland, Tor Arne
Leirbruveien 24, 7026 Trondheim, Norway — Cross Country Skier
Hetrick, Jennifer
A K A Talent, 6310 San Vicente Blvd, #200, Los Angeles CA 90048, USA — Actress
Hetson, Greg
Goldstar Public Relations, PO Box 130, Ross on Wye HR9 6WY, England — Guitarist (Red Kross, Circle Jerks)
Hettich, Georg
Albert-Schweitzer-Str 1, 78186 Schonach, Germany — Nordic Combined Skier
Hetzel, Eric P
2271 Hetzel Road, Crowley LA 70526, USA — Baseball Player
Hetzel, Fred
40290 Iron Liege Court, Leesburg VA 20176, USA — Basketball Player
Heuer, Rolf
C E R N, Large Hadron Collider, 1211 Geneva 23, Switzerland — Physicist
Heuring, Lori
B/W/R, 9100 Wilshire Blvd, #500W, Beverly Hills CA 90212 USA — Actress
Heusinger, Patrick
Group Entertainment, 115 W 29th St, #1102, New York NY 10001, USA — Actor
Heward, Jamie
159 Bentley Dr, Regina SK S4N 4S7, Canada — Ice Hockey Player
Hewer, Mitch
United Agents, 12-26 Lexington St, London W1F 0LE, England — Actor
Hewett, Howard
Universal Attractions, 135 W 26th St, #1200, New York NY 10001 USA — Singer (Shalamar)
Hewish, Anthony
Pryor's Cottage, Kingston, Cambridge CB3 7NQ, England — Nobel Physics Laureate
Hewitt, Angela
Opus 3 Artists, 470 Park Ave S, #900N, New York NY 10016 USA — Concert Pianist
Hewitt, Jennifer Love
10015 Toluca Lake Ave, Toluca Lake CA 91602, USA — Actress, Singer
Hewitt, Lleyton
PO Box 1235, North Sydney NSW 2059, Australia — Tennis Player
Hewitt, Martin
1147 Horn Ave, #3, West Hollywood CA 90069, USA — Actor
Hewitt, Paul
Georgia Institute of Technology, Athletic Dept, Atlanta GA 30332, USA — Basketball Coach
Hewitt, Peter
Casorotto Ramsay, Waverley House, 7-12 Noel St, London W1F 8GQ, England — Director
Hewlett, David
Northern Exposure Talent, 2888 Birch St, Vancouver BC V6H 2T6, Canada — Actor
Hewlett, Jamie C
Nasty Little Man, 110 Greene St, #605, New York NY 10012 USA — Cartoonist (Tank Girl)
Hewson, John
A B N Amro Australia, 10 Spring St, #14, Sydney NSW 2000, Australia — Government Official, Australia
Hewson, John G (Jack)
114 Tahlequah Lane, Loudon TN 37774, USA — Basketball Player
Hextall, Dennis H
2631 Harvest Hill Dr, Brighton MI 48114, USA — Ice Hockey Player
Hextall, Ronald (Ron)
570 29th St, Manhattan Beach CA 90266, USA — Ice Hockey Player

Hexum, Nicholas L (Nick) — Singer, Songwriter (311)
311 Hive, 8904 Florence Dr, Omaha NE 68147, USA

Hey, Virginia — Actress
Anthony Williams Mgmt, 50 Oxford St, Paddington NSW 2021, Australia

Heydeman, Gregory G (Greg) — Baseball Player
702 Ramona Ave, Monterey CA 93940, USA

Heyer, Ingeburg — Astronomer
PO Box 143, Burtonsville MD 20866, USA

Heyerdahl, Christopher — Actor
Kirk Talent Agencies, 134 Abbott St, #402, Vancouver BC V6B 2K4, Canada

Heyland, Rob — Actor
United Agents, 12-26 Lexington St, London W1F 0LE, England

Heyman, David — Producer
Bloom Hergott Diemer, 150 S Rodeo Dr, #300, Beverly Hills CA 90212 USA

Heyman, Mark — Writer
Protozoa Pictures, 104 N 7th St, Brooklyn NY 11211, USA

Heyman, Richard — Geneticist
Ligand Pharmaceuticals, 9393 Town Center Dr, #100, San Diego CA 92121, USA

Heywood, Anne — Actress
9966 Liebe Dr, Beverly Hills CA 90210, USA

Hiassen, Carl — Writer
Knopf Publishers, 1745 Broadway, New York NY 10019 USA

Hiatt, Andrew — Molecular Biologist
Scripps Research Foundation, 10666 N Torrey Pines Road, La Jolla CA 92037, USA

Hiatt, Fred — Journalist
Washington Post, Editorial Dept, 1150 15th St NW, Washington DC 20071 USA

Hiatt, Jack E — Baseball Player
715 E 1st St, Coquille OR 97423, USA

Hiatt, John — Singer, Guitarist, Songwriter
United Talent Agency, 9336 Civic Center Dr, Beverly Hills CA 90210 USA

Hiatt, Philip A (Phil) — Baseball Player
30 Littleton St, Cantonment FL 32533, USA

Hiatt, Shana — Model
Shandrew Public Relations, 1050 S Stanley Ave, Los Angeles CA 90019 USA

Hibbard, J Gregory (Greg) — Baseball Player
5287 Conifer View Lane, Lakeland TN 38002, USA

Hibbert, Edward — Actor
TalentWorks, 3500 W Olive Ave, #1400, Burbank CA 91505 USA

Hibbert, Roy D — Basketball Player
Indiana Pacers, Conseco Fieldhouse, 125 S Pennsylvania, Indianapolis IN 46204 USA

Hibbs, James K (Jim) — Baseball Player
4659 Foothill Road, Ventura CA 93003, USA

Hibel, Edna — Artist
1530 53rd St, West Palm Beach FL 33407, USA

Hick, Graeme A — Cricketer
Worcestershire County Cricket Club, New Road, Worcester WR2 4QQ, England

Hickam, Homer H, Jr — Writer
9532 Hemlock Dr SE, Huntsville AL 35803, USA

Hicke, Ernie — Ice Hockey Player
5287 S Sugarberry Court, Gilbert AZ 85298, USA

Hickerson, Bryan D — Baseball Player
275 S Hunters Ridge, Warsaw IN 46582, USA

Hickey, David L — Labor Leader
Security Police Fire Professional Union, 25510 Kelly Road, Roseville MI 48066, USA

Hickey, John Benjamin — Actor
Paradigm Agency, 360 N Crescent Dr, North Building, Beverly Hills CA 90210 USA

Hickey, Thomas H (Bo) — Football Player
94 Field Crest Road, New Canaan CT 06840, USA

Hickey, Thomas J — Air Force General
2127 Bobbyber Dr, Vienna VA 22182, USA

Hickey, William V — Businessman
Sealed Air Corp, Park 80 E, Saddle Brook NJ 07663, USA

Hickland, Catherine — Actress
255 W 84th St, #2A, New York NY 10024, USA

Hickman, Ana — Model
I D Model Mgmt, 137 Varick St, New York NY 10013, USA

Hickman, Dallas M — Football Player
6521 E Dreyfus Dr, Scottsdale AZ 85254, USA

Hickman, Darryl — Actor
171 Hermosillo Road, Santa Barbara CA 93108, USA

Hickman, Dwayne — Actor
PO Box 17226, Encino CA 91416, USA

Hickman, Fred — Sportscaster
Atlanta Braves, Turner Field, 755 Hank Aaron Dr, Atlanta GA 30315 USA

Hickman, James L (Jim) — Baseball Player
PO Box 455, Henning TN 38041, USA

Hickman, Johnny — Singer, Guitarist (Cracker)
Back Bay Mgmt, 397 Little Neck Road, #305, Virginia Beach VA 23452 USA

Hickman, Sara — Singer, Songwriter
Valdenn, RR 12 Box 13801, #202, Wimberley TX 78676, USA

Hickox, Anthony — Director
United Agents, 12-26 Lexington St, London W1F 0LE, England

Hickox, Marc — Actor
Butler Ruston Bell, 10 Saint Mary St, #308, Toronto ON M4Y 1P9, Canada

Hicks, Artis — Football Player
1804 Woods Edge Dr NE, Leesburg VA 20176, USA

Hicks, Bill — Fiddler (Red Clay Ramblers)
Keith Case Assoc, 1025 17th Ave S, #200, Nashville TN 37212 USA

Hicks, Catherine — Actress
Margrit Polak Mgmt, 1411 Carroll Ave, Los Angeles CA 90026, USA

Hicks, Clifford W (Cliff), Jr — Football Player
8967 Windham Court, Spring Valley CA 91977, USA

Hicks, Dan — Singer
Leslie Wiener, PO Box 245, Sausalito CA 94966, USA

Hicks, Dan — Sportscaster
NBC-TV, Sports Dept, 30 Rockefeller Plaza, #270E, New York NY 10112 USA

Hicks, Dwight
PO Box 342, Sierra Madre CA 91025, USA — Football Player

Hicks, Elizabeth (Betty)
669 Canyon View Dr, Laguna Beach CA 92651, USA — Golfer

Hicks, Eric D
6714 W 148th Terrace, Overland Park KS 66223, USA — Football Player

Hicks, India A C
Storm Model Agency, 5 Jubilee Place, Chelsea, London SW3 3TD, England — Model, Interior Designer

Hicks, J Stephen
2445 Kanan Road, Agoura Hills CA 91301, USA — Photographer

Hicks, James E (Jim)
9331 Portal Dr, Houston TX 77031, USA — Baseball Player

Hicks, John C, Jr
3287 Green Cook Road, Johnstown OH 43031, USA — Football Player

Hicks, Michelle
Domain Talent, 9229 W Sunset Blvd, #710, West Hollywood CA 90069 USA — Actress, Model

Hicks, Robert
Warner Books, 1271 Ave of Americas, New York NY 10020 USA — Writer

Hicks, Scott
PO Box 824, Kent Town 5071, South Africa — Director, Writer

Hicks, Taylor
19 Entertainment, 8560 W Sunset Blvd, #900, West Hollywood CA 90069, USA — Singer

Hicks, Thomas L (Tom)
207 Rivershire Lane, #106, Lincolnshire IL 60069, USA — Football Player

Hicks, W Joseph (Joe)
2707 Brookmere Road, Charlottesville VA 22901, USA — Baseball Player

Hicks, Wayne W
7726 E Buteo Dr, Scottsdale AZ 85255, USA — Ice Hockey Player

Hicks, Wilmer Kenzie (W K)
10149 Kemp Forest Dr, Houston TX 77080, USA — Football Player

Hickson, James E (J J), Jr
Portland Trail Blazers, Rose Garden, 1 N Center Court St, Portland OR 97227 USA — Basketball Player

Hidalgo, David
Gold Mountain, 3940 Laurel Canyon Blvd, #444, Studio City CA 91604 USA — Singer (Los Lobos), Songwriter

Hidalgo, John
Mays Valentine Davenport Moore, 1899 L St NW, Washington DC 20036, USA — Government Official

Hiddleston, Thomas W (Tom)
W M E Entertainment, 9601 Wilshire Blvd, #300, Beverly Hills CA 90210 USA — Actor

Hide, Herbie
Lionheart Boxing, 415 Argyle Road, #5M, Brooklyn NY 11218, USA — Boxer

Hide, Raymond
17 Clinton Ave, East Molesey, Surrey KT8 0HS, England — Geophysicist

Hieb, Richard J
N A S A, Johnson Space Center, 2101 NASA Road, Houston TX 77058 USA — Astronaut

Hiebert, Erwin N
40 Payson Road, Belmont MA 02478, USA — Historian

Hiegel, Catherine
Artmedia, 20 Ave Rapp, 75007 Paris, France — Actress

Hier, Marvin
Simon Wiesenthal Holocaust Center, 9766 W Pico Blvd, Los Angeles CA 90035, USA — Religious Leader, Rabbi, Social Activist

Hieronymus, Clara W
50 Spring St, Savannah TN 38372, USA — Journalist

Hietpas, Joe
611 E Timberline Dr, Appleton WI 54913, USA — Baseball Player

Higareda, Martha
I C M Partners, 10250 Constellation Blvd, #900, Los Angeles CA 90067 USA — Actress

Higdon, Bruce
210 Canvasback Court, Murfreesboro TN 37130, USA — Cartoonist

Higgenson, Tom
One Moment Mgmt, PO Box 55156, Sherman Oaks CA 91413 USA — Singer, Songwriter (Plain White T's)

Higginbotham, Joan E
1409 Mija Lane, Seabrook TX 77586, USA — Astronaut

Higginbotham, Patrick E
US Court of Appeals, US Courthouse, 1100 Commerce St, Dallas TX 75242, USA — Judge

Higgins, Alan J
Creative Artists Agency, 2000 Ave of Stars, #100, Los Angeles CA 90067 USA — Producer

Higgins, Anthony
I C M Partners, 10250 Constellation Blvd, #900, Los Angeles CA 90067 USA — Actor

Higgins, Bertie
5775 Peachtree Dunwoody Road NE, Atlanta GA 30342, USA — Singer, Songwriter

Higgins, Chester, Jr
New York Times, Editorial Dept, 229 W 43rd St, New York NY 10036, USA — Photographer

Higgins, David Anthony
Stone Manners Salners, 9911 W Pico Blvd, #1400, Los Angeles CA 90035 USA — Actor, Writer, Producer

Higgins, Dennis D
1123 Boonville Road, Jefferson Cty MO 65109, USA — Baseball Player

Higgins, J Kenneth
Boeing Commercial Airplane Group, PO Box 3707, Seattle WA 98124, USA — Test Pilot

Higgins, Jack
September Tide, Mont de la Roque, Jersey, Channel Islands JE3 8BQ, England — Writer

Higgins, Jack
59 Waverly Ave, Clarendon Hills IL 60514, USA — Editorial Cartoonist

Higgins, Joel
Gage Group, 315 W 57th St, #4H, New York NY 10019 USA — Actor, Singer

Higgins, John
40 Williams Dr, Annapolis MD 21401, USA — Swimmer, Swimming Coach

Higgins, John Michael
Magnolia Entertainment, 9595 Wilshire Blvd, #601, Beverly Hills CA 90212, USA — Actor

Higgins, Melissa (Missy)
John Watson Mgmt, PO Box 281 Surry Hills NSW 2010, Australia — Singer, Songwriter

Higgins, Michael D
President's Office, 'Aras an Uachtarain, Phoenix Park, Dublin 8, Ireland — President, Ireland

Higgins, Michael S (Mike)
137 48th Ave, Greeley CO 80634, USA — Basketball Player

Higgins, Robert
Fleet Boston Corp, PO Box 55850, Boston MA 02205, USA — Businessman

H

Higgins, Roderick D (Rod) 743 Mendenhall Court, Fort Mill SC 29715, USA	Basketball Player
Higgins, Rosalyn International Court of Justice, Peace Palace, 2517 KJ Hague, Netherlands	Judge
Higgins, Steve Creative Artists Agency, 2000 Ave of Stars, #100, Los Angeles CA 90067 USA	Actor
Higginson, John 16 Sundew Road, Savannah GA 31411, USA	Pathologist
Higginson, Torri Don Buchwald/Fortitude, 6500 Wilshire Blvd, #2200, Los Angeles CA 90048 USA	Actress
Higgs, Kenny 746 Sargent Dr, Owensboro KY 42301, USA	Basketball Player
Higgs, Mark D 45 NW 156th Lane, Pembroke Pines FL 33028, USA	Football Player
Higgs, Peter W 2 Darnaway St, Edinburgh EH3 6BG, Scotland	Physicist
Higham, Scott Washington Post, Editorial Dept, 1150 15th St NW, Washington DC 20071 USA	Journalist
Highmore, Freddie Artist Rights Group, 4 Great Portland Place, London W1W 8PA, England	Actor
Highsmith, Alonzo W 3703 E Valley Dr, Missouri City TX 77459, USA	Football Player
Hightower, Chelsie K Abrams Artists, 9200 W Sunset Blvd, #1125, West Hollywood CA 90069 USA	Dancer
Hightower, Dont'a New England Patriots, 1 Patriot Place, Foxboro MA 02035 USA	Football Player
Hightower, John B 394 Emily Dickinson N, Newport News VA 23606, USA	Museum Director
Hightower, Rosetta Lustig Talent, PO Box 770850, Orlando FL 32877 USA	Singer (Orlons)
Higuera, Joel Tucanes Inc, 6055 E Washington Blvd, #455, Commerce CA 90040, USA	Singer (Los Tucanes de Tijuana)
Higuera, Teodoro V 1567 S Sycamore Place, Chandler AZ 85286, USA	Baseball Player
Hijuelos, Oscar Hofstra University, English Dept, 10000 Fulton Ave, Hempstead NY 11550, USA	Writer
Hilario, Maybyner R (Nene) 300 W 11th Ave, #18C, Denver CO 80204, USA	Basketball Player
Hilbert, Andy 419 N Michigan Ave, Howell MI 48843, USA	Ice Hockey Player
Hildebrand, Roger H University of Chicago, Fermi Institute, 5640 S Ellis Ave, Chicago IL 60637, USA	Astronomer, Astrophysicist
Hildebrandt, Greg Spiderweb Art, 5 Waterloo Road, Hopatcong NJ 07843, USA	Cartoonist (Terry & the Pirates)
Hildreth, Eugene A 2000 Cambridge Ave, #129, Reading PA 19610, USA	Physician
Hildreth, Mark Characters Talent Agency, 8 Elm St, Toronto ON M5G 1G7, Canada	Actor
Hilfiger, Tommy Tommy Hilfiger USA, 601 W 26th St, #500, New York NY 10001, USA	Fashion Designer
Hilgenberg, Jay W 1296 Kimmer Court, Lake Forest IL 60045, USA	Football Player
Hilgenberg, Joel 2027 Ridgeway Dr, Iowa City IA 52245, USA	Football Player
Hilgenbrinck, Tad Innovative Artists, 1505 10th St, Santa Monica CA 90401 USA	Actor
Hilgendorf, Thomas E (Tom) PO Box 124, Camanche IA 52730, USA	Baseball Player
Hilger, Russell T (Rusty) 2625 SW 67th St, Oklahoma City OK 73159, USA	Football Player
Hiljus, Eric K 2253 Demaray Dr, Grants Pass OR 97527, USA	Baseball Player
Hill Smith, Marilyn Music International, 13 Ardilaun Road, Highbury, London N5 2QR, England	Opera Singer
Hill, Aaron W 4741 W Addisyn Court, Visalia CA 93291, USA	Baseball Player
Hill, Achim Dahmestr 94, 12526 Berlin, Germany	Rowing Athlete
Hill, Al D 4807 Margaret Lane, Harrisburg PA 17110, USA	Ice Hockey Player
Hill, Amy J G M, 15 Lexham Mews, London W8 6JW, England	Actress
Hill, Anita Brandeis University, Heller Law School, Waltham MA 02254, USA	Educator
Hill, Armond G 1626 Laurens Way SW, Atlanta GA 30311, USA	Basketball Player
Hill, Bernard Optimism Entertainment, 3383 Robertson Place, #2, Los Angeles CA 90034, USA	Actor
Hill, Bob 205 Rio Cordillera, Boerne TX 78006, USA	Basketball Coach
Hill, Brendan C C C3 Presents, 98 San Jacinto Blvd, #400, Austin TX 78701, USA	Drummer (Blues Traveler)
Hill, Brian Detroit Pistons, Palace, 4 Championship Dr, Auburn Hills MI 48326 USA	Basketball Coach
Hill, Bruce E 1919 E Citation Lane, Tempe AZ 85284, USA	Football Player
Hill, Calvin 10300 Walker Lake Dr, Great Falls VA 22066, USA	Football Player, Executive
Hill, Carolyn 5906 Summer Point Blvd S, Gulfport FL 33707, USA	Golfer
Hill, Damon G D B R D C, Silverstone, Towcester, Northamptonshire NN12 8TN, England	Auto Racing Driver
Hill, Dan Paquin Entertainment, 1067 Sherwin Road, Winnipeg MB R3H 1C1, Canada	Singer, Songwriter
Hill, Dave C E S D, 10635 Santa Monica Blvd, #130, Los Angeles CA 90025 USA	Actor, Comedian

Hill, David
13844 Buckhart St, Corona CA 92880, USA — Football Player

Hill, David B (Dave)
125 Jenny Lind Dr, Hendersonvlle NC 28791, USA — Baseball Player

Hill, David H (Dave)
402 Le Grand Dr, Panama City Beach FL 32413, USA — Football Player

Hill, Donald E (Donnie)
6 Knob Hill, Laguna Niguel CA 92677, USA — Baseball Player

Hill, Draper
1818 Northbrook Dr, Lancaster PA 17601, USA — Editorial Cartoonist

Hill, Dule
I C M Partners, 10250 Constellation Blvd, #900, Los Angeles CA 90067 USA — Actor

Hill, Dusty
Sanctuary Mgmt, 15301 Ventura Blvd, Building B, Sherman Oaks CA 91403, USA — Singer, Bassist (ZZ Top)

Hill, Eddie
Eddie Hill's Fun Cycles, 401 N Scott Ave, Wichita Falls TX 76306, USA — Drag Racing Driver

Hill, Edwin D
International Brotherhood of Electrical Workers, 1125 15th St NW, Washington DC 20005, USA — Labor Leader

Hill, Eric D
PO Box 870637, New Orleans LA 70187, USA — Football Player

Hill, Erica R
CNN-TV, 190 Marietta Ave SW, Atlanta GA 30303 USA — Commentator

Hill, Faith
Creative Artists Agency, 2000 Ave of Stars, #100, Los Angeles CA 90067 USA — Singer, Actress

Hill, Frederick G (Fred)
31441 Paseo Riobo, San Juan Capistrano CA 92675, USA — Football Player

Hill, Garry A
9602 Willowglen Trail, Charlotte NC 28215, USA — Baseball Player

Hill, Gary
Donald Young Gallery, 224 S Michigan Ave, #266, Chicago IL 60604, USA — Artist

Hill, Geoffrey W
Boston University, University Professors, 745 Commonwealth St, Boston MA 02215, USA — Writer

Hill, George J, Jr
Indiana Pacers, Conseco Fieldhouse, 125 S Pennsylvania, Indianapolis IN 46204 USA — Basketball Player

Hill, Gerald A (Jerry)
300 Hudson St, #202, Denver CO 80220, USA — Football Player

Hill, Glenallen
2913 Cortez Court, College Station TX 77845, USA — Baseball Player

Hill, Grant H
9600 McCormick Place, Windermere FL 34786, USA — Basketball Player

Hill, Gregory M (Greg)
8014 Downington Court, Spring TX 77379, USA — Football Player

Hill, Harlon
PO Box 428, Killen AL 35645, USA — Football Player

Hill, Harry
4225 Shore Dr, #147, Virginia Beach VA 23455, USA — Hero

Hill, Ian
Trinifold Mgmt, 12 Oval Road, #300, Camden, London NW1 7DH, England — Bassist (Judist Priest)

Hill, J D
2375 W Comstock Dr, Chandler AZ 85224, USA — Football Player

Hill, Jack
5310 Clear Run Dr, Wilmington NC 28403, USA — Director, Producer, Writer

Hill, James C
US Court of Appeals, PO Box 52598, Jacksonville FL 32201, USA — Judge

Hill, Jane H
University of Arizona, Language Dept, Tucson AZ 85721, USA — Language Educator

Hill, Jeremy D
10050 Gooding Dr, Dallas TX 75229, USA — Baseball Player

Hill, Jim
4120 Parva Ave, Los Angeles CA 90027, USA — Football Player, Sportscaster

Hill, Jody
Rough House, 1722 Whitley Ave, Los Angeles CA 90028, USA — Actor, Producer, Director

Hill, John S
2005 Boyce Bridge Road, Creedmoor NC 27522, USA — Football Player

Hill, Jon Michael
Cornerstone Talent Agency, 37 West 20th St, #1108, New York NY 10011, USA — Actor

Hill, Jonah
W M E Entertainment, 9601 Wilshire Blvd, #300, Beverly Hills CA 90210 USA — Actor

Hill, Jordan
143/Atlantic Records, 9229 W Sunset Blvd, #900, West Hollywood CA 90069, USA — Singer, Songwriter

Hill, Jordan
Los Angeles Lakers, Staples Center, 1111 S Figueroa St, Los Angeles CA 90015 USA — Basketball Player

Hill, Julia Butterfly
Circle of Life Foundation, PO Box 6747, Albany CA 94706, USA — Environmentalist

Hill, Kenneth W (Ken)
1360 Shady Oaks Dr, Southlake TX 76092, USA — Baseball Player

Hill, Kenneth W (Kenny)
121 Hawkins Place, Boonton NJ 07005, USA — Football Player

Hill, Kent A
630 Hawthorne Place, Fayetteville GA 30214, USA — Football Player

Hill, Kim
Ambassador Artist Agency, PO Box 50358, Nashville TN 37205, USA — Singer, Guitarist

Hill, Koyie D
1704 NW 146th St, Edmond OK 73013, USA — Baseball Player

Hill, Lauren Michelle
Playboy Promotions, 2706 Media Center Dr, Los Angeles CA 90065 USA — Model, Actress

Hill, Lauryn
D A S Communications, 83 Riverside Dr, New York NY 10024, USA — Rap Artist (Fugees), Actress

Hill, Marc K
203 Maple St, Elsberry MO 63343, USA — Baseball Player

Hill, Mike
6750 Jefferson Road, Brooklyn MI 49230, USA — Golfer

Hill, Mike
Paradigm Agency, 360 N Crescent Dr, North Building, Beverly Hills CA 90210 USA — Editor

Hill, Milton G (Milt)
8401 Avalon Court, Cumming GA 30041, USA — Baseball Player

H

Hill, Pat California State University, Athletic Dept, Fresno CA 93740, USA	Football Coach
Hill, Randal T 5360 SW 130th Terrace, Miramar FL 33027, USA	Football Player
Hill, Richard J (Rich) 17 Spafford Road, Milton MA 02186, USA	Baseball Player
Hill, Ron PO Box 11, Hyde, Cheshire SK14 1RD, England	Track Athlete
Hill, Sean 2735 E Carob Dr, Chandler AZ 85286, USA	Ice Hockey Player
Hill, Shaun 4956 Shorewood Dr, Osage Beach MO 65065, USA	Football Player
Hill, Simmie, Jr 1470 Elizabeth Blvd, Pittsburgh PA 15221, USA	Basketball Player
Hill, Steven 18 Jill Lane, Monsey NY 10952, USA	Actor
Hill, Susan E Longmoor Farmhouse, Ebrington, Chipping Campden, Gloucestershire GL55 6NW, England	Writer
Hill, Talmaldga L (Ike) 412 Randolph St, Oak Park IL 60302, USA	Football Player
Hill, Terence 3 Los Pinos Road, Santa Fe NM 87507, USA	Actor
Hill, Terrell L 5320 Fox Hollow Road, Eugene OR 97405, USA	Biophysicist, Chemist
Hill, Thomas (Tom) 428 Elmcrest Dr, Norman OK 73071, USA	Track Athlete
Hill, Tim Gersh Agency, 9465 Wilshire Blvd, #600, Beverly Hills CA 90212 USA	Director, Producer, Writer
Hill, Tyrone Atlanta Hawks, Centennial Tower, 101 Marietta St NW, #1900, Atlanta GA 30303 USA	Basketball Player
Hill, Virgil Timothy Downey, PO Box 442, Oceanville NJ 08231, USA	Boxer
Hill, Virgil L, Jr 1000 Glendevon Court, Ambler PA 19002, USA	Navy Admiral, Educator
Hill, W Robert (Bobby) 1874 Dry Creek Road, San Jose CA 95124, USA	Baseball Player
Hill, Walter 836 Greenway Dr, Beverly Hills CA 90210, USA	Director
Hill, Warren Narada/Blue Note Productions, 150 5th Ave, #600, New York NY 10011, USA	Jazz Saxophonist
Hill, Winston C 1900 E Girard Place, #605, Englewood CO 80113, USA	Football Player
Hillaby, John Constable Co, Lanchesters, 102 Fulham Palace Road, London W6 9ER, England	Writer
Hillary, Barbara Playboy Promotions, 2706 Media Center Dr, Los Angeles CA 90065 USA	Model
Hillcoat, John Creative Artists Agency, 2000 Ave of Stars, #100, Los Angeles CA 90067 USA	Director
Hille, Bertil 10630 Lakeside Ave NE, Seattle WA 98125, USA	Physiologist
Hille, Einar 8862 La Jolla Scenic Dr N, La Jolla CA 92037, USA	Mathematician
Hillebrand, Gerald J (Jerry) 23 Madison Circle, Davenport IA 52806, USA	Football Player
Hillebrecht, Rudolf F H Gneiststr 7, 30169 Hanover, Germany	Architect
Hillegas, Shawn P 870 Rockville Road, South Fork PA 15956, USA	Baseball Player
Hillel, Shlomo 14 Gelber St, Jerusalem 96755, Israel	Government Official, Israel
Hillen, Bobby, Jr Donleavy Racing, 5011 Midlothian Turnpike, Richmond VA 23225, USA	Auto Racing Driver
Hillenbrand, Daniel A Hillenbrand Industries, 700 State RR 46 E, Batesville IN 47006, USA	Businessman
Hillenbrand, Laura Jankow & Nesbitt, 445 Park Ave, New York NY 10022, USA	Writer
Hillenbrand, Shea 2614 E Via De Palmas, Gilbert AZ 85298, USA	Baseball Player
Hiller, Arthur 1218 Benedict Canyon, Beverly Hills CA 90210, USA	Director
Hiller, David D Chicago Tribune, Publisher's Office, 435 N Michigan Ave, Chicago IL 60611, USA	Publisher
Hiller, John F W8085 Becker Dr, Iron Mountain MI 49801, USA	Baseball Player
Hillerman, John Prager & Hillerman, 12424 Wilshire Blvd, #1000, Los Angeles CA 90025, USA	Actor
Hilliard, Dalton 23 Hermitage Dr, Destrehan LA 70047, USA	Football Player
Hilliard, Isaac J (Ike) 17020 SW 74th Ave, Palmetto Bay FL 33157, USA	Football Player
Hillier, Bevis Maggie Noach Literary Agency, 21 Redan St, London W14 0AB, England	Writer
Hillier, Paul D Hazard Chase, 25 City Road, Cambridge CB1 1DP, England	Concert Singer, Music Director
Hillier, Steve Primary Talent, 2-12 Petonville Road, London N1 9PL, England	Keyboardist (Dubstar)
Hillis, Ali Luber Rocklin Entertainment, 8530 Wilshire Blvd, #555, Beverly Hills CA 90211 USA	Actress
Hillis, David M University of Texas, Computational Biology Center, Austin TX 78712, USA	Integrative Biologist
Hillis, Peyton Kansas City Chiefs, 1 Arrowhead Dr, Kansas City KS 64129 USA	Football Player
Hillis, W Daniel (Danny) Applied Minds, 1209 Grand Central Ave, Glendale CA 91201, USA	Computer Scientist
Hillman, Chris Entertainment Unlimited, 72 N Village Ave, #3, Rockville Centre NY 11570, USA	Singer, Bassist (Byrds)

Hillman, Darius D (Dave)
849 Mimosa Dr, Kingsport TN 37660, USA — Baseball Player
Hillman, Darnell
6011 Medora Dr, Indianapolis IN 46228, USA — Basketball Player
Hillman, J Eric
157 Bellaire St, Denver CO 80220, USA — Baseball Player
Hillman, Larry M
57 Westland St, Saint Catharines ON L2S 3W8, Canada — Ice Hockey Player
Hills, Carla A
3125 Chain Bridge Road NW, Washington DC 20016, USA — Secretary, Housing & Urban Development
Hills, Douglas
Douglas Hills Assoc, 920 S Waukegan Road, #300, Lake Forest IL 60045, USA — Architect
Hills, Hollis H
570 Marnie Circle, Melbourne FL 32904, USA — WW II Navy Air Force Hero
Hills, Roderick M
Mudge Rose Guthrie Alexander Ferdon, 1200 19th St NW, Washington DC 20036, USA — Businessman, Government Official
Hilmers, David C
2846 Bellefontaine St, Houston TX 77025, USA — Astronaut
Hilmes, Jerome B
4900 Windsor Park, Sarasota FL 34235, USA — Army General
Hilson, Keri
I C M Partners, 10250 Constellation Blvd, #900, Los Angeles CA 90067 USA — Singer, Songwriter
Hilton, Barron
Hilton Hotels Corp, 7930 Jones Branch Dr, #100, McLean VA 22102, USA — Businessman
Hilton, J David (Dave)
4910 E Sunnyside Dr, Scottsdale AZ 85254, USA — Baseball Player
Hilton, John J
3911 S Fairway Dr, Powhatan VA 23139, USA — Football Player
Hilton, Paris
Paris Hilton Entertainment, 250 N Canon Dr, #100, Beverly Hills CA 90210, USA — Model, Actress
Hilton, Roy L
8332 Merrymount Dr, Windsor Mill MD 21244, USA — Football Player
Hilton, Tyler
Emblem Mgmt, 22315 Mulholland Highway, Calabasas CA 91302, USA — Actor, Singer
Hilty, Megan
One Entertainment, 12 W 57th St, #PH, New York NY 10019, USA — Actress, Singer
Hiltz, Nichole
Sanders/Armstrong/Caserta Mgmt, 2120 Colorado Ave, #120, Santa Monica CA 90404 USA — Actress
Hiltzik, Michael A
Los Angeles Times, Editorial Dept, 202 W 1st St, Los Angeles CA 90012 USA — Journalist
Himelstein, Aaron
Innovative Artists, 1505 10th St, Santa Monica CA 90401 USA — Actor
Himes Gomez, Margaret
Gomez Assoc, 504 E 74th St, #300, New York NY 10021, USA — Interior Designer
Himes, Richard D (Dick)
431 Prairie Lane, Luxemburg WI 54217, USA — Football Player
Hinault, Bernard
Quest Levure, 7 Rue de la Sauvaie, 21 Sud-Est, 35000 Rennes, France — Cyclist
Hinch, Andrew Jay (A J)
8415 Avenida de las Ondas, La Jolla CA 92037, USA — Baseball Player
Hinchcliffe, James
Andretti Audiosport, 7615 Zionsville Road, Indianapolis IN 46268, USA — Auto Racing Driver
Hinchliffe, Dickon
First Artists Mgmt, 4764 Park Granada, #210, Calabasas CA 91302 USA — Composer
Hindle, Art
Independent Artists, 9601 Wilshire Blvd, #750, Beverly Hills CA 90210 USA — Actor
Hindman, Stanley C (Stan)
824 Creed Road, Oakland CA 94610, USA — Football Player
Hindmarch, Anya
Plough Brewery, 516 Wandsworth Road, London SW8 3JX, England — Fashion Designer
Hinds, Aisha
Greene Assoc, 1901 Ave of Stars, #130, Los Angeles CA 90067 USA — Actress
Hinds, Brent
Pinnacle Entertainment, 30 Glenn St, White Plains NY 10603, USA — Guitarist, Singer (Mastodon)
Hinds, Ciaran
Dalzell & Beresford, 26 Astwood Mews, London SW7 4DE, England — Actor
Hinds, David
Steel Pulse Ltd, 33 Kersley Road, London N16 0NT, England — Singer, Guitarist (Steel Pulse)
Hinds, Samuel A A
Prime Minister's Office, Wights Lane, Georgetown, Guyana — Prime Minister, Guyana
Hinds, Samuel R (Sam)
320 S 56th Terrace, Hollywood FL 33023, USA — Baseball Player
Hinds, William E (Bill)
1301 Spring Oaks Circle, Houston TX 77055, USA — Cartoonist (Tank McNamara)
Hine, Maynard K
1121 W Michigan St, Indianapolis IN 46202, USA — Dentist
Hine, Patrick
Lloyd's Bank, Cox's & Kings, 7 Pall Mall, London SW1 5NA, England — Air Force Marshal, England
Hiner, Glen H, Jr
Owens-Corning, 1 Owens Corning Parkway, Toledo OH 43659, USA — Businessman
Hines, Brendan
TalentWorks, 3500 W Olive Ave, #1400, Burbank CA 91505 USA — Actor
Hines, Cheryl
W M E Entertainment, 9601 Wilshire Blvd, #300, Beverly Hills CA 90210 USA — Actress, Comedienne
Hines, Deni
Peter Rix Mgmt, 49 Hume St, #200, Crows Nest NSW 2065, Australia — Singer
Hines, Garrett
US Bobsled/Skeleton Federation, 1631 Mesa Ave, #A, Colorado Springs CO 80906 USA — Bobsled Athlete
Hines, Glen R
861 N Queen Annes Lace Dr, Fayetteville AR 72704, USA — Football Player
Hines, Mimi
Scott Stander Assoc, 4533 Van Nuys Blvd, #401, Sherman Oaks CA 91403 USA — Actress, Comedienne
Hingis, Martina
Inselweg 28, 8640 Hurden, Switzerland — Tennis Player
Hingorani, Narain G
835 W Big Sand Place, Oro Valley AZ 85755, USA — Electrical Engineer

H

Hingsen, Jurgen
655 Circle Dr, Santa Barbara CA 93108, USA — Football Player

Hinkle, Bryan E
1402 Missouri Ave, Bridgeville PA 15017, USA — Football Player

Hinkle, George A
4998 Willowford Road, Robertsville MO 63072, USA — Golfer

Hinkle, Lon
PO Box 1347, Bigfork MT 59911, USA — Actress

Hinkle, Marin
I/D Public Relations, 7060 Hollywood Blvd, #800, Los Angeles CA 90028 USA — Football Player

Hinnant, Michael W (Mike)
43 Ashford Way, Schwenksville PA 19473, USA — Government Official

Hinners, Noel
7 Greyswood Court, Potomac MD 20854, USA — Fashion Designer

Hino, Kazuyoshi
Hino & Malee Inc, 3701 N Ravenswood Ave, Chicago IL 60613, USA — Judge

Hinojosa, Ricardo H
US District Court, PO Box 5007, McAllen TX 78502, USA — Singer, Songwriter

Hinojosa, Tish
PO Box 3304, Austin TX 78764, USA — Ice Hockey Player

Hinote, Daniel C (Dan)
4323 Forest Park Ave, Saint Louis MO 63108, USA — Basketball Player

Hinrich, Kirk J
1886 Hilltop Lane, Bannockburn IL 60015, USA — Actor

Hinrichs, Fabian
Heppeler Agency, Steinstr 54, 81667 Munich, Germany — Ice Hockey Player

Hinse, Andre
PO Box 237, Fort Cobb OK 73038, USA — Baseball Player

Hinske, Eric S
10222 E Southwind Lane, #1041, Scottsdale AZ 85262, USA — Actress

Hinson, Jordan D
Inphenate, 9701 Wilshire Blvd, #1000, Beverly Hills CA 90212 USA — Golfer

Hinson, Larry
3179 Highway 32 E, Douglas GA 31533, USA — Basketball Player

Hinson, Roy M
8167 Quail Meadow Way, West Palm Beach FL 33412, USA — Skier

Hinterseer, Ernst
Hahnenkammstr, 6370 Kitzbuhel, Austria — Baseball Player

Hinton, Charles E (Chuck), Jr
6330 16th St NW, Washington DC 20011, USA — Football Player

Hinton, Christopher J (Chris)
374 Citadella Court, Alpharetta GA 30022, USA — Football Player

Hinton, Eddie
34 Auburn Ridge, Spring Branch TX 78070, USA — Model

Hinton, Jessa
Playboy Promotions, 2706 Media Center Dr, Los Angeles CA 90065 USA — Baseball Player

Hinton, Richard M (Rich)
7447 Hawkins Road, Sarasota FL 34241, USA — Writer

Hinton, Susan Eloise (S E)
Delacorte Press, 1540 Broadway, New York NY 10036, USA — Businessman

Hintz, Donald C
Entergy Corp, 10055 Grogans Mill Road, #150, Spring TX 77380, USA — Model, Actress

Hinze, Kristy
Ford Models Inc, 111 5th Ave, #900, New York NY 10003 USA — Baseball Player

Hinzo, Thomas L (Tommy)
635 Imperial Beach Blvd, Imperial Beach CA 91932, USA — Architect

Hiort, Esbjorn
Bel Colles Farm, Parkvej 6, 2960 Rungsted Kyst, Denmark — Actor

Hipp, Paul
Stone Manners Salners, 9911 W Pico Blvd, #1400, Los Angeles CA 90035 USA — Football Player

Hipple, Eric E
7155 Driftwood Dr, Fenton MI 48430, USA — Astronaut

Hire, Kathryn P (Kay)
PO Box 580146, Houston TX 77258, USA — Ice Hockey Player

Hirsch, Corey
Saint Louis Blues, Scott Trade Center, 1401 Clark Ave, Saint Louis MO 63103 USA — Educator

Hirsch, E D, Jr
University of Virginia, Education Dept, Charlottesville VA 22906, USA — Actor

Hirsch, Emile
Collective, 8383 Wilshire Blvd, #1050, Beverly Hills CA 90211 USA — Actress

Hirsch, Hallee
B/W/R, 9100 Wilshire Blvd, #500W, Beverly Hills CA 90212 USA — Interior Designer

Hirsch, Howard
Hirsch/Bedner Assoc, 3216 Nebraska Ave, Santa Monica CA 90404, USA — Writer, Producer

Hirsch, Janis
Creative Artists Agency, 2000 Ave of Stars, #100, Los Angeles CA 90067 USA — Actor

Hirsch, Judd
Joan Sittenfield Mgmt, 1064 S Ogden Dr, Los Angeles CA 90019, USA — Businessman

Hirsch, Laurence E
Centex Corp, 2728 N Harwood, #200, Dallas TX 75201, USA — Inventor (Surgical Stapler)

Hirsch, Leon C
150 Glover Ave, Norwalk CT 06850, USA — Editor

Hirsch, Paul
Innovative Artists, 1505 10th St, Santa Monica CA 90401 USA — Actor

Hirsch, Robert P
1 Place du Palais Bourbon, 75007 Paris, France — Writer, Religious Leader, Rabbi

Hirsch, Sherre
Canyon Ranch, 8600 E Rockcliffe Road, Tucson AZ 85750, USA — Baseball Umpire

Hirschbeck, Mark
12 Isinglass Terrace, Trumbull CT 06611, USA — Director, Actor

Hirschbiegel, Oliver
United Talent Agency, 9336 Civic Center Dr, Beverly Hills CA 90210 USA — Cinematographer

Hirschfeld, Gerald J
826 Pavilion Place, Ashland OR 97520, USA — Businessman

Hirschfield, Alan J
PO Box 7443, Jackson WY 83002, USA

Hingsen - Hirschfield

Hirschfield, Bradley — Religious Leader, Rabbi
Center for Learning & Leadership, 440 Park Ave S, #400, New York NY 10016, USA
Hirschman, Albert O — Economist
3486 Lawrenceville Road, Princeton NJ 8540, USA
Hirst, Damien — Sculptor
White Cube Gallery, Saint James's, 44 Duke St, London SW1Y 6DD, England
Hirtz, Dagmar — Director
Jollystr 45, 81545 Munich, Germany
Hiscock, Norm — Producer
Vanguarde Artists Mgmt, 119 Spadina Ave, #501, Toronto ON M5V 2L1, Canada
Hiser, Gene T — Baseball Player
1450 Caldwell Lane, Hoffman Estates IL 60169, USA
Hiskey, Bryant (Babe) — Golfer
4046 Pirates Beach, Galveston TX 77554, USA
Hisle, Larry E — Baseball Player
312 W Saddleworth Court W, Thiensville WI 53092, USA
Hitchcock, Ken — Ice Hockey Coach
11118 Valleydale Dr, #C, Dallas TX 75230, USA
Hitchcock, Robyn — Singer (Soft Boys), Songwriter
Agency Group Ltd, 142 W 57th St, #600, New York NY 10019 USA
Hitchcock, Russell — Singer (Air Supply)
PO Box 3367, Beverly Hills CA 90212, USA
Hitchcock, Sterling A — Baseball Player
255 Yucca Road, Naples FL 34102, USA
Hitchcock, Sylvia L — Beauty Queen
Miss Universe Organization, 1370 Ave of Americas, #1600, New York NY 10019 USA
Hite, Robert L — WW II Army Air Corps Hero
112 Elaine Ave, Camden AR 71701, USA
Hite, Shere D — Writer
75 Haywood St, #312, Asheville NC 28801, USA
Hite, William P — Labor Leader
United Plumbing/Pipefitters Assn, 3 Park Place, Annapolis MD 21401, USA
Hitsujia, Shirotama — Director
Yubiwa Hotel, 4-41-15-701, Yoyogi Shibuyaku, Tokyo 151 0053, Japan
Hitt, John C — Educator
University of Central Florida, President's Office, Orlando FL 32816, USA
Hix, Charles — Fashion Expert, Writer
Simon & Schuster, 1230 Ave of Americas, Concourse 1, New York NY 10020, USA
Hjejle, Iben — Actress
Art Management ApS, Kronprinsensgade 9A, 1114 CPH Copenhagen K, Denmark
Hjorth, Maria A (Mimmi) — Golfer
608 Henley Circle, Davenport FL 33896, USA
Hlinka, Nichol — Ballerina
New York City Ballet, Lincoln Center Plaza, New York NY 10023 USA
Hnatiuk, Glen — Golfer
8746 Mississippi Run, Weeki Wachee FL 34613, USA
Hnidy, Shane — Ice Hockey Player
1704 Silvermere Court, Duluth GA 30097, USA
Ho, David — Medical Researcher
Aaron Diamond AIDS Research Center, 455 1st Ave, New York NY 10016, USA
Ho, Derek K — Surfer
Assn of Surfing Professionals, PO Box 309, Huntington Beach CA 92648, USA
Ho, Josie — Actress
I C M Partners, 10250 Constellation Blvd, #900, Los Angeles CA 90067 USA
Ho, Tao — Architect
499 King's Road, #8/B, North Point, Hong Kong Special Region, China
Hoag, Jan — Actress
Amsel Eisenstadt Frazier, 5055 Wilshire Blvd, #865, Los Angeles CA 90036 USA
Hoag, Judith W — Actress
Bauman Redanty Shaul Agency, 5757 Wilshire Blvd, #473, Los Angeles CA 90036 USA
Hoag, Peter C — Test Pilot
3655 Little Rock Dr, Provo UT 84604, USA
Hoag, Tami — Writer
Bantam/Dell Books, 1745 Broadway, New York NY 10019, USA
Hoage, Terrell L (Terry) — Football Player
870 Arbor Road, Paso Robles CA 93446, USA
Hoagland, Edward — Writer
PO Box 51, Barton VT 05822, USA
Hoagland, Jimmie L (Jim) — Journalist
Washington Post, Editorial Dept, 1150 15th St NW, Washington DC 20071, USA
Hoaglin, G Frederick (Fred) — Football Player, Coach
7 Governors Road, Hilton Head SC 29928, USA
Hoak, Richard j (Dick) — Football Player
162 Crest View Dr, Greensburg PA 15601, USA
Hoar, Joseph P — Marine Corps General
386 13th St, Del Mar CA 92014, USA
Hoard, Leroy — Football Player
13141 NW 8th Court, Sunrise FL 33325, USA
Hoare, C Antony R — Computer Engineer
Oxford University, Computing Laboratory, Parks Road, Oxford OX1 3QD, England
Hobaugh, Charles O — Astronaut
N A S A, Johnson Space Center, 2101 NASA Road, Houston TX 77058 USA
Hobault, John — Space Scientist
15 Piper Road, #K319, Scarborough ME 04074, USA
Hobbie, Glen F — Baseball Player
RR 2 Box 234A, Ramsey IL 62080, USA
Hobbs, Becky — Singer, Pianist
Entertainment Artists, PO Box 120824, Nashville TN 37212 USA
Hobbs, Chelsea — Actress
Paradigm Agency, 360 N Crescent Dr, North Building, Beverly Hills CA 90210 USA
Hobbs, David — Auto Racing Driver, Sportscaster
David Hobbs Honda, 6100 N Green Bay Ave, Glendale WI 53209, USA
Hobbs, Ellis, III — Football Player
8885 Old Southwick Pass, Alpharetta GA 30022, USA
Hobbs, Jeff — Writer
Simon & Schuster, 1230 Ave of Americas, Concourse 1, New York NY 10020 USA

H

Hirschfield - Hobbs

H

Hobbs, John D (Jack) — Baseball Player
3 Wade Dr, Cherry Hill NJ 08034, USA
Hoberman, David — Producer
Mandeville Films, 500 S Buena Vista St, Animation Building 2G, Burbank CA 91521, USA
Hobert, Billy J — Football Player
255 Portofino Way, Redondo Beach CA 90277, USA
Hoblit, Gregory (Greg) — Director
W M E Entertainment, 9601 Wilshire Blvd, #300, Beverly Hills CA 90210 USA
Hobolt, John C — Space Scientist
15 Piper Road, #K319, Scarborough ME 04074, USA
Hobson, Clell L (Butch) — Baseball Player, Manager
6302 Catarata St, Bakersfield CA 93311, USA
Hobson, Helen — Actress
Gavin Barker Assoc, 2D Wimpole St, London W1G 0EB, England
Hobson, Jeff — Illusionist
Jack Grenier Productions, 32630 Concord Dr, Madison Heights MI 48071 USA
Hobson, Victor B — Football Player
505 Gracelyn Court SW, Atlanta GA 30331, USA
Hoch, Carin — Golfer
International Mgmt Group, 1 Erieview Plaza, 1360 E 9th St, Cleveland OH 44114 USA
Hoch, Danny — Performance Artist, Actor
Gersh Agency, 9465 Wilshire Blvd, #600, Beverly Hills CA 90212 USA
Hoch, Scott — Golfer
9239 Cypress Cove Dr, Orlando FL 32819, USA
Hochevar, Luke A — Baseball Player
2452 Glen Meadow Road, Knoxville TN 37909, USA
Hochhuth, Rolf — Writer
PO Box 661, 4002 Basel, Switzerland
Hochschorner, Pavol — Canoeing Athlete
Lesna 8, 81104 Bratislava, Slovakia
Hochstein, Russ — Football Player
10 Sidney St, Plainville MA 2762, USA
Hochwald, Bari — Actress
Herb Tannen, 10801 National Blvd, #101, Los Angeles CA 90064 USA
Hock, Dee Ward — Businessman
Visa International, 900 Metro Center Blvd, Foster City CA 94404, USA
Hocke, Stefan — Ski Jumper
Sportgymnasium, Am Harzwald 3, 98558 Oberhof, Germany
Hockenbery, Charles M (Chuck) — Baseball Player
1546 Birka Lane, Onalaska WI 54650, USA
Hockfield, Susan — Educator
Massachusetts Institute of Technology, President's Office, Cambridge MA 02139, USA
Hocking, Amanda — Writer
Saint Martin's Press, 175 5th Ave, #400, New York NY 10010 USA
Hocking, Dennis L (Denny) — Baseball Player
7384 E Villanueva Dr, Orange CA 92867, USA
Hockney, David — Artist, Photographer
Tradhart Ltd, 19B Buckingham Ave, Slough SL1 4QB, England
Hodder, Kane W — Actor, Stuntman
Amsel Eisenstadt Frazier, 5055 Wilshire Blvd, #865, Los Angeles CA 90036 USA
Hoddle, Glenn — Soccer Player, Manager
Football Assn, 16 Lancaster Gate, London W2 3LW, England
Hodel, Donald P — Secretary, Energy; Labor
1801 Sara Dr, #L, Chesapeake VA 23320, USA
Hodel, Nathan W — Football Player
2411 Goldenrod Way, Wauconda IL 60084, USA
Hodge, Aldis — Actor
Paradigm Agency, 360 N Crescent Dr, North Building, Beverly Hills CA 90210 USA
Hodge, Chad — Writer, Producer
W M E Entertainment, 9601 Wilshire Blvd, #300, Beverly Hills CA 90210 USA
Hodge, Charles E (Charlie) — Ice Hockey Player
27111 25A Ave, Aldergrove BC V4W 3N4, Canada
Hodge, Daniel A (Dan) — Freestyle Wrestler
914 Jackson St, Perry OK 73077, USA
Hodge, Douglas — Actor
United Agents, 12-26 Lexington St, London W1F 0LE, England
Hodge, Ed O — Baseball Player
127 Jedwell St, Johnson City TN 37601, USA
Hodge, Edwin — Actor
Luber Rocklin Entertainment, 8530 Wilshire Blvd, #555, Beverly Hills CA 90211 USA
Hodge, John — Producer
United Agents, 12-26 Lexington St, London W1F 0LE, England
Hodge, Kenneth R (Ken), Sr — Ice Hockey Player
13 Longfellow Dr, Newburyport MA 01950, USA
Hodge, Patricia — Actress
I C M Partners, Marlborough House, 10 Earlham St, #300, London WC2H 9LNP, England
Hodge, Sedrick J — Football Player
120 Victoria Place, Fayetteville GA 30214, USA
Hodges, Bill — Basketball Coach
Georgia College, Athletic Dept, Milledgeville GA 31061, USA
Hodges, Craig A — Basketball Player
67 Elm St, Park Forest IL 60466, USA
Hodges, J T — Singer, Songwriter
Show Dog-Universal Music, 2303 21st Ave S, #400, Nashville TN 37212 USA
Hodges, Mike — Director
Wesley Farm, Durweston, Blanford Forum, Dorset DT11 0QG, England
Hodges, Robert H, Jr — Judge
US Claims Court, 717 Madison Place NW, Washington DC 20439, USA
Hodges, Ronald W (Ron) — Baseball Player
110 Hajo Lane, Rocky Mount VA 24151, USA
Hodges, Roneeka — Basketball Player
Indiana Fever, Conseco Fieldhouse, 125 S Pennsylvania, Indianapolis IN 46204 USA
Hodges, Trey — Baseball Player
19506 Kuykendahl Road, Spring TX 77379, USA
Hodgins, William — Interior Designer
232 Clarendon St, Boston MA 02116, USA

Hobbs - Hodgins

Hodgman, John
United Talent Agency, 9336 Civic Center Dr, Beverly Hills CA 90210 USA — Actor, Writer

Hodgson, James D
28802 Grayfox St, Malibu CA 90265, USA — Secretary, Labor

Hodgson, Nicholas J D (Nick)
Red Light Mgmt, 8439 Sunset Blvd, West Hollywood CA — Singer, Drummer (Kaiser Chiefs)

Hodgson, Roger
Agency Group Ltd, 142 W 57th St, #600, New York NY 10019 USA — Guitarist (Supertramp)

Hoechlin, Tyler
United Talent Agency, 9336 Civic Center Dr, Beverly Hills CA 90210 USA — Actor

Hoeg, Peter
Farrar Straus Giroux, 18 W 18th St, #700, New York NY 10011 USA — Writer

Hoeks, Sylvia
Copper En Co, Wamondstraat 73-1, 1058 KR Amsterdam, Netherlands — Actress

Hoelsher, Vanessa
Playboy Promotions, 2706 Media Center Dr, Los Angeles CA 90065 USA — Model

Hoelzer, Margaret
535 N Coast Highway, Laguna Beach CA 92651, USA — Swimmer

Hoenig, Heinz
Society Relations, Mundsburger Damm 2, 22087 Hamburg, Germany — Actor

Hoenig, Thomas M
615 W Meyer Blvd, Kansas City MO 64113, USA — Government Official, Financier

Hoest, Bunny
William Hoest Enterprises, 27 Watch Way, Lloyd Neck, Huntington NY 11743, USA — Cartoonist (Lockhorns)

Hoewing, Gerald L
Navy Mutual Aid Assn, 29 Carpenter Road, Arlington VA 22214, USA — Navy Admiral

Hoey, George W
13635 Clermont Court, Thornton CO 80602, USA — Football Player

Hofer, Paul D
981 June Road, Memphis TN 38119, USA — Football Player

Hoff, Kathryn (Katie)
106 Kenilworth Park, #4D, Towson MD 21204, USA — Swimmer

Hoff, Lawrence C
8720 Cypress Club Dr, Raleigh NC 27615, USA — Businessman

Hoff, Marcian E (Ted), Jr
26541 Taafe Road, Los Altos Hills CA 94022, USA — Inventor (Microprocessor)

Hoff, Michael
University of Nebraska, Art & Art History Dept, 120 Richards Hall, Lincoln NE 68588, USA — Art Historian

Hoff, Philip H
Hoff Wilson Powell Lang, PO Box 123, Essex Junction VT 05453, USA — Governor, VT

Hoffa, James P
2593 Hounds Chase Dr, Troy MI 48098, USA — Labor Leader

Hoffman, Alan J
I B M Research Center, PO Box 218, Yorktown Heights NY 10598, USA — Mathematician

Hoffman, Alice
32 Lowell Road, Concord MA 1742, USA — Writer

Hoffman, Basil
26 Aller Court, Glendale CA 91206, USA — Actor

Hoffman, Charley
Professional Golfer's Assn, PO Box 109601, Palm Beach Gardens FL 33410 USA — Golfer

Hoffman, Darleane C
Lawrence Berkeley Laboratory, 1 Cyclotron Road, Berkeley CA 94720, USA — Nuclear Physicist

Hoffman, Dustin L
Punch Productions, 11661 San Vicente Blvd, #222, Los Angeles CA 90049, USA — Actor

Hoffman, Gaby
Innovative Artists, 235 Park Ave S, #1000, New York NY 10003 USA — Actress

Hoffman, Glenn E
201 S Old Bridge Road, Anaheim CA 92808, USA — Baseball Player, Manager

Hoffman, Guy A
313 Fairway Dr, #S, Bloomington IL 61701, USA — Baseball Player

Hoffman, Jackie
Don Buchwald/Fortitude, 6500 Wilshire Blvd, #2200, Los Angeles CA 90048 USA — Actress

Hoffman, Jeffrey A
US Embassy, 2 Ave Gabriel, PSC 116/NASA, 75382 Paris Cedex, France — Astronaut

Hoffman, John Robert
Creative Artists Agency, 2000 Ave of Stars, #100, Los Angeles CA 90067 USA — Director, Writer

Hoffman, Matt
D D K Talent, 16255 Ventura Blvd, #525, Encino CA 91436, USA — Actor

Hoffman, Michael
United Talent Agency, 9336 Civic Center Dr, Beverly Hills CA 90210 USA — Director, Writer

Hoffman, Philip Seymour
Paradigm Agency, 360 Park Ave S, #1600, New York NY 10010 USA — Actor

Hoffman, Reid G
LinkedIn, 2029 Stierlin Court, #200, Mountain Valley CA 94043, USA — Businessman

Hoffman, Rick
Framework Entertainment, 9057 Nemo St, #C, West Hollywood CA 90069 USA — Actor

Hoffman, Robert James, III
Impression Entertainment, 9229 W Sunset Blvd, #700, Los Angeles CA 90069, USA — Actor

Hoffman, Ted, Jr
1568 Partarian Way, San Jose CA 95129, USA — Bowling Executive

Hoffman, Thom
Anne Alvares Correa, 34 Rue Jouffroy d'Abbans, 75017 Paris, France — Actor

Hoffman, William M
190 Prince St, New York NY 10012, USA — Lyricist, Writer

Hoffmann, Ambrosi
Talstrasse 63, 7250 Davos Dorf, Switzerland — Alpine Skier

Hoffmann, Christian
Frunwald 7, 4160 Aigen, Austria — Cross Country Skier

Hoffmann, Gaby
I C M Partners, 10250 Constellation Blvd, #900, Los Angeles CA 90067 USA — Actress

Hoffmann, Jan
Ice Skating Union, Menzinger Str 68, 80992 Munich, Germany — Figure Skater

Hoffmann, Jules A
Biologie Moléculaire & Cellulaire Institut, 15 Rue Descartes, 67084 Strasbourg Cedex, France — Nobel Medicine Laureate

Hoffmann, Roald
4 Sugarbush Lane, Ithaca NY 14850, USA — Nobel Chemistry Laureate

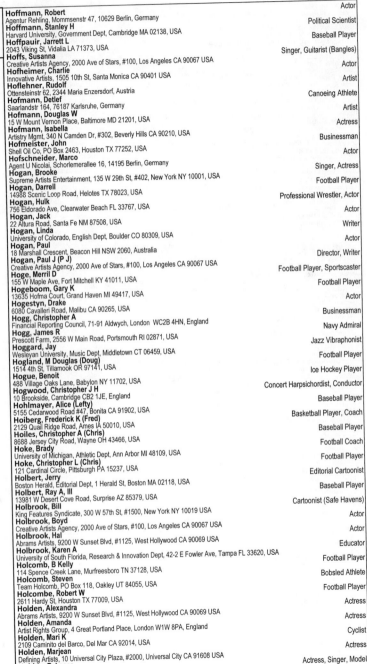

Hoffmann, Robert
Agentur Rehling, Mommsenstr 47, 10629 Berlin, Germany — Actor
Hoffmann, Stanley H
Harvard University, Government Dept, Cambridge MA 02138, USA — Political Scientist
Hoffpauir, Jarrett L
2043 Viking St, Vidalia LA 71373, USA — Baseball Player
Hoffs, Susanna
Creative Artists Agency, 2000 Ave of Stars, #100, Los Angeles CA 90067 USA — Singer, Guitarist (Bangles)
Hofheimer, Charlie
Innovative Artists, 1505 10th St, Santa Monica CA 90401 USA — Actor
Hoflehner, Rudolf
Ottensteinstr 62, 2344 Maria Enzersdorf, Austria — Artist
Hofmann, Detlef
Saarlandstr 164, 76187 Karlsruhe, Germany — Canoeing Athlete
Hofmann, Douglas W
15 W Mount Vernon Place, Baltimore MD 21201, USA — Artist
Hofmann, Isabella
Artistry Mgmt, 340 N Camden Dr, #302, Beverly Hills CA 90210, USA — Actress
Hofmeister, John
Shell Oil Co, PO Box 2463, Houston TX 77252, USA — Businessman
Hofschneider, Marco
Agent U Nicolai, Schorlemerallee 16, 14195 Berlin, Germany — Actor
Hogan, Brooke
Supreme Artists Entertainment, 135 W 29th St, #402, New York NY 10001, USA — Singer, Actress
Hogan, Darrell
14988 Scenic Loop Road, Helotes TX 78023, USA — Football Player
Hogan, Hulk
756 Eldorado Ave, Clearwater Beach FL 33767, USA — Professional Wrestler, Actor
Hogan, Jack
22 Altura Road, Santa Fe NM 87508, USA — Actor
Hogan, Linda
University of Colorado, English Dept, Boulder CO 80309, USA — Writer
Hogan, Paul
18 Marshall Crescent, Beacon Hill NSW 2060, Australia — Actor
Hogan, Paul J (P J)
Creative Artists Agency, 2000 Ave of Stars, #100, Los Angeles CA 90067 USA — Director, Writer
Hoge, Merril D
155 W Maple Ave, Fort Mitchell KY 41011, USA — Football Player, Sportscaster
Hogeboom, Gary K
13635 Hofma Court, Grand Haven MI 49417, USA — Football Player
Hogestyn, Drake
6080 Cavalleri Road, Malibu CA 90265, USA — Actor
Hogg, Christopher A
Financial Reporting Council, 71-91 Aldwych, London WC2B 4HN, England — Businessman
Hogg, James R
Prescott Farm, 2556 W Main Road, Portsmouth RI 02871, USA — Navy Admiral
Hoggard, Jay
Wesleyan University, Music Dept, Middletown CT 06459, USA — Jazz Vibraphonist
Hogland, M Douglas (Doug)
1514 4th St, Tillamook OR 97141, USA — Football Player
Hogue, Benoit
488 Village Oaks Lane, Babylon NY 11702, USA — Ice Hockey Player
Hogwood, Christopher J H
10 Brookside, Cambridge CB2 1JE, England — Concert Harpsichordist, Conductor
Hohlmayer, Alice (Lefty)
5155 Cedarwood Road #47, Bonita CA 91902, USA — Baseball Player
Hoiberg, Frederick K (Fred)
2129 Quail Ridge Road, Ames IA 50010, USA — Basketball Player, Coach
Hoiles, Christopher A (Chris)
8688 Jersey City Road, Wayne OH 43466, USA — Baseball Player
Hoke, Brady
University of Michigan, Athletic Dept, Ann Arbor MI 48109, USA — Football Coach
Hoke, Christopher L (Chris)
121 Cardinal Circle, Pittsburgh PA 15237, USA — Football Player
Holbert, Jerry
Boston Herald, Editorial Dept, 1 Herald St, Boston MA 02118, USA — Editorial Cartoonist
Holbert, Ray A, III
13981 W Desert Cove Road, Surprise AZ 85379, USA — Baseball Player
Holbrook, Bill
King Features Syndicate, 300 W 57th St, #1500, New York NY 10019 USA — Cartoonist (Safe Havens)
Holbrook, Boyd
Creative Artists Agency, 2000 Ave of Stars, #100, Los Angeles CA 90067 USA — Actor
Holbrook, Hal
Abrams Artists, 9200 W Sunset Blvd, #1125, West Hollywood CA 90069 USA — Actor
Holbrook, Karen A
University of South Florida, Research & Innovation Dept, 42-2 E Fowler Ave, Tampa FL 33620, USA — Educator
Holcomb, B Kelly
114 Spence Creek Lane, Murfreesboro TN 37128, USA — Football Player
Holcomb, Steven
Team Holcomb, PO Box 118, Oakley UT 84055, USA — Bobsled Athlete
Holcombe, Robert W
2611 Hardy St, Houston TX 77009, USA — Football Player
Holden, Alexandra
Abrams Artists, 9200 W Sunset Blvd, #1125, West Hollywood CA 90069 USA — Actress
Holden, Amanda
Artist Rights Group, 4 Great Portland Place, London W1W 8PA, England — Actress
Holden, Mari K
2109 Caminito del Barco, Del Mar CA 92014, USA — Cyclist
Holden, Marjean
Defining Artists, 10 Universal City Plaza, #2000, Universal City CA 91608 USA — Actress
Holden, Rebecca
Box Office, 5207 Rustic Way, Old Hickory TN 37138, USA — Actress, Singer, Model
Holden, Robert L (Bob)
Webster University, Political Science Dept, 470 E Lockwood Ave, Saint Louis MO 63119, USA — Governor, MO
Holden, Steven A (Steve)
1202 N Nevada Way, Mesa AZ 85203, USA — Football Player

Holden, Warrick D
17202 Stratford Green Dr, Sugar Land TX 77498, USA — Football Player

Holden-Reid, Kris
Oscars Abrams Zimel, 438 Queen St E, Toronto ON M5A 1T4, Canada — Actress

Holder, Eric
Justice Department, 10th St & Constitution Ave NW, Washington DC 20530 USA — Attorney General

Holder, Geoffrey
Innovative Artists, 235 Park Ave S, #1000, New York NY 10003 USA — Actor, Dancer

Holdsclaw, Chamique
San Antonio Silver Stars, 1 AT&T Center, San Antonio TX 78219 USA — Basketball Player

Holdsworth, Frederick W (Fred)
578 Upland Hills Dr, Chelsea MI 48118, USA — Baseball Player

Holecek, John F
1828 Prairie St, Glenview IL 60025, USA — Football Player

Holiday, Phillip
Pacific Boxing Club, 14 Channel St, Cleveland QLD, Australia — Boxer

Holl, Steven M
Steven Holl Architects, 435 Hudson St, #400, New York NY 10014, USA — Architect

Holladay, Wilhelmina Cole
National Museum of Women in Arts, 1250 New York NW, Washington DC 20005, USA — Museum Executive

Holland, Agnieszka
Field Entertainment, 1240 N Wetherly Dr, Los Angeles CA 90069, USA — Director, Writer

Holland, Alfred W (Al)
443 Lewiston St NW, Roanoke VA 24017, USA — Baseball Player

Holland, Brian
9912 Cozy Glen Circle, Las Vegas NV 89117, USA — Songwriter

Holland, Darius J
13972 Meadowbrook Dr, Broomfield CO 80020, USA — Football Player

Holland, Dexter
Rebel Waltz, 31652 2nd Ave, Laguna Beach CA 92651, USA — Singer (Offspring)

Holland, Edward (Eddie), Jr
555 S Burlingame Ave, Los Angeles CA 90049, USA — Songwriter

Holland, J Bradley (Brad)
1374 Sparrow Road, Carlsbad CA 92011, USA — Basketball Player, Coach

Holland, James F
Mount Sinai Medical Center, Oncology Dept, 1190 5th Ave, New York NY 10029, USA — Oncologist

Holland, Jamie L
4025 Jonesville Road, Wake Forest NC 27587, USA — Football Player

Holland, Johnny R
3303 Prestwick Square, Missouri City TX 77459, USA — Football Player, Coach

Holland, Jolie
Rare Artists, 794 44th Ave, San Francisco CA 94121, USA — Singer (Be Good Tanyas), Songwriter

Holland, Julian M (Jools)
One Fifteen, Globe House, Middle Lane Mews, London N8 8PN, England — Pianist (Squeeze, The The)

Holland, Kimberly
Playboy Promotions, 2706 Media Center Dr, Los Angeles CA 90065 USA — Model

Holland, Montrae R
1096 Sendero Dr, Keller TX 76248, USA — Football Player

Holland, Richard J
Screen Talent Agency, Rich Mix Building, 35-47 Bethnal Green Road, London E1 6LA, England — Art Director

Holland, Tara Dawn
9050 Carothers Parkway, #104, Franklin TN 37067, USA — Beauty Queen

Holland, Terry
East Carolina University, Athletic Dept, Greenville NC 27858, USA — Basketball Player, Coach, Administrator

Holland, Todd
3 Arts Entertainment, 9460 Wilshire Blvd, #700, Beverly Hills CA 90212 USA — Director, Producer

Holland, Tom
Dead Rabbit Films, 215 Zelley Ave, Moorestown NJ 08057 08057, USA — Director

Holland, Wilbur
538 Georgia Dr, Columbus GA 31907, USA — Basketball Player

Holland, Willa
Gersh Agency, 9465 Wilshire Blvd, #600, Beverly Hills CA 90212 USA — Actress, Model

Holland, Willard R, Jr
FirstEnergy Corp, 76 S Main St, Akron OH 44308, USA — Businessman

Hollande, Francois G G
Palais de l'Elysee, 55 Rue Faubourg Saint Honore, 75008 Paris, France — President, France

Hollander, Edmund D
Hollander Landscape Design, 200 Park Ave S, New York NY 10003, USA — Landscape Architect

Hollander, John
Yale University, English Dept, New Haven CT 06520, USA — Writer

Hollander, Lorin
I C M Artists, 40 W 57th St, #1800, New York NY 10019 USA — Concert Pianist

Hollander, Nicole
Sylvia Syndicate, 1440 N Dayton St, Chicago IL 60642, USA — Cartoonist (Sylvia)

Hollander, Tom
Independent Talent Group, Oxford House, 76 Oxford St, London W1D 1BS, England — Actor, Producer, Writer

Hollandsworth, Todd M
1310 MacAlpin Court, Inverness IL 60010, USA — Baseball Player

Hollas, Donald W
1811 Mayweather Lane, Richmond TX 77406, USA — Football Player

Holldobler, Berthold K
University of Wurzburg, Zoology Dept, Am Nubland, 97074 Wurzburg, Germany — Writer, Biologist, Zoologist

Holle, Gary C
820 5th Ave, Watervliet NY 12189, USA — Baseball Player

Hollein, Hans
Eiskellerstr 1, 40213 Dusseldorf, Germany — Pritzker Architectural Laureate

Holler, J Edward (Ed)
4500 Ivy Hall Dr, Columbia SC 29206, USA — Football Player

Holleran, Leslie
United Talent Agency, 9336 Civic Center Dr, Beverly Hills CA 90210 USA — Producer

Hollerer, Walter F
Heerstr 99, 14055 Berlin, Germany — Writer

Holliday, Cheryl
W M E Entertainment, 9601 Wilshire Blvd, #300, Beverly Hills CA 90210 USA — Writer, Producer

Holliday, D Giovonni (Vonnie)
1060 Canter Road NE, Atlanta GA 30324, USA — Football Player

H

Holden - Holliday

Holliday, Jennifer Y Pyramid Entertainment, 377 Rector Place, #21A, New York NY 10280 USA	Singer, Actress
Holliday, Matthew T (Matt) 4 Ravenswood Road, Englewood CO 80113, USA	Baseball Player
Holliday, Polly D Blake Agency, 23441 Malibu Colony Road, Malibu CA 90265 USA	Actress, Singer
Hollier, Dwight L 5012 Woodview Lane, Matthews NC 28104, USA	Football Player
Holliger, Heinz Konzertgellschaft, Hochstr 51, 4002 Basel, Switzerland	Concert Oboist, Composer
Holliman, Earl PO Box 1969, Studio City CA 91614, USA	Actor
Hollimon, Mike 9922 Glenn Canyon Dr, Dallas TX 75243, USA	Baseball Player
Hollings, Michael R Saint Mary of Angels, Moorhouse Road, Bayswater, London W2 5DJ, England	Religious Leader
Hollingsworth, David S Orbital Sciences Corp, 21839 Atlantic Blvd, Dulles VA 20166, USA	Space Scientist
Hollinquest, Lamont 13709 S San Pedro St, Los Angeles CA 90061, USA	Football Player
Hollins, David M (Dave) 3221 Southwestern Blvd, Orchard Park NY 14127, USA	Baseball Player
Hollins, Lionel E 7594 Tagg Dr, Germantown TN 38138, USA	Basketball Player, Coach
Hollis, Essie B 9102 NW 48th St, Sunrise FL 33351, USA	Basketball Player
Hollis, Michael S (Mike) 124 Sawbill Palm Dr, Ponte Vedra Beach FL 32082, USA	Football Player
Hollister, Dave I C M Partners, 10250 Constellation Blvd, #900, Los Angeles CA 90067 USA	Singer
Holloman, Gus M 2489 County Road 139, Cameron TX 76520, USA	Football Player
Holloman, Laurel Sanders/Armstrong/Caserta Mgmt, 2120 Colorado Ave, #120, Santa Monica CA 90404 USA	Actress
Holloway, Brenda Universal Attractions, 135 W 26th St, #1200, New York NY 10001 USA	Singer
Holloway, Brian D 4110 Heritage Lake Court, Lutz FL 33558, USA	Football Player
Holloway, Glen L 2737 N Columbus Blvd, #6, Tucson AZ 85712, USA	Football Player
Holloway, James L, III 4800 Fillmore Ave, #1058, Alexandria VA 22311, USA	Navy Admiral
Holloway, Jennifer I M G Artists, 152 W 57th St, #500, New York NY 10019 USA	Opera Singer
Holloway, Joshua L (Josh) Brillstein Entertainment Partners, 9150 Wilshire Blvd, #350, Beverly Hills CA 90212 USA	Actor, Model
Holloway, Ken World Class/Berry Mgmt, 1848 Tyne Blvd, Nashville TN 37215, USA	Singer
Holloway, Matt Creative Artists Agency, 2000 Ave of Stars, #100, Los Angeles CA 90067 USA	Writer
Holloway, Robin G Gonville & Caius College, Music Dept, Cambridge CB2 1TA, England	Composer
Holloway, William J, Jr US Court of Appeals, PO Box 1767, Oklahoma City OK 73101, USA	Judge
Hollweg, Ryan 190 John Olds Dr, #212, Manchester CT 06042, USA	Ice Hockey Player
Holly, Jeffrey O (Jeff) 1201 Walnut Ave, #57, Tustin CA 92780, USA	Baseball Player
Holly, Lauren Gilbertson Entertainment, 1334 3rd St Promenade, #207, Santa Monica CA 90401, USA	Actress
Hollyday, Christopher Ted Kurland, 173 Brighton Ave, Allston MA 02134 USA	Jazz Saxophonist
Holm, Anders United Talent Agency, 9336 Civic Center Dr, Beverly Hills CA 90210 USA	Actor, Writer
Holm, Dorthe Elisabeth Curling Assn, Idraettens Hus, 2605 Brondby, Denmark	Curling Athlete
Holm, Ian Markham & Froggatt, Julian House, 4 Windmill St, London W1P 1HF, England	Actor
Holm, Joan 3639 S 61st Court, Cicero IL 60804, USA	Bowler
Holm, Peter 1 Rue de Fer Achevel Port Grimaud, 83310 Cogolin, France	Singer
Holman, Brian S 15821 Parkhill St, Overland Park KS 66221, USA	Baseball Player
Holman, C Ray Mallinckrodt Inc, 675 McDonnell Blvd, Saint Louis MO 63134, USA	Businessman
Holman, Clare United Agents, 12-26 Lexington St, London W1F 0LE, England	Actress
Holman, Gary R 3269 Maricopa Ave, #114, Lake Havasu City AZ 86406, USA	Baseball Player
Holman, Marshall 288 Island Pointe Dr, Medford OR 97504, USA	Bowler
Holman, R Scott 177 E Wilson St, Santa Rosa Beach FL 32459, USA	Baseball Player
Holman, Ralph T 3900 Bethel Dr, Saint Paul MN 55112, USA	Biochemist
Holman, Rodney A 41460 Herwig Bluff Road, Slidell LA 70461, USA	Football Player
Holman, Shawn L 105 Edgewood Road, Sewickley PA 15143, USA	Baseball Player
Holmberg, Jonas M O B Agency, 6404 Wilshire Blvd, #505, Los Angeles CA 90048 USA	Drummer (Komeda)
Holmberg, Marcus M O B Agency, 6404 Wilshire Blvd, #505, Los Angeles CA 90048 USA	Bassist (Komeda)
Holmberg, Robert A (Rob) 611 Richfield Court, Greensburg PA 15601, USA	Football Player

Holmes, Amy M (A M)   Writer
Princeton University, Creative Writing Program, Princeton NJ 08544, USA

Holmes, Andre (PaDre)   Musician (Fishbone)
Silverback Mgmt, 9469 Jefferson Blvd, #101, Culver City CA 90232, USA

Holmes, Ashton   Actor
B/W/R, 9100 Wilshire Blvd, #500W, Beverly Hills CA 90212 USA

Holmes, Clint   Singer
Conversation Co, 1044 Northern Blvd, #304, Roslyn NY 11576 USA

Holmes, D Brainerd   Space Engineer, Businessman
Bay Colony Corp Center, 950 Winter St, #4350, Waltham MA 02451, USA

Holmes, Darren L   Baseball Player
1 Emerald Court, Arden NC 28704, USA

Holmes, David   Music Producer, Composer
First Artists Mgmt, 4764 Park Granada, #210, Calabasas CA 91302 USA

Holmes, Earl L   Football Player
2978 Stonybrook Court, Tallahassee FL 32309, USA

Holmes, J B   Golfer
5175 Latrobe Dr, Windermere FL 34786, USA

Holmes, J Patrick (Pat)   Football Player
221 Mack Hollimon Dr, Kerrville TX 78028, USA

Holmes, Jennifer   Actress
PO Box 6303, Carmel CA 93921, USA

Holmes, Jerry   Football Player
107 Chatham Terrace, Hampton VA 23666, USA

Holmes, Katie   Actress
Creative Artists Agency, 2000 Ave of Stars, #100, Los Angeles CA 90067 USA

Holmes, Kelly   Track Athlete
Talk Mgmt, 26/28 Hammersmith Grove, London W6 7BA, England

Holmes, Kenneth (Kenny)   Football Player
6103 Aqua Ave, #PH #, Miami Beach FL 33141, USA

Holmes, Larry   Boxer
228 W Canal St, Easton PA 18042, USA

Holmes, Lester   Football Player
3760 Motor Ave, Los Angeles CA 90034, USA

Holmes, Pete   Actor
W M E Entertainment, 9601 Wilshire Blvd, #300, Beverly Hills CA 90210 USA

Holmes, Priest A   Football Player
9937 Spring Beauty, San Antonio TX 78254, USA

Holmes, Robert   Sculptor
PO Box 244, Sheep Ranch CA 95246, USA

Holmes, Rupert   Singer, Songwriter, Writer
Creative Artists Agency, 2000 Ave of Stars, #100, Los Angeles CA 90067 USA

Holmes, Santonio, Jr   Football Player
PO Box 1959, Burleson TX 76097, USA

Holmes, Tina   Actress
Abrams Artists, 9200 W Sunset Blvd, #1125, West Hollywood CA 90069 USA

Holmgren, Michael G (Mike)   Football Coach, Executive
Cleveland Browns, 76 Lou Groza Blvd, Berea OH 44017 USA

Holmgren, Paul H   Ice Hockey Player, Coach
724 Southwick Circle, Somerdale NJ 08083, USA

Holmquest, Donald L   Astronaut
205 Princeton Road, Menlo Park CA 94025, USA

Holmstrom, B Tomas   Ice Hockey Player
43479 McLean Court, Novi MI 48375, USA

Holmstrom, Bengt R   Economist
Massachusetts Institute of Technology, Economics Dept, Cambridge MA 02139, USA

Holofcener, Nicole   Director
United Talent Agency, 9336 Civic Center Dr, Beverly Hills CA 90210 USA

Holohan, Peter J (Pete)   Football Player
2945 Curie St, San Diego CA 92122, USA

Holonyak, Nick, Jr   Inventor (Light Emitting Diode)
101 W Windsor Road, Urbana IL 61802, USA

Holroyd, Michael D   Writer
85 Saint Marks Road, London W10 6JS England

Holroyd, Scott   Actor
Stone Manners Salners, 9911 W Pico Blvd, #1400, Los Angeles CA 90035 USA

Holscher, Mark   Attorney
O'Melveny & Meyers, 400 S Hope St, Los Angeles CA 90071, USA

Holsinger, James W, Jr   Physician
University of Kentucky Medical School, Public Health College, Lexington KY 40506, USA

Holst, Per   Producer
Per Holst Film A/S, Rentemestervej 69A, 2400 Copenhagen NV, Denmark

Holt, Christopher M (Chris)   Baseball Player
152 Hollywood Dr, Coppell TX 75019, USA

Holt, David Lee   Guitarist (Mavericks)
AristoMedia, 1620 16th Ave S, Nashville TN 37212, USA

Holt, Issiac, III   Football Player
4028 Fairmont Place, Birmingham AL 35207, USA

Holt, James W (Jim)   Baseball Player
150 Judge Sharpe Road, Graham NC 27253, USA

Holt, Lester   Commentator
NBC-TV, News Dept, 30 Rockefeller Plaza, #270E, New York NY 10112 USA

Holt, Pierce   Football Player
5101 County Road 430, San Angelo TX 76901, USA

Holt, Sandrine   Actress
A P A Talent/Literary Agency, 405 S Beverly Dr, #300, Beverly Hills CA 90212 USA

Holt, Terrence   Football Player
9924 Thoughtful Spot Way, Raleigh NC 27614, USA

Holt, Torrance J (Torry)   Football Player
2604 Prosser Court, Raleigh NC 27614, USA

Holten, Kasper   Director
Royal Danish Theatre, Postbox 2185, 1017 Copenhagen K, Denmark

Holtermann, E Louis, Jr   Publisher
Glamour, Publisher's Office, 350 Madison Ave, New York NY 10017, USA

Holton, A Linwood, Jr   Governor, VA
3883 Black Stump Road, Weems VA 22576, USA

H

Holton, Brian J 3214 Estate Dr, Oakdale PA 15071, USA	Baseball Player
Holton, Gerald 64 Francis Ave, Cambridge MA 02138, USA	Physicist
Holton, Michael D 5822 NW Redfox Dr, Portland OR 97229, USA	Basketball Player, Coach
Holtz, Louis L (Lou) 9201 Cromwell Park Place, Orlando FL 32827, USA	Football Coach, Sportscaster
Holtz, Michael J (Mike) 243 Goodridge Road, Northern Cambria PA 15714, USA	Baseball Player
Holtzman, David Washington University Medical Center, 660 S Euclid Ave, Saint Louis MO 63110, USA	Neurologist
Holtzman, Kenneth D (Ken) 256 Waterside Dr, Grover MO 63040, USA	Baseball Player
Holub, Emil Joe (E J) 2311 S County Road 1120, Midland TX 79706, USA	Football Player
Holub, Robert C University of Massachusetts, Chancellor's Office, Whitmore Building, Amherst MA 01003, USA	Educator
Holum, Dianne 2835 W 32nd Ave, #89, Denver CO 80211, USA	Speed Skater
Holum, Kristin 2835 W 32nd Ave, #89, Denver CO 80211, USA	Speed Skater
Holway, Jerome F 448 Spruce Dr, Exton PA 19341, USA	Cinematographer
Holyfield, Evander 794 Evander Holyfield Highway, #279, Fayetteville GA 30214, USA	Boxer
Holz, Gordon F (Gordy) 730 S Plaza Dr, #222, Saint Paul MN 55120, USA	Football Player
Holzemer, Mark H 10044 S MacAlister Trail, Littleton CO 80129, USA	Baseball Player
Holzer, Helmut 2403 Little Cove Road, Owens Crossroads AL 35763, USA	Space Scientist
Holzer, Jenny 80 Hewitt Road, Hoosick Falls NY 12090, USA	Artist
Holzinger, Brian A 1005 Ledgemont Dr, Broadview Heights OH 44147, USA	Ice Hockey Player
Holzmair, Wolfgang Augstein & Hahn, Tal 28, 80331 Munich, Germany	Opera Singer
Holzman, Malcolm Hardy Holzman Pfeiffer, 902 Broadway, #1900, New York NY 10010, USA	Architect
Homan, Dennis 1950 Charlotte Court, Florence AL 35630, USA	Football Player
Homewrecker, Suzi The Kirby Organization, 9200 Sunset Blvd, #600, Los Angeles CA 90069, USA	Singer, Guitarist (Civet)
Homfeld, Conrad Sandron, 11744 Marblestone Court, Wellington FL 33414, USA	Equestrian
Homme, Joshua M (Josh) The Firm, 2049 Century Park E, #2550, Los Angeles CA 90067 USA	Guitarist (Queens of the Stone Age)
Hon, John T Cardinal Catholic Diocese Center, 12F, 16 Caine Road, Hong Kong, China	Religious Leader
Honda, Yuka Billions Corp, 3522 W Armitage Ave, Chicago IL 60647, USA	Singer (Cibo Matto)
Honeck, Manfred Pittsburgh Symphony, Heinz Hall, 600 Penn Ave, Pittsburgh PA 15222, USA	Conductor
Honeycutt, Frederick W (Rick) 207 Forrest Road, Fort Oglethorpe GA 30742, USA	Baseball Player
Honeycutt, Van B Computer Sciences Corp, 2100 E Grand Ave, El Segundo CA 90245, USA	Businessman
Honeyghan, Lloyd 50 Barnfield Wood Road, Park Langley, Beckenham, Kent BR3 6SZ, England	Boxer
Hong Chih Kuo Seattle Mariners, Safeco Field, PO Box 4100, Seattle WA 98194 USA	Baseball Player
Hong, James Stage 9 Talent 1249 N Lodi Place, Hollywood CA 90038, USA	Actor, Producer, Director
Hongsakula, Apasra (Pook) Slimming Spa, 95 Ladprao Soi 23, Chatuchak, Bangkok 10900, Thailand	Beauty Queen
Honore, Jean Cardinal Archeveche, BP 1117, 27 Rue Jules-Simon, 37011 Tours Cedex, France	Religious Leader
Honore, Russel L Keppler Speakers, 4350 N Fairfax Dr, #700, Arlington VA 22203, USA	Army General
Honrubia, Samuel Montpellier Agglomeration H B, 1000 Ave du val de Montferrand, 34090 Montpellier, France	Handball Player
Honti, Zolton Gersh Agency, 9465 Wilshire Blvd, #600, Beverly Hills CA 90212 USA	Cinematographer
Hood, Donald H (Don) 20753 Charing Cross Circle, Estero FL 33928, USA	Baseball Player
Hood, Estus, III 2105 W Grace St, Kankakee IL 60901, USA	Football Player
Hood, Gavin Anonymous Content, 3532 Hayden Ave, Culver City CA 90232 USA	Director
Hood, Kenneth 5799 Bloomfield Ave, Verona NJ 07044, USA	Religious Leader
Hood, Leroy E Institutions for Systems Biology, 1441 N 34th St, Seattle WA 98103, USA	Inventor (DNA Sequencer), Geneticist
Hood, Robin 6705 Shoal Creek Dr, Arlington TX 76001, USA	Golfer
Hood, Walter Hood Studio, 3016 Filbert St, Oakland CA 94608, USA	Landscape Designer
Hood, Winford D 79 Anderson Ave NW, Atlanta GA 30314, USA	Football Player
Hook, James W (Jay) PO Box 90, Maple City MI 49664, USA	Baseball Player
Hooker, Charles R 28 Whippingham Road, Brighton, Sussex BN2 3PG, England	Artist
Hooker, Fair, Jr 3728 Rutherford Court, Inglewood CA 90305, USA	Football Player

Hooker, Jake — Journalist
New York Times, Editorial Dept, 229 W 43rd St, New York NY 10036 USA
Hooks, Bell — Writer
291 W 12th St, New York NY 10014, USA
Hooks, Brian — Actor
Don Buchwald/Fortitude, 6500 Wilshire Blvd, #2200, Los Angeles CA 90048 USA
Hooks, Jan — Actress, Comedienne
Innovative Artists, 1505 10th St, Santa Monica CA 90401 USA
Hooks, Kevin — Director, Producer
Gyre Entertainment, 4119 W Burbank Blvd, Burbank CA 91505, USA
Hooks, Robert — Actor
145 N Valley St, Burbank CA 91505, USA
Hooks, Roland — Football Player
3724 Calgary Dr, Reno NV 89511, USA
Hookstratten, Edward G — Attorney
Ed Hookstratten Mgmt, 9536 Wilshire Blvd, #500, Beverly Hills CA 90212, USA
Hooper, Bobby Joe — Basketball Player
825 Ivywood St, #4, Dayton OH 45420, USA
Hooper, Brandon — Actor, Writer, Producer
United Talent Agency, 9336 Civic Center Dr, Beverly Hills CA 90210 USA
Hooper, C Darrow — Track Athlete
6 Braemore Place, Dallas TX 75230, USA
Hooper, Ella — Singer (Killing Heidi)
Harbour Agency, 135 Forbes St, Woolloomooloo NSW 2011, Australia
Hooper, Kay — Writer
Bantam/Dell Books, 1745 Broadway, New York NY 10019, USA
Hooper, Thomas G (Tom) — Director
I C M Partners, 10250 Constellation Blvd, #900, Los Angeles CA 90067 USA
Hooper, Tobe — Director
Gersh Agency, 9465 Wilshire Blvd, #600, Beverly Hills CA 90212 USA
Hoopes, Chad — Concert Violinist
I M G Artists, 152 W 57th St, #500, New York NY 10019 USA
Hooser, Carroll L — Basketball Player
925 Edgefield Trail, Flower Mound TX 75028, USA
Hooton, Burt C — Baseball Player
3619 Granby Court, San Antonio TX 78217, USA
Hoover, Alice — Baseball Player
340 Roosevelt Ave, Reading PA 19605, USA
Hoover, Bradley R (Brad) — Football Player
2130 Climbing Rose Lane, Matthews NC 28104, USA
Hoover, Houston R — Football Player
1216 Mareed Ave, Yazoo City MS 39194, USA
Hoover, Paul C — Baseball Player
2320 Anderson Road, Cuyahoga Falls OH 44221, USA
Hoover, Richard — Scenic Designer
I C M Partners, 10250 Constellation Blvd, #900, Los Angeles CA 90067 USA
Hoover, Robert A (Bob) — Test Pilot
Bob Hoover Airshows, 1100 E Imperial Ave, El Segundo CA 90245, USA
Hoover, Thomas L (Tom) — Basketball Player
9 Apple Manor Lane, East Brunswick NJ 08816, USA
Hopcroft, John E — Computer Scientist
Cornell University, Engineering College, Carpenter Hall, Ithaca NY 14853, USA
Hope, Alec D — Writer
PO Box 7949, Alice Springs NT 0871, Australia
Hope, Amanda — Model
Playboy Promotions, 2706 Media Center Dr, Los Angeles CA 90065 USA
Hope, David (Dave) — Bassist (Kansas)
Immanuel Angelican Church, 250 Indian Bayou Trail, Destin FL 32541, USA
Hope, Jim — Producer, Writer
A P A Talent/Literary Agency, 405 S Beverly Dr, #300, Beverly Hills CA 90212 USA
Hope, Leslie — Actress
Oscars Abrams Zimel, 438 Queen St E, Toronto ON M5A 1T4, Canada
Hope, Maurice — Boxer
582 Kingsland Road, London E8, England
Hope, William (Bill) — Actor
Ken McReddie Assoc, 11 Connaught Place, London W2 2ET, England
Hopkins, Anthony — Actor
United Talent Agency, 9336 Civic Center Dr, Beverly Hills CA 90210 USA
Hopkins, Antony — Composer, Writer
Woodyard Cottage, Ashridge Park, Little Gaddesden, Berkhamsted HP4 1PS, England
Hopkins, Bo — Actor
6628 Ethel Ave, North Hollywood CA 91606, USA
Hopkins, Bradley D (Brad) — Football Player
95 Timberline Dr, Nashville TN 37221, USA
Hopkins, Donald (Don) — Baseball Player
PO Box 8817, Benton Harbor MI 49023, USA
Hopkins, Emma — Actress
Associated International Mgmt, Fairfax House, Fulwood Place, London WC1V 6HU, England
Hopkins, Gail E — Baseball Player
120 Canterbury Dr, Parkersburg WV 26104, USA
Hopkins, Godfrey T — Photographer
Wilmington Cottage, Wilmington Road, Seaford, East Sussex BN25 2EH, England
Hopkins, Jan — Commentator
CNN-TV, 190 Marietta Ave SW, Atlanta GA 30303 USA
Hopkins, Jennifer — Tennis Player
4312 W 110 St, Leawood KS 66211, USA
Hopkins, Jerry W — Football Player
1025 Burberry, Woodway TX 76712, USA
Hopkins, John — Bassist (Zac Brown Band)
Shore Fire Media, 32 Court St, #1600, Brooklyn NY 11201 USA
Hopkins, Josh — Actor
Gersh Agency, 9465 Wilshire Blvd, #600, Beverly Hills CA 90212 USA
Hopkins, Joshua — Opera Singer
I M G Artists, Hogarth Business Park, Chiswick, London W4 2TH, England
Hopkins, Kaitlin — Actress
Gage Group, 315 W 57th St, #4H, New York NY 10019 USA

Hopkins, Linda 2055 N Ivar St, #PH 21, Los Angeles CA 90068, USA	Singer
Hopkins, Michael J 27 Broadley Terrace, London NW1 6LG, England	Architect
Hopkins, Paul Edna Talent Mgmt, 318 Dundas St W, Toronto ON M5T 1G5, Canada	Actor
Hopkins, Robert M (Bob) 8421 SE 71st St, Mercer Island WA 98040, USA	Basketball Player
Hopkins, Stephen J Creative Artists Agency, 2000 Ave of Stars, #100, Los Angeles CA 90067 USA	Director
Hopkins, Sy Paramount Entertainment, 12 Kosakowski Dr, Morris Plains NJ 07590 USA	Singer (Five Satins)
Hopkins, Telma Innovative Artists, 1505 10th St, Santa Monica CA 90401 USA	Actress, Singer
Hopkins, Tom 7531 E 2nd St, Scottsdale AZ 85251, USA	Writer
Hopkins, Wesley (Wes) 7412 White Oak Road, Fairfield AL 35064, USA	Football Player
Hoppe, Fred PO Box 42, Milford NE 68405, USA	Sculptor
Hoppe, Wolfgang Dieterstedter Str 11, 99510 Apolda, Germany	Bobsled Athlete
Hoppen, David D (Dave) 16341 Webster St, Omaha NE 68118, USA	Basketbal Player
Hopper, Heather Baron Entertainment, 13848 Ventura Blvd, #A, Sherman Oaks CA 91423, USA	Actress
Hopper, Norris S 902 Hampton St, Shelby NC 28152, USA	Baseball Player
Hopperdeitz, Anna Agentur Fuhrmann, Lindenstr 8A, 84424 Isen-Pemmering, Germany	Actress
Hoppus, Mark 14015 Chestnut Hill Lane, San Diego CA 92128, USA	Bassist (Blink-182, +44)
Hopson, Dennis 7229 Donnybrook Dr, Dublin OH 43017, USA	Basketball Player
Hora, Jeremy Union Entertainment, 1323 Newbury Road, #104, Newbury Park CA 91320, USA	Guitarist (Default)
Horan, Dennis, Jr 32458 Galatina St, Temecula CA 92592, USA	Bowler
Horan, James Angel City Talent, 8318 Kirkwood Dr, Los Angeles CA 90046, USA	Actor
Horan, Michael W (Mike) 7235 E La Cumbre Dr, Orange CA 92869, USA	Football Player
Horan, Monica Creative Artists Agency, 2000 Ave of Stars, #100, Los Angeles CA 90067 USA	Actress
Hordges, Cedrick T 237 W 127th St, #28, New York NY 10027, USA	Basketball Player
Horecker, Bernard L 16517 Cypress Villa Lane, Fort Myers FL 33908, USA	Biochemist
Horford Reynoso, Alfred J (Al) Atlanta Hawks, Centennial Tower, 101 Marietta St NW, #1900, Atlanta GA 30303 USA	Basketball Player
Horgan, Joe 2039 Kellogg Way, Rancho Cordova CA 95670, USA	Baseball Player
Horgan, Patrick I C M Partners, 10250 Constellation Blvd, #900, Los Angeles CA 90067 USA	Actor
Horgan, Sharon United Agents, 12-26 Lexington St, London W1F 0LE, England	Actress, Comedienne
Horinek, Ramon A 184 National Blvd, Universal City TX 78148, USA	Vietnam War Air Force Hero
Horlen, Joel E (Joe) 3718 Chartwell Dr, San Antonio TX 78230, USA	Baseball Player
Horlock, John H 2 The Avenue, Ampthill, Bedford MK45 2NR, England	Mechanical Engineer, Educator
Horn, Donald G (Don) 2229 Wynterbrook Dr, Littleton CO 80126, USA	Football Player
Horn, Gyula Parliament, Kossuth Lajos Ter 1/3, 1055 Budapest, Hungary	Prime Minister, Hungary
Horn, Joseph (Joe) 2408 Shenley Park Court, Duluth GA 30097, USA	Football Player
Horn, Marian Blank US Claims Court, 717 Madison Place NW, Washington DC 20439, USA	Judge
Horn, Paul J 4601 Leyns Road, Victoria BC V8N 3A1, Canada	Jazz Flutist, Saxophonist
Horn, Samuel L (Sam) 1305 Narragansett Blvd, Cranston RI 02905, USA	Baseball Player
Hornacek, Jeffrey J (Jeff) 5821 N 37th St, Paradise Valley AZ 85253, USA	Basketball Player
Hornaday, Jeffrey I C M Partners, 10250 Constellation Blvd, #900, Los Angeles CA 90067 USA	Choreographer
Hornaday, Ronald (Ron), Jr 116 Courtney Lane, Mooresville NC 28117, USA	Truck, Auto Racing Driver
Hornbacher, Scott United Talent Agency, 9336 Civic Center Dr, Beverly Hills CA 90210 USA	Producer
Hornbuckle, Linda Mark Young, 3303 NE Stanton St, Portland OR 97212, USA	Singer
Hornby, Nick Penguin Books, 80 Stand, London WC2R 0RL, England	Writer
Horne, Jimmy Bo Talent Consultants International, 105 Shad Row, #B, Piermont NY 10968 USA	Singer, Dancer
Horne, John R Navistar International, PO Box 1488, Warrenville IL 60555, USA	Businessman
Horne, Marilyn Marilyn Horne Foundation, 315 W 86th St, #2D, New York NY 10024, USA	Opera Singer
Horne, Steve Tasman Motor Sports Group, 4192 Weaver Court, Hilliard OH 43026, USA	Auto Racing Executive
Horneber, Petra Ringstr 77, 85402 Kranzberg, Germany	Markswoman

Hopkins - Horneber

Horneff, Will — Actor
Abrams Artists, 9200 W Sunset Blvd, #1125, West Hollywood CA 90069 USA
Horner, Alex Kapp — Actress
Innovative Artists, 1505 10th St, Santa Monica CA 90401 USA
Horner, Charles A (Chuck) — Air Force General
2824 Jack Nicklaus Way, Shalimar FL 32579, USA
Horner, Craig — Actor
Marquee Mgmt, 188 Oxford St, Paddington NSW 2021, Australia
Horner, J Robert (Bob) — Baseball Player
209 Steeplechase Dr, Irving TX 75062, USA
Horner, James — Composer
Gorfaine/Schwartz, 4111 W Alameda Ave, #509, Burbank CA 91505 USA
Horner, John R (Jack) — Paleontologist
70 Cougar Dr, Bozeman MT 59718, USA
Horner, Martina S — Educator, Businesswoman
T I A A-C R E F, 730 3rd Ave, New York NY 10017, USA
Hornig, Donald F — Chemist
1 Little Pond Cove Road, Little Compton RI 02837, USA
Hornish, Samuel J (Sam), Jr — Auto Racing Driver
Penske Championship Racing, 220 Penske Way, Mooresville NC 28115, USA
Hornlein, Horst — Luge Athlete
Tambascherstr 13, 98559 Oberhoff, Germany
Hornsby, Bruce — Singer, Pianist
PO Box 3545, Williamsburg VA 23187, USA
Hornsby, David — Actor
Schachter Entertainment, 1157 S Beverly Dr, #200, Los Angeles CA 90035 USA
Hornsby, Russell — Actor
Paradigm Agency, 360 N Crescent Dr, North Building, Beverly Hills CA 90210 USA
Hornung, Paul V — Football Player
3115 Arden Road, Louisville KY 40222, USA
Horovitz, Adam (King Ad-Rock) — Rap Artist (Beastie Boys)
Capitol Records, 810 7th Ave, New York NY 10019 USA
Horovitz, Israel A — Writer
Washington Square Arts, 310 Bowery, #200, New York NY 10012, USA
Horovitz, Joseph — Composer
Royal College of Music, Prince Consort Road, London SW7 2BS, England
Horovitz, Rachael — Producer, Actress
Creative Artists Agency, 2000 Ave of Stars, #100, Los Angeles CA 90067 USA
Horowitz, Ben — Drummer (Gaslight Anthem)
Esther Creative Group, 27 W 24th St, #404, New York NY 10010, USA
Horowitz, David C — Commentator
Fight Back Productions, 139 S Beverly Dr, #233, Beverly Hills CA 90210, USA
Horowitz, Jerome P — Internist
Wayne State University Medical School, 540 E Canfield Ave, Detroit MI 48201, USA
Horowitz, Paul — Physicist, Electrical Engineer
111 Chilton St, Cambridge MA 02138, USA
Horowitz, Sari — Journalist
Washington Post, Editorial Dept, 1150 15th St NW, Washington DC 20071 USA
Horowitz, Scott J — Astronaut
5491 Freestyle Way, Park City UT 84098, USA
Horrigan, Sam — Actor, Producer
Prestige Talent Agency, 1615 16th St, Santa Monica CA 90404, USA
Horrocks, Jane — Actress, Singer
United Agents, 12-26 Lexington St, London W1F 0LE, England
Horry, Robert K — Basketball Player
2618 Sara Ridge Lane, Katy TX 77450, USA
Horsey, David — Editorial Cartoonist
King Features Syndicate, 300 W 57th St, #1500, New York NY 10019 USA
Horsford, Anna Maria — Actress
Innovative Artists, 1505 10th St, Santa Monica CA 90401 USA
Horsley, Jack — Swimmer
608 N Sampson St, Ellensburg WA 98926, USA
Horsley, Lee A — Actor
Central Artists, 3310 W Burbank Blvd, Burbank CA 91505, USA
Horsman, Vincent S J (Vince) — Baseball Player
1941 Pinehurst Dr, Clearwater FL 33763, USA
Horton, Anthony D (Tony) — Baseball Player
17001 Livorno Dr, Pacific Palisades CA 90272, USA
Horton, Ethan S — Football Player
4602 Fairvista Dr, Charlotte NC 28269, USA
Horton, Frank E — Educator
288 River Ranch Circle, Bayfield CO 81122, USA
Horton, Gregory K (Greg) — Football Player
1053 Lytle St, Redlands CA 92374, USA
Horton, Peter — Actor
W M E Entertainment, 9601 Wilshire Blvd, #300, Beverly Hills CA 90210 USA
Horton, Raymond A (Ray) — Football Player
3400 S Water St, Pittsburgh PA 15203, USA
Horton, Ricky N — Baseball Player
16026 Aston Court, Chesterfield MO 63005, USA
Horton, Robert — Actor
5317 Andasol Ave, Encino CA 91316, USA
Horton, William W (Willie) — Baseball Player
5655 Woodland Pass, Bloomfield Hills MI 48301, USA
Horvath, Bronco J — Ice Hockey Player
27 Oliver St, South Yarmouth MA 02664, USA
Horvitz, H Robert — Nobel Medicine Laureate
34 Pilgrim Road, Wellesley Hills MA 02481, USA
Horvitz, Louis J — Director
Gersh Agency, 9465 Wilshire Blvd, #600, Beverly Hills CA 90212 USA
Horwitz, Dominique — Actress, Singer
Agentur Patricia Horwitz, Erdmannstra 10, 22765 Hamburg, Germany
Horwitz, Morton J — Attorney, Educator
Harvard University, Law School, Cambridge MA 02138, USA
Horwitz, Tony — Journalist, Writer
PO Box 5056, Vineyard Haven MA 02568, USA

Hosey, Dwayne S — Baseball Player
164 N Plum Ave, Ontario CA 91764, USA
Hoshide, Akihiko (Aki) — Astronaut
J A X A, Tsukuba Space Center, 2-1-1 Sengen, Tsukubashi, Ibaraki 305 8505, Japan
Hosket, Wilmer F (Bill) — Basketball Player
4721 Bayford Court, Columbus OH 43220, USA
Hoskins, Bob — Actor
United Agents, 12-26 Lexington St, London W1F 0LE, England
Hoskins, Derrick — Football Player
10491 Road 842, Philadelphia MS 39350, USA
Hosley, Timothy K (Tim) — Baseball Player
112 Elena Dr, Moore SC 29369, USA
Hosmer, Bradley C (Brad) — Air Force General
PO Box 1128, Cedar Crest NM 87008, USA
Hospodar, Edward D (Ed) — Ice Hockey Player
217 Orchard Way, Wayne PA 19087, USA
Hossa, Marian — Ice Hockey Player
270 E Pearson St, #1402, Chicago IL 60611, USA
Hossack, Allison — Actress
Characters Talent Mgmt, 8 Elm St, Toronto ON M5G 1G7, Canada
Hossein, Robert — Actor, Director
Ghislaine de Wing, 10 Rue du Docteur Roux, 75015 Paris, France
Hosseini, Khaled — Writer
Riverhead/Penguin Group, 375 Hudson St, Basement 1, New York NY 10014, USA
Hostak, Martin — Ice Hockey Player
Ceska Televize, Kavci Hory, 14070 Prague 4, Czech Republic
Hostetler, David A (Dave) — Baseball Player
3404 Steeplechase Trail, Arlington TX 76016, USA
Hostetler, David L — Sculptor
PO Box 989, Athens OH 45701, USA
Hostetler, Jeff W — Football Player
2032 Magnolia Dr, Morgantown WV 26508, USA
Hostetter, G Richard — Religious Leader
Presbyterian Church in America, 1852 Century Place NE, #201, Atlanta GA 30345, USA
Hotani, Hirokazu — Microbiotics Engineer
Teikyo University, Biosciences Dept, Toyosatodai, Utsunomiya 320 0003, Japan
Hotchkiss, Rob — Guitarist (Train)
Jon Landau, 150 Rowayton Ave, Norwalk CT 06853, USA
Hotez, Peter — Microbiologist, Immunologist
Sabin Vaccine Institute, 2000 Pennsylvania Ave NW, #7100, Washington DC 20006, USA
Hottelet, Richard C — Commentator
120 Chestnut Hill Road, Wilton CT 06897, USA
Hotten, Terry — Chemist
Eli Lilly Wood Laboratory, Windlesham, Surrey GO20 6PH, England
Hottman, Kenneth (Ken) — Baseball Player
9537 2nd Ave, Elk Grove CA 95624, USA
Hoty, Dee — Actress, Singer
Gage Group, 315 W 57th St, #4H, New York NY 10019 USA
Hotz, Kenneth J (Kenny) — Actor, Director, Writer
Paradigm Agency, 360 N Crescent Dr, North Building, Beverly Hills CA 90210 USA
Hou, Ya-Ming — Biologist
Massachusetts Institute of Technology, Biology Dept, Cambridge MA 02139, USA
Houbregs, Robert J (Bob) — Basketball Player
1949 Arena Court SE, Olympia WA 98501, USA
Houcke, Sara — Circus Animal Trainer
Ringling Bros Barnum & Bailey, 8607 Westwood Circle Dr, Vienna VA 22182 USA
Hough, Charles O (Charlie) — Baseball Player
2266 Shade Tree Circle, Brea CA 92821, USA
Hough, Derek — Dancer, Choreographer
Brillstein Entertainment Partners, 9150 Wilshire Blvd, #350, Beverly Hills CA 90212 USA
Hough, James H (Jim) — Football Player
2440 Christian Dr, Chaska MN 55318, USA
Hough, Joseph C, Jr — Educator
Union Theological Seminary, President's Office, New York NY 10027, USA
Hough, Julianne M — Dancer, Singer, Actress
Creative Artists Agency, 2000 Ave of Stars, #100, Los Angeles CA 90067 USA
Hough, Stephen A G — Concert Pianist
C M Artists, 127 W 96th St, #13B, New York NY 10025 USA
Houghton, Frances — Rowing Athlete
Tyrian Club, 6 Lower Mall, Hammersmith W6 9DJ, England
Houghton, Israel — Singer, Songwriter, Guitarist
Integrity Music, 1000 Cody Road, Mobile AL 36695, USA
Houghton, James R — Businessman
36 Spencer Hill Road, Corning NY 14830, USA
Houghton, John T — Physicist, Climatologist
Hadley Center, London Broad, Bracknell, Berkshire RG12 2SZ, England
Houghton, Katharine — Actress
Ambrosio/Mortimer, 165 W 46th St, New York NY 10036 USA
Houghton, Michael — Geneticist
Chiron Corp, 4560 Horton St, Emeryville CA 94608, USA
Hougland, William (Bill) — Basketball Player
PO Box 2629, Edwards CO 81632, USA
Houle, Rejean — Ice Hockey Player
7941 Boul Lasalle, Lasalle QC H8P 3R1, Canada
Hoult, Nicholas — Actor
Independent Talent Group, Oxford House, 76 Oxford St, London W1D 1BS, England
Houlton, D J — Baseball Player
2357 N Campus Ave, Upland CA 91784, USA
Houngbo, Gilbert — Prime Minister, Togo
Prime Minister's Office, BP 5618, Lome, Togo
Hounsou, Djimon — Actor, Model
Creative Artists Agency, 2000 Ave of Stars, #100, Los Angeles CA 90067 USA
House, David (Dave) — Businessman
Nortel Networks Corp, 8200 Dixie Road, Brampton ON L6T 5P6, Canada
House, Edward L (Eddie) — Basketball Player
Miami Heat, American Airlines Arena, 601 Biscayne Blvd, Miami FL 33132 USA

House, James R (J R)
34 River Ridge Trail, Ormond Beach FL 32174, USA — Baseball Player
House, James S
University of Michigan, Social Research Institute, Ann Arbor MI 48106, USA — Psychologist
House, Karen Eliot
58 Cleveland Lane, Princeton NJ 08540, USA — Journalist
House, Thomas R (Tom)
12794 Via Felino, Del Mar CA 92014, USA — Baseball Player
House, Yoanna
I M G Models, 304 Park Ave S, #PH-North, New York NY 10010 USA — Model
Householder, Paul W
521 N Swinton Ave, Delray Beach FL 33444, USA — Baseball Player
Houser, Jerry
12995 Galewood St, Studio City CA 91604, USA — Actor
Houser, John W, Jr
2197 Creekside Dr, Solvang CA 93463, USA — Football Player
Houser, Kevin J
941 Montclair Circle, Westlake OH 44145, USA — Football Player
Houser, Randy
W M E Entertainment, 1600 Division St, #300, Nashville TN 37203 USA — Singer, Songwriter
Houshmandzadeh, Touraj (T J), Jr
16703 Greenbrook Circle, Cerritos CA 90703, USA — Football Player
Housley, Phil
2877 Itasca Ave S, Lakeland MN 55043, USA — Ice Hockey Player
Houston, Allan W
Allan Houston Foundation, 350 5th Ave, #5900, New York NY 10118, USA — Basketball Player
Houston, Bobby
4640 Vendue Range Dr, Raleigh NC 27604, USA — Football Player
Houston, Byron D
3108 Birch Land, Edmond OK 73034, USA — Basketball Player
Houston, Cissy
Nippy Inc, 60 Park Place, #1800, Newark NJ 07102, USA — Singer
Houston, James E (Jim)
925 Trimble Place, Northfield OH 44067, USA — Football Player
Houston, Kenneth R (Ken)
3603 Forest Village Dr, Kingwood TX 77339, USA — Football Player
Houston, Marques B
Pyramid Entertainment, 377 Rector Place, #21A, New York NY 10280 USA — Singer, Actor
Houston, Penelope
Absolute Artists, 8490 W Sunset Blvd, #403, West Hollywood CA 90069, USA — Singer
Houston, Russell
General Delivery, Eagar AZ 85925, USA — Artist
Houston, Stephen D
Brown University, Anthropology Dept, Providence RI 02912, USA — Anthropologist, Social Scientist
Houston, Thelma
4296 Mount Vernon Dr, Los Angeles CA 90008, USA — Singer
Houston, Tyler S
325 Pleasant Summit Dr, Henderson NV 89012, USA — Baseball Player
Houston, Wade
University of Tennessee, Athletic Dept, Knoxville TN 37901, USA — Basketball Coach
Hout, Michael
University of California, Demography Center, 2538 Channing, Berkeley CA 94720, USA — Demographer
Hovan, Christopher J (Chris)
17301 Ladera Estates Blvd, Lutz FL 33548, USA — Football Player
Hove, Andrew C (Skip), Jr
Promontory Financial Group, 1201 Pennsylvania NW, #617, Washington DC 20004, USA — Government Official, Financier
Hovind, David J
Paccar Inc, 777 106th Ave NE, Bellevue WA 98004, USA — Businessman
Hovland, Tim
Association of Volleyball Professionals, 960 Knox St, #A, Torrance CA 90502 USA — Volleyball Player
Hovsepian, Vatche
Armenian Church of America West, 1201 N Vine St, Los Angeles CA 90038, USA — Religious Leader
Howard, Adina
I C M Partners, 730 5th Ave, New York NY 10019 USA — Singer
Howard, Alan M
Julian Belfrage Assoc, 9 Argyll St, #300, London W1F 7TG, England — Actor
Howard, Andrew
Julian Belfrage Assoc, 9 Argyll St, #300, London W1F 7TG, England — Actor
Howard, Ann
Stafford Law Assoc, 6 Barham Close, Weybridge, Surrey KT13 9PR, England — Opera Singer
Howard, Arliss
Innovative Artists, 235 Park Ave S, #1000, New York NY 10003 USA — Actor, Director
Howard, Barbara
PO Box 459, Chelsea MI 48118, USA — Actress
Howard, Bruce E
8705 Misty Creek Dr, Sarasota FL 34241, USA — Baseball Player
Howard, Bryce Dallas
Management 360, 9111 Wilshire Blvd, Beverly Hills CA 90210 USA — Actress
Howard, Christian (Chris)
11 Hawser Lane, Swampscott MA 01907, USA — Baseball Player
Howard, Christopher H (Chris)
8655 Jones Road, #301, Houston TX 77065, USA — Baseball Player
Howard, Clark
WSB-AM, 1601 West Peachtree St, Atlanta GA 30309, USA — Entertainer
Howard, Clint
4286 Clybourn Ave, Burbank CA 91505, USA — Actor
Howard, David
5516 E Rosedale St, Fort Worth TX 76112, USA — Football Player
Howard, David W
22846 Chesterview Loop, #111, Land O Lakes FL 34639, USA — Baseball Player
Howard, Desmond K
Prince Promotions, 9663 Santa Monica Blvd, #324, Beverly Hills CA 90210, USA — Football Player
Howard, Douglas L (Doug)
8038 Deer Creek Road, Salt Lake City UT 84121, USA — Baseball Player
Howard, Dwight D
3565 Rice Lake Loop, Longwood FL 32779, USA — Basketball Player

V.I.P. Address Book

H

Howard, Eugene (Gene)	Football Player
11051 Lavender Ave, Fountain Valley CA 92708, USA	
Howard, Frank O	Baseball Player
24178 Lenah Woods Place, Aldie VA 20105, USA	
Howard, George	Bowler
8415 Brookwood Dr, Portage MI 49024, USA	
Howard, George	Jazz Saxophonist
David Rubinson, PO Box 411197, San Francisco CA 94141, USA	
Howard, Greg	Basketball Player
4517 W 16th Place, #2, Los Angeles CA 90019, USA	
Howard, Greg	Cartoonist (Sally Forth)
3403 W 28th St, Minneapolis MN 55416, USA	
Howard, Harry N	Historian
6508 Greentree Road, Bradley Hills Grove, Bethesda MD 20817, USA	
Howard, Hobie	Singer (Sawyer Brown)
O-Seven Artist Mgmt, PO Box 210586, Nashville TN 37221, USA	
Howard, James J, III	Businessman
Northern States Power, 414 Nicollett Mall, Minneapolis MN 55401, USA	
Howard, James Newton	Composer
Gorfaine/Schwartz, 4111 W Alameda Ave, #509, Burbank CA 91505 USA	
Howard, Jan	Singer, Songwriter
Tessier-Marsh Talent, 2825 Blue Brick Dr, Nashville TN 37214, USA	
Howard, Jason	Opera Singer
I M G Artists, Hogarth Business Park, Chiswick, London W4 2TH, England	
Howard, Jeffrey R	Judge
US Court of Appeals, US Courthouse, 55 Pleasant St, Concord NH 03301, USA	
Howard, Jeremy	Actor
Stone Manners Salners, 9911 W Pico Blvd, #1400, Los Angeles CA 90035 USA	
Howard, John W	Prime Minister, Australia
GPO Box 59, Sydney NSW 2001, Australia	
Howard, Joshua J (Josh)	Basketball Player
6306 Linden Lane, Dallas TX 75230, USA	
Howard, Juwan A	Basketball Player
11714 Bistro Lane, Houston TX 77082, USA	
Howard, Ken	Actor, Labor Leader
Screen Actors Guild, 5757 Wilshire Blvd, Los Angeles CA 90036, USA	
Howard, Kyle	Actor, Writer, Director
United Talent Agency, 9336 Civic Center Dr, Beverly Hills CA 90210 USA	
Howard, Linda	Writer
Ballatine Books, 1745 Broadway, New York NY 10019 USA	
Howard, Michael	Government Official, England
House of Lords, Westminster, London SW1A 0PW, England	
Howard, Michelle J	Navy Admiral
Deputy Commander, Fleet Forces Command, 1562 Mitscher Ave, Norfolk VA 23551 USA	
Howard, Miki	Singer
Gardiner Entertainment, 5683 Hazelcrest Circle, Westlake Village CA 91362, USA	
Howard, Otis	Basketball Player
231 Manhattan Ave, Oak Ridge TN 37830, USA	
Howard, Paul G	Football Player
10859 W 85th Place, Arvada CO 80005, USA	
Howard, Rance	Actor
4286 Clybourn Ave, Burbank CA 91505, USA	
Howard, Rebecca Lynn	Singer
W M E Entertainment, 1600 Division St, #300, Nashville TN 37203 USA	
Howard, Reginald C (Reggie)	Football Player
PO Box 382666, Germantown TN 38183, USA	
Howard, Richard	Writer
23 Waverly Place, #5X, New York NY 10003, USA	
Howard, Robert E	Cartoonist (Conan)
Dark House Publishing, 10956 SE Main St, Portland OR 97222, USA	
Howard, Ronald F (Ron)	Football Player
14701 NE 61st Court, Redmond WA 98052, USA	
Howard, Ronald W (Ron)	Actor, Director
Imagine Entertainment, 9465 Wilshire Blvd, #700, Beverly Hills CA 90212, USA	
Howard, Russ	Curling Athlete
Curling Assn, 1660 Vimont Court, Cumberland ON K4A 4J4, Canada	
Howard, Ryan J	Baseball Player
1630 Bentshire Court, Ballwin MO 63011, USA	
Howard, Sherri	Track Athlete
14059 Bridle Ridge Road, Sylmar CA 91342, USA	
Howard, Sophie	Model
International Model Mgmt, Elysium Gate, 126-128 New Kings Road, London SW6 4LZ, England	
Howard, Steven B (Steve)	Baseball Player
4712 Shetland Ave, Oakland CA 94605, USA	
Howard, Susan	Actress
PO Box 1456, Boerne TX 78006, USA	
Howard, Terrence D	Actor
Creative Artists Agency, 2000 Ave of Stars, #100, Los Angeles CA 90067 USA	
Howard, Thomas S	Baseball Player
822 8th Ave, Middletown OH 45044, USA	
Howard, Tish	Model
Playboy Promotions, 2706 Media Center Dr, Los Angeles CA 90065 USA	
Howard, Traylor	Actress
John Carrabino Mgmt, 5900 Wilshire Blvd, #406, Los Angeles CA 90036 USA	
Howard, Walker	Actor
Stone Manners Salners, 9911 W Pico Blvd, #1400, Los Angeles CA 90035 USA	
Howard, Walter I (Todd)	Football Player
1300 Bienville Ave, Ruston LA 71270, USA	
Howard, Wilbur L	Baseball Player
643 Walston Lane, Houston TX 77060, USA	
Howard, William W, Jr	Association Executive
National Wildlife Federation, 11100 Wildlife Center Dr, Reston VA 20190, USA	
Howarth, Elgar	Composer
27 Cromwell Ave, London N6 5HN, England	
Howarth, James E (Jim)	Baseball Player
PO Box 401, 1 Hancock Plaza, Gulfport MS 39502, USA	

Howarth, Roger — Actor
K & H, 1212 Ave of Americas, #3, New York NY 10036, USA
Howarth, Thomas — Architect
University of Toronto, 230 College St, Toronto ON M5S 1R1, Canada
Howatch, Susan — Writer
Aitken & Stone, 29 Fernshaw Road, London SW10 0TG, England
Howe of Aberavon, R E Geoffrey — Government Official, England
Barclays Bank, Cavendish Square Branch, 4 Vere St, London W1, England
Howe, Arthur — Journalist
Philadelphia Inquirer, Editorial Dept, 400 N Broad St, Philadelphia PA 19130, USA
Howe, Arthur H (Art), Jr — Baseball Player, Manager
17214 Calico Peak Way, Cypress TX 77433, USA
Howe, Brian — Singer (Bad Company)
Union Entertainment, 1323 Newbury Road, #104, Newbury Park CA 91320, USA
Howe, Daniel Walker — Writer
Oxford University Press, 198 Madison Ave, #800, New York NY 10016 USA
Howe, Gordon (Gordie) — Ice Hockey Player
9 Inverness Lane, Jackson NJ 8527, USA
Howe, Jonathan T — Navy Admiral
Arthur Vining Davis Foundation, 225 Water St, #1510, Jacksonville FL 32202, USA
Howe, Mark S — Ice Hockey Player
106 Barrington Road, Bloomfield Hills MI 48302, USA
Howe, Michael — Actor
Associated International Mgmt, Fairfax House, Fulwood Place, London WC1V 6HU, England
Howe, Oscar — Artist
5900 S Prairie View Court, Sioux Falls SD 57108, USA
Howe, Tina — Writer
333 W End Ave, New York NY 10023, USA
Howell, Alex — Cartoonist (Butch & Dougie)
King Features Syndicate, 300 W 57th St, #1500, New York NY 10019 USA
Howell, Anthony — Actor
Ken McReddie Assoc, 11 Connaught Place, London W2 2ET, England
Howell, Bailey E — Basketball Player
1989 S Montgomery St, Starkville MS 39759, USA
Howell, C Thomas — Actor
Glick Agency, 1321 7th St, #203, Santa Monica CA 90401 USA
Howell, Charles, III — Golfer
5187 Vardon Dr, Windermere FL 34786, USA
Howell, Delles R — Football Player
1907 Crescent Dr, Monroe LA 71202, USA
Howell, Henry V (Harry) — Ice Hockey Player
401-49 Robinson St, Hamilton ON L8P 1Y7, Canada
Howell, Jack R — Baseball Player
822 S Lehigh Dr, Tucson AZ 85710, USA
Howell, James P (J P) — Baseball Player
808 46th St, Sacramento CA 95819, USA
Howell, Jay C — Baseball Player
4560 Colony Point, Suwanee GA 30024, USA
Howell, Jefferson D, Jr — Marine Corps General
2207 Villa Rose Dr, Houston TX 77062, USA
Howell, John T — Football Player
8276 San Dollar Dr, Windsor CO 80528, USA
Howell, Kathleen — Aeronautical Engineer
Purdue University, Aeronautical Engineering Dept, West Lafayette IN 47907, USA
Howell, Kenneth (Ken), Jr — Baseball Player
29512 Bradmoor Court, Farmington Hills MI 48334, USA
Howell, Margaret — Fashion Designer
5 Garden House, 8 Battersea Park Road, London SW8 4BG, England
Howell, Margaret — Actress
Chateau/Billings Agency, 8489 W 3rd St, #1032, Los Angeles CA 90048, USA
Howell, Michael L (Mike) — Football Player
200 Charlotte St, Monroe LA 71202, USA
Howell, Pat G — Football Player
7692 N Kincaid Ave, Fresno CA 93711, USA
Howell, Porter — Guitarist (Little Texas)
Splash Public Relations, 1520 16th Ave S, #2, Nashville TN 37212, USA
Howell, Roy L — Baseball Player
PO Box 1734, Lompoc CA 93438, USA
Howell, William R — Businessman
J C Penney Co, PO Box 10001, Dallas TX 75301, USA
Howells, Anne E — Opera Singer
Milestone, Broom Close, Esher, Surrey KT10 9NP, England
Howerdel, Billy — Guitarist (Perfect Circle), Songwriter
The Firm, 2049 Century Park E, #2550, Los Angeles CA 90067 USA
Howerton, Glenn — Producer, Writer, Actor
W M E Entertainment, 9601 Wilshire Blvd, #300, Beverly Hills CA 90210 USA
Howes, Sally Ann — Actress, Singer
Palm Beach Theater Guild, PO Box 667, Palm Beach FL 33480, USA
Howey, Steve — Actor
United Talent Agency, 9336 Civic Center Dr, Beverly Hills CA 90210 USA
Howfield, Robert (Bobby) — Football Player
5529 S Lowell Blvd, Littleton CO 80123, USA
Howison, Ryan — Golfer
245 Barbados Dr, Jupiter FL 33458, USA
Howitt, Dann P J — Baseball Player
PO Box 565, Douglas MI 49406, USA
Howitt, Peter — Director
Industry Entertainment, 955 Carillo Dr, #300, Los Angeles CA 90048 USA
Howland, Ben — Basketball Coach
University of California, Athletic Dept, Los Angeles CA 90024, USA
Howland, Beth — Actress, Singer
Michael J Pollard, 520 S Burnside Ave, #12A, Los Angeles CA 90036, USA
Howland, Rick — Actor
Oscars Abrams Zimel, 438 Queen St E, Toronto ON M5A 1T4, Canada
Howle, Paul — Cartoonist (In Their Own Words)
United Feature Syndicate, PO Box 5610, Cincinnati OH 45201 USA

Howlett, Liam P
Midi Mgmt, Jenkins Lane, Great Hallinsbury, Essex CM22 7QL, England — Musician (Prodigy), Composer

Howley, Charles L (Chuck)
Happy Hollow Ranch, 26875 FM 47, Wills Point TX 75169, USA — Football Player

Howley, Peter M
Harvard Medical School, 200 Longwood Ave, Boston MA 02115, USA — Pathologist

Howry, Bobby D (Bob)
24108 N 73rd Lane, Peroia AZ 85383, USA — Baseball Player

Howson, Peter
Flowers East, 82 Kingsland Road, London E2 8DP, England — Artist

Howton, William H (Bill)
1796 County Road 10, Plainview TX 79072, USA — Football Player

Howze, Leonard Earl
Kritzer Levine Wilkins Griffin, 11872 La Grange Ave, #100, Los Angeles CA 90025 USA — Actor

Hoy, Christopher A (Chris)
British Cycling Centre, Stuart St, Manchester M11 4DQ, England — Cyclist

Hoy, Peter A
26 Woods Dr, Canton NY 13617, USA — Baseball Player

Hoying, Robert C (Bobby)
Crawford Hoying Real Estate, 555 Metro Place N, #600, Dublin OH 43017, USA — Football Player

Hoyle, Dan
Gersh Agency, 41 Madison Ave, #3301, New York NY 10010 USA — Actor, Comedian

Hoyt, D LaMarr
1594 Lost Creek Dr, Columbia SC 29212, USA — Baseball Player

Hozumi, Masako
Skating Federation, 1-1-1 Jinnan, #414, Shibuyaku, Tokyo 150-8050, Japan — Speed Skater

HR
Agency Group Ltd, 142 W 57th St, #600, New York NY 10019 USA — Singer (Bad Brains)

Hrabosky, Alan T (Al)
9 Frontenac Estates Dr, Saint Louis MO 63131, USA — Baseball Player, Sportscaster

Hrabowski, Freeman A, III
University of Maryland Baltimore County, President's Office, 1000 Hilltop Circle, Baltimore MD 21250, USA — Educator

Hrbaty, Dominik
Octagon Worldwide, 7100 Forest Ave, #201, Richmond VA 23226 USA — Tennis Player

Hrbek, Kent A
Hrbek Outdoors, 5500 Lincoln Dr, #150, Edina MN 55436, USA — Baseball Player

Hrdy, Sarah Blaffer
University of California, Anthropology Dept, Davis CA 95616, USA — Anthropologist

Hriniak, Walter J (Walt)
18 Stacy Dr, North Andover MA 01845, USA — Baseball Player

Hristov, Momchil
Hristo Vakavelski Str Bl 5, #3, 1700 Sofia, Bulgaria — Photographer

Hrkac, Tony
6904 W Lantern Lane, Mequon WI 53092, USA — Ice Hockey Player

Hrudey, Kelly
CBC-TV, PO Box 500, Station A, Toronto ON M5W 1E6, Canada — Ice Hockey Player

Hrusa, Jakub
I M G Artists, Hogarth Business Park, Chiswick, London W4 2TH, England — Conductor

Hruska, Carrie B
Mayo Clinic, Biomedical Engineering Dept, 200 1st St SW, Rochester MN 55905, USA — Biomedical Engineer

Hsiang, Wu-chung
Princeton University, Mathematics Dept, Princeton NJ 08544, USA — Mathematician

Hsiao, Rita
W M E Entertainment, 9601 Wilshire Blvd, #300, Beverly Hills CA 90210 USA — Writer

Hsuan Yu Chen
Taiwan University Medical Center, Roosevelt Road, Taipei 10517, Taiwan — Oncologist

Hu Jintao
Chairman's Office, Zhongnanhai, Beijing 100017, China — President, China

Hu Qili
Consultative Conference, 23 Taipingqiao St, Beijing 100283, China — Government Official, China

Hu Shuli
Caijing Media, Winterless Center, 1 Xidawanglu, Chaoyang District, Beijing 100026 PR, China — Editor

Hu, Ann
C E S D, 10635 Santa Monica Blvd, #130, Los Angeles CA 90025 USA — Director, Writer

Hu, Kelly
Paul Kohner, 9300 Wilshire Blvd, #555, Beverly Hills CA 90212 USA — Actress

Huang Qun
Global Athletics/Marketing, 611 Tremont St, #400, Boston MA 02118, USA — Gymnast

Huang, Helen
I C M Artists, 40 W 57th St, #1800, New York NY 10019 USA — Concert Pianist

Huang, Henry
Washington University, McDonnell Pediatrics Dept, Saint Louis MO 63110, USA — Inventor (DNA Sequencer), Biologist

Huang, James
Kazarian/Spencer/Ruskin, 11969 Ventura Blvd, #300, Studio City CA 91604 USA — Actor, Producer

Huang, Kerson
Massachusetts Institute of Technology, Physics Dept, 77 Massachusetts, #6309, Cambridge 02139, USA — Physicist

Huang, Ying
Columbia Artists Mgmt Inc, 1790 Broadway, #702, New York NY 10019 USA — Opera Singer

Huard, Damon P
9508 NE 18th St, Clyde Hill WA 98004, USA — Football Player

Huarte, John G
14959 La Cumbre Dr, Pacific Palisades CA 90272, USA — Football Player

Hub
W M E Entertainment, 1325 Ave of Americas, New York NY 10019 USA — Bassist (Roots)

Hubbard, Elizabeth (Liz)
Liebman Entertainment, 25 E 21st St, #PH, New York NY 10010, USA — Actress

Hubbard, Erica
Pantheon Talent, 1801 Century Park E, #1910, Los Angeles CA 90067, USA — Actress

Hubbard, Glenn D
1515 Kings Crossing, Stone Mountain GA 30087, USA — Baseball Player

Hubbard, Gregg (Hobie)
O-Seven Artist Mgmt, PO Box 210586, Nashville TN 37221, USA — Singer, Keyboardist (Sawyer Brown)

Hubbard, John
Chilcombe House, Chilcombe near Bridport, Dorset DT6 4PN, England — Artist

Hubbard, Marvin R (Marv)
5804 Dawn View Court, Castro Valley CA 94552, USA — Football Player

V.I.P. Address Book

Hubbard, Michael W (Mike)
2552 Brookstone Lane, Richmond VA 23233, USA — Baseball Player
Hubbard, Phillip G (Phil)
5130 Pleasant Forest Dr, Centreville VA 20120, USA — Basketball Player, Coach
Hubbard, R Glenn
Columbia University, Graduate Management School, New York NY 10027, USA — Government Official, Economist
Hubbard, Robert
353 Piper Road, West Springfield MA 01089, USA — Basketball Player
Hubbard, Trenidad A (Trent)
4206 Clearwater Court, Missouri City TX 77459, USA — Baseball Player
Hubbard, William N, Jr
3634 Woodcliff Dr, Kalamazoo MI 49008, USA — Businessman
Hubby, Sandra
Playboy Promotions, 2706 Media Center Dr, Los Angeles CA 90065 USA — Model
Hubel, David H
98 Collins Road, Waban MA 02468, USA — Nobel Medicine Laureate
Huber, Anke
Dieselstr 10, 76689 Karlsdorf-Neuthard, Germany — Tennis Player
Huber, Gunther
Olympic Committee, Foro Italico, Largo Lauro de Bosis 15, 00135 Rome, Italy — Bobsled Athlete
Huber, Jon
4409 S Angeline St, Seattle WA 98118, USA — Baseball Player
Huber, Robert
Planck Biochemie Institut, Am Klopferspitz, 82152 Martinsried, Germany — Nobel Chemistry Laureate
Hubert, Janet L
Michael Slessinger, 8730 W Sunset Blvd, #220W, West Hollywood CA 90069 USA — Actress
Hubley, Season
47 Pleasant St, Essex Junction VT 05452, USA — Actress
Hubley, Whip
Geddes Agency, 8430 Santa Monica Blvd, #201, West Hollywood CA 90069 USA — Actor
Huck, A Francis (Fran)
313-2505 11th Ave, Regina SK S4P 0K6, Canada — Ice Hockey Player
Huck, John Lloyd
233 Lion's Hill Road, State College PA 16803, USA — Businessman
Huckabee, Cooper
Kazarian/Spencer/Ruskin, 11969 Ventura Blvd, #300, Studio City CA 91604 USA — Actor
Huckabee, Michael (Mike)
Fox-TV, News Dept, 5151 Wisconsin Ave NW, #100, Washington DC 20016 USA — Governor, AR
Huckaby, Ken
4490 S Rio Dr, Chandler AZ 85249, USA — Baseball Player
Hucknall, Michael J (Mick)
Sideways Mgmt, Junction Mews, Paddington, London WC1E 7EA, England — Singer (Simply Red)
Huckstep, Ronald L
108 Sugarloaf Crescent, Castlecrag, Syndey NSW 2068, Australia — Orthopedic Surgeon
Hucles, Angela
8 Worcester Square, #1, Boston MA 02118, USA — Soccer Player
Hucul, Fred
4550 N Flowing Wells Road, #226, Tucson AZ 85705, USA — Ice Hockey Player
Hudd, Roy
A Z A Artists, 652 Finchley Road, London NW11 7NT, England — Actor
Huddleston, David
9200 W Sunset Blvd, #612, West Hollywood CA 90069, USA — Actor
Huddleston, Mark W
University of New Hampshire, President's Office, Durham NH 03824, USA — Educator
Huddy, Charlie
9114 100 A Ave, Edmonton AB T5H 4N7, Canada — Ice Hockey Player
Hudecek, Vaclav
Londynska 25, 120 00 Prague 2, Czech Republic — Concert Violinist
Hudek, John R
7603 Shady Way Dr, Sugar Land TX 77479, USA — Baseball Player
Hudepohl, Joe
10437 Greendale Dr, Tampa FL 33626, USA — Swimmer
Hudgens, David M (Dave)
5802 E Windsor Ave, Scottsdale AZ 85257, USA — Baseball Player
Hudgens, Vanessa A
Untitled Entertainment, 350 S Beverly Dr, #200, Beverly Hills CA 90212 USA — Singer, Actress, Model
Hudler, Jiri
555 S Old Woodward Ave, Birmingham MI 48009, USA — Ice Hockey Player
Hudler, Rex A
11745 Riehl Ave, Tustin CA 92782, USA — Baseball Player
Hudlin, Reginald
Paradigm Agency, 360 N Crescent Dr, North Building, Beverly Hills CA 90210 USA — Actor, Director, Writer
Hudner, Thomas J, Jr
31 Allen Farm Lane, Concord MA 01742, USA — Korean War Navy Hero (CMH)
Hudson, C B, Jr
Torchmark Corp, 2001 3rd Ave S, Birmingham AL 35233, USA — Businessman
Hudson, Cary
Michelle Roche Media Relations, 360 University Circle, Athens GA 30605, USA — Singer, Songwriter
Hudson, Charles (Charlie)
32 W Hooker Ave, Coalgate OK 74538, USA — Baseball Player
Hudson, Charles L
PO Box 368, Oakwood TX 75855, USA — Baseball Player
Hudson, Clifford G
Securities Investor Protection, 805 15th St NW, #800, Washington DC 20005, USA — Financier
Hudson, Ernie
TalentWorks, 3500 W Olive Ave, #1400, Burbank CA 91505 USA — Actor
Hudson, Garth
Skyline Music, 32 Clayton St, Portland ME 04103, USA — Organist (Band)
Hudson, Gordon L
5350 Edgewood Circle, Salt Lake City UT 84117, USA — Football Player
Hudson, Hugh
Jenks & Partners, 37 W 28th St, #7, New York NY 10001, USA — Director
Hudson, James
Harvard Medical School, Psychiatry Dept, 25 Shattuck St, Boston MA 02115, USA — Psychiatrist
Hudson, James C (Jim)
215 Mallet Court, Austin TX 78737, USA — Football Player

H

Hubbard - Hudson

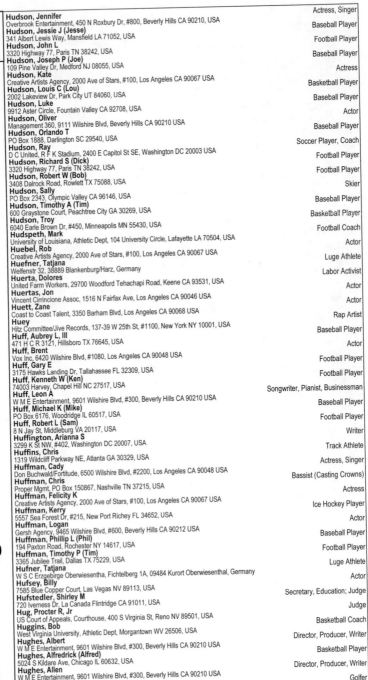

Hudson, Jennifer — Actress, Singer
Overbrook Entertainment, 450 N Roxbury Dr, #800, Beverly Hills CA 90210, USA

Hudson, Jessie J (Jesse) — Baseball Player
341 Albert Lewis Way, Mansfield LA 71052, USA

Hudson, John L — Football Player
3320 Highway 77, Paris TN 38242, USA

Hudson, Joseph P (Joe) — Baseball Player
109 Pine Valley Dr, Medford NJ 08055, USA

Hudson, Kate — Actress
Creative Artists Agency, 2000 Ave of Stars, #100, Los Angeles CA 90067 USA

Hudson, Louis C (Lou) — Basketball Player
2002 Lakeview Dr, Park City UT 84060, USA

Hudson, Luke — Baseball Player
9912 Aster Circle, Fountain Valley CA 92708, USA

Hudson, Oliver — Actor
Management 360, 9111 Wilshire Blvd, Beverly Hills CA 90210 USA

Hudson, Orlando T — Baseball Player
PO Box 1888, Darlington SC 29540, USA

Hudson, Ray — Soccer Player, Coach
D C United, R F K Stadium, 2400 E Capitol St SE, Washington DC 20003 USA

Hudson, Richard S (Dick) — Football Player
3320 Highway 77, Paris TN 38242, USA

Hudson, Robert W (Bob) — Football Player
3408 Dalrock Road, Rowlett TX 75088, USA

Hudson, Sally — Skier
PO Box 2343, Olympic Valley CA 96146, USA

Hudson, Timothy A (Tim) — Baseball Player
600 Graystone Court, Peachtree City GA 30269, USA

Hudson, Troy — Basketball Player
6040 Earle Brown Dr, #450, Minneapolis MN 55430, USA

Hudspeth, Mark — Football Coach
University of Louisiana, Athletic Dept, 104 University Circle, Lafayette LA 70504, USA

Huebel, Rob — Actor
Creative Artists Agency, 2000 Ave of Stars, #100, Los Angeles CA 90067 USA

Huefner, Tatjana — Luge Athlete
Welfenstr 32, 38889 Blankenburg/Harz, Germany

Huerta, Dolores — Labor Activist
United Farm Workers, 29700 Woodford Tehachapi Road, Keene CA 93531, USA

Huertas, Jon — Actor
Vincent Cirrincione Assoc, 1516 N Fairfax Ave, Los Angeles CA 90046 USA

Huett, Zane — Actor
Coast to Coast Talent, 3350 Barham Blvd, Los Angeles CA 90068 USA

Huey — Rap Artist
Hitz Committee/Jive Records, 137-39 W 25th St, #1100, New York NY 10001, USA

Huff, Aubrey L, III — Baseball Player
471 H C R 3121, Hillsboro TX 76645, USA

Huff, Brent — Actor
Vox Inc, 6420 Wilshire Blvd, #1080, Los Angeles CA 90048 USA

Huff, Gary E — Football Player
3175 Hawks Landing Dr, Tallahassee FL 32309, USA

Huff, Kenneth W (Ken) — Football Player
74003 Harvey, Chapel Hill NC 27517, USA

Huff, Leon A — Songwriter, Pianist, Businessman
W M E Entertainment, 9601 Wilshire Blvd, #300, Beverly Hills CA 90210 USA

Huff, Michael K (Mike) — Baseball Player
PO Box 6176, Woodridge IL 60517, USA

Huff, Robert L (Sam) — Football Player
8 N Jay St, Middleburg VA 20117, USA

Huffington, Arianna S — Writer
3299 K St NW, #402, Washington DC 20007, USA

Huffins, Chris — Track Athlete
1319 Wildcliff Parkway NE, Atlanta GA 30329, USA

Huffman, Cady — Actress, Singer
Don Buchwald/Fortitude, 6500 Wilshire Blvd, #2200, Los Angeles CA 90048 USA

Huffman, Chris — Bassist (Casting Crowns)
Proper Mgmt, PO Box 150867, Nashville TN 37215, USA

Huffman, Felicity K — Actress
Creative Artists Agency, 2000 Ave of Stars, #100, Los Angeles CA 90067 USA

Huffman, Kerry — Ice Hockey Player
5557 Sea Forest Dr, #215, New Port Richey FL 34652, USA

Huffman, Logan — Actor
Gersh Agency, 9465 Wilshire Blvd, #600, Beverly Hills CA 90212 USA

Huffman, Phillip L (Phil) — Baseball Player
194 Paxton Road, Rochester NY 14617, USA

Huffman, Timothy P (Tim) — Football Player
3365 Jubilee Trail, Dallas TX 75229, USA

Hufner, Tatjana — Luge Athlete
W S C Erzgebirge Oberwiesentha, Fichtelberg 1A, 09484 Kurort Oberwiesenthal, Germany

Hufsey, Billy — Actor
7585 Blue Copper Court, Las Vegas NV 89113, USA

Hufstedler, Shirley M — Secretary, Education; Judge
720 Iverness Dr, La Canada Flintridge CA 91011, USA

Hug, Procter R, Jr — Judge
US Court of Appeals, Courthouse, 400 S Virginia St, Reno NV 89501, USA

Huggins, Bob — Basketball Coach
West Virginia University, Athletic Dept, Morgantown WV 26506, USA

Hughes, Albert — Director, Producer, Writer
W M E Entertainment, 9601 Wilshire Blvd, #300, Beverly Hills CA 90210 USA

Hughes, Alfredrick (Alfred) — Basketball Player
5024 S Kildare Ave, Chicago IL 60632, USA

Hughes, Allen — Director, Producer, Writer
W M E Entertainment, 9601 Wilshire Blvd, #300, Beverly Hills CA 90210 USA

Hughes, Bradley — Golfer
204 Easton Court, Simpsonville SC 29680, USA

Hughes, Bronwen — Director
Gersh Agency, 9465 Wilshire Blvd, #600, Beverly Hills CA 90212 USA

Hughes, Chris New Republic, 1400 K St NW, #1200, Washington DC 20005, USA	Businessman, Publisher, Editor
Hughes, Clara Speed Skating Canada, 2781 Lancaster Road, #402, Ottawa ON K1B 1A7, Canada	Speed Skater, Cyclist
Hughes, Dan San Antonio Silver Stars, 1 AT&T Center, San Antonio TX 78219 USA	Basketball Coach, Executive
Hughes, David A 5307 240th Ave NE, Redmond WA 98053, USA	Football Player
Hughes, Eddie 4253 Deerfield Hills Road, Colorado Springs CO 80916, USA	Basketball Player
Hughes, Ernest L (Ernie) 2116 Camino Brazos, Pleasanton CA 94566, USA	Football Player
Hughes, Finola Harrison Stokes, 8730 W Sunset Blvd, #270, West Hollywood CA 90069, USA	Actress
Hughes, Frank John A P A Talent/Literary Agency, 405 S Beverly Dr, #300, Beverly Hills CA 90212 USA	Actor
Hughes, H Richard 47 Chiswick Quay, London W4 3UR, England	Architect
Hughes, Harold R (Harry) Patton Boggs Blow, 2550 M St NW, #500, Washington DC 20037, USA	Governor, MD
Hughes, J Randell (Randy) 17608 Cedar Creek Canyon Dr, Dallas TX 75252, USA	Football Player
Hughes, James M (Jim) 7526 El Manor Ave, Los Angeles CA 90045, USA	Baseball Player
Hughes, John 317 Laudholm Farm Road, Wells ME 04090, USA	Ice Hockey Player
Hughes, Karen Harper Collins Publishers, 10 E 53rd St, Cellar 1, New York NY 10022 USA	Government Official
Hughes, Kate 275 Merlot Lane, Saint Albans MO 63073, USA	Golfer
Hughes, Kathleen 8818 Rising Glen Place, Los Angeles CA 90069, USA	Actress
Hughes, Keith W 176 Sycamore Road, Havertown PA 19083, USA	Baseball Player
Hughes, Kim G 5203 Bluemound Road, Rolling Hills Estates CA 90274, USA	Basketball Player, Coach
Hughes, Larry D 3 Hanna Court, Cleveland OH 44108, USA	Basketball Player
Hughes, Mervyn G Australian Cricket Board, 90 Jollimant St, Melbourne VIC 3002, Australia	Cricketer
Hughes, Miko Jamieson Assoc, 53 Sunrise Road, Superior MT 59872, USA	Actor
Hughes, Nicola Gavin Barker Assoc, 2D Wimpole St, London W1G 0EB, England	Actress
Hughes, Pat 8388 Webster Hills Road, Dexter MI 48130, USA	Ice Hockey Player
Hughes, Phil 275 Bayshore Blvd, #501, Tampa FL 33606, USA	Baseball Player
Hughes, Richard D Agency Group Ltd, 361-373 City Road, London EC1V 2QA, England	Drummer (Keane)
Hughes, Richard H (Dick) PO Box 598, Stephens AR 71764, USA	Baseball Player
Hughes, Sally Associated International Mgmt, Fairfax House, Fulwood Place, London WC1V 6HU, England	Actress
Hughes, Sarah E John Hughes, 12 Channel Dr, Great Neck NY 11024, USA	Figure Skater
Hughes, Terry Creative Artists Agency, 2000 Ave of Stars, #100, Los Angeles CA 90067 USA	Director
Hughes, Terry W 532 Pierpoint Avenue Extension, Spartanburg SC 29303, USA	Baseball Player
Hughes, Thomas E (Tom) 610 Kimswick Court, Deer Park TX 77536, USA	Baseball Player
Hughes, Thomas J, Jr 400 Mar Vista Dr, #4, Monterey CA 93940, USA	Navy Admiral
Hughes, Tom C E S D, 10635 Santa Monica Blvd, #130, Los Angeles CA 90025 USA	Actor
Hughes, Tyrone C 5812 W Deer Park Blvd, New Orleans LA 70127, USA	Football Player
Hughes, W Patrick (Pat) 4 Woodside Dr, Stratham NH 03885, USA	Football Player
Hughes, Wendy I C M Partners, 10250 Constellation Blvd, #900, Los Angeles CA 90067 USA	Actress
Hughes-Fulford, Millie Veterans Affairs Dept, Medical Center, 4150 Clement St, San Francisco CA 94121, USA	Astronaut
Hughey, Gary H Deputy CinC, US Transportation Command, Scott Air Force Base IL 62225 USA	Marine Corps General
Hughley, D L I C M Partners, 10250 Constellation Blvd, #900, Los Angeles CA 90067 USA	Actor, Comedian
Hugo, Chad Virgin Records, 338 N Foothill Road, Beverly Hills CA 90210 USA	Singer, Rap Artist (NERD)
Huguenin, G Richard Millitech Corp, 5 North St, South Deerfield MA 01373, USA	Inventor (Portable Gun Detector Camera)
Huh, John Professional Golfer's Assn, PO Box 109601, Palm Beach Gardens FL 33410 USA	Golfer
Huisgen, Rolf Kaulbachstr 10, 80539 Munich, Germany	Chemist
Huish, Justin 3475 Indian Mesa Dr, Thousand Oaks CA 91360, USA	Archer
Huisman, Justin R 8713 Forest Glen Court, Saint John IN 46373, USA	Baseball Player
Huisman, Michiel Conway Van Gelder Grant, 8-12 Broadwick St, #300, London W1F 8HW, England	Actor
Huisman, Richard A (Rick) 17W25 Oak Lane, Bensenville IL 60106, USA	Baseball Player
Huismann, Mark L 5751 NW Plantation Lane, Lees Summit MO 64064, USA	Baseball Player

V.I.P. Address Book

Humphrey, Terryal G (Terry) 7 Oakmont, Trabuco Canyon CA 92679, USA	Baseball Player
Humphreys, Matthew Don Buchwald/Fortitude, 6500 Wilshire Blvd, #2200, Los Angeles CA 90048 USA	Actor
Humphreys, Michael B (Mike) 1402 Lost Creek Dr, De Soto TX 75115, USA	Baseball Player
Humphreys, Robert W (Bob) 1803 Oakwood St, Bedford VA 24523, USA	Baseball Player
Humphries, J Jay 22107 N 37th Terrace, Phoenix AZ 85050, USA	Basketball Player
Humphries, Kaillie Alberta Bobsled, Niven Center, 140 Canada Olympic Road, Calgary AB T3B 5RS, Canada	Bobsled Athlete
Humphries, Stefan G 8708 E Redwood Lane, Spokane WA 99217, USA	Football Player
Humphries, W Stanley (Stan) 4100 Chauvin Lane, Monroe LA 71201, USA	Football Player
Humphry, Derek Euthanasia Research & Guidance Organization, 24828 Norris Lane, Junction City OR 97448, USA	Social Activist
Hun Sen, Samdech Prime Minister's Office, Supreme National Council, Phnom Penh, Cambodia	Prime Minister, Cambodia
Hundley, C Randolph (Randy) 122 E Forest Lane, Palatine IL 60067, USA	Baseball Player
Hundley, Rodney C (Hot Rod) 29769 N 130th Dr, Peoria AZ 85383, USA	Basketball Player, Sportscaster
Hundley, Todd R PO Box 2502, Glenview IL 60025, USA	Baseball Player
Hundt, Reed E 6416 Brookside Dr, Chevy Chase MD 20815, USA	Government Official
Hung, Sammo Blue Stone Entertainment, 9000 Sunset Blvd, #515, Los Angeles CA 90069, USA	Actor
Hunger, Daniela S V Preussen, Hansastr 190, 13088 Berlin, Germany	Swimmer
Hunger, Sophie Agency Group Ltd, 142 W 57th St, #600, New York NY 10019 USA	Singer
Huniford, James Huniford Design Studio, 210 11th Ave, #601, New York NY 10001, USA	Interior Designer, Architect
Hunkapiller, Michael Applied Biosystems, 850 Lincoln Centre Dr, Foster City CA 94404, USA	Inventor (DNA Sequencer), Biochemist
Hunley, Leann Mitchell K Stubbs Assoc, 8695 W Washington Blvd, #204, Culver City CA 90232 USA	Actress
Hunley, Rickard C (Ricky) 4435 Circle View Blvd, Los Angeles CA 90043, USA	Football Player
Hunnam, Charlie Creative Artists Agency, 2000 Ave of Stars, #100, Los Angeles CA 90067 USA	Actor
Hunnicutt, Gayle 174 Regents Park Road, London NW1 8XP, England	Actress
Hunold, Joachim Air Berlin PLC, Saatwinkler Damm 42-43, 13627 Berlin, Germany	Businessman
Hunt, Bonnie W M E Entertainment, 9601 Wilshire Blvd, #300, Beverly Hills CA 90210 USA	Actress, Director
Hunt, Bruce I C M Partners, 10250 Constellation Blvd, #900, Los Angeles CA 90067 USA	Director
Hunt, Bryan 9 White St, New York NY 10013, USA	Artist, Sculptor
Hunt, Byron R PO Box 281, Rutherford NJ 07070, USA	Football Player
Hunt, Caroline R 100 Crescent Court, #1700, Dallas TX 75201, USA	Businesswoman
Hunt, Cletidus M 3744 Misty Oak Dr, Memphis TN 38125, USA	Football Player
Hunt, Courtney W M E Entertainment, 9601 Wilshire Blvd, #300, Beverly Hills CA 90210 USA	Writer
Hunt, Crystal Don Buchwald/Fortitude, 6500 Wilshire Blvd, #2200, Los Angeles CA 90048 USA	Actress
Hunt, Darlene United Talent Agency, 9336 Civic Center Dr, Beverly Hills CA 90210 USA	Producer, Writer, Actress
Hunt, David Ken McReddie Assoc, 11 Connaught Place, London W2 2ET, England	Actor, Director
Hunt, Helen Creative Artists Agency, 2000 Ave of Stars, #100, Los Angeles CA 90067 USA	Actress
Hunt, J Randall (Randy) 324 Holly Ridge Dr, Montgomery AL 36109, USA	Baseball Player
Hunt, James B, Jr Womble Carlyle Sandridge Rice, 150 Fayetteville St Mall, Raleigh NC 27601, USA	Governor, NC
Hunt, Johnny M First Baptist Church, 11905 Highway 92, Woodstock GA 30188, USA	Religious Leader
Hunt, Joseph (Joe) Iron Workers Union, 1750 New York Ave NW, #400, Washington DC 20006, USA	Labor Leader
Hunt, Linda W M E Entertainment, 9601 Wilshire Blvd, #300, Beverly Hills CA 90210 USA	Actress
Hunt, Nelson Bunker Hunt Resources Corp, Fountain Place, 1445 Ross at Field, Dallas TX 75202, USA	Businessman
Hunt, R Kevin 11 Royal Lane, Londonderry NH 03053, USA	Football Player
Hunt, R Timothy Rose Cottage, Ridge, Herts EN6 3LH, England	Nobel Medicine Laureate
Hunt, Rameck Three Doctors Foundation, 65 Hazelwood Ave, Newark NJ 07106, USA	Physician
Hunt, Richard H 1017 W Lill Ave, Chicago IL 60614, USA	Sculptor
Hunt, Robert K (Bobby) 5928 Bentway Dr, Charlotte NC 28226, USA	Football Player
Hunt, Ronald K (Ron) 2806 Jackson Road, Wentzville MO 63385, USA	Baseball Player
Hunt, Samuel K (Sam) 1708 Eliza St, Nacogdoches TX 75961, USA	Football Player

Hunt, Stephanie
Innovative Artists, 1505 10th St, Santa Monica CA 90401 USA — Actress

Hunten, Donald M
1828 E Barn Swallow Lane, Green Valley AZ 85614, USA — Astronomer

Hunter, Anthony R (Tony)
4578 Vista de la Patria, Del Mar CA 92014, USA — Molecular Biologist

Hunter, Brian L
8349 S Aberdeen St, Chicago IL 60620, USA — Baseball Player

Hunter, Brian R
12141 Centralia St, #219, Lakewood CA 90715, USA — Baseball Player

Hunter, Charles D
295 N Rural Road, #153, Chandler AZ 85226, USA — Businessman

Hunter, Charlie
Figurehead Mgmt, 3470 19th St, San Francisco CA 94110, USA — Jazz Guitarist (Charlie Hunter Quartet)

Hunter, Daniel L
210 N Lakeview Dr, Farmerville LA 71241, USA — Football Player

Hunter, Dave
53350 Range Road 220, Androssan AB T8E 2B5, Canada — Ice Hockey Player

Hunter, G William (Billy)
104 E Seminary Ave, Lutherville MD 21093, USA — Baseball Player, Manager

Hunter, Harold J (Buddy)
14616 Fir Circle, Plattsmouth, NE 68048, USA — Baseball Player

Hunter, Holly
Special Artists Agency, 9465 Wilshire Blvd, #820, Beverly Hills CA 90212 USA — Actress

Hunter, Ian
Helter Skelter, 347-353 Chiswick High Road, London W4 4HS, England — Singer, Songwriter (Mott the People)

Hunter, J Scott
6386 Dolive Court, Daphne AL 36526, USA — Football Player

Hunter, James
Monterey International, 200 W Superior St, #202, Chicago IL 60654 USA — Singer, Guitarist

Hunter, James M (Jim)
12939 Penshurst Lane, Windermere FL 34786, USA — Baseball Player

Hunter, Jeffrey O (Jeff)
2004 Barton Court, Augusta GA 30906, USA — Football Player

Hunter, Jesse
Friedman & LaRosa, 1334 Lexington Ave, New York NY 10128, USA — Singer, Guitarist

Hunter, Jim
Jungle Jim Hunter Mgmt, 864 Woodpark Way SW, Calgary AB T2W 2V8, Canada — Skier

Hunter, John
Lawrence Livermore Laboratory, 7000 East St, Livermore CA 94550, USA — Rocket Engineer

Hunter, Leslie (Les)
8712 W 92nd St, Overland Park KS 66212, USA — Basketball Player

Hunter, Lindsey B
4355 Hickory Ridge Court, Plymouth MI 48170, USA — Basketball Player

Hunter, Mark
London Knights, 99 Dundas St, London ON N6A 6K1, Canada — Ice Hockey Player

Hunter, Patrick E
8901 S 10th Dr, Phoenix AZ 85041, USA — Football Player

Hunter, Rachel
23 Beverly Park Terrace, Beverly Hills CA 90210, USA — Model, Actress

Hunter, Robert
Agency Group Ltd, 1880 Century Park E, #711, Los Angeles CA 90067 USA — Songwriter (Grateful Dead)

Hunter, Simon
United Talent Agency, 9336 Civic Center Dr, Beverly Hills CA 90210 USA — Director

Hunter, Stephen
Washington Post, Editorial Dept, 1150 15th St NW, Washington DC 20071 USA — Writer

Hunter, T Othello
Atlanta Hawks, Centennial Tower, 101 Marietta St NW, #1900, Atlanta GA 30303 USA — Basketball Player

Hunter, Tab
PO Box 50308, Santa Barbara CA 93150, USA — Actor, Singer

Hunter, Tim
Toronto Maple Leafs, AirCanada Center, 40 Bay St, Toronto ON M5J 2K2, Canada — Ice Hockey Player

Hunter, Tim
A P A Talent/Literary Agency, 250 W 57th St, #1701, New York NY 10107 USA — Director

Hunter, Torii K
7164 Richmond Dr, Frisco TX 75035, USA — Baseball Player

Hunter, Willard M
2562 Poppleton Ave, Omaha NE 68105, USA — Baseball Player

Hunter-Gault, Charlayne
News Hour Show, 2700 S Quincy St, #250, Arlington VA 22206, USA — Commentator, Writer

Hunthausen, Raymond G
Catholic Archdiocese of Seattle, 710 9th Ave, Seattle WA 98104, USA — Religious Leader

Huntington, Sam
United Talent Agency, 9336 Civic Center Dr, Beverly Hills CA 90210 USA — Actor

Huntington-Whiteley, Rosie
Women Model Mgmt, 199 Lafayette St, #700, New York NY 10012 USA — Model, Actress

Huntley, Joni
7148 SW 4th Ave, Portland OR 97219, USA — Track Athlete

Huntley, Richard E
7123 Rumple Road, Charlotte NC 28262, USA — Football Player

Huntsman, Jon M, Jr
Brookings Institute, 1775 Massachusetts Ave NW, Washington DC 20036 USA — Diplomat; Governor, UT

Huntsman, Stanley H
5532 Timbercrest Trail, Knoxville TN 37909, USA — Track Coach

Huntz, Stephen M (Steve)
3303 Linden Road, #405, Rocky River OH 44116, USA — Baseball Player

Hunyadfi, Steven
838 Ridgewood Dr, #12, Fort Wayne IN 46805, USA — Swimming Coach

Hunyady, Emese
Beim Spitzriegel 1/2/9, 2500 Baden, Austria — Speed Skater

Hunziker, Terry
208 3rd Ave S, Seattle WA 98104, USA — Interior Designer

Hupp, Jana Marie
A P A Talent/Literary Agency, 405 S Beverly Dr, #300, Beverly Hills CA 90212 USA — Actress

Huppert, David B (Dave)
6732 Stephens Path, Zephyrhills FL 33542, USA — Baseball Player

Huppert, Isabelle	Actress
Voyez Mon Agent, 20 Ave Rapp, 75007 Paris, France	
Hurd of Westwell, Douglas R	Government Official, England
Hawkpoint, Crosby Court, 4 Great Saint Helens, London EC3A 6HA, England	
Hurd, Gale Anne	Producer
Valhalla Motion Pictures, 3201 Cahuenga Blvd W, Los Angeles CA 90068, USA	
Hurd, Michelle	Actress
T M T Entertainment, 648 Broadway, #1002, New York NY 10012, USA	
Hurdle, Clinton M (Clint)	Baseball Player, Manager
9068 Sturbridge Place, Littleton CO 80129, USA	
Hurd-Wood, Rachel C	Actress
Troika, 74 Clerkenwell Road, #300, London EC1M 5QA, England	
Hurford, Peter J	Concert Organist
Broom House, Saint Bernard's Road, Saint Albans, Hertfordshire AL3 5RA, England	
Hurlbert, Jacquline (Jackie)	Artist
Studio Ten XIII, 16396 SW Kimball Ave, Lake Oswego OR 97035, USA	
Hurlbut, Laura	Golfer
24741 Calle Conejo, Calabasas CA 91302, USA	
Hurley, Alfred F	Educator, Historian
3505 Turtle Creek Blvd, #6A, Dallas TX 75219, USA	
Hurley, Andrew (Andy)	Drummer (Fall Out Boy)
PO Box 219, 1187 Wilmette Ave, Wilmette IL 60091, USA	
Hurley, Bob	Basketball Coach
Saint Anthony High School, Athletic Dept, 175 8th St, Jersey City NJ 07302, USA	
Hurley, Bob	Surfing Executive
Hurley International, 1945 Placentia Ave, Costa Mesa CA 92627, USA	
Hurley, Chad	Businessman
YouTube, 1000 Cherry Ave, #200, San Bruno CA 94066, USA	
Hurley, Craig	Actor
Avo Talent, 8500 Melrose Ave, #212, West Hollywood CA 90069, USA	
Hurley, Douglas G	Astronaut
1848 Lake Landing Dr, League City TX 77573, USA	
Hurley, Elizabeth	Model, Actress
United Talent Agency, 9336 Civic Center Dr, Beverly Hills CA 90210 USA	
Hurley, Robert M (Bobby)	Basketball Player
1410 Shoreline Way, Hollywood FL 33019, USA	
Hurn, David	Photographer
Prospect Cottage, Tintern, Chepstow, Gwent NP16 6SG, Wales	
Hurnik, Ilja	Concert Pianist, Composer
Cesky Rozhlas, Vinohradska 12, 120 99 Prague 2, Czech Republic	
Hurran, Nick	Director
Independent Talent Group, Oxford House, 76 Oxford St, London W1D 1BS, England	
Hurst, Bruce V	Baseball Player
1080 N Riata St, Gilbert AZ 85234, USA	
Hurst, Geoff	Soccer Player
Dragonwyck, Saint George's Hill, Weybridge, Surrey KT13 0PY, England	
Hurst, Maurice R	Football Player
3520 Leonidas St, New Orleans LA 70118, USA	
Hurst, Michael	Actor, Director, Producer
Johnson & Laird Mgmt, PO Box 78340, Grey Lynn, Auckland 1245, New Zealand	
Hurst, Pat	Golfer
730 Camino Amigo, Danville CA 94526, USA	
Hurst, Rick	Actor
1230 N Horn Road, West Hollywood CA 90069, USA	
Hurst, Ryan D	Actor
Piper Kaniecki Mgmt, 13273 Ventura Blvd, #104, Studio City CA 91604, USA	
Hurst, William H (Bill)	Baseball Player
9331 SW 192nd Dr, Cutler Bay FL 33157, USA	
Hurston, Charles F (Chuck)	Football Player
9360 Prestwick Club Dr, Duluth GA 30097, USA	
Hurt, Frank	Labor Leader
Bakery Confectionery Tobacco Union, 10401 Connecticut, Kensington MD 20895, USA	
Hurt, John	Actor
Independent Talent Group, Oxford House, 76 Oxford St, London W1D 1BS, England	
Hurt, Mary Beth	Actress
I C M Partners, 10250 Constellation Blvd, #900, Los Angeles CA 90067 USA	
Hurt, Weston	Opera Singer
Opus 3 Artists, 470 Park Ave S, #900N, New York NY 10016 USA	
Hurt, William	Actor
I C M Partners, 10250 Constellation Blvd, #900, Los Angeles CA 90067 USA	
Hurtado Larrea, Oswaldo	President, Ecuador
Suecia 277 y Av Los Shyris, Quito, Ecuador	
Hurtado, Edwin A	Baseball Player
1202 15th Ave N, Lake Worth FL 33460, USA	
Hurvich, Leo M	Psychologist
276 5th Ave, #306, New York NY 10001, USA	
Hurwitz, Charles E	Businessman
Maxxam Inc, 1330 Post Oak Blvd, #2000, Houston TX 77056, USA	
Hurwitz, Jerard	Molecular Biologist
Memorial Sloan Kettering Cancer Center, 1275 York Ave, New York NY 10065, USA	
Hurwitz, Jon	Director, Producer, Writer
Creative Artists Agency, 2000 Ave of Stars, #100, Los Angeles CA 90067 USA	
Hurwitz, Mitchell (Mitch)	Producer, Writer
Tantamount, 10202 W Washington Blvd, Astaire Building, Culver City CA 90202, USA	
Husa, Karel J	Composer, Conductor
3417 Foy Glen Court, Apex NC 27539, USA	
Husar, Lubomyr Cardinal	Religious Leader
Ploscha Sviatoho Jura 5, 290000 Lviv, Ukraine	
Huscroft, Jamie	Ice Hockey Player
3024 38th St SE, Puyallup WA 98374, USA	
Huselius, Kristian	Ice Hockey Player
Columbus Blue Jackets, Arena, 200 W Nationwide Blvd, #1, Columbus OH 43215 USA	
Husen, Torsten	Educator
Armfeltsgatan 10, 115 34 Stockholm, Sweden	
Husmann, Edward E (Ed)	Football Player
27266 Orth Lane, Conroe TX 77385, USA	

H

Huppert - Husmann

Huson, Jeffrey K (Jeff)	Baseball Player
10349 Rowlock Way, Parker CO 80134, USA	
Hussey, Olivia	Actress
Frozen Frame Entertainment, 3115 Foothill Blvd, #247, La Crescenta CA 91214, USA	
Husted, Wayne D	Artist
Keep Homestead Museum, Ely Road, Monson MA 01057, USA	
Huster, Marc	Weightlifter
Grundstr 111, 0132 Dresden, Germany	
Huston, Anjelica	Actress, Director
57 Windward Ave, Venice CA 90291, USA	
Huston, Daniel (Danny)	Director, Actor
Julian Belfrage Assoc, 9 Argyll St, #300, London W1F 7TG, England	
Huston, Geoff A	Basketball Player
1960 Ellis Ave, Bronx NY 10472, USA	
Huston, Jack	Actor
United Talent Agency, 9336 Civic Center Dr, Beverly Hills CA 90210 USA	
Huston, John	Golfer
1134 Skye Lane, Palm Harbor FL 34683, USA	
Hutcherson, Josh	Actor
I C M Partners, 10250 Constellation Blvd, #900, Los Angeles CA 90067 USA	
Hutcherson, Robert (Bobby)	Jazz Vibraphonist
Blue Note Records, 6920 W Sunset Blvd, Los Angeles CA 90028 USA	
Hutchins, Melvin R (Mel)	Basketball Player
160 Sherri Lane, Oceanside CA 92054, USA	
Hutchins, Will	Actor
PO Box 371, Glen Head NY 11545, USA	
Hutchinson, Barbara	Labor Leader
American Federation of Labor, 815 15th St NW, Washington DC 20005, USA	
Hutchinson, Chad M	Football, Baseball Player
1388 Elder Ave, Menlo Park CA 94025, USA	
Hutchinson, Eric	Singer, Pianist, Songwriter
Warner Bros Records, 3300 Warner Blvd, Burbank CA 91505 USA	
Hutchinson, Frederick E	Educator
University of Maine, President's Office, Orono ME 04469, USA	
Hutchinson, J Maxwell	Architect
58 Hatton Garden, London EC1N 8LX, England	
Hutchinson, Scott R	Football Player
1223 Northern Way, Winter Springs FL 32708, USA	
Hutchinson, Steven J (Steve)	Football Player
16119 Crosby Cove Road, Wayzata MN 55391, USA	
Hutchison, Dave	Ice Hockey Player
Re/Max Realty, 3922 Hamilton Road, Dorchester ON N0L 1G2, Canada	
Hutchison, Fiona	Actress
Don Buchwald/Fortitude, 6500 Wilshire Blvd, #2200, Los Angeles CA 90048 USA	
Huth, Edward J	Editor, Physician
1124 Morris Ave, Bryn Mawr PA 19010, USA	
Huther, Bruce A	Football Player
1156 N Bonnie Brae St, Denton TX 76201, USA	
Hutman, Jon	Production Designer
Gersh Agency, 9465 Wilshire Blvd, #600, Beverly Hills CA 90212 USA	
Hutsell, Melanie	Actress, Comedienne
Greene Assoc, 1901 Ave of Stars, #130, Los Angeles CA 90067 USA	
Hutshing, Joe	Editor
Gersh Agency, 9465 Wilshire Blvd, #600, Beverly Hills CA 90212 USA	
Hutson, G Herbert (Herb)	Baseball Player
7203 W Sugar Tree Court, Savannah GA 31410, USA	
Hutson, Martin	Actor
Ken McReddie Assoc, 11 Connaught Place, London W2 2ET, England	
Hutt, Peter B	Attorney
124 S Fairfax St, Alexandria VA 22314, USA	
Hutter, Mark	Actor
Judy Fox Mgmt, 1525 ½ S Beverly Dr, Los Angeles, CA 90035, USA	
Hutter, Sidney	Artist
Sidney Hutter Glass & Light, 225 Riverside Ave, Auburndale MA 02466, USA	
Hutto, James N (Jim)	Baseball Player
1317 John Carroll Dr, Pensacola FL 32504, USA	
Hutton, Danny	Singer (Three Dog Night)
2437 Horseshoe Canyon Road, Los Angeles CA 90046, USA	
Hutton, Lauren	Model, Actress
Untitled Entertainment, 350 S Beverly Dr, #200, Beverly Hills CA 90212 USA	
Hutton, Mark S	Baseball Player
6 Corfu Court, Westlakes, Adelaide SA 5021, Australia	
Hutton, Thomas G (Tommy)	Baseball Player, Sportscaster
18 Huntly Dr, Palm Beach Gardens FL 33418, USA	
Hutton, Timothy	Actor
W M E Entertainment, 9601 Wilshire Blvd, #300, Beverly Hills CA 90210 USA	
Hutton, W Thomas (Tom)	Football Player
85 Pinehurst St, Memphis TN 38117, USA	
Huxhold, Kenneth W (Ken)	Football Player
5007 Prairie Rose Court, Middleton WI 53562, USA	
Huxley, Hugh E	Biologist
349 Nashawtuc Road, Concord MA 01742, USA	
Huxtable, Ada Louise	Architectural Critic
969 Park Ave, New York NY 10028, USA	
Huyck, Willard	Director, Writer
39 Oakmont Dr, Los Angeles CA 90049, USA	
Hvorostovsky, Dmitri	Opera Singer
Askonas Holt, Lincoln House, 300 High Holborn, London WC1V 7JH, England	
Hwang Seok-Ho	Soccer Player
Football Assn, 1-131 Sinmunno, 2-Ga Jongno-Gu, Seoul 110 062, South Korea	
Hwang, David Henry	Writer
Bobbi Thompson Mgmt, 870 Galloway St, Pacific Palisades CA 90272, USA	
Hyams, Peter	Director
627 San Lorenzo St, Santa Monica CA 90402, USA	
Hyatt, Fred P (Freddie)	Football Player
19350 SE 52nd Place, Morriston FL 32668, USA	

Hyatt, Joel Z
Hyatt Legal Services, 1215 Superior Ave E, Cleveland OH 44114, USA — Attorney, Businessman

Hybl, William J
El Pomar Foundation, 10 Lake Circle, Colorado Springs CO 80906, USA — Foundation, Sports Executive

Hyche, Heath
Brillstein Entertainment Partners, 9150 Wilshire Blvd, #350, Beverly Hills CA 90212 USA — Actor, Comedian

Hyde, Christopher
Onyx Penguin Putnam, 375 Hudson St, New York NY 10014, USA — Writer

Hyde, Glenn T
955 Eudora St, #201, Denver CO 80220, USA — Football Player

Hyde, James
Innovative Artists, 1505 10th St, Santa Monica CA 90401 USA — Actor

Hyde, Jonathan
Artist Rights Group, 4 Great Portland Place, London W1W 8PA, England — Actor

Hyde, Richard E (Dick)
1506 Cambridge Dr, Champaign IL 61821, USA — Baseball Player

Hyder, Greg
16228 Wato Road, #A, Apple Valley CA 92307, USA — Basketball Player

Hyde-White, Alex
Amsel Eisenstadt Frazier, 5055 Wilshire Blvd, #865, Los Angeles CA 90036 USA — Actor

Hyers, Timothy J (Tim)
241 Ridge Road, Covington GA 30016, USA — Baseball Player

Hyland, Brian
Paradise Artists, PO Box 1821, Ojai CA 93024 USA — Singer

Hyland, Robert J (Bob)
30 Colonial Road, White Plains NY 10605, USA — Football Player

Hyland, Sarah
R K M, 400 N Mansfield Ave, Los Angeles CA 90036, USA — Actress

Hylton, James
15 Avalon Road, Martin GA 30557, USA — Auto Racing Driver

Hylton, Thomas J
Pottstown Mercury, Editorial Dept, Hanover & King Sts, Pottstown PA 19464, USA — Journalist

Hyman, Earle
Manhattan Towers, 484 W 43rd St, #33E, New York NY 10036, USA — Actor

Hyman, Misty
3826 E Lupine Ave, Phoenix AZ 85028, USA — Swimmer

Hyman, Richard R (Dick)
Abby Hoffer, 223 1/2 E 48th St, New York NY 10017 USA — Jazz Pianist, Composer

Hyman, Timothy
62 Muddelton Square, London EC1, England — Artist

Hymes, Dell H
20 Mountvue Dr, Charlottesville VA 22901, USA — Anthropologist

Hynd, Noel
I C M Partners, 10250 Constellation Blvd, #900, Los Angeles CA 90067 USA — Writer

Hynd, Ronald
Fern Cottage, U Somerton, Bury Saint Edmonds, Suffolk IP29 4ND, England — Ballet Dancer, Choreographer

Hynde, Christine E (Chrissie)
Gailforce Mgmt, 91 Peterborough Road, London SW6 3BU, England — Singer, Guitarist, Songwriter

Hynes, Garry
Druid Theater Co, Druid Lane & Flood St, North County Galway, Ireland — Director

Hynes, Jessica
Independent Talent Group, Oxford House, 76 Oxford St, London W1D 1BS, England — Actress, Comedienne, Writer

Hynes, Samuel
130 Moore St, Princeton NJ 08540, USA — Writer

Hynes, Tyler
A P A Talent/Literary Agency, 405 S Beverly Dr, #300, Beverly Hills CA 90212 USA — Actor

Hynoski, Henry, Jr
New York Giants, Meadowlands Stadium, 102 Route 120, East Rutherford NJ 07073 USA — Football Player

Hysong, Nick
10424 N 38th St, Phoenix AZ 85028, USA — Track Athlete

Hytner, Nicholas R
United Agents, 12-26 Lexington St, London W1F 0LE, England — Director

Hyzdu, Adam
7823 E Red Hawk Circle, Mesa AZ 85207, USA — Baseball Player

I Coco Blame — Singer, Songwriter
Universal Music, 364-366 Kensington High St, London W14 8NS, England

Iacavazzi, Cosmo J — Football Player
90 Vine St, Taylor PA 18517, USA

Iacobellis, Sam F — Businessman, Aeronautical Engineer
Rockwell International, PO Box 5090, Costa Mesa CA 92628, USA

Iacocca, Lido A (Lee) — Businessman
75252 Pepperwood Dr, Indian Wells CA 92210, USA

Iaconio, Frank — Auto Racing Driver
250 US Highway 206, Flanders NJ 07836, USA

Iafrate, Al A — Ice Hockey Player
17320 Fairfield St, Livonia MI 48152, USA

Ian, Janis — Singer, Songwriter
PO Box 150099, Nashville TN 37215, USA

Iannetta, Christopher D (Chris) — Baseball Player
7422 E 7th Ave, #14, Denver CO 80230, USA

Iassonga, Daniel (Dan) — Baseball Umpire
1501 Bailey Farm Court SW, Marietta GA 30064, USA

Iavarone, Michael — Thoroughbred Racing Executive
I E A H Stables, 595 Stewart Ave, #450, Garden City NY 11530, USA

Iavaroni, Marcus J (Marc) — Basketball Player, Coach
8129 N Via de Lago, Scottsdale AZ 85258, USA

Ibaka, Serge J — Basketball Player
Oklahoma City Thunder, 211 N Robinson Ave, #300, Oklahoma City OK 73102 USA

Ibanez, Raul J — Baseball Player
210 Quisset Lane, Wayne PA 19087, USA

Ibbetson, Bruce — Rowing Athlete
424 San Bernardino Ave, Newport Beach CA 92663, USA

Ibragimov, Sultan — Boxer
Warrior's Boxing Promotions, 5397 Orange Dr, #202, Davie FL 33314, USA

Ibrahim, Abdullah, (Dollar Brand) — Jazz Pianist, Composer
Brad Simon Organization, 155 W 46th St, #500, New York NY 10036 USA

Icahn, Carl C — Businessman
Icahn Co, 445 Hamilton Ave, #1210, White Plains NY 10601, USA

Ice Cube — Rap Artist, Actor, Director
Cube Vision, 9000 W Sunset Blvd, West Hollywood CA 90069, USA

Ice T — Rap Artist, Actor
Jorge Hinojosa Mgmt, 6606 Maryland Dr, Los Angeles CA 90048, USA

Ickx, Jacques B (Jacky) — Auto Racing Driver
171 Chaussee de la Hulpe, 1170 Brussels, Belgium

Idle, Eric — Actor, Comedian (Monty Python)
Mayday Mgmt, 68A Delancey St, Camden Town, London NW1 7RY, England

Idol, Billy — Singer, Songwriter
East End Mgmt, 8209 Melrose Ave, #200, Los Angeles CA 90046, USA

Idowu, Phillips — Track Athlete
Belgrave Harriers, Denmark Road, London SW19 4PG, England

Idziak, Slawomir — Cinematographer
Ul Wazow 1-Z, Warsaw 01-986, Poland

Ielemia, Apisai — Prime Minister, Tuvalu
Prime Minister's Office, Vaiaku, Funafuti, Tuvalu

Ifans, Rhys — Actor
Brillstein Entertainment Partners, 9150 Wilshire Blvd, #350, Beverly Hills CA 90212 USA

Ifill, Gwen — Commentator
Public Broadcasting System, 1320 Braddock Place, Alexandria VA 22314 USA

Iger, Robert A — Businessman
Walt Disney Co, 500 S Buena Vista St, Burbank CA 91521, USA

Iginla, Jarome A A — Ice Hockey Player
Newport Sports, 601-201 City Centre Dr, Mississauga ON L58 2T4, Canada

Iglesias, Enrique — Singer
2345 Lake Ave, Sunset Isle 3, Miami Beach FL 33140, USA

Iglesias, Gabriel — Comedian, Actor
Creative Artists Agency, 2000 Ave of Stars, #100, Los Angeles CA 90067 USA

Iglesias, Julio — Singer
1177 Kane Concourse, Bay Harbor Islands FL 33154, USA

Iglesias, Julio, Jr — Singer, Songwriter
Mathews Mgmt, 8730 Sunset Blvd, #200, Los Angeles CA 90069, USA

Ignarro, Louis J — Nobel Medicine Laureate
C H A, 10833 La Conte Ave, Los Angeles CA 90095, USA

Ignasiak, Michael J (Mike) — Baseball Player
8473 Dixie Highway, Ira MI 48023, USA

Ignatius Zakka I Iwas, Patriarch — Religious Leader
Syrian Orthodox Patriarchate, Bab Touma, BP 914, Damascus, Syria

Ignatius, David — Writer, Columnist
W W Norton, 500 5th Ave, #600, New York NY 10110 USA

Ignatius, Paul R — Government Official
2700 Calvert St NW, #416, Washington DC 20008, USA

Ignizo, Mildred — Bowler
241 Shore Acres Dr, Rochester NY 14612, USA

Iguodala, Andre T — Basketball Player
1111 Riverview Lane, West Conshohocken PA 19428, USA

Igwebuike, Donald A — Football Player
1118 Tumlin Court, Lawrenceville GA 30045, USA

Iha, James Y — Guitarist (Smashing Pumpkins)
Spivak Sobol Entertainment, 11845 W Olympic Blvd, #1125, Los Angeles CA 90064, USA

Ihara, Michio — Sculptor
63 Wood St, Concord MA 01742, USA

Ihle, Andreas — Canoeing Athlete
Wiesenweg 5, 39114 Magedburg, Germany

Ikeda, Daisaku — Religious Leader, Philosopher
Soka Gakkai, 32 Shinanomachi, Shinjuku, Tokyo 160 8583, Japan

Ikeda, Kazuyosi — Physicist, Writer
Nisi 7-7-11, Aomadani Minoo-si, Osaka 562 0023, Japan

Ikenberry, Stanley O — Educator
University of Illinois, Education Dept, 1310 S 6th St, Champaign IL 61820, USA

Ikola, Willard — Ice Hockey Player, Coach
5697 Green Circle Drive, #316, Hopkins MN 55343, USA

Iler, Robert B/W/R, 9100 Wilshire Blvd, #500W, Beverly Hills CA 90212 USA	Actor
Iles, Greg Creative Artists Agency, 2000 Ave of Stars, #100, Los Angeles CA 90067 USA	Writer
Ilg, Raymond P 1830 Fountain Dr, #1505, Reston VA 20190, USA	Navy Admiral
Ilgauskas, Zydrunas 32654 Lake Road, Avon Lake OH 44012, USA	Basketball Player
Iliff, Peter Don Buchwald/Fortitude, 6500 Wilshire Blvd, #2200, Los Angeles CA 90048 USA	Director, Writer
Ilitch, Michael (Mike) 23670 Woodlyne Dr, Bingham Farms MI 48025, USA	Ice Hockey, Baseball Executive
Ilken, Tunch A 2610 Cedarvue Dr, Pittsburgh PA 15241, USA	Football Player
Ilonzeh, Annie Vincent Cirrincione Assoc, 1516 N Fairfax Ave, Los Angeles CA 90046 USA	Actress
Ilunga-Mbenga, Didier (D J) Los Angeles Lakers, Staples Center, 1111 S Figueroa St, Los Angeles CA 90015 USA	Basketball Player
Ilves, Toomas Hendrik President's Office, 39 Av Weizenbergi, 15050 Tallinn, Estonia	President, Estonia
Imada, Ryuji 16204 Sierra de Avila, Tampa FL 33613, USA	Golfer
Imai, Nobuko Irene Witmer Mgmt, Leidsegracht 42, 1016 CM Amsterdam, Netherlands	Concert Violist
Iman Essex House, 160 Central Park S, New York NY 10019, USA	Model, Actress
Iman, Chanel Beatrice International Models, Via Vincenzo Monti 47, 20123 Milan, Italy	Model
Imants, Marcis Bamberger Symphony Orchestra, Postfach 110146, 96029 Bamberger, Germany	Conductor
Imbruglia, Natalie Merlin Elite, Hammersmith Studios, 55 Yelman Road, London W6 8JF, England	Singer, Songwriter, Actress
Imhoff, Darrall T 3637 Sterling Woods Dr, Eugene OR 97408, USA	Basketball Player
Imhoff, Gary Samantha Group, 300 S Raymond Ave, Pasadena CA 91105, USA	Actor
Immelman, Trevor J 5174 Vardon Dr, Windermere FL 34786, USA	Golfer
Immelt, Jeffrey (Jeff) General Electric Co, 3135 Easton Turnpike, Fairfield CT 06828, USA	Businessman
Imperioli, Michael T N T Entertainment Group, 648 Broadway, #1002, New York NY 10012, USA	Actor
Imrie, Celia Rights House, 34-43 Russell St, London WC2B 5HA, England	Actress
Imus, Don I C M Partners, 10250 Constellation Blvd, #900, Los Angeles CA 90067 USA	Actor
In Kyung Kim Ladies Pro Golf Assn, 100 International Golf Dr, Daytona Beach FL 32124 USA	Golfer
Inaba, Carrie Ann EnterMediArts, 800 S Main St, #200, Burbank CA 91506, USA	Dancer, Choreographer, Singer
Inamori, Kazuo R D D I Corp, 3-22 Nishi-Shinjuku, Shinjuku, Tokyo 163 8003, Japan	Businessman
Inarritu, Alejandro Gonzalez Gang Tyrer Ramer, 132 S Rodeo Dr, #306, Beverly Hills CA 90212 USA	Director
Inbal, Eliahu Askonas Holt, Lincoln House, 300 High Holborn, London WC1V 7JH, England	Conductor
Incandela, Joseph (Joe) University of California, Physics Dept, Broida Hall, Santa Barbara CA 93106, USA	Particle Physicist
Incaviglia, Peter J (Pete) PO Box 1047, Argyle TX 76226, USA	Baseball Player
Incognito, Richard D (Richie) 3231 NW 125th Ave, Sunrise FL 33323, USA	Football Player
Indelicato, Mark Station 3, 8522 National Blvd, #108, Culver City CA 90232, USA	Actor
India Granada Entertainment, 480 NE 30th St, #101, Miami FL 33137, USA	Singer
India.Arie Creative Artists Agency, 2000 Ave of Stars, #100, Los Angeles CA 90067 USA	Singer, Guitarist, Songwriter
Indiana, Robert Star of Hop, Press Box 464, Vinalhaven ME 04863, USA	Artist
Indovina, Lorenza Carol Levi Mgmt, Via G Pisanelli 2, 00196 Rome, Italy	Actress
Indurain, Miguel Avenida Villava, 31013 Pamplona, Navarra, Spain	Cyclist
Infante, Lindy 6780 A1A S, Saint Augustine FL 32080, USA	Football Coach
Infante, Omar R Detroit Tigers, Comerica Park, 2100 Woodward Ave, Detroit MI 48201 USA	Baseball Player
Ingarfield, Earl, Sr 1715 Lakehill Crescent S, Lethbridge AB T1K 3R2, Canada	Ice Hockey Player
Inge, C Brandon 5003 Windsong Trail, Salem SC 29676, USA	Baseball Player
Ingels, Marty 4531 Noeline Way, Encino CA 91436, USA	Actor, Comedian
Ingelsby, Tom 1507 Canterbury Lane, Berwyn PA 19312, USA	Basketball Player
Ingersoll, Andrew P California Institute of Technology, Geological/Planetary Sciences Division, Pasadena CA 91125, USA	Meteorologist, Climatologist
Inghram, Mark G PO Box 771721, Eagle River AK 99577, USA	Physicist
Ingle, Doug Entertainment Services International, 6400 Pleasant Park Dr, Chanhassen MN 55317 USA	Singer, Keyboardist (Iron Butterfly)
Ingman, Einar H, Jr W4053 N Silver Lake Road, Irma WI 54442, USA	Korean War Army Hero (CMH)
Ingraham, Laura Sirius XM Radio, 1221 Ave of Americas, New York NY 10020, USA	Commentator

Ingram, Alfred — Baseball Player
983 Oakland Dr. Atlanta GA 30315, USA
Ingram, Brian D — Football Player
4805 White Oak Path, Stone Mountain GA 30088, USA
Ingram, Jack — Auto Racing Driver
699 Brevard Road, Asheville NC 28806, USA
Ingram, James — Singer, Songwriter
867 S Muirfield Road, Los Angeles CA 90005, USA
Ingram, Marv — Singer (Four Preps)
4339 Ensenada Dr, Woodland Hills CA 91364, USA
Ingram, Melvin — Football Player
San Diego Chargers, 4020 Murphy Canyon Road, San Diego CA 92123 USA
Ingram, Preston — Baseball Player
174 Douglas St SE, Atlanta GA 30317, USA
Ingrassia, Paul J — Journalist
111 Division Ave, New Providence NJ 07974, USA
Inkeles, Alex — Sociologist
32 Plaza Dr, Berkeley CA 94705, USA
Inkster, Juli Simpson — Golfer
23140 Mora Glen Dr, Los Altos Hills CA 94024, USA
Inman, Bobby Ray — Navy Admiral, Government Official
Arboretum Plaza, 9442 N Capital of Texas Highway, #685, Austin TX 78759, USA
Inman, John S — Golfer
2210 Chase St, Durham NC 27707, USA
Inman, Joseph C (Joe), Jr — Golfer
3599 Tuckers Farm SE, Marietta GA 30067, USA
Innauer, Anton (Toni) — Ski Jumper, Coach
Steinbruckstr 8/II, 6024 Innsbruck, Austria
Innaurato, Albert F — Writer
325 W 22nd St, New York NY 10011, USA
Innes, Laura — Actress
Creative Artists Agency, 2000 Ave of Stars, #100, Los Angeles CA 90067 USA
Innis, Jeffrey D (Jeff) — Baseball Player
4920 Woodlong Lane, Cumming GA 30040, USA
Innis, Roy E A — Civil Rights Activist
817 Broadway, New York NY 10003, USA
Inogradov, Pavel — Cosmonaut
Cosmonaut Training Center, Star City, 141160 Zvezdny Gorodok, Moscow Oblast, Russia
Inoni, Ephraim — Prime Minister, Cameroon Republic
Palais de L'Unite, Rue de l'Exploratour, Yaounde, Cameroon
Inoue, Rena — Figure Skater
Lee Marshall Mgmt, 199 E Garfield Road, Aurora OH 44202, USA
Inoue, Shinya — Biologist, Photographer
Marine Biological Laboratory, 167 Water St, Woods Hole MA 02543, USA
Inouye, Daniel K — Senator, HI; WW II Army Hero (CMH)
300 Ala Moana Blvd, #7-212, Honolulu HI 96850, USA
Inouye, Lisa — Actress
Media Artists Group, 8222 Melrose Ave, #203, Los Angeles CA 90048 USA
Insalaco, Kim — Ice Hockey Player
USA Hockey, 1775 Bob Johnson Dr, Colorado Springs CO 80906 USA
Insko, Delmer M (Del) — Harness Racing Driver
2360 Fischer Road, South Beloit IL 61080, USA
Insley, Will — Artist
231 Bowery, New York NY 10002, USA
Inspectah Deck — Rap Artist (Wu-Tang Clan)
A&E Entertainment, 13280 NE Freeway, #F328, Houston TX 77040, USA
Insulza, Jose Miguel — Government Official, Chile
Organization of American States, 17th St & Constitution Ave, Washington DC 20006, USA
Intriligator, Michael D — Economist
140 Foxtail Dr, Santa Monica CA 90402, USA
Inui, Kumiko — Architect
Showa Women's University, 1-7 Taishide, Satagayaku, Tokyo 154 8533, Japan
Inzaghi, Filippo (Pippo) — Soccer Player
F C Milan, Via Filippo Turati 3, 20121 Milan, Italy
Inzko, Valentin — High Representative, Bosnia-Herzegovia
Emerika Bluma 1, 71000 Sarajevo, Bosnia-Herzegovina
Iommi, F Anthony (Tony) — Guitarist (Black Sabbath), Songwriter
Sharon Osborne Mgmt, 8899 Beverly Blvd, #905, West Hollywood CA 90048, USA
Iooss, Walter — Photographer
152 DeForest Road, Montauk NY 11954, USA
Iorg, Dane C — Baseball Player
5358 W Evergreen Circle, American Fork UT 84003, USA
Iorg, Garth R — Baseball Player
10635 Alameda Dr, Knoxville TN 37932, USA
Iovine, Vicki — Writer, Columnist, Model
Trident Media Group, 41 Madison Ave, #3600, New York NY 10010, USA
Ipcar, Dahlov — Illustrator, Artist, Writer
Thomas Crotty Frost Gully Gallery, 1159 US Route 1, Freeport ME 04032, USA
Iraheta, Allison — Singer
Jive Records, 137-39 W 25th St, #1100, New York NY 10001 USA
Irani, Ray R — Businessman
Occidental Petroleum, 10889 Wilshire Blvd, #1000, Los Angeles CA 90024, USA
Irbe, Arturs — Ice Hockey Player
10733 Trego Trail, Raleigh NC 27614, USA
Irby, Michael C — Actor
Greene Assoc, 1901 Ave of Stars, #130, Los Angeles CA 90067 USA
Iredale, Randle W — Architect
1151 W 8th Ave, Vancouver BC V6H 1C5, Canada
Ireland, Dan — Director, Producer, Writer
Gersh Agency, 9465 Wilshire Blvd, #600, Beverly Hills CA 90212 USA
Ireland, Julius W (Buck) — WW II Marine Corps Hero
4389 Malaai St, #324, Honolulu HI 96818, USA
Ireland, Kathy — Model, Actress
Guttman Assoc, 118 S Beverly Dr, #201, Beverly Hills CA 90212 USA
Ireland, Marin — Actress
I C M Partners, 10250 Constellation Blvd, #900, Los Angeles CA 90067 USA

Ireland, Patricia
Katz Kutter Haigler Assoc, 801 Pennsylvania Ave NW, #750, Washington DC 20004, USA — Association Executive

Irglova, Marketa
Billions Corp, 3522 W Armitage Ave, Chicago IL 60647 USA — Actress, Pianist, Songwriter

Irigoyen, Adam
Coast to Coast Talent, 3350 Barham Blvd, Los Angeles CA 90068 USA — Actor

Irimia, Gabriela
Concorde International, 101 Shepherds Bush Road, London W6 7LP, England — Singer (Cheeky Girls)

Irimia, Monica
Concorde International, 101 Shepherds Bush Road, London W6 7LP, England — Singer (Cheeky Girls)

Irina
Marilyn Model Agency, 32 Union Square E, #PH, New York NY 10003 USA — Model

Iris, Donnie
807 Darlington Road, Beaver Falls PA 15010, USA — Singer, Songwriter

Iron & Wine
Warner Bros Records, 3300 Warner Blvd, Burbank CA 91505 USA — Singer, Guitarist, Songwriter

Irons, Gerald D
30010 E Legends Trail Court, Spring TX 77386, USA — Football Player

Irons, Grant M
30010 E Legends Trail Court, Spring TX 77386, USA — Football Player

Irons, Jeremy
Ken McReddie Assoc, 11 Connaught Place, London W2 2ET, England — Actor

Ironside, Michael
Abrams Artists, 9200 W Sunset Blvd, #1125, West Hollywood CA 90069 USA — Actor

Irrera, Domenick J (Dom)
Don Buchwald/Fortitude, 6500 Wilshire Blvd, #2200, Los Angeles CA 90048 USA — Actor, Comedian

Irvan, V Earnest (Ernie)
9939 Troutman Road, Midland NC 28107, USA — Auto Racing Driver

Irvin, Cal
1311 Julian St, Greensboro NC 27406, USA — Baseball Player, Basketball Coach

Irvin, John
6 Lower Common South, London SW15 1BP, England — Director

Irvin, Kenneth P (Ken)
8151 Nesbit Ferry Road, Atlanta GA 30350, USA — Football Player

Irvin, LeRoy, Jr
2905 Ruby Dr, #C, Fullerton CA 92831, USA — Football Player

Irvin, Michael J
2339 Aberdeen Bend, Carrolton TX 75007, USA — Football Player, Sportscaster

Irvin, Monford M (Monte)
1815 Enclave Parkway, #6203, Houston TX 77077, USA — Baseball Player

Irvin, Sandora
San Antonio Silver Stars, 1 AT&T Center, San Antonio TX 78219 USA — Basketball Player

Irvine, Edmund (Eddie), Jr
Jaguar Racing, Browns Lane, Allesley Coventry CV5 9DR, England — Auto Racing Driver

Irvine, Edward A (Ted)
5-2727 Portage Ave, Winnipeg MB R3J 0R2, Canada — Ice Hockey Player

Irvine, Jeremy
Hatton McEwan, 3 Chocolate Studios, 7 Shepherdess Place, London N1 7LJ, England — Actor

Irving, Amy
TalentWorks, 3500 W Olive Ave, #1400, Burbank CA 91505 USA — Actress

Irving, John W
Turnbull Agency, PO Box 757, Dorset VT 05251, USA — Writer

Irving, K Stuart (Stu)
93 Hart St, Beverly MA 01915, USA — Ice Hockey Player

Irving, Kyrie A
Cleveland Cavaliers, Gund Arena, 1 Center Court, Cleveland OH 44115 USA — Basketball Player

Irving, Paul H
Manatt Phelps Phillips, 11355 W Olympic Blvd, #20, Los Angeles CA 90064, USA — Attorney

Irwin, Elaine
Innovative Artists, 1505 10th St, Santa Monica CA 90401 USA — Model

Irwin, Hale S
5720 N Saguaro Road, Paradise Valley AZ 85253, USA — Golfer

Irwin, Heath S
5530 N 115th St, Longmont CO 80504, USA — Football Player

Irwin, Jay
Artists Agency, 1180 S Beverly Dr, #301, Los Angeles CA 90035 USA — Actor, Writer

Irwin, Jennifer
Gersh Agency, 9465 Wilshire Blvd, #600, Beverly Hills CA 90212 USA — Actress

Irwin, Mark
1260 Coast Village Circle, Santa Barbara CA 93108, USA — Cinematographer

Irwin, Paul G
Humane Society of the United States, PO Box 9100, League City TX 77574, USA — Association Executive

Irwin, Robert W
501 S Beverly Dr, Beverly Hills CA 90212, USA — Artist

Irwin, Timothy E (Tim)
5512 River Point Cove Road, Knoxville TN 37919, USA — Football Player

Irwin, Tom, II
Don Buchwald/Fortitude, 6500 Wilshire Blvd, #2200, Los Angeles CA 90048 USA — Actor

Irwin, William M (Bill)
20 1st Ave, Nyack NY 10960, USA — Clown, Actor

Isaac, Oscar
United Talent Agency, 9336 Civic Center Dr, Beverly Hills CA 90210 USA — Actor

Isaacks, Levie C
6634 Sunnyslope Ave, Van Nuys CA 91401, USA — Cinematographer

Isaacs, Jason
Gersh Agency, 9465 Wilshire Blvd, #600, Beverly Hills CA 90212 USA — Actor

Isaacs, Jeremy I
Royal Opera House, Covent Garden, Bow St, London WC2E 9DD, England — Director

Isaacs, Levie
Innovative Artists, 1505 10th St, Santa Monica CA 90401 USA — Cinematographer

Isaacs, Susan
Harper Collins Publishers, 10 E 53rd St, Cellar 2, New York NY 10022, USA — Writer

Isaacson, Walter S
I C M Partners, 10250 Constellation Blvd, #900, Los Angeles CA 90067 USA — Journalist

Isaak, Chris
I F A Talent Agency, 8730 W Sunset Blvd, #490, West Hollywood CA 90069 USA — Singer, Songwriter, Actor

Isacco, Jennifer — Bobsled Athlete
Olympic Committee, Foro Italico, Largo Lauro de Bosis 15, 00135 Rome, Italy
Isacksen, Peter — Actor
Sutton-Barth Vennari, 145 S Fairfax Ave, #310, Los Angeles CA 90036 USA
Isaksson, Irma Sara — Singer, Songwriter
United Stage Artists, PO Box 11029, 100 61, Stockholm, Sweden
Isbell, Jason — Singer, Guitarist, Songwriter
Ground Control Touring, 20 Jay St, #826, Brooklyn NY 11201 USA
Isbell, Stewart — Photographer
Retna, 24 W 25th St, #1200, New York NY 10010, USA
Isbin, Sharon — Concert Guitarist
Columbia Artists Mgmt Inc, 1790 Broadway, #702, New York NY 10019 USA
Isbister, Brad — Ice Hockey Player
1818 Lakeview Dr, Fort Wayne IN 46808, USA
Iscove, Robert (Rob) — Director
Course Mgmt, 15159 Greenleaf St, Sherman Oaks CA 91403, USA
Isdell, E Neville — Businessman
International Business Leaders Forum, 15 Cornwall Terrace, London NW1 4QP, England
Isham, Mark — Composer
23679 Calabasas Road, #522, Calabasas CA 91302, USA
Ishibashi, Brittany — Actress
Abrams Artists, 9200 W Sunset Blvd, #1125, West Hollywood CA 90069 USA
Ishida, Jim — Actor
871 N Vail Ave, Montebello CA 90640, USA
Ishida, Nobuhiro — Boxer
Golden Boy Promotions, 626 Wilshire Blvd, #350, Los Angeles CA 90017 USA
Ishiguro, Kazuo — Writer
Rogers Coleridge White, 20 Powis Mews, London W11 1JN, England
Ishii, Ken — Composer
3-5-12 Yakumo, Meguroku, Tokyo 152 0023, Japan
Ishikawa, Shigeru — Economist
19-8-4 Chome Kugayama, Suginamiku, Tokyo 168 0082, Japan
Ishikawa, Travis T — Baseball Player
12 Narcissus Court, Danville CA 94506, USA
Ishimaru, Akira — Electrical Engineer
2913 165th Place NE, Bellevue WA 98008, USA
Ishizaka, Kimishige — Allergist
Allergy/Immunology Institute, 11149 N Torrey Pines Road, La Jolla CA 92037, USA
Ishizaka, Teruko — Allergist
Good Samaritan Hospital, 5601 Loch Raven Blvd, Baltimore MD 21239, USA
Isikoff, Michael — Writer, Journalist
6209 Meadowbrook Lane, Chevy Chase MD 20815, USA
Isinbayeva, Yelena G — Track Athlete
Podium Group, 3 Ave de Grande Bretagne, 98000 Monte Carlo, Monaco
Iskander, Fazil A — Writer
Leningradski Prosp Korp 2, #67, 125040 Moscow, Russia
Isler, Jennifer (J J) — Yachtswoman
6828 Country Club Dr, La Jolla CA 92037, USA
Isley, Ronald (Ron) — Singer (Isley Brothers)
Ron Weisner Mgmt, PO Box 261640, Encino CA 91426, USA
Ismael, Gerard — Actor
Agents Associes, 201 Rue du Faubourg Saint Honore, 75008 Paris, France
Ismail, Qadry R — Football Player
1506 Sunningdale Way, Bel Air MD 21015, USA
Ismail, Raghib R (Rocket) — Football Player
7423 Marigold Dr, Irving TX 75063, USA
Isner, John — Tennis Player
5700 Saddlebrook Way, Wesley Chapel FL 33543, USA
Ison, Christopher J — Journalist
Minneapolis-Saint Paul Star Tribune, 425 Portland Ave, Minneapolis MN 55488, USA
Isozaki, Arata — Architect
5-12-9 Akasaka, Minatoku, Tokyo 107 0052, Japan
Israel, Steven D (Steve) — Football Player
14039 Lissadell Circle, Charlotte NC 28277, USA
Israel, Werner — Physicist
2323 Hamiota St, #401, Victoria BC V8R 2N1, Canada
Isringhausen, Jason D — Baseball Player
550 E Lake Dr, Tarpon Springs FL 34688, USA
Issel, Daniel P (Dan) — Basketball Player, Coach, Executive
325 E Palace Ave, Santa Fe NM 87501, USA
Isserlis, Steven — Concert Cellist
I M G Artists, Hogarth Business Park, Chiswick, London W4 2TH, England
Italeli, Iakoba T — Governor General, Tuvalu
Governor General's Office, Government House, Vaiaku, Funafuti, Tuvalu
Itin, Ilya — Concert Pianist
Jonathan Wentworth Assoc, 10 Fiske Place, #530, Mount Vernon NY 10550 USA
Ito, Lance — Judge
Los Angeles Superior Court, 210 W Temple St, #M6, Los Angeles CA 90012, USA
Ito, Midori — Figure Skater
Prince Hotel Skate Club, 3-4 Shin Yokohama, Kanagawa 222 8533, Japan
Ito, Robert — Actor
843 N Sycamore Ave, Los Angeles CA 90038, USA
Ito, Takenobu — Businessman
Honda Motor Co, 2-1-1 Minami-Aoyama, Minatoku, Tokyo 107 8556, Japan
Itzin, Gregory — Actor
S M S Talent, 8383 Wilshire Blvd, #230, Beverly Hills CA 90211 USA
Iu, Carolyn — Interior Designer
Iu & Bibliowicz, 57 E 11th St, #700, New York NY 10003, USA
Ivanchenkov, Aleksandr S — Cosmonaut
Cosmonaut Training Center, Star City, 141160 Zvezdny Gorodok, Moscow Oblast, Russia
Ivanek, Zeljko — Actor
Leading Artists, 145 W 45th St, #1000, New York NY 10036, USA
Ivanisevic, Goran — Tennis Player
Alijnoviceva 28, 58000 Split, Serbia
Ivanishvili, Bidzina — President, Georgia
President's Office, 1 M Abdushelishvili St, 103 Tbilisi, Georgia

Isacco - Ivanishvili

Ivanov, Georgi I
Air Sofia Ltd, Sofia Airport, 1 Brussels Blvd, 1540 Sofia, Bulgaria
Cosmonaut, Bulgaria

Ivanov, Gjorge
President's Office, Villa Vodno, Aco Karamanov BB, 1000 Skopje, Macedonia
President, Macedonia

Ivanov, Igor S
Moscow State Institute, Vernadskogo Prospekt 76, 119454 Moscow, Russia
Government Official, Russia

Ivanov, Kalina
Marsh-Best Assoc, 9150 Wilshire Blvd, #220, Beverly Hills CA 90212 USA
Actress, Designer, Art Director

Ivanov, Vyacheslav V
University of California, Slavic Languages Dept, Los Angeles CA 90024, USA
Philologist, Linguist

Ivanovic, Ana
D H Mgmt, Holeestra 86, 4054 Basel, Switzerland
Tennis Player

Ivanov-Smolensky, Kirill
Octagon Worldwide, 1751 Pinnacle Dr, #1500, McLean VA 22102 USA
Tennis Player

Ivar, Stan
Borinstein Oreck Bogart, 3172 Dona Susana Dr, Studio City CA 91604 USA
Actor

Ivens, Terri
Paul Kohner, 9300 Wilshire Blvd, #555, Beverly Hills CA 90212 USA
Actress

Iveri, Tamar
I M G Artists, Hogarth Business Park, Chiswick, London W4 2TH, England
Opera Singer

Ivers, Eileen
Roots Agency, 177 Woodland Ave, Westwood NJ 07675, USA
Fiddler

Iversen, Leslie M
Oxford University, Pharmacology Dept, Oxford OX1 3QT, England
Pharmacologist

Iverson, Allen
308 Harper Dr, #210, Moorestown NJ 8057, USA
Basketball Player

Iverson, Becky
4723 Poplar Creek Dr, Madison WI 53718, USA
Golfer

Ivery, Eddie Lee
1080 Wrightsboro Road, Thomson GA 30824, USA
Football Player

Ivey, Dana
Paradigm Agency, 360 N Crescent Dr, North Building, Beverly Hills CA 90210 USA
Actress

Ivey, James B (Jim)
5840 Dahlia Dr, #7, Orlando FL 32807, USA
Editorial Cartoonist

Ivey, Judith
Abrams Artists, 9200 W Sunset Blvd, #1125, West Hollywood CA 90069 USA
Actress

Ivey, Royal T
6080 Indian Wood Circle SE, Mableton GA 30126, USA
Basketball Player

Ivey, Susan
Reynolds American, PO Box 2990, Winston-Salem NC 27102, USA
Businesswoman

Ivie, Michael W (Mike)
PO Box 1565, Loganville GA 30052, USA
Baseball Player

Ivins, Marsha S
2811 Timber Briar Circle, Houston TX 77059, USA
Astronaut

Ivins, Michael L
World's Fair Mgmt, 1208 Chowning Ave, Edmond OK 73034, USA
Bassist, Keyboardist (Flaming Lips)

Ivory, Horace O
5321 Diaz Ave, Fort Worth TX 76107, USA
Football Player

Ivory, James (Sap)
3026 Wenonah Park Road SW, Birmingham AL 35211, USA
Baseball Player

Ivory, James F
18 Patroon St, Claverack NY 12513, USA
Director, Producer

Ivosev, Aleksandra
Sluzbeni put Zavoda 5, Careva Cuprija, 11030 Belgrade, Serbia
Markswoman

Ivy Queen
I C M Partners, 10250 Constellation Blvd, #900, Los Angeles CA 90067 USA
Reggaeton, Rap Artist, Songwriter

Ivy, Corey T
8412 Seven Coves Court, Tampa FL 33634, USA
Football Player

Iwabuchi, Mana
Football Assn, 3-10-15 Hongo, Bunkyoku, Tokyo 113 0033 Japan
Soccer Player

Iwamura, Akinori
623 Saxony Road, Saint Petersburg FL 33716, USA
Baseball Player

Iwan, Dafydd
Carrog, Rhos-Bach, Caeathro, Caernarfon, Gwynedd LL55 2TF, Wales
Singer, Songwriter

Iwaniec, Henryk
Rutgers State University, Mathematics Dept, New Brunswick NJ 08903, USA
Mathematician

Iwashimizu, Azusa
Football Assn, 3-10-15 Hongo, Bunkyoku, Tokyo 113 0033 Japan
Soccer Player

Iwata, Satoru
Nintendo, 11-1 Kamitoba Hokotatecho, Minamiku, Kyoto 601 8501, Japan
Businessman

Iwatani, Toru
Tokyo Polytechnic University, 1583 Iiyama, Atsugi Kanagawa 243 0297, Japan
Computer Game Inventor

Iwerks, Donald W
Iwerks Entertainment, 4520 W Valerio St, Burbank CA 91505, USA
Businessman

Iwuoma, Chidi
4616 Benton St, Antioch CA 94531, USA
Football Player

Izambard, Sebastien
Octagon, 81-83 Fulham High St, London SW6 3JW, England
Singer (Il Divo)

Izo, George W
PO Box 325, Alexandria VA 22313, USA
Football Player

Izon, David
Stanley Levin, 226 Palafox Place, Pensacola FL 32502, USA
Boxer

Izturis, Cesar D
375 Douglas Ave, Clearwater FL 33755, USA
Baseball Player

Izzard, Eddie
United Talent Agency, 9336 Civic Center Dr, Beverly Hills CA 90210 USA
Actor, Comedian

Izzo, Lawrence A (Larry)
1 Snowbird Place, Spring TX 77381, USA
Football Player

Izzo, Tom
Michigan State University, Athletic Dept, Breslin Center, East Lansing MI 48824, USA
Basketball Coach

J Splif — Singer (Far East Movement)
Stampede Mgmt, 12530 Beatrice St, Los Angeles CA 90066, USA

Ja Rule — Pop, Rap Artist; Actor
Universal Media Artists, 8222 Melrose Ave, #203, Los Angeles CA 90048, USA

Jaafari, Ibrahim al- — Prime Minister, Iraq
Parliament, Karradat Mariam, Baghdad, Iraq

Jaar, Alfredo — Photographer, Sculptor, Filmmaker
252 Lafayette St, #3G, New York NY 10012, USA

Jablonski, Joseph — Concert Pianist
Carlscrona Chamber Music Festival, Verstorp Skarfva, 371 91 Karlskrona, Sweden

Jablonski, Patrick D (Pat) — Ice Hockey Player
18814 Wimbledon Circle, Lutz FL 33558, USA

Jabs, Matthias — Guitarist
M J Guitars, Pariser Str 32, 81667 Munich, Germany

Jace, Michael — Actor
Blueprint Mgmt, 5670 Wilshire Blvd, #2525, Los Angeles CA 90036, USA

Jack, Jarrett M — Basketball Player
Golden State Warriors, 1011 Broadway, Oakland CA 94605 USA

Jacke, Christopher L (Chris) — Football Player
1158 S Taylor St, #C, Green Bay WI 54304, USA

Jackee — Actress
Metropolitan Talent Agency, 7020 La Presa Dr, Los Angeles CA 90068 USA

Jackendoff, Ray S — Language Educator
Brandies University, Linguistics & Cognitive Dept, Waltham MA 02254, USA

Jackiw, Roman W — Physicist
Massachusetts Institute of Technology, Physics Dept, Cambridge MA 02139, USA

Jackiw, Stefan — Concert Violinist
Opus 3 Artists, 470 Park Ave S, #900N, New York NY 10016 USA

Jacklin, Bill — Artist
62 Bank St, New York NY 10014, USA

Jacklin, Tony — Golfer, Sportscaster
1175 51st St W, Bradenton FL 34209, USA

Jackman, Hugh — Actor, Singer, Dancer
W M E Entertainment, 9601 Wilshire Blvd, #300, Beverly Hills CA 90210 USA

Jackson Hoye, Rose — Actress
Haldeman Business Mgmt, 1137 2nd St, #119, Santa Monica CA 90403, USA

Jackson Nelson, Marjorie — Track Athlete
Athletics Australia, 431 Saint Kilda Road, Melbourne VIC 3004, Australia

Jackson, Ed, Jr — Architect
ArchD Consulting, PO Box 1345, Fairfax VA 22038

Jackson, Alan — Singer, Guitarist, Songwriter
Creative Artists Agency, 2000 Ave of Stars, #100, Los Angeles CA 90067 USA

Jackson, Alfred — Football Player
1811 Kirby Dr, Houston TX 77019, USA

Jackson, Alvin N (Al) — Baseball Player
3221 SE Morningside Blvd, Port Saint Lucie FL 34952, USA

Jackson, Andrea — Actress
Daily Buzz, 34 Skyline Dr, Lake Mary FL 32746, USA

Jackson, Anne — Actress
TalentWorks, 3500 W Olive Ave, #1400, Burbank CA 91505 USA

Jackson, Arthur J — WW II Marine Corps Hero (CMH)
1290 E Spring Court, Boise ID 83712, USA

Jackson, Barry — Actor
Angel & Frances, 12 D'Arblay St, London W1F 8DU, England

Jackson, Betty — Fashion Designer
Betty Jackson Ltd, 1 Netherwood Place, London W14 0BW, England

Jackson, Bobby — Basketball Player
Houston Rockets, 1730 Jefferson St, Houston TX 77003 USA

Jackson, Brandon T — Actor
Class Clown Entertainment, 14622 Ventura Blvd, #1002, Sherman Oaks CA 91403, USA

Jackson, Calvin B — Football Player
250 SW 28th Terrace, Fort Lauderdale FL 33312, USA

Jackson, Charles L (Chuck) — Baseball Player
15821 SE 175th Place, Renton WA 98058, USA

Jackson, Charles M — Football Player
PO Box 888285, Atlanta GA 30356, USA

Jackson, Cheyenne — Actor
Schiff Co, 8440 Warner Dr, #B1, Culver City CA 90232 USA

Jackson, Chuck — Singer
Universal Attractions, 135 W 26th St, #1200, New York NY 10001 USA

Jackson, Colin R — Track Athlete
4 Jackson Close, Rhoose, Vale of Glamorgan CF62 3DQ, England

Jackson, Danny L — Baseball Player
16332 Larsen St, Overland Park KS 66062, USA

Jackson, Darrell L — Football Player
Darrell Jackson Family Foundation, 720 E Fletcher Ave, #202, Tampa FL 33612, USA

Jackson, Darrell P — Baseball Player
PO Box 4424, Downey CA 90241, USA

Jackson, Darrin J — Baseball Player
432 E Mead Dr, Chandler AZ 85249, USA

Jackson, DeSean — Football Player
Philadelphia Eagles, 1 Novacare Way, Philadelphia PA 19145 USA

Jackson, Earnest (Ernie) — Football Player
938 Pisgah N, Eads TN 38028, USA

Jackson, Eddie — Bowler
3961 Glenmore Ave, Cincinnati OH 45211, USA

Jackson, Edwin — Baseball Player
6955 Setter Dr, Columbus GA 31909, USA

Jackson, Elly — Singer, Keyboardist (La Roux)
Beatnik Public Relations, 5 Little Portland St, London W1W 7JD, England

Jackson, Eric (E J) — Canoeing Athlete
Jackson Kayak, 325 Iris Dr, Sparta TN 38583, USA

Jackson, Francis A — Concert Organist, Composer
Nether Garth, East Acklam, Malton North Yorkshire YO17 9RG, England

Jackson, Frank H — Football Player
2812 Boll St, Dallas TX 7504, USA

Jackson, Freddie — Singer, Songwriter
Orpheus, 630 9th Ave, #1101, New York NY 10036, USA
Jackson, Gildart — Actor
Innovative Artists, 1505 10th St, Santa Monica CA 90401 USA
Jackson, Glenda — Actress
Crouch Assoc, 9-15 Neal St, London WC2H 9PF, England
Jackson, Grady O — Football Player
PO Box 841, Braselton GA 30517, USA
Jackson, Grant D — Baseball Player
212 Mesa Circle, Pittsburgh PA 15241, USA
Jackson, Harold — Journalist
57 Fox Hollow Lane, Sewell NJ 08080, USA
Jackson, Harold L — Football Player, Coach
6144 Flight Ave, Los Angeles CA 90056, USA
Jackson, James A (Jim) — Basketball Player
17827 Windflower Way, Dallas TX 75252, USA
Jackson, Janet — Singer, Actress, Dancer
Guttman Assoc, 118 S Beverly Dr, #201, Beverly Hills CA 90212 USA
Jackson, Jaren — Basketball Player
16813 Hoffman Manor Dr, Silver Spring MD 20905, USA
Jackson, Javon — Jazz Saxophonist
Palmetto Records, 67 Hill Road, Redding CT 06896, USA
Jackson, Jeff — Basketball Coach
Furman University, Athletic Dept, Greenville SC 29613, USA
Jackson, Jeff — Ice Hockey Player
1119 Parkview Dr, Griffin GA 30224, USA
Jackson, Jeremy — Actor
Mary Grady Agency, 269 S Beverly Dr, #1088, Beverly Hills CA 90212 USA
Jackson, Jermaine — Singer, Guitarist, Songwriter
468 N Camden Dr, #200, Beverly Hills CA 90210, USA
Jackson, Jesse L — Civil Rights Activist, Evangelist
Operation Push, 930 E 50th St, Chicago IL 60615, USA
Jackson, Joanne — Swimmer
Nova Centurion S C, Beechdale Road, Bilborough, Nottingham NG8 3LL, England
Jackson, Joe — Singer, Pianist, Songwriter
Agency Group Ltd, 142 W 57th St, #600, New York NY 10019 USA
Jackson, Joe M — Vietnam War Air Force Hero (CMH)
25320 38th Ave S, Kent WA 98032, USA
Jackson, John — Baseball Player
PO Box 898, Hodge LA 71247, USA
Jackson, John — Football Player
8183 Alpine Aster Court, Liberty Township OH 45044, USA
Jackson, John David — Boxer
1022 S State St, Tacoma WA 98405, USA
Jackson, Jonathan — Actor
One Entertainment, 9220 Sunset Blvd, #306, Los Angeles CA 90069 USA
Jackson, Joshua — Actor
Creative Artists Agency, 2000 Ave of Stars, #100, Los Angeles CA 90067 USA
Jackson, Julian — Boxer
Sugar Estate Branc, PO Box 10246, Charlotte Amalie VI 00801, USA
Jackson, Kate — Actress
Greater Talent Network, 437 5th Ave, #700, New York NY 10016, USA
Jackson, Keith J — Football Player
PO Box 241695, Little Rock AR 72223, USA
Jackson, Keith M — Sportscaster
ABC-TV, Sports Dept, 77 W 66th St, New York NY 10023 USA
Jackson, Kenneth B (Ken) — Baseball Player
PO Box 613, Waskom TX 75692, USA
Jackson, Kevin — Freestyle Wrestler
7215 Montarbor Dr, Colorado Springs CO 80918, USA
Jackson, Kirby — Football Player
2301 Cameron Dr, Buford GA 30518, USA
Jackson, Larron D — Football Player
20000 Mitchell Place, #56, Denver CO 80249, USA
Jackson, Larry R — Labor Leader
Grain Millers Federation, 14115 Lincoln St NE, #200, Andover MN 55304, USA
Jackson, LaToya — Singer, Model
Chuck Jones Public Relations, 150 W 51st, #802, New York NY 10019, USA
Jackson, Lauren — Basketball Player
Seattle Storm, Key Arena, 351 Elliott Ave W, #500, Seattle WA 98119 USA
Jackson, Lillian — Baseball Player
1050 W Camino Velesquez, Green Valley AZ 85622, USA
Jackson, Lisa — Writer
Signet Books, 375 Hudson St, New York NY 10014 USA
Jackson, Lisa P — Government Official
Environmental Protection Agency, 1200 Pennsylvania NW, Washington DC 20004, USA
Jackson, Lucious B (Luke) — Basketball Player
4580 Cartwright St, Beaumont TX 77707, USA
Jackson, Luke R — Basketball Player
7711 County Road 511, Rosharon TX 77583, USA
Jackson, Mannie — Basketball Player, Executive
Harlem Globetrotters, 400 E Van Buren, #300, Phoenix AZ 85004, USA
Jackson, Mark A — Basketball Player, Coach
25548 Kingston Court, Calabasses CA 91302, USA
Jackson, Mark A — Football Player
4351 Flandes St, Las Vegas NV 89121, USA
Jackson, Marlin T — Football Player
Philadelphia Eagles, 1 Novacare Way, Philadelphia PA 19145 USA
Jackson, Mary Ann — Actress
30108 Village 30, #30, Camarillo CA 93012, USA
Jackson, Matthew Day — Artist
Hauser & Wirth, 32 E 69th St, New York NY 10021, USA
Jackson, Mel — Actor
101 E 119th St, #2D, New York NY 10035, USA
Jackson, Melvin (Mel), Jr — Football Player
4345 Enoro Dr, Los Angeles CA 90008, USA

Jackson, Mervin P (Merv) — Basketball Player
16638 Kildare Court, Tinley Park IL 60477, USA
Jackson, Michael A — Football Player
PO Box 473, Tangiaphoa LA 70465, USA
Jackson, Michael R (Mike) — Baseball Player
17214 Oak Dale Dr, Spring TX 77379, USA
Jackson, Mick — Director
1349 Berea Place, Pacific Palisades CA 90272, USA
Jackson, Millie — Singer, Songwriter, Actress
Keishval Enterprises, 133 Cedar Lane, Teaneck NJ 07666, USA
Jackson, Monte C — Football Player
7646 Westbrook Ave, San Diego CA 92139, USA
Jackson, Noah D — Football Player
1640 Milburne Road, Lake Forest IL 60045, USA
Jackson, Peter — Director, Producer
Wing Nut Films, PO Box 15208, Miramar, Wellington 6003, New Zealand
Jackson, Philip — Actor
Markham & Froggatt, Julian House, 4 Windmill St, London W1P 1HF, England
Jackson, Philip D (Phil) — Basketball Player, Coach
18942 Medicine Rock Lane, Lakeside MT 59922, USA
Jackson, Quinton (Rampage) — Ultimate Fighter, Actor
Roar Mgmt, 9701 Wilshire Blvd, #800, Beverly Hills CA 90212 USA
Jackson, R Graham — Architect
Calhoun Tungate Jackson Dill Architects, 6200 Savoy Dr, Houston TX 77036, USA
Jackson, Ralph A — Basketball Player
3235 W 11th Place, Inglewood CA 90303, USA
Jackson, Randall B (Randy) — Football Player
747 Musago Run, Lake Mary FL 32746, USA
Jackson, Randy — Actor, Producer
Harriet Sternberg Mgmt, 4530 Gloria Ave, Encino CA 91436, USA
Jackson, Ransom J (Randy) — Baseball Player
250 Hunnicutt Dr, Athens GA 30606, USA
Jackson, Rebbie — Singer, Songwriter
Groove Entertainment, 1005 N Alfred St, #2, West Hollywood CA 90069, USA
Jackson, Reginald M (Reggie) — Baseball Player
305 Amador Ave, Seaside CA 93955, USA
Jackson, Richard Lee — Actor
1815 Butler Ave, #120, Los Angeles CA 90025, USA
Jackson, Rickey A — Football Player
2744 Hyde Park Ave N, Harvey LA 70058, USA
Jackson, Roger — Football Player
3762 Oxford Dr, Macon GA 31204, USA
Jackson, Roland T (Sonny) — Baseball Player
117 Palm Bay Dr, #B, Palm Beach Gardens FL 33418, USA
Jackson, Ronald Shannon — Jazz Drummer
Natalie Shannon Jackson, 175 W 87th St, #30C, New York NY 10024, USA
Jackson, Ronnie D (Ron) — Baseball Player
515 White Road, Fayetteville GA 30214, USA
Jackson, Roy Lee — Baseball Player
8269 Lee Road 54, Auburn AL 36830, USA
Jackson, S Randall (Randy) — Singer
Big J Productions, 854 Florida Blvd, New Orleans LA 70124 USA
Jackson, Samuel L — Actor
Anonymous Content, 3532 Hayden Ave, Culver City CA 90232 USA
Jackson, Sharisse (Shar) — Actress, Singer
Sovereign Talent Group, 8421 Wilshire Blvd, #200, Beverly Hills CA 90211, USA
Jackson, Sherry — Actress
800 N Lucia Ave, #A, Redondo Beach CA 90277, USA
Jackson, Shirley Ann — Educator, Theoretical Physicist
Rensselaer Polytechnic Institute, President's Office, Troy NY 12180, USA
Jackson, Stephen J — Basketball Player
10541 Titan Run, Carmel IN 46032, USA
Jackson, Steven W (Steve) — Football Player
43752 Lees Mill Square, Leesburg VA 20176, USA
Jackson, Stonewall — Singer, Guitarist, Songwriter
6007 Cloverland Dr, Brentwood TN 37027, USA
Jackson, Stoney — Actor
1602 N Fuller Ave, #102, Los Angeles CA 90046, USA
Jackson, Stu — Basketball Coach, Executive
National Basketball Assn, 645 5th Ave, #1900, New York NY 10022, USA
Jackson, Tarvaris F — Football Player
11171 Sun Center Dr, #290, Rancho Cordova CA 95670, USA
Jackson, Terence L (Terry) — Football Player
2269 Glenmore Terrace, Rockville MD 20850, USA
Jackson, Thomas (Tom) — Football Player, Sportscaster
7475 Brill Road, Cincinnati OH 45243, USA
Jackson, Thomas Penfield — Judge
US District Court, 333 Constitution Ave NW, #4400, Washington DC 20001, USA
Jackson, Tiffany — Basketball Player
Tulsa Shock, B O K Center, 200 S Denver, Tulsa OK 74103 USA
Jackson, Tito — Singer (Jackson Five)
2467 Taylor Ave, Corona CA 92882, USA
Jackson, Tony — Basketball Player
1009 Trevey Point, Lexington KY 40515, USA
Jackson, Tracey — Writer
Arlook Group, 205 S Beverly Drive, #209, Beverly Hills CA 90212, USA
Jackson, Trina — Swimmer
9271 Saltwater Way, Jacksonville FL 32256, USA
Jackson, Tyoka — Football Player
16312 Birkdale Dr, Odessa FL 33556, USA
Jackson, Vestee, II — Football Player
2800 S Eastern Ave, #410, Las Vegas NV 89169, USA
Jackson, Victoria — Actress, Comedienne
Breen Agency, 25 Music Square W, Nashville TN 37203, USA
Jackson, Vincent — Football Player
Tampa Bay Buccaneers, 1 W Buccaneer Place, Tampa FL 33607 USA

Jackson, Vincent E (Bo) 100 Oak Ridge Dr, Burr Ridge IL 60527, USA	Football, Baseball Player
Jackson, Wanda Wanda Jackson Enterprises, 11700 S Western Ave, Oklahoma City OK 73170, USA	Singer
Jackson, Wardell PO Box 164142, Columbus OH 43216, USA	Basketball Player
Jackson, Wilbur PO Box 1571, Ozark AL 36361, USA	Football Player
Jackson, Willie B, Jr PO Box 12643, Gainesville FL 32604, USA	Football Player
Jackson, Zach 7630 Menler Dr, Austin TX 78735, USA	Baseball Player
Jaco, Charles PO Box 220182, Saint Louis MO 63122, USA	Commentator, Writer
Jacob, Francois 15 Rue de Conde, 75006 Paris, France	Nobel Medicine Laureate
Jacob, Irene Paradigm Agency, 360 N Crescent Dr, North Building, Beverly Hills CA 90210 USA	Actress
Jacob, Jacob-Farj-Rafael (J F R) Roli Press, M-75 Greater Kailash 2 Market, New Delhi 110048, India	Indian Army General
Jacob, John E Anheuser-Busch, 1 Busch Place, Saint Louis MO 63118, USA	Civil Rights Activist
Jacob, Stanley W 1055 SW Westwood Court, Portland OR 97239, USA	Surgeon
Jacobellis, Lindsey 30648 E Ski Bowl Way, Government Camp OR 97028, USA	Snowboard Athlete
Jacobi, Derek G Independent Talent Group, Oxford House, 76 Oxford St, London W1D 1BS, England	Actor
Jacobi, Walter 2004 Max Luther Dr NW, #419, Huntsville AL 35810, USA	Space Scientist
Jacobs, Allen W 3050 Tolcate Lane, Salt Lake City UT 84121, USA	Football Player
Jacobs, Arnold S (A J), Jr Simon & Schuster, 1230 Ave of Americas, Concourse 1, New York NY 10020 USA	Writer
Jacobs, Brandon San Francisco 49ers, 4949 Centennial Blvd, Santa Clara CA 95054 USA	Football Player
Jacobs, David J (Dave) 8388 Glen Eagle Dr, Manlius NY 13104, USA	Football Player
Jacobs, Debbie T-Best Talent Agency, 508 Honey Lake Court, Danville CA 94506 USA	Singer
Jacobs, Dennis G US Appeals Court, Moynihan Courthouse, 500 Pearl St, New York NY 10007, USA	Judge
Jacobs, Emma Rhubarb Agency, Chiswick, 1A Devonshire Road, London W4 2EU, England	Actress
Jacobs, Gillian United Talent Agency, 9336 Civic Center Dr, Beverly Hills CA 90210 USA	Actress
Jacobs, Glenn World Wrestling Entertainment, Titan Towers, 1241 E Main St, Stamford CT 06902 USA	Professional Wrestler
Jacobs, H Ray 2402 W 5th Ave, Corsicana TX 75110, USA	Football Player
Jacobs, Harry E 108 Lenora Dr, Hamburg NY 14075, USA	Football Player
Jacobs, Howard L Forgie Jacobs Leonard, 4165 E Thousand Oaks Blvd, Westlake Village CA 91362, USA	Attorney
Jacobs, Irwin M Qualcomm Inc, 5775 Morehouse Dr, San Diego CA 92121, USA	Businessman
Jacobs, Jack H Bankers Trust Co, 1 Appold St, London EC2A 2HE, England	Vietnam War Army Hero (CMH)
Jacobs, Jeremy M 1300 N Davis Road, East Aurora NY 14052, USA	Businessman, Hockey Executive
Jacobs, Jim Ronald Taft, 18 W 55th St, New York NY 10019, USA	Writer, Composer, Actor
Jacobs, Julien I US Tax Court, 400 2nd St NW, Washington DC 20217, USA	Judge
Jacobs, Kate East Central One, All Saints Road, Suffolk 1P6 8PR, England	Singer, Guitarist, Songwriter
Jacobs, Katie Heel & Toe Films, 2058 Broadway, Santa Monica CA 90404, USA	Writer, Producer
Jacobs, Lamar G (Jake) 2925 Terra Ceia Bay Blvd, Palmetto FL 34221, USA	Baseball Player
Jacobs, Lawrence-Hilton PO Box 67905, Los Angeles CA 90067, USA	Actor
Jacobs, Lloyd A University of Toledo, President's Office, 2801 Bancroft, Toledo OH 43606, USA	Educator
Jacobs, Marc Louis Vuitton, 2 Rue du Pont Neuf, 75001 Paris, France	Fashion Designer
Jacobs, Michael J (Mike) 1583 Hikers Trail Dr, Chula Vista CA 91915, USA	Baseball Player
Jacobs, Paul E Qualcomm, 5775 Morehouse Dr, San Diego CA 92121, USA	Businessman
Jacobs, Proverb G 4369 Detroit Ave, Oakland CA 94619, USA	Football Player
Jacobs, Robert Nathan Gersh Agency, 9465 Wilshire Blvd, #600, Beverly Hills CA 90212 USA	Writer
Jacobs, Taylor H 8083 Longmeadow Dr, Tallahassee FL 32312, USA	Football Player
Jacobs, Timothy J (Tim) 7306 Finns Lane, Lanham MD 20706, USA	Football Player
Jacobsen, Anders Ringkollen Skilubb, Owrensgt 28, 3510 Honefoss, Norway	Ski Jumper
Jacobsen, Casey G 24622 Cresta Court, Laguna Hills CA 92653, USA	Basketball Player
Jacobsen, Hugh Newell Hugh Newell Jacobsen Architect, 2529 P St NW, Washington DC 20007, USA	Architect
Jacobsen, Peter 27771 Marina Pointe Dr, Bonita Springs FL 34134, USA	Golfer

Jacobsen, Stephanie — Actress
1 Mgmt, 9000 W Sunset Blvd, #1550, Los Angeles CA 90069 USA

Jacobs-Lorena, Marcelo — Molecular Microbiologist
Johns Hopkins University, Malaria Research Institute, Baltimore MD 21218, USA

Jacobson, D D — Bowler
8261 Rees St, Playa del Rey CA 90293, USA

Jacobson, Danny — Writer
Brillstein Entertainment Partners, 9150 Wilshire Blvd, #350, Beverly Hills CA 90212 USA

Jacobson, Herbert L — Diplomat, Journalist
Apartado 160, Escazu, Costa Rica

Jacobson, Nina — Producer
Color Force, 1524 Cloverfield Blvd, #C, Santa Monica CA 90404, USA

Jacobson, Peter — Actor
Innovative Artists, 235 Park Ave S, #1000, New York NY 10003 USA

Jacoby, Brook W — Baseball Player
21825 N Dobson Road, Scottsdale AZ 85255, USA

Jacoby, Joe — Football Player
Jacoby Jeep/Eagle/Chrysler, 7308 Cedar Run Dr, Warrenton VA 20187, USA

Jacoby, Mark — Actor, Singer
TalentWorks, 3500 W Olive Ave, #1400, Burbank CA 91505 USA

Jacoby, Scott — Actor
PO Box 5569, Sherman Oaks CA 91413, USA

Jacome, Jason J — Baseball Player
5115 N Camino Esplendora, Tucson AZ 85718, USA

Jacot, Christopher — Actor
Lauren Levitt Assoc, 425 4 5th Ave, #300, Vancouver BC V6J 1TS, Canada

Jacot, Michele — Alpine Skier
Residence du Brevent, 74 Chamonix, France

Jacott, Carlos — Actor
Thruline Entertainment, 9250 Wilshire Blvd, #100, Beverly Hills CA 90212 USA

Jacox, Kendyl L — Football Player
50 Schubach Dr, Sugar Land, TX 77479, USA

Jacquemard, Simonne — Writer
Le Verdier, 24520 Sireuil, France

Jacques, Patrick T (Pat) — Baseball Player
4430 Annandale Dr, Stockton CA 95219, USA

Jacques, Russell K — Sculptor
38 Drake St, Newport Beach CA 92663, USA

Jacquot, Benoit — Director
Voyez Mon Agent, 20 Ave Rapp, 75007 Paris, France

Jaczko, Gregory B — Government Official
US Nuclear Regulatory Commission, Mail Stop 0-16G4, Washington DC 20555, USA

Jadakiss — Rap Artist (Ruff Ryders)
J Erving Group, 555 Whitehall St SW, #N, Atlanta GA 30303, USA

Jaeckel, Paul H — Baseball Player
328 W 7th St, Claremont CA 91711, USA

Jaeckin, Just — Director
8 Villa Mequillet, 92200 Neuilly/Seine, France

Jaeger, Andrea — Tennis Player
Kids Stuff Foundation, Silver Lining Ranch, 1490 S Ute Ave, Aspen CO 81611, USA

Jaeger, Jeff T — Football Player
3026 Sahalee Dr W, Sammamish WA 98074, USA

Jaeger, Sam — Actor
D/F Management, 315 S Beverly Dr, #201, Beverly Hills CA 90212 USA

Jaeggi, Andreas — Opera Singer
I M G Artists, Hogarth Business Park, Chiswick, London W4 2TH, England

Jaenicke, Hannes — Actor
Goetherstr 17, 80336 Munich, Germany

Jaenisch, Rudolf — Biologist
Massachusetts Institute of Technology, Biology Dept, 9 Cambridge Center, Cambridge MA 02142, USA

Jaffe, Arthur M — Mathematical Physicist
27 Lancaster St, Cambridge MA 02140, USA

Jaffe, Harold W — Epidemiologist
Centers for Disease Control, 1600 Clifton Road NE, Atlanta GA 30329 USA

Jaffe, Robert L — Theoretical Physicist
Massachusetts Institute of Technology, Physics Dept, Cambridge MA 02139, USA

Jaffe, Stanley R — Producer, Director
152 W 57th St, #5200F, New York NY 10019, USA

Jaffe, Susan — Ballerina
American Ballet Theatre, 890 Broadway, #300, New York NY 10003 USA

Jaffrey, Raza — Actor
United Agents, 12-26 Lexington St, London W1F 0LE, England

Jaffrey, Saeed — Actor, Comedian
503 Sejal New Link Road, Andheri, Mumbai MS 400058, India

Jagendorf, Andre T — Plant Physiologist
455 Savage Farm Dr, Ithaca NY 14850, USA

Jager, Thomas (Tom) — Swimmer
1416 Chinook St, Moscow ID 83843, USA

Jagge, Finn Christian — Alpine Skier
Michelets Vei 108, 1320 Stabekk, Norway

Jagger, Bianca — Actress, Model
Media Artists Group, 8222 Melrose Ave, #203, Los Angeles CA 90048 USA

Jagger, Elizabeth (Lizzy) — Model
Tess Mgmt, 9-10 Market Place, #400, London W1W 8AQ, England

Jagger, Michael (Mick) — Singer (Rolling Stones)
Jagged Films, 1041 N Formosa Ave, West Hollywood CA 90046, USA

Jagland, Thorbjoern — Prime Minister, Norway
Stortinget, Karl Johans Gate 22, 0026 Oslo, Norway

Jaglom, Henry — Director
9165 W Sunset Blvd, #300, West Hollywood CA 90069, USA

Jagr, Jaromir — Ice Hockey Player
HC Avangard-Omsk, Dekabristov 91, 644010 Omsk, Russia

Jaha, John E — Baseball Player
12776 SE Geneva Way, Happy Valley OR 97086, USA

Jahan, Marine — Actress, Dancer
Media Artists Group, 8222 Melrose Ave, #203, Los Angeles CA 90048 USA

Jaheim
Universal Attractions, 135 W 26th St, #1200, New York NY 10001 USA — Singer
Jahn, Helmut
Murphy/Jahn, 33 E Wacker Dr, #300, Chicago IL 60601, USA — Architect
Jahn, Robert G
Princeton University, Aerospace Sciences Dept, Princeton NJ 08544, USA — Aeronautical Engineer
Jahn, Sigmund
Fontanestr 35, 15344 Strausberg, Germany — Cosmonaut, East Germany; General
Jaidah, Ali Mohammed
Qatar Petroleum Corp, PO Box 3212, Doha, Qatar — Government Official, Qatar
Jakel, Bernd
Salvador-Allende-Str 48, 12559 Berlin, Germany — Yachtsman
Jakes, John
445 Meadow Lark Dr, Sarasota FL 34236, USA — Writer
Jakes, T D
T D Jakes Ministries, PO Box 763518, Dallas TX 75376, USA — Religious Leader
Jakes, Van K
305 Worthing Lane, McDonough GA 30253, USA — Football Player
Jakobs, Marco
Oststr 1B, 59427 Unna, Germany — Bobsled Athlete
Jakobson, Max
Rahapajankatu 3B 17, 00160 Helsinki 16, Finland — Journalist; Government Official, Finland
Jakobsson, Johan M
Aalborg Handbold, Willy Brandts Vej 31, 9220 Aalborg Ost, Denmark — Handball Player
Jakopin, John
57 Samana Dr, Miami FL 33133, USA — Ice Hockey Player
Jakosits, Michael
Karlsbergstr 140, 66424 Homburg/Saar, Germany — Marksman
Jakub, Lisa
Lafeaver Talent, 785 Carlaw Ave, #101, Toronto ON M4K 3L1, Canada — Actress
Jakubowicz, Jonathan
Creative Artists Agency, 2000 Ave of Stars, #100, Los Angeles CA 90067 USA — Director, Producer, Writer
Jalal, Farida
3B Nandini Unik Housing Society, Andheri, Mumbai MS 400058, India — Actress
Jalali, Bahram
University of California, Electrical Engineering Dept, Los Angeles CA 90024, USA — Electrical Engineer
Jamail, Joseph D, Jr
Jamail & Kolius, 500 Dallas St, #3434, Houston TX 77002, USA — Attorney
Jamal, Ahmad
Ellora Mgmt, PO Box 755, 11 Brook St, Lakeville CT 06039, USA — Jazz Pianist
Jamelia
Shalit Global Mgmt, 7 Moor St, London W1D 5NB, England — Singer, Songwriter
James, Aaron (A J)
3057 Orrin Ave, Youngstown OH 44505, USA — Basketball Player
James, Anthony
C N A Assoc, 1875 Century Park East, #2250, Los Angeles CA 90067 USA — Actor
James, Arthur (Art)
6935 Brown Dr S, Fairburn GA 30213, USA — Baseball Player
James, Boney
Barbara Rose Entertainment, 4203 Bellaire Ave, Studio City CA 91604, USA — Saxophonist, Songwriter
James, Bradie D
2509 Silver Table Dr, Lewisville TX 75056, USA — Football Player
James, Brett
Starstruck Entertainment, 40 Music Square W, Nashville TN 37203, USA — Singer, Guitarist, Songwriter
James, Brian D'Arcy
Thruline Entertainment, 9250 Wilshire Blvd, #100, Beverly Hills CA 90212 USA — Actor
James, Charity
C E S D, 10635 Santa Monica Blvd, #130, Los Angeles CA 90025 USA — Actress
James, Charles H (Chuck)
4840 Golden Dr SW, Mableton GA 30126, USA — Baseball Player
James, Charles W (Charlie)
3303 Tanglewood Way, Fulton MO 65251, USA — Baseball Player
James, Charmayne
Gold Buckle Ranch, 2100 N Highway 360, #1207, Grand Prairie TX 75050, USA — Rodeo Rider
James, Cheryl (Salt)
Entertainment Artists, PO Box 120824, Nashville TN 37212 USA — Rap Artist (Salt'N'Pepa)
James, Clifton
500 W 43rd St, #26J, New York NY 10036, USA — Actor
James, Colton
James/Levy Mgmt, 3500 W Olive Ave, #1470, Burbank CA 91505 USA — Actor
James, D Christopher (Chris)
1040 County Road 2707, Alto TX 75925, USA — Baseball Player
James, D Clayton
106 Wagon Wheel Trail, Moneta VA 24121, USA — Historian
James, Dalton
Coast to Coast Talent, 3350 Barham Blvd, Los Angeles CA 90068 USA — Actor
James, Daniel J, III
Director, Air National Guard, HqUSAF, Pentagon, Washington DC 20330, USA — Air Force General
James, Dion
5 Shelter Point Court, Sacramento CA 95831, USA — Baseball Player
James, Don
7047 Chanticleer Ave SE, Snoqualmie WA 98065, USA — Football Coach
James, Donald M
Vulcan Materials Co, 1200 Urban Center Dr, Birmingham AL 35242, USA — Businessman
James, E L
Vintage Books, 1745 Broadway, New York NY 10019 USA — Writer
James, Edgerrin T
1853 Cross Green Way, Orange Park FL 32003, USA — Football Player
James, Elgin
Brillstein Entertainment Partners, 9150 Wilshire Blvd, #350, Beverly Hills CA 90212 USA — Director
James, Eloisa
Mary Bly, Fordham University, English Dept, Lincoln Center Campus, New York NY 10023, USA — Writer
James, Forrest H (Fob), Jr
39 Alabama Road, Lehigh Acres FL 33936, USA — Governor, AL
James, Frances C
Florida State University, Biological Sciences Dept, Tallahassee FL 32306, USA — Biologist

V.I.P. Address Book

James, G William (Bill) — Baseball Writer, Statistician
625 Ohio St, Lawrence KS 66044, USA

James, Geraldine — Actress
Denville Hall, 62 Ducks Hill Road, Northwood, Middlesex HA6 2SB, England

James, Godfrey — Actor
Shack, Western Road, Pevensey Bay, East Sussex BN23 6HG, England

James, Henry C — Basketball Player
527 E Leith St, Fort Wayne IN 46806, USA

James, J Craig — Football Player, Sportscaster
12714 W FM 455, Celina TX 75009, USA

James, James (Boney) — Jazz Saxophonist
Direct Mgmt Group, 947 N La Cienega Blvd, #G, West Hollywood CA 90069, USA

James, Jenorris (Jeno) — Football Player
1620 NW 117th Ave, Plantation FL 33323, USA

James, Jesse — Actor
Dino May Mgmt, 6362 Hollywood Blvd, #PH 422, Los Angeles CA 90028, USA

James, Jesse G — Producer
West Coast Choppers, 718 W Anaheim St, Long Beach CA 90813, USA

James, Jessica R (Jessie) — Singer, Songwriter
Show Dog/Universal Music, 2303 21st Ave S, #400, Nashville TN 37212, USA

James, Jimmy — Singer (Jimmy James & the Vagabonds)
Barry Collings, PO Box 2112, Hockley, Essex SS5 4WD, England

James, John — Actor
PO Box 9, Cambridge NY 12816, USA

James, John P (Johnny) — Baseball Player
6037 E Larkspur Dr, Scottsdale AZ 85254, USA

James, John W, Jr — Football Player
23108 NE 69th Ave, Melrose FL 32666, USA

James, Joni — Singer
Silent Angels Productions, 439 E 74th St, #5FW, New York NY 10021, USA

James, Joshua — Singer
Creative Artists Agency, 2000 Ave of Stars, #100, Los Angeles CA 90067 USA

James, Kate — Model
Men/Women Model Inc, 199 Lafayette St, New York NY 10012, USA

James, Kevin, III — Illusionist, Actor
Jeff Sussman Mgmt, 603 W 115th St, #282, New York NY 10025, USA

James, LeBron R — Basketball Player
Miami Heat, American Airlines Arena, 601 Biscayne Blvd, Miami FL 33132 USA

James, Leela — Singer, Songwriter
R D K Music Mgmt, PO Box 11611, Beverly Hills CA 90213, USA

James, Lennie — Actor
Principal Entertainment, 130 W 42nd St, #614, New York NY 10036, USA

James, Lionel — Football Player
199 Woodbury Dr, Sterret AL 35147, USA

James, M William (Billy) — Basketball Player
12 S Sunset Dr, Lexington IN 47138, USA

James, Marco — Actor
Don Buchwald/Fortitude, 6500 Wilshire Blvd, #2200, Los Angeles CA 90048 USA

James, Marianne — Jazz Guitarist, Composer
89 Ave Charles de Gaulle, 92575 Neuilly-sur-Seine Cedex, France

James, Michael E (Mike) — Baseball Player
115 Austin Court, Mary Esther FL 32569, USA

James, Oliver — Actor
Independent Talent Group, Oxford House, 76 Oxford St, London W1D 1BS, England

James, Oliver — Psychologist, Writer
Gillon Aitken Assoc, 18-21 Cavaye Place, London SW10 9PT, England

James, P D — Writer
Greene & Heaton Ltd, 37A Goldhawk Road, London W12 8QQ, England

James, Pell — Actress
I C M Partners, 730 5th Ave, New York NY 10019 USA

James, Robert (Bob) — Jazz Keyboardist (Bob James Trio)
Monterey International, 200 W Superior St, #202, Chicago IL 60654 USA

James, Robert D — Football Player
1511 N Highland Ave, Murfreesboro TN 37130, USA

James, Robert H (Bob) — Baseball Player
15844 Cindy Court, Canyon Country CA 91387, USA

James, Roland O — Football Player
19 Spring Lane, Sharon MA 02067, USA

James, Shannon — Model
Playboy Promotions, 2706 Media Center Dr, Los Angeles CA 90065 USA

James, Sheryl — Journalist
Saint Petersburg Times, Editorial Dept, 490 1st Ave, Saint Petersburg FL 33701, USA

James, Sonny — Singer, Guitarist, Songwriter
W M E Entertainment, 1600 Division St, #300, Nashville TN 37203 USA

James, Thomas (Tom) — Rowing Athlete
Molesey Boat Club, Barge Walk, East Molesey, Surrey KT8 9AJ, England

James, Tommy — Singer (Shondells)
Lustig Talent, PO Box 770850, Orlando FL 32877 USA

James, Tory S — Football Player
70 N Gary Glen Circle, Spring TX 77382, USA

James-Collier, Rob — Actor
Independent Talent Group, Oxford House, 76 Oxford St, London W1D 1BS, England

James-Kuehl, Sheila — Actress
3201 Pearl St, Santa Monica CA 90405, USA

Jameson, Keith — Opera Singer
Columbia Artists Mgmt Inc, 1790 Broadway, #702, New York NY 10019 USA

Jameson, Nick — Actor
Danis Panaro Nist, 9201 W Olympic Blvd, Beverly Hills CA 90212, USA

James-Rodman, Charmayne — Rodeo Rider
General Delivery, Clayton NM 88415, USA

Jamieson, Janet — Baseball Player
6324 212th St SW, #3, Lynnwood WA 98036, USA

Jamieson, John K — Businessman
10313 Stanley Circle, Minneapolis MN 55437, USA

Jamison, Antawn C — Basketball Player
6041 Providence Country Club Dr, Charlotte NC 28277, USA

Jamison, George R, Jr
3430 Vineyard Hill Dr, Rochester MI 48306, USA — Football Player
Jamison, Judith
Alvin Ailey American Dance Foundation, 405 W 55th St, New York NY 10019, USA — Dancer, Choreographer
Jammeh, Yahya A J J
President's Office, Private Mail Bag, State House, Banjul, Gambia — Head of State, Gambia; Army Officer
Jammer, Quentin T
7815 Sendero Angelica, San Diego CA 92127, USA — Football Player
Jampolsky, Gerald
Celestial Arts, 6001 Shellmound St, #400, Emeryville CA 94608, USA — Writer
Janas, Elizabeth
Don Buchwald/Fortitude, 6500 Wilshire Blvd, #2200, Los Angeles CA 90048 USA — Actress
Janaszak, Steve
42 Montrose Ave, Babylon NY 11702, USA — Ice Hockey Player
Jance, J A
William Morrow, 1350 Ave of Americas, New York NY 10019, USA — Writer
Jancso, Miklos
Eszter U 17, 1022 Budapest, Hungary — Director
Janda, Krystyna
Teatr Powszechny, Ul Zamoyskiego 20, 03 801 Warsaw, Poland — Actress
Jane, Thomas
Creative Artists Agency, 2000 Ave of Stars, #100, Los Angeles CA 90067 USA — Actor
Janes, Dominic
Rising Talent Mgmt, 137 S Spalding Drive, #406, Beverly Hills CA 90212, USA — Actor
Janeski, Gerald J (Gerry)
28901 Via Buena Vista, San Juan Capistrano CA 92675, USA — Baseball Player
Janetti, Gary
W M E Entertainment, 9601 Wilshire Blvd, #300, Beverly Hills CA 90210 USA — Producer, Writer
Janeway, Michael C
Columbia University, Graduate Journalism School, New York NY 10027, USA — Editor, Educator, Writer
Janeway, Richard
PO Box 188, Blowing Rock NC 28605, USA — Physician
Jang, Jeong (J J)
8749 The Esplanade, #33, Orlando FL 32836, USA — Golfer
Janic, Adrienne
Bleu Entertainment, 5225 Wilshire Blvd, #401, Los Angeles CA 90036, USA — Actress
Janikowski, Sebastian
11958 Brady Road, Jacksonville FL 32223, USA — Football Player
Janis, Byron
Phillips Records, 810 7th Ave, New York NY 10019 USA — Concert Pianist
Janis, Conrad
Hardwick-Tolman Mgmt, PO Box 11697, Nashville TN 37222, USA — Actor, Jazz Trombonist
Janish, Paul R
11926 Deep Woods Dr, Cypress TX 77429, USA — Baseball Player
Janitz, John A
Textron Inc, 40 Westminster St, #500, Providence RI 02903, USA — Businessman
Janka, Carlo
Ski & Sports Club Obersaxen, PO Box 4, 7134 Obersaxen Meierhof, Switzerland — Alpine Skier
Jankovic, Jelena
Octagon Worldwide, 1751 Pinnacle Dr, #1500, McLean VA 22102 USA — Tennis Player
Jankovic, Joseph
Baylor College of Medicine, Neurology Dept, Baylor Plaza, Houston TX 77030, USA — Neurologist
Jankowska-Cieslak, Jadwiga
Film Polski, Ul Mazewiecka 6/8, 00-950 Warsaw, Poland — Actress
Jankowski, Gene F
American Film Institute, 901 15th St NW, #700, Washington DC 20005, USA — Businessman
Jankowski, Peter
United Talent Agency, 9336 Civic Center Dr, Beverly Hills CA 90210 USA — Producer
Jann, Michael Patrick
Creative Artists Agency, 2000 Ave of Stars, #100, Los Angeles CA 90067 USA — Director, Producer, Actor
Jannazzo, Izzy
6924 62nd Ave, Middle Village NY 11379, USA — Boxer
Janney, Allison
W M E Entertainment, 9601 Wilshire Blvd, #300, Beverly Hills CA 90210 USA — Actress
Janney, Craig H
4424 N 59th Place, Phoenix AZ 85018, USA — Ice Hockey Player
Jannot, Mark
Popular Science, Editorial Dept, 2 Park Ave, #900, New York NY 10016, USA — Editor
Janotta, Howard (Howie)
18118 Brookwood Forest, San Antonio TX 78258, USA — Basketball Player
Janov, Arthur
1205 Abbot Kinney Blvd, Venice CA 90291, USA — Psychologist, Psychotherapist
Janovitz, Bill
Agency Group Ltd, 142 W 57th St, #600, New York NY 10019 USA — Singer, Guitarist (Buffalo Tom)
Janowicz, Josh
1 Mgmt, 9000 W Sunset Blvd, #1550, Los Angeles CA 90069 USA — Actor
Janowitz, Gundula
3072 Kasten 75, Austria — Opera Singer
Janowitz, Tama
Random House, 1745 Broadway, #1800, New York NY 10019 USA — Writer
Janowski, Marek
Columbia Artists Mgmt Inc, 1790 Broadway, #702, New York NY 10019 USA — Conductor
Jansa, Janez
Prime Minister's Office, Gregorciceva St 20, 61000 Ljubljana, Slovenia — Prime Minister, Slovenia
Jansch, Heather
Knowle, Rundlerohy, Newton Abbot, Devon TQ12 2PJ, England — Artist
Jansen, Daniel E (Dan)
PO Box 3354, Mooresville NC 28117, USA — Speed Skater
Jansen, Janine
Harrison/Parrott, 5-6 Albion Court, London W6 0QT, England — Concert Violinist
Janson, Karin Stahre
Royal Carribean Int'l, 1111 S Arroyo Parkway, #450, Pasadena CA 91105, USA — Cruise Ship Captain
Jansons, Mariss
Opus 3 Artists, 470 Park Ave S, #900N, New York NY 10016 USA — Conductor
Jansrud, Kjetil
Vinstra, 2640 Gudbrandsdalen, Norway — Alpine Skier

V.I.P. Address Book

Janssen, Daniel
La Ronciere, 108 Ave Ernest Solvay, 1310 La Hulpe, Belgium — Businessman

Janssen, Famke
Brookside Artist Mgmt, 250 W 57th St, #2303, New York NY 10107 USA — Actress, Model

Janssen, Marlene
Playboy Promotions, 2706 Media Center Dr, Los Angeles CA 90065 USA — Model, Actress

Janssen, R Casey
8461 Spring Circle Huntington Beach CA 92646, USA — Baseball Player

Janssens, Mark
115 Central Park W, #17A, New York NY 10023, USA — Ice Hockey Player

Jantz, Richard
University of Tennessee, Anthropology Dept, Knoxville TN 37996, USA — Anthropologist

January, Briann J
Indiana Fever, Conseco Fieldhouse, 125 S Pennsylvania, Indianapolis IN 46204 USA — Basketball Player

January, Donald R (Don)
5006 Village Place, Dallas TX 75248, USA — Golfer

Jany, Alexandre (Alex)
104 Blvd Livon, 13007 Marseille, France — Swimmer

Janzen, Daniel H
Parque Nacional Santa Rosa, #169, Liberia, Guanacaste Province, Costa Rica — Biologist

Janzen, Edmund
General Conference of Mennonite Brethren, 8000 W 21st St, Wichita KS 67205, USA — Religious Leader

Janzen, Lee M
9088 Point Cypress Dr, Orlando FL 32836, USA — Golfer

Janzen, Rhoda
Hope College, English Dept, Holland MI 49422, USA — Writer

Jaquess, Lindel G (Pete)
631 Cunningham Lane, El Cajon CA 92019, USA — Football Player

Jaquiss, Nigel
Willamette Week, Editorial Dept, 822 SW 10th Ave, Portland OR 97205, USA — Journalist

Jaramillo. Jason C
6111 Madeline Lane, Caledonia WI 53108, USA — Baseball Player

Jardine, Alan C (Al)
Edge Mgmt, 10850 Wilshire Blve, #380, Los Angeles CA 90024, USA — Singer, Guitarist (Beach Boys)

Jardine, Ray
Ray-Way Products, PO Box 2153, Arizona City AZ 85123, USA — Mountaineer, Hiker, Cyclist, Rower

Jarecki, Andrew
Creative Artists Agency, 2000 Ave of Stars, #100, Los Angeles CA 90067 USA — Director

Jarman, Claude, Jr
16 Tamal Vista Lane, Axminster, Kentfield CA 94904, USA — Actor

Jarmusch, Jim
Cinetic Mgmt, 555 W 25th St, #400, New York NY 10001, USA — Director

Jarosz, Sarah
Paradigm Agency, 404 W Franklin St, Monterey CA 93940 USA — Singer, Songwriter, Musician

Jarre, Jean M A
Creme-Creative Mgmt, 8 Rue de Levis, 75017 Paris, France — Composer

Jarreau, Alwyn L (Al)
Tsunami Entertainment, 2525 Hyperion Ave, Los Angeles CA 90027, USA — Singer

Jarrell, Jessica
Island Def Jam Records, 8920 W Sunset Blvd, #200, West Hollywood CA 90069 USA — Singer

Jarrett, Dale A
1510 46th Ave NE, Hickory NC 28601, USA — Auto Racing Driver

Jarrett, Douglas W (Doug)
3486 Maisonneuve Ave, Windsor ON N9E 1Y8, Canada — Ice Hockey Player

Jarrett, Gabriel
Hervey/Grimes Talent, 10561 Missouri Ave, #2, Los Angeles CA 90025 USA — Actor

Jarrett, Gary W
9662 E Peak View Road, Scottsdale AZ 85262, USA — Ice Hockey Player

Jarrett, Keith
Stephen Cloud Presentation, PO Box 578, Santa Ynez CA 93460, USA — Jazz Pianist, Composer

Jarrett, Ned M
3182 Ninth Tee Dr, Newton NC 28658, USA — Auto Racing Driver

Jarriel, Thomas E (Tom)
ABC-TV, News Dept, 77 W 66th St, New York NY 10023 USA — Commentator

Jarrin, Jaime
Los Angeles Dodgers, Stadium, 1000 Elysian Park Ave, Los Angeles CA 90090 USA — Sportscaster

Jarrold, Julian
W M E Entertainment, 9601 Wilshire Blvd, #300, Beverly Hills CA 90210 USA — Director, Producer, Actor

Jarryd, Anders
Maaneskoldsgatan 37, 531 00 Lidkoping, Sweden — Tennis Player

Jaruzelski, Wojciech
Biuro Bylego, Al Jerozolimskie 91, 02 001 Warsaw, Poland — President, Poland; Army General

Jarvi, Kristjan
I M G Artists, Hogarth Business Park, Chiswick, London W4 2TH, England — Conductor

Jarvi, Neeme
Harrison/Parrott, 5-6 Albion Court, London W6 0QT, England — Conductor

Jarvi, Paavo
Orchestre de Paris, Salle Pleyel, 252 rue du Faubourg Saint-Honore, 75008 Paris, France — Conductor

Jarvik, Robert K
Jarvick Heart Inc, 333 W 52nd St, New York NY 10019, USA — Surgeon, Inventor (Artificial Heart)

Jarvis, Doug
Montreal Canadiens, 1275 Saint Antoine St W, Montreal QC H3C 5L2, Canada — Ice Hockey Player

Jarvis, James C (Jim)
PO Box 154, Asotin WA 99402, USA — Basketball Player

Jarvis, Katie
Artist Rights Group, 4 Great Portland Place, London W1W 8PA, England — Actress

Jarvis, Kevin T
1613 Whispering Hills Dr, Franklin TN 37069, USA — Baseball Player

Jarvis, L Raeminton (Ray)
19155 Hi View Dr, Brookfield WI 53045, USA — Football Player

Jarvis, R Patrick (Pat)
4201 Providence Lane, Tucker GA 30084, USA — Baseball Player

Jarvis, Wes
National Training Rinks, 1115 Stellar Dr, Newmarket ON L3Y 7B8, Canada — Ice Hockey Player

Jason, David
Richard Stone Partnership, 85 New Cavendish St, London W1W 6XD, England — Actor, Comedian

Jasontek, Rebecca
1201 Retswood Dr, Loveland OH 45140, USA — Synchronized Swimmer
Jasper, Edward V (Ed)
113 N Price St, Troup TX 75789, USA — Football Player
Jaster, Larry E
1105 Mill Creek Dr, Saint Johns FL 32259, USA — Baseball Player
Jastremski, Chet
927 S Baldwin Dr, Bloomington IN 47401, USA — Swimmer
Jastrow, Kenneth M, II
Temple-Inland Inc, 303 S Temple Dr, Diboll TX 75941, USA — Businessman
Jastrow, Terry L
13201 Old Oak Lane, Los Angeles CA 90049, USA — Director
Jata, Paul
117 Hidden Ridge Court, Highland Heights KY 41076, USA — Baseball Player
Jaugstetter, Robert
619 Mandeville St, #3, New Orleans LA 70117, USA — Rowing Athlete
Jaumotte, Andre
33 Ave Jeanne, Bte 17, 1050 Brussels, Belgium — Mechanical Engineer
Jauron, Dick M
Cleveland Browns, 76 Lou Groza Blvd, Berea OH 44017 USA — Football Player, Coach
Javan, Ali
12 Hawthorne St, Cambridge MA 02138, USA — Physicist, Inventor
Javed Miandad Khan
Cricket Control Board, Gaddafi Stadium, Lahore, Pakistan — Cricketer
Javerbaum, David
3 Arts Entertainment, 9460 Wilshire Blvd, #700, Beverly Hills CA 90212 USA — Writer
Javier Liranzo, M Julian
PO Box 71, San Francisco de Marcoris, Dominican Republic — Baseball Player
Javier, Stanley J A (Stan)
5798 Hammock Isles Dr, Naples FL 34119, USA — Baseball Player
Jawara, Dawda K
15 Birchen Lane, Haywards Heath, West Sussex RH16 1RY, England — President, Gambia
Jaworski, Marian Cardinal
Lviv Archdiocese Curia, Katedralna Square, 79008 Lviv, Ukraine — Religious Leader
Jaworski, Ronald V (Ron)
18 Brookwood Dr, Medford NJ 08055, USA — Football Player, Sportscaster
Jax, J Garth
12014 E Lake Circle, Greenwood Village CO 80111, USA — Football Player
Jay, Anjali
Independent Talent Group, Oxford House, 76 Oxford St, London W1D 1BS, England — Actress
Jay, Joseph R (Joey)
7209 Battenwood Court, Tampa FL 33615, USA — Baseball Player
Jay, Ken
Warner Bros Records, 3300 Warner Blvd, Burbank CA 91505 USA — Drummer (Static-X)
Jay, Martin E
University of California, History Dept, Berkeley CA 94720, USA — Historian
Jay, Peter
Hensington Farmhouse, Woodstock, Oxfordshire OX20 1LH, England — Government Official, England
Jay, Ricky
W M E Entertainment, 9601 Wilshire Blvd, #300, Beverly Hills CA 90210 USA — Illusionist, Actor
Jay, Vincent
Ski Federation, 50 Rue des Marquisats, BP 2451, 74011 Annecy Cedex, France — Biathlete
Jayner, Travis
US Speed Skating, PO Box 18370, Kearns UT 84118, USA — Speed Skater
Jayston, Michael
Michael Whitehall, 125 Gloucester Road, London SW7 4TE, England — Actor
Jealous, Benjamin Todd
N A A C P, 4805 Mount Hope Dr, Baltimore MD 21215, USA — Association Executive
Jean, B C
Intellectual Artists Mgmt, 10585 Santa Monica Blvd, #135, Los Angeles CA 90025, USA — Singer, Songwriter
Jean, Christiane
C D A Studio Di Nardo, Via Cavour 171, 00184 Rome, Italy — Actress
Jean, Kenneth
Columbia Artists Mgmt Inc, 1790 Broadway, #702, New York NY 10019 USA — Conductor
Jean, Michaelle
Governor General's Office, 1 Sussex Dr, Ottawa ON K1A 0A2, Canada — Governor General, Canada
Jean, Nikki
Creative Artists Agency, 2000 Ave of Stars, #100, Los Angeles CA 90067 USA — Singer, Songwriter
Jean, Olivier
Speed Skating Canada, 2781 Lancaster Road, #402, Ottawa ON K1B 1A7, Canada — Speed Skater
Jean, Vadim
United Agents, 12-26 Lexington St, London W1F 0LE, England — Director
Jean, Wyclef
W M E Entertainment, 1325 Ave of Americas, New York NY 10019, USA — Rap Artist, Actor
Jean-Baptiste, Marianne R
Independent Talent Group, Oxford House, 76 Oxford St, London W1D 1BS, England — Actress
Jeangerard, Robert E (Bob)
1930 Belmont Ave, San Carlos CA 94070, USA — Basketball Player
Jean-Gilles, Max
Philadelphia Eagles, 1 Novacare Way, Philadelphia PA 19145 USA — Football Player
Jean-Louis, Jimmy
Ken McReddie Assoc, 11 Connaught Place, London W2 2ET, England — Actor
Jeanmaire, Zizi
Ballets Roland Petit, 20 Blvd Gabes, 13008 Marseille, France — Ballerina, Actress
Jeanrenaud, Joan
Kronos Quartet, 1235 9th Ave, San Francisco CA 94122, USA — Concert Cellist (Kronos Quartet)
Jeantot, Philippe
Jeantot Organization, BP 01, 85100 Les Sables D'Olonne, France — Yachtsman, Explorer
Jee, Elizabeth
Commercials Unlimited, 190 N Canon Dr, #202, Beverly Hills, CA 90210 USA — Actress
Jee, M James
Johns Hopkins University, Astronomy Dept, Baltimore MD 21218, USA — Astronomer
Jeelani, Abdul Q
W515 State Road 59, Palmyra WI 53156, USA — Basketball Player
Jeetendra
26 Gulmohar Cross Road 5, JVPD Scheme, Mumbai MS 400049, India — Actor

J

Jeezy
Def Jam Records, 160 Varick St, #1200, New York NY 10013 USA — Rap Artist

Jeffcoat, Donald L (Donnie)
Antrim Street Entertainment, 5225 Wilshire Blvd, #424, Los Angeles CA 90036, USA — Actor

Jeffcoat, J Michael (Mike)
4224 Oak Springs Dr, Arlington TX 76016, USA — Baseball Player

Jeffcoat, James W (Jim)
5135 Summit Hill Dr, Dallas TX 75287, USA — Football Player

Jefferies, Gregory S (Greg)
7806 Bernal Ave, Pleasanton CA 94588, USA — Baseball Player

Jeffers, Eve
I C M Partners, 10250 Constellation Blvd, #900, Los Angeles CA 90067 USA — Actress

Jeffers, Patrick C
5810 Buckpasser Cove, Austin TX 78746, USA — Football Player

Jefferson, Al
Utah Jazz, Energy Solutions Arena, 301 W South Temple, Salt Lake City UT 84101 USA — Basketball Player

Jefferson, Herb, Jr
California Paralyzed Veterans, 5901 E 7th St, Building 150, Long Beach CA 90822, USA — Actor

Jefferson, James A, III
11220 NE 53rd St, Kirkland WA 98033, USA — Football Player

Jefferson, John L
43590 Merchant Mill Terrace, Leesburg VA 20176, USA — Football Player

Jefferson, Margo
New York Times, Editorial Dept, 229 W 43rd St, New York NY 10036, USA — Journalist

Jefferson, Reginal J (Reggie)
1881 Raymond Tucker Road, Tallahassee FL 32311, USA — Baseball Player

Jefferson, Richard A
San Antonio Spurs, Alamodome, 1 AT&T Center Parkway, San Antonio TX 78219 USA — Basketball Player

Jefferson, Roy L
8813 Queen Elizabeth Blvd, Annandale VA 22003, USA — Football Player

Jefferson, Stanley (Stan)
2420 Hunter Ave, #3E, Bronx NY 10475, USA — Baseball Player

Jefferts Schori, Katharine
Espicopal Church Center, 815 2nd Ave, New York NY 10017, USA — Religious Leader

Jeffires, Haywood F
2601 Courtyard Lane, Pearland TX 77584, USA — Football Player

Jeffre, Justin P
D A S Communications, 83 Riverside Dr, New York NY 10024, USA — Singer (98 Degrees)

Jeffrey, Arthur F
7305 Englewood Hill Place, Yakima WA 98908, USA — WW II Army Air Corps Hero

Jeffrey, P Michael
Governor General's Office, Government House, Canberra ACT 2600, Australia — Governor General, Australia

Jeffrey, Richard C
55 Patton Ave, Princeton NJ 08540, USA — Philosopher

Jeffreys, Alec J
Leicester University, Biochemistry Dept, University Road, Leicester LE1 7RH, England — Inventor (Genetic Fingerprinting)

Jeffreys, Anne
121 S Bentley Ave, Los Angeles CA 90049, USA — Actress

Jeffries, Chris
Toronto Raptors, Air Canada Center, 20 Bay St, Toronto ON M5J 2N8, Canada — Basketball Player

Jeffries, Edward (Dean)
Jeffries Studio of Style, 3077 Cahuenga Blvd, Los Angeles CA 90028, USA — Custom Car Painter, Stuntman

Jeffries, Fran
Terry M Hill, 41910 Boardwalk, #A2, Palm Desert CA 92211 USA — Singer, Actress, Model

Jeffries, Herbert (Herb)
Terry M Hill, 41910 Boardwalk, #A2, Palm Desert CA 92211 USA — Singer, Actor

Jeffries, John T
1652 E Camino Cielo, Tucson AZ 85718, USA — Astronomer

Jeffries, Sabrina
Pocket Star Books, 1230 Ave of Americas, New York NY 10020, USA — Writer

Jeffries, Tony
Amateur Boxing Assn, National Sports Centre, London SE19 2B8, England — Boxer

Jeffs, Christine
United Talent Agency, 9336 Civic Center Dr, Beverly Hills CA 90210 USA — Director, Writer

Jeinsen, Elke E W
Playboy Promotions, 2706 Media Center Dr, Los Angeles CA 90065 USA — Model

Jelen, Ben
555 W 53rd St, #1252, New York NY 10019, USA — Singer, Musician, Songwriter

Jelic, Christopher J (Chris)
33 Allegheny Ave, #5, Cuddy PA 15031, USA — Baseball Player

Jelinek, Elfriede
Jupiterweg 40, 1140 Vienna, Austria — Nobel Literature Laureate

Jellis, Paul
Ken McReddie Assoc, 11 Connaught Place, London W2 2ET, England — Actor

Jeltz, L Steven (Steve)
608 W 28th Place, Lawrence KS 66046, USA — Baseball Player

Jemison, Eddie
Don Buchwald/Fortitude, 6500 Wilshire Blvd, #2200, Los Angeles CA 90048 USA — Actor

Jemison, Mae C
Dartmouth College, Environmental Studies Dept, Hanover NH 03755, USA — Astronaut

Jencks, William P
11 Revere St, Lexington MA 02420, USA — Biochemist

Jendresen, Erik
W M E Entertainment, 9601 Wilshire Blvd, #300, Beverly Hills CA 90210 USA — Writer

Jenes, Theodore G, Jr
809 169th Place SW, Lynnwood WA 98037, USA — Army General

Jenkin of Roding, Patrick F
703 Howard House, Dolphin Square, London SW1V 3PQ, England — Government Official, England

Jenkin, Warren
Harbour Agency, 135 Forbes St, Woolloomooloo NSW 2011, Australia — Bassist (Killing Heidi)

Jenkins, Alfred D
4267 Janice Dr, Atlanta GA 30337, USA — Football Player

Jenkins, Billy L
4761 S Atchison Court, Aurora CO 80015, USA — Football Player

Jenkins, Carter
InMomentum Mgmt, 14622 Ventura Blvd, #778, Sherman Oaks CA 91403, USA — Actor

Jeezy - Jenkins

Jenkins, Charles H, Jr — Businessman
Publix Super Markets, PO Box 407, Lakeland FL 33802, USA
Jenkins, Charles L (Charlie) — Track Athlete, Coach
12826 Forest Creek Court, Sykesville MD 21784, USA
Jenkins, Cullen D — Football Player
49124 Peninsular Dr, Belleville MI 48111, USA
Jenkins, Daniel — Actor
S M S Talent, 8383 Wilshire Blvd, #230, Beverly Hills CA 90211 USA
Jenkins, David W — Figure Skater
5947 S Atlanta Ave, Tulsa OK 74105, USA
Jenkins, Don J — Vietnam War Army Hero (CMH)
3783 Bowling Green Road, Morgantown KY 42261, USA
Jenkins, Eddie J (Ed) — Football Player
PO Box 190278, Boston MA 02119, USA
Jenkins, Ferguson A (Fergie), Jr — Baseball Player
3655 W Anthem Way, #A109, Anthem AZ 85086, USA
Jenkins, Geoffrey S (Geoff) — Baseball Player
6683 E Judson Road, Paradise Valley AZ 85253, USA
Jenkins, George — Physician
Three Doctors Foundation, 65 Hazelwood Ave, Newark NJ 07106, USA
Jenkins, Hayes Alan — Figure Skater
3183 Regency Place, Westlake OH 44145, USA
Jenkins, Izel, Jr — Football Player
5106 Masters Lane N, Wilson NC 27896, USA
Jenkins, Jerry B — Writer
Tyndale House Publishers, 351 Executive Dr, PO Box 80, Wheaton IL 60187, USA
Jenkins, John L — Basketball Player
Atlanta Hawks, Centennial Tower, 101 Marietta St NW, #1900, Atlanta GA 30303 USA
Jenkins, Katherine — Singer
Nettwerk Mgmt, 59-65 Worship St, London EC2A 2DU, England
Jenkins, Ken — Actor
Paradigm Agency, 360 N Crescent Dr, North Building, Beverly Hills CA 90210 USA
Jenkins, Kerry C — Football Player
5492 Scout Trace Lane, Birmingham AL 35244, USA
Jenkins, Kristopher R-C (Kris) — Football Player
9525 Sweetleaf Place, Charlotte NC 28278, USA
Jenkins, Larry Flash — Actor
B/W/R, 9100 Wilshire Blvd, #500W, Beverly Hills CA 90212 USA
Jenkins, Loren — Journalist
Washington Post, Editorial Dept, 1150 15th St NW, Washington DC 20071, USA
Jenkins, Michael G — Football Player
4817 Basingstoke Dr, Suwanee GA 30024, USA
Jenkins, Noam — Actor
Glick Agency, 1321 7th St, #203, Santa Monica CA 90401 USA
Jenkins, Patricia L (Patty) — Director, Writer
Creative Artists Agency, 2000 Ave of Stars, #100, Los Angeles CA 90067 USA
Jenkins, Richard — Actor
Gersh Agency, 9465 Wilshire Blvd, #600, Beverly Hills CA 90212 USA
Jenkins, Robert L — Football Player
2878 Fieldview Terrace, San Ramon CA 94583, USA
Jenkins, Sandra — Curling Athlete
Curling Assn, 1660 Vimont Court, Cumberland ON K4A 4J4, Canada
Jenkins, Stephan D — Singer, Guitarist (Third Eye Blind)
Eric Godtland Mgmt, 1040 Mariposa St, #200, San Francisco CA 94107, USA
Jenkins, Tamara — Director
Cinetic Mgmt, 555 W 25th St, #400, New York NY 10001 USA
Jenkins, Thomas (Tomi) — Singer (Cameo)
Red Entertainment, 481 8th Ave, #824, New York NY 10001, USA
Jenks, Downing B — Businessman
1 McKnight Place, #115, Saint Louis MO 63124, USA
Jenks, Robert S (Bobby) — Baseball Player
8383 Wilshire Blvd, #500, Beverly Hills CA 90211, USA
Jenner, Brody — Entertainer, Model
I C M Partners, 10250 Constellation Blvd, #900, Los Angeles CA 90067 USA
Jenner, Bruce — Track Athlete, Actor
Commercial Talent, 9255 Sunset Blvd, #505, West Hollywood CA 90069, USA
Jenness, James — Businessman
Kellogg Co, 1 Kellogg Square, PO Box 3599, Battle Creek MI 49016, USA
Jennings, Alex — Actor
Royal National Theater, South Park, London SE1 9PX, England
Jennings, Brandon — Basketball Player
Milwaukee Bucks, Bradley Center, 1001 N 4th St, #2, Milwaukee WI 53203 USA
Jennings, Brian L — Football Player
San Francisco 49ers, 4949 Centennial Blvd, Santa Clara CA 95054 USA
Jennings, David T (Dave) — Football Player
1 Briarcliff Road, Upper Saddle River NJ 07458, USA
Jennings, Garth — Director
Hammer & Tongs, Holborn Studios, 49-50 Eagle Wharf Road, London N1 7ED, England
Jennings, Greg, Jr — Football Player
977 Green Ridge Road, De Pere WI 54115, USA
Jennings, J Douglas (Doug) — Baseball Player
PO Box 812692, Boca Raton FL 33481, USA
Jennings, Jason R — Baseball Player
5274 Monterey Dr, Frisco TX 75034, USA
Jennings, Jim — Architect
Jim Jennings Architect, 49 Rodgers Alley, San Francisco CA 94103, USA
Jennings, Jonas D — Football Player
123 Davis Road, Fayetteville GA 30215, USA
Jennings, Keith O — Football Player
119 Axtell Dr, Summerville SC 29485, USA
Jennings, Keith R — Basketball Player
808 Lakeland Court, Culpeper VA 22701, USA
Jennings, Kelly J — Football Player
Seattle Seahawks, 12 Seahawks Way, Renton WA 98056 USA
Jennings, Paul — Writer
PO Box 1459, Warrnambool VIC 3280, Australia

Jennings, Paul C — Civil Engineer
640 S Grand Ave, Pasadena CA 91105, USA
Jennings, Robert B — Pathologist
Duke University, Medical Center, Pathology Dept, Durham NC 27710, USA
Jennings, Shooter — Singer
208 Bibb St, Campbellsville KY 42718, USA
Jennings, Stanford J — Football Player
215 Jasmine Way, Alpharetta GA 30004, USA
Jennings, Wilbur (Will) — Composer, Songwriter
B M I, 8730 W Sunset Blvd, #300, Los Angeles CA 90069 USA
Jenrette, Richard H — Businessman
67 E 93rd St, New York NY 10128, USA
Jens, Salome — Actress
C E S D, 10635 Santa Monica Blvd, #130, Los Angeles CA 90025 USA
Jens, Walter — Writer
Sonnenstr 5, 72076 Tubingen, Germany
Jensen, Ashley — Actress, Comedienne
Hamilton Hodell, 66-68 Margaret St, London W1W 8SR, England
Jensen, David — Entertainer
Capital Gold, 30 Leicester Square, London WC2H 7LA, England
Jensen, Debra — Model
31441 Santa Margarita Parkway, #322, Rancho Santa Margarita CA 92688, USA
Jensen, Derrick — Football Player
147 Downing St, Panama City FL 32413, USA
Jensen, Eivind Gullberg — Conductor
Ophelias Public Relations for Culture, Lucile-Grahn-Str 37, 81675 Munich, Germany
Jensen, Elwood V — Biochemist
National Institutes of Health, Fogarty International Center, Bethesda MD 20892, USA
Jensen, Jacob — Industrial Designer
Bang Olufsen, Peter Bangs Vej 15, PO Box 40, DK 7600 Struer, Denmark
Jensen, James — Geologist
Brigham Young University, Geology Dept, Provo UT 84602, USA
Jensen, James C (Jim) — Football Player
9811 N Oak Knoll Circle, Davie FL 33324, USA
Jensen, James D (Jim) — Football Player
1972 Cayman Dr, Windsor CO 80550, USA
Jensen, James W, Jr — Cinematographer
28853 Garnet Hill Court, Agoura Hills CA 91301, USA
Jensen, Jonathan W (Jon) — Football Player
36771 Allder School Road, Purcellville VA 20132, USA
Jensen, Liz — Writer
Gillon Aitken Assoc, 18-21 Cavaye Place, London SW10 9PT, England
Jensen, Marcus C — Baseball Player
19550 N Grayhawk Dr, #1134, Scottsdale AZ 85255, USA
Jenson, Victoria (Vicky) — Director, Animator
Creative Artists Agency, 2000 Ave of Stars, #100, Los Angeles CA 90067 USA
Jenssen, Amanda — Singer
Sony Music Sweden, Box 3187, 103 63 Stockholm, Sweden , USA
Jent, Chris — Basketball Player
445 Retreat Lane W, Powell OH 43065, USA
Jentsch, Julia — Actress
Agentur Vogel, Katzbachstr 8, 10965 Berlin, Germany
Jeon Da-Hye — Speed Skater
Skating Union, 88 Bangyee-Dong, Songpaku, Seoul 138 749, South Korea
Jeong, Ken — Actor, Comedian
United Talent Agency, 9336 Civic Center Dr, Beverly Hills CA 90210 USA
Jepsen, Carly Rae — Singer, Songwriter
Simkin Artist Mgmt, 165 W Broadway, #101-1001, Vancouver BC V6H 4E4, Canada
Jepsen, Kevin M — Baseball Player
425 Cannon Green Dr, #H, Goleta CA 93117, USA
Jepsen, Les — Basketball Player
8075 9th Street Way N, Saint Paul MN 55128, USA
Jepsen, Roger W — Senator, IA
3542 Pennyroyal Road, Port Charlotte FL 33953, USA
Jepson, Mary Lou — Computer Scientist, Social Activist
Massachusetts Institute of Technology, Media Laboratory, Cambridge MA 02139, USA
Jepson, Mikael — Guitarist (The Ark)
Live Nation, Linnegatan 89, Box 21451, 104 51 Stockholm, Sweden
Jeremiah, David E — Navy Admiral
2898 Melanie Lane, Oakton VA 22124, USA
Jeremih — Singer
Def Jam Records, 160 Varick St, #1200, New York NY 10013 USA
Jeremy — Singer, Guitarist (Chad & Jeremy)
Icon Performing Arts, 1557 Westwood Blvd, #242, Los Angeles CA 90024, USA
Jerins, Ruby — Actress
Management 360, 9111 Wilshire Blvd, Beverly Hills CA 90210 USA
Jerkens, H Allen — Thoroughbred Racing Trainer
9509 242nd St, Floral Park NY 11001, USA
Jerkins, Rodney (Darkchild) — Music Producer
Paradigm Agency, 360 N Crescent Dr, North Building, Beverly Hills CA 90210 USA
Jernigan, Tamara E (Tammy) — Astronaut
4268 Brindisi Place, Pleasanton CA 94566, USA
Jernstedt, Ken — WW II Marine Corps Hero
911 Pine St, Hood River OR 97031, USA
Jeru the Damaja — Rap Artist
W M E Entertainment, 1325 Ave of Americas, New York NY 10019 USA
Jerusalem, Siegfried — Opera Singer
Sudring 9, 90542 Eckental, Germany
Jervey, Travis R — Football Player
22 Sand Dolalr Dr, Isle of Palms SC 29451, USA
Jerzak, Stephen — Singer, Songwriter
Agency Group Ltd, 142 W 57th St, #600, New York NY 10019 USA
Jerzembeck, Michael J (Mike) — Baseball Player
10625 S Hall Dr, Charlotte NC 28270, USA
Jeselnik, Anthony — Actor, Comedian
Mosiac Media Group, 9200 W Sunset Blvd, #1000, Los Angeles CA 90069 USA

Jessee, Michael A — Government Official, Financier
Federal Home Loan Bank, 1 Financial Center, #2000, Boston MA 02111, USA

Jessen, Gene Nora — Astronaut Candidate
630 S Tiburon Ave, Meridian ID 83642, USA

Jessie J — Singer, Songwriter
Universal Republic Records, 1755 Broadway, #700, New York NY 10019, USA

Jessup, Bill (Billy0 — Football Player
13341 Saint Andrews Dr, #137D, Seal Beach CA 90740, USA

Jesus, Juan — Soccer Player
Confederacion de Futebol, Rua Victor Civita 66, #1, Rio de Janeiro 22775 044, Brazil

Jet Li — Actor
Current Entertainment, 9378 Wilshire Blvd, #210, Beverly Hills CA 90212, USA

Jeter, Derek S — Baseball Player
845 United Nations Plaza, #888, New York NY 10017, USA

Jeter, Gary M — Football Player
3612 Quail Ridge Dr, Plainsboro NJ 8536, USA

Jeter, John (Johnny) — Baseball Player
1012 N 5th St, Monroe LA 71201, USA

Jetsun Pema — Queen, Bhutan
Royal Palace, Tashichhodzong, Thimphu, Bhutan

Jett, Brent W — Astronaut
2529 Goldsmith St, Houston TX 77030, USA

Jett, James — Football Player, Track Athlete
PO Box 430, Kearneysville WV 25430, USA

Jett, Joan — Singer, Guitarist, Songwriter
Blackheart Records, 636 Broadway, New York NY 10012, USA

Jett, John — Football Player
177 Crowder Point Dr, Reedville VA 22539, USA

Jeunet, Jean-Pierre — Director
I C M Partners, 10250 Constellation Blvd, #900, Los Angeles CA 90067 USA

Jevanord, Oystein — Drummer (A-Ha)
Bandana Mgmt, 11 Elvaston Place, #300, London SW7 5QC, England

Jewel — Singer, Songwriter, Actress
Front Line Mgmt, 1100 Glendon Ave, #2000, Los Angeles CA 90024 USA

Jewell, Buddy, Jr — Singer, Songwriter
PO Box 58, Antioch TN 37011, USA

Jewison, Norman F — Director, Producer
Yorktown Productions, 300 W Olympic Blvd, #1314, Santa Monica CA 90401, USA

Jhabvala, Ruth Prawer — Writer
400 E 52nd St, New York NY 10022, USA

Ji Dong-Won — Soccer Player
Football Assn, 1-131 Sinmunno, 2-Ga Jongno-Gu, Seoul 110 062, South Korea

Ji Yai-Shin — Golfer
Ladies Pro Golf Assn, 100 International Golf Dr, Daytona Beach FL 32124 USA

Ji Young Oh — Golfer
Ladies Pro Golf Assn, 100 International Golf Dr, Daytona Beach FL 32124 USA

Jia, Li — Hematologist
Duke University Medical Center, Hematology Dept, Durham NC 27708, USA

Jia, Ran — Concert Pianist
I M G Artists, Hogarth Business Park, Chiswick, London W4 2TH, England

Jiang Tiefeng — Artist
Jiang Publishing, 1329 San Carlos Road, Arcadia CA 91006, USA

Jiear, Alison — Singer, Actress
United Agents, 12-26 Lexington St, London W1F 0LE, England

Jiggets, Daniel M (Dan) — Football Player
4751 RFD, Long Grove IL 60047, USA

Jiles, Dwayne — Football Player
3712 Churchill Court, Plano TX 75075, USA

Jillian, Ann — Actress
PO Box 57739, Sherman Oaks CA 91413, USA

Jim Yong Kim — Physician
Partners in Health, 641 Huntington Ave, #100, Boston MA 02115, USA

Jimenez Rodriguez, Raul A — Soccer Player
Federacion de Futbol, Colima 373 Colonia Roma, Delegacion Cuauhtemoc Mexico DF 06700, Mexico

Jimenez, Carlos — Architect
Jimenez Architectural Design Studio, 1116 Willard St, Houston TX 77006, USA

Jimenez, Flaco — Singer/Accordionist (Texas Tornados)
Fiesta Records, PO Box 241388, San Antonio TX 78224, USA

Jimenez, Gladys — Actress
Stone Manners Salners, 9911 W Pico Blvd, #1400, Los Angeles CA 90035 USA

Jimenez, Jessica — Actress
A P A Talent/Literary Agency, 405 S Beverly Dr, #300, Beverly Hills CA 90212 USA

Jimenez, Miguel Angel — Golfer
Advantage International, 1025 Thomas Jefferson NW, #450, Washington DC 20007 USA

Jimenez, Nicario — Artist
5531 Teak Wood Dr NW, Naples FL 34119, USA

Jimenez, Penelope — Model
Playboy Promotions, 2706 Media Center Dr, Los Angeles CA 90065 USA

Jimenez, Santiago, Jr — Singer, Accordian Player
Folklore Productions, PO Box 7003, Santa Monica CA 90406, USA

Jimerson, Charlton — Baseball Player
22048 Betlen Way, Castro Valley CA 94546, USA

Jiminez, Joe — Golfer
29243 Enchanted Glen, Boerne TX 78015, USA

Jiminez, Miguel A — Baseball Player
16 Shelley Court, Middletown NY 10941, USA

Jimmy Jam — Businessman, Producer, Composer
Universal Attractions, 135 W 26th St, #1200, New York NY 10001 USA

Jimoh, Ade — Football Player
41782 Bristow Manor Dr, Ashburn VA 20148, USA

Jin — Rap Artist, Actor
American Talent Agency, 26 Finney Farm Road, Croton on Hudson NY 10520, USA

Jin Sun Yu — Speed Skater
Skating Union, 88 Bangyee-Dong, Songpaku, Seoul 138 749, South Korea

Jing Haipeng — Taikonaut
Satellite Launch Center, Jiuquan, Guangzhou Province, China

Jinks, Dan — Producer
Dan Jinks Co, 4024 Radford Ave, Bungalow 9, Studio City CA 91604, USA

Jiricna, Eva M — Architect
Jiricna Architects, 38 Warren St, #300, London W1T 6AE, England

Jirov, Vassili — Boxer
Thell Torrence, 5449 S Eastern Ave, #3, Las Vegas NV 89119, USA

Jirtle, Randy L — Geneticist
Duke University Medical Center, Radiation Oncology Dept, Durham NC 27708, USA

J-Kwon — Rap Artist
Universal Attractions, 135 W 26th St, #1200, New York NY 10001 USA

Jo, Sumi — Opera Singer
Askonas Holt, Lincoln House, 300 High Holborn, London WC1V 7JH, England

Jo, Timothy W (Tim) — Actor
Innovative Artists, 1505 10th St, Santa Monica CA 90401 USA

Joannou, Chris — Bassist (Silverchair)
John Watson Mgmt, PO Box 281, Sunny Hills NSW 2010, Australia

Joanou, Phil — Director
Todd Smith Assoc, 11835 W Olympic Blvd, #640, Los Angeles CA 90064, USA

Job, Brian — Swimmer
PO Box 70427, Sunnyvale CA 94086, USA

Jobe, Emmett — Auto Racing Executive
Phoenix International Raceway, 125 S Avondale Blvd, #200, Avondale AZ 85323, USA

Jobe, Frank W — Sports Orthopedic Surgeon
Kerlan-Jobe Orthopedic Clinic, 501 E Hardy St, #200, Inglewood CA 90301, USA

Jobert, Marlene — Actress
8-10 Blvd de Courcelles, 75008 Paris, France

Jobrani, Maz — Actor
Levity Entertainment, 6701 Center Drive W, #1111, Los Angeles CA 90045 USA

Jobson, Richard — Director, Producer, Writer
Curtis Brown Group, 28-29 Haymarket St, #500, London SW1Y 4SP, England

Jodat, James S (Jim) — Football Player
25032 Mammoth Circle, Lake Forest CA 92630, USA

Jodie, Brett — Baseball Player
1359 Corley Mill Road, Lexington SC 29072, USA

Jodorowsky, Alejandro — Director, Producer, Composer
Agence Josiane Stroh, 3 Allee Marie Laurent, 75020 Paris, France

Jodzio, Rick — Ice Hockey Player
31202 Boca Raton Place, Laguna Niguel CA 92677, USA

Joe — Singer, Songwriter, Record Producer
Kedar Entertainment, 21 W 39th St, #600, New York NY 10018, USA

Joe, Leon M — Football Player
7917 Woodyard Road, Clinton MD 20735, USA

Joe, William (Billy) — Football Player, Coach
3964 Butler Springs Way, Birmingham AL 35226, USA

Joel, Billy — Singer, Songwriter
Maritime Inc, 34 Audrey Ave, #4, Oyster Bay NY 11771, USA

Joel, Richard M — Educator
Yeshiva University, President's Office, 500 W 185th St, New York NY 10033, USA

Joerres, Jeffrey — Businessman
Manpower Inc, 600 A B Data Dr, Milwaukee WI 53217, USA

Joey Z — Guitarist (Life of Agony, Stereomud)
Agency Group Ltd, 142 W 57th St, #600, New York NY 10019 USA

Joffe, Roland V — Director, Producer
Baumgartan Mgmt, 406 Wilshire Blvd, Santa Monica CA 90401, USA

Joffin, Jon — Cinematographer
Dattner Dispoto, 10635 Santa Monica Blvd, #165, Los Angeles CA 90025, USA

Jofre, Eder — Boxer
Alamo de Ministero Rocha, Azevedo 373, C Cesar 21-15, Sao Paulo, Brazil

Jogia, Avan — Actor
United Talent Agency, 9336 Civic Center Dr, Beverly Hills CA 90210 USA

Johannesen, Lena — Body Builder, Model
PO Box 325, Culver City CA 90232, USA

Johannsen, Jake — Actor
Paradigm Agency, 360 N Crescent Dr, North Building, Beverly Hills CA 90210 USA

Jóhannsson, Jóhann — Composer
Agency Group Ltd, 142 W 57th St, #600, New York NY 10019 USA

Johannsson, Kristjan — Opera Singer
Herbert Breslin, 119 W 57th St, #1505, New York NY 10019 USA

Johansen, Iris — Writer
Jane Rotrosen Agency, 318 E 51st St, New York NY 10022, USA

Johansen, Roy — Writer
Jane Rotrosen Agency, 318 E 51st St, New York NY 10022, USA

Johanson, Donald C — Anthropologist
Arizona State University, Human Origins Institute, Tempe AZ 85287, USA

Johanson, Jai Johnny (Jaimoe) — Drummer (Allman Brothers Band)
Allman Brothers Band Inc, 18 Tamworth Road, Waban MA 02468, USA

Johanson, Sue — Educator, Writer, Commentator
Sunday Night Sex Show, 42 Pardee Ave, Toronto ON M6K 3H5, Canada

Johansson, Calle — Ice Hockey Player
1708 Mayfair Place, Crofton MD 21114, USA

Johansson, Jean — Actress
Associated International Mgmt, Fairfax House, Fulwood Place, London WC1V 6HU, England

Johansson, Kathy — Model, Body Builder
PO Box 43351, Tucson AZ 85733, USA

Johansson, Lars-Olof — Guitarist, Keyboardist (Cardigans)
Talent Trust, Kungsgatan 9C, 411 19 Gothenburg, Sweden

Johansson, Paul — Actor
Innovative Artists, 1505 10th St, Santa Monica CA 90401 USA

Johansson, Per-Ulik — Golfer
18710 SE Pineneedle Lane, Jupiter FL 33469, USA

Johansson, Scarlett — Actress, Model, Singer
Melanie Johansson Mgmt, 7135 Hollywood Blvd, #804, Los Angeles CA 90046, USA

Johansson, Stefan — Auto Racing Driver
3546 Crownridge Dr, Sherman Oaks CA 91403, USA

Johaug, Therese — Cross Country Skier
Nansen I L Ski, Toini Berg Brynhildsvoll, Dalsbygda, 2550 Os I Osterdalen, Norway

Johjima, Kenji
2412 109th Ave SE, Bellevue WA 98004, USA — Baseball Player
John, Chris
Harry's Gym, 14 Cressall Road, Balcatta, Perth WA 6021, Australia — Boxer
John, David D
7 Cyncoed Ave, Cardiff CF2 6ST, Wales — Museum Executive, Explorer
John, Elton
Twenty-First Artists, 1 Blythe Road, London W14 0HG, England — Singer, Songwriter
John, Thomas E (Tommy)
6202 Seton House Lane, Charlotte NC 28277, USA — Baseball Player
John, Tylyn
813 Harbor Blvd, #133, West Sacramento CA 95691, USA — Model, Actress
Johnagin, Tommy
Avalon Mgmt, 4a Exmoor St, London W10 6BD, England — Actor, Comedian
Johncock, Gordon
649 S Fall River Dr, Coldwater MI 49036, USA — Auto Racing Driver
John-Jules, Danny
Jonathan Altaras Assoc, 11 Garrick St, London WC2E 9AR, England — Actor
Johnny A
Rosebud Agency, PO Box 170429, San Francisco CA 94117 USA — Guitarist
Johnny O
Universal Attractions, 135 W 26th St, #1200, New York NY 10001 USA — Singer
Johnova, Andriena
Nad Kralovskou Oborou 278/15, 170 00 Prague 7, Czech Republic — Artist
John-Roger
Movement of Spiritual InnerAwareness, PO Box 513935, Los Angeles CA 90051, USA — Religious Leader
Johns, Chris
National Geographic, Editorial Dept, 1145 17th St NW, Washington DC 20036 USA — Editor
Johns, Daniel
John Watson Mgmt, PO Box 281, Sunny Hills NSW 2010, Australia — Singer, Guitarist (Silverchair)
Johns, Douglas A (Doug)
1131 SW 72nd Ave, Plantation FL 33317, USA — Baseball Player
Johns, Glynis
2051 N Highland Ave, Los Angeles CA 90068, USA — Actress
Johns, Jasper
97 Low Road, #642, Sharon CT 06069, USA — Artist
Johns, Lori
PO Box 3667, Corpus Christi TX 78463, USA — Drag Racing Driver
Johns, R Keith
1525 Suzanne Ridge Court, Glencoe MO 63038, USA — Baseball Player
Johns, Raymond E, Jr
Commander, Air Mobility Command, Scott Air Force Base IL 62225 USA — Air Force General
Johns, Simon
Duophonic Records, PO Box 3787, London SE22 9DZ, England — Bassist (Stereolab)
Johnson Pucci, Gail
2132 Ward Dr, Walnut Creek CA 94596, USA — Synchronized Swimmer
Johnson, Aaron
3810 Gabrielle Dr, Dublin OH 43016, USA — Ice Hockey Player
Johnson, Aaron
Hamilton Hodell, 66-68 Margaret St, London W1W 8SR, England — Actor
Johnson, Addison
King Features Syndicate, 300 W 57th St, #1500, New York NY 10019 USA — Cartoonist (Bringing Up Father)
Johnson, Alexander (Alex)
18425 Bretton Dr, Detroit MI 48223, USA — Baseball Player
Johnson, Alexzander S (Alexz)
W M E Entertainment, 9601 Wilshire Blvd, #300, Beverly Hills CA 90210 USA — Actress
Johnson, Allen
Octagon Worldwide, 7100 Forest Ave, #201, Richmond VA 23226 USA — Track Athlete
Johnson, Amy Jo
Burstein Co, 15304 Sunset Blvd, #208, Pacific Palisades CA 90272, USA — Actress, Singer, Songwriter
Johnson, Anderson J (Andy)
PO Box 6828, Athens GA 30604, USA — Football Player
Johnson, Andre L
Houston Texans, 2 Reliant Park, Houston TX 77054 USA — Football Player
Johnson, Andreas
International Talent Booking, Ariel House, 74A Charlotte St, #100 London W1T 4QJ, England — Singer
Johnson, Anne-Marie
Diverse Talent Group, 9911 Pico Blvd, #350W, Los Angeles CA 90035 USA — Actress
Johnson, Anthony C (Tony)
4446 Janssen Dr, Memphis TN 38128, USA — Baseball Player
Johnson, Anthony M
5162 Inwood Place, Mableton GA 30126, USA — Basketball Player
Johnson, Anthony S
752 Peppervine Ave, Saint Johns FL 32259, USA — Football Player
Johnson, Arte
2725 Bottlebrush Dr, Los Angeles CA 90077, USA — Actor, Comedian
Johnson, Arthur
5735 E Waltann Lane, Scottsdale AZ 85254, USA — Hero
Johnson, Ashley
Anonymous Content, 3532 Hayden Ave, Culver City CA 90232 USA — Actress
Johnson, Avery
Brooklyn Nets, 15 Metro Tech Center, #1100, Brooklyn NY 11201 USA — Basketball Player, Coach
Johnson, Bart
B/W/R, 9100 Wilshire Blvd, #500W, Beverly Hills CA 90212 USA — Actor
Johnson, Ben
4 Saint Peter's Wharf, Hammersmith Terrace, London W6 9UD, England — Artist
Johnson, Benjamin F (Ben)
112 Locksley Dr, Greenwood SC 29649, USA — Baseball Player
Johnson, Benjamin S (Ben), Jr
Ed Futerman, 2 Saint Clair Ave E, #1500, Toronto ON M4T 2R1, Canada — Track Athlete
Johnson, Bernie
15 Carriage Way, Scarborough ME 04074, USA — Ice Hockey Player
Johnson, Betsey L
Betsey Johnson Co, 498 Fashion Ave, #2103, New York NY 10018, USA — Fashion Designer
Johnson, Beverly
PO Box 1474, Rancho Mirage CA 92270, USA — Model, Actress

Johjima - Johnson

Johnson, Bjorn
TalentWorks, 3500 W Olive Ave, #1400, Burbank CA 91505 USA — Actor, Director

Johnson, Brad
Metropolitan Talent Agency, 7020 La Presa Dr, Los Angeles CA 90068 USA — Model, Actor

Johnson, Brandon H
1541 W Coquina Dr, Gilbert AZ 85233, USA — Football Player

Johnson, Brent
808 N Florida St, Arlington VA 22205, USA — Ice Hockey Player

Johnson, Brian
Alberts Music, 9 Rangers Road, Neutral Bay, Sydney NSW 2089, Australia — Singer (AC/DC)

Johnson, Brian D
1405 Balmoral Dr, Detroit MI 48203, USA — Baseball Player

Johnson, Bryant A
5749 Legends Club Circle, Braselton GA 30517, USA — Football Player

Johnson, Bryce
Untitled Entertainment, 350 S Beverly Dr, #200, Beverly Hills CA 90212 USA — Actor

Johnson, Buck
701 Pine Grove Road, Harvest AL 35749, USA — Basketball Player

Johnson, C Barth (Bart)
1929 N Newland Ave, Chicago IL 60707, USA — Baseball Player

Johnson, C Stephen (Steve)
9715 SW Quail Post Road, Portland OR 97219, USA — Basketball Player

Johnson, Calvin, Jr
185 Roscommon Court, Tyrone GA 30290, USA — Football Player

Johnson, Carolyn Dawn
R P M Mgmt, 209 10th Ave S, #229, Nashville TN 37203, USA — Singer, Songwriter

Johnson, Chad J J
Miami Dolphins, 7500 SW 30th St, Davie FL 33314 USA — Football Player

Johnson, Charles
Carolina Panthers, Ericsson Stadium, 800 S Mint St, Charlotte NC 28202 USA — Football Player

Johnson, Charles E
6549 Wakefalls Dr, Wake Forest NC 27587, USA — Football Player

Johnson, Charles E
12301 NW 7th St, Plantation FL 33325, USA — Baseball Player

Johnson, Charles L (Charley)
PO Box 1312, Mesilla NM 88046, USA — Football Player

Johnson, Charles R
University of Washington, English Dept, Seattle WA 98105, USA — Writer

Johnson, Cheryl L
United American Nurses, 8515 Georgia Ave, Silver Spring MD 20910, USA — Labor Leader

Johnson, Chris J
A P A Talent/Literary Agency, 405 S Beverly Dr, #300, Beverly Hills CA 90212 USA — Actor

Johnson, Christa
6210 W Sunset Road, Tucson AZ 85743, USA — Golfer

Johnson, Clark
United Talent Agency, 9336 Civic Center Dr, Beverly Hills CA 90210 USA — Actor, Director

Johnson, Clemon
835 N Waukeenah St, Monticello FL 32344, USA — Basketball Player

Johnson, Clifford (Cliff)
9618 Mediator Pass, Converse TX 78109, USA — Baseball Player

Johnson, Corey
Another Tongue, 10-11 D'Arblay St, London W1F 8DS, England — Actor

Johnson, Cornelius O
603 Dale St, Highland Springs VA 23075, USA — Football Player

Johnson, Courtney
408 Tharp Dr, Moraga CA 94556, USA — Water Polo Player

Johnson, Craig
812 Island Dr, #A, Alameda CA 94502, USA — Ice Hockey Player

Johnson, Craig A
Penguin Books, 375 Hudson St, Basement 1, New York NY 10014 USA — Writer

Johnson, Curtis W
2015 Calumet Ave, Toledo OH 43607, USA — Football Player

Johnson, Curtis, Jr
Tulane University, Athletic Dept, New Orleans LA 70118, USA — Football Coach

Johnson, Daniel R (Dan)
3355 134th Ave NE, Andover MN 55304, USA — Baseball Player

Johnson, Darren
University of Oregon, Chemistry Dept, Eugene OR 97403, USA — Chemist

Johnson, Darrius D
402 Thomas St, Terrell TX 75160, USA — Football Player

Johnson, Dave
United Garment Workers, 4207 Lebanon Road, Hermitage TN 37076, USA — Labor Leader

Johnson, David A (Davey)
1064 Howell Branch Road, Winter Park FL 32789, USA — Baseball Player, Manager

Johnson, David Allen (D J)
500 Tripoli St, Pittsburgh PA 15212, USA — Football Player

Johnson, David C (Dave)
3202 Woodhollow Circle, Abilene TX 79606, USA — Baseball Player

Johnson, David Cay
New York Times, Editorial Dept, 229 W 43rd St, New York NY 10036 USA — Journalist

Johnson, David G
5500 S Shore Dr, #1406, Chicago IL 60637, USA — Economist

Johnson, David W
Campbell Soup Co, 1 Campbell Place, Camden NJ 08103, USA — Businessman

Johnson, David W (Dave)
7101 Mount Vista Road, Kingsville MD 21087, USA — Baseball Player

Johnson, Demetrios
840 Garonne Dr, Ballwin MO 63021, USA — Football Player

Johnson, DerMarr M
14610 Man O War Dr, Bowie MD 20721, USA — Basketball Player

Johnson, Derrick O
524 Private Road 4450, Uvalde TX 78801, USA — Football Player

Johnson, Diane
Creative Artists Agency, 2000 Ave of Stars, #100, Los Angeles CA 90067 USA — Writer

Johnson, Don
Don Johnson Productions, 9663 Santa Monica Blvd, #278, Beverly Hills CA 90210, USA — Actor

Johnson, Donald (Groundhog) 3935 King Place, Cincinnati OH 45223, USA	Baseball Player
Johnson, Donald R (Don) 1529 NE 21st Ave, #205, Portland OR 97232, USA	Baseball Player
Johnson, Dwayne D (The Rock) White Buffalo Entertainment, One State Street Plaza, #2400, New York NY 10004, USA	Actor, Professional Wrestler
Johnson, Dwight O 1812 King Cole Dr, Waco TX 76705, USA	Football Player
Johnson, Earvin (Magic), Jr Magic Johnson Foundation, 9100 Wilshire Blvd, #700E, Beverly Hills CA 90212, USA	Basketball Player, Coach
Johnson, Echo L 2402 Jarratt Ave, #B, Austin TX 78703, USA	Model
Johnson, Edward (Eddie) Seattle Sounders, 12 Seahawks Way, Renton WA 98056 USA	Soccer Player
Johnson, Edward A (Eddie) 6133 N 61st Place, Paradise Valley AZ 85253, USA	Basketball Player
Johnson, Edward L (Eddie), Jr PO Box 542, Weirsdale FL 32195, USA	Basketball Player
Johnson, Edward S (Tre), III 680 Harrison Ave, Peekskill NY 10566, USA	Football Player
Johnson, Emma Columbia Artists Mgmt Inc, 1790 Broadway, #702, New York NY 10019 USA	Concert Clarinetist
Johnson, Eric Gotham Group, 7250 Melrose Ave, Los Angeles CA 90046, USA	Writer
Johnson, Eric 893 Chateau Meadows Dr, Eugene OR 97401, USA	Golfer
Johnson, Eric Monterey International, 200 W Superior St, #202, Chicago IL 60654 USA	Guitarist
Johnson, Eric A P A Talent/Literary Agency, 405 S Beverly Dr, #300, Beverly Hills CA 90212 USA	Actor
Johnson, Erik Colorado Avalanche, Pepsi Center, 1000 Chopper Circle, Denver CO 80204 USA	Ice Hockey Player
Johnson, Ernest T (Ernie), Jr TNT-TV, Sports Dept, 1050 Techwood Dr, Atlanta GA 30318 USA	Sportscaster
Johnson, Ervin Minnesota Timberwolves, Target Center, 600 1st Ave N, Minneapolis MN 55403 USA	Basketball Player
Johnson, Essex L 1633 E Dimondale Dr, Carson CA 90746, USA	Football Player
Johnson, Ezra R 330 Millhaven Landing, Fayetteville GA 30215, USA	Football Player
Johnson, Frank King Features Syndicate, 300 W 57th St, #1500, New York NY 10019 USA	Cartoonist (Bringing Up Father)
Johnson, Frank A 1151 Cypress Hill Lane, Stockton CA 95206, USA	Baseball Player
Johnson, Franklin L (Frank) 4320 N 40th St, Phoenix AZ 85018, USA	Basketball Player, Coach
Johnson, Fred 5501 Camelia St, Pittsburgh PA 15201, USA	Singer (Marcels)
Johnson, Gary 50 Tallwood Court, Atherton CA 94027, USA	Baseball Player
Johnson, Gene Modern Mgmt, 1625 Broadway, #600, Nashville TN 37203, USA	Guitarist, Mandolin Player (Diamond Rio)
Johnson, Georgann 218 Glenroy Place, Los Angeles CA 90049, USA	Actress
Johnson, George Green Light Talent Agency, PO Box 3172, Beverly Hills CA 90212 USA	Singer, Guitarist (Brothers Johnson)
Johnson, George 2860 Brookford Lane SW, Atlanta GA 30331, USA	Golfer
Johnson, George T 630 Highland Overlook, Atlanta GA 30349, USA	Basketball Player
Johnson, George W George Mason University, President's Office, Fairfax VA 22030, USA	Educator
Johnson, Glen DiBella Entertainment, 350 7th Ave, #800, New York NY 10001, USA	Boxer
Johnson, Gregory C N A S A, Johnson Space Center, 2101 NASA Road, Houston TX 77058 USA	Astronaut
Johnson, Gregory C (Greg) 1058 Runyon Road, Rochester Hills MI 48306, USA	Ice Hockey Player
Johnson, Gregory H N A S A, Johnson Space Center, 2101 NASA Road, Houston TX 77058 USA	Astronaut
Johnson, Hansford T U S A A Capital Corp, 9800 Fredericksburg Road, San Antonio TX 78240, USA	Air Force General
Johnson, Harold 2964 N Bambrey St, Philadelphia PA 19132, USA	Boxer
Johnson, Haynes B University of Maryland, Journalism Dept, College Park MD 20742, USA	Journalist
Johnson, Holly Wolfgang Kuhle Artist Mgmt, PO Box 425, London SW6 3TX, England	Singer (Frankie Goes to Hollywood)
Johnson, Howard M (Hojo) 8597 SE Coconut St, Hobe Sound FL 33455, USA	Baseball Player
Johnson, Hugh T Mirisch Agency, 8840 Wilshire Blvd, #100, Beverly Hills CA 90211 USA	Director, Cinematographer
Johnson, I Birger 1508 Barclay Place, Schenectady NY 12309, USA	Electrical Engineer
Johnson, Ian Wall Street Journal, Editorial Dept, 1 World Financial Center, New York NY 10281, USA	Journalist
Johnson, J Bradley (Brad) 1911 Nellie Gray Court, Athens GA 30606, USA	Football Player
Johnson, J Curley 5512 Wedgefield Road, Granbury TX 76049, USA	Football Player
Johnson, J Seward Sculpture Foundation, 2525 Michigan Ave, #A6, Santa Monica CA 90404, USA	Sculptor
Johnson, Jack Partisan Arts, PO Box 5085, Larkspur CA 94977, USA	Singer, Guitarist, Songwriter
Johnson, James A Perseus LLC, 1325 Ave of Americas, #2500, New York NY 10019, USA	Government Official, Financier

V.I.P. Address Book

	Football Player
Johnson, James E (Jimmy) 656 Amaranth Blvd, Mill Valley CA 94941, USA	Football Coach, Sportscaster
Johnson, James W (Jimmy) Fox-TV, Sports Dept, 205 W 67th St, New York NY 10065 USA	Singer, Songwriter
Johnson, Jamey Mercury Records, 54 Music Square E, #300, Nashville TN 37203 USA	Football Player
Johnson, Jarret W 437 Evans Road, Niceville FL 32578, USA	Baseball Player
Johnson, Jason M 18122 Emerald Bay St, Tampa FL 33647, USA	Actor, Comedian, Ventrioquist
Johnson, Jay Comedians USA, 1308 Sumac Drive, Knoxville TN 37919, USA	Actor
Johnson, Jay Kenneth A P A Talent/Literary Agency, 405 S Beverly Dr, #300, Beverly Hills CA 90212 USA	Navy Admiral, Businessman
Johnson, Jay L General Dynamics, 2941 Fairview Park Dr, #100, Falls Church VA 22042, USA	Swimmer, Coach
Johnson, Jenna University of Tennessee, Athletic Dept, PO Box 15016, Knoxville TN 37901, USA	Producer, Writer
Johnson, Jennifer W M E Entertainment, 9601 Wilshire Blvd, #300, Beverly Hills CA 90210 USA	Navy Admiral
Johnson, Jerome L Navy-Marine Corps Relief Society, 801 N Randolph St, Arlington VA 22203, USA	Baseball Player
Johnson, Jerry M 16670 Espola Road, Poway CA 92064, USA	Football Player
Johnson, Jesse 102 Rosegill Road, Richmond VA 23236, USA	Auto Racing Driver
Johnson, Jimmie K PO Box 4283, Mooresville NC 28117, USA	Cartoonist (Arlo & Janis)
Johnson, Jimmy United Media Syndicate, PO Box 5610, Cincinnati OH 45201 USA	Basketball Player
Johnson, Joe M 1639 Academy Square, Atlanta GA 30337, USA	Actress
Johnson, Johari H W A Talent, 3500 W Olive Ave, #1400, Burbank CA 91505 USA	Basketball Player
Johnson, John H 4751 N 18th St, Milwaukee WI 53209, USA	Baseball Player
Johnson, John Henry 3345 Delna, Sparks NV 89431, USA	Ice Hockey Player
Johnson, John J L (Jack), III Los Angeles Kings, Staples Center, 1111 S Figueroa St, Los Angeles CA 90015 USA	Football Player
Johnson, Johnnie, Jr 3540 W Sahara Ave, #780, Las Vegas NV 89102, USA	Football Player
Johnson, Johnny PO Box 13301, Tempe AZ 85284, USA	Baseball Player
Johnson, Jonathan K 101 Broad Bluff Point, Irmo SC 29063, USA	Physician
Johnson, Joseph E, III 187 Sea Hammock Way, Ponte Vedra Beach FL 32082, USA	Baseball Player
Johnson, Joshua M (Josh) 10855 S 94th East Place, Tulsa OK 74133, USA	Baseball Player
Johnson, K Lance 5712 Foxfire Road, Mobile AL 36618, USA	Actress
Johnson, Kate Lang Innovative Artists, 1505 10th St, Santa Monica CA 90401 USA	Gymnast
Johnson, Kathy 2102 Clubside D, Longwood FL 32779, USA	Labor Leader
Johnson, Keith Woodworkers of America Union, 1622 N Lombard St, Portland OR 97217, USA	Actor
Johnson, Kenneth A (Kenny) Paradigm Agency, 360 N Crescent Dr, North Building, Beverly Hills CA 90210 USA	Basketball Player
Johnson, Kenneth H (Ken) 1401 N Wheeler Ave, Portland OR 97227, USA	Baseball Player
Johnson, Kenneth T (Ken) 121 Myrtlewood Dr, Pineville LA 71360, USA	Basketball Player, Sportscaster, Mayor
Johnson, Kevin M Mayor's Office, City Hall, 915 I St, #500, Sacramento CA 95814, USA	Football Player, Sportscaster
Johnson, Keyshawn 19232 Northfleet Way, Tarzana CA 91356, USA	Model
Johnson, Kylie Playboy Promotions, 2706 Media Center Dr, Los Angeles CA 90065 USA	Dancer, Model
Johnson, Kym Rothman Patino Andres Entertainment, 4370 Tujunga Ave, #120, Studio City CA 91604, USA	Baseball Player
Johnson, Lamar 4105 Sangre Trail, Arlington TX 76016, USA	Football Player
Johnson, Landon T 1915 Mountain Trail Dr, Charlotte NC 28214, USA	Football Player
Johnson, Larry A, Jr 340 Glengarry Lane, State College PA 16801, USA	Basketball Player
Johnson, Larry D Larry Johnson's R W A C, 15303 Dallas Parkway, #970, Addison TX 75001, USA	Baseball Player
Johnson, Larry D 5111 Hector Ave, #405, Cleveland OH 44127, USA	Actress
Johnson, Laura Geddes Agency, 8430 Santa Monica Blvd, #201, West Hollywood CA 90069 USA	Composer
Johnson, Laurie Priority House, Camp Hill, Stanmore, Middlesex HA7 3JQ, England	Football Player
Johnson, LeShon E 15102 Beverly St, Overland Park KS 66223, USA	Football Player
Johnson, Levi 1202 Craig Dr, Westland MI 48186, USA	Poker Player
Johnson, Linda Poker Gives, PO Box 434, Conyers NY 10920, USA	Football Player
Johnson, Lonnie D 8500 Amber Ridge Court, Sanford FL 32771, USA	Singer, Bassist (Brothers Johnson)
Johnson, Louis Green Light Talent Agency, PO Box 3172, Beverly Hills CA 90212 USA	

Johnson, Louis B (Lou)
4532 Valley Ridge Ave, Los Angeles CA 90008, USA — Baseball Player

Johnson, Lynn-Holly
2109 S Wilbur Ave, Walla Walla WA 99362, USA — Actress

Johnson, Manuel H, Jr
Johnson Smick Int'l, 2099 Pennsylvania Ave NW, #950, Washington DC 20006, USA — Government Official, Economist

Johnson, Marc
Word of Mouth Music, 235 E 22nd St, #9F, New York NY 10010, USA — Jazz Bassist, Composer

Johnson, Marcia Thornton
Scholastic Press, 555 Broadway, New York NY 10012 USA — Writer

Johnson, Margaret A
825 Country Club Dr SE, #1D, Rio Rancho NM 87124, USA — Baseball Player

Johnson, Mark
Gran Via Productions, 1888 Century Park E, #1400, Los Angeles CA 90067, USA — Producer

Johnson, Mark
Milwaukee Journal Sentinel, Editorial Dept, PO Box 371, Milwaukee WI 53201 USA — Journalist

Johnson, Mark
1204 Howison Place SW, Washington DC 20081, USA — Boxer

Johnson, Mark E
1609 Hidden Hill Dr, Verona WI 53593, USA — Ice Hockey Player

Johnson, Mark P
40 Helen Ave, Rye NY 10580, USA — Baseball Player

Johnson, Mark Steven
Creative Artists Agency, 2000 Ave of Stars, #100, Los Angeles CA 90067 USA — Director, Writer

Johnson, Marques K
5133 Dawn View Place, Los Angeles CA 90043, USA — Basketball Player

Johnson, Marvin
5452 Turfway Circle, Indianapolis IN 46228, USA — Boxer

Johnson, Marvin M
3055 SE Bison Road, Bartlesville OK 74006, USA — Chemical Engineer

Johnson, Matt
Free Trade Agency, Chapel Place, Rivington St, London EC2A 3DQ, England — Singer, Guitarist (The The); Songwriter

Johnson, Michael
A R T R A-Artists Mgmt, 130 S Canal St, #211, Chicago IL 60606, USA — Singer, Guitarist, Songwriter

Johnson, Michael D
Baylor University, Athletic Dept, 150 Bear Run, Waco TX 76711, USA — Track Athlete

Johnson, Michael K (Mike)
446 23rd Place, Manhattan Beach CA 90266, USA — Baseball Player

Johnson, Michael M (Butch)
9719 S Red Oakes Dr, Littleton CO 80126, USA — Football Player

Johnson, Michelle
Angel City Talent, 4741 Laurel Canyon Blvd, Valley Village CA 91607, USA — Actress, Model

Johnson, Mike
Paradigm Agency, 360 N Crescent Dr, North Building, Beverly Hills CA 90210 USA — Animator, Director

Johnson, Monte C
2349 Hurst Dr NE, Atlanta GA 30305, USA — Football Player

Johnson, N James (Jim)
Interactive Coaching, 34522 N Scottsdale Road, #D8, Scottsdale AZ 85266, USA — Ice Hockey Player

Johnson, Neil A
821 Plymouth Lane, Virginia Beach VA 23451, USA — Basketball Player

Johnson, Nicholas R (Nick)
8008 Sacramento St, Fair Oaks CA 95628, USA — Baseball Player

Johnson, Nicole Randall
Greene Assoc, 1901 Ave of Stars, #130, Los Angeles CA 90067 USA — Actress

Johnson, Norman D (Norm)
8523 NW Anderson Hill Road, Silverdale WA 98383, USA — Football Player

Johnson, Ollie
1700 Spring Garden St, Philadelphia PA 19130, USA — Basketball Player

Johnson, Ora J
General Baptists Ministries, 100 Stinson Dr, Poplar Bluff MO 63901, USA — Religious Leader

Johnson, Paatricia M (Trish)
Encompass, 121 Hook Road, Epsom, Surrey KT19 8TU, England — Golfer

Johnson, Patricia (Tish)
Professional Bowlers Assn, 719 2nd Ave, #701, Seattle WA 98104 USA — Bowler

Johnson, Patrick
A P A Talent/Literary Agency, 405 S Beverly Dr, #300, Beverly Hills CA 90212 USA — Actor

Johnson, Paul
Georgia Institute of Technology, Athletic Dept, Atlanta GA 30332, USA — Football Coach

Johnson, Paul B
29 Newton Road, London W2 5JR, England — Historian

Johnson, Paul H
1719 Yale Ave, Burley ID 83318, USA — Ice Hockey Player

Johnson, Penny
Mitchell K Stubbs Assoc, 8695 W Washington Blvd, #204, Culver City CA 90232 USA — Actress

Johnson, Pete
6304 Misty Cove Lane, Columbus OH 43231, USA — Football Player

Johnson, R E
Train Dispatchers Assn, 4239 W 150th St, #1, Cleveland OH 44135, USA — Labor Leader

Johnson, R Keith
PO Box 4122, Park City UT 84060, USA — Baseball Player

Johnson, Rafer L
4217 Woodcliff Road, Sherman Oaks CA 91403, USA — Track Athlete, Actor

Johnson, Randall D (Randy)
8404 N El Maro Circle, Paradise Valley AZ 85253, USA — Baseball Player

Johnson, Raylee T
2010 Black Fox Dr NE, Atlanta GA 30345, USA — Football Player

Johnson, Rebecca
United Agents, 12-26 Lexington St, London W1F 0LE, England — Actress

Johnson, Reed C
10008 Mirada Dr, Las Vegas NV 89144, USA — Baseball Player

Johnson, Reggie D (Sweet)
Puglistic Drama, 1029 Highway 6 N, #650-150, Houston TX 77079, USA — Boxer

Johnson, Reginald R (Reggie)
17907 Souter Lane, Land O'Lakes FL 34638, USA — Football Player

Johnson, Richard
234 Route 197, Woodstock CT 06281, USA — Archer

Johnson, Richard A (Dick) 5001 E Main St, #762, Mesa AZ 85205, USA	Baseball Player
Johnson, Richard J 926 Peachwood Bend Dr, Houston TX 77077, USA	Football Player
Johnson, Richard K Conway Van Gelder Grant, 8-12 Broadwick St, #300, London W1F 8HW, England	Actor
Johnson, Richard S Professional Golfer's Assn, PO Box 109601, Palm Beach Gardens FL 33410 USA	Golfer
Johnson, Rob C 26635 Aracena Dr, Mission Viejo CA 92691, USA	Football Player
Johnson, Robert D (Bob) 650 Caves Highway, Cave Junction OR 97523, USA	Baseball Player
Johnson, Robert D (Bob) 165 Magnolia Ave, Cincinnati OH 45246, USA	Football Player
Johnson, Robert G (Junior), Jr 3200 Seven Eagles Road, Charlotte NC 28210, USA	Auto Racing Driver, Executive
Johnson, Robert L Black Entertainment TV, 1900 W Place NE, Washington DC 20018, USA	Businessman, Basketball Executive
Johnson, Robert Sherlaw Omnibus Press, 14/15 Berners St, London W1T 3LJ, England	Composer, Concert Pianist
Johnson, Robert W (Bob) 1474 Barclay St, Saint Paul MN 55106, USA	Baseball Player
Johnson, Romina Mission Control, City Business Center, Lower Road, London SE16 2XB, England	Singer
Johnson, Ron J C Penny Co, 650 Legacy Dr, Plano TX 75024, USA	Businessman
Johnson, Ron, Sr 1080 Stafford Place, Detroit MI 48207, USA	Football Player
Johnson, Ronald A (Ron) 226 Summit Ave, Summit NJ 07901, USA	Football Player
Johnson, Roy Roofers & Waterproofers Union, 1125 17th St NW, Washington DC 20036, USA	Labor Leader
Johnson, Rudi A 5177 Rollman Estates Dr, Cincinnati OH 45236, USA	Football Player
Johnson, Rupert Franklin Resources, 277 Mariners Island Blvd, San Mateo CA 94404, USA	Financier
Johnson, Russell Professor's Place, PO Box 11198, Bainbridge Island WA 98110, USA	Actor
Johnson, Samuel L (Sammy) 142 Old Mill Road, #B, High Point NC 27265, USA	Football Player
Johnson, Sandy Playboy Promotions, 2706 Media Center Dr, Los Angeles CA 90065 USA	Model, Actress
Johnson, Sankey Anton (S A) 109 Boca de la Playa, #B, San Clemente CA 92672, USA	Businessman
Johnson, Scott PO Box 195222, Winter Springs FL 32719, USA	Gymnast
Johnson, Scott W M E Entertainment, 1600 Division St, #300, Nashville TN 37203 USA	Guitarist (Gin Blossoms/Low Watts)
Johnson, Scott Tzadik Records, 200 E 10th St, Box 126, New York, NY 10003, USA	Composer
Johnson, Seleena Shanachie Records, 37 E Clinton St, #1, Newton NJ 07860 USA	Singer, Songwriter
Johnson, Shawn 5910 Ashworth Road, PO Box 227, West Des Moines IA 50266, USA	Gymnast
Johnson, Sonia 3318 2nd St S, Arlington VA 22204, USA	Women's, Religious Activist
Johnson, Spencer G P Putnam's Sons, 375 Hudson St, New York NY 10014 USA	Writer
Johnson, Stanley L (Stan) 56 Moringside Dr, Daly City CA 94015, USA	Baseball Player
Johnson, Steffond 10525 Marsh Lane, Dallas TX 75229, USA	Basketball Player
Johnson, Syl Blue Sky Artists, 761 Washington Ave N, Minneapolis MN 55401, USA	Singer, Songwriter
Johnson, Syleena Rodgers Redding, PO Box 4603, Macon GA 31208 USA	Singer, Songwriter
Johnson, Ted C 10 Appletree Lane, Wayland MA 01778, USA	Football Player
Johnson, Temeko Phoenix Mercury, American West Arena, 201 E Jefferson St, Phoenix AZ 85004 USA	Basketball Player
Johnson, Terry Endev Energy, 200-207 9th Ave SW, Calgary AB T2P 1K3, Canada	Ice Hockey Player
Johnson, Terry (Buzzy) Resort Attractions, 2375 E Tropicana Ave, #304, Las Vegas NV 89119, USA	Singer (Flamingos)
Johnson, Thomas (Pepper) New England Patriots, 1 Patriot Place, Foxboro MA 02035 USA	Football Player
Johnson, Thomas F 1611 Constitution Blvd, Rock Hill SC 29732, USA	Baseball Player
Johnson, Thomas R (Tom) 2700 Knox Ave N, Minneapolis MN 55411, USA	Baseball Player
Johnson, Timothy (Tim) 2839 Dorell Ave, Orlando FL 32814, USA	Football Player
Johnson, Timothy E (Tim) 2550 E River Road, #3205, Tucson AZ 85718, USA	Baseball Player, Manager
Johnson, Tom Ardmore Sound, Ardmore Studios, Herbert Road, Bray, County Wicklow, Ireland	Sound Editor
Johnson, Tommy Green Light Talent Agency, PO Box 3172, Beverly Hills CA 90212 USA	Musician (Brothers Johnson)
Johnson, Torrence V Jet Propulsion Laboratory, 4800 Oak Grove Dr, Pasadena CA 91109 USA	Astronomer, Space Scientist
Johnson, Trent Stanford University, Athletic Dept, Stanford CA 94305, USA	Basketball Coach
Johnson, Vance E 679 Curecanti Circle, Grand Junction CO 81507, USA	Football Player
Johnson, Vaughan M 4915 Arendell St, #253, Morehead City NC 28557, USA	Football Player

Johnson, Victoria	
V J International, PO Box 1744, Lake Oswego OR 97035, USA	Physical Fitness Instructor
Johnson, Vincent (Vinnie)	
5236 Elmsgate Dr, Orchard Lake MI 48324, USA	Basketball Player
Johnson, Virginia	
Dance Theatre of Harlem, 466 W 152nd St, New York NY 10031, USA	Ballerina
Johnson, Virginia E	
Johnson Assoc, 800 Holland Road, Ballwin MO 63021, USA	Sex Therapist, Psychologist
Johnson, W Bruce	
Sears Holdings, 3333 Beverly Road, Hoffman Estates IL 60179, USA	Businessman
Johnson, W Leon	
813 Vine Arden Road, Morganton NC 28655, USA	Football Player
Johnson, W Russell (Russ)	
3542 Russell Road, Green Cove Springs FL 32043, USA	Baseball Player
Johnson, Wallace D	
5210 S Campbell Ave, Chicago IL 60632, USA	Baseball Player
Johnson, Wallace E (Mickey)	
3642 W Grenshaw St, Chicago IL 60624, USA	Basketball Player
Johnson, Warren	
Warren Johnson Enterprises, 700 N Price Road, Sugar Hill GA 30518, USA	Auto Racing Driver
Johnson, Warren C	
946 Bellclair Road SE, Grand Rapids MI 49506, USA	Chemist
Johnson, Wendy	
126 Red Brook Lane, Mooresville NC 28117, USA	Auto Racing Driver
Johnson, William A (Billy White Shoes)	
3701 Whitney Place, Duluth GA 30096, USA	Football Player
Johnson, William B	
Ritz-Carlton Hotels, 4445 Willard Ave, #800, Chevy Chase MD 20815, USA	Businessman
Johnson, William E (Bill)	
3399 Hartwood Road, Cleveland Heights OH 44112, USA	Football Player
Johnson, William Merritt	
Creative Artists Agency, 2000 Ave of Stars, #100, Los Angeles CA 90067 USA	Writer
Johnson, William R	
H J Heinz Co, PO Box 57, Pittsburgh PA 15230, USA	Businessman
Johnson, Zach	
267 Saint Andrews, Saint Simons Island GA 31522, USA	Golfer
Johnson-Scharpf, Brandy	
Brandy Johnson's Global Gymnastics, 1945 Don Wickham Dr, Clermont FL 34711, USA	Gymnast
Johnsson, Kim	
5308 Oaklawn Ave, Minneapolis MN 55424, USA	Ice Hockey Player
Johnstad, Kurt	
W M E Entertainment, 9601 Wilshire Blvd, #300, Beverly Hills CA 90210 USA	Writer
Johnston McKay, Mary H	
University of Tennessee, Space Institute, Tullahoma TN 37388, USA	Astronaut
Johnston, Allen H	
Bishop's House, 3 Wymer Terrace, PO Box 21, Chartwell, Hamilton 3210, New Zealand	Religious Leader
Johnston, Bruce	
I C M Partners, 10250 Constellation Blvd, #900, Los Angeles CA 90067 USA	Singer (Beach Boys)
Johnston, Daryl P (Moose)	
4414 Woodfin Dr, Dallas TX 75220, USA	Football Player
Johnston, Freedy	
High Road Touring, 751 Bridgeway, #200, Sausalito CA 94965 USA	Singer, Songwriter
Johnston, Gerald A	
McDonnell Douglas Corp, PO Box 516, Saint Louis MO 63166, USA	Businessman
Johnston, Gerald E	
Clorox Co, 1221 Broadway, Oakland CA 94612, USA	Businessman
Johnston, Harold S	
285 Franklin St, Harrisonburg VA 22801, USA	Chemist
Johnston, J Bennett, Jr	
Johnston Assoc, 900 19th St NW, #800, Washington DC 20006, USA	Senator, LA
Johnston, Jimmy	
Pro's Inc, 9 S 12th St, #300, Richmond VA 23219, USA	Golfer
Johnston, Joanna	
Independent Talent Group, Oxford House, 76 Oxford St, London W1D 1BS, England	Costume Designer
Johnston, Joel R	
1318 Meadowview Dr, #M, Pottstown PA 19464, USA	Baseball Player
Johnston, John Dennis	
S D B Partners, 1801 Ave of Stars, #902, Los Angeles CA 90067 USA	Actor
Johnston, Kristen	
Paradigm Agency, 360 N Crescent Dr, North Building, Beverly Hills CA 90210 USA	Actress
Johnston, L Marshall	
3933 Waville Road NE, Bemidji MN 56601, USA	Ice Hockey Player
Johnston, Lynn	
Universal Press Syndicate, 4520 Main St, #700, Kansas City MO 64111 USA	Cartoonist (For Better or For Worse)
Johnston, Mark R	
609 Carolyn Ave, Austin TX 78705, USA	Football Player
Johnston, Nate	
8870 Fontainbleau Blvd, #301, Miami FL 33172, USA	Basketball Player
Johnston, Rebecca	
Cornell University, Ithaca NY 14853 USA	Ice Hockey Player
Johnston, Rex D	
15117 Illinois Ave, Paramount CA 90723, USA	Football, Baseball Player
Johnston, S K, Jr	
Coca-Cola Enterprises, 2500 Windy Ridge Parkway, #700, Atlanta GA 30339, USA	Businessman
Johnston, Steven E (Stevie)	
Silverhawk Boxing, 10120 S Eastern Ave, #200, Henderson NV 89052, USA	Boxer
Johnstone, John W	
9330 Clubside Circle, #3305, Sarasota FL 34238, USA	Baseball Player
Johnstone, John W (Jay), Jr	
853 Chapea Road, Pasadena CA 91107, USA	Baseball Player
Johnstone, John W, Jr	
467 Carter St, New Canaan CT 06840, USA	Businessman
Johnstone, Parker, III	
Parker Johnstone Honda, 30600 SW Parkway Ave, Wilsonville OR 97070, USA	Auto Racing Driver
Johnston-Forbes, Cathy	
5104 Lunar Dr, Kitty Hawk NC 27949, USA	Golfer

Johnson - Johnston-Forbes

Johnston-Ulrich, Kim — Actress
S D B Partners, 1801 Ave of Stars, #902, Los Angeles CA 90067 USA

Joiner, Charles (Charlie), Jr — Football Player, Coach
16935 W Bernardo Dr, #107, San Diego CA 92127, USA

Joiner, J Russell (Rusty) — Actor, Model
TalentWorks, 3500 W Olive Ave, #1400, Burbank CA 91505 USA

JoJo — Singer, Songwriter, Actress
Universal Records, 70 Universal City Plaza, Universal City CA 91608 USA

Jokinen, Jussi — Ice Hockey Player
Carolina Hurricanes, R B C Center, 1400 Edwards Mills Road, Raleigh NC 27607 USA

Jokinen, Olli — Ice Hockey Player
6501 N Federal Highway, #2, Boca Raton FL 33487, USA

Jokubonis, Gediminas — Sculptor
V Kudirkos 4-3, 2009 Vilnius, Lithuania

Jolas, Betsy M — Composer
Nat Superieur Musique Conservatoire, 209 Ave Jaures, 75019 Paris, France

Joli, France — Singer
Brothers Mgmt, 141 Dunbar Ave, Fords NJ 08863 USA

Jolicoeur, David — Rap Artist (DeLaSoul)
Entertainment Artists, PO Box 120824, Nashville TN 37212 USA

Jolie, Angelina — Actress, Model, Director
I F A Talent Agency, 8730 W Sunset Blvd, #490, West Hollywood CA 90069 USA

Joliff, Howard (Howie) — Basketball Player
2346 Fallen Oak Circle NE, Massillon OH 44646, USA

Joliot, Pierre A — Biologist
16 Rue de la Glaciere, 75013 Paris, France

Jollett, Mikel — Singer, Guitarist (Airborne Toxic Event)
Island Def Jam Records, 8920 W Sunset Blvd, #200, West Hollywood CA 90069 USA

Jolley, Gordon H — Football Player
1459 Navajo Dr, Saint George UT 84790, USA

Jolly, Allison — Yachtswoman
27122 Benidorm, Mission Viejo CA 92692, USA

Jolly, E Grady — Judge
US Court of Appeals, Eastland Courthouse, 245 E Capitol St, Jackson MS 39201, USA

Jolovitz, Jenna — Actress, Writer
Creative Artists Agency, 2000 Ave of Stars, #100, Los Angeles CA 90067 USA

Joltz, Joachim — Electrical Engineer
A M Forsthof 16, 42119 Wuppertal, Germany

Jon B — Singer, Songwriter
Entertainment Artists, PO Box 120824, Nashville TN 37212 USA

Jonas, Joseph A (Joe) — Singer, Guitarist (Jonas Brothers)
Philymack Inc, 11661 San Vicente Blvd, #609, Los Angeles CA 90049, USA

Jonas, Nicholas J (Nick) — Singer, Guitarist (Jonas Brothers)
Jonas Group, 6725 W Sunset Blvd, #350, Los Angeles CA 90028, USA

Jonas, P Kevin — Singer, Guitarist (Jonas Brothers)
Philymack Inc, 11661 San Vicente Blvd, #609, Los Angeles CA 90049, USA

Jonathan, Wesley — Actor
Marsh Entertainment, 12444 Ventura Blvd, #203, Studio City CA 91604, USA

Jones, Aaron D, II — Football Player
7677 Torino Court, Orlando FL 32835, USA

Jones, Adam B (Pacman) — Football Player
4282 N Chapel Road, Franklin TN 37067, USA

Jones, Adam L — Baseball Player
Baltimore Orioles, Oriole Park, 333 W Camden St, Baltimore MD 21201 USA

Jones, Adam T — Guitarist (Tool)
Volcano Records, 3575 Cahuenga Blvd W, #590, Los Angeles CA 90068, USA

Jones, Aled — Singer
Agency Group Ltd, 361-373 City Road, London EC1V 2QA, England

Jones, Alex S — Journalist
1 Waterhouse St, #61, Cambridge MA 02138, USA

Jones, Alfornia (Al) — Baseball Player
1339 Brussels St, San Francisco CA 94134, USA

Jones, Alfred — Boxer
19610 Northbrook Dr, Southfield MI 48076, USA

Jones, Allen C — Artist
41 Charterhouse Square, London EC1M 6EA, England

Jones, Andruw R — Baseball Player
2931 Grey Moss Pass, Duluth GA 30097, USA

Jones, Angus T — Actor
Paradigm Agency, 360 N Crescent Dr, North Building, Beverly Hills CA 90210 USA

Jones, Anthony H — Basketball Player
44 Hempstead Dr, Newark DE 19702, USA

Jones, Antonia — Actress
Buzz Halliday, 8899 Beverly Blvd, #620, Los Angeles CA 90048 USA

Jones, Asjha T — Basketball Player
Connecticut Sun, 1 Mohegan Sun Blvd, Uncasville CT 06382 USA

Jones, Barry L — Baseball Player
411 S Morton Ave, Centerville IN 47330, USA

Jones, Ben — Representative, GA; Actor
Cooter's Place, 157 Parkway, Gatlinburg TN 37738, USA

Jones, Bertram H (Bert) — Football Player
1492 Madera Sr, Ruston LA 71270, USA

Jones, Bill T — Choreographer
219 W 19th St, New York NY 10011, USA

Jones, Booker T — Singer, Guitarist (Booker T & the MG's)
Wenig-LaMonica Associates, 580 White Plains Road, Tarrytown NY 11591, USA

Jones, Brad — Bassist (Jazz Passengers)
Cross Road Mgmt, 45 W 11th St, #7B, New York NY 10011, USA

Jones, Brad — Ice Hockey Player
International Hockey League, PO Box 175, Bedford MI 49020, USA

Jones, Brandon V — Football Player
1070 Randall Road, Texarkana TX 75501, USA

Jones, Brent M — Football Player, Sportscaster
756 El Pintado Road, Danville CA 94526, USA

Jones, Caldwell — Basketball Player
625 Edgecombe, Stockbridge GA 30281, USA

Jones, Caleb Landry
Paradigm Agency, 360 N Crescent Dr, North Building, Beverly Hills CA 90210 USA — Actor

Jones, Calvin (Fuzz)
J W Entertainment, PO Box 78904, Atlanta GA 30357, USA — Singer, Musician (Legendary Blues Band)

Jones, Calvin D
2815 Butterfield Stage Road, Lewisville TX 75077, USA — Baseball Player

Jones, Carnetta
C E S D, 10635 Santa Monica Blvd, #130, Los Angeles CA 90025 USA — Actress

Jones, Cedric D
804 Hawkesbury Park, Norman OK 73072, USA — Football Player

Jones, Chandler J
New England Patriots, 1 Patriot Place, Foxboro MA 02035 USA — Football Player

Jones, Charles A
304 Chestnut St, Elizabethtown KY 42701, USA — Basketball Player

Jones, Cherry
W M E Entertainment, 9601 Wilshire Blvd, #300, Beverly Hills CA 90210 USA — Actress

Jones, Christine
Abrams Artists, 275 7th Ave, #2600, New York NY 10001 USA — Scenic Designer

Jones, Claude Earl
Henderson/Hogan, 850 7th Ave, #1003, New York NY 10019 USA — Actor

Jones, Cleon J
751 Edwards St, Mobile AL 36610, USA — Baseball Player

Jones, Cleve
Names Project Foundation, 637 Hope St, Atlanta GA 30310, USA — Social Activist

Jones, Clinton (Clint)
16555 Sherman Way, #C, Lake Balboa CA 91406, USA — Football Player

Jones, Cobi
501 N Edinburgh Ave, Los Angeles CA 90048, USA — Soccer Player, Coach

Jones, Courtney J L
National Skating Assn, 15-27 Gee St, London EC1V 3RE, England — Figure Skating Executive

Jones, Cullen A
Premier Management Group, 1100 Crescent Green, #104, Cary, NC 27518 USA — Swimmer

Jones, Dahntay L
PO Box 9984, Trenton NJ 8650, USA — Basketball Player

Jones, Dale
PO Box 2716, Boone NC 28607, USA — Football Player

Jones, Damon
10703 Karter Court, Houston TX 77064, USA — Basketball Player

Jones, Damon
12690 Copper Springs Road, Jacksonville Fl 32246, USA — Football Player

Jones, Daniel W
University of Mississippi, Chancellor's Office, 1848 University Circle, Oxford MS 38677, USA — Educator

Jones, Dante D
328 Partridge Run Dr, Duncanville TX 75137, USA — Football Player

Jones, Darryl
Rascoff/Zysblat Organization, 250 W 57th St, New York NY 10107 USA — Bassist (Rolling Stones)

Jones, Darryl L
15628 King Dr, Meadville PA 16335, USA — Baseball Player

Jones, David
Owen White Mgmt, 22 Brunswick Terrace, Hove, East Sussex BN3 1HJ, England — Conductor

Jones, David (Deacon)
715 S Canyon Mist Lane, Anaheim CA 92808, USA — Football Player, Executive

Jones, David A
Humana Corp, 500 W Main St, Louisville KY 40202, USA — Businessman

Jones, David C
46661 Algonian Parkway, #106, Sterling VA 20165, USA — Air Force General

Jones, Davy
T R W Racing, 2000 Jaguar Dr, Valparaiso IN 46383, USA — Auto Racing Driver

Jones, Dax X
10021 W Suddard Place, Beach Park IL 60087, USA — Baseball Player

Jones, Dean
Dean Jones Productions, PO Box 570276, Tarzana CA 91357, USA — Actor, Singer

Jones, Denise R M
Blanton Harrell Cooke Corzine, 1014 Cross Bow Court, Hendersonville TN 37075 USA — Singer (Point of Grace)

Jones, Dhani M
10300 Gary Road, Potomac MD 20854, USA — Football Player

Jones, Dick (Dickie)
17744 Romar St, Northridge CA 91325, USA — Actor

Jones, Donell
Universal Attractions, 135 W 26th St, #1200, New York NY 10001 USA — Singer, Songwriter

Jones, Dot-Marie
Levin Agency, 8484 Wilshire Blvd, #750, Beverly Hills CA 90211, USA — Actress

Jones, Doug
Coolwaters Productions, 10061 Riverside Dr, Box 531, Toluca Lake CA 91602 USA — Actor

Jones, Douglas R (Doug)
129 E Navilla Place, Covina CA 91723, USA — Baseball Player

Jones, Dwight E
20119 Mayfair Park Lane, Spring TX 77379, USA — Basketball Player

Jones, Eddie
Gage Group, 14724 Ventura Blvd, #505, Sherman Oaks CA 91403 USA — Actor

Jones, Eddie
Jones Studio, 4450 N 12th St, Phoenix AZ 85014, USA — Architect

Jones, Eddie C
3400 Paddock Road, Weston FL 33331, USA — Basketball Player

Jones, Edith H
US Court of Appeals, US Courthouse, 515 Rusk Ave, #12015, Houston TX 77002, USA — Judge

Jones, Edward L (Too Tall)
1 Lost Valley Dr, Dallas TX 75234, USA — Football Player

Jones, Edward M
Jones Studios, 4450 N 12th St, Phoenix AZ 85014, USA — Architect

Jones, Edward P
Amistad/Harper Collins Publishers, 10 E 53rd St, New York NY 10022, USA — Writer

Jones, Ernest L (Ernie)
17410 SW 109th Ave, Miami FL 33157, USA — Football Player

Jones, Evan
A P A Talent/Literary Agency, 405 S Beverly Dr, #300, Beverly Hills CA 90212 USA — Actor

Jones, Fay
Grover Thurston Gallery, 309 Occidental Ave S, Seattle WA 98104, USA — Artist

Jones, Felicity
Independent Talent Group, Oxford House, 76 Oxford St, London W1D 1BS, England — Actress

Jones, Freddie R, Jr
151 S 111th Place, Mesa AZ 85208, USA — Football Player

Jones, Frederick T (Fred)
Los Angeles Clippers, Staples Center, 1111 S Figueroa St, Los Angeles CA 90015 USA — Basketball Player

Jones, Gary D
250 E Highway 67, #4207, Duncanville TX 75137, USA — Football Player

Jones, Gemma
Conway Van Gelder Grant, 8-12 Broadwick St, #300, London W1F 8HW, England — Actress

Jones, George
Top Notch Talent, PO Box 250, Gladeville TN 37071, USA — Singer, Guitarist, Songwriter

Jones, Glenn
Andi Howard Entertainment, 100 N Crescent Dr, #275, Beverly Hills CA 90210, USA — Singer

Jones, Gordon
18919 Fishermans Bend Dr, Lutz FL 33558, USA — Football Player

Jones, Grace
Wall of Sound, 24 Farm Lane Trading, London SW6 1QJ, England — Model, Actress, Singer

Jones, Greg
PO Box 500, Tahoe City CA 96145, USA — Skier

Jones, Greg P
2331 S Fenton Dr, Lakewood CO 80227, USA — Football Player

Jones, Grover W (Deacon)
1015 Goldfinch Ave, Sugar Land TX 77478, USA — Baseball Player

Jones, Gwyneth
Opera et Concert, 37 Rue de la Chaussee d'Antin, 75009 Paris, France — Opera Singer

Jones, Harold M (Hal)
4125 Palmyra Road, Los Angeles CA 90008, USA — Baseball Player

Jones, Hassan A
1010 Eldridge St, Clearwater FL 33755, USA — Football Player

Jones, Hayes W
408 Stonewood Dr, Peachtree City GA 30269, USA — Track Athlete

Jones, Homer C
408 S Texas St, Pittsburg TX 75686, USA — Football Player

Jones, Horace A
7925 Hobart Ave, Pensacola FL 32534, USA — Football Player

Jones, Howard
F M L, 33 Alexander Road, Aylesbury, Buckinghamshire HP20 2NR, England — Singer, Songwriter

Jones, J Dalton
4688 S Dixon Lane, Liberty MS 39645, USA — Baseball Player

Jones, Jack
48892 Orchard Dr, Indio CA 92201, USA — Singer

Jones, Jacque D
347 Saint Rita Court, San Diego CA 92113, USA — Baseball Player

Jones, James (Jimmy)
319 Salinas Dr, Henderson NV 89014, USA — Basketball Player

Jones, James A (J J)
PO Box 22694, Kansas City MO 64113, USA — Football Player

Jones, James C (Jimmy)
3054 Newcastle Dr, Dallas TX 75220, USA — Baseball Player

Jones, James C (Jimmy)
2 Odyssey Dr, Tinley Park IL 60477, USA — Football Player

Jones, James Earl
Paradigm Agency, 360 N Crescent Dr, North Building, Beverly Hills CA 90210 USA — Actor

Jones, James R
18130 Palm Breeze Dr, Tampa FL 33647, USA — Football Player

Jones, Jamie
Big Machine Media, 575 Lexington Ave, #400, New York NY 10022, USA — Singer (All-4-One)

Jones, Jamison
Jay D Schwartz, 3151 Cahuenga Blvd W, #220, Los Angeles CA 90068 USA — Actor

Jones, Janet
9100 Wilshire Blvd, #1000W, Beverly Hills CA 90212, USA — Actress

Jones, January
Mosiac Media Group, 9200 W Sunset Blvd, #1000, Los Angeles CA 90069, USA — Actress

Jones, Jason
United Talent Agency, 9336 Civic Center Dr, Beverly Hills CA 90210 USA — Actor, Writer

Jones, Jason D
Seattle Seahawks, 12 Seahawks Way, Renton WA 98056 USA — Football Player

Jones, Jeffrey A (Jeff)
2200 Ready Road, Carleton MI 48117, USA — Baseball Player

Jones, Jeffrey D
S M S Talent, 8383 Wilshire Blvd, #230, Beverly Hills CA 90211 USA — Actor

Jones, Jenny
600 Plum Tree Road, Barrington IL 60010, USA — Entertainer, Comedienne

Jones, Jerrauld C (Jerry)
4400 Preston Road, Dallas TX 75205, USA — Football Executive

Jones, Jill Marie
D2 Mgmt, 9255 Sunset Blvd, #600, West Hollywood CA 90069, USA — Actress

Jones, Jim
A&M Entertainment, 13280 NW Freeway, #F328, Houston TX 77040, USA — Rap Artist

Jones, Jimmie
2658 Unicorn Court, Herndon VA 20171, USA — Football Player

Jones, Jimmie S
204 Moss Dr, Cedar Hill TX 75104, USA — Football Player

Jones, John E, III
US District Court, Federal Building, 240 W 3rd St, Williamsport PA 17701, USA — Judge

Jones, John Paul
Opium Arts, 49 Portland Road, London W11 4LJ, England — Bassist, Keyboardist (Led Zeppelin)

Jones, Johnny (Lam)
1903 Pachea Trail, Round Rock TX 78665, USA — Football Player, Track Athlete

Jones, Julia
Untitled Entertainment, 350 S Beverly Dr, #200, Beverly Hills CA 90212 USA — Actress

Jones, Julius A M
517 Northwood Trail, Southlake TX 76092, USA — Football Player

Jones, June S, III	Football Player, Coach
Southern Methodist University, Athletic Dept, Dallas TX 75275, USA	
Jones, Junior	Boxer
Golden Boy Promotions, 626 Wilshire Blvd, #350, Los Angeles CA 90017, USA	
Jones, Kelly	Singer, Guitarist (Stereophonics)
Marsupial Mgmt, Home Farm, Welfor, Newbury, Berkshire RG20 8HR, England	
Jones, Ken	Football Player
4455 Porter Road, Niagara Falls NY 14305, USA	
Jones, Kenneth V	Actor
P R S, 29/33 Berners St, London W1P 4AA, England	
Jones, Kim R	Football Player
1396 Madison Ave, #150, Loveland CO 80537, USA	
Jones, Kimberly	Sportscaster
YES Network, 405 Lexington Ave, #3600, New York NY 10174, USA	
Jones, Kirk	Director
Creative Artists Agency, 2000 Ave of Stars, #100, Los Angeles CA 90067 USA	
Jones, L Q	Actor
2144 1/2 N Cahuenga Blvd, Los Angeles CA 90068, USA	
Jones, Larry	Basketball Player
1442 Cottingham Court, Columbus OH 43209, USA	
Jones, Larry W (Chipper)	Baseball Player
5015 Heatherwood Court, Roswell GA 30075, USA	
Jones, LeRoy	Football Player
347 Kantor Blvd, Casselberry FL 32707, USA	
Jones, Leslie	Actress
I C M Partners, 10250 Constellation Blvd, #900, Los Angeles CA 90067 USA	
Jones, Levi J	Football Player
1448 W Bahia Court, Gilbert AZ 85233, USA	
Jones, Luka	Actor, Comedian
3 Arts Entertainment, 9460 Wilshire Blvd, #700, Beverly Hills CA 90212 USA	
Jones, Lupita	Beauty Queen
Miss Universe Organization, 1370 Ave of Americas, #1600, New York NY 10019 USA	
Jones, Lynn M	Baseball Player
9959 Dicksonburg Road, Conneautville PA 16406, USA	
Jones, M Donta'	Football Player
4495 Jimmy Greens Place, La Plata MD 20646, USA	
Jones, Major J B	Basketball Player
2475 Brandy Mill Road, Houston TX 77067, USA	
Jones, Marcus	Baseball Player
20375 Longbay Dr, Yorba Linda CA 92887, USA	
Jones, Marcus E	Football Player
18701 Pepper Pike, Lutz FL 33558, USA	
Jones, Marilyn	Actress
Kaplan-Stahler Agency, 8383 Wilshire Blvd, #923, Beverly Hills CA 90211, USA	
Jones, Marion L	Track Athlete, Basketball Player
PO Box 3065, Cary NC 27519, USA	
Jones, Marvin	Baseball Player
4134 12th St, Ecorse MI 48229, USA	
Jones, Marvin M	Football Player
8891 Brighton Lane, #114, Bonita Springs FL 34135, USA	
Jones, Matt	Actor
Paradigm Agency, 360 N Crescent Dr, North Building, Beverly Hills CA 90210 USA	
Jones, Matthew (Matt)	Football Player
13838 Bella Riva Lane, Jacksonville FL 32225, USA	
Jones, Maxine	Singer (En Vogue)
East West Records, 75 Rockefeller Plaza, #1200, New York NY 10019, USA	
Jones, Michael D (Mike)	Football Player
422 Davis Road, Lebanon TN 37087, USA	
Jones, Michael D (Mike)	Football Player
Lincoln University, Athletic Dept, Jefferson MO 65101, USA	
Jones, Michael G (Mick)	Singer, Guitarist (Clash, Foreigner)
Function, 8330 W 3rd St, Los Angeles CA 90048, USA	
Jones, Mickey	Actor, Musician
Shoestring Productions, PO Box 940321, Simi Valley CA 93094, USA	
Jones, Nate	Boxer
7801 South Shore Dr, Chicago IL 60649, USA	
Jones, Nathaniel R	Judge
201 E 5th St, #1700, Cincinnati OH 45202, USA	
Jones, Newton B	Labor Leader
International Brotherhood of Boilermakers, 753 State Ave, #570, Kansas City KS 66101, USA	
Jones, Norah	Singer, Pianist; Songwriter
Creative Artists Agency, 2000 Ave of Stars, #100, Los Angeles CA 90067 USA	
Jones, Odell	Baseball Player
5831 Opal Ave, Palmdale CA 93552, USA	
Jones, Orlando	Actor
Paradigm Agency, 360 N Crescent Dr, North Building, Beverly Hills CA 90210 USA	
Jones, P J	Auto Racing Driver
Gurney Racing, 2334 S Broadway, #2186, Santa Ana CA 92707, USA	
Jones, Parnelli	Auto Racing Driver, Executive
20550 Earl St, Torrance CA 90503, USA	
Jones, Paul	Guitarist (Elastica)
Chatto & Linnit, 123A King's Road, London SW3 4PL, England	
Jones, Perry J, III	Basketball Player
Oklahoma City Thunder, 211 N Robinson Ave, #300, Oklahoma City OK 73102 USA	
Jones, Pete	Director, Writer
Creative Artists Agency, 2000 Ave of Stars, #100, Los Angeles CA 90067 USA	
Jones, Quentin	Actor
Associated International Mgmt, Fairfax House, Fulwood Place, London WC1V 6HU, England	
Jones, Quincy D, Jr	Composer, Conductor
Quincy Jones Productions, 6671 W Sunset Blvd, #1574A, Los Angeles CA 90028, USA	
Jones, Quintorris L (Julio)	Football Player
Atlanta Falcons, 4400 Falcon Parkway, Flowery Branch GA 30542 USA	
Jones, Randall L (Randy)	Baseball Player
2638 Cranston Dr, Escondido CA 92025, USA	
Jones, Randy	Bobsled Athlete
US Bobsled/Skeleton Federation, 1631 Mesa Ave, #A, Colorado Springs CO 80906 USA	

Jones, Rashida — Actress, Writer
United Talent Agency, 9336 Civic Center Dr, Beverly Hills CA 90210 USA
Jones, Renee — Actress
256 S Robertson Blvd, #700, Beverly Hills CA 90211, USA
Jones, Rhydian — Actor
Associated International Mgmt, Fairfax House, Fulwood Place, London WC1V 6HU, England
Jones, Richard T — Actor
Don Buchwald/Fortitude, 6500 Wilshire Blvd, #2200, Los Angeles CA 90048 USA
Jones, Richard W (Rich) — Basketball Player
101 Luna Way, #232, Las Vegas NV 89145, USA
Jones, Rickie Lee — Singer, Songwriter
Publicity Conn, Haversham Lodge, Melrose Ave, London NW2 4JS, England
Jones, Robbie — Actor
Untitled Entertainment, 350 S Beverly Dr, #200, Beverly Hills CA 90212 USA
Jones, Robert (K C) — Basketball Player, Coach
13405 NW Spirit Court W, Silverdale WA 98383, USA
Jones, Robert C (Bobby) — Basketball Player
7413 Valleybrook Road, Charlotte NC 28270, USA
Jones, Robert E (Bobby) — Football Player
6824 Stewart Sharon Road, Brookfield OH 44403, USA
Jones, Robert J (Bobby) — Baseball Player
10222 N Whitney Ave, Fresno CA 93730, USA
Jones, Robert L — Football Player
728 Barton Creek Blvd, Austin TX 78746, USA
Jones, Robert M (Bobby) — Baseball Player
32 Elm St, Rutherford NJ 07070, USA
Jones, Robert O (Bobby) — Baseball Player
7809 S Oxford Ave, Tulsa OK 74136, USA
Jones, Rod — Guitarist (Idlewild)
Agency Group Ltd, 361-373 City Road, London EC1V 2QA, England
Jones, Roderick W (Rod) — Football Player
517 Tealridge Lane, DeSoto TX 75115, USA
Jones, Roger C — Football Player
712 Trebor Dr, Goodlettsville TN 37072, USA
Jones, Ronald J (Popeye) — Basketball Player
29 Bass Pond Dr, Frisco TX 75034, USA
Jones, Rondell T — Football Player
423 Competition Road, Raleigh NC 27603, USA
Jones, Rosie — Model
Samantha Bond Mgmt, Elysium Gate, 126-128 New Kings Road, London SW6 4LZ, England
Jones, Rosie — Golfer
4895 High Point Road, Atlanta GA 30342, USA
Jones, Ross A — Baseball Player
4135 Eastridge Circle, Pompano Beach FL 33064, USA
Jones, Roy, Jr — Boxer
4590 Isbella Ingram Dr, Pensacola FL 32504, USA
Jones, Rulon K — Football Player
4003 N 3775 E, Eden UT 84310, USA
Jones, Rupert Penry — Actor
Artist Rights Group, 4 Great Portland Place, London W1W 8PA, England
Jones, Ruppert S — Baseball Player
17925 Valle de Lobo Dr, Poway CA 92064, USA
Jones, Sam J — Actor
Creative Artists Agency, 2000 Ave of Stars, #100, Los Angeles CA 90067 USA
Jones, Sam, III — Actor
A P A Talent/Literary Agency, 405 S Beverly Dr, #300, Beverly Hills CA 90212 USA
Jones, Samuel (Sam) — Basketball Player
338 S Hampton Club Way, Saint Augustine FL 32092, USA
Jones, Sarah — Actress
Greene Assoc, 1901 Ave of Stars, #130, Los Angeles CA 90067 USA
Jones, Scott A — Inventor (LED Video Animation)
Dittoe Public Relations, 2815 E 62nd St, #300, Indianapolis IN 46220, USA
Jones, Sean — Football Player
4602 McKeever Lane, Missouri City TX 77459, USA
Jones, Serene — Educator
Union Theological Seminary, President's Office, 3041 Broadway, New York NY 10027, USA
Jones, Sharon — Singer
Motormouth Media, 2525 Hyperion Ave, #1, Los Angeles CA 90027, USA
Jones, Shirley — Actress, Singer
Suite One Productions, 16400 Ventura Blvd, #335, Encino CA 91436, USA
Jones, Simon — Actor
Innovative Artists, 1505 10th St, Santa Monica CA 90401 USA
Jones, Solomon — Basketball Player
New Orleans Hornets, 1250 Poydras St, #101, New Orleans LA 70113 USA
Jones, Stacy — Singer, Guitarist, Songwriter
Crush Music, 584 Broadway, #1102, New York NY 10012, USA
Jones, Stephen — Attorney
Jones & Wyatt, PO Box 472, Enid OK 73702, USA
Jones, Stephen H (Steve) — Basketball Player
26 Kingwood Greens Dr, Kingwood TX 77339, USA
Jones, Stephen J M — Fashion Designer
Steve Jones Millinery, 36 Great Queen St, London WC1E 6BT, England
Jones, Steve — Golfer
Whirlwind Golf Club, 5200 Grand Del Mar Way, San Diego CA 92130, USA
Jones, Steve — Guitarist (Sex Pistols)
Solo Agency, 53-55 Fulham High St, #200, London SW6 3JJ, England
Jones, Steve H — Football Player
12774 Fee Fee Road, Saint Louis MO 63146, USA
Jones, Steven — Physicist
Brigham Young University, Physics Dept, Provo UT 84602, USA
Jones, Steven H (Steve) — Baseball Player
8116 Kingsdale Dr, Knoxville TN 37919, USA
Jones, Stewart — Architect
Meyer/Gifford/Jones, 270 Lafayette St, New York NY 10012, USA
Jones, T Frederick (Rick) — Baseball Player
6319 Nancy Dr, Jacksonville FL 32244, USA

J

Jones, Tamala — Actress
Imparato Fay Mgmt, 1126 Roxbury Dr, Los Angeles CA 90035 USA
Jones, Taylor — Cartoonist
Times-Mirror Syndicate, Times-Mirror Square, Los Angeles CA 90053 USA
Jones, Tebucky S — Football Player
11 Salisbury Way, Farmington CT 6032, USA
Jones, Terrence — Basketball Player
Houston Rockets, 1730 Jefferson St, Houston TX 77003 USA
Jones, Terry — Animator, Director (Monty Python)
Python Pictures, 34 Thistlewaite Road, London E5 QQQ, England
Jones, Thomas D — Astronaut
N A S A, Johnson Space Center, 2101 NASA Road, Houston TX 77058 USA
Jones, Thomas Q — Football Player
2742 Clinch Haven Road, Big Stone Gap VA 24219, USA
Jones, Thomas V — Businessman
1050 Moraga Dr, Los Angeles CA 90049, USA
Jones, Timothy B (Tim) — Baseball Player
6049 Roloff Way, Orangevale CA 95662, USA
Jones, Toby — Actor
United Talent Agency, 9336 Civic Center Dr, Beverly Hills CA 90210 USA
Jones, Todd B G — Baseball Player
421 Eagle Point Dr, Pell City AL 35128, USA
Jones, Tom — Singer
W M E Entertainment, 9601 Wilshire Blvd, #300, Beverly Hills CA 90210 USA
Jones, Tommy Lee — Actor, Director
Creative Artists Agency, 2000 Ave of Stars, #100, Los Angeles CA 90067 USA
Jones, Tracy D — Baseball Player
101 Harbor Green Dr, #602, Bellevue KY 41073, USA
Jones, Trevor — Composer
46 Ave Road, Highgate, London N6 5DR, England
Jones, Tyler Patrick — Actor
House of Representatives, 1434 6th St, #1, Santa Monica CA 90401 USA
Jones, Vaughan F R — Mathematician
University of California, Mathematics Dept, Berkeley CA 94720, USA
Jones, Victor P — Football Player
17727 Sedona Way, Cornelius NC 28031, USA
Jones, Victor T — Football Player
PO Box 132241, Dallas TX 75313, USA
Jones, Vinnie — Actor
Cole Kitchenn Personal Mgmt, 212 Strand, London WC2R 1AP, England
Jones, W Timothy (Tim) — Baseball Player
30 Chicot Dr, Maumelle AR 72113, USA
Jones, Wallace C (Wah-Wah) — Basketball Player
512 Chinoe Road, Lexington KY 40502, USA
Jones, Walter (Wali) — Basketball Player
3160 SW 132nd Ave, Miramar FL 33027, USA
Jones, Walter J — Football Player
520 Raymond Place NW, Renton WA 98057, USA
Jones, Wesley — Architect
Holt Hinshaw Jones, 320 Florida St, San Francisco CA 94110, USA
Jones, Wilbert (Wil) — Basketball Player
3360 Idlecreek Way, Decatur GA 30034, USA
Jones, William A (Dub) — Football Player
904 Glendale Dr, Ruston LA 71270, USA
Jones, Zoe Lister — Actress, Writer
W M E Entertainment, 9601 Wilshire Blvd, #300, Beverly Hills CA 90210 USA
Jones-Doxey, Marilyn — Baseball Player
5058 Red Oak Place, Bradenton FL 34207, USA
Jong, Erica M — Writer
PO Box 1414, New York NY 10021, USA
Jongh, John P — Governor, VI
Governor's Office, 21-2 Kongens Gade, Charlotte Amalie, Saint Thomas VI 00802 USA
Jonrowe, Dee Dee — Dog Sled Racer
PO Box 272, Willow AK 99688, USA
Jonsen, Albert R — Physician
1383 Jones St, #502, San Francisco CA 94109, USA
Jonsson, U P Jorgen — Ice Hockey Player
Anaheim Ducks, 2695 E Katella Ave, Anaheim CA 92806 USA
Jonze, Spike — Director, Actor
Creative Artists Agency, 2000 Ave of Stars, #100, Los Angeles CA 90067 USA
Joo Min-Jin — Speed Skater
Skating Union, 88 Bangyee-Dong, Songpaku, Seoul 138 749, South Korea
Joop, Jette — Fashion Designer
Jette Design Group, Parkallee 53, 20144 Hamburg, Germany
Joop, Wolfgang — Fashion Designer
Joop!, Harvestehuder Weg 22, 20149 Hamburg, Germany
Jopling of Alnderby Quernhow, T Michael — Government Official, England
Ainderby Hall, Thirsk, North Yorkshire YO7 4HZ, England
Joppy, William T — Boxer
5107 Cansing Dr, Camp Springs MD 20748, USA
Jorda, Claude J C — Judge
International Criminal Tribunal, PO Box 13888, 2501 Hague, Netherlands
Jordan, Alex — Interior Designer
Gregga Jordan Smieszny, 1225 N State Parkway, Chicago IL 60610, USA
Jordan, Alexis — Singer
Roc Nation, 1411 Broadway, #3800, New York NY 10018, USA
Jordan, Brian O — Football, Baseball Player
2631 Trailing Ivy Way, Buford GA 30519, USA
Jordan, Claudia — Model, Entertainer
C E S D, 10635 Santa Monica Blvd, #130, Los Angeles CA 90025 USA
Jordan, Curtis W — Football Player
629 Surfside Ave, Virginia Beach VA 23451, USA
Jordan, Darin G — Football Player
44 Connell Dr, Stoughton MA 02072, USA
Jordan, Don D — Businessman
Reliant Energy, 1111 Louisiana Ave, Houston TX 77002, USA

Jones - Jordan

V.I.P. Address Book
493

Jordan, Edward M (Eddie) — Basketball Player, Coach
158 Monroe Ave, Belle Mead NJ 08502, USA
Jordan, Glenn — Director
9401 Wilshire Blvd, #700, Beverly Hills CA 90212, USA
Jordan, Gregor — Director
H L A Mgmt, PO Box 1536, Strawberry Hills, Sydney NSW 2012, Australia
Jordan, H DeAndre, Jr — Basketball Player
Los Angeles Clippers, Staples Center, 1111 S Figueroa St, Los Angeles CA 90015 USA
Jordan, Jeremy — Actor, Singer
Lacam Management, 283 W Montecito Ave, Sierra Madre CA 91024, USA
Jordan, Jeremy — Actor
I C M Partners, 10250 Constellation Blvd, #900, Los Angeles CA 90067 USA
Jordan, Kathy — Tennis Player
114 Walter Hays Dr, Palo Alto CA 94303, USA
Jordan, Kevin W — Baseball Player
127 Ney St, San Francisco CA 94112, USA
Jordan, LaMont D — Football Player
1407 Alberta Dr, District Heights MD 20747, USA
Jordan, Lee Roy — Football Player
7710 Caruth Blvd, Dallas TX 75225, USA
Jordan, Leslie — Actor
Michael Slessinger, 8730 W Sunset Blvd, #220W, West Hollywood CA 90069 USA
Jordan, Marc — Singer, Songwriter
Agency Group Ltd, 142 W 57th St, #600, New York NY 10019 USA
Jordan, Mary — Journalist
Washington Post, Editorial Dept, 1150 15th St NW, Washington DC 20071 USA
Jordan, Michael B — Actor
United Talent Agency, 9336 Civic Center Dr, Beverly Hills CA 90210 USA
Jordan, Michael J — Basketball Player
David Falk Mgmt, 5335 Wisconsin Ave, #850, Washington DC 20015, USA
Jordan, Montell — Singer, Songwriter
Evolution Talent Agency, 1501 Broadway, #1301, New York NY 10036 USA
Jordan, Neil P — Director
2 Martello Terrace, Strand Road, Bray, County Wicklow, Ireland
Jordan, P Buford — Football Player
11 Acadia St, Kenner LA 70065, USA
Jordan, Paul S (Ricky) — Baseball Player
5691 Power Inn Road, #A, Sacramento CA 95824, USA
Jordan, Philippe — Conductor
I M G Artists, Hogarth Business Park, Chiswick, London W4 2TH, England
Jordan, Randy L — Football Player
514 Mountain Laurel, Chapel Hill NC 27517, USA
Jordan, Ronny — Jazz Guitarist
Universal Attractions, 135 W 26th St, #1200, New York NY 10001 USA
Jordan, Sass — Singer, Songwriter
Agency Group Ltd, 142 W 57th St, #600, New York NY 10019 USA
Jordan, Scott A — Baseball Player
265 Great Oak Dr, Athens GA 30605, USA
Jordan, Sheila J — Singer, Songwriter
F A M, 4102 Rue Saint Urbain, Montreal QC H2W 1V3, Canada
Jordan, Shelby L — Football Player
29208 Posey Way, Rancho Palos Verdes CA 90275, USA
Jordan, Stanley — Jazz Guitarist
S J Productions, 2370 W Highway 89A, #11, Sedona AZ 86336, USA
Jordan, Steven R (Steve) — Football Player
581 W San Marcos Dr, Chandler AZ 85225, USA
Jordan, Thomas J (Tom) — Baseball Player
2909 S Wyoming Ave, Roswell NM 88203, USA
Jordan, Tina Marie — Model
Playboy Promotions, 2706 Media Center Dr, Los Angeles CA 90065 USA
Jordan, Vernon E, Jr — Civil Rights Activist
2940 Benton Place NW, Washington DC 20008, USA
Jordanova, Vera — Actress, Model
Special Artists Agency, 9465 Wilshire Blvd, #820, Beverly Hills CA 90212 USA
Jorge, Seu — Singer, Songwriter, Actor
Windish Agency, 1658 N Milwaukee Ave, #211, Chicago IL 60647, USA
Jorgensen, Anker — Prime Minister, Denmark
Borgbjergvej 1, 2450 SV Copenhagen, Denmark
Jorgensen, Michael (Mike) — Baseball Player, Manager
1820 Harbor Mill Dr, Fenton MO 63026, USA
Jorgensen, Roger K — Basketball Player
642 Woodcrest Dr, Pittsburgh PA 15205, USA
Jorgensen, Terry A — Baseball Player
1493 S Sugar Bush Road, Luxemburg WI 54217, USA
Jorgenson, Dale W — Economist
1010 Memorial Dr, #14C, Cambridge MA 02138, USA
Jorgenson, John — Guitarist (Desert Rose Band)
T G Squared Artist Representation, 201 Rainbow Dr, Carrboro NC 27510, USA
Jorginho — Soccer Player
Rua Levi Carreiro 420, Barra de Tijuca, Brazil
Jorndt, L Daniel — Businessman
Walgreen Co, 200 Wilmot Road, Deerfield IL 60015, USA
Jose, D Felix A — Baseball Player
9825 Equus Circle, Boynton Beach FL 33472, USA
Jose, Jose — Singer
Joyce Agency Entertainment Services, 370 Harrison Ave, Harrison NY 10528, USA
Josefowicz, Leila — Concert Violinist
C M Artists, 127 W 96th St, #13B, New York NY 10025 USA
Joseph Wenzel — Prince, Liechtenstein
Prince's Residence, Schloss Vaduz, 9490 Vaduz, Liechtenstein
Joseph, Amin — Actor
Jay Schachter Entertainment, 28994 Sam Place, Canyon Country CA 91387, USA
Joseph, Curtis S — Ice Hockey Player
Newport Sports Mgmt, 601-201 City Centre, Mississauga ON L5B 2T4, Canada
Joseph, Daryl J — Astronaut
615 Peachtree Court, Campbell CA 95008, USA

Joseph, James
8942 Stoneridge Place, Montgomery AL 36117, USA — Football Player

Joseph, Johnathan
Houston Texans, 2 Reliant Park, Houston TX 77054 USA — Football Player

Joseph, Joseph E, III
University of Michigan, Taubman Center, Ann Arbor MI 48109, USA — Physician

Joseph, Kimberly
Creative Representation, 1/44 Derby St, Collingwood VIC 3065, Australia — Actress, Director, Writer

Joseph, R Christopher (Chris)
17 L'Hirondelle Court, Saint Albert AB T8N 5X9, Canada — Ice Hockey Player

Joseph, Shalrie
New England Revolution, 1 Patriot Place, Foxboro MA 02035 USA — Soccer Player

Joseph, Stephen
New York City Health Department, 125 Worth St, New York NY 10013, USA — Physician

Joseph, William
1071 NE 107th St, Miami FL 33161, USA — Football Player

Josephson, Brian D
Cavendish Laboratory, Madingley Road, Cambridge CB3 0HE, England — Nobel Physics Laureate

Josephson, Karen
1923 Junction Dr, Concord CA 94518, USA — Synchronized Swimmer

Josephson, Lester J (Josey)
5388 N Genematas Dr, Tucson AZ 85704, USA — Football Player

Josephson, Sarah
1923 Junction Dr, Concord CA 94518, USA — Synchronized Swimmer

Joshi, Indira
B B C Artist Mail, PO Box 116, Belfast BT2 7AJ, Northern Ireland — Singer

Joshi, Pallavi
23 Veer Savarkar Road, Mahim, Mumbai MS 400016, India — Actress, Entertainer

Joshua, Von E
20922 E Glen Haven Circle, Northville MI 48167, USA — Baseball Player

Josipovic, Ivo
Presidential Palace, Banski Dvori, Zagreb 10000, Croatia — President, Croatia

Jospin, Lionel R
Parti Socialiste, 10 Rue de Solfarino, 75333 Paris Cedex 07, France — Prime Minister, France

Josserand, Marion
Ski Federation, 50 Rue des Marquisats, BP 2451 , 74011 Annecy Cedex, France — Freestyle Cross Skier

Joubert, Beverly
National Geographic, Editorial Dept, 1145 17th St NW, Washington DC 20036 USA — Photographer

Joubert, Dereck
National Geographic, Editorial Dept, 1145 17th St NW, Washington DC 20036 USA — Photographer

Joulwan, George A
1348 S 19th St, Arlington VA 22202, USA — Army General

Jourdain, Michel, Jr
Team Rahal, 4601 Lyman Dr, Hilliard OH 43026, USA — Auto Racing Driver

Jourdan, Louis
1139 Maybrook Dr, Beverly Hills CA 90210, USA — Actor

Jourgensen, Al
First Row Talent, 6220 Lemona Ave, #8, Van Nuys CA 91411, USA — Singer, Guitarist (Ministry)

Journell, Jimmy
1511 Eastgate Road, Springfield OH 45503, USA — Baseball Player

Jousset, Anne
Artmedia, 20 Ave Rapp, 75007 Paris, France — Actress

Jovanotti
Trident Mgmt, Corso Europa 13, 20122 Milan, Italy — Singer, Rap Artist, Songwriter, Actor

Jovanovich, Brandon
I M G Artists, Hogarth Business Park, Chiswick, London W4 2TH, England — Opera Singer

Jovanovich, Peter W
Pearson Education, 1 Lake St, Upper Saddle River NJ 07458, USA — Publisher

Jovanovski, Edward (Ed)
5224 NW 27th Court, Margate FL 33063, USA — Ice Hockey Player

Jovich, John B
1342 Rosepointe Dr, York PA 17404, USA — Historian

Jovovich, Milla
Untitled Entertainment, 350 S Beverly Dr, #200, Beverly Hills CA 90212 USA — Actress, Model, Singer

Joy, Mike
111 Mystic Lake Loop, Mooresville NC 28117, USA — Sportscaster

Joyal, Edward A (Eddie)
6469 Wandermere Dr, San Diego CA 92120, USA — Ice Hockey Player

Joyce, Andrea
Arts & Entertainment, 235 E 45th St, #200, New York NY 10017, USA — Sportscaster, Commentator

Joyce, James A
9785 SW 167th Place, Beaverton OR 97007, USA — Baseball Umpire

Joyce, Joan
20024 Back Nine Dr, Boca Raton FL 33498, USA — Softball Player, Golfer

Joyce, John T (Jack)
Bricklayers & Allied Craftsmen, 815 15th St NW, Washington DC 20005, USA — Labor Leader

Joyce, Kara Lynn
5973 Cedar Ridge Dr, Ann Arbor MI 48103, USA — Swimmer

Joyce, Kevin F
420 W Olive St, #9, Long Beach NY 11561, USA — Basketball Player

Joyce, Matt
6330 E Wilshire Dr, Scottsdale AZ 85257, USA — Football Player

Joyce, Matthew R (Matt)
Tampa Bay Rays, 1 Tropicana Dr, Saint Petersburg FL 33705 USA — Baseball Player

Joyce, Tom
21 Likely Road, Santa Fe NM 87508, USA — Sculptor

Joyce, William
2911 Centenary Blvd, PO Box 4188, Shreveport LA 71104, USA — Artist, Writer

Joyce, William H
Union Carbide, 39 Old Ridgebury Road, #1, Danbury CT 06810, USA — Businessman

Joyeux, Odette
Agents Associes, 201 Rue du Faubourg Saint Honore, 75008 Paris, France — Actress

Joyner, Alrederick (Al)
10500 Crosspoint Blvd, Indianapolis IN 46256, USA — Track Athlete

Joyner, Harry C (Butch)
9127 W Stageline Road, Payson AZ 85541, USA — Basketball Player

Joyner, Michelle — Actress
Kritzer Levine Wilkins Griffin, 11872 La Grange Ave, #100, Los Angeles CA 90025 USA
Joyner, Seth — Football Player, Sportscaster
5138 N 79th Place, Scottsdale AZ 85250, USA
Joyner, Wallace K (Wally) — Baseball Player
516 E 2800 S, Mapleton UT 84664, USA
Joyner-Kersee, Jacqueline (Jackie) — Track Athlete
1049 Bristol Manor Dr, Ballwin MO 63011, USA
Jozwiak, Brian J — Football Player, Coach
203 Ruby Lake Lane, Winter Haven FL 33884, USA
J-Ro — Rap Artist
Likwit Entertainment, PO Box 360713, Los Angeles CA 90036, USA
Ju Ming — Sculptor
208 No 2 She-shi-hu, Chin-shan, Taipei, Taiwan
Juan Carlos I — King, Spain
Palacio de la Zarzuela, 28671 Madrid, Spain
Juanes — Singer, Guitarist
Fernan Martinez Mgmt, 4141 NE 2nd Ave, #106C, Miami FL 33137, USA
Juantorena Danger, Alberto — Track Athlete
National Institute for Sports, Sports City, Havana, Cuba
Juarez, Ricardo (Rocky) — Boxer
3916 Weems St, Houston TX 77009, USA
Juby, Marcus L — Religious Leader
Reformed Church of Latter-Day Saints, 801 E 23rd St, Independence MO 64055, USA
Juchhelm, Alwin M, Jr — WW II Army Air Corps Hero
939 Ave of Pines, Grenada MS 38901, USA
Judah, Zab — Boxer
Prize Fight Boxing, 7160 Tchulahoma Road, #A1, Southhaven MS 38671, USA
Judd, Ashley — Actress, Model
PO Box 1569, Franklin TN 37065, USA
Judd, Bob — Writer
Harper Collins Publishers, 10 E 53rd St, Cellar 1, New York NY 10022 USA
Judd, Jackie — Commentator
ABC-TV, News Dept, 77 W 66th St, New York NY 10023 USA
Judd, Michael G (Mike) — Baseball Player
9805 Shadow Road, La Mesa CA 91941, USA
Judd, Naomi — Singer (Judds), Songwriter
Big Enterprises, 819 18th Ave S, Nashville TN 32703, USA
Judd, Wynonna — Singer, Guitarist
Big Enterprises, PO Box 682708, Franklin TN 37068, USA
Juden, Jeffrey D (Jeff) — Baseball Player
85 Proctor St, Salem MA 01970, USA
Judge, George — Economist
University of California, Economics Dept, Berkeley CA 94720, USA
Judge, Mike — Animator (Beavis & Butt-Head), Actor
3 Arts Entertainment, 9460 Wilshire Blvd, #700, Beverly Hills CA 90212 USA
Judkins, Jeffrey R (Jeff) — Basketball Player, Coach
3471 S 3570 E, Salt Lake City UT 84109, USA
Judson, Howard K (Howie) — Baseball Player
239 Fairway Circle NE, Winter Haven FL 33881, USA
Judson, William T — Football Player
652 Sinclair Way, Jonesboro GA 30238, USA
Jue, Blawoh P — Football Player
4514 Billingham St, Fairfax VA 22030, USA
Juergensen, Heather — Actress
Paradigm Agency, 360 N Crescent Dr, North Building, Beverly Hills CA 90210 USA
Jugnauth, Anerood — President, Mauritius
President's Office, Government Centre, Port Louis, Mauritius
Jugnot, Gerard — Director, Actor
J G P M, 11 Rue Chavez, 75016 Paris, France
Ju-Ju — Rap Artist (Beatnuts)
Agency Group Ltd, 142 W 57th St, #600, New York NY 10019 USA
Julavits, Heidi — Writer
G P Putnam's Sons, 375 Hudson St, New York NY 10014 USA
Julian, Alexander, II — Fashion Designer
323 Florida Hill Road, Ridgefield CT 6877, USA
Julian, Janet — Actress
Metropolitan Talent Agency, 7020 La Presa Dr, Los Angeles CA 90068 USA
Julien, Claude — Ice Hockey Player, Coach
3 Myrna Road, Lexington MA 02420, USA
Julius, DeAnne — Economist
Bank of England, Threadneedle St, London EC2R 8AH, England
July, Miranda — Actor, Director, Writer
United Talent Agency, 9336 Civic Center Dr, Beverly Hills CA 90210 USA
Jumaliyev, Kubanychbek M — Prime Minister, Kyrgyzstan
Transport Ministry, Isanova Str 42, 720017 Bishkek, Kyrgyzstan
Junck, Mary E — Businesswoman
Lee Enterprises, 201 N Harrison St, #600, Davenport IA 52801, USA
Juncker, Jean-Claude — Prime Minister, Luxembourg
Prime Minister's Office, 33 Boul Roosevelt, 1728 Luxembourg-Ville, Luxembourg
June, Carl H — Pathologist
University of Pennsylvania Medical School, 421 Curie Blvd, Philadelphia PA 19104, USA
June, Cato N — Football Player
13500 Van Brady Road, Upper Marlboro MD 20772, USA
Juneau, Joseph (Joe) — Ice Hockey Player
Harlem Technologies, 100-2 Rue du Jardin, Pont Rouge QC G3H 3R7, Canada
Jung Sung-Ryong — Soccer Player
Football Assn, 1-131 Sinmunno, 2-Ga Jongno-Gu, Seoul 110 062, South Korea
Jung Woo-Young — Soccer Player
Football Assn, 1-131 Sinmunno, 2-Ga Jongno-Gu, Seoul 110 062, South Korea
Jung, Andrea — Businesswoman
Avon Products, 1345 Ave of Americas Basement Concourse 9, New York NY 10105, USA
Jung, Ernst — Writer
88515 Lagenensligen/Wiltlingen, Germany
Jung, Richard — Neurologist
Waldhofstr 42, 71691 Freiburg, Germany

Junge, Daniel — Director
Milkhaus/Jungefilm, 3059 Vine St, Denver Co 80205, USA

Junger, Gil — Director
A P A Talent/Literary Agency, 405 S Beverly Dr, #300, Beverly Hills CA 90212 USA

Junger, Sebastian — Writer, Director
United Talent Agency, 9336 Civic Center Dr, Beverly Hills CA 90210 USA

Junior, Ester J (E J) — Football Player
911 W Summit St, Bolivar MO 65613, USA

Junior, Marvin — Singer (Dells)
Associated Booking Corp, 501 Madison Ave, #603, New York NY 10022 USA

Junker, Steve N — Football Player
5660 Julmar Dr, Cincinnati OH 45238, USA

Junkie XL — Keyboardist, Guitarist, Drummer
3D Mgmt, 1555 N Vine St, #230, Los Angeles CA 90028, USA

Junkin, Abner K (Trey) — Football Player
5 Lakeside Lane, Newport AR 72112, USA

Junkin, Michael W (Mike) — Football Player
1002 Whitehall Dr, Doylestown PA 18901, USA

Junqueira, Bruno — Auto Racing Driver
3669 Royal Palm Ave, Miami FL 33133, USA

Juntunen, Helena — Opera Singer
Harrison/Parrott, 5-6 Albion Court, London W6 0QT, England

Juppe, Alain M — Prime Minister, France
Mairie, Place Pey-Berland, 33077 Bordeaux Cedex, France

Jur, Jeffrey — Cinematographer
4438 Wortser Ave, Studio City CA 91604, USA

Jurado, Jeanette L — Singer (Expose), Songwriter
Richard Walters, PO Box 2789, Toluca Lake CA 91610 USA

Jurak, Edward J (Ed) — Baseball Player
3650 S Walker Ave, San Pedro CA 90731, USA

Jurasik, Peter — Actor
2109 S Wilbur Ave, Walla Walla WA 99362, USA

Jurevicius, Joseph M (Joe) — Football Player
3310 Brainard Road, Pepper Pike OH 44142, USA

Jurgens, Udo — Singer, Pianist, Songwriter
Freddy Burger Mgmt, Carmentstr 12, 8030 Zurich, Switzerland

Jurgensen, Christian A (Sonny), III — Football Player
6963 Greentree Dr, Naples FL 34108, USA

Jurgensmeier-Carroll, Margaret — Baseball Player
5245 Rowena Dr, Roscoe IL 61073, USA

Jurin, Michael — Guitarist (Stellarstar)
+1 Management/Public Relations, 242 Wythe Ave, #6, Brooklyn NY 11211, USA

Jurkovic, John I — Football Player
2212 June Dr, Schereville IN 46375, USA

Jurowski, Michail — Conductor
Amalienhof 20, 13581 Berlin, Germany

Jurowski, Vladimir — Conductor
I M G Artists, Hogarth Business Park, Chiswick, London W4 2TH, England

Jurrjens, Jair F — Baseball Player
Atlanta Braves, Turner Field, 755 Hank Aaron Dr, Atlanta GA 30315 USA

Just, Ward S — Writer
Janklow & Nesbit Assoc, 445 Park Ave, #1300, New York NY 10022 USA

Juster, Norton — Writer, Architect
55 Kellogg Ave, Amherst MA 01002, USA

Justice, David C — Baseball Player
18570 Old Coach Way, Poway CA 92064, USA

Justice, Victoria — Actress, Singer
United Talent Agency, 9336 Civic Center Dr, Beverly Hills CA 90210 USA

Justin, Kerry J — Football Player
13331 W Marlette Court, Litchfield Park AZ 85340, USA

Justman, Seth — Singer, Keyboardist (J Geils Band)
Nick Ben-Meir, 652 N Doheny Dr, West Hollywood CA 90069, USA

Jutze, Alfred H (Skip) — Baseball Player
3395 Zephry Court, Wheat Ridge CO 80033, USA

Juvenile — Rap Artist
Pretty Special, 200 W 72nd St, #64, New York NY 10023, USA

K7 — Rap Artist
AM/PM Entertainment Concepts, 415 63rd St, #200, Brooklyn NY 11220, USA

Kaake, Jeff — Actor
2533 N Carson St, #3105, Carson City NV 89706, USA

Kaas, Carmen — Model
Men/Women Model Inc, 199 Lafayette St, #700, New York NY 10012 USA

Kaas, Patricia — Singer
Attitude, 71 Rue Robespierre, 93100 Montreuil, France

Kaat, James L (Jim) — Baseball Player
PO Box 1130, Port Salerno FL 34992, USA

Kabakov, Ilya — Artist
Gladstone Gallery, 515 W 52nd St, New York NY 10019, USA

Kaberle, Frantisek — Ice Hockey Player
3105 Briar Stream Run, Raleigh NC 27612, USA

Kaberle, Tomas — Ice Hockey Player
Montreal Canadiens, 1275 Saint Antoine St W, Montreal QC H3C 5L2, Canada

Kabila, Joseph — President, Congo; Army General
President's Office, Mont Ngaliema, Kinshasa, Congo Democratic Republic

Kabui, Frank — Governor General, Soloman Islands
Governor General's House, Box 252, Honiara, Guadacanal, Solomon Islands

Kac, Eduardo — Artist
Chicago Art Institute, 112 S Michigan Ave, #400, Chicago IL 60603, USA

Kaci — Singer
Morey Management Group, 1100 Glendon Ave, PH 1, Los Angeles CA 90024, USA

Kacyvenski, Isaiah J — Football Player
1081 Beacon St, #8, Brookline MA 02446, USA

Kaczmarek, Jane — Actress
Greenlight Mgmt, 13848 Valleyheart Drive, Sherman Oaks CA 91423, USA

Kaczur, Nick — Football Player
17K Marie Dr, Attleboro MA 02703, USA

Kad — Actor, Writer, Director
1 Mgmt, 9000 W Sunset Blvd, #1550, Los Angeles CA 90069 USA

Kadanoff, Leo P — Physicist
5421 S Cornell Ave, Chicago IL 60615, USA

Kadare, Ismail — Writer
40 Rue Violet, 75015 Paris, France

Kadenyuk, Leonid K — Cosmonaut
Cosmonaut Training Center, Star City, 141160 Zvezdny Gorodok, Moscow Oblast, Russia

Kadish, Michael S (Mike) — Football Player
7941 Sudbury Lane SE, Ada MI 49301, USA

Kadison, Joshua — Singer, Songwriter, Pianist
Nick Bode, 1265 Electric Ave, Venice CA 90291, USA

Kaeding, Nate — Football Player
1528 1st Ave, #A, Coralville IA 52241, USA

Kaestle, Carl F — Historian
35 Charlesfield St, Providence RI 02906, USA

Kaesviharn, Kevin R — Football Player
6334 Merrimac Lane N, Osseo MN 55311, USA

Kafatos, Fotis C — Biologist
Imperial College, Cell/Molecular Biology Dept, London SW7 2AZ, England

Kafelnikov, Yevgeny A — Tennis Player
International Mgmt Group, 26 Riverside Dr, Rumson NJ 07760, USA

Kaftan, George A — Basketball Player
2591 Lantern Light Way, Manasquan NJ 08736, USA

Kagan, Daryn — Commentator
CNN-TV, 190 Marietta Ave SW, Atlanta GA 30303 USA

Kagan, Elaine — Actress, Writer
Greene Assoc, 1901 Ave of Stars, #130, Los Angeles CA 90067 USA

Kagan, Elena — Supreme Court Justice
US Supreme Court, 1 1st St NE, Washington DC 20543 USA

Kagan, Henri Boris — Chemist
Universite Paris-Sud, Institut de Chimie Moleculaire, 91405 Orsay, France

Kagan, Jeremy Paul — Director
2024 N Curson Ave, Los Angeles CA 90046, USA

Kagan, Robert A — Attorney, Educator
University of California, Law School, Boalt Hall, Berkeley CA 94720, USA

Kagasoff, Daren — Actor
Anderson Group Public Relations, 8060 Melrose Ave, #400, Los Angeles CA 90046, USA

Kagge, Erling — Polar Skier
Munkedamsveien 86, 0270 Oslo, Norway

Kahane, Gabriel — Composer
I M G Artists, Hogarth Business Park, Chiswick, London W4 2TH, England

Kahane, Jeffrey — Concert Pianist, Conductor
C M Artists, 127 W 96th St, #13B, New York NY 10025 USA

Kahin, Brian — Educator
Harvard University, Information Infrastructure Project, Cambridge MA 02138, USA

Kahin, Dahir Riyale — President, Somaliland Republic
President's Office, Hargiesa, Somaliland Republic

Kahler, Eric — Educator
University of Minnesota, President's Office, 176 N Mississippi River Blvd, Saint Paul MN 55104, USA

Kahn, David R — Publisher
New Yorker, Publisher's Office, 4 Times Square, New York NY 10036, USA

Kahn, Harold — Businessman
Wet Seal Inc, 26972 Burbank, Foothill Ranch CA 92610, USA

Kahn, Joseph — Journalist
New York Times, Editorial Dept, 229 W 43rd St, New York NY 10036 USA

Kahn, Joseph — Director
I C M Partners, 10250 Constellation Blvd, #900, Los Angeles CA 90067 USA

Kahn, Michael — Editor
Gersh Agency, 9465 Wilshire Blvd, #600, Beverly Hills CA 90212 USA

Kahn, Nikki — Photographer
Washington Post, Editorial Dept, 1150 15th St NW, Washington DC 20071 USA

Kahn, Oliver — Soccer Player
Playce AG, Osterwaldstr 10, 80805 Munich, Germany

Kahn, Robert E — Inventor (Internet Protocol)
909 Lynton Place, McLean VA 22102, USA

Kahn, Roger
PO Box 556, Stone Ridge NY 12484, USA — Writer

Kahn, Si
Real People's Music, 520 Clinton, Oak Park IL 60304, USA — Singer, Musician, Songwriter

Kahne, Kasey K
265 Cayuga Dr, Mooresville NC 28117, USA — Auto Racing Driver

Kahneman, Daniel
70 E 10th St, #HD, New York NY 10003, USA — Nobel Economics Laureate

Kaifu, Toshiki
House of Representatives, Diet, Tokyo 100 0014, Japan — Prime Minister, Japan

Kaihori, Ayumi
Football Assn, 3-10-15 Hongo, Bunkyoku, Tokyo 113 0033 Japan — Soccer Player

Kain, Karin A
National Ballet of Canada, 470 Queens Quay, Toronto ON M5V 3K4, Canada — Ballet Dancer

Kain, Khalil
Envision Entertainment, 8840 Wilshire Blvd, Beverly Hills CA 90211 USA — Actor

Kaine, Whitney
Playboy Promotions, 2706 Media Center Dr, Los Angeles CA 90065 USA — Model

Kaipanen, Aume H
Sinebrychffinkatu 11B 17, Helsinki 12, Finland — Writer

Kaiser, A Dale
832 Santa Fe Ave, Stanford CA 94305, USA — Biochemist

Kaiser, George B
Bank of Oklahoma, Bank of Oklahoma Tower, PO Box 2300, Tulsa OK 74102, USA — Financier

Kaiser, Jeffrey P (Jeff)
26227 James Dr, Grosse Isle MI 48138, USA — Baseball Player

Kaiser, Joseph
I M G Artists, 152 W 57th St, #500, New York NY 10019 USA — Opera Singer, Actor

Kaiser, Michael M
Kennedy Center for Performing Arts, 2700 F St NW, Washington DC 20566, USA — Concert Executive

Kaiser, R Thomas (Tom)
8 Independence Way, Southampton NJ 08088, USA — Baseball Player

Kaiser, Raf
University of Hawaii, Physical Chemistry Dept, Honolulu HI 96822, USA — Physical Chemist

Kaiser, Suki
Greene Assoc, 1901 Ave of Stars, #130, Los Angeles CA 90067 USA — Actress

Kaiser, Tim
Vision Art Mgmt, 530 N Larchmont Blvd, #2, Los Angeles CA 90004, USA — Producer

Kaiser-Brown, Natasha
2601 Hickman Road, Des Moines IA 50310, USA — Track Athlete

Kaiserman, William
29 W 56th St, New York NY 10019, USA — Fashion Designer

Kaji, Gautam S
World Bank Group, 1818 H St NW, Washington DC 20433, USA — Government Official, Financier

Kajlich, Bianca
United Talent Agency, 9336 Civic Center Dr, Beverly Hills CA 90210 USA — Model, Actress

Kajol
Usha Kiran, Altamount Road, Mumbai MS 400026, India — Actress

Kaka, Ricardo
F C Milan, Via Filippo Turati 3, 20121 Milan, Italy — Soccer Player

Kakhidze, Djansug I
Leselidze St 18, 380005 Tbilisi, Georgia — Conductor

Kaku, Michio
City University of New York, Physics Dept, New York NY 10031, USA — Theoretical Physicist

Kakutani, Michiko
New York Times, Editorial Dept, 229 W 43rd St, New York NY 10036, USA — Journalist

Kalainov, Samuel C
American Mutual Life, 611 5th Ave, Des Moines IA 50309, USA — Businessman

Kalashnikov, Mikhail T
Sovietskaya Ul 21A, #KV 46, 426076 Izhevsk, Russia — Weapon Designer (AK-47), Army General

Kalb, Marvin
1717 Massachusetts Ave NW, #610, Washington DC 20036, USA — Commentator, Educator

Kaldor, Connie
Fleming Artists, 543 N Main St, Ann Arbor MI 48104, USA — Singer, Songwriter

Kalem, Toni
Creative Artists Agency, 2000 Ave of Stars, #100, Los Angeles CA 90067 USA — Actress

Kalember, Patricia
Innovative Artists, 1505 10th St, Santa Monica CA 90401 USA — Actress

Kalen, Herbert D
General Delivery, Angel Fire NM 87710, USA — Vietnam War Air Force Hero

Kaleri, Aleksandr Y (Sasha)
141 160 Svyosdny Gorodok, Moskovskoi Oblasti, Potchta Kosmonavtor, Russia — Cosmonaut

Kalesniko, Michael
Creative Artists Agency, 2000 Ave of Stars, #100, Los Angeles CA 90067 USA — Director, Writer

Kalichstein, Joseph
Opus 3 Artists, 470 Park Ave S, #900N, New York NY 10016 USA — Concert Pianist

Kalikow, Peter S
H J Kalikow Co, 101 Park Ave, #2500, New York NY 10178, USA — Publisher

Kalil, Matt
Minnesota Vikings, 9520 Viking Dr, Eden Prairie MN 55344 USA — Football Player

Kalin, Tom
Creative Artists Agency, 2000 Ave of Stars, #100, Los Angeles CA 90067 USA — Director, Writer

Kalina, Mike
Travelin' Gourmet Show, PBS-TV, 1320 Braddock Place, Alexandria VA 22314, USA — Chef

Kalina, Richard
44 King St, New York NY 10014, USA — Artist

Kaline, Albert W (Al)
3613 York Court, Bloomfield Hills MI 48301, USA — Baseball Player

Kaling, Mindy
United Talent Agency, 9336 Civic Center Dr, Beverly Hills CA 90210 USA — Actress, Comedienne, Writer

Kalinin, Dmitri
555 Pleasantville Road, #210N, Briarcliff NY 10510, USA — Ice Hockey Player

Kalis, Todd A
900 Bayview Court, Cranberry Township PA 16066, USA — Football Player

Kalish, Martin
School Administrators Federation, 853 Broadway, New York NY 10003, USA — Labor Leader

Kalish, Robert P — Government Official, Financier
Government National Mortgage Assn, 451 7th St SW, Washington DC 20410, USA
Kalitta, Connie — Auto Racing Driver
Kalitta Motorsports, 1010 James L Hart Parkway, Ypsilanti MI 48197, USA
Kaljuste, Tonu — Conductor
Konzertdirektion Hortnagel, Oranienburgen Str 50D, 10117 Berlin, Germany
Kalla, Charlotte — Cross Country Skier
Swedish Ski Federation, Riksskidstadion, 791 19 Falun, Sweden
Kallaugher, Kevin (Kall) — Editorial Cartoonist
Baltimore Sun, Editorial Dept, 501 N Calvert St, Baltimore MD 21278, USA
Kallen, Jackie — Boxing Manager
Trident Media, 41 Madison Ave, #3600, New York NY 10010, USA
Kallen, Kitty — Singer, Actress
35 Winthrop Place, Englewood NJ 07631, USA
Kallin, Catherine — Physicist
224 Hillcrest Ave, Hamilton ON L8P 2X5, Canada
Kallisch, Cornelia — Opera Singer
Kunstler Sekretariat am Gasteig, Rosenheimer Str 52, 81669 Munich, Germany
Kallita, Doug — Auto Racing Driver
Kalitta Motorsports, 1010 James L Hart Parkway, Ypsilanti MI 48197, USA
Kallosh, Renata — Physicist
Stanford University, Physics Dept, Stanford CA 94305, USA
Kallur, Anders — Ice Hockey Player
Utsiktsvagen 14, 791 31 Falun, Sweden
Kalman, Rudolf E — Mathematician
E T H Zentrum, 8092 Zurich, Switzerland
Kalonji, Sizzla — Singer
Agency Group Ltd, 142 W 57th St, #600, New York NY 10019 USA
Kalpokas, Donald M — Prime Minister, Vanuatu
Vanuaaku Pati, PO Box 472, Port Vila, Vanuatu
Kalu, Ndukwe D (N D) — Football Player
3719 Popular Springs Dr, Missouri City TX 77459, USA
Kalule, Ayub — Boxer
Palie, Skjulet, Bagsvaert 12, Copenhagen 2880, Denmark
Kalyan, Adhir — Actor
Abrams Artists, 9200 W Sunset Blvd, #1125, West Hollywood CA 90069 USA
Kamal, Gray — Keyboardist (Roots)
Helter Skelter, 347-353 Chiswick High Road, London W4 4HS, England
Kamali, Norma — Fashion Designer
O M O Norma Kamali, 11 W 56th St, New York NY 10019, USA
Kaman, Christopher Z (Chris) — Basketball Player
300 N Dianthus St, Manhattan Beach CA 90266, USA
Kamano, Stacy — Actress, Model
Vision Mgmt, 8500 Steller Dr, Building 8, Culver City CA 90232, USA
Kamarck, Andrew M — Financier, Diplomat
PO Box 1267, Brewster MA 02631, USA
Kamarck, Martin A — Government Official, Financier
Export-Import Bank, 811 Vermont Ave NW, Washington DC 20571, USA
Kamb, Alexander — Geneticist
300 Alberta Way, Hillsborough CA 94010, USA
Kamen, Dean — Inventor (Portable Dialysis Machine)
D E K A Research & Development, 340 Commercial St, Manchester NH 03101, USA
Kamen, Robert Mark — Writer
Paradigm Agency, 360 N Crescent Dr, North Building, Beverly Hills CA 90210 USA
Kamensky, Valeri — Ice Hockey Player
4 Stonehedge Dr S, Greenwich CT 06831, USA
Kamieniecki, Scott A — Baseball Player
7800 Somerhill Lane, Clarkston MI 48348, USA
Kamin, Aaron K — Guitarist (Calling), Songwriter
The Firm, 2049 Century Park E, #2550, Los Angeles CA 90067 USA
Kamin, Blair — Architectural Critic
Chicago Tribune, Editorial Dept, 350 N Orleans St, Chicago IL 60654 USA
Kaminir, Lisa — Actress
Ellis Talent Group, 4705 Laurel Canyon Blvd, #300, Valley Village CA 91607, USA
Kaminski, Janusz Z — Cinematographer
23801 Calabasas Road, #2004, Calabasas CA 91302, USA
Kaminski, Larry M — Football Player
31423 State Highway 3 NE, Poulsbo WA 98370, USA
Kaminski, Marek — Explorer
Ul Dickmana 14/15, 80 339 Gdansk, Poland
Kaminsky, Arthur C — Sports Attorney
Athletes & Artists, 888 7th Ave, #3700, New York NY 10106, USA
Kaminsky, James — Editor
Maxim, Dennis Publishing, 1040 Ave of Americas, #1500, New York NY 10018, USA
Kaminsky, Kevin S — Ice Hockey Player
162 Dryad Woods Road, Raymond ME 04071, USA
Kaminsky, Walter — Chemist
Hamburg University, Chemistry Dept, Martin-Luther-King Platz 6, 20146 Hamburg, Germany
Kamisar, Yale — Attorney, Educator
2910 Daleview Dr, Ann Arbor MI 48105, USA
Kamm, Henry — Journalist
New York Times, Editorial Dept, 229 W 43rd St, New York NY 10036, USA
Kammen, Michael G — Historian
Cornell University, History Dept, McGraw Hall, Ithaca NY 14853, USA
Kammer, Jerry — Journalist
San Diego Union-Tribune, Editorial Dept, 350 Camino Reina, San Diego CA 92108 USA
Kammerer, Carlton C (Carl) — Football Player
6941 Brooks Road, Highland MD 20777, USA
Kammerlander, Hansjorg (Hans) — Mountaineer
6274 Aschau, #69A, Zillertal (T), Austria
Kamp, Alexandra — Actress, Model
Agentur Aziel, Torkelweg 8, 78224 Singen, Germany
Kampelman, Max M — Government Official
3131 Connecticut Ave NW, #2811, Washington DC 20008, USA
Kampman, Aaron A — Football Player
3999 Chicora Wood Place, Jacksonville FL 32224, USA

Kampmeier, Deborah
I C M Partners, 10250 Constellation Blvd, #900, Los Angeles CA 90067 USA — Director, Writer
Kamu, Okko T
Calle Mozart 7, Rancho Domingo, 29639 Benalmedina Pueblo, Spain — Conductor
Kan, Yuet Wai
20 Yerba Buena Ave, San Francisco CA 94127, USA — Geneticist
Kanaan, Tony
K V Racing Technology, 4001 Methanol Lane, Indianapolis IN 46268, USA — Auto Racing Driver
Kanakaredes, Melina
W M E Entertainment, 9601 Wilshire Blvd, #300, Beverly Hills CA 90210 USA — Actress
Kanal, Tony
Rebel Waltz, 31652 2nd Ave, Laguna Beach CA 92651, USA — Bassist, Songwriter (No Doubt)
Kanaly, Steve
C E S D, 10635 Santa Monica Blvd, #130, Los Angeles CA 90025 USA — Actor
Kanamori, Hiroo
California Institute of Technology, Geophysics Dept, Pasadena CA 91125, USA — Geophysicist
Kanan, Sean
Stone Manners Salners, 9911 W Pico Blvd, #1400, Los Angeles CA 90035 USA — Actor
Kananin, Roman G
Joint-Stock Mosprojekt, 13/14 1 Brestkaya Str, 125190 Moscow, Russia — Architect
Kancheli, Giya A (Georgy)
Tovstonogov Str 6, 380064 Tbilisi, Georgia — Composer
Kandel, Eric R
9 Sigma Place, Bronx NY 10471, USA — Nobel Medicine Laureate
Kander, John H
146 Central Park W, #14D, New York NY 10023, USA — Composer
Kandil, Hesham
Prime Minister's Office, PO Box 191, 1 Majlis El-Shaab St, Cairo, Egypt — Prime Minister, Egypt
Kane Elson, Marion
4669 Badger Road, Santa Rosa CA 95409, USA — Synchronized Swimmer
Kane, Carol
Glick Agency, 1321 7th St, #203, Santa Monica CA 90401 USA — Actress
Kane, Chelsea
United Talent Agency, 9336 Civic Center Dr, Beverly Hills CA 90210 USA — Actress
Kane, Christian
Sutton-Barth Vennari, 145 S Fairfax Ave, #310, Los Angeles CA 90036 USA — Actor, Singer, Songwriter
Kane, Howie
T C I, 105 Shad Row, #D, Piermont NY 10968, USA — Singer (Jay & the Americans)
Kane, John C
Cardinal Health, 7000 Cardinal Place, Dublin OH 43017, USA — Businessman
Kane, Kelly
D H Talent, 1800 N Highland Ave, #300, Los Angeles CA 90028 USA — Actress
Kane, Lorie
101-5397 Eglinton Ave W, Etobicoke ON M9C 5K6, Canada — Golfer
Kane, Nick
AstroMedia, 1620 16th Ave S, Nashville TN 37212, USA — Singer (Mavericks)
Kane, Patrick T
213 McKinley Parkway, Buffalo NY 14220, USA — Ice Hockey Player
Kane, Robert H
University of Texas, Philosophy Dept, Austin TX 78712, USA — Philosopher
Kanell, Daniel P (Danny)
4631 NE 25th Ave, Fort Lauderdale FL 33308, USA — Football Player
Kanellis, Maria
World Wrestling Entertainment, Titan Towers, 1241 E Main St, Stamford CT 06902 USA — Professional Wrestler, Model
Kanengiser, William
Besen Arts, 77 Park Ave, #128, Hoboken NJ 07030, USA — Guitarist (LAGQ)
Kaneswaran, Siva
Industry Music Group, 128 Regent Road, Hanley Stoke, Trent ST1 3AY, England — Singer (Wanted), Model
Kang, Dong-Suk
Clarion/Seven Muses, 47 Whitehall Park, London N19 3TW, England — Concert Violinist
Kang, Jimin
8539 E Cactus Wren Circle, Scottsdale AZ 85266, USA — Golfer
Kang, Tim
Vincent Cirrincione Assoc, 1516 N Fairfax Ave, Los Angeles CA 90046 USA — Actor
Kanicki, James H (Jim)
Tackle Hill Farm, 4590 Schramling Road, Pierpont OH 44082, USA — Football Player
Kanievska, Marek
I C M Partners, 10250 Constellation Blvd, #900, Los Angeles CA 90067 USA — Director
Kanin, Fay
653 Palisades Beach Road, Santa Monica CA 90402, USA — Writer
Kann Valar, Paula
34 Hubertus Ring, Franconia NH 03580, USA — Alpine Skier
Kann, Peter R
Dow Jones Co, 1 World Financial Center, #900, New York NY 10281, USA — Businessman, Publisher, Journalist
Kanne, Michael S
US Court of Appeals, PO Box 1340, Lafayette IN 47902, USA — Judge
Kannenberg, Bernd
Sportschule, 87527 Sonthofen/Allgau, Germany — Track Athlete
Kanouse, Lyle
Gage Group, 14724 Ventura Blvd, #505, Sherman Oaks CA 91403 USA — Actor
Kantner, Paul L
Mission Control, 15030 Ventura Blvd, #300, Sherman Oaks CA 91403, USA — Guitarist (Jefferson Airplane, Starship)
Kantor, Michael (Mickey)
2709 Olive Ave NW, Washington DC 20007, USA — Secretary, Commerce
Kao, Archie
C E S D, 10635 Santa Monica Blvd, #130, Los Angeles CA 90025 USA — Actor
Kao, Charles K
Yee Foundation, 1 Harbour Road, #1708, Wan Chai, Hong Kong, China — Nobel Physics Laureate
Kao, Min H
Garmin International, 1200 E 151st St, Olathe KS 66062, USA — Businessman
Kapadia, Asif
Independent Talent Group, Oxford House, 76 Oxford St, London W1D 1BS, England — Actor, Writer, Director
Kapadia, Dimple
201A Vastu Building, Military Road Juhu, Mumbai MS 400049, India — Actress
Kapanen, Niko K P
Ak Bars Kazan, Tatneff Arena, Kazan, Tatarstan, Russia — Ice Hockey Player

V.I.P. Address Book

K

Kahn - Kapanen

Kapanen, Sami H K — Ice Hockey Player
Kalpa Hockey, Sairaalakatu 15, 70110 Kuopio, Finland

Kapches, Ko — Singer, Songwriter
Agency Group Ltd, 142 W 57th St, #600, New York NY 10019 USA

Kapelos, John — Actor
Axiom Mgmt, 10701 Wilshire Blvd, #1202, Los Angeles CA 90024, USA

Kapilow, Robert (Rob) — Conductor, Composer
I M G Artists, Hogarth Business Park, Chiswick, London W4 2TH, England

Kapinos, Tom — Producer, Writer
Creative Artists Agency, 2000 Ave of Stars, #100, Los Angeles CA 90067 USA

Kapioitas, John — Businessman
I T T Sheraton Corp, 1111 Westchester Ave, West Harrison NY 10604, USA

Kaplan, Gabe — Actor, Comedian
9551 Hidden Valley Road, Beverly Hills CA 90210, USA

Kaplan, Janice — Editor, Writer
Parade Magazine, Editor's Office, 711 3rd Ave, New York NY 10017, USA

Kaplan, Jonathan S — Director
4323 Ben Ave, Studio City CA 91604, USA

Kaplan, Justin — Writer
PO Box 219, Truro MA 02666, USA

Kaplan, Kyle — Actor
Greene Assoc, 1901 Ave of Stars, #130, Los Angeles CA 90067 USA

Kaplan, Marvin — Actor
PO Box 1522, Burbank CA 91507, USA

Kaplan, Nathan O — Biochemist
8587 La Jolla Scenic Dr, La Jolla CA 92037, USA

Kaplan, Paul — Singer, Songwriter
Old Coat Music, 203 Heatherstone Road, Amherst MA 01002, USA

Kaplansky, Lucy — Singer, Guitarist, Songwriter
Fleming Artists, 543 N Main St, Ann Arbor MI 48104, USA

Kapler, Gabriel S (Gabe) — Baseball Player
18316 Palomar Place, Tarzana CA 91356, USA

Kaplow, Herbert E — Commentator
211 N Van Buren St, Falls Church VA 22046, USA

Kapnek, Emily — Producer, Wrtiter
Gotham Group, 9255 Sunset Blvd, #515, Los Angeles CA 90069, USA

Kapoor, Anil — Actor
I C M Partners, 10250 Constellation Blvd, #900, Los Angeles CA 90067 USA

Kapoor, Kareena — Actress
2B/110/1201 Excellency 4th Cross Road, Mumbai MS 400058, India

Kapoor, Karisma — Actress
1101/1201 4th Cross Road, Andheri W, Mumbai MS 400048, India

Kapoor, Rishi — Actor
27 Krishna Raj, Pali Hill Bandra, Mumbai MS 400058, India

Kapoor, Shashi — Actor
112 Atlas Apartments, Mumbai 400006, India

Kapor, Mitchell D — Computer Programmer
Open Source Application Foundation, 177 Post St, #900, San Francisco CA 94108, USA

Kapp, Joseph (Joe) — Football Player, Coach
PO Box 1973, Los Gatos CA 95031, USA

Kappe, Ron — Architect
715 Brooktree Road, Pacific Palisades CA 90272, USA

Kapranos, Alexander P (Alex) — Singer, Guitarist (Franz Ferdinand)
M A M A Group, 59-65 Worship St, London EC2A 2DU, England

Kaprisky, Valerie — Actress
Artmedia, 20 Ave Rapp, 75007 Paris, France

Kapture, Mitzi — Actress
Lovett Mgmt, 1327 Brinkley Ave, Los Angeles CA 90049 USA

Kapur, Shekhar — Director
Sentient Entertainment, 1617 Broadway, Mezzanine, Santa Monica CA 90404, USA

Karabits, Kirill — Conductor
Bournemouth Symphony Orchestra, 2 Seldown Lane, Poole, Dorset BH15 1UF, England

Karadaglic, Milos — Concert Guitarist
I M G Artists, Hogarth Business Park, Chiswick, London W4 2TH, England

Karaev, Anatol — Concert Violinist
I M G Artists, Hogarth Business Park, Chiswick, London W4 2TH, England

Karageorghis, Vassos — Archaeologist
Foundation Anastasios Leventis, 28 Sofoulis St, Nicosia, Cyprus

Karagias, Evan — Professional Wrestler
2009 Tomshire Dr, Gastonia NC 28056, USA

Karamanov, Alemdar S — Composer
Voykova Str 2, #4, Simferopol, Crimea, Ukraine

Karamesines, Chris — Drag Racing Driver
7444 S Claremont Ave, Chicago IL 60636, USA

Karan, Amara — Actress
Curtis Brown Group, 28-29 Haymarket St, #500, London SW1Y 4SP, England

Karan, Donna — Fashion Designer
Donna Karan Co, 361 Newbury St, Boston MA 02115, USA

Karathanasis, Sotirios K — Physiologist
Harvard Medical School, 25 Shattuck St, Boston MA 02115, USA

Karchner, Matthew D (Matt) — Baseball Player
401 E 2nd St, Berwick PA 18603, USA

Kardashian, Khloe — Reality TV Actress
W M E Entertainment, 9601 Wilshire Blvd, #300, Beverly Hills CA 90210 USA

Kardashian, Kimberly (Kim) — Actress, Model
W M E Entertainment, 9601 Wilshire Blvd, #300, Beverly Hills CA 90210 USA

Kardashian, Kourtney — Reality TV Actress
W M E Entertainment, 9601 Wilshire Blvd, #300, Beverly Hills CA 90210 USA

Karelin, Alesander A — Greco-Roman Wrestler
State Duma, Yedinstvo Faction, Okhotny Ryad 1, 103265 Moscow, Russia

Karelskaya, Rimma K — Ballerina
Bolshoi Theater, Teatralnaya Pl 1, 103009 Moscow, Russia

Karen, James — Actor
Amsel Eisenstadt Frazier, 5055 Wilshire Blvd, #865, Los Angeles CA 90036 USA

Karieva, Bernara — Ballerina
National Ballet Theater, 28 MK Otaturk St, 700029 Tashkent, Uzbekistan

Karim, Jawed
YouTube, 1000 Cherry Ave, #200, San Bruno CA 94066, USA — Businessman

Karim-Lamrani, Mohammed
Rue du Mont Saint Michel, Anfa Superieur, Casablanca 21300, Morocco — Prime Minister, Morocco

Karimov, Islom M
President's Office, Uzbekistansky Prosp 45, 700163 Tashkent, Uzbekistan — President, Uzbekistan

Karina, Anna
Artmedia, 20 Ave Rapp, 75007 Paris, France — Actress

Kariya, Paul T
2493 Aquasanta, Tustin CA 92782, USA — Ice Hockey Player

Karkovice, Ronald J (Ron)
3201 Oakstand Lane, Orlando FL 32812, USA — Baseball Player

Karl, Benjamin M
Snowboard Federation, Olympic St 10, 6010 Innsbruck, Austria — Snowboarding Athlete

Karl, George M
245 S Krameria St, Denver CO 80224, USA — Basketball Coach, Executive

Karl, R Scott
6446 Lilium Lane, Carlsbad CA 92011, USA — Baseball Player

Karle, Isabella
6304 Lakeview Dr, Falls Church VA 22041, USA — Chemist

Karle, Jerome
6304 Lakeview Dr, Falls Church VA 22041, USA — Nobel Chemistry Laureate

Karlen, John
Gersh Agency, 9465 Wilshire Blvd, #600, Beverly Hills CA 90212 USA — Actor

Karlic, Estanislao E Cardinal
Monte Caseris 77, 3100 Parana (Entre Rios), Argentina — Religious Leader

Karlin, Ben
United Talent Agency, 9336 Civic Center Dr, Beverly Hills CA 90210 USA — Writer, Producer

Karlis, Richard J (Rich)
13807 E Greenwood Dr, Aurora CO 80014, USA — Football Player

Karlsson, Erik
Ottawa Senators, Scotia Bank Place, Kanata ON K2V 1A5, Canada — Ice Hockey Player

Karlsson, Lena
M O B Agency, 6404 Wilshire Blvd, #505, Los Angeles CA 90048 USA — Singer (Komeda)

Karlstad, Geir
Hamarveien 5A, 1472 Fjellhamar, Norway — Speed Skater

Karlzen, Mary
Little Big Man, 155 Ave of Americas, #700, New York NY 10013, USA — Singer, Songwriter

Karman, Tawakul
Al-Islah Party, Parliament Building, Sana's, Yemen — Nobel Peace Laureate

Karmann, Sam
Les Films A4, 41 Rue Vivienne 75002 Paris, France — Actor

Karmanos, Peter, Jr
Compuware Corp, 1 Campus Martius, Detroit MI 48226, USA — Businessman, Hockey Executive

Karmazin, Mel
Sirius Satelite Radio, 1221 Avenue of Americas, #3600, New York NY 10020, USA — Businessman

Karmi, Ram
Karmi Architects, 17 Kaplan St, Tel Aviv 64734, Israel — Architect

Karmi-Melamede, Ada
Karmi Architects, 17 Kaplan St, Tel Aviv 64734, Israel — Architect

Karn, Richard
Stone Manners Salners, 9911 W Pico Blvd, #1400, Los Angeles CA 90035 USA — Actor

Karnes, David K
9639 Oak Circle, Omaha NE 68124, USA — Senator, NE

Karnes, Jay
Innovative Artists, 1505 10th St, Santa Monica CA 90401 USA — Actor

Karneus, Katarina
Ingpen & Williams, 131 Putney Bridge Road, London SW15 2PA, England — Opera Singer

Karnow, Stanley
10850 Spring Knolls Dr, Potomac MD 20854, USA — Historian

Karnuth, Jason
2822 Helding Park Court, Katy TX 77494, USA — Baseball Player

Karolyi, Bela
454 Forest Service 200 Road, Huntsville TX 77340, USA — Gymnastics Coach

Karolyi, Marta
World Gymnastics Academy, 1937 W Parker Road, Plano TX 75023, USA — Gymnastics Coach

Karon, Jan
7060 Esmont Farm, Esmont VA 22937, USA — Writer

Karp, Peter
Agency Group Ltd, 142 W 57th St, #600, New York NY 10019 USA — Singer, Songwriter

Karp, Richard M
University of Washington, Computer Science Dept, Seattle WA 98195, USA — Computer Scientist, Engineer

Karpati, Gyorgy
Il Liva Utca 1, 1025 Budapest, Hungary — Water Polo Player

Karpatkin, Rhoda H
280 Riverside Drive, New York NY 10025, USA — Publisher

Karpluk, Erin
Play Mgmt, 807 Powell St, #220, Vancouver BC V6A 1H7, Canada — Actress

Karplus, Martin
Harvard University, Chemistry Dept, Cambridge MA 02138, USA — Chemist

Karponosov, Gennadiy
146 Dallam Road, Newark DE 19711, USA — Ice Dancer, Coach

Karpovsky, Alex
Mosiac Media Group, 9200 W Sunset Blvd, #1000, Los Angeles CA 90069 USA — Actor, Director

Karr, Mary
Syracuse University, English Dept, Syracuse NY 13244, USA — Writer

Karrass, Chester L
1633 Stanford St, Santa Monica CA 90404, USA — Writer

Karros, Eric P
1170 Longfellow Dr, Manhattan Beach CA 90266, USA — Baseball Player

Karrys, George
Curling Assn, 1660 Vimont Court, Cumberland ON K4A 4J4, Canada — Curling Athlete

Karsay, Stefan A (Steve)
20244 N 102nd Place, Scottsdale AZ 85255, USA — Baseball Player

Karsenty, Gerard
Columbia University Medical Center, 701 W 168th St, #1602A, New York NY 10032, USA — Geneticist

Karsh, Jonathan — Producer, Director
Relativity Real, 1040 N Las Palmas Ave, Los Angeles CA 90038, USA
Karst, Kenneth L — Attorney, Educator
University of California, Law School, PO Box 951476, Los Angeles CA 90095, USA
Karstens, Jeffrey W (Jeff) — Baseball Player
212 S Moody Ave, #3, Tampa FL 33609, USA
Kartheiser, Vincent P — Actor
Paradigm Agency, 360 N Crescent Dr, North Building, Beverly Hills CA 90210 USA
Kartz, Keith L — Football Player
19232 E Hinsdale Lane, Centennial CO 80016, USA
Karume, Amani Abeid — President, Zanzibar
President's Office, State House, PO Box 776, Zanzibar, Tanzania
Karusseit, Ursula — Actress
Agentur Astrid Rhn, Nazarethkirchstr 53, 13347 Berlin, Germany
Karvan, Claudia — Actress
United Talent Agency, 9336 Civic Center Dr, Beverly Hills CA 90210 USA
Karyo, Tcheky — Actor
Artmedia, 20 Ave Rapp, 75007 Paris, France
Karzai, Hamid — President, Afghanistan
President's Office, Shar Rahi Sedarat, Kabul, Afghanistan
Kasaks, Sally Frame — Businesswoman
AnnTaylor Stores, 7 Times Square, #4, New York NY 10036, USA
Kasarova, Vesselina — Opera Singer
Opera et Concert, 37 Rue de la Chaussee d'Antin, 75009 Paris, France
Kasatkina, Natalya K — Ballerina, Choreographer
Karietny Riad. H 5/10, #37, 103006 Moscow, Russia
Kasatonov, Alexei V — Ice Hockey Player
153 Eagle Rock Way, Montclair NJ 07042, USA
Kasay, John D — Football Player
8812 Covey Rise Court, Charlotte NC 28226, USA
Kasch, Cody — Actor
TalentWorks, 3500 W Olive Ave, #1400, Burbank CA 91505 USA
Kasch, Max — Actor
Abrams Artists, 9200 W Sunset Blvd, #1125, West Hollywood CA 90069 USA
Kasdan, Jacob (Jake) — Director, Actor
W M E Entertainment, 9601 Wilshire Blvd, #300, Beverly Hills CA 90210 USA
Kasdan, Lawrence E — Director, Writer
Kasdan Pictures, PO Box 17578, Beverly Hills CA 90209, USA
Kaselawski, Bradley R (Brad) — Auto Racing Driver
K Auto Motorsports, 2790 Auburn Road, Auburn Hills MI 48326, USA
Kasem, Casey — Entertainer, Actor
138 N Mapleton Dr, Los Angeles CA 90077, USA
Kasem, Jean — Actress
138 N Mapleton Dr, Los Angeles CA 90077, USA
Kaseman, Keith — Architect
Kaseman Beckman Advanced Strategies, 408 Vine St, #2B, Philadelphia PA 19106, USA
Kaser, Helmut A — Soccer Executive
Hitzigweg 11, 8032 Zurich, Switzerland
Kasha, Al — Composer, Lyricist
458 N Oakhurst Dr, #102, Beverly Hills CA 90210, USA
Kasher, Tim — Singer, Guitarist (Cursive)
Ground Control Touring, 20 Jay St, #826, Brooklyn NY 11201 USA
Kashiwara, Masaki — Mathematician
Mathematical Science Institute, Kyoto University, Kyoto 606 8502, Japan
Kashkari, Neel — Financier, Government Official
Treasury Department, 1500 Pennsylvania Ave NW, Washington DC 20220 USA
Kashkashian, Kim — Concert Violist
Musicians Corporate Mgmt, PO Box 825, Highland NY 12528, USA
Kaskey, Raymond J — Sculptor, Architect
2221 Hiatt Place NW, Washington DC 20007, USA
Kasko, Edward M (Eddie) — Baseball Player, Manager
32 Major Ginter Court, Richmond VA 23227, USA
Kasler, James — WW II Army Air Corps Hero
8993 E 1500N Road, Momence IL 60954, USA
Kasling, Dagmar Luhenschloss — Track Athlete
Hollehocjstr 27E, 39110 Magdeburg, Germany
Kasman, Yakov — Concert Pianist
Jonathan Wentworth Assoc, 10 Fiske Place, #530, Mount Vernon NY 10550 USA
Kasparov, Garry K — Chess Player
Kasparov Agency, 3114 45th St, #8, West Palm Beach FL 33407, USA
Kasper, Kevin J — Football Player
2211 Spartina Lane, Naperville IL 60564, USA
Kasper, Steve — Ice Hockey Player, Coach
6 Swan Lane, Andover MA 01810, USA
Kasper, Walter Cardinal — Religious Leader
Consiglio per L'Unita dei Crostoamo, Via dell'Erba 1, 00193 Rome, Italy
Kaspszyk, Jacek — Conductor
Teatr Wielki, Pl Teatralny 1, 00 077 Warsaw, Poland
Kasrashvili, Makvala — Opera Singer
Bolshoi Theater, Teatralnaya Pl 1, 103009 Moscow, Russia
Kass, Carmen — Model
Women Model Mgmt, 199 Lafayette St, #700, New York NY 10012 USA
Kass, Daniel (Danny) — Snowboard Skier
4315 NE Laurelhurst Place, Portland OR 97213, USA
Kass, Leon R — Bioethicist
1150 17th St NW, #AE1, Washington DC 20036, USA
Kassay, Jacob — Artist
Eleven Rivington, 11 Rivington St & 195 Chrystie St, New York NY 10002, USA
Kassebaum, Nancy Landon — Senator, KS
Robert Wood Johnson Foundation, College Road E, Princeton NJ 08543, USA
Kassell, Brad — Football Player
20117 Rancho Cielo Court, Lago Vista TX 78645, USA
Kassell, Carl — Commentator
National Public Radio, 635 Massachusetts Ave NW, #1, Washington DC 20001, USA
Kassell, Nicole — Director, Writer
Washington Square Arts, 1041 N Formosa Ave, Formosa Building, West Hollywood CA 90046, USA

Kassen, Mark — Actor
Creative Artists Agency, 2000 Ave of Stars, #100, Los Angeles CA 90067 USA

Kassir, John — Actor
Vincent Cirrincione Assoc, 1516 N Fairfax Ave, Los Angeles CA 90046 USA

Kassoma, A Paulo — Prime Minister, Angola
National Assemby, Rua do 1 Confresso do M P L A, CP 1204 Luanda, Angola

Kassorla, Irene C — Psychologist
908 N Roxbury Dr, Beverly Hills CA 90210, USA

Kassovitz, Mathieu — Actor, Director
M N P Enterprise, 18 Rue Du Fabourge du Temple, 75011 Paris, France

Kasten, Robert W, Jr — Senator, WI
Kasten Co, 888 16th St NW, #700, Washington DC 20006, USA

Kastor, Deena — Track Athlete
1208 Majestic Pines Dr, Mammoth Lakes CA 93546, USA

Kasulke, Benjamin — Cinematographer
United Talent Agency, 9336 Civic Center Dr, Beverly Hills CA 90210 USA

Kasyanov, Mikhail M — Prime Minister, Russia
House of Government, Krasnopresneskaya Nab 2, 103274 Moscow, Russia

Katainen, Jyrki T — Prime Minister, Finland
Prime Minister's Office, Snellmaninkatu 1A, 00170, Helsinki, Finland

Katchor, Ben — Cartoonist (Julius Knipl)
Wylie Agency, 250 W 57th St, #2114, New York NY 10107 USA

Kate — Duchess of Cambridge
Clarence House, Stable Yard Gate, London SW1A 1BA, England

Katehi, Linda P B — Educator
University of California, Chancellor's Office, 1 Shields Ave, Davis CA 95616, USA

Kates, Kimberley — Actress
David Talent, 116 S Gardner St, Los Angeles CA 90036, USA

Kates, Robert W — Geographer
1081 Bar Harbor Road, Trenton ME 04605, USA

Kathpalia, Rajeev — Architect
Vastu Shilpa Consultants, Sangath, Thaltej Road, Ahmedabad 380054, India

Katic, Stana J — Actress
Third Hill Entertainment, 195 S Beverly Dr, #400, Beverly Hills CA 90212, USA

Katims, Jason — Producer
Creative Artists Agency, 2000 Ave of Stars, #100, Los Angeles CA 90067 USA

Katin, Peter R — Concert Pianist
4 Clarence Road, Croydon, Surrrey CR0 2EN, England

Katleman, Michael — Director
United Talent Agency, 9336 Civic Center Dr, Beverly Hills CA 90210 USA

Kato, Masaya — Actor
Paceline Entertainment, 12444 Ventura Blvd, #103, Studio City CA 91604 USA

Katon, Rosanne — Actress, Model
407 Ocean Front Walk, #5, Venice CA 90291, USA

Katona, Kerry J E — Entertainer, Singer
Flood Bumstead McCready McCarthy, 1700 Hayes St, #304, Nashville TN 37203 USA

Katritzky, Alan R — Chemist
1221 SW 21st Ave, Gainesville FL 32601, USA

Katsoudas, Stella — Singer (Sister Soleil), Songwriter
Ashley Talent, 2002 Hogback Road, #20, Ann Arbor MI 48105 USA

Katt, Nicholas L (Nicky) — Actor
Sloss Law Office, 555 W 25th St, #400, New York NY 10001, USA

Katt, William — Actor
Home Agency, 4420 W Lovers Lane, Dallas TX 75209, USA

Kattan, Chris — Actor, Comedian
A P A Talent/Literary Agency, 405 S Beverly Dr, #300, Beverly Hills CA 90212 USA

Kattan, Mohammed Imad — Architect
PO Box 950846, Amman 11195, Jordan

Kattus, J Eric — Football Player
854 Adams Road, Loveland OH 45140, USA

Katula, Matthew C (Matt) — Football Player
14 Victoria Court, #21, Reisterstown MD 21136, USA

Katz, Abraham — Diplomat
US Council for International Business, 1212 Ave of Americas, New York NY 10036, USA

Katz, Alex — Artist
435 W Broadway, New York NY 10012, USA

Katz, Bernard — Sculptor
PO Box 41064, Philadelphia PA 19127, USA

Katz, Donald L — Petroleum Engineer
2011 Washtenaw Ave, Ann Arbor MI 48104, USA

Katz, Douglas J (Doug) — Navy Admiral
1530 Gordon Cove Dr, Annapolis MD 21403, USA

Katz, Harold — Basketball Executive
Philadelphia 76ers, 1st Union Center, 3601 S Broad St, Philadelphia PA 19148 USA

Katz, Hilda — Artist
915 W End Ave, #5D, New York NY 10025, USA

Katz, Jonathan — Actor, Comedian, Animator
Creative Artists Agency, 2000 Ave of Stars, #100, Los Angeles CA 90067 USA

Katz, Michael — Pediatrician
200 E 57th St, #11K, New York NY 10022, USA

Katz, Omri — Actor
J H Productions, 23679 Calabasas Road, #333, Calabasas CA 91302, USA

Katz, Ross — Producer, Director, Writer
Ross Katz Films, 200 Park Ave S, #800, New York NY 10003, USA

Katz, Samuel L — Pediatrician
1917 Wildcat Creek Road, Chapel Hill NC 27516, USA

Katz, Stanley N — Attorney, Educator
American Council on Learned Societies, 228 E 45th St, New York NY 10017, USA

Katz, Stephen M — Cinematographer
C E S D, 10635 Santa Monica Blvd, #130, Los Angeles CA 90025 USA

Katzenberg, David — Producer, Writer
Katz/Smith Productions, 8447 Wilshire Blvd, #210, Beverly Hills CA 90211, USA

Katzenberg, Jeffrey — Businessman
DreamWorks SKG, 100 Flower St, Glendale CA 91201, USA

Katzenmoyer, Andrew W (Andy) — Football Player
5764 Salem Dr, Westerville OH 43082, USA

Katzmann, Robert A — Judge
US Court of Appeals, Moynihan Courthouse, 500 Pearl St, New York NY 10007, USA
Katzur, Klaus — Swimmer
Robert-Siewart-Str 76, 0912 Chemnitz, Germany
Kauffman, Marta — Writer, Producer
W M E Entertainment, 9601 Wilshire Blvd, #300, Beverly Hills CA 90210 USA
Kauffman, Stuart A A — Biologist
Biocomplexity Institute, 2500 University NW, Calgary AB T2N 1N4, Canada
Kaufman, Adam — Actor
S D B Partners, 1801 Ave of Stars, #902, Los Angeles CA 90067 USA
Kaufman, Bel — Writer
1020 Park Ave, New York NY 10028, USA
Kaufman, Charles S (Charlie) — Director, Producer, Writer
W M E Entertainment, 9601 Wilshire Blvd, #300, Beverly Hills CA 90210 USA
Kaufman, Dan S — Hematologist
University of Wisconsin Medical School, Hematology Dept, Madison WI 53706, USA
Kaufman, Donald — Writer
United Talent Agency, 9336 Civic Center Dr, Beverly Hills CA 90210 USA
Kaufman, Henry — Financier
Henry Kaufman Co, 65 E 55th St, New York NY 10022, USA
Kaufman, Moises — Director, Writer
Gersh Agency, 41 Madison Ave, #3301, New York NY 10010 USA
Kaufman, Napoleon — Football Player
1913 Via Di Salerno, Pleasanton CA 94566, USA
Kaufman, Philip — Director, Writer
I C M Partners, 10250 Constellation Blvd, #900, Los Angeles CA 90067 USA
Kaufman, Thomas C (Thom) — Biologist
Indiana University, Biology Dept, Bloomington IN 47405, USA
Kaufmann, Christine — Actress
Zentralburo, Kleiner Griechenmarkt 81, 50676 Cologne, Germany
Kaufmann, Robert (Bob) — Basketball Player
1677 Rivermist Dr SW, Lilburn GA 30047, USA
Kaukonen, Jorma L, Jr — Guitarist (Jefferson Airplane, Hot Tuna)
Fur Peach Ranch, 39495 Saint Clair Road, Pomeroy OH 45769, USA
Kaunda, Kenneth D — President, Zambia
21A Serval Road, Private Bag E501, Lusaka, Zambia
Kaurismaki, Aki — Director
Sputnik, Museokato 13A, 00100 Helsinki, Finland
Kausalya — Actress
15A-2 Akshar, Palace Road, Bangalore AJ 52, India
Kaushal, Kamini — Actress, Dancer
B2 Anita Mount Pleasant Road, Malabar Hill, Mumbai MS 400006, India
Kauth, Kathleen — Ice Hockey Player
13 Hillcrest Lane, Saratoga Springs NY 12866, USA
Kava, Caroline — Actress
TalentWorks, 3500 W Olive Ave, #1400, Burbank CA 91505 USA
Kavanaugh, Brett M — Judge
US Appellate Court, 333 Constitution Ave NW, #4400, Washington DC 20001, USA
Kavanaugh, John — Actor
The Agency, 9 Upper Fitzwilliam St, 2 Dublin, Ireland
Kavandi, Janet L — Astronaut
3907 Park Circle Way, Houston TX 77059, USA
Kavner, Julie — Actress
I C M Partners, 10250 Constellation Blvd, #900, Los Angeles CA 90067 USA
Kavovit, Andrew — Actor
Thruline Entertainment, 9250 Wilshire Blvd, #100, Beverly Hills CA 90212 USA
Kavrakos, Dimitri — Opera Singer
Columbia Artists Mgmt Inc, 1790 Broadway, #702, New York NY 10019 USA
Kawakubo, Rei — Fashion Designer
Comme des Garcons, 16 Place Vendome, 75001 Paris, France
Kawasumi, Nahomi — Soccer Player
Football Assn, 3-10-15 Hongo, Bunkyoku, Tokyo 113 0033 Japan
Kay, Alan C — Computer Scientist
Viewpoints Research Institute, 1209 Grand Capital Ave, Glendale CA 91201, USA
Kay, Clarence H — Football Player
1648 Lansing St, Aurora CO 80010, USA
Kay, Dianne — Actress
1565 Calle Del Estribo, Pacific Palisades CA 90272, USA
Kay, Dominic Scott — Actor
Paradigm Agency, 360 N Crescent Dr, North Building, Beverly Hills CA 90210 USA
Kay, Herma H — Attorney, Educator
University of California, Law School, Boalt Hall, Berkeley CA 94720, USA
Kay, Jason (Jay) — Singer (Jamiroquai)
Nettwerk Mgmt, 6525 W Sunset Blvd, #800, Los Angeles CA 90028 USA
Kay, John — Singer, Guitarist (Steppenwolf)
Lustig Talent, PO Box 770850, Orlando FL 32877 USA
Kay, Lesli — Actress
Innovative Artists, 1505 10th St, Santa Monica CA 90401 USA
Kay, Stephen T — Actor
I C M Partners, 10250 Constellation Blvd, #900, Los Angeles CA 90067 USA
Kaye, Carol — Guitarist, Bassist
25852 McBean Parkway, #200, Valencia CA 91355, USA
Kaye, Jonathan — Golfer
328 W El Camino, Phoenix AZ 85021, USA
Kaye, Paul — Actor
Richard Stone Partnership, 85 New Cavendish St, London W1W 6XD, England
Kaye, Thorsten — Actor
I C M Partners, 10250 Constellation Blvd, #900, Los Angeles CA 90067 USA
Kayne — Singer, Songwriter
Agency Group Ltd, 142 W 57th St, #600, New York NY 10019 USA
Kayser, Manfred — Molecular Biologist
Erasmus University Medical Center, 3013 Rotterdam GE, Netherlands
Kazan, Lainie — Singer, Actress
TalentWorks, 3500 W Olive Ave, #1400, Burbank CA 91505 USA
Kazan, Zoe — Actress
Gersh Agency, 9465 Wilshire Blvd, #600, Beverly Hills CA 90212 USA

Kazankina, Tatyana
Hoshimina St, 111211 Saint Petersburg, Russia — Track Athlete

Kazanski, Theodore S (Ted)
1544 Dormie Dr, Gladwin MI 48624, USA — Baseball Player

Kazee, Steve
Innovative Artists, 1505 10th St, Santa Monica CA 90401 USA — Actor

Kazer, Beau
139A N San Fernando Blvd, Burbank CA 91502, USA — Actor

Kazmaier, Richard W (Dick), Jr
261 Park Lane, Concord MA 01742, USA — Football Player

Kazmir, Scott E
16619 Rose Bay Trail, Cypress TX 77429, USA — Baseball Player

Kazurinsky, Tim
Geddes Agency, 1633 N Halsted St, #300, Chicago IL 60614, USA — Actor, Comedian

Keach, James
Catfish Productions, 23852 Pacific Coast Highway, #313, Malibu CA 90265, USA — Actor

Keach, Stacy
Diamond Mgmt, 31 Percy St, London W1T 2DD, England — Actor

Keady, L Eugene (Gene)
Saint John's University, Athletic Dept, 8000 Utopia Parkway, Queens NY 11439, USA — Basketball Coach

Keaggy, Phil
Ray Ware Artist Mgmt, 3108 Saint Stephens Way, Franklin TN 37064, USA — Guitarist

Kealey, Steven W (Steve)
1080 1700 Ave, Abilene KS 67410, USA — Baseball Player

Kean, Jane
Sutton-Barth Vennari, 145 S Fairfax Ave, #310, Los Angeles CA 90036 USA — Actress

Kean, Laurel
11831 Forest Mere Dr, Bonita Springs FL 34135, USA — Golfer

Kean, Thomas H
PO Box 332, Far Hills NJ 07931, USA — Governor, NJ; Educator

Keanan, Staci
Vox Inc, 6420 Wilshire Blvd, #1080, Los Angeles CA 90048 USA — Actress

Keane, Dolores
Kieren Cavanaugh, PO Box 5339, Dublin 4, Ireland — Singer, Musician

Keane, Glen
Walt Disney Studios, Animation Dept, 500 S Buena Vista St, Burbank CA 91521, USA — Animator

Keane, John
Bloomsbury Publishing, 36 Soho Square, London W1D 3Q4, England — Writer

Keane, John M
United Talent Agency, 9336 Civic Center Dr, Beverly Hills CA 90210 USA — Film Composer

Keane, John M (Jack)
General Dynamics, 2941 Fairview Park Dr, #100, Falls Church VA 22042, USA — Army General

Keane, Kerrie
S D B Partners, 1801 Ave of Stars, #902, Los Angeles CA 90067 USA — Actress

Keane, Louis M (Dillie)
Gavin Barker Assoc, 2D Wimpole St, London W1G 0EB, England — Actress, Singer, Comedienne

Keane, Roy M
Manchester United, Busby Way, Old Trafford, Manchester M16 0RA, England — Soccer Player

Keane, Sean
Macklam/Feldman Mgmt, 1505 W 2nd Ave, #200, Vancouver BC V6H 3Y4, Canada — Fiddler (Chieftains)

Keane, William
C E S D, 10635 Santa Monica Blvd, #130, Los Angeles CA 90025 USA — Actor

Kear, David
34 W End, Ohope 3121, New Zealand — Geologist

Kearney, Hannah
Waterville Valley B B T S, Box 277, Waterville Valley NH 03215, USA — Moguls Skier

Kearney, James L (Jim)
1817 E 59th St, Kansas City MO 64130, USA — Football Player

Kearney, Mat
Tri-Star Sports & Entertainment, 450 N Roxbury Dr, #602, Beverly Hills CA 90210, USA — Singer, Songwriter

Kearney, Robert H (Bob)
4155 Elizabeth Dr, Stevensville MI 49127, USA — Baseball Player

Kearney, Timothy E (Tim)
2144 Dartmouth Gate Court, Ballwin MO 63011, USA — Football Player

Kearns, Austin R
719 Haverhill Dr, Lexington KY 40503, USA — Baseball Player

Kearns, Dennis M
1292 Esquimalt Ave, West Vancouver BC V7T 1K3, Canada — Ice Hockey Player

Kearse, Amalya L
US Court of Appeals, Moynihan Courthouse, 500 Pearl St, New York NY 10007, USA — Judge

Kearse, Jevon
61 Whitworth Blvd, Nashville TN 37205, USA — Football Player

Kearse, NaShawn
Leverage Mgmt, 3030 Pennsylvania Ave, Santa Monica CA 90404 USA — Actor

Keaser, Lloyd (Butch)
43960 Tavern Dr, Ashburn VA 20147, USA — Freestyle Wrestler

Keating, Charles
Don Buchwald/Fortitude, 10 E 44th St, New York NY 10017 USA — Actor

Keating, Christopher P (Chris)
741 Canton Ave, Milton MA 02186, USA — Football Player

Keating, Dominic
TalentWorks, 3500 W Olive Ave, #1400, Burbank CA 91505 USA — Actor

Keating, Francis A (Frank), II
American Life Insurers, 101 Constitution Ave NW, #700W, Washington DC 20001, USA — Governor, OK

Keating, Paul J
GPO Box 1265, Potts Point NSW 1335, Australia — Prime Minister, Australia

Keating, Ronan
Outside Organization, 180-182 Tottenham Court, London W1P 9LE, England — Singer (Boyzone)

Keating, Thomas A (Tom)
3725 W St NW, Washington DC 20007, USA — Football Player

Keating, Timothy J
7443 Collins Meade Way, Alexandria VA 22315, USA — Navy Admiral

Keaton, Danielle
Paceline Entertainment, 12444 Ventura Blvd, #103, Studio City CA 91604 USA — Actress

Keaton, Diane
15260 Ventura Blvd, #1040, Sherman Oaks CA 91403, USA — Actress, Director

K

Keaton, Michael — Actor
Colomby/Keaton Productions, 2110 Main St, #302, Santa Monica CA 90405, USA
Keats, Donald H — Composer
University of Denver, Music School, Denver CO 80208, USA
Keb' Mo' — Singer, Songwriter
Monterey International, 200 W Superior St, #202, Chicago IL 60654 USA
K'eba, Miftah Muhammed — General Secretary, Libya
General Secretary's Office, Bab el Asiziya Barracks, Tripoli, Libya
Kebbel, Arielle — Actress
Paradigm Agency, 360 N Crescent Dr, North Building, Beverly Hills CA 90210 USA
Kebbell, Toby — Actor
Independent Talent Group, Oxford House, 76 Oxford St, London W1D 1BS, England
Kebede, Liya — Model, Actress
I M G Models, 304 Park Ave S, #PH-North, New York NY 10010 USA
Kebich, Vyacheslav F — Prime Minister, Belarus
National Assembly, K Marksa Str 38, Dom Urada, 220016 Minsk, Belarus
Keck, Donald B — Inventor (Silica Optical Waveguide)
2877 Chequers Circle, Big Flats NY 14814, USA
Keck, Howard B — Philanthropist
600 Wilshire Blvd, #17, Los Angeles CA 90017, USA
Keczmer, Daniel L (Dan) — Ice Hockey Player
9533 Sanctuary Place, Brentwood TN 37027, USA
Kedah — Sultan, Kedah
Istana Anak Bukit, Alor Setar, Kedah, Darul Aman, Malaysia
Kee, John P — Singer
A&M Entertainment, 13280 NW Freeway, #328, Houston,TX 77040, USA
Keefe, Adam T — Basketball Player
15933 Alcima Ave, Pacific Palisades CA 90272, USA
Keefe, Mike — Editorial Cartoonist
Denver Post, Editorial Dept, PO Box 1709, Denver CO 80201, USA
Keefer, Don — Actor
4146 Allott Ave, Sherman Oaks CA 91423, USA
Keeffe, Bernard — Conductor
153 Honor Oak Road, London SE23 3RN, England
Keegan, Andrew — Actor
FilmEngine, 345 Maple Dr, #222, Beverly Hills CA 90210, USA
Keegan, Kevin J — Soccer Player, Executive
Manchester City F C, Maine Road, Moss Side, Manchester M14 7WN, England
Keegan, Robert J — Businessman
Goodyear Tire & Rubber, 1144 E Market St, Akron OH 44316, USA
Keegan, Scarlett — Model
C E S D, 10635 Santa Monica Blvd, #130, Los Angeles CA 90025 USA
Keehne, Virginya — Actress
Craig Mgmt, 2240 Miramonte Circle E, #C, Palm Springs CA 92264 USA
Keel, Alton G, Jr — Diplomat, Businessman
Atlantic Partners, 2891 S River Road, Stanardsville VA 22973, USA
Keelaghan, James — Singer, Songwriter
Jensen Music International, PO Box 3445, Charlottetown PE C1A 8W5, Canada
Keeler, Jesse F — Electronic Musician (Mstrkrft)
Biz 3 Publicity, 1321 N Milwaukee Ave, #452, Chicago IL 60622, USA
Keeler, William H Cardinal — Religious Leader
National Conference of Catholic Bishops, 3211 4th St, Washington DC 20017, USA
Keeley, Edmund L — Writer
140 Littlebrook Road, Princeton NJ 08540, USA
Keeley, Robert V — Diplomat
3814 Livingston St NW, Washington DC 20015, USA
Keeley, Sam — Actor
Paradigm Agency, 360 N Crescent Dr, North Building, Beverly Hills CA 90210 USA
Keelor, Greg — Singer, Guitarist (Blue Rodeo)
Starfish Entertainment, 906A Logan Ave, Toronto ON M4K 3E4, Canada
Keen, Robert Earl — Singer, Songwriter
C3 Presents, 98 San Jacinto Blvd, #400, Austin TX 78701, USA
Keen, Sam — Writer, Philosopher
16331 Norrbom Road, Sonoma CA 95476, USA
Keena, Monica — Actress
Greater Vision Agency, 8981 Sunset Blvd, #101, Los Angeles CA 90069, USA
Keenan, Edward L — Historian
Harvard University, History Dept, Robinson Hall, Cambridge MA 02138, USA
Keenan, Joseph D — Labor Leader
2727 29th St NW, Washington DC 20008, USA
Keenan, Larry — Ice Hockey Player
132 Gordon Dr, North Bay ON P1B 8B2, Canada
Keenan, Maynard James — Singer (Tool, Perfect Circle)
The Firm, 2049 Century Park E, #2550, Los Angeles CA 90067 USA
Keenan, Michael E (Mike) — Ice Hockey Coach
PO Box 175, 1975 Duval St, Key West FL 33041, USA
Keene Cherot, Kyera — Producer, Writer
C C A, 7 Saint Georges Square, London SW1V 2HX, England
Keene, Donald L — Language Educator
Columbia University, Language Dept, Kent Hall, New York NY 10027, USA
Keene, Phillip P — Actor
A K A Talent, 6310 San Vicente Blvd, #200, Los Angeles CA 90048 USA
Keene, Tommy — Singer, Guitarist, Songwriter
Black Park Mgmt, PO Box 107, Sunbury NC 27979, USA
Keener, Catherine — Actress
Gersh Agency, 9465 Wilshire Blvd, #600, Beverly Hills CA 90212 USA
Keener, Joseph D (Joe) — Baseball Player
26849 Lompac Ave, Barstow CA 92311, USA
Keenlyside, Simon — Opera Singer
Askonas Holt, Lincoln House, 300 High Holborn, London WC1V 7JH, England
Keenum, Mark E — Educator
Mississippi State University, President's Office, Allen Hall, Mississippi State MS 39762, USA
Keeny, Spurgeon M, Jr — Association Executive
3600 Albemarle St NW, Washington DC 20008, USA
Keeslar, Matt — Actor
Martin Berneman Mgmt, 5820 Wilshire Blvd, #200, Los Angeles CA 90036 USA

Keezer, Geoff — Jazz Pianist
D L Media, 124 N Highland Ave, Bala Cynwyd PA 19004, USA
Keflezighi, Mebrahtom (Meb) — Track Athlete
Mammoth Track Club, PO Box 7552, Mammoth Lakes CA 93546, USA
Kegel, Oliver — Canoeing Athlete
Am Bogen 23, 13589 Berlin, Germany
Kegeles, Gerson — Chemist
RR 1 Box 156, Groveton NH 03582, USA
Keggi, Caroline — Golfer
807 Westlake Dr, Ormond Beach FL 32174, USA
Kehler, C Robert (Bob) — Air Force General
Commander, US Space Command, Peterson Air Force Base CO 80914 USA
Kehoe, Rick — Ice Hockey Player, Coach
1027 Highland Dr, Cincinnati OH 45211, USA
Kehoe, Robert (Bob) — Soccer Player, Coach
4848 Towne South Road, Saint Louis MO 63128, USA
Keibler, Stacy — Actress, Model, Wrestler
W M E Entertainment, 9601 Wilshire Blvd, #300, Beverly Hills CA 90210 USA
Keifer, C Tom — Singer, Guitarist (Cinderella)
Union Entertainment Group, 1323 Newbury Road, #104, Thousand Oaks CA 91320, USA
Keifer, Elizabeth — Actress
Stone Manners Salners, 9911 W Pico Blvd, #1400, Los Angeles CA 90035 USA
Keightley, David N — Historian
University of California, History Dept, Berkeley CA 94720, USA
Keilis-Borok, Vladimir I — Geophysicist, Mathematician
Earthquake Prediction Institute, Warshavskoye 79, 113556 Moscow, Russia
Keillor, Garrison E — Actor, Writer, Producer
Prairie Home Productions, 480 Cedar St, Saint Paul MN 55101, USA
Keineg, Katell — Singer
Headline Agency, 39 Churchfields, Milltown, Dublin 14, Ireland
Keisel, Brett — Football Player
2015 W Grove Dr, Gibsonia PA 15044, USA
Keisler, Randy — Baseball Player
6842 Durango Creek Dr, Magnolia TX 77354, USA
Keita, Ibrahim Boubacar — Prime Minister, Mali
Alliance pour la Demoractie au Mali, BP 1791, Bamako-Coura, Mali
Keita, Salif — Singer, Composer
Mad Minute Music, 5-7 Rue Paul Bert, 93400 Saint Ouen, France
Keitel, Harvey — Actor
Finch & Partners, 35 Heddon St, #PH, London W1B 4BR, England
Keith, Damon J — Judge
US Court of Appeals, US Courthouse, 231 W Lafayette Blvd, Detroit MI 48226, USA
Keith, David — Actor
125 S Barrington Place, Los Angeles CA 90049, USA
Keith, Louis — Physician
333 E Superior St, #476, Chicago IL 60611, USA
Keith, Penelope — Actress
66 Berkeley House, Hay Hill, London SW3, England
Keith, Toby — Singer, Actor
Show Dog-Universal Music, 2303 21st Ave S, #400, Nashville TN 37212 USA
Kekalainen, Jarmo — Ice Hockey Player, Executive
Jokerit H C, Areenankuja 1, 00240 Helsinki, Finland
Keker, John — Attorney
710 Sansome St, San Francisco CA 94111, USA
Kekich, Michael D (Mike) — Baseball Player
4942 Kolopelli Dr, Rio Rancho NM 87144, USA
Kekilli, Sibel — Actress
Wasted Mgmt, Diffenbachstr 33, 10967 Berlin, Germany
Kelcher, J Louie — Football Player
10204 Carlotta Cove, Austin TX 78733, USA
Kele — Singer, Musician
Agency Group Ltd, 142 W 57th St, #600, New York NY 10019 USA
Keleti, Agnes — Gymnast
Wingate Institute for Physical Education & Sport, Netanya 42902, Israel
Kelif, Atmen — Actor
Artmedia, 20 Ave Rapp, 75007 Paris, France
Kelis — Singer
Creative Artists Agency, 2000 Ave of Stars, #100, Los Angeles CA 90067 USA
Kell, Ayla — Actress
Savage Agency, 6212 Banner Ave, Los Angeles CA 90038 USA
Kell, Everett L (Skeeter) — Baseball Player
PO Box 10113, Conway AR 72034, USA
Kellar-Duke, Rebecca D (Becky) — Ice Hockey Player
Team Canada, 2424 University Dr NW, Calgary AB T2N 3Y9, Canada
Kellaway, Roger — Composer, Jazz Pianist
Joel Chriss, 60 E 8th St, #34N, New York NY 10003 USA
Kelleher, Herbert D — Businessman
144 Thelma Dr, San Antonio TX 78212, USA
Kelleher, Michael D (Mick) — Baseball Player
1451 Alamo Pintado Road, Solvang CA 93463, USA
Kelleher, Tim — Actor
Paradigm Agency, 360 N Crescent Dr, North Building, Beverly Hills CA 90210 USA
Keller, Bill — Journalist
New York Times, Editorial Dept, 229 W 43rd St, New York NY 10036, USA
Keller, Erhard — Speed Skater
Sudliche Munchneustr 6A, 82031 Grunwald, Germany
Keller, Jason — Auto Racing Driver
Progressive Motorsports, 177 Knob Hill Road, Mooresville NC 28117, USA
Keller, Joseph B — Mathematician
820 Sonoma Terrace, Stanford CA 94305, USA
Keller, Julia — Journalist
Chicago Tribune, Editorial Dept, 350 N Orleans St, Chicago IL 60654 USA
Keller, Kasey — Soccer Player
Seattle Sounders, 12 Seahawks Way, Renton WA 98056 USA
Keller, Klete — Swimmer
3015 N Hozoni Road, Prescott AZ 86305, USA

Keller, Marthe — Actress
Lemonstr 9, 81679 Munich, Germany
Keller, Mary Page — Actress
S M S Talent, 8383 Wilshire Blvd, #230, Beverly Hills CA 90211 USA
Keller, Nino — Drummer (Caesars)
Paradigm Agency, 360 Park Ave, #1600, New York NY 10022 USA
Keller, Robert P — Marine Corps General
6367 Kirby Oaks Dr, Memphis TN 38119, USA
Keller, Shawn — Animator
C A A T Studios, 36 King Eider Lane, Aliso Viejo CA 92656, USA
Keller, Thomas — Chef
French Laundry, 6540 Washington St, Yountville CA 94599, USA
Kellerman, Ernie J — Football Player
90 Glenview Dr, Aurora OH 44202, USA
Kellerman, Faye — Writer
Karpfinger Agency, 357 W 20th St, #A, New York NY 10011, USA
Kellerman, Jonathan S — Writer
Karpfinger Agency, 357 W 20th St, #A, New York NY 10011, USA
Kellerman, Martin — Cartoonist (Rocky)
Krukmakargatan 29, 118 51 Stockhom, Sweden
Kellerman, Max — Sportscaster, Commentator
Fox-TV, Sports Dept, PO Box 900, Beverly Hills CA 90213 USA
Kellerman, Sally — Actress
Polimedia Communications, 1010 Wilshire Blvd, Los Angeles CA 90017, USA
Kellermann, Susan — Actress
Stone Manners Salners, 9911 W Pico Blvd, #1400, Los Angeles CA 90035 USA
Kelley, Brian L — Football Player
98 Constitution Way, Basking Ridge NJ 07920, USA
Kelley, David E — Producer, Writer
David E Kelley Productions, 1600 Rosecrans Ave, Manhattan Beach CA 90266, USA
Kelley, Dean — Basketball Player
5900 Longleaf Dr, Lawrence KS 66049, USA
Kelley, Donald R — Historian
45 Jefferson Ave, New Brunswick NJ 08901, USA
Kelley, E Allen (Al) — Basketball Player
5900 Longleaf Dr, Lawrence KS 66049, USA
Kelley, Elijah — Actor, Singer
Schiff Co, 8440 Warner Dr, #B1, Culver City CA 90232 USA
Kelley, Gaynor N — Businessman
Perkin-Elmer Corp, 710 Bridgeport Ave, Shelton CT 06484, USA
Kelley, Harold H — Psychologist
21634 Rambla Vista St, Malibu CA 90265, USA
Kelley, Josh — Singer, Songwriter
Wilspro Mgmt, 1335 Martin Ave, Point Pleasant NJ 08742, USA
Kelley, Kitty — Writer
1228 Eton Court NW, Washington DC 20007, USA
Kelley, Malcolm David — Actor
Amsel Eisenstadt Frazier, 5055 Wilshire Blvd, #865, Los Angeles CA 90036 USA
Kelley, Nathalie — Actress
Innovative Artists, 1505 10th St, Santa Monica CA 90401 USA
Kelley, Paul X — Marine Corps General
1600 N Oak St, #1619, Arlington VA 22209, USA
Kelley, Richard R (Rich) — Basketball Player
314 Raymundo Dr, Woodside CA 94062, USA
Kelley, Robert O — Educator
University of North Dakota, President's Office, Grand Forks ND 58202, USA
Kelley, Ryan J — Actor
A P A Talent/Literary Agency, 405 S Beverly Dr, #300, Beverly Hills CA 90212 USA
Kelley, S R — Sculptor
PO Box 682, Mendocino CA 95460, USA
Kelley, Sheila — Actress
I F A Talent Agency, 8730 W Sunset Blvd, #490, West Hollywood CA 90069 USA
Kelley, Steve — Editorial Cartoonist
Creators Syndicate, 737 3rd St, Hermosa Beach CA 90254 USA
Kelley, Thomas G — Vietnam War Navy Hero (CMH)
600 Washington St, #1100, Boston MA 02111, USA
Kelley, Thomas H (Tom) — Baseball Player
710 11th Ave S, North Myrtle Beach SC 29582, USA
Kelley, William G — Businessman
Consolidated Stores, 1105 N Market St, Wilmington DE 19801, USA
Kelliher, Bill — Guitarist, Singer (Mastodon)
Pinnacle Entertainment, 30 Glenn St, White Plains NY 10603, USA
Kellis, Manolis — Electrical Engineer
Massachusetts Institute of Technology, Engineering Dept, Cambridge MA 02139, USA
Kellman, Barnet — Director
Paradigm Agency, 360 N Crescent Dr, North Building, Beverly Hills CA 90210 USA
Kellmeyer, Fern L (Peachy) — Tennis Executive
Women's Tennis Assn, 1 Progress Plaza, #1500, Saint Petersburg FL 33701 USA
Kellner, Lawrence (Larry) — Businessman
Continental Airlines, PO Box 4607, Houston TX 77210, USA
Kellogg, Allan J, Jr — Vietnam War Marine Air Hero (CMH)
250 Ilihau St, Kailua HI 96734, USA
Kellogg, Clark C — Basketball Player, Sportscaster
5423 Medallion Dr E, Westerville OH 43082, USA
Kellogg, David — Director
I C M Partners, 10250 Constellation Blvd, #900, Los Angeles CA 90067 USA
Kellogg, William S — Businessman
Kohl's Corp, N56W17000 Ridgewood Dr, Menomonee Falls WI 53051, USA
Kellum, Marvin L (Marv) — Football Player
235 Jamaica Ave, Pittsburgh PA 15229, USA
Kelly, Annese — Bowler
3812 Bach Way, North Las Vegas NV 89032, USA
Kelly, Arvesta — Basketball Player
1040 Oxford St N, Saint Paul MN 55103, USA
Kelly, Brendan — Actor
Allman/Rea Mgmt, 141 Barrington Walk, #E, Los Angeles CA 90049, USA

Kelly, Brian K University of Notre Dame, Athletic Dept, Notre Dame IN 46556, USA	Football Coach
Kelly, Daniel Hugh Innovative Artists, 1505 10th St, Santa Monica CA 90401 USA	Actor
Kelly, David Patrick Paradigm Agency, 360 N Crescent Dr, North Building, Beverly Hills CA 90210 USA	Actor
Kelly, Eamon M 3122 Octavia St, New Orleans LA 70125, USA	Educator
Kelly, Ellsworth PO Box 151, Spencertown NY 12165, USA	Artist
Kelly, Gary C Southwest Airlines, PO Box 36647, Dallas TX 75235, USA	Businessman
Kelly, J Thomas (Tom) 1643 Currie St N, Saint Paul MN 55119, USA	Baseball Player, Manager
Kelly, James E (Jim) 6 Woodcrest Dr, Orchard Park NY 14127, USA	Football Player
Kelly, James M (Jim) 403 S Northfield St, Mediapolis IA 52637, USA	Astronaut
Kelly, Jean Louisa Levine/Okwu/Erickson, 6363 Wilshire Blvd, #300, Los Angeles CA 90048, USA	Actress
Kelly, Jerry 531 Farwell Dr, Madison WI 53704, USA	Golfer
Kelly, Joanne Domain Talent, 9229 W Sunset Blvd, #710, West Hollywood CA 90069 USA	Actress
Kelly, John E M I America Records, 6920 W Sunset Blvd, Los Angeles CA 90028 USA	Singer (Kelly Family)
Kelly, John H John Kelly Consulting, 1808 Over Lake Dr SE, #D, Conyers GA 30013, USA	Diplomat
Kelly, Joseph W (Joe) PO Box 6335, Cincinnati OH 45206, USA	Football Player
Kelly, Krista Playboy Promotions, 2706 Media Center Dr, Los Angeles CA 90065 USA	Model
Kelly, Laura Michelle Dalzell & Beresford, 26 Astwood Mews, London SW7 4DE, England	Actress
Kelly, Leonard P (Red) 30 Dunvegan, Toronto ON M4V 2P6, Canada	Ice Hockey Player, Coach
Kelly, Leroy 91 Club House Dr, Willingboro NJ 8046, USA	Football Player
Kelly, Lisa W M E Entertainment, 9601 Wilshire Blvd, #300, Beverly Hills CA 90210 USA	Singer (Celtic Woman)
Kelly, Lisa Robin Metropolitan Talent Agency, 7020 La Presa Dr, Los Angeles CA 90068 USA	Actress
Kelly, Mark E 2121 Barrington Dr, League City TX 77573, USA	Astronaut
Kelly, Michael J Liebman Entertainment, 35 E 21st St, #PH, New York NY 10010, USA	Actor
Kelly, Michael R (Mike) 5072 S Serpentine Road, Flagstaff AZ 86001, USA	Baseball Player
Kelly, Minka Creative Artists Agency, 2000 Ave of Stars, #100, Los Angeles CA 90067 USA	Actress
Kelly, Moira Gersh Agency, 9465 Wilshire Blvd, #600, Beverly Hills CA 90212 USA	Actress
Kelly, Patrick F (Pat) 3519 Capri Court, Philadelphia PA 19145, USA	Baseball Player
Kelly, Paul One Louder Entertainment, PO Box 989, Darlinghurst NSW 1300, Australia	Singer, Guitarist, Songwriter
Kelly, Paul J, Jr US Appeals Court, 120 S Federal Plaza, Santa Fe NM 87501, USA	Judge
Kelly, R Creative Artists Agency, 2000 Ave of Stars, #100, Los Angeles CA 90067 USA	Rap Artist, Singer, Songwriter
Kelly, Raymond Police Commissioner's Office, 1 Police Plaza, New York NY 10038, USA	Law Enforcement Official
Kelly, Richard Darko Entertainment, 1041 N Formosa Ave, West Hollywood CA 90046, USA	Director, Writer
Kelly, Robert Bank of New York Mellon Corp, 1 Wall St, New York NY 10005, USA	Financier
Kelly, Robert J (Bob) 10 Peyton Court, Marlton NJ 08053, USA	Ice Hockey Player
Kelly, Roberto C (Bobby) 510 Franklin Dr, Arlington TX 76011, USA	Baseball Player
Kelly, Sam Richard Stone Partnership, 85 New Cavendish St, London W1W 6XD, England	Actor
Kelly, Sarah I C M Partners, 10250 Constellation Blvd, #900, Los Angeles CA 90067 USA	Singer
Kelly, Scott J 315 N Abrego Dr, Green Valley AZ 85614, USA	Astronaut
Kelly, Shane J Fairsy Consultancy, 25 Kerran Crescent, Lanceston TAS 7249, Australia	Cyclist
Kelly, Thomas J (Tom) 241 Deer Run, Miami Springs FL 33166, USA	Thoroughbred Racing Trainer
Kelly, Thomas J (Tom), III PO Box 2208, Sanatoga Branch, Pottstown PA 19464, USA	Photojournalist
Kelly, Thomas J, Jr Memorial Sloan Kettering Cancer Center, 1275 York Ave, New York NY 10065, USA	Molecular Biologist
Kelly, Thomas P 1518 Thurber Road, Corning NY 14830, USA	Sculptor
Kelly, Van H 11 Beauregard Dr, Spencer NC 28159, USA	Baseball Player
Kelm, Larry D 67 Driftoak Circle, Spring TX 77381, USA	Football Player
Kelman, Arthur 1406 Springmoor Circle, Raleigh NC 27615, USA	Plant Pathologist
Kelman, James Weidenfeld-Nicolson, Upper Saint Martin's Lane, London WC2H 9EA, England	Writer
Kelser, Gregory (Greg) 30400 Forest Dr, Franklin MI 48025, USA	Basketball Player

Kelsey, Frances O — Pharmacologist
Federal Drug Administration, 5600 Fishers Lane, Rockville MD 20852, USA

Kelsey, Linda — Actress
500 S Sepulveda Blvd, #500, Los Angeles CA 90049, USA

Kelsey, Quinn — Opera Singer
Columbia Artists Mgmt Inc, 1790 Broadway, #702, New York NY 10019 USA

Kelso, Ben — Basketball Player
1877 Midchester Dr, West Bloomfield MI 48324, USA

Kelso, Frank B, II — Navy Admiral
102 Golf Dr, Fayetteville NC 28314, USA

Kelso, Mark A — Football Player
897 Luther Road, East Aurora NY 14052, USA

Kelso, Megan — Cartoonist, Writer
4416 S Othello St, Seattle WA 98118, USA

Kelton, David W — Baseball Player
515 Riverside Road, LaGrange GA 30240, USA

Kem — Singer, Keyboardist, Songwriter
Paradise Group, 8721 Sunset Blvd, #210, Los Angeles CA 90069, USA

Kemal, Yashar — Writer
P K 14 Basinkoy, 34360 Istanbul, Turkey

Kemme, Thomas — Labor Leader
Stove Furnace & Appliance Union, 2929 S Jefferson Ave, Saint Louis MO 63118, USA

Kemmer, Heike — Equestrian
Am Amselhof 4, 47495 Rheinberg, Germany

Kemmerer, Russell P (Russ) — Baseball Player
6335 Colebrook Dr, Indianapolis IN 46220, USA

Kemner, Caren — Volleyball Player
2045 Elm St, Quincy IL 62301, USA

Kemoeatu, Ma'ake T — Football Player
22729 Zulla Chase Place, Ashburn VA 20148, USA

Kemp, Charlotte — Model
Playboy Promotions, 2706 Media Center Dr, Los Angeles CA 90065 USA

Kemp, Gary — Guitarist (Spandau Ballet)
International Talent Group, 729 7th Ave, #1600, New York NY 10019 USA

Kemp, Jeffrey A (Jeff) — Football Player
22101 NE 66th Place, Redmond WA 98053, USA

Kemp, Jeremy — Actor
Marina Martin, 12/13 Poland St, London W1V 3DE, England

Kemp, Matthew R (Matt) — Baseball Player
28814 Deodar Place, Santa Clarita CA 91390, USA

Kemp, Perry C — Football Player
PO Box 78, Westland PA 15378, USA

Kemp, Ross — Actor, Producer
Brillstein Entertainment Partners, 9150 Wilshire Blvd, #350, Beverly Hills CA 90212 USA

Kemp, Shawn T — Basketball Player
Oskar's Kitchen, 621 1/2 Queen Anne Ave, Seattle WA 98109, USA

Kemp, Steven (Steve) F — Baseball Player
1428 Colony Plaza, Newport Beach CA 92660, USA

Kemp, Will — Actor, Dancer, Model
United Agents, 12-26 Lexington St, London W1F 0LE, England

Kemper, David W, II — Financier
Commerce Bancshares, 1000 Walnut St, Kansas City MO 64106, USA

Kemper, Ellie — Actress
Mosiac Media Group, 9200 W Sunset Blvd, #1000, Los Angeles CA 90069 USA

Kemper, Hunter C — Triathlete
330 Golf Brook Circle, #208, Longwood FL 32779, USA

Kemper, J Mariner, Jr — Financier
U M B Financial Corp, 1010 Grand Ave, Kansas City MO 64106, USA

Kemper, Randolph E (Randy) — Fashion Designer
Randy Kemper Corp, 530 Fashion Ave, #1400, New York NY 10018, USA

Kemper, Victor J — Cinematographer
Mirisch Agency, 8840 Wilshire Blvd, #100, Beverly Hills CA 90211 USA

Kempf, Cecil J — Navy Admiral
831 Olive Ave, Coronado CA 92118, USA

Kempf, Freddy — Concert Pianist
I M G Artists, Hogarth Business Park, Chiswick, London W4 2TH, England

Kempner, Patty — Swimmer
1605 Harris Dr, Fort Collins CO 80524, USA

Kempner, Walter — Nutritionist
1505 Virginia Ave, Durham NC 27705, USA

Kempthorne, Dirk A — Secretary, Interior; Governor, Senator
2081 S White Pine Lane, Boise ID 83706, USA

Kempton, Timothy J (Tim) — Basketball Player
4131 N 43rd St, Phoenix AZ 85018, USA

Kenan, Gil — Director, Animator
W M E Entertainment, 9601 Wilshire Blvd, #300, Beverly Hills CA 90210 USA

Kendal, Felicity — Actress
Chatto & Linnit, 123A King's Road, London SW3 4PL, England

Kendall, A Bruce — Yachtsman
6 Pedersen Place, Bucklands Beach, Auckland 2012, New Zealand

Kendall, Barbara — Yachtswoman
Kendall Distributing, 26 Great South Road, Otahuhu 1062, New Zealand

Kendall, David — Producer
Rothman Brecher Agency, 9465 Wilshire Blvd, #840, Beverly Hills CA 90212 USA

Kendall, Donald M — Businessman
PepsiCo Inc, Anderson Hill Road, Purchase NY 10577, USA

Kendall, Fred L — Baseball Player
57575 Johnston Road, Anza CA 92539, USA

Kendall, Jason D — Baseball Player
11730 Stonehenge Lane, Los Angeles CA 90077, USA

Kendall, Jeannie — Singer (Kendalls)
Joe Taylor Artist Agency, PO Box 279, Williamstown NJ 37068 USA

Kendall, Kerri — Model
4128 Catalina Place, San Diego CA 92107, USA

Kendall, Skip — Golfer
8406 Kemper Lane, Windermere FL 34786, USA

Kendall, Tom
International Motor Sports Assn, 1394 Broadway Ave, Braselton GA 30517, USA — Auto Racing Driver
Kenders, Albert D G (Al)
8744 Matilija Ave, Panorama City CA 91402, USA — Baseball Player
Kendler, Bob
US Handball Assn, 4101 Dempster St, Skokie IL 60076, USA — Handball, Raquetball Player
Kendrick, Alex
Sherwood Baptist Church, 2201 Whispering Pines Road, Albany GA 31707, USA — Religious Leader, Filmmaker, Writer
Kendrick, Anna
Creative Artists Agency, 2000 Ave of Stars, #100, Los Angeles CA 90067 USA — Actress, Singer
Kendrick, Frank E
8355 Providence Dr, Fishers IN 46038, USA — Basketball Player
Kendrick, Howard J (Howie)
4030 E Anderson Dr, Phoenix AZ 85032, USA — Baseball Player
Kendrick, Rodney
Carolyn McClair, 410 W 53rd St, #128C, New York NY 10019, USA — Singer, Jazz Pianist, Composer
Kendrick, Stephen
Sherwood Baptist Church, 2201 Whispering Pines Road, Albany GA 31707, USA — Religious Leader, Writer
Keneally, Thomas M
24 Serpentine, Bilgola Beach NSW 2107, Australia — Writer
Kenilorea, Peter
Kalala House, PO Box 535, Honiara, Guadacanal, Solomon Islands — Prime Minister, Solomon Islands
Kenn, Michael L (Mike)
360 Bardolier, Alpharetta GA 30022, USA — Football Player
Kenna, E Douglas (Doug)
Carlisle Companies, 250 S Clinton Square, Syracuse NY 13202, USA — Businessman, Football Player
Kennard, Derek C
15849 S 35th Way, Phoenix AZ 85048, USA — Football Player
Kennard, William E (Bill)
Carlyle Group, 1001 Pennsylvania Ave NW, #220S, Washington DC 20004, USA — Government Official
Kennedy, Adam T
5025 Windhill Dr, Riverside CA 92507, USA — Baseball Player
Kennedy, Adrienne
I C M Partners, 10250 Constellation Blvd, #900, Los Angeles CA 90067 USA — Writer
Kennedy, Alan D
Tupperware Corp, PO Box 2353, Orlando FL 32802, USA — Businessman
Kennedy, Anthony M
US Supreme Court, 1 1st St NE, Washington DC 20543 USA — Supreme Court Justice
Kennedy, Cam
Dark Horse Publishing, 10956 SE Main St, Portland OR 97222 USA — Cartoonist
Kennedy, Caroline B
John F Kennedy Presidential Library & Museum, Columbia Point, Boston MA 02125, USA — Writer, Attorney
Kennedy, Cornelia G
US Court of Appeals, US Courthouse, 231 W Lafayette Blvd, Detroit MI 48226, USA — Judge
Kennedy, Cortez
121 Gary Lynn Dr, Osceola AR 72370, USA — Football Player
Kennedy, Courtney
13 Whispering Hill Road, Woburn MA 01801, USA — Ice Hockey Player
Kennedy, David
Ken McReddie Assoc, 11 Connaught Place, London W2 2ET, England — Actor
Kennedy, David M
Stanford University, History Dept, Stanford CA 94305, USA — Historian
Kennedy, Dean
General Delivery, Pincher Creek AB T0K 1W0, Canada — Ice Hockey Player
Kennedy, Delicious
Universal Attractions, 135 W 26th St, #1200, New York NY 10001 USA — Singer (All-4-One)
Kennedy, Diana S
Clarkson Potter/Crown Publishing Group, 1745 Broadway, New York NY 10019, USA — Chef, Writer
Kennedy, Donald
Stanford University, International Studies Institute, Stanford CA 94305, USA — Educator
Kennedy, Ethel
PO Box 328, Hyannis Port MA 02647, USA — Wife of Robert Kennedy
Kennedy, Eugene (Gene)
8218 Westrock Dr, Dallas TX 75243, USA — Basketball Player
Kennedy, Forbes T
20 Oakland Dr, Charlottetown PE C1C 1P4, Canada — Ice Hockey Player
Kennedy, George
Orange Grove Group, 12178 Ventura Blvd, #205, Studio City CA 91604, USA — Actor
Kennedy, Ian
1204 Suncast Lane, #2, El Dorado Hills CA 95762, USA — Baseball Player
Kennedy, James C
1601 W Peachtree St NE, Atlanta GA 30309, USA — Businessman
Kennedy, James E (Jim)
13940 SW Lisa Lane, Beaverton OR 97005, USA — Baseball Player
Kennedy, Jamie
3 Arts Entertainment, 9460 Wilshire Blvd, #700, Beverly Hills CA 90212 USA — Actor, Comedian
Kennedy, Jason
United Talent Agency, 9336 Civic Center Dr, Beverly Hills CA 90210 USA — Actor
Kennedy, Jimmy W
New York Giants, Meadowlands Stadium, 102 Route 120, East Rutherford NJ 07073 USA — Football Player
Kennedy, Joey D (Joe), Jr
1635 11th Place S, Birmingham AL 35205, USA — Journalist
Kennedy, John E
2 Rodney Road, Peabody MA 01960, USA — Baseball Player
Kennedy, John Milton
5711 Reseda Blvd, #204, Tarzana CA 91356, USA — Actor
Kennedy, Junior R
6001 Eucalyptus Dr, #215, Bakersfield CA 93306, USA — Baseball Player
Kennedy, Kathleen
Kennedy-Marshall Co, 619 Arizona Ave, Santa Monica CA 90401, USA — Producer
Kennedy, Kevin
R W S H Agency, 1107 1/2 Glendon Ave, Los Angeles CA 90024, USA — Producer, Writer
Kennedy, Kevin C
Fox-TV, Sports Dept, 205 W 67th St, New York NY 10065 USA — Baseball Player, Manager
Kennedy, Lee
Equifax Inc, 1550 Peachtree St NE, Atlanta GA 30309, USA — Businessman

Kennedy, Leon Isaac — Actor
859 N Hollywood Way, #384, Burbank CA 91505, USA

Kennedy, M Peter — Figure Skater
7650 SE 41st, Mercer Island WA 98040, USA

Kennedy, Maria Doyle — Actress, Singer
United Agents, 12-26 Lexington St, London W1F 0LE, England

Kennedy, Maura — Singer (Kennedys)
PO Box 1298, New York NY 10276, USA

Kennedy, Mimi — Actress
Justice & Ponder, PO Box 480033, Los Angeles CA 90048, USA

Kennedy, Myles R — Singer, Guitarist
Wind-Up Records, 72 Madison Ave, #800, New York NY 10016 USA

Kennedy, Nigel — Concert Violinist
Russells, Regency House, 1-4 Warwick St, London W1R 5WB, England

Kennedy, Paul M — Historian
409 Humphrey St, New Haven CT 06511, USA

Kennedy, Pete — Singer (Kennedys)
PO Box 1298, New York NY 10276, USA

Kennedy, Randall L — Attorney, Educator
Harvard University, Law School, Cambridge MA 02138, USA

Kennedy, Ray F — Businessman
Masco Corp, 21001 Van Born Road, Taylor MI 48180, USA

Kennedy, Robert A — Educator
University of Maine, President's Office, 5703 Alumni Hall, Orono ME 04469, USA

Kennedy, Rory — Director, Producer
Moxie Firecracker Films, 232 3rd St, #B403, Brooklyn NY 11215, USA

Kennedy, T Lincoln, Jr — Football Player
3555 E Jasmine Circle, Mesa AZ 85213, USA

Kennedy, Terrence E (Terry) — Baseball Player
333 N Pennington Dr, #23, Chandler AZ 85224, USA

Kennedy, William J — Writer
New York State Writers Institute, 1400 Washington Ave, Albany NY 12222, USA

Kennedy, William R (Pickles) — Basketball Player
9927 Galleon Dr, West Palm Beach FL 33411, USA

Kennedy, X Joseph (X J) — Writer
22 Revere St, Lexington MA 02420, USA

Kennedy-Powell, Kathleen — Judge
Los Angeles Municipal Court, 110 N Grand Ave, Los Angeles CA 90012, USA

Kennerly, David Hume — Photojournalist
1015 18th St, Santa Monica CA 90403, USA

Kennerty, Michael B (Mike) — Singer, Guitarist (All-American Rejects)
Interscope Records, 2220 Colorado Ave, Santa Monica CA 90404 USA

Kenney, Emma — Actress
Innovative Artists, 1505 10th St, Santa Monica CA 90401 USA

Kenney, Gerald T (Jerry) — Baseball Player
1980 Harrison Ave, Beloit WI 53511, USA

Kenney, Kerri — Actress, Comedienne
Gersh Agency, 9465 Wilshire Blvd, #600, Beverly Hills CA 90212 USA

Kenney, Stephen F (Steve) — Football Player
1105 Silver Oaks Court, Raleigh NC 27614, USA

Kenney, William P (Bill) — Football Player
2808 SW Arthur Dr, Lees Summit MO 64082, USA

Kenniebrew, Dolores (Dee Dee) — Singer (Crystals)
Superstars Unlimited, PO Box 371371, Las Vegas NV 89137, USA

Kennison, Eddie J, III — Football Player
14813 Sherwood Road, Overland Park KS 66224, USA

Kenny G — Saxophonist
Front Line Mgmt, 1100 Glendon Ave, #2000, Los Angeles CA 90024 USA

Kenny, Andrew — Singer (American Analog Set), Songwriter
Flower Booking, 1532 N Milwaukee Ave, #201, Chicago IL 60622, USA

Kenny, Enda — Prime Minister, Ireland
Taoiseach's Office, Gov't Buildings, Upper Merrion St, Dublin 2, Ireland

Kenny, Jason — Cyclist
Ashwood Laboratories, Brockhall Village, Blackburn, Lancashire BB6 8BB, England

Kenny, Shirley Strum — Educator
State University of New York, President's Office, Stony Brook NY 11794, USA

Kenny, Tom — Actor, Comedian
Innovative Artists, 1505 10th St, Santa Monica CA 90401 USA

Kenny, Yvonne — Opera Singer
I M G Artists, Burlington Lane, Chiswick, London W4 2TH, England

Kenon, Larry J — Basketball Player
25057 Toutant Beauregard Road, San Antonio TX 78255, USA

Kenseth, Matthew R (Matt) — Auto Racing Driver
111 Stonewall Beach Lane, Mooresville NC 28117, USA

Kensing, Logan F — Baseball Player
450 Rodalyn Dr, Boerne TX 78006, USA

Kensit, Patsy — Actress, Singer
A P A Talent/Literary Agency, 405 S Beverly Dr, #300, Beverly Hills CA 90212 USA

Kent — Duke, England
York House, Saint James's Palace, London SW1A 1BQ, England

Kent, Allegra — Ballerina
New York City Ballet, Lincoln Center Plaza, New York NY 10023 USA

Kent, Arthur — Commentator
2184 Torringford St, Torrington CT 06790, USA

Kent, Jean — Actress
London Mgmt, 2-4 Noel St, London W1V 3RB, England

Kent, Jeffrey A (Jeff) — Baseball Player
550 Chaparral Court, Altadena CA 91001, USA

Kent, Jonathan — Director
International Talent Booking, Ariel House, 74A Charlotte St, #100 London W1T 4QJ, England

Kent, Julie — Ballerina
American Ballet Theatre, 890 Broadway, #300, New York NY 10003 USA

Kent, Muhtar — Businessman
Coca-Cola Co, 1 Coca-Cola Plaza, 310 North Ave NW, Atlanta GA 30313, USA

Kent, Stacey — Singer
Ted Kurland, 173 Brighton Ave, Allston MA 02134 USA

Kent, Steve — Baseball Player
3118 Minthorn Dr, Killeen TX 76542, USA
Kentridge, William — Artist
David Krut Projects, Box 892, Houghton, 2041 Johannesburg, South Africa
Kenty, Hilmer — Boxer
Escot Boxing, 19260 Bretton Dr, Detroit MI 48223, USA
Kenville, William M (Bill) — Basketball Player
59 Crary Ave, Binghamton NY 13905, USA
Keny-Guyer, Neal L — Association Executive
Mercy Corps, 45 SW Ankeny St, Portland OR 97204, USA
Kenyon, Melvin E (Mel) — Auto Racing Driver
2645 S 25th West, Lebanon IN 46052, USA
Kenyon, Sherrilyn — Writer
Pocket Books, 1230 Ave of Americas, New York NY 10020 USA
Kenzo — Fashion Designer
54 Rue Etienne Marcel, 75002 Paris, France
Keogh, Lainey — Fashion Designer
42 Dawson St, Dublin 2, Ireland
Keoghan, Phil — Entertainer
International Mgmt Group, 1 Erieview Plaza, 1360 E 9th St, Cleveland OH 44114 USA
Keon, David M (Dave) — Ice Hockey Player
115 Brackenwood Road, Palm Beach Gardens FL 33418, USA
Keough, Donald R (Don) — Financier
200 Galleria Parkway, #970, Atlanta GA 30339, USA
Keough, Matthew L (Matt) — Baseball Player
12 Shire, Trabuco Canyon CA 92679, USA
Keough, Riley — Model, Actress
W M E Entertainment, 9601 Wilshire Blvd, #300, Beverly Hills CA 90210 USA
Keppinger, Jeffrey S (Jeff) — Baseball Player
1578 Cordillo Court, Dacula GA 30019, USA
Kepros, Nicholas — Actor
TalentWorks, 3500 W Olive Ave, #1400, Burbank CA 91505 USA
Kercheval, Ken — Actor
PO Box 3371, Granada Hills CA 91634, USA
Kerdyk, Tracy — Golfer
441 Valencia Ave, #401, Coral Gables FL 33134, USA
Keresztes, K Sandor — Architect
Fo Utca 44/50, 1011 Budapest, Hungary
Kerfeld, Charles P (Charlie) — Baseball Player
PO Box 1666, Gig Harbor WA 98335, USA
Kerger, Paula — Government Official
Public Broadcasting System, 1320 Braddock Dr, Alexandria VA 22314, USA
Kerim, Srgjan — Government Official, Macedonia
United Nations, General Assembly, New York NY 10017, USA
Kerkeling, Hape — Actor
Postfach 200257, 13512 Berlin, Germany
Kerkorian, Kirk — Businessman
M G M/U A Communications, 2500 Broadway St, Santa Monica CA 90404, USA
Kerkovich, Rob — Actor
I C M Partners, 10250 Constellation Blvd, #900, Los Angeles CA 90067 USA
Kerlikowske, R Gil — Government, Law Enforcement Official
National Drug Control Policy Office, White House, Washington DC 20500, USA
Kern, Geof — Photographer
1355 Conant St, Dallas TX 75207, USA
Kern, James L (Jim) — Baseball Player
6009 Amberwood Court, Arlington TX 76016, USA
Kern, Joey — Actor
Paradigm Agency, 360 Park Ave S, #1600, New York NY 10010 USA
Kern, Olga — Concert Pianist
Columbia Artists Mgmt Inc, 1790 Broadway, #702, New York NY 10019 USA
Kern, Otto — Fashion Designer
Augustastr 1, 67655 Kaiserslautern, Germany
Kern, Paul J — Army General
A M Industries, 105 N Niles Ave, South Bend IN 46617, USA
Kern, Rex W — Football Player
2816 Avenida de Autlan, Camarillo CA 93010, USA
Kernan, William F (Buck) — Army General
30 Pinewild Dr, Pinehurst NC 28374, USA
Kernek, George B — Baseball Player
16423 Cotton Gin Ave, Wayne OK 73095, USA
Kernen, Joe — Commentator
CNBC-TV, 2200 Fletcher Ave, #600, Fort Lee NJ 07024, USA
Kernochan, Sarah — Writer, Director, Producer
Mange-Ment, 1103 1/2 Glendon Ave, Los Angeles CA 90024, USA
Kerns, David V, Jr — Microbiotics Engineer
Vanderbilt University, Electrical Engineering Dept, Nashville TN 37235, USA
Kerns, Joanna — Actress
Paradigm Agency, 360 N Crescent Dr, North Building, Beverly Hills CA 90210 USA
Keropian, Michael — Sculptor
Keropian Sculpture LLC, 392 Gipsy Trail Road, Carmel NY 10512, USA
Kerr, Allen — Plant Pathologist
419 Carrington St, Adelaide SA 5000, Australia
Kerr, Anita — Singer
235 W 36th St, #321M, New York NY 10018, USA
Kerr, Brook — Actress
Precision Entertainment, 6338 Wilshire Blvd, Los Angeles CA 90048, USA
Kerr, Cristie — Golfer
10810 E Addy Way, Scottsdale AZ 85262, USA
Kerr, Donald M, Jr — Physicist
Science Applications International, 1241 Cave St, La Jolla CA 92037, USA
Kerr, Edward — Actor
A K A Talent, 6310 San Vicente Blvd, #200, Los Angeles CA 90048 USA
Kerr, Graham — Food Expert, Writer
Kerr Corp, 1020 N Sunset Dr, Camano Island WA 98282, USA
Kerr, John G — Actor
2975 Monterey Road, San Marino CA 91108, USA

Kerr, Judy — Actress
4139 Tujunga Ave, Studio City CA 91604, USA
Kerr, Kristen — Actress
Innovative Artists, 1505 10th St, Santa Monica CA 90401 USA
Kerr, Miranda — Model
I M G Models, 304 Park Ave S, #PH-North, New York NY 10010 USA
Kerr, Pat — Fashion Designer
Pat Kerr Inc, 200 Wagner Place, Memphis TN 38103, USA
Kerr, Philip — Writer
Independent Talent Group, Oxford House, 76 Oxford St, London W1D 1BS, England
Kerr, Tim — Ice Hockey Player
335 Tom Brown Road, Moorestown NJ 08057, USA
Kerr, William T — Businessman
Meredith Corp, 1716 Locust St, Des Moines IA 50309, USA
Kerrey, J Robert (Bob) — Governor, Senator; Vietnam Hero (CMH)
278 W 4th St, New York NY 10014, USA
Kerrigan, Joseph T (Joe) — Baseball Player, Manager
450 Forest Lane, North Wales PA 19454, USA
Kerrigan, Nancy A — Figure Skater
40 Salem St, #101, Lynnfield MA 01940, USA
Kerrigan, Pamela — Golfer
3205 Truckers Lane, Hingham MA 02043, USA
Kerry, Alexandra — Actress, Producer, Director
Tar Art Media, 304 Hudson St, #600, New York NY 10013, USA
Kerry, James — Astronaut
N A S A, Johnson Space Center, 2101 NASA Road, Houston TX 77058 USA
Kersee, Bob — Track Coach
University of California, Athletic Dept, Los Angeles CA 90024, USA
Kersey, Jerome — Basketball Player
24140 SW Peters Mountain Road, West Linn OR 97068, USA
Kersey, Paul — Actor
TalentWorks, 3500 W Olive Ave, #1400, Burbank CA 91505 USA
Kersh, David — Singer
Mark Hybner Entertainment, 50 Music Square W, #802, Nashville TN 37203, USA
Kershaw, Clayton E — Baseball Player
Los Angeles Dodgers, Stadium, 1000 Elysian Park Ave, Los Angeles CA 90090 USA
Kershaw, Douglas J (Doug) — Singer, Fiddler, Songwriter
Cooking Vinyl, 10 Allied Way, London W3 0RQ, England
Kershaw, Sammy — Singer
Sammy Kershaw Mgmt, 38 Music Square E, #111, Nashville TN 37203, USA
Kertesz, Imre — Nobel Literature Laureate
Rowohit Verlage, Hamburger Str 17, 21465 Reinbeck, Germany
Kerwin, Brian — Actor
Paradigm Agency, 360 Park Ave S, #1600, New York NY 10010 USA
Kerwin, Cornelius — Educator
American University, President's Office, Washington DC 20006, USA
Kerwin, Joseph P — Astronaut
10411 River Road, College Station TX 77845, USA
Kerwin, Lance — Actor
26331 Osborne Lane, Homeland CA 92548, USA
Kerwin, Larkin — Physicist
2166 Bourboniere Park, Sillery QC G1T 1B4, Canada
Kerwin, Thomas V (Tom) — Basktbal Player
283 Salter Path Road, #114, Atlantic Beach NC 28512, USA
Keselowski, Bradley R (Brad) — Auto Racing Driver
Penske Racing, 200 Penske Way, Mooresville, NC 28115 28115, USA
Kesha — Singer, Songwriter
Paradigm Agency, 360 Park Ave S, #1600, New York NY 10010 USA
Keshen, Christine — Curling Athlete
Curling Assn, 1660 Vimont Court, Cumberland ON K4A 4J4, Canada
Keshishian, Alek — Director
Creative Artists Agency, 2000 Ave of Stars, #100, Los Angeles CA 90067 USA
Kesler, Ryan — Ice Hockey Player
Vancouver Canucks, 800 Griffiths Way, Vancouver BC V6B 6G1, Canada
Kessel, Philip J (Phil), Jr — Ice Hockey Player
500 Atlantic Ave, #198, Boston MA 02210, USA
Kessinger, Donald E (Don) — Baseball Player, Manager
1306 Pelican Loop, Oxford MS 38655, USA
Kessler, David A — Physician, Government Official
University of California Medical School, Dean's Office, San Francisco CA 94143, USA
Kessler, Glenn D — Producer, Writer
Creative Artists Agency, 2000 Ave of Stars, #100, Los Angeles CA 90067 USA
Kessler, Jeffrey L — Attorney
Dewey Ballantine, 1301 Ave of Americas, Basement 3, New York NY 10019, USA
Kessler, Mikkel — Boxer
Bettina Palle, Frederiksberg Alle 76, 1820 Frederiksberg C, Denmark
Kessler, Ron — Writer
Newsman.com, PO Box 20989, West Palm Beach FL 33416, USA
Kessler, Stephen — Director
Nikki Weiss Co, 754 N La Jolla Ave, Los Angeles CA 90046, USA
Kessler, Todd A — Producer, Writer
Creative Artists Agency, 2000 Ave of Stars, #100, Los Angeles CA 90067 USA
Kester, Richard L (Rick) — Baseball Player
PO Box 623, Gardnerville NV 89410, USA
Kestner, Boyd — Actor
Mirisch Agency, 8840 Wilshire Blvd, #100, Beverly Hills CA 90211 USA
Ketchum, Hal — Singer, Songwriter
602 Wayside Dr, Wimberley TX 78676, USA
Ketchum, Howard — Color Engineer
3800 Washington Road, West Palm Beach FL 33405, USA
Ketchum, Robert Glenn — Photographer
Art Source, 11901 Santa Monica Blvd, Los Angeles CA 90025, USA
Ketelsen, Kyle — Opera Singer
I M G Artists, 152 W 57th St, #500, New York NY 10019 USA
Ketilsson, Jon — Opera Singer
I M G Artists, Hogarth Business Park, Chiswick, London W4 2TH, England

Ketterle, Wolfgang — Nobel Physics Laureate
25 Bellingham Dr, Brookline MA 02446, USA
Kettle, Roger — Cartoonist (Man Called Horse)
King Features Syndicate, 300 W 57th St, #1500, New York NY 10019 USA
Kettner, Carla — Producer, Writer
W M E Entertainment, 9601 Wilshire Blvd, #300, Beverly Hills CA 90210 USA
Kev Nish — Singer (Far East Movement)
Stampede Mgmt, 12530 Beatrice St, Los Angeles CA 90066, USA
Keves, Gyorgy — Architect
Keves es Epitesztarsai Rt, Melinda Utca 21, 1121 Budapest, Hungary
Key, A Wade — Football Player
PO Box 857, Hondo TX 78861, USA
Key, James E (Jimmy) — Baseball Player
128 Talavera Place, Palm Beach Gardens FL 33418, USA
Key, John — Prime Minister, New Zealand
Prime Minister's Office, Parliament Buildings, Wellington 6160, New Zealand
Keyes, Daniel — Writer
7491 N Federal Highway, #C5-110, Boca Raton FL 33487, USA
Keyes, James W — Businessman
Blockbuster Inc, 3704 Stratford Ave, Dallas TX 75205, USA
Keyes, Leroy — Football Player
3935 Glen Eagles Place, West Lafayette IN 47906, USA
Keyes, Nathan — Actor
Creative Artists Agency, 2000 Ave of Stars, #100, Los Angeles CA 90067 USA
Keyes, Robert W — Physicist, Engineer
I B M Research Division, PO Box 218, Yorktown Heights NY 10598, USA
Keyfitz, Nathan — Statistician
1580 Massachusetts Ave, #7C, Cambridge MA 02138, USA
Keynes, Skander — Actor
Hamilton Hodell, 66-68 Margaret St, London W1W 8SR, England
Keys, Alicia — Singer, Songwriter, Pianist
M B K Entertainment, 519 8th Ave, #1900, New York NY 10001, USA
Keys, Brady, Jr — Football Player
2931 Banchory Road, Winter Park FL 32792, USA
Keys, Donald — Educator
Planetary Citizens, 777 United Nations Plaza, New York NY 10017, USA
Keys, Rudy — Basketball Player
4308 Ludi Mae Court, Charlotte NC 28227, USA
Keys, Tyrone P — Football Player
5708 Clouds Peak Dr, Lutz FL 33558, USA
Keyser, F Ray, Jr — Governor, VT
64 Warner Ave, Proctor VT 05765, USA
Keyser, Richard L — Businessman
W W Grainger Inc, 14441 W Illinois Route 60, Lake Forest IL 60045, USA
Keyworth, Jonathan K (Jon) — Football Player
1722 E Ridgefield Road, Spanish Fork UT 84660, USA
Khabibulin, Nikolai I — Ice Hockey Player
6451 E El Maro Circle, Paradise Valley AZ 85253, USA
Khajag Barsamian — Religious Leader
Armenian Church of America, Eastern Diocese, 630 2nd Ave, New York NY 10016, USA
Khaled — Singer
G L P Artist Marketing, Huetteldorfer Str 259, 1140 Vienna, Austria
Khalfoun, Franck — Actor, Director
United Talent Agency, 9336 Civic Center Dr, Beverly Hills CA 90210 USA
Khali, Simbi — Actress
I C M Partners, 10250 Constellation Blvd, #900, Los Angeles CA 90067 USA
Khalifa, Sam — Baseball Player
1050 N Camino Seco, #1044, Tucson AZ 85710, USA
Khalifa, Sheikh Hamad bin Isa al- — Emir, Bahrain
Rifa's Palace, PO Box 555, Manama, Bahrain
Khalifa, Sheikh Khalifa bin Sulman, al- — Prime Minister, Bahrain
Prime Minister's Office, Government House, PO Box 1000, Manama, Bahrain
Khalifa, Sheikh Salman bin Hamad al- — Crown Prince, Bahrain
Defense Ministry, PO Box 245, West Rif'a, Bahrain
Khalifa, Wiz — Rap Artist
Atlantic Records, 9229 W Sunset Blvd, #900, West Hollywood CA 90069 USA
Khama, K Ian — President, Botswana; Army General
President's Office, State House, Private Bag 001, Gaborone, Botswana
Khamenei, Hojatolislam Sayyed Ali — President, Iran
President's Office, Pastor Ave, Teheran, Iran
Khan, Aamir — Actor
11 Bela Vista Apartments, Pali Hill Bandra, Mumbai MS 400050, India
Khan, Amir I — Boxer
Golden Boy Promotions, 626 Wilshire Blvd, #350, Los Angeles CA 90017 USA
Khan, Amjad Ali — Sarod Player, Composer
3 Sadhna Enclave, Panchsheel Park, New Delhi 110 017, India
Khan, Chaka — Singer, Actress
Management for Advancement of Artists, 9100 Wilshire Blvd, #450E, Beverly Hills CA 90212, USA
Khan, Irrfan — Actor
Paradigm Agency, 360 N Crescent Dr, North Building, Beverly Hills CA 90210 USA
Khan, Nareem — Fashion Designer
Deborah Hughes, 311 W 43rd St, #1102, New York NY 10036, USA
Khan, Niazi Imran — Cricketer
Pakistan Tehreek-e-Insaf, Street #84, Ho 2, Sector G-6/4, Islamabad, Pakistan
Khan, Salman — Actor
3 Galaxy Apartments, B J Road, Band Stand Bandra, Mumbai MS 400050, India
Khan, Salman A (Sal) — Educator
Khan Academy Discovery Laboratory, 151 Laura Lane, Palo Alto CA 94303, USA
Khan, Shahrukh — Actor
Amrit Apartments, #700, 15th Carter Road Bandra, Mumbai MS 400050, India
Khan, Ustad Sultan — Sarangi Musician
Agency Group Ltd, 1880 Century Park E, #711, Los Angeles CA 90067, USA
Khanh, Emmanuelle — Fashion Designer
Emmanuelle Khanh International, 39 Ave Victor Hugo, 75116 Paris, France
Khanna, Akshay — Actor
13/C Elplaza, Little Gibs Road, Malabar Hill, Mumbai MS 400026, India

Khanna, Rinke — Actress
201A Vastu Building, Military Road Juhu, Mumbai MS 400049, India
Khanna, Vinod — Actor
11 Palazo, #1300, Malabar Hill, Mumbai MS 400006, India
Khanzadian, Vahan — Opera Singer
PO Box 137, Jewett NY 12444, USA
Kharbanda, Kulbhushan — Actor
501 Silver Cascade, Mount Mary Road, Bandra, Mumbai MS 400050, India
Khashoggi, Adnan M — Businessman
La Baraka, 29604 Marbella, Spain
Khavin, Vladimir Y — Architect
Glavmosarchitectura, Triumfalnaya Square 1, 103001 Moscow, Russia
Khayat, Edward (Eddie) — Football Player, Coach
7813 Haydenberry Cove, Nashville TN 37221, USA
Khayat, Robert C (Bob) — Educator, Football Player
PO Box 677, Oxford MS 38655, USA
Kher, Anupam — Actor
402 Marina, Juhu Tara Road Juhu Beach, Mumbai MS 400049, India
Khmylev, Yuri A — Ice Hockey Player
8236 Oakway Lane, Buffalo NY 14221, USA
Khokhlov, Boris — Ballet Dancer
Myaskovsky St 11-13, #102, 121019 Moscow, Russia
Khondji, Darius — Cinematographer
Independent Talent Group, Oxford House, 76 Oxford St, London W1D 1BS, England
Khorkina, Svetlana — Gymnast
Gymnastics Federation, Lujnetskaya Nabererynaya 8, 119270 Moscow, Russia
Khosla, Vinod — Businessman
Khosla Ventures, 3000 Sand Hill Road, Building 3, Menlo Park CA 94025, USA
Khouri, Callie — Director, Writer
Creative Artists Agency, 2000 Ave of Stars, #100, Los Angeles CA 90067 USA
Khoury, Raymond — Writer
Penguin Books, 375 Hudson St, Basement 1, New York NY 10014 USA
Khristenko, Viktor — Prime Minister, Russia
Prime Minister's Office, Krasnopresneskaya Nab 2, 103274 Moscow, Russia
Khristich, Dmitri — Ice Hockey Player
5002 N Convent Lane, #E, Philadelphia PA 19114, USA
Khrushchev, Sergei — Writer
3 Laurelhurst Road, Cranston RI 02920, USA
Khush, Gurdev S — Agricultural Researcher
International Rice Institute, Box 3127, Makati City 1271, Philippines
Ki Sung-Yueng — Soccer Player
Football Assn, 1-131 Sinmunno, 2-Ga Jongno-Gu, Seoul 110 062, South Korea
Kiarostami, Abbas — Director
Zeitgeist Films, 247 Center St, #203, New York NY 10013, USA
Kibaki, Mwai — President, Kenya
President's Office, Harambee House, Harambee Ave, Nairobi, Kenya
Kiberlain, Sandrine — Actress, Singer
Voyez Mon Agent, 20 Ave Rapp, 75007 Paris, France
Kibrick, Anne — Medical Educator
381 Seminary Ave, #221, Auburndale MA 02466, USA
Kid Capri — DJ Musician
Central Entertainment Group, 166 5th Ave, #400, New York NY 10010, USA
Kid Frost — Rap Artist
Green Light Talent Agency, PO Box 3172, Beverly Hills CA 90212 USA
Kid Rock — Rap Artist
Creative Artists Agency, 2000 Ave of Stars, #100, Los Angeles CA 90067 USA
Kidd, Jason F — Basketball Player
367 Cottonwood Way, Mahwah NJ 07430, USA
Kidd, Jodie — Model
I M G Models, 131-151 Great Titchfield St, London W1W 5BB, England
Kidd, M John — Football Player
4204 Moorland Dr, Midland MI 48640, USA
Kidd, Warren L — Basketball Player
313 River Road, Harpersville AL 35078, USA
Kidd, William W (Billy) — Alpine Skier
Billy Kidd Racing, 2305 Mount Werner Circle, Steamboat Springs CO 80487, USA
Kidder Lee, Barbara — Alpine Skier
1308 W Highland, Phoenix AZ 85013, USA
Kidder, Margot — Actress
Muse Mgmt, 1541 Ocean Ave, #200, Santa Monica CA 90401, USA
Kidder, Tracy — Writer
Random House, 1745 Broadway, #1800, New York NY 10019 USA
Kidd-Gilchrist, Michael — Basketball Player
Charlotte Bobcats, 333 E Trade St, #A, Charlotte NC 28202 USA
Kidjo, Angelique — Singer, Songwriter
Vector Mgmt, PO Box 120479, Nashville TN 37212 USA
Kidron, Beeban — Director, Producer, Writer
Independent Talent Group, Oxford House, 76 Oxford St, London W1D 1BS, England
Kieber, Walter — Head of Government, Liechtenstein
Landstra 22, 9494 Schaan, Liechtenstein
Kiechel, Walter, III — Editor
929 Washington St, Hoboken NJ 07030, USA
Kiecker, Dana E — Baseball Player
4104 Prairie Ridge Road, Saint Paul MN 55123, USA
Kiedis, Anthony — Singer (Red Hot Chili Peppers)
Untitled Entertainment, 350 S Beverly Dr, #200, Beverly Hills CA 90212 USA
Kiefel, Ronald — Cyclist
3893 Field Dr, Wheat Ridge CO 80033, USA
Kiefer, Adolph G — Swimmer, Coach
42125 N Hunt Club Road, Wadsworth IL 60083, USA
Kiefer, Mark A — Baseball Player
11832 Old Fashion Way, Garden Grove CA 92840, USA
Kiefer, Nicolas — Tennis Player
B L A Z, Bonner Str 12A, 30173 Hanover, Germany
Kiefer, Steven G (Steve) — Baseball Player
12389 Cloudburst Trail, Moreno Valley CA 92555, USA

Kieffer, James M
422 Stoutenburgh Lane, Pittsford NY 14534, USA — Businessman

Kiehl, Marina
Hermie-Bland Str 11, 81545 Munich, Germany — Alpine Skier

Kiehl, Stuart
4193 Concord Ave, Santa Rosa CA 95407, USA — Cinematographer

Kiel, Richard
1056 Loyola Ave, Clovis CA 93619, USA — Actor

Kielty, Robert M (Bobby)
21504 Appaloosa Court, Canyon Lake CA 92587, USA — Baseball Player

Kiely, Mark
Diverse Talent Group, 9911 Pico Blvd, #350W, Los Angeles CA 90035 USA — Actor

Kier, Udo
Richard Schwartz Mgmt, 2934 N Beverly Glen Circle, #107, Los Angeles CA 90077 USA — Actor

Kiermayer, Susanne
Amthofplatz 5, 94259 Kirchberg, Germany — Markswoman

Kieschnick, M Brooks
210 Joliet Ave, #A, San Antonio TX 78209, USA — Baseball Player

Kiesel, Theresia
Stifterstr 24, 4050 Truan, Austria — Track Athlete

Kiffin, Irv
1441 Trellis Lane, Pembroke Pines FL 33026, USA — Basketball Player

Kiffin, Lane M
University of Southern California, Athletic Dept, Los Angeles CA 90089, USA — Football Player, Coach

Kigeli V Ndagindurwa
Kigeli Foundation, Fairfax Towers, 9941 Oak Creek Place, Oakton VA 22124, USA — King, Rwanda

Kightlinger, Laura
Avalon Mgmt, 8332 Melrose Ave, #200, Los Angeles CA 90069, USA — Actress, Comedienne

Kihlstedt, Rya
Brookside Mgmt, 250 W 57th St, #2303, New York NY 10107, USA — Actress

Kihn, Greg
Riot Mgmt, PO Box 8553, Berkeley CA 94707, USA — Singer, Guitarist (Greg Kihn Band)

Kihune, Robert K U
1428 Aunauna St, Kailua HI 96734, USA — Navy Admiral

Kiick, James F (Jim)
2900 S University Dr, #9112, Davie FL 33328, USA — Football Player

Kiir Mayardit, Salva
President Office, Juba, Southern Sudan — President, South Sudan

Kiiskinen, Kalle
Curling Assn, Kalatorppa 2A62, 02230 Espoo, Finland — Curling Athlete

Kikuchi, Rinko
Anore, 6-17-15-9F Jingumae, Shibuya, Tokyo 150 0001, Japan — Actress

Kikuchi, Rioko
Japanese Aerospace Exploration Agency, 2-1-1 Sengen, Tsukuba-shi, Ibaraki 305 8505, Japan — Astronaut, Japan; Photographer

Kikwete, Jakaya Mrisho
President's Office, State House, PO Box 9120, Dar es Salaam, Tanzania — President, Tanzania

Kilar, Jason
Hulu, 12312 W Olympic Blvd, Los Angeles CA 90064, USA — Businessman

Kilar, Wojciech
Ul Kosciuszki 165, 40 524 Katowice, Poland — Composer

Kilbane, Pat
Amsel Eisenstadt Frazier, 5055 Wilshire Blvd, #865, Los Angeles CA 90036 USA — Actor

Kilbey, Steven J
M O B Agency, 6404 Wilshire Blvd, #505, Los Angeles CA 90048 USA — Singer, Guitarist (Church); Songwriter

Kilborn, Craig
Don Buchwald/Fortitude, 6500 Wilshire Blvd, #2200, Los Angeles CA 90048 USA — Actor, Comedian, Writer, Producer

Kilbourne, Wendy
9200 W Sunset Blvd, #612, West Hollywood CA 90069, USA — Actress

Kilburn, Terry
Oakland University, Meadowbrook Theatre, Walton & Squirrel, Rochester MI 48063, USA — Actor

Kilcher, Q'Orianka
R-Dog, 100 5th Ave, #1100, New York NY 10011, USA — Actress

Kilcline, Thomas J (Tom), Jr
Commander, Naval Air Force Pacific, NAS North Island, San Diego CA 92135 USA — Navy Admiral

Kilcullen, Robert B (Bob)
400 E Division St, Pilot Point TX 76258, USA — Football Player

Kildea, Bobby
Ground Control Touring, 20 Jay St, #826, Brooklyn NY 11201 USA — Guitarist, Bassist (Belle & Sebastian)

Kiley, Ariel
Untitled Entertainment, 350 S Beverly Dr, #200, Beverly Hills CA 90212 USA — Actress

Kilgallon, Robert D
662 Park Ave, Meadville PA 16335, USA — Environmental Researcher

Kilgore, Jerry
T B A Artist Mgmt, 300 10th Ave S, Nashville TN 37203, USA — Singer, Songwriter

Kilgore, Jon
2422 Glen Oaks Court NE, Atlanta GA 30345, USA — Football Player

Kilgus, Paul N
968 Threewood Circle, Bowling Green KY 42103, USA — Baseball Player

Kilius, Marika
Postfach 201151, 63271 Dreieich, Germany — Figure Skater

Kilkenny, Michael D (Mike)
274 Holland St W, Bradford ON L3Z 1J1, Canada — Baseball Player

Kill, Jerry
Legacy Agency, 230 Park Ave, #851, New York NY 10169 USA — Football Coach

Killam, Taran
A P A Talent/Literary Agency, 405 S Beverly Dr, #300, Beverly Hills CA 90212 USA — Actor

Killar, Wojciech
Ul Ksciuszki 165, 40 524 Katowice, Poland — Composer

Killeen, Denise
803 Golden Wood Trace, Canton GA 30114, USA — Golfer

Killeen, Evans H
PO Box 885, Westhampton Beach NY 11978, USA — Baseball Player

Killen, Kyle
W M E Entertainment, 9601 Wilshire Blvd, #300, Beverly Hills CA 90210 USA — Producer, Writer

Killens, Terry D
5665 Water Spring Way, Mason OH 45040, USA — Football Player

K

Killer Mike J L Entertainment, 18653 Ventura Blvd, #340, Tarzana CA 91356 USA	Rap Artist
Killing, Laure Agence Christine Parat, 9 Rue de Maubeuge, 75009 Paris, France	Actress
Killip, Christopher D Harvard University, Visual Studies Dept, 24 Quincy St, Cambridge MA 02138, USA	Photographer
Killum, Ernie 710 Pennybrook Lane, Stone Mountain GA 30087, USA	Basketball Player
Killy, Jean-Claude Villa Les Oiseaux 13 Chemin Bellefontaine, 1223 Cologny GE, Switzerland	Alpine Skier
Kilman, Sato Prime Minister's Office, PO Box 053, Port Vila, Vanuatu	Prime Minister, Vanuatu
Kilmer, Val PO Box 364, Rowe NM 87562, USA	Actor
Kilmer, William O (Billy) 1853 Monte Carlo Way, #36, Coral Springs FL 33071, USA	Football Player
Kilmore, Chris Variety Artists, 793 Higuera St, #6, San Luis Obispo CA 93401 USA	DJ Musician, Keyboardist (Incubus)
Kilner, Clare Gersh Agency, 9465 Wilshire Blvd, #600, Beverly Hills CA 90212 USA	Director, Writer
Kilner, Kevin Innovative Artists, 1505 10th St, Santa Monica CA 90401 USA	Actor
Kllpatrick, Carl 10517 23rd Street Court E, Edgewood WA 98372, USA	Basketball Player
Kilrain, Susan L 625 Cedar Lane, Virginia Beach VA 23452, USA	Astronaut
Kilrea, Brian 2192 Saunderson Dr, Ottawa ON K1G 2G4, Canada	Ice Hockey Player, Coach
Kilts, James M Centerview Partners, 31 W 52nd St, #2200, New York NY 10019, USA	Businessman
Kilzer, Louis C (Lon) Minneapolis-Saint Paul Star-Tribune, 425 Portland Ave, Minneapolis MN 55488, USA	Journalist
Kim Bo-Kyung Football Assn, 1-131 Sinmunno, 2-Ga Jongno-Gu, Seoul 110 062, South Korea	Soccer Player
Kim Chang-Soo Football Assn, 1-131 Sinmunno, 2-Ga Jongno-Gu, Seoul 110 062, South Korea	Soccer Player
Kim Dong Sung Skating Union, 88 Bangyee-Dong, Songpaku, Seoul 138 749, South Korea	Speed Skater
Kim Hyun-Sung Football Assn, 1-131 Sinmunno, 2-Ga Jongno-Gu, Seoul 110 062, South Korea	Soccer Player
Kim Jong-Pil 340-38, Sindang 4-Dongku, Seoul, South Korea	Prime Minister, South Korea; General
Kim Jong-Un President's Office, Pyongyang, North Korea	President Designate, North Korea
Kim Kee-Hee Football Assn, 1-131 Sinmunno, 2-Ga Jongno-Gu, Seoul 110 062, South Korea	Soccer Player
Kim Ki-Hoon Skating Union, 88 Bangyee-Dong, Songpaku, Seoul 138 749, South Korea	Speed Skater
Kim Seoung Il Skating Union, 88 Bangyee-Dong, Songpaku, Seoul 138 749, South Korea	Speed Skater
Kim So Hui Skating Union, 88 Bangyee-Dong, Songpaku, Seoul 138 749, South Korea	Speed Skater
Kim Young-Gwon Football Assn, 1-131 Sinmunno, 2-Ga Jongno-Gu, Seoul 110 062, South Korea	Soccer Player
Kim Young-Sam 7-6-1 Sangdo, Dongjakku, Seoul 156 743, South Korea	President, South Korea
Kim Yu-Na Toronto C S C C, 141 Wilson Ave, Toronto ON M5M 3A3, Canada	Figure Skater
Kim Yun-Mi Skating Union, 88 Bangyee-Dong, Songpaku, Seoul 138 749, South Korea	Speed Skater
Kim, Anthony Professional Golfer's Assn, PO Box 109601, Palm Beach Gardens FL 33410 USA	Golfer
Kim, Byung Hyun 4601 E Skyline Dr, #1302, Tucson AZ 85718, USA	Baseball Player
Kim, Christina Ladies Pro Golf Assn, 100 International Golf Dr, Daytona Beach FL 32124 USA	Golfer
Kim, Daniel Dae A P A Talent/Literary Agency, 405 S Beverly Dr, #300, Beverly Hills CA 90212 USA	Actor
Kim, Grace Playboy Promotions, 2706 Media Center Dr, Los Angeles CA 90065 USA	Model
Kim, Jacqueline Innovative Artists, 1505 10th St, Santa Monica CA 90401 USA	Actress
Kim, Jaegwon Brown University, Philosophy Dept, Providence RI 02912, USA	Philosopher
Kim, Jim Yong World Bank Group, 1818 H St NW, Washington DC 20433, USA	Financier, Educator
Kim, John J Chicago Sun-Times, Editorial Dept, 401 N Wabash Ave, Chicago IL 60611 USA	Journalist
Kim, Kathleen Harrison/Parrott, 5-6 Albion Court, London W6 0QT, England	Opera Singer
Kim, Kwang Soo McLean Hospital, Molecular Neurobiology Laboratory, 115 Mill St, Belmont MA 02478, USA	Neuroscientist, Psychiatrist
Kim, Nelli V 2480 Cobblehill, #A, Alcove, Woodbury MN 55125, USA	Gymnast
Kim, Peter S Whitehead Institute, 9 Cambridge Center, Cambridge MA 02142, USA	Biochemist, Geneticist
Kim, Yunjin Ace Mgmt, 11359 Chalon Road, Los Angeles CA 90049, USA	Actress
Kimball, Bobby Monterey International, 200 W Superior St, #202, Chicago IL 60654 USA	Singer (Toto)
Kimball, Christopher Public Broadcasting System, 1320 Braddock Place, Alexandria VA 22314 USA	Chef
Kimball, Dick 1540 Waltham Dr, Ann Arbor MI 48103, USA	Diver, Diving Coach
Kimball, Jeffrey Paradigm Agency, 360 N Crescent Dr, North Building, Beverly Hills CA 90210 USA	Cinematographer

Kimball, Lynnda
Playboy Promotions, 2706 Media Center Dr, Los Angeles CA 90065 USA — Model

Kimball, Thomas (Toby)
6859 Avenida Andorra, La Jolla CA 92037, USA — Basketball Player

Kimball, Warren F
2540 Otter Lane, Johns Island SC 29455, USA — Historian

Kimble, Avis
Playboy Promotions, 2706 Media Center Dr, Los Angeles CA 90065 USA — Model

Kimble, Gregory K (Bo)
100 Poe Court, North Wales PA 19454, USA — Basketball Player

Kimble, Warren
RR 3 Box 1038, Brandon VT 05733, USA — Artist

Kimbrel, Craig M
Atlanta Braves, Turner Field, 755 Hank Aaron Dr, Atlanta GA 30315 USA — Baseball Player

Kimbrough, Charles
255 Amalfi Dr, Santa Monica CA 90402, USA — Actor, Singer

Kimbrough, Elbert L
886 W 2nd St, Galesburg IL 61401, USA — Football Player

Kimbrough, R Shane
N A S A, Johnson Space Center, 2101 NASA Road, Houston TX 77058 USA — Astronaut

Kimbrough, Stan
3922 Elm Ave, Cincinnati OH 45236, USA — Basketball Player

Kimery, James L
Veterans of Foreign Wars, 405 W 34th St, Kansas City MO 64111, USA — Association Executive

Kimm, Bruce E
3168 121st St, Amana IA 52203, USA — Baseball Player, Manager

Kimmel, Jimmy
J K Live, El Capitan Center, 6834 Hollywood Blvd, Los Angeles CA 90028, USA — Actor, Comedian

Kimmelman, Michael
New York Times, Editorial Dept, 229 W 43rd St, New York NY 10036 USA — Art Critic

Kimmet, Brian
Geddes Agency, 8430 Santa Monica Blvd, #201, West Hollywood CA 90069 USA — Actor

Kimmins, Kenneth
A K A Talent Agency, 6310 San Vicente Blvd, #200, Los Angeles CA 90048, USA — Actor

Kimura, Doreen
211 Madison Ave, Toronto ON M5R 2S6, Canada — Psychologist

Kimura, Kazuo
Japan Design Foundation, 2-2 Cenba Chuo, Higashiku, Osaka 541 0046, Japan — Industrial Designer

Kinard, A Terance (Terry)
207 Navigators Dr, Pawleys Island SC 29585, USA — Football Player

Kinard, William R (Billy)
PO Box 680944, Fort Payne AL 35968, USA — Football Player

Kincaid, Jamaica
College Road, North Bennington VT 05257, USA — Writer

Kinchen, Arif S
Xpose Talent Agency, 1055 E Colorado Blvd, #5, Pasadena CA 91106, USA — Actor

Kinchen, Brian D
19502 E Pinnacle Circle, Baton Rouge LA 70810, USA — Football Player

Kinchen, Todd W
247 Guava Dr, Baton Rouge LA 70808, USA — Football Player

Kinchla, Chandler (Chan)
C3 Presents, 98 San Jacinto Blvd, #400, Austin TX 78701, USA — Guitarist (Blues Traveler)

Kinchla, Thaddeus A (Tad)
C3 Presents, 98 San Jacinto Blvd, #400, Austin TX 78701, USA — Bassist (Blues Traveler)

Kincses, Veronika
Hungarian State Opera, Andrassy Utca 22, 1061 Budapest, Hungary — Opera Singer

Kind, Richard
Foster Entertainment, 12533 Woodgreen St, Building B, Los Angeles CA 90066, USA — Actor

Kind, Roslyn
Randy Johnson Co, PO Box 69A18, West Hollywood CA 90069, USA — Actress, Singer

Kindall, Gerald D (Jerry)
7220 E Grey Fox Lane, Tucson AZ 85750, USA — Baseball Player

Kinder, Donald R
University of Michigan, Political Science Dept, Ann Arbor MI 48109, USA — Political Scientist

Kinder, Melvyn
1951 San Ysidro Dr, Beverly Hills CA 90210, USA — Psychologist, Writer

Kinder, Richard D
Kinder-Morgan Inc, 500 Dallas St, #1000, Houston TX 77002, USA — Businessman

Kindig, Howard W, Jr
8740 Bayside Ave, Baton Rouge LA 70806, USA — Football Player

Kindler, Damian
H2F Entertainment, 644 N Cherokee Ave, Los Angeles CA 90004, USA — Producer, Writer

Kindler, Jeffrey B
Pfizer Inc, 235 E 42nd St, New York NY 10017, USA — Businessman

Kindrachuk, Orest
106 Meeshaway Trail, Medford Lakes NJ 08055, USA — Ice Hockey Player

Kindred, David A
Atlanta Constitution, 223 Perimeter Center Parkway NE, Atlanta GA 30346, USA — Sportswriter

Kiner, Kevin
First Artists Mgmt, 4764 Park Granada, #210, Calabasas CA 91302 USA — Composer

Kiner, Ralph M
19 Doubling Road, Greenwich CT 06830, USA — Baseball Player, Sportscaster

Kiner, Steven A (Steve)
112 N Ole Hickory Trail, Carrollton GA 30117, USA — Football Player

King Hogue, Maxine (Micki)
3509 Colt Neck Lane, Lexington KY 40502, USA — Diver

King Tee
Keith Case Assoc, 1025 17th Ave S, #200, Nashville TN 37212 USA — Rap Artist

King, Albert
88 Sturbridge Circle, Wayne NJ 07470, USA — Basketball Player

King, Angelo T
2922 W Royal Lane, #2090, Irving TX 75063, USA — Football Player

King, Anthony S
Mill House, Middle Green, Wakes Colne, Colchester, Essex CP6 2BP, England — Political Scientist

King, B B
W M E Entertainment, 9601 Wilshire Blvd, #300, Beverly Hills CA 90210 USA — Singer, Guitarist

K

Kahn - King

King, Ben E
Chaplin Entertainment, 1650 Broadway, #303, New York NY 10019, USA — Singer

King, Bernard
307 Jupiter Hills Dr, Duluth GA 30097, USA — Basketball Player

King, Billie Jean
World Team Tennis, 1776 Broadway, #600, New York NY 10019, USA — Tennis Player

King, Brent
I F A Talent Agency, 8730 W Sunset Blvd, #490, West Hollywood CA 90069 USA — Actor

King, Carole
660 Wild Iris Lane, Santa Cruz CA 95060, USA — Composer, Singer, Pianist

King, Carolyn Dineen
US Court of Appeals, US Courthouse, 515 Rusk Ave, #12015, Houston TX 77002, USA — Judge

King, Charles G (Chick)
4036 Highway 54, Paris TN 38242, USA — Baseball Player

King, Cheryl
CLInc Talent, 843 N Sycamore Ave, Los Angeles CA 90038, USA — Actress

King, Claude
House of Talent, 9 Lucy Lane, Sherwood AR 72120, USA — Singer, Guitarist

King, Colbert
Washington Post, Editorial Dept, 1150 15th St NW, Washington DC 20071 USA — Journalist

King, Curtis E
2538 Beechwood Dr, Vineland NJ 08361, USA — Baseball Player

King, Dana
CBS-TV, News Dept, 524 W 57th St, New York NY 10019, USA — Commentator

King, Daniel (Dan)
4320 Hickoryview Dr, Louisville KY 40299, USA — Basketball Player

King, David A
20 Glisson Road, Cambridge CB1 2EW, England — Chemist

King, Dennis
108 Andrew Court, Mount Shasta CA 96067, USA — Artist

King, Derek
8184 E Wingspan Way, Scottsdale AZ 85255, USA — Ice Hockey Player

King, Dexter Scott
Martin Luther King Nonviolent Social Change Center, 449 Auburn Ave NE, Atlanta GA 30312, USA — Association Executive

King, Diana
Associated Booking Corp, 501 Madison Ave, #603, New York NY 10022 USA — Singer, Songwriter

King, Don
Don King Productions, 501 Fairway Dr, Deerfield Beach FL 33441, USA — Boxing Promoter

King, Donald W (Don)
1621 Fox Hall Road, Savannah GA 31406, USA — Football Player

King, Edward E (Ed)
9903 North Blvd, Cleveland OH 44108, USA — Football Player

King, Elizabeth (Betsy)
7418 E Alta Sierra Dr, Scottsdale AZ 85266, USA — Golfer

King, Emanuel
Hollywood Christian High School, 1708 N 60th Ave, Hollywood FL 33021, USA — Football Player

King, Eric S
1063 Stanford Dr, Simi Valley CA 93065, USA — Baseball Player

King, Erik
Burstein Co, 15304 W Sunset Blvd, #208, Pacific Palisades CA 90272 USA — Actor

King, Evelyn (Champagne)
T-Best Talent Agency, 508 Honey Lake Court, Danville CA 94506 USA — Singer

King, Fallon
Capitol Records, 810 7th Ave, New York NY 10019 USA — Singer (Cherish)

King, Farrah
Capitol Records, 810 7th Ave, New York NY 10019 USA — Singer (Cherish)

King, Felisha
Capitol Records, 810 7th Ave, New York NY 10019 USA — Singer (Cherish)

King, G Stephen (Steve)
45 Chipping Stone Road, North Atteboro MA 02760, USA — Football Player

King, Gary
Harvard University, Quantitative Social Science Institute, Cambridge MA 02138, USA — Political Scientist

King, Georgia
Paradigm Agency, 360 N Crescent Dr, North Building, Beverly Hills CA 90210 USA — Actress

King, Gordon D
2641 Highwood Dr, Roseville CA 95661, USA — Football Player

King, Graham
G K Films, 1540 2nd St, #200, Santa Monica CA 90401, USA — Writer, Producer

King, Harold (Hal)
828 Geneva Dr, Oviedo FL 32765, USA — Baseball Player

King, Horace E
884 Fairburn Road NW, Atlanta GA 30331, USA — Football Player

King, Jaime
Gersh Agency, 9465 Wilshire Blvd, #600, Beverly Hills CA 90212 USA — Actress, Model

King, James
Rounder Records, 1 Rounder Way, Burlington MA 01803 USA — Singer

King, James H (Jim)
720 Stokenbury Road, Elkins AR 72727, USA — Baseball Player

King, Jamie Thomas
3 Arts Entertainment, 9460 Wilshire Blvd, #700, Beverly Hills CA 90212 USA — Actor

King, Jeff
PO Box 48, Denali National Park AK 99755, USA — Dog Sled Racer

King, Jeffrey F (Jeff)
Creative Artists Agency, 2000 Ave of Stars, #100, Los Angeles CA 90067 USA — Producer, Director, Writer

King, Jeffrey W (Jeff)
50401 Highway 278, Wisdom MT 59761, USA — Baseball Player

King, Joanne
T N Enterprises, 14 Beach Grove, Blackrock County, Dublin, Ireland — Actress

King, Joe
A2 Mgmt, 624 Davis St, #200, Evanston IL 60201, USA — Singer, Guitarist (Fray)

King, Joey
Coast to Coast Talent, 3350 Barham Blvd, Los Angeles CA 90068 USA — Actress

King, Jon
Story Worldwide, Primrose Hill, 15B Saint George's Mews, London NW1 8XC, England — Singer (Gang of Four)

King, Kaki
Big Hasssle, 44 Wall St, #2200, New York NY 10005, USA — Singer, Guitarist

King, Kathryn (Katie) Ice Hockey Player
3 Birchwood Road, Salem NH 3079, USA
King, Kevin R Baseball Player
RR 1 Box 107, Braggs OK 74423, USA
King, Kris Ice Hockey Player
National Hockey League, 50 Bay St, #1100, Toronto ON M5J 2X8, Canada
King, Kristin Ice Hockey Player
USA Hockey, 1775 Bob Johnson Dr, Colorado Springs CO 80906 USA
King, Lamar Football Player
5082 Springhouse Circle, Rosedale MD 21237, USA
King, Larry Commentator, Columnist
Media Talent Group, 9200 Sunset Blvd, #550, West Hollywood CA 90069, USA
King, Linden K Football Player
1130 S Flower St, #416, Los Angeles CA 90015, USA
King, Loyd Basketball Player
118 Wilde Brook Dr, Asheville NC 28806, USA
King, Mark Singer, Bassist (Level 42)
Level 42, PO Box 23, Sandown P036 0QL, Canada
King, Mark Artist
King Griffin Inc, 8665 Miralani Dr, #100, San Diego CA 92126, USA
King, Mary E Equestrian Rider
Matford Park Farm, Exminster, Exeter, Devon EX6 8AT, England
King, Mary-Claire Geneticist
University of Washington Medical School, Genetics Dept, Seattle WA 98195, USA
King, Mervyn A Economist
Bank of England, Threadneedle St, London EC2R 8AH, England
King, Michael Patrick Director, Writer
Creative Artists Agency, 2000 Ave of Stars, #100, Los Angeles CA 90067 USA
King, Michelle Producer, Writer
Paradigm Agency, 360 N Crescent Dr, North Building, Beverly Hills CA 90210 USA
King, Morgana Singer, Actress
13327 Cheltenham Dr, Sherman Oaks CA 91423, USA
King, Neosha Singer (Cherish)
Capitol Records, 810 7th Ave, New York NY 10019 USA
King, Perry Actor
3647 Wrightwood Dr, Studio City CA 91604, USA
King, Peter Sportscaster, Sportswriter
NBC-TV, Sports Dept, 30 Rockefeller Plaza, #270E, New York NY 10112 USA
King, Phillip Sculptor
Royal College of Arts, Kensington Gore, London SW7 2EU, England
King, Raymond K (Ray) Baseball Player
4220 N 161st Ave, Goodyear AZ 85395, USA
King, Regina Actress
I C M Partners, 10250 Constellation Blvd, #900, Los Angeles CA 90067 USA
King, Reginald B (Reggie) Basketball Player
4716 Chouteau St, Shawnee KS 66226, USA
King, Richard L Businessman
Albertson's Inc, 250 E Parkcenter Blvd, Boise ID 83706, USA
King, Robert Producer, Writer
Paradigm Agency, 360 N Crescent Dr, North Building, Beverly Hills CA 90210 USA
King, Robert B Judge
US Court of Appeals, 300 Virginia St E, #2630, Charleston WV 25301, USA
King, Ronette Interior Designer
Gensler Assoc, 600 California St, #1000, San Francisco CA 94108, USA
King, Shaun E Football Player, Sportscaster
1270 Orange Ave E, Winter Park FL 32789, USA
King, Stephen E Writer
Juliann Eugley, 49 Florida Ave, Bangor ME 04401, USA
King, Stephenson T Prime Minister, Saint Lucia
Prime Minister's Office, Greaham Louisy Building, #500, Waterfront, Castries, Saint Lucia
King, Theodore W (Ted) Actor
Brady Brannon Rich, 5670 Wilshire Blvd, #820, Los Angeles CA 90036, USA
King, Thomas J (Tom) Government Official, England
House of Commons, Westminster, London SW1A 0AA, England
King, Thomas V (Tom) Basketball Player
4930 Sea Witch Dr, Fernandina Beach FL 32034, USA
King, W David (Dave) Ice Hockey Coach
Phoenix Coyotes, 6751 N Sunset Blvd, #200, Glendale AZ 85305 USA
King, William (Bill) Trumpeter (Commodores)
Management Assoc, 1920 Benson Ave, Saint Paul MN 55116, USA
King, Woodie, Jr Producer
417 Convent Ave, New York NY 10031, USA
Kinga, Yukari Soccer Player
Football Assn, 3-10-15 Hongo, Bunkyoku, Tokyo 113 0033 Japan
Kingdom, Roger Track Athlete
146 S Fairmont St, #1, Pittsburgh PA 15206, USA
Kingery, Michael S (Mike) Baseball Player
51923 298th St, Grove City MN 56243, USA
King-Hele, Desmond G Writer
7 Hilltops Court, 65 North lane, Buriton, Hampshire GU31 5RS, England
Kingman, Brian P Baseball Player
8825 5th Ave, Hesperia CA 92345, USA
Kingman, David A (Dave) Baseball Player
PO Box 209, Glenbrook NV 89413, USA
Kingrea, Richard O (Rick) Football Player
102 N Bayview St, Fairhope AL 36532, USA
Kingsale, Eugene H (Gene) Baseball Player
105 Angelfish Lane, Jupiter FL 33477, USA
Kingsbury, Gina Ice Hockey Player
Team Canada, 2424 University Dr NW, Calgary AB T2N 3Y9, Canada
Kingsbury, Tim Musician (Arcade Fire)
Billions Corp, 3522 W Armitage Ave, Chicago IL 60647 USA
Kingsley, Ben Actor
New Penworth House, Stratford upon Avon, Warwickshire 0V3 7QX, England
Kingsolver, Barbara E Writer
PO Box 160, Meadowview VA 24361, USA

K

Kahn - Kingsolver

Kingston, Alex — Actress
Principal Entertainment, 1964 Westwood Blvd, #400, Los Angeles CA 90025 USA

Kingston, George — Ice Hockey Coach
235 W Camino Descanso, Palm Springs CA 92264, USA

Kingston, Kenny — Astrologer
C E S D, 10635 Santa Monica Blvd, #130, Los Angeles CA 90025 USA

Kingston, Maxine Hong — Writer
University of California, English Dept, Berkeley CA 94720, USA

Kingston, Sean — Rap Artist, Songwriter, Actor
I C M Partners, 10250 Constellation Blvd, #900, Los Angeles CA 90067 USA

Kinkade, Mike — Baseball Player
3005 SE Spyglass Dr, Vancouver WA 98683, USA

Kinkel, Klaus — Government Official, Germany
Auswartiges Amt, Adenauerallee 101, 53113 Bonn, Germany

Kinley, Heather — Singer (Kinleys)
PO Box 128501, Nashville TN 37212, USA

Kinley, Jennifer — Singer (Kinleys)
Sony Records, 2100 Colorado Ave, Santa Monica CA 90404 USA

Kinmont, Kathleen — Actress
9929 Sunset Blvd, #310, Los Angeles CA 90069, USA

Kinnally, Jon — Writer, Producer
W M E Entertainment, 9601 Wilshire Blvd, #300, Beverly Hills CA 90210 USA

Kinnaman, Joel — Actor
United Talent Agency, 9336 Civic Center Dr, Beverly Hills CA 90210 USA

Kinnear, Dominic — Soccer Coach
Houston Dynamo, 1415 Louisiana, #3400, Houston TX 77002 USA

Kinnear, Greg — Actor, Comedian
Creative Artists Agency, 2000 Ave of Stars, #100, Los Angeles CA 90067 USA

Kinnear, James W, III — Businessman
149 Taconic Road, Greenwich CT 06831, USA

Kinnebrew, Larry D — Football Player
216 Kingston Ave NE, Rome GA 30161, USA

Kinnell, Galway — Writer
110 Bleecker St, #6D, New York NY 10012, USA

Kinney, Dallas — Photojournalist
13010 Silver Sands Dr, Fort Myers FL 33913, USA

Kinney, Dennis P — Baseball Player
125 Olde Towne Way, #1, Myrtle Beach SC 29588, USA

Kinney, Erron Q — Football Player
1103 State Blvd, Franklin TN 37064, USA

Kinney, Jeff — Writer, Cartoonist
Harry N Abrams/Amulet Publishers, 115 W 18th St, New York NY 10011, USA

Kinney, Jeffrey B (Jeff) — Football Player
2720 W 161st Terrace, Stilwell KS 66085, USA

Kinney, Kathy — Actress
C E S D, 10635 Santa Monica Blvd, #130, Los Angeles CA 90025 USA

Kinney, Matt — Baseball Player
12 Owens Way, Hermon ME 04401, USA

Kinney, Sean H — Drummer (Alice in Chains)
Atmosphere Artists Mgmt, 6523 California Ave SW, #348, Seattle WA 98136, USA

Kinney, Terry — Actor
Steppenwolf Films, 813 Gaffield Place, Evanston IL 60201, USA

Kinnock, Neil G — Government Official, England
European Communities Commission, 200 Rue de Loi, 1049 Brussels, Belgium

Kinnunen, Michael J (Mike) — Baseball Player
5818 McKinley Place N, Seattle WA 98103, USA

Kinsella, John P — Swimmer
PO Box 3067, Sumas WA 98295, USA

Kinsella, Thomas — Writer
639 Addison St, Philadelphia PA 19147, USA

Kinsella, William Patrick (W P) — Writer
9442 Nowell, Chilliwack BC V2P 4X7, Canada

Kinser, Steve — Auto Racing Driver
Kinser Racing, 280 E Smithville Road, Bloomington IN 47401, USA

Kinsey, Angela — Actress
United Talent Agency, 9336 Civic Center Dr, Beverly Hills CA 90210 USA

Kinsey, Donald — Singer, Guitarist (Kinsey Report)
Jay Reil Assoc, 3490 Bayberry Dr, Northbrook IL 60062, USA

Kinsey, James L — Chemist
Rice University, Natural Sciences School, Houston TX 77005, USA

Kinsey, Kenneth — Bassist (Kinsey Report)
Jay Reil Assoc, 3490 Bayberry Dr, Northbrook IL 60062, USA

Kinsey, Ralph (Woody) — Drummer (Kinsey Report)
Jay Reil Assoc, 3490 Bayberry Dr, Northbrook IL 60062, USA

Kinshofer-Guthlein, Christa — Alpine Skier
Munchnerstr 44, 83026 Rosenheim, Germany

Kinski, Nastassja — Actress, Model
1000 Bel Air Place, Los Angeles CA 90077, USA

Kinsler, Ian M — Baseball Player
4029 Westmont Court, Bedford TX 76021, USA

Kinsley, Michael E — Editor, Commentator
14150 NE 20th St, #527, Bellevue WA 98007, USA

Kinsman, Brent — Actor
Coast to Coast Talent, 3350 Barham Blvd, Los Angeles CA 90068 USA

Kinsman, Shane — Actor
Coast to Coast Talent, 3350 Barham Blvd, Los Angeles CA 90068 USA

Kinsman, T James (Jim) — Vietnam War Army Hero (CMH)
111 Howe Road E, Toledo WA 98591, USA

Kiper, Mel, Jr — Sportscaster
ESPN-TV, ESPN Plaza, 935 Middle St, Bristol CT 06010 USA

Kipketer, Wilson — Track Athlete
Atletik Forbund, Idraettens Hus, Brondby Stadion 20, 2605 Brondby, Denmark

Kiplinger, Austin H — Publisher
Montevideo, 1680 River Road, Poolesville MD 20837, USA

Kipnis, David M — Physician
710 S Hanley Road, #15A, Saint Louis MO 63105, USA

Kipniss, Robert Hudson House, PO Box 112, Ardsley on Hudson NY 10503, USA	Artist
Kipper, Robert W (Bob) 117 Tuscany Way, Greer SC 29650, USA	Baseball Player
Kiprusoff, Miikka S Calgary Flames, PO Box 1540, Station M, Calgary AB T2P 3B9, Canada	Ice Hockey Player
Kiraly, Charles F (Karch) 307 Boca del Canon, San Clemente CA 92672, USA	Volleyball Player, Coach
Kiraly, John Lynn Roberts, 2410 Avenue A, Bradenton Beach FL 34217, USA	Artist
Kirby, Bruce 629 N Orlando Ave, #3, West Hollywood CA 90048, USA	Actor
Kirby, Luke Gersh Agency, 9465 Wilshire Blvd, #600, Beverly Hills CA 90212 USA	Actor
Kirby, Peter Bobsled Canada, 140 Canada Olympic Road SW, Calgary AB T3B 5R5, Canada	Bobsled Athlete
Kirby, Ronald H PO Box 337, Melville, 2109 Johannesburg, South Africa	Architect
Kirby, Terry G 744 Michelle Dr, Newport News VA 23601, USA	Football Player
Kirby, Wayne L 320 Kenya Road, Las Vegas NV 89123, USA	Baseball Player
Kirch, Patrick V University of California, Anthropology Dept, Kroeber Hall, Berkeley CA 94720, USA	Archaeologist
Kirchbach, Gunar Georgi-Dobrowolski-Str 10, 15517 Furstenwalde, Germany	Canoeing Athlete
Kirchberger, Sonja Calle C'An Sanc 14, 07001 Palma de Mallorca, Baleares, Spain	Actress
Kircheisen, Bjorn Georg-Baumgarten-Str 4, 08349 Johanngeorgenstadt, Germany	Nordic Combined Skier
Kirchen, Bill 6935 Chinook Dr, Austin TX 78736, USA	Guitarist (Twangbangers)
Kirchhoff, Ulrich Hoven 258, 48720 Rosendahl, Germany	Equestrian
Kirchner, Cristina F Casa de Gobierno, Balcarce 50, Buenos Aires 1064, Argentina	President, Agentina
Kirchner, Jamie Lee Gersh Agency, 41 Madison Ave, #3301, New York NY 10010 USA	Actress
Kirchner, Mark Hauptstr 74A, 98749 Scheibe-Alsbach, Germany	Biathlete
Kirchschlager, Angelika Mastroianni Assoc, 161 W 61st St, #32B, New York NY 10023, USA	Opera Singer
Kirilenko, Andrei G 1406 Perrys Hollow Road, Salt Lake City UT 84103, USA	Basketball Player
Kirilenko, Maria Y Women's Tennis Assn, 1 Progress Plaza, #1500, Saint Petersburg FL 33701 USA	Tennis Player, Model
Kirk, Jemima Creative Artists Agency, 2000 Ave of Stars, #100, Los Angeles CA 90067 USA	Actress
Kirk, Justin Management 360, 9111 Wilshire Blvd, Beverly Hills CA 90210 USA	Actor
Kirk, Rahsaan Roland Atlantic Records, 9229 W Sunset Blvd, #900, West Hollywood CA 90069 USA	Jazz Musician
Kirk, Tammy Joe 732 Peek Road, Dalton GA 30721, USA	Motorcyle Racing Rider, Auto Driver
Kirk, Thomas B Brookhaven National Laboratory, Physics Dept, 2 Center St, Upton NY 11973, USA	Physicist
Kirk, Tommy 833 Beacon Ave, Los Angeles CA 90017, USA	Actor
Kirk, Walton (Walt), Jr 2355 Coventry Parkway, #B202, Dubuque IA 52001, USA	Basketball Player
Kirkby, Emma Consort of Music, 54A Leamington Road Villas, London W11 1HT, England	Opera, Concert Singer
Kirke, Simon Alan Cottam Agency, 8 Cabin End Row, Knuzden, Blackburn BB1 2DP, England	Drummer (Free, Bad Company)
Kirkeby, Per Margarete Roeder Gallery, 545 Broadway, New York NY 10012, USA	Artist
Kirkland, Douglas 9060 Wonderland Park Ave, Los Angeles CA 90046, USA	Photographer
Kirkland, Gelsey Dube Zakin Mgmt, 67 Riverside Dr, #3B, New York NY 10024, USA	Ballerina
Kirkland, L Levon 316 Carters Creek Court, Simpsonville SC 29681, USA	Football Player
Kirkland, Mike Bob Flick Productions, 300 Vine St, #14, Seattle WA 98121, USA	Singer, Banjo Player (Brothers Four)
Kirkland, Ric Fortune Magazine, Time & Life Building, Rockefeller Center, New York NY 10020, USA	Editor
Kirkland, Sally Greene Assoc, 1901 Ave of Stars, #130, Los Angeles CA 90067 USA	Actress
Kirkland, Wilbur 127 Kimberwick Circle, Glenmoore PA 19343, USA	Basketball Player
Kirkland, Willie C 19374 Northrup St, Detroit MI 48219, USA	Baseball Player
Kirkman, Rick King Features Syndicate, 300 W 57th St, #1500, New York NY 10019 USA	Cartoonist (Baby Blues)
Kirkpatrick, Chris Wright Entertainment, PO Box 590009, Orlando FL 32859 USA	Singer ('N Sync)
Kirkpatrick, D/Andre L (Dre) Cincinnati Bengals, 1 Paul Brown Stadium, Cincinnati OH 45202 USA	Football Player
Kirkpatrick, Kevin Stone Manners Salners, 9911 W Pico Blvd, #1400, Los Angeles CA 90035 USA	Actor
Kirkpatrick, Maggie Karen Kay Mgmt, PO Box 446, Auckland 1140, New Zealand	Actress
Kirkwood, Curt High Road Touring, 751 Bridgeway, #200, Sausalito CA 94965 USA	Singer (Meat Puppets)
Kirkwood, Donald P (Don) 455 W Elmwood Ave, Clawson MI 48017, USA	Baseball Player

K

Kahn - Kirkwood

Kirla, John A — WW II Army Air Corps Hero
447 Main St, PO Box 396, Deep River CT 06417, USA

Kirn, Walter — Writer
Creative Artists Agency, 2000 Ave of Stars, #100, Los Angeles CA 90067 USA

Kirner, Gary B — Football Player
3507 Senasac Ave, Long Beach CA 90808, USA

Kirrane, John J (Jack), Jr — Ice Hockey Player
3 Country Road, Chestnut MA 02467, USA

Kirrene, Joseph J (Joe) — Baseball Player
2557 Kilpatrick Court, San Ramon CA 94583, USA

Kirsch, Russell — Inventor (Square Pixels)
4610 SW Greenhills Way, Portland OR 97221, USA

Kirsch, Stan — Actor
Stan Kirsch Studios, 6671 Sunset Blvd, #1584-A, Los Angeles CA 90028, USA

Kirschke, Travis — Football Player
10196 Crooked Stick Trail, Lone Tree CO 80124, USA

Kirschner, Carl — Educator
Rutgers State University College, President's Office, New Brunswick NJ 08093, USA

Kirschner, David M — Animator, Producer
David Kirschner Productions, 400 S June St, Los Angeles CA 90020, USA

Kirschner, Marc W — Cell Biologist
Harvard Medical School, Cell Biology Dept, 25 Shattuck St, Boston MA 02115, USA

Kirschstein, Ruth L — Physician
6 West Dr, Bethesda MD 20814, USA

Kirshbaum, Laurence J — Publisher
Warner Books, Time-Life Building, Rockefeller Center, New York NY 10020, USA

Kirshbaum, Ralph — Concert Cellist
Ingpen & Williams, 131 Putney Bridge Road, London SW15 2PA, England

Kirshner, Mia — Actress
Gersh Agency, 9465 Wilshire Blvd, #600, Beverly Hills CA 90212 USA

Kirst, Michael W — Educator
Stanford University, Education School, Stanford CA 94305, USA

Kirstein, Peter T — Computer Scientist
University College, Computer Science Dept, London WC1E 6BT, England

Kirszenstein Szewinska, Irena — Track Athlete
Ul Bagno 5 m 80, 00 112 Warsaw, Poland

Kirtadze, Nino — Actress
GoDigital Media Group, 233 Wilshire Blvd, #100, Santa Monica CA 90401, USA

Kirton, Mark R — Ice Hockey Player
251 N Service Road W, Oakville ON L6M 3E7, Canada

Kirvesniemi, Harri — Cross Country Skier
Karhu Ski, Henrikinkatu 2, 21100 Naantali, Finland

Kirwan, Larry — Singer, Guitarist (Black 47)
Skyline Music, 28 Union St, Whitefield NH 03598, USA

Kirwan, William E, II — Educator
3112 Old Court Road, Pikesville MD 21208, USA

Kisabaka, Lisa — Track Athlete
Franz-Hitze-Str 22, 51372 Leverkusen, Germany

Kiser, Garland R — Baseball Player
267 Carr Dr, Blountville TN 37617, USA

Kiser, Terry — Actor
Innovative Artists, 1505 10th St, Santa Monica CA 90401 USA

Kishlansky, Mark A — Historian
Harvard University, History Dept, Cambridge MA 02138, USA

Kisio, Kelly W — Ice Hockey Player
Calgary Hitmen, PO Box 1420 Station Main, Calgary AB T2P 3B9, Canada

Kisner, Jacob — Writer
245 Park Ave S, #PH F, New York NY 10003, USA

Kison, Bruce E — Baseball Player
1403 Riverview Circle, Bradenton FL 34209, USA

Kissane, James J (Jim) — Basketball Player
6 Mellen Lane, Wayland MA 01778, USA

Kissin, Evgeni I — Concert Pianist
I M G Artists, 152 W 57th St, #500, New York NY 10019 USA

Kissinger, Henry A — Secretary, State; Nobel Peace Laureate
PO Box 38, South Kent CT 06785, USA

Kissling, Conny — Freestyle Skier
Hubel, 3254 Messen, Switzerland

Kistler, Darci — Ballerina
New York City Ballet, Lincoln Center Plaza, New York NY 10023 USA

Kita, Toshiyuki — Industrial Designer
TS Bild 2F, 3-1-2 Tenma, Kitauku, Osaka 530 0043, Japan

Kitaen, Tawny — Actress
Brady Brannon Rich, 5670 Wilshire Blvd, #820, Los Angeles CA 90036 USA

Kitamura, Ryuhei — Director
Capitol Motion Pictures, 610 Brazos, #300D, Austin TX 78701, USA

Kitano, Takeshi — Actor, Director, Writer
Office Kitano, 5-4-14 Akasaka Minataku, 107 0052 Tokyo, Japan

Kitaro — Musician, Composer
Agency Group Ltd, 142 W 57th St, #600, New York NY 10019 USA

Kitayenko, Dmitri G — Conductor
Chalet Kalimor, 1652 Botterens, Switzerland

Kitbunchu, M Michai Cardinal — Religious Leader
122 Soi Naaksuwan, Thanon Nonsi, Yannawa, Bangkok 10120, Thailand

Kitchell, Sonya — Singer, Songwriter
Monterey International, 200 W Superior St, #202, Chicago IL 60654 USA

Kitchen, Curtis — Basketball Player
343 19th Ave, Seattle WA 98122, USA

Kitchen, Michael — Actor
Rights House, 34-43 Russell St, London WC2B 5HA, England

Kitchen, Mike — Ice Hockey Player, Coach
5570 NE Trieste Way, Boca Raton FL 33487, USA

Kite, Gregory F (Greg) — Basketball Player
3060 Seigneury Dr, Windermere FL 34786, USA

Kite, Jonathan — Actor
Full Circle Mgmt, 4932 Lankershim Blvd, #202, North Hollywood CA 91601, USA

Kite, Thomas O (Tom), Jr — Golfer
907 Terrace Mountain Dr, West Lake Hills TX 78746, USA

Kitsch, Taylor — Actor
Rogers & Cowan, 8687 Melrose Ave, #G700, West Hollywood CA 90069 USA

Kitson, Linda F — Artist
1 Argyll Mansions, Kings Road, London SW3 5ER, England

Kitsopoulos, Constantine — Conductor
I M G Artists, Hogarth Business Park, Chiswick, London W4 2TH, England

Kitt, A J — Alpine Skier
Colt Realty Group, 509 Cascade Ave, #A, Hood River OR 97031, USA

Kittel, Charles — Physicist
University of California, Physics Dept, Berkeley CA 94720, USA

Kittinger, Joseph W (Joe), Jr — Parachutist, Balloonist
608 Mariner Way, Altamonte Springs FL 32701, USA

Kittle, Ronald D (Ron) — Baseball Player
1840 Tour Trace, Chesterton IN 46304, USA

Kittles, Tory — Actor
Paradigm Agency, 360 N Crescent Dr, North Building, Beverly Hills CA 90210 USA

Kittredge, William A — Writer
42 Brookside Way, Missoula MT 59802, USA

Kivelson, Margaret Galland — Physicist
University of California, Earth & Space Sciences Dept, Los Angeles CA 90024, USA

Kiwanuka, Mathias K — Football Player
456 9th St, #13, Hoboken NJ 07030, USA

Kiyosaki, Robert T — Writer
Cashflow Technologies, 4330 N Civic Center Plaza, #100, Scottsdale AZ 85251, USA

Kizer, Carolyn A — Writer
University of Arizona, English Dept, Tucson AZ 85721, USA

Kjus, Lasse — Alpine Skier
Rugdeveien 2C, 1404 Siggerud, Norway

Klabunde, Charles S — Artist
68 W 3rd St, New York NY 10012, USA

Klammer, Franz — Alpine Skier
Mooswald 22, 9712 Friesach, Austria

Klaplisch, Cedric — Director, Writer
Ce Qui Me Meut Motion Pictures, 23 Passage de la Main d'Or, 75011 Paris, France

Klapman, Lia — Sculptor
2581 Mission St, Santa Cruz CA 95060, USA

Klarik, Jeffrey — Producer, Writer
W M E Entertainment, 9601 Wilshire Blvd, #300, Beverly Hills CA 90210 USA

Klas, Eri — Conductor
C M Artists, 127 W 96th St, #13B, New York NY 10025 USA

Klassen, Daniel V (Danny) — Baseball Player
28925 N 111th Place, Scottsdale AZ 85262, USA

Klatt, Trent — Ice Hockey Player
267 SW 12th Ave, Grand Rapids MN 55744, USA

Klaus, Vaclav — President, Czechoslovakia
President's Office, Prague Castle, Prazsky Hrad, Hradecek, 119 08 Prague 1, Czech Republic

Klausing, Chuck — Football Coach
2115 Lazor St, Indiana PA 15701, USA

Klausner, Julie — Actress, Writer
Avalon Mgmt, 8332 Melrose Ave, #200, Los Angeles CA 90069, USA

Klausner, Richard D — Cell Biologist
Column Group, 1700 Owens Street, #500, San Francisco CA 94158, USA

Klavan, Andrew — Writer
Gersh Agency, 9465 Wilshire Blvd, #600, Beverly Hills CA 90212 USA

Klaveno, Mariana — Actress
A P A Talent/Literary Agency, 405 S Beverly Dr, #300, Beverly Hills CA 90212 USA

Klawe, Maria — Educator
Harvey Mudd College, President's Office, Claremont CA 91711, USA

Klawitter, Thomas C (Tom) — Baseball Player
605 Foxglove Lane, Whitewater WI 53190, USA

Klaws, Alexander — Singer, Actor
19 Music & Mgmt, 35-37 Parkgate Road, London SW11 4NP, England

Klecko, Daniel R (Dan) — Football Player
234 Cedar Road, Mullica Hill NJ 08062, USA

Klecko, Joseph E (Joe) — Football Player
6 Victorian Way, Colts Neck NJ 07722, USA

Klee, Ken — Ice Hockey Player
78 W Ranch Trail, Morrison CO 80465, USA

Klees, Christian — Marksman
Eutiner Sportschutzen, Schutzenweg 26, 23701 Eutin, Germany

Kleibrink, Shannon — Curling Athlete
Curling Assn, 1660 Vimont Court, Cumberland ON K4A 4J4, Canada

Klein, Abigail — Actress
Brillstein Entertainment Partners, 9150 Wilshire Blvd, #350, Beverly Hills CA 90212 USA

Klein, Calvin R — Fashion Designer
650 Meadow Lane, Southampton NY 11968, USA

Klein, Chris — Actor
I C M Partners, 10250 Constellation Blvd, #900, Los Angeles CA 90067 USA

Klein, Dale E — Government Official
US Nuclear Regulatory Commission, 11555 Rockville Pike, Rockville MD 20852, USA

Klein, Danny — Bassist (J Geils Band)
Nick Ben-Meir, 652 N Doheny Dr, West Hollywood CA 90069, USA

Klein, David — Geneticist
National Child Health Institute, 49 Convent Dr, Bethesda MD 20892, USA

Klein, Edward — Writer
Random House, 1745 Broadway, #1800, New York NY 10019 USA

Klein, Emilee — Golfer
7660 Beverly Blvd, #315, Los Angeles CA 90036, USA

Klein, George — Tumor Biologist
Kottlavagen 10, 181 61 Lidingo, Sweden

Klein, Jess — Singer, Guitarist, Songwriter
Invasion Group, 133 W 25th St, #500, New York NY 10001, USA

Klein, Joe — Journalist, Writer
Time, Editorial Dept, Time-Life Building, 1271 Ave of Americas, New York NY 10020, USA

Klein, Joel	Attorney, Government Official, Educator
New York City Schools, Chancellor's Office, 110 Livingston, Brooklyn NY 11201, USA	
Klein, Lawrence R	Nobel Economics Laureate
1400 Waverly Road, #B035, Gladwyne PA 19035, USA	
Klein, Lester A	Urologist
Scripps Clinic, Urology Dept, 10666 N Torrey Pines Road, La Jolla CA 92037, USA	
Klein, Marci	Producer
Slate Public Relations, 9000 Sunset Blvd, #915, West Hollywood CA 90069 USA	
Klein, Richard G	Paleoanthropologist
Stanford University, Anthropologist Services Dept, Stanford CA 94305, USA	
Klein, Robert	Actor, Comedian
67 Ridgecrest Road, Briarcliff Manor NY 10510, USA	
Klein, Robert O (Bob)	Football Player
15263 Friends St, Pacific Palisades CA 90272, USA	
Kleine, Joseph W (Joe)	Basketball Player
53 Hickory Hills Circle, Little Rock AR 72212, USA	
Kleinendorst, Kurt	Ice Hockey Player, Coach
30833 Sunny Beach Road, Grand Rapids MN 55744, USA	
Kleinert, Harold E	Microsurgeon
225 Abraham Flexner Way, #700, Louisville KY 40202, USA	
Kleinfeld, Andrew J	Judge
US Court of Appeals, Courthouse Square, 250 Cushman St, Fairbanks AK 99701, USA	
Kleinman, Arthur M	Anthropologist, Psychiatrist
Harvard University, Anthropology Dept, Cambridge MA 02138, USA	
Kleinrock, Leonard	Computer Scientist
318 N Rockingham Ave, Los Angeles CA 90049, USA	
Kleinsasser, Jimmy C (Jim)	Football Player
6835 Cardinal Cove Dr, Mound MN 55364, USA	
Kleinsmith, Bruce	Cartoonist
PO Box 1083, San Juan Bautista CA 95045, USA	
Kleintank, Luke	Actor
Robert Stein Management, 345 N Maple Dr, #317, Beverly Hills CA 90210, USA	
Kleiser, Randal	Director
3050 Runyan Canyon Road, Los Angeles CA 90046, USA	
Kleiza, Linas	Basketball Player
Toronto Raptors, Air Canada Center, 20 Bay St, Toronto ON M5J 2N8, Canada	
Klembaum, Sharon	Religious Leader, Rabbi
Congregation Beth Simchat Torah, 57 Bethune St, New York NY 10014, USA	
Klemm, Adrian W	Football Player
13600 Marina Pointe Dr, #1908, Marina del Rey CA 90292, USA	
Klemm, Jon	Ice Hockey Player
400 61st St, Willowbrook IL 60527, USA	
Klemmer, John	Jazz Saxophonist
Boardman, 10548 Clearwood Court, Los Angeles CA 90077, USA	
Klemperer, William	Chemist
53 Shattuck Road, Watertown MA 02472, USA	
Klemt, Becky	Attorney
Pence & MacMillan, PO Box 1285, Laramie WY 82073, USA	
Klesko, Ryan A	Baseball Player
735 Henderson Mill Road, Covington GA 30014, USA	
Klesla, Rostislav	Ice Hockey Player
6751 N Sunset Blvd, #200, Glendale AZ 85305, USA	
Klett, Peter	Guitarist (Candlebox)
Novi Entertainment, 201 N Robertson Blvd, #201, Beverly Hills CA 90211, USA	
Klever, Victor K (Rocky)	Football Player
3829 W 42nd St, Anchorage AK 99517, USA	
Kley, Chaney	Actor
Paradigm Agency, 360 N Crescent Dr, North Building, Beverly Hills CA 90210 USA	
Klibanoff, Hank	Journalist, Historian
Emory University, Journalism Dept, 201 Dowman Drive, Atlanta GA 30322, USA	
Klim, Michael	Swimmer
177 Bridge Road, Richmond VIC 3121, Australia	
Klima, Petr	Ice Hockey Player
1000 Forest Lane, Bloomfield Hills MI 48301, USA	
Klimchock, Louis S (Lou)	Baseball Player
8876 S Myrtle Ave, Tempe AZ 85284, USA	
Klimisch, Dick	Inventor (Auto Catalytic Converter)
43 Fairfold Road, Grosse Pointe Shores MI 48236, USA	
Klimke, Ingrid	Equestrian Rider
Kanalstr 340, 48159 Munster, Germany	
Klimke, Reiner	Equestrian Rider
Krumme Str 3, 48143 Munster, Germany	
Klimova, Marina V	Ice Dancer
Sharks Ice, 1500 S 10th St, San Jose CA 95112, USA	
Klimuk, Pyotr I	Cosmonaut, Air Force General
Cosmonaut Training Center, Star City, 141160 Zvezdny Gorodok, Moscow Oblast, Russia	
Kline, J Robert (Bobby)	Baseball Player
6656 31st Way S, Saint Petersburg FL 33712, USA	
Kline, Jeff	Writer, Producer
Creative Artists Agency, 2000 Ave of Stars, #100, Los Angeles CA 90067 USA	
Kline, Kevin D	Actor
1636 3rd Ave, #309, New York NY 10128, USA	
Kline, Richard	Actor
Osgood Mgmt, 43 Lennox Terrace, West Orange NJ 07052, USA	
Kline, Richard H	Cinematographer
1015 Manning Ave, Los Angeles CA 90024, USA	
Kline, Steven J (Steve)	Baseball Player
PO Box 1525, Chelan WA 98816, USA	
Kline-Randall, Maxine	Baseball Player
105 Nottingham Road, Bloomsberg PA 17815, USA	
Kling, Anja	Actress
Agentur Margarita Kling, Amselweg 6, 14557 Wilhelmhorst, Germany	
Kling, Gerit	Actress
Agentur Margarita Kling, Amselweg 6, 14557 Wilhelmshorst, Germany	
Klingbeil, Charles (Chuck)	Football Player
47921 US Highway 41, Houghton MI 49931, USA	

Klingenbeck, Scott E
6230 Kincora Court, Cincinnati OH 45233, USA — Baseball Player
Klingensmith, Michael J
Entertainment Weekly, Rockefeller Center, New York NY 10020, USA — Publisher
Klingler, David R
Dallas Theological Seminary, 6000 Dale Carnegie Lane, Houston TX 77036, USA — Football Player
Klinsmann, Jurgen
F C Bayern Munich, Postfach 900451, 81504 Munich, Germany — Soccer Player, Coach
Klitschko, Vitali V
Klitschko Management Group, Borselstr 28, Haus 1, 22765 Hamburg, Germany — Boxer
Klitschko, Wladimir
Klitschko Management Group, Borselstr 28, Haus 1, 22765 Hamburg, Germany — Boxer
Klooparens, Beth
Klooparens Inc, 250 5th Ave, New York NY 10001, USA — Architect
Klop, Cody
Curtis Talent Management, 9607 Arby Dr, Beverly Hills CA 90210, USA — Actor
Klose, Miroslav
A S B W Sports Marketing, Ubierring 7, 50678 Colgone, Germany — Soccer Player
Kloser, Harald
Gorfaine/Schwartz, 4111 W Alameda Ave, #509, Burbank CA 91505 USA — Composer
Kloss, Karlie E
Next Model Mgmt, 23 Watts St, New York NY 10013 USA — Model
Klotz, Frank G
Commander, Air Global Strike Force Command, Barksdale Air Force Base LA 71110, USA — Air Force General
Klotz, H Louis (Red)
114 S Osbourne Ave, Margate City NJ 08402, USA — Basketball Player, Coach
Klotz, Irving M
1500 Sheridan Road, #7D, Wilmette IL 60091, USA — Chemist, Biochemist
Klotz, John S (Jack)
729 E 25th St, Chester PA 19013, USA — Football Player
Klous, Patricia
2539 Benedict Canyon Dr, Beverly Hills CA 90210, USA — Actress
Kloves, Steve
Creative Artists Agency, 2000 Ave of Stars, #100, Los Angeles CA 90067 USA — Director, Writer
Klueh, Duane
252 Francis Avenue Court, Terre Haute IN 47804, USA — Basketball Player, Coach
Klug, Aaron
70 Cavendish Ave, Cambridge CB1 4OT, England — Nobel Chemistry Laureate
Klug, Chris
Chris Klug Foundation, 182 Riverdown Dr, Aspen CO 81611, USA — Snowboard Skier
Kluger, Richard
Random House, 1745 Broadway, #1800, New York NY 10019 USA — Writer
Klugh, Earl
I C M Partners, 10250 Constellation Blvd, #900, Los Angeles CA 90067 USA — Jazz Guitarist
Klugman, Jack
20700 Quedo Dr, Woodland Hills CA 91364, USA — Actor
Klum, Heidi
W M E Entertainment, 9601 Wilshire Blvd, #300, Beverly Hills CA 90210 USA — Model, Actress
Klum, Mattias
Svanliden, Hammarskog, 755 91 Uppsala, Sweden — Photographer
Klunk, William E
Alzheimer's Disease Laboratory, 200 Lothrop St, Pittsburgh PA 15213, USA — Neurologist
Klutts, Gene E (Mickey)
6136 Maple Ave, Lake Isabella CA 93240, USA — Baseball Player
Kluttz, Lonnie
183 Greenwing Lane, Saint Matthews SC 29135, USA — Basketball Player
Kluwe, Christopher J (Chris)
13026 Ottawa Dr, Savage MN 55378, USA — Football Player
Klyszewski, Waclaw
Ul Gornoslaska 16 m 15A, 00-432 Warsaw, Poland — Architect
Kmak, Joseph R (Joe)
1021 Hatteras Court, Foster City CA 94404, USA — Baseball Player
K'Maro
Warner Music, Alter Wandrahm 14, 20457 Hamburg, Germany — Singer, Rap Artist, Songwriter
KMG the Illustrator
Green Light Talent Agency, PO Box 3172, Beverly Hills CA 90212 USA — Rap Artist (Above the Law)
K'Naan
Paquin Entertainment, 206B-219 Dufferin St, Toronto ON M6K 3J1, Canada — Rap Artist, Singer, Guitarist
Knackert, Brent B
16802 Leafwood Circle, Huntington Beach CA 92647, USA — Baseball Player
Knafelc, Gary
2147 Burley Ave, Clermont FL 34711, USA — Football Player
Knaifel, Alexander A
Skobelevski Pr 5, #130, 194214 Saint Petersburg, Russia — Composer
Knape Lindberg, Ulrike
Drostvagen 7, 691 33 Karlskoga, Sweden — Diver
Knapp, Charles B
120 Brookview Circle N, Atlanta GA 30339, USA — Educator
Knapp, Cleon T
Talewood Corp, 8939 S Sepulveda Blvd, #110, Los Angeles CA 90045, USA — Publisher
Knapp, Jennifer L
Gotee Records, 1746 General George Patton Dr, Brentwood TN 37027, USA — Singer
Knapp, John W
Virginia Military Institute, Superintendent's Office, Lexington VA 24450, USA — Educator, Army General
Knapp, R Christian (Chris)
788 Rich Dr, Oviedo FL 32765, USA — Baseball Player
Knapp, Steven
George Washington University, President's Office, Washington DC 20052, USA — Educator
Knaus, Chad A
149 Pin Oak Lane, Mooresville NC 28117, USA — Auto Racing Crew Chief
Knaus, William A
University of Virginia, Medical School, Public Health Service Dept, Charlottesville VA 22908, USA — Physician, Medical Activist
Knauss, Hans
Fastenberg 60, 8970 Schladming, Austria — Alpine Skier
Knauss, Melania
T Mgmt, 91 5th Ave, #300, New York NY 10003 USA — Model

K

Kneale, R Bryan C — Sculptor
10A Muswell Road, London N10 2BG, England

Knebel, John A — Secretary, Agriculture
1418 Laburnum St, McLean VA 22101, USA

Knepper, Robert — Actor
Innovative Artists, 1505 10th St, Santa Monica CA 90401 USA

Knepper, Robert W (Bob) — Baseball Player
5704 Callcott Way, #E, Alexandria VA 22312, USA

Kness, Richard M — Opera Singer
240 Central Park South, #16M, New York NY 10019, USA

Kneuer, Cameo — Physical Fitness Expert
Starshape by Cameo, 2554 Lincoln Blvd, #640, Venice CA 90291, USA

Knibb, Sean — Landscape Architect
Knibb Design, 141 S Barrington Ave, Los Angeles CA 90049, USA

Knicely, Alan L — Baseball Player
PO Box 433, Dayton VA 22821, USA

Knickman, Roy — Cyclist
436 Fallbrook Ave, Newbury Park CA 91320, USA

Knight, Beverly — Singer, Songwriter
D W L, 53 Goodge St, #200, London W1T 1TG, England

Knight, Brandon — Basketball Player
Detroit Pistons, Palace, 4 Championship Dr, Auburn Hills MI 48326 USA

Knight, Brandon M — Baseball Player
191 S Pacific Ave, #B, Ventura CA 93001, USA

Knight, Brevin — Basketball Player
3226 Bedford Lane, Germantown TN 38139, USA

Knight, C Ray — Baseball Player, Manager
PO Box 129, Auburn AL 36831, USA

Knight, Charles F — Businessman
Emerson Electric Co, 8000 W Florissant Ave, Box 41000, Saint Louis MO 63136, USA

Knight, Chris — Singer, Songwriter
Rick Alter Mgmt, 1018 17th Ave S, #12, Nashville TN 37212, USA

Knight, Christopher — Actor
Identity Talent Agency, 9107 Wilshire Blvd, #450, Beverly Hills CA 90210 USA

Knight, David R — Football Player
2600 Farm Road, Alexandria VA 22302, USA

Knight, Gladys — Singer
Shakeji, 3221 La Mirada Ave, Las Vegas NV 89120, USA

Knight, Hilary — Ice Hockey Player
USA Hockey, 1775 Bob Johnson Dr, Colorado Springs CO 80906 USA

Knight, Jean — Singer
Acts Nashville, 1103 Bell Grimes Lane, Nashville TN 37207, USA

Knight, Jonathan — Singer (New Kids on the Block)
90 Apple St, Essex MA 01929, USA

Knight, Jordan — Singer (New Kids on the Block)
Central Entertainment Group, 166 5th Ave, #400, New York NY 10010, USA

Knight, Keith — Cartoonist (K Chronicles)
PO Box 341862, Los Angeles CA 90034, USA

Knight, L Curtis (Curt), Jr — Football Player
7230 Rio Flora Place, Downey CA 90241, USA

Knight, Negele — Basketball Player
18624 N 4th Ave, Phoenix AZ 85027, USA

Knight, Philip H — Businessman
Nike Inc, 1 SW Bowerman Dr, Beaverton OR 97005, USA

Knight, Robert M (Bobby) — Basketball Coach
8003 County Road 6910, Lubbock TX 79407, USA

Knight, Ronald E (Ron) — Basketball Player
1426 Ellsmere Ave, Los Angeles CA 90019, USA

Knight, Shirley — Actress
Diamond Mgmt, 31 Percy St, London W1T 2DD, England

Knight, Sterling — Actor
Greene Assoc, 1901 Ave of Stars, #130, Los Angeles CA 90067 USA

Knight, Steven — Writer
Creative Artists Agency, 2000 Ave of Stars, #100, Los Angeles CA 90067 USA

Knight, T R — Actor
Innovative Artists, 1505 10th St, Santa Monica CA 90401 USA

Knight, Thomas L (Tommy) — Football Player
70 Overington Ave, Marlton NJ 08053, USA

Knight, Toby — Basketball Player
106 Claywood Dr, Brentwood NY 11717, USA

Knight, Travis J — Basketball Player
3159 Millcreek Road, Pleasant Grove UT 84062, USA

Knight, Tuesday — Actress
Stephany Hurkos Mgmt, 11935 Kling St, #10, Valley Village CA 91607 USA

Knight, Wayne — Actor, Comedian
Brillstein Entertainment Partners, 9150 Wilshire Blvd, #350, Beverly Hills CA 90212 USA

Knight, William R (Billy) — Basketball Player, Executive
1051 Bluffhaven Way NE, Atlanta GA 30319, USA

Knightley, Keira — Actress
United Agents, 12-26 Lexington St, London W1F 0LE, England

Knighton, Zachary — Actor
3 Arts Entertainment, 9460 Wilshire Blvd, #700, Beverly Hills CA 90212 USA

Knight-Pulliam, Keshia — Actress
PO Box 866, Teaneck NJ 07666, USA

Knights, Dave — Bassist (Procol Harum)
195 Sandycombe Road, Kew TW9 2EW, England

Knisley, Sam — Basketball Player
14808 Hanover Pike, Upperco MD 21155, USA

Knoblauch, E Charles (Chuck) — Baseball Player
11702 Forest Glen St, Houston TX 77024, USA

Knoff, Kurt — Football Player
11121 Bluestem Lane, Eden Prairie MN 55347, USA

Knol, Monique — Cyclist
Draarlier 6, 3766 Et Soest, Netherlands

Knoll, Andrew H — Paleontologist
Harvard University, Botanical Museum, 26 Oxford St, Cambridge MA 02138, USA

Knoll, Jozsef
Semmelweis Medical University, Pharmacology Dept, 1445 Budapest, Hungary — Pharmacologist

Knoop, Robert F (Bobby)
2543 E Mountain Sky Ave, Phoenix AZ 85048, USA — Baseball Player

Knopf, Sascha
Stone Manners Salners, 9911 W Pico Blvd, #1400, Los Angeles CA 90035 USA — Actress, Model

Knopfler, David
Damage Mgmt, 16 Lambton Place, London W11 2SH, England — Guitarist (Dire Straits)

Knopfler, Mark
Paul Crockford Mgmt, 272 Latimer Road, London W10 6QY, England — Singer, Guitarist (Dire Straits)

Knorr, Randy D
3200 Arville St, #279, Las Vegas NV 89102, USA — Baseball Player

Knotts, Gary
18 Covey Road, Decatur, AL 35603 35603, USA — Baseball Player

Knowles, Beyonce
Music World Entertainment, 1505 Hadley St, Houston TX 77002, USA — Singer, Actress, Model

Knowles, Darold D
1515 Whisper Wind Lane, Oldsmar FL 34677, USA — Baseball Player

Knowles, Michael R
University of North Carolina Medical School, Pulmonary & Critical Care Dept, Chapel Hill NC 27599, USA — Medical Researcher

Knowles, Rodney
3592 Island Dr, North Topsail Beach NC 28460, USA — Basketball Player

Knowles, Sabrina
3824 SW Morgan St, Seattle WA 98126, USA — Artist

Knowles, Solange
Hansen Jacobson Teller, 450 N Roxbury Dr, #800, Beverly Hills CA 90210 USA — Actress, Singer

Knowlson, Elizabeth
Bloomsbury Publishing, 36 Soho Square, London W1D 3Q4, England — Writer

Knowlson, James
Bloomsbury Publishing, 36 Soho Square, London W1D 3Q4, England — Writer

Knowlton, Steve R
Palmer Yeager Assoc, 6600 E Hampden Ave, #210, Denver CO 80224, USA — Skier

Knox, Charles R (Chuck)
48711 San Vicente St, La Quinta CA 92253, USA — Football Coach

Knox, Deborah
Curling Assn, 14 Donnelly Dr, Bedford MK4 9TU, England — Curling Athlete

Knox, Heather
Playboy Promotions, 2706 Media Center Dr, Los Angeles CA 90065 USA — Model

Knox, John C
3701 W Oak Shores Dr, Crossroads TX 76227, USA — Baseball Player

Knox, Kenny
3813 Dills Road, Monticello FL 32344, USA — Golfer

Knox, Ruth A
Wesleyan College, President's Office, 4760 Forsyth Road, Macon GA 31210, USA — Educator

Knox, Taylor
Pro Surfing Mgmt, 320 High Tide Dr, #101, Saint Augustine FL 32080 USA — Surfer

Knox, Terence
House of Representatives, 1434 6th St, #1, Santa Monica CA 90401 USA — Actor

Knox-Johnston, W R P (Robin)
26 Sefton St, Putney, London SW15, England — Yachtsman

Knoxville, Johnny
Creative Artists Agency, 2000 Ave of Stars, #100, Los Angeles CA 90067 USA — Actor, Comedian

Knuble, Michael (Mike)
2107 San Lu Rae Dr SE, Grand Rapids MI 49506, USA — Ice Hockey Player

Knudsen, Lars
United Talent Agency, 9336 Civic Center Dr, Beverly Hills CA 90210 USA — Producer

Knudson, Alfred G, Jr
Institute for Cancer Research, 7701 Burholme Ave, Philadelphia PA 19111, USA — Geneticist

Knudson, Mark R
881 W 100th Ave, Northglenn CO 80260, USA — Baseball Player

Knudson, Thomas J
Sacramento Bee, Editorial Dept, 21st & Q Sts, Sacramento CA 95852, USA — Journalist

Knuppe, Franziska
Model Mgmt, Hartungstr 5, 20146 Hamburg, Germany — Model

Knussen, S Oliver
BBC Symphony Orchestra, BBC Maida Vale Studios, Delaware Road, London W9 2LG, England — Conductor, Composer

Knuth, Donald E
Stanford University, Computer Science Dept, Gates Building, Stanford CA 94305, USA — Computer Scientist; Kyoto Laureate

Knuth, Shay
Playboy Promotions, 2706 Media Center Dr, Los Angeles CA 90065 USA — Model

Ko Gi Hyun
Skating Union, 88 Bangyee-Dong, Songpaku, Seoul 138 749, South Korea — Speed Skater

Ko Un
Anseong, Gyeonggi-do 456 600, South Korea — Writer

Koback, Nicholas N (Nick)
71 Hopmeadow St, #9A-1, Weatogue CT 06089, USA — Baseball Player

Kobayashi, Makoto
High Energy Accelerator Research, 1-1 Oho, Tsukuba 305 0801, Japan — Nobel Physics Laureate

Kobel, Kevin R
7650 E Williams Dr, #1072, Scottsdale AZ 85255, USA — Baseball Player

Kober, Jeff
4544 Ethel Ave, Studio City CA 91604, USA — Actor

Kobilka, Brian K
Stanford University Medical School, 300 Pasteur Drive, Palo Alto CA 94304, USA — Nobel Chemistry Laureate

Koblik, Steven
Huntington Library & Art Gallery, 1151 Oxford Road, San Marino CA 91108, USA — Museum Executive, Educator

Kobrin, Alex
I M G Artists, Hogarth Business Park, Chiswick, London W4 2TH, England — Concert Pianist

Kobylt, John
248 Oceano Dr, Los Angeles CA 90049, USA — Entertainer

Koch, Alan G
1714 Pebble Creek Dr, Prattville AL 36066, USA — Baseball Player

Koch, Carin
2000 Auburn Dr, #330, Beachwood OH 44122, USA — Golfer

Koch, Charles G
Koch Industries, PO Box 2256, Wichita KS 67201, USA — Businessman

K

Kahn - Koch

K

Koch, Christopher (Chris) — Director
United Talent Agency, 9336 Civic Center Dr, Beverly Hills CA 90210 USA

Koch, David H — Businessman
Koch Industries, 4111 E 37th St N, Wichita KS 67220, USA

Koch, Ed — Artist
1211 NW Ogden Ave, Bend OR 97701, USA

Koch, Edward I — Mayor, New York City
Robinson Silverman Pearce, 1290 Ave of Americas, #3300, New York NY 10104, USA

Koch, Gary — Golfer
2934 W Lawn Ave, Tampa FL 33611, USA

Koch, Gregory M (Greg) — Football Player
34 Valley Oaks Circle, Spring TX 77382, USA

Koch, James V — Educator, Economist
Old Dominion University, Economics Dept, Norfolk VA 23529, USA

Koch, Peter A (Pete) — Football Player
866 W 16th St, Newport Beach CA 92663, USA

Koch, Sebastian — Actor
Anne Alvares Correa, 34 Rue Jouffroy d'Abbans, 75017 Paris, France

Koch, Sophie — Opera Singer
I M G Artists, Hogarth Business Park, Chiswick, London W4 2TH, England

Koch, William (Bill) — Nordic Skier
PO Box 115, Ashland OR 97520, USA

Koch, William C (Billy) — Baseball Player
3160 Tusket Ave, North Port FL 34286, USA

Koch, William I (Bill) — Yachtsman, Businessman
Oxbow Corp, 1601 Forum Place, West Palm Beach FL 33401, USA

Kocherga, Anatoli I — Opera Singer
Gogolevskaho 37 Korp 2, #47, 254053 Kiev, Ukraine

Kocherry, Thomas — Social Activist
Kerala Swatantra Matsyathozhilali Federation, Kerala 69508, India

Kochi, Jay K — Chemist
4372 Faculty Lane, Houston TX 77004, USA

Kocourek, David A — Football Player
1170 Cara Court, Marco Island FL 34145, USA

Kocsis, Zoltan — Concert Pianist, Composer
Ringlo Utica 60/A, 1116 Budapest, Hungary

Kocur, Joey — Ice Hockey Player
2830 Vero Dr, Highland MI 48356, USA

Kodes, Jan — Tennis Player
I C L T K Tennis Club, Ostrov Stvanice, 170 00 Prague 7, Czech Republic

Kodjoe, Boris — Model, Actor
Untitled Entertainment, 350 S Beverly Dr, #200, Beverly Hills CA 90212 USA

Koechner, David — Actor
Creative Artists Agency, 2000 Ave of Stars, #100, Los Angeles CA 90067 USA

Koelle, George B — Pharmacologist
3300 Darby Road, #3310, Haverford PA 19041, USA

Koelling, Brian W — Baseball Player
20230 Augusta Dr, Lawrenceburg IN 47025, USA

Koen, Karleen — Writer
Random House, 1745 Broadway, #1800, New York NY 10019 USA

Koenekamp, Fred — Cinematographer
9222 Corbin Ave, #402, Northridge CA 91324, USA

Koenig, Ezra — Singer, Guitarist (Vampire Weekend)
Monotone Inc, 820 Seward St, Los Angeles CA 90038, USA

Koenig, Walter — Actor
PO Box 4395, Valley Village CA 91617, USA

Koepp, David — Director, Writer
Creative Artists Agency, 2000 Ave of Stars, #100, Los Angeles CA 90067 USA

Koester, Helmut H K E — Theologian
12 Flintlock Road, Lexington MA 02420, USA

Koffigoh, Joseph Kokou — Prime Minister, Togo
Regional Integration Ministry, Lome, Togo

Kofler, Andreas — Ski Jumper
A-Sponsoring, Spengergasse 37/3, 1050 Vienna, Austria

Kofoed, Bart — Basketball Player
10161 Foxhall Dr, Charlotte NC 28210, USA

Kofoed, Seana — Actress
Greene Assoc, 1901 Ave of Stars, #130, Los Angeles CA 90067 USA

Kogan, Pavel L — Concert Violinist, Conductor
Bryusov Per 8/10, #19, 103009 Moscow, Russia

Kogan, Theo — Singer (Lunachicks), Actress
Wilhelmina Creative Mgmt, 300 Park Ave S, #200, New York NY 10010, USA

Kogen, Jay K — Producer, Writer, Actor
Paradigm Agency, 360 N Crescent Dr, North Building, Beverly Hills CA 90210 USA

Kohan, David — Producer
Vision Art Mgmt, 530 N Larchmont Blvd, #2, Los Angeles CA 90004, USA

Kohde-Kilsch, Claudia — Tennis Player
Elsa-Brandstrom-Str 22, 66119 Saarbrucken, Germany

Kohl, Ernest — Singer
Nocturnal Artists, 170 W End Ave, #3T, New York NY 10023, USA

Kohl, Helmut — Chancellor, Germany
Marbacherstr 11, 67071 Ludwigshafen/Rhein-Obbersheim, Germany

Kohlberg, Jerome, Jr — Financier
155 Crow Hill Road, Mount Kisco NY 10549, USA

Kohlbrand, Joe — Football Player
3709 Indian River Dr, Cocoa FL 32926, USA

Kohler, Juliane — Actress
Agentur Jarzyk-Holter, Sophienstr 21, 10178 Berlin, Germany

Kohler, Jurgen — Soccer Player
V f R Aalen, Gmunder Str 16, 73430 Aalen, Germany

Kohler, Sheila — Writer
Margaret Hanbury, 27 Walcott Square, London SE11 4UB, England

Kohlmeier, Ryan — Baseball Player
301 Vine St, Cottonwood Falls KS 66845, USA

Kohls, Kris — Drummer (Adema)
Novi Entertainment, PO Box 17077, Beverly Hills CA 90209, USA

K

Kohlsaat, Peter
420 N 5th St, #707, Minneapolis MN 55401, USA — Cartoonist (Single Slices)
Kohn, A Eugene
Kohn Pedersen Fox Assoc, 111 W 57th St, #300, New York NY 10019, USA — Architect
Kohn, Joseph J
32 Sturges Way, Princeton NJ 08540, USA — Mathematician
Kohn, Mike
US Bobsled/Skeleton Federation, 1631 Mesa Ave, #A, Colorado Springs CO 80906 USA — Bobsled Athlete
Kohn, Walter
236 La Vista Grande, Santa Barbara CA 93103, USA — Nobel Chemistry Laureate
Kohner, Susan
John Weitz Inc, 3 E 66th St, #2C, New York NY 10065, USA — Actress
Kohoutek, Lubos
Corthumstr 5, 21029 Hamburg, Germany — Astronomer
Kohrs, Robert H (Bob)
2910 E Nance St, Mesa AZ 85213, USA — Football Player
Koirala, Manisha
302 Beachwood Towers, Yari Rd, Versova, Andheri (W), Mumbai 400061, India — Actress
Koivu, Mikko S
Minnesota Wild, XCel Energy Arena, 1275 Saint Antoine W, Saint Paul MN 55104 USA — Ice Hockey Player
Koivu, Saku A
2200-201 Portage Ave, Winnipeg MB R3B 3L3, Canada — Ice Hockey Player
Kojac, George
33 Arboles del Norte, Fort Pierce FL 34951, USA — Swimmer
Kojima, Ariko
Miss Universe Organization, 1370 Ave of Americas, #1600, New York NY 10019 USA — Beauty Queen
Kojis, Donald R (Don)
8186 Commercial St, La Mesa CA 91942, USA — Basketball Player
Kojovic, Lora
Craig Wyckoff Assoc, 11350 Ventura Blvd, #100, Studio City CA 91604, USA — Actress
Kok Oudegeest, Mary
Escuela Nacional de Natacion, Izarra, Alava, Spain — Swimmer
Kok, Willem (Wim)
Dijsselhofplantsoen 12, 1077 BL, Amersterdam, Netherlands — Prime Minister, Netherlands
Kokesh, Chris
1111B NW 131st Way, Vancouver WA 98685, USA — Singer, Fiddle Player (Misty River)
Kokonin, Vladimir
Bolshoi Theater, Teatralnaya Pl 1, 103009 Moscow, Russia — Opera, Ballet Executive
Kolander, Steve
Sussman Assoc, 1222 16th Ave S, #300, Nashville TN 37212, USA — Singer, Guitarist, Songwriter
Kolb Thomas, Claudia A
Stanford University, Athletic Dept, Stanford CA 94305, USA — Swimmer, Coach
Kolb, Brandon
2043 Pine Oak Place, Danville CA 94506, USA — Baseball Player
Kolb, Edward W (Rocky)
Fermi National Accelerator Laboratory, PO Box 500, Batavia IL 60510 USA — Cosmologist
Kolb, Gary A
5143 Hopewell Dr, Charleston WV 25313, USA — Baseball Player
Kolb, Jon P
1775 McDowell St, Sharon PA 16146, USA — Football Player
Kolbe, James T (Jim)
German Marshall Fund, 1744 R St NW, Washington DC 20009, USA — Representative, AZ
Kolber, Suzy
ESPN-TV, ESPN Plaza, 935 Middle St, Bristol CT 06010 USA — Sportscaster
Kolbert, Kathryn
Center for Reproductive Law & Policy, 120 Wall St, New York NY 10005, USA — Attorney
Kolden, Scott
293 N State College Blvd, #1025, Orange CA 92868, USA — Actor
Kole, Kelly
PO Box 226, Hartsdale NY 10530, USA — Actress, Model
Kole, Warren
Paul Kohner, 9300 Wilshire Blvd, #555, Beverly Hills CA 90212 USA — Actor
Kolehmaisen, Mikko
Poppelitie 18, 50130 Mikkeli, Finland — Canoeing Athlete
Kolen, J Michael (Mike)
1613 Manchester Lane, Birmingham AL 35243, USA — Football Player
Kolirin, Eran
I C M Partners, 10250 Constellation Blvd, #900, Los Angeles CA 90067 USA — Director
Kolius, John
103 S Y St, La Porte TX 77571, USA — Yachtsman
Kollar, Trudi Eberle
Pozsar's Gymnastics Academy, 2709 El Camino Ave, Sacramento CA 95821, USA — Gymnast
Koller, Arnold
Steinegg, Gschwendes 8, 9050 Appenzell, Switzerland — President, Switzerland
Kollhoff, Hans
Kurfursendamm 178-179, 10707 Berlin, Germany — Architect
Kollner, Eberhard
An der Trainierbahn 7, 11536 Neuenhagen, Germany — Cosmonaut, East Germany
Kollo, Rene
Pran Event Gmbh, Ralf Sellelberg, An der Brucke 18, 26180 Rastede, Germany — Opera Singer
Kolm, Henry V
Weir Meadow Road, Wayland MA 01778, USA — Electrical Engineer (Magnetic Train)
Kolodner, Richard D
Dana-Farber Cancer Institute, 44 Binney St, Boston MA 02115, USA — Biochemist, Cancer Researcher
Kolodziej, Ross A
1123 Sandalwood Dr, Lawrenceville GA 30043, USA — Football Player
Koloskov, Alex
2320 Rose Walk Dr, Alpharetta GA 30005, USA — Photographer
Kolpakova, Irina A
American Ballet Theatre, 890 Broadway, #300, New York NY 10003 USA — Ballerina
Kolstad, Dean
15492 Brooklodge Road, Hickory Corners MI 49060, USA — Ice Hockey Player
Kolstad, Harold E (Hal)
15149 Bel Escou Dr, San Jose CA 95124, USA — Baseball Player
Kolsti, Paul
Dallas News, Editorial Dept, Communications Center, Dallas TX 75265, USA — Editorial Cartoonist

K

Koltai, Lajos
Gersh Agency, 9465 Wilshire Blvd, #600, Beverly Hills CA 90212 USA — Cinematographer, Director

Kolvenbach, Peter-Hans
Borgo Santo Spirito 5, CP 6139, 00195 Rome, Italy — Religious Leader

Kolzig, Olaf
2030 Carolina Ave NE, Saint Petersburg FL 33703, USA — Ice Hockey Player

Koman, William J (Bill)
5 Upper Ladue Road, Saint Louis MO 63124, USA — Football Player

Komar, Vitaly
55 Lisspenard St, New York NY 10013, USA — Artist

Komenich, Kim
111 Cornelia Ave, Mill Valley CA 94941, USA — Photojournalist

Kometani, Pam
4342 Kilauea Ave, Honolulu HI 96816, USA — Golfer

Komine, Shane
641 8th Ave, Honolulu HI 96816, USA — Baseball Player

Komleva, Gabriela T
Fontanka Nab 116, #34, 198005 Saint Petersburg, Russia — Ballerina

Komlos, Peter
Sport-U 6, 2083 Solymar, Hungary — Concert Violinist

Komminski, Brad L
688 Fallside Lane, Westerville OH 43081, USA — Baseball Player

Komorowski, Bronislaw M
Palac Prezydencki, Ul Krakowskie Przedmiescie 48, 00 071 Warsaw, Poland — President, Poland

Komsic, Zeljko
President's Office, Marsala Titz 7, 71000 Sarajevo, Bosnia & Herzegovina — President, Bosnia & Herzegovina

Komunyakaa, Yusef
900 W State St, Trenton NY 08618, USA — Writer

Kon Artis
Coast to Coast Talent, 3350 Barham Blvd, Los Angeles CA 90068 USA — Rap Artist (D-12)

Koncak, Jon
PO Box 10040, Jackson WY 83002, USA — Basketball Player

Koncar, Mark
447 N Alpine Blvd, Alpine UT 84004, USA — Football Player

Konchalovsky, Andrei
Weissmann Wolff Bergman, 9665 Wilshire Blvd, #900, Beverly Hills CA 90212, USA — Director

Kondakova, Elena V
Scientific Industrial Assn, Utica Lenina 4A, 141070 Kaliningrad, Russia — Cosmonaut

Kondla, Thomas A (Tom)
3517 Cleveland Ave, Brookfield IL 60513, USA — Basketball Player

Kondo, Jun
A I S T, Tsukuba Central 2, Tsukuba, Ibaraki 305 8568, Japan — Theoretical Physicist

Kondrattyeva, Marina V
Bolshoi Theater, Teatralnaya Pl 1, 103009 Moscow, Russia — Ballerina

Kondratyev, Dmitri Y
Cosmonaut Training Center, Star City, 141160 Zvezdny Gorodok, Moscow Oblast, Russia — Cosmonaut

Konerko, Paul J
8053 E Leaning Rock Road, Scottsdale AZ 85266, USA — Baseball Player

Kong, Venice
Playboy Promotions, 2706 Media Center Dr, Los Angeles CA 90065 USA — Model, Actress

Konieczny, Douglas J (Doug)
9503 Dundalk St, Spring TX 77379, USA — Baseball Player

Konik, George
1027 Savannah Road, Saint Paul MN 55123, USA — Ice Hockey Player

Konitz, Lee
Bennett Morgan, 1022 RR 376, #3, Wappinger Falls NY 12590 USA — Jazz Saxophonist

Konkol, Mark
Chicago Sun-Times, Editorial Dept, 401 N Wabash Ave, Chicago IL 60611 USA — Journalist

Kono, Tamio (Tommy)
98-2025 Hapaki St, Aiea HI 96701, USA — Weightlifter

Kononenko, Oleg D
Cosmonaut Training Center, Star City, 141160 Zvezdny Gorodok, Moscow Oblast, Russia — Cosmonaut

Konrad, Cathy
Tree Line Films, 1708 Berkeley St, Santa Monica CA 90404, USA — Producer

Konrad, John H
Hughes Space-Communications Group, PO Box 92919, Los Angeles CA 90009, USA — Astronaut

Konrad, Robert L (Rob), Jr
11884 Windmill Lake Dr, Boynton Beach FL 33473, USA — Football Player

Konroyd, Steve
317 S Park Ave, Hinsdale IL 60521, USA — Ice Hockey Player

Konstantinov, Vladimir
6782 Enclave, West Bloomfield MI 48322, USA — Ice Hockey Player

Kont, Paul
Doblinger Music, Dorotheergasse 10, 1011 Vienna, Austria — Composer

Kontos, Christopher (Chris)
40 Beck Blvd, Penetanguishene ON L9M 1E1, Canada — Hockey Player

Konuszewski, Dennis J
3054 Yorkshire Dr, Bay City MI 48706, USA — Baseball Player

Konyukhov, Fedor F
Tourism/Sports Union, Studeniy Proyezd 7, 129282 Moscow, Russia — Explorer

Kool Moe Dee
Celebrity Talent Agency, 111 E 14th St, #249, New York NY 10003 USA — Rap Artist

Koolhaas, Rem
Metropolitan Architecture, Heer Bokelweg 149, 3032 Rotterdam, Netherlands — Architect

Koolman, Olindo
Governor's Office, L G Smith Blvd 76, Oranjestad, Aruba — Governor, Aruba

Koonce, George E, Jr
925 E Wells St, #217, Milwaukee WI 53202, USA — Football Player

Koonce, Graham
2474 Pimlico Place, Alpine CA 91901, USA — Baseball Player

Koones, Charles C
Variety Inc, Publisher's Office, 360 Park Ave S, New York NY 10010, USA — Publisher

Koons, Jeff
Jeff Koons Productions, 601 W 29th St, New York NY 10001, USA — Artist, Sculptor

Koontz, Dean R
PO Box 9529, Newport Beach CA 92658, USA — Writer

Koop, C Everett
3 Ivy Pointe Way, Hanover NH 03755, USA — Physician, Government Official

Kooper, Al
Concerted Efforts, PO Box 440326, Somerville MA 02144 USA — Singer, Guitarist

Koopman, A Ton G M
Meerweg 23, 1405 BC Bussu, Netherlands — Conductor, Concert Keyboardist

Koopmans-Kint, Cor
Pacific Sands C''Van Park, Nambucca Heads NSW 2448, Australia — Swimmer

Kooser, Ted
1820 Branched Oak Road, Garland NE 68360, USA — Writer

Koosman, Jerry M
2483 State Road 35, Osceola WI 54020, USA — Baseball Player

Kopacz, George F
14150 Somerset Court, Orland Park IL 60467, USA — Baseball Player

Kopatchinskaja, Patricia
Maren Borchers, Schlüterstrasse 36, 10629 Berlin, Germany — Concert Violinist

Kopay, David M (Dave)
100 W Highland Dr, #102, Seattle WA 98119, USA — Football Player

Kopecky, Tomas
4401 N Federal Highway, #201, Boca Raton FL 33431, USA — Ice Hockey Player

Kopell, Bernard M (Bernie)
Amsel Eisenstadt Frazier, 5055 Wilshire Blvd, #865, Los Angeles CA 90036 USA — Actor

Kopeloff, Eric
I C M Partners, 10250 Constellation Blvd, #900, Los Angeles CA 90067 USA — Producer

Kopelson, Arnold
Kopelson Entertainment, 8560 Sunset Blvd, West Hollywood CA 90069, USA — Producer

Koper, Herbert L (Bud)
1225 Lakeshore Dr, #118, Edmond OK 73013, USA — Basketball Player

Kopervas, Gary
King Features Syndicate, 300 W 57th St, #1500, New York NY 10019 USA — Cartoonist (Out on a Limb)

Kopicki, Joseph G (Joe)
47608 Cheryl Court, Shelby Township MI 48315, USA — Basketball Player

Kopins, Karen
Sutton-Barth Vennari, 145 S Fairfax Ave, #310, Los Angeles CA 90036 USA — Actress

Kopit, Arthur
207 W 106th St, #7D, New York NY 10025, USA — Writer

Koplan, Jeffrey
Emory University, Academic Health Affairs Dept, Atlanta GA 30322, USA — Medical Administrator

Koplitz, Howard D (Howie)
623 Boyd St, Oshkosh WI 54901, USA — Baseball Player

Koplitz, Lynne
Paradigm Agency, 360 N Crescent Dr, North Building, Beverly Hills CA 90210 USA — Actress

Koplove, Michael P (Mike)
3235 Chaucer St, Philadelphia PA 19145, USA — Baseball Player

Kopp, Jeffrey B (Jeff)
13752 Deer Chase Place, Jacksonville FL 32224, USA — Football Player

Kopp, Wendy
Teach for America Foundation, 315 W 36th St, #700, New York NY 10018, USA — Association Executive

Koppel, Ted
3505 Belfont Dr, Ellicot City MD 21043, USA — Commentator

Koppelman, Brian
Creative Artists Agency, 2000 Ave of Stars, #100, Los Angeles CA 90067 USA — Director, Writer

Koppelman, Chaim
141 Wooster St, #6C, New York NY 10012, USA — Artist

Koppen, Daniel (Dan)
1807 Old Bridge Lane, Bellingham MA 02019, USA — Football Player

Kopper, Hilmar
DaimlerChrysler AG, Mercedestr 137, 70237 Stuttgart, Germany — Financier

Kopperud, Gunnar
Bloomsbury Publishing, 36 Soho Square, London W1D 3Q4, England — Writer

Koppes, Peter
M O B Agency, 6404 Wilshire Blvd, #505, Los Angeles CA 90048 USA — Guitarist (Church)

Kopple, Barbara J
Inphenate, 9701 Wilshire Blvd, #1000, Beverly Hills CA 90212 USA — Director

Kopra, Timothy L
4912 Cross Creek Lane, League City TX 77573, USA — Astronaut

Koprowski, Hilary
334 Fairhill Road, Wynnewood PA 19096, USA — Microbiologist

Koptchak, Sergei
Robert Lombardo Assoc, Harkness Plaza, 61 W 62nd St, #6F, New York NY 10023 USA — Opera Singer

Korab, Jamie
Curling Assn, 1660 Vimont Court, Cumberland ON K4A 4J4, Canada — Curling Athlete

Korab, Jerry
Korab Inc, 960 N Weigel Ave, Elmhurst IL 60126, USA — Ice Hockey Player

Koralek, Paul G
7 Chalcot Road, #1, London NW1 8LH, England — Architect

Korbut, Olga V
16356 N Thompson Peak Parkway, #2024, Scottsdale AZ 85260, USA — Gymnast

Korcheck, Stephen J (Steve)
6424 98th St E, Bradenton FL 34202, USA — Baseball Player

Korcia, Laurent
E M I Records, 18 Rue de la Convention, 75-15 Paris, France — Concert Violinist

Kord, Kazimierz
Ul Nadarzynska 37A, 05 805 Kanie-Otrebusy, Poland — Conductor

Korda, Jessica
Ladies Pro Golf Assn, 100 International Golf Dr, Daytona Beach FL 32124 USA — Golfer

Korda, Michael V
Simon & Schuster, 1230 Ave of Americas, Concourse 1, New York NY 10020, USA — Writer

Korda, Petr
4909 61st Ave Dr W, Bradenton FL 34210, USA — Tennis Player

Korder, Howard
I C M Partners, 10250 Constellation Blvd, #900, Los Angeles CA 90067 USA — Writer

Korec, Jan Chryzostom Cardinal
Biskupstvo Nitra, PP 46A, 95050 Nitra, Slovakia — Religious Leader

Korecky, Robert J (Bobby)
209 Culver Road, Monmouth Junction NJ 08852, USA — Baseball Player

K

Koren, Christine (Chris) — Model
Playboy Promotions, 2706 Media Center Dr, Los Angeles CA 90065 USA
Koren, Edward B — Cartoonist
PO Box 464, Brookfield VT 05036, USA
Koren, Steve — Writer, Producer
Creative Artists Agency, 2000 Ave of Stars, #100, Los Angeles CA 90067 USA
Korf, Mia — Actress
Don Buchwald/Fortitude, 6500 Wilshire Blvd, #2200, Los Angeles CA 90048 USA
Korie, Michael — Librettist
I C M Partners, 10250 Constellation Blvd, #900, Los Angeles CA 90067 USA
Korince, George E — Baseball Player
710-610 Lake St, Saint Catherines ON L2N 5T1, Canada
Korine, Harmony — Director
Creative Artists Agency, 2000 Ave of Stars, #100, Los Angeles CA 90067 USA
Kormakur, Baltasar — Director
Blueeyes Productions, Seljaveg 2, 101 Reykjavik, Iceland
Korman, Maxime Carlot — Prime Minister, Vanuatu
PO Box 698, Port Vila, Vanuatu
Kormann, Manuela — Curling Athlete
Curling Assn, PO Box 606, 3000 Bern, Switzerland
Korn, Jim — Ice Hockey Player
19679 Sweetwater Curve, Excelsior MN 55331, USA
Korn, Lester B — Businessman
466 Lexington Ave, #237, New York NY 10017, USA
Kornberg, Roger D — Nobel Chemistry Laureate
345 Walsh Road, Atherton CA 94027, USA
Kornet, Frank — Basketball Player
9580 Stanton Road, Lantana TX 76226, USA
Kornfeld, Stuart A — Hematologist
Washington University Medical School, Clinical Science Dept, Saint Louis MO 63110, USA
Kornheiser, Anthony I (Tony) — Sportswriter, Sportscaster
ESPN-TV, ESPN Plaza, 935 Middle St, Bristol CT 06010 USA
Koroll, Cliff — Ice Hockey Player
23W569 Glendale Terrace, Roselle IL 60172, USA
Koroma, Ernest Bai — President, Sierra Leone
President's Office, State House, Independence Ave, Freetown, Sierra Leone
Koronka, John — Baseball Player
1403 10th St, Clermont FL 34711, USA
Korot, Alla — Actress
Stone Manners Salners, 9911 W Pico Blvd, #1400, Los Angeles CA 90035 USA
Kors, Michael — Fashion Designer
11 W 42nd St, #2000, New York NY 10036, USA
Kortas, Kenneth C (Ken) — Football Player
466 Brooks Lane, Simpsonville KY 40067, USA
Korte, Steven J (Steve) — Football Player
137 Dunleith Lane, Mandeville LA 70471, USA
Korver, Kyle E — Basketball Player
1483 Wesleys Run, Gladwyne PA 19035, USA
Korver, Paul — Actor
Gersh Agency, 9465 Wilshire Blvd, #600, Beverly Hills CA 90212 USA
Korzeniowski, Abel — Composer
Evolution Music Partners, 1680 N Vine St, #500, Los Angeles CA 90028 90028, USA
Korzun, Valery G — Cosmonaut
Cosmonaut Training Center, Star City, 141160 Zvezdny Gorodok, Moscow Oblast, Russia
K-OS — Rap Artist, Songwriter
Agency Group Ltd, 142 W 57th St, #600, New York NY 10019 USA
Kosar, Bernie J, Jr — Football Player
PO Box 8, Nashport OH 43830, USA
Kosar, Scott — Writer
Gotham Group, 9255 Sunset Blvd. Suite 515. Los Angeles, CA 90069, USA
Kosco, Andrew J (Andy) — Baseball Player
10324 Springfield Road, Youngstown OH 44514, USA
Koshalek, Richard — Museum Executive
Museum of Contemporary Art, 250 S Grand Ave, Los Angeles CA 90012, USA
Koshansky, Joseph S (Joe) — Baseball Player
13314 Point Pleasant Dr, Fairfax VA 22033, USA
Koshiba, Masatoshi — Nobel Physics Laureate
University of Tokyo, 7-3-1 Hongo, Nunkyoku, Tokyo 113 8654, Japan
Koshiro, Matsumoto, IV — Kabuki Actor, Dancer
Kabukiza Theatre, 12-15-4 Ginza, Chuoku, Tokyo 104 0061, Japan
Kosier, Kyle B — Football Player
8943 E Calle del Palo Verde, Scottsdale AZ 85255, USA
Koski, Tony — Basketball Player
143 King James Dr, South Dennis MA 02660, USA
Koski, William J (Bill) — Baseball Player
1120 Valencia Court, Modesto CA 95350, USA
Koskie, Cordel L (Corey) — Baseball Player
161 Primrose Lane, Hamel MN 55340, USA
Koskinen, John — Government Official
Federal Home Loan Mortgage Corp, 8100 Jones Branch Dr, McLean VA 22102, USA
Koskoff, Sarah — Actress
Anonymous Content, 3532 Hayden Ave, Culver City CA 90232 USA
Koslofski, Kevin C — Baseball Player
1910 Shore Oak Dr, Decatur IL 62521, USA
Koslow, Lauren — Actress
Michael Bruno, 13576 Cheltenham Dr, Sherman Oaks CA 91423, USA
Kosmalski, Lenonard J (Len) — Basketball Player
404 Washington Ave, #PH 8, Miami Beach FL 33139, USA
Kosminsky, Peter — Director
United Agents, 12-26 Lexington St, London W1F 0LE, England
Koss, Alan — Actor
I C M Partners, 10250 Constellation Blvd, #900, Los Angeles CA 90067 USA
Koss, Johann Olav — Speed Skater
Dagaliveien 21, 0387 Oslo, Norway
Koss, John C — Inventor
Koss Corp, 4129 N Port Washington Ave, Milwaukee WI 53212, USA

Koren - Koss

Kostabi, Mark Kostabi World, 514 W 24th St, New York NY 10011, USA	Artist, Sculptor, Composer
Kostadinova, Stefka Rue Anghel Kantchev 4, 1000 Sofia, Bulgaria	Track Athlete
Kostelecki, David Palackeho 127, 66461 Holasice, Czech Republic	Marksman
Kostelic, Ivica Trg Sportova 11, 10000 Zagreb, Croatia	Alpine Skier
Kostelic, Janica Medvedgradsken 45A, 10000 Zagreb, Croatia	Alpine Skier
Koster, Steven J 26881 Goya Circle, Mission Viejo CA 92691, USA	Cinematographer
Kostic, Goran Agence Christine Parat 9 Rue de Maubeuge 75009 Paris France	Actor
Kostomarov, Roman Skating Federation, Luchnesksaia Nab 8, 119871 Moscow, Russia	Ice Dancer
Kostov, Ivan Blvd Rakovski 134, 1000 Sofia, Bulgaria	Prime Minister, Bulgaria
Kostova, Elizabeth J Little Brown, 3 Center Plaza, #100, Boston MA 02108 USA	Writer
Kostro, Frederick C (Frank) 3161 S Jasmine Way, Denver CO 80222, USA	Baseball Player
Kostroff, Michael Zero Gravity Mgmt, 10 Universal City Plaza, #2000, Universal City CA 91608, USA	Actor
Kosugi, Kane Destiny Production, 3-19-2 Shiba, Minatoku, Tokyo 105 0014, Japan	Actor
Kosugi, Sho Sho Kosugi Productions, 6381 Hollywood Blvd, #280, Los Angeles CA 90028, USA	Actor
Koszelak, Stanley N 1125 Mendocino Way, Redlands CA 92374, USA	Biochemist
Kotalik, Ales 17681 Hackberry Court, Eden Prairie MN 55347, USA	Ice Hockey Player
Kotb, Hoda NBC-TV, News Dept, 30 Rockefeller Plaza, #270E, New York NY 10112 USA	Commentator
Kotcheff, W Theodore (Ted) Baumgarten Management & Productions, 406 Wilshire Blvd, Santa Monica CA 90401, USA	Director
Kotchman, Casey J 8442 125th Court, Seminole FL 33776, USA	Baseball Player
Koteas, Elias United Talent Agency, 9336 Civic Center Dr, Beverly Hills CA 90210 USA	Actor
Kotelnik, Andreas Universum Boxing Promotion, Am Stadtrand 27, 22047 Hamburg, Germany	Boxer
Koterba, Jeff Omaha World Herald, Editorial Dept, 14th & Dodge St, Omaha NE 68102, USA	Sports, Editorial Cartoonist
Kotite, Richard E (Rich) 241 Fanning St, Staten Island NY 10314, USA	Football Player, Coach
Kotlarek, Gene 4910 Walking Horse Point, Colorado Springs CO 80923, USA	Skier
Kotlayakov, Vladimir M Profsoyuznaya St 43-1-80, 117420 Moscow, Russia	Geographer, Glacierologist
Kotov, Oleg V Cosmonaut Training Center, Star City, 141160 Zvezdny Gorodok, Moscow Oblast, Russia	Cosmonaut
Kotova, Nina I M G Artists, Hogarth Business Park, Chiswick, London W4 2TH, England	Concert Cellist
Kotsay, Mark S 6659 Calle Ponte Bella, Rancho Santa Fe CA 92091, USA	Baseball Player
Kotsonis, Ieronymous Archdiocese of Athens, Hatzichristou 8, Athens 402, Greece 53212, USA	Religious Leader
Kottaras, George 167 Cartmel Dr, Markham ON L3S 1W6, Canada	Baseball Player
Kottke, Leo Chuck Morris Entertainment, 930 W 7th Ave, Denver CO 80204, USA	Singer, Songwriter, Guitarist
Kotto, Yaphet F Rival Agency, 9157 Sunset Blvd, #212, West Hollywood CA 90069, USA	Actor
Kotulak, Ronald Chicago Tribune, Editorial Dept, 435 N Michigan Ave, #1, Chicago IL 60611, USA	Editor
Kotzky, Alex S 25 Highfield Road, Glen Cove NY 11542, USA	Cartoonist (Apartment 3-G)
Kouchner, Bernard L'Action d'Humanitaire, 8 Ave de Segur, 75350 Paris, France	Physician; Government Official, France
Koudelka, Josef Magnum Photos, 19 Rue Hegesippe Moneau, 75018 Paris, France	Photographer
Koufax, Sanford (Sandy) 106 Amy Ann Lane, Vero Beach FL 32963, USA	Baseball Player
Koufos, Konstantine D (Kosta) Denver Nuggets, Pepsi Center, 1000 Chopper Circle, Denver CO 80204 USA	Basketball Player
Kournikova, Anna 2345 Lake Ave, Sunset Isle 3, Miami Beach FL 33140, USA	Tennis Player, Model
Koutouvides, Niko S 129 9th Lane, Kirkland WA 98033, USA	Football Player
Kouzmanoff, Kevin 28606 Evergreen Manor Dr, Evergreen CO 80439, USA	Baseball Player
Kovacevich, Stephen C M Artists, 127 W 96th St, #13B, New York NY 10025 USA	Concert Pianist, Conductor
Kovach, Bill Harvard University, Nieman Fellows Program, Cambridge MA 02138, USA	Editor, Foundation Executive
Kovacic, Ernst Im Muehlfeld 3, 2102 Bisamberg, Austria	Concert Violinist
Kovacs, Andras Magyar Jakobinusok Ter 2/3, 1122 Budapest, Hungary	Director
Kovacs, Denes Iranyi Utca 12, 1053 Budapest V, Hungary	Concert Violinist
Kovacs, Istvan (Koko) Box Utca, Bajcsy Zs, Ut 21, 1065 Budapest, Hungary	Boxer
Kovalainen, Heikki J Caterham Motorsport Kennet Road Dartford Kent DA1 4QN, England	Auto Racing Driver

V.I.P. Address Book

K

Kahn - Kovalainen

Kovalchuk, Ilja V — Ice Hockey Player
5509 Long Island Dr NW, Atlanta GA 30327, USA

Kovalenko, Andrei — Ice Hockey Player
Kontinental Hockey League, 20/2 Ovchinnikovskaya, 115035 Moscow, Russia

Kovalenok, Vladimir S — Cosmonaut, Air Force General
3 Hovanskaya St, #22, 129515 Moscow, Russia

Kovalev, Alexei V — Ice Hockey Player
676 Riversville Road, Greenwich CT 6831, USA

Kovalevsky, Jean — Astronomer
Villa La Padovane, 8 Rue Saint Michel, Saint-Antoine, 06130 Grasse, France

Kovatchev, Julian — Conductor
I M G Artists, Hogarth Business Park, Chiswick, London W4 2TH, England

Kove, Martin — Actor
Rogues Gallery, 9107 Wilshire Blvd, #450, Beverly Hills CA 90210, USA

Kowal, Charles T — Astronomer
Space Telescope Science Institute, Homewood Campus, Baltimore MD 21218, USA

Kowalczyk, Ed — Singer, Guitarist (Live)
Monterey Peninsula Artists, 404 W Franklin St, Monterey CA 93940 USA

Kowalczyk, Jozef — Religious Leader
Nuncjatura Apostolska, Al J Ch Szucha 12, #163, 00 582 Warsaw, Poland

Kowalczyk, Justyna — Cross Country Skier
Budynek Poiskiego Radia, Ul Karkonoska 10, 53 015 Wroclaw, Poland

Kowalczyk, Walter J (Walt) — Football Player
144 W Maryknoll Road, Rochester Hills CA 48309, USA

Kowalewicz, Ben — Singer (Billy Talent)
Big Machine Media, 579 Lexington Ave, #400, New York NY 10022, USA

Kowalik, Trent — Actor
Gersh Agency, 41 Madison Ave, #3301, New York NY 10010 USA

Kowalkowski, Scott T — Football Player
3995 Kelsey Road, Lake Orion MI 48360, USA

Kowitz, Brian M — Baseball Player
1657 Bullock Circle, Owings Mills MD 21117, USA

Koy, Ernest M (Ernie), Jr — Football Player
PO Box 6, Kenney TX 77452, USA

Koy, J Theo (Ted) — Football Player
1225 County Road 155, Georgetown TX 78626, USA

Koy, Jo — Actor, Comedian, Writer
Creative Artists Agency, 2000 Ave of Stars, #100, Los Angeles CA 90067 USA

Koyagialo, Louis Alphonse — Premier, Congo Democratic Republic
Prime Minister's Office, Kinshasa, Congo Democratic Republic

Koyama, Debbie — Golfer
118 Tranquila Dr, Camarillo CA 93012, USA

Koyamada, Shin — Actor
Shannon Murphy, 8224A Santa Monica Blvd, #721, West Hollywood CA 90046, USA

Koz, Dave — Jazz Saxophonist, Flutist
5850 W 3rd St, #307, Los Angeles CA 90036, USA

Kozak, Donald (Don) — Ice Hockey Player
1510 E Beacon Dr, Gilbert AZ 85234, USA

Kozak, Harley Jane — Actress
TalentWorks, 3500 W Olive Ave, #1400, Burbank CA 91505 USA

Kozak, Scott A — Football Player
18617 S Grasle Road, Oregon City OR 97045, USA

Kozar, Heather — Model, Actress
C E S D, 10635 Santa Monica Blvd, #130, Los Angeles CA 90025 USA

Kozeev, Konstantin M — Cosmonaut
Cosmonaut Training Center, Star City, 141160 Zvezdny Gorodok, Moscow Oblast, Russia

Kozelko, Thomas W (Tom) — Basketball Player
6200 Peninsula Dr, Traverse City MI 49686, USA

Kozena, Magdalena — Opera Singer
Narodni Divadlo, Dvorakova 11, 60000 Brno, Czech Republic

Kozerski, Bruce — Football Player
3088 Waterbury Court, Edgewood KY 41017, USA

Kozinski, Alex — Judge
US Court of Appeals, 125 S Grand Ave, Pasadena CA 91105, USA

Koziol, John C — Air Force General
Deputy CinC, Intelligence & Surveillance, HqUSAF, Pentagon, Washington DC 20330 USA

Kozlicki, Ronald F (Ron) — Basketball Player
5002 Hidden Branches Dr, Atlanta GA 30338, USA

Kozlov, Akexey S — Jazz Saxophonist, Band Leader, Composer
Shchepkin Str 25, #28, 129090 Moscow, Russia

Kozlov, Viktor N — Ice Hockey Player
363 Merlin Way, Plantation FL 33324, USA

Kozlov, Vyacheslav A — Ice Hockey Player
H C Dynamo Moscow, Ul East 2, Building 2, 125167 Moscow, Russia

Kozlova, Valentina — Ballerina
New York City Ballet, Lincoln Center Plaza, New York NY 10023 USA

Kozlowski, Ben — Baseball Player
9083 Briarwood Dr, Seminole FL 33772, USA

Kozlowski, Brian S — Football Player
61 E Shore Dr, Niantic CT 06357, USA

Kozlowski, Glen A — Football Player
455 Belmont Place, #262, Provo UT 84606, USA

Kozlowski, Linda — Actress
Bedford & Pearce, 19 Abbotsford Road, Katoomba NSW 2780, Australia

Kozlowski, Michael J (Mike) — Football Player
932 NW 110th Ave, Plantation FL 33324, USA

Koznick, Kristina — Alpine Skier
PO Box 85, Wolcott CO 81655, USA

Kozol, Jonathan — Writer
PO Box 145, Byfield MA 01922, USA

Kraatz, Victor — Figure Skater
Connecticut Skating Center, 300 Alumni Road, Newington CT 06111, USA

Kraayeveld, Cathrine H — Basketball Player
Atlanta Dream, 83 Walton St NW, #400, Atlanta, GA 30303 USA

Krabbe, Jeroen — Actor
Van Eeghaustraat 107, 1071 EZ Amsterdam, Netherlands

Krabbe, Tim
Bloomsbury Publishing, 36 Soho Square, London W1D 3Q4, England — Writer

Krabbe-Zimmermann, Katrin
Dorfstr 9, 17091 Pinnow, Germany — Track Athlete

Krackow, Jurgen
Schumannstr 100, 40237 Dusseldorf, Germany — Businessman

Kraemer, Harry J
Baxter International, 1 Baxter Parkway, Deerfield IL 60015, USA — Businessman

Kraemer, Joseph W (Joe)
3212 NE 401st Circle, La Center WA 98629, USA — Baseball Player

Kraft, Christopher C (Chris), Jr
14919 Village Elm St, Houston TX 77062, USA — Space Administrator

Kraft, Craig A
931 R St NW, Washington DC 20001, USA — Artist, Sculptor

Kraft, Greg
14820 Rue de Bayonne, #302, Clearwater FL 33762, USA — Golfer

Kraft, Leo A
45 Hill Park Ave, #3E, Great Neck NY 11021, USA — Composer

Kraft, Robert
4722 Noeline Ave, Encino CA 91436, USA — Composer

Kraft, Robert P
University of California, Lick Observatory, Santa Cruz CA 95064, USA — Astrophysicist

Kragen, Greg
1447 Boulevard Way, Walnut Creek CA 94595, USA — Football Player

Kraggerud, Henning
I M G Artists, Hogarth Business Park, Chiswick, London W4 2TH, England — Concert Violinist

Kragthorpe, Steve
University of Louisville, Athletic Dept, Louisville KY 40292, USA — Football Coach

Kraguly, Radovan
Llwyngarth Fawr, Comin Coch, Builth Wells, Powys LD2 3PP, Wales — Artist

Krajicek, Richard
Krajicek Foundation, Olympisch Stadion 3, 1076 DE Amsterdam, Netherlands — Tennis Player

Krakau, Mervin F (Merv)
706 Prairie St, Guthrie Center IA 50115, USA — Football Player

Krakoff, Reed
831 Madison Ave, New York NY 10021, USA — Fashion Designer

Krakoski, Joseph A (Joe)
560 Village Blvd, #37, Incline Village NV 89451, USA — Football Player

Krakowski, Jane
United Talent Agency, 9336 Civic Center Dr, Beverly Hills CA 90210 USA — Actress, Singer

Krall, Diana
S L Feldman Mgmt, 1505 W 2nd Ave, #200, Vancouver BC V6H 3Y4, Canada — Singer, Pianist, Songwriter

Kraly, Steven C (Steve)
12 Davis Ave, Johnson City NY 13790, USA — Baseball Player

Kramarsky, David
1630 Berkeley St, #1, Santa Monica CA 90404, USA — Director

Kramek, Robert E
43 Firefall Court, Spring TX 77380, USA — Coast Guard Admiral

Kramer, Barry D
101 Deanna Court, Schenectady NY 12309, USA — Basketball Player

Kramer, Billy J
Mars Talent, 27 L'Ambiance Court, Nanuet NY 10954 USA — Singer (Billy J Kramer & the Dakotas)

Kramer, Chris
Lucas Talent, 100 W Pender St, #700, Vancouver BC V6B 1RB, Canada — Actor

Kramer, Clare
S M S Talent, 8383 Wilshire Blvd, #230, Beverly Hills CA 90211 USA — Actress

Kramer, Eric Allen
Stone Manners Salners, 9911 W Pico Blvd, #1400, Los Angeles CA 90035 USA — Actor

Kramer, Gerald L (Jerry)
11768 W Chinden Blvd, Garden City ID 83714, USA — Football Player

Kramer, Jeffrey
Innovative Artists, 1505 10th St, Santa Monica CA 90401 USA — Director, Writer

Kramer, Jim
I C M Partners, 10250 Constellation Blvd, #900, Los Angeles CA 90067 USA — Writer

Kramer, Joel B
3817 E Highland Ave, Phoenix AZ 85018, USA — Basketball Player

Kramer, Joseph M (Joey)
Front Line Mgmt, 1100 Glendon Ave, #2000, Los Angeles CA 90024 USA — Drummer (Aerosmith)

Kramer, Kent D
200 Troon Road, McKinney TX 75070, USA — Football Player

Kramer, Larry
Gay Men's Health Crisis, 119 W 24th St, Lobby 1, New York NY 10011, USA — Social Activist, Writer

Kramer, Randall J (Randy)
143 Camino Pacifico, Aptos CA 95003, USA — Baseball Player

Kramer, Stepfanie
Teitelbaum Artists Group, 8840 Wilshire Blvd, #200, Beverly Hills CA 90211, USA — Actress

Kramer, Thomas F (Tommy)
806 Emerald Bay, San Antonio TX 78260, USA — Football Player

Kramer, Thomas J (Tom)
10665 Hamilton Ave, Cincinnati OH 45231, USA — Baseball Player

Kramer, W Erik
5950 Kingham Court, Agoura Hills CA 91301, USA — Football Player

Kramer, Wayne
W M E Entertainment, 9601 Wilshire Blvd, #300, Beverly Hills CA 90210 USA — Director

Kramer, Wayne
I C M Partners, 730 5th Ave, New York NY 10019 USA — Jazz Guitarist (Was Not Was, MC5)

Kramlich, Richard S
Deputy CofS, Installations/Logistics, HqUSMC, Navy St, Washington DC 20380 USA — Marine Corps General

Kramnik, Vladimir
Russian Chess Federation, Luchnetskaya 8, 119270 Moscow, Russia — Chess Player

Kranepool, Edward E (Ed)
M E Promotions, 177 High Pond Dr, Jericho NY 11753, USA — Baseball Player

Krantz, Judith T
166 Groverton Place, Los Angeles CA 90077, USA — Writer

Kranz, Eugene (Gene)
1108 Shady Oak Lane, Dickinson TX 77539, USA — Space Scientist

K

Kranz, Fran — Actor
United Talent Agency, 9336 Civic Center Dr, Beverly Hills CA 90210 USA
Krapek, Karl — Businessman
United Technologies Corp, United Technologies Building, Hartford CT 06101, USA
Krasinski, John — Actor, Comedian
W M E Entertainment, 9601 Wilshire Blvd, #300, Beverly Hills CA 90210 USA
Krasniqi, Luan — Boxer
Oschleweg 10, 78628 Rottweil, Germany
Krasnoff, Eric — Businessman
Pall Corp, 25 Harbor Park Dr, Port Washington NY 11050, USA
Krasny, Yuri — Artist
Sloane Gallery, Oxford Office Building, 1612 17th St, Denver CO 80202, USA
Kratch, Robert A (Bob) — Football Player
10685 County Road 24, Watertown MN 55388, USA
Kratochvilova, Jarmila — Track Athlete
Pod Vysehradem 207, 582 82 Golcuv Jenikov, Czech Republic
Kratzert, Bill — Golfer
7470 Founders Way, Ponte Vedra FL 32082, USA
Kraulis, Andrew — Actor
Rosenthal Agency, 204-14 Prince Arthur Ave, Toronto ON M5R 1A9, Canada
Kraus, Alanna — Speed Skater
Speed Skating Canada, 2781 Lancaster Road, #402, Ottawa ON K1B 1A7, Canada
Kraus, Daniel J (Dan) — Basketball Player
10101 Governor Warfield Parkway, #222, Columbia MD 21044, USA
Kraus, Nicola — Writer
Atria Books, 1230 Ave of Americas, New York NY 10020 USA
Krause, Brian — Actor, Director, Producer
Glick Agency, 1321 7th St, #203, Santa Monica CA 90401 USA
Krause, Chester L — Publisher
Krause Publications, 700 E State St, Iola WI 54990, USA
Krause, Paul J — Football Player
Pinewood Golf Course, Real Estate Dept, 18150 Waco St NW, Elk River MN 55330, USA
Krause, Peter — Actor
Creative Artists Agency, 2000 Ave of Stars, #100, Los Angeles CA 90067 USA
Krause, Richard M — Immunologist
4000 Cathedral Ave NW, #134B, Washington DC 20016, USA
Kraushaar-Pielach, Silke — Luge Athlete
Gorkistr 22, 96515 Sonneberg, Germany
Krauss, Alison — Singer, Fiddler
Arcieri Assoc, 305 Madison Ave, #2315, New York NY 10165 USA
Krauss, Barry — Football Player
5346 Creekbend Dr, Carmel IN 46033, USA
Krauss, Lawrence M (Larry) — Astrophysicist
Case Western Reserve University, Physics Dept, Cleveland OH 44106, USA
Krauss, Nicole — Writer
W W Norton, 500 5th Ave, #600, New York NY 10110 USA
Krauss, Robert M — Psychologist
Columbia University, Psychology Dept, Schermerhorn Hall, New York NY 10027, USA
Krausse, Lewis B (Lew), Jr — Baseball Player
12811 NE 186th St, Holt MO 64048, USA
Krausse, Stefan — Luge Athlete
Karl-Zink-Str 2, 96883 Ilmenau, Germany
Krauthammer, Charles — Columnist
Washington Post Writers Group, 1150 15th St NW, Washington DC 20071, USA
Kravchuk, Igor A — Ice Hockey Player
Harrington College, Athletic Dept, 300 Riviere Rouge, Harrington QC J8G 2S7, Canada
Kravchuk, Leonid M — President, Ukraine
Verkhovna Rada, M Hruspevskoho 5, 252019 Kiev, Ukraine
Kravec, Kenneth P (Ken) — Baseball Player
6752 Taeda Dr, Sarasota FL 34241, USA
Kravitz, Daniel (Danny) — Baseball Player
8810 Route 487, Dushore PA 18614, USA
Kravitz, Lee — Editor
Parade, Editorial Dept, 711 3rd Ave, New York NY 10017, USA
Kravitz, Lenny — Singer, Songwriter, Musician
Creative Artists Agency, 2000 Ave of Stars, #100, Los Angeles CA 90067 USA
Krawczyk, Raymond A (Ray) — Baseball Player
67 Cloudcrest, Aliso Viejo CA 92656, USA
Krayer, Otto H — Pharmacologist
4140 E Cooper St, Tucson AZ 85711, USA
Krayzelburg, Lenny — Swimmer
55 Oceana Dr E, #5H, Brooklyn NY 11235, USA
Krayzie Bone — Rap Artist (Bone Thugs-N-Harmony)
Life Entertainment, 15441 Red Hill Ave, #G, Tustin CA 92780, USA
Kreamer, Ann — Writer
W M E Entertainment, 9601 Wilshire Blvd, #300, Beverly Hills CA 90210 USA
Krebbs, John — Auto Racing Driver
Diamond Ridge, 3232 Amoruso Way, Roseville CA 95747, USA
Krebs, Robert D — Businessman
Burlington North/Santa Fe, 2650 Lou Menk Dr, Fort Worth TX 76131, USA
Krebs, Susan — Actress
6019 Buffalo Ave, #A, Van Nuys CA 91401, USA
Kredel, Elmar Maria — Religious Leader
Obere Karolinenstra 5, 96033 Bamber, Germany
Kregel, Kevin R — Astronaut
2601 Bay Shore Dr, Seabrook TX 77586, USA
Kreider, Dan — Football Player
1069 Iron Bridge Road, Mount Joy PA 17552, USA
Kreider, Steve K — Football Player
350 Harrow Lane, Blue Bell PA 19422, USA
Kreis, Jason — Soccer Player, Coach
Real Salt Lake, 9256 S State St, Sandy UT 84070 USA
Kreitling, Richard A (Rich) — Football Player
24017 Trout Lake Road, Bovey MN 55709, USA
Kreklow, Wayne — Basketball Player
4001 S Old Mill Creek Road, Columbia MO 65203, USA

Krementz, Jill — Photographer
620 Sagaponack Main St, Southampton NY 11968, USA
Kremer, Andrea — Sportscaster
NBC-TV, Sports Dept, 30 Rockefeller Plaza, #270E, New York NY 10112 USA
Kremer, Arthur — Drummer (Stellarstarr*)
+1 Management/Public Relations, 242 Wythe Ave, #6, Brooklyn NY 11211, USA
Kremer, Gidon — Concert Violinist
Opus 3 Artists, 470 Park Ave S, #900N, New York NY 10016 USA
Kremer, J Kendall (Ken) — Football Player
6116 Double Eagle Court, Kansas City MO 64152, USA
Kremers, James E (Jimmy) — Baseball Player
6209 W Orlando St, Broken Arrow OK 74011, USA
Kremmel, James L (Jim) — Baseball Player
524 W 18th Ave, Spokane WA 99203, USA
Krens, Thomas — Museum Executive
Solomon R Guggenheim Museum, 1071 5th Ave, New York NY 10128, USA
Krentz, Jayne Ann (Amanda Quick) — Writer
Axelrod Agency, 66 Church St, Lenox MA 01240, USA
Krenz, Jan — Conductor, Composer
Al J Ch Szucha 16, 00 582 Warsaw, Poland
Kreps, David M — Economist
Stanford University, Graduate Business School, Stanford CA 94305, USA
Kresa, Kent — Businessman
General Motors Corp, 100 Renaissance Center, Detroit MI 48243, USA
Kresge, Chris — Golfer
834 Trailwood Dr, Apopka FL 32712, USA
Kreskin — Illusionist
444 2nd St, Pitcairn PA 15140, USA
Kress, Charles S (Charlie) — Baseball Player
1705 Pine St, #104, Sandpoint ID 83864, USA
Kress, Nathan — Actor
A P A Talent/Literary Agency, 405 S Beverly Dr, #300, Beverly Hills CA 90212 USA
Kressley, Carson — Entertainer
Untitled Entertainment, 350 S Beverly Dr, #200, Beverly Hills CA 90212 USA
Kretchmer, Arthur — Editor
Playboy, Editorial Dept, 680 N Lake Shore Dr, Chicago IL 60611, USA
Kretschmann, Thomas — Actor
Hoestermann Mgmt, Gneisenaustr 94, 10961 Berlin, Germany
Kreuger, Richard A (Rick) — Baseball Player
4664 Sheldon Court, Hudsonville MI 49426, USA
Kreuk, Kristin L — Actress
Gersh Agency, 9465 Wilshire Blvd, #600, Beverly Hills CA 90212 USA
Kreuter, Chadden M (Chad) — Baseball Player
6737 SW 77th Terrace, South Miami FL 33143, USA
Kreutz, Olin G — Football Player
750 S Southmeadow Lane, Lake Forest IL 60045, USA
Kreutzer, Franklin J (Frank) — Baseball Player
921 Windwhisper Lane, Annapolis MD 21403, USA
Kreutzmann, Bill — Drummer (Grateful Dead)
Arista Records, 8750 Wilshire Blvd, #300, Beverly Hills CA 90211 USA
Kreviazuk, Chantal — Singer, Pianist, Songwriter
S L Feldman Mgmt, 1505 W 2nd Ave, #200, Vancouver BC V6H 3Y4, Canada
Kribel, Joel — Golfer
26254 N 46th St, Phoenix AZ 85050, USA
Krick, Jaynie — Baseball Player
1522 Azalea Dr, Arlington TX 76013, USA
Krickstein, Aaron — Tennis Player
7559 Fairmont Court, Boca Raton FL 33496, USA
Krieg, Arthur M — Immunologist
University of Iowa Medical College, Immunology Dept, Iowa City IA 52242, USA
Krieg, David M (Dave) — Football Player
2439 E Desert Willow Dr, Phoenix AZ 85048, USA
Krieger, Ellie — Dietician, Entertainer
Flutie Entertainment, 9320 Wilshire Blvd, #202, Beverly Hills CA 90212, USA
Krieger, Lee Toland — Director
72nd Street Productions, 1041 N Formosa Ave, West Hollywood CA 90046, USA
Krieger, Robby — Guitarist (Doors), Songwriter
Doors Music, 8899 Beverly Blvd, #812, Los Angeles CA 90048, USA
Krier, Leon — Architect
8 Rue des Chapeliers, 83830 Claviers, France
Kriewaldt, Clint — Football Player
W3189 Center Valley Road, Freedom WI 54165, USA
Krige, Alice — Actress
Diamond Mgmt, 31 Percy St, London W1T 2DD, England
Krikalev, Sergei K — Cosmonaut
Cosmonaut Training Center, Star City, 141160 Zvezdny Gorodok, Moscow Oblast, Russia
Krim, Mathilde — Philanthropist, Medical Activist
AmfAR Foundation for AIDS Research, 5900 Wilshire Blvd, Los Angeles CA 90036, USA
Kring, Tim — Writer, Producer
W M E Entertainment, 9601 Wilshire Blvd, #300, Beverly Hills CA 90210 USA
Krinsky, Yehuda — Religious Leader, Rabbi
Chabad-Lubavitch, 841 Ocean Parkway, Brooklyn NY 11230, USA
Kripke, Eric — Writer, Director, Producer
Principato-Young, 9465 Wilshire Blvd, #880, Beverly Hills CA 90212 USA
Kripke, Saul A — Philosopher
Princeton University, Philosophy Dept, Princeton NJ 08544, USA
Krislov, Marvin — Educator
Oberlin College, President's Office, 70 N Professor St, Oberlin OH 44074, USA
Kriss, Gerard A — Astronomer
Johns Hopkins University, Astronomy Dept, Baltimore MD 21218, USA
Kristen, Marta — Actress
475 Mesa Dr, Santa Monica CA 90402, USA
Kristensen, Tom — Auto Racing Driver
Autosport International, Broom Road, Teddington Middlesex TW11 9BE, England
Kristiansen, Ingrid — Track Athlete
Nils Collett Vogts Vei 51B, 0765 Oslo, Norway

K

Kristiansen, Kjeld Kirk Lego Group, 7190 Billund, Denmark	Businessman, Educator
Kristine W Diva Central, 7510 W Sunset Blvd, #1445, Los Angeles CA 90046, USA	Singer
Kristmanson, Kyrie Agency Group Ltd, 142 W 57th St, #600, New York NY 10019 USA	Singer, Songwriter
Kristof, Emory National Geographic, Editorial Dept, 1145 17th St NW, Washington DC 20036 USA	Photographer
Kristof, Joe 4290 Meadowview Court, Columbus OH 43224, USA	Bowler
Kristof, Kathy M Los Angeles Times, Editorial Dept, 202 W 1st St, Los Angeles CA 90012 USA	Columnist
Kristof, Nicholas D New York Times, Editorial Dept, 229 W 43rd St, New York NY 10036, USA	Journalist
Kristofferson, Kris Tony Cee Assoc, PO Box 410, Utica NY 13503, USA	Singer, Songwriter, Actor
Krivda, Rick M 112 Dolores Dr, Irwin PA 15642, USA	Baseball Player
Krivokrasov, Sergei V 16500 Collins Ave, #1556, Sunny Island Beach FL 33160, USA	Ice Hockey Player
Kriwet, Heinz Thyssen AG, August-Thyssen-Str 1, 40211 Dusseldorf, Germany	Businessman
Krmpotich, David 128 Archbishop Dr, Conshocken PA 19428, USA	Rowing Athlete
Kroeger, Chad R Union Entertainment Group, 1323 Newbury Road, #104, Newbury Park CA 91320, USA	Singer, Guitarist (Nickelback)
Kroeger, Gary 10474 Santa Monica Blvd, #380, Los Angeles CA 90025, USA	Actor, Comedian
Kroeger, Josh 1007 Wildlife Road, San Diego CA 92131, USA	Baseball Player
Kroeger, Michael D H (Mike) Union Entertainment Group, 1323 Newbury Road, #104, Newbury Park CA 91320, USA	Bassist (Nickelback)
Kroemer, Herbert University of California, Electrical Engineering Dept, Santa Barbara CA 93106, USA	Nobel Physics Laureate
Kroenig, Brad Ford Models Inc, 111 5th Ave, #900, New York NY 10003 USA	Model
Kroes, Doutzen D N A Model Mgmt, 555 W 25th St, New York NY 10001, USA	Model
Kroes, Neelie European Commission, 200 Rue de la Loi, 1049 Brussels, Belgium	Government Official, Netherlands
Krofft, Marty 700 Greentree Road, Pacific Palisades CA 90272, USA	Puppeteer
Krofft, Sid 7710 Woodrow Wilson Dr, Los Angeles CA 90046, USA	Puppeteer
Kroft, Steve CBS-TV, News Dept, 51 W 52nd St, New York NY 10019 USA	Commentator
Krol, Joachim Above the Line, Goethestr 17, 80336 Munich, Germany	Actor
Kroll, Alexander S (Alex) 581 Whalley Road, Charlotte VT 05445, USA	Football Player, Businessman
Kroll, Gary M 9038 E 40th St, Tulsa OK 74145, USA	Baseball Player
Kroll, Lucien Ave Louis Berlaimont 20, Boite 9, 1160 Brussels, Belgium	Architect
Kroll, Nick Mosiac Media Group, 9200 W Sunset Blvd, #1000, Los Angeles CA 90069 USA	Actor, Comedian
Kromm, Richard (Rich) 1935 Cheyenne Dr, Evansville IN 47715, USA	Ice Hockey Player
Kron, Elizabeth S (Lisa) I C M Partners, 10250 Constellation Blvd, #900, Los Angeles CA 90067 USA	Actress
Kronberger, Petra Ellmautal 37, 5452 Pfarrwerfen, Austria	Alpine Skier
Krone, Julie 7305 Marine Place, Carlsbad CA 92011, USA	Thoroughbred Racing Jockey
Kronwall, H Niklas 22235 Picadilly Circle, Novi MI 48375, USA	Ice Hockey Player
Kropf, Susan Avon Products, 1251 Ave of Americas, #C2-63, New York NY 10020, USA	Businesswoman
Kropfeld, Jim Hydroplanes Inc, 9117 Zoellner Dr, Cincinnati OH 45251, USA	Boat Racing Driver
Kropfelder, Nicholas 13803 Lighthouse Ave, Ocean City MD 21842, USA	Soccer Player
Kropp, Tom 1811 W 41st St, Kearney NE 68845, USA	Basketball Player
Kross, David Schulze & Heyn, Rosa-Luxemburg-Str 17, 10178 Berlin, Germany	Actor
Kroszner, Randall Federal Reserve Board, 20th St & Constitution Ave NW, Washington DC 20551, USA	Government Official, Economist
Krot, Alexander N University of Hawaii-Manoa, Geophysics Institute, 1680 East-West Road, #602, Honolulu HI 96822, USA	Astrobiologist, Cosmochemist
Kroto, Harold W Sussex University, Chemistry Dept, Falmer, Brighton BN1 9QJ, England	Nobel Chemistry Laureate
Krsnich, Rocco P (Rocky) 5701 W 92nd St, Overland Park KS 66207, USA	Baseball Player
KRS-One Richard Walters, PO Box 2789, Toluca Lake CA 91610 USA	Rap Artist
Krstic, Nenad Boston Celtics, 226 Causeway St, #4, Boston MA 02114 USA	Basketball Player
Kruczek, Michael (Mike) 4028 Gilder Rose Place, Winter Park FL 32792, USA	Football Player
Krueck, Ronald Krueck & Sexton Architects, 221 W Erie, Chicago IL 60654, USA	Architect
Krueger, Alan B White House, 1600 Pennsylvania Ave NW, Washington DC 20500 USA	Government Official, Economist
Krueger, Anne O Stanford University, Economics Dept, Stanford CA 94305, USA	Economist

Kristiansen - Krueger

Krueger, Charles A (Charlie)
44 Regency Dr, Clayton CA 94517, USA — Football Player

Krueger, James G
Rockefeller University Medical Center, 1230 York Ave, New York NY 10065 USA — Dermatologist

Krueger, Ralph
Edmonton Oilers, 11230 110th St, Edmonton AB T5G 3H7, Canada — Ice Hockey Coach

Krueger, Robert C (Bob)
PO Box 311717, New Braunfels TX 78131, USA — Senator, TX; Diplomat

Krueger, Rolf F
6502 Lake Circle, Wallis TX 77485, USA — Football Player

Krueger, William C (Bill)
30132 SE Redmond Fall City Road, Fall City WA 98024, USA — Baseball Player

Kruger, Diane
U B B A, 6 Rue de Braque, 75003 Paris, France — Actress, Model

Kruger, Hardy
Agence Elizabeth Simpson, 62 Blvd du Montparnasse, 75015 Paris, France — Actor

Kruger, Kelly
Glick Agency, 1321 7th St, #203, Santa Monica CA 90401 USA — Actress

Kruger, Lon
University of Oklahoma, Athletic Dept, Norman OK 73019, USA — Basketball Coach

Krugman, Paul R
70 Lambert Dr, Princeton NJ 08540, USA — Nobel Economics Laureate

Kruk, John M
PO Box 7847, Naples FL 34101, USA — Baseball Player, Sportscaster

Krukow, Michael E (Mike)
6094 Madbury Court, San Luis Obispo CA 93401, USA — Baseball Player

Krulak, Charles C
4801 Bonita Bay Blvd, Bonita Springs FL 34134, USA — Marine Corps General

Krulwich, Robert
CBS-TV, News Dept, 524 W 57th St, New York NY 10019, USA — Commentator

Krumholtz, David
Collective, 8383 Wilshire Blvd, #1050, Beverly Hills CA 90211 USA — Actor

Krumrie, Timothy A (Tim)
21215 Bucking Way, Oak Creek CO 80467, USA — Football Player

Krupa, Joanna
Major Model Mgmt, 419 Park Ave, #1201, New York NY 10016, USA — Model, Actress

Krupp, Uwe
3716 Strand, Manhattan Beach CA 90266, USA — Ice Hockey Player

Krushelnyski, Mike
7080 Holiday Dr, Bloomfield Hills MI 48301, USA — Ice Hockey Player

Kruspe, Richard Z
Pilgrim Mgmt, PO Box 540101, 10042 Berlin, Germany — Guitarist (Rammstein)

Krylova, Angelika
Skating Assn, Luchnesksaia Nab 8, 119871 Moscow, Russia — Ice Dancer

Krynzel, Dave
951 Derringer Lane, Henderson NV 89014, USA — Baseball Player

Krypreos, Nick
9209 Copenhaven Dr, Potomac MD 20854, USA — Ice Hockey Player

Krystkowiak, Larry B
2343 S Dallin St, Salt Lake City UT 84109, USA — Basketball Player, Coach

Krzyzewski, Michael W (Mike)
4406 W Cornwallis Road, Durham NC 27705, USA — Basketball Coach

K's Choice
Sharpe's Entertainment Services, 683 Palmera Ave, Pacific Palisades CA 90272, USA — Rock Musical Group

Kuba, Filip
17216 Emerald Chase Dr, Tampa FL 33647, USA — Ice Hockey Player

Kuban, Bob
17626 Lasiandra Dr, Chesterfield MO 63005, USA — Singer, Drummer

Kubasov, Valeri N
Cosmonaut Training Center, Star City, 141160 Zvezdny Gorodok, Moscow Oblast, Russia — Cosmonaut

Kubek, Anthony C (Tony)
121 E Water St, #120, Appleton WI 54911, USA — Baseball Player, Sportscaster

Kubel, Jason J
21031 Ventura Blvd, #1000, Woodland Hills CA 91364, USA — Baseball Player

Kube-McDowell, Michael P
4403 Cherry Hill Dr, Okemos MI 48864, USA — Writer

Kubenka, Jeffrey S (Jeff)
6935 FM 957, Schulenburg TX 78956, USA — Baseball Player

Kuberski, Robert K (Bob), Jr
13 Forwood Dr, Garnet Valley PA 19060, USA — Football Player

Kuberski, Stephen P (Steve)
91 Lawson Road, Winchester MA 01890, USA — Basketball Player

Kubiak, Gary
14 Woods Edge Lane, Houston TX 77024, USA — Football Player, Coach

Kubiak, Leo
2638 N Prestwick Way, Lecanto FL 34461, USA — Basketball Player

Kubiak, Teresa M
Indiana University, Jacobs Music School, Bloomington IN 47405, USA — Opera Singer

Kubiak, Theodore R (Ted)
11956 Bernando Plaza Dr, San Diego CA 92128, USA — Baseball Player

Kubilius, Andrius
Prime Minister's Office, Turno-Vaizganto 2, 01511 Vilnius, Lithuania — Prime Minister, Lithuania

Kubina, Pavel
1145 81st St S, Saint Petersburg FL 33707, USA — Ice Hockey Player

Kubinski, Timothy M (Tim)
384 Santa Maria Ave, San Luis Obispo CA 93405, USA — Baseball Player

Kubski, Gilbert T (Gil)
4542 Scenario Dr, Huntington Beach CA 92649, USA — Baseball Player

Kucek, John A C (Jack)
8220 Blue Heron Lane, Canfield OH 44406, USA — Baseball Player

Kucera, Frantisek
Sportovni, Tupolevova Ul 669, 19900 Prague Letnany 9, Czech Republic — Ice Hockey Player

Kuchar, Matthew G (Matt)
1909 Dixon Lann, Saint Simons Island GA 31522, USA — Golfer

Kucinich, Dennis J
14518 Drake Road, Strongsville OH 44136, USA — Representative, OH; Mayor, Cleveland

K

Kahn - Kucinich

Kucks, John C (Johnny) 15 Oakland St, Hillsdale NJ 07642, USA	Baseball Player
Kuczenski, Bruce J 135 Southshire Dr, Southington CT 06489, USA	Basketball Player
Kuczynski Godard, Pedro-Pablo Premier's Office, Urb Corpac, Calle 1 Oeste, San Isidro, Lima 27, Peru	Prime Minister, Peru
Kuczynski, Betty 4515 Prescott Ave, Lyons IL 60534, USA	Bowler
Kudelka, James A National Ballet of Canada, 470 Queens Quay W, Toronto ON M5V 3K4, Canada	Ballet Choreographer, Dancer
Kudelski, Bob 93 Copperleaf Dr, Cody WY 82414, USA	Ice Hockey Player
Kuder, Mary Kuder Art Studio, 539 Navahopi Road, Sedona AZ 86336, USA	Artist
Kudlow, Lawrence A Kudlow Co, 301 Tahmore Dr, Fairfield CT 06825, USA	Government Official, Economist
Kudrna, Julius Sekaninova 36, 120 00 Prague 2, Czech Republic	Canoeing Athlete
Kudrow, Lisa Is or Isn't Entertainment, 8391 Beverly Blvd, #125, Los Angeles CA 90048, USA	Actress
Kuebler, David Haydn Rawstron, 36 Station Road, London SE20 7BQ, England	Opera Singer
Kuechenberg, Robert J (Bob) 2519 Arbor Dr, Fort Lauderdale FL 33312, USA	Football Player
Kuechenberg, Rudolph B (Rudy) 2928 SE 20th Ave, Cape Coral FL 33904, USA	Football Player
Kuehn, Enrico B S D, An der Schiesstatte 4, 83471 Berchtesgaden, Germany	Bobsled Athlete
Kuehne, Hank 11117 Green Bayberry Dr, Palm Beach Gardens FL 33418, USA	Golfer
Kuehne, Kelli 245 Kings Peak Court, Heber City UT 84032, USA	Golfer
Kuerten, Gustavo Octagon Worldwide, 1751 Pinnacle Dr, #1500, McLean VA 22102 USA	Tennis Player
Kuerti, Julian I M G Artists, Hogarth Business Park, Chiswick, London W4 2TH, England	Conductor
Kuester, John D, Jr 105 Carnoustie Way, Media PA 19063, USA	Basketball Player, Coach
Kufeldt, James Winn-Dixie Stores, 5050 Edgewood Court, Jacksonville FL 32254, USA	Businessman
Kufuor, John Agyekum President's Office, Golden Jubilee House, PO Box 1627, Accra, Ghana	President, Ghana
Kugler, Pete D 33 Peach Court, Marco Island FL 34145, USA	Football Player
Kuhaulua, Fred M 89-203 Ualakahiki Place, Waianae HI 96792, USA	Baseball Player
Kuhaulua, Jesse Azumazeki Stable, 4-6-4 Higashi Komagata, Ryogoku, Tokyo, Japan	Sumo Wrestler
Kuhl, Patrick Sudring 2, 76532 Baden-Baden, Germany	Swimmer
Kuhlman, Arkadi I N G Direct, PO Box 80, Saint Cloud MN 56302, USA	Financier
Kuhlman, Ron 5738 Willis Ave, Van Nuys CA 91411, USA	Actor
Kuhlmann, Kathleen M International Management Group, 54 Ave Marceau, 75008 Paris, France	Opera Singer
Kuhlmann-Wilsdorf, Doris University of Virginia, Materials Science Dept, Charlottesville VA 22901, USA	Physicist
Kuhn, David E Plum TV, 419 Lafayette St, #700, New York NY 10003, USA	Animator
Kuhn, Gustav Winkel 25, 6343 Ere, Austria	Conductor
Kuhn, Stephen L (Steve) Berkeley Agency, 2608 9th St, #301, Berkeley CA 94710 USA	Jazz Pianist, Composer
Kuhne-Schiemann, Rita Rosenweg 8, 14542 Werder/Havel, Germany	Track Athlete
Kuiper, Duane E 3665 Deer Trail Dr, Danville CA 94506, USA	Baseball Player
Kuipers, Andre European Space Centre, 8-10 Rue Mario Nikis, 75738 Paris Cedex, France	Astronaut
Kuisma, Antti Olympic Committee, Radiokatu 20, 00240 Helsinki, Finland	Nordic Combined Skier
Kukoc, Toni 1850 Hybernia Dr, Highland Park IL 60035, USA	Basketball Player
Kula, Irwin Center for Learning & Leadership, 440 Park Ave S, #400, New York NY 10016, USA	Religious Leader, Rabbi, Writer
Kuleshov, Valery Musicians Corporate Mgmt, PO Box 825, Highland NY 12528, USA	Concert Pianist
Kulich, Vladimir Jeff Goldberg Mgmt, 817 Monte Leon Dr, Beverly Hills CA 90210, USA	Actor
Kulick, Kelly Professional Bowlers Assn, 719 2nd Ave, #701, Seattle WA 98104 USA	Bowler
Kulik, Ilia Rita Meyers, 21230 SE 268th Place, Maple Valley WA 98038, USA	Figure Skater
Kulka, Konstanty A Filharmonia Narodowa, Ul Jasna 5, 00 007 Warsaw, Poland	Concert Violinist
Kulkarni, Shrinivas R California Institute of Technology, Astronomy Dept, Pasadena CA 91125, USA	Astronomer
Kullberg, Duane R 6444 N 79th St, Scottsdale AZ 85250, USA	Businessman
Kullman, Ellen E I DuPont de Nemours, 1007 Market St, Wilmington DE 19895, USA	Businesswoman
Kulov, Feliks S Prime Minister's Office, Ul Perromayskaya 57, 720003 Bishkek, Kyrgyzstan	Prime Minister, Kyrgyzstan
Kuma, Kengo Kengo Kuma Assoc, 2-12-12, Minamiaoyama, Minatoku, Tokyo 107 0062, Japan	Architect

Kumagai, Saki — Soccer Player
Football Assn, 3-10-15 Hongo, Bunkyoku, Tokyo 113 0033 Japan
Kumanyika, Shiriki K — Nutritionist
University of Illinois, Nutrition & Dietetics Dept, Chicago IL 60607, USA
Kumar, Akshay — Actor
Benzer Lokhandwala Complex Andheri (W), 203A Wing, Mumbai MS 400053, India
Kumar, Dilip — Actor
34/B Palli Hill, Nargis Dutt Road Bndra (W), Mumbai MS 400050, India
Kumar, Manoj — Actor, Director, Producer
Lakshmi Villa Grount, Tagore Road Santacruz (W), Mumbai MS 400050, India
Kumbernuss, Astrid — Track Athlete
Max Adrian Str 1, 17034 Neubrandenburg, Germany
Kumble, Roger — Director, Actor, Writer
United Talent Agency, 9336 Civic Center Dr, Beverly Hills CA 90210 USA
Kume, John M — Baseball Player
6810 Woodard Road, Andover OH 44003, USA
Kumin, Maxine W — Writer
30 W Joppa Road, Warner NH 03278, USA
Kummer, Glenn F — Businessman
Fleetwood Enterprises, 3125 Myers St, Riverside CA 92503, USA
Kump, Ernest J — Architect
Villa Boecklin, Jupiterstr 15, 8032 Zurich, Switzerland
Kundera, Milan — Writer
Gallimard, 5 Rue Sebastien-Bottin, 75007 Paris, France
Kundla, John A — Basketball Coach
909 Main St NE, #208, Minneapolis MN 55413, USA
Kunerth, Mark J — Writer, Producer
Broder Webb Chervin Silbermann, 9242 Beverly Blvd, Beverly Hills CA 90210 USA
Kunes, Ellen — Editor
Oprah Magazine, Editor's Office, 224 W 57th St, #900, New York NY 10019, USA
Kung, Candie — Golfer
Ladies Pro Golf Assn, 100 International Golf Dr, Daytona Beach FL 32124 USA
Kung, Hans — Theologian
Waldhauserstr 23, 72076 Tubingen, Germany
Kung, Patrick C — Pharmacologist
T Cell Sciences, 119 4th Ave, Needham MA 02494, USA
Kunin, Madeline M — Governor, VT
60 Southwind Dr, Burlington VT 05401, USA
Kunis, Mila — Actress
Creative Artists Agency, 2000 Ave of Stars, #100, Los Angeles CA 90067 USA
Kunkel, Jeffrey W (Jeff) — Baseball Player
4921 County Road 605, Burleson TX 76028, USA
Kunkel, Louis M — Pediatrician
Children's Hospital, 300 Longwood Ave, Boston MA 02115, USA
Kunkle, John F — Religious Leader
Evangelical Methodist Church, 3000 W Kellogg Dr, Wichita KS 67213, USA
Kunnert, Kevin R — Basketball Player
8286 SW Wilderland Court, Portland OR 97224, USA
Kunstler, Morton — Artist, Illustrator
137 Cove Neck Road, Oyster Bay NY 11771, USA
Kuntz, Russell J (Rusty) — Baseball Player
10102 W 152nd Terrace, Overland Park KS 66221, USA
Kunz, Edward C (Eddie) — Baseball Player
1500 SW Pleasant View Dr, #151, Gresham OR 97080, USA
Kunz, George J — Football Player
8215 S Bermuda Road, Las Vegas NV 89123, USA
Kunze, Terry D — Basketball Player
6931 Halifax Ave N, Minneapolis MN 55429, USA
Kunzru, Hari — Writer
E P Dutton, 375 Hudson St, New York NY 10014 USA
Kupchak, Mitchell (Mitch) — Basketball Player
361 Fordyce Road, Los Angeles CA 90049, USA
Kupcinet, Kari — Actress
1660 Mill Trail, Highland Park IL 60035, USA
Kupec, Charles J — Basketball Player
6448 River Run, Columbia MD 21044, USA
Kupets, Courtney — Gymnast
133 Falling Shoals Dr, Athens GA 30605, USA
Kupfer, Abraham (Avi) — Immunologist
Johns Hopkins University Medical School, Immunobiology Dept, 733 N Broadway, Baltimore MD 21205, USA
Kupfer, Carl — Ophthalmologist
National Institutes of Health, 10 Center Dr, Bethesda MD 20892, USA
Kupfer, Harry — Director
Komische Oper, Behrenstr 55-57, 10117 Berlin, Germany
Kupferberg, Sabine — Ballerina
Dans Theater 3, Scheldoekshaven 60, 2511 EN Gravenhage, Netherlands
Kupp, Jacob R (Jake) — Football Player
4801 Snowmountain Road, Yakima WA 98908, USA
Kupperman, Joel J — Philosopher
115 E 9th St, #15E, New York NY 10003, USA
Kurant, Willy — Cinematographer
Lyons Sheldon Agency, 800 S Robertson Blvd, #6, Los Angeles CA 90035, USA
Kuras, Ellen M — Cinematographer
54 Summit St, Nyack NY 10960, USA
Kureishi, Hanif — Writer
Rogers Coleridge White, 20 Powis Mews, London W11 1JN, England
Kurek, Ralph E — Football Player
1311 Lime Pond Road, South Royalton VT 05068, USA
Kurita, Toyomichi — Cinematographer
Sandra Marsh Assoc, 9150 Wilshire Blvd, #220, Beverly Hills CA 90212 USA
Kurkova Emmons, Katerina — Markswoman
US Olympic Committee, 1 Olympic Plaza, Building 6, Colorado Springs CO 80909 USA
Kurkova, Karolina I — Model, Actress
S S & M Model Mgmt, C/Provenca 286-288, 08008 Barcelona, Spain
Kurland, Robert A (Bob) — Basketball Player
1024 Kings Crown Dr, Sanibel FL 33957, USA

Kahn - Kurland

Kurlander, Tom — Actor
Independent Artists Agency, 9601 Wilshire Blvd, #750, Beverly Hills CA 90210, USA
Kuroda, Emily — Actress
Stone Manners Salners, 9911 W Pico Blvd, #1400, Los Angeles CA 90035 USA
Kuroda, Hiroki — Baseball Player
New York Yankees, Yankee Stadium, E 161st St & River Ave, Bronx NY 10451 USA
Kurosaki, Ryan Y — Baseball Player
3324 Huelani Dr, Honolulu HI 96822, USA
Kurrat, Klaus-Dieter — Track Athlete
Am Hochwald 30, 28460, 14532 Kleinmachnow, Germany
Kurri, Jari P — Ice Hockey Player
Hockey Hall of Fame, B C E Place, 30 Yonge St, Toronto ON M5E 1X8, Canada
Kursinski, Anne — Equestrian
107 Spring Hill Road, Frenchtown NJ 08825, USA
Kurstin, Gregory A (Greg) — Keyboardist (Bird & the Bee)
Blue Note Records, 6920 W Sunset Blvd, Los Angeles CA 90028 USA
Kurtag, Gyorgy — Composer
Lihego V3, 2621 Veroce, Hungary
Kurtenbach, Orland J — Ice Hockey Player
14066 29A Ave, Surrey BC V4P 2J8, Canada
Kurth, Wallace (Wally) — Actor, Singer
C E S D, 10635 Santa Monica Blvd, #130, Los Angeles CA 90025 USA
Kurtha, Akbar — Actor
United Agents, 12-26 Lexington St, London W1F 0LE, England
Kurtis, Bill — Commentator
Kurtis Productions, 400 W Erie St, #500, Chicago IL 60654, USA
Kurtis, Darlene — Model, Actress
Playboy Promotions, 2706 Media Center Dr, Los Angeles CA 90065 USA
Kurtova, Karolina — Model
D N A Model Mgmt, 555 W 25th St, #600, New York NY 10001 USA
Kurtz, Harold J (Hal) — Baseball Player
511 Flat Iron Square Road, Church Hill MD 21623, USA
Kurtz, Swoosie — Actress, Singer
Innovative Artists, 1505 10th St, Santa Monica CA 90401 USA
Kurtze, Andrew — Businessman
Sprint P C S Group, 6391 Sprint Parkway, Overland Park KS 66251, USA
Kurtzig, Sandra L — Businesswoman
E-Benefits, 2420 Sand Hill Road, #201, Menlo Park CA 94025, USA
Kurtzman, Alex — Writer, Producer
Kurtzman Orci Paper Products, 100 Universal Plaza, Building 5171, Universal City CA 91608, USA
Kurupt — Rap Artist, Songwriter, Actor
United Talent Agency, 9336 Civic Center Dr, Beverly Hills CA 90210 USA
Kurvers, Tom — Ice Hockey Player
10146 Birch Grove Road, Brainerd MN 56401, USA
Kurylenko, Olga — Actress, Model
Tavistock Wood, 45 Conduit St, London W1S 2YN, England
Kurys, Sophie M — Baseball Player
8301 E Fairmount Ave, Scottsdale AZ 85251, USA
Kurzak, Aleksandra — Opera Singer
I M G Artists, Hogarth Business Park, Chiswick, London W4 2TH, England
Kurzweil, Raymond — Inventor (Computer-Generated Voice)
Capel & Land, 29 Wardour St, London W1D 6PS, England
Kusama, Karyn — Director
I C M Partners, 10250 Constellation Blvd, #900, Los Angeles CA 90067 USA
Kusatsu, Clyde — Actor
Stone Manners Salners, 9911 W Pico Blvd, #1400, Los Angeles CA 90035 USA
Kuschak, Metropolitan Andrei — Religious Leader
Ukranian Orthodox Church in America, 3 Davenport Ave, New Rochelle NY 10805, USA
Kush, Rod R — Football Player
45 Willow Point Dr, Ashland NE 68003, USA
Kushboo — Actress
20/1 Arch Bishop, Mathiyas Ave, Boat Club Road, Chennai TN 600028, India
Kushell, Lisa — Actress
Abrams Artists, 9200 W Sunset Blvd, #1125, West Hollywood CA 90069 USA
Kushner, Harold S — Religious Leader, Rabbi, Writer
Temple Israel, 145 Hartford St, Natick MA 01760, USA
Kushner, Robert E — Artist
D C Moore Gallery, 724 5th Ave, #800, New York NY 10019, USA
Kuske, Kevin — Bobsled Athlete
B S R Rennsteig Oberhof, Alte Ohrdufer Str 6, 98559 Oberhof, Germany
Kusnyer, Arthur W (Art) — Baseball Player
6598 Taeda Dr, Sarasota FL 34241, USA
Kustra, Robert W — Educator
Boise State University, President's Office, Boise ID 83725, USA
Kusturica, Emir — Director, Writer, Actor
Fondazione Cultural Edison, Largo VIII Marzo 9, 43100 Parma, Italy
Kutcher, Ashton — Actor
Katalyst Films, 6806 Lexington Ave, Los Angeles CA 90038, USA
Kutcher, Randy S — Baseball Player
3016 Purple Sage Lane, Palmdale CA 93550, USA
Kuti, Fela A — Singer
Rosebud Agency, PO Box 170429, San Francisco CA 94117 USA
Kuttner, Stephan G — Historian
2270 Le Conte Ave, #601, Berkeley CA 94709, USA
Kutyna, Donald J — Air Force General, Businessman
4818 Kenyon Court, Colorado Springs CO 80917, USA
Kutyna, Marion J (Marty) — Baseball Player
2255 NW 14th St, Delray Beach FL 33445, USA
Kutzler, Jerry S — Baseball Player
9500 81st St, #311, Pleasant Prairie WI 53158, USA
Kuusela, Armi H — Beauty Queen
6241 Waverly Ave, La Jolla CA 92037, USA
Kuykendall, Fulton G — Football Player
1497 Rucker Circle, Woodstock GA 30188, USA
Kuzava, Robert L (Bob) — Baseball Player
1118 Vinewood St, Wyandotte MI 48192, USA

Kuziel, Robert C (Bob) — Football Player
3375 Walnut Dr, Ellicott City MD 21043, USA
Kuzmina, Anastasiya V — Biathlete
Biathlon Assn, Partizánska Cesta 71, 974 01 Banska Bystrica, Slovakia
Kuznetsoff, Alexei — Concert Pianist
Columbia Artists Mgmt Inc, 1790 Broadway, #702, New York NY 10019 USA
Kuznetsova, Svetlana A — Tennis Player
Women's Tennis Assn, 1 Progress Plaza, #1500, Saint Petersburg FL 33701 USA
Kuznetsoya, Dina — Opera Singer
Harrison/Parrott, 5-6 Albion Court, London W6 0QT, England
Kuzyk, Mimi — Actress
Characters Talent Mgmt, 8 Elm St, Toronto ON M5G 1G7, Canada
Kvapil, Radoslav — Concert Pianist
Hradecka 5, 13000 Prague 3, Czech Republic
Kvapil, Travis — Auto, Truck Racing Driver
141 Silverleaf Lane, Mooresville NC 28115, USA
Kvasha, Oleg V — Ice Hockey Player
22 Bluff Road, Glen Cove NY 11542, USA
Kvitova, Petra — Tennis Player
Women's Tennis Assn, 1 Progress Plaza, #1500, Saint Petersburg FL 33701 USA
Kwak Yoon Gy — Speed Skater
Skating Union, 88 Bangyee-Dong, Songpaku, Seoul 138 749, South Korea
Kwalick, Thaddeus J (Ted) — Football Player
755 Purdue Court, Santa Clara CA 95051, USA
Kwan, Jennie — Actress
Innovative Artists, 1505 10th St, Santa Monica CA 90401 USA
Kwan, Michelle W — Figure Skater
Tufts University, Fletcher Law/Diplomacy School, Medford MA 02155, USA
Kwan, Nancy — Actress
Marlin, 252 7th Ave, #9P, New York NY 10001, USA
Kwanten, Ryan — Actor
Orly Adelson Productions, 2900 Olympic Blvd, Los Angeles CA 90404, USA
Kwapis, Ken — Director, Producer, Actor
United Talent Agency, 9336 Civic Center Dr, Beverly Hills CA 90210 USA
Kwasniewski, Aleksander — President, Poland
Kancelaria Prezydenta RP, Ul Wiejska 4/8, 00 902 Warsaw, Poland
Kweli, Talib — Rap Artist (Black Star), Songwriter
Susan Blond Inc, 50 W 57th St, #1400, New York NY 10019 USA
Kweller, Ben — Singer, Songwriter
C 3 Presents, 98 San Jacinto Blvd, #400, Austin TX 78701, USA
Kwiatkowski, Joel — Ice Hockey Player
2020 Tall Pines Dr SE, Grand Rapids MI 49546, USA
Kwoh, Yik San — Electrical Engineer, Inventor
Hi-Tech Medical Systems, 17155 Newhope St, Fountain Valley CA 92708, USA
Kwolek, Stephanie L — Inventor (Kevlar)
312 Spalding Road, Wilmington DE 19803, USA
Kwouk, Burt — Actor
QVoice, Holborn Hall, 193-197 High Holborn, London WC1V 7BD, England
Kyd, Gerald — Actor
Ken McReddie Assoc, 11 Connaught Place, London W2 2ET, England
Kydland, Finn E — Nobel Economics Laureate
169 Noble Lane, Worthington PA 16262, USA
Kyle, Aaron D — Football Player
8544 Townley Road, #2M, Huntersville NC 28078, USA
Kyle, David L — Businessman
O N E O K Inc, 100 W 5th St, PO Box 871, Tulsa OK 74102, USA
Kyle, Jason C — Football Player
19109 W Catawba Ave, #200, Cornelius NC 28031, USA
Kyle, Kaylyn — Soccer Player
Canadian Soccer, Place Soccer Canada, 237 Metcalfe St, Ottawa ON K2P 1R2, Canada
Kylian, Jiri — Ballet Dancer
Netherlands Dance Theater, Schedeldoekshaven 60, 2501 CH Den Haag, Netherlands
Kynaston, Nicholas — Concert Organist
25 High Park Road, Richmond-upon-Thames, Surrey TW9 4BH, England
Kyo, Machiko — Actress
Olimpia Copu, 6-35 Jingumae, Shibuyaku, Tokyo 151 0001, Japan
Kyrillos, Jean-Paul — Publisher
Food & Wine, Publisher's Office, 1120 Ave of Americas, New York NY 10036, USA
Kyte, Jim — Ice Hockey Player
226 Sherwood Dr, Ottawa ON K1Y 3V8, Canada

K

Kahn - Kyte

L

Name	Occupation
Laage, Gerhart	Architect
Schulterblatt 36, 20357 Hamburg, Germany	
Laaksonen, Antti	Ice Hockey Player
9225 Red Oak Dr, Victoria MN 55386, USA	
Laaveg, Paul M	Football Player
PO Box 406, Berryville VA 22611, USA	
LaBar, Jeffrey P (Jeff)	Singer, Guitarist (Cinderella)
Union Entertainment Group, 1323 Newbury Road, #104, Thousand Oaks CA 91320, USA	
Labarthe, Samuel	Actor
Cineart, 36 Rue de Ponthieu, 75008 Paris, France	
LaBelle, Patti	Singer
I C M Partners, 10250 Constellation Blvd, #900, Los Angeles CA 90067 USA	
LaBeouf, Shia S	Actor
John Crosby Mgmt, 1310 N Spaulding Ave, Los Angeles CA 90046 USA	
Labeque, Katia	Concert Pianist
Askonas Holt, Lincoln House, 300 High Holborn, London WC1V 7JH, England	
Labeque, Marielle	Concert Pianist
Askonas Holt, Lincoln House, 300 High Holborn, London WC1V 7JH, England	
Labine, Tyler	Actor
Creative Artists Agency, 2000 Ave of Stars, #100, Los Angeles CA 90067 USA	
Labis, Attilo	Ballet Dancer, Choreographer
13 Ave Rubens, 78400 Chateau, France	
Labonte, Justin	Auto Racing Driver
PO Box 843, Trinity NC 27370, USA	
Labonte, Robert A (Bobby)	Auto Racing Driver
Bobby Labonte Racing, PO Box 358, Trinity NC 27370, USA	
Labonte, Terrance L (Terry)	Auto, Truck Racing Driver
PO Box 370, Trinity NC 27370, USA	
Laborde, Alden J	Businessman
63 Oriole St, New Orleans LA 70124, USA	
Labounty, Matthew J (Matt)	Football Player
360 W 17th Ave, Eugene OR 97401, USA	
LaBour, Fred (Too Slim)	Singer, Bassist (Riders in the Sky)
New Frontier Mgmt, 1921 Broadway, Nashville TN 37203, USA	
Labourier, Dominique	Actress
Agence Elisabeth Simpson, 62 Blvd du Montparnasse, 75015 Paris, France	
LaBoy, Travis J	Football Player
1567 E Prescott Court, Chandler AZ 85249, USA	
Labre, Yvon	Ice Hockey Player
7812 Tilmont Ave, Parkville MD 21234, USA	
LaBute, Neil	Director, Writer
Contemptible Entertainment, 1202 Poinsettia Drive, West Hollywood CA 90046, USA	
Labyorteaux, Matthew	Actor
167 W 72nd St, #3R, New York NY 10023, USA	
Labyorteaux, Patrick	Actor
C E S D, 10635 Santa Monica Blvd, #130, Los Angeles CA 90025 USA	
Lace, Jerry E	Figure Skating Executive
10214 Pine Glade Dr, Colorado Springs CO 80920, USA	
Lacey, Deborah	Actress
A K A Talent, 6310 San Vicente Blvd, #200, Los Angeles CA 90048 USA	
Lacey, Jesse T	Singer (Taking Back Sunday, Brand New)
Stunt Company Media, 20 Jay St, #208, Brooklyn NY 11201, USA	
Lacey, Robert J (Bob)	Baseball Player
1717 20th St NW, #308, Washington DC 20009, USA	
Lach, Elmer J	Ice Hockey Player
89 Bayview Ave, Pointe Claire QC H9S 5C4, Canada	
Lachance, Michel (Mike)	Harness Racing Driver
183 Sweetmans Lane, Millstone Township NJ 08535, USA	
LaChance, Scott	Ice Hockey Player
15 Meadow View Lane, Andover MA 01810, USA	
LaChapelle, David	Photographer
Venus Entertainment, 3630 Eastham Dr, Culver City CA 90232 USA	
Lachemann, Marcel E	Baseball Player, Manager
529 Fieldview Place, Arroyo Grande CA 93420, USA	
Lachemann, Rene G	Baseball Player, Manager
7500 E Boulders Parkway, #68, Scottsdale AZ 85266, USA	
Lacher, Blaine	Ice Hockey Player
29 Shannon Crescent SE, Medicine Hat AB T1B 4C2, Canada	
Lachey, Andrew J (Drew)	Singer (98 Degrees), Actor
Core Entertainment, 14742 Ventura Blvd, #PH, Sherman Oaks CA 91403, USA	
Lachey, James M (Jim)	Football Player
1445 Roxbury Road, Columbus OH 43212, USA	
Lachey, Nicholas S (Nick)	Singer (98 Degrees)
Front Line Mgmt, 1100 Glendon Ave, #2000, Los Angeles CA 90024 USA	
LaChiusa, Michael John	Composer, Librettist
Abrams Artists, 9200 W Sunset Blvd, #1125, West Hollywood CA 90069 USA	
Lachman, Dichen	Actress
Gersh Agency, 9465 Wilshire Blvd, #600, Beverly Hills CA 90212 USA	
Lachman, Gary Valentine	Writer, Musician
Tarcher/Penguin Books, 375 Hudson St, Basement 1, New York NY 10014, USA	
Lacina, Corbin	Football Player
1550 Skyline Court, Saint Paul MN 55121, USA	
Lack, Andrew	Businessman
Sony/BMG Music Entertainment, 550 Madison Ave, #600, New York NY 10022, USA	
Lackberg, Camilla	Writer
Nordin Agency, Gotgatan 58, 102 61 Stockholm, Sweden	
Lacke, Elizabeth (Beth)	Actress
Aria Model & Talent Mgmt, 1017 W Washington, #2C, Chicago IL 60607, USA	
Lacker, Jeffrey	Financier, Government Official
Federal Reserve Board, 701 E Byrd St, #200, Richmond VA 23219, USA	
Lackey, Elizabeth (Lisa)	Actress
Marquee Mgmt, Gate House, 188 Oxford St, Paddington NSW 2021, Australia	
Lackey, John D	Baseball Player
10 Shore Walk, Newport Coast CA 92657, USA	
Laclavere, Georges	Geophysicist
53 Ave de Breteuil, 70075 Paris, France	

Laage - Laclavere

Laclotte, Michel R	Museum Executive
10 Bis Rue du Pre-aux-Clerc, 75007 Paris, France	
Lacock, R Pierre (Pete)	Baseball Player
10019 Mackey Circle, Overland Park KS 66212, USA	
Lacombe, Francois	Ice Hockey Player
Webster Hockey Academy, 22 Hampton Gardens, Point Claire QC H9S 5B8, Canada	
Lacombe, Henri	Oceanographer
20 Bis Ave de Lattre de Tassigny, 92340 Bourg la Reine, France	
Lacorte, Frank J	Baseball Player
1667 El Dorado Dr, Gilroy CA 95020, USA	
Lacoste, Catherine	Golfer
Calle B6, #4, El Soto de la Moraleja Alcobendas, Madrid, Spain	
Lacroix, Andre J	Ice Hockey Player
115 S Franklin St, Chagrin Falls OH 44022, USA	
Lacroix, Christian M M	Fashion Designer
73 Rue du Faubourg Saint Honore, 75008 Paris, France	
Lacroix, Daniel	Ice Hockey Player
New York Islanders, 1255 Hempstead Turnpike, Uniondale NY 11553 USA	
Lacroix, Eric	Ice Hockey Player
10463 Meadowleaf Way, Highlands Ranch CO 80126, USA	
Lacy, Alan	Businessman
Sears Roebuck Co, 3333 Beverly Blvd, Hoffman Estates IL 60179, USA	
Lacy, Edgar E	Basketball Player
215 6th St, #D, West Sacramento CA 95605, USA	
Lacy, Jake	Actor
I C M Partners, 10250 Constellation Blvd, #900, Los Angeles CA 90067 USA	
Lacy, Jeffrey S (Jeff)	Boxer
5718 Eaglemount Dr, Lithia FL 33547, USA	
Lacy, Jerry	Actor
Sutton-Barth Vennari, 145 S Fairfax Ave, #310, Los Angeles CA 90036 USA	
Lacy, Leondaus (Lee)	Baseball Player
6130 Nevada Ave, #E420, Woodland Hills CA 91367, USA	
Ladd, Alan W, Jr	Producer
706 N Arden Dr, Beverly Hills CA 90210, USA	
Ladd, Andrew	Ice Hockey Player
550 N Saint Clair St, #2403, Chicago IL 60611, USA	
Ladd, Cheryl	Actress
Don Buchwald/Fortitude, 6500 Wilshire Blvd, #2200, Los Angeles CA 90048 USA	
Ladd, David	Actor
9212 Hazen Dr, Beverly Hills CA 90210, USA	
Ladd, Diane	Actress
Scott Hart Mgmt, 14622 Ventura Blvd, #746, Sherman Oaks CA 91403, USA	
Ladd, Peter L (Pete)	Baseball Player
239 Town Farm Road, New Gloucester ME 04260, USA	
Laderman, Ezra	Composer
Yale University, Music School, New Haven CT 06520, USA	
Ladin, Eric	Actor
Innovative Artists, 1505 10th St, Santa Monica CA 90401 USA	
Ladner, Benjamin	Educator
American University, President's Office, Washington DC 20016, USA	
Ladouceur, Randy	Ice Hockey Player
1221 Cross Creek Circle, #F7, Greenville NC 27834, USA	
Lady Gaga	Singer, Songwriter
135 W 70th St, #1A, New York NY 10023, USA	
Lady Sovereign	Rap Artist
Paradigm Agency, 360 N Crescent Dr, North Building, Beverly Hills CA 90210 USA	
Laemmle, Carla	Actress
645 N Serrano Blvd, Los Angeles CA 90004, USA	
Laettner, Christian D	Basketball Player
1041 Ponte Vedra Blvd, Ponte Vedra Beach FL 32082, USA	
Lafayette, John	Actor
Greene Assoc, 1901 Ave of Stars, #130, Los Angeles CA 90067 USA	
Lafayette, Nathan	Ice Hockey Player
Travel Guard Canada, 145 Welligton St W, Toronto ON M5J 1H8, Canada	
Laffer, Arthur B	Economist
24255 Pacific Coast Highway, Malibu CA 90263, USA	
Lafferty, James	Actor, Director, Producer
United Talent Agency, 9336 Civic Center Dr, Beverly Hills CA 90210 USA	
Lafferty, Stuart	Actor
Paceline Entertainment, 12444 Ventura Blvd, #103, Studio City CA 91604 USA	
Lafforgue, Laurent	Mathematician
I H E S, Mathematics Dept, 91440 Bures sur Yvette, France	
LaFlamme, David	Violinist (It's a Beautiful Day)
Tabletop Productions, PO Box 698, Carson City NV 89702, USA	
Lafleur, Gregory L (Greg)	Football Player
PO Box 612, Baton Rouge LA 70821, USA	
Lafleur, Guy D	Ice Hockey Player
14 Place du Moulin, L'Ile Bizard QC H9E 1N2, Canada	
Lafley, Alan G	Businessman
Clayton Dubilier Rice, 375 Park Ave, #1800, New York NY 10152, USA	
Laflin, Bonnie-Jill	Model, Entertainer
C E S D, 10635 Santa Monica Blvd, #130, Los Angeles CA 90025 USA	
LaFontaine, Patrick (Pat)	Ice Hockey Player
3 Beach Dr, Lloyd Harbor NY 11743, USA	
Laforet, Marie	Actress
Agents Associes, 201 Rue du Faubourg Saint Honore, 75008 Paris, France	
Lafrance, Noemie	Choreographer
148 Classon Ave, Brooklyn NY 11205, USA	
Lafreniere, Roger	Ice Hockey Player
110 Eugene Road, North Bay ON P1B 8B7, Canada	
LaFrentz, Raef A	Basketball Player
PO Box 88, Decorah IA 52101, USA	
Laga, Michael R (Mike)	Baseball Player
148 Maple Ridge Road, Florence MA 01062, USA	
Lagarde, Christine	Financier
International Monetary Fund, 700 19th Ave NW, Washington DC 20431, USA	

LaGarde, Thomas J (Tom)
3809 E Greensboro Chapel Hill Road, Snow Camp NC 27349, USA — Basketball Player

Lagardere, Arnaud
Airbus Industrie, Ronde Point Maucie Bellont 1, 31707 Blagnac, France — Businessman

Lagasse, Emeril
829 Saint Charles Ave, New Orleans LA 70130, USA — Chef, Restauranteur

Lagat, Bernard
9121 E Cottonwood Court, Tucson AZ 85749, USA — Track Athlete

Lagattuta, Bill
CBS-TV, News Dept, 7800 Beverly Blvd, Los Angeles CA 90036, USA — Commentator

Lageman, Jeffrey D (Jeff)
PO Box 364, Basye VA 22810, USA — Football Player

Lagerberg, Bengt F A
Talent Tust, Kungsgaten 9C, 411 19 Gothenburg, Sweden — Drummer (Cardigans)

Lagerfeld, Karl
31 Blvd de la Maubourg, 75007 Paris, France — Fashion Designer, Photographer

Lago, Clara
Kuranda Mgmt, Santo Angel 84, 28043 Madrid, Spain — Actress

Lagoo, Shreeram
3 Gold Mist, 36 Carter Road, Bandra, Mumbai MS 400050, India — Actor

Lagos Escobar, Ricardo
Club de Madrid, C/Goya 5-7, Pasaje 2, 28001 Madrid, Spain — President, Chile

LaGravenese, Richard
Creative Artists Agency, 2000 Ave of Stars, #100, Los Angeles CA 90067 USA — Director, Writer

LaGrossa, Stephanie
42 Caldwell Dr, Toms River NJ 08757, USA — Actress

Lagrow, Lerrin H
12271 E Turquoise Ave, Scottsdale AZ 85259, USA — Baseball Player

Laguna, Frederica de
10 S Bryn Mawr Ave, Bryn Mawr PA 19010, USA — Anthropologist

LaHaie, Dick
Kalitta Motorsports, 1010 James L Hart Parkway, Ypsilanti MI 48197, USA — Drag Racing Driver

LaHaye, Tim
Tyndale House Publishers, 351 Executive Dr, PO Box 80, Wheaton IL 60187, USA — Writer

Lahbib, Simone
Ken McReddie Assoc, 11 Connaught Place, London W2 2ET, England — Actress

Lahiri, Jhumpa
Knopf Publishers, 1745 Broadway, New York NY 10019 USA — Writer

Lahm, Philipp
Rinab Grill, Rathausstr 39, 83734 Hausham, Germany — Soccer Player

LaHood, Ray
Transportation Department, 400 7th St SW, Washington DC 20590 USA — Secretary, Transporation

Lahoud, Joseph M (Joe)
90 Tinker Hill Road, New Preston Marble Dale CT 06777, USA — Baseball Player

Lahti, Christine
Management 360, 9111 Wilshire Blvd, Beverly Hills CA 90210 USA — Actress, Director

Lahti, Jeffrey A (Jeff)
4632 Tyler Dr, Hood River OR 97031, USA — Baseball Player

Lai, Francis
23 Rue Franklin, 75016 Paris, France — Composer

Laidlaw, R Scott
2286 Franklin Pike, Lewisburg TN 37091, USA — Football Player

Laidlaw, Tom
Laidlaw Sports Mgmt, 32 Ridge Blvd, Port Chester NY 10573, USA — Ice Hockey Player

Laimbeer, William (Bill)
470 Gray Court, Marco Island FL 34145, USA — Basketball Player

Laine, Cleo
Old Rectory, Wavendon, Milton Keynes MK17 8LT, England — Singer

Laine, Denny
I C M Partners, 10250 Constellation Blvd, #900, Los Angeles CA 90067 USA — Singer, Guitarist (Moody Blues)

Laing, Richard
Ken McReddie Assoc, 11 Connaught Place, London W2 2ET, England — Actor

Laingen, L Bruce
5627 Old Chester Road, Bethesda MD 20814, USA — Diplomat

Lair, Michael J
Hyco Kid, 87 Oyster Cove Landing, Hartfield VA 23071, USA — Actor

Laird, Bruce A
1405 Margarette Ave, Towson MD 21286, USA — Football Player

Laird, Gerald L, III
13735 E Yucca St, Scottsdale AZ 85259, USA — Baseball Player

Laird, Martin
Professional Golfer's Assn, PO Box 109601, Palm Beach Gardens FL 33410 USA — Golfer

Laird, Melvin R
1730 Rhode Island Ave NW, #406, Washington DC 20036, USA — Secretary, Defense; Businessman

Laird, Peter
PO Box 417, Haydenville MA 01039, USA — Cartoonist (Ninja Turtles)

Laird, Ronald (Ron)
4706 Diane Dr, Ashtabula OH 44004, USA — Track Athlete

Laitman, Jeffrey
Mount Sinai Medical Center, Anatomy Dept, 1 Levy Place, New York NY 10029, USA — Anatomist

Lajoie, Jonathan
United Talent Agency, 9336 Civic Center Dr, Beverly Hills CA 90210 USA — Actor, Writer

LaJoie, Randall (Randy)
PO Box 3478, Westport CT 06880, USA — Auto Racing Driver

Lajolo, Giovanni Cardinal
Pontifical Commission for Vatican City State, 00120 Vatican City — Religious Leader

Lake, Antwan T
1032 Bluebell Dr, Dacula GA 30019, USA — Football Player

Lake, Carnell A
PO Box 55048, Irvine CA 92619, USA — Football Player

Lake, Don
Divine Mgmt, 3822 Latrobe Ave, Los Angeles CA 90031, USA — Actor, Writer

Lake, Greg
Asia, 9 Hillgate St, London W8 7SP, England — Singer, Bassist (Emerson Lake Palmer)

Lake, James A
University of California, Molecular Biology Institute, Los Angeles CA 90024, USA — Molecular Biologist

L

Lake - Lambiel

Lake, Oliver E D L Media, 124 N Highland Ave, Bala Cynwyd PA 19004, USA	Jazz Saxophonist, Synthesizer Player
Lake, Ricki W M E Entertainment, 9601 Wilshire Blvd, #300, Beverly Hills CA 90210 USA	Actress
Lake, Sanoe Jet Set Talent Agency, 2160 Avenida de la Playa, La Jolla CA 92037, USA	Actress
Lake, Stephen M (Steve) 7402 N 177th Ave, Waddel AZ 85355, USA	Baseball Player
Laker, Jim Oak End, 9 Portinscale Road, Putney, London SW15, England	Cricketer
Laker, Timothy J (Tim) 673 Azure Hills Dr, Simi Valley CA 93065, USA	Baseball Player
Lakes, Gary I C M Artists, 40 W 57th St, #1800, New York NY 10019 USA	Opera Singer
Lake-Tack, Louise A Governor General's Office, Government House, St John's, Antigua & Barbuda	Governor General, Antigua & Barbuda
Lakin, Christine Don Buchwald/Fortitude, 6500 Wilshire Blvd, #2200, Los Angeles CA 90048 USA	Actress
Lakner, Yehoshua Postfach 7851, 6000 Lucerne 7, Switzerland	Composer
Lakshmi, Padma B/W/R, 9100 Wilshire Blvd, #500W, Beverly Hills CA 90212 USA	Actress, Model, Writer
Lal, Devendra 4445 Via Precipicio, San Diego CA 92122, USA	Oceanographer
Lala, Joe I C M Partners, 10250 Constellation Blvd, #900, Los Angeles CA 90067 USA	Singer, Percussionist (Blues Image)
LaLande, Hector (Hec) 848 McIntyre St E, North Bay ON P1B 1G1, Canada	Ice Hockey Player
Lalas, Alexi 1007 Maybrook Dr, Beverly Hills CA 90210, USA	Soccer Player, Executive, Sportscaster
Laliberte, Guy Cirque du Soleil, 8400 2nd Ave, Montreal QC H1Z 4M6, Canada	Businessman, Circus Executive, Astronaut
LaLiberte, Nicole Click Model Mgmt, 881 7th Ave, New York NY 10019 USA	Model
Laliberte-Bourque, Andree Musee du Quebec, 1 Ave Wolfe-Montcalm, Quebec QC G1R 5H3, Canada	Museum Executive
Lalime, Patrick 70 Rive du Golf, Grand Mere QC G9T 5K4, Canada	Ice Hockey Player
Lalla Salma Palais Royal, Le Mechouar, Rabat, Morocco	Princess Consort, Morocco
Lalonde, R Lawrence (Larry) Creative Artists Agency, 2000 Ave of Stars, #100, Los Angeles CA 90067 USA	Guitarist (Primus)
Lalonde, Robert P (Bobby) 523 Broadgreen St, Pickering ON L1W 3E8, Canada	Ice Hockey Player
Lam, Derek Jeffrey Lam Co, 446 W 13th St, New York NY 10014, USA	Fashion Designer
Lam, Mei-Ling Playboy Promotions, 2706 Media Center Dr, Los Angeles CA 90065 USA	Model
Lam, Sal Kit Malaysia University, Microbiolgy Dept, 50603 Kuala Lumpur, Malaysia	Virologist
Lamar, Dwight (Bo) 103 Claire St, Lafayette LA 70507, USA	Basketball Player
LaMarr, Phil TalentWorks, 3500 W Olive Ave, #1400, Burbank CA 91505 USA	Actor, Comedian
Lamas, Lorenzo Sutton-Barth Vennari, 145 S Fairfax Ave, #310, Los Angeles CA 90036 USA	Actor
Lamb, Allan J Lamb Assoc, 4 Saint Giles St, #400, Northampton NN1 1JB, England	Cricketer
Lamb, Brian P C-Span Network, 400 N Capitol St NW, #650, Washington DC 20001, USA	Businessman
Lamb, Dennis 19 Rue de Franqueville, 75016 Paris, France	Diplomat
Lamb, Jeremy Oklahoma City Thunder, 211 N Robinson Ave, #300, Oklahoma City OK 73102 USA	Basketball Player
Lamb, Larry MacFarlane Chard Assoc, 33 Percy St, London W1T 2DF, England	Actor
Lamb, Michael Bobby Roberts, 3050 Business Park Circle, #303, Goodlettsville TN 37221 USA	Guitarist (Confederate Railroad)
Lamb, Mike 17 Meadow Wood Dr, Trabuco Canyon CA 92679, USA	Baseball Player
Lamb, Raymond R (Ray) 3 Corte Tallista, San Clemente CA 92673, USA	Baseball Player
Lamberg, Adam M Innovative Artists, 1505 10th St, Santa Monica CA 90401 USA	Actor
Lambert, Adam M 19 Music & Mgmt, 35-37 Parkgate Road, London SW11 4NP, England	Singer, Songwriter
Lambert, Chloe Artmedia, 20 Ave Rapp, 75007 Paris, France	Actress
Lambert, Christophe A P A Talent/Literary Agency, 405 S Beverly Dr, #300, Beverly Hills CA 90212 USA	Actor
Lambert, John E 884 Dolphin Dr, Danville CA 94526, USA	Basketball Player
Lambert, John H (Jack) PO Box 512, Worthington PA 16262, USA	Football Player
Lambert, Lane 258 E Washington St, Jefferson WI 53549, USA	Ice Hockey Player, Coach
Lambert, Mary M Don Buchwald/Fortitude, 6500 Wilshire Blvd, #2200, Los Angeles CA 90048 USA	Director
Lambert, Miranda W M E Entertainment, 1600 Division St, #300, Nashville TN 37203 USA	Singer, Guitarist, Songwriter
Lambert, Nathalie Speed Skating Canada, 2781 Lancaster Road, #402, Ottawa ON K1B 1A7, Canada	Speed Skater
Lambert, Phyllis Centre d'Architecture, 1920 Rue Baile, Montreal QC H3H 2S6, Canada	Architect
Lambiel, Stephane Route de Praz Berard 3A, 1844 Villeneuve, Switzerland	Figure Skater

Lambo, T Adeoye — Psychiatrist
Lambo Foundation, 11 Olatunsbosun St, Ikeja, Lagos State, Nigeria
Lambrecht, Dietrich R — Electrical Engineer
Rathenaustr 11, 45470 Mulheim an der Ruhr, Germany
Lambrecht, Yves — Actor
Artmedia, 20 Ave Rapp, 75007 Paris, France
Lambro, Phillip — Composer, Pianist
Trigram Music, 1888 Century Park East, #10, Los Angeles CA 90067, USA
Lamm, Norman — Educator, Religious Leader, Rabbi
Eicharen Theological Seminary, 2540 Amsterdam Ave, New York NY 10033, USA
Lamm, Richard D — Governor, CO
University of Denver, Public Policy Center, Denver CO 80208, USA
Lamm, Robert W — Singer, Keyboardist (Chicago)
Front Line Mgmt, 1100 Glendon Ave, #2000, Los Angeles CA 90024 USA
Lammers, Esmee — Director, Writer
Features Creative Mgmt, Entrepotdok 76A, 101 AD Amsterdam, Netherlands
Lammons, Peter S (Pete), Jr — Football Player
5006 E Fallen Bough Dr, Houston TX 77041, USA
Lamonica, Daryle P — Football Player
All Star Warehouse, 2860 S East Ave, Fresno CA 93725, USA
Lamont, Gene W — Baseball Player, Manager
5194 Siesta Woods Dr, Sarasota FL 34242, USA
Lamont, Norman S H — Government Official, England
Balli Group PLC, 5 Stanhope Gate, London W1Y 5LA, England
Lamontagne, Ray — Singer, Songwriter
Mick Mgmt, 35 Washington St, Brooklyn NY 11201 USA
Lamoriello, Louis (Lou) — Ice Hockey Executive, Coach
New Jersey Devils, Arena, 50 State Route 120, East Rutherford NJ 07073 USA
Lamott, Anne — Writer
Wylie Agency, 250 W 57th St, #2114, New York NY 10107 USA
LaMotta, Jake — Boxer
Raging Bull Enterprises, 400 E 57th St, New York NY 10022, USA
Lamp, Dennis P — Baseball Player
30824 La Miranda, #228, Rancho Santa Margarita CA 92688, USA
Lamp, Jeffrey A (Jeff) — Basketball Player
4971 Credit River Dr, Savage MN 55378, USA
Lampanelli, Lisa — Actress, Comedienne
Parallel Artists Mgmt, 9420 Wilshire Blvd, #250, Beverly Hills CA 90212, USA
Lampard, C Keith — Baseball Player
6124 Highway 6 N, Houston TX 77084, USA
Lamparski, Richard — Writer
4202 Calle Real, #245, Santa Barbara CA 93110, USA
Lampert, Edward S — Businessman
E S L Investments, 200 Greenwich Ave, #3, Greenwich CT 06830, USA
Lampert, Zohra — Actress
Don Buchwald/Fortitude, 6500 Wilshire Blvd, #2200, Los Angeles CA 90048 USA
Lampkin, Thomas M (Tom) — Baseball Player
3810 SE 153rd Court, Vancouver WA 98683, USA
Lampley, James (Jim) — Sportscaster
3325 Caminito Daniella, Del Mar CA 92014, USA
Lamprey, Zane — Actor, Comedian
W M E Entertainment, 9601 Wilshire Blvd, #300, Beverly Hills CA 90210 USA
Lampson, Butler W — Computer Engineer
Microsoft Corp, 1 Microsoft Way, Redmond WA 98052, USA
Lampton, Michael — Astronaut
University of California, Space Science Laboratory, Berkeley CA 94720, USA
Lamsma, Simone — Concert Violinist
I M G Artists, Hogarth Business Park, Chiswick, London W4 2TH, England
Lamy, Pascal L F — Government Official, France
World Trade Organization, Rue Lausanne 154, 1211 Geneva 21, Switzerland
LaNasa, Katherine — Actress
I F A Talent Agency, 8730 W Sunset Blvd, #490, West Hollywood CA 90069 USA
Lancashire, Sarah — Actress
Talents Artists, 59 Snyder Road, London N16 7UF, England
Lancaster, Lester W (Les) — Baseball Player
PO Box 1105, Dothan AL 36302, USA
Lancaster, Mark — Artist
Cunningham Dance Foundation, 55 Bethune St, New York NY 10014, USA
Lancaster, Neal — Golfer
6 Quail Run, Smithfield NC 27577, USA
Lance, Dirk — Bassist (Incubus)
Variety Artists, 793 Higuera St, #6, San Luis Obispo CA 93401 USA
Lancelotti, Richard A (Rick) — Baseball Player
5190 Thompson Road, Clarence NY 14031, USA
Landau, Juliet — Actress
Miss Juliet Productions, PO Box 2792, Los Angeles CA 90078, USA
Landau, Martin — Actor
PO Box 10959, Beverly Hills CA 90213, USA
Landau, Russ — Composer
Evolution Music Partners, 1680 Vine St, #500, Los Angeles CA 90028 USA
Landau, Saul — Writer
Institute for Policy Studies, 1601 Connecticut Ave NW, Washington DC 20009, USA
Landau, Tina — Director
I C M Partners, 10250 Constellation Blvd, #900, Los Angeles CA 90067 USA
Landeau, Alexsia — Actress
Agents Associes, 201 Rue du Faubourg Saint Honore, 75008 Paris, France
Landecker, Amy — Actress
C E S D, 257 Park Ave S, #950, New York NY 10010 USA
Lander, David L — Actor
918 S Tremaine Ave, Los Angeles CA 90019, USA
Lander, Eric Steven — Mathematician, Biologist
Broad Institute, 9 Cambridge Circle, Cambridge MA 02142, USA
Landers, Andy — Basketball Coach
University of Georgia, Athletic Dept, Athens GA 30602, USA
Landers, Audrey — Actress, Singer
Landers Productions, 4048 Las Palmas Dr, Sarasota FL 34238, USA

Landers, Judy — Actress
Landers Productions, 4048 Las Palmas Dr, Sarasota FL 34238, USA
Landers, Larry — Golfer
PO Box 497, Azle TX 76098, USA
Landers, Paul H — Guitarist (Rammstein)
Pilgrim Mgmt, PO Box 540101, 10042 Berlin, Germany
Landes, David S — Historian
1010 Memorial Dr, #11E, Cambridge MA 02138, USA
Landes, Michael — Actor
Creative Artists Agency, 2000 Ave of Stars, #100, Los Angeles CA 90067 USA
Landestoy, Rafael — Baseball Player
PO Box 940755, Miami FL 33194, USA
Landeta, Sean E — Football Player
137 Powerhouse Road, #7W, Roslyn Heights NY 11577, USA
Landis, Floyd — Cyclist
4632 Felton St, #2, San Diego CA 92116, USA
Landis, James H (Jim) — Baseball Player
203 Alchemy Way, Napa CA 94558, USA
Landis, John D — Director
Gersh Agency, 9465 Wilshire Blvd, #600, Beverly Hills CA 90212 USA
Landis, William H (Bill) — Baseball Player
525 E Sycamore Dr, Hanford CA 93230, USA
Lando, Joe — Actor
Jay D Schwartz & Assoc, 6767 Forest Lawn Dr, #211, Los Angeles CA 90068, USA
Landon, Jennifer — Actress
Collective, 8383 Wilshire Blvd, #1050, Beverly Hills CA 90211 USA
Landon, Laurene — Actress
Dale Garrick, 1017 N La Cienega Blvd, #109, West Hollywood CA 90069 USA
Landreaux, Kenneth F (Ken) — Baseball Player
1510 N Siesta Ave, La Puente CA 91746, USA
Landress, Ilene S — Producer
Creative Artists Agency, 2000 Ave of Stars, #100, Los Angeles CA 90067 USA
Landrieu, Moon — Secretary, Housing & Urban Development
4301 S Prieur St, New Orleans LA 70125, USA
Landrum, T William (Bill) — Baseball Player
840 Silver Point Road, Chapin SC 29036, USA
Landrum, Terry L (Tito) — Baseball Player
428 E 50th St, Garden, New York NY 10022, USA
Landry, Carl C — Basketball Player
New Orleans Hornets, 1250 Poydras St, #101, New Orleans LA 70113 USA
Landry, Dawan F — Football Player
309 Kennedy St, Ama LA 70031, USA
Landry, Gregory P (Greg) — Football Player, Coach
133 Melanie Lane, Troy MI 48098, USA
Landry, Karen — Actress
Don Buchwald/Fortitude, 6500 Wilshire Blvd, #2200, Los Angeles CA 90048 USA
Landry, LaRon L — Football Player
New York Jets, 1 Jets Dr, Florham Park NJ 07932 USA
Landsberger, Mark W — Basketball Player
1702 8th Ave SE, Saint Cloud MN 56304, USA
Landsbergis, Vytautas — President, Lithuania
European Parliament, Bat Altiero Spinelli, Wiertzstraat 60, 1047 Brussels, Belgium
Landsburg, Valerie — Actress
PO Box 1617, Topanga CA 90290, USA
Landshamer, Christina — Opera Singer
Kunstler Sekretariat am Gasteig, Rosenheimer Str 52, 81669 Munich, Germany
Landsman, Mark — Producer, Director
Hirsch Wallerstein Hayum, 10100 Santa Monica Blvd, #1700, Los Angeles CA 90067 USA
Landy, Bernard — Government Official, Canada
Gouvement du Quebec, 885 Grand Allee Est, Quebec QC GLA 1A2, Canada
Lane, Abbe — Singer, Actress
500 Bel Air Road, Los Angeles CA 90077, USA
Lane, Akira — Model
PO Box 8052, Laguna Hills CA 92654, USA
Lane, Cristy — Singer
L S Records, PO Box 654, Madison TN 37116, USA
Lane, David P — Oncologist
Dundee Medical Center, Molecular Research Dept, Dundee DD1 9SY, Scotland
Lane, Diane — Actress
Hyler Mgmt, 20 Ocean Park Blvd, #25, Santa Monica CA 90405 USA
Lane, Gord — Ice Hockey Player
8 Magnolia Dr, Brandon MB R7A 0Y9, Canada
Lane, John R (Jack) — Museum Executive
San Francisco Museum of Modern Art, 151 3rd St, San Francisco CA 94103, USA
Lane, Kenneth Jay — Fashion Designer
Kenneth Jay Lane Inc, 20 W 37th St, #900, New York NY 10018, USA
Lane, Lilas — Actress
TalentWorks, 3500 W Olive Ave, #1400, Burbank CA 91505 USA
Lane, MacArthur — Football Player
3238 Knowland Ave, Oakland CA 94619, USA
Lane, Malcolm D — Biological Chemist
717 Maiden Choice Lane, #525, Catonsville MD 21228, USA
Lane, Marvin (Marv) — Baseball Player
40164 Gulliver Dr, Sterling Heights MI 48310, USA
Lane, Matthew — Golfer
Links Mgmt, 5068 W Plano Parkway, #256, Plano TX 75093, USA
Lane, Max A — Football Player
16 Strong St, Newburyport MA 1950, USA
Lane, Mike — Editorial Cartoonist
Baltimore Sun, Editorial Dept, 501 N Calvert St, Baltimore MD 21278, USA
Lane, Nathan — Actor, Singer
I C M Partners, 10250 Constellation Blvd, #900, Los Angeles CA 90067 USA
Lane, Richard H (Dick) — Baseball Player
2717 Legend Dr, Las Vegas NV 89134, USA
Lane, Robert W — Businessman
Deere Co, 1 John Deere Place, Moline IL 61265, USA

Lane, Robin — Dancer, Choreographer
Do Jump Co, Echo Theater, 1515 SE 37th Ave, Portland OR 97214, USA
Lanegan, Mark — Singer, Guitarist (Queens of Stone Age)
The Firm, 2049 Century Park E, #2550, Los Angeles CA 90067 USA
Laneuville, Eric — Actor, Director
5138 W Slauson Ave, Los Angeles CA 90056, USA
Laney, James T — Educator, Diplomat
2015 Grand Prix Dr NE, Atlanta GA 30345, USA
Laney, Sandra E — Businesswoman
Cadre Computer Resources, 255 E 5th St, #1200, Cincinnati OH 45202, USA
Lang Lang — Concert Pianist
Bedlam Mgmt, PO Box 34449, London W6 0RT, England
Lang, Andrew C — Basketball Player
1048 Woodruff Plantation Parkway SE, Marietta GA 30067, USA
Lang, Antonio M — Basketball Player
2255 Barretts Lane, Mobile AL 36617, USA
Lang, Belinda — Actress
Ken McReddie Assoc, 11 Connaught Place, London W2 2ET, England
Lang, Brittany — Golfer
Gaylord Sports Mgmt, 13845 N Northsight Blvd, #200, Scottsdale AZ 85260 USA
Lang, David — Composer
Red Poppy Music, 66 Greene St, #500, New York NY 10012, USA
Lang, Gene E — Football Player
11526 Azalea Trace, Gulfport MS 39503, USA
Lang, Helmut — Fashion Designer
Michele Morgan, 184 Rue Saint-Maur, 75010 Paris, France
Lang, Jack M E — Government Official, France
Mairie, 41000 Blois, France
Lang, Jonny — Singer, Guitarist
Vector Mgmt, 1607 17th Ave S, Nashville TN 37212, USA
lang, k d — Singer, Actress
Paradigm Agency, 404 W Franklin St, Monterey CA 93940 USA
Lang, Katherine Kelly — Actress, Model
Edmonds Entertainment Group, 1635 N Cahuenga Blvd, Los Angeles CA 90028, USA
Lang, Kenard D — Football Player
1781 Oakbrook Dr, Longwood FL 32779, USA
Lang, Michelle — Actress
Paceline Entertainment, 12444 Ventura Blvd, #103, Studio City CA 91604 USA
Lang, Perry — Actor
A P A Talent/Literary Agency, 405 S Beverly Dr, #300, Beverly Hills CA 90212 USA
Lang, Robert — Ice Hockey Player
PO Box 633, Diablo CA 94528, USA
Lang, Stephen — Actor, Director, Writer
Innovative Artists, 1505 10th St, Santa Monica CA 90401 USA
Langan, Kevin — Opera Singer
Columbia Artists Mgmt Inc, 1790 Broadway, #702, New York NY 10019 USA
Langbein, John H — Attorney, Educator
Yale University, Law School, 127 Wall St, New Haven CT 06511, USA
Langbo, Arnold G — Businessman
Kellogg Co, 1 Kellogg Square, PO Box 3599, Battle Creek MI 49016, USA
Langdon, Darren — Ice Hockey Player
1 Oake's Road, Deer Lake NF A8K 1X5, Canada
Langdon, Harry — Photographer
501 Center St, #6, El Segundo CA 90245, USA
Langdon, Sue Ane — Actress
4618 Park Mirasol, Calabasas CA 91302, USA
Lange, Allison — Actress
Stone Manners Salners, 9911 W Pico Blvd, #1400, Los Angeles CA 90035 USA
Lange, Andre — Bobsled Athlete
Team Andre Lange, Robert-Schumann-Str 14B, 98529 Suhl, Germany
Lange, Artie — Actor, Comedian
3 Arts Entertainment, 9460 Wilshire Blvd, #700, Beverly Hills CA 90212 USA
Lange, Eric — Actor
Domain Talent, 9229 W Sunset Blvd, #710, West Hollywood CA 90069 USA
Lange, Jessica — Actress
Untitled Entertainment, 350 S Beverly Dr, #200, Beverly Hills CA 90212 USA
Lange, Niklaus — Actor
A P A Talent/Literary Agency, 405 S Beverly Dr, #300, Beverly Hills CA 90212 USA
Lange, Otto L — Botanist
Leitengraben 37, 97084 Wuerzburg, Germany
Lange, Richard O (Dick) — Baseball Player
39744 Salvatore Dr, Sterling Heights MI 48313, USA
Lange, Ted — Actor
House of Representatives, 1434 6th St, #1, Santa Monica CA 90401 USA
Lange, Thomas — Rowing Athlete
Ratzeburger Ruderclub, Domhof 57, 23909 Ratzburg, Germany
Langella, Frank — Actor
I C M Partners, 10250 Constellation Blvd, #900, Los Angeles CA 90067 USA
Langen, Christoph — Bobsled Athlete
B C Unterhaching, Ottobrunner Str 16, 82008 Unterhaching, Germany
Langenbrunner, Jaime — Ice Hockey Player
94096 Warloe Shore Lane, Moose Lake MN 55767, USA
Langenkamp, Heather — Actress
Malibu Gum Co, 23852 Pacific Coast Highway, #655, Malibu CA 90265, USA
Langer, A J — Actress
Valeo Entertainment, 8265 Sunset Blvd, #103, Los Angeles CA 90046, USA
Langer, Alois A — Inventor (Implantable Defibrillator)
111 Saddlebrook Dr, Harrison City PA 15636, USA
Langer, Bernhard — Golfer
3667 Princeton Place, Boca Raton FL 33496, USA
Langer, James J (Jim) — Football Player
14280 Wolfram St NW, Anoka MN 55303, USA
Langer, James S — Physicist
1130 Las Canoas Lane, Santa Barbara CA 93105, USA
Langer, Robert S, Jr — Inventor (Controlled Drug Delivery)
Massachusetts Institute of Technolgy, Langer Laboratory, Cambridge MA 02139, USA

Langerhans, Ryan D — Baseball Player
PO Box 1026, Round Rock TX 78680, USA
Langevin, David (Dave) — Ice Hockey Player
1090 W Circle Court, Saint Paul MN 55118, USA
Langfield, Camille — Actress
PO Box 254, Carmel by the Sea CA 93921, USA
Langford, J Rick — Baseball Player
8330 9th Avenue Terrace NW, Bradenton FL 34209, USA
Langham, C Antonio — Football Player
PO Box 232, Town Creek AL 35672, USA
Langham, Franklin — Golfer
PO Box 3428, Peachtree City GA 30269, USA
Langham, Wallace — Actor
Imperium 7 Talent, 5455 Wilshire Blvd, #1706, Los Angeles CA 90036, USA
Langhorne, Reginald D (Reggie) — Football Player
12260 Smiths Neck Road, Carrollton VA 23314, USA
Langkow, Daymond R — Ice Hockey Player
11549 E Cochise Dr, Scottsdale AZ 85259, USA
Langlands, Robert P — Mathematician
60 Battle Road, Princeton NJ 08540, USA
Lang-Lessing, Sebastian — Conductor
I M G Artists, Hogarth Business Park, Chiswick, London W4 2TH, England
Langlois, Albert, Jr — Ice Hockey Player
2473 Crest View Dr, Los Angeles CA 90046, USA
Langlois, Paul — Guitarist (Tragically Hip)
Bobby Breen Mgmt, 13 Blackburn St, #300, Toronto ON M4M 2B3, Canada
Langmaid, Ben — Singer, Songwriter (La Roux)
Beatnik Public Relations, 5 Little Portland St, London W1W 7JD, England
Langmann, Thomas — Producer, Actor
La Petite Reine, 20 Rue de Saint-Petersbourg, 75008 Paris, France
Langridge, Matthew — Rowing Athlete
Leander Club, Henley on Thames, Leander RG9 2LP, England
Langston, J William — Neurologist
Parkinson's Foundation, 2444 Moorpark Ave, San Jose CA 95128, USA
Langston, Mark E — Baseball Player
56 Golden Eagle, Irvine CA 92603, USA
Langston, Murray — Actor, Comedian
Entertainment Alliance, PO Box 4734, Santa Rosa CA 95402, USA
Langton, Brooke — Actress
Gersh Agency, 9465 Wilshire Blvd, #600, Beverly Hills CA 90212 USA
Langway, Rod C — Ice Hockey Player
8260 Powhickery Dr, Mechanicsville VA 23116, USA
Lanier, Cathy L — Law Enforcement Official
Metropolitan Police Dept, 300 Indiana Ave NW, Washington DC 20001, USA
Lanier, Harold C (Hal) — Baseball Player, Manager
3270 Countryside View Dr, Saint Cloud FL 34772, USA
Lanier, Jaron — Computer Engineer (Virtual Reality)
Advanced Network Services, 200 Business Park Dr, Armonk NY 10504, USA
Lanier, Kenneth W (Ken) — Football Player
21923 E Ridge Trail Circle, Aurora CO 80016, USA
Lanier, Robert J (Bob), Jr — Basketball Player, Coach
13027 E Saddlehorn Trail, Scottsdale AZ 85259, USA
Lanier, Willie E — Football Player
2911 E Brigstock Road, Midlothian VA 23113, USA
Lanig, Hans-Peter — Alpine Skier
Omachstr 11, 87541 Hindelang, Germany
Lankford, Frank G — Baseball Player
104 Lakeview Ave NE, Atlanta GA 30305, USA
Lankford, Kim — Actress
House of Representatives, 1434 6th St, #1, Santa Monica CA 90401 USA
Lankford, Paul J — Football Player
3838 Biggin Church Road W, Jacksonville FL 32224, USA
Lankford, Raymond L (Ray) — Baseball Player
1520 Lake Whitney Dr, Windermere FL 34786, USA
Lanners, Bouli — Actor
Voyez Mon Agent, 20 Ave Rapp, 75007 Paris, France
Lanois, Daniel — Singer, Musician, Songwriter
Monterey Peninsula Artists, 404 W Franklin St, Monterey CA 93940 USA
Lanoue, Virginie — Actress
Artmedia, 20 Ave Rapp, 75007 Paris, France
Lansbury, Angela — Actress, Singer
Don Buchwald/Fortitude, 6500 Wilshire Blvd, #2200, Los Angeles CA 90048 USA
Lansbury, David — Actor
Don Buchwald/Fortitude, 6500 Wilshire Blvd, #2200, Los Angeles CA 90048 USA
Lansdale, Joe R — Writer
199 County Road 508, Nacogdoches TX 75961, USA
Lansford, Alex J (Buck) — Football Player
PO Box 905, Lampasas TX 76550, USA
Lansford, Carney R — Baseball Player
43736 Pocahontas Road, Baker City OR 97814, USA
Lansford, Joseph D (Jody) — Baseball Player
3691 Warbler Ave, Santa Clara CA 95051, USA
Lansford, Michael J (Mike) — Football Player
6200 E Canyon Rim Road, #205, Grants Pass OR 97526, USA
Lansing, Michael T (Mike) — Baseball Player
9691 S Sun Meadow St, Littleton CO 80129, USA
Lansing, P J — Model
Playboy Promotions, 2706 Media Center Dr, Los Angeles CA 90065 USA
Lansing, Sherry L — Producer
10741 Levico Way, Los Angeles CA 90077, USA
Lanter, Matt — Actor
Emerald Talent Group, 15260 Ventura Blvd, #1200, Sherman Oaks CA 91403
Lantz, Stuart B (Stu) — Basketball Player
5270 Mount Burnham Dr, San Diego CA 92111, USA
Lanvin, Bernard — Fashion Designer
22 Rue du Faubourg Saint Honore, 70008 Paris, France

Lanvin, Gerard — Actor
Voyez Mon Agent, 20 Ave Rapp, 75007 Paris, France
Lanz, Rick — Ice Hockey Player
18962 20th Ave, Surrey BC V3S 9V2, Canada
Lanza, Manuel — Opera Singer
I C M Artists, 40 W 57th St, #1800, New York NY 10019 USA
Lanza, Suzanne — Model, Actress
Greater Visions Artists Talent Agency, 8981 W Sunset Blvd, #101, West Hollywood CA 90069 USA
Laoretti, Larry — Golfer
10567 SW Whooping Crane Way, Palm City FL 34990, USA
LaPaglia, Anthony — Actor
400 N Bristol Ave, Los Angeles CA 90049, USA
LaPaglia, Jonathan — Actor
Untitled Entertainment, 350 S Beverly Dr, #200, Beverly Hills CA 90212 USA
Laperriere, Ian — Ice Hockey Player
415 Washington Ave, Haddonfield NJ 8033, USA
Laperriere, J Jacques H — Ice Hockey Player
1490 Rue Bergeron, Quebec QC G3E 1G5, Canada
Lapham, David A (Dave) — Football Player
8254 Sunfish Lane, Maineville OH 45039, USA
Lapham, Lewis H — Editor
Harper's, Editorial Dept, 666 Broadway, New York NY 10012, USA
Lapierre, Dominique — Historian
Les Bignoles, 83350 Ramatuelle, France
Lapine, James E — Writer, Director
85 Mill River Road, South Salem NY 10590, USA
Lapira, Liza — Actress
Paradigm Agency, 360 N Crescent Dr, North Building, Beverly Hills CA 90210 USA
LaPlaca, Alison — Actress
1614 N Argyle Ave, Los Angeles CA 90028, USA
LaPlanche, Rosemary — Actress, Beauty Queen
13914 Hartsook St, Sherman Oaks CA 91423, USA
LaPlant, Rob — Producer
Lighthearted Entertainment, 4111 W Alameda Ave, #409, Burbank CA 91505, USA
LaPlante, Lynda — Writer, Actress
LaPlante Productions, 162-170 Wardour St, London W1V 3AT, England
Lapoint, David J (Dave) — Baseball Player
11704 Stonewood Gate Dr, Riverview FL 33579, USA
Lapointe, Claude — Ice Hockey Player
805 Stony Creek Court, Lansdale PA 19446, USA
Lapointe, Guy G — Ice Hockey Player
Minnesota Wild, XCel Energy Arena, 1275 Saint Antoine W, Saint Paul MN 55104 USA
LaPorte, Danny — Motorcycle Racing Rider
18033 S Santa Fe Ave, Compton CA 90221, USA
LaPorte, Juan — Boxer, Trainer
77 Front St, Brooklyn NY 11201, USA
Laposata, Joseph S — Army General
Battle Monuments Commission, 20 Massachusetts, Washington DC 20314, USA
Lapotaire, Jane — Actress
92 Oxford Gardens, #C, London W10, England
Lappalainen, Markku — Bassist (Hoobastank)
Island Def Jam Records, 8920 W Sunset Blvd, #200, West Hollywood CA 90069 USA
Lappas, Steve — Basketball Coach
Villanova University, Athletic Dept, Villanova PA 19085, USA
Laprade, Edgar — Ice Hockey Player
12 Shuniah St, Thunder Bay ON P7A 2Y8, Canada
LaPraed, Ronald (Ron) — Bassist, Trumpeter (Commodores)
Management Assoc, 1920 Benson Ave, Saint Paul MN 55116, USA
Laqueur, Walter — Historian
Journal of Contemporary History, 4 Devonshire St, London W1N 2BH, England
Lara, Alexandra Maria — Actress
Players Agentur Mgmt, Sophienstra 21, 10178 Berlin-Mitte, Germany
Lara, Brian C — Cricketer
West Indies Cricket Club, PO Box 616, Saint John's, Antigua
Lara, Joanne — Actress
Abraxas Talent, 4260 Troost Ave, #1, Studio City CA 91604, USA
Laragh, John H — Physician
435 E 70th St, New York NY 10021, USA
Lardner, George, Jr — Journalist
Washington Post, Editorial Dept, 1150 15th St NW, Washington DC 20071, USA
Lardo, Vincent — Writer
G P Putnam's Sons, 375 Hudson St, New York NY 10014 USA
Laresca, Vincent — Actor
TalentWorks, 3500 W Olive Ave, #1400, Burbank CA 91505 USA
Larese, York B — Basketball Player, Coach
22 Grove Place, #15, Winchester MA 01890, USA
Largent, Steve M — Football Player; Representative, OK
3835 N Randolph Court, Arlington VA 22207, USA
Larholm, Jonas — Handball Player
Aalborg Handbold, Willy Brandts Vej 31, 9220 Aalborg Ost, Denmark
Larionov, Igor N — Ice Hockey Player
2363 Tilbury Place, Bloomfield Hills MI 48301, USA
Lariviere, Richard W — Museum Executive, Educator
Field Museum of Natural History, 1400 S Lake Shore Dr, Chicago IL 60605, USA
Lark, Maria — Actress
Coast to Coast Talent, 3350 Barham Blvd, Los Angeles CA 90068 USA
Larkin, Barry L — Baseball Player
5410 Osprey Isle Lane, Orlando FL 32819, USA
Larkin, Christopher (Chris) — Actor
Ken McReddie Assoc, 11 Connaught Place, London W2 2ET, England
Larkin, Eugene T (Gene) — Baseball Player
9496 Abbott Court, Eden Prairie MN 55347, USA
Larkin, Stephen K — Baseball Player
9178 Solon Dr, Cincinnati OH 45242, USA
Larmer, Steve — Ice Hockey Player
1664 Poplar Point Road, RR 4, Peterborough ON K9J 6X5, Canada

Larmore, Jennifer — Opera Singer
I M G Artists, 152 W 57th St, #500, New York NY 10019 USA
Laro, David — Judge
US Tax Court, 400 2nd St NW, Washington DC 20217, USA
LaRoche, Andrews C (Andy) — Baseball Player
815 W 18th St, Fort Scott KS 66701, USA
LaRoche, David E (Dave) — Baseball Player
815 W 18th St, Fort Scott KS 66701, USA
LaRocque, Gene R — Government Official, Navy Admiral
5015 Macomb St NW, Washington DC 20016, USA
Laroque, Michele — Actress
Agents Associes, 201 Faubourg Saint Honore, 75008 Paris, France
LaRosa, Julius — Singer
67 Sycamore Lane, Irvington NY 10533, USA
LaRosa, Paul — Opera Singer
I M G Artists, Hogarth Business Park, Chiswick, London W4 2TH, England
Larose, Claude D — Ice Hockey Player
5060 NW 54th St, Coconut Creek FL 33073, USA
Larose, H John — Baseball Player
99 Roland St, Cumberland RI 02864, USA
LaRose, M Daniel (Danny) — Football Player
4873 N Raymond Road, Luther MI 49656, USA
Larose, Victor R (Vic) — Baseball Player
2908 E Sylvia St, Phoenix AZ 85032, USA
LaRouche, Lyndon H, Jr — Political Activist
18520 Round Top Lane, Round Hill VA 20141, USA
Larouche, Pierre — Ice Hockey Player
112 Vanderbilt Dr, Pittsburgh PA 15243, USA
Larrabee, Martin G — Biophysicist
11630 Glen Arm Road, #V54, Glen Arm MD 21057, USA
Larrieux, Amel — Singer
Blisslife Records, 725 River Road, #32-215, Edgewater NJ 07020, USA
Larroquette, John — Actor
Brillstein Entertainment Partners, 9150 Wilshire Blvd, #350, Beverly Hills CA 90212 USA
Larry the Cable Guy — Actor, Comedian
Parallel Entertainment, 9420 Wilshire Blvd, #250, Beverly Hills CA 90212 USA
Larry, Wendy — Basketball Coach
Old Dominion University, Institutional Advancement Office, Norfolk VA 23529, USA
Larsen, Art — Tennis Player
203 Lorraine Blvd, San Leandro CA 94577, USA
Larsen, Blaine — Singer, Songwriter
Morris Management Group, 818 19th Ave S, Nashville TN 37203, USA
Larsen, Don J — Baseball Player
C M G Worldwide, 10500 Crosspoint Blvd, Indianapolis IN 46256, USA
Larsen, Gary L — Football Player
4317 San Juan St NE, Olympia WA 98516, USA
Larsen, Jack Lenor — Textile Designer
Long Island Reserve, 133 Hands Creek Road, East Hampton NY 11937, USA
Larsen, Libby — Composer
2205 Kenwood Parkway, Minneapolis MN 55405, USA
Larsen, Marit — Singer, Songwriter (M-2-M)
United Stage, Box 11029, 100 61 Stockholm, Sweden
Larsen, Ralph S — Businessman
100 Albany St, #200, New Brunswick NJ 08901, USA
Larsen, Terrance A — Financier
75 Bryn Mawr Ave, Lansdowne PA 19050, USA
Larson, Brie — Actress
Gersh Agency, 9465 Wilshire Blvd, #600, Beverly Hills CA 90212 USA
Larson, Charles R (Chuck) — Navy Admiral
591 Coover Road, Annapolis MD 21401, USA
Larson, Daniel J (Dan) — Baseball Player
797 Oxen St, Paso Robles CA 93446, USA
Larson, Edward J (Ed) — Historian
24346 Baxter Dr, Malibu CA 90265, USA
Larson, Erik — Writer
Crown Publishing Group, 1745 Broadway, New York NY 10019 USA
Larson, Gary — Cartoonist (Far Side)
FarWorks, 601 Union St, #620, Seattle WA 98101, USA
Larson, Glen A — Producer, Writer, Singer
5125 Kelvin Ave, Woodland Hills CA 91364, USA
Larson, Gregory K (Greg) — Football Player
PO Box 393, Nisswa MN 56468, USA
Larson, Jack E — Actor
449 N Skyewiay Road, Los Angeles CA 90049, USA
Larson, Jill — Actress
Innovative Artists, 1505 10th St, Santa Monica CA 90401 USA
Larson, Lance — Swimmer
1131 La Limonar Road, Santa Ana CA 92705, USA
Larson, Peter N — Businessman
Brunswick Corp, 1 N Field Court, Lake Forest IL 60045, USA
Larson, Reed — Ice Hockey Player
14334 Fairway Dr, Eden Prairie MN 55344, USA
Larson, Wolf — Actor
11969 Ventura Blvd, #300, Studio City CA 91604, USA
Larsson, Dean — Golfer
Advantage International, 1025 Thomas Jefferson NW, #450, Washington DC 20007 USA
Larter, Ali — Actress, Model
Water Street Mgmt, 5225 Wilshire Blvd, #615, Los Angeles CA 90036, USA
LaRue, Eva — Actress
Stone Manners Salners, 9911 W Pico Blvd, #1400, Los Angeles CA 90035 USA
LaRue, Florence — Singer (Fifth Dimension), Actress
W M E Entertainment, 1325 Ave of Americas, New York NY 10019 USA
Larue, M Jason — Baseball Player
30020 Twin Ridge Dr, Bulverde TX 78163, USA
LaRussa, Anthony (Tony), Jr — Baseball Player, Manager
338 Golden Meadow Place, Alamo CA 94507, USA

LaRusso, Vincent — Actor
419 Park Ave S, #1009, New York NY 10016, USA
Lary, Frank S — Baseball Player
11813 Baseball Dr, Northport AL 35475, USA
Lary, R Yale — Football Player
6366 Lansdale Road, Fort Worth TX 76116, USA
LaSala, James — Labor Leader
Amalgamated Transit Union, 5025 Wisconsin Ave NW, Washington DC 20016, USA
LaSalle, Eriq — Actor, Director
Principato-Young, 9465 Wilshire Blvd, #880, Beverly Hills CA 90212 USA
Lascarro, Juanita — Opera Singer
Harrison/Parrott, 5-6 Albion Court, London W6 0QT, England
Lascher, David — Actor
Amatruda Benson Assoc, 9107 Wilshire Blvd, #500, Beverly Hills CA 90210, USA
Lash, Bill — Skier
17438 Bothell Way NE, #C305, Bothell WA 98011, USA
Lash, James V (Jim) — Football Player
597 Van Everett Ave, Akron OH 44306, USA
Laskey, William A (Bill) — Baseball Player
PO Box 1556, Burlingame CA 94011, USA
Laskey, William G (Bill) — Football Player
PO Box 734, 3257 N Manitou Trail, Leland MS 49654, USA
Laskin, Larissa — Actress
Marshak/Zachary, 8840 Wilshire Blvd, #100, Los Angeles CA 90211, USA
Laslavic, James E (Jim) — Football Player
648 A Ave, Coronado CA 92118, USA
LaSorda, Thomas — Businessman
Daimler-Chrysler Group, 100 Chrysler Dr, Auburn Hills MI 48326, USA
Lasorda, Thomas C (Tommy) — Baseball Player, Manager, Executive
1473 W Maxzim Ave, Fullerton CA 92833, USA
Lassally, Walter — Cinematographer
6 Ladbroke Gardens, London W11 2PT, England
Lasse, Richard S (Dick) — Football Player
111 Windcrest Court, Beaver Falls PA 15010, USA
Lasser, Louise — Actress, Comedienne
200 E 71st St, #20C, New York NY 10021, USA
Lasseter, John — Director, Animator
Pixar Animation, 1200 Park Ave, Emeryville CA 94608, USA
Lassetter, Donald O (Don) — Baseball Player
379 Old Carrollton Road, Newnan GA 30263, USA
Lassez, Sarah — Actress
Untitled Entertainment, 350 S Beverly Dr, #200, Beverly Hills CA 90212 USA
Lassiter, Isaac T (Ike) — Football Player
2812 Rawson St, Oakland CA 94619, USA
Lassiter, Kwamie — Football Player
122 W Sunrise Place, Chandler AZ 85248, USA
Last, James — Orchestra Leader
Schone Aussicht 16, 22085 Hamburg, Germany
Laster, Danny B — Animal Research Scientist
Hruska Meat Animal Research Center, PO Box 166, Clay Center NE 68933, USA
Lastra, Pilar — Model, Actress
Playboy Promotions, 2706 Media Center Dr, Los Angeles CA 90065 USA
Latana, Valerie — Editor
Shape, Editorial Dept, 1 Park Ave, New York NY 10016, USA
Lateef, Yusef — Jazz Saxophonist, Flutist, Composer
Rhino Records, 10635 Santa Monica Blvd, Los Angeles CA 90025 USA
Latham, Louise — Actress
300 Hot Springs Road, Santa Barbara CA 93108, USA
Lathan, Sanaa — Actress
John Carrabino Mgmt, 5900 Wilshire Blvd, #406, Los Angeles CA 90036 USA
Lathan, Stan — Director, Producer, Writer
Simmons Latham Media Group, 6100 Wilshire Blvd, #1111, Los Angeles CA 90048, USA
Lathrop, Kit D — Football Player
3412 E Windsong Dr, Phoenix AZ 85048, USA
Latimer, Don B — Football Player
562 S Kalispell Way, Aurora CO 80017, USA
Latimore — Singer, Keyboardist
Rodgers Redding, PO Box 4603, Macon GA 31208 USA
Latimore, Jacob — Actor
Creative Artists Agency, 2000 Ave of Stars, #100, Los Angeles CA 90067 USA
Latimore, Joseph — Actor
Innovative Artists, 1505 10th St, Santa Monica CA 90401 USA
Latman, A Barry — Baseball Player
2726 Shelter Island Dr, PO Box 519, San Diego CA 92106, USA
Lattimore, Kenny — Singer
Ten 2 One Entertainment, 5225 Wilshire Blvd, #400, Los Angeles CA 90036, USA
Lattin, David (Big Daddy) — Basketball Player
8230 Twin Tree Lane, Houston TX 77071, USA
Lattisaw, Stacy — Singer
Walter Reeder Productions, PO Box 27641, Philadelphia PA 19118, USA
Lattner, John J (Johnny) — Football Player
1700 Riverwoods Dr, #503, Melrose Park IL 60160, USA
Laub, Larry — Bowler
5380 W Eaglestone Loop, Tucson AZ 85742, USA
Lauby, Chantal — Actress
Voyez Mon Agent, 20 Ave Rapp, 75007 Paris, France
Lauda, Andreas-Nikolaus (Niki) — Auto Racing Driver
San Costa de Baix, Santa Eulalia del Rio, 07840 Ibiza, Spain
Lauder, Leonard A — Businessman
Estee Lauder Companies, 767 5th Ave, Basement 1, New York NY 10153, USA
Lauder, Ronald S — Businessman, Diplomat
Estee Lauder Companies, 767 5th Ave, Basement 1, New York NY 10153, USA
Lauderdale, Jim — Singer, Songwriter
Agency Group Ltd, 142 W 57th St, #600, New York NY 10019 USA
Laudner, Timothy J (Tim) — Baseball Player
PO Box 10, Hamel MN 55340, USA

Laudrup, Brian
2960 Rungsted Kyst, Denmark — Soccer Player
Lauer, Andrew
Motive Entertainment, 1149 3rd St, Santa Monica CA 90403, USA — Actor
Lauer, Bonnie
525 Via Laguna Vista, San Luis Obispo CA 93405, USA — Golfer
Lauer, Martin
D L V, Alsfeder Str 17, 64289 Darmstadt, Germany — Track Athlete
Lauer, Matt
2301 Deerfield Road, Sag Harbor NY 11963, USA — Commentator
Lauer, Tod R
6471 N Tierra de Las Catalina, Tucson AZ 85718, USA — Astronomer
Laughlin, John
Laughlin Enterprises, 13116 Albers St, Sherman Oaks CA 91401, USA — Actor
Laughlin, Robert B
960 Mears Court, Stanford CA 94305, USA — Nobel Physics Laureate
Laughlin, Thomas R (Tom)
PO Box 840, Moorpark CA 93020, USA — Actor, Director
Laukkanen, Janne K
Tampa Bay Lightning, 401 Channelside Dr, Tampa FL 33602 USA — Ice Hockey Player
Lauper, Cyndi
So What Mgmt, 890 W End Ave, #1A, New York NY 10025, USA — Singer, Songwriter
Laurance, Dale R
Occidental Petroleum, 10889 Wilshire Blvd, #1000, Los Angeles CA 90024, USA — Businessman
Laurance, Matthew W
1951 Hillcrest Road, Los Angeles CA 90068, USA — Actor
Laure, Carole
Voyez Mon Agent, 20 Ave Rapp, 75007 Paris, France — Singer, Actress
Laurel, Richard (Rich)
706 Antelope Way, Kissimmee FL 34759, USA — Basketball Player
Lauren, Joy
Paradigm Agency, 360 N Crescent Dr, North Building, Beverly Hills CA 90210 USA — Actress
Lauren, Ralph
867 Madison Ave, New York NY 10021, USA — Fashion Designer
Lauren, Tammy
Glick Agency, 1321 7th St, #203, Santa Monica CA 90401 USA — Actress
Laurence, Ashley
Imperium 7 Artists, 5455 Wilshire Blvd, #1706, Los Angeles CA 90036 USA — Actress
Laurens, Camille
Bloomsbury Publishing, 36 Soho Square, London W1D 3Q4, England — Writer
Laurent, Melanie
U B B A, 6 Rue de Braque, 75003 Paris, France — Actress
Laurer, Joanie (Chyna)
Esterman Entertainment, 12333 Pretoria Dr, Silver Spring MD 20904 USA — Professional Wrestler, Model
Lauria, Dan
Marshak/Zachary Co, 8840 Wilshire Blvd, #100, Beverly Hills CA 90211 USA — Actor
Lauria, Matt
Bauman Assoc, 250 W 57th St, #2223, New York NY 10107 USA — Actor
Lauricella, Francis E (Hank)
1200 S Clearview Parkway, #1166, New Orleans LA 70123, USA — Football Player
Lauridsen, Morten
University of Southern California, Music Dept, Los Angeles CA 90089, USA — Composer, Musician
Laurie, Harry
540 Bramhall Ave, #3, Jersey City NJ 07304, USA — Basketball Player
Laurie, Hugh
Hamilton Hodell, 66-68 Margaret St, London W1W 8SR, England — Actor, Comedian, Writer
Laurie, Miracle
Diverse Talent Group, 9911 Pico Blvd, #350W, Los Angeles CA 90035 USA — Actress
Laurie, Piper
Don Buchwald/Fortitude, 6500 Wilshire Blvd, #2200, Los Angeles CA 90048 USA — Actress
Laurinaitis, James R
Saint Louis Rams, 901 N Broadway, Saint Louis MO 63101 USA — Football Player
Laursen, Jeppe (Senior)
Festival Network Mgmt, 30 Irving Place, #600, New York NY 10003, USA — Singer, Keyboardist (Junior Senior)
Lauter, Ed
Sutton-Barth Vennari, 145 S Fairfax Ave, #310, Los Angeles CA 90036 USA — Actor
Lauterbach, Robert E
118 Dowling Dr, Pittsburgh PA 15215, USA — Businessman
Lautner, Georges C
9 Chemin des Basses Ribes, 06130 Grasse, France — Director
Lautner, Taylor D
Management 360, 9111 Wilshire Blvd, Beverly Hills CA 90210 USA — Actor
Lavadour, James
Umatilla Indian Reservation Confederated Tribles, Pendleton OR 97801, USA — Artist
Lavalliere, Michael E (Mike)
216 81st St W, Bradenton FL 34209, USA — Baseball Player
Lavanant, Dominique
Voyez Mon Agent, 20 Ave Rapp, 75007 Paris, France — Actress
Lave, Lester B
1008 Devonshire Road, Pittsburgh PA 15213, USA — Economist
Laveikin, Aleksandr I
Cosmonaut Training Center, Star City, 141160 Zvezdny Gorodok, Moscow Oblast, Russia — Cosmonaut
Lavelle, Gary R
1100 Worthington Court, Virginia Beach VA 23464, USA — Baseball Player
Lavelle, Rosanna
Hamilton Hodell, 66-68 Margaret St, London W1W 8SR, England — Actress
Lavender, Jay
Verve Talent, 9696 Culver Blvd, #301, Culver City CA 90232, USA — Producer, Director, Writer
Lavender, Joseph (Joe)
1929 W Erie Ave, Philadelphia PA 19140, USA — Football Player
Laventhol, Henry L (Hank)
445 Heritage Hills, #F, Somers NY 10589, USA — Artist
Laver, Rodney G (Rod)
PO Box 4798, Hilton Head Island SC 29938, USA — Tennis Player
Lavergne, Didier
Mirisch Agency, 8840 Wilshire Blvd, #100, Beverly Hills CA 90211 USA — Makeup Artist

Laverick, Elise — Rowing Athlete
Thames Rowing Club, Putney Embankment, London SW15 1LB, England

Lavery, Sean — Ballet Dancer, Choreographer
New York City Ballet, Lincoln Center Plaza, New York NY 10023 USA

LaVette, Bettye — Singer
Rosebud Agency, PO Box 170429, San Francisco CA 94117 USA

Lavi, Daliah — Actress
Dahlienweg 2, 58313 Herdecke, Germany

Lavia, Gabriele — Actor
Carol Levi Mgmt, Via G Pisanelli 2, 00196 Rome, Italy

Lavigne, Avril — Singer, Songwriter
Nettwerk Mgmt, 1650 W 2nd Ave, Vancouver BC V6J, Canada

Lavin, Leonard H — Businessman
Alberto-Culver, 2525 Armitage Ave, Melrose Park IL 60160, USA

Lavin, Linda — Actress, Singer
R J Productions, 401 E 74th St, #145, New York NY 10021, USA

Laviolette, Peter — Ice Hockey Player, Coach
7000 Firehouse Road, Longboat Key FL 34228, USA

Lavoine, Marc — Actor
Voyez Mon Agent, 20 Ave Rapp, 75007 Paris, France

LaVorgna, Adam — Actor
Hartig-Hilepo Agency, 54 W 21st St, #610, New York NY 10010 USA

Lavoy, Robert W (Bob) — Basketball Player
4902 Bayshore Blvd, #605, Tampa FL 33611, USA

Lavrosky, Mikhail L — Ballet Dancer
Voznesesenky Per 16/4, #7, 103009 Moscow, Russia

Lavrsen, Helena Blach — Curling Athlete
Curling Assn, Idraettens Hus, 2605 Brondby, Denmark

Law, Bernard F Cardinal — Religious Leader
Saint Mary Major Basilica, 00120 Vatican City

Law, Bob — Artist, Sculptor
Warehouse, 18 Bread St, Penzance, Cornwall TR18 2EG, England

Law, Jude — Actor
Julian Belfrage Assoc, 9 Argyll St, #300, London W1F 7TG, England

Law, Kelley — Curling Athlete
Curling Assn, 1660 Vimont Court, Cumberland ON K4A 4J4, Canada

Law, Tajuan E (Ty) — Football Player
10862 Hawks Vista St, Plantation FL 33324, USA

Law, Vance A — Baseball Player
1682 N 1950 W, Provo UT 84604, USA

Law, Vernon S (Vern) — Baseball Player
Bace Sports, 5699 Kanan Road, #157, Agoura Hills CA 91301, USA

Lawanson, Ruth — Volleyball Player
2050 Dickerson Road, Reno NV 89503, USA

Lawler, Jerry — Professional Wrestler, Sportscaster
415 Saint Nick Dr, Memphis TN 38117, USA

Lawler, John (King) — Professional Wrestler
415 Saint Nick Dr, Memphis TN 38117, USA

Lawless, Blackie — Singer, Guitarist (WASP)
Chipster, 800 Village Square Crossing, Palm Beach Gardens FL 33410 USA

Lawless, Lucy — Actress
Valeo Entertainment, 8265 Sunset Blvd, #103, Los Angeles CA 90046, USA

Lawless, Paul — Ice Hockey Player
4231 N Winfield Scott Plaza, #1, Scottsdale AZ 85251, USA

Lawless, R Burton — Football Player
2035 Oak Glen Dr, McGregor TX 76657, USA

Lawless, Robert W — Educator
University of Tulsa, President's Office, Tulsa OK 74104, USA

Lawless, Thomas J (Tom) — Baseball Player
1238 Laura St, Casselberry FL 32707, USA

Lawn, John C — Law Enforcement Official
New York Yankees, Yankee Stadium, E 161st St & River Ave, Bronx NY 10451 USA

Lawrence, Andrew (Andy) — Actor
Rebel Entertainment Partners, 5700 Wilshire Blvd, #456, Los Angeles CA 90036, USA

Lawrence, Bill — Producer, Director
I C M Partners, 10250 Constellation Blvd, #900, Los Angeles CA 90067 USA

Lawrence, Carol — Actress, Singer
Orange Grove Group, 12178 Ventura Blvd, #205, Studio City CA 91604, USA

Lawrence, Carolyn — Actress
W M E Entertainment, 9601 Wilshire Blvd, #300, Beverly Hills CA 90210 USA

Lawrence, Francis — Director
3 Arts Entertainment, 9460 Wilshire Blvd, #700, Beverly Hills CA 90212 USA

Lawrence, Henry — Football Player
401 17th St W, Palmetto FL 34221, USA

Lawrence, James (Loz) — Guitarist (Strawberry Blondes)
PO Box 33, Pontypool, Gwent NP4 6YU, England

Lawrence, James R (Jim) — Baseball Player
225 Haddington St, Caledonia ON N3W 1G1, Canada

Lawrence, Jennifer — Actress
Creative Artists Agency, 2000 Ave of Stars, #100, Los Angeles CA 90067 USA

Lawrence, Joseph (Joey) — Actor
Abrams Artists, 9200 W Sunset Blvd, #1125, West Hollywood CA 90069 USA

Lawrence, Josie — Actress
International Artists, 193-97 High Holborn, London WC1V 7BD, England

Lawrence, Marc — Director, Producer, Writer
United Talent Agency, 9336 Civic Center Dr, Beverly Hills CA 90210 USA

Lawrence, Martin F — Actor, Comedian
Collective, 8383 Wilshire Blvd, #1050, Beverly Hills CA 90211 USA

Lawrence, Matthew W — Actor
TalentWorks, 3500 W Olive Ave, #1400, Burbank CA 91505 USA

Lawrence, Nina — Publisher
W Magazine, Publisher's Office, 3500 Piedmont Road, #505, Atlanta GA 30305, USA

Lawrence, Rebecca — Actress
I C M Partners, 10250 Constellation Blvd, #900, Los Angeles CA 90067 USA

Lawrence, Richard D — Army General
7301 Valburn Dr, Austin TX 78731, USA

Lawrence, Robert S — Physician
Highfield House, 4000 N Charles St, #1112, Baltimore MD 21218, USA
Lawrence, Robert Z — Government Official, Economist
Harvard University, Cambridge MA 02138 USA
Lawrence, Rolland D — Football Player
317 Sugarcreek Dr, Franklin PA 16323, USA
Lawrence, Scott — Actor
Ellis Talent Gorup, 4705 Laurel Canyon Blvd, #300, Valley Village CA 91607, USA
Lawrence, Sean C — Baseball Player
336 S Poplar Ave, Elmhurst IL 60126, USA
Lawrence, Sharon — Actress
A P A Talent/Literary Agency, 405 S Beverly Dr, #300, Beverly Hills CA 90212 USA
Lawrence, Steve — Singer
944 Pinehurst Dr, Las Vegas NV 89109, USA
Lawrence, Steven Anthony — Actor
Axiom Mgmt, 10701 Wilshire Blvd, #1202, Los Angeles CA 90024, USA
Lawrence, Tracy — Singer, Songwriter
Bobby Roberts, PO Box 1547, Goodlettsville TN 37070, USA
Lawrence, Vicki — Actress, Comedienne, Singer
6000 Lido Ave, Long Beach CA 90803, USA
Lawrence, Wendy B — Astronaut
National Reconnaissance Office, 14675 Lee Road, Chantilly VA 20151, USA
Lawrie, Nathan E (Nate) — Football Player
1157 Melville Ave, Fairfield CT 06825, USA
Lawrie, Paul S — Golfer
Code:4 Sports Ltd, Milton Gate, 60 Chiswell St, London EC1Y 4AG, England
Lawson of Blaby, Nigel — Government Official, England
32 Sutherland Walk, London SE17, England
Lawson, Ben — Actor
Untitled Entertainment, 350 S Beverly Dr, #200, Beverly Hills CA 90212 USA
Lawson, Bianca — Actress
Don Buchwald/Fortitude, 6500 Wilshire Blvd, #2200, Los Angeles CA 90048 USA
Lawson, Denis — Actor
Independent Talent Group, Oxford House, 76 Oxford St, London W1D 1BS, England
Lawson, Doyle — Mandolinist
Sugar Hill Records, 3322 West End Ave, #1100, Nashville TN 37203 USA
Lawson, Joshua (Josh) — Actor
Management 360, 9111 Wilshire Blvd, Beverly Hills CA 90210 USA
Lawson, Kara — Basketball Player
Connecticut Sun, 1 Mohegan Sun Blvd, Uncasville CT 06382 USA
Lawson, Leigh — Actor
CornerStone Talent Agency, 37 W 20th St, #1107, New York NY 10011, USA
Lawson, Maggie — Actress
Gersh Agency, 9465 Wilshire Blvd, #600, Beverly Hills CA 90212 USA
Lawson, Manny — Football Player
Cincinnati Bengals, 1 Paul Brown Stadium, Cincinnati OH 45202 USA
Lawson, Michael — Writer
C E S D, 10635 Santa Monica Blvd, #130, Los Angeles CA 90025 USA
Lawson, Nigella — Chef, Writer
Creative Artists Agency, 2000 Ave of Stars, #100, Los Angeles CA 90067 USA
Lawson, Richard — Actor
Gage Group, 14724 Ventura Blvd, #505, Sherman Oaks CA 91403 USA
Lawson, Richard L — Air Force General
6910 Clifton Road, Clifton VA 20124, USA
Lawson, Sonia — Artist
Royal Academy, Burlington House, Piccadilly, London W1V 0DS, England
Lawson, Tywon R (Ty) — Basketball Player
Denver Nuggets, Pepsi Center, 1000 Chopper Circle, Denver CO 80204 USA
Lawton, Brian R — Ice Hockey Player
5012 Oak Bend Lane, Minneapolis MN 55436, USA
Lawton, Mary — Cartoonist (Nowhere to Hide)
Chronicle Features, 901 Mission St, San Francisco CA 94103, USA
Lawton, Matthew (Matt), III — Baseball Player
27264 Highway 67, Saucier MS 39574, USA
Lax, Benjamin — Physicist
Massachusetts Institute of Technology, Physics Dept, Cambridge MA 02139, USA
Lax, Melvin — Physicist
12 High St, Summit NJ 07901, USA
Lax, Peter D — Abel Mathematics Laureate
Courant Math Institute, 251 Mercer St, #910, New York NY 10012, USA
Laxalt, Paul D — Governor, Senator, NV
801 Pennsylvania Ave NW, #750, Washington DC 20004, USA
Laxton, Brett — Baseball Player
6922 Springwood Blvd, Denham Springs LA 70726, USA
Laxton, William H (Bill) — Baseball Player
261 Mansion Ave, Audubon NJ 08106, USA
Laybourne, Geraldine (Gerry) — Businessman
Oxygen Media, 75 9th Ave, #700, New York NY 10011, USA
Layer, Friedemann — Conductor
I M G Artists, Hogarth Business Park, Chiswick, London W4 2TH, England
Layton, Dennis (Mo) — Basketball Player
872 S 14th St, Newark NJ 07108, USA
Layton, Donald H — Financier
Federal Home Loan Mortgage Corp, 8100 Jones Branch Dr, McLean VA 22102, USA
Layton, Lester K (Les) — Baseball Player
8780 E McKellips Road, #27, Scottsdale AZ 85257, USA
Layton, Peter — Artist
London Glassblowing, 7 Leather Market, Weston St, London SE1 3ER, England
Layzie Bone — Rap Artist (Bone Thugs-N-Harmony)
Green Light Talent Agency, PO Box 3172, Beverly Hills CA 90212 USA
Lazar, Aaron — Actor
Abrams Artists, 9200 W Sunset Blvd, #1125, West Hollywood CA 90069 USA
Lazar, J Dan (Danny) — Baseball Player
8444 Oakwood Ave, Munster IN 46321, USA
Lazarev, Alexander N — Conductor
Christopher Tennant Artists, 39 Tadema Road, #2, London SW10 0PY, England

Lazarus, Mell — Cartoonist (Miss Peach, Momma)
Creators Syndicate, 737 3rd St, Hermosa Beach CA 90254 USA
Lazarus, Rochelle B (Shelly) — Businesswoman
106 E 78th St, New York NY 10075, USA
Lazear, Edward P — Government Official, Economist
277 Old Spanish Trail, Portola Valley CA 94028, USA
Lazenby, George — Actor
Hervey/Grimes Talent, 10561 Missouri Ave, #2, Los Angeles CA 90025 USA
Lazetich, Peter G (Pete) — Football Player
185 Martin St, Reno NV 89509, USA
Lazier, Robert (Buddy) — Auto Racing Driver
386 Hanson Ranch Road, Vail CO 81657, USA
Lazlo, Viktor — Actress, Singer
56 Rue de Lisbonne, 75008 Paris, France
Lazorko, Jack T — Baseball Player
1360 Meandering Way, Rockwall TX 75087, USA
Lazuktin, Alexander I — Cosmonaut
Cosmonaut Training Center, Star City, 141160 Zvezdny Gorodok, Moscow Oblast, Russia
Lazure, Gabrielle — Actress
A C T 1, 83 Rue Saint Honore, 75001 Paris, France
Le Toya — Singer (Destiny's Child)
Creative Artists Agency, 2000 Ave of Stars, #100, Los Angeles CA 90067 USA
Lea, Nicholas — Actor
Global Artists Agency, 6253 Hollywood Blvd, #508, Los Angeles CA 90028 USA
Leach, Jalal — Baseball Player
3718 Phillip Island Road, West Sacramento CA 95691, USA
Leach, Michael C (Mike) — Football Coach
Washington State University, Athletic Dept, Pullman WA 99164, USA
Leach, Penelope — Child Psychologist
3 Tanza Lane, London NW3 2UA, England
Leach, Reginald J (Reggie) — Ice Hockey Player
263 Thomas Jefferson Terrace, Elkton MD 21921, USA
Leach, Richard M (Rick) — Baseball Player
593 Layman Creek Circle, Grand Blanc MI 48439, USA
Leach, Robin — Producer, Entertainer
Celebrity Consultants, 3340 Ocean Park Blvd, #1005, Santa Monica CA 90405 USA
Leach, Rosemary — Actress
Felix de Wolfe, 51 Maida Vale, London W9 1SD, England
Leach, Sheryl — Animator (Barney)
Lyons Group, 300 E Bethany Road, Allen TX 75002, USA
Leach, Stephen (Steve) — Ice Hockey Player
197 South St, Reading MA 01867, USA
Leach, T Vonta — Football Player
5409 White Oak Dr, Lumberton NC 28358, USA
Leach, Terry H — Baseball Player
2135 SW Locks Road, Stuart FL 34997, USA
Leachman, Cloris — Actress
410 S Barrington Ave, #307, Los Angeles CA 90049, USA
Leader, George M — Governor, PA
1528 Sand Hill Road, Hummelstown PA 17036, USA
Leader, Tom — Architect
537 Golden Gate Ave, Richmond CA 94801, USA
Leadon, Bernie — Singer, Guitarist (Eagles)
Northstar Entertainment, 501 S Reino Road, #1-380, Thousand Oaks CA 91320, USA
Leaf, Alexander — Physician
100 Newbury Court, #5515, Concord MA 1742, USA
League, Brandon P — Baseball Player
2385 Lake Heather Heights Court, Dunedin FL 34698, USA
Leah, Rachelle — Model, Actress
W M E Entertainment, 9601 Wilshire Blvd, #300, Beverly Hills CA 90210 USA
Leahy, Pat — Ice Hockey Player
1 Bristol Dr, Duxbury MA 02332, USA
Leahy, Patrick J (Pat) — Football Player
717 Chamblee Lane, Saint Louis MO 63141, USA
Leak, Jennifer — Actress
James D'Auria Assoc, PO Box 2219, Amagansett NY 11930, USA
Leak, Justice — Actor
C E S D, 10635 Santa Monica Blvd, #130, Los Angeles CA 90025 USA
Leakes, Nene — Actress
Collective, 8383 Wilshire Blvd, #1050, Beverly Hills CA 90211 USA
Leakey, Meave G — Paleontologist
PO Box 24926, Nairobi 00502, Kenya
Leakey, Richard E F — Paleonotolgist
PO Box 24926, Nairobi 00502, Kenya
Leaks, Manny — Basketball Player
9912 North Blvd, Cleveland OH 44108, USA
Leaks, Roosevelt, Jr — Football Player
Roosevelt Leaks Properties, 11525 Glen Falloch Court, Austin TX 78754, USA
Leal, Sharon — Actress, Singer
Alchemy Entertainment, 7024 Melrose Blvd, #420, Los Angeles CA 90038, USA
Leanderson, Matthew — Rowing Athlete
1301 N Highlands Parkway, #110, Tacoma WA 98406, USA
Leandro Alfonso de Borbon — Infante, Spain
Ediciones Martinez Rocca, Paseo de Recoletos 4, 28001 Madrid, Spain
Lear, Amanda — Singer
Cineta, 15 Rue Chapon, 75003 Paris, France
Lear, Harold C (Hal) — Basketball Player
11321 E Sunnyside Dr, Scottsdale AZ 85259, USA
Lear, Norman M — Producer, Director
100 N Crescent Dr, #120, Beverly Hills CA 90210, USA
Learned, Michael — Actress
Gage Group, 14724 Ventura Blvd, #505, Sherman Oaks CA 91403 USA
Leary, Denis — Actor, Comedian, Producer
Apostle, 568 Broadway, #301, New York NY 10012, USA
Leary, Paul — Guitarist, Singer (Butthole Surfers)
Kork Agency, 1880 Century Park E, #711, Los Angeles CA 90067, USA

Leary, Timothy J (Tim) — Baseball Player
2461 Santa Monica Blvd, Santa Monica CA 90404, USA

Leaud, Jean-Pierre — Actor
Artmedia, 20 Ave Rapp, 75007 Paris, France

Leavell, Alan F — Basketball Player
7007 Windy Pines Dr, Spring TX 77379, USA

Leavenworth, Scott — Actor
Curtis Talent Mgmt, 9607 Arby Dr, Beverly Hills CA 90210, USA

Leavitt, Judith W — Historian
University of Wisconsin, Medical History Dept, Madison WI 53706, USA

Leavitt, Phil — Singer (Diamonds)
Lustig Talent, PO Box 770850, Orlando FL 32877 USA

Leavy, Edward — Judge
US Court of Appeals, Pioneer Courthouse, 555 SW Yamhill St, Portland OR 97204, USA

Lebadang — Artist
Circle Gallery, 303 E Wacker Dr, Chicago IL 60601, USA

LeBar, Joshua — Actor, Director, Writer
Glick Agency, 1321 7th St, #203, Santa Monica CA 90401 USA

LeBaron, Edward W (Eddie), Jr — Football Player
7524 Pineridge Lane, Fair Oaks CA 95628, USA

LeBeau, C Richard (Dick) — Football Player, Coach
10405 Stone Court, Cincinnati OH 45242, USA

LeBeau, Patrick-Michael — Ice Hockey Player
610 Vanier, Saint Jerome QC J7Z 6B4, Canada

LeBeauf, Sabrina — Actress
11 Asbury Road, Asheville NC 28804, USA

Lebedev, Valentin V — Cosmonaut
Cosmonaut Training Center, Star City, 141160 Zvezdny Gorodok, Moscow Oblast, Russia

LeBel, B Harper — Football Player
3379 Scadlock Lane, Sherman Oaks CA 91403, USA

Leber, Ben — Football Player
4457 35th Ave S, Minneapolis MN 55406, USA

LeBlanc, Christian — Actor
Glick Agency, 1250 6th St, #100, Santa Monica CA 90401, USA

Leblanc, Jean-Paul (J P) — Ice Hockey Player
120 Gadwall Lane, Manlius NY 13104, USA

LeBlanc, Karina — Soccer Player
Canadian Soccer, Place Soccer Canada, 237 Metcalfe St, Ottawa ON K2P 1R2, Canada

LeBlanc, Matt — Actor
W M E Entertainment, 9601 Wilshire Blvd, #300, Beverly Hills CA 90210 USA

LeBlanc, Sherri — Ballerina
New York City Ballet, Lincoln Center Plaza, New York NY 10023 USA

LeBlanc-Boucher, Anouk — Speed Skater
Speed Skating Canada, 2781 Lancaster Road, #402, Ottawa ON K1B 1A7, Canada

Lebo, Jeffrey B (Jeff) — Basketball Player, Coach
500 Hidden Lake Way, Santa Rosa Beach FL 32459, USA

Leboeuf, Laurence — Actress
K L Benzakein Talent, 1155 Rene-Levesque Blvd W, #2500, Montreal QC H3B 2K4, Canada

LeBoeuf, Raymond W — Businessman
P P G Industries, 1 P P G Place, Pittsburgh PA 15272, USA

LeBon, Simon — Singer, Songwriter (Duran Duran)
D D Productions, 93A Westbourne Park Villas, London W2 5ED, England

LeBon, Yasmin — Model
Place Model Mgmt, Am Feld 29, 22765 Hamburg, Germany

LeBor, Adam — Journalist, Writer
Bloomsbury Publishing, 36 Soho Square, London W1D 3Q4, England

Lebovitz, Nolan — Director, Writer
Paradigm Agency, 360 N Crescent Dr, North Building, Beverly Hills CA 90210 USA

Lebowitz, Fran — Actress, Producer, Writer
Random House, 1745 Broadway, #1800, New York NY 10019 USA

Lebowitz, Joel L — Mathematician
Rutgers University, Math Sciences Center, New Brunswick NJ 08903, USA

Leboyer, Frederick — Physician
Georges Borchardt, 136 E 57th St, #1400, New York NY 10022, USA

LeBrock, Kelly — Actress, Model
Kazarian/Spencer/Ruskin, 11969 Ventura Blvd, #300, Studio City CA 91604 USA

LeBrun, Christopher M — Artist
Marlborough Fine Art, 6 Albermarle St, London W1X 4BY, England

LeBrun, Denis — Cartoonist (Blondie)
King Features Syndicate, 300 W 57th St, #1500, New York NY 10019 USA

LeCarre, John — Writer
9 Gainsborough Gardens, London NW3 1BJ, England

LeCause, Carl D — Harness Racing Driver, Owner
124 Ashbury Ave, Freehold NJ 07728, USA

Lecavalier, Vincent — Ice Hockey Player
401 Channelside Dr, Tampa FL 33602, USA

Lechleiter, John — Businessman
Eli Lilly Co, Lilly Corporate Center, Indianapolis IN 46285, USA

Lechler, E Shane — Football Player
4608 Sandyford Court, Dublin CA 94568, USA

Lechter, Sharon L — Writer
Cashflow Technologies, 4330 N Civic Center Plaza, #100, Scottsdale AZ 85251, USA

Lechtman, Heather N — Historian
Massachusetts Institute of Technology, History Dept, Cambridge MA 02139, USA

Leckey, Nicholas N (Nick) — Football Player
1056 E Windsor Dr, Gilbert AZ 85296, USA

Leckie, Mike — Sculptor
PO Box 5718, Eugene OR 97405, USA

Leckner, Eric — Basketball Player
608 27th St, Manhattan Beach CA 90266, USA

LeClair, James M (Jim) — Football Player
32 4th Ave NE, Mayville ND 58257, USA

LeClair, John C — Ice Hockey Player
108 Tunbridge Circle, Haverford PA 19041, USA

LeClerc, Jean — Actor
19 W 44th St, #1500, New York NY 10036, USA

LeClerc, Mike — Ice Hockey Player
473 Abbie Way, Costa Mesa CA 92627, USA
LeClerc, Paul — Librarian
New York Public Library, 5th Ave & 42nd St, New York NY 10018, USA
Leclerc, Roger A — Football Player
257 Elm St, Agawam MA 01001, USA
LeClezio, Jean-Marie Gustave — Nobel Literature Laureate
Editions Gallimard, 5 Rue Sebastien-Bottin, 75007 Paris, France
Lecomte, Benoit — Swimmer
Cross Atlantic Swimming Challenge, 3005 S Lamar, #D109-353, Austin TX 78704, USA
Leconte, Henri — Tennis Player
International Mgmt Group, Pier House, Chiswick, London W4M 3NN, England
Leconte, Patrice — Director
Artmedia, 20 Ave Rapp, 75007 Paris, France
Lecount, Terry J — Football Player
1288 Branchfield Court, Riverdale GA 30296, USA
LeCroy, Matt — Baseball Player
11314 Cedar Pointe Dr N, Hopkins MN 55305, USA
L'Ecuyer, John — Director
Paradigm Agency, 360 N Crescent Dr, North Building, Beverly Hills CA 90210 USA
Ledbetter, Lilly — Social Activist
PO Box 72, Jacksonville AL 36265, USA
Ledee, Ricardo A (Ricky) — Baseball Player
D29 Calle Antonio Ledee Rivera, Extension Carmen, Salinas PR 00751, USA
Leder, Mimi — Director
Creative Artists Agency, 2000 Ave of Stars, #100, Los Angeles CA 90067 USA
Leder, Philip — Geneticist
Harvard Medical School, Genetics Dept, 77 Ave Louis Pasteur, Boston MA 02115, USA
Leder, Steven — Religious Leader, Rabbi
Wilshire Boulevard Temple, 3663 Wilshire Blvd, Los Angeles CA 90010, USA
Lederman, Leon M — Nobel Physics Laureate
Illinois Math Science Academy, 1500 W Sullivan Road, Aurora IL 60506, USA
Ledesma, Aaron D — Baseball Player
241 Grove Circle S, Dunedin FL 34698, USA
Ledford, Brandy — Actress, Model
Ellis Talent Group, 4705 Laurel Canyon Blvd, #300, Valley Village CA 91607, USA
Ledford, Frank F, Jr — Army General, Physician
Southwest Biomed Research Foundation, PO Box 760549, San Antonio TX 78245, USA
Ledisi — Singer, Songwriter
PO Box 99735, Oakland CA 94662, USA
Ledoyen, Virginie — Actress, Model
80 Ave Gen Charles de Gaulle, 92200 Neuilly, France
Ledyard, Grant — Ice Hockey Player
5072 Old Goodrich Road, Clarence NY 14031, USA
Lee Beom-Young — Soccer Player
Football Assn, 1-131 Sinmunno, 2-Ga Jongno-Gu, Seoul 110 062, South Korea
Lee Bo-Kyung — Soccer Player
Football Assn, 1-131 Sinmunno, 2-Ga Jongno-Gu, Seoul 110 062, South Korea
Lee Byung-Chun — Veternarian
National University, San 56-1, Shillim-Dong, Seoul 151-742, South Korea
Lee Hong-Koo — Prime Minister, South Korea
Club de Madrid, C/Goya 5-7, Pasaje 2, 28001 Madrid, Spain
Lee Ho-Suk — Speed Skater
Skating Union, 88 Bangyee-Dong, Songpaku, Seoul 138 749, South Korea
Lee Hsien Loong — Prime Minister, Singapore
Premier's Office, Istana Annexe, Istana, 238823 Singapore, Singapore
Lee Myung Bak — President, South Korea
President's Office, Chong Wa Dae, 1 Sejong-no, Seoul 110 820, South Korea
Lee Sang Hwa — Speed Skater
Skating Union, 88 Bangyee-Dong, Songpaku, Seoul 138 749, South Korea
Lee Seung Hoon — Speed Skater
Skating Union, 88 Bangyee-Dong, Songpaku, Seoul 138 749, South Korea
Lee Ufan — Artist
Ecole Superieure des Beaux-Arts, 14 Rue Bonaparte, 75006 Paris, France
Lee, Alexondra — Actress
Sanders/Armstrong/Caserta Mgmt, 2120 Colorado Ave, #120, Santa Monica CA 90404 USA
Lee, Alfred (Butch) — Basketball Player
6616 Bluestone Court, Charlotte NC 28212, USA
Lee, Amos — Singer, Songwriter
Red Light Mgmt, 44 Wall St, #2200, New York NY 10005, USA
Lee, Amy — Singer, Musician (Evanescence)
Dennis Rider Mgmt, 931 Hilldale Ave, West Hollywood CA 90069, USA
Lee, Andrew P (Andy) — Football Player
San Francisco 49ers, 4949 Centennial Blvd, Santa Clara CA 95054 USA
Lee, Ang — Director
Creative Artists Agency, 2000 Ave of Stars, #100, Los Angeles CA 90067 USA
Lee, Anthonia W (Amp) — Football Player
990 Brickyard Road, Chipley FL 32428, USA
Lee, Ben — Singer (Luna), Songwriter
Gold Village Entertainment, 72 Madison Ave, #800, New York NY 90016, USA
Lee, Beverly — Singer (Shirelles)
Bevi Corp, PO Box 100, Clifton NJ 07015, USA
Lee, Bobby — Actor
Creative Artists Agency, 2000 Ave of Stars, #100, Los Angeles CA 90067 USA
Lee, Brenda — Singer
Brenda Lee Productions, 2175 Carson St, Nashville TN 37211, USA
Lee, Brook A M — Beauty Queen, Actress
A K A Talent, 6310 San Vicente Blvd, #200, Los Angeles CA 90048 USA
Lee, Carl, III — Football Player
1 Stonegate Dr, Hurricane WV 25526, USA
Lee, Carlos N — Baseball Player
1400 N 11th Ave, Melrose Park IL 60160, USA
Lee, Change Rae — Writer
Princeton University, English Dept, Princeton NJ 08544, USA
Lee, Charles R — Businessman
Marathon Petroleum Corp, 539 S Main St, Findlay OH 45840, USA

Lee, Charles S (C S) — Actor
Peter Strain, 5455 Wilshire Blvd, #1812, Los Angeles CA 90036 USA
Lee, Christopher F C — Actor
5 Sandown House, Wheat Field Terrace, London W4, England
Lee, Clifton P (Cliff) — Baseball Player
5706 Riviera Dr, Benton AR 72019, USA
Lee, Clyde W — Basketball Player
1118 Crater Hill Dr, Nashville TN 37215, USA
Lee, Corey W — Baseball Player
278 Lancashire Run, Smithfield NC 27577, USA
Lee, Courtney — Basketball Player
Houston Rockets, 1730 Jefferson St, Houston TX 77003 USA
Lee, David — Basketball Player
Golden State Warriors, 1011 Broadway, Oakland CA 94605 USA
Lee, David — Director, Writer
Grub Street Productions, 5555 Melrose Ave, #101, Los Angeles CA 90038, USA
Lee, David A — Football Player
2518 N Waverly Dr, Bossier City LA 71111, USA
Lee, David E — Baseball Player
56 Terrace Dr, Pittsburgh PA 15205, USA
Lee, David G (Dave) — Basketball Player
2580 Rampart Terrace, Reno NV 89519, USA
Lee, David H — Astronomer
Plenum Publishing Group, 233 Spring St, #600, New York NY 10013, USA
Lee, David L — Businessman
Global Crossing Ltd, Wessex House, 45 Reid St, Hamilton HM 12, Bermuda
Lee, David M — Nobel Physics Laureate
Cornell University, Physics Dept, Clark Hall, Ithaca NY 14853, USA
Lee, Dennis — Director
I C M Partners, 10250 Constellation Blvd, #900, Los Angeles CA 90067 USA
Lee, Derek G — Baseball Player
8834 Liatris Dr, Frankfort IL 60423, USA
Lee, Derrek L — Baseball Player
3576 Brittany Way, El Dorado Hills CA 95762, USA
Lee, Dickey — Singer
Cape Entertainment, 8432 NW 31st Court, Sunrise FL 33351, USA
Lee, Don — Writer
Ploughshares, Emerson College, 120 Boylston St, #414, Boston MA 02116, USA
Lee, Donald E (Don) — Baseball Player
9101 E Palm Tree Dr, Tucson AZ 85710, USA
Lee, Doug — Basketball Player
10770 Procyon St, Las Vegas NV 89141, USA
Lee, Gary L — Interior Designer
Gary Lee Partners, 360 W Superior, #1, Chicago IL 60654, USA
Lee, Geddy — Singer, Bassist (Rush)
S L Feldman Mgmt, 1505 W 2nd Ave, #200, Vancouver BC V6H 3Y4, Canada
Lee, Grandma — Actress, Comedienne
Lee Strong, 626 Staffordshire Dr, Jacksonville FL 32225, USA
Lee, Gregory S (Greg) — Basketball Player
8077 Wild Flower Way, San Diego CA 92120, USA
Lee, Harper — Writer
PO Box 278, Monroeville AL 36461, USA
Lee, Ho Wang — Virologist
Life Sciences Institute, 388 Poongnap-Dong, Seoul 138 736, South Korea
Lee, Howard V — Vietnam War Marine Corps Hero (CMH)
529 King Arthur Dr, Virginia Beach VA 23464, USA
Lee, Jack R (Jacky) — Football Player
6306 Mid Pines Dr, Houston TX 77069, USA
Lee, James Kyson — Actor
S M S Talent, 8383 Wilshire Blvd, #230, Beverly Hills CA 90211 USA
Lee, Janice Y K — Writer
Park Literary Group, 270 Lafayette St, #1504, New York NY 10012, USA
Lee, Jared B — Cartoonist
Jared B Lee Studio, 2942 Hamilton Road, Lebanon OH 45036, USA
Lee, Jason — Actor
Ribisi Entertainment Group, 3278 Wilshire Blvd, #702, Los Angeles CA 90010, USA
Lee, Jason Scott — Actor
Untitled Entertainment, 350 S Beverly Dr, #200, Beverly Hills CA 90212 USA
Lee, Jeanette — Billards Player
Octagon Worldwide, 1751 Pinnacle Dr, #1500, McLean VA 22102 USA
Lee, Jenny — Golfer
1705 Canyon Edge Dr, Austin TX 78733, USA
Lee, Jieho — Director, Writer
United Talent Agency, 9336 Civic Center Dr, Beverly Hills CA 90210 USA
Lee, Jim — Cartoonist
Wildstorm Productions, 888 Prospect St, #240, La Jolla CA 92037, USA
Lee, Joe — Businessman
Darden Restaurants, 1000 Darden Center Dr, Orlando FL 32837, USA
Lee, Johnny — Singer, Guitarist, Songwriter
W I F T Mgmt, 2317 Pecan, Dickinson,TX 77539, USA
Lee, Jonathan (Jon) — Actor, Singer (S Club 7)
Elinor Hilton Assoc, 1 Goodwins Court, London WC2N 4LL, England
Lee, Jonna — Actress
8721 W Sunset Blvd, #103, West Hollywood CA 90069, USA
Lee, Keith D — Basketball Player
11653 Metz Place, Eads TN 38028, USA
Lee, Kristin — Concert Violinist
I C M Artists, 40 W 57th St, #1800, New York NY 10019 USA
Lee, Kurk — Basketball Player
2745 Scarborough Circle, Windsor Mill MD 21244, USA
Lee, Larry D — Football Player
PO Box 3889, Highland Park MI 48203, USA
Lee, Laura — Singer
Lee Magid, 15414 Ridgewood Dr, Sonora CA 95370, USA
Lee, Lela — Actress
S M S Talent, 8383 Wilshire Blvd, #230, Beverly Hills CA 90211 USA

Lee, Leron — Baseball Player
8150 Warren Court, Granite Bay CA 95746, USA

Lee, Luanne — Actress, Model
Playboy Promotions, 2706 Media Center Dr, Los Angeles CA 90065 USA

Lee, Malcolm D — Director
Creative Artists Agency, 2000 Ave of Stars, #100, Los Angeles CA 90067 USA

Lee, Manuel L (Manny) — Baseball Player
321 NW 31st St, Miami FL 33127, USA

Lee, Mark D — Guitarist (Third Day), Songwriter
Creative Trust, 5141 Virginia Way, #320, Brentwood TN 37027, USA

Lee, Mark A — Football Player
3610 208th St SE, Bothell WA 98021, USA

Lee, Mark C — Astronaut
79 S Player Crest Circle, Spring TX 77382, USA

Lee, Mark L — Baseball Player
130 N Rosemont St, Amarillo TX 79106, USA

Lee, Mark O — Baseball Player
3580 Brunswick Dr, Colorado Springs CO 80920, USA

Lee, Michele — Actress, Singer
Michele Lee Productions, 10866 Wilshire Blvd, #1100, Los Angeles CA 90024, USA

Lee, Nikki S — Photographer
Sikkema Jenkins Co, 530 W 22nd St, New York NY 10011, USA

Lee, Nina — Concert Cellist
David Rowe Artists, 24 Beesom St, #2, Marblehead MA 01945, USA

Lee, Patrick — Golfer
Links Mgmt, 5068 W Plano Parkway, #256, Plano TX 75093, USA

Lee, Rachel — Concert Violinist
I M G Artists, 152 W 57th St, #500, New York NY 10019 USA

Lee, Reggie — Actor
David Shapira Assoc, 193 N Robertson Blvd, Beverly Hills CA 90211 USA

Lee, Rex — Actor
Stone Manners Salners, 9911 W Pico Blvd, #1400, Los Angeles CA 90035 USA

Lee, Robert D (Bob) — Baseball Player
PO Box 1589, Lake Havasu City AZ 86405, USA

Lee, Robert M (Bob) — Football Player
363 Parker Ave, San Francisco CA 94118, USA

Lee, Robinne — Actress
Abrams Artists, 9200 W Sunset Blvd, #1125, West Hollywood CA 90069 USA

Lee, Rock A — Basketball Player
4616 Blackfoot Ave, San Diego CA 92117, USA

Lee, Ronald V (Ronnie) — Football Player
139 Shady Trail, McGregor TX 76657, USA

Lee, RonReaco — Actor
Principato-Young, 9465 Wilshire Blvd, #880, Beverly Hills CA 90212 USA

Lee, Russell E — Basketball Player
1457 Smokehouse Lane, Stone Mountain GA 30088, USA

Lee, Ruta — Actress
2623 Laurel Canyon Road, Los Angeles CA 90046, USA

Lee, Samuel (Sammy) — Diver, Coach
16537 Harbour Lane, Huntington Beach CA 92649, USA

Lee, Sandra — Cook, Writer
Food Network, 1180 Ave of Americas, #1200, New York NY 10036 USA

Lee, Sandra — Style Expert
W M E Entertainment, 9601 Wilshire Blvd, #300, Beverly Hills CA 90210 USA

Lee, Shannon E — Actress
Innovative Artists, 1505 10th St, Santa Monica CA 90401 USA

Lee, Sheryl — Actress
Brillstein Entertainment Partners, 9150 Wilshire Blvd, #350, Beverly Hills CA 90212 USA

Lee, Spike — Director
Forty Acres & A Mule Filmworks, 75 S Elliott Place, Brooklyn NY 11217, USA

Lee, Stan — Publisher, Cartoonist
Pow Entertainment, 9440 Santa Monica Blvd, #620, Beverly Hills CA 90210, USA

Lee, Sung Hi — Actress, Model
Marshak/Zachary Co, 8840 Wilshire Blvd, #100, Beverly Hills CA 90211 USA

Lee, Terry J — Baseball Player
4650 Wendover St, Eugene OR 97404, USA

Lee, Tommy — Drummer, Singer (Motley Crue)
Immortal Entertainment, 1620 26th St, #1060N, Santa Monica CA 90404, USA

Lee, Travis R — Baseball Player
PO Box 231081, Encinitas CA 92023, USA

Lee, Tsung-Dao — Nobel Physics Laureate
512 Clinton St, Brooklyn NY 11231, USA

Lee, Wayne — Space Engineer
Jet Propulsion Laboratory, 4800 Oak Grove Dr, Pasadena CA 91109 USA

Lee, Will Yun — Actor
A P A Talent/Literary Agency, 405 S Beverly Dr, #300, Beverly Hills CA 90212 USA

Lee, William F (Bill) — Baseball Player
305 Common View Dr, Craftsbury VT 05826, USA

Lee, William Gregory — Actor
Berneman Mgmt, 5820 Wilshire Blvd, #200, Los Angeles CA 90036, USA

Lee, Yuan T — Nobel Chemistry Laureate
19 Las Piedras, Orinda CA 94563, USA

Leebron, David W — Educator
Rice University, President's Office, Houston TX 77005, USA

Leech, Allen — Actor
Finch Partners, 4-8 Heddon St, London W1B 4BS, England

Leech, Beverly — Actress
House of Representatives, 1434 6th St, #1, Santa Monica CA 90401 USA

Leech, Kenneth — Theologian, Social Activist
Centrepoint, Central House, 25 Camperdown St, London E1 8DZ, England

Leech, Richard — Opera Singer
Thea Dispeker Artists, 59 E 54th St, New York NY 10022 USA

Leede, Ed — Basketball Player
307 Roca Place, Castle Rock CO 80108, USA

Leek, Eugene H (Gene) — Baseball Player
2722 E Parker Court, Visalia CA 93292, USA

Leeman, Gary — Ice Hockey Player
15 Willow Fern Dr, Barrie ON L4N 0Z9, Canada
Leemans, Kimberly — Model, Actress
New Wave Entertainment, 2660 W Olive Ave, Burbank CA 91505, USA
Leen, Bill — Bassist (Gin Blossoms)
W M E Entertainment, 1600 Division St, #300, Nashville TN 37203 USA
Leeper, David D (Dave) — Baseball Player
23997 Kaleb Dr, Corona CA 92883, USA
Leerhuber, Brian — Opera Singer
I M G Artists, Hogarth Business Park, Chiswick, London W4 2TH, England
Leese, Howard — Guitarist, Keyboardist (Heart)
1770 N Highland Ave, #H-482, Los Angeles CA 90028, USA
Leestma, David C — Astronaut
4314 Lake Grove Dr, Seabrook TX 77586, USA
Leetch, Brian J — Ice Hockey Player
40 Battery St, #PH 12, Boston MA 02109, USA
Leeuwenburg, Jay R — Football Player
6268 S Coventry Lane W, Littleton CO 80123, USA
Leeves, Jane — Actress
23501 Malibu Colony Road, Malibu CA 90265, USA
Lefcourt, Gerald — Attorney
211 Central Park W, New York NY 10024, USA
Lefcourt, Peter — Actor
Creative Artists Agency, 2000 Ave of Stars, #100, Los Angeles CA 90067 USA
LeFebure, Estelle — Model, Actress
Cineart, 36 Rue de Ponthieu, 75008 Paris, France
Lefebvre, James K (Jim) — Baseball Player, Manager
10160 E Whispering Wind Dr, Scottsdale AZ 85255, USA
Lefebvre, Joseph H (Joe) — Baseball Player
PO Box 16658, Hooksett NH 03106, USA
Lefebvre, Sylvain — Ice Hockey Player
Colorado Avalanche, Pepsi Center, 1000 Chopper Circle, Denver CO 80204 USA
Lefevre, Rachelle — Actress
W M E Entertainment, 9601 Wilshire Blvd, #300, Beverly Hills CA 90210 USA
Lefferts, Craig L — Baseball Player
40820 N Laurel Valley Way, Anthem AZ 85086, USA
Lefkofsky, Eric — Businessman
Groupon Inc, 600 W Chicago Ave, #620, Chicago IL 60654, USA
Lefkovitz, Keili — Actress
Metropolitan Talent Agency, 7020 La Presa Dr, Los Angeles CA 90068 USA
Lefkowitz, Robert J — Nobel Chemistry Laureate
Duke University Medical Center, Chemistry Dept, PO Box 3821, Durham NC 27702, USA
Lefley, Chuck — Ice Hockey Player
PO Box 65, Grosses Isle MB R0C 1G0, Canada
Leflore, Ronald (Ron) — Baseball Player
6263 93rd Terrace, #4206, Pinellas Park FL 33782, USA
Leftwich, Byron A — Football Player
1322 Charter Court E, Jacksonville FL 32225, USA
Leftwich, Phillip D (Phil) — Baseball Player
15819 S 31st St, Phoenix AZ 85048, USA
Legace, Emmanuel F (Manny) — Ice Hockey Player
40708 Village Oaks, Novi MI 48375, USA
Legace, Jean-Guy — Ice Hockey Player
126 Casa Grande Lane, Santa Rosa Beach FL 32459, USA
Legato, Robert (Rob) — Visual Effects Artist
W M E Entertainment, 9601 Wilshire Blvd, #300, Beverly Hills CA 90210 USA
Legend, John — Singer, Pianist, Songwriter, Actor
Creative Artists Agency, 2000 Ave of Stars, #100, Los Angeles CA 90067 USA
Legette, Tyrone C — Football Player
1304 Hancock St, Columbia SC 29205, USA
Legg, Gregory L (Greg) — Baseball Player
1920 E View Dr, Norman OK 73071, USA
Leggero, Natasha — Actress, Comedienne, Writer
Brillstein Entertainment Partners, 9150 Wilshire Blvd, #350, Beverly Hills CA 90212 USA
Leggett, Anthony J — Nobel Physics Laureate
607 W Pennsylvania Ave, Urbana IL 61801, USA
Legien, Waldemar — Judo Athlete
Ul Grottgera 10, 41 902 Bytom, Poland
Legler, Timothy E (Tim) — Basketball Player
20 W Woodland Ave, Cape May Court House NJ 08210, USA
Legrand, Michel — Composer, Conductor, Concert Pianist
Kraft-Engel Mgmt, 15233 Ventura Blvd, #200, Sherman Oaks CA 91403 USA
Legrande, Larry E, Sr — Baseball Player
1331 Leon St NW, Roanoke VA 24017, USA
Legree, Lance — Football Player
25 Ardmore Ave, Clifton NJ 07012, USA
Legris, Manuel C — Ballet Dancer
National Theater of Paris Opera, 8 Rue Scribe, 75009 Paris, France
LeGros, James — Actor
I F A Talent Agency, 8730 W Sunset Blvd, #490, West Hollywood CA 90069 USA
LeGuin, Ursula K — Writer
3321 NW Thurman St, Portland OR 97210, USA
Leguizamo, John — Actor, Comedian
United Talent Agency, 9336 Civic Center Dr, Beverly Hills CA 90210 USA
Lehan, Michael — Football Player
418 Madison Ave S, Hopkins MN 55343, USA
Lehane, Dennis — Writer
341 Kerrville South Dr, Kerrville TX 78028, USA
Lehew, James A (Jim) — Baseball Player
3086 Fairview Road, Grantsville MD 21536, USA
Lehman, I Robert — Biochemist
895 Cedro Way, Stanford CA 94305, USA
Lehman, Kristin — Actress, Dancer
Oscars Abrams Zimel, 438 Queen St E, Toronto ON M5A 1T4, Canada
Lehman, Thomas E L (Tom) — Golfer
9820 E Thompson Peak Parkway, #704, Scottsdale AZ 85255, USA

L

Leeman - Lehman

Lehmann, Edie — Actress
24844 Malibu Road, Malibu CA 90265, USA

Lehmann, Jens — Soccer Player
Rosenthaler Str 40-41, Hackesche Hofe, 10179 Berlin, Germany

Lehmann, Jens — Cyclist
V f B Stuttgart, Mercedesstr 109, 70372 Stuttgart, Germany

Lehmann, Karl Cardinal — Religious Leader
Bischofliches Ordinariat, PF 1560, Bischofsplatz 2A, 55116 Mainz, Germany

Lehmann, Michael — Director
Industry Entertainment, 955 Carillo Dr, #300, Los Angeles CA 90048 USA

Lehman-Smith, Debra — Interior Designer
Lehman-Smith & McLeish, 1212 Banks St NW, Washington DC 20007, USA

Lehmberg, Stanford E — Historian
1005 Calle Largo, Santa Fe NM 87501, USA

Lehn, Jean-Marie P — Nobel Chemistry Laureate
6 Rue des Pontonniers, 67000 Strasbourg, France

Lehne, Fredric — Actor
Bauman Assoc, 250 W 57th St, #2223, New York NY 10107 USA

Lehninger, Albert L — Biochemist
15020 Tanyard Road, Sparks MD 21152, USA

Lehr, Charles L (Justin) — Baseball Player
6015 Nagel St, La Mesa CA 91942, USA

Lehr, John — Actor, Writer
Grade A Entertainment, 149 S Barrington Ave, #719, Los Angeles CA 90049, USA

Lehrer, James C (Jim) — Commentator, Writer
News Hour Show, 2700 S Quincy St, #250, Arlington VA 22206, USA

Lehrer, Scott — Sound Designer
I C M Partners, 10250 Constellation Blvd, #900, Los Angeles CA 90067 USA

Lehrer, Thomas A (Tom) — Pianist, Comedian
11 Sparks St, Cambridge MA 02138, USA

Lehtinen, Dexter — Attorney, Government Official
US Attorney's Office, Justice Dept, 155 S Miami Ave, Miami FL 33130, USA

Lehtinen, Jere K — Ice Hockey Player
622 Stratford Lane, Coppell TX 75019, USA

Lehtonen, Kari — Ice Hockey Player
3230 Bryn Mawr Dr, Dallas TX 75225, USA

Leibman, Ron — Actor
27 W 87th St, #2, New York NY 10024, USA

Leibovitz, Annie — Photographer
68 River Road, Rhinebeck NY 12572, USA

Leibovitz, Mitchell G — Businessman
Pep Boys-Manny Moe & Jack, 3111 W Allegheny Ave, Philadelphia PA 19132, USA

Leibrandt, Charles L (Charlie) — Baseball Player
1235 Stuart Ridge, Alpharetta GA 30022, USA

Leicester, Jon — Baseball Player
937 12th St, #204, Santa Monica CA 90403, USA

Leick, Hudson — Actress
Paradigm Agency, 360 Park Ave S, #1600, New York NY 10010 USA

Leifer, Carol — Actress, Comedienne
A P A Talent/Literary Agency, 405 S Beverly Dr, #300, Beverly Hills CA 90212 USA

Leifer, Neil — Photographer
235 W 56th St, #21B, New York NY 10019, USA

Leiferkus, Sergei P — Opera Singer
5 The Paddocks, Abberbury Road, Iffley, Oxford OX4 4ET, England

Leifheit, Sylvia — Model
Agentur Reed, Treppendorfer Weg 13, 12527 Berlin, Germany

Leigh, Chyler — Actress
N2N Entertainment, 1230 Montana Ave, #303, Santa Monica CA 90403 USA

Leigh, Danni — Singer
Cramden Coach Corp, PO Box 463, Austin TX 78767, USA

Leigh, Doug — Figure Skating Coach
Mariposa Skating School, PO Box 444, Barrie ON L4M 4T7, Canada

Leigh, Jennifer Jason — Actress
United Talent Agency, 9336 Civic Center Dr, Beverly Hills CA 90210 USA

Leigh, Mike — Director
37 Marylebone Lane, London W1U 2NW, England

Leigh, Mitch — Composer
29 W 57th St, #1000, New York NY 10019, USA

Leigh, Monica — Model
Playboy Promotions, 2706 Media Center Dr, Los Angeles CA 90065 USA

Leigh, Nikki — Model
Playboy Promotions, 2706 Media Center Dr, Los Angeles CA 90065 USA

Leigh, Regina — Singer (Regina Regina)
Buddy Lee Attractions, 38 Music Square E, #300, Nashville TN 37203 USA

Leigh, Vince — Actor
Ken McReddie Assoc, 11 Connaught Place, London W2 2ET, England

Leighton, Laura — Actress
A P A Talent/Literary Agency, 405 S Beverly Dr, #300, Beverly Hills CA 90212 USA

Leighton, Roberta — Actress
20700 Ventura Blvd, #240, Woodland Hills CA 91364, USA

Leija, James (Jesse) — Boxer
116 Cas Hills Dr, San Antonio TX 78213, USA

Leiker, Anthony W (Tony) — Football Player
411 E 21st St, Hays KS 67601, USA

Leimkuehler, Paul — Amputee Skier, Businessman
351 Darbys Run, Bay Village OH 44140, USA

Leinart, Matthew S (Matt) — Football Player
22 E Oakwood Hills Dr, Chandler AZ 85248, USA

Leiner, Danny — Director, Producer, Writer
I C M Partners, 10250 Constellation Blvd, #900, Los Angeles CA 90067 USA

Leiper, David P (Dave) — Baseball Player
3312 E Glenrosa Ave, Phoenix AZ 85018, USA

Leipheimer, Levi — Cyclist
1755 Crystal Springs Court, Santa Rosa CA 95404, USA

Leishman, Marc — Golfer
Professional Golfer's Assn, PO Box 109601, Palm Beach Gardens FL 33410 USA

Leister, John W
304 Devon Dr, Saint Louis MI 48880, USA — Baseball Player

Leisure, David
Vincent Cirrincione Assoc, 1516 N Fairfax Ave, Los Angeles CA 90046 USA — Actor

Leitch, Matthew
Diamond Mgmt, 31 Percy St, London W1T 2DD, England — Actor

Leiter, Alois T (Al)
181 E 90th St, #9B, New York NY 10128, USA — Baseball Player

Leiter, Mark E
121 Carriage Way, Forked River NJ 8731, USA — Baseball Player

Leiter, Michael E
National Counterterrorism Center, 1505 Tysons McLean Blvd, McLean VA 22102, USA — Government Official

Leiter, Robert E (Bob)
1921 Shorepoint Village, Gimli BC R0C 1B0, Canada — Ice Hockey Player

Leith, Prudence M
94 Kensington Park Road, London W11 2PN, England — Food Expert

Leithauser, Hamilton
Mick Mgmt, 35 Washington St, Brooklyn NY 11201 USA — Singer, Guitarist (Walkmen)

Leitner, Patric-Fritz
Gesprachsstoff Marketing, Scholssstr 9B, 82140 Olching, Germany — Luge Athlete

Leitso, Tyron
Lucas Talent, 6-1238 Homer St, Vancouver BC V6B 2YB, Canada — Actor

Leitzel, Joan
University of Nebraska, President's Office, Lincoln NE 68588, USA — Educator

Leius, Scott T
12620 42nd Place N, Minneapolis MN 55442, USA — Baseball Player

Lekang, Anton
47 Pratt St, Winsted CT 06098, USA — Ski Jumper

Lekman, Jens
Agency Group Ltd, 142 W 57th St, #600, New York NY 10019 USA — Singer, Songwriter

Leland, David
Creative Artists Agency, 2000 Ave of Stars, #100, Los Angeles CA 90067 USA — Director

Lelie, Ashley J
501 Hahaione St, #13H, Honolulu HI 96825, USA — Football Player

Lelliott, Jeremy
Joan Green Mgmt, 1836 Courtney Terrace, Los Angeles CA 90046, USA — Actor

Lellouche, Gilles
U B B A, 6 Rue de Braque, 75003 Paris, France — Actor

Lelong, Pierre J
9 Place de Rungis, 75013 Paris, France — Mathematician

Lelouch, Claude
15 Ave Hoche, 75008 Paris, France — Director

Lelouch, Salome
Artmedia, 20 Ave Rapp, 75007 Paris, France — Actress

Lelyveld, Joseph
Wylie Agency, 250 W 57th St, #2114, New York NY 10107 USA — Editor

LeMaho, Yvon
Centre for Ecological & Evolutionary Synthesis, PO Box 1066 Blindern, 0316 Oslo, Norway — Ecologist

Lemaire, Jacques G
PO Box 1207, Palmetto FL 34220, USA — Ice Hockey Player, Coach

Lemanczyk, David L (Dave)
24 Lehigh Court, Rockville Centre NY 11570, USA — Baseball Player

LeMarche, Maurice
Danis Panaro Nist, 9201 W Olympic Blvd, Beverly Hills CA 90212 USA — Actor

Lemaster, Denver C (Denny)
4833 Carlene Way SE, Lilburn GA 30047, USA — Baseball Player

LeMaster, Frank P
PO Box 159, Birchrunville PA 19421, USA — Football Player

Lemaster, Johnnie L
PO Box 943, Paintsville KY 41240, USA — Baseball Player

Lemasters, Braden
Paradigm Agency, 360 N Crescent Dr, North Building, Beverly Hills CA 90210 USA — Actor

LeMat, Paul
6300 Wilshire Blvd, #1460, Los Angeles CA 90048, USA — Actor

Lematta, Wes
PacWest Racing Group, PO Box 1717, Bellevue WA 98009, USA — Auto Racing Executive

Lemay, Richard P (Dick)
1741 Holland Lane, Wichita KS 67212, USA — Baseball Player

LeMay-Doan, Catriona A
Landmark Sport Group, 277 Richmond St W, Toronto ON M54 1X1, Canada — Speed Skater

Lembeck, Michael
Principato-Young, 9465 Wilshire Blvd, #880, Beverly Hills CA 90212 USA — Director, Actor

Lembo, Joseph
220 Riverside Blvd, #16V, New York NY 10069, USA — Interior Designer

Leme, Sebasitao Carvalho
Av Pedro de Toledo 1114, Banzato Marilia, Sao Paulo 17509 021, Brazil — Photographer

Lemelin, Reggie
10 Benevenuto Circle, Peabody MA 01960, USA — Ice Hockey Player

Lemelin, Stephanie
Paradigm Agency, 360 N Crescent Dr, North Building, Beverly Hills CA 90210 USA — Actress

Lemercier, Valerie
Artmedia, 20 Ave Rapp, 75007 Paris, France — Actress

Lemieux, Claude P
4802 E Ray Road, Phoenix AZ 85044, USA — Ice Hockey Player

LeMieux, George S
Gunster Yoakley, 450 E Las Olas Blvd, Fort Lauderdale FL 30301, USA — Senator, FL

Lemieux, Jocelyn
2004 E Glenn Dr, Phoenix AZ 85020, USA — Ice Hockey Player

Lemieux, Joseph H
Owens-Illinois Inc, 1 Sea Gate, Toledo OH 43666, USA — Businessman

Lemieux, Laurence
Coleman Lemieux Compagnie, 304 Parliament St, Toronto ON M5A 3A4, Canada — Dancer

Lemieux, Mario
630 Academy St, Sewickley PA 15143, USA — Ice Hockey Player

Lemieux, Raymond U
7602 119th St, Edmonton AB T6G 1W3, Canada — Chemist

L

Lemke, Mark A
3 Olena Dr, Whitesboro NY 13492, USA — Baseball Player

Lemme, Steve
United Talent Agency, 9336 Civic Center Dr, Beverly Hills CA 90210 USA — Actor, Comedian, Writer, Producer

Lemmon, Chris
80 Murray St, South Glastonbury CT 06073, USA — Actor

Lemmons, Kasi
Gersh Agency, 9465 Wilshire Blvd, #600, Beverly Hills CA 90212 USA — Director, Writer, Actress

Lemon, Chester E (Chet)
38150 Timberlane Dr, Umatilla FL 32784, USA — Baseball Player

Lemon, George (Meadowlark), III
6501 E Greenway Parkway, #1206, Scottsdale AZ 85254, USA — Basketball Player

Lemon, Peter C
Lemco Enterprises, PO Box 49025, Colorado Springs CO 80949, USA — Vietnam War Army Hero (CMH)

LeMond, Gregory J (Greg)
3000 Willow Dr, Hamel MN 55340, USA — Cyclist

Lemonds, David L (Dave)
1501 Aringill Lane, Matthews NC 28104, USA — Baseball Player

Lemper, Ute
Les Visiteurs du Soir, 40 Rue de la Folie Regnault, 75011 Paris, France — Singer, Actress, Dancer

Lenahan, Edward P
Fortune, Publisher's Office, Rockefeller Center, New York NY 10020, USA — Publisher

Lenard, Michael B
US Olympic Committee, 1 Olympic Plaza, Building 6, Colorado Springs CO 90909 USA — Olympics Executive

Lenard, Voshon K
22694 Nottingham Lane, Southfield MI 48033, USA — Basketball Player

Lenchewski, Andrew
Creative Artists Agency, 2000 Ave of Stars, #100, Los Angeles CA 90067 USA — Producer, Writer

Lendl, Ivan
400 5 1/2 Mile Road, Goshen CT 06756, USA — Tennis Player

Lenehan, Nancy
Meghan Schumacher Mgmt, 12551D Riverside Dr, #387, Sherman Oaks CA 91423, USA — Actress

Lenfant, Claude J M
PO Box 65278, Vancouver WA 98665, USA — Physician

Lengies, Vanessa
Gersh Agency, 9465 Wilshire Blvd, #600, Beverly Hills CA 90212 USA — Actress

Lenhardt, Donald E (Don)
1513 Timberlake Manor Parkway, Chesterfield MO 63017, USA — Baseball Player

Lenk, Hans
Neubrunnenschlag 15, 76337 Waldbronn, Germany — Rowing Athlete, Philosopher

Lenk, Thomas
Gemeinde Braunsbach, 74542 Schloss Tierberg, Germany — Sculptor

Lenk, Tom
Vanguard Management Group, 8060 Melrose Ave, #400, Los Angeles CA 90046, USA — Actor, Writer, Producer

Lenka
Agency Group Ltd, 142 W 57th St, #600, New York NY 10019 USA — Singer, Songwriter

Lenkaitis, William E (Bill)
26 Rose Court Way, East Walpole MA 02032, USA — Football Player

Lenkov, Peter M
Creative Artists Agency, 2000 Ave of Stars, #100, Los Angeles CA 90067 USA — Producer, Writer

Lenkus, Linnea
820 Gladys Ave, Long Beach CA 90804, USA — Photographer

Lennix, Harry J
Brookside Artist Mgmt, 250 W 57th St, #2303, New York NY 10107, USA — Actor

Lennon, Diane
1984 State Highway 165, Branson MO 65616, USA — Singer (Lennon Sisters)

Lennon, Janet
1984 State Highway 165, Branson MO 65616, USA — Singer (Lennon Sisters)

Lennon, Julian
Man from Another Room, 20 Bulstrode St, London W1M 5FR, England — Singer, Songwriter

Lennon, Kathy
Overlook Dr, #10, Branson MO 65616, USA — Singer (Lennon Sisters)

Lennon, Patrick O
60 Meister Blvd, Freeport NY 11520, USA — Baseball Player

Lennon, Peggy
1984 State Highway 165, Branson MO 65616, USA — Singer (Lennon Sisters)

Lennon, Richard G
Archdiocese of Boston, 66 Brooks Dr, Braintree MA 02184, USA — Religious Leader

Lennon, Sean
KillerMoxie Mgmt, 5890 W Jefferson Blvd, #J, Los Angeles CA 90016, USA — Singer, Actor

Lennon, Thomas (Tom)
Creative Artists Agency, 2000 Ave of Stars, #100, Los Angeles CA 90067 USA — Actor, Comedian

Lennox, Annie
19 Music & Mgmt, 35-37 Parkgate Road, London SW11 4NP, England — Singer (Eurythmics), Songwriter

Lennox, Kai
TalentWorks, 3500 W Olive Ave, #1400, Burbank CA 91505 USA — Actor

Lennox, William J, Jr
University of Nevada, President's Office, Las Vegas NV 89154, USA — Army General, Educator

Leno, Jay
I C M Partners, 10250 Constellation Blvd, #900, Los Angeles CA 90067 USA — Actor, Comedian

Lenoir, Noemie
U B B A, 6 Rue de Braque, 75003 Paris, France — Model

Lenon, Paris M
1505 Taylor St, Lynchburg VA 24504, USA — Football Player

Lenormand, Marie
Columbia Artists Mgmt Inc, 1790 Broadway, #702, New York NY 10019 USA — Opera Singer

Lenox, Jack, Jr
2362 Haddington Court, The Villages FL 32162, USA — WW II Army Air Corps Hero

Lenska, Rula
David Daley Assoc, 586A Kings Road, London SW6 2DX, England — Model, Actress

Lentine, James M (Jim)
1066 Calle del Cerro, #1411, San Clemente CA 92672, USA — Baseball Player

Lentz, Larry L (Leary)
1309 Whispering Pines Dr, Houston TX 77055, USA — Basketball Player

Lenz, Kay
Kritzer Levine Wilkins, 8840 Wilshire Blvd, #100, Beverly Hills CA 90211, USA — Actress

Lemke - Lenz

Lenz, Kim
Mark Pucia Media, 5000 Oak Bluff Court, Atlanta GA 30350, USA — Singer, Songwriter

Lenz, Rick
12955 Calvert St, Van Nuys CA 91401, USA — Actor

Leo, Melissa C
Creative Artists Agency, 2000 Ave of Stars, #100, Los Angeles CA 90067 USA — Actress

Leon
Stone Manners Salners, 9911 W Pico Blvd, #1400, Los Angeles CA 90035 USA — Actor, Singer (Young Lions)

Leon, Eduardo A (Eddie)
5285 N Strada de Rubino, Tucson AZ 85750, USA — Baseball Player

Leon, Kenny
W M E Entertainment, 1325 Ave of Americas, New York NY 10019 USA — Director

Leon, Valerie
Essanay Ltd, 2 Conduit St, London W1R 9TG, England — Actress

Leonard, Isabel
I M G Artists, Hogarth Business Park, Chiswick, London W4 2TH, England — Opera Singer

Leonard, Bob
1241 Hillcrest Dr, Carmel IN 46033, USA — Basketball Player

Leonard, Brett
Quattro Media, 171 Pier Ave, #328, Santa Monica CA 90405, USA — Director, Producer, Writer

Leonard, Brian
20 Countryside Court Dr, Gouverneur NY 13642, USA — Football Player

Leonard, Dennis P
4102 SW Evergreen Lane, Blue Springs MO 64015, USA — Baseball Player

Leonard, Elmore
2192 Yarmouth Road, Bloomfield Village MI 48301, USA — Writer

Leonard, Gary
2406 Ridgefield Road, Columbia MO 65203, USA — Basketball Player

Leonard, J Wayne
Entergy Corp, 10055 Grogans Mill Road, #150, Spring TX 77380, USA — Businessman

Leonard, James F (Jim)
119 Cress Road, Santa Cruz CA 95060, USA — Football Player

Leonard, Joanne
University of Michigan, Art Dept, Ann Arbor MI 48109, USA — Photographer

Leonard, Joe
PO Box 194, Gasoline Alley, Indianapolis IN 46222, USA — Motorcycle Racing Rider, Auto Driver

Leonard, Joshua
Collective, 8383 Wilshire Blvd, #1050, Beverly Hills CA 90211 USA — Actor

Leonard, Justin
3700 Euclid Ave, Dallas TX 75205, USA — Golfer

Leonard, Mark D
22042 Hibiscus Dr, Cupertino CA 95014, USA — Baseball Player

Leonard, Myers
Portland Trail Blazers, Rose Garden, 1 N Center Court St, Portland OR 97227 USA — Basketball Player

Leonard, Ray C (Sugar Ray)
PO Box 1433, Pacific Palisades CA 90272, USA — Boxer

Leonard, Robert Sean
W M E Entertainment, 9601 Wilshire Blvd, #300, Beverly Hills CA 90210 USA — Actor

Leonard, William R (Slick)
5398 Baltimore Court, Carmel IN 46033, USA — Basketball Player, Coach

Leonard, Zoe
Paula Cooper Gallery, 534 W 21st St, New York NY 10011, USA — Photographer

Leonardini, Jean-Pierre
U B B A, 6 Rue de Braque, 75003 Paris, France — Actor

Leonardis, Tom
Whoop/One Ho Productions, 333 W 52nd St, #600, New York NY 10019, USA — Producer

Leone, Justin
5605 Dawnbreak Dr, Las Vegas NV 89149, USA — Baseball Player

Leone, Marianne
Paradigm Agency, 360 N Crescent Dr, North Building, Beverly Hills CA 90210 USA — Actress

Leonetti, John R
Montana Artists Agency, 9150 Wilshire Blvd, #100, Beverly Hills CA 0212, USA — Cinematographer

Leonetti, Matthew F, Jr
1362 Bella Oceana Vista, Pacific Palisades CA 90272, USA — Cinematographer

Leong, Page
C N A Assoc, 1875 Century Park East, #2250, Los Angeles CA 90067 USA — Actress

Leonhard, David P (Dave)
87 Corning St, Beverly MA 01915, USA — Baseball Player

Leonhardt, David
New York Times, Editorial Dept, 229 W 43rd St, New York NY 10036 USA — Journalist

Leonhardt, Ulf
Saint Andrews University, Physics Dept, Fife KY16 9AJ, Scotland — Theoretical Physicist

Leonhart, William
119 Oak Terrace, Lake Bluff IL 60044, USA — Diplomat

Leoni, Tea
United Talent Agency, 9336 Civic Center Dr, Beverly Hills CA 90210 USA — Actress

Leonov, Aleksei A
Alfa Capital, Masha Porivaeva Ul 11, 107078 Moscow, Russia — Cosmonaut, Air Force General

Leonskaja, Elisabeth
I M G Artists, Hogarth Business Park, Chiswick, London W4 2TH, England — Concert Pianist

Leonti, Nikki
W M E Entertainment, 9601 Wilshire Blvd, #300, Beverly Hills CA 90210 USA — Singer

Leopardi, Chauncey
Abrams Artists, 9200 W Sunset Blvd, #1125, West Hollywood CA 90069 USA — Actor

Leopold, Jordan
10988 Mississippi Dr N, Champlin MN 55316, USA — Ice Hockey Player

Leopold, Leroy J (Bobby)
4221 W Spruce St, #1404, Tampa FL 33607, USA — Football Player

Leopold, Tom
Gersh Agency, 9465 Wilshire Blvd, #600, Beverly Hills CA 90212 USA — Actor, Comedian, Producer

Lepage, Robert
103 Dalhousie, Quebec City QC G1K 4B9, Canada — Actor, Director

Lepcio, Thaddeus S (Ted)
263 Greenlodge St, Dedham MA 02026, USA — Baseball Player

LePelley, Guernsey
35 Saint Germain St, Boston MA 02115, USA — Editorial Cartoonist

LePen, Marine — Government Official, France
National Front, 76-78 Rue des Suisses, 92000 Nanterre, France

LePichon, Xavier — Geologist
Ecole Normale Superieure, 24 Rue Lhomond, 75005 Paris Cedex 05, France

Lepore, Nanette — Fashion Designer
225 W 35th St, #1700, New York NY 10001, USA

Lepore, Tatiana — Actress
Carol Levi Mgmt, Via G Pisanelli 2, 00196 Rome, Italy

Leppard, Raymond J — Conductor
Indianapolis Symphony, 32 E Washington St, #600, Indianapolis IN 46204, USA

Leppert, Don E — Baseball Player
1630 Epping Forest Dr, Southaven MS 38671, USA

Leppert, Donald G (Don) — Baseball Player
317 Sunrise Cay, #201, Naples FL 34114, USA

LePrevost, Nicholas — Actor
Ken McReddie Assoc, 11 Connaught Place, London W2 2ET, England

Lepsis, Matthew S (Matt) — Football Player
1833 Broken Bend Dr, Westlake TX 76262, USA

Lerach, William (Bill) — Attorney
Milberg Weiss Hynes Lerach, 1600 W Broadway, #1800, San Diego CA 92101, USA

Lerch, Randy L — Baseball Player
19490 Monterey Rd, Morgan Hill CA 95037, USA

Lerche, Sondre — Singer, Guitarist, Songwriter
Macklam/Feldman Mgmt, 1505 W 2nd Ave, #200, Vancouver BC V6H 3Y4, Canada

Lerchen, George E — Baseball Player
354 E Rose Ave, Garden City MI 48135, USA

Lerew, Anthony A — Baseball Player
6 Summer Dr, Dillsburg PA 17019, USA

Lerman, Logan — Actor
Creative Artists Agency, 2000 Ave of Stars, #100, Los Angeles CA 90067 USA

Lerner, Dan — Director
Paradigm Agency, 360 N Crescent Dr, North Building, Beverly Hills CA 90210 USA

Lerner, Michael — Religious Leader, Rabbi
Tikkun, 2342 Shattuck Ave, #1200, Berkeley CA 94704, USA

Lerner, Michael — Actor
Abrams Artists, 9200 W Sunset Blvd, #1125, West Hollywood CA 90069 USA

LeRoux, Francois — Opera Singer
I M G Artists, Burlington Lane, Chiswick, London W4 2TH, England

Leroux, Francois — Ice Hockey Player
507 Hickory Grade Road, Bridgeville PA 15017, USA

Leroux, Sydney R — Soccer Player
Atlanta Beat, 1955 Vaughn Road, #209, Kennesaw GA 30144 USA

LeRoy, Gloria — Actress
TalentWorks, 3500 W Olive Ave, #1400, Burbank CA 91505 USA

Leroy-Beauliey, Philippine — Actress
Artmedia, 20 Ave Rapp, 75007 Paris, France

Les, James A (Jim) — Basketball Player, Coach
4030 Shadybrook Court, Granite Bay CA 95746, USA

Lesar, David — Businessman
Halliburton Co, Lincoln Plaza, 500 N Akard St, Dallas TX 75201, USA

LeSaunier, Jacqueline — Actress
Angentur Retzlaff, Kurfuerstenstra 34, 10785 Berlin, Germany

Lesch, James R — Businessman
15840 Malibu E, Willis TX 77318, USA

Leschin, Luisa — Actress, Writer, Producer
W M E Entertainment, 9601 Wilshire Blvd, #300, Beverly Hills CA 90210 USA

Leschyshyn, Curtis — Ice Hockey Player
40 Laurel Mountain Dr, Littleton CO 80127, USA

Lescroart, John T — Writer
Penguin Books, 375 Hudson St, Basement 1, New York NY 10014 USA

Lesh, Phil — Bassist (Grateful Dead)
Paradigm Agency, 360 N Crescent Dr, North Building, Beverly Hills CA 90210 USA

LeShana, David C — Educator
8246 E Hoverland Road, Scottsdale AZ 85255, USA

Lesher, Brian H — Baseball Player
217 Vassar Dr, Newark DE 19711, USA

LeSieyr, Michael — Producer, Writer
Creative Artists Agency, 2000 Ave of Stars, #100, Los Angeles CA 90067 USA

Leskanic, Curtis J (Curt) — Baseball Player
2032 Alaqua Dr, Longwood FL 32779, USA

Leskanich, Katrina — Singer (Katrina & the Waves)
Barry Collins, PO Box 2112, Hockley, Essex SS4 4WD, England

Leslie, A Ryan — Singer, Songwriter, Producer
Laine Mgmt, 131 Victoria Road, Salford M6 8LF, England

Leslie, Fred W — Astronaut
2038 Springhouse Road SE, Huntsville AL 35802, USA

Leslie, Joan — Actress
2228 N Catalina St, Los Angeles CA 90027, USA

Leslie, Lisa — Basketball Player, Model
PO Box 452447, Los Angeles CA 90045, USA

Leslie, Ryan — Rap Artist
W M E Entertainment, 9601 Wilshire Blvd, #300, Beverly Hills CA 90210 USA

Lesnie, Andrew — Cinematographer
United Talent Agency, 9336 Civic Center Dr, Beverly Hills CA 90210 USA

Lespert, Jalil — Actor
Artmedia, 20 Ave Rapp, 75007 Paris, France

Lessac, Michael — Director
Creative Artists Agency, 2000 Ave of Stars, #100, Los Angeles CA 90067 USA

Lessard, Stefan — Bassist (Dave Matthews Band), Songwriter
Red Light Mgmt, PO Box 520, Crozet VA 22932, USA

Lessin, Robert H — Financier
Smith Barney Inc, 590 Madison Ave, #1100, New York NY 10022, USA

Lessing, Doris M — Nobel Literature Laureate
11 Kingscroft Road, #3, London NW2 3QE, England

Lester of Herne Hill, Anthony P — Attorney
Blackstone Chambers, Blackstone House, Temple, London EC4Y 9BW, England

Lester, Adrian — Actor
Medavoy Mgmt, 10203 Santa Monica Blvd, #400, Los Angeles CA 90067 USA
Lester, Jonathan T (Jon) — Baseball Player
Boston Red Sox, Fenway Park, 4 Yawkey Way, Boston MA 02215 USA
Lester, Joseph (Joe) — Keyboardist (Silversun Pickups)
Ink Tank Public Relations, 1824 W Sunset Blvd, #102, Los Angeles CA 90026, USA
Lester, Ketty — Actress, Singer
5931 Comey Ave, Los Angeles CA 90034, USA
Lester, Mark L — Director
American World Pictures, 21700 Oxnard St, #1770, Woodland Hills CA 91367, USA
Lester, Richard (Dick) — Director
Petersham Lodge, River Lane, Richmond Surrey TW10 7AG, England
Lester, Ronnie — Basketball Player, Executive
PO Box 2187, Manhattan Beach CA 90267, USA
Lester, Timothy L (Tim) — Football Player
1160 Bream Dr, Alpharetta GA 30004, USA
Lester, Tom — Actor
PO Box 363, Laurel MS 39441, USA
Lesuk, Bill — Ice Hockey Player
40 Bracken Ave, East Saint Paul MB R2E 0K2, Canada
Lesure, James — Actor
Wolman Wealth Mgmt, 10640 Rochester Ave, Los Angeles CA 90024, USA
Letarte, Pierre — Cinematographer
551 W Pinacle, Abercorn QC J0E 1B0, Canada
Letarte, Steve — Auto Racing Mechanic
18420 Nantz Road, Cornelius NC 28031, USA
Letbetter, R Steve — Businessman
Reliant Energy, 1111 Louisiana, Houston TX 77002, USA
Leterme, Yves C D — Prime Minister, Belgium
Prime Minister's Office, 16 Rue de la Loi, 1000 Brussels, Belgium
Leterrier, Louis — Director
Management 360, 9111 Wilshire Blvd, Beverly Hills CA 90210 USA
Lethem, Jonathan — Writer
McSweeney's Books, 372 5th Ave, Brooklyn NY 11215, USA
Letheren, Mark — Actor
Ken McReddie Assoc, 11 Connaught Place, London W2 2ET, England
Letherman, Lindze L — Actress
Lovett Mgmt, 1327 Brinkley Ave, Los Angeles CA 90049, USA
Letizia — Crown Princess, Spain
Palacio de la Zarzuela, 28080 Madrid, Spain
Leto, Jared — Actor
Untitled Entertainment, 350 S Beverly Dr, #200, Beverly Hills CA 90212 USA
Letowski, Trevor — Ice Hockey Player
3612 Lion Ridge Court, Raleigh NC 27612, USA
Letscher, Matthew (Matt) — Actor
Sanders/Armstrong/Caserta Mgmt, 2120 Colorado Ave, #120, Santa Monica CA 90404 USA
Letsie III — King, Lesotho
Royal Palace, PO Box 524, Maseru, Lesotho
Letsinger, Robert L — Chemist
4400 Stone Way N, #223, Seattle WA 98103, USA
Lett, Clifford — Basketball Player
7067 Rampart Way, Pensacola FL 32505, USA
Lett, Leon, Jr — Football Player
2 Longleaf Circle, Fairhope AL 36532, USA
Letteri, Joseph (Joe) — Special Effects Designer
Weta Digital, 9-11 Manuka St, Miramar, Wellington 6022, New Zealand
Letterman, David — Entertainer, Comedian
Worldwide Pants, 1697 Broadway, #3000, New York NY 10019, USA
Letts, Tracy — Writer
1756 W School St, Chicago IL 60657, USA
Leung Chiu Wai, Tony — Actor
Jet Tone Films, 180 Tung Le Wan Road, #21F, Hong Kong, China
Leung, Ken — Actor
Hartig-Hilepo Agency, 54 W 21st St, #610, New York NY 10010 USA
Leuthard, Doris — President, Switzerland
Federal Chancellery, Bundeshaus-W, Bundesgasse, 3033 Berne, Switzerland
Levada, William J Cardinal — Religious Leader
Doctrine of Faith Congregation, Palazzo del Uffizio 11, 00193 Rome, Italy
Leval, Pierre N — Judge
US Court of Appeals, Moynihan Courthouse, 500 Pearl St, New York NY 10007, USA
Levane, Andrew J — Basketball Player, Coach
14 Northstone Court, Irmo SC 29063, USA
Levant, Brian — Director
W M E Entertainment, 9601 Wilshire Blvd, #300, Beverly Hills CA 90210 USA
LeVay, Simon — Neuroscientist
970 Palm Ave, West Hollywood CA 90069, USA
Leveaux, David — Director
Simpson Fox Assoc, 52 Shaftesbury Ave, London W1V 7DE, England
Leven, Jeremy — Director, Writer
Paradigm Agency, 360 N Crescent Dr, North Building, Beverly Hills CA 90210 USA
Levene, Ben — Artist
Royal Academy of Arts, Piccadilly, London W1V 0DS, England
Levens, H Dorsey — Football Player
4249 Olde Mille Lane NE, Atlanta GA 30342, USA
Leveque, Michel — Minister of State, Monaco
57 Rue de l'Universite, 75007 Paris, France
Lever, Don — Ice Hockey Player
247 Quail Hollow Lane, East Amherst NY 14051, USA
Lever, Lafayette (Fat) — Basketball Player
50 Regency Park Circle, #12107, Sacramento CA 95835, USA
Levering, Kate — Actress
Paradigm Agency, 360 N Crescent Dr, North Building, Beverly Hills CA 90210 USA
Leverington, Shelby — Actress
C E S D, 10635 Santa Monica Blvd, #130, Los Angeles CA 90025 USA
LeVert, Edward (Eddie) — Singer (O'Jays)
Pyramid Entertainment, 377 Rector Place, #21A, New York NY 10280 USA

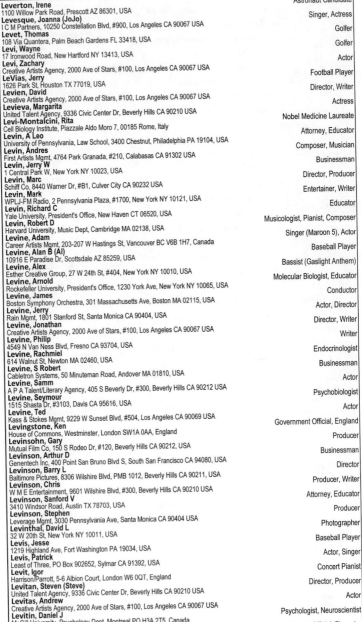

L

Leverton - Levrault

Leverton, Irene 1100 Willow Park Road, Prescott AZ 86301, USA	Astronaut Candidate
Levesque, Joanna (JoJo) I C M Partners, 10250 Constellation Blvd, #900, Los Angeles CA 90067 USA	Singer, Actress
Levet, Thomas 108 Via Quantera, Palm Beach Gardens FL 33418, USA	Golfer
Levi, Wayne 17 Ironwood Road, New Hartford NY 13413, USA	Golfer
Levi, Zachary Creative Artists Agency, 2000 Ave of Stars, #100, Los Angeles CA 90067 USA	Actor
LeVias, Jerry 1626 Park St, Houston TX 77019, USA	Football Player
Levien, David Creative Artists Agency, 2000 Ave of Stars, #100, Los Angeles CA 90067 USA	Director, Writer
Levieva, Margarita United Talent Agency, 9336 Civic Center Dr, Beverly Hills CA 90210 USA	Actress
Levi-Montalcini, Rita Cell Biology Institute, Piazzale Aldo Moro 7, 00185 Rome, Italy	Nobel Medicine Laureate
Levin, A Leo University of Pennsylvania, Law School, 3400 Chestnut, Philadelphia PA 19104, USA	Attorney, Educator
Levin, Andres First Artists Mgmt, 4764 Park Granada, #210, Calabasas CA 91302 USA	Composer, Musician
Levin, Jerry W 1 Central Park W, New York NY 10023, USA	Businessman
Levin, Marc Schiff Co, 8440 Warner Dr, #B1, Culver City CA 90232 USA	Director, Producer
Levin, Mark WPLJ-FM Radio, 2 Pennsylvania Plaza, #1700, New York NY 10121, USA	Entertainer, Writer
Levin, Richard C Yale University, President's Office, New Haven CT 06520, USA	Educator
Levin, Robert D Harvard University, Music Dept, Cambridge MA 02138, USA	Musicologist, Pianist, Composer
Levine, Adam Career Artists Mgmt, 203-207 W Hastings St, Vancouver BC V6B 1H7, Canada	Singer (Maroon 5), Actor
Levine, Alan B (Al) 10916 E Paradise Dr, Scottsdale AZ 85259, USA	Baseball Player
Levine, Alex Esther Creative Group, 27 W 24th St, #404, New York NY 10010, USA	Bassist (Gaslight Anthem)
Levine, Arnold Rockefeller University, President's Office, 1230 York Ave, New York NY 10065, USA	Molecular Biologist, Educator
Levine, James Boston Symphony Orchestra, 301 Massachusetts Ave, Boston MA 02115, USA	Conductor
Levine, Jerry Rain Mgmt, 1801 Stanford St, Santa Monica CA 90404, USA	Actor, Director
Levine, Jonathan Creative Artists Agency, 2000 Ave of Stars, #100, Los Angeles CA 90067 USA	Director, Writer
Levine, Philip 4549 N Van Ness Blvd, Fresno CA 93704, USA	Writer
Levine, Rachmiel 614 Walnut St, Newton MA 02460, USA	Endocrinologist
Levine, S Robert Cabletron Systems, 50 Minuteman Road, Andover MA 01810, USA	Businessman
Levine, Samm A P A Talent/Literary Agency, 405 S Beverly Dr, #300, Beverly Hills CA 90212 USA	Actor
Levine, Seymour 1515 Shasta Dr, #3103, Davis CA 95616, USA	Psychobiologist
Levine, Ted Kass & Stokes Mgmt, 9229 W Sunset Blvd, #504, Los Angeles CA 90069 USA	Actor
Levingstone, Ken House of Commons, Westminster, London SW1A 0AA, England	Government Official, England
Levinsohn, Gary Mutual Film Co, 150 S Rodeo Dr, #120, Beverly Hills CA 90212, USA	Producer
Levinson, Arthur D Genentech Inc, 400 Point San Bruno Blvd S, South San Francisco CA 94080, USA	Businessman
Levinson, Barry L Baltimore Pictures, 8306 Wilshire Blvd, PMB 1012, Beverly Hills CA 90211, USA	Director
Levinson, Chris W M E Entertainment, 9601 Wilshire Blvd, #300, Beverly Hills CA 90210 USA	Producer, Writer
Levinson, Sanford V 3410 Windsor Road, Austin TX 78703, USA	Attorney, Educator
Levinson, Stephen Leverage Mgmt, 3030 Pennsylvania Ave, Santa Monica CA 90404 USA	Producer
Levinthal, David L 32 W 20th St, New York NY 10011, USA	Photographer
Levis, Jesse 1219 Highland Ave, Fort Washington PA 19034, USA	Baseball Player
Levis, Patrick Least of Three, PO Box 902652, Sylmar CA 91392, USA	Actor, Singer
Levit, Igor Harrison/Parrott, 5-6 Albion Court, London W6 0QT, England	Concert Pianist
Levitan, Steven (Steve) United Talent Agency, 9336 Civic Center Dr, Beverly Hills CA 90210 USA	Director, Producer
Levitas, Andrew Creative Artists Agency, 2000 Ave of Stars, #100, Los Angeles CA 90067 USA	Actor
Levitin, Daniel J McGill University, Psychology Dept, Montreal PQ H3A 2T5, Canada	Psychologist, Neuroscientist
Levitt, Arthur, Jr Carlyle Group, 1001 Pennsylvania Ave NW, #220S, Washington DC 20004, USA	Government Official, Financier
Levitt, George 82 Via Del Corso, Palm Beach Gardens FL 33418, USA	Chemist
Levitt, Steven D University of Chicago, Economics Dept, Chicago IL 60637, USA	Economist, Writer
LeVox, Gary Turner & Nichols, 49 Music Square W, #500, Nashville TN 37203, USA	Singer (Rascal Flatts)
Levrault, Allen 5 Granada Dr, Westport MA 02790, USA	Baseball Player

Levrone, Kevin
Beacon Talent, 170 Apple Ridge Road, Woodcliff Lake NJ 07677, USA — Body Builder, Actor

Levy, Barrington
Agency Group Ltd, 142 W 57th St, #600, New York NY 10019 USA — Singer

Levy, Bernard-Henri
Editions Grasset/Fasquelle, 61 Rue des Saint-Peres, 75006 Paris, France — Philosopher

Levy, Clifford J
New York Times, Editorial Dept, 229 W 43rd St, New York NY 10036 USA — Journalist

Levy, Dan
Great North Artists Mgmt, 350 Dupont St, Toronto ON M5R 1V9, Canada — Actor, Comedian

Levy, David H
Mount Palomar Observatory, 35899 Canfield Road, Palomar Mountain CA 92060, USA — Astronomer

Levy, Eugene
Anonymous Content, 3532 Hayden Ave, Culver City CA 90232 USA — Actor, Comedian, Director

Levy, Jane
Suskin Management, 2 Charlton St, #5K, New York NY 10014, USA — Actress

Levy, Jean-Bernard
Vivendi, 42 Ave de Friedland, 75380 Paris Cedex 08, France — Businessman

Levy, Kenneth
K L A-Tencor Corp, 160 Rio Robles, San Jose CA 95134, USA — Businessman

Levy, Marvin D (Marv)
National Pro Athletes Organization, 1806 Watermere Lane, Windermere FL 34786, USA — Football Coach

Levy, Marvin David
Sheldon Sofer Mgmt, 130 W 56th St, New York NY 10019, USA — Composer

Levy, Naomi
Academy of Jewish Religion, 574 Hilgard Ave, Los Angeles CA 90024, USA — Religious Leader, Rabbi

Levy, Peter
I C M Partners, 10250 Constellation Blvd, #900, Los Angeles CA 90067 USA — Cinematographer

Levy, Shawn
21 Laps Entertainment, 10201 W Pico Blvd, Building 41, Los Angeles CA 90035, USA — Director

Levy, William
W M E Entertainment, 9601 Wilshire Blvd, #300, Beverly Hills CA 90210 USA — Actor

Lew, Jacob J (Jack)
White House, 1600 Pennsylvania Ave NW, Washington DC 20500 USA — Government Official

Lew, Scott
Principato-Young, 9465 Wilshire Blvd, #880, Beverly Hills CA 90212 USA — Director

Lewin, Gene
GrooveLily, PO Box 11570, Glendale CA 91226, USA — Drummer, Singer (GrooveLily)

Lewin, Josh
1081 W Winding Creek Dr, Grapevine TX 76051, USA — Sportscaster

Lewis, Aaron
The Firm, 2049 Century Park E, #2550, Los Angeles CA 90067 USA — Singer, Guitarist (Staind)

Lewis, Albert R
3532 Macedonia Road, Centreville MS 39631, USA — Football Player

Lewis, Ananda
Britto Agency, 234 W 56th St, #PH, New York NY 10019, USA — Actress

Lewis, Andrew L (Drew)
PO Box 70, Lederach PA 19450, USA — Secretary, Transportation; Businessman

Lewis, Anthony
New York Times, Editorial Dept, 2 Faneuil Hall, Boston MA 02109, USA — Columnist

Lewis, Barbara
Hello Stranger Productions, PO Box 300488, Casselberry FL 32730, USA — Singer

Lewis, Bernard
Princeton University, Near Eastern Studies Dept, Princeton NJ 08544, USA — Historian

Lewis, Blake C
PO Box 806, Lynnwood WA 98046, USA — Singer, Songwriter

Lewis, Bob
63910 E Squash Blossom Lane, Tucson AZ 85739, USA — Basketball Player

Lewis, Bobby
Lustig Talent, PO Box 770850, Orlando FL 32877 USA — Singer

Lewis, Charlotte
2814 N Sheridan Road, Peoria IL 61604, USA — Basketball Player

Lewis, Clea
Innovative Artists, 1505 10th St, Santa Monica CA 90401 USA — Actress

Lewis, Colby P
14800 Orchard Crest Ave, Bakersfield CA 93314, USA — Baseball Player

Lewis, Crystal
Creative Artists Agency, 2000 Ave of Stars, #100, Los Angeles CA 90067 USA — Singer, Rap Artist

Lewis, Cynthia R
Harper's Bazaar, Publisher's Office, 1770 Broadway, New York NY 10019, USA — Publisher

Lewis, Damaris
Elite Model Mgmt, 404 Park Ave S, #900, New York NY 10016 USA — Model

Lewis, Damian
Markham & Froggatt, Julian House, 4 Windmill St, London W1P 1HF, England — Actor

Lewis, Damione R
9601 Gato del Sol Court, Waxhaw NC 28173, USA — Football Player

Lewis, Daniel N (Dan)
460 S Park St, Detroit MI 48215, USA — Football Player

Lewis, Darren J
2212 Rosemount Lane, San Ramon CA 94582, USA — Baseball Player

Lewis, Dave
2040 Ranch Road, Holly MI 48442, USA — Ice Hockey Player, Coach

Lewis, David
Bang & Olufsen A/S, Peter Bangs Vej 15, PO Box 40, 7600 Stuer, Denmark — Industrial Designer

Lewis, David Levering
Rutgers University, History Dept, East Rutherford NJ 07073, USA — Writer

Lewis, David R (Dave)
406 142nd St, Ocean City MD 21842, USA — Football Player

Lewis, Dawnn
Stone Manners Salners, 9911 W Pico Blvd, #1400, Los Angeles CA 90035 USA — Actress

Lewis, De'Andre D (D D)
10230 125th Ave NE, Kirkland WA 98033, USA — Football Player

Lewis, Denise
Outside Organization, 177-8 Tottenham Court Road, London W1T 7NY, England — Heptathlete

Lewis, Dwight D (D D)
P C S Sales, 1624 Northcrest Dr, Plano TX 75075, USA — Football Player

L

Levrone - Lewis

Lewis, Emmanuel — Actor
Orange Grove Group, 12178 Ventura Blvd, #205, Studio City CA 91604, USA
Lewis, F Carlton (Carl) — Track Athlete
528 Palisades Dr, Pacific Palisades CA 90272, USA
Lewis, Frank D — Football Player
118 Presque Isle Dr, Houma LA 70363, USA
Lewis, Frederick L (Fritz) — Basketball Player
4122 Illinois Ave NW, Washington DC 20011, USA
Lewis, Gary — Singer (Gary Lewis & the Playboys)
701 Balin Court, Nashville TN 37221, USA
Lewis, Geoffrey — Actor
5210 Collier Place, Woodland Hills CA 91364, USA
Lewis, Herschell Gordon — Director
Lewis Enterprises, 451 Heritage Dr, #215, Pompano Beach FL 33060, USA
Lewis, Huey — Singer, Actor
Hulex Corp, PO Box 819, Mill Valley CA 94942, USA
Lewis, J L — Golfer
2504 Orleans Dr, Cedar Park TX 78613, USA
Lewis, Jamal L — Football Player
10614 Lee Ave, Cleveland OH 44106, USA
Lewis, James M (Jim) — Baseball Player
5311 Hansel Ave, #D12, Orlando FL 32809, USA
Lewis, James S (Jim) — Baseball Player
676 Sparks St, Jackson MI 49202, USA
Lewis, Jasmine — Actress
Evolution Entertainment, 901 N Highland Ave, Los Angeles CA 90038 USA
Lewis, Jason — Actor
Untitled Entertainment, 350 S Beverly Dr, #200, Beverly Hills CA 90212 USA
Lewis, Jenifer — Actress, Singer
Innovative Artists, 1505 10th St, Santa Monica CA 90401 USA
Lewis, Jensen D — Baseball Player
1278 W 9th St, #928, Cleveland OH 44113, USA
Lewis, Jermaine E — Football Player
4919 Pleasant Grove Road, Reisterstown MD 21136, USA
Lewis, Jerry — Actor, Comedian, Director
Jerry Lewis Films, 3160 W Sahara Ave, #C16, Las Vegas NV 89102, USA
Lewis, Jerry Lee — Singer, Pianist, Composer
PO Box 206, Old Hickory TN 37138, USA
Lewis, Jim — Composer
I C M Partners, 10250 Constellation Blvd, #900, Los Angeles CA 90067 USA
Lewis, Jonathan Guy — Actor
Ken McReddie Assoc, 11 Connaught Place, London W2 2ET, England
Lewis, Juliette — Actress
B L Mgmt, 840 Country Club Dr, Burbank CA 91501, USA
Lewis, Karen — Writer
Sarnoff Co, 10 Universal City Plaza, #2000, Universal City CA 91608, USA
Lewis, Kevin — Football Player
4417 Roy St, Orlando FL 32812, USA
Lewis, Lennox — Boxer
Gainsborough House, 81 Oxford St, #206, London W1D 2EU, England
Lewis, Leo, III — Football Player
10116 Ivywood Court, Eden Prairie MN 55347, USA
Lewis, Lisa — Boxer
7242 N Wheeler Ave, Fresno CA 93722, USA
Lewis, Marcedes A — Football Player
3725 Bouton Dr, Lakewood CA 90712, USA
Lewis, Mark D — Baseball Player
1246 Cleveland Ave, Hamilton OH 45013, USA
Lewis, Marvin — Football Coach
Cincinnati Bengals, 1 Paul Brown Stadium, Cincinnati OH 45202 USA
Lewis, Michael — Writer
Creative Artists Agency, 2000 Ave of Stars, #100, Los Angeles CA 90067 USA
Lewis, Michael H (Mike) — Football Player
3350 Blodgett St, Houston TX 77004, USA
Lewis, Mike — Basketball Player
490 Windsor Park Road, Kernersville NC 27284, USA
Lewis, Monica — Singer, Actress
Lang, 1100 Alta Loma Road, #16A, West Hollywood CA 90069, USA
Lewis, Morris C (Mo) — Football Player
22012 Gardner Dr, Alpharetta GA 30009, USA
Lewis, Neville — Interior Designer
Ted Moudis Assoc, 79 Madison Ave, #1000, New York NY 10016, USA
Lewis, Phill — Actor
Kritzer Levine Wilkins Griffin, 11872 La Grange Ave, #100, Los Angeles CA 90025 USA
Lewis, Ramsey E, Jr — Jazz Pianist, Composer
7655 N Sheridan Road, Chicago IL 60626, USA
Lewis, Rashard Q — Basketball Player
9 E Rivercrest Dr, Houston TX 77042, USA
Lewis, Ray A — Football Player
2401 Tufton Ave, Reisterstown MD 21136, USA
Lewis, Richard — Actor, Comedian
Bauman Assoc, 250 W 57th St, #2223, New York NY 10107 USA
Lewis, Richie T — Baseball Player
13209 E Country Road 700 S, Losantville IN 47354, USA
Lewis, Robert Lloyd — Producer
Gersh Agency, 9465 Wilshire Blvd, #600, Beverly Hills CA 90212 USA
Lewis, Russell T — Businessman, Publisher
New York Times Co, Publisher's Office, 229 W 43rd St, New York NY 10036, USA
Lewis, Sally Sirkin — Interior Designer
502 N Oak St, Inglewood CA 90302, USA
Lewis, Scott E — Baseball Player
2584 Fairway Dr, Costa Mesa CA 92627, USA
Lewis, Sherman — Football Player, Coach
45822 Bristol Circle, Novi MI 48377, USA
Lewis, Stacy — Golfer
Sterling Sports Mgmt, 7650 Rivers Edge Dr, Columbus OH 43235, USA

Lewis, Stephen R, Jr 222 S 9th St, #440, Minneapolis MN 55402, USA	Educator	**L**
Lewis, T United Feature Syndicate, PO Box 5610, Cincinnati OH 45201 USA	Cartoonist (Over the Hedge)	
Lewis, Tom I C M Partners, 10250 Constellation Blvd, #900, Los Angeles CA 90067 USA	Singer	
Lewis, Vaughan A West Indies University, International Relations Institute, Saint Augustine, Trinidad & Tobago	Prime Minister, Saint Lucia	
Lewis, Vicki Stone Manners Salners, 9911 W Pico Blvd, #1400, Los Angeles CA 90035 USA	Actress, Comedienne	
Lewis, Victor Joanne Klein, 130 W 28th St, New York NY 10001, USA	Jazz Drummer	
Lewis, Walter 7915 Park Dr, Saint Louis MO 63117, USA	Ethnobotanist	
Lewis, William J (Bill) University of Notre Dame, Athletic Dept, Notre Dame IN 46556 USA	Football Coach	
Lewiston, Denis C 13700 Tahiti Way, #24, Marina del Rey CA 90292, USA	Cinematographer	
Ley, Terrence R (Terry) 2955 SE Custer Road, Prineville OR 97754, USA	Baseball Player	
Leyden, Paul Paradigm Agency, 360 N Crescent Dr, North Building, Beverly Hills CA 90210 USA	Actor	
Leygue, Louis Georges 6 Rue de Docteur Blanche, 75016 Paris, France	Sculptor	
Leyla Model Management Group, 1024 6th Ave, #201, New York NY 10018, USA	Model, Actress	
Leyland, James R (Jim) Detroit Tigers, Comerica Park, 2100 Woodward Ave, Detroit MI 48201 USA	Baseball Manager	
Leyritz, James J (Jim) 11060 Cameron Court, #304, Davie FL 33324, USA	Baseball Player	
Leyton, John 53 Keyes House, Dolphin Square, London SW1V 3NA, England	Actor, Singer	
Leyva, Nicholas T (Nick) 1098 Tilghman Road, Chesterbrook PA 19087, USA	Baseball Manager	
Lezak, Jason E 3 Galena, Irvine CA 92602, USA	Swimmer	
Lezcano, Carlos 415 W Boxelder Place, Chandler AZ 85225, USA	Baseball Player	
Lezcano, Sixto J 7828 Bardmoor Chill Circle, Orlando FL 32835, USA	Baseball Player	
Lhuillier, Monique 1201 S Grand Ave, #300, Los Angeles CA 90015, USA	Fashion Designer	
Li Hongzhi Universe Publishing, PO Box 193, Gillette NJ 07933, USA	Religious Leader	
Li Jiajun Skating Assn, 56 Zhongguancun South St, Haidian, Beijing 100044, China	Speed Skater	
Li Ka Shing 70/F Cheung Kong Center, 2 Queen's Road, Cental Region, Hong Kong, China	Businessman	
Li Keyu 21 Gong-Jian Hutong, Di An-Men, Beijing 100009, China	Fashion Designer	
Li Lanqing Communist Party Central Committee, Zhonganahai, Beijing 100017, China	Government Official, China	
Li Na Women's Tennis Assn, 1 Progress Plaza, #1500, Saint Petersburg FL 33701 USA	Tennis Player	
Li Peng Communist Party Central Committee, Zhonganahai, Beijing 100017, China	Premier, China	
Li, Frederick Dana-Farber Cancer Institute, 44 Binney St, Boston MA 02115, USA	Molecular Biologist	
Liagigre, Christian 122 Rue de Grenelle, 75007 Paris, France	Interior Designer	
Liakhovich, Sergei Central Boxing Gym, 1755 W Van Buren St, Phoenix AZ 85007, USA	Boxer	
Liano, Jennifer Playboy Promotions, 2706 Media Center Dr, Los Angeles CA 90065 USA	Model	
Liao, Sheri Xiaoyi Global Village, 86 Bei Yuan Road, Jiaming District, Beijing 100101, China	Environmental Activist	
Libano Christo, Carlos A Escola Dominicana de Teologia, Rua Atibaia 420, Sao Paulo SP 01235 010, Brazil	Social Activist, Writer	
Libatique, Matthew J 4524 Ambrose Ave, Los Angeles CA 90027, USA	Cinematographer	
Libby, Wendy B Stetson University, President's Office, 421 N Woodland Blvd, DeLand FL 32723, USA	Educator	
Liberato, Liana Creative Artists Agency, 2000 Ave of Stars, #100, Los Angeles CA 90067 USA	Actress	
Liberman, Avigdor Knesset, Kiryat Ben Gurion, Israel 91950, Israel	Government Official, Israel	
Libertini, Richard 2313 McKinley Ave, Venice CA 90291, USA	Actor	
Libeskind, Daniel Studio Daniel Libeskund, Windscheidstr 18, 10627 Berlin, Germany	Architect	
Libett, Nick 4272 N McNay Court, West Bloomfield MI 48323, USA	Ice Hockey Player	
Libman, Leslie I C M Partners, 10250 Constellation Blvd, #900, Los Angeles CA 90067 USA	Director, Writer	
Liboiron, Landon Characters Talent Mgmt, 8 Elm St, Toronto ON M5G 1G7, Canada	Actor	
Libor, Christiane I M G Artists, Hogarth Business Park, Chiswick, London W4 2TH, England	Opera Singer	
Libran, Frankie 100 Calle Principe, #1, Mayaguez PR 00680, USA	Baseball Player	
Libutti, Frank New York City Deputy Commissioner's Office, 1 Police Plaza, New York NY 10038, USA	Marine Corps General, Police Official	
Licht, Jeremy 4355 Clybourn Ave, Toluca Lake CA 91602, USA	Actor	
Licht, Louis Ecoltree, 3017 Valley View Lane NE, North Liberty IA 52317, USA	Environmental Scientist	**Lewis - Licht**

Lichtblau, Eric — Journalist
New York Times, Editorial Dept, 229 W 43rd St, New York NY 10036 USA

Lichtenberg, Byron K — Astronaut
5701 Impala South Road, Athens TX 75752, USA

Lichtenberger, H W — Businessman
Praxair Inc, 39 Old Ridgebury Road, #7, Danbury CT 06810, USA

Lichtenstein, Harvey — Music Executive
Brooklyn Academy of Music, 30 Lafayette Ave, Brooklyn NY 11217, USA

Lichti, Todd S — Basketball Player
2331 Holly View Dr, Martinez CA 94553, USA

Lick, Dale W — Mathematician, Computer Scientist
348 Remington Run Loop, Tallahassee FL 32312, USA

Lick, Dennis A — Football Player
6140 S Knox Ave, Chicago IL 60629, USA

Lickliter, Frank, II — Golfer
846 S Main St, Franklin OH 45005, USA

Lickliter, Todd — Basketball Coach
Marian University, Athletic Dept, 3200 Cold Spring Road, Indianapolis IN 46222, USA

Licon, Jeffrey (Jeff) — Director, Actor
Innovative Artists, 1505 10th St, Santa Monica CA 90401 USA

Lidback, Jenny — Golfer
1130 Graystone Crossing, Alpharetta GA 30005, USA

Liddell, Chuck — Wrestler, Mixed Martial Athlete
Zinkin Entertainment, 5 E River Park Place W, #203, Fresno CA 93720, USA

Liddell, David A (Dave) — Baseball Player
2631 Preakness Way, Norco CA 92860, USA

Liddy, G Gordon — Watergate Figure, Actor
9112 Riverside Dr, Fort Washington MD 20744, USA

Lidell, Jamie — Singer
Agency Group Ltd, 361-373 City Road, London EC1V 2QA, England

Lidge, Bradley T (Brad) — Baseball Player
4833 Front St, Castle Rock CO 80104, USA

Lidov, Arthur — Artist
Pleasant Ridge Road, Poughquag NY 12570, USA

Lidstrom, Nicklas E — Ice Hockey Player
47725 Bellagio Dr, Northville MI 48167, USA

Lieber, Charles M — Chemist
Harvard University, Chemistry Dept, Cambridge MA 02138, USA

Lieber, Jonathan R (Jon) — Baseball Player
3060 Isle of Palms Dr W, Mobile AL 36695, USA

Lieber, Larry — Cartoonist (Amazing Spider-Man)
King Features Syndicate, 300 W 57th St, #1500, New York NY 10019 USA

Lieber, Mimi — Actress
TalentWorks, 3500 W Olive Ave, #1400, Burbank CA 91505 USA

Lieber, Rob — Writer, Actor
Anonymous Content, 3532 Hayden Ave, Culver City CA 90232 USA

Lieberman, Myron — Educator
910 17th St NW, #800, Washington DC 20006, USA

Lieberman, Robert — Director
A P A Talent/Literary Agency, 405 S Beverly Dr, #300, Beverly Hills CA 90212 USA

Lieberman, Todd — Producer
Mandeville Films, 500 S Buena Vista St, Animation Building 2G, Burbank CA 91521, USA

Lieberman, Wendy — Actress, Comedienne
Art/Work Entertainment, 5900 Wilshire Blvd, #1720, Los Angeles CA 9003, USA

Lieberman-Cline, Nancy — Basketball Player
2636 Creekway Dr, Carrollton TX 75010, USA

Lieberstein, Paul B — Actor, Comedian, Writer, Producer
Creative Artists Agency, 2000 Ave of Stars, #100, Los Angeles CA 90067 USA

Liebert, Ottmar — Guitarist, Composer
Kelly Anderson, 551 West Cordova Road, #809, Santa Fe NM 87505, USA

Lieberthal, Michael S (Mike) — Baseball Player
1740 Larkfield Ave, Westlake Village CA 91362, USA

Liebeskind, John — Brain Surgeon, Psychologist
University of California Medical Center, Surgery Dept, Los Angeles CA 90024, USA

Liebesman, Jonathan — Director
Principato-Young, 9465 Wilshire Blvd, #880, Beverly Hills CA 90212 USA

Liebman, David — Jazz Saxophonist
2206 Brislin Road, Stroudsberg PA 18360, USA

Liebowitz, Ronald D, Jr — Educator
Middlebury College, President's Office, 9 Old Chapel Road, Middlebury VT 05753, USA

Liefeld, Rob — Cartoonist (Youngblood)
1440 N Harbor Blvd, #305, Fullerton CA 92835, USA

Liefer, Jeff — Baseball Player
1116 W Bay Ave, Newport Beach CA 92661, USA

Liekens, Koen — Drummer (K's Choice)
Sharpe Entertainment Services, 683 Palmera Ave, Pacific Palisades CA 90272, USA

Lien, Jennifer — Actress
Abrams Artists, 9200 W Sunset Blvd, #1125, West Hollywood CA 90069 USA

Lienhard, William (Bill) — Basketball Player
1320 Lawrence Ave, Lawrence KS 66049, USA

Liepa, Andris — Ballet Dancer
Bryusov Per 17, #13, 103009 Moscow, Russia

Liepa, Ilsa — Ballerina
Bryusov Per 17, #12, 103009 Moscow, Russia

Liepmann, Hans W — Aeronautical Engineer, Physicist
55 Haverstock Road, La Canada Flintridge CA 91011, USA

Lietzke, Bruce — Golfer
PO Box 177, Larue TX 75770, USA

Lifeson, Alex — Guitarist (Rush)
S L Feldman Mgmt, 1505 W 2nd Ave, #200, Vancouver BC V6H 3Y4, Canada

Ligety, Ted — Alpine Skier
US Ski Team, PO Box 100, Park City UT 84060, USA

Light, John — Actor
Markham & Froggatt, Julian House, 4 Windmill St, London W1P 1HF, England

Light, Judith — Actress
Gersh Agency, 9465 Wilshire Blvd, #600, Beverly Hills CA 90212 USA

Light, Matthew C (Matt)
261 East St, Foxboro MA 02035, USA — Football Player

Lightbody, Gary
Big Life Mgmt, 67-69 Charlton St, London NW1 1HY, England — Singer, Songwriter (Snow Patrol)

Lightfoot, Edwin N
University of Wisconsin, Chemical Engineering Dept, 1415 Engineering Dr, Madison WI 53706, USA — Chemical, Biological Engineer

Lightfoot, Gordon
Early Morning, 1365 Yonge St, #207, Toronto ON M4T 2P7, Canada — Singer, Guitarist, Songwriter

Lightman, Alan P
Harvard University, Humanities Dept, Cambridge MA 02138, USA — Physicist, Writer

Lightman, Toby
Nettwerk Mgmt, 345 7th Ave, #2400, New York NY 10001, USA — Singer, Songwriter

Lightner, Candace L (Candy)
1216 Portner Road, Alexandria VA 22314, USA — Social Activist

Ligon, Bill
PO Box 1432, Gallatin TN 37066, USA — Basketball Player

Ligouri, James A
Iona College, President's Office, New Rochelle NY 10801, USA — Educator

Ligtenberg, Kerry
9274 Albright Court, Inver Grove Heights MN 55077, USA — Baseball Player

Lijn, Liliane
99 Camden Mews, London NW1 9BU, England — Sculptor

Likens, Gene E
Ecosystem Studies Institute, PO Box AB, Millbrook NY 12545, USA — Ecologist, Biologist

Lil Bow Wow
Central Entertainment Group, 251 W 39st, #700, New York NY 10018, USA — Rap Artist

Lil' Fame
Pyramid Entertainment, 377 Rector Place, #21A, New York NY 10280 USA — Rap Artist (MOP)

Lil' J
Thruline Entertainment, 9250 Wilshire Blvd, #100, Beverly Hills CA 90212 USA — Rap Artist

Lil' JJ
W M E Entertainment, 9601 Wilshire Blvd, #300, Beverly Hills CA 90210 USA — Actor, Comedian

Lil Jon
Susan Blond Inc, 50 W 57th St, #1400, New York NY 10019 USA — Rap Artist, Songwriter

Lil' Kim
Richard De La Font, 4845 Sheridan Road, #505, Tulsa OK 74145, USA — Rap Artist

Lil Mama
F Y I Public Relations, 45 E 20th St, #5B, New York NY 10003, USA — Rap Artist

Lil' Wayne
Bryant Mgmt, 800 Brickell Ave, #550, Miami FL 33131, USA — Rap Artist (Hot Boys), Actor

Liles, John-Michael
1540 E Shore Dr, Culver IN 46511, USA — Ice Hockey Player

Liles, Robert L
19520 Tiber Court, Montgomery Village MD 20886, USA — WW II Army Air Corps Hero

Lilienfeld, Abraham M
3203 Old Post Dr, Pikesville MD 21208, USA — Epidemiologist

Lilja, Andreas
6501 N Federal Highway, #2, Boca Raton FL 33487, USA — Ice Hockey Player

Lilja, George V
8 Driftwood Dr, Warren PA 16365, USA — Football Player

Lill, Dennis
Ken McReddie Assoc, 11 Connaught Place, London W2 2ET, England — Actor

Lillard, Bill
5418 Imogene St, Houston TX 77096, USA — Bowler

Lillard, Damian
Portland Trail Blazers, Rose Garden, 1 N Center Court St, Portland OR 97227 USA — Basketball Player

Lillard, Matthew
Paradigm Agency, 360 N Crescent Dr, North Building, Beverly Hills CA 90210 USA — Actor

Lillee, Dennis K
Swan Sport, PO Box 158, Byron Bay NSW 2481, Australia — Cricketer

Lilley, Chris
Princess Pictures, 11 Princes St, Saint Kilda VIC 3182, Australia — Producer, Writer, Actor

Lilley, James R
2801 New Mexico Ave NW, #407, Washington DC 20007, USA — Diplomat

Lilley, John M
Baylor University, President's Office, 1 Bear Place, Waco TX 76798, USA — Educator

Lillibridge, Brent S
22714 43rd Dr SE, Bothell WA 98021, USA — Baseball Player

Lilliquist, Derek J
226 10th Ave, Vero Beach FL 32962, USA — Baseball Player

Lillis, Robert P (Bob)
5107 Cherry Tree Lane, Orlando FL 32819, USA — Baseball Player, Manager

Lilly, Evangeline
Creative Artists Agency, 2000 Ave of Stars, #100, Los Angeles CA 90067 USA — Actress, Model

Lilly, Kristine
10 Bradford Terrace, #2, Brookline MA 02446, USA — Soccer Player

Lilly, Robert L (Bob)
3310 Drexel Dr, Dallas TX 75205, USA — Football Player

Lilly, Theodore R (Ted), III
1305 W Waveland Ave, Chicago IL 60613, USA — Baseball Player

Lim Chwen Jeng
Bartlett Architecture School, 22 Gordon St, London WC1H 0QB, England — Architect

Lim Siew Al
304 Morning Sun Dr, Birmingham AL 35242, USA — Golfer

Lim, H J
Harrison/Parrott, 5-6 Albion Court, London W6 0QT, England — Concert Pianist

Lima, Adriana
D N A Model Mgmt, 520 Broadway, #1100, New York NY 10012, USA — Model

Lima, Devin
LFO/BMG Records, 8750 Wilshire Blvd, Beverly Hills CA 90211, USA — Singer, Rap Artist (Lyte Funky Ones)

Lima, Kevin
W M E Entertainment, 9601 Wilshire Blvd, #300, Beverly Hills CA 90210 USA — Director, Producer

Liman, Doug
Dutch Oven, 12233 W Olympic Blvd, #256, Los Angeles CA 90064, USA — Director

Limbaugh, Rush
PO Box 2795, Palm Beach FL 33480, USA — Entertainer

L

Light - Limbaugh

Limbert, Deborah (Deb) — Explorer, Speleologist
British Cave Research Assn, Old Methodist Chapel, Great Hucklow, Buxton SK17 8RG, England
Limbert, Howard — Explorer, Speleologist
British Cave Research Assn, Old Methodist Chapel, Great Hucklow, Buxton SK17 8RG, England
Lime-Fedderson, Yvonne — Actress
15757 N 78th St, Scottsdale AZ 85260, USA
Limos, Tiffany — Actress
Vincent Cirrincione Assoc, 1516 N Fairfax Ave, Los Angeles CA 90046 USA
Lin Ching Hsia — Actress
Taiwan Cinema-Drama Assn, 196 Chunghua Road, 10/F, Sec 1 Taipei, Taiwan
Lin, Bridget — Actress
8 Fei Ngo Shan Road, Kowloon, Hong Kong, China
Lin, Cho-Liang — Concert Violinist
Juilliard School, 60 Lincoln Center Plaza, New York NY 10023, USA
Lin, Jeremy S — Basketball Player
Houston Rockets, 1730 Jefferson St, Houston TX 77003 USA
Lin, Justin — Director
Trailing Johnson Productions, 2100 Sawtell Blvd, Los Angeles CA 90025, USA
Lin, Maya Ying — Architect, Sculptor
Sidney Janis Gallery, 120 E 75th St, #6A, New York NY 10021, USA
Lin, Yu Ping — Golfer
Jerry Wong, 1450 Subtropic Dr, La Habra Heights CA 90631, USA
Lincecum, Timothy L (Tim) — Baseball Player
16062 SE 4th St, Belluvue WA 98008, USA
Lincicome, Brittany G — Golfer
7971 Idlewild Lane, Seminole FL 33777, USA
Lincoln, Andrew — Actor
Markham & Froggatt, Julian House, 4 Windmill St, London W1P 1HF, England
Lincoln, Craig — Diver
20930 Almazan Road, Woodland Hills CA 91364, USA
Lincoln, Jeremy A — Football Player
3411 W Lincolnshire Blvd, Toledo OH 43606, USA
Lincoln, Keith P — Football Player
550 SE Crestview St, Pullman WA 99163, USA
Lincoln, Lar Park — Actress
Premiere Artists Agency, 1875 Century Park E, #2250, Los Angeles CA 90067 USA
Lincoln, Michael G (Mike) — Baseball Player
8269 Moss Oak Ave, Citrus Heights CA 95610, USA
Lincoln, Todd — Director, Writer
Creative Artists Agency, 2000 Ave of Stars, #100, Los Angeles CA 90067 USA
Lind, Adam A — Baseball Player
6520 Turf Way, Anderson IN 46013, USA
Lind, Don L — Astronaut
51 N 376 E, Smithfield UT 84335, USA
Lind, Heather — Actress
I C M Partners, 10250 Constellation Blvd, #900, Los Angeles CA 90067 USA
Lind, Jackson H (Jack) — Baseball Player
6132 E Redmont Dr, Mesa AZ 85215, USA
Lind, Joan — Rowing Athlete
240 Euclid Ave, Long Beach CA 90803, USA
Lind, Jose — Baseball Player
18 Brisas del Plata, Dorado PR 00646, USA
Lind, Juha P — Ice Hockey Player
Montreal Canadiens, 1275 Saint Antoine St W, Montreal QC H3C 5L2, Canada
Lind, Marshall L — Educator
University of Alaska, Chancellor's Office, Fairbanks AK 99775, USA
Lind, Zach — Drummer (Jimmy Eat World)
S A M, 722 Seward St, Los Angeles CA 90038, USA
Lindahl, Cathrine — Curling Athlete
Curling Assn, Idrottshuser, Marbackagatan 19, 123 43 Farsta, Sweden
Lindahl, George, III — Businessman
Anadarko Petroleum Corp, 1201 Lake Robbins Dr, Spring TX 77380, USA
Lindahl, Margaretha — Curling Athlete
Curling Assn, Idrottshuser, Marbackagatan 19, 123 43 Farsta, Sweden
Lindbeck, Assar — Economist
50 Ostermalmsgatan, 114 26 Stockholm, Sweden
Lindbeck, George A — Theologian
Yale University, Divinity School, New Haven CT 06520, USA
Lindberg, Athena — Model
Playboy Promotions, 2706 Media Center Dr, Los Angeles CA 90065 USA
Lindberg, Chad — Actor
Creative Partners Group, 1522 2nd St, Santa Monica CA 90401, USA
Lindbergh, Peter — Photographer
Camerawork AG, Kantstr 149, 10623 Berlin, Germany
Lindelind, Liv — Model
PO Box 1029, Frazier Park CA 93225, USA
Lindell, Rian D — Football Player
45 Stoughton Lane, Orchard Park NY 14127, USA
Lindeman, James W (Jim) — Baseball Player
2278 S Scott St, Des Plaines IL 60018, USA
Lindemann, Til — Singer (Rammstein)
Pilgrim Mgmt, PO Box 540101, 10042 Berlin, Germany
Linden, Eugene — Writer
Penguin Books, 375 Hudson St, Basement 1, New York NY 10014 USA
Linden, Hal — Actor
Stone Manners Salners, 9911 W Pico Blvd, #1400, Los Angeles CA 90035 USA
Linden, Jamie — Director, Writer
Paradigm Agency, 360 N Crescent Dr, North Building, Beverly Hills CA 90210 USA
Linden, Todd — Baseball Player
7825 NW Anderson Hill Road, Silverdale WA 98383, USA
Linden, Trevor — Ice Hockey Player
1362 23rd St SE, Medicine Hat AB T1A 2C9, Canada
Linden, Walter C (Walt) — Baseball Player
4432 Harvey Ave, Western Springs IL 60558, USA
Lindenlaub, Karl W — Cinematographer
3021 Nichols Canyon Road, Los Angeles CA 90046, USA

Linder, Kate
Siegal Co, 9025 Wilshire Blvd, #400, Beverly Hills CA 90211, USA — Actress
Linderman, Earl W
5005 E Camelback Road, Phoenix AZ 85018, USA — Artist
Lindes, Hal
Damage Mgmt, 16 Lambton Place, London W11 2SH, England — Guitarist (Dire Straits)
Lindh, Hilary
PO Box 33036, Juneau AK 99803, USA — Alpine Skier
Lindholm, Ingvar N
Hringe Hages Vag 33, 144 00 Ronninge, Sweden — Composer
Lindhome, Riki
Principato-Young, 9465 Wilshire Blvd, #880, Beverly Hills CA 90212 USA — Actress
Lindig, Bill M
Sysco Corp, 1390 Enclave Parkway, Houston TX 77077, USA — Businessman
Lindley, Christina
Esterman Entertainment, 12333 Pretoria Dr, Silver Spring MD 20904, USA — Model, Actress
Lindley, David
Rosebud Agency, PO Box 170429, San Francisco CA 94117 USA — Guitarist
Lindley, John W
PO Box 351, 15332 Antioch St, Pacific Palisades CA 90272, USA — Cinematographer
Lindman, Karl
Wilhelmina Models, 300 Park Ave S, #200, New York NY 10010 USA — Model
Lindner, William G
Transport Workers Union, 80 W End Ave, New York NY 10023, USA — Labor Leader
Lindo, Delroy
Innovative Artists, 1505 10th St, Santa Monica CA 90401 USA — Actor
Lindon, Vincent
Artmedia, 20 Ave Rapp, 75007 Paris, France — Actor
Lindquist, Barbara M (Barb)
215 Targhee Towne Road, Alta WY 83414, USA — Triathlete
Lindquist, Susan L
Whitehead Institute, 9 Cambridge Circle, Cambridge MA 02142, USA — Biologist
Lindqvist, David
Paradigm Agency, 360 Park Ave, #1600, New York NY 10022 USA — Bassist (Caesars)
Lindros, Eric B
1 Morton Square, #6BE, New York NY 10014, USA — Ice Hockey Player
Lindroth, Eric
13151 Dufresne Place, San Diego CA 92129, USA — Water Polo Player
Lindsay, Bill
700 NW 7th Ave, Boca Raton FL 33486, USA — Ice Hockey Player
Lindsay, Elvin (Lin)
6220 E Broadway Road, #347, Mesa AZ 85206, USA — WW II Navy Air Force Hero
Lindsay, Everett E
101 Wildwood Beach Road, #11, Saint Paul MN 55115, USA — Football Player
Lindsay, James J
676 Azalea Dr, Vass NC 28394, USA — Army General
Lindsay, Mark
Lustig Talent, PO Box 770850, Orlando FL 32877 USA — Singer, Songwriter
Lindsay, R B Theodore (Ted)
2598 Invitational Dr, Oakland MI 48363, USA — Ice Hockey Player
Lindsay, Robert
Hamilton Hodell, 66-68 Margaret St, London W1W 8SR, England — Actor, Singer
Lindsay-Abaire, David
W M E Entertainment, 9601 Wilshire Blvd, #300, Beverly Hills CA 90210 USA — Writer
Lindsey, James E (Jim)
1165 E Joyce Blvd, Fayetteville AR 72703, USA — Football Player
Lindsey, M Douglas (Doug)
2410 Silver Spur Lane, Leander TX 78641, USA — Baseball Player
Lindsey, P Dale
4020 Murphy Canyon Road, San Diego CA 92123, USA — Football Player
Lindsey, Steven W
3217 W Yarrow Circle, Superior CO 80027, USA — Astronaut
Lindsey, Tracy
651B N Kilkea Dr, Los Angeles CA 90048, USA — Actress
Lindsey, William D (Bill)
1317 Winterberry Dr, Reidsville NC 27320, USA — Baseball Player
Lindskog, Par
Maxine Robertson Mgmt, 14 Forge Dr, Claygate KT10 0HR, England — Opera Singer
Lindsley, Blake
Shelter Entertainment, 9454 Wilshire Blvd, #715, Beverly Hills CA 90212 USA — Actress
Lindsley, Donald B
517 11th St, Santa Monica CA 90402, USA — Psychologist, Physiologist
Lindstrand, Per
Thunder & Colt, Maesbury Road, Oswestry, Shropshire SY10 8HA, England — Balloonist
Lindstrom Breer, Murle
7008 Sand Road, Savannah GA 31410, USA — Golfer
Lindstrom, Charles W (Charlie)
PO Box 486, Atlanta IL 61723, USA — Baseball Player
Lindstrom, Christopher A (Chris)
70 Dudley Hill Road, Dudley MA 01571, USA — Football Player
Lindstrom, David A (Dave)
11562 Hardy St, Overland Park KS 66210, USA — Football Player
Lindstrom, Jack
United Feature Syndicate, PO Box 5610, Cincinnati OH 45201 USA — Cartoonist (Executive Suite)
Lindstrom, Jon
Innovative Artists, 1505 10th St, Santa Monica CA 90401 USA — Actor
Lindstrom, Matthew J (Matt)
316 Mohawk Ave, Rexburg ID 83440, USA — Baseball Player
Lindvall, Angela
Rogue Entertainment, 10900 Wilshire Blvd, #1400, Los Angeles CA 90024, USA — Model, Actress
Lineback, Richard
S M S Talent, 8383 Wilshire Blvd, #230, Beverly Hills CA 90211 USA — Actor
Linebrink, Scott
2100 County Road 156, Granger TX 76530, USA — Baseball Player
Linehan, Marsha M
University of Washington, Behavioral Research/Therapy Clinic, Seattle WA 98195, USA — Psychologist

Linehan, Scott — Football Coach
Detroit Lions, 222 Republic Dr, Allen Park MI 48101 USA

Lineker, Gary W — Soccer Player
Markee UK, 6 Saint George St, Nottingham NG1 3BE, England

Lininger, Jerry M — Astronaut
550 S Stoney Point Road, Suttons Bay MI 49682, USA

Lines, Aaron — Singer
Agency Group Ltd, 142 W 57th St, #600, New York NY 10019 USA

Lines, Richard G (Dick) — Baseball Player
1716 Pebble Beach Lane, Lady Lake FL 32159, USA

Ling — Model
I M G Models, 304 Park Ave S, #PH-North, New York NY 10010 USA

Ling, Jahja — Conductor
Opus 3 Artists, 470 Park Ave S, #900N, New York NY 10016 USA

Ling, Lisa — Commentator
W M E Entertainment, 1325 Ave of Americas, New York NY 10019 USA

Ling, Sergei S — Prime Minister, Belarus
Belarus Mission, United Nations, 136 E 67th St, New York NY 10065, USA

Ling, Victor — Biophysicist
5671 Trafalgar St, Vancouver BC V6N 1C2, Canada

Lingenfelter, Steven R (Steve) — Basketball Player
17378 Ithaca Court, Lakeville MN 55044, USA

Linger, Andreas — Luge Athlete
Bettelwurfsiedlung 9, 6067 Absam, Austria

Linger, Wolfgang — Luge Athlete
Bettelwurfsiedlung 9, 6067 Absam, Austria

Lingner, Adam J — Football Player
8395 Norwood Lane N, Maple Grove MN 55369, USA

Linhart, Anton H (Toni) — Football Player
13 Summer Run Court, Luther Timonium MD 21093, USA

Linhart, Carl J — Baseball Player
2647 Delmar Ave, Granite City IL 62040, USA

Lini, Ham — Prime Minister, Vanuatu
Prime Minister's Office, PO Box 053, Port Vila, Vanuatu

Liniak, Cole E — Baseball Player
PO Box 235625, Encinitas CA 92023, USA

Linichuk, Natalia — Ice Dancer, Coach
146 Dallam Road, Newark DE 19711, USA

Link, Caroline — Director
Just Publicity, Erhardstr 8, 80469 Munich, Germany

Linker, Amy — Actress
Lemack Co, 508 Gerona Ave, San Gabriel CA 91775, USA

Linklater, Hamish — Actor, Writer
I C M Partners, 10250 Constellation Blvd, #900, Los Angeles CA 90067 USA

Linklater, Richard — Director, Writer
Creative Artists Agency, 2000 Ave of Stars, #100, Los Angeles CA 90067 USA

Linkletter, Nicole — Model
Elite Model Mgmt, 404 Park Ave S, #900, New York NY 10016 USA

Linley, Cody — Actor
C E S D, 10635 Santa Monica Blvd, #130, Los Angeles CA 90025 USA

Linn, Rex — Actor
Vox Inc, 6420 Wilshire Blvd, #1080, Los Angeles CA 90048 USA

Linn, Richard — Judge
US Court of Appeals, 717 Madison Place NW, Washington DC 20439, USA

Linn, Teri Ann — Actress
Sutton-Barth Vennari, 145 S Fairfax Ave, #310, Los Angeles CA 90036 USA

Linn-Baker, Mark — Actor
27702 Fairweather St, Canyon Country CA 91351, USA

Linnehan, Richard M — Astronaut
1501 Copperfield Parkway, #216, College Station TX 77845, USA

Linney, Laura — Actress
Brillstein Entertainment Partners, 9150 Wilshire Blvd, #350, Beverly Hills CA 90212 USA

Linseman, Ken — Ice Hockey Player
1070 Ocean Blvd, Hampton NH 03842, USA

Linson, Art — Director, Producer
I C M Partners, 10250 Constellation Blvd, #900, Los Angeles CA 90067 USA

Lintel, Michelle — Actress
Kazarian/Spencer/Ruskin, 11969 Ventura Blvd, #300, Studio City CA 91604 USA

Linteris, Gregory T — Astronaut
US Commerce Dept, Fire Science Division, Gaithersburg MD 20899, USA

Linton, Douglas W (Doug) — Baseball Player
201 Ellison St, Rochester NY 14609, USA

Linton, Tom — Guitarist (Jimmy Eat World)
S A M, 722 Seward St, Los Angeles CA 90038, USA

Lintu, Hannu — Conductor
Tampere Philharmonic Orchestra, PL 16, 33101 Tampere, Finland

Lintz, Larry — Baseball Player
8529 Sun Sprite Way, Elk Grove CA 95624, USA

Linville, Joanne — Actress
Special Artists Agency, 9465 Wilshire Blvd, #820, Beverly Hills CA 90212 USA

Linz, Alex D — Actor
Innovative Artists, 1505 10th St, Santa Monica CA 90401 USA

Linz, Philip F (Phil) — Baseball Player
20 Rocky Rapids Road, Stamford CT 06903, USA

Linzy, Frank A — Baseball Player
38947 E 151st St S, Coweta OK 74429, USA

Lioeanjie, Rene — Labor Leader
National Maritime Union, 1150 17th St NW, Washington DC 20036, USA

Lionetti, Donald M — Army General
4517 W Rosemere Road, Tampa FL 33609, USA

Lions, Pierre-Louis — Mathematician
Paris University, Mathematics Dept, Place Marechal Lattre-de-Tessigny, 75775 Paris, France

Liotta, Ray — Actor
United Talent Agency, 9336 Civic Center Dr, Beverly Hills CA 90210 USA

Lipa, Elisabeta — Rowing Athlete
Str Reconstructiei 1, #78, Bucharest, Romania

Lipes, Jody Lee
Sheldon Prosnit Agency, 800 S Robertson Blvd, Los Angeles CA 90035, USA — Cinematographer
Lipetri, N Angelo
150 Yoakum Ave, Farmingdale NY 11735, USA — Baseball Player
Lipez, Kermit V
US Court of Appeals, 537 Congress St, Portland ME 04101, USA — Judge
Lipinski, Ann Marie
Chicago Tribune, Editorial Dept, 435 N Michigan Ave, #1, Chicago IL 60611, USA — Journalist
Lipinski, Tara
Thumbs Up Enterprises, PO Box 1487, Sugar Land TX 77487, USA — Figure Skater, Actress
Lipman, Elinor
Houghton Mifflin Harcourt, 215 Park Ave S, #1200, New York NY 10003 USA — Writer
Lipnicki, Jonathan
Greene Assoc, 1901 Ave of Stars, #130, Los Angeles CA 90067 USA — Actor
Lipovsek, Marjana
Kunstleragentur Raab & Bohm, Plankengasse 7, 1010 Vienna, Austria — Opera Singer
Lippard, Stephen J
975 Memorial Dr, #602, Cambridge MA 02138, USA — Chemist
Lippett, Ronald G (Ronnie)
610 Foundry St, South Easton MA 02375, USA — Football Player
Lippincott, Philip E
Campbell Soup Co, Campbell Place, Camden NJ 08103, USA — Businessman
Lipps, Louis A
17 Brilliant Ave, #100, Pittsburgh PA 15215, USA — Football Player
Lipscomb, Steve
World Poker Tour Enterprises, 5700 Wilshire Blvd, #350, Los Angeles CA 90036 USA — Poker Executive
Lipski, Robert P (Bob)
1 Snook St, Scranton PA 18505, USA — Baseball Player
Lipton, Martin
Wachtell Lipton Rosen Katz, 51 W 52nd St, New York NY 10019, USA — Attorney
Lipton, Peggy
Saint Martin's Press, 175 5th Ave, #400, New York NY 10010 USA — Actress
Liquori, Martin (Marty)
2915 NW 58th Blvd, Gainesville FL 32606, USA — Track Athlete, Sportscaster
Liriano, Francisco
2900 Thomas Ave S, Minneapolis MN 55416, USA — Baseball Player
Liriano, Nelson A
Burlington Royals, PO Box 1143, Burlington NC 27216, USA — Baseball Player
Lisa Lisa
4-Star Entertainment, 1675 York Ave, #32C, New York NY 10128 USA — Singer (Lisa Lisa & Cult Jam)
LisaRaye
C E S D, 10635 Santa Monica Blvd, #130, Los Angeles CA 90025 USA — Actress
Lisbe, Mike
I C M Partners, 10250 Constellation Blvd, #900, Los Angeles CA 90067 USA — Writer, Producer
Lisch, Russell J (Rusty)
206 Country Club Lane, Belleville IL 62223, USA — Football Player
Liscio, Anthony F (Tony)
10348 Trailcliff Dr, Dallas TX 75238, USA — Football Player
Lisi, Ricardo P E (Rick)
1207 N Wren Dr, Rogers AR 72756, USA — Baseball Player
Lisi, Virna
Voyez Mon Agent, 20 Ave Rapp, 75007 Paris, France — Actress
Lisiecki, Jan
I M G Artists, Hogarth Business Park, Chiswick, London W4 2TH, England — Concert Pianist
Lisitsa, Valentina
Columbia Artists Mgmt Inc, 1790 Broadway, #702, New York NY 10019 USA — Concert Pianist
Liske, Peter A (Pete)
116 E Mountain Brook Lane, Wenatchee WA 98801, USA — Football Player
Liskevych, Taras
Oregon State University, Athletic Dept, Corvallis OR 97331, USA — Volleyball Player, Coach
Liskov, Barbara H
Massachusetts Institute of Technology, Computer Science Laboratory, Cambridge MA 02139, USA — Computer Engineer
Lissack, Russell D
Coalition Mgmt, 12 Barley Mow Passage, London W4 4PH, England — Guitarist (Bloc Party)
Lissner, Stephane M
Theatre du Chatelet, 2 Rue Edouourd Colonne, 75001 Paris, France — Director
Lissoni, Piero
Lissoni Assoc, Via Goito 9, 20121 Milan, Italy — Interior Designer
List, Peyton
Schreck Rose Dapello, 1790 Broadway, #2000, New York NY 10019 USA — Actress
List, Peyton R
Paradigm Agency, 360 N Crescent Dr, North Building, Beverly Hills CA 90210 USA — Actress, Model
List, Robert F
1660 Catalpa Lane, Reno NV 89511, USA — Governor, NV
List, Spencer
Paradigm Agency, 360 N Crescent Dr, North Building, Beverly Hills CA 90210 USA — Actor
Listach, Patrick A (Pat)
6030 Durande Dr, Baton Rouge LA 70820, USA — Baseball Player
Lister, Alton L
5413 Kirkridge Place, Garland TX 75044, USA — Basketball Player
Lister, Tommy (Tiny)
Abrams Artists, 9200 W Sunset Blvd, #1125, West Hollywood CA 90069 USA — Actor, Wrestler
Liston, Ian
Hiss & Boo, 7 Nyes Hill, Wineham Lane, Bolney, W Sussex RH17 5SD, England — Actor
Liteky, Angelo J (Charles)
Medal of Honor Society, 40 Patriots Point Road, Mount Pleasant SC 29464, USA — Vietnam War Army Chaplain (CMH)
Lithgow, John
W M E Entertainment, 9601 Wilshire Blvd, #300, Beverly Hills CA 90210 USA — Actor, Singer
Litsch, Jesse A
6948 80th Terrace, Pinellas Park FL 33781, USA — Baseball Player
Littell, Jonathan
Harper Collins Publishers, 10 E 53rd St, Cellar 1, New York NY 10022 USA — Writer
Littell, Mark A
21001 N Tatum Blvd, #1630511, Phoenix AZ 85050, USA — Baseball Player
Littell, Robert
Penguin Books, 375 Hudson St, Basement 1, New York NY 10014, USA — Writer

L

Littenberg, Barbara — Architect
Peterson/Littenberg Architecture, 13 E 66th St, New York NY 10065, USA

Litterell, Brian — Singer (Backstreet Boys)
The Firm, 2049 Century Park E, #2550, Los Angeles CA 90067 USA

Little Anthony — Singer
Universal Attractions, 135 W 26th St, #1200, New York NY 10001 USA

Little Richard — Singer
Hyatt Sunset Hotel, 8401 W Sunset Blvd, West Hollywood CA 90069, USA

Little Steven — Singer, Musician, Actor
Premier Talent, 3 E 54th St, #1100, New York NY 10022 USA

Little, Carole — Fashion Designer
Carole Little Inc, PO Box 77917, Los Angeles CA 90007, USA

Little, Chad — Auto Racing Driver
8718 Statesville Road, Charlotte NC 28269, USA

Little, Charles L — Labor Leader
United Transportation Union, 24950 Country Club Blvd, North Olmsted OH 44070, USA

Little, D Jeffrey (Jeff) — Baseball Player
5711 W Camper Road, Genoa OH 43430, USA

Little, D Scott — Baseball Player
1726 Carolina Lane, Cape Girardeau MO 63701, USA

Little, Dwight H — Director
A P A Talent/Literary Agency, 405 S Beverly Dr, #300, Beverly Hills CA 90212 USA

Little, Floyd D — Football Player
34505 5th Place SW, Federal Way WA 98023, USA

Little, Larry C — Football Player, Coach
14761 SW 169th Lane, Miami FL 33187, USA

Little, Leonard A — Football Player
4 Rainier Pointe Court, Saint Charles MO 63301, USA

Little, Natasha — Actress
Hamilton Hodell, 66-68 Margaret St, London W1W 8SR, England

Little, Rich — Actor, Comedian
C E S D, 10635 Santa Monica Blvd, #130, Los Angeles CA 90025 USA

Little, Robert A — Chef
49 Firth St, London W1V 5TE, England

Little, Sally — Golfer
3210 S Ocean Blvd, #702, Highland Beach FL 33487, USA

Little, Steve — Actor
Odenkirk Provissiero Entertainment, 650 N Bronson Ave, #B145, Los Angeles, CA 90004, USA

Little, Tasmin E — Concert Violinist
Chamber Music Society, 70 Lincoln Center Plaza, Front 2, New York NY 10023, USA

Little, Tawny Godin — Entertainer, Beauty Queen
17941 Sky Park Circle, #F, Irvine CA 92614, USA

Little, W Grady — Baseball Manager
13115 Odell Heights Dr, Mint Hill NC 28227, USA

Littlefield, John A — Baseball Player
1935 Ramar Road, Bullhead City AZ 86442, USA

Littlefield, Warren — Businessman, Producer
Littlefield Co, 500 S Buena Vista St, #1835, Burbank CA 91521, USA

Littleford, Beth — Actress, Comedienne
Domain Talent, 9229 W Sunset Blvd, #710, West Hollywood CA 90069 USA

Littlejohn, Dennis G — Baseball Player
6813 Klamath Way, #D, Bakersfield CA 93309, USA

Littler, Gene A — Golfer
PO Box 1949, Rancho Santa Fe CA 92067, USA

Littles, Eugene S (Gene) — Basketball Player, Coach
6421 E Beck Lane, Scottsdale AZ 85254, USA

Littleton, Harvey K — Sculptor
232 E Ridge Dr, Spruce Pine NC 28777, USA

Littleton, Wes A — Baseball Player
30085 Clear Water Dr, Canyon Lake CA 92587, USA

Littman, Jonathan — Producer
Jerry Bruckheimer Films, 1631 10th St, Santa Monica CA 90404, USA

Litton, Andrew — Conductor
I M G Artists, Burlington Lane, Chiswick, London W4 2TH, England

Litton, Bruce — Auto Racing Driver
10184 E US Highway 136, Clermont IN 46234, USA

Litton, Drew — Editorial Cartoonist
Rocky Mountain News, Editorial Dept, 101 W Colfax Ave, #500, Denver CO 80202, USA

Litton, J Gregory (Greg) — Baseball Player
22 Hillbrook Way, Pensacola FL 32503, USA

Littrell, Brian T — Singer
The Firm, 2049 Century Park E, #2550, Los Angeles CA 90067 USA

Littrell, Gary L — Vietnam War Army Hero (CMH)
4302 Belle Vista Dr, Saint Pete Beach FL 33706, USA

Litwack, Leon F — Historian
University of California, History Dept, Berkeley CA 94720, USA

Liu Boming — Taikonaut
Satellite Launch Center, Jiuquan, Guangzhou Province, China

Liu Chao Shiuan — Prime Minister, Taiwan
Premier's Office, 1 Chunghsiao East Road, Section 1, Taipei, Taiwan

Liu Chunhong — Weightlifter
9 Tiyuguan Road, Beijing 100763, China

Liu, Dyana — Actress
Greene Assoc, 1901 Ave of Stars, #130, Los Angeles CA 90067 USA

Liu, Lucy — Actress, Model
United Talent Agency, 9336 Civic Center Dr, Beverly Hills CA 90210 USA

Liukin, Nastia — Gymnast
World Olympic Gymnastics Academy, 1937 W Parker Road, Plano TX 75023, USA

Liukin, Valeri — Gymnast, Coach
World Olympic Gymnastics Academy, 1937 W Parker Road, Plano TX 75023, USA

Liut, Michael D (Mike) — Ice Hockey Player
26011 German Mill Road, Franklin MI 48025, USA

Livadiotti, Massimo — Artist
Piazza Vittorio Emanuele II, #31, 00185 Rome, Italy

Livage, Jacques — Chemist
College de France, 11 Place M Berthelot, 75231 Paris Cedex 05, France

Littenberg - Livage

Lively, Blake
Untitled Entertainment, 350 S Beverly Dr, #200, Beverly Hills CA 90212 USA — Actress

Lively, Everett A (Bud)
8605 Esslinger Court SE, Huntsville AL 35802, USA — Baseball Player

Lively, Penelope M
Duck End, Great Rollright, Chipping, Northern Oxfordshire OX7 5SB, England — Writer

Lively, Pierce
US Court of Appeals, PO Box 1226, Danville KY 40423, USA — Judge

Lively, Robyn
Don Buchwald/Fortitude, 6500 Wilshire Blvd, #2200, Los Angeles CA 90048 USA — Actress

Livengood, Ed
Vamp Music Source, 902 W Franklin Ave, #15, Minneapolis MN 55405, USA — Drummer (Jucifer)

Liveris, Andrew N
Dow Chemical, 2030 Dow Center, Midland MI 48674, USA — Businessman

Livermore, Ann
Hewlett-Packard Co, 300 Hanover St, Palo Alto CA 94304, USA — Businesswoman

Livermore, Brooks
Associated International Mgmt, Fairfax House, Fulwood Place, London WC1V 6HU, England — Actor

Liverpool, Nicholas J O
President's Office, Morne Bruce, Victoria St, Rouseau, Dominica — President, Dominica

Livers, Virgil C, Jr
313 Clearview Ave, Bowling Green KY 42101, USA — Football Player

Livier, Ruth
C E S D, 10635 Santa Monica Blvd, #130, Los Angeles CA 90025 USA — Actress

Livingston, Andrew L (Andy)
650 E Century Ave, Gilbert AZ 85296, USA — Football Player

Livingston, Barry
T G M D Agency, 6267 Forest Lawn Dr, #101, Los Angeles CA 90068, USA — Actor

Livingston, David M
Dana-Farber Cancer Institute, 44 Binney St, Boston MA 02115 USA — Internist

Livingston, James E
3146 Pignatelli Crescent, Mount Pleasant SC 29466, USA — Vietnam Marine Hero (CMH), General

Livingston, John
Defining Artists, 10 Universal City Plaza, #2000, Universal City CA 91608, USA — Actor

Livingston, Michael P (Mike)
8181 Monrovia St, Lenexa KS 66215, USA — Football Player

Livingston, Robert L, Jr
Livingston Group, 499 S Capitol St SW, #600, Washington DC 20003, USA — Representative, LA

Livingston, Ron
United Talent Agency, 9336 Civic Center Dr, Beverly Hills CA 90210 USA — Actor

Livingston, Shaun
7334 Trask Ave, Playa del Rey CA 90293, USA — Basketball Player

Livingston, Stanley
PO Box 1782, Studio City CA 91614, USA — Actor

Livingston, Warren
308 E Malibu Dr, Tempe AZ 85282, USA — Football Player

Livingstone, Scott L
3504 Sunrise Ranch Road, Southlake TX 76092, USA — Baseball Player

Livio, Mario
Hubble Space Technology Institute, 3700 San Martin Dr, Baltimore MD 21218, USA — Astrophysicist

Livni, Tzipi
Foreign Ministry, 9 Yitzhak Rubin Road, Jerusalem 91035, Israel — Acting Prime Minister, Israel

Livsey, William J
230 Carriage Chase, Fayetteville GA 30214, USA — Army General

Liwienski, Chris
6721 Pointe Lake Lucy, Chanhassen MN 55317, USA — Football Player

Lizer, Kari
Jackoway Tyerman Wertheimer, 1925 Century Park E, #2200, Los Angeles CA 90067 USA — Actress, Producer

Ljungberg, K Fredrik (Freddie)
Seattle Sounders, 12 Seahawks Way, Renton WA 98056 USA — Model, Soccer Player

Ljungberg, Lasse 'Leari'
Live Nation, Linnegatan 89, Box 21451, 104 51 Stockholm, Sweden — Bassist (The Ark)

Ljungqvist, Ida
Playboy Promotions, 2706 Media Center Dr, Los Angeles CA 90065 USA — Model

LL Cool J
Alchemy Entertainment, 7024 Melrose Ave, #420, Los Angeles CA 90038 USA — Rap Artist, Actor

Llamosa, Carlos
13803 Via Lido, #300, Newport Beach CA 92663, USA — Soccer Player

Llenas, Winston E
Apartado 92, Santiago, Dominican Republic — Baseball Player

Llewellyn, John A
University of South Florida, Chemical/Biomedical Engineering Dept, 4202 E Fowler Ave, Tampa FL 33620, USA — Astronaut

Llewellyn, Robert
United Agents, 12-26 Lexington St, London W1F 0LE, England — Actor, Writer

Llewelyn, Doug
Rebel Entertainment Partners, 5700 Wilshire Blvd, #456, Los Angeles CA 90036, USA — Actor

Lloyd
Island Records, 925 8th St, New York NY 10019 USA — Singer, Songwriter

Lloyd Webber, Andrew
Really Useful Group, 19/22 Tower St, London WC2H 9TW, England — Composer

Lloyd Webber, Julian
I M G Artists, Burlington Lane, Chiswick, London W4 2TH, England — Concert Cellist

Lloyd, Brandon M
5112 NW Downing St, Blue Springs MO 64015, USA — Football Player

Lloyd, Carli
Atlanta Beat, 1955 Vaughn Road, #209, Kennesaw GA 30144, USA — Soccer Player

Lloyd, Charles
Joel Chriss, 60 E 8th St, #34N, New York NY 10003 USA — Jazz Saxophonist, Composer

Lloyd, Cher
Epic Records, 550 Madison Ave, #600, New York NY 10022 USA — Singer, Songwriter

Lloyd, Clive H
Harefield, Harefield Dr, Wilmslow, Cheshire SK9 1NJ, England — Cricketer

Lloyd, David A (Dave)
24432 County Road 3107, Gladewater TX 75647, USA — Football Player

Lloyd, Earl F
PO Box 1976, Crossville TN 38558, USA — Basketball Player, Coach

Lloyd, Emily — Actress
Rights House, Drury House, 34-43 Russell St, London WC2B 5HA, England

Lloyd, Eric — Actor
Osbrink Talent Agency, 4343 Lankershim Blvd, #100, North Hollywood CA 91602 USA

Lloyd, Geoffrey E R — Philosopher
2 Prospect Row, Cambridge CB1 1DU, England

Lloyd, Georgina — Writer
Bantam Books, 1745 Broadway, New York NY 10019 USA

Lloyd, Graeme J — Baseball Player
455 Oceanview Ave, Palm Harbor FL 34683, USA

Lloyd, Gregory L (Greg) — Football Player
805 Glynn St, #127, Box 305, Fayetteville GA 30214, USA

Lloyd, Jake — Actor
Osbrink Talent, 4343 Lankershim Blvd, #100, North Hollywood CA 91602, USA

Lloyd, James — Keyboardist (Pieces of a Dream)
23309 Commerce Park Road, Cleveland OH 44122, USA

Lloyd, Kathleen — Actress
House of Representatives, 1434 6th St, #1, Santa Monica CA 90401 USA

Lloyd, Lewis K — Basketball Player
1038 N Pallas St, Philadelphia PA 19104, USA

Lloyd, Madison — Actress
Osbrink Talent, 4343 Lankershim Blvd, #100, North Hollywood CA 91602, USA

Lloyd, Norman — Actor
1813 Old Ranch Road, Los Angeles CA 90049, USA

Lloyd, Phyllida — Director
Annette Stone Assoc, 97 Mortimer St, London W1W 7SU, England

Lloyd, Robert A — Opera Singer
67B Fortis Green, London SE1 9HL, England

Lloyd, Sabrina — Actress
Don Buchwald/Fortitude, 6500 Wilshire Blvd, #2200, Los Angeles CA 90048 USA

Lloyd, Sam — Actor
Sloat Entertainment, 27631 Belmonte, Mission Viejo CA 92692, USA

Lloyd, Scott G — Basketball Player
6838 Alexander Dr, Dallas TX 75214, USA

Lloyd, Walt — Cinematographer
22287 Mulholland Highway, #393, Calabasas CA 91302, USA

Lloyd-Jones, David M — Conductor
94 Whitelands House, Cheltenham Terrace, London SW3 4RA, England

Lo, Ismael — Singer, Composer
Syllart/Next Music, 52 Rue Paul Lescop, 92000 Nanterre, France

Loach, Kenneth (Ken) — Director
Sixteen Films, 187 Wardour St, #200, London W1F 8ZB, England

Loach, Lonnie — Ice Hockey Player
1263 Colby Dr, Saint Peters MO 63376, USA

Loader, Danyon J — Swimmer
9 Prince Albert Road, Saint Kilda, Dunedin, New Zealand

Loaiza Veyna, Esteban A — Baseball Player
2871 Gate Three Place, Chula Vista CA 91914, USA

Lobacheva, Irina — Ice Dancer
Skating Federation, Luchnesksaia Nab 8, 119871 Moscow, Russia

Lobdell, Frank — Artist
2754 Octavia, San Francisco CA 94123, USA

Lobel, Anita — Writer
Greenwillow/William Morrow, 1350 Ave of Americas, New York NY 10019, USA

LoBianco, Tony — Actor
David Shapira Assoc, 193 N Robertson Blvd, Beverly Hills CA 90211 USA

Lobkowicz, Nicholas — Philosopher
Am Kirchberg 6, 91804 Mornsheim, Germany

Lobo — Singer, Songwriter
14432 Clubhouse Dr, Bokeelia FL 33922, USA

Lobo Sosa, Porfirio — President, Honduras
Casa Presidencial, Blvd Juan Pablo II, Tegucigalpa MDC, Honduras

Lobo, Rebecca — Basketball Player
PO Box 734, Granby CT 06035, USA

Loca, Jean-Louie — Actor
Jean-François Pignard de Marthod, 11 Rue Chanez, 75781 Paris Cedex 16, France

Locane, Amy — Actress
McCabe Group, 3211 Cahuenga Blvd W, #104, Los Angeles CA 90068, USA

LoCascio, Luigi — Actor
Media Art Mgmt, C/ Castelló 82, 2 Derecha, 28006 Madrid, Spain

Loceff, Michael — Producer
Paradigm Agency, 360 N Crescent Dr, North Building, Beverly Hills CA 90210 USA

Locher, Richard (Dick) — Editorial Cartoonist
Chicago Tribune, Editorial Dept, 435 N Michigan Ave, #1, Chicago IL 60611, USA

Lochmueller, Robert L (Bob) — Basketball Player
18 William Tell Blvd, Tell City IN 47586, USA

Lochner, Philip R, Jr — Government Official, Businessman
Time Warner Inc, 1 Time Warner Center, New York NY 10019, USA

Lochner, Rudolf (Rudi) — Bobsled Athlete
Hofreiterstr 15, 83471 Schonau/Konigsee, Germany

Lochte, Ryan — Swimmer
120 Brookside Dr, Port Orange FL 32128, USA

Lock, Donald W (Don) — Baseball Player
11725 W Alderny Court, #42, Wichita KS 67212, USA

Lockbaum, Gordon C (Gordie) — Football Player
35 Brookshire Road, Worcester MA 01609, USA

Locke, Bruce — Actor
Vox Inc, 6420 Wilshire Blvd, #1080, Los Angeles CA 90048 USA

Locke, Charles E (Chuck) — Baseball Player
1560 Haven Hills Road, Poplar Bluff MO 63901, USA

Locke, Gary F — Secretary, Commerce; Governor, WA
Commerce Department, 14th St & Constitution Ave NW, Washington DC 20230 USA

Locke, Lawrence D (Bobby) — Baseball Player
194 Eight 80 Acres Road, Dunbar PA 15431, USA

Locke, Ronald T (Ron) — Baseball Player
15 Lewiston Ave, West Kingston RI 02892, USA

Locke, Sondra
7465 Hillside Ave, Los Angeles CA 90046, USA — Actress, Director

Locke, Spencer
A P A Talent/Literary Agency, 405 S Beverly Dr, #300, Beverly Hills CA 90212 USA — Actress

Locker, Jacob C (Jake)
Tennessee Titans, 460 Great Circle Road, Nashville TN 37228 USA — Football Player

Locker, Robert A (Bob)
1561 Rancho View Road, Lafayette CA 94549, USA — Baseball Player

Lockett, Kevin E
1319 W Xyler St, Tulsa OK 74127, USA — Football Player

Lockhart, Anne
Linda McAlister Agency, 100 Oak Lane, Waxahachie TX 75167, USA — Actress

Lockhart, Dennis
Federal Reserve Bank, 1000 Peachtree St NE, Atlanta GA 30309, USA — Government Official, Financier

Lockhart, Eugene, Jr
2215 High Country Dr, Carrollton TX 75007, USA — Football Player

Lockhart, Ian
Q25 Calle Excelsa Villas del Cafetal II, Yauco PR 00698, USA — Basketball Player

Lockhart, James
105 Woodcock Hill, Harrow, Middx HA3 0JJ, England — Conductor

Lockhart, June
PO Box 3207, Will Rogers Unit 261, Santa Monica CA 90408, USA — Actress

Lockhart, Keith
Boston Pops Orchestra, Symphony Hall, 301 Massachusetts Ave, Boston MA 02115, USA — Conductor

Lockhart, Keith V
3330 McKinley Point Dr, Dacula GA 30019, USA — Baseball Player

Lockhart, Paul S
8605 Cross View, Fairfax Station VA 22039, USA — Astronaut

Lockhart, Sharon
Barbara Gladstone Gallery, 515 W 24th St, New York NY 10011, USA — Photographer, Filmmaker

Lockington, David
C M Artists, 127 W 96th St, #13B, New York NY 10025 USA — Conductor

Locklear, Gene
1811 Penasco Road, El Cajon CA 92019, USA — Baseball Player

Locklear, Heather
I C M Partners, 10250 Constellation Blvd, #900, Los Angeles CA 90067 USA — Actress, Model

Locklear, Samuel J, III
Commander, 3rd Fleet San Diego, FPO AP 96601 USA — Navy Admiral

Locklear, Sean H
New York Giants, Meadowlands Stadium, 102 Route 120, East Rutherford NJ 07073 USA — Football Player

Locklin, Stuart C (Stu)
532 Carfax Place SW, Albuquerque NM 87121, USA — Baseball Player

Lockwood, Claude E (Skip), Jr
47 John Druce Lane, Wrentham MA 02093, USA — Baseball Player

Lockwood, Gary
3083 1/2 Rambla Pacifica, Malibu CA 90265, USA — Actor

Locorriere, Dennis
Artists International Mgmt, 9850 Sandalwood Blvd, #458, Boca Raton FL 33428, USA — Singer, Guitarist (Dr Hook)

Loder, Kevin
505 W 4th St, Mishawaka IN 46544, USA — Basketball Player

Lodge, David J
University of Birmingham, English Dept, Birmingham B15 2TT, England — Writer

Lodge, Roger
Paradigm Agency, 360 N Crescent Dr, North Building, Beverly Hills CA 90210 USA — Entertainer

Lodish, Harvey F
195 Fisher Ave, Brookline MA 02445, USA — Biologist

Lodish, Michael T (Mike)
171 E Lincoln St, Birmingham MI 48009, USA — Football Player

LoDuca, Joseph
1117 Isabel St, Burbank CA 91506, USA — Composer

LoDuca, Paul
3227 Medaris Lane, San Antonio TX 78258, USA — Baseball Player

Lodwick, Todd
Winter Sports Club, 845 Howelsen Hill Parkway, Steamboat Springs CO 84077, USA — Nordic Combined Skier

Loe, Harald A
National Dental Research Institute, 9000 Rockville Pike, Bethesda MD 20892, USA — Dentist

Loe, Kameron D
2323 N Houston St, #312, Dallas TX 75219, USA — Baseball Player

Loeb, Abraham (Avi)
Harvard University, Theory & Computation Institute, Cambridge MA 02138, USA — Theoretical Physicist

Loeb, Allan
Scarlet Fire Entertainment, 561 28th Ave, Venice CA 90291, USA — Writer

Loeb, Caroline
A A C Agence Artistique, 10 Ave George V, 75009 Paris, France — Actress

Loeb, Damian
49 Lispenard St, New York NY 10013, USA — Artist

Loeb, Jerome T
May Department Stores, 611 Olive St, #2076, Saint Louis MO 63101, USA — Businessman

Loeb, John L, Jr
John L Loeb Jr Assoc, 50 Broad St, #1137, New York NY 10004, USA — Diplomat, Financier

Loeb, Lisa
Untitled Entertainment, 350 S Beverly Dr, #200, Beverly Hills CA 90212 USA — Singer, Songwriter, Actress

Loeb, Marshall R
41 E 72nd St, New York NY 10021, USA — Editor, Writer, Columnist

Loeb, Sebastien
I S C, 6 Saint Catherine's Mews, Milner St, London SW3 2PX, England — Auto Racing Driver

Loeffler, Pete
In De Goot Entertainment, 119 W 23rd St, #609, New York NY 10011, USA — Singer, Guitarist (Chevelle)

Loeffler, Sam
In De Goot Entertainment, 119 W 23rd St, #609, New York NY 10011, USA — Drummer (Chevelle)

Loeillet, Sylvie
Agence Laurence Bagoe, 11 Rue Delambre, 75014 Paris, France — Actress

Loengard, John
20 W 86th St, New York NY 10024, USA — Photographer

Loescher, Peter
Siemens AG, Wittelsbacherplatz 2, 80333 Munich, Germany — Businessman

Loewen, James W — Historian
Catholic University, History Dept, Washington DC 20064, USA
Loewer, Carlton E — Baseball Player
PO Box 3590, Alpine WY 83128, USA
Lofgren, Nils — Singer, Guitarist, Songwriter
Anson Smith Mgmt, 8012 Old Georgetown Road, Bethesda MD 20814, USA
Loftin, R Bowen — Educator
Texas A&M University, President's Office, College Station TX 77843, USA
Lofton, Curtis T — Football Player
New Orleans Saints, 5800 Airline Highway, Metairie LA 70003 USA
Lofton, Fred C — Religious Leader
Progressive National Baptist Convention, 601 50th St NE, Washington DC 20019, USA
Lofton, James — Baseball Player
14103 Cerise Ave, #18, Hawthorne CA 90250, USA
Lofton, James D — Football Player
13177 Via Mesa Dr, San Diego CA 92129, USA
Lofton, Kenneth (Kenny) — Baseball Player
PO Box 68473, Tucson AZ 85737, USA
Logan, David R — Football Player
5875 S Dry Creek Court, Greenwood Village CO 80121, USA
Logan, Ernest E (Ernie) — Football Player
609 Francis Court, Spring Lake NC 28390, USA
Logan, Exavier (Nook) — Baseball Player
19410 Creek Bend Dr, Spring TX 77388, USA
Logan, Jack — Singer
W M E Entertainment, 1325 Ave of Americas, New York NY 10019 USA
Logan, James K — Judge
US Court of Appeals, PO Box 790, 1 Patrons Plaza, Olathe KS 66061, USA
Logan, Jerry D — Football Player
1624 Hillcrest Dr, Graham TX 76450, USA
Logan, John — Writer, Producer
Creative Artists Agency, 2000 Ave of Stars, #100, Los Angeles CA 90067 USA
Logan, John (Johnny) — Baseball Player
6115 W Cleveland Ave, Milwaukee WI 53219, USA
Logan, Lara — Commentator
CBS-TV, News Dept, 51 W 52nd St, New York NY 10019 USA
Logan, Marc A — Football Player
2501 Glascow Lane, Lexington KY 40511, USA
Logan, Melissa — Singer (Chicks in Speed)
K Records, 924 Jefferson St SE, #101, Olympia WA 98501, USA
Logan, Phyllis — Actress
47 Courtfield Road, #9, London SW7 4DB, England
Logan, Randolph (Randy) — Football Player
330 W Fornance St, Norristown PA 19401, USA
Logan, Samuel, Jr — Relgious Leader
World Reformed Fellowship, 430 Montier Road, Glenside PA 19038, USA
Logano, Joseph T (Joey) — Auto Racing Driver
Joe Gibbs Racing, 13415 Reese Blvd W, Huntersville NC 28078, USA
Loges, Stephan — Opera Singer
Hazard Chase, 72 Charlotte St, London W1T 4QQ, England
Logg, Charles P, Jr — Rowing Athlete
3634 Shady Oak Trail, Gainesville GA 30506, USA
Loggia, Robert — Actor
323 W Grand Ave, El Segundo CA 90245, USA
Loggins, Kenny — Singer, Songwriter
670 Oak Springs Lane, Santa Barbara CA 93108, USA
Logue, Antonia — Writer
Bloomsbury Publishing, 36 Soho Square, London W1D 3Q4, England
Logue, Donal — Actor
Kipperman Mgmt, 420 W End Ave, #1G, New York NY 10024 USA
Logunov, Anatoly A — Physicist
High Energy Research Center, 142281 Protvino, Moscow Region, Russia
Loh, John M (Mike) — Air Force General
125 Captain Graves, Williamsburg VA 23185, USA
Loh, Sandra Tsing — Entertainer, Writer, Activist
Crown Publishing Group, 1745 Broadway, New York NY 10019 USA
Loh, Wallace D — Educator
University of Maryland, President's Office, College Park MD 20742, USA
Lohan, Aliana D (Ali) — Singer
B/W/R, 9100 Wilshire Blvd, #500W, Beverly Hills CA 90212 USA
Lohan, Lindsay — Actress, Singer, Model
Untitled Entertainment, 350 S Beverly Dr, #200, Beverly Hills CA 90212 USA
Lohan, Sinead — Singer, Songwriter
Pat Egan Sound, Merchant's Court, 24 Merchant's Quay, Dublin, Ireland
Lohas, Brad A — Basketball Player
55 Tartan Dr, North Liberty IA 52317, USA
Lohman, Alison — Actress
Principato-Young, 9465 Wilshire Blvd, #880, Beverly Hills CA 90212 USA
Lohmiller, John M (Chip) — Football Player
PO Box 810, Crosslake MN 56442, USA
Lohr, Bob — Golfer
8225 Breeze Cove Lane, Orlando FL 32819, USA
Lohse, Kyle M — Baseball Player
8613 E Artisan Pass, Scottsdale AZ 85266, USA
Loiola, Jose G — Volleyball Player
1135 23rd St, Manhattan Beach CA 90266, USA
Loiret, Anne — Actress
Agence Artiste Adequet, 80 Rue d'Amsterdam, 75009 Paris, France
Loiseau, Sebastien — Actor
Cineart, 36 Rue de Ponthieu, 75008 Paris, France
Loiselie, Richard F (Rich) — Baseball Player
560 Timber Dr, Harvard IL 60033, USA
Loiselle, Claude — Ice Hockey Player
3 Warren St, Hudson Falls NY 12839, USA
Loken, James B — Judge
US Court of Appeals, 300 S 4th St, Minneapolis MN 55415, USA

Loken, Kristanna — Actress, Model
Levity Entertainment Group, 6701 Center Drive W, #1111, Los Angeles CA 90045, USA
Lokoloko, Tore — Governor General, Papua New Guinea
PO Box 5622, Port Moresby, Papua New Guinea
Lolene — Singer, Songwriter
Creative Artists Agency, 2000 Ave of Stars, #100, Los Angeles CA 90067 USA
Lolich, Michael S (Mickey) — Baseball Player
6252 Robin Hill, Washington MI 48094, USA
Lollobrigida, Gina — Actress
Via Appia Antica 223, 00178 Rome, Italy
Loman, Douglas E (Doug) — Baseball Player
25 Lincoln St, Bakersfield CA 93305, USA
Lomas, Barbara Joyce — Singer (BT Express)
Star-Vest Mgmt, 102 Ryders Lane, East Brunswick NJ 08816, USA
Lomas, Mark A — Football Player
PO Box 17781, Irvine CA 92623, USA
Lomasney, Steven J (Steve) — Baseball Player
7 Arnold Road, Peabody MA 01960, USA
Lomax, Michael — Foundation Executive, Educator
United Negro Fund, 500 E 62nd St, New York NY 10065, USA
Lomax, Neil V — Football Player
13060 Knaus Road, Lake Oswego OR 97034, USA
Lomax, Noah — Actor
Amsel Eisenstadt Frazier, 5055 Wilshire Blvd, #865, Los Angeles CA 90036 USA
Lombard, George P — Baseball Player
2275 Rhinehill Road NE, Atlanta GA 30315, USA
Lombard, Karina — Actress, Model
Genesis Entertainment Partners, 152 S Kilkea Dr, Los Angeles CA 90048, USA
Lombard, Louise — Actress
Paradigm Agency, 360 N Crescent Dr, North Building, Beverly Hills CA 90210 USA
Lombardi, Louis — Actor
TalentWorks, 3500 W Olive Ave, #1400, Burbank CA 91505 USA
Lombardi, Michael (Mike) — Actor
A P A Talent/Literary Agency, 405 S Beverly Dr, #300, Beverly Hills CA 90212 USA
Lombardi, Philip A (Phil) — Baseball Player
26440 Brooks Circle, Stevenson Ranch CA 91381, USA
Lombardozzi, Domenick — Actor
Gersh Agency, 9465 Wilshire Blvd, #600, Beverly Hills CA 90212 USA
Lombardozzi, Stephen P (Steve) — Baseball Player
12404 Hall Shop Road, Fulton MD 20759, USA
Lombreglio, Ralph — Writer
Doubleday Press, 1540 Broadway, New York NY 10036, USA
Lomon, Kevin D — Baseball Player
13397 Morris Loop, Cameron OK 74932, USA
Lomonaco, Michael — Restauranteur, Chef
Porter House, Time Warner Center, 10 Columbus Circle, #400, New York NY 10019, USA
Lomotey, Lofi — Educator
Southern University, Chancellor's Office, Baton Rouge LA 70813, USA
Lonard, Peter — Golfer
Links Sports, PO Box 6111, Lake Munmorah NSW 2259, Australia
Lonborg, James R (Jim) — Baseball Player
498 First Parish Road, Scituate MA 02066, USA
Loncar, Amanda — Actress
Gersh Agency, 9465 Wilshire Blvd, #600, Beverly Hills CA 90212 USA
Lonchakov, Yuri V — Cosmonaut
Cosmonaut Training Center, Star City, 141160 Zvezdny Gorodok, Moscow Oblast, Russia
Loncraine, Richard — Director
Casorotto Ramsay, Waverley House, 7-12 Noel St, London W1F 8GQ, England
London, Alexandra — Actress
Artmedia, 20 Ave Rapp, 75007 Paris, France
London, Antonio M — Football Player
404 SW Atlantic St, Tullahoma TN 37388, USA
London, Daniel — Actor
Paradigm Agency, 360 N Crescent Dr, North Building, Beverly Hills CA 90210 USA
London, Irving M — Physician
Harvard-M I T Health Sciences, 77 Massachusetts Ave, Cambridge MA 02139, USA
London, Jason — Actor
A K A Talent, 6310 San Vicente Blvd, #200, Los Angeles CA 90048 USA
London, Jeremy — Actor
Media Artists Group, 8222 Melrose Ave, #203, Los Angeles CA 90048 USA
London, Jonathan — Writer
Chronicle Books, 680 2nd St, San Francisco CA 94107 USA
London, Lauren — Actress
John Carrabino Mgmt, 5900 Wilshire Blvd, #406, Los Angeles CA 90036 USA
London, Lisa — Actress, Model
Brooke Dunn Oliver, 9169 W Sunset Blvd, #202, West Hollywood CA 90069 USA
London, Rick — Cartoonist
Artistic Licensing Agency, 126 Oriole St, #516, Hot Springs AR 71901, USA
Lone, John — Actor
Sussman Assoc, 1222 16th Ave S, #300, Nashville TN 37212, USA
Lonergan, Kenneth — Director, Writer, Actor
Creative Artists Agency, 2000 Ave of Stars, #100, Los Angeles CA 90067 USA
Loney, James A — Baseball Player
4926 Birdsong Lane, Missouri City TX 77459, USA
Loney, Troy — Ice Hockey Player
4245 Glasgow Road, Valencia PA 16059, USA
Long, Anthony A — Educator
1088 Telvin St, Albany CA 94706, USA
Long, Barry — Ice Hockey Player
San Jose Sharks, San Jose Arena, 525 W Santa Clara St, San Jose CA 95113 USA
Long, Charles F (Chuck), II — Football Player, Coach
2504 Walnut Road, Norman OK 73072, USA
Long, Dallas — Track Athlete
PO Box 355, Whitefish MT 59937, USA
Long, David F (Dave) — Football Player
177 E Kaibab Way, Cochise AZ 85606, USA

Long, Grant A — Basketball Player
8501 Morton Taylor Road, Belleville MI 48111, USA
Long, Howie — Football Player, Sportscaster, Actor
I C M Partners, 10250 Constellation Blvd, #900, Los Angeles CA 90067 USA
Long, Jeoffry J (Jeoff) — Baseball Player
11 Flower Court, Lakeside Park KY 41017, USA
Long, Jodi — Actress
Innovative Artists, 1505 10th St, Santa Monica CA 90401 USA
Long, John E (Johnny) — Basketball Player
11976 Hunt St, Romulus MI 48174, USA
Long, Justin — Actor
Creative Artists Agency, 2000 Ave of Stars, #100, Los Angeles CA 90067 USA
Long, Kathy — Actress
G Williams Agency, 525 S 4th St, #365, Philadelphia PA 19147, USA
Long, Matthew (Matt) — Actor
United Talent Agency, 9336 Civic Center Dr, Beverly Hills CA 90210 USA
Long, Melvin (Mel), Sr — Football Player
837 Imani Circle, Toledo OH 43604, USA
Long, Nia — Actress
One Talent Mgmt, 9220 Sunset Blvd, #306, Los Angeles CA 90069, USA
Long, Robert A J (Bob) — Football Player
3695 Stonebrook Court, Brookfield WI 53005, USA
Long, Robert E (Bob) — Baseball Player
3648 Willow Lake Circle, Chattanooga TN 37419, USA
Long, Robert M — Businessman
Longs Drug Stores, 1 C V S Dr, Woonsocket RI 02895, USA
Long, Robert W (Bob) — Football Player
1413 W Via de la Gloria, Green Valley AZ 85622, USA
Long, Ryan M — Baseball Player
3102 Winchester Ranch Trail, Katy TX 77493, USA
Long, Shelley — Actress, Comedienne
Stone Manners Salners, 9911 W Pico Blvd, #1400, Los Angeles CA 90035 USA
Long, Terrence D — Baseball Player
4208 Abrams Dr, Millbrook AL 36054, USA
Long, William D (Bill) — Baseball Player
7699 Dimmick Road, Cincinnati OH 45241, USA
Long, William Ivey — Costume Designer
I C M Partners, 730 5th Ave, New York NY 10019 USA
Longet, Claudine — Actress
Ronald D Austin, 6000 E Hopkins, Aspen CO 81611, USA
Longley, Lucien J (Luc) — Basketball Player
500 Marquette Ave NW, #400, Albuquerque NM 87102, USA
Longmire, Anthony E (Tony) — Baseball Player
419 Fleming Ave E, Vallejo CA 94591, USA
Longo, Jeannie Ciprelli- — Cyclist
Federation de Cyclisme, 5 Rue de Rome, 93561 Rosny-sous-Bois, France
Longo, Lenny — Singer (Box Tops)
Texas Sounds, PO Box 1644, Dickinson TX 77539, USA
Longo, Robert — Artist, Sculptor
Longo Studio, 224 Center St, New York NY 10013, USA
Longo, Tony — Actor
310 Tahiti Way, #209, Marina del Rey CA 90292, USA
Longoria, Eva — Actress, Model
Unbelievable Entertainment, 7095 Hollywood Blvd, #797, Hollywood CA 90028, USA
Longoria, Evan M — Baseball Player
1211 E Cumberland Ave, #1403, Tampa FL 33602, USA
Longwell, Ryan W — Football Player
5169 Fairway Oaks Dr, Windermere FL 34786, USA
Lonich, Yogi — Guitarist (Buckcherry)
10th Street Mgmt, 700 N San Vicente Blvd, #G410, West Hollywood CA 90069, USA
Lonnett, Joseph D (Joe) — Baseball Player
126 Duncan Circle, Beaver PA 15009, USA
Lonow, Claudia — Actress, Comedienne, Producer
W M E Entertainment, 9601 Wilshire Blvd, #300, Beverly Hills CA 90210 USA
Lonsdale, Gordon C — Cinematographer
4513 W 10600 N, Highland UT 84003, USA
Lonsdale, Michael — Actor
France Degand, 25 Rue du General Foy, 75008 Paris, France
Loob, P Hakan — Ice Hockey Player
Farjestads BK, Box 318, 65108 Karlstad, Sweden
Look, Bruce M — Baseball Player
4298 Maitland Road, Williamsburg MI 49690, USA
Look, Dean Z — Baseball, Football Player
80 Victorian Hills Dr, Okemos MI 48864, USA
Looker, Dane A — Football Player
7213 41st Avenue Court E, Tacoma WA 98443, USA
Lookinland, Mike — Actor
PO Box 9968, Salt Lake City UT 84109, USA
Lookstein, Haskel — Religious Leader, Rabbi
Congregation Kehilath Jeshurun, Ramaz School, 60 E 78th St, New York NY 10075, USA
Loomer, Lisa — Writer
Abrams Artists, 9200 W Sunset Blvd, #1125, West Hollywood CA 90069 USA
Loomis, Rick — Journalist
Los Angeles Times, Editorial Dept, 202 W 1st St, Los Angeles CA 90012 USA
Looney, Brian J — Baseball Player
188 Romulus Road, Cheshire CT 06410, USA
Looney, Shelley — Ice Hockey Player
31 Beaman Lane, North Falmouth MA 02556, USA
Looper, Aaron J — Baseball Player
1405 Manchester, Shawnee OK 74804, USA
Looper, Braden L — Baseball Player
16253 Wynncrest Ridge Court, Chesterfield MO 63005, USA
Loose, Michael K — Navy Admiral
Deputy CNO, Fleet Readiness/Logistics, HqUSN, Pentagon, Washington DC 20350 USA
Lopardo, Frank — Opera Singer
7 Suzanne B Court, Massapequa NY 11758, USA

Lopata, Stanley E (Stan)
2239 Leisure World, Mesa AZ 85206, USA — Baseball Player

Loper, Daniel R
1115 Stillwater Trail, Hendersonville TN 37075, USA — Football Player

Lopert, Tanya
Cineart, 36 Rue de Ponthieu, 75008 Paris, France — Actress

Lopes, David E (Davey)
309 San Elijo St, San Diego CA 92106, USA — Baseball Player, Manager

Lopes, Leila
Miss Universe Organization, 1370 Ave of Americas, #1600, New York NY 10019 USA — Beauty Queen

Lopez de Ayala, Pilar
Media Art Mgmt, C/ Castelló 82, 2 Derecha, 28006 Madrid, Spain — Actress

Lopez Lujan, Leonardo
Museo del Templo Mayor, 8 Seminario Ave, Mexico City DF 06060, Mexico — Archaeologist

Lopez Rodriguez, Nicolas de J Cardinal
Archdiocese of Santo Domingo, Santo Domingo, AP 186, Dominican Republic — Religious Leader

Lopez Rodriquez, Arturo
16056 English Oaks Ave, #C, Bowie MD 20716, USA — Baseball Player

Lopez, Albert A (Albie)
2887 E Palo Verde Court, Gilbert AZ 85296, USA — Baseball Player

Lopez, Brook R
Brooklyn Nets, 15 Metro Tech Center, #1100, Brooklyn NY 11201 USA — Basketball Player

Lopez, Danny (Little Red)
16531 Aquamarine Court, Chino Hills CA 91709, USA — Boxer

Lopez, Felipe
2142 Walden Park Circle, #204, Kissimmee FL 34744, USA — Baseball Player

Lopez, George
Creative Artists Agency, 2000 Ave of Stars, #100, Los Angeles CA 90067 USA — Actor, Comedian

Lopez, Gerry
PO Box 1202, Bend OR 97709, USA — Surfer, Executive

Lopez, Javier A
4824 Quaker Lane, Golden CO 80403, USA — Baseball Player

Lopez, Jennifer
Nuyorican Productions, 1100 Glendon Ave, #920, Los Angeles CA 90024, USA — Actress, Singer, Model

Lopez, Juan Manuel
P R Best Promotions, Cond Santa Juanita L58, Bayamon PR 00956, USA — Boxer

Lopez, Lourdes
Miami City Ballet, Roca Center, 2200 Liberty Ave, Miami Beach FL 33139, USA — Ballerina, Ballet Executive

Lopez, Luis A
636 40th St, Brooklyn NY 11232, USA — Baseball Player

Lopez, Luis S
1701 Pleasant Run Road, Carrollton TX 75006, USA — Baseball Player

Lopez, Mario
TalentWorks, 3500 W Olive Ave, #1400, Burbank CA 91505 USA — Actor

Lopez, Mickey
17430 SW 117th Ave, Miami FL 33177, USA — Baseball Player

Lopez, Nancy
2308 Tara Dr, Albany GA 31721, USA — Golfer

Lopez, Nano
96 Frontage Road, Walla Walla WA 99362, USA — Sculptor

Lopez, Oscar
Agency Group Ltd, 1880 Century Park E, #711, Los Angeles CA 90067 USA — Guitar Player

Lopez, Priscilla
Stone Manners Salners, 9911 W Pico Blvd, #1400, Los Angeles CA 90035 USA — Actress

Lopez, Raul
Memphis Grizzlies, 191 Beale St, Memphis TN 38103 USA — Basketball Player

Lopez, Robert S
41 Richmond Ave, New Haven CT 06515, USA — Historian

Lopez, Robin B
Phoenix Suns, 201 E Jefferson St, Phoenix AZ 85004 USA — Basketball Player

Lopez, Sal
DePaz Mgmt, 2011 N Vermont Ave, Los Angeles CA 90027, USA — Actor

Lopez, Sandra
Columbia Artists Mgmt Inc, 1790 Broadway, #702, New York NY 10019 USA — Opera Singer

Lopez, Sergi
Artmedia, 20 Ave Rapp, 75007 Paris, France — Actor

Lopez, Steve
G P Putnam's Sons, 375 Hudson St, New York NY 10014 USA — Writer

Lopez, Steven
Elite Taekwondo Center, 9707 S Highway 6, Sugar Land TX 77498, USA — Taekwondo Athlete

Lopez, T Joseph
Lexington Institute, 1600 Wilson Blvd, #900, Arlington VA 22209 USA — Navy Admiral

Lopez, Tim G
One Moment Mgmt, PO Box 55156, Sherman Oaks CA 91413 USA — Bassist (Plain White T's)

Lopez, Tony (Tiger)
3221 Sweet Maple Way, Sacramento CA 95833, USA — Boxer

Lopez, Trini
1139 Abrigo Road, Palm Springs CA 92262, USA — Singer, Actor, Orchestra Leader

Lopez-Alegria, Michael E
1919 Tangle Press Court, Houston TX 77062, USA — Astronaut

Lopez-Cobos, Jesus
8 Chemin de Bellerive, 1007 Lausanne, Switzerland — Conductor

Lopez-Gallego, Gonzalo
I C M Partners, 10250 Constellation Blvd, #900, Los Angeles CA 90067 USA — Director

Lopez-Garcia, Antonio
Galeria Marlborough, Orfila 5, 28010 Madrid, Spain — Artist

Loquasto, Santo
Paradigm Agency, 360 N Crescent Dr, North Building, Beverly Hills CA 90210 USA — Lighting, Costume Designer

Lorca, Daniel
M-Square Mgmt, 201 W 72nd St, #12G, New York NY 10023, USA — Bassist (Nada Surf)

Lorch, George A
Armstrong World, 313 W Liberty St, Lancaster PA 17603, USA — Businessman

Lorch, Karl P, Jr
92-861 Palailai St, Kapolei HI 96707, USA — Football Player

Lorcy, Julian
BoBoxe, 68 Blvd Henri Barbusse, 78800 Houilles, France — Boxer

Lord, Albert L — Businessman
S L M Corp, 12061 Bluemont Dr, Reston VA 20190, USA

Lord, M G — Editorial Cartoonist
Janklow & Nesbit Assoc, 445 Park Ave, #1300, New York NY 10022 USA

Lord, Marjorie — Actress
1110 Maytor Place, Beverly Hills CA 90210, USA

Lord, Mary Lou — Singer
Agency Group Ltd, 142 W 57th St, #600, New York NY 10019 USA

Lord, Peter — Animator, Director
Aardman Animations, Gas Ferry Road, Bristol BS1 6UN, England

Lord, Winston — Diplomat
740 Park Ave, New York NY 10021, USA

Lordi, Mr — Singer (Lordi)
Le Kepi Rouge, PL 285, 02601 Espoo, Finland

Lords, Traci — Actress
Innovative Artists, 1505 10th St, Santa Monica CA 90401 USA

Loren, Josie — Actress
Ellen Meyer Mgmt, 8899 Beverly Blvd, #612, West Hollywood CA 90048, USA

Loren, Natalie — DJ Musician, Model
Leni's Model Mgmt, 55E Hatton Garden, London EC1N 8HP, England

Loren, Sophia — Actress
Casa Postale 430, 1211 Geneva 12, Switzerland

Lorentz, Jim — Ice Hockey Player
2555 Staley Road, Grand Island NY 14072, USA

Lorenz, Christian (Flake) — Keyboardist (Rammstein)
Pilgrim Mgmt, PO Box 540101, 10042 Berlin, Germany

Lorenz, Ericka — Water Polo Player
2604 Fulton St, Berkeley CA 94704, USA

Lorenz, Lee — Cartoonist
PO Box 131, Easton CT 06612, USA

Lorenzen, Fred — Auto Racing Driver
64 E Elm St, #4, Chicago IL 60611, USA

Lorenzo, Blas — Actor
PO Box 2127, Los Angeles CA 90078, USA

Lorenzoni, Andrea — Astronaut, Italy
Via B Vergine del Carmelo 168, 00144 Rome, Italy

Loretta, Mark D — Baseball Player
7844 Sendora Angelica, San Diego CA 92127, USA

Loria, Christopher (Gus) — Astronaut
102 Sea Mist Dr, League City TX 77573, USA

Lorick, W Anthony (Tony) — Football Player
349 Burney Lane, Kerrville TX 78028, USA

Lorimer, Bob — Ice Hockey Player
24 Cranberry Lane, Aurora ON L4G 5Y3, Canada

Loring, Gloria — Singer, Actress
PO Box 1243, Cedar Glen CA 92321, USA

Loring, John R — Artist
621 Avon Road, West Palm Beach FL 33401, USA

Loring, Lynn — Actress
4910 Petit Ave, Encino CA 91436, USA

Lorius, Claude — Glaciologist
Glaciologies Laboratoire, Rue Moliere, 38402 Saint-Martin d'Heres, France

Lorraine, Andrew J — Baseball Player
10436 E Acoma Dr, Scottsdale AZ 85255, USA

Lorre, Chuck — Producer
I C M Partners, 10250 Constellation Blvd, #900, Los Angeles CA 90067 USA

Lortie, Louis — Concert Pianist
Seldy Cramer Artists, 3436 Springhill Road, Lafayette CA 94549, USA

Lortkipanidze, Vazha G — Minister of State, Georgia
Government House, Ingorokva 7, 380034 Tbilsi, Georgia

Losada, Isabel — Writer
Curtis Brown Group, 28-29 Haymarket St, #500, London SW1Y 4SP, England

LoSchiavo, Francesca — Set Decorator
Via delle Querce 51, 47842 San Giovanni in Marignano, Italy

Loscutoff, James (Jim) — Basketball Player, Coach
166 Jenkins Road, Andover MA 01810, USA

Losick, Richard M — Molecular Biologist
Harvard Medical School, 25 Shattuck St, Boston MA 02115, USA

Losier, Michele — Opera Singer
I M G Artists, Hogarth Business Park, Chiswick, London W4 2TH, England

Losman, Jonathan P (J P) — Football Player
70 Oakland Place, Buffalo NY 14222, USA

Loss, Harold — Religious Leader, Rabbi
Temple Israel, 5725 Walnut Lake Road, West Bloomfield MI 48323, USA

Lotan, Jonah — Actor
Gersh Agency, 9465 Wilshire Blvd, #600, Beverly Hills CA 90212 USA

Lothamer, Edward D (Ed) — Football Player
14545 W 183rd St, Olathe KS 66062, USA

LoTruglio, Joe — Actor
United Talent Agency, 9336 Civic Center Dr, Beverly Hills CA 90210 USA

Lott, Felicity A — Opera Singer
Augstein & Hahn, Tal 28, 80331 Munich, Hermany

Lott, Ronald M (Ronnie) — Football Player, Sportscaster
2965 Woodside Road, Woodside CA 94062, USA

Lotti, Helmut — Singer, Songwriter
Bevrijdinstraat 39, 2300 Turnhout, Belgium

Lotton, Gerald — Artist
Lotton Glass, 24760 Country Lane, Crete IL 60417, USA

Lotz, Anne Graham — Religious Leader
AnGeL Ministries, 515 Hollyridge Dr, Raleigh NC 27612, USA

Lotz, Dick — Golfer
2058 Riesling Way, Shingle Springs CA 95682, USA

Louboutin, Christian — Footwear Designer
19 Rue Jean-Jacques Rousseau, 75001 Paris, France

Loucks, Scott G — Baseball Player
1801 Viola Dr, Sierra Vista AZ 85635, USA

Loucks, Vernon R, Jr
Baxter Healthcare Corp, 1450 Waukegan Road, Waukegan IL 60085, USA — Businessman
Louderback, Thomas F (Tom)
15 Leopard Road, #1G, Berwyn PA 19312, USA — Football Player
Loudon, Aarnout A
Rembrandt Kaan 16, 6881 CS Velp, Netherlands — Businessman
Loudon, Rodney
3 Gaston St, East Bergholt, Colchester, Essex CO7 6SD, England — Theoretical Physicist
Loueke, Lionel
Blue Note Records, 6920 W Sunset Blvd, Los Angeles CA 90028 USA — Jazz Guitarist
Louganis, Gregory E (Greg)
Premier Management Group, 1100 Crescent Green, #104, Cary, NC 27518 USA — Diver
Loughery, Kevin M (Murph)
4474 Club Dr NE, Atlanta GA 30319, USA — Basketball Player, Coach, Executive
Loughlin, Lori
United Talent Agency, 9336 Civic Center Dr, Beverly Hills CA 90210 USA — Actress, Singer
Loughlin, Mary Anne
WTBS-TV, News Dept, 1050 Techwood Dr NW, Atlanta GA 30318, USA — Commentator
Loughnane, Lee David
Front Line Mgmt, 1100 Glendon Ave, #2000, Los Angeles CA 90024 USA — Trumpeter (Chicago), Songwriter
Loughran, James
34 Cleveden Dr, Glasgow G12 0RX, Scotland — Conductor
Louis C K
3 Arts Entertainment, 9460 Wilshire Blvd, #700, Beverly Hills CA 90212 USA — Director, Writer, Actor
Louis, Murray
Nikolais/Louis Foundation, 375 W Broadway, New York NY 10012, USA — Dancer, Choreographer
Louisa, Maria
Next Model Mgmt, 23 Watts St, New York NY 10013, USA — Model
Louisa-Godett, Mima
Premier's Office, Fort Amsterdam 17, Willemstad, Netherlands Antilles — Premier, Netherlands Antilles
Louis-Dreyfus, Julia
Hofflund/Polone, 9465 Wilshire Blvd, #420, Beverly Hills CA 90212 USA — Actress, Comedienne
Louise, Tina
310 E 46th St, #24G, New York NY 10017, USA — Actress, Singer
Louiso, Todd
Anonymous Content, 3532 Hayden Ave, Culver City CA 90232 USA — Actor, Director, Writer
Louisy, C Pearlette
Governor General's Office, Government House, Box 216, Morne Fortune, Castries, Saint Lucia — Governor General, Saint Lucia
Loukos, Yorgos
Lyon Opera Ballet, Place de la Comédie, 69001 Lyon, France — Ballet Executive
Loun, Donald N (Don)
9095 Wexford Dr, Vienna VA 22182, USA — Baseball Player
Lourdusamy, D Simon Cardinal
Palazzo dei Convertendi, 64 Via della Conciliazione, 00193 Rome, Italy — Religious Leader
Lourie, Alan D
US Court of Appeals, 717 Madison Place NW, Washington DC 20439, USA — Judge
Louris, Gary
Sussman Assoc, 1222 16th Ave S, #300, Nashville TN 37212, USA — Singer, Songwriter (Jayhawks)
Lousma, Jack R
2722 Roseland St, Ann Arbor MI 48103, USA — Astronaut
Loutfi, Ali Mahmoud
29 Ahmed Heshmat St, Zamalek, Cairo, Egypt — Prime Minister, Egypt
Louvier, Alain
53 Ave Victor Hugo, 92100 Boulogne-Billancourt, France — Composer
Louwerse, Mirusia
PO Box 3169, Birkdale QLD 4159, Australia — Opera, Concert Singer
Loux, Shane L
3105 E Sparrow Place, Chandler AZ 85286, USA — Baseball Player
Lovano, Joe
66 Beaver Brook Road, New Windsor NY 12553, USA — Jazz Saxophonist, Composer
Lovato, Demi
Creative Artists Agency, 2000 Ave of Stars, #100, Los Angeles CA 90067 USA — Actress, Singer
Love, Courtney
M V O Ltd, 307 7th Ave, #907, New York NY 10001, USA — Singer (Hole), Actress, Songwriter
Love, Darlene
American Mgmt, 19948 Mayal St, Chatsworth CA 91311, USA — Singer, Actress
Love, Davis, III
Love Golf Design, 100 Brunswick Ave, Saint Simons Island GA 31522, USA — Golfer
Love, Duval L
8985 Yuba River Ave, Fountain Valley CA 92708, USA — Football Player
Love, Faizon
I C A Talent, 818 12th St, #9, Santa Monica CA 90403 USA — Actor, Comedian
Love, Gerald
High Road Touring, 751 Bridgeway, #200, Sausalito CA 94965 USA — Bassist (Teenage Fanclub)
Love, Kevin W
Minnesota Timberwolves, Target Center, 600 1st Ave N, Minneapolis MN 55403 USA — Basketball Player
Love, Loni
Innovative Artists, 1505 10th St, Santa Monica CA 90401 USA — Actress, Comedienne
Love, Michael D (Mike)
24563 Ebelden Ave, Newhall CA 91321, USA — Singer (Beach Boys)
Love, Randy
2202 Fairlands Dr, Garland TX 75040, USA — Football Player
Love, Stanley G
4315 Indian Sunrise Court, Houston TX 77059, USA — Astronaut
Love, Stanley S (Stan)
1950 Egan Way, Lake Oswego OR 97034, USA — Basketball Player
Love, Terence P
Curtin University, Design Dept, GPO Box U1987, Perth WA 6845, Australia — Educator
Lovelace, James L
Deputy Chief of Staff, Operations Plans, HqUSA, Pentagon, Washington DC 20310 USA — Army General
Lovelace, Vance O
5608 12th Ave S, Tampa FL 33619, USA — Baseball Player
Loveless, Patty
Mike Robertson Mgmt, PO Box 120073, Nashville TN 37212, USA — Singer, Songwriter
Lovell, Jacqueline
8707 Shirley Ave, Northridge CA 91324, USA — Actress, Model

Lovell, James A, Jr — Astronaut
Lovell Communications, PO Box 49, Lake Forest IL 60045, USA
Lovell, Robert R — Space Scientist
Orbital Sciences Corp, 21839 Atlantic Blvd, Dulles VA 20166, USA
Lovellette, Clyde E — Basketball Player
8 Woodspoint Circle, North Manchester IN 46962, USA
Lovelock, James E — Chemist, Inventor
Coombe Mill, Saint Giles on Heath, Launceston, Cornwall PL15 9RY, England
Lovely, Randy — Editor
Arizona Republic, Editorial Dept, 200 E Van Buren St, Phoenix AZ 85004 USA
Lover, Seth — Inventor, Engineer (Humbucking Pickup)
4 Village Dr, Saint Louis MO 63146, USA
Lovering, David — Singer, Drummer (Pixies)
X-Ray Touring, 77-79 Great Eastern St, #A, London EC2A 3HU, England
Loverne, David — Football Player
2307 Amber Falls Dr, Rocklin CA 95765, USA
LoVetere, John M — Football Player
PO Box 2901, Lebanon TN 37088, USA
Lovett, Lyle — Singer, Songwriter
Vector Mgmt, 1100 Glendon Ave, #2000, Los Angeles CA 90024, USA
Lovett, Ruby — Singer
Myers Media, PO Box 378, Canton NY 13617, USA
Loviglio, John P (Jay) — Baseball Player
23 3rd Ave, East Islip NY 11730, USA
Loville, Derek K — Football Player
D B L Financial, 3020 E Camelback Road, #301, Phoenix AZ 85016, USA
Loving, Candy — Model, Actress
8560 W Sunset Blvd, #600, West Hollywood CA 90069, USA
Lovins, Amory B — Physicist
Hypercar Inc, 3768 Highway 82, #204, Glenwood Springs CO 81601, USA
Lovitz, Jon — Actor, Comedian
Chuck Binder Mgmt, 1465 Lindacrest Dr, Beverly Hills CA 90210 USA
Lovland, Rolf — Pianist (Secret Garden), Composer
Thranesgate 2B, Oslo 473, Norway
Lovretta, Michelle A — Producer, Writer
Alpern Group, 15645 Royal Oak Road, Encino CA 91436, USA
Lovrich, Peter (Pete) — Baseball Player
19626 Beechnut Dr, Mokena IL 60448, USA
Lovullo, Salvatore A (Torey) — Baseball Player
32108 Sailview Lane, Westlake Village CA 91361, USA
Low, Francis E — Physicist
7102 Plantation Lane, Rockville MD 20852, USA
Low, Stephen — Diplomat
8300 Burdette Road, #556, Bethesda MD 20817, USA
Lowder, Kyle — Actor
Kazarian/Spencer/Ruskin, 11969 Ventura Blvd, #300, Studio City CA 91604 USA
Lowdermilk, R Kirk — Football Player
9475 Apollo Road NE, Kensington OH 44427, USA
Lowe, Barry — Writer
315 Audley St, London W1, England
Lowe, Chad — Actor
Anonymous Content, 3532 Hayden Ave, Culver City CA 90232 USA
Lowe, Chan — Editorial Cartoonist
Fort Lauderdale Sun-Sentinel, Editorial Dept, 200 E Las Olas Blvd, Fort Lauderdale FL 33301, USA
Lowe, Christopher S (Chris) — Keyboardist (Pet Shop Boys)
W M E Entertainment, 9601 Wilshire Blvd, #300, Beverly Hills CA 90210 USA
Lowe, Derek C — Baseball Player
12711 Terabella Way, Fort Myers FL 33912, USA
Lowe, Gary R — Football Player
16940 Lauderdale Ave, Beverly Hills MI 48025, USA
Lowe, J Sean — Baseball Player
802 Oak Dr, Mesquite TX 75149, USA
Lowe, Kevin — Ice Hockey Player, Coach, Executive
Edmonton Oilers, 11230 110th St, Edmonton AB T5G 3H7, Canada
Lowe, Nicholas D (Nick) — Singer, Songwriter, Guitarist
M V O Ltd, 307 7th Ave, #807, New York NY 10001, USA
Lowe, Paul E — Football Player
3906 Marine View Ave, San Diego CA 92113, USA
Lowe, Rob — Actor
W M E Entertainment, 9601 Wilshire Blvd, #300, Beverly Hills CA 90210 USA
Lowe, Sidney R — Basketball Player, Coach
2631 Wallingford Road, Winston-Salem NC 27101, USA
Lowe, Stephanie — Golfer
2004 Delancey Dr, Norman OK 73071, USA
Lowe, Woodrow — Football Player, Coach
PO Box 988, Alabaster AL 35007, USA
Lowell, Abbe D — Attorney
700 12th St NW, Washington DC 20005, USA
Lowell, Charles D (Charlie) — Keyboardist (Jars of Clay)
Nettwerk Mgmt, 1650 W 2nd Ave, Vancouver BC V6J 4R3, Canada
Lowell, Chris — Actor
Thruline Entertainment, 9250 Wilshire Blvd, #100, Beverly Hills CA 90212 USA
Lowell, Elizabeth — Writer
Avon Books, 1350 Ave of Americas, New York NY 10019 USA
Lowell, Michael A (Mike) — Baseball Player
620 Santurce Ave, Coral Gables FL 33143, USA
Lowell, Scott — Actor
Evolution Entertainment, 901 N Highland Ave, Los Angeles CA 90038 USA
Lowenstein, John L — Baseball Player
7017 Via Locanda Ave, Las Vegas NV 89131, USA
Lowery, Corey — Bassist (Stereo Mud)
Agency Group Ltd, 142 W 57th St, #600, New York NY 10019 USA
Lowery, David — Singer, Guitarist (Cracker), Songwriter
Back Bay Mgmt, 397 Little Neck Road, #305, Virginia Beach VA 23452 USA
Lowery, Dominic G (Nick) — Football Player
8416 E Via de Jardin, Scottsdale AZ 85258, USA

Lowery, Steve
1073 Royal Mile, Birmingham AL 35242, USA — Golfer
Lowman, Nate
Carlson Gallery, 55 S Audley St, London W1K 2QH, England — Artist
Lown, Bernard
Lown Cardiovascular Group, 21 Longwood Ave, Brookline MA 02446, USA — Cardiologist
Lown, Omar J (Turk)
1106 Van Buren St, Pueblo CO 81004, USA — Baseball Player
Lowndes, Jessica
Creative Artists Agency, 2000 Ave of Stars, #100, Los Angeles CA 90067 USA — Actress
Lowrie, Jed C
1895 Evergreen Ave NE, Salem OR 97301, USA — Baseball Player
Lowry, Glenn D
Museum of Modern Art, Director's Office, 11 W 53rd St, New York NY 10019, USA — Museum Executive
Lowry, Kyle
Toronto Raptors, Air Canada Center, 20 Bay St, Toronto ON M5J 2N8, Canada — Basketball Player
Lowry, Lois
205 Brattle St, Cambridge MA 02138, USA — Writer
Lowry, Noah
2621 Matera Lane, San Diego CA 92108, USA — Baseball Player
Lowry, Shanti
Don Buchwald/Fortitude, 6500 Wilshire Blvd, #2200, Los Angeles CA 90048 USA — Actress
Loy, James M
L-1 Identity Solutions, 177 Broad St, #1200, Stamford CT 06901, USA — Coast Guard Admiral, Government Official
Loy, Rory J
Rangers F C, Ibrox Stadium, 150 Edmiston Dr, Glasgow G51 2XD, Scotland — Soccer Player
Loynd, Michael W (Mike)
19 Randall Dr, Short Hills NJ 07078, USA — Baseball Player
Lozano Barragan, Javier Cardinal
Health Care Workers Assistance, Via Conciliazione 3, 00193 Rome, Italy — Religious Leader
Lozano, Conrad
Gold Mountain, 3940 Laurel Canyon Blvd, #444, Studio City CA 91604 USA — Singer, Bassist (Los Lobos)
Lozano, Florencia
Paradigm Agency, 360 N Crescent Dr, North Building, Beverly Hills CA 90210 USA — Actress
Lozano, Silvia
Ballet Folklorico, 31 Esq Con Riva Palacio, Col Guerrero, Mexico DF CP 06300, Mexico — Choreographer
Lu Qihui
100-301, 398 Xin-Pei Road, Xin-Zuan, Shanghai, China — Sculptor
Lu, Edward T (Ed)
18222 Bal Harbour Dr, Houston TX 77058, USA — Astronaut
Luan Jujie
146 Shuang-Le Yuan, #301, Qin-Huai Region, Nanjing 210009, China — Fencer
Lubanski, Ed
5326 Christi Dr, Warren MI 48091, USA — Bowler
Lubatti, Henri
S D B Partners, 1801 Ave of Stars, #902, Los Angeles CA 90067 USA — Actor
Lubbers, Rudolphus F M (Ruud)
Lambertweg 4, Rotterdam RA 3062, Netherlands — Prime Minister, Netherlands
Lubchenco, Jane
Oregon State University, Marine Biology Dept, Corvallis OR 97331, USA — Marine Biologist, Zoologist
Lubezki, Emmanuel
I C M Partners, 10250 Constellation Blvd, #900, Los Angeles CA 90067 USA — Cinematographer
Lubich, Bronko
3146 Whitemarsh Circle, Dallas TX 75234, USA — Professional Wrestler
Lubin, Barry (Grandma)
Big Apple Circus, 505 8th Ave, #1900, New York NY 10018 USA — Clown
Lubin, Gilson
Law Talent Agency, 5 Ambleside Ave, Toronto ON M8Z 2H5, Canada — Actor, Comedian
Lubin, Steven
State University of New York, School of Arts, Purchase NY 10577, USA — Concert Pianist
Lubotsky, Mark
Overtoom 329 III, 1054 JM Amsterdam, Netherlands — Concert Violinist
Lubovitch, Lar
Lar Lubovitch Dance Co, 229 W 42nd St, #8, New York NY 10036, USA — Dancer, Choreographer
Lubratich, Steven G (Steve)
24 Sackett Road, Lee NH 03861, USA — Baseball Player
Lubs, Herbert A
5133 SW 71st Place, Miami FL 33155, USA — Geneticist
Luby, Thia
2918 Marion Dr, Colorado Springs CO 80909, USA — Writer, Yoga Instructor
Luc, Tone
Headline Talent, PO Box 131518, Staten Island NY 10313 USA — Rap Artist, Actor
Lucado, Max
Oak Hills Church of Christ, 6929 Camp Bullis Road, San Antonio TX 78256, USA — Writer
Lucas, Adetokunbo Oulmide
25 Adebajo St, Kongi, PO Box 30917, Sec Bo, Ibadan, Nigeria — Physician
Lucas, Ben C
Creative Artists Agency, 2000 Ave of Stars, #100, Los Angeles CA 90067 USA — Director, Producer, Writer
Lucas, Craig
Peikoff Law Office, 173 E Broadway, #C1, New York NY 10002, USA — Lyricist, Writer
Lucas, Gary P
1511 High St, Rice Lake WI 54868, USA — Baseball Player
Lucas, George
LucasFilm, 5858 Lucas Valley Road, Nicasio CA 94946, USA — Director, Producer
Lucas, Isabel
United Talent Agency, 9336 Civic Center Dr, Beverly Hills CA 90210 USA — Actress
Lucas, Jerry R
Dr Memorabilia, 231 E 2nd St, Chillicothe OH 45601, USA — Basketball Player
Lucas, Jessica
Thruline Entertainment, 9250 Wilshire Blvd, #100, Beverly Hills CA 90212 USA — Actress
Lucas, John H, Jr
21 Pin Oak Estates, Bellaire TX 77401, USA — Basketball Player, Coach, Executive
Lucas, Josh
Principato-Young, 9465 Wilshire Blvd, #880, Beverly Hills CA 90212 USA — Actor
Lucas, Kenneth C (Ken)
404 Oakmont Lane, Waxhaw NC 28173, USA — Football Player

V.I.P. Address Book

Lucas, Marne Aalto Lounge, 3356 SE Belmont St, Portland OR 97214, USA	Photographer
Lucas, Matthew R (Matt) Troika, 74 Clerkenwell Road, #300, London EC1M 5QA, England	Actor
Lucas, Richard J (Richie) 1269 Estate Dr, West Chester PA 19380, USA	Football Player
Lucas, Robert E, Jr 5448 S East View Park, #3, Chicago IL 60615, USA	Nobel Economics Laureate
Lucas, Sarah Sadie Coles, 35 Heddon St, London W1B 4BP, England	Artist
Lucas, Timothy B (Tim) 5081 S Florence Dr, Greenwood Village CO 80111, USA	Football Player
Lucchesi, Bruno 30 5th Ave, New York NY 10011, USA	Sculptor
Lucchesi, Frank J 4703 Mill Creek Dr, Colleyville TX 76034, USA	Baseball Player, Manager
Lucchesini, Andrea Arts Manangement Group, 1133 Broadway, #1025, New York NY 10010, USA	Concert Pianist
Lucci, Michael G (Mike) 3184 Middlebelt Road, West Bloomfield MI 48323, USA	Football Player
Lucci, Susan Rogers & Cowan, 8687 Melrose Ave, #G700, West Hollywood CA 90069 USA	Actress
Luce, Derrel J 4112 Green Oak Dr, Waco TX 76710, USA	Football Player
Luce, Don 67 Tartan Lane, Buffalo NY 14221, USA	Ice Hockey Player
Luce, Richard N House of Lords, Westminster, London SW1A 0PW, England	Governor, Gibralta
Luce, William (Bill) PO Box 370, Depoe Bay OR 97341, USA	Writer
Lucero, Carlos F US Court of Appeals, 1929 Stout St, Denver CO 80294, USA	Judge
Luchini, Fabrice Voyez Mon Agent, 20 Ave Rapp, 75007 Paris, France	Actor
Luchko, Klara S Kotelmicheskaya Nab 1/15 Korp B, #308, 109240 Moscow, Russia	Actress
Luchsinger, Susie Psalm Ministries, 406 W 10th St, Atoka OK 74525, USA	Singer
Lucic, Zeljko I M G Artists, Hogarth Business Park, Chiswick, London W4 2TH, England	Opera Singer
Lucid, Shannon W 1622 Gunwale Road, Houston TX 77062, USA	Astronaut, Biophysicist
Lucier, Louis J (Lou) 7 Jaclyn Rae Dr, Millbury MA 01527, USA	Baseball Player
Lucio, Shannon Filament Pictures, 2104 N Cahuenga Blvd, #303, Los Angeles CA 90068, USA	Actress
Luck, Andrew A Indianapolis Colts, 7001 W 56th St, Indianapolis IN 46254 USA	Football Player
Luck, Frank Lerchenweg 9, 98587 Springstille, Germany	Biathlete
Luck, Gary E S A A H Foundation, 1147 N Clark St, #2044, West Hollywood CA 90069, USA	Army General
Luckett, LeToya A P A Talent/Literary Agency, 405 S Beverly Dr, #300, Beverly Hills CA 90212 USA	Singer
Luckey, Ken Greene Assoc, 1901 Ave of Stars, #130, Los Angeles CA 90067 USA	Actor
Luckhurst, Michael C W (Mick) 2757 Dawsons Chase, Duluth GA 30097, USA	Football Player
Luckinbill, Lawrence PO Box 330, Georgetown CT 06829, USA	Actor
Luckovich, Mike Atlanta Constitution, 223 Perimeter Center Parkway NE, Atlanta GA 30346, USA	Editorial Cartoonist
Lucy, Donny 3674 Oakcliff Dr, Fallbrook CA 92028, USA	Baseball Player
Lucy, Tom Leander Club, Henley on Thames, Leander RG9 2LP, England	Rowing Athlete
Luczo, Stephen J Seagate Technology, 920 Disc Dr, Scotts Valley CA 95066, USA	Businessman
Ludacris Creative Artists Agency, 2000 Ave of Stars, #100, Los Angeles CA 90067 USA	Rap Artist, Actor
Luddington, Camilla Progressive Artists Agency, 1041 N Formosa Ave, West Hollywood CA 90046 USA	Actress
Luder, Owen H Communication in Construction, 2 Smith Square, London SW1P 3HS, England	Architect
Ludes, John T Fortune Brands Inc, 300 Tower Parkway, Lincolnshire IL 60069, USA	Businessman
Luding-Rothenburger, Christa Dresdener Eisspot-Club, Pieschener Allee 1, 01067 Dresden, Germany	Speed Skater, Cyclist
Ludington, Ronald (Ron) 611 Thompson Station Road, Newark DE 19711, USA	Figure Skater
Ludwick, Ryan A 115 Roberts Circle, Georgetown TX 78633, USA	Baseball Player
Ludwig, Alexander Lucas Talent, 100 W Pender St, #700, Vancouver BC V6B 1R8, Canada	Actor
Ludwig, Christa 1458 Ter, Chemin des Colles, 06740 Chateau-neuf de Grasse, France	Opera Singer
Ludwig, Craig 421 River St, Eagle River WI 54521, USA	Ice Hockey Player
Ludwig, George H University of Iowa, Physics & Astronomy Dept, Iowa City IA 52242, USA	Physicist
Ludwig, Ken Gersh Agency, 9465 Wilshire Blvd, #600, Beverly Hills CA 90212 USA	Writer
Lue, Tyronn J 2926 Montessouri St, Las Vegas NV 89117, USA	Basketball Player
Luebber, Stephen L (Steve) 3302 Moorehead Dr, Joplin MO 64804, USA	Baseball Player

Luebbers, Larry C
844 Isaac Shelby Circle E, Frankfort KY 40601, USA — Baseball Player
Lueck, William M (Bill)
409 E Bird Lane, Litchfield Park AZ 85340, USA — Football Player
Luecken, Richard F (Rick)
2902 Fontana Dr, East Providence RI 02915, USA — Baseball Player
Lueders, Pierre
Bobsled Canada, 140 Canada Olympic Road SW, Calgary AB T3B 5R5, Canada — Bobsled Athlete
Luft, Lorna
Stiletto Entertainment, 8295 S La Cienega Blvd, Inglewood CA 90301, USA — Actress, Singer
Lugansky, Nicolai
Harrison/Parrott, 5-6 Albion Court, London W6 0QT, England — Concert Pianist
Lugbill, Jon
8810 Wishart Road, Richmond VA 23229, USA — Canoeing Athlete
Luger, Gery
Hinterfeld 598, 6861 Alberschwende, Austria — Photographer
Lugo, Julio
1555 Gants Circle, Kissimmee FL 34744, USA — Baseball Player
Luhrmann, Baz
Bazmark Inq, PO Box 430, Kings Cross NSW 2011, Australia — Director
Luisi, Fabio
Zurich Opera House, Falkenstr 1, 8008 Zurich, Switzerland — Conductor
Luisotti, Nicola
I M G Artists, Hogarth Business Park, Chiswick, London W4 2TH, England — Conductor
Lujack, John C (Johnny)
6321 Crow Valley Dr, Bettendorf IA 52722, USA — Football Player
Lujan, Manuel, Jr
Manuel Lujan Agencies, PO Box 3727, Albuquerque NM 87190, USA — Secretary, Interior
Lukachyk, Robert J
100 High St, Woodbridge NJ 07095, USA — Baseball Player
Lukas, D Wayne
1034 Oak Canyon Lane, Glendora CA 91741, USA — Thoroughbred Racing Trainer
Lukashenko, Aleksandr
President's Office, Karl Marx Str 38, 220016 Minsk, Belarus — President, Belarus
Lukasiewicz, Mark
8035 Fir Dr, Clay NY 13041, USA — Baseball Player
Lukather, Steve (Luke)
Fitzgerald Hartley, 1964 Wedgewood Ave, Nashville TN 37212 USA — Musician (Toto)
Luke, Derek
W M E Entertainment, 9601 Wilshire Blvd, #300, Beverly Hills CA 90210 USA — Actor
Luke, John A, Jr
Westvaco Corp, 299 Park Ave, #1300, New York NY 10171, USA — Businessman
Luke, Mathew C (Matt)
5262 Eucalyptus Hill Road, Yorba Linda CA 92886, USA — Baseball Player
Lukeba, Merveille
Independent Talent Group, Oxford House, 76 Oxford St, London W1D 1BS, England — Actor
Luken, Thomas J (Tom)
8036 Cast A Way, Mason OH 45040, USA — Football Player
Lukens, Max L
Baker Hughes Inc, PO Box 4740, Houston TX 77210, USA — Businessman
Luketic, Robert
Mosiac Media Group, 9200 W Sunset Blvd, #1000, Los Angeles CA 90069 USA — Director
Lukin, Matt
Legends of 21st Century, 7 Trinity Row, Florence MA 01062, USA — Bassist (Mudhoney)
Lukin, Valery
Arctic/Antarctic Research Institute, 38 Bering Str, 199397 Saint Petersburg, Russia — Oceanographer
Lukis, Adrian
Ken McReddie Assoc, 11 Connaught Place, London W2 2ET, England — Actor
Lukowich, Brad
3400 Craig Dr, #721, McKinney TX 75070, USA — Ice Hockey Player
Luksic, Igor
Prime Minister's Office, Jovana Tomasevica BB, Podgorica, Montenegro — Prime Minister, Montenegro
Lulu
Concorde International, 101 Shepherds Bush Road, London W6 7LP, England — Singer, Actress
Lum, Michael K (Mike)
3476 Cochise Dr SE, Atlanta GA 30339, USA — Baseball Player
Lumbly, Carl W
Brady Brannon Talent, 204 N Rossmore Ave, Los Angeles CA 90004, USA — Actor
Lumenti, Raphael A (Ralph)
9 Tomaso Road, Milford MA 01757, USA — Baseball Player
Lumidee
Universal Music Group, 2220 Colorado Ave, Santa Monica CA 90404, USA — Singer
Lumley, Dave
PO Box 610, Murfreesboro AR 71958, USA — Ice Hockey Player
Lumley, Joanna
Independent Talent Group, Oxford House, 76 Oxford St, London W1D 1BS, England — Actress
Lumley, John L
743 Snyder Hill Road, Ithaca NY 14850, USA — Physicist
Lumme, Jyrki O
9646 E Laurel Lane, Scottsdale AZ 85260, USA — Ice Hockey Player
Lumpe, Jerry D
732 S Pearson Dr, Springfield MO 65809, USA — Baseball Player
Lumpkin, Sean F
4708 Virginia Lane, Minneapolis MN 55424, USA — Football Player
Lumpp, Raymond G (Ray)
21 Hewlett Dr, East Williston NY 11596, USA — Basketball Player
Lumsden, David J
Melton House, Soham, Cambridgeshire CB7 5DB, England — Conductor, Concert Organist
Luna, Barbara
18026 Rodarte Way, Encino CA 91316, USA — Actress
Luna, Diego
Canana Films, San Luis Potosi #211 Piso 8, Colonia Roma, Mexico City DF 06700, Mexico — Actor
Lunar, Fernando
3125 Zuni Place, Alamogordo NM 88310, USA — Baseball Player
Lund, Corb
Agency Group Ltd, 142 W 57th St, #600, New York NY 10019 USA — Singer, Songwriter

Lund, Deanna — Actress
Fred Eichelman, 545 Howard Dr, Salem VA 24153, USA

Lund, Donald A (Don) — Baseball Player
1299 Laurel View Dr, Ann Arbor MI 48105, USA

Lund, Eva — Curling Athlete
Curling Assn, Idrottshuser, Marbackagatan 19, 123 43 Farsta, Sweden

Lund, Gordon T — Baseball Player
1602 S Harvard Ave, Arlington Heights IL 60005, USA

Lund, Katia — Director
Gersh Agency, 9465 Wilshire Blvd, #600, Beverly Hills CA 90212 USA

Lundaas, Terje — Artist, Sculptor
Glass Art & Design, 7003 N Waterway Dr, #201, Miami FL 33133, USA

Lundberg, Anders — Physiologist
Goteberg University, Physiology Dept, Box 33031, 40 033 Goteborg, Sweden

Lundberg, Athena — Model
Playboy Promotions, 2706 Media Center Dr, Los Angeles CA 90065 USA

Lundberg, Fred Borre — Nordic Combined Skier
Skogbrynet 11, 9250 Bardu, Norway

Lunden, Joan — Commentator
Celebrity Consultants, 3340 Ocean Park Blvd, #1005, Santa Monica CA 90405 USA

Lundgren, Dolph — Actor
Baumgarten Mgmt, 11925 Wilshire Blvd, #310, Los Angeles CA 90025, USA

Lundgren, Terry — Businessman
Federated Department Stores, 151 W 34th St, New York NY 10001, USA

Lundholm, Johan (Bengt) — Ice Hockey Player
Torsgatan 16, 11362 Stockholm, Sweden

Lundi, Monika — Actress
Ortlindestr 2, 81927 Munich, Germany

Lundquist, David B (Dave) — Baseball Player
714 12th Ave NE, Hickory NC 28601, USA

Lundquist, Stephen (Steve) — Swimmer
246 Northwest Dr, Stockbridge GA 30281, USA

Lundquist, Verne — Sportscaster
1710 Natches Way, Steamboat Springs CO 80487, USA

Lundqvist, Alex — Model
Wilhelmina Models, 300 Park Ave S, #200, New York NY 10010 USA

Lundqvist, B Henrik — Ice Hockey Player
310 W 52nd St, #PHD, New York NY 10019, USA

Lundstedt, Thomas R (Tom) — Baseball Player
9813 Brookside Lane, Ephraim WI 54211, USA

Lundstrom, Tord G — Ice Hockey Player
Brynas Byggnads AB, 801 33 Gavle, Sweden

Lundy, Carmen — Singer
Abby Hoffer, 223 1/2 E 48th St, New York NY 10017 USA

Lundy, Jessica — Actress
Metropolitan Talent Agency, 7020 La Presa Dr, Los Angeles CA 90068 USA

Lundy, Victor A — Architect
Victor A Lundy Assoc, 701 Mulberry Lane, Bellaire TX 77401, USA

Lunenfeld, Bruno — Endocrinologist
7 Rav Ashi St, Tel Aviv 69395, Israel

Luner, Jaime — Actress
Berneman Mgmt, 5820 Wilshire Blvd, #200, Los Angeles CA 90036, USA

Lunghi, Cherie — Actress
C A M, 111 Shoreditch High St, #400, London E1 6JN, England

Lunka, Zoltan — Boxer
Weinheimer Str 2, 69198 Schriesheim, Germany

Lunke, Hilary — Golfer
11701 Broad Oaks Dr, Austin TX 78759, USA

Lunn, Bob — Golfer
PO Box 1495, Woodbridge CA 95258, USA

Lunney, Glenn — Space Scientist
United Space Alliance, 1150 Gemini Dr, Houston TX 77058, USA

Lunsford, Trey — Baseball Player
3955 Nail Road, Southaven MS 38672, USA

Luongo, Aldo — Artist
883 Westbourne Ave, West Hollywood CA 90069, USA

Luongo, Christopher J (Chris) — Ice Hockey Player
103 Arabian Dr, Madison AL 35758, USA

Luongo, Roberto — Ice Hockey Player
7280 Lemon Grass Dr, Parkland FL 33076, USA

Lupberger, Edwin A — Businessman
Nesher Investments, 2010 NE 164th St, North Miami Beach FL 33162, USA

Lupica, Mike — Sportswriter
87 Bald Hill Road, New Canaan CT 06840, USA

Lupien, Gilles — Ice Hockey Player
Sports Prospects, 77 Rue de Bleury, Rosemere QC J7A 4L9, Canada

Luplow, Alvin D (Al) — Baseball Player
4250 Lakecress Dr E, Saginaw MI 48603, USA

Lupo, Janet P — Model
PO Box 6232, Hoboken NJ 07030, USA

LuPone, Patti — Singer, Actress
235 Park Ave S, #700, New York NY 10003, USA

Lupu, Radu — Concert Pianist
Opus 3 Artists, 470 Park Ave S, #900N, New York NY 10016 USA

Lupus, Peter — Actor, Bodybuilder, Model
Greene Assoc, 1901 Ave of Stars, #130, Los Angeles CA 90067 USA

Lurie, Alison — Writer
Cornell University, English Dept, Ithaca NY 14850, USA

Lurie, Jeffrey — Football Executive
312 Llanfair Road, Wynnewood PA 19096, USA

Lurie, Ranan R — Editorial Cartoonist
Cartoonnews International, 375 Park Ave, #1301, New York NY 10152, USA

Lurie, Rod — Director, Producer
Battleplan Productions, 1041 N Formosa Ave, Santa Monica W Building, West Hollywood CA 90046, USA

Lurtsema, Robert R (Bob) — Football Player
16920 Judicial Road, Lakeville MN 55044, USA

Lurz, Dagmar International Skating Union, Chemin du Primerose 2, 1007 Lausanne, Switzerland	Figure Skater
Lusader, Scott E 4169 Bold Meadows, Oakland Township MI 48306, USA	Baseball Player
Lusardi, Linda E3 Artists, 56 Shorts Gardens, London WC2H 9AN, England	Model
Lush, Billy Mary Erickson Entertainment, 2122 Hillhurst Ave, #A, Los Angeles CA 90027, USA	Actor
Lusis, Janis Vesetas 8-3, 1013 Riga, Latvia	Track Athlete
Lussier, Patrick Paradigm Agency, 360 N Crescent Dr, North Building, Beverly Hills CA 90210 USA	Director
Lussier, Sheila Wilson Assoc, 5418 Wilshire Blvd, #510, Los Angeles CA 90036, USA	Actress
Lust, Reimar Bellevue 49, 22301 Hamburg, Germany	Physicist
Lusteg, G Booth 1100 SW 111th Way, Davie FL 33324, USA	Football Player
Lustig, M Bruce Washington Hebrew Congregation, 3935 Macomb St NW, Washington DC 20016, USA	Religious Leader, Rabbi
Lustig, William 15016 Marble Dr, Sherman Oaks CA 91403, USA	Producer, Director, Actor
Lusztig, George 106 Grant Ave, Newton MA 02459, USA	Mathematician
Lute, Douglas E National Security Council, 1600 Pennsylvania Ave NW, Washington DC 20500, USA	Army General
Luter, Fred, Jr Franklin Avenue Baptist Church, 2515 Franklin Ave, New Orleans LA 70117, USA	Religious Leader
Lutes, Eric Special Artists Agency, 9465 Wilshire Blvd, #820, Beverly Hills CA 90212 USA	Actor
Luther, Edward A (Ed) 30486 Le Port, Laguna Niguel CA 92677, USA	Football Player
Luttrell, Rachel S M S Talent, 8383 Wilshire Blvd, #230, Beverly Hills CA 90211 USA	Actress
Lutz, Bob 101 Via Ensueno, San Clemente CA 92672, USA	Tennis Player
Lutz, Joleen H David Moss, 733 Seward St, #PH, Los Angeles CA 90038 USA	Actress
Lutz, Kellan B/W/R, 9100 Wilshire Blvd, #500W, Beverly Hills CA 90212 USA	Actor
Lutz, Lisa Levine Greenberg Literary Agency, 307 7th Ave, #2407, New York NY 10001, USA	Writer
Lutz, Robert A 3966 Pleasant Lake Road, Ann Arbor MI 48103, USA	Businessman
Lux, Danny I C M Partners, 10250 Constellation Blvd, #900, Los Angeles CA 90067 USA	Composer
Lux, Loretta Yossi Milo Gallery, 555 W 24th St, New York NY 10011, USA	Photographer
Luxon, Benjamin M Mazet, Relubbus Lane, Saint Hilary, Penzance, Cornwall TR20 9DS, England	Opera Singer
Luyendyk, Arie 9915 N Copper Ridge Trail, Fountain Hills AZ 85268, USA	Auto Racing Driver
Luyties, Ricci 2215 Hartford St, San Diego CA 92110, USA	Volleyball Player
Luzinski, Gregory M (Greg) 25680 Streamlet Court, Bonita Springs FL 34135, USA	Baseball Player
Lwin, Annabella M O B Agency, 6404 Wilshire Blvd, #505, Los Angeles CA 90048 USA	Singer (Bow Wow Wow)
Lyakhov, Vladimir A Cosmonaut Training Center, Star City, 141160 Zvezdny Gorodok, Moscow Oblast, Russia	Cosmonaut
Lyall, John A John Lyall Architects, 13-19 Curtain Road, London EC2A 3LT, England	Architect
Lyden, Mitchell S (Mitch) 227 Shore Court, Lauderdale by the Sea FL 33308, USA	Baseball Player
Lydman, Toni 6035 Corinne Lane, Clarence Center NY 14032, USA	Ice Hockey Player
Lydon, Alexa Gersh Agency, 9465 Wilshire Blvd, #600, Beverly Hills CA 90212 USA	Actress
Lydon, James (Jimmy) 3538 Lomacitas Lane, Bonita CA 91902, USA	Actor
Lydon, John (Johnny Rotten) 31962 Pacific Coast Highway, Malibu CA 90265, USA	Singer, Musician (Sex Pistols)
Lydon, Malcolm 1429 Jaudon Road, Dover FL 33527, USA	Astronaut
Lydy, D Scott 4278 S Leoma Lane, Chandler AZ 85249, USA	Baseball Player
Lyght, Todd W 912 Camino Ibiza, San Clemente CA 92672, USA	Football Player
Lyle, Gary T 222 Beach Dr NE, Saint Petersburg FL 33701, USA	Football Player
Lyle, Kami D S Mgmt, 2814 12th Ave S, #202, Nashville TN 37204, USA	Singer, Trumpeter, Songwriter
Lyle, Keith A 9615 Maypan Place, Seminole FL 33777, USA	Football Player
Lyle, Sandy 4904 Duck Creek Lane, #450, Ponte Vedra Beach FL 32082, USA	Golfer
Lyles, A C 2115 Linda Flora Dr, Los Angeles CA 90077, USA	Producer
Lyles, Lester E 6315 14th St NW, Washington DC 20011, USA	Football Player
Lyles, Lester L (Les) United Services Automobile Assn, U S A A Building, San Antonio TX 78288, USA	Air Force General
Lyles, Robert D 1012 Merritt Road, #C, West Point NY 10996, USA	Football Player
Lyman, Dorothy Stone Manners Salners, 9911 W Pico Blvd, #1400, Los Angeles CA 90035 USA	Actress

L

Lurz - Lyman

L

Lyman - Lynne

Lyman, Dustin S — Football Player
10529 Dacre Place, Lone Tree CO 80124, USA

Lynam, Jim — Basketball Coach, Executive
Philadelphia 76ers, 1st Union Center, 3601 S Broad St, Philadelphia PA 19148 USA

Lynch, Allen J — Vietnam War Army Hero (CMH)
438 Belle Plaine Ave, Gurnee IL 60031, USA

Lynch, Charles A — Businessman
24 Susan Gale Court, Menlo Park CA 94025, USA

Lynch, Claire — Singer
PO Box 926, Hermitage TN 37076, USA

Lynch, Dan — Editorial Cartoonist
Fort Wayne Journal-Gazette, Editorial Dept, 600 W Main St, Fort Wayne IN 46802, USA

Lynch, David K — Director
David Lynch Foundation, PO Box 93158,Los Angeles CA 90093, USA

Lynch, Edele — Singer (B*Witched)
Clintons, 55 Drury Lane, Covent Garden, London WC2B 5SQ, England

Lynch, Edward F (Ed) — Baseball Player
7832 E Parkview Lane, Scottsdale AZ 85255, USA

Lynch, Francis X (Fran) — Football Player
2553 Lake Vista Dr, Broomfield CO 80023, USA

Lynch, George D, III — Basketball Player
1000 Phils Creek Road, Chapel Hill NC 27516, USA

Lynch, Jair — Gymnast
9207 Three Oaks Dr, Silver Spring MD 20901, USA

Lynch, James E (Jim) — Football Player
1717 W 91st Place, Kansas City MO 64114, USA

Lynch, Jane — Actress, Comedienne
Domain Talent, 9229 W Sunset Blvd, #710, West Hollywood CA 90069 USA

Lynch, Jennifer Chambers — Writer, Director
Anthem Entertainment, 5225 Wilshire Blvd, #615, Los Angeles CA 90036 USA

Lynch, Jessica — Iraqi War Army Hero
Gregory Lynch, RR 1, Palestine WV 26160, USA

Lynch, John — Actor
Markham & Froggatt, Julian House, 4 Windmill St, London W1P 1HF, England

Lynch, John Carroll — Actor
Abrams Artists, 9200 W Sunset Blvd, #1125, West Hollywood CA 90069 USA

Lynch, John T, Jr — Football Player
13 Sandy Lake Road, Englewood CO 80113, USA

Lynch, Keavy — Singer (B*Witched)
Clintons, 55 Drury Lane, Covent Garden, London WC2B 5SQ, England

Lynch, Kelly — Model, Actress
TalentWorks, 3500 W Olive Ave, #1400, Burbank CA 91505 USA

Lynch, Lorenzo — Football Player
864 Bentwater Parkway, Cedar Hill TX 75104, USA

Lynch, Marshawn T — Football Player
17159 SE 100th St, Renton WA 98059, USA

Lynch, Peter S — Financier
27 State St, Boston MA 02109, USA

Lynch, Sandra L — Judge
US Court of Appeals, 1 Courthouse Way, Boston MA 02210, USA

Lynch, Shane — Singer (Boyzone), Actor
Associated International Mgmt, Fairfax House, Fulwood Place, London WC1V 6HU, England

Lynch, Susan — Actress
Troika, 74 Clerkenwell Road, #300, London EC1M 5QA, England

Lynch, Thomas C — Navy Admiral
751 Eagle Farm Road, Villanova PA 19085, USA

Lynch, Thomas W (Tom) — Producer
Tom Lynch Co, 1801 Ave of Stars, #710, Los Angeles CA 90067, USA

Lynde, Stan — Cartoonist (Rick O'Shay)
252 Ashley, Kalispell MT 59901, USA

Lynden-Bell, Donald — Astronomer
Institute of Astronomy, Madingley Road, Cambridge CB3 0HA, England

Lyndon, Frank — Singer (Belmonts)
Paramount Entertainment, 12 Kosakowski Dr, Morris Plains NJ 07590 USA

Lynds, Roger — Astronomer
Kitt Peak National Observatory, Tucson AZ 85726, USA

Lyne, Adrian — Director
W M E Entertainment, 9601 Wilshire Blvd, #300, Beverly Hills CA 90210 USA

Lyngstad, Anni-Frida — Singer (ABBA), Songwriter
Mono Music, Sodra Brobaeken 41A, 111 49 Stockholm, Sweden

Lynn Salomon, Janet — Figure Skater
PO Box 1026, Haymarket VA 20168, USA

Lynn, Cheryl — Singer, Actress
PO Box 667, Smithtown NY 11787, USA

Lynn, Frederic M (Fred) — Baseball Player
7336 El Fuerte St, Carlsbad CA 92009, USA

Lynn, Greg — Architect
University of California, Architecture School, Los Angeles CA 90024, USA

Lynn, Johnny R — Football Player
6 Steuben Bay, Alameda CA 94502, USA

Lynn, Jonathan — Director
United Agents, 12-26 Lexington St, London W1F 0LE, England

Lynn, Loretta — Singer, Guitarist, Songwriter
44 Hurricane Mills Road, Hurricane Mills TN 37078, USA

Lynn, Meredith Scott — Actress
Bauman Redanty Shaul Agency, 5757 Wilshire Blvd, #473, Los Angeles CA 90036 USA

Lynn, Theresa — Actress
243 Hamilton Ave, #2, Clifton NJ 7011, USA

Lynn, Vera — Actress, Singer
Hampers Croft, Common Lane, Ditchling, East Sussex BN6 8TJ, England

Lynne, Gillian — Dance Director, Choreographer
Lean-2 Productions, 18 Rutland St, Knightsbridge, London SW7 1EF, England

Lynne, Gloria — Singer
Universal Attractions, 135 W 26th St, #1200, New York NY 10001 USA

Lynne, Jeff — Singer, Guitarist, Songwriter
Front Line Mgmt, 1100 Glendon Ave, #2000, Los Angeles CA 90024 USA

Lynne, Rockie
Universal Records, 1755 Broadway, #600, New York NY 10019 USA — Singer, Songwriter

Lynne, Shelby
High Road, 751 Bridgeway, #200, Sausalito CA 94965, USA — Singer, Fiddle Player, Songwriter

Lynskey, Melanie
Susan Smith, 1344 N Wetherly Dr, Los Angeles CA 90069 USA — Actress

Lyon, Brandon J
4291 S Iowa St, Chandler AZ 85248, USA — Baseball Player

Lyon, Sue
Rudman, 1317 N Whitnall Highway, Burbank CA 91505, USA — Actress

Lyonne, Natasha
A P A Talent/Literary Agency, 405 S Beverly Dr, #300, Beverly Hills CA 90212 USA — Actress

Lyons, Barry S
527 Front Beach Dr, #71, Ocean Springs MS 39564, USA — Baseball Player

Lyons, Ben
W M E Entertainment, 9601 Wilshire Blvd, #300, Beverly Hills CA 90210 USA — Film Critic, Columnist

Lyons, Curt R
124 Virginia Dr, Richmond KY 40475, USA — Baseball Player

Lyons, David
Anonymous Content, 3532 Hayden Ave, Culver City CA 90232 USA — Actor

Lyons, Elena
Innovative Artists, 1505 10th St, Santa Monica CA 90401 USA — Actress

Lyons, James A, Jr
9481 Piney Mountain Road, Warrenton VA 20186, USA — Navy Admiral

Lyons, Martin A (Marty)
8 White Pine Court, Smithtown NY 11787, USA — Football Player

Lyons, Mitchell W (Mitch)
8344 Woodcrest Dr NE, Rockford MI 49341, USA — Football Player

Lyons, Phyllis
Bauman Redanty Shaul Agency, 5757 Wilshire Blvd, #473, Los Angeles CA 90036 USA — Actress

Lyons, Robert F
3810 Magnolia Blvd, PO Box 1292, Burbank CA 91507, USA — Actor

Lyons, Stephen K (Steve)
8196 E Del Platino Dr, Scottsdale AZ 85258, USA — Baseball Player

Lyons, Thomas L (Tommy)
2814 Drummond Point SE, Atlanta GA 30339, USA — Football Player

Lysacek, Evan F
Toyota Sports Center, 555 N Nash St, El Segundo CA 90245, USA — Figure Skater

Lysenko, Tatiana
Harris Agency, 17814 Lillian St, Omaha NE 68136, USA — Gymnast

Lysiak, Thomas J (Tom)
1050 Cedar Grove Road, Buckhead GA 30625, USA — Ice Hockey Player

Lyst, John H
Indianapolis Newspapers Inc, PO Box 145, Indianapolis IN 46206, USA — Editor

Lythgoe, Nigel
Nigel Lythgoe Productions, 8560 W Sunset Blvd, #900, West Hollywood CA 90069, USA — Producer, Director, Writer

Lyttle, James L (Jim)
751 Camino Lakes Circle, Boca Raton FL 33486, USA — Baseball Player

Lyttle, Kevin
Nene Musik Productions, 1460 SW Santiago Ave, Port Saint Lucie FL 34953 USA — Singer

Lyttle, Sancho
Atlanta Dream, 83 Walton St NW, #400, Atlanta, GA 30303 USA — Basketball Player

Lyubimov, Yuri P
M Nikitskaya Str 16-21, 121069 Moscow, Russia — Director, Actor

Lyubshin, Stanislav A
Vernadskogo Prosp 123, #171, 117571 Moscow, Russia — Actor

L

Lynne - Lyubshin

M I A
2:30 Publicity, 304 Hudson St, #700, New York NY 10013, USA — Rap Artist

Ma Ying Jeou
President's Office, Chieshshou Hall, Chongcing S Road, Taipei 100, Taiwan — President, Taiwan

Ma, Tzi
A P A Talent/Literary Agency, 405 S Beverly Dr, #300, Beverly Hills CA 90212 USA — Actor

Ma, Yo-Yo
Musichall Ltd, Vicarage Way, Ringmer BN8 5LA, England — Concert Cellist, Composer

Maas, Kevin C
PO Box 21019, Castro Valley CA 94546, USA — Baseball Player

Maas, William T (Bill)
653 N Shoreline Dr, Lees Summit MO 64064, USA — Football Player, Sportscaster

Maazel, Lorin V
Z des Aubris, Tal 15 5th Floor, 80331 Munich, Germany — Conductor, Concert Violinist

Mabbs, Edward C
21 Stonehedge Road, Lincoln MA 01773, USA — Businessman

Mabe, Ricky
Collective, 8383 Wilshire Blvd, #1050, Beverly Hills CA 90211 USA — Actor

Mabeus, Chris
151 Shady Lane, Soldotna AK 99669, USA — Baseball Player

Mabius, Eric
I C M Partners, 10250 Constellation Blvd, #900, Los Angeles CA 90067 USA — Actor

Mably, Luke
United Agents, 12-26 Lexington St, London W1F 0LE, England — Actor

Mabrey, Sunny
Paradigm Agency, 360 N Crescent Dr, North Building, Beverly Hills CA 90210 USA — Actress

Mabry, John S
715 Bellerive Manor Dr, Saint Louis MO 63141, USA — Baseball Player

Mabus, Raymond E, Jr
Secretary of Navy, HqUSN, Pentagon, Washington DC 20350, USA — Governor, MS

MacAdam, Al
PO Box 232, Morrell PE C0A 1S0, Canada — Ice Hockey Player

MacAfee, Kenneth A (Ken), II
154 South St, Needham MA 02492, USA — Football Player

Macal, Zdenek
Opus 3 Artists, 470 Park Ave S, #900N, New York NY 10016 USA — Conductor

Macarron Jaime, Ricardo
Agustin de Bethencourt 7, Madrid 3, Spain — Artist

MacArthur, Ellen
Whitegates, Arctic Road, Cowes, Isle of Wight PO31 7PG, England — Yachtswoman

MacArthur, Hayes
Creative Artists Agency, 2000 Ave of Stars, #100, Los Angeles CA 90067 USA — Actor

Macat, Julio G
Paradigm Agency, 360 N Crescent Dr, North Building, Beverly Hills CA 90210 USA — Cinematographer

Macaulay, Stewart
University of Wisconsin, Law School, 975 Bascom Mall, #6107, Madison WI 53706, USA — Attorney, Educator

MacAvoy, Paul W
920 Indian Beach Dr, Sarasota FL 34234, USA — Economist

Maccarinelli, Enzo
13 Hengoed Hall Dr, Cefn, Hengoed, Mid Glamorgan CF8 7JW, Wales — Boxer

Macchio, Ralph
Don Buchwald/Fortitude, 6500 Wilshire Blvd, #2200, Los Angeles CA 90048 USA — Actor

Maccioni, Sirio
Le Cirque 200, 151 E 58th St, Front 1, New York NY 10022, USA — Restauranteur, Chef

MacDermid, Paul
81 Lakeland Dr, Sauble Beach ON N0H 2G0, Canada — Ice Hockey Player

MacDermot, Galt
MacDermot Assoc, 12 Silver Lake Road, Staten Island NY 10301, USA — Composer

Macdissi, Peter
United Talent Agency, 9336 Civic Center Dr, Beverly Hills CA 90210 USA — Actor

MacDonald, Amy
Melodramatic Records, PO Box 623, Weybridge KT13 3DE, England — Singer, Songwriter

MacDonald, C Parker
3 Miller Road, Northford CT 06472, USA — Ice Hockey Player

Macdonald, Hettie
Independent Talent Group, Oxford House, 76 Oxford St, London W1D 1BS, England — Director

MacDonald, Julien
Haydens Place, 447A Portobello Road, London W11 1LT, England — Fashion Designer

Macdonald, Kelly
Independent Talent Group, Oxford House, 76 Oxford St, London W1D 1BS, England — Actress

Macdonald, Kevin
United Agents, 12-26 Lexington St, London W1F 0LE, England — Director

Macdonald, Norm
Gersh Agency, 9465 Wilshire Blvd, #600, Beverly Hills CA 90212 USA — Actor, Comedian

MacDonald, Parker
3 Miller Road, Northford CT 06472, USA — Ice Hockey Player

Macdonald, Richard
213 Galisteo St, Santa Fe NM 87501, USA — Sculptor

Macdonald, Robert (Bob)
522 Harbor Grove Circle, Safety Harbor FL 34695, USA — Baseball Player

Macdonald, Shauna
United Agents, 12-26 Lexington St, London W1F 0LE, England — Actress

Macdougal, R Meiklejohn (Mike)
2429 N Travis St, Mesa AZ 85207, USA — Baseball Player

MacDowell, Andie
Schiff Co, 8440 Warner Dr, #B1, Culver City CA 90232 USA — Model, Actress

MacEachern, David
Bobsled Canada, 140 Canada Olympic Road SW, Calgary AB T3B 5R5, Canada — Bobsled Athlete

Macek, Donald M (Don)
3615 Monte Real, Escondido CA 92029, USA — Football Player

Macer, Sterling, Jr
Gage Group, 14724 Ventura Blvd, #505, Sherman Oaks CA 91403 USA — Actor, Director, Writer

MacFadyen, Angus
Alchemy Entertainment, 7024 Melrose Ave, #420, Los Angeles CA 90038 USA — Actor

MacFadyen, Matthew
Hamilton Hodell, 66-68 Margaret St, London W1W 8SR, England — Actor

Macfarlane, Luke — Actor
Management 360, 9111 Wilshire Blvd, Beverly Hills CA 90210 USA
MacFarlane, Michael A (Mike) — Baseball Player
7421 Woodside Ave, Stockton CA 95207, USA
MacFarlane, Seth — Animator, Producer, Writer
Fuzzy Door Productions, 5700 Wilshire Blvd, #325, Los Angeles CA 90036, USA
MacGraw, Ali — Actress
Relatively Mgmt, 8899 Beverly Blvd, #509, Los Angeles CA 90048, USA
MacGregor, Bruce — Ice Hockey Player
8112 NW 133rd St, Edmonton AB T5R 0B1, Canada
MacGregor, Jeff — Writer
ESPN-TV, ESPN Plaza, 935 Middle St, Bristol CT 06010 USA
MacGregor, Joanna C — Concert, Jazz Pianist
SoundCircus Records, PO Box 57, Reading, Berkshire BG1 5TX, England
Mach, David S — Sculptor
64 Canonbie Road, Forest Hill, London SE23 3AG, England
Macha, Kenneth E (Ken) — Baseball Player, Manager
1118 Winnie Way, Latrobe PA 15650, USA
Machada, Lesley Ann — Actress
Principato-Young, 9465 Wilshire Blvd, #880, Beverly Hills CA 90212 USA
Machado Fajardo, Alicia — Beauty Queen, Actress, Model
Miss Universe Organization, 1370 Ave of Americas, #1600, New York NY 10019 USA
Machado Ventura, Jose Ramon — Vice President, Cuba
Palacio de Gobierno, Cibsejo de la Ravolucion, Havana, Cuba
Machado, China — Model
I M G Models, 304 Park Ave S, #PH-North, New York NY 10010 USA
Machado, Justina — Actress
Allman/Rhea Mgmt, 141 S Barrington Ave, #E, Los Angeles CA 90049, USA
Machado, Rodolfo — Architect
Machado & Silvetti, 500 Harrison Ave, Boston MA 02118, USA
Macharski, Franciszak Cardinal — Religious Leader
Metropolita Krakowski, Ul Franciszkanska 3, 31 004 Krakow, Poland
Machen, J Bernard — Educator
University of Florida, President's Office, Tigert Hall, Gainesville FL 32611, USA
Machlis, Gail — Cartoonist (Quality Time)
Gail Machlis Illustrations, 1 Arcade Ave, Berkeley CA 94708, USA
Machover, Tod — Composer
Massachusetts Institute of Technology, Media Laboratory, Cambridge MA 02139, USA
Macht, Gabriel S — Actor
I C M Partners, 10250 Constellation Blvd, #900, Los Angeles CA 90067 USA
Macht, Stephen — Actor
248 S Rodeo Dr, Beverly Hills CA 90212, USA
Machungo, Mario F de Graca — Prime Minister, Mozambique
Banco International, Avda Zedequias, Mananhela 478, Maputo, Mozambique
Maclellan, Brian — Ice Hockey Player
Washington Capitals, 627 N Glebe Road, #850, Arlington VA 22203 USA
MacInnis, Allan (Al) — Ice Hockey Player, Executive
1132 Highland Point Dr, Saint Louis MO 63131, USA
MacInnis, Frank T — Businessman
E M C O R Group, 301 Merritt Seven, #600, Norwalk CT 06851, USA
MacIntosh, Craig — Cartoonist (Sally Forth)
3403 W 28th St, Minneapolis MN 55416, USA
Macintyre, Carter — Actor
United Talent Agency, 9336 Civic Center Dr, Beverly Hills CA 90210 USA
MacIsaac, Martha — Actress
A M I Artists Mgmt, 464 King St E, Toronto ON M5A 1L7, Canada
MacIver, Norm — Ice Hockey Player
2119 Ponderosa Circle, Duluth MN 55811, USA
MacIvor, Daniel — Actor
I C M Partners, 10250 Constellation Blvd, #900, Los Angeles CA 90067 USA
Mack, Allison — Actress
Industry Entertainment, 955 Carillo Dr, #300, Los Angeles CA 90048 USA
Mack, Bill — Sculptor
Erin Taylor Editions, 5222 W 78th St, Minneapolis MN 55435, USA
Mack, Cedric M — Football Player
116 Chestnut St, Lake Jackson TX 77566, USA
Mack, Consuelo — Commentator
WealthTrack, PO Box 20485, Dag Hammarskjold Convenience Center, New York NY 10017, USA
Mack, J Kevin — Football Player
29359 Hummingbird Circle, Westlake OH 44145, USA
Mack, John J — Financier
Morgan Stanley Co, 1585 Broadway, Lower B, New York NY 10036, USA
Mack, Lonnie — Singer, Guitarist
Concerted Efforts, PO Box 440326, Somerville MA 02144 USA
Mack, Shane L — Baseball Player
35324 Marsh Lane, Wildomar CA 92595, USA
Mack, Stacey L — Football Player
4885 Raleigh St, #6, Orlando Fl 32811, USA
Mack, Thomas I (Tom) — Football Player
52 Grand Miramar Dr, Henderson NV 89011, USA
Mackall, Michelle — Golfer
2057 Oxford Ave, Cardiff CA 92007, USA
Mackanin, Peter (Pete), Jr — Baseball Player, Manager
11563 E Bronco Trail, Scottsdale AZ 85255, USA
Mackay, David — Director, Producer
Gersh Agency, 9465 Wilshire Blvd, #600, Beverly Hills CA 90212 USA
Mackay, Harvey — Writer
Mackay Envelope Corp, 2100 Elm St SE, Minneapolis MN 55414, USA
MacKay-Lyons, Brian — Architect
MacKay-Lyons Architect Inc, 2188 Gottingen St, Halifax NS B3K 3B4, Canada
Macke, Richard C — Navy Admiral
1887 Alaweo St, Honolulu HI 96821, USA
Mackenzie, Alastair — Actor
Ken McReddie Assoc, 11 Connaught Place, London W2 2ET, England
MacKenzie, David — Director
United Agents, 12-26 Lexington St, London W1F 0LE, England

MacKenzie, J Barry — Ice Hockey Player
Minnesota Wild, XCel Energy Arena, 1275 Saint Antoine W, Saint Paul MN 55104 USA

MacKenzie, Kenneth P (Ken) — Baseball Player
15 Fair St, Guilford CT 06437, USA

MacKenzie, Peter — Actor
Precision Entertainment, 6338 Wilshire Blvd, Los Angeles CA 90048, USA

Mackey, Cindy — Golfer
1190 Millstone Run, Bogart GA 30622, USA

Mackey, Lance — Dog Sled Racer
PO Box 75015, Fairbanks AK 99707, USA

Mackey, Malcolm M — Basketball Player
504 Hemphill Ave, Chattanooga TN 37411, USA

Mackey, Rick — Dog Sled Racer
5938 Four Mile Road, Nenana AK 99760, USA

Mackie, Allison — Actress
A P A Talent/Literary Agency, 405 S Beverly Dr, #300, Beverly Hills CA 90212 USA

Mackie, Anthony — Actor
Inspire Entertainment, 1517 S Bentley Ave, #202, Los Angeles CA 90025, USA

Mackie, Robert G (Bob) — Fashion Designer
Bob Mackie Ltd, 530 Fashion Ave, New York NY 10018, USA

Mackin, Sean — Violinist (Yellowcard)
Capitol Records, 1750 N Vine St, Los Angeles CA 90028 USA

MacKinnon, Catherine — Attorney, Social Activist
University of Michigan, Law School, 625 S State St, Ann Arbor MI 48109, USA

MacKinnon, Roderick — Nobel Chemistry Laureate
53 Winchester St, #2, Brookline MA 2446, USA

MacKinnon, Simmone J — Actress
Mark Morrissey Assoc, 45 Oxford St, Bondi Junction NSW 2022, Australia

Mackintosh, Cameron A — Producer
Cameron Mackintosh Ltd, 1 Bedford Square, London WC1B 3RA, England

Mackintosh, Steven — Actor
Independent Talent Group, Oxford House, 76 Oxford St, London W1D 1BS, England

Macklin, David — Actor
Wilson, 5410 Wilshire Blvd, #510, Los Angeles CA 90036, USA

Macknowski, John A — Basketball Player
1902 Garnet Lane, Dandridge, TN 37225, USA

Macknowski, Stephen — Canoeing Athlete
462 Kimball Ave, Yonkers NY 10704, USA

Mackowiak, Robert W (Rob) — Baseball Player
2414 W Superior St, Chicago IL 60612, USA

Mackrides, William (Bill) — Football Player
1060 Beverly Lane, Newtown Square PA 19073, USA

MacLachlan, Kyle — Actor
Gersh Agency, 9465 Wilshire Blvd, #600, Beverly Hills CA 90212 USA

Maclachlan, Patricia — Writer
21 Unquomonk Road, Williamsburg MA 01096, USA

MacLaine, Shirley — Actress
MacLaine Enterprises, PO Box 33950, Santa Fe NM 87594, USA

MacLean, Donald J (Don) — Basketball Player
216 Los Padres Dr, Thousand Oaks CA 91361, USA

MacLean, Doug — Ice Hockey Coach
466 Notre Dame St, Summerside PE C1N 1T3, Canada

MacLean, John — Ice Hockey Player, Coach
44 Old Farm Road, Basking Ridge NJ 7920, USA

MacLean, Paul A — Ice Hockey Player, Coach
41544 Glade Road, Canton MI 48187, USA

MacLean, Steven G — Astronaut, Canada
N A S A, Johnson Space Center, 2101 NASA Road, Houston TX 77058 USA

MacLeish, Richard G (Rick) — Ice Hockey Player
5612 Bay Ave, Ocean City NJ 08226, USA

Macleod, Carla — Ice Hockey Player
Team Canada, 2424 University Dr NW, Calgary AB T2N 3Y9, Canada

MacLeod, Gavin — Actor
70070 Frank Sinatra Dr, #7, Rancho Mirage CA 92270, USA

MacLeod, Joanna — Actress
Associated International Mgmt, Fairfax House, Fulwood Place, London WC1V 6HU, England

MacLeod, John M — Basketball Coach
4610 E Fanfol Dr, Phoenix AZ 85028, USA

Macleod, Thomas W (Tom) — Football Player
15412 N Hazard Road, Spokane WA 99208, USA

MacMaster, Natalie — Fiddler
Columbia Artists Mgmt Inc, 1790 Broadway, #702, New York NY 10019 USA

MacMillan, John S — Ice Hockey Player
2672 W Conifer Dr, Eagle ID 83616, USA

MacMillan, Robert L (Bob) — Ice Hockey Player
Sport Page, PO Box 908 Station Central, Charlottetown PE C1A 3Z6, Canada

MacMillan, William S (Billy) — Ice Hockey Player
Upper Meadowbank Road, RR 2, Cornwall PE C0A 1H0, Canada

MacMurray, William — Electrical Engineer
200 Deer Run Road, Schaghticoke NY 12154, USA

Macnee, Patrick — Actor
7 Mount Holyoke, Rancho Mirage CA 92270, USA

MacNeil, Allister W (Al) — Ice Hockey Player, Coach
151 Parkview Way SE, Calgary AB T2J 4N3, Canada

MacNeil, Robert B W — Commentator
2700 S Quincy St, Arlington VA 22206, USA

MacNeille, Tress — Actress
Sutton-Barth Vennari, 145 S Fairfax Ave, #310, Los Angeles CA 90036 USA

MacNicol, Peter — Actor
Principato-Young, 9465 Wilshire Blvd, #880, Beverly Hills CA 90212 USA

Macomber, Debbie — Writer
PO Box 1458, Port Orchard WA 98366, USA

Macomber, Dick — Thoroughbred Racing Jockey
6720 NW 28th Terrace, Fort Lauderdale FL 33309, USA

Macomber, George B N — Skier
1 Design Center Place, #600, Boston MA 02210, USA

Macoun, Jamie
J M A C Drilling, 1313 10th St, Misku AB T3E 2X3, Canada — Ice Hockey Player
MacPherson, Duncan I
Toronto Star, Editorial Dept, 1 Yonge St, Toronto ON M5E 1E6, Canada — Editorial Cartoonist
Macpherson, Elle
Don Buchwald/Fortitude, 6500 Wilshire Blvd, #2200, Los Angeles CA 90048 USA — Model
Macpherson, Wendy
PO Box 93433, Henderson NV 89009, USA — Bowler
MacQuitty, Jonathan
Abingworth Mgmt Inc, 3000 Sand Hill Road, #4-135, Menlo Park CA 94025, USA — Inventor (Immunodeficient Mouse)
MacRae, Sheila
666 W End Ave, #10H, New York NY 10025, USA — Actress, Singer
MacTavish, Craig
3 Quail Hollow Court, Voorhees NJ 08043, USA — Ice Hockey Player, Coach
Macurdy, John
Columbia Artists Mgmt Inc, 1790 Broadway, #702, New York NY 10019 USA — Opera Singer
MacWhorter, Keith
75 Martin St, Rehoboth MA 02769, USA — Baseball Player
Macy, Geoffrey W
University of California, Integrative Planetary Center, Berkeley CA 94720, USA — Astronomer
Macy, Kyle R
3320 Overbrook Dr, Lexington KY 40502, USA — Basketball Player, Coach
Macy, William H (Bill)
Creative Artists Agency, 2000 Ave of Stars, #100, Los Angeles CA 90067 USA — Actor
Madden, Beezie
3908 Stone Bridge Road, Cazenovia NY 13035, USA — Equestrian
Madden, Benji L
A Fein Martini, 37 W 20th St, #1008, New York NY 10011, USA — Singer, Guitarist (Good Charlotte)
Madden, Dave
4790 Blossom Dr, Delray Beach FL 33445, USA — Actor, Comedian
Madden, Joel R
Girlie Action, 59 W 19th St, #4B, New York NY 10011, USA — Singer (Good Charlotte)
Madden, John
6 Briarcliff Road, Montville NJ 07045, USA — Ice Hockey Player
Madden, John E
5095 Coronado Blvd, Pleasanton CA 94588, USA — Football Player, Coach, Sportscaster
Madden, John P
Casorotto Ramsay, Waverley House, 7-12 Noel St, London W1F 8GQ, England — Director
Madden, Michael A (Mike)
4733 Frankfort Way, Denver CO 80239, USA — Baseball Player
Madden, Mickey
J Records, 745 5th Ave, #600, New York NY 10151 USA — Bassist (Maroon 5)
Madden, Morris D
105 Jennings St, Laurens SC 29360, USA — Baseball Player
Maddin, Guy
Loeb & Loeb, 10100 Santa Monica Blvd, #2200, Los Angeles CA 90067, USA — Director
Maddon, Joseph J (Joe)
2560 N Lindsay Road, #32, Mesa AZ 85213, USA — Baseball Manager
Maddow, Rachel A
Napoli Mgmt, 8844 W Olympic Blvd, #100, Beverly Hills CA 90211, USA — Commentator
Maddox, David M
2301 Fort Scott Dr, Arlington VA 22202, USA — Army General
Maddox, Elliott
980 Coral Ridge Dr, #104, Coral Springs FL 33071, USA — Baseball Player
Maddox, Eva
Eva Maddox Assoc, 333 N Wabash Ave, #3600, Chicago IL 60611, USA — Interior Designer
Maddox, Jerry G
20647 Thundersky Circle, Riverside CA 92508, USA — Baseball Player
Maddox, Mark A
100 W Washington St, #1900, Phoenix AZ 85003, USA — Football Player
Maddox, Rachel
MSNBC, News Dept, 22 Fletcher Ave, Fort Lee NJ 07024, USA — Commentator
Maddox, Thomas A (Tommy)
210 Ridge View Lane, Roanoke TX 76262, USA — Football Player
Maddux, Gregory A (Greg)
36 Innisbrook Ave, Las Vegas NV 89113, USA — Baseball Player
Madeley, Anna
Independent Talent Group, Oxford House, 76 Oxford St, London W1D 1BS, England — Actress
Mader, Rebecca
Innovative Artists, 1505 10th St, Santa Monica CA 90401 USA — Actress
Madfai, Kahtan al
22 Vassileos Constantinou, 11635 Athens, Greece — Architect
Madi, Hamada (Bolero)
Prime Minister's Office, BP 421, Moroni, Comoros — Prime Minister, Comoros
Madigan, Amy
Industry Entertainment, 955 Carillo Dr, #300, Los Angeles CA 90048 USA — Actress
Madigan, Kathleen
A P A Talent/Literary Agency, 405 S Beverly Dr, #300, Beverly Hills CA 90212 USA — Actress, Comedienne
Madigan, Martha
730 Carpenter Lane, Philadelphia PA 19119, USA — Photographer
Madinier, Bruno
Agence Artiste Adequet, 80 Rue d'Amsterdam, 75009 Paris, France — Actor
Madison, C Scott (Scotty)
5397 Thornapple Lane NW, Acworth GA 30101, USA — Baseball Player
Madison, Holly
Entertainment Fusion Group, 8899 Beverly Blvd, #412, West Hollywood CA 90046, USA — Model, Actress
Madison, Samuel A (Sam)
13153 SW 25th Place, Davie FL 33325, USA — Football Player
Madkins, Gerald
528 W 8th St, Merced CA 95341, USA — Basketball Player
Madlock, Bill, Jr
1565 Calle del Estribo, Pacific Palisades CA 90272, USA — Baseball Player
Madobe, Sheikh Adeb Mohamed Nor
President's Office, People's Palace, Mogadishu, Somalia — President, Somalia
Madonna
Untitled Entertainment, 350 S Beverly Dr, #200, Beverly Hills CA 90212 USA — Singer, Actress

M

Madrigal, Al — Actor
Creative Artists Agency, 2000 Ave of Stars, #100, Los Angeles CA 90067 USA

Madrigali, Jeff — Yachtsman
6212 Greenblower Lane, Clinton WA 98236, USA

Madritsch, Bobby — Baseball Player
8628 Linder Ave, Burbank IL 60459, USA

Madsen, Loren W — Sculptor
428 Broome St, New York NY 10013, USA

Madsen, Mark E — Basketball Player
10132 Gristmill Ridge, Eden Prairie MN 55347, USA

Madsen, Michael — Actor
Madsen International Mgmt, 9000 Sunset Blvd, Los Angeles CA 90069, USA

Madsen, Ole Christian — Director
Nimbus Film Productions, Hauchsvej 17, 1825 Frederiksberg, Denmark

Madsen, Virginia — Actress
Untitled Entertainment, 350 S Beverly Dr, #200, Beverly Hills CA 90212 USA

Madson, Ryan M — Baseball Player
75 Mullen Dr, Sicklerville NJ 08081, USA

Maduro, Calvin G — Baseball Player
793 Springdale Dr, Millersville MD 21108, USA

Mae, Audra — Singer, Songwriter
Agency Group Ltd, 142 W 57th St, #600, New York NY 10019 USA

Maedizossian, Prelate Moushegh — Religious Leader
Armenian Apostolic Church, 4401 Russell Ave, Los Angeles CA 90027, USA

Maese, Joseph M (Joe) — Football Player
4738 W Krystal Way, Glendale AZ 85308, USA

Maestri, Hector A — Baseball Player
581 SW 89th Court, Miami FL 33174, USA

Maestro, Mia — Actress
I C M Partners, Marlborough House, 10 Earlham St, #300, London WC2H 9LNP, England

Maeve, Stella — Actress
Abrams Artists, 9200 W Sunset Blvd, #1125, West Hollywood CA 90069 USA

Maffei, Lamberto — Neurobiologist
National Research Council, Piazzale Aldo Moro 7, 00185 Rome, Italy

Maffett, Debra Sue (Debbie) — Beauty Queen
1525 McGavock St, Nashville TN 37203, USA

Maffia, Roma — Actress
Nancy Iannios Public Relations, PO Box 430, Signal Mountain TN 37377 USA

Magadan, David J (Dave) — Baseball Player
3733 Johnathon Ave, Palm Harbor FL 34685, USA

Magaw, John W — Law Enforcement Official
Transportation Security Administration, 400 7th St SW, Washington DC 20590, USA

Magee, Dave — Harness Racing Driver
5S350 Deer Ridge Path, Big Rock IL 60511, USA

Magee, Herb — Basketball Coach
Philadelphia University, Athletic Dept, Philadelphia PA 19144, USA

Magee, Kenneth — Actor
11491 Riverside Dr, Los Angeles CA 91602, USA

Magee, Wendell E, Jr — Baseball Player
6500 Muskogee Cove, Leeds AL 35094, USA

Maggard, Dave — Track Athlete, Sports Executive
University of Houston, Athletic Dept, Houston TX 77204, USA

Maggenti, Maria — Director
Paradigm Agency, 360 N Crescent Dr, North Building, Beverly Hills CA 90210 USA

Maggert, Jeff — Golfer
62 W Bracebridge Circle, Spring TX 77382, USA

Maggette, Corey A — Basketball Player
Detroit Pistons, Palace, 4 Championship Dr, Auburn Hills MI 48326 USA

Maggs, Donald J (Don) — Football Player
26525 Amhearst Circle, #106, Beachwood OH 44122, USA

Magic Dick (Salwitz) — Harmonica Player (J Geils Band)
Nick Ben-Meir, 652 N Doheny Dr, West Hollywood CA 90069, USA

Magill, Frank J — Judge
US Court of Appeals, Federal Building, 657 2nd Ave N, Fargo ND 58102, USA

Magilton, Gerard E (Jerry) — Astronaut
Martin Marietta Astro Space, 100 Campus Dr, Newtown PA 18940, USA

Magimel, Benoit — Actor
Intertalent, 48 Rue Gay-Lussac, 75005 Paris, France

Maginn, Matt — Bassist (Cursive)
Ground Control Touring, 20 Jay St, #826, Brooklyn NY 11201 USA

Maginnes, John — Golfer
612 Topwater Lane, Greensboro NC 27455, USA

Magloire, Jamaal D — Basketball Player
Toronto Raptors, Air Canada Center, 20 Bay St, Toronto ON M5J 2N8, Canada

Magnani, Olivia — Actress
Agents Associes, 201 Rue du Faubourg Saint Honore, 75008 Paris, France

Magnante, Michael A (Mike) — Baseball Player
5305 Via Quinto, Newbury Park CA 91320, USA

Magnanti, Brooke — Writer, Epidemiologist
Orion Publishing, 5 Upper Saint Martin's Lane, London WC2H 9EA, England

Magni, James — Architect, Interior Designer
Magni Design, Pacific Design Center, 8687 Melrose Ave, West Hollywood CA 90069, USA

Magnus, Edie — Commentator
NBC-TV, News Dept, 30 Rockefeller Plaza, #270E, New York NY 10112 USA

Magnus, Sandra H (Sandy) — Astronaut
3477 Vinings North Trail SE, Smyrna GA 30080, USA

Magnuson, Ann — Actress
1317 Maltman Ave, Los Angeles CA 90026, USA

Magnussen-Ceila, Karen K — Figure Skater
2852 Thorndiff Dr, North Vancouver BC V7R 2S5, Canada

Magowan, Kate — Actress
United Agents, 12-26 Lexington St, London W1F 0LE, England

Magrane, Joseph D (Joe) — Baseball Player
705 Guisando de Avila, Tampa FL 33613, USA

Magri, Charles G (Charlie) — Boxer
345 Bethnal Green Road, Bethnal Green, London E2 6LG, England

V.I.P. Address Book

Magris, Claudio — Writer, Journalist
Via Carpaccio 2, 34127 Trieste, Italy
Magruder, Christopher J (Chris) — Baseball Player
1740 Leisure Lane, Yakima WA 98908, USA
Magsamen, Sandra — Writer, Artist
Orchard Books/Scholastic, 557 Broadway, New York NY 10012, USA
Maguire, Adrian E — Thoroughbred Racing Jockey
17 Willes Close, Faringdon, Oxfordshire SN7 7DU, England
Maguire, Albert M — Surgeon
Children's Hospital, 34th St & Civic Center Blvd, Philadelphia PA 19104, USA
Maguire, Joseph — Navy Admiral
National Counterterrorism Center, 1505 Tysons McLean Blvd, McLean VA 22102, USA
Maguire, Les — Pianist (Gerry & the Pacemakers)
Barry Collins, 21A Cliftown Road, Southend-on-Sea, Essex SS1 1AB, England
Maguire, Michael — Actor, Singer
Epstein-Wyckoff, 280 S Beverly Blvd, #400, Beverly Hills CA 90212 USA
Maguire, Paul L — Sportscaster, Football Player
707 Ocean Blvd, Isle of Palms SC 29451, USA
Maguire, Richard W — Cinematographer
605 Summer Mesa Dr, Las Vegas NV 89144, USA
Maguire, Sean — Actor
Paul Kohner, 9300 Wilshire Blvd, #555, Beverly Hills CA 90212 USA
Maguire, Sharon — Director, Producer, Writer
United Talent Agency, 9336 Civic Center Dr, Beverly Hills CA 90210 USA
Maguire, Tobey — Actor
W M E Entertainment, 9601 Wilshire Blvd, #300, Beverly Hills CA 90210 USA
Maguire, Zak — Actor
A&J Mgmt, 242A The Ridgeway, Botany Bay, Enfield EN2 8AP, England
Mahaffey, John D, Jr — Golfer
594 Sawdust Road, #229, Spring TX 77380, USA
Mahaffey, Randolph (Randy) — Basketball Player
25 Berkeley Road, Avondale Estates GA 30002, USA
Mahaffey, Valerie — Actress
Innovative Artists, 1505 10th St, Santa Monica CA 90401 USA
Mahaffrey, Arthur (Art) — Baseball Player
PO Box 1212, Allentown PA 18105, USA
Mahal, Taj — Singer, Musician, Songwriter
Monterey International, 200 W Superior St, #202, Chicago IL 60654 USA
Mahalanabis, Dilip — Physician
Applied Studies Society, 108 Manicktata Main Road, Kolkata 700054, India
Mahalic, Drew A — Football Player
2114 W Sunset Dr, Portland OR 97239, USA
Mahama, John D — President, Ghana
President's Office, Golden Jubilee House, PO Box 1627, Accra, Ghana
Mahan, Hunter — Golfer
3316 Snowmass Lane, McKinney TX 75070, USA
Mahan, Lawrence (Larry) — Rodeo Rider
PO Box 119, Sunset TX 76270, USA
Mahan, Sean C — Football Player
4202 E 116th Place, Tulsa OK 74137, USA
Mahanthappa, Rudresh — Jazz Saxophonist, Composer
338 Prospect Place, #3J, Brooklyn NY 11238, USA
Mahar, Kevin — Baseball Player
2506 E Wheeler St, Midland MI 48642, USA
Maharidge, Dale D — Writer
Stanford University, Communications Dept, Stanford CA 94305, USA
Mahay, Ronald M (Ron) — Baseball Player
13177 E Cochise Road, Scottsdale AZ 85259, USA
Maher, Bill — Commentator, Comedian
Creative Artists Agency, 2000 Ave of Stars, #100, Los Angeles CA 90067 USA
Maher, Chris — Photographer
PO Box 5, Lambertville MI 48144, USA
Maher, Sean — Actor
S D B Partners, 1801 Ave of Stars, #902, Los Angeles CA 90067 USA
Mahinmi, Ian — Basketball Player
Indiana Pacers, Conseco Fieldhouse, 125 S Pennsylvania, Indianapolis IN 46204 USA
Mahler, Michael J (Mickey) — Baseball Player
7911 Quirt St, San Antonio TX 78227, USA
Mahohato Mohato Seeiso — Queen, Lesotho
Royal Palace, PO Box 524, Maseru 100, Lesotho
Maholm, Paul G — Baseball Player
518 Village Green Blvd W, Mars PA 16046, USA
Mahomes, Patrick L (Pat) — Baseball Player
1834 Ridgeline Road, Tyler TX 75703, USA
Mahon, Sean — Actor
Principal Entertainment, 1964 Westwood Blvd, #400, Los Angeles CA 90025 USA
Mahone, Ed — Boxer
Marvin Millett, 6548 Whitney Ave, Saint Louis MO 63133, USA
Mahoney, Brian C — Basketball Player
96 Greystone Road, Rockville Center NY 11570, USA
Mahoney, James T (Jim) — Baseball Player
345 Hawthorne Ave, #2, Hawthorne NJ 07506, USA
Mahoney, John — Actor
I C M Partners, 10250 Constellation Blvd, #900, Los Angeles CA 90067 USA
Mahoney, Margaret E — Foundation Executive
M E H Assoc, 421 5th Ave, #2010, New York NY 10016, USA
Mahoney, Maureen — Attorney
Latham & Watkins, 555 7th St NW, Washington DC 20004, USA
Mahoney, Mike — Baseball Player
4412 98th St, Urbandale IA 50322, USA
Mahoney, Roger — Cartoonist (Millie)
2 Sussex Cottages, Emsworth Common Road, Emsworth, Hampshire, England
Mahoney, Tim — Guitarist (311), Songwriter
311 Hive, 8904 Florence Dr, Omaha NE 68147, USA
Mahony, Roger Cardinal — Religious Leader
Archdiocese of Los Angeles, 3424 Wilshire Blvd, Los Angeles CA 90010, USA

Mahorn, Derrick A (Rick) — Basketball Player, Coach
44 Gordon Lane, East Hartford CT 06118, USA
Mahovlich, Francis W (Frank) — Ice Hockey Player
2-954 Ave Road, Toronto ON M5P 2K8, Canada
Mahovlich, Peter J (Pete) — Ice Hockey Player
116 Farr Lane, Queensbury NY 12804, USA
Mahr, Joe — Journalist
Toledo Blade, Editorial Dept, 541 N Superior St, Toledo OH 43660, USA
Mahre, Phillip (Phil) — Alpine Skier
1041 Red Sky Dr, Yakima WA 98903, USA
Mahre, Steve — Alpine Skier
1041 Red Sky Dr, Yakima WA 98903, USA
Mahumdi, Baghadadi al- — General Secretary, Libya
General Secretary's Office, Bab el Asiziya Barracks, Tripoli, Libya
Maida, Adam J Cardinal — Religious Leader
Archdiocese of Detroit, 1234 Washington Blvd, #1, Detroit MI 48226, USA
Maiden-Naccarato, Jeanne — Bowler
1 N Stadium Way, #4, Tacoma WA 98403, USA
Maier, Hermann — Alpine Skier
Reitdorf 106, 5542 Flachau, Austria
Maier, Mitchell W (Mitch) — Baseball Player
435 Amelia Circle, South Lyon MI 48178, USA
Maier, Pauline R — Historian
60 Larchwood Dr, Cambridge MA 02138, USA
Maier, Sepp — Soccer Player
Lindenstra 12, 85664 Hohenlinden, Germany
Maiga, Hamchetou — Basketball Player
Sacramento Monarchs, Arco Arena, 1 Sports Parkway, Sacramento CA 95834 USA
Maiga, Ousmane Issoufi — Prime Minister, Mali
Prime Minister's Office, BP 97, Bamako, Mali
Maikki, Susanna — Conductor
Ensemble Intercontemporain, 223 Ave Jean-Jaurès 75019 Paris, France
Mailhouse, Robert — Actor
Stone Manners Salners, 9911 W Pico Blvd, #1400, Los Angeles CA 90035 USA
Maillard, Carol — Singer (Sweet Honey in the Rock)
I C M Partners, 10250 Constellation Blvd, #900, Los Angeles CA 90067 USA
Main, Frank — Journalist
Chicago Sun-Times, Editorial Dept, 401 N Wabash Ave, Chicago IL 60611 USA
Main, Ravinder — Rheumatologist
Charing Cross Hospital, Saint Dunstan's Road, London W6 8RP, England
Maine, John K — Baseball Player
129 Richards Ferry Road, Fredericksburg VA 22406, USA
Maines, Natalie — Singer (Dixie Chicks)
Strategic Artist Mgmt, 1100 Glendon Ave, #1000, Los Angeles CA 90024, USA
Maino — Rap Artist
Hustle Hard Records, 1290 Ave of Americas, Concourse 3, New York NY 10104, USA
Mair, Adam — Ice Hockey Player
25 San Fernando Lane, East Amherst NY 14051, USA
Mairena, Oswaldo — Baseball Player
160 E 6th Place, Mesa AZ 85201, USA
Maisel, Harvey — Educator
University of Nebraska, Chancellor's Office, Lincoln NE 68588, USA
Maisel, Jay — Photographer
190 Bowery, New York NY 10012, USA
Maisenberg, Olega — Concert Pianist
In Der Gugl 9, 3400 Klosterneuburg, Austria
Maisky, Mischa M — Concert Cellist
138 Meerlaan, 1900 Overijse, Belgium
Maisuradze, Badri — Opera Singer
I M G Artists, Hogarth Business Park, Chiswick, London W4 2TH, England
Maitland, Beth — Actress
Epstein-Wyckoff, 280 S Beverly Dr, #400, Beverly Hills CA 90212 USA
Maiwenn — Actress, Director, Writer
Agence Artiste Adequet, 80 Rue d'Amsterdam, 75009 Paris, France
Majdarzavyn Ganzorig — Cosmonaut, Mongolia
Academy of Sciences, Peace Ave 54B, Ulan Bator 51, Mongolia
Majerle, Daniel L (Dan) — Basketball Player
4534 E Oregon Ave, Phoenix AZ 85018, USA
Majerus, Rick — Basketball Coach, Sportscaster
Saint Louis University, Athletic Dept, Saint Louis MO 63103, USA
Majewski, Gary W — Baseball Player
1103 Chamboard Lane, Houston TX 77018, USA
Majewski, Janusz — Director, Writer
Ul Forteczna 1A, 01 540 Warsaw, Poland
Majkowski, Donald V (Don) — Football Player
1593 Bayhill Dr, Duluth GA 30097, USA
Majoli, Iva — Tennis Player
International Mgmt Group, 1 Erieview Plaza, 1360 E 9th St, Cleveland OH 44114 USA
Major, Clarence L — Writer
University of California, English Dept, Voorhies Hall, Davis CA 95616, USA
Major, Jason — Actor, Writer
Principato-Young, 9465 Wilshire Blvd, #880, Beverly Hills CA 90212 USA
Major, John — Prime Minister, England
8 Stukeley Road, Huntingdon, Cambridgeshire PE29 6HQ, England
Major, Malvina L — Opera Singer
PO Box 11-175, Manners St, Te Aero, Wellington 6011, New Zealand
Major, Reema — Singer
Agency Group Ltd, 142 W 57th St, #600, New York NY 10019 USA
Majorino, Tina — Actress
Leverage Mgmt, 3030 Pennsylvania Ave, Santa Monica CA 90404 USA
Majors, John T (Johnny) — Football Player, Coach
4207 Beechwood Road, Knoxville TN 37920, USA
Majors, Lee — Actor
1831 Rocking Horse Dr, Simi Valley CA 93065, USA
Majumder, Shaun — Actor
Paradigm Agency, 360 N Crescent Dr, North Building, Beverly Hills CA 90210 USA

Makarov, Askold A — Ballet Dancer
Plutalova Str 18-4, 197136 Saint Petersburg, Russia
Makarov, Sergei M — Ice Hockey Player
4072 Teale Ave, San Jose CA 95117, USA
Makarova, Natalia R — Ballerina
Herbert Breslin, 119 W 57th St, #1505, New York NY 10019 USA
Makela, P Helena — Immunologist
National Public Health Service, Mannerheimintie 166, Helsinki, Finland
Makela, Wille — Curling Athlete
Curling Assn, Kalatorppa 2A62, 02230 Espoo, Finland
Makela-Nummela, Satu — Markswoman
Radiokatu 20, 00240 Helsinki, Finland
Makerov, Julie — Opera Singer
Columbia Artists Mgmt Inc, 1790 Broadway, #702, New York NY 10019 USA
Makhalina, Yulia V — Ballerina
Kirov Ballet Theater, 1 Pl Iskusstr, 190000 Saint Petersburg, Russia
Maki, Chico — Ice Hockey Player
Norfolk County Sports Hall of Fame, 95 Culver, Simcoe ON N3Y 2V5, Canada
Maki, Fumihiko — Pritzker Architectural Laureate
5-16-22 Higashi-Gotanda, Shinagawaku, Tokyo 141 0022, Japan
Makings, Elizabeth — Golfer
1500 N Markdale, #12, Mesa AZ 85201, USA
Makkena, Wendy — Actress
Schumacher Mgmt, 1122 San Vicente Blvd, Santa Monica CA 90402, USA
Mako, C Gene — Tennis Player
430 S Burnside Ave, #MC, Los Angeles CA 90036, USA
Makoare, Lawrence — Actor
Robert Bruce Agency, 218 Richmond Road, Grey Lynn, Auckland, New Zealand
Maksimova, Yekaterina S — Ballerina
Smolenskaya Naberezhnaya 5/13-62, 121099 Moscow, Russia
Maksudian, Michael B (Mike) — Baseball Player
12148 E San Simeon Dr, Scottsdale AZ 85259, USA
Maksymiuk, Jerzy — Conductor
Gdanska 2 m 14, 01 633 Warsaw, Poland
Maktoum, Mohammed bin Rashid Al — Prime Minister, United Arab Emirates
Prime Minister's Office, Manhal Palace, Abu Dhabi, United Arab Emirates
Malachi, Carolyn — Singer
Clarke & Assoc, 2020 Pennsylvania Ave NW, #271, Washington DC 20006, USA
Malahide, Patrick — Actor
I C M Partners, Marlborough House, 10 Earlham St, #300, London WC2H 9LNP, England
Malakhov, Vladimir I — Ice Hockey Player
PO Box 420536, Kissimmee FL 34742, USA
Malakian, Daron V — Singer, Guitarist (System of a Down)
Velvet Hammer Music, 9014 Melrose Ave, West Hollywood CA 90069, USA
Malamala, Siupeli — Football Player
122 110th Ave SE, Bellevue WA 98004, USA
Malandrino, Catherine — Fashion Designer
468 Bromme St, New York NY 10013, USA
Malarchuk, Clint — Ice Hockey Player
1308 Myers Dr, Gardnerville NV 89410, USA
Malaret Contreras, Marisol — Beauty Queen, Actress
Miss Universe Organization, 1370 Ave of Americas, #1600, New York NY 10019 USA
Malarkey, Donald G — WW II Army Hero
2233 Juneau Court S, Salem OR 97302, USA
Malaska, Mark — Baseball Player
3823 Cumberland Dr, Youngstown OH 44515, USA
Malchow, Tom — Swimmer
10220 NW Edgewood Dr, Portland OR 97229, USA
Malco, Romany — Actor
Principato-Young, 9465 Wilshire Blvd, #880, Beverly Hills CA 90212 USA
Malcom, Shirley M — Association Executive
Science Advancement Assn, 1200 New York Ave NW, Washington DC 20005, USA
Malcomson, Paula — Actress
I C M Partners, 10250 Constellation Blvd, #900, Los Angeles CA 90067 USA
Maldacena, Juan — Physicist
Harvard University, Physics Dept, Cambridge MA 02138, USA
Maldini, Paolo — Soccer Player
F C Milan, Via Filippo Turati 3, 20121 Milan, Italy
Maldonado, Candido (Candy) — Baseball Player
HC 2 Box 16800, Arecibo PR 00612, USA
Malee, Chompoo — Fashion Designer
Hino & Malee Inc, 3701 N Ravenswood Ave, Chicago IL 60613, USA
Maleeva, Katerina — Tennis Player
Mladostr 1, #45, NH 14, Sofia 1174, Bulgaria
Maleeva-Fragniere, Manuela — Tennis Player
Bourg-Dessous 28, 1814 La Tour de Peitz, Switzerland
Malek, Rami — Actor
W M E Entertainment, 9601 Wilshire Blvd, #300, Beverly Hills CA 90210 USA
Malenchenko, Yuri I — Cosmonaut
Cosmonaut Training Center, Star City, 141160 Zvezdny Gorodok, Moscow Oblast, Russia
Maler, James M (Jim) — Baseball Player
1758 NE 177th St, North Miami Beach FL 33162, USA
Malerba, Franco E — Astronaut
Italian Space Agency, Viale Liegi 26, 00198 Rome, Italy
Malfitano, Catherine — Opera Singer
I M G Artists, Burlington Lane, Chiswick, London W4 2TH, England
Malgarini, Ryan — Actor
Savage Agency, 6212 Banner Ave, Los Angeles CA 90038 USA
Malhotra, Manny — Ice Hockey Player
1210 Oakland Ave, Columbus OH 43212, USA
Malice — Rap Artist (Clipse)
American Talent Agency, 26 Finney Farm Road, Croton on Hudson NY 10520, USA
Malick, Terrence F — Director, Writer
Creative Artists Agency, 2000 Ave of Stars, #100, Los Angeles CA 90067 USA
Malick, Wendie — Actress, Model
Innovative Artists, 1505 10th St, Santa Monica CA 90401 USA

M

Malicki-Sanchez, Keram TalentWorks, 3500 W Olive Ave, #1400, Burbank CA 91505 USA	Actor
Malielegaoi, Tuila'epa L Sa'ilele Prime Minister's Office, PO Box L1861, Vailima, Apia, Samoa	Prime Minister, Samoa
Malignaggi, Paulie 1620 80th St, Brooklyn NY 11214, USA	Boxer
Malik, Art 18 Sydney Mews, London SW3 6HL, England	Actor
Malik, Marek 919 Anchorage Road, Tampa FL 33602, USA	Ice Hockey Player
Maliki, Nouri al- Prime Minister's Office, Karradat Mariam, Baghdad, Iraq	Prime Minister, Iraq
Malina, Joshua I F A Talent Agency, 8730 W Sunset Blvd, #490, West Hollywood CA 90069 USA	Actor
Malinchak, William J (Bill) 6422 NW 65th Way, Parkland FL 33067, USA	Football Player
Malini, Hema 17 Jai Hind Society, 12th Road Juhu Scheme, Mumbai MS 400049, India	Actress
Malinvaud, Edmond 42 Ave de Saxe, 75007 Paris, France	Economist
Maliponte, Adrianna Gorlinsky Promotions, 35 Darer, London W1, England	Opera Singer
Malizia, Mike 570 SE Southwood Trail, Stuart FL 34997, USA	Golfer
Malkin, Evgeni Pittsburgh Penguins, Consol Energy Center, 1001 5th Ave, Pittsburgh PA 15219 USA	Ice Hockey Player
Malkin, Max Skouras Agency, 1149 3rd St, #300, Santa Monica CA 90403, USA	Cinematographer
Malkmus, Robert E (Bobby) 400 Wallingford Terrace, Union NJ 07083, USA	Baseball Player
Malkovich, John Mr Mudd, 137 N Larchmont, Box 113, Los Angeles CA 90004, USA	Actor
Mallary, Robert PO Box 97, Conway MA 01341, USA	Sculptor
Mallette, Alfred J 7040 Quail Hill Road, Charlotte NC 28210, USA	Army General
Malley, Kenneth C 136 Riverside Road, Edgewater MD 21037, USA	Navy Admiral
Malley, M Matthew (Matt) Direct Mgmt, 947 N La Cienega Blvd, #G, West Hollywood CA 90069, USA	Bassist (Counting Crowes), Songwriter
Mallick, Don 42045 N Tilton Dr, Lancaster CA 93536, USA	Test Pilot
Mallicoat, Robbin D (Rob) 2050 SE Larson Court, Hillsboro OR 97123, USA	Baseball Player
Mallon, Meg 5105 N Ocean Blvd, #C, Boynton Beach FL 33435, USA	Golfer
Mallon, Thomas 801 25th St NW, Washington DC 20037, USA	Writer
Mallory, Brenda Julie Nelson Gallery, 1280 Iron Horse Dr, Park City UT 84060, USA	Artist
Mallory, Carole Pocket Books, 1230 Ave of Americas, New York NY 10020 USA	Actress
Mallory, Glynn C, Jr 19221 Heather Forest, San Antonio TX 78258, USA	Army General
Malloy, Edward A University of Notre Dame, President's Office, Notre Dame IN 46556, USA	Educator
Malloy, Tom Stone Manners Salners, 9911 W Pico Blvd, #1400, Los Angeles CA 90035 USA	Actor, Writer
Malo, Raul AristoMedia, 1620 16th Ave S, Nashville TN 37212, USA	Singer (Mavericks), Songwriter
Malone, Ben (Benny) 49 E Broadway Road, Tempe AZ 85282, USA	Football Player
Malone, Brendan Orlando Magic, 8701 Maitland Summit Blvd, Orlando FL 32810 USA	Basketball Coach
Malone, Charles R (Chuck) 310 Liberty St, Marked Tree AR 72365, USA	Baseball Player
Malone, James W Catholic Bishops Conference, 1312 Massachusetts Ave NW, Washington DC 20005, USA	Religious Leader
Malone, Jeffrey N (Jeff) 415 Lee Road 313, Smiths Station AL 36877, USA	Basketball Player
Malone, Jena Gersh Agency, 9465 Wilshire Blvd, #600, Beverly Hills CA 90212 USA	Actress
Malone, John C Liberty Media Corp, 12300 Liberty Blvd, Englewood CO 80112, USA	Businessman
Malone, Karl 105 W Charter St, Farmerville LA 71241, USA	Basketball Player
Malone, Kype D G C/Interscope Records, 2220 Colorado Ave, Santa Monica CA 90404, USA	Singer (TV on the Radio)
Malone, Maicel 4064 Bothwell Terrace, Tallahassee FL 32317, USA	Track Athlete
Malone, Mark M 850 W Adams St, #3F, Chicago IL 60607, USA	Football Player
Malone, Moses E 310 S Keswick Court, Sugar Land TX 77478, USA	Basketball Player
Malone, Nancy 8857 W Olympic Blvd, #201, Beverly Hills CA 90211, USA	Actress
Malone, Patricia Bruno Magli USA, 75 Triangle Blvd, Carlstadt NJ 07072, USA	Businesswoman
Malone, Ryan 5210 Terraceview Lane N, Minneapolis MN 55446, USA	Ice Hockey Player
Malone, Thomas F 275 Steele Road, #B504, West Hartford CT 06117, USA	Geophysicist
Malone, Wallace D, Jr SouthTrust Corp, 420 20th St N, Birmingham AL 35203, USA	Financier
Malone, William A P A Talent/Literary Agency, 405 S Beverly Dr, #300, Beverly Hills CA 90212 USA	Director

Malicki-Sanchez - Malone

Maloney, Dan — Ice Hockey Player, Coach, Executive
Sutton Group Realty, 241 Minet's Point Road, Barrie ON L4N 4C4, Canada
Maloney, David W (Dave) — Ice Hockey Player
122 Dolphin Cove Quay, Stamford CT 06902, USA
Maloney, Donald M (Don) — Ice Hockey Player, Executive
21 Guilford Lane, Greenwich CT 06831, USA
Maloney, James W (Jim) — Baseball Player
7027 N Teilman Ave, #102, Fresno CA 93711, USA
Maloney, Michael — Actor
Markham & Froggatt, Julian House, 4 Windmill St, London W1P 1HF, England
Maloney, William R — Marine Corps General
Navy Mutual Aid Assn, Henderson Hall, 29 Carpenter Road, Arlington VA 22214, USA
Malouf, David G J — Writer
Mobbs, 35A Sutherland Crescent, Darling Point, Sydney NSW 2027, Australia
Malsby, Lynn — Keyboardist (Klymaxx)
R D M J Entertainment Mgmt, 3619 Rose Ave, Long Beach CA 90807 USA
Maltbie, Roger — Golfer, Sportscaster
179 Longmeadow Dr, Los Gatos CA 95032, USA
Maltby, Kirk — Ice Hockey Player
58 Putnam Place, Grosse Pointe Shores MI 48236, USA
Maltby, Richard E, Jr — Lyricist, Director
200 E 89th St, #16B, New York NY 10128, USA
Malter, Arnold S — Attorney
301 N Lake Ave, #810, Pasadena CA 91101, USA
Malthouse, Matthew — Actor
Gavin Barker Assoc, 2D Wimpole St, London W1G 0EB, England
Maltin, Leonard — Film, TV Critic, Producer
10424 Whipple St, Toluca Lake CA 91602, USA
Maltzan, Michael — Architect
2801 Hyperion Ave, Los Angeles CA 90027, USA
Malyshev, Yuri V — Cosmonaut
Cosmonaut Training Center, Star City, 141160 Zvezdny Gorodok, Moscow Oblast, Russia
Malysz, Adam H — Ski Jumper
K S Wisla Ustronianka, ul Wyzwolenia 67, 43 460 Wisla, Poland
Malzone, Frank J — Baseball Player
16 Aletha Road, Needham MA 02492, USA
Mamby, Saoul — Boxer
20 W Mosholu Parkway S, #17, Bronx NY 10468, USA
Mamet, David A — Writer, Director
2 Northfield Plaza, #200, Northfield IL 60093, USA
Mamet, Zosia — Actress
United Talent Agency, 9336 Civic Center Dr, Beverly Hills CA 90210 USA
Mamula, Michael B (Mike) — Football Player
4 Ithan Woods Lane, Villanova PA 19085, USA
Manabe, Syukuro — Meteorologist
Princeton University, Atmospheric Sciences Dept, Princeton NJ 08540, USA
Manahan, George — Conductor
Columbia Artists Mgmt Inc, 1790 Broadway, #702, New York NY 10019 USA
Manakov, Gennadi M — Cosmonaut
Cosmonaut Training Center, Star City, 141160 Zvezdny Gorodok, Moscow Oblast, Russia
Manarov, Musa C — Cosmonaut
Khovanskeya 3, 129515 Moscow, Russia
Mancham, James R M — President, Seychelles
PO Box 29, Mahe, Seychelles
Manchester, Melissa — Singer, Songwriter
4915 Tyrone Ave, #123, Sherman Oaks CA 91423, USA
Manchevski, Milcho — Director
A P A Talent/Literary Agency, 405 S Beverly Dr, #300, Beverly Hills CA 90212 USA
Mancina, Mark — Composer
Gorfaine/Schwartz, 4111 W Alameda Ave, #509, Burbank CA 91505 USA
Mancini, Ray (Boom Boom) — Boxer, Actor
12524 Indianapolis St, Los Angeles CA 90066, USA
Mancuso, Frank G — Businessman
201 N Canon Dr, #328, Beverly Hills CA 90210, USA
Mancuso, Julia — Alpine Skier
US Ski Team, 1500 Kearns Blvd, #100, Park City UT 84060 USA
Mancuso, Nick — Actor
Law Talent Agency, 5 Ambleside Ave, Toronto ON M8Z 2H5, Canada
Mandabach, Caryn — Producer
Oxygen Media, 75 9th Ave, New York NY 10011, USA
Mandarich, Ante J (Tony) — Football Player
12767 E Altadena Dr, Scottsdale AZ 85259, USA
Mandel, Howie — Actor
Alvey Productions, 23679 Calabasas Road, #180, Calabasas CA 91302, USA
Mandel, Johnny — Composer
2401 Main St, Santa Monica CA 90405, USA
Mandel, Robert C — Director
I C M Partners, 10250 Constellation Blvd, #900, Los Angeles CA 90067 USA
Mandela, N Winnie Madikizela- — Social Activist
Orlando West, Soweto, Johannesburg 1804, South Africa
Mandela, Nelson R — President, South Africa; Nobel Laureate
Private Bag X70000, Houghton 2041, South Africa
Mandella, Richard E — Thoroughbred Racing Trainer
285 W Huntington Dr, Arcadia CA 91007, USA
Mandelstam, Stanley — Physicist
1800 Spruce St, Berkeley CA 94709, USA
Manderino, Joey — Actor, Comedian, Writer
Creative Artists Agency, 2000 Ave of Stars, #100, Los Angeles CA 90067 USA
Manders, David F (Dave) — Football Player
1504 Silverlake Road, McKinney TX 75070, USA
Mandler, George — Psychologist
1406 La Jolla Knoll, La Jolla CA 92037, USA
Mandler, Jean M — Psychologist
1406 La Jolla Knoll, La Jolla CA 92037, USA
Mandley, William H (Pete) — Football Player
103 E Smoke Tree Road, Gilbert AZ 85296, USA

Mandlikova, Hana — Tennis Player
Octagon Worldwide, 1751 Pinnacle Dr, #1500, McLean VA 22102 USA
Mandoki, Luis — Director
Paradigm Agency, 360 N Crescent Dr, North Building, Beverly Hills CA 90210 USA
Mandrell, Barbara — Singer, Actress
2020 Fieldstone Parkway, Franklin TN 37069, USA
Mandrell, Erline — Singer
544 W Main St, Gallatin TN 37066, USA
Mandrell, Louise — Singer
Mandrell Inc, 1101 Hunters Lane, Ashland City TN 37015, USA
Mandvi, Aasif — Actor, Writer
I C M Partners, 10250 Constellation Blvd, #900, Los Angeles CA 90067 USA
Mandylor, Costas — Actor
Kritzer Levine Wilkins Griffin, 11872 La Grange Ave, #100, Los Angeles CA 90025 USA
Mane, Gucci — Rap Artist
Susan Blond Inc, 50 W 57th St, #1400, New York NY 10019 USA
Manea, Marius — Opera Singer
I M G Artists, Hogarth Business Park, Chiswick, London W4 2TH, England
Manea, Norman — Writer
201 W 70th St, #101, New York NY 10023, USA
Manery, Randy — Ice Hockey Player
6587 Garrett Road, Buford GA 30518, USA
Manetti, Larry — Actor
Epstein-Wyckoff, 280 S Beverly Dr, #400, Beverly Hills CA 90212 USA
Manfredi, Michael — Architect, Sculpter
Weiss/Manfredi, 130 W 29th St, #1200, New York NY 10001, USA
Manfredini, Harry — Composer
Soundtrack Music, 2229 Cloverfield Blvd, Santa Monica CA 90405, USA
Manganiello, Joe — Actor
Creative Artists Agency, 2000 Ave of Stars, #100, Los Angeles CA 90067 USA
Mangels, Andy — Writer
PO Box 3226, Portland OR 97208, USA
Mangelsdorf, David — Geneticist
Salk Institute, 10100 N Torrey Pines Road, La Jolla CA 92037 USA
Mangieri, Dino M — Football Player
108 Lamport Blvd, #3C, Staten Island NY 10305, USA
Mangione, Chuck — Jazz Trumpeter, Composer
Gates Music, 23 W 73rd St, #915, New York NY 10023, USA
Mangold, James — Director, Producer, Writer
Tree Line Films, 1708 Berkeley St, Santa Monica CA 90404, USA
Mangold, Nick — Football Player
361 Shunpike Road, Chatham NJ 07928, USA
Mangold, Sylvia P — Artist
1 Bull Road, Washingtonville NY 10992, USA
Mangrum, James L (Jim Dandy) — Singer (Black Oak Arkansas)
Lustig Talent, PO Box 770850, Orlando FL 32877 USA
Mangual, Jose M (Pepe) — Baseball Player
2325 Calle Tabonuco, Ponce PR 00716, USA
Mangue Gonzalez, Marta — Handball Player
Z R K Zajecar, Dositejeva 11, 19000 Zajecar, Serbia
Mangum, John W, Jr — Football Player
150 Summerwood Dr, Pearl MS 39208, USA
Mangum, Kristofer T (Kris) — Football Player
16720 Krishna Lane, Charlotte NC 28277, USA
Manh, Nong Duc — General Secretary, Vietnam
General's Secretary Office, Hoang Hoa Tham St, Hanoi, Vietnam
Manheim, Camryn — Actress
United Talent Agency, 9336 Civic Center Dr, Beverly Hills CA 90210 USA
Maniago, Cesare — Ice Hockey Player
19-788 Citadel Dr, Port Coquitlam BC V3C 6G9, Canada
Maniatis, Thomas P — Genetics Engineer, Molecular Biologist
Harvard University, Biochemistry Dept, 7 Divinity St, Cambridge MA 02138, USA
Manigault-Stallworth, Omarosa — Actress
Don Buchwald/Fortitude, 6500 Wilshire Blvd, #2200, Los Angeles CA 90048 USA
Manilow, Barry — Singer, Songwriter
Stiletto Entertainment, 8295 S LaCienega Blvd, Inglewood CA 90301, USA
Manion, Daniel A — Judge
US Court of Appeals, 204 S Main St, South Bend IN 46601, USA
Maniscalco, Sebastian — Actor, Comedian
Levity Entertainment Group, 6701 Center Drive W, #1111, Los Angeles CA 90045, USA
Manji, Rizwan — Actor
Don Buchwald/Fortitude, 6500 Wilshire Blvd, #2200, Los Angeles CA 90048 USA
Mankell, Henning — Writer
Leopard Forlag AB, Paulsgatan 11, 118 46 Stockholm, Sweden
Mankins, Logan L — Football Player
1 Mockingbird Lane, North Attleboro MA 02760, USA
Mankiw, N Gregory — Government Official, Economist
45 Chestnut St, Wellesley MA 02481, USA
Mankoff, Robert — Cartoonist
New Yorker, Editorial Dept, 4 Times Square, Basement C1B, New York NY 10036 USA
Mankowski, Philip A (Phil) — Baseball Player
2280 Southwestern Blvd, Buffalo NY 14224, USA
Manley, Christopher — Cinematographer
Sheldon Prosnit Agency, 800 S Robertson Blvd, Los Angeles CA 90035, USA
Manley, Dexter — Football Player
2350 Atascocita Road, Humble TX 77396, USA
Manley, Elizabeth — Figure Skater
Marco Enterprises, 74830 Velie Dr, #A, Palm Desert CA 92260, USA
Manlove, William B (Bill), Jr — Football Coach
Delaware Valley College, Athletic Dept, 700 East Butler Ave, Doylestown PA 18901, USA
Mann, Aimee — Singer ('Til Tuesday); Songwriter
SuperEgo Records, 511 Ave of Americas, #197, New York NY 10011, USA
Mann, Barry — Composer
1010 Laurel Way, Beverly Hills CA 90210, USA
Mann, Byron — Actor
Metropolitan Talent Agency, 7020 La Presa Dr, Los Angeles CA 90068 USA

Mann, Carol A 6 Cape Chestnut Dr, Spring TX 77381, USA	Golfer
Mann, Charles 1518 Night Shade Court, Vienna VA 22182, USA	Football Player
Mann, Claude Artmedia, 20 Ave Rapp, 75007 Paris, France	Actor
Mann, Cuonzo 111 Wiggins St, #8, West Lafayette IN 47906, USA	Basketball Player
Mann, Danny Danis Panaro Nist, 9201 W Olympic Blvd, Beverly Hills CA 90212 USA	Actor
Mann, David W 10550 S 200 W, Columbia City IN 46725, USA	Religious Leader
Mann, Dick American Motorcycle Assn, 13515 Yarmouth Dr, Pickerington OH 43147 USA	Motorcycle Racing Rider
Mann, Errol D 5521 Bonanza Place, Missoula MT 59808, USA	Football Player
Mann, Gabriel A P A Talent/Literary Agency, 405 S Beverly Dr, #300, Beverly Hills CA 90212 USA	Actor, Model
Mann, H Thompson 34 Titcomb St, #2, Newburyport MA 1950, USA	Swimmer
Mann, James (Jim) 197 N Franklin St, Holbrook MA 02343, USA	Baseball Player
Mann, John W Mosiac Media Group, 9200 W Sunset Blvd, #1000, Los Angeles CA 90069 USA	Actor
Mann, Kelly J 1335 Franklin St, #4, Santa Monica CA 90404, USA	Baseball Player
Mann, Kristen C Washington Mystics, Verizon Center, 401 9th St NW, #750, Washington DC 20004 USA	Basketball Player
Mann, Leslie Creative Artists Agency, 2000 Ave of Stars, #100, Los Angeles CA 90067 USA	Actress
Mann, Manfred E M I Records, 43 Brook Green, London W6 7EF, England	Keyboardist
Mann, Michael K Forward Pass, 12233 W Olympic Blvd, #340, Los Angeles CA 90064, USA	Producer, Director
Mann, Nieko C E S D, 10635 Santa Monica Blvd, #130, Los Angeles CA 90025 USA	Actress
Mann, Shelley I 1301 S Scott St, #638S, Arlington VA 22204, USA	Swimmer
Mann, Terrance V 138 W 118th St, #2, New York NY 10026, USA	Actor, Director
Mann, Thomas E Brookings Institute, 1775 Massachusetts Ave NW, Washington DC 20036 USA	Political Scientist
Mannelly, J Patrick 1128 Kildare Ave, Libertyville IL 60048, USA	Football Player
Manning Mims, Madeline 7477 E 48th St, #83-4, Tulsa OK 74145, USA	Track Athlete
Manning, Daniel R (Danny) 205 Running Ridge Road, Lawrence KS 66049, USA	Basketball Player
Manning, Dennis J Guardian Life Insurance, 7 Hanover Square, New York NY 10004, USA	Businessman
Manning, Donald Fast Lane International, 4856 Haygood Road, #200, Virginia Beach VA 23455, USA	Singer (Abyssinians)
Manning, E Archie, III 1420 1st St, New Orleans LA 70130, USA	Football Player, Sportscaster
Manning, Elisha N (Eli) 1500 Hudson St, #1000, Hoboken NJ 07030, USA	Football Player
Manning, James B (Jim) 41 Fox Run Dr, Weaverville NC 28787, USA	Baseball Player
Manning, Jane 2 Wilton Square, London N1 3DL, England	Opera Singer
Manning, Linford Fast Lane International, 4856 Haygood Road, #200, Virginia Beach VA 23455, USA	Singer (Abyssinians)
Manning, Paul C British Cycling Centre, Stuart St, Manchester M11 4DQ, England	Cyclist
Manning, Peyton W Denver Broncos, 13655 E Broncos Parkway, Englewood CO 80112 USA	Football Player
Manning, Richard (Ricky), Jr Oakland Raiders, 1220 Harbor Bay Parkway, Alameda CA 94502 USA	Football Player
Manning, Richard E (Rick) 22447 N 49th Place, Phoenix AZ 85054, USA	Baseball Player
Manning, Rob Jet Propulsion Laboratory, 4800 Oak Grove Dr, Pasadena CA 91109 USA	Space Engineer
Manning, Taryn A P A Talent/Literary Agency, 405 S Beverly Dr, #300, Beverly Hills CA 90212 USA	Singer (Boomkat), Actress
Manningham, Mario C San Francisco 49ers, 4949 Centennial Blvd, Santa Clara CA 95054 USA	Football Player
Mannion, Pace S 4190 Achilles Dr, Salt Lake City UT 84124, USA	Basketball Player
Manoff, Dinah TalentWorks, 3500 W Olive Ave, #1400, Burbank CA 91505 USA	Actress
Manojlovic, Miki Artmedia, 20 Ave Rapp, 75007 Paris, France	Actor
Manon, Julio 4726 15th Ave S, Saint Petersburg FL 33711, USA	Baseball Player
Manor, Brison 3 Campden Hill Road, Sherwood AR 72120, USA	Football Player
Manos, James, Jr James Manos Jr Productions, 215 W 6th St, #PH-15, Los Angeles CA 90014, USA	Producer, Director, Writer
Manoux, J P Bauman Redanty Shaul Agency, 5757 Wilshire Blvd, #473, Los Angeles CA 90036 USA	Actor
Mansell, Clinton D (Clint) First Artists, 1631 N Bristol St, #B20, Santa Ana CA 92706 USA	Composer
Mansell, Kevin Kohl's Corp, N56W17000 Ridgewood Dr, Menomonee Falls WI 53051, USA	Businessman
Mansell, Nigel Old House Farm, North Dean, High Wycombe, Bucks HP14 4NL, England	Auto Racing Driver

M

Manser, Michael J — Architect
Manser Practice, Hammersmith Bridge, London W6 9DA, England
Mansfield, E Von — Football Player
1711 Lynwood Court, Flossmoor IL 60422, USA
Mansfield, Peter — Nobel Medicine Laureate
Nottingham University, Physics Dept, Nottingham NG7 2RD, England
Manson, Dave — Ice Hockey Player
Dallas Stars, 2601 Ave of Stars, #100, Frisco TX 75034 USA
Manson, Marilyn — Singer (Marilyn Manson)
Creative Artists Agency, 2000 Ave of Stars, #100, Los Angeles CA 90067 USA
Manson, Shirley — Singer (Garbage), Actress
Untitled Entertainment, 350 S Beverly Dr, #200, Beverly Hills CA 90212 USA
Mansouri, Lotfi — Director
San Francisco Opera House, 301 Van Ness Ave, San Francisco CA 94102, USA
Mantalis, George — Singer (Four Coins)
309 Winners Circle, Canonsburg PA 15317, USA
Mantee, Paul — Actor
PO Box 687, Malibu CA 90265, USA
Mantegna, Joe — Actor
I C M Partners, 10250 Constellation Blvd, #900, Los Angeles CA 90067 USA
Mantei, Matthew B (Matt) — Baseball Player
4709 Chicago Path, Stevensville MI 49127, USA
Mantel, Hilary M — Writer
A M Heath, 79 Saint Martin's Lane, London WC2N 4AA, England
Mantello, Joe — Director
Creative Artists Agency, 2000 Ave of Stars, #100, Los Angeles CA 90067 USA
Mantha, Moe — Ice Hockey Player
1538 Scio Ridge Road, Ann Arbor MI 48103, USA
Mantilla, Felix — Baseball Player
6973 N Tacoma St, Milwaukee WI 53224, USA
Mantis, Nick — Basketball Player
1344 Autumn Dr, Crown Point IN 46307, USA
Mantle, Anthony Dod — Cinematography
I C M Partners, 10250 Constellation Blvd, #900, Los Angeles CA 90067 USA
Manto, Jeffrey P (Jeff) — Baseball Player
725 Radcliffe St, Bristol PA 19007, USA
Mantooth, Randolph — Actor
6210 Rodgerton Dr, Los Angeles CA 90068, USA
Mantreola, Patricia — Singer, Model, Actress
B M G, 1540 Broadway, #9E, New York NY 10036, USA
Mantz, Michael — Astronaut
1940 Elanita Dr, San Pedro CA 90732, USA
Mantzoukas, Jason — Actor, Writer
United Talent Agency, 9336 Civic Center Dr, Beverly Hills CA 90210 USA
Manuel, Barry P — Baseball Player
805 Oak St, Mamou LA 70554, USA
Manuel, Charles F (Chuck) — Baseball Player, Manager
1496 Mira Vista Circle, Weston FL 33327, USA
Manuel, Jerry — Baseball Player, Manager
5556 Ridge Park Dr, Loomis CA 95650, USA
Manuel, Lionel — Football Player
827 E Cedar Dr, Chandler AZ 85249, USA
Manuel, Marquand A — Football Player
3672 Churchill Downs Dr, Davie FL 33328, USA
Manuelidis, Laura — Neuropathologist
Yale University Medical School, Neuropathology Dept, New Haven CT 06520, USA
Manumaleuna, Brandon M — Football Player
1218 Koleeta Dr, Harbor City CA 90710, USA
Manusky, Gregory (Greg) — Football Player
11537 Willow Springs Dr, Zionsville IN 46077, USA
Manuwai, Vince K — Football Player
4495 Ecton Lane E, Jacksonville FL 32246, USA
Manwaring, Kurt D — Baseball Player
20 Prospect Ridge, Horseheads NY 14845, USA
Manx, Harry — Singer, Guitar Player
Agency Group Ltd, 142 W 57th St, #600, New York NY 10019 USA
Manz, Wolfgang — Concert Pianist
Pasteuralle 55, 30655 Hanover, Germany
Manzanero, Armando — Singer
Pro Art, Paz Soldan 170, #903, San Isidro, Lima 27, Peru
Manzanillo, Josias (Jose) — Baseball Player
274 Kennebec St, Mattapan MA 02126, USA
Manzano, Leonel (Leo) — Track Athlete
Lenihan Group, 3915 Rockledge Dr, Austin TX 78731, USA
Manzarek, Ray — Keyboardist (Doors)
1145 Hedgeside Ave, Napa CA 94558, USA
Manzi, Catello — Harness Racing Driver
1 Hickory Lane, Freehold NJ 07728, USA
Manzi, Rocco — Harness Racing Executive
112 Willow Meadow Way, Oneida NY 13421, USA
Manzie, Jim — Composer
649 Platt Circle, El Dorado Hills CA 95762, USA
Manzini, Antonio — Actor
Carol Levi Mgmt, Via G Pisanelli 2, 00196 Rome, Italy
Manzoni, Giacomo — Composer
Viale Papiniano 31, 20123 Milan, Italy
Maple, Edward R (Eddie) — Thoroughbred Racing Jockey
Rose Hill Plantation Boarding Center, 1 Rose Hill Dr, Bluffton SC 29910, USA
Maples, David — Producer, Writer
Manage-Ment, 1103 1/2 Glendon Ave, Los Angeles CA 90024, USA
Mara, Kate — Actress
United Talent Agency, 9336 Civic Center Dr, Beverly Hills CA 90210 USA
Mara, Mary — Actress
Greene Assoc, 1901 Ave of Stars, #130, Los Angeles CA 90067 USA
Mara, Paul — Ice Hockey Player
500 Commercial St, #D, Boston MA 02109, USA

Manser - Mara

Mara, Rooney — Actress
W M E Entertainment, 9601 Wilshire Blvd, #300, Beverly Hills CA 90210 USA
Marais, Jessica — Actress
United Talent Agency, 9336 Civic Center Dr, Beverly Hills CA 90210 USA
Marak, Paul P — Baseball Player
1211 Comanche Trail, Alamogordo NM 88310, USA
Maramorosch, Karl — Entomologist
1050 George St, New Brunswick NJ 08901, USA
Maran, Josie — Model, Actress
Global Creative, 1051 N Cole Ave, #B, Los Angeles CA 90038, USA
Maraniss, David — Journalist
Washington Post, Editorial Dept, 1150 15th St NW, Washington DC 20071, USA
Maratos-Flier, Elfetheria — Geneticist
Joslin Diabetes Center, 1 Joslin Place, Boston MA 02215, USA
Marber, Patrick — Writer
Judy Daish Assoc, 2 Saint Charles Place, London W10 6EG, England
Marbley, Harlan — Boxer
6113 Parkview Lane, Clinton MD 20735, USA
Marboeuf, Julie — Actress
Intertalent, 48 Rue Gay Lussac, 75005 Paris, France
Marbury, Stephon X — Basketball Player
4 Sycamore Court, Purchase NY 10577, USA
Marc 7 — Rap Artist
Vision Entertainment Group, 1100 Glendon Ave, #1100, Los Angeles CA 90024, USA
Marc, Alessandra — Opera Singer
Clarisse B Kampel Foundation, 330 E 63rd St, New York NY 10065, USA
Marceau, Sophie — Actress
Special Artists Agency, 9465 Wilshire Blvd, #820, Beverly Hills CA 90212 USA
Marcell, Joseph — Actor
Markham & Froggatt, Julian House, 4 Windmill St, London W1P 1HF, England
Marcello, Vince — Director, Writer, Actor
Gersh Agency, 9465 Wilshire Blvd, #600, Beverly Hills CA 90212 USA
March, Jane — Actress, Model
International Talent Mgmt, 31 Harley St, London W1G 9QS, England
March, Little Peggy — Singer
Cape Entertainment, 8432 NW 31st Court, Sunrise FL 33351, USA
March, Stephanie — Actress
Gersh Agency, 9465 Wilshire Blvd, #600, Beverly Hills CA 90212 USA
Marchal, Olivier — Actor, Director
Artmedia, 20 Ave Rapp, 75007 Paris, France
Marchand, Guy — Actor
Voyez Mon Agent, 20 Ave Rapp, 75007 Paris, France
Marchant, Todd — Ice Hockey Player
10448 Caribou Way, Tustin CA 92782, USA
Marchetti, Gino J — Football Player
324 Devon Way, West Chester PA 19380, USA
Marchibroda, Theodore J (Ted) — Football Player, Coach, Executive
90 Orchard Point Dr, Weems VA 22576, USA
Marchionne, Sergio — Businessman
Fiat SpA, Via Nizza 250, 10126 Turin, Italy
Marchisano, Francesco Cardinal — Religious Leader
Cancelleria Apostolica Palazzo, Piazza Cancelleria 1, 00186 Rome, Italy
Marchlewski, Frank C — Football Player
428 Toledo Dr, New Kensington PA 15068, USA
Marchment, Bryan — Ice Hockey Player
San Jose Sharks, San Jose Arena, 525 W Santa Clara St, San Jose CA 95113 USA
Marchuk, Guri I — Applied Mathematician
Numerical Mathematics Institute, Gubkin Str 8, 117333 Moscow, Russia
Marchuk, Yevhen K — Prime Minister, Ukraine; General
Verkovna Rada, M Hrushevskoho Str 5, 252008 Kiev, Ukraine
Marciano, David — Actor
Don Buchwald/Fortitude, 6500 Wilshire Blvd, #2200, Los Angeles CA 90048 USA
Marcikic, Ivan — Physicist, Inventor (Unbreakable Codes)
Geneva University, 24 Rue du General Dufour, 1211 Geneva 4, Switzerland
Marcil, Vanessa — Actress
Paradigm Agency, 360 N Crescent Dr, North Building, Beverly Hills CA 90210 USA
Marcinkiewicz, Kazimierz — Prime Minister, Poland
European Bank for Reconstruction/Development, 1 Exchange Square, London EC2A 2JN, England
Marcis, Dave — Auto Racing Driver
Marcis Auto Racing, PO Box 645, Skyland NC 28776, USA
Marciulionis, R Sarunas — Basketball Player
Hotel Sarunas, Raitininku St 4, 2051 Vilnius, Lithuania
Marcol, Czeslaw C (Chester) — Football Player
PO Box 94, Dollar Bay MI 49922, USA
Marcon, Andre — Actor
Artmedia, 20 Ave Rapp, 75007 Paris, France
Marcos, Imelda R — First Lady, Philippines
Leyte Providencia Dept, Tolosa Leyte, Philippines
Marcotte, Don — Ice Hockey Player
12 Cote St, Amesbury MA 01913, USA
Marcovicci, Andrea — Actress, Singer
Bauman Redanty Shaul Agency, 5757 Wilshire Blvd, #473, Los Angeles CA 90036 USA
Marcum, Art — Writer
Creative Artists Agency, 2000 Ave of Stars, #100, Los Angeles CA 90067 USA
Marcum, Joseph L — Financier
609 Lake Dr, Vero Beach FL 32963, USA
Marcum, Shaun M — Baseball Player
1413 Jill Lane, Excelsior Springs MO 64024, USA
Marcus Schaffer, Jackie — Producer, Director, Writer
United Talent Agency, 9336 Civic Center Dr, Beverly Hills CA 90210 USA
Marcus, Bernard — Businessman
Home Depot Inc, 2455 Paces Ferry Road SE, Atlanta GA 30339, USA
Marcus, Egerton — Boxer
Atlas Boxing Centre, 849 Saint Clair Ave W, Toronto ON M6C 1C1, Canada
Marcus, Jurgen — Singer
Pestalozzistr 23A, 80469 Munich, Germany

M

Marcus, Ken — Photographer
Ken Marcus Studio, 6916 Melrose Ave, Los Angeles CA 90038, USA
Marcus, Rudolph A — Nobel Chemistry Laureate
331 S Hill Ave, Pasadena CA 91106, USA
Marcus, Stanley — Judge
US Court of Appeals, 36 NE 1st St, #300, Miami FL 33132, USA
Marcus, Trula M — Actress
Artists Agency, 1180 S Beverly Dr, #301, Los Angeles CA 90035 USA
Marcy, Geoffrey W (Geoff) — Astronomer
University of California, Astronomy Dept, Berkeley CA 94720, USA
Mardall, Cyril L — Architect
5 Boyne Terrace Mews, London W11 3LR, England
Marden, Brice — Artist
6 Saint Lukes Place, New York NY 10014, USA
Marden, Matthew — Actor
Mosiac Media Group, 9200 W Sunset Blvd, #1000, Los Angeles CA 90069 USA
Mardones, Benny — Singer
Tony Cee, PO Box 410, Utica NY 13503, USA
Mare, Olindo F — Football Player
106 Wescoe Dr, Mooresville NC 28117, USA
Maree, Sydney — Track Athlete
2 Braxton Road, Bryn Mawr PA 19010, USA
Maren, Jerry — Actor
PO Box 90010, San Diego CA 92169, USA
Marentette, Leo J — Baseball Player
33606 Beechwood St, Westland MI 48185, USA
Maretska, Maria — Sculptor
730 W 14th St, Medford OR 97501, USA
Margaglio, Maurizio — Ice Dancer
Ice Sports Federation, Via Piransi 44B, 20137 Milan, Italy
Margarito Montiel, Antonio — Boxer
Top Rank Inc, 3908 Howard Hughes Parkway, #580, Las Vegas NV 89169 USA
Margera, Brandon C (Bam) — Actor, Skateboarder
PO Box 671, Westtown PA 19395, USA
Margerum, Kenneth (Ken) — Football Player
494 Riverview Dr, Capitola CA 95010, USA
Margiela, Martin — Fashion Designer
Maison Martin Margiela, 163 Rue Saint Maur, 75011 Paris, France
Margison, Richard — Opera Singer
George Martynuk, 352 7th Ave, New York NY 10001, USA
Margo, Philip — Singer, Pianist, Drummer (Tokens)
American Mgmt, 19948 Mayall St, Chatsworth CA 91311, USA
Margolin, Phillip M — Writer, Actor
United Talent Agency, 9336 Civic Center Dr, Beverly Hills CA 90210 USA
Margolin, Stuart — Actor
House of Representatives, 1434 6th St, #1, Santa Monica CA 90401 USA
Margolis, Cindy — Model, Actress
12711 Ventura Blvd, #400, Studio City CA 91604, USA
Margolis, Laura — Actress
Artists Mgmt, 1119 Colorado Ave, #12, Santa Monica CA 90401, USA
Margolis, Lawrence S — Judge
US Claims Court, 717 Madison Place NW, Washington DC 20439, USA
Margolis, Mark — Actor
Abrams Artists, 9200 W Sunset Blvd, #1125, West Hollywood CA 90069 USA
Margolyes, Miriam — Actress
United Agents, 12-26 Lexington St, London W1F 0LE, England
Margon, Bruce H — Astronomer
University of Washington, Astronomy Dept, PO Box 351580, Seattle WA 98195, USA
Margoneri, Joseph E (Joe) — Baseball Player
341 Turkeytown Road, West Newton PA 15089, USA
Margoyles, Miriam — Actress
Innovative Artists, 1505 10th St, Santa Monica CA 90401 USA
Margrave, John L — Chemist
4511 Vrone, Bellaire TX 77401, USA
Margrethe II — Queen, Denmark
Amalienborg Palace, 1257 Copenhagen K, Denmark
Margulies, Donald — Writer
Yale University, English Dept, New Haven CT 06520, USA
Margulies, James H (Jimmy) — Editorial Cartoonist
Hackensack Record, Editorial Dept, 150 River St, Hackensack NJ 07601, USA
Margulies, Julianna L — Actress
W M E Entertainment, 9601 Wilshire Blvd, #300, Beverly Hills CA 90210 USA
Maria Teresa — Grand Duchess Consort, Luxembourg
Palais Grand-Ducal, 17 Rue du Marche-aux-Herbes, 1728 Luxembourg-Ville, Luxembourg
Mariam, Mengistu Haile — President, Ethiopia; Army General
PO Box 1536, Gunhill Enclave, Harare, Zimbabwe
Marianelli, Dario — Composer
Air Edel, 8687 Melrose Ave, #900, Los Angeles CA 90069 USA
Mariani, Carlo M — Artist
117 W 171st St, #12E, New York NY 10023, USA
Mariano, Jarah — Model
I M G Models, 304 Park Ave S, #PH-North, New York NY 10010 USA
Mariategui Chiappe, Sandro — Prime Minister, Peru
Ave Ramirez Gaston 375, Miraflores, Lima, Peru
Marichal, Juan A S — Baseball Player
9458 NW 54th Doral Circle Lane, Doral FL 33178, USA
Marie — Princess, Liechtenstein
Schloss Vaduz, 9490 Vaduz, Liechtenstein
Marie, Constance — Actress
C E S D, 10635 Santa Monica Blvd, #130, Los Angeles CA 90025 USA
Marimow, William K — Journalist
777 S Broad St, #214, Philadelphia PA 19147, USA
Marin, Carlos — Singer (Il Divo)
Octagon, 81-83 Fulham High St, London SW6 3JW, England
Marin, John W (Jack) — Basketball Player
3909 Regent Road, Durham NC 27707, USA

M

Marin, Maguy 10 Blvd de Lattre de Tassigny, 69143 Rillieux-la-Pape Cedex, France	Choreographer
Marin, Richard A (Cheech) Chicano Collection, 923 E 3rd St, #203, Los Angeles CA 90013, USA	Actor, Comedian (Cheech & Chong)
Marinaro, Edward F (Ed) Amsel Eisenstadt Frazier, 5055 Wilshire Blvd, #865, Los Angeles CA 90036 USA	Actor, Football Player
Marinca, Anamaria Conway Van Gelder Grant, 8-12 Broadwick St, #300, London W1F 8HW, England	Actress
Marinelli, Rod Chicago Bears, 1000 Football Dr, Lake Forest IL 60045 USA	Football Coach
Marini, Gilles S D B Partners, 1801 Ave of Stars, #902, Los Angeles CA 90067 USA	Actor, Model
Marinin, Maxim V Skating Federation, Luznetskaya Nabererhnya 8, 119871 Moscow, Russia	Figure Skater
Marino, Cathy 6313 Willowdale Dr, Plano TX 75093, USA	Golfer
Marino, Daniel C (Dan), Jr 3415 Stallion Lane, Weston FL 33331, USA	Football Player, Sportscaster
Marino, Ken A P A Talent/Literary Agency, 405 S Beverly Dr, #300, Beverly Hills CA 90212 USA	Actor
Marino, Peter 150 E 58th St, #3600, New York NY 10155, USA	Architect
Mario Sony Records, 2100 Colorado Ave, Santa Monica CA 90404 USA	Singer, Actor
Mario, Ernest 20 Greenhouse Dr, Princeton NJ 08540, USA	Businessman, Pharmacist
Marion, Brock E 10 NW 42nd St, Ocala FL 34475, USA	Football Player
Marion, Frank N 15920 SW 99th Court, Miami FL 33157, USA	Football Player
Marion, Fred D 10032 Oak Quarry Dr, Orlando FL 32832, USA	Football Player
Marion, Shawn D 5434 E Cannon Dr, Paradise Valley AZ 85253, USA	Basketball Player
Mariotti, Ray Austin American-Statesman, Editor's Office, 166 E Riverside, Austin TX 78704, USA	Editor
Marisol 427 Washington St, #700, New York NY 10013, USA	Sculptor
Mariucci, Steve 15940 Romita Court, Monte Sereno CA 95030, USA	Football Coach, Sportscaster
Mariye, Lily C E S D, 10635 Santa Monica Blvd, #130, Los Angeles CA 90025 USA	Actress
Mariza Musicas do Mundo, Rua Dalmprensa Nacional, #34, 1250 126 Lisbon, Portugal	Singer
Marjanovic, Zana Troika, 74 Clerkenwell Road, #300, London EC1M 5QA, England	Actress
Mark, Hans M 1715 Scenic Dr, Austin TX 78703, USA	Government Official, Physicist, Educator
Mark, Heidi 8730 W Sunset Blvd, #270, West Hollywood CA 90069, USA	Actress, Model
Mark, Mary Ellen Mary Ellen Mark Library, 134 Spring St, #502, New York NY 10012, USA	Photographer
Markakis, Nicholas W (Nick) 949 E Piney Hill Road, Monkton MD 21111, USA	Baseball Player
Markarian, Andranik N Prime Minister's Office, Ul Nalbandyyrna 32, 375010 Yerevan, Armenia	Prime Minister, Armenia
Marker, Laurie Cheetah Conservation Fund, PO Box 1380, Ojai CA 93024, USA	Animal Activist, Biologist
Marker, Steve Borman Entertainment, 1250 6th St, #401, Santa Monica CA 90401, USA	Guitarist (Garbage)
Markey, James A Agency Group Ltd, 142 W 57th St, #600, New York NY 10019 USA	Guitarist (Concrete Blonde)
Markey, Lucille P 18 La Gorce Circle Lane, La Gorce Island, Miami Beach FL 33141, USA	Thoroughbred Racing Breeder
Markey, Mary Jo Paradigm Agency, 360 N Crescent Dr, North Building, Beverly Hills CA 90210 USA	Editor
Markgraf, Kate Octagon Worldwide, 1751 Pinnacle Dr, #1500, McLean VA 22102 USA	Soccer Player
Markham, Monte PO Box 607, Malibu CA 90265, USA	Actor
Markin, David R 2671 Brackett Ave, Kalamazoo MI 49004, USA	Businessman
Markle, C Wilson Colorization Inc, 26 Soho St, Toronto ON M5T 1Z7, Canada	Film Engineer
Markle, Peter F Blue Line Productions, 212 26th St, #295, Santa Monica CA 90402, USA	Director
Marklund, E Elisabeth (Liza) Piratforlaget AB, Kaptensgatab 6, 114 57 Stockholm, Sweden	Writer
Markov, Alexey I M G Artists, Hogarth Business Park, Chiswick, London W4 2TH, England	Opera Singer
Markov, Daniil (Danny) 17875 Collins Ave, Sunny Isles Beach FL 33160, USA	Ice Hockey Player
Markowitz, Barry Paradigm Agency, 360 N Crescent Dr, North Building, Beverly Hills CA 90210 USA	Cinematographer
Markowitz, Harry M 1010 Turquoise St, #245, San Diego CA 92109, USA	Nobel Economics Laureate
Markowitz, Robert Paradigm Agency, 360 N Crescent Dr, North Building, Beverly Hills CA 90210 USA	Director, Producer
Marks, Albert J Miss America Organization, 1370 Ave of Americas, #1600, New York NY 10019 USA	Beauty Pageant Executive
Marks, Bruce Boston Ballet Co, 19 Clarendon St, Boston MA 02116, USA	Ballet Dancer, Artistic Director
Marks, David J Marks Barfield Architects, 50 Bromells Road, London SW4 0BG, England	Architect
Marks, John G 2733 47th St S, #205, Fargo ND 58104, USA	Ice Hockey Player

Marin - Marks

Marks, Michael E — Businessman
Flextronics International, 2090 Fortune St, San Jose CA 95131, USA
Marks, Miko — Singer, Guitarist
Mirrome Records, 2923 Verde Vista Dr, #C, Santa Barbara CA 93105, USA
Marks, Paul A — Oncologist, Cell Biologist
25680 Military Road, Watertown NY 13601, USA
Marks, Sean A — Basketball Player
2702 Circle Dr, Newport Beach CA 92663, USA
Markstein, Gary — Editorial Cartoonist
Milwaukee Journal, Editorial Dept, 333 W State St, Milwaukee WI 53203, USA
Markwart, Nevin — Ice Hockey Player
24 Old Barn Road, Hanover MA 02339, USA
Marleau, Patrick D — Ice Hockey Player
12021 Magnolia Court, Saratoga CA 95070, USA
Marley, Damian (Jr Gong) — Singer, Songwriter
Bob Marley Music, 76 9th Ave, #1110, New York NY 10011, USA
Marley, Ziggy — Singer, Songwriter
Ziggy Marley Mgmt, 269 S Beverly Dr, #175, Beverly Hills CA 90212, USA
Marlin, Sterling — Auto Racing Driver
Phoenix Racing, 195 Jones Road, Spartanburg SC 29307, USA
Marlind, Mans — Director
Zero Gravity Mgmt, 9255 Sunset Blvd, #1010, Los Angeles CA 90069 USA
Marling, Brit — Actress, Writer
Creative Artists Agency, 2000 Ave of Stars, #100, Los Angeles CA 90067 USA
Marlohe, Berenice — Actress
I C M Partners, 10250 Constellation Blvd, #900, Los Angeles CA 90067 USA
Marlowe, Andrew W — Producer, Screenwriter
Creative Artists Agency, 2000 Ave of Stars, #100, Los Angeles CA 90067 USA
Marm, Walter J, Jr — Vietnam War Army Hero (CMH)
PO Box 2017, Fremont NC 27830, USA
Marmel, Steve — Producer, Writer
Gersh Agency, 9465 Wilshire Blvd, #600, Beverly Hills CA 90212 USA
Marmol, Carlos A — Baseball Player
1500 Robin Circle, #218, Hoffman Estates IL 60169, USA
Marmont, Louise — Curling Athlete
Curling Assn, Idrottshuser, Marbackagatan 19, 123 43 Farsta, Sweden
Marohn, William D — Businessman
Whirlpool Corp, 2000 N State St, RR 63, Benton Harbor MI 49022, USA
Marois, Mario — Ice Hockey Player
Chicago Blackhawks, United Center, 1901 W Madison St, Chicago IL 60612 USA
Maroney, Laurence — Football Player
12560 Grandview Forest Dr, Saint Louis MO 63127, USA
Maroon, Paul — Guitarist, Pianist (Walkmen)
Mick Mgmt, 35 Washington St, Brooklyn NY 11201 USA
Marosz, Tom — Artist
Botanical Enclosures, 606 Concepion Ave, La Mesa CA 91941, USA
Maroth, Michael W (Mike) — Baseball Player
909 Johns Pointe Dr, Oakland FL 34787, USA
Maroulis, Constantine — Actor, Singer
David Passick Entertainment, 12 Kent St, New City NY 10956, USA
Marozsan, Erika — Actress
Scenario Agentur, Rambergstr 5, 80799 Munich, Germany
Marquette, Christopher (Chris) — Actor
United Talent Agency, 9336 Civic Center Dr, Beverly Hills CA 90210 USA
Marquette, Sean — Actor
A K A Talent, 6310 San Vicente Blvd, #200, Los Angeles CA 90048 USA
Marquez, Alfonso — Baseball Umpire
4103 S Skyline Court, Gilbert AZ 85297, USA
Marquez, Juan Manuel — Boxer
961 Everett St, Los Angeles CA 90026, USA
Marquez, Martin — Actor
United Agents, 12-26 Lexington St, London W1F 0LE, England
Marquez, Rafael — Boxer
Romanza Gym, Regina St 252, Deligacion, Colonia Iztacalco, Mexico City DF 07300, Mexico
Marquez, Raul — Boxer
729 Evanston St, Houston TX 77015, USA
Marquis, Jason S — Baseball Player
300 Vogel Ave, Staten Island NY 10309, USA
Marrero, Elieser (Eli) — Baseball Player
10230 SW 64th St, Miami FL 33173, USA
Marriner, Neville — Conductor
Academy Saint Martin in Fields, Raine St, London E1 9RG, England
Marriott, J Willard, Jr — Businessman
Marriott International, 10400 Fernwood Road, Bethesda MD 20817, USA
Marriott, Richard E — Businessman
Host Marriott Corp, 10400 Fernwood Road, Bethesda MD 20817, USA
Marron, Donald B — Financier
U B S PaineWebber, 1285 6th Ave, New York NY 10019, USA
Marrone, Doug — Football Player, Coach
6100 Waitsfield Dr S, Jamesville NY 13078, USA
Marrs, Audrey M — Producer
Representational Pictures, 75 E 4th St, #83, New York NY 10003, USA
Mars, Bruno — Singer, Songwriter
Elektra Records, 75 Rockefeller Plaza, 1700, New York NY 10019 USA
Mars, Chris — Drummer (Replacements)
PO Box 24631, Minneapolis MN 55424, USA
Mars, Susannah — Singer, Actress
L M L Music Records, PO Box 48081, Los Angeles CA 90048, USA
Marsalis, Branford — Jazz Saxophonist, Composer
Columbia Artists Mgmt Inc, 1790 Broadway, #702, New York NY 10019 USA
Marsalis, Ellis — Jazz Pianist
Management Ark, 116 Village Blvd, #200, Princeton NJ 08540, USA
Marsalis, James (Jim) — Football Player
101 Royal Oak Lane, Kathleen GA 31047, USA
Marsalis, Wynton — Jazz Trumpeter, Composer
Management Ark, 116 Village Blvd, #200, Princeton NJ 08540, USA

Marsan, Eddie
Paradigm Agency, 360 N Crescent Dr, North Building, Beverly Hills CA 90210 USA — Actor
Marsden, Gerard (Gerry)
Barry Collins, 21A Cliftown Road, Southend on Sea, Essex SS1 1AB, England — Singer, Guitarist (Gerry & Pacemakers)
Marsden, James P
W M E Entertainment, 9601 Wilshire Blvd, #300, Beverly Hills CA 90210 USA — Actor
Marsden, Roy
Ken McReddie Assoc, 11 Connaught Place, London W2 2ET, England — Actor
Marsden, Russell
Pias Entertainment Group, Trading Centre, 101 Farm Lane, #24, London SW6 1QJ, England — Singer, Guitarist (Band of Skulls)
Marsh of Mannington, Richard W
House of Lords, Westminster, London SW1A 0PW, England — Government Official, England
Marsh, Brad
Ottawa Senators, Scotia Bank Place, Kanata ON K2V 1A5, Canada — Ice Hockey Player
Marsh, Doug
629 Forest Ave, Saint Louis MO 63135, USA — Football Player
Marsh, Graham
Marsh Golf Design, 29 Commerce Dr, Box 300, Robina QED 4226, Australia — Golfer
Marsh, James
Independent Talent Group, Oxford House, 76 Oxford St, London W1D 1BS, England — Documentary Producer, Director
Marsh, Jean
52 Shaftesbury Ave, London W1V 7DE, England — Actress
Marsh, Jeff (Swampy)
Disney Channel, Phineas & Ferb Show, 500 S Buena Vista St, Burbank, CA 91521, USA — Producer, Animator
Marsh, Jodie
News International, Editorial Dept, 1 Virginia St, London E98 1XY, England — Model
Marsh, Kym
Safe Mgmt, 111 Guildford Road, Lightwater, Surrey GU18 5RA, England — Singer (Hear'say)
Marsh, Linda
170 W End Ave, #22P, New York NY 10023, USA — Actress
Marsh, Michael (Mike)
2425 Holly Hall St, #152, Houston TX 77054, USA — Track Athlete
Marsh, Michelle
Neon Mgmt, 34 Clare Lane, London N1 3DB, England — Model
Marsh, Miles L
Fort James Corp, 1919 S Broadway, Green Bay WI 54304, USA — Businessman
Marsh, Robert T
20550 Falcons Landing Circle, #5106, Sterling VA 20165, USA — Air Force General, Businessman
Marsh, Terry
69 Ingaway, Langdon Hills, Basildon SS16 5QJ, England — Boxer
Marsh, Thomas O (Tom)
9140 Summerfield Road, Temperance MI 48182, USA — Baseball Player
Marshal, Lyndsey
Troika, 74 Clerkenwell Road, #300, London EC1M 5QA, England — Actress
Marshall, Albert L (Bert)
Calgary Flames, PO Box 1540, Station M, Calgary AB T2P 3B9, Canada — Ice Hockey Player
Marshall, Amanda L
Creative Artists Agency, 2000 Ave of Stars, #100, Los Angeles CA 90067 USA — Singer, Actress
Marshall, Arthur J
4821 Rocky Shoals Circle, Evans GA 30809, USA — Football Player
Marshall, Barry J
Charles Gairdner Hospital, Verdun St, Nedlands WA 6009, Australia — Nobel Medicine Laureate
Marshall, Brian A
Agency Group Ltd, 142 W 57th St, #600, New York NY 10019 USA — Bassist (Creed, Alter Bridge)
Marshall, David L (Dave)
4802 E Centralia St, Long Beach CA 90808, USA — Baseball Player
Marshall, Donald (Don)
5887 SE Riverboat Dr, Stuart FL 34997, USA — Ice Hockey Player
Marshall, Donny E
410 N 63rd St, Seattle WA 98103, USA — Basketball Player
Marshall, Donyell L
55 Ridgecreek Trail, Chagrin Falls OH 44022, USA — Basketball Player
Marshall, F Ray
PO Box Y, Austin TX 78713, USA — Secretary, Labor
Marshall, Frank W
Kennedy/Marshall Co, 619 Arizona Ave, Santa Monica CA 90401, USA — Producer
Marshall, Garry K
Henderson Productions, 4252 Riverside Dr, Burbank CA 91505, USA — Director, Actor
Marshall, Grant
General Delivery, North Rustico PE C0A 1X0, Canada — Ice Hockey Player
Marshall, Henry H
68-1745 Waikoloa Road, #101, Waikoloa HI 96738, USA — Football Player
Marshall, James
Susan J Talent Agency, 12501 Riverside Dr, #211, Studio City CA 91607, USA — Actor
Marshall, James L (Jim)
4241 Basswood Road, Minneapolis MN 55416, USA — Football Player
Marshall, Jason
438 Begonia Ave, Corona del Mar CA 92625, USA — Ice Hockey Player
Marshall, John
S E T I Institute, 515 N Whitman Road, Mountain View CA 94043, USA — Geologist
Marshall, Keith A
334 Beckwith Road, Pine City NY 14871, USA — Baseball Player
Marshall, Ken
Special Artists, 9465 Wilshire Blvd, #880, Beverly Hills CA 90212, USA — Actor
Marshall, Kendall D
Phoenix Suns, 201 E Jefferson St, Phoenix AZ 85004 USA — Basketball Player
Marshall, Kris
Independent Talent Group, Oxford House, 76 Oxford St, London W1D 1BS, England — Actor
Marshall, Lawrence E (Larry)
1044 Washington St, Kansas City MO 64105, USA — Football Player
Marshall, Leonard A
PO Box 272016, Boca Raton FL 33427, USA — Football Player
Marshall, Margaret A
Woodside, Main St, Gargunnock, Stirling FKS 3BP, Scotland — Opera Singer
Marshall, Michael A (Mike)
1280 W Desert Sun Dr, Yuma AZ 85365, USA — Baseball Player

Marshall, Michael G (Mike) — Baseball Player
38324 Jendral Ave, Zephyrhills FL 33542, USA

Marshall, Neil — Director
I C M Partners, 10250 Constellation Blvd, #900, Los Angeles CA 90067 USA

Marshall, Paula — Actress
Innovative Artists, 1505 10th St, Santa Monica CA 90401 USA

Marshall, Penny — Actress, Director, Producer
Shelter Entertainment, 9454 Wilshire Blvd, #715, Beverly Hills CA 90212, USA

Marshall, Peter — Entertainer
PO Box 261999, Encino CA 91426, USA

Marshall, R James (Jim) — Baseball Player, Manager
19700 N 76th St, #1091, Scottsdale AZ 85255, USA

Marshall, Ray — Economist
University of Texas, L B Johnson Public Affairs School, Dallas TX 78713, USA

Marshall, Richard — Football Player
11232 Colonial Country Lane, Charlotte NC 28277, USA

Marshall, Rob — Director; Choreographer
Creative Artists Agency, 2000 Ave of Stars, #100, Los Angeles CA 90067 USA

Marshall, Tom — Publisher
Sunset, Publisher's Office, 80 Willow Road, Menlo Park CA 94025, USA

Marshall, Tonie — Director
Artmedia, 20 Ave Rapp, 75007 Paris, France

Marshall, W W (Bones) — Air Force General, Hero
4389 Malia St, #429, Honolulu HI 96821, USA

Marshall, Wilber B — Football Player
3016 E Main St, Mims FL 32754, USA

Marshall, Willie — Ice Hockey Player
2110 Acorn Court, Lebanon PA 17042, USA

Marshall-Green, Logan — Actor
Gersh Agency, 9465 Wilshire Blvd, #600, Beverly Hills CA 90212 USA

Marshburn, Thomas H (Tom) — Astronaut
N A S A, Johnson Space Center, 2101 NASA Road, Houston TX 77058 USA

Marson, Louis G (Lou) — Baseball Player
6631 E Wilshire Dr, Scottsdale AZ 85257, USA

Marsters, James — Actor
Amanda Howard, 74 Clerkenwell Road, London EC1M 5QA, England

Marston, Joshua M — Director, Writer
W M E Entertainment, 9601 Wilshire Blvd, #300, Beverly Hills CA 90210 USA

Marta — Soccer Player
Dois Riachas, Alagoas, Brazil

Marte, Judy — Actress
Gold Levin, 8424A Santa Monica Blvd, #706, Los Angeles CA 90069, USA

Martel, Arlene — Actress
2109 S Wilbur Ave, Walla Walla WA 99362, USA

Martel, Christiane — Beauty Queen, Actress
Miss Universe Organization, 1370 Ave of Americas, #1600, New York NY 10019 USA

Martel, Yann — Writer
Houghton Mifflin Harcourt, 215 Park Ave S, #1200, New York NY 10003 USA

Martell, Arthur E — Chemist
4047 Martinshire Dr, Houston TX 77025, USA

Martell, Donna — Actress
PO Box 3335, Granada Hills CA 91394, USA

Martella, Vincent — Actor
C E S D, 10635 Santa Monica Blvd, #130, Los Angeles CA 90025 USA

Martelly, J Michel (Sweet Micky) — President, Haiti
President's Office, Palais Nacional, Champ de Mars, Port-au-Prince, Haiti

Martens, Wilfried — Prime Minister, Belgium
Europese Volkspartij, Rue D'Arlon 67, 1040 Brussels, Belgium

Martha, J Paul — Football Player
5008 Starfish Way, San Diego CA 92154, USA

Marthouret, Francois — Actor
Artmedia, 20 Ave Rapp, 75007 Paris, France

Martika — Singer
Entertainment Artists, PO Box 120824, Nashville TN 37212 USA

Martikan, Michal — Canoeing Athlete
K T K Dukla Liptovsky, Nabrezie J Krala 8, Liptovsky Mikulas, Slovakia

Martin Chase, Deborah (Debra) — Producer
Martin Chase Productions, 500 S Buena Vista St, Burbank CA 91521, USA

Martin, Aaron B — Football Player
3605 Seth Court, Springdale MD 20774, USA

Martin, Albert S (Al) — Baseball Player
400N Cornado St, #1062, Chandler AZ 85224, USA

Martin, Andrea — Actress, Comedienne
Innovative Artists, 1505 10th St, Santa Monica CA 90401 USA

Martin, Ann M — Writer
Chronicle Books, 85 2nd St, San Francisco CA 94105, USA

Martin, Anne-Marie — Actress
Creative Artists Agency, 2000 Ave of Stars, #100, Los Angeles CA 90067 USA

Martin, Anthony I (Amos) — Football Player
11824 Duane Point Circle, #201, Louisville KY 40243, USA

Martin, Billy — Jazz Percussionist, Composer
Creative Artists Agency, 2000 Ave of Stars, #100, Los Angeles CA 90067 USA

Martin, Boris M (Babe) — Baseball Player
114 N Holloway Road, Ballwin MO 63011, USA

Martin, Boyce F, Jr — Judge
US Court of Appeals, US Courthouse, 601 W Broadway, Louisville KY 40202, USA

Martin, Brad — Singer
I C M Partners, 10250 Constellation Blvd, #900, Los Angeles CA 90067 USA

Martin, Brian — Luge Athlete
777 San Antonio Road, #132, Palo Alto CA 94303, USA

Martin, Carolyn (Biddy) — Educator
University of Wisconsin, Chancellor's Office, 500 Lincoln Dr, Madison WI 53706, USA

Martin, Casey — Golfer
University of Oregon, Athletic Dept, 2727 Harris Parkway, Eugene OR 97405, USA

Martin, Catherine — Scenic, Costume Designer
Bazmark Films, PO Box 430, Kings Cross NSW 1340, Australia

Martin, Cedric — Singer, Bassist (Con Funk Shun)
Thrill Entertainment, 9530 Hageman St, #B278, Bakersfield CA 93312 USA

Martin, Chris William — Actor
A P A Talent/Literary Agency, 405 S Beverly Dr, #300, Beverly Hills CA 90212 USA

Martin, Christoper A J (Chris) — Singer (Coldplay)
Paradigm Agency, 360 N Crescent Dr, North Building, North Building, North Building, North Building, Beverly Hills CA 90210 USA

Martin, Christopher (Chris) — Football Player
15760 Horton Court, Overland Park KS 66223, USA

Martin, Christy — Boxer
2015 University Heights Lane, Charlotte NC 28213, USA

Martin, Cuonzo L — Basketball Player
4315 Thistlewood Way, Knoxville TN 37919, USA

Martin, Curtis — Football Player
100 Hilton Ave, #PH 1, Garden City NY 11530, USA

Martin, D Renie — Baseball Player
509 Little Eagle Court, Valrico FL 33594, USA

Martin, Darnell — Director
I C M Partners, 10250 Constellation Blvd, #900, Los Angeles CA 90067 USA

Martin, Darnell — Director, Writer
Paradigm Agency, 360 N Crescent Dr, North Building, Beverly Hills CA 90210 USA

Martin, David — Commentator
CBS-TV, News Dept, 2020 M St NW, Washington DC 20036 USA

Martin, Demetri E — Actor, Comedian, Producer
Creative Artists Agency, 2000 Ave of Stars, #100, Los Angeles CA 90067 USA

Martin, Dewey — Actor
1371 East Ave de los Arboles, Thousand Oaks CA 91360, USA

Martin, Donald J (Don) — Football Player
1003 Hilltop Dr, Carrolton MO 64633, USA

Martin, Doug — Football Player
17115 NE 183rd Place, Woodinville WA 98072, USA

Martin, Doug — Golfer
Golf Ranch, 5390 Limaburg Road, Burlington KY 41005, USA

Martin, Doug — Football Player
Tampa Bay Buccaneers, 1 W Buccaneer Place, Tampa FL 33607 USA

Martin, Duane — Actor
Paul Kohner, 9300 Wilshire Blvd, #555, Beverly Hills CA 90212 USA

Martin, Ed F — Actor
Talent Synidcate, 1680 Vine St, #1018, Los Angeles CA 90028, USA

Martin, Edward H — Navy Admiral
729 Guadalupe Ave, Coronado CA 92118, USA

Martin, Eric W — Football Player
111 Windfall Place, Clinton MS 39056, USA

Martin, G Steven — Biochemist, Biologist
University of California, Biological Sciences Dept, Barker Hall, Berkeley CA 94720, USA

Martin, G Wayne — Football Player
408 Rue de la Rivere, Kenner LA 70065, USA

Martin, George C — Aeronautical Engineer
900 University St, #5P, Seattle WA 98101, USA

Martin, George D — Football Player
50 Cheshire Lane, Ringwood NJ 07456, USA

Martin, George H — Businessman, Lyricist
Lynhurst Road, Hampstead, London NW3 5NG, England

Martin, George R R — Writer
103 San Salvador, Santa Fe NM 87501, USA

Martin, Gerald W — Football Player
New Orleans Saints, 5800 Airline Highway, Metairie LA 70003 USA

Martin, Graham Patrick — Actor
TalentWorks, 3500 W Olive Ave, #1400, Burbank CA 91505 USA

Martin, Grant — Ice Hockey Player
Nejanilini Lake Lodge, 19 Av Brooke, Collingwood ON L9Y 5L2, Canada

Martin, Greg — Singer, Musician (Kentucky Headhunters)
Bobby Roberts, 3050 Business Park Circle, #303, Goodlettsville TN 37221 USA

Martin, Harold — President, New Caledonia
President's Office, Artillerie 8 Rt des Artfices, BP M2, 98849 Noumea Cedex, New Caledonia

Martin, Henry R — Cartoonist (Good News Bad News)
1382 Newtown Langhorne Road, #G206, Newtown PA 18940, USA

Martin, J Michael (Mike) — Baseball Player
7904 Waterfalls Ave, Las Vegas NV 89128, USA

Martin, J William (Billy) — Football Player
PO Box 2969, Cumming GA 30028, USA

Martin, Jacques — Ice Hockey Coach
Jacques Martin Hockey School, 198 Daventry Crescent, Nepean ON K2J 4N1, Canada

Martin, James G — Governor, NC
Carolinas Medical Center, PO Box 32861, Charlotte NC 28232, USA

Martin, Jerry L — Baseball Player
109 Chelton Court, Columbia SC 29212, USA

Martin, Jesse L — Actor, Singer
I C M Partners, 730 5th Ave, New York NY 10019 USA

Martin, Joe — Cartoonist (Mister Boffo)
King Features Syndicate, 300 W 57th St, #1500, New York NY 10019 USA

Martin, John H — Educator
J H M Corp, 3930 RCA Blvd, #3240, Palm Beach Gardens FL 33410, USA

Martin, Joseph C (J C) — Baseball Player
112 Oakmont Court, Advance NC 27006, USA

Martin, Judith (Miss Manners) — Journalist
1651 Harvard St NW, Washington DC 20009, USA

Martin, Kellie — Actress, Producer
Thruline Entertainment, 9250 Wilshire Blvd, #100, Beverly Hills CA 90212 USA

Martin, Kelvin B — Football Player
608 Guadalupe Road, Keller TX 76248, USA

Martin, Kenyon L — Basketball Player
23104 Dolorosa St, Woodland Hills CA 91367, USA

Martin, Kevin — Curling Athlete
Curling Assn, 1660 Vimont Court, Cumberland ON K4A 4J4, Canada

Martin, Kevin — Singer, Guitarist (Candlebox)
Novi Entertainment, PO Box 17077, Beverly Hills CA 90209, USA

M

Martin, LaRue	Basketball Player
1236 Harvest Lane, University Park IL 60484, USA	
Martin, Luci	Singer (Chic)
Lustig Talent, PO Box 770850, Orlando FL 32877 USA	
Martin, Lynn M	Secretary, Labor
Harry Walker Agency, 355 Lexington Ave, #2100, New York NY 10017, USA	
Martin, Madeleine	Actress
I C M Partners, 10250 Constellation Blvd, #900, Los Angeles CA 90067 USA	
Martin, Marilyn	Singer
Atlantic Records, 9229 W Sunset Blvd, #900, West Hollywood CA 90069 USA	
Martin, Mark A	Auto Racing Driver
D E I, 1675 Coddle Creek Highway, Mooresville NC 28115, USA	
Martin, Marsha P	Government Official, Financier
Farm Credit Administration, 1501 Farm Credit Dr, #3600, McLean VA 22102, USA	
Martin, Millicent	Actress, Singer
London Mgmt, 2-4 Noel St, London W1V 3RB, England	
Martin, Nicholas	Director
United Agents, 12-26 Lexington St, London W1F 0LE, England	
Martin, Norberto E (Paco)	Baseball Player
5905 Ricker Road, Raleigh NC 27610, USA	
Martin, Pamela Sue	Actress
PO Box 2278, Hailey ID 83333, USA	
Martin, Paul	Ice Hockey Player
3401 Annandale Dr, Presto PA 15142, USA	
Martin, Paul C (Jake)	Baseball Player
1529 33rd St, San Diego CA 92102, USA	
Martin, Phillip R (Phil)	Basketball Player
6937 Vineridge Dr, Dallas TX 75248, USA	
Martin, R Bruce	Chemist
University of Virginia, Chemistry Dept, Charlottesville VA 22903, USA	
Martin, Ray	Billiards Player
11-05 Cadmus Place, Fair Lawn NJ 07410, USA	
Martin, Raymond J (Ray)	Baseball Player
383 Adams St, Quincy MA 02169, USA	
Martin, Rhona	Curling Athlete
Curling Assn, 14 Donnelly Dr, Bedford MK4 9TU, England	
Martin, Ricky	Actor, Singer
PO Box 13345, Santurce Station, San Juan PR 00908, USA	
Martin, Roderick D (Rod)	Football Player
PO Box 23, Manhattan Beach CA 90267, USA	
Martin, Rudolf	Actor
Don Buchwald/Fortitude, 6500 Wilshire Blvd, #2200, Los Angeles CA 90048 USA	
Martin, Sandy	Actress
TalentWorks, 3500 W Olive Ave, #1400, Burbank CA 91505 USA	
Martin, Sarah	Singer, Violinist (Belle & Sebastian)
Ground Control Touring, 20 Jay St, #826, Brooklyn NY 11201 USA	
Martin, Seth	Ice Hockey Player
1200 Heather Place, Trail BC V1R 4Y2, Canada	
Martin, Steve	Actor, Comedian, Writer
Martin/Stein Co, 1528 N Curson Ave, Los Angeles CA 90046, USA	
Martin, Sylvia Wene	Bowler
2701 Clark Towers Court, #125, Las Vegas NV 89102, USA	
Martin, T J	Producer
Principato-Young, 9465 Wilshire Blvd, #880, Beverly Hills CA 90212 USA	
Martin, Terry G	Ice Hockey Player
184 Hampton Hill Dr, Buffalo NY 14221, USA	
Martin, Thomas E (Tom)	Baseball Player
8001 Surf Dr, Panama City FL 32408, USA	
Martin, Todd C	Tennis Player
156 Coach Lamp Way, Ponte Vedra FL 32082, USA	
Martin, Tony D	Football Player
1198 B Green Road, Boston GA 31626, USA	
Martin, Walter	Organist, Bassist (Walkmen)
Mick Mgmt, 35 Washington St, Brooklyn NY 11201 USA	
Martindale, Margo	Actress
Gersh Agency, 41 Madison Ave, #3301, New York NY 10010 USA	
Martindale, Wink	Entertainer, Singer
5744 Newcastle Lane, Calabasas CA 91302, USA	
Martinelli Berrocal, Ricardo A	President, Panama
Palacio Presidencial, Valija 50, Panama City 1, Panama	
Martines, Alessandra	Actress
Artmedia, 20 Ave Rapp, 75007 Paris, France	
Martinez Sistach, Lluis Cardinal	Religious Leader
Arzobispado, Carrer del Bisbe 5, 08002 Barcelona, Spain	
Martinez Somalo, Eduardo Cardinal	Religious Leader
Palazzo delle Congregazioni, Piazza Pio XII 3, 00193 Rome, Italy	
Martinez, A	Actor
David Shapira Assoc, 193 N Robertson Blvd, Beverly Hills CA 90211 USA	
Martinez, Alfredo (Fred)	Baseball Player
2346 Thomas St, Los Angeles CA 90031, USA	
Martinez, Ana Maria	Opera Singer
J F Mastroianni, 161 W 61st St, #17E, New York NY 10023, USA	
Martinez, Angela	Actress
Abrams Artists, 9200 W Sunset Blvd, #1125, West Hollywood CA 90069 USA	
Martinez, Benito	Actor
Platform Public Relations, 2666 N Beachwood Dr, Los Angeles CA 90068, USA	
Martinez, Carmelo	Baseball Player
32 Brisas del Plata, Dorado PR 00646, USA	
Martinez, Conchita	Tennis Player
511 Westminster Dr, Cardiff by the Sea CA 92007, USA	
Martinez, Constantino (Tino)	Baseball Player
2705 W Kathleen St, Tampa FL 33607, USA	
Martinez, Daniel J	Artist
Robert Berman/B1 Gallery, 2525 Michigan Ave, Santa Monica CA 90404, USA	
Martinez, David (Dave)	Baseball Player
3315 Enterprise Road E, Safety Harbor FL 34695, USA	

Martinez, Douglas V (S A)
311 Hive, 8904 Florence Dr, Omaha NE 68147, USA — Singer, DJ Musician (311), Songwriter

Martinez, Edgar
3036 249th Ave SE, Sammamish WA 98075, USA — Baseball Player

Martinez, Felix A (Tippy)
1524 Dellsway Road, Towson MD 21286, USA — Baseball Player

Martinez, J Dennis
9400 SW 63rd Court, Miami FL 33156, USA — Baseball Player

Martinez, John A (Buck)
10315 Long Beach Blvd, Long Beach Township NJ 08008, USA — Baseball Player, Manager

Martinez, Jose A
14601 SW 33rd Court, Miramar FL 33027, USA — Baseball Player

Martinez, Melquiades R (Mel)
D L A Piper, 500 8th St NW, Washington DC 20004, USA — Secretary, Housing & Urban Development

Martinez, Natalie
W M E Entertainment, 9601 Wilshire Blvd, #300, Beverly Hills CA 90210 USA — Actress, Model

Martinez, Olivier
Gersh Agency, 9465 Wilshire Blvd, #600, Beverly Hills CA 90212 USA — Actor

Martinez, Pedro J
3029 Birkdale Dr, Weston FL 33332, USA — Baseball Player

Martinez, Ramon J
3029 Birkdale Dr, Weston FL 33332, USA — Baseball Player

Martinez, Rene O
Serca Music, 2020 W Houston Ave, McAllen TX 78501, USA — Drummer (Intocable)

Martinez, Robert (Bob)
4647 W San Jose St, Tampa FL 33629, USA — Government Official; Governor, FL

Martinez, Vincent
Artmedia, 20 Ave Rapp, 75007 Paris, France — Actor

Martini, Steve
Plume/GP Putnam's Sons, 375 Hudson St, New York NY 10014, USA — Writer

Martinie, Ryan
Agency Group Ltd, 142 W 57th St, #600, New York NY 10019 USA — Bassist (Mudvayne)

Martinkovic, John G
1001 Ernst Dr, Green Bay WI 54304, USA — Football Player

Martino, Pat
2318 S 16th St, Philadelphia PA 19145, USA — Jazz Guitarist, Composer

Martino, Renato R Cardinal
Justice & Peace Curia, Piazzo S Calisto 16, 00120 Vatican City — Religious Leader

Martins, Jean-Pierre
Sophie Lemaitre, 22 Rue Nollet, 75017 Paris, France — Actor

Martins, Peter
New York City Ballet, Lincoln Center Plaza, New York NY 10023 USA — Ballet Dancer, Artistic Director

Martinson, Leslie H
2288 Coldwater Canyon Dr, Beverly Hills CA 90210, USA — Director

Marton, Eva
International Artists Group, 201 E 87th St, #21E, New York NY 10128 USA — Opera Singer

Martorella, Mildred (Millie)
Professional Bowlers Assn, 719 2nd Ave, #701, Seattle WA 98104 USA — Bowler

Marts, Lonnie
13650 Bromley Point Dr, Jacksonville FL 32225, USA — Football Player

Marty, Martin E
175 E Delaware Place, #8508, Chicago IL 60611, USA — Theologian

Martzke, Rudy
USA Today, Editorial Dept, 1000 Wilson Blvd, Arlington VA 22209, USA — Sportswriter

Maruk, Dennis
2624 Garfield Ave, Minneapolis MN 55408, USA — Ice Hockey Player

Marusha
Kaiser-Friedrich-Str 41, 10627 Berlin, Germany — Techno Musician

Maruyama, Karen
Rooster Films, 5225 Wilshire Blvd, #406, Los Angeles CA 90036, USA — Actress

Maruyama, Karina
Football Assn, 3-10-15 Hongo, Bunkyoku, Tokyo 113 0033 Japan — Soccer Player

Maruyama, Shigeki
15210 Antelo Place, Los Angeles CA 90077, USA — Golfer

Marve, Eugene R
4510 S Cameron Ave, Tampa FL 33611, USA — Football Player

Marvel, Jonathan
Rogers Marvel Architects, 145 Hudson St, #304, New York NY 10013, USA — Architect

Marvin, Gisele
USA Hockey, 1775 Bob Johnson Dr, Colorado Springs CO 80906 USA — Ice Hockey Player

Marvin, Hank B
Universal Music, 364-366 Kensington High St, London W14 8NS, England — Guitarist (Shadows)

Marx, Gilda
Gilda Marx Industries, 11755 Exposition Blvd, Los Angeles CA 90064, USA — Fashion Designer

Marx, Jeffrey A
Lexington Herald-Leader, Editorial Dept, Main & Midland, Lexington KY 40507, USA — Journalist

Marx, Michael
Northwest Fencing Center, 4950 SW Western Ave, Beaverton OR 97005, USA — Fencer

Marx, Richard
Wayne Isaak, 352 Atlantic Ave, #3, Brooklyn NY 11217, USA — Singer, Songwriter

Marzich, Andy
25141 Whitespring, Mission Viejo CA 92692, USA — Bowler

Marzoli, Andrea
Berkeley Geochronolgy Center, 2455 Ridge Road, Berkeley CA 94709, USA — Geologist

Masak, Ron
Arlent Thornton Agency, 12711 Ventura Blvd, 490, Studio City CA 91604, USA — Actor

Masakayan, Liz
2864 Palomino Circle, La Jolla CA 92037, USA — Volleyball Player

Masako
Imperial Palace, 1-1 Chiyoda, Chiyodaku, Tokyo 100, Japan — Crown Princess, Japan

Masaoka, Onan K S
1323 Auwae Road, Hilo HI 96720, USA — Baseball Player

Mascarenas, Andi
1984 Nova Road, Pine CO 80470, USA — Sculptor

Maschio, Robert
Stone Manners Salners, 9911 W Pico Blvd, #1400, Los Angeles CA 90035 USA — Actor

Masco, Judit — Model
S S & M Model Mgmt, C/Provenca 286-88, 08008 Barcelona, Spain
Masekela, Hugh R — Jazz Trumpeter, Singer
Ritmo Artists, PO Box 684705, Austin TX 78768, USA
Mashburn, Jamal — Basketball Player
5625 Pine Tree Dr, Miami Beach FL 33140, USA
Mashburn, Jesse — Track Athlete
8520 S Pennsylvania Ave, Oklahoma City OK 73159, USA
Masire, Quett K J — President, Botswana
PO Box 70, Gaborone, Botswana
Masius, John — Producer, Writer
John Masius Productions, 1785 Westridge Road, Los Angeles CA 90049, USA
Maskaev, Oleg — Boxer
Gleason's Boxing Gym, 75 Front St, New York NY 10005, USA
Maskawa, Toshihide — Nobel Physics Laureate
Koyoto Sangyo University, Kamigamo, Kitaku, Kyoto City 603 8553, Japan
Maske, Henry — Boxer
Tocardo, Neuer Wamdrahm 1, Speicherstadt, 20457 Hamburg, Germany
Maskin, Eric S — Nobel Economics Laureate
112 Mercer St, Princeton NJ 08540, USA
Maslansky, Paul — Producer, Director
Bamberger Business, 10850 Wilshire Blvd, #575, Los Angeles CA 90024, USA
Maslin, Janet — Writer, Journalist
New York Times, Editorial Dept, 229 W 43rd St, New York NY 10036 USA
Maslow, James — Actor
Creative Artists Agency, 2000 Ave of Stars, #100, Los Angeles CA 90067 USA
Masohn, Mercedes — Actress
Greene Assoc, 1901 Ave of Stars, #130, Los Angeles CA 90067 USA
Mason of Barnsley, Roy — Government Official, England
12 Victoria Ave, Barnsley, South Yorks S7O 2BH, England
Mason, Andrew — Businessman
Groupon Inc, 600 W Chicago Ave, #620, Chicago IL 60654, USA
Mason, Anthony G D — Basketball Player
9 Brownstone Way, #308, Englewood NJ 07631, USA
Mason, B John — Meteorologist
64 Christchurch Road, East Sheen, London SW14, England
Mason, Birny, Jr — Chemical Engineer
2208 Theall Road, Rye NY 10580, USA
Mason, Bob — Ice Hockey Player
9549 Yukon Ave S, Minneapolis MN 55438, USA
Mason, Bobbie Ann — Writer
PO Box 518, Lawrenceburg KY 40342, USA
Mason, Brent — Singer
Mercury Records, 54 Music Square E, #300, Nashville TN 37203 USA
Mason, Chris — Ice Hockey Player
PO Box 12465, Saint Louis MO 63132, USA
Mason, Dave — Singer, Guitarist (Traffic); Songwriter
3130 E Ojai Ave, Ojai CA 93023, USA
Mason, Derrick J — Football Player
9640 Portofino Dr, Brentwood TN 37027, USA
Mason, Desmond T — Basketball Player
6440 N Lake Dr, Milwaukee WI 53217, USA
Mason, Henry (Hank) — Baseball Player
5004 W Leyburn Court, #102, Henrico VA 23228, USA
Mason, Jackie — Actor, Comedian
W M E Entertainment, 1325 Ave of Americas, New York NY 10019, USA
Mason, James P (Jim) — Baseball Player
11410 Queens Way, Theodore AL 36582, USA
Mason, Larry B — Vietnam War Air Force Hero
826 Cinebar Road, Cinebar WA 98533, USA
Mason, Lawrence — Actor
Kazarian/Spencer/Ruskin, 11969 Ventura Blvd, #300, Studio City CA 91604 USA
Mason, Lindsey M — Football Player
8665 Ritchboro Road, District Heights MD 20747, USA
Mason, Marlyn — Actress, Singer
27 Glen Oak Court, Medford OR 97504, USA
Mason, Marsha — Actress
Innovative Artists, 1505 10th St, Santa Monica CA 90401 USA
Mason, Michael P (Mike) — Baseball Player
2711 Piper Ridge Lane, Excelsior MN 55331, USA
Mason, Monica — Ballerina, Ballet Director
Royal Opera House, Convent Garden, Bow St, London WC2, England
Mason, Nick — Drummer (Pink Floyd)
One Fifteen, Globe House, Middle Lane Mews, London N8 8PN, England
Mason, Roger L — Baseball Player
322 Park St, Bellaire MI 49615, USA
Mason, Ron — Ice Hockey Coach
Michigan State University, Athletic Dept, East Lansing MI 48224, USA
Mason, Sally — Educator
University of Iowa, President's Office, Iowa City IA 52242, USA
Mason, Thomas C (Tommy) — Football Player
240 S Orange Acres Dr, Anaheim CA 92807, USA
Mason, Tom — Actor
Hartig-Hilepo Agency, 54 W 21st St, #610, New York NY 10010 USA
Mason, Valerie Denise — Model
Playboy Promotions, 2706 Media Center Dr, Los Angeles CA 90065 USA
Mason, Vince — Rap Artist (De La Soul)
Richard Walters, PO Box 2789, Toluca Lake CA 91610 USA
Masopust, Josef — Soccer Player
Koulova 11, 160 00 Prague 6, Czech Republic
Masri, Tahir Nashat al- — Prime Minister, Jordan
PO Box 5550, Amman 11183, Jordan
Mass, Chris — Writer, Producer, Actor
Untitled Entertainment, 350 S Beverly Dr, #200, Beverly Hills CA 90212 USA
Mass, Wayne — Football Player
71 Eagle View, Durango CO 81303, USA

Massa, Felipe
Caixa Postal 19091, Sao Paulo SP 04505 970, Brazil — Auto Racing Driver
Massard, Didier
Julie Saul Gallery, 535 W 22nd St, #6F, New York NY 10011, USA — Photographer
Massari, Lea
Viale Parioli 59, 00197 Rome, Italy — Actress
Massenburg, Tony A
1120 Fowler Road, Owings MD 20736, USA — Basketball Player
Massenburg, Walter B
Commander, Naval Air Systems Command, Patuxent River MD 20670 USA — Navy Admiral
Masset, Andrew
People Store Talent Agency, 645 Lambert Dr, Atlanta GA 30324, USA — Actor
Masset, Nicholas A (Nick)
14575 W Mountain View Blvd, #11107, Surprise AZ 85374, USA — Baseball Player
Massevitch, Alla G
6 Pushkurev Per, #4, 103045 Moscow, Russia — Astronomer
Massey, Debbie
PO Box 116, Cheboygan MI 49721, USA — Golfer
Massey, Kent
4085 Foothill Road, Carpinteria CA 93013, USA — Yachtsman
Massey, Robert L
6746 Terry Lane, Charlotte NC 28215, USA — Football Player
Massey, Walter E
Bank of America Corp, 100 N Tryon St, #220, Charlotte NC 28202, USA — Educator, Physicist, Financier
Massie, Robert K
52 W Clinton Ave, Irvington NY 10533, USA — Writer
Massimino, Michael J
15814 Elk Park Lane, Houston TX 77062, USA — Astronaut
Massimino, Rolland V (Rollie)
18578 SE Ferland Court, Jupiter FL 33469, USA — Basketball Coach
Massimov, Karim K
Dom Pravieelstva, Plaza im VI Lenina, 148008 Astana, Kazakhstan — Prime Minister, Kazakhstan
Massof, Robert W
Wilmer Ophthalmological Institute, 550 N Broadway, #600, Baltimore MD 21205, USA — Inventor (Seeing Eye Apparatus)
Massoglia, Chris
Zero Gravity Mgmt, 1531 14th St, Santa Monica CA 90404, USA — Actor
Massu, Nicolas A
Association of Tennis Professionals, 200 Tournament Road, Ponte Vedra Beach FL 32082 USA — Tennis Player
Mast, Richard K (Rick)
390 E Midland Trail, Lexington VA 24450, USA — Auto Racing Driver
Masta Killa
A&M Entertainment, 13280 NE Freeway, #F328, Houston TX 77040, USA — Rap Artist (Wu-Tang Clan)
Mastalli, Chiara
Agenzie Fabrizia Mancuso, Piazza Benedetto Cairoli 6, 00186 Rome, Italy — Actress
Master P
Silverstone Entertainment USA, 10 Universal City Plaza, #2400, Universal City CA 91608, USA — Rap Artist, Actor, Producer
Masters, Blake
Brant Rose Agency, 6671 Sunset Blvd, #1584B, Los Angeles CA 90028, USA — Writer, Producer, Director
Masters, William J (Billy)
501 SW Silver Spur Circle, Lees Summit MO 64081, USA — Football Player
Masterson, Chase
Masterson Entertainment, 12400 Ventura Blvd, #1200, Studio City CA 91604, USA — Actress
Masterson, Danny
Masterson Mgmt, 1566 Hillcrest Ave, Glendale CA 91202, USA — Actor
Masterson, Fay
Global Artists Agency, 6253 Hollywood Blvd, #508, Los Angeles CA 90028 USA — Actress
Masterson, Mary Stuart
Don Buchwald/Fortitude, 10 E 44th St, New York NY 10017 USA — Actress
Masterson, Peter
1165 5th Ave, #15A, New York NY 10029, USA — Writer, Director, Producer
Masterson, Valerie
Music International, 13 Ardilaun Road, London N5 2QR, England — Opera Singer
Maston, Le'Shai E
7856 Overridge Dr, Dallas TX 75232, USA — Football Player
Mastracchio, Richard A (Rick)
1910 Hillside Oak Lane, Houston TX 77062, USA — Astronaut
Mastrangelo, Carlo
Paramount Entertainment, 12 Kosakowski Dr, Morris Plains NJ 07590 USA — Singer (Dion & the Belmonts)
Mastrantonio, Mary Elizabeth
Lou Coulson Assoc, 37 Berwick St, London W1V 8RS, England — Actress, Singer
Mastrogiacomo, Gina
Pakula/King, 9229 W Sunset Blvd, #315, West Hollywood CA 90069 USA — Actress
Mastroianni, Armand
Creative Artists Agency, 2000 Ave of Stars, #100, Los Angeles CA 90067 USA — Director
Mastroianni, Chiara
Zelig Films, 57 Rue Reaumur, 75002 Paris, France — Actress
Masui, Yoshio
32 Overton Crescent, Don Mills, North York ON M3B 2V2, Canada — Zoologist
Masur, Kurt
Masur Music, Ansonia, 790 Riverside Dr, #6N, New York NY 10032, USA — Conductor
Masur, Richard
Susan Smith, 1344 N Wetherly Dr, Los Angeles CA 90069 USA — Actor
Masvidal, Paul A
Season of Mist Records, 111 Route de Valentinell, 13011 Marseille, France — Singer, Guitarist (Cynic, Aeon Spoke)
Mata, Victor J
New York Yankees, Yankee Stadium, E 161st St & River Ave, Bronx NY 10451 USA — Baseball Player
Matalin, Mary
325 Fishers Road, Maureltown VA 22644, USA — Political Consultant
Matalon, J Rolando (Roly)
Congregation B'nai Jeshurun, 2109 Broadway, #2034, New York NY 10023, USA — Religious Leader, Rabbi
Matane, Paulius N
Governor General's Office, PO Box 79, Port Moresby 121, Papua New Guinea — Governor General, Papua New Guinea
Matarazzo, Heather
Don Buchwald/Fortitude, 10 E 44th St, New York NY 10017 USA — Actress
Matarazzo, Leonard (Len)
2715 Carlisle St, New Castle. PA 16105, USA — Baseball Player

Mataskelekele, Kalkot — President, Vanuata; Judge
President's Office, Port Vila, Vanuatu

Matchefts, John — Ice Hockey Player
2415 Chelton Road, Colorado Springs CO 80909, USA

Matchett, Kari — Actress
Paradigm Agency, 360 N Crescent Dr, North Building, Beverly Hills CA 90210 USA

Matchick, J Thomas (Tom) — Baseball Player
7700 Pillod Road, Holland OH 43528, USA

Mateparae, Jeremiah (Jerry) — Governor General, New Zealand
Governor General's Office, Government House, Private Bag 39995, Wellington 5045, New Zealand

Matheny, Eric — Actor
Don Buchwald/Fortitude, 6500 Wilshire Blvd, #2200, Los Angeles CA 90048 USA

Matheny, Logan — Drummer (Roman Candle)
Russell Carter Artist Mgmt, 567 Ralph Magill Blvd, Atlanta GA 30312 USA

Matheny, Skip — Singer, Guitarist (Roman Candle)
Russell Carter Artist Mgmt, 567 Ralph Magill Blvd, Atlanta GA 30312 USA

Matheny, Timshel — Organist (Roman Candle)
Russell Carter Artist Mgmt, 567 Ralph Magill Blvd, Atlanta GA 30312 USA

Mather, John C — Nobel Physics Laureate
3400 Rosemary Lane, Hyattsville MD 20782, USA

Mathers, Jerry — Actor
McInerney Business Mgmt, 26372 Calle Lucana, San Juan Capistrano CA 92675, USA

Matheson, Diana — Soccer Player
Canadian Soccer, Place Soccer Canada, 237 Metcalfe St, Ottawa ON K2P 1R2, Canada

Matheson, Hans — Actor
Lou Coulson Assoc, 37 Berwick St, London W1V 8RS, England

Matheson, Tim — Actor, Director
Generate Mgmt, 1545 26th St, #200, Santa Monica CA 90404, USA

Mathew, Suleka — Actress
Abrams Artists, 9200 W Sunset Blvd, #1125, West Hollywood CA 90069 USA

Mathews, F David — Secretary, Health Education & Welfare
6050 Mad River Road, Dayton OH 45459, USA

Mathews, Gregory I (Greg) — Baseball Player
11721 Old Ballas Road, #107, Saint Louis MO 63141, USA

Mathews, Harlan — Senator, TN
420 Hunt Club Road, Nashville TN 37221, USA

Mathews, Jessica T — Foundation Executive
Carnegie Int'l Peace Endowment, 1779 Massachusetts NW, Washington DC 20036, USA

Mathews, Raymond D (Ray) — Football Player
PO Box 108, Harrisville PA 16038, USA

Mathews, Timothy J (T J) — Baseball Player
839 Autumn Rise Lane, Columbia IL 62236, USA

Mathieson, John — Cinematographer
Independent Talent Group, Oxford House, 76 Oxford St, London W1D 1BS, England

Mathieu, Marquis — Ice Hockey Player
113 W Lake Shore Dr, Hallandale FL 33009, USA

Mathieu, Philip — Concert Guitarist
Lindy S Martin Mgmt, 1007 Lakewater Dr, Henrico VA 23229, USA

Mathilde — Crown Princess, Belgium
Koninklijk Palace, Rue de Brederode, 1000 Brussels, Belgium

Mathis, Rashean — Football Player
26200 Marsh Landing Parkway, Ponte Vedra FL 32082, USA

Mathis, Buster, Jr — Boxer
4409 Carol Ave SW, Wyoming MI 49519, USA

Mathis, Chester A — Radiologist
University of Pittsburgh Medical Center, P E T Facility, Radiology Dept, Pittsburgh PA 15213, USA

Mathis, Clint — Soccer Player
Los Angeles Galaxy, Home Depot Center, 18400 Avalon Blvd, Carson CA 90746 USA

Mathis, Evan B — Football Player
11938 N 113th Place, Scottsdale AZ 85259, USA

Mathis, Jeffrey S (Jeff) — Baseball Player
4420 Spring Valley Dr, Marianna FL 32448, USA

Mathis, Johnny — Singer
1469 Stebbins Terrace, Los Angeles CA 90069, USA

Mathis, Samantha — Actress
Paradigm Agency, 360 N Crescent Dr, North Building, Beverly Hills CA 90210 USA

Mathis, Terance — Football Player
3415 Camellia Lane, Suwanee GA 30024, USA

Mathis, William H (Bill) — Football Player
43 Paces West Dr NW, Atlanta GA 30327, USA

Mathis-Eddy, Darlene — Writer
1409 W Cardinal St, Muncie IN 47303, USA

Mathison, Cameron — Actor
Innovative Artists, 1505 10th St, Santa Monica CA 90401 USA

Matisi, John R — Baseball Player
98-1616 Hoolauae St, Aiea HI 96701, USA

Matisyahu — Singer
Agency Group Ltd, 142 W 57th St, #600, New York NY 10019 USA

Matkevich, Mark — Actor
TalentWorks, 3500 W Olive Ave, #1400, Burbank CA 91505 USA

Matlack, Jonathan T (Jon) — Baseball Player
2495 Sawdust Road, #1101, Spring TX 77380, USA

Matlin, Marlee — Actress
Solo Productions, 8205 Santa Monica Blvd, #1279, West Hollywood CA 90046, USA

Matlock, Glen — Bassist (Sex Pistols)
Solo Agency, 53-55 Fulham High St, #200, London SW6 3JJ, England

Matlock, Jack F, Jr — Diplomat
940 Princeton-Kingston Road, Princeton NJ 08540, USA

Matlock, John J — Football Player
127 Seagrape Dr, #102, Jupiter FL 33458, USA

Matola, Sharon — Zoo Director, Conservationist
Belize Zoo & Tropical Education Center, PO Box 1787, Belize City, Belize

Matorin, Vladimir A — Opera Singer
Ulansky Per 21, Korp 1, #53, 103045 Moscow, Russia

Matos, Eddie — Actor
Schumacher Mgmt, 10323 Santa Monica Blvd, #101, Los Angeles CA 90024, USA

M

Matos, Elisabete — Opera Singer
Opera et Concert, 37 Rue de la Chaussee d'Antin, 75009 Paris, France
Matranga, Jonah — Singer, Songwriter
Agency Group Ltd, 142 W 57th St, #600, New York NY 10019 USA
Matronic, Ana — Singer (Scissors Sisters), Songwriter
Girlie Action, 59 W 19th St, #4B, New York NY 10011 USA
Matshikiza, Pumeza — Opera Singer
I M G Artists, Hogarth Business Park, Chiswick, London W4 2TH, England
Matson, J Randel (Randy) — Track Athlete
1002 Park Place, College Station TX 77840, USA
Matsos, Emil G (Archie) — Football Player
1410 Coventry Close St, East Lansing MI 48823, USA
Matsui, Hideki — Baseball Player
845 United Nations Plaza, #52C, New York NY 10017, USA
Matsui, Kazuo (Kaz) — Baseball Player
229 N Almont Dr, Beverly Hills CA 90211, USA
Matsui, Keiko — Jazz Pianist
Ted Kurland, 173 Brighton Ave, Allston MA 02134 USA
Matsuzaka, Daisuke — Baseball Player
Boston Red Sox, Fenway Park, 4 Yawkey Way, Boston MA 02215 USA
Matsuzaki, Yuki — Actor
Williams-Michael Relations, 3940 Laurel Canyon, #785, Studio City CA 91604, USA
Matt, Mike — Rodeo Rider
111 S 24th St W, #9125, Billings MT 59102, USA
Matta, Thad — Basketball Coach
Ohio State University, Athletic Dept, Columbus OH 43210, USA
Matte, Thomas R (Tom) — Football Player
11309 Old Carriage Road, Glen Arm MD 21057, USA
Mattea, Kathy — Singer, Guitarist
International Music Network, 278 Main St, #400, Gloucester MA 01930 USA
Mattei, Frank — Singer (Danny & the Juniors)
Joe Taylor Mgmt, PO Box 1017, Blackwood NJ 08012, USA
Mattes, Eva — Actress
Agentur Carola Studlar, Neurieder Str, #1C, 92152 Planegg, Germany
Mattes, Ronald A (Ron) — Football Player
1718 Moreland Wood Trail NW, Concord NC 28027, USA
Mattes, Troy — Baseball Player
2932 Lexington St, Sarasota FL 34231, USA
Matteson, John — Writer
W W Norton, 500 5th Ave, #600, New York NY 10110 USA
Matteson, Troy — Golfer
6518 Old Shadburn Ferry Road, Buford GA 30518, USA
Matthes, Roland — Swimmer
Luitpoldstr 35A, 97828 Marktheidenfeld, Germany
Matthes, Ulrich — Actor
Bleibtreustr 8, 10623 Berlin, Germany
Matthew, Catriona I — Golfer
I M G, Pier House, Strand-on-Green, Chiswick, London W4 3NN, England
Matthews, Alvin L (Al) — Football Player
19451 Diablo Dr, Pflugerville TX 78660, USA
Matthews, Bruce R — Football Player
6423 Oilfield Road, Sugar Land TX 77479, USA
Matthews, Casey C — Football Player
Philadelphia Eagles, 1 Novacare Way, Philadelphia PA 19145 USA
Matthews, Cerys — Singer (Catatonia)
M R M Productions, 5 Kirby St, London EC1N 8TS, England
Matthews, Chris — Commentator
9 E Kirke St, Chevy Chase MD 20815, USA
Matthews, Dakin — Actor
Henderson/Hogan, 850 7th Ave, #1003, New York NY 10019 USA
Matthews, Dave — Singer, Guitarist (Dave Matthews Band)
A T O Records, 157 Chambers St, #1200, New York NY 10007, USA
Matthews, DeLane — Actress
Don Buchwald/Fortitude, 6500 Wilshire Blvd, #2200, Los Angeles CA 90048 USA
Matthews, Eric — Singer, Songwriter
Empyrean/WishingTree Records, PO Box 197, Warren RI 02885, USA
Matthews, Francis — Actor
Scott Marshall Partners, 15 Little Portland, #200, London W1W 8BW, England
Matthews, Gary N, Jr — Baseball Player
Cincinnati Reds, Great American Ball Park, 100 Main St, Cincinnati OH 45202 USA
Matthews, Gary N, Sr — Baseball Player
1542 W Jackson Blvd, Chicago IL 60607, USA
Matthews, Ian — Singer, Guitarist
Geoffrey Blumenauer Artists, PO Box 343, Burbank CA 91503 USA
Matthews, Keith — Astronomer
California Institute of Technology, Astronomy Dept, Pasadena CA 91125, USA
Matthews, Liesel — Actress
Creative Artists Agency, 2000 Ave of Stars, #100, Los Angeles CA 90067 USA
Matthews, Lisa — Model, Actress
Playboy Promotions, 2706 Media Center Dr, Los Angeles CA 90065 USA
Matthews, Mike — Baseball Player
14326 Bakerwood Place, Haymarket VA 20169, USA
Matthews, Pat Stanley — Actress
210 Stanton St, Walla Walla WA 99362, USA
Matthews, Robert C O — Economist
Clare College, Economics Dept, Cambridge CB2 1TL, England
Matthews, Sally — Opera Singer
Maxine Robertson Mgmt, 14 Forge Dr, Claygate KT1O 0HR, England
Matthews, Shane — Football Player
848 NW 136th St, Agoura Hills CA 91301, USA
Matthews, Vincent (Vince) — Track Athlete
6755 193rd Lane, Fresh Meadows NY 11365, USA
Matthews, W Clay, III — Football Player
Green Bay Packers, 1265 Lombardi Ave, Green Bay WI 54304 USA
Matthews, W Clay, Jr — Football Player
6068 Canterbury Dr, Agoura Hills CA 91301, USA

Matos - Matthews

Matthies, Nina — Volleyball Player, Coach
Pepperdine University, Athletic Dept, Malibu CA 90265, USA

Matthiesen, Mads — Director, Writer
Paradigm Agency, 360 N Crescent Dr, North Building, Beverly Hills CA 90210 USA

Matthiessen, Peter — Writer, Naturalist
527 Bridge Lane, Sagaponack NY 11962, USA

Mattiace, Len — Golfer
12802 Hunt Club Road N, Jacksonville FL 32224, USA

Mattila, Karita M — Opera Singer
45B Croxley Road, London W9 3HJ, England

Mattingly, Ashley — Model
Playboy Promotions, 2706 Media Center Dr, Los Angeles CA 90065 USA

Mattingly, Donald A (Don) — Baseball Player, Manager
7601 Newburgh Road, Evansville IN 47715, USA

Mattingly, Mack F — Senator, GA; Diplomat
4315 10th St, East Beach, Saint Simons Island GA 31522, USA

Mattingly, Thomas K, II — Astronaut, Navy Admiral
Rocket Development Co, 1501 Quail St, #102, Newport Beach CA 92660, USA

Mattis, James N — Marine Corps General
Commander, Central Command, 7115 S Boundary, MacDill Air Force Base FL 33621 USA

Mattscherodt, Katrin — Speed Skater
Sportclub Berlin, Weissenseer Weg 53, 13053 Berlin, Germany

Mattson, Riley C — Football Player
12 Coconut Grove Lane, Lahaina HI 96761, USA

Mattson, Robin — Actress
Stan Kamens Mgmt, 7772 Torreyson Dr, Los Angeles CA 90046, USA

Mattsson, Helena — Actress
United Talent Agency, 9336 Civic Center Dr, Beverly Hills CA 90210 USA

Matuszek, Leonard J (Len) — Baseball Player
10326 Deerfield Road, Cincinnati OH 45242, USA

Matvichuk, Richard — Ice Hockey Player
1203 Earlston Court, Southlake TX 76092, USA

Matz, Michael R — Equestrian, Thoroughbred Racing Trainer
2953 Hurlinham Dr, Wellington FL 33414, USA

Matzdorf, Pat — Track Athlete
1252 Bainbridge Dr, Naperville IL 60563, USA

Matzner, Jason — Director
Paradigm Agency, 360 N Crescent Dr, North Building, Beverly Hills CA 90210 USA

Mau, Bruce — Multimedia Designer
197 Spadina Ave, #501, Toronto ON M5T 2C8, Canada

Maualuga, Rey — Football Player
Cincinnati Bengals, 1 Paul Brown Stadium, Cincinnati OH 45202 USA

Mauboy, Jessica — Actress
R G M Associates, 64-76 Kippax St, #202, Surry Hills NSW 2010, Australia

Mauceri, John — Conductor
I C M Artists, 40 W 57th St, #1800, New York NY 10019 USA

Mauck, Carl F — Football Player
2129 Winthrop Hill Road, Argyle TX 76226, USA

Maudsley, Tony — Actor
United Agents, 12-26 Lexington St, London W1F 0LE, England

Mauer, Joseph P (Joe) — Baseball Player
671 Lexington Parkway N, Saint Paul MN 55104, USA

Maultsby, Nancy — Opera Singer
I M G Artists, Hogarth Business Park, Chiswick, London W4 2TH, England

Mauney, Carl V — Navy Admiral
Deputy Commander, US Strategic Command, Offutt Air Force Base NE 68113, USA

Maupin, Armistead J, Jr — Writer
Literary Bent, PO Box 4109990, #528, San Francisco CA 94141, USA

Maura, Carmen — Actress
Ramon Pilaces, C/Hortaleza 20, #1 Izqda, 28004 Madrid, Spain

Maurel, Julien — Actor
Artmedia, 20 Ave Rapp, 75007 Paris, France

Maurer, Andrew L (Andy) — Football Player
30 Perrydale Ave, Medford OR 97501, USA

Maurer, Ingo — Inventor, Lighting Designer
Team Ingo Maurer, Kaiserstr 47, 80801 Munich, Germany

Maurer, Robert D — Inventor (Silica Optical Waveguide)
2572 W 28th Ave, Eugene OR 97405, USA

Maurer, Robert J (Rob) — Baseball Player
3114 E Gum St, Evansville IN 47714, USA

Mauresmo, Amelie — Tennis Player
Athleteline, 2 Rue du Chemin Vert, 92110 Clichy, France

Maurice, Paul — Ice Hockey Coach
Carolina Hurricanes, R B C Center, 1400 Edwards Mills Road, Raleigh NC 27607 USA

Mauriello, Tammy — Boxer
1148 E 81st St, Brooklyn NY 11236, USA

Maurier, Claire — Actress
Anne Alvares Correa, 34 Rue Jouffroy d'Abbans, 75017 Paris, France

Mauroy, Pierre — Prime Minister, France
17-19 Rue Voltaire, 59000 Lille, France

Maurstad, Toralv — Director, Actor
Thorleif, Hangsvei 20, 0712 Voksenkollen, Norway

Mauser, Timothy E (Tim) — Baseball Player
114 Shadow Creek Lane, Aledo TX 76008, USA

Mauz, Henry H (Hank), Jr — Navy Admiral
1608 Viscaine Road, Pebble Beach CA 93953, USA

Maven, Max — Illusionist
PO Box 1298, La Mesa CA 91944, USA

Mawae, Kevin J — Football Player, Labor Leader
3704A Estes Road, Nashville TN 37215, USA

Mawby, Russell G — Foundation Executive
W K Kellogg Foundation, 1 Michigan Ave E, Battle Creek MI 49017, USA

Max, Peter — Artist
118 Riverside Dr, New York NY 10024, USA

Maxcy, D Brian — Baseball Player
982 Cobble Creek Dr, Birmingham AL 35226, USA

Maxi Jazz	Rap Artist (Faithless)
Helter Skelter, 347-353 Chiswick High Road, London W4 4HS, England	
Maxie, Brett D	Football Player
1702 Richbourg Park Dr, Brentwood TN 37027, USA	
Maximova, Elena	Opera Singer
I M G Artists, Hogarth Business Park, Chiswick, London W4 2TH, England	
Maxsom, Alvin E	Football Player
3215 S Danube St, Aurora CO 80013, USA	
Maxvill, C Dalian (Dal)	Baseball Player
1115 Eagle Creek Road, Chesterfield MO 63005, USA	
Maxwell	Singer
W M E Entertainment, 9601 Wilshire Blvd, #300, Beverly Hills CA 90210 USA	
Maxwell, Arthur E	Oceanographer
PO Box 31249, Santa Fe NM 87594, USA	
Maxwell, Brad	Ice Hockey Player
27285 Natchez Ave, Elko MN 55020, USA	
Maxwell, Cedric B (Cornbread)	Basketball Player
151 Tremont St, #25H, Boston MA 02111, USA	
Maxwell, Charles R (Charlie)	Baseball Player
730 Mapleview Ave, Paw Paw MI 49079, USA	
Maxwell, Kevin F H	Publisher
Moulsford Manor, Moulsford Oxon OX10 9HO, England	
Maxwell, Robert D	WW II Army Hero (CMH)
1001 SE 15th St, #44, Bend OR 97702, USA	
Maxwell, Ronald F (Ron)	Director, Writer
Weissmann Wolff Bergman, 9665 Wilshire Blvd, #900, Beverly Hills CA 90212, USA	
Maxwell, Thomas M (Tommy)	Football Player
1634 Rockview Dr, Granbury TX 76049, USA	
Maxwell, Vernon	Basketball Player
2601 NW 23rd Blvd, #170, Gainesville FL 32605, USA	
Maxwell, Vernon L	Football Player
1955 E Citation Lane, Tempe AZ 85284, USA	
May of Oxford, Robert M M	Biologist
Royal Society, 6 Carlton House Terrace, London SW1Y 5AG, England	
May, Antoinette	Writer
William Morrow Publishers, 1350 Ave of Americas, New York NY 10019 USA	
May, Arthur	Architect
Kohn Pedersen Fox Assoc, 111 W 57th St, #300, New York NY 10019, USA	
May, B Deems	Football Player
3922 Ayscough Road, Charlotte NC 28211, USA	
May, Bob	Golfer
420 Grand Augusta Lane, Las Vegas NV 89144, USA	
May, Brad	Ice Hockey Player
9167 E Mountain Spring Road, Scottsdale AZ 85255, USA	
May, Brian	Guitarist (Queen), Songwriter
Old Bakehouse, 16A High St, Barnes, London SW13, England	
May, Darrell K	Baseball Player
747 Minthorne Road, Rogue River OR 97537, USA	
May, Deborah	Actress
Artists Agency, 1180 S Beverly Dr, #301, Los Angeles CA 90035 USA	
May, Derrick B	Baseball Player
2 Jaymar Road, Newark DE 19702, USA	
May, Donald J (Don)	Basketball Player
1128 Colwick Dr, Dayton OH 45420, USA	
May, Elaine	Actress, Comedienne, Director
146 Central Park West, #5D, New York NY 10023, USA	
May, Imelda	Singer, Guitarist, Songwriter
Neil O'Brien Entertainment, 26 Eastcastle St, #300, London W1W 8DQ, England	
May, James	Actor
Arlington Enterprises, 1-3 Charlotte St, London W1T 1RD, England	
May, Lee A	Baseball Player
2200 Manatee Ave W, Bradenton FL 34205, USA	
May, Mark E	Football Player, Sportscaster
3557 E Minton St, Mesa AZ 85213, USA	
May, Mathilda	Actress
Voyez Mon Agent, 20 Ave Rapp, 75007 Paris, France	
May, Milton S (Milt)	Baseball Player
2200 Manatee Ave W, Bradenton FL 34205, USA	
May, Phillip (Phil)	Singer (Pretty Things)
Talent Consultants International, 105 Shad Row, #B, Piermont NY 10968 USA	
May, Ralphie	Actor, Comedian, Producer
United Talent Agency, 9336 Civic Center Dr, Beverly Hills CA 90210 USA	
May, Ray	Football Player
1921 Wellington Road, Los Angeles CA 90016, USA	
May, Richard H	WW II Navy Air Hero
3732 E Pasadena Ave, Phoenix AZ 85018, USA	
May, Rudolph (Rudy), Jr	Baseball Player
8090 N Augusta St, Fresno CA 93720, USA	
May, Scott G	Basketball Player
2001 E Hillside Dr, Bloomington IN 47401, USA	
May, Sean G	Basketball Player
2001 E Hillside Dr, Bloomington IN 47401, USA	
May, Torsten	Boxer
Frankfurt Boxing Ring, Kieler Str 9, 15234 Frankfurt/Oder, Germany	
Mayall, John	Singer, Keyboardist, Composer
30844 Grenoble Court, Westlake Village CA 91362, USA	
Mayall, Rik	Actor, Comedian
Brunskill Mgmt, 169 Queen's Gate, London SW7 5HE, England	
Mayasich, John E	Ice Hockey Player
77 E Missouri Ave Unit 45, Phoenix AZ 85012, USA	
Maybank, Anthuan	Track Athlete
171 N Porter St, Elgin IL 60120, USA	
Mayberry, E Anthony (Tony)	Football Player
15704 Cochester Road, Tampa FL 33647, USA	
Mayberry, Jermane T	Football Player
2208 Court del Rey, Round Rock TX 78681, USA	

Mayberry, John C — Baseball Player
11115 W 121st Terrace, Overland Park KS 66213, USA
Mayberry, O Lee — Basketball Player
4115 E 36th St N, Tulsa OK 74115, USA
Maybin, Cameron K — Baseball Player
85 Brompton Road, Arden NC 28704, USA
Maybury, John — Director
Independent Talent Group, Oxford House, 76 Oxford St, London W1D 1BS, England
Mayer H, Jurgen — Architect
Bleibtreystr 54, 10623 Berlin, Germany
Mayer, Christian — Alpine Skier
Siedlerweg 18, 9584 Finkelstein, Austria
Mayer, Edwin D (Ed) — Baseball Player
440 Oakdale Ave, Corte Madera CA 94925, USA
Mayer, Gene — Tennis Player
115 South St, Glenn Dale MD 20769, USA
Mayer, H Robert — Judge
US Court of Appeals, 717 Madison Place NW, Washington DC 20439, USA
Mayer, John — Singer, Songwriter
Mick Mgmt, 35 Washington St, Brooklyn NY 11201, USA
Mayer, Joseph E — Chemical Physicist
2345 Via Siena, La Jolla CA 92037, USA
Mayer, Marissa — Businesswoman
Yahoo Inc, 701 1st Ave, Sunnyvale CA 94089, USA
Mayer, Michael — Director
Creative Artists Agency, 2000 Ave of Stars, #100, Los Angeles CA 90067 USA
Mayer, Travis — Freestyle Skier
37050 Williams St, Steamboat Springs CO 80487, USA
Mayers, Jamal — Ice Hockey Player
9 Terrace Gardens, Saint Louis MO 63131, USA
Mayes, Rueben — Football Player
2953 Lord Byron Place, Eugene OR 97408, USA
Mayfair, Billy — Golfer
PO Box 25490, Scottsdale AZ 85255, USA
Mayfield, Jeremy A — Auto Racing Driver
Mayfield Motorsports, 2220 Highway 49 N, Harrisburg NC 28075, USA
Mayfield, Les — Director, Producer
Creative Artists Agency, 2000 Ave of Stars, #100, Los Angeles CA 90067 USA
Mayhew of Twysden, Patrick B B — Government Official, England
House of Lords, Westminster, London SW1A 0PW, England
Mayhew, Lauren C — Singer, Actress
Abrams Artists, 9200 W Sunset Blvd, #1125, West Hollywood CA 90069 USA
Mayhew, Martin — Football Player
4035 Sonnet Dr, Tallahassee FL 32303, USA
Mayle, Peter — Writer
Knopf Publishers, 201 E 50th St, New York NY 10022, USA
Maynard, Bradley A (Brad) — Football Player
4915 Sage Lane, Long Grove IL 60047, USA
Maynard, Mimi — Actress
Schiowitz Connor, 1680 N Vine St, #1016, Los Angeles CA 90028 USA
Mayne, Brent D — Baseball Player
1863 Parkglen Circle, Costa Mesa CA 92627, USA
Mayne, D Roger — Photographer
Colway Manor, Colway Lane, Lyme Regis, Dorset DT7 3HD, England
Mayne, Kenny — Sportscaster
ESPN-TV, ESPN Plaza, 935 Middle St, Bristol CT 06010 USA
Mayne, Thomas — Pritzker Architectual Laureate
Morphosis Architects, 3444 Wesley St, Culver City CA 90232, USA
Maynor, Asa — Actress
PO Box 1469, Beverly Hills CA 90213, USA
Maynor, Eric — Basketball Player
Oklahoma City Thunder, 211 N Robinson Ave, #300, Oklahoma City OK 73102 USA
Maynor, Stephanie — Golfer
5205 Bordeaux Cove, Ellicott City MD 21043, USA
Mayo, John L (Jackie) — Baseball Player
450 Boardman Poland Road, Youngstown OH 44512, USA
Mayo, O J — Basketball Player
3576 Golf Walk Circle, Memphis TN 38125, USA
Mayock, Michael F (Mike) — Sportscaster
607 Georges Lane, Ardmore PA 19003, USA
Mayopoulos, Timothy J — Businessman, Government Official
Federal National Mortgage Association, 3900 Wisconsin Ave NW, Washington DC 20016, USA
Mayor Zaragoza, Federico — Government Official, Spain
Ma Caribe 15, Interland, Majadahonda, 28220 Madrid, Spain
Mayor, Michel G E — Astronomer
University of Geneva, Geneva Observatory, 1211 Geneva 4, Switzerland
Mayotte, Timothy S (Tim) — Tennis Player
266 W 115th St, #4A, New York NY 10026, USA
Mayron, Melanie — Actress, Director
1435 N Ogden Dr, Los Angeles CA 90046, USA
Mays, Alvoid — Football Player
3903 Cape Vista Dr, Bradenton FL 34209, USA
Mays, Daniel — Actor
Curtis Brown Group, 28-29 Haymarket St, #500, London SW1Y 4SP, England
Mays, Jayma — Actress
United Talent Agency, 9336 Civic Center Dr, Beverly Hills CA 90210 USA
Mays, Joseph E (Joe) — Baseball Player
10314 Riverbank Terrace, Bradenton FL 34212, USA
Mays, Lyle — Jazz Pianist
Ted Kurland, 173 Brighton Ave, Allston MA 02134 USA
Mays, Melinda — Model
2221 Peachtree Road NE, #D440, Atlanta GA 30309, USA
Mays, Willie H — Baseball Player
51 Mount Vernon Lane, Atherton CA 94027, USA
May-Treanor, Misty — Volleyball Player
460 NW 115th Way, Coral Springs FL 33071, USA

Mayweather, Floyd, Jr — Boxer
4720 Laguna Vista St, Las Vegas NV 89147, USA
Mayweather, Roger — Boxer, Trainer
2784 Trotwood Lane, Las Vegas NV 89108, USA
Mazach, John J — Navy Admiral
1137 Quail Roost Court, Virginia Beach VA 23451, USA
Mazar, Debi — Actress
Framework Entertainment, 9057 Nemo St, #C, West Hollywood CA 90069 USA
Mazelle, Kym — Singer
Concorde International, 101 Shepherds Bush Road, London W6 7LP, England
Mazer, Dan — Writer
United Agents, 12-26 Lexington St, London W1F 0LE, England
Mazeroski, William S (Bill) — Baseball Player
281 Walton Tea Room Road, Greensburg PA 15601, USA
Mazor, Stanley (Stan) — Inventor (Microprocessor)
F T I/Teklicon, 3031 Tisch Way, San Jose CA 95128, USA
Mazowiecki, Tadeusz — Prime Minister, Poland
Sejm R P, Ul Qiejska 4/6/8, 00-902 Warsaw, Poland
Mazur, Jay J — Labor Leader
Industrial Textile Employees Needletrades, 1710 Broadway, New York NY 10019, USA
Mazur, Monet — Actress
Innovative Artists, 1505 10th St, Santa Monica CA 90401 USA
Mazurok, Yuri A — Opera Singer
Bolshoi State Theater, Teatralnaya Pl 1, 103009 Moscow, Russia
Mazursky, Paul — Director
614 26th St, Santa Monica CA 90402, USA
Mazza, Marc — Actor
S N Bellefaye, 30 Rue Saint Marc, 75002 Paris, France
Mazza, Valeria — Model
Riccardo Ga, 8/10 Via Revere, 20123 Milan, Italy
Mazzante, Kelly — Basketball Player
New York Liberty, Madison Square Garden, 2 Penn Plaza, New York NY 10121 USA
Mazzanti, Jerry E — Football Player
1712 S Lakeshore Dr, Lake Village AR 71653, USA
Mazzara, Glen — Producer, Writer
Creative Artists Agency, 2000 Ave of Stars, #100, Los Angeles CA 90067 USA
Mazzello, Joseph — Actor
J J M Productions, 9560 Wilshire Blvd, #500, Beverly Hills CA 90212, USA
Mazzie, Marin — Actress, Singer
Mitchell K Stubbs Assoc, 8695 W Washington Blvd, #204, Culver City CA 90232 USA
Mazzilli, Lee L — Baseball Player, Manager
67 Stonehedge Dr S, Greenwich CT 06831, USA
Mazzo, Kay — Ballerina
School of American Ballet, 70 Lincoln Center Plaza, New York NY 10012, USA
Mazzucco, Raphael — Photographer
Micon, 270 W 17th St, #6D, New York NY 10011, USA
Mbatha-Raw, Gugu — Actress
Curtis Brown Group, 28-29 Haymarket St, #500, London SW1Y 4SP, England
Mbeki, Thabo M — President, South Africa
Postal Box X1000, Pretoria 0001, South Africa
Mbenga, D J — Basketball Player
6112 Winton St, Dallas TX 75214, USA
Mbete, Baleka M — President, South Africa
PO Box 15, Cape Town, South Africa
M'Bow, Amadou-Mahtar — Government Official, Senegal
BP 5276, Dakar-Fann, Senegal
MC Lyte — Rap Artist
C E S D, 10635 Santa Monica Blvd, #130, Los Angeles CA 90025 USA
McAdam, Gary — Ice Hockey Player
34 Meadow Lane, Portland ME 04103, USA
McAdams, Rachel — Actress
Magnolia Entertainment, 9595 Wilshire Blvd, #601, Beverly Hills CA 90212, USA
McAdoo, Robert A (Bob) — Basketball Player, Coach
16710 SW 82nd Ave, Village of Palmetto Bay FL 33157, USA
McAfee, Stephanie — Writer
New American Library, 1633 Broadway, New York NY 10019 USA
McAlear, Nancy — Actress
Fountainhead Talent, 121 Davenport Road, Toronto ON M5R 1HZ, Canada
McAlister, Christopher J (Chris) — Football Player
8206 Pumpkin Hill Court, Pikesville MD 21208, USA
McAlister, Dulumus J (Deuce) — Football Player
2177 Doc Webb Road, Lena MS 39094, USA
McAlpine, Christopher W (Chris) — Ice Hockey Player
4390 Reiland Lane, Saint Paul MN 55126, USA
McAlpine, Donald M — Cinematographer
377 Placer Creek Lane, Henderson NV 89014, USA
McAnally, Mac — Singer, Songwriter
Mailboat Records, 10866 Wilshire Blvd, #200, Los Angeles CA 90024, USA
McAnally, Ron — Thoroughbred Racing Trainer
18653 Paso Nuevo Dr, Tarzana CA 91356, USA
McAnany, James (Jim) — Baseball Player
1723 Cochran St, #G, Simi Valley CA 93065, USA
McAndrew, James C (Jim) — Baseball Player
17917 N 93rd St, Scottsdale AZ 85255, USA
McAndrew, Nell — Model
One the Stablings, Barnet Lane, Elstree, Herts WD6 3HJ, England
McAnuff, Des — Director
W M E Entertainment, 9601 Wilshire Blvd, #300, Beverly Hills CA 90210 USA
McAnulty, Paul — Baseball Player
921 Palomar Way, Oxnard CA 93033, USA
McArdle, Andrea — Actress, Singer
111 W 117th St, New York NY 10026, USA
McArthur, Alex — Actor
9443 Hillrose St, Sunland CA 91040, USA
McArthur, Derek — Photographer
73 Strathaven Road, Kirkmuirhill, Lanark ML11 9RW, Scotland

McArthur, James D, Jr	Navy Admiral
Commander, Network Warfare Command, 2465 Guadalcanal, Norfolk VA 23521, USA	
McArthur, John H	Educator
8 Kettle Lane, Weston MA 2493, USA	
McArthur, K Megan	Astronaut
N A S A, Johnson Space Center, 2101 NASA Road, Houston TX 77058 USA	
McArthur, William S (Bill), Jr	Astronaut
2512 Mountain Falls Court, Friendswood TX 77546, USA	
McAslan, John R	Architect
McAslan Partners, 202 Kensington Church St, London W8 4DP, England	
McAuley, Alphonso	Actor
Paradigm Agency, 360 N Crescent Dr, North Building, Beverly Hills CA 90210 USA	
McAuliffe, Callan	Actor
R G M Associates, 64-76 Kippax St, #202, Surry Hills NSW 2010, Australia	
McAuliffe, Dennis P	Army General
9160 Belvoir Woods Parkway, Fort Belvoir VA 22060, USA	
McAuliffe, Richard J (Dick)	Baseball Player
32 Worthington Dr, Farmington CT 06032, USA	
McAvoy, James	Actor
United Agents, 12-26 Lexington St, London W1F 0LE, England	
McAvoy, Thomas J (Tom)	Baseball Player
2 Clinton Court, Stillwater NY 12170, USA	
McBain, Andrew	Ice Hockey Player
87 Balsam Ave, Toronto ON M4E 3B8, Canada	
McBain, Fiona	Singer, Guitarist, Songwriter
High Road Touring, 751 Bridgeway, #200, Sausalito CA 94965 USA	
McBain, Nicko	Drummer (Iron Maiden)
Sanctuary Music Mgmt, 82 Bishop's Bridge Road, London W2 6BB, England	
McBath, Michael S (Mike)	Football Player
5044 Sailwind Circle, Orlando FL 32810, USA	
McBean, Alvin O (Al)	Baseball Player
PO Box 4475, Saint Thomas VI 00801, USA	
McBee, Rives	Golfer
1504 Canyon Oaks Dr, Irving TX 75061, USA	
McBeth, Marcus A	Baseball Player
42052 W Sunland Dr, Maricopa AZ 85138, USA	
McBrayer, Jack	Actor, Comedian
United Talent Agency, 9336 Civic Center Dr, Beverly Hills CA 90210 USA	
McBriar, Mat	Football Player
4020 Buena Vista St, Dallas TX 75204, USA	
McBride, Arnold R (Bake)	Baseball Player
4077 Reliant Circle, Owensboro KY 42301, USA	
McBride, Brian	Soccer Player
Chicago Fire, 700 S Harlem Ave, Bridgeview IL 60455 USA	
McBride, Chi	Actor
United Talent Agency, 9336 Civic Center Dr, Beverly Hills CA 90210 USA	
McBride, Christian	Jazz Bassist
Ted Kurland, 173 Brighton Ave, Allston MA 02134 USA	
McBride, Daniel F (Danny)	Actor, Comedian
Rough House, 1722 Whitley Ave, Los Angeles CA 90028, USA	
McBride, Jeff	Illusionist
Innovative Artists, 1505 10th St, Santa Monica CA 90401 USA	
McBride, Joe	Singer, Keyboardist
Universal Attractions, 135 W 26th St, #1200, New York NY 10001 USA	
McBride, Jon A	Astronaut
Image Development Group, 1018 Kanawha Blvd, #901, Charleston WV 25301, USA	
McBride, Justin T	Rodeo Rider
1714 Revard Ave, Pawhuska OK 74056, USA	
McBride, Kenneth F (Ken)	Baseball Player
3446 Cypress Ave, Cleveland OH 44109, USA	
McBride, Martina	Singer
Bruce Allen Talent, 425 Carrall St, #500, Vancouver BC V6B 6E3, Canada	
McBride, Patricia	Ballerina
Sharon Wagner Artists, 150 W End Ave, New York NY 10023, USA	
McBride, Will	Photographer
Neuve Schonhauser Str 10, 10178 Berlin, Germany	
McBridge, Macay	Baseball Player
Detroit Tigers, Comerica Park, 2100 Woodward Ave, Detroit MI 48201 USA	
McBroom, Amanda	Singer, Songwriter
Kazarian/Spencer/Ruskin, 11969 Ventura Blvd, #300, Studio City CA 91604 USA	
McBurney, Simon	Director, Writer, Actor
Troika, 74 Clerkenwell Road, #300, London EC1M 5QA, England	
McCabe, Bryan	Ice Hockey Player
6120 Via Venetia S, Delray Beach FL 33484, USA	
McCabe, Eamonn P	Photographer
Guardian, 119 Farrington Road, London EC1R 3ER, England	
McCabe, Frank	Basketball Player
6712 N White Fir Dr, Edwards IL 61528, USA	
McCabe, Joe R	Baseball Player
3932 E 79th St, Indianapolis IN 46240, USA	
McCabe, John	Composer, Concert Pianist
Novello Co, 8/9 Firth St, London W1V 5TZ, England	
McCabe, Patrick	Writer
Picador, Macmillan Books, 25 Eccleston Place, London SW1W 9NF, England	
McCabe, Zia	Singer, Guitarist (Dandy Warhols)
Monqui Mgmt, PO Box 5908, Portland OR 97228, USA	
McCafferty, Donald F (Don), Jr	Football Coach
167 E Shore Road, Halesite NY 11743, USA	
McCaffrey, Barry R	Army General, Government Official
McCaffrey Assoc, 1800 Diagonal Road, #600, Alexandria VA 22314, USA	
McCaffrey, Edward T (Ed)	Football Player
321 Paragon Way, Castle Rock CO 80108, USA	
McCahill, Crystal	Model
Playboy Promotions, 2706 Media Center Dr, Los Angeles CA 90065 USA	
McCain, Edwin	Singer, Songwriter
Harrington Mgmt, PO Box 1267, Decatur GA 30031, USA	

McCain, Frances Lee — Actress
8075 W 3rd St, #303, Los Angeles CA 90048, USA
McCain, Howard — Director, Writer
Circle of Confusion, 10723 71st Road, #300, Forest Hills NY 11375, USA
McCall, Brian A — Baseball Player
550 Tremont Ave, #200, London NW1 8HH, England
McCall, C W — Singer, Songwriter
PO Box E, Ouray CO 81427, USA
McCall, Darrell — Singer, Songwriter
Texas Sounds Entertainment, 633 Davis Road, League City TX 77573, USA
McCall, John W (Windy) — Baseball Player
8043 E Ragweed Dr, Tucson AZ 85710, USA
McCall, Mitzi — Actress
C E S D, 10635 Santa Monica Blvd, #130, Los Angeles CA 90025 USA
McCall, Oliver — Boxer
Warrior's Boxing Promotions, 5397 Orange Dr, #202, Davie FL 33314, USA
McCall, Reese — Football Player
1311 1st Ave N, Bessemer AL 35020, USA
McCall, Ross — Actor
Stone Manners Salners, 9911 W Pico Blvd, #1400, Los Angeles CA 90035 USA
McCallany, Holt — Actor
Mosiac Media Group, 9200 W Sunset Blvd, #1000, Los Angeles CA 90069 USA
McCallister, Blaine — Golfer
1878 Epping Forest Way S, Jacksonville FL 32217, USA
McCallum, David — Actor
Abrams Artists, 275 7th Ave, #2600, New York NY 10001, USA
McCallum, Napoleon A — Football Player
314 Doe Run Circle, Henderson NV 89012, USA
McCament, L Randall (Randy) — Baseball Player
17338 N Del Webb Blvd, Sun City AZ 85373, USA
McCamus, Tom — Actor
Gary Goddard Agency, 10 Sainte Mary St, #305, Toronto ON M4Y 1P9, Canada
McCandless, Bruce, II — Astronaut
210932 Pleasant Park Dr, Conifer CO 80433, USA
McCanlies, Tim — Director, Producer, Writer
Gotham Group, 9255 W Sunset Blvd, #515, Los Angeles CA 90069, USA
McCann, Brendan M — Basketball Player
599 Shinnecock Lane, Green Cove Springs FL 32043, USA
McCann, Brian M — Baseball Player
869 Big Horn Hollow, Sun City AZ 85373, USA
McCann, Leslie C (Les) — Jazz Singer, Pianist, Composer
De Leon Artists, PO Box 21329, Piedmont CA 94620 USA
McCann, Renetta E — Businesswoman
Starcom MediaVest Group, 35 W Wacker Dr, Chicago IL 60601, USA
McCann, Sean — Singer (Great Big Sea)
Fleming Assoc, 167 Little Lake Dr, Ann Arbor MI 48103, USA
McCardell, Keenan W — Football Player
4918 Newpoint Dr, Fresno TX 77545, USA
McCareins, Justin — Football Player
7707 Andes Lane, Parkland FL 33067, USA
McCarley, Erin — Singer, Guitarist, Songwriter
Mick Mgmt, 35 Washington St, Brooklyn NY 11201, USA
McCarney, P Daniel (Dan) — Football Coach
North Texas University, Athletic Dept, 1155 Union Circle, Denton TX 76203, USA
McCarren, Laurence A (Larry) — Football Player
520 W Chickadee Lane, Green Bay WI 54313, USA
McCarrick, Theodore E Cardinal — Religious Leader
Archdiocesan Pastoral Center, 5001 Eastern Ave, Washington DC 20017, USA
McCarron, Christopher (Chris) — Thoroughbred Racing Jockey
4158 Paris Pike, Georgetown KY 40324, USA
McCarron, Douglas J — Labor Leader
Carpenters/Joiners Brotherhood, 101 Connecticut Ave NW, Washington DC 20001, USA
McCarron, Scott — Golfer
78225 Calle Cadiz, La Quinta CA 92253, USA
McCarry, Charles — Writer
Random House, 1745 Broadway, #1800, New York NY 10019 USA
McCartan, John W (Jack) — Ice Hockey Player
15504 Almond Lane, Eden Prairie MN 55347, USA
McCarter, Andre E — Basketball Player
3257 Kibbe Court, Lawrenceville GA 30044, USA
McCarthy, Andrew — Actor
4708 Vesper Ave, Sherman Oaks CA 91403, USA
McCarthy, Cormac — Writer
1101 N Mesa, El Paso TX 79002, USA
McCarthy, Dennis — Composer
First Artists Mgmt, 4764 Park Granada, #210, Calabasas CA 91302 USA
McCarthy, Jenny — Model, Actress
Untitled Entertainment, 350 S Beverly Dr, #200, Beverly Hills CA 90212 USA
McCarthy, John J (Johnny) — Basketball Player
1350 Union Road, #2F, West Seneca NY 14224, USA
McCarthy, Julianna — Actress
Stone Manners Salners, 9911 W Pico Blvd, #1400, Los Angeles CA 90035 USA
McCarthy, Justin D — Navy Admiral
Director, Material Readiness/Logistics, HqUSN, Pentagon, Washington DC 20350, USA
McCarthy, Kevin — Ice Hockey Player, Coach
1139 Warf Road, Lexington NC 27292, USA
McCarthy, Laurie — Producer
United Talent Agency, 9336 Civic Center Dr, Beverly Hills CA 90210 USA
McCarthy, Melissa — Actress
Creative Artists Agency, 2000 Ave of Stars, #100, Los Angeles CA 90067 USA
McCarthy, Mike — Football Coach
Green Bay Packers, 1265 Lombardi Ave, Green Bay WI 54304 USA
McCarthy, Nicholas A (Nick) — Singer, Guitarist (Franz Ferdinand)
M A M A Group, 57-65 Worship Ave, London EC2A 2DU, England
McCarthy, Steve — Ice Hockey Player
1019 W Jackson Blvd, #3F, Chicago IL 60607, USA

McCarthy, Thomas J (Tom) — Actor, Director
Gersh Agency, 9465 Wilshire Blvd, #600, Beverly Hills CA 90212 USA

McCarthy, Thomas M (Tom) — Baseball Player
PO Box 38, Limington ME 04049, USA

McCarthy-Miller, Beth — Director
Creative Artists Agency, 2000 Ave of Stars, #100, Los Angeles CA 90067 USA

McCartney, James L — Singer, Guitarist, Songwriter
Engine Company Records, 334 Bleeker St, #K144, New York NY 10014, USA

McCartney, Jesse — Actor, Singer
Sugar Beats Entertainment, 12129 Maxwellton Ave, Studio City CA 91604, USA

McCartney, Paul — Singer (Beatles); Songwriter
M P L Communications Ltd, 1 Soho Square, London W1V 6BQ, England

McCartney, Stella — Fashion Designer
34-36 Perrymount Road, Haywards Heath, West Susex RH16 3DN, England

McCarty, Darren — Ice Hockey Player
McCarthy Cancer Foundation, PO Box 1874, Royal Oak MI 48066, USA

McCarty, David A — Baseball Player
110 Waldo Ave, Piedmont CA 94611, USA

McCarty, Walter L — Basketball Player
7525 Pine Valley Lane, Indianapolis IN 46250, USA

McCarver, J Timothy (Tim) — Baseball Player, Sportscaster
5825 Riegels Harbor Road, Sarasota FL 34242, USA

McCary, Michael — Singer (Boyz II Men)
Spectrum Talent, 9107 Wilshire Blvd, #450, Beverly Hills CA 90210, USA

McCashin, Constance — Actress
66 Fountain St, West Newton MA 02465, USA

McCaskill, Kirk E — Baseball Player
33985 Cape Cove, Dana Point CA 92629, USA

McCaslin, Donny — Jazz Saxophonist
Greenleaf Records, PO Box 477364, Chicago IL 60647 USA

McCatty, Steven E (Steve) — Baseball
1075 Woodbriar Dr, Oxford MI 48371, USA

McCauley, Barry — Opera Singer
598 Ridgewood Road, Oradell NJ 07649, USA

McCauley, Donald F (Don), Jr — Football Player
Rams Club, PO Box 2446, Chapel Hill NC 27515, USA

McCauley, James Michael — Actor, Composer, Director
Stone Manners Salners, 9911 W Pico Blvd, #1400, Los Angeles CA 90035 USA

McCauley, William F — Navy Admiral
670 Margarita Ave, Coronado CA 92118, USA

McCaw, Bruce — Auto Racing Executive
PacWest Racing Group, PO Box 1717, Bellevue WA 98009, USA

McCay, Peggy — Actress
2714 Carmar Dr, Los Angeles CA 90046, USA

McClain Johnson, Katrina — Basketball Player
1907 Carlton St, North Charleston SC 29405, USA

McClain, Cady — Actress
Innovative Artists, 235 Park Ave S, #1000, New York NY 10003 USA

McClain, Charly — Singer
John Lentz, PO Box 198888, Nashville TN 37219, USA

McClain, China Anne — Actress
Paradigm Agency, 360 N Crescent Dr, North Building, Beverly Hills CA 90210 USA

McClain, Dewey L — Football Player
1032 Flagg Way, Lawrenceville GA 30044, USA

McClain, Johnathan — Actor
Innovative Artists, 1505 10th St, Santa Monica CA 90401 USA

McClain, Scott M — Baseball Player
660 Golden Gate Point, #61, Sarasota FL 34236, USA

McClain, Theodore (Ted) — Basketball Player
104 Eaton Court, Nashville TN 37218, USA

McClairen, Jack (Cy) — Football Player, Basketball Coach
1337 Idlewild Dr, Daytona Beach FL 32114, USA

McClamon, Zahn — Actor
Amsel Eisenstadt Frazier, 5055 Wilshire Blvd, #865, Los Angeles CA 90036 USA

McClanahan, Brent A — Football Player
1100 Sayword Court, Bakersfield CA 93312, USA

McClanahan, Randall D (Randy) — Football Player
8107 W Via del Sol, Peoria AZ 85383, USA

McClanahan, Robert B (Rob) — Ice Hockey Player
3310 Watertown Road, Long Lake MN 55356, USA

McClary, Thomas (Tom) — Guitarist, Singer (Commodores)
Management Assoc, 1920 Benson Ave, Saint Paul MN 55116, USA

McClatchy, J D — Writer, Editor
15 Grand St, Stonington CT 06378, USA

McClean, Lalisha — Singer (Allure)
Universal Attractions, 135 W 26th St, #1200, New York NY 10001 USA

McClelland, Kevin — Ice Hockey Player
2886 Keeley Cove, Southaven MS 38671, USA

McClellin, Sheamus L (Shea) — Football Player
Chicago Bears, 1000 Football Dr, Lake Forest IL 60045 USA

McClements, Robert, Jr — Businessman
31 Cardinal Lane, Key Largo FL 33037, USA

McClenathan, Cory — Drag Racing Driver
1681 E Northfield Dr, Brownsburg IN 46112, USA

McClendon, Lloyd G — Baseball Player, Manager
1082 Mission Hills Court, Chesterton IN 46304, USA

McClendon, Reiley — Actor
Innovative Artists, 1505 10th St, Santa Monica CA 90401 USA

McCleon, Dexter K — Football Player
1901 Post Oak Blvd, #509, Houston TX 77056, USA

McClintock, Eddie — Actor
I C M Partners, 10250 Constellation Blvd, #900, Los Angeles CA 90067 USA

McClintock, William — Space Scientist
University of Colorado, Atmospheric/Space Physics Dept, Boulder CO 80309, USA

McClinton, Curtis R — Football Player
McClinton Development, 11714 Jefferson St, Kansas City MO 64114, USA

McClinton, Delbert PO Box 159008, Nashville TN 37215, USA	Singer, Musician, Songwriter
McCloskey, Jim 221 Witherspoon St, Princeton NJ 08542, USA	Social Activist
McCloskey, Paul N (Pete), Jr 580 Mountain Home Road, Woodside CA 94062, USA	Representative, CA
McCloskey, Robert J 84 Old Black Point Road, Niantic CT 06357, USA	Diplomat
McCloud, George A 19501 W Country Club Dr, #1603, Aventura FL 33180, USA	Basketball Player
McCloughan, Kent A 2241 Woody Creek Circle, Loveland CO 80538, USA	Football Player
McClover, Darrell A, II 6120 SW 19th St, Pompano Beach FL 33068, USA	Football Player
McClure, Larry Morgan-McClure Motorsports, 26502 Newbanks Road, Abingdon VA 24210, USA	Auto Racing Executive
McClure, Marc Amsel Eisenstadt Frazier, 5055 Wilshire Blvd, #865, Los Angeles CA 90036 USA	Actor
McClure, Robert C (Bob) 3834 SE Fairway E, Stuart FL 34997, USA	Baseball Player
McClure, Tane Don Gerler, 3349 Cahuenga Blvd W, #1, Los Angeles CA 90068 USA	Actress
McClure, Todd Atlanta Falcons, 4400 Falcon Parkway, Flowery Branch GA 30542 USA	Football Player
McClure, Wilbert (Skeeter) 57 Broadlawn Park, #26, Newton MA 02467, USA	Boxer
McClurg, Edie Peyrot Lagnese Mucci, 5750 Wilshire Blve, #580, Los Angeles CA 90036, USA	Actress
McClurkin, Donnie Lone Oak Entertainment, 116 Huntington Place, Hendersonville TN 37075, USA	Singer
McColgan, Elizabeth (Liz) Marquee UK, 6 George St, Nottingham NG1 3BE, England	Track Athlete
McColl, William F (Bill), Jr 5166 Chelsea St, La Jolla CA 92037, USA	Football Player
McCollough, Jack Proenza Schouler, 120 Walker St, #1600, New York NY 10013, USA	Fashion Designer
McColluh, Thayne M Gonzaga University, President's Office, 502 E Boone Ave, Spokane WA 99258, USA	Educator
McCollum, Andrew J (Andy) 3933 Autumn Farms Dr, Pacific MO 63069, USA	Football Player
McCollum, Rick Rascoff/Zysblat Organization, 250 W 57th St, New York NY 10107 USA	Guitarist (Afghan Whigs)
McColm, Matt ReBar Mgmt, 10061 Riverside Dr, #722, Toluca Lake CA 91602, USA	Actor
McComas, Brian Leon Medica Mgmt, 187 Hidden Lake Road, Hendersonville TN 37075, USA	Singer, Songwriter
McComb, Heather 1 Mgmt, 9000 W Sunset Blvd, #1550, Los Angeles CA 90069 USA	Actress
McComb, William (Bill) Liz Clairborne Inc, 1441 Broadway, New York NY 10018, USA	Businessman
McConathy, John R 2320 Belmont Blvd, Bossier City LA 71111, USA	Basketball Player
McConaughey, Matthew Creative Artists Agency, 2000 Ave of Stars, #100, Los Angeles CA 90067 USA	Actor
McConkey, Jim C 505 W 54th St, #PH 12, New York NY 10019, USA	Cinematographer
McConkey, Philip J (Phil) 1856 Viking Way, La Jolla CA 92037, USA	Football Player
McConnell, Denise Playboy Promotions, 2706 Media Center Dr, Los Angeles CA 90065 USA	Model
McConnell, Harden M Stanford University, Chemistry Dept, Stanford CA 94305, USA	Chemist
McConnell, Michael W US Court of Appeals, 2480 Cowper St, Palo Alto CA 94301, USA	Judge
McConnell, Page Dionysian Productions, 431 Pine St, Burlington VT 05401, USA	Keyboardist (Phish)
McConnell-Serio, Suzanne (Suzie) 2590 Rossmoore Dr, Pittsburgh PA 15241, USA	Basketball Player, Coach
McCoo, Marilyn Brokaw Co, 9255 W Sunset Blvd, #804, West Hollywood CA 90069 USA	Singer (Fifth Dimension), Actress
McCook, John Abrams Artists, 9200 W Sunset Blvd, #1125, West Hollywood CA 90069 USA	Actor
McCool, William J (Billy) 9250 SE 121st Loop, Summerfield FL 34491, USA	Baseball Player
McCord, AnnaLynne Innovative Artists, 1505 10th St, Santa Monica CA 90401 USA	Actress
McCord, Bob 11540 N Donley Dr, Parker CO 80138, USA	Ice Hockey Player
McCord, Darris P 6160 W Surrey Road, Bloomfield Hills MI 48301, USA	Football Player
McCord, Gary D PO Box 1964, Edwards CO 81632, USA	Golfer, Sportscaster
McCord, Joe Milton University of Colorado, Waring Institute, 4200 E 9th Ave, Denver CO 80262, USA	Biochemist
McCord, Keith R 1609 Five Acre Road, Dolomite AL 35061, USA	Basketball Player
McCord, Kent 1738 N Orange Grove Ave, Los Angeles CA 90046, USA	Actor
McCormack, Catherine 120 Riverside Dr, #7G, New York NY 10024, USA	Actress
McCormack, Donald R (Don) 866 Glenfield Dr, Palm Harbor FL 34684, USA	Baseball Player
McCormack, Eric I C M Partners, 10250 Constellation Blvd, #900, Los Angeles CA 90067 USA	Actor
McCormack, Mary Gersh Agency, 9465 Wilshire Blvd, #600, Beverly Hills CA 90212 USA	Actress

McCormack, Michael J (Mike)	Football Player, Coach, Executive
11518 SE 309th St, Auburn WA 98092, USA	
McCormack, Patty	Actress, Model
Rothman Patino Andres, 4360 Tujunga Ave, Studio City CA 91604, USA	
McCormack, Will	Actor, Writer
United Talent Agency, 9336 Civic Center Dr, Beverly Hills CA 90210 USA	
McCormick, Carolyn	Actress
TalentWorks, 220 E 23rd St, #303, New York NY 10010, USA	
McCormick, Kelly	Actress
I C M Partners, 10250 Constellation Blvd, #900, Los Angeles CA 90067 USA	
McCormick, Maureen	Actress, Singer
Rebel Entertainment Partners, 5700 Wilshire Blvd, #456, Los Angeles CA 90036, USA	
McCormick, Michael F (Mike)	Baseball Player
1600 Morganton Road, #U9, Pinehurst NC 28374, USA	
McCormick, Patricia J (Pat)	Diver
92 Riversea Road, Seal Beach CA 90740, USA	
McCormick, Timothy D (Tim)	Basketball Player
2500 Leroy Lane, West Bloomfield MI 48324, USA	
McCorvey, Bill	Singer (Pirates of the Mississippi)
Third Coast Talent, PO Box 110225, Nashville TN 37222, USA	
McCorvey, Norma	Litigant
11343 Cactus Lane, Dallas TX 75238, USA	
McCouch, Grayson	Actor
A P A Talent/Literary Agency, 405 S Beverly Dr, #300, Beverly Hills CA 90212 USA	
McCoughtry, Angel	Basketball Player
Atlanta Dream, 83 Walton St NW, #400, Atlanta, GA 30303 USA	
McCourt, Frank	Baseball Executive
22426 Pacific Coast Highway, Malibu CA 90265, USA	
McCoury, Del	Singer, Guitarist (Del McCoury Band)
R S Entertainment, 329 Rockland Road, Hendersonville TN 37075, USA	
McCoury, Robbie	Banjo Player (Del McCoury Band)
R S Entertainment, 329 Rockland Road, Hendersonville TN 37075, USA	
McCoury, Ronnie	Mandolin Player (Del McCoury Band)
R S Entertainment, 329 Rockland Road, Hendersonville TN 37075, USA	
McCovey, Willie L	Baseball Player
PO Box 620342, Redwood City CA 94062, USA	
McCowan, Dustin M	Baseball Player
PO Box 1281, Ludowici GA 31316, USA	
McCowen, Alec	Actor
Conway Van Gelder Grant, 8-12 Broadwick St, #300, London W1F 8HW, England	
McCown, Joshusa T (Josh)	Football Player
1312 Lookout Circle, Waxhaw NC 28173, USA	
McCown, Lucas P (Luke)	Football Player
30963 US Highway 69 N, Rusk TX 75785, USA	
McCoy, Glenn	Editorial Cartoonist
Belleville News-Democrat, Editorial Dept, 120 S Illinois, Bellville IL 62220, USA	
McCoy, Jason	Singer, Songwriter
Agency Group Ltd, 142 W 57th St, #600, New York NY 10019 USA	
McCoy, Jennifer	Photographer, Artist
Postmasters Gallery, 459 W 19th St, New York NY 10011, USA	
McCoy, Jordan	Singer
Bad Boy Entertainment, 1440 Broadway, #16, New York NY 10018 USA	
McCoy, Kevin	Photographer, Artist
New York University, Steinhardt Art School, New York NY 10003, USA	
McCoy, Larry S	Baseball Umpire
5758 Highway 139, Greenway AR 72430, USA	
McCoy, Matt	Actor
A K A Talent, 6310 San Vicente Blvd, #200, Los Angeles CA 90048 USA	
McCoy, Michael C (Mike)	Football Player
PO Box 464263, Lawrenceville GA 30042, USA	
McCoy, Michael P (Mike)	Football Player
2224 Cotton Gin Row, Jefferson GA 30549, USA	
McCoy, Mike (Mouse)	Director
Bandito Brothers, 3115 S La Cienega Blvd, Los Angeles CA 10016, USA	
McCoy, Neal	Singer
Cherry Miller Kane Entertainment, 53 Concord Park E, Nashville TN 37205, USA	
McCoy, Sandra	Actress
Main Title Mgmt, 8383 Wilshire Blvd, #408, Beverly Hills CA 90211 USA	
McCoy, Sherilyn S	Businesswoman
Avon Products, 1345 Ave of Americas, Basement Concourse 9, New York NY 10105, USA	
McCracken, Quinton A	Baseball Player
11308 E Autumn Sage Dr, Scottsdale AZ 85255, USA	
McCrackin, Daisy	Actress
Stone Manners Salners, 9911 W Pico Blvd, #1400, Los Angeles CA 90035 USA	
McCrane, Paul	Actor
United Talent Agency, 9336 Civic Center Dr, Beverly Hills CA 90210 USA	
McCraney, Tarell Alvin	Writer
I C M Partners, 10250 Constellation Blvd, #900, Los Angeles CA 90067 USA	
McCrary, Darius	Actor
Diverse Talent Group, 9911 W Pico Blvd, #350W, Los Angeles CA 90035, USA	
McCrary, Fred D	Football Player
134 Grandmar Chase, Clermont FL 34711, USA	
McCrary, Joel	Actor
C E S D, 10635 Santa Monica Blvd, #130, Los Angeles CA 90025 USA	
McCrary, Michael C	Football Player
9907 Chase Hill Court, Vienna VA 22182, USA	
McCraw, Tommy L (Tom)	Baseball Player
3142 SE Monte Vista Court, Port Saint Lucie FL 34952, USA	
McCray, Bobby L, Jr	Football Player
14907 SW 52nd St, Miramar FL 33027, USA	
McCray, Nikki	Basketball Player
4278 Fox Hills Dr, Louisville TN 37777, USA	
McCray, Prentice	Football Player
2109 N Argonaut St, Stockton CA 95204, USA	
McCray, Rodney E	Basketball Player
33 Bonita Vista Road, Mount Vernon NY 10552, USA	

McCrea, John | Singer (Cake), Songwriter
Umbrella Group, 1 West St, #3506, New York NY 10004, USA
McCready, Malinda G (Mindy) | Singer
Creative Artists Agency, 3310 W End Ave, #500, Nashville TN 37203 USA
McCready, Mike | Guitarist (Pearl Jam)
Curtis Mgmt, 1900 S Corgiat Dr, Seattle WA 98108, USA
McCreary, Bear | Composer
3622 Clarington Ave, #5, Los Angeles CA 90034, USA
McCreary, William (Bill), Sr | Ice Hockey Player, Coach
4318 Highcrest Dr, #1, Brighton MI 48116, USA
McCree, Marlon T | Football Player
2109 N Argonaut St, Windermere FL 34786, USA
McCrory, Glenn | Boxer
Yetholm Place, Newiggin Hall, Newcastle upon Tyne NE5 4EB, England
McCrory, Helen | Actress
Independent Talent Group, Oxford House, 76 Oxford St, London W1D 1BS, England
McCrory, Milton (Milt) | Boxer
Escot Boxing Enterprises, 19244 Bretton Dr, Detroit MI 48223, USA
McCrory, Robert (Bob) | Baseball Player
30 Rebecca Lane, Hattiesburg MS 39402, USA
McCuigan, Paul | Director
Fallout Entertainment, 3100 Airport Ave, Santa Monica CA 90405, USA
McCullagh, Peter | Mathematician, Statistician
University of Chicago, Statistics Dept, 5734 University Ave, Chicago IL 60637, USA
McCullers, Lance G | Baseball Player
3309 Hoedt Road, Tampa FL 33618, USA
McCulley, Michael J | Astronaut
365 Private Road 652, Bay City TX 77414, USA
McCullin, Donald (Don) | Photographer
Hamiltons Gallery, 13 Carlos Place, London W1, England
McCulloch, Bruce | Actor, Writer, Producer
United Talent Agency, 9336 Civic Center Dr, Beverly Hills CA 90210 USA
McCulloch, Earl | Football Player, Track Athlete
2108 Santa Fe Ave, #15, Long Beach CA 90810, USA
McCulloch, Ed (Ace) | Auto Racing Driver
1397 Cherry Tree Road, Avon IN 46123, USA
McCullough, Bernard J (Barry), III | Navy Admiral
Commander, Cyber Command & 10th Fleet, Fort George C Meade MD 20755, USA
McCullough, Colleen | Writer
PO Box 333, Norfolk Island NSW 2899, Australia
McCullough, David | Writer, Entertainer
Creative Artists Agency, 2000 Ave of Stars, #100, Los Angeles CA 90067 USA
McCullough, Kimberly | Actress, Singer, Dancer
Brillstein Entertainment Partners, 9150 Wilshire Blvd, #350, Beverly Hills CA 90212 USA
McCullough, Wayne | Boxer
Sky Sports, Grants Way, Isleworth, Middlesex TW7 5QD, England
McCullum, Samuel C (Sam) | Football Player
7701 88th Place SE, Mercer Island WA 98040, USA
McCumber, Mark | Golfer, Sportscaster
527 Le Master Dr, Ponte Vedra Beach FL 32082, USA
McCune, Don | Bowler
3551 Coventry Gardens Dr, Las Vegas NV 89135, USA
McCurdy, Jennette | Actress, Singer
Management 360, 9111 Wilshire Blvd, Beverly Hills CA 90210 USA
McCurry, Jeffrey D (Jeff) | Baseball Player
9015 Linkmeadow Lane, Houston TX 77025, USA
McCurry, Margaret | Architect
Tigerman McCurry Architects, 444 N Wells St, #206, Chicago IL 60654, USA
McCurry, Mike | Government Official, Journalist
CNN-TV, 190 Marietta Ave SW, Atlanta GA 30303 USA
McCurry, Steve | Photographer
2 5th Ave, New York NY 10011, USA
McCusker, James B (Jim) | Football Player
209 N Main St, Jamestown NY 14701, USA
McCusker, Joan | Curling Athlete
Curling Assn, 1660 Vimont Court, Cumberland ON K4A 4J4, Canada
McCutchen, Andrew S | Baseball Player
Pittsburgh Pirates, P N C Park, 115 Federal St, #115B, Pittsburgh PA 15212 USA
McCutcheon, Daylon | Football Player
4393 Hiwassee, Claremont CA 91711, USA
McCutcheon, Hugh | Volleyball Coach
US Olympic Committee, 1 Olympia Plaza, Building 6, Colorado Springs CO 80909, USA
McCutcheon, Lawrence | Football Player
19981 Weems Lane, Huntington Beach CA 92646, USA
McCutcheon, Linda | Publisher
A A R P Publications, Director's Office, 601 E St NW, Washington DC 20049, USA
McCutcheon, Martine | Actress, Singer
Amanda Howard, 74 Clerkenwell Road, London EC1M 5QA, England
McDaniel, Chris | Keyboardist (Confederate Railroad)
Bobby Roberts, 3050 Business Park Circle, #303, Goodlettsville TN 37221 USA
McDaniel, Edward (Ed) | Football Player
13111 Brenwood Trail, Hopkins MN 55343, USA
McDaniel, James | Actor
Innovative Artists, 1505 10th St, Santa Monica CA 90401 USA
McDaniel, John (Johnny) | Football Player
608 Andalusia Trail, De Soto TX 75115, USA
McDaniel, Lyndall D (Lindy) | Baseball Player
16641 E 1550 Road, Hollis OK 73550, USA
McDaniel, Randall C | Football Player
20405 Manor Road, Excelsior MN 55331, USA
McDaniel, Terence L (Terry) | Football Player
730 Shenandoah, Cedar Hill TX 75104, USA
McDaniel, Xavier M | Basketball Player
2 Oakmist Court, Blythewood SC 29016, USA
McDaniels, Darryl (Darryl M) | Rap Artist (Run-DMC)
Richard Walters, PO Box 2789, Toluca Lake CA 91610 USA

McDaniels, James R (Jim) — Basketball Player
2549 Smallhouse Road, Bowling Green KY 42104, USA
McDaniels, Josh — Football Coach
Saint Louis Rams, 901 N Broadway, Saint Louis MO 63101 USA
McDaniels, Pellom — Football Player
333 W Meyer Blvd, #608, Kansas City MO 64113, USA
McDavid, Ray D — Baseball Player
1245 Market St, #1348, San Diego CA 92101, USA
McDavis, Roderick J — Educator
Ohio University, President's Office, Athens OH 45701, USA
McDermott, Anne-Marie — Concert Pianist
Opus 3 Artists, 470 Park Ave S, #900N, New York NY 10016 USA
McDermott, Charlie — Actor
Kritzer Levine Wilkins, 8840 Wilshire Blvd, #100, Beverly Hills CA 90211, USA
McDermott, Colleen — Actress
C E S D, 10635 Santa Monica Blvd, #130, Los Angeles CA 90025 USA
McDermott, Dean — Actor, Writer, Producer
United Talent Agency, 9336 Civic Center Dr, Beverly Hills CA 90210 USA
McDermott, Dylan — Actor
Schiff Co, 8440 Warner Dr, #B1, Culver City CA 90232 USA
McDermott, John — Singer, Songwriter
Artistopia, PO Box 6691, Woodbridge VA 22195, USA
McDermott, R Terrance (Terry) — Speed Skater
5078 Chainbridge Dr, Bloomfield Hills MI 48304, USA
McDermott, Terence K (Terry) — Baseball Player
7205 Sunlight Peak Dr NE, Rio Rancho NM 87144, USA
McDiarmid, Ian — Actor
Independent Talent Group, Oxford House, 76 Oxford St, London W1D 1BS, England
McDill, Alan — Baseball Player
244 Richwoods Road, Arkadelphia AR 71923, USA
McDivitt, James A (Jim) — Astronaut, Air Force General
3530 E Calle Puerta de Acero, Tucson AZ 85718, USA
McDole, Roland O (Ron) — Football Player
2083 Lockes Mill Road, Berryville VA 22611, USA
McDonagh, John Michael — Director, Producer, Writer
United Talent Agency, 9336 Civic Center Dr, Beverly Hills CA 90210 USA
McDonagh, Martin — Writer, Director
Creative Artists Agency, 2000 Ave of Stars, #100, Los Angeles CA 90067 USA
McDonald, Alvin B (Ab) — Ice Hockey Player
419 Thompson Dr, Winnipeg MB R3J 3E7, Canada
McDonald, Arthur B — Physicist
Queen's University, Physics Dept, Kingston ON K7L 3N6, Canada
McDonald, Audra — Actress, Singer
W M E Entertainment, 1325 Ave of Americas, New York NY 10019 USA
McDonald, Ben — Baseball Player
8780 Henderson Road, Denham Springs LA 70726, USA
McDonald, Christopher — Actor
Gersh Agency, 9465 Wilshire Blvd, #600, Beverly Hills CA 90212 USA
McDonald, Country Joe — Singer, Guitarist
PO Box 7054, Berkeley CA 94707, USA
McDonald, Glenn S — Basketball Player
2135 Vuelta Grande Ave, Long Beach CA 90815, USA
McDonald, James L (Jim) — Baseball Player
PO Box 995, Brea CA 92822, USA
McDonald, James Z — Baseball Player
Los Angeles Dodgers, Stadium, 1000 Elysian Park Ave, Los Angeles CA 90090 USA
McDonald, Jiggs — Sportscaster
8331 Arborfield Court, Fort Myers FL 33912, USA
McDonald, John J — Baseball Player
3546 Michigan Ave, Cincinnati OH 45208, USA
McDonald, L Benard (Ben) — Baseball Player
8780 Henderson Road, Denham Springs LA 70726, USA
McDonald, Lanny — Ice Hockey Player
23 Springside St, Calgary AB T3Z 3M1, Canada
McDonald, Mackey J — Businessman
V F Corp, 628 Green Valley Road, Greensboro NC 27408, USA
McDonald, Michael — Singer, Songwriter
I C M Partners, 10250 Constellation Blvd, #900, Los Angeles CA 90067 USA
McDonald, Miriam — Actress
Innovative Artists, 1505 10th St, Santa Monica CA 90401 USA
McDonald, Paul B — Football Player
1815 Tradewinds Lane, Newport Beach CA 92660, USA
McDonald, Richie — Singer (Lonestar)
PO Box 128648, Nashville TN 37212, USA
McDonald, Robert M — Businessman
Procter & Gamble, 1 Procter & Gamble Plaza, Cincinnati OH 45202, USA
McDonald, Thomas F (Tommy) — Football Player
537 W Valley Forge Road, King of Prussia PA 19406, USA
McDonald, Timothy (Tim) — Football Player
2432 Lexington Ave, Clovis CA 93619, USA
McDonell, Thomas — Actor
W M E Entertainment, 9601 Wilshire Blvd, #300, Beverly Hills CA 90210 USA
McDonnell, Dirk — Photographer
Throckmorton Fine Art, 145 E 57th St, #300, New York NY 10022, USA
McDonnell, John F — Businessman
McDonnell Douglas Corp, PO Box 516, Saint Louis MO 63166, USA
McDonnell, Mary — Actress
Innovative Artists, 1505 10th St, Santa Monica CA 90401 USA
McDonnell, Patrick — Cartoonist (Mutts)
King Features Syndicate, 300 W 57th St, #1500, New York NY 10019 USA
McDonough, Mary — Actress
6858 Canteloupe Ave, Van Nuys CA 91405, USA
McDonough, Matthew (Spag) — Drummer (Mudvayne)
Agency Group Ltd, 142 W 57th St, #600, New York NY 10019 USA
McDonough, Michael — Cinematographer
Sheldon Prosnit Agency, 800 S Robertson Blvd, Los Angeles CA 90035, USA

McDonough, Neal — Actor
Paradigm Agency, 360 N Crescent Dr, North Building, Beverly Hills CA 90210 USA
McDonough, Sean — Sportscaster
ABC-TV, Sports Dept, 77 W 66th St, New York NY 10023 USA
McDonough, William — Architect
700 E Jefferson St, Charlottesville VA 22902, USA
McDonough, William J — Government Official, Financier
Public Company Accounting Oversight Board, 1666 K NW, Washington DC 20006, USA
McDorman, Jake — Actor
United Talent Agency, 9336 Civic Center Dr, Beverly Hills CA 90210 USA
McDormand, Frances — Actress
D/F Mgmt, 270 Lafayette St, #402, New York NY 10012 USA
McDougal, R Meiklejohn (Mike) — Baseball Player
Kansas City Royals, Kauffman Stadium, 1 Royal Way, Kansas City MO 64129 USA
McDougall, Charles — Director, Writer
United Agents, 12-26 Lexington St, London W1F 0LE, England
McDougall, Walter A — Historian
University of Pennsylvania, History Dept, Philadelphia PA 19104, USA
McDowell, Jack B — Baseball Player
3104 Del Rey Ave, Carlsbad CA 92009, USA
McDowell, Leonard (Bubba) — Football Player
6353 Richmond Ave, Houston TX 77057, USA
McDowell, Oddibe — Baseball Player
5240 SW 18th St, West Park FL 33023, USA
McDowell, Roger A — Baseball Player
2690 Pete Shaw Road, Marietta GA 30066, USA
McDowell, Ronnie — Singer, Guitarist
PO Box 53, Portland TN 37148, USA
McDowell, Samuel E (Sam) — Baseball Player
City of Legends, 1925 Don Wickham Dr, Clermont FL 34711, USA
McDuffie, Matthew — Writer
Paradigm Agency, 360 N Crescent Dr, North Building, Beverly Hills CA 90210 USA
McDuffie, Otis J (O J) — Football Player
1333 NW 121st Ave, Plantation FL 33323, USA
McDuffie, Robert — Concert Violinist, Conductor
Columbia Artists Mgmt Inc, 1790 Broadway, #702, New York NY 10019 USA
McDyess, Antonio K — Basketball Player
30 Cranbrook Road, Bloomfield Hills MI 48304, USA
McEachern, Shawn — Ice Hockey Player
71 Beach St, Marblehead MA 01945, USA
McEldowney, Brooke — Cartoonist (9 Chickwood Lane)
United Feature Syndicate, PO Box 5610, Cincinnati OH 45201 USA
McElhenney, Rob — Producer, Writer, Actor
3 Arts Entertainment, 9460 Wilshire Blvd, #700, Beverly Hills CA 90212 USA
McElhenny, Hugh E — Football Player
3013 Via Venezia, Henderson NV 89052, USA
McElhone, Natascha — Actress
Paradigm Agency, 360 N Crescent Dr, North Building, Beverly Hills CA 90210 USA
McElligott, Dominique — Actress
Creative Artists Agency, 2000 Ave of Stars, #100, Los Angeles CA 90067 USA
McElmury, James D (Jim) — Ice Hockey Player
9122 78th Street S, Cottage Grove MN 55016, USA
McElroy, Charles D (Chuck) — Baseball Player
1049 Nederland Ave, Port Arthur TX 77640, USA
McElroy, Reginald L (Reggie) — Football Player
RR 1 Box 109A, Preston MO 65732, USA
McElroy, Vann W — Football Player
524 Private Road 4450, Uvalde TX 78801, USA
McEnaney, William H (Will) — Baseball Player
1055 SW 3rd St, Boca Raton FL 33486, USA
McEnery, Peter R — Actor
Richard Stone Partnership, 85 New Cavendish St, London W1W 6XD, England
McEnroe, John P, Jr — Tennis Player, Sportscaster
1080 5th Ave, New York NY 10128, USA
McEntire, Reba — Singer, Actress
W M E Entertainment, 9601 Wilshire Blvd, #300, Beverly Hills CA 90210 USA
McEuen, John — Musician (Nitty Gritty Dirt Band)
New Frontier Touring, 1921 Broadway, Nashville TN 37203, USA
McEwan, Geraldine — Actress
Independent Talent Group, Oxford House, 76 Oxford St, London W1D 1BS, England
McEwan, Ian R — Writer
15 Park Town, Oxford OX2 6SN, England
McEwen, Mark — Commentator
CBS-TV, News Dept, 51 W 52nd St, New York NY 10019 USA
McEwen, Mike — Ice Hockey Player
3712 N Peniel Ave, Bethany OK 73008, USA
McEwen, Tom — Drag Racing Driver
17368 Buttonwood St, Fountain Valley CA 92708, USA
McEwing, Joseph E (Joe) — Baseball Player
630 Deerbrook Dr, Yardley PA 19067, USA
McFadden, Bryan N — Singer, Pianist, Songwriter
Concorde International, 101 Shepherds Bush Road, London W6 7LP, England
McFadden, Cynthia — Commentator
ABC-TV, News Dept, 77 W 66th St, New York NY 10023 USA
McFadden, Daniel L — Nobel Economics Laureate
41 Southampton Ave, Berkeley CA 94707, USA
McFadden, Darren — Football Player
Oakland Raiders, 1220 Harbor Bay Parkway, Alameda CA 94502 USA
McFadden, Davenia — Actress
Don Buchwald/Fortitude, 6500 Wilshire Blvd, #2200, Los Angeles CA 90048 USA
McFadden, Gates — Actress
Innovative Artists, 1505 10th St, Santa Monica CA 90401 USA
McFadden, Katy — Sculptor, Ceramist
313 SW Maricara St, Portland OR 97219, USA
McFadden, Leon — Baseball Player
8617 S 10th Ave, Inglewood CA 90305, USA

McFadden, Mary J — Fashion Designer
525 E 72nd St, #2A, New York NY 10021, USA

McFadden, Paul — Football Player
7395 Christopher Dr, Youngstown OH 44514, USA

McFadden, Robert D — Journalist
New York Times, Editorial Dept, 229 W 43rd St, New York NY 10036, USA

McFadden-Rusynyk, Betty Jean — Baseball Player
7267 W 130th St, Cleveland OH 44130, USA

McFadyen, Jack — Artist
284 Globe Road, London E2 0NS, England

McFarland, Anthony D — Football Player
7733 Still Lakes Dr, Odessa FL 33556, USA

McFarland, Dennis — Writer
Henry Holt, 175 5th Ave, #400, New York NY 10010 USA

McFarland, James D (Jim) — Football Player
5102 S 90th St, Lincoln NE 68526, USA

McFarland, Michael C — Educator
Holy Cross University, President's Office, 1 College St, Worcester MA 01610, USA

McFarland, R Kay — Football Player
7394 Monaco St, Centennial CO 80112, USA

McFarlane, Robert C — Government Official
2010 Prospect St NW, Washington DC 20037, USA

McFarlane, Todd — Cartoonist (Spawn)
Todd McFarlane Entertainment, 1711 W Greentree Dr, Tempe AZ 85284, USA

McFarling, Ursula Lee — Journalist
Los Angeles Times, Editorial Dept, 202 W 1st St, Los Angeles CA 90012 USA

McFaull, David — Yachtsman
109 Poloke Place, Honolulu HI 96822, USA

McFeely, William S — Historian, Writer
35 Mill Hill Road, Wellfleet MA 02667, USA

McFerrin, Bobby — Singer, Songwriter
W M E Entertainment, 9601 Wilshire Blvd, #300, Beverly Hills CA 90210 USA

McG — Director
W M E Entertainment, 9601 Wilshire Blvd, #300, Beverly Hills CA 90210 USA

McGaffigan, Andrew J (Andy) — Baseball Player
6243 Forestwood Dr E, Lakeland FL 33811, USA

McGahee, Willis A, III — Football Player
225 NE Mizner Blvd, #685, Boca Raton FL 33432, USA

McGahey Heinzler, Kathleen — Field Hockey Player
7427 W 81st St, Los Angeles CA 90045, USA

McGann, Michelle — Golfer
1200 Singer Dr, West Palm Beach FL 33404, USA

McGann, Paul — Actor
Ken McReddie Assoc, 11 Connaught Place, London W2 2ET, England

McGann, Stephen — Actor
Associated International Mgmt, Fairfax House, Fulwood Place, London WC1V 6HU, England

McGarity, Vernon — WW II Army Hero (CMH)
6901 Andrews Road, Memphis TN 38135, USA

McGarrahan, J Scott — Football Player
4704 Monte Carmelo Place, Austin TX 78738, USA

McGarrigle, Anna — Singer, Songwriter
Concerted Efforts, PO Box 440326, Somerville MA 02144 USA

McGarry, Steve — Cartoonist (Pop Culture)
United Feature Syndicate, PO Box 5610, Cincinnati OH 45201 USA

McGaughey, Claude R (Shug), III — Thoroughbred Racing Trainer
1927 Keene Road, Nicholasville KY 40356, USA

McGee, Benjamin (Ben) — Football Player
35 Castle Cove, Jackson MS 39212, USA

McGee, Jack — Actor
C E S D, 10635 Santa Monica Blvd, #130, Los Angeles CA 90025 USA

McGee, Marcus — Actor
Brooks Murphy Stevens, 5619 N Lankershim Blvd, North Hollywood CA 91601 USA

McGee, Michael B (Mike) — Football Player
22710 Uncompahgre Road, Montrose CO 81403, USA

McGee, Willie D — Baseball Player
2081 Lupine Road, Hercules CA 94547, USA

McGegan, Nicholas — Conductor
Schwalbe Partners, 170 E 61st St, #500, New York NY 10065, USA

McGehee, Scott — Director, Producer
Oasis Media Group, 8730 W Sunset Blvd, #700, West Hollywood CA 90069, USA

McGeorge, Missie — Golfer
1836 Willow Springs Court, Haslet TX 76052, USA

McGeorge, Richard E (Rich) — Football Player
2200 Trail Wood Dr, Durham NC 27705, USA

McGerr, Jason — Drummer (Death Cab for Cutie)
Zeitgeist Artist Mgmt, 660 York St, #216, San Francisco CA 94110, USA

McGhee, Carla — Basketball Player
103 Indigo Chase, Columbia SC 29229, USA

McGhee, Kanavis — Football Player
Challenge Earl College High School, 5601 West Loop S, Houston TX 77081, USA

McGhee-Anderson, Kathleen — Writer, Producer
A P A Talent/Literary Agency, 405 S Beverly Dr, #300, Beverly Hills CA 90212 USA

McGilberry, Randall K (Randy) — Baseball Player
2110 Foxford St, Cantonment FL 32533, USA

McGill, Anthony — Concert Clarinetist
Metropolitan Opera Orchestra, Lincoln Center Plaza, New York NY 10023, USA

McGill, Bill (Billy) — Basketball Player
5129 W 58th Place, Los Angeles CA 90056, USA

McGill, Bob — Ice Hockey Player
116 Oriole Dr, Holland Landing ON L9N 1H1, Canada

McGill, Bruce — Actor
Stone Manners Salners, 9911 W Pico Blvd, #1400, Los Angeles CA 90035 USA

McGill, C Leonard (Lenny) — Football Player
3516 W 125th Circle, Broomfield CO 80020, USA

McGill, Don — Producer, Writer
W M E Entertainment, 9601 Wilshire Blvd, #300, Beverly Hills CA 90210 USA

McGill, Jill 3765 Carmel View Road, #3, San Diego CA 92130, USA	Golfer
McGill, Michael (Mickey) Associated Booking Corp, 501 Madison Ave, #603, New York NY 10022 USA	Singer (Dells)
McGill, Michael Patrick C E S D, 10635 Santa Monica Blvd, #130, Los Angeles CA 90025 USA	Actor, Comedian
McGill, Michael R (Mike) 8930 Louis Court, Saint John IN 46373, USA	Football Player
McGillion, Paul Amanda Howard, 74 Clerkenwell Road, London EC1M 5QA, England	Actor
McGillis, Dan 9 Country Club Dr, Chatham NJ 07928, USA	Ice Hockey Player
McGillis, Kelly David Williams Mgmt, 9614 Olympic Blvd, #F, Beverly Hills CA 90212, USA	Actress
McGinest, William L (Willie) 20382 Tramore Lane, Strongsville OH 44149, USA	Football Player
McGinley, John C W M E Entertainment, 9601 Wilshire Blvd, #300, Beverly Hills CA 90210 USA	Actor
McGinley, Raymond High Road Touring, 751 Bridgeway, #200, Sausalito CA 94965 USA	Guitarist (Teenage Fanclub)
McGinley, Ted Innovative Artists, 1505 10th St, Santa Monica CA 90401 USA	Actor
McGinn, Bernard J 5702 Kenwood Ave, Chicago IL 60637, USA	Theologian
McGinn, Colin 4779 Collins Ave, #4302, Miami Beach FL 33140, USA	Philosopher
McGinn, Daniel M (Dan) 1309 S 189th Court, Omaha NE 68130, USA	Baseball Player
McGinnis, Dave 3526 E Equestrian Trail, Phoenix AZ 85044, USA	Football Coach
McGinnis, George F 11245 Marlin Road, Indianapolis IN 46239, USA	Basketball Player
McGinnis, Joe Janklow & Nesbit, 445 Park Ave, #1300, New York NY 10022, USA	Writer
McGinnis, Joe, Jr I C M Partners, 10250 Constellation Blvd, #900, Los Angeles CA 90067 USA	Writer
McGinnis, Russell B (Russ) 1110 N Judd Place, Chandler AZ 85226, USA	Baseball Player
McGirt, James (Buddy), Jr Elite Youth Program, 104 Day Dr, Sebastian FL 32958, USA	Boxer, Manager
McGlocklin, Jon P 5281 State Road, #83, Hartland WI 53029, USA	Basketball Player
McGlone, Mike Don Buchwald/Fortitude, 6500 Wilshire Blvd, #2200, Los Angeles CA 90048 USA	Actor
McGlothin, Ezra M (Pat) 1454 Kenesaw Ave, Knoxville TN 37919, USA	Baseball Player
McGlynn, Richard A (Dick) 38 Rock Glen Road, Medford MA 02155, USA	Ice Hockey Player
McGonagle, Marta Charles Sherman, 8306 Wilshire Blvd, #2017, Beverly Hills CA 90211, USA	Actress
McGoon, Dwight C 840 9th Ave SW, Rochester MN 55902, USA	Surgeon
McGovern, Elizabeth Rights House, Drury House, 34-43 Russell St, London WC2B 5HA, England	Actress
McGovern, James D (Jim) 900 Amaryllis Ave, Oradell NJ 07649, USA	Golfer
McGovern, Maureen Jennifer Howe, 12087 Evergreen St NW, Minneapolis MN 55448, USA	Singer
McGowan, Patrick R (Pat) PO Box 88, Southern Pines NC 28388, USA	Golfer
McGowan, Zach Innovative Artists, 1505 10th St, Santa Monica CA 90401 USA	Actor
McGrady, Charles Sierra Club, 85 2nd St, #200 San Francisco CA 94105, USA	Environmentalist
McGrady, Tracy L 23 Beacon Hill, Sugar Land TX 77479, USA	Basketball Player
McGrain, Peter 207 Maple St, White Salmon WA 98672, USA	Artist
McGrath, C Peter State University of New York, President's Office, 4400 Vestal Parkway E, Binghamton NY 13902, USA	Educator
McGrath, Douglas Creative Artists Agency, 2000 Ave of Stars, #100, Los Angeles CA 90067 USA	Director, Actor, Writer
McGrath, James Yale University, Genetics Dept, New Haven CT 06520, USA	Geneticist
McGrath, Jeremy J R Motorsports 801 SW Ordnance Road, Ankeny IA 50023, USA	Motorcycle Racing Rider
McGrath, Judy MTV Networks, 1515 Broadway, New York NY 10036, USA	Businesswoman
McGrath, Mark Pinnacle Entertainment, 30 Glenn St, White Plains NY 10603, USA	Singer (Sugar Ray), Entertainer
McGrath, Mike 738 Colusa Ave, El Cerrito CA 94530, USA	Bowler
McGrath, Robert E (Bob) Bob McGrath Productions, 295 Frances St, Teaneck NJ 07666, USA	Actor, Writer
McGraw, Joseph 416 Alissa Lane, Burlington MA 98233, USA	WW II Navy Air Hero
McGraw, Melinda Domain Talent, 9229 W Sunset Blvd, #710, West Hollywood CA 90069 USA	Actress
McGraw, Michael S (Mike) PO Box 529, Medicine Bow WY 82329, USA	Football Player
McGraw, Muffet University of Notre Dame, Athletic Dept, Notre Dame IN 46556, USA	Basketball Coach
McGraw, Phillip C (Dr Phil) 1008 Lexington Road, Beverly Hills CA 90210, USA	Entertainer, Psychologist
McGraw, Tim Creative Artists Agency, 2000 Ave of Stars, #100, Los Angeles CA 90067 USA	Singer

McGregor, Ewan United Agents, 12-26 Lexington St, London W1F 0LE, England	Actor
McGregor, Gilbert R (Gil) 3700 Orleans Ave, #4411, New Orleans LA 70119, USA	Basketball Player
McGregor, Scott H 1514 Providence Road, #A, Towson MD 21286, USA	Baseball Player
McGriff, Frederick S (Fred) 16314 Millan de Avila, Tampa FL 33613, USA	Baseball Player
McGriff, Hershel General Delivery, Green Valley AZ 85622, USA	Auto Racing Driver
McGriff, Terence R (Terry) 2905 Langston Dr, Fort Pierce FL 34946, USA	Baseball Player
McGruder, Aaron Universal Press Syndicate, 4520 Main St, #700, Kansas City MO 64111 USA	Cartoonist (Boondocks)
McGuane, Thomas F, III 410 S 3rd Ave, Bozeman MT 59715, USA	Writer
McGuckin, Aislin Ken McReddie Assoc, 11 Connaught Place, London W2 2ET, England	Actress
McGuigan, Paul Ignition Mgmt, 54 Linhope St, London NW1 6HL, England	Bassist (Oasis)
McGuigan, Paul Fallout Entertainment Group, 3100 Airport Ave, Santa Monica CA 90405, USA	Director
McGuinn, Roger PO Box 2022, Windermere FL 34786, USA	Singer, Guitarist (Byrds), Songwriter
McGuinness, James (Jay) Industry Music Group, 128 Regent Road, Hanley Stoke, Trent ST1 3AY, England	Singer (Wanted)
McGuinness, Martin Sinn Fein, 170 Falls Road, Belfast BT12 4PD, Northern Ireland	Government Official, Northern Ireland
McGuire, Betty H David Moss, 733 Seward St, #PH, Los Angeles CA 90038 USA	Actress
McGuire, Christine 100 Rancho Circle, Las Vegas NV 89107, USA	Singer (McGuire Sisters)
McGuire, Jack American Red Cross, 431 18th St NW, Washington DC 20006, USA	Association Executive
McGuire, M C Adolfus (Mickey) 1521 Middle Park Dr, Dayton OH 45414, USA	Baseball Player
McGuire, Patti 1962 E Valley Road, Santa Barbara CA 93108, USA	Model
McGuire, Phyllis 100 Rancho Circle, Las Vegas NV 89107, USA	Singer (McGuire Sisters)
McGuire, Ryan B 171 Great Lawn, Irvine CA 92620, USA	Baseball Player
McGuire, W Eugene (Gene) 3229 Country Club Dr, Lynn Haven FL 32444, USA	Football Player
McGuire, Willard H National Education Assn, 1201 16th St NW, Washington DC 20036, USA	Labor Leader
McGuire, William Biff Gage Group, 14724 Ventura Blvd, #505, Sherman Oaks CA 91403 USA	Actor
McGwire, Mark D PO Box 165, 4521 Campus Dr, East Irvine CA 92650, USA	Baseball Player
McHaffie Vidal, Deborah Tony Criscuolo, 8425 NW 222nd Ave, Alachua FL 32615, USA	Golfer
McHale, Joel W M E Entertainment, 9601 Wilshire Blvd, #300, Beverly Hills CA 90210 USA	Actor, Comedian
McHale, Kevin Greene Assoc, 1901 Ave of Stars, #130, Los Angeles CA 90067 USA	Actor
McHale, Kevin E 20 Blue Jay Lane, Saint Paul MN 55127, USA	Basketball Player, Executive, Coach
McHattie, Stephen Christopher Wright Mgmt, 3207 Winnie Dr, Los Angeles CA 90068, USA	Actor
McHenry, Donald F Georgetown University, Foreign Service School, Washington DC 20057, USA	Diplomat
McHenry, Vance L 2396 Brown St, Durham CA 95938, USA	Baseball Player
McHugh, Heather University of Washington, English Dept, PO Box 354330, Seattle WA 98195, USA	Writer
McHugh, John M Secretary's Office, HqUSA, Pentagon, Washington DC 20310, USA	Secretary, Army; Representative, NY
McIlhenny, Donald B (Don) 8505 Edgemere Road, #101, Dallas TX 75225, USA	Football Player
McIlrath, Tim Agency Group Ltd, 142 W 57th St, #600, New York NY 10019 USA	Singer, Guitarist (Rise Against)
McIlravy, Lincoln 4220 210th St NE, Solon IA 52333, USA	Freestyle Wrestler
McIlroy, Rory Holywood Golf Club, Nuns Walk, Demesne Road, Holywood, County Down BT18 9LE, Northern Ireland	Golfer
McIlvaine, James M (Jim) Camp Anokijig, W5639 Anokijig Lane, Plymouth WI 53073, USA	Basketball Player
McInally, Patrick J (Pat) 19321 Ocean Heights Lane, Huntington Beach CA 92648, USA	Football Player
McInerney, John B (Jay), Jr I C M Partners, 10250 Constellation Blvd, #900, Los Angeles CA 90067 USA	Writer
McInnis, Jeff L 3404 Lazy Day Lane, Charlotte NC 28269, USA	Basketball Player
McInnis, Marty 21 Peter Hobart Dr, Hingham MA 02043, USA	Ice Hockey Player
McIntosh, Damion A 1221 SW Summit Crossing Dr, Lees Summit MO 64081, USA	Football Player
McIntosh, Roger A (Rocky) Washington Redskins, 21300 Redskin Park Dr, Ashburn VA 20147 USA	Football Player
McIntosh, Timothy A (Tim) 1815 S Talbott Place, Waynesboro VA 22980, USA	Baseball Player
McIntyre, Guy M 257 Arrowhead Way, Hayward CA 94544, USA	Football Player
McIntyre, Joey Management by Jaffe, 68 Ridgewood Ave, Glen Ridge NJ 07028, USA	Singer (New Kids on the Block)

McIver, Everett A — Football Player
1205 Avignon Dr SW, Conyers GA 30094, USA

McKagan, Duff — Bassist (Guns N' Roses)
Sanctuary Mgmt, 15301 Ventura Blvd, Building B, Sherman Oaks CA 91403, USA

McKart, Bronco — Boxer
Scott Beard, 11343 Telegraph Road, #A, Erie PA 48133, USA

McKay, Adam — Actor, Director, Writer
Gary Sanchez Productions, 729 Seward St, #200, Los Angeles CA 90038, USA

McKay, Al — Guitarist (Earth Wind Fire), Songwriter
Spirit Media, PO Box 43591, Phoenix AZ 85080, USA

McKay, Ami — Writer
PO Box 146, Canning NS B0P 1H0, Canada

McKay, Caroline — Drummer (Glasvegas)
Sony Music, 9 Derry St, London W8 5HY, England

McKay, Christian — Actor
Ken McReddie Assoc, 11 Connaught Place, London W2 2ET, England

McKay, David L (Dave) — Baseball Player
9702 W La Posada Circle, Scottsdale AZ 85255, USA

McKay, Heather — Squash, Racquetball Player
48 Nesbitt Dr, Toronto ON M4W 2G3, Canada

McKay, Mhairi — Golfer
898 W Ashbourne Dr, Eagle ID 83616, USA

McKay, Monroe G — Judge
US Court of Appeals, Federal Building, 125 S State St, Salt Lake City UT 84138, USA

McKay, Nellie — Singer, Pianist, Songwriter
Creative Artists Agency, 2000 Ave of Stars, #100, Los Angeles CA 90067 USA

McKay, Peggy — Actress
8811 Wonderland Ave, Los Angeles CA 90046, USA

McKay, Randy — Ice Hockey Player
44640 US Highway 41, Chassell MI 49916, USA

McKay, Ritchie — Basketball Coach
Liberty University, Athletic Dept, Lynchburg VA 24502, USA

McKay, Robert C (Bob) — Football Player
4110 Bluffridge Dr, Austin TX 78759, USA

McKeague, David W — Judge
US Appellate Court, 315 W Allegan St, Lansing MI 48933, USA

McKean, James G (Jim) — Baseball Umpire
740 Sand Pine Dr NE, Saint Petersburg FL 33703, USA

McKean, Michael J — Actor, Comedian
A P A Talent/Literary Agency, 405 S Beverly Dr, #300, Beverly Hills CA 90212 USA

McKechnie, Walt — Ice Hockey Player
McKeck's Place, PO Box 752, Haliburton ON K0M 1S0, Canada

McKee, Frank S — Labor Leader
United Steelworkers Union, 60 Blvd of Allies, #5, Pittsburgh PA 15222, USA

McKee, Gina — Actress
United Agents, 12-26 Lexington St, London W1F 0LE, England

McKee, Jay — Ice Hockey Player
1423 Topping Road, Saint Louis MO 63131, USA

McKee, Kinnaird R — Navy Admiral
7100 Wheeler Park Circle, Easton MD 21601, USA

McKee, Maria — Singer, Songwriter
Geffen Records, 10900 Wilshire Blvd, #1000, Los Angeles CA 90024 USA

McKee, Theodore A — Judge
US Appeals Court, US Courthouse, 601 Market St, #20614, Philadelphia PA 19106, USA

McKee, Todd — Actor
316 N Flores St, Los Angeles CA 90048, USA

McKellar, Danica — Actress
C E S D, 10635 Santa Monica Blvd, #130, Los Angeles CA 90025 USA

McKellen, Ian — Actor
2act, Mirza Co, 826 Garratt Lane, London SW17 0LZ, England

McKeller, T Keith — Football Player
1972 Waccamaw Path, Winston Salem NC 27127, USA

McKelvey, Rob — Golfer
1814 Duke Road, Atlanta GA 30341, USA

McKenna, Bruce C — Writer, Journalist, Producer
Flashpoint Entertainment, 9150 Wilshire Blvd, #247, Beverly Hills CA 90212, USA

McKenna, Chris — Actor
Stone Manners Salners, 9911 W Pico Blvd, #1400, Los Angeles CA 90035 USA

McKenna, Kevin R — Basketball Player
15387 Nicholas St, Omaha NE 68154, USA

McKenna, Lori — Songwriter
Gorfaine/Schwartz, 4111 W Alameda Ave, #509, Burbank CA 91505 USA

McKenna, Stephen F — Artist
Crocknafeola, Killybegs, County Donegal, Ireland

McKenna, Virginia — Actress
8 Buckfast Court, Runcorn, Cheshire WA7 1QJ, England

McKenney, Donald H (Don) — Ice Hockey Player
16 Edgewater Dr, Norton MA 02766, USA

McKennitt, Lorena — Singer, Songwriter
Quinlan Road, PO Box 933, Stratford ON N5A 7M3, Canada

McKenny, James C (Jim) — Ice Hockey Player
City-TV, 299 Queen St W, Toronto ON M5V 2Z5, Canada

McKenzie Smith, Ian — Artist
70 Hamilton Place, Aberdeen AB15 5BA, Scotland

McKenzie, Benjamin (Ben) — Actor
Management 360, 9111 Wilshire Blvd, Beverly Hills CA 90210 USA

McKenzie, Bret — Singer (Flight of the Conchords), Actor
Creative Artists Agency, 2000 Ave of Stars, #100, Los Angeles CA 90067 USA

McKenzie, Dan P — Geologist
Bullard Labs, Madingley Rise, Madingley Road, Cambridge CB3 0EZ, England

McKenzie, Derrick — Drummer (Jamiroquai)
Nettwerk Mgmt, 6525 W Sunset Blvd, #800, Los Angeles CA 90028 USA

McKenzie, Forrest D W — Basketball Player
2516 S Laurelwood, Santa Ana CA 92704, USA

McKenzie, Jacqueline — Actress
Robyn Gardiner Mgmt, 397 Riley St, Surry Hills NSW 2010, Australia

McKenzie, James P (Jim) — Ice Hockey Player
9266 Chevoit Dr, Brentwood TN 37027, USA

McKenzie, John — Ice Hockey Player
10 Clearview Road, Stoneham MA 02180, USA

McKenzie, Julia — Actress
Ken McReddie Assoc, 11 Connaught Place, London W2 2ET, England

McKenzie, Kevin — Ballet Dancer
American Ballet Theatre, 890 Broadway, #300, New York NY 10003 USA

McKenzie, Raleigh — Football Player
715 Huntsman Place, Herndon VA 20170, USA

McKenzie, Reggie — Football Player, Executive
411 Carta Road, Knoxville TN 37914, USA

McKenzie, Reginald (Reggie) — Football Player
13853 Trumbull St, Highland Park MI 48203, USA

McKenzie, Stanley (Stan) — Basketball Player
8316 Governor Grayson Way, Ellicott City MD 21043, USA

McKeon, Doug — Actor
4644 Arriba Dr, Tarzana CA 91356, USA

McKeon, Joel J — Baseball Player
1901 Pierce St, Hollywood FL 33020, USA

McKeon, John A (Jack) — Baseball Player, Manager
1529 Charleigh Court, Elon NC 27244, USA

McKeon, Nancy — Actress
Stone Manners Salners, 9911 W Pico Blvd, #1400, Los Angeles CA 90035 USA

McKeown, Bob — Commentator
CBS-TV, News Dept, 51 W 52nd St, New York NY 10019 USA

McKeown, M Margaret — Judge
2447 Ardath Road, La Jolla CA 92037, USA

McKernan, John R, Jr — Governor, ME
77 Sanderson Road, Cumberland Foreside ME 04110, USA

McKey, Derrick W — Basketball Player
8 Woodard Place, Zionsville IN 46077, USA

McKidd, Kevin — Actor
Independent Talent Group, Oxford House, 76 Oxford St, London W1D 1BS, England

McKie, Aaron F — Basketball Player
1400 Youngs Ford Road, Gladwyne PA 19035, USA

McKie, Jason A — Football Player
4431 W Lawn Ave, Waukegan IL 60085, USA

McKinley, Alvin J — Football Player
45274 W Miraflores St, Maricopa AZ 85139, USA

McKinley, Craig R — Air Force General
Chief, National Guard Bureau, HqUSAF, Pentagon, Washington DC 20330 USA

McKinley, John — Rowing Athlete
952 Bloomfield Village, Auburn Hills MI 48326, USA

McKinley, John K — Businessman
1 Canterbury Green, #800, Stamford CT 06901, USA

McKinley, Robin — Writer
Writer's House, 21 W 26th St, New York NY 10010, USA

McKinley-Uselmann, Therese — Baseball Player
1644 N Greenwood Ave, Park Ridge IL 60068, USA

McKinnely, Philip B (Phil) — Football Player
585 Edgehill Place, Alpharetta GA 30022, USA

McKinney, C Richard (Rich) — Baseball Player
2495 E Peterson Road, Troy OH 45373, USA

McKinney, DeMetria — Actress
Don Buchwald/Fortitude, 6500 Wilshire Blvd, #2200, Los Angeles CA 90048 USA

McKinney, Kennedy — Boxer
187 B & R Lane, Golden Meadow LA 70357, USA

McKinney, Kurt — Actor
5003 Tilden Ave, #206, Sherman Oaks CA 91423, USA

McKinney, Mark — Actor, Comedian, Writer
Oscars Abrams Zimel, 438 Queen St E, Toronto ON M5A 1T4, Canada

McKinney, Odis, Jr — Football Player
23126 Collins St, Woodland Hills CA 91367, USA

McKinney, Richard (Rick) — Archery Athlete
549 E Silver Creek Road, Gilbert AZ 85296, USA

McKinney, Seth A — Football Player
2403 Crown Court, College Station TX 77845, USA

McKinney, Stephen M (Steve) — Football Player
335 County Road 201, Centerville TX 75833, USA

McKinney, Tamara — Alpine Skier
4395 Parkers Mill Road, Lexington KY 40513, USA

McKinnie, Bryant D — Football Player
12535 Stoneway Court, Davie FL 33330, USA

McKinnon, Bruce — Editorial Cartoonist
Halifax Chronicle Herald, 1650 Argyle St, Halifax NS B3J 2T2, Canada

McKinnon, Daniel D (Dan) — Ice Hockey Player
610 Riverdale Dr NE, Warroad MN 56763, USA

McKinnon, Dennis L — Football Player
1016 Adams St, North Chicago IL 60064, USA

McKinnon, Ray — Actor
Creative Artists Agency, 2000 Ave of Stars, #100, Los Angeles CA 90067 USA

McKinnon, Ronald (Ron) — Football Player
1063 Grand Oaks Dr, Bessemer AL 35022, USA

McKissack, Patricia — Writer
Scholastic Press, 555 Broadway, New York NY 10012 USA

McKissick, John — Football Coach
Summerville High School, Athletic Dept, Summerville SC 29484, USA

McKittrick, Rob — Director, Writer
Creative Artists Agency, 2000 Ave of Stars, #100, Los Angeles CA 90067 USA

McKnight, Anthony (Tony) — Baseball Player
406 Dundee Road, Texarkana AR 71854, USA

McKnight, Brian — Singer, Songwriter
Universal Attractions, 135 W 26th St, #1200, New York NY 10001 USA

McKnight, Clarence E, Jr — Army General
1624 Linway Park Dr, McLean VA 22101, USA

McKnight, Ira — Baseball Player
608 S Summit Dr, #1, South Bend IN 46619, USA
McKnight, James — Football Player
16705 Berkshire Court, Southwest Ranches FL 33331, USA
McKnight, Jefferson A (Jeff) — Baseball Player
3296 Highway 92 W, Bee Branch AR 72013, USA
McKnight, John — Singer, Musician (Fishbone)
Silverback Mgmt, 9469 Jefferson Blvd, #101, Culver City CA 90232, USA
McKnight, Steven L — Molecular Biologist
8513 Swananoah Road, Dallas TX 75209, USA
McKnight, Theodore R (Ted) — Football Player
10236 Cedarbrooke Lane, Kansas City MO 64131, USA
McKnight, Thomas F — Artist
30 Peck Road, #2201, Torrington CT 06790, USA
Mckown, Zack — Interior Designer
Tsao-McKorn Design, 20 Vandam St, #1000, New York NY 10013, USA
McKuen, Rod — Singer, Songwiter, Writer
C E S D, 10635 Santa Monica Blvd, #130, Los Angeles CA 90025 USA
McKyer, Timothy B (Tim) — Football Player
11201 Golden Dr, Charlotte NC 28216, USA
McLachlan, Craig D — Actor, Singer
Neil Clugston Organisation, 11A Wigham Road, Glebe NSW 2037, Australia
McLachlan, Sarah — Singer, Songwriter
Nettwerk Mgmt, 1650 W 2nd Ave, Vancouver BC V6J 4R3, Canada
McLafferty, Fred W — Chemist
103 Needham Place, Ithaca NY 14850, USA
McLaglen, Andrew V — Director
Stanmore Productions, PO Box 1056, Friday Harbor WA 98250, USA
McLain, Dennis D (Denny) — Baseball Player
4432 Golf View Dr, Brighton MI 48116, USA
McLane, James P (Jimmy), Jr — Swimmer
97 Mount Vernon St, #1, Boston MA 02108, USA
McLaren, Brandon Jay — Actor
Pakula/King, 9229 W Sunset Blvd, #315, West Hollywood CA 90069 USA
McLaren, John L — Baseball Manager
Washington Nationals, 1500 S Capitol St SE, Washington DC 20003 USA
McLaren, Kyle E — Ice Hockey Player
6582 Skyfarm Dr, San Jose CA 95120, USA
McLaughlin, Ann Dore — Secretary, Labor
Rand Corp, 1200 S Hayes St, #400, Arlington VA 22202, USA
McLaughlin, Audrey — Government Official, Canada
410 Hoge St, Whitehorse, Yukon Y1A 1W2, Canada
McLaughlin, Brian — Actor
Brooks Murphy Stevens, 5619 N Lankershim Blvd, North Hollywood CA 91601 USA
McLaughlin, Byron S — Baseball Player
7030 Alamitos Ave, San Diego CA 92154, USA
McLaughlin, David — Association Executive
American Red Cross, 431 18th St NW, Washington DC 20006, USA
McLaughlin, Emma — Writer
Atria Books, 1230 Ave of Americas, New York NY 10020 USA
McLaughlin, Jake — Actor
Paradigm Agency, 360 N Crescent Dr, North Building, Beverly Hills CA 90210 USA
McLaughlin, Jim — Architect
McLaughlin Assoc, PO Box 479, Sun Valley ID 83353, USA
McLaughlin, Joey R — Baseball Player
1611 S Troost Ave, Tulsa OK 74120, USA
McLaughlin, John — Jazz Guitarist, Composer
International Music Network, 278 Main St, #400, Gloucester MA 01930 USA
McLaughlin, John E — Government Official
Central Intelligence Agency, Deputy Director's Office, Washington DC 20505, USA
McLaughlin, John J — Commentator
McLaughlin Group, 1717 Rhode Island Ave NW, #640, Washington DC 20036, USA
McLaughlin, Joseph J (Joe) — Football Player
65 Pells Fishing Road, Brewster MA 02631, USA
McLaughlin, Joseph M — Judge
US Court of Appeals, Moynihan Courthouse, 500 Pearl St, New York NY 10007, USA
McLaughlin, Michael (Mike) — Auto Racing Driver
PO Box 45, Waterloo NY 13165, USA
McLaughlin, Michael D (Bo) — Baseball Player
536 N Grand, Mesa AZ 85201, USA
McLean, A J — Singer (Backstreet Boys), Actor
Podwell Entertainment, 710 N Orlando Ave, #203, West Hollywood CA 90069, USA
McLean, Don — Singer, Songwriter
M P I, 9255 W Sunset Blvd, #407, West Hollywood CA 90069, USA
McLean, Greg — Director, Writer
W M E Entertainment, 9601 Wilshire Blvd, #300, Beverly Hills CA 90210 USA
McLean, Hayley — Singer, Songwriter
Agency Group Ltd, 142 W 57th St, #600, New York NY 10019 USA
McLean, Jane — Actress
Oscars Abrams Zimel, 438 Queen St E, Toronto ON M5A 1T4, Canada
McLean, Kirk — Ice Hockey Player
Burnaby Express, 3676 Kensington Ave, Burnaby BC V5B 4Z6, Canada
McLean, Michelle — Beauty Queen
McLean Children's Trust, PO Box 97428, Maerua Mall, Windhoek, Namibia
McLean, Rene — Jazz Saxophonist, Flutist
Brad Simon Organization, 155 W 46th St, #500, New York NY 10036 USA
McLean, Robert (Barney) — Skier, Ski Jumper
9555 W 59th Ave, #303, Arvada CO 80004, USA
McLean, Sally — Actress, Producer
Salmac Mgmt, PO Box 526, Mount Martha VIC 3934, Australia
McLean-Ross, Lucella — Baseball Player
401-5107 47th St, Lloydminster AB T9V 0G1, Canada
McLellan, Zoe — Actress
Metropolitan Talent Agency, 7020 La Presa Dr, Los Angeles CA 90068 USA
McLemore, Dana — Football Player
125 Seagate Dr, San Mateo CA 94403, USA

M

McLemore, LaMonte	Singer (Fifth Dimension)
Brokaw Co, 9255 W Sunset Blvd, #804, West Hollywood CA 90069 USA	
McLemore, Mark T	Baseball Player
533 S White Chapel Blvd, Southlake TX 76092, USA	
McLendon-Covey, Wendi	Actress, Producer, Writer
John Carrabino Management, 5900 Wilshire, #406, Los Angeles CA 90036, USA	
McLennan, Jamie	Ice Hockey Player
Calgary Flames, PO Box 1540, Station M, Calgary AB T2P 3B9, Canada	
McLeod, Erin	Soccer Player
Canadian Soccer, Place Soccer Canada, 237 Metcalfe St, Ottawa ON K2P 1R2, Canada	
McLeod, R J Jackie	Ice Hockey Player
13 John Hair Court, Saskatoon SK S7J 2K6, Canada	
McLeod, Robert D (Bob)	Football Player
600 Spring Creek Blvd, Brenham TX 77833, USA	
McLerie, Allyn Ann	Actress, Dancer
3344 Campanil Dr, Santa Barbara CA 93109, USA	
McLish, Rachel	Actress, Body Builder
Ron Samuels Entertainment, 100 Wilshire Blvd, #750, Santa Monica CA 90401, USA	
McLlwain, Dave	Ice Hockey Player
Yacht Club Woods, Grand Bend ON N0M 1T0, Canada	
McLoughlin, Tom	Director
Paradigm Agency, 360 N Crescent Dr, North Building, Beverly Hills CA 90210 USA	
McLouth, Nathan R (Nate)	Baseball Player
6116 W Fieldstone Hills Dr SE, Caldedonia MI 49316, USA	
McLure, Charles E, Jr	Government Official
250 Yerba Santa Ana, Los Altos CA 94022, USA	
McMahan, Jack W	Baseball Player
131 Forest View Circle, Hot Springs AR 71913, USA	
McMahon, Andrew R	Singer, Pianist, Songwriter
Sanctuary Artist Mgmt, 9255 Sunset Blvd, #200, Los Angeles CA 90069 USA	
McMahon, Donald A	Businessman
63 W Wieuca Road NE, #1, Atlanta GA 30342, USA	
McMahon, James R (Jim)	Football Player
22431 N Violetta Dr, Scottsdale AZ 85255, USA	
McMahon, Julian	Actor
W M E Entertainment, 9601 Wilshire Blvd, #300, Beverly Hills CA 90210 USA	
McMahon, Michael E (Mike)	Football Player
313 Oak Grove Court, Wexford PA 15090, USA	
McMahon, Stacy	Model
White Tiger Modeling, PO Box 5298, South Melbourne VIC 3205, Australia	
McMahon, Vincent K, Jr	Professional Wrestling Executive
World Wrestling Entertainment, Titan Towers, 1241 E Main St, Stamford CT 06902 USA	
McMakin, John G	Football Player
608 Longview Ave, Anacortes WA 98221, USA	
McManus, James M (Jim)	Baseball Player
2352 Hopkins Mill Road, Duluth GA 30096, USA	
McManus, Michaela	Actress
United Talent Agency, 9336 Civic Center Dr, Beverly Hills CA 90210 USA	
McMartin, John	Actor, Singer
Artists Agency, 1180 S Beverly Dr, #301, Los Angeles CA 90035 USA	
McMath, Jimmy L	Baseball Player
3321 22nd St, Tuscaloosa AL 35401, USA	
McMenamin, Mark A S	Geologist
Mount Holyoke College, Geology Dept, South Hadley MA 01075, USA	
McMichael, Gregory W (Greg)	Baseball Player
240 Parkside Club Court, Duluth GA 30097, USA	
McMichael, Randy H	Football Player
361 17th St NW, Atlanta GA 30363, USA	
McMichael, Steve D	Football Player
1268 Holiday Dr, Somonauk IL 60552, USA	
McMillan, Caroline Pierce	Golfer
7625 E Phantom Way, Scottsdale AZ 85255, USA	
McMillan, Ernest C (Ernie)	Football Player
14816 Sycamore Manor Court, Chesterfield MO 63017, USA	
McMillan, Lewis L (Randy)	Football Player
6832 Hayley Ridge Way, Baltimore MD 21209, USA	
McMillan, Nathaniel (Nate)	Basketball Player, Coach
3525 Ghiglieri Court, West Linn OR 97068, USA	
McMillan, Terry L	Writer
PO Box 2408, Danville CA 94526, USA	
McMillan, Thomas E (Tommy)	Baseball Player
712 Spring Lake Road, Thomasville GA 31792, USA	
McMillan, William (Bill)	Marksman
1930 Sandstone Vista, Encinitas CA 92024, USA	
McMillen, C Thomas (Tom)	Representative, MD; Basketball Player
Homeland Security Capital Corp, 1005 N Glebe Road, #550, Arlington VA 22201, USA	
McMillen, Robert	Track Athlete
5708 Golden West Ave, Temple City CA 91780, USA	
McMillian, Audray G	Football Player
1230 Hahlo St, Houston TX 77020, USA	
McMillian, James M (Jim)	Basketball Player
4804 Tara Dr, Greensboro NC 27410, USA	
McMillian, Michael	Actor
Innovative Artists, 1505 10th St, Santa Monica CA 90401 USA	
McMillin, James R (Jim)	Football Player
7985 Westview Dr, Lakewood CO 80214, USA	
McMillon, William (Billy)	Baseball Player
1516 Lost Creek Dr, Columbia SC 29212, USA	
McMonagle, Donald R	Astronaut
7737 E Shadow Vista Court, Tucson AZ 85750, USA	
McMorrow, James Vincent	Singer, Songwriter
Agency Group Ltd, 142 W 57th St, #600, New York NY 10019 USA	
McMullen, Curtis T	Mathematician
Harvard University, Science Center, Cambridge MA 02138, USA	
McMullen, Kenneth L (Ken)	Baseball Player
10 Estaban Dr, Camarillo CA 93010, USA	

McLemore - McMullen

McMullian, Amos R	Businessman
Flowers Industries, 200 US Highway 19 S, Thomasville GA 31792, USA	
McMullin, Ernan V	Philosopher
University of Notre Dame, Philosophy Dept, Notre Dame IN 46556, USA	
McMurray, James C (Jamie)	Auto Racing Driver
211 Milford Circle, Mooresville NC 28117, USA	
McMurtry, Gregory W (Greg)	Football Player
755 Oak Point Lane, Madison Heights MI 48071, USA	
McMurtry, J Craig	Baseball Player
2835 Bottoms East Road, Troy TX 76579, USA	
McMurtry, James	Singer, Songwriter
High Road Touring, 751 Bridgeway, #200, Sausalito CA 94965 USA	
McMurtry, Larry	Writer
PO Box 552, Archer City TX 76351, USA	
McMurtry, Tom	Test Pilot
PO Box 273, Edwards CA 93523, USA	
McNab, Mercedes	Actress, Model
Stone Manners Salners, 9911 W Pico Blvd, #1400, Los Angeles CA 90035 USA	
McNab, Peter M	Ice Hockey Player
10311 Rancho Montecito, Parker CO 80138, USA	
McNabb, Donovan	Football Player
21800 Towncenter Plaza, #266A, Sterling VA 20164, USA	
McNabb, Duncan J	Air Force General
Commander, US Transportation Command, Scott Air Force Base IL 62225, USA	
McNairy, Scoot	Actor
I C M Partners, 10250 Constellation Blvd, #900, Los Angeles CA 90067 USA	
McNally, Andrew, IV	Publisher
Rand McNally Co, 9855 Woods Dr, Skokie IL 60077, USA	
McNally, David (Dave)	Director, Producer, Writer
W M E Entertainment, 9601 Wilshire Blvd, #300, Beverly Hills CA 90210 USA	
McNally, Kevin	Actor
Hatton McEwan, 3 Chocolate Studios, 7 Shepherdess Place, London N1 7LJ, England	
McNally, Shannon	Singer, Songwriter
Capitol Records, 1750 N Vine St, Los Angeles CA 90028 USA	
McNally, Stephen (Ste)	Singer, Guitarist (BBMak)
Spirit Media, PO Box 43591, Phoenix AZ 85080, USA	
McNally, Terrence	Writer, Actor
Gersh Agency, 9465 Wilshire Blvd, #600, Beverly Hills CA 90212 USA	
McNamara, Brian	Actor
TalentWorks, 3500 W Olive Ave, #1400, Burbank CA 91505 USA	
McNamara, Eileen	Journalist
Boston Globe, Editorial Dept, 135 William Morrissey Blvd, Dorchester MA 02125 USA	
McNamara, Gerry	Ice Hockey Player
213-350 Mill Road, Etobicoke ON M9C 5R7, Canada	
McNamara, James P (Jim)	Baseball Player
15317 Surrey House Way, Centreville VA 20120, USA	
McNamara, John F	Baseball Player, Manager
1206 Beech Hill Road, Brentwood TN 37027, USA	
McNamara, Julianne L	Gymnast, Actress
Todd Zeile, 5445 Via Nicola, Newbury Park CA 91320, USA	
McNamara, Katherine	Actress
Stewart Talent, 318 West 53rd St, #201, New York NY 10019, USA	
McNamara, Mark R C	Basketball Player
PO Box 134, Strawberry CA 95375, USA	
McNamara, Melissa	Golfer
7715 S Quebec Ave, Tulsa OK 74136, USA	
McNamara, Robert M (Bob)	Baseball Player
4764 Dalea Place, Oceanside CA 92057, USA	
McNamara, Sean	Director
A P A Talent/Literary Agency, 405 S Beverly Dr, #300, Beverly Hills CA 90212 USA	
McNamara, William (Billy)	Actor
Venture I A B, 3211 Cahuenga Blvd W, #104, Los Angeles CA 90068, USA	
McNamee, Jessica	Actress
United Talent Agency, 9336 Civic Center Dr, Beverly Hills CA 90210 USA	
McNanie, Sean	Football Player
14915 Rancho Real, Del Mar CA 92014, USA	
McNaught, Judith	Writer
Random House, 1745 Broadway, #1800, New York NY 10019 USA	
McNaughton, John D	Director, Producer, Writer
Gersh Agency, 9465 Wilshire Blvd, #600, Beverly Hills CA 90212 USA	
McNaughton, Robert F, Jr	Computer Scientist
2511 15th St, Troy NY 12180, USA	
McNeal, Donald (Don)	Football Player
3311 Toledo Plaza, Coral Gables FL 33134, USA	
McNeal, Travis	Football Player
4707 40th Place N, Birmingham AL 35217, USA	
McNealy, Scott G	Businessman
Sun Microsystems, 4150 Network Circle, Santa Clara CA 95054, USA	
McNeely, Jeffrey L (Jeff)	Baseball Player
405 Everette St, Monroe NC 28112, USA	
McNeil, Clifton A	Football Player
1001 Westbury Dr, #98, Mobile AL 36609, USA	
McNeil, Freeman	Football Player
PO Box 62, Greenlawn NY 11740, USA	
McNeil, Kate	Actress
1743 N Dillon St, Los Angeles CA 90026, USA	
McNeil, Lori	Tennis Player
International Mgmt Group, 1 Erieview Plaza, 1360 E 9th St, Cleveland OH 44114 USA	
McNeil, Patrick (Pat)	Football Player
2117 US Highway 80 E, Mesquite TX 75150, USA	
McNeil, Ryan D	Football Player
315 14th St NW, Atlanta GA 30318, USA	
McNeill, Corbin A, Jr	Businessman
P E C O Energy Co, 2301 Market St, Philadelphia PA 19103, USA	
McNeill, Frederick A (Fred)	Football Player
3500 W Manchester Blvd, #320, Inglewood CA 90305, USA	

M

McMullian - McNeill

McNeill, Robert Duncan — Actor
Rothman Agency, 9250 Wilshire Blvd, #PH, Beverly Hills CA 90212, USA

McNeill, Robert J (Bob) — Basketball Player
1318 Wooded Way, Bryn Mawr PA 19010, USA

McNeill, Thomas G (Tom) — Football Player
31019 Torrey Road, Waller TX 77484, USA

McNeill, W Donald (Don) — Tennis Player
2165 15th Ave, Vero Beach FL 32960, USA

McNerney, W James, Jr — Businessman
Boeing Co, 100 N Riverside, Chicago IL 60606, USA

McNertney, Gerald E (Jerry) — Baseball Player
1124 10th St, Nevada IA 50201, USA

McNichol, Kristy — Actress
Good Guy Entertainment, 3733 Oakfield Dr, Sherman Oaks CA 91423, USA

McNish, Allan — Auto Racing Driver
C S S Stellar Mgmt, 34-43 Russell St, London WC2B 5HA, England

McNiven, Julie — Actress
Don Buchwald/Fortitude, 6500 Wilshire Blvd, #2200, Los Angeles CA 90048 USA

McNorton, Bruce E — Football Player
PO Box 672, Bloomfield Hills MI 48303, USA

McNutt, Stephen F — Cinematographer
Innovative Artists, 1505 10th St, Santa Monica CA 90401 USA

McOmie, Maggie — Actress
Arthouse Talent, 107 SE Washington St, #156, Portland OR 97214, USA

M'Cormack, Adetokumboh — Actor
Hofflund/Polone, 9465 Wilshire Blvd, #420, Beverly Hills CA 90212 USA

McPartland, Marian M — Jazz Pianist
D L Media, 124 N Highland Ave, Bala Cynwyd PA 19004, USA

McPartlin, Ryan — Actor, Model
Evolution Entertainment, 901 N Highland Ave, Los Angeles CA 90038 USA

McPeak, Merrill A (Tony) — Air Force General
123 Furnace St, Lake Oswego OR 97034, USA

McPhee, John A — Writer
475 Drake's Corner Road, Princeton NJ 08540, USA

McPhee, Jonathan — Conductor
PO Box 1425, Marblehead MA 01945, USA

McPhee, Katharine H — Singer, Actress
Schiff Co, 9465 Wilshire Blvd, #480, Beverly Hills CA 90212, USA

McPhee, Kodi Smit — Actor
I C M Partners, 10250 Constellation Blvd, #900, Los Angeles CA 90067 USA

McPhee, Martha — Writer
Wylie Agency, 250 W 57th St, #2114, New York NY 10107 USA

McPhee, Mike — Ice Hockey Player
16 Brook Point Road, Tantallon NS B3Z 2R3, Canada

McPherson, Charles — Jazz Saxophonist
Joel Chriss, 60 E 8th St, #34N, New York NY 10003 USA

McPherson, Dallas L — Baseball Player
219 Gold Crest Dr, Braselton GA 30517, USA

McPherson, Donald G (Don) — Football Player
Sports Leadership Institute, Adelphi University, Garden City NY 11530, USA

McPherson, James A — Writer
Little Brown, 3 Center Plaza, #100, Boston MA 02108 USA

McPherson, James M — Historian
15 Randall Road, Princeton NJ 08540, USA

McPherson, John — Cartoonist (Close to Home)
Universal Press Syndicate, 4520 Main St, #700, Kansas City MO 64111 USA

McPherson, Kristy — Golfer
Ladies Pro Golf Assn, 100 International Golf Dr, Daytona Beach FL 32124 USA

McQuarrie, Christopher — Writer, Diector, Producer
Invisible Ink, 9696 Culver Blvd, #203, Culver City CA 90232, USA

McQuarters, Robert W (R W) — Football Player
1548 E 54th St N, Tulsa OK 74126, USA

McQueen, Chad — Actor
8306 Wilshire Blvd, #438, Beverly Hills CA 90211, USA

McQueen, Cozell — Basketball Player
100 E Charing Cross, Cary NC 27513, USA

McQueen, Michael R (Mike) — Baseball Player
6623 Lost Horizon Dr, Austin TX 78759, USA

McQueen, Steven R — Actor
Schiff Co, 8440 Warner Dr, #B1, Culver City CA 90232 USA

McQueen, Steven R (Steve) — Artist, Director
Casorotto Ramsay, Waverley House, 7-12 Noel St, London W1F 8GQ, England

McQueen, Tanya — Actress
Generate, 1545 26th St, #200, Santa Monica CA 90404, USA

McQuilken, Kim E — Football Player
360 Highgrove Dr, Fayetteville GA 30215, USA

McRae, Basil — Ice Hockey Player
759 Hyde Park Road, #252, London ON N6H 3S2, Canada

McRae, Benjamin P (Bennie) — Football Player
532 W 143rd St, #63, New York NY 10031, USA

McRae, Charles E — Football Player
PO Box 30527, Knoxville TN 37930, USA

McRae, Harold O (Hal) — Baseball Player, Manager
519 Sand Crane Court, Bradenton FL 34212, USA

McRae, Shane — Actor
Gersh Agency, 9465 Wilshire Blvd, #600, Beverly Hills CA 90212 USA

McRaney, Gerald — Actor
217 Keller St, Bay Saint Louis MS 39520, USA

McReynolds, Lawrence J (Larry), III — Sportscaster, Auto Racing Mechanic
123 Mystic Lake Loop, Mooresville NC 28117, USA

McReynolds, W Kevin — Baseball Player
2 Country Place, Roland AR 72135, USA

McRobbie, Michael A — Educator
Indiana University, President's Office, 107 S Indiana, Bloomington IN 47405, USA

McRoy, Spike — Golfer
742 Mira Vista Dr SE, Huntsville AL 35802, USA

McShane, Ian
McShane Productions, 30 New Bridge St, London EC4V 6BJ, England — Actor

McShane, Jamie
Select Artists, 1138 12th St, #1, Santa Monica CA 90403 USA — Actor

McShane, Jennifer
Pallas Mgmt, 12535 Chandler Blvd, #1, Valley Village CA 91607, USA — Actress

McShera, Sophie
Curtis Brown Group, 28-29 Haymarket St, #500, London SW1Y 4SP, England — Actress

McSorley, Gerard
Insight Mgmt, 1134 S Cloverdale Ave, Los Angeles CA 90019 USA — Actor

McSorley, Marty
3301 The Strand, Hermosa Beach CA 90254, USA — Ice Hockey Player

McSwain, Rodney (Rod)
5393 Stonewood Dr, Hickory NC 28602, USA — Football Player

McTavish, Graham
Stone Manners Salners, 9911 W Pico Blvd, #1400, Los Angeles CA 90035 USA — Actor

McTeer, Janet
Rights House, 34-43 Russell St, London WC2B 5HA, England — Actress

McTeigue, James
Creative Artists Agency, 2000 Ave of Stars, #100, Los Angeles CA 90067 USA — Director

McTiernan, John
Paradigm Agency, 360 N Crescent Dr, North Building, Beverly Hills CA 90210 USA — Director

McVey, Robert P
3333 NE 34th St, #1522, Fort Lauderdale FL 33308, USA — Ice Hockey Player

McVicar, Daniel
1704 Oak St S, Santa Monica CA 90405, USA — Actor

McVie, Christine
406 Poplar Dr, Wilmette IL 60091, USA — Singer (Fleetwood Mac), Songwriter

McVie, John
4224 Waialae Ave, Honolulu HI 96816, USA — Bassist (Fleetwood Mac), Songwriter

McVie, Tom
5713 Willow Springs Highway, Ferndale WA 98248, USA — Ice Hockey Coach

McWhirter, Jillian
PO Box 6308, Beverly Hills CA 90212, USA — Actress

McWilliams, Brian
Longshoremen/Warehousemen Union, 1188 Franklin St, San Francisco CA 94109, USA — Labor Leader

McWilliams, Eric L
798 Hearst Way, Corona CA 92882, USA — Basketball Player

McWilliams, Fleming
Michael Dixon Mgmt, 119 Pebble Creek Road, Franklin TN 37064, USA — Singer

McWilliams, Johnny
4540 E Blue Spruce Lane, Gilbert AZ 85298, USA — Football Player

McWilliams, Larry D
4102 Beckley Court, Colleyville TX 76034, USA — Baseball Player

McWilliams, Robert H, Jr
US Court of Appeals, US Courthouse, 1929 Stout St, Denver CO 80294, USA — Judge

McWilliams-Franklin, Taj
Washington Mystics, Verizon Center, 401 9th St NW, #750, Washington DC 20004 USA — Basketball Player

Meacham, John
Newsweek Magazine, Editorial Dept, 308 E 50th St, New York NY 10022, USA — Writer

Meacham, Robert A (Bobby)
20610 Prince Creek Dr, Katy TX 77450, USA — Baseball Player

Meacham, Russell L (Rusty)
1906 Eden Glen Lane, Pearland TX 77581, USA — Baseball Player

Meachem, Robert
San Diego Chargers, 4020 Murphy Canyon Road, San Diego CA 92123 USA — Football Player

Mead, Chuck
Thirty Tigers, 1604 8th Ave S, #200, Nashville TN 37203, USA — Guitarist (BR5-149)

Mead, Courtland
I C M Partners, 10250 Constellation Blvd, #900, Los Angeles CA 90067 USA — Actor

Mead, Dana G
300 Boylston St, #1103, Boston MA 02116, USA — Businessman

Mead, Lee S
Artist Rights Group, 4 Great Portland Place, London W1W 8PA, England — Actor, Singer

Mead, Shepherd
53 Rivermead Court, London SW6 3RY, England — Writer

Meade, Angela
I M G Artists, Hogarth Business Park, Chiswick, London W4 2TH, England — Opera Singer

Meade, Carl J
15013 Live Oak Springs Canyon Road, Canyon Country CA 91387, USA — Astronaut

Meador, Eddie D (Ed)
1135 Padgett Hill Road, Natural Bridge VA 24578, USA — Football Player

Meadows, Brian
917 Butter & Egg Road, Troy AL 36081, USA — Baseball Player

Meadows, Jayne
16185 Woodvale Road, Encino CA 91436, USA — Actress

Meadows, Michael R (Louie)
110 Heavens Lane, Maysville NC 28555, USA — Baseball Player

Meadows, Shane
Casorotto Ramsay, Waverley House, 7-12 Noel St, London W1F 8GQ, England — Director

Meadows, Stephen
1760 Courtney Ave, Los Angeles CA 90046, USA — Actor

Meadows, Tim
A P A Talent/Literary Agency, 405 S Beverly Dr, #300, Beverly Hills CA 90212 USA — Actor, Comedian

Meadows, William H
Wilderness Society, President's Office, 1615 M St NW, Washington DC 20036, USA — Association Executive

Meads, D Donald (Don)
3220 Cypress Way, Santa Rosa CA 95405, USA — Baseball Player

Meads, Johnny s
9419 Pine Lilly Court, Navarre FL 32566, USA — Football Player

Meagher, Mary T
404 Vanderwall, Peachtree City GA 30269, USA — Swimmer

Meagher, Rick
2698 Innisfil Road, Mississauga ON L5M 4J2, Canada — Ice Hockey Player

Mealing, Amanda
Curtis Brown Group, 28-29 Haymarket St, #500, London SW1Y 4SP, England — Actress

Meaney, Colm — Actor
Innovative Artists, 1505 10th St, Santa Monica CA 90401 USA

Meaney, Kevin — Actor, Comedian, Writer
OmniPop Talent Group, 4605 Lankershim Blvd, #201, Toluca Lake CA 91602 USA

Means, David — Writer
Wylie Agency, 250 W 57th St, #2114, New York NY 10107 USA

Means, Natrone J — Football Player
14602 Greenpoint Lane, Huntersville NC 28078, USA

Means, Winslow — Basketball Player
1336 Arch St, Zanesville OH 43701, USA

Meany, Colm — Actor
Troika, 74 Clerkenwell Road, #300, London EC1M 5QA, England

Meara, Anne — Actress, Comedienne
118 Riverside Dr, #5A, New York NY 10024, USA

Meares, Patrick J (Pat) — Baseball Player
8405 E Bridlewood St, Wichita KS 67206, USA

Mears, Casey J — Auto Racing Driver
5020 Carmel Park Dr, Charlotte NC 28226, USA

Mears, Derek — Actor
Kazarian/Spencer/Ruskin, 11969 Ventura Blvd, #300, Studio City CA 91604 USA

Mears, F Gary — Singer, Guitarist (Casuals)
12170 Country Road 215, Tyler TX 75707, USA

Mears, Rick R — Auto Racing Driver
1536 NW Buttonbush Circle, Palm City FL 34990, USA

Mears, Roger, Sr — Truck Racing Driver
PO Box 520, Terrell NC 28682, USA

Mears, Walter R — Journalist
Associated Press, Editorial Dept, 2021 K St NW, #600, Washington DC 20006, USA

Meat Loaf — Singer, Actor
Sanders/Armstrong/Caserta Mgmt, 2120 Colorado Ave, #120, Santa Monica CA 90404 USA

Mebane, Brandon J — Football Player
2310 SE 2nd Court, Renton WA 98056, USA

Mecchi, Irene — Writer
Abrams Artists, 9200 W Sunset Blvd, #1125, West Hollywood CA 90069 USA

Meche, Gilbert A (Gil) — Baseball Player
6513 Ridge Road, Kansas City MO 64152, USA

Mechem, Charles S, Jr — Golf Executive, Businessman
United States Show, 1 Eastwood Dr, Cincinnati OH 45227, USA

Mechler, Pia — Actress
Stacey Castro Media, 4009 Leeward Ave, Los Angeles CA 90005 USA

Mechlowicz, Scott — Actor
Management 360, 9111 Wilshire Blvd, Beverly Hills CA 90210 USA

Meciar, Vladimir — Prime Minister, Slovakia
Urad Vlady SR, Nam Slobody 1, 81370 Bratislava, Slovakia

Mecir, James M (Jim) — Baseball Player
3679 Annis Circle, Pleasanton CA 94588, USA

Mecir, Miloslav — Tennis Player
Julova 1, 83101 Bratislava, Czech Republic

Mecklenburg, Karl B — Football Player
6372 S Zenobia Court, Littleton CO 80123, USA

Medak, Peter — Director
Gersh Agency, 9465 Wilshire Blvd, #600, Beverly Hills CA 90212 USA

Medders, Brandon E — Baseball Player
9732 Charolais Dr, Tuscaloosa AL 35405, USA

Meddick, Jim — Cartoonist (Monty)
United Feature Syndicate, PO Box 5610, Cincinnati OH 45201 USA

Medeiros, Glenn — Singer
PO Box 8, Lawai HI 96765, USA

Medford, Paul J — Actor, Choreographer
Gavin Barker Assoc, 2D Wimpole St, London W1G 0EB, England

Mediate, Rocco — Golfer
2548 Medina Circle, Medina WA 98039, USA

Medich, George F (Doc) — Baseball Player
3007 Woodfield Dr, Aliquippa PA 15001, USA

Medina Estevez, Jorge Arturo Cardinal — Religious Leader
Congregation for Divine Worship, Piazza Pio XII 10, 00193 Rome, Italy

Medina Sanchez, Dasnilo — President, Dominican Republic
Palacio Nacional, Calle Moises Garcia, Ave Mexico, Santo Domingo, Dominican Republic

Medlen, Kris — Baseball Player
2161 Technology Place, Long Beach CA 90810, USA

Medley, Bill — Singer (Righteous Brothers)
Barry Rillera, 9841 Hot Springs Dr, Huntington Beach CA 92646, USA

Medoff, Mark H — Writer
PO Box 3072, Las Cruces NM 88003, USA

Medved, Aleksandr V — Freestyle Wrestler
Belarussian State Univeristy, Sports Excellence Dept, 220030 Minsk, Belarus

Medved, Ronald G (Ron) — Football Player
6615 239th Ave E, Buckley WA 98321, USA

Medvedenko, Stanislav (Slava) — Basketball Player
1700 Ruhland Ave, Manhattan Beach CA 90266, USA

Medvedev, Andrei — Tennis Player
Association of Tennis Professionals, 200 Tournament Road, Ponte Vedra Beach FL 32082 USA

Medvedev, Dmitry A — Prime Minister, Russia
Prime Minister's Office, Krasnopresnenskaya Nab 2, 103274 Moscow, Russia

Medvedev, Zhores A — Biologist
4 Osborn Gardens, London NW7 1DY, England

Medvin, Scott H — Baseball Player
673 Lynbrook Ave, Tonawanda NY 14150, USA

Medway, Heather — Actress
A P A Talent/Literary Agency, 405 S Beverly Dr, #300, Beverly Hills CA 90212 USA

Medwin, Michael — Actor
I C M Partners, Marlborough House, 10 Earlham St, #300, London WC2H 9LNP, England

Mee, L Darnell — Basketball Player
2005 Westland Dr SW, #1201, Cleveland TN 37311, USA

Meehan, Gerald M (Gerry) — Ice Hockey Player
2 Dafoe Court, Aurora ON L4G 7C8, Canada

Meehan, Martin T (Marty) — Educator; Representative, MA
University of Massachusetts, Chancellor's Office, Lowell MA 01854, USA
Meeke, Brent — Ice Hockey Player
11331 Whitetail Run St NW, Bolivar OH 44612, USA
Meeker, Howie — Ice Hockey Player, Coach, Sportscaster
979 Dickinson Way, Parksville BC V9P 1Z7, Canada
Meeks, Robert E (Bob) — Football Player
PO Box 29734, Denver CO 80229, USA
Meeler, C Philip (Phil) — Baseball Player
102 Pine St, Knightdale NC 27545, USA
Meely, Cliff — Basketball Player
3240 Iris Ave, #204, Boulder CO 80301, USA
Meena — Actress
58 2nd St, Venkatesh Nagar, Virugambakkam, Chennai TN 600092, India
Meents, Scott — Basketball Player
4231 155th Place SE, Bellevue WA 98006, USA
Meese, Edwin, III — Attorney General
1075 Spring Hill Road, McLean VA 22102, USA
Meester, Bradley R (Brad) — Football Player
7644 Chipwood Lane, Jacksonville FL 32256, USA
Meester, Leighton — Actress, Singer
W M E Entertainment, 9601 Wilshire Blvd, #300, Beverly Hills CA 90210 USA
Meeuwsen, Terry A — Beauty Queen, Singer, Entertainer
Pat Robertson's 700 Club, 977 Centerville Turnpike, Virginia Beach VA 23463, USA
Megaton, Olivier — Director
W M E Entertainment, 9601 Wilshire Blvd, #300, Beverly Hills CA 90210 USA
Meggysey, David M (Dave) — Football Player
2528 Benvenue Ave, Berkeley CA 94704, USA
MeGrew, Mike — Baseball Player
25 Karen Dr, Hope Valley RI 02832, USA
Mehl, Lance A — Football Player
44920 Kacsmar Estates Dr, Saint Clairsville OH 43950, USA
Mehldau, Brad — Jazz Pianist
Merlin Company, 16574 Bosque Dr, Encino CA 91436, USA
Mehra, Smirti — Golfer
4038 Greystone Dr, Clermont FL 34711, USA
Mehrabian, Robert — Educator
Carnegie Mellon University, President's Office, Pittsburgh PA 15213, USA
Mehring, Sona — Social Activist
CaringBridge, PO Box 6032, Albert Lea MN 56007, USA
Mehringer, David M — Astronomer
University of Illinois, Astronomy Dept, Champaign IL 61820, USA
Mehta, Deepa — Director, Writer
I C M Partners, 10250 Constellation Blvd, #900, Los Angeles CA 90067 USA
Mehta, Sujata — Actress
56 Dev Chhaya Tardeo Haji Ali Road, Tardeo, Mumbai MS 400034, India
Mehta, Ved P — Writer
139 E 79th St, New York NY 10075, USA
Mehta, Zubin — Conductor
27 Oakmont Dr, Los Angeles CA 90049, USA
Meidani, Rexhep — President, Albania
Club de Madrid, C/Goya 5-7, Pasaje 2, 28001 Madrid, Spain
Meier, David K (Dave) — Baseball Player
523 W Stuart Ave, Fresno CA 93704, USA
Meier, Dieter — Synthesizer Player (Yello)
Creative Artists Agency, 2000 Ave of Stars, #100, Los Angeles CA 90067 USA
Meier, Raymond — Photographer
Raymond Meier Photography, 532 Broadway, #800, New York NY 10012, USA
Meier, Richard A — Pritzker Architectural Laureate
Richard Meier Partners, 475 10th Ave, #600, New York NY 10018, USA
Meier, Robert J D (Rob) — Football Player
7551 Scarlet Ibis Lane, Jacksonville FL 32256, USA
Meier, Shadley B (Shad) — Football Player
4001 Skyline Dr, Nashville TN 37215, USA
Meier, Waltraud — Opera Singer
Hilbert Artists Mgmt, Maximilanstr 22, 80539 Munich, Germany
Meieran, Andrew — Director, Producer
W M E Entertainment, 9601 Wilshire Blvd, #300, Beverly Hills CA 90210 USA
Meiers, Shallan A — Model
Playboy Promotions, 2706 Media Center Dr, Los Angeles CA 90065 USA
Meighan, Tom — Singer (Kasabian)
International Talent Booking, Ariel House, 74A Charlotte St, #100 London W1T 4QJ, England
Meigs, Montgomery C — Army General
Business Executives for National Security, 1030 15th NW, Washington DC 20005, USA
Meili, Launi — Markswoman
2001 Wagon Gap Trail, Monument CO 80132, USA
Meilinger, Steven F (Steve) — Football Player
719 Camino Road, Lexington KY 40502, USA
Meindl, James D — Electrical Engineer
Georgia Institute of Technology, Microelectronics Center, Atlanta GA 30332, USA
Meine, Klaus — Singer, Guitarist (Scorpions)
Und Verlags, Bohlenweg 8, 30835 Langenhagen, Germany
Meineke, Donald E (Don) — Basketball Player
329 Silvertree Court, Dayton OH 45459, USA
Meinwald, Jerrold — Chemist
429 Warren Road, Ithaca NY 14850, USA
Meirelles, Fernando — Director
O2 Films, Rua Heliopolis 410, Vila Hamburguesa, Sao Paulo SP 05318 010, Brazil
Meisel, Stephen — Photographer
64 Wooster St, New York NY 10012, USA
Meiselas, Susan — Photographer
256 Mott St, New York NY 10012, USA
Meisner, Gregory P (Greg) — Football Player
229 Carr Dr, Ligonier PA 15658, USA
Meisner, Joachim Cardinal — Religious Leader
Archbishop's Diocese, Marzellenstr 32, 50668 Cologne, Germany

Meisner, Randy — Bassist, Singer (Eagles, Poco)
Rick Alter Mgmt, 1018 17th Ave S, #12, Nashville TN 37212, USA
Meister, Élisabeth — Opera Singer
I M G Artists, Hogarth Business Park, Chiswick, London W4 2TH, England
Meixler, Edward (Ed) — Football Player
13812 Hastings Farm Road, Huntersville NC 28078, USA
Meja — Singer (Legacy of Sound), Composer
Basic Music Mgmt, Norrtullsgatan 51, 113 45 Stockholm, Sweden
Mejia, Jorge Maria Cardinal — Religious Leader
Biblioteca Apostolica Vaticina, 00120 Vatican City
Mejia, Paul R — Ballet Dancer, Choreographer
Fort Worth Ballet, 6848 Green Oaks Road, Fort Worth TX 76116, USA
Mejias, Roman G — Baseball Player
27325 Terrytown Road, Sun City CA 92586, USA
Mekka, Eddie — Actor
8217 San Ramon Dr, Las Vegas NV 89147, USA
Mekki, Smail — Actor
Cineart, 36 Rue de Ponthieu, 75008 Paris, France
Melamed, Lisa — Producer
Paradigm Agency, 360 N Crescent Dr, North Building, Beverly Hills CA 90210 USA
Melamid, Aleksander — Artist
53 Lisspenard St, New York NY 10013, USA
Melancon, Charles J (Charlie) — Representative, LA
International Franchise Assn, 1501 K St NW, #350, Washington DC 20005, USA
Melancon, Mei — Actress
Essential Entertainment, 5225 Wilshire Blvd, #702, Los Angeles CA 90036, USA
Melanie — Singer, Guitarist, Songwriter
53 Baymont St, #5, Clearwater Beach FL 33767, USA
Melano, Fabrizio — Director
Columbia Artists Mgmt Inc, 1790 Broadway, #702, New York NY 10019 USA
Melanson, Roland (Rollie) — Ice Hockey Player
728 Rue Pierre Biard, Boucherville QC J4B 7R3, Canada
Melato, Mariangela — Actress
Via dei Coronari 44, 00186 Rome, Italy
Melcher, John — Senator, MT
2519 Wylie Ave, Missoula MT 59802, USA
Melchionni, Gary D — Basketball Player
1040 Grandview Blvd, Lancaster PA 17601, USA
Melchionni, William P (Bill) — Basketball Player
115 Whitehall Blvd, Garden City NY 11530, USA
Melchior, Ib — Writer
8228 Marymount Lane, Los Angeles CA 90069, USA
Mele, Sabath A (Sam) — Baseball Player, Manager
340 Adams St, Quincy MA 02169, USA
Mele-Mel — Rap Artist
Groove Entertainment, 1005 N Alfred St, #2, West Hollywood CA 90069, USA
Melendez, John (Stuttering) — Actor, Comedian
Paradigm Agency, 360 N Crescent Dr, North Building, Beverly Hills CA 90210 USA
Melendez, Ron — Actor
Jay D Schwartz Assoc, 3151 Cahuenga Blvd W, #220, Los Angeles CA 90068, USA
Melhuse, Adam — Baseball Player
758 Center St, San Luis Obispo CA 93405, USA
Melinda — Illusionist
M Entertainment, 4041 Audrie St, #A, Las Vegas NV 89109, USA
Melini, Angela — Model, Actress
Playboy Promotions, 2706 Media Center Dr, Los Angeles CA 90065 USA
Mellanby, Scott — Ice Hockey Player
2548 Town and Country Lane, Saint Louis MO 63131, USA
Mellekas, John S — Football Player
498 Broadway, Newport RI 02840, USA
Mellencamp, John — Singer, Songwriter
Belmont Mall Studio, 5087 Lower Schooner Road, Nashville IN 47448, USA
Mello, Craig C — Nobel Medicine Laureate
25 Fessenden Road, Barrington RI 02806, USA
Mello, Tamara — Actress
A P A Talent/Literary Agency, 405 S Beverly Dr, #300, Beverly Hills CA 90212 USA
Mellons, Ken — Singer, Guitarist, Songwriter
PO Box 8293, Hermitage TN 37076, USA
Mellor, James R — Businessman
23 Shreve Dr, Laguna Beach CA 92651, USA
Mellor, Thomas R (Tom) — Ice Hockey Player
63 Spoonhill Ave, Marlborough MA 01752, USA
Melman, Jeffrey (Jeff) — Director, Producer
I C M Partners, 10250 Constellation Blvd, #900, Los Angeles CA 90067 USA
Melnick, Bruce E — Astronaut
Boeing Aerospace, PO Box 21233, Kennedy Space Center, Orlando FL 32815, USA
Melnick, Valeriya — Model
Fashion Model Mgmt, Via Monterosa 80, 20149 Milan, Italy
Melnyk, Larry — Ice Hockey Player
1748 Sugarpine Court, Coquitlam BC V3E 3E4, Canada
Melo, Brian — Singer, Songwriter
Agency Group Ltd, 142 W 57th St, #600, New York NY 10019 USA
Melo, Fabricio P (Fab) — Basketball Player
Boston Celtics, 226 Causeway St, #4, Boston MA 02114 USA
Meloan, Jonathan M (Jon) — Baseball Player
8017 Lichtenauer Dr, Lenexa KS 66219, USA
Meloche, Gilles — Ice Hockey Player
Pittsburgh Penguins, Consol Energy Center, 1001 5th Ave, Pittsburgh PA 15219 USA
Meloni, Christopher — Actor
Gersh Agency, 9465 Wilshire Blvd, #600, Beverly Hills CA 90212 USA
Meloy, Colin P H — Singer, Guitarist (Decemberists)
Big Hassle, 44 Wall St, #2200, New York NY 10005, USA
Melrose, Barry J — Ice Hockey Player, Coach
10 Windy Ridge, Glens Falls NY 12801, USA
Melroy, Pamela A — Astronaut
920 N Barton St, Arlington VA 22201, USA

Melton, Barry
PO Box 890983, Sacramento CA 95798, USA — Singer (Country Joe & the Fish)
Melton, William E (Bill)
333 E 35th St, Chicago IL 60616, USA — Baseball Player
Meltzer, Allan L
Carnegie Mellon University, Economics Dept, Pittsburgh PA 15260, USA — Economist
Meltzer, Brad
20533 Biscayne Blvd, #371, Aventura FL 33180, USA — Writer
Melua, Katie
Dramatico Ltd, PO Box 214, Farnham, Surrey GU10 5AL, England — Singer, Songwriter
Meluskey, Mitchell W (Mitch)
26 Meadowbrooke Road, Yakima WA 98903, USA — Baseball Player
Melvill, Michael W
24120 Jacaranda Dr, Tehachapi CA 93561, USA — Astronaut, Test Pilot
Melvin, Leland D
N A S A, Johnson Space Center, 2101 NASA Road, Houston TX 77058 USA — Astronaut
Melvin, Robert P (Bob)
5637 E Canyon Ridge North Dr, Cave Creek AZ 85331, USA — Baseball Player, Manager
Melvoin, Wendy
Girl Brothers, 9454 Wilshire Blvd, #711, Beverly Hills CA 90212, USA — Singer, Guitarist
Melzack, Ronald
51 Banstead Road, Montreal QC H4X 1P1, Canada — Psychologist
Meminger, Dean P
45 W 139th St, #16E, New York NY 10037, USA — Basketball Player
Memory, Thara
American Music Program, 116 NE 29th Ave, Portland OR 97232, USA — Jazz Trumpeter
Memphis Bleek
Green Light Talent Agency, PO Box 3172, Beverly Hills CA 90212 USA — Rap Artist
Menand, Louis
New Yorker, Editorial Dept, 4 Times Square, Basement C1B, New York NY 10036 USA — Historian
Menard, Paul
T R G Motorsports, 292 Rolling Hill Road, Mooresville NC 28117, USA — Auto Racing Driver
Menaul, Christopher S
United Agents, 12-26 Lexington St, London W1F 0LE, England — Director
Mench, Kevin F
1305 Danbury Parks Dr, Keller TX 76248, USA — Baseball Player
Menchaca, Penelope
Telemundo Network Group, 2470 W 8th Ave, Hialeah FL 33010 USA — Entertainer
Menchu Tum, Rigoberta
Av Simeon Canas 4-04 Zona 2, Ciudad de Guatemala, Guatemala — Nobel Peace Laureate
Mencia, Carlos
Brillstein Entertainment Partners, 9150 Wilshire Blvd, #350, Beverly Hills CA 90212 USA — Actor, Comedian, Writer
Menczer, Pauline
6 Burra Burra CL, Ocean Shores NSW 2483, Australia — Surfer
Mendel, Nathan G (Nate)
S A M, 722 Seward St, Los Angeles CA 90038, USA — Bassist (Foo Fighters)
Mendelsohn, Ben
Untitled Entertainment, 350 S Beverly Dr, #200, Beverly Hills CA 90212 USA — Actor
Mendelsohn, Carol
W M E Entertainment, 9601 Wilshire Blvd, #300, Beverly Hills CA 90210 USA — Producer, Writer
Mendenhall, John R
PO Box 532, Cullen LA 71021, USA — Football Player
Mendenhall, Ken E
1708 S Rankin St, Edmond OK 73013, USA — Football Player
Mendes, Eva
Management 360, 9111 Wilshire Blvd, Beverly Hills CA 90210 USA — Actress, Model
Mendes, Sam
Independent Talent Group, Oxford House, 76 Oxford St, London W1D 1BS, England — Director
Mendes, Sergio
A P A Talent/Literary Agency, 405 S Beverly Dr, #300, Beverly Hills CA 90212 USA — Pianist
Mendez, Akissa
Universal Attractions, 135 W 26th St, #1200, New York NY 10001 USA — Singer (Allure)
Mendler, Bridgit
Gersh Agency, 9465 Wilshire Blvd, #600, Beverly Hills CA 90212 USA — Actress
Mendoza Moncada, Dayana S
Trump Model Agency, 91 5th Ave, #300, New York NY 10003 USA — Beauty Queen, Model
Mendoza, Cristobal R (Minnie)
2866 Charlotte Dr, Murrells Inlet SC 29576, USA — Baseball Player
Mendoza, Linda
A P A Talent/Literary Agency, 405 S Beverly Dr, #300, Beverly Hills CA 90212 USA — Director, Producer
Mendoza, Mark (Animal)
Rebellion Entertainment, 2440 Broadway, #111, New York NY 10024, USA — Singer, Bassist (Twisted Sister)
Mendoza, Martha
Associated Press, 450 W 33rd St, #1500, New York NY 10001 USA — Journalist
Mendoza, Michael J (Mike)
14207 S 20th St, Phoenix AZ 85048, USA — Baseball Player
Mendoza, Natalie J
R G M Associates, 64-76 Kippax St, #202, Surry Hills NSW 2010, Australia — Actress, Singer
Mendoza, Ramiro
18706 Pepper Pike, Lutz FL 33558, USA — Baseball Player
Menechino, Frank
522 Arlene St, Staten Island NY 10314, USA — Baseball Player
Meneses, Alex
Abrams Artists, 275 7th Ave, #2600, New York NY 10001 USA — Actress
Meneses, Antonio
Concert/Spectacle Agency, 29 Rue Coulouneriere, 1204 Geneva, Switzerland — Concert Cellist
Meneve, Russ
C H Entertainment, 6 W 14th St, New York NY 10011, USA — Actor, Comedian
Menez, Bernard
119 Blvd de Grenelle, 75015 Paris, France — Actor, Singer
Menges, Chris
Claire Best Assoc, 736 Seward St, Los Angeles CA 90038, USA — Cinematographer, Director
Menhart, Paul G
725 Kelsall Dr, Richmond Hill GA 31324, USA — Baseball Player
Menichetti, Roberto
Via Perugina 88, Gubbio (PG), Italy — Fashion Designer

V.I.P. Address Book

M

Menke, Denis J
1246 Berkshire Lane, Tarpon Springs FL 34688, USA — Baseball Player

Menken, Alan
Mason Co, 1212 Ave of Americas, #1400, New York NY 10036, USA — Composer

Mennea, Pietro
Via Cassia 1041, 00189 Rome, Italy — Track Athlete

Menon, Mambillikalathil G K
C63 Tarang Apts, Mother Dairy Road, Patparganj, Delhi 110092, India — Physicist

Menounos, Maria
W M E Entertainment, 9601 Wilshire Blvd, #300, Beverly Hills CA 90210 USA — Actress, Model

Mensah, Peter
Abrams Artists, 9200 W Sunset Blvd, #1125, West Hollywood CA 90069 USA — Actor

Menshov, Vladimir V
3D Tverskaya-Yamskaya 52, #29, 125047 Moscow, Russia — Actor, Director

Mentzer, Ethan
Sharp & Focused Mgmt, 323 Broadway St, Cambridge MA 02139, USA — Bassist (Click Five)

Menuicucci, Pier Marino
Co-Regent's Office, Government Palace, 47031 San Marino — Co-Regent, San Marino

Menzel, Idina
One Entertainment, 12 W 57th St, #PH 1, New York NY 10019 USA — Actress, Singer

Menzel, Jiri
Divadlo na Vinchradech, Namesti Miru 7, 12000 Prague 2, Czech Republic — Director

Menzer, Ina
Spotlight Boxing, Am Stadtrand 27, 22047 Hamburg, Germany — Boxer

Menzies, Heather
PO Box 1645, Park City UT 84060, USA — Actress

Menzies, Marvin
New Mexico State University, Athletic Dept, Las Cruces NM 88003, USA — Basketball Coach

Menzies, Peter G, Jr
903 Tahoe Blvd, #802, Incline Village NV 89451, USA — Cinematographer

Meola, Tony
488 Forest St, Kearny NJ 07032, USA — Soccer Player

Meoli, Rudolph B (Rudy)
1211 San Gabriel Ave, Henderson NV 89002, USA — Baseball Player

Meow, Meow
I M G Artists, Hogarth Business Park, Chiswick, London W4 2TH, England — Opera Singer

Meraz, Alex
Innovative Artists, 1505 10th St, Santa Monica CA 90401 USA — Actor

Merbold, Ulf
Am Sonnenhang 4, 53721 Siegburg, Germany — Astronaut, Germany

Mercader, Julio
University of Calgary, Archaeology Dept, Calgary AB T2N 1N4, Canada — Archaeologist

Mercado, Orlando L
12021 W Louise Court, Sun City AZ 85373, USA — Baseball Player

Merced Villaneuva, Orlando L
PO Box 190494, San Juan PR 00919, USA — Baseball Player

Mercein, Charles S (Chuck)
59 Club Pointe Dr, White Plains NY 10605, USA — Football Player

Mercer, James R
Nasty Little Man, 110 Greene St, #605, New York NY 10012 USA — Singer, Guitarist (Shins)

Mercer, Kelvin
Richard Walters, PO Box 2789, Toluca Lake CA 91610 USA — Rap Artist (De La Soul)

Mercer, Michael (Mike)
64463 McGrath Road, Bend OR 97701, USA — Football Player

Mercer, Robert E
11 Island Estates Parkway, Palm Coast FL 32137, USA — Businessman

Mercer, Toby
Mercer Studios, 316 E Reserve Dr, Kalispell MT 59901, USA — Artist

Merchant, J Anderson (Andy)
PO Box 8, Malcolm AL 36556, USA — Baseball Player

Merchant, Larry
470 20th St, Santa Monica CA 90402, USA — Boxing Sportscaster

Merchant, Natalie
Indian Love Bride Music, PO Box 716, Lake Katrine NY 12449, USA — Singer, Songwriter

Merchant, Stephen
W M E Entertainment, 9601 Wilshire Blvd, #300, Beverly Hills CA 90210 USA — Producer, Comedian, Actor

Mercier, Michele
Residence Cape di Monte, 06400 Cannes, France — Actress

Mercilus, Whitney
Houston Texans, 2 Reliant Park, Houston TX 77054 USA — Football Player

Mercker, Kent H
5340 Muirfield Court, Dublin OH 43017, USA — Baseball Player

Merckx, Eddy
S'Herenweg 11, 1860 Meise, Belgium — Cyclist

Mercurio, Jed
Simon & Schuster, 1230 Ave of Americas, Concourse 1, New York NY 10020 USA — Writer

Mercurio, Paul
Beyond Films, 53-55 Brisbane St, Sunnyhills, Sydney NSW 2010, Australia — Actor, Singer

Meredith, O Claiborne (Cla), III
3807 Kensington Ave, Richmond VA 23221, USA — Baseball Player

Meredith, Richard O (Dick)
26580 Hickory Blvd, Bonita Springs FL 34134, USA — Ice Hockey Player

Meridith, Ronald K (Ron)
308 Via Promesa, San Clemente CA 92673, USA — Baseball Player

Meriweather, Joe C
5316 NW 84th Terrace, Kansas City MO 64154, USA — Basketball Player

Meriwether, Elizabeth (Liz)
W M E Entertainment, 9601 Wilshire Blvd, #300, Beverly Hills CA 90210 USA — Writer, Producer

Meriwether, Lee
12139 Jeanette Place, Granada Hills CA 91344, USA — Actress, Beauty Queen

Merkel, Angela
Bundeskanzlerant, Willy-Brandt-Str 1, 10557 Berlin, Germany — Chancellor, Germany

Merkens, Guido A
8101 Research Forest Dr, Spring TX 77382, USA — Football Player

Merkerson, S Epatha
I C M Partners, 10250 Constellation Blvd, #900, Los Angeles CA 90067 USA — Actress, Singer

Menke - Merkerson

654

V.I.P. Address Book

Merkosky, Glenn — Ice Hockey Player
113 Farr Lane, Queensbury NY 12804, USA
Merle, Carole — Alpine Skier
Chalet La Calette, 04400 Super-Sauze, France
Merletti, Lewis C — Law Enforcement Official
Cleveland Browns, 76 Lou Groza Blvd, Berea OH 44017 USA
Merlin, Jan — Actor
347 N California St, Burbank CA 91505, USA
Merlo, James L (Jim) — Football Player
1547 E Starpass Dr, Fresno CA 93730, USA
Merloni, Louis W (Lou) — Baseball Player
29 Wild Hunter Road, Dennis MA 02638, USA
Mero, Rena (Sable) — Wrestler, Model, Actress
Rena Productions, 760 Valley Stream Dr, Geneva FL 32732, USA
Meron, Neil — Producer
Storyline Entertainment, 8335 Sunset Blvd, #207, West Hollywood CA 90069, USA
Merow, James F — Judge
US Claims Court, 717 Madison Place NW, Washington DC 20439, USA
Merrell, Barry — Ice Hockey Player
253 Raquette St, Winnipeg MB R3K 1M9, Canada
Merrells, Jason — Actor
QVoice, 8 Kings St, London WC2E 8HN, England
Merrick, Doris — Actress
609 Desert West Dr, Rancho Mirage CA 92270, USA
Merrick, Marge — Bowler
Professional Bowlers Assn, 719 2nd Ave, #701, Seattle WA 98104 USA
Merrick, Robert — Yachtsman
470 Sea Meadow Dr, Portsmouth RI 02871, USA
Merrick, Wayne — Ice Hockey Player
68 Chesham Court, London ON N6G 3T4, Canada
Merrill, Catherine — Artist
Old Church Pottery, 1456 Florida St, San Francisco CA 94110, USA
Merrill, Dina — Actress
TalentWorks, 3500 W Olive Ave, #1400, Burbank CA 91505 USA
Merrill, Edward W — Chemical Engineer
90 Somerset St, Belmont MA 02478, USA
Merrill, Mark C — Football Player
782 Mimosa Lane, Saint Paul MN 55112, USA
Merrill, Robbie — Bassist (Godsmack, Everclear)
Front Line Mgmt, 1100 Glendon Ave, #2000, Los Angeles CA 90024 USA
Merrill, Stephen E (Steve) — Governor, NH
562 Main St, Farmington NH 03835, USA
Merriman, Ryan — Actor
W K T Public Relations, 9350 Wilshire Blvd, #450, Beverly Hills CA 90212 USA
Merriman, Shawne D — Football Player
7821 Vanity Fair Dr, Greenbelt MD 20770, USA
Merriott, Ronald — Diver
1271 McDole Dr, Sugar Grove IL 60554, USA
Merritt, Chris — Opera Singer
Askonas Holt, Lincoln House, 300 High Holborn, London WC1V 7JH, England
Merritt, Courtney — Actress
Coast to Coast Talent, 3350 Barham Blvd, Los Angeles CA 90068 USA
Merritt, Gilbert S — Judge
US Court of Appeals, US Courthouse, 701 Broadway, Nashville TN 37203, USA
Merritt, Jack N — Army General
US Army Assn, 2425 Wilson Blvd, #100, Arlington VA 22201, USA
Merritt, James J (Jim) — Baseball Player
2777 Blue Spruce Dr, Hemet CA 92545, USA
Merriweather, Michael L (Mike) — Football Player
PO Box 8351, Stockton CA 95208, USA
Merrow, Jeffrey C (Jeff) — Football Player
5989 Shadburn Ferry Road, Buford GA 30518, USA
Merrow, Susan — Association Executive
Sierra Club, 85 2nd St, #200, San Francisco CA 94105, USA
Merten, Alan G — Educator
George Mason University, President's Office, 4400 University Dr, Fairfax VA 22030, USA
Merten, Lauri — Golfer
1010 Del Harbour Dr, Delray Beach FL 33483, USA
Mertens, Alan — Auto Racing Executive
PacWest Racing Group, PO Box 1717, Bellevue WA 98009, USA
Mertens, Francois — Cyclist
79 Bonnie Vue Lane, New Milford CT 06776, USA
Mertens, Jerome W (Jerry) — Football Player
465 Woodside Dr, Woodside CA 94062, USA
Merton, Robert C — Nobel Economics Laureate
75 Cambridge Parkway, #E1108, Cambridge MA 02142, USA
Mertz, Barbara — Writer
M P M, PO Box 57, Myersville MD 21773, USA
Mertz, Edwin T — Biochemist
1504 Via Della Scala, Henderson NV 89052, USA
Mertz, Francis J — Educator
54 Woodcrest Dr, Morristown NJ 07960, USA
Merullo, Matthew B (Matt) — Baseball Player
8 Fox Run Road, Madison CT 06443, USA
Merwin, John D — Governor, VI
PO Box 1029, Hudson OH 44236, USA
Merwin, William Stanley (W S) — Writer
Steven Barclay Agency, 12 Western Ave, Petaluma CA 94952, USA
Merz, Curtis (Curt) — Football Player
1111 W Seminole St, Springfield MO 65807, USA
Merz, Suzanne (Sue) — Ice Hockey Player
5 Douglas Dr, Greenwich CT 06831, USA
Mesa, Jose R N — Baseball Player
PO Box 112207, Miami FL 33111, USA
Meschery, Thomas N (Tom) — Basketball Player
1216 Versailles Ave, Alameda CA 94501, USA

Meselson, Matthew S — Biochemist
Harvard University, Fairchild Biochemistry Laboratories, Cambridge MA 02138, USA
Mesereau, Thomas D — Attorney
1875 Century Park E, Los Angeles CA 90067, USA
Mesguich, Daniel — Actor, Director
Agence Monita Derrieux, 17-21 Rue Duret, 75116 Paris, France
Mesina Stanley, Dianne — Producer, Writer
Paradigm Agency, 360 N Crescent Dr, North Building, Beverly Hills CA 90210 USA
Mesquida, Roxane — Actress
Agence Elisabeth Simpson, 62 Boulevard Du Montparnasse, 75015 Paris, France
Messenger, Randall J (Randy) — Baseball Player
455 Market St, #2240, San Francisco CA 94105, USA
Messer, L Dale — Football Player
5449 N Brooks Ave, Fresno CA 93711, USA
Messer, Thomas M — Museum Executive
35 Sutton Place, New York NY 10022, USA
Messerschmid, Ernst — Astronaut, Germany
Universitat Stuttgart, Pfaffenwaldring 31, 70569 Stuttgart, Germany
Messerschmidt, J Alexander (Andy) — Baseball Player
200 Lagunita Dr, Soquel CA 95073, USA
Messi, Lionel A (Leo) — Soccer Player
F C Barcelona, Aristides Maillo S/N, 08028 Barcelona, Spain
Messier, Eric — Ice Hockey Player
9671 Timber Hawk Circle, #22, Littleton CO 80126, USA
Messier, Mark D — Ice Hockey Player
45 Birchwood Dr, Greenwich CT 06831, USA
Messina, Chris — Actor
Brillstein Entertainment Partners, 9150 Wilshire Blvd, #350, Beverly Hills CA 90212 USA
Messina, Jim — Singer, Songwriter
Director Management Group, 947 N La Cienega Blvd, #G, West Hollywood CA 90069, USA
Messina, Jo Dee — Singer, Songwriter
Sanctuary Mgmt, 15301 Ventura Blvd, Building B, Sherman Oaks CA 91403, USA
Messing, Debra — Actress
3 Arts Entertainment, 9460 Wilshire Blvd, #700, Beverly Hills CA 90212 USA
Messinger, Rina — Beauty Queen
Miss Universe Organization, 1370 Ave of Americas, #1600, New York NY 10019 USA
Messner, Heinrich (Heini) — Alpine Skier
Huebenweg 11, 6150 Steinach, Austria
Messner, Johnny — Actor
Zero Gravity Mgmt, 9255 Sunset Blvd, #1010, Los Angeles CA 90069 USA
Messner, Reinhold — Explorer, Mountaineer
Firmian, Sigmudskronerstr 53, 39100 Bozen, Italy
Meszaros, Andrej — Ice Hockey Player
Philadelphia Flyers, 1st Union Center, 3601 S Broad St, Philadelphia PA 19148 USA
Meszaros, Marta — Director
MalFilm Studio, Lumumba Utca 174, 1149 Budapest, Hungary
Metcalf, Eric Q — Football Player
6027 S Redwing St, Seattle WA 98118, USA
Metcalf, John — Writer
128 Lewis St, Ottawa ON K2P 0S7, Canada
Metcalf, Laurie — Actress
W M E Entertainment, 9601 Wilshire Blvd, #300, Beverly Hills CA 90210 USA
Metcalf, Ryan — Actor
Red Letter Entertainment, 437 W 48th St, #D, New York NY 10036, USA
Metcalf, Terrance R (Terry) — Football Player
5112 S Fountain St, Seattle WA 98178, USA
Metcalf, Terrence O — Football Player
1524 Jackson Ave E, #9, Oxford MS 38655, USA
Metcalfe, Jesse — Actor
Gersh Agency, 9465 Wilshire Blvd, #600, Beverly Hills CA 90212 USA
Metcalfe, Robert M — Inventor (Ethernet), Computer Scientist
Polaris Venture Partners, 1000 Winter St, #3350, Waltham MA 02451, USA
Metcalf-Lindenburger, Dorothy M — Astronaut
N A S A, Johnson Space Center, 2101 NASA Road, Houston TX 77058 USA
Metheny, Patrick B (Pat) — Jazz Guitarist, Composer
Ted Kurland, 173 Brighton Ave, Allston MA 02134 USA
Method Man — Rap Artist (Wu-Tang Clan), Actor
Smart Girl Productions, 8335 Sunset Blvd, #222, West Hollywood CA 90069, USA
Metrano, Art — Actor
C E S D, 10635 Santa Monica Blvd, #130, Los Angeles CA 90025 USA
Metro, Charles (Charlie) — Baseball Player, Manager
7890 Indiana St, Arvada CO 80007, USA
Metropolit, Glen — Ice Hockey Player
1070 Redwine Cove Road SW, Dalton GA 30720, USA
Mette-Marit — Princess, Norway
Det Kongelige, Slottet, Drammensvein 1, 0010 Oslo, Norway
Mettifogo, Roberto — Photographer
Via Montorio 54, 37131 Verona, Italy
Metzelaars, Peter H (Pete) — Football Player
10640 Pine Valley Path, Indianapolis IN 46234, USA
Metzger, Clarence E (Butch) — Baseball Player
641 Rivergate Way, Sacramento CA 95831, USA
Metzger, Roger H — Baseball Player
3560 Bluebonnet Blvd, Brenham TX 77833, USA
Metzger, Stephane — Actor
Agence Artiste Adequet, 80 Rue d'Amsterdam, 75009 Paris, France
Metzner, Raven — Producer, Writer
W M E Entertainment, 9601 Wilshire Blvd, #300, Beverly Hills CA 90210 USA
Meuli, Daniela — Snowboard Athlete
Muehlstra 26, 7260 Davos Dorf, Switzerland
Meunier-Lebouc, Patricia — Golfer
110 Dalena Way, Palm Beach Gardens FL 33418, USA
Mew — Keyboardist (Elastica)
C E O Mgmt, Ransomes Dock, 35-37 Parkgate Road, London SW11 4NP, England
Mewes, Jason — Actor
C E S D, 10635 Santa Monica Blvd, #130, Los Angeles CA 90025 USA

Mey, Uwe-Jens
Vulkanstr 22, 10367 Berlin, Germany — Speed Skater

Meyer Reyes, Deborah E (Debbie)
PO Box 2076, Carmichael CA 95609, USA — Swimmer

Meyer, Aaron
PO Box 25486, Portland OR 97298, USA — Concert, Rock Violinist; Composer

Meyer, Breckin
Gersh Agency, 9465 Wilshire Blvd, #600, Beverly Hills CA 90212 USA — Actor

Meyer, Dakota L
1384 Brockman Keltner Road, Greensburg KY 42743, USA — Afghanistan War Hero (CMH)

Meyer, Daniel J
7655 Annesdale Dr, Cincinnati OH 45243, USA — Businessman

Meyer, Daniel L (Dan)
433 Cedar Lane, Mickleton NJ 08056, USA — Baseball Player

Meyer, Daniel T (Dan)
11540 Marsh Creek Road, Clayton CA 94517, USA — Baseball Player

Meyer, Dina
TalentWorks, 3500 W Olive Ave, #1400, Burbank CA 91505 USA — Actress

Meyer, Dirk
Advanced Micro Devices, 1 A M D Place, PO Box 3453, Sunnyvale CA 94088, USA — Businessman

Meyer, Don
Northern State University, Athletic Dept, Aberdeen SD 57401, USA — Basketball Coach

Meyer, Edgar
I M G Artists, 152 W 57th St, #500, New York NY 10019 USA — Concert Double Bassist, Composer

Meyer, Edward C
1101 S Arlington Ridge Road, #1116, Arlington VA 22202, USA — Army General

Meyer, John
Meyer/Gifford/Jones, 270 Lafayette St, New York NY 10012, USA — Architect

Meyer, Laurence H
Federal Reserve Board, 20th St & Constitution Ave NW, Washington DC 20551, USA — Economist, Government Official

Meyer, Loren H
3577 330th St, Ruthven IA 51358, USA — Basketball Player

Meyer, Nicholas
Creative Artists Agency, 2000 Ave of Stars, #100, Los Angeles CA 90067 USA — Director, Writer

Meyer, Ron
Universal Studios, 100 Universal City Plaza, Universal City CA 91608, USA — Businessman

Meyer, Stephenie
Little Brown/Mysterious Press/Warner, 1271 Ave of Americas, New York NY 10020 USA — Writer

Meyer, Urban
8562 SW 12th Lane, Gainesville FL 32607, USA — Football Coach

Meyer, Yves F
Ecole Normale Superieure, 61 Ave President Wilson, 94235 Cachan, France — Mathematician

Meyerowitz, Joel
817 W End Ave, #11D, New York NY 10025, USA — Photographer

Meyerriecks, Jeffrey
Lindy Martin Mgmt, 1007 Lakewater Dr, Henrico VA 23229, USA — Concert Guitarist

Meyers Drysdale, Ann E
235 W Main St, Los Gatos CA 95030, USA — Basketball Player, Sportscaster

Meyers Tikalsky, Linda
RR 5 Box 265T, Santa Fe NM 87506, USA — Skier

Meyers, Anne Akiko
Colbert Artists, 111 W 57th St, #1416, New York NY 10019 USA — Concert Violinist

Meyers, Ari
Holly Lebed Personal Mgmt, 10535 Wilshire Blvd, #808, Los Angeles CA 90024, USA — Actress

Meyers, August (Augie)
Texas Re-Cord Co, PO Box 78163, Bulverde TX 78163, USA — Singer, Organist (Sir Douglas Quintet)

Meyers, Chad W
816 Summit Ridge Dr, Papillion NE 68046, USA — Baseball Player

Meyers, David
Creative Artists Agency, 2000 Ave of Stars, #100, Los Angeles CA 90067 USA — Director, Writer

Meyers, David W (Dave)
40629 Carmelina Circle, Temecula CA 92591, USA — Basketball Player

Meyers, Josh
Paul Kohner, 9300 Wilshire Blvd, #555, Beverly Hills CA 90212 USA — Actor, Comedian

Meyers, Nancy
W M E Entertainment, 9601 Wilshire Blvd, #300, Beverly Hills CA 90210 USA — Director, Producer

Meyers, Seth
Brillstein Entertainment Partners, 9150 Wilshire Blvd, #350, Beverly Hills CA 90212 USA — Actor, Comedian

Meyfarth, Ulrike Nasse-
Buschweg 53, 51519 Odenthal, Germany — Track Athlete

Meyjes, Menno
Casorotto Ramsay, Waverley House, 7-12 Noel St, London W1F 8GQ, England — Director, Writer

Meyrowitz, Carol M
T J X Companies, 770 Conchituate Road, Framingham MA 01701, USA — Businesswoman

Meyssignac, Emmanuelle
Artmedia, 20 Ave Rapp, 75007 Paris, France — Actress

Meyyappan, Meyya
Ames Research Center, Nanotechnology Center, Moffett Field CA 94035, USA — Nanotechnologist

Mezentseva, Galina
Kirov Ballet Theater, 1 Pl Iskusstr, 190000 Saint Petersburg, Russia — Ballerina

Mezlekia, Nega
Picador USA Books, 175 5th Ave, New York NY 10010, USA — Writer

Mezzogiorno, Giovanna
Media Art Mgmt, C/ Castelló 82, 2 Derecha, 28006 Madrid, Spain — Actress

Mfume, Kweisi
3000 Druid Park Dr, Baltimore MD 21215, USA — Association Executive

MGMT
Paradigm Agency, 404 W Franklin St, Monterey CA 93940 USA — Pop, Rock Music Duo

Mhyre, Wencke S
Im Vendia 22, 1315 Nesoya, Norway — Singer, Actress

Mi Hyun Kim
Ladies Pro Golf Assn, 100 International Golf Dr, Daytona Beach FL 32124 USA — Golfer

Miano, Richard J (Rich)
Miano Sports Bar, 7168 Makaa St, Honolulu HI 96825, USA — Football Player

Miartusova, Nella
Club Nella, PO Box 25, 182 00 Prague 8, Czech Republic — Model

M

Mica, Daniel L — Representative, FL
Credit Union National Assn, 601 Pennsylvania NW, #600W, Washington DC 20004, USA
Micarelli, Lucia — Concert, Jazz Violinist
Colomby Group, 2110 Main St, #202, Santa Monica CA 90405, USA
Miceli, Daniel (Danny) — Baseball Player
1712 Cottonwood Creek Place, Lake Mary FL 32746, USA
Miceli, Justine — Actress
Paradigm Agency, 360 N Crescent Dr, North Building, Beverly Hills CA 90210 USA
Michael — King, Romania
Villa Serena, 77 Chemin Louis-Degallier, 1290 Versoix-Geneva, Switzerland
Michael, Eugene R (Gene) — Baseball Player, Manager, Executive
49 Union Ave, Upper Saddle River NJ 07458, USA
Michael, George — Singer, Guitarist, Songwriter
2 Elgin Mews, London W9 1NN, England
Michael, M Blane — Judge
US Appeals Court, 300 Virginia St E, #7602, Charleston WV 25301, USA
Michael, Ralph — Actor
Michael Slessinger, 8730 W Sunset Blvd, #220W, West Hollywood CA 90069 USA
Michael, Richard J (Rich) — Football Player
957 S Van Ness Ave, San Francisco CA 94110, USA
Michaell, Monnae — Actress
Geddes Agency, 8430 Santa Monica Blvd, #201, West Hollywood CA 90069 USA
Michaels, Alan R (Al) — Sportscaster
401 S Bristol Ave, Los Angeles CA 90049, USA
Michaels, Bret — Singer (Poison)
W M E Entertainment, 9601 Wilshire Blvd, #300, Beverly Hills CA 90210 USA
Michaels, Ellen — Model, Photographer
PO Box 1757, New York NY 10021, USA
Michaels, Fern — Writer
9 David Court, Edison NJ 08820, USA
Michaels, Jason D — Baseball Player
5019 Avenue Avignon, Lutz FL 33558, USA
Michaels, Julie — Actress
PO Box 7304, #149, North Hollywood CA 91603, USA
Michaels, Lorne — Producer, Screenwriter
Broadway Video, 1619 Broadway, #900, New York NY 10019, USA
Michaels, Louis A (Lou) — Football Player
69 Grace St, Kingston PA 18704, USA
Michaels, Marilyn — Singer
185 W End Ave, New York NY 10023, USA
Michaels, Walter (Walt) — Football Player, Coach
282 Michaels Road, Shickshinny PA 18655, USA
Michaelsen, Kari — Actress
Silver Star AG Ltd, 3905 Auto Mall Dr, Westlake Village CA 91362, USA
Michaels-Moore, Anthony — Opera Singer
I M G Artists, Burlington Lane, Chiswick, London W4 2TH, England
Michaelson, Ingrid — Singer, Pianist/Songwriter
Paradigm Agency, 360 N Crescent Dr, North Building, Beverly Hills CA 90210 USA
Michalak, Christian M (Chris) — Baseball Player
1108 Mockingbird Lane, Keller TX 76248, USA
Michaleczewski, Dariusz — Boxer
Ul Rajska 4C, Gdansk 80-850, Poland
Michalek, Zbynek — Ice Hockey Player
3160 Annandale Dr, Presto PA 15142, USA
Michalka, Alyson (Aly) — Singer, Actress
Prospect Park, 2049 Century Park E, #2550, Los Angeles CA 90067, USA
Michalka, Amanda J (A J) — Singer, Actress, Songwriter
Prospect Park, 2049 Century Park E, #2550, Los Angeles CA 90067, USA
Michals, Duane — Photographer
109 E 19th St, New York NY 10003, USA
Micheaux, Larry W — Basketball Player
2914 Calendar Lake Dr, Missouri City TX 77459, USA
Micheaux, Nikki — Actress
Don Buchwald/Fortitude, 6500 Wilshire Blvd, #2200, Los Angeles CA 90048 USA
Micheel, Shaun — Golfer
1267 Dubray Lake Circle, Collierville TN 38017, USA
Michel, F Curtis — Astronaut
2101 University Blvd, Houston TX 77030, USA
Michel, Hartmut — Nobel Chemistry Laureate
Max Planck Biophysics Institute, 60438 Frankfurt am Main, Germany
Michel, James A — President, Seychelles
President's Office, State House, PO Box 655, Victoria, Mahe, Seychelles
Michel, Jean-Louis — Underwater Scientist
I F R E M E R, Center de Toulon, 83500 La Seyne dur Mer, Toulon, France
Michel, Paul R — Judge
US Court of Appeals, 717 Madison Place NW, Washington DC 20439, USA
Michel, Pras — Rap Artist, Actor
Blue Train Entertainment, 9333 Wilshire Blvd, G Level, Beverly Hills CA 90210 USA
Michele, Chrisette — Singer, Songwriter
I C M Partners, 10250 Constellation Blvd, #900, Los Angeles CA 90067 USA
Michele, Michael — Actress
Innovative Artists, 1505 10th St, Santa Monica CA 90401 USA
Micheler, Elisabeth — Canoeing Athlete
Gruntenstr 45, 86163 Augsburg, Germany
Micheletti Bain, Roberto — President, Honduras
Casa Presidencial, Blvd Juan Pablo II, Tegucigalpa MDC, Honduras
Michell, Keith — Actor
Chatto & Linnit, 123A King's Road, London SW3 4PL, England
Michell, Roger — Director
Independent Talent Group, Oxford House, 76 Oxford St, London W1D 1BS, England
Michelle — Singer, Actress
Buro Michelle, Wallstr 16, 10179 Berlin, Germany
Michelle, Candice — Model, Wrestler, Actress
Abraxas Talent, 4260 Troost Ave, #1, Studio City CA 91604, USA
Michels, John J — Football Player
504 Matterhorn Dr, Gatlinburg TN 37738, USA

Michels, Stephanie — Actress
C E S D, 10635 Santa Monica Blvd, #130, Los Angeles CA 90025 USA

Michelson, Claudia — Actress
Agentur Hoestermann, Gneisenaustr 94, 10961 Berlin, Germany

Michie, David A R — Artist
17 Gilmour Road, Edinburgh EH16 5NS, England

Michiko — Empress, Japan
Imperial Palace, 1-1 Chiyoda, Chiyodaku, Tokyo 100, Japan

Michos, Anastas N — Cinematographer
I C M Partners, 10250 Constellation Blvd, #900, Los Angeles CA 90067 USA

Mick — Drummer (Dave Dee Dozy Beaky Mick Tich)
Gerd Kehren Mgmt, Postfach 1408, 41804 Erkelenz, Germany

Mickell, Darren — Football Player
9250 Chelsea Dr, Miramar FL 33025, USA

Mickelson Cummins, Anna — Rowing Athlete
Cummins Chiropractic & Wellness, 4122 Factoria Blvd SE #202 Bellevue WA 98006, USA

Mickelson, Philip A (Phil) — Golfer
Gaylord Sports Mgmt, 13845 N Northsight Blvd, #200, Scottsdale AZ 85260, USA

Mickens, Terry K — Football Player
5725 Martin Road, #4256, Plano TX 75024, USA

Middendorf, Tracy — Actress
Bauman Redanty Shaul Agency, 5757 Wilshire Blvd, #473, Los Angeles CA 90036 USA

Middlebrook, Jason — Baseball Player
3309 Glenview Ave, Austin TX 78703, USA

Middlebrooks, Willie F — Football Player
18775 SW 78th Court, Cutler Bay FL 33157, USA

Middleditch, Thomas — Actor
W M E Entertainment, 9601 Wilshire Blvd, #300, Beverly Hills CA 90210 USA

Middleton, Darren — Guitarist (Powderfinger)
Secret Service, PO Box 401, Fortitude Valley QLD 4006, Australia

Middleton, Richard (Rick) — Ice Hockey Player
PO Box 1161, Hampton NH 03843, USA

Middleton, Terdell — Football Player
1893 Prospect St, Memphis TN 38106, USA

Midgley, John — Sound Mixer
Creative Media Mgmt, Ealing Studio, Ealing Green, London W5 5EP, England

Midkiff, Dale — Actor
Amsel Eisenstadt Frazier, 5055 Wilshire Blvd, #865, Los Angeles CA 90036 USA

Midler, Bette — Singer, Actress
Creative Artists Agency, 2000 Ave of Stars, #100, Los Angeles CA 90067 USA

Midori — Concert Violinist
Midori Foundation, 850 7th Ave, #705, New York NY 10019, USA

Miechur, Thomas F — Labor Leader
Cement & Allied Workers Union, 2500 Brickdale, Elk Grove Village IL 60007, USA

Miele, Rudolf — Businessman
Miele & Cie, Carl-Miele-Str 29, 33332 Guterslh, Germany

Mientkiewicz, Douglas A (Doug) — Baseball Player
810 Lugo Ave, Coral Gables FL 33156, USA

Miers, Harriet E — Government Official, Attorney
Locke Liddell Sapp, 901 15th St NW, #900, Washington DC 20005, USA

Mies, Richard W — Navy Admiral
Navy Mutual Aid Assn, Directors Board, 29 Carpenter Road, Arlington VA 22214, USA

Mieske, Matthew T (Matt) — Baseball Player
2199 E Bombay Road, Midland MI 48642, USA

Miettinen, Antti — Ice Hockey Player
Tampa Bay Lightning, 401 Channelside Dr, Tampa FL 33602 USA

Mifsud Bonnici, Ugo — President, Malta
18 Erin Serracino Inglott Road, Cospicua, Malta

Migay, Rudolph J (Rudy) — Ice Hockey Player
485 Belrose Road, Thunder Bay ON P7G 1K1, Canada

Migenes, Julia — Opera Singer
Les Visiteurs du Soir, 40 Rue de la Folie Regnault, 75011 Paris, France

Miggins, Lawrence E (Larry) — Baseball Player
2405 Kingston St, Houston TX 77019, USA

Migliore, Richard — Thoroughbred Racing Jockey
48 Killearn Road, Millbrook NY 12545, USA

Mignola, Mike — Cartoonist (Hellboy)
Dark Horse Publishing, 10956 SE Main St, Portland OR 97222 USA

Miguel — Singer, Songwriter
R C A Records, 8750 Wilshire Blvd, Beverly Hills CA 90211 USA

Miguel, Luis — Singer
Warner Music International Records, 3300 Warner Blvd, Burbank CA 91505, USA

Mihm, Christopher S (Chris) — Basketball Player
4708 Peace Pipe Path, Austin TX 78746, USA

Mihok, Dash — Actor
Gersh Agency, 9465 Wilshire Blvd, #600, Beverly Hills CA 90212 USA

Mijares, Cristian — Boxer
DiBella Entertainment, 350 7th Ave, #800, New York NY 10001, USA

Mika — Singer, Songwriter
Fuerte Group, 1775 Broadway, #2300, New York NY 10019, USA

Mikan, G Lawrence (Larry) — Basketball Player
891 Carmona Court, Chula Vista CA 91910, USA

Mikati, Najib A — Prime Minister, Lebanon
Premier's Office, Serail, Place de l'Etoile, Beirut, Lebanon

Mike-Mayer, Istvan (Steve) — Football Player
681 Lincoln Ave, Glen Rock NJ 07452, USA

Mike-Mayer, Nicholas (Nick) — Football Player
681 Lincoln Ave, Glen Rock NJ 07452, USA

Mikhalchenko, Alla A — Ballerina
Malaya Gruzinskaya St 12/18, 123242 Moscow, Russia

Mikhalkov, Nikita S — Director
Maly Kozikhinsky Per 4, #16-17, 103001 Moscow, Russia

Mikita, Stanley (Stan) — Ice Hockey Player
57 Chesterfield Court, Burr Ridge IL 60527, USA

Mikkelsen, A Verner A (Vern) — Basketball Player, Golfer
17715 Breconville Road, Wayzata MN 55391, USA

M

Mikkelsen, Lars	Actor
Conway Van Gelder Grant, 8-12 Broadwick St, #300, London W1F 8HW, England	
Mikkelsen, Mads	Actor
Arts Mgmt, Kronprinsensgade 9A, 1114 Copenhagen K, Denmark	
Mikkelson, Meaghan	Ice Hockey Player
Ice Complex, Winter Park, 88 Canada Olympic Road SW, Calgary AB T3B 5R5, Canada	
Mikkelson, William R (Bill)	Ice Hockey Player
47 Glen Meadow Crescent, Saint Aliber AB T8N 3A2, Canada	
Miko, Izabella	Actress
Affirmative Entertainment, 425 N Robertson Blvd, Los Angeles CA 90048, USA	
Mikolaj, Aga	Opera Singer
Künstleragentur Augstein & Hahn, Tal 28 80331 Munich, Germany	
Miksis, Alfonse K (Al)	Basketball Player
522 E Algonquin Road, #203, Schaumburg IL 60173, USA	
Mikva, Abner J	Judge
442 New Jersey Ave SE, Washington DC 20003, USA	
Milacki, Robert (Bob)	Baseball Player
1873 Martinique Dr, Lake Havasu City AZ 86406, USA	
Milano, Alyssa	Actress
Creative Artists Agency, 2000 Ave of Stars, #100, Los Angeles CA 90067 USA	
Milano, Dan	Producer, Writer, Actor
Gersh Agency, 9465 Wilshire Blvd, #600, Beverly Hills CA 90212 USA	
Milanov, Rossen	Conductor
Princeton Symphony Orchestra, 575 Ewing St, Princeton, NJ 08540, USA	
Milanovic, Zoran	Prime Minister, Croatia
Prime Minister's Office, Radicev Trg 7, 41000 Zagreb, Croatia	
Milbern, David	Actor
Bauman Redanty Shaul Agency, 5757 Wilshire Blvd, #473, Los Angeles CA 90036 USA	
Milbourne, Lawrence W (Larry)	Baseball Player
747 Yale Terrace, Lake Havasu City AZ 86406, USA	
Milbrett, Tiffeny	Soccer Player
1902 SW Broadleaf Dr, Portland OR 97219, USA	
Milburn, Brendan	Pianist (GrooveLily), Songwriter
GrooveLily, PO Box 11570, Glendale CA 91226, USA	
Milburn, Glyn C	Football Player
8815 S 2nd Ave, Inglewood CA 90305, USA	
Milburn, H Theodore	Judge
440 Alexian Way, #37, Signal Mountain TN 37377, USA	
Milbury, Mike	Ice Hockey Player, Coach
61 Edwardel Road, Needham MA 02492, USA	
Milch, David	Producer, Writer
Red Board Productions, 3000 W Olympic Blvd, Building 4, Santa Monica CA 90404, USA	
Milchan, Arnon	Producer
Regency Enterprises, 4000 Warner Blvd, #66, Burbank CA 91522, USA	
Miledi, Ricardo	Neurobiologist
9 Gibbs Court, Irvine CA 92617, USA	
Miles, Aaron W	Baseball Player
1716 San Jose Dr, Davenport IA 52807, USA	
Miles, Darius L	Basketball Player
1906 Llewellyn Road, Bellevue IL 62223, USA	
Miles, Heather	Singer, Songwriter
Rounder Records, 1 Rounder Way, Burlington MA 01803 USA	
Miles, Joanna	Actress
2062 N Vine St, Los Angeles CA 90068, USA	
Miles, John R (Jack)	Writer
3568 Mountain View Ave, Pasadena CA 91107, USA	
Miles, John W	Geophysicist
1764 Overlook Lane, Santa Barbara CA 93103, USA	
Miles, Leslie E (Les)	Football Coach
Lousiana State University, Athletic Dept, Baton Rouge LA 70803, USA	
Miles, Sarah	Actress
Chithurst Manor, Trotten near Petersfield, Hampshire GU31 5EU, England	
Miles, Sylvia	Actress
A P A Talent/Literary Agency, 405 S Beverly Dr, #300, Beverly Hills CA 90212 USA	
Miles, Vera	Actress
PO Box 1599, Palm Desert CA 92261, USA	
Miles-Clark, Jearl	Track Athlete
J J Clark, University of Florida, Athletic Dept, Gainesville FL 32604, USA	
Milhoan, Michael	Actor
TalentWorks, 3500 W Olive Ave, #1400, Burbank CA 91505 USA	
Mili, Itula	Football Player
4468 Glenmoor Hills Dr, South Jordan UT 84095, USA	
Milian, Christina	Singer, Actress, Songwriter
Milian Mgmt, 16830 Ventura Blvd, #501, Encino CA 91436, USA	
Miliband, David W	Government Official, England
Foreign Secretary's Office, 11 Downing St, London SW1A 2AA, England	
Milicevic, Ivana	Actress, Model
A P A Talent/Literary Agency, 405 S Beverly Dr, #300, Beverly Hills CA 90212 USA	
Milicic, Darko	Basketball Player
5460 Whitehall Blvd, Oakland Township MI 48306, USA	
Milinchik, Joseph M (Joe)	Football Player
653 Ryan Dr, Allentown PA 18103, USA	
Milinovich, Gia M	Producer, Presenter
Sue Rider Mgmt, PO Box 49175, London SW19 3WY, England	
Militello, Sam S	Baseball Player
3217 W Saint John St, Tampa FL 33607, USA	
Militzok, Nathan (Nat)	Basketball Player
78 Blue Lagoon, Laguna Beach CA 92651, USA	
Milius, John F	Director, Writer
I C M Partners, 10250 Constellation Blvd, #900, Los Angeles CA 90067 USA	
Milk, Barry	Educator
Bowdoin College, President's Office, Brunswick ME 04011, USA	
Milk, Chris	Photographer
Anonymous Content, 3532 Hayden Ave, Culver City CA 90232 USA	
Milk, Mike	DJ Dance Musician
Future Music, Bayerstr 77A, 80335 Munich, Germany	

Mikkelsen - Milk

Milken, Michael R — Financier, Philanthropist
4543 Tara Dr, Encino CA 91436, USA
Milla, Roger — Soccer Player
Federation Camerounaise de Football, BP 1116, Yaounde, Cameroon
Millan, Amy — Singer
Agency Group Ltd, 142 W 57th St, #600, New York NY 10019 USA
Millan, Cesar — Psychologist
Dog Psychology Center, PO Box 1130, Canyon Country CA 91386, USA
Millan, Felix B — Baseball Player
G16 Calle Camarero Parq Ecusetre, Carolina PR 00987, USA
Millar, Jeffrey L (Jeff) — Cartoonist (Tank McNamara)
1301 Spring Oaks Circle, Houston TX 77055, USA
Millar, Kevin C — Baseball Player
14200 Flat Top Ranch Road, Austin TX 78732, USA
Millar, Miles — Producer, Writer
Millar/Gough Ink, 500 S Buena Vista St, Animations Building, Burbank CA 91521, USA
Millard, Bart — Singer (MercyMe)
Brickhouse Entertainment, 106 Mission Court, #1202, Franklin TN 37067, USA
Millard, Bryan J — Football Player
507 Sabine St, #1001, Austin TX 78701, USA
Millard, Keith — Football Player
3739 Oakhurst Way, Dublin CA 94568, USA
Millardet, Patricia — Actress
Agents Associes, 201 Rue du Faubourg Saint Honore, 75008 Paris, France
Milledge, Lastings D — Baseball Player
11114 Sailbrooke Dr, Riverview FL 33579, USA
Millegan, Eric — Actor
Don Buchwald/Fortitude, 6500 Wilshire Blvd, #2200, Los Angeles CA 90048 USA
Millen, Greg — Ice Hockey Player
980 Orch, Bridgenorth ON K0L 1H0, Canada
Millen, Hugh B — Football Player
6836 Cascade Ave SE, Snoqualmie WA 98065, USA
Millen, Matt G — Football Player, Executive, Sportscaster
862 Durham Road, Riegelsville PA 18077, USA
Millepied, Benjamin — Ballet Dancer, Choreographer
New York City Ballet, Lincoln Center Plaza, New York NY 10023 USA
Miller, Aaron — Ice Hockey Player
147 Appletree Point Road, Burlington VT 05408, USA
Miller, Alan — Journalist
Los Angeles Times, Editorial Dept, 202 W 1st St, Los Angeles CA 90012 USA
Miller, Alan R — Football Player
3118 Erie Dr, Orchard Lake MI 48324, USA
Miller, Alice — Golfer
2 Log Church Road, Wilmington DE 19807, USA
Miller, Allison — Actress
Beth Goldstein Mgmt, 4433 Colbath Ave, #34, Sherman Oaks CA 91423, USA
Miller, Alyssa — Model
Mous Model Mgmt, 117 N Robertson Blvd, Los Angeles CA 90048, USA
Miller, Amara — Actress
United Talent Agency, 9336 Civic Center Dr, Beverly Hills CA 90210 USA
Miller, Andre L — Basketball Player
Denver Nuggets, Pepsi Center, 1000 Chopper Circle, Denver CO 80204 USA
Miller, Andrea — Choreographer/Dance Executive
Gallim Dance, 304 W 75th St, New York NY 10023, USA
Miller, Anthony — Basketball Player
1083 Superior St, Benton Harbor MI 49022, USA
Miller, Bebe — Choreographer, Dancer
Bebe Miller Dance Co, 54 W 21st St, #502, New York NY 10010, USA
Miller, Bennett — Director
Creative Artists Agency, 2000 Ave of Stars, #100, Los Angeles CA 90067 USA
Miller, Billy R — Football Player
13745 Elkton Court, Moorpark CA 93021, USA
Miller, Bode — Alpine Skier
63 Eastern Valley Road, Franconia NH 03580, USA
Miller, Bradley A (Brad) — Basketball Player
2731 Marl Oak Dr, Highland Park IL 60035, USA
Miller, Bruce — Producer
Jackoway Tyerman Wertheimer, 1925 Century Park E, #2200, Los Angeles CA 90067 USA
Miller, Buddy — Guitarist, Songwriter
Vector Mgmt, PO Box 120479, Nashville TN 37212 USA
Miller, C Arden — Pediatrician
350 Carolina Meadows Villa, Chapel Hill NC 27517, USA
Miller, Carol — Bowler
Professional Bowlers Assn, 719 2nd Ave, #701, Seattle WA 98104 USA
Miller, Cheryl D — Basketball Player, Coach
3206 Ellington Dr, Los Angeles CA 90068, USA
Miller, Christa — Actress
I C M Partners, 10250 Constellation Blvd, #900, Los Angeles CA 90067 USA
Miller, Christine Cook — Judge
US Claims Court, 717 Madison Place NW, Washington DC 20439, USA
Miller, Christopher J (Chris) — Football Player
701 W Hackberry Dr, Chandler AZ 85248, USA
Miller, Cleophus (Cleo), Jr — Football Player
16613 Raymond St, Maple Heights OH 44137, USA
Miller, Colleen M (Coco) — Basketball Player
Los Angeles Sparks, 888 S Figueroa St, #2010, Los Angeles CA 90017 USA
Miller, Corky A P — Baseball Player
1115 7th St, Calimesa CA 92320, USA
Miller, Damian D — Baseball Player
N1276 Wuensch Road, La Crosse WI 54601, USA
Miller, Dan — Singer (O-Town)
J Records, 745 5th Ave, #600, New York NY 10151 USA
Miller, Darrell K — Baseball Player
21159 Via Alisa, Yorba Linda CA 92887, USA
Miller, David — Cartoonist (Dave)
Back 40 Design, PO Box 7985, Edmond OK 73083, USA

M

Miller, David Alan — Conductor
Opus 3 Artists, 470 Park Ave S, #900N, New York NY 10016 USA
Miller, Dennis — Actor, Comedian
Brillstein Entertainment Partners, 9150 Wilshire Blvd, #350, Beverly Hills CA 90212 USA
Miller, Denny — Actor
9612 Gavin Stone Ave, Las Vegas NV 89145, USA
Miller, Dyar K — Baseball Player
8816 Admirals Bay Dr, Indianapolis IN 46236, USA
Miller, E Heath — Football Player
1304 Hidden Canyon Court, Sewickley PA 15143, USA
Miller, Edward L (Eddie) — Baseball Player
1819 Alfreda Blvd, San Pablo CA 94806, USA
Miller, Everett — Hero
13655 Ahwahnee Way, Poway CA 92064, USA
Miller, Frank — Cartoonist (Sin City, Dark Knight)
Dark Horse Publishing, 10956 SE Main St, Portland OR 97222 USA
Miller, Frank — Actor, Writer
Shapiro-Lichtman, 8827 Beverly Blvd, Los Angeles CA 90048 USA
Miller, Fred D — Football Player
4535 Black Rock Road, Upperco MD 21155, USA
Miller, Fred J — Football Player
7143 Sawmill Trail, Houston TX 77040, USA
Miller, Gabrielle — Actress
Oscars Abrams Zimel, 438 Queen St E, Toronto ON M5A 1T4, Canada
Miller, George D — Air Force General
20 Phillips Pond South, Natick MA 01760, USA
Miller, George T (Kennedy) — Director, Producer
30 Orwell St, King's Cross, Sydney NSW 2011, Australia
Miller, Howard S — Actor
Endurance Talent Mgmt, 2920 W Olive Ave, #202, Burbank CA 91505, USA
Miller, James A — Oncologist
1822 Masters Lane, Madison WI 53719, USA
Miller, James C, III — Government Official
Citizens for Sound Economy, 1250 H St NW, Washington DC 20005, USA
Miller, James D (Jim) — Football Player
9916 King Road, Davisburg MI 48350, USA
Miller, James G (Jim) — Football Player
PO Box 863, Ripley MS 38663, USA
Miller, Jamir M — Football Player
6717 E Meadowlark Lane, Paradise Valley AZ 85253, USA
Miller, Jeff — Bassist (Caedmon's Call)
Breen Agency, 25 Music Square W, Nashville TN 37203, USA
Miller, Jeremy — Actor
Acumen Entertainment Partners, 15915 Ventura Blvd, #304, Encino CA 91436, USA
Miller, Jerry — Navy Admiral
Smithsonian Institution Press, 750 9th St NW, #4300, Washington DC 20560, USA
Miller, Jody — Singer
PO Box 413, Blanchard OK 73010, USA
Miller, Joel McKinnon — Actor
Greene Assoc, 1901 Ave of Stars, #130, Los Angeles CA 90067 USA
Miller, John — Commentator
ABC-TV, News Dept, 77 W 66th St, New York NY 10023 USA
Miller, John A — Baseball Player
5105 River Ave, #A, Newport Beach CA 92663, USA
Miller, John E — Baseball Player
13443 Old Annapolis Road, Mount Airy MD 21771, USA
Miller, John L (Johnny) — Golfer, Sportscaster
Johnny Miller Enterprises, PO Box 2260, Napa CA 94558, USA
Miller, John W — Educator
Central Connecticut State University, President's Office, New Britain CT 06050, USA
Miller, Jon — Sportscaster, Baseball Player
ESPN-TV, ESPN Plaza, 935 Middle St, Bristol CT 06010 USA
Miller, Jonathan W — Director
Royce Carlton, 866 United Nations Plaza, New York NY 10017, USA
Miller, Jonny Lee — Actor
Independent Talent Group, Oxford House, 76 Oxford St, London W1D 1BS, England
Miller, Joshua H (Josh) — Football Player
572 Macleod Dr, Gibsonia PA 15044, USA
Miller, Joshua J (Josh) — Actor, Director, Writer
Gersh Agency, 9465 Wilshire Blvd, #600, Beverly Hills CA 90212 USA
Miller, Julie — Singer, Songwriter
Vector Mgmt, PO Box 120479, Nashville TN 37212 USA
Miller, Justin M — Football Player
Arizona Cardinals, PO Box 888, Phoenix AZ 85001 USA
Miller, Justin M — Baseball Player
2087 Bonnie Ave, Palm Harbor FL 34683, USA
Miller, Keith A — Baseball Player
190 Water St, #2, Milford MI 48381, USA
Miller, Keith H — Governor, AK
3705 Arctic Blvd, Anchorage AK 99503, USA
Miller, Kelly — Basketball Player
New York Liberty, Madison Square Garden, 2 Penn Plaza, New York NY 10121 USA
Miller, Kelly D — Ice Hockey Player
3783 Chippendale Circle, Okemos MI 48864, USA
Miller, Kevin — Drummer (Fuel)
Media Five Entertainment, 3005 Brodhead Road, #170, Bethlehem PA 18020, USA
Miller, Kevin B — Ice Hockey Player
4243 Redbud Trail, Williamston MI 48895, USA
Miller, Kristen — Actress, Comedienne
Special Artists Agency, 9465 Wilshire Blvd, #820, Beverly Hills CA 90212 USA
Miller, Kurt E — Baseball Player
1511 Iroquois Circle, Carrollton TX 75007, USA
Miller, L Anthony — Football Player
2302 Villa Camille, San Dimas CA 91773, USA
Miller, Lajos — Opera Singer
Hegyalja Utca 32, 3232 Matrafured, Hungary

Miller, Larry — Actor, Comedian
Brillstein Entertainment Partners, 9150 Wilshire Blvd, #350, Beverly Hills CA 90212 USA
Miller, Lawrence J (Larry) — Basketball Player
311 Mulberry St, Catasauqua PA 18032, USA
Miller, Linda Lael — Writer
Harlequin Enterprises, 225 Duncan Mill Road, Don Mills ON MJB JK9, Canada
Miller, Marcus — Jazz Bassist, Composer
I C M Partners, 10250 Constellation Blvd, #900, Los Angeles CA 90067 USA
Miller, Marisa — Actress, Model
Cartel Mgmt, 665 N Lillian Way, Los Angeles CA 90004, USA
Miller, Mark — Singer (Sawyer Brown)
O-Seven Artist Mgmt, PO Box 210586, Nashville TN 37221, USA
Miller, Marlin — Opera Singer
I M G Artists, Hogarth Business Park, Chiswick, London W4 2TH, England
Miller, Marvin J — Labor Leader
211 E 70th St, New York NY 10021, USA
Miller, McKaley — Actress
Osbrink Talent Agency, 4343 Lankershim Blvd, #100, North Hollywood CA 91602 USA
Miller, Michael L (Mike) — Basketball Player
2869 Ladbrook Way, Thousand Oaks CA 91361, USA
Miller, Mildred — Opera Singer
PO Box 110108, Pittsburgh PA 15232, USA
Miller, Mulgrew — Jazz Pianist
3725 Farmersville Road, Easton PA 18045, USA
Miller, N Keith — Baseball Player
1831 W Alamosa Dr, Terrell TX 75160, USA
Miller, Nancy (Ann) — Writer, Producer
W M E Entertainment, 9601 Wilshire Blvd, #300, Beverly Hills CA 90210 USA
Miller, Nate — Boxer
1943 N Uber St, Philadelphia PA 19121, USA
Miller, Nicole J — Fashion Designer
780 Madison Ave, Front 1, New York NY 10065, USA
Miller, Norman C (Norm) — Baseball Player
43 Columbia Crest Place, Spring TX 77382, USA
Miller, Oliver J — Basketball Player
2912 S Meadow Dr, Fort Worth TX 76133, USA
Miller, Omar Benson — Actor
A P A Talent/Literary Agency, 405 S Beverly Dr, #300, Beverly Hills CA 90212 USA
Miller, Paul — Actor
Fountainhead Talent, 131 Davenport Road, Toronto ON M5R 1H8, Canada
Miller, Paul D — Navy Admiral, Businessman
Teledyne Technologies, 1049 Camino Dos Rios, Thousand Oaks CA 91360, USA
Miller, Penelope Ann — Actress
A P A Talent/Literary Agency, 405 S Beverly Dr, #300, Beverly Hills CA 90212 USA
Miller, Peter North — Businessman
Quinneys, Camilla Dr, Westhumble, Dorking, Surrey RH5 6BU, England
Miller, Randall S (Randy) — Baseball Player
22523 Oak Mist Lane, Katy TX 77494, USA
Miller, Raymond R (Ray) — Baseball Manager
PO Box 41, New Athens OH 43981, USA
Miller, Rebecca — Actress, Director, Writer
Creative Artists Agency, 2000 Ave of Stars, #100, Los Angeles CA 90067 USA
Miller, Reginald W (Reggie) — Basketball Player, Sportscaster
3785 Puerco Canyon Road, Malibu CA 90265, USA
Miller, Rhett — Singer (Old 97's), Songwriter
Paradigm Agency, 360 N Crescent Dr, North Building, Beverly Hills CA 90210 USA
Miller, Richard A (Rick) — Baseball Player
12790 Silverthorn Court, Bonita Springs FL 34135, USA
Miller, Risa — Writer
Saint Martin's Press, 175 5th Ave, #400, New York NY 10010 USA
Miller, Robert (Steve) — Businessman
Delphi Automotive Systems, 5725 Delphi Dr, Troy MI 48098, USA
Miller, Robert Ellis — Director
1901 Ave of Stars, #1040, Los Angeles CA 90067, USA
Miller, Robert G — Businessman
Albertsons, 250 E Parkcenter Blvd, Boise ID 83706, USA
Miller, Robert G (Bob) — Baseball Player
1702 Keim Trail, Saint Charles IL 60174, USA
Miller, Robert J (Bob) — Baseball Player
1202 Andover Circle, Commerce Township MI 48390, USA
Miller, Robert J (Bob) — Governor, NV
Jones Vargas, 3773 S Howard Hughes Parkway, #300S, Las Vegas NV 89169, USA
Miller, Robert L — Football Player
5403 Augusta Trail, Fort Collins CO 80528, USA
Miller, Ryan — Singer, Guitarist (Guster)
Nettwerk Mgmt, 345 7th Ave, #2400, New York NY 10001, USA
Miller, Sam — Director
Independent Talent Group, Oxford House, 76 Oxford St, London W1D 1BS, England
Miller, Scott P — Football Player
1570 NW 128th Dr, #306, Sunrise FL 33323, USA
Miller, Sean — Basketball Coach
University of Arizona, Athletic Dept, Tucson AZ 85721, USA
Miller, Selvia (Junior) — Football Player
3051 Agate Court, Lincoln NE 68516, USA
Miller, Shannon — Gymnast
Shannon Miller Lifestyle, 4319 Salisbury Road, #4, Jacksonville FL 32218, USA
Miller, Shawn V — Football Player
3070 W Old Highway Road, Morgan UT 84050, USA
Miller, Sienna A — Actress, Model
United Agents, 12-26 Lexington St, London W1F 0LE, England
Miller, Steve — Singer, Songwriter, Orchestra Leader
PO Box 12680, Seattle WA 98111, USA
Miller, Stuart L (Stu) — Baseball Player
3701 Ocaso Court, Cameron Park CA 95682, USA
Miller, Susan — Model, Actress
Playboy Promotions, 2706 Media Center Dr, Los Angeles CA 90065 USA

Miller, Tangi — Actress, Producer, Writer
Olivia Entertainment, PO Box 19398, Los Angeles CA 90019, USA
Miller, Taylor — Actress
Innovative Artists, 1505 10th St, Santa Monica CA 90401 USA
Miller, Travis E — Baseball Player
51 Whisper Way, Eaton OH 45320, USA
Miller, Trever D — Baseball Player
24155 Hideout Trail, Land O Lakes FL 34639, USA
Miller, Troy — Producer, Director
Dakota Pictures, 4133 Lankershim Blvd, North Hollywood CA 91602, USA
Miller, Valerie Rae — Actress
United Talent Agency, 9336 Civic Center Dr, Beverly Hills CA 90210 USA
Miller, Von — Football Player
Denver Broncos, 13655 E Broncos Parkway, Englewood CO 80112 USA
Miller, Wade T — Baseball Player
12 Woods Way, Reading PA 19610, USA
Miller, Webb — Biologist
Pennsylvania State University, Biology Dept, Wartik Laboratory, University Park PA 16802
Miller, Wentworth — Actor
I C M Partners, 10250 Constellation Blvd, #900, Los Angeles CA 90067 USA
Miller, Wiley — Cartoonist (Non Sequitur/Us & Them)
8 Granite Heights Road, Kennebunkport ME 04046, USA
Miller, William J (Bill) — Football Player
701 Belden Court, Saint Augustine FL 32086, USA
Miller, Willie T — Football Player
6290 Walnut Dr, Pinson AL 35126, USA
Miller, Zachary P (Zach) — Football Player
Seattle Seahawks, 12 Seahawks Way, Renton WA 98056 USA
Miller-Lawrence, Christa — Actress
I C M Partners, 10250 Constellation Blvd, #900, Los Angeles CA 90067 USA
Millett, Kate — Women's Activist, Writer
20 Old Overlook Road, Poughkeepsie NY 12603, USA
Millett, Terroon — Boxer
6548 Whitney Ave, Saint Louis MO 63133, USA
Millhauser, Steven — Writer
235 Caroline St, Saratoga Springs NY 12866, USA
Millian, Felix Bernardo — Baseball Player
Calle 13R14, El Conquistador, Trujillo AH PR 00760, USA
Millican, Clay — Auto Racing Driver
545 Watson Road, Atoka TN 38004, USA
Milligan, Dustin — Actor
Red Mgmt, 415 W Esplanade, #3, North Vancouver BC V7M 1A6, Canada
Milligan, Joseph — Guitarist (Anberlin)
Arson Media Group, 23 N Summerlin Ave, #200, Orlando FL 32801, USA
Milligan, Randy A — Baseball Player
6905 Real Princess Lane, Gwynn Oak MD 21207, USA
Milliken, Angie — Actress
Polaris Entertainment, 8048 W 3rd St, #300, Los Angeles CA 90048, USA
Milliken, James B — Educator
University of Nebraska, President's Office, Lincoln NE 68588, USA
Million, Mike — Director, Producer, Writer
Brucks/McDonald Entertainment, 1635 N Cahuenga Blvd, #400, Los Angeles CA 90028, USA
Millman, Gabriel — Actor
Harvest Talent Mgmt, 124 W 80th St, #1, New York NY 10024, USA
Millner, F Ann — Educator
Weber State University, President's Office, 3848 Harrison Blvd, Ogden UT 84408, USA
Millns, James G (Jim), Jr — Ice Dancer
7603 Dunbridge Dr, Odessa FL 33556, USA
Milo, Aprile E — Opera Singer
Columbia Artists Mgmt Inc, 1790 Broadway, #702, New York NY 10019 USA
Milloy, Lawyer M — Football Player
57 Chapman Loop, Steilacom WA 98388, USA
Mills, Alan B — Baseball Player
1811 Bellgrove St, Lakeland FL 33805, USA
Mills, Alley — Actress
Stone Manners Salners, 9911 W Pico Blvd, #1400, Los Angeles CA 90035 USA
Mills, Barry — Educator
Bowdoin College, President's Office, Brunswick ME 04011, USA
Mills, Christopher (Chris) — Basketball Player
2223 Camden Ave, Los Angeles CA 90064, USA
Mills, Crispian — Singer, Guitarist (Kula Shakur)
Little Big Man, 39A Grammercy Park N, #1C, New York NY 10010, USA
Mills, Donna — Actress
TalentWorks, 3500 W Olive Ave, #1400, Burbank CA 91505 USA
Mills, Ernest L (Ernie) — Football Player
PO Box 2435, Dunnellon FL 34430, USA
Mills, Hayley — Actress, Singer
Chatto & Linnit, 123A King's Road, London SW3 4PL, England
Mills, J Bradley (Brad) — Baseball Player, Manager
4746 W Buena Vista Court, Visalia CA 93291, USA
Mills, John Henry — Football Player
755 Bahia Circle, Ocala FL 34472, USA
Mills, Judson — Actor
Dino May Mgmt, 11262 Ventura Blvd, #PH, Studio City CA 91604, USA
Mills, Juliet — Actress
Diamond Management, 31 Percy St, London W1T 2DD, England
Mills, Mary — Golfer
310 S Ocean Blvd, #106, Boca Raton FL 33432, USA
Mills, Mary — Opera Singer
I M G Artists, Hogarth Business Park, Chiswick, London W4 2TH, England
Mills, Michael E (Mike) — Bassist (REM)
REM/Athens Ltd, PO Box 8032, Athens GA 30603, USA
Mills, Mike — Director
United Talent Agency, 9336 Civic Center Dr, Beverly Hills CA 90210 USA
Mills, Phoebe — Gymnast
Harris Agency, 17814 Lillian St, Omaha NE 68136, USA

M

Mills, Stephanie	Singer, Actress
Left Bank Mgmt, 9255 W Sunset Blvd, #200, West Hollywood CA 90069 USA	
Mills, Terry R	Basketball Player
37840 Scott Pine Dr, New Boston MI 48164, USA	
Mills, William H (Bill)	Baseball Player
4344 Commercial St, Port Charlotte FL 33953, USA	
Mills, William M (Billy)	Track Athlete
7760 Winding Way, #722, Fair Oaks CA 95628, USA	
Mills, Zach	Actor
Paradigm Agency, 360 N Crescent Dr, North Building, Beverly Hills CA 90210 USA	
Millwood, Kamla	Model
Impact Model Mgmt, 324-326 Regent St, #104, London W1B 3HH, England	
Millwood, Kevin A	Baseball Player
1204 Suncast Lane, #2, El Dorado Hills CA 95762, USA	
Milne, Brian F	Football Player
1411 Beacon St, Cincinnati OH 45230, USA	
Milner, Anthony F D	Composer
147 Heythorp St, Southfields, London SW18 5BT, England	
Milner, Edward J (Eddie)	Baseball Player
491 Stambaugh Ave, Columbus OH 43207, USA	
Milner, Martin	Actor
3106 Azahar St, Carlsbad CA 92009, USA	
Milnes, Sherrill E	Opera Singer
Herbert Barrett, 266 W 37th St, #2000, New York NY 10018 USA	
Milnor, John W	Abel Mathematics Laureate
3 Laurel Lane, Setauket NY 11733, USA	
Milos, Sofia	Actress
Rogers & Cowan, 8687 Melrose Ave, #G700, West Hollywood CA 90069 USA	
Miloszewski, Steve	Guitarist (Reveille)
David Levy Mgmt, 200 W 57th St, #308, New York NY 10019, USA	
Milot, Richard P (Rich)	Football Player
15840 Hunton Lane, Haymarket PA 20169, USA	
Milsap, Ronnie	Singer, Pianist, Songwriter
Ronnie Milsap Enterprises, PO Box 40665, Nashville TN 37204, USA	
Milsome, Douglas	Cinematographer
Mirisch Agency, 8840 Wilshire Blvd, #100, Beverly Hills CA 90211 USA	
Milstead, Roderick L (Rod), Jr	Football Player
6674 Fenwick Road, Bryans Road MD 20616, USA	
Milton, Eric R	Baseball Player
1133 Asquith Dr, Arnold MD 21012, USA	
Milton, Peter W	Artist
2 New Hampshire Turnpike S, Francestown NH 03043, USA	
Milton-Jones, DeLisha	Basketball Player
Los Angeles Sparks, 888 S Figueroa St, #2010, Los Angeles CA 90017 USA	
Mimbs, Michael R (Mike)	Baseball Player
2761 Mimbs Road, Alamo GA 30411, USA	
Mimica-Gezzan, Sergio	Director, Producer
United Talent Agency, 9336 Civic Center Dr, Beverly Hills CA 90210 USA	
Mimieux, Yvette	Actress
Howard Ruby Photography, 2222 Corinth Ave, Los Angeles CA 90064, USA	
Mimoun, Alain	Track Athlete
27 Ave Edouard-Jenner, 94500 Champigny sur Marne, France	
Mims-Flowers, Tairia	Softball Player
Amateur Softball, 2801 NE 50th St, Oklahoma City OK 73111, USA	
Mina, Denise	Writer
Little Brown, 3 Center Plaza, #100, Boston MA 02108 USA	
Mincy, Charles A	Football Player
2227 W 24th St, #7, Los Angeles CA 90018, USA	
Mindel, Lee F	Architect
Shelton Mindel Assoc, 56 W 22nd St, #1200, New York NY 10010, USA	
Minear, Tim	Writer, Producer
W M E Entertainment, 9601 Wilshire Blvd, #300, Beverly Hills CA 90210 USA	
Minenkov, Andrei	Ice Dancer
Skating Federation, Luchnesskaia Nab 8, 119871 Moscow, Russia	
Miner, Rachel	Actress
Untitled Entertainment, 350 S Beverly Dr, #200, Beverly Hills CA 90212 USA	
Miner, Steve	Director
Gersh Agency, 9465 Wilshire Blvd, #600, Beverly Hills CA 90212 USA	
Ming Tsai	Chef
Food Network, 1180 Ave of Americas, #1200, New York NY 10036 USA	
Mingenbach, Louise	Costume Designer
United Talent Agency, 9336 Civic Center Dr, Beverly Hills CA 90210 USA	
Minghella, Max	Actor
Creative Artists Agency, 2000 Ave of Stars, #100, Los Angeles CA 90067 USA	
Mingiedi, Mawangu	Percussionist, Likembe Player
Concerted Efforts, PO Box 440326, Somerville MA 02144 USA	
Ming-Na Wen	Actress
Gersh Agency, 9465 Wilshire Blvd, #600, Beverly Hills CA 90212 USA	
Mingo, Eugene L (Gene)	Football Player
5701 E Colorado Ave, Denver CO 80224, USA	
Minh Tran	Dancer, Choreographer
2014 NE 47th Ave, Portland OR 97213, USA	
Miniefield, Kevin L	Football Player
11733 E Starflower Dr, Chandler AZ 85249, USA	
Minkoff, Rob	Director, Producer, Animator
Oasis Media Group, 8730 W Sunset Blvd, #700, West Hollywood CA 90069, USA	
Minkowski, Marc	Conductor
Deutsche Grammaphon Records, 810 7th Ave, New York NY 10019 USA	
Minnelli, Liza	Actress, Singer
150 E 69th St, #21G, New York NY 10021, USA	
Minnette, Dylan	Actor
C E S D, 10635 Santa Monica Blvd, #130, Los Angeles CA 90025 USA	
Minnick, Walter C (Walt)	Representative, ID
The Majority Group LLP, 1701 Pennsylvania Ave NW, #300, Washington DC 20006, USA	
Minnifield, Dirk D	Basketball Player
10902 Little Gap Court, Sugar Land TX 77498, USA	

Mills - Minnifield

Minnifield, Frank D — Football Player
4809 Chaffey Lane, Lexington KY 40515, USA
Minnillo, Vanessa — Entertainer
B/W/R, 9100 Wilshire Blvd, #500W, Beverly Hills CA 90212 USA
Minns, Martyn — Religious Leader
Truro Church, Rector's Office, 10520 Main St, Fairfax VA 22030, USA
Minogue, Danii — Singer
PO Box 46824, London SW11 3WS, England
Minogue, Kylie — Singer, Actress
Primary Talent International, 10-11 Jockey's Fields, London WC1R 4BN, England
Minor, Blas, Jr — Baseball Player
7139 N Dean St, Winton CA 95388, USA
Minor, Greg M — Basketball Player
6543 Merrick Landing Blvd, Windermere FL 34786, USA
Minor, Jerry — Actor
United Talent Agency, 9336 Civic Center Dr, Beverly Hills CA 90210 USA
Minor, Shane — Singer
E S P Mgmt, 838 N Doheny Dr, #302, West Hollywood CA 90069, USA
Minor, Travis D — Football Player
PO Box 1635, Hallandale FL 33008, USA
Minoso, Saturino O A A (Minnie) — Baseball Player
3700 N Lake Shore Dr, #303, Chicago IL 60613, USA
Minot, Eliza — Writer
Knopf Publishers, 1745 Broadway, New York NY 10019 USA
Minow, Newton N — Government Official
179 E Lake Shore Dr, #15W, Chicago IL 60611, USA
Minshall, James E (Jim) — Baseball Player
615 Manatee Ave, Ellenton FL 34222, USA
Minsky, Charles D — Cinematographer
202 Toro Canyon Road, Carpinteria CA 93013, USA
Minsky, Marvin L — Computer Scientist
Massachusetts Institute of Technology, Computer Science Dept, Cambridge MA 02139, USA
Minter, Alan — Boxer
Fighting Talk, 30 Peterborough Way, Fellgate, Jarrow NE32 4XD, Canada
Minter, Barry A — Football Player
2626 Garcitas Creek, Richmond TX 77406, USA
Minter, Kristin — Actress
Lovett Mgmt, 1327 Brinkley Ave, Los Angeles CA 90049, USA
Minter, Michael C)Mike) — Football Player
506 N East Ave, Kannapolis NC 28083, USA
Minton, Gregory B (Greg) — Baseball Player
690 N Muleshoe Road, Apache Junction AZ 85119, USA
Minton, Yvonne F — Opera Singer
Organisation Int'l Artistique, 16 Ave F D Roosevelt, 75008 Paris, France
Mintz, Beatrice — Embryologist
Fox Chase Cancer Center, 333 Cottman Ave, Philadelphia PA 19111, USA
Mintz, Daniel (Dan) — Actor, Writer
Creative Artists Agency, 2000 Ave of Stars, #100, Los Angeles CA 90067 USA
Mintz, Shlomo — Concert Violinist, Conductor
Kunstleragentur Raab & Bohm, Plankengasse 7, 1010 Vienna, Austria
Mintz-Plasse, Christopher — Actor
United Talent Agency, 9336 Civic Center Dr, Beverly Hills CA 90210 USA
Minutelli, Gino M — Baseball
3305 Foxtrot Court, Spring Hill TX 76639, USA
Mio, Eddie — Ice Hockey Player
PO Box 252745, West Bloomfield MI 48325, USA
Miou-Miou — Actress
U B B A, 6 Rue de Braque, 75003 Paris, France
Mir, Isabelle — Alpine Skier
65170 Saint-Lary, France
Mira, George — Football Player
19225 SW 128th Court, Miami FL 33177, USA
Mirabella, Erin — Cyclist
914 N Idaho St, La Habra CA 90631, USA
Mirabella, Grace — Editor, Publisher
Mirabella, Editor's Office, 200 Madison Ave, New York NY 10016, USA
Mirabella, Paul T — Baseball Player
125 Jenks Road, Morristown NJ 07960, USA
Mirabelli, Douglas A (Doug) — Baseball Player
9788 Edgewood Ave, Traverse City MI 49685, USA
Miraldi, Dean M — Football Player
14015 Live Oak Lane, Grass Valley CA 95945, USA
Miranda, Claudio — Cinematographer
Dattner Disposto, 10635 Santa Monica Blvd, #165, Los Angeles CA 90025, USA
Miranda, Lin-Manuel — Lyricist, Actor, Singer
W M E Entertainment, 9601 Wilshire Blvd, #300, Beverly Hills CA 90210 USA
Miranda, Pia — Actress
United Mgmt, 61 Marlborough St, #400-45, Surry Hills NSW 2010, Australia
Mirchoff, Beau — Actor
A P A Talent/Literary Agency, 405 S Beverly Dr, #300, Beverly Hills CA 90212 USA
Mirer, Rick F — Football Player
820 Braxton Court, Goshen IN 46526, USA
Mirich, Rex L — Football Player
620 W Yaqui Dr, Tucson AZ 85704, USA
Miricioiu, Nelly — Opera Singer
53 Midhurst Ave, Muswell Hill, London N10 3EP, England
Mirikitani, Janice — Writer
Celestial Arts Press, 6001 Shellmound St, #400, Emeryville CA 94608, USA
Mirisch, Walter M — Producer
647 Warner Ave, Los Angeles CA 90024, USA
Mirkin, David — Director, Producer, Writer
Gersh Agency, 9465 Wilshire Blvd, #600, Beverly Hills CA 90212 USA
Mirman, Eugene — Actor
I C M Partners, 10250 Constellation Blvd, #900, Los Angeles CA 90067 USA
Mirmira, Raghavendra G — Biochemist, Molecular Biologist
University of Virginia Medical School, Charlottesville VA 22903, USA

Mironov, Boris O	Ice Hockey Player
2911 Bayview Ave, North York ON M2K 1E8, Canada	
Mironov, Dmitri O	Ice Hockey Player
2911 Bayview Ave, North York ON M2K 1E8, Canada	
Mirren, Helen	Actress
Ken McReddie Assoc, 11 Connaught Place, London W2 2ET, England	
Mirrione, Stephen	Editor
I C M Partners, 10250 Constellation Blvd, #900, Los Angeles CA 90067 USA	
Mirrlees, James A	Nobel Economics Laureate
Trinity College, Economics Dept, Cambridge CB2 1TQ, England	
Mirziyoyev, Shavkat M	Prime Minister, Uzbekistan
Prime Minister's Office, Mustariik 5, 70008 Tashkent, Uzbekistan	
Miscavige, David	Religious Leader
Scientology Religious Tech Center, 1710 Ivar St, #1100, Los Angeles CA 90028, USA	
Misch, Patrick T J	Baseball Player
725 N Dobson Road, #255, Chandler AZ 85224, USA	
Mischak, Robert M (Bob)	Football Player
73 Brookwood Road, #12, Orinda CA 94563, USA	
Mischer, Don	Producer, Director, Writer
Don Mischer Productions, 8899 Beverly Blvd, #902, Los Angeles CA 90048, USA	
Mischka, James	Fashion Designer
Badgley Mischka, 215 W 40th St, New York NY 10018, USA	
Misersky, Antje	Biathlete
Grenzgraben 3A, 98714 Stutzerbach, Germany	
Mishkin, Frederic	Government Official, Economist
Columbia University, Economics Dept, New York NY 10027, USA	
Misiano, Christopher (Chris)	Director, Producer
Creative Artists Agency, 2000 Ave of Stars, #100, Los Angeles CA 90067 USA	
Misiano, Vincent	Director
Creative Artists Agency, 2000 Ave of Stars, #100, Los Angeles CA 90067 USA	
Miskulin, Joey (Cowpolka King)	Singer, Accordionist (Riders in the Sky)
New Frontier Mgmt, 1921 Broadway, Nashville TN 37203, USA	
Misner, Susan	Actress
One Entertainment, 12 W 57th St, #PH 1, New York NY 10019 USA	
Misrach, Richard L	Photographer
1420 45th St, Emeryville CA 94608, USA	
Missick, Dorian	Actor
A P A Talent/Literary Agency, 405 S Beverly Dr, #300, Beverly Hills CA 90212 USA	
Mistry, Jimi	Actor
Brillstein Entertainment Partners, 9150 Wilshire Blvd, #350, Beverly Hills CA 90212 USA	
Mistry, Kaizad	Computer Chip Engineer
Intel Corp, 5200 NE Elam Parkway, Hillsboro OR 97124, USA	
Mitalipov, Shoukhrat	Reproductive Biologist
3075 NW Overlook Dr, Hillsboro OR 97124, USA	
Mitchard, Jacquelyn	Writer
Penguin Books, 375 Hudson St, Basement 1, New York NY 10014 USA	
Mitchell, Aidan D	Actor
Stone Manners Salners, 9911 W Pico Blvd, #1400, Los Angeles CA 90035 USA	
Mitchell, Andrea	Commentator
2710 Chain Bridge Road NW, Washington DC 20016, USA	
Mitchell, Augie	Guitarist (Intruders)
Billy Paul Mgmt, 8215 Winthrop St, Philadelphia PA 19136, USA	
Mitchell, Betsy	Swimmer
Laurel High School, Athletic Dept, 1 Lyman Circle, Beachwood OH 44122, USA	
Mitchell, Bobby	Golfer
435 Wimbish Dr, Danville VA 24541, USA	
Mitchell, Brandon P	Football Player
806 Schlessinger St, Abbeville LA 70510, USA	
Mitchell, Brian K	Football Player
5435 Chandley Farm Circle, Centreville VA 20120, USA	
Mitchell, Brian Stokes	Actor, Singer
Paradigm Agency, 360 N Crescent Dr, North Building, Beverly Hills CA 90210 USA	
Mitchell, Daryl M (Chill)	Actor
United Talent Agency, 9336 Civic Center Dr, Beverly Hills CA 90210 USA	
Mitchell, Donald R	Football Player
5620 Minner Dr, Beaumont TX 77708, USA	
Mitchell, Dryden	Bassist, Pianist (Alien Ant Farm)
Creative Artists Agency, 2000 Ave of Stars, #100, Los Angeles CA 90067 USA	
Mitchell, Edgar D	Astronaut
PO Box 540037, Greenacres FL 33454, USA	
Mitchell, Elizabeth	Actress
I F A Talent Agency, 8730 W Sunset Blvd, #490, West Hollywood CA 90069 USA	
Mitchell, Elizabeth R (Liz)	Singer (Boney M)
International Artists, PO Box 100334, 47563 Goch, Germany	
Mitchell, Finesse	Actor, Comedian
I C M Partners, 10250 Constellation Blvd, #900, Los Angeles CA 90067 USA	
Mitchell, George	Guitarist (Intruders)
Billy Paul Mgmt, 8215 Winthrop St, Philadelphia PA 19136, USA	
Mitchell, George J	Senator, ME
D L A Piper, 1251 Ave of Americas, #C2-75, New York NY 10020, USA	
Mitchell, George P	Businessman, Philanthropist
Mitchell Energy & Development, PO Box 4000, The Woodlands TX 77387, USA	
Mitchell, James H (Jim)	Football Player
120 Twin Creek Terrace, Forest VA 24551, USA	
Mitchell, Jessie J (Mitch)	Baseball Player
1964 Cherry Ave, Birmingham AL 35214, USA	
Mitchell, John	Baseball Player
1708 Castleberry Way, Birmingham AL 35214, USA	
Mitchell, John Cameron	Actor, Director, Writer
Creative Artists Agency, 2000 Ave of Stars, #100, Los Angeles CA 90067 USA	
Mitchell, John K	Baseball Player
5017 Hasty Dr, Nashville TN 37211, USA	
Mitchell, Johnny	Football Player
7617 Courtyard Run W, Boca Raton FL 33433, USA	
Mitchell, Joni	Singer, Songwriter
624 Funchal Road, Los Angeles CA 90077, USA	

Mitchell, Kawika U — Football Player
971 N Lake Sybelia Dr, Maitland FL 32751, USA
Mitchell, Keith — Actor
A P A Talent/Literary Agency, 405 S Beverly Dr, #300, Beverly Hills CA 90212 USA
Mitchell, Keith A — Baseball Player
731 S 42nd St, San Diego CA 92113, USA
Mitchell, Kenneth — Actor
Innovative Artists, 1505 10th St, Santa Monica CA 90401 USA
Mitchell, Kevin D — Baseball Player
3869 Ocean View Blvd, San Diego CA 92113, USA
Mitchell, Kim — Singer
41 Britain St, #305, Toronto ON M5A 1R, Canada
Mitchell, Kirsty L — Actress
Conway Van Gelder Grant, 8-12 Broadwick St, #300, London W1F 8HW, England
Mitchell, Leland — Basketball Player
RR 5 Box 4, Starkville MS 39759, USA
Mitchell, Leona — Opera Singer
Columbia Artists Mgmt Inc, 1790 Broadway, #702, New York NY 10019 USA
Mitchell, Leroy — Football Player
6598 N Pinewood Dr, Parker CO 80134, USA
Mitchell, Lydell D — Football Player
702 Reservoir St, Baltimore MD 21217, USA
Mitchell, Lyvonia A (Stump) — Football Player, Coach
43091 Old Gallivan Terrace, Ashburn VA 20147, USA
Mitchell, Mack H — Football Player
PO Box 741, Diboll TX 75941, USA
Mitchell, Mike — Director, Actor, Writer
Creative Artists Agency, 2000 Ave of Stars, #100, Los Angeles CA 90067 USA
Mitchell, Murray C — Basketball Player
401 Northshore Blvd, #905, Portland TX 78374, USA
Mitchell, Paul M — Baseball Player
23 Carr Road, Berlin MA 01503, USA
Mitchell, Peter C (Pete) — Football Player
125 Sawbill Palm Dr, Ponte Vedra Beach FL 32082, USA
Mitchell, Radha — Actress
Shanahan Mgmt, PO Box 1509, Darlinghurst NSW 1300, Australia
Mitchell, Robert — Baseball Player
2009 Elmwood Ave, Tampa FL 33605, USA
Mitchell, Robert C (Bobby) — Football Player, Executive
36 Hollyberry Court, Rockville MD 20852, USA
Mitchell, Robert Vance (Bobby) — Baseball Player
8697 Tiogawoods Dr, Sacramento CA 95828, USA
Mitchell, Roland E — Football Player
PO Box 5701, Lake Charles LA 70606, USA
Mitchell, Roscoe E, Jr — Jazz Reeds Player, Composer
S R O Artists, 6629 University Ave, #206, Middleton WI 53562, USA
Mitchell, Samuel E (Sam), Jr — Basektball Player, Coach
73 Smokerise Point, Peachtree City GA 30269, USA
Mitchell, Sasha — Actor
Flick East-West, 9057 Nemo St, #A, West Hollywood, CA 90069 USA
Mitchell, Shareen — Actress
Independent Artists Agency, 9601 Wilshire Blvd, #750, Beverly Hills CA 90210, USA
Mitchell, Sharmba — Boxer
819 Hayward Ave, Takoma Park MD 20912, USA
Mitchell, Shay — Actress
A P A Talent/Literary Agency, 405 S Beverly Dr, #300, Beverly Hills CA 90212 USA
Mitchell, Silas Weir — Actor
Greene Assoc, 1901 Ave of Stars, #130, Los Angeles CA 90067 USA
Mitchell, Steven Long (Steve) — Writer, Producer, Director
Imagiquest Entertainment, 10200 Riverside Dr, #201, Toluca Lake CA 91602, USA
Mitchell, Thomas G (Tom) — Football Player
1421 SW 49th Terrace, Cape Coral FL 33914, USA
Mitchell, Todd — Basketball Player
4134 Emmajean Road, Toledo OH 43607, USA
Mitchell, Tony — Cinematographer, Director
United Agents, 12-26 Lexington St, London W1F 0LE, England
Mitchell, W Scott — Football Player
2375 S State St, Springville UT 84663, USA
Mitchell, Warren — Actor
Shanahan Mgmt, 91 Campbell St, #300, Surry Hills NSW 2010, Australia
Mitchell, William R (Willie) — Ice Hockey Player
Los Angeles Kings, Staples Center, 1111 S Figueroa St, Los Angeles CA 90015 USA
Mitchell-Smith, Ilan — Actor
10460 Queens Blvd, #10C, Forest Hills NY 11375, USA
Mitchison, N Avrion — Zoologist, Anatomist
14 Belitha Villas, London N1 1PD, England
Miti, Carlotta — Actress
Carol Levi Mgmt, Via G Pisanelli 2, 00196 Rome, Italy
Mitra, Rhona — Actress
Untitled Entertainment, 350 S Beverly Dr, #200, Beverly Hills CA 90212 USA
Mitre, Sergio A — Baseball Player
1707 Summer Sky St, Chula Vista CA 91915, USA
Mitsotakis, Konstantinos — Prime Minister, Greece
1 Aravintinou St, 106 74 Athens, Greece
Mittal, Lakshmi N — Businessman
L N M Group, Hofplein 20, #1500, Rotterdam 3032, Netherlands
Mitte, R J — Actor
Bauman Redanty Shaul Agency, 5757 Wilshire Blvd, #473, Los Angeles CA 90036 USA
Mittermaier-Neureuther, Rosi — Alpine Skier
Winkelmoosalm, 83242 Reit Im Winkel, Germany
Mittermayer, Tatjana — Freestyle Moguls Skier
Bucha 2A, 83661 Lenggries, Germany
Mitterrutzner, Martin — Opera Singer
Kunstler Sekretariat am Gasteig, Rosenheimer Str 52, 81669 Munich, Germany
Mitterwald, George E — Baseball Player
1721 Murdock Blvd, Orlando FL 32825, USA

Mittleman, Steve — Actor, Comedian
A K A Talent, 6310 San Vicente Blvd, #200, Los Angeles CA 90048 USA
Mitts, Heather — Soccer Player, Sportscaster
Atlanta Beat, 1955 Vaughn Road, #209, Kennesaw GA 30144, USA
Mitz, Alonzo L — Football Player
2609 NE 4th St, #216, Renton WA 98056, USA
Mivelaz, Betty — Bowler
1543 Grand Ave, Medford OR 97504, USA
Mix, Bryant L — Football Player
37 Greenwood Plantation Road, Natchez MS 39120, USA
Mix, Ronald J (Ron) — Football Player
7840 Mission Center Court, #104, San Diego CA 92108, USA
Mix, Steven C (Steve) — Basketball Player
25743 Willowbend Road, Perrysburg OH 43551, USA
Mix, Timothy — Opera Singer
I M G Artists, Hogarth Business Park, Chiswick, London W4 2TH, England
Mixon, Katy — Actress
W M E Entertainment, 9601 Wilshire Blvd, #300, Beverly Hills CA 90210 USA
Mixon, Kenneth J (Kenny) — Football Player
175 Bayridge Lane, Weston FL 33326, USA
Mixson, J Wayne — Governor, FL
2219 Demeron Road, Tallahassee FL 32308, USA
Miyamoto, Shigeru — Video Game Designer
Nintendo, 11-1 Kamitoba, Hokotatecho Minamiku, Kyoto 601-8501, Japan
Miyamura, Hiroshi H — Korean War Army Hero (CMH)
659 Kaimalino St, Kailua HI 96734, USA
Miyazaki, Hayao — Animator
Studio Ghibli, 1-4-25 Kajinocho, Koganeishi 184, Japan
Miyazato, Ai — Golfer
Ladies Pro Golf Assn, 100 International Golf Dr, Daytona Beach FL 32124 USA
Miyori, Kim — Actress
Susan Smith, 1344 N Wetherly Dr, Los Angeles CA 90069 USA
Mize, John D — Vietnam War Air Force Hero
112 Sunset Dr, Belmond IA 50421, USA
Mize, Larry — Golfer
106 Graystone Court, Columbus GA 31904, USA
Mize, Ola L — Korean War Army Hero (CMH)
211 Hartwood Dr, Gadsden AL 35901, USA
Mizerock, John J — Baseball Player, Manager
1189 Leasure Run Road, Rochester Mills PA 15771, USA
Mizota, Diane — Actress
Paradise Group, PO Box 69451, West Hollywood CA 90069, USA
Mizrahi, Isaac — Fashion Designer
1516 S Canfield Ave, Los Angeles CA 90035, USA
MJG — Rap Artist (8Ball & MJG)
J L Entertainment, 18653 Ventura Blvd, #340, Tarzana CA 91356 USA
Mleczko-Griswold, Allison J (A J) — Ice Hockey Player
3 Hinckley Lane, Nantucket MA 02554, USA
Mlicki, David J (Dave) — Baseball Player
5350 Reserve Dr, Dublin OH 43017, USA
Mnookin, Robert H — Attorney, Educator
10 Follen St, Cambridge MA 02138, USA
Mnouchkine, Ariane — Director
Theatre du Soleil, Cartoucherie, 75012 Paris, France
Mo Yan — Nobel Literature Laureate
Meutheun, 215 Vauxhall Bridge Road, London SW1V 1EJ, England
Moakes, Gordon P — Guitarist (Bloc Party)
Coalition Mgmt, 12 Barley Mow Passage, London W4 4PH, England
Moakler, Shanna L — Beauty Queen, Actress, Model
Global Artists Agency, 6253 Hollywood Blvd, #508, Los Angeles CA 90028 USA
Moalem, Sharon — Writer
Harper Collins Publishers, 10 E 53rd St, Cellar 1, New York NY 10022 USA
Moates, David A (Dave) — Baseball Player
7924 24th Ave W, Bradenton FL 34209, USA
Moats, David — Journalist
Rutland Herald, Editorial Dept, PO Box 668, Rutland VT 05702, USA
Moats, Sanford K — Air Force General, WW II Hero
59-635 Akanoho Place, Haleiwa HI 96712, USA
Mobley, Cuttino R — Basketball Player
PO Box 11319, Beverly Hills CA 90213, USA
Mobley, John U — Football Player
3512 Legacy Hills Court, Longwood FL 32779, USA
Mobley, Mary Ann — Actress, Beauty Queen
Corsa Agency, 11704 Wilshire Blvd, #204, Los Angeles CA 90025, USA
Mobley, Orson O — Football Player
400 S 24th Ave, Hattiesburg MS 39401, USA
Moby — Singer, Guitarist
Fresh & Clean Media, 12701 Venice Blvd, Los Angeles CA 90066, USA
Moceanu, Dominique — Gymnast
Medialine Communications, 7300 York Ave S, #204, Edina MN 55435, USA
Mochrie, Colin — Actor, Comedian
385 Adelaide St W, Toronto ON M5V 1S4, Canada
Mock Garrett — Baseball Player
13650 Maisemore Road, Houston TX 77015, USA
Mock, Geraldine F (Jerrie) — Aviatrix
343 E King St, Quincy FL 32351, USA
Mockett, Cathy — Golfer
1601 Antigua Way, Newport Beach CA 92660, USA
Mocumbi, Pascoal M — Prime Minister, Mozambique
1874 Ave Armando Tivane, Maputo, Mozambique
Modano, Michael (Mike) — Ice Hockey Player
6424 Mimosa Lane, Dallas TX 75230, USA
Modell, Frank — Cartoonist
115 Three Mile Course, Guilford CT 06437, USA
Modin, Fredrik — Ice Hockey Player
8955 Dunn Curt, Dublin OH 43017, USA

Modine, Matthew — Actor
Untitled Entertainment, 350 S Beverly Dr, #200, Beverly Hills CA 90212 USA
Modry, Jaroslav — Ice Hockey Player
1724 Malvern Hill Place, Duluth GA 30097, USA
Modrzejewski, Robert J — Vietnam War Marine Corps Hero (CMH)
4725 Oporto Court, San Diego CA 92124, USA
Modzelewski, Richard B (Dick) — Football Player
1357 Fox Run Dr, #105, Willoughby OH 44094, USA
Moe, Douglas E (Doug) — Basketball Player, Coach
13 Arnold Palmer, San Antonio TX 78257, USA
Moe, Thomas S (Tommy) — Alpine Skier
1556 Hidden Lane, Anchorage AK 99501, USA
Moegle, Richard L (Dicky) — Football Player
4207 DeForest Ridge Circle, Katy TX 77494, USA
Moehler, Brian M — Baseball Player
269 Woodlawn Dr NE, Marietta GA 30067, USA
Moehringer, J R — Journalist
Los Angeles Times, Editorial Dept, 202 W 1st St, Los Angeles CA 90012 USA
Moe-Humphreys, Karen — Swimmer, Swimming Coach
505 Augusta Dr, Moraga CA 94556, USA
Moeller, Chad E — Baseball Player
11058 E Raintree Dr, Scottsdale AZ 85255, USA
Moeller, Chet — Football Player
Wilson Price Information Technology, 3815 Interstate Court, Montgomery AL 36109, USA
Moeller, David — Luge Athlete
Meet Success, Auf der Eierwiese 1, 82031 Gruenwald, Germany
Moeller, Dennis L — Inventor
147 Florence Dr, Jupiter FL 33458, USA
Moeller, Dennis M — Baseball Player
24979 Constitution Ave, #536, Valencia CA 91381, USA
Moeller, Edward — Basketball Player
1011 Kelton College Way, Morrisville NC 27560, USA
Moeller, Joseph D (Joe) — Baseball Player
1505 Avenida de Nogales, San Clemente CA 92672, USA
Moeller, Robert T — Navy Admiral
Deputy Commander, Military Operations, US Africa Command, APO AE 09751, USA
Moellering, John H — Army General
United Services Automobile Assn, USAA Building, San Antonio TX 78288, USA
Moen, John — Drummer (Decemberists)
Big Hassle, 44 Wall St, #2200, New York NY 10005, USA
Moennig, Katherine — Actress
Framework Entertainment, 9057 Nemo St, #C, West Hollywood CA 90069 USA
Moffat, Katherine (Kitty) — Actress
Henderson/Hogan, 850 7th Ave, #1003, New York NY 10019 USA
Moffatt, Henry K — Mathematical Physicist
6 Banhams Close, Cambridge CB4 1HX, England
Moffatt, Katy — Singer, Guitarist, Songwriter
PO Box 334, O Fallon IL 62269, USA
Moffett, D W — Actor
3 Arts Entertainment, 9460 Wilshire Blvd, #700, Beverly Hills CA 90212 USA
Moffett, Donald — Artist
Anthony Meier Fine Arts, 1969 California St, San Francisco CA 94109, USA
Moffitt, John — Track Athlete
Vector Sports Mgmt, 417 Keller Parkway, Keller TX 76248, USA
Moffitt, Peggy — Model
Browns, 23-27 S Moulton St, London W1K 5RD, England
Moffitt, Randall J (Randy) — Baseball Player
1725 Baltic Ave, Prescott AZ 86301, USA
Mofford, Rose — Governor, AZ
330 W Maryland Ave, #104, Phoenix AZ 85013, USA
Mogenburg, Dietmar — Track Athlete
Alter Garfen 34, 51371 Leverkusen, Germany
Mogilny, Alexander G — Ice Hockey Player
10225 Collins Ave, #2202, Bal Harbour FL 33154, USA
Mogis, Michael R (Mike) — Musician (Bright Eyes)
Press Here, 138 W 25th St, #700, New York NY 10001, USA
Mohacsi, Mary — Bowler
15445 Sunset St, Livonia MI 48154, USA
Mohamed Khouna, Cheikh El Avia Ould — Prime Minister, Mauritania
Prime Minister's Office, Nouakchott, Mauritania
Mohammed VI — King, Morocco
Royal Palais, Dar Al Mahkzen, Rabat, Morocco
Mohapatra, Bibhu — Fashion Designer
270 W 38th St, #1100, New York NY 10018, USA
Mohler, Michael R (Mike) — Baseball Player
1627 S Shirley Ave, Gonzales LA 70737, USA
Mohoric, Dale R — Baseball Player
15501 Rockside Road, Maple Heights OH 44137, USA
Mohr, Christopher G (Chris) — Football Player
3260 Surrey Road, Thomson GA 30824, USA
Mohr, Dustan — Baseball Player
103 Parkwood Dr, Hattiesburg MS 39402, USA
Mohr, Jay — Actor, Comedian
New Wave Entertainment, 2660 W Olive Ave, Burbank CA 91505, USA
Mohri, Mamoru — Astronaut, Japan
Japanese Aerospace Exploration Agency, 2-1-1 Sengen, Tsukuba-shi, Ibaraki 305 8505, Japan
Mohseni, Saad — Businessman
Moby Group, 3 Street 12, Wazir Akbar Khan, District 10, Kabul, Afghanistan
Mohyeldin, Ayman — Journalist
Al Jazeera, PO Box 23127, Doha, Qatar
Moir, Richard — Actor
Shanahan Mgmt, PO Box 1509, Darlinghurst NSW 1300, Australia
Moir, Scott — Ice Skater
Ilderton Skating Club, Box 33, Ilderton, ON N0M 2A0, Canada
Moiso, Jerome — Basketball Player
Cleveland Cavaliers, Gund Arena, 1 Center Court, Cleveland OH 44115 USA

M

Mojsiejenko, Ralf	Football Player
11334 Baldwin Road, Bridgman MI 49106, USA	
Mok, Karen	Actress
Creative Artists Agency, 2000 Ave of Stars, #100, Los Angeles CA 90067 USA	
Mokeski, Paul K	Basketball Player
4004 Crestwood Dr, Carrolton TX 75007, USA	
Mokosak, Carl	Ice Hockey Player
8073 Rum Creek Trail NE, Rockford MI 49341, USA	
Mokri, Amir M	Cinematographer
Gersh Agency, 9465 Wilshire Blvd, #600, Beverly Hills CA 90212 USA	
Mol, Gretchen	Actress
John Carrabino Mgmt, 5900 Wilshire Blvd, #406, Los Angeles CA 90036 USA	
Molale, Brandon	Actor
Coolwaters Productions, 10061 Riverside Dr, Box 531, Toluca Lake CA 91602 USA	
Molden, Alex M	Football Player
2083 Wellington Dr, West Linn OR 97068, USA	
Moldovan, Diana	Model
Yes Model Mgmt, 2 Bibescu Voda BL P5, #26, Bucharest, Romania	
Mole, Fenton L	Baseball Player
738 Glen Eagle Court, Danville CA 94526, USA	
Molina, Alfred	Actor, Singer
Lou Coulson, 37 Berwick St, London W1V 3RF, England	
Molina, Angela	Actress
Agents Associes, 201 Rue du Faubourg Saint Honore, 75008 Paris, France	
Molina, Benjamin J (Bengie)	Baseball Player
6475 E Crantree Place, Yuma AZ 85365, USA	
Molina, Jose B	Baseball Player
Tampa Bay Rays, 1 Tropicana Dr, Saint Petersburg FL 33705 USA	
Molina, Mario J	Nobel Chemistry Laureate
PO Box 12406, La Jolla CA 92039, USA	
Molina, Yadier B	Baseball Player
1005 Bluff Pointe Court, Caseyville IL 62232, USA	
Molinari, Anna	Fashion Designer
Via G Ferraris 13/15/15/15A, 411012 Carpi (Modena), Italy	
Molinaro, Al	Actor
1530 Arboles Dr, Glendale CA 91207, USA	
Molinaro, Robert J (Bob)	Baseball Player
1 Harbourside Dr, #2312, Delray Beach FL 33483, USA	
Molitor, Paul L	Baseball Player
6725 Iroquois Circle, Minneapolis MN 55439, USA	
Molko, Brian	Singer, Guitarist (Placebo), Songwriter
Riverman Records, George House, Brecon Road, London W6 8PY, England	
Moll, John L	Electronics Engineer
4111 Old Trace Road, Palo Alto CA 94306, USA	
Moll, Kurt	Opera Singer
Gross Theaterstr 34, 20354 Hamburg, Germany	
Moll, Richard	Actor
Studio Talent Group, 1328 12th St, Santa Monica CA 90401, USA	
Molla, Jordi	Actor
Paradigm Agency, 360 N Crescent Dr, North Building, Beverly Hills CA 90210 USA	
Moller, Paul	Inventor (Sky Car), Engineer
Moller International, 1222 Research Park Dr, Davis CA 95618, USA	
Moller, Randy	Ice Hockey Player
3950 NW 23rd Terrace, Boca Raton FL 33431, USA	
Moller-Gladisch, Silke	Track Athlete
Lange Str 6, 18055 Rostock, Germany	
Mollo, John	Costume Designer
Dower House, Church St, West Hanney, Wantage OX12 0LW, England	
Mollo-Christensen, Erik L	Oceanographer
10 Barberry Road, Lexington MA 02421, USA	
Molloy, Irene	Actress
Gersh Agency, 9465 Wilshire Blvd, #600, Beverly Hills CA 90212 USA	
Molloy, Matt	Flutist (Chieftains)
Macklam/Feldman Mgmt, 1505 W 2nd Ave, #200, Vancouver BC V6H 3Y4, Canada	
Moloney, Janel	Actress
Gersh Agency, 9465 Wilshire Blvd, #600, Beverly Hills CA 90212 USA	
Moloney, Paddy	Singer (Chieftains)
Macklam/Feldman Mgmt, 1505 W 2nd Ave, #200, Vancouver BC V6H 3Y4, Canada	
Moloney, Richard H (Rich)	Baseball Player
125 Mallard Way, Waltham MA 02452, USA	
Moltmann, Jurgen	Theologian
Liebermeister Str 12, 72076 Tubingen, Germany	
Molyneux, Juan Pablo	Architect
J P Molyneux Studio, 29 E 69th St, New York NY 10021, USA	
Mom Rajawong Sirikit Kitiyarara	Queen, Thailand
Royal Residence, Chitralada Villa, 9 Rama VI Road, Soi 30, Bangkok 10400, Thailand	
Momaday, N Scott	Writer
University of Arizona, English Dept, Tucson AZ 85721, USA	
Momesso, Sergio	Ice Hockey Player
Momesso Caffe, 3669 Boul St Jean, Dollard les Ormeaux QC H9G 1X2, Canada	
Momoa, Jason	Actor, Model
A P A Talent/Literary Agency, 405 S Beverly Dr, #300, Beverly Hills CA 90212 USA	
Momsen, Taylor	Actress
Das Communications, 83 Riverside Dr, New York NY 10024, USA	
Monacelli, Amleto	Bowler
Professional Bowlers Assn, 719 2nd Ave, #701, Seattle WA 98104 USA	
Monaco, Kara	Model
Dino May Mgmt, 11262 Ventura Blvd, #PH, Studio City CA 91604, USA	
Monaco, Kelly M	Actress, Model, Dancer
W M E Entertainment, 9601 Wilshire Blvd, #300, Beverly Hills CA 90210 USA	
Monae, Janelle	Singer
W M E Entertainment, 9601 Wilshire Blvd, #300, Beverly Hills CA 90210 USA	
Monaghan, Cameron	Actor
C E S D, 10635 Santa Monica Blvd, #130, Los Angeles CA 90025 USA	
Monaghan, Dominic	Actor
A P A Talent/Literary Agency, 405 S Beverly Dr, #300, Beverly Hills CA 90212 USA	

Mojsiejenko - Monaghan

Monaghan, Kris — Golfer
54 Golf Course Dr, Ranchos de Taos NM 87557, USA

Monaghan, Marjorie — Actress
John Crosby Mgmt, 1310 N Spaulding Ave, Los Angeles CA 90046 USA

Monaghan, Michelle — Actress
I C M Partners, 10250 Constellation Blvd, #900, Los Angeles CA 90067 USA

Monahan, Dan — Actor
Cuzzings Mgmt, 1425 N Detroit St, #304, Los Angeles CA 90046, USA

Monahan, David H — Actor, Director
Bauman Redanty Shaul Agency, 5757 Wilshire Blvd, #473, Los Angeles CA 90036 USA

Monahan, Garry — Ice Hockey Player
4665 Piccadilly N, West Vancouver BC V7W 1E3, Canada

Monahan, Gretchen (Gretta) — Entertainer
Food Network, 1180 Ave of Americas, #1200, New York NY 10036 USA

Monahan, Pat — Singer (Train)
Jon Landau, 150 Rowayton Ave, Norwalk CT 06853, USA

Monahan, Shane H — Baseball Player
624 Stickley Oak Way, Woodstock GA 30189, USA

Monahan, William — Writer, Director
W M E Entertainment, 9601 Wilshire Blvd, #300, Beverly Hills CA 90210 USA

Monastyrska, Liudmyla — Opera Singer
I M G Artists, Hogarth Business Park, Chiswick, London W4 2TH, England

Monbouquette, William C (Bill) — Baseball Player
46 Doonan St, Medford MA 02155, USA

Moncrief, Sidney A — Basketball Player
9842 Audelia Road, #1109, Dallas TX 75238, USA

Moncrieff, Karen — Actress, Director, Writer
Pitbull Pictures, 4116 Dundee Dr, Los Angeles CA 90027, USA

Mond, Josh — Producer
United Talent Agency, 9336 Civic Center Dr, Beverly Hills CA 90210 USA

Mondale, Walter F — Vice President; Senator, MN
Dorsey & Whitney, 50 S 6th St, #1500, Minneapolis MN 55402, USA

Monday, Kenneth D (Kenny) — Freestyle Wrestler
4119 W Deer Crossing Dr, Stillwater OK 74074, USA

Monday, Robert J (Rick) — Baseball Player, Sportscaster
811 Gayfeather Lane, Vero Beach FL 32963, USA

Mondey, Fawnia — Actress, Model
631 N Stephanie St, #162, Henderson NV 89014, USA

Mondou, Pierre — Ice Hockey Player
239 Rue Wildor Larochelle, Sorel Tracy QC J3P 6R2, Canada

Mone, Michelle — Fashion Designer
M J M International, 8 Redwood Crescent, Peel Park, Glasgow G74 5PA, Scotland

Moneo, J Rafael — Pritzker Architectural Laureate
Calle Mino 5, Madrid 28002, Spain

Monet, Daniella — Actress
Paradigm Agency, 360 N Crescent Dr, North Building, Beverly Hills CA 90210 USA

Money, Eddie — Singer
I C M Partners, 730 5th Ave, New York NY 10019 USA

Money, Eric V — Basketball Player
457 S Harvard Ave, Tucson AZ 85710, USA

Money, Ken — Astronaut, Canada
D C I E M, 1133 Sheppard Ave W, #2000, Downsview ON M3M 3B9, Canada

Monger, Christopher — Director
I C M Partners, 10250 Constellation Blvd, #900, Los Angeles CA 90067 USA

Monger, Matthew L (Matt) — Football Player
10219 S Canton Ave, Tulsa OK 74137, USA

Monheit, Jane — Singer, Songwriter
N-Coded Music/Warlock Records, 126 5th Ave, #200, New York NY 10011, USA

Monica — Singer
Spirit Media, PO Box 43591, Phoenix AZ 85080, USA

Mo'Nique — Actress, Comedienne
Spectrum Talent Agency, 520 W 43rd St, New York NY 10036, USA

Moniz, Wendy — Actress
Innovative Artists, 1505 10th St, Santa Monica CA 90401 USA

Monk, Arthur (Art) — Football Player, Sportscaster
10896 Lake Windemere Dr, Great Falls VA 22066, USA

Monk, Debra — Actress, Singer
Gage Group, 315 W 57th St, #4H, New York NY 10019 USA

Monk, Meredith J — Choreographer, Composer
228 W Broadway, New York NY 10013, USA

Monk, Sophie — Singer, Actress
A P A Talent/Literary Agency, 405 S Beverly Dr, #300, Beverly Hills CA 90212 USA

Monninger, Nikki — Bassist, Singer (Silversun Pickups)
Ink Tank Public Relations, 1825 W Sunset Blvd, #102, Los Angeles CA 90026, USA

Monoharova, Taitana — Opera Singer
I M G Artists, Hogarth Business Park, Chiswick, London W4 2TH, England

Monoson, Lawrence — Actor
Ovation Mgmt, 12028 National Blvd, Los Angeles CA 90064, USA

Monroe, Ashley — Singer, Songwriter
Spalding Entertainment, 1025 16th Ave, #303, Nashville TN 30312, USA

Monroe, Craig K — Baseball Player
4123 Lynn Dr, Texarkana TX 75503, USA

Monroe, Jordan — Model
Playboy Promotions, 2706 Media Center Dr, Los Angeles CA 90065 USA

Monroe, Kimber — Actress
1230 N Horn, #728, West Hollywood CA 90069, USA

Monroe, Lawrence J (Larry) — Baseball Player
725 N Hundley St, Hoffman Estates IL 60169, USA

Monroe, Maika — Actress
W M E Entertainment, 9601 Wilshire Blvd, #300, Beverly Hills CA 90210 USA

Monroe, Meredith — Actress
Abrams Artists, 9200 W Sunset Blvd, #1125, West Hollywood CA 90069 USA

Monroe, Mircea — Actress
Innovative Artists, 1505 10th St, Santa Monica CA 90401 USA

Monroe, V Earl (Pearl) — Basketball Player
1925 Adam Clayton Powell Jr Blvd, #6D, New York NY 10026, USA

Monroe, Zachary C (Zach) 1 Sandalwood Lane, Bartonville IL 61607, USA	Baseball Player
Monson, Dan California State University, Athletic Dept, Long Beach CA 90840, USA	Basketball Coach
Monson, Thomas S Church of Latter-Day Saints, 47 E South Temple, Salt Lake City UT 84150, USA	Religious Leader
Montador, Steve 5857 NW 122nd Terrace, Coral Springs FL 33076, USA	Ice Hockey Player
Montag, Heidi Innovator Mgmt, 8899 Beverly Blvd, #622, Los Angeles CA 90048, USA	Actress, Singer, Model
Montagnier, Luc World AIDS Research Foundation, Castello 4930, 30122 Venice, Italy	Nobel Medicine Laureate
Montague, Diana 91 Saint Martin's Lane, London WC2, England	Opera Singer
Montague, Emily TalentWorks, 3500 W Olive Ave, #1400, Burbank CA 91505 USA	Actress
Montague, John E 52 Northshore Circle, Dadeville AL 36853, USA	Baseball Player
Montaigne, Lawrence 1827 Morganton Dr, Henderson NV 89052, USA	Actor
Montalbano, Chuck 4725 Farmdale Ave, North Hollywood CA 91602, USA	Golfer
Montana, Claude 131 Rue Saint-Denis, 75001 Paris, France	Fashion Designer
Montana, Joseph C (Joe), Jr 9010 Franz Valley Road, Calistoga CA 94515, USA	Football Player
Montana, Manny S D B Partners, 1801 Ave of Stars, #902, Los Angeles CA 90067 USA	Actor
Montanaro, Carlo I M G Artists, Hogarth Business Park, Chiswick, London W4 2TH, England	Conductor
Montanez, Guillermo N (Willie) HC 5 Box 52020, Caguas PR 00725, USA	Baseball Player
Montefusco, John J 1 Oakdale Dr, Middletown NJ 07748, USA	Baseball Player
Monteith, Hank 35 William St, Stratford ON N5A 4X9, Canada	Ice Hockey Player
Monteith, Kelly PO Box 11669, Knoxville TN 37939, USA	Actor, Comedian
Montelone, Richard (Rich) 441 Lucerne Ave, Tampa FL 33606, USA	Baseball Player
Monterey, Judi Playboy Promotions, 2706 Media Center Dr, Los Angeles CA 90065 USA	Model
Montero, Gabriela I M G Artists, Hogarth Business Park, Chiswick, London W4 2TH, England	Concert Pianist
Montero, Miguel A Arizona Diamondbacks, Chase Field, 401 E Jefferson, Phoenix AZ 85003 USA	Baseball Player
Montero, Pablo Televisa, Blvd A Lopez Mateos 232, Colonia San Angel, DF CP 01060, Mexico	Singer, Actor
Montes, Marisa E M I Records, 150 5th Ave, #700, New York NY 10011 USA	Singer, Guitarist
Montevecchi, Liliane Fifi Oscard, 110 W 40th St, #1601, New York NY 10018, USA	Singer, Actress, Dancer
Monteverde, Alejandro Gomez Metanoia Films, 2950 Los Feliz Blvd, #204, Los Angeles CA 90039, USA	Writer, Director, Producer
Montez, Chris Mars Talent, 27 L'Ambiance Court, Nanuet NY 10954 USA	Singer
Montgomerie, Colin S International Mgmt Group, Pier House, Strand on the Green, London W4 3NN, England	Golfer
Montgomery, Alton 441 N 9th St, Griffin GA 30223, USA	Football Player
Montgomery, Anne ESPN-TV, ESPN Plaza, 935 Middle St, Bristol CT 06010 USA	Sportscaster
Montgomery, Belinda Epstein-Wyckoff, 280 S Beverly Dr, #400, Beverly Hills CA 90212 USA	Actress
Montgomery, Chuck Don Buchwald/Fortitude, 6500 Wilshire Blvd, #2200, Los Angeles CA 90048 USA	Actor
Montgomery, Cleotha (Cleo) 1801 Crape Myrtle Circle, Irving TX 75063, USA	Football Player
Montgomery, D Lamont (Monty) 3011 Pecan Way Court, Richmond TX 77406, USA	Football Player
Montgomery, Eddie Parallel Entertainment, 209 10th Ave S, #506, Nashville TN 37203, USA	Singer (Montgomery Gentry)
Montgomery, Gregory H (Greg), Jr 2112 Brentwood Dr, Baton Rouge LA 70809, USA	Football Player
Montgomery, J Michael (Mike) 4224 High Star Lane, Dallas TX 75287, USA	Football Player
Montgomery, James P (Jim) 1537 Bella Vista Dr, Dallas TX 75218, USA	Swimmer, Coach
Montgomery, Janet Hamilton Hodell, 66-68 Margaret St, London W1W 8SR, England	Actress
Montgomery, Jeffrey T (Jeff) 3701 W 140th St, Overland Park KS 66224, USA	Baseball Player
Montgomery, Jim Rensselaer Polytechnic Institute, Athletic Dept, 110 8th St, Troy NY 12180, USA	Ice Hockey Player
Montgomery, John Michael Average Joe's Entertainment Group, 209 10th Ave S, #337, Nashville TN 37203, USA	Singer
Montgomery, Kevin Brooks Murphy Stevens, 5619 N Lankershim Blvd, North Hollywood CA 91601 USA	Actor
Montgomery, Marvin J (Marv) 1509 S Macon St, Aurora CO 80012, USA	Football Player
Montgomery, Melba Billy Deaton Talent, 1214 16th Ave S, Nashville TN 37212 USA	Singer
Montgomery, Mike University of California, Athletic Dept, Berkeley CA 94720, USA	Basketball Coach
Montgomery, Monty B 807 Corn Tassel Trail, Martinsville VA 24112, USA	Baseball Player

Montgomery, Poppy — Actress
United Talent Agency, 9336 Civic Center Dr, Beverly Hills CA 90210 USA

Montgomery, Robert A — Surgeon
Johns Hopkins University Medical Center, Transplantation Center, Baltimore MD 21218, USA

Montgomery, Robert E (Bob) — Baseball Player
2 Parkway Dr, Saugus MA 01906, USA

Montgomery, Steven L (Steve) — Baseball Player
13731 Mercado Dr, Del Mar CA 92014, USA

Montgomery, Sy — Writer
Ballatine Books, 1745 Broadway, New York NY 10019 USA

Montgomery, Wilbert N — Football Player
3116 Fox Valley Dr, West Friendship MD 21794, USA

Monti, Mario — Prime Minister, Italy
Prime Minister's Office, Palazzo Chigi, Piazza Colonna 370, 00187 Rome, Italy

Montiel, Dito — Director, Writer
Underground Films & Mgmt, 447 S Highland Ave, Los Angeles CA 90036, USA

Montler, Michael R (Mike) — Football Player
479 Tiara Vista Dr, Grand Junction CO 81507, USA

Montminy, Marc R — Neurochemist
Salk Institute, 10100 N Torrey Pines Road, La Jolla CA 92037 USA

Montoya, Craig — Bassist (Everclear)
Pinnacle Entertainment, 30 Glenn St, White Plains NY 10603, USA

Montoya, Juan — Interior Designer
330 E 59th St, #200, New York NY 10022, USA

Montoya, Juan Pablo — Auto Racing Driver
Earnhardt Ganassi Racing, 8500 Westmoreland Dr, Concord NC 28027, USA

Montoya, Max, Jr — Football Player
2110 Williams Road, Hebron KY 41048, USA

Montoyo, Jose Carlos (Charlie) — Baseball Player
438 Summer Sails Dr, Valrico FL 33594, USA

Montross, Eric S — Basketball Player
4668 S NC Highway 150, Lexington NC 27295, USA

Montsho Este — Rap Artist (Arrested Development)
Agency Group Ltd, 142 W 57th St, #600, New York NY 10019 USA

Montvidas, Edgaras — Opera Singer
Maxine Robertson Mgmt, 14 Forge Dr, Claygate KT1O 0HR, England

Montville, Leigh — Sportswriter
I C M Partners, 10250 Constellation Blvd, #900, Los Angeles CA 90067 USA

Monty, Peter C (Pete) — Football Player
PO Box 338, Wellington CO 80549, USA

Moock, Joseph G (Joe) — Baseball Player
12432 Pecos Ave, Greenwell Springs LA 70739, USA

Moodie, Janice — Golfer
19746 Woodchase Circle, Orlando FL 32836, USA

Moody, Eric — Baseball Player
336 Gleneagle Circle, Irmo SC 29063, USA

Moody, Keith M — Football Player
4632 Riverview Court, Tracy CA 95377, USA

Moody, Lynne — Actress
Gersh Agency, 9465 Wilshire Blvd, #600, Beverly Hills CA 90212 USA

Moody, Ron — Actor
Ingleside, 41 The Green, Southgate, London N14, England

Moody-Luckhurst, Teri — Golfer
103 Pierrepont Isle, Duluth GA 30097, USA

Moog, Andy — Ice Hockey Player
530 Rolling Hills Road, Coppell TX 75019, USA

Moomaw, Donn D — Football Player
3124 Corda Dr, Los Angeles CA 90049, USA

Moon, Elizabeth — Writer
Jabberwocky Literary Agency, PO Box 4558, Sunnyside NY 11104, USA

Moon, H Warren — Football Player
Seattle Seahawks, 12 Seahawks Way, Renton WA 98056 USA

Moon, Jamario R — Basketball Player
Charlotte Bobcats, 333 E Trade St, #A, Charlotte NC 28202 USA

Moon, Philip — Actor
Don Buchwald/Fortitude, 6500 Wilshire Blvd, #2200, Los Angeles CA 90048 USA

Moon, Sheri — Actress
Dimension Films, 345 Hudson St, #1300, New York NY 10014, USA

Moon, Wallace W (Wally) — Baseball Player
3801 E Crest Dr, #6401, Bryan TX 77802, USA

Mooney, Beth E — Businesswoman
KeyCorp, 127 Public Square, Cleveland OH 44114, USA

Mooney, Debra — Actress
Principal Entertainment, 1964 Westwood Blvd, #400, Los Angeles CA 90025 USA

Mooney, Edward K (Ed) — Football Player
4105 63rd St, Lubbock TX 79413, USA

Mooney, John — Singer, Guitarist
Intrepid Artists, Midtown Plaza, 1300 Baxter St, #405, Charlotte NC 28204, USA

Mooney, John J — Inventor (3-Way Catalytic Converter)
85 Colgate Ave, Wyckoff NJ 07481, USA

Mooneyham, William C (Bill) — Baseball Player
5731 White Crane Road, Atwater CA 95301, USA

Moonves, Leslie — Businessman, Producer
Columbia Broadcasting System Inc, 7800 Beverly Blvd, Los Angeles CA 90036, USA

Moore, Abra — Singer
Leslie Turner Mgmt, PO Box 60053, Nashville TN 37206, USA

Moore, Alan — Cartoonist, Writer
Top Shelf, PO Box 1282, Marietta GA 30061, USA

Moore, Alvin — Football Player
1111 W Lark Dr, Chandler AZ 85286, USA

Moore, Alvin E (Junior) — Baseball Player
3728 Wall Ave, Richmond CA 94804, USA

Moore, Andre M — Basketball Player
12137 S Justine St, Chicago IL 60643, USA

Moore, Angelo C — Singer, Saxophonist (Fishbone)
Silverback Mgmt, 9469 Jefferson Blvd, #101, Culver City CA 90232, USA

Moore, Ann S — Publisher
Time-Life, Chairwoman's Office, Time-Life Building, New York NY 10020, USA
Moore, Archie F — Baseball Player
201 Courtland Road, Indiana PA 15701, USA
Moore, Balor L — Baseball Player
6301 Almeda Road, #717, Houston TX 77021, USA
Moore, Barbara — Actress, Model
Playboy Promotions, 2706 Media Center Dr, Los Angeles CA 90065 USA
Moore, Benjamin P — Artist
3123 39th Place S, Seattle WA 98144, USA
Moore, Billie — Basketball Coach
2247 Meadow Lane, Fullerton CA 92831, USA
Moore, Bradley A (Brad) — Baseball Player
3135 Challenger Point Dr, Loveland CO 80538, USA
Moore, Brandon — Football Player
Enter-Sports Mgmt, 5 Concourse Parkway, #3000, Atlanta GA 30328, USA
Moore, Calvin C — Mathematician
1408 Eagle Pointe Court, Lafayette CA 94549, USA
Moore, Chante — Singer, Songwriter
Creative Artists Agency, 2000 Ave of Stars, #100, Los Angeles CA 90067 USA
Moore, Charles W (Charlie) — Baseball Player
342 County Road 276, Cullman AL 35057, USA
Moore, Charles, Jr — Track Athlete
10 Barclay St, #39C, New York NY 10007, USA
Moore, Chris — Producer, Director, Actor
Hansen Jacobson Teller, 450 N Roxbury Dr, #800, Beverly Hills CA 90210 USA
Moore, Christina — Actress
C E S D, 10635 Santa Monica Blvd, #130, Los Angeles CA 90025 USA
Moore, Clinton R (Mikki) — Basketball Player
Golden State Warriors, 1011 Broadway, Oakland CA 94605 USA
Moore, Corey A — Football Player
Cincinnati Bengals, 1 Paul Brown Stadium, Cincinnati OH 45202 USA
Moore, Corwin — Writer, Actor
Creative Artists Agency, 2000 Ave of Stars, #100, Los Angeles CA 90067 USA
Moore, David E (Dave) — Football Player
PO Box 174, Macon NC 27551, USA
Moore, Demi — Actress
Creative Artists Agency, 2000 Ave of Stars, #100, Los Angeles CA 90067 USA
Moore, Dick — Cartoonist (Our Gang)
Dick Moore Assoc, 1560 Broadway, New York NY 10036, USA
Moore, Dylan — Actress
Stone Manners Salners, 9911 W Pico Blvd, #1400, Los Angeles CA 90035 USA
Moore, E McNeil — Football Player
1212 Woodlawn Dr, Center TX 75935, USA
Moore, Eric P — Football Player
2225 Lindsay Lane, Florissant MO 63031, USA
Moore, Ezekiel (Zeke), Jr — Football Player
3422 Prudence Court, Houston TX 77045, USA
Moore, Gary D — Baseball Player
7985 Roundrock Road, Dallas TX 75248, USA
Moore, Geoff — Singer, Songwriter
United Talent Agency, 9336 Civic Center Dr, Beverly Hills CA 90210 USA
Moore, Gerald H (Jerry) — Football Coach
Appalachian State University, Athletic Dept, Boone NC 28608, USA
Moore, Harold G (Hal) — Army General, Writer, Hero
585 Moores Mill Road, Auburn AL 36830, USA
Moore, Herman J — Football Player
3160 Fallen Oaks Court, #605, Rochester Hills MI 48309, USA
Moore, Jackie — Singer
T-Best Talent Agency, 508 Honey Lake Court, Danville CA 94506 USA
Moore, Jackie S — Baseball Player, Manager
2721 Laurel Valley Lane, Arlington TX 76006, USA
Moore, James — Baseball Player
2624 Abner Place NW, Atlanta GA 30318, USA
Moore, James E, Jr — Army General
18940 Joaquin Court, Salinas CA 93908, USA
Moore, Jason — Director
W M E Entertainment, 9601 Wilshire Blvd, #300, Beverly Hills CA 90210 USA
Moore, Joel David — Actor
I C M Partners, 10250 Constellation Blvd, #900, Los Angeles CA 90067 USA
Moore, Jonathan Patrick — Actor
Management 360, 9111 Wilshire Blvd, Beverly Hills CA 90210 USA
Moore, Josh — Keyboardist (Caedmon's Call)
Breen Agency, 25 Music Square W, Nashville TN 37203, USA
Moore, Joshua Logan — Actor
Innovative Artists, 1505 10th St, Santa Monica CA 90401 USA
Moore, Julianne — Actress, Model
Management 360, 9111 Wilshire Blvd, Beverly Hills CA 90210 USA
Moore, Kellen — Football Player
Detroit Lions, 222 Republic Dr, Allen Park MI 48101 USA
Moore, Kelvin O — Baseball Player
75 Stoney Point Terrace, Covington GA 30014, USA
Moore, Langston — Football Player
1022 W Estrella Dr, Chandler AZ 85224, USA
Moore, Leonard E (Lenny) — Football Player
8815 Stonehaven Road, Randallstown MD 21133, USA
Moore, LeRoy M — Football Player
24 Mary Day Ave, Pontiac MI 48341, USA
Moore, Loree — Basketball Player
New York Liberty, Madison Square Garden, 2 Penn Plaza, New York NY 10121 USA
Moore, Lorrie — Writer
University of Wisconsin, English Dept, Madison WI 53706, USA
Moore, Lucille — Baseball Player
6450 Miami Circle, South Bend IN 46614, USA
Moore, Mandy — Singer, Actress, Model
Storefront Entertainment, 528 1/2 N San Vicente Blvd, West Hollywood CA 90048, USA

M

Moore - Moore

Moore, Marcus R — Baseball Player
254 Warren Way, Pittsburg CA 94565, USA

Moore, Mary — Baseball Player
4225 Lake Grove Court, White Lake MI 48383, USA

Moore, Mary Tyler — Actress
510 E 86th St, #21A, New York NY 10028, USA

Moore, Maulty J — Football Player
5781 S Sable Circle, Margate FL 33063, USA

Moore, Maya A — Basketball Player
Minnesota Lynx, Target Center, 600 1st Ave N, Minneapolis MN 55403 USA

Moore, Melanie Deanne — Actress
James/Levy Mgmt, 3500 W Olive Ave, #1470, Burbank CA 91505 USA

Moore, Melba — Singer, Actress
Greg Purcott Productions, PO Box 276005, Boca Raton FL 33427, USA

Moore, Melissa Anne — Actress
PO Box 55, Versailles KY 40383, USA

Moore, Mewelde J C — Football Player
6345 Riverine Dr, Baton Rouge LA 70820, USA

Moore, Michael (Mike) — Attorney
Attorney General's Office, PO Box 220, Jackson MS 39205, USA

Moore, Michael F — Director
Dog Eat Dog Films, 430 W 14th St, #401, New York NY 10014, USA

Moore, Michael W (Mike) — Baseball Player
1472 E Calle de Caballos, Tempe AZ 85284, USA

Moore, Nathaniel (Nat) — Football Player
Nat Moore Assoc, 16911 NE 6th Ave, North Miami Beach FL 33162, USA

Moore, Patrick — Astronomer, Writer
Farthings, 39 West St, Selsey, Sussex PO20 9AAD, England

Moore, Patrick — Golfer
4638 E Dartmouth St, Mesa AZ 85205, USA

Moore, R Barry — Baseball Player
6702 Conifer Circle, Indian Trail NC 28079, USA

Moore, Red — Baseball Player
2450 Perry Blvd NW, Atlanta GA 30318, USA

Moore, Richard W (Dickie) — Ice Hockey Player
4955 Chemin Saint Francois, Saint Laurent QC H4S 1P3, Canada

Moore, Robert A — Football Player
1906 E Gate Dr, Stone Mountain GA 30087, USA

Moore, Robert D (Bob) — Baseball Player
1641 Chelsea Road, Palos Verdes Estates CA 90274, USA

Moore, Robert R (Bob) — Football Player
20 Sally Ann Road, Orinda CA 94563, USA

Moore, Robert S (Rob) — Football Player
14239 S 8th St, Phoenix AZ 85048, USA

Moore, Robert V (Bobby) — Baseball Player
3703 Hyde Park Ave, Cincinnati OH 45209, USA

Moore, Roger — Actor
Diamond Mgmt, 31 Percy St, London W1T 2DD, England

Moore, Ronald L (Ron) — Football Player
5730 N Oakwood St, Spencer TX 73084, USA

Moore, Samuel D (Sam) — Singer (Sam & Dave)
I'ma Da Wife Enterprises, 7119 E Shea Blvd, #109-436, Scottsdale AZ 85254, USA

Moore, Scott A — Baseball Player
Baltimore Orioles, Oriole Park, 333 W Camden St, Baltimore MD 21201 USA

Moore, Shemar — Actor
Innovative Artists, 1505 10th St, Santa Monica CA 90401 USA

Moore, Stephen — Actor
Markham & Froggatt, Julian House, 4 Windmill St, London W1P 1HF, England

Moore, Stephen Campbell — Actor
Untitled Entertainment, 350 S Beverly Dr, #200, Beverly Hills CA 90212 USA

Moore, Thomas — Writer
Harper/Collins Publishers, 10 E 53rd St, Cellar 1, New York NY 10022, USA

Moore, Thomas M (Tom) — Football Player
1038 Forest Harbor Dr, Hendersonville TN 37075, USA

Moore, Thurston — Singer, Guitarist (Sonic Youth)
Silva Artist Mgmt, 722 Seward St, Los Angeles CA 90038, USA

Moore, Tracy L — Basketball Player
12116 E 37th Place, Tulsa OK 74146, USA

Moore, Trevor P — Actor, Comedian, Writer, Director
Creative Artists Agency, 2000 Ave of Stars, #100, Los Angeles CA 90067 USA

Moore, Warren N (Trey) — Baseball Player
5128 Bellerive Bend Dr, College Station TX 77845, USA

Moorehead, Aaron M — Football Player
725 Cowper St, #36, Palo Alto CA 94301, USA

Moorehead, Emery M — Football Player
1005 Sussex Dr, Northbrook IL 60062, USA

Moorehead, Kindal J — Football Player
10011 Montrose Dr, Charlotte NC 28269, USA

Moorer, Allison — Singer, Songwriter, Actress
Deep South Entertainment, 188 Wind Chime Court, #104, Raleigh, NC 27615, USA

Moore-Warner, Eleanor — Baseball Player
2172 Kinney Ave NW, Grand Rapids MI 49534, USA

Moore-Watkins, Pauline — Actress
4077 SW Sunset Dr, #202, Lake Oswego OR 97035, USA

Moorhouse, Jocelyn — Director, Producer, Writer
Creative Artists Agency, 2000 Ave of Stars, #100, Los Angeles CA 90067 USA

Moorman, Brian D — Football Player
4 Woodbine Court, Orchard Park NY 14127, USA

Moorman, Maurice F (Mo), Jr — Football Player
9641 Shelbyville Road, Simpsonville KY 40067, USA

Mora Gramunt, Gabriel — Architect
Mora-Sanvisens Arquitectes, 24 Herzegovina, Pal 1, 08006 Barcelona 08006, Spain

Mora, Gene — Cartoonist (Graffiti)
United Feature Syndicate, PO Box 5610, Cincinnati OH 45201 USA

Mora, James L (Jim), Jr — Football Coach
University of California, Athletic Dept, Los Angeles CA 90024, USA

Mora, Melvin — Baseball Player
2316 Willow Vale Dr, Fallston MD 21047, USA
Mora, Naima — Model
Ford Models Inc, 111 5th Ave, #900, New York NY 10003 USA
Morabito, Timothy R (Tim) — Football Player
98 Myrtle Ave, Edgewater NJ 07020, USA
Moraes, Adrian — Rodeo Bull Rider
Professional Bull Riders Assn, 6 S Tejon St, #700, Colorado Springs CO 80903, USA
Moraga, David — Baseball Player
608 Peach Court, Fairfield CA 94534, USA
Morahan, Christopher T — Director
Highcombe, Devil's Punchbowl, Thursley, Godalming, Surrey GU8 6NS, England
Morales Ayma, Juan Evo — President, Bolivia
President's Office, Palacio de Gobierno, Plaza Murilla, La Paz, Bolivia
Morales Elvira, Erik I — Boxer
Miguel Diaz, 9483 Bondeno St, Las Vegas NV 89123, USA
Morales Hernandez, Jose M — Baseball Player
PO Box 770985, Winter Garden FL 34777, USA
Morales, Esai — Actor
Innovative Artists, 1505 10th St, Santa Monica CA 90401 USA
Morales, P Pablo — Swimmer
University of Nebraska, Athletic Dept, Lincoln NE 68588, USA
Morales, Richard A (Rich) — Baseball Player
1650 Rosita Road, Pacifica CA 94044, USA
Morales-Rhodes, Natalie L — Actress, Producer, Commentator
United Talent Agency, 9336 Civic Center Dr, Beverly Hills CA 90210 USA
Moran, Erin — Actress
The Agency, 3711 Ocean Front Walk, #1, Marina del Rey CA 90292 USA
Moran, Ian — Ice Hockey Player
427 Bay Road, Duxbury MA 02332, USA
Moran, J Kevin — Navy Admiral
Investor Relations Group, 11 Stone St, #300, New York NY 10003, USA
Moran, Jason — Jazz Pianist
Vision Arts Mgmt, 16 Clintfinger Road, Saugerties NY 12477, USA
Moran, Julie — Sportscaster, Actress
Creative Artists Agency, 2000 Ave of Stars, #100, Los Angeles CA 90067 USA
Moran, Nick — Actor, Director
Ken McReddie Assoc, 11 Connaught Place, London W2 2ET, England
Moran, R Alan (Al) — Baseball Player
34134 Banbury St, Farmington Hills MI 48331, USA
Moran, Richard J (Rich) — Football Player
7252 Mimosa Dr, Carlsbad CA 92011, USA
Moran, Sean F — Football Player
13577 W 84th Dr, Arvada CO 80005, USA
Moran, Terry — Commentator
ABC-TV, News Dept, 77 W 66th St, New York NY 10023 USA
Moran, Thomas L (Tommy) — Producer, Writer
Creative Artists Agency, 2000 Ave of Stars, #100, Los Angeles CA 90067 USA
Moran, William N (Billy) — Baseball Player
PO Box 82, Luthersville GA 30251, USA
Morandi, Piergiorgio — Conductor
I M G Artists, Hogarth Business Park, Chiswick, London W4 2TH, England
Morandini, Michael R (Mickey) — Baseball Player
242 Crabapple Lane, Valparaiso IN 46383, USA
Moranis, Rick — Actor, Comedian
Bailey Brand Mgmt, 506 Santa Monica Blvd, #327, Santa Monica CA 90401, USA
Morano Walker, Reed — Cinematographer
Gersh Agency, 9465 Wilshire Blvd, #600, Beverly Hills CA 90212 USA
Morante, Laura — Actress
Media Art Mgmt, C/ Castelló 82, 2 Derecha, 28006 Madrid, Spain
Morariu, Ana Caterina — Actress
Cristiano Cucchini Mgmt, Lungotevere dei Mellini 10, 00193 Rome, Italy
Morath, Max — Singer
Producers Inc, 11806 N 56th St, Tampa FL 33617 USA
Moravcik, Jozef — Prime Minister, Slovakia
Primacialne Ham 1, Box 192, 81422 Bratislava, Slovakia
Moravec, Ivan — Concert Pianist
Pod Vyhidkou 520, 160 00 Prague 6, Czech Republic
Morawetz, Cathleen S — Mathematician
251 Mercer St, New York NY 10012, USA
Morbito, Paul — Guitarist (Chesterfield Kings)
Agency Group Ltd, 142 W 57th St, #600, New York NY 10019 USA
Morceli, Noureddine — Track Athlete
Youth & Sports Ministry, 3 Rue Mohamed Belouizdad, Algiers, Algeria
Mordecai, Michael H (Mike) — Baseball Player
10 Cross Creek Lane, Dothan AL 36303, USA
Mordente, Tony — Actor, Dancer, Choreographer
31 Bay Harbor Dr, Bigfork MT 59911, USA
Mordkovitch, Lydia — Concert Violinist
25B Belsize Ave, London NW3 3BL, England
More, Camilla — Actress
Sharon Kemp, 477 S Robertson Blvd, #204, Beverly Hills CA 90211 USA
More, Jayson — Ice Hockey Player
9532 Thoroughbred Way, Brentwood TN 37027, USA
More, Michelle — Volleyball Player, Model
Association of Volleyball Professionals, 960 Knox St, #A, Torrance CA 90502 USA
Moreau, Ethan B — Ice Hockey Player
Columbus Blue Jackets, Arena, 200 W Nationwide Blvd, #1, Columbus OH 43215 USA
Moreau, Jeanne — Actress
Artmedia, 20 Ave Rapp, 75007 Paris, France
Morehead, David M (Dave) — Baseball Player
13872 Glenmere Dr, Santa Ana CA 92705, USA
Moreira, Airto — Jazz Percussionist
Universal Attractions, 135 W 26th St, #1200, New York NY 10001 USA
Morel, Eric — Boxer
7119 Tree Lane, Madison WI 53717, USA

M

Morel, Francois — Composer, Conductor, Concert Pianist
Laval University, 1055 Av du Seminaire, Quebec PQ G1V 0A6, Canada
Morel, Pierre — Director, Cinematographer
Sentient Entertainment, 1617 Broadway, Mezzanine Suite, Santa Monica CA 90404, USA
Moreland, B Keith — Baseball Player
4209 Hidden Canyon Cove, Austin TX 78746, USA
Morell, Michael J — Government Official
Central Intelligence Agency, Director's Office, Washington DC 20505, USA
Morello, Thomas B (Tom) — Singer, Guitarist
G A S Entertainment, 722 Seward St, Los Angeles CA 90038, USA
Moreno, Belita — Actress
Paradigm Agency, 360 N Crescent Dr, North Building, Beverly Hills CA 90210 USA
Moreno, Catalina Sandino — Actress
Principal Entertainment, 1964 Westwood Blvd, #400, Los Angeles CA 90025, USA
Moreno, Chino — Singer, Guitarist (Deftones)
Velvet Hammer Music, 9911 W Pico Blvd, #350, Los Angeles CA 90035, USA
Moreno, Ezekiel A (Zeke) — Football Player
1881 Harris Mill Ave, Chula Vista CA 91913, USA
Moreno, Jorge — Singer
Forward Motion Records, 3456 N Miami Ave, Miami FL 33127, USA
Moreno, Luis Alberto — Financier, Government Official
Inter-America Development Bank, 1300 New York Ave NW, Washington DC 20577, USA
Moreno, Mario — Bassist (Los Tucanes de Tijuana)
Tucanes Inc, 6055 E Washington Blvd, #455, Commerce CA 90040, USA
Moreno, Orber — Baseball Player
4833 Kingston Circle, Kissimmee FL 34746, USA
Moreno, Rita — Actress, Singer
David Belenzon Mgmt, PO Box 1298, La Mesa CA 91944, USA
Moreno, Roberto — Auto Racing Driver
252 Montclaire Circle, Weston FL 33326, USA
Moreno-Ocampo, Luis — Attorney
International Criminal Court, Maanweg 174, 2516 AB, Hague, Netherlands
Morenstein, Harley — Actor, Comedian
Gersh Agency, 9465 Wilshire Blvd, #600, Beverly Hills CA 90212 USA
Moresco, Robert (Bobby) — Producer, Director, Writer, Actor
Moresco Productions, 4231 W National Ave, Burbank CA 91505, USA
Moret, Rogelio (Roger) — Baseball Player
HC 1 Box 5225, Guaynabo PR 00971, USA
Moretti, Fabrizio — Drummer (Strokes)
M V O Ltd, 370 7th Ave, #807, New York NY 10001, USA
Moretz, Chloe — Actress
W M E Entertainment, 9601 Wilshire Blvd, #300, Beverly Hills CA 90210 USA
Morey, Bill — Actor
Kazarian/Spencer/Ruskin, 11969 Ventura Blvd, #300, Studio City CA 91604 USA
Morey, Sean J — Football Player
63 McCosh Circle, Princeton NJ 8540, USA
Morga, Tom — Actor, Stuntman
Stuntmen Assn, 10660 Riverside Dr, #200E, Toluca Lake CA 91602, USA
Morgan, Abi — Writer
Creative Artists Agency, 2000 Ave of Stars, #100, Los Angeles CA 90067 USA
Morgan, Alexandra P (Alex) — Soccer Player
Wasserman Media Group, 10960 Wilshire Blvd, #2200, Los Angeles CA 90024, USA
Morgan, Anthony E — Football Player
10306 Reno Ave, Cleveland OH 44105, USA
Morgan, Barbara R — Astronaut
2996 S Rookery Lane, Boise ID 83706, USA
Morgan, Chad — Actor
S M S Talent, 8383 Wilshire Blvd, #230, Beverly Hills CA 90211 USA
Morgan, Craig — Singer, Guitarist, Songwriter
Neostar Mgmt, 2 S University Dr, #325, Plantation FL 33324, USA
Morgan, Daniel T (Dan), Jr — Football Player
1915 Funny Cide Dr, Waxhaw NC 28173, USA
Morgan, Debbi — Actress
Mitchell K Stubbs Assoc, 8695 W Washington Blvd, #204, Culver City CA 90232 USA
Morgan, Debelah — Singer, Songwriter
D A S Communications, 83 Riverside Dr, New York NY 10024, USA
Morgan, Donald M — Cinematographer
15826 Mayall St, North Hills CA 91343, USA
Morgan, Edmund S — Historian
Yale University Press, 302 Temple St, New Haven, CT 06511, USA
Morgan, Gil — Golfer
PO Box 806, Edmond OK 73083, USA
Morgan, Glen — Director, Producer, Writer
Creative Artists Agency, 2000 Ave of Stars, #100, Los Angeles CA 90067 USA
Morgan, James N — Economist
1217 Bydding Road, Ann Arbor MI 48103, USA
Morgan, Jane — Singer
27740 Pacific Coast Highway, Malibu CA 90265, USA
Morgan, Jaye P — Singer, Actress
1185 La Grange Ave, Newbury Park CA 91320, USA
Morgan, Jeffrey Dean — Actor
United Talent Agency, 9336 Civic Center Dr, Beverly Hills CA 90210 USA
Morgan, John G, Jr — Navy Admiral
Deputy CNO, Operations/Plans/Strategy, HqUSN, Pentagon, Washington DC 20350 USA
Morgan, Joseph — Actor
Richard Konigsberg Mgmt, 400 N Mansfield Ave, Los Angeles CA 90036, USA
Morgan, Joseph L (Joe) — Baseball Player
3523 Country Club Place, Danville CA 94506, USA
Morgan, Joseph M (Joe) — Baseball Player, Manager
15 Oak Hill Dr, Walpole MA 02081, USA
Morgan, Kevin L — Baseball Player
205 Yearling Road, #A, Duson LA 70529, USA
Morgan, Lorrie — Singer
Robert Thomas Agency, 42350 Niagara Dr, Sterling Heights MI 48313, USA
Morgan, Marabel — Writer
Total Woman Inc, 1300 NW 167th St, Miami FL 33169, USA

Morgan, Michael — Geneticist
Wellcome Trust, 183 Euston Road, London NW1 2BE, England

Morgan, Michele — Actress, Singer
Agents Associes C Volte, 201 Faubourg Saint Honore, 75008 Paris, France

Morgan, Mike — Baseball Player
PO Box 681130, Park City UT 84068, USA

Morgan, Mike — Cartoonist (For Heaven's Sake)
Trinity United Methodist Church, 814 West Ave, Cartersville GA 30120, USA

Morgan, Peter — Writer, Director
Independent Talent Group, Oxford House, 76 Oxford St, London W1D 1BS, England

Morgan, Piers — Commentator
CNN-TV, News Dept, 820 1st St NE, #1000, Washington DC 20002 USA

Morgan, Quincy D E — Football Player
2715 Taylorcrest, Missouri City TX 77459, USA

Morgan, Robert B — Senator, NC
PO Box 377, Lillington NC 27546, USA

Morgan, Robert M (Bobby) — Baseball Player
3004 Stoneybrook Road, Oklahoma City OK 73120, USA

Morgan, Robin E — Editor, Writer
Ms Magazine, Editorial Dept, 230 Park Ave, New York NY 10169, USA

Morgan, Shelly Taylor — Actress
Pakula/King, 9229 W Sunset Blvd, #315, West Hollywood CA 90069 USA

Morgan, Stanley D — Football Player
PO Box 383048, Germantown TN 38183, USA

Morgan, Thomas R — Marine Corps General
8105 Haddington Court, Fairfax Station VA 22039, USA

Morgan, Tim — Auto Racing Executive
Morgan-McClure Motorsports, 26502 Newbanks Road, Abingdon VA 24210, USA

Morgan, Tracy — Actor, Comedian
3 Arts Entertainment, 9460 Wilshire Blvd, #700, Beverly Hills CA 90212 USA

Morgan, Trevor — Actor
I F A Talent Agency, 8730 W Sunset Blvd, #490, West Hollywood CA 90069 USA

Morgan, Walter — Golfer
15536 Fishermans Rest Court, Cornelius NC 28031, USA

Morgan, William N — Architect
William Morgan Architects, 220 E Forsyth St, Jacksonville FL 32202, USA

Morganna — Entertainer, Model
PO Box 20281, Columbus OH 43220, USA

Morgenson, Gretchen C — Journalist
New York Times, Editorial Dept, 229 W 43rd St, New York NY 10036 USA

Morgenstern, Joe — Journalist
Wall Street Journal, Editorial Dept, 1 World Financial Center, New York NY 10281 USA

Morgenstern, Julie — Writer
Julie Morgenstern Enterprises, 850 7th Ave, New York NY 10019, USA

Morgenthau, Kramer — Cinematographer
1632 Maltman Ave, Los Angeles CA 90026, USA

Morgenthau, Robert M — Attorney
1085 Park Ave, New York NY 10128, USA

Morhardt, Meredith G (Moe) — Baseball Player
219 Spencer Hill Road, Winsted CT 06098, USA

Mori, Barbara — Actress
Caliber Media, 9229 W Sunset Blvd, #705, West Hollywood CA 90069, USA

Mori, Emanuel (Manny) — President, Miconesia
President's Office, Palikir, Kolonia, Pohnpei FM 96941, Micronesia

Mori, Hanae — Fashion Designer
Veronique de Moussai, 5 Place de l'Alma, 75008 Paris, France

Mori, Riyo — Beauty Queen
Miss Universe Organization, 1370 Ave of Americas, #1600, New York NY 10019 USA

Mori, Yoshiro — Prime Minister, Japan
House of Representatives, 1-7-1 Nagatacho, Chiyoda ku, Tokyo 100 0014, Japan

Morial, Marc H — Social Activist; Mayor, New Orleans
National Urban League, 120 Wall St, #700, New York NY 10005, USA

Moriarty, Erin — Actress
Jordan Gill Dornbaum, 1133 Broadway, #623, New York NY 10010, USA

Moriarty, Laura — Writer
University of Kansas, Lawrence KS 66045 USA

Moriarty, Michael — Actor
Actor International, Via Fosso del Poggio 141, 00189 Rome, Italy

Moriarty, Mike — Baseball Player
5 E Oleander Dr, Mount Laurel NJ 08054, USA

Moriarty, Thomas (Tom), Jr — Football Player
28800 Fairmount Blvd, Cleveland OH 44124, USA

Moriarty-Gentile, Cathy — Actress
Liebman Entertainment, 235 Park Ave S, #1000, New York NY 10003, USA

Moric, Nina — Model, Singer
New York Model Mgmt, 596 Broadway, #701, New York NY 10012 USA

Morillon, Philippe — Army General, France
Ministere de la Defense, 14 Rue Saint-Dominique, 75700 Paris, France

Morin, Catherine — Actress
Artmedia, 20 Ave Rapp, 75007 Paris, France

Morin, James C (Jim) — Editorial Cartoonist
Miami Herald, Editorial Dept, 1 Herald Plaza, Miami FL 33132 USA

Morin, Lee M E — Astronaut
10 Marys Creek Lane, Friendswood TX 77546, USA

Moringstar, Darren — Basketball Player
1515 W Ingomar Road, Pittsburgh PA 15237, USA

Morissette, Alanis — Singer, Songwriter
Creative Artists Agency, 2000 Ave of Stars, #100, Los Angeles CA 90067 USA

Moritz, Louisa — Actress
405 S Cliffwood Ave, Los Angeles CA 90049, USA

Moriyama, Raymond — Architect
32 Davenport Road, Toronto ON M5R 1H3, Canada

Mork, Truis — Concert Cellist
Harrison/Parrott, 5-6 Albion Court, London W6 0QT, England

Morkis, Dorothy — Equestrian
17 Farm St, Dover MA 02030, USA

Morlan, John G — Baseball Player
3290 Belgreen St, Grove City OH 43123, USA
Morland, David — Golfer
5531 Oxford Moor Blvd, Windermere FL 34786, USA
Morley, Joanne — Golfer
I M G, Pier House, Strand-on-the-Green, Chiswick, London W4 3NN England
Morley, Lawrence W — Geophysicist
90 Hemlock St, Saint Thomas ON N5R 1X9, Canada
Morley, Malcolm — Artist, Sculptor
Sperone Westwater, 415 W 13th St, #200, New York NY 10014, USA
Morman, Alvin — Baseball Player
117 Philadelphia Dr, Rockingham NC 28379, USA
Morman, Russell L (Russ) — Baseball Player
3209 S Mark Twain Ave, Blue Springs MO 64015, USA
Mornas, Pierre-Olivier — Actor
Art 7, 11 Rue Du Bouloi, 75001 Paris, France
Morneau, Justin E G — Baseball Player
1829 Forestview Lane N, Minneapolis MN 55441, USA
Moroder, Giorgio — Composer
Soundtrack Music Assoc, 1460 4th St, #308, Santa Monica CA 90401 USA
Moronko, Jeffrey R (Jeff) — Baseball Player
3903 Bartons Court, Sugar Land TX 77479, USA
Moroski, Michael H (Mike) — Football Player
1214 Pine Lane, Davis CA 95616, USA
Morozov, Akeksei A — Ice Hockey Player
Pittsburgh Penguins, Consol Energy Center, 1001 5th Ave, Pittsburgh PA 15219 USA
Morozov, Vladimir M — Opera Singer
Kirov Ballet Theater, 1 Pl Iskusstr, 190000 Saint Petersburg, Russia
Morrall, Earl E — Football Player
2751 68th St SW, Naples FL 34105, USA
Morrell, David — Writer, Producer
United Talent Agency, 9336 Civic Center Dr, Beverly Hills CA 90210 USA
Morricone, Andrea — Composer
Gorfaine/Schwartz, 4111 W Alameda Ave, #509, Burbank CA 91505 USA
Morricone, Ennio — Composer
Viale della Letterature, #30, 00144 Rome, Italy
Morris, Betty — Bowler
2169 Donovan Dr, Lincoln CA 95648, USA
Morris, Byron (Bam) — Football Player
251 NE 4th St, Cooper TX 75432, USA
Morris, Carol — Beauty Queen
Miss Universe Organization, 1370 Ave of Americas, #1600, New York NY 10019 USA
Morris, Christopher V (Chris) — Basketball Player
3097 Milford Chase SW, Marietta GA 30008, USA
Morris, Danny W — Baseball Player
802 E Main St, Petersburg IN 47567, USA
Morris, Derek — Ice Hockey Player
9820 E Thompson Peak Parkway, #718, Scottsdale AZ 85255, USA
Morris, Doug — Businessman
Universal Music Group, 100 Universal City Plaza, Universal City CA 91608, USA
Morris, Edmund — Writer, Educator
222 Central Park S, #14A, New York NY 10019, USA
Morris, Errol — Director
W M E Entertainment, 9601 Wilshire Blvd, #300, Beverly Hills CA 90210 USA
Morris, Eugene E (Mercury) — Football Player
11315 SW 243rd Terrace, Homestead FL 33032, USA
Morris, Garrett — Actor, Singer
Agency Group, 9348 Civic Center Dr, #200, Beverly Hills CA 90210 USA
Morris, Gary — Singer
Gurley Co, PO Box 150657, Nashville TN 37215 USA
Morris, Iain — Writer
Creative Artists Agency, 2000 Ave of Stars, #100, Los Angeles CA 90067 USA
Morris, Isaiah — Basketball Player
4308 W Cermak Road, Chicago IL 60623, USA
Morris, James P — Opera Singer
Columbia Artists Mgmt Inc, 1790 Broadway, #702, New York NY 10019 USA
Morris, James S (Jim) — Baseball Player
2216 Rock Creek Dr, Kerrville TX 78028, USA
Morris, James T — Government Official
World Food Programme, Via Cesare Giulio Viola 68, 00148 Rome, Italy
Morris, Jan — Writer
Trefan Morys, Llanystumdwy, Criccieth, Gwynedd LL52 0LP, Wales
Morris, Jason N — Judo Athlete
575 Swaggertown Road, Schenectady NY 12302, USA
Morris, Jay Hunter — Opera Singer
I M G Artists, 152 W 57th St, #500, New York NY 10019 USA
Morris, Jenny — Singer
Artist & Event Mgmt, PO Box 537, Randwick NSW 2031, Australia
Morris, Jessica — Actress
Michael Bruno Group, 13576 Cheltenham Dr, Sherman Oaks CA 91423, USA
Morris, John — Curling Athlete
Curling Assn, 1660 Vimont Court, Cumberland ON K4A 4J4, Canada
Morris, John C — Neurologist
Memory Diagnostic Center, 4488 Forest Park Ave, Saint Louis MO 63108, USA
Morris, John D — Baseball Player
2645 Elm Dr, North Bellmore NY 11710, USA
Morris, John S (Jack) — Baseball Player
7993 100th St N, Saint Paul MN 55110, USA
Morris, Johnny E — Football Player
753 Shoreline Road, Lake Barrington IL 60010, USA
Morris, Jon — Ice Hockey Player
16 Gail St, Chelmsford MA 01824, USA
Morris, Jon N — Football Player
10 Berkeley Court, Bluffton SC 29910, USA
Morris, Joseph E (Joe) — Football Player
307 Mark Twain Way, Mahwah NJ 07430, USA

Morris, Julian — Actor
Brillstein Entertainment Partners, 9150 Wilshire Blvd, #350, Beverly Hills CA 90212 USA
Morris, Kathryn — Actress
Mosiac Media Group, 9200 W Sunset Blvd, #1000, Los Angeles CA 90069 USA
Morris, Keith — Singer (Black Flag, Circle Jerks)
Agency Group, 1880 Century Park E, #711, Los Angeles CA 90067, USA
Morris, Larry — Sculptor
105 N Union St, #4, Alexandria VA 22314, USA
Morris, Lawrence C (Larry) — Football Player
4737 Upper Berkshire Road, Flowery Branch GA 30542, USA
Morris, Marianne — Golfer
4013 Lisa Lane, Middletown OH 45042, USA
Morris, Mark W — Choreographer, Dancer
Mark Morris Dance Group, 3 Lafayette Ave, #504, Brooklyn NY 11217, USA
Morris, Matthew C (Matt) — Baseball Player
397 Old Jupiter Beach Road, Jupiter FL 33477, USA
Morris, Maurice A — Football Player
772 Golden Eagle Dr, Conway SC 29527, USA
Morris, Michael S (Mike) — Football Player
5421 Oriole Dr, Farmington MN 55024, USA
Morris, Nathan — Singer (Boyz II Men)
Selverne Co, 3450 Cahuenga Blvd W, #906, Los Angeles CA 90068, USA
Morris, Oswald (Ossie) — Cinematographer
Holbrook, Church St, Fontmell Magna, Shaftesbury SP7 0NY, England
Morris, Phil — Actor
Innovative Artists, 1505 10th St, Santa Monica CA 90401 USA
Morris, Raheem — Football Coach
Washington Redskins, 21300 Redskin Park Dr, Ashburn VA 20147 USA
Morris, Redmond — Producer
Independent Talent Group, Oxford House, 76 Oxford St, London W1D 1BS, England
Morris, Reginald H — Cinematographer
255 Bambaugh Circle, #308, Scarborough ON M1W 3T6, Canada
Morris, Robert — Sculptor
PO Box 100, Gardiner NY 12525, USA
Morris, Ronald (Ron) — Track Athlete
330 S Reese Place, Burbank CA 91506, USA
Morris, Sarah Jane — Actress
Gersh Agency, 9465 Wilshire Blvd, #600, Beverly Hills CA 90212 USA
Morris, Shellee — Singer (Twister Alley)
6117 Highway 135, Lake City AR 72437, USA
Morris, Trevor — Film Composer
Trevor Morris Studios, 1550 18th St, Santa Monica CA 90404, USA
Morris, W Harold (Hal) — Baseball Player
6138 Payne Stewart Dr, Windermere FL 34786, USA
Morris, Warren R — Baseball Player
1215 Wilshire Dr, Alexandria LA 71303, USA
Morris, Wayna — Singer (Boyz II Men)
Wright Entertainment Group, PO Box 590009, Orlando FL 32859, USA
Morris, Wayne L — Football Player
5715 Old Ox Road, Dallas TX 75241, USA
Morrison, Adam J — Basketball Player
7301 Vista del Mar, #11, Playa del Rey CA 90293, USA
Morrison, Christopher W (Mink) — Director, Writer
I C M Partners, 10250 Constellation Blvd, #900, Los Angeles CA 90067 USA
Morrison, Denise M — Businesswoman
Campbell Soup Co, 1 Campbell Place, Camden NJ 08103, USA
Morrison, Denny — Speed Skater
Speed Skating Canada, 2781 Lancaster Road, #402, Ottawa ON K1B 1A7, Canada
Morrison, Don A — Football Player
10191 FM 512, Wolfe City TX 75496, USA
Morrison, Fred L — Football Player
38189 Greywalls Dr, Murrieta CA 92562, USA
Morrison, Grant — Cartoonist
I C M Partners, 10250 Constellation Blvd, #900, Los Angeles CA 90067 USA
Morrison, Ian (Scotty) — Ice Hockey Executive, Referee
Kennisis Lake, RR 1 PO Box 314, Haliburton ON K0M 1S0, Canada
Morrison, James — Actor
Sutton-Barth Vennari, 145 S Fairfax Ave, #310, Los Angeles CA 90036 USA
Morrison, James — Singer, Songwriter
412 S Pueblo Ave, Ojai CA 93023, USA
Morrison, James F (Jim) — Baseball Player
8715 11th Ave Place NW, Bradenton FL 34209, USA
Morrison, Jennifer — Actress
John Carrabino Mgmt, 5900 Wilshire Blvd, #406, Los Angeles CA 90036 USA
Morrison, Jim — Ice Hockey Player
1 Potts Lane, Port Hope ON L1A 0A4, Canada
Morrison, Kathryn — Model
Playboy Promotions, 2706 Media Center Dr, Los Angeles CA 90065 USA
Morrison, Lew — Ice Hockey Player
406 Souris St, Harntey MB R0M 0X0, Canada
Morrison, Mark — Singer
Atlantic Records, 1290 Ave of Americas, Concourse 3, New York NY 10104 USA
Morrison, Matthew J — Actor
Creative Artists Agency, 2000 Ave of Stars, #100, Los Angeles CA 90067 USA
Morrison, Michael F (Mike) — Basketball Player
113 Rivanna Lane, Greenville SC 29607, USA
Morrison, Phil — Director, Producer
Management 360, 9111 Wilshire Blvd, Beverly Hills CA 90210 USA
Morrison, Shayne — Bassist (Perfect Stranger)
Great American Talent, PO Box 2476, Hendersonville TN 37077, USA
Morrison, Shelley — Actress
Don Gerler, 3349 Cahuenga Blvd W, #1, Los Angeles CA 90068 USA
Morrison, Steven C (Steve) — Football Player
4485 Lake Forest Dr E, Ann Arbor MI 48108, USA
Morrison, Temuera — Actor
Robert Bruce Agency, 218 Richmond, Grey Lynn, Auckland 2, New Zealand

M

Morris - Morrison

Morrison, Tommy — Boxer
Tommy Morrison Children's Foundation, 6801 N Tyler Road, Maize KS 67101, USA
Morrison, Toni — Nobel Literature Laureate
185 Nassau St, Princeton NJ 08542, USA
Morrison, Van — Singer, Guitarist, Songwriter
115A Glenthorne, Hammersmith, London W6 OLJ, England
Morriss, Guy W — Football Player
3825 Cocanougher Road, Perryville KY 40468, USA
Morrissey — Singer, Songwriter
Paradigm Agency, 360 N Crescent Dr, North Building, Beverly Hills CA 90210 USA
Morrissey, David — Actor
Troika, 74 Clerkenwell Road, #300, London EC1M 5QA, England
Morrissey, James M (Jim) — Football Player
48 Fox Trail, Lincolnshire IL 60069, USA
Morrissey, Neil — Actor
Independent Talent Group, Oxford House, 76 Oxford St, London W1D 1BS, England
Morrone, Joe — Soccer Coach
University of Connecticut, Athletic Dept, Storrs Mansfield CT 06269, USA
Morrow, Bobby Joe — Track Athlete
2022 Elmwood Dr, Harlingen TX 78550, USA
Morrow, Brenden — Ice Hockey Player
3528 Centenary Ave, Dallas TX 75225, USA
Morrow, Bruce (Cousin Brucie) — Entertainer
CBS Radio Network, 51 W 52nd St, New York NY 10019, USA
Morrow, Harold, Jr — Football Player
126 Golden Isles Dr, #62A, Hallandale Beach FL 33009, USA
Morrow, Joshua — Actor
Marv Dauer Mgmt, 11661 San Vicente Blvd, #104, Los Angeles CA 90049, USA
Morrow, Kenneth (Ken) — Ice Hockey Player
6732 NW Monticello Dr, Kansas City MO 64152, USA
Morrow, Mari — Actress
C E S D, 10635 Santa Monica Blvd, #130, Los Angeles CA 90025 USA
Morrow, Rob — Actor
Hofflund/Polone, 9465 Wilshire Blvd, #420, Beverly Hills CA 90212 USA
Morrow, Steve — Soccer Coach
F C Dallas, 9200 World Cup Way, #202, Frisco TX 75034 USA
Morse, C Jeremy — Financier
102A Drayton Gardens, London SW10 9RJ, England
Morse, Catherine C (Cathy) — Golfer
6228 Celadon Circle, West Palm Beach FL 33418, USA
Morse, David — Guitarist (Air Supply)
PO Box 3367, Beverly Hills CA 90212, USA
Morse, David — Actor
United Talent Agency, 9336 Civic Center Dr, Beverly Hills CA 90210 USA
Morse, David E — Publisher
Christian Science Monitor, Publisher's Office, 1 Norway St, Boston MA 02136, USA
Morse, F Bradford — Representative, MA
411 E 53rd Ave, #18C, New York NY 10022, USA
Morse, Helen — Actress
International Casting Service, 218 Crown St, #2, Darlinghurst, NSW 2010, Australia
Morse, John P — Golfer
9291 17 Mile Road, Marshall MI 49068, USA
Morse, Michael J (Mike) — Baseball Player
417 NW 97th Ave, Plantation FL 33324, USA
Morse, Robert — Actor
Bauman Redanty Shaul Agency, 5757 Wilshire Blvd, #473, Los Angeles CA 90036 USA
Morse, Steve — Guitarist, Songwriter
Agency Group Ltd, 142 W 57th St, #600, New York NY 10019 USA
Morsi Isa al-Ayyat, Mohammed — President, Egypt
Presidential Palace, Abdin, Qasr El-Nile St, Cairo 002, Egypt
Mort, Cynthia — Writer, Producer, Director
W M E Entertainment, 9601 Wilshire Blvd, #300, Beverly Hills CA 90210 USA
Mortensen, Chris (Mort) — Sportscaster
ESPN-TV, ESPN Plaza, 935 Middle St, Bristol CT 06010 USA
Mortensen, Dale T — Nobel Economics Laureate
Northwestern University, Economics Dept, Evanston IL 60208, USA
Mortensen, Daniel E (Dan) — Rodeo Saddle Bronc Rider
945 Noblewood Dr, Billings MT 59101, USA
Mortensen, Jesper (Junior) — Singer, Guitarist (Junior Senior)
Festival Network Mgmt, 30 Irving Place, #600, New York NY 10003, USA
Mortensen, Viggo — Actor
Rawlings Co, 3933 Patrick Henry Place, Agoura Hills CA 91301, USA
Mortier, Gerard — Director
Kultur Ruhr, Leifhestr 35, 45886 Gelsenkirchen, Germany
Mortier, Koen — Director, Producer, Writer
New School Media, 9229 Sunset Blvd, #301, West Hollywood CA 90069, USA
Mortimer Barrett, Angela — Tennis Player
Oaks, Coombe Hill, Beverly Lane, Kingston on Thames, Surrey, England
Mortimer, Emily — Actress
Independent Talent Group, Oxford House, 76 Oxford St, London W1D 1BS, England
Morton, Bruce A — Commentator
CNN-TV, News Dept, 820 1st St NE, #1000, Washington DC 20002 USA
Morton, Chad A — Football Player
50 State Route 120, East Rutherford NJ 07073, USA
Morton, Euan — Actor, Singer
Innovative Artists, 1505 10th St, Santa Monica CA 90401 USA
Morton, Guy, Jr — Baseball Player
567 Ferndale Ave, Vermillion OH 44089, USA
Morton, Joe — Actor
TalentWorks, 220 E 23rd St, #400, New York NY 10010, USA
Morton, Johnnie J — Football Player
2911 Oakwood Lane, Torrance CA 90505, USA
Morton, Judee — Actress
2386 Sunset Heights Dr, Los Angeles CA 90046, USA
Morton, K Elaine — Model, Actress
PO Box 965, Lahaina HI 96767, USA

M

Morton, Kristopher (Colt) — Baseball Player
3245 Santa Barbara Dr, Wellington FL 33414, USA
Morton, L Craig — Football Player
450 E Strawberry Dr, #1, Mill Valley CA 94941, USA
Morton, Lewis — Producer, Writer
Creative Artists Agency, 2000 Ave of Stars, #100, Los Angeles CA 90067 USA
Morton, Margaret — Curling Athlete
Curling Assn, 14 Donnelly Dr, Bedford MK4 9TU, England
Morton, Mark — Guitarist (Lamb of God)
Entertainment Services, 1000 Main Street Plaza, #303, Voorhees NJ 08043, USA
Morton, Michael D — Football Player
5254 Strike the Gold Lane, Wesley Chapel FL 33544, USA
Morton, Richard — Basketball Player
1111 Gilman Ave, San Francisco CA 94124, USA
Morton, Samantha — Actress
Principato-Young, 9465 Wilshire Blvd, #880, Beverly Hills CA 90212 USA
Mortson, Gus — Ice Hockey Player
Central Gas Ontario, PO Box 1456, Timmins ON P4N 7X4, Canada
Morukov, Boris V — Cosmonaut
Cosmonaut Training Center, Star City, 141160 Zvezdny Gorodok, Moscow Oblast, Russia
Mosby, Bernice — Basketball Player
Washington Mystics, Verizon Center, 401 9th St NW, #750, Washington DC 20004 USA
Moschen, Michael — Juggler
PO Box 178, Cornwall Bridge CT 06754, USA
Moschenko, Sergei I — Cosmonaut
Cosmonaut Training Center, Star City, 141160 Zvezdny Gorodok, Moscow Oblast, Russia
Moschitto, Rosario A (Ross) — Baseball Player
1633 SW Harbour Isles Circle, Port Saint Lucie FL 34986, USA
Moscow, David — Actor
Robert Stein Mgmt, PO Box 3797, Beverly Hills CA 90212, USA
Mosebar, Donald H (Don) — Football Player
1713 Walnut Ave, Manhattan Beach CA 90266, USA
Moseby, Lloyd A — Baseball Player
9140 Los Lagos Circle S, Granite Bay CA 95746, USA
Moseley, Bill — Actor
Judy Fox Mgmt, 1525 1/2 S Beverly Dr, Los Angeles CA 90035, USA
Moseley, Dustin A — Baseball Player
1602 Line Ferry Road, Texarkana AR 71854, USA
Moseley, Jonny — Freestyle Moguls Skier
167 Trinidad Dr, Belvedere Tiburon CA 94920, USA
Moseley, Mark D — Football Player
7250 Middle Road, Middletown VA 22645, USA
Moseley, William — Actor
A P A Talent/Literary Agency, 405 S Beverly Dr, #300, Beverly Hills CA 90212 USA
Moseley-Braun, Carol — Senator, IL
Ambassador Organics, 1634 E 53rd St, #200, Chicago IL 60615, USA
Moser, Barry — Illustrator
155 Pantry Road, North Hatfield MA 01066, USA
Moser, Johannes — Concert Cellist
I M G Artists, Hogarth Business Park, Chiswick, London W4 2TH, England
Moser, Michele — Curling Athlete
Curling Assn, PO Box 606, 3000 Bern, Switzerland
Moser, Richard A (Rick) — Football Player
24040 Camino del Avion, Dana Point CA 92629, USA
Moser-Proll, Annemarie — Alpine Skier
Moser Cafe-Bar #92, 5602 Kleinarl 115, Austria
Moses, Albert — Actor
15 Overstone Road, Harpenden Hertfordshire AL5 5PN, England
Moses, Edwin C — Track Athlete
1184 Daventry Way NE, Atlanta GA 30319, USA
Moses, Gerald B (Jerry) — Baseball Player
PO Box 2153, Wolfeboro NH 03894, USA
Moses, Haven C — Football Player
1140 Cherokee St, #604, Denver CO 80204, USA
Moses, Mark — Actor
Innovative Artists, 1505 10th St, Santa Monica CA 90401 USA
Moses, Rick — Actor, Singer
Calder Agency, 19919 Redwing St, Woodland Hills CA 91364 USA
Moses, Robert (Bob) — Educator, Social Activist
99 Bishop Allen Dr, Cambridge MA 02139, USA
Moses, William R — Actor
Amsel Eisenstadt Frazier, 5055 Wilshire Blvd, #865, Los Angeles CA 90036 USA
Moshe, Guy — Director, Writer
Creative Artists Agency, 2000 Ave of Stars, #100, Los Angeles CA 90067 USA
Mosher, Gregory D — Director, Producer
I C M Partners, 730 5th Ave, New York NY 10019 USA
Mosimann, Anton — Chef
Mosimann's, 11B W Halkin St, London SW1X 8JL, England
Mosisili, B Pakalitha — Prime Minister, Lesotho
Chairman's Office, Military Council, PO Box 527, Maseru 100, Lesotho
Moskau, Paul R — Baseball Player
5041 N Apache Hills Trail, Tucson AZ 85750, USA
Moskovitz, Dustin — Businessman
Asana Inc, 3180 18th St, San Francisco CA 94110, USA
Moskowitz, Robert S — Artist
81 Leonard St, New York NY 10013, USA
Mosley, Lacey N — Singer (Flyleaf)
W M E Entertainment, 9601 Wilshire Blvd, #300, Beverly Hills CA 90210 USA
Mosley, Max R — Auto Racing Executive
International Automobile Federation, 8 Place de la Concorde, 75008 Paris, France
Mosley, Roger E — Actor
4470 W Sunset Blvd, #107-342, Los Angeles CA 90027, USA
Mosley, Shane (Sugar) — Boxer
Chrome Enterprise, PO Box 1924, Pomona CA 91769, USA
Mosley, Walter — Writer
37 Carmine St, #275, New York NY 10014, USA

Morton - Mosley

Mosquera, Julio A — Baseball Player
1419 Stone Creek Dr, Tarpon Springs FL 34689, USA
Moss, Cynthia — Animal Conservationist
African Wildlife Foundation, Mara Road, PO Box 48177, Nairobi, Kenya
Moss, Damian — Baseball Player
1877 Georgia Highway 19 South, Dublin GA 31021, USA
Moss, Eddie B — Football Player
15404 Eagle Estates Lane, Florissant MO 63034, USA
Moss, Elisabeth G — Actress
Ribisi Entertainment Group, 3278 Wilshire Blvd, #702, Los Angeles CA 90010, USA
Moss, Eric Owen — Architect
8557 Higuera St, Culver City CA 90232, USA
Moss, Geoffrey — Cartoonist, Illustrator
315 E 68th St, New York NY 10065, USA
Moss, J Lester (Les) — Baseball Player
420 Tullis Ave, Longwood FL 32750, USA
Moss, Kate — Model
Colegrave House, 70 Berners St, London W1T 3NL, England
Moss, P Buckley — Artist
1 Popular Grove Lane, Mathews VA 23109, USA
Moss, Paige — Actress
Marshak/Zachary Co, 8840 Wilshire Blvd, #100, Beverly Hills CA 90211 USA
Moss, Perry — Golfer
5660 S Lakeshore Dr, #505, Shreveport LA 71119, USA
Moss, Perry L — Football Player, Coach
420 Caddie Dr, Debary FL 32713, USA
Moss, Perry V — Basketball Player
165 Columbia Dr, Amherst MA 01002, USA
Moss, Randy G — Football Player
5060 Via de Amalfi Dr, Boca Raton FL 33496, USA
Moss, Ronn — Actor, Bassist
2401 Nottingham Ave, Los Angeles CA 90027, USA
Moss, Santana T — Football Player
7262 SW 123rd Place, Miami FL 33183, USA
Moss, Shirley — Sculptor
Moss Studios, PO Box 18104, Anaheim CA 92817, USA
Moss, Sinorice T — Football Player
156 Blue Heron Dr, Secaucus NJ 07094, USA
Moss, Stirling — Auto Racing Driver
Stirling Moss Ltd, 46 Shephard St, Mayfair, London W1Y 8JN, England
Moss, Winston N — Football Player
914 Thornberry Creek Dr, Hobart WI 54155, USA
Moss, Zefross P — Football Player
126 Kensington Dr, Madison AL 35758, USA
Moss-Bachrach, Ebon — Actor
Innovative Artists, 1505 10th St, Santa Monica CA 90401 USA
Mossbauer, Rudolf L — Nobel Physics Laureate
Stumpflingstr 6A, 82031 Grunwald, Germany
Mosser, Jonell — Singer
Phil Mayo Co, PO Box 304, Bomoseen VT 05732, USA
Mosshart, Alison — Singer, Guitarist (Kills), Songwriter
Third Man Records, 623 7th Ave S, Nashville TN 37203, USA
Mossi, Donald L (Don) — Baseball Player
23250 Canyon Lane, Caldwell ID 83607, USA
Most, Donny — Actor
28451 Foothill Dr, Agoura Hills CA 91301, USA
Mostert, Dutch — Artist
93696 Mallard Lane, North Bend OR 97459, USA
Mostow, George D — Mathematician
300 Audubon Court, New Haven CT 06510, USA
Mostow, Jonathan — Director
W M E Entertainment, 9601 Wilshire Blvd, #300, Beverly Hills CA 90210 USA
Mota, Jose M — Baseball Player
19058 E La Crosse St, Glendora CA 91741, USA
Mota, Manuel R (Manny) — Baseball Player
PO Box 2820, Toluca Lake CA 91610, USA
Mota, Rosa — Track Athlete
R Teatro 194 4 Esq, 4100 Porto, Portugal
Mote, Bobby — Rodeo Rider
6510 SW King Lane, Culver OR 97734, USA
Mote, Kelley H — Football Player
75 Baldwin Ave, Point Lookout NY 11569, USA
Mothersbaugh, Mark A — Singer, Keyboardist (Devo), Songwriter
Mutato Muzika, 8760 W Sunset Blvd, West Hollywood CA 90069, USA
Motion, Andrew — Writer
University of East Anglia, English Dept, Norwich NR4 7TJ, England
Motlanthe, Kgalema P — President, South Africa
PO Box 61884, Marshalltown 2107, South Africa
Motley, Darryl D — Baseball Player
10800 W 65th St, Shawnee KS 66203, USA
Mott, Darwin — Ice Hockey Player
11 Palenchuk Place, Meadow Lake SK S9X 1H2, Canada
Mott, Morris K — Ice Hockey Player
9 Elmdale Blvd, Brandon MB R7B 1B5, Canada
Mott, W Stephen (Steve), III — Football Player
7108 N Highfield Dr, Birmingham AL 35242, USA
Mott, William I (Bill) — Horse Tracing Trainer
WinStar Farms, 3301 Pisgah Pike, Versailles KY 40383, USA
Motta, J Richard (Dick) — Basketball Coach
423 Highway 89, Fish Haven ID 83287, USA
Mottau, Mike — Ice Hockey Player
57 Herring Weir Road, Duxbury MA 2332, USA
Mottelson, Ben R — Nobel Physics Laureate
Nordita, Blegdamsvej 17, 2100 Copenhagen 0, Denmark
Mottola, Charles E (Chad) — Baseball Player
6479 Lake Pembroke Place, Orlando FL 32829, USA

Mottola, Greg — Director, Writer
United Talent Agency, 9336 Civic Center Dr, Beverly Hills CA 90210 USA

Mottola, Thomas D — Businessman
Casablanca Records, 8255 W Sunset Blvd, West Hollywood CA 90046, USA

Motz, Diana Gribbon — Judge
US Appeals Court, 101 W Lombard St, #3625, Baltimore MD 21201, USA

Mouawad, Jerry — Director
Imago Theater, PO Box 15182, Portland OR 97293, USA

Mouchawar, Alan — Water Polo Player
1943 Port Trinity Place, Newport Beach CA 92660, USA

Mouglalis, Anna — Actress
Agents Associes, 201 Rue du Faubourg Saint Honore, 75008 Paris, France

Moulay Hassan — Crown Prince, Morocco
Royal Palace, Rabat, Morocco

Mould, Bob — Singer, Guitarist, Songwriter
High Road Touring, 751 Bridgeway, #200, Sausalito CA 94965 USA

Moulder-Brown, John — Actor
Spotlight, 7 Leicester Place, London WC2H 7RJ, England

Moulds, Eric S — Football Player
30 Brownstone Court, East Amherst NY 14051, USA

Mouli — Actress
12 Srinivasa Ave, Chennai TN 600028, India

Moulton, Alexander E — Bicycle Engineer
Hall, Bradford on Avon, Wilts BA15 1AJ, England

Moulton, Sara — Chef
Sara Moulton Enterprises, 130 W 24th St, #3B, New York NY 10011, USA

Moultrie, Arnett N — Basketball Player
Philadelphia 76ers, 1st Union Center, 3601 S Broad St, Philadelphia PA 19148 USA

Mounce, Anthony D (Tony) — Baseball Player
237 Cotton Bayou Lane, Kenner LA 70065, USA

Mounsey, Tara — Ice Hockey Player
22 Forge Pond, #B, Canton MA 02021, USA

Mount, Anson — Actor
Innovative Artists, 1505 10th St, Santa Monica CA 90401 USA

Mount, Richard C (Rick) — Basketball Player
904 Hopkins Road, Lebanon IN 46052, USA

Mountcastle, Vernon B, Jr — Neurophysiologist
6605 Walnutwood Circle, Baltimore MD 21212, USA

Moura, Wagner — Actor
United Talent Agency, 9336 Civic Center Dr, Beverly Hills CA 90210 USA

Mourinho, Jose — Soccer Player, Coach
F C Inter Milan, Via Durini 24, 20122 Milan, Italy

Mourning, Alonzo — Basketball Player
3525 Anchorage Way, Miami FL 33133, USA

Mouskouri, Nana J — Singer, Songwriter
Elli's Mgmt, Hausteigstr 64, 70180 Stuttgart 2, Germany

Moussa, Amre M — Government Official, Egypt
Arab League, PO Box 11642, Tahrir Square, Cairo, Egypt

Mouton, James R — Baseball Player
4710 Lakeside Meadow Court, Missouri City TX 77459, USA

Mouton, Lyle J — Baseball Player
4101 Auston Way, Palm Harbor FL 34685, USA

Movsessian-Lamoriello, Victoria (Viki) — Ice Hockey Player
17 Webb St, Lexington MA 02420, USA

Mowat, Farley M — Writer, Naturalist
18 King St, Port Hope ON L1A 2R4, Canada

Mowatt, Ezekial (Zeke) — Football Player
Mowatt Inc, 194 Passaic St, #2A, Hackensack NJ 07601, USA

Mowers, Mark — Ice Hockey Player
10 Pollock Dr, Middleton MA 01949, USA

Mowerson, Robert — Swimmer
2601 Kenzie Terrace, #324, Minneapolis MN 55418, USA

Mowins, Beth — Sportscaster
ESPN-TV, ESPN Plaza, 935 Middle St, Bristol CT 06010 USA

Mowrey, Caitlin — Actress
Innovative Artists, 1505 10th St, Santa Monica CA 90401 USA

Mowrey, Dude — Singer
Joe Taylor Artist Agency, PO Box 279, Williamstown NJ 37068 USA

Mowry, Tahj D — Actor
Felker Toczak Gellman, 10880 Wilshire Blvd, #2070, Los Angeles CA 90024 USA

Mowry, Tia — Actress
Kritzer Levine Wilkins Griffin, 11872 La Grange Ave, #100, Los Angeles CA 90025 USA

Mowry-Housley, Tamera — Actress
United Talent Agency, 9336 Civic Center Dr, Beverly Hills CA 90210 USA

Moxey, Jim — Ice Hockey Player
7 Blue Heron Dr, Orangeville ON L9W 5K6, Canada

Moxey, John Llewellyn — Director
Shapiro-Lichtman, 8827 Beverly Blvd, Los Angeles CA 90048 USA

Moya, Carlos — Tennis Player
Ave Diagonal 618 3D, 08021 Barcelona, Spain

Moyer, Jamie — Baseball Player
5500 34th St W, Badenton FL 34210, USA

Moyer, Kenneth W (Ken) — Football Player
3896 Magma Court, Mason OH 45040, USA

Moyer, Paul S — Football Player
9411 NE 32nd St, Clyde Hill WA 98004, USA

Moyer, Stephen — Actor, Director
United Agents, 12-26 Lexington St, London W1F 0LE, England

Moyers, Bill D — Commentator
151 Central Park W, #5N, New York NY 10023, USA

Moyet, Alison — Singer
Agency Group Ltd, 142 W 57th St, #600, New York NY 10019 USA

Moyle, Allan — Director, Writer
Becsey Wisdom Kalajian, 849 S Wooster St, #7, Los Angeles CA 90035, USA

Moynahan, Bridget — Actress, Model
Brillstein Entertainment Partners, 9150 Wilshire Blvd, #350, Beverly Hills CA 90212 USA

M

Moynihan, Bobby — Actor, Comedian
United Talent Agency, 9336 Civic Center Dr, Beverly Hills CA 90210 USA
Moynihan, Christopher (Chris) — Actor, Producer, Writer
Domain Talent, 9229 W Sunset Blvd, #710, West Hollywood CA 90069 USA
Moynihan, Colin B — Government Official, England
Crown Reach, 16 Grosvenor Road, London SW1V 3JV, England
Moyse, Heather — Bobsled Athlete
Alberta Bobsled, Niven Center, 140 Canada Olympic Road, Calgary AB T3B 5RS, Canada
Mozilo, Angelo R — Financier
Countrywide Credit Industries, 4500 Park Granada, Calabasas CA 91302, USA
Mr Cheeks — Rap Artist (Lost Boyz)
Agency Group Ltd, 142 W 57th St, #600, New York NY 10019 USA
Mraz, Jason — Singer, Songwriter
Bill Silva Mgmt, 8225 Santa Monica Blvd, West Hollywood CA 90046, USA
Mrazek, Jerome — Ice Hockey Player
3133 Mountain Road, Glen Allen VA 23060, USA
Mrazovich, Chuck — Basketball Player
7260 W 12th Ave, Hialeah FL 33014, USA
Mroudjae, Ali — Prime Minister, Comoros
BP 58, Rond Point Gobadjou, Moroni, Comoros
Mrozik, Rick — Ice Hockey Player
2234 Kelly Ave, Cloquet MN 55720, USA
Mruczkowski, Scott A — Football Player
10701 Mountview Ave, Cleveland OH 44125, USA
Msamati, Lucian — Actor
Diamond Mgmt, 31 Percy St, London W1T 2DD, England
Mswati III, Makhosetive — King, Swaziland
Lozitha Palace, PO Box 1, Mbabane, Swaziland
Muccino, Gabriele — Director
Creative Artists Agency, 2000 Ave of Stars, #100, Los Angeles CA 90067 USA
Muckalt, Bill — Ice Hockey Player
3001 Civic Center Circle NE, Rio Rancho NM 87144, USA
Mucke, Manuela — Canoeing Athlete
Charlottenstr 13, 10315 Berlin, Germany
Muckensturm, Jerry R — Football Player
4209 Hickory Lane, Jonesboro AR 72401, USA
Muckler, John — Ice Hockey Executive, Coach
387 Woods Acres Dr, East Amherst NY 14051, USA
Mudd, Daniel — Government Official, Financier
Federal National Mortgage Assn, 3900 Wisconsin Ave NW, Washington DC 20016, USA
Mudd, Howard E — Football Player, Coach
15933 Reserve Dr SE, North Bend WA 98045, USA
Mudd, Roger H — Commentator
7167 Old Dominion Dr, McLean VA 22101, USA
Mudge, Jennifer — Actress
Group Entertainment, 115 W 29th St, #1102, New York NY 10001, USA
Mudra, Darrell — Football Coach
424 Tiger Hammock Road, Crawfordville FL 32327, USA
Muehe, Anna Maria — Actress
Fitz & Skoglund, Linienstr 130, 10115 Berlin, Germany
Mueller, Edward — Businessman
Qwest Communications, 1801 California St, #5200, Denver CO 80202, USA
Mueller, George E — Electrical Engineer, Missile Scientist
Kistler Aerospace Corp, 3760 Carillon Point, Kirkland WA 98033, USA
Mueller, Gerd — Soccer Player
Neuestr 21, 81479 Munich, Germany
Mueller, Leah Poulos — Speed Skater
11455 N Mulberry Dr, Mequon WI 53092, USA
Mueller, Lisel — Writer
Louisiana State University Press, PO Box 25053, Baton Rouge LA 70894, USA
Mueller, Niels — Director
W M E Entertainment, 9601 Wilshire Blvd, #300, Beverly Hills CA 90210 USA
Mueller, Robert S, III — Law Enforcement Official
Federal Bureau of Investigation, 9th & Pennsylvania NW, Washington DC 20535, USA
Mueller, Vance A — Football Player
8141 Damico Dr, El Dorado Hills CA 95762, USA
Mueller, Willard L (Willie) — Baseball Player
2320 Tolbert Lane, West Bend WI 53090, USA
Mueller, William R (Bill) — Baseball Player
570 W Canyon Way, Chandler AZ 85248, USA
Mueller-Stahl, Armin — Actor
I C M Partners, 10250 Constellation Blvd, #900, Los Angeles CA 90067 USA
Muench, David — Photographer
PO Box 30500, Santa Barbara CA 93130, USA
Mugabe, Robert G — President, Zimbabwe
President's Office, Munhumutapa Bldg, Samora Machel Ave, Harare, Zimbabwe
Mugabi, John — Boxer
PO Box 246, Main Beach, Gold Coast QLD, Australia
Mughelli, Ovie P — Football Player
3485 Moye Trail, Duluth GA 30097, USA
Mugler, Thierry — Fashion Designer
Patrick Alaux, 4 Rue Faubourg Saint Honore, 75008 Paris, France
Muhammad, Eddie Mustafa — Boxer
9030 W Sahara Blvd, Las Vegas NV 89117, USA
Muhlbach, Donald L (Don), Jr — Football Player
711 Pinetree Lane, Lufkin TX 75904, USA
Muhtadee Billah al- — Prince Heir Apparent, Brunei
Istana Nural Iman, Bandar Seri Begawan 1100, Brunei Darussalam, Brunei
Muir DeGraad, Karen — Swimmer
Applebosch State Hospital, Ozwatini, Natal, South Africa
Muirhead, Oliver — Actor
Don Buchwald/Fortitude, 6500 Wilshire Blvd, #2200, Los Angeles CA 90048 USA
Mujica, Jose Pepe — President, Uruguay
Chacra El Paso de la Arena, Montevideo, Uruguay
Mujurawar, Ali Mohammed — Prime Minister, Republic of Yemen
Premier's Office, Street of 26th September, Sana'a, Yemen Arab Republic

Mukai, Chiaki Naito- — Astronaut, Japan
100 Cyberonics Blvd, #201, Houston TX 77058, USA
Mukherjee, Bharati — Writer
130 Rivoli St, San Francisco CA 94117, USA
Mukherjee, Pranab K — President, India
President's Office, Bharat Ka, Rashtrapti Bhavan, New Delhi 110004, India
Mukherjee, Siddhartha — Writer
Charles Scribner's Sons, 866 3rd Ave, New York NY 10022 USA
Mula, Inva — Opera Singer
Columbia Artists Mgmt Inc, 1790 Broadway, #702, New York NY 10019 USA
Mulally, Alan R — Businessman
Ford Motor Co, Dearborn Road, Dearborn MI 48121, USA
Mulari, Tarja — Speed Skier
Motion Oy, Vanhan Mankkaantie 33, 02180 Espoo, Finland
Mularkey, Mike — Football Player, Coach
4411 Meadow Club Dr, Suwanee GA 30024, USA
Mulcahy, Kathleen — Artist, Sculptor
260 Whittengale Road, Oakdale PA 15071, USA
Mulcahy, Russell — Director
A P A Talent/Literary Agency, 405 S Beverly Dr, #300, Beverly Hills CA 90212 USA
Muldaur, Diana — Actress
20 Cummings Way, Edgartown MA 02539, USA
Muldaur, Geoff — Singer, Guitarist
Nancy Fly Agency, PO Box 90306, Austin TX 78709, USA
Muldaur, Maria — Singer, Songwriter
Piedmont Talent, PO Box 680006, Charlotte NC 28216, USA
Mulder, Karen — Model
Metropolitan Modeling Agency, 5 Union Square W, #500, New York NY 10003, USA
Mulder, Mark — Baseball Player
10295 E Cholla St, Scottsdale AZ 85260, USA
Muldoon, Patrick — Actor, Model
Eclectic Pictures, 7119 Sunset Blvd, #375, Los Angeles CA 90046, USA
Muldoon, Paul B — Writer
Princeton University, Creative Writing Progam, Princeton NJ 08544, USA
Muldowney, Dominic J — Composer
Carlin Music, 3 Bridge Approach, Chalk Farm, London NW1 8BD, England
Muldowney, Shirley — Auto Racing Driver
8680 Willow Road, Willis MI 48191, USA
Mulgrew, Kate — Actress
Innovative Artists, 1505 10th St, Santa Monica CA 90401 USA
Mulhern, Matt — Actor
Don Buchwald/Fortitude, 6500 Wilshire Blvd, #2200, Los Angeles CA 90048 USA
Mulhern, Richard — Ice Hockey Player
397 Walpole Ave, Beaconsfield QC H9W 2G6, Canada
Mulhern, Ryan — Ice Hockey Player
42 Faculty Circle, Kingston RI 02881, USA
Mulhern, Sinead — Opera Singer
Guy Barzilay Artists, 420 W 25th St, #4F, New York NY 10001, USA
Mulholland, John F — Army General
Army Special Operations Command, 2929 Desert Storm Dr, Fort Bragg NC 28310, USA
Mulholland, Terence J (Terry) — Baseball Player
11655 N 18th Place, Phoenix AZ 85020, USA
Mulitalo, Edwin M — Football Player
12587 Moonlite Hill Court, Herriman UT 84096, USA
Mulkerin, Ted — Writer
Creative Artists Agency, 2000 Ave of Stars, #100, Los Angeles CA 90067 USA
Mulkey, Chris — Actor
Don Buchwald/Fortitude, 6500 Wilshire Blvd, #2200, Los Angeles CA 90048 USA
Mulkey-Robertson, Kim — Basketball Player, Coach
Baylor University, Athletic Dept, Waco TX 76798, USA
Mull, Carter — Photographer
Marc Foxx Gallery, 6150 Wilshire Blvd, #5, Los Angeles CA 90048, USA
Mull, Martin — Actor
Anonymous Content, 3532 Hayden Ave, Culver City CA 90232 USA
Mullady, Thomas S (Tom) — Football Player
2855 Crooked Oak Dr, Germantown TN 38138, USA
Mullally, Megan — Actress, Singer
United Talent Agency, 9336 Civic Center Dr, Beverly Hills CA 90210 USA
Mullan, Carrie — Actress
United Agents, 12-26 Lexington St, London W1F 0LE, England
Mullan, Peter — Actor, Director
Markham & Froggatt, Julian House, 4 Windmill St, London W1P 1HF, England
Mullane, Richard M (Mike) — Astronaut
1301 Las Lomas Road NE, Albuquerque NM 87106, USA
Mullaney, Mark A — Football Player
17448 Frondell Court, Eden Prairie MN 55347, USA
Mullavey, Greg — Actor
31 Tiemann Place, #48, New York NY 10027, USA
Mullen, Brian — Ice Hockey Player
124 Berkeley Circle, Basking Ridge NJ 07920, USA
Mullen, Ford P (Moon) — Baseball Player
20505 Marine Dr, #3, Stanwood WA 98292, USA
Mullen, Joseph P (Joey) — Ice Hockey Player
36 Friends Lane, South Dennis MA 02660, USA
Mullen, Larry, Jr — Drummer (U-2)
Principle Mgmt, 30-32 Sir John Rogerson Quay, Dublin 2, Ireland
Mullen, M David — Cinematographer
3930 Wade St, Los Angeles CA 90066, USA
Mullen, Michael G (Mike) — Navy Admiral
Chairman, Joint Chiefs of Staff, Pentagon, Washington DC 20318 USA
Mullen, Nicole C — Singer, Songwriter
Creative Artists Agency, 2000 Ave of Stars, #100, Los Angeles CA 90067 USA
Mullen, Scott — Baseball Player
73 Walling Grove Road, Beaufort SC 29907, USA
Mullen, Thomas — Writer
I C M Partners, 10250 Constellation Blvd, #900, Los Angeles CA 90067 USA

Mullens, Byron J (B J) — Basketball Player
Charlotte Bobcats, 333 E Trade St, #A, Charlotte NC 28202 USA

Muller, Egon — Motorcycle Racing Rider
Dorfstr 17, 24247 Rodenbek/Kiel, Germany

Muller, Gerd — Soccer Player
Heinrich-Vogel-Str 10A, 81479 Munich, Germany

Muller, Ina — Singer, Actress
105 Music, Hopfensack 20, 20457 Hamburg, Germany

Muller, Jorg — Auto Racing Driver
Insert Motorsport, Fassoldshof 1, 95336 Mainleus, Germany

Muller, K Alex — Nobel Physics Laureate
Haldenstr 54, 8909 Hedingen, Switzerland

Muller, Kirk — Ice Hockey Player, Coach
Calgary Flames, PO Box 1540, Station M, Calgary AB T2P 3B9, Canada

Muller, Lillian — Model, Actress
PO Box 20029-414, Encino CA 91416, USA

Muller, Michel — Actor
Artmedia, 20 Ave Rapp, 75007 Paris, France

Muller, Peter — Alpine Skier
Haldenstr 18, 8134 Adliswil, Switzerland

Muller, Richard S — Electrical, Microbiotics Engineer
University of California, Sensor/Actuator Center, Berkeley CA 94720, USA

Muller, Robby — Cinematographer
Mirisch Agency, 8840 Wilshire Blvd, #100, Beverly Hills CA 90211 USA

Muller-Brachmann, Hanno — Opera Singer
Kunstler Sekretariat am Gasteig, Rosenheimer Str 52, 81669 Munich, Germany

Muller-Schott, Daniel — Concert Violist
Konzertdirektion Schmid, Konigstra 36, 30175 Hannover, Germany

Muller-Westernhagen, Marius — Singer, Actor
Motor Entertainment, Brunnenstr 24, 10119 Berlin, Germany

Mulligan, Brian — Opera Singer
I M G Artists, Hogarth Business Park, Chiswick, London W4 2TH, England

Mulligan, Carey H — Actress
Julian Belfrage Assoc, 9 Argyll St, #300, London W1F 7TG, England

Mulligan, Deanna M — Businesswoman
Guardian Life Insurance, 7 Hanover Square, New York NY 10004, USA

Mulligan, Gerry — Writer
3 Arts Entertainment, 9460 Wilshire Blvd, #700, Beverly Hills CA 90212 USA

Mulligan, Richard C — Molecular Biologist, Geneticist
Children's Hospital, Genetics Dept, 320 Longwood Ave, Boston MA 02115, USA

Mulligan, Sean P — Baseball Player
24474 Eastgate Dr, Diamond Bar CA 91765, USA

Mulligan, Wayne E — Football Player
2410 The Haul Over, Johns Island SC 29455, USA

Mulliken, William (Bill) — Swimmer
4216 N Keeler Ave, Chicago IL 60641, USA

Mullin, Christopher P (Chris) — Basketball Player
116 Laurelwood Dr, Danville CA 94506, USA

Mullin, Reed D — Drummer (Corrosion of Conformity)
Chipster, 800 Village Square Crossing, Palm Beach Gardens FL 33410 USA

Mulliniks, S Rance — Baseball Player
2614 S Peppertree St, Visalia CA 93277, USA

Mullins, Aimee — Model, Athlete
Authentic Talent/Literary Mgmt, 45 Main St, #1004, Brooklyn NY 11201, USA

Mullins, Gerald B (Gerry) — Football Player
PO Box 523, Saxonburg PA 16056, USA

Mullins, Gregory E (Greg) — Baseball Player
PO Box 443, Florahome FL 32140, USA

Mullins, Jeffrey V (Jeff) — Basketball Player, Coach
8866 N Sea Oaks Way, #202, Vero Beach FL 32963, USA

Mullins, Shawn — Singer, Songwriter
Russell Carter Artist Mgmt, 567 Ralph Mcgill Blvd NE, Atlanta GA 30312, USA

Mullis, Kary B — Nobel Chemistry Laureate
400 Goldenrod Ave, Corona del Mar CA 92625, USA

Mullova, Viktoria Y — Concert Violinist
Kunstler Sekretariat am Gasteig, Rosenheimer Str 52, 81669 Munich, Germany

Mulloy, Gardner P — Tennis Player
800 NW 9th Ave, Miami FL 33136, USA

Muloin, Wayne — Ice Hockey Player
2991 Hayes St, Avon OH 44011, USA

Mulroney, Dermot — Actor
W M E Entertainment, 9601 Wilshire Blvd, #300, Beverly Hills CA 90210 USA

Mulroney, Kieran — Actor, Writer
Management 360, 9111 Wilshire Blvd, Beverly Hills CA 90210 USA

Mulroney, M Brian — Prime Minister, Canada
47 Forden Crescent, Westmount QC H3Y 2Y5, Canada

Mulrooney, Richard — Soccer Player
Houston Dynamo, 1415 Louisiana, #3400, Houston TX 77002 USA

Mulva, James J — Businessman
ConocoPhillips Inc, 600 N Daisy Ashford, Houston TX 77079, USA

Mulvey, Grant — Ice Hockey Player
70 E Scott St, #706, Chicago IL 60610, USA

Mulvey, Kevin — Baseball Player
24 Eric Court, Parlin NJ 08859, USA

Mulvey, Paul — Ice Hockey Player
8009 Oak Hollow Lane, Fairfax Station VA 22039, USA

Mulvihill, Robert — Basketball Player
53 Pike Dr, #1C, Wayne NJ 07470, USA

Mumba, Samantha — Singer, Actress
Helter Skelter, 347-353 Chiswick High Road, London W4 4HS, England

Mumford, Eloise — Actress
Paradigm Agency, 360 N Crescent Dr, North Building, Beverly Hills CA 90210 USA

Mumley, Nicholas (Nick) — Football Player
1432 Audubon Dr, Columbus IN 47203, USA

Mumphrey, Jerry W — Baseball Player
7709 FM 850, Tyler TX 75705, USA

Mumy, Billy — Actor
PO Box 433, 11333 Moorpark St, North Hollywood CA 91603, USA

Munchak, Michael A (Mike) — Football Player, Coach
9155 Saddlebow Dr, Brentwood TN 37027, USA

Muncie, Harry V (Chuck) — Football Player
3013 S Apple Court, Antioch LA 94509, USA

Muncrief, Kevin — Golfer
939 S Flood Ave, Norman OK 73069, USA

Mundae, Misty — Actress
El Independent Cinema, PO Box 132, Butler NJ 07405, USA

Mundell, Robert A — Nobel Economics Laureate
35 Clarement Ave, New York NY 10027, USA

Mundy, Carl E, Jr — Marine Corps General
9308 Ludgate Dr, Alexandria VA 22309, USA

Mundy, Chris — Producer, Writer
United Talent Agency, 9336 Civic Center Dr, Beverly Hills CA 90210 USA

Mundy, John H — Historian
29 Claremont Ave, New York NY 10027, USA

Mungle, Matthew W — Make-Up Artist
Milton Agency, 6715 Hollywood Blvd, #206, Los Angeles CA 90028, USA

Muni, Craig — Ice Hockey Player
9291 Via Cimato Dr, Clarence Center NY 14032, USA

Munitz, Barry — Foundation Executive
J Paul Getty Trust, 1200 Getty Center Dr, #400, Los Angeles CA 90049, USA

Muniz, Armando — Boxer
6657 45th St, Riverside CA 92509, USA

Muniz, Frankie — Actor
Paradigm Agency, 360 N Crescent Dr, North Building, Beverly Hills CA 90210 USA

Muniz, Vik — Photographer
169 Bond St, Brooklyn NY 11217, USA

Munk, Chris — Basketball Player
14 Hillview Court, San Francisco CA 94124, USA

Munk, Walter H — Geophysicist
9530 La Jolla Shores Dr, La Jolla CA 92037, USA

Munn, Allison — Actress
Innovative Artists, 1505 10th St, Santa Monica CA 90401 USA

Munninghoff, Scott A — Baseball Player
866 Laverty Lane, Cincinnati OH 45230, USA

Munns, Allen G — Navy Admiral
Commander, Submarine Command Atlantic, 7958 Blandy Road, Norfolk VA 23511 USA

Munoz, J Oscar — Baseball Player
14161 Leaning Pine Dr, Hialeah FL 33014, USA

Munoz, M Anthony — Football Player, Sportscaster
7575 Rockeby Court, Cincinnati OH 45241, USA

Munoz, Michael A (Mike) — Baseball Player
1000 Carroll Meadows Court, Southlake TX 76092, USA

Munoz, Ricardo J (Ricky) — Singer, Accordian Player (Intocable)
Serca Music, 2020 W Houston Ave, McAllen TX 78501, USA

Munoz, Roberto (Bobby) — Baseball Player
9040 NW 20th St, Pembroke Pines FL 33024, USA

Munro, Alice — Writer
PO Box 1133, Clinton ON N0M 1L0, Canada

Munro, Caroline — Actress
5 Paddington St, London W1M 3LA, England

Munro, Lochlyn — Actor
Innovative Artists, 1505 10th St, Santa Monica CA 90401 USA

Munro, Peter D — Baseball Player
4311 Westmoreland St, Little Neck NY 11363, USA

Munroe, George B — Basketball Player
870 United Nations Plaza, #31E, New York NY 10017, USA

Munroe, Odessa — Actress
Carrier Talent Mgmt, 1080 Howe St, #705, Vancouver BC V6Z 2T1, Canada

Munsel, Patrice — Opera Singer
PO Box 472, Schroon Lake NY 12870, USA

Munson, Eric W — Baseball Player
5550 Wilshire Blvd, #314, Los Angeles CA 90036, USA

Munson, John — Bassist (Semisonic)
Monterey Peninsula Artists, 404 W Franklin St, Monterey CA 93940 USA

Munter, Leilani — Auto Racing Driver, Social Activist
PO Box 3355, Mooresville NC 38117, USA

Munter, Scott — Baseball Player
13024 Jessie Ave, Omaha NE 68164, USA

Muntyan, Mikhail — Opera Singer
16 N Iorga Str, #13, 277012 Chisnau, Moldova

Mura, Stephen A (Steve) — Baseball Player
31892 Old Oak Road, Trabuco Canyon CA 92679, USA

Murad, Ferid — Nobel Medicine Laureate
3409 Wilson Blvd, Arlington VA 22201, USA

Murakami, Haruki — Writer
I C M Partners, 730 5th Ave, New York NY 10019 USA

Murakami, Masanori — Baseball Player
1-4-15-1506 Nisho Ohi Shinagawaku, Tokyo 140 0015, Japan

Murakami, Ryu — Writer
Kodansha Books, 2-12-21 Otowa, Bunkyoku, Tokyo 112 8001, Japan

Murakami, Takashi — Artist
Management 360, 9111 Wilshire Blvd, Beverly Hills CA 90210 USA

Murat, Bernard — Actor
Artmedia, 20 Ave Rapp, 75007 Paris, France

Murat, Stephanie — Actress
Artmedia, 20 Ave Rapp, 75007 Paris, France

Murayama, Makio — Biochemist
5010 Benton Ave, Bethesda MD 20814, USA

Murayama, Tomiichi — Prime Minister, Japan
3-2-2 Chiyomachi, Oita, Oita 870, Japan

Murchison, Ira — Track Athlete
10113 S Sangamon St, Chicago IL 60643, USA

Murciano, Enrique — Actor
Untitled Entertainment, 350 S Beverly Dr, #200, Beverly Hills CA 90212 USA
Murcutt, Glenn — Pritzker Architectural Laureate
Neeson Murcutt Architects, 71 York St, #500, Sydney NSW 2000, Australia
Murdoch, Don — Ice Hockey Player
Hockey in the Rockies School, PO Box 383, Cranbrook BC V1C 4H9, Canada
Murdoch, K Rupert — Publisher
News America Publishing, 1211 Ave of Americas, #500, New York NY 10036, USA
Murdoch, Robert (Bob) — Ice Hockey Player
410 11th Ave S, Cranbrook BC V1C 2P9, Canada
Murdoch, Robert J (Bob) — Ice Hockey Player, Coach
1330 Angelo Dr, Beverly Hills CA 90210, USA
Murdoch, Stuart L — Singer, Songwriter (Belle & Sebastian)
Ground Control Touring, 20 Jay St, #826, Brooklyn NY 11201 USA
Murdoch, William W — Population Ecologist
University of California, Ecology Evolution Marine Biology Dept, Santa Barbara CA 93106, USA
Murdock, David H — Businessman
10900 Wilshire Blvd, #1600, Los Angeles CA 90024, USA
Murdock, George P — Anthropologist
107 E Wynnewood Road, Wynnewood PA 19096, USA
Murdock, Shirley — Singer
PO Box 26249, Dayton OH 45426, USA
Muresan, Gheorghe — Basketball Player, Actor
12250 Glen Road, Potomac MD 20854, USA
Muresan, Lucian Cardinal — Religious Leader
Archdiocese, Fagaras & Alba Iulia, Str Petro Pavel Aron 2, 515400 Blaj AB, Romania
Muriel, Xavier — Drummer (Buckcherry)
10th Street Mgmt, 700 N San Vicente Blvd, #G410, West Hollywood CA 90069, USA
Murino, Caterina — Actress
Soli Associati, Viale Dei Parioli 44, 00197 Rome, Italy
Muris, Timothy J — Government Official
George Mason University, Law School, Fairfax VA 22030, USA
Murkoff, Heidi — Writer
What To Expect Foundation, 211 W 80th St, Lower Level, New York, NY 10024, USA
Murley, Matt — Ice Hockey Player
32 Hialeah Dr, Troy NY 12182, USA
Muro, J Michael — Cinematographer
Gersh Agency, 9465 Wilshire Blvd, #600, Beverly Hills CA 90212 USA
Murofushi, Koji A — Track Athlete
World Athletics Mgmt, Untersperr 4A, 4644 Scharnstein, Austria
Murphey, Christopher — Producer, Writer
Rothman Brecher Agency, 920 Wilshire Blvd, #PH, Beverly Hills CA 90212, USA
Murphey, Michael Martin — Singer, Songwriter
Artra Artists, 130 S Canal St, #211, Chicago IL 60606, USA
Murphy, Ben — Actor
2690 Rambla Pacifico St, Malibu CA 90265, USA
Murphy, Bob — Golfer
12005 Dunes Road, Boynton Beach FL 33436, USA
Murphy, Calvin J — Basketball Player, Executive
8218 Cliffshire Court, Houston TX 77083, USA
Murphy, Carolyn — Model, Actress
W M E Entertainment, 9601 Wilshire Blvd, #300, Beverly Hills CA 90210 USA
Murphy, Caryle M — Journalist
Washington Post, Editorial Dept, 1150 15th St NW, Washington DC 20071, USA
Murphy, Charles S — Government Official
100 Bluff View Dr, #503C, Belleair Bluffs FL 33770, USA
Murphy, Charlie Q — Actor, Comedian
I C M Partners, 10250 Constellation Blvd, #900, Los Angeles CA 90067 USA
Murphy, Cillian — Actor
Lisa Richards Agency, 108 Upper Leeson St, Dublin 4, Ireland
Murphy, Dale B — Baseball Player
467 Aspen Ridge Lane, Alpine UT 84004, USA
Murphy, Daniel F (Danny) — Baseball Player
5030 Champion Blvd, #6226, Boca Raton FL 33496, USA
Murphy, Daniel T — Baseball Player
2878 Dickie Court, Jacksonville FL 32216, USA
Murphy, David Lee — Singer
D Mgmt, 1102 18th Ave S, Nashville TN 37212, USA
Murphy, David M — Baseball Player
3708 Sunrise Ranch Road, Southlake TX 76092, USA
Murphy, Diana E — Judge
US Court of Appeals, 300 S 4th St, #11E, Minneapolis MN 55415, USA
Murphy, Donald — Actor
PO Box 904, Ranchester WY 82839, USA
Murphy, Donald R (Donnie) — Baseball Player
10211 Willow Bend Circle, #18, Charlotte NC 28210, USA
Murphy, Donna — Actress, Singer, Dancer
Brookside Artists Mgmt, 250 W 57th St, #2303, New York NY 10107, USA
Murphy, Dwayne K — Baseball Player
1811 S Karen Dr, Chandler AZ 85286, USA
Murphy, Eddie — Actor, Comedian
Eddie Murphy Productions, 9601 Wilshire Blvd, #300, Beverly Hills CA 90210, USA
Murphy, Erin — Actress
Commercial Talent, 9255 Sunset Blvd, #505, West Hollywood CA 90069, USA
Murphy, Glenn — Businessman
Gap Inc, 2 Folsom St, San Francisco CA 94105, USA
Murphy, Gord — Ice Hockey Player
10041 Cartgate Court, Dublin OH 43017, USA
Murphy, Joe — Ice Hockey Player
10292 Horton Road, Goodrich MI 48438, USA
Murphy, Jonathan — Actor
Innovative Artists, 1505 10th St, Santa Monica CA 90401 USA
Murphy, Kevin — Producer, Writer
W M E Entertainment, 9601 Wilshire Blvd, #300, Beverly Hills CA 90210 USA
Murphy, Kim — Journalist
Los Angeles Times, Editorial Dept, 202 W 1st St, Los Angeles CA 90012 USA

Murphy, Lawrence T (Larry) — Ice Hockey Player
1167 Connaught Dr, Ennismore ON K0L 1T0, Canada
Murphy, Mark H — Singer
Abby Hoffer, 223 1/2 E 48th St, New York NY 10017 USA
Murphy, Mark H — Football Player
935 N Broadway, DePere WI 54115, USA
Murphy, Mark S — Football Player
3699 Myersville Road, Uniontown OH 44685, USA
Murphy, Michael — Actor
Paul Kohner, 9300 Wilshire Blvd, #555, Beverly Hills CA 90212 USA
Murphy, Michael R — Judge
US Court of Appeals, Federal Building, 125 S State St, Salt Lake City UT 84138, USA
Murphy, Mike — Ice Hockey Player, Coach
National Hockey League, 50 Bay St, #1100, Toronto ON M5J 2X8, Canada
Murphy, Nate — Paleontologist
Judith River Dinosaur Institute, PO Box 51177, Billings MT 59105, USA
Murphy, Nick — Director, Producer, Writer
Independent Talent Group, Oxford House, 76 Oxford St, London W1D 1BS, England
Murphy, Peter J — Singer (Bauhaus)
Satellite Mgmt, 34 Salisbury St, London NW8 8QE, England
Murphy, Reg — Editor, Publisher
National Geographic Society, 1145 17th St NW, Washington DC 20036, USA
Murphy, Richard L (Dick) — Baseball Player
6890 Connie Dr, Avon IN 46123, USA
Murphy, Rob — Ice Hockey Player
Hockey Stall, 35 Mika St, Stittsville ON K2S 1K8, Canada
Murphy, Robert A (Rob) — Baseball Player
44 S Sewalls Point Road, Stuart FL 34996, USA
Murphy, Ron — Ice Hockey Player
1 Valley Road, Nanticoke ON N0H 1L0, Canada
Murphy, Ronald T (Ronnie) — Basketball Player
14800 Hanover Pike, Upperco MD 21155, USA
Murphy, Rosemary — Actress
Don Buchwald/Fortitude, 6500 Wilshire Blvd, #2200, Los Angeles CA 90048 USA
Murphy, Ryan — Director, Producer, Writer
Creative Artists Agency, 2000 Ave of Stars, #100, Los Angeles CA 90067 USA
Murphy, Sean P — Golfer
1004 June Place, Lovington NM 88260, USA
Murphy, Thomas (Tom) — Writer
4 Garville Road, Dublin 6, County Dublin, Ireland
Murphy, Thomas A (Tom) — Baseball Player
26561 Via Sacramento, Capistrano Beach CA 92624, USA
Murphy, Thomas F (Tommy) — Baseball Player
1824 Dunsford Road, Jacksonville FL 32207, USA
Murphy, Thomas S — Businessman
Capital Cities/ABC, 77 W 66th St, New York NY 10023, USA
Murphy, Tod J — Basketball Player
23 Parsons Hill Road, Wenham MA 01984, USA
Murphy, Troy B — Basketball Player
Dallas Mavericks, Pavilion, 2909 Taylor St, Dallas TX 75226 USA
Murphy, William E (Billy) — Baseball Player
5309 66th Ave Court W, University Place WA 98467, USA
Murphy, William P, Jr — Inventor (Disposable Metal Trays)
25 SW 24th Road, Miami FL 33129, USA
Murphy-O'Connor, Cormac Cardinal — Religious Leader
Archbishop's House, Ambrosden Ave, London SW1P 1QJ, England
Murray, Andrew (Andy) — Tennis Player
Association of Tennis Professionals, Palliser Road, London W14 9EB, England
Murray, Andy — Ice Hockey Coach
5765 232nd St W, Faribault MN 55021, USA
Murray, Ann — Opera Singer
Augstein & Hahn, Tal 28, 80331 Munich, Germany
Murray, Anne — Singer
Box 69030, 12 Sainte Claire Ave E, Toronto, ON M4T 1KO, Canada
Murray, Bill — Actor, Comedian
Ziffren Brittenham Branca, 1801 Century Park W, #700, Los Angeles CA 90067 USA
Murray, Brian — Actor
Paradigm Agency, 360 Park Ave S, #1600, New York NY 10010 USA
Murray, Brian Doyle — Actor
Abrams Artists, 9200 W Sunset Blvd, #1125, West Hollywood CA 90069 USA
Murray, Bruce C — Planetary Scientist, Geologist
Jet Propulsion Laboratory, 4800 Oak Grove Dr, Pasadena CA 91109, USA
Murray, Bryan C — Ice Hockey Coach, Executive
2215 NE 32nd Ave, Fort Lauderdale FL 33305, USA
Murray, Calvin D — Baseball Player
17434 Courtney Pine Circle, Spring TX 77379, USA
Murray, Chad Michael — Actor, Model
Brillstein Entertainment Partners, 9150 Wilshire Blvd, #350, Beverly Hills CA 90212 USA
Murray, Cherry A — Physicist
Lucent Technologies, 700 Mountain Ave, New Providence NJ 07974, USA
Murray, Chris — Chemist
I B M Watson Research Center, PO Box 218, Yorktown Heights NY 10598 USA
Murray, Dale A — Baseball Player
5695 FM 2718, Yorktown TX 78164, USA
Murray, Dave — Guitarist (Iron Maiden)
Sanctuary Music Mgmt, 82 Bishop's Bridge Road, London W2 6BB, England
Murray, David K — Jazz Saxophonist, Orchestra Leader
Joel Chriss, 60 E 8th St, #34N, New York NY 10003 USA
Murray, Devon — Actor
PO Box 814, Maynooth, County Kildare, Ireland
Murray, Don — Actor
1201 La Patera Canyon Road, Goleta CA 93117, USA
Murray, Doug — Cartoonist ('Nam)
Marvel Comic Group, 10 E 40th St, #900, New York NY 10016, USA
Murray, Eddie C — Baseball Player
15609 Bronco Dr, Canyon Country CA 91387, USA

M

Murray, Edward P (Eddie) 1070 Forest Bay Dr, Waterford MI 48328, USA	Football Player
Murray, Glen 1320 10th St, Manhattan Beach CA 90266, USA	Ice Hockey Player
Murray, Hannah Troika, 74 Clerkenwell Road, #300, London EC1M 5QA, England	Actress
Murray, Iain International Management Group, 75490 Fairway Dr, Indian Wells CA 92210, USA	Yachtsman
Murray, James D University of Washington, Applied Mathematics Dept, PO Box 352420, Seattle WA 98195, USA	Biologist
Murray, Jennifer Polar First, Onslow Gardens, #2, London SW7 3LX, England	Aviatrix, Explorer
Murray, Jim 37 Viceroy Crescent, Brandon MB R7B 3R7, Canada	Ice Hockey Player
Murray, Joel Abrams Artists, 9200 W Sunset Blvd, #1125, West Hollywood CA 90069 USA	Actor
Murray, Jonathan Bunim/Murray Productions, 6007 Sepulveda Blvd, Van Nuys CA 91411, USA	Producer, Director, Writer
Murray, Joseph E 108 Abbott Road, Wellesley Hills MA 02481, USA	Nobel Medicine Laureate
Murray, Keith Richard Walters, PO Box 2789, Toluca Lake CA 91610 USA	Rap Artist
Murray, Larry 3200 Round Hill Dr, Hayward CA 94542, USA	Baseball Player
Murray, Matthew M (Matt) 109 Greenwood Ave, Swampscott MA 01907, USA	Baseball Player
Murray, Peg 800 Light House Road, Southold NY 11971, USA	Actress
Murray, Randy Royal Lepage Foothills, 50-805 5th Ave SW, Calgary AB T2P 0N6, Canada	Ice Hockey Player
Murray, Rob Providence Bruins, 1 La Salle Square, Providence RI 02903, USA	Ice Hockey Player
Murray, Robert (Bob) Anaheim Ducks, 2695 E Katella Ave, Anaheim CA 92806 USA	Ice Hockey Player, Executive
Murray, Ronald (Flip) Atlanta Hawks, Centennial Tower, 101 Marietta St NW, #1900, Atlanta GA 30303 USA	Basketball Player
Murray, Sean Unified Mgmt, 4231 National Ave, Burbank CA 91505, USA	Actor
Murray, Stuart Stuart Murray Assoc, 144 High St, North Sydney NSW 2060, Australia	Architect
Murray, Terence R (Terry) 11 Kirkwood Road, Scarborough ME 04074, USA	Ice Hockey Player, Coach
Murray, Terrence (Terry) Fleet Boston Corp, PO Box 55850, Boston MA 02205, USA	Financier
Murray, Tracy L 2419 Tour Edition Dr, Henderson NV 89074, USA	Basketball Player
Murray, Troy Chicago Blackhawks, United Center, 1901 W Madison St, Chicago IL 60612, USA	Ice Hockey Player
Murray, Ty 1660 Private Road 1213, Stephenville TX 76401, USA	Rodeo Rider
Murray-Leslie, Alex K Records, 924 Jefferson St SE, #101, Olympia WA 98501, USA	Singer (Chicks in Speed)
Murrell, Adrian 17236 Green Dolphin Lane, Cornelius NC 28031, USA	Football Player
Murrett, Robert B National Geospatial Intelligence Agency, 7500 Geoint Dr, Springfield VA 22150 USA	Navy Admiral
Murrey, Dorie S 230 NE 178th St, Shoreline WA 98155, USA	Basketball Player
Murro, Noam Management 360, 9111 Wilshire Blvd, Beverly Hills CA 90210 USA	Director, Producer
Murtagh, Kate 5104 Greenbush Ave, Sherman Oaks CA 91423, USA	Actress
Murton, Matthew H (Matt) 2304 Silver Palm Dr, #302, Kissimmee FL 34747, USA	Baseball Player
Murzyn, Dana 41 Sunset Way SE, Calgary AB T2X 3H6, Canada	Ice Hockey Player
Musabayev, Talgat A Cosmonaut Training Center, Star City, 141160 Zvezdny Gorodok, Moscow Oblast, Russia	Cosmonaut
Musante, Tony 38 Bedford St, New York NY 10014, USA	Actor
Musburger, Brent W 286 Locha Dr, Jupiter FL 33458, USA	Sportscaster
Muse, Arizona Next Model Mgmt, 23 Watts St, New York NY 10013 USA	Model, Actress
Muser, Anthony J (Tony) 1122 Martha Ann Dr, Los Alamitos CA 90720, USA	Baseball Player, Manager
Museveni, Yoweri K President's Office, PO Box 7108, Kampala, Uganda	President, Uganda; Army General
Musgrave, F Story 8572 Sweetwater Trail, Kissimmee FL 34747, USA	Astronaut
Musgrave, Mandy Innovative Artists, 1505 10th St, Santa Monica CA 90401 USA	Actress
Musgrave, R Kenton US Court of International Trade, 1 Federal Plaza, New York NY 10278, USA	Judge
Musgrave, Ted Ultra Motorsports, 22 Raceway Dr, Mooresville NC 28115, USA	Auto, Truck Racing Driver
Musgrave, Thea Novello Co, 8/9 Firth St, London W1V 5TZ, England	Composer, Conductor
Musgrave, William S (Bill) 4062 Leprechan Way, Duluth GA 30097, USA	Football Player
Musgraves, Dennis E 17100 N Highway 24, Centralia MO 65240, USA	Baseball Player
Musharraf, Pervez President's Office, Aiwan-e-Sadr, Mall & Mayo Roads, Islamabad, Pakistan	President, Pakistan; Army General
Mushok, Mike The Firm, 2049 Century Park E, #2550, Los Angeles CA 90067 USA	Guitarist (Staind)

Musial, Stanley F (Stan)	Baseball Player
1650 Des Peres Road, #125, Saint Louis MO 63131, USA	
Musil, Frantisek (Frank)	Ice Hockey Player
Edmonton Oilers, 11230 110th St, Edmonton AB T5G 3H7, Canada	
Musiol, Bogdan	Bobsled Athlete
Fitness-Studio, Talstr 50, 98544 Zella-Mehlis, Germany	
Musiq	Singer
Island/Def Soul Records, 825 8th Ave, #2700, New York NY 10019, USA	
Musk, Elon	Businessman
SpaceX, 1 Rocket Road, Hawthorne CA 90250, USA	
Musker, John	Animator, Director
Creative Artists Agency, 2000 Ave of Stars, #100, Los Angeles CA 90067 USA	
Musselman, Jeffrey J (Jeff)	Baseball Player
1842 Port Tiffin Place, Newport Beach CA 92660, USA	
Musselwhite, Charlie	Singer, Harmonica Player, Guitarist
Rosebud Agency, PO Box 170429, San Francisco CA 94117 USA	
Mussenden, Isis	Costume Designer
Messina Baker Entertainment, 955 Carrillo Dr, #100, Los Angeles CA 90048 USA	
Mussina, Michael C (Mike)	Baseball Player
737 White Church Road, Muncy PA 17756, USA	
Musso, Mitchel T	Actor
Principato-Young, 9465 Wilshire Blvd, #880, Beverly Hills CA 90212 USA	
Mustafaa, Najee	Football Player
4265 Jailette Road, Atlanta GA 30349, USA	
Mustaine, David S (Dave)	Guitarist (Metallica, Megadeth)
E S P Mgmt, 838 N Doheny Dr, #302, West Hollywood CA 90069, USA	
Mustard, Chad A	Football Player
6329 S 171st St, Omaha NE 68135, USA	
Muster, Brad W	Football Player
2017 Stony Oak Court, Santa Rosa CA 95403, USA	
Muster, Thomas	Tennis Player
370 Felter Ave, Hewlett NY 11557, USA	
Mustin, Henry C	Navy Admiral
2347 S Rolfe St, Arlington VA 22202, USA	
Mustonen, Olli	Concert Pianist, Conductor, Composer
Hazard Chase, 25 City Road, Cambridge CB1 1DP, England	
Mutchnick, Max	Producer
VisionArt Mgmt, 530 N Larchmont Blvd, #2, Los Angeles CA 90004, USA	
Mutebi II, Ronald Muwenda	King, Uganda
Mengo Palace, PO Box 58, Kampala, Uganda	
Muth, Rene	Basketball Coach
Pennsylvania State University, Athletic Dept, University Park PA 16802, USA	
Muti, Ornella	Actress
33 Via Porta de Pinta, 24100 Bergamo, Italy	
Muti, Riccardo	Conductor
Via Corti Alle Mura 25, 48100 Ravenna, Italy	
Mutombo, Dikembe	Basketball Player
4787 Northside Dr NW, Atlanta GA 30327, USA	
Mutscheller, James F (Jim)	Football Player
12350 Rosslare Ridge Road, #102, Lutherville Timonium MD 21093, USA	
Mutter, Anne-Sophie	Concert Violinist
Effnerstr 48, 81925 Munich, Germany	
Muxworthy, Jake	Actor
Innovative Artists, 1505 10th St, Santa Monica CA 90401 USA	
Muzzatti, Jason	Ice Hockey Player
4581 Dunmorrow Dr, Okemos MI 48864, USA	
Mwampembwa, Godfrey (Gado)	Editorial Cartoonist
Sasa Serna Productions, PO Box 13956, Nairobi, Kenya	
Mya	Singer, Actress, Songwriter
Media Artists Group, 8222 Melrose Ave, #203, Los Angeles CA 90048 USA	
Myasnikovich, Mikhail U	Prime Minister, Belarus
Prime Minister's Office, Karl Marx Str 38, 220016 Minsk, Belarus	
Myers, Barton	Architect
949 Toro Canyon Road, Santa Barbara CA 93108, USA	
Myers, Billie	Singer, Actress
R J O Artist Relations & Mgmt, H S B C Bank, 101 W 14th St, New York NY 10011, USA	
Myers, Brett A	Baseball Player
385 Summerset Dr, Saint Johns FL 32259, USA	
Myers, Chris	Sportscaster
Fox-TV, Sports Dept, 205 W 67th St, New York NY 10065 USA	
Myers, Cynthia	Model, Actress
PO Box 10, Llano CA 93544, USA	
Myers, Dale D	Space Engineer
Dale Myers Assoc, 7835 Rush Rose Dr, #214, Carlsbad CA 92009, USA	
Myers, Danny	Auto Racing Driver
Childress Racing, PO Box 1189, Industrial Dr, Welcome NC 27374, USA	
Myers, Gregory J (Greg)	Football Player
2915 S Deframe Way, Lakewood CO 80228, USA	
Myers, Gregory R (Greg)	Baseball Player
7917 Brasado Way, Riverside CA 92508, USA	
Myers, Jack D	Physician
14 Prout Road, Freeport ME 04032, USA	
Myers, Joel Philip	Glass Artist
151 W Market St, Marietta PA 17547, USA	
Myers, John M (Jack)	Football Player
25 Biltmore Lane, Menlo Park CA 94025, USA	
Myers, Lisa	Commentator
NBC-TV, News Dept, 4001 Nebraska Ave NW, Washington DC 20016 USA	
Myers, Margaret J (Dee Dee)	Government Official, Commentator
Vanity Fair, Conde Nast Publications, 4 Times Square, New York NY 10036, USA	
Myers, Michael	Opera Singer
Opera et Concert, 37 Rue de la Chaussee d'Antin, 75009 Paris, France	
Myers, Michael S (Mike)	Baseball Player
337 High Ridge Way, Castle Rock CO 80108, USA	
Myers, Mike	Actor, Comedian
W M E Entertainment, 9601 Wilshire Blvd, #300, Beverly Hills CA 90210 USA	

M

Musial - Myers

Myers, Norman — Environmental Scientist, Conservationist
Upper Meadow, Old Road, Headington, Oxford OX3 8SZ, England
Myers, Peter E (Pete) — Basketball Player
19W011 13th St, Lombard IL 60148, USA
Myers, Randall K (Randy) — Baseball Player
15525 NE Caples Road, Brush Prairie WA 98606, USA
Myers, Richard B (Dick) — Air Force General
Kansas State University, History Dept, Manhattan KS 66506, USA
Myers, Roderick D — Baseball Player
1816 S 3rd St, Conroe TX 77301, USA
Myers, Rodney L — Baseball Player
229 E Tanya Road, Phoenix AZ 85086, USA
Myers, Russell — Cartoonist (Broom Hilda)
Tribune Media Services, 435 N Michigan Ave, #1500, Chicago IL 60611 USA
Myers, Terry-Jo — Golfer
11592 Timberline Circle, Fort Myers FL 33966, USA
Myers, Thomas P (Tom) — Football Player
6015 Rapid Creek Court, Kingwood TX 77345, USA
Myers, Walter Dean — Photographer
Miriam Altshuler Literary Agency, 53 Old Post Road N, Red Hook NY 12571, USA
Myerson, Bess — Beauty Queen, Actress, Consumer Activist
453 7th St, Santa Monica CA 90402, USA
Myerson, Mike — Guitarist (Heartland)
Country Thunder Records, 1016 17th Ave S, Nashville TN 37212, USA
Myerson, Roger B — Nobel Economics Laureate
1219 Elmwood Ave, Wilmette IL 60091, USA
Myers-Tikalsky, Linda — Skier
RR 5 Box 2651, Santa Fe NM 87506, USA
Myette, Aaron — Baseball Player
14277 101A Ave, Surry BC V0B 2G2, Canada
Mygind, Peter — Actor
Elmer Dahl Agencies, Kanneworff Overgaard, Square 8B, 5600 Faabourg, Denmark
Myhre, John — Art Director, Production Designer
Sandra Marsh & Associates, 9150 Wilshire Blvd, #220, Beverly Hills CA 90212, USA
Myhrvold, Nathan — Businessman
Intellectual Ventures, 3150 139th Ave SE, Building 4, Bellevue WA 98005, USA
Myles, Alannah — Singer, Guitarist, Songwriter
Miracle Prestige, 1 Water Lane, Camden Town, London NW1 8N2, England
Myles, Heather — Singer
Heather Hotline, 5165 Brighton Dr, Riverside CA 92504, USA
Myles, Sophia — Actress
Gersh Agency, 9465 Wilshire Blvd, #600, Beverly Hills CA 90212 USA
Mylnikov, Sergei A — Ice Hockey Player
Kuzkin Cup Hockey, Ul Talalikkin VI 28, 109029 Moscow, Russia
Myre, Philippe (Phil) — Ice Hockey Player
39270 Heatherbrook Dr, Farmington Hills MI 48331, USA
Myrick, Daniel — Director
Media Talent Group, 9200 W Sunset Blvd, #550, West Hollywood CA 90069 USA
Myrtle, Charles J (Chip), Jr — Football Player
7500 E Quincy Ave, #E110, Denver CO 80237, USA
Myslinski, Thomas J (Tom), Jr — Football Player
1762 Dickens Cove, Germantown TN 38139, USA
Mystikal — Rap Artist
Richard Walters, PO Box 2789, Toluca Lake CA 91610 USA

Na Yeon Choi
Ladies Pro Golf Assn, 100 International Golf Dr, Daytona Beach FL 32124 USA — Golfer

Na, Kevin
Professional Golfer's Assn, PO Box 109601, Palm Beach Gardens FL 33410 USA — Golfer

Naacke, Lisa
Z B F Agentur, Friedrichstr 39, 10969 Berlin, Germany — Actress

Naber, John P
PO Box 50107, Pasadena CA 91115, USA — Swimmer

Nabholz, Christopher W (Chris)
1 Cottage Hill W, Pottsville PA 17901, USA — Baseball Player

Nabokov, Evgeni V
5763 Poppy Hills Place, San Jose CA 95138, USA — Ice Hockey Player

Nabors, Jim
PO Box 10364, Honolulu HI 96816, USA — Actor, Singer

Nachamkin, Boris A
350 E 62nd St, #5J, New York NY 10065, USA — Basketball Player

Nachbaur, Donald K (Don)
671 Clermont Dr, Richland WA 99352, USA — Ice Hockey Player

Nachmanoff, Jeffrey
Creative Artists Agency, 2000 Ave of Stars, #100, Los Angeles CA 90067 USA — Director, Writer

Nachtwey, James
First Run/Icarus Films, 32 Court St, #2007, Brooklyn NY 11201, USA — Photojournalist

Nadal, Rafael
International Management Group, Via Augusta 200, 08021 Barcelona, Spain — Tennis Player

Nadeau, Gary
First Wave, 319 E 85th St, #200, New York NY 10028, USA — Director

Nader, Laura
University of California, Anthropology Dept, Kroeber Hall, Berkeley CA 94720, USA — Anthropologist

Nader, Michael
Paradigm Agency, 360 N Crescent Dr, North Building, Beverly Hills CA 90210 USA — Actor

Nader, Ralph
1600 20th St NW, Washington DC 20009, USA — Consumer Activist

Nadig, Marie-Theres
Haus Olympia, 8897 Flumserberg, Switzerland — Alpine Skier

Nadingar, Emmanuel D
Prime Minister's Office, La Primature, Vale Royal, N'Djamena, Chad — Prime Minister, Chad

Nady, Xavier C, VI
11320 Wild Meadow Place, San Diego CA 92131, USA — Baseball Player

Nafzger, Carl
General Delivery, Olton TX 79064, USA — Thoroughbred Racing Trainer

Nafziger, Dana A
251 El Dorado Way, Pismo Beach CA 93449, USA — Football Player

Nagalla, Srinivasa R
Oregon Health Science University, 3181 SW Jackson Park Dr, Portland OR 97239 USA — Pediatrician

Nagano, Kent G
Berkeley Symphony Orchestra, 1942 University Ave, #207, Berkeley CA 94704, USA — Conductor

Nagashima, Shigeo
3-29-19 Denenchofu, Ohtaku, Tokyo 145, Japan — Baseball Player, Manager

Nagel, Sidney R
4913 S Kimbark Ave, Chicago IL 60615, USA — Physicist

Nagel, Steven R
3801 Eagle View Court, Columbia MO 65203, USA — Astronaut

Nagel, Thomas
New York University, Law School, 40 Washington Square S, New York NY 10012, USA — Philosopher

Nagle, Browning
2281 Birchton Dr, Germantown TN 38139, USA — Football Player

Nagler, R Gern
73595 Agave Lane, Palm Desert CA 92260, USA — Football Player

Nagra, Parminder
Protea Group International, 23975 Park Sorrento, #365, Calabasas CA 91302, USA — Actress

Nagy, Charles H
60 Robin Road, Westbury NY 11590, USA — Baseball Player

Nagy, Michael
Kunstler Sekretariat am Gasteig, Rosenheimer Str 52, 81669 Munich, Germany — Opera Singer

Nagy, Michael T (Mike)
8 Indian Trail, Bronx NY 10465, USA — Baseball Player

Nagy, Stanislaw Cardinal
Priests of Sacred Heart, Via Casale S Piov 20, 00165 Rome, Italy — Religious Leader

Naharin, Ohad
Batsheva Dance Co, 6 Yechieli St, Tel-Aviv 65149, Israel — Choreographer

Nahodha, Shamsi Vuai
Chief Minister's Office, PO Box 239, Zanzibar, Tanzania — Chief Minister, Zanzibar

Nahon, Chris
Hansen Jacobson Teller, 450 N Roxbury Dr, #800, Beverly Hills CA 90210, USA — Director

Nahorodny, William G (Bill)
1948 Rainbow Dr, Clearwater FL 33765, USA — Baseball Player

Nahrgang, Jim
18283 Parkshore Dr, Northville MI 48168, USA — Ice Hockey Player

Nahyan, Khalifa bin Zayed Al
Manhal Palace, Abu Dhabi, United Arab Emirates — President, United Arab Emirates

Naidu, Ajay
Global Artists Agency, 6253 Hollywood Blvd, #508, Los Angeles CA 90028, USA — Actor, Director, Writer

Naidus, Alex
Slumberland Records, PO Box 19029, Oakland CA 94619, USA — Bassist (Pains of Being Pure at Heart)

Naifeh, Steven W
335 Sumter St SE, Aiken SC 29801, USA — Writer

Nail, David
Universal Records, 70 Universal City Plaza, Universal City CA 91608 USA — Singer

Nail, Jimmy
Independent Talent Group, Oxford House, 76 Oxford St, London W1D 1BS, England — Actor

Nailatikau, Epeli
President's Office, Government House, Berkeley Crescent, PO Box 2513, Suva, Viti Levu, Fiji — President, Fiji; Brigadier General

Nails, Jamie M
PO Box 667291, Pompano Beach FL 33066, USA — Football Player

Naima
Ford Models Inc, 111 5th Ave, #900, New York NY 10003 USA — Model

Naimoli, Vincent — Baseball Executive
16616 Villalenda de Avila, Tampa FL 33613, USA
Naipaul, V S — Nobel Literature Laureate
Gillon Aitken Ltd, 29 Fernshaw Road, London SW10 0TG, England
Nair, Mira — Director
Cinetic Mgmt, 555 W 25th St, #400, New York NY 10001 USA
Nairne, Robert C (Rob) — Football Player
2611 Colt Road, Rancho Palos Verdes CA 90275, USA
Naisbitt, John — Writer
Spittelauer Platz 5A3A, 1090 Vienna, Austria
Naish, Bronwen — Concert Double Bass Player
Moelfre, Cwm Pennant, Garndolbenmaen, Gwunedd, North Wales LL5 9AX, Wales
Najee — Jazz Saxophonist
Pyramid Entertainment, 377 Rector Place, #21A, New York NY 10280 USA
Najera, Eduardo A — Basketball Player
Charlotte Bobcats, 333 E Trade St, #A, Charlotte NC 28202 USA
Najiib Tun Razak — Prime Minister, Malaysia
Prime Minister's Office, Jalan Dato Onn, 50502 Kuala Lumpur, Malaysia
Najimy, Kathy — Actress
One Entertainment, 12 W 57th St, #PH 1, New York NY 10019 USA
Najita, Tetsuo — Historian
University of Chicago, History Dept, 1126 E 59th St, Chicago IL 60637, USA
Nakache, Olivier — Director
Creative Artists Agency, 2000 Ave of Stars, #100, Los Angeles CA 90067 USA
Nakajima, Tadashi — Astronomer
California Institute of Technology, Astronomy Dept, Pasadena CA 91125, USA
Nakajima, Tsuneyuki (Tommy) — Golfer
International Management Group, 7-18-18 Roppongi, Minatoku, Tokyo 106 0032 Japan
Nakama, Keo — Swimmer
1344 9th Ave, Honolulu HI 96816, USA
Nakamatsu, Jon — Concert Pianist
Van Cliburn Foundation, 2525 Ridgmar Blvd, #307, Fort Worth TX 76116, USA
Nakamura, Kuniwo — President, Palau
Ta Belau Party, Olbiil era Kelulau, Koror PW 96940, Palau
Nakamura, Shuji — Inventor (Blue & White LED Lasers)
University of California, Engineering College, Santa Barbara CA 93106, USA
Nakamura, Suzy — Actress
Innovative Artists, 1505 10th St, Santa Monica CA 90401 USA
Nakanishi, Koji — Chemist
560 Riverside Dr, New York NY 10027, USA
Nakata, Hideo — Director
I C M Partners, 10250 Constellation Blvd, #900, Los Angeles CA 90067 USA
Nakata, Hidetoshi — Soccer Player
A C Parma, Viale Partigiani d'Italia, 43100 Parma, Italy
Nakatani, Corey — Thoroughbred Racing Jockey
PO Box 7673, Louisville KY 40257, USA
Naked, Bif — Singer, Songwriter
Crazed Mgmt, PO Box 356, Jamison PA 18929, USA
Nakhirunkanok, Porntip (Bui) — Beauty Queen
Angels Wings Foundation, 1482 E Valley Road, #428, Montecito CA 93108, USA
Nalbandian, David — Tennis Player
Association of Tennis Professionals, 200 Tournament Road, Ponte Vedra Beach FL 32082 USA
Nalder, Eric C — Journalist
Seattle Times, Editorial Dept, 1120 John St, Seattle WA 98109 USA
Nalen, Thomas A (Tom) — Football Player
4081 Preserve Parkway N, Greenwood Village CO 80121, USA
Nalick, Anna — Singer, Songwriter
Jane Johnson, 21731 Ventura Blvd, #300, Woodland Hills CA 91364, USA
Nalin, David R — Pharmacologist
100 Luck Hill Road, West Chester PA 19382, USA
Nall, Benita — Actress
C E S D, 10635 Santa Monica Blvd, #130, Los Angeles CA 90025 USA
Nall, N Anita — Swimmer
PO Box 872505, Tempe AZ 85287, USA
Nalluri, Bharat — Director
Independent Talent Group, Oxford House, 76 Oxford St, London W1D 1BS, England
Nam Tae-Hee — Soccer Player
Football Assn, 1-131 Sinmunno, 2-Ga Jongno-Gu, Seoul 110 062, South Korea
Nama, George A — Artist, Sculptor
RR 1 Box 72, Montauk NY 11954, USA
Namaliu, Rabbie L — Prime Minister, Papua New Guinea
PO Box 6655, National Capital District, Boroko, Papua New Guinea
Namath, Joseph W (Joe) — Football Player, Actor
Namanco Productions, 300 E 51st St, #7D, New York NY 10022, USA
Nambu, Yoichiro — Nobel Physics Laureate
University of Chicago, Fermi Institute, 5640 S Ellis Ave, Chicago IL 60637, USA
Nance, John J — Writer
4512 8th Ave, Tacoma WA 98405, USA
Nance, Todd — Drummer (Widespread Panic)
Brown Cat Inc, 400 Foundry St, Athens GA 30601 USA
Nanne, Louis V (Lou) — Ice Hockey Player
6982 Tupa Dr, Minneapolis MN 55439, USA
Nannini, Alessandro — Auto Racing Driver
Via Massetana Romana 56, 53199 Siena, Italy
Nannini, Gianna — Singer, Songwriter
Cose di Musica, Via Plinio 15, 20129 Milan, Italy
Nantis, Rich — Ice Hockey Player
9585 Rue Jourdain, Quebec QC G2K 1K5, Canada
Nanty, Isabelle — Actress
Voyez Mon Agent, 20 Ave Rapp, 75007 Paris, France
Nantz, James W (Jim), III — Sportscaster
CBS-TV, Sports Dept, 51 W 52nd St, New York NY 10019 USA
Napier, John — Designer
M L R, Douglas House, 16-18 Douglas St, London SW1P 4PB, England
Napier, Mark — Ice Hockey Player, Executive
National Hockey League Alumni Assn, 170 Attwell Dr, #650, Toronto ON M9W 5Z5, Canada

Napier, Wilfrid F Cardinal
Archbishop's House, 154 Gordon Road, Greyville 4023, South Africa — Religious Leader

Napoles, Jose A
Cerrada Tizapan 9-303 Ediciov, Codigo Postel 06080 Mexico City DF, Mexico — Boxer

Napoli, Michael A (Mike)
2010 NW 118th Ave, Pembroke Pines FL 33026, USA — Baseball Player

Napolitano, Christopher
Playboy, Editor's Office, 680 N Lake Shore Dr, Chicago IL 60611, USA — Editor

Napolitano, Giorgio
President's Office, Palazzo del Quirinale, Via Nazionale 190, 00184 Rome, Italy — President, Italy

Napolitano, Janet
Homeland Security Department, Washington DC 20528 USA — Secretary, Homeland Security

Napolitano, Johnette
Agency Group Ltd, 142 W 57th St, #600, New York NY 10019 USA — Singer (Concrete Blonde), Songwriter

Naragon, Harold R (Hal)
1521 Hagey Dr, Barberton OH 44203, USA — Baseball Player

Narain, Nicole
8033 W Sunset Blvd, #224, West Hollywood CA 90046, USA — Model, Actress

Naranjo, Gerardo
Creative Artists Agency, 2000 Ave of Stars, #100, Los Angeles CA 90067 USA — Director

Narayen, Shantanu
Adobe Systems, 345 Park Ave, San Jose CA 95110, USA — Businessman

Narcisse, Daniel
T H W Kiel Handball, Ziegelteich 30, 24103 Kiel, Germany — Handball Player

Nardelli, Robert L
Chrysler Corp, 100 Chrysler Dr, Auburn Hills MI 48326, USA — Businessman

Narducci, Kathrine
Greene Assoc, 1901 Ave of Stars, #130, Los Angeles CA 90067 USA — Actress

Narducci, Tim
Artist Group International, 9560 Wilshire Blvd, #400, Beverly Hills CA 90212 USA — Singer, Guitarist (Systematic)

Nares, James
Paul Kasmin Gallery, 511 W 27th St, New York NY 10001, USA — Artist

Narita, Hiro
2262 Magnolia Ave, Petaluma CA 94952, USA — Cinematographer

Narleski, Raymond E (Ray)
1183 Chews Landing Road, Clementon NJ 08021, USA — Baseball Player

Narron, Jerry A
304 Ashworth Dr, Goldsboro NC 27530, USA — Baseball Player, Manager

Naruhito
Imperial Palace, 1-1 Chiyoda, Chiyoda-ku, Tokyo 100, Japan — Crown Prince, Japan

Narvekar, Prabhakar R
4701 Willard Ave, Chevy Chase MD 20815, USA — Government Official, Financier

Narveson, Chris
1804 Kenwyck Manor Way, Raleigh NC 27612, USA — Baseball Player

Nasar, Sylvia
Columbia University, 2950 Broadway, Front 1, New York NY 10027, USA — Writer

Nascimento, Milton
Feinstein Mgmt, 8560 W Sunset Blvd, West Hollywood CA 90069, USA — Singer, Songwriter

Nash Whitaker, Keisha
344 E 59th St, New York NY 10022, USA — Fashion Designer

Nash, Charles F (Cotton)
600 Summershade Circle, Lexington KY 40502, USA — Basketball, Baseball Player

Nash, David
Capel Rhiw, Blanau, Ffestiniog, Gwynedd Wales LL41 3NT, Wales — Sculptor

Nash, Graham W
Creative Artists Agency, 2000 Ave of Stars, #100, Los Angeles CA 90067 USA — Singer, Songwriter

Nash, James E (Jim)
4383 White Surrey Dr NW, Kennesaw GA 30144, USA — Baseball Player

Nash, Jamia S
Carson-Adler Agency, 250 W 57 St, #2030, New York NY 10107, USA — Actress, Singer

Nash, John F, Jr
Princeton University, Economics Dept, Fine Hall, Princeton NJ 08544, USA — Nobel Economics Laureate

Nash, Johnny
I C M Partners, 730 5th Ave, New York NY 10019 USA — Singer, Songwriter

Nash, Joseph A (Joe)
15 Colgate Road, Wellesley MA 02482, USA — Football Player

Nash, Kate
13 Artists, 11-14 Kensington St, Brighton BN1 4AJ, England — Singer, Songwriter

Nash, Kenny
1336 NE 16th Terrace, Fort Lauderdale FL 33304, USA — Singer

Nash, Leigh
Nettwerk Mgmt, 1201 Villa Place, #206, Nashville TN 37212 USA — Singer (Sixpence None the Richer)

Nash, Niecy
Principato-Young, 9465 Wilshire Blvd, #880, Beverly Hills CA 90212 USA — Actress, Comedienne

Nash, Noreen
719 N Maple Dr, Beverly Hills CA 90210, USA — Actress

Nash, Rick
57 Deerfield Crescent, Brampton ON L6T 1K8, Canada — Ice Hockey Player

Nash, Robert L (Bob)
659 Kahiau Loop, Honolulu HI 96821, USA — Basketball Player

Nash, Steven J (Steve)
6602 E Indian Bend Road, Paradise Valley AZ 85253, USA — Basketball Player

Nash, Tyson
16895 SW 91st Ave, #17, Portland OR 97223, USA — Ice Hockey Player

Naslund, Markus
Mike Gillis Assoc, 154 Earl St, Kingston ON K7L 2H2, Canada — Ice Hockey Player

Naslund, Mats T
General Delivery, 6963 Pregassona, Switzerland — Ice Hockey Player

Naslund, Ronald A (Ron)
2600 Cheyenne Circle, Hopkins MN 55305, USA — Ice Hockey Player

Nasr, Seyyed Hossein
George Washington University, Gelman Library, Washington DC 20052, USA — Theologian

Nastase, Ilie
Calea Plevnei 14, Bucharest, Hungary — Tennis Player

Natal, Robert M (Bob)
3913 Cockrill Dr, McKinney TX 75070, USA — Baseball Player

Natali, Vincenzo — Director, Writer
Creative Artists Agency, 2000 Ave of Stars, #100, Los Angeles CA 90067 USA

Natalicio, Diana S — Educator
University of Texas, President's Office, El Paso TX 79968, USA

Natanson, Agathe — Actress
Artmedia, 20 Ave Rapp, 75007 Paris, France

Nater, Swen E — Basketball Player
4125 248th Court SE, Issaquah WA 98029, USA

Nathan, David G — Physician
Dana-Farber Cancer Institute, 44 Binney St, Boston MA 02115, USA

Nathan, Joseph A — Businessman
Compuware Corp, 1 Campus Martius, Detroit MI 48226, USA

Nathan, Joseph M (Joe) — Baseball Player
19066 Vogel Farm Road, Eden Prairie MN 55347, USA

Nathan, Sellapan Ramanathan (S R) — President, Singapore
President's Office, Orchard Road, Istana, 238823 Singapore, Singapore

Nathan, Tony C — Football Player, Coach
15110 Dunbarton Place, Hialeah FL 33016, USA

Nathaniel (Popp), Bishop — Religious Leader
Romanian Orthodox Episcopate, 2522 Grey Tower Road, Jackson MI 49201, USA

Nathanson, Jeff — Director, Producer, Writer
United Talent Agency, 9336 Civic Center Dr, Beverly Hills CA 90210 USA

Nathanson, Matt — Singer, Songwriter
Crush Mgmt, 60-62 E 11th St, #7, New York NY 10003 USA

Nathman, John B — Navy Admiral
Commander, Fleet Forces Command, 1562 Mitscher Ave, Norfolk VA 23551 USA

Natonski, Richard F — Marine Corps General
Commander, Marine Forces Command, 1468 Ingram St, Norfolk VA 23511 USA

Natori, Josie C — Fashion Designer
Natori Co, 40 E 34th St, New York NY 10016, USA

Natsuki, Shizuko — Writer
2-6-1 Ooile, Mini-amiku, Fukuokashi 815 0073, Japan

Natt, Calvin L — Basketball Player
25201 E Indore Dr, Aurora CO 80016, USA

Natter, Robert J — Navy Admiral
Robert J Natter Assoc, 507 Rutile Dr, Porte Vedre FL 32082, USA

Nattiel, Ricky R — Football Player
835 NW 119th St, Gainesville FL 32606, USA

Nattress, Eric J (Ric) — Ice Hockey Player
Stoney Creek Warriors, 467 Charlton Ave E, Hamilton ON L8W 2Z9, Canada

Naughton, David — Actor
14955 Dickens St, #208, Sherman Oaks CA 91403, USA

Naughton, James — Actor, Singer
Paradigm Agency, 360 N Crescent Dr, North Building, Beverly Hills CA 90210 USA

Naughton, Naturi — Singer (3LW), Actress
Innovative Artists, 1505 10th St, Santa Monica CA 90401 USA

Naulls, William D (Willie) — Basketball Player
511 S Carondelet St, #403, Los Angeles CA 90057, USA

Nault, Marie-Eve — Soccer Player
Canadian Soccer, Place Soccer Canada, 237 Metcalfe St, Ottawa ON K2P 1R2, Canada

Nauman, Bruce L — Sculptor, Artist
4630 Rising Hill Road, Altadena CA 91001, USA

Nause, Martha — Golfer
13206 Patterson Trail, Minocqua WI 54548, USA

Nauta, Katie — Actress, Singer, Model
L A Talent, 8335 W Sunset Blvd, #200, Los Angeles CA 90069 USA

Nava, Gregory — Director
I C M Partners, 10250 Constellation Blvd, #900, Los Angeles CA 90067 USA

Nava, Michael — Writer
California Supreme Court, 350 McAllister St, San Francisco CA 94102, USA

Navarrete, Ximena — Beauty Queen, Model
Miss Universe Organization, 1370 Ave of Americas, #1600, New York NY 10019 USA

Navarro Cintron, Jaime — Baseball Player
8100 Oak Park Road, Orlando FL 32819, USA

Navarro Vivas, Dioner F — Baseball Player
13243 Pike Lake Dr, Riverview FL 33579, USA

Navarro, Carlos — Boxer
1722 W 59th Place, Los Angeles CA 90047, USA

Navarro, David M (Dave) — Guitarist, Pianist (Jane's Addiction)
Armada Partners, 815 Moraga Drive, Los Angeles CA 90049, USA

Navarro, Guillermo J — Cinematographer
Sheldon Prosnit Agency, 800 S Robertson Blvd, #6, Los Angeles CA 90035, USA

Navarro, Juan Carlos — Basketball Player
19545 S Ashglen Circle, Collierville TN 38107, USA

Navies, Hannibal C — Football Player
2356 Bransley Place, Duluth GA 30097, USA

Navka, Tatiana A — Ice Dancer
Skating Federation, Luchnesksaia Nab 8, 119871 Moscow, Russia

Navon, Itzhak — President, Israel
39 Jabotinsky St, Jerusalem, Israel

Navratilova, Martina — Tennis Player
Women's Tennis Assn, 1 Progress Plaza, #1500, Saint Petersburg FL 33701 USA

Naylor, Gloria — Writer
One Way Productions, 638 2nd St, Brooklyn NY 11215, USA

Naylor, Phyllis Reynolds — Writer
401 Russell Ave, #713, Gaithersburg MD 20877, USA

Naymark, Lola — Actress
Agence Artiste Adequet, 80 Rue d'Amsterdam, 75009 Paris, France

Nayyar, Kunal — Actor, Comedian
Innovative Artists, 1505 10th St, Santa Monica CA 90401 USA

Nazarbayev, Nursultan A — President, Kazakhstan
President's Office, 11 Beybitshilik St, 473000 Astana, Kazakhstan

Nazario, Sonia — Journalist
Los Angeles Times, Editorial Dept, 202 W 1st St, Los Angeles CA 90012 USA

NdegeOcello, Me'Shell — Singer, Bassist, Songwriter
Evolution Music Partners, 1680 N Vine St, #500, Los Angeles CA 90028, USA

N'Dour, Youssou — Singer
Konzertagentur Berthold Seliger, Nonnengasse 15, 36037 Fulda, Germany

Neagle, Dennis E (Denny), Jr — Baseball Player
16254 Sandstone Dr, Morrison CO 80465, USA

Neal, Blaine — Baseball Player
256 Dowdy Dr, Gibbstown NJ 08027, USA

Neal, Diane — Actress
Socially Awkward Productions, 344 Grove St, #117, Jersey City NJ 07302, USA

Neal, Dylan — Actor
Metropolitan Talent Agency, 7020 La Presa Dr, Los Angeles CA 90068 USA

Neal, Elise — Actress
A P A Talent/Literary Agency, 405 S Beverly Dr, #300, Beverly Hills CA 90212 USA

Neal, Fred (Curly) — Basketball Player
1639 Tiverton St, Winter Springs FL 32708, USA

Neal, Lloyd — Basketball Player
905 NE Mariners Loop, Portland OR 97211, USA

Neal, Lorenzo L — Football Player
10520 Waterbury Dr, Stockton CA 95209, USA

Neal, Richard I — Marine Corps General
Military Officers Assn, 201 N Washington St, Alexandria VA 22314, USA

Neal, Stephen M (Steve) — Football Player
126 Fales Road, North Attleboro MA 02760, USA

Neal, T Daniel (Dan) — Football Player
711 Homestead Blvd, Louisville KY 40207, USA

Neale, Harry — Ice Hockey Coach
224 Quail Hollow Lane, East Amherst NY 14051, USA

Nealon, Kevin — Actor, Comedian
Gersh Agency, 41 Madison Ave, #3301, New York NY 10010 USA

Nealy, Eddie C (Ed) — Basketball Player
702 Lightstone Dr, San Antonio TX 78258, USA

Neame, Christopher — Actor
Borinstein Oreck Bogart, 3172 Dona Susana Dr, Studio City CA 91604 USA

Near, Holly — Singer, Songwriter, Actress
PO Box 236, Ukiah CA 95482, USA

Neary, Martin G J — Concert Organist, Conductor
71 Clancarty Road, Fulham, London SW6 3BB, England

Neaton, Patrick (Pat) — Ice Hockey Player
3519 Olde Dominion Dr, #2, Brighton MI 48114, USA

Neblett, Carol — Opera Singer
Sardos Artists, 180 W End Ave, New York NY 10023, USA

Nebout, Claire — Actress
Artmedia, 20 Ave Rapp, 75007 Paris, France

Necas, Petr — Prime Minister, Czech Republic
Premier's Office, Nabrezi Edvarda Benese 4, 118 01 Prague 1, Czech Republic

Necciai, Ronald A (Ron) — Baseball Player
6261 Overlook Lane, Belle Vernon PA 15012, USA

Nece, Ryan C — Football Player
4401 W Kennedy Blvd, #300, Tampa FL 33609, USA

Nechita, Alexandra — Artist
Wentworth Gallery, 1118 NW 159th Dr, Miami FL 33169, USA

Neckar, Stanislav (Stan) — Ice Hockey Player
10255 Waterside Oaks Dr, Tampa FL 33647, USA

Nederlander, James M — Producer
Nederlander Organization, 1450 Broadway, #2000, New York NY 10018, USA

Nedjari, Al — Actor
Grantham-Hazekdune, 5 Blenheim St, London W1S 1LD, England

Nedney, Joseph T (Joe) — Football Player
121 Lauren Circle, Scotts Valley CA 95066, USA

Nedomansky, Vaclav — Ice Hockey Player
6600 Beachview Dr, #204, Rancho Palos Verdes CA 90275, USA

Nedved, Pavel — Soccer Player
F C Juventus, Corso Galilo Ferraris 32, 10128 Turin, Italy

Nedved, Petr — Ice Hockey Player
H C Bili Tygri Liberec, Tipsport Arena, Jeronymova 494/20, 460 07 Liberec, Czech Republic

Nee, Adam — Actor
Brillstein Entertainment Partners, 9150 Wilshire Blvd, #350, Beverly Hills CA 90212 USA

Needham, Connie — Actress
126 Laurent, Newport Beach CA 92660, USA

Needham, Hal — Director
Laura Lizer Assoc, PO Box 46609, Los Angeles CA 90046, USA

Needham, Tracey — Actress
Stone Manners Salners, 9911 W Pico Blvd, #1400, Los Angeles CA 90035 USA

Needleman, Herbert L — Cardiologist, Pharmacologist
Pittsburgh University Medical School, 3811 O'Hara St, Pittsburgh PA 15213, USA

Needleman, Jacob — Philosopher
841 Wawona Ave, Oakland CA 94610, USA

Neel, Troy L — Baseball Player
PO Box 1582, El Campo TX 77437, USA

Neely, Bob — Ice Hockey Player
72 Squire Bakers Lane, Markham ON L3P 3H2, Canada

Neely, Cam — Ice Hockey Player, Executive
76 Davison Dr, Lincoln MA 01773, USA

Neely, Mark E, Jr — Historian
Oxford University Press, 198 Madison Ave, #800, New York NY 10016, USA

Neely, Ralph E — Football Player
6943 Sperry St, Dallas TX 75214, USA

Neeman, Calvin A (Cal) — Baseball Player
93 Champagne Dr, Lake Saint Louis MO 63367, USA

Neeson, Liam — Actor
A R G, 4 Great Portland St, London W1W 8PA, England

Nef, John U — Historian
2726 N St NW, Washington DC 20007, USA

Nef, Sonja — Alpine Skier
Halten 345, 9035 Grub, Switzerland

Neff, Garrett — Model
Click Model Mgmt, 881 7th Ave, New York NY 10019 USA

Neff, Lucas — Actor
Untitled Entertainment, 350 S Beverly Dr, #200, Beverly Hills CA 90212 USA
Neff, Steve — Bowler
3655 S Suncoast Blvd, Homosassa FL 34448, USA
Negay, Notah — Golfer
Professional Golfer's Assn, PO Box 109601, Palm Beach Gardens FL 33410 USA
Negishi, Takashi — Economist
2-10-5-301 Motoazabu, Minatoku, Tokyo 106, Japan
Negray, Ronald A (Ron) — Baseball Player
587 W Nimisila Road, Akron OH 44319, USA
Negreanu, Daniel — Poker Player
World Poker Tour Enterprises, 5700 Wilshire Blvd, #350, Los Angeles CA 90036 USA
Negri Sembilan, Yang Di-Pertuan Besar — Ruler, Malaysia
Yang Di-Pertuan Agong's Residence, Serembam, Malaysia
Negron, Chuck — Singer (Three Dog Night)
Paradise Artists, PO Box 1821, Ojai CA 93024 USA
Negron, Taylor — Actor
Stone Manners Salners, 9911 W Pico Blvd, #1400, Los Angeles CA 90035 USA
Negroponte, John D — Government Official
Yale University, International Affairs Dept, New Haven CT 06520, USA
Negroponte, Nicholas — Computer Engineer
69 Mount Vernon St, Boston MA 02108, USA
Nehamas, Alexander — Philosopher
Princeton University, Philosophy Dept, Princeton NJ 08544, USA
Nehberg, Rudiger — Explorer, Adventurer
Grossenseer Str 1A, 22929 Rausdorf, Germany
Nehemiah, Renaldo — Track Athlete, Football Player
15515 Owens Glen Terrace, North Potomac MD 20878, USA
Neher, Erwin — Nobel Medicine Laureate
Domane 11, 37120 Bovenden, Germany
Nehmer, Meinhard — Bobsled Athlete
Varnkevitz, 18556 Altenkirchen, Germany
Nehy, Regine — Actress
Innovative Artists, 1505 10th St, Santa Monica CA 90401 USA
Neibauer, Gary W — Baseball Player
146 Delta Ave, Bismarck ND 58504, USA
Neid, Silvia — Soccer Player
Betramstr 18, 60320 Frankfurt/Main, Germany
Neidert, John T — Football Player
4731 Placid Circle, Sarasota FL 34231, USA
Neidich, Charles — Conductor, Concert Clarinetist
Diane Saldick Mgmt, 225 E 36th St, New York NY 10016, USA
Neil, Andrew F — Editor
Glenburn Enterprises, PO Box 584, London SW7 3QY, England
Neil, Dan — Automobile Critic
Los Angeles Times, Editorial Dept, 202 W 1st St, Los Angeles CA 90012 USA
Neil, Deanna — Writer, Actress
EcoSeekers, PO Box 637, Nyack NY 10960, USA
Neil, Hildegarde — Actress
Associated International Mgmt, Fairfax House, Fulwood Place, London WC1V 6HU, England
Neil, Vince — Singer (Motley Crue)
Ashley Talent, 2002 Hogback Road, #20, Ann Arbor MI 48105 USA
Neill, Michael R (Mike) — Baseball Player
17 Cape May Point, Greensboro NC 27455, USA
Neill, Noel — Actress
2295 Belgrade Road, Metropolis IL 62960, USA
Neill, Sam — Actor
Rights House, 34-43 Russell St, London WC2B 5HA, England
Neils, Steven L (Steve) — Football Player
1329 Waterford Road, Saint Paul MN 55125, USA
Neilson, Jim — Ice Hockey Player
907-525 Sainte Mary Ave, Winnipeg MB R3C 3X3, Canada
Neilson-Bell, Sandra — Swimmer
3101 Mistyglen Circle, Austin TX 78746, USA
Neinas, Charles M (Chuck) — Football Executive
5344 Westridge Dr, Boulder CO 80301, USA
Neis, Reagan Dale — Actress
Curtis Talent Mgmt, 9607 Arby Drive, Beverly Hills CA 90210, USA
Nelligan, Kate — Actress
Innovative Artists, 235 Park Ave S, #1000, New York NY 10003 USA
Nellis, M Duane — Educator
University of Idaho, President's Office, Administration Building, Moscow ID 83844, USA
Nellis, William J — Physicist
Lawrence Livermore Laboratory, 7000 East Ave, Livermore CA 94550, USA
Nelly — Rap Artist (Saint Lunatics), Actor
ItGirl Public Relations, 5225 Wilshire Blvd, #718, Los Angeles CA 90036, USA
Nelms, Michael (Mike) — Football Player
11331 Fawn Lake Parkway, Spotsylvania VA 22551, USA
Nelsen, William K (Bill) — Football Player
13512 Dornoch Dr, Orlando FL 32828, USA
Nelson, Albert (Al) — Football Player
660 Boas St, #918, Harrisburg PA 17102, USA
Nelson, Alvin — Rodeo Rider
1441 W Beicegel Creek Road, Grassy Butte ND 58634, USA
Nelson, Azumah — Boxer
Trustworthy Boxing, PO Box 939, Mamprobi, Accra, Ghana
Nelson, Bob — Actor
I C M Partners, 10250 Constellation Blvd, #900, Los Angeles CA 90067 USA
Nelson, C Shane — Football Player
115 Knoll Trail, Sandia TX 78383, USA
Nelson, Cailin — Astrophysicist
Lawrence Livermore Laboratory, 7000 East Ave, Livermore CA 94550, USA
Nelson, Charles L (Chuck) — Football Player
3028 162nd Place SE, Mill Creek WA 98012, USA
Nelson, Colette — Model, Bodybuilder
PO Box 1122, Seaford NY 11783, USA

Nelson, Craig Richard
Borinstein Oreck Bogart, 3172 Dona Susana Dr, Studio City CA 91604 USA — Actor
Nelson, Craig T
Paradigm Agency, 360 N Crescent Dr, North Building, Beverly Hills CA 90210 USA — Actor
Nelson, Cynthia (Cindy)
PO Box 1699, 0171 Larkspur Lane, Vail CO 81658, USA — Alpine Skier
Nelson, Darrin M
9116 1/2 S Manhattan Place, Los Angeles CA 90047, USA — Football Player
Nelson, David A
US Court of Appeals, Courthouse Building, 425 Walnut St, Cincinnati OH 45202, USA — Judge
Nelson, David E (Dave)
12213 Clubhouse Dr, Bradenton FL 34202, USA — Baseball Player
Nelson, Deborah
Seattle Times, Editorial Dept, 1120 John St, Seattle WA 98109 USA — Journalist
Nelson, Dennis R
612 East St S, Kewanee IL 61443, USA — Football Player
Nelson, Diane
Curling Assn, 1660 Vimont Court, Cumberland ON K4A 4J4, Canada — Curling Athlete
Nelson, Donald A (Nellie)
2284 S Kihei Road, Kihei HI 96753, USA — Basketball Player, Coach, Executive
Nelson, Dorothy W
US Court of Appeals, 125 S Grand Ave, Pasadena CA 91105, USA — Judge
Nelson, Edmund C (Ed)
1160 Billings Dr, Pittsburgh PA 15241, USA — Football Player
Nelson, Edward
Fletcher Jacob, 5 Chapel Place, Rivington St, London EC2A 3DQ, England — Actor
Nelson, Edwin S (Ed)
4568 Peeples Road, Oak Ridge NC 27310, USA — Actor
Nelson, George D
A A A S Project, 1200 New York Ave NW, #100, Washington DC 20005, USA — Astronaut
Nelson, Jameer
Orlando Magic, 8701 Maitland Summit Blvd, Orlando FL 32810 USA — Basketball Player
Nelson, James
PO Box 32, Kells, County Meath, Ireland — Singer (Celtic Tenors)
Nelson, James (Jim)
Gentlemen's Quarterly, Editor's Office, 350 Madison Ave, New York NY 10017, USA — Editor
Nelson, James E
Baha'i Faith, 536 Sheridan Road, Wilmette IL 60091, USA — Religious Leader
Nelson, Jeffrey A (Jeff)
8270 Stone Crop Dr, #N, Ellicott City MD 21043, USA — Baseball Player
Nelson, Jennifer Yuh
DreamWorks Animation, 1000 Flower St, Glendale CA 91201, USA — Director, Animator
Nelson, John
I C M Partners, 10250 Constellation Blvd, #900, Los Angeles CA 90067 USA — Visual Effects Artist
Nelson, John Allen
4960 Fulton Ave, Sherman Oaks CA 91423, USA — Actor
Nelson, John R
1111 Hermann Dr, #19A, Houston TX 77004, USA — Theologian
Nelson, Joseph G (Joe)
2407 Azure Circle, Highland CA 92346, USA — Baseball Player
Nelson, Judd
Don Buchwald/Fortitude, 6500 Wilshire Blvd, #2200, Los Angeles CA 90048 USA — Actor
Nelson, Judith
2600 Buena Vista Way, Berkeley CA 94708, USA — Opera, Concert Singer
Nelson, Keith E
10th Street Mgmt, 700 N San Vicente Blvd, #G410, West Hollywood CA 90069, USA — Guitarist (Buckcherry), Songwriter
Nelson, Kirsten
Mitchell K Stubbs Assoc, 8695 W Washington Blvd, #204, Culver City CA 90232 USA — Actress
Nelson, Larry
421 Oakmont Circle, Marietta GA 30067, USA — Golfer
Nelson, Lauren
Miss America Organization, 1370 Ave of Americas, #1600, New York NY 10019 USA — Beauty Queen
Nelson, Lee M
23 Lindley Ave NW, Marietta GA 30064, USA — Football Player
Nelson, Liza
G P Putnam's Sons, 375 Hudson St, New York NY 10014 USA — Writer
Nelson, Marilyn Carlson
Carlson Companies, Carlson Parkway, PO Box 59159, Minneapolis MN 55459, USA — Businesswoman
Nelson, Mark
TalentWorks, 3500 W Olive Ave, #1400, Burbank CA 91505 USA — Actor
Nelson, Melvin F (Mel)
27420 Fisher St, Highland CA 92346, USA — Baseball Player
Nelson, Ralph A
Carle Foundation Hospital, 611 W Park St, #1, Urbana IL 61801, USA — Nutritionist
Nelson, Ricky L
2599 E Desert Broom Place, Chandler AZ 85286, USA — Baseball Player
Nelson, Robert A (Bob)
125 Nelson, Lakeside OR 97449, USA — Artist
Nelson, Robert A (Rob)
312 Alta Vista Ave, South Pasadena CA 91030, USA — Baseball Player
Nelson, Roger E
4113 Limerick Dr, Lake Wales FL 33859, USA — Baseball Player
Nelson, Scott
800 Sara Dr, Coshocton OH 43812, USA — Baseball Umpire
Nelson, Sean C
Barsuk Records, PO Box 22546, Seattle WA 98122, USA — Singer, Keyboardist (Harvey Danger)
Nelson, Steven L (Steve)
143 Saddleworth Way, Middleboro MA 02346, USA — Football Player, Coach
Nelson, Terry L
3393 Highway 51 N, Arkadelphia AR 71923, USA — Football Player
Nelson, Tim Blake
Gateway Management, 860 Via de la Paz, #F10, Pacific Palisades CA 90272, USA — Actor, Director
Nelson, Todd
Atlanta Thrashers, 101 Marietta St NW, #1900, Atlanta GA 30303 USA — Ice Hockey Player
Nelson, Tracy
Scott Carlson Entertainment, 5739 Bucknell Ave, Valley Village CA 91607, USA — Actress

Nelson, W Eugene (Gene)
PO Box 946, Dade City FL 33526, USA
Baseball Player

Nelson, William H (Bill)
PO Box 9235, Pahrump NV 89060, USA
Football Player

Nelson, Willie
Creative Artists Agency, 2000 Ave of Stars, #100, Los Angeles CA 90067 USA
Singer, Guitarist, Songwriter

Nemchinov, Sergei L
53 Walker Ave, Rye NY 10580, USA
Ice Hockey Player

Nemcova, Petra
Innovative Artists, 1505 10th St, Santa Monica CA 90401 USA
Model, Actress

Nemec, Corin
Abrams Artists, 9200 W Sunset Blvd, #1125, West Hollywood CA 90069 USA
Actor

Nemechek, Joseph F (Joe), III
128 S Iredell Industrial Park Road, Mooresville NC 28115, USA
Auto, Truck Racing Driver

Nemelka, Richard
6108 S 1300 E, Salt Lake City UT 84121, USA
Basketball Player

Nemeth, Miklos
Keszi U 7, 1029 Budapest II, Hungary
Prime Minister, Hungary

Nemov, Alexei
Gymnastics Federation, Lujnetskaya Nabereynaya 8, 119270 Moscow, Russia
Gymnast

Nen, Richard L (Dick)
48 Via Barcaza, Trabuca Canyon CA 92679, USA
Baseball Player

Nen, Robert A (Robb)
8 S View, Trabuco Canyon CA 92679, USA
Baseball Player

Nepomniaschy, Alex
Innovative Artists, 1505 10th St, Santa Monica CA 90401 USA
Cinematographer

Nerem, Robert M
9435 Creekside Trail, Stone Mountain GA 30087, USA
Mechanical Engineer

Neri Vela, Rodolfo
Playa Copacabana 131, Col Marte, Mexico City DF 08830, Mexico
Astronaut, Mexico

Neri, Francesca
Blue Train Entertainment, 798 Brooktree Road, Pacific Palisades CA 90272, USA
Actress

Neri, Manuel
Charles Cowes Gallery, 210 11th Ave, #500, New York NY 10001, USA
Sculptor

Nerlove, Marc L
University of Maryland, Economics Research Dept, College Park MD 20742, USA
Economist

Nero, Franco
Muse Mgmt, 1541 Ocean Ave, #200, Santa Monica CA 90401, USA
Actor

Nero, Peter
202 Hidden Acres Lane, Media PA 19063, USA
Pianist, Conductor

Nerud, John
19 Pound Hollow Road, Glen Head NY 11545, USA
Thoroughbred Racing Executive, Trainer

Nesbitt, Christine
Landmark Sport Group, 1 City Centre Drive, #605, Mississauga ON L5B 1M2, Canada
Speed Skater

Nesbitt, James
Artist Rights Group, 4 Great Portland Place, London W1W 8PA, England
Actor

Nesbitt, Mairead
W M E Entertainment, 9601 Wilshire Blvd, #300, Beverly Hills CA 90210 USA
Fiddler, Violinist (Celtic Woman)

Nesbo, Jo
Svartensgatan 4, 116 20 Stockholm, Sweden
Writer

Nesby, Ann
Pyramid Entertainment, 377 Rector Place, #21A, New York NY 10280 USA
Singer

Nesher, Avi
Gersh Agency, 9465 Wilshire Blvd, #600, Beverly Hills CA 90212 USA
Director, Producer, Writer

Nesic, Alex
Principato-Young, 9465 Wilshire Blvd, #880, Beverly Hills CA 90212 USA
Actor

Nesmith, Michael (Mike)
Videoranch, 1793 Catalina St, Seaside CA 93955, USA
Singer, Guitarist (Monkees)

Nespoli, Paolo A
2011 Dawn Crest Court, Kemah TX 77565, USA
Astronaut

Nespral, Jackie
NBC-TV, News Dept, 30 Rockefeller Plaza, #270E, New York NY 10112 USA
Commentator

Ness, Mike
Relentless Artist Mgmt, 1922 Placentia, #A, Costa Mesa CA 92627, USA
Singer, Guitarist (Social Distortion)

Ness, Rick
Metropolitan Entertainment Group, 2 Penn Plaza, #1500, New York NY 10121, USA
Singer, Guitarist (Fig Dish)

Nessen, Ronald H (Ron)
6409 Walhonding Road, Bethesda MD 20816, USA
Government Official, Journalist

Nessler, Brad
ABC-TV, Sports Dept, 77 W 66th St, New York NY 10023 USA
Sportscaster

Nesta, Alessandro
Lazio F C, Via di Santa Cornelia 14, 00060 Formello, Italy
Soccer Player

Nester, Eugene W
Washington University, Microbiology Dept, Seattle WA 98195, USA
Microbiolgist

Nesterenko, Eric
PO Box 1025, Vail CO 81658, USA
Ice Hockey Player

Nesterenko, Yevgeny Y
Fruzenskaya Nab 24 Korp 1, #178, 119146 Moscow, Russia
Opera Singer

Nesterovic, Radoslav (Rasho)
11 Sanctuary Dr, San Antonio TX 78248, USA
Basketball Player

Nestico, Samuel A (Sammy)
1731 Blackbird Circle, Carlsbad CA 92011, USA
Composer, Arranger

Netanyahu, Benjamin
Prime Minister's Office, 3 Rehov Kaplan, Jerusalem 91919, Israel
Prime Minister, Israel

Nethercott, Acer
Oxford Brooks University Club, 69 Yamells Hill, Oxford OX2 9BG, England
Rowing Athlete

Netherland, Joseph H
F M C Corp, 200 E Randolph Dr, Chicago IL 60601, USA
Businessman

Netolicky, Robert (Bob)
PO Box 531, Carmel IN 46082, USA
Basketball Player

Netravali, Arun N
10 Byron Court, Westfield NJ 07090, USA
Engineer

Netrebko, Anna Y
Centre Stage Artist Mgmt, Stralauer Allee 1, 10245 Berlin, Germany
Opera Singer

Nettles, G Douglas (Doug)
13105 Quail Creek Court, Silver Spring MD 20904, USA
Football Player

Nettles, Graig
11217 Carmel Creek Road, #2, San Diego CA 92130, USA — Baseball Player
Nettles, James A (Jim)
3817 Mandeville Canyon Road, Los Angeles CA 90049, USA — Football Player
Nettles, James W (Jim)
4632 N Darien Dr, Tacoma WA 98407, USA — Baseball Player
Nettles, Jennifer
Gail Gellman Mgmt, 23852 Pacific Coast Highway, #920, Malibu CA 90265, USA — Singer (Sugarland)
Nettles, John
Saraband Assoc, 265 Liverpool Road, London N1 1NL, England — Actor
Neu, Michael D (Mike)
406 Fraga Court, Martinez CA 94553, USA — Baseball Player
Neufeld, Elizabeth F
University of California Medical School, Biology Dept, Los Angeles CA 90024, USA — Biochemist
Neufeld, Ray
Selkirk Steelers, 1011 Manitoba Ave, Selkirk MB R1A 3T7, Canada — Ice Hockey Player
Neufeld, Sarah
Billions Corp, 3522 W Armitage Ave, Chicago IL 60647 USA — Violinist (Arcade Fire)
Neugebauer, Gerry
California Institute of Technology, Astrophysics Dept, Pasadena CA 91125, USA — Astrophysicist
Neugebauer, Marcia
7519 S Elliot Lane, Tucson AZ 85747, USA — Physicist
Neugebauer, Nick
101 S Sahuaro Dr, Gilbert AZ 85233, USA — Baseball Player
Neuharth, Allen H
Freedom Forum, 1101 Wilson Blvd, #2300, Arlington VA 22209, USA — Publisher
Neuhauser, Duncan V B
PO Box 932, Blue Hill ME 04614, USA — Epidemiologist
Neuheisel, Richard (Rick)
3601 Winding Creek Road, Sacramento CA 95864, USA — Football Player, Coach
Neumann, Liselotte
11003 Muirfield Dr, Rancho Mirage CA 92270, USA — Golfer
Neumann, Randy
600 E Crescent Ave, #104, Upper Saddle River NJ 7458, USA — Boxer, Referee
Neumann, Wolfgang
Metropolitan Opera Assn, Lincoln Center Plaza, New York NY 10023 USA — Opera Singer
Neumannova, Katerina
Svantlova 1803, 39701 Pisek, Czech Republic — Cross Country Skier
Neumeier, Daniel G (Dan)
N2635 County Road V, Lodi WI 53555, USA — Baseball Player
Neumeier, John
Hamburg Ballet, 54 Caspar-Voght-Str, 20535 Hamburg, Germany — Choreographer
Neuner, Magdalena
Postfach 1354, 82145 Planegg, Germany — Biathlete
Neuvic, Thierry
Artmedia, 20 Ave Rapp, 75007 Paris, France — Actor
Neuwelt, Edward A
Oregon Health Sciences University, 3181 SW Jackson Park Dr, Portland OR 97201, USA — Neurologist
Neuwirth, Bebe
144 Prospect Ave, Princeton NJ 08540, USA — Actress, Dancer, Singer
Nevarez, Alfred
Universal Attractions, 135 W 26th St, #1200, New York NY 10001 USA — Singer (All-4-One)
Neveldine, Mark
United Talent Agency, 9336 Civic Center Dr, Beverly Hills CA 90210 USA — Director, Writer
Neves, Jose Maria P
Prime Minister's Office, Varzea CP 304, Cidade da Praia, Ilha de Santiago, Cape Verde — Prime Minister, Cape Verde
Neville, Aaron
1090 Millwood Court, Brentwood TN 37027, USA — Singer
Neville, Arthel
1840 Victory Blvd, Glendale CA 91201, USA — Entertainer
Neville, Bill
506 Oakdale Road, Jamestown NC 27282, USA — Cartoonist (Tiny Toons)
Neville, Robert C
Boston University, Theology School, Boston MA 02215, USA — Theologian
Neville, Thomas O (Tom), Jr
PO Box 11175, Montgomery AL 36111, USA — Football Player
Nevin, Bob
61 River Court Blvd, East York ON M4K 3A3, Canada — Ice Hockey Player
Nevin, Brooke
TalentWorks, 3500 W Olive Ave, #1400, Burbank CA 91505 USA — Actress
Nevin, Phil J
18795 Heritage Dr, Poway CA 92064, USA — Baseball Player
Nevins, David
Showtime Networks, 10880 Wilshire Blvd, #1600, Los Angeles CA 90024, USA — Producer, Writer
Nevinson, Nancy
23 Mill Close, Fishbourne, Chichester, England — Actress
Nevitt, Charles G (Chuck)
3124 Cartwright Dr, Raleigh NC 27612, USA — Basketball Player
Newacheck, Kyle
United Talent Agency, 9336 Civic Center Dr, Beverly Hills CA 90210 USA — Actor, Writer, Producer, Director
Newbern, George
Leslie Allan-Rice Mgmt, 1007 Maybrook Dr, Beverly Hills CA 90210, USA — Actor
Newberry, Jeremy D
1225 Almondwood Dr, Antioch VA 94509, USA — Football Player
Newberry, Thomas (Tom)
PO Box 9299, Tavernier FL 33070, USA — Football Player
Newborn, Ira
Vangelos Mgmt, 15233 Ventura Blvd, #200, Sherman Oaks CA 91403 USA — Composer
Newcombe, Donald (Don)
1448 Young St, #705, Honolulu HI 96814, USA — Baseball Player
Newcombe, John D
Newcombe's Tennis Ranch, 325 Mission Valley Road, New Braunfels TX 78132, USA — Tennis Player
Newell, Catharine
Bullseye Gallery, 300 NW 13th Ave, Portland OR 97209, USA — Sculptor
Newell, Homer E
2567 Nicky Lane, Alexandria VA 22311, USA — Physicist

Newell, Mike 50 Canon Entertainment, Oxford House, 76 Oxford St, London W1D 1BS, England	Director
Newell, Thomas D (Tom) 9525 Cordoba Blvd, Sparks NV 89441, USA	Baseball Player
Newfield, Heidi Curb Records, 48 Music Square E, Nashville TN 37203 USA	Singer, Guitarist (Trick Pony)
Newfield, Marc A 5591 Selkirk Dr, Huntington Beach CA 92649, USA	Baseball Player
Newhart, Bob 420 Amapola Lane, Los Angeles CA 90077, USA	Actor, Comedian
Newhouse, Donald E Advance Publications, 950 W Fingerboard Road, Staten Island NY 10305, USA	Publisher
Newhouse, Frederick (Fred) 3003 Pine Lake Trail, Houston TX 77068, USA	Track Athlete
Newhouse, Robert F 6847 Truxton Dr, Dallas TX 75231, USA	Football Player
Newhouse, Samuel I, Jr Advance Publications, 950 W Fingerboard Road, Staten Island NY 10305, USA	Publisher
Newlin, Michael F (Mike) 1414 Horseshoe Dr, Sugar Land TX 77478, USA	Basketball Player
Newman, Albert D (Al) 1044 Laroda, Ontario CA 91762, USA	Baseball Player
Newman, Alec Relativity Mgmt, 8899 Beverly Blvd, #510, Los Angeles CA 90048, USA	Actor
Newman, Anthony I C M Artists, 40 W 57th St, #1800, New York NY 10019 USA	Concert Harpsichordist, Conductor
Newman, Barry N2N Entertainment, 1230 Montana Ave, #303, Santa Monica CA 90403 USA	Actor
Newman, Dan 192 E County Road 27, RR 1, Cottam ON N0R 1B0, Canada	Ice Hockey Player
Newman, David First Artists Mgmt, 4764 Park Granada, #210, Calabasas CA 91302 USA	Composer
Newman, Edward K (Ed) 10100 SW 140th St, Miami FL 33176, USA	Football Player
Newman, Jaime Ray Debby O'Connor, PO Box 16212, Irvine CA 92623, USA	Actress
Newman, James Cassell-Levy Talent Agency, 843 N Sycamore Ave, Los Angeles CA 90038, USA	Actor
Newman, James H 18583 Martinique Dr, Houston TX 77058, USA	Astronaut
Newman, Jeffrey L (Jeff) 10133 N 103rd St, Scottsdale AZ 85258, USA	Baseball Player, Manager
Newman, Jimmy C 2802 Opryland Dr, Nashville TN 37214, USA	Singer, Songwriter
Newman, Jon O US Court of Appeals, 450 Main St, #218, Hartford CT 06103, USA	Judge
Newman, Josh 5909 Canyon Creek Dr, Dublin OH 43016, USA	Baseball Player
Newman, Kevin ABC-TV, News Dept, 77 W 66th St, New York NY 10023 USA	Commentator
Newman, Kyle Fire Thief Films, 15260 Ventura Blvd, #2100, Sherman Oaks CA 91403, USA	Director, Producer
Newman, Laraine TalentWorks, 3500 W Olive Ave, #1400, Burbank CA 91505 USA	Actress, Comedienne
Newman, Nanette Seven Pines, Wentworth, Surrey GU25 4QP, England	Actress
Newman, Oscar Community Design Analysis Institute, 66 Clover Dr, Great Neck NY 11021, USA	Architect, Urban Planner
Newman, Pauline US Court of Appeals, 717 Madison Place NW, Washington DC 20439, USA	Judge
Newman, Phyllis 211 Central Park West, #19E, New York NY 10024, USA	Actress, Singer
Newman, Randy Cathy Kerr Mgmt, 7715 W Sunset Blvd, #100, Los Angeles CA 90046, USA	Singer, Pianist, Composer
Newman, Ryan J Stewart-Haas Racing, 6001 Haas Way, Kannapolis NC 28081, USA	Auto, Truck Racing Driver
Newman, Terence 2817 Park Bridge Court, Dallas TX 75219, USA	Football Player
Newman, Thomas M Gorfaine/Schwartz, 4111 W Alameda Ave, #509, Burbank CA 91505 USA	Composer
Newman, Zeb Framework Entertainment, 9057 Nemo St, #C, West Hollywood CA 90069 USA	Actor
Newmar, Julie 204 S Carmelina Ave, Los Angeles CA 90049, USA	Actress
Newmark, Craig A Craigslist, PO Box 225159, San Francisco CA 94122, USA	Businessman
Newmark, Dave 545 Pierce St, #2301, Albany CA 94706, USA	Basketball Player
Newsom, David Thruline Entertainment, 9250 Wilshire Blvd, #100, Beverly Hills CA 90212 USA	Actor
Newsom, Gavin E Mayor's Office, 400 S Van Ness Ave, San Francisco CA 94103, USA	Mayor, San Francisco
Newsom, Joanna Billions Corp, 3522 W Armitage Ave, Chicago IL 60647 USA	Singer, Harpist
Newsome, Craig 200 Johnson St, Holmen WI 54636, USA	Football Player
Newsome, Harry K, Jr 213 Hawthorne Lane, Cheraw SC 29520, USA	Football Player
Newsome, Ozzie 6 Padonia Woods Court, Cockeysville MD 21030, USA	Football Player, Executive
Newsome, Timothy A (Timmy) 7005 Quartermile Lane, Dallas TX 75248, USA	Football Player
Newsome, Vincent K (Vince) 5308 Woodnote Lane, Columbia MD 21044, USA	Football Player
Newsome, William R (Billy) PO Box 2001, Shreveport LA 71166, USA	Football Player

Newson, Warren D — Baseball Player
13232 Padre Ave, Keller TX 76244, USA

Newsted, Jason — Bassist (Metallica)
205 Alamo View Place, Walnut Creek CA 94595, USA

Newton, Becki — Actress
United Talent Agency, 9336 Civic Center Dr, Beverly Hills CA 90210 USA

Newton, Bill R — Basketball Player
15 Brixworth Lane, #6, Nashville TN 37205, USA

Newton, C M — Basketball Coach, Administrator
524 Currie Way, Birmingham AL 35209, USA

Newton, Cameron J (Cam) — Football Player
Carolina Panthers, Ericsson Stadium, 800 S Mint St, Charlotte NC 28202 USA

Newton, Chris — Cyclist
National Cycling Centre, Stuart St, Manchester M11 4DQ, England

Newton, Christopher — Director
22 Prideaux St, Niagara-on-the-Lake ON L0S 1J0, Canada

Newton, Juice — Singer, Guitarist, Songwriter
O J Mgmt, 4321 Reyes Dr, Tarzana CA 91356, USA

Newton, Matthew — Actor
Robyn Gardiner Mgmt, 397 Riley St, Surry Hills NSW 2010, Australia

Newton, Nathaniel (Nate), Jr — Football Player
1921 White Oak Clearing, Southlake TX 76092, USA

Newton, Richard Y (Dick), III — Air Force General
Deputy CofS, Manpower/Personnel, HqUSAF, Pentagon, Washington DC 20330, USA

Newton, Robert L (Bob) — Football Player
37701 Hollister Dr, Palm Desert CA 92211, USA

Newton, Roger — Medical Researcher
Esperion Therapeutics, 695 K M S Place, 3621 S State St, Ann Arbor MI 48108, USA

Newton, Thandie — Actress
Independent Talent Group, Oxford House, 76 Oxford St, London W1D 1BS, England

Newton, Thomas R (Tom) — Football Player
169 Park Road, Rochester NY 14622, USA

Newton, Wayne — Singer, Actor
Wayne Newton Mgmt, 6730 S Pecos Road, Las Vegas NV 89120, USA

Newton-John, Olivia — Singer, Actress
104 Lighthouse Dr, Jupiter Inlet Colony FL 33469, USA

Neyelova, Marina M — Actress
Potapovsky Per 12, 117333 Moscow, Russia

Neymar — Soccer Player
Confederacion de Futebol, Rua Victor Civita 66, #1, Rio de Janeiro 22775 044, Brazil

Ne-Yo — Rap Artist, Singer, Songwriter
W M E Entertainment, 9601 Wilshire Blvd, #300, Beverly Hills CA 90210 USA

Nezhat, Camran — Endocrinologist
Fertility/Endocrinology Center, 5555 Peachtree Dunwoody Road NE, Atlanta GA 30342, USA

Ngata, E Haloti — Football Player
Baltimore Ravens, Ravens Stadium, 1 Winning Dr, Baltimore MD 21230 USA

Nguyen Khanh — Prime Minister, South Vietnam; General
1 Hoang Van Thu, Hanoi, Vietnam

Nguyen Minh Triet — President, Vietnam
President's Palace, 1 Hoang Hoa Tham, Hanoi, Vietnam

Nguyen Tan Dung — Prime Minister, Vietnam
State Bank of Vietnam, 47-49 Thai To, Hanoi, Vietnam

Nguyen, Dat T — Football Player
2111 Wayside Dr, Bryan TX 77802, USA

Nguyen, Dustin — Actor
1051 S Dunsmuir Ave, Los Angeles CA 90019, USA

Nguyen, Navia — Model
Don Buchwald/Fortitude, 10 E 44th St, New York NY 10017 USA

Nhamadjo, Manuel Serifo — Acting President, Guinea-Bissau
President's Office, Palacio Presidential, Bissau, Guinea-Bissau

Niccol, Andrew — Writer, Director, Producer
Creative Artists Agency, 2000 Ave of Stars, #100, Los Angeles CA 90067 USA

Nichanian, Veronique — Fashion Designer
Hermes, 24 Rue Faubourg Saint Honore, 75008 Paris, France

Nichol, Gene R, Jr — Educator
University of North Carolina, Law School, Chapel Hill NC 27599, USA

Nichol, Scott B — Ice Hockey Player
612 Ladyhawk Lane, Victor NY 14564, USA

Nicholas, Alison — Golfer
Pat Darby, Badgar Farm House, Badgar near Wolverhampton WV6 7LS, England

Nicholas, Denise — Actress
932 S Longwood Ave, Los Angeles CA 90019, USA

Nicholas, Henry — Labor Leader
Hospital & Health Care Union, 330 W 42nd St, #1905, New York NY 10036, USA

Nicholas, J D — Singer, Guitarist (Commodores)
Management Assoc, 1920 Benson Ave, Saint Paul MN 55116, USA

Nicholas, Nicholas J, Jr — Publisher
Pluggers Inc, 1000 SW Broadway, #1850, Portland OR 97205, USA

Nicholas, Peter M — Businessman
Boston Scientific Corp, 1 Boston Scientific Place, Natick MA 01760, USA

Nicholas, Thomas Ian — Actor
Innovative Artists, 1505 10th St, Santa Monica CA 90401 USA

Nicholls, Bernie — Ice Hockey Player
17101 Planters Row, Addison TX 75001, USA

Nicholls, Craig — Singer (Vines)
Winterman-Goldstein, 17 Holdsworth St, Newtown NSW 2042, Australia

Nicholls, David A — Writer
Curtis Brown Group, 28-29 Haymarket St, #500, London SW1Y 4SP, England

Nichols, Austin — Actor
United Talent Agency, 9336 Civic Center Dr, Beverly Hills CA 90210 USA

Nichols, Carl E — Baseball Player
901 E Artesia Blvd, Compton CA 90221, USA

Nichols, David C, Jr — Navy Admiral
Deputy Commander, US Central Command, MacDill Air Force Base, Tampa FL 33621, USA

Nichols, Dorothy L — Government Official, Financier
Farm Credit Administration, 1501 Farm Credit Dr, #3600, McLean VA 22102, USA

Nichols, Gates — Guitarist (Confederate Railroad)
Bobby Roberts, 3050 Business Park Circle, #303, Goodlettsville TN 37221 USA
Nichols, Hamilton J, Jr — Football Player
11015 Kirkmead Dr, Houston TX 77089, USA
Nichols, Jeff — Director, Producer, Writer
Creative Artists Agency, 2000 Ave of Stars, #100, Los Angeles CA 90067 USA
Nichols, Joe — Singer
Show Dog-Universal Music, 2303 21st Ave S, #400, Nashville TN 37212 USA
Nichols, John — Writer
New Press, 38 Greene St, #400, New York NY 10013, USA
Nichols, Kenwood C — Businessman
Champion International Corp, 1 Champion Plaza, Stamford CT 06921, USA
Nichols, Kyra — Ballerina
Peter Diggins Assoc, 133 W 71st St, New York NY 10023, USA
Nichols, Larry — Rubik Cube Designer
Moleculon Research Corp, 139 Main St, Cambridge MA 02142, USA
Nichols, Lorrie — Bowler
1251 Lexington Dr, Algonquin IL 60102, USA
Nichols, Marisol — Actress
Paradigm Agency, 360 N Crescent Dr, North Building, Beverly Hills CA 90210 USA
Nichols, Mark — Curling Athlete
Curling Assn, 1660 Vimont Court, Cumberland ON K4A 4J4, Canada
Nichols, Mark S — Football Player
5905 Penn Station Lane, Bakersfield CA 93311, USA
Nichols, Michael (Nick) — Photographer
National Geographic, Editorial Dept, 1145 17th St NW, Washington DC 20036 USA
Nichols, Mike — Director, Comedian
Creative Artists Agency, 2000 Ave of Stars, #100, Los Angeles CA 90067 USA
Nichols, Nichelle — Actress
23281 Leonora Dr, Woodland Hills CA 91367, USA
Nichols, Peter R — Writer
Alan Brodie, 211 Piccadilly, London W1V 9LD, England
Nichols, Rachel — Actress
Management 360, 9111 Wilshire Blvd, Beverly Hills CA 90210 USA
Nichols, Robert H (Bobby) — Golfer
8681 Glenlyon Court, Fort Myers FL 33912, USA
Nichols, Rodney L (Rod) — Baseball Player
1570 Elk Trail, Helena MT 59601, USA
Nichols, Stephen — Actor
PO Box 82231, Athens GA 30608, USA
Nichols, T Reid — Baseball Player
5473 Wild Cherry Circle, Milwaukee WI 53214, USA
Nicholson, Andrew — Basketball Player
Orlando Magic, 8701 Maitland Summit Blvd, Orlando FL 32810 USA
Nicholson, David L (Dave) — Baseball Player
15316 Lakepoint Dr, Benton IL 62812, USA
Nicholson, Jack — Actor
Bresler Kelly Assoc, 11500 W Olympic Blvd, #400, Los Angeles CA 90064 USA
Nicholson, Julianne — Actress
Creative Artists Agency, 2000 Ave of Stars, #100, Los Angeles CA 90067 USA
Nicholson, Scott — Writer
1888 Bernard Bledsoe Lane, Todd NC 28684, USA
Nichting, Christopher T (Chris) — Baseball Player
7151 Gracely Dr, Cincinnati OH 45233, USA
Nickel, Scott — Cartoonist (Eek, Team Bob, His & Hers)
Paws Inc, 5440 E County Road 450, Albany IN 47320, USA
Nickerson, Donald A, Jr — Religious Leader
Episcopal Church, 815 2nd Ave, Basement, New York NY 10017, USA
Nickerson, Hardy O — Football Player
6288 Ruthland Road, Oakland CA 94611, USA
Nickey, Donnie O — Football Player
3491 General Hood Trail, Nashville TN 37204, USA
Nicklaus, Jack W — Golfer
Golf Podium, Infinity Sports, 5500 Military Trail, #22-294, Jupiter FL 33458, USA
Nickle, Doug — Baseball Player
19440 Victoria Court, #R2, Sonoma CA 95476, USA
Nicks, Carl, Jr — Football Player
Tampa Bay Buccaneers, 1 W Buccaneer Place, Tampa FL 33607 USA
Nicks, Hakeem — Football Player
New York Giants, Meadowlands Stadium, 102 Route 120, East Rutherford NJ 07073 USA
Nicks, O Carl — Basketball Player
10200 Yosemite Lane, Indianapolis IN 46234, USA
Nicks, Regina — Singer (Regina Regina)
Buddy Lee Attractions, 38 Music Square E, #300, Nashville TN 37203 USA
Nicks, Stevie — Singer, Songwriter
PO Box 112083, Carrollton, Texas 75011
Nickson, Julia — Actress
Metropolitan Talent Agency, 7020 La Presa Dr, Los Angeles CA 90068 USA
Nickulas, Eric — Ice Hockey Player
PO Box 507, West Barnstable MA 2668, USA
Nicolaou, Kyriacos Costa — Chemist
Scripps Research Institute, 10550 N Torrey Pines Road, La Jolla CA 92037 USA
Nicole, Ellyn — Actress
Creative Management, 2050 S Bundy Dr, #280, Los Angeles CA 90025, USA
Nicole, Jasika — Actress
Abrams Artists, 9200 W Sunset Blvd, #1125, West Hollywood CA 90069 USA
Nicole, Jayde — Model
Playboy Promotions, 2706 Media Center Dr, Los Angeles CA 90065 USA
Nicolet, Danielle — Actress
A P A Talent/Literary Agency, 405 S Beverly Dr, #300, Beverly Hills CA 90212 USA
Nicol-Fox, Helen — Baseball Player
432 E Cornell Dr, Tempe AZ 85283, USA
Nicollier, Claude — Astronaut, Switzerland
18710 Martinique Dr, Houston TX 77058, USA
Nicolodi, Daria — Actress
Carol Levi Mgmt, Via G Pisanelli 2, 00196 Rome, Italy

Nicolson, Steve — Actor
Ken McReddie Assoc, 11 Connaught Place, London W2 2ET, England
Nicora, Attilio Cardinal — Religious Leader
Patrimony of Apostolic See, Palazzo Apostolico, 00120 Vatican City
Nicosia, Steven R (Steve) — Baseball Player
190 Northshore Crossing, Dallas GA 30157, USA
Nidetch, Jean — Businesswoman
Weight Watchers International, 3860 Crenshaw Blvd, Los Angeles CA 90008, USA
Nie Haishen — Taikonaut
Satellite Launch Center, Jiuquan, Guangzhou Province, China
Nieberg, Lars — Equestrian
Gestit Waldershausen, 35315 Homberg, Germany
Nied, David G — Baseball Player
211 Masters Lane, Midlothian TX 76065, USA
Niedenfuer, Thomas E (Tom) — Baseball Player
3933 Losillias Dr, Sarasota FL 34238, USA
Nieder, William H (Bill) — Track Athlete
PO Box 310, Mountain Ranch CA 95246, USA
Niederauer, Duncan — Financier
N Y S E Euronext, 11 Wall St, New York NY 10005, USA
Niederhoffer, Victor — Squash Player
Niederhoffer Cross Zeckhauser, 757 3rd Ave, New York NY 10017, USA
Niedermayer, Robert W (Rob) — Ice Hockey Player
49 Belcourt Dr, Newport Beach CA 92660, USA
Niedermayer, Scott — Ice Hockey Player
49 Belcourt Dr, Newport Beach CA 92660, USA
Niedernhuber, Barbara — Luge Athlete
Schwarzeckstr 58, 83486 Ramsau, Germany
Niehaus, Leonard (Lennie) — Composer, Jazz Saxophonist
Soundtrack Music Assoc, 1460 4th St, #308, Santa Monica CA 90401 USA
Niehoff, Robert T (Rob) — Football Player
4874 Sandalwood Court, Mason OH 45040, USA
Niekamp, Jim — Ice Hockey Player
3511 E Cochise Dr, Phoenix AZ 85028, USA
Niekro, Lance — Baseball Player
3822 Cheverly Dr E, Lakeland FL 33813, USA
Niekro, Philip H (Phil) — Baseball Player
6382 Nichols Road, Flowery Branch GA 30542, USA
Nielsen, Brian — Boxer
Bettina Palle, 12 Skjulet, 2800 Bagsvend, Denmark
Nielsen, Brigitte — Actress, Model
Almond Talent Mgmt, 8217 Beverly Blvd, #8, West Hollywood CA 90048, USA
Nielsen, Connie — Actress
United Talent Agency, 9336 Civic Center Dr, Beverly Hills CA 90210 USA
Nielsen, Gerald A (Jerry) — Baseball Player
4631 Kewanee St, Fair Oaks CA 95628, USA
Nielsen, J Scott — Baseball Player
2898 Valley View Ave, Salt Lake City UT 84117, USA
Nielsen, Jeffrey M (Jeff) — Ice Hockey Player
6113 Birchcrest Dr, Minneapolis MN 55436, USA
Nielsen, Rick — Singer, Guitarist (Cheap Trick)
Oakie Dokie Mgmt, 6090 Central Ave, Saint Petersburg FL 33707, USA
Nielsen, S Gifford — Football Player
10 Sarahs Cove, Sugar Land TX 77479, USA
Nielsen, William Johnk — Actor
Panorama Agency, ApS Ryesgade 103B, 2100 Copenhagen, Denmark
Niemann, Jeffrey W (Jeff) — Baseball Player
5922 Jason St, Houston TX 77074, USA
Niemann, Randall H (Randy) — Baseball Player
1585 SW Harbour Isles Circle, Port Saint Lucie FL 34986, USA
Niemann, Richard W (Rich) — Basketball Player
7911 Stanford Ave, Saint Louis MO 63130, USA
Niemann-Stirnemann, Gunda — Speed Skater
Postfach 503, 99010 Erfurt, Germany
Niemeyer, Paul V — Judge
US Court of Appeals, 101 W Lombard St, #3625, Baltimore MD 21201, USA
Niemi, Lisa — Actress
Flick East-West, 9057 Nemo St, #A, West Hollywood, CA 90069 USA
Nieminen, Minna — Rowing Athlete
Vuoksen Soutajat Ry, Koskenparras 10, 55100 Imatra, Finland
Nieminen, Toni — Ski Jumper
Landen Kanava 99, Vesijarvenkatu 74, 15140 Lahti, Finland
Nieminen, Ville — Ice Hockey Player
Saint Louis Blues, Scott Trade Center, 1401 Clark Ave, Saint Louis MO 63103 USA
Nierman, Leonardo — Artist, Sculptor
Amsterdam 43 PH, Mexico City 11 DF, Mexico
Nies, Eric — Actor, Model
Don Buchwald/Fortitude, 6500 Wilshire Blvd, #2200, Los Angeles CA 90048 USA
Nieson, Charles B (Chuck) — Baseball Player
8681 Carriage Hill Draw, Savage MN 55378, USA
Nieto, Thomas A (Tom) — Baseball Player
22446 Eagles Watch Dr, Land O Lakes FL 34639, USA
Nieuwendyk, Joseph (Joe) — Ice Hockey Player, Executive
3204 Drexel Dr, Dallas TX 75205, USA
Nieuwenhuis, Hans — Director
Columbia Artists Mgmt Inc, 1790 Broadway, #702, New York NY 10019 USA
Nieves, Joe — Actor
TalentWorks, 3500 W Olive Ave, #1400, Burbank CA 91505 USA
Nieves, Melvin R (Mel) — Baseball Player
6131 Seven Lakes W, West End NC 27376, USA
Nigam, Anjul — Actor, Writer, Producer
Brittany House Pictures, 1680 N Vine St, #326, Los Angeles CA 90028, USA
Nigh, George P — Governor, OK; Educator
University of Central Oklahoma, President's Office, Edmond OK 73034, USA
Nightingale, Maxine — Singer
Diva Central, 7510 W Sunset Blvd, #1445, Los Angeles CA 90046 USA

Nighy, Bill — Actor
W M E Entertainment, 9601 Wilshire Blvd, #300, Beverly Hills CA 90210 USA
Nighy, Jo-Anne — Actress
Associated International Mgmt, Fairfax House, Fulwood Place, London WC1V 6HU, England
Nigrelli, Ross F — Pathologist
29 Barracuda Road, East Quogue NY 11942, USA
Nihalani, Govind — Director, Producer
139 Aradhana, Bandra (E), Mumbai MS 400051, India
Niinimaa, Janne H — Ice Hockey Player
2200-201 Portage Ave, Winnipeg MB R3B 3L3, Canada
Niinisto, Sauli V — President, Finland
President's Office, Mariankatu 2, 00170 Helsinki, Finland
Niittymaki, Antero — Ice Hockey Player
1751 Pinnacle Dr, #1500, McLean VA 22102, USA
Niklason, Laura E — Tissue Engineer
Duke University, Medical School, Anesthesia Dept, Durham NC 27706, USA
Nikolas, Alexa — Actress
Gersh Agency, 9465 Wilshire Blvd, #600, Beverly Hills CA 90212 USA
Nikolishin, Andrei I — Ice Hockey Player
105 Bloomfield Ave, Hartford CT 06105, USA
Niksic, Nermin — Prime Minister, Bosnia-Herzegovia
Prime Minister's Office, Alipasina 1, 71000 Sarajevo, Bosnia & Herzegovina
Nilan, Christopher J (Chris) — Ice Hockey Player
577 Adams St, #D, Milton MA 02186, USA
Niland, John H — Football Player
16058 Chalfont Court, Dallas TX 75248, USA
Niles, Prescott — Bassist (Knack)
Edge Mgmt, 10850 Wilshire Blvd, #300, Los Angeles CA 90024, USA
Nill, Jim — Ice Hockey Player
20837 Dundee Dr, Novi MI 48375, USA
Nilsen, John — Composer, Pianist
Magic Wing Music, PO Box 222, West Linn OR 97068, USA
Nilsen, Kurt E — Singer, Guitarist, Songwriter
Playroom, Sandakerveien 24D, #F2, 0473 Oslo, Norway
Nilsmark, Catrin — Golfer
187 Commodore Dr, Jupiter FL 33477, USA
Nilsson, David W (Dave) — Baseball Player
34 Lawnhill Road, Nelang QLD 4211, Australia
Nilsson, Kent — Ice Hockey Player
9034 Crichton Woods Dr, Orlando FL 32819, USA
Nilsson, Lennart — Photographer
Engelbrektsgatan 18, 114 32 Stockholm, Sweden
Nilsson, Sandra — Model
Playboy Promotions, 2706 Media Center Dr, Los Angeles CA 90065 USA
Nilsson, Ulf — Ice Hockey Player
QBrick AB, Sodra Hamnvagen 22, Stockholm 11 541, Sweden
Nimmannitya, Suchitra — Epidemiologist, Pediatrician
Children's Hospital, Rajvithee Road, Bangkok 10400, Thailand
Nimmo, Dirk — Actor
Michael Whitehall, 125 Gloucester Road, London SW7 4TE, England
Nimoy, Leonard — Actor, Director
Gersh Agency, 9465 Wilshire Blvd, #600, Beverly Hills CA 90212 USA
Nimphius, Kurt A — Basketball Player
750 Dry Creek Road, Sedona AZ 86336, USA
Nimri, Najwa — Actress
Kuranda Mgmt, Santo Angel 84, 28043 Madrid, Spain
Ninowski, James (Jim), Jr — Football Player
2715 Melcombe Circle, #302, Troy MI 48084, USA
Nipar, Yvette — Actress
Irv Schechter, 9460 Wilshire Blvd, #300, Beverly Hills CA 90212 USA
Nipon, Albert — Fashion Designer
Leslie Faye Co, Albert Nipon Div, 1400 Broadway, #1600, New York NY 10018, USA
Nipper, Albert S (Al) — Baseball Player
401 White Birch Valley Court, Chesterfield MO 63017, USA
Nippert, Merlin L — Baseball Player
1015 N Michigan Ave, Mangum OK 73554, USA
Nirenberg, Louis — Mathematician
221 W 82nd St, New York NY 10024, USA
Nirmala, Sister — Religious Leader
Missionaries of Charity, 54A Lower Circular Road, Kolkata 700016, India
Nisbet, Robert A — Historian, Sociologist
6131 Purple Aster Lane NE, Albuquerque NM 87111, USA
Nisbett, Richard E — Psychologist
University of Michigan, Culture & Cognition Program, Ann Arbor MI 48109, USA
Nischwitz, Ronald L (Ron) — Baseball Player
17 S Saint Clair St, #330, Dayton OH 45402, USA
Nishani, Bujar F — President, Albania
President's Office, Bulevardi Deshmoret E Kombit, Tirana, Albania
Nishizawa, Junichi — Electronics Engineer, Inventor
Semiconductor Research Institute, Kawauchi, Aobaku, Sendai 980 0862, Japan
Nishizawa, Ryue — Pritzker Architect Laureate
Sanaa Ltd, 2-2-35-6B Higashi-Shinagawa, Tokyo 140 0002, Japan
Nishizuka, Yasutomi — Biochemist, Pharmacologist
Kobe University Medical School, Pharmacology Dept, 650 0017 Kobe, Japan
Nishkian, Byron — Skier
150 4th St, #PH, San Francisco CA 94103, USA
Nispel, Marcus — Director
Stone Soup, 12200 W. Olympic Blvd, #140, Los Angeles CA 90064, USA
Nissalke, Thomas E (Tom) — Basketball Coach
3075 Kennedy Dr, #406, Salt Lake City UT 84108, USA
Nissen, Steve — Cardiologist
817 Hanover Road, Gates Mills OH 44040, USA
Nistico, Louis (Lou) — Ice Hockey Player
404 Westbury Crescent, Thunder Bay ON P7C 4N4, Canada
Nitkowski, Christopher J (C J) — Baseball Player
205 Townsend Lane, Alpharetta GA 30004, USA

Nittmann, David
PO Box 19065, Boulder CO 80308, USA — Artist
Nitzkowski, Monte
7041 Seal Circle, Huntington Beach CA 92648, USA — Swimming Coach
Niven, David, Jr
1100 Alta Loma Road, #1004, West Hollywood CA 90069, USA — Actor, Businessman
Niven, Kip
9000 W Sunset Blvd, #801, West Hollywood CA 90069, USA — Actor
Niven, Laurence V (Larry)
11874 Macoda Lane, Chatsworth CA 91311, USA — Writer
Nivola, Alessandro
Management 360, 9111 Wilshire Blvd, Beverly Hills CA 90210 USA — Actor
Niwa, Gail
Siegel Artist Mgmt, 1416 Hinman Ave, Evanston IL 60201, USA — Concert Pianist
Niwano, Nikkyo
Rissho Kosei-kai, 2-11-1 Wada Suginamiku, Tokyo 166-8537, Japan — Religious Leader
Nix, A Kent
2732 Colonial Parkway, Fort Worth TX 76109, USA — Football Player
Nix, Jayson T
Toronto Blue Jays, Skydome, 1 Blue Jay Way, Toronto ON M5V 1J1, Canada — Baseball Player
Nix, Laynce M
1506 Princeton Ave, Midland TX 79701, USA — Baseball Player
Nix, Matthew E (Matt)
W M E Entertainment, 9601 Wilshire Blvd, #300, Beverly Hills CA 90210 USA — Producer, Director, Writer
Nix, Steve E
Devil Dolls Booking, 3505 S Lamar Blvd, #1050, Austin TX 78704, USA — Guitarist (Briefs)
Nix, William D
Stanford University, Materials Science/Engineering Dept, Stanford CA 94305, USA — Engineer
Nixo, Livinia H
Laurel Bergman Mgmt, 389 Malvern Road, South Yarra VIC 3141, Australia — Actress
Nixon, Agnes E
774 Conestoga Road, Bryn Mawr PA 19010, USA — Producer, Writer
Nixon, Amy
Curling Assn, 1660 Vimont Court, Cumberland ON K4A 4J4, Canada — Curling Athlete
Nixon, C Trotman (Trot)
1023 Ocean Ridge Dr, Wilmington NC 28405, USA — Baseball Player
Nixon, Cynthia
Innovative Artists, 1505 10th St, Santa Monica CA 90401 USA — Actress
Nixon, Kimberley
United Talent Agency, 9336 Civic Center Dr, Beverly Hills CA 90210 USA — Actress
Nixon, Marni
Harden-Curtis, 850 7th Ave, #903, New York NY 10019, USA — Singer, Actress
Nixon, Nicholas
25 Waverly St, Brookline MA 02445, USA — Photographer
Nixon, Norman E (Norm)
607 Marguerita Ave, Santa Monica CA 90402, USA — Basketball Player
Nixon, Otis J, Jr
400 Bass Way NW, Kennesaw GA 30144, USA — Baseball Player
Nixon, Russell E (Russ)
4265 Tee Pee Lane, Las Vegas NV 89129, USA — Baseball Player, Manager
Nixon, Torran B (Tory)
PO Box 308, Colfax CA 95713, USA — Football Player
Niznik, Stephanie
TalentWorks, 3500 W Olive Ave, #1400, Burbank CA 91505 USA — Actress
Njue, John Cardinal
Archdiocese of Nairobi, PO Box 14231, Nairobi, Kenya — Religious Leader
Nkurunziza, Pierre
President's Office, Kiriri Presidential Palace, Bujumbura, Burundi — President, Burundi
Noah, Joakim
Chicago Bulls, United Center, 1901 W Madison St, Chicago IL 60612 USA — Basketball Player
Noah, John M
3315 W Prairiewood Dr S, Fargo ND 58103, USA — Ice Hockey Player
Noah, Max W
552 Douty Hill Road, Sangerville ME 04479, USA — Army General
Noah, Trevor
Levity Entertainment Group, 6701 Center Drive W, #1111, Los Angeles CA 90045, USA — Actor, Comedian, Writer
Noah, Yannick
20 Rue Billancourt, 92100 Boulogne, France — Tennis Player, Coach
Nobacon, Danbent
Doug Smith Assoc, PO Box 1151, London W3 8ZJ, England — Singer, Keyboardist (Chumbawamba)
Nobilo, Frank
10209 Atterbury Court, Orlando FL 32827, USA — Golfer
Nobis, Thomas H (Tommy), Jr
40 S Battery Place NE, Atlanta GA 30342, USA — Football Player, Executive
Noble
Agency Group Ltd, 361-373 City Road, London EC1V 2QA, England — Guitarist, Pianist (British Sea Power)
Noble, Adrian K
Askonas Holt, Lincoln House, 300 High Holborn, London WC1V 7JH, England — Director
Noble, Brandon P
184 Low Country Loop, Murrells Inlet SC 29576, USA — Football Player
Noble, Brian D
2400 Luberon Dr, Henderson NV 89044, USA — Football Player
Noble, Charles E (Chuck)
3585 W Beechwood Ave, #106, Fresno CA 93711, USA — Basketball Player
Noble, Chelsea
Insight Mgmt, 9818 Arkansas St, Bellflower CA 90706, USA — Actress
Noble, Cheryl
Curling Assn, 1660 Vimont Court, Cumberland ON K4A 4J4, Canada — Curling Athlete
Noble, James
Paradigm Agency, 360 Park Ave S, #1600, New York NY 10010 USA — Actor
Noble, John
Coast to Coast Talent, 3350 Barham Blvd, Los Angeles CA 90068 USA — Actor
Noble, Richard
Richard Noble Consulting, Hunters, Headley Road, Grayshott, Surrey GU26 6DL, England — Auto Speed Racing Driver
Noblitt, Niles L
Biomet Inc, Airport Industrial Park, PO Box 587, Warsaw IN 46581, USA — Businessman

Nobu — Chef, Restaurateur
Nobu's, 105 Hudson St, New York NY 10013, USA
Noce, Paul D — Baseball Player
913 W Maumee St, Adrian MI 49221, USA
Nocera, Daniel G — Chemist
Massachusetts Institute of Technology, Chemistry Dept, Cambridge MA 02139, USA
Nochlin, Linda — Art Historian
New York University, Fine Arts Institute, New York NY 10012, USA
Nocioni, Andres — Basketball Player
2281 Royal Ridge Dr, Northbrook IL 60062, USA
Nock, George V — Football Player
1025 Nine North Dr, #H, Alpharetta GA 30004, USA
Noda, Yoshihiko — Prime Minister, Japan
Prime Minister's Office, 1-6-1 Nagatoicho, Chiyodaku, Tokyo 100 8968, Japan
Noddle, Jeffrey — Businessman
SuperValu Inc, 11840 Valley View Parkway, Eden Prairie MN 55344, USA
Noe, Gaspar — Director
W M E Entertainment, 9601 Wilshire Blvd, #300, Beverly Hills CA 90210 USA
Noel, Chris — Vietnam Radio Personality, Actress
291 NE 19th Ave, Boynton Beach FL 33435, USA
Noel, Monique — Model, Actress
Playboy Promotions, 2706 Media Center Dr, Los Angeles CA 90065 USA
Noel, Philip W — Governor, RI
345 Channel View, #105, Warwick RI 02889, USA
Noghaideli, Zurab — Prime Minister, Georgia
Premier's Office, Government House, Ingorokva 7, 380034 Tbilsi, Georgia
Noguchi, Soichi — Astronaut
N A S A, Johnson Space Center, 2101 NASA Road, Houston TX 77058 USA
Noguchi, Thomas T — Pathologist
1110 Avoca Ave, Pasadena CA 91105, USA
Nogulich, Natalia — Actress
Geddes Agency, 8430 Santa Monica Blvd, #201, West Hollywood CA 90069 USA
Noiega Gomez, Eduardo — Actor
Joserra Cadinanos, Plaza de los Mostenses 11, #612, 28015 Madrid, Spain
Nojima, Minoru — Concert Pianist
John Gingrich Mgmt, PO Box 515, New York NY 10023, USA
Nokelainen, Petteri — Ice Hockey Player
Montreal Canadiens, 1275 Saint Antoine St W, Montreal QC H3C 5L2, Canada
Nokes, Matthew D (Matt) — Baseball Player
2255 Oxford Ave, Cardiff by the Sea CA 92007, USA
Nokio — Singer (Dru Hill)
I C M Partners, 10250 Constellation Blvd, #900, Los Angeles CA 90067 USA
Noko — Musician (Apollo440)
X L Talent, Reverb House, Bennett St, London W4 2AH, England
Nolan, Barry — Entertainer
I C M Partners, 10250 Constellation Blvd, #900, Los Angeles CA 90067 USA
Nolan, Christopher — Director, Writer
W M E Entertainment, 9601 Wilshire Blvd, #300, Beverly Hills CA 90210 USA
Nolan, Deanna — Basketball Player
Tulsa Shock, B O K Center, 200 S Denver, Tulsa OK 74103 USA
Nolan, Gary L — Baseball Player
97 Acacia Ave, Oroville CA 95966, USA
Nolan, Jonathan — Writer
W M E Entertainment, 9601 Wilshire Blvd, #300, Beverly Hills CA 90210 USA
Nolan, Joseph W (Joe) — Baseball Player
9515 Alix Dr, Saint Louis MO 63123, USA
Nolan, Kathleen (Kathy) — Actress
House of Representatives, 1434 6th St, #1, Santa Monica CA 90401 USA
Nolan, Kenny — Singer, Songwriter
Creative Artists Agency, 2000 Ave of Stars, #100, Los Angeles CA 90067 USA
Nolan, Martin F — Editor
Boston Globe, Editorial Dept, 135 W T Morrissey Blvd, Dorchester MA 02125, USA
Nolan, Michelle — Actress
Hofflund/Polone, 9465 Wilshire Blvd, #420, Beverly Hills CA 90212 USA
Nolan, Mike — Football Coach
Atlanta Falcons, 4400 Falcon Parkway, Flowery Branch GA 30542 USA
Nolan, Norma B — Beauty Queen
Miss Universe Organization, 1370 Ave of Americas, #1600, New York NY 10019 USA
Nolan, Owen L — Ice Hockey Player
3402 Crestmoor Dr, Saint Paul MN 55125, USA
Nolan, Ted — Ice Hockey Player, Coach
269 Queen St E, Sault Sainte Marie ON P6A 1Y9, Canada
Nolan, Thomas B — Geologist
2219 California St NW, Washington DC 20008, USA
Nolan, Tom — Actor
1335 N Ontario St, Burbank CA 91505, USA
Noland, Robert L — Businessman
5555 Eastlake Blvd, Washoe Valley NV 89704, USA
Nolasco, Amaury — Actor
W M E Entertainment, 9601 Wilshire Blvd, #300, Beverly Hills CA 90210 USA
Nolasco, C Enrique (Ricky) — Baseball Player
824 Challenge Ave, Beaumont CA 92223, USA
Noles, Dickie R — Baseball Player
20 Dougherty Blvd, #I2, Glen Mills PA 19342, USA
Nolet, Simon — Ice Hockey Player
1342 Rue de la Belle Vue, Cap Rouge QC G1Y 2T1, Canada
Nolfi, George — Director, Producer, Writer
W M E Entertainment, 9601 Wilshire Blvd, #300, Beverly Hills CA 90210 USA
Nolin, Gena Lee — Actress, Model
Shandrew Public Relations, 1050 S Stanley Ave, Los Angeles CA 90019, USA
Noll, Charles H (Chuck) — Football Player, Coach
23680 Merano Court, #202, Bonita Springs FL 34134, USA
Nolte, Claudia — Government Official, Germany
Mulgarten 28, 98693 Ilmenau, Germany
Nolte, Eric C — Baseball Player
23885 Noelle Ave, Murrieta CA 92562, USA

Nolte, Nick — Actor
6714 Bonsall Dr, Malibu CA 90265, USA
Nolting, Paul F — Religious Leader
Church of Lutheran Confession, 620 E 50th St, Loveland CO 80538, USA
Nomina, Thomas J (Tom) — Football Player
20700 Park Place, Estero FL 33928, USA
Nomura, Masayasu — Molecular Biologist
74 Whitman Court, Irvine CA 92617, USA
Nomvete, Pamela — Actress
Ken McReddie Assoc, 11 Connaught Place, London W2 2ET, England
Nong Duc Manh — General Secretary, Vietnam
General Secretary's Office, Hoang Hoa Tham St, Hanoi, Vietnam
Nool, Erki — Track Athlete
Regati 1, Tallinn 119871, Estonia
Noonan, Brian — Ice Hockey Player
262 W Eggleston Ave, Elmhurst IL 60126, USA
Noonan, Chris — Director
Creative Artists Agency, 2000 Ave of Stars, #100, Los Angeles CA 90067 USA
Noonan, Daniel N (Danny) — Football Player
19501 Woolworth Circle, Omaha NE 68130, USA
Noonan, John T, Jr — Judge
US Court of Appeals, Court Building, 95 7th St, San Francisco CA 94103, USA
Noonan, Karl P — Football Player
7149 Oxford Hunt Dr, Stanley NC 28164, USA
Noonan, Pat — Soccer Player
Columbus Crew, 1 Black & Gold Blvd, Columbus OH 43211 USA
Noonan, Patrick F — Association Executive, Conservationist
3553 Hamlet Place, Chevy Chase MD 20815, USA
Noonan, Peggy — Writer
Greater Talent Network, 437 5th Ave, #700, New York NY 10016, USA
Noonan, Timothy J — Businessman
Rite Aid Corp, 30 Hunter Lane, Camp Hill PA 17011, USA
Noone, Kathleen — Actress
130 W 42nd St, #1804, New York NY 10036, USA
Noone, Nora Jane — Actress
Gavin Barker Assoc, 2D Wimpole St, London W1G 0EB, England
Noone, Peter — Singer (Herman's Hermits), Actor
Bensky Entertainment, 15021 Ventura Blvd, #343, Sherman Oaks CA 91403, USA
Noor Al-Hussein — Queen Mother, Jordan
Royal Hashemite Court, PO Box 5166, 11183 Amman, Jordan
Nooteboom, Cees — Writer
Suhrkamp Verlag, Linderstr 29, 60325 Frankfurt/Main, Germany
Nooyi, Indra — Businesswoman
PepsiCo, 700 Anderson Hill Road, Purchase NY 10577, USA
Norberg, Anette — Curling Athlete
Talaforum, Norr Malarstrand 6, 112 20 Stockholm, Sweden
Norcross, Clayton — Actor
1327 Linda Way, Arcadia CA 91006, USA
Nordenberg, Mark A — Educator
University of Pittsburgh, Chancellor's Office, Pittsburgh PA 15261, USA
Nordenstrom, Bjorn — Cancer Radiologist
Karolinska Institute, Radiology Dept, 171 77 Stockholm, Sweden
Nordhaus, William D — Economist
Yale University, Economics Dept, New Haven CT 06520, USA
Nordli, Odvar — Prime Minister, Norway
Snarveien 4, 2312 Ottestad, Norway
Nordling, Jeffrey — Actor
A P A Talent/Literary Agency, 405 S Beverly Dr, #300, Beverly Hills CA 90212 USA
Nordmann, Robert — Basketball Player
631 E Sherwood Road, Williamstown MI 48895, USA
Nordquist, Mark A — Football Player
3495 Seacrest Dr, Carlsbad CA 92008, USA
Nordqvist, Anna — Golfer
Ladies Pro Golf Assn, 100 International Golf Dr, Daytona Beach FL 32124 USA
Nordsieck, Kenneth H — Astronomer
University of California, Astronomy Dept, Santa Cruz CA 95060, USA
Nordstrom, John E — Composer
Gorfaine/Schwartz, 4111 W Alameda Ave, #509, Burbank CA 91505 USA
NORE — Rap Artist
Don Buchwald/Fortitude, 6500 Wilshire Blvd, #2200, Los Angeles CA 90048 USA
Noren, Irving A (Irv) — Baseball, Basketball Player
3154 Camino Crest Dr, Oceanside CA 92056, USA
Noren, Lars — Writer
Ostermalmsgatan 33, 114 26 Stockholm, Sweden
Norgard, Erik C — Football Player
60 Harbor View Dr, Sugar Land TX 77479, USA
Noriega, Carlos I — Astronaut
4630 Silhouette Dr, Katy TX 77493, USA
Noris, Joe — Ice Hockey Player
1111 Via Carolina, La Jolla CA 92037, USA
Norman, Chris — Singer
Denis Vaughan Mgmt, PO Box 28286, London N21 3WT, England
Norman, Daniel E (Dan) — Baseball Player
430 McBroom Ave, Barstow CA 92311, USA
Norman, Edie Jo — Bowler
3544 Mariner Blvd, Spring Hill FL 34609, USA
Norman, Gregory J (Greg) — Golfer
Great White Shark Enterprises, 2041 Vista Parkway, West Palm Beach FL 33411, USA
Norman, Hayley Marie — Actress
Underground Films & Mgmt, 447 S Highland Ave, Los Angeles CA 90036, USA
Norman, Jessye — Concert Singer
L'Orchidee, PO Box South, Crugers NY 10521, USA
Norman, Kenneth D (Ken) — Basketball Player
19020 Kedzie Ave, Homewood IL 60430, USA
Norman, Marc — Writer
I C M Partners, 10250 Constellation Blvd, #900, Los Angeles CA 90067 USA

Norman, Marsha — Writer
W M E Entertainment, 9601 Wilshire Blvd, #300, Beverly Hills CA 90210 USA

Norman, Michael — Astrophysicist
University of California, Astronomy Dept, La Jolla CA 90293, USA

Norman, Monty — Composer
P R S, 29/33 Berners St, London W1P 4AA, England

Norman, Nelson A — Baseball Player
6135 Long Key Lane, Boynton Beach FL 33472, USA

Norman, Pettis B — Football Player
1430 Bar Harbor Circle, Dallas TX 75232, USA

Normandy, Jim — Guitar Designer
Normandy Guitars, PO Box 3564, Salem OR 97302, USA

Norodom Sihamoni — King, Cambodia
Khemarind Palace, Phnom Penh, Cambodia

Noronen, Mika — Ice Hockey Player
65 S Autumn Dr, Rochester NY 14626, USA

Norrena, Fredrik — Ice Hockey Player
1750 Barrington Road, Columbus OH 43221, USA

Norrington, Roger A C — Conductor
Camerata Academica Salzburg, Bergstr 22, 5020 Salzburg, Austria

Norrington, Stephen (Steve) — Director
W M E Entertainment, 9601 Wilshire Blvd, #300, Beverly Hills CA 90210 USA

Norris, Alan E — Judge
US Court of Appeals, US Courthouse, 85 Marconi Blvd, Columbus OH 43215, USA

Norris, Bruce — Writer
Steppenwolf Theater, 758 W North Ave, #400, Chicago IL 60610, USA

Norris, C Dwayne — Ice Hockey Player
850 Eastlake Court, Oxford MI 48371, USA

Norris, Carli — Actress
Gavin Barker Assoc, 2D Wimpole St, London W1G 0EB, England

Norris, Christopher — Actress
Sutton-Barth Vennari, 145 S Fairfax Ave, #310, Los Angeles CA 90036 USA

Norris, Chuck — Actor
Kritzer Levine Wilkins Griffin, 11872 La Grange Ave, #100, Los Angeles CA 90025 USA

Norris, Daran — Actor
I C M Partners, 10250 Constellation Blvd, #900, Los Angeles CA 90067 USA

Norris, David Owen — Concert Pianist
17 Manor Road, Andover, Hantsfordshire SP10 3JS, England

Norris, Dean J — Actor
Bauman Redanty Shaul Agency, 5757 Wilshire Blvd, #473, Los Angeles CA 90036 USA

Norris, Elwood G (Woody) — Inventor (Hypersonic Sound Technology)
American Technology Corp, 13112 Evening Creek Dr S, San Diego CA 92128, USA

Norris, Hermione — Actress
Artist Rights Group, 4 Great Portland Place, London W1W 8PA, England

Norris, Jack — Ice Hockey Player
PO Box 332, Delisle SK S0L 0P0, Canada

Norris, James F (Jim) — Baseball Player
6375 Oak Hollow Dr, Burleson TX 76028, USA

Norris, James R, Jr — Chemist
University of Chicago, Chemistry Dept, 5735 S Ellis Ave, Chicago IL 60637, USA

Norris, Lee — Actor
Don Buchwald/Fortitude, 6500 Wilshire Blvd, #2200, Los Angeles CA 90048 USA

Norris, Michael K (Mike) — Baseball Player
6228 Ridgemont Dr, Oakland CA 94619, USA

Norris, Michele — Commentator
National Public Radio, 635 Massachusetts Ave NW, #1, Washington DC 20001, USA

Norris, Patricia — Costume Designer
Murtha Agency, 4240 Promenade Way, #232, Marina del Rey CA 90292, USA

Norris, Paul J — Businessman
W R Grace Co, 7500 Grace Dr, Columbia MD 21044, USA

Norris, Terry — Boxer
3668 Syracuse St, La Jolla CA 92122, USA

Norris, Thomas R — Vietnam War Navy Hero (CMH)
33593 E Hayden Lake Road, Hayden ID 83835, USA

Norris, Tim — Golfer
1604 Little Kitten Ave, Manhattan KS 66503, USA

Norris, William A — Judge
US Court of Appeals, 312 N Spring St, #G33, Los Angeles CA 90012, USA

Norstrom, Mattias — Ice Hockey Player
3516 Amherst Ave, Dallas TX 75225, USA

Norsworthy, Lamar — Businessman
2828 N Harwood St, #100, Dallas TX 75201, USA

North, Andrew S (Andy) — Golfer
3289 High Point Road, Madison WI 53719, USA

North, Douglass C — Nobel Economics Laureate
7569 Homestead Road, Benzonia MI 49616, USA

North, Gary L — Air Force General
Commander, Pacific Air Force, Hickam Air Force Base HI 96853 USA

North, Jay — Actor
290 NE 1st Ave, Lake Butler FL 32054, USA

North, Nolan — Actor, Comedian
Origin Talent, 4705 Laurel Canyon Blvd. #306, Studio City CA 91607, USA

North, Oliver L — Government Official, Marine Officer
Freedom Alliance, 22570 Markley Circle, #240, Sterling VA 20166, USA

North, William A (Billy) — Baseball Player
5523 106th Ave NE, Kirkland WA 98033, USA

Northam, Jeremy — Actor
Rights House, 34-43 Russell St, London WC2B 5HA, England

Northcutt, Dennis L — Football Player
1 Park Plaza, #970, Irvine CA 92614, USA

Northey, Scott R — Baseball Player
9920 Bankside Dr, Roswell GA 30076, USA

Northrop, Wayne — Actor
37900 Road 800, Raymond CA 93653, USA

Northrup, Anne M — Representative, KY
Consumer Product Safety Commission, 4330 East West Hwy, Bethesda MD 20814, USA

Northway, Douglas (Doug) — Swimmer
3239 E 3rd St, Tucson AZ 85716, USA
Norton, Brad — Ice Hockey Player
7 Great Road, Acton MA 01720, USA
Norton, Edward — Actor
W M E Entertainment, 9601 Wilshire Blvd, #300, Beverly Hills CA 90210 USA
Norton, Graham — Actor, Comedian
United Talent Agency, 9336 Civic Center Dr, Beverly Hills CA 90210 USA
Norton, Gregory B (Greg) — Baseball Player
11130 Eliot Court, Denver CO 80234, USA
Norton, James A (Jim) — Football Player
2550 S Ellsworth Road, #13, Mesa AZ 85209, USA
Norton, Jeff — Ice Hockey Player
285 Saint George St, Duxbury MA 02332, USA
Norton, Jerry R — Football Player
6901 Chevy Chase Ave, Dallas TX 75225, USA
Norton, Kenneth H (Ken) — Boxer, Actor
Donald Hennesey, PO Box 491, Jacksonville IL 62651, USA
Norton, Kenneth H (Ken), Jr — Football Player, Sportscaster
135 Union Jack Mall, Marina del Rey CA 90292, USA
Norton, Peter — Computer Software Designer
225 Arizona Ave, #200W, Santa Monica CA 90401, USA
Norton, Richard E (Rick) — Football Player
901 W Mahoney St, Plant City FL 33563, USA
Norton, Thomas J (Tom) — Baseball Player
4900 Southwood Dr, Sheffield Lake OH 44054, USA
Norton, Virginia — Bowler
11706 Mindanao St, Cypress CA 90630, USA
Norton-Taylor, Judy — Actress, Model
Tisherman Agency, 6767 Forest Lawn Dr, #101, Los Angeles CA 90068 USA
Norville, Deborah — Commentator
PO Box 426, Mill Neck NY 11765, USA
Norwich, Craig R — Ice Hockey Player
11448 Welters Way, Eden Prairie MN 55347, USA
Norwood, Dorothy — Singer
Universal Attractions, 135 W 26th St, #1200, New York NY 10001 USA
Norwood, Lee C — Ice Hockey Player
28876 Olson St, Livonia MI 48150, USA
Norwood, Scott A — Football Player
41955 Blue Flag Terrace, Stone Ridge VA 20105, USA
Norwood, Willie B — Basketball Player
414 W 122nd St, #B, Los Angeles CA 90061, USA
Noseworthy, Jack — Actor
Don Buchwald/Fortitude, 6500 Wilshire Blvd, #2200, Los Angeles CA 90048 USA
Nossal, Gustav J V — Immunologist, Pathologist
46 Fellows St, Kew VIC 3101, Australia
Nosseck, Noel — Director
1435 San Ysidro Dr, Beverly Hills CA 90210, USA
Nossek, Joseph R (Joe) — Baseball Player
630 Sunrise Dr, Amherst OH 44001, USA
Nossiter, Jonathan — Director, Producer, Writer
United Talent Agency, 9336 Civic Center Dr, Beverly Hills CA 90210 USA
Notaro, Phyllis — Bowler
11123 Maritime Court, Wellington FL 33449, USA
Noth, Christopher — Actor
Sanders/Armstrong/Caserta Mgmt, 2120 Colorado Ave, #120, Santa Monica CA 90404 USA
Nothstein, Marty — Cyclist
1019 Village Round, Allentown PA 18106, USA
Notkin, Richard T — Sculptor
PO Box 698, Helena MT 59624, USA
Notkins, Abner L — Virologist
National Institute of Dental Research, 9000 Rockville Pike, Bethesda MD 20892, USA
Noto, Lucio A — Businessman
Mobil Corp, 3225 Gallows Road, Fairfax VA 22037, USA
Nott Cunningham, Tara — Weightlifter
Olympic Training Center, 1 Olympic Plaza, Building 4, Colorado Springs CO 80909, USA
Nott, John W F — Government Official, England
31 Walpole St, London SW3 4QS, England
Nottage, Lynn — Writer
Gersh Agency, 9465 Wilshire Blvd, #600, Beverly Hills CA 90212 USA
Nottebohm, Andreas — Artist
17496 7th St E, Sonoma CA 95476, USA
Nottingham, Donald R (Don) — Football Player
5750 NE 36th Avenue Road, Ocala FL 34479, USA
Nouri, Michael — Actor
Burstein, 15304 W Sunset Blvd, #208, Pacific Palisades CA 90272, USA
Noury, Alain — Actor
Domaine de Hurlevents, 26400 Soyans Crest-Sud, France
Nouvel, Jean — Pritzker Architecture Laureate
Architectures Jean Nouvel, 10 Cite d'Angouleme, 75011 Paris, France
Nova, Heather — Singer
Free Trade Agency, 9 Chapel Place, Rivington St, London EC2A 3DQ, England
Novacek, Jay M — Football Player
PO Box 471490, Fort Worth TX 76147, USA
Novack, K J — Businessman
America Online, 22000 A O L Way, Sterling VA 20166, USA
Novak Popper, Ilona — Swimmer
Il Orso Utca 23, Budapest, Hungary
Novak, Benjamin J (B J) — Actor, Comedian, Writer
B/W/R, 9100 Wilshire Blvd, #500W, Beverly Hills CA 90212 USA
Novak, John R — Inventor (Air Cleaning Radiator)
Engelhard Corp, Automotive Emissions Systems, 101 Wood Ave, Iselin NJ 08830, USA
Novak, Kim — Actress
Cameron Enterprises, 10100 Santa Monica Blvd, #1060, Los Angeles CA 90067, USA
Novak, Michael — Theologian
5050 Ave Maria Blvd, Ave Maria FL 34142, USA

Novakovic, Bojana — Actress
Creative Artists Agency, 2000 Ave of Stars, #100, Los Angeles CA 90067 USA

Novaro, Jean-Claude — Sculptor
32 Chemin Hautes Vignasses, 06410 Biot, France

Novello, Antonia C — Physician, Government Official
1616 Foss Ave, Orlando FL 32814, USA

Novello, Don (Father Guido Sarducci) — Actor, Comedian
Elizabeth Rush Agency, 82 Cumberland Ave, Verona NJ 07044, USA

Noveskey, Matt — Bassist (Blue October)
Rainmaker Artists, PO Box 551665, Dallas TX 75355, USA

Novitsky, Oleg — Cosmonaut
Cosmonaut Training Center, Star City, 141160 Zvezdny Gorodok, Moscow Oblast, Russia

Novoa, Rafael — Actor
Univision, 605 3rd Ave, #1200, New York NY 10158 USA

Novoa, Rafael A — Baseball Player
3420 N 47th Way, Phoenix AZ 85018, USA

Novotna, Jana — Tennis Player
7834 Montvale Way, McLean VA 22102, USA

Novotny, Dave — Bassist (Saliva)
Helter Skelter, 347-353 Chiswick High Road, London W4 4HS, England

Nowak, Piotr (Peter) — Soccer Player, Coach
Philadelphia Union, Union Field, Seaport Dr, Chester PA 19013 USA

Nowatzke, Thomas M (Tom) — Football Player
4335 Diuble Road, Ann Arbor MI 48103, USA

Nowell, Peter C — Pathologist, Biologist
9 Foxcroft Lane, Media PA 19063, USA

Nowicki, Tom — Actor
Davis Mgmt, 4111 Lankershim Blvd, North Hollywood CA 91602, USA

Nowitzki, Dirk — Basketball Player
10735 Strait Lane, Dallas TX 75229, USA

Nowra, Louis — Writer
Level 18, Plaza 11, 500 Oxford St, Bondi Junction NSW 2011, Australia

Nowrasteh, Cyrus — Director, Writer
Creative Artists Agency, 2000 Ave of Stars, #100, Los Angeles CA 90067 USA

Noxon, Marti — Producer, Writer
W M E Entertainment, 9601 Wilshire Blvd, #300, Beverly Hills CA 90210 USA

Noyce, Phillip — Director
United Talent Agency, 9336 Civic Center Dr, Beverly Hills CA 90210 USA

Noyori, Ryoji — Nobel Chemistry Laureate
135-417 Shinden, Umemoricho, Nisshin, Aichi 470 0132, Japan

Nozieres, Philippe P G F — Physicist
15 Route de Saint Nizier, 38180 Seyssins, France

Nozuka, Justin — Singer, Songwriter
Agency Group Ltd, 142 W 57th St, #600, New York NY 10019 USA

Nsibambi, Apolo — Prime Minister, Uganda
Premier's Office, Parliament Building, PO Box 341, Kampala, Uganda

Ntombi — Queen Regent, Swaziland
Royal Residence, PO Box 1, Lobamba, Swaziland

Nuami, Sheikh Humaid IV ibin Rashid, Al — Ruler, Ajman
Royal Palace, PO Box 1, Ajman, United Arab Emirates

Nubiola, Esther — Actress
Cineart, 36 Rue de Ponthieu, 75008 Paris, France

Nucci, Danny — Actor
TalentWorks, 3500 W Olive Ave, #1400, Burbank CA 91505 USA

Nucci, Leo — Opera Singer
Opera Art, Via Isolalta Forette 11, 37068 Vigasio VR, Italy

Nuce, Ted — Rodeo Bull Rider
12606 Victory Ave, Oakdale CA 95361, USA

Nugent, Michael (Mike) — Football Player
Cincinnati Bengals, 1 Paul Brown Stadium, Cincinnati OH 45202 USA

Nugent, Nelle — Producer
Foxboro Entertainment, 133 E 58th St, #301, New York NY 10022, USA

Nugent, Theodore A (Ted) — Singer, Guitarist, Songwriter
4008 W Michigan Ave, Jackson MI 49202, USA

Nugent-Hopkins, Ryan J — Ice Hockey Player
Edmonton Oilers, 11230 110th St, Edmonton AB T5G 3H7, Canada

Null, Jason — Guitarist (Saving Abel), Songwriter
Virgin Records, 338 N Foothill Road, Beverly Hills CA 90210 USA

Numan, Gary — Singer, Songwriter
86 Staines Road, Wraysbury, North Staines, Middx TW19 5A, England

Nu-Mark — Rap Artist
Vision Entertainment Group, 1100 Glendon Ave, #1100, Los Angeles CA 90024, USA

Numbers, Ronald L — Historian
University of Wisconsin, History of Science & Health Dept, Madison WI 53706, USA

Numminen, Teppo K — Ice Hockey Player
5975 Tipperary Manor, Clarence Center NY 14032, USA

Nunez, Edwin — Baseball Player
2618 E Locust Dr, Chandler AZ 85286, USA

Nunez, Joseph (Joe) — Actor
TalentWorks, 3500 W Olive Ave, #1400, Burbank CA 91505 USA

Nunez, Miguel A, Jr — Actor
Raw Talent Mgmt, 9615 Brighton Way, #300, Beverly Hills CA 90210 USA

Nunez, Oscar — Actor
A P A Talent/Literary Agency, 405 S Beverly Dr, #300, Beverly Hills CA 90212 USA

Nunez, Victor — Director
Gersh Agency, 9465 Wilshire Blvd, #600, Beverly Hills CA 90212 USA

Nunley, Frank H — Football Player
2131 Mulberry Circle, San Jose CA 95125, USA

Nunn, Michael — Boxer
314 E 13th St, #1, Davenport IA 52803, USA

Nunn, Samuel A (Sam) — Senator, GA
75 14th St NE, #4810, Atlanta GA 30309, USA

Nunn, Terri — Singer (Berlin)
M O B Agency, 6404 Wilshire Blvd, #505, Los Angeles CA 90048 USA

Nunn, Trevor R — Director
Royal National Theater, South Bank, London SE1 9PX, England

Nunnally, Jonathan K (Jon) — Baseball Player
36550 Chester Road, #504, Avon OH 44011, USA
Nunnari, Talmadge — Baseball Player
7101 Joy St, #A8, Pensacola FL 32504, USA
Nurse, Paul M — Nobel Medicine Laureate
Clare Hall Laboratories, Cell Cycle Control Laboratory, Hertsfordshire EN6 3LD, England
Nussbaum, Danny — Actor
Conway Van Gelder Grant, 8-12 Broadwick St, #300, London W1F 8HW, England
Nussbaum, Karen — Labor Activist
9-5 National Working Women Assn, 231 W Wisconsin, #900, Milwaukee WI 53203, USA
Nussbaum, Martha C — Philosopher
University of Chicago, Law School, 111 E 60th St, Chicago IL 60637, USA
Nussle, James A (Jim) — Government Official, Representative, IA
PO Box 445, Marion IA 52302, USA
Nusslein-Volhard, Christiane — Nobel Medicine Laureate
Klosttermuhle 15, 72074 Tubingen, Germany
Nutini, Paolo — Singer
Atlantic Records, 1290 Ave of Americas, Concourse 3, New York NY 10104 USA
Nutt, Amy Ellis — Journalist
Newark Star-Ledger, Editorial Dept, 1 Star-Ledger Plaza, Newark NJ 07102, USA
Nutt, Jim — Artist
1035 Greenwood Ave, Wilmette IL 60091, USA
Nuttall, Amy — Actress, Singer
Merlin Elite, 37 Lower Belgrave St, London SW1W 0LS, England
Nutten, Thomas R (Tom) — Football Player
431 S Creek Dr, Osprey FL 34229, USA
Nutter, Alice — Singer, Percussionist (Chumbawamba)
Doug Smith Assoc, PO Box 1151, London W3 8ZJ, England
Nutter, David — Director
W M E Entertainment, 9601 Wilshire Blvd, #300, Beverly Hills CA 90210 USA
Nutting, Wallace H — Army General
6 Schooner Way, Saco ME 04072, USA
Nutzle, Futzie — Artist, Cartoonist
PO Box 325, Aromas CA 95004, USA
Nuveman, Stacey — Softball Player
USA Softball, 2801 NE 50th St, Oklahoma City OK 73111, USA
Nuwer, Hank — Writer, Journalist, Educator
Franklin College, Shirk Hall, 1100 Branigin Blvd, Franklin IN 46131, USA
Nuyen, France — Actress
1800 Franklin Canyon Terrace, Beverly Hills CA 90210, USA
Nuzorewa, Abel Tendekayi — Prime Minister, Zimbabwe
United African National Council, 40 Charter Road, Harare, Zimbabwe
Nyad, Diana — Swimmer, Sportscaster
870 5th Ave, Los Angeles CA 90005, USA
Nyberg, Frederik — Alpine Skier
Kaptensgatan 2C, 832 00 Froson, Sweden
Nyberg, Karen L — Astronaut
1848 Lake Landing Dr, League City TX 77573, USA
Nyberg, Katarina — Curling Athlete
Curling Assn, Idrottshuser, Marbackagatan 19, 123 43 Farsta, Sweden
Nye, Bill — Actor
W M E Entertainment, 9601 Wilshire Blvd, #300, Beverly Hills CA 90210 USA
Nye, Blaine F — Football Player
1200 Bay Laurel Dr, Menlo Park CA 94025, USA
Nye, Erle A — Businessman
6924 Desco, Dallas TX 75225, USA
Nye, Robert — Writer
Thornfield, Kingsland, Ballinghassig, County Cork, Ireland
Nye, Ryan C — Baseball Player
3319 Golf Course Dr, Alma AR 72921, USA
Nyers, C Richard (Dick) — Football Player
4055 N Riverside Dr, Columbus IN 47203, USA
Nyers, Rezso — Secretary General, Hungary
Ozgida Utca 22/A, 1025 Budapest, Hungary
Nygaard, Richard L — Judge
US Court of Appeals, 1st National Bank Building, 717 State St, Erie PA 16501, USA
Nyland, William L — Marine Corps General
2750 Semoran Circle, Pensacola FL 32503, USA
Nylander, Michael — Ice Hockey Player
8813 Mayberry Court, Potomac MD 20854, USA
Nylund, Gary — Ice Hockey Player
3504 154th St, Surry BC V3S 0R3, Canada
Nyman, Michael L — Composer, Pianist
Michael Nyman Ltd, PO Box 430, High Wycombe HP13 5QT, England
Nyqvist, Michael — Actor
W M E Entertainment, 9601 Wilshire Blvd, #300, Beverly Hills CA 90210 USA
Nystedt, Knut — Composer, Conductor
Det Norske Musikforlag A/S, Postbuks 1499 Bika, Oslo 0116, Norway
Nystrom, Eric — Ice Hockey Player
475 Berry Road, Syosset NY 11791, USA
Nystrom, Joakim — Tennis Player
Torsgatan 194, 931 00 Skelfefteaa, Sweden
Nyswaner, Ronald L (Ron) — Writer, Producer, Director
United Talent Agency, 9336 Civic Center Dr, Beverly Hills CA 90210 USA

O, Karen — Singer (Yeah Yeah Yeahs), Songwriter
Yeah Yeah Yeahs, 249 Metropolitan Ave, Brooklyn NY 11211, USA
Oakenfold, Paul — DJ Musician
PO Box 19788, London SW15 2FT, England
Oakes, W Warren — Drummer (Against Me)
Boca Fiesta Restaurant, 232 SE 1st St, Gainesville FL 32601, USA
Oakley, Charles — Basketball Player
700 Park Regency Place NE, #1105, Atlanta GA 30326, USA
Oates, Adam R — Ice Hockey Player, Coach
53570 Del Gato Dr, La Quinta CA 92253, USA
Oates, Bart S — Football Player, Sportscaster
2 Silverbrook Road, Morristown NJ 07960, USA
Oates, John — Singer (Hall & Oates), Songwriter
Doyle-Kos Entertainment, 1 Penn Plaza, 2107, New York NY 10119, USA
Oates, Joyce Carol — Writer
McClelland & Stewart, 75 Sherbourne St, #500, Toronto ON M5A 2P9, Canada
Oats, Carleton — Football Player
10605 E Coralbell Ave, Mesa AZ 85208, USA
Obama, Barack H, II — President, United States; Nobel Laureate
White House, 1600 Pennsylvania Ave NW, Washington DC 20500 USA
Obama, Michelle — Wife of US President
White House, 1600 Pennsylvania Ave NW, Washington DC 20500 USA
Obando Bravo, Miguel Cardinal — Religious Leader
Arzobispado, Apartado 3058, Managua, Nicaragua
O'Bannon, Edward C (Ed) — Basketball Player
1397 Minuet St, Henderson NV 89052, USA
Obasanjo, Olusegun — President, Nigeria; Army General
Obasanjo Farms Nigeria, PO Box 90, Otta, Ogun State, Nigeria
Obato, Gyo — Architect
100 N Broadway, Saint Louis MO 63102, USA
Obeid, Atef M — Prime Minister, Egypt
Arab International Bank, 35 Abdel Khalek Sarwat St, Cairo, Egypt
Obeidat, Ahmad Abdul-Majeed — Prime Minister, Jordan
Law & Arbitration Center, PO Box 926544, Amman, Jordan
Oben, Roman D — Football Player
11476 Creekstone Lane, San Diego CA 92128, USA
Oberg, Margo — Surfer
Margo Oberg Surf School, Poipu Beach, Koloa HI 96756, USA
Obergfoll, Christina — Track Athlete
Alsfelder Str 27, 64289 Darmstadt, Germany
Oberholser, Arron — Golfer
5901 E Via Los Caballos, Paradise Valley AZ 85253, USA
Oberkfell, Kenneth R (Ken) — Baseball Player
1335 W Welsford Dr, Spring TX 77386, USA
Obermeyer, Klaus F — Fashion Designer
Sport Obermeyer, 115 Atlantic Ave, Aspen CO 81611, USA
Obermueller, Wesley M (Wes) — Baseball Player
7031 27th Ave, Newhall IA 52315, USA
Oberoi, Vivek — Actor
5 Krta Kunj Golden Beach, Ruia Park Juhu, Mumbai MS 400049, India
O'Berry, Carl G — Air Force General
Boeing Co, PO Box 4921, 3370 Miraloma Ave, Anaheim CA 92806, USA
O'Berry, P Michael (Mike) — Baseball Player
5977 S Fork Dr, Hoover AL 35244, USA
Oberst, Conor M — Singer, Guitarist (Bright Eyes)
Untitled Entertainment, 350 S Beverly Dr, #200, Beverly Hills CA 90212 USA
Oberto, Fabricio R J — Basketball Player
901 15th St, #1605, Arlington VA 22202, USA
Obiang Nguema Mbasogo, Teodoro — President, Equatorial Guinea
President's Office, Palacio de la Presidencia, Malabo, Equatorial Guinea
O'Boyle, Maureen — Entertainer
1600 Meadowood Lane, Charlotte NC 28211, USA
Obradors, Jacqueline — Actress
A P A Talent/Literary Agency, 405 S Beverly Dr, #300, Beverly Hills CA 90212 USA
O'Bradovich, Edward (Ed) — Football Player
235 N Smith St, #207, Palatine IL 60067, USA
Obradovich, James R (Jim) — Football Player
2601 Morningside Dr, Lomita CA 90717, USA
Obraztsova, Elena V — Opera Singer
Bolshoi Theater, Teatralnaya Pl 1, 103009 Moscow, Russia
Obreht, Tea — Writer
Random House, 1745 Broadway, #1800, New York NY 10019 USA
O'Brian, Hugh — Actor
O'Brian Youth Leadership, 31255 Cedar Valley, #327, Westlake Village CA 91362, USA
O'Brien, Bill — Football Coach
Pennsylvania State University, Athletic Dept, University Park PA 16802, USA
O'Brien, Carl (Cubby) — Actor
39919 NE 127th Court, Amboy WA 98601, USA
O'Brien, Cathy — Track Athlete
19 Foss Farm Road, Durham NH 03824, USA
O'Brien, Charles H (Charlie) — Baseball Player
4932 E 38th Place, Tulsa OK 74135, USA
O'Brien, Conan — Entertainer
W M E Entertainment, 9601 Wilshire Blvd, #300, Beverly Hills CA 90210 USA
O'Brien, Dan — Track Athlete
8390 E Via de Ventura, #110, Scottsdale AZ 85258, USA
O'Brien, Dennis — Ice Hockey Player
31 Hope St N, Port Hope ON L1A 2N4, Canada
O'Brien, Edna — Writer
David Godwin Assoc, 55 Monmouth St, London WC2H 9DG, England
O'Brien, Edward J (Eddie) — Baseball Player
522 Alder St, #101, Edmonds WA 98020, USA
O'Brien, Edwin F Cardinal — Religious Leader
Equestrian Order, 00120 Vatican City
O'Brien, G Dennis — Educator
PO Box 510, Middlebury VT 05753, USA

O'Brien, Jack	Director, Choreographer
Gersh Agency, 9465 Wilshire Blvd, #600, Beverly Hills CA 90212 USA	
O'Brien, Keith M P Cardinal	Religious Leader
Archbishop's House, 42 Greenhill Gardens, Edinburgh EH10 4B5, Scotland	
O'Brien, Kenneth J (Ken), Jr	Football Player
201 Manhattan Ave, Manhattan Beach CA 90266, USA	
O'Brien, Margaret	Actress
14840 Valerio St, Van Nuys CA 91405, USA	
O'Brien, Maureen	Actress
United Agents, 12-26 Lexington St, London W1F 0LE, England	
O'Brien, Michael	Labor Leader
Transport Workers Union, 1700 Broadway, #200, New York NY 10019, USA	
O'Brien, Pat	Sportscaster, Entertainer
I C M Partners, 10250 Constellation Blvd, #900, Los Angeles CA 90067 USA	
O'Brien, Peter M (Pete)	Baseball Player
5509 Montclair Dr, Colleyville TX 76034, USA	
O'Brien, Richard	Composer, Lyricist
TimeWarp, 1 Elm Grove, Hildenborough, Tonbridge Kent TN11 9HE, England	
O'Brien, Ron	Diving Coach
80450 Overseas Highway, #401, Islamorada FL 33036, USA	
O'Brien, Soledad	Commentator
Spivak Mgmt, 6222 Wilshire Blvd, #240, Los Angeles CA 90048, USA	
O'Brien, Terrence L	Judge
US Court of Appeals, 2120 Capitol Ave, #2131, Cheyenne WY 82001, USA	
O'Brien, Tim	Singer
W N S Group, 6 Rolyn Hills Dr, Orangeburg NY 10962, USA	
O'Brien, Tim	Writer
Minnesota West Technical College, English Dept, Worthington MN 56187, USA	
O'Brien, Tina	Actress
Shepherd Mgmt, 45 Maddox St, #400, London W1S 2PE, England	
O'Brien, Tom	Football Coach
North Carolina State University, Athletic Dept, Raleigh NC 27695, USA	
O'Brien, Trever	Actor
Luber Rocklin Entertainment, 8530 Wilshire Blvd, #555, Beverly Hills CA 90211 USA	
O'Bryan, Sean	Actor
Domain Talent, 9229 W Sunset Blvd, #710, West Hollywood CA 90069 USA	
Obst, Lynda	Producer, Writer
Lynda Obst Productions, 5555 Melrose Ave, Astaire Building, Los Angeles CA 90038, USA	
O'Byrne, Brian F	Actor
Lisa Richards Agency, 108 Upper Leeson St, Dublin 4, Ireland	
O'Callahan, John (Jack)	Ice Hockey Player
101 Linden Ave, Glencoe IL 60022, USA	
Ocampo Uria, Adriana C	Geologist, Planetary Scientist
National Aeronautics/Space Administration, 300 E St SW, Washington DC 20546, USA	
Ocampo, Miguel	Artist
Wood Street Gallery, 601 Wood St, Pittsburgh PA 15222, USA	
O'Caroll, Sinead	Singer (B*Witched)
Clintons, 55 Drury Lane, Covent Garden, London WC2B 5SQ, England	
O'Carroll, Brendan	Actor
Kaplan-Stahler Agency, 8383 Wilshire Blvd, #923, Beverly Hills CA 90211 USA	
Ocasek, Ric	Singer, Guitarist (Cars); Songwriter
Lookout Mgmt, 1460 4th St, #300, Santa Monica CA 90401 USA	
Occhilupo, Mark	Surfer
Billabong, 1 Billabong Place, Burleigh Heads QLD 4220, Australia	
Ocean, Billy	Singer, Songwriter
Laurie Jay Enterprises, 32 Willesden Lane, London NW6 7ST, England	
Ochiai, Masayuki	Director
Director's Guild, Shibuya Goto Building, 3-2 Maruyama, #5, Shibuya, Tokyo 150 0044, Japan	
Ochiltree, Dianne	Writer
716 Tropical Circle, Sarasota FL 34242, USA	
Ochirbat, Punsalmaagiin	President, Mongolia
Tengeriin Tsag Co, Olympic St 14, Ulan Bator, Mongolia	
Ochman, Wieslaw	Opera Singer
Ul Miaczynska 46B, 02-637 Warsaw, Poland	
Ochoa, Alex	Baseball Player
14526 NW 83rd Passage, Hialeah FL 33016, USA	
Ochoa, Ellen	Astronaut
4515 Sterling Wood Way, Houston TX 77059, USA	
Ochoa, Lorena	Golfer
Ladies Pro Golf Assn, 100 International Golf Dr, Daytona Beach FL 32124 USA	
Ochowicz, James L (Jim)	Cyclist
945 Hutchinson Ave, Palo Alto CA 94301, USA	
Ockels, Wubbo	Astronaut, Netherlands
E S T E C, Postbus 299, 2200 AG Noordwijk, Netherlands	
O'Connell, Brian	Bassist
Junoon, Sidco Tower, #A-10/2, Strachen Road, Karachi 74200, Pakistan	
O'Connell, Carol	Writer
Berkley Publishing Group, 375 Hudson St, Basement 1, New York NY 10014 USA	
O'Connell, Deirdre	Actress
Innovative Artists, 1505 10th St, Santa Monica CA 90401 USA	
O'Connell, Jack	Actor
Conway Van Gelder Grant, 8-12 Broadwick St, #300, London W1F 8HW, England	
O'Connell, Jerry	Actor, Director
3 Arts Entertainment, 9460 Wilshire Blvd, #700, Beverly Hills CA 90212 USA	
O'Connell, Maura	Singer
S A D Mgmt, 218 Sawyer Road, Sherburne NY 13460, USA	
O'Connell, Mike	Ice Hockey Player, Coach
17 Border St, Cohasset MA 02025, USA	
O'Connell, Robbie	Singer
Producers Inc, 11806 N 56th St, Tampa FL 33617 USA	
O'Connor, Brian	Baseball Player
3054 Inwood Dr, Cincinnati OH 45241, USA	
O'Connor, Bridget	Writer
Michelle Kass & Assoc, 85 Charing Cross Road, London WC2H 0AA, England	
O'Connor, Bryan D	Astronaut
1305 Lafayette Dr, Alexandria VA 22308, USA	

O

Owen - O'Connor

O'Connor, Christy, Jr — Golfer
Gaylord Sports Mgmt, 13845 N Northsight Blvd, #200, Scottsdale AZ 85260 USA
O'Connor, Derrick — Actor
Markham & Froggatt, Julian House, 4 Windmill St, London W1P 1HF, England
O'Connor, Edmund F — Army General
1169 Ironsides Ave, Melbourne FL 32940, USA
O'Connor, Erin — Model
2pm Model Mgmt, Norregade 2, 1165 Copenhagen K, Denmark
O'Connor, Frances — Actress
Gersh Agency, 9465 Wilshire Blvd, #600, Beverly Hills CA 90212 USA
O'Connor, Gavin — Actor, Director, Writer
Solaris, 12 Washington Blvd, #200, Venice CA 90292, USA
O'Connor, Glynnis — Actress
Bauman Redanty Shaul Agency, 5757 Wilshire Blvd, #473, Los Angeles CA 90036 USA
O'Connor, J Dennis — Educator
Smithsonian Institution, Provost's Office, Washington DC 20560, USA
O'Connor, Jack W — Baseball Player
PO Box 430, Yucca Valley CA 92286, USA
O'Connor, Jane — Writer
Harper Collins Publishers, 10 E 53rd St, Cellar 1, New York NY 10022 USA
O'Connor, Kelley — Opera Singer
I M G Artists, Hogarth Business Park, Chiswick, London W4 2TH, England
O'Connor, Kevin J — Actor
Innovative Artists, 1505 10th St, Santa Monica CA 90401 USA
O'Connor, Mark — Fiddler, Violinist
Columbia Artists Mgmt Inc, 1790 Broadway, #702, New York NY 10019 USA
O'Connor, Mary Anne — Basketball Player
60 Romanock Place, Fairfield CT 06825, USA
O'Connor, Michael — Costume Designer
Dench Arnold Agency, 10 Newburgh St, London W1F 7RN, England
O'Connor, Myles — Ice Hockey Player
O'Connors Fine Footwear, 1415 1st St SW, Calgary AB T2R 0V9, Canada
O'Connor, Patrick — Actor
Paradigm Agency, 360 N Crescent Dr, North Building, Beverly Hills CA 90210 USA
O'Connor, Patrick D (Pat) — Director, Writer
United Agents, 12-26 Lexington St, London W1F 0LE, England
O'Connor, Renee — Actress
R O R Productions, 1601 N Sepulveda Blvd, #768, Manhattan Beach CA 90266, USA
O'Connor, Sandra Day — Supreme Court Justice, Educator
College of William & Mary, Chancellor's Office, Williamsburg VA 23187, USA
O'Connor, Sinead — Singer, Songwriter
Paradigm Agency, 360 N Crescent Dr, North Building, Beverly Hills CA 90210 USA
O'Connor, Thom — Artist
Moss Road, Voorheesville NY 12186, USA
O'Connor, Timothy J (Tim) — Actor
House of Representatives, 1434 6th St, #1, Santa Monica CA 90401 USA
O'Connor, William F (Bill) — Football Player
1905-40 Richview Road, Toronto ON M9A 5C1, Canada
O'Conor, John — Concert Pianist
Columbia Artists Mgmt Inc, 1790 Broadway, #702, New York NY 10019 USA
Odadjian, Sharvarsh S (Shavo) — Bassist (System of a Down)
Velmet Hammer Music, 9911 W Pico Blvd, #360W, Los Angeles CA 90035, USA
Odar, Baran Bo — Director, Producer, Writer
United Talent Agency, 9336 Civic Center Dr, Beverly Hills CA 90210 USA
O'Dassey, Seregon — Actress, Model
545 8th Avem #401, New York NY 10018, USA
O'Day, Alan — Singer, Songwriter
Talent Consultants International, 105 Shad Row, #B, Piermont NY 10968 USA
O'Day, Aubrey M — Singer (Danity Kane), Songwriter, Model
Bad Boy Entertainment, 1440 Broadway, #16, New York NY 10018 USA
O'Day, George — Yachtsman
6 Turtle Lane, Dover MA 02030, USA
Oddleifson, Christopher R (Chris) — Ice Hockey Player
1950 Westover Road, North Vancouver BC V7J 3J3, Canada
Odelein, Lyle — Ice Hockey Player
12569 Winding Hollow Lane, Frisco TX 75033, USA
Odelein, Selmar — Ice Hockey Player
Farm, Quill Lake SK S0A 3E0, Canada
Odell, Bob H — Football Player, Coach
911 Stenton Place, Ocean City NJ 08226, USA
O'Dell, Nancy — Actress
W M E Entertainment, 9601 Wilshire Blvd, #300, Beverly Hills CA 90210 USA
O'Dell, Tony — Actor
417 N Griffith Park Dr, Burbank CA 91506, USA
O'Dell, William O (Billy) — Baseball Player
225 Odelll Road, Newberry SC 29108, USA
Oden, McDonald — Football Plater
480 Chimneytop Dr, Antioch TN 37013, USA
Oden, Robert — Surgeon, Skiing Physician
PO Box 660, Aspen CO 81612, USA
Oden, Robert A, Jr — Educator
Carleton College, President's Office, 1 N College St, Northfield MN 55057, USA
Odgers, Jeff — Ice Hockey Player
Farm, Spy Hill SK S0A 3W0, Canada
Odhiambo, David — Writer
7 8th Ave, Lake Pleasant MA 01347, USA
Odierno, Raymond T — Army General
Chief of Staff, HqUSA, Pentagon, Washington DC 20310 USA
Odjick, Gino — Ice Hockey Player
Musquem Gold Academy, 3904 51st Ave W, Vancouver BC V6N 3W1, Canada
Odjig, Daphne — Artist
7841 Highway 97 North, #182, Kelowna BC V4V 1E7, Canada
Odmark, Matthew T (Matt) — Guitarist (Jars of Clay)
Nettwerk Mgmt, 1650 W 2nd Ave, Vancouver BC V6J 4R3, Canada
Odom, Antwan — Football Player
4562 Raynor Court, Mason OH 45040, USA

Odom, Clifton L (Cliff) — Football Player
6708 Marthas Vineyard Dr, Arlington TX 76001, USA
Odom, Johnny Lee (Blue Moon) — Baseball Player
10343 Slater Ave, #204, Fountain Valley CA 92708, USA
Odom, Lamar J — Basketball Player
21731 Ventura Blvd, #300, Woodland Hills CA 91364, USA
Odom, Stephen T (Steve) — Football Player
1482 Lincoln St, Berkeley CA 94702, USA
Odomes, Nathaniel B (Nate) — Football Player
900 Quail Creek Dr, Columbus GA 31907, USA
Odoms, Riley M — Football Player
16731 Quail Park Dr, Missouri City TX 77489, USA
O'Donnell, Andrew — Basketball Player
3310 Lincoln Ave, Allentown PA 18103, USA
O'Donnell, Annie — Actress
Kazarian/Spencer/Ruskin, 11969 Ventura Blvd, #300, Studio City CA 91604 USA
O'Donnell, Chris — Actor
W M E Entertainment, 9601 Wilshire Blvd, #300, Beverly Hills CA 90210 USA
O'Donnell, Daniel — Singer
Brockwell, 90B Lagan Road, Dublin Industrial Estate, Dublin 11, Ireland
O'Donnell, Fred — Ice Hockey Player
690 Carnaby St, Kingston ON K0H 2H0, Canada
O'Donnell, George D — Baseball Player
70 Crusaders Road, Springfield IL 62704, USA
O'Donnell, Joseph R (Joe) — Football Player
447 Bodley Crescent, Milan MI 48160, USA
O'Donnell, Keir — Actor
United Talent Agency, 9336 Civic Center Dr, Beverly Hills CA 90210 USA
O'Donnell, Neil K — Football Player
5329 Stanford Dr, Nashville TN 37215, USA
O'Donnell, Rosie — Actress
W M E Entertainment, 9601 Wilshire Blvd, #300, Beverly Hills CA 90210 USA
O'Donnell, Sean — Ice Hockey Player
1656 Manhattan Ave, Hermosa Beach CA 90254, USA
O'Donnell, William (Bill) — Harness Racing Driver
569 Penn Estate, East Stroudsburg PA 18301, USA
O'Donoghue, Colin — Actor
Alchemy Entertainment, 7024 Melrose Ave, #420, Los Angeles CA 90038 USA
O'Donoghue, John E — Baseball Player
5246 Far Oak Circle, Sarasota FL 34238, USA
O'Donoghue, Neil — Football Player
1118 Flushing Ave, Clearwater FL 33764, USA
O'Donohue, John F — Actor
Don Buchwald/Fortitude, 6500 Wilshire Blvd, #2200, Los Angeles CA 90048 USA
O'Dowd, Chris — Actor
United Talent Agency, 9336 Civic Center Dr, Beverly Hills CA 90210 USA
Odrowski, Gerry — Ice Hockey Player
PO Box 126, Trout Creek ON P0H 2L0, Canada
Oduber, Nelson O — Prime Minister, Aruba
Prime Minister's Office, L G Smith Blvd 76, Oranjestad, Aruba
Oduye, Adepero — Actress
Washington Square Arts, 1041 N Formosa Ave, Formosa Building, West Hollywood CA 90046, USA
O'Dwyer, Billy — Ice Hockey Player
11 Fox Hill Dr, Braintree MA 02184, USA
Oe, Kenzaburo — Nobel Literature Laureate
585 Seijo-Machi, Setagayaku, Tokyo, Japan
Oedekerk, Steve — Director
W M E Entertainment, 9601 Wilshire Blvd, #300, Beverly Hills CA 90210 USA
Oefelein, William A — Astronaut
Adventure Write, PO Box 113074, Anchorage AK 99511, USA
Oelkers, Bryan A — Baseball Player
3404 Taylor Ave, Bridgeton MO 63044, USA
Oelze, Christiane — Opera Singer
Augstein & Hahn, Tal 28, 80331 Munich, Germany
Oester, Ronald J (Ron) — Baseball Player
3760 Nine Mile-Tobasco Road, Cincinnati OH 45255, USA
Oetiker, Phil — Cinematographer
422 10th St, Brooklyn NY 11215, USA
Oettinger, Anthony G — Mathematician
65 Elizabeth Road, Belmont MA 02478, USA
Offerdahl, John A — Football Player
2749 NE 37th Dr, Fort Lauderdale FL 33308, USA
Offerman, Jose A — Baseball Player
10720 Moorpark St, North Hollywood CA 91602, USA
Offerman, Nick — Actor
United Talent Agency, 9336 Civic Center Dr, Beverly Hills CA 90210 USA
Office, Rowland J (Rollie) — Baseball Player
1028 Lake Glen Way, Sacramento CA 95822, USA
Ofili, Chris — Artist
Victoria Miro Gallery, 21 Cork St, London W1X 1HB, England
O'Flaherty, Gerry — Ice Hockey Player
5446 Cortez Crescent, North Vancouver BC V7R 4R4, Canada
Ogando, Alexi — Baseball Player
Texas Rangers, Ameriquest Field, 1000 Ballpark Way, #306, Arlington TX 76011 USA
Ogato, Sadako — Government Official, Japan
United Nations Office for Refugees, CP 2500, 1211 Geneva 2, Switzerland
Ogbogu, Eric O — Football Player
16814 Harbour Town Dr, Silver Spring MD 20905, USA
Ogden, Carlos (Bud) — Basketball Player
3324 S 4th St, Springfield IL 62703, USA
Ogden, Jonathan P (Jon) — Football Player
3330 Georgia Ave NW, Washington DC 20010, USA
Ogden, Raymond D (Ray) — Football Player
188 Anderson Dr, Brunswick GA 31520, USA
Ogea, Chad W — Baseball Player
3233 Plantation Court, Baton Rouge LA 70820, USA

O

Owen - Ogea

Ogi, Adolf	President, Switzerland
United Nations, Palais des Nations, #C119, 1211 Geneva 10, Switzerland	
Ogier, Bulle	Actress
Artmedia, 20 Ave Rapp, 75007 Paris, France	
Ogilvie, Brian H	Ice Hockey Player
4708 60th St, Red Deer AB T4N 7C7, Canada	
Ogilvie, Lana	Model
Company Models, 17 Little West 12th St, #333, New York NY 10014, USA	
Ogilvie, N Joseph (Joe)	Golfer
10 Cicero Lane, Austin TX 78746, USA	
Ogilvy, Geoff C	Golfer
8355 E Hartford Dr, #105, Scottsdale AZ 85255, USA	
Ogilvy, Ian	Actor
Julian Belfrage Assoc, 9 Argyll St, #300, London W1F 7TG, England	
Ogimi, Yuki Nagasato	Soccer Player
F F C Turbine Potsdam, Am Luftschiffhafen 2, #33, 14471 Potsdam, Germany	
Ogio, Michel	Governor General, Papua New Guinea
Governor General's Office, PO Box 79, Port Moresby 121, Papua New Guinea	
Ogle, Brett	Golfer
Advantage International, 1751 Pinnacle Dr, #1500, McLean VA 22102 USA	
Oglivie, Benjamin A (Ben)	Baseball Player
1012 E Sandpiper Dr, Tempe AZ 85283, USA	
O'Grady, Gail	Actress
Shelter Entertainment, 9454 Wilshire Blvd, #715, Beverly Hills CA 90212 USA	
O'Grady, Sean	Boxer
5808 NW 117th Terrace, Oklahoma City OK 73162, USA	
Ogren, Jayce	Conductor
I M G Artists, 152 W 57th St, #500, New York NY 10019 USA	
Ogrin, David	Golfer
2321 Common St, #102, New Braunfels TX 78130, USA	
Ogrodnick, John	Ice Hockey Player
37034 Aldgate Court, Farmington Hills MI 48335, USA	
Ogunleye, Adewale	Football Player
19113 NW 23rd Court, Pembroke Pines FL 33029, USA	
Ogwumike, Nnemkadi (Nnenka)	Basketball Player
Los Angeles Sparks, 888 S Figueroa St, #2010, Los Angeles CA 90017 USA	
Oh Jae-Seok	Soccer Player
Football Assn, 1-131 Sinmunno, 2-Ga Jongno-Gu, Seoul 110 062, South Korea	
Oh, Sadaharu	Baseball Player
Fukuoka Dome Daiei Hawks, 2-2-2 Jigyohama, Chuoku Fukuoka 810 0065, Japan	
Oh, Sandra	Actress
Principal Entertainment, 1964 Westwood Blvd, #400, Los Angeles CA 90025 USA	
Oh, Soon Teck	Actor
Lee Assoc, 8961 W Sunset Blvd, #V, West Hollywood CA 90069, USA	
O'Hair, Sean	Golfer
PO Box 127, Pocopson PA 19366, USA	
Ohakete, Ifeanyi	Football Player
11912 Crosswind Court, Reston VA 20194, USA	
O'Hanlon, Francis B (Fran)	Basketball Player
27 W Wayne Ave, Easton PA 18042, USA	
O'Hara, Catherine	Actress, Comedienne
I C M Partners, 10250 Constellation Blvd, #900, Los Angeles CA 90067 USA	
O'Hara, Kelli	Actress, Singer
One Entertainment, 12 W 57th St, #PH, New York NY 10019, USA	
O'Hara, M Kelley	Soccer Player
Soccer Federation, 1801 S Prairie Ave, Chicago IL 60616 USA	
O'Hara, Maureen	Actress
Artists Agency, 1180 S Beverly Dr, #301, Los Angeles CA 90035 USA	
O'Hare, Damian	Actor
Innovative Artists, 1505 10th St, Santa Monica CA 90401 USA	
O'Hare, Denis	Actor, Singer
Innovative Artists, 1505 10th St, Santa Monica CA 90401 USA	
O'Haver, Tommy	Director, Writer, Actor
Media Talent Group, 9200 W Sunset Blvd, #550, West Hollywood CA 90069 USA	
Oher, Michael J	Football Player
Baltimore Ravens, Ravens Stadium, 1 Winning Dr, Baltimore MD 21230 USA	
Ohkuchi, Shunichi	Businessman
Nippon Suisan Kaisha Ltd, 2-6-2 Otemachi, Chiyoda, Tokyo 100-8686, Japan	
Ohl, Donald J (Don)	Basketball Player
2 E Lockhaven Court, Edwardsville IL 62025, USA	
Ohlde, Nicole	Basketball Player
Tulsa Shock, B O K Center, 200 S Denver, Tulsa OK 74103 USA	
Ohlendorf, C Ross	Baseball Player
2300 Barton Creek Blvd, #40, Austin TX 78735, USA	
Ohlsson, Garrick	Concert Pianist
Opus 3 Artists, 470 Park Ave S, #900N, New York NY 10016 USA	
Ohlund, K Mattias	Ice Hockey Player
Tampa Bay Lightning, 401 Channelside Dr, Tampa FL 33602 USA	
Ohman, Jack	Editorial Cartoonist (Mixed Media)
Portland Oregonian, Editorial Dept, 1320 SW Broadway, Portland OR 97201, USA	
Ohman, William M (Will)	Baseball Player
8939 E Norwood Circle, Mesa AZ 85207, USA	
Ohme, Kevin A	Baseball Player
805 Starlifter Lane, Valrico FL 33594, USA	
Ohnishi, Minoru	Businessman
Fuji Photo Film, 26-30 Nishiazabu, Minatoku, Tokyo 106-8620, Japan	
Ohno, Apolo Anton	Speed Skater
Dreams Inc, 2 S University Dr, #325, Plantation FL 33324 USA	
Ohno, Shinobu	Soccer Player
Football Assn, 3-10-15 Hongo, Bunkyoku, Tokyo 113 0033 Japan	
Ohno, Yumiko	Singer, Bassist (Buffalo Daughter)
W M E Entertainment, 9601 Wilshire Blvd, #300, Beverly Hills CA 90210 USA	
Ohr, Fred	WW II Army Air Corps Hero
6401 Newburg Road, #211, Rockford IL 61108, USA	
Ohrner, Tommy (Tommi)	Actor
Ortlinder 6, 81927 Munich, Germany	

Ohta, Tomoko — Geneticist
20-20 Hatsunedai, Mishimashi, Shizuokaken 411-0018, Japan
Ohtani, Monshu Koshin — Religious Leader
Horikawa-Dori, Hanayachosagaru, Shimogyoku, Kyoto 600-8501, Japan
O'Hurley, John — Actor
Marv Dauer Mgmt, 11661 San Vicente Blvd, #104, Los Angeles CA 90049, USA
Ohuruogu, Christine I — Track Athlete
N & E Beagles, 281 Prince Regent Lane, London E13 8SD, England
Oistrakh, Igor D — Concert Violinist
Novolesnaya Str 3, Korp 2, #10, Moscow, Russia
Ojala, Kirt S — Baseball Player
1902 Forest Lake Dr SE, Grand Rapids MI 49546, USA
Ojeda, Eddie — Singer, Guitarist (Twisted Sister)
Rebellion Entertainment, 2440 Broadway, #111, New York NY 10024, USA
Ojeda, O Augie — Baseball Player
5351 W Morgan Place, Chandler AZ 85226, USA
Ojeda, Robert M (Bob) — Baseball Player
20 Somerset Dr, Rumson NJ 07760, USA
Oka, Masi — Actor
United Talent Agency, 9336 Civic Center Dr, Beverly Hills CA 90210 USA
Oka, Takeshi — Chemist
1463 E Park Place, Chicago IL 60637, USA
Okabe, Nororki — Engineer, Architect
Kansai Airport, 1 Banchi Senshu-Kuko Kita, Izumisanoshi, Osaka 549, Japan
Okafor, Chukwuemeka N (Emeka) — Basketball Player
840 Tchoupitoulas St, #102, New Orleans LA 70130, USA
Okajima, Hideki — Baseball Player
303 3rd St, #704, Cambridge MA 2142, USA
Okamoto, Ayako — Golfer
22627 Ladeene Ave, Torrance CA 90505, USA
Okamoto, Tao — Actress
I C M Partners, 10250 Constellation Blvd, #900, Los Angeles CA 90067 USA
Oke, Janette — Writer
Baker Publishing Group, PO Box 6287, Grand Rapids MI 49516, USA
Okeafor, Chikezie R (Chike) — Football Player
8340 N Ridgeview Dr, Paradise Valley AZ 85253, USA
O'Keefe, Jeremiah J, Sr — WW II Marine Corps Air Force Hero
202 White Blvd, Ocean Springs MS 39564, USA
O'Keefe, Jodie Lyn — Actress
Vincent Cirrincione Assoc, 1516 N Fairfax Ave, Los Angeles CA 90046 USA
O'Keefe, Laurence (Larry) — Composer
I C M Partners, 10250 Constellation Blvd, #900, Los Angeles CA 90067 USA
O'Keefe, Michael — Actor
Paradigm Agency, 360 N Crescent Dr, North Building, Beverly Hills CA 90210 USA
O'Keefe, Miles — Actor
Sharp/Karrys, 117 N Orlando Ave, Los Angeles CA 90048, USA
O'Keefe, Sean — Educator, Governmemt Official
E A D S North America, 1616 N Fort Myer Dr, #1600, Arlington VA 22209, USA
O'Keefe, Thomas V (Tommy) — Basketball Player
1000 Potomac Lane, Alexandria VA 22308, USA
Okeniyi, Dayo — Actor
United Talent Agency, 9336 Civic Center Dr, Beverly Hills CA 90210 USA
Okereke, Kelechukwu R (Kele) — Singer, Guitarist (Bloc Party)
Coalition Mgmt, 12 Barley Mow Passage, London W4 4PH, England
Okhotnikoff, Nikolai P — Opera Singer
Canal Griboedova 109, #13, 190068 Saint Petersburg, Russia
Okobi, Chukwunweze S (Chukky) — Football Player
5516 Maple Heights Court, Pittsburgh PA 15232, USA
Okogie, Anthony Olubunmi Cardinal — Religious Leader
Archdiocese, PO Box 8, 19 Catholic Mission St, Lagos, Nigeria
Okolowicz, Jeff — Guitarist (Chesterfield Kings)
Agency Group Ltd, 142 W 57th St, #600, New York NY 10019 USA
Okolowicz, Ted — Guitarist (Chesterfield Kings)
Agency Group Ltd, 142 W 57th St, #600, New York NY 10019 USA
Okonedo, Sophie — Actress
Hamilton Hodell, 66-68 Margaret St, London W1W 8SR, England
Okoniewski, J Stephen (Steve) — Football Player
222 S Oakland Ave, Oconto Falls WI 54154, USA
O'Koren, Michael F (Mike) — Basketball Player
109 Quaker Road, Mickleton NJ 08056, USA
Okoye, Christian E — Football Player
10082 Big Pine Dr, Rancho Cucamonga CA 91737, USA
Okrie, Leonard J (Len) — Baseball Player
2636 Burke Lane, Fayetteville NC 28306, USA
Okumoto, Yuji — Actor
Kono Kitchen, 8501 5th Ave NE, Seattle WA 98115, USA
Okumura, Tomohiro — Concert Violinist
Jecklin Assoc, 2717 Nichols Lane, Davenport IA 52803, USA
Okun, Daniel A — Environmental Engineer
204 Carol Woods, 750 Weaver Dairy Road, Chapel Hill NC 27514, USA
Okur, Mehmet — Basketball Player
1387 Perrys Hollow Road, Salt Lake City UT 84103, USA
Olagundoye, Toks — Actress
Glick Agency, 1321 7th St, #203, Santa Monica CA 90401 USA
Olah, George A — Nobel Chemistry Laureate
2252 Gloaming Way, Beverly Hills CA 90210, USA
Olajuwon, Hakeem A — Basketball Player
1305 N Horseshoe Dr, Sugar Land TX 77478, USA
Olander, Edwin (Ed) — WW II Marine Corps Air Force Hero
85 N Maple St, Florence MA 01062, USA
Olander, James B (Jim) — Baseball Player
8421 S Triangle R Ranch Place, Vail AZ 85641, USA
Olander, Jimmy — Guitarist (Diamond Rio)
Modern Mgmt, 1625 Broadway, #600, Nashville TN 37203, USA
Olandt, Ken — Actor
3216 Allegheny Court, Westlake Village CA 91362, USA

Olazabel, Jose Maria — Golfer
Real Club Golf de San Sebastian, Baserritar Etorbidea 1, 20280 Hondarribia, Gipuzkoa, Spain
Olberding, Mark A — Basketball Player
4131 Cliff Oaks St, San Antonio TX 78229, USA
Olbermann, Keith T — Sportscaster, Commentator
I C M Partners, 10250 Constellation Blvd, #900, Los Angeles CA 90067 USA
Olczyk, Ed — Ice Hockey Player, Coach
4581 Pamela Court, Long Grove IL 60047, USA
Olden, Paul — Sportscaster
68 Dean St, #3F, Brooklyn NY 11201, USA
Oldenburg, Brandon — Animator
Moonbot Studios, 2031 Kings Highway, #102, Shreveport LA 71103, USA
Oldenburg, Claes T — Sculptor
556 Broome St, New York NY 10013, USA
Oldenburg, Richard E — Museum Executive
447 E 57th St, New York NY 10022, USA
Olderman, Murray — Sportswriter
832 Inverness Dr, Rancho Mirage CA 92270, USA
Oldershaw, Kelsey — Actress
Darren Goldberg Mgmt, 5225 Wilshire Blvd, #419, Los Angeles CA 90036, USA
Oldfield, Bruce — Fashion Designer
27 Beauchamp Place, London SW3 1 NJ, England
Oldfield, Mike — Singer, Songwriter
PO Box 2031, Blandford DT11 9YB, England
Oldfield, Sally — Singer
Global Artists Mgmt, Willy-Brandt-Str 39, 50374 Erftstadt, Germany
Oldham, Christopher M (Chris) — Football Player
8701 E Wilshire Dr, Scottsdale AZ 85257, USA
Oldham, John H — Baseball Player
1845 Anne Way, San Jose CA 95124, USA
Oldham, John O (Johnny) — Basketball Player, Coach
2127 Sycamore Dr, Bowling Green KY 42104, USA
Oldham, Todd — Fashion Designer
120 Wooster St, New York NY 10012, USA
Oldis, Robert C (Bob) — Baseball Player
7414 Pohick Road, Lorton VA 22079, USA
Oldman, Gary — Actor, Director
A P A Talent/Literary Agency, 405 S Beverly Dr, #300, Beverly Hills CA 90212 USA
Oldring, Peter — Actor, Comedian
Schumacher Mgmt, 10323 Santa Monica Blvd, #101, Los Angeles CA 90024, USA
Olds, Gabriel — Actor
Stone Manners Salners, 9911 W Pico Blvd, #1400, Los Angeles CA 90035 USA
Oldstone, Michael B A — Neuropharmacologist
Scripps Research Institute, Neuropharmacology Dept, La Jolla CA 92037, USA
Olear, Doug — Actor
Progressive Artists Agency, 1041 N Formosa Ave, West Hollywood CA 90046 USA
O'Leary, Brian T — Astronaut
Future Focus on Human Potential, 5136 E Karen Dr, Scottsdale AZ 85254, USA
O'Leary, Hazel R — Secretary, Energy; Educator
Fisk University, President's Office, 1000 17th Ave N, Nashville TN 37208, USA
O'Leary, John — Actor
Gage Group, 14724 Ventura Blvd, #505, Sherman Oaks CA 91403 USA
O'Leary, Matthew — Actor
I C M Partners, 10250 Constellation Blvd, #900, Los Angeles CA 90067 USA
O'Leary, Michael — Actor
38 Prospect Ave, Montclair NJ 07042, USA
O'Leary, Troy F — Baseball Player
1060 W Norwood St, Rialto CA 92377, USA
Olejnik, Craig — Actor
Robert Stein Mgmt, PO Box 3797, Beverly Hills CA 90212, USA
Oleksy, Jozef — Prime Minister, Poland
Sejm R P, Ul Wiejska 4/6/8, 00 902 Warsaw, Poland
Ole-Moiyol, Onesmo — Molecular Biologist, Immunologist
Insect Physiologist Centre, Nyayo Stadium, PO Box 30772, Nairobi, Kenya
Olerud, John G — Baseball Player
PO Box 606, Medina WA 98039, USA
Olesz, Rostislav — Ice Hockey Player
8687 Melrose Ave, #7, West Hollywood CA 90069, USA
Olevsky, Julian — Concert Violinist
68 Blue Hills Road, Amherst MA 01002, USA
Oleynik, Larisa — Actress
Savage Agency, 6212 Banner Ave, Los Angeles CA 90038 USA
Olin, Ken — Actor
Innovative Artists, 1505 10th St, Santa Monica CA 90401 USA
Olin, Laurie — Landscape Architect
227 S 6th St, Philadelphia PA 19106, USA
Olin, Lena — Actress
Paradigm Agency, 360 N Crescent Dr, North Building, Beverly Hills CA 90210 USA
Oliphant, Patrick B (Pat) — Editorial Cartoonist
Susan Conway Gallery, 1214 13th St, Washington DC 20005, USA
Olitzky, Kerry M — Religious Leader, Rabbi
Jewish Outreach Institute, 1270 Broadway, #609, New York NY 10001, USA
Oliva, Ignazio — Actor
Carol Levi Mgmt, Via G Pisanelli 2, 00196 Rome, Italy
Oliva, L Jay — Educator
Skirball Performing Arts Center, 60 Washington Square S, New York NY 10012, USA
Oliva, Pedro (Tony) — Baseball Player
212 Spring Valley Dr, Minneapolis MN 55420, USA
Olivares Palqu, Omar — Baseball Player
PO Box 1328, San German PR 00683, USA
Olivares, Ruben — Boxer
Geno Productions, PO Box 113, Montebello CA 90640, USA
Olivas, John D — Astronaut
595 36th St, Manhattan Beach CA 90266, USA
Olive, Jason — Actor
Innovative Artists, 1505 10th St, Santa Monica CA 90401 USA

Olive, John 8652 Harjoan Ave, San Diego CA 92123, USA	Basketball Player
Oliveira, Elmar C M Artists, 127 W 96th St, #13B, New York NY 10025 USA	Concert Violinist
Oliver, Albert (Al) PO Box 1466, Portsmouth OH 45662, USA	Baseball Player
Oliver, Brian Creative Artists Agency, 2000 Ave of Stars, #100, Los Angeles CA 90067 USA	Producer
Oliver, Christian House of Representatives, 1434 6th St, #1, Santa Monica CA 90401 USA	Actor
Oliver, Clarence H (Clancy) 233 Springview, Irvine CA 92620, USA	Football Player
Oliver, Daniel T 318 Prince St, #6, Alexandria VA 22314, USA	Navy Admiral
Oliver, Darren C 1804 Larkspur Court, Southlake TX 76092, USA	Baseball Player
Oliver, Dean 21386 Notus Road, Greenleaf ID 83626, USA	Rodeo Rider
Oliver, Hubert (Hubie) 136 Blake St, Elyria OH 44035, USA	Football Player
Oliver, Jamie PO Box 51372, London N1 7WX, England	Chef
Oliver, John W M E Entertainment, 9601 Wilshire Blvd, #300, Beverly Hills CA 90210 USA	Actor, Writer, Producer
Oliver, Joseph M (Joe) 5223 Oak Island Road, Belle Isle FL 32809, USA	Baseball Player
Oliver, Louis, III 5082 SW 167th Ave, Miramar FL 33027, USA	Football Player
Oliver, Mary Molly Malone Cook Agency, PO Box 1071, Sweet Briar VA 24595, USA	Writer
Oliver, Murray C 5505 McGuire Road, Minneapolis MN 55439, USA	Ice Hockey Player
Oliver, Nancy United Talent Agency, 9336 Civic Center Dr, Beverly Hills CA 90210 USA	Producer, Writer
Oliver, Nathaniel (Nate) 4403 Oak Hill Road, Oakland CA 94605, USA	Baseball Player
Oliver, Pam Ken Lindner Assoc, 2049 Century Park East, #1000, Los Angeles CA 90067, USA	Sportscaster
Oliver, Robert L (Bob) 1716 G St, Rio Linda CA 95673, USA	Baseball Player
Oliver, Winslow P 2027 Summerall Court, Richmond TX 77406, USA	Football Player
Oliveri, Nick The Firm, 2049 Century Park E, #2550, Los Angeles CA 90067 USA	Bassist (Queens of the Stone Age)
Olivero, Chris Innovative Artists, 1505 10th St, Santa Monica CA 90401 USA	Actor
Olivia Ozone Productions, PO Box 4153 Point Dume Station, Malibu CA 90265, USA	Artist, Illustrator
Olivier, Philip Associated International Mgmt, Fairfax House, Fulwood Place, London WC1V 6HU, England	Actor
Olivieri, Dawn A P A Talent/Literary Agency, 405 S Beverly Dr, #300, Beverly Hills CA 90212 USA	Actress
Olivo, America Northern Exposure Talent, 570 Granville St, #503, Vancouver BC V6C 3P1, Canada	Actress, Model
Olivo, Joey 9628 Poinciana St, Pico Rivera CA 90660, USA	Boxer
Olivo, Karen Liebman Entertainment, 12 E 46th St, #500, New York NY 10017, USA	Actress, Dancer
Olivo, Miguel E 10004 Plaza de Oro Dr, Oakdale CA 95361, USA	Baseball Player
Olivor, Jane Ed Keane, 32 Saint Edwards Road, Boston MA 02128, USA	Singer
Oliwa, Krzystof 4 Meeker Dr, Florham Park NJ 07932, USA	Ice Hockey Player
Olkewicz, Neal T 1028 Summer Lane, Pottstown PA 19465, USA	Football Player
Olkewicz, Walter Commercial Talent, 9255 Sunset Blvd, #505, Los Angeles CA 90069, USA	Actor
Ollie, Kevin J 210 Thompson St, South Glastonbury CT 06073, USA	Basketball Player
Ollila, Jorma Royal Dutch Shell, Carel v Bylandtlaan 16, 2596 HR Den Haag, Netherlands	Businessman
Ollom, James D (Jim) 10916 27th Ave SE, Everett WA 98208, USA	Baseball Player
Olmedo, Alex 5067 Woodley Ave, Encino CA 91436, USA	Tennis Player
Olmert, Ehud 29 November Road, Jerusalem 92105, Israel	Prime Minister, Israel
Olmi, Paolo I M G Artists, Hogarth Business Park, Chiswick, London W4 2TH, England	Conductor
Olmo, Luis F R (Jibaro) 620 Calle Jose Ramon Figueroa, San Juan PR 00907, USA	Baseball Player
Olmos, Edward James Olmos Productions, 500 S Buena Vista St, Old Animation Building, Burbank CA 91521, USA	Actor
Olmstead, Alan R (Al) 1008 Pinecone Trail, Florissant MO 63031, USA	Baseball Player
Olmstead, M Bert 2-1512 High Country Dr NW, High River AB T1V 1V9, Canada	Ice Hockey Player, Coach
Olmstead, Matt W M E Entertainment, 9601 Wilshire Blvd, #300, Beverly Hills CA 90210 USA	Producer
Olney, Claude W Olney A' Seminars, PO Box 686, Scottsdale AZ 85252, USA	Educator
Olofsson-Zidek, Anna Carin Margareta Silver, Jamtlandsgatan 8, 842 32 Sveg, Sweden	Biathlete
Olojede, Dele New York Newsday, Editorial Dept, 235 Pinelawn Road, Melville NY 11747 USA	Journalist

O'Loughlin, Alex — Actor
Linston Morris Mgmt, 3 Gladstone St, #301, Newtown 2042, Australia
O'Loughlin, Gerald S — Actor
23388 Mulholland Dr, #204, Woodland Hills CA 91364, USA
O'Loughlin, Sean — Conductor, Composer
I M G Artists, 152 W 57th St, #500, New York NY 10019 USA
Olowokandi, Michael — Basketball Player
10061 SW 60th Court, Miami FL 33156, USA
Olsavsky, Jerome D (Jerry) — Football Player
92 Lake Shore Dr, Youngstown OH 44511, USA
Olsdal, Stefan A B — Bassist, Guitarist (Placebo)
Riverman Records, George House, Brecon Road, London W6 8PY, England
Olsen, Andrew H (Andy) — Baseball Umpire
451 93rd Ave N, Saint Petersburg FL 33702, USA
Olsen, Ashley — Actress
DualStar Entertainment Group, 3760 Robertson Blvd, Los Angeles CA 90067, USA
Olsen, Bud — Basketball Player
1602 Gardiner Lane, #130, Louisville KY 40205, USA
Olsen, Elizabeth — Actress
Gersh Agency, 41 Madison Ave, #3301, New York NY 10010 USA
Olsen, Eric Christian — Actor
United Talent Agency, 9336 Civic Center Dr, Beverly Hills CA 90210 USA
Olsen, Gregory (Greg) — Tourist Cosmonaut
Sensors Unlimited, 3490 US Route 1, Building 12, Princeton NJ 08540, USA
Olsen, Kevin — Baseball Player
3353 Dales Dr, Norco CA 92860, USA
Olsen, Mark V — Producer, Writer
Creative Artists Agency, 2000 Ave of Stars, #100, Los Angeles CA 90067 USA
Olsen, Mary Kate — Actress
DualStar Entertainment Group, 3760 Robertson Blvd, Los Angeles CA 90067, USA
Olsen, Olaf — Archaeologist
Strevelsjovedvej 2, Alro, 8300 Oder, Denmark
Olsen, Paul E — Geologist
Columbia University, Lamont-Doherty Geological Laboratory, New York NY 10027, USA
Olsen, Phillip V (Phil) — Football Player
112 Hitching Post Road, Bozeman MT 59715, USA
Olsen, Scott M — Baseball Player
2991 NE 185th St, #1701, Aventura FL 33180, USA
Olsen, Stanford — Opera Singer
Columbia Artists Mgmt Inc, 1790 Broadway, #702, New York NY 10019 USA
Olshansky, Igor — Football Player
PO Box 5000, Rancho Santa Fe CA 92067, USA
Olshwanger, Ron — Photojournalist
1447 Meadowside Dr, Saint Louis MO 63146, USA
Olson, Allen I — Governor, ND
631 Broken Arrow Road, Chanhassen MN 55317, USA
Olson, Benjamin D (Benji) — Football Player
2211 Old Natchez Trace, Franklin TN 37069, USA
Olson, Candice — Interior Designer
Fusion Television, 145 Front St E, #L1, Toronto ON M5A 1E3, Canada
Olson, Dennis — Ice Hockey Player
521 1st Ave S, Kenora ON P9N 1W6, Canada
Olson, Eric T — Navy Admiral
Commander, US Special Operations Command, MacDill Air Force Base FL 33621 USA
Olson, Gale — Model
Playboy Promotions, 2706 Media Center Dr, Los Angeles CA 90065 USA
Olson, Greggory W (Gregg) — Baseball Player
1996 Port Nelson Place, Newport Beach CA 92660, USA
Olson, Gregory W (Greg) — Baseball Player
18592 Saint Mellion Place, Eden Prairie MN 55347, USA
Olson, Harold V — Football Player
1622 Holly Springs Road NE, Marietta GA 30062, USA
Olson, Heather — Actress
T C M Model & Talent, 2200 6th Ave, #530, Seattle WA 98121, USA
Olson, Hope — Model
Playboy Promotions, 2706 Media Center Dr, Los Angeles CA 90065 USA
Olson, James — Actor
29122 Cliffside Dr, Malibu CA 90265, USA
Olson, Josh — Writer, Director
BenderSpink, 5870 W Jefferson Blvd, #E, Los Angeles CA 90016 USA
Olson, Kaitlin — Actress
Flutie Entertainment, 9320 Wilshire Blvd, #202, Beverly Hills CA 90212 USA
Olson, Karl A — Baseball Player
1417 Pin Oak Dr, Gardnerville NV 89410, USA
Olson, Lisa — Sportswriter
New York Daily News, Editorial Dept, 220 E 42nd St, New York NY 10017 USA
Olson, Mancur — Economist
4316 Claggett Pine Way, University Park MD 20782, USA
Olson, Mark — Singer, Songwriter (Jayhawks)
Sussman Assoc, 1222 16th Ave S, #300, Nashville TN 37212, USA
Olson, Mark W — Government Official, Economist
Public Accounting Oversight Board, 1666 K St NW, #800, Washington DC 20006, USA
Olson, Nancy — Actress
945 N Alpine Dr, Beverly Hills CA 90210, USA
Olson, Peter W — Businessman, Publisher
Random House, 1745 Broadway, #1800, New York NY 10019 USA
Olson, R Lute — Basketball Coach
5831 E Finisterra, Tucson AZ 85750, USA
Olson, Theodore B — Government Official
Gibson Dunn Crutcher, 1050 Connecticut Ave NW, #300, Washington DC 20036, USA
Olson, Timothy L (Tim) — Baseball Player
5416 Pebble Court, McKinney TX 75070, USA
Olson, Weldon N (Weldy) — Ice Hockey Player
2623 Goldenrod Lane, Findlay OH 45840, USA
Olsson, Christian — Track Athlete
F S D Internet Tjanster, Box 5026, 250 03 Helsinborg, Sweden

Olsson, Curt G — Financier
Skandinaviska Enskilda Banken, 106 40 Stockholm, Sweden
Olsson, Johan — Cross Country Skier
Asarna Idrottsklubb, Box 79, 840 31 Asarna, Sweden
Olsson, Paul J (P J) — Singer, Songwriter
Good Times Music, 506 Shelden Ave, Houghton MI 49931, USA
Olsson, Staffan — Handball Player, Coach
Hammarby I F, Mandagen Den 27/10, 2008 KL Hammarby, Sweden
Olszewski, Jan F — Prime Minister, Poland
Biuro Poselskie, Al Ujazdowskie 13, 00 567 Warsaw, Poland
Olwine, Edward R (Ed) — Baseball Player
223 Spanish Lakes Dr, Nokomis FL 34275, USA
Olyphant, Timothy — Actor
Brillstein Entertainment Partners, 9150 Wilshire Blvd, #350, Beverly Hills CA 90212 USA
O'Malley, Mike — Actor
Creative Artists Agency, 2000 Ave of Stars, #100, Los Angeles CA 90067 USA
O'Malley, Peter — Baseball Executive
515 S Figueroa St, #1988, Los Angeles CA 90071, USA
O'Malley, Robert E — Vietnam War Marine Corps Hero (CMH)
PO Box 775, Goldthwaite TX 76844, USA
O'Malley, Sean P Cardinal — Religious Leader
Archdiocese of Boston, 66 Brooks Dr, Braintree MA 02184, USA
O'Malley, Susan — Basketball Executive
Washington Wizards, M C I Centre, 601 F St NW, Washington DC 20004 USA
O'Malley, Thomas D — Businessman
Tosco Corp, 1700 E Putnam Ave, #500, Old Greenwich CT 06870, USA
O'Malley, Thomas P (Tom) — Baseball Player
10 Carriage Square, Montoursville PA 17754, USA
O'Mara, Jason — Actor
Independent Talent Group, Oxford House, 76 Oxford St, London W1D 1BS, England
O'Mara, Kate — Actress
Michael Ladkin Mgmt, 1 Duchess St, #1, London W1N 3DE, England
O'Mara, Mark — Harness Racing Driver, Trainer
6882 NW 65th Terrace, Parkland FL 33067, USA
Omarion — Singer (B2K), Songwriter, Actor
Pyramid Entertainment, 377 Rector Place, #21A, New York NY 10280 USA
O'Meara, Mark F — Golfer
2000 Auburn Dr, #330, Beachwood OH 44122, USA
O'Meara, Peter — Actor
Roar Mgmt, 9701 Wilshire Blvd, #800, Beverly Hills CA 90212 USA
Omeyer, Thierry — Handball Player
T H W Kiel Handball, Ziegelteich 30, 24103 Kiel, Germany
Omidyar, Pierre M — Businessman
Omidyar Network, 2145 Hamilton Ave, San Jose CA 95125, USA
Omundson, Timothy — Actor
S M S Talent, 8383 Wilshire Blvd, #230, Beverly Hills CA 90211 USA
Omura, Satoshi — Organic Chemist
Kitasato Institute, 9-1-5 Shirokane, Tokyo 108, Japan
Onaiyekan, John O — Religious Leader
Archbishop's House, Area 3, Section 2, PO Box 286, Garki, Abuja FCT, Nigeria
O'Nan, Stewart — Writer
Viking Press, 375 Hudson St, New York NY 10014 USA
Ondaatje, Michael — Writer
Glendon College, English Dept, 2275 Bayview, Toronto ON M4N 3M6, Canada
Ondricek, Miroslav — Cinematographer
Nad Pomnikem 1, 15200 Prague 5 Smichow, Czech Republic
O'Neal, Alexander — Singer, Songwriter
Green Light Talent Agency, PO Box 3172, Beverly Hills CA 90212 USA
O'Neal, Carlton (Carol) — Model
Playboy Promotions, 2706 Media Center Dr, Los Angeles CA 90065 USA
O'Neal, Deltha L, III — Football Player
10225 Meadowknoll Dr, Loveland OH 45140, USA
O'Neal, E Stanley — Financier
Merrill Lynch Co, World Financial Center, 2 Vesey St, New York NY 10007, USA
O'Neal, Griffin — Actor
21368 Pacific Coast Highway, Malibu CA 90265, USA
O'Neal, Jamie — Singer, Songwriter
Momentum Label Group, 8161 Highway 100, #179, Nashville TN 37221, USA
O'Neal, Jermaine — Basketball Player
1500 Ocean Dr, #1206, Miami Beach FL 33139, USA
O'Neal, Leslie C — Football Player
4951 Yerba Santa Dr, San Diego CA 92115, USA
O'Neal, Ralph T — Chief Minister, British Virgin Islands
Chief Minister's Office, Road Town, Tortola, British Virgin Islands
O'Neal, Randall J (Randy) — Baseball Player
10015 Honey Tree Court, Orlando FL 32836, USA
O'Neal, Ryan — Actor
David Shapira Assoc, 193 N Robertson Blvd, Beverly Hills CA 90211 USA
O'Neal, Shaquille R — Basketball Player
9927 Giffin Court, Windermere FL 34786, USA
O'Neal, Steve — Football Player
2914 Coronado Dr, College Station TX 77845, USA
O'Neal, Tatum — Actress
Untitled Entertainment, 350 S Beverly Dr, #200, Beverly Hills CA 90212 USA
O'Neil, Edward W (Ed) — Football Player
6691 Aiken Road, Lockport NY 14094, USA
O'Neil, Lawrence — Director
I C M Partners, 10250 Constellation Blvd, #900, Los Angeles CA 90067 USA
O'Neil, Linda — Actress, Model
C E S D, 10635 Santa Monica Blvd, #130, Los Angeles CA 90025 USA
O'Neil, Melissa C — Singer
19 Entertainment, 8560 W Sunset Blvd, #900, Los Angeles CA 90069 USA
O'Neil, Tricia — Actress
David Shapira Assoc, 193 N Robertson Blvd, Beverly Hills CA 90211 USA
O'Neill of Bengarve, O Sylvia — Philosopher
Newham College, Philosophy Dept, Cambridge CB3 9DF, England

O'Neill, Brian — Ice Hockey Executive
2600-1800 McGill College Ave, Montreal QC H3A 3J6, Canada

O'Neill, Dan — Association Executive
Mercy Corps, 45 SW Ankeny St, Portland OR 97204, USA

O'Neill, Dan — Cartoonist (Odd Bodkins, O'Neill)
PO Box 1297, Nevada City CA 95959, USA

O'Neill, Doug — Thoroughbred Racing Trainer
Doug O'Neill Stable, Hollywood Park, 1050 S Prairie Ave, Inglewood CA 90301, USA

O'Neill, Ed — Actor
I C M Partners, 10250 Constellation Blvd, #900, Los Angeles CA 90067 USA

O'Neill, Eugene F — Communications Engineer
394 Dogford Road, Etna NH 03750, USA

O'Neill, Jennifer — Actress, Model
Jennifer O'Neill Ministries, 30 Hillenglade Dr, Nashville TN 37207, USA

O'Neill, Kevin — Basketball Coach
University of Southern California, Athletic Dept, Heritage Hall, Los Angeles CA 90089, USA

O'Neill, Maggie — Actress
Independent Talent Group, Oxford House, 76 Oxford St, London W1D 1BS, England

O'Neill, Michael E — Financier
Citigroup Inc, 55 E 52nd St, New York NY 10055, USA

O'Neill, Morgan — Director, Writer, Actor
Paradigm Agency, 360 N Crescent Dr, North Building, Beverly Hills CA 90210 USA

O'Neill, Paul A — Baseball Player
7785 Hartford Hill Lane, Cincinnati OH 45242, USA

O'Neill, Paul H — Secretary, Treasury
3 Von Lent Place, Pittsburgh PA 15232, USA

O'Neill, Susan (Susie) — Swimmer
Elite Sports Properties, 326 Seaview Road, Henley Beach SA 5022, Australia

Ong, John D — Businessman, Diplomat
230 Aurora St, Hudson OH 44236, USA

Onkotz, Dennis H — Football Player
270 Walker Dr, State College PA 16801, USA

Ono, Takashi — Gymnast
Gymnastics Assn, Kishi Hall, 1-1 Jinnan Shibuyaku, Tokyo 150-8050, Japan

Ono, Yoko — Filmmaker, Singer, Artist
Dakota Hotel, 1 W 72nd St, #1, New York NY 10023, USA

Onopka, Snejana — Model
Women Model Mgmt, 199 Lafayette St, #700, New York NY 10012 USA

O'Nora, Brian — Baseball Umpire
5265 Nashua Dr, Youngstown OH 44515, USA

Onorati, Peter — Actor
Liberman/Zerman Mgmt, 252 N Larchmont Blvd, #200, Los Angeles CA 90004 USA

Ontiveros, Steven (Steve) — Baseball Player
9970 E Charter Oak Road, Scottsdale AZ 85260, USA

Ontiveros, Steven R (Steve) — Baseball Player
18061 N 87th Dr, #2127, Peoria AZ 85382, USA

Ontkean, Michael — Actor
PO Box 51, Kilauea HI 96754, USA

Onufriyenko, Yuri I — Cosmonaut
Cosmonaut Training Center, Star City, 141160 Zvezdny Gorodok, Moscow Oblast, Russia

Onweagba, Oluchi — Model
D N A Model Mgmt, 555 W 25th St, #600, New York NY 10001 USA

Onyali, Mary — Track Athlete
Kurt Varricchio, 23861 El Toro Road, #700, Lake Forest CA 92630, USA

Oosterhuis, Peter — Golfer
2823 Providence Road, #182, Charlotte NC 28211, USA

Opacic, Paul — Actor
Associated International Mgmt, Fairfax House, Fulwood Place, London WC1V 6HU, England

Opasik, Jim — Artist
1914 Beverly Road, Catonsville MD 21228, USA

Opertti Baddan, Didier — Government Official, Uruguay
A L A D I, Calle Cebollati 1461, Montevideo CP 11200, Uruguay

Ophuls, Marcel — Director
10 Rue Ernest Deloison, 92200 Neuilly-sur-Seine, France

Opie, Alan — Opera Singer
I M G Artists, Hogarth Business Park, Chiswick, London W4 2TH, England

Opik, Ernst J — Astronomer
University of Maryland, Physics & Astronomy Dept, College Park MD 20742, USA

Oppegard, Peter — Figure Skater
East West Ice Palace, 11446 Artesia Blvd, Artesia CA 90701, USA

Oppenheim, Irwin — Chemical Physicist
140 Upland Road, Cambridge MA 02140, USA

Oppenheim-Barnes of Gloucester, Sally — Government Official, England
Quietways, Highlands, Painswick, Gloustershire, England

Oppenheimer, Alan — Actor
1207 Beverly Green Dr, Beverly Hills CA 90212, USA

Oppenheimer, Benjamin R — Astronomer
Columbia University, Astronomy Dept, New York NY 10027, USA

Oppenheimer, Deborah — Producer, Writer
N B C Universal, 100 Universal City Plaza, Universal City CA 91608, USA

Oppewall, Jeannine Claudia — Art Director
Gersh Agency, 9465 Wilshire Blvd, #600, Beverly Hills CA 90212 USA

Oquendo, Jose M R G — Baseball Player
13219 Selma Road, De Soto MO 63020, USA

O'Quinn, Terry — Actor
I F A Talent Agency, 8730 W Sunset Blvd, #490, West Hollywood CA 90069 USA

Oquist, Michael L (Mike) — Baseball Player
1910 Raton Ave, La Junta CO 81050, USA

Orakpo, Brian N — Football Player
Washington Redskins, 21300 Redskin Park Dr, Ashburn VA 20147 USA

Oram, Tara — Singer
Agency Group Ltd, 142 W 57th St, #600, New York NY 10019 USA

Oramo, Sakari M — Conductor
Royal Stockholm Symphony Orchestra, Konserthus, Hotorget 8, Box 7083, 103 87 Stockholm, Sweden

Orange, Walter (Clyde) — Singer, Drummer (Commodores)
Management Assoc, 1920 Benson Ave, Saint Paul MN 55116, USA

Orbach, Raymond L — Educator
4004 Petra Path, Austin TX 78731, USA
Orban, Viktor — Prime Minister, Hungary
Prime Minister's Office, Kossuth Lajos Ter 1-3, 1055 Budapest, Hungary
Orbit, William — Keyboardist, Guitarist, Songwriter
Creative Artists Agency, 2000 Ave of Stars, #100, Los Angeles CA 90067 USA
Ord, Robert L (Bob), III — Army General
3020 Ribera Road, Carmel CA 93923, USA
Ordonez, Magglio J — Baseball Player
181 Nurmi Dr, Fort Lauderdale FL 33301, USA
Ordonez, Pilar — Actress
Hac de Pavones 169, 28030 Madrid, Spain
Ordonez, Rey — Baseball Player
16501 NW 84th Ave, Hialeah FL 33016, USA
Ordway, Frederick I, III — Writer
3423 Lookout Dr SE, Huntsville AL 35801, USA
O'Ree, William E (Willie) — Ice Hockey Player
7961 Anders Circle, La Mesa CA 91942, USA
O'Reilly Werry, Heather A — Soccer Player
Soccer Federation, 1801 S Prairie Ave, Chicago IL 60616 USA
O'Reilly, Ahna — Actress
W M E Entertainment, 9601 Wilshire Blvd, #300, Beverly Hills CA 90210 USA
O'Reilly, Anthony J F — Businessman, Publisher
H J Heinz Co, PO Box 57, Pittsburgh PA 15230, USA
O'Reilly, Bill — Commentator
O'Reilly Factor, Fox-TV, 1211 Ave of Americas, New York NY 10036, USA
O'Reilly, David J — Businessman
Chevron Corp, 6001 Bollinger Canyon Road, San Ramon CA 94583, USA
O'Reilly, Genevieve — Actress
PO Box 128, Surry Hills NSW 2010, Australia
O'Reilly, Terry — Ice Hockey Player
PO Box 5544, Salisbury MA 01952, USA
O'Reilly, Tim — Publisher, Businessman
O'Reilly Media, 1005 Gravenstein Highway N, Sebastopol CA 95472, USA
Oremans, Miriam — Tennis Player
Octagon Worldwide, 1751 Pinnacle Dr, #1500, McLean VA 22102 USA
Orenstein, Andrew — Producer, Writer
Paradigm Agency, 360 N Crescent Dr, North Building, Beverly Hills CA 90210 USA
Oresko, Nicholas — WW II Army Hero (CMH)
3 Tenakill Park E, #111, Cresskill NJ 7626, USA
Oreskovich, Alesha — Model
Playboy Promotions, 2706 Media Center Dr, Los Angeles CA 90065 USA
Orie, Kevin L — Baseball Player
190 Shadow Ridge Dr, Pittsburgh PA 15238, USA
Origliasso, Jessica — Singer (Vernoicas), Actress
Harbour Agency, 135 Forbes St, Woolloomooloo NSW 2011, Australia
Origliasso, Lisa — Singer (Veronicas), Actress
Harbour Agency, 135 Forbes St, Woolloomooloo NSW 2011, Australia
O'Riordan, Dolores M E — Singer (Cranberries), Songwriter
Creative Artists Agency, 2000 Ave of Stars, #100, Los Angeles CA 90067 USA
Oritz, John — Actor
Gersh Agency, 9465 Wilshire Blvd, #600, Beverly Hills CA 90212 USA
Orland, Frank J — Oral Microbiologist, Dentist
519 Jackson Blvd, Forest Park IL 60130, USA
Orlandi, Luca — Fashion Designer
Luca Luca, 19 W 36th St, #400, New York NY 10018, USA
Orlando, Gates — Ice Hockey Player
252 Bennington Hills Court, West Henrietta NY 14586, USA
Orlando, Tony — Singer
Brokaw Co, 9255 W Sunset Blvd, #804, West Hollywood CA 90069 USA
Orlean, Susan — Writer
New Yorker, Editorial Dept, 4 Times Square, Basement C1B, New York NY 10036 USA
Orleans, Joan — Singer
PO Box 2596, New York NY 10009, USA
Orloff, John — Producer, Writer
Creative Artists Agency, 2000 Ave of Stars, #100, Los Angeles CA 90067 USA
Orlovsky, Daniel J (Dan) — Football Player
2 Reliant Park, Houston TX 77054, USA
Orman, Suze — Writer
Suze Orman Financial Group, 2000 Powell St, #1605, Emeryville CA 94608, USA
Ormond, Julia — Actress
Gersh Agency, 9465 Wilshire Blvd, #600, Beverly Hills CA 90212 USA
Orms, Barry D — Basketball Player
3 Loudon Dr, #8, Fishkill NY 12524, USA
Ornish, Dean — Cardiologist
Preventive Medicine Research Institute, 900 Bridgeway, #2, Sausalito CA 94965, USA
Ornstein, Donald S — Mathematician
857 Tolman Dr, Stanford CA 94305, USA
Ornstein, Norman J — Political Scientist
2212 Wyoming Ave NW, Washington DC 20008, USA
Orosco, Jesse R — Baseball Player
16242 Winecreek Road, San Diego CA 92127, USA
O'Rourke, James P (Charlie) — Baseball Player
15612 N Little Spokane Dr, Spokane WA 99208, USA
O'Rourke, Tom — Actor
TalentWorks, 3500 W Olive Ave, #1400, Burbank CA 91505 USA
Orozco, Gabriel — Sculptor
Marian Goodman Gallery, 124 W 57th St, New York NY 10019, USA
Orozco-Estrada, Andres — Conductor
I M G Artists, Hogarth Business Park, Chiswick, London W4 2TH, England
Orpik, R Brooks — Ice Hockey Player
2396 Hilltop Road, Presto PA 15142, USA
Orr, James F, III — Businessman
U N U M Provident Corp, 2211 Congress St, Portland ME 04122, USA
Orr, John M (Johnny) — Basketball Coach, Administrator
5736 Gallery Court, West Des Moines IA 50266, USA

Orr, Kay S — Governor, NE
1425 H St, Lincoln NE 68508, USA
Orr, Louis M — Basketball Player, Coach
1333 Pine Valley Dr, Bowling Green OH 43402, USA
Orr, Peterson T (Pete) — Baseball Player
400 Rannie Road, Newmarket ON L3X 2N3, Canada
Orr, Robert G (Bobby) — Ice Hockey Player
Orr Hockey Group, PO Box 290836, Charlestown MA 02129, USA
Orr, Shantee D — Football Player
PO Box 20301, Houston TX 77225, USA
Orr, Terrance F (Terry) — Football Player
2710 Kellogg Ave, Dallas TX 75216, USA
Orr, Terrence S — Ballet Dancer, Executive
Pittsburgh Ballet Theater, 2900 Liberty Ave, Pittsburgh PA 15201, USA
Orrall, Robert Ellis — Singer
3 E 54th St, #1400, New York NY 10022, USA
Orr-Cahall, Christina — Museum Director
Museum & Library Service Institute, 1800 M St NW, #900, Washington DC 20036, USA
Orrell, Thomas M — Biologist
Smithsonian Natural History Museum, 10th & Constitution, Washington DC 20560, USA
Orr-Ewing, Hamish — Businessman
Fox Mill, Purton near Swindon, Wilts SN5 9EF, England
Orrico, Stacie — Singer, Actress
Creative Artists Agency, 2000 Ave of Stars, #100, Los Angeles CA 90067 USA
Orser, Brian — Figure Skater
I M G Canada, 175 Bloor St E, #400S, Toronto ON M4W 3R8, Canada
Orser, Leland — Actor
Gersh Agency, 9465 Wilshire Blvd, #600, Beverly Hills CA 90212 USA
Orsini, Myrna J — Sculptor
Orsini Studios, 4411 N 7th St, Tacoma WA 98406, USA
Orsino, John J — Baseball Player
6141 Terra Mere Circle, Boynton Beach FL 33437, USA
Orsulak, Joseph M (Joe) — Baseball Player
29 Keansburg Road, Parsippany NJ 07054, USA
Orszag, Peter R — Government Official
Office of Management/Budget, 1600 Pennsylvania Ave NW, Washington DC 20500, USA
Orta, Jorge — Baseball Player
1201 Heather Hill Crescent, Flossmoor IL 60422, USA
Ortega Gaona, Amancio — Businessman
Inditex SA, Avenida de la Diputacion, 15142 Arteixo, La Coruna, Spain
Ortega Saavedra, J Daniel — President, Nicaragua
President's Office, Casa de Gobierno, Barrio El Carmen, #2398, Managua, Nicaragua
Ortega y Alamino, Jaime L Cardinal — Religious Leader
Apartado 594, Calle Habana 152, Havana 10100, Cuba
Ortega, Bill — Baseball Player
4635 NW 95th Ave, Doral FL 33178, USA
Ortega, Chico P (Chick) — Actor
Artmedia, 20 Ave Rapp, 75007 Paris, France
Ortega, Fernando — Singer, Songwriter
Breen Agency, 25 Music Square W, Nashville TN 37203, USA
Ortega, Kenny — Director, Choreographer
Paradigm Agency, 360 N Crescent Dr, North Building, Beverly Hills CA 90210 USA
Ortega, Lindi — Singer, Songwriter
Agency Group Ltd, 142 W 57th St, #600, New York NY 10019 USA
Ortenberg, Arthur — Businessman
Liz Claiborne Inc, 1441 Broadway, New York NY 10018, USA
Ortenzio, Frank J — Baseball Player
2357 Oak Forest St, Jacksonville FL 32250, USA
Orth, Viviane — Model
Louisa Models, Ebersbergerstr 9, 81679 Munich, Germany
Ortiz, Adalberto C (Junior) — Baseball Player
296 Strayer St, Johnstown PA 15906, USA
Ortiz, Ana — Actress
G E F Entertainment, 122 N Clark Dr, #401, Los Angeles CA 90048, USA
Ortiz, Carlos — Boxer
2050 Seward Ave, #3L, Bronx NY 10473, USA
Ortiz, Cristina — Concert Pianist
Harrison/Parrott, 5-6 Albion Court, London W6 0QT, England
Ortiz, David A — Baseball Player
296 Strayer St, Johnstown PA 15906, USA
Ortiz, Domingo — Percussionist (Widespread Panic)
Brown Cat Inc, 400 Foundry St, Athens GA 30601 USA
Ortiz, Javier V — Baseball Player
19520 SW 39th Court, Miramar FL 33029, USA
Ortiz, John — Actor
Gersh Agency, 41 Madison Ave, #3301, New York NY 10010 USA
Ortiz, Russell R (Russ) — Baseball Player
4040 E McClellan Road, #13, Mesa AZ 85205, USA
Ortiz, Shalim — Actor
C E S D, 10635 Santa Monica Blvd, #130, Los Angeles CA 90025 USA
Ortlieb, Patrick — Alpine Skier
Hotel Montana, Oberlech, 6764 Lech, Austria
Ortmeier, Dan — Baseball Player
2121 Fairmont Dr, Flower Mound TX 75028, USA
Ortmeyer, Jed — Ice Hockey Player
1421 S 52nd St, Omaha NE 68106, USA
Ortner, Bev — Bowler
PO Box 436, Odebolt IA 51458, USA
Orton, Beth — Singer
Paradigm Agency, 360 Park Ave S, #1600, New York NY 10010 USA
Orton, John A — Baseball Player
2929 E Dublin St, Gilbert AZ 85295, USA
Orton, Kyle R — Football Player
3114 Coates Crossing, Baton Rouge LA 70810, USA
Orvis, Herbert V (Herb) — Football Player
1235 Autumn Court, Longmont CO 80504, USA

Osborn, Danny L — Baseball Player
7620 Knox Court, Westminster CO 80030, USA
Osborn, David V (Dave) — Football Player
18067 Judicial Way N, Lakeville MN 55044, USA
Osborn, John Jay, Jr — Writer
14 Fair Oaks St, San Francisco CA 94110, USA
Osborn, Kassidy — Singer (SheDaisy)
L G B Media, 1228 Pineview Lane, Nashville TN 37211, USA
Osborn, Kelsi — Singer (SheDaisy)
L G B Media, 1228 Pineview Lane, Nashville TN 37211, USA
Osborn, Kristyn — Singer (SheDaisy), Songwriter
L G B Media, 1228 Pineview Lane, Nashville TN 37211, USA
Osborne, Anders — Singer, Guitarist, Songwriter
Universal Music Group, 54 Music Square E, #300, Nashville TN 37203 USA
Osborne, Donovan A — Baseball Player
1851 Brightstone Court, Reno NV 89521, USA
Osborne, James H (Jim) — Football Player
4 Canyon Court, Algonquin IL 60102, USA
Osborne, Jeffrey — Singer, Songwriter
Green Light Talent Agency, PO Box 3172, Beverly Hills CA 90212 USA
Osborne, Joan — Singer, Songwriter
Monterey Peninsula Artists, 404 W Franklin St, Monterey CA 93940 USA
Osborne, Keith — Ice Hockey Player
Niagara Falls Hockey, 6570 Frederica St, Niagara Falls ON L2G 1C9, Canada
Osborne, Kent — Actor
Creative Management Entertainment Group, 2050 S Bundy Dr, #280, Los Angeles CA 90025, USA
Osborne, Lawrence — Writer
Farrar Straus Giroux, 18 W 18th St, #700, New York NY 10011 USA
Osborne, Mark — Director, Animator
W M E Entertainment, 9601 Wilshire Blvd, #300, Beverly Hills CA 90210 USA
Osborne, Mark — Ice Hockey Player
28 Princess Anne Crescent, Etobicoke ON M9A 2P1, Canada
Osborne, Mary — Surfer, Model
Patagonia, 8550 White Fir St, Reno NV 89523 USA
Osborne, Mary Pope — Writer
Random House, 1745 Broadway, #1800, New York NY 10019 USA
Osborne, Thomas W (Tom) — Football Coach; Representative, NE
5400 Trotter Road, Lincoln NE 68516, USA
Osbourne, Jack — Actor
W M E Entertainment, 9601 Wilshire Blvd, #300, Beverly Hills CA 90210 USA
Osbourne, John M (Ozzy) — Singer, Songwriter
Sharon Osbourne Mgmt, 8899 Beverly Blvd, #905, Los Angeles CA 90048, USA
Osbourne, Kelly — Singer, Actress
B/W/R, 9100 Wilshire Blvd, #500W, Beverly Hills CA 90212 USA
Osbourne, Sharon — Businesswoman, Entertainer
W M E Entertainment, 9601 Wilshire Blvd, #300, Beverly Hills CA 90210 USA
Osburn, Julie — Actress
S M S Talent, 8383 Wilshire Blvd, #230, Beverly Hills CA 90211 USA
Osburn, L Pat — Baseball Player
208 64th Street Court NW, Bradenton FL 34209, USA
Osby, Greg — Jazz Saxophonist
Bridge Agency, 35 Clark St, #A5, Brooklyn Heights NY 11201, USA
O'Scannlain, Diarmuid F — Judge
US Court of Appeals, Pioneer Courthouse, 555 SW Yamhill St, Portland OR 97204, USA
Oscar, Carlos — Actor, Comedian
Heidi Rotbart Management, 1810 Malcolm Ave, #207, Los Angeles CA 90025, USA
Osgood, Charles — Commentator
CBS-TV, News Dept, 524 W 57th St, New York NY 10019, USA
Osgood, Charles E — Psychologist
30 E Main St, Champaign IL 61820, USA
Osgood, Chris — Ice Hockey Player
1445 Penniman Ave, Plymouth MI 48170, USA
Osgood, Kassim A — Football Player, Actor
Gersh Agency, 9465 Wilshire Blvd, #600, Beverly Hills CA 90212 USA
O'Shannon, Daniel T (Dan) — Producer, Writer
Gendler & Kelly, 450 N Roxbury Dr, #1000, Beverly Hills CA 90210, USA
O'Shea, Daniel P (Danny) — Ice Hockey Player
7343 Colfax Ave S, Minneapolis MN 55423, USA
O'Shea, Michael D — Cinematographer
Murtha Agency, 4240 Promenade Way, #232, Marina del Rey CA 90292, USA
O'Shea, Milo — Actor
Bancroft Hotel, 40 W 72nd St, #17A, New York NY 10023, USA
Osheroff, Douglas D — Nobel Physics Laureate
75 Ranch Road, Woodside CA 94062, USA
Oshima, Hiromi — Model
Playboy Promotions, 2706 Media Center Dr, Los Angeles CA 90065 USA
Oshima, Nagisa — Director
4-11-5 Kugenuma-Matsugaoka, Fujisawa-shi 251, Kangawa Province, Japan
Osiecki, Mark — Ice Hockey Player
7482 New Albany Links Dr, New Albany OH 43054, USA
Osik, Keith R — Baseball Player
5 Pal Court, Shoreham NY 11786, USA
Osin, Roman — Cinematographer
Independent Talent Group, Oxford House, 76 Oxford St, London W1D 1BS, England
Osinski, Daniel (Dan) — Baseball Player
9723 W Amber Trail, Sun City AZ 85351, USA
Oslin, K T — Singer
Consortium, 49 Music Square W, #210, Nashville TN 37203, USA
Osman, H P — Marine Corps General
Deputy CofS, Manpower/Reserves, HqUSMC, 2 Navy St, Washington DC 20380, USA
Osman, Mat — Bassist (Suede)
Interceptor Enterprises, 98 White Lion St, London N1 9PF, England
Osman, Osman Ahmed — Civil Engineer
Osman Ahmed Osman Co, 34 Adly St, Cairo, Egypt
Osmanski, Joy — Actress
TalentWorks, 3500 W Olive Ave, #1400, Burbank CA 91505 USA

Osmar - Oswald

Osmar, Dean PO Box 32, Clam Gulch AK 99568, USA	Dog Sled Racer
Osment, Emily J Creative Artists Agency, 2000 Ave of Stars, #100, Los Angeles CA 90067 USA	Actress
Osment, Haley Joel Paradigm Agency, 360 N Crescent Dr, North Building, Beverly Hills CA 90210 USA	Actor
Osmond, Alan Tony Denton, 19 S Molton Lane, Mayfair, London W1K 5LE, England	Singer (Osmonds)
Osmond, Cliff 630 Benvenida Ave, Pacific Palisades CA 90272, USA	Actor, Director
Osmond, Donny Donny Osmond Entertainment, 1329 South 800 East, Orem UT 84097, USA	Singer
Osmond, Jay Tony Denton, 19 S Molton Lane, Mayfair, London W1K 5LE, England	Singer (Osmonds)
Osmond, Ken 9863 Wornom Ave, Sunland CA 91040, USA	Actor
Osmond, Marie Rogers & Cowan, 8687 Melrose Ave, #G700, West Hollywood CA 90069 USA	Singer, Actress
Osmond, Merrill Tony Denton, 19 S Molton Lane, Mayfair, London W1K 5LE, England	Singer (Osmonds)
Osmond, Wayne Tony Denton, 19 S Molton Lane, Mayfair, London W1K 5LE, England	Singer (Osmonds)
Osorio, Jorge Federico Columbia Artists Mgmt Inc, 1790 Broadway, #702, New York NY 10019 USA	Concert Pianist
Osrin, Raymond H Cleveland Plain Dealer, Editorial Dept, 1801 Superior Ave, Cleveland OH 44114, USA	Editorial Cartoonist
Oss, Arnold, Jr 25601 N Abajo Dr, Rio Verde AZ 85263, USA	Ice Hockey Player
Ossana, Diana Anonymous Content, 3532 Hayden Ave, Culver City CA 90232 USA	Writer, Producer
Ost, Friedheim Vermogensberatungs AG, Querstr 1, 60322 Frankfurt/Main, Germany	Government Official, Germany
Ostaseski, Frank Zen Hospice Project, 273 Page St, San Francisco CA 94102, USA	Hospice Director
Osteen, Claude W 2313 Duncan Perry Road, Grand Prairie TX 75050, USA	Baseball Player
Osteen, Joel S H Lakewood Church, 3700 Southwest Freeway, Houston TX 77027, USA	Religious Leader
Osterhage, Jeff C E S D, 10635 Santa Monica Blvd, #130, Los Angeles CA 90025 USA	Actor
Osterkorn, Walter R (Wally) 3202 E Medlock Dr, Phoenix AZ 85018, USA	Basketball Player
Osterman, Catherine L (Cat) PO Box 77084, Houston TX 77084, USA	Softball Player
Ostertag, Gregory D (Greg) 8434 E Havasupai Dr, Scottsdale AZ 85255, USA	Basketball Player
Ostheim, Michael Louisa Models, Ebersberger Str 9, 81679 Munich, Germany	Model
Ostholt, Frank Vohren 31, 48231 Warendorf, Germany	Equestrian
Ostin, Michael (Mo) DreamWorks SKG, 1000 Flower St, Glendale CA 91201, USA	Businessman
Osting, Jimmy 927 Lakeside Dr, Taylorsville KY 40071, USA	Baseball Player
Ostman, Arnold Haydn Rawstron, 36 Station Road, London SE20 7BQ, England	Conductor
Ostriker, Jeremiah P 33 Philip Dr, Princeton NJ 08540, USA	Astrophysicist
Ostroff, Dawn C W Television Network, 4000 Warner Blvd, Burbank CA 91522, USA	Businesswoman
Ostroski, Gerald (Jerry), Jr 6926 E 115th Place S, Bixby OK 74008, USA	Football Player
Ostrosky, Beth Don Buchwald/Fortitude, 10 E 44th St, New York NY 10017 USA	Model, Actress
Ostrosser, Brian L 27 Chelsea Crescent, Stoney Creek ON L8E 5R7, Canada	Baseball Player
Ostrum, Peter 6065 Duncan Road, Glenfield NY 13343, USA	Actor
O'Sullevan, Peter J 37 Cranmer Court, London SW3 3HW, England	Sportswriter, Sportscaster
O'Sullivan, Adele Health Care for the Homeless, 220 S 12th Ave, Phoenix AZ 85007, USA	Physician, Social Activist
O'Sullivan, Chris 114 Elmer Road, Dorchester Center MA 02124, USA	Ice Hockey Player
O'Sullivan, Daniel J (Dan) 33 Crescent Ave, Summit NJ 07901, USA	Basketball Player
O'Sullivan, Gilbert Park Promotions, PO Box 651, Park Road, Oxford OX2 9RB, England	Singer, Songwriter
O'Sullivan, Shawn Cabbagetown Boxing Club, 2 Lancaster Ave, Toronto ON M4X 1C1, Canada	Boxer
O'Sullivan, Sonia Kim McDonald, 201 High St, Hampton Hill, Middx TW12 1NL, England	Track Athlete
O'Sullivan, Terence Laborers International Union, 905 16th St NW, #600, Washington DC 20006, USA	Labor Leader
Osuna, Alfonso (Al) 8256 Via Rosa, Orlando FL 32836, USA	Baseball Player
Osuna, P Antonio 10345 W Olympic Blvd, Los Angeles CA 90064, USA	Baseball Player
Osvart, Andrea Innovative Artists, 1505 10th St, Santa Monica CA 90401 USA	Actress
Oswald, Mark Don Schumacher Racing, 1681 E Northfield Dr, #A, Brownsburg IN 46112, USA	Drag Racing Driver
Oswald, Mark Herbert Barrett, 266 W 37th St, #2000, New York NY 10018 USA	Opera Singer
Oswald, Stephen S N A S A, Johnson Space Center, 2101 NASA Road, Houston TX 77058, USA	Astronaut

Name	Profession
Oswalt, Roy E 107 Oakmont Road, Starkville MS 39759, USA	Baseball Player
Oszajca, John Interscope Records, 2220 Colorado Ave, Santa Monica CA 90404 USA	Singer
Otanez, Willis A 7904 March Brown Ave, Las Vegas NV 89149, USA	Baseball Player
Otellini, Paul S Intel Corp, 2200 Mission College Blvd, Santa Clara CA 95054, USA	Businessman
Oteri, Cheri Gersh Agency, 9465 Wilshire Blvd, #600, Beverly Hills CA 90212 USA	Actress, Comedienne
Othenin-Girard, Dominque 327 S Church Lane, Los Angeles CA 90049, USA	Director
Otis, Amos J 8930 Tiger Shale Way, Las Vegas NV 89123, USA	Baseball Player
Otis, Carre Dash Group, 550 N Larchmont Blvd, #201, Los Angeles CA 90004, USA	Actress, Model
Otis, Glenn K 3 Tioga Lane, Carlisle PA 17015, USA	Army General
Otis, James L (Jim) 14795 Greenleaf Valley Dr, Chesterfield MO 63017, USA	Football Player
O'Toole, Annette I C M Partners, 10250 Constellation Blvd, #900, Los Angeles CA 90067 USA	Actress
O'Toole, James J (Jim) 1010 Lanette Dr, Cincinnati OH 45230, USA	Baseball Player
O'Toole, Peter S Chartwell Ink Mgmt, 7319 Beverly Blvd, #10, Los Angeles CA 90036, USA	Actor
O'Toole, Shane 68 Irishtown Road, Dublin 4, Ireland	Architect
Otstott, Charles P 6152 Pohick Station Dr, Fairfax Station VA 22039, USA	Army General
Otsuka, Akinori 891 Fairway Dr, Boulder City NV 89005, USA	Baseball Player
Ott, Alice Sara Harrison/Parrott, 5-6 Albion Court, London W6 0QT, England	Concert Pianist
Ott, Mirjam Curling Assn, PO Box 606, 3000 Bern, Switzerland	Curling Athlete
Ott, Mona Asuka Harrison/Parrott, 5-6 Albion Court, London W6 0QT, England	Concert Pianist
Ott, Steve 2758 Saint Clair, Pointe Aux Roches ON N0R 1N0, Canada	Ice Hockey Player
Otten, James E (Jim) 1417 N Forest, Mesa AZ 85203, USA	Baseball Player
Ottenbrite, Anne Swimming Canada, 2197 Riverside Dr, #700, Ottawa ON K1H 7X3, Canada	Swimmer
Ottey-Page, Merlene Jamaican Olympic Committee, PO Box 544, Kingston 10, Jamaica	Track Athlete
Ottke, Sven Anke Luetkenhorst, Maastricherstr 38, 80672 Cologne, Germany	Boxer
Otto, August J (Gus) 8705 Leeward Dr, Las Vegas NV 89117, USA	Football Player
Otto, David A (Dave) 1383 Shady Lane, Wheaton IL 60187, USA	Baseball Player
Otto, Frei P Berghalde 19, 7250 Leonberg, 71229 Warmbroun, Germany	Architect, Structural Engineer
Otto, Gotz Z B F Agentur, Friedrichstr 39, 10969 Berlin, Germany	Actor
Otto, James Raybaw/Warner Bros Records, 20 Music Square East, Nashville TN 37203, USA	Singer, Songwriter
Otto, James E (Jim) 00 Estates Dr, Auburn CA 95602, USA	Football Player
Otto, Joel 7144 Sues Dr, Pequot Lakes MN 56472, USA	Ice Hockey Player
Otto, John E Flip/Interscope Records, 8733 Sunset Blvd, #205, West Hollywood CA 90069, USA	Drummer (Limp Bizkop)
Otto, Kristin Z D F Sportedaktion, Postfach 4040, 55100 Mainz, Germany	Swimmer
Otto, Michael Wandsbeker Str 3-7, 22179 Hamburg, Germany	Businessman
Otto, Miranda United Agents, 12-26 Lexington St, London W1F 0LE, England	Actress
Otto, Sylke Egersdorfer Str 3, 90513 Zirndorf, Germany	Luge Athlete
Otunbayeva, Roza I Social Democratic Party, Ul Shabdan Baatyr, #D4B, 720003 Bishkek, Kyrgyzstan	President, Kyrgyzstan
Ouattara, Alassane D International Monetary Fund, 700 19th St NW, #12-300H, Washington DC 20431, USA	President, Cote d'Ivorie; Financier
Oubre, Louis B, III 12345 I 10 Service Road, #2403, New Orleans LA 70128, USA	Football Player
Ouchi, William G University of California, Graduate Management School, Los Angeles CA 90024, USA	Educator
Oue, Eiji I M G Artists, Hogarth Business Park, Chiswick, London W4 2TH, England	Conductor
Ouedraogo, Gerard Kango 01 BP 347, Ouagadougou, Burkina Faso	Prime Minister, Burkina Faso
Ouedraogo, Idrissa 01 BP 2524, Ouagadougou, Burkina Faso	Director
Ouellet, Marc Cardinal Archdiocese of Quebec, 2 Rue Port-Dauphin, Quebec PQ G1R 4R6, Canada	Religious Leader
Ouellette, Caroline Team Canada, 2424 University Dr NW, Calgary AB T2N 3Y9, Canada	Ice Hockey Player
Ouellette, Philip R (Phil) 7421 Poppy St, Corona CA 92881, USA	Baseball Player
Oukach, Zineb Anthony Assoc, PO Box 910, New York NY 10108, USA	Actress
Ouma, Kassim Peltz Boxing Promotions, 2501 Brown St, Philadelphia PA 19130, USA	Boxer

O

Owen - Ouma

Oumarou, Seyni — Prime Minister, Niger
Prime Minister's Office, State House, BP 353, Abuja, Niger

Oundjian, Peter — Conductor
Toronto Symphony Orchestra, 6-212 King St E, Toronto ON M58 1K5, Canada

Ousland, Borge — Trans Polar Skier
Axel Huitfeldts V5, 1170 Oslo, Norway

Ousset, Cecile — Concert Pianist
Intermusica Artists Mgmt, 16 Duncan Terrace, London N1 8B7, England

Outerbridge, Peter — Actor
O A Z, 438 Queen St E, Toronto ON M5A 1T4, Canada

Outhwaite, Tamzin — Actress
Conway Van Gelder Grant, 8-12 Broadwick St, #300, London W1F 8HW, England

Outlaw, Charles (Bo) — Basketball Player
Orlando Magic, 8701 Maitland Summit Blvd, Orlando FL 32810 USA

Outman, Joshua S (Josh) — Baseball Player
5273 Seasonbrooks Lane, Imperial MO 63052, USA

Outman, Tim — Sculptor
2863 Lydick Way, Eugene OR 97401, USA

Outtara, Alassane D — President, Ivory Coast
President's Office, Presidential Palace, N'Gokro, Yamoussoukro, Cote d'Ivoire

Ouyahia, Ahmed — Prime Minister, Algeria
Prime Minister's Office, 32 Ave Souidani Boudiemad, Algiers, Algeria

Ovadia, Moni — Composer, Writer
Promo Music, Via Della Volto 21, 40131 Bologna (BO), Italy

Ovchinikov, Vladimir P — Concert Pianist
Manygate, 13 Cotswold Mews, 30 Battersea Square, London SW11 3RA, England

Ovechkin, Alexander M — Ice Hockey Player
6301 Osprey Terrace, Coconut Creek FL 33073, USA

Overall, Park — Actress
1374 Ripley Island Road, Afton TN 37616, USA

Overath, Wolfgang — Soccer Player
Auf Dem Hummerich 5, 53721 Siegburg, Germany

Overbay, Lyle S — Baseball Player
107 Captain Lane, Centralia WA 98531, USA

Overbeck, Carla — Soccer Player
205 Zaoata Lane, Chapel Hill NC 27517, USA

Overbeek, Jan T G — Physical Chemist
Zweerslaan 35, 3723 HN Bilthoven, Netherlands

Overbey, Kellie — Actress
Stone Manners Salners, 9911 W Pico Blvd, #1400, Los Angeles CA 90035 USA

Overend, Ned — Cyclist
Boure Bicycle Clothing, 98 Everett St, Durango CO 81303, USA

Overgard, Robert M — Religious Leader
Church of Lutheran Brethren, PO Box 655, Fergus Falls MN 56538, USA

Overhauser, Albert W — Physicist
236 Pawnee Dr, West Lafayette IN 47906, USA

Overman, Ion — Actress
Don Buchwald/Fortitude, 6500 Wilshire Blvd, #2200, Los Angeles CA 90048 USA

Overman, Larry E — Chemist
University of California, Chemistry Dept, Irvine CA 92717, USA

Overmyer, Eric — Writer, Producer
Creative Artists Agency, 2000 Ave of Stars, #100, Los Angeles CA 90067 USA

Overstreet, Chord — Actor
W M E Entertainment, 9601 Wilshire Blvd, #300, Beverly Hills CA 90210 USA

Overstreet, Paul — Singer, Songwriter
Scarlet Moon Records, PO Box 320, Pegram TN 37143, USA

Overstreet, Tommy — Singer, Songwriter
Capitol Mgmt Group, 1214 16th Ave S, Nashville TN 37212, USA

Overton, David — Businessman, Restauranteur
Cheesecake Factory Inc, 26901 Malibu Hills Road, Agoura Hills CA 91301, USA

Overton, Kelly — Actress
Management 360, 9111 Wilshire Blvd, Beverly Hills CA 90210 USA

Overy, H Michael (Mike) — Baseball Player
3010 N 152nd Lane, Goodyear AZ 85395, USA

Ovitz, Michael S — Businessman
1234 Benedict Canyon Dr, Beverly Hills CA 90210, USA

Ovredal, Andre — Director
W M E Entertainment, 9601 Wilshire Blvd, #300, Beverly Hills CA 90210 USA

Ovsyannikov, Oleg — Ice Dancer
Skating Assn, Luchnesskaia Nab 8, 119871 Moscow, Russia

Owchar, Dennis — Ice Hockey Player
154 Krieghoff Ave, Markham ON L3R 1W1, Canada

Owchinko, Robert D (Bob) — Baseball Player
15111 N Hayden Road, #160-357, Scottsdale AZ 85260, USA

Owen, Beverly — Actress
Tony Greco, 1435 Bellaire Place, Pittsburgh PA 15226, USA

Owen, Chris — Actor
J L A Talent Agency, 9151 Sunset Blvd, West Hollywood CA 90069, USA

Owen, Clive — Actor
42 West, 220 W 42nd St, #1200, New York NY 10036, USA

Owen, Dave — Baseball Player
1921 FM 3136, Cleburne TX 76031, USA

Owen, David A L — Government Official, Educator
78 Narrow St, Limehouse, London E14 8BP, England

Owen, Gary — Actor
I C M Partners, 10250 Constellation Blvd, #900, Los Angeles CA 90067 USA

Owen, Joshua R (Jake) — Singer
Dale Morris Assoc, 818 19th Ave S, Nashville TN 37203, USA

Owen, Lawrence T (Larry) — Baseball Player
804 White Pine St, New Carlisle OH 45344, USA

Owen, Lloyd — Actor
Hamilton Hodell, 66-68 Margaret St, London W1W 8SR, England

Owen, Michael — Soccer Player
Liverpool F C, Anfield Road, Liverpool L4 0TH, England

Owen, Priscilla R — Judge
US Court of Appeals, 903 San Jacinto Blvd, #400, Austin TX 78701, USA

Owen, Randy Y — Singer, Guitarist (Alabama)
Alabama Band Promotions, PO Box 680529, Fort Payne AL 35968, USA

Owen, Spike D — Baseball Player
11211 Musket Rim St, Austin TX 78738, USA

Owen, W Thomas (Tom) — Football Player
PO Box 3, Albany OK 74721, USA

Owens, Billy E — Basketball Player
608 Canary Dr, Carlisle PA 17013, USA

Owens, C Burgess, Jr — Football Player
1430 Telegraph Road, West Chester PA 19380, USA

Owens, Daniel W (Dan) — Football Player
280 Selkirk Lane, Duluth GA 30097, USA

Owens, Edwin (Cotton) — Auto Racing Driver, Owner
Cotton Owens Enterprises, 7921 Valley Falls Road, Spartanburg SC 29303, USA

Owens, Eric B — Baseball Player
22431 N 54th St, Phoenix AZ 85054, USA

Owens, Gary — Entertainer
I C M Partners, 10250 Constellation Blvd, #900, Los Angeles CA 90067 USA

Owens, James P (Jim) — Baseball Player
1426 Ramada Dr, Houston TX 77062, USA

Owens, Joseph T (Joe) — Football Player
2754 Highway 13 N, Columbia MS 39429, USA

Owens, Loren E (Steve) — Football Player
3700 W Robinson, #230, Norman OK 73072, USA

Owens, Luke — Football Player
3330 Warrensville Center Road, #502, Shaker Heights OH 44122, USA

Owens, Mel T — Football Player
13603 Marina Pointe Dr, #A612, Marina del Rey CA 90292, USA

Owens, Morris L — Football Player
4156 W Michigan Ave, Glendale AZ 85308, USA

Owens, Rena — Actress, Model
Ken Belling, PO Box 300471, Casselberry FL 32730, USA

Owens, Robert G, Jr — WW II Marine Corps Air Force Hero
730 Amicus Ave, Newport Beach CA 92610, USA

Owens, Terrell E — Football Player
5207 Sandy Shores Court, Lithonia GA 30038, USA

Owens, Terry W — Football Player
2524 Poovey Road SE, Decatur GA 35603, USA

Owens, Thomas W (Tom) — Basketball Player
19788 Wildwood Dr, West Linn OR 97068, USA

Owings, Micah B — Baseball Player
3208 Druid Hills Reserve Dr NE, Atlanta GA 30329, USA

Owsley, Douglas — Anthropologist
Smithsonian Institution, 17th & M Sts NW, Washington DC 20036, USA

Oxenberg, Catherine — Actress
Power Entertainment, 9100 Wilshire Blvd, Beverly Hills CA 90212, USA

Oxtoby, David W — Educator
Pomona College, President's Office, 120 E Bonita, Claremont CA 91711, USA

Oxy Moron, Monty — Keyboardist (Damned)
Leave Home Booking, 10 W Broadway, #608, Salt Lake City UT 84101, USA

Oyakawa, Yoshinobu (Yoshi) — Swimmer
4171 Hutchinson Road, Cincinnati OH 45248, USA

Oyaya, Mary — Actress
Coolwaters Productions, 10061 Riverside Dr, Box 531, Toluca Lake CA 91602 USA

Oyelowo, David O — Actor
Hamilton Hodell, 66-68 Margaret St, London W1W 8SR, England

Oz, Amos — Writer
Ben Gurion University, PO Box 653, 84105 Beersheva, Israel

Oz, Frank R — Puppeteer, Director
36 Herrick Road, Sharon CT 06069, USA

Ozaki, Masashi — Golfer
Bridgestone Sports, 14230 Lochridge Blvd, #G, Covington GA 30014, USA

Ozaki, Satoshi — Physicist
Brookhaven National Lab, Heavy Ion Collider, 2 Center St, Upton NY 11973, USA

Ozawa, Ichiro — Government Official, Japan
2-38 Fukuromachi, Mizusawashi, Iwateken 023-0814, Japan

Ozawa, Seiji — Conductor
Vienna State Opera, Opernrig 2, 1010 Vienna, Austria

Ozbek, Rifat — Fashion Designer
Ozbek Ltd, 18 Haunch of Venison Yard, London W1Y 1AF, England

Ozick, Cynthia — Writer
34 Soundview St, New Rochelle NY 10805, USA

Ozio, David — Bowler
6110 Barrington Ave, Beaumont TX 77706, USA

Ozolinsh, Sandis — Ice Hockey Player
701 Golf Club Dr, Castle Rock CO 80108, USA

Ozuk, Charles, Jr — WW II Army Air Corps Hero
5740 Churchill Lane, Libertyville IL 60048, USA

Ozuna, Fritz — Artist
6769 State Highway 27, Comfort TX 78013, USA

Ozzie, Raymond (Ray) — Computer Software Designer
50 Harbor St, Manchester MA 01944, USA

O

Owen - Ozzie

Paabo, Svante — Zoo Executive
Evolutionary Anthropology Inst, Deutscher Platz 6, 04103 Leipzig, Germany
Paasikivi, Lilli — Opera Singer
Harrison/Parrott, 5-6 Albion Court, London W6 0QT, England
Paavo, Jarvi — Conductor
Cincinnati Symphony Orchestra, 1241 Elm St, Cincinnati OH 45202, USA
Pabo, Carl O — Biologist
Protean Futures, 475 Gate 5 Road, #210A, Sausalito CA 94965, USA
Pabst, Augie — Auto Racing Driver
Race Legends, 5410 Highway 73, Marshall WI 53559, USA
Pacar, Johnny — Actor
Collective, 8383 Wilshire Blvd, #1050, Beverly Hills CA 90211 USA
Pace, Betty D — Molecular Chemist
University of Texas Medical Center, 900 W Campbell Road, Richardson TX 75080, USA
Pace, Calvin L — Football Player
4044 Lyon Blvd SW, Atlanta GA 30331, USA
Pace, Darrell O — Archery Athlete
4394 Princeton Road, Hamilton OH 45011, USA
Pace, Dominic — Actor
Shapiro-Lichtman, 8827 Beverly Blvd, Los Angeles CA 90048 USA
Pace, Judy — Actress
4139 Cloverdale Ave, Los Angeles CA 90008, USA
Pace, Lee — Actor
Management 360, 9111 Wilshire Blvd, Beverly Hills CA 90210 USA
Pace, Norman R, Jr — Microbiologist
University of Colorado, Molecular Cellular Dept, Boulder CO 80309, USA
Pace, Orlando L — Football Player
939 Tucker Lane, Saint Louis MO 63131, USA
Pace, Stanley C — Businessman
16561 Merrill Court, Chagrin Falls OH 44023, USA
Pacella, John L — Baseball Player
1500 Abbotsford Green Dr, Powell OH 43065, USA
Pacey, Steven — Actor
Ken McReddie Assoc, 11 Connaught Place, London W2 2ET, England
Pachal, Clayton — Ice Hockey Player
230 Laycoe Crescent, Saskatoon SK S7S 1H5, Canada
Pachauri, Rajendra K — Climatologist
Tata Energy Reseach Institute, Habitat Place, New Delhi 110003, India
Pacheco, Ferdie — Sportscaster
4151 Gate Lane, Miami FL 33137, USA
Pacheco, Johnny — Musician, Composer
Universal Attractions, 135 W 26th St, #1200, New York NY 10001 USA
Pachulia, Zaur (Zaza) — Basketball Player
Atlanta Hawks, Centennial Tower, 101 Marietta St NW, #1900, Atlanta GA 30303 USA
Pacino, Al — Actor
I C M Partners, 730 5th Ave, New York NY 10019 USA
Paciorek, James J (Jim) — Baseball Player
9641 E Waters Edge Place, Tucson AZ 85749, USA
Paciorek, Thomas M (Tom) — Baseball Player
2389 Broad Creek Dr, Stone Mountain GA 30087, USA
Packard, Kelly — Actress, Model
21071 Placerita Canyon Road, Newhall CA 91321, USA
Packer, A William (Billy) — Sportscaster
Bazel Group, 115 Penn Warren Dr, #300, Brentwood TN 37027, USA
Packer, Ann — Writer
Random House, 1745 Broadway, #1800, New York NY 10019 USA
Packer, David — Actor
Creative Artists Agency, 2000 Ave of Stars, #100, Los Angeles CA 90067 USA
Packham, Jenny — Fashion Designer
Spectrum House, 32-34 Gordon House Road, #A, London NW5 1LP, England
Packwood, Robert W (Bob) — Senator, OR
Sunrise Research, 2201 Wisconsin Ave NW, #C120, Washington DC 20007, USA
Pacquiano, Alberto D (Bobby) — Boxer
Top Rank Inc, 3908 Howard Hughes Parkway, #580, Las Vegas NV 89169, USA
Pacquiao, Emanuel D (Manny) — Boxer
4th St, Seaview Heights, Lawaan, Talisay City, Cebu PH 6045, Philippines
Pacula, Joanna — Actress
Chuck Binder Mgmt, 1465 Lindacrest Dr, Beverly Hills CA 90210 USA
Padalecki, Jared — Actor
Industry Entertainment, 955 Carillo Dr, #300, Los Angeles CA 90048 USA
Padalka, Gennady I — Cosmonaut
Cosmonaut Training Center, Star City, 141160 Zvezdny Gorodok, Moscow Oblast, Russia
Padbury, Wendy — Actress
Evans & Reiss, 100 Fawe Park Road, London SW15 2EA, England
Paddio, Gerald — Basketball Player
2801 Crystal Bay Dr, Las Vegas NV 89117, USA
Paddock, John — Ice Hockey Player, Coach, Executive
Philadelphia Flyers, 1st Union Center, 3601 S Broad St, Philadelphia PA 19148 USA
Padgett, Jason — Actor
G V A Talent Agency, 8981 W Sunset Blvd, #101, West Hollywood CA 90069, USA
Padilha, Jose — Director, Producer, Writer
Creative Artists Agency, 2000 Ave of Stars, #100, Los Angeles CA 90067 USA
Padilla, Douglas (Doug) — Track Athlete
182 N 555 W, Orem UT 84057, USA
Padilla, Vicente D — Baseball Player
1816 O'Henry Court, Arlington TX 76006, USA
Padjean, Gary A — Football Player
9314 Tower Bridge Road, Indianapolis IN 46240, USA
Padma-Nathan, Harin — Urologist
1245 16th St, #312, Santa Monica CA 90404, USA
Padmore, Mark — Opera Singer
Maxine Robertson Mgmt, 14 Forge Dr, Claygate KT10 0HR, England
Paek, Jim — Ice Hockey Player
119 Alexander Dr, Elyria OH 44035, USA
Paerson, Anja — Alpine Skier
Bjorkvagen 9, 920 64 Tarnaby, Sweden

Paetkau, David — Actor
Precision Entertainment, 6338 Wilshire Blvd, Los Angeles CA 90048, USA
Paetz, Robert — Space Scientist
7203 Macy Court, Riverside CA 92503, USA
Paez, Jorge (Maromero) — Boxer
Call G 650-4, Col Nueva, Mexicali 21100 , Baja, Mexico
Paez, Richard A — Judge
US Appellate Court, Court Building, 125 S Grand Ave, Pasadena CA 91105, USA
Paez, Rodolfo (Fito) — Pianist
Sony Records, 550 Madison Ave, #600, New York NY 10022 USA
Pafko, Andrew (Andy) — Baseball Player
1890 W Glenlord Road, Stevensville MI 49127, USA
Pagac, Frederick (Fred) — Football Player
10261 Normandy Crest, Eden Prairie MN 55347, USA
Pagan, David P (Dave) — Baseball Player
504 10th Ave W, Nipawin SK S0E 1E0, Canada
Pagan, Michael J — Actor
Innovative Artists, 1505 10th St, Santa Monica CA 90401 USA
Pagano, Charles D (Chuck) — Football Coach
Indianapolis Colts, 7001 W 56th St, Indianapolis IN 46254 USA
Pagano, Lindsay — Singer
Azoff Music, 1100 Glendon Ave, #2000, Los Angeles CA 90024, USA
Pagano, Walter — Actor
Artmedia, 20 Ave Rapp, 75007 Paris, France
Page, Alan C — Football Player, Judge
Page Education Foundation, PO Box 581254, Minneapolis MN 55458, USA
Page, Anthony — Director
I C M Partners, 10250 Constellation Blvd, #900, Los Angeles CA 90067 USA
Page, Ashley — Ballet Dancer, Choreographer
Scottish Ballet, Tramway, 25 Albert Dr, Glasgow G41 2PE, Scotland
Page, David C — Geneticist
Massachusetts Institute of Techonolgy, Genetics Dept, Cambridge MA 02139, USA
Page, Ellen — Actress
W M E Entertainment, 9601 Wilshire Blvd, #300, Beverly Hills CA 90210 USA
Page, Erika — Actress
Progressive Artists Agency, 1041 N Formosa Ave, West Hollywood CA 90046 USA
Page, Frank S — Religious Leader
First Baptist Church, 200 W Main St, Taylors SC 29687, USA
Page, Genevieve — Actress
52 Rue de Vaugirard, 75006 Paris, France
Page, Harrison — Actor
S D B Partners, 1801 Ave of Stars, #902, Los Angeles CA 90067 USA
Page, Jimmy — Singer (Yardbirds/Led Zeppelin)
Trinifold Mgmt, 12 Oval Road, London NW1 7DH, England
Page, Joanna — Actress
Independent Talent Group, Oxford House, 76 Oxford St, London W1D 1BS, England
Page, Larry — Businessman, Computer Scientist
Google Inc, 1600 Amphitheatre Parkway, #41, Mountain View CA 94043, USA
Page, Michael — Equestrian
PO Box 229, North Salem NY 10560, USA
Page, Michael R (Mike) — Baseball Player
599 Briarcliff Dr, Woodruff SC 29388, USA
Page, Michelle — Actress
Framework Entertainment, 9057 Nemo St, #C, West Hollywood CA 90069 USA
Page, Patti — Singer, Actress
404 Loma Larga Dr, Solana Beach CA 92075, USA
Page, Pierre — Ice Hockey Coach
Anaheim Ducks, 2695 E Katella Ave, Anaheim CA 92806 USA
Page, Sam — Actor
Inphenate, 9701 Wilshire Blvd, #1000, Beverly Hills CA 90212 USA
Page, Solomon — Football Player
9302 Vista Circle, Irving TX 75063, USA
Page, Steven — Singer, Guitarist (Barenaked Ladies)
Nettwerk Mgmt, 6525 W Sunset Blvd, #800, Los Angeles CA 90028 USA
Page, Tim — Journalist
Washington Post, Editorial Dept, 1150 15th St NW, Washington DC 20071, USA
Pagel, Karl D — Baseball Player
2698 N Ellis St, Chandler AZ 85224, USA
Pagel, Mike J — Football Player
11981 Coopers Run, Strongsville OH 44149, USA
Pagels, Elaine H — Theologian
Princeton University, Religion Dept, Princeton NJ 08544, USA
Pagett, Nicola — Actress
Art Work Entertainment, 5900 Wilshire Blvd, #2900, Los Angeles CA 90036, USA
Paglia, Camille — Writer, Educator
University of the Arts, Humanities Dept, 320 S Broad St, Philadelphia PA 19102, USA
Pagliarulo, Michael T (Mike) — Baseball Player
11 Fieldstone Dr, Winchester MA 01890, USA
Pagnozzi, Thomas A (Tom) — Baseball Player
4760 E Maywood Road, Fayetteville AR 72703, USA
Pagonis, William G — Army General
202 Smalstig Road, Evans City PA 16033, USA
Pahang — Sultan, Malaysia
Istana Abu Bakar, Pekan, Pahang, Malaysia
Pahlavi, Fara Diba — Empress, Iran
Kambiz Atabai, PO Box 2931, New York NY 10185, USA
Pahlsson, O Samuel (Sammy) — Ice Hockey Player
9429 Tartan Ridge Blvd, Dublin OH 43017, USA
Pahud, Emmanuel — Concert Flutist
Opus 3 Artists, 470 Park Ave S, #900N, New York NY 10016 USA
Pahukoa, Jeff K — Football Player
2612 79th Ave NE, Everett WA 98258, USA
Paich, David F — Singer, Keyboardist (Toto)
Monterey International, 200 W Superior St, #202, Chicago IL 60654 USA
Paiement, Rosaire W — Ice Hockey Player
3351 S Palm Aire Dr, #301, Pompano Beach FL 33069, USA

Paiement, Wilf	Ice Hockey Player
1064 Streambank Dr, Mississauga ON L5H 3Z1, Canada	
Paige Kent, Heather	Actress
Don Buchwald/Fortitude, 6500 Wilshire Blvd, #2200, Los Angeles CA 90048 USA	
Paige, Amanda	Model
Playboy Promotions, 2706 Media Center Dr, Los Angeles CA 90065 USA	
Paige, Elaine	Singer, Actress
Douglas Gorman Rothacker Wilhelm, 1501 Broadway, #703, New York NY 10036 USA	
Paige, Janis	Actress
1700 Rising Glen Road, Los Angeles CA 90069, USA	
Paige, Jennifer	Singer, Songwriter
Great Scott Productions, 4750 Lincoln Blvd, #229, Marina del Rey CA 90292, USA	
Paige, Peter	Actor
Creative Artists Agency, 2000 Ave of Stars, #100, Los Angeles CA 90067 USA	
Paige, Stephone	Football Player
8293 N Paula Ave, Fresno CA 93720, USA	
Paige, Tony	Footbal Player
208 Mowbray Road, Silver Spring MD 20904, USA	
Paik Kun Woo	Concert Pianist
Worldwide Artists, 12 Rosebery, Thornton Heath, Surrey CR7 8PT, England	
Pailes, William A	Astronaut
411 S Cedar Ridge Circle, Robinson TX 76706, USA	
Paine, John	Singer, Guitarist (Brothers Four)
Bob Flick Productions, 300 Vine St, #14, Seattle WA 98121, USA	
Painter, John Mark	Musician (Fleming & John)
Michael Dixon Mgmt, 119 Pebblecreek Road, Franklin TN 37064, USA	
Painter, Lance T	Baseball Player
2683 E Pinto Dr, Gilbert AZ 85296, USA	
Pais, Josh	Actor
Innovative Artists, 1505 10th St, Santa Monica CA 90401 USA	
Paisley, Brad	Singer
W M E Entertainment, 1600 Division St, #300, Nashville TN 37203 USA	
Paisley, David	Actor
Associated International Mgmt, Fairfax House, Fulwood Place, London WC1V 6HU, England	
Paisley, Ian R K	First Minister, Northern Ireland
Parsonage, 17 Cyprus Ave, Belfast BT5 5NT, Northern Ireland	
Pak, Charles	Medical Researcher
University of Texas Southwestern Medical Center, 5323 Harry Hines Blvd, Dallas TX 75390, USA	
Pak, Se Ri	Golfer
7926 Versilia Dr, Orlando FL 32836, USA	
Paksas, Rolandus	President, Lithuania
Liberal Union, Radvilaites Srt 1, #210, 2000 Vilnius, Lithuania	
Palahniuk, Chuck	Writer, Actor
United Talent Agency, 9336 Civic Center Dr, Beverly Hills CA 90210 USA	
Palance, Holly	Actress
98 Millstone Road, Brewster MA 02631, USA	
Palast, Greg	Writer
E P Dutton, 375 Hudson St, New York NY 10014 USA	
Palastra, Joseph T, Jr	Army General
RR 1 Box 267, Myrtle MO 65778, USA	
Palau, Doug	Producer, Writer
A P A Talent/Literary Agency, 405 S Beverly Dr, #300, Beverly Hills CA 90212 USA	
Palau, Luis	Evangelist
Luis Palau Evangelistic Assn, 1500 NW 167th Place, Beaverton OR 97006, USA	
Palazzari, Doug	Ice Hockey Player, Executive
4370 Dynasty Dr, Colorado Springs CO 80918, USA	
Palazzi, Togo A	Basketball Player
84 Framingham Road, Southborough MA 01772, USA	
Palden Namgyal	Prince, Sikkim
J P Morgan Chase, 270 Park Ave, #1200, New York NY 10017, USA	
Paleczny, Piotr	Concert Pianist
Chopin Music Academy, Ul Okolnik 2, 00 368 Warsaw, Poland	
Palekar, Amol	Actor, Director
Chire Bandee, 10th N S Road, J V P D Scheme, Mumbai MS 400049, India	
Palelei, Si'ulagi J (Lonnie)	Football Player
1808 SW Chief Circle, Blue Springs MO 64015, USA	
Palermaa, Osku	Bowler
Storm Products, 165 S 8th W, Brigham City UT 84302, USA	
Palermo, Stephen M (Steve)	Baseball Umpire
5102 W 143rd Terrace, Overland Park KS 66224, USA	
Paley, Albert R	Sculptor
Paley Studio, 25 N Washington St, Rochester NY 14614, USA	
Paley, Michael	Religious Leader, Rabbi
Jewish Resource Center, 130 E 59th St, New York NY 10022, USA	
Palffy, Zigmund (Ziggy)	Ice Hockey Player
H K 36 Skalica Clementisova 50, 90901 Skalica, Slovakia	
Palicki, Adrianne	Actress
United Talent Agency, 9336 Civic Center Dr, Beverly Hills CA 90210 USA	
Palin, Michael E	Actor, Comedian, Writer (Monty Python)
Gumby Corp, 34 Tavistock St, London WC2E 7PB, England	
Palin, Sarah L H	Governor, Alaska
Alive Communications, 7680 Goddard St, #200, Colorado Springs CO 80920, USA	
Palis, Jacob	Mathematician
Instituto Matematica, Estrada Castornina 110, Rio de Janeiro 22460 320 RJ, Brazil	
Palkiewicz, Jacek	Explorer
Via Filzi 18, 36022 Cassola Vicenza, Italy	
Pall, Donn S	Baseball Player
8001 Waterford Lakes Dr, #2311, Charlotte NC 28210, USA	
Pall, Olga	Alpine Skier
Fahrenweg 28, 6060 Absam, Austria	
Palladino, Aleksa	Actress, Singer
Gersh Agency, 9465 Wilshire Blvd, #600, Beverly Hills CA 90212 USA	
Palladino, Daniel	Producer, Writer
Creative Artists Agency, 2000 Ave of Stars, #100, Los Angeles CA 90067 USA	
Palladino, Erik	Actor, Producer, Writer
Coronel Group, 1100 Glendon Ave, #1700, Los Angeles CA 90046, USA	

Palladio, Sam — Actor
W M E Entertainment, 9601 Wilshire Blvd, #300, Beverly Hills CA 90210 USA

Pallavi — Actress
14A Director Colony, Kodambakkam, Chennai TN 600024, India

Palleroni, Sergio — Architect
University of Texas, Architecture School, Austin TX 78712, USA

Palli, Anne-Marie — Golfer
7477 E Cannon Dr, Scottsdale AZ 85258, USA

Pallone, David M (Dave) — Baseball Umpire
1610 Little Raven St, #515, Denver CO 80202, USA

Pally, Adam — Actor
Creative Artists Agency, 2000 Ave of Stars, #100, Los Angeles CA 90067 USA

Palm, Richard P (Mike) — Baseball Player
21 Riverview Place, Scituate MA 02066, USA

Palm, Siegfried — Concert Cellist
Gerhild Baron Mgmt, Dornbacher Str 41/III/3, 1170 Vienna, Austria

Palmade, Pierre — Actor
Voyez Mon Agent, 20 Ave Rapp, 75007 Paris, France

Palmateer, Mike — Ice Hockey Player
30 Simmons Crescent, Aurora ON L4G 6B5, Canada

Palmaz, Julio C — Inventor (Intravascular Stent)
University of Texas Health & Science Center, 7703 Floyd Curl Dr, San Antonio TX 78229, USA

Palmeiro Corrales, Rafael C — Baseball Player
5216 Reims Court, Colleyville TX 76034, USA

Palmeiro, Orlando — Baseball Player
11991 SW 103rd Terrace, Miami FL 33186, USA

Palmer, Amanda — Singer, Songwriter
Agency Group Ltd, 1880 Century Park E, #711, Los Angeles CA 90067 USA

Palmer, Arnold D — Golfer
9007 Bay Hill Blvd, Orlando FL 32819, USA

Palmer, Betsy — Actress
3 Glen Hill Road, #304, Danbury CT 6811, USA

Palmer, Brad — Ice Hockey Player
Box 544, Lake Cowichan BC V0R 2G0, Canada

Palmer, Bud — Basketball Player
1200 S Flagler Dr, #303, West Palm Beach FL 33401, USA

Palmer, Carl — Drummer (Emerson Lake & Palmer, Asia)
Siren Artist Mgmt, 4446 W 169th St, Lawndale CA 90260, USA

Palmer, Carson — Football Player
25052 Adelanto Dr, Laguna Niguel CA 92677, USA

Palmer, Chris — Football Player, Coach
Houston Texans, 2 Reliant Park, Houston TX 77054 USA

Palmer, Dave R — Army General, Educator
4531 Blue Ridge Dr, Belton TX 76513, USA

Palmer, David L — Football Player
PO Box 310871, Birmingham AL 35231, USA

Palmer, David W — Baseball Player
61 Sherman Ave, Glens Falls NY 12801, USA

Palmer, Dean W — Baseball Player
3907 W Millers Bridge Road, Tallahassee FL 32312, USA

Palmer, Diana — Writer
Harlequin Enterprises, 225 Duncan Mill Road, Don Mills ON MJB JK9, Canada

Palmer, Geoffrey — Actor
Marmont Mgmt, Langham House, 302/8 Regent St, London W1R 5AL, England

Palmer, Geoffrey W R — Prime Minister, New Zealand
63 Roxburgh St, Mount Victoria, Wellington 6011, New Zealand

Palmer, Gregg — Actor
5726 Graves Ave, Encino CA 91316, USA

Palmer, James A (Jim) — Baseball Player, Sportscaster
239 Sanford Ave, Palm Beach FL 33480, USA

Palmer, Jesse J — Football Player, Sportscaster
8052 Hopkins Lane, Indianapolis IN 46250, USA

Palmer, Keke — Actress
W M E Entertainment, 9601 Wilshire Blvd, #300, Beverly Hills CA 90210 USA

Palmer, Patsy — Actress
International Artistes, 193-97 High Holborn, London WC1V 7BD, England

Palmer, Peter W — Actor
PO Box 482, Simpsonville KY 40067, USA

Palmer, Russell E — Financier
Palmer Group, 3600 Market St, #530, Philadelphia PA 19104, USA

Palmer, Ryan H — Golfer
4909 Rockrimmon Court, Colleyville TX 76034, USA

Palmer, Sandra — Golfer
498 Peralta Ave, Long Beach CA 90803, USA

Palmer, Teresa — Actress
Management 360, 9111 Wilshire Blvd, Beverly Hills CA 90210 USA

Palmer, Violet — Basketball Referee
N B A Referees Assn, 1455 Pennsylvania Ave NW, #225, Washington DC 20004, USA

Palmer, Walter — Basketball Player
87 South St, Rockport MA 01966, USA

Palmer, William R — Publisher
Detroit News, Publisher's Office, 615 W Lafayette Blvd, Detroit MI 48226, USA

Palmer, Zoie — Actress
Characters Talent Mgmt, 8 Elm St, Toronto ON M5G 1G7, Canada

Palmieri, Eddie — Jazz Pianist, Singer
Universal Attractions, 135 W 26th St, #1200, New York NY 10001 USA

Palminteri, Chazz — Actor
W M E Entertainment, 9601 Wilshire Blvd, #300, Beverly Hills CA 90210 USA

Palmisano, Samuel J — Businessman
I B M Corp, 1 North Castle Dr, #2, Armonk NY 10504, USA

Palombi, Ron — Bowler
227 E 29th St, Erie PA 16504, USA

Palomino, Carlos — Boxer
4200 Longridge Ave, Studio City CA 91604, USA

Palsson, Thorsteinn — Prime Minister, Iceland
Hateigsvegur 40, 105 Reykjavik, Iceland

Paltrow, Gwyneth — Actress, Model, Singer
Brillstein Entertainment Partners, 9150 Wilshire Blvd, #350, Beverly Hills CA 90212 USA

Paltrow, Jake — Director
United Talent Agency, 9336 Civic Center Dr, Beverly Hills CA 90210 USA

Palumba, Joseph C (Joe) — Football Player
927 Old Garth Road, Charlottesville VA 22901, USA

Palys, Stanley F (Stan) — Baseball Player
RR 6 Box 6119, Moscow PA 18444, USA

Pampling, Rodney (Rod) — Golfer
9 Campbell Court, Lewisville TX 75077, USA

Pamuk, Orhan — Nobel Literature Laureate
Purtelas Mah Beyoglu, Beyoglu Istanbul, Turkey

Pan Hong — Actress
Omei Film Studio, Tonghui Menwai, Chengdu City, Sichuan Province, China

Panabaker, Danielle — Actress
Management 360, 9111 Wilshire Blvd, Beverly Hills CA 90210 USA

Panabaker, Kay — Actress
Sanders/Armstrong/Caserta Mgmt, 2120 Colorado Ave, #120, Santa Monica CA 90404 USA

Panafieu, Bernard L A Cardinal — Religious Leader
Archdiocese, 14 Place du Colonel-Edon, 13284 Marseille Cedex 07, France

Pancake, Sam — Actor
Pakula/King, 9229 W Sunset Blvd, #315, West Hollywood CA 90069 USA

Pandey, Chunky — Actor
1 A/B Monisha Apts, Saint Andrews Road, Bandra, Mumbai MS 400050, India

Pandolfo, Jay — Ice Hockey Player
3 Meadowcroft Road, Burlington MA 01803, USA

Pandor, Henk — Artist
3422 Harrison St SE, Portland OR 97214, USA

Panetta, Leon E — Government Official; Representative, NY
Defense Department, Pentagon, Washington DC 20301 USA

Panettiere, Hayden — Actress, Singer
Brookside Artists Mgmt, 250 W 57th St, #2303, New York NY 10107, USA

Panettiere, Jansen — Actor
C E S D, 10635 Santa Monica Blvd, #130, Los Angeles CA 90025 USA

Pang Qing — Figure Skater
Skating Assn, 56 Zhongguancun South St, Haidian, Beijing 100044, China

Pang, Darren — Ice Hockey Player
1009 Mississippi Ave, #G, Saint Louis MO 63104, USA

Panic, Milan — Prime Minister, Yugoslavia; Businessman
I C N Pharmaceuticals, 3300 Hyland Ave, Costa Mesa CA 92626, USA

Panichas, George A — Writer
PO Box AB, College Park MD 20741, USA

Panichgul, Thakoon — Fashion Designer
270 Lafayette St, #810, New York NY 10012, USA

Panikkar, Sean — Opera Singer
I M G Artists, Hogarth Business Park, Chiswick, London W4 2TH, England

Panis, Olivier — Auto Racing Driver
Bar Team, Box 5014, Brackley, Northhamptonshire NN13, England

Panish, Morton B — Physical Chemist
52 Baldwin Road, Freeport ME 04032, USA

Panjabi, Archana (Archie) — Actress
Biscuit Boy Productions, PO Box 13467, London NW4 1WQ, England

Panke Reithofer, Norbert — Businessman
Bayerische Motoren Werke, Petuelring 130, 80788 Munich, Germany

Pankey, Irvin L (Irv) — Football Player
348 Walker St, Aberdeen MD 21001, USA

Pankin, Stuart — Actor
Abrams Artists, 9200 W Sunset Blvd, #1125, West Hollywood CA 90069 USA

Pankovits, James F (Jim) — Baseball Player
6014 Catalina Dr, #115, North Myrtle Beach SC 29582, USA

Pankow, James C — Trombone Player (Chicago), Songwriter
3826 Bowsprit Circle, Westlake Village CA 91361, USA

Pankow, John — Actor
Gersh Agency, 9465 Wilshire Blvd, #600, Beverly Hills CA 90212 USA

Panni, Marcello — Conductor, Composer
3 Piazza Borghese, 00186 Rome, Italy

Panoff, Robert — Nuclear Engineer
1140 Connecticut Ave NW, Washington DC 20036, USA

Panos, Zois (Joe) — Football Player
31010 Chequamegon Dr, Hartland WI 53029, USA

Panova, Elena — Circus Aerialist
Cirque du Soleil, 8400 2nd Ave, Montreal QC H1Z 4M6, Canada

Panozzo, Chuck — Bassist (Styx)
Alliance Artists, 1225 Northmeadow Parkway, #100, Roswell GA 30076, USA

Panteleev, Grigori — Ice Hockey Player
5 Commonwealth Road, Natick MA 01760, USA

Pantoliano, Joe — Actor
Principal Entertainment, 130 W 42nd St, #614, New York NY 10036, USA

Panula, Jorma — Conductor, Composer
Sibelius Academy, P Rautatiekatu 9, 00100 Helsinki 10, Finland

Paola — Queen, Belgium
Koninklijk Palais, Rue de Brederode, 1000 Brussels, Belgium

Paoli, Cecile — Actress
Agents Associes, 201 Rue du Faubourg Saint Honore, 75008 Paris, France

Paolini, Christopher — Writer
Random House, 1745 Broadway, #1800, New York NY 10019 USA

Paolo, Connor — Actor
Abrams Artists, 9200 W Sunset Blvd, #1125, West Hollywood CA 90069 USA

Papa, Bob — Sportscaster
N F L Network, 10950 Washington Blvd, #100, Culver City CA 90232 USA

Papa, John P — Baseball Player
275 Mary Ave, Stratford CT 06614, USA

Papa, Tom — Actor, Comedian
3 Arts Entertainment, 9460 Wilshire Blvd, #700, Beverly Hills CA 90212 USA

Papamichael, Phedon M — Cinematographer
Innovative Artists, 1505 10th St, Santa Monica CA 90401 USA

Papas, Irene
Anne Alvares Correa, 34 Rue Jouffroy d'Abbans, 75017 Paris, France — Actress
Papazian, Marty
Chasen Agency, 8899 Beverly Blvd, #716, Los Angeles CA 90048 USA — Actor
Pape, Rene
Artists Mgmt, Dahlmannstra 9, 10629 Berlin, Germany — Opera, Concert Singer, Actor
Papert, Seymour S
Learning Barn, PO Box 387, Blue Hill ME 04614, USA — Mathematician
Papi, Stanley G (Stan)
1111 W Sierra Madre Ave, Fresno CA 93705, USA — Baseball Player
Papis, Massimiliano (Max)
10855 NW 33rd St, Miami FL 33172, USA — Auto Racing Driver
Papo, Brandon
C E S D, 10635 Santa Monica Blvd, #130, Los Angeles CA 90025 USA — Actor
Papoulias, Karolos
President's Office, Presidential Palace, Herodes Atticus St, 10674 Athens, Greece — President, Greece
Papp, Robert J, Jr
Commandant, US Coast Guard, 2100 2nd St SW, Washington DC 20593 USA — Coast Guard Admiral
Pappalardi, Felix
Skyline Music, 2270 Maiden Lane SW, Roanoke VA 24015, USA — Singer, Bassist (Mountain)
Pappano, Antonio
I M G Artists, Hogarth Business Park, Chiswick, London W4 2TH, England — Conductor
Pappas, Deane
2930 S College Dr, Fayetteville AR 72701, USA — Golfer
Pappas, George
21108 Blakely Shores Dr, Cornelius NC 28031, USA — Bowler
Pappas, Milton S (Milt)
319 Aspen Dr, Beecher IL 60401, USA — Baseball Player
Pappin, James J (Jim)
48947 Greasewood Lane, Palm Desert CA 92260, USA — Ice Hockey Player
Paquette, Craig H
16626 S Magenta Road, Phoenix AZ 85048, USA — Baseball Player
Paquin, Anna
W M E Entertainment, 9601 Wilshire Blvd, #300, Beverly Hills CA 90210 USA — Actress
Paradis, Vanessa
Agence Artiste Adequet, 80 Rue d'Amsterdam, 75009 Paris, France — Model, Singer, Actress
Paradise, Robert (Bob)
1303 Beechwood Place, Saint Paul MN 55116, USA — Ice Hockey Player
Parazaider, Walter
Front Line Mgmt, 1100 Glendon Ave, #2000, Los Angeles CA 90024 USA — Woodwind Musician (Chicago)
Parazynski, Scott E
2015 Wroxton Road, Houston TX 77005, USA — Astronaut
Parcells, Duane C (Bill)
Miami Dolphins, 7500 SW 30th St, Davie FL 33314 USA — Football Coach, Executive
Pardee, Arthur B
987 Memorial Dr, #271, Cambridge MA 02138, USA — Biochemist
Pardee, John
Paradigm Agency, 360 N Crescent Dr, North Building, Beverly Hills CA 90210 USA — Producer
Pardee, John P (Jack)
Hawks Hill Ranch, PO Box 272, Gause TX 77857, USA — Football Player, Coach
Pardes, Herbert
New York Presbyterian Hospital, 161 Fort Washington Ave, New York NY 10032, USA — Psychiatrist
Pardo, Don
NBC-TV, News Dept, 30 Rockefeller Plaza, #270E, New York NY 10112 USA — Commentator
Pardo, Etela
Gavin Barker Assoc, 2D Wimpole St, London W1G 0EB, England — Actress
Pardo, Jimmy
Gersh Agency, 9465 Wilshire Blvd, #600, Beverly Hills CA 90212 USA — Actor, Comedian
Pardue, Kip
Roar Mgmt, 9701 Wilshire Blvd, #800, Beverly Hills CA 90212 USA — Actor
Pardue, Mary-Lou
Massachusetts Institute of Technology, Biology Dept, Cambridge MA 02139, USA — Biologist
Pare, Jessica
United Talent Agency, 9336 Civic Center Dr, Beverly Hills CA 90210 USA — Actress
Pare, Michael
Stolen Thunder Mgmt, 7950 W Sunset Blvd, #516, Los Angeles CA 90046, USA — Actor
Pare, Richard
174 Park St, Montclair NJ 07042, USA — Photographer
Paredes, Marisa
Alsire Garcia Maroto, Pl Espana 18, #15, 28008 Madrid, Spain — Actress
Parekh, Asha
Azad Road, Juhu, Mumbai MS 400049, India — Actress
Paremski, Natasha
I M G Artists, Hogarth Business Park, Chiswick, London W4 2TH, England — Concert Pianist
Parent, Bernard M (Bernie)
Schooner Island Marina, 5100 Lake Road, #H-01, Wildwood NJ 08260, USA — Ice Hockey Player
Parent, Mark A
8829 Midview Dr, Palo Cedro CA 96073, USA — Baseball Player
Parent, Monique
PO Box 3458, Ventura CA 93006, USA — Actress, Model
Paret, Peter
Institute for Advanced Studies, Historical Studies School, Princeton NJ 08540, USA — Historian
Paretsky, Sara N
5831 S Blackstone Ave, Chicago IL 60637, USA — Writer
Parfit, Derek A
All Souls College, Philosophy Dept, Oxford OX1 4AL, England — Philosopher
Parfitt, Judy
Conway Van Gelder Grant, 8-12 Broadwick St, #300, London W1F 8HW, England — Actress
Pargo, Jannero
3280 Timberwood Lane, Riverwoods IL 60015, USA — Basketball Player
Parham, Lennon
Mosiac Media Group, 9200 W Sunset Blvd, #1000, Los Angeles CA 90069 USA — Producer, Writer, Actress
Parillaud, Anne
Artmedia, 20 Ave Rapp, 75007 Paris, France — Actress
Parilli, Vito (Babe)
8060 E Girard Ave, #218, Denver CO 80231, USA — Football Player, Coach

Paris, Jhevon Agency Group Ltd, 142 W 57th St, #600, New York NY 10019 USA	Singer, Songwriter
Paris, Kelly J 1515 Redwood Circle, Thousand Oaks CA 91360, USA	Baseball Player
Paris, Mica Richard Walters, PO Box 2789, Toluca Lake CA 91610 USA	Singer
Paris, Myrna Columbia Artists Mgmt Inc, 1790 Broadway, #702, New York NY 10019 USA	Opera Singer
Paris, Twila T P Productions, PO Box 20, Elm Springs AR 72728, USA	Singer, Songwriter
Paris, William (Bubba) 4096 Beacon Place, Discovery Bay CA 94505, USA	Football Player
Parise, Jean-Paul (J P) 3814 Raspberry Ridge Road NW, Prior Lake MN 55372, USA	Ice Hockey Player
Parise, Vanessa Lara Rosenstock Mgmt, 8371 Blackburn Ave, #1, Los Angeles CA 90048, USA	Actress
Parise, Zachary J (Zach) 78 Blackburne Terrace, West Orange NJ 07052, USA	Ice Hockey Player
Parish, Diane C A M, 111 Shoreditch High St, #400, London E1 6JN, England	Actress
Parish, Robert L 18730 Peninsula Circle Dr, Cornelius NC 28031, USA	Basketball Player
Parish, Sarah Another Tongue, 10-11 D'Arblay St, London W1F 8DS, England	Actress
Parisi, Angelo Judo Institute, 21-25 Ave de la Porte de Chatillon, 75680 Paris, France	Judo Athlete
Parisot, Dean Creative Artists Agency, 2000 Ave of Stars, #100, Los Angeles CA 90067 USA	Director, Producer, Writer
Parisse, Annie Gersh Agency, 9465 Wilshire Blvd, #600, Beverly Hills CA 90212 USA	Actress
Parizeau, Michel G 250 Rue Chauveau, Drummondville QC J2C 6L2, Canada	Ice Hockey Player
Park Chu-Young Football Assn, 1-131 Sinmunno, 2-Ga Jongno-Gu, Seoul 110 062, South Korea	Soccer Player
Park Hye-Won Skating Union, 88 Bangyee-Dong, Songpaku, Seoul 138 749, South Korea	Speed Skater
Park Jong-Woo Football Assn, 1-131 Sinmunno, 2-Ga Jongno-Gu, Seoul 110 062, South Korea	Soccer Player
Park, Chan Ho 10 Hallcrest Dr, Ladera Ranch CA 92694, USA	Baseball Player
Park, D Bradford (Brad) 20 Stanley Road, Lynnfield MA 01940, USA	Ice Hockey Player
Park, Ernest C (Ernie) 3160 Private Road 1101, Clyde TX 79510, USA	Football Player
Park, Grace Untitled Entertainment, 350 S Beverly Dr, #200, Beverly Hills CA 90212 USA	Actress
Park, Grace 8298 E Tallfeather Dr, Scottsdale AZ 85255, USA	Golfer
Park, Inbee Ladies Pro Golf Assn, 100 International Golf Dr, Daytona Beach FL 32124 USA	Golfer
Park, James T 11 Bradford Road, Weston MA 02493, USA	Microbiologist
Park, Linda Seven Summits, 8906 W Olympic Blvd, Beverly Hills CA 90211, USA	Actress
Park, Megan Paradigm Agency, 360 N Crescent Dr, North Building, Beverly Hills CA 90210 USA	Actress
Park, Merle F Royal Ballet School, 144 Talgarth Road, London W14 9DE, England	Ballerina
Park, Michael Innovative Artists, 1505 10th St, Santa Monica CA 90401 USA	Actor
Park, Nicholas W (Nick) Aardvark Animation, Gas Ferry Road, Bristol B51 6UN, England	Animator, Director
Park, Ray Priluck Co, 1230 Montana Ave, Santa Monica CA 90403, USA	Actor
Park, Richard 6416 Vista Pacifica, Rancho Palos Verdes CA 90275, USA	Ice Hockey Player
Park, Steve 261 Indian Trail Road, Mooresville NC 28117, USA	Auto Racing Driver
Park, Sydney 3 Arts Entertainment, 9460 Wilshire Blvd, #700, Beverly Hills CA 90212 USA	Actress
Parke, Dorothy A K A Talent Agency, 6310 San Vicente Blvd, #200, Los Angeles CA 90048, USA	Actress
Parke, Evan Essential Talent, 6399 Wilshire Blvd, #400, Los Angeles CA 90048, USA	Actor
Parkening, Christopher I M G Artists, 152 W 57th St, #500, New York NY 10019 USA	Concert Guitarist
Parker Kennedy, Jessica Play Mgmt, 807 Powell St, #220, Vancouver BC V6A 1H7, Canada	Actress
Parker, Alan W United Talent Agency, 9336 Civic Center Dr, Beverly Hills CA 90210 USA	Director
Parker, Andrea A P A Talent/Literary Agency, 405 S Beverly Dr, #300, Beverly Hills CA 90212 USA	Actress
Parker, B Frank RR 4 Box 83-2, Broken Bow OK 74728, USA	Football Player
Parker, Barrington D, Jr US Court of Appeals, Moynihan Courthouse, 500 Pearl St, New York NY 10007, USA	Judge
Parker, Candace Los Angeles Sparks, 888 S Figueroa St, #2010, Los Angeles CA 90017 USA	Basketball Player
Parker, Caryl Mack Rancho Divine Productions , 9 Music Square S, #108, Nashville TN 37203, USA	Singer
Parker, Christian 10101 Mesa Arriba Ave NE, Albuquerque NM 87111, USA	Baseball Player
Parker, Christopher I C M Partners, 10250 Constellation Blvd, #900, Los Angeles CA 90067 USA	Actor
Parker, Clarence M (Ace) 210 Snead's Fairway, Portsmouth VA 23701, USA	Football, Baseball Player

Parker, Craig — Actor
Karen Kay Mgmt, PO Box 446, Auckland 1140, New Zealand
Parker, David G (Dave) — Baseball Player
Cobra Industries, 4038 Oak Tree Court, Loveland OH 45140, USA
Parker, Denise — Archery Athlete
131 W 4300 N, Ogden UT 84414, USA
Parker, Eleanor — Actress
2195 La Paz Way, Palm Springs CA 92264, USA
Parker, Eugene N — Physicist
1006 Gardner Road, Flossmoor IL 60422, USA
Parker, Franklin — Writer
Western Carolina University, Education & Psychology Dept, Cullowhee NC 28723, USA
Parker, Glenn A — Football Player, Sportscaster
5420 N Campbell Ave, Tucson AZ 85718, USA
Parker, Graham — Singer, Guitarist
Performers of the World, 5657 Wilshire Blvd, #280, Los Angeles CA 90036 USA
Parker, Harry W — Baseball Player
7180 Ellerson Mill Circle, #B, Mechanicsville VA 23111, USA
Parker, Jameson — Actor
1604 N Vista Ave, Los Angeles CA 90046, USA
Parker, Jamie — Actor
Rights House, 34-43 Russell St, London WC2B 5HA, England
Parker, Jeff — Editorial Cartoonist
Florida Today, Editorial Dept, 1 Gannett Plaza, Melbourne FL 32940, USA
Parker, Jo Ellen Johnson — Educator
Sweet Briar College, President's Office, Sweet Briar VA 24595, USA
Parker, Jon Kimura — Concert Pianist
Opus 3 Artists, 470 Park Ave S, #900N, New York NY 10016 USA
Parker, Kelly — Soccer Player
Canadian Soccer, Place Soccer Canada, 237 Metcalfe St, Ottawa ON K2P 1R2, Canada
Parker, Kristal — Golfer
5675 E Bent Tree Dr, Scottsdale AZ 85266, USA
Parker, Lara — Actress
PO Box 1254, Topanga CA 90290, USA
Parker, Lucinda — Artist
Laura Russo Gallery, 805 NW 21st St, Portland OR 97209, USA
Parker, Maceo — Jazz Saxophonist
Central Entertainment Services, 109 W Newark Ave, Wildwood NJ 08260, USA
Parker, Mark — Businessman
Nike Inc, 1 SW Bowerman Dr, Beaverton OR 97005, USA
Parker, Mary-Louise — Actress
W M E Entertainment, 1325 Ave of Americas, New York NY 10019 USA
Parker, Molly — Actress
D/F Mgmt, 270 Lafayette St, #402, New York NY 10012 USA
Parker, Nate — Actor
Simmons & Scott Entertainment, 7942 Mulholland Dr, Los Angeles CA 90046, USA
Parker, Nathaniel — Actor
Independent Talent Group, Oxford House, 76 Oxford St, London W1D 1BS, England
Parker, Nicole Ari — Actress
Gersh Agency, 41 Madison Ave, #3301, New York NY 10010 USA
Parker, Noelle — Actress
9300 Wilshire Blvd, #555, Beverly Hills CA 90212, USA
Parker, Oliver — Director
76 Oxford St, London W1N 0AX, England
Parker, Paula Jai — Actress
Levity Entertainment, 6701 Center Drive W, #1111, Los Angeles CA 90045 USA
Parker, Ray, Jr — Singer, Guitarist
Paradise Artists, 2002 Hogback Road, Ann Arbor MI 48015, USA
Parker, Richard A (Rick) — Baseball Player
2641 NE 74th St, Kansas City MO 64119, USA
Parker, Riddick T, Jr — Football Player
11226 NE 68th St, #212B, Kirkland WA 98033, USA
Parker, Robert — Singer, Saxophonist
Jeff Hubbard, PO Box 26334, Indianapolis IN 46226, USA
Parker, Robert A R — Astronaut
N A S A, Johnson Space Center, 2101 NASA Road, Houston TX 77058 USA
Parker, Sage — Actress
Kazarian/Spencer/Ruskin, 11969 Ventura Blvd, #300, Studio City CA 91604 USA
Parker, Sarah Jessica — Actress, Model
Pretty Matches Productions, 1100 Ave of Americas, #G26, New York NY 10026, USA
Parker, Scott — Motorcycle Racing Rider
6096 Grand Blanc Road, Swartz Creek MI 48473, USA
Parker, Scott — Ice Hockey Player
1253 S Perry Park Road, Sedalia CO 80135, USA
Parker, T Jefferson — Writer
E P Dutton, 375 Hudson St, New York NY 10014 USA
Parker, Thomas A (Tom) — Singer, Guitarist (Wanted)
Industry Music Group, 128 Regent Road, Hanley Stoke, Trent ST1 3AY, England
Parker, Trey, II — Animator, Writer
Important Films, 12910 Culver Blvd, #A, Los Angeles CA 90066, USA
Parker, Vaughn A — Football Player
2500 6th Ave, #107, San Diego CA 92103, USA
Parker, W Anthony (Tony) — Basketball Player
11214 Anaqua Springs, Boerne TX 78006, USA
Parker, W Douglas (Doug) — Businessman
America West Airlines, 4000 E Sky Harbor Blvd, Phoenix AZ 85034, USA
Parker, William — Surgeon
Duke University, Medical School, Trent Dr, Durham NC 27710, USA
Parker, William N (Willie) — Football Player
9327 Kai Dr, Beach City TX 77523, USA
Parker, Willie E — Football Player
Washington Redskins, 21300 Redskin Park Dr, Ashburn VA 20147 USA
Parker-Bowles, Camilla — Duchess of Cornwall, England
Buckingham Palace, London SW1A 1AA, England
Parkhill, Barry — Basketball Player
3429 Cesford Grange, Keswick VA 22947, USA

Parkhurst, Carolyn — Writer
Little Brown, 3 Center Plaza, #100, Boston MA 02108 USA

Parkhurst, Heather-Elizabeth — Actress
8491 W Sunset Blvd, #440, West Hollywood CA 90069, USA

Parkins, Barbara — Actress
Bis Mgmt, 12115 San Vicente Blvd, #109, Los Angeles CA 90049, USA

Parkinson, Bradford W — Businessman, Inventor
2360 Camino Edna, San Luis Obispo CA 93401, USA

Parkinson, Dian — Entertainer, Model
Jo-Ann Geffem, 3151 Cahuenga Blvd, #235, Los Angeles CA 90068, USA

Parkinson, Robert L, Jr — Businessman
Abbott Laboratories, 100 Abbott Park Road, North Chicago IL 60064, USA

Parks, Cherokee B — Basketball Player
PO Box 11525, Las Vegas NV 89111, USA

Parks, David W (Dave) — Football Player
12113 Palisades Parkway, Austin TX 78732, USA

Parks, Francine — Model
Playboy Promotions, 2706 Media Center Dr, Los Angeles CA 90065 USA

Parks, Maxie — Track Athlete
4545 E Norwich Ave, Fresno CA 93726, USA

Parks, Michael — Actor
1618 N Vine St, #614, Los Angeles CA 90028, USA

Parks, Suzan-Lori — Writer
Steven Barclay Agency, 12 Western Ave, Petaluma CA 94952, USA

Parks, Van Dyke — Singer, Composer
2141 Layton St, Pasadena CA 91104, USA

Parlow, Cindy — Soccer Player
3911 Tamarron Circle, #101, Memphis TN 38125, USA

Parmalee, Bernard A (Bernie) — Football Player
9208 158th St, Overland Park KS 66221, USA

Parmenter, Charles S — Chemist
Indiana University, Chemistry Dept, Bloomington IN 47405, USA

Parmet, Philip (Phil) — Cinematographer
Paradigm Agency, 360 N Crescent Dr, North Building, Beverly Hills CA 90210 USA

Parnell, Bobby — Baseball Player
2265 Barger Road, Salisbury NC 28146, USA

Parnell, Chris — Actor, Comedian
Mosiac Media Group, 24 Music Square W, #100, Nashville TN 37203, USA

Parnell, Lee Roy — Singer, Guitarist
Mike Robertson Mgmt, 1227 17th Ave S, #3, Nashville TN 37212, USA

Parnevik, Jesper — Golfer
17553 SE Conch Bar Ave, Jupiter FL 33469, USA

Parodi, Starr — Composer
Evolution Music, 1680 Vine St, #500, Los Angeles CA 90028, USA

Parol, Tina — Singer, Songwriter
Motown Records, 6255 W Sunset Blvd, Los Angeles CA 90028 USA

Paronto, Chad M — Baseball Player
617 Benedict Road, Pittsfield MA 01201, USA

Parque, James V (Jim) — Baseball Player
4109 Crystal Ridge Dr SE, Puyallup WA 98372, USA

Parr, Carolyn Miller — Judge
US Tax Court, 400 2nd St NW, Washington DC 20217, USA

Parr, Ralph S — Korean & Vietnam War Air Force Hero
2294 Common St, #442, New Braunfels TX 78130, USA

Parr, Robert G — Chemist
701 Kenmore Road, Chapel Hill NC 27514, USA

Parra, Derek — Speed Skater
14927 Treseder St, Draper UT 84020, USA

Parra, Manuel A (Manny) — Baseball Player
3142 Halverson Way, Roseville CA 95661, USA

Parrella, John L — Football Player
8161 Regency Dr, Pleasanton CA 94588, USA

Parrett, Jeffrey D (Jeff) — Baseball Player
2765 Pinckard Pike, Versailles KY 40383, USA

Parrett, William — Businessman
Deloitte Touche Tohmatsu, 433 Country Club Road, New Canaan CT 06840, USA

Parrilla, Lana — Actress
I F A Talent Agency, 8730 W Sunset Blvd, #490, West Hollywood CA 90069 USA

Parris, Fred — Singer (Five Satins)
Paramount Entertainment, 12 Kosakowski Dr, Morris Plains NJ 07590 USA

Parris, Gary T — Football Player
5170 9th St, Vero Beach FL 32966, USA

Parris, Steven M (Steve) — Baseball Player
403 Rookery Court, Joliet IL 60431, USA

Parrish, Bernard P (Bernie) — Football Player
4129 NW 32nd St, Gainesville FL 32605, USA

Parrish, Hunter — Actor
Management 360, 9111 Wilshire Blvd, Beverly Hills CA 90210 USA

Parrish, John H — Baseball Player
325 Charles Road, Lancaster PA 17603, USA

Parrish, Lance M — Baseball Player
1101 Chateau Lane, Nashville TN 37215, USA

Parrish, Larry A — Baseball Player, Manager
234 Green Haven Lane W, Dundee FL 33838, USA

Parrish, Lemar R — Football Player
52 Brittany Way, Palmetto GA 30268, USA

Parros, Peter — Actor
Amsel Eisenstadt Frazier, 5055 Wilshire Blvd, #865, Los Angeles CA 90036 USA

Parros, Rick U — Football Player
15932 E Lehigh Circle, Aurora CO 80013, USA

Parrott, Andrew H — Conductor
Allied Artists, 42 Montpelier Square, London SW7 1JZ, England

Parrott, Michael E A (Mike) — Baseball Player
PO Box 1264, Lyons CO 80540, USA

Parry, Craig — Golfer
5139 Latrobe Dr, Windemere FL 34786, USA

Parry, Edward (Ed)
6152 Benoit Road, Clay MI 48001, USA — Basketball Player

Parry, Richard Reed
Billions Corp, 3522 W Armitage Ave, Chicago IL 60647 USA — Musician (Arcade Fire)

Parry, Robert T
11362 Barranca Road, Santa Rosa Valley CA 93012, USA — Government Official, Financier

Parseghian, Ara R
51767 Oakbrook Court, Granger IN 46530, USA — Football Coach, Sportscaster

Parshall, George W
2401 Pennsylvania Ave, #714, Wilmington DE 19806, USA — Chemist

Parsky, Gerald L
Aurora Capital Partners, 1800 Century Park East, Los Angeles CA 90067, USA — Attorney

Parsley, Ambrosia
Zoe/Rounder Records, 1 Rounder Way, Burlington MA 01803, USA — Singer (Shivaree)

Parsley, Clifford D (Cliff)
7601 E 134th Terrace, Grandview MO 64030, USA — Football Player

Parsons, Alan
Band Guru Mgmt, PO Box 11192, Denver CO 80211, USA — Musician

Parsons, Charles D
22 Hancock St, Cambridge MA 02139, USA — Philosopher

Parsons, David
Parsons Dance Foundation, 476 Broadway, New York NY 10013, USA — Choreographer

Parsons, David (Dave)
Front Line Mgmt, 1100 Glendon Ave, #2000, Los Angeles CA 90024 USA — Bassist (Bush)

Parsons, Estelle
Paradigm Agency, 360 Park Ave S, #1600, New York NY 10010 USA — Actress

Parsons, Jim
Creative Artists Agency, 2000 Ave of Stars, #100, Los Angeles CA 90067 USA — Actor, Comedian

Parsons, John T
1456 Brigadoon Court, Traverse City MI 49686, USA — Inventor (Machine Numerical Control)

Parsons, Karyn
Lesher Entertainment, 1134 S Cloverdale Ave, Los Angeles CA 90019, USA — Actress

Parsons, Nicholas
Quarry Cottage, Windrush near Burford, England — Actor

Parsons, Phil
18801 Coveside Lane, Cornelius NC 28031, USA — Auto Racing Driver

Parsons, Robert H (Bob)
1098 Stanton Road, Lake Zurich IL 60047, USA — Football Player

Parsons, Robert K
Jackson & Kelly, PO Box 553, Charleston,WV 25322, USA — Astronaut

Part, Arvo
Universal Edition, 48 Great Marlborough St, London S1F 7BB, England — Composer

Partee, Barbara H
50 Hobart Lane, Amherst MA 01002, USA — Educator

Partee, Dennis F
604 E Rusk St, Marshall TX 75670, USA — Football Player

Parten, Ty D
2926 W Eastman Dr, Anthem AZ 85086, USA — Football Player

Parton, Dolly
Dollywood Co, 2700 Dollywood Parks Blvd, Pigeon Forge TN 37863, USA — Singer, Actress, Songwriter

Parton, Stella
PO Box 120871, Nashville TN 37212, USA — Singer

Partridge, Alex
Leander Club, Henley on Thames, Leander RG9 2LP, England — Rowing Athlete

Partridge, John A
Cudham Court, Cudham near Sevenoaks, Kent TN14 7QF, England — Architect

Partridge, Leah
Columbia Artists Mgmt Inc, 1790 Broadway, #702, New York NY 10019 USA — Opera Singer

Partridge, Richard B (Rick)
707 Reeder Road, Paramus NJ 07652, USA — Football Player

Partridge, Wendy
Paradigm Agency, 360 N Crescent Dr, North Building, Beverly Hills CA 90210 USA — Costume Designer

Paruzzi, Gabriella
Via Cardorna 47, 33010 Fuzine UR, Italy — Cross Country Skier

Pasanella, Giovanni
Pasanella & Klein, 330 W 42nd St, New York NY 10036, USA — Architect

Pasanella, Marco
Pasanella Co, 45 W 18th St, New York NY 10011, USA — Furniture Designer

Pasarell, Charles
78200 Miles Ave, Indian Wells CA 92210, USA — Tennis Player

Pascal, Adam
Innovative Artists, 1505 10th St, Santa Monica CA 90401 USA — Actor, Singer

Pascal, Olivia
Agentur Alexander, Lamonstr 9, 81679 Munich, Germany — Actress

Pascal, Pedro
Innovative Artists, 235 Park Ave S, #1000, New York NY 10003 USA — Actor

Pascal-Trouillot, Ertha
Christ Roi 21, Port-au-Prince, Haiti — President, Haiti

Paschall, William H (Bill)
7926 Windspray Dr, Summerfield NC 27358, USA — Baseball Player

Pasco, Richard
Michael Whitehall, 125 Gloucester Road, London SW7 4TE, England — Actor

Pascoal, Hermeto
Brasil Universo Prod, RVN Vitor Guisard 209, Rio de Janerio 21832, Brazil — Jazz Musician

Pascual, Camilo A
7741 SW 32nd St, Miami FL 33155, USA — Baseball Player

Pascual, Luis
Theatre de l'Europe, 1 Place Paul Claudel, 75006 Paris, France — Director

Pascual, Mercedes
University of Michigan, Ecology & Biology Dept, Ann Arbor MI 48109, USA — Ecologist, Evolutionary Biologist

Pasdar, Adrian
I C M Partners, 10250 Constellation Blvd, #900, Los Angeles CA 90067 USA — Actor

Pasek, Justine
Physical Modelos, Edificia Parque Uracaca Av, Balboa, Panama City, Panama — Beauty Queen, Model

Pash, Jim
624 Sistine St, Las Vegas NV 89144, USA — Singer (Surfaris)

Pashnick, Larry J
506 Highland St, Wyandotte MI 48192, USA — Baseball Player

Pashos, Anthony G (Tony)
23 30th Ave, Jacksonville Beach FL 32250, USA — Football Player

Pasian, Karina
Def Jam Records, 160 Varick St, #1200, New York NY 10013 USA — Singer

Pasillas, Jose A, II
Variety Artists, 793 Higuera St, #6, San Luis Obispo CA 93401 USA — Drummer (Incubus)

Pasin, Dave
787 Holly Oak Dr, Palo Alto CA 94303, USA — Ice Hockey Player

Paskai, Laszlo Cardinal
Uri Utca 62, 1014 Budapest, Hungary — Religious Leader

Paslawski, Greg
10 Topping Lane, Saint Louis MO 63131, USA — Ice Hockey Player

Pasqua, Daniel A (Dan)
45 Silo Ridge Road E, Orland Park IL 60467, USA — Baseball Player

Pasquale, Steven
I C M Partners, 10250 Constellation Blvd, #900, Los Angeles CA 90067 USA — Actor

Pasqualino, Luke
B W H Agency, 117 Shaftesbury Ave, London WC2H 8AD, England — Actor

Pasqualoni, Paul
University of Connecticut, Storrs CT 06269 USA — Football Coach

Pasquette, Didier
15 Ave du Stade, 10400 Trainelfrance, France — Circus Tightrope Walker

Pasquin, John R
Paradox Productions, 801 Tarcuto Way, Los Angeles CA 90077, USA — Director, Producer

Pass, Patrick D
57 Revere Terrace, Attleboro MA 02703, USA — Football Player

Passarelli, Pasquale
Pfalzer Waldweg 5, 68753 Waghausel, Germany — Greco-Roman Wrestler

Passer, Ivan
Innovative Artists, 1505 10th St, Santa Monica CA 90401 USA — Director

Passmore, John A
6 Jansz Crescent, Manuka ACT 2603, Australia — Philosopher

Passmore, Matt
W M E Entertainment, 9601 Wilshire Blvd, #300, Beverly Hills CA 90210 USA — Actor

Passos Coelho, Pedro M M
Prime Minister's Office, Rua du Imprensa a Estrela 8, 1249 068 Lisbon, Portugal — Prime Minister, Portugal

Pastan, Linda
11710 Beall Mountain Road, Potomac MD 20854, USA — Writer

Pastides, Harris
University of South Carolina, President's Office, Osborne Building, Columbia SC 29208, USA — Educator

Pastis, Stephan
1 Snoopy Place, Santa Rosa CA 95403, USA — Cartoonist

Pastner, Josh
University of Memphis, Athletic Dept, 570 Normal St, Memphis TN 38152, USA — Basketball Coach

Pastore, Frank E
1542 Francis Way, Upland CA 91786, USA — Baseball Player

Pastore, Vincent
PO Box 207, Bronx NY 10464, USA — Actor

Pastorini, Dante A (Dan), Jr
2323 McCue Road, #1909, Houston TX 77056, USA — Football Player

Pastrana, Al
1628 Ridout Road, Annapolis MD 21409, USA — Football Player

Patat, Frederic
Faculte de Medecine, 2 Bis Blvd Tonnelle, 37032 Tours Cedex, France — Spatinaut, France

Patch, Karen
United Talent Agency, 9336 Civic Center Dr, Beverly Hills CA 90210 USA — Costume Designer

Patchett, Ann
Saint Martin's Press, 175 5th Ave, #400, New York NY 10010 USA — Writer

Pate, Jerome K (Jerry)
5 Hyde Park Road, Pensacola FL 32503, USA — Golfer

Pate, Jonas
W M E Entertainment, 9601 Wilshire Blvd, #300, Beverly Hills CA 90210 USA — Director, Writer

Pate, Josh
W M E Entertainment, 9601 Wilshire Blvd, #300, Beverly Hills CA 90210 USA — Director, Writer

Pate, Steve
1034 Brookview Ave, Westlake Village CA 91361, USA — Golfer

Patek, Frederick J (Freddie)
5408 NE Wedgewood Lane, Lees Summit MO 64064, USA — Baseball Player

Patekar, Nana
304 Sheetal Apna Ghar Soc, Samarth Nagar Andgeri, Mumbai MS 400058, India — Actor

Patel, C Kumar N
1171 Roberto Lane, Los Angeles CA 90077, USA — Inventor (Carbon Dioxide Laser)

Patel, Dev
Curtis Brown Group, 28-29 Haymarket St, #500, London SW1Y 4SP, England — Actor

Pateman, Carole
University of California, Political Science Dept, Los Angeles CA 90024, USA — Political Scientist

Patera, John A (Jack)
82 Osprey Dr, Cle Elum WA 98922, USA — Football Player, Coach

Patera, Ken
6932 Stratford Road, Saint Paul MN 55125, USA — Weightlifter

Paterson, Bill
Kerry Gardner, 15 Kensington High St, London W8 5NP, England — Actor

Paterson, D Rick
Anaheim Ducks, 2695 E Katella Ave, Anaheim CA 92806 USA — Ice Hockey Player, Executive

Paterson, David A
WOR Radio, 111 Broadway, #300, New York NY 10006, USA — Governor, NY

Paterson, Jodi Ann
Playboy Promotions, 2706 Media Center Dr, Los Angeles CA 90065 USA — Model

Paterson, Joseph A (Joe)
49 Sullivan Place, Lake George NY 12845, USA — Ice Hockey Player

Paterson, Katherine
70 Wildersburg Common, Barre VT 05641, USA — Writer

Patey, Larry J
2713 Autumn Run Court, Chesterfield MO 63005, USA — Ice Hockey Player

Pathon, Jerome
611 Carrotwood Terrace, Plantation FL 33324, USA — Football Player
Patil, Pratibha
President's Office, Bharat Ka, Rashtrapti Bhavan, New Delhi 110004, India — President, India
Patinkin, Mandy
Planetarium Station, PO Box 64, New York NY 10024, USA — Actor, Singer
Patitz, Tatjana
Trump Model Agency, 91 5th Ave, #300, New York NY 10003 USA — Model, Actress
Patkau, John
Patkau Architects, 560 Beaty St, #L110, Vancouver BC V6B 2L3, Canada — Architect
Pato, Alexandre
F C Milan, Via Filippo Turati 3, 20121 Milan, Italy — Soccer Player
Patriarco, Earle
Askonas Holt, Lincoln House, 300 High Holborn, London WC1V 7JH, England — Opera Singer
Patric, Jason
Creative Artists Agency, 2000 Ave of Stars, #100, Los Angeles CA 90067 USA — Actor
Patrick, Bill
NBC-TV, Sports Dept, 30 Rockefeller Plaza, #270E, New York NY 10112 USA — Sportscaster
Patrick, Butch
15701 Redington Dr, Redington Beach FL 33708, USA — Actor
Patrick, Craig
113 Royston Road, Pittsburgh PA 15238, USA — Ice Hockey Player
Patrick, Danica
Danica Racing, PO Box 155, Roscoe IL 61073, USA — Auto Racing Driver, Model
Patrick, James
5024 Red Tail Run, Buffalo NY 14221, USA — Ice Hockey Player
Patrick, Kyle
Sharp & Focused Mgmt, 323 Broadway St, Cambridge MA 02139, USA — Singer, Guitarist (Click Five)
Patrick, Mike
ESPN-TV, ESPN Plaza, 935 Middle St, Bristol CT 06010 USA — Sportscaster
Patrick, Nicholas J M
10811 Oak Creek St, Houston TX 77024, USA — Astronaut
Patrick, Robert
Coronel Group, 1100 Glendon Ave, #1700, Los Angeles CA 90046, USA — Actor
Patrick, Ruth
Academy of Natural Sciences, 19th & Parkway, Philadelphia PA 19103, USA — Educator
Patrick, Thomas M
Peoples Energy Corp, 130 E Randolph Dr, #300, Chicago IL 60601, USA — Businessman
Patridge, Audrina
I C M Partners, 10250 Constellation Blvd, #900, Los Angeles CA 90067 USA — Actress
Patron, Javier
I C M Partners, 10250 Constellation Blvd, #900, Los Angeles CA 90067 USA — Director
Patten of Barnes, Christopher F
Oxford University, Chancellor's Office, Oxford OX1 2JD, England — Governor General, Hong Kong; Educator
Patten, Cassandra
Stockport Metro, 12 Grand Central Square, Stockport SK1 3TA, England — Swimmer
Patten, David
333 Oak Creek Circle, Columbia SC 29223, USA — Football Player
Patten, John L (Joel), II
13415 Marble Rock Dr, Chantilly VA 20151, USA — Football Player
Patterson, Berman
605 Universe Blvd, #T1212, Juno Beach FL 33408, USA — Singer (Cleftones)
Patterson, Carly
3401 Therondunn Dr, Plano TX 75023, USA — Gymnast
Patterson, Christian
Ken McReddie Assoc, 11 Connaught Place, London W2 2ET, England — Actor
Patterson, Colin
Just in Case Fire, 11979 40th St SE, Calgary AB T2Z 4M3, Canada — Ice Hockey Player
Patterson, D Corey
1115 Gordon Combs Road NW, Marietta GA 30064, USA — Baseball Player
Patterson, Daryl A
20145 Tollhouse Road, Clovis CA 93619, USA — Baseball Player
Patterson, Elvis V
8915 Allman Road, Lenexa KS 66219, USA — Football Player
Patterson, Francine G (Penny)
Gorilla Foundation, PO Box 620640, Redwood City CA 94062, USA — Animal Psychologist (Koko Trainer)
Patterson, Gary
Patterson International, 25208 Malibu Road, Malibu CA 90265, USA — Cartoonist
Patterson, Gary
Texas Christian University, Athletic Dept, Fort Worth TX 76129, USA — Football Coach
Patterson, James
10 Red Horse Hill Road, Sharon CT 06069, USA — Writer, Businessman
Patterson, James T
Brown University, History Dept, Providence RI 02912, USA — Historian
Patterson, John H
2709 Country Club Dr, Orange TX 77630, USA — Baseball Player
Patterson, John M
Court of Judiciary, PO Box 30155, Montgomery AL 36103, USA — Governor, AL
Patterson, K Shawn
15711 E Avenida del Ville Court, Chandler AZ 85249, USA — Football Player
Patterson, Kenneth B (Ken)
1202 Maverick Trail, McGregor TX 76657, USA — Baseball Player
Patterson, Lorna
23852 Pacific Coast Highway, #355, Malibu CA 90265, USA — Actress
Patterson, Marnette
Abrams Artists, 9200 W Sunset Blvd, #1125, West Hollywood CA 90069 USA — Actress
Patterson, Michael
J P Morgan Chase, 270 Park Ave, #1200, New York NY 10017, USA — Financier
Patterson, Richard North
PO Box 183, West Tisbury MA 02575, USA — Writer
Patterson, Robert C (Bob)
3106 47th Avenue Lane NE, Hickory NC 28601, USA — Baseball Player
Patterson, Robert M
907 Ironwood Dr, Henderson KY 42420, USA — Vietnam War Army Air Hero (CMH)
Patterson, Ross
B/W/R, 9100 Wilshire Blvd, #500W, Beverly Hills CA 90212 USA — Actor

Patterson, Scott
Hofflund/Polone, 9465 Wilshire Blvd, #420, Beverly Hills CA 90212 USA — *Actor*

Patterson, Scott R
148 Tall Maple Court, Freeburg IL 62243, USA — *Baseball Player*

Patti, Sandi
PO Box 6, Pendleton IN 46064, USA — *Singer, Pianist*

Patti, Thomas
10 Federico Dr, Pittsfield MA 01201, USA — *Artist*

Pattillo, Charles C
11514 Little Bay Harbor Way, Spotsylvania VA 22551, USA — *Air Force General, WW II Hero*

Pattillo, Linda
CNN-TV, News Dept, 820 1st St NE, #1000, Washington DC 20002 USA — *Commentator*

Pattin, Martin W (Marty)
3401 Sweetgrass Court, Lawrence KS 66049, USA — *Baseball Player*

Pattinson, Robert
Curtis Brown Group, 28-29 Haymarket St, #500, London SW1Y 4SP, England — *Actor*

Patton, Carl V
Georgia State University, President's Office, Atlanta GA 30303, USA — *Educator*

Patton, Marvcus R
110 Gallatin St NW, Washington DC 20011, USA — *Football Player*

Patton, Melvin (Mel)
2312 Via del Aguagate, Fallbrook CA 92028, USA — *Track Athlete*

Patton, Mike
Ipecac Records, PO Box 1778, Orinda CA 94563, USA — *Singer (Faith No More)*

Patton, Paula
W M E Entertainment, 9601 Wilshire Blvd, #300, Beverly Hills CA 90210 USA — *Actress*

Patton, Ricky R
1454 Brookline Court SE, Mableton GA 30126, USA — *Football Player*

Patton, Troy J
33635 W Decker Dr, Magnolia TX 77355, USA — *Baseball Player*

Patton, William C (Will)
Paradigm Agency, 360 N Crescent Dr, North Building, Beverly Hills CA 90210 USA — *Actor*

Patty, J Edward (Budge)
La Marne, 14 Ave de Jurigoz, 1006 Lausanne, Switzerland — *Tennis Player*

Patulski, Walter G (Walt)
420 Kimber Road, Syracuse NY 13224, USA — *Football Player*

Patzaichin, Ivan
S C Sportiv Unirea Tricolor, Soseaua Stefan Cel Mare 9, Bucharest, Romania — *Canoeing Athlete*

Patzakis, Michele
Prappas Co, 9201 Wilshire Blvd, #204, Beverly Hills CA 90210, USA — *Opera Singer*

Pau, Peter
Gersh Agency, 9465 Wilshire Blvd, #600, Beverly Hills CA 90212 USA — *Cinematographer*

Pauk, Gyorgy
27 Armitage Road, London NW11 8QT, England — *Concert Violinist*

Paul, Aaron M
United Talent Agency, 9336 Civic Center Dr, Beverly Hills CA 90210 USA — *Actor*

Paul, Adrian
Filmblips, 4968 Yonge St, #2911, Toronto ON M2N 7G9, Canada — *Actor*

Paul, Alexandra
Forster Entertainment, 12533 Woodgreen St, Building B, Los Angeles CA 90036, USA — *Actress*

Paul, Billy
8215 Winthrop St, Philadelphia PA 19136, USA — *Singer*

Paul, Christi
CNN-TV, 190 Marietta Ave SW, Atlanta GA 30303 USA — *Commentator*

Paul, Christiane
Players Agentur Mgmt, Sophienstr 21, 10178 Berlin-Mille, Germany — *Actress*

Paul, Christopher E (Chris)
749 Fountain Brook Lane, Lewisville NC 27023, USA — *Basketball Player*

Paul, Don Michael
A P A Talent/Literary Agency, 405 S Beverly Dr, #300, Beverly Hills CA 90212 USA — *Director, Writer, Actor*

Paul, Henry
Debra McCloud Accounting, 1400 18th Ave S, #C3, Nashville TN 37212, USA — *Singer (BlackHawk), Songwriter*

Paul, Jarrad
Principato-Young, 9465 Wilshire Blvd, #880, Beverly Hills CA 90212 USA — *Actor, Writer*

Paul, Joshua W (Josh)
4126 Canoga Park Dr, Brandon FL 33511, USA — *Baseball Player*

Paul, Kevin
Jana Luker Agency, 1923 1/2 Westwood Blvd, #3, Los Angeles CA 90025, USA — *Actor*

Paul, Markus D
2322 Oliver Court, Mahwah NJ 07430, USA — *Football Player*

Paul, Michael G (Mike)
5121 N Circulo Sobrio, Tucson AZ 85718, USA — *Baseball Player*

Paul, Robert
10675 Rochester Ave, Los Angeles CA 90024, USA — *Figure Skater*

Paul, Sean
Susan Blond Inc, 50 W 57th St, #1400, New York NY 10019 USA — *Rap Artist (Youngbloodz)*

Paul, Tito J
2394 Ness Court, Powell OH 43065, USA — *Football Player*

Paul, Tommy
3578 Village Green Dr, Sarasota FL 34239, USA — *Boxer*

Paul, Vinnie
Concrete Mgmt, 361 W Broadway, #200, New York NY 10013, USA — *Drummer (Pantera)*

Paul, Whitney
6802 Thornwild Road, Missouri City TX 77489, USA — *Football Player*

Paul, Wolfgang J
Postfach 1324, 59939 Olsberg-Bigge, Germany — *Soccer Player*

Paula, Alejandro F (Jandi)
Premier's Office, Fort Amsterdam 17, Willemstad, Netherlands Antilles — *Prime Minister, Netherlands Antilles*

Paulauskas, Arturas
Seimas, Gedimino Pr 53, LT 2600 Vilnius, Lithuania — *President, Lithuania*

Pauley, Jane
I C M Partners, 10250 Constellation Blvd, #900, Los Angeles CA 90067, USA — *Commentator*

Paulino, Ronny A
129 Cardinal Circle, Pittsburgh PA 15237, USA — *Baseball Player*

Pauls, Raymond
Veidenbaum Str 41/43, #26, 226001 Riga, Latvia — *Jazz Pianist, Composer*

V.I.P. Address Book

Paulsen, Gary
126 Bookout NE, Tularosa NM 88352, USA — Writer
Paulsen, Robert (Rob)
Sutton-Barth Vennari, 145 S Fairfax Ave, #310, Los Angeles CA 90036 USA — Actor
Paulsen, Tiffany
Creative Artists Agency, 2000 Ave of Stars, #100, Los Angeles CA 90067 USA — Actress
Paulson, Carl
8211 Tibet Butler Dr, Windermere FL 34786, USA — Golfer
Paulson, Dainard A
2904 Main St, Union Gap WA 98903, USA — Football Player
Paulson, Dennis J
1872 Shadetree Dr, San Marcos CA 92078, USA — Golfer
Paulson, Henry M (Hank), Jr
401 N Michigan Ave, #3100, Chicago IL 60611, USA — Secretary, Treasury; Financier
Paulson, Jay
Ira Belgrade Mgmt, 5850E W 3rd St, Los Angeles CA 90036, USA — Actor
Paulson, Kenneth
Newseum, 555 Pennsylvania Ave NW, Washington DC 20001, USA — Editor, Foundation Executive
Paulson, Richard L
Potlatch Corp, 601 W Riverside Ave, #1100, Spokane WA 99201, USA — Businessman
Paulson, Sarah
United Talent Agency, 9336 Civic Center Dr, Beverly Hills CA 90210 USA — Actress
Paultz, William E (Billy)
1914 Waters Edge Lane, Seabrook TX 77586, USA — Basketball Player
Paulus, Diane
Gersh Agency, 9465 Wilshire Blvd, #600, Beverly Hills CA 90212 USA — Director, Writer
Paup, Bryce E
4300 Oak Ridge Circle, De Pere WI 54115, USA — Football Player
Pausini, Laura
Gentemusic Mgmt, Piazza della Conciliazione 5, 20123 Milano, Italy — Singer, Songwriter
Pavan, Marisa
4 Allee des Brouillards, 75018 Paris, France — Actress
Pavan, Sarah L
University of Nebraska, Athletic Dept, Lincoln NE 68588, USA — Volleyball Player
Pavano, Carl A
PO Box 1307, Thomasville GA 31799, USA — Baseball Player
Pavelich, Mark T
19 E Norwood Shores, Lutsen MN 55612, USA — Ice Hockey Player
Pavelich, Martin N (Marty)
1709 Forest Lane, Bloomfield Hills MI 48301, USA — Ice Hockey Player
Pavese, James P (Jim)
65 Whittier Dr, Kings Park NY 11754, USA — Ice Hockey Player
Pavia, Ria
TalentWorks, 3500 W Olive Ave, #1400, Burbank CA 91505 USA — Actress
Pavin, Corey
4332 Gilbert Ave, Dallas TX 75219, USA — Golfer
Pavlas, David L
PO Box 1224, Shiner TX 77984, USA — Baseball Player
Pavletich, Donald S (Don)
13645 Adelaide Lane, Brookfield WI 53005, USA — Baseball Player
Pavlik, Kelly (Ghost)
949 Cornell Ave, Youngstown OH 44502, USA — Boxer
Pavlik, Roger A
622 Beaver Bend Road, Houston TX 77037, USA — Baseball Player
Pavlo
Agency Group Ltd, 142 W 57th St, #600, New York NY 10019 USA — Guitar Player
Pavlovic, Aleksandar (Sasha)
Boston Celtics, 226 Causeway St, #4, Boston MA 02114 USA — Basketball Player
Pawelczyk, James A (Jim)
N A S A, Johnson Space Center, 2101 NASA Road, Houston TX 77058 USA — Astronaut
Pawlak, Waldemar
Zarzad Glowny ZOSP RP, Ul Obozna 1, 00 340 Warsaw, Poland — Prime Minister, Poland
Pawlenty, Timothy J (Tim)
Financial Services Roundtable, 1001 Pennsylvania Ave NW, #500 South, Washington DC 20004, USA — Governor, MN
Pawlikowski, Pawel
Creative Artists Agency, 2000 Ave of Stars, #100, Los Angeles CA 90067 USA — Director
Pawlowski, John
257 Mill Branch Way, North Augusta SC 29860, USA — Baseball Player
Pawson, Anthony J
Mount Sinai Hospital, 600 University Ave, Toronto ON M5G 1X5, Canada — Microbiologist
Pawson, John
70-78 York Way, #B, London N1 9AG, England — Architect
Paxon, L William (Bill)
Akin Gump Strauss Hauer, 1333 New Hampshire NW, #400, Washington DC 20036, USA — Representative, NY
Paxson, James E (Jim)
3225 Southdale Dr, #1, Dayton OH 45409, USA — Basketball Player
Paxson, John M
125 Boardman Court, Lake Bluff IL 60044, USA — Basketball Player, Executive
Paxton, Leonitas E (Lonie), III
2495 Oak Vista Court, Castle Rock CO 80104, USA — Football Player
Paxton, Michael D (Mike)
1145 S Indian Wells Dr, Collierville TN 38017, USA — Baseball Player
Paxton, Robert O
460 Riverside Dr, #72, New York NY 10027, USA — Historian
Paxton, Sara
United Talent Agency, 9336 Civic Center Dr, Beverly Hills CA 90210 USA — Actress
Paxton, Tom
Fleming Tamulevich Assoc, 733 N Main St, Ann Arbor MI 48104, USA — Singer, Songwriter
Paxton, William A (Bill)
W M E Entertainment, 9601 Wilshire Blvd, #300, Beverly Hills CA 90210 USA — Actor
Payer, Serge
2343 Lorraine St, RR 1, Rockland ON K4K 1K7, Canada — Ice Hockey Player
Payette, Julie
Space Agency, Rockliffe Base, Ottawa ON K1A 1A1, Canada — Astronaut, Canada
Paymah, Karl
PO Box 4268, Culver City CA 90231, USA — Football Player

P

Paymer, David — Actor
A P A Talent/Literary Agency, 405 S Beverly Dr, #300, Beverly Hills CA 90212 USA

Payne, Alexander — Director, Producer, Writer
Ad Hominem Enterprises, 506 Santa Monica Blvd, #400, Santa Monica CA 90401, USA

Payne, Allen — Actor
Harrison Stokes, 8730 W Sunset Blvd, #270, West Hollywood CA 90069, USA

Payne, Anthony E — Composer
2 Wilton Square, London N1 3DL, England

Payne, Bruce — Actor
Gilbertson Entertainment, 1334 3rd Street Promenade, #201, Santa Monica CA 90401 USA

Payne, C Ladell — Educator
Randolph-Macon College, President's Office, Ashland VA 23005, USA

Payne, David N — Optical Fiber Engineer
Southampton University, Electronics Dept, Highfield, Southampton SO17 1BJ, England

Payne, Dougie — Bassist (Travis)
Wildlife Entertainment, 21 Heathmans Road, London SW6 4TJ, England

Payne, Freda — Singer, Actress
Scott Stander Assoc, 4533 Van Nuys Blvd, #401, Sherman Oaks CA 91403 USA

Payne, Harry C — Educator
Williams College, President's Office, Williamstown MA 01267, USA

Payne, Henry — Editorial Cartoonist
Detroit News, Editorial Dept, 615 W Lafayette, Detroit MI 48226, USA

Payne, Julie — Actress
Pakula/King, 9229 W Sunset Blvd, #315, West Hollywood CA 90069 USA

Payne, Keith — Vietnam War Australian Army Hero (VC)
2 Saint Bee's Ave, Bucasia QLD 4740, Australia

Payne, Keri-Anne — Swimmer
Stockport Metro, 12 Grand Central Square, Stockport SK1 3TA, England

Payne, Roger S — Biologist, Conservationist
191 Western Road, Lincoln MA 01773, USA

Payne, Seth C — Football Player
PO Box 787, Portville NY 14770, USA

Payne, Steven J (Steve) — Ice Hockey Player
N6497 County Road N, Beldenville WI 54003, USA

Payne, Tom — Actor
Paradigm Agency, 360 N Crescent Dr, North Building, Beverly Hills CA 90210 USA

Payne, Waylon — Singer, Actor
Nine Yards Entertainment, 8530 Wilshire Blvd, #500, Beverly Hills CA 90211 USA

Pays, Amanda — Actress
Origin Talent, 4705 Laurel Canyon Blvd, #306 , Studio City CA 91607, USA

Payton, Benjamin F — Educator
20200 Chapel Trace, Estero FL 33928, USA

Payton, Christian — Actor
Grossman & Jack Talent, 33 W Grand Ave, #402, Chicago IL 60654, USA

Payton, Edward (Eddie) — Football Player
118 Woodland Hills Blvd, Madison MS 39110, USA

Payton, Gary D — Basketball Player
2745 S Monte Cristo Way, Las Vegas NV 89117, USA

Payton, Gary E — Astronaut
2367 Diamond Creek Dr, Colorado Springs CO 80921, USA

Payton, Jason L (Jay) — Baseball Player
3000 Cone Manor Lane, Raleigh NC 27613, USA

Payton, Nicholas — Jazz Trumpeter
Management Ark, 116 Village Blvd, #200, Princeton NJ 08540, USA

Payton, Sean — Football Player, Coach
2006 Brazos Court, Westlake TX 76262, USA

Pazienza, Vinny — Boxer
54 Tivoli Court, Warwick RI 02886, USA

Peace, Terry — Actor
PO Box 74, Allison Park PA 15101, USA

Peaches — Singer, Songwriter
Butterscotch Castle, 535 Geary St, #612, San Francisco CA 94102, USA

Peacock, Alice — Singer, Songwriter
Aware Records, 1316 Sherman Ave, #215, Evanston IL 60201, USA

Peacock, Andrew S — Government Official, Australia
19 Queens Road, Melbourne VIC 3004, Australia

Peake, Don — Guitarist, Composer
Marcelli Co, 11333 Moorpark, #411, Studio City CA 91602, USA

Peake, Pat — Ice Hockey Player
327 Hecht Dr, Madison Heights MI 48071, USA

Peake, Ryan A — Singer, Guitarist (Nickelback)
Union Entertainment Group, 17737 Ventura Blvd, #208, Encino CA 91316, USA

Peaker, E J — Actress
4935 Densmore Ave, Encino CA 91436, USA

Pear, David L (Dave) — Football Player
3126 199th Ave SE, Sammamish WA 98075, USA

Pearce, Guy — Actor
Shanahan Mgmt, PO Box 1509, Darlinghurst NSW 1300, Australia

Pearce, Jacqueline — Actress
Rhubarb Personal Mgmt, 6 Langley St, #41, London WC2H 9JA, England

Pearce, Oscar — Actor
Ken McReddie Assoc, 11 Connaught Place, London W2 2ET, England

Pearce, Reynold — Fashion Designer
Pearce Fionda, Loft, 27 Horsell Road, Highbury, London N5 1XL, England

Pearce, Stephen — Religious Leader, Rabbi
Congregation Emanuel, 2 Lake St, San Francisco CA 94118, USA

Pearce, Steven W (Steve) — Baseball Player
1928 E Gachet Blvd, Lakeland FL 33813, USA

Pearcy, Stephen — Singer (Ratt)
Paradise Artists, PO Box 1821, Ojai CA 93024 USA

Pearl, Barry — Actor
Coolwaters Productions, 10061 Riverside Dr, Box 531, Toluca Lake CA 91602 USA

Pearl, Judea — Computer Scientist, Statistician
University of California, Computer Science Dept, Los Angeles CA 90024, USA

Pearlstein, Philip — Artist
361 W 36th St, New York NY 10018, USA

Pearlstein, Randy	Actor
Bleeker Street Entertainment, 853 Broadway, #1214, New York NY 10003, USA	
Pearlstein, Steven	Journalist
Washington Post, Editorial Dept, 1150 15th St NW, Washington DC 20071 USA	
Pearlstine, Norman	Editor
Carlyle Group, 1000 Pennsylvania Ave NW, Washington DC 20003, USA	
Pearman, F Alvin, Jr	Football Player
5601 Chadfort Lane, Charlotte NC 28226, USA	
Pearson, Albert G (Albie)	Baseball Player
55473 Oakhill, La Quinta CA 92253, USA	
Pearson, Allison	Writer
Knopf Publishers, 1745 Broadway, New York NY 10019 USA	
Pearson, Becky	Golfer
1630 SW 8th Ave, Boca Raton FL 33486, USA	
Pearson, David G	Auto Racing Driver
290 Burnett Road, Boiling Springs SC 29316, USA	
Pearson, Drew	Football Player
3721 Mount Vernon Way, Plano TX 75025, USA	
Pearson, Jayice (J C)	Football Player
721 SW Winterhill Lane, Lees Summit MO 64081, USA	
Pearson, Keir	Writer, Editor, Producer
Management 360, 9111 Wilshire Blvd, Beverly Hills CA 90210 USA	
Pearson, Larry	Auto Racing Driver
Buckshot Racing, 182 Belue Road, Spartansburg SC 29303, USA	
Pearson, Mike Parker	Archaeologist
Sheffield University, Archaeology Dept, Sheffield S1 4ET, England	
Pearson, Preston J	Football Player
Pro Style Assoc, 9104 Moss Farm Lane, Dallas TX 75243, USA	
Pearson, Ralph G	Chemist
715 Grove Lane, Santa Barbara CA 93105, USA	
Pearson, Richard (Rick)	Editor
I C M Partners, 10250 Constellation Blvd, #900, Los Angeles CA 90067 USA	
Pearson, Ridley	Writer
Dell Books, 1745 Broadway, New York NY 10019 USA	
Pearson, Robert G	Ice Hockey Player
Beyond the Point, 467 Meadow St, Oshawa ON L1L 1B9, Canada	
Pearson, Scott	Ice Hockey Player
Medassets Inc, 100 N Point Center E, #200, Alpharetta GA 30022, USA	
Pearson, T R	Writer
Crown Publishing Group, 1745 Broadway, New York NY 10019 USA	
Peart, Neal	Drummer (Rush)
S L Feldman Mgmt, 1505 W 2nd Ave, #200, Vancouver BC V6H 3Y4, Canada	
Pease, Patsy	Actress
15432 Hartland St, Van Nuys CA 91406, USA	
Pease, Rendel S	Physicist
Poplars, West Isley, Newbury, Berks RG20 7AW, England	
Peavy, Jacob E (Jake)	Baseball Player
PO Box 346, Catherine AL 36728, USA	
Peay, Francis	Football Player, Coach
541 Morgan St, Pittsburgh PA 15219, USA	
Peca, Michael A (Mike)	Ice Hockey Player
46 Golden Pheasant Dr, Getzville NY 14068, USA	
Pechstein, Claudia	Speed Skater
Powerplay Mgmt, Seeburger Chaussee 2, 14467 Gross Glienicke, Germany	
Peck, Austin	Actor
Stone Manners Salners, 9911 W Pico Blvd, #1400, Los Angeles CA 90035 USA	
Peck, Carolyn	Basketball Player, Coach
University of Florida, Athletic Dept, Gainesville FL 32611, USA	
Peck, Cecilia	Actress
Cabin Creek Films, 270 Lafayette St, #710, New York NY 10012, USA	
Peck, Ethan	Actor
I C M Partners, 10250 Constellation Blvd, #900, Los Angeles CA 90067 USA	
Peck, J Eddie	Actor
Thirdhill Entertainment, 195 S Beverly Dr, #400, Beverly Hills CA 90212, USA	
Peck, Josh	Actor
Collective, 8383 Wilshire Blvd, #1050, Beverly Hills CA 90211 USA	
Peck, Raoul	Director, Producer, Writer
United Talent Agency, 9336 Civic Center Dr, Beverly Hills CA 90210 USA	
Peck, Richard E	Educator, Writer
96 Homesteads Road, Placitas NM 87043, USA	
Peck, Robert Newton	Writer
500 Sweetwater Club Circle, Longwood FL 32779, USA	
Peck, Tom	Auto Racing Driver
417 E North St, McConnellsburg PA 17233, USA	
Pecker, David J	Publisher
American Media, 600 S East Coast Ave, Lantana FL 33462, USA	
Pecker, Jean-Claude	Astronomer
Pusat-Tasek, Les Corbeaux, 85350 L'lle d'Yeu, France	
Peckovam Dagmar	Opera Singer
Na Pankraci 101, 140 00 Prague 4, Czech Republic	
Pecota, William J (Bill)	Baseball Player
332 NE Warrington Court, Lees Summit MO 64064, USA	
Pecqueur, Mario	Actor
Artmedia, 20 Ave Rapp, 75007 Paris, France	
Pedersen, Allen (Al)	Ice Hockey Player
2261 Fieldcrest Dr, Colorado Springs CO 80921, USA	
Pedersen, William	Architect
Kohn Pedersen Fox Assoc, 111 W 57th St, #300, New York NY 10019, USA	
Pedersen-Bieri, Maya	Skeleton Athlete
Saeter, 3818 Oyer, Norway	
Pedersen, Barry A	Ice Hockey Player
18 Cutting Road, Swampscott MA 01907, USA	
Pedersen, Denis E	Ice Hockey Player
74 Cummings Circle, West Orange NJ 07052, USA	
Pedersen, Douglas I (Doug)	Football Player
12 Gladwynne Terrace, Moorestown NJ 08057, USA	

P

Paetkau - Pederson

Pederson, Mark
151 Equestrian Lane, Kalispell MT 59901, USA — Ice Hockey Player

Pedrad, Nasim
Principato-Young, 9465 Wilshire Blvd, #880, Beverly Hills CA 90212 USA — Actor, Comedian

Pedregon, Cruz
Cruz Pedregon Racing, 462 South Point Circle, #A, Brownsburg IN 46112, USA — Drag Racing Driver

Pedregon, Frank
Frank Pedregon Racing, 6174 Cabernet Place, Alta Loma CA 91766, USA — Drag Racing Driver

Pedretti, Adam
Harbour Agency, 135 Forbes St, Woolloomooloo NSW 2011, Australia — Drummer (Killing Heidi)

Pedrique, Alfredo J (Al)
10382 E Oakbrook St, Tucson AZ 85747, USA — Baseball Player

Pedro, James A (Jimmy)
52 Valley St, Wakefield MA 01880, USA — Judo Athlete

Pedroia, Dustin L
26425 S 116th St, Chandler AZ 85249, USA — Baseball Player

Pedroni, Simone
Pro Arte, Fosswinckelsgt 9, 5007 Bergen, Norway — Concert Pianist

Peebles, Ann
Bullseye Blues, 1 Rounder Way, Burlington MA 01803, USA — Singer

Peebles, P James E
24 Markham Road, Princeton NJ 08540, USA — Physicist, Educator

Peek, Antwan M
19555 E Kerry Place, Strongsville OH 44149, USA — Football Player

Peeler, Anthony E
4502 E 48th St, Kansas City MO 64130, USA — Basketball Player

Peelle, Justin M
14040 Iris Lane, Poway CA 92064, USA — Football Player

Peeples, George
1032 Loma Lisa Lane, Arcadia CA 91006, USA — Basketball Player

Peeples, Lewis
Paramount Entertainment, 12 Kosakowski Dr, Morris Plains NJ 07590 USA — Singer (Five Satins)

Peeples, Nia
Levity Entertainment Group, 6701 Center Drive W, #1111, Los Angeles CA 90045, USA — Actress, Singer

Peerce, Larry
225 W 34th St, #1012, New York NY 10122, USA — Director

Peers, Holly J
Samantha Bond Mgmt, Elysium Gate, 126-128 New Kings Road, London SW6 4LZ, England — Model

Peet, Amanda
Management 360, 9111 Wilshire Blvd, Beverly Hills CA 90210 USA — Actress

Peete, Calvin
128 Garden Gate Dr, Ponte Vedra Beach FL 32082, USA — Golfer

Peete, Rodney
11964 Crest Place, Beverly Hills CA 90210, USA — Football Player

Peeters, Pete
Peeters Farm, Namao AB T0A 2N0, Canada — Ice Hockey Player

Pegg, Simon
United Talent Agency, 9336 Civic Center Dr, Beverly Hills CA 90210 USA — Actor, Comedian, Writer

Pegram, Erric D
5913 Sterling Trail, McKinney TX 75071, USA — Football Player

Pei, Ieoh Ming (I M)
11 Sutton Place, New York NY 10022, USA — Pritzker Architectural Laureate

Peinemann, Edith
Pro Musicis, Ruetistr 38, 8032 Zurich, Switzerland — Concert Pianist

Peirce, Kimberly
Creative Artists Agency, 2000 Ave of Stars, #100, Los Angeles CA 90067 USA — Director, Producer, Writer

Peirse, Sarah
R G M Associates, 64-76 Kippax St, #202, Surry Hills NSW 2010, Australia — Actress

Peirsol, Aaron
4110 Shoal Creek Blvd, Austin TX 78756, USA — Swimmer

Peirson, John
3 Steepletree Lane, Wayland MA 01778, USA — Ice Hockey Player, Sportscaster

Peizewat, Gwendal
Sports de Glace Federation, 35 Rue Felicien David, 75016 Paris, France — Ice Dancer

Pejman, Bob
Pejman Gallery, 509 Millburn Ave, Short Hills NJ 07078, USA — Artist

Pekarkova, Iva
Farrar Straus Giroux, 18 W 18th St, #700, New York NY 10011 USA — Writer

Peldon, Ashley
Marshak/Zachary Co, 8840 Wilshire Blvd, #100, Beverly Hills CA 90211 USA — Actress

Peldon, Courtney
Bartels Co, PO Box 57593, Sherman Oaks CA 91413, USA — Actress

Pele
Rua Riachuelo 121-3, Andar-Fones 34-1633/35 Santos SP, Brazil — Soccer Player

Pelecanos, George P
Little Brown, 3 Center Plaza, #100, Boston MA 02108 USA — Writer

Pelen, Perrine
31 Ave de l'Eygala, 38700 Corens Mont Fleury, France — Alpine Skier

Pelfrey, Michael A (Mike)
1204 Suncast Lane, #2, El Dorado Hills CA 95762, USA — Baseball Player

Pelikan, Lisa
Diamond Mgmt, 31 Percy St, London W1T 2DD, England — Actress

Pelini, Mark (Bo)
University of Nebraska, Athletic Dept, Lincoln NE 68588, USA — Football Coach

Pell, George Cardinal
Archdiocese, Polding Centre, 133 Liverpool St, Sydney NSW 2000, Australia — Religious Leader

Pell, Paula
W M E Entertainment, 9601 Wilshire Blvd, #300, Beverly Hills CA 90210 USA — Writer

Pellea, Oana
Ken McReddie Assoc, 11 Connaught Place, London W2 2ET, England — Actress

Pellegrini, Margaret
5018 N 61st Ave, Glendale AZ 85301, USA — Actress

Pellegrino, Edmund D
5610 Wisconsin Ave, Chevy Chase MD 20815, USA — Physician

Pellegrino, Mark
Domain Talent, 9229 W Sunset Blvd, #710, West Hollywood CA 90069 USA — Actor

Pellerin, Scott — Ice Hockey Player
10 Dunraven Road, Windham NH 03087, USA
Pelletier, David J — Ice Dancer
12116 NW 128th St, Edmonton AB T5L 1C3, Canada
Pelletier, Marcel — Ice Hockey Player
Boston Bruins, 100 Legends Way, #250, Boston MA 02114 USA
Pelletreau, Robert H, Jr — Diplomat
State Department, 2201 C St NW, Washington DC 20520 USA
Pelley, Scott — Commentator
CBS-TV, News Dept, 51 W 52nd St, New York NY 10019 USA
Pelli, Cesar A — Architect
Cesar Pelli Assoc, 1056 Chapel St, New Haven CT 06510, USA
Pellington, Mark — Director
United Talent Agency, 9336 Civic Center Dr, Beverly Hills CA 90210 USA
Pelluer, Steven C (Steve) — Football Player
2632 W Lake Sammamish Parkway NE, Redmond WA 98052, USA
Pelphrey, John — Basketball Coach
University of Arkansas, Athletic Dept, Fayetteville AR 72701, USA
Peltason, Jack W — Educator
18 Whistler Court, Irvine CA 92617, USA
Pelton, M Lee — Educator
Willamette University, President's Office, 900 State St, Salem OR 97301, USA
Peltonen, Ville — Ice Hockey Player
Dynamo Minsk, Minsk Arena, Pr Pobeditelei 111, 220116 Minsk, Belarus
Peltz, J Russell — Boxing Promoter
Peltz Boxing Promotions, 2501 Brown St, Philadelphia PA 19130, USA
Peltz, Nelson — Businessman
Triarc Companies, 900 3rd Ave, New York NY 10022, USA
Peluce, Meeno — Actor
PO Box 3743, Glendale CA 91221, USA
Peluso, Lisa — Actress
Shauna Sickenger, PO Box 301, Ramona CA 92065, USA
Peluso, Michael D (Mike) — Ice Hockey Player
3616 W Fuller St, Edina, MN 55410, USA
Pelyk, Michael J (Mike) — Ice Hockey Player
56-385 East Mall, Toronto ON M9B 6J4, Canada
Pelzer, Dave — Writer
D-Esprit, PO Box 1846, Rancho Mirage CA 92270, USA
Pemberton, Johnny — Actor
Principato-Young, 9465 Wilshire Blvd, #880, Beverly Hills CA 90212 USA
Pena Martinez, Geronimo — Baseball Player
KM 17 7 Pista Duarte, Los Alcarrizzos, Dominican Republic
Pena Nieto, Enrique — President, Mexico
Palacio Nacional, Los Pinos, Puerto 1, 11850 Mexico City DF, Mexico
Pena Padilla, Antonio F (Tony) — Baseball Player, Manager
New York Yankees, Yankee Stadium, E 161st St & River Ave, Bronx NY 10451 USA
Pena Vasquez, Alejandro — Baseball Player
12635 Etris Road, Roswell GA 30075, USA
Pena, Anthony — Actor
Sha'Lin Talent Mgmt, PO Box 11411, Burbank CA 91510, USA
Pena, Carlos F — Baseball Player
4248 Cascada Circle, Hollywood FL 33024, USA
Pena, Elizabeth — Actress
Bauman Redanty Shaul Agency, 5757 Wilshire Blvd, #473, Los Angeles CA 90036 USA
Pena, Federico F — Secretary, Transportation, Energy
362 Detroit St, #A, Denver CO 80206, USA
Pena, Jennifer M — Singer
C E S D, 10635 Santa Monica Blvd, #130, Los Angeles CA 90025 USA
Pena, Michael A — Actor
Management 360, 9111 Wilshire Blvd, Beverly Hills CA 90210 USA
Pena, Orlando G — Baseball Player
1750 W 46th St, #416, Hialeah FL 33012, USA
Pena, Paco — Concert Guitarist, Composer
Wim Visser Ruysdaelkade 5, 1072 AG Amsterdam, Netherlands
Pena, Wilfredo M (Wily Mo) — Baseball Player
27250 Breakers Dr, Wesley Chapel FL 33544, USA
Penacoli, Jerry — Entertainer
I C M Partners, 10250 Constellation Blvd, #900, Los Angeles CA 90067 USA
Penate, Jack — Singer, Songwriter
United Agents, 12-26 Lexington St, London W1F 0LE, England
Pence, Hunter A — Baseball Player
10301 Wagon Road W, Austin TX 78736, USA
Penchion, Robert E (Bob) — Football Player
110 Elliott Ave, Muscle Shoals AL 35661, USA
Pendatchanska, Alexandrina — Opera Singer
Opera et Concert, 37 Rue de la Chaussee d'Antin, 75009 Paris, France
Pender, Melvin (Mel) — Track Athlete
2330 Goodwood Blvd SE, Smyrna GA 30080, USA
Penderecki, Krzysztof — Composer, Conductor
Ul Cisowa 22, 30-229 Cracow, Poland
Pendergrass, Henry P — Physician
Vanderbilt University Medical School, 1621 21st Ave S, Nashville TN 37212, USA
Penders, Tom — Basketball Coach
George Washington University, Athletic Dept, Washington DC 20052, USA
Pendleton, Moses — Dancer, Choreographer
Momix, PO Box 35, Washington CT 06794, USA
Pendleton, Terry L — Baseball Player
332 Grassmeade Way, Snellville GA 30078, USA
Pendleton, Victoria — Cyclist
Three60 Sports Mgmt, 158-160 North Gower St, London NW1 2ND, England
Penghlis, Thaao — Actor
Metropolitan Talent Agency, 7020 La Presa Dr, Los Angeles CA 90068 USA
Pengily, Kirk — Guitarist, Saxophonist, Singer (INXS)
8 Hayes St, #1, Neutral Bay 20891 NSW, Australia
Pengo, Polycarp Cardinal — Religious Leader
PO Box 167, Dar-es-Salaam, Tanzania

Penhall, Joe — Director, Writer
Judy Daish Assoc, 2 Saint Charles Place, London W10 6EG, England
Penicheiro, Ticha — Basketball Player
Los Angeles Sparks, 888 S Figueroa St, #2010, Los Angeles CA 90017 USA
Penick, Trevor — Singer (O-Town)
Trans Continental Records, 127 W Church St, #350, Orlando FL 32801, USA
Penikett, Tahmoh — Actor
Lucas Talent, Sun Tower, 100 W Pender, #700, Vancouver BC V6B 1RB, Canada
Peniston, CeCe — Singer
250 W 57th St, #821, New York NY 10107, USA
Penky, Joseph F — Chemical Engineer
Purdue University, Chemical Engineering Dept, West Lafayette IN 47907, USA
Penn, (Jillette) — Comedian, Illusionist (Penn & Teller)
A P A Talent/Literary Agency, 405 S Beverly Dr, #300, Beverly Hills CA 90212 USA
Penn, Christopher A (Chris) — Football Player
PO Box 123, South Coffeyville OK 74072, USA
Penn, Kal — Actor
Gersh Agency, 9465 Wilshire Blvd, #600, Beverly Hills CA 90212 USA
Penn, Michael — Singer, Songwriter
H K Mgmt, 9200 W Sunset Blvd, #530, West Hollywood CA 90069 USA
Penn, Sean — Actor, Director
Creative Artists Agency, 2000 Ave of Stars, #100, Los Angeles CA 90067 USA
Penn, Zak — Director, Producer, Writer, Actor
Zak Penn's Co, 6240 W 3rd St, #421, Los Angeles CA 90036, USA
Pennacchio, Len A — Geneticist
Stanford University, Human Genome Center, Stanford CA 94305, USA
Penner, Dustin — Ice Hockey Player
117 E Balboa Blvd, Newport Beach, CA 92661, USA
Penner, Jonathan — Actor
I C M Partners, 10250 Constellation Blvd, #900, Los Angeles CA 90067 USA
Penner, Stanford S — Aeronautical Engineer
5912 Avenida Chamnez, La Jolla CA 92037, USA
Penney, Steve — Ice Hockey Player
155 Rue Notre Dame, Saint Pereol des Neiges QC G0A 3R0, Canada
Pennie, Collins — Actor
Untitled Entertainment, 350 S Beverly Dr, #200, Beverly Hills CA 90212 USA
Pennie, Michael W — Sculptor
117 Bradford Road, Atworth, Melksham, Wilts SN12 8HY, England
Pennington, Brad L — Baseball Player
7220 E State Road 160, Salem IN 47167, USA
Pennington, Cliff — Baseball Player
23603 Hartwick Lane, San Antonio TX 78259, USA
Pennington, Clifford (Cliff) — Ice Hockey Player
9960 5th St N, #203, Saint Petersburg FL 33702, USA
Pennington, J Chad — Football Player
133 Willbrook Lane, Clinton TN 37716, USA
Pennington, Janice — Model, Actress
PO Box 11402, Beverly Hills CA 90213, USA
Pennington, Julia — Actress
Judy Schoen, 606 N Larchmont Blvd, #309, Los Angeles CA 90004 USA
Pennington, Michael — Actor
41 Marlborough Hill, London NW8 0NG, England
Pennington, Ty — Actor
Agency S G H, 6525 Sunset Blvd, #900-PH, Los Angeles CA 90028, USA
Pennison, Jay L — Football Player
3007 W Autumn Run Circle, Sugar Land TX 77479, USA
Pennock of Norton, Raymond — Businessman
Morgan Grenfell Group, 23 Great Winchester St, London EC2P 2AX, England
Pennock, Chris — Actor
25150 1/2 Malibu Road, Malibu CA 90265, USA
Penny, Bradley W (Brad) — Baseball Player
25071 Abercrombie Lane, Calabasas CA 91302, USA
Penny, Daniel — Geoscientist
University of Sydney, Geoscience Dept, Sydney NSW 2006, Australia
Penny, Joe — Actor
Gage Group, 14724 Ventura Blvd, #505, Sherman Oaks CA 91403 USA
Penny, Roger P — Businessman
Bethlehem Steel, 1655 Valley Center Parkway, #200, Bethlehem PA 18017, USA
Penny, Sydney — Actress
Stone Manners Salners, 9911 W Pico Blvd, #1400, Los Angeles CA 90035 USA
Pennyfeather, William N (Will) — Baseball Player
333 Rector St, #6D, Perth Amboy NJ 08861, USA
Penot, Jacques — Actor
9 Rue de l'Isly, 75008 Paris, France
Penrose, Patricia (Tricia) — Actress, Singer
International Artists, 193-197 High Holborn, London WC1V 7BD, England
Penry-Jones, Rupert — Actor
Artist Rights Group, 4 Great Portland Place, London W1W 8PA, England
Penske, Roger S — Auto Racing Driver, Executive
Penske Racing, Penske Plaza, 366 Riverfront, Reading PA 19602, USA
Pentecost, Del — Actor
Paradigm Agency, 360 N Crescent Dr, North Building, Beverly Hills CA 90210 USA
Pentland, Alex P — Computer Scientist
Massachusetts Institute of Technology, Media Laboratory, Cambridge MA 02139, USA
Penzias, Arno A — Nobel Physics Laureate
New Enterprise Assoc, 2855 Sand Hill Road, Menlo Park CA 94025, USA
Peoples, David — Golfer
2545 Cedarwood Dr, Germantown TN 38138, USA
Peoples, David Webb — Director, Writer
Creative Artists Agency, 2000 Ave of Stars, #100, Los Angeles CA 90067 USA
Peoples, John — Physicist
Fermi Nat Acceleration Laboratory, C D F Collaboration, PO Box 500, Batavia IL 60510, USA
Peper, Tim — Actor
Paradigm Agency, 360 N Crescent Dr, North Building, Beverly Hills CA 90210 USA
Pepitone, Joseph A (Joe) — Baseball Player
27 Roosevelt Blvd, Massapequa NY 11758, USA

Peplinski, Jim — Ice Hockey Player
Peplinski Auto Leasing, 212 Meridian Road NE, Calgary AB T2A 2N6, Canada
Peplowski, Ken — Jazz Saxophonist, Clarinetist
Columbia Artists Mgmt Inc, 1790 Broadway, #702, New York NY 10019 USA
Pepoy, Andrew — Cartoonist (Annie)
Tribune Media Services, 435 N Michigan Ave, #1500, Chicago IL 60611 USA
Pepper Mochrie, Dorothy (Dottie) — Golfer
PO Box 623, Saratoga Springs NY 12866, USA
Pepper, Barry — Actor
Paul Kohner, 9300 Wilshire Blvd, #555, Beverly Hills CA 90212 USA
Pepper, Beverly — Sculptor
Torre Gentile Di Todi (PG), Italy
Pepper, Cynthia — Actress
219 Friendly Court, Henderson NV 89052, USA
Pepper, John E, Jr — Businessman
Walt Disney Co, 500 S Buena Vista St, Burbank CA 91521, USA
Pepperberg, Irene M — Writer
Harper Collins Publishers, 10 E 53rd St, Cellar 1, New York NY 10022 USA
Peppers, Julius F — Football Player
173 Rehoboth Lane, Mooresville NC 28117, USA
Peppler, Mary Jo — Volleyball Player
Coast Volleyball Club, 11526 Sorrento Valley Road, San Diego CA 92121, USA
Pera, Renee Reijo — Human Reproductive Biologist
University of California Medical Center, 505 Parnassus, San Francisco CA 94122, USA
Perabo, Piper — Actress
United Talent Agency, 9336 Civic Center Dr, Beverly Hills CA 90210 USA
Perahia, Murray — Concert Pianist
Askonas Holt, Lincoln House, 300 High Holborn, London WC1V 7JH, England
Peralta Fabi, Ricardo — Astronaut, Mexico
Ciudad Universitaria, Instituto de Ingenieria, Circuito Escolar Sn, CP 04510, Mexico DF, Mexico
Peralta Morones, Oribe P — Soccer Player
Federacion de Futbol, Colima 373 Colonia Roma, Delegacion Cuauhtemoc Mexico DF 06700, Mexico
Peralta, Jhonny A — Baseball Player
27940 Berringer Run, Westlake OH 44145, USA
Percival, Brian — Director
Gotham Group, 9255 Sunset Blvd, #515, Los Angeles CA 90069, USA
Percival, Lance — Actor
Rhubarb Agency, 1A Devonshire Road, #100, London W4 2EU, England
Percival, Mac L — Football Player
6710 Flowermound Dr, Sugar Land TX 77479, USA
Percival, Troy E — Baseball Player
1090 Coronet Dr, Riverside CA 92506, USA
Perconte, John P (Jack) — Baseball Player
6197 Hinterlong Court, Lisle IL 60532, USA
Perdue, William E (Will) — Basketball Player
6310 Innisbrook Dr, Prospect KY 40059, USA
Perec, Marie-Jose — Track Athlete
H S International Sports Mgmt, 9871 Irvine Center Dr, Irvine CA 92618, USA
Peregrym, Missy — Actress
Gersh Agency, 9465 Wilshire Blvd, #600, Beverly Hills CA 90212 USA
Pereira, Mike — Football Executive, Sportscaster
National Football League, 280 Park Ave, #12W, New York NY 10017, USA
Perek, Lubos — Astronomer
Kourimska 28, 130 00 Prague 3, Czech Republic
Perelman, Ronald O — Businessman
Revlon Group, 35 E 62nd St, New York NY 10065, USA
Perelman, Vadim — Director, Writer
Rumble Media, 1620 Broadway, Santa Monica CA 90403, USA
Perenyi, Miklos — Concert Violinist
Liszt Academy of Music, PO Box 206, Liszt Ter 8, 1391 Budapest, Hungary
Peres, Shimon — Nobel Peace Laureate; President, Israel
President's Office, Beit Hanassi, 3 Hanassi St, Jerusalem 92188, Israel
Peress, Gilles — Photographer
48 Great Jones St, #2SE, New York NY 10012, USA
Peretokin, Mark — Ballet Dancer
Bolshoi Theater, Teatralnaya Pl 1, 103009 Moscow, Russia
Peretz, Jesse — Director
United Talent Agency, 9336 Civic Center Dr, Beverly Hills CA 90210 USA
Pereyra, Marianela — Actress
Brady Brannon Rich, 5670 Wilshire Blvd, #820 , Los Angeles CA 90036, USA
Perez Batista, Manuel M (Manny) — Actor
Don Buchwald/Fortitude, 6500 Wilshire Blvd, #2200, Los Angeles CA 90048 USA
Perez de Cuellar, Javier — Secretary General, United Nations
Avenida Aurelio Miro Quesada 1071, San Isifro, Lima 2, Peru
Perez Esquivel, Adolfo — Nobel Peace Laureate
Servicio Paz y Justicia, Piedras 730, 1070 Buenos Aires, Argentina
Perez Fernandez, Pedro — Government Official, Spain
Partido Socialista Obrero Espanol, Ferraz 68 y 70, 28008 Madrid, Spain
Perez Molina, Otto F — President, Guatemala
President's Office, Palacio Nacional, 6 Avenida 419, Guatemala City, Guatemala
Perez, Amanda — Singer, Songwriter
Paradigm Agency, 360 N Crescent Dr, North Building, Beverly Hills CA 90210 USA
Perez, Antonio M — Businessman
Eastman Kodak Co, 343 State St, Rochester NY 14650, USA
Perez, Atanasio R (Tony) — Baseball Player, Manager
1717 N Bayshore Dr, #3246, Miami FL 33132, USA
Perez, Carmen — Actress
Evolution Entertainment, 901 N Highland Ave, Los Angeles CA 90038 USA
Perez, Chris — Guitarist, Orchestra Leader, Actor
Big F D Entertainment, 301 Arizona Ave, #200, Santa Monica CA 90401, USA
Perez, Christopher R (Chris) — Baseball Player
Cleveland Indians, Jacobs Field, 2401 Ontario St, Cleveland OH 44115 USA
Perez, Eduardo A — Baseball Player
113 Calle Las Flores, San Juan PR 00911, USA
Perez, Hugo E — Soccer Player
22018 Newbridge Dr, Lake Forest CA 92630, USA

Perez, Jossie Columbia Artists Mgmt Inc, 1790 Broadway, #702, New York NY 10019 USA	Opera Singer
Perez, Luiz (Louie) Gold Mountain, 3940 Laurel Canyon Blvd, #444, Studio City CA 91604 USA	Drummer, Singer (Los Lobos)
Perez, Manny Don Buchwald/Fortitude, 6500 Wilshire Blvd, #2200, Los Angeles CA 90048 USA	Actor
Perez, Martin R (Marty), Jr 30 Willowick Dr, Decatur GA 30034, USA	Baseball Player
Perez, Melido T G Nigua KM 21 1/2, Santo Domingo, Dominican Republic	Baseball Player
Perez, Rosie Authentic Talent Mgmt, 45 Main St, #1000, Brooklyn NY 11201, USA	Actress, Singer
Perez, Timothy Paul Three Moons Entertainment, 5441 E Beverly Blvd, #G, Los Angeles CA 90022, USA	Actor
Perez, Vincent United Agents, 12-26 Lexington St, London W1F 0LE, England	Actor, Director
Pergine, John S 5 Jody Dr, Plymouth Meeting PA 19462, USA	Football Player
Perillo, Gregory 2 Blackwell Road, Nesconset NY 11767, USA	Artist
Perine, Kelly Mark Holder Mgmt, 5225 Wilshire Blvd, #600, Los Angeles CA 90036 USA	Actor, Comedian
Perisho, Matthew A (Matt) 1462 W Cardinal Way, Chandler AZ 85286, USA	Baseball Player
Perkin, J D Laura Russo Gallery, 805 NW 21st St, Portland OR 97209, USA	Sculptor
Perkins, Broderick P 5367 San Vicente Blvd, #237, Los Angeles CA 90019, USA	Baseball Player
Perkins, Carl C 1401 15th St, Huntington WV 25701, USA	Representative, KY
Perkins, Courtland D 400 Hilltop Terrace, Alexandria VA 22301, USA	Aeronautical Engineer
Perkins, Donald A (Don) 808 Vassar Dr NE, Albuquerque NM 87106, USA	Football Player
Perkins, Edward J 2801 New Mexico Ave NW, #1407, Washington DC 20007, USA	Diplomat
Perkins, Elizabeth Gersh Agency, 9465 Wilshire Blvd, #600, Beverly Hills CA 90212 USA	Actress
Perkins, Emily Wales University, Film Studies, Aberystwuth, Ceredigion SY23 3AJ, Wales	Actress
Perkins, Glen W 19775 Jersey Ave, Lakeville MN 55044, USA	Baseball Player
Perkins, Gregory S (Tex) MajorBox Music, PO Box 1164, Windsor VIC 3181, Australia	Singer, Songwriter
Perkins, Homer G 372 S Shore Road, Pascoag RI 02859, USA	Businessman
Perkins, Jack A&E Network, 235 E 45th St, New York NY 10017, USA	Commentator
Perkins, John M 1655 Saint Charles St, Jackson MS 39209, USA	Civil Rights Activist
Perkins, Kathleen Rose Trademark Talent, 144 S Beverly Dr, #404, Beverly Hills CA 90212, USA	Actress
Perkins, Kendrick 137 Fox Road, Waltham MA 02451, USA	Basketball Player
Perkins, Kieren GPO Box 232, Brisbane QED 4001, Australia	Swimmer
Perkins, Lawrence B, Jr 4 Rectory Lane, Scarsdale NY 10583, USA	Architect
Perkins, Lucian 3103 17th St NW, Washington DC 20010, USA	Photojournalist
Perkins, Millie 2511 Canyon Dr, Los Angeles CA 90068, USA	Actress
Perkins, Oz Greene Assoc, 1901 Ave of Stars, #130, Los Angeles CA 90067 USA	Actor
Perkins, Polly Associated International Mgmt, Fairfax House, Fulwood Place, London WC1V 6HU, England	Actress
Perkins, Samuel B (Sam) 14901 Bellbrook Dr, Dallas TX 75254, USA	Basketball Player
Perkins, Stephen A DeMann Entertainment, 9465 Wilshire Blvd, #426, Beverly Hills CA 90212, USA	Drummer (Jane's Addiction), Songwriter
Perkins, Susan Y 23 Winsor Way, Weston MA 02493, USA	Beauty Queen
Perkins, Travis Abraxas Talent, 4260 Troost Ave, #1, Studio City CA 91604, USA	Actor
Perkins, W Ray 57 Honors Lane, Hattiesburg MS 39402, USA	Football Player, Coach
Perkins, Warren C (Red) 717 Fairfield Ave, Gretna LA 70056, USA	Basketball Player
Perkowski, Harold W (Harry) 211 McGinnis St, Beckley WV 25801, USA	Baseball Player
Perks, Craig 321 Thibodeaux Dr, Lafayette LA 70503, USA	Golfer
Perl, Frank J 5020 Biloxi Ave, North Hollywood CA 91601, USA	Cinematographer
Perl, Martin L 3737 El Centro Ave, Palo Alto CA 94306, USA	Nobel Physics Laureate
Perlich, Max Anthem Entertainment, 5225 Wilshire Blvd, #615, Los Angeles CA 90036, USA	Actor
Perlini, Fred 409 Albert St W, Sault Sainte Marie ON P6A 1C2, Canada	Ice Hockey Player
Perlman, Harvey University of Nebraska, Chancellor's Office, Lincoln NE 68588, USA	Educator
Perlman, Itzhak I M G Artists, Hogarth Business Park, Chiswick, London W4 2TH, England	Concert Violinist, Conductor
Perlman, Jonathan S (Jon) 3225 Bryn Mawr Dr, Dallas TX 75225, USA	Baseball Player

Perlman, Lawrence — Businessman
Ceridian Corp, 3311 E Old Shakopee Road, Minneapolis MN 55425, USA
Perlman, Navah — Concert Pianist
I M G Artists, Hogarth Business Park, Chiswick, London W4 2TH, England
Perlman, Rhea — Actress
8665 Burton Way, #507, Los Angeles CA 90048, USA
Perlman, Ron — Actor
Kritzer Levine Wilkins Griffin, 11872 La Grange Ave, #100, Los Angeles CA 90025 USA
Perlmutter, Saul — Nobel Physics Laureate
Lawrence Berkeley National Laboratory, 1 Cycloton Road, Berkeley CA 94720 USA
Perlozzo, Samuel B (Sam) — Baseball Player, Manager
18101 Emerald Bay St, Tampa FL 33647, USA
Perls, Tom — Physician
2 Harrington Lane, Weston MA 02493, USA
Perman, Jay A — Educator
University of Maryland, President's Office, 220 Arch St, Baltimore MD 21201, USA
Pernel, Florence — Actress
Artmedia, 20 Ave Rapp, 75007 Paris, France
Pernice, Tom, Jr — Golfer
38390 Shoal Creek Dr, Murrieta CA 92562, USA
Pero, Anthony J (A J) — Singer, Drummer (Twisted Sister)
Rebellion Entertainment, 2440 Broadway, #111, New York NY 10024, USA
Peron, Carlos — Synthesizer Player (Yello)
Creative Artists Agency, 2000 Ave of Stars, #100, Los Angeles CA 90067 USA
Perot, Edward J (Petey) — Football Player
2401 Hillside Road, Ruston LA 71270, USA
Perot, H Ross — Businessman, Presidential Candidate
Perot Systems, 2300 W Plano Parkway, Plano TX 75075, USA
Perot, Henry Ross, Jr — Aviator
Perot Group, Lakeside Square, 12377 Merit Dr, #1700, Dallas TX 75251, USA
Perranoski, Ronald P (Ron) — Baseball Player
3805 Indian River Dr, Vero Beach FL 32963, USA
Perrault, Dominique — Architect
Perrault Architecte, 26 Rue Brunneseau, 75629 Paris Cedex 13, France
Perreau, Gigi — Actress
5841 Cantaloupe Ave, Van Nuys CA 91401, USA
Perreault, Annie — Speed Skater
Speed Skating Canada, 2781 Lancaster Road, #402, Ottawa ON K1B 1A7, Canada
Perreault, Gilbert (Gil) — Ice Hockey Player
4 Rue de la Serenite, Victoriaville QC G6S 1J4, Canada
Perreault, Yanic — Ice Hockey Player
4303 E Cactus Road, #345, Phoenix AZ 85032, USA
Perrella, James E — Businessman
Ingersoll-Rand Co, PO Box 6820, Piscataway NJ 08855, USA
Perren, Diego — Curling Athlete
Curling Assn, PO Box 606, 3000 Bern, Switzerland
Perret, Craig — Thoroughbred Racing Jockey
825 Antioch Road, Shelbyville KY 40065, USA
Perretta, Ralph J — Football Player
1305 Calle Scott, Encinitas CA 92024, USA
Perrette, Pauley — Actress
S D B Partners, 1801 Ave of Stars, #902, Los Angeles CA 90067 USA
Perri, Christina — Singer, Songwriter
Atlantic Records, 9229 W Sunset Blvd, #900, West Hollywood CA 90069 USA
Perrier, Mireille — Actress
Jean-François Pignard de Marthod, 11 Rue Chanez, 75781 Paris Cedex 16, France
Perriman, Brett R — Football Player
PO Box 83337, Conyers GA 30013, USA
Perrine, Valerie — Actress
Bensky Entertainment, 15030 Ventura Blvd, #343, Sherman Oaks CA 91403, USA
Perrineau, Harold, Jr — Actor
A P A Talent/Literary Agency, 405 S Beverly Dr, #300, Beverly Hills CA 90212 USA
Perrotta, Tom — Writer
Saint Martin's Press, 175 5th Ave, #400, New York NY 10010 USA
Perry, A Joseph (Joe) — Guitarist (Aerosmith), Songwriter
Front Line Mgmt, 1100 Glendon Ave, #2000, Los Angeles CA 90024 USA
Perry, Alex — Fashion Designer
104/106 The Strand, 412-414 George St, Sydney NSW 2000, Australia
Perry, Anne — Writer
Tyrn Vawr, Seafield, Portmahomack, Rosshire IV20 1RE, Scotland
Perry, Barry W — Businessman
Engelhard Corp, 101 Wood Ave, Iselin NJ 08830, USA
Perry, Bradley Steven — Actor
Coast to Coast Talent, 3350 Barham Blvd, Los Angeles CA 90068 USA
Perry, Curtis R — Basketball Player
1222 I St NE, Washington DC 20002, USA
Perry, Darren — Football Player
801 Volvo Parkway, #109, Chesapeake VA 23320, USA
Perry, Edward L (Ed) — Football Player
1583 SW 161st Ave, Pembroke Pines FL 33027, USA
Perry, Elliott L — Basketball Player
3230 Scheibler Road, Memphis TN 38128, USA
Perry, Felton — Actor
Hollywood Book, 6562 Hollywood Blvd, Los Angeles CA 90028, USA
Perry, Gaylord J — Baseball Player
All Sports USA, PO Box 489, Spruce Pine NC 28777, USA
Perry, Gerald — Football Player
2940 Dell Dr, Columbia SC 29209, USA
Perry, Gerald E — Football Player
336 5th St, Manhattan Beach CA 90266, USA
Perry, Gerald J — Baseball Player
1348 Waterford Green Close, Marietta GA 30068, USA
Perry, Herbert E (Herb), Jr — Baseball Player
978 N Fletcher Ave, Mayo FL 32066, USA
Perry, J Christopher (Chris) — Golfer
170 Valley Run Dr, Powell OH 43065, USA

Perry, J Kenneth (Kenny) — Golfer
418 Quail Ridge Road, Franklin KY 42134, USA

Perry, James E (Jim) — Baseball Player
155 Porters Glen, New London NC 28127, USA

Perry, Jeff — Actor
2029 Century Park E, #1060, Los Angeles CA 90067, USA

Perry, John Bennett — Actor
Greene Assoc, 1901 Ave of Stars, #130, Los Angeles CA 90067 USA

Perry, John R — Philosopher
Stanford University, Language/Information Study Center, Stanford CA 94305, USA

Perry, Katy — Singer, Songwriter
Direct Management Group, 947 N La Cienega Blvd, #G, West Hollywood CA 90069, USA

Perry, Keith — Singer, Fiddler, Songwriter
Curb Records, 48 Music Square E, Nashville TN 37203 USA

Perry, Lee (Scratch) — Singer (Upsetters)
Agency Group Ltd, 142 W 57th St, #600, New York NY 10019 USA

Perry, Linda — Singer (Four Non Blondes), Songwriter
Rockstar/Interscope Records, 2220 Colorado Ave, Santa Monica CA 90404, USA

Perry, Luke — Actor
Himber Entertainment, PO Box 950, South Orange NJ 07079 USA

Perry, Matthew — Actor
Creative Artists Agency, 2000 Ave of Stars, #100, Los Angeles CA 90067 USA

Perry, Melvin G (Bob) — Baseball Player
445 Fox Chase Village, New Bern NC 28562, USA

Perry, Michael Dean — Football Player
1029 Sedgewood Circle, Charlotte NC 28211, USA

Perry, Michael R — Writer, Producer
United Talent Agency, 9336 Civic Center Dr, Beverly Hills CA 90210 USA

Perry, Michelle — Concert French Horn Player
Columbia Artists Mgmt Inc, 1790 Broadway, #702, New York NY 10019 USA

Perry, Robert P — Molecular Biologist
1808 Bustleton Pike, Southampton PA 18966, USA

Perry, Rodney C (Rod) — Football Player
40 E Bloomfield Lane, Westfield IN 46074, USA

Perry, Scott E — Football Player
2807 Graysby Ave, San Pedro CA 90732, USA

Perry, Stephen H (Steve) — Singer (Cherry Poppin Daddies)
Paradise Artists, PO Box 1821, Ojai CA 93024 USA

Perry, Stephen P (Steve) — Singer (Journey), Songwriter
Perry S Oretzky, 10880 Wilshire Blvd, #920, Los Angeles CA 90024, USA

Perry, Steve — Writer
959 E Cinnamon Dr, Lemoore CA 93245, USA

Perry, Todd J — Football Player
13805 Brittle Road, Alpharetta GA 30004, USA

Perry, Troy D — Religious Leader
Metropolitan Churches Fellowship, 5300 Santa Monica Blvd, Los Angeles CA 90029, USA

Perry, Tyler — Actor, Director, Writer
Tyler Perry Co, 541 10th St NW, #172, Atlanta GA 30318, USA

Perry, Vernon, Jr — Football Player
PO Box 842201, Houston TX 77284, USA

Perry, W Patrick (Pat) — Baseball Player
1115 W Franklin St, Taylorville IL 62568, USA

Perry, William A (Refrigerator) — Football Player
2885 Old Camp Long Road, Aiken SC 29805, USA

Perry, William J — Secretary, Defense
11210 Hooper Lane, Los Altos Hills CA 94024, USA

Perryman, Jill — Actress
4 Hillside Crescent, Gooseberry Hill WA 6076, Australia

Perryman, Robert L (Bob) — Football Player
PO Box 8543, Haverhill MA 01835, USA

Persad-Bissessar, Kamla — Prime Minister, Trinidad & Tobago
Prime Minister's Office, Whitehall, Maraval Road, Port of Spain, Trinidad & Tobago

Persbrandt, Mikael — Actor
I C M Partners, 10250 Constellation Blvd, #900, Los Angeles CA 90067 USA

Pershing, Jennifer — Model
Playboy Promotions, 2706 Media Center Dr, Los Angeles CA 90065 USA

Persoff, Nehemiah — Actor
5670 Moonstone Dr, Cambria CA 93428, USA

Person, Chuck C — Basketball Player
2022 Ruhland Ave, Redondo Beach CA 90278, USA

Person, Robert A — Baseball Player
25 Bellerive Acres, Saint Louis MO 63121, USA

Person, Wesley L — Basketball Player
PO Box 481, Brantley AL 36009, USA

Personen, Richard M — Football Player
765 Pine Hills Place, The Villages FL 32162, USA

Persons, Peter — Golfer
1153 Saint Andrews Dr, Macon GA 31210, USA

Persson, Elisabeth — Curling Athlete
Curling Assn, Idrottshuser, Marbackagatan 19, 123 43 Farsta, Sweden

Persson, Jorgen — Cinematographer
Rydbolundsvagen 7, 185 31 Vaxholm, Sweden

Persson, Nina E — Singer (Cardigans), Songwriter
Talent Trust, Kungsgatan 9C, 411 19 Gothenburg, Sweden

Persson, Ricard — Ice Hockey Player
2200-201 Portage Ave, Winnipeg MB R3B 3L3, Canada

Persson, Stefan — Businessman
Hennes & Mauritz AB, Sverigekontoret, 106 38 Stockholm, Sweden

Persson, Torsten — Economist
Stockholm University, International Economic Studies Institute, 106 91 Stockholm, Sweden

Pert, Candace — Neuroscientist
Georgetown University, New Medicine Institute, Washington DC 20057, USA

Perzanowski, Stanley (Stan) — Baseball Player
PO Box 133, New Park PA 17352, USA

Pescatelli, Tammy — Actress, Comedienne
Parallel Entertainment, 9420 Wilshire Blvd, #250, Beverly Hills CA 90212 USA

Pesce, Gaetano
543 Broadway, #5, New York NY 10012, USA — Interior Designer

Pesch, Dorothee (Doro)
Postfach 105313, 40044 Dusseldorf, Germany — Singer (Warlock)

Pesci, Joe
Jay Julien Mgmt, 1501 Broadway, #2600, New York NY 10036, USA — Actor

Pescia, Lisa
Coast to Coast Talent, 3350 Barham Blvd, Los Angeles CA 90068 USA — Actress

Pescucci, Gabriella
Sandra Marsh & Associates, 9150 Wilshire Blvd, #220, Beverly Hills CA 90212, USA — Costume Designer

Pesek, Libor
I M G Artists, Hogarth Business Park, Chiswick, London W4 2TH, England — Conductor

Pess, Katalin
Names Model Mgmt, Via Savona 53, 20144 Milan, Italy — Model

Pestka, Sidney
Robert Wood Johnson Medical School, 675 Hoes Lane, Piscataway NJ 08854, USA — Molecular Geneticist

Pestova, Daniela
Next Model Mgmt, 9 Boul de la Madeleine, 75001 Paris, France — Model

Pesut, George
1008-415 Michigan St, Victoria BC V8V 1R8, Canada — Ice Hockey Player

Petagine, Roberto A
1098 Hunting Lodge Dr, Miami Springs FL 33166, USA — Baseball Player

Peter, Valentine J
Father Flanagan's Boys Town, 14100 Crawford St, Boys Town NE 68010, USA — Religious Leader, Social Worker

Peterek, Jeffrey A (Jeff)
8073 Elm Valley Road, Three Oaks MI 49128, USA — Baseball Player

Peterle, Lozje
Slovenian Christian Democrats, Beethovnova 4, 1000 Ljubljana, Slovenia — Prime Minister, Slovenia

Peterman, D Brian
Commander, US Coast Guard Atlantic, 4131 Crawford St, Portsmouth VA 23704 USA — Coast Guard Admiral

Peterman, Melissa
A P A Talent/Literary Agency, 405 S Beverly Dr, #300, Beverly Hills CA 90212 USA — Actress

Peterman, Steven
Jackoway Tyerman Wertheimer, 1925 Century Park E, #2200, Los Angeles CA 90067 USA — Producer

Peters, Anthony L (Tony)
2402 Boston St, Muskogee OK 74401, USA — Football Player

Peters, Bernadette
323 W 80th St, New York NY 10024, USA — Singer, Actress

Peters, Bob
Bemidji State University, Athletic Dept, Bemidji MN 56601, USA — Ice Hockey Coach

Peters, Christopher M (Chris)
613 Chessbriar Dr, Three Oaks MI 49128, USA — Baseball Player

Peters, Clarke
Stone Manners Salners, 9911 W Pico Blvd, #1400, Los Angeles CA 90035 USA — Actor

Peters, Clayre
Playboy Promotions, 2706 Media Center Dr, Los Angeles CA 90065 USA — Model

Peters, Dan
Legends of 21st Century, 7 Trinity Row, Florence MA 01062, USA — Drummer (Mudhoney)

Peters, Devereaux
Minnesota Lynx, Target Center, 600 1st Ave N, Minneapolis MN 55403 USA — Basketball Player

Peters, Emmitt
General Delivery, Ruby AK 99768, USA — Dog Sled Racer

Peters, Evan
Creative Artists Agency, 2000 Ave of Stars, #100, Los Angeles CA 90067 USA — Actor

Peters, Garry
3020 Eastview, Saskatoon SK S7J 3J2, Canada — Ice Hockey Player

Peters, Gary C
7121 N Serenoa Dr, Sarasota FL 34241, USA — Baseball Player

Peters, Gretchen
Purple Crayon Mgmt, PO Box 331242, Nashville TN 37203, USA — Singer, Songwriter

Peters, Jan
959 7th St, Beaver PA 15009, USA — Singer

Peters, Jason R
95 Stroughton Lane, Orchard Park NY 14127, USA — Football Player

Peters, Jim, Jr
Vermont Academy, PO Box 500, Saxtons River VT 05154, USA — Ice Hockey Player

Peters, Jon
9941 Tower Lane, Beverly Hills CA 90210, USA — Producer

Peters, Maria Liberia
Prime Minister's Office, Fort Amsterdam, Willemstad, Netherlands Antilles — Prime Minister, Netherlands Antilles

Peters, Mary
Willowtree Cottage, River Road, Dunmurray, Belfast, Northern Ireland — Track Athlete

Peters, Mike
PO Box 957, Bradenton FL 34206, USA — Editorial Cartoonist

Peters, Ralph
Trident Media Group, 41 Madison Ave, #3600, New York NY 10010 USA — Writer

Peters, Rick
TalentWorks, 3500 W Olive Ave, #1400, Burbank CA 91505 USA — Actor

Peters, Roberta
19356 Cedar Glen Dr, Boca Raton FL 33434, USA — Opera Singer, Actress

Peters, Russell
Seven Summits Mgmt, 8906 W Olympic Blvd, Beverly Hills CA 90211 USA — Actor, Comedian

Peters, Scott
Rothman Brecher Agency, 9465 Wilshire Blvd, #840, Beverly Hills CA 90212 USA — Producer, Writer

Peters, Timothy
B H R, PO Box 1708, Mount Juliet TN 37121, USA — Auto, Truck Racing Drivier

Peters, Tom
Tom Peters Group, 555 Hamilton Ave, Palo Alto CA 94301, USA — Writer, Management Consultant

Peters, Vicki
Playboy Promotions, 2706 Media Center Dr, Los Angeles CA 90065 USA — Model, Actress

Peters, Volney M
325 Lancaster Road, Walnut Creek CA 94595, USA — Football Player

Petersen, Byron E
University of Florida Medical School, PO Box 100275, Gainesville FL 32610, USA — Pathologist

Petersen, Chris
Boise State University, Athletic Dept, Boise ID 83725, USA — Football Coach

Petersen, Christopher R (Chris) — Baseball Player
242 Timberland Ave, Longwood FL 32750, USA

Petersen, Cole — Actor
Simmons & Scott, 7942 Mulholland Dr, Los Angeles CA 90046, USA

Petersen, John D — Educator
University of Tennessee, President's Office, Holt Tower, Knoxville TN 37996, USA

Petersen, Kurt D — Football Player
5520 Linmore Lane, Plano TX 75093, USA

Petersen, Paul — Actor, Singer
A Minor Consideration, 14530 Denker Ave, Gardena CA 90247, USA

Petersen, Suzann — Golfer
Gladengveien 3B, 0661 Oslo, Norway

Petersen, Theodore H (Ted) — Football Player
1195 N 17000E, Momence IL 60954, USA

Petersen, Toby — Ice Hockey Player
2529 Bryant Ave S, Minneapolis MN 55405, USA

Petersen, William L — Actor
High Horse Films, 100 Universal City Plaza, Building 2128, Universal City CA 91608, USA

Petersen, Wolfgang — Director
Paradigm Agency, 360 N Crescent Dr, North Building, Beverly Hills CA 90210 USA

Peterson, Adam C — Baseball Player
6401 NE 14th St, Vancouver WA 98665, USA

Peterson, Adrian L — Football Player
9212 Cold Stream Lane, Eden Prairie MN 55347, USA

Peterson, Anthony W (Tony) — Football Player
1124 Lakewood Circle, Naperville IL 60540, USA

Peterson, Bob — Writer
Pixar, 1200 Park Ave, Emeryville CA 94608, USA

Peterson, Buzz — Basketball Coach
University of Tennessee, Athletic Dept, Knoxville TN 37996, USA

Peterson, Calvin E (Cal) — Football Player
22646 Ingomar St, Canoga Park CA 91304, USA

Peterson, Chase N — Educator
910 S Donner Way, #201, Salt Lake City UT 84108, USA

Peterson, David C — Photojournalist
4805 Pinehurst Court, Pleasant Hill IA 50327, USA

Peterson, Debbi — Singer, Drummer (Bangles)
Russell Carter Artist Mgmt, 567 Ralph Mcgill Blvd, Atlanta GA 30312, USA

Peterson, Donald H — Astronaut
Aerospace Operations Consultants, 427 Pebblebrook Dr, Seabrook TX 77586, USA

Peterson, Fred I (Fritz) — Baseball Player
PO Box 137, East Dubuque IL 61025, USA

Peterson, George P (Bud) — Educator
Georgia Institute of Technology, President's Office, Atlanta GA 30332, USA

Peterson, J Todd — Football Player
135 Bellacree Road, Duluth GA 30097, USA

Peterson, John — Freestyle Wrestler
457 19th Ave, Comstock WI 54826, USA

Peterson, Julian T — Football Player
3655 Peachtree Road NE, #403, Atlanta GA 30319, USA

Peterson, Melvin L (Mel) — Basketball Player
2896 Evergreen Lane, Aurora IL 60502, USA

Peterson, Morris, Jr — Basketball Player
909 Lafayette St, #12, New Orleans LA 70113, USA

Peterson, Patrick D — Football Defensive Back
Arizona Cardinals, PO Box 888, Phoenix AZ 85001 USA

Peterson, Peter G — Secretary of Commerce, Financier
Blackstone Group, 345 Park Ave, Basement LB4, New York NY 10154, USA

Peterson, Steven — Architect
Peterson/Littenberg Architecture, 131 E 66th St, #1B, New York NY 10065, USA

Peterson, Sylvia — Singer (Chiffons)
Lustig Talent, PO Box 770850, Orlando FL 32877 USA

Peterson, Vicki — Singer, Guitarist (Bangles)
Russell Carter Artist Mgmt, 567 Ralph Mcgill Blvd, Atlanta GA 30312, USA

Peterson, William W (Bill) — Football Player
13536 Mijo Lane, Lakeside CA 92040, USA

Petersson, Tom — Singer, Bassist (Cheap Trick, Swag)
Oakie Dokie Mgmt, 6090 Central Ave, Saint Petersburg FL 33707, USA

Petey Pablo — Rap Artist
Spring Mgmt, 404 Carroll Canal, Venice CA 90291, USA

Petit, Michel — Ice Hockey Player
129 Latches Lane, Media PA 19063, USA

Petit, Philippe — High Wire Walker
Cathedral of Saint John the Devine, 1047 Amsterdam Ave, New York NY 10025, USA

Petitbon, Richard A (Richie) — Football Player, Coach
9628 Percussion Way, Vienna VA 22182, USA

Petitgout, Lewis G (Luke) — Football Player
5221 S Nichol St, Tampa FL 33611, USA

Petke, Mike — Soccer Player
Red Bulls New York, 600 Cape May St, Harrison, NJ 07029 USA

Peto, Richard — Epidemiologist
Radcliffe Infirmary, Harkness Building, Oxford ON OX2 6HE, England

Petra, Yvon — Tennis Player
Residence du Prieure, 78100 Saint Germain-en-Laye, France

Petraglia, John (Johnny) — Bowler
25 Turnbridge Court, Jackson NJ 08527, USA

Petralli, Eugene J (Geno) — Baseball Player
119 Laser Lane, Weatherford TX 76087, USA

Petrella, Robert (Bob) — Football Player
116 Aberdeen Way, Rio Grande NJ 08242, USA

Petrenko, Vasily — Conductor
I M G Artists, Hogarth Business Park, Chiswick, London W4 2TH, England

Petrenko, Viktor — Figure Skater
Ice Vault Arena, 10 Nevins Road, Wayne NJ 07470, USA

Petri, Michala — Concert Recorder Player
Nordskraenten 3, 2980 Kokkedal, Denmark

Petri, Nina — Actress
Agentur Carola Studlar, Agnesstr 47, 80798 Munich, Germany
Petrich, Robert M (Bob) — Football Player
1391 Silverberry Court, El Cajon CA 92019, USA
Petrick, Benjamin W (Ben) — Baseball Player
1553 NE Jackson School Road, Hillsboro OR 97124, USA
Petrie, Daniel M, Jr — Director
Enderby Entertainment, 18034 Ventura Blvd, #445, Encino CA 91316, USA
Petrie, Donald — Director
Gersh Agency, 9465 Wilshire Blvd, #600, Beverly Hills CA 90212 USA
Petrie, Geoff M — Basketball Player, Executive
3675 Holly Hill Lane, Loomis CA 95650, USA
Petro, Johan — Basketball Player
Brooklyn Nets, 15 Metro Tech Center, #1100, Brooklyn NY 11201 USA
Petrocelli, Americo P (Rico) — Baseball Player
37 Green Heron Lane, Nashua NH 03062, USA
Petrone, Shana — Singer
Epic Records, 34 Music Square E, Nashville TN 37203, USA
Petroni, Michael — Director, Writer, Actor
W M E Entertainment, 9601 Wilshire Blvd, #300, Beverly Hills CA 90210 USA
Petronio, Stephen — Dancer, Choreographer
95 Saint Marks Place, New York NY 10009, USA
Petroro, Marisa — Actress
House of Representatives, 1434 6th St, #1, Santa Monica CA 90401 USA
Petroske, John E (Jack) — Ice Hockey Player
PO Box 366, Side Lake MN 55781, USA
Petrov, Denis A — Figure Skater
World Ice Arena, 1881th Bao'an Road, Luohu District, Shenzhen 518001, China
Petrova, Nadia — Tennis Player
Women's Tennis Assn, 1 Progress Plaza, #1500, Saint Petersburg FL 33701 USA
Petrovic, Tim — Golfer
11602 Turtle Lane, Austin TX 78726, USA
Petrovicky, Ronald — Ice Hockey Player
3236 Birkdale Ave, Duluth, GA 30097, USA
Petrovics, Emil — Composer
Attila Utca 29, 1013 Budapest, Hungary
Petruska, Richard — Basketball Player
4704 Pine Oak Park, #636, Houston TX 77081, USA
Petry, Daniel J (Dan) — Baseball Player
30715 Mystic Forest Dr, Farmington Hills MI 48331, USA
Petry, Leroy A — Afghanistan War Army Hero (CMH)
Public Affairs Office, PO Box 339500, Joint Base Lewis-McChord WA 98433, USA
Petsko, Gregory A — Chemist, Biochemist
8 Jason Road, Belmont MA 02478, USA
Pett, Joel — Editorial Cartoonist
PO Box 174, Wilmore KY 40390, USA
Pettengill, Gordon H — Planetary Physicist
Massachusetts Institute of Technology, Space Research Center, Cambridge MA 02139, USA
Pettersen, Suzann — Golfer
R&A Group Services, Beach House, Golf Place, Saint Andrews Fife KY16 9JA, Scotland
Pettersson, Carl — Golfer
2208 Oak Lawn Way, Wake Forest NC 27587, USA
Pettet, Joanna — Actress
Paradigm Agency, 360 N Crescent Dr, North Building, Beverly Hills CA 90210 USA
Pettie, Jim — Ice Hockey Player
81 Kirk Road, Rochester NY 14612, USA
Pettiford, Valerie — Actress, Singer
TalentWorks, 3500 W Olive Ave, #1400, Burbank CA 91505 USA
Pettigrew, Gary L — Football Player
2707 E 27th Ave, #2B, Spokane WA 99223, USA
Pettigrew, L Eudora — Educator
State University of New York, President's Office, Old Westbury NY 11568, USA
Pettinger, Matt — Ice Hockey Player
3075 Eastdowne Road, Victoria BC V8R 5S1, Canada
Pettini, Joseph P (Joe) — Baseball Player
112 Logan Court, Bethany WV 26032, USA
Pettis, Gary G — Baseball Player
3129 Crestline Court, Antioch CA 94531, USA
Pettis, Madison — Actress
Coast to Coast Talent, 3350 Barham Blvd, Los Angeles CA 90068 USA
Pettit, Donald R — Astronaut
2014 Country Ridge Dr, Houston TX 77062, USA
Pettit, G W Paul — Baseball Player
928 Sarazen St, Hemet CA 92543, USA
Pettit, Robert E (Bob), Jr — Basketball Player
7 Garden Lane, New Orleans LA 70124, USA
Pettitte, Andrew E (Andy) — Baseball Player
2222 W Lawther Dr, Deer Park TX 77536, USA
Petty, J T — Director, Writer
Creative Artists Agency, 2000 Ave of Stars, #100, Los Angeles CA 90067 USA
Petty, Kyle E — Auto Racing Driver
135 Longfield Dr, Mooresville NC 28115, USA
Petty, Lori — Actress
Intellectual Property Group, 10585 Santa Monica Blvd, #140, Los Angeles CA 90025, USA
Petty, Richard L — Auto Racing Driver
Richard Petty Motorsports, 7065 Zephyr Place, Concord NC 28027, USA
Petty, Tom — Singer, Guitarist, Songwriter
East End Mgmt, 13721 Ventura Blvd, #200, Sherman Oaks CA 91423, USA
Pettyfer, Alex — Actor
W M E Entertainment, 9601 Wilshire Blvd, #300, Beverly Hills CA 90210 USA
Peugeot, Roland — Businessman
170 Ave Victor Hugo, 75116 Paris, France
Pevec, Katja — Actress
Greene Assoc, 1901 Ave of Stars, #130, Los Angeles CA 90067 USA
Peyroux, Madeline — Singer, Songwriter
Rounder Records, 1 Rounder Way, Burlington MA 01803 USA

Peyser, Penny — Actress
22039 Alizondo Dr, Woodland Hills CA 91364, USA

Peyton, Brad — Director
Verve Talent & Literary Agency, 9696 Culver Blvd, #301, Culver City CA 90232, USA

Pfaff, Judy — Sculptor
319 Greenwich St, #5L, New York NY 10013, USA

Pfahl, John — Photographer
Janet Borden, 560 Broadway, #601, New York NY 10012, USA

Pfann, George R — Football Player, Coach
120 Warwick Place, Ithaca NY 14850, USA

Pfeiffer, Meg — Singer
Kuka, Bolschestr 20, 12587 Berlin, Germany

Pfeiffer, Michelle — Actress
Management 360, 9111 Wilshire Blvd, Beverly Hills CA 90210 USA

Pfeiffer, Norman — Architect
Hardy Holzman Pfeiffer, 811 W 7th St, #430, Los Angeles CA 90017, USA

Pfeil, Robert R (Bobby) — Baseball Player
2358 Pheasant Run Circle, Stockton CA 95207, USA

Pfell, Mark — Golfer
2565 Chelsea Road, Palos Verdes Estates CA 90274, USA

Pfister, Daniel A (Dan) — Baseball Player
322 Nevada St, Hollywood FL 33019, USA

Pfister, Wally — Cinematographer
2500 Jupiter Dr, Los Angeles CA 90046, USA

Pflug, Jo Ann — Actress
PO Box 3292, Jupiter FL 33469, USA

Pfund, Leroy H (Lee) — Baseball Player
130 Windsor Park Dr, #C214, Carol Stream IL 60188, USA

Pfund, Randy — Basketball Coach, Executive
50 S Pointe Dr, #608, Miami Beach FL 33139, USA

Phair, Liz — Singer, Songwriter, Actress
A2 Mgmt, 624 Davis St, #200, Evanston IL 60201, USA

Pham Minh Man, Jean-Baptiste Cardinal — Religious Leader
Toa Tonggiam Muc, 180 Nguyen Dink Chieu, Thanh-Pho Ho Chi Minh, Vietnam

Pham Tuan — Cosmonaut, Vietnam
4C-1000-Soc Son, Hanoi, Vietnam

Phaneuf, Dion — Ice Hockey Player
271 Heath Road NW, Edmonton AB T6R 1V3, Canada

Pharr, Tommy L — Football Player
314 Harrison Lane, Winder GA 30680, USA

Phegley, Roger D — Basketball Player
43 Timberlane Dr, Morton IL 61550, USA

Phelan, James J (Jim) — Basketball Player, Coach
16579 Old Emmitsburg Road, Emmitsburg MD 21727, USA

Phelps, Doug — Singer, Bassist (Kentucky Headhunters)
Webster & Assoc Public Relations, PO Box 23015, Nashville TN 37202, USA

Phelps, Edmund S — Nobel Economics Laureate
45 E 89th St, #28B, New York NY 10128, USA

Phelps, James — Actor
United Agents, 12-26 Lexington St, London W1F 0LE, England

Phelps, Jaycie — Gymnast
1443 Persimmon Circle, Greenfield IN 46140, USA

Phelps, Kelly Joe — Singer, Guitarist, Songwriter
Fleming Artists, 543 N Main St, Ann Arbor MI 48104, USA

Phelps, Kenneth A (Ken) — Baseball Player
6030 E Foothill Dr N, Paradise Valley AZ 85253, USA

Phelps, Michael E — Neuroscientist, Inventor
16720 Huerta Road, Encino CA 91436, USA

Phelps, Michael F — Swimmer
PO Box 65239, Baltimore MD 21209, USA

Phelps, Oliver — Actor
United Agents, 12-26 Lexington St, London W1F 0LE, England

Phelps, Richard F (Digger) — Basketball Coach, Sportscaster
Lordly & Dane, 1344 Main St, Waltham MA 02451, USA

Phelps, Ricky Lee — Singer, Musician (Kentucky Headhunters)
Webster & Assoc Public Relations, PO Box 23015, Nashville TN 37202, USA

Phifer, Mekhi — Actor
Facilitator Films, 4000 Warner Blvd, Building 17, Burbank CA 91522, USA

Philaret, Patriarch — Religious Leader
10 Osvobozdeniya St, 220004 Minsk, Belarus

Philbin, Gerald J (Gerry) — Football Player
9976 Marsala Way, Delray Beach FL 33446, USA

Philbin, Joseph (Joe) — Football Coach
Miami Dolphins, 7500 SW 30th St, Davie FL 33314 USA

Philbin, Regis — Entertainer
101 W 67th St, #51A, New York NY 10023, USA

Philbrick, Denise — Golfer
5364 Carnegie Loop, Livermore CA 94550, USA

Philcox, Todd S — Football Player
1156 Creeks Edge Court, Ponte Vedra FL 32082, USA

Philip — Prince, England; Duke of Edinburgh
Buckingham Palace, Westminster, London SW1A 1AA, England

Philip, George M — Educator
State University of New York, President's Office, 1400 Washington Ave, Albany NY 12222, USA

Philip, Primate — Religious Leader
Antiochian Orthodox Christian Church, 358 Mountain Road, Englewood NJ 07631, USA

Philippe — Crown Prince, Belgium
Koninklijk Palais, Rue de Brederode, 1000 Brussels, Belgium

Philippoussis, Mark — Tennis Player
Octagon Worldwide, 1751 Pinnacle Dr, #1500, McLean VA 22102 USA

Philipps, Busy — Actress
I C M Partners, 10250 Constellation Blvd, #900, Los Angeles CA 90067 USA

Philips, Chuck — Journalist
Los Angeles Times, Editorial Dept, 202 W 1st St, Los Angeles CA 90012 USA

Philips, Gina — Actress
Kritzer Levine Wilkins Griffin, 11872 La Grange Ave, #100, Los Angeles CA 90025 USA

Phillipoff, Harold
736 Georgia St SE, Albuquerque NM 87108, USA   Ice Hockey Player

Phillippe, Ryan
Schiff Co, 8440 Warner Dr, #B1, Culver City CA 90232 USA   Actor

Phillips, Andre L P
Edison High School, 1425 Center St, Stockton CA 95206, USA   Track Athlete

Phillips, Anthony
Solo Agency, 53-55 Fulham High St, #200, London SW6 3JJ, England   Guitarist (Genesis), Songwriter

Phillips, Arianne
United Talent Agency, 9336 Civic Center Dr, Beverly Hills CA 90210 USA   Costume Designer

Phillips, Bijou
Untitled Entertainment, 350 S Beverly Dr, #200, Beverly Hills CA 90212 USA   Singer, Model, Actress

Phillips, Bill
Muscle Media, 444 Corporate Circle, Golden CO 80401, USA   Physical Fitness Expert

Phillips, Bobbie
Kelly Agency, 3001 Heavenly Ridge St, Thousand Oaks CA 91362, USA   Actress

Phillips, Brandon E
586 Rowland Road, Stone Mountain GA 30083, USA   Baseball Player

Phillips, Britta
Don Buchwald/Fortitude, 6500 Wilshire Blvd, #2200, Los Angeles CA 90048 USA   Bassist (Luna, Dean & Britta)

Phillips, Caryl
A P Watt Ltd, 20 John St, London WC1N 2DR, England   Writer

Phillips, Charles W
915 N Holliston Ave, Pasadena CA 91104, USA   Football Player

Phillips, Chynna
Duryea Entertainment, 54 Danbury Road, #367, Ridgefield CT 06877, USA   Singer, Actress

Phillips, Clarence G (J R)
12210 N Rio Vista Dr, Sun City AZ 85351, USA   Baseball Player

Phillips, D Eugene (Gene)
11606 Whisper Willow St, San Antonio TX 78230, USA   Basketball Player

Phillips, Derek
Evolution Entertainment, 901 N Highland Ave, Los Angeles CA 90038 USA   Actor

Phillips, Dwight
USA Track & Field, RCA Dome, PO Box 140, Indianapolis IN 46225 USA   Track Athlete

Phillips, Eddie L
800 McCary St SW, Birmingham AL 35211, USA   Basketball Player

Phillips, Emo
Harbour Agency, 63 William St, #300, East Sydney NSW 1022, Australia   Actor, Comedian

Phillips, Erin V
Indiana Fever, Conseco Fieldhouse, 125 S Pennsylvania, Indianapolis IN 46204 USA   Basketball Player

Phillips, Ethan
TalentWorks, 3500 W Olive Ave, #1400, Burbank CA 91505 USA   Actor

Phillips, G Andrew (Andy)
5206 Glenfair Circle, Northport AL 35475, USA   Baseball Player

Phillips, Gersha
Paradigm Agency, 360 N Crescent Dr, North Building, Beverly Hills CA 90210 USA   Costume Designer

Phillips, Grant-Lee
Cooking Vinyl, 10 Allied Way, London W3 OrQ, England   Singer, Guitarist, Songwriter, Actor

Phillips, Howard
Conservative Caucus, 47 West St, Boston MA 02111, USA   Public Policy Analyst

Phillips, J Dixon, Jr
US Court of Appeals, 100 Europa Dr, Chapel Hill NC 27517, USA   Judge

Phillips, James J (Red)
67 Lakeview Dr, #10D, Alexander City AL 35010, USA   Football Player

Phillips, Jason C
7111 DeFranzo Loop, Fort George G Meade MD 20755, USA   Baseball Player

Phillips, Jason H
1702 Aden Mist Dr, Houston TX 77003, USA   Football Player

Phillips, Jason L
1777 Tara Way, San Marcos CA 92078, USA   Baseball Player

Phillips, Jay
I C M Partners, 10250 Constellation Blvd, #900, Los Angeles CA 90067 USA   Actor

Phillips, Jermaine
11802 Derbyshire Dr, Tampa FL 33626, USA   Football Player

Phillips, Jess W, Jr
2820 San Antonio St, Beaumont TX 77701, USA   Football Player

Phillips, John
University of Tulsa, Athletic Dept, Tulsa OK 74104, USA   Basketball Coach

Phillips, John L
154 Canoe Cove Lane, Sandpoint ID 83864, USA   Astronaut

Phillips, Joseph C
Don Buchwald/Fortitude, 6500 Wilshire Blvd, #2200, Los Angeles CA 90048 USA   Actor

Phillips, Joseph G (Joe)
4080 SE 39th Circle, Ocala FL 34480, USA   Football Player

Phillips, Judith
Bernardo Beach Native Plant Farm, 1 Sanchez Dr, Veguita NM 87062, USA   Landscape Architect

Phillips, Julianne
3 Arts Entertainment, 9460 Wilshire Blvd, #700, Beverly Hills CA 90212 USA   Actress

Phillips, K Anthony (Tony)
13341 E Cochise Road, Scottsdale AZ 85259, USA   Baseball Player

Phillips, Kate
Houghton Mifflin Harcourt, 215 Park Ave S, #1200, New York NY 10003 USA   Writer

Phillips, Kenneth (Kenny)
New York Giants, Meadowlands Stadium, 102 Route 120, East Rutherford NJ 07073 USA   Football Player

Phillips, Kevin
A P A Talent/Literary Agency, 405 S Beverly Dr, #300, Beverly Hills CA 90212 USA   Actor

Phillips, Kevin P
Grand Central Publishing, 237 Park Ave, #1300, New York NY 10017, USA   Political Analyst

Phillips, Kimberly
Playboy Promotions, 2706 Media Center Dr, Los Angeles CA 90065 USA   Model

Phillips, Kristie
610 1st Ave, Asbury Park NJ 07712, USA   Gymnast

Phillips, Lawrence L
9527 Langdon Ave, North Hills CA 91343, USA   Football Player

Phillips, Leslie S
78 Maida Vale, London W9 1PR, England   Actor

P

Paetkau - Phillips

Phillips, Lisa Ann — Actress
Don Buchwald/Fortitude, 6500 Wilshire Blvd, #2200, Los Angeles CA 90048 USA

Phillips, Lou Diamond — Actor
Global Artists Agency, 6253 Hollywood Blvd, #508, Los Angeles CA 90028, USA

Phillips, Loyd W — Football Player
739 Sands Road, Cave Springs AR 72718, USA

Phillips, Mackenzie — Actress
S D B Partners, 1801 Ave of Stars, #902, Los Angeles CA 90067 USA

Phillips, Melvin (Mel), Jr — Football Player
6368 Milk Wagon Lane, Hialeah FL 33014, USA

Phillips, Michael D (Mike) — Baseball Player
3322 Ridgefield St, Irving TX 75062, USA

Phillips, Michelle — Singer (Mamas & Papas), Actress
Rebel Entertainment Partners, 5700 Wilshire Blvd, #456, Los Angeles CA 90036, USA

Phillips, Nathan — Actor
Principato-Young, 9465 Wilshire Blvd, #880, Beverly Hills CA 90212 USA

Phillips, Norma — Social Activist
Mothers Against Drunk Driving, PO Box 819100, Dallas TX 75381, USA

Phillips, Oail Andres (Bum) — Football Coach, Sportscaster
2981 S Riverside Lane, Goliad TX 77963, USA

Phillips, Owen M — Geophysical Engineer
462 Heron Point, Chestertown MD 21620, USA

Phillips, Paul A — Baseball Player
507 N Main Ave, Demopolis AL 36732, USA

Phillips, Peter C B — Economist
PO Box 208281, New Haven CT 06520, USA

Phillips, Phil — Singer, Songwriter
PO Box 105, Jennings LA 70546, USA

Phillips, Preston T — Architect
Preston T Phillips Architect, PO Box 3037, Bridgehampton NY 11932, USA

Phillips, Reginald K — Football Player
8300 W Airport Blvd, #906, Houston TX 77071, USA

Phillips, Richard — Captain, Maersk Alabama Cargo Ship
211 River Road, Underhill VT 05489, USA

Phillips, Sam — Singer, Songwriter
High Road Touring, 751 Bridgeway, #200, Sausalito CA 94965 USA

Phillips, Sean — Cartoonist
153 Petherton Road, Highbury, London N5 2RS, England

Phillips, Sian — Actress
Dalzell & Beresford, 26 Astwood Mews, London SW7 4DE, England

Phillips, Susanna — Opera Singer
I M G Artists, Hogarth Business Park, Chiswick, London W4 2TH, England

Phillips, T Scott — Drummer (Creed, Alter Bridge)
Wind-Up Records, 72 Madison Ave, #800, New York NY 10016 USA

Phillips, Todd — Director, Writer
Green Hat Productions, 4000 Warner Blvd, Building 66, Burbank CA 91522, USA

Phillips, W Taylor (Tay) — Baseball Player
594 Mein Mitchell Road, Hiram GA 30141, USA

Phillips, Wade — Football Coach
6115 Norway Road, Dallas TX 75230, USA

Phillips, Warren H — Publisher
Bridge Works Publications, PO Box 1798, Bridgehampton NY 11932, USA

Phillips, Wendy — Actress
Stone Manners Salners, 9911 W Pico Blvd, #1400, Los Angeles CA 90035 USA

Phillips, William D — Nobel Physics Laureate
13409 Chestnut Oak Dr, Gaithersburg MD 20878, USA

Phillips, Zara A E — Princess, England; Equestrian
Gatecombe Park, Minchinhampton, Stroud GL6 9AT, England

Phillipson, Don — Soccer Executive
5014 Gladiola Way, Golden CO 80403, USA

Philo, Phoebe — Fashion Designer
Chloe, 54-56 Rue du Faubourg Saint Honore, 75008 Paris, France

Philp, Tom — Journalist
Sacramento Bee, Editorial Dept, 2100 Q St, Sacramento CA 95816 USA

Phinney, Davis — Cyclist, Sportscaster
470 Juniper Ave, Boulder CO 80304, USA

Phipps, Michael E (Mike) — Football Player
2748 NE 25th St, Lighthouse Point FL 33064, USA

Phipps, William E — Actor
Commercial Talent, 9255 Sunset Blvd, #505, Los Angeles CA 90069, USA

Phoebus, Thomas H (Tom) — Baseball Player
2822 SW Lakemont Place, Palm City FL 34990, USA

Phoenix, Joaquin R — Actor, Singer, Guitarist
Patricola Public Relations, 9171 Wilshire Blvd, #441, Beverly Hills CA 90210 USA

Piano, Renzo — Pritzker Architectural Laureate
Renzo Piano Building Workshop, Via Rubens 29, 16158 Genoa, Italy

Piat, Jean — Actor
Artmedia, 20 Ave Rapp, 75007 Paris, France

Piatkowski, Eric T — Basketball Player
2125 S 189th Circle, Omaha NE 68130, USA

Piatkowski, Walter (Walt) — Basketball Player
5263 Autumn Place, Rapid City SD 57702, USA

Piau, Sandrine — Opera Singer
I M G Artists, Hogarth Business Park, Chiswick, London W4 2TH, England

Piazza, Michale J (Mike) — Baseball Player
1000 S Pointe Dr, #3101, Miami Beach FL 33139, USA

Piazza, Vincent — Actor
Gersh Agency, 9465 Wilshire Blvd, #600, Beverly Hills CA 90212 USA

Picard, Geoffrey — Rowing Athlete
2020 W Lake Blvd, Tahoe City CA 96145, USA

Picard, J Noel — Ice Hockey Player
3636 Wilmington Ave, Saint Louis MO 63116, USA

Picard, Robert R J — Ice Hockey Player
4718 Grand Cypress Circle N, Coconut Creek FL 33073, USA

Picardo, Robert — Actor
Sovereign Talent Group, 8421 Wilshire Blvd, #200, Beverly Hills CA 90211, USA

Picasso, Paloma
Quintana Ron Ltd, 291A Brompton Road, London SW3 2DY, England — Jewelry Designer, Actress

Picatto, Alexandra
Abrams Artists, 9200 W Sunset Blvd, #1125, West Hollywood CA 90069 USA — Actress

Piccard, Bertrand
Winds of Hope, Ave de Florimont 20, 1006 Lausanne, Switzerland — Balloonist

Picciolo, Robert M (Rob)
11773 Invierno Dr, San Diego CA 92124, USA — Baseball Player

Piccoli, Michel
11 Rue des Lions Saint Paul, 75004 Paris, France — Actor

Piccolo, Ottavia
Anne Alvares Correa, 34 Rue Jouffroy d'Abbans, 75017 Paris, France — Actress

Piccolo, Rina
King Features Syndicate, 300 W 57th St, #1500, New York NY 10019 USA — Cartoonist (Six Chix, Tina's Groove)

Piccone, Louis J (Lou)
325 N Forest Road, Buffalo NY 14221, USA — Football Player

Piccone, Robin
Piccone Apparel Corp, 1424 Washington Blvd, Venice CA 90291, USA — Fashion Designer

Pichardo, Hipolito
21218 Saint Andrews Blvd, #305, Boca Raton FL 33433, USA — Baseball Player

Pichette, Dave
4751 Rue Escoffier, Quebec QC G1Y 3J4, Canada — Ice Hockey Player

Pick, Amelie
Artmedia, 20 Ave Rapp, 75007 Paris, France — Actress

Pickard, Nancy
7258 Mastin St, Shawnee KS 66203, USA — Writer

Pickel, William G (Bill)
9 Autumn Ridge Road, South Salem NY 10590, USA — Football Player

Pickens, Carl M
3085 Sugarloaf Club Dr, Duluth GA 30097, USA — Football Player

Pickens, James, Jr
Wright Entertainment, 3207 Winnier Dr, Los Angeles CA 90068, USA — Actor

Pickens, Jo Ann
Norman McCann Artists, 56 Lawrie Park Gardens, London SE26 6XJ, England — Opera Singer

Pickens, T Boone, Jr
B P Capital, 8117 Preston Road, #260, Dallas TX 75225, USA — Businessman

Pickering, Jeff
King Features Syndicate, 300 W 57th St, #1500, New York NY 10019 USA — Cartoonist (Spats)

Pickering, Thomas R
2318 Kimbro St, Alexandria VA 22307, USA — Diplomat, Businessman

Pickett, Cecil L (Ricky)
1017 Wood Ridge Dr, Azle TX 76020, USA — Baseball Player

Pickett, Cindy
Shelter Entertainment, 9454 Wilshire Blvd, #715, Beverly Hills CA 90212 USA — Actress

Pickett, Rex
A P A Talent/Literary Agency, 405 S Beverly Dr, #300, Beverly Hills CA 90212 USA — Director, Writer

Pickett, Ryan L
Green Bay Packers, 1265 Lombardi Ave, Green Bay WI 54304 USA — Football Player

Pickford, Kevin P
6006 N Harcourt Dr, Coeur D'Alene ID 83815, USA — Baseball Player

Pickitt, John L
38 Sunrise Point Road, Clover SC 29710, USA — Air Force General

Pickler, Kellie
Fitzgerald Hartley, 1908 Wedgewood Ave, Nashville TN 37212, USA — Singer, Songwriter

Pickles, Christina
Domain Talent, 9229 W Sunset Blvd, #710, West Hollywood CA 90069 USA — Actress

Pickles, Vivian
91 Regent St, London W1R 8RU, England — Actress

Pickup, Ronald
54 Crouch Hall Road, London N8 8HG, England — Actor

Picolotti, Romina
Human Rights Center, Gen Paz 186, 10 Mo Pisa A, Cordoba 5000, Argentina — Social Activist

Picoult, Jodi
PO Box 508, Etna NH 03750, USA — Writer

Pictor, Bruce
Variety Artists, 793 Higuera St, #6, San Luis Obispo CA 93401 USA — Drummer (Association)

Piddock, Jim
Amsel Eisenstadt Frazier, 5055 Wilshire Blvd, #865, Los Angeles CA 90036 USA — Actor

Pidgeon, Rebecca
Ken McReddie Assoc, 11 Connaught Place, London W2 2ET, England — Actress, Singer

Pidhirny, Harry
1880 Valley Farm Road, Pickering ON L1V 6B3, Canada — Ice Hockey Player

Piech, Ferdinand
Volkswagenwerk AG, 38436 Wolfsburg, Germany — Businessman

Piedmont, Matt
Creative Artists Agency, 2000 Ave of Stars, #100, Los Angeles CA 90067 USA — Director, Producer, Writer

Piedra, Jorge
2208 Vaquero Estates Blvd, Westlake TX 76262, USA — Baseball Player

Pielmeier, John
Creative Artists Agency, 2000 Ave of Stars, #100, Los Angeles CA 90067 USA — Writer, Actor, Producer

Pienaar, Jacobus F
Rugby Football Union, PO Box 99, Newlands 7725, South Africa — Rugby Player

Piene, Otto
383 Old Ayer Road, Groton MA 01450, USA — Sculptor, Artist

Pier, Christina
I M G Artists, Hogarth Business Park, Chiswick, London W4 2TH, England — Opera Singer

Pierce, Allison
Paradigm Agency, 360 N Crescent Dr, North Building, Beverly Hills CA 90210 USA — Singer, Guitarist (Pierces)

Pierce, Catherine
Paradigm Agency, 360 N Crescent Dr, North Building, Beverly Hills CA 90210 USA — Singer (Pierces)

Pierce, Chester M
17 Prince St, Jamaica Plain MA 02130, USA — Psychiatrist

Pierce, David Hyde
2400 Inverness Ave, Los Angeles CA 90027, USA — Actor, Singer

Pierce, Donald R (Don)
340 Neptune Ave, Encinitas CA 92024, USA — Thoroughbred Racing Jockey

Pierce, Edward J (Ed) — Baseball Player
702 E Laurel Ave, Glendora CA 91741, USA

Pierce, Jeffrey — Actor
Don Buchwald/Fortitude, 6500 Wilshire Blvd, #2200, Los Angeles CA 90048 USA

Pierce, Jeffrey C (Jeff) — Baseball Player
1046 Lantern Lanes, Circle Pines MN 55014, USA

Pierce, Jill — Actress
Extreme Team Productions, 15941 S Harlem, #319, Tinley Park IL 60477, USA

Pierce, Jonathan — Singer
Muse Assoc, 330 Franklin Road, #135-8, Brentwood TN 37027, USA

Pierce, Kirstin — Actress
Don Buchwald/Fortitude, 6500 Wilshire Blvd, #2200, Los Angeles CA 90048 USA

Pierce, L Jack — Baseball Player
1002 Cortez St, Laredo TX 78040, USA

Pierce, Lincoln — Cartoonist (Big Nate)
United Feature Syndicate, PO Box 5610, Cincinnati OH 45201 USA

Pierce, Mary — Tennis Player
Women's Tennis Assn, 1 Progress Plaza, #1500, Saint Petersburg FL 33701 USA

Pierce, Paul A — Basketball Player
79 Winter St, Lincoln MA 01773, USA

Pierce, Randy — Ice Hockey Player
178 Five Arches Dr, RR 2, Pakenham ON K0A 2X0, Canada

Pierce, Ron — Harness Racing Driver
PO Box 361, Clarksburg NJ 08510, USA

Pierce, Tamora — Writer
Random House, 1745 Broadway, #1800, New York NY 10019 USA

Pierce, W William (Billy) — Baseball Player
1321 Baileys Crossing Dr, Lemont IL 60439, USA

Pierce, Wendell — Actor
Paradigm Agency, 360 N Crescent Dr, North Building, Beverly Hills CA 90210 USA

Pierce-Roberts, Tony — Cinematographer
1 Princes Gardens, London W5 1SD, England

Piercy, Marge — Writer
PO Box 1473, Wellfleet MA 02667, USA

Piercy, Scott — Golfer
Professional Golfer's Assn, PO Box 109601, Palm Beach Gardens FL 33410 USA

Pierpoint, Eric — Actor
2199 Topanga Skyline Dr, Topanga CA 90290, USA

Pierre, Juan D — Baseball Player
6148 NW 65th Terrace, Parkland FL 33067, USA

Pierre-Paul, Jason — Football Player
New York Giants, Meadowlands Stadium, 102 Route 120, East Rutherford NJ 07073 USA

Piers, Julie — Golfer
Ladies Pro Golf Assn, 100 International Golf Dr, Daytona Beach FL 32124 USA

Piersall, James A (Jimmy) — Baseball Player
1105 Oakview Dr, Wheaton IL 60187, USA

Pierson, Emma — Actress
Independent Talent Group, Oxford House, 76 Oxford St, London W1D 1BS, England

Pierson, Geoffrey — Actor
Stone Manners Salners, 9911 W Pico Blvd, #1400, Los Angeles CA 90035 USA

Pierson, Jack — Photographer, Sculptor
Cheim & Read, 547 W 25th St, New York NY 10001, USA

Pierson, Kate — Singer, Organist (B-52's)
Lazy Meadow Motel, 5191 Route 28, Mount Tremper NY 12457, USA

Pierson, Markus — Artist, Sculptor
OutWest, 7216 Washington St NE, #A, Albuquerque NM 87109, USA

Pierson, Peter S (Pete) — Football Player
17646 Jamestown Way, #D, Lutz FL 33558, USA

Pierson, Plenette — Basketball Player
New York Liberty, Madison Square Garden, 2 Penn Plaza, New York NY 10121 USA

Pierson, Reggie L — Football Player
17566 Elderberry Circle, Carson CA 90746, USA

Pierzynski, Anthony J (A J) — Baseball Player
2139 N Clifton Ave, Chicago IL 60614, USA

Pieterse, Sasha — Actress
A P A Talent/Literary Agency, 405 S Beverly Dr, #300, Beverly Hills CA 90212 USA

Pietkiewicz, Stanley T (Stan) — Basketball Player
2213 Venetian Way, Winter Park FL 32789, USA

Pietrangeli, Nicola (Nicky) — Tennis Player
Via Eustachio Manfredi 15, 00197 Rome, Italy

Pietrangelo, Frank — Ice Hockey Player
6371 Moretta Dr, Niagara Falls ON L2E 4H7, Canada

Pietrus, Mickael — Basketball Player
13420 Bonica Way, Windermere FL 34786, USA

Pietruski, John M, Jr — Businessman
27 E Corsica Court, Farmingdale NJ 07727, USA

Pietrzak, James M (Jim) — Football Player
8807 Citrus Village Dr, #108, Tampa FL 33626, USA

Pietrzykowski, Zbigniew — Boxer
Ul Gomicza 5, Bielsko-Blata 43 409, Poland

Pietz, Amy — Actress
Innovative Artists, 1505 10th St, Santa Monica CA 90401 USA

Pifferini, Robert M (Bob), Jr — Football Player
1731 Granite Hill Road, Placerville CA 95667, USA

Pigford, Eva — Model, Actress
Ford Models Inc, 111 5th Ave, #900, New York NY 10003 USA

Pigg, Landon — Singer, Songwriter
R C A Records, 8750 Wilshire Blvd, Beverly Hills CA 90211 USA

Piggott, Lester K — Thoroughbred Racing Jockey
Beech Tree House, Tostock, Bury Saint Edmonds, Suffolk 1P30 9NY, England

Piggott, Marcus — Photographer
Art Partner, 155 6th Ave, #1500, New York NY 10013, USA

Pignatano, Joseph B (Joe) — Baseball Player
150 78th St, Brooklyn NY 11209, USA

Pigott-Smith, Tim — Actor
Conway Van Gelder Grant, 8-12 Broadwick St, #300, London W1F 8HW, England

V.I.P. Address Book

Pihlman, Tuomas
105 Spit Brook Road, Nashua NH 03062, USA — Ice Hockey Player
Pike, Gary
10031 Benares Place, Sun Valley CA 91352, USA — Singer (Lettermen)
Pike, Jim
M P I Talent Agency, 1801 Ave of Stars, #1420, Los Angeles CA 90067, USA — Singer (Lettermen)
Pike, Mike H (Mark)
508 Marywood Court, Edgewood KY 41017, USA — Football Player
Pike, Nicholas
First Artists Mgmt, 4764 Park Granada, #210, Calabasas CA 91302 USA — Composer
Pike, Rosamund
United Agents, 12-26 Lexington St, London W1F 0LE, England — Actress
Pilarczyk, Daniel E
100 E 8th St, #800, Cincinnati OH 45202, USA — Religious Leader
Pilati, Stefano
Yves Saint Laurent, 7 Ave George V, 75008 Paris, France — Fashion Designer
Pileggi, Mitch
Pakula/King, 9229 W Sunset Blvd, #315, West Hollywood CA 90069 USA — Actor
Pileggi, Nicholas
Bloom Hergott Diemer, 150 S Rodeo Dr, #300, Beverly Hills CA 90212 USA — Writer, Producer
Pilger, John R
57 Hambatt Road, London SW4 9EQ, England — Journalist, Filmmaker, Environmentalist
Pilgrim, Evan B
1787 Cobblestone Dr, Provo UT 84604, USA — Football Player
Piligian, Craig
Pilgrim Films, 12020 Chandler Blvd, #200, North Hollywood CA 91607, USA — Producer
Pilkington, Lorraine
Another Tongue, 10-11 D'Arbay St, London W1F 8DS, England — Actress
Pill, Alison
Burstein Co, 15304 W Sunset Blvd, #208, Pacific Palisades CA 90272 USA — Actress
Pilla, Anthony M
Catholic Bishops National Conference, 3211 4th St, Washington DC 20017, USA — Religious Leader
Pillari, Ross
B P America Inc, 535 Madison Ave, #200, New York NY 10022, USA — Businessman
Piller Cottrer, Pietro
Borgo Gran Villa 76, 32047 Sappada, Italy — Cross Country Skier
Piller, Zachery P (Zach)
23 Colonel Winstead Dr, Brentwood TN 37027, USA — Football Player
Pillers, Lawrence D
140 David Clemons Road, Quincy FL 32352, USA — Football Player
Pilliod, Charles J, Jr
49 Twin Oaks Road, #2, Akron OH 44313, USA — Diplomat, Businessman
Pillitteri, Lynn J
Western Washington University, Biology Dept, 516 High St, Bellingham WA 98225, USA — Biologist
Pillow, Ray
Joe Taylor Artist Agency, PO Box 279, Williamstown NJ 37068 USA — Singer, Songwriter
Pilote, Pierre P
PO Box 247, Wyevale ON L0L 2T0, Canada — Ice Hockey Player
Pimenta, Simon Ignatius Cardinal
Archbishop's House, 21 Nathalal Parekh Marg, Mumbai 400 039, India — Religious Leader
Pinault, Francois
Artemis SA, 5 Blvd de Latour-Maubourg, 75007 Paris, France — Businessman
Pincay, Laffit, Jr
719 Carriage House Dr, Arcadia CA 91006, USA — Thoroughbred Racing Jockey
Pinchak, Jimmy (Jax)
Stone Manners Salners, 9911 W Pico Blvd, #1400, Los Angeles CA 90035 USA — Actor
Pinchot, Bronson
Amsel Eisenstadt Frazier, 5055 Wilshire Blvd, #865, Los Angeles CA 90036 USA — Actor
Pinckney, Edward L (Ed)
3350 SW 27th Ave, #1004, Miami FL 33133, USA — Basketball Player
Pinckney, Sandra
Food Network, 1180 Ave of Americas, #1200, New York NY 10036 USA — Chef
Pincling, Andrew (Pinch)
Leave Home Booking, 1400 S Foothill Dr, #34, Salt Lake City UT 84108, USA — Drummer (Damned)
Pincus, Henry
Principato-Young, 9465 Wilshire Blvd, #880, Beverly Hills CA 90212 USA — Director
Pinda, Mizengo
Prime Minister's Office, PO Box 980, Dodoma, Tanzania — Prime Minister, Tanzania
Pinder, A Geraold (Gerry)
320 39th Ave SW, Calgary AB T2S 0W7, Canada — Ice Hockey Player
Pinder, Cyril C
7137 S Luella Ave, Chicago IL 60649, USA — Football Player
Pinder, Lucy
Neon Models, 34 Clare Lane, London N1 3DB, England — Model
Pinder, Michael (Mike)
Moody Blues, 53-55 High St, Cobham, Surrey KT11 3DP, England — Keyboardist (Moody Blues)
Pine, Chris
Creative Artists Agency, 2000 Ave of Stars, #100, Los Angeles CA 90067 USA — Actor
Pine, Courtney
Collaboration, 23 Ave Crescent, London W3 8ET, England — Jazz Saxophonist
Pine, Linda
Abrams-Rubaloff Lawrence, 8075 W 3rd St, #303, Los Angeles CA 90048 USA — Actress
Pine, Robert
4212 Ben Ave, Studio City CA 91604, USA — Actor
Pineau-Valencienne, Didier
63 Rue de la Boetie, 75008 Paris, France — Businessman
Pineda, Michael F
New York Yankees, Yankee Stadium, E 161st St & River Ave, Bronx NY 10451 USA — Baseball Player
Pineiro, Joel A
3410 Poinciana Ave, Miami FL 33133, USA — Baseball Player
Piñera Echenique, M J Sebastian
President's Office, Palacio de la Monedo, Santiago, Chile — President, Chile
Pinera, Mike
Neal Hollander Agency, 9966 Majorca Place, Boca Raton FL 33434 USA — Singer, Guitarist
Pines, Alexander
University of California, Chemistry Dept, Hildebrand Hall, Berkeley CA 94720, USA — Chemist

Pinette, John
Luber Rocklin Entertainment, 8530 Wilshire Blvd, #555, Beverly Hills CA 90211 USA — Actor, Comedian

Pinger, Mark
5201 Orduna Dr, #6, Coral Gables FL 33146, USA — Swimmer

Pini, Daniela
I M G Artists, Hogarth Business Park, Chiswick, London W4 2TH, England — Opera Singer

Piniella, Louis V (Lou)
1005 Taray de Avila, Tampa FL 33613, USA — Baseball Player, Manager

Pinkel, Donald P
275 Marlene Dr, San Luis Obispo CA 93405, USA — Pediatrician

Pinkel, Gary
University of Missouri, Athletic Dept, Columbia MO 64211, USA — Football Coach

Pinker, Steven A
Harvard University, Psychology Dept, Cambridge MA 01238, USA — Psychologist

Pinkett Smith, Jada
I C M Partners, 10250 Constellation Blvd, #900, Los Angeles CA 90067 USA — Actress

Pinkett, Allen J
320 W 8th Place, Hobart IN 46342, USA — Football Player

Pinkins, Tonya
Warren Cowan, 8899 Beverly Blvd, #918, Los Angeles CA 90048 USA — Actress, Singer

Pinkney, V Reginald (Reggie)
518 Rock Canyon Dr, Fayetteville NC 28303, USA — Football Player

Pinkston, Rob
Momentum Talent, 9401 Wilshire Blvd, #501, Beverly Hills CA 90212, USA — Actor

Pinkston, Ryan
A P A Talent/Literary Agency, 405 S Beverly Dr, #300, Beverly Hills CA 90212 USA — Actor

Pinkwater, Julie
Ladies' Home Journal, Publisher's Office, 125 Park Ave, New York NY 10017, USA — Publisher

Pinner, Artose D
102 Big Blue Court, Hopkinsville KY 42240, USA — Football Player

Pinney, Raymond E (Ray)
6529 NE Windermere Road, #B, Seattle WA 98105, USA — Football Player

Pinnock, Trevor
35 Gloucester Crescent, London NW1 7DL, England — Conductor, Concert Harpsichordist

Pino, Danny
G E F Entertainment, 122 N Clark Dr, #401, Los Angeles CA 90048, USA — Actor

Pino, Mario
10305 Kingsway Court, Ellicott City MD 21042, USA — Thoroughbred Racing Jockey

Pinol, Jacqueline
TalentWorks, 3500 W Olive Ave, #1400, Burbank CA 91505 USA — Actress

Pinon, Dominique
Agence Artiste Adequet, 80 Rue d'Amsterdam, 75009 Paris, France — Actor

Pinos, Carmen
Av Diagonal 490, #3/2, 08026 Barcelona, Spain — Architect

Pinsent, Gordon E
Noble Caplan Abrams, 1260 Yonge St, #200, Toronto ON M4T 1W6, Canada — Actor

Pinsent, Matthew
British International Rowing Office, 6 Lower Mall, London W6 9DJ, England — Rowing Athlete

Pinsky, Drew
Dr Drew Productions, 14742 Ventura Blvd, #PH, Sherman Oaks CA 91403, USA — Actor, Moive Producer

Pinsky, Robert N
Boston University, Creative Writing Dept, 236 Bay State Road, Boston MA 02215, USA — Writer

Pinson, Bobby O
Susan Niles Public Relations, 726 Bresslyn Road, Nashville TN 37205, USA — Singer, Guitarist, Songwriter

Pinson, Julie
13576 Cheltenham Dr, Sherman Oaks CA 91423, USA — Actress

Pintat Santolaria, Albert
President's Office, Casa de la Valle, Andorra la Vella, Andorra — Head of Government, Andorra

Pintauro, Danny
Preston Entertainment, 8033 Sunset Blvd, #2750, Los Angeles CA 90046, USA — Actor

Pinter, Mark
Gage Group, 14724 Ventura Blvd, #505, Sherman Oaks CA 91403 USA — Actor

Pinto, Freida
Creative Artists Agency, 2000 Ave of Stars, #100, Los Angeles CA 90067 USA — Actress, Model

Pinto, Inbal
Inbal Pinto Dance Co, 5 Yechley St, Neve Tzedek, Tel-Aviv 65149, Israel — Dancer, Choreographer

Pinto, Mandie
27660 Heather Ridge Way, Canyon Country CA 91351, USA — Singer

Pinto, Maria
133 N Jefferson St, #600, Chicago IL 60601, USA — Fashion Designer

Pintscher, Matthias
Grennenau, Fischerweg 2, 34302 Guxhagen, Germany — Composer, Conductor

Piollet, Marc
Kunstler Sekretariat am Gasteig, Rosenheimer Str 52, 81669 Munich, Germany — Conductor

Piotrovsky, Mikhail B
State Hermitage Museum, 2 Dvortsovaya, 190000 Saint Petersburg, Russia — Museum Executive

Piotrowski, Tom
80 Clarks Landing Road, Port Republic, NJ 08241, USA — Basketball Player

Piovanelli, Silvano Cardinal
Piazzi S Giovanni 3, 50129 Florence, Italy — Religious Leader

Piovani, Nicola
Via G Veroese 103, 00146 Rome, Italy — Composer

Piper, Billie P
Rights House, Drury House, 34-43 Russell St, London WC2B 5HA, England — Singer, Actress

Piper, Cherie
Team Canada, 2424 University Dr NW, Calgary AB T2N 3Y9, Canada — Ice Hockey Player

Piper, Jacki
Rob Groves Mgmt, 33 Glasshouse St, Soho, London W1B 5DG, England — Actress

Piper, Roddy
Super Artists, 2910 Main St, #200, Santa Monica CA 90405, USA — Professional Wrestler, Actor

Pipes, Leah
Untitled Entertainment, 350 S Beverly Dr, #200, Beverly Hills CA 90212 USA — Actress

Pipes, R Byron
4509 Sugar Maple Dr, Lafayette IN 47905, USA — Educator

Pipkin, Joyce C (J C)
1026 Stone Stack Dr, Bethlehem PA 18015, USA — Football Player

Pippen, Scottie
2571 Del Lago Dr, Fort Lauderdale FL 33316, USA — Basketball Player
Pippig, Uta
Take the Magic Step, 777 NW 51st St, #309, Boca Raton FL 33431, USA — Track Athlete
Pippy, Katelyn
A P A Talent/Literary Agency, 405 S Beverly Dr, #300, Beverly Hills CA 90212 USA — Actress
Piquet, Nelson
Autodromo, SEN/CDPM, Rua da Gasolina #01, 7007-400 Brasilia DF, Brazil — Auto Racing Driver
Piraro, Dan
534 Wilcox Ave, Los Angeles CA 90004, USA — Cartoonist (Bizarro)
Pires de Miranda, Pedro
Avenida da India 10, 1300 Lisbon, Portugal — Government Official, Portugal
Pires do Nascimento, Alexandre
E M I Records, 150 5th Ave, #700, New York NY 10011 USA — Singer
Pires, Cleo
Ascend Entertainment, 950 10th St, #A, Santa Monica CA 90403, USA — Actress
Pires, Mary Joao
Herzberger Artists, 't Woud 1, 3862 PM Nijkerk, Netherlands — Concert Pianist
Pirkis, Max
I C M Partners, 10250 Constellation Blvd, #900, Los Angeles CA 90067 USA — Actor
Pirkl, Gregory D (Greg)
6822 Emerald Bay Lane, Indianapolis IN 46237, USA — Baseball Player
Pirner, Dave
Monterey Peninsula Artists, 404 W Franklin St, Monterey CA 93940 USA — Singer (Soul Asylum), Songwriter
Piro, Stephanie
PO Box 605, Hampton NH 03843, USA — Cartoonist (Six Chix)
Pirtie, Gerald E (Gerry)
30306 E 59th St, Broken Arrow OK 74014, USA — Baseball Player
Pirus, Alex
15W222 Concord St, Elmhurst IL 60126, USA — Ice Hockey Player
Pisapia, Joe
Nettwerk Mgmt, 345 7th Ave, #2400, New York NY 10001, USA — Singer, Bassist (Guster)
Pisarcik, Joseph A (Joe)
27 Compass Circle, Mount Laurel NJ 08054, USA — Football Player
Pisarev, Andrei
I M G Artists, Hogarth Business Park, Chiswick, London W4 2TH, England — Concert Pianist
Pischetsrider, Bernd
Volkswagen AG, Brieffach 1849, 38436 Wolfsburg, Germany — Businessman
Pisciotta, Marc G
867 Village Green NW, Marietta GA 30064, USA — Baseball Player
Piscitelli, Sabitino C (Sabby), Jr
500 NW 15th Court, Boca Raton FL 33486, USA — Football Player
Piscopo, Joe
Amsel Eisenstadt Frazier, 5055 Wilshire Blvd, #865, Los Angeles CA 90036 USA — Actor, Comedian
Pister, Karl S
University of California, Chancellor's Office, Santa Cruz CA 95064, USA — Educator
Pistone, Tom
7858 Old Concord Road, Charklotte NC 28213, USA — Auto Racing Driver
Pistor, Ludger
Stacey Castro Media, 4009 Leeward Ave, Los Angeles CA 90005 USA — Actor
Pitbull
Media Artists Group, 8255 Sunset Blvd, Los Angeles CA 90046, USA — Rap Artist
Pitchford, Dean
8491 W Sunset Blvd, PO Box 111, West Hollywood CA 90069, USA — Lyricist, Writer
Pitcock, Joan
341 E Lester Ave, Fresno CA 93720, USA — Golfer
Pitel, Piyush
Cabletron Systems, 35 Industrial Way, Rochester NY 14614, USA — Businessman
Pithart, Petr
Drazickeho Nam 10/65, 11800 Prague 1, Czech Republic — Government Official, Czech Republic
Pitillo, Maria
Karen Foreman Mgmt, 17547 Ventura Blvd, Encino CA 91316, USA — Actress
Pitino, Richard (Rick)
214 Mockingbird Gardens Dr, Louisville KY 40207, USA — Basketball Coach
Pitkamaki, Tero
P L 42, 60511 Hyllykallo, Finland — Track Athlete
Pitkanen, Joni
1214 Cobble Creek Circle, Cherry Hill NJ 08003, USA — Ice Hockey Player
Pitko, Alexander (Alex)
2689 Sports Village Loop, #12, Pinetop AZ 85935, USA — Baseball Player
Pitlick, Lance
5010 Shenandoah Lane N, Minneapolis MN 55446, USA — Ice Hockey Player
Pitlock, Lee E (Skip)
215 Prospect St, Seguin TX 78155, USA — Baseball Player
Pitman, Jennifer S
Owls Barn, Kintbury, Hungerford, Berks RG17 9XS, England — Thoroughbred Racing Trainer
Pitof
A P A Talent/Literary Agency, 405 S Beverly Dr, #300, Beverly Hills CA 90212 USA — Director, Writer
Pitou Zimmerman, Penny
560 Sanborn Road, Sanbornton NH 03269, USA — Alpine Skier
Pitre, Louise
Paquin Entertainment, 395 Notre Dame Ave, Winnipeg MB R3B 1R2, Canada — Singer, Actress
Pitt, Brad
Brillstein Entertainment Partners, 9150 Wilshire Blvd, #350, Beverly Hills CA 90212 USA — Actor, Producer
Pitt, Eugene S
Neal Hollander Agency, 9966 Majorca Place, Boca Raton FL 33434 USA — Singer (Jive Five)
Pitt, Harvey L
Kalorama Partners, 1130 Connecticut Ave NW, #800, Washington DC 20036, USA — Government Official, Financier
Pitt, Michael
W M E Entertainment, 9601 Wilshire Blvd, #300, Beverly Hills CA 90210 USA — Actor
Pittaro, Christopher F (Chris)
42 Pintinalli Dr, Trenton NJ 08619, USA — Baseball Player
Pittas, Dimitri
Columbia Artists Mgmt Inc, 1790 Broadway, #702, New York NY 10019 USA — Opera Singer
Pittin, Alessandro
G S Fiamme Gialle, Via alle Coste 14, 38037 Predazzo (TN), Italy — Nordic Combined Skier

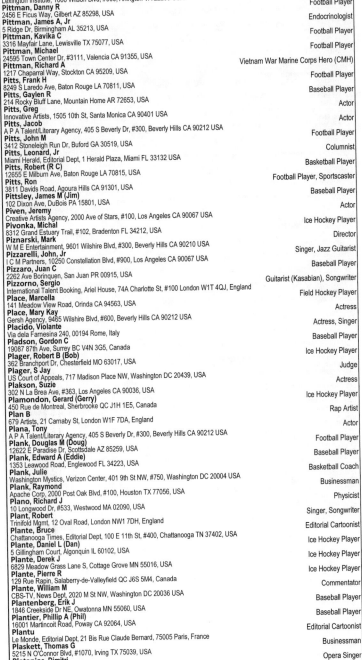

Pittman, Charles H
Lexington Institute, 1600 Wilson Blvd, #900, Arlington VA 22209 USA — Marine Corps General

Pittman, Danny R
2456 E Ficus Way, Gilbert AZ 85298, USA — Football Player

Pittman, James A, Jr
5 Ridge Dr, Birmingham AL 35213, USA — Endocrinologist

Pittman, Kavika C
3316 Mayfair Lane, Lewisville TX 75077, USA — Football Player

Pittman, Michael
24595 Town Center Dr, #3111, Valencia CA 91355, USA — Football Player

Pittman, Richard A
1217 Chaparral Way, Stockton CA 95209, USA — Vietnam War Marine Corps Hero (CMH)

Pitts, Frank H
8249 S Laredo Ave, Baton Rouge LA 70811, USA — Football Player

Pitts, Gaylen R
214 Rocky Bluff Lane, Mountain Home AR 72653, USA — Baseball Player

Pitts, Greg
Innovative Artists, 1505 10th St, Santa Monica CA 90401 USA — Actor

Pitts, Jacob
A P A Talent/Literary Agency, 405 S Beverly Dr, #300, Beverly Hills CA 90212 USA — Actor

Pitts, John M
3412 Stoneleigh Run Dr, Buford GA 30519, USA — Football Player

Pitts, Leonard, Jr
Miami Herald, Editorial Dept, 1 Herald Plaza, Miami FL 33132 USA — Columnist

Pitts, Robert (R C)
12655 E Milburn Ave, Baton Rouge LA 70815, USA — Basketball Player

Pitts, Ron
3811 Davids Road, Agoura Hills CA 91301, USA — Football Player, Sportscaster

Pittsley, James M (Jim)
102 Dixon Ave, DuBois PA 15801, USA — Baseball Player

Piven, Jeremy
Creative Artists Agency, 2000 Ave of Stars, #100, Los Angeles CA 90067 USA — Actor

Pivonka, Michal
8312 Grand Estuary Trail, #102, Bradenton FL 34212, USA — Ice Hockey Player

Piznarski, Mark
W M E Entertainment, 9601 Wilshire Blvd, #300, Beverly Hills CA 90210 USA — Director

Pizzarelli, John, Jr
I C M Partners, 10250 Constellation Blvd, #900, Los Angeles CA 90067 USA — Singer, Jazz Guitarist

Pizzaro, Juan C
2262 Ave Borinquen, San Juan PR 00915, USA — Baseball Player

Pizzorno, Sergio
International Talent Booking, Ariel House, 74A Charlotte St, #100 London W1T 4QJ, England — Guitarist (Kasabian), Songwriter

Place, Marcella
141 Meadow View Road, Orinda CA 94563, USA — Field Hockey Player

Place, Mary Kay
Gersh Agency, 9465 Wilshire Blvd, #600, Beverly Hills CA 90212 USA — Actress

Placido, Violante
Via dela Farnesina 240, 00194 Rome, Italy — Actress, Singer

Pladson, Gordon C
19087 87th Ave, Surrey BC V4N 3G5, Canada — Baseball Player

Plager, Robert B (Bob)
362 Branchport Dr, Chesterfield MO 63017, USA — Ice Hockey Player

Plager, S Jay
US Court of Appeals, 717 Madison Place NW, Washington DC 20439, USA — Judge

Plakson, Suzie
302 N La Brea Ave, #363, Los Angeles CA 90036, USA — Actress

Plamondon, Gerard (Gerry)
450 Rue de Montreal, Sherbrooke QC J1H 1E5, Canada — Ice Hockey Player

Plan B
679 Artists, 21 Carnaby St, London W1F 7DA, England — Rap Artist

Plana, Tony
A P A Talent/Literary Agency, 405 S Beverly Dr, #300, Beverly Hills CA 90212 USA — Actor

Plank, Douglas M (Doug)
12622 E Paradise Dr, Scottsdale AZ 85259, USA — Football Player

Plank, Edward A (Eddie)
1353 Leawood Road, Englewood FL 34223, USA — Baseball Player

Plank, Julie
Washington Mystics, Verizon Center, 401 9th St NW, #750, Washington DC 20004 USA — Basketball Coach

Plank, Raymond
Apache Corp, 2000 Post Oak Blvd, #100, Houston TX 77056, USA — Businessman

Plano, Richard J
10 Longwood Dr, #533, Westwood MA 02090, USA — Physicist

Plant, Robert
Trinifold Mgmt, 12 Oval Road, London NW1 7DH, England — Singer, Songwriter

Plante, Bruce
Chattanooga Times, Editorial Dept, 100 E 11th St, #400, Chattanooga TN 37402, USA — Editorial Cartoonist

Plante, Daniel L (Dan)
5 Gillingham Court, Algonquin IL 60102, USA — Ice Hockey Player

Plante, Derek J
6829 Meadow Grass Lane S, Cottage Grove MN 55016, USA — Ice Hockey Player

Plante, Pierre R
129 Rue Rapin, Salaberry-de-Valleyfield QC J6S 5M4, Canada — Ice Hockey Player

Plante, William M
CBS-TV, News Dept, 2020 M St NW, Washington DC 20036 USA — Commentator

Plantenberg, Erik J
1846 Creekside Dr NE, Owatonna MN 55060, USA — Baseball Player

Plantier, Phillip A (Phil)
16001 Martincoit Road, Poway CA 92064, USA — Baseball Player

Plantu
Le Monde, Editorial Dept, 21 Bis Rue Claude Bernard, 75005 Paris, France — Editorial Cartoonist

Plaskett, Thomas G
5215 N O'Connor Blvd, #1070, Irving TX 75039, USA — Businessman

Platanias, Dimitri
I M G Artists, Hogarth Business Park, Chiswick, London W4 2TH, England — Opera Singer

Plater-Zyberk, Elizabeth M
Duany & Plater-Zyberk Architects, 1023 SW 25th Ave, Miami FL 33135, USA — Architect

Platini, Michel
F I F A, Hitugweg 11, PO Box 85, 8030 Zurich 30, Switzerland — Soccer Player

Platov, Evgeni
Princeton Sports Center, PO Box 155, Blawenburg NJ 08504, USA — Ice Dancer

Platt, Campion A
Campion A Platt Architect, 152 Madison Ave, #900, New York NY 10016, USA — Architect

Platt, Howard
Shirley Hamilton, 333 E Ontario, #302, Chicago IL 60611, USA — Actor

Platt, Marc E
Marc Platt Productions, 100 Universal City Plaza, Bungalow 5163, Universal City CA 91608, USA — Producer

Platt, Oliver
W M E Entertainment, 9601 Wilshire Blvd, #300, Beverly Hills CA 90210 USA — Actor

Player, Gary J
Blair Atholl Farm, Lanseria, Fourways near Johannesburg, Gauteng 2068, South Africa — Golfer

Player, Scott D
330 N Shore Circle, #1113, Saint Augustine FL 32092, USA — Football Player

Playfair, James (Jim)
200-99 Station St, Saint John NB E2L 4X4, Canada — Ice Hockey Player, Coach

Playfair, Larry
724 Ransom Road, Grand Island NY 14072, USA — Ice Hockey Player

Plaza, Aubrey
Creative Artists Agency, 2000 Ave of Stars, #100, Los Angeles CA 90067 USA — Actress, Comedienne

Pleasant, Anthony D
17249 Connor Quay Court, Cornelius NC 28031, USA — Football Player

Pleasant, Marquis A
3549 Rio Grande Circle, Dallas TX 75233, USA — Football Player

Pleau, Lawrence W (Larry)
650 Spyglass Summit Dr, Chesterfield MO 63017, USA — Ice Hockey Player, Executive

Plec, Julie
W M E Entertainment, 9601 Wilshire Blvd, #300, Beverly Hills CA 90210 USA — Producer, Writer

Pleis, William (Bill)
16744 4th Ave NE, Bradenton FL 34212, USA — Baseball Player

Plemons, Jesse
TalentWorks, 3500 W Olive Ave, #1400, Burbank CA 91505 USA — Actor

Plesac, Daniel T (Dan)
245 White Thorne Lane, Valpariso IN 46383, USA — Baseball Player

Pleshette, John
Lynn Pleshette Literary Agency, 2700 N Beachwood Dr, Los Angeles CA 90068, USA — Actor, Director

Pless, Rance
5528 Asheville Highway, Greenville TN 37743, USA — Baseball Player

Pletcher, Eldon
210 Canberra Court, Slidell LA 70458, USA — Editorial Cartoonist

Pletcher, Todd A
Todd Pletcher Racing Stables, PO Box 30066, Elmont NY 11003, USA — Thoroughbred Racing Trainer

Pletnev, Mikhail V
Russian National Orchestra, Garibaldi 19, 117335 Moscow, Russia — Conductor, Concert Pianist

Plett, Willi
Willi Plett Sports Park, 1248 Harris Commons Place, Roswell GA 30076, USA — Ice Hockey Player

Plevneliev, Rosen A
President's Office, 2 Dondukov Blvd, 1123 Sofia, Bulgaria — President, Bulgaria

Plews, Herbert E (Herb)
350 Ponca Place, Boulder CO 80303, USA — Baseball Player

Pliego, Cesar
Marcella C Public Relations, 646 S Barrington Ave, #206, Brentwood CA 90049, USA — Bassist (Kinky)

Plies
Multi Entertainment, 4044 W Lake Mary Blvd, #104-324, Lake Mary FL 32746, USA — Rap Artist

Plimpton, Martha
Innovative Artists, 1505 10th St, Santa Monica CA 90401 USA — Actress

Plisetskaya, Maya M
Tverskaya 25/9, #31, 103050 Moscow, Russia — Ballerina

Pliska, Paul
George M Martynuk, 352 7th Ave, New York NY 10001, USA — Opera Singer

Plitmann, Hila
I M G Artists, Hogarth Business Park, Chiswick, London W4 2TH, England — Opera Singer

Plodinec, Timothy A (Tim)
23251 Gilmore St, West Hills CA 91307, USA — Baseball Player

Ploeger, Kurt A
6451 E Nance St, Mesa AZ 85215, USA — Football Player

Ploenchit, Saen Sor
Songchai Co, 71/23 Setsiri Rd, Sams Payathai, Bangkok 10400, Thailand — Boxer

Plotkin, Stanley A
3940 Delancey St, Philadelphia PA 19104, USA — Virologist

Plotnick, Jack
Stone Manners Salners, 9911 W Pico Blvd, #1400, Los Angeles CA 90035 USA — Actor

Plott, Charles R
881 El Campo Dr, Pasadena CA 91107, USA — Economist

Plowden, David
609 Cherry St, Winnetka IL 60093, USA — Writer, Photographer

Plowright, Joan A
Malthouse, Horsham Road, Ashurst, Steyning, West Sussex BN44 3AR, England — Actress

Plowright, Rosalind A
83 Saint Mark's Ave, Salisbury, Wilts SP1 3DW, England — Opera Singer

Pluhar, Erika
Huschkgasse 5, 1190 Vienna, Austria — Actress

Plum, Milton R (Milt)
1104 Oakside Court, Raleigh NC 27609, USA — Football Player

Plumb
FlatRock Mgmt, 2021 21st Ave S, #B104, Nashville TN 37212, USA — Singer

Plumb, Eve
Clear Talent Group, 325 W 38th St, #1203, New York NY 10018, USA — Actress

Plumb, Ron
975 Auden Park Dr, Kingston ON K7M 7T9, Canada — Ice Hockey Player

Plumer, Patricia (PattiSue)
USA Track & Field, 4341 Starlight Dr, Indianapolis IN 46239 USA — Track Athlete

Plumlee, Miles C
Indiana Pacers, Conseco Fieldhouse, 125 S Pennsylvania, Indianapolis IN 46204 USA — Basketball Player

Plummer, Ahmed K — Football Player
PO Box 30147, Columbus OH 43230, USA

Plummer, Amanda — Actress
Artist Group, 1650 Broadway, #1105, New York NY 10019 , USA

Plummer, Bruce E — Football Player
712 Fairmont Park Dr, Dacula GA 30019, USA

Plummer, Christopher — Actor, Singer
49 Wampum Hill Road, Weston CT 06883, USA

Plummer, Gary L — Football Player
10374 Rue Chamberry, San Diego CA 92131, USA

Plummer, Glenn — Actor
Innovative Artists, 1505 10th St, Santa Monica CA 90401 USA

Plummer, Jason S (Jake) — Football Player
282 Winterberry Way, Sandpoint ID 83864, USA

Plummer, William F (Bill) — Baseball Player, Manager
8504 Oak Terrace Lane, Millville CA 96062, USA

Plunk, Eric V — Baseball Player
9500 Pats Point Dr, Corona CA 92883, USA

Plunkett, Arthur S (Art) — Football Player
332 Santa Monica Dr, Henderson NV 89014, USA

Plunkett, Gerard — Actor
M A Mgmt, 1947 Pendrell St, #106, Vancouver BC V6G 1T5, Canada

Plunkett, James W (Jim), Jr — Football Player
51 Kilroy Way, Atherton CA 94027, USA

Plunkett, Marcella — Actress
Lisa Richards Agency, 108 Upper Leeson St, Dublin 4, Ireland

Plunkett, Maryann — Actress
Davis Spylios Mgmt, 244 W 54th St, #707, New York NY 10019, USA

Plushenko, Evgeny — Figure Skater
Flashlight Artists Agency, Via Enrico Fermi 18, 39100 Bolzano (BZ), Italy

Ply, Robert V (Bobby) — Football Player
8616 Ash Ave, Raytown MO 64138, USA

Plympton, Jeffrey H (Jeff) — Baseball Player
8 Robin St, Plainville MA 02762, USA

Plyushch, Ivan S — Head of State, Ukraine
Verkhovna Rada, M Hrushevskoho 5, 252019 Kiev, Ukraine

P-Nut — Bassist (311)
311 Hive, 8904 Florence Dr, Omaha NE 68147, USA

Poapst, Steve — Ice Hockey Player
502 Kelly Court, Lombard IL 60148, USA

Pocklington, Peter H — Ice Hockey Executive
Edmonton Oilers, 11230 110th St, Edmonton AB T5G 3H7, Canada

Pocoroba, Biff B — Baseball Player
3445 Broxton Mill Way, Snellville GA 30039, USA

Pocza, Harvie — Ice Hockey Player
135 Sun Harbour Close Road, Calgary AB T2X 3C4, Canada

Podein, Shjon — Ice Hockey Player
4350 Browndale Ave, Minneapolis MN 55424, USA

Podell, Eyal — Actor
Paul Kohner, 9300 Wilshire Blvd, #555, Beverly Hills CA 90212 USA

Podesta, John D — Government Official
3743 Brandywine St, Washington DC 20016, USA

Podesta, Rossana — Actress
Via Bartolomeo Ammanatti 8, 00187 Rome, Italy

Podeswa, Jeremy — Director
Rebelfilms, 317 Manning Ave, Toronto ON M6J 2K8, Canada

Podewell, Cathy — Actress
17328 S Crest Dr, Los Angeles CA 90035, USA

Podhoretz, Norman — Editor, Writer
Commentary, Editor's Office, 165 E 56th St, New York NY 10022, USA

Podlesh, Adam — Football Player
1302 Hackberry Court, Libertyville IL 60048, USA

Podloski, Ray — Ice Hockey Player
13323 118th St NW, Edmonton AB T5E 5L6, Canada

Podolak, Edward J (Ed) — Football Player
2227 Emma Road, Basalt CO 81621, USA

Podowski, Debbie — Actress
Red Mgmt, Box 3, 415 W Esplanade, North Vancouver BC V7M 1A6, Canada

Podsednik, Scott E — Baseball Player
6613 Herbert Road, Colleyville TX 76034, USA

Poe — Singer, Songwriter
Nettwerk Mgmt, 1650 W 2nd Ave, Vancouver BC V6J 4R3, Canada

Poe, Dontari — Football Player
Kansas City Chiefs, 1 Arrowhead Dr, Kansas City KS 64129 USA

Poe, Johnnie E — Football Player
1102 Colas Ave, East Saint Louis IL 62207, USA

Poehler, Amy — Actress, Comedienne
W M E Entertainment, 9601 Wilshire Blvd, #300, Beverly Hills CA 90210 USA

Poelvoorde, Benoit — Actor
Voyez Mon Agent, 20 Ave Rapp, 75007 Paris, France

Poepping, Michael H (Mike) — Baseball Player
13791 250th Ave, Pierz MN 56364, USA

Poesy, Clemence — Actress
Agence Elizabeth Simpson, 62 Blvd du Montparnasse, 75015 Paris, France

Poff, John W — Baseball Player
2786 Mishler Road, Mio MI 48647, USA

Poggioli, Sylvia — Commentator
National Public Radio, 635 Massachusetts Ave NW, #1, Washington DC 20001, USA

Pogorelich, Ivo — Concert Pianist
Columbia Artists Mgmt Inc, 1790 Broadway, #702, New York NY 10019 USA

Pogostkina, Alina — Concert Violinist
Harrison/Parrott, 5-6 Albion Court, London W6 0QT, England

Pogrebin, Letty Cottin — Editor, Writer, Social Activist
33 W 67th St, New York NY 10023, USA

Pogue, Donald W — Judge
US Court of International Trade, 1 Federal Plaza, New York NY 10278, USA

Pogue, William R
15 Wesley Dr, Bella Vista AR 72715, USA — Astronaut
Pohamba, Hifikepunye L
President's Office, State House, Mugabe Ave, Windhoek 9000, Namibia — President, Namibia
Pohl, Don
903 E Bellows St, Mount Pleasant MI 48858, USA — Golfer
Pohl, Frederick G, Jr
855 S Harvard Dr, Palatine IL 60067, USA — Writer
Pohl, John (Johnny)
2382 Clover Lane, Red Wing MN 55066, USA — Ice Hockey Player
Pohlman, Jenny
3824 SW Morgan St, Seattle WA 98126, USA — Artist
Poile, David R
Nashville Predators, 501 Broadway, Nashville TN 37203 USA — Ice Hockey Executive
Poile, Don
165 Woodford Dr SW, Calgary AB T2W 4C2, Canada — Ice Hockey Player
Poinar, George O, Jr
Oregon State University, Entomology Dept, Corvallis OR 97331, USA — Entomologist
Poindexter, Buster
Agency Group Ltd, 142 W 57th St, #600, New York NY 10019 USA — Singer
Poindexter, John M
10 Barrington Fare, Rockville MD 20850, USA — Navy Admiral, Government Official
Poindexter, Larry
TalentWorks, 3500 W Olive Ave, #1400, Burbank CA 91505 USA — Actor
Pointer, Aaron E
4902 N Scenic View Lane, Tacoma WA 98407, USA — Baseball Player
Pointer, Anita
12060 Crest Court, Beverly Hills CA 90210, USA — Singer (Pointer Sisters)
Pointer, Bonnie
T-Best Talent Agency, 508 Honey Lake Court, Danville CA 94506 USA — Singer (Pointer Sisters)
Pointer, Noel
Headline Talent, PO Box 131518, Staten Island NY 10313 USA — Jazz Violinist
Pointer, Priscilla
213 16th St, Santa Monica CA 90402, USA — Singer (Pointer Sisters)
Pointer, Ruth
Morey Management Group, 1100 Glendon Ave, #1100, Los Angeles CA 90024 USA — Singer (Pointer Sisters)
Poirot, Pierre
Artmedia, 20 Ave Rapp, 75007 Paris, France — Actor
Poisel, Philipp
Holunder Records, Waldhornlestr 18, 72072 Tuebingen, Germany — Singer
Poison Ivy
Leave Home Booking, 10 W Broadway, #608, Salt Lake City UT 84101, USA — Bassist (Cramps), Songwriter
Poitier, Sidney
Creative Artists Agency, 2000 Ave of Stars, #100, Los Angeles CA 90067 USA — Actor
Poitier, Sydney Tamiia
Paradigm Agency, 360 N Crescent Dr, North Building, Beverly Hills CA 90210 USA — Actress
Polaha, Kristoffer
Medavoy Mgmt, 10203 Santa Monica Blvd, #400, Los Angeles CA 90067 USA — Actor
Polamalu, Troy A
1761 Colgate Circle, La Jolla CA 92037, USA — Football Player
Polanco, Placido E
8950 SW 63rd Court, Miami FL 33156, USA — Baseball Player
Polanski, Roman
Chalet Milky Way, 3780 Gstaad, Switzerland — Director, Writer
Polansky, Mark L
2010 Hillside Oak Lane, Houston TX 77062, USA — Astronaut
Polanyi, John C
University of Toronto, Chemistry Dept, Toronto ON M5S 3H6, Canada — Nobel Chemistry Laureate
Polchinski, Joseph G
University of California, Physics Institute, Santa Barbara CA 93106, USA — Physicist
Pole, Richard H (Dick)
5124 Marsh Field Lane, Sarasota FL 34235, USA — Baseball Player
Polee, Dwayne L
1169 E 60th St, Los Angeles CA 90001, USA — Basketball Player
Polegato, Brett
International Mgmt Group, Pier House, Strand on the Green, London W4 3NN, England — Opera, Concert Singer
Polenzani, Matthew
I M G Artists, Hogarth Business Park, Chiswick, London W4 2TH, England — Opera Singer
Polese, Kim
Marimba Inc, 440 Clyde Ave, Mountain View CA 94043, USA — Businesswoman
Poleshchuk, Alexander F
Cosmonaut Training Center, Star City, 141160 Zvezdny Gorodok, Moscow Oblast, Russia — Cosmonaut
Poletiek, Noah
Don Buchwald/Fortitude, 6500 Wilshire Blvd, #2200, Los Angeles CA 90048 USA — Actor
Poletto, Severino Cardinal
Via Arcivescovado 12, 10121 Torino, Italy — Religious Leader
Poleway, Christopher J
Fortune Group, Time & Life Building, Rockefeller Center, New York NY 10020, USA — Businessman
Polic, Henry, II
Sutton-Barth Vennari, 145 S Fairfax Ave, #310, Los Angeles CA 90036 USA — Actor
Policarpo, Jose da Cruz Cardinal
Curia Parriarcal, Campo di Saint Clara, 1100 473 Lisbon, Portugal — Religious Leader
Polich, Mike
825 3rd St NE, Osseo MN 55369, USA — Ice Hockey Player
Polinsky, Alexander
C E S D, 10635 Santa Monica Blvd, #130, Los Angeles CA 90025 USA — Actor
Polish, Mark
United Talent Agency, 9336 Civic Center Dr, Beverly Hills CA 90210 USA — Actor, Producer, Writer
Polish, Michael
Creative Artists Agency, 2000 Ave of Stars, #100, Los Angeles CA 90067 USA — Director, Producer, Writer
Polito, Jon
Domain Talent, 9229 W Sunset Blvd, #710, West Hollywood CA 90069 USA — Actor
Politte, Clifford A (Cliff)
6306 Sprig Oak Court, #C, Saint Louis MO 63128, USA — Baseball Player
Politzer, H David
1145 Linda Vista Ave, Pasadena CA 91103, USA — Nobel Physics Laureate

Polk, Carlos D — Football Player
922 Saint Germain Road, Chula Vista CA 91913, USA

Polk, DaShon L — Football Player
3503 Cornwall Court, Missouri City TX 77459, USA

Polk, Steven R — Air Force General
Inspector General, HqUSAF, Pentagon, Washington DC 20330 USA

Polkinghorne, John C — Theologian, Templeton Laureate
Queen's College, Cambridge University, Cambridge CB3 9ET, England

Poll, Jon — Director, Producer
Gersh Agency, 9465 Wilshire Blvd, #600, Beverly Hills CA 90212 USA

Polla, Dennis L — Microbiotics Engineer
University of Minnesota, Electrical Engineering Dept, Minneapolis MN 55455, USA

Pollack, Andrea — Swimmer
S S V, Postfach 420140, 34070 Kassel, Germany

Pollack, Daniel — Concert Pianist
University of Southern California, Music Dept, Los Angeles CA 90089, USA

Pollack, Frank — Football Player
41 Tyrrel Court, Danville CA 94526, USA

Pollack, Jeffrey N — Poker Executive
Federated Sports & Gaming, Palms Casino & Resort, 4301 W Flamingo Road, Las Vegas NV 89103, USA

Pollack, Kevin — Actor
Don Buchwald/Fortitude, 6500 Wilshire Blvd, #2200, Los Angeles CA 90048 USA

Pollak, Avshalom — Dancer, Choreographer
Inbal Pinto Dance Co, 5 Yechley St, Neve Tzedek, Tel-Aviv 65149, Israel

Pollak, Cheryl A — Actress
PO Box 761460, Los Angeles CA 90076, USA

Pollak, Kevin — Actor, Comedian
Leverage Mgmt, 3030 Pennsylvania Ave, Santa Monica CA 90404 USA

Pollak, Lisa — Journalist
Baltimore Sun, Editorial Dept, 501 N Calvert St, Baltimore MD 21278, USA

Pollak, Michael D (Mike) — Football Player
Carolina Panthers, Ericsson Stadium, 800 S Mint St, Charlotte NC 28202 USA

Pollan, Tracy — Actress
Gersh Agency, 9465 Wilshire Blvd, #600, Beverly Hills CA 90212 USA

Pollard, Bernard K — Football Player
5605 Fairhaven Ave, Woodland Hills CA 91367, USA

Pollard, Frank D, Jr — Football Player
113 L C R 474, Mexia TX 76667, USA

Pollard, Marcus L — Football Player
673 Meadow Lakes Dr, Pine Mountain GA 31822, USA

Pollard, Michael J — Actor
520 S Burnside Ave, #12A, Los Angeles CA 90036, USA

Pollard, Robert — Singer, Musician, Songwriter
Manage This, PO Box 256, Old Chelsea Station, New York NY 10113, USA

Pollard, Robert L (Bob) — Football Player
8987 Washington Blvd, Beaumont TX 77707, USA

Pollard, Scot — Basketball Player
10389 Windemere, Carmel IN 46032, USA

Pollen, Arabella R H — Fashion Designer
Canham Mews, #8, Canham Road, London W3 7SR, England

Polley, Sarah — Actress, Director
10 Mary St, #308, Toronto ON M4Y 1P9, Canada

Pollini, Armando — Fashion Designer
Via Gambolina 51/6, 27029 Vigevano (PV), Italy

Pollini, Maurizio — Concert Pianist
R E S I A, Via Manzoni 31, 20120 Milan, Italy

Pollock, Alex J — Government Official, Financier
Federal Home Loan Bank, 111 E Wacker Dr, #800, Chicago IL 60601, USA

Pollock, David M — Football Player
Cincinnati Bengals, 1 Paul Brown Stadium, Cincinnati OH 45202 USA

Pollock, Griselda — Artist
Leeds University, Fine Arts Dept, Leeds LS2 9JT, England

Pollock, J C — Writer
I C M Partners, 10250 Constellation Blvd, #900, Los Angeles CA 90067 USA

Polo, Ana Maria — Commentator
Telemundo Network Group, 2470 W 8th Ave, Hialeah FL 33010 USA

Polo, Joseph (Joe) — Curling Athlete
Curling Assn, 5525 Clem's Way, Stevens Point WI 54482 USA

Polo, Teri — Actress, Model
Gersh Agency, 9465 Wilshire Blvd, #600, Beverly Hills CA 90212 USA

Polone, Gavin — Actor, Producer
Pariah, 9744 Wilshire Blvd, #205, Beverly Hills CA 90212, USA

Poloni, John P — Baseball Player
1714 Polo Club Dr, Tarpon Springs FL 34689, USA

Polonich, Dennis — Ice Hockey Player
70 Varsity Estates Close NW, Calgary AB T3B 5J1, Canada

Poloujadoff, Michel E — Electrical Engineer
8 Rue Roches, 77760 Buthiers, France

Polshek, James Stewart — Architect
Polshak Partnership, 320 W 134th St, #800, New York NY 10030, USA

Polson, John — Actor, Director, Producer
Creative Artists Agency, 2000 Ave of Stars, #100, Los Angeles CA 90067 USA

Polson, Ralph M — Basketball Player
3846 S Eagle Lane, Spokane WA 99206, USA

Polyakov, Valeri V — Cosmonaut
Health Ministry, Choroshevskoye Chaussee 76A, 123007 Moscow, Russia

Polynice, Olden — Basketball Player
PO Box 220339, Newhall CA 91322, USA

Pomakov, Robert — Opera Singer
I M G Artists, Hogarth Business Park, Chiswick, London W4 2TH, England

Pomeroy, Earl R — Representative, ND
Alston & Bird LLP, 950 F St NW, Washington DC 20004, USA

Pomers, Scarlett — Actress, Singer
D M G Talent, 4804 Laurel Canyon Blvd, Valley Village CA 91607, USA

Pominville, Jason — Ice Hockey Player
9123 Curry Lane, Clarence Center NY 14032, USA

V.I.P. Address Book

Pommier, Jean-Bernard — Concert Pianist, Conductor
Musike Academies, 12 Rte Praz Gilliard, 1000 Lausanne, Switzerland

Pomodora, Arnaldo — Sculptor
Via Vigevano 5, 20144 Milan, Italy

Pompeo, Ellen — Actress
John Carrabino Mgmt, 5900 Wilshire Blvd, #406, Los Angeles CA 90036 USA

Pomplun, Raquel — Model
Playboy Promotions, 2706 Media Center Dr, Los Angeles CA 90065 USA

Ponazecki, Joe — Actor
Don Buchwald/Fortitude, 10 E 44th St, New York NY 10017 USA

Ponce Enrile, Juan — Government Official, Philippines
2305 Morado St, Dasmarinas Village, Makati, Metro Manila, Philippines

Ponce, Carlos — Singer, Actor
Luber Rocklin Entertainment, 8530 Wilshire Blvd, #555, Beverly Hills CA 90211 USA

Ponce, Miguel A — Soccer Player
Federacion de Futbol, Colima 373 Colonia Roma, Delegacion Cuauhtemoc Mexico DF 06700, Mexico

Ponce, Poncie — Actor
13501 Delano St, Van Nuys CA 91401, USA

Ponce, Walter — Concert Pianist
University of California, Music Dept, Los Angeles CA 90024, USA

Poncia, Vincent (Vinnie), Jr — Singer, Songwriter
Joel Faden, 250 W 57th St, New York NY 10107, USA

Ponder, David E (Dave) — Football Player
1818 Sandalwood Lane, Grapevine TX 76051, USA

Ponder, Moana — Sculptor
Art Inc, 9401 San Pedro, San Antonio TX 78216, USA

Pondexter, Cappie — Basketball Player
New York Liberty, Madison Square Garden, 2 Penn Plaza, New York NY 10121 USA

Pondexter, Clifton (Cliff) — Basketball Player
1135 W Stuart Ave, Fresno CA 93711, USA

Ponomarenko, Sergei V — Ice Dancer
Sharks Ice, 1500 S 10th St, San Jose CA 95112, USA

Pons, B Stanley — Chemist
University of Utah, Chemistry Dept, Eyring Building, Salt Lake City UT 84112, USA

Pons, Juan — Opera Singer
Herbert Breslin, 119 W 57th St, #1505, New York NY 10019 USA

Ponson, Sidney A — Baseball Player
2541 NE 35th Dr, Fort Lauderdale FL 33308, USA

Ponta, Victor-Viorel (Vic) — Prime Minister, Romania
Prime Minister's Office, Piata Vicotriei 1, 71201 Bucharest, Romania

Pontbriand, Ryan D — Football Player
3044 Forest Lake Dr, Westlake OH 44145, USA

Pontes, Marcos C — Astronaut, Brazil
Cosmonaut Training Center, Star City, 141160 Zvezdny Gorodok, Moscow Oblast, Russia

Ponti, Michael — Concert Pianist
Heubergstr 32, 83565 Eschenlohe, Germany

Pontius, Chris — Actor
Untitled Entertainment, 350 S Beverly Dr, #200, Beverly Hills CA 90212 USA

Pontois, Noella-Chantal — Ballerina
25 Rue de Maubeuge, 75009 Paris, France

Ponty, Jean-Luc — Jazz Violinist, Composer
10340 Santa Monica Blvd, Los Angeles CA 90025, USA

Pook, Christopher R (Chris) — Auto Racing Executive
Championship Auto Racing, 5350 Lakeview Parkway S Dr, Indianapolis IN 46268 USA

Pook, Jocelyn — Composer
Kraft-Engel Mgmt, 15233 Ventura Blvd, #200, Sherman Oaks CA 91403 USA

Pool, David A — Football Player
8120 Walcot Lane, #D, Cincinnati OH 45249, USA

Pool, James L — Pharmacologist
Baylor Medical Center, 1200 Moursand Ave, Houston TX 77030 USA

Pool, John L — Cancer Surgeon
1011 Charles St, #C, Fredericksbrg VA 22401, USA

Pool, Kenneth R (Bud) — WW II Army Air Corps Hero
6840 Kilimanjaro Dr, Evergreen CO 80439, USA

Poole, Brian — Singer (Tremeloes)
Jason West Agency, Gables House, Saddlebow, Kings Lynn PE34 3AR, England

Poole, David J — Artist
Trinity Flint Barn, Weston Lane, Petersfield Hants GU32 3NN, England

Poole, James R (Jim) — Baseball Player
605 Falls Lake Dr, Alpharetta GA 30022, USA

Poole, Keith R S — Football Player
4100 S Arizona Ave, #4, Chandler AZ 85248, USA

Poole, Nathan L — Football Player
8686 Longwood St, San Diego CA 92126, USA

Poole, Tyrone — Football Player
3415 Rivers Call Blvd, Atlanta GA 30339, USA

Poole, William — Government Official, Economist
Federal Reserve Bank, PO Box 442, Saint Louis MO 63166, USA

Pooler, Rosemary S — Judge
US Court of Appeals, Lee Courthouse, 100 S Clinton St, Syracuse NY 13202, USA

Pooley, Don — Golfer
5251 N Camino Sumo, Tucson AZ 85718, USA

Pooley, Emma — Cyclist
Girhaldenstr 71, Zurich, Switzerland

Poons, Larry — Artist
Salander O'Reilly Galleries, 20 E 79th St, New York NY 10075, USA

Poots, Imogen — Actress
Independent Talent Group, Oxford House, 76 Oxford St, London W1D 1BS, England

Pop, Iggy — Singer, Songwriter, Actor
Susan Blond Inc, 50 W 57th St, #1400, New York NY 10019 USA

Popa Chubby — Singer, Guitarist
Concerted Efforts, PO Box 440326, Somerville MA 02144 USA

Popcorn, Faith — Businesswoman
Brain Reserve, 1 Dag Hammarskjold Plaza, #1600, New York NY 10017, USA

Pope, Carly — Actress
Kritzer Levine Wilkins Griffin, 11872 La Grange Ave, #100, Los Angeles CA 90025 USA

P

Pope - Porter

Pope, Clarence C, Jr Fort Worth Episcopal Church Diocese, 6300 Ridlea Place, Fort Worth TX 76116, USA	Religious Leader
Pope, Dick Independent Talent Group, Oxford House, 76 Oxford St, London W1D 1BS, England	Cinematographer
Pope, Edwin Miami Herald, Editorial Dept, 1 Herald Plaza, Miami FL 33132 USA	Sportswriter
Pope, Manley Albewanin, 156 5th Ave, #904, New York NY 10010 10010, USA	Actor
Pope, Marquez P PO Box 470487, San Francisco CA 94147, USA	Football Player
Pope, Odeon MarsJazz Booking, 1006 Ashby Place, Charlottesville VA 22901, USA	Jazz Saxophonist, Orchestra Leader
Pope, Tim I C M Partners, 10250 Constellation Blvd, #900, Los Angeles CA 90067 USA	Director
Popein, Larry 80-650 Harrington Road, Kamloops BC V2B 6T7, Canada	Ice Hockey Player
Popiel, Jan V 2501 Peppermill Ridge Dr, Chesterfield MO 63005, USA	Ice Hockey Player
Popiel, Poul P 2501 Peppermill Ridge Dr, Chesterfield MO 63005, USA	Ice Hockey Player
Popoff, A Jay Sepeyts Entertainment, 5543 Edmondson Pike, #8A, Nashville TN 37211, USA	Singer (Lit)
Popoff, Frank P Indiana University, Kelly Business School, 1309 East St, Bloomington IN 47405, USA	Businessman
Popoff, Jeremy A Sepetys Entertainment, 5543 Edmondson Pike, #8A, Nashville TN 37211, USA	Guitarist (Lit)
Popov, Aleksandr International Olympic Committee, Chateau de Vidy, 1007 Lausanne, Switzerland	Swimmer
Popov, Dmytro I M G Artists, Hogarth Business Park, Chiswick, London W4 2TH, England	Opera Singer
Popov, Leonid I Cosmonaut Training Center, Star City, 141160 Zvezdny Gorodok, Moscow Oblast, Russia	Cosmonaut
Popovac, Gwynn 17270 Robin Ridge, Sonora CA 95370, USA	Artist, Sculptor
Popovic, Bojana Petrovic Z R K Buducnost T-Mobile, Ivan Milutinovic B B, 81000 Podgorica, Montenegro	Handball Player
Popovic, Mark 30 New Mountain Road, Stoney Creek ON L8G 2R7, Canada	Ice Hockey Player
Popovich, Gregg 41 Vineyard Dr, San Antonio TX 78257, USA	Basketball Executive, Coach
Popovich, Gregory Planet Hollywood Theater Resort, 3667 Las Vegas Blvd S, Las Vegas NV 89109, USA	Animal Trainer, Comedian
Popovich, Paul E 2604 Woodlawn Road, Northbrook IL 60062, USA	Baseball Player
Poppen, Christoph Deutsche Radio Philharmonie, Saint Johanner Markt 27, 66111 Saarbrücken, Germany	Conductor
Popper, John Hard Head Productions, PO Box 651, New York NY 10014, USA	Singer, Musician (Blues Traveler)
Popplewell, Anna I C M Partners, 10250 Constellation Blvd, #900, Los Angeles CA 90067 USA	Actress
Popson, David G (Dave) 82 Fall St, Ashley PA 18706, USA	Basketball Player
Poquette, Benedict J (Ben) 17917 N Shore Estates Road, Spring Lake MI 49456, USA	Basketball Player
Poquette, Thomas A (Tom) 3411 Ridgeway Dr, Eau Claire WI 54701, USA	Baseball Player
Poranski, Jason Ba Da Bing Records, 181 Clermont Ave, #403, Brooklyn NY 11205, USA	Guitarist, Mandolin Player (Beirut)
Porcaro, Steven M (Steve) 13596 Contour Dr, Sherman Oaks CA 91423, USA	Composer, Keyboardist (Toto)
Porcellino, John PO Box 881, Elgin IL 60121, USA	Cartoonist (King-Cat)
Porcello, Frederick A (Rick), III PO Box 27, Oldwick NJ 08858, USA	Baseball Player
Porch, Colleen Amsel Eisenstadt Frazier, 5055 Wilshire Blvd, #865, Los Angeles CA 90036 USA	Actress
Porch, Michelle Vincent Cirrincione Assoc, 1516 N Fairfax Ave, Los Angeles CA 90046 USA	Actress
Porcher, Robert PO Box 691464, Orlando FL 32869, USA	Football Player
Porfilio, John C US Court of Appeals, 1919 Stout St, Denver CO 80294, USA	Judge
Porizkova, Paulina One Entertainment, 12 W 57th St, #PH 1, New York NY 10019, USA	Model, Actress
Porretta, Matthew A K A Talent, 6310 San Vicente Blvd, #200, Los Angeles CA 90048 USA	Actor
Port, Christopher C (Chris) 432 Walnut St, New Orleans LA 70118, USA	Football Player
Port, Whitney Creative Artists Agency, 2000 Ave of Stars, #100, Los Angeles CA 90067 USA	Producer, Actress
Portenoy, Russell K Beth Israel Medical Center, Pain Medicine Dept, 1st Ave & 16th St, New York NY 10003, USA	Neurologist
Porter, Andrew (Andy) 2502 W 117th St, Hawthorne CA 90250, USA	Baseball Player
Porter, Billy Industry Entertainment, 955 Carillo Dr, #300, Los Angeles CA 90048 USA	Singer, Actor
Porter, Charles W (Chuck) 9321 Snyder Lane, Perry Hall MD 21128, USA	Baseball Player
Porter, Daniel E (Dan) 7360 Cowles Mountain Road, San Diego CA 92119, USA	Baseball Player
Porter, Daryl M 9053 W Sunrise Blvd, Plantation FL 33322, USA	Football Player
Porter, David H Skidmore College, President's Office, Saratoga Springs NY 12866, USA	Educator
Porter, Gary Milwaukee Journal Sentinel, Editorial Dept, PO Box 371, Milwaukee WI 53201 USA	Journalist

Porter, Gayle
Gaston-Porter Health Improvement Center, 8612 Timber Hill, Potomac MD 20854, USA — Psychologist, Social Activist
Porter, Greg
God's Katrina Kitchen, 554 Camp Ave, Gulfport MS 39501, USA — Social Activist
Porter, J W (Jay)
9677 Heather Circle W, Palm Beach Gardens FL 33410, USA — Baseball Player
Porter, Jody
Big Hassle, 157 Chambers St, #1200, New York NY 10007, USA — Singer (Fountains of Wayne), Guitarist
Porter, John E
Hogan & Hartson, 555 13th Ave NW, #800E, Washington DC 20004, USA — Representative, IL
Porter, Joseph E (Joey)
9523 Laramie Ave, Bakersfield CA 93314, USA — Football Player
Porter, Kalan
Agency Group Ltd, 142 W 57th St, #600, New York NY 10019 USA — Singer, Songwriter
Porter, Kevin J
1070 County Road 551, Lanett AL 36863, USA — Football Player
Porter, Lee
1604 Birch Lane, Greensboro NC 27408, USA — Golfer
Porter, Lorena
R D M J Entertainment Mgmt, 3619 Rose Ave, Long Beach CA 90807 USA — Singer (Klymaxx)
Porter, Marquis D (Bo)
1226 N Teal Estates Circle, Fresno TX 77545, USA — Baseball Player
Porter, R Kalan
B M G Canada, 190 Liberty St, #100, Toronto ON M6K 3L5, Canada — Singer
Porter, Randy
Laughlin Racing, 113 Pride Dr, Simpsonville SC 29681, USA — Auto Racing Driver
Porter, Richard A (Ricky)
24 Wyegate Court, Owings Mills MD 21117, USA — Football Player
Porter, Robert L (Bob)
771 Pueblo Ave, Napa CA 94558, USA — Baseball Player
Porter, Ronald D (Ron)
3960 NW 99th Ave, Coral Springs FL 33065, USA — Football Player
Porter, Rufus
20403 Amberlight Lane, Katy TX 77450, USA — Football Player
Porter, Scott
Brillstein Entertainment Partners, 9150 Wilshire Blvd, #350, Beverly Hills CA 90212 USA — Actor
Porterfield, Ellary
Gersh Agency, 9465 Wilshire Blvd, #600, Beverly Hills CA 90212 USA — Actress
Porter-King, Mary Bea
6412 Kalama Road, Kapaa HI 96746, USA — Golfer
Portes, Alejandro
Princeton University, Sociology Dept, Princeton NJ 08544, USA — Sociologist
Portes, Andrea
I C M Partners, 10250 Constellation Blvd, #900, Los Angeles CA 90067 USA — Writer
Portes, Richard D
London Business School, Regent's Park, London NW1 4SA, England — Economist
Portillo, Michael D X
House of Commons, Westminster, London SW1A 0AA, England — Government Official, England
Portis, Charles
7417 Kingwood Road, Little Rock AR 72207, USA — Writer
Portis, Clinton E
3510 NE 156th Ave, Gainesville FL 32609, USA — Football Player
Portisch, Lajos
Chess Federation, Nephadsereg Utca 10, 1055 Budapest, Hungary — Chess Player
Portman, John C, Jr
303 Peachtree Center Ave NE, #575, Atlanta GA 30303, USA — Architect
Portman, Natalie
Brillstein Entertainment Partners, 9150 Wilshire Blvd, #350, Beverly Hills CA 90212 USA — Actress
Portman, Rachel
Independent Talent Group, Oxford House, 76 Oxford St, London W1D 1BS, England — Composer
Portman, Robert M (Bob)
1412 Winter Sweet Place, Hillsborough NC 27278, USA — Basketball Player
Portnoy, Darin
Doctors Without Borders, PO Box 5030, Hagerstown MD 21741, USA — Association Executive, Physician
Porto, James
601 W 26th St, #1321, New York NY 10001, USA — Photographer
Portugal, Mark S
65 Serpentine Road, Warren RI 02885, USA — Baseball Player
Portwich, Ramona
K C Limmer, Stockhardtweg 3, 30453 Hanover, Germany — Canoeing Athlete
Porvari, Jukka
Pohjola Vahinkovakuutus Oy Ostoreskonta E1, Pohjola 00013, Finland — Ice Hockey Player
Poryes, Michael
Paradigm Agency, 360 N Crescent Dr, North Building, Beverly Hills CA 90210 USA — Producer
Porzio, L Michael (Mike)
PO Box 2242, Westport CT 06880, USA — Baseball Player
Posa, Victor
162 Bonny Meadows Dr, Aurora ON L4G 6N1, Canada — Ice Hockey Player
Posada Villeta, Jorge R
300 E 77th St, #11B, New York NY 10075, USA — Baseball Player
Posada, Leopold J (Leo)
8200 Grand Canal Dr, Miami FL 33144, USA — Baseball Player
Posavad, Mike
Compass Flooring, 6390 Kestral Road, Mississauga ON L5T 1Z3, Canada — Ice Hockey Player
Pose, Scott V
1216 Kintail Dr, Raleigh NC 27613, USA — Baseball Player
Posehn, Brian
Gersh Agency, 9465 Wilshire Blvd, #600, Beverly Hills CA 90212 USA — Actor, Comedian
Posen, Zac
Outspoken LLC, 13 Laight St, #17, New York NY 10013, USA — Fashion Designer
Poses, Frederic M
AlliedSignal Inc, PO Box 4000, Morristown NJ 07962, USA — Businessman
Posey, Gerald D (Buster), III
San Francisco Giants, AT&T Park, 24 Willie Mays Plaza, San Francisco CA 94107 USA — Baseball Player
Posey, James M M
3471 Main Highway, #515, Miami FL 33133, USA — Basketball Player

Posey, Parker — Actress
Untitled Entertainment, 350 S Beverly Dr, #200, Beverly Hills CA 90212 USA

Posey, Parker McKenna — Actress
Osbrink Talent Agency, 4343 Lankershim Blvd, #100, North Hollywood CA 91602 USA

Posin, Arie — Director, Producer, Writer
W M E Entertainment, 9601 Wilshire Blvd, #300, Beverly Hills CA 90210 USA

Posluszny, Paul M — Football Player
12023 Wynnfield Lakes Circle, Jacksonville FL 32246, USA

Posner, David M — Religious Leader, Rabbi
Temple Emanuel, 1 E 65th St, New York NY 10065, USA

Posner, Mike — Singer, Songwriter
Sony Records, 550 Madison Ave, #600, New York NY 10022 USA

Posner, Richard A — Judge
US Court of Appeals, 219 S Dearborn St, #2302B, Chicago IL 60604, USA

Posokhin, Mikhail M — Architect
Mosproyekt-2, 2 Brestskaya Str 5, 123056 Moscow, Russia

Post, Avery D — Religious Leader
80 Lyme Road, #246, Hanover NH 03755, USA

Post, Glen F, III — Businessman
CenturyLink, 100 Century Tel Dr, Monroe LA 71203, USA

Post, Louise L — Singer, Guitarist
S T C Entertainment, 5627 Sepulveda Blvd, #230, Van Nuys CA 91411, USA

Post, Markie — Actress
Glick Agency, 1260 6th St, #100, Santa Monica CA 90401, USA

Post, Mike — Composer
Mike Post Productions, 1007 W Olive Ave, Burbank CA 91506, USA

Post, Richard M (Dickie) — Football Player
1229 Seminole St, Los Alamos NM 87544, USA

Post, Ron — Association Executive
Medical Teams International, 14150 SW Milton Court, Portland OR 97224, USA

Post, Sandra — Golfer
Sandra Post Golf School, 15731 Regional Road 50, Cakedin ON L7E 3H9, Canada

Post, Ted — Director
11815 Dorothy St, #12, Los Angeles CA 90049, USA

Postell, Lavor — Basketball Player
2201 Lady Marion Lane, Albany GA 31707, USA

Postema, Pam — Baseball Umpire
242 Kansas Ave, Henderson NV 89015, USA

Poster, Steven B (Steve) — Cinematographer
W M E Entertainment, 9601 Wilshire Blvd, #300, Beverly Hills CA 90210 USA

Postlewait, Kathy — Golfer
111 Saint Johns Landing Dr, Winter Spings FL 32708, USA

Postman, Marc — Astronomer
3303 Lightfoot Dr, Pikesville MD 21208, USA

Poteat, Henry M (Hank), II — Football Player
19 Welsford Way, Mount Holly NJ 08060, USA

Potente, Franka — Actress
Gersh Agency, 9465 Wilshire Blvd, #600, Beverly Hills CA 90212 USA

Pothier, Brian — Ice Hockey Player
1537 Morton Ave, New Bedford MA 02745, USA

Poti, Thomas E (Tom) — Ice Hockey Player
2 Honey Locust Lane, Sandwich MA 02563, USA

Potrykus, Ingo — Plant Scientist
Eidgenossische Tech Hochschule, Plant Science Dept, 8093 Zurich, Switzerland

Potter, Carol — Actress
Pakula/King, 9229 W Sunset Blvd, #315, West Hollywood CA 90069 USA

Potter, Chris — Saxophonist
Vision Arts Mgmt, 16 Clint Fingers Road, Saugerties NY 12477, USA

Potter, Christopher J (Chris) — Actor
565 Orwell St, Missisgauga ON L5A 2W4, Canada

Potter, Cynthia (Cindy) — Diver, Sportscaster
2628 Winding Lane NE, Atlanta GA 30319, USA

Potter, Dan M — Religious Leader
21 Forest Dr, Albany NY 12205, USA

Potter, Grace — Singer (Nocturnals)
Paradigm Agency, 404 W Franklin St, Monterey CA 93940 USA

Potter, Huntington — Molecular Biologist
Florida Alzheimer's Disease Research Center, 12901 Bruce Downs Blvd, Tampa, FL 33612, USA

Potter, John — Government Official
US Postal Service, 475 L'Enfant Plaza SW, #3138, Washington DC 20260, USA

Potter, Madeleine — Actress
Ken McReddie Assoc, 11 Connaught Place, London W2 2ET, England

Potter, Martin — Surfer
Gotcha International, 32 Journey, #250, Aliso Viejo CA 92656, USA

Potter, Michael G (Mike) — Baseball Player
21582 Archer Circle, Huntington Beach CA 92646, USA

Potter, Monica — Actress
Schiff Co, 8440 Warner Dr, #B1, Culver City CA 90232 USA

Potter, Philip A — Religious Leader
Bishop Barbel Wartenberg-Potter, Plessenstr 5A, 24837 Schleswig, Germany

Potter, Richard — Saxophonist (Eve Unbound)
United Talent Agency, 9336 Civic Center Dr, Beverly Hills CA 90210 USA

Potter, Ryan — Actor
C E S D, 10635 Santa Monica Blvd, #130, Los Angeles CA 90025 USA

Potter, Sally — Actress, Director, Writer
Creative Artists Agency, 2000 Ave of Stars, #100, Los Angeles CA 90067 USA

Potter, Ted, Jr — Golfer
Professional Golfer's Assn, PO Box 109601, Palm Beach Gardens FL 33410 USA

Pottios, Myron J (Mike) — Football Player
4234 Hilaria Way, Newport Beach CA 92663, USA

Potts, Annie — Actress
Innovative Artists, 1505 10th St, Santa Monica CA 90401 USA

Potts, Cliff — Actor
PO Box 131, Topanga CA 90290, USA

Potts, Michael L (Mike) — Baseball Player
604 18th St, Butner NC 27509, USA

Potts, Paul R
Creative Artists Agency, 2000 Ave of Stars, #100, Los Angeles CA 90067 USA — Opera Singer

Potts, Roosevelt B
113 Mounger Road, Rayville LA 71269, USA — Football Player

Potvin, Denis
6820 NW 101st Terrace, Parkland FL 33076, USA — Ice Hockey Player

Potvin, Felix
Les Cantonniers de Magog, 100 Saint-Alphones, Magoh QC J1X 3Y5, Canada — Ice Hockey Player

Potvin, Jean R
24 Longwood Dr, Huntington Station NY 11746, USA — Ice Hockey Player

Potzsch, Oliver
Ullstein, Friedrichstr 126, 10117 Berlin, Germany — Writer

Poul, Alan
Boku Films, 14545 Victory Blvd, Van Nuys CA 91411, USA — Producer, Actor

Poulin, Dave
46 E Cedar St, #1, Chicago IL 60611, USA — Ice Hockey Player, Coach

Poulin, Patrick
Burger King, 415 25E Ave, Saint-Eustache QC J7P 4Y1, Canada — Ice Hockey Player

Poullain, Frankie
Whitehouse Mgmt, PO Box 43829, London NW6 3PJ, England — Bassist (Darkness)

Poulos, Leah
11455 B Mulberry Dr, Mequon WI 53092, USA — Speed Skater

Poulsen, Ken S
PO Box 1699, Oakhurst CA 93644, USA — Baseball Player

Pound, Richard W D
87 Arlington Ave, Westmount QC H3Y 2W5, Canada — Olympics Executive

Pounder, C C H
Mitchell K Stubbs Assoc, 8695 W Washington Blvd, #204, Culver City CA 90232 USA — Actress

Pounder-O'Toole, Cheryl
Team Canada, 2424 University Dr NW, Calgary AB T2N 3Y9, Canada — Ice Hockey Player

Pounds, Darryl L
4613 Lambert Place, Alexandria VA 22311, USA — Football Player

Poundstone, Paula
11812 San Vicente Blvd, #400, Los Angeles CA 90049, USA — Actress, Comedienne

Poupard, Paul Cardinal
Piazza San Calisto 16, 00120 Vatican City — Religious Leader

Poupaud, Pierre
Artmedia, 20 Ave Rapp, 75007 Paris, France — Actor

Pournelle, Jerry E
12051 Laurel Terrace, Studio City CA 91604, USA — Writer

Pousette, Lena
Atkins Assoc, 8040 Ventura Canyon Ave, Panorama City CA 91402 USA — Actress

Poussaint, Alvin F
Judge Baker Guidance Center, 53 Parker Hill Ave, Roxbury Crossing MA 02120, USA — Psychiatrist

Poust, Tracy
W M E Entertainment, 9601 Wilshire Blvd, #300, Beverly Hills CA 90210 USA — Producer, Writer

Povenmire, Daniel K (Dan)
Disney Channel, Phineas & Ferb Show, 500 S Buena Vista St, Burbank, CA 91521, USA — Producer, Animator

Povetkin, Aleksandr V
Sauerland Event, Hanns-Braun-Str, 14053 Berlin, Germany — Boxer

Povich, Maury R
Creative Artists Agency, 2000 Ave of Stars, #100, Los Angeles CA 90067 USA — Commentator, Entertainer

Povinelli, Mark
Kazarian/Spencer/Ruskin, 11969 Ventura Blvd, #300, Studio City CA 91604 USA — Actor

Powe, Leon, Jr
45 Kings Way, Waltham MA 02451, USA — Basketball Player

Powell, A J Philip
16 Little Boltons, London SW10 9LP, England — Architect

Powell, Alonzo S
220 N Patterson Blvd, Dayton OH 45402, USA — Baseball Player

Powell, Arthur L (Art)
1304 City Lights Dr, Aliso Viejo CA 92656, USA — Football Player

Powell, Brittney
Amsel Eisenstadt Frazier, 5055 Wilshire Blvd, #865, Los Angeles CA 90036 USA — Actress, Model

Powell, Cecil
220 Villa Verde Dr SE, Rio Rancho NM 87124, USA — Test Pilot

Powell, Charles E (Charley)
4119 Aralia Road, Altadena CA 91001, USA — Football Player

Powell, Cincinnatus (Cincy)
2541 Brookside Dr, Irving TX 75063, USA — Basketball Player

Powell, Clifton
Opus Entertainment, 5225 Wilshire Blvd, #905, Los Angeles CA 90036, USA — Actor

Powell, Colin L
1317 Ballantrae Farm Dr, McLean VA 22101, USA — Army General, Secretary of State

Powell, D Dwane, Jr
Raleigh News Observer, Editorial Dept, 215 S McDowell, Raleigh NC 27601, USA — Editorial Cartoonist

Powell, Dennis C
1743 Eastgate Ave, Upland CA 91784, USA — Baseball Player

Powell, Donald D
Powell Kleinschmidt, PO Box 1130, Libertyville IL 60048, USA — Interior Designer

Powell, Earl A (Rusty), III
National Gallery of Art, Constitution Ave & 4th St NW, Washington DC 20565, USA — Museum Executive

Powell, Eric
2401 Cairo Bend Road, Lebanon TN 37087, USA — Cartoonist (Goon)

Powell, Esteban
C E S D, 10635 Santa Monica Blvd, #130, Los Angeles CA 90025 USA — Actor, Producer

Powell, Hosken
1289 Tamara St, Pensacola FL 32504, USA — Baseball Player

Powell, J Mac
Creative Trust, 5141 Virginia Way, #320, Brentwood TN 37027, USA — Singer, Guitarist (Third Day)

Powell, James R
Plus Ultra Technologies, 180 Harbor Road, Stony Brook NY 11790, USA — Inventor (Magnetic Levitation Train)

Powell, James W (Jay)
155 Butler Dr, Ridgeland MS 39157, USA — Baseball Player

Powell, Jane
150 W End Ave, #26C, New York NY 10023, USA — Singer, Actress

Powell, Jeremy R — Baseball Player
3022 W Summit Walk Court, Anthem AZ 85086, USA

Powell, Jerome (Jay) — Government Leader, Financier
Federal Reserve System, 20th St & Constitution Ave NW, Washington DC 20551, USA

Powell, Jesse — Singer, Songwriter
Universal Attractions, 135 W 26th St, #1200, New York NY 10001 USA

Powell, Jimmy — Golfer
49895 Lago Dr, La Quinta CA 92253, USA

Powell, John — Composer
Kraft-Engel Mgmt, 15233 Ventura Blvd, #200, Sherman Oaks CA 91403 USA

Powell, John G — Track Athlete
5545 Sobb Ave, Las Vegas NV 89118, USA

Powell, John W (Boog) — Baseball Player
Boog's Barbeque, 333 W Camden St, Baltimore MD 21201, USA

Powell, Josh — Basketball Player
Atlanta Hawks, Centennial Tower, 101 Marietta St NW, #1900, Atlanta GA 30303 USA

Powell, L Dante — Baseball Player
5715 W Walton St, Long Beach CA 90815, USA

Powell, Luke — Football Player
Indiana State University, Athletic Dept, 401 N 4th St, Terre Haute IN 47809, USA

Powell, Marvin, Jr — Football Player
5441 8th Ave, Los Angeles CA 90043, USA

Powell, Michael (Mike) — Track Athlete
7676 N Fresno St, #27, Fresno CA 93720, USA

Powell, Michael K — Government Official
College of William & Mary, PO Box 8795, Williamsburg VA 23187, USA

Powell, Monroe — Singer (Platters)
Personality Presents, 880 E Sahara Ave, #101, Las Vegas NV 89104, USA

Powell, Renee — Golfer
PO Box 30196, East Canton OH 44730, USA

Powell, Robert — Actor
Diamond Mgmt, 31 Percy St, London W1T 2DD, England

Powell, Sandy — Costume Designer
Independent Talent Group, Oxford House, 76 Oxford St, London W1D 1BS, England

Powell, Susan — Actress
6333 Bryn Mawr Dr, Los Angeles CA 90068, USA

Power, Cat — Singer, Pianist, Guitarist
Ground Control, 108 E Main St, #8, Carrboro NC 27510, USA

Power, Dave — Actor
Bauman Redanty & Shaul, 5757 Wilshire Blvd, #473, Los Angeles CA 90036, USA

Power, J D (Dave) — Businessman
J D Power Associates, 2625 Townsgate Road, Westlake Village CA 91361, USA

Power, Lawrence — Concert Viola Player
Ingpen & Williams, 131 Putney Bridge Road, London SW15 2PA, England

Power, Susan — Writer
G P Putnam's Sons, 375 Hudson St, New York NY 10014 USA

Power, Ted H — Baseball Player
1165 Tahiti Parkway, Sarasota FL 34236, USA

Power, Udana — Actress, Writer
Iatia Well Inc, 1050 S Hayworth Ave, Los Angeles CA 90035, USA

Power, Will — Writer, Composer, Actor
I C M Partners, 10250 Constellation Blvd, #900, Los Angeles CA 90067 USA

Power, Will — Auto Racing Driver
Penske Racing, Penske Plaza, 366 Riverfront, Reading PA 19602, USA

Powers, Clyde J — Football Player
6020 NW Williams Ave, Lawton OK 73505, USA

Powers, James B — Religious Leader
American Baptist Assn, 4605 N State Line, Texarkana TX 75503, USA

Powers, Richard — Writer
University of Illinois, English Dept, Champaign IL 61820, USA

Powers, Ross — Snowboard Skier
PO Box 186, Londonderry VT 05148, USA

Powers, Stefanie — Actress
PO Box 5087, Sherman Oaks CA 91413, USA

Powers, Warren A — Football Player
14742 Thornbird Manor Parkway, Chesterfield MO 63017, USA

Powers, Williams, Jr — Educator
University of Texas, Austin TX 78712 USA

Powis, Lynn — Ice Hockey Player
2669 S Columbine St, Denver CO 80210, USA

Powter, Daniel P — Singer, Pianist, Songwriter
Gary Stamler Mgmt, 3055 Overland Ave, #200, Los Angeles CA 90034, USA

Powter, Susan — Physical Fitness Expert, Writer
Stop the Insanity, 6250 Ridgewood Road, Saint Cloud MN 56395, USA

Poza, Jorge — Actor
Televisa, Blvd A Lopez Mateos 232, Colonia San Angel, DF CP 01060, Mexico

Pozsgay, Imre — Government Official, Hungary
Parliament Buildings, Kossuth Lajos Ter 1, 1055 Budapest, Hungary

Prabaya, Adrian — Conductor
Harrison/Parrott, 5-6 Albion Court, London W6 0QT, England

Prabhakar, Arati — Financier
US Venture Partners, 2735 Sand Hill Road, Menlo Park CA 94025, USA

Prada, Aura Helena — Actress
Gabriel Blanco, Rio Balsas 35-32, Colonia Cuauhtemoc DF 6500, Mexico

Prada, Miuccia — Fashion Designer
Galleria Vittorio Emanuele 60-65, 20121 Milan, Italy

Prado, Edgar — Thoroughbred Racing Jockey
1519 Shoreline Way, Hollywood FL 33019, USA

Prado, Edward C — Judge
US Court of Appeals, 755 E Mulberry Ave, San Antonio TX 78212, USA

Prady, Bill — Producer / Writer / Actor
Rothman Brecher Agency, 9250 Wilshire Blvd, #PH, Beverly Hills CA 90212, USA

Prammanasudh, Stacy — Golfer
5016 S Toledo Ave, #18-O, Tulsa OK 74135, USA

Pran — Actor
25 Union Park, Khar, Mumbai MS 400052, India

Prance, Ghillean T
Old Vicarage, Silver St, Lyme Regis, Dorset DT7 3HS, England — Botanist

Prantera, Amanda
Bloomsbury Publishing, 36 Soho Square, London W1D 3Q4, England — Writer

Pras
I C M Partners, 10250 Constellation Blvd, #900, Los Angeles CA 90067 USA — Rap Artist (Fugees)

Prasad, Sunand
Penoyre & Prasad, 28-42 Banner St, London EC1Y 8QE, England — Architect

Prasad, Udayan
United Talent Agency, 9336 Civic Center Dr, Beverly Hills CA 90210 USA — Director, Actor

Prasong Tuchinda
Phya-Thai II Hospital, 943 Phaholythin, Phayatha Bangkok 10400, Thailand — Pediatrician

Pratchett, Terry
Colin Smythe, PO Box 6, Gerrards Cross, Bucks SL9 8XA, England — Writer

Prather, Joan
31647 Sea Level Dr, Malibu CA 90265, USA — Actress

Pratiwi Sudarmono P
Universitas Indonesia, Microbiology Dept, Salemba Raya, Jakata 10430, Indonesia — Astronaut, Indonesia

Pratt, Awadagin
C M Artists, 127 W 96th St, #13B, New York NY 10025 USA — Concert Pianist

Pratt, Chris
Creative Artists Agency, 2000 Ave of Stars, #100, Los Angeles CA 90067 USA — Actor

Pratt, Deborah
Bruce Clute, 8205 Santa Monica Blvd, #1-299, West Hollywood CA 90046, USA — Actress

Pratt, George C
55 Sugar Tom Ridge, East Norwich NY 11732, USA — Judge

Pratt, Judson
2585 N Fountain Arbor Way, Orange CA 92867, USA — Actor

Pratt, Kelly
Ba Da Bing Records, 181 Clermont Ave, #403, Brooklyn NY 11205, USA — Trumpeter (Beirut)

Pratt, Kelly
23 Lombard Crescent, Saint Albert AB T8N 3N1, Canada — Ice Hockey Player

Pratt, Keri Lynn
Innovative Artists, 1505 10th St, Santa Monica CA 90401 USA — Actress

Pratt, Michael P (Mike)
14603 Landon Court, Louisville KY 40245, USA — Basketball Player

Pratt, Robert H (Bob), Jr
4322 Monument Park, Richmond VA 23230, USA — Football Player

Pratt, Roger
10 Nightingale Lane, Hornsey, London N8 7QU, England — Cinematographer

Pratt, Todd A
5950 Dorset Bridge Road, Douglasville GA 30135, USA — Baseball Player

Pratt, Tracy
1705-15038 101st Ave, Surrey BC V3R 0N2, Canada — Ice Hockey Player

Pratt, Victoria
Don Buchwald/Fortitude, 6500 Wilshire Blvd, #2200, Los Angeles CA 90048 USA — Actress

Praver, Tori
I M G Models, 304 Park Ave S, #PH-North, New York NY 10010 USA — Model

Preate, Ernest D, Jr
Attorney General's Office, 4th & Walnut, Harrisburg PA 17120, USA — Attorney, Government Official

Prebble, Lucy
Rod Hall Agency, 7 Mallow St, London EC1Y 8RQ, England — Producer, Writer

Precourt, Charles J
1960 Shoshone Dr, Ogden UT 84403, USA — Astronaut

Predock, Antoine
Antoine Predock Architect, 300 12th St, Albuquerque NM 87102, USA — Architect

Preece, Steven P (Steve)
2723 NW Monte Vista Terrace, Portland OR 97210, USA — Football Player

Pregenzer, John A
6314 104th St E, Puyallup WA 98373, USA — Baseball Player

Pregerson, Harry
US Court of Appeals, 21800 Oxnard St, Woodland Hills CA 91367, USA — Judge

Pregulman, Mervin (Merv)
4 Cherokee Blvd, #517, Chattanooga TN 37405, USA — Football Player

Preisler, Gary
I C M Partners, 10250 Constellation Blvd, #900, Los Angeles CA 90067 USA — Director

Preissing, Thomas J (Tom)
1824 Anglers Dr, Steamboat Springs CO 80487, USA — Ice Hockey Player

Prejean, Patrick
Agence Babette Pouget, 3 Rue de Ponthieu, 75008 Paris, France — Actor

Prejean, Sister Helen
3009 Grand Route Saint John, #6, New Orleans LA 70119, USA — Social Activist, Writer

Prelutsky, Jack
PO Box 366, 7683 SE 27th St, Mercer Island WA 98040, USA — Writer

Premji, Azim
Wipro Ltd, Doddakannelli, Sarjapur Road, Bangalore 560035, India — Businessman, Philanthropist

Prentice, Dean S
350 Doon Valley Dr, Kitchener ON N2P 2M9, Canada — Ice Hockey Player

Prepon, Laura
Gersh Agency, 9465 Wilshire Blvd, #600, Beverly Hills CA 90212 USA — Actress

Prescott, Edward C
2308 Lake Place, Minneapolis MN 55405, USA — Nobel Economics Laureate

Prescott, John L
365 Saltshouse Road, Sutton on Hull, North Humberside, England — Government Official, England

Prescott, Jon
Abrams Artists, 9200 W Sunset Blvd, #1125, West Hollywood CA 90069 USA — Actor

Prescott, Kathryn
Curtis Brown Group, 28-29 Haymarket St, #500, London SW1Y 4SP, England — Actress

Prescott, Robert T
Innovative Artists, 1505 10th St, Santa Monica CA 90401 USA — Actor

Presko, Joseph E (Joe)
1612 NE 77th Terrace, Kansas City MO 64118, USA — Baseball Player

Presle, Micheline
6 Rue Antoine Dubois, 75006 Paris, France — Actress

Presley, Angaleena
Ten Ten Music Group, 33 Music Square W, #110, Nashville TN 37203, USA — Singer/Songwriter

Presley, Brian — Actor
I/D Public Relations, 7060 Hollywood Blvd, #800, Los Angeles CA 90028 USA

Presley, James A (Jim) — Baseball Player
2449 Bonanza Dr, Cantonment FL 32533, USA

Presley, Lisa Marie — Actress, Singer
Front Line Mgmt, 1100 Glendon Ave, #2000, Los Angeles CA 90024 USA

Presley, Priscilla — Actress
1167 Summit Dr, Beverly Hills CA 90210, USA

Presley, Reg — Singer (Troggs)
Stan Green, PO Box 4, Dartmouth, Devon TQ6 0YD, England

Presley, Richard — Guitarist (Breeders)
W M E Entertainment, 9601 Wilshire Blvd, #300, Beverly Hills CA 90210 USA

Presley, Wayne — Ice Hockey Player
1339 Kingsway Dr, Highland MI 48356, USA

Press, Bill — Commentator
CNN-TV, 190 Marietta Ave SW, Atlanta GA 30303 USA

Press, Frank — Geophysicist
2500 Virginia Ave, #616 South, Washington DC 20037, USA

Press, Natalie — Actress
United Agents, 12-26 Lexington St, London W1F 0LE, England

Pressel, Morgan — Golfer
3111 Clint Moore Road, #101, Boca Raton FL 33496, USA

Pressey, Paul M — Basketball Player, Coach
782 Haddonstone Circle, Lake Mary FL 32746, USA

Pressler, H Paul — Attorney, Judge
3711 San Felipe St, #9J, Houston TX 77027, USA

Pressler, Larry L — Senator, SD
1666 K St NW, #500, Washington DC 20006, USA

Pressler, Menahem M J — Concert Pianist
Melvin Kaplan, 115 College St, #4, Burlington VT 05401, USA

Pressley, Dominic I — Basketball Player
1406 Whooping Court, Upper Marlboro MD 20774, USA

Pressley, Harold — Basketball Player
6470 Matheny Way, Citrus Heights CA 95621, USA

Pressley, Robert — Auto, Truck Racing Driver
6 Forestdale Dr, Asheville NC 28803, USA

Pressman, Edward R — Producer
Edward R Pressman Films, 1639 11th St, #251, Santa Monica CA 90404, USA

Pressman, Lawrence — Actor
15033 Encanto Dr, Sherman Oaks CA 91403, USA

Pressman, Michael — Director
Glick Agency, 1321 7th St, #203, Santa Monica CA 90401 USA

Pressman, Sally — Actress
United Talent Agency, 9336 Civic Center Dr, Beverly Hills CA 90210 USA

Prestel, James F (Jim) — Football Player
6150 N Hurricane Court, Parker CO 80134, USA

Prestia, Francis (Rocco) — Bassist (Tower of Power)
Air Tight Mgmt, 115 West Road, Winchester Center CT 06098, USA

Preston, Carrie — Actress
Innovative Artists, 1505 10th St, Santa Monica CA 90401 USA

Preston, Douglas — Writer
Editions L'Archipel, 34 Rue des Bourdonnais, 75001 Paris, France

Preston, Duncan — Actor
46 Hilltop House, Hornsey Lane, London N6 5NW, England

Preston, J A — Actor
Paradigm Agency, 360 N Crescent Dr, North Building, Beverly Hills CA 90210 USA

Preston, Kelly — Actress, Model
Creative Artists Agency, 2000 Ave of Stars, #100, Los Angeles CA 90067 USA

Preston, Mike — Actor
House of Representatives, 1434 6th St, #1, Santa Monica CA 90401 USA

Preston, R David (Dave) — Football Player
PO Box 16511, Golden CO 80402, USA

Preston, Raymond N (Ray), Jr — Football Player
820 Regulo Place, #1811, Chula Vista CA 91910, USA

Preston, Simon J — Concert Organist, Choirmaster
Little Hardwick, Langton Green, Tunbridge Wells, Kent TN3 0EY, England

Preston, Steven C — Secretary of Housing & Urban Development
Small Business Administration, 409 3rd St SW, Washington DC 20024, USA

Prestridge, Luke E — Football Player
17802 Island Spring Lane, Tomball TX 77377, USA

Pretre, Georges — Conductor
Chateau de Vaudricourt, A Naves, 81100 Par Castres, France

Prettyman, Tristan — Singer, Songwriter
Paradigm Agency, 404 W Franklin St, Monterey CA 93940 USA

Preus, David W — Religious Leader
2481 Como Ave, Saint Paul MN 55108, USA

Previn, Andre G — Conductor, Composer, Jazz Pianist
180 W 80th St, #206, New York NY 10024, USA

Prevost, Greg — Singer, Musician (Chesterfield Kings)
Agency Group Ltd, 142 W 57th St, #600, New York NY 10019 USA

Prevost, Josette — Actress
Levin Agency, 8484 Wilshire Blvd, #745, Beverly Hills CA 90211, USA

Prew, William A — Swimmer, Businessman
30600 Telegraph Road, #3110, Bingham Farms MI 48025, USA

Preziosi, Alessandro — Actor
Carol Levi Mgmt, Via G Pisanelli 2, 00196 Rome, Italy

Price, Alan — Singer, Organist (Animals), Songwriter
Lustig Talent, PO Box 770850, Orlando FL 32877 USA

Price, Antony — Fashion Designer
17 Langton St, London SW10 0JL, England

Price, Armintie A — Basketball Player
Atlanta Dream, 83 Walton St NW, #400, Atlanta, GA 30303 USA

Price, Elex D — Football Player
2833 J B Mance Ave, Jackson MS 39213, USA

Price, Frank — Film Executive
Price Entertainment, 527 Spoleto Dr, Pacific Palisades CA 90272, USA

Price, H Brent — Basketball Player
1111 W Wynona Ave, Enid OK 73703, USA
Price, Hilary — Cartoonist (Rhymes with Orange)
221 Pine St, #414, Florence MA 01062, USA
Price, Jack — Ice Hockey Player
39 Waterloo St S, Goderich ON N7A 3P1, Canada
Price, James G — Physician, Columnist
12205 Mohawk Road, Leawood KS 66209, USA
Price, Jimmie W (Jim) — Baseball Player
57152 Willow Way, Washington MI 48094, USA
Price, Joseph W (Joe) — Baseball Player
1874 Arabian Court, Hebron KY 41048, USA
Price, Katie (Jordan) — Model, Singer
Volition, Raleigh Studios, 1600 Rosecrans Ave, #400, Manhattan Beach CA 90266, USA
Price, Kelly — Singer
J L Entertainment, 18653 Ventura Blvd, #340, Tarzana CA 91356, USA
Price, Larry C — Photojournalist
930 S Garfield St, Denver CO 80209, USA
Price, Lia Scott — Actress, Producer, Writer
Lia Scott Price Productions, 4455 Torrance Blvd, #866, Torrance CA 90503, USA
Price, Lindsay — Actress
Management 360, 9111 Wilshire Blvd, Beverly Hills CA 90210 USA
Price, Lloyd — Singer, Pianist, Songwriter
95 Horseshoe Hill Road, Pound Ridge NY 10576, USA
Price, M V Leontyne — Opera Singer
9 Vandam St, New York NY 10013, USA
Price, Marc — Actor
8444 Magnolia Dr, Los Angeles CA 90046, USA
Price, Megyn — Actress
A P A Talent/Literary Agency, 405 S Beverly Dr, #300, Beverly Hills CA 90212 USA
Price, Michael F — Financier
Franklin Mutual Advisors, 57 John F Kennedy Parkway, Short Hills NJ 07078, USA
Price, Mike — Football Coach
University of Texas, Athletic Dept, El Paso TX 79968, USA
Price, Mike — Basketball Player
4415 Thorleigh Dr, Indianapolis IN 46226, USA
Price, Mitchell L — Football Player
9944 Candlestick Lane, Pensacola FL 32514, USA
Price, Molly — Actress
Gersh Agency, 9465 Wilshire Blvd, #600, Beverly Hills CA 90212 USA
Price, Nichoas R L (Nick) — Golfer
Nick Price Group, 900 S US Highway 1, #105, Jupiter FL 33477, USA
Price, Noel — Ice Hockey Player
21 Windeyer Crescent, Kanata ON K2K 2P6, Canada
Price, Pat — Ice Hockey Player
PO Box 3, Robson BC V0G 1X0, Canada
Price, Paul B — Physicist
1056 Overlook Road, Berkeley CA 94708, USA
Price, Peerless L — Football Player
5658 Legends Club Circle, Braselton GA 30517, USA
Price, Phoebe — Actress
P Mgmt, 11666 Montana Ave, Los Angeles CA 90049, USA
Price, Ray — Singer, Guitarist
Billy Deaton Talent, 1214 16th Ave S, Nashville TN 37212 USA
Price, Richard — Writer
Creative Artists Agency, 2000 Ave of Stars, Los Angeles CA 90067, USA
Price, Willard D — Explorer
PO Box 2783, Laguna Hills CA 92654, USA
Priddy, Nancy — Actress
11223 Sunshine Terrace, Studio City CA 91604, USA
Priddy, Robert S (Bob) — Baseball Player
136 Shingiss St, #214, McKees Rocks PA 15136, USA
Pride, Charley — Singer, Guitarist, Baseball Player
Cecca Productions, PO Box 670507, Dallas TX 75367, USA
Pride, Curtis J — Baseball Player
1288 Lake Breeze Dr, Wellington FL 33414, USA
Pride, Dicky — Golfer
4645 Cason Cove Dr, Windermere FL 34786, USA
Pridemore, L Thomas (Tom), Jr — Football Player
3935 Poplar Springs Road, Gainesville GA 30507, USA
Priesand, Sally J — Religious Leader
32 Fernwood Dr, Asbury Park NJ 07712, USA
Priest, Eddie Lee (Ed), Jr — Baseball Player
445 Ballard Road, Altoona AL 35952, USA
Priest, Maxi — Singer
Virgin Records, 150 5th Ave, Front 3, New York NY 10011 USA
Priest, Steve — Singer, Bassist (Sweet)
D C M International, 296 Nether St, Finchley, London N3 1RJ, England
Priestlay, Ken — Ice Hockey Player
5438 Crescent Dr, Delta BC V4K 2C9, Canada
Priestley, Jason — Actor
A P A Talent/Literary Agency, 405 S Beverly Dr, #300, Beverly Hills CA 90212 USA
Priestley, Thomas (Tom), Jr — Director
Paradigm Agency, 360 N Crescent Dr, North Building, Beverly Hills CA 90210 USA
Prieto, Ariel — Baseball Player
15325 SW 53rd St, Miami FL 33185, USA
Prieto, Chris — Baseball Player
3450 Fisher Place, Carmel CA 93923, USA
Prieto, Rodrigo — Cinematographer
PO Box 3338, Beverly Hills CA 90212, USA
Primack, Joel R — Astronomer
University of California, Astronomy Dept, Santa Cruz CA 95064, USA
Primakov, Yevgeny M — Prime Minister, Russia
Federation Chamber of Commerce, Ilyinka Str 6, 103684 Moscow, Russia
Primeau, Keith — Ice Hockey Player
2 Danforth Dr, Voorhees NJ 08043, USA

Primeau, Wayne — Ice Hockey Player
Toronto Maple Leafs, AirCanada Center, 40 Bay St, Toronto ON M5J 2K2, Canada
Primes, Robert — Cinematographer
Innovative Artists, 1505 10th St, Santa Monica CA 90401 USA
Primrose, Neil — Drummer (Travis)
Wildlife Entertainment, 21 Heathmans Road, London SW6 4TJ, England
Prince — Singer, Guitarist, Songwriter
Paisley Park Enterprises, 7801 Audubon Road, Chanhassen MN 55317, USA
Prince, Bart — Architect
3501 Monte Vista NE, Albuquerque NM 87106, USA
Prince, Donald M (Don) — Baseball Player
11143 James B White Highway S, Whiteville NC 28472, USA
Prince, Faith — Actress, Singer
Hart Mgmt, 1900 Ave of Stars, #1800, Los Angeles CA 90067, USA
Prince, Harold S (Hal) — Producer, Director
Directors Company, 311 W 43rd St, #307, New York NY 10036, USA
Prince, Jonathan — Actor, Producer, Writer
United Talent Agency, 9336 Civic Center Dr, Beverly Hills CA 90210 USA
Prince, Larry L — Businessman
Genuine Parts Co, 2999 Circle 75 Parkway, Atlanta GA 30339, USA
Prince, Peter — Writer
Bloomsbury Publishing, 36 Soho Square, London W1D 3Q4, England
Prince, Richard — Artist, Photographer
Michael Kohn Gallery, 8071 Beverly Blvd, Los Angeles CA 90048, USA
Prince, Tayshaun D — Basketball Player
5550 Leeds Court, Oakland Township MI 48306, USA
Prince, Thomas A (Tom) — Baseball Player
6816 10th Ave NW, Bradenton FL 34209, USA
Prince-Bythewood, Gina — Writer, Director, Producer
Creative Artists Agency, 2000 Ave of Stars, #100, Los Angeles CA 90067 USA
Principal, Victoria — Actress
23852 Pacific Coast Highway, #785, Malibu CA 90265, USA
Principe, Joe — Bassist (Rise Against)
Agency Group Ltd, 142 W 57th St, #600, New York NY 10019 USA
Prine, Andrew — Actor
3364 Longridge Ave, Sherman Oaks CA 91423, USA
Prine, John — Singer, Songwriter
Al Bunetta Mgmt, 33 Music Square W, #102B, Nashville TN 37203, USA
Pringle, Joan — Actress
TalentWorks, 3500 W Olive Ave, #1400, Burbank CA 91505 USA
Prinosil, David — Tennis Player
T C Wolfsberg, Am Schanzl 3, 92224 Amberg, Germany
Prinz, Bret R — Baseball Player
15471 N 88th Ave, Peoria AZ 85382, USA
Prinze, Freddie, Jr — Actor
Brillstein Entertainment Partners, 9150 Wilshire Blvd, #350, Beverly Hills CA 90212 USA
Prinzi, Frank — Cinematographer
571 W 113th St, #24, New York NY 10025, USA
Prioleau, Pierson O — Football Player
2221 Santee River Road, Saint Stephen SC 29479, USA
Prior of Brampton, James M L — Government Official, England
36 Morpeth Mansions, London SW1, England
Prior, Anthony E — Football Player
3529 Holding St, Riverside CA 92501, USA
Prior, Madeleine E (Maddy) — Singer
Park Promotions, PO Box 651, Park Road, Oxford OX2 9RB, England
Prior, Mark W — Baseball Player
10284 Waddell Circle, San Diego CA 92124, USA
Prior, Michael R (Mike) — Football Player
14511 Quail Pointe Dr, Carmel IN 46032, USA
Priory, Richard B — Businessman
Duke Energy Co, 526 S Church St, Charlotte NC 28202, USA
Pritchard, Barry — Singer, Guitarist (Fortunes)
Lustig Talent, PO Box 770850, Orlando FL 32877 USA
Pritchard, Connor — Producer, Writer
I C M Partners, 10250 Constellation Blvd, #900, Los Angeles CA 90067 USA
Pritchard, David E — Physicist
Massachusetts Institute of Technology, Physics Dept, Cambridge MA 02139, USA
Pritchard, Harold W (Buddy) — Baseball Player
507 E Sunny Hills Road, Fullerton CA 92835, USA
Pritchard, Michael R (Mike) — Football Player
PO Box 93114, Las Vegas NV 89193, USA
Pritchard, Ronald D ((Ron) — Football Player
495 E Coconino Dr, Chandler AZ 85249, USA
Pritchett, Christopher D (Chris) — Baseball Player
959 Fir Tree Place, Carlsbad CA 92011, USA
Pritchett, Kelvin B — Football Player
46679 Pinehurst Circle, Stone Mountain GA 30087, USA
Pritchett, Matthew (Matt) — Cartoonist (Matt)
London Daily Telegraph, 181 Marsh Wall, London E14 9SR, England
Pritchett, Stanley J — Football Player
523 Monteagle Trace, Stone Mountain GA 30087, USA
Pritko, Steven (Steve) — Football Player
328 Chanticlair Dr, Apex NC 27502, USA
Probst, Jeff — Producer, Director, Actor
W M E Entertainment, 9601 Wilshire Blvd, #300, Beverly Hills CA 90210 USA
Probst, Lawrence F (Larry), III — Businessman
US Olympic Committee, 1 Olympic Plaza, Building 6, Colorado Springs CO 80909 USA
Prochaska, Andreas — Director
Spielkind-Mattias Frik, Zimmerstr 11, 10969 Berlin, Germany
Prochazka, Martin — Ice Hockey Player
H C Kladno, Petra Bezruc 2531, 272 80 Kladno, Czech Republic
Prochnow, Jurgen — Actor
Innovative Artists, 1505 10th St, Santa Monica CA 90401 USA
Prock, Markus — Luge Athlete
Tyrolean Luge Assn, Olympia World, Olympiastr 10, 6020 Innsbruck, Austria

Procter, Emily
Paradigm Agency, 360 N Crescent Dr, North Building, Beverly Hills CA 90210 USA — Actress, Model

Proctor, James A (Jim)
2 Westmoreland Place, Saint Louis MO 63108, USA — Baseball Player

Proctor, Phillip
C E S D, 10635 Santa Monica Blvd, #130, Los Angeles CA 90025 USA — Actor

Proctor, Robert N
Stanford University, History Dept, Stanford CA 94305, USA — Scientific Historian

Proctor, Scott C
428 NE Bayberry Lane, Jensen Beach FL 34957, USA — Baseball Player

Prodi, Romano
Prime Minister's Office, Palazzo Chigi, Piazza Colonna 370, 00187 Rome, Italy — Prime Minister, Italy

Proehl, Richard S (Ricky)
3504 Bromley Wood Lane, Greensboro NC 27410, USA — Football Player

Proenza, William (Bill)
US National Weather Service, 11691 SW 17th St, Miami FL 33165, USA — Climatologist, Government Official

Professor Griff
Brookes Co, 3710 S Robertson Blvd, #100, Culver City CA 90232, USA — Rap Artist (Public Enemy)

Prohgress
Stampede Mgmt, 12530 Beatrice St, Los Angeles CA 90066, USA — Singer (Far East Movement)

Prokop, Joseph M (Joe)
1042 N Mountain Ave, Upland CA 91786, USA — Football Player

Prokop, Matt
Management 360, 9111 Wilshire Blvd, Beverly Hills CA 90210 USA — Actor

Proly, Michael J (Mike)
21 Hollander Dr, Taylors SC 29687, USA — Baseball Player

Promuto, Vincent L (Vince)
9 Island Dr, Norwalk CT 06855, USA — Football Player

Pronger, Christopher R (Chris)
345 S Hinchman Ave, Haddonfield NJ 08033, USA — Ice Hockey Player

Pronger, Sean J
1229 Firwood Dr, Pittsburgh PA 15243, USA — Ice Hockey Player

Pronovost, Andre J A
1-412 46 E Eue, Shawinigan QC G9N 5B8, Canada — Ice Hockey Player

Pronovost, J Jean D
Hockey Ministries, 1100 La Gauchetiere St W, Montreal QC H3B 2S2, Canada — Ice Hockey Player

Pronovost, Peter
Johns Hopkins University Medical Center, Baltimore MD 21218 USA — Intensive Care Physician

Pronovost, R Marcel
4620 Dali Court, Windsor ON N9G 2M8, Canada — Ice Hockey Player, Coach

Propes, Duane
Splash Public Relations, 1520 16th Ave S, #2, Nashville TN 37212, USA — Guitarist (Little Texas)

Prophet, Billy
Paramount Entertainment, 12 Kosakowski Dr, Morris Plains NJ 07590 USA — Singer (Jive Five)

Propp, Brian
2320 Riverton Road, Cinnaminson NJ 08077, USA — Ice Hockey Player

Prose, Francine
P E N American Center, 588 Broadway, #303, New York NY 10012, USA — Writer

Prospal, Vaclav
6301 Osprey Terrace, Coconut Creek FL 33073, USA — Ice Hockey Player

Prosser, James
Refugee Mgmt, 209 10th Ave S, #347, Cummins Station, Nashville TN 37203, USA — Singer

Prosser, Robert
Cumberland Presbyterian Church, 1978 Union Ave, Memphis TN 38104, USA — Religious Leader

Prost, Alain M P
11 Ave de la Gare, 1260 Nyon, Switzerland — Auto Racing Driver

Prost, Sharon
US Court of Appeals, 717 Madison Place NW, Washington DC 20439, USA — Judge

Protopopov, Oleg A
Chalet Hubel, 3818 Grindelwald, Switzerland — Figure Skater

Proulx, Brooklynn
Global Creative, 1051 N Cole Ave, #B, Los Angeles CA 90038, USA — Actress

Proulx, E Annie
PO Box 789, Saratoga WY 82331, USA — Writer

Prout, Brian
Modern Mgmt, 1625 Broadway, #600, Nashville TN 37203, USA — Drummer (Diamond Rio)

Prout, Kirsten
Alchemy Entertainment, 7024 Melrose Ave, #420, Los Angeles CA 90038 USA — Actress

Proval, David
Glick Agency, 1260 6th St, #100, Santa Monica CA 90401, USA — Actor

Provence, Andrew C
224 Providence Road, Fayetteville GA 30215, USA — Football Player

Provenza, Paul
Metropolitan Talent Agency, 7020 La Presa Dr, Los Angeles CA 90068 USA — Actor, Director

Provost, Jon
627 Montclair Ave, Santa Rosa CA 95409, USA — Actor

Prowse, David
Spotlight, 7 Leicester Place, London WC2H 7BP, England — Actor

Proyas, Alex
Creative Artists Agency, 2000 Ave of Stars, #100, Los Angeles CA 90067 USA — Director, Producer, Writer

Prpic, Joel
2586 S Shore Road, Sudbury ON P3G 1M3, Canada — Ice Hockey Player

Prucha, Petr
6122 S Cypress Point Dr, Chandler AZ 85249, USA — Ice Hockey Player

Prudhomme, Christian
A S O, 2 Rue Rouget de l'Isle, 92130 Issy Les Mouoimeaux, France — Cycling Executive

Prudhomme, Don
Don Prudhomme Racing, 1232 Distribution Way, Vista CA 92081, USA — Drag Racing Driver

Prudhomme, Paul
2424 Chartres St, New Orleans LA 70117, USA — Chef

Pruett, Jeanne
Joe Taylor Artist Agency, PO Box 279, Williamstown NJ 37068 USA — Singer, Songwriter

Pruett, Scott
9743 W Bray Creek St, Star ID 83669, USA — Auto Racing Driver

Pruetz, Jill
Iowa State University, Anthropology Dept, Ames IA 50011, USA — Primatologist, Anthropologist

Pruitt, Gregory D (Greg) — Football Player
13851 Larchmere Blvd, Cleveland OH 44120, USA

Pruitt, James B — Football Player
PO Box 244483, Boynton Beach FL 33424, USA

Pruitt, Jordan L — Singer
Black Angel Records, PO Box 54, Fairview TN 37862, USA

Pruitt, Michael L (Mike) — Football Player
20568 Kelsey Lane, Strongsville OH 44149, USA

Pruitt, Mickey A — Football Player
15647 Dante Dr, South Holland IL 60473, USA

Pruitt, Ronald R (Ron) — Baseball Player
3632 Turnberry Dr, Medina OH 44256, USA

Prunariu, Dumitru D — Cosmonaut, Romania
Str Sf Spiridon 12, #4, 70231 Bucharest, Romania

Prunskiene, Kazimiera D — Prime Minister, Lithuania
Kriviu 53A-13, 2007 Vilnius, Lithuania

Prusiner, Stanley B — Nobel Medicine Laureate
University of California, Biochemistry Dept, San Francisco CA 94143, USA

Pruzansky, Mark E — Orthopedic Surgeon
975 Park Ave, New York NY 10028, USA

Pryce, Jonathan — Actor, Singer
Julian Belfrage Assoc, 9 Argyll St, #300, London W1F 7TG, England

Pryce, Malcolm — Writer
Bloomsbury Publishing, 36 Soho Square, London W1D 3Q4, England

Pryce, Trevor W — Football Player
12057 Open Run Road, Ellicott City MD 21042, USA

Prydz, Eric — DJ Musician
Ministry of Sound, 103 Gaunt St, London SE1 6DP, England

Prynoski, Chris — Animator, Producer
Titmouse, 6616 Lexington Ave, Los Angeles CA 90038, USA

Pryor, Aaron — Boxer
2964 High Forest Lane, #345, Cincinnati OH 45223, USA

Pryor, David H — Senator, Governor, AR
507 N 11th St, Paragould AR 72450, USA

Pryor, Gregory R (Greg) — Baseball Player
9726 W 115th Terrace, Overland Park KS 66210, USA

Pryor, Nicholas — Actor
S D B Partners, 1801 Ave of Stars, #902, Los Angeles CA 90067 USA

Prystai, Dymtro (Metro) — Ice Hockey Player
77 Crestwood Crescent, Yorkton SK S3N 2P2, Canada

Przybilla, Joel A — Basketball Player
21890 SW 109th Terrace, Tualtin OR 97062, USA

Psycho Les — Rap Artist (Beatnuts)
Agency Group Ltd, 142 W 57th St, #600, New York NY 10019 USA

Ptacek, Louis J — Geneticist
University of California Medical Center, Fu & Ptacek Laboratories, 1550 4th St, San Francisco CA 94158, USA

Ptashne, Mark S — Biochemist
Harvard University, Biochemistry Dept, Cambridge MA 02138, USA

Pucci, Lou Taylor — Actor
United Talent Agency, 9336 Civic Center Dr, Beverly Hills CA 90210 USA

Pucillo, Michael (Mike) — Football Player
9402 Council Rock Court, Riverview FL 33578, USA

Puck, Wolfgang — Chef
805 N Sierra Dr, Beverly Hills CA 90210, USA

Puckett, Gary — Singer, Songwriter
10710 Seminole Blvd, #3, Largo FL 33778, USA

Pudi, Danny — Actor, Writer
United Talent Agency, 9336 Civic Center Dr, Beverly Hills CA 90210 USA

Puenzo, Luis A — Director
Cinematografia Nacional Instituto, Lima 319, 1073 Buenos Aires, Argentina

Puerta, Joe — Singer, Guitarist (Ambrosia)
Lustig Talent, PO Box 770850, Orlando FL 32877 USA

Puett, Tommy — Actor
16621 Cerulean Court, Chino Hills CA 91709, USA

Puetz, Garry S — Football Player
1779 Robinson Road, Dahlonega GA 30533, USA

Puffer, Brandon — Baseball Player
1546 Haynie Bend, Round Rock TX 78665, USA

Pugacheva, Alla B — Singer
State Variety Theater, Bersenevskaya Nab 20/2, 109072 Moscow, Russia

Puget, Jade E — Guitarist (AFI)
S A M, 722 Seward St, Los Angeles CA 90038, USA

Puget, Jean-Loup — Astrophysicist
Institut d'Astrophysique Spatiale, Paris-Sud, 91898 Orsay Cedex, France

Pugh, Gareth — Fashion Designer
Mandi Lennard Publicity, 2 Hoxton St, London N1 6NG, England

Pugh, Jethro, Jr — Football Player
Gifts Inc, 329 E Colorado Blvd, #505, Dallas TX 75203, USA

Pugh, Larry — Football Player
RR 4, New Castle PA 16101, USA

Pugh, Timothy D (Tim) — Baseball Player
8015 N 187th East Ave, Owasso OK 74055, USA

Pugsley, Don — Actor
Lichtman/Salners, 15865 Royal Haven Place, Sherman Oaks CA 91403 USA

Puhl, Terrance S (Terry) — Baseball Player
918 Gondola St, Sugar Land TX 77478, USA

Pujats, Janis Cardinal — Religious Leader
Metropolijas Kurija, Maza Pils Iela 2/A, 1050 Riga, Latvia

Pujol, Laetitia — Ballerina
Paris Opera Ballet, Place de l'Opera, 75009 Paris, France

Pujols Alcantara, J Albert — Baseball Player
102 Grand Meridien Forest, Chesterfield MO 63005, USA

Pujols, Luis B — Baseball Player, Manager
3867 Jonathans Way, Boynton Beach FL 33436, USA

Puleo, Charles M (Charlie) — Baseball Player
3202 Miser Station Road, Louisville TN 37777, USA

Puleston-Davies, Ian — Actor
Ken McReddie Assoc, 11 Connaught Place, London W2 2ET, England

Pulford, Robert J (Bob) — Ice Hockey Player, Coach
78 Coventry Road, Northfield IL 60093, USA

Pulgram, William — Interior Designer
3747 Peachtree Road NE, #1425, Atlanta GA 30319, USA

Pulido, J Carlos — Baseball Player
PO Box 25323, Miami FL 33102, USA

Puljic, Vinko Cardinal — Religious Leader
Nadbiskupski Ordinarijat, Kaptol 7, 71000 Sarajevo, Bosnia & Herzegovina

Pulkkinen, David — Ice Hockey Player
5095 Croatia Road, Sudbury ON P3G 1L5, Canada

Pullen, Melanie Clark — Actress
Julian Belfrage Assoc, 9 Argyll St, #300, London W1F 7TG, England

Pulliam, Harvey J — Baseball Player
2009 Mount Hamilton Dr, Antioch CA 94531, USA

Pulliam, Keshia Knight — Actress
A P A Talent/Literary Agency, 405 S Beverly Dr, #300, Beverly Hills CA 90212 USA

Pullman, Bill — Actor
I C M Partners, 10250 Constellation Blvd, #900, Los Angeles CA 90067 USA

Pullman, Philip — Writer
24 Templar Road, Oxford OX2 8LT, England

Pulsford, K H Nigel — Singer, Guitarist (Bush)
Front Line Mgmt, 1100 Glendon Ave, #2000, Los Angeles CA 90024 USA

Pulsipher, Lindsay — Actress
I C M Partners, 10250 Constellation Blvd, #900, Los Angeles CA 90067 USA

Pulsipher, William T (Bill) — Baseball Player
1986 SW Certosa Road, Port Saint Lucie FL 34953, USA

Pulver, Lara — Actress
Independent Talent Group, Oxford House, 76 Oxford St, London W1D 1BS, England

Pulver, Liselotte — Actress
Villa Bip, 1166 Perroy, Kanton Vaudois, Switzerland

Pulz, Penny — Golfer
10315 W Winninger Circle, Sun City AZ 85351, USA

Puna, Henry T — Prime Minister, Cook Islands
Prime Minister's Office, Avarua, Rarotonga, Cook Islands

Punch, Lucy — Actress
United Agents, 12-26 Lexington St, London W1F 0LE, England

Punsalan Swallow, Elizabeth — Ice Dancer, Coach
Detroit Skating Club, 888 Denison Court, Bloomfield Hills MI 48302, USA

Punto, Nicholas P (Nick) — Baseball Player
19550 N Grayhawk Dr, #1122, Scottsdale AZ 85255, USA

Puppa, Daren — Ice Hockey Player
4526 Cheval Blvd, Lutz FL 33558, USA

Pupunu, Alfred S (Al) — Football Player
415 Conestoga Road, Moscow ID 83843, USA

Purcell, Dominic — Actor
Untitled Entertainment, 350 S Beverly Dr, #200, Beverly Hills CA 90212 USA

Purcell, James N — Government Official
5113 W Running Brook Road, Columbia MD 21044, USA

Purcell, Lee — Actress
Coast to Coast Talent, 3350 Barham Blvd, Los Angeles CA 90068 USA

Purcell, Patrick B — Publisher
Boston Herald, Publisher's Office, 1 Herald St, Boston MA 02118, USA

Purcell, Sarah — Actress
6525 Esplanade St, Playa del Rey CA 90293, USA

Purcell, William — Astrophysicist
Northwestern University, Astrophysics Dept, Evanston IL 60208, USA

Purdee, Nathan — Actor
Irv Schechter, 9460 Wilshire Blvd, #300, Beverly Hills CA 90212 USA

Purdy, Alfred — Writer
Harbour Publishing, PO Box 219, Madeira Park BC V0N 2H0, Canada

Purdy, Joe — Singer, Songwriter
Agency Group Ltd, 142 W 57th St, #600, New York NY 10019 USA

Purdy, Jolene — Actress
Innovative Artists, 1505 10th St, Santa Monica CA 90401 USA

Purdy, Robert — Actor
Associated International Mgmt, Fairfax House, Fulwood Place, London WC1V 6HU, England

Purdy, Ted — Golfer
14259 N 2nd Ave, Phoenix AZ 85023, USA

Purefoy, James — Actor
Independent Talent Group, Oxford House, 76 Oxford St, London W1D 1BS, England

Puri, Om — Actor
703 Trishul 2, Seven Bungalows, Andheri-W, Mumbai 61, India

Purim, Flora — Singer
Airflow Productions, 3940 Laurel Canyon Blvd, #179, Studio City CA 91604, USA

Purinton, Dale — Ice Hockey Player
2045 Cowichan Bay Road, Cowichan Bay BC V0R 1N1, Canada

Puri, Linda — Actress
Momentum Talent Mgmt, 13935 Burbank Blvd, #102, Valley Glen CA 91401, USA

Purtzer, Tom — Golfer
9828 E Desert Cove Ave, Scottsdale AZ 85260, USA

Purvanov, Georgi — President, Bulgaria
President's Office, 2 Dondukov Blvd, 1123 Sofia, Bulgaria

Purves, William — Financier
100 Ebury Mews, London SW1 9NX, England

Purvis, Jeffrey (Jeff) — Auto Racing Driver
1157 Dunbar Cove Road, Clarksville TN 37043, USA

Purvis, Neal — Writer, Producer
United Talent Agency, 9336 Civic Center Dr, Beverly Hills CA 90210 USA

Puryear, Martin — Sculptor
Drysdale Gallery, 700 New Hampshire Ave NW, #917, Washington DC 20037, USA

Puscau, Alina — Model, Singer, Actress
I M G Models, 304 Park Ave S, #PH-North, New York NY 10010 USA

Pusch, Alexander — Fencer
Lindenweg 39, 97941 Tauberbischofsheim, Germany

P

Paetkau - Pusch

Pusey, Chris — Ice Hockey Player
287 Brantwood Park Road, Brantford ON N3P 1H6, Canada

Pusha T — Rap Artist (Clipse)
American Talent Agency, 26 Finney Farm Road, Croton on Hudson NY 10520, USA

Pushelberg, Glenn — Interior Designer
Yabu Pushelberg, 138 Spring St, #400, New York NY 10012, USA

Pushor, Jamie — Ice Hockey Player
29 Jay Road W, Lake George NY 12845, USA

Puskaric, Ljubomir — Opera Singer
I M G Artists, Hogarth Business Park, Chiswick, London W4 2TH, England

Putch, John — Actor
I C M Partners, 10250 Constellation Blvd, #900, Los Angeles CA 90067 USA

Putilin, Nikolai G — Opera Singer
Mariinsky Theater, Teatralnaya Square 1, 190000 Saint Petersburg, Russia

Putin, Vladimir V — President, Russia
President's Office, Kremlin, Staraya Pl 4, 103132 Moscow, Russia

Putman, P Edward (Ed) — Baseball Player
PO Box 3366, Mesquite NV 89024, USA

Putnam, Ashley — Opera Singer
Maurice Mayer, 201 W 54th St, #1C, New York NY 10019, USA

Putnam, C Duane — Football Player
1545 Magnolia Ave, Ontario CA 91762, USA

Putnam, Hilary W — Philosopher
31 Cleveland St, Arlington MA 2474, USA

Putnam, Patrick E (Pat) — Baseball Player
4040 Staley Road, Fort Myers FL 33905, USA

Putterman, Seth J — Physicist
University of California, Physics Dept, Los Angeles CA 90024, USA

Puttnam, David T — Producer
Enigma Productions, 29A Tufton St, London SW1P 3QL, England

Putz, Joseph J (J J) — Baseball Player
8375 W La Caille, Peoria AZ 85383, USA

Putze, Martin — Bobsled Athlete
B S R Rennsteig Oberhof, Alte Ohrdrufer Str 6, 98559 Oberhof, Germany

Putzier, Jebediah L (Jeb) — Football Player
2641 W 131st Terrace, Leawood KS 66209, USA

Putzulu, Bruno — Actor
Voyez Mon Agent, 20 Ave Rapp, 75007 Paris, France

Puyana, Rafael — Concert Harpsichordist
Hacienda La Chucua, Carrera 4, #87-21, Santa Fe de Bogota, Colombia

Puzzuoli, P David (Dave) — Football Player
22214 Rock Creek Circle, Strongsville OH 44149, USA

Pyatt, F Nelson — Ice Hockey Player
1680 Arthur St W, Thunder Bay ON P7K 1A8, Canada

Pyavko, Vladislav I — Opera Singer
Bryusov Per 2/14, #27, 103009 Moscow, Russia

Pye, R Edward (Eddie) — Baseball Player
307 Polk St, Columbia TN 38401, USA

Pyfrom, Shawn C — Actor
Podwall Entertainment, 710 N Orlando Ave, #203, West Hollywood CA 90069, USA

Pygram, Wayne — Actor
Peachtree Services, 1805 134th Ave SE, #27, Bellevue WA 98005, USA

Pyle, Andy — Bassist (Kinks)
Larry Page, 29 Ruston Mews, London W11 1RB, England

Pyle, Chuck — Singer, Guitarist, Songwriter
Stewart Management & Booking, PO Box 27581, Denver CO 80227, USA

Pyle, Michael J (Mike) — Football Player
2436 Saranac Court, Glenview IL 60026, USA

Pyle, Missi — Actress
McKeon-Myrones Mgmt, 3500 Olive Ave, #770, Burbank CA 91505 USA

Pyle, Thomas D (Artimus) — Drummer (Lynyrd Skynyrd)
Lustig Talent, PO Box 770850, Orlando FL 32877 USA

Pyle, W Palmer — Football Player
14808 N Olympic Way, Fountain Hills AZ 85268, USA

Pynchon, Thomas — Writer
Henry Holt, 175 5th Ave, #400, New York NY 10010 USA

Pyne, Natasha — Actress
Kate Feast, Primrose Hill Studios, Fitzroy Road, London NW1 8TR, England

Pyne, Stephen J — Historian
Arizona State University, History Dept, Tempe AZ 85287, USA

Pysnarski, Timothy M (Tim) — Baseball Player
10716 S Austin Ave, Chicago Ridge IL 60415, USA

Pytka, Joseph (Joe) — Director, Actor
United Talent Agency, 9336 Civic Center Dr, Beverly Hills CA 90210 USA

Q

Def Jam Records, 160 Varick St, #1200, New York NY 10013 USA — Singer (112)

Q, Maggie
Echelon Talent Mgmt, 3674 Oxford St, Vancouver BC V5K 1P3, Canada — Actress

Q, Maggie
Creative Artists Agency, 2000 Ave of Stars, #100, Los Angeles CA 90067 USA — Actress, Model

Qabus ibin Sa'id al Sa'id
Diwan, PO Box 632, Muscat 113, Oman — Sultan, Oman

Qasimi, Sheikh Dr Sultan ibn Muhammad Al
Ruler's Palace, Sharjah, United Arab Emirates — Ruler, Sharjah

Qasimi, Sheikh Saqr ibn Muhammad Al
Ruler's Palace, Ras Al Khaimah, United Arab Emirates — Ruler, Ras Al Khaimah

Q-Tip
Creative Artists Agency, 2000 Ave of Stars, #100, Los Angeles CA 90067 USA — Rap Artist

Quagmire, Joshua
PO Box 2221, Los Angeles CA 90078, USA — Cartoonist (Cutey Bunny)

Quaid, Dennis
W M E Entertainment, 9601 Wilshire Blvd, #300, Beverly Hills CA 90210 USA — Actor

Quaid, Jack
United Talent Agency, 9336 Civic Center Dr, Beverly Hills CA 90210 USA — Actor

Quaid, Randy
PO Box 1513, Marfa TX 79843, USA — Actor

Quaintance, Rachel
OmniPop Talent Group, 4605 Lankershim Blvd, #201, Toluca Lake CA 91602 USA — Actress, Comedienne

Qualls, Chad M
8416 Big View Dr, Austin TX 78730, USA — Baseball Player

Qualls, D J
Paul Kohner, 9300 Wilshire Blvd, #555, Beverly Hills CA 90212 USA — Actor

Qualls, James R (Jim)
410 N Country Road 950, Sutter IL 62373, USA — Baseball Player

Quance, Kristine
1320 Moncado Dr, Glendale CA 91207, USA — Swimmer

Quann Jendrick, Megan
11602 135th Street Court E, Puyallup WA 98374, USA — Swimmer

Quant, Mary
Mary Quant Ltd, 7 Montpelier St, Knightsbridge, London SW7 1EX, England — Fashion Designer

Quantrill, Paul J
334 E Lake Road, Palm Harbor FL 34685, USA — Baseball Player

Quarles, Shelton E
17019 Candeleda de Avila, Tampa FL 33613, USA — Football Player

Quarrie, Donald (Don)
Jamaican Amateur Athletic Assn, PO Box 272, Kingston 5, Jamaica — Track Athlete

Quarterman, Saundra
Stone Manners Salners, 9911 W Pico Blvd, #1400, Los Angeles CA 90035 USA — Actress

Quasthoff, Thomas
C M Artists, 127 W 96th St, #13B, New York NY 10025 USA — Concert Singer

Quatro, Suzi
Cape Entertainment, 8432 NW 31st Court, Fort Lauderdale FL 33351, USA — Singer, Songwriter, Actress

Quayle, Anna
Caroline Dawson, 125 Gloucester Road, London SW7 4TE, England — Actress

Quayle, J Danforth (Dan)
Laura Mintner, 7001 N Scottsdale Road, Scottsdale AZ 85253, USA — Vice President

Quayle, Steven
Gersh Agency, 9465 Wilshire Blvd, #600, Beverly Hills CA 90212 USA — Director

Queen Ida
Traditional Arts Services, 3661 Albion Place N, #2, Seattle WA 98103, USA — Singer, Accordian Player

Queen Latifah
Flavor Unit Entertainment, 155 Morgan St, Jersey City NJ 07302, USA — Rap Artist, Actress, Model

Queen, Jeffrey R (Jeff)
4765 Canterbury Court, Oceanside CA 92056, USA — Football Player

Queffelec, Anne
15 Ave Corneille, 78600 Maisons-Laffitte, France — Concert Pianist

Queler, Eve
Opera Orchestra of New York, 344 E 63rd St, #B1, New York NY 10065, USA — Conductor

Quenneville, Joel N
835 S Park Ave, Hinsdale IL 60521, USA — Ice Hockey Player, Coach

Querim, Molly
CBS-TV, Sports Dept, 51 W 52nd St, New York NY 10019 USA — Sportscaster

Query, Jeff L
93 Woodlily Place, Spring TX 77382, USA — Football Player

Questlove
Paradigm Agency, 360 N Crescent Dr, North Building, Beverly Hills CA 90210 USA — Drummer (Roots), DJ

Questrom, Allen I
J C Penney Co, 6501 Legacy Dr, Plano TX 75024, USA — Businessman

Quezada, Milly
Wilson Sanchez Entertainment, 10852 38th Ave, Corona NY 11368, USA — Singer

Quick, Diana
Independent Talent Group, Oxford House, 76 Oxford St, London W1D 1BS, England — Actress

Quick, James E (Jim)
6061 Keeble Lane, Camino CA 95709, USA — Baseball Umpire

Quick, Jonathan D (Jon)
Los Angeles Kings, Staples Center, 1111 S Figueroa St, Los Angeles CA 90015 USA — Ice Hockey Player

Quick, Michael A (Mike)
13 Slab Branch Road, Marlton NJ 08053, USA — Football Player

Quie, Albert H (Al)
4209 Christy Lane, Minnetonka MN 55345, USA — Governor, MN

Quigley, Dana C
2670 Tecumseh Dr, West Palm Beach FL 33409, USA — Golfer

Quigley, Laura
1111B NW 131st Way, Vancouver WA 98685, USA — Singer, Bassist (Misty River)

Quigley, Linnea
Purrfect Productions, PO Box 1771, Pompano Beach, FL 33061 USA — Actress

Quilici, Frank R
3413 E 126th St, Burnsville MN 55337, USA — Baseball Player, Manager

Quill, Timothy E
University of Rochester, Medical & Dentistry School, Rochester NY 14642, USA — Social Activist, Internist

Q

Q - Quill

Q

Quillan, Frederick D (Fred) 2924 Bailey Lane, Eugene OR 97401, USA	Football Player
Quin, Sara K Paquin Entertainment, 395 Notre Dame Ave, Winnipeg MB R3B 1R2, Canada	Singer (Tegan & Sara), Songwriter
Quince, Dolvett Rogers & Cowan, 8687 Melrose Ave, #G700, West Hollywood CA 90069 USA	Physical Fitness Instructor, Actor
Quindlen, Anna M I C M Partners, 10250 Constellation Blvd, #900, Los Angeles CA 90067 USA	Columnist
Quinlan, Kathleen PO Box 6728, Malibu CA 90264, USA	Actress
Quinlan, Maeve Beech Park Entertainment, 2934 Beverly Glen Circle, #333, Los Angeles CA 90077, USA	Actress
Quinlan, Thomas R (Tom) 1061 Sterling St S, Saint Paul MN 55119, USA	Baseball Player
Quinlan, William D (Bill) 393 Mount Vernon St, Lawrence MA 01843, USA	Football Player
Quinn, Aidan Paradigm Agency, 360 N Crescent Dr, North Building, Beverly Hills CA 90210 USA	Actor
Quinn, Aileen 12747 Riverside Dr, #208, Valley Village CA 91607, USA	Actress
Quinn, Brayden T (Brady) 5889 Connolly Court, Dublin OH 43016, USA	Football Player
Quinn, Brian Brian Quinn Soccer School, 9606 Aero Dr, #3500, San Diego CA 92123, USA	Soccer Player, Coach
Quinn, Carmel Michael J Lannon, 5830 McKenzie Road, North Olmsted OH 44070, USA	Singer
Quinn, Colin A P A Talent/Literary Agency, 405 S Beverly Dr, #300, Beverly Hills CA 90212 USA	Actor, Comedian
Quinn, Cynthia Momix, PO Box 35, Washington CT 06794, USA	Dancer
Quinn, DeClan 22 Cherry Ave, Cornwall on Hudson NY 12520, USA	Cinematographer
Quinn, Ed I C M Partners, 10250 Constellation Blvd, #900, Los Angeles CA 90067 USA	Actor
Quinn, J B Patrick (Pat) Edmonton Oilers, 11230 110th St, Edmonton AB T5G 3H7, Canada	Ice Hockey Player, Coach
Quinn, Jane Bryant Newsweek, Editorial Dept, 251 W 57th St, New York NY 10019, USA	Columnist
Quinn, Jonathan G (Jonny) Big Life Mgmt, 67-69 Charlton St, London NW1 1HY, England	Drummer (Snow Patrol)
Quinn, Jonathan R 8409 W 145th Terrace, Overland Park KS 66223, USA	Football Player
Quinn, Kimberly Verve Entertainment, 5900 Wilshire Blvd, #1720, Los Angeles CA 90036, USA	Actress
Quinn, Martha 11684 Ventura Blvd, #453, Studio City CA 91604, USA	Actress, Model
Quinn, Michael P (Mike) 10703 Del Monte Dr, Houston TX 77042, USA	Football Player
Quinn, Molly C Ellen Meyer Mgmt, 8899 Beverly Blvd, #612, West Hollywood CA 90048, USA	Actress
Quinn, Noelle Washington Mystics, Verizon Center, 401 9th St NW, #750, Washington DC 20004 USA	Basketball Player
Quinn, Patricia Jonathan Altaras Assoc, 11 Garrick St, London WC2E 9AR, England	Actress
Quinn, Sally 3014 N St NW, Washington DC 20007, USA	Journalist
Quinones August, Denise M Untitled Entertainment, 350 S Beverly Dr, #200, Beverly Hills CA 90212 USA	Beauty Queen, Actress
Quinones Torruellas, Luis R 5821 Calle San Bruno Urb Santa Teresita, Ponce PR 00730, USA	Baseball Player
Quinones, John ABC-TV, News Dept, 77 W 66th St, New York NY 10023 USA	Commentator
Quint, Deron T 13 Littlehale Road, Durham NH 03824, USA	Ice Hockey Player
Quintal, Stephane 1356A Rue La Fontaine, Montreal QC H2L 1T5, Canada	Ice Hockey Player
Quintana, Carlos DiBella Entertainment, 350 7th Ave, #800, New York NY 10001, USA	Boxer
Quinto, Zachary Creative Artists Agency, 2000 Ave of Stars, #100, Los Angeles CA 90067 USA	Actor
Quirk, James P (Jamie) 310 W 123rd Terrace, Kansas City MO 64145, USA	Baseball Player
Quirk, Matthew Hatchette Book Group, 3 Center Plaza, Boston MA 02108, USA	Writer
Quiroga, Elena Agencia Balcells, Diagonal 580, 08021 Barcelona, Spain	Writer
Quist, Janet 13446 Poway Road, #239, Poway CA 92064, USA	Model
Quivar, Florence Columbia Artists Mgmt Inc, 1790 Broadway, #702, New York NY 10019 USA	Opera Singer
Quivers, Robin O Sirius Satellite Radio, 1221 Ave of Americas, New York NY 10020, USA	Entertainer
Quock, Audrey New York Model Mgmt, 596 Broadway, #701, New York NY 10012 USA	Model, Actress
Quon, Xian Otto Models, 2901 W Coast Highway, #350, Newport Beach CA 92663, USA	Model
Qureshi, Aisam Octagon Worldwide, 1751 Pinnacle Dr, #1500, McLean VA 22102 USA	Tennis Player
Qvist, Trine Curling Assn, Idraettens Hus, 2605 Brondby, Denmark	Curling Athlete

Quillan - Qvist

Raab, Marc A
8500 Sea Pines Place, McKinney TX 75070, USA — Football Player
Raabe, Brian C
38760 Kost Trail, North Branch MN 55056, USA — Baseball Player
Raabe, Max
Klimperkasten, Thuyring 63, 12101 Berlin, Germany — Opera Singer
Raakhee
Muktangan Sarojini, Naidu Road, Santacruz, Mumbai MS 400054, India — Actress
Raba, Robert (Bob)
16066 Acre St, North Hills CA 91343, USA — Football Player
Rabach, Casey E
5707 Bay Shore Dr, Sturgeon Bay WI 54235, USA — Football Player
Rabal, Liberto
Anne Alvares Correa, 34 Rue Jouffroy d'Abbans, 75017 Paris, France — Actor
Raban, Jonathan
Pantheon Books, 1745 Broadway, New York NY 10019, USA — Writer
Rabe, Charles H (Charlie)
6059 E Sierra Blanca St, Mesa AZ 85215, USA — Baseball Player
Rabe, David W
Creative Artists Agency, 2000 Ave of Stars, #100, Los Angeles CA 90067 USA — Writer
Rabe, Lily
Framework Entertainment, 9057 Nemo St, #C, West Hollywood CA 90069 USA — Actress
Rabe, Pamela
Shanahan Mgmt, PO Box 1509, Darlinghurst NSW 1300, Australia — Actress
Rabelo, Mike
5813 N 17th St, Tampa FL 33610, USA — Baseball Player
Rabemananjara, Charles
Premier's Office, BP 248, Mahazoarivo, 101 Antananarivo, Madagascar — Prime Minister, Madagascar
Rabin, Trevor
Kraft-Engel Mgmt, 15233 Ventura Blvd, #200, Sherman Oaks CA 91403 USA — Composer
Rabinovitch, B Seymour
116 Fairview Ave N, #832, Seattle WA 98109, USA — Chemist
Rabinowitz, Dorothy
Wall Street Journal, Editorial Dept, 1 World Financial Center, New York NY 10281 USA — Journalist
Rabinowitz, Jesse C
University of California, Molecular & Cell Biology Dept, Berkeley CA 94720, USA — Biochemist
Rabinyan, Dorit
Bloomsbury Publishing, 36 Soho Square, London W1D 3Q4, England — Writer
Rabkin, Mitchell T
Beth Israel Deaconess Medical Center, 330 Brookline Ave, Boston MA 02215, USA — Physician
Raboteau, Albert J
Princeton University, Religion School, Princeton NJ 08544, USA — Religious Historian
Rabourdin, Olivier
J F P M, 11 Rue Chavez, 75781 Paris Cedex 16, France — Actor
Raboy, Marcus
Modus Entertaiment, 8730 W Sunset Blvd, #290, West Hollywood CA 90069, USA — Director
Raburn, Ryan N
6612 Ike Smith Road, Plant City FL 33565, USA — Baseball Player
Raby, Stuart
Ohio State University, Physics Dept, Columbus OH 43210, USA — Physicist
Racette, Patricia
Opus 3 Artists, 470 Park Ave S, #900N, New York NY 10016 USA — Opera Singer
Rachel, Allyn
Creative Artists Agency, 2000 Ave of Stars, #100, Los Angeles CA 90067 USA — Actress
Rachel, Leah
W M E Entertainment, 9601 Wilshire Blvd, #300, Beverly Hills CA 90210 USA — Actress, Writer
Rachins, Alan
TalentWorks, 3500 W Olive Ave, #1400, Burbank CA 91505 USA — Actor
Rachlin, Julian
Askonas Holt, Lincoln House, 300 High Holborn, London WC1V 7JH, England — Concert Violinist
Racicot, Marc F
28013 Swan Cove Dr, Bigfork MT 59911, USA — Governor, MT
Racimo, Victoria
Marion Rosenberg, PO Box 69826, West Hollywood CA 90069 USA — Actress
Racine, Yves
Arizona Capital Inc, 1515 Ave Saint Jean Baptiste, Quebec QC G2E 5E2, Canada — Ice Hockey Player
Rackers, Neil W
2577 E Locust Dr, Chandler AZ 85286, USA — Football Player
Rackley, Derek L
2770 Shumard Oak Dr, Braselton GA 30517, USA — Football Player
Rackley, Marvin E (Marv)
512 S Bibb St, Westminster SC 29693, USA — Baseball Player
Raczka, Michael (Mike)
72 Foley Dr, Southington CT 06489, USA — Baseball Player
Radachowsky, George J, Jr
63 Lake Place N, Danbury CT 06810, USA — Football Player
Radcliffe, Daniel
Artist Rights Group, 4 Great Portland Place, London W1W 8PA, England — Actor
Rade, John A
611 Deertrail Dr, Hailey ID 83333, USA — Football Player
Rademacher, Ingo
S D B Partners, 1801 Ave of Stars, #902, Los Angeles CA 90067 USA — Actor
Rademacher, T Peter (Pete)
5585 River Styx Road, Medina OH 44256, USA — Boxer
Rademacher, William S (Bill)
5409 Maple Ridge, Haslett MI 48840, USA — Football Player
Rader, David M (Dave)
14413 Westdale Dr, Bakersfield CA 93314, USA — Baseball Player
Rader, Dotson C
Parade Magazine, Editorial Dept, 750 3rd Ave, New York NY 10017, USA — Writer
Rader, Douglas L (Doug)
3332 SE Court Dr, Stuart FL 34997, USA — Baseball Player, Manager
Rader, Paul A
Ashbury College, President's Office, 1 Macklem Dr, Wilmore KY 40390, USA — Religious Leader, Educator
Rader, Randall R
US Appeals Court, 717 Madison Place NW, Washington DC 20439, USA — Judge

R

Rader-Shieber, Chas — Director
Columbia Artists Mgmt Inc, 1790 Broadway, #702, New York NY 10019 USA
Radford, Mark J — Basketball Player
3423 NE 22nd Ave, Portland OR 97212, USA
Radford, Michael — Director
Intellectual Artists Mgmt, 10585 Santa Monica Blvd, #135, Los Angeles CA 90025, USA
Radigan, Terry — Singer, Songwriter
Frank Callari Corp, PO Box 331549, Nashville TN 37203, USA
Radinsky, Scott D — Baseball Player
2974 Santiago St, Westlake Village CA 91362, USA
Radke, Brad W — Baseball Player
125 18th St, Belleair Beach FL 33786, USA
Radko, Christopher — Artist
PO Box 536, Elmsford NY 10523, USA
Radmanovic, Nebojsa — President, Bosnia & Herzegovina
President's Office, Marsala Titz 7, 71000 Sarajevo, Bosnia & Herzegovina
Radmanovic, Vladimir — Basketball Player
Chicago Bulls, United Center, 1901 W Madison St, Chicago IL 60612 USA
Radner, Roy — Economist
30711 Overlook Run, Buena Vista CO 81211, USA
Radnor, Josh — Actor
Gersh Agency, 9465 Wilshire Blvd, #600, Beverly Hills CA 90212 USA
Radojevic, Danilo — Ballet Dancer
American Ballet Theatre, 890 Broadway, #300, New York NY 10003 USA
Radovich, Frank R — Basketball Player
121 Lakewood Dr, Statesboro GA 30458, USA
Radtke, Ed — Director, Writer
Parseghian/Planco, 388 2nd Ave, #506, New York, NY 10010 USA
Radulov, Alexander — Ice Hockey Player
2600 Hillsboro Pike, #322, Nashville TN 37212, USA
Radvanovsky, Sondra — Opera Singer
I M G Artists, Hogarth Business Park, Chiswick, London W4 2TH, England
Radwanska, Agnieszka — Tennis Player
Women's Tennis Assn, 1 Progress Plaza, #1500, Saint Petersburg FL 33701 USA
Rady, Michael — Actor
Gersh Agency, 9465 Wilshire Blvd, #600, Beverly Hills CA 90212 USA
Rae, Brenda — Opera Singer
Columbia Artists Mgmt Inc, 1790 Broadway, #702, New York NY 10019 USA
Rae, Cassidy — Actress
24708 Riverchase Dr, #B213, Valencia CA 91355, USA
Rae, Charlotte — Actress
C E S D, 10635 Santa Monica Blvd, #130, Los Angeles CA 90025 USA
Rae, Corinne Bailey — Singer, Songwriter
Creative Artists Agency, 2000 Ave of Stars, #100, Los Angeles CA 90067 USA
Rae, Patricia — Actress
Rebel Entertainment Partners, 5701 Wilshire Blvd, #456, Los Angeles CA 90036, USA
Raether, Harold H (Hal) — Baseball Player
6105 Lincoln Dr, #133, Minneapolis MN 55436, USA
Rafalski, Brian C — Ice Hockey Player
4709 Rue Belle Mer, Sanibel FL 33957, USA
Rafelson, Bob — Director
1543 Dog Team Road, New Haven VT 05472, USA
Raffarin, Jean-Pierre — Prime Minister, France
7 Route de Saint-Georges, 86360 Chasseneuil-du-Poitou, France
Rafferty, Thomas M (Tom) — Football Player
1526 Mount Gilead Road, Roanoke TX 76262, USA
Rafikov, Mars Z — Cosmonaut
Ul M Gorkova 59, KV 44, 480 002 Almaty, Kazakhstan
Rafsanjani, Hojatoleslam H — President, Iran
Expediency Council of Islamic Order, Majilis, Teheran, Iran
Rafter, Patrick — Tennis Player
S F X Sports, PO Box 1235, North Sydney NSW 2059, Australia
Ragan, David — Auto Racing Driver
Roush Fenway Racing, 4600 Roush Place, Concord NC 28027, USA
Ragin, John S — Actor
5706 Briarcliff Road, Los Angeles CA 90068, USA
Raglan, Herb — Ice Hockey Player
335 King St, Peterborough ON K9J 2S8, Canada
Ragnarsson, Marcus — Ice Hockey Player
Hallonstigen 2, Bjorklinge 74 030, Sweden
Rago, Joseph — Journalist
Wall Street Journal, Editorial Dept, 1 World Financial Center, New York NY 10281 USA
Ragogna, Mike — Singer, Guitarist, Songwriter
PO Box 2331, Fairfield IA 52556, USA
Ragonese, Isabella — Actress
Officine Artistiche, Via Francesco Domenico Guerrazzi 7, 00152 Rome, Italy
Ragsdale, William — Actor
Stone Manners Salners, 9911 W Pico Blvd, #1400, Los Angeles CA 90035 USA
Rahal, Robert W (Bobby) — Auto Racing Driver, Owner
Team Rahal Racing, 4601 Lyman Dr, Hilliard OH 43026, USA
Rahim, Tahar — Actor
A U R A Agency, 34/36 Rue du Louvre, 75001 Paris France
Rahlves, Daron — Alpine Skier
11655 Mount Rose View Dr, Truckee CA 96161, USA
Rahm, Kevin — Actor
Gersh Agency, 9465 Wilshire Blvd, #600, Beverly Hills CA 90212 USA
Rahman Khan, Ataur — Prime Minister, Bangladesh
Bangladesh Jatiya League, 500A Dhanmondi R/A, Road 7, Dhaka, Bangladesh
Rahman, Allah Rakkha (A R) — Composer
Panchthan Recording Inn, 5 4th St, Dr Subbaraya Nagar, Kodambakkam, Chennai 24, India
Rahzel — Rap Artist, Percussionist (Roots)
Agency Group Ltd, 142 W 57th St, #600, New York NY 10019 USA
Rai, Aishwarya — Beauty Queen, Actress
Canyon Entertainment, PO Box 256, Palm Springs CA 92263, USA
Raible, Steve C — Football Player
18 W Raye St, Seattle WA 98119, USA

Raich, Eric J — Baseball Player
3963 Edward Dr, Brunswick OH 44212, USA
Raichle, Marcus E — Neurologist, Radiologist
Washington University Medical School, Radiology Dept, Saint Louis MO 63110, USA
Raiken, Sherwin H — Basketball Player
2400 McClellan Blvd, #E1208, Pennsauken NJ 08109, USA
Raikkonen, Kimi — Auto Racing Driver
Team Lotus, Hethel Industrial Estate, Potash Lane, Hethel, Norfolk NR14 8EY, England
Railsback, Steve — Actor
11684 Ventura Blvd, #581, Studio City CA 91604, USA
Raimey, David E (Dave) — Football Player
2212 W 2nd St, Dayton OH 45417, USA
Raimi, Sam — Director, Producer, Actor
Stars Road Entertainment, 10202 W Washington Blvd, Lean Building, Culver City CA 90232, USA
Raimi, Ted — Actor
Liberman/Zerman Mgmt, 252 N Larchmont Blvd, #200, Los Angeles CA 90004 USA
Raimond, Jean-Bernard — Government Official, France
12 Rue des Poissonniers, 92200 Neuilly-sur-Seine, France
Raimondi, Ruggero — Opera Singer
M Gromof, 140 Bis Rue Lecourbe, 75015 Paris, France
Raine, Craig A — Writer
New College, English Dept, Oxford OX1 3BN, England
Rainer, Luise — Actress
34 Eaton Mews North, London SW1 XAS, England
Rainer, Wali R — Football Player
8119 Braidstone Terrace, Chesterfield VA 23838, USA
Raines, F Anthony (Tony) — Auto, Truck Racing Driver
Front Row Motorsports, 3536 Denver Dr, Denver NC 28037, USA
Raines, Shirley C — Educator
University of Memphis, President's Office, Administration Building, Memphis TN 38152, USA
Raines, Timothy (Tim) — Baseball Player
1242 Saint Albans Loop, Lake Mary FL 32746, USA
Rainey, Charles D (Chuck) — Baseball Player
6484 Del Cerro Blvd, San Diego CA 92120, USA
Rainey, James — Pianist (Stamps Quartet)
PO Box 1471, Brentwood TN 37024, USA
Rainey, Matt — Photojournalist
Star-Ledger, Editorial Dept, 1 Star-Ledger Plaza, Newark NJ 07102, USA
Rainford, Rob — Chef
Agency Group, 9348 Civic Center Dr, #200, Beverly Hills CA 90210 USA
Rains, Traver — Fashion Designer
Heatherette, 111 E 7th St, New York NY 10009, USA
Rainwater, Keech — Drummer (Lonestar)
Borman Entertainment, 4322 Harding Pike, #429, Nashville TN 37205, USA
Rainwater, Marvin — Singer
36968 295th St, Aitkin MN 56431, USA
Raiola, Dominic — Football Player
7940 Barnsbury Ave, West Bloomfield MI 48324, USA
Raisa, Francia — Actress
Abrams Artists, 9200 W Sunset Blvd, #1125, West Hollywood CA 90069 USA
Raisman, Alexandra R (Aly) — Gymnast
Octagon Worldwide, 1751 Pinnacle Dr, #1500, McLean VA 22102 USA
Raison, Miranda — Actress
Ken McReddie Assoc, 11 Connaught Place, London W2 2ET, England
Raitt, Bonnie L — Singer, Songwriter
Gold Mountain, 3940 Laurel Canyon Blvd, #444, Studio City CA 91604 USA
Raja Permaisuri Agong XIII — Sultana, Malaysia
Sultan's Palace, Istana Bukit Serene, 50502 Kuala Lumpur, Malaysia
Rajapakse, Mahinda — President, Sri Lanka
President's Office, Republic Square, Sri Jayewardenepura Kotte, Sri Lanka
Rajasulochana — Actress
70 G N Chetty Road, T Nagar, Chennai TN 600017, India
Rajat, Kapoor — Actor, Director
140 Andheri Indl Est, Andheri (W), Mumbai MS 400053, India
Rajna, Thomas — Concert Pianist, Composer
10 Wyndover Road, Claremont, Cape Town, West Cape 7708, South Africa
Rajoelina, Audray — President, Madagascar
President's Office, 11 Oktomvri BB, 101 Antananarivo, Madagascar
Rajsich, Gary L — Baseball Player
6510 Charleston Dr, Colleyville TX 76034, USA
Rajskub, Mary Lynn — Actress
Innovative Artists, 1505 10th St, Santa Monica CA 90401 USA
Rakaa Iriscience — Rap Artist (Dilated Peoples)
Zzonked, Stratford Workshops, Burford Road, London E15 2SP, England
Rakers, Jason P — Baseball Player
547 Hickory Hollow Dr, Canfield OH 44406, USA
Rakhmonov, Imomali S — President, Tajikistan
President's Office, Rudaki Prospect 80, 734051 Dusanabe, Tajikistan
Rakim — Rap Artist (Eric B & Rakim)
Susan Blond Inc, 50 W 57th St, #1400, New York NY 10019 USA
Rakoczy, Gregg A — Football Player
8709 Hidden Green Lane, Tampa FL 33647, USA
Rakove, Jack N — Historian, Writer
Stanford University, History Dept, Stanford CA 94305, USA
Rales, Steven M — Businessman
Danaher Corp, 1250 24th St NW, Washington DC 20037, USA
Rall, J Edward — Physician
9901 Longs Mill Road, Rocky Ridge MD 21778, USA
Rall, Ted — Editorial Cartoonist
Chronicle Features, 901 Mission St, San Francisco CA 94103 USA
Ralph, Richard P — Governor, Falkland Islands
Governor's Office, Government House, Stanley, Falkland Islands
Ralph, Sheryl Lee — Actress, Singer
S M S Talent, 8383 Wilshire Blvd, #230, Beverly Hills CA 90211 USA
Ralston, Dennis — Tennis Player
203 Wellwood Lane, Conroe TX 77304, USA

R

Ralston, John R — Football Player, Coach
8245 Claret Court, San Jose CA 95135, USA
Ralston, Steve — Soccer Player
New England Revolution, 1 Patriot Place, Foxboro MA 02035 USA
Ram, C Venkata — Physician
Texas Southwestern Medical Center, 5323 Harry Hines Blvd, Dallas TX 75390, USA
Rama IX — King, Thailand
Chitralada Villa, Bangkok, Thailand
Ramachandran, Vilayanur S — Neuroscientist
University of California San Diego, Brain/Cognition Center, 9500 Gilman Drive, La Jolla CA 92093, USA
Ramage, Rob — Ice Hockey Player
16127 Wilson Manor Dr, Chesterfield MO 63005, USA
Ramahatra, Victor — Prime Minister, Madagascar; Army General
PO Box 6004, 101 Antananarivo, Madagascar
Ramakrishnan, Venkatraman — Nobel Chemistry Laureate
M R C Molecular Biology Laboratory, Hills Road, Cambridge CB2 0QH, England
Ramamurthy, Sendhil — Actor
Levine Okwu Erickson, 6363 Wilshire Blvd, #300, Los Angeles CA 90048, USA
Ramazzotti, Eros — Singer
Via Vittoria Colonna, 20149 Milan, Italy
Rambahadur Limbu — Vietnam War Borneo Army Hero (VC)
Box 420, Bandar Seri Begawan, Negara Brunei Darussalam, Brunei
Rambis, D Kurt — Basketball Player, Coach
20 Chatham, Manhattan Beach CA 90266, USA
Rambola, Tony — Guitarist (Godsmack)
Front Line Mgmt, 1100 Glendon Ave, #2000, Los Angeles CA 90024 USA
Ramenofsky Wingfield, Marilyn — Swimmer
1240 NW 116th St, Seattle WA 98177, USA
Ramey, Samuel E — Opera Singer
320 Central Park West, New York NY 10025, USA
Ramgoolam, Navinchandra — Prime Minister, Mauritius
Prime Minister's Office, Government Center, Port Louis, Mauritius
Ramirez Vazquez, Pedro — Architect
Avenida de la Fuentes 170, Mexico City 01900 DF, Mexico
Ramirez, Aramis N — Baseball Player
1440 N Lake Shore Dr, #10EG, Chicago IL 60610, USA
Ramirez, Cierra — Actress
Corsa Agency, 11704 Wilshire Blvd, #204, Los Angeles CA 90025, USA
Ramirez, Dania — Actress
I C M Partners, 10250 Constellation Blvd, #900, Los Angeles CA 90067 USA
Ramirez, Edgar — Actor
Creative Artists Agency, 2000 Ave of Stars, #100, Los Angeles CA 90067 USA
Ramirez, Efren — Actor
Clear Talent Group, 10950 Ventura Blvd, Studio City, CA 91604, USA
Ramirez, Hanley — Baseball Player
2903 Lake Ridge Lane, Weston FL 33332, USA
Ramirez, Horacio — Baseball Player
6424 Queens Court Trace, Mableton GA 30126, USA
Ramirez, Manuel A (Manny) — Baseball Player
13737 NW 18th Court, Pembroke Pines FL 33028, USA
Ramirez, Marisa — Actress
Vanguard Management Group, 8060 Melrose Ave, #400, Los Angeles CA 90046, USA
Ramirez, Michael P (Mike) — Editorial Cartoonist
Investor's Business Daily, 19 W 44th St, #1804, New York NY 10036, USA
Ramirez, Pedro J — Editor
El Mundo, Editor's Office, Calle Pradillo 42, 28002 Madrid, Spain
Ramirez, Raul — Tennis Player
Avenida Ruiz, 65 Sur Ensenada, Baja California, Mexico
Ramirez, Sara — Actress
Mitchell K Stubbs Assoc, 8695 W Washington Blvd, #204, Culver City CA 90232 USA
Ramis, Harold A — Actor, Director, Writer
United Talent Agency, 9336 Civic Center Dr, Beverly Hills CA 90210 USA
Ramo, Simon — Businessman
1221 Ocean Ave, #1003, Santa Monica CA 90401, USA
Ramon, Haim — Government Official, Israel
Knesset, Kiryat Ben-Gurion, Jerusalem 91950, Israel
Ramone, Phil — Businessman, Songwriter
Gorfaine/Schwartz, 4111 W Alameda Ave, #509, Burbank CA 91505 USA
Ramos Guerra, Pedro G (Pete) — Baseball Player
6637 W 22nd Lane, Hialeah FL 33016, USA
Ramos Ricciardi, Tabare R (Tab) — Soccer Player
Tab Ramos Soccer Programs, 17 Blair Road, Aberdeen NJ 07747, USA
Ramos, Constance (Connie) — Actress
Paradigm Agency, 360 N Crescent Dr, North Building, Beverly Hills CA 90210 USA
Ramos, Del — Singer (Association)
Variety Artists, 793 Higuera St, #6, San Luis Obispo CA 93401 USA
Ramos, Domingo A — Baseball Player
Carr Duarte KM 8 1/2, Ucey al Medio, Santiago, Dominican Republic
Ramos, Fidel V — President, Philippines; Army General
120 Maria Cristina St, AAVA Muntinlupa City, Philippines
Ramos, Hilario (Larry), Jr — Singer, Guitarist (Association)
Variety Artists, 793 Higuera St, #6, San Luis Obispo CA 93401 USA
Ramos, Melvin J (Mel) — Artist
5941 Ocean View Dr, Oakland CA 94618, USA
Ramos, Patrick — Drummer (Versus)
Ground Control Touring, 20 Jay St, #838, Brooklyn NY 11201, USA
Ramos, Roberto (Bobby) — Baseball Player
8945 Lake Irma Point, Orlando FL 32817, USA
Ramos, Rudy — Actor, Singer
Craig Wyckoff Mgmt, 11300 Ventura Blvd, #100, Studio City CA 91604, USA
Ramos, Sarah — Actress
I C M Partners, 10250 Constellation Blvd, #900, Los Angeles CA 90067 USA
Ramos-Horta, Jose — Nobel Laureate; President, Timor-Leste
President's Office, Dili, Timor-Leste
Ramotar, Donald — President, Guyana
President's Office, Brickham, New Garden & South Sts, Georgetown, Guyana

Ramphele, Mamphela A
International Bank of Reconstruction/Development, 1818 H St NW, Washington DC 20433, USA — Educator

Rampling, Charlotte
Les Visiteurs du Soir, 40 Rue de la Folie Regnault, 75011 Paris, France — Actress

Ramsay, Anne
A P A Talent/Literary Agency, 405 S Beverly Dr, #300, Beverly Hills CA 90212 USA — Actress

Ramsay, Craig
10602 Plantation Bay Dr, Tampa FL 33647, USA — Ice Hockey Player, Coach

Ramsay, Gordon
G R Holdings, 68 Royal Hospital Road, London SW3 4HP, England — Chef, Entertainer

Ramsay, John T (Jack)
11118 Gulf Shore Dr, #904, Naples FL 34108, USA — Basketball Coach, Executive

Ramsay, Laymon
2417 Princeton Ave SW, Birmingham AL 35211, USA — Baseball Player

Ramsay, Lynne
W M E Entertainment, 9601 Wilshire Blvd, #300, Beverly Hills CA 90210 USA — Director, Writer

Ramsay, Marshall
Copley News Service, 123 Camino de la Reina, San Diego CA 92108, USA — Cartoonist

Ramsey, Anessa
Mitchell K Stubbs Assoc, 8695 W Washington Blvd, #204, Culver City CA 90232 USA — Actress

Ramsey, Calvin (Cal)
New York University, Alumni Office, 181 Mercer St, New York NY 10012, USA — Basketball Player

Ramsey, David
A P A Talent/Literary Agency, 405 S Beverly Dr, #300, Beverly Hills CA 90212 USA — Actor

Ramsey, Derrick K
C M R 445 Box 23, APO AE 09046, USA — Football Player

Ramsey, Fernando D
2501 Sandy Trail, Keller TX 76248, USA — Baseball Player

Ramsey, Frank V, Jr
PO Box 363, Madisonville KY 42431, USA — Basketball Player, Coach

Ramsey, James R
University of Louisville, President's Office, Louisville KY 40292, USA — Educator

Ramsey, Laura
Luber Rocklin Entertainment, 8530 Wilshire Blvd, #555, Beverly Hills CA 90211 USA — Actress

Ramsey, Lowell W (Chuck), Jr
17519 Martel Road, Lenoir City TN 37772, USA — Football Player

Ramsey, Mary
Geffen Records, 10900 Wilshire Blvd, #1000, Los Angeles CA 90024 USA — Singer (10000 Maniacs)

Ramsey, Michael
2120 Welch St, Houston TX 77019, USA — Attorney

Ramsey, Michael (Mike)
Ramsey's Gold Medal Sports, 445 W 79th St, Chanhassen MN 55317, USA — Ice Hockey Player

Ramsey, Michael Jeffrey (Mike)
11564 92nd Way N, Largo FL 33773, USA — Baseball Player

Ramsey, Nathan L (Nate)
1938 Cambridge St, Philadelphia PA 19130, USA — Football Player

Ramsey, Patrick A
515 Toma Lodge Dr, Ruston LA 71270, USA — Football Player

Ramsey, Wesley (Wes)
Abrams Artists, 9200 W Sunset Blvd, #1125, West Hollywood CA 90069 USA — Actor

Ramsey, William E
825 Bayshore Dr, Pensacola FL 32507, USA — Navy Admiral

Ramsfjell, Bent Aanund
Curling Assn, Sognsveien 75, Serviceboks 1, 0840 Oslo, Norway — Curling Athlete

Ramson, Eason L
3526 Bayberry Dr, Walnut Creek CA 94598, USA — Football Player

Ramstein, Marco
Curling Assn, PO Box 606, 3000 Bern, Switzerland — Curling Athlete

Ran, Shulamit
University of Chicago, Music Dept, 5845 S Ellis Ave, Chicago IL 60637, USA — Composer

Ranaldo, Lee
Silva Artist Mgmt, 722 Steward St, Los Angeles CA 90038, USA — Guitarist (Sonic Youth)

Rand Reese, Mary
6650 Los Gatos, Atascadero CA 93422, USA — Track Athlete

Rand, A Barry
American Association of Retired Persons, 601 E St NW, Washington DC 20049, USA — Association Executive, Businessman

Rand, Robert W
Good Samaritan Hospital, Neurosciences Institute, Los Angeles CA 90017, USA — Neurosurgeon, Educator

Randa, Joseph G (Joe)
6436 Ensley Lane, Mission Hills KS 66208, USA — Baseball Player

Randall, Alice
McCormick & Williams, 37 W 20th St, New York NY 10011, USA — Writer, Songwriter

Randall, Anne
10526 W Tropicana Circle, Sun City AZ 85351, USA — Actress, Model

Randall, Carolyn D
US Court of Appeals, 515 Rusk St, #12015, Houston TX 77002, USA — Judge

Randall, Claire
9965 W Royal Oak Road, #1214, Sun City AZ 85351, USA — Religious Leader

Randall, Frankie
1210 Ashwood Dr, Jefferson City TN 37760, USA — Boxer

Randall, James O (Sap)
158 Heather Lane, Ruston LA 71270, USA — Baseball Player

Randall, Jon
Joe's Garage, 4405 Belmont Park Terrace, Nashville TN 37215, USA — Singer, Songwriter

Randall, Josh
I F A Talent Agency, 8730 W Sunset Blvd, #490, West Hollywood CA 90069 USA — Actor

Randall, Lisa
Harvard University, Physics Dept, Cambridge MA 02138, USA — Physicist

Randall, Semeka C
Michigan State University, Athletic Dept, East Lansing MI 48824, USA — Basketball Player, Coach

Randazzo, Mike
585 Gatewood Dr, Greenwood IN 46143, USA — Actor

Randi, James
201 SE 12th St, Fort Lauderdale FL 33316, USA — Illusionist

Randle El, Antwaan
PO Box 3247, Leesburg VA 20177, USA — Football Player

Ramphele - Randle El

Randle, E Tate — Football Player
11116 Sea Hero Lane, Austin TX 78748, USA

Randle, Ervin L — Football Player
900 Spring Creek Dr, Grapevine TX 76051, USA

Randle, John A — Football Player
375 Calamus Circle, Hamel MN 55340, USA

Randle, Leonard S (Lenny) — Baseball Player
39461 Cozumel Court, Murrieta CA 92563, USA

Randle, Theresa — Actress
Agency Group, 9348 Civic Center Dr, #200, Beverly Hills CA 90210 USA

Randle, Tom — Opera Singer
I M G Artists, Hogarth Business Park, Chiswick, London W4 2TH, England

Randolph, A Raymond — Judge
US Court of Appeals, 333 Constitution NW, #4400, Washington DC 20001, USA

Randolph, Alvin C (Al) — Football Player
319 Roble Ave, Redwood City CA 94061, USA

Randolph, Anthony E, Jr — Basketball Player
Denver Nuggets, Pepsi Center, 1000 Chopper Circle, Denver CO 80204 USA

Randolph, Carl — Bassist (Reveille)
David Levin Mgmt, 200 W 57th St, #308, New York NY 10019, USA

Randolph, Joyce — Actress
295 Central Park West, #18A, New York NY 10024, USA

Randolph, Leo — Boxer
17020 20th Ave E, Spanaway WA 98387, USA

Randolph, Robert — Guitarist
Warner Bros Records, 3300 Warner Blvd, Burbank CA 91505 USA

Randolph, Sam — Golfer
5285 Heightsview Lane E, #322, Fort Worth TX 76132, USA

Randolph, Stephen — Baseball Player
3706 Apache Forest Dr, Austin TX 78739, USA

Randolph, Willie I — Baseball Player, Manager
715 Jenney Trail, Franklin Lakes NJ 07417, USA

Randolph, Zachary (Zach) — Basketball Player
Memphis Grizzlies, 191 Beale St, Memphis TN 38103 USA

Randrup, Michael — Test Pilot
10 Fairlawn Road, Lythamst, Annes, Lancashire FY8 5PT, England

Rands, Bernard — Composer, Conductor
Harvard University, Music Dept, Cambridge MA 02138, USA

Raney, Sue — Singer
5114 Ranchito Ave, Sherman Oaks CA 91423, USA

Ranford, William (Bill) — Ice Hockey Player
670 Vista Lago Circle N, Palm Desert CA 92211, USA

Ranheim, Paul S — Ice Hockey Player
12128 N Reflection Ridge Dr, Oro Valley AZ 85755, USA

Rania al-Abdullah — Queen, Jordan
Royal Palace, Royal Hashemite Court, Amman, Jordan

Raniere, Sandro — Soccer Player
Confederacion de Futebol, Rua Victor Civita 66, #1, Rio de Janeiro 22775 044, Brazil

Ranieri, Luisa — Actress
Media Art Mgmt, C/ Castelló 82, 2 Derecha, 28006 Madrid, Spain

Ranis, Gustav — Economist
7 Mulberry Road, Woodbridge CT 06525, USA

Ranken, Andrew — Drummer (Pogues)
Agency Group Ltd, 361-373 City Road, London EC1V 2QA, England

Ranki, Dezso — Concert Pianist
Ordogorom Lejto 11/B, 1112 Budapest, Hungary

Rankin, Alfred M, Jr — Businessman
N A C C O Industries, 5875 Landerbrook Dr, #300, Cleveland OH 44124, USA

Rankin, Chris — Actor
Stacey Castro Media, 4009 Leeward Ave, Los Angeles CA 90005 USA

Rankin, Judy — Golfer
2715 Racquet Club Dr, Midland TX 79705, USA

Rankin, Kevin — Actor
Abrams Artists, 9200 W Sunset Blvd, #1125, West Hollywood CA 90069 USA

Rankine, Terry — Architect
Cambridge Seven Assoc, 1050 Massachusetts Ave, Cambridge MA 02138, USA

Ranks, Shabba — Singer
Sony Records, 2100 Colorado Ave, Santa Monica CA 90404 USA

Rannazzisi, Stephen — Actor
United Talent Agency, 9336 Civic Center Dr, Beverly Hills CA 90210 USA

Rannells, Andrew — Actor
Abrams Artists, 9200 W Sunset Blvd, #1125, West Hollywood CA 90069 USA

Ransey, Kelvin — Basketball Player
3195 Monterey Dr, Tupelo MS 38801, USA

Ransom, B Cody — Baseball Player
3146 E Boston St, Gilbert AZ 85295, USA

Ransom, Derrick W, Jr — Football Player
505 Sawgrass Dr, Akron OH 44333, USA

Ransom, Jeffrey D (Jeff) — Baseball Player
2131 Curtis St, Berkeley CA 94702, USA

Ransone, James (P J) — Actor
Management 360, 9111 Wilshire Blvd, Beverly Hills CA 90210 USA

Rao, C N Ramachandra — Chemist
J N C President's House, Indian Science Institute, Bangalor 560012, India

Rao, Calyampudi R — Mathematician, Statistician
29 Old Orchard St, Buffalo NY 14221, USA

Rao, Michael — Educator
Virginia Commonwealth University, President's Office, Richmond VA 23284, USA

Rapace, Noomi — Actress
Agentfirman Planthaber/Kilden, Drottninggatan 55, 111 21 Stockholm, Sweden

Rapada, Clayton A (Clay) — Baseball Player
2737 Fenway Ave, Chesapeake VA 23323, USA

Rapaport, Michael — Actor
Paradigm Agency, 360 N Crescent Dr, North Building, Beverly Hills CA 90210 USA

Raphael — Singer, Actor
Los Rosales #7, Monteprincipe, 28668 Boadilla del Monte, Madrid, Spain

Raphael, Fredric M — Writer, Director
Steve Kenis Co, Royalty House, 72-74 Dean St, London WID 3SG, England
Raphael, Sally Jessy — Entertainer, Actress
249 Quaker Hill Road, Pawling NY 12564, USA
Rapinoe, Megan A — Soccer Player
Seattle Sounders, 12 Seahawks Way, Renton WA 98056 USA
Rapoport, Ellen — Writer, Producer
Management 360, 9111 Wilshire Blvd, Beverly Hills CA 90210 USA
Rapp, Adam — Writer, Director
United Talent Agency, 9336 Civic Center Dr, Beverly Hills CA 90210 USA
Rapp, Anthony D — Actor, Singer
Untitled Entertainment, 23 E 22nd St, #300, New York NY 10010 USA
Rapp, Patrick L (Pat) — Baseball Player
2554 Pete Seay Road, Sulphur LA 70663, USA
Rapp, Vernon F (Vern) — Baseball Player, Manager
1559 Redwing Lane, Broomfield CO 80020, USA
Rappaport, Ben — Actor
Gersh Agency, 9465 Wilshire Blvd, #600, Beverly Hills CA 90212 USA
Rappeneau, Jean-Paul — Director, Writer
24 Rue Henri Barbusse, 75005 Paris, France
Rapping 4-Tay — Rap Artist
Richard Walters, PO Box 2789, Toluca Lake CA 91610 USA
Rarick, Cindy — Golfer
PO Box 30001, Tucson AZ 85751, USA
Rasby, Walter H — Football Player
6413 Brookbury Court, Charlotte NC 28226, USA
Rasche, David — Actor
Innovative Artists, 1505 10th St, Santa Monica CA 90401 USA
Rascoe, Robert B (Bobby) — Basketball Player
523 Sumpter Ave, Bowling Green KY 42101, USA
Rascon, Alfred V — Vietnam War Army Hero (CMH)
10397 Derby Dr, Laurel MD 20723, USA
Rash, Jim — Actor, Writer
Creative Artists Agency, 2000 Ave of Stars, #100, Los Angeles CA 90067 USA
Rash, Ron — Writer
320 Princess Grace Ave, Clemson SC 29631, USA
Rash, Steve — Director
Gersh Agency, 9465 Wilshire Blvd, #600, Beverly Hills CA 90212 USA
Rashad, Ahmad — Football Player, Sportscaster
13220 Verdun Dr, Palm Beach Gardens FL 33410, USA
Rashad, Phylicia — Actress
Parseghian/Planco, 388 2nd Ave, #506, New York, NY 10010 USA
Rasheeda — Rap Artist
I C M Partners, 10250 Constellation Blvd, #900, Los Angeles CA 90067 USA
Rasizade, Artur T — Prime Minister, Azerbaijan
Prime Minister's Office, Lermontov Str 68, 370066 Baku, Azerbaijan
Raskin, Alex — Journalist
Los Angeles Times, Editorial Dept, 202 W 1st St, Los Angeles CA 90012 USA
Rasley, Rocky — Football Player
1747 W Harbor Dr, Isleton CA 95641, USA
Rasmussen, Anders Fogh — Prime Minister, Denmark
N A T O Headquarters, Blvd Leopold III, 1110 Brussels, Belgium
Rasmussen, Blair A — Basketball Player
3258 74th Ave SE, Mercer Island WA 98040, USA
Rasmussen, Dennis L — Baseball Player
PO Box 547341, Orlando FL 32854, USA
Rasmussen, Eric R — Baseball Player
237 SW 45th St, Cape Coral FL 33914, USA
Rasmussen, Erik — Ice Hockey Player
16705 50th Court N, Minneapolis MN 55446, USA
Rasmussen, Gerry B — Cartoonist (Bub Slug, Betty)
10716 69th Ave NW, Edmonton AB T6H 2E1, Canada
Rasmussen, Poul Nyrup — Prime Minister, Denmark
Allegade 6A, 2000 Frederiksberg, Denmark
Rasmussen, Randall L (Randy) — Football Player
81 Grumman Hill Road, Wilton CT 06897, USA
Rasmussen, Randy R — Football Player
3990 114th Lane NW, Minneapolis MN 55433, USA
Rasmussen, Rie — Actress, Director
McCue Sussmane Zapfel, 521 Fifth Ave, #2800, New York NY 10175, USA
Rasmussen, Wayne F — Football Player
9000 E Maple St, Brandon SD 57005, USA
Raspberry, Larry — Singer (Gentrys)
Craig Nowag Attractions, 2095 Exeter Road, Germantown TN 38138, USA
Rasuk, Victor — Actor
Gersh Agency, 9465 Wilshire Blvd, #600, Beverly Hills CA 90212 USA
Ratajkowski, Emily — Actress, Model
C E S D, 10635 Santa Monica Blvd, #130, Los Angeles CA 90025 USA
Ratchford, Jeremy — Actor
Fountainhead Talent, 131 Davenport Road, Toronto ON M5R 1H8, Canada
Ratchuk, Peter — Ice Hockey Player
218 Ruskin Road, Buffalo NY 14226, USA
Ratcliffe, John A — Radio Astronomer
193 Huntingdon Road, Cambridge CB3 0DL, England
Ratelle, J G Y Jean — Ice Hockey Player
1200 Salem St, #111, Lynnfield MA 01940, USA
Rath, A Gary — Baseball Player
202 James Dr, Long Beach MS 39560, USA
Rath, Meaghan — Actress
Rain Mgmt, 1800 Stanford St, Santa Monica CA 90404, USA
Rathbone, Jackson — Actor
Cutler Mgmt, 165 Little Park Lane, Los Angeles CA 90049, USA
Rather, Dan — Commentator
45 E 80th St, #26A, New York NY 10075, USA
Rather, David E (Bo) — Football Player
4050 W Centre Ave, #215, Portage MI 49024, USA

Rathje, Mike — Ice Hockey Player
14850 Blossom Hill Road, Los Gatos CA 95032, USA

Rathke, Henrich K M H — Religious Leader
Schleifmuhlenweg 11, 19061 Schwering, Germany

Rathman, Thomas D (Tom) — Football Player
2762 Bloomfield Crossing, Bloomfield Hills MI 48304, USA

Ratleff, W Edward (Ed) — Basketball Player
4202 Paseo de Oro, Cypress CA 90630, USA

Ratley, Sarah Lee — Astronaut Candidate
PO Box 6973, Leawood KS 66206, USA

Ratliff, Jeremiah J (Jay) — Football Player
Dallas Cowboys, 1 Cowboys Parkway, Irving TX 75063 USA

Ratliff, Paul H — Baseball Player
78 Campton Place, Laguna Niguel CA 92677, USA

Ratliff, Theo C — Basketball Player
1180 Mount Paran Road NW, Atlanta GA 30327, USA

Ratliffe, Lisa — Model
New York Model Mgmt, 596 Broadway, #701, New York NY 10012 USA

Ratner, Brett — Director
Rat Entertainment, 100 Universal City Plaza, Bungalow 5196, Universal City CA 91608, USA

Ratner, Marina — Mathematician
University of California, Mathematics Dept, Berkeley CA 94720, USA

Ratner, Mark A — Chemist
615 Greenleaf Ave, Glencoe IL 60022, USA

Ratser, Dmitri — Concert Pianist
Naxim Gershunoff, 1401 NE 9th St, #38, Fort Lauderdale FL 33304, USA

Rattay, Timothy F (Tim) — Football Player
2556 W Princeville Dr, Anthem AZ 85086, USA

Rattle, Simon D — Conductor
Askonas Holt, Lincoln House, 300 High Holborn, London WC1V 7JH, England

Ratushinskaya, Irina B — Writer
Vargius Publishing House, Kazakova Str 18, 107005 Moscow, Russia

Ratzenberger, John — Actor
Management Squared, 10900 Wilshire Blvd, #1400, Los Angeles CA 90024, USA

Rau, Douglas J (Doug) — Baseball Player
RR 1 Box 154A, Columbus TX 78934, USA

Rauch, Jasen — Guitarist, Composer (Red)
Paradigm Agency, 404 W Franklin St, Monterey CA 93940 USA

Rauch, Jon — Baseball Player
14081 N Old Forest Trail, Oro Valley AZ 85755, USA

Rauch, Melissa — Actress
Gersh Agency, 9465 Wilshire Blvd, #600, Beverly Hills CA 90212 USA

Raup, David M — Paleontologist
423 Johnson Dr, Washington Island WI 54246, USA

Rausse, Errol — Ice Hockey Player
338 Rosslare Dr, Arnold MD 21012, USA

Rautins, Leo R — Basketball Player
202 Litchfield Dr, Syracuse NY 13224, USA

Rautzhan, Clarence G (Lance) — Baseball Player
2472 Covington Dr, Myrtle Beach SC 29579, USA

Ravali — Actress
159 Thirupathi Nagar, Valasaravakkam, Chennai TN 600087, India

Ravanello, Rick — Actor
Greene Assoc, 1901 Ave of Stars, #130, Los Angeles CA 90067 USA

Raven, Eddy — Singer, Guitarist, Songwriter
Birds of a Feather, PO Box 2476, Hendersonville TN 37077, USA

Raven, Marion — Singer (M-2-M), Songwriter
10th Street Mgmt, 700 N San Vicente Blvd, #G410, West Hollywood CA 90069, USA

Raven, Peter H — Botanist
Missouri Botanical Garden, 4355 Shaw Blvd, Saint Louis MO 63110, USA

Raven-Symone — Actress, Singer
United Talent Agency, 9336 Civic Center Dr, Beverly Hills CA 90210 USA

Raver, Kim — Actress
Mosiac Media Group, 9200 W Sunset Blvd, #1000, Los Angeles CA 90069 USA

Ravera, Gina — Actress
Kass & Stokes Mgmt, 9229 W Sunset Blvd, #504, Los Angeles CA 90069 USA

Ravich, Rand — Director, Producer, Writer
Creative Artists Agency, 2000 Ave of Stars, #100, Los Angeles CA 90067 USA

Ravitch, Diane S — Historian
New York University, Press Building, Washington Place, New York NY 10003, USA

Ravlich, Matt — Ice Hockey Player
15 Appletree Lane, Dalton MA 01226, USA

Ravony, Francisque — Prime Minister, Madagascar
Union des Forces Vivas Democratiques, Antananarivo, Madagascar

Rawat, Navi — Actress
Innovative Artists, 1505 10th St, Santa Monica CA 90401 USA

Rawi, Raad — Actor
Ken McReddie Assoc, 11 Connaught Place, London W2 2ET, England

Rawles, James Wesley — Writer
Trident Media Group, 41 Madison Ave, #3600, New York NY 10010 USA

Rawley, Shane W — Baseball Player
4587 Cherrybark Court, Sarasota FL 34241, USA

Rawlings, Florence — Singer, Songwriter
Agency Group Ltd, 361-373 City Road, London EC1V 2QA, England

Rawlins, Adrian — Actor
Ken McReddie Assoc, 11 Connaught Place, London W2 2ET, England

Rawlinson, Johnnie B — Judge
US Court of Appeals, US Courthouse, 333 Las Vegas Blvd S, Las Vegas NV 89101, USA

Rawls, Elizabeth E (Betsy) — Golfer
101 Lynthwaite Farm Lane, Wilmington DE 19803, USA

Rawls, Sam — Cartoonist (Pops Place)
King Features Syndicate, 300 W 57th St, #1500, New York NY 10019 USA

Ray J — Singer, Songwriter, Actor
Norwood & Norwood, 22817 Ventura Blvd, #432, Woodland Hills CA 91364, USA

Ray, Amy — Singer (Indigo Girls), Songwriter
Russell Carter Artist Mgmt, 567 Ralph Mcgill Blvd, Atlanta GA 30312, USA

R

Ray, Billy Management 360, 9111 Wilshire Blvd, Beverly Hills CA 90210 USA	Director, Writer
Ray, Chris 15311 Winding Creek Dr, Tampa FL 33613, USA	Baseball Player
Ray, Clifford (Cliff) Boston Celtics, 226 Causeway St, #4, Boston MA 02114 USA	Basketball Player, Coach
Ray, Darrol A 13000 Doriath Way, Oklahoma City OK 73170, USA	Football Player
Ray, Edward B (Eddie) 219 W Oak Lane, Lake Charles LA 70605, USA	Football Player
Ray, Edward J Oregon State University, President's Office, Corvallis OR 97331, USA	Educator
Ray, J Earl 446 N Lowell St, Casper WY 82601, USA	Basketball Player
Ray, Jimmy Epic Records, 9830 Wilshire Blvd, Beverly Hills CA 90212 USA	Singer
Ray, John Gucci Group, 1 Amstelplein, 1096 HA Amsterdam, Netherlands	Fashion Designer
Ray, John C (Johnny) 12470 S 432, Chouteau OK 74337, USA	Baseball Player
Ray, Lisa Characters Talent Mgmt, 8 Elm St, Toronto ON M5G 1G7, Canada	Actress
Ray, Marguerite 1329 N Vista St, #106, Los Angeles CA 90046, USA	Actress
Ray, Rachael W M E Entertainment, 1325 Ave of Americas, New York NY 10019 USA	Chef
Ray, Rob 289 Sausalito Dr, East Amherst NY 14051, USA	Ice Hockey Player
Ray, Robert D Blue Cross/Blue Shield of Iowa, 636 Grand Ave, Des Moines IA 50309, USA	Governor, IA
Ray, Ronald E 2670 Saint Andrews Blvd, Tarpon Springs FL 34688, USA	Vietnam War Army Hero (CMH)
Ray, Terry 42559 Angel Wing Way, Ashburn WA 20148, USA	Football Player
Raycroft, Andrew Vancouver Canucks, 800 Griffiths Way, Vancouver BC V6B 6G1, Canada	Ice Hockey Player
Raye, Collin Agency Group Ltd, 142 W 57th St, #600, New York NY 10019 USA	Singer
Rayford, Floyd K 11701 Pointe Circle, Fort Myers FL 33908, USA	Baseball Player
Rayl, James R (Jim) 201 W Boulevard, Kokomo IN 46902, USA	Basketball Player
Raymer, Cory G 34900 Delia Court, Round Hill VA 20141, USA	Football Player
Raymo, Maureen Boston University, Geology Dept, Boston MA 02215, USA	Geologist
Raymond, Corey 106 Carter St, New Iberia LA 70560, USA	Football Player
Raymond, J Claude 3 De la Citiere, #911, Saint Luc QC J0J 2A0, Canada	Baseball Player
Raymond, Janice Playboy Promotions, 2706 Media Center Dr, Los Angeles CA 90065 USA	Model
Raymond, Lisa Octagon Worldwide, 1751 Pinnacle Dr, #1500, McLean VA 22102 USA	Tennis Player
Raymond, Ralph USA Softball, 1 Olympia Plaza, Colorado Springs CO 80909, USA	Softball Coach
Raymonde, Tania A P A Talent/Literary Agency, 405 S Beverly Dr, #300, Beverly Hills CA 90212 USA	Actress
Raymond-James, Michael TalentWorks, 3500 W Olive Ave, #1400, Burbank CA 91505 USA	Actor
Raymund, Steven A Tech Data Corp, 5350 Tech Data Dr, Clearwater FL 33760, USA	Businessman
Raynaud, Jean-Pierre 12 Ave Rhin et Danube, 92250 La Gareene Colombes, France	Sculptor
Rayner, Adam Innovative Artists, 1505 10th St, Santa Monica CA 90401 USA	Actor
Raynor, Bruce Unite, 275 7th Ave, #1100, New York NY 10001, USA	Labor Leader
Raz, Joseph Oxford University, Balliol College, Oxford OX1 3BJ, England	Philosopher
Raz, Kavi Dale Garrick, 1017 N La Cienega Blvd, #109, West Hollywood CA 90069 USA	Actor
Razah Def Jam Records, 160 Varick St, #1200, New York NY 10013 USA	Singer, Songwriter
Raz-B Pyramid Entertainment, 377 Rector Place, #21A, New York NY 10280 USA	Singer (B2K)
Razborov, A A Princeton University, Mathematics Dept, Princeton NJ 08540, USA	Mathematician
Raziano, Barry J 1315 4th St, Kenner LA 70062, USA	Baseball Player
Re, Giovanni Battisti Cardinal Palazzina dell-Arciprete, 00120 Vatican City	Religious Leader
Rea, Chris Real Life, 122 Holland Park Ave, London W11 4UA, England	Singer, Guitarist, Songwriter
Rea, Connie M 13 Marina Dr, Winter Haven FL 33881, USA	Basketball Player
Rea, Stephen Barking Dog Entertainment, 609 Greenwich St, #600, New York NY 10014, USA	Actor
Read, Dolly 30765 Pacific Coast Highway, #103, Malibu CA 90265, USA	Model, Actress
Read, James Pakula/King, 9229 W Sunset Blvd, #315, West Hollywood CA 90069 USA	Actor
Read, Richard Portland Oregonian, Editorial Dept, 1320 SW Broadway, Portland OR 97201, USA	Journalist
Read, Sister Joel Alverno College, President's Office, PO Box 343922, Milwaukee WI 53234, USA	Educator

Ray - Read

R

Readdy, William F (Bill) — Astronaut
N A S A, Johnson Space Center, 2101 NASA Road, Houston TX 77058 USA

Reader, Ted — Chef
Agency Group, 9348 Civic Center Dr, #200, Beverly Hills CA 90210 USA

Readman, Andrew — Actor
Ken McReddie Assoc, 11 Connaught Place, London W2 2ET, England

Ready, Randy M — Baseball Player
4410 Enfield Dr, Dallas TX 75220, USA

Reagan, Nancy D — Wife of US President, Actress
10880 Wilshire Blvd, #870, Los Angeles CA 90024, USA

Reagon, Bernice Johnson — Singer (Sweet Honey in the Rock)
American University, History Dept, Washington DC 20016, USA

Reagor, W Montae — Football Player
3 Fox Glen Run, Frisco TX 75034, USA

Reale, Willie — Writer, Lyricist
Creative Artists Agency, 2000 Ave of Stars, #100, Los Angeles CA 90067 USA

Reality, Maxim — Singer, Emcee (Prodigy)
Midi Mgmt, Jenkins Lane, Great Hallinsbury, Essex CM22 7QL, England

Reames, Britt — Baseball Player
806 Dalton Road, Seneca SC 29678, USA

Reardon, Jeffrey J (Jeff) — Baseball Player
5 Marlwood Lane, Palm Beach Gardens FL 33418, USA

Reaser, Elizabeth — Actress
United Talent Agency, 9336 Civic Center Dr, Beverly Hills CA 90210 USA

Reason, Rex — Actor
Roadside Productions, 20105 Rhapsody Road, Walnut Creek CA 91789, USA

Reasoner, Marty — Ice Hockey Player
9427 Crystal Beach Road, Hammondsport NY 14840, USA

Reasons, Gary P — Football Player
805 Glendevon Dr, McKinney TX 75071, USA

Reaume, Marc A — Ice Hockey Player
299 Laurier Dr, LaSalle ON N9J 1L7, Canada

Reaves, Kenneth M (Ken) — Football Player
413 Oakside Dr SW, Atlanta GA 30331, USA

Reaves, T Johnson (John) — Football Player, Coach
4825 W San Miguel St, Tampa FL 33629, USA

Reavie, Chez — Golfer
Gaylord Sports Mgmt, 13845 N Northsight Blvd, #200, Scottsdale AZ 85260 USA

Reavis, David C (Dave) — Football Player
5495 S Newport Circle, Greenwich Village CO 80111, USA

Reavley, Thomas M — Judge
3830 Wickersham Lane, Houston TX 77027, USA

Rebek, Julius, Jr — Chemist
2330 Calle de Oro, La Jolla CA 92037, USA

Rebekah — Singer
International Talent Booking, Ariel House, 74A Charlotte St, #100 London W1T 4QJ, England

Reberger, Frank B — Baseball Player
439 Sunset View Lane, Hope ID 83836, USA

Rebhorn, James — Actor
S M S Talent, 8383 Wilshire Blvd, #230, Beverly Hills CA 90211 USA

Reboulet, Jeffrey A (Jeff) — Baseball Player
3776 Grand Oak Trail, Dayton OH 45440, USA

Rebraca, Zeljko — Basketball Player
1550 8th St, Manhattan Beach CA 90266, USA

Recasner, Eldridge D — Basketball Player
6159 164th Ave SE, Bellevue WA 98006, USA

Recchi, Mark — Ice Hockey Player
114 Fairway Lane, Pittsburgh PA 15238, USA

Rechichar, Albert D (Bert) — Football Player
141 W McClain Road, Belle Vernon PA 15012, USA

Reckell, Peter — Actor
Mattie Mgmt, 415 N Camden Dr, #203, Beverly Hills CA 90210, USA

Rector, Jeff — Actor
10748 Aqua Vista St, North Hollywood CA 91602, USA

Redahl, Gordon (Gord) — Ice Hockey Player
201 Milton St, Flin Flon MB R8A 0H8, Canada

Redbone, Leon — Singer, Guitarist
Pathfinder Mgmt, PO Box 159006, Nashville TN 37215, USA

Redd, Glenn H — Football Player
4526 W 1500 N, Ogden UT 84404, USA

Redd, Michael W — Basketball Player
2 Crescent Pond, New Albany OH 43054, USA

Redden, Barry D — Football Player
PO Box 6501, Katy TX 77491, USA

Redden, Wade — Ice Hockey Player
Newport Sports, 601-201 City Centre Dr, Mississauga ON L5B 2T4, Canada

Reddick, Cat — Soccer Player
2620 Altadena Road, Birmingham AL 35243, USA

Reddick, Jaret R — Singer, Guitarist (Bowling for Soup)
Rainmaker Artists, PO Box 551665, Dallas TX 75355, USA

Reddick, Lance — Actor
Innovative Artists, 1505 10th St, Santa Monica CA 90401 USA

Reddicliffe, Steven — Editor
TV Guide, Editorial Dept, 100 Matsonford Road, Wayne PA 19080, USA

Redding, Cory B — Football Player
Indianapolis Colts, 7001 W 56th St, Indianapolis IN 46254 USA

Redding, Timothy J (Tim) — Baseball Player
1801 E Palm Valley Blvd, Round Rock TX 78664, USA

Reddout, Franklin P (Frank) — Basketball Player
379 Niblick Circle, Winter Haven FL 33881, USA

Reddy, D Raj — Computer Scientist
Robotics Institute, Carnegie-Mellon University, Pittsburgh PA 15213, USA

Reddy, Helen — Singer, Actress
269 S Beverly Dr, #1181, Beverly Hills CA 90212, USA

Redeker, Quinn — Actor
8075 3rd Ave, #303, Los Angeles CA 90048, USA

Readdy - Redeker

Redfern, Peter I (Pete)	Baseball Player
12516 Haddon Ave, Sylmar CA 91342, USA	
Redford, Amy Hart	Actress
Paradigm Agency, 360 N Crescent Dr, North Building, Beverly Hills CA 90210 USA	
Redford, J A C	Composer
Gorfaine/Schwartz, 4111 W Alameda Ave, #509, Burbank CA 91505 USA	
Redford, Robert	Actor, Director
Sundance Institute, 5900 Wilshire Blvd, #800, Los Angeles CA 90036, USA	
Redgrave, Jemma	Actress
Conway Van Gelder Grant, 8-12 Broadwick St, #300, London W1F 8HW, England	
Redgrave, Steven G	Rowing Athlete
Athole Still Mgmt, 25-27 Westow St, London SE19 3RY, England	
Redgrave, Vanessa	Actress, Singer
Gavin Barker Assoc, 2D Wimpole St, London W1G 0EB, England	
Redick, Jonathan Clay (J J)	Basketball Player
315 E New England Ave, #13, Winter Park FL 32789, USA	
Reding, Juli	Actress, Model
PO Box 1806, Beverly Hills CA 90213, USA	
Redman	Rap Artist
One Entertainment, 12 W 57th St, #PH 1, New York NY 10019 USA	
Redman, Amanda	Actress
Lip Service Casting, 60-66 Wardour St, London W1F 0TA, England	
Redman, Chris J	Football Player
15410 Beckley Crossing Dr, Louisville KY 40245, USA	
Redman, Joshua	Jazz Saxophonist, Composer
Wilkins Mgmt, 323 Broadway, Cambridge MA 02139, USA	
Redman, Julian (Tike)	Baseball Player
W155N6984 Amberleigh Circle, Menomonee Falls WI 53051, USA	
Redman, Mark A	Baseball Player
6818 E 109th St, Tulsa OK 74133, USA	
Redman, Michele	Golfer
3410 Queensland Lane N, Minneapolis MN 55447, USA	
Redman, Richard C (Rick)	Football Player
8953 Windham Court NE, Lacey WA 98516, USA	
Redman, Susie	Golfer
30442 Wayside Dr, Spanish Fort AL 36527, USA	
Redmann, Teal	Actress
Innovative Artists, 1505 10th St, Santa Monica CA 90401 USA	
Redmayne, Eddie	Actor
United Agents, 12-26 Lexington St, London W1F 0LE, England	
Redmond, H Wayne	Baseball Player
18061 Sussex St, Detroit MI 48235, USA	
Redmond, Markus	Actor
Stagecoach Entertainment, 1223 Wilshire Blvd, #1560, Santa Monica CA 90403, USA	
Redmond, Marlon B	Basketball Player
441 Oak St, San Francisco CA 94102, USA	
Redmond, Michael E (Mickey)	Ice Hockey Player
30699 Harlincin Court, Franklin MI 48025, USA	
Redmond, Michael P (Mike)	Baseball Player
13506 S Bluegrouse Lane, Spokane WA 99224, USA	
RedOne	Songwriter, Record Producer
Paradigm Agency, 360 N Crescent Dr, North Building, Beverly Hills CA 90210 USA	
Redpath, Jean	Singer
Sunny Knowe, Promenade, Leven, Fife, Scotland	
Redquest, Greg	Ice Hockey Player
139 Springdale Dr, Barrie ON L4M 4Y1, Canada	
Redstone, Sumner M	Businessman
98 Baldpate Hill Road, Newton MA 02459, USA	
Redus, Gary E	Baseball Player
2202 Mallard Lane SE, Decatur AL 35601, USA	
Reece, Beasley	Football Player, Sportscaster
17 Stirling Way, Lumberton NJ 08048, USA	
Reece, Daniel L (Danny)	Football Player
5519 S Corning Ave, Los Angeles CA 90056, USA	
Reece, Gabrielle (Gabby)	Volleyball Player, Model
PO Box 2227, Malibu CA 90265, USA	
Reece, Maynard	Artist
5315 Robertson Dr, Des Moines IA 50312, USA	
Reed, Alvin D	Football Player
3910 Abbeywood Dr, Pearland TX 77584, USA	
Reed, Alyson	Actress, Singer, Dancer
Opus Entertainment, 5225 Wilshire Blvd, #905, Los Angeles CA 90036, USA	
Reed, Andre D	Football Player
3865 Torrey Hill Lane, San Diego CA 92130, USA	
Reed, Anthony W (Tony)	Football Player
14068 Mount Tabor Road, Odessa MO 64076, USA	
Reed, Brandy	Basketball Player
Los Angeles Sparks, 888 S Figueroa St, #2010, Los Angeles CA 90017 USA	
Reed, Brian	Guitarist (EvinRudes), Songwriter
Turner Management Group, 9200 W Sunset Blvd, #600, West Hollywood CA 90069, USA	
Reed, Darren D	Baseball Player
8101 Santa Ana Road, Ventura CA 93001, USA	
Reed, Edward E (Ed), Jr	Football Player
4703 Avatar Lane, Owings Mills MD 21117, USA	
Reed, Frank R	Football Player
6989 Windstone Lane, Stone Mountain GA 30087, USA	
Reed, Hubert F (Hub)	Basketball Player
46601 Garretts Lake Road, Shawnee OK 74804, USA	
Reed, Ishmael S	Writer
1446 6th St, #C, Berkeley CA 94710, USA	
Reed, Jeff S	Baseball Player
259 Sunrise Dr, Elizabethton TN 37643, USA	
Reed, Jeffrey M (Jeff)	Football Player
1702 S Shore Court, Pittsburgh PA 15203, USA	
Reed, Jeremy T	Baseball Player
977 Hormel Ave, La Verne CA 91750, USA	

Reed, Jerry M — Baseball Player
13964 106th Ave, Largo FL 33774, USA

Reed, Jody E — Baseball Player
3539 Lake Padgett Dr, Land O'Lakes FL 34639, USA

Reed, John Shedd — Financier
Citigroup Inc, 55 E 52nd St, New York NY 10055, USA

Reed, Johnny — Singer (Orioles)
Jackson Artists, 7251 Lowell Dr, #200, Overland Park KS 66204, USA

Reed, Joseph B (Joe) — Football Player
106 Whitechapel Court, Cedar Park TX 78613, USA

Reed, Joshua B (Josh) — Football Player
7333 Camelia Way Court, Baton Rouge LA 70808, USA

Reed, Lou — Singer (Velvet Undergound), Songwriter
I C M Partners, 10250 Constellation Blvd, #900, Los Angeles CA 90067 USA

Reed, Mark A — Physicist
Syracuse University, Engineering/Applied Science Dept, Syracuse NY 13244, USA

Reed, Mitchell — Bassist, Fiddle Player (BeauSoleil)
Rosebud Agency, PO Box 170429, San Francisco CA 94117 USA

Reed, Nikki — Actress, Writer
Thruline Entertainment, 9250 Wilshire Blvd, #100, Beverly Hills CA 90212 USA

Reed, Oscar L — Football Player
700 Elizabeth Lane, Minneapolis MN 55411, USA

Reed, Pamela — Actress
Innovative Artists, 1505 10th St, Santa Monica CA 90401 USA

Reed, Patrick — Director
White Pine Pictures, 822 Richmond St W, #301, Toronto ON M6J 1C9, Canada

Reed, Peter (Pete) — Rowing Athlete
Leander Club, Henley on Thames, Leander RG9 2LP, England

Reed, Peyton — Director, Producer, Writer, Actor
W M E Entertainment, 9601 Wilshire Blvd, #300, Beverly Hills CA 90210 USA

Reed, Ralph — Religious Leader
1801 Sarah Dr, #L, Chesapeake VA 23320, USA

Reed, Rex T — Film Critic
Dakota Hotel, 1 W 72nd St, #86, New York NY 10023, USA

Reed, Richard A (Rick) — Baseball Player
9604 County Road 107, #7, Proctorville OH 45669, USA

Reed, Ronald L (Ron) — Baseball, Basketball Player
2613 Cliffview Dr, Lilburn GA 30047, USA

Reed, Shanna — Actress
1327 Brinkley Ave, Los Angeles CA 90049, USA

Reed, Stephen V (Steve) — Baseball Player
5335 Pine Ridge Road, Golden CO 80403, USA

Reed, Thomas C — Government Official
Quaker Hill Development Corp, PO Box 2240, Healdsburg CA 95448, USA

Reed, W Jake — Football Player
PO Box 1848, Frisco TX 75034, USA

Reed, Willis, Jr — Basketball Player, Coach, Executive
PO Box 1779, Ruston LA 71273, USA

Reeder, Serena — Actress
Hess Entertainment, 250 S Beverly Dr, #201, Beverly Hills CA 90212, USA

Reeds, Mark — Ice Hockey Player
7823 Cardinal Ridge Court, Saint Louis MO 63119, USA

Reedus, Norman — Actor, Model
Industry Entertainment, 955 Carillo Dr, #300, Los Angeles CA 90048 USA

Reekie, Joe — Ice Hockey Player
622 Sean Dr, Annapolis MD 21401, USA

Reep, Jon — Actor, Comedian
Gersh Agency, 9465 Wilshire Blvd, #600, Beverly Hills CA 90212 USA

Rees, Andrew — Opera Singer
Musichall Ltd, Vicarage Way, Ringmer BN8 5LA, England

Rees, Clifford H (Ted), Jr — Air Force General
1620 Mayflower Court, #B414, Winter Park FL 32792, USA

Rees, Dai — Fashion Designer
6 Blackstock Mews, Blackstock Road, London N4 2BT, England

Rees, Eberhard — Physicist
69 Revere Way, Huntsville AL 35801, USA

Rees, Jed — Musician, Actor
Paradigm Agency, 360 N Crescent Dr, North Building, Beverly Hills CA 90210 USA

Rees, John W — Bassist (Men at Work)
Fish Creek, Gippsland VIC 3959, Australia

Rees, Martin J — Astronomer
King's College, Astronomy Institute, Cambridge CB2 1ST, England

Rees, Mina — Mathematician
301 E 66th St, New York NY 10065, USA

Rees, Roger — Actor
Innovative Artists, 1505 10th St, Santa Monica CA 90401 USA

Reese, Calvin (Pokey) — Baseball Player
12416 Sylvan Oak Way, Charlotte NC 28273, USA

Reese, Della — Singer, Actress
Lett-Reese International Promotions, 1910 Bel Air Road, Los Angeles CA 90077, USA

Reese, Izell — Football Player
10270 Willeo Creek Trace, Roswell GA 30075, USA

Reese, Jeff — Ice Hockey Player
697 Maple Ave, Haddonfield NJ 08033, USA

Reese, Kevin P — Baseball Player
1221 Willow St, San Diego CA 92106, USA

Reese, Mason — Actor
Nowbar, 22 7th Ave S, New York NY 10014, USA

Reese, Richard B (Rich) — Baseball Player
PO Box 2339, Carefree AZ 85377, USA

Reese, Tracy — Fashion Designer
T R Designs, 260 W 39th St, #1900, New York NY 10018, USA

Reeser, Autumn — Actress
Kritzer Levine Wilkins Griffin, 11872 La Grange Ave, #100, Los Angeles CA 90025 USA

Reeser, Morgan — Yachtsman
1948 Coral Gardens Dr, Wilton Manors FL 33306, USA

Reeves, Bryant — Basketball Player
11648 S 4710 Road, Muldrow OK 74948, USA
Reeves, Daniel E (Dan) — Football Player, Coach; Sportscaster
785 W Conway Dr SW, Atlanta GA 30327, USA
Reeves, Dianne — Singer
PO Box 66, Englishtown NJ 07726, USA
Reeves, Jacques D — Football Player
619 Scenic Dr, Irving TX 75039, USA
Reeves, Julie — Singer
PO Box 300, Russell KY 41169, USA
Reeves, Keanu — Actor
3 Arts Entertainment, 9460 Wilshire Blvd, #700, Beverly Hills CA 90212 USA
Reeves, Khalid — Basketball Player
11519 140th St, Jamaica NY 11436, USA
Reeves, Martha — Singer (Martha & the Vandellas)
Ideal Entertainment, 1674 Broadway, #300, New York NY 10019, USA
Reeves, Matt — Director, Producer, Writer
Creative Artists Agency, 2000 Ave of Stars, #100, Los Angeles CA 90067 USA
Reeves, Perrey — Actress
Paradigm Agency, 360 N Crescent Dr, North Building, Beverly Hills CA 90210 USA
Reeves, Richard — Columnist
Universal Press Syndicate, 4520 Main St, #700, Kansas City MO 64111 USA
Reeves, Robert (Bobby) — Singer (Adema)
Novi Entertainment, PO Box 17077, Beverly Hills CA 90209, USA
Reeves, Saskia — Actress
Markham & Froggatt, Julian House, 4 Windmill St, London W1P 1HF, England
Reeves, Scott — Actor, Singer (Blue County)
House of Representatives, 1434 6th St, #1, Santa Monica CA 90401 USA
Reeves, Walter J — Football Player
PO Box 16171, Fort Worth TX 76162, USA
Refaeli, Bar — Model
One Model Mgmt, 424 W Broadway, #200, New York NY 10012 USA
Refn, Nicolas Winding — Director
W M E Entertainment, 9601 Wilshire Blvd, #300, Beverly Hills CA 90210 USA
Regalado, Rudolph V (Rudy) — Baseball Player
PO Box 475, Borrego Springs CA 92004, USA
Regalado, Victor — Golfer
Tijuana Country Club, 2630 E Point Beyer Blvd, #106, San Ysidro CA 92703, USA
Regalbuto, Joe — Actor
Stone Manners Salners, 9911 W Pico Blvd, #1400, Los Angeles CA 90035 USA
Regan, Brian — Actor, Comedian, Writer
Gersh Agency, 9465 Wilshire Blvd, #600, Beverly Hills CA 90212 USA
Regan, Bridget — Actress
Gersh Agency, 41 Madison Ave, #3301, New York NY 10010 USA
Regan, Fionn — Singer, Songwriter
Agency Group Ltd, 361-373 City Road, London EC1V 2QA, England
Regan, Judith — Writer, Entertainer
New Enterprises, 1211 Ave of Americas, Lower C31, New York NY 10036, USA
Regan, Philip R (Phil) — Baseball Player, Manager
1375 108th St, Byron Center MI 49315, USA
Regat, Jacques — Sculptor
13830 Jarvi Dr, Anchorage AK 99515, USA
Regat, Mary — Sculptor
13830 Jarvi Dr, Anchorage AK 99515, USA
Regehr, Duncan — Actor
2501 Main St, Santa Monica CA 90405, USA
Regen, Elizabeth — Actress
Don Buchwald/Fortitude, 6500 Wilshire Blvd, #2200, Los Angeles CA 90048 USA
Regen, Richard — Writer, Producer
United Talent Agency, 9336 Civic Center Dr, Beverly Hills CA 90210 USA
Reger, Nate — Writer
I C M Partners, 10250 Constellation Blvd, #900, Los Angeles CA 90067 USA
Reggio, Godfrey — Director
Regional Education Institute, PO Box 2404, Santa Fe NM 87504, USA
Regilio, Nicholas D (Nick) — Baseball Player
6505 Raham Court, Port Orange FL 32128, USA
Regis, John — Track Athlete
67 Fairby Road, London SE12 8JP, England
Regner, Thomas E (Tom) — Football Player
2231 Big Trail Circle, Reno NV 89521, USA
Regnier, Charles — Actor, Director
Neherstr 7, 81675 Munich, Germany
Rehberg, Scott J — Football Player
1153 Thistle Lane, Lebanon OH 45036, USA
Reherman, Lee — Actor
Ellis Talent Group, 4705 Laurel Canyon Blvd, #300, Valley Village CA 91607 91607, USA
Rehm, Fred — Basketball Player
19340 W Stonehedge Dr, #A, Brookfield WI 53045, USA
Rehm, Jack D — Publisher
19 Neponset Ave, #9A, Old Saybrook CT 06475, USA
Rehr, Frank — Cartoonist (Ferd'nand)
United Feature Syndicate, PO Box 5610, Cincinnati OH 45201 USA
Reibsten, Janet — Psychologist
Bloomsbury Publishing, 36 Soho Square, London W1D 3Q4, England
Reich, Charles A — Attorney, Educator, Writer
Crown Publishing Group, 1745 Broadway, New York NY 10019 USA
Reich, Frank M — Football Player
12551 Glendurgan Dr, Carmel IN 46032, USA
Reich, Robert B — Secretary, Labor
1230 Bonita Ave, Berkeley CA 94709, USA
Reich, Stephen M (Steve) — Composer
Howard Stokar Mgmt, 870 W End Ave, New York NY 10025, USA
Reichardt, Frederic C (Rick) — Baseball Player
2404 NW 63rd Terrace, Gainesville FL 32606, USA
Reichardt, Louis F (Lou) — Mountaineer, Physiologist
University of California, Rock Hall, 1550 4th St, San Francisco, 94158, USA

R

Reichel, Robert	Ice Hockey Player
Toronto Maple Leafs, AirCanada Center, 40 Bay St, Toronto ON M5J 2K2, Canada	
Reichenbach, J Michael (Mike)	Football Player
2230 Cloverly Circle, Jamison PA 18929, USA	
Reichert, Daniel R (Dan)	Baseball Player
445 Cornell Dr, Turlock CA 95382, USA	
Reichert, David G (Dave)	Law Enforcement Official, Representative
PO Box 53322, Bellevue WA 98015, USA	
Reichert, Jack F	Businessman, Bowling Executive
580 Douglas Dr, Lake Forest IL 60045, USA	
Reichert, Tanja	Actress
Pacific Artists, 1404-510 W Hastings St, Vancouver BC V6B 1L8, Canada	
Reichl, Ruth M	Editor, Columnist
Gourmet, Editorial Dept, 4 Times Square, New York NY 10036, USA	
Reichle, Luke	Costume Designer
Innovative Artists, 1505 10th St, Santa Monica CA 90401 USA	
Reichman, Fred	Artist
1235 Stanyan St, San Francisco CA 94117, USA	
Reichow, Garet N (Jerry)	Football Player
9 Meredith Dr, Santa Fe NM 87506, USA	
Reichs, Kathleen (Kathy)	Writer, Anthropologist
University of North Carolina, English Dept, Charlotte NC 28223, USA	
Reid, Andy	Football Player, Coach
1215 Page Terrace, Villanova PA 19085, USA	
Reid, Clifford A	Research Scientist, Businessman
Complete Genomics, 2071 Stierlin Court, Mountain View CA 94043, USA	
Reid, Daphne Maxwell	Actress
1 New Millenium Dr, Peterburg VA 23805, USA	
Reid, Dave	Ice Hockey Player
1522 Hawkswood Dr, RR 1, Ennismore ON K0L 1T0, Canada	
Reid, Don S	Singer (Statler Brothers), Songwriter
American Major Talent, 8747 Highway 304, Hernando MS 38632, USA	
Reid, Harold W	Singer (Statler Brothers), Songwriter
American Major Talent, 8747 Highway 304, Hernando MS 38632, USA	
Reid, Herman (J R)	Basketball Player
121 Cemetary St, Chester SC 29706, USA	
Reid, Jim	Singer, Guitarist (Jesus & Mary Chain)
Paradise Artists, PO Box 1821, Ojai CA 93024 USA	
Reid, Michael B (Mike)	Football Player, Composer
825 Overton Lane, Nashville TN 37220, USA	
Reid, Mike	Golfer
1220 Chadwick Dr, Westminster MD 21158, USA	
Reid, Ogden R	Journalist, Diplomat
Ophir Hill, Purchase NY 10577, USA	
Reid, Richard	Actor
Kritzer Levine Wilkins Griffin, 11872 La Grange Ave, #100, Los Angeles CA 90025 USA	
Reid, Robert K	Basketball Player, Coach
Washington Wizards, M C I Centre, 601 F St NW, Washington DC 20004 USA	
Reid, Sebastian (Sam)	Actor
Rights House, 34-43 Russell St, London WC2B 5HA, England	
Reid, Shauna	Writer
Harper Collins Publishers, 10 E 53rd St, Cellar 1, New York NY 10022 USA	
Reid, Tanya	Actress
Edna Talent Mgmt, 318 Dundas St W, Toronto ON M5T 1G5, Canada	
Reid, Tara	Actress, Model
Glick Agency, 1321 7th St, #203, Santa Monica CA 90401 USA	
Reid, Terry	Singer
Geoffrey Blumenauer Artists, PO Box 343, Burbank CA 91503 USA	
Reid, Tim	Actor, Director
1 New Millennium Dr, Petersburg VA 23805, USA	
Reid, Tom	Ice Hockey Player
603 Hawthorne Woods Dr, Saint Paul MN 55123, USA	
Reid, Vernon	Guitarist (Living Colour)
Entertainment Artists, PO Box 120824, Nashville TN 37212 USA	
Reid, William	Singer, Guitarist (Jesus & Mary Chain)
Paradise Artists, PO Box 1821, Ojai CA 93024 USA	
Reiff, Ethan	Writer, Director
United Talent Agency, 9336 Civic Center Dr, Beverly Hills CA 90210 USA	
Reiff, Riley	Football Player
Detroit Lions, 222 Republic Dr, Allen Park MI 48101 USA	
Reifsnyder, Robert H (Bob)	Football Player
681 Ocean Parkway, Berlin MD 21811, USA	
Reightler, Kenneth S, Jr	Astronaut
1602 Honeysuckle Ridge Court, Annapolis MD 21401, USA	
Reihner, George A	Football Player
1010 Electric St, Scranton PA 18509, USA	
Reilly, Gabrielle	Model, Commentator
14117 W 53rd Terrace, Shawnee KS 66216, USA	
Reilly, James F, II	Astronaut
15903 Lake Lodge Dr, Houston TX 77062, USA	
Reilly, John	Actor
Sovereign Talent Group, 8421 Wilshire Blvd, #200, Beverly Hills CA 90211 USA	
Reilly, John C	Actor
Framework Entertainment, 9057 Nemo St, #C, West Hollywood CA 90069 USA	
Reilly, Kelly	Actress
I C M Partners, 10250 Constellation Blvd, #900, Los Angeles CA 90067 USA	
Reilly, Michael E (Mike)	Baseball Umpire
131 Smithfield Road, Battle Creek MI 49015, USA	
Reilly, William K	Government Official
Stanford University, International Studies Institute, Stanford CA 94305, USA	
Reimann, Aribert	Composer, Concert Pianist
Hohenzollerndamm 97, 10717 Berlin, Germany	
Reimer, Dennis J (Denny)	Army General
2602 N Brandywine St, Arlington VA 22207, USA	
Reimers, Bruce M	Football Player
2206 W River Dr, Humboldt IA 50548, USA	

Rein, Andrew
31 Acorn Dr, Hawthorn Woods IL 60047, USA — Freestyle Wrestler

Reinders, Kate
Paradigm Agency, 360 N Crescent Dr, North Building, Beverly Hills CA 90210 USA — Singer, Actress

Reineck, Thomas
Graf-Bernadotte-Str 4, 45133 Essen, Germany — Canoeing Athlete

Reineke, Chad
1904 Tanglewood Dr, Defiance OH 43512, USA — Baseball Player

Reinemund, Steven S
PepsiCo Inc, 700 Anderson Hill Road, Purchase NY 10577, USA — Businessman

Reiner, Carl
714 N Rodeo Dr, Beverly Hills CA 90210, USA — Actor, Writer, Director

Reiner, Rob
Castle Rock Entertainment, 335 N Maple Dr, #350, Beverly Hills CA 90210, USA — Director, Actor

Reinert, Sean
Season of Mist Records, 111 Rt de la Valebtinell, 13011 Marseille, France — Drummer (Cynic)

Reinfeldt, J Fredrik
Prime Minister's Office, Rosenbad 4, 103 33 Stockholm, Sweden — Prime Minister, Sweden

Reinfeldt, Michael R (Mike)
1204 Waterstone Blvd, Franklin TN 37069, USA — Football Player

Reinhardt, John E
3154 Gracefield Road, #417, Silver Spring MD 20904, USA — Diplomat

Reinhardt, Nicole
Agentur Koster, Alsterdorfer Str 208, 22297 Hamburg, Germany — Canoeing Athlete

Reinhardt, Stephen R
US Court of Appeals, 312 N Spring St, #G33, Los Angeles CA 90012, USA — Judge

Reinhart, Gregory
I M G Artists, Hogarth Business Park, Chiswick, London W4 2TH, England — Opera Singer

Reinhart, Haley
19 Entertainment, 8560 W Sunset Blvd, #900, Los Angeles CA 90069 USA — Singer

Reinhart, Paul
2911 Altamont Crescent, West Vancouver BC V7V 3B9, Canada — Ice Hockey Player

Reinharz, Jehuda
131 Sewall Ave, #71, Brookline MA 2446, USA — Educator

Reinhold, Judge
Optimism Entertainment, 303 N La Peer Dr, #205, Beverly Hills CA 90211, USA — Actor, Director

Reinking, Ann
5912 E Sapphire Lane, Phoenix AZ 85253, USA — Actress, Dancer, Choreographer, Director

Reinprecht, Steven E
45 S Garfield St, Denver CO 80209, USA — Ice Hockey Player

Reirden, Todd
17 Herons Bill Dr, Bluffton SC 29909, USA — Ice Hockey Player

Reise, Leo C, Jr
27 Cumming Court, Ancaster ON L9G 1V4, Canada — Ice Hockey Player

Reiser, Jerry
28 S Washington Ave, Dobbs Ferry NY 10522, USA — Architect

Reiser, Paul
Nuance Productions, 4049 Radford Ave, Studio City CA 91604, USA — Actor

Reisman, Garrett E
1715 Hedgecroft Dr, Seabrook TX 77586, USA — Astronaut

Reiss, Albert J, Jr
600 Prospect St, #7A, New Haven CT 06511, USA — Sociologist

Reiss, Howard
16656 Oldham St, Encino CA 91436, USA — Chemist

Reisz, Michael
Mosiac Media Group, 9200 W Sunset Blvd, #1000, Los Angeles CA 90069 USA — Actor

Reiter, Mario
Hauselweg 5, 6830 Rankweil, Austria — Alpine Skier

Reiter, Stanley
425 Davis St, #425, Evanston IL 60201, USA — Economist

Reiter, Thomas
European Space Center, Linder Hohe, Box 906096, 51127 Cologne, Germany — Astronaut, Germany

Reith, Brian E
9706 54th Court E, Parrish FL 34219, USA — Baseball Player

Reitman, Ivan
900 Cold Springs Road, Santa Barbara CA 93108, USA — Director, Producer

Reitman, Jason
W M E Entertainment, 9601 Wilshire Blvd, #300, Beverly Hills CA 90210 USA — Director, Writer

Reitman, Joseph D (Joe)
TalentWorks, 3500 W Olive Ave, #1400, Burbank CA 91505 USA — Actor

Reitsma, Chris
6050 Jim Davis Road, Parrish FL 34219, USA — Baseball Player

Reitz, Bruce A
Falk CV Research Center, 300 Pasteur Dr, Stanford CA 94305, USA — Cardiac Surgeon

Reitz, Donald L
PO Box 206, Clarkdale AZ 86324, USA — Artist

Reitz, Kenneth J (Ken)
2833 Fairways Circle, Lutz FL 33558, USA — Baseball Player

Rekar, Bryan R
4326 Waterville Ave, Wesley Chapel FL 33543, USA — Baseball Player

Reklow, Jesse
2415 College Ave, #20, Berkeley CA 94704, USA — Cartoonist (Slow Wave)

Relaford, Desmond L (Desi)
12483 Highview Dr, Jacksonville FL 32225, USA — Baseball Player

Rellford, Richard A
28 Balfour Road W, Palm Beach Gardens FL 33418, USA — Basketball Player

Relman, Arnold S
New England Journal of Medicine, 860 Winter St, #2, Waltham MA 02451, USA — Editor, Physician

Relyea, John
Opus 3 Artists, 470 Park Ave S, #900N, New York NY 10016 USA — Singer

Remar, James
Gersh Agency, 9465 Wilshire Blvd, #600, Beverly Hills CA 90212 USA — Actor

Rembert, John L (Johnny)
2564 Willow Creek Dr, Orange Park FL 32003, USA — Football Player

Remedios, Alberto T
Stuart Trotter, 21 Lanhill Road, London W9 2BS, England — Opera Singer

Remek, Vladimir — Cosmonaut, Czech Republic
Veletrzni 17, Prague 7 17000, Czech Republic

Remigino, Lindy — Track Athlete
22 Paris Lane, Newington CT 06111, USA

Remini, Leah M — Actress
United Talent Agency, 9336 Civic Center Dr, Beverly Hills CA 90210 USA

Remlinger, Michael J (Mike) — Baseball Player
18331 N 93rd Way, Scottsdale AZ 85255, USA

Remnick, David J — Writer, Editor
257 W 86th St, #11A, New York NY 10024, USA

Rempe, Jim — Billiards Player
60 George Dr, Jefferson Township PA 18436, USA

Remy, Gerald P (Jerry) — Baseball Player
1403 Wisteria Way, Wayland MA 01778, USA

Renaud, Line — Singer, Actress
5 Rue de Bois de Boulogne, 75016 Paris, France

Renaud, Mark — Ice Hockey Player
11788 Tecumseh Road E, Windsor ON N8N 1L7, Canada

Renault, Dennis — Editorial Cartoonist
Sacramento Bee, Editorial Dept, 21st & Q Sts, Sacramento CA 95852, USA

Renbourn, John — Guitarist (Pentangle)
Folklore Inc, PO Box 7003, Santa Monica CA 90406, USA

Rencher, Terrence L — Basketball Player
2001 S Mo Pac Expressway, #924, Austin TX 78746, USA

Rendall, Mark — Actor
TalentWorks, 3500 W Olive Ave, #1400, Burbank CA 91505 USA

Rendell of Barbergh, Ruth B — Writer
26 Cornwall Terrace Mews, London NW1 5LL, England

Rendell, Edward G (Ed) — Governor, PA
Ballard Sahr, 1755 Market St, #5100, Philadelphia PA 19103, USA

Rendell, Marjorie O — Judge
US Court of Appeals, US Courthouse, 601 Market St, Philadelphia PA 19106, USA

Renee, Leah — Actress
Paradigm Agency, 360 N Crescent Dr, North Building, Beverly Hills CA 90210 USA

Renee, Lyne — Actress
Don Buchwald/Fortitude, 6500 Wilshire Blvd, #2200, Los Angeles CA 90048 USA

Renes, Lawrence — Conductor
Harrison/Parrott, 5-6 Albion Court, London W6 0QT, England

Renfrew of Kaimsthorn, Andrew C — Archaeologist
McDonald Archaeological Institute, Downing St, Cambridge CB2 3ER, England

Renfro, Melvin L (Mel) — Football Player
Renfro Bridge Foundation, 8211 Hunnicut Road, Dallas TX 75228, USA

Renfro, Mike R — Football Player
PO Box 93073, Southlake TX 76092, USA

Renfroe, Cohen W (Laddie) — Baseball Player
236 Hickory Lane, Batesville MS 38606, USA

Renfroe, Jeff — Director
Characters Talent Agency, 1505 W 2nd Ave, #200, Vancouver BC V6H 3Y4, Canada

Renick, W Richard (Rick) — Baseball Player
7320 Hawkins Road, Sarasota FL 34241, USA

Renier, Jeremie — Actor
A C T 1, 83 Rue Saint Honore, 75001 Paris, France

Renko, Steven (Steve) — Baseball Player
15812 W 136th St, Olathe KS 66062, USA

Renna, William B (Bill) — Baseball Player
1476 Lesher Court, San Jose CA 95125, USA

Renne, Paul — Geologist
Berkeley Geochronology Center, 2445 Ridge Road, Berkeley CA 94709, USA

Renner, Jeremy — Actor
Creative Artists Agency, 2000 Ave of Stars, #100, Los Angeles CA 90067 USA

Rennert, Laurence H (Dutch) — Baseball Umpire
2560 46th Road, Vero Beach FL 32966, USA

Rennert, Wolfgang — Conductor
Holbeinstr 58, 12203 Berlin, Germany

Renney, Tom — Ice Hockey Coach
Detroit Red Wings, Joe Louis Arena, 600 Civic Center Dr, Detroit MI 48226 USA

Rennie, Callum Keith — Actor
A P A Talent/Literary Agency, 405 S Beverly Dr, #300, Beverly Hills CA 90212 USA

Reno, Janet — Attorney General
11200 N Kendall Dr, Miami FL 33176, USA

Reno, Jean — Actor
Gaumont, 30 Ave Charles de Gaulle, 92200 Neuilly Sur Seine, France

Reno, Loren M — Air Force General
Deputy CofS, Logistics/Installations, HqUSAF, Pentagon, Washington DC 20330 USA

Reno, William H — Army General
2706 S Ives St, Arlington VA 22202, USA

Renoth, Heidi — Snowboard Skier
Lercheckerweg 23, 83471 Berchtesgaden, Germany

Rensberger, Scott — Journalist
914 7th St NE, Washington DC 20002, USA

Rense Noland, Paige — Editor
Architectural Digest, Editorial Dept, 5900 Wilshire Blvd, Los Angeles CA 90036, USA

Renshaw, Jeannine — Actress, Producer
I C M Partners, 10250 Constellation Blvd, #900, Los Angeles CA 90067 USA

Renteria, Richard A (Rich) — Baseball Player
43310 Calle Nacido, Temecula CA 92592, USA

Rentmeester, Co — Photographer
PO Box 1562, Westhampton Beach NY 11978, USA

Renton of Mount Harry, R Timothy — Government Official, England
Mount Harry House, Offham, Lewes, East Sussex BN7 3QW, England

Rentzel, T Lance — Football Player
12014 Monument Dr, #354, Fairfax VA 22033, USA

Rentzepis, Peter M — Chemist
University of California, Chemistry Dept, Irvine CA 92717, USA

Renuart, V Eugene (Gene), Jr — Air Force General
Commander, US Northern Command, Peterson Air Force Base CO 80914 USA

Renzetti, Donato — Conductor
Columbia Artists Mgmt Inc, 1790 Broadway, #702, New York NY 10019 USA

Renzi, Andrea — Actor
Carol Levi Mgmt, Via G Pisanelli 2, 00196 Rome, Italy

Renzulli, Frank — Producer, Writer
Creative Artists Agency, 2000 Ave of Stars, #100, Los Angeles CA 90067 USA

Repin, Vadim V — Concert Violinist
Eckholdtweg 2A, 23566 Lubeck, Germany

Repko, Jason E — Baseball Player
93005 E Chelsea Road, Kennewick WA 99338, USA

Requa, John — Writer, Director
W M E Entertainment, 9601 Wilshire Blvd, #300, Beverly Hills CA 90210 USA

Rerych, Stephen (Steve) — Swimmer
1142 Ridgewood Dr, Point Pleasant WV 25550, USA

Resch, Alexander — Luge Athlete
Gesprachsstoff Marketing, Scholssstr 9B, 82140 Olching, Germany

Resch, Glenn A (Chico) — Ice Hockey Player
607 8th St, Lyndhurst NJ 07071, USA

Rescher, Nicholas — Philosopher
1033 Milton St, Pittsburgh PA 15218, USA

Reske, Hans-Joachim — Track Athlete
Sinshimer Str 18, 69226 Nussloch, Germany

Reskin, Barbara — Sociologist
University of Washington, Sociology Dept, Seattle WA 98195, USA

Resnais, Alain — Director
Intertalent, 48 Rue Gay Lussac, 75005 Paris, France

Resnick, Marcia — Photographer
2 Grove St, #1F, New York NY 10014, USA

Resnik, Regina — Opera Singer
American Guild of Musical Arts, 1430 Broadway, #1404, New York NY 10018, USA

Resop, Chris — Baseball Player
2152 Harlans Run, Naples FL 34105, USA

Resor, Helen — Ice Hockey Player
22 N Stanwich Road, Greenwich CT 06831, USA

Ressler, Glenn E — Football Player
1524 Woodcreek Dr, Mechanicsburg PA 17055, USA

Restani, Jane A — Judge
US Court of International Trade, 1 Federal Plaza, New York NY 10278, USA

Restovich, Michael — Baseball Player
710 11th St SW, Rochester MN 55902, USA

Resweber, Carroll C — Motorcycle Racing Rider
2440 Imhoff Ave, Port Arthur TX 77642, USA

Reswick, James B — Engineer
PO Box 549, Crozet VA 22932, USA

Retondo, Mike — Guitarist (Plain White T's)
One Moment Mgmt, PO Box 55156, Sherman Oaks CA 91413 USA

Retore, Guy — Theater Executive
Theatre de l'Est Parisien, 159 Ave Gambetta, 75020 Paris, France

Rettenmund, Mervin W (Merv) — Baseball Player
1860 San Carlos Ave, San Carlos CA 94070, USA

Retton, Mary Lou — Gymnast
110 Kennywood Dr, Fairmont WV 26554, USA

Retzer, Kenneth L (Ken) — Baseball Player
746 Harvard Dr, Edwardsville IL 62025, USA

Retzer, Otto W — Director
Justinus-Kerner-Str 10, 80686 Munich, Germany

Retzlaff, Palmer (Pete) — Football Player
669 New Road, Gilbertsville PA 19525, USA

Reuben, David R — Psychiatrist
Scott Meredith, 1675 Broadway, New York NY 10019, USA

Reuben, Gloria — Actress
Great Northern Artists, 350 Dupont St, Toronto ON M5R 1V9, Canada

Reubens, Paul — Comedian, Actor
W M E Entertainment, 9601 Wilshire Blvd, #300, Beverly Hills CA 90210 USA

Reuschel, Paul R — Baseball Player
1143 Stacy Lane, Macomb IL 61455, USA

Reuschel, Ricky E (Rick) — Baseball Player
PO Box 143, Renfrew PA 16053, USA

Reuss, Jerry — Baseball Player
1 Line Dr, Des Moines IA 50309, USA

Reuten, Thekla — Actress
Innovative Artists, 1505 10th St, Santa Monica CA 90401 USA

Reutimann, David — Auto Racing Driver
Tommy Baldwin Racing, 296 Cayuga Road, Mooresville NC 28117, USA

Reutter, Katherine — Speed Skater
Q Sports Marketing, 534 W Evergreen St, Wheaton IL 60187, USA

Reveiz, Fuad Y — Football Player
PO Box 22430, Knoxville TN 37933, USA

Revell, Graeme — Composer
Kraft-Engel Mgmt, 15233 Ventura Blvd, #200, Sherman Oaks CA 91403 USA

Revere, Paul — Pianist (Paul Revere & the Raiders)
Richard De La Font Agency, 4845 S Sheridan Road, #505, Tulsa OK 74145 USA

Reverho, Christine — Actress
Artmedia, 20 Ave Rapp, 75007 Paris, France

Revering, David A (Dave) — Baseball Player
1063 Crows Wing Way, Ivins UT 84738, USA

Revill, Clive — Actor
15029 Encanto Dr, Sherman Oaks CA 91403, USA

Revin, Sergei N — Cosmonaut
Cosmonaut Training Center, Star City, 141160 Zvezdny Gorodok, Moscow Oblast, Russia

Rex, Simon — Actor, Producer
Luber Rocklin Entertainment, 8530 Wilshire Blvd, #555, Beverly Hills CA 90211 USA

Rey, Antonia — Actress
Alvarado Rey Agency, 7906 Santa Monica Blvd, #205, West Hollywood CA 90046, USA

Rey, Reynaldo — Actor, Comedian, Writer
Starwil Talent, 433 N Camden Dr, #400, Beverly Hills CA 90210, USA

R

Renzetti - Rey

Reyes Rosales, Diego Antonio — Soccer Player
Federacion de Futbol, Colima 373 Colonia Roma, Delegacion Cuauhtemoc Mexico DF 06700, Mexico
Reyes, Anthony L — Baseball Player
8929 Watson Ave, Whittier CA 90605, USA
Reyes, Carlos A — Baseball Player
23811 Butterfly Landing Dr, Land O'Lakes FL 34638, USA
Reyes, Eddie — Guitarist
Helter Skelter, 347-353 Chiswick High Road, London W4 4HS, England
Reyes, Franc — Director
Collective, 8383 Wilshire Blvd, #1050, Beverly Hills CA 90211 USA
Reyes, Jose B — Baseball Player
24 Stone Hill Dr S, Manhasset NY 11030, USA
Reyes, Joseph A (Jo-Jo) — Baseball Player
9554 Paradise Place, Riverside CA 92508, USA
Reyes, Judy — Actress
Leverage Mgmt, 3030 Pennsylvania Ave, Santa Monica CA 90404 USA
Reynolds Booth, Nancy — Skier
3197 Padaro Lane, Carpinteria CA 93013, USA
Reynolds, Albert — Prime Minister, Ireland
18 Nilesbury Road, Ballsbridge, Dublin 4, Ireland
Reynolds, Anna — Opera Singer
Peesten 9, 95359 Kasendorf, Germany
Reynolds, Archie E — Baseball Player
1828 Pinecrest Dr, Tyler TX 75701, USA
Reynolds, Burt — Actor
Kritzer Levine Wilkins Griffin, 11872 La Grange Ave, #100, Los Angeles CA 90025 USA
Reynolds, Carolyn — Artist
1440 Catalina, Laguna Beach CA 92651, USA
Reynolds, Corey — Actor
New Wave Entertainment, 2660 W Olive Ave, Burbank, CA 91505, USA
Reynolds, Dean — Commentator
ABC-TV, News Dept, 5010 Creston St, Hyattsville MD 20781 USA
Reynolds, Debbie — Actress, Singer
6514 Lankershim Blvd, North Hollywood CA 91606, USA
Reynolds, Derrick S (Ricky) — Football Player
37540 Church Ave, Dade City FL 33525, USA
Reynolds, Donald E (Don) — Baseball Player
6035 NE 35th Place, Portland OR 97211, USA
Reynolds, Edward (Ed) — Football Player
2387 Country Side Dr, Fleming Isle FL 32003, USA
Reynolds, G Craig — Baseball Player
4210 Hidden Links Court, Kingwood TX 77339, USA
Reynolds, Gene — Actor, Producer
2034 Castillian Dr, Los Angeles CA 90068, USA
Reynolds, Glenn F — Inventor (Proscar Drug)
242 Edgewood Ave, Westfield NJ 07090, USA
Reynolds, Harold C — Baseball Player, Sportscaster
2890 NW Angelica Dr, Corvallis OR 97330, USA
Reynolds, James — Actor
1925 Hanscom Dr, South Pasadena CA 91030, USA
Reynolds, James N (Jim), IV — Baseball Umpire
708 Highpoint Dr, Rocky Hill CT 06067, USA
Reynolds, Jeff — Basketball Coach
US Air Force Academy, Athletic Dept, Colorado Springs CO 80840, USA
Reynolds, Jerry O — Basketball Coach, Executive
Sacramento Kings, Arco Arena, 1 Sports Parkway, Sacramento CA 95834 USA
Reynolds, John Brently — Actor
Hansen Jacobson Teller, 450 N Roxbury Dr, #800, Beverly Hills CA 90210 USA
Reynolds, John H — Physicist, Educator
University of California, Physics Dept, Berkeley CA 94720, USA
Reynolds, John S (Jack) — Football Player
11480 SW 102nd St, Miami FL 33176, USA
Reynolds, Kenneth L (Ken) — Baseball Player
182 Greenwood St, Marlborough MA 01752, USA
Reynolds, Kevin — Director
W M E Entertainment, 9601 Wilshire Blvd, #300, Beverly Hills CA 90210 USA
Reynolds, Patrick — Actor, Social Activist
260 S Rodeo Dr, Beverly Hills CA 90212, USA
Reynolds, R Shane — Baseball Player
3540 Marantha Dr, Sugar Land TX 77479, USA
Reynolds, Robert — Bassist (Mavericks, Swag)
AristoMedia, 1620 16th Ave S, Nashville TN 37212, USA
Reynolds, Robert A (Bob) — Baseball Player
952 SW Campus Dr, #2603, Federal Way WA 98023, USA
Reynolds, Roger L — Composer
University of California, Music Department, La Jolla CA 92093, USA
Reynolds, Ronn D — Baseball Player
1410 N Armour St, Wichita KS 67206, USA
Reynolds, Ryan — Actor
Dark Trick Films, PO Box 10605, Beverly Hills CA 90213, USA
Reynolds, Sheldon — Guitarist (Earth Wind & Fire)
Great Scott Productions, 4750 Lincoln Blvd, #229, Marina del Rey CA 90292, USA
Reynolds, Thomas A, Jr — Attorney
Winston & Strawn, 1 First National Plaza, 45 W Wacker Dr, Chicago IL 60601, USA
Reynolds, Thomas D (Tommie) — Baseball Player
640 Jinks Crossing Road, Bainbridge GA 39819, USA
Reynolds, Tim — Instrumentalist
Paradigm Agency, 360 N Crescent Dr, North Building, Beverly Hills CA 90210 USA
Reynolds, W Ann — Educator
University of Alabama, Outreach Development Center, Birmingham AL 35294, USA
Reynoso, Armando R — Baseball Player
PO Box 442, Scottsdale AZ 85252, USA
Reza, Yasmina — Writer, Actresss, Comedienne
Gersh Agency, 9465 Wilshire Blvd, #600, Beverly Hills CA 90212 USA
Reznikoff, William S — Biochemist
University of Wisconsin, Biochemistry Dept, 433 Babcock Dr, Madison WI 53706, USA

Reznor, M Trent W M E Entertainment, 9601 Wilshire Blvd, #300, Beverly Hills CA 90210 USA	Singer (Nine Inch Nails)
Rhames, Ving Innovative Artists, 1505 10th St, Santa Monica CA 90401 USA	Actor
Rhea, Caroline Kipperman Mgmt, 420 W End Ave, #1G, New York NY 10024 USA	Actress, Comedienne
Rheaume, Manon Manon Rheaume Foundation, PO Box 701816, Plymouth MI 48170, USA	Ice Hockey Player
Rhett, Errict U 6 NW 108th Terrace, Plantation FL 33324, USA	Football Player
Rhey, Ashley 1220 Airport Freeway, #G456, Bedford TX 76022, USA	Actress, Model
Rhimes, Shonda I C M Partners, 10250 Constellation Blvd, #900, Los Angeles CA 90067 USA	Writer, Producer
Rhine, Kendall L, Sr 6240 State Route 127 N, Alto Pass IL 62905, USA	Basketball Player
Rhines, Peter B 5753 61st Ave NE, Seattle WA 98105, USA	Oceanographer
Rhoads, James B 1300 Fox Run Trail, Platte City MO 64079, USA	Archivist
Rhoads, Paul Iowa State University, Athletic Dept, Ames IA 50011, USA	Football Coach
Rhoda, Hilary I M G Models, 304 Park Ave S, #PH-North, New York NY 10010 USA	Model
Rhoden, Richard A (Rick) 8009 Whisper Lake Lane E, Ponte Vedra FL 32082, USA	Baseball Player
Rhodes, Arthur L, Jr 14114 Phoenix Road, Phoenix MD 21131, USA	Baseball Player
Rhodes, Cynthia 15260 Ventura Blvd, #2100, Sherman Oaks CA 91403, USA	Actress, Dancer
Rhodes, Damian (Dusty) 8595 Sanctuary Dr, Mentor OH 44060, USA	Ice Hockey Player
Rhodes, Donnelly Northern Exposure Talent Management Group, 570 Granville St, Vancouver BC V6C 3P1, Canada	Actor
Rhodes, Eugene S (Gene) 132 N Peterson Ave, #8, Louisville KY 40206, USA	Basketball Player
Rhodes, Frank H T Cornell University, Geology Dept, Snee Hall, Ithaca NY 14853, USA	Geologist, Educator
Rhodes, Jewell Parker Arizona State University, English Dept, Tempe AZ 85287, USA	Writer
Rhodes, Karl D (Dusty) 4230 Cedar Bend Dr, Missouri City TX 77459, USA	Baseball Player
Rhodes, Kerry Arizona Cardinals, PO Box 888, Phoenix AZ 85001 USA	Football Player
Rhodes, Kim Stone Manners Salners, 9911 W Pico Blvd, #1400, Los Angeles CA 90035 USA	Actress
Rhodes, Nick D D Productions, 93A Westbourne Park Villas, London W2 5ED, England	Keyboardist (Duran Duran)
Rhodes, Philip W M E Entertainment, 1600 Division St, #300, Nashville TN 37203 USA	Drummer (Gin Blossoms, Pharaohs)
Rhodes, Ray 1507 Juliet Dr, Allen TX 75013, USA	Football Player, Coach
Rhodes, Richard L Janklow & Nesbit, 445 Park Ave, #1300, New York NY 10022, USA	Writer
Rhodes, Robert Robert Rhodes Associates Architects, 330 W 42nd St, New York NY 10036, USA	Architect
Rhodes, Rodrick PO Box 17704, Sugar Land TX 77496, USA	Basketball Player
Rhodes, Tom OmniPop Talent Group, 4605 Lankershim Blvd, #201, Toluca Lake CA 91602 USA	Actor, Comedian
Rhodes, Zandra L 79-85 Bermondsey St, London SE1 3XF, England	Fashion Designer
Rhodri, Steffan Ken McReddie Assoc, 11 Connaught Place, London W2 2ET, England	Actor
Rhomberg, Kevin J 9692 Executive Court, Mentor OH 44060, USA	Baseball Player
Rhome, Gerald B (Jerry) 3883 Morning Meadow Lane, Buford GA 30519, USA	Football Player, Coach
Rhone, Earnest C (Earnie) 3603 Potomac Ave, Texarkana TX 75503, USA	Football Player
Rhyan, Dick 111 Camp Dr, Georgetown TX 78633, USA	Golfer
Rhymes, Busta T C A/Jed Root, 9220 Sunset Blvd, #315, Los Angeles CA 90069, USA	Rap Artist, Actor
Rhys Meyers, Jonathan Brillstein Entertainment Partners, 9150 Wilshire Blvd, #350, Beverly Hills CA 90212 USA	Actor
Rhys, Matthew W M E Entertainment, 9601 Wilshire Blvd, #300, Beverly Hills CA 90210 USA	Actor
Rhys, Paul Markham & Froggatt, Julian House, 4 Windmill St, London W1P 1HF, England	Actor
Rhys, Phillip Independent Talent Group, Oxford House, 76 Oxford St, London W1D 1BS, England	Actor
Rhys-Davies, John Just Voices Agency, 140 Buckingham Palace Road, London SW1W 9SA, England	Actor
Ribant, Dennis J 46 Sidra Cove, Newport Coast CA 92657, USA	Baseball Player
Ribble, Pat 23 Cheyenne Court, Leamington ON N8H 5E2, Canada	Ice Hockey Player
Ribbs, Willy T 2343 Ribbs Lane, San Jose CA 95116, USA	Auto Racing Driver
Ribeau, Sidney A Howard University, President's Office, Washington DC 20059, USA	Educator
Ribeiro, Alfonso Creative Talent Group, 1900 Ave of Stars, #2475, Los Angeles CA 90067, USA	Actor
Ribeiro, Ignacio Clements Ribeiro Ltd, 48 S Molton St, London W1X 1HE, England	Fashion Designer

Ribeiro, Michael T (Mike) — Ice Hockey Player
5609 Monterey Dr, Frisco TX 75034, USA
Ribes, Jean-Michel — Actor
Artmedia, 20 Ave Rapp, 75007 Paris, France
Ribisi, Giovanni — Actor
Management 360, 9111 Wilshire Blvd, Beverly Hills CA 90210 USA
Ribisi, Marissa — Actress
United Talent Agency, 9336 Civic Center Dr, Beverly Hills CA 90210 USA
Ricard, Adrian — Actress
Amsel Eisenstadt Frazier, 5055 Wilshire Blvd, #865, Los Angeles CA 90036 USA
Ricard, Alan C — Football Player
10306 Ripple Lake Dr, Houston TX 77065, USA
Ricard, Jean-Pierre B Cardinal — Religious Leader
Archdiocese of Bordeaux, 183 Cours de la Somme, 33034 Bordeaux, France
Ricardo, Benito C (Benny) — Football Player, Actor, Comedian
3012 Harding Way, Costa Mesa CA 92626, USA
Ricci, Christina — Actress
Management 360, 9111 Wilshire Blvd, Beverly Hills CA 90210 USA
Ricci, Mike — Ice Hockey Player
286 Mountain Laurel Lane, Los Gatos CA 95032, USA
Rice, Andrew (Andy) — Football Player
801 N Main St, Hallettsville TX 77964, USA
Rice, Anne — Writer
9 Monte Carlo Dr, Kenner LA 70065, USA
Rice, Bobby G — Singer
505 Canton Pass, Madison TN 37115, USA
Rice, Buddy — Auto Racing Driver
Panther Racing, 5740 Decatur Blvd, Indianapolis IN 46241, USA
Rice, Condoleezza — Secretary, State
Stanford University, Hoover Institution, Stanford CA 94305, USA
Rice, Damien — Singer, Guitarist, Songwriter
Paradigm Agency, 360 N Crescent Dr, North Building, Beverly Hills CA 90210 USA
Rice, Elizabeth — Actress
TalentWorks, 3500 W Olive Ave, #1400, Burbank CA 91505 USA
Rice, Gigi — Actress
Bamboo Mgmt, 17 Buccaneer St, Marina Del Rey CA 90292, USA
Rice, Glen A — Basketball Player
8920 SW 162nd Terrace, Palmetto Bay FL 33157, USA
Rice, James E (Jim) — Baseball Player
35 Bobby Jones Dr, Andover MA 01810, USA
Rice, James R — Geophysicist
Harvard University, Applied Science Division, Cambridge MA 02138, USA
Rice, Jerry L — Football Player
267 Atherton Ave, Atherton CA 94027, USA
Rice, John L — Baseball Umpire
2666 E 73rd St, #12W, Chicago IL 60649, USA
Rice, Kenneth E (Ken) — Football Player
10619 Big Canoe, Big Canoe GA 30143, USA
Rice, Luanne — Writer
I C M Partners, 10250 Constellation Blvd, #900, Los Angeles CA 90067 USA
Rice, Patrick E (Pat) — Baseball Player
4090 Zurich Dr, Colorado Springs CO 80920, USA
Rice, Raymell M (Ray) — Football Player
Baltimore Ravens, Ravens Stadium, 1 Winning Dr, Baltimore MD 21230 USA
Rice, Ronald W (Ron) — Football Player
22880 Twyckingham Ave, Southfield MI 48034, USA
Rice, Sidney R — Football Player
Seattle Seahawks, 12 Seahawks Way, Renton WA 98056 USA
Rice, Simeon J — Football Player
371 Channelside Walkway, #301, Tampa FL 33602, USA
Rice, Stephanie — Swimmer
Saint Peters Swim Club, Box 598, Indooroopilly QLD 4068, Australia
Rice, Steven (Steve) — Ice Hockey Player
99 Duncairn Ave, Kitchener ON N2M 4S5, Canada
Rice, Stuart A — Chemist
5517 S Kimbark Ave, Chicago IL 60637, USA
Rice, Susan E — Government Official, Diplomat
US Mission, United Nations Plaza, New York NY 10017, USA
Rice, Thomas M — Theoretical Physicist
Theoretische Physik, ETH-Honggerberg, 8093 Zurich, Switzerland
Rice, Timothy M B (Tim) — Lyricist
Chilterns, France-Hill Dr, Camberley, Surrey GU153-30A, England
Rich, Adam — Actor
Jeff Ballard Public Relations 4814 Lemona Ave, Sherman Oaks CA 91403, USA
Rich, Alexander — Molecular Biologist
2 Walnut Ave, Cambridge MA 02140, USA
Rich, Allan — Actor
Greater Vision Agency, 9229 W Sunset Blvd, #320, West Hollywood CA 90069, USA
Rich, Christopher — Actor
Bresler Kelly Assoc, 11500 W Olympic Blvd, #400, Los Angeles CA 90064 USA
Rich, David Lowell — Director
721 Royal Anne Lane, #201, Raleigh NC 27615, USA
Rich, Frank H — Drama Critic, Columnist
New York Times, Editorial Dept, 229 W 43rd St, New York NY 10036 USA
Rich, John — Singer, Guitarist, Songwriter
Morris Management Group, 818 19th Ave S, Nashville TN 37203, USA
Rich, Katie — Actress
10100 Santa Monica Blvd, #2490, Los Angeles CA 90067, USA
Rich, Tommy — Basketball Player
1348 Clubview Court, Venice FL 34292, USA
Rich, Tony — Singer, Keyboardist, Songwriter
Prestige, 220 E 23rd St, #303, New York NY 10010, USA
Richard of Ammanford, Ivor S — Government Official, England
11 South Square, Gray's Inn, London WC1R 5EU, England
Richard, Cecile — Association Executive
Planned Parenthood Federation, 434 W 33rd St, New York NY 10001, USA

Richard, Chris
11389 Ironwood Road, San Diego CA 92131, USA — Baseball Player

Richard, Cliff
Harley House, Portsmouth Road, Box 46C, Esher, Surrey KT10 9AA, England — Singer

Richard, Dawn
Playboy Promotions, 2706 Media Center Dr, Los Angeles CA 90065 USA — Model, Actress

Richard, Dawn A
Bad Boy Entertainment, 1440 Broadway, #16, New York NY 10018 USA — Singer (Danity Kane)

Richard, Deb
736 Port Charlotte Dr, Ponte Vedra FL 32081, USA — Golfer

Richard, Henri
905-4300 Place de Cageux, Ile Paton Laval QC H7W 4Z3, Canada — Ice Hockey Player

Richard, James Rodney (J R)
Mary Olive Baptist Church, 2804 McGowan St, Houston TX 77004, USA — Baseball Player

Richard, Lee E (Bee Bee)
1621 14th St, Port Arthur TX 77640, USA — Baseball Player

Richard, Nathalie
Voyez Mon Agent, 20 Ave Rapp, 75007 Paris, France — Actress

Richard, Pierre
Artmedia, 20 Ave Rapp, 75007 Paris, France — Actor

Richards, Ariana
Don Buchwald/Fortitude, 6500 Wilshire Blvd, #2200, Los Angeles CA 90048 USA — Actress

Richards, Bradley G (Brad)
101 Warren St, #3150, New York NY 10007, USA — Ice Hockey Player

Richards, Brooke
Playboy Promotions, 2706 Media Center Dr, Los Angeles CA 90065 USA — Model

Richards, Dakota Blue
Artist Rights Group, 4 Great Portland Place, London W1W 8PA, England — Actress

Richards, David R (Dave)
4209 San Carlos St, Dallas TX 75205, USA — Football Player

Richards, Denise
P M K-B N C, 8687 Melrose Ave, #800, Los Angeles CA 90069 USA — Actress, Model

Richards, Duane L
PO Box 54, Palestine OH 45352, USA — Baseball Player

Richards, Emilie
PO Box 228, Chautauqua NY 14722, USA — Writer

Richards, Eugene
Many Voices, 472 13th St, Brooklyn NY 11215, USA — Photographer

Richards, Fred C
1760 Dodge Dr NW, Warren OH 44485, USA — Baseball Player

Richards, George Maxwell
President's House, Botanical Garden Area, Port of Spain, Trinidad & Tobago — President, Trinidad & Tobago

Richards, J August
I C M Partners, 10250 Constellation Blvd, #900, Los Angeles CA 90067 USA — Actor

Richards, J Golden
7274 Winesap Court, Salt Lake City UT 84121, USA — Football Player

Richards, J R
W M E Entertainment, 1325 Ave of Americas, New York NY 10019 USA — Singer (Dishwalla)

Richards, Keith
25 Walden Woods Lane, Weston CT 06883, USA — Singer (Rolling Stones), Songwriter

Richards, Kim
10326 Orton Ave, Los Angeles CA 90064, USA — Actress

Richards, Lucille
17 Stonemeadow Dr, Bridgewater MA 2324, USA — Baseball Player

Richards, Mark
Mark Richards Surfboards, 755 Hunter St, Newcastle NSW 2302, Australia — Surfer

Richards, Michael
Abrams Artists, 275 7th Ave, #2600, New York NY 10001 USA — Actor, Comedian

Richards, Paul L
University of California, Physics Dept, LeConte Hall, Berkeley CA 94720, USA — Physicist

Richards, Paul W
N A S A, Johnson Space Center, 2101 NASA Road, Houston TX 77058 USA — Astronaut

Richards, Renee
1604 Union St, San Francisco CA 94123, USA — Tennis Player

Richards, Rex E
13 Woodstock Close, Oxford OX2 8DB, England — Chemist

Richards, Richard N
N A S A, Johnson Space Center, 2101 NASA Road, Houston TX 77058 USA — Astronaut

Richards, Robert E (Bob)
76782 Interstate 20, Gordon TX 76453, USA — Track Athlete

Richards, Robert G (Bobby)
2881 Fairplay Road, Rutledge GA 30663, USA — Football Player

Richards, Russell E (Rusty)
1193 Spring Sage St, Henderson NV 89011, USA — Baseball Player

Richards, Stephanie
H David Moss, 733 Seward St, #PH, Los Angeles CA 90038 USA — Actress

Richards, Todd M
Columbus Blue Jackets, Arena, 200 W Nationwide Blvd, #1, Columbus OH 43215 USA — Ice Hockey Player, Coach

Richards, Warren J
9075 S 700 E, #109, Sandy UT 84070, USA — Writer

Richardson, Alpete (Al)
PO Box 371105, Decatur GA 30037, USA — Football Player

Richardson, Ashley
Jason Weinberg Assoc, 451 Greenwich St, New York NY 10013, USA — Model

Richardson, Cameron
Paradigm Agency, 360 N Crescent Dr, North Building, Beverly Hills CA 90210 USA — Model, Actress

Richardson, Clint D
1207 9th Ave NW, Puyallup WA 98371, USA — Basketball Player

Richardson, Damien A
1300 E Cromwell Ave, Fresno CA 93720, USA — Football Player

Richardson, Dan
Agency Group Ltd, 142 W 57th St, #600, New York NY 10019 USA — Drummer (Stereo Mud)

Richardson, Dave
62 Agassie Dr, Winnipeg MB R3T 2K7, Canada — Ice Hockey Player

Richardson, Derek
I C M Partners, 10250 Constellation Blvd, #900, Los Angeles CA 90067 USA — Actor

Richardson, Donna
Anchor Bay Entertainment, 1699 Stutz Dr, Troy MI 48084, USA — Physical Fitness Expert

Richardson, Dorothy (Dot)
1120 W Lakeshore Dr, Clermont FL 34711, USA — Softball Player

Richardson, Emma
Pias Entertainment Group, Trading Centre, 101 Farm Lane, #24, London SW6 1QJ, England — Singer, Bassist (Band of Skulls)

Richardson, Gloster V
9143 S Euclid Ave, Chicago IL 60617, USA — Football Player

Richardson, Gordon C (Gordie)
23 Saint Paul Church Road, Colquitt GA 39837, USA — Baseball Player

Richardson, Greg
382 Camden Ave, Youngstown OH 44505, USA — Boxer

Richardson, Jack
12171 Sunset Ave, Grass Valley CA 95945, USA — Artist

Richardson, Jake
Untitled Entertainment, 350 S Beverly Dr, #200, Beverly Hills CA 90212 USA — Actor

Richardson, Jane S
Duke University, Biochemistry Dept, Durham NC 27708, USA — Biochemist

Richardson, Jason A
75 Dahlia St, Denver CO 80220, USA — Basketball Player

Richardson, Jeffrey S (Jeff)
11779 W Fordson Dr, Marana AZ 85653, USA — Baseball Player

Richardson, Jeremy T
Orlando Magic, 8701 Maitland Summit Blvd, Orlando FL 32810 USA — Basketball Player

Richardson, Jerome (Pooh)
23434 Sherman Way, West Hills CA 91307, USA — Basketball Player

Richardson, Jerome J (Jerry)
Carolina Panthers, Ericsson Stadium, 800 S Mint St, Charlotte NC 28202 USA — Football Player, Executive

Richardson, Joely
Ken McReddie Assoc, 11 Connaught Place, London W2 2ET, England — Actress

Richardson, John E
3053 Eagles Claw Ave, Thousand Oaks CA 91362, USA — Football Player

Richardson, Ken
Pfizer Laboratories, Ramsgate Road, Sandwich Kent CT13 9NJ, England — Chemist, Inventor

Richardson, Ken
Hockey Heritage, 400 Government Road W, Kirkland Lake ON P2N 3M6, Canada — Ice Hockey Player

Richardson, Kevin Michael
C E S D, 10635 Santa Monica Blvd, #130, Los Angeles CA 90025 USA — Actor

Richardson, Kevin S
The Firm, 2049 Century Park E, #2550, Los Angeles CA 90067 USA — Singer (Backstreet Boys)

Richardson, Kyle D
3516 Balmar Mews Road, Baltimore MD 21211, USA — Football Player

Richardson, LaTanya
Framework Entertainment, 9057 Nemo St, #C, West Hollywood CA 90069 USA — Actress

Richardson, Linda
Musichall Ltd, Vicarage Way, Ringmer BN8 5LA, England — Opera Singer

Richardson, Mark
13 Artists, 11-14 Kensington St, Brighton BN1 4AJ, England — Drummer (Skunk Anansie)

Richardson, Michael C (Mike)
723 Owen Ave, #C, Huntington Beach CA 92648, USA — Football Player

Richardson, Michael W (Mike)
7310 Covewood Dr, Garland TX 75044, USA — Football Player

Richardson, Micheal Ray
6089 S Ukraine Circle, Aurora CO 80015, USA — Basketball Player

Richardson, Mike
Dark Horse Publishing, 10956 SE Main St, Portland OR 97222 USA — Publisher

Richardson, Miranda
Independent Talent Group, Oxford House, 76 Oxford St, London W1D 1BS, England — Actress

Richardson, Nolan
4057 N Hughmount Road, Fayetteville AR 72704, USA — Basketball Coach

Richardson, Patricia
Innovative Artists, 1505 10th St, Santa Monica CA 90401 USA — Actress

Richardson, Quentin L
Minnesota Timberwolves, Target Center, 600 1st Ave N, Minneapolis MN 55403 USA — Basketball Player

Richardson, Robert B
Skouras Agency, 1149 3rd St, #300, Santa Monica CA 90403 USA — Cinematographer

Richardson, Robert C
4 Hunter Lane, Ithaca NY 14850, USA — Nobel Physics Laureate

Richardson, Robert C (Bobby)
47 Adams Ave, Sumter SC 29150, USA — Baseball Player

Richardson, Robert, Jr
PO Box 523, McKinney TX 75070, USA — Auto Racing Driver

Richardson, Sam
4121 Sequoyah Road, Oakland CA 94605, USA — Sculptor

Richardson, Terry
3598 Rosemary Heights Crescent, Surrey BC V3S 0P2, Canada — Ice Hockey Player

Richardson, Trent
Cleveland Browns, 76 Lou Groza Blvd, Berea OH 44017 USA — Football Player

Richardson, William C
W K Kellogg Foundation, 1 Michigan Ave E, Battle Creek MI 49017, USA — Foundation Executive, Educator

Richardson, William R
8612 Dixie Place, McLean VA 22102, USA — Army General

Richardson, Willie L
5928 Waverly Dr, Jackson MS 39206, USA — Football Player

Richardson-Whitfield, Salli
Innovative Artists, 1505 10th St, Santa Monica CA 90401 USA — Actress

Richards-Ross, Sanya (Sandie)
Octagon Worldwide, 1751 Pinnacle Dr, #1500, McLean VA 22102 USA — Track Athlete

Richen, John M
Contemporary Fine Arts Gallery, 7946 Ivanhoe Ave, La Jolla CA 92037, USA — Sculptor

Richer, Stephane
Club de Golf Montpelier, 440 Ave S Richaer, Montpelier QC J0V 1M0, Canada — Ice Hockey Player

Richert, Peter G (Pete)
80 La Cerra Dr, Rancho Mirage CA 92270, USA — Baseball Player

Richey, Cliff
2936 Cumberland Dr, San Angelo TX 76904, USA — Tennis Player

V.I.P. Address Book

Richey, Jennifer
C E S D, 10635 Santa Monica Blvd, #130, Los Angeles CA 90025 USA — Actress
Richey, Kim
209 10th Ave S, #322, Nashville TN 37203, USA — Singer, Songwriter
Richey, Wade E
207 Bayonne Dr, Lafayette LA 70507, USA — Football Player
Richie, Lionel
L B R Entertainment, 9903 Santa Monica Blvd, #529, Beverly Hills CA 90212, USA — Singer, Songwriter
Richie, Nicole
Paradigm Agency, 360 N Crescent Dr, North Building, Beverly Hills CA 90210 USA — Actress, Producer
Richie, Robert E (Bob)
1835 Meadowvale Way, Sparks NV 89431, USA — Baseball Player
Richie, Shane
International Artistes, 193-197 High Holborn, London WC1V 7BD, England — Singer, Actor
Richings, Julian
Gary Goddard Agency, 10 St Mary's St, #305, Toronto ON M4Y 1P9, Canada — Actor
Richling, Greg
B K Entertainment Group, 15300 Ventura Blvd, #203, Sherman Oaks CA 91403, USA — Singer, Bassist (Wallflowers)
Richman, Caryn
1805 Via Arriba, Palos Verdes Estates CA 90274, USA — Actress
Richman, Jason
W M E Entertainment, 9601 Wilshire Blvd, #300, Beverly Hills CA 90210 USA — Producer, Writer
Richman, Jonathan
High Road Touring, 751 Bridgeway, #200, Sausalito CA 94965 USA — Singer, Guitarist (Modern Lovers), Actor
Richman, Peter Mark
5114 Del Moreno Dr, Woodland Hills CA 91364, USA — Actor
Richmond, Anthony B
United Talent Agency, 9336 Civic Center Dr, Beverly Hills CA 90210 USA — Cinematograhper
Richmond, Branscombe
PO Box 881095, Pukalani HI 96788, USA — Actor
Richmond, Deon
Innovative Artists, 1505 10th St, Santa Monica CA 90401 USA — Actor
Richmond, Geri
University of Oregon, Chemistry Dept, Eugene OR 97403, USA — Chemist
Richmond, Mitchell J (Mitch)
25374 Prado de la Felicidad, Calabasas CA 91302, USA — Basketball Player
Richmond, Steve
21290 W Pepper Dr, Lake Zurich IL 60047, USA — Ice Hockey Player
Richt, Mark
University of Georgia, Athletic Dept, PO Box 1472, Athens GA 30603, USA — Football Coach
Richter, Allen G (Al)
3810 Atlantic Ave, #703, Virginia Beach VA 23451, USA — Baseball Player
Richter, Andy
Creative Artists Agency, 2000 Ave of Stars, #100, Los Angeles CA 90067 USA — Actor, Comedian
Richter, Barry
7202 Timberwood Dr, Madison WI 53719, USA — Ice Hockey Player
Richter, Burton
620 Sand Hill Road, #206C, Palo Alto CA 94304, USA — Nobel Physics Laureate
Richter, Gerhard
Bismarckstr 50, 50672 Cologne, Germany — Artist
Richter, Jason James
Aqua Talent, 9000 Sunset Blvd, #700, Los Angeles CA 90069, USA — Actor
Richter, John F
2740 Narcissa Road, Plymouth Meeting PA 19462, USA — Basketball Player
Richter, Michael T (Mike)
61 Cutler Road, Greenwich CT 06831, USA — Ice Hockey Player
Richter, Pat V
11111 Bardon Road, Woodruff WI 54568, USA — Football Player, Administrator
Richwine, Maria
Acme Talent Agency, 4727 Wilshire Blvd, #333, Los Angeles CA 90010 USA — Actress
Rickard, Joe
Paradigm Agency, 404 W Franklin St, Monterey CA 93940 USA — Drummer (Red)
Rickard, Robbie
Professional Bowlers Assn, 719 2nd Ave, #701, Seattle WA 98104 USA — Bowler
Rickards, Ashley
United Talent Agency, 9336 Civic Center Dr, Beverly Hills CA 90210 USA — Actress
Ricker, Maelle D
Agenda Sport Marketing, 318 11th Ave SE, #340, Calgary AB T2G 0Y2 Canada T2G — Snowboarding Athlete
Ricketts, Thomas G (Tom), Jr
720 Warrendale Bayne Road, Wexford PA 15090, USA — Football Player
Rickhards, Dominic
Gavin Barker Assoc, 2D Wimpole St, London W1G 0EB, England — Actor
Rickles, Don
10249 Century Woods Dr, Los Angeles CA 90067, USA — Actor, Comedian
Rickman, Alan
Independent Talent Group, Oxford House, 76 Oxford St, London W1D 1BS, England — Actor
Ricks, Christopher B
Lasborough Park near Tetbury, Gloucestershire GL8 8UF, England — Writer, Educator
Ricks, Mikhael R
5024 Lincoln St, Hollywood FL 33021, USA — Football Player
Rickter, Alicia
Innovative Artists, 1505 10th St, Santa Monica CA 90401 USA — Model, Actress
Rico, Alfredo C (Fred)
7720 Ensign Ave, Sun Valley CA 91352, USA — Baseball Player
Rida, Flo
Susan Blond Inc, 50 W 57th St, #1400, New York NY 10019 USA — Rap Artist
Riddell, Derek
Hamilton Hodell, 66-68 Margaret St, London W1W 8SR, England — Actor
Riddick, Frank A, Jr
150 Broadway St, #709, New Orleans LA 70118, USA — Physician
Riddick, Robbert L (Robb)
111 Lilli Lane, Woodstock GA 30188, USA — Football Player
Riddick, Steven (Steve)
PO Box 1892, Norfolk VA 23501, USA — Track Athlete
Riddiford, Lynn M
40733 Manor House Road, Leesburg VA 20175, USA — Zoologist

R

Riddleberger, Dennis M (Denny) — Baseball Player
35785 Hunter Ave, Westland MI 48185, USA
Riddles, Libby — Dog Sled Racer
PO Box 15253, Fritz Creek AK 99603, USA
Riddoch, Gregory L (Greg) — Baseball Player, Manager
703 Windflower Dr, Longmont CO 80504, USA
Rider, Isaiah (J R) — Basketball Player
PO Box 121R, Montchanin DE 19710, USA
Ridge, Thomas J (Tom) — Secretary, Home Security; Governor, PA
Westwood Estate Dr, Erie PA 16506, USA
Ridgeley, Andrew — Singer, Guitarist (Wham!)
8800 W Sunset Blvd, #401, West Hollywood CA 90069, USA
Ridgeway, Angie — Golfer
419 Glen Crest Dr, Moore SC 29369, USA
Ridgeway, Frank — Cartoonist (Mr Abernathy)
King Features Syndicate, 300 W 57th St, #1500, New York NY 10019 USA
Ridgway, Jeff — Baseball Player
9041 Parlor Dr, Ladson SC 29456, USA
Ridgway, Stan — Singer, Songwriter
Agency Group Ltd, 142 W 57th St, #600, New York NY 10019 USA
Ridker, Paul — Cardiologist
Brigham & Women's Hospital, 75 Francis St, Boston MA 02115, USA
Ridley, John — Writer, Director, Producer
Creative Artists Agency, 2000 Ave of Stars, #100, Los Angeles CA 90067 USA
Ridley, Mike — Ice Hockey Player
Home Run Sports, 1005 St Mary's Road, Winnipeg MB R2M 3S4, Canada
Ridlon, James A (Jim) — Football Player
4468 E Lake Road, Cazenovia NY 13035, USA
Ridnour, Lukas R (Luke) — Basketball Player
Milwaukee Bucks, Bradley Center, 1001 N 4th St, #2, Milwaukee WI 53203 USA
Riedel, Lars — Track Athlete
Trinitatis Str 20, 09130 Chemnitz, Germany
Riedel, Oliver (Ollie) — Bassist (Rammstein)
Pilgrim Mgmt, PO Box 540101, 10042 Berlin, Germany
Riedlbauch, Vaclav — Composer
Revolucni 6, 110 00 Prague 1, Czech Republic
Riedling, John — Baseball Player
2118 Homestead Lane, Franklin TN 37064, USA
Rieffel, Lisa — Actress
A P A Talent/Literary Agency, 405 S Beverly Dr, #300, Beverly Hills CA 90212 USA
Riegert, Peter — Actor
Don Buchwald/Fortitude, 10 E 44th St, New York NY 10017 USA
Riegger, John — Golfer
768 Tossa de Mar Ave, Henderson NV 89002, USA
Riegle, Gene — Harness Racing Driver, Trainer
818 Chestnut Circle, Greenville OH 45331, USA
Riehle, Richard — Actor
Stone Manners Salners, 9911 W Pico Blvd, #1400, Los Angeles CA 90035 USA
Riemersma, A Jay — Football Player
3067 Regency Parkway, Zeeland MI 49464, USA
Riendeau, Vincent — Ice Hockey Player
Harrington College, Che Riviere Rouge, Harrington QC JBG 2S7, Canada
Rienstra, John W — Football Player
5056 Briscoglen Dr, Colorado Springs CO 80906, USA
Ries, Christopher D — Artist
Keelersburg Road, Tunkhannock PA 18657, USA
Ries, Julien Cardinal — Religious Leader
Diocese, 1 Rue de l'Eveche, 5000 Namur, Belgium
Riesch, Maria Hoefl- — Alpine Skier
Postfach 1728, 82467 Garmisch-Partenkirchen, Germany
Riesco, Armando — Actor
Liebman Entertainment, 12 E 46th St, #500, New York NY 10017, USA
Riesenberg, Douglas J (Doug) — Football Player
25068 Starr Creek Road, Corvallis OR 97333, USA
Riesgo, D Nikco — Baseball Player
29625 Bermuda Lane, Southfield MI 48076, USA
Riesgraf, Beth — Actress, Director, Writer
Insight Entertainment, 1134 S Coverdale Ave, Los Angeles CA 90019, USA
Riess, Adam G — Nobel Physics Laureate
Space Telescope Science Institute, 3700 San Martin Dr, Baltimore MD 21218, USA
Riessen, Marty — Tennis Player
PO Box 5444, Santa Barbara CA 93150, USA
Rieu, Andre L M N — Concert Violinist, Conductor, Composer
Polygram Holland, Mozartlaan 25, 1217 CM Hilversum, Netherlands
Riffenburgh, Beau — Historian
Bloomsbury Publishing, 36 Soho Square, London W1D 3Q4, England
Rifkin, Arnold — Producer
Cheyenne Enterprises, 406 Wilshire Blvd, Santa Monica CA 90401, USA
Rifkin, Jeremy — Writer, Social Activist
1660 L St NW, #216, Washington DC 20036, USA
Rifkin, Joshua — Concert Pianist, Conductor
100 Montgomery St, Cambridge MA 02140, USA
Rifkin, Ron — Actor, Singer
Innovative Artists, 235 Park Ave S, #1000, New York NY 10003 USA
Rigazio, Donald — Ice Hockey Player
8514 Cheffield Dr, Louisville KY 40222, USA
Rigby McCoy, Cathleen R (Cathy) — Gymnast, Actress
McCoy Rigby Entertainment, 22601 La Palma Ave, #105, Yorba Linda CA 92887, USA
Rigby, Amy — Singer, Songwriter
Press Network, 1229 17th Ave S, Nashville TN 37212, USA
Rigby, Jean P — Opera Singer
John Coast Mgmt, Manfield House, 3769 Strand, London WC1, England
Rigby, Randall L, Jr — Army General
869 Oak Hill Road, Lake Barrington IL 60010, USA
Rigg, Diana — Actress
Artist Rights Group, 4 Great Portland Place, London W1W 8PA, England

Riggan, Jerrod Baseball Player
PO Box 1019, Brewster WA 98812, USA
Riggans, Shawn Baseball Player
5700 Hancock Road, Southwest Ranches FL 33330, USA
Riggin, Patrick M (Pat) Ice Hockey Player
112 Fairlane Ave, London ON N6K 3E6, Canada
Riggins, John Football Player, Sportscaster
8000 Riverside Dr, Cabin John MD 20818, USA
Riggle, Rob Actor, Comedian
Principato-Young, 9465 Wilshire Blvd, #880, Beverly Hills CA 90212 USA
Riggleman, James D (Jim) Baseball Player, Manager
14950 Gulf Blvd, #1003, Madeira Beach FL 33708, USA
Riggs, Adam D Baseball Player
26 Pebble Hollow Court, Spring TX 77381, USA
Riggs, Chandler Actor
East Coast Talent Agency, 3 Central Plaza, #344, Rome GA 30161, USA
Riggs, Gerald Football Player
2574 Bright Court, Decatur GA 30034, USA
Riggs, Lorrin A Psychologist
80 Lyme Road, #104, Hanover NH 03755, USA
Riggs, R Scott Auto, Truck Racing Driver
216 Preston Andrews Road, Bahama NC 27503, USA
Righetti, Amanda Actress
United Talent Agency, 9336 Civic Center Dr, Beverly Hills CA 90210 USA
Righetti, David A (Dave) Baseball Player
552 Magdalena Ave, Los Altos Hills CA 94024, USA
Rigoni, Benito Bobsled Athlete
Olympic Committee, Foro Italico, Largo Lauro de Bosis 15, 00135 Rome, Italy
Rihanna Singer
W M E Entertainment, 1325 Ave of Americas, New York NY 10019 USA
Riis, Bjarne L Cyclist
Riis Cycling, Firskovej 36, 2800 KGS Lyngby, Denmark
Rijker, Lucia Boxer, Kickboxer, Actress
Sports Placement Service, 6671 W Sunset Blvd, #1521, Los Angeles CA 90028, USA
Rijo, Jose A Baseball Player
2127 Brickell Ave, #2101, Miami FL 33129, USA
Rikaart, Greg Actor
S D B Partners, 1801 Ave of Stars, #902, Los Angeles CA 90067 USA
Riker, Albert J Plant Pathologist
2760 E 8th St, Tucson AZ 85716, USA
Riker, Robin Actress
Stone Manners Salners, 9911 W Pico Blvd, #1400, Los Angeles CA 90035 USA
Riker, Thomas E (Tom) Basketball Player
600 Fines Creek Road, Clyde NC 28721, USA
Riklis, Meshulam Businessman
Riklis Family Corp, 2901 Las Vegas Blvd S, Las Vegas NV 89109, USA
Riles, Ernest Baseball Player
221 Asante Dr, Ellenwood GA 30294, USA
Riley, Amber Actress
P M K-B N C, 8687 Melrose Ave, #800, Los Angeles CA 90069 USA
Riley, Bridget L Artist
Karsten Schubert, 47 Lexington St, London W1R 3LG, England
Riley, Chris Golfer
2289 Surrey Meadows Ave, Henderson NV 89052, USA
Riley, E Theodore (Teddy) Songwriter, Singer (Blackstreet)
Richard Walters, PO Box 2789, Toluca Lake CA 91610 USA
Riley, Elaine Actress
405 N Bay Front, Newport Beach CA 92662, USA
Riley, Eric Basketball Player
6601 Sands Point Dr, #4, Houston TX 77074, USA
Riley, Gerald (Jerry) Dog Sled Racer
General Delivery, Nenana AK 99760, USA
Riley, Jack Actor
C E S D, 10635 Santa Monica Blvd, #130, Los Angeles CA 90025 USA
Riley, James C Army General
Commanding General, V Corps, APO AE 09079 USA
Riley, James G (Jim) Football Player
2201 Cardinal Dr, Edmond OK 73013, USA
Riley, Jeannie C Singer
906 Granville Road, Franklin TN 37064, USA
Riley, John P (Jack), Jr Ice Hockey Player, Coach
PO Box 1302, Marstons Mills MA 02648, USA
Riley, Kenneth J (Ken) Football Player
1035 Carver Ave, Bartow FL 33830, USA
Riley, Lawrence (Larry) Football Player
8 Daley Road, Poughkeepsie NY 12603, USA
Riley, Madison Actress
Emerald Talent Group, 15260 Ventura Blvd, #1200, Sherman Oaks CA 91403, USA
Riley, Matthew P (Matt) Baseball Player
17169 W Ironwood St, Surprise AZ 85388, USA
Riley, Michael Actor
Thruline Entertainment, 9250 Wilshire Blvd, #100, Beverly Hills CA 90212 USA
Riley, Mike Football Coach
Oregon State University, Athletic Dept, Corvallis OR 97331, USA
Riley, Patrick J (Pat) Basketball Player, Coach, Executive
180 Arvida Parkway, Miami FL 33156, USA
Riley, Richard D Association Executive
16 Boathouse Road, Laconia NH 03246, USA
Riley, Richard W Secretary, Education; Governor, SC
Nelson Mullins Riley Scarborough, 104 S Main St, #900, Greenville SC 29601, USA
Riley, Ruth Basketball Player
Metis Sports Management, 132 N Old Woodward Ave, Birmingham MI 48009
Riley, Sam Actor
Creative Artists Agency, 2000 Ave of Stars, #100, Los Angeles CA 90067 USA
Riley, Steve B Football Player
7 Via Cancion, San Clemente CA 92673, USA

Riley, Talulah
Independent Talent Group, Oxford House, 76 Oxford St, London W1D 1BS, England — Actress

Riley, Tarrus
Agency Group Ltd, 142 W 57th St, #600, New York NY 10019 USA — Singer

Riley, Terry M
Shri Moonshine Ranch, 13699 Moonshine Road, Camptonville CA 95922, USA — Composer, Pianist

Riley, Tom
I C M Partners, 10250 Constellation Blvd, #900, Los Angeles CA 90067 USA — Actor

Riley, Victor A
1430 Bavand Circle, #107, Rock Hill SC 29732, USA — Football Player

Riley, Victor J, Jr
100 Elm St, Williamstown MA 01267, USA — Financier

Riley, William (Bill)
286 Buckingham Ave, Riverview NB E1B 2P2, Canada — Ice Hockey Player

Riley, William J
US Court of Appeals, Federal Building, PO Box 307, Omaha NE 68101, USA — Judge

Rilling, Helmuth
Opus 3 Artists, 470 Park Ave S, #900N, New York NY 10016 USA — Conductor, Concert Organist

Rimes, LeAnn
PO Box 150667, Nashville TN 37215, USA — Singer

Rimington, Dave B
125 W 110th St, #5A, New York NY 10026, USA — Football Player

Rimington, Stella
PO Box 1604, London SW1P 1XB, England — Government Official, England

Rimmel, James E
Evangelical Presbyterian Church, 26049 Five Mile Road, Redford MI 48239, USA — Religious Leader

Rinaldi, Kathy
Advantage International, 1025 Thomas Jefferson NW, #450, Washington DC 20007 USA — Tennis Player

Rinaldi, Richard P (Rich)
1117 Perry Lane, Collegeville PA 19426, USA — Basketball Player

Rinaldo, Benjamin
Ski World, 2680 Buena Park Dr, Studio City CA 91604, USA — Skier

Rincon, Juan M
5150 Lincoln Dr, Minneapolis MN 55436, USA — Baseball Player

Rinehart, Kenneth
University of Illinois, Chemistry Dept, Urbana IL 61801, USA — Chemist

Ring, R Royce
PO Box 2184, El Cajon CA 92021, USA — Baseball Player

Ring, Timothy M
C F Bard Co, 730 Central Ave, Murray Hill NJ 07974, USA — Businessman

Ringenberg, Jason
American Frontier, PO Box 2445, Northbrook IL 60065, USA — Singer (Jason & the Scorchers)

Ringer, Jennifer
New York City Ballet, Lincoln Center Plaza, New York NY 10023 USA — Ballerina

Ringer, Noah
Creative Artists Agency, 2000 Ave of Stars, #100, Los Angeles CA 90067 USA — Actor

Ringgold, Faith
Simon & Schuster, 1230 Ave of Americas, Concourse 1, New York NY 10020 USA — Writer, Artist

Ringle, William M
Davidson College, Anthropolgy Dept, Chambers Hall, Davidson NC 28035, USA — Anthropologist

Ringwald, Molly
Untitled Entertainment, 350 S Beverly Dr, #200, Beverly Hills CA 90212 USA — Actress

Rinker, Laurie A
PO Box 550, Jensen Beach FL 34958, USA — Golfer

Rinker, Lee C
1151 Egret Circle S, #380, Jupiter FL 33458, USA — Golfer

Rinna, Lisa
Paradigm Agency, 360 N Crescent Dr, North Building, Beverly Hills CA 90210 USA — Actress, Model

Rinne, Pekka
Nashville Predators, 501 Broadway, Nashville TN 37203 USA — Ice Hockey Player

Rinsch, Carl
Brillstein Entertainment Partners, 9150 Wilshire Blvd, #350, Beverly Hills CA 90212 USA — Director, Producer, Writer

Rintoul, David
Ken McReddie Assoc, 11 Connaught Place, London W2 2ET, England — Actor

Rintoul, Steve
17506 Osprey Manor Way, Lithia FL 33547, USA — Golfer

Rintzler, Marius A
Friedingstr 18, 40625 Dusseldorf, Germany — Opera Singer

Rinzler, Lisa
Gersh Agency, 9465 Wilshire Blvd, #600, Beverly Hills CA 90212 USA — Cinematographer

Riopelle, Howard
4 Beechmont Crescent, Gloucester ON K1B 4B1, Canada — Ice Hockey Player

Riordan, Michael W (Mike)
140 Inwood Road, Stevensville MD 21666, USA — Basketball Player

Riordan, Richard J
141 N Bristol Ave, Los Angeles CA 90049, USA — Mayor, Los Angeles

Rios Montt, J Efrain
6A Avenida A 3-18 Zona 1, Guatamela City, Guatemala — President, Guatemala; Army General

Rios, Alberto
Arizona State University, English Dept, Tempe AZ 85287, USA — Writer

Rios, Armando
790 Ridenhour Circle, Orlando FL 32809, USA — Baseball Player

Rios, Brandon L
Top Rank Inc, 3908 Howard Hughes Parkway, #580, Las Vegas NV 89169 USA — Boxer

Rios, Daniel (Danny)
2523 W 9th Lane, Hialeah FL 33010, USA — Baseball Player

Rios, Emily
Kass & Stokes Mgmt, 9229 W Sunset Blvd, #504, Los Angeles CA 90069 USA — Actress

Rios, Marcelo
International Mgmt Group, Via Augusta 200, #400, 08021 Barcelona, Spain — Tennis Player

Rios, Mark
Rios Clementi Hale Studios, 639 N Larchmont Blvd, #101, Los Angeles CA 90004, USA — Architect

Rios, Susan
Try Art Galleries, 3100 Porter St, Soquel CA 95073, USA — Artist

Riotta, Vincent
Untitled Entertainment, 350 S Beverly Dr, #200, Beverly Hills CA 90212 USA — Actor

Rioux, Gerry	
213 Grosvenor, Iroquois Falls ON P0K 1G0, Canada	Ice Hockey Player
Ripa, Kelly	
Milojo Productions, 270 Lafayette St, #702, New York NY 10012, USA	Actress, Model
Ripert, Eric	
Le Bernardin, 787 7th Ave, Concourse 1, New York NY 10019, USA	Chef
Ripken, Calvin E (Cal), Jr	
1427 Clarkview Road, #100, Baltimore MD 21209, USA	Baseball Player
Ripken, William O (Bill)	
900 Mount Soma Court, Fallston MD 21047, USA	Baseball Player
Ripley, Alice	
Thruline Entertainment, 9250 Wilshire Blvd, #100, Beverly Hills CA 90212 USA	Actress, Singer
Ripley, Allen S	
50 Dunham St, Attleboro MA 02703, USA	Baseball Player
Rippey, Rodney Allan	
3941 Veselich Ave, #4-251, Los Angeles CA 90039, USA	Actor
Ripple, Kenneth F	
US Court of Appeals, 204 S Main St, South Bend IN 46601, USA	Judge
Rippy, Leon	
Greene Assoc, 1901 Ave of Stars, #130, Los Angeles CA 90067 USA	Actor
Rippy, Nicolas	
Wilhelmina Models, 300 Park Ave S, #200, New York NY 10010 USA	Model
Ris, Hans	
2116 Madison St, Madison WI 53711, USA	Zoologist
RisCassi, Robert W	
Spectrum Group, 11 Canal Center Plaza, #103, Alexandria VA 22314, USA	Army General
Riseborough, Andrea	
Independent Talent Group, Oxford House, 76 Oxford St, London W1D 1BS, England	Actress
Risebrough, Doug	
5809 Schaefer Road, Minneapolis MN 55436, USA	Ice Hockey Player, Coach
Risen, James	
New York Times, Editorial Dept, 229 W 43rd St, New York NY 10036 USA	Journalist
Risien, Cody L	
505 Bulian Lane, Austin TX 78746, USA	Football Player
Riske, David R	
2771 Culloden Ave, Henderson NV 89044, USA	Baseball Player
Risley, William C (Bill)	
1160 Prim Rose Circle, Greenwood AR 72936, USA	Baseball Player
Rison, Andre P	
6293 N Jennings Road, Mount Morris MI 48458, USA	Football Player
Rispoli, Michael	
Principal Entertainment, 130 W 42nd St, #614, New York NY 10036, USA	Actor
Risser, Paul G	
Natural History Museum, Director's Office, PO Box 37012, Washington DC 20013, USA	Educator
Rissling, Gary	
7905 Tilmont Ave, Parkville MD 21234, USA	Ice Hockey Player
Riszdorfer, Michal	
Bratislava Ul M Scho SKP, Trnasvkeho 2/A, 84446 Bratislava, Slovakia	Canoeing Athlete
Riszdorfer, Richard	
Bratislava Ul M Scho SKP, Trnasvkeno 2/A, 84446 Bratislava, Slovakia	Canoeing Athlete
Ritcher, James A (Jim)	
8620 Bournemouth Dr, Raleigh NC 27615, USA	Football Player
Ritchie, Brian	
Good Feelings Artist Mgmt, PO Box 6632, Minneapolis MN 55406, USA	Bassist (Violent Femmes)
Ritchie, Darren	
A P A Talent/Literary Agency, 405 S Beverly Dr, #300, Beverly Hills CA 90212 USA	Actor
Ritchie, Guy	
Creative Artists Agency, 2000 Ave of Stars, #100, Los Angeles CA 90067 USA	Director
Ritchie, Ian	
110 Three Colt St, London E14 8A2, England	Architect
Ritchie, Jay S	
8275 Highway 52, Rockwell NC 28138, USA	Baseball Player
Ritchie, Jill	
Wallman Public Relations, 10323 Santa Monica Blvd, #109, Los Angeles CA 90025, USA	Actress
Ritchie, Jim	
Adelson Galleries, Mark Hotel, 19 E 82nd St, New York NY 10028, USA	Sculptor
Ritchie, John H	
Mount, Heswall, Wirral L60 4RD, England	Architect
Ritchie, Jon D	
2302 Claridge Court, Enola PA 17025, USA	Football Player
Ritchie, Todd E	
114 Hulan Dr, Kerens TX 75144, USA	Baseball Player
Ritchson, Alan	
United Talent Agency, 9336 Civic Center Dr, Beverly Hills CA 90210 USA	Actor
Ritenour, Lee M	
11808 Dorothy St, #108, Los Angeles CA 90049, USA	Jazz Guitarist, Singer, Composer
Ritger, Dick	
804 Valley View Dr, River Falls WI 54022, USA	Bowler
Rittenhouse, Lenore	
295 Bellhaven Dr, Carthage NC 28327, USA	Golfer
Ritter, C Dowd	
AmSouth Bancorp, AmSouth Sonat Tower, 1900 5th Ave N, Birmingham AL 35203, USA	Financier
Ritter, Huntley	
Stafford Films, 9701 Wilshire Blvd, #1000, Beverly Hills CA 90212, USA	Actor
Ritter, Jason	
I C M Partners, 730 5th Ave, New York NY 10019 USA	Actor
Ritter, Josh	
Powerplay, 5434 W Sample Road, PM Box 533, Margate FL 33073, USA	Singer, Songwriter
Ritter, Krysten	
Group Entertainment, 115 West 29th St, #1102, New York NY 10001, USA	Actress
Ritter, Reggie B	
1564 Estep Road, Donaldson AR 71941, USA	Baseball Player
Ritter, Tyson J	
Creative Artists Agency, 2000 Ave of Stars, #100, Los Angeles CA 90067 USA	Singer, Bassist (All-American Rejects)
Rittinger, Al	
5423 Wallace Ave, Delta BC V4M 3V4, Canada	Ice Hockey Player

Ritts, Jim — Golf Executive
Ladies Pro Golf Assn, 100 International Golf Dr, Daytona Beach FL 32124 USA

Ritz, Kevin D — Baseball Player
68559 8th Street Road, Cambridge OH 43725, USA

Ritzman, Alice — Golfer
614 S Foys Lake Dr, Kalispell MT 59901, USA

Riva, Diana-Maria — Actress
Jonas Public Relations, 240 26th St, #3, Santa Monica CA 90402 USA

Riva, Emmanuelle — Actress
Anne Alvares Correa, 34 Rue Jouffroy d'Abbans, 75017 Paris, France

Rivaldo — Soccer Player
F C Milan, Via Filippo Turati 3, 20121 Milan, Italy

Rivas, Daniel Louis — Actor
A P A Talent/Literary Agency, 405 S Beverly Dr, #300, Beverly Hills CA 90212 USA

Rivera Carrera, Norberto Cardinal — Religious Leader
Curia Arzobispal, Aptdo Postal 24-4-33, Mexico City DF 06700, Mexico

Rivera Mendoza, Zuleyka J — Beauty Queen
Miss Universe Organization, 1370 Ave of Americas, #1600, New York NY 10019 USA

Rivera Pedraza, Luis A — Baseball Player
16 Calle Lazaro Ramos, Cidra PR 00739, USA

Rivera, Ana Liz — Actress
Televisa, Blvd A Lopez Mateos 232, Colonia San Angel, DF CP 01060, Mexico

Rivera, Chita — Actress, Singer, Dancer
Shopiro & Lobel, 220 W 42nd St, #1900, New York NY 10036, USA

Rivera, Geraldo — Entertainer
17 Annett Ave, Edgewater NJ 07020, USA

Rivera, Jerry — Singer
P M Talent, 8815 Conroy Windermere Road, #110, Orlando FL 32835, USA

Rivera, Jessica — Opera Singer
I M G Artists, Hogarth Business Park, Chiswick, London W4 2TH, England

Rivera, Jose — Writer, Producer
I C M Partners, 10250 Constellation Blvd, #900, Los Angeles CA 90067 USA

Rivera, Jose Antonio — Boxer
7 Rodi Circle, Worcester MA 01603, USA

Rivera, Manuel J (Jim) — Baseball Player
2311 Abbey Dr, #7, Fort Wayne IN 46835, USA

Rivera, Marco A — Football Player
1854 Rue de Isabelle, Flower Mound TX 75022, USA

Rivera, Mariano — Baseball Player
147 Anderson Hill Road, Purchase NY 10577, USA

Rivera, Michael — Actor
Innovative Artists, 1505 10th St, Santa Monica CA 90401 USA

Rivera, Michael R (Mike) — Baseball Player
2814 Harwood Court, Kissimmee FL 34744, USA

Rivera, Robert — Artist
21 Sandia Lane, Placitas NM 87043, USA

Rivera, Ronald E (Ron) — Football Player, Coach
14420 Rancho del Prado Trail, San Diego CA 92127, USA

Rivero, Jorge — Actor
H David Moss, 733 Seward St, #PH, Los Angeles CA 90038 USA

Rivers, Austin J — Basketball Player
New Orleans Hornets, 1250 Poydras St, #101, New Orleans LA 70113 USA

Rivers, David L — Basketball Player
10509 Greensprings Dr, Tampa FL 33626, USA

Rivers, Glenn A (Doc) — Basketball Player, Coach
5 Isle Of Sicily, Winter Park FL 32789, USA

Rivers, J Milton (Mickey) — Baseball Player
350 NW 48th St, Miami FL 33127, USA

Rivers, Jamie A — Football Player
40 Waterman Place, Saint Louis MO 63112, USA

Rivers, Joan — Entertainer, Comedienne
Larry Thompson Organization, 9663 Santa Monica Blvd, #801, Beverly Hills CA 90210, USA

Rivers, Johnny — Singer, Songwriter
3141 Coldwater Canyon Lane, Beverly Hills CA 90210, USA

Rivers, Keith — Football Player
Cincinnati Bengals, 1 Paul Brown Stadium, Cincinnati OH 45202 USA

Rivers, Marcellus — Football Player
12003 Eden Lane, Frisco TX 75034, USA

Rivers, Melissa — Actress, Producer
Larry Thompson Organization, 9663 Santa Monica Blvd, #801, Beverly Hills CA 90210, USA

Rivers, Philip — Football Player
San Diego Chargers, 4020 Murphy Canyon Road, San Diego CA 92123 USA

Rivers, Reginald C (Reggie) — Football Player
407 Corona St, Denver CO 80218, USA

Rivers, Samuel R (Sam) — Bassist (Limp Bizkit)
Flip/Interscope Records, 8733 Sunset Blvd, #205, West Hollywood CA 90069, USA

Rivers, Wayne — Ice Hockey Player
7736 Cedar Lake Ave, San Diego CA 92119, USA

Rives, Donald E (Don) — Football Player
4910 Oldfield Dr, Arlington TX 76016, USA

Rivest, Ronald L — Computer Scientist
Massachusetts Institute of Technology, Electrical Engineering Dept, Cambridge MA 02139, USA

Rivette, Jacques — Director
Voyez Mon Agent, 20 Ave Rapp, 75007 Paris, France

Riviere, Jean-Max — Composer
6 Rue Choron, 75009 Paris, France

Rivlin, Alice M — Government Official
2842 Chesterfield Place, Washington DC 20008, USA

Rix, J Simon — Bassist (Kaiser Chiefs)
Red Light Mgmt, 8439 Sunset Blvd, West Hollywood CA 90069, USA

Rizzi, Darren — Football Player, Coach
University of Rhode Island, Athletic Dept, Kingston RI 02881, USA

Rizzo, Jerry — Basketball Player
2548 126th St, #1, Flushing NY 11354, USA

Rizzo, Joseph V (Joe) — Football Player
6131 Dorsett Place, Wilmington NC 28403, USA

Rizzo, Patrice (Patti)
1033 NE 17th Way, #2004, Fort Lauderdale FL 33304, USA — Golfer
Rizzo, Pietro
I M G Artists, Hogarth Business Park, Chiswick, London W4 2TH, England — Conductor
Rizzo, Todd M
7 Williamsburg Court, Sewell NJ 08080, USA — Baseball Player
Rizzo, Willy
Paul Smith Gallery, 9 Albermarle St, London W1, England — Photographer, Furniture Designer
Rizzotti, Jennifer
University of Hartford, Athletic Dept, West Hartford CT 06117, USA — Basketball Player, Coach
Rizzuto, Garth
109 13th Ave S, Cranbrook BC B1C 2V6, Canada — Ice Hockey Player
Roa, Joseph R (Joe)
677 E Brickley Ave, Hazel Park MI 48030, USA — Baseball Player
Roach, Jason G
6004 Delaval Lane, Raleigh NC 27614, USA — Baseball Player
Roach, Jay
Everyman Pictures, 3000 W Olympic Blvd, #1500, Santa Monica CA 90404, USA — Director
Roach, John G
4101 San Carlos St, Dallas TX 75205, USA — Football Player
Roach, Melvin E (Mel)
4131 Southhaven Road, Richmond VA 23235, USA — Baseball Player
Roach, Steve
Hearts of Space, PO Box 5916, Sausalito CA 94966, USA — Musician
Roache, Linus
I C M Partners, 10250 Constellation Blvd, #900, Los Angeles CA 90067 USA — Actor
Roaches, Carl E
1314 Twining Oaks Lane, Missouri City. TX 77489, USA — Football Player
Roaf, William L (Willie)
208 Cypress Bayou Lane, Kenner LA 70065, USA — Football Player
Roan, Michael P
11275 Green Valley Road, Sebastopol CA 95472, USA — Football Player
Roan, Oscar B, III
9 Pringle Lane, Rockwall TX 75087, USA — Football Player
Roark, Terry P
1752 Edward Dr, Laramie WY 82072, USA — Educator
Roarke, Michael T (Mike)
940 Quaker Lane, #2302, East Greenwich RI 02818, USA — Baseball Player
Robards, Karen
Pocket Books, 1230 Ave of Americas, New York NY 10020 USA — Writer
Robards, Sam
Paradigm Agency, 360 N Crescent Dr, North Building, Beverly Hills CA 90210 USA — Actor
Robb, AnnaSophia
Creative Artists Agency, 2000 Ave of Stars, #100, Los Angeles CA 90067 USA — Actress
Robb, Charles S
George Mason University, Law School, 3301 N Fairfax Dr, Arlington VA 22201, USA — Governor, Senator, VA
Robb, David
Hobson's International, 62 Chiswick High Road, London W4 1SY, England — Actor
Robb, Douglas (Doug)
Creative Artists Agency, 2000 Ave of Stars, #100, Los Angeles CA 90067 USA — Singer (Hoobastank)
Robb, Peter
Bloomsbury Publishing, 36 Soho Square, London W1D 3Q4, England — Writer
Robb, Walter L
1358 Ruffner Road, Schenectady NY 12309, USA — Businessman, Inventor
Robbie, Margot
Creative Artists Agency, 2000 Ave of Stars, #100, Los Angeles CA 90067 USA — Actress
Robbins, Austin D
4627 Hilltop Terrace SE, Washington DC 20019, USA — Football Player
Robbins, Barret G
25773 Perlman Place, #B, Stevenson Ranch CA 91381, USA — Football Player
Robbins, Brian
Varsity Pictures, 1040 N Las Palmas Ave, Building 2, Los Angeles CA 90038, USA — Director, Producer, Actor
Robbins, Deanna
630 N Keystone St, Burbank CA 91506, USA — Actress
Robbins, Jake
14208 Castle Abbey Lane, Charlotte NC 28277, USA — Baseball Player
Robbins, James E (Tootie)
3600 W Ray Road, #1031, Chandler AZ 85226, USA — Football Player
Robbins, Jane
Scott Marshall Mgmt, 44 Perry Road, London W3 7NA, England — Actress
Robbins, Kelly
1025 Lincoln Dr, Weidman MI 48893, USA — Golfer
Robbins, Randy
583 E Palo Verde St, Casa Grande AZ 85122, USA — Football Player
Robbins, Tim
Actor's Gang, 9070 Venice Blvd, Culver City CA 90232, USA — Actor, Director
Robbins, Tom
PO Box 338, La Conner WA 98257, USA — Writer
Robbins, Tony
Jennifer Martinez, 9888 Carroll Centre Road, #100, San Diego CA 92126, USA — Writer
Robelot, Jane
CBS-TV, News Dept, 51 W 52nd St, New York NY 10019 USA — Commentator
Roberge, Bertrand R (Bert)
267 Sunderland Dr, Auburn ME 04210, USA — Baseball Player
Roberge, Kalyna
Speed Skating Canada, 2781 Lancaster Road, #402, Ottawa ON K1B 1A7, Canada — Speed Skater
Roberson, Antoinette
Diva Central, 7510 W Sunset Blvd, #1445, Los Angeles CA 90046 USA — Singer, Songwriter, Record Producer
Roberson, James W
PO Box 121013, Big Bear Lake CA 92315, USA — Cinematographer
Roberson, Rick
635 W West Ave, Fullerton CA 92832, USA — Basketball Player
Robert, Alain (Spiderman)
Maverick House Publishing, Dunboyne Business Park, Dunboyne, County Meath, Ireland — Rock, Urban Climber
Robert, Jacques F
14 Villa Saint-Georges, 92160 Antony, France — Attorney, Educator

R

Robert, Rene P 8-5490 Glen Erin Dr, Mississauga ON L5M 5R4, Canada	Ice Hockey Player
Roberto, Phillip J (Phil) 5238 Ottawa Ave, Niagara Falls ON L2E 4Y8, Canada	Ice Hockey Player
Roberts, Alfredo 4001 Tolbert Place, Carmel IN 46074, USA	Football Player
Roberts, Ashley A K A Talent, 6310 San Vicente Blvd, #200, Los Angeles CA 90048 USA	Singer (Pussycat Dolls), Actress
Roberts, Bernard Uwchlaw'r Coed, Llanbedr, Gwynedd LL45 2NA, Wales	Concert Pianist
Roberts, Bradley K (Brad) Agency Group Ltd, 142 W 57th St, #600, New York NY 10019 USA	Singer, Guitarist (Crash Test Dummies)
Roberts, Brian L Comcast Corp, 1500 Market St, #800W, Philadelphia PA 19102, USA	Businessman
Roberts, Brian M 11326 E Mimosa Dr, Scottsdale AZ 85262, USA	Baseball Player
Roberts, Bruce Gorfaine/Schwartz, 4111 W Alameda Ave, #509, Burbank CA 91505 USA	Singer, Songwriter
Roberts, Cecil United Mine Workers, 8315 Lee Highway, #500, Fairfax VA 22031, USA	Labor Leader
Roberts, Corrine (Cokie) 5315 Bradley Blvd, Bethesda MD 20814, USA	Commentator
Roberts, Craig W M E Entertainment, 9601 Wilshire Blvd, #300, Beverly Hills CA 90210 USA	Actor
Roberts, Dallas Dontanville/Frattaroli Mgmt, 315 S Beverly Dr, #201, Beverly Hills CA 90212, USA	Actor
Roberts, Dan Agency Group Ltd, 142 W 57th St, #600, New York NY 10019 USA	Bassist (Crash Test Dummies)
Roberts, David (Dave) 14310 SW 73rd Ave, Archer FL 32618, USA	Track Athlete
Roberts, David L (Dave) 43690 Algonquin Dr, #26, Novi MI 48375, USA	Ice Hockey Player
Roberts, David L (Dave) 9705 Sam Bass Trail, Keller TX 76244, USA	Baseball Player
Roberts, David R (Dave) 1208 Crestview Dr, Cardiff by the Sea CA 92007, USA	Baseball Player
Roberts, David W (Dave) 6937 Laurel Valley Dr, Fort Worth TX 76132, USA	Baseball Player
Roberts, Dee 2012 N 19th St, Boise ID 83702, USA	Artist
Roberts, Doris 6225 Quebec Dr, Los Angeles CA 90068, USA	Actress
Roberts, Emma R Sweeney Entertainment, 6253 Hollywood Blvd, #201, Los Angeles CA 90028 90028, USA	Actress, Singer
Roberts, Eric A Triple E Management, 20750 Ventura Blvd, #342, Woodland Hills CA 91364, USA	Actor
Roberts, Eugene L, Jr New York Times, Editorial Dept, 229 W 43rd St, New York NY 10036, USA	Editor
Roberts, Frederick C (Fred) 463 Knight Circle, Alpine UT 84004, USA	Basketball Player
Roberts, Gary 2095 Lake Shore Blvd, Toronto ON M8V 4G4, Canada	Ice Hockey Player
Roberts, Gene University of Maryland, Journalism Dept, College Park MD 20742, USA	Editor, Historian
Roberts, Gordon R 445 Ward-Koebel Road, Oregonia OH 45054, USA	Vietnam War Army Hero (CMH)
Roberts, Ian W M E Entertainment, 9601 Wilshire Blvd, #300, Beverly Hills CA 90210 USA	Actor
Roberts, Jake (The Snake) Prince Marketing Group, 18 Carillon Circle, Livingston NJ 07039 USA	Professional Wrestler
Roberts, James A (Jim) 137 Ridgecrest Dr, Chesterfield MO 63017, USA	Ice Hockey Player, Coach
Roberts, John Creative Artists Agency, 2000 Ave of Stars, #100, Los Angeles CA 90067 USA	Director
Roberts, John CBS-TV, News Dept, 51 W 52nd St, New York NY 10019 USA	Commentator
Roberts, John US Supreme Court, 1st St NE, Washington DC 20543, USA	Chief Justice, Supreme Court
Roberts, John D California Institute of Technology, Crellin Laboratory, Pasadena CA 91125, USA	Chemist
Roberts, John D (J D) 6708 Trevi Court, Oklahoma City OK 73116, USA	Football Player, Coach
Roberts, Jonathan Abrams Artists, 9200 W Sunset Blvd, #1125, West Hollywood CA 90069 USA	Dancer
Roberts, Jordan Creative Artists Agency, 2000 Ave of Stars, #100, Los Angeles CA 90067 USA	Director, Writer, Actor
Roberts, Joseph (Joe) 10975 Elvessa St, Oakland CA 94605, USA	Basketball Player
Roberts, Julia Creative Artists Agency, 2000 Ave of Stars, #100, Los Angeles CA 90067 USA	Actress
Roberts, Julie Mercury Records, 54 Music Square E, #300, Nashville TN 37203, USA	Singer
Roberts, Kenny K R Marketing, 419 Medina Road, Medina OH 44256, USA	Motorcycle Racing Rider
Roberts, Kevin J Saatchi & Saatchi Worldwide, 375 Hudson St, Basement 3, New York NY 10014, USA	Businessman
Roberts, Larry PO Box 663, Bandon OR 97411, USA	Sculptor
Roberts, Lawrence G Caspian Networks, 170 Baytech Dr, San Jose CA 95134, USA	Computer Scientist
Roberts, Leon J (Bip) PO Box 170299, Arlington TX 76003, USA	Baseball Player
Roberts, Leon K 4711 Chapel Springs Court, Arlington TX 76017, USA	Baseball Player
Roberts, Leonard Luber Rocklin Entertainment, 8530 Wilshire Blvd, #555, Beverly Hills CA 90211 USA	Actor

Roberts, Loren 8429 Orchard Hill Dr, Germantown TN 38138, USA	Golfer
Roberts, Lynn 42 Vespers Way, Okatie SC 29909, USA	Singer, Actress
Roberts, M Brigitte Gillon Atkin, 29 Fernshaw Road, London SW10 0TG, England	Writer
Roberts, Marcus R C A Records, 8750 Wilshire Blvd, Beverly Hills CA 90211 USA	Jazz Pianist
Roberts, Marvin J (Marv) 6202 Carriage Gate Lane SE, Mableton GA 30126, USA	Basketball Player
Roberts, Michele Henry Holt, 175 5th Ave, #400, New York NY 10010 USA	Writer
Roberts, Nicola M Concorde International, 101 Shepherds Bush Road, London W6 7LP, England	Singer (Girls Aloud)
Roberts, Nora 19239 Burnside Bridge Road, Keedysville MD 21756, USA	Writer
Roberts, Patricia (Trish) 218 Carver Dr, Monroe GA 30655, USA	Basketball Player
Roberts, Paul H PO Box 951567, Los Angeles CA 90095, USA	Mathematician
Roberts, R Michael 2213 Hominy Branch Court, Columbia MO 65201, USA	Animal Scientist
Roberts, Richard J New England Biolabs, 240 County Road, Ipswich MA 01938, USA	Nobel Medicine Laureate
Roberts, Richard L Oral Roberts University, President's Office, 7777 S Lewis Ave, Tulsa OK 74171, USA	Educator
Roberts, Rick Gary Goddard Agency, 10 Sainte Mary's St, #305, Toronto ON M4Y 5QD, Canada	Actor
Roberts, Robin ESPN-TV, ESPN Plaza, 935 Middle St, Bristol CT 06010 USA	Sportscaster, Commentator
Roberts, Ryan A 6017 Avalon St, North Richland Hills TX 76180, USA	Baseball Player
Roberts, Sam Agency Group Ltd, 142 W 57th St, #600, New York NY 10019 USA	Singer
Roberts, Shawn Gersh Agency, 9465 Wilshire Blvd, #600, Beverly Hills CA 90212 USA	Actor
Roberts, Stanley C 1192 Congaree Road, Hopkins SC 29061, USA	Basketball Player
Roberts, Stephen I M G Artists, Hogarth Business Park, Chiswick, London W4 2TH, England	Opera Singer
Roberts, Tanya Good Guy Entertainment, 3733 Oakfield Dr, Sherman Oaks CA 91423, USA	Actress
Roberts, Tiffany 2772 Ascot Dr, San Ramon CA 94583, USA	Soccer Player
Roberts, Tony 970 Park Ave, #8N, New York NY 10028, USA	Actor
Roberts, Walter (Walt) 268 Kenbrook Circle, San Jose CA 95111, USA	Football Player
Roberts, William H (Bill) 18520 NW 67th Ave, #141, Hialeah FL 33015, USA	Football Player
Roberts, Willis A 11501 Harts Road, Jacksonville FL 32218, USA	Baseball Player
Roberts, Xavier PO Box 1438, Cleveland GA 30528, USA	Businessman, Doll Designer
Robertson of Port Ellen, George I M House of Lords, Westminster, London SW1A 0PW, England	Government Official, England
Robertson, Alvin C 2919 Biering Peak, San Antonio TX 78247, USA	Basketball Player
Robertson, Andre L 2229 Cross Lane, Orange TX 77630, USA	Baseball Player
Robertson, Belinda B R Cashmere, 22 Palmerston Place, Edinburgh EH12 5AL, Scotland	Fashion Designer
Robertson, Brittany (Britt) Innovative Artists, 1505 10th St, Santa Monica CA 90401 USA	Actress
Robertson, Dale PO Box 850707, Yukon OK 73085, USA	Actor
Robertson, Daryl B 52 Princeton Dr, Midvale UT 84047, USA	Baseball Player
Robertson, David Opus 3 Artists, 470 Park Ave S, #900N, New York NY 10016 USA	Conductor
Robertson, David A New York Yankees, Yankee Stadium, E 161st St & River Ave, Bronx NY 10451 USA	Baseball Player
Robertson, Davis Joffrey Ballet, 70 E Lake St, #1300, Chicago IL 60601, USA	Dancer
Robertson, DeWayne 26 Green St, Newbury MA 01951, USA	Football Player
Robertson, Donald A (Don) 5715 W Monte Vista Road, Phoenix AZ 85035, USA	Baseball Player
Robertson, Ed Nettwerk Mgmt, 6525 W Sunset Blvd, #800, Los Angeles CA 90028 USA	Guitarist (Barenaked Ladies), Songwriter
Robertson, Finlay Independent Talent Group, Oxford House, 76 Oxford St, London W1D 1BS, England	Actor
Robertson, Geordie 1 Scarborough Park, Rochester NY 14625, USA	Ice Hockey Player
Robertson, Isiah B 906 Mill Spring Dr, Garland TX 75040, USA	Football Player
Robertson, Jenny Shelter Entertainment, 9454 Wilshire Blvd, #715, Beverly Hills CA 90212 USA	Actress
Robertson, Joseph E, Jr Oregon Health Science University, President's Office, Portland OR 97201, USA	Ophthalmologist, Educator
Robertson, Kathleen Untitled Entertainment, 350 S Beverly Dr, #200, Beverly Hills CA 90212 USA	Actress
Robertson, Kimmy Innovative Artists, 1505 10th St, Santa Monica CA 90401 USA	Actress
Robertson, Leslie E 100 Riverside Blvd, #18D, New York NY 10069, USA	Structural Engineer

R

Roberts - Robertson

R

Robertson, M G (Pat) — Evangelist
Christian Broadcast Network, 100 Centerville Turnpike, Virginia Beach VA 23463, USA

Robertson, Marcus A — Football Player
3320 Spinnaker Lane, #18C, Detroit MI 48207, USA

Robertson, Mike — Snowboarding Athlete
Snowboard Federation, 301-333 Terminal Avenue, Vancouver BC V6A 4C1, Canada

Robertson, Nathan D (Nate) — Baseball Player
7918 W 53rd St N, Maize KS 67101, USA

Robertson, Oscar P — Basketball Player
621 Tusculum Ave, Cincinnati OH 45226, USA

Robertson, Richard P (Rich) — Baseball Player
1201 Crescent Terrace, Sunnyvale CA 94087, USA

Robertson, Richard W (Rich) — Baseball Player
32202 Sandwedge Dr, Waller TX 77484, USA

Robertson, Robbie — Singer, Guitarist (Band); Songwriter
Special Artists Agency, 9465 Wilshire Blvd, #820, Beverly Hills CA 90212 USA

Robertson, Robert E (Bob) — Baseball Player
10015 Shinnamon Dr SW, Cumberland MD 21502, USA

Robertson, Ruth — Artist, Photographer
602 3rd St, Herndon VA 20170, USA

Robertson, Shirley A — Yachtswoman
Lynx Sports Mgmt, Lymington Road, Lymington, Hampshire SO41 5S5, England

Roberts-Smith, Benjamin — Afghanistan War Air Hero (VC)
Victoria Cross Assn, Old Admiralty Building, London SW1A 2BL, England

Robes, Ernest C (Bill) — Ski Jumper
3 Mile Road, Etna NH 03750, USA

Robey, Frederick R (Rick) — Basketball Player
2108 Club Vista Place, Louisville KY 40245, USA

Robidoux, William J (Billy Joe) — Baseball Player
2 King George Dr, Ware MA 01082, USA

Robillard, Duke — Guitarist, Orchestra Leader
Rosebud Agency, PO Box 170429, San Francisco CA 94117 USA

Robin, Cynthia — Archaeologist
Northwestern University, Anthropology Dept, 1812 Hillman, Evanston IL 60208, USA

Robin, Muriel — Actress
Voyez Mon Agent, 20 Ave Rapp, 75007 Paris, France

Robinowitz, Joseph R — Editor, Publisher
TV Guide, Editorial Dept, 100 Matsonford Road, Wayne PA 19080, USA

Robins, Craig — Businessman
Dacra Development Corp, 3841 NE 2nd Ave, #400, Miami FL 33137, USA

Robins, Laila — Actress
Paradigm Agency, 360 N Crescent Dr, North Building, Beverly Hills CA 90210 USA

Robinson Peete, Holly — Actress
Innovative Artists, 1505 10th St, Santa Monica CA 90401 USA

Robinson, Alex J — Singer, Songwriter
Agency Group Ltd, 142 W 57th St, #600, New York NY 10019 USA

Robinson, Alexia — Actress
Heylee Winters Assoc, 8491 W Sunset Blvd, #268, West Hollywood CA 90069, USA

Robinson, Andrew J — Actor
2671 Byron Place, Los Angeles CA 90046, USA

Robinson, Ann — Actress
1357 Elysian Park Dr, Los Angeles CA 90026, USA

Robinson, Anne — Entertainer
Penrose Media, 19 Victoria Grove, London W8 5RW, England

Robinson, Brooks C — Baseball Player
9210 Baltimore National Pike, Ellicot MD 21042, USA

Robinson, Bruce — Writer, Actor, Director
Paradigm Agency, 360 N Crescent Dr, North Building, Beverly Hills CA 90210 USA

Robinson, Bruce P — Baseball Player
1310 Dellcrest Lane, La Jolla CA 92037, USA

Robinson, Bumper — Actor
Collective, 8383 Wilshire Blvd, #1050, Beverly Hills CA 90211 USA

Robinson, Charles — Actor
Stone Manners Salners, 9911 W Pico Blvd, #1400, Los Angeles CA 90035 USA

Robinson, Chip — Auto Racing Driver
3034 Lake Forest Dr, Augusta GA 30909, USA

Robinson, Chris — Actor
Daniel Hoff Agency, 5455 Wilshire Blvd, #1100, Los Angeles CA 90036, USA

Robinson, Christopher M (Chris) — Singer, Guitarist (Black Crowes)
Angelus Entertainment, 16000 Ventura Blvd, #600, Encino CA 91436, USA

Robinson, Clarence (Arnie) — Track Athlete
2904 Ocean View Blvd, San Diego CA 92113, USA

Robinson, Clifford R — Basketball Player
702 Sandia Place, Franklin Lakes NJ 07417, USA

Robinson, Clifford T (Cliff) — Basketball Player
98 S Bardsbrook Circle, Spring TX 77382, USA

Robinson, Craig — Actor, Comedian
3 Arts Entertainment, 9460 Wilshire Blvd, #700, Beverly Hills CA 90212 USA

Robinson, Craig G — Baseball Player
648 Picketts Mill Dr, Shreveport LA 71115, USA

Robinson, David M — Basketball Player
PO Box 691207, San Antonio TX 78269, USA

Robinson, Dawn S — Singer (En Vogue, Lucy Pearl)
Creative Artists Agency, 2000 Ave of Stars, #100, Los Angeles CA 90067 USA

Robinson, Don A — Baseball Player
1215 86th Court NW, Bradenton FL 34209, USA

Robinson, Doug — Ice Hockey Player
6 Tiffany Court, Saint Catherines ON L2M 7N3, Canada

Robinson, E Rafael — Football Player
4312 Forest Hill Circle, Forest Hill TX 76140, USA

Robinson, Eddie J — Football Player
6315 E Mystic Meadow, Houston TX 77021, USA

Robinson, Emily Erwin — Singer (Dixie Chicks); Songwriter
Strategic Artists Mgmt, 1100 Glendon Ave, #1100, Los Angeles CA 90024, USA

Robinson, Fatima — Dancer, Choreographer, Video Director
PO Box 833, 8306 Wilshire Blvd, Beverly Hills CA 90213, USA

Robinson, Floyd A
PO Box 152419, San Diego CA 92195, USA — Baseball Player

Robinson, Flynn J
11875 Manor Dr, #1, Hawthorne CA 90250, USA — Basketball Player

Robinson, Frank
15557 Aqua Verde Dr, Los Angeles CA 90077, USA — Baseball Player, Manager

Robinson, Fred C
Yale University, English Dept, New Haven CT 06520, USA — Educator

Robinson, Gerald
4708 Scarborough Place, Stone Mountain GA 30087, USA — Football Player

Robinson, Glenn
Franklin & Marshall College, Athletic Dept, Lancaster PA 17604, USA — Basketball Coach

Robinson, Ivan
140 W Roselyn St, Philadelphia PA 19120, USA — Boxer

Robinson, Jackie
130 W Harcourt St, Long Beach CA 90805, USA — Basketball Player

Robinson, James P (Jimmy)
4326 Fox Hollow Court, Oneida WI 54155, USA — Football Player

Robinson, Janice
Flavor Unit Entertainment, 119 Washington Ave, Miami Beach FL 33139, USA — Singer (Livin' Joy)

Robinson, Jay
13757 Milbank Ave, Sherman Oaks CA 91423, USA — Actor

Robinson, Jeffrey D (Jeff)
27 Weber Lane, Trabuco Canyon CA 92679, USA — Baseball Player

Robinson, Jeffrey M (Jeff)
2103 Monarch Ridge Dr, El Cajon CA 92019, USA — Baseball Player

Robinson, Jeffrey W (Jeff)
1020 W Ruffner St, Seattle WA 98119, USA — Football Player

Robinson, Jerry D
2398 Julio Lane, Santa Rosa CA 95401, USA — Football Player

Robinson, John
Paradigm Agency, 360 N Crescent Dr, North Building, Beverly Hills CA 90210 USA — Actor

Robinson, John A
1513 Village View Road, Encinitas CA 92024, USA — Football Coach

Robinson, Johnny N
3209 S Grand St, Monroe LA 71202, USA — Football Player

Robinson, Keith D
Collective, 8383 Wilshire Blvd, #1050, Beverly Hills CA 90211 USA — Actor, Singer

Robinson, Ken
Washington Speakers Bureau, 1663 Prince St, Alexandria VA 22314, USA — Educator

Robinson, Kerry K
133 Vlasis Dr, Ballwin MO 63011, USA — Baseball Player

Robinson, Koren
109 Hasselwood Dr, Cary NC 27518, USA — Football Player

Robinson, Larry
10709 Winding Stream Way, Bradenton FL 34212, USA — Ice Hockey Player, Coach

Robinson, Laura
Henderson/Hogan, 850 7th Ave, #1003, New York NY 10019 USA — Actress

Robinson, Laurent
Jacksonville Jaguars, 1 AllTel Stadium Place, Jacksonville FL 32202 USA — Football Player

Robinson, Marcus A
PO Box 1924, Fort Valley GA 31030, USA — Football Player

Robinson, Marilynne
University of Iowa, Iowa Writers' Workshop, Dey House, Iowa City IA 52242, USA — Writer

Robinson, Mark L
303 Pennsylvania Ave, Palm Harbor FL 34683, USA — Football Player

Robinson, Mary T W
Aras an Uachtarain, Phoenix Park, Dublin 8, Ireland — President, Ireland

Robinson, Matthew (Matt)
M C S Agency, 47 Dean St, London W1D 5BE, England — Director, Producer

Robinson, Matthew G (Matt)
12374 Mandarin Road, Jacksonville FL 32223, USA — Football Player

Robinson, Melvin D (Bo)
PO Box 2323, Coppell TX 75019, USA — Football Player

Robinson, Morris
Opus 3 Artists, 470 Park Ave S, #900N, New York NY 10016 USA — Singer

Robinson, Nathaniel C (Nate)
Chicago Bulls, United Center, 1901 W Madison St, Chicago IL 60612 USA — Basketball Player

Robinson, Nick
Savage Agency, 6212 Banner Ave, Los Angeles CA 90038 USA — Actor

Robinson, Nicole
Stone Manners Salners, 9911 W Pico Blvd, #1400, Los Angeles CA 90035 USA — Actress

Robinson, Oliver L
9640 Eastpointe Circle, Birmingham AL 35217, USA — Basketball Player

Robinson, Patrick
Harper Collins Publishers, 10 E 53rd St, Cellar 1, New York NY 10022 USA — Writer

Robinson, Patrick
Gap Inc, 2 Folsom St, San Francisco CA 94105, USA — Fashion Designer

Robinson, Paul H
1303 W 26th St, Safford AZ 85546, USA — Football Player

Robinson, Phil Alden
Academy of Motion Picture Arts & Sciences, 8949 Wilshire Blvd, Beverly Hills CA 90211, USA — Director, Writer

Robinson, R David (Dave)
406 S Rose Blvd, Akron OH 44320, USA — Football Player

Robinson, Randall
African American Registry, PO Box 19441, Minneapolis MN 55419, USA — Social Activist, Writer

Robinson, Rich
Angelus Entertainment, 16000 Ventura Blvd, #600, Encino CA 91436, USA — Guitarist (Black Crowes), Songwriter

Robinson, Rob
23466 Greening Dr, Novi MI 48375, USA — Ice Hockey Player

Robinson, Ronald D (Ron)
3128 E Race Ave, Visalia CA 93292, USA — Baseball Player

Robinson, Ronnie
4169 S Germantown Road, Memphis TN 38125, USA — Basketball Player

Robinson, Shawna
Performance One, 545 Pitts School Road NW, #C, Concord NC 28027, USA — Auto, Truck Racing Driver

Robinson, Shelton D
18725 20th Dr SE, Bothell WA 98012, USA — Football Player

Robinson, Smokey
Public Relations Partners, 12702 Landale St, Studio City CA 91604, USA — Singer, Songwriter

Robinson, Stephen K
2405 Airline Dr, Friendswood TX 77546, USA — Astronaut

Robinson, Thomas E
Sacramento Kings, Arco Arena, 1 Sports Parkway, Sacramento CA 95834 USA — Basketball Player

Robinson, Todd
Paradigm Agency, 360 N Crescent Dr, North Building, Beverly Hills CA 90210 USA — Director, Writer

Robinson, Tony
Kate Feast, Primrose Hill Studios, Fitzroy Road, London NW1 8TR, England — Actor

Robinson, Twyla
Columbia Artists Mgmt Inc, 1790 Broadway, #702, New York NY 10019 USA — Opera Singer

Robinson, V Gene
Diocesan House, 63 Green St, Concord NH 03301, USA — Religious Leader

Robinson, W Dunta
485 Vincent Dr, Athens GA 30607, USA — Football Player

Robinson, W Edward (Eddie)
6104 Cholla Dr, Fort Worth TX 76112, USA — Baseball Player

Robinson, Wayne L
2341 Main Highway, Breaux Bridge LA 70517, USA — Football Player

Robinson, Wendy Raquel
TalentWorks, 3500 W Olive Ave, #1400, Burbank CA 91505 USA — Actress

Robinson, Zuleikha
Gersh Agency, 41 Madison Ave, #3301, New York NY 10010 USA — Actress

Robisch, David G (Dave)
1401 Guemes Court, Springfield IL 62702, USA — Basketball Player

Robiskie, Terry J
333 Las Olas Way, #910, Fort Lauderdale FL 33301, USA — Football Player, Coach

Robison, Bruce
Artist Envoy Agency, 1016 16th Ave S, #101, Nashville TN 37212, USA — Singer, Songwriter

Robison, Charlie
Steve Hoiberg Organization, 864 Pinnacle Hill Road, Kingston Springs TN 37082, USA — Singer, Songwriter

Robison, Paula
Musicians Corporate Mgmt, PO Box 825, Highland NY 12528, USA — Concert Flutist

Robitaille, Luc
1750 14th St, #D, Santa Monica CA 90404, USA — Ice Hockey Player, Executive

Robitaille, Mike
121 Ransom Oaks Dr, East Amherst NY 14051, USA — Ice Hockey Player

Robitaille, Pat
Agency Group Ltd, 142 W 57th St, #600, New York NY 10019 USA — Singer, Songwriter

Robitaille, Randy
632 Seyton Dr, Nepean ON K2H 7X5, Canada — Ice Hockey Player

Robles Ortega, Francisco Cardinal
Apartado 7, Zuazva 1100, Monterrey NL 64000, Mexico — Religious Leader

Robles, Marisa
38 Luttrell Ave, London SW15 6PE, England — Concert Harpist

Robles, Mike
I C M Partners, 10250 Constellation Blvd, #900, Los Angeles CA 90067 USA — Actor, Comedian, Producer

Robson, Bryan
Middlesbrough F C, Riverside Stadium, Middlebrough TS3 6RS, England — Soccer Player

Robson, Thomas J (Tom)
7331 W Morrow Dr, Glendale AZ 85308, USA — Baseball Player

Robuchon, Joel
Societe de Gestion Culinaire, 67 Blvd Gen M Valin, 75015 Paris, France — Chef

Robyn
D E F Mgmt, 51 Lonsdale Road, Queens Park, London NW6 6RA, England — Singer

Rocard, Michel L L
Hotel de Ville, 63 Rue M Berteaux, 78700 Conflans-Sainte-Honorine, France — Prime Minister, France

Rocca, Constantino
Golf Products International, 5719 Lake Lindero Dr, Agoura Hills CA 91301, USA — Golfer

Rocca, Maurice A (Mo)
Gersh Agency, 9465 Wilshire Blvd, #600, Beverly Hills CA 90212 USA — Actor, Comedian, Writer

Rocca, Patrick
Artmedia, 20 Ave Rapp, 75007 Paris, France — Actor

Rocca, Peter
534 Hazel Ave, San Bruno CA 94066, USA — Swimmer

Rocchigiani, Ralf
Rocky's Gym, Grabenstr 200A, 47057 Duisburg, Germany — Boxer

Rocco Yim
38/F A I A Tower, 183 Electric Road, North Point, Hong Kong SAR, China — Architect

Rocco, Alex
Sovereign Talent Group, 10474 S Santa Monica Blvd, #301, Los Angeles CA 90025, USA — Actor

Rocco, Rinaldo
Cristiano Cucchini Mgmt, Lungotevere del Mellini 10, 00193 Rome, Italy — Actor

Rocha, John
12-13 Temple Lane, Dublin 2, Ireland — Fashion Designer

Roche, Alden S, Jr
1082 Farragut St, New Orleans LA 70114, USA — Football Player

Roche, Anthony D (Tony)
5 Kapiti St, Saint Ives NSW 2075, Australia — Tennis Player

Roche, E Kevin
Roche Dinkeloo Assoc, 20 Davis St, Hamden CT 06517, USA — Pritzker Architectural Laureate

Roche, John M
191 Clayton Lane, #303, Denver CO 80206, USA — Basketball Player

Rochefort, Jean
Le Chene Rogneaux, 078125 Grosvre, France — Actress

Rochefort, Julien
Artmedia, 20 Ave Rapp, 75007 Paris, France — Actor

Rochefort, Leon J F
1661 Rue Notre Dame, Sainte Marthe du Cap QC G8T 4J9, Canada — Ice Hockey Player

Rochefort, Normand
7704 Camminare Dr, Sarasota FL 34238, USA — Ice Hockey Player

Rochelle, Michael D
Deputy CofS Manpower & Personnel, HqUSA, Pentagon, Washington DC 20310, USA — Army General

R

Rocher, Guy
4911 Chemin de la Cote-des-Neiges, #409, Montreal QC H3V 1H7, Canada — Sociologist

Rochester, Paul G
9209 Sweet Berry Dr, Jacksonville FL 32256, USA — Football Player

Rochford, Michael J (Mike)
5185 Cougars Prowl, Lake Worth FL 33449, USA — Baseball Player

Rochon, Lela
Brillstein Entertainment Partners, 9150 Wilshire Blvd, #350, Beverly Hills CA 90212 USA — Actress

Rock, Angela
4771 Vista Lane, San Diego CA 92116, USA — Volleyball Player

Rock, Antonio (Tony)
Bleu Entertainment, 4935 Whitsett Ave, #8, Valley Village CA 91607, USA — Actor, Comedian

Rock, Chris
I C M Partners, 10250 Constellation Blvd, #900, Los Angeles CA 90067 USA — Actor, Comedian, Director

Rock, Pete
Reach Global, 3500 Rose Crest Lane, Fairfax VA 22033 USA — Rap Artist

Rock, Walter W (Walt)
1030 Highams Court, Woodbridge VA 22191, USA — Football Player

Rockburne, Dorothea G
140 Grand St, #2WF, New York NY 10013, USA — Artist, Sculptor

Rockefeller, David
1 Chase Manhattan Plaza, New York NY 10005, USA — Financier

Rockefeller, James S
425 Park Ave, New York NY 10022, USA — Financier

Rockell
T-Best Talent Agency, 508 Honey Lake Court, Danville CA 94506 USA — Singer, Songwriter

Rocker, John L
1223 Manor Oaks Court, Atlanta GA 30338, USA — Baseball Player

Rocker, Lee
Susan Blond Inc, 50 W 57th St, #1400, New York NY 10019 USA — Bassist (Stray Cats)

Rocker, Tracy Q
1792 Northumberland Dr, Brentwood TN 37027, USA — Football Player

Rockett, Patrick E (Pat)
17107 Eagle Hollow Dr, San Antonio TX 78248, USA — Baseball Player

Rockett, Richard A (Rikki)
Front Line Mgmt, 1100 Glendon Ave, #2000, Los Angeles CA 90024 USA — Drummer (Poison)

Rockette, Joannie
International Management Group, 767 5th Ave, #4500, New York NY 10153, USA — Figure Skater

Rockwell, David
Rockwell Group, 5 Union Square W, New York NY 10003, USA — Architect

Rockwell, Martha
Dartmouth College, PO Box 9, Hanover NH 03755, USA — Skier, Coach

Rockwell, Sam
Arcieri Assoc, 305 Madison Ave, #2315, New York NY 10165 USA — Actor

Rodan, Jay
Brillstein Entertainment Partners, 9150 Wilshire Blvd, #350, Beverly Hills CA 90212 USA — Actor

Rodas, Richard M (Rick)
6877 Bergano Place, Rancho Cucamonga CA 91701, USA — Baseball Player

Rodat, Robert
Gersh Agency, 9465 Wilshire Blvd, #600, Beverly Hills CA 90212 USA — Producer, Writer

Roday, James
Principal Entertainment, 1964 Westwood Blvd, #400, Los Angeles CA 90025 USA — Actor

Rodd, Marcia
12315 Tiara St, Valley Village CA 91607, USA — Actress

Roddam, Francis G (Franc)
Independent Talent Group, Oxford House, 76 Oxford St, London W1D 1BS, England — Director

Roddick, Andrew S (Andy)
140 Shermans Mill Dr, Ingram TX 78025, USA — Tennis Player

Rode, Franc Cardinal
Consecrated Life Institutes, Piazza del Uffizio 11, 00193 Rome, Italy — Religious Leader

Roden, Karel
W M E Entertainment, 9601 Wilshire Blvd, #300, Beverly Hills CA 90210 USA — Actor

Rodenhauser, Mark T
1451 Charlotte Highway, York SC 29745, USA — Football Player

Rodenheiser, Richard P (Dick)
186 State St, Framingham MA 01702, USA — Ice Hockey Player

Roderick, Brande
Prince Marketing Group, 18 Carillon Circle, Livingston NJ 07039 USA — Model, Actress

Rodger, Kate
J K A Talent Agency, 12725 Ventura Blvd, #H, Studio City CA 91604, USA — Actress, Model

Rodgers of Quarry Bank, William T
43 North Road, London N6 4BE, England — Government Official, England

Rodgers, Aaron C
2360 Crown Pointe Blvd, Suamico WI 54173, USA — Football Player

Rodgers, Derrick A
5550 SW 192nd Terrace, Southwest Ranches FL 33332, USA — Football Player

Rodgers, Jimmie
42230 Sandy Bay Road, Bermuda Dunes CA 92203, USA — Singer, Songwriter

Rodgers, Joan
113 Sotheby Road, London N5 2UT, England — Opera Singer

Rodgers, John S (Johnny)
PO Box 11172, Omaha NE 68111, USA — Football Player

Rodgers, Michael E
Innovative Artists, 1505 10th St, Santa Monica CA 90401 USA — Actor

Rodgers, Nile G
Lustig Talent, PO Box 770850, Orlando FL 32877 USA — Guitarist (Chic), Businessman

Rodgers, Paul
Work Hard, 19D Pinhold Road, London SW16 5GD, England — Singer (Free, Bad Company), Songwriter

Rodgers, Phil
Grand Del Mar, 5200 Grand Del Mar Way, San Diego CA 92130, USA — Golfer

Rodgers, Robert L (Buck)
5181 West Knoll Dr, Yorba Linda CA 92886, USA — Baseball Player, Manager

Rodgers, William H (Bill)
Bill Rodgers Running Center, 1 N Market St, #353, Boston MA 02109, USA — Track Athlete

Rodgers-Cromartie, Dominique R
Philadelphia Eagles, 1 Novacare Way, Philadelphia PA 19145 USA — Football Player

Roditi, Claudio — Trumpeter
McClair Public Relations, PO Box 55, Radio Station, New York NY 10101, USA

Rodl, Henrik — Basketball Player
A L B A Berlin, Olympischer Platz 4, 14053 Berlin, Germany

Rodman, Dennis K — Basketball Player, Actor
Rodman Group, 4910 Campus Dr, Newport Beach CA 92660, USA

Rodman, Howard A — Writer, Producer, Director
University of Southern California, Cinematic Arts Dept, Los Angeles CA 90089, USA

Rodney, Fernando — Baseball Player
Tampa Bay Rays, 1 Tropicana Dr, Saint Petersburg FL 33705 USA

Rodnina, Irina — Figure Skater
13243 Fiji Way, #B, Marina del Rey CA 90292, USA

Rodrigue, George — Journalist
Dallas News, Editorial Dept, 508 Young St, Dallas TX 75202, USA

Rodrigue, George — Artist
Rodrigue Studio, 1434 S College Road, Lafayette LA 70503, USA

Rodrigues, Charlie — Cartoonist (Charlie)
Tribune Media Services, 435 N Michigan Ave, #1500, Chicago IL 60611 USA

Rodriguez — Singer, Songwriter
Agency Group Ltd, 142 W 57th St, #600, New York NY 10019 USA

Rodriguez Madariaga, Oscar A Cardinal — Religious Leader
Conferencia Episcopal, Lavreles, Comayaguela 3121, Tegucigalpa, Honduras

Rodriguez Romero, Jose Antonio — Soccer Player
Federacion de Futbol, Colima 373 Colonia Roma, Delegacion Cuauhtemoc Mexico DF 06700, Mexico

Rodriguez Zapatero, Jose Luis — Prime Minister, Spain
Council of State, C/Mayor 79, 28013 Madrid, Spain

Rodriguez, Adam — Actor
Global Artists Agency, 1648 Wilcox Ave, #3, Los Angeles CA 90028, USA

Rodriguez, Alexander E (Alex) — Baseball Player
171 E Sunrise Ave, Coral Gables FL 33133, USA

Rodriguez, Alfredo — Concert Pianist
I M G Artists, Hogarth Business Park, Chiswick, London W4 2TH, England

Rodriguez, Amy J — Soccer Player
Philadelphia Independence, Union Field, Seaport Dr, Chester PA 19013 USA

Rodriguez, Anthony — Golfer
13602 Summer Glen Dr, San Antonio TX 78247, USA

Rodriguez, Arturo S — Labor Leader
United Farm Workers, 29700 Woodford Tehachapi Road, Keene CA 93531, USA

Rodriguez, Carlos — Baseball Player
10139 Snyder Church Road, Baltimore OH 43105, USA

Rodriguez, Carrie — Singer, Fiddle Player, Songwriter
Rosebud Agency, PO Box 170429, San Francisco CA 94117 USA

Rodriguez, Daniel — Opera Singer
SueBMusic, 30 Stonycrest Dr, #13, Middletown CT 06457, USA

Rodriguez, David M — Army General
I S A Force, N A T O Hdqs, Blvd Leopold III, Brussells 1110, Belgium , USA

Rodriguez, Davinia — Opera Singer
I M G Artists, Hogarth Business Park, Chiswick, London W4 2TH, England

Rodriguez, Edwin — Baseball Player, Manager
7901 30th Ave N, Saint Petersburg FL 33710, USA

Rodriguez, Freddy — Actor
Kass & Stokes Mgmt, 9229 W Sunset Blvd, #504, Los Angeles CA 90069 USA

Rodriguez, Genesis — Actress
I C M Partners, 10250 Constellation Blvd, #900, Los Angeles CA 90067 USA

Rodriguez, Gina — Actress
A P A Talent/Literary Agency, 405 S Beverly Dr, #300, Beverly Hills CA 90212 USA

Rodriguez, Ivan (Pudge) — Baseball Player
15530 SW 70th Terrace, Miami FL 33193, USA

Rodriguez, Jennifer (Jen) — Speed Skater
Q Sports Marketing, 534 W Evergreen St, Wheaton IL 60187 USA

Rodriguez, Johnny — Singer, Guitarist, Songwriter
240 S Wilson Blvd, Nashville TN 37205, USA

Rodriguez, Jose Luis — Actor
T G A Voice, 100 Lincoln Road, #928, Miami Beach FL 33178, USA

Rodriguez, Juan (Chi Chi) — Golfer
Chi Chi Rodriguez Academy, 3030 N McMullen Booth Road, Clearwater FL 33761, USA

Rodriguez, Marco — Actor
Ellis Talent Group, 4705 Laurel Canyon Blvd, #300 Valley Village CA 91607, USA

Rodriguez, Michelle — Actress
Untitled Entertainment, 350 S Beverly Dr, #200, Beverly Hills CA 90212 USA

Rodriguez, Narciso — Fashion Designer
50 Bond St, #700, New York NY 10012, USA

Rodriguez, Paul — Actor, Comedian
Rodriguez Entertainment, 3940 Laurel Canyon Blvd, #1159, Studio City CA 91604, USA

Rodriguez, Ramon — Actor
Collective, 8383 Wilshire Blvd, #1050, Beverly Hills CA 90211 USA

Rodriguez, Raul — Float Designer
Fiesta Floats, 9362 Lower Azusa Road, Temple City CA 91780, USA

Rodriguez, Richard A (Rich) — Football Coach, Sportscaster
University of Arizona, Athletic Dept, Tucson AZ 85721, USA

Rodriguez, Richard A (Rich) — Baseball Player
14578 Corkwood Dr, Moorpark CA 93021, USA

Rodriguez, Rico — Actor
Clear Talent Group, 10950 Ventura Blvd, Studio City CA 91604, USA

Rodriguez, Rita M — Financier
Academy for Educational Development, 1825 Connecticut Ave NW, Washington DC 20006, USA

Rodriguez, Robert — Director
Trouble Maker Studios, 4900 Old Manor Road, Austin TX 78723, USA

Rodriguez, Sergio — Basketball Player
New York Knicks, Madison Square Garden, 2 Penn Plaza, New York, NY 10121 USA

Rodriguez, Valente — Actor
TalentWorks, 3500 W Olive Ave, #1400, Burbank CA 91505 USA

Rodriguez-Lopez, Omar — Guitarist (Mars Volta), Composer
Agency Group Ltd, 142 W 57th St, #600, New York NY 10019 USA

Roe, Alex — Actor
Associated International Mgmt, Fairfax House, Fulwood Place, London WC1V 6HU, England

Roe, Allison P
34 Martin Crescent, Northcote, Auckland 0627, New Zealand — Track Athlete

Roe, John H
Bemis Co, Northstar Center, 222 S 9th St, Minneapolis MN 55402, USA — Businessman

Roe, Marty
Modern Mgmt, 1625 Broadway, #600, Nashville TN 37203, USA — Singer, Guitarist (Diamond Rio)

Roe, Tommy
PO Box 5092, Beverly Hills CA 90209, USA — Singer, Songwriter

Roebuck, Daniel
Leslie Allen-Rice Mgmt, 1007 Maybrook Dr, Beverly Hills CA 90210, USA — Actor

Roebuck, Edward J (Ed)
3434 Warwood Road, Lakewood CA 90712, USA — Baseball Player

Roeder, Robert G
504 E 63rd St, #33P, New York NY 10065, USA — Biochemist

Roeg, Nicolas J
Luc Roeg Artists, 32 Tavustick St, London WC2, England — Director

Roehm, Carolyn J
Carolyn Roehm Inc, 257 W 39th St, #400, New York NY 10018, USA — Fashion Designer

Roekker, Heinz
Zietenstr 21, 26131 Oldenburg, Germany — WW II German Luftwaffe Hero

Roelandts, Willem P
Xilinx, PO Box 240010, San Jose CA 95154, USA — Businessman

Roelofs, Wendell L
4 Crescence Dr, Geneva NY 14456, USA — Biochemist, Entomologist

Roemer, John E
University of California, Economics Dept, Davis CA 95616, USA — Economist

Roemer, Sarah
Luber Rocklin Entertainment, 8530 Wilshire Blvd, #555, Beverly Hills CA 90211 USA — Actress

Roenick, Jeremy
8525 E Dixileta Dr, Scottsdale AZ 85266, USA — Ice Hockey Player

Roenicke, Gary S
11023 Rough and Ready Road, Rough and Ready CA 95975, USA — Baseball Player

Roenicke, Ronald J (Ron)
2212 Avenida Las Ramblas, Chino Hills CA 91709, USA — Baseball Player, Manager

Roerig, Zach
Innovative Artists, 1505 10th St, Santa Monica CA 90401 USA — Actor

Roesch, Michael
Im Kohlhau 6, 01773 Zinwald, Germany — Biathlete

Roesky, Herbert W
Gottingen University, Inorganic Chemistry Dept, 37077 Gottingen, Germany — Chemist

Roethlisberger, Ben
200 Fernwood Dr, Clinton PA 15026, USA — Football Player

Roethlisberger, Nadia
Curling Assn, PO Box 606, 3000 Bern, Switzerland — Curling Athlete

Roffe-Steinrotter, Diann
248 N 29th St, Camp Hill PA 17011, USA — Alpine Skier

Rogan, Joe
W M E Entertainment, 9601 Wilshire Blvd, #300, Beverly Hills CA 90210 USA — Actor, Comedian

Roge, Pascal
17 Ave des Cavaliers, 1224 Geneva, Switzerland — Concert Pianist

Rogen, Seth
Principal Entertainment, 1964 Westwood Blvd, #400, Los Angeles CA 90025 USA — Actor, Comedian, Writer

Rogers of Riverside, Richard G
Rogers Partnership, Thames Wharf, Rainville Road, London W6 9HA, England — Pritzker Architectural Laureate

Rogers, Carlos C
San Francisco 49ers, 4949 Centennial Blvd, Santa Clara CA 95054 USA — Football Player

Rogers, Carlos D
Indiana Pacers, Conseco Fieldhouse, 125 S Pennsylvania, Indianapolis IN 46204 USA — Basketball Player

Rogers, Erik
Agency Group Ltd, 142 W 57th St, #600, New York NY 10019 USA — Singer (Stereo Mud)

Rogers, George W, Jr
1007 Lofty Pine Dr, Columbia SC 29212, USA — Football Player

Rogers, Gil
Don Buchwald/Fortitude, 10 E 44th St, New York NY 10017 USA — Actor

Rogers, Ingrid
Flick East-West, 9057 Nemo St, #A, West Hollywood, CA 90069 USA — Actress

Rogers, James B (J B)
Reflection Pictures, 2001 Wilshire Blvd, #250, Santa Monica CA 90403, USA — Director

Rogers, James E
Duke Energy, 212 S Tryon St, #400, Charlotte NC 28281, USA — Businessman

Rogers, John M
US Court of Appeals, US Courthouse, 100 E 5th St, #3100, Cincinnati OH 45202, USA — Judge

Rogers, Judith W
US Court of Appeals, 717 Madison Place NW, Washington DC 20439, USA — Judge

Rogers, June Scobee
Challenger Center, 1250 N Pitt St, #1, Alexandria VA 22314, USA — Writer

Rogers, Kenneth A (Kenny)
1730 Ottinger Road, Roanoke TX 76262, USA — Baseball Player

Rogers, Lynn L
145 W Conan St, Ely MN 55731, USA — Wildlife Biologist, Ecologist

Rogers, Melody
C E S D, 10635 Santa Monica Blvd, #130, Los Angeles CA 90025 USA — Actress

Rogers, Melvin N
3113 S Manitoba Dr, Santa Ana CA 92704, USA — Football Player

Rogers, Michele
Playboy Promotions, 2706 Media Center Dr, Los Angeles CA 90065 USA — Model

Rogers, Mimi
Collective, 8383 Wilshire Blvd, #1050, Beverly Hills CA 90211 USA — Actress

Rogers, Nick
Royal Yachting Squadron, Castle Cowles, Isle of Wight PO31 7QT, England — Yachtsman

Rogers, Paul
9 Hillside Gardens, Highgate, London N6 5SU, England — Actor

Rogers, Randy
W M E Entertainment, 1600 Division St, #300, Nashville TN 37203 USA — Singer

Rogers, Rob
Pittsburgh Post-Gazette, Editorial Dept, 23 Blvd Allies, Pittsburgh PA 15222, USA — Editorial Cartoonist

Rogers, Robert
Rogers Marvel Architects, 145 Hudson St, #304, New York NY 10013, USA — Architect

Rogers, Rosemary
Avon Books, 959 8th Ave, New York NY 10019, USA — Writer

Rogers, Shaun C O
New York Giants, Meadowlands Stadium, 102 Route 120, East Rutherford NJ 07073 USA — Football Player

Rogers, Stephen D (Steve)
2 Lenape Lane, Princeton Junction NJ 08550, USA — Baseball Player

Rogers, Tracy D
1011 Tam O'Shanter Dr, Bakersfield CA 93309, USA — Football Player

Rogers, Tristan
C E S D, 10635 Santa Monica Blvd, #130, Los Angeles CA 90025 USA — Actor

Rogers, Wayne
11828 La Grange Ave, Los Angeles CA 90025, USA — Actor

Rogers, William C (Bill)
123 Eaton St, #104, San Antonio TX 78209, USA — Golfer

Rogge, Jacques
International Olympic Committee, Chateau de Vidy, 1007 Lausanne, Switzerland — Sports Executive

Roggenburk, Garry E
33550 Streamview Dr, Avon OH 44011, USA — Baseball Player

Rogoff, Ilan
Apdo 1098, 07080 Palma de Mallorca, Spain — Concert Pianist

Rogoff, Kenneth S
11 Hillside Ave, Cambridge MA 02140, USA — Economist

Rogombe, Rose Francine
Senate President's Office, BP 546, Libreville, Gabon — President, Gabon

Rohbock, Shauna
Q Sports Marketing, 534 W Evergreen St, Wheaton IL 60187 USA — Bobsled Athlete

Rohde, David
Christian Science Monitor, Editorial Dept, 1 Norway St, Boston MA 02136 USA — Journalist

Rohde, Hillary
Hillary Rohde Cashmere, 22 Moray Place, Edinburgh EH3 6DB, Scotland — Fashion Designer

Rohde, Leonard E (Len)
324 Alta Vista Ave, Los Altos Hills CA 94022, USA — Football Player

Rohde, Lisa
9807 Whitehorn Dr, Charlotte NC 28277, USA — Rowing Athlete

Rohlander, Uta
Liebigstr 9, 06237 Leuna, Germany — Track Athlete

Rohlf, F James
State University of New York, Ecology & Evolution Dept, Stony Brook NY 11794, USA — Biometrician

Rohm, Elisabeth
A P A Talent/Literary Agency, 405 S Beverly Dr, #300, Beverly Hills CA 90212 USA — Actress

Rohr, James E
P N C Bank Corp, 1 P N C Plaza, 249 5th Ave, Pittsburgh PA 15222, USA — Financier

Rohrer, Heinrich
Rebbergstr 9D, 8832 Wollerau, Switzerland — Nobel Physics Laureate

Rohrer, Katherine
Columbia Artists Mgmt Inc, 1790 Broadway, #702, New York NY 10019 USA — Opera Singer

Roiphe, Anne
Bloomsbury Publishing, 36 Soho Square, London W1D 3Q4, England — Writer

Roizman, Bernard
5555 S Everett Ave, Chicago IL 60637, USA — Virologist

Roizman, Owen
17533 Magnolia Blvd, Encino CA 91316, USA — Cinematographer

Rojas Medrano, Melquiades (Mel)
15645 Collins Ave, #802, North Miami Beach FL 33160, USA — Baseball Player

Rojas Rivas, Octavio R (Cookie)
19195 Mystic Pointe Dr, #3002, Aventura FL 33180, USA — Baseball Player, Manager

Rojas, Tito (El Gallo)
Universal Attractions, 135 W 26th St, #1200, New York NY 10001 USA — Singer, Orchestra Leader

Rojcewicz, Susan (Sue)
16360 Blackie Road, Salinas CA 93907, USA — Basketball Player

Rojeski, Shawn
510 11th St NW, Chisholm MN 55719, USA — Curling Athlete

Roker, Al
W M E Entertainment, 1325 Ave of Americas, New York NY 10019 USA — Entertainer

Rokke, Ervin J
810 Dolan Dr, Monument CO 80132, USA — Air Force General

Roland, Edgar E (Ed), Jr
Creative Artists Agency, 2000 Ave of Stars, #100, Los Angeles CA 90067 USA — Singer (Collective Soul), Songwriter

Roland, Johnny E
10339 Corbell Dr, #C, Saint Louis MO 63146, USA — Football Player, Coach

Roland, M Dean
Creative Artists Agency, 2000 Ave of Stars, #100, Los Angeles CA 90067 USA — Guitarist, Keyboardist (Collective Soul)

Rolandi, Gianna
New York City Opera, Lincoln Center Plaza, New York NY 10023, USA — Opera Singer

Rolen, Scott B
11711 N Pennsylvania St, #250, Carmel IN 46032, USA — Baseball Player

Roles-Williams, Barbara
3790 Leisure Lane, Las Vegas NV 89103, USA — Figure Skater

Rolfe Johnson, Anthony
Ulf Tornqvist, Sankt Eriksgatan 100, 113 31 Stockholm, Sweden — Opera Singer

Rolfe, Dale
365 Hughson St, Gravehurst ON P1P 1G8, Canada — Ice Hockey Player

Roll, Dean M
Shark Stuff, PO Box 752073, Dayton OH 45475, USA — Wrestler

Rolle
Helter Skelter, 347-353 Chiswick High Road, London W4 4HS, England — Musician (Fearless)

Rolle, Antrel R
28232 SW 158th Court, Homestead FL 33033, USA — Football Player

Rolle, Donald D (Butch)
17822 NW 15th St, Pembroke Pines FL 33029, USA — Football Player

Rolle, Samari T
16201 Quiet Vista Circle, Delray Beach FL 33446, USA — Football Player

Roller, David E (Dave)
1110 Anthony Court, Suwanee GA 30024, USA — Football Player

Rolling, Henry L	Football Player
8256 Garnet Canyon Lane, Las Vegas NV 89129, USA	
Rollins, Edward J (Ed)	Political Consultant
Dilenschneider Group, 200 Park Ave, MetLife Building, New York NY 10166, USA	
Rollins, Henry	Singer, Songwriter, Actor
Evolution Entertainment, 901 N Highland Ave, Los Angeles CA 90038 USA	
Rollins, James C (Jimmy)	Baseball Player
120 Fox Chase Court, Swedesboro NJ 08085, USA	
Rollins, John	Golfer
5501 Montclair Dr, Colleyville TX 76034, USA	
Rollins, Richard J (Rich)	Baseball Player
4146 Evergreen Lane, Richfield OH 44286, USA	
Rollins, Theodore W (Sonny)	Jazz Saxophonist, Composer
Ted Kurland, 173 Brighton Ave, Allston MA 02134 USA	
Rollins, Wayne M (Tree)	Basketball Player, Coach
PO Box 681971, Orlando FL 32868, USA	
Rolston, Brian	Ice Hockey Player
301 White Oak Ridge Road, Short Hills NJ 07078, USA	
Rolston, Holmes III	Philosopher, Templeton Religion Laureate
1712 Concord Dr, Fort Collins CO 80526, USA	
Rolston, Matthew	Photographer
United Talent Agency, 9336 Civic Center Dr, Beverly Hills CA 90210 USA	
Roman, John G	Football Player
327 Abbey Road, Berwyn PA 19312, USA	
Roman, Lauren E	Actress
1086 Blue Heron Ave NE, Bainbridge Island WA 98110, USA	
Roman, Petre	Prime Minister, Romania
Str Gogol 2, Sector 1, 012017 Bucharest, Romania	
Romanchych, Larry	Ice Hockey Player
3989 206A St, Langley BC V3A 7A8, Canada	
Romanek, Mark	Director, Writer
Creative Artists Agency, 2000 Ave of Stars, #100, Los Angeles CA 90067 USA	
Romanenko, Roman Y	Cosmonaut
Cosmonaut Training Center, Star City, 141160 Zvezdny Gorodok, Moscow Oblast, Russia	
Romanenko, Yuri V	Cosmonaut
Cosmonaut Training Center, Star City, 141160 Zvezdny Gorodok, Moscow Oblast, Russia	
Romano, Chris	Actor, Writer, Producer
United Talent Agency, 9336 Civic Center Dr, Beverly Hills CA 90210 USA	
Romano, Christy Carlson	Actress, Singer
Rebel Entertainment Partners, 5700 Wilshire Blvd, #456, Los Angeles CA 90036, USA	
Romano, Jason A	Baseball Player
1411 Willow Oak Circle, Bradenton FL 34209, USA	
Romano, John	Psychiatrist
212 Valley Road, Merion Station PA 19066, USA	
Romano, John A (Johnny), Jr	Baseball Player
160 W Pago Pago Dr, Naples FL 34113, USA	
Romano, Larry	Actor
C E S D, 10635 Santa Monica Blvd, #130, Los Angeles CA 90025 USA	
Romano, Pete	Cinematographer
HydroFlex Inc, 301 E El Segundo Blvd, El Segundo CA 90245, USA	
Romano, Ray	Actor, Comedian, Producer
I C M Partners, 10250 Constellation Blvd, #900, Los Angeles CA 90067 USA	
Romano, Rino	Actor
6931 Paseo del Serra, Los Angeles CA 90068, USA	
Romano, Roberto	Ice Hockey Player
5865 Rue Brossard, Saint-Leonard QC H1T 3R6, Canada	
Romanov, Pyotr V	Government Official, Russia
Pr Mira 108, 660017 Krasnoyarsk, Russia	
Romanov, Stephanie	Actress
Untitled Entertainment, 350 S Beverly Dr, #200, Beverly Hills CA 90212 USA	
Romanowski, William T (Bill)	Football Player
390 Hampton Road, Piedmont CA 94611, USA	
Romans, Ben	Keyboardist (Click Five)
Soundtrack Music, 1460 4th St, #308, Santa Monica CA 90401, USA	
Romanus, Richard	Actor
14011 Ventura Blvd, #213, Sherman Oaks CA 91403, USA	
Romar, Lorenzo	Basketball Player, Coach
4408 164th Lane SE, Issaquah WA 98027, USA	
Romario	Soccer Player
Adelaide F C, PO Box 620, Hindmarsh SA 5007, Australia	
Romashin, Anatoliy V	Actor
Vspolny Per 16 Korp 1, #60, 103101 Moscow, Russia	
Romatowski, Jenny	Softball, Baseball Player
3116 Highlands Blvd, Palm Harbor FL 34684, USA	
Romberg, Brett C	Football Player
Atlanta Falcons, 4400 Falcon Parkway, Flowery Branch GA 30542 USA	
Rome, Jim	Actor, Writer
Creative Artists Agency, 2000 Ave of Stars, #100, Los Angeles CA 90067 USA	
Rome, Sydne	Actress
Isabella Gull Assoc, Vicolo del Buon Consiglio, 00184 Rome, Italy	
Romeike, Hinrich	Equestrian
Moholzu, 24809 Nubbel, Germany	
Romensky, Anka	Model
PO Box 3897, Hallandale FL 33008, USA	
Romeo, Paolo Cardinal	Religious Leader
Archdiocese of Palermo, Corso Vittorio Emanuel 461, 90134 Palermo, Italy	
Romeo, Robin	Bowler
Professional Bowlers Assn, 719 2nd Ave, #701, Seattle WA 98104 USA	
Romer, Christina D	Government Official, Economist
University of California, Economics Dept, Evans Hall, Berkeley CA 94720, USA	
Romer, Roy R	Governor, CO; Educator
Los Angeles School District, 333 S Beaudry Ave, #209, Los Angeles CA 90017, USA	
Romero, Anders	Golfer
Professional Golfer's Assn, PO Box 109601, Palm Beach Gardens FL 33410 USA	
Romero, Angel	Concert Guitarist
Richard Gilkerson, 1737 Whitley Ave, #200, Los Angeles CA 90028, USA	

Romero, Celino — Concert Guitarist
Columbia Artists Mgmt Inc, 1790 Broadway, #702, New York NY 10019 USA

Romero, Danny, Jr — Boxer
800 Salida Sandia SW, Albuquerque NM 87105, USA

Romero, Edgardo (Ed) — Baseball Player
1380 Wood Row Way, Wellington FL 33414, USA

Romero, George A — Director
Gersh Agency, 9465 Wilshire Blvd, #600, Beverly Hills CA 90212 USA

Romero, Ned — Actor
19438 Lassen Ave, Northridge CA 91324, USA

Romero, Pepe — Concert Guitarist
Columbia Artists Mgmt Inc, 1790 Broadway, #702, New York NY 10019 USA

Romero, Randy P — Thoroughbred Racing Jockey
1019 Kaliste Saloom Road, #905, Lafayette LA 70508, USA

Romero, Rebecca J — Cyclist, Rowing Athlete
National Cycling Centre, Stewart St, Manchester M11 4DQ, England

Rometty, Virginia M — Businesswoman
I B M Corp, 1 North Castle Dr, #2, Armonk NY 10504, USA

Romig, Joseph H (Joe) — Football Player
1300 Plaza Court N, Lafayette CO 80026, USA

Romijn, Rebecca — Model, Actress
United Talent Agency, 9336 Civic Center Dr, Beverly Hills CA 90210 USA

Romine, Kevin A — Baseball Player
8750 Rogue River Ave, Fountain Valley CA 92708, USA

Rominger, Kent V — Astronaut
2714 Bridgeport Ave, Salt Lake City UT 84121, USA

Romney, Hervin A R — Architect
1556 San Benito Ave, Coral Gables FL 33134, USA

Romo, Antonio R (Tony) — Football Player
Dallas Cowboys, 1 Cowboys Parkway, Irving TX 75063 USA

Romo, Daniela — Actress
Televisa, Blvd A Lopez Mateos 232, Colonia San Angel, DF CP 01060, Mexico

Romulo — Soccer Player
Confederacion de Futebol, Rua Victor Civita 66, #1, Rio de Janeiro 22775 044, Brazil

Rona, Jeff — Composer
Rykodisc Records, 30 Irving Place, #300, New York NY 10003 USA

Ronaldinho — Soccer Player
F C Milan, Via Filippo Turati 3, 20121 Milan, Italy

Ronaldo — Soccer Player
S C Corinthians Paulista, Fazendinha, Sao Paulo SP, Brazil

Ronaldo, Christiano — Soccer Player
Gestifute, Oceans 3/15/02 #D, 2 Office, United Park, 1990-197 Lisbon, Portugal

Ronan, Edward (Ed) — Ice Hockey Player
70 Jefferson Road, Franklin MA 02038, USA

Ronan, Saoirse — Actress
Macfarlane Chard, 7 Adelaide St, Dun Laoghaire, Dublin, Ireland

Ronan, William J — Railway Engineer
525 S Flagler Dr, West Palm Beach FL 33401, USA

Rondo, Rajon P — Basketball Player
9 Fridolin Hill, Lincoln MA 01773, USA

Ronney, Paul D — Astronaut
613 Ranchito Road, Monrovia CA 91016, USA

Ronning, Clifford J (Cliff) — Ice Hockey Player
7130 Kitchener St, Burnaby BC V5A 1L3, Canada

Ronningen, Jon — Greco-Roman Wrestler
Mellomasveien 132, 1414 Trollasen, Norway

Rono, Peter — Track Athlete
Mount Saint Mary's College, Athletic Dept, Emmitsburg MD 21727, USA

Ronson, Leonard K (Len) — Ice Hockey Player
2006 SW Eastwood Ave, Gresham OR 97080, USA

Ronstadt, Linda M — Singer
Krost-Chapin, 912 N West Knoll Dr, West Hollywood CA 90069 USA

Ronty, Paul — Ice Hockey Player
2300 Commonwealth Ave, #3-4, Auburndale MA 02466, USA

Roof, Phillip A (Phil) — Baseball Player
1301 Pillar Chase, Paducah KY 42001, USA

Rook, Susan — Commentator
CNN-TV, 190 Marietta Ave SW, Atlanta GA 30303 USA

Rooker, James P (Jim) — Baseball Player
2378 Windchime Dr, Jacksonville FL 32224, USA

Rooker, Michael — Actor
Kritzer Levine Wilkins Griffin, 11872 La Grange Ave, #100, Los Angeles CA 90025 USA

Rooney — Rock Music Group
Agency Group Ltd, 1880 Century Park E, #711, Los Angeles CA 90067 USA

Rooney, Daniel M (Dan) — Football Executive, Diplomat
940 N Lincoln Ave, Pittsburgh PA 15233, USA

Rooney, Joe Don — Singer, Guitarist (Rascal Flatts)
Turner & Nichols, 49 Music Square W, #500, Nashville TN 37203, USA

Rooney, Kathleen — Writer
University of Arkansas Press, 105 N McIlroy Ave, Fayetteville AR 72701, USA

Rooney, Kevin — Actor
Emptage Hallett, 14 Rathbone Place, London W1T 1HT, England

Rooney, Mercy — Model, Actress
Playboy Promotions, 2706 Media Center Dr, Los Angeles CA 90065 USA

Rooney, Mickey — Actor
741 S Garfield Ave, Alhambra CA 91801, USA

Rooney, Patrick E (Pat) — Baseball Player
4825 Lighthouse Dr, Racine WI 53402, USA

Rooney, Steven P (Steve) — Ice Hockey Player
5 Helen Dr, Canton MA 02021, USA

Roos, Don — Director, Writer
Is or Isn't Entertainment, 8391 Beverly Blvd, #125, Los Angeles CA 90048, USA

Roos, Michael (Mike) — Football Player
500 Madison Ave, #103, Nashville TN 37208, USA

Root, Amanda — Actress
I C M Partners, 10250 Constellation Blvd, #900, Los Angeles CA 90067 USA

Root, Stephen
Gersh Agency, 9465 Wilshire Blvd, #600, Beverly Hills CA 90212 USA — Actor
Root, William J (Bill)
33 Hamilton Hall Dr, Markham ON L3P 3L5, Canada — Ice Hockey Player
Roper, Dee Dee (Spinderella)
Next Plateau Records, 1650 Broadway, #1103, New York NY 10019, USA — Rap Artist (Salt'N'Pepa)
Roper, John A
4213 Alice St, Houston TX 77021, USA — Football Player
Roponun, Riitta-Liise
Oulu Ski Club, Sammonkatu 6, 90570 Oulu, Finland — Cross Country Skier
Rorem, Ned
PO Box 764, Nantucket MA 02554, USA — Composer, Writer
Rosa, Angela Alvarado
Marshak/Zachary Co, 8840 Wilshire Blvd, #100, Beverly Hills CA 90211 USA — Actress
Rosa, John W, Jr
Citadel, President's Office, Charleston SC 29409, USA — Air Force General, Educator
Rosa, Robi Draco (Robby)
Creative Artists Agency, 2000 Ave of Stars, #100, Los Angeles CA 90067 USA — Singer, Producer, Composer
Rosado, Eduardo
Calle 3, Ave Cupules 112A, Col G Giberes, Menda, Yucatan 97070, Mexico — Opera Singer
Rosales, Gaudencio B Cardinal
Archdiocese of Manila, 121 Arzobispo St, 1099 Manila, Philippines — Religious Leader
Rosales, Jennifer (Jenny)
265 S Vine St, Anaheim CA 92805, USA — Golfer
Rosamilia, Alex
Esther Creative Group, 27 W 24th St, #404, New York NY 10010, USA — Guitarist (Gaslight Anthem)
Rosand, David
560 Riverside Dr, New York NY 10027, USA — Art Historian
Rosas, Cesar
Gold Mountain, 3940 Laurel Canyon Blvd, #444, Studio City CA 91604 USA — Singer, Songwriter (Los Lobos)
Rosato, Genesia
Royal Ballet, Covent Garden, Bow St, London WC2E 9DD, England — Ballerina
Rosberg, Keke E
7 Rue Gabian, 9800 Monte Carlo, Monaco — Auto Racing Driver
Rosborough, Patty
OmniPop Talent Group, 4605 Lankershim Blvd, #201, Toluca Lake CA 91602 USA — Actress, Comedienne
Roschkov, Victor
Toronto Star, Editorial Dept, 1 Yonge St, Toronto ON M5E 1E5, Canada 90068, USA — Editorial Cartoonist
Rose Marie
6916 Chisholm Ave, Van Nuys CA 91406, USA — Actress, Singer
Rose, Adam
Stone Manners Salners, 9911 W Pico Blvd, #1400, Los Angeles CA 90035 USA — Actor
Rose, Andrew
1620 Ashland Ave, Santa Monica CA 90405, USA — Composer
Rose, Anika Noni
David Williams Mgmt, 9614 Olympic Blvd, #F, Beverly Hills CA 90212, USA — Actress, Singer
Rose, Axl
5055 Latigo Canyon Road, Malibu CA 90265, USA — Singer (Guns N' Roses), Songwriter
Rose, Bernard
Casorotto Ramsay, Waverley House, 7-12 Noel St, London W1F 8GQ, England — Director, Writer, Cinematographer
Rose, Brian
5 Ashland St, South Dartmouth MA 02748, USA — Baseball Player
Rose, Charles (Charlie)
Rose Communications, 499 Park Ave, #1500, New York NY 10022, USA — Commentator, Producer, Actor
Rose, Chris
Fox-TV, Sports Dept, PO Box 900, Beverly Hills CA 90213 USA — Sportscaster
Rose, Clarence
106 Harding Place, Goldsboro NC 27534, USA — Golfer
Rose, Cristine
S M S Talent, 8383 Wilshire Blvd, #230, Beverly Hills CA 90211 USA — Actress
Rose, Derrick M
Chicago Bulls, United Center, 1901 W Madison St, Chicago IL 60612 USA — Basketball Player
Rose, Donovan J
103 Lenox Court, Yorktown VA 23693, USA — Football Player
Rose, Irwin
14900 1st Ave NE, #230, Shoreline WA 98155, USA — Nobel Chemistry Laureate
Rose, Jalen
Three Tier Entertainment, 645 W 9th St, #406, Los Angeles CA 90015, USA — Basketball Player
Rose, Jamie
Marshak/Zachary Co, 8840 Wilshire Blvd, #100, Beverly Hills CA 90211 USA — Actress
Rose, Jessica
Hirsch Wallerstein Hayum, 10100 Santa Monica Blvd, #1700, Los Angeles CA 90067 USA — Actress
Rose, John
King Features Syndicate, 300 W 57th St, #1500, New York NY 10019 USA — Cartoonist (Snuffy Smith)
Rose, Joseph H (Joe)
3293 SW 138th Way, Davie FL 33330, USA — Football Player
Rose, Justin R
4sports & Entertainment, 8 Celbridge Mews, London W2 6EU, England — Golfer
Rose, Kenny F (Ken)
1736 Bronzewood Court, Newbury Park CA 91320, USA — Football Player
Rose, Lee
Broder Webb Chervin Silberman, 9242 Beverly Blvd, Beverly Hills CA 90210 USA — Director, Producer
Rose, Lela
224 W 30th St, #1400, New York NY 10001, USA — Fashion Designer
Rose, Michael
Agency Group, 9348 Civic Center Dr, #200, Beverly Hills CA 90210 USA — Singer (Black Uhuru)
Rose, Pam
PO Box 50362, Nashville TN 37205, USA — Singer (Kennedy Rose)
Rose, Peter E (Pete)
13348 Chandler Blvd, Sherman Oaks CA 91401, USA — Baseball Player, Manager
Rose, Peter E (Pete), Jr
3921 Legendary Ridge Lane, Cleves OH 45002, USA — Baseball Player
Rose, Sherrie
1758 Laurel Canyon Blvd, Los Angeles CA 90046, USA — Actress, Model
Roseanne
904 Silver Spur Road, #433, Rolling Hills Estates CA 90274, USA — Actress, Comedienne

Roseau, Maurice E D — Mechanical Engineer
144 Bis Ave du General Leclerc, 92330 Sceaux, France
Roselle, David P — Educator
14 Laurel Ridge Road, Wilmington DE 19807, USA
Rosellini, Anne — Film Producer, Writer
Gersh Agency, 9465 Wilshire Blvd, #600, Beverly Hills CA 90212 USA
Rosello Rodriguez, David (Dave) — Baseball Player
HC 1 Box 8125, Hormigueros PR 00660, USA
Rosemont, Romy — Actress
Main Title Mgmt, 8383 Wilshire Blvd, #408, Beverly Hills CA 90211 USA
Rosen, Albert L (Al) — Baseball Player, Executive
15 Mayfair Dr, Rancho Mirage CA 92270, USA
Rosen, Beatrice — Actress
Cinetalent, 18 Rue Seguier, 75006 Paris, France , USA
Rosen, Charles W — Concert Pianist
Owen/White Mgmt, 59 Landsdowne Place, Hove, East Sussex BN3 1FL, England
Rosen, Dan — Director
Modus Entertainment, 8569 Holloway Dr, #1, West Hollywood CA 90069, USA
Rosen, Harold A — Engineer, Inventor
Rosen Electrical Equipment, 8401 Slauson Ave, Pico Rivera CA 90660, USA
Rosen, Milton W — Engineer, Physicist
5610 Alta Vista Road, Bethesda MD 20817, USA
Rosen, Nathaniel — Concert Cellist
3273 SW Avalon Way, #B, Seattle WA 98126, USA
Rosen, Ralph — WW II Navy Air Force Hero
35 Maynard Road, Northampton MA 01060, USA
Rosenbaum, Edward E — Physician
333 NW 23rd St, Portland OR 97210, USA
Rosenbaum, Michael — Actor
A P A Talent/Literary Agency, 405 S Beverly Dr, #300, Beverly Hills CA 90212 USA
Rosenberg, Alan — Actor
Innovative Artists, 1505 10th St, Santa Monica CA 90401 USA
Rosenberg, Howard — Music Critic
5859 Larboard Lane, Agoura Hills CA 91301, USA
Rosenberg, Pierre M — Museum Executive
Musee du Louvre, 34-36 Quai du Louvre, 75068 Paris, France
Rosenberg, Scott — Writer
W M E Entertainment, 9601 Wilshire Blvd, #300, Beverly Hills CA 90210 USA
Rosenberg, Steven A — Oncologist, Surgeon
National Cancer Institute, 31 Center Dr, Building 10, Bethesda MD 20892, USA
Rosenberg, Tina — Writer
New School for Social Research, World Policy Institute, New York NY 10011, USA
Rosenblath, Marshall N — Physicist
2311 Via Siena, La Jolla CA 92037, USA
Rosenblatt, Dana — Boxer
39 Cleveland Road, Chestnut Hill MA 02467, USA
Rosenbluth, Leonard R (Lennie) — Basketball Player
124 Meadowmont Village Circle, Chapel Hill NC 27517, USA
Rosenburg, Saul A — Oncologist
Stanford University Medical School, Oncology Division, 300 Pasteur Dr, Stanford CA 94305, USA
Rosendahl, Heidemarie (Heide) Ecker- — Track Athlete
Burscheider Str 426, 51381 Leverkusen, Germany
Rosenfeld, Irene B — Businesswoman
Kraft Foods, 3 Lakes Dr, Northfield IL 60093, USA
Rosenfeld, Isadore — Clinical Physician
Warner Books, 1271 Ave of Americas, New York NY 10020 USA
Rosenfels, Sage J — Football Player
19651 Hickory St, Omaha NE 68130, USA
Rosenfelt, David — Writer
Warner Books, 1271 Ave of Americas, New York NY 10020 USA
Rosenfield, John Max — Educator
1573 Cambridge St, #711, Cambridge MA 2138, USA
Rosengrant, John — Visual Effects Designer
Legacy Effects, 340 Parkside Dr, San Fernando CA 91340, USA
Rosengren, Eric — Government Official, Financier
Federal Reserve Bank, 500 Atlantic Ave, Boston MA 02210, USA
Rosenquist, James A — Artist
PO Box 4, 420 Broadway, Aripeka FL 34679, USA
Rosenstein, Samuel M — Judge
US Court of International Trade, 2200 S Ocean Lane, Fort Lauderdale FL 33316, USA
Rosenthal, Amy Krouse — Writer
Harper Collins Publishers, 10 E 53rd St, Cellar 1, New York NY 10022 USA
Rosenthal, David S — Director, Writer
W M E Entertainment, 9601 Wilshire Blvd, #300, Beverly Hills CA 90210 USA
Rosenthal, Jacob (Jack) — Journalist
New York Times, Editorial Dept, 229 W 43rd St, New York NY 10036, USA
Rosenthal, Jody Anschutz — Golfer
18938 E McDowell Mountain Dr, Rio Verde AZ 85263, USA
Rosenthal, Mark D — Director, Producer, Writer
Verve Talent, 9696 Culver Blvd, #301, Culver City CA 90232, USA
Rosenthal, Philip — Producer, Writer, Actor
Creative Artists Agency, 2000 Ave of Stars, #100, Los Angeles CA 90067 USA
Rosenthal, Rachel — Performance Artist
2847 S Robertson Blvd, Los Angeles CA 90034, USA
Rosenthal, Rick — Director
Whitewater Films, 11264 La Grange Ave, Los Angeles CA 90025, USA
Rosenthal, Robert J — Editor
Philadelphia Inquirer, Editorial Dept, 400 N Broad St, Philadelphia PA 19130, USA
Rosenzweig, Barney — Producer
2311 Fisher Island Dr, Miami Beach FL 33109, USA
Rosenzweig, Robert M — Educator
1462 Dana Ave, Palo Alto CA 94301, USA
Roses, Allen D — Neurologist
Glaxo Wellcome, 5 Moore Dr, Durham NC 27709, USA
Rosewall, Ken — Tennis Player
Turramurra, 111 Pentacost Ave, Sydney NSW 2074, Australia

Roshan, Hrithik
Filmkraft Mayur, Tilak Road, Santa Cruz (W), Mumbai MS 400054, India — Actor
Roshan, Rakesh
Kavita 10th Road, J V P D Scheme, Mumbai MS 400049, India — Director, Producer, Actor
Rosin, Dino
Arte Studio, Fondamento Manin 40, 30141 Murano, Italy — Sculptor
Rosinski, Edward J
1308 Kellogg Ave, Utica NY 13502, USA — Inventor (Zeolite Catalytic Cracking)
Rosman, Mark
Paradigm Agency, 360 N Crescent Dr, North Building, Beverly Hills CA 90210 USA — Director
Rosner, Robert
4950 S Greenwood Ave, Chicago IL 60615, USA — Astrophysicist
Rosnes, Renee
Integrity Talent, 1 Westcroft Court, Cockeysville MD 21030 USA — Jazz Pianist
Rosovsky, Henry
130 Mount Auburn St, #506, Cambridge MA 02138, USA — Economist
Ross Fairbanks, Anne
995 Lombardy Lane, Denver CO 80215, USA — Swimmer
Ross Naess, Evan
Kritzer Levine Wilkins Griffin, 11872 La Grange Ave, #100, Los Angeles CA 90025 USA — Actor
Ross, Aaron J
13001 Bay Hill Dr, Beltsville MD 20705, USA — Football Player
Ross, Annie
Virginia Wicks Entertainment, 2737 Edwin Place, Los Angeles CA 90046, USA — Actress
Ross, Atticus
Costa Communications, 8265 Sunset Blvd, #101, Los Angeles CA 90046, USA — Composer
Ross, Ben
Brillstein Entertainment Partners, 9150 Wilshire Blvd, #350, Beverly Hills CA 90212 USA — Director
Ross, Betsy
ESPN-TV, ESPN Plaza, 935 Middle St, Bristol CT 06010 USA — Sportscaster
Ross, Charlotte
Untitled Entertainment, 350 S Beverly Dr, #200, Beverly Hills CA 90212 USA — Actress
Ross, Chris
John Watson Mgmt, PO Box 281, Surry Hills NSW 2010, Australia — Bassist, Keyboardist (Wolfmother)
Ross, Christopher
Independent Talent Group, Oxford House, 76 Oxford St, London W1D 1BS, England — Cinematographer
Ross, Cody J
21469 N 83rd St, Scottsdale AZ 85255, USA — Baseball Player
Ross, David A
Whitney Museum of American Art, 945 Madison Ave, New York NY 10021, USA — Museum Director
Ross, David W (Dave)
2768 Millstone Plantation Road, Tallahassee FL 32312, USA — Baseball Player
Ross, Diana
Sunshine Sachs Assoc, 149 5th Ave, #700, New York NY 10010, USA — Singer, Actress
Ross, Don
PO Box 981, Venice CA 90294, USA — Body Builder
Ross, Donald R
US Court of Appeals, Federal Building, PO Box 307, Omaha NE 68101, USA — Judge
Ross, Evan
Kritzer Levine Wilkins Griffin, 11872 La Grange Ave, #100, Los Angeles CA 90025 USA — Actor
Ross, F Robert (Bob)
862 Bergamo Ave, San Jacinto CA 92583, USA — Baseball Player
Ross, Gary
Creative Artists Agency, 2000 Ave of Stars, #100, Los Angeles CA 90067 USA — Director, Writer
Ross, Gary D
1729 Cuadro Vista, San Marcus CA 92078, USA — Baseball Player
Ross, Ian M
2592 Morningstar Road, Manasquan NJ 08736, USA — Electrical Engineer
Ross, Jeffrey (Jeff)
Thruline Entertainment, 9250 Wilshire Blvd, #100, Beverly Hills CA 90212 USA — Actor, Comedian
Ross, Jerry L
N A S A, Johnson Space Center, 2101 NASA Road, Houston TX 77058 USA — Astronaut
Ross, John
620 Sand Hill Road, #402B, Palo Alto CA 94304, USA — Chemist
Ross, Jonathan
Off the Kerb Productions, 22 Thornhill Crescent, London N1 1BJ, England — Actor
Ross, Karie
ESPN-TV, ESPN Plaza, 935 Middle St, Bristol CT 06010 USA — Sportscaster
Ross, Katharine
33050 Pacific Coast Highway, Malibu CA 90265, USA — Actress
Ross, Kevin L
537 Beacon St, Camden NJ 08105, USA — Football Player
Ross, Kyla B
Gym-Max Academy, 2969 Century Place, Costa Mesa CA 92626, USA — Gymnast
Ross, Liberty
Storm Model Agency, 5 Jubilee Place, Chelsea, London SW3 3TD, England — Model
Ross, Lonny
Thruline Entertainment, 9250 Wilshire Blvd, #100, Beverly Hills CA 90212 USA — Actor, Comedian
Ross, Marion
C E S D, 10635 Santa Monica Blvd, #130, Los Angeles CA 90025 USA — Actress
Ross, Mark J
1747 N Wild Hyacinth Dr, Tucson AZ 85715, USA — Baseball Player
Ross, Marv
Pacific Talent Agency, PO Box 19145, Portland OR 97280, USA — Guitarist (Quarterflash)
Ross, Matt
I C M Partners, 10250 Constellation Blvd, #900, Los Angeles CA 90067 USA — Actor
Ross, Rick
Multi Entertainment, 4044 W Lake Mary Blvd, #104-324, Lake Mary FL 32746, USA — Rap Artist
Ross, Ricky
Impressive Public Relations, 9 Jeffreys Place, London NW1 9PP, England — Singer (Deacon Blue)
Ross, Rindy
Pacific Talent Agency, PO Box 19145, Portland OR 97280, USA — Singer, Saxophonist (Quarterflash)
Ross, Terrence
Toronto Raptors, Air Canada Center, 20 Bay St, Toronto ON M5J 2N8, Canada — Basketball Player
Ross, Thomas W, Sr
University of North Carolina, 910 Raleigh Road, PO Box 2688, Chapel Hill NC 27514, USA — Educator

R

R

Ross, Tracee Ellis — Actress
I C M Partners, 10250 Constellation Blvd, #900, Los Angeles CA 90067 USA
Ross, Wilburn K — WW II Army Hero (CMH)
819 Haskell St, Dupont WA 98327, USA
Ross, William — Composer
Gorfaine/Schwartz, 4111 W Alameda Ave, #509, Burbank CA 91505 USA
Rossant, Colette — Writer
Bloomsbury Publishing, 36 Soho Square, London W1D 3Q4, England
Rossdale, Gavin M — Singer, Songwriter (Bush); Actor
Creative Artists Agency, 2000 Ave of Stars, #100, Los Angeles CA 90067 USA
Rosselli, Joe — Baseball Player
6231 Le Sage Ave, Woodland Hills CA 91367, USA
Rossellini, Isabella — Model, Actress
Ancieri Assoc, 305 Madison Ave, #2315, New York NY 10165, USA
Rossen, Carol — Actress
15450 Longbow Dr, Sherman Oaks CA 91403, USA
Rosser, James M — Educator
California State University, President's Office, Los Angeles CA 90032, USA
Rosser, Ronald E — WW II Army Hero (CMH)
36 James St, Roseville OH 43777, USA
Rosset, Marc — Tennis Player
Michel Rosset, Rue Albert Gos 16, 1206 Geneva, Switzerland
Rossi, Anni — Violist
Agency Group Ltd, 142 W 57th St, #600, New York NY 10019 USA
Rossi, Derrick J — Pathologist
Harvard University, Stem Cell Institute, 124 Mount Auburn St, Cambridge MA 02138, USA
Rossi, Paolo — Soccer Player
F C Juventus, Corso Galilo Ferraris 32, 10128 Turin, Italy
Rossi, Theo — Actor
Greene Assoc, 1901 Ave of Stars, #130, Los Angeles CA 90067 USA
Rossi, Valentino — Motorcycle Racing Rider
Via C Basti 5/A, 61010 Tavullia (PU), Italy
Rossington, Gary R — Guitarist (Lynyrd Skynyrd)
Vector Mgmt, PO Box 120479, Nashville TN 37212 USA
Rossini, Bianca — Actress
Arlene Thornton, 12001 Ventura Blvd, #201, Studio City CA 91604, USA
Rossio, Terry — Writer, Producer
Dodie Gold Mgmt, 9165 Alcott St, Los Angeles CA 90035, USA
Rossiter, Martin — Singer, Pianist (Gene)
Agency Group Ltd, 361-373 City Road, London EC1V 2QA, England
Rossiter, Robert E — Businessman
Lear Corp, 21557 Telegraph Road, Southfield MI 48033, USA
Rosskopf, Joerg — Table Tennis Player
Tischtennisbund, Otto-Fleck-Schneise 12A, 60528 Frankfurt/Maim, Germany
Rossman, Michael G — Biochemist
1208 Wiley Dr, West Lafayette IN 47906, USA
Rosso, Louis T — Businessman
4300 N Harbor Blvd, Fullerton CA 92835, USA
Rossouw, Jacques — Physician
National Institutes of Health, Women's Health Initiative, 6701 Rockledge Dr, Bethesda MD 20817, USA
Rossovich, Rick — Actor
Schumacher Mgmt, 10323 Santa Monica Blvd, #101, Los Angeles CA 90024, USA
Rossovich, Timothy J (Tim) — Football Player, Actor
19811 Wildwood West Dr, Penn Valley CA 95946, USA
Rossum, Allen B L — Football Player
5669 Legends Club Circle, Braselton GA 30517, USA
Rossum, Emmy — Actress, Singer
Schiff Co, 8440 Warner Dr, #B1, Culver City CA 90232 USA
Rossy, Elam J (Rico) — Baseball Player
A7 Calle Atenas, Repto Flamingo, Ext Forest Hills, Bayamon PR 00959, USA
Rost, Andrea — Opera Singer
Nefelejes U 27, Budaors 2040, Hungary
Roszak, Thomas — Architect
Roszak/A D C, PO Box 8528, Northfield IL 60093, USA
Rota, Darcy — Ice Hockey Player
2510 Ashurst Ave, Coquitlam BC V3K 5T4, Canada
Rotas, Nikiphoros G — Composer
15 Astydamantos St, Athens 116 34, Greece
Roth, Andrea — Actress
Domain Talent, 9229 W Sunset Blvd, #710, West Hollywood CA 90069 USA
Roth, Ann — Costume Designer
Road 3, Box 3124, Bangor PA 18013, USA
Roth, Arnold — Cartoonist (Poor Arnold's Almanac)
National Cartoonists Society, 9 Ebony Court, Brooklyn NY 11229, USA
Roth, David Lee — Singer (Van Halen), Songwriter
455 Bradford St, Pasadena CA 91105, USA
Roth, Doug — Basketball Player
9975 Spillway Circle, #201, Cordova TN 38016, USA
Roth, Eli — Actor, Director, Writer
Creative Artists Agency, 2000 Ave of Stars, #100, Los Angeles CA 90067 USA
Roth, Eric — Writer
Creative Artists Agency, 2000 Ave of Stars, #100, Los Angeles CA 90067 USA
Roth, Jack A — Molecular Biologist
M D Anderson Medical Center, 1515 Holcombe Blvd, #207, Houston TX 77030 USA
Roth, Jane R — Judge
US Court of Appeals, 333 Constitution Ave NW, #3128, Washington DC 20001, USA
Roth, Jesse — Endocrinologist
National Institute of Arthritis, 9000 Rockville Pike, Bethesda MD 20892, USA
Roth, Joe — Businessman
Creative Artists Agency, 2000 Ave of Stars, #100, Los Angeles CA 90067 USA
Roth, John A — Businessman
Nortel Networks Corp, 8200 Dixie Road, Brampton ON L6T 5P6, Canada
Roth, Klaus F — Mathematician
Colbost, 16A Drummond Road, Iverness IV2 4NB, Scotland
Roth, Mark S — Bowler
13 Wellesley Road, Montclair NJ 07043, USA

Roth, Matt
Bauman Redanty Shaul Agency, 5757 Wilshire Blvd, #473, Los Angeles CA 90036 USA — Actor
Roth, Matthew M (Matt)
14081 SW 54th St, Miramar FL 33027, USA — Football Player
Roth, Michael S
Wesleyan University, President's Office, Wesleyan Station, Middletown CT 06459, USA — Educator
Roth, Philip
Wylie Agency, 250 W 57th St, #2114, New York NY 10107, USA — Writer
Roth, Rachel
Amsel Eisenstadt Frazier, 5055 Wilshire Blvd, #865, Los Angeles CA 90036 USA — Actress
Roth, Tim
Markham & Froggatt, Julian House, 4 Windmill St, London W1P 1HF, England — Actor, Director
Rothberg, Patti
Steve Kurtz Marquee Mgmt, 274 Madison Ave, #1900, New York NY 10016, USA — Singer, Songwriter
Rothenberg, Andres
Global Artists Agency, 6253 Hollywood Blvd, #508, Los Angeles CA 90028 USA — Actor
Rothman, James E
Memorial Sloan Kettering Cancer Center, 1275 York Ave, New York NY 10065 USA — Cellular Biochemist, Biophysicist
Rothman, John
Don Buchwald/Fortitude, 10 E 44th St, New York NY 10017 USA — Actor
Rothman, Les
11854 Fountainside Circle, Boynton Beach FL 33437, USA — Basketball Player
Rothman, Stephanie
11925 Mayfield Ave, #4, Los Angeles CA 90049, USA — Director
Rothrock, Cynthia
20670 Callon Dr, Topanga CA 90290, USA — Actress
Rothschild, Lawrence L (Larry)
4508 W Culbreath Ave, Tampa FL 33609, USA — Baseball Player, Manager
Rothstein, Ronald (Ron)
60 Edgewater Dr, #4E, Coral Gables FL 33133, USA — Basketball Coach
Rotimi
W M E Entertainment, 9601 Wilshire Blvd, #300, Beverly Hills CA 90210 USA — Singer, Songwriter, Actor
Rotter, Stephen A
Paradigm Agency, 360 N Crescent Dr, North Building, Beverly Hills CA 90210 USA — Editor
Rottet, Lauren
D M J M/Rottet, 515 S Flower St, 800, Los Angeles CA 90071, USA — Interior Designer
Rottino, Vincent A (Vinny)
4939 Crystal Spring, Racine WI 53406, USA — Baseball Player
Rottner, Marvin (Mickey)
5757 N Sheridan Road, #88, Chicago IL 60660, USA — Basketball Player
Rouco Varela, Antonio Maria Cardinal
Arzobispado, Called San Justo 2, 28071 Madrid, Spain — Religious Leader
Rouen, Thomas F (Tom), Jr
20343 N Hayden Road, #105, Scottsdale AZ 85255, USA — Football Player
Roughead, Gary
Chief of Naval Operations, HqUSN, Pentagon, Washington DC 20350 USA — Navy Admiral
Rouleau, Joseph-Alfred
32 Lakeshore Road, Beaconsfield QC H9W 4H3, England — Opera Singer
Roulston, Tom
6814 E 25th St, #N, Wichita KS 67226, USA — Ice Hockey Player
Roundtree, Raleigh C
2001 Roosevelt Dr, Augusta GA 30904, USA — Football Player
Roundtree, Richard
4441 Cahuenga Blvd, #A, Toluca Lake CA 91602, USA — Actor
Roundtree, Saudia
University of Central Florida, Athletic Dept, 4000 Central Florida Blvd, Orlando FL 32816, USA — Basketball Player, Coach
Rounsaville, V Gene
537 Red Rome Lane, Brentwood CA 94513, USA — Baseball Player
Rourke, James P (Jim)
466 Plymouth St, Abington MA 02351, USA — Football Player
Rourke, Mickey
I C M Partners, 10250 Constellation Blvd, #900, Los Angeles CA 90067 USA — Actor
Rouse, Bob
19135 74th Ave, RR 15, Surrey BC V4N 3G5, Canada — Ice Hockey Player
Rouse, Christopher
University of Rochester, Eastman Music School, 26 Gibbs St, Rochester NY 14604, USA — Composer
Rouse, Christopher
W M E Entertainment, 9601 Wilshire Blvd, #300, Beverly Hills CA 90210 USA — Editor
Rouse, Curtis L
710 Heatherhurst Court, Clarksville TN 37043, USA — Football Player
Rouse, Irving
509 Rockavon Road, Narberth PA 19072, USA — Anthropologist
Rouse, Jeffrey (Jeff)
600 Sharon Park Dr, #B208, Menlo Park CA 94025, USA — Swimmer
Rouse, Mitch
Paradigm Agency, 360 N Crescent Dr, North Building, Beverly Hills CA 90210 USA — Actor, Director, Writer
Roush, Jack
Roush Racing, 4600 Roush Place, Concord NC 28027, USA — Auto Racing Executive
Rouson, C Lee
20 Main St, Flanders NJ 07836, USA — Football Player
Rousseau, J J Robert (Bobby)
Golf Club, PO Box 222 Suc Bureau Chef, Louiseville QC J5V 2L6, Canada — Ice Hockey Player
Rousseff, Dilma V
Palacio do Planalto, Praca dos 3 Poderas, 70 150 Brasilia DF, Brazil — President, Brazil
Roussel, Dominic
Success Hockey, 1717 Rue Fleetwood, Laval QC H7N 4B2, Canada — Ice Hockey Player
Roussel, Nathalie
Artmedia, 20 Ave Rapp, 75007 Paris, France — Actress
Roussel, Thomas J (Tom)
13 Heron Lane, Mandeville LA 70471, USA — Football Player
Rousselot, Philippe
Gersh Agency, 9465 Wilshire Blvd, #600, Beverly Hills CA 90212 USA — Cinematographer
Route, Ronald A
Inspector General, HqUSN, Pentagon, Washington DC 20350 USA — Navy Admiral
Routh, Brandon
Main Title Mgmt, 8383 Wilshire Blvd, #408, Beverly Hills CA 90211 USA — Actor

Routledge, Alison — Actress
Marmont Mgmt, Langham House, 302/8 Regent St, London W1R 5AL, England

Routledge, Patricia — Actress
Marmont Mgmt, Langham House, 302/8 Regent St, London W1R 5AL, England

Routt, Stanford B — Football Player
Kansas City Chiefs, 1 Arrowhead Dr, Kansas City KS 64129 USA

Rouvali, Santtu-Matias — Conductor
Tapiola Sinfonietta, PO Box 3262, 02070 City of Espoo, Finland

Rouve, Jean-Paul — Actor
U B B A, 6 Rue de Braque, 75003 Paris, France

Rouvel, Catherine — Actress
Artmedia, 20 Ave Rapp, 75007 Paris, France

Rouviere, Koby — Actor
C E S D, 10635 Santa Monica Blvd, #130, Los Angeles CA 90025 USA

Roux, Albert H — Chef
Le Gavroche, 43 Upper Brook St, London W1Y 1PF, England

Roux, Jean-Louis — Director, Actor
4145 Blueridge Crescent, #2, Montreal QC H3H 1S7, Canada

Roux, Michel A — Chef
Waterside Inn, Ferry Road, Bray, Berks SL6 2AT, England

Rove, Karl C — Government Official
1333 New Hampshire Ave NW, #600, Washington DC 20036, USA

Rovero, Jennifer — Model
Playboy Promotions, 2706 Media Center Dr, Los Angeles CA 90065 USA

Rovner, Ilana D — Judge
US Court of Appeals, 219 S Dearborn St, Chicago IL 60604, USA

Rovner, Michael — Photographer, Artist
640 Broadway, #7E, New York NY 10012, USA

Rowan, Kelly — Actress
Untitled Entertainment, 350 S Beverly Dr, #200, Beverly Hills CA 90212 USA

Rowan, Peter — Singer, Guitarist
Keith Case Assoc, 1025 17th Ave S, #200, Nashville TN 37212 USA

Rowand, Aaron R — Baseball Player
34 Meadowhawk Lane, Las Vegas NV 89135, USA

Rowbotham, Stephen — Rowing Athlete
Leander Club, Henley on Thames, Leander RG9 2LP, England

Rowden, William H — Navy Admiral
55 Pinewood Court, Lancaster VA 22503, USA

Rowdon, Wade L — Baseball Player
230 Crooked Tree Trail, Deland FL 32724, USA

Rowe, Brad — Actor
Domain Talent, 9229 W Sunset Blvd, #710, West Hollywood CA 90069 USA

Rowe, David H (Dave) — Football Player
980 Sherwood Ave, Asheboro NC 27205, USA

Rowe, Jack — Writer
Pocket Books, 1230 Ave of Americas, New York NY 10020 USA

Rowe, John W — Businessman
Exelon Corp, 10 S Dearborn St, #4800, Chicago IL 60603, USA

Rowe, Misty — Actress, Model
2193 River Road, Egg Harbor Cay NJ 08215, USA

Rowe, Nicholas — Actor
Julian Belfrage Assoc, 9 Argyll St, #300, London W1F 7TG, England

Rowe, Robert B (Bob) — Football Player
1754 Highview Circle Court, Ballwin MO 63021, USA

Rowe, Sandra M — Editor
Portland Oregonian, Editorial Dept, 1320 SW Broadway, Portland OR 97201, USA

Rowe, Thomas J (Tom) — Ice Hockey Player
1121 Park West Blvd, Mount Pleasant SC 29466, USA

Rowell, Victoria — Actress
Third Hill Entertainment, 195 S Beverly Dr, #400, Beverly Hills CA 90212, USA

Rowland, Dave — Singer (Dave & Sugar)
PO Box 121089, Nashville TN 37212, USA

Rowland, Derrick — Basketball Player
3 Island View Road, Cohoes NY 12047, USA

Rowland, J David — Businessman
6 Danbury St, London N1 8JU, England

Rowland, James Anthony — Governor General, Australia; Marshal
17 Pindari Ave, Mosman NSW 2088, Australia

Rowland, Kelly — Singer (Destiny's Child), Actress
Collective, 8383 Wilshire Blvd, #1050, Beverly Hills CA 90211 USA

Rowland, Landon H — Businessman
Kansas City Southern, PO Box 219335, Kansas City MO 64121, USA

Rowland, Mark — Track Athlete, Coach
Oregon Track Club, PO Box 11364, Eugene OR 97440, USA

Rowland, Richard G (Rich) — Baseball Player
593 E 1st St, Cloverdale CA 95425, USA

Rowlands, Gena — Actress
7917 Woodrow Wilson Dr, Los Angeles CA 90046, USA

Rowlands, Tom — Singer, Musician (Chemical Brothers)
9PR, 65-69 White Lion St, London N1 9PR, England

Rowley, Cynthia — Fashion Designer
W M E Entertainment, 9601 Wilshire Blvd, #300, Beverly Hills CA 90210 USA

Rowley, Janet D — Physician
5310 S University Ave, Chicago IL 60615, USA

Rowling, J K (Jo) — Writer
PO Box 27036, Edinburgh EH10 5WB, Scotland

Rowlinson, John S — Chemist
12 Pullens Field, Headington OX3 0BU, England

Rowny, Edward L — Army General
6200 Oregon Ave NW, #345, Washington DC 20015, USA

Rowser, John F — Football Player
17564 Alta Vista Dr, Southfield MI 48075, USA

Roxburgh, Richard — Actor
United Agents, 12-26 Lexington St, London W1F 0LE, England

Roy — Animal Illusionist (Siegfried & Roy)
Kirvin Doak Communications, 7935 W Sahara Ave, #201, Las Vegas NV 89117, USA

Roy C
Carolina Record Distributors, 229 Augusta Highway, Allendale SC 29810, USA — Singer, Songwriter

Roy, Alfred
2708 Range Road, Los Angeles CA 90065, USA — Songwriter, Lyricist

Roy, Andre
Calgary Flames, PO Box 1540, Station M, Calgary AB T2P 3B9, Canada — Ice Hockey Player

Roy, Aruna
Mazdoor Kisan Shakti Sangathan, Village Devdoongri, Post Brar, Rajsamand, Rajasthan, India — Political, Social Activist

Roy, Arundhati
India Ink Publishing, C1 Soami Nagar, New Delhi 110 017, India — Writer

Roy, Brandon
19807 183rd Way SE, Renton WA 98058, USA — Basketball Player

Roy, Derek
100 Rivermist Dr, Buffalo NY 14202, USA — Ice Hockey Player

Roy, Drew
United Talent Agency, 9336 Civic Center Dr, Beverly Hills CA 90210 USA — Actor

Roy, Jean-Pierre
407 Rue des Harfangs, Saint-Nicolas QC G7A 3H4, Canada — Baseball Player

Roy, John
Galloways One, 15 Lexham Mews, London W8 6JW, England — Actor, Comedian

Roy, Jonathan
Agency Group Ltd, 142 W 57th St, #600, New York NY 10019 USA — Singer

Roy, Lesley
Jive Records, 137-39 W 25th St, #1100, New York NY 10001 USA — Singer

Roy, Loriene
American Library Assn, 50 E Huron, Chicago IL 60611, USA — Association Executive, Librarian

Roy, Patrick
201 Chemin de la Plage Saint Laurent, Quebec QC G1Y 1W6, Canada — Ice Hockey Player

Roy, Reena
Pam Villa D'Monte Park Road, Bandra, Mumbai MS 400050, India — Actress

Royal, Bert V
Paradigm Agency, 360 N Crescent Dr, North Building, Beverly Hills CA 90210 USA — Producer, Writer

Royal, Billy Joe
Bobby Roberts, 3050 Business Park Circle, #303, Goodlettsville TN 37221 USA — Singer; Songwriter

Royal, Lauren
PO Box 52932, Irvine CA 92619, USA — Writer

Royal, Segolene
Parti Socialiste, 10 Rue de Solferino, 75333 Paris, France — Government Official, France

Royals, Mark A
4035 Courtside Way, Tampa FL 33618, USA — Football Player

Royce Da 5'9"
I C M Partners, 10250 Constellation Blvd, #900, Los Angeles CA 90067 USA — Rap Artist

Roye, Orpheus M
12955 NW 18th Manor, Pembroke Pines FL 33028, USA — Football Player

Royer, Stanley D (Stan)
9301 Christopher Lake Dr, Columbia IL 62236, USA — Baseball

Royo Sanchez, Aristides
Morgan & Morgan, PO Box 1824, Panama City 1, Panama — President, Panama

Royo, Andre
Don Buchwald/Fortitude, 6500 Wilshire Blvd, #2200, Los Angeles CA 90048 USA — Actor

Royo, Jose
Triad Art Group, 44 E Belmont Dr, Romeoville IL 60446, USA — Artist

Royo-Torres, Rafael
Teruel-Dinopolis Museum, Poligono de los Planos, 44002 Teruel, Spain — Paleontologist

Royster, Jeron K (Jerry)
1 Brewers Way, Milwaukee WI 53214, USA — Baseball Player, Manager

Royster, Willie A
229 55th St NE, Washington DC 20019, USA — Baseball Player

Rozanov, Evgeny G
International Architecture Academy, 2nd Brestskaya Str 4, 103104 Moscow, Russia — Architect

Rozbruch, S Robert
Cornell University Weill Medical College, 519 E 72nd St, New York NY 10021, USA — Orthopedic Surgeon

Rozema, David S (Dave)
1560 N Renaud Road, Grosse Pointe Woods MI 48236, USA — Baseball Player

Rozema, Patricia
Creative Artists Agency, 2000 Ave of Stars, #100, Los Angeles CA 90067 USA — Director

Rozhdestvensky, Gennady N
Victor Hochhauser Ltd, 4 Oak Hill Way, London NW3, England — Conductor

Rozier, Clifford G
PO Box 1194, Palmetto FL 34220, USA — Basketball Player

Rozier, Michael M (Mike)
9 Hidden Hollow Lane, Sicklerville NJ 08081, USA — Football Player

Roznovsky, Victor S (Vic)
266 W Bluff Ave, Fresno CA 93711, USA — Baseball Player

Rozsival, Michal
19417 N 101st St, Scottsdale AZ 85255, USA — Ice Hockey Player

Ruah, Daniela
Gersh Agency, 9465 Wilshire Blvd, #600, Beverly Hills CA 90212 USA — Actress

Ruano Pascual, Virginia
Women's Tennis Assn, 1 Progress Plaza, #1500, Saint Petersburg FL 33701 USA — Tennis Player

Rubalcaba, Gonzalo
Eardrums Music, PO Box 173304, Hialeah FL 33017, USA — Jazz Pianist, Composer

Rubbia, Carlo
C E R N, Particle Physics Laboratory, 1211 Geneva 23, Switzerland — Nobel Physics Laureate

Ruben, Joseph P (Joe)
Paradigm Agency, 360 N Crescent Dr, North Building, Beverly Hills CA 90210 USA — Director

Rubens, Sibylla
Kunstler Sekretariat am Gasteig, Rosenheimer Str 52, 81669 Munich, Germany — Opera Singer

Rubenstein, Ann
NBC-TV, News Dept, 30 Rockefeller Plaza, #270E, New York NY 10112 USA — Commentator

Rubenstein, Edward
Stanford University Medical School, Surgery Dept, Stanford CA 94305, USA — Physician

Ruberto, John E (Sonny)
207 Ambridge Court, #204, Chesterfield MO 63017, USA — Baseball Player

Rubiano Saenz, Pedro Cardinal
Arzubispado, Carrera 7 N 10-20, Santa Fe de Bogota DC 1, Colombia — Religious Leader

Roy C - Rubiano Saenz

Rubick, Robin J (Rob) — Football Player
PO Box 63, Curtis MI 49820, USA
Rubik, Erno — Inventor (Rubik Cube)
Rubik Studio, Varosmajor Utca 74, 1122 Budapest, Hungary
Rubin, Amy — Actress
Hervey/Grimes Talent, 10561 Missouri Ave, #2, Los Angeles CA 90025 USA
Rubin, Chandra — Tennis Player
708 S Saint Antoine St, Lafayette LA 70501, USA
Rubin, Gloria — Actress
I C M Partners, 10250 Constellation Blvd, #900, Los Angeles CA 90067 USA
Rubin, Harry — Biologist
University of California, Molecular Biology Dept, Berkeley CA 94720, USA
Rubin, Jennifer — Actress, Model
Charles Riley Public Relations, 7122 Beverly Blvd, #F, Los Angeles CA 90036, USA
Rubin, Leigh — Cartoonist (Rubes)
Creators Syndicate, 737 3rd St, Hermosa Beach CA 90254 USA
Rubin, Louis D, Jr — Writer
702 Gimghoul Road, Chapel Hill NC 27514, USA
Rubin, Richard — Actor, Musician
Metropolitan Talent Agency, 7020 La Presa Dr, Los Angeles CA 90068 USA
Rubin, Robert — Medical Researcher
Massachusetts General Hospital, 32 Fruit St, Boston MA 02114, USA
Rubin, Robert E — Secretary, Treasury; Financier
Citigroup Inc, 55 E 52nd St, New York NY 10055, USA
Rubin, Tibor (Ted) — Korean War Army Hero (CMH)
5442 Marietta Ave, Garden Grove CA 92845, USA
Rubin, Vanessa — Singer
Joel Chriss, 60 E 8th St, #34N, New York NY 10003 USA
Rubin, Vera C — Astronomer
Carnegie Institution, 5241 Broad Branch Road NW, Washington DC 20015, USA
Rubinek, Saul — Actor, Director, Producer
Great Northern Artists Mgmt, 350 Dupont St, Toronto ON M5R 1V9, Canada
Rubino, Frank A — Attorney
1001 Brickell Bay Dr, #2206, Miami FL 33131, USA
Rubinoff, Ira — Biologist
Smithsonian Tropical Research Institute, Unit 0848, APO AA 34002, USA
Rubinstein, John A — Actor
4417 Leydon Ave, Woodland Hills CA 91364, USA
Rubinstein, Jonathan J (Jon) — Businessman, Computer Scientist
Palm Inc, 950 W Maude Ave, Sunnyvale CA 94085, USA
Rubinstein, Peter J — Religious Leader, Rabbi
Central Synagogue, 123 E 55th St, New York NY 10022, USA
Rubin-Vega, Daphne — Actress, Singer
Paradigm Agency, 360 N Crescent Dr, North Building, Beverly Hills CA 90210 USA
Rubio, Paulina — Singer
Sanctuary Artist Management, 15301 Ventura Blvd, #400 Bldg B, Sherman Oaks CA 91403, USA
Rubio, Ricard (Ricky) — Basketball Player
Minnesota Timberwolves, Target Center, 600 1st Ave N, Minneapolis MN 55403 USA
Ruby, Sterling — Artist
Xavier Hufkens, 6-8 Rue Saint-Georges, 1050 Brussels, Belgium
Rucchin, Steve — Ice Hockey Player
614 Acacia Ave, Corona del Mar CA 92625, USA
Rucci, Ralph — Fashion Designer, Artist
Chado Ralph Rucci, 536 Broadway, #6, New York NY 10012, USA
Rucci, Todd L — Football Player
5 Southview Lane, Lititz PA 17543, USA
Ruccolo, Richard — Actor
A P A Talent/Literary Agency, 405 S Beverly Dr, #300, Beverly Hills CA 90212 USA
Rucinski, Artur — Opera Singer
I M G Artists, Hogarth Business Park, Chiswick, London W4 2TH, England
Rucinsky, Martin — Ice Hockey Player
8025 Bonhomme Ave, Saint Louis MO 63105, USA
Ruck, Alan — Actor
Innovative Artists, 1505 10th St, Santa Monica CA 90401 USA
Ruckelshaus, William D — Businessman, Government Official
Pugent Sound Partnership, PO Box 47500, Olympia WA 98504, USA
Ruckenstein, Eli — Chemical Engineer
755 Renaissance Dr, #203, Buffalo NY 14221, USA
Rucker, Anja — Track Athlete
T U S Jena, Wollnitzer Str 42, 07749 Jena, Germany
Rucker, Darius — Singer (Hootie & the Blowfish)
Capitol Records, 3322 West End Ave, #1100, Nashville TN 37203 USA
Rucker, David M (Dave) — Baseball Player
18602 Piper Place, Yorba Linda CA 92886, USA
Rucker, Michael D (Mike) — Football Player
5971 Rolling Ridge Dr, Kannapolis NC 28081, USA
Rucker, Reginald J (Reggie) — Football Player
4517 Saint Germain Blvd, Cleveland OH 44128, USA
Rudakova, Natalya — Actress
Don Buchwald/Fortitude, 10 E 44th St, New York NY 10017 USA
Rudbottom, Roy R, Jr — Diplomat
7831 Park Lane, #213A, Dallas TX 75225, USA
Rudd, Delaney — Basketball Player
422 Chesham Dr, Kernersville NC 27284, USA
Rudd, Dwayne D — Football Player
22 Williams Road, Trenton SC 29847, USA
Rudd, John — Basketball Player
4440 Sweet Bay Dr, Lake Charles LA 70611, USA
Rudd, Paul — Actor
United Talent Agency, 9336 Civic Center Dr, Beverly Hills CA 90210 USA
Rudd, Phillip H N (Phil) — Drummer (AC/DC)
Alberts Music, 9 Rangers Road, Neutral Bay, Sydney NSW 2089, Australia
Rudd, Ricky — Auto Racing Driver
Entertainment Marketing, 124 Summerville Dr, Mooresville NC 28115, USA
Ruddle, Francis H — Biologist, Geneticist
Yale University, Biology Dept, Kline Biology Tower, New Haven CT 06511, USA

Ruddy, Timothy D (Tim)	Football Player
3885 Vale View Lane, Mead CO 80542, USA	
Rudel, Julius	Conductor
101 Central Park West, #11A, New York NY 10023, USA	
Rudenstine, Neil L	Educator
A W Mellon Foundation, 140 E 62nd St, New York NY 10065, USA	
Rudi, Joseph O (Joe)	Baseball Player
17667 Deer Park Loop, Baker City OR 97814, USA	
Rudin, Scott	Producer
Scott Rudin Productions, 120 W 45th St, #1001, New York NY 10036, USA	
Rudisha, David	Track Athlete
Saint Patrick's High School, PO Box 310, 30700 Iten, Keiyo District, Rift Valley Province, Kenya	
Rudman, Warren B	Senator, NH
327 10th St SE, Washington DC 20003, USA	
Rudnay, John C (Jack)	Football Player
7219 Whipperwill Road, Versailles MO 65084, USA	
Rudner, Rita	Actress, Comedienne, Writer
2877 Paradise Dr, #1605, Los Angeles CA 90032, USA	
Rudnick, Paul	Writer
Creative Artists Agency, 2000 Ave of Stars, #100, Los Angeles CA 90067 USA	
Rudolf, Kevin	Singer, Musician, Songwriter
Cash Money/Motown Records, 6255 W Sunset Blvd, Los Angeles CA 90028, USA	
Rudolph, Alan S	Director
William J Goldstein, 15760 Ventura Blvd, #1600, Encino CA 91436, USA	
Rudolph, Benjamin (Ben)	Football Player
561 E General Gorgas Dr, Mobile AL 36617, USA	
Rudolph, Council, Jr	Football Player
8310 Lago Vista Dr, Tampa FL 33614, USA	
Rudolph, John L (Jack)	Football Player
2211 Glynndale Dr, Valdosta GA 31602, USA	
Rudolph, Kenneth V (Ken)	Baseball Player
9969 E Bayview Dr, Scottsdale AZ 85258, USA	
Rudolph, Lars	Actor
Gunda Kniggendorff Mgmt, Postfach 440414, 12004 Berlin, Germany	
Rudolph, Maya	Actress, Comedienne
3 Arts Entertainment, 9460 Wilshire Blvd, #700, Beverly Hills CA 90212 USA	
Rudometkin, John	Basketball Player
6181 Wise Road, Newcastle CA 95658, USA	
Rudorfler, Erich	German Air Force Hero
Bismarkstr 3A, 23677 Bad Schwarteau, Germany	
Rudzinski, Witold	Composer
Ul Narbutta 50 m 6, 02 541 Warsaw, Poland	
Rue, Sara	Actress, Comedienne
Alan David Mgmt, 8840 Wilshire Blvd, #200, Beverly Hills CA 90211, USA	
Ruebell, Matthew A (Matt)	Baseball Player
7509 W Augusta Blvd, Yorktown IN 47396, USA	
Ruegamer, C Grey	Football Player
7380 E Eastern Ave, #124, Las Vegas NV 89123, USA	
Ruehl, Mercedes	Actress
Innovative Artists, 1505 10th St, Santa Monica CA 90401 USA	
Ruel, Claude	Ice Hockey Coach
102-1450 Rue Beauhamois, Longueuil QC J4M 1X2, Canada	
Ruelas, Gabriel (Gabe)	Boxer
1119 S Hudson Ave, Los Angeles CA 90019, USA	
Ruell, Aaron	Actor, Director, Writer
Universal Media Artists, 8222 Melrose Ave, #203, Los Angeles CA 90048, USA	
Ruelle, David P	Mathematician
1 Ave Charles-Comar, 91440 Bures-sur-Yvette, France	
Rueter, Kirk W	Baseball Player
46 Pheasant Ridge Court, Nashville IL 62263, USA	
Ruether, Mike A	Football Player
23014 Gardner Dr, Alpharetta GA 30009, USA	
Ruether, Rosemary R	Theologian
530 Mayflower Road, Claremont CA 91711, USA	
Ruettgers, Kenneth F (Ken)	Football Player
16897 Golden Stone Dr, Sisters OR 97759, USA	
Ruettiger, Daniel E (Rudy)	Football Player
293 Goldstar St, Henderson NV 89012, USA	
Ruff, Howard J	Financial Analyst, Writer
PO Box 441, Orem UT 84059, USA	
Ruff, Lindy	Ice Hockey Player, Coach
5006 Winding Lane, Clarence NY 14031, USA	
Ruff, Matt	Writer
Harper Collins Publishers, 10 E 53rd St, Cellar 1, New York NY 10022 USA	
Ruff, Orlando B	Football Player
202 S Raymond Ave, #304, Pasadena CA 91105, USA	
Ruffalo, Mark	Actor
Brillstein Entertainment Partners, 9150 Wilshire Blvd, #350, Beverly Hills CA 90212 USA	
Ruffcorn, Scott P	Baseball Player
2137 Barton Hills Dr, Austin TX 78704, USA	
Ruffin, Bruce W	Baseball Player
3410 Pawnee Pass S, Austin TX 78738, USA	
Ruffin, Jimmy	Singer
Star-Vest, 102 Ryders Lane, East Brunswick NJ 08816, USA	
Ruffin, Johnny R	Baseball Player
4229 Trumpworth Court, Valrico FL 33596, USA	
Ruffner, Paul	Basketball Player
3352 N 100 E, #210, Provo UT 84604, USA	
Ruge, John A	Cartoonist
240 Bronxville Road, #B4, Bronxville NY 10708, USA	
Rugers, Martin	Astronomer
University of Washington, Astronomy Dept, Seattle WA 98195, USA	
Ruggiano, Justin M	Baseball Player
8711 Tallwood Dr, Austin TX 78759, USA	
Ruggiero, Angela	Ice Hockey Player
196 Old Military Road, Lake Placid NY 12946, USA	

Ruhe, Martin — Cinematographer
Esther Kurle Mgmt, Tucholskystr 45, 10117 Berlin, Germany
Ruhl, Sarah — Writer
Bret Adams Artists Agency, 448 W 44th St, New York NY 10036, USA
Ruhnke, Kent — Ice Hockey Player
Felsenrainstr 11, Zurich 8052, Switzerland
Ruhsam, John W — WW II Marine Corps Air Force Hero
1010 American Eagle Blvd, #346, Sun City Center FL 33573, USA
Ruini, Camillo Cardinal — Religious Leader
Vicar of Rome, 00120 Vatican City
Ruivivar, Anthony M — Actor
Gersh Agency, 9465 Wilshire Blvd, #600, Beverly Hills CA 90212 USA
Ruiz Anchia, Juan — Cinematographer
Gersh Agency, 9465 Wilshire Blvd, #600, Beverly Hills CA 90212 USA
Ruiz, Hector — Businessman
Advanced Micro Devices, 1 A M D Place, PO Box 3453, Sunnyvale CA 94088, USA
Ruiz, John — Boxer
11009 Salford Dr, Las Vegas NV 89144, USA
Ruiz, Manuel (Chico) — Baseball Player
267 Calle Tapia, San Juan PR 00912, USA
Ruiz-Corforte, Tracie L — Synchronized Swimmer
B T O Foundation, 312 Sweet Cherry Court, Hollidaysburg PA 16648, USA
Rukeyser, William S — Publisher
1509 Rudder Lane, Knoxville TN 37919, USA
Rule, Ann — Writer
PO Box 98846, Seattle WA 98198, USA
Rule, Bobby F (Bob) — Basketball Player
4303 Kansas Ave, Riverside CA 92507, USA
Ruley, Amy — Basketball Coach
North Dakota State University, Athletic Dept, Fargo ND 58105, USA
Rulin, Olesya — Actress
Paul Kohner, 9300 Wilshire Blvd, #555, Beverly Hills CA 90212 USA
Rullo, Gerenoso C (Jerry) — Basketball Player
300 Brookline Blvd, Havertown PA 19083, USA
Rumer — Singer, Songwriter
Agency Group Ltd, 361-373 City Road, London EC1V 2QA, England
Rummells, Dave — Golfer
1820 Harbor Blvd, Kissimmee FL 34744, USA
Rummenigge, Karl-Heinz — Soccer Player
Eichleite 4, 80231 Grunwald, Germany
Rumph, Michael J (Mike) — Football Player
4686 SW 179th Way, Miramar FL 33029, USA
Rumsfeld, Donald H — Secretary, Defense; Businessman
1718 M St NW, #366, Washington DC 20036, USA
Runager, Max C — Football Player
109 Roger Smith, Williamsburg VA 23185, USA
Runcie, James — Writer
David Godwin Assoc, 55 Monument St, London WC2H 9DG, England
Runco, Mario, Jr — Astronaut
207 Lakeshore Dr, Seabrook TX 77586, USA
Rundgren, Todd — Singer, Songwriter
Panacea Entertainment, 13587 Andalusia Dr E, Camarillo CA 93012, USA
Runge, Brian — Baseball Umpire
8225 E County Dr, El Cajon CA 92021, USA
Runge, Paul W — Baseball Player
1719 W Community Dr, Jupiter FL 33458, USA
Runnells, Thomas W (Tom) — Baseball Player, Manager
6045 Settlers Ridge Circle, Sylvania OH 43560, USA
Runnicles, Donald — Conductor
Opus 3 Artists, 470 Park Ave S, #900N, New York NY 10016 USA
Running, Steve — Ecologist
1419 Khanabad Dr, Missoula MT 59802, USA
Runyan, Joe — Dog Sled Racer
Rt 1, 314.5 Parks Highway, Nenana AK 99760, USA
Runyan, Jon D — Football Player
262 Mount Laurel Road, #1, Mount Laurel NJ 08054, USA
Runyan, Marla — Track Athlete
5135 Center Way, Eugene OR 97405, USA
Runyan, Sean D — Baseball Player
1958 Bermuda Pointe Dr, Haines City FL 33844, USA
Runyon, Edwin — Religious Leader
General Baptists Assn, 100 Stinson Dr, Poplar Bluff MO 63901, USA
Ruotsalainen, Reijo J — Ice Hockey Player
Jukurit Mikkeli Raviradantie 1, Mikkeli 50100, Finland
RuPaul — Entertainer
RuCo, 332 Bleecker St, #F22, New York NY 10014, USA
Rupe, Joshua M (Josh) — Baseball Player
225 Arrowfield Road, Virginia Beach VA 23454, USA
Rupe, Ryan K — Baseball Player
2 Windflower Place, Spring TX 77381, USA
Rupert, Michael — Actor, Composer, Director
Don Buchwald/Fortitude, 10 E 44th St, New York NY 10017 USA
Rupp, Debra Jo — Actress
Stone Manners Salners, 9911 W Pico Blvd, #1400, Los Angeles CA 90035 USA
Rupp, Duane — Ice Hockey Player
2446 McMonagle Ave, Pittsburgh PA 15216, USA
Rupp, Michael (Mike) — Ice Hockey Player
3936 Medford Square, Hilliard OH 43026, USA
Ruppel, Adam — Guitarist (Systematic)
Artist Group International, 9560 Wilshire Blvd, #400, Beverly Hills CA 90212 USA
Ruprecht, Tom — Writer
United Talent Agency, 9336 Civic Center Dr, Beverly Hills CA 90210 USA
Rusch, Glendon J — Baseball Player
6428 Chaffee St, Tujunga CA 91042, USA
Rusch, Kristine Kathryn — Writer
PO Box 479, Lincoln City OR 97367, USA

Ruscha, Edward J — Artist
35 S Venice Blvd, Venice CA 90291, USA
Ruscio, Kenneth — Educator
Washington & Lee University, President's Office, Lexington VA 24450, USA
Ruse, Michael — Philosopher
651 E 6th Ave, Tallahassee FL 32303, USA
Rusedski, Greg — Tennis Player
Association of Tennis Professionals, 200 Tournament Road, Ponte Vedra Beach FL 32082 USA
Rusesabagina, Paul — Humanitarian
Baron Albert d'Huartlaan 124, 1950 Kraainem, Belgium
Rush, Barbara — Actress
House of Representatives, 1434 6th St, #1, Santa Monica CA 90401 USA
Rush, Brandon L — Basketball Player
Golden State Warriors, 1011 Broadway, Oakland CA 94605 USA
Rush, Deborah — Actress
Gersh Agency, 9465 Wilshire Blvd, #600, Beverly Hills CA 90212 USA
Rush, Geoffrey — Actor
Shanahan Mgmt, PO Box 1509, Darlinghurst NSW 1300, Australia
Rush, Gerald M (Jerry) — Football Player
17536 Oak Dr, Detroit MI 48221, USA
Rush, Jennifer — Singer
Armin Rahm Agency, Dreimuhlenstr 7, 80469 Munich, Germany
Rush, Kareem L — Basketball Player
2805 E 62nd St, Kansas City MO 64130, USA
Rush, Merrilee — Singer, Songwriter
M G W Advertising, 408 NE 40th, Seattle WA 98105, USA
Rush, Otis — Singer, Guitarist
Concerted Efforts, PO Box 440326, Somerville MA 02144 USA
Rush, Richard W — Director, Producer
821 Stradella Road, Los Angeles CA 90077, USA
Rush, Robert J (Bob) — Football Player
420 Mary Lane, Auburn AL 36830, USA
Rush, Robert R (Bob) — Baseball Player
444 S Higley Road, #116, Mesa AZ 85206, USA
Rushbrook, Claire — Actress
Troika, 74 Clerkenwell Road, #300, London EC1M 5QA, England
Rushdie, A Salman — Writer
United Talent Agency, 9336 Civic Center Dr, Beverly Hills CA 90210 USA
Rushing, Marion G — Football Player
4520 Galum Church Road, Pinckneyville IL 62274, USA
Rushlow, Timothy A (Tim) — Singer, Guitarist (Rushlow Harris)
K M G Records, 3631 W End Ave, Nashville TN 37205, USA
Ruskin, Joseph — Actor
13840 Kittridge St, Van Nuys CA 91405, USA
Ruskowski, Terry — Ice Hockey Player
2542 Silent Shore Court, Richmond TX 77406, USA
Russ, Tim — Actor
C E S D, 10635 Santa Monica Blvd, #130, Los Angeles CA 90025 USA
Russ, William — Actor
26500 Agoura Road, Calabasas CA 91302, USA
Russell Beale, Simon — Actor
Richard Stone Partnership, 85 New Cavendish St, London W1W 6XD, England
Russell, Adam W — Baseball Player
627 Mariner Village, Huron OH 44839, USA
Russell, Allison — Singer (Po' Girl)
Emerging Music, Horns Cross, Bidesford, Devon EX39 5DW, England
Russell, Betsy — Actress
Marshak/Zachary Co, 8840 Wilshire Blvd, #100, Beverly Hills CA 90211 USA
Russell, Brenda — Singer, Songwriter, Keyboardist
S K M Artist Mgmt, PO Box 25906, Los Angeles CA 90025, USA
Russell, Bryon D — Basketball Player
22451 Cass Ave, Woodland Hills CA 91364, USA
Russell, C Andrew (Andy) — Football Player
230 Glen Abbey Court, Presto PA 15142, USA
Russell, Catherine — Actress
Rights House, 34-43 Russell St, London WC2B 5HA, England
Russell, Cazzie L — Basketball Player
Savannah College of Art & Design, Athletic Dept, Savannah GA 31402, USA
Russell, Charles O (Chuck) — Director
Gersh Agency, 9465 Wilshire Blvd, #600, Beverly Hills CA 90212 USA
Russell, Christopher T — Geophysicist
University of California, Institute of Geophysics & Planetary Physics, Los Angeles CA 90024, USA
Russell, Clive — Actor
Shepherd Mgmt, 45 Maddox St, #400, London W1S 2PC, England
Russell, David O — Director, Writer
Creative Artists Agency, 2000 Ave of Stars, #100, Los Angeles CA 90067 USA
Russell, Graham — Singer (Air Supply)
PO Box 3367, Beverly Hills CA 90212, USA
Russell, Hugh — Opera Singer
Columbia Artists Mgmt Inc, 1790 Broadway, #702, New York NY 10019 USA
Russell, JaMarcus — Football Player
13111 Skyline Road, Oakland CA 94619, USA
Russell, James T — Inventor
14589 51st St, Bellevue WA 98006, USA
Russell, Jay — Director
A P A Talent/Literary Agency, 405 S Beverly Dr, #300, Beverly Hills CA 90212 USA
Russell, Jeffrey L (Jeff) — Baseball Player
2325 Oak Knoll Dr, Colleyville TX 76034, USA
Russell, Jena — Actress, Singer
United Agents, 12-26 Lexington St, London W1F 0LE, England
Russell, John W — Baseball Player, Manager
1709 NE Woodland Shores Court, Lees Summit MO 64086, USA
Russell, Keri — Actress, Model
Burstein Co, 15304 W Sunset Blvd, #208, Pacific Palisades CA 90272 USA
Russell, Kimberly — Actress
14622 Ventura Blvd, Sherman Oaks CA 91403, USA

Russell, Kurt 1417 Capri Dr, Pacific Palisades CA 90272, USA	Actor
Russell, Leon PO Box 24455, New Orleans LA 70184, USA	Singer, Pianist, Songwriter
Russell, Liane B 130 Tabor Road, Oak Ridge TN 37830, USA	Geneticist
Russell, Lucy Hamilton Hodell, 66-68 Margaret St, London W1W 8SR, England	Actress, Model
Russell, M Campanella (Campy) 66 Earlmoor Blvd, Pontiac MI 48341, USA	Basketball Player
Russell, Margaret A Architectural Digest, Editorial Dept, 5900 Wilshire Blvd, Los Angeles CA 90036, USA	Editor
Russell, Mark PO Box 9904, Washington DC 20016, USA	Actor, Comedian
Russell, Phil 590 Wind Drift Lane, Spring Lake MI 49456, USA	Ice Hockey Player
Russell, Sharman Apt Western New Mexico State University, English Dept, Silver City NM 88062, USA	Writer
Russell, Theresa Scott Zimmerman Mgmt, 1644 Courtney Ave, Los Angeles CA 90046, USA	Actress
Russell, Tom Shout Factory, 2042A Armacost Ave, Los Angeles CA 90025, USA	Singer, Songwriter
Russell, Twan S 212 Lakeside Circle, Sunrise FL 33326, USA	Football Player
Russell, William E (Bill) 27982 Red Pine Court, Valencia CA 91354, USA	Baseball Player, Manager
Russell, William F (Bill) 9415 SE 52nd St, Mercer Island WA 98040, USA	Basketball Player, Coach
Russell, Willy Casorotto Ramsay, Waverley House, 7-12 Noel St, London W1F 8GQ, England	Writer
Russi, Bernhard Postfach 107, 5620 Bremgarten, Switzerland	Alpine Skier
Russo, Daniel Agents Associes, 201 Rue du Faubourg Saint Honore, 75008 Paris, France	Actor
Russo, David Rugolo Entertainment, 195 S Beverly Drive, #400, Beverly Hills CA 90212, USA	Director, Writer, Actor
Russo, Dominic I C M Partners, 10250 Constellation Blvd, #900, Los Angeles CA 90067 USA	Producer, Writer
Russo, Gianni Sanders Agency, 9014 Melrose Ave, West Hollywood CA 90069, USA	Actor
Russo, James 8306 Wilshire Blvd, #438, Beverly Hills CA 90211, USA	Actor, Writer
Russo, John 216 Euclid Ave, Glassport PA 15045, USA	Writer
Russo, Martin A Cassidy & Assoc, 700 13th Ave NW, #400, Washington DC 20005, USA	Representative, IL
Russo, Rene John Crosby Mgmt, 1310 N Spaulding Ave, Los Angeles CA 90046 USA	Actress, Model
Russo, Richard Knopf Publishers, 1745 Broadway, New York NY 10019 USA	Writer
Rut, Tomasz 1909 Tigertail Blvd, Dania Beach FL 33004, USA	Artist
Rutan, Elbert L (Burt) 14329 Rutan Road, Mojave CA 93501, USA	Airplane Designer
Rutan, Richard G (Dick) 2833 Delmar Ave, Mojave CA 93501, USA	Experimental Airplane Pilot, Designer
Rutgens, Joseph C (Joe) 227 W Devlin St, Spring Valley IL 61362, USA	Football Player
Ruth, Lauren PO Box 200206, New Haven CT 06520, USA	Cartoonist
Ruth, Michael J (Mike) 8222 Kirkbride Dr, Danvers MA 01923, USA	Football Player
Rutherford, Emily Paradigm Agency, 360 N Crescent Dr, North Building, Beverly Hills CA 90210 USA	Actress
Rutherford, James E (Jim) 2542 Village Manor Way, Raleigh NC 27614, USA	Ice Hockey Player
Rutherford, John S (Johnny), III 4919 Black Oak Lane, River Oaks TX 76114, USA	Auto Racing Driver
Rutherford, Kelly Luber Rocklin Entertainment, 8530 Wilshire Blvd, #555, Beverly Hills CA 90211 USA	Actress
Rutherford, Mike Solo Agency, 53-55 Fulham High St, #200, London SW6 3JJ, England	Guitarist (Genesis)
Rutherfurd, Emily Paradigm Agency, 360 N Crescent Dr, North Building, Beverly Hills CA 90210 USA	Actress
Ruthven, Richard D (Dick) 13480 Providence Lake Dr, Alpharetta GA 30004, USA	Baseball Player
Rutigliano, Sam 9671 Metcalf Road, Willoughby OH 44094, USA	Football Coach
Rutkowski, Edward J A (Ed) 47 Brenton Lane, Hamburg NY 14075, USA	Football Player
Rutland, Robert A Tulsa University, History Dept, Tulsa OK 74101, USA	Historian
Rutledge, Jeffrey R (Jeff) 6102 W Gary Dr, Chandler AZ 85226, USA	Football Player, Coach
Rutledge, Johnny B, Jr 756 SW 10th St, Belle Glade FL 33430, USA	Football Player
Rutledge, Justin Agency Group Ltd, 142 W 57th St, #600, New York NY 10019 USA	Singer, Songwriter
Rutledge, Roderick A (Rod) 1254 4th Way, Pleasant Grove AL 35127, USA	Football Player
Rutsala, Vern A 2494 NE 24th St, Portland OR 97212, USA	Writer
Rutschman, Adolph (Ad) 2142 NW Pinehurst Dr, McMinnville OR 97128, USA	Football Coach
Rutschow-Stomporowski, Katrin Rosenthaler Str 34-35, 10178 Berlin, Germany	Rowing Athlete

Ruttan, Susan — Actress
TalentWorks, 3500 W Olive Ave, #1400, Burbank CA 91505 USA
Rutter, John M — Composer, Conductor
Old Lacey's, Saint John's St, Duxford, Cambridge CB2 4RA, England
Ruud, Barrett J — Football Player
1821 S 33rd St, Lincoln NE 68506, USA
Ruud, Thomas R (Tom) — Football Player
1821 S 33rd St, Lincoln NE 68506, USA
Ruuska Percy, Sylvia — Swimmer
4216 College View Way, Carmichael CA 95608, USA
Ruusuvuori, Aarno E — Architect
Annankatu 15 B 10, 00120 Helsinki 12, Finland
Ruuttu, Christian — Ice Hockey Player
Phoenix Coyotes, 6751 N Sunset Blvd, #200, Glendale AZ 85305 USA
Ruutu, Jarko — Ice Hockey Player
Ottawa Senators, Scotia Bank Place, Kanata ON K2V 1A5, Canada
Ruutu, Tuomo I — Ice Hockey Player
Carolina Hurricanes, R B C Center, 1400 Edwards Mills Road, Raleigh NC 27607 USA
Ruzek, Roger B — Football Player
6404 Penina Trail, Denton TX 76210, USA
Ruzowitsky, Stefan — Director
United Agents, 12-26 Lexington St, London W1F 0LE, England
Ryal, Mark D — Baseball Player
204 E University Dr, Auburn AL 36832, USA
Ryan, Amy — Actress
Gersh Agency, 9465 Wilshire Blvd, #600, Beverly Hills CA 90212 USA
Ryan, Bob — Sportswriter
Boston Globe, Editorial Dept, 135 William Morrissey Blvd, Dorchester MA 02125 USA
Ryan, Cathy Cahlin — Actress
Seven Summits Mgmt, 8906 W Olympic Blvd, Beverly Hills CA 90211 USA
Ryan, Debbie — Basketball Coach
University of Virginia, Athletic Dept, PO Box 400827, Charlottesville VA 22904, USA
Ryan, Ed — Harness Racing Executive
PO Box 6249, Freehold NJ 07728, USA
Ryan, Frank B — Football Player
PO Box 185, Grafton VT 05146, USA
Ryan, Heather — Model
Playboy Promotions, 2706 Media Center Dr, Los Angeles CA 90065 USA
Ryan, James D (Buddy) — Football Coach
819 Abingdon Lane, Shelbyville KY 40065, USA
Ryan, James J (Jim) — Football Player
1726 C St NE, Washington DC 20002, USA
Ryan, James L — Judge
US Court of Appeals, US Courthouse, 231 W Lafayette Blvd, Detroit MI 48226, USA
Ryan, Jay — Actor
United Talent Agency, 9336 Civic Center Dr, Beverly Hills CA 90210 USA
Ryan, Jeri L — Actress
I C M Partners, 10250 Constellation Blvd, #900, Los Angeles CA 90067 USA
Ryan, Kay — Writer
College of Marin, English Dept, 835 College Ave, Kentfield CA 94904, USA
Ryan, Kenneth E (Ken) — Baseball Player
45 Tanager Road, Seekonk MA 02771, USA
Ryan, Kevin — Actor
I C M Partners, 10250 Constellation Blvd, #900, Los Angeles CA 90067 USA
Ryan, Kwame — Conductor
Orchestre National Bordeaux Aquataine, Place de Comédie, BP 90095, 33025 Bordeaux Cedex, France
Ryan, L Nolan, Jr — Baseball Player
237 Escalera Parkway, Georgetown TX 78628, USA
Ryan, Lee — Singer, Songwriter, Actor
Independent Talent Group, Oxford House, 76 Oxford St, London W1D 1BS, England
Ryan, Lisa Dean — Actress
1327 Brinkley Ave, Los Angeles CA 90049, USA
Ryan, Matt — Actor
W M E Entertainment, 9601 Wilshire Blvd, #300, Beverly Hills CA 90210 USA
Ryan, Matthew T (Matt) — Football Player
3268 Bransley Way, Duluth GA 30097, USA
Ryan, Meg — Actress
United Talent Agency, 9336 Civic Center Dr, Beverly Hills CA 90210 USA
Ryan, Michael E (Mike) — Air Force General
United Services Automobile Assn, 9800 Fredericksburg Road, San Antonio TX 78288, USA
Ryan, Michael J (Mike) — Baseball Player
592 Stoneham Road, Wolfeboro NH 03894, USA
Ryan, Michael S — Baseball Player
521 Water St, Indiana PA 15701, USA
Ryan, Michelle — Actress
Independent Talent Group, Oxford House, 76 Oxford St, London W1D 1BS, England
Ryan, Mitchell — Actor
C E S D, 10635 Santa Monica Blvd, #130, Los Angeles CA 90025 USA
Ryan, Norbert R, Jr — Navy Admiral
Military Officers Assn, 201 N Washington St, Alexandria VA 22314, USA
Ryan, Patrick L (Pat) — Football Player
6930 Old Kent Dr, Knoxville TN 37919, USA
Ryan, Rebecca — Model, Actress
United Agents, 12-26 Lexington St, London W1F 0LE, England
Ryan, Rex — Football Coach
New York Jets, 1 Jets Dr, Florham Park NJ 07932 USA
Ryan, Robert V (B J), Jr — Baseball Player
1211 Perdenalas Trail, Westlake TX 76262, USA
Ryan, Roz — Actress
Gage Group, 315 W 57th St, #4H, New York NY 10019 USA
Ryan, Shawn — Producer, Writer
MiddKid Productions, 10201 W Pico Blvd, Los Angeles CA 90035, USA
Ryan, Thomas M — Businessman
C V S/Caremark Corp, 1 C V S/Caremark Dr, Woonsocket RI 02895, USA
Ryan, Tim — Actor
S M S Talent, 8383 Wilshire Blvd, #230, Beverly Hills CA 90211 USA

Ryan, Tom K — Cartoonist (Tumbleweeds)
North American Syndicate, 235 E 45th St, New York NY 10017 USA

Ryans, DeMeco — Football Player
Philadelphia Eagles, 1 Novacare Way, Philadelphia PA 19145 USA

Ryazanov, Eldar A — Director
Bolshoi Tishinski Per 12, #70, 123557 Moscow, Russia

Rybczynski, Witold — Writer
Charles Scribner's Sons, 866 3rd Ave, New York NY 10022 USA

Rybkin, Ivan P — Government Official, Russia
Administration of President, Staraya Pl 4, 103132 Moscow, Russia

Rychel, Warren — Ice Hockey Player
Windsor Spitfires, 334 Wyandotte St E, Windsor ON N9A 3H6, Canada

Rychlec, Thomas R (Tom) — Football Player
71 Round Hill Road, Southington CT 06489, USA

Rycroft Strickland, Melissa K — Actress
W M E Entertainment, 9601 Wilshire Blvd, #300, Beverly Hills CA 90210 USA

Rycroft, Carter — Curling Athlete
Curling Assn, 1660 Vimont Court, Cumberland ON K4A 4J4, Canada

Ryczek, Daniel S (Dan) — Football Player
3714 Monitor Place, Olney MD 20832, USA

Ryczek, Paul A — Football Player
9335 Scott Road, Roswell GA 30076, USA

Rydal, Emma — Actress
Rights House, 34-43 Russell St, London WC2B 5HA, England

Rydalch, Ronald J (Ron) — Football Player
500 E Durfee St, Grantsville UT 84029, USA

Rydell, Bobby — Singer, Actor
917 Bryn Mawr Ave, Penn Valley PA 19072, USA

Rydell, Christopher — Actor
911 N Sweetzer, #C, West Hollywood CA 90069, USA

Rydell, Mark — Director
Concourse Productions, 435 N Oakhurst Dr, #602, Beverly Hills CA 90210, USA

Ryder, Mitch — Singer
Hoffman Talent Agency, PO Box 26037, Minneapolis MN 55426, USA

Ryder, Norman B — Sociologist
Princeton University, Sociology Dept, Princeton NJ 08544, USA

Ryder, Thomas O — Publisher
Reader's Digest Assn, Publisher's Office, PO Box 100, Pleasantville NY 10570, USA

Ryder, Winona — Actress
Gersh Agency, 9465 Wilshire Blvd, #600, Beverly Hills CA 90212 USA

Ryding, Yvonne A — Beauty Queen
Anderzson Care, PO Box 160, SE 271 24 Ystad, Sweden

Rydze, Richard — Diver
383 Kane Blvd, Pittsburgh PA 15243, USA

Ryerson, Ann — Actress
Abrams Artists, 9200 W Sunset Blvd, #1125, West Hollywood CA 90069 USA

Rykiel, Sonia F — Fashion Designer
175 Blvd Saint Germain, 75006 Paris, France

Rylance, Georgina — Actress
Markham & Froggatt, Julian House, 4 Windmill St, London W1P 1HF, England

Rylance, Mark — Director, Actor
Hamilton Hodell, 66-68 Margaret St, London W1W 8SR, England

Rylko, Stanislaw Cardinal — Religious Leader
Pontifical Council for Laity, Piazza S Calisto 16, 00153 Rome, Italy

Ryman, Robert T — Artist
17 W 16th St, New York NY 10011, USA

Rymer, Charlie — Golfer, Sportscaster
11721 Camden Park Dr, Windermere FL 34786, USA

Rymsha, Andy — Ice Hockey Player
8124 Huntington Road, Huntington Woods MI 48070, USA

Rynkiewicz, Mariusz — Sculptor
12401 Alexander Road, Everett WA 98204, USA

Rypdal, Terje — Guitarist, Flutist, Composer
P J P As, Utragata 16, 5700 Voss, Norway

Rypien, Mark R — Football Player
8817 N Warren St, Spokane WA 99208, USA

Ryu, So Yeon — Golfer
Ladies Pro Golf Assn, 100 International Golf Dr, Daytona Beach FL 32124 USA

Ryumin, Valery V — Cosmonaut
Cosmonaut Training Center, Star City, 141160 Zvezdny Gorodok, Moscow Oblast, Russia

Ryun, James R (Jim) — Track Athlete; Representative, KS
132 D St SE, Washington DC 20003, USA

Ryzhkov, Nikolai I — Premier, Russia
Federation Council, Bolshaya Dmitrovka Str 26, 103009 Moscow, Russia

RZA — Rap Artist (Wu-Tang Clan), Actor
I C M Partners, 10250 Constellation Blvd, #900, Los Angeles CA 90067 USA

Saadiq, Raphael — Singer, Songwriter
Universal Attractions, 135 W 26th St, #1200, New York NY 10001 USA
Saar, Bettye — Artist
8074 Willow Glen Road, Los Angeles CA 90046, USA
Saar, Eric — Writer
Penguin Books, 375 Hudson St, Basement 1, New York NY 10014 USA
Saarinen, Aino-Kalsa — Cross Country Skier
Suomen Hiihtoliitto, Radiokatu 20, 00093 Slu, Finland
Saarinen, Tero — Dancer, Choreographer
Tero Saarinen Co, Bulevardi 23-27, 00180 Helsinki, Finland
Saarloos, Kirk C — Baseball Player
8608 E Sunnywalk Lane, Anaheim CA 92808, USA
Saatchi, Charles — Businessman
36 Golden Square, London W1R 4EE, England
Saatchi, Maurice — Businessman
36 Golden Square, London W1R 4EE, England
Sabah IV, Sheikh Ahmad Jabar al-Sabah — Emir, Kuwait
Darwa Salwa Palace, Amiry Diwan, Kuwait City, Kuwait
Sabah, Sheikh Nasser Al Mohammed al- — Prime Minister, Kuwait
Prime Minister's Office, PO Box 4, Safat 13001, Kuwait City, Kuwait
Saban, Louis H (Lou) — Football Player, Coach
2087 Appalachee Circle, Tavares FL 32778, USA
Saban, Nick — Football Coach
University of Alabama, Athletic Dept, Tuscaloosa AL 35487, USA
Sabara, Daryl — Actor
A P A Talent/Literary Agency, 405 S Beverly Dr, #300, Beverly Hills CA 90212 USA
Sabates, Felix — Auto Racing Executive
Ganassi Racing, 600 E Laburnum Ave, Richmond VA 23222, USA
Sabathia, Carsten C (C C) — Baseball Player
PO Box 30, Alpine NJ 07620, USA
Sabatini, David D — Cell Biologist, Biochemist
New York University, Cell Biology/Biochemistry Dept, New York NY 10012, USA
Sabatini, Gabriela — Tennis Player
35/35 Grosvenor St, London W1K 4QX, England
Sabatino, Joe — Actor
Acme Talent Agency, 4727 Wilshire Blvd, #333, Los Angeles CA 90010 USA
Sabatino, Michael — Actor
13538 Valleyheart Dr, Sherman Oaks CA 91423, USA
Sabato, Antonio, Jr — Actor, Model
Global Artists Agency, 6253 Hollywood Blvd, #508, Los Angeles CA 90028 USA
Sabbatini, Rory — Golfer
9472 Sagrada Park, Fort Worth TX 76126, USA
Sabelle — Singer, Songwriter
Sarmast Entertainment, 241 W 36th St, #2R, New York NY 10018, USA
Saberhagen, Bret W — Baseball Player
Make a Difference Foundation, 6520 Platt Ave, #566, West Hills CA 91307, USA
Sabo, Christopher A (Chris) — Baseball Player
7455 Stonemeadow Lane, Cincinnati OH 45242, USA
Sabol, Edward E (Ed) — Producer, Filmmaker
N F L Films, 330 Fellowship Road, Mount Laurel NJ 08054, USA
Sabourin, Gary B — Ice Hockey Player
54 Holland Ave, Chatham ON N7M 2C7, Canada
Saca Gonzalez, E Antonio (Tony) — President, El Salvador
Casa Presidencial, Calle Dario Gonzales 806, San Salvador, El Salvador
Sacca, Anthony J (Tony) — Football Player
11 Heather Glen Lane, Riverside NJ 08075, USA
Sacco, Joe — Ice Hockey Player, Coach
1001 Southbury Place, Littleton CO 80129, USA
Sacco, Joe — Cartoonist
305 SE Ankeny St, Portland OR 97233, USA
Saccone, Viviana — Actress
Telefe, Pavon 2444, (C1248AAT) Buenos Aires, Argentina
Sachar, Louis — Writer
Delacorte Press, 1540 Broadway, New York NY 10036 USA
Sacharuk, Lawrence W (Larry) — Ice Hockey Player
HG Tiroler Wasserkraft, Olumpiastr 10, Innsbruck 6020, Austria
Sachdev, Asha — Actress
18B Sunset Heights, 59 Pali Hill Bandra, Mumbai MS 400050, India
Sachenbacher-Stehle, Evi — Cross Country Skier
Birnbacher Str 1, 83242 Reit im Winkl, Germany
Sachs, Andrew — Actor
Richard Stone Partnership, 85 New Cavendish St, London W1W 6XD, England
Sachs, Ira — Director, Writer
Marie Therese Guirgis Mgmt, 125 Riverside Dr, #8C, New York NY 10024, USA
Sachs, Jeffrey D — Economist
Harvard University, International Development Institute, Cambridge MA 02138, USA
Sack, Kevin — Journalist
Los Angeles Times, Editorial Dept, 202 W 1st St, Los Angeles CA 90012 USA
Sack, Robert D — Judge
US Court of Appeals, Moynihan Courthouse, 500 Pearl St, New York NY 10007, USA
Sack, Steve — Cartoonist (Professor Doodle's)
Minneapolis Star-Tribune, 425 Portland Ave, Minneapolis MN 55488, USA
Sackheim, Daniel — Director
Creative Artists Agency, 2000 Ave of Stars, #100, Los Angeles CA 90067 USA
Sackhoff, Katee — Actress
Bleu Entertainment, 5225 Wilshire Blvd, #336, Los Angeles CA 90036, USA
Sacko, Soumana — Prime Minister, Mali
Villa 14 Bis 48, Sema Gexco, Bamako, Mali
Sacks, Greg — Auto Racing Driver
6092 Sabal Creek Blvd, Port Orange FL 32128, USA
Sacks, Jonathan H — Religious Leader
735 High Road, London N12 0US, England
Sacks, Oliver W — Writer, Physician, Neurologist
2 Horatio St, #3G, New York NY 10014, USA
Sacramone, Alicia M — Gymnast
Frederick Sacramone, 41 Hastings Road, Winchester MA 01890, USA

Sadat, Jehan El- — Social Activist
University of Maryland, International Development Center, College Park MD 20742, USA
Sade — Singer, Songwriter
R D W M, 37 Limestone St, London SW10 0BQ, England
Sadecki, Raymond M (Ray) — Baseball Player
4237 E Clovis Ave, Mesa AZ 85206, USA
Sadek, Michael G (Mike) — Baseball Player
6741 Quartz Mine Road, Mountain Ranch CA 95246, USA
Sadier, Laetitia — Singer, Musician (Stereolab)
Duophonic Records, PO Box 3787, London SE22 9DZ, England
Sadik, Nafis — Government Official, Pakistan
300 E 56th St, #9J, New York NY 10022, USA
Sadiq Al-Mahedi — Prime Minister, Sudan
Club de Madrid, C/Goya 5-7, Pasaje 2, 28001 Madrid, Spain
Sadler, Donnie L — Baseball Player
802 Sadler Road, Valley Mills TX 76689, USA
Sadler, Elliott W B — Auto, Truck Racing Driver
108 Conway Court, Mooresville NC 28117, USA
Sadler, Herman M (Hermie), III — Auto Racing Driver
PO Box 32, Emporia VA 23847, USA
Sadler, William — Actor
Don Buchwald/Fortitude, 6500 Wilshire Blvd, #2200, Los Angeles CA 90048 USA
Sadoski, Thomas — Actor
United Talent Agency, 9336 Civic Center Dr, Beverly Hills CA 90210 USA
Sadoyan, Isabelle — Actress
Artmedia, 20 Ave Rapp, 75007 Paris, France
Saenz, Olmedo — Baseball Player
4300 W Ford City Dr, #1002, Chicago IL 60652, USA
Saez Conde, Inez L — Beauty Queen
Miss Universe Organization, 1370 Ave of Americas, #1600, New York NY 10019 USA
Safdie, Moshe — Architect
100 Rev Nazareno Properzi Way, Somerville MA 02143, USA
Safer, Morley — Commentator
CBS-TV, News Dept, 524 W 57th St, New York NY 10019, USA
Saffiotti, Umberto — Pathologist
5114 Wissioming Road, Bethesda MD 20816, USA
Saffo, Paul — Non-Profit Executive, Journalist
Institute for the Future, 27740 Sand Hill Road, Menlo Park CA 94025, USA
Safin, Marat M — Tennis Player
T C Weiden am Postkeller, Schirmitzer Weg, 92637 Weiden, Germany
Safina, Carl — Marine Biologist
Blue Spring Institute, 250 Lawrence Hill Road, Cold Spring Harbor NY 11724, USA
Safina, Dinara M — Tennis Player
Women's Tennis Assn, 1 Progress Plaza, #1500, Saint Petersburg FL 33701 USA
Safiq, Ahmed M — Prime Minister, Egypt
Prime Minister's Office, PO Box 191, 1 Majlis El-Shaab St, Cairo, Egypt
Safran, Joshua — Director, Writer
United Talent Agency, 9336 Civic Center Dr, Beverly Hills CA 90210 USA
Safuto, Dominick (Randy) — Singer (Randy & the Rainbows)
Brothers Mgmt, 141 Dunbar Ave, Fords NJ 08863 USA
Safuto, Frank — Singer (Randy & the Rainbows)
Brothers Mgmt, 141 Dunbar Ave, Fords NJ 08863 USA
Sagal, Jean — Actress
Progressive Artists Agency, 1041 N Formosa Ave, West Hollywood CA 90046 USA
Sagal, Katey — Actress
B & B Mgmt, 1041 N Formosa Ave, West Hollywood CA 90046, USA
Saganiuk, Rocky — Ice Hockey Player
13252 Lake Mary Dr, Plainfield IL 60585, USA
Sagdeev, Roald Z — Physicist
University of Maryland, East-West Space Center, College Park MD 20742, USA
Sage, Bill — Actor
Don Buchwald/Fortitude, 6500 Wilshire Blvd, #2200, Los Angeles CA 90048 USA
Sage, Halston — Actress
Creative Artists Agency, 2000 Ave of Stars, #100, Los Angeles CA 90067 USA
Sage, Wendy — Actress
Bobby Ball Agency, 4116 W Magnolia Blvd, #205, Burbank CA 91505, USA
Sage, William (Bill) — Actor
Don Buchwald/Fortitude, 6500 Wilshire Blvd, #2200, Los Angeles CA 90048 USA
Sagebrecht, Marianne — Actress
Postfach 1454, 80539 Munich, Germany
Sagemiller, Melissa — Actress
Paradigm Agency, 360 N Crescent Dr, North Building, Beverly Hills CA 90210 USA
Sager, Anthony J (A J) — Baseball Player
10310 Belmont Meadows Lane, Perrysburg OH 43551, USA
Sager, Carole Bayer — Singer, Songwriter
10779 Bellagio Road, Los Angeles CA 90077, USA
Sager, Craig — Sportscaster
Jock Jill & Frankie's Sports Grill, 5600 Roswell Road NE, #M3, Atlanta GA 30342, USA
Saget, Robert L (Bob) — Actor, Comedian
Brillstein Entertainment Partners, 9150 Wilshire Blvd, #350, Beverly Hills CA 90212 USA
Sagnier, Ludivine — Actress
Agence Elizabeth Simpson, 62 Blvd de Montparnasse, 75015 Paris, France
Sagona, Katie — Actress
Wilhelmina Creative Mgmt, 300 Park Ave S, #200, New York NY 10010, USA
Sagripanti, Giacomo — Conductor
I M G Artists, Hogarth Business Park, Chiswick, London W4 2TH, England
Sahagun, Elena — Actress
Artists Agency, 1180 S Beverly Dr, #301, Los Angeles CA 90035 USA
Sahakyan, Bako — President, Nagorno-Karabakh
President's Office, Nagorno-Karabakh, Stepanakert, Nahorni, Azerbaijan
Sahanaja, Darian — Keyboardist (Wondermints)
Paradise Artists, PO Box 1821, Ojai CA 93024 USA
Sahay, Vikram (Vik) — Actor
Don Buchwald/Fortitude, 6500 Wilshire Blvd, #2200, Los Angeles CA 90048 USA
Sahl, Mort — Actor, Comedian
1441 3rd Ave, #12C, New York NY 10028, USA

Said, Ali Ahmad (Adonis) — Writer
Green Inter Books, 6022 Wilshire Blvd, #200A, Los Angeles CA 90036, USA
Said, Boris — Auto, Truck Racing Driver
15 Avalon Road, Martin GA 30557, USA
Sailors, Kenneth L (Ken) — Basketball Player
2119 E Grand Ave, #6, Laramie WY 82070, USA
Saimes, George — Football Player, Executive
2307 Beechmoor Dr NW, North Canton OH 44720, USA
Saini, Rajiv — Architect, Interior Designer
Rajiv Saini Assoc, 9 Jer Mansion, Bandra (W), Mumbai 400050, India
Sainsbury of Preston Candover, John D — Businessman
J Sainsbury PLC, 33 Holborn, London EC1N 2HT, England
Sainsbury of Turville, David J — Businessman
Eagle House, 110 Jermyn St, London SW1Y 6EE, England
Sainsbury, R Mark — Philosopher
King's College, Philosophy Dept, London WC2R 2LS, England
Saint Claire, Randy A — Baseball Player
7117 State Route 8, Brant Lake NY 12815, USA
Saint James, Susan — Actress
174 West St, #54, Litchfield CT 06759, USA
Saint, Crosbie E — Army General
1116 N Pitt St, Alexandria VA 22314, USA
Saint, Eva Marie — Actress
I C M Partners, 10250 Constellation Blvd, #900, Los Angeles CA 90067 USA
Sainte-Marie, Buffy — Singer, Guitarist, Songwriter
RR 1 Box 368, Kapaa HI 96746, USA
Saint-Subber, Arnold — Producer
116 E 64th St, New York NY 10065, USA
Sainz Gall de Perez, Ines — Journalist
TV Azteca, Periferico 4121, Colonia Fuentes Pedregal, DF CP 14141, Mexico
Sainz, Salvador — Actor, Director
Ave Prat de la Riba 43, 43201 Reus (Tarragona), Spain
Saipe, Mike E — Baseball Player
4191 Combe Way, San Diego CA 92122, USA
Sajak, Pat — Entertainer
Wheel of Fortune Show, 3400 Riverside Dr, #201, Burbank CA 91505, USA
Sajko, Kristina — Model
D N A Model Mgmt, 555 W 25th St, #600, New York NY 10001 USA
Sakaguchi, Mizuho — Soccer Player
Football Assn, 3-10-15 Hongo, Bunkyoku, Tokyo 113 0033 Japan
Sakamoto, Ryoichi — Composer, Musician
Creative Artists Agency, 2000 Ave of Stars, #100, Los Angeles CA 90067 USA
Sakamura, Ken — Computer Scientist, Inventor
University of Tokyo, Information Science Dept, 7-3-1 Hongo, Bunkyoku, Tokyo 113-0033, Japan
Sakata, Lenn H — Baseball Player
2490 2nd Ave, Merced CA 95340, USA
Sakato, George T — WW II Army Hero (CMH)
8369 Katherine Way, Denver CO 80221, USA
Sakharov, Alik — Cinematographer
Global Artists Agency, 6253 Hollywood Blvd, #508, Los Angeles CA 90028 USA
Sakic, Joseph S (Joe) — Ice Hockey Player
4785 S Franklin St, Englewood CO 80113, USA
Sakmann, Bert — Nobel Medicine Laureate
Max Planck Institute, Jahnstr 39, 69120 Heidelberg, Germany
Saks, Gene — Director, Actor
I C M Partners, 730 5th Ave, New York NY 10019 USA
Sakshaug, Eugene C — Electrical Engineer
18 Grove Ave, Pittsfield MA 01201, USA
Sala, Edoardo — Actor
Agenzia Paola Bonelli, Via Parioli 50, 00197 Rome, Italy
Sala, Richard — Cartoonist (Peculia)
3131 College Ave, Berkeley CA 94705, USA
Sala, Sharon — Writer
Mira/Harlequin, 225 Duncan Mill Road, Don Mills ON MJB JK9, CA
Salaam, Ephraim M — Football Player
8868 Chadbury Place, Elk Grove CA 95758, USA
Salaam, Rashaan I — Football Player
8132 Brookhaven Road, San Diego CA 92114, USA
Saladino, John F — Interior Designer
Saladino Group, 200 Lexington Ave, #1600, New York NY 10016, USA
Salans, Lester B — Physician
Sandoz Research Institute, RR 10, East Hanover NJ 07936, USA
Salas, Mark B — Baseball Player
1302 6th St SE, Ruskin FL 33570, USA
Salazar, Alberto — Track Athlete
Nike Inc, 1 SW Bowerman Dr, Beaverton OR 97005, USA
Salazar, Angel — Actor, Comedian
OmniPop Talent Group, 4605 Lankershim Blvd, #201, Toluca Lake CA 91602 USA
Salazar, Kenneth L (Ken) — Secretary, Interior; Senator, CO
Interior Department, 1849 C St NW, Washington DC 20240 USA
Salazar, Luis E — Baseball Player
20808 Cabrillo Way, Boca Raton FL 33428, USA
Salcido Flores, Carlos A — Soccer Player
Federacion de Futbol, Colima 373 Colonia Roma, Delegacion Cuauhtemoc Mexico DF 06700, Mexico
Saldana, Theresa — Actress
B D P Assoc, 10637 Burbank Blvd, North Hollywood CA 91601 USA
Saldana, Zoe — Actress
I C M Partners, 10250 Constellation Blvd, #900, Los Angeles CA 90067 USA
Saldanha, Carlos — Animator, Director
Blue Sky Studios, 44 S Broadway, #1700, White Springs NY 10601, USA
Saldi, J Jay, IV — Football Player
303 Donley Court, Southlake TX 76092, USA
Saldivar, Lou — Graphic Artist
Milwaukee Journal Sentinel, Editorial Dept, PO Box 371, Milwaukee WI 53201 USA
Sale, Jamie R — Ice Dancer
12116 NW 128th St, Edmonton AB T5L 1C3, Canada

Saleaumua, R Daniel (Dan)
1603 Morning Breeze Lane, National City CA 91950, USA — Football Player

Saleh, Karim
Ken McReddie Assoc, 11 Connaught Place, London W2 2ET, England — Actor

Salem, Dahlia
Anthem Entertainment, 5225 Wilshire Blvd, #615, Los Angeles CA 90036 USA — Actress

Salem, Harvey M
25 Menlo Place, Berkeley CA 94707, USA — Football Player

Salem, Kario
Creative Artists Agency, 2000 Ave of Stars, #100, Los Angeles CA 90067 USA — Writer, Actor

Salenger, Meredith
Shelter Entertainment, 9454 Wilshire Blvd, #715, Beverly Hills CA 90212 USA — Actress

Salerno-Sonnenberg, Nadja
Opus 3 Artists, 470 Park Ave S, #900N, New York NY 10016 USA — Concert Violinist

Sales, Nykesha
Connecticut Sun, 1 Mohegan Sun Blvd, Uncasville CT 06382 USA — Basketball Player

Saleski, Don
1800 N Ridley Creek Road, Media PA 19063, USA — Ice Hockey Player

Salfati, Pierre-Henri
Artmedia, 20 Ave Rapp, 75007 Paris, France — Actor

Salgado, Curtis
Odaglas, 22660 NW Dogwood St, Hillsboro OR 97124, USA — Singer, Harmonica Player

Salgado, Sebastiano R, Jr
Instituto Terra, Bulcao Farm Land Institute, PO Box 005, 35200 000 Aimores MG, Brazil — Photographer

Saliers, Emily
Russell Carter Artist Mgmt, 567 Ralph Mcgill Blvd, Atlanta GA 30312, USA — Singer (Indigo Girls), Songwriter

Salim, Salim Ahmed
Organization of African Unity, PO Box 3243, Addis Ababa, Ethiopia — Prime Minister, Tanzania

Salinger, Diane
The Agency, 3711 Ocean Front Walk, #1, Marina del Rey CA 90292 USA — Actress

Salinger, Matt
Bresler Kelly Assoc, 11500 W Olympic Blvd, #400, Los Angeles CA 90064 USA — Actor

Salisbury, Laney
Random House, 1745 Broadway, #1800, New York NY 10019 USA — Writer

Salisbury, R Sean
5823 Brushy Creek Trail, Dallas TX 75252, USA — Football Player

Salkeld, Roger W
27834 Ridgegrove Dr, Santa Clarita CA 91350, USA — Baseball Player

Salkind, Ilya
Pinewood Studios, Iverheath, Iver, Bucks SL0 0NH, England — Producer

Sallah, Michael D
Toledo Blade, Editorial Dept, 541 N Superior St, Toledo OH 43660, USA — Journalist

Salle, David
Deitch-Boone Gallery, 541 W 24th St, New York NY 10011, USA — Artist

Salle, Jerome
U B B A, 6 Rue de Braque, 75003 Paris, France — Director, Writer

Salles, Walter, Jr
VideoFilmes, Rua Do Russel 270 - Gloria, Rio de Janeiro RJ 22210 110, Brazil — Director

Salley, John T
4619 Caritina Dr, Tarzana CA 91356, USA — Basketball Player, Sportscaster, Actor

Sallinen, Aulis H
Teosto, Lauttasaarentie 1, 00200 Helsinki 20, Finland — Composer

Salling, Mark
Momentum Talent, 9401 Wilshire Blvd, #501, Beverly Hills CA 90212, USA — Actor

Sallis, Peter
Jonathan Altaras Assoc, 11 Garrick St, London WC2E 9AR, England — Actor

Sally, Jerome E
4107 Roxbury Court, Columbia MO 65203, USA — Football Player

Salminen, Matti
Mariedi Anders Artists, 3030 Baker St, San Francisco CA 94123 USA — Opera Singer

Salming, Borje
Box 45438, 104 31 Stockholm, Sweden — Ice Hockey Player

Salmoiraghi, Franco
PO Box 61708, Honolulu HI 96839, USA — Photographer

Salmon, Timothy J (Tim)
6061 E Sunnside Dr, Scottsdale AZ 85254, USA — Baseball Player

Salmons, John R
909 Waverly Road, Bryn Mawr PA 19010, USA — Basketball Player

Salmons, Stephen (Steve)
1717 N El Dorado Ave, Ontario CA 91764, USA — Volleyball Player

Salo, Mika J
Sauber Racing, Wildbachstr 9, 8340 Hinwil, Switzerland — Auto Racing Driver

Salo, Ola
Live Nation, Linnegatan 89, Box 21451, 104 51 Stockholm, Sweden — Singer, Guitarist, Pianist (The Ark)

Salo, Sami
Vancouver Canucks, 800 Griffiths Way, Vancouver BC V6B 6G1, Canada — Ice Hockey Player

Salo, Teemu
Curling Assn, Kalatorppa 2A62, 02230 Espoo, Finland — Curling Athlete

Salo, Tommy M
Lefksands I F, Box 118, 793 23 Leksand, Sweden — Ice Hockey Player

Salome, Jean-Paul
Voyez Mon Agent, 20 Ave Rapp, 75007 Paris, France — Director

Salomon, Leon E (Lee)
2795 Kipps Colony Dr S, Saint Petersburg FL 33707, USA — Army General

Salomon, Mikael
Creative Artists Agency, 2000 Ave of Stars, #100, Los Angeles CA 90067 USA — Director, Cinematographer

Salonen, Esa-Pekka
Cathy Nelson, Court House, Dorstone, Herefordshire HR3 6AW, England — Conductor, Composer

Salonga, Lea
Atlantic Records, 1290 Ave of Americas, Concourse 3, New York NY 10104 USA — Singer, Actress

Salopek, Paul
Chicago Tribune, Editorial Dept, 350 N Orleans St, Chicago IL 60654 USA — Journalist

Salt, Charlotte
Seven Summits Mgmt, 8906 W Olympic Blvd, Beverly Hills CA 90211 USA — Actress

Salt, Jennifer
3742 Sheridge Dr, Sherman Oaks CA 91403, USA — Actress

Saltalamacchia, Jarrod S — Baseball Player
12688 Headwater Circle, Wellington FL 33414, USA
Salter, Bryant J — Football Player
16810 SW 88th Court, Village of Palmetto Bay FL 33157, USA
Salter, James — Writer
Knopf Publishers, 1745 Broadway, New York NY 10019 USA
Salter, Russell D — Immunologist
University of Pittsburgh Medical School, Immunology Dept, Pittsburgh PA 15260, USA
Saltykov, Aleksey A — Director
Institute Mosfilmovsky Per 4A, #104, 119285 Moscow, Russia
Saltykov, Boris G — Economist; Government Official, Russia
Russian Technologies, Bryusov Per 11, 103009 Moscow, Russia
Salva, Victor — Director
Gersh Agency, 9465 Wilshire Blvd, #600, Beverly Hills CA 90212 USA
Salvador, Bryce — Ice Hockey Player
1059 Lawrence Ave, Westfield NJ 07090, USA
Salvadori, Al — Basketball Player
1204 Lenox Dr, Bethel Park PA 15102, USA
Salvatore, Diane J — Editor
Ladies' Home Journal, Editor's Office, 125 Park Ave, New York NY 10017, USA
Salvatore, Robert A (R A) — Writer
Tom Doherty Assoc, 175 5th Ave, New York NY 10010, USA
Salvay, Bennett — Composer
Gorfaine/Schwartz, 4111 W Alameda Ave, #509, Burbank CA 91505 USA
Salvino, Carmen — Bowler
65 Stevens Dr, Schaumburg IL 60173, USA
Salwen, Hal — Director
Gersh Agency, 9465 Wilshire Blvd, #600, Beverly Hills CA 90212 USA
Salzman, Mark — Writer
Random House, 1745 Broadway, #1800, New York NY 10019 USA
Sam the Sham — Singer
6123 Old Brunswick Road, Arlington TN 38002, USA
Samaras, Antonis — Prime Minister, Greece
Prime Minister's Office, Maximos Mansion, 19 Irodou Attikou St, 10674 Athens, Greece
Samaras, Lucas — Sculptor, Photographer
Pace Wildenstein Gallery, 32 E 57th St, #400, New York NY 10022, USA
Samardzija, Jeff — Baseball Player
3351 N Southport Ave, Chicago IL 60657, USA
Samberg, Andy — Actor
United Talent Agency, 9336 Civic Center Dr, Beverly Hills CA 90210 USA
Samberg, D Andrew (Andy) — Actor, Comedian
Mosiac Media Group, 9200 W Sunset Blvd, #1000, Los Angeles CA 90069 USA
Sambito, Joseph C (Joe) — Baseball Player
23 Modesto, Irvine CA 92602, USA
Sambora, Richard S (Richie) — Singer, Songwriter (Bon Jovi)
Bon Jovi Mgmt, 809 Elder Circle, Austin TX 78733, USA
Samcoff, Edward W (Ed) — Baseball Player
8153 Maderia Port Lane, Fair Oaks CA 95628, USA
Sameshima, Aya — Soccer Player
Football Assn, 3-10-15 Hongo, Bunkyoku, Tokyo 113 0033 Japan
Samet, Jonathan M — Epidemiologist
Johns Hopkins University, Bloomberg Public Health School, Baltimore MD 21205, USA
Samford, Ronald E (Ron) — Baseball Player
2174 Kessler Court, Dallas TX 75208, USA
Samie, Catherine — Actress
Artmedia, 20 Ave Rapp, 75007 Paris, France
Samios, Nicholas P — Science Administrator, Physicist
Brookhaven National Laboratory, Director's Office, 2 Center St, Upton NY 11973, USA
Sammons, Clint — Baseball Player
732 King Sword Court SE, Mableton GA 30126, USA
Sammons, Mary F — Businesswoman
Rite Aid Corp, 30 Hunter Lane, Camp Hill PA 17011, USA
Samms, Emma — Actress
2934 1/2 N Beverly Glen Circle, #417, Los Angeles CA 90077, USA
Samoilova, Tatiana Y — Actress
Spiridonyevsky Per 8/11, 103104 Moscow, Russia
Samokutyaev, Alexander M — Cosmonaut
Cosmonaut Training Center, Star City, 141160 Zvezdny Gorodok, Moscow Oblast, Russia
Sampen, William A (Bill) — Baseball Player
11 Carnaby Court, Brownsburg IN 46112, USA
Sampey, Angelle — Motorcycle Racing Rider, Auto Driver
Star Racing, PO Box 1241, Americus GA 31709, USA
Sample, Joseph L (Joe) — Jazz Pianist
I C M Partners, 10250 Constellation Blvd, #900, Los Angeles CA 90067 USA
Sample, Steven B — Educator
211 S Orange Grove Blvd, #14, Pasadena CA 91105, USA
Sample, William A (Billy) — Baseball Player
10 Pascack Road, Township of Washington NJ 07676, USA
Sampler, Philece — Actress
Vox Inc, 6420 Wilshire Blvd, #1080, Los Angeles CA 90048 USA
Samples, Keith — Writer
Characters Talent Mgmt, 8 Elm St, Toronto ON M5G 1G7, Canada
Sampleton, Lawrence — Football Player
2900 Bunny Run, Austin TX 78746, USA
Sampras, Peter (Pete) — Tennis Player
2552 Via Anita, Palos Verdes Estates CA 90274, USA
Sampson, Benjamin D (Benji) — Baseball Player
8312 Flat Rock Court, North Richland Hills TX 76182, USA
Sampson, Gary — Ice Hockey Player
Alaska Sportsman's Lodge, PO Box 231985, Anchorage AK 99523, USA
Sampson, Kelvin — Basketball Coach
Milwaukee Bucks, Bradley Center, 1001 N 4th St, #2, Milwaukee WI 53203 USA
Sampson, R Gregory (Greg) — Football Player
3286 Highland Dr, Carlsbad CA 92008, USA
Sampson, Ralph L, Jr — Basketball Player, Coach
530 Myrtle St, Harrisonburg VA 22802, USA

S

Sams, Dean Borman Entertainment, 4322 Harding Pike, #429, Nashville TN 37205, USA	Keyboardist (Lonestar)
Sams, Judy 2603 Wells Ave, Sarasota FL 34232, USA	Golfer
Sams, Russell TalentWorks, 3500 W Olive Ave, #1400, Burbank CA 91505 USA	Actor
Samsonov, Sergei V 2896 Croftshire Court, Rochester MI 48306, USA	Ice Hockey Player
Samuel, Amado R 1931 Yale Dr, Louisville KY 40205, USA	Baseball Player
Samuel, Asante T 19340 SW 54th St, Miramar FL 33029, USA	Football Player
Samuel, Juan M 777 S Eden St, Baltimore MD 21231, USA	Baseball Player
Samuell, Yann Films Talents, 34 Rue Du Louvre, 75001 Paris, France	Director, Writer
Samuels, Chris 8415 Fredericksburg Road, #906, San Antonio TX 78229, USA	Football Player
Samuels, Roger N 4865 Tampico Way, San Jose CA 95118, USA	Baseball Player
Samuelsson, Bengt I Karolinska Institute, Chemistry Dept, 171 77 Stockholm, Sweden	Nobel Medicine Laureate
Samuelsson, K Mikael 44751 Roundview Dr, Novi MI 48375, USA	Ice Hockey Player
Samuelsson, Kjell 5 Simsbury Dr, Voorhees NJ 08043, USA	Ice Hockey Player
Samuelsson, Ulf 19175 N 95th Place, Scottsdale AZ 85255, USA	Ice Hockey Player, Coach
Sanada, Hiroyuki Lighthouse Entertainment, 9220 W Sunset Blvd, #200, West Hollywood CA 90069 USA	Actor
Sanborn, David Patrick Rains Assoc, 1255 5th Ave, #7J, New York NY 10029, USA	Jazz Saxophonist, Composer
Sanches, Brian 903 N 31st St, Nederland TX 77627, USA	Baseball Player
Sanches, Stacy Playboy Promotions, 2706 Media Center Dr, Los Angeles CA 90065 USA	Model, Actress
Sanchez Azuara, Rocio TV Azteca, Periferico 4121, Colonia Fuentes Pedregal, DF CP 14141, Mexico	Actress
Sanchez Vicario, Arantxa Sabino de Arana 28, #6-1A, 08028 Barcelona, Spain	Tennis Player
Sanchez Vicario, Emilio A Sabino de Arana 28, #6-1A, 08028 Barcelona, Spain	Tennis Player
Sanchez, Alejandro A (Alex) 1400 Mellissa Circle, Antioch CA 94509, USA	Baseball Player
Sanchez, Ana Maria Opera et Concert, 37 Rue de la Chaussee d'Antin, 75009 Paris, France	Opera Singer
Sanchez, Ashlyn Osbrink Talent Agency, 4343 Lankershim Blvd, #100, North Hollywood CA 91602 USA	Actress
Sanchez, David Addeo Music International, 37 W 26th St, #315, New York NY 10010, USA	Saxophonist
Sanchez, Duaner 56748 Eastvue Dr, Osceola IN 46561, USA	Baseball Player
Sanchez, Eduardo Haxan Films, PO Box 261370, Encino CA 91426, USA	Director, Producer, Writer
Sanchez, Frederick P (Freddy), Jr 2494 E Cloud Dr, Chandler AZ 85249, USA	Baseball Player
Sanchez, Gabriel (Gaby) 5621 SW 130th Place, Miami FL 33183, USA	Baseball Player
Sanchez, Hector Acero Shelly Finkel Mgmt, 110 Greene St, #403, New York NY 10012 USA	Boxer
Sanchez, Humberto A 3825 Glenford Dr, Clermont FL 34711, USA	Baseball Player
Sanchez, Keram Malicki Nine Yards Entertainment, 8530 Wilshire Blvd, #500, Beverly Hills CA 90211 USA	Actor
Sanchez, Kiele Industry Entertainment, 955 Carillo Dr, #300, Los Angeles CA 90048 USA	Actress
Sanchez, Marco Stone Manners Salners, 9911 W Pico Blvd, #1400, Los Angeles CA 90035 USA	Actor
Sanchez, Mark D New York Jets, 1 Jets Dr, Florham Park NJ 07932 USA	Football Player
Sanchez, Pedro Columbia University, Earth Institute, New York NY 10027, USA	Soil Scientist
Sanchez, Poncho PO Box 59236, Norwalk CA 90652, USA	Jazz Drummer
Sanchez, Roselyn A P A Talent/Literary Agency, 405 S Beverly Dr, #300, Beverly Hills CA 90212 USA	Actress
Sanchez, Samuel Euskadi-Fundacio Ciolista, C/Iparragirre 46-1, 48010 Bilboa, Spain	Cyclist
Sanchez-Gijon, Aitana Alsira Garcia Maroto, Gran Via 63, #3 Izda, 28013 Madrid, Spain	Actress
Sanchez-Vilella, Roberto 414 Ave Munoz Rivera, #7A, Stop 31-1/2, San Juan PR 00918, USA	Governor, Puerto Rico
Sand, Paul Paradigm Agency, 360 N Crescent Dr, North Building, Beverly Hills CA 90210 USA	Actor
Sand, Todd 2973 Harbor Blvd, #468, Costa Mesa CA 92626, USA	Figure Skater
Sanda, Dominique Agence Metropolitan Paris, 23 Blvd des Capucines, 75002 Paris, France	Actress
Sandberg of Passfield, Michael G R Waterside, Passfield, Liphook, Hants GU30 7RT, England	Financier
Sandberg, Ryne D 26 Biltmore Estates, Phoenix AZ 85016, USA	Baseball Player
Sande, Emeli Virgin Records, Kensal House, 533-79 Harrow Road, London W10 4RH, England	Singer, Musician, Songwriter
Sandelin, Scott 4880 Adrian Lane, Hermantown MN 55811, USA	Ice Hockey Player, Coach

Sams - Sandelin

Sandeman, William S (Bill) — Football Player
PO Box 203, Homewood CA 96141, USA
Sandeno, Kaitlin — Swimmer
78 Townsend, Irvine CA 92620, USA
Sander, Anne — Golfer
1261 Parkside Dr E, Seattle WA 98112, USA
Sander, Casey — Actor
Leavitt Talent Group, 11500 W Olympic Blvd, #400, Los Angeles CA 90064, USA
Sander, Ian — Producer, Director, Actor
Sander/Moses Productions, 500 S Buena Vista St, Burbank CA 91521, USA
Sander, Jil — Fashion Designer
Osterfeldstr 32-34, 22529 Hamburg, Germany
Sander, Judith M — Artist
25218 Oak Lane, Philomath OR 97370, USA
Sanders, Anthony M — Baseball Player
7881 E McGee Mountain Road, Tucson AZ 85750, USA
Sanders, Barry D — Football Player
PO Box 81336, Rochester MI 48308, USA
Sanders, Beverly — Actress
12218 Morrison St, Valley Village CA 91607, USA
Sanders, Bill — Cartoonist
PO Box 661, Milwaukee WI 53201, USA
Sanders, C J — Actor
Abrams Artists, 9200 W Sunset Blvd, #1125, West Hollywood CA 90069 USA
Sanders, Charles A (Charlie) — Football Player, Coach
3418 Palm Aire Court, Rochester Hills MI 48309, USA
Sanders, Chris — Director
W M E Entertainment, 9601 Wilshire Blvd, #300, Beverly Hills CA 90210 USA
Sanders, David A — Baseball Player
10411 S Ellen St, Mulvane KS 67110, USA
Sanders, Deion L — Football, Baseball Player, Sportscaster
1280 N Preston Road, Prosper TX 75078, USA
Sanders, Doug — Golfer
1311 Nantucket Dr, Houston TX 77057, USA
Sanders, Eric D — Football Player
9325 Tailey Circle, Duluth GA 30097, USA
Sanders, Erin — Actress
C E S D, 10635 Santa Monica Blvd, #130, Los Angeles CA 90025 USA
Sanders, Frank V — Football Player
4551 E Desert Trumpet Road, Phoenix AZ 85044, USA
Sanders, Franklyn B (Frank) — Ice Hockey Player
613 Lake View Dr, Saint Paul MN 55129, USA
Sanders, James B — Football Player
Arizona Cardinals, PO Box 888, Phoenix AZ 85001 USA
Sanders, Jay O — Actor
Innovative Artists, 1505 10th St, Santa Monica CA 90401 USA
Sanders, Jeff — Basketball Player
PO Box 374, South Holland IL 60473, USA
Sanders, John F — Baseball Player
3004 Cheshire Court, Woodstock GA 30189, USA
Sanders, Jonathan (Jon) — Yachtsman
Riverview Gardens, 20 Dean St, #95, Claremont, Perth WA 6010, Australia
Sanders, Kenneth G (Ken) — Baseball Player
12141 Parkview Lane, Hales Corners WI 53130, USA
Sanders, Kenneth R (Ken) — Football Player
3067 FM 217, Valley Mills TX 76689, USA
Sanders, Marlene — Commentator
175 Riverside Dr, New York NY 10024, USA
Sanders, Pharoah — Jazz Saxophonist
Lady U Productions, 484 W 43rd St, #29F, New York NY 10036, USA
Sanders, Reginald L (Reggie) — Baseball Player
122 Vista Del Mar Lane, #102, Myrtle Beach SC 29572, USA
Sanders, Richard — Actor
4954 Strohm Ave, North Hollywood CA 91601, USA
Sanders, Ricky W — Football Player
4822 Rockwood Dr, Houston TX 77004, USA
Sanders, Scott G — Baseball Player
315 Belmont Dr, Thibodaux LA 70301, USA
Sanders, Summer — Swimmer, Sportscaster
731 Martingale Lane, Park City UT 84098, USA
Sanders, Susan (Sue) — Golfer
3888 Cheyenne Place, Sedalia CO 80135, USA
Sanders, Thomas D — Football Player
2030 Appleton Dr, Missouri City TX 77489, USA
Sanders, Thomas E (Satch) — Basketball Player, Executive
114 Fenway, Boston MA 02115, USA
Sanders, Troy — Singer, Bassist (Mastodon)
Pinnacle Entertainment, 30 Glenn St, White Plains NY 10603, USA
Sanders, W J (Jerry), III — Businessman
Advanced Micro Devices, 1 A M D Place, PO Box 3453, Sunnyvale CA 94088, USA
Sanderson, Cael S — Freestyle Wrestler
Pennsylvania State University, Athletic Dept, University Park PA 16802, USA
Sanderson, Derek M — Ice Hockey Player
Howland Capital Mgmt, 75 Federal St, Boston MA 02110, USA
Sanderson, Geoff M — Ice Hockey Player
Philadelphia Flyers, 1st Union Center, 3601 S Broad St, Philadelphia PA 19148 USA
Sanderson, Peter — Artist
1105 Shell Gate Plaza, Alameda CA 94501, USA
Sanderson, Scott D — Baseball Player
945 Newcastle Dr, Lake Forest IL 60045, USA
Sanderson, Theresa (Tessa) — Track Athlete
Performing Artistes, 24A High St, Cobham KT11 3EB, England
Sanderson, William — Actor
TalentWorks, 3500 W Olive Ave, #1400, Burbank CA 91505 USA
Sandeson, William S — Editorial Cartoonist
2230 Muskoday Pass, Fort Wayne IN 46809, USA

Sandford, Ed — Ice Hockey Player
18 Clearwater Road, Winchester MA 01890, USA
Sandford, John — Writer, Journalist
I C M Partners, 730 5th Ave, New York NY 10019 USA
Sandiford, L Erskine — Prime Minister, Barbados
Hillvista, Porters, Saint James, Barbados
Sandin, Daniel J — Inventor (Cave Electronic Visualization)
University of Illinois, Electronic Visualization Laboratory, 842 W Taylor St, Chicago IL 60607, USA
Sandlak, Jim — Ice Hockey Player
74 Green Hedge Lane, London ON N6H 5A6, Canada
Sandler, Adam — Actor, Comedian
Brillstein Entertainment Partners, 9150 Wilshire Blvd, #350, Beverly Hills CA 90212 USA
Sandler, Herbert M — Financier
Sandler Foundation, 121 Steuart St, San Francisco CA 94105, USA
Sandler, Tony — Singer (Sandler & Young)
Ralton Productions, PO Box 4915, Palm Springs CA 92263, USA
Sandlock, Michael J (Mike) — Baseball Player
81 Bible St, Cos Cob CT 06807, USA
Sandlund, Debra — Actress
Innovative Artists, 1505 10th St, Santa Monica CA 90401 USA
Sandoval Iniguez, Juan Cardinal — Religious Leader
Arzobispado, Liceo 17, #1-331, 44100 Guadalajara, Mexico
Sandoval, Arturo — Jazz Trumpeter
PO Box 143936, Coral Gables FL 33114, USA
Sandoval, Eugene — Architect
Zimmer Gunner Frasca Partnership, 320 SW Oak St, #500, Portland OR 97204, USA
Sandoval, Hope — Singer (Mazzy Star, Going Home)
Rough Trade Mgmt, 66 Golbarne Road, London W10 5PS, England
Sandoval, Miguel — Actor
Innovative Artists, 1505 10th St, Santa Monica CA 90401 USA
Sandoval, Sonny — Singer (POD)
Atlantic Records, 9229 W Sunset Blvd, #900, West Hollywood CA 90069 USA
Sandow, Nicholas J (Nick) — Actor
Stone Manners Salners, 9911 W Pico Blvd, #1400, Los Angeles CA 90035 USA
Sandrelli, Stefania — Actress
T N A, Viale Parioli 41, 00197 Rome, Italy
Sandri, Leonardo Cardinal — Religious Leader
Oriental Churches Congregation, Palazzo del Bramante, 00193 Rome, Italy
Sandrich, Jay H — Director
Creative Artists Agency, 2000 Ave of Stars, #100, Los Angeles CA 90067 USA
Sands, Charles D (Charlie) — Baseball Player
28940 Bermuda Pointe Circle, #103, Bonita Springs FL 34134, USA
Sands, Julian — Actor
S D B Partners, 1801 Ave of Stars, #902, Los Angeles CA 90067 USA
Sands, Stark — Actor
Management 360, 9111 Wilshire Blvd, Beverly Hills CA 90210 USA
Sands, Terdell D — Football Player
PO Box 2217, Chattanooga TN 37409, USA
Sands, Tommy — Singer, Actor
Gallup Entertainment, 9340 Queens Blvd, Rego Park NY 11374, USA
Sandt, Thomas J (Tom) — Baseball Player
15265 Boones Way, Lake Oswego OR 97035, USA
Sandusky, Alexander B (Alex) — Football Player
22 Floral Ave, Key West FL 33040, USA
Sandusky, Michael G (Mike) — Football Player
2786 Amberwood Court, Naples FL 34120, USA
Sandvig, Jake — Actor
Innovative Artists, 1505 10th St, Santa Monica CA 90401 USA
Sandy B — Singer
Atlantic Entertainment Group, 2922 Atlantic Ave, #200, Atlantic City NJ 08401, USA
Sandy, Gary — Actor
PO Box 818, Cynthiana KY 41031, USA
Sane, Justin — Singer, Songwriter
Agency Group Ltd, 142 W 57th St, #600, New York NY 10019 USA
Sanejouand, Jean Michel — Artist
Belle-Ville, 49150 Vaulandry, France
Sanford, Arlene — Director, Producer, Writer
Anonymous Content, 3532 Hayden Ave, Culver City CA 90232 USA
Sanford, Chance S — Baseball Player
15028 Bardwell Lane, Frisco TX 75035, USA
Sanford, Ed — Ice Hockey Player
18 Clearwater Road, Winchester MA 01890, USA
Sanford, J Frederick (Fred) — Baseball Player
1046 W 600 N, Salt Lake City UT 84116, USA
Sanford, Lucius M — Football Player
1350 Allegheny St SW, Atlanta GA 30310, USA
Sanford, Meredith L (Mo) — Baseball Player
2800 Highway 389, Starkville MS 39759, USA
Sanford, O Leo — Football Player
3044 Gorton Road, Columbia MD 21046, USA
Sanford, Richard M (Rick) — Football Player
110 Oak Park Dr, #B, Irmo SC 29063, USA
Sanford, Ron — Basketball Player
3129 Santana Lane, Plano TX 75023, USA
Sang Hun Choe — Journalist
Associated Press, 450 W 33rd St, #1500, New York NY 10001 USA
Sangay, Lonsang — Prime Minister, Tibet Exile Government
Tibet Government in Exile, Kashag, Dharmsala 176205 H P, India
Sanger, Frederick — Nobel Chemistry Laureate
Far Leys, Fen Lane, Swaffham Bulbeck, Cambridge CB5 0NJ, England
Sangheli, Andrei — Prime Minister, Moldova
Parliament House, Prosp 105, 277073 Kishineau, Moldova
SanGiacomo, Laura — Actress
I C M Partners, 10250 Constellation Blvd, #900, Los Angeles CA 90067 USA
Sangster, Thomas — Actor
Marcus & McCrimmon, 4 Fitzwarren Gardens, London N19 3TP, England

Sanguillen, Manny — Baseball Player
2838 SW 4th St, Boynton Beach FL 33435, USA
Sanguinetti Coirolo, Julio Maria — President, Uruguay
Partido Colorado, Andres Martinez Trueba 1271, Montevideo, Uruguay
SanMiguel, Renay — Commentator
CNN-TV, 190 Marietta Ave SW, Atlanta GA 30303 USA
Sano, Roy I — Religious Leader
United Methodist Church, 100 Maryland Ave NE, #300, Washington DC 20002, USA
Sansa, Maya — Actress
Markham & Froggatt, Julian House, 4 Windmill St, London W1P 1HF, England
Sansom, Chip — Cartoonist (Born Loser)
204 Long Beach Road, Centerville MA 02632, USA
Sansweet, Steven J — Writer
PO Box 2009, San Rafael CA 94912, USA
Sant, Alfred — Prime Minister, Malta
National Labor Center, Mills End Road, Hanrum, Malta
Santa Rosa, Gilberto — Singer
Universal Attractions, 135 W 26th St, #1200, New York NY 10001 USA
Santana, Carlos — Guitarist, Singer, Songwriter
Santana Mgmt, 121 Jordan St, San Rafael CA 94901, USA
Santana, Harmony — Actress
Gray Krauss Des Rochers, 207 W 25th Street, #600, New York NY 10001, USA
Santana, Johan A — Baseball Player
10471 Via Lombardia Court, Miromar Lakes FL 33913, USA
Santana, Manuel — Tennis Player
International Tennis Hall of Fame, 194 Bellevue Ave, Newport RI 02840, USA
Santana, Rafael F — Baseball Player
3220 SE 1st Ave, Cape Coral FL 33904, USA
Santangello, Frank P (F P) — Baseball Player
3602 Rocky Ridge Way, El Dorado Hills CA 95762, USA
Santaolalla, Gustavo — Guitarist, Composer
Columbia Artists Mgmt Inc, 1790 Broadway, #702, New York NY 10019 USA
Santer, Jacques — Prime Minister, Luxembourg
69 Rue J P Huberty, 1742 Luxembourg-Ville, Luxembourg
Santiago, Benito R — Baseball Player
PO Box 5759, Lighthouse Point FL 33074, USA
Santiago, Christina L — Model
Playboy Promotions, 2706 Media Center Dr, Los Angeles CA 90065 USA
Santiago, Jose — Baseball Player
690 Calle Cesar Gonzalez, #2108, San Juan PR 00918, USA
Santiago, Joseph A (Joey) — Guitarist (Pixies)
X-Ray Touring, 77-79 Great Eastern St, #A, London EC2A 3HU, England
Santiago, Otis J (O J) — Football Player
8780 NW 37th Place, Hollywood FL 33024, USA
Santiago, Ray — Actor
Innovative Artists, 1505 10th St, Santa Monica CA 90401 USA
Santiago, Saundra — Actress
C E S D, 257 Park Ave S, #950, New York NY 10010 USA
Santiago-Hudson, Ruben — Actor
Vincent Cirrincione Assoc, 1516 N Fairfax Ave, Los Angeles CA 90046 USA
Santigold — Singer, Songwriter
Roc Nation Mgmt, 1411 Broadway New York NY 10018, USA
SantoDomingo, Rafael — Baseball Player
PO Box 21, Orocovis PR 00720, USA
Santoni, Reni — Actor
Geddes Agency, 8430 Santa Monica Blvd, #201, West Hollywood CA 90069 USA
Santora, Nick — Producer
W M E Entertainment, 9601 Wilshire Blvd, #300, Beverly Hills CA 90210 USA
Santorelli, Frank — Actor
Bleecker Street Entertainment, 853 Broadway, #1214, New York NY 10003, USA
Santorini, Alan J (Al) — Baseball Player
100 Wescott Dr, Clemson SC 29631, USA
Santoro, Rodrigo — Actor
I C M Partners, 10250 Constellation Blvd, #900, Los Angeles CA 90067 USA
Santos Ordonez, Elvin E — President, Honduras
Casa Presidencial, Blvd Juan Pablo II, Tegucigalpa MDC, Honduras
Santos, Anthony (Romeo) — Singer, Songwriter
Sony Music Miami, 605 Lincoln Road Road, #700, Miami Beach FL 33139 USA
Santos, Joe — Actor
Amsel Eisenstadt Frazier, 5055 Wilshire Blvd, #865, Los Angeles CA 90036 USA
Santos, Jose — Thoroughbred Racing Jockey
620 SW 99th Ave, Pembroke Pines FL 33025, USA
Santos, Juan Manuel — President, Colombia
Palacio de Narino, Plaza de Bolivar, Santa Fe, Bogota DE, Colombia
Santos, Rick — Drag Racing Driver
S&S Automotive, 14127 Washington Ave, San Leandro CA 94578, USA
SantosDeOliveira, Alessandra — Basketball Player
Washington Mystics, Verizon Center, 401 9th St NW, #750, Washington DC 20004 USA
Santovenia, Nelson G — Baseball Player
14642 SW 141st Court, Miami FL 33186, USA
Sanz, Alejandro — Singer, Songwriter
Creative Artists Agency, 2000 Ave of Stars, #100, Los Angeles CA 90067 USA
Sanz, Horatio — Actor, Comedian
United Talent Agency, 9336 Civic Center Dr, Beverly Hills CA 90210 USA
Saperstein, David — Religious Leader, Rabbi, Writer
Religious Action Center, 2027 Massachusetts Ave NW, Washington DC 20036, USA
Sapienza, Al — Actor
Independent Talent Group, Oxford House, 76 Oxford St, London W1D 1BS, England
Sapolu, M Jesse — Football Player
1123 Buckingham Dr, #B, Costa Mesa CA 92626, USA
Sapp, Gerome D — Football Player
4654 Riverstone Dr, Owings Mills MD 21117, USA
Sapp, Marvin — Singer
Sony Records, 2100 Colorado Ave, Santa Monica CA 90404 USA
Sapp, Theron C — Football Player
892 N Belair Road, Augusta GA 30909, USA

Sapp, Warren H — Football Player, Sportscaster
11049 Bridge House Road, Windermere FL 34786, USA

Sapphire — Writer
Viking Press, 375 Hudson St, New York NY 10014 USA

Saprykin, Oleg — Ice Hockey Player
15802 N 71st St, #301, Scottsdale AZ 85254, USA

Sara, Mia — Actress
Gersh Agency, 9465 Wilshire Blvd, #600, Beverly Hills CA 90212 USA

Sarafyan, Angela — Actress
Innovative Artists, 1505 10th St, Santa Monica CA 90401 USA

Saraiva Martins, Jose Cardinal — Religious Leader
Palazzo delle Congregazioni, Piazzo Pio XII, 00193 Rome, Italy

Saralegui, Cristina — Commentator
T G A Voice, 100 Lincoln Road, #928, Miami Beach FL 33178, USA

Sarandon, Chris — Actor
Stone Manners Salners, 9911 W Pico Blvd, #1400, Los Angeles CA 90035 USA

Sarandon, Susan — Actress, Model
I C M Partners, 10250 Constellation Blvd, #900, Los Angeles CA 90067 USA

Saraste, Jukka-Pekka — Conductor
Columbia Artists Mgmt Inc, 1790 Broadway, #702, New York NY 10019 USA

Sarasvuo, Virpi Kuitunen — Cross Country Skier
Ilmarisentie 26B, 03100 Nummela, Finland

Sarbanes, Paul S — Senator, MD
320 Suffolk Road, Baltimore MD 21218, USA

Sardinha, Dane — Baseball Player
156 Kuuhei Road, Kailua HI 96734, USA

Sardo, Michael — Producer, Writer
Creative Artists Agency, 2000 Ave of Stars, #100, Los Angeles CA 90067 USA

Sardou, Michel — Singer
Artmedia, 20 Ave Rapp, 75007 Paris, France

Sarelle, Leilani — Actress
Affinity Artists Agency, 5724 W 3rd St, #511, Los Angeles CA 90036, USA

Sarfati, Alain — Architect
43 Rue Maurice Ripoche, 75014 Paris, France

Sargent, Ben — Editorial Cartoonist
Austin American-Statesman, 166 E Riverside Dr, Austin TX 78704, USA

Sargent, Joseph D — Producer, Director
27432 Latigo Bay View Dr, Malibu CA 90265, USA

Sargent, Thomas J (Tom) — Nobel Economics Laureate
New York University, New York NY 10012 USA

Sargsyan, Serzh A — President, Armenia
President's Office, Marshal Bagramian Prosp 19, 375010 Yerevan, Armenia

Sargysan, Tigran — Prime Minister, Armenia
Prime Minister's Office, Ul Nalbandyyrna 32, 375010 Yerevan, Armenia

Sarich, Cory — Ice Hockey Player
19322 Autumn Woods Ave, Tampa FL 33647, USA

Sarkisian, Steve — Football Player, Coach
University of Washington, Athletic Dept, Seattle WA 98195, USA

Sarne, Tanya — Fashion Designer
Ghost Ltd, The Chapel, 263 Kensal Road, London W10 5DB, England

Sarner, Craig B — Ice Hockey Player
1375 Brown Road S, Wayzata MN 55391, USA

Sarno, Joe — Writer
5941 W Irving Park Road, Chicago IL 60634, USA

Sarnoff, Elizabeth (Liz) — Producer, Writer
W M E Entertainment, 9601 Wilshire Blvd, #300, Beverly Hills CA 90210 USA

Sarr, Theodore-Adrien Cardinal — Religious Leader
Archevech, BP 1908, Avenue Jean XXIII, Dakar, Senegal

Sarsgaard, Peter — Actor
Creative Artists Agency, 2000 Ave of Stars, #100, Los Angeles CA 90067 USA

Sartain, Dan — Singer, Songwriter
Agency Group Ltd, 142 W 57th St, #600, New York NY 10019 USA

Sasaki, Kazuhiro — Baseball Player
Seattle Mariners, Safeco Field, PO Box 4100, Seattle WA 98194 USA

Saskamoose, Fred — Ice Hockey Player
PO Box 225, Shell Lake SK S0J 2G0, Canada

Sasselov, Dimitar — Astronomer
Harvard-Smithsonian Astrophysics Center, 60 Garden St, Cambridge MA 02138, USA

Sasser, Clarence E — Vietnam War Army Hero (CMH)
13414 FM 521, Rosharon TX 77583, USA

Sasser, Grant — Ice Hockey Player
1949 SE Orient Dr, Gresham OR 97080, USA

Sasser, James R (Jim) — Senator, TN; Diplomat
601 Mainstream Dr, Nashville TN 37228, USA

Sasser, Mack D (Mackey) — Baseball Player
19 Harrington Lane, Dothan AL 36305, USA

Sasso, Will — Actor, Comedian
Paradigm Agency, 360 N Crescent Dr, North Building, Beverly Hills CA 90210 USA

Sasson, Deborah — Opera, Pop Singer
Erlenhaupstr 10, 64625 Bensheim, Germany

Sassoon, Beverly — Model
2533 Benedict Canyon Dr, Beverly Hills CA 90210, USA

Sassoon, David — Fashion Designer
Bellville Sassoon, 18 Culford Gardens, London SW3 2ST, England

Sassou-Nguesso, Denis — President, Congo People's Republic
Palais du Peuple, Quartier Plateau, Brazzaville, Congo Republic

Sastre Candil, Carlos — Cyclist
Team Geox, Via Feltrina Centro 16, 31044 Biadene de Montebelluna, Italy

Sastre, Ines — Model, Actress
Paradigm Agency, 360 N Crescent Dr, North Building, Beverly Hills CA 90210 USA

Sata, Michael C — President, Zambia
President's Office, State House, PO Box 30208, Lusaka, Zambia

Satan, Miroslav — Ice Hockey Player
46 Kettlepond Road, Jericho NY 11753, USA

Satcher, David M — Navy Admiral, Government Official
Morehouse College, Medical School, Atlanta GA 30314, USA

Satcher, Robert L (Bobby), Jr — Astronaut
N A S A, Johnson Space Center, 2101 NASA Road, Houston TX 77058 USA
Sater, Steven — Lyricist, Writer, Producer
Creative Artists Agency, 2000 Ave of Stars, #100, Los Angeles CA 90067 USA
Sather, Glen C — Ice Hockey Player, Executive
77380 Vista Rosa, La Quinta CA 92253, USA
Sato, Kazuo — Economist
300 E 71st St, #15H, New York NY 10021, USA
Sato, Yuka — Figure Skater
Detroit Figure Skating Club, 888 Denison Court, Bloomfield Hills MI 48302, USA
Satra, Sonia — Actress
C E S D, 257 Park Ave S, #950, New York NY 10010 USA
Satrapi, Marjane — Writer, Director, Actress
United Talent Agency, 9336 Civic Center Dr, Beverly Hills CA 90210 USA
Satriani, Joe — Singer, Guitarist
PO Box 429094, San Francisco CA 94142, USA
Satriano, Thomas V (Tom) — Baseball Player
5320 Otis Ave, Tarzana CA 91356, USA
Satterfield, Paul — Actor
8323 W 1st St, Los Angeles CA 90048, USA
Sattler, John F — Marine Corps General
Director, Strategic Plans/Policy, Joint Staff, Pentagon, Washington DC 20310 USA
Saturday, Jeffrey B (Jeff) — Football Player
2437 Londonberry Blvd, Carmel IN 46032, USA
Saturno, William — Archaeologist
University of New Hampshire, Anthropology Dept, Durham NH 03824, USA
Saturova, Simona — Opera Singer
Kunstler Sekretariat am Gasteig, Rosenheimer Str 52, 81669 Munich, Germany
Saucier, Kevin A — Baseball Player
2316 Silversides Loop, Pensacola FL 32526, USA
Saud, Prince Sultan Bin Abdulaziz al — Government Official, Saudi Arabia
Defense Ministry, PO Box 26731, Airport Road, Riyadh 11165, Saudi Arabia
Saudek, Jan — Photographer
Blodkova 6, 130 00 Prague 3, Czech Republic
Sauer, Craig C — Football Player
6926 Pagenkopf Road, Maple Plain MN 55359, USA
Sauer, George H, Jr — Football Player
1297 Amberlea Dr E, Columbus OH 43230, USA
Sauer, Louis — Architect
3472 Marlowe St, Montreal QC H4A 3L7, Canada
Sauer, Richard J — Educator, Association Executive
National 4-H Council, 7100 Connecticut Ave, Chevy Chase MD 20815, USA
Sauerbeck, Scott W — Baseball Player
1818 4th St W, Palmetto FL 34221, USA
Sauerbrun, Todd S — Football Player
8201 N Oleander Ave, Niles IL 60714, USA
Sauerbrunn, Rebecca E (Becky) — Soccer Player
D C United, R F K Stadium, 2400 E Capitol St SE, Washington DC 20003 USA
Sauerlander, Willibald P W — Art Historian
Victoriastr II, 80803 Munich, Germany
Sauers, Gene — Golfer
9 Judsons Court, Savannah GA 31410, USA
Saul, David J — Prime Minister, Bermuda
Rocky Ledge, 18 Devonshire Bay Road, DV 07, Bermuda
Saul, John W, III — Writer
The Firm, 2049 Century Park E, #2550, Los Angeles CA 90067 USA
Saul, Ralph S — Businessman
1400 Waverly Road, #V57, Gladwyne PA 19035, USA
Saul, Ronald R (Ron) — Football Player
78 Sleepy Hollow Circle, Charles Town WV 25414, USA
Saul, Stephanie — Journalist
Newsday, Editorial Dept, 235 Pinelawn Road, Melville NY 11747, USA
Saulters, Glynn — Basketball Player
240 Country Lane, Quitman LA 71268, USA
Saum, Sherri M — Actress
Shandrew Public Relations, 1050 S Stanley Ave, Los Angeles CA 90019 USA
Saunders, Bernie — Ice Hockey Player
150 Pinecrest Dr, Hastings on Hudson NY 10706, USA
Saunders, George — Writer
Syracuse University, Creative Writing Program, Syracuse NY 13244, USA
Saunders, Jennifer — Actress
United Agents, 12-26 Lexington St, London W1F 0LE, England
Saunders, John — Sportscaster
ESPN-TV, ESPN Plaza, 935 Middle St, Bristol CT 06010 USA
Saunders, John R — Auto Racing Executive
Watkins Glen Speedway, PO Box 500F, Watkins Glen NY 14891, USA
Saunders, Joseph F (Joe) — Baseball Player
1415 E Grand Canyon Dr, Chandler AZ 85249, USA
Saunders, Martha Dunagin — Educator
Southern Mississippi University, President's Office, Hattiesburg MS 39406, USA
Saunders, Pamela — Model, Actress
Playboy Promotions, 2706 Media Center Dr, Los Angeles CA 90065 USA
Saunders, Phillip (Flip) — Basketball Coach
Washington Wizards, M C I Centre, 601 F St NW, Washington DC 20004 USA
Saunders, Tony — Baseball Player
PO Box 434, Severna Park MD 21146, USA
Saunders, Townsend — Freestyle Wrestler
733 Chantilly Dr, Sierra Vista AZ 85635, USA
Saura, Carlos — Director
Antonio Duran, Calle Arturo Soria 52, #Edif 2, 1-5A, 28027 Madrid, Spain
Sauter, Johnathan J (Johnny) — Auto, Truck Racing Driver
779 S Washburn St, #8, Oshkosh WI 54904, USA
Sauve, Robert (Bob) — Ice Hockey Player
Jandec Inc, 803-3080 Boul le Carrefour, Laval QC H7T 2R5, Canada
Sauveur, Richard D (Rich) — Baseball Player
3312 47th Ave E, Bradenton FL 34203, USA

Savage, Ben — Actor
Diane Roberts Mgmt, 73 Market St, Venice CA 90291, USA

Savage, Chantay — Singer
Universal Attractions, 135 W 26th St, #1200, New York NY 10001 USA

Savage, Charlie — Journalist
Boston Globe, Editorial Dept, 135 William Morrissey Blvd, Dorchester MA 02125 USA

Savage, Don — Basketball Player
53 Park Edge, #1E, Berkeley Heights NJ 07922, USA

Savage, Fred — Actor, Director
Creative Artists Agency, 2000 Ave of Stars, #100, Los Angeles CA 90067 USA

Savage, J Robert (Bob) — Baseball Player
63 High Acres Road, Randolph NH 03593, USA

Savage, John — Actor
5584 Bonneville Road, Hidden Hills CA 91302, USA

Savage, John J (Jack) — Baseball Player
9920 White Blossom Blvd, Louisville KY 40241, USA

Savage, Paul — Curling Athlete
Curling Assn, 1660 Vimont Court, Cumberland ON K4A 4J4, Canada

Savage, Rick — Bassist (Def Leppard)
Front Line Mgmt, 1100 Glendon Ave, #2000, Los Angeles CA 90024 USA

Savage, Stephanie — Producer
W M E Entertainment, 9601 Wilshire Blvd, #300, Beverly Hills CA 90210 USA

Savage, Theodore E (Ted) — Baseball Player
1510 Mallard Landing Court, Chesterfield MO 63017, USA

Savage-Rumbaugh, Susan — Primatologist
Great Ape Trust, 4200 SE 44th Ave, Des Moines, Iowa 50320 50320, USA

Saval, Dany — Actress
131 Rue de l'Universite, 75007 Paris, France

Savant, Doug — Actor
S M S Talent, 8383 Wilshire Blvd, #230, Beverly Hills CA 90211 USA

Savard, Andre — Ice Hockey Player
Pittsburgh Penguins, Consol Energy Center, 1001 5th Ave, Pittsburgh PA 15219 USA

Savard, Denis — Ice Hockey Player, Coach
8307 Regency Court, Willow Springs IL 60480, USA

Savard, Marc — Ice Hockey Player
197 8th St, #511, Charlestown MA 02129, USA

Savard, Serge A — Ice Hockey Player, Executive
1790 Champs du Golf, RR 1, Saint Bruno QC J3V 4P6, Canada

Savary, Jerome — Director
Opera Comique, 5 Rue Favart, 75002 Paris, France

Savchenko, Aliona — Figure Skater
Eisstadion Ingo Steuer, Wittgensdorfer Str 2A, 09114 Chemnitz, Germany

Savchenko, Arkadiy M — Opera Singer
8-358 Storozhovskaya Str, 220002 Minsk, Belarus

Saverine, Robert P (Bob) — Baseball Player
228 Slice Dr, Stamford CT 06907, USA

Savery, Uffe — Percussion Musician (Safri Duo)
P D H Music, Dag Hammarskjold Alle 42 G, 2100 Copenhagen 0, Denmark

Savic, Maja — Handball Player
Z R K Buducnost T-Mobile, Ivan Milutinovic B B, 81000 Podgorica, Montenegro

Savident, John — Actor
Granada Television, Quay St, Manchester M60 9EA, England

Savidge, Jennifer — Actress
TalentWorks, 3500 W Olive Ave, #1400, Burbank CA 91505 USA

Saville, Curtis — Long Distance Rower, Explorer
RFD Box 44, West Charleston VT 05872, USA

Saville, Kathleen — Long Distance Rower, Explorer
RFD Box 44, West Charleston VT 05872, USA

Savini, Tom — Actor, Special Effects Artist
311 Taylor St, Pittsburgh PA 15224, USA

Savinykh, Viktor P — Cosmonaut
Moscow State University, Aerophotogrammetry Institute, Gorokhovskiy 4, 103064 Moscow, Russia

Saviola, Camille — Actress
Kazarian/Spencer/Ruskin, 11969 Ventura Blvd, #300, Studio City CA 91604 USA

Savitskaya, Svetlana Y — Cosmonaut
Russian Association, Khovanskaya Str 3, 129515 Moscow, Russia

Savitt, Richard (Dick) — Tennis Player
19 E 80th St, New York NY 10075, USA

Savoy, Guy — Chef
101 Blvd Pereire, 75017 Paris, France

Savransky, Morris (Moe) — Baseball Player
128 Dorset Dr, Boca Raton FL 33434, USA

Savre, Danielle — Actress, Singer
TalentWorks, 3500 W Olive Ave, #1400, Burbank CA 91505 USA

Sawa, Devon — Actor
Gersh Agency, 9465 Wilshire Blvd, #600, Beverly Hills CA 90212 USA

Sawa, Homare — Soccer Player
Football Assn, 3-10-15 Hongo, Bunkyoku, Tokyo 113 0033 Japan

Sawalha, Julia — Actress
Associated International Mgmt, Fairfax House, Fulwood Place, London WC1V 6HU, England

Sawalha, Nadia — Entertainer
Associated International Mgmt, Fairfax House, Fulwood Place, London WC1V 6HU, England

Sawalha, Nadim — Actor
Associated International Mgmt, Fairfax House, Fulwood Place, London WC1V 6HU, England

Sawallisch, Wolfgang — Conductor, Concert Pianist
Hinterm Bichl 2, 83224 Grassau, Germany

Sawyer, Alan L — Basketball Player
117 San Juan Dr, Sequim WA 98382, USA

Sawyer, Diane — Commentator
147 Columbus Ave, #300, New York NY 10023, USA

Sawyer, Forrest — Commentator
NBC-TV, News Dept, 30 Rockefeller Plaza, #270E, New York NY 10112 USA

Sawyer, John W — Football Player
23637 Sunnyside Lane, Zachary LA 70791, USA

Sawyer, Kevin — Ice Hockey Player
5118 N Ivy Court, Spokane Valley WA 99206, USA

Sawyer, Ray Work Hard Public Relations, 35 Farm Ave, London SW16 2UT, England	Singer, Guitarist (Dr Hook)
Sawyer, Talance M 6150 Brookhaven Dr, Bastrop LA 71220, USA	Football Player
Sax, David J (Dave) 3352 Eaton Dr, Roseville CA 95661, USA	Baseball Player
Sax, Geoffrey I C M Partners, 10250 Constellation Blvd, #900, Los Angeles CA 90067 USA	Director
Sax, Stephen L (Steve) 201 Wesley Court, Roseville CA 95661, USA	Baseball Player
Saxe, Adrian A 4835 N Figueroa St, Los Angeles CA 90042, USA	Artist
Saxon, Edward Edward Saxon Productions, 1526 14th St, #105, Santa Monica CA 90404, USA	Producer
Saxon, James E 28500 Fox Hollow Dr, Hayward CA 94542, USA	Football Player
Saxon, John Beacon Talent, 9250 Sunset Blvd, #727, Los Angeles CA 90069, USA	Actor
Saxon, Michael E (Mike) 211 Winding Hollow Lane, Coppell TX 75019, USA	Football Player
Saxton, Charlie Creative Artists Agency, 2000 Ave of Stars, #100, Los Angeles CA 90067 USA	Actor
Saxton, James E (Jimmy) 5000 Mission Oaks Blvd, #52, Austin TX 78735, USA	Football Player
Sayako Imperial Palace, 1-1 Chiyoda, Chiyodaku, Tokyo 100, Japan	Princess, Japan
Sayalero Fernandez, Maritza Aveida Ruiz, 65 Sun Ensenada, Baja California, Mexico	Beauty Queen
Sayed, Mostafa Amr El 579 Westover Dr NW, Atlanta GA 30305, USA	Chemist
Sayer, Leo Harbour Agency, 135 Forbes St, Woolloomooloo NSW 2011, Australia	Singer, Songwriter
Sayers, Gale E 1313 N Ritchie Court, #407, Chicago IL 60610, USA	Football Player
Saykally, Richard J University of California, Chemistry Dept, Latimer Hall, Berkeley CA 94720, USA	Chemist
Sayles, John T 210 13th St, Hoboken NJ 07030, USA	Director
Saylor, Edward J 14010 99th Ave E, Puyallup WA 98373, USA	WW II Army Air Corps Hero
Scacchi, Greta Shanahan Mgmt, PO Box 1509, Darlinghurst NSW 1300, Australia	Actress
Scaggs, William R (Boz) W M E Entertainment, 9601 Wilshire Blvd, #300, Beverly Hills CA 90210 USA	Singer, Songwriter
Scaglione, Josefina Untitled Entertainment, 350 S Beverly Dr, #200, Beverly Hills CA 90212 USA	Actress, Singer
Scagliotti, Allison Schiff Co, 8440 Warner Dr, #B1, Culver City CA 90232 USA	Actress
Scaife, Oliver L (Bo), III 6505 Banbury Crossing, Brentwood TN 37027, USA	Football Player
Scala, Tina Jack Scagneti Talent, 5118 Vineland Ave, #101, North Hollywood CA 91601, USA	Actress
Scalabrine, Brian 1513 Griffin Ave, Enumclaw WA 98022, USA	Basketball Player
Scalapino, Douglas J University of California, Physics Dept, Santa Barbara CA 93106, USA	Physicist
Scales, Bobby L 3547 Archgate Court, Alpharetta GA 30004, USA	Baseball Player
Scales, Charles A (Charley) 4035 Vistaview St, West Mifflin PA 15122, USA	Football Player
Scales, Dwight A 6112 Roosevelt Circle NW, Huntsville AL 35810, USA	Football Player
Scales, Prunella M Conway Van Gelder Grant, 8-12 Broadwick St, #300, London W1F 8HW, England	Actress
Scalia, Antonin US Supreme Court, 1 1st St NE, Washington DC 20543 USA	Supreme Court Justice
Scalia, Jack 16260 Ventura Blvd, Encino CA 91436, USA	Actor
Scallions, Bret Media Five Entertainment, 3005 Brodhead Road, #170, Bethlehem PA 18020, USA	Singer, Guitarist (Fuel)
Scalzo, Tony Russell Carter Artists, 315 Ponce de Leon Blvd, #755, Decatur GA 30030, USA	Singer, Bassist (Fastball)
Scamarcio, Riccardo Cineart, 36 Rue de Ponthieu, 75008 Paris, France	Actor
Scaminace, Joseph M Sherwin-Williams Co, 101 W Prospect Ave, #1020, Cleveland OH 44115, USA	Businessman
Scamurra, Peter (Pete) 15 Guinevere Court, Getzville NY 14068, USA	Ice Hockey Player
Scancarelli, Jim Mark J Cohen, PO Box 1892, Santa Rosa CA 95402, USA	Cartoonist (Gasoline Alley)
Scandiuzzi, Roberto Atelier Fedelli, Via Casekke 76, 40068 San Lazzaro Savena (Bo), Italy	Opera Singer
Scanlan, Robert G (Bob), Jr 12400 Montecito Road, #315, Seal Beach CA 90740, USA	Baseball Player
Scanlan, Teresa Miss America Organization, 1370 Ave of Americas, #1600, New York NY 10019 USA	Beauty Queen
Scanlon, J Patrick (Pat) 7400 Portland Ave S, Minneapolis MN 55423, USA	Baseball Player
Scanlon, Thomas M, Jr Harvard University, Philosophy Dept, Cambridge MA 02138, USA	Philosopher
Scannell, Susan 247 S Beverly Dr, #102, Beverly Hills CA 90212, USA	Actress
Scarabelli, Michele Characters Talent Agency, 8 Elm St, Toronto ON M5G 1G7, Canada	Actress
Scarbath, John C (Jack) 736 Calvert Road, Rising Sun MD 21911, USA	Football Player

Scarbery, Randy J — Baseball Player
5010 E Lewis Ave, Fresno CA 93727, USA

Scarborough, C Joseph (Joe) — Commentator; Representative, FL
MSNBC-TV, 900 Sylvan Ave, Englewood Cliffs NJ 07632, USA

Scarce, G McCurdy (Mac) — Baseball Player
1010 Richmond Glen Circle, Alpharetta GA 30004, USA

Scardapane, Dario — Producer, Writer
Management 360, 9111 Wilshire Blvd, Beverly Hills CA 90210 USA

Scardelletti, Robert A — Labor Leader
Transportation Communications Union, 3 Research Place, Rockville MD 20850, USA

Scardino, Don — Director
Creative Artists Agency, 2000 Ave of Stars, #100, Los Angeles CA 90067 USA

Scarf, Herbert E — Economist
88 Blake Road, Hamden CT 06517, USA

Scarface — Rap Artist (Geto Boys)
J L Entertainment, 18653 Ventura Blvd, #340, Tarzana CA 91356 USA

Scarfe, Gerald A — Cartoonist
Jane Asher Party Cakes, 22-24 Cale St, London SW3 3QU, England

Scarfe, Jonathan — Actor
Gary Goddard Agency, 10 Saint Mary's St, #305, Toronto ON M4Y 1P9, Canada

Scargill, Arthur — Labor Leader
National Union of Mineworkers, 2 Huddersfield Road, Barnsley, England

Scarimbolo, Adam — Actor
C E S D, 10635 Santa Monica Blvd, #130, Los Angeles CA 90025 USA

Scarlett, Noel — Football Player
1306 Quail Meadow Dr, Wylie TX 75098, USA

Scarpati, Joseph H (Joe), Jr — Football Player
32 Lexington Circle, Marlton NJ 08053, USA

Scarpitto, Robert F (Bob) — Football Player
117 White Oaks Lane, Carmel Valley CA 93924, USA

Scarr, Sandra W — Psychologist
77-6222 Kaunmakamalu Dr, Holualoa HI 96725, USA

Scarry, Elaine — Educator
Harvard University, English Dept, Cambridge MA 02138, USA

Scarsone, Steven W (Steve) — Baseball Player
3935 E Rough Rider Road, #1158, Phoenix AZ 85050, USA

Scarwid, Diana E — Actress
Committed Artists Entertainment, 2600 W Olive Ave, #500, Burbank CA 91505, USA

Scatchard, Dave — Ice Hockey Player
8312 N 50th St, Paradise Valley AZ 85253, USA

Scates, Allen E — Volleyball Coach
8433 Apple Hill Court, Las Vegas NV 89128, USA

Scattini, Monica — Actress
Carol Levi Mgmt, Via G Pisanelli 2, 00196 Rome, Italy

Scelzi, Gary — Drag Racing Driver
Alan Johnson Racing, 2772 S Cherry Ave, Fresno CA 93706, USA

Scerbo, Cassie — Actress
Strong Management, 9350 Wilshire Blvd. #224, Beverly Hills CA 90212, USA

Schaaf-Behle, Petra — Biathlete
Am Rodeland 22, 34508 Willingen, Germany

Schaal, Kristen — Actress, Writer
United Talent Agency, 9336 Civic Center Dr, Beverly Hills CA 90210 USA

Schaal, Paul — Baseball Player
68-1962 Puu Nui St, Waikoloa HI 96738, USA

Schaal, Richard — Actor
612 Gulf Blvd, #9, Indian Rocks Beach FL 33785, USA

Schaal, Wendy — Actress
Gage Group, 14724 Ventura Blvd, #505, Sherman Oaks CA 91403 USA

Schacher, Mel — Bassist (Grand Funk Railroad)
Lustig Talent, PO Box 770850, Orlando FL 32877 USA

Schachman, Howard K — Molecular Biochemist
University of California, Molecular Biology Dept, Berkeley CA 94720, USA

Schacht, Henry B — Businessman
Lucent Technologies Inc, 600 Mountain Ave, New Providence NJ 07974, USA

Schachter-Shalomi, Zalman — Religious Leader, Rabbi
Yesod Foundation, PO Box 48, Boulder CO 80306, USA

Schacker, Harold (Hal) — Baseball Player
4609 N Matanzas Ave, Tampa FL 33614, USA

Schacter, Beth — Director, Writer
Anonymous Content, 3532 Hayden Ave, Culver City CA 90232 USA

Schacter-Shalomi, Zalman — Religious Leader
Spiritual Eldering Institute, 535 W S Boulder Road, Lafayette CO 80026, USA

Schade, Frank — Basketball Player
826 Nicolet Ave, Oshkosh WI 54901, USA

Schaden, Rick — Businessman
Quiznos, 1975 Lawrence St, #400, Denver CO 80202, USA

Schadler, Bernard R (Ben) — Basketball Player
808 Bauer Dr, San Carlos CA 94070, USA

Schadler, Jay — Commentator
ABC-TV, News Dept, 77 W 66th St, New York NY 10023 USA

Schaech, Jonathan — Actor
A P A Talent/Literary Agency, 405 S Beverly Dr, #300, Beverly Hills CA 90212 USA

Schaefer, Henry F, III — Chemist
University of Georgia, Computational Quantum Chemistry Center, Athens GA 30602, USA

Schaefer, Jeffrey S (Jeff) — Baseball Player
2110 Woodbend Trail, Fort Mill SC 29708, USA

Schaefer, Roberto — Cinematographer
Innovative Artists, 1505 10th St, Santa Monica CA 90401 USA

Schaeffer, Eric — Actor, Director, Producer
Paradigm Agency, 360 N Crescent Dr, North Building, Beverly Hills CA 90210 USA

Schaeffer, Frank — Writer
Carroll & Graf, 245 W 17th St, #1100, New York NY 10011, USA

Schaeffer, Leonard — Businessman
WellPoint Health Networks, 1 Wellpoint Way, Westlake Village CA 91362, USA

Schaeffer, Mark P — Baseball Player
18261 Parthenia St, Northridge CA 91325, USA

Schaeffer, William — Hero
1865 Paseo de Oro, Colorado Springs CO 80904, USA

Schaetzel, John R — Writer
3050 Military Road NW, #555, Washington DC 20015, USA

Schafer, Christine — Opera Singer
Columbia Artists Mgmt Inc, 1790 Broadway, #702, New York NY 10019 USA

Schafer, Edward T (Ed) — Secretary, Agriculture; Governor, ND
1131 N 4th St, Bismarck ND 58501, USA

Schafer, Hans — Soccer Player
D F B, Postfach 710265, 60492 Frankfurt, Germany

Schafer, Jordan J — Baseball Player
80 Pine Forest Dr, Haines City FL 33844, USA

Schaffel, Lewis — Basketball Executive
Miami Heat, American Airlines Arena, 601 Biscayne Blvd, Miami FL 33132 USA

Schaffel, Maria — Actress
Stone Manners Salners, 9911 W Pico Blvd, #1400, Los Angeles CA 90035 USA

Schaffer, Eric — Concert Executive
Kennedy Center for Performing Arts, 2700 F St NW, Washington DC 20566, USA

Schaffer, Jimmie R (Jim) — Baseball Player
655 Birch Terrace, Coopersburg PA 18036, USA

Schafrath, Richard P (Dick) — Football Player
704 Ashland Road, Mansfield OH 44905, USA

Schaible, Michael — Interior Designer
Bray-Schnaible Design, 80 W 40th St, #800, New York NY 10018, USA

Schaitber, Harold A — Labor Leader
International Fire Fighters, 1750 New York Ave NW, #300, Washington DC 20006, USA

Schajris Rodriguez, Noel — Singer, Guitarist (Sin Bandera)
Westwood Mgmt, Maria de Teresa 250, San Angel, Mexico City 01040, Mexico

Schakper, Alison — Producer, Writer
W M E Entertainment, 9601 Wilshire Blvd, #300, Beverly Hills CA 90210 USA

Schall, Alvin A — Judge
US Appeals Court, 717 Madison Place NW, Washington DC 20439, USA

Schaller, George B — Zoologist
90 Sentry Hill Road, Roxbury CT 06783, USA

Schaller, Willie — Soccer Player
3283 S Indiana St, Lakewood CO 80228, USA

Schallert, William — Actor
14920 Ramos Place, Pacific Palisades CA 90272, USA

Schallock, Arthur L (Art) — Baseball Player
749 Crocus Dr, Sonoma CA 95476, USA

Schally, Andrew V — Nobel Medicine Laureate
3801 Collins Ave, Miami Beach FL 33140, USA

Schama, Simon M — Historian, Writer
Columbia University, Art History Dept, Fairweather Hall, Cambridge MA 02138, USA

Schamehorn, Kevin — Ice Hockey Player
5536 Stoney Brook Road, Kalamazoo MI 49009, USA

Schamus, James — Director, Producer
Creative Artists Agency, 2000 Ave of Stars, #100, Los Angeles CA 90067 USA

Schanberg, Sydney H — Journalist
PO Box 236, Rifton NY 12471, USA

Schankweiler, Scott B — Football Player
11 Bartley Court, Nottingham MD 21236, USA

Schanley, Tom — Actor
Maverick Artists, 6100 Wilshire Blvd, #550, Los Angeles CA 90048, USA

Schapiro, Mary L — Financier, Government Official
Securities & Exchange Commission, 100 F St NE, Washington DC 20549, USA

Schapp, Dick — Sportscaster
ESPN-TV, ESPN Plaza, 935 Middle St, Bristol CT 06010 USA

Scharansky, Natan — Social Activist, Computer Scientist
Shalem Center, 13 Yehoshua Bin-Nun St, Jersalem 93145, Israel

Scharer, Erich — Bobsled Athlete
Grutstra 63, 8074 Herrliberg, Switzerland

Scharping, Rudolf — Government Official, Germany
Wilhelmstr 5, 56112 Lahnstein, Germany

Schattinger, Jeffrey C (Jeff) — Baseball Player
PO Box 134, Lake Arrowhead CA 92352, USA

Schatz, Howard — Photographer
435 W Broadway, #200, New York NY 10012, USA

Schatz, Mark — Bassist (Nickel Creek)
Q-Prime South, 131 S 11th St, Nashville TN 37206 USA

Schatzberg, Jerry N — Director
I C M Partners, 10250 Constellation Blvd, #900, Los Angeles CA 90067 USA

Schatzeder, Daniel E (Dan) — Baseball Player
186 River Mist Dr, Oswego IL 60543, USA

Schatzman, Evry — Astrophysicist
11 Rue de l'Eglise, Dompierre, 60420 Maignelay-Montigny, France

Schaub, Matthew R (Matt) — Football Player
3300 Irvine Ave, #300, Newport Beach CA 92660, USA

Schaudt, Martin — Equestrian
Gerhardstr 10/2, 72461 Albstadt, Germany

Schauer, Frederick F — Attorney, Educator
Harvard University, Kennedy Government School, Cambridge MA 02138, USA

Schaufuss, Peter — Ballet Dancer, Director
Papoutsis Representation, 18 Sundial Ave, London SE25 4BX, England

Schaukowitch, Carl — Football Player
11700 Bishops Content Road, Bowie MD 20721, USA

Schayes, Adolph (Dolph) — Basketball Player, Coach
PO Box 156, Syracuse NY 13214, USA

Schayes, Daniel L (Danny) — Basketball Player
8586 E Krail St, Scottsdale AZ 85250, USA

Schazad, Graziella — Singer
Warner Music Group, Alter Wandraham 14, 20457 Hamburg, Germany , USA

Schechtman, Daniel — Nobel Chemistry Laureate
Technion Institute of Technology, Haifa 32000, Israel

Scheck, Barry — Attorney, Educator
Yeshiva University, Law School, 55 5th Ave, #600, New York NY 10003, USA

Scheckter, Jody D — Auto Racing Driver
Home Farm, Laverstoke Park, Overton, Hampshire RG25 3DR, England
Scheckter, Tomas — Auto Racing Driver
11412 Divers Cove Court, Indianapolis IN 46236, USA
Schedeen, Anne — Actress
Metropolitan Talent Agency, 7020 La Presa Dr, Los Angeles CA 90068 USA
Scheer, Paul — Actor, Comedian, Writer
Principato-Young, 9465 Wilshire Blvd, #880, Beverly Hills CA 90212 USA
Scheffer, Will — Producer, Writer
Creative Artists Agency, 2000 Ave of Stars, #100, Los Angeles CA 90067 USA
Schefter, Adam — Sportscaster
ESPN-TV, ESPN Plaza, 935 Middle St, Bristol CT 06010 USA
Scheib, Carl A — Baseball Player
2922 Old Ranch Road, San Antonio TX 78217, USA
Scheibel, Arnold B — Psychiatrist
100 Bay Place, #804, Oakland CA 94610, USA
Scheid, Eusebio Oscar Cardinal — Religious Leader
Archdiocese, Rua Benjamin Constant 23/502, 20241 Rio de Janeiro, Brazil
Scheid, Richard P (Rich) — Baseball Player
402 Grant Ave, Hightstown NJ 08520, USA
Scheinblum, Richard A (Richie) — Baseball Player
1308 Woodstock Dr, Palm Harbor FL 34684, USA
Schekman, Randy W — Medical Researcher
Howard Hughes Institute, 4000 Jones Bridge Road, Chevy Chase MD 20815, USA
Schell, Catherine — Actress
Postfach 800504, 51005 Cologne, Germany
Schell, Jozef S — Geneticist
College de France, 11 Pl Marcelin-Berthelot, 75231 Paris Cedex 05, France
Schell, Maximilian — Actor
16501 Ventura Blvd, #304, Encino CA 91436, USA
Schellenberg, August — Actor
TalentWorks, 3500 W Olive Ave, #1400, Burbank CA 91505 USA
Schellhase, David G (Dave) — Basketball Player
862 Walnut Ridge E, Logansport IN 46947, USA
Schelling, Thomas C — Nobel Economics Laureate
4506 Wetherill Road, Bethesda MD 20816, USA
Schellman, John A — Chemist
65 W 30th Ave, #508, Eugene OR 97405, USA
Schelmerding, Kirk — Auto Racing Mechanic
Childress Racing, PO Box 1189, Industrial Dr, Welcome NC 27374, USA
Schelotto, Guillermo Barros — Soccer Player
Columbus Crew, 1 Black & Gold Blvd, Columbus OH 43211 USA
Schemansky, Norbert — Weightlifter
24826 New York St, Dearborn MI 48124, USA
Schenker, Rudolf — Guitarist (Scorpions)
Und Verlags, Bohlenweg 8, 30835, Germany
Schenkkan, Robert F, Jr — Writer, Actor
W M E Entertainment, 9601 Wilshire Blvd, #300, Beverly Hills CA 90210 USA
Schenkman, Eric — Musician (Spin Doctors)
D A S Communications, 83 Riverside Dr, New York NY 10024 USA
Schepisi, Frederic A (Fred) — Director
PO Box 743, South Yarra VIC 3141, Australia
Scheraga, Harold A — Chemist
223 Savage Farm Dr, Ithaca NY 14850, USA
Scherbachenko, Ekaterina — Opera Singer
I M G Artists, Hogarth Business Park, Chiswick, London W4 2TH, England
Scherbo, Vitali — Gymnast
8308 Aqua Spray Ave, Las Vegas NV 89128, USA
Scherer, Frederic M — Economist
53 Standish St, #2, Cambridge MA 02138, USA
Scherer, Odilo P Cardinal — Religious Leader
Avenida Higienopolis 890, 02138-908 Sao Paulo SP, Brazil
Scherman, Frederick J (Fred) — Baseball Player
7454 S Tipp Cowlesville Road, Tipp City OH 45371, USA
Scherman, Nossom — Religious Leader, Rabbi, Editor
ArtScroll/Mesorah Publications, 4514 11th Ave, Brooklyn NY 11219, USA
Scherrer, Jean-Louis — Fashion Designer
51 Ave du Montaigne, 75008 Paris, France
Scherrer, Tom — Golfer
2608 Drommore Lane, Raleigh NC 27614, USA
Scherrer, William J (Bill) — Baseball Player
222 Fareway Lane, Grand Island NY 14072, USA
Scherza, Chuck — Ice Hockey Player
51 Manistee St, Pawtucket RI 02861, USA
Scherzinger, Nicole — Singer (Eden's Crush, Pussycat Dolls)
W M E Entertainment, 9601 Wilshire Blvd, #300, Beverly Hills CA 90210 USA
Scheuer, Paul J — Chemist
3217 Melemele Place, Honolulu HI 96822, USA
Schiano, Gregory E (Greg) — Football Coach
Tampa Bay Buccaneers, 1 W Buccaneer Place, Tampa FL 33607 USA
Schiavo, Mary — Government Official, Social Activist
Ohio State University, Public Policy Dept, Columbus OH 43210, USA
Schiavo, Richard J — Thoroughbred Racing Executive
I E A H Stables, 595 Stewart Ave, #450, Garden City NY 11530, USA
Schiavone, Francesca — Tennis Player
Women's Tennis Assn, 1 Progress Plaza, #1500, Saint Petersburg FL 33701 USA
Schickel, Richard — Writer, Film Critic
9051 Dicks St, West Hollywood CA 90069, USA
Schickele, Peter — Composer, Comedian
Opus 3 Artists, 470 Park Ave S, #900N, New York NY 10016 USA
Schiebold, Hans — Artist
13705 SW 118th Court, Portland OR 97223, USA
Schieffer, Bob — Commentator
CBS-TV, News Dept, 2020 M St NW, Washington DC 20036 USA
Schierholtz, Nathan J (Nate) — Baseball Player
7500 E Deer Valley Road, #118, Scottsdale AZ 85255, USA

Schiff, Andras
Terry Harrison Mgmt, Market St, Charlbury, Oxon OX7 3PJ, England — Concert Pianist

Schiff, Heinrich
Astrid Schoerke, Monckegergallee 41, 30453 Hanover, Germany — Concert Cellist, Conductor

Schiff, Mark
Gail Stocker Presents, 1025 N Kings Road, #113, West Hollywood CA 90069, USA — Actor, Comedian

Schiff, Richard
I F A Talent Agency, 8730 W Sunset Blvd, #490, West Hollywood CA 90069 USA — Actor

Schiff, Stacy
Little Brown, 1271 Ave of Americas, New York NY 10020, USA — Writer

Schiffer, Claudia
Aussenwall 94, 47495 Rheinberg, Germany — Model, Actress

Schiffer, Michael
Ballpark Pictures, PO Box 508, Venice CA 90294, USA — Writer, Producer

Schiffman, Guillaume
20 Rue Saulnier, 75009 Paris, France — Cinematographer

Schiffman, Mark
National Cancer Institute, 6120 Executive Blvd, Bethesda MD 20892, USA — Physician, Epidemiologist

Schiffman, Michael
Harvest Mgmt, PO Box 279, Jefferson Valley NY 10535, USA — Actor

Schiffrin, Andre
New Press, 450 W 41st St, New York NY 10036, USA — Publisher

Schifrin, Lalo
710 N Hillcrest Road, Beverly Hills CA 90210, USA — Composer

Schild, Marlies
Weikersbach 9, 5760 Saalfelden, Austria — Alpine Skier

Schiller, Lawrence J
10 W End Ave, #30B, New York NY 10023, USA — Producer, Director, Writer

Schiller, Rob
A P A Talent/Literary Agency, 405 S Beverly Dr, #300, Beverly Hills CA 90212 USA — Director

Schilling, Charles T (Chuck)
907 Caroline Court, New Bern NC 28560, USA — Baseball Player

Schilling, Curtis M (Curt)
7 Woodridge Road, Medfield MA 02052, USA — Baseball Player

Schilling, Taylor
Gersh Agency, 9465 Wilshire Blvd, #600, Beverly Hills CA 90212 USA — Actress

Schimberni, Mario
Armando Curcio Editore SpA, Via IV Novembre, 00187 Rome, Italy — Businessman

Schimmel, Paul R
Scripps Research Institute, 10550 N Torrey Pines Road, La Jolla CA 92037, USA — Biologist, Biochemist

Schindelholz, Lorenz
Hardstr 184, 4715 Herbetswil, Switzerland — Bobsled Athlete

Schinkel, Kenneth (Ken)
19927 Beaulieu Court, Fort Myers FL 33908, USA — Ice Hockey Player

Schipper, Jessicah
Swimming Australia, 12/7 Beissel St, Belconnen ACT 2617, Australia — Swimmer

Schirripa, Steve R
Innovative Artists, 1505 10th St, Santa Monica CA 90401 USA — Actor

Schisgal, Murray J
I C M Partners, 730 5th Ave, New York NY 10019 USA — Writer

Schissler, Les
3060 E Bridge St, #20, Brighton CO 80601, USA — Bowler

Schlafly, Phyllis S
68 Fairmount Ave, Alton IL 62002, USA — Women's Activist

Schlamme, Thomas (Tommy)
Creative Artists Agency, 2000 Ave of Stars, #100, Los Angeles CA 90067 USA — Director

Schlatter, Charlie
Sutton-Barth Vennari, 145 S Fairfax Ave, #310, Los Angeles CA 90036 USA — Actor

Schleeh, Russ
21634 Paseo Maravia, Mission Viejo CA 92692, USA — Test Pilot

Schlegel, Hans W
European Space Center, Linder Hohe, Box 906096, 51127 Cologne, Germany — Astronaut, Germany

Schlegel, Sylvester
Live Nation, Linnegatan 89, Box 21451, 104 51 Stockholm, Sweden — Drummer (The Ark)

Schlereth, Mark F
9479 S Shadow Hill Circle, Lone Tree CO 80124, USA — Football Player

Schlesinger, Adam
Big Hassle, 157 Chambers St, #1200, New York NY 10007, USA — Singer (Fountains of Wayne), Songwriter

Schlesinger, Cory M
36 Bradford Court, Dearborn MI 48126, USA — Football Player

Schlesinger, James R
Georgetown University, 1800 K St NW, #400, Washington DC 20006, USA — Secretary, Defense; Energy

Schlessinger, Laura
3201 Campanil Dr, Santa Barbara CA 93109, USA — Radio Psychologist, Physiologist

Schlichtmann, Jan
359 Hale St, Beverly Farms MA 01915, USA — Attorney

Schlink, Bernhard
Heilbronner Str 3, 10779 Berlin, Germany — Writer

Schlitt, John W
112 Glen Haven Lane, Franklin TN 37069, USA — Singer (Petra, Head East)

Schlondorff, Volker O
Studio Babelsberg, Postfach 900361, 14439 Potsdam, Germany — Director

Schloredt, Robert S (Bob)
Nestle-Beich, 1827 N 167th St, Shoreline WA 98133, USA — Football Player

Schlossberg, Hayden
Creative Artists Agency, 2000 Ave of Stars, #100, Los Angeles CA 90067 USA — Director, Writer

Schlueter, Dale W
15555 SW Harcourt Terrace, Portland OR 97224, USA — Basketball Player

Schluter, Poul H
Frederiksberg Allee 66, 1820 Frederiksberg C, Denmark — Prime Minister, Denmark

Schmautz, Robert J (Bobby)
19866 N 90th Ave, Peoria AZ 85382, USA — Ice Hockey Player

Schmeichel, Peter
Aston Villa, Villa Park, Trinity Road, Birmingham B6 6HE, England — Soccer Player

Schmelz, Alan G (Al)
7406 E Camino Rayo de Luz, Scottsdale AZ 85266, USA — Baseball Player

Schmemann - Schmoeller

Schmemann, Serge New York Times, Editorial Dept, 229 W 43rd St, New York NY 10036, USA	Journalist
Schmid, Benjamin Harrison/Parrott, Lucile-Grahn-Stra 37, 81675 Munich, Germany	Concert, Jazz Violinist
Schmid, Daniel J (Dan) Paradise Artists, PO Box 1821, Ojai CA 93024 USA	Bassist (Cherry Poppin' Daddies)
Schmid, Harald Schulstr 11, 63594 Hasselroth, Germany	Track Athlete
Schmid, Kyle Glick Agency, 1321 7th St, #203, Santa Monica CA 90401 USA	Actor
Schmid, Sigi Seattle Sounders, 12 Seahawks Way, Renton WA 98056 USA	Soccer Coach
Schmidgall-Potter, Jennifer L 3640 Wooddale Ave S, #103, Minneapolis MN 55416, USA	Ice Hockey Player
Schmidly, David J University of New Mexico, President's Office, Albuquerque NM 87131, USA	Educator
Schmidt, Andreas Fossredder 51, 22359 Hamburg, Germany	Opera Singer
Schmidt, Benno C, Jr Edison Project, 375 Park Ave, New York NY 10152, USA	Educator
Schmidt, Brian P Australian National University, Mount Stromlo Observatory, Canberra ACT 0200, Australia	Nobel Physics Laureate
Schmidt, David J (Dave) 7172 N Serenoa Dr, Sarasota FL 34241, USA	Baseball Player
Schmidt, Eric E Google Inc, 1600 Amphitheatre Parkway, #41, Mountain View CA 94043, USA	Businessman, Computer Engineer
Schmidt, Frederick A (Freddy) 128 Constitution Ave, Wind Gap PA 18091, USA	Baseball Player
Schmidt, Helmut Neuberger Weg 80, 22419 Hamburg, Germany	Chancellor, West Germany
Schmidt, Henry J (Hank) 4641 Mission Bell Lane, La Mesa CA 91941, USA	Football Player
Schmidt, Jason D 6539 E Cheney Dr, Paradise Valley AZ 85253, USA	Baseball Player
Schmidt, Joseph P (Joe) 226 Norcliff Dr, Bloomfield Hills MI 48302, USA	Football Player
Schmidt, Kathryn (Kate) 1008 Dexter St, Los Angeles CA 90042, USA	Track Athlete
Schmidt, Kenneth Coast to Coast Talent, 3350 Barham Blvd, Los Angeles CA 90068 USA	Actor
Schmidt, Klaus German Archaeological Institute, Inonu Caddesi 10, 34437 Istanbul, Turkey	Archeologist
Schmidt, Maarten California Institute of Technology, Astronomy Dept, Pasadena CA 91125, USA	Astronomer
Schmidt, Michael J (Mike) 373 Eagle Dr, Jupiter FL 33477, USA	Baseball Player
Schmidt, Milton C (Milt) 10 Longwood Dr, #376, Westwood MA 02090, USA	Ice Hockey Player
Schmidt, Richard University of Pennsylvania Hospital, 3400 Spruce St, Philadelphia PA 19104, USA	Surgeon
Schmidt, Rob Gersh Agency, 9465 Wilshire Blvd, #600, Beverly Hills CA 90212 USA	Director
Schmidt, Robert M (Bob) 10005 Sky View Way, #2106, Fort Myers FL 33913, USA	Football Player
Schmidt, Roy L 1844 Highpoint Road, Snellville GA 30078, USA	Football Player
Schmidt, Sam Sam Schmidt Racing, 6803 Coffman Road, Indianapolis IN 46208, USA	Auto Racing Driver
Schmidt, Sophie Canadian Soccer, Place Soccer Canada, 237 Metcalfe St, Ottawa ON K2P 1R2, Canada	Soccer Player
Schmidt, Susan Washington Post, Editorial Dept, 1150 15th St NW, Washington DC 20071 USA	Journalist
Schmidt, Terry R 2 Stone River Dr, Asheville NC 28804, USA	Football Player
Schmidt, Walter Wilhelm Raabe Weg 23, 38110 Brauschweig, Germany	Track Athlete
Schmidt, William (Bill) 1809 Devonwood Court, Knoxville TN 37922, USA	Track Athlete
Schmidt, Wolfgang Birkheckenstr 116B, 70599 Stuttgart, Germany	Track Athlete
Schmiegel, Klaus K 4507 Staughton Dr, Indianapolis IN 46226, USA	Inventor (Prozac)
Schmiesing, Joseph F (Joe) 19460 County Road 2, Sauk Centre MN 56378, USA	Football Player
Schmirler, Sandra Curling Assn, 1660 Vimont Court, Cumberland ON K4A 4J4, Canada	Curling Athlete
Schmit, Timothy B W M E Entertainment, 1325 Ave of Americas, New York NY 10019 USA	Singer, Bassist (Eagles)
Schmitt, Arnd Rheinuferweg 59B, 47495 Bornheim, Germany	Fencer
Schmitt, Harrison H (Jack) PO Box 90730, Albuquerque NM 87199, USA	Senator, NM; Astronaut
Schmitt, Janis Playboy Promotions, 2706 Media Center Dr, Los Angeles CA 90065 USA	Model
Schmitt, John C 2 Mayflower Road, Glen Head NY 11545, USA	Football Player
Schmitt, Martin W W P Group, Lustenauerstra 64, 6850 Dornbirn, Austria	Ski Jumper
Schmitt, Maximilian Kunstler Sekretariat am Gasteig, Rosenheimer Str 52, 81669 Munich, Germany	Opera Singer
Schmitt, Pal President's Office, Kossuth Lajos Ter 1-3, 1055 Budapest, Hungary	President, Hungary
Schmock, Jonathan A P A Talent/Literary Agency, 405 S Beverly Dr, #300, Beverly Hills CA 90212 USA	Actor, Director
Schmoeller, David 3910 Woodhill Ave, Las Vegas NV 89121, USA	Director

Schmoll, Steve
4758 Chastain Dr, Melbourne FL 32940, USA — Baseball Player

Schnabel, Julian
Cinetic Mgmt, 555 W 25th St, #400, New York NY 10001 USA — Artist, Director

Schnackenberg, Roy L
180 E Pearson St, Chicago IL 60611, USA — Artist, Sculptor

Schnarre, Monika
Alex Stevens, 137 N Larchmont, #259, Los Angeles CA 90004, USA — Model, Actress

Schnebel, Dieter
Hektorstr 15, 10711 Berlin, Germany — Composer

Schnebli, Dolf
Sudstr 45, 8008 Zurich, Switzerland — Architect

Schneck, David L (Dave)
3891 Lehigh Dr, Northampton PA 18067, USA — Baseball Player

Schneck, Michael L (Mike)
2006 Condor Lane, Gibsonia PA 15044, USA — Football Player

Schneerson, Rachel
National Institutes of Health, 9000 Rockville Pike, Bethesda MD 20892, USA — Immunologist

Schneider, Aaron
Anonymous Content, 3532 Hayden Ave, Culver City CA 90232 USA — Cinematographer

Schneider, Bob
Agency Group Ltd, 142 W 57th St, #600, New York NY 10019 USA — Singer, Songwriter

Schneider, Brian D
130 Playa Rienta Way, Palm Beach Gardens FL 33418, USA — Baseball Player

Schneider, Christoph (Doom)
Pilgrim Mgmt, PO Box 54101, 10042 Berlin, Germany — Drummer (Rammstein)

Schneider, Cory
Vancouver Canucks, 800 Griffiths Way, Vancouver BC V6B 6G1, Canada — Ice Hockey Player

Schneider, Daniel J (Dan)
W M E Entertainment, 9601 Wilshire Blvd, #300, Beverly Hills CA 90210 USA — Actor, Director, Producer

Schneider, Daniel L (Dan)
PO Box 30940, Tucson AZ 85751, USA — Baseball Player

Schneider, Eliza
W M E Entertainment, 9601 Wilshire Blvd, #300, Beverly Hills CA 90210 USA — Actress

Schneider, Fred
Direct Management Group, 947 N La Cienega Blvd, #G, West Hollywood CA 90069, USA — Singer, Songwriter (B-52s)

Schneider, Jeffrey T (Jeff)
268 Pin Oak Dr, Geneseo IL 61254, USA — Baseball Player

Schneider, John
Trail's End, 4607 Lakeview Canyon Road, #569, Westlake Village CA 91361, USA — Actor, Singer

Schneider, Lew
United Talent Agency, 9336 Civic Center Dr, Beverly Hills CA 90210 USA — Producer, Writer, Actor

Schneider, Mathieu
1311 6th St, Manhattan Beach CA 90266, USA — Ice Hockey Player

Schneider, Max
W M E Entertainment, 9601 Wilshire Blvd, #300, Beverly Hills CA 90210 USA — Actor

Schneider, Paul
MacMillan, 1177 Ave of Americas, #1965, New York NY 10036 USA — Writer

Schneider, Paul A
Creative Artists Agency, 2000 Ave of Stars, #100, Los Angeles CA 90067 USA — Actor

Schneider, Rob
Gersh Agency, 9465 Wilshire Blvd, #600, Beverly Hills CA 90212 USA — Actor, Comedian

Schneider, Robert
Billions Corp, 3522 W Armitage Ave, Chicago IL 60647 USA — Singer, Guitarist (Apples in Stereo)

Schneider, Vreni
Dorf, 8767 Elm, Switzerland — Alpine Skier

Schneider, William C (Buzz)
5656 Turtle Lake Road, Saint Paul MN 55126, USA — Ice Hockey Player

Schneiderman, David A
I C M Partners, 10250 Constellation Blvd, #900, Los Angeles CA 90067 USA — Publisher, Editor

Schneier, Arthur
Appeal of Conscience Foundation, 119 W 57th St, #820, New York NY 10019, USA — Religious Leader, Association Executive

Schnelker, Robert B (Bob)
85 Silver Oaks Circle, Naples FL 34119, USA — Football Player

Schnelldorfer, Manfred
Seydlitzstr 55, 80993 Munich, Germany — Figure Skater

Schnellenberger, Howard
118 SE 25th Ave, Boynton Beach FL 33435, USA — Football Coach

Schnetzer, Stephen
Liebman Entertainment, 25 E 21st St, #PH, New York NY 10010, USA — Actor

Schnieders, Richard
Sysco Corp, 1390 Enclave Parkway, Houston TX 77077, USA — Businessman

Schnitker, J Michael (Mike)
PO Box 968, Conifer CO 80433, USA — Football Player

Schnittker, Richard D (Dick)
2303 E Las Granadas, Green Valley AZ 85614, USA — Basketball Player

Schobel, Aaron R
1024 Yaupon Creek Estuary, Columbus TX 78934, USA — Football Player

Schobel, Matthew T (Matt)
PO Box 1276, Columbus TX 78934, USA — Football Player

Schobel, Robert E (Bo)
112 Fairview St, Columbus TX 78934, USA — Football Player

Schoch, Philipp
Waldheim, 8496 Steg, Switzerland — Snowboarding Athlete

Schochet, Bob
6 Sunset Road, Highland Mills NY 10930, USA — Cartoonist

Schock, Gina
Direct Managment Group, 947 N La Cienega Blvd, #G, West Hollywood CA 90069, USA — Singer, Drummer (Go-Go's)

Schock, Ron
1360 Whalen Road, Penfield NY 14526, USA — Ice Hockey Player

Schockemohle, Alwin
Kreis Diepholz/Niedersachsen, 49453 Muhlen, Germany — Equestrian

Schoeller, Pierre
Agence Associes, 82 Rue de Rennes, 75006 Paris, France — Director, Writer

Schoen, Gerald T (Gerry)
110 Mark Twain Dr, #21, New Orleans LA 70123, USA — Baseball Player

Schoen, Max H — Dentist
123 Wellfleet Circle, Folsom CA 95630, USA

Schoenaerts, Matthias — Actor
Lisa Richards Agency, 108 Upper Leeson St, Dublin 4, Ireland

Schoenbaechler, Andreas — Aerials Skier
Muhlrutistr 2, 8910 Affoltern a A, Switzerland

Schoenborn, Christoph Cardinal — Religious Leader
Wollzeile 2, 1010 Vienna, Austria

Schoendienst, Albert F (Red) — Baseball Player, Manager
1105 Jo Carr Dr, Town and Country MO 63017, USA

Schoene, Russ — Basketball Player
1136 205th Ave NE, Sammamish WA 98074, USA

Schoeneweis, Scott D — Baseball Player
14420 E Kern Court, Fountain Hills AZ 85268, USA

Schoenfeld, Jim — Ice Hockey Player, Coach
45 W 60th St, #18D, New York NY 10023, USA

Schoenfield, Al — Swimming Executive
75 Santa Rosa St, San Luis Obispo CA 93405, USA

Schoenke, Raymond F (Ray), Jr — Football Player
21151 Woodfield Road, Gaithersburg MD 20882, USA

Schofield, David — Actor
Ken McReddie Assoc, 11 Connaught Place, London W2 2ET, England

Schofield, Dwight — Ice Hockey Player
9024 Cardinal Terrace, Saint Louis MO 63144, USA

Schofield, J Richard (Dick) — Baseball Player
138 Circle Dr, Springfield IL 62703, USA

Schofield, John — Jazz Guitarist, Composer
International Music Network, 278 Main St, Gloucester MA 01930, USA

Schofield, Oscar — Oceanographer
Marine Biology/Ocean Optics Center, 71 Dudley Road, New Brunswick NJ 08901, USA

Schofield, Richard C (Dick) — Baseball Player
17703 Gardenview Place Court, Glencoe MO 63038, USA

Scholes, Myron S — Nobel Economics Laureate
34 Stern Lane, Atherton CA 94027, USA

Scholl, Andreas — Opera Singer
I M G Artists, Hogarth Business Park, Chiswick, London W4 2TH, England

Schollander, Donald A (Don) — Swimmer
3576 Lakeview Blvd, Lake Oswego OR 97035, USA

Scholten, Jim — Singer, Bassist (Sawyer Brown)
O-Seven Artist Mgmt, PO Box 210586, Nashville TN 37221, USA

Scholtz, Bruce D — Football Player
6607 Cypress Point N, Austin TX 78746, USA

Scholtz, Robert J (Bob) — Football Player
6721 S 71st East Ave, Tulsa OK 74133, USA

Schomberg, A Thomas — Sculptor
4923 S Snowberry Lane, Evergreen CO 80439, USA

Schon, Jan Hendrik — Inventor (Molecule Transistor)
Lucent Technology Bell Laboratory, 600 Mountain Ave, New Providence NJ 07974, USA

Schon, Kyra — Actress
930 N Sheridan Ave, Pittsburgh PA 15206, USA

Schon, Neal J — Guitarist (Journey)
Front Line Mgmt, 1100 Glendon Ave, #2000, Los Angeles CA 90024 USA

Schonberg, Claude-Michel — Composer
Cameron Mackintosh Ltd, 1 Bedford Square, London WC1B 3RA, England

Schonert, Turk L — Football Player
7 Sugar Mill Court, Lancaster NY 14086, USA

Schonherr, Ivonne — Actress
Sascha Wunsch Artists Mgmt, Stubenrauchstr 57, 12161 Berlin, Germany

Schonhuber, Franz — Commentator
Europaburo, Fraunhoferstr 23, 80469 Munich, Germany

Schoofs, Mark — Journalist
Village Voice, Editorial Dept, 32 Cooper Square, New York NY 10003, USA

Schooler, Michael R (Mike) — Baseball Player
519 N Buttonwood St, Anaheim CA 92805, USA

Schoolnik, Gary — Microbiologist
Stanford University Medical School, Microbiology Dept, Stanford CA 94305, USA

Schools, Dave — Bassist (Widespread Panic)
Brown Cat Inc, 400 Foundry St, Athens GA 30601 USA

Schoomaker, Peter J (Pete) — Army General
Special Operations Warrior Foundation, PO Box 13483, Tampa FL 33681, USA

Schopf, J William — Paleobiologist
University of California, Study of Evolution Center, Los Angeles CA 90024, USA

Schorer, Jane — Journalist
Des Moines Register, Editorial Dept, PO Box 957, Des Moines IA 50306, USA

Schorr, Bill — Cartoonist (Phoebe's Place)
United Feature Syndicate, PO Box 5610, Cincinnati OH 45201 USA

Schorske, Carl E — Historian, Writer
45 Meadow Lakes, #1, Hightstown NJ 08520, USA

Schott, Ben — Photographer, Writer
Rogers Coleridge White, 20 Powis Mews, London W11 1JN, England

Schottenheimer, Martin E (Marty) — Football Coach, Sportscaster
19825 Northcove Road, #B, Cornelius NC 28031, USA

Schourek, Peter A (Pete) — Baseball Player
13761 Balmoral Greens Ave, Clifton VA 20124, USA

Schrader, Kenneth (Ken) — Auto, Truck Racing Driver
Ken Schrader Racing, 4403 Stough Road, Concord NC 28027, USA

Schrader, Maria — Actress
Davien Littlefield Mgmt, 477 Madison Ave, New York NY 10022, USA

Schrader, Paul J — Director, Writer
Parseghian/Planco, 388 2nd Ave, #506, New York, NY 10010 USA

Schrag, Ariel — Writer
Peikoff Law Office, 173 E Broadway, #C1, New York NY 10002, USA

Schram, Bitty — Actress
1 Mgmt, 9000 W Sunset Blvd, #1550, Los Angeles CA 90069 USA

Schram, Jessica (Jessy) — Actress
C E S D, 10635 Santa Monica Blvd, #130, Los Angeles CA 90025 USA

Schramka, Paul E — Baseball Player
W180N9923 Riversbend Circle W, Germantown WI 53022, USA
Schramm, David — Actor
Gersh Agency, 9465 Wilshire Blvd, #600, Beverly Hills CA 90212 USA
Schranz, Karl — Alpine Skier
Hotel Garni, 6580 Saint Anton, Austria
Schreiber, Adam B — Football Player
PO Box 27085, Panama City FL 32411, USA
Schreiber, Lawrence A (Larry) — Football Player
388 Albion Ave, Woodside CA 94062, USA
Schreiber, Liev — Actor, Director
Creative Artists Agency, 2000 Ave of Stars, #100, Los Angeles CA 90067 USA
Schreiber, Martin J — Governor, WI
2700 S Shore Dr, #B, Milwaukee WI 53207, USA
Schreiber, Pablo — Actor
I C M Partners, 10250 Constellation Blvd, #900, Los Angeles CA 90067 USA
Schreiber, Stuart L — Chemist
Harvard University, Chemistry Dept, Cambridge MA 02138, USA
Schreiber, Theodore H (Ted) — Baseball Player
116 Nantucket Isle, Centerville GA 31028, USA
Schreier, Peter — Opera Singer, Conductor
Peter McCann Ltd, 56 Lawrie Park Gardens, London SE26 6XY, England
Schremmer, Patty — Golfer
5547 Avenida del Mare, Sarasota FL 34242, USA
Schremp, Rob — Ice Hockey Player
303 Phillips St, Fulton NY 13069, USA
Schrempf, Detlef — Basketball Player
9735 NE 1st St, Bellevue WA 98004, USA
Schrempp, Jurgen E — Businessman
Daimler-Chrysler AG, Plieningerstra, 70546 Stuttgart, Germany
Schreyer, Cynthia (Cindy) — Golfer
208 Brushy Hill Road, Danbury CT 06810, USA
Schreyer, Edward R — Governor General, Canada
250 Wellington Crescent, #401, Winnipeg MB R3M 0B3, Canada
Schrieffer, John R — Nobel Physics Laureate
22465 Tuna Place, Boca Raton FL 33428, USA
Schrimshaw, Nevin S — Nutritionist
Sandwich Notch Farm, Thornton NH 03223, USA
Schrock, Richard R — Nobel Chemistry Laureate
15 Cabot St, Winchester MA 01890, USA
Schroder, Ernst A — Actor
Podere Montalto, Castellina In Chianti, 53011 Siena, Italy
Schroder, Rick — Actor, Director
Hofflund/Polone, 9465 Wilshire Blvd, #420, Beverly Hills CA 90212 USA
Schroeder, A William (Bill) — Baseball Player
S75W17724 Harbor Circle, Muskego WI 53150, USA
Schroeder, Barbet G — Director, Producer
Creative Artists Agency, 2000 Ave of Stars, #100, Los Angeles CA 90067 USA
Schroeder, Carly — Actress
Innovative Artists, 1505 10th St, Santa Monica CA 90401 USA
Schroeder, Eugene W (Gene) — Football Player
918 Aaron Court, Crown Point IN 46307, USA
Schroeder, Gerhard — Chancellor, Germany
Buro Bundeskanzler, Unter den Linden 50, 10117 Berlin, Germany
Schroeder, Jay B — Football Player
730 E Grinnell Dr, Burbank CA 91501, USA
Schroeder, Jim — Bowler
3 Greenhaven Terrace, Tonawanda NY 14150, USA
Schroeder, John H — Educator
University of Wisconsin, Chancellor's Office, Milwaukee WI 53211, USA
Schroeder, Manfred R — Physicist
Rieswartenweg 8, 37077 Gottingen, Germany
Schroeder, Mary M — Judge
US Court of Appeals, 230 N 1st Ave, #101, Phoenix AZ 85003, USA
Schroeder, Patricia S — Representative, CO
621 Nadina Place, Kissimmee FL 34747, USA
Schroeder, Paul W — Historian
University of Illinois, History Dept, 810 S Wright St, Urbana IL 61801, USA
Schroeder, Steven A — Foundation Executive, Physician
10 Paseo Mirasol, Belvedere Tiburon CA 94920, USA
Schroeder, Terry — Water Polo Player, Coach
North Ranch Chiropractic, 31225 La Baya Dr, #206, Westlake Village CA 91362, USA
Schroeder, William F (Bill) — Football Player
2176 Shady Lane, Green Bay WI 54313, USA
Schrom, Kenneth M (Ken) — Baseball Player
1002 Black Diamond Court, Portland TX 78374, USA
Schroy, Kenneth M (Ken) — Football Player
79 Russell Road, Garden City NY 11530, USA
Schroyer, Heath — Basketball Coach
University of Wyoming, Athletic Dept, Laramie WY 82071, USA
Schruefer, John J — Gynecologist
3800 Reservoir Road NW, Washington DC 20007, USA
Schu, Richard S (Rick) — Baseball Player
2013 Driftwood Circle, El Dorado Hills CA 95762, USA
Schuba, Beatrice (Trixi) — Figure Skater
Giorgengasse 2/1/8, Vienna 1190, Austria
Schubert, Christoph — Ice Hockey Player
Atlanta Thrashers, 101 Marietta St NW, #1900, Atlanta GA 30303 USA
Schubert, Richard F — Association Executive
6615 Madison-McLean Dr, McLean VA 22101, USA
Schubert, Steven W (Steve) — Football Player
7 Douglas Dr, Candia NH 03034, USA
Schuchmacher, John — Football Player
6000 Reims Road, #3006, Houston TX 77036, USA
Schuck, Anett — Canoeing Athlete
Defoestry 6A, 04159 Leipzig, Germany

Schuck, John — Actor
Douglas Gorman Rothacker Wilhelm, 1501 Broadway, #703, New York NY 10036, USA
Schuck, Walter — WW II German Luftwaffe Hero
Tekstr 55, 66424 Homburg/Saar, Germany
Schueler, Ronald R (Ron) — Baseball Player
3201 E Camino Sin Nombre, Paradise Valley AZ 85253, USA
Schuffenhauer, Bill — Bobsled Athlete
2888 Marilyn Dr, Ogden UT 84403, USA
Schuh, Harry F — Football Player
2309 Massey Road, Memphis TN 38119, USA
Schuh, Jeffrey J (Jeff) — Football Player
5550 Vagabond Lane N, Minneapolis MN 55446, USA
Schuhl, Jean Jacques — Writer
Editions Gallimard, 5 Rue Sebastien Bottin, 75007 Paris, France
Schul, Robert (Bob) — Track Athlete
320 Wisteria Dr, Dayton OH 45419, USA
Schuldt, Travis — Actor
Stone Manners Salners, 9911 W Pico Blvd, #1400, Los Angeles CA 90035 USA
Schuler, Carolyn J — Swimmer
26552 Via del Sol, Mission Viejo CA 92691, USA
Schull, Amanda — Ballerina, Actress
San Francisco Ballet, 455 Franklin St, San Francisco CA 94102, USA
Schull, Rebecca — Actress
9300 Wilshire Blvd, #410, Beverly Hills CA 90212, USA
Schuller, Grete — Sculptor
8 Barstow Road, #7G, Great Neck NY 11021, USA
Schuller, Gunther — Composer, Conductor
Margun Music, 167 Dudley Road, Newton Center MA 02459, USA
Schuller, Robert H — Evangelist
464 S Esplanade St, Orange CA 92869, USA
Schult, Arthur W (Art) — Baseball Player
9255 SW 90th St, Ocala FL 34481, USA
Schult, Jurgen — Track Athlete
Drosselweg 6, 19069 Leuna, Germany
Schulters, Lance A — Football Player
594 Grant Ave, Roselle NJ 07203, USA
Schultz, C Budd (Buddy) — Baseball Player
6510 N 59th St, Paradise Valley AZ 85253, USA
Schultz, Carl — Director
I C M Partners, 10250 Constellation Blvd, #900, Los Angeles CA 90067 USA
Schultz, Connie — Journalist
Cleveland Plain Dealer, Editorial Dept, 801 Superior Ave, Cleveland OH 44113 USA
Schultz, Dave — Ice Hockey Player
505 Alpine Court, Mays Landing NJ 08330, USA
Schultz, Dean — Government Official, Financier
Federal Home Loan Bank, 1079 Hutchinson Road, Walnut Creek CA 94598, USA
Schultz, Dwight — Actor
Media Partners, 8306 Wilshire Blvd, #337, Beverly Hills CA 90211, USA
Schultz, George W (Barney) — Baseball Player
400 Fern Brook Lane, #218, Mount Laurel NJ 08054, USA
Schultz, Howard — Businessman
Starbucks Corp, 2401 Utah Ave S, #800, Seattle WA 98134, USA
Schultz, John — Director, Producer, Writer
Creative Artists Agency, 2000 Ave of Stars, #100, Los Angeles CA 90067 USA
Schultz, Michael A — Director
Chrystalite Productions, PO Box 1940, Santa Monica CA 90406, USA
Schultz, Nick — Ice Hockey Player
201 Downey St, Strasbourg SK S9G 4V0, Canada
Schultz, Peter C — Inventor (Silica Optical Waveguide)
Heraeus Amersil Inc, 3473 Satellite Blvd, #300, Duluth GA 30096, USA
Schultz, Peter G — Chemist
Salk Research Institute, 10550 N Torrey Pine Road, La Jolla CA 92037, USA
Schultz, Philip — Writer
Houghton Mifflin Harcourt, 215 Park Ave S, #1200, New York NY 10003 USA
Schultz, Richard D — Association Executive
US Olympic Committee, 1 Olympic Plaza, Building 6, Colorado Springs CO 80909 USA
Schultz, Stanley G — Physiologist
4955 Heatherglen Dr, Houston TX 77096, USA
Schultz, William (Bill) — Football Player
9954 Hidden Falls Circle, Fishers IN 46037, USA
Schultze, Charles L — Government Official, Economist
5520 33rd St NW, Washington DC 20015, USA
Schulweis, Harold M — Religious Leader, Rabbi
Congregation Valley Beth Shalom, 15739 Ventura Blvd, Encino CA 91436, USA
Schulz, Axel — Boxer
Bliss Media, Nuhrenstr 23, 15234 Frankfurt, Germany
Schulz, Jeffrey A (Jeff) — Baseball Player
1167 N Stockwell Road, Evansville IN 47715, USA
Schulz, Jody J — Football Player
222 Schulz Lane, Chester MD 21619, USA
Schulz, Kurt E — Football Player
5075 Rockledge Dr, Clarence NY 14031, USA
Schulz, Ted — Golfer
94 Persimmon Ridge Dr, Louisville KY 40245, USA
Schulze, Donald A (Don) — Baseball Player
20558 Geer Ave, Hilmar CA 95324, USA
Schulze, Matt — Actor
Principato-Young, 9465 Wilshire Blvd, #880, Beverly Hills CA 90212 USA
Schulze, Paul — Actor
Kyle Friz Mgmt, 6325 Heather Dr, Los Angeles CA 90068, USA
Schulze, Richard M — Businessman
Best Buy Co, 7601 Penn Ave S, Minneapolis MN 55423, USA
Schumacher, Joel — Director
Joel Schumacher Productions, 10960 Wilshire Blvd, #1900, Los Angeles CA 90024, USA
Schumacher, Michael — Auto Racing Driver
Postfach 308, 1234 Vufflens-le-Chateau, Switzerland

Schumacher, Ralf
Williams B M W, Grove Wantage, Oxfordshire OX12 0DQ, England — Auto Racing Driver

Schumacher, Tony
Schumacher Racing, 1681 E Northfield Dr, #A, Brownsburg IN 46112, USA — Drag Racing Driver

Schumacher, William (Billy)
U-37 Racing Team, 2819 20th Ave W, Seattle, WA 98199, USA — Boat Racing Driver

Schumaker, Jared M (Skip)
8877 Tulare Dr, #310B, Huntington Beach CA 92646, USA — Baseball Player

Schumann, Jochen
Birkenstr 88, 48336 Penzberg, Germany — Yachtsman

Schumann, Ralf
Steomach 22, 97640 Stockheim, Germany — Marksman

Schur, Michael
United Talent Agency, 9336 Civic Center Dr, Beverly Hills CA 90210 USA — Producer, Writer, Actor

Schurman, Maynard F
301 Beaver St, Summerside PE C1N 2A2, Canada — Ice Hockey Player

Schurmann, Petra
Max-Emanuel-Str 7, 82319 Starnberg, Germany — Swimmer

Schurr, Harry W
1178 Davis Dr, Fairborn OH 45324, USA — Vietnam War Air Force Hero

Schurr, Wayne A
10030 W 500 S, Hudson IN 46747, USA — Baseball Player

Schussler Fiorenza, Elisabeth
Notre Dame University, Theology Dept, Notre Dame IN 46556, USA — Writer, Theologian

Schutz, Carl J
PO Box 162, French Settlement LA 70733, USA — Baseball Player

Schutz, Dana
Friedrich Petzel Gallery, 537 W 22nd St, New York NY 10011, USA — Artist

Schutz, Klaus
9 Konstanzerstr, 10707 Berlin, Germany — Mayor, Berlin; Government Official

Schutz, Susan Polis
Blue Mountain Arts Inc, PO Box 4549, Boulder CO 80306, USA — Writer

Schutz, William N (Bill)
9954 Hidden Falls Circle, Fishers IN 46037, USA — Football Player

Schutze, Jim
Avon Books, 1350 Ave of Americas, New York NY 10019, USA — Writer, Journalist

Schuur, Diane
Stiletto Entertainment, 8295 S La Cienega Blvd, Inglewood CA 90301, USA — Singer

Schwab, Charles R
Charles Schwab Co, 101 Montgomery St, #200, San Francisco CA 94104, USA — Financier

Schwab, Corey
20633 76th Ave SE, Snohomish WA 98296, USA — Ice Hockey Player

Schwabe, Michael S (Mike)
304 36th St, Newport Beach CA 92663, USA — Baseball Player

Schwahn, Mark
W M E Entertainment, 9601 Wilshire Blvd, #300, Beverly Hills CA 90210 USA — Producer, Writer

Schwall, Donald B (Don)
2000 Lake Marshall Dr, Gibsonia PA 15044, USA — Baseball Player

Schwaller, Andreas
Curling Assn, PO Box 606, 3000 Bern, Switzerland — Curling Athlete

Schwaller, Christof
Curling Assn, PO Box 606, 3000 Bern, Switzerland — Curling Athlete

Schwantz, James W (Jim)
1047 W Chatham Dr, Palatine IL 60067, USA — Football Player

Schwantz, Kevin
Kevin Schwantz School, 3446 Winder Highway, #M234, Flowery Branch GA 30542, USA — Motorcycle Racing Rider

Schwarthoff, Florian
Fischweiher 51, 64646 Heppenheim, Germany — Track Athlete

Schwartz, Alan
Bear Stearns Co, 383 Madison Ave, New York NY 10179, USA — Financier

Schwartz, Ben
W M E Entertainment, 9601 Wilshire Blvd, #300, Beverly Hills CA 90210 USA — Actor, Comedian, Writer

Schwartz, Bryan L
14805 Silver Feather Circle, Broomfield CO 80023, USA — Football Player

Schwartz, D Randall (Randy)
757 El Rancho Dr, El Cajon CA 92019, USA — Baseball Player

Schwartz, Jim
Detroit Lions, 222 Republic Dr, Allen Park MI 48101 USA — Football Coach

Schwartz, Josh
W M E Entertainment, 9601 Wilshire Blvd, #300, Beverly Hills CA 90210 USA — Writer, Producer

Schwartz, Lloyd
27 Pennsylvania Ave, Somerville MA 02145, USA — Journalist

Schwartz, Maite
TalentWorks, 3500 W Olive Ave, #1400, Burbank CA 91505 USA — Actress

Schwartz, Martha
Martha Schwartz Partners, 147 Sherman St, #200A, Cambridge MA 02140, USA — Landscape Architect

Schwartz, Maxime
Institut Pasteur, 25-28 Rue du Docteur-Roux, 75724 Paris Cedex 15, France — Medical Administrator

Schwartz, Neena B
450 Davis St, Evanston IL 60201, USA — Endocrinologist

Schwartz, Norton A
Chief of Staff, HqUSAF, Pentagon, Washington DC 20330 USA — Air Force General

Schwartz, Scott
19111 Arminta St, Reseda CA 91335, USA — Actor

Schwartz, Stephen L
Andrew Freedman Public Relations, 9127 Thrasher Ave, Los Angeles CA 90069, USA — Composer, Lyricist, Singer

Schwartz, Thomas A
Military Child Education Coalition, PO Box 2519, Harker Heights TX 76548, USA — Army General

Schwartzbach, Gerald
655 Redwood Highway, #277, Mill Valley CA 94941, USA — Attorney

Schwartzel, Charl A J L
International Sports Mgmt, Cherry Tree Farm, Rostherne, Cheshire WA14 3RZ, England — Golfer

Schwartzman, John
Murtha Agency, 1025 Colorado Ave, Santa Monica CA 90401, USA — Cinematographer, Director

Schwartzman, Robert
I C M Partners, 10250 Constellation Blvd, #900, Los Angeles CA 90067 USA — Actor

S

Schwary, Ronald L
W M E Entertainment, 9601 Wilshire Blvd, #300, Beverly Hills CA 90210 USA — Actor, Producer, Director

Schwarz, Gerard R
Royal Liverpool Orchestra, Hope St, Liverpool L1 9BP, England — Conductor

Schwarz, Hanna
Opera et Concert, 37 Rue de la Chaussee d'Antin, 75009 Paris, France — Opera Singer

Schwarz, Julian
C M Artists, 127 W 96th St, #13B, New York NY 10025 USA — Concert Cellist

Schwarzbein, Diana
Health Communications, 3201 SW 15th St, Deerfield Beach FL 33442, USA — Physician, Writer

Schwarzenegger, Arnold A
Creative Artists Agency, 2000 Ave of Stars, #100, Los Angeles CA 90067 USA — Body Builder, Actor; Governor, CA

Schwarzkopf, H Norman
Black Summit, 301 W Platt St, Tampa FL 33606, USA — Army General

Schwarzman, Stephen A
Blackstone Group, 345 Park Ave, Basement Lobby B4, New York NY 10154, USA — Financier

Schwarz-Schilling, Christian
Am Dohlberg 10, 63564 Budingen, Germany — Government Official, Germany

Schweickart, Russell L
C T A Commercial Systems, 6116 Executive Blvd, #800, Rockville MD 20852, USA — Astronaut

Schweiger, Til
Barefoot Films, Saarbrueckerstra 36, 10405 Berlin, Germany — Actor

Schweigert, Stuart E
4825 Gratiot Road, Saginaw MI 48638, USA — Football Player

Schweiker, Richard S (Dick)
8890 Windy Ridge Way, McLean VA 22102, USA — Secretary, Health & Human Services

Schweikher, Paul
3222 E Missouri Ave, Phoenix AZ 85018, USA — Architect

Schweitz, John E
813 Smith Dr, Florence SC 29501, USA — Basketball Player

Schwentke, Robert
Creative Artists Agency, 2000 Ave of Stars, #100, Los Angeles CA 90067 USA — Director

Schwer, William (Billy)
5 Grange Ave, Luton LU4 9AS, England — Boxer

Schwertsik, Kurt
Penzinger Str 26, 1140 Vienna, Austria — Composer

Schwery, Henri Cardinal
CP 2334, 1950 Sion 2, Switzerland — Religious Leader

Schwimmer, David
Creative Artists Agency, 2000 Ave of Stars, #100, Los Angeles CA 90067 USA — Actor, Director

Schwimmer, Rusty
Meghan Schumacher Mgmt, 13351D Riverside Dr, #387, Sherman Oaks CA 91423, USA — Actress

Schwinden, Ted
401 N Fee St, Helena MT 59601, USA — Governor, MT

Schwitters, Roy F
1718 Cromwell Hill, Austin TX 78703, USA — Physicist

Schygulla, Hanna
Agents Associes Marie Chen, Rue Faubourg St Honore, 75008 Paris, France — Actress

Schypinski, Gerald A (Jerry)
28014 Shadowwood Lane, Harrison Township MI 48045, USA — Baseball Player

Scialfa, Patty
1224 Benedict Canyon, Beverly Hills CA 90210, USA — Singer (E Street Band)

Sciarra, John M
404 Morning Star Lane, Newport Beach CA 92660, USA — Football Player

Scifres, Michael T (Mike)
13100 Dear Canyon Court, San Diego CA 92131, USA — Football Player

Scio, Yvonne
Artmedia, 20 Ave Rapp, 75007 Paris, France — Actress, Model

Scioli, Brad E
106 Steinbright Dr, Collegeville PA 19426, USA — Football Player

Sciorra, Anabella
A P A Talent/Literary Agency, 405 S Beverly Dr, #300, Beverly Hills CA 90212 USA — Actress

Scioscia, Michael L (Mike)
1915 Falling Star Ave, Westlake Village CA 91362, USA — Baseball Player, Manager

Scirica, Anthony J
US Court of Appeals, 601 Market St, #22614, Philadelphia PA 19106, USA — Judge

Sclisizzi, Enio
100 Millside Dr, Milton ON L9T 5E2, Canada — Ice Hockey Player

Scob, Edith
Agence Artistes Cinetea, 15 Rue Chapon, 75003 Paris, France — Actress

Scobee, Joshua T (Josh)
11686 Blackstone River Dr, Jacksonville FL 32256, USA — Football Player

Scobey, Josh
1372 E Mead Dr, Chandler AZ 85249, USA — Football Player

Scodelario, Kaya
Curtis Brown Group, 28-29 Haymarket St, #500, London SW1Y 4SP, England — Actress

Scofidio, Ricardo
Diller Scofidio Renfro, 601 W 26th St, #1815, New York NY 10001, USA — Architect

Scofield, John
Verve Records, 1755 Broadway, #600, New York NY 10019 USA — Jazz Electric Guitarist

Scofield, Richard M (Dick)
3251 Country Club Parkway, Castle Rock CO 80108, USA — Air Force General

Scoggins, Matt
4900 Calhoun Canyon Loop, Austin TX 78735, USA — Diving Coach

Scoggins, Tracy
Metropolitan Talent Agency, 7020 La Presa Dr, Los Angeles CA 90068 USA — Actress

Scola Balvoa, Luis A
11801 Sea Shadow Bend, Pearland TX 77584, USA — Basketball Player

Scola, Angelo Cardinal
Archdiocese, S Marco 320/A, 30124 Venice, Italy — Religious Leader

Scola, Ettore
Via Bertoloni 1/E, 00197 Rome, Italy — Director

Scolari, Peter
C E S D, 10635 Santa Monica Blvd, #130, Los Angeles CA 90025 USA — Actor

Scolnick, Edward M
1201 Magnolia Dr, Wayland MA 01778, USA — Geneticist, Virologist

Schwary - Scolnick

866   V.I.P. Address Book

Sconiers, Daryl A
16775 S Paine St, #1, Fontana CA 92336, USA — Baseball Player

Scorcio, Michael (Mike)
10360 SE Waverly Court, #405, Portland OR 97222, USA — WW II Army Air Corps Hero

Score, Michael (Mike)
Lustig Talent, PO Box 770850, Orlando FL 32877 USA — Singer, Keyboardist (Flock of Seagulls)

Scorpio
Universal Attractions, 135 W 26th St, #1200, New York NY 10001 USA — Rap Artist (Furious Five)

Scorsese, Martin
Sikelia Productions, 110 W 57th St, #500, New York NY 10019, USA — Director

Scorupco, Izabella
Mikas Stockholm, Bredgrand 2, 111 30 Stockholm, Sweden — Actress, Singer, Model

Scott Brown, Denise
Venturi Scott Brown Assoc, 4236 Main St, Philadelphia PA 19127, USA — Architect

Scott Thomas, Kristin A
Agence Artiste Adequet, 80 Rue d'Amsterdam, 75009 Paris, France — Actress

Scott, A David (Dave)
3151 Robindale Road, Decatur GA 30034, USA — Football Player

Scott, Adam
Creative Artists Agency, 2000 Ave of Stars, #100, Los Angeles CA 90067 USA — Actor

Scott, Adam
Professional Golfer's Assn, PO Box 109601, Palm Beach Gardens FL 33410 USA — Golfer

Scott, Alvin L
5786 W Townley Ave, Glendale AZ 85302, USA — Basketball Player

Scott, Andy
D C M International, 296 Nether St, Finchley, London N3 1RJ, England — Guitarist (Sweet)

Scott, Anthony (Tony)
120 Seay St, Spartanburg SC 29306, USA — Baseball Player

Scott, April
C E S D, 10635 Santa Monica Blvd, #130, Los Angeles CA 90025 USA — Actress

Scott, Ashley
Don Buchwald/Fortitude, 6500 Wilshire Blvd, #2200, Los Angeles CA 90048 USA — Actress

Scott, B James
10127 Chisholm Trail, Dallas TX 75243, USA — Football Player

Scott, Bartholomew E (Bart)
6 Kings Court, Morristown NJ 07960, USA — Football Player

Scott, Brian
Joe Gibbs Racing, 6001 Haas Way, Kannapolis NC 28127, USA — Truck Racing Driver

Scott, Byron A
668 Euclid Ave, #527, Cleveland OH 44114, USA — Basketball Player, Coach

Scott, Camilla
23773 Via Canon, #201, Newhall CA 91321, USA — Actress

Scott, Campbell
Paradigm Agency, 360 N Crescent Dr, North Building, Beverly Hills CA 90210 USA — Actor

Scott, Chad O
18526 Reliant Dr, Gaithersburg MD 20879, USA — Football Player

Scott, Charles T (Charlie)
300 Chastain Manor Dr, Norcross GA 30071, USA — Basketball Player

Scott, Clarence R, Jr
216 Sisson Ave NE, Atlanta GA 30317, USA — Football Player

Scott, Clyde L (Smackover)
12840 Rivercrest Dr, Little Rock AR 72212, USA — Football Player, Track Athlete

Scott, Darnay
18551 Patton St, Detroit MI 48219, USA — Football Player

Scott, Dave
3080 Valmont Road, #242, Boulder CO 80301, USA — Triathlete, Coach

Scott, David R
Merces, V C Johnson, 30 Hackamore Lane, #1, Bell Canyon CA 91307, USA — Astronaut

Scott, Deborah Lynn
Innovative Artists, 1505 10th St, Santa Monica CA 90401 USA — Costume Designer

Scott, Dennis E
5425 Palm Lake Circle, Orlando FL 32819, USA — Basketball Player

Scott, DeQuincy
681 Country Place Dr, Pearl MS 39208, USA — Football Player

Scott, Desiree R M
Canadian Soccer, Place Soccer Canada, 237 Metcalfe St, Ottawa ON K2P 1R2, Canada — Soccer Player

Scott, Donald M (Donnie)
6042 114th Terrace N, Pinellas Park FL 33782, USA — Baseball Player

Scott, Donovan
Judy Fox Mgmt, 1525 1/2 S Beverly Dr, Los Angeles CA 90035, USA — Actor

Scott, Doug
Warwick Mill Center, Weck Bridge, Carlisle Cumbria CA4 8RR, England — Mountaineer

Scott, Dougray
W M E Entertainment, 9601 Wilshire Blvd, #300, Beverly Hills CA 90210 USA — Actor

Scott, Freddie L
PO Box 197, Coahoma MS 38617, USA — Football Player

Scott, Gary T
25 W Elm St, #47, Greenwich CT 06830, USA — Baseball Player

Scott, Gloria Dean Randle
Bennett College, President's Office, Greensboro NC 27401, USA — Educator

Scott, Herbert C, Jr
605 Rawhide Court, Plano TX 75023, USA — Football Plyaer

Scott, Hillary
Capitol Records, 810 7th Ave, New York NY 10019 USA — Singer, Songwriter (Lady Antebellum)

Scott, Irene F
US Tax Court, 400 2nd St NW, Washington DC 20217, USA — Judge

Scott, J Raymond (Ray)
5318 Indian Trail, Ypsilanti MI 48197, USA — Basketball Player, Coach

Scott, Jack
34039 Coachwood Dr, Sterling Heights MI 48312, USA — Singer, Songwriter

Scott, Jacob E (Jake), Jr
32 Seaside South Court, Key West FL 33040, USA — Football Player

Scott, Jacqueline
Lichtman/Salners, 15865 Royal Haven Place, Sherman Oaks CA 91403 USA — Actress

Scott, Jake
Black Dog Films, 42-44 Beak St, London W1F 9RH, England — Director

S

Sconiers - Scott

Scott, Jake
PO Box 18106, Encino CA 91416, USA
Singer, Guitarist

Scott, Jason Shane
Commercial Talent, 9255 Sunset Blvd, #505, Los Angeles CA 90069, USA
Actor

Scott, Jean Bruce
Autry National Center, 4700 Western Heritage Way, Los Angeles CA 90027, USA
Actress

Scott, Jerry
Creators Syndicate, 737 3rd St, Hermosa Beach CA 90254 USA
Cartoonist (Baby Blues, Zits)

Scott, Jill
I C M Partners, 10250 Constellation Blvd, #900, Los Angeles CA 90067 USA
Singer, Songwriter, Actress

Scott, Jimmy
Maxine Harvard, 7942 W Bell Road, #C5, Glendale AZ 85308 USA
Singer

Scott, Jonathan R
Chicago Bears, 1000 Football Dr, Lake Forest IL 60045 USA
Football Player

Scott, Josey
Helter Skelter, 347-353 Chiswick High Road, London W4 4HS, England
Singer (Saliva)

Scott, Kathryn Leigh
3236 Bennett Dr, Los Angeles CA 90068, USA
Actress

Scott, Klea
Sovereign Talent Group, 8421 Wilshire Blvd, #200, Beverly Hills CA 90211, USA
Actress

Scott, LaToucha
Richard Walters, PO Box 2789, Toluca Lake CA 91610 USA
Singer (Xscape)

Scott, Lizabeth
8277 Hollywood Blvd, Los Angeles CA 90069, USA
Actress

Scott, Lorna
Tyler Kjar, 10153 1/2 Riverside Dr, #255, Toluca Lake CA 91602 USA
Actress

Scott, Luke B
PO Box 39, De Leon Springs FL 32130, USA
Baseball Player

Scott, Manda
Delacorte Press, 1540 Broadway, New York NY 10036 USA
Writer

Scott, Mark (Gus)
Global Star Productions, 103 Godwin Ave, #225, Midland Park NJ 07432, USA
Drummer (Trixter)

Scott, Melody Thomas
12068 Crest Court, Beverly Hills CA 90210, USA
Actress

Scott, Michael W (Mike)
28355 Chat Dr, Laguna Niguel CA 92677, USA
Baseball Player

Scott, Mike
Agency Group Ltd, 142 W 57th St, #600, New York NY 10019 USA
Singer (Waterboys), Songwriter

Scott, Pippa
10 Ocean Park Blvd, #1, Santa Monica CA 90405, USA
Actress

Scott, Randolph C (Randy)
1440 Woodland Lake Dr, Snellville GA 30078, USA
Football Player

Scott, Reid
Impression Entertainment, 9229 W Sunset Blvd, #700, Los Angeles CA 90069, USA
Actor

Scott, Richard U (Dick)
3369 Upland Court, Adamstown MD 21710, USA
Football Player

Scott, Ridley
632 N La Peer Dr, West Hollywood CA 90069, USA
Director

Scott, Robert B (Bobby)
801 McKinley Pointe Lane, Knoxville TN 37934, USA
Football Player

Scott, Rodney
Domain Talent, 9229 W Sunset Blvd, #710, West Hollywood CA 90069 USA
Actor

Scott, Rodney D
4206 Priscilla Ave, Indianapolis IN 46226, USA
Baseball Player

Scott, Seann William
Elephant Pictures, 1466 N Milwaukee Ave, #2, Chicago IL 60622, USA
Actor

Scott, Sherie Rene
Principal Entertainment, 1964 Westwood Blvd, #400, Los Angeles CA 90025 USA
Actress, Singer

Scott, Spencer
PO Box 461177, Los Angeles CA 90046, USA
Model

Scott, Stuart
ESPN-TV, ESPN Plaza, 935 Middle St, Bristol CT 06010 USA
Sportscaster

Scott, Tamika
Richard Walters, PO Box 2789, Toluca Lake CA 91610 USA
Singer (Xscape)

Scott, Thomas C (Tom)
3259 Kirkwood Court, Keswick VA 22947, USA
Football Player

Scott, Timothy
50 Clare Court, Judd St, London WC1H 9QW, England
Sculptor

Scott, Timothy D (Tim)
956 W Julia Way, Hanford CA 93230, USA
Baseball Player

Scott, Todd C
5605 Avenue P, Galveston TX 77551, USA
Football Player

Scott, Tom Everett
Paradigm Agency, 360 N Crescent Dr, North Building, Beverly Hills CA 90210 USA
Actor

Scott, Walter B
1991 Edgefield Road, Trenton SC 29847, USA
Football Player

Scott, Willard H, Jr
NBC-TV, News Dept, 30 Rockefeller Plaza, #270E, New York NY 10112 USA
Entertainer

Scott, Willie L, Jr
1123 Long St, Newberry SC 29108, USA
Football Player

Scott, Winston E
PO Box 1192, Cape Canaveral FL 32920, USA
Astronaut

Scotti, Benjamin J (Ben)
715 N Beverly Dr, Beverly Hills CA 90210, USA
Football Player

Scotti, Nick
Untitled Entertainment, 350 S Beverly Dr, #200, Beverly Hills CA 90212 USA
Actor, Singer

Scotto, Renata
3 Stone Hallow Way, Armonk NY 10504, USA
Opera Singer

Scottoline, Lisa
Harper Collins Publishers, 10 E 53rd St, Cellar 1, New York NY 10022 USA
Writer

Scotty, Ludwig
President's Office, Government Offices, Yaren, Nauru
President, Nauru

Scovell, Nell
Paradigm Agency, 360 N Crescent Dr, North Building, Beverly Hills CA 90210 USA
Producer

Scowcroft, Brent
900 17th St NW, #500, Washington DC 20006, USA
Government Official, Air Force General

Scrafford, Kirk T — Football Player
19400 US Highway 93 N, Florence MT 59833, USA

Scranton, James D (Jim) — Baseball Player
27519 Hammack Ave, Perris CA 92570, USA

Scranton, Nancy — Golfer
1816 Forest Glen Way, Saint Augustine FL 32092, USA

Scranton, William W — Governor, PA; Ambassador to UN
Marquette University, Dentistry School, 604 N 16th St, Milwaukee WI 53233, USA

Scribner, William C (Bucky) — Football Player
246 Porter Mill Bend Dr, Camdenton MO 65020, USA

Scrimm, Angus — Actor
PO Box 5193, North Hollywood CA 91616, USA

Scrimshaw, Nevin S — Nutritionist
Sandwich Mountain Farm, PO Box 330, Campton NH 03223, USA

Scrivener, Wayne A (Chuck) — Baseball Player
1766 Hazel St, Birmingham AL 48009, USA

Scroggins, Tracy L — Football Player
6001 N Ocean Dr, #707, Hollywood FL 33019, USA

Scruggs, Anthony R (Tony) — Baseball Player
11621 Braddock Dr, #17, Culver City CA 90230, USA

Scruggs, Randy — Singer, Songwriter
Creative Artists Agency, 3310 W End Ave, #500, Nashville TN 37203 USA

Scudamore, Peter — Steeplechase Racing Jockey
Mucky Cottage, Grangehill, Naunton, Cheltenham, Glos GL54 3AY, England

Scudder, W Scott — Baseball Player
943 Farm Road 1499, Paris TX 75460, USA

Scuderi, Robert J (Rob) — Ice Hockey Player
16 Old Colony Dr, Dover MA 02030, USA

Scudero, Joseph A (Joe) — Football Player
2534 N Railroad Way, Hernando FL 34442, USA

Scullion, Mary — Social Activist
Project Home, 1515 Fairmount Ave, Philadelphia PA 19130, USA

Scully, John F, Jr — Football Player
3500 Bankview Dr, Joliet IL 60431, USA

Scully, Vincent E (Vin) — Sportscaster
25090 Jim Bridger Road, Hidden Hills CA 91302, USA

Scully-Power, Paul D — Astronaut
US Navy Underwater Systems Lab, 33A Code, New London CT 06320, USA

Sculthorpe, Peter J — Composer
91 Holdsworth St, Woollahra, NSW 2025, Australia

Scurlock, Clifton T (Kliph) — Drummer (Flaming Lips)
World's Fair Mgmt, 1208 Chowing Ave, Edmond OK 73034, USA

Scurry, Briana — Soccer Player
11610 137th Ave N, Dayton MN 55327, USA

Scurti, John — Actor
Gersh Agency, 41 Madison Ave, #3301, New York NY 10010 USA

Scutaro, Marcos H (Marco) — Baseball Player
19877 E Country Club Dr, #3503, Miami FL 33180, USA

Sea, Daniela — Actress
Mange-ment, 1103 1/2 Glendon Ave, Los Angeles CA 90024, USA

Seacrest, Ryan — Entertainer
Creative Artists Agency, 2000 Ave of Stars, #100, Los Angeles CA 90067 USA

Seaforth-Hayes, Susan — Actress
Hayforth Enterprises, 11333 Moorpark St, #368, Studio City CA 91602, USA

Seaga, Edward P G — Prime Minister, Jamaica
24-26 Grenada Crescent, New Kingston, Kingston 5, Jamaica

Seagal, Steven — Actor
9325 E Brahma Road, Scottsdale AZ 85262, USA

Seagrave, Jocelyn — Actress
Perspective Film, 15030 Ventura Blvd, Sherman Oaks CA 91403, USA

Seagren, Robert L (Bob) — Track Athlete, Actor
24710 Palermo Dr, Calabasas CA 91302, USA

Seagrove, Jenny — Actress
Rights House, 34-43 Russell St, London WC2B 5HA, England

Seal — Singer, Songwriter
Creative Artists Agency, 2000 Ave of Stars, #100, Los Angeles CA 90067 USA

Seal, Mark — Writer
Viking Press, 375 Hudson St, New York NY 10014 USA

Seal, Paul N — Football Player
21599 Hidden Rivers Dr N, Southfield MI 48075, USA

Seale, Bobby — Political Activist (Black Panthers)
Cafe Society, 302 W Chelton Ave, Philadelphia PA 19144, USA

Seale, John C — Cinematographer
Mirisch Agency, 1801 Century Park E, Los Angeles CA 90067, USA

Seale, Samuel R (Sam) — Football Player
1818 Da Gama Court, Escondido CA 92026, USA

Seals, George E — Football Player
1101 1st St, #204, Coronado CA 92118, USA

Seals, James — Singer, Songwriter (Seals & Crofts)
Star Entertainment, 1675 York Ave, #32C, New York NY 10128, USA

Seals, Raymond B (Ray) — Football Player
664 NW Shaw Glen, Lake City FL 32055, USA

Seaman, Christopher — Conductor
Symphony Australia, 1 Oxford Street, #5-2, Darlinghurst NSW 2010, Australia

Seaman, David — Soccer Player
Arsenal London, Avenell Road, Highbury, London N5 1BU, England

Seanez, Rudy C — Baseball Player
1422 McCabe Cove Road, El Centro CA 92243, USA

Searage, Raymond M (Ray) — Baseball Player
9737 Pine Lake Trail, Saint Petersburg FL 33708, USA

Searcy, Leon, Jr — Football Player
3841 Biggin Church Road, Jacksonville FL 32224, USA

Searcy, Nick — Actor
Abrams Artists, 275 7th Ave, #2600, New York NY 10001, USA

Searcy, W Stephen (Steve) — Baseball Player
5112 Gouffon Road, Knoxville TN 37918, USA

Searfoss, Richard A — Astronaut
24480 Silver Creek Way, Tehachapi CA 93561, USA

Sears, Joe — Actor
Gersh Agency, 9465 Wilshire Blvd, #600, Beverly Hills CA 90212 USA

Sears, Kenneth R (Ken) — Basketball Player
40 Cutter Dr, Watsonville CA 95076, USA

Sears, Paul B — Ecologist
17 Las Milpas, Taos NM 87571, USA

Seasick Steve — Singer, Songwriter
Agency Group Ltd, 1880 Century Park E, #711, Los Angeles CA 90067 USA

Seaver, G Thomas (Tom) — Baseball Player
1761 Diamond Mountain Road, Calistoga CA 94515, USA

Seavey, David — Editorial Cartoonist
USA Today, Editorial Dept, 1000 Wilson Blvd, Arlington VA 22209, USA

Seay, Robert M (Bobby) — Baseball Player
1591 Oak Circle N, Sarasota FL 34232, USA

Sebastian, Cuthbert M — Governor General, Saint Kitts & Nevis
Governor General's House, 6 Canyon St, Basseterre, Saint Kitts & Nevis

Sebastian, John — Singer, Songwriter
2431 Briarcrest Road, Beverly Hills CA 90210, USA

Sebastiani, Sergio Cardinal — Religious Leader
Palazzo delle Congregazioni, Lardo del Colonnato 3, 00193 Rome, Italy

Sebelius, Kathleen G — Secretary, Health; Governor, KS
Health/Human Services Dept, 200 Independence Ave SW, Washington DC 20201 USA

Sebestyen, Marta — Singer, Flutist
Konzertagentur Berthold Seliger, Nonnengasse 15, 36037 Fulda, Germany

Sebold, Alice — Writer
Dunow Carlson Lerner Literary Agency, 27 W 20th St, #1107, New York NY 10011, USA

Sebra, Robert B (Bob) — Baseball Player
20 Misners Trail, Ormond Beach FL 32174, USA

Secada, Jon — Singer, Songwriter
Okie Dokie Mgmt, 6090 Central Ave, Saint Petersburg FL 33707, USA

Seckel, Danny — Actor, Comedian
OmniPop Talent Group, 4605 Lankershim Blvd, #201, Toluca Lake CA 91602 USA

Secor, Kyle — Actor
Brillstein Entertainment Partners, 9150 Wilshire Blvd, #350, Beverly Hills CA 90212 USA

Secord, Al — Ice Hockey Player
950 Ginger Court, Southlake TX 76092, USA

Secord, John — Singer, Guitarist, Songwriter
Making Texas Music, Old Putnam Bank Building, PO Box 1013, Putnam TX 76469, USA

Secord, Richard V — Army General
Computerized Thermal Imaging, 1719 W 2800 S, Ogden UT 84401, USA

Secrest, Meryle — Writer
Bloomsbury Publishing, 36 Soho Square, London W1D 3Q4, England

Secrest, Wayne — Bassist (Confederate Railroad)
Bobby Roberts, 3050 Business Park Circle, #303, Goodlettsville TN 37221 USA

Seda, Jon — Actor
I C M Partners, 10250 Constellation Blvd, #900, Los Angeles CA 90067 USA

Sedaka, Neil — Singer, Pianist, Songwriter
Neal Sedaka Music, 730 5th Ave, #950, New York NY 10019, USA

Sedaris, Amy — Actress, Comedienne
Paradigm Agency, 360 N Crescent Dr, North Building, Beverly Hills CA 90210 USA

Sedaris, David — Writer
64 Thompson St, New York NY 10012, USA

Seddon, Margaret Rhea — Astronaut
1709 Shagbark Trail, Murfreesboro TN 37130, USA

Sedelmaier, J Josef (Joe) — Director; Animator
Sedelmaier Film Productions, 858 W Armitage Ave, #267, Chicago IL 60614, USA

Sedgman, Frank A — Tennis Player
28 Bolton Ave, Hampton VIC 3188, Australia

Sedgwick, Kyra — Actress
United Talent Agency, 9336 Civic Center Dr, Beverly Hills CA 90210 USA

Sedin, Daniel — Ice Hockey Player
1233 Nanton Ave, Vancouver BC V6H 2C7, Canada

Sedin, Henrik — Ice Hockey Player
C A A Hockey, 822 11th Ave SW, #204, Calgary AB T2R 0E5, Canada

Sedlbauer, Ronald A (Ron) — Ice Hockey Player
4231 Lakeshore Road, Burlington ON L7L 1A5, Canada

Sedney, Jules — Prime Minister, Suriname
May St 34, Paramaribo, Suriname

Sedykh, Yuri G — Track Athlete
Light Athletics Federation, Luzhnetskaya Nab 8, 119270 Moscow, Russia

See, Carolyn — Writer
930 3rd St, #203, Santa Monica CA 90403, USA

See, Lisa — Writer
El Pueblo Monument Authority, 125 Paseo de Plaza, #400, Los Angeles CA 90012, USA

See, Marshall — Basketball Player
1138 S Canal Circle, Camp Verde AZ 86322, USA

See, R Laurence (Larry) — Baseball Player
1913 W Remington Dr, Chandler AZ 85286, USA

Seear, Beatrice N S — Government Official, England
189B Kennington Road, London SE11 6ST, England

Seear, Noot — Model, Actress
Innovative Artists, 1505 10th St, Santa Monica CA 90401 USA

Seedorf, Clarence — Soccer Player
F C Milan, Via Filippo Turati 3, 20121 Milan, Italy

Seeger, Anthony — Ethnomusicologist
University of California, Music Dept, Los Angeles CA 90024, USA

Seeger, Pete — Singer, Banjoist, Songwriter
PO Box 431, Dutchess Junction, Beacon NY 12508, USA

Seehofer, Horst L — President, Germany
Bundeskanzlerant, Schlossplatz 1, 10178 Berlin, Germany

Seehorn, Rhea — Actress
Untitled Entertainment, 350 S Beverly Dr, #200, Beverly Hills CA 90212 USA

Seelbach, Charles F (Chuck) — Baseball Player
13800 Fairhill Road, #501, Cleveland OH 44120, USA

Seeler, Uwe — Soccer Player
H S V, Rothenbaumchaussee 125, 20149 Hamburg, Germany

Seeley, Andrew M E (Drew) — Actor, Singer, Songwriter
PO Box 250, 522 S Hunt Club Blvd, Apopka FL 32704, USA

Seeley, Thomas D — Biologist
Cornell University, Biological Sciences Division, Ithaca NY 14853, USA

Seeling, Angelle — Motorcycle Racing Rider
G Smith Motorsports, 10567 Airline Dr, Saint Rose LA 70087, USA

Seely, Jeannie — Singer, Songwriter
Tessier-Marsh Talent, 2825 Blue Book Dr, Nashville TN 37214 USA

Seezer, Maurice — Singer, Composer
Bloomsbury Publishing, 36 Soho Square, London W1D 3Q4, England

Sefcki, Kevin J — Baseball Player
16921 Steeplechase Parkway, Orland Park IL 60467, USA

Seffrin, John R — Association Executive
American Cancer Society, 1599 Clifton Road NE, Atlanta GA 30329, USA

Sefolosha, Thabo — Basketball Player
910 Colony Dr, Salisbury MD 21804, USA

Sega, Ronald M — Astronaut, Electrical Engineer
711A Massey Lane, Alexandria VA 22314, USA

Segal, Fred — Fashion Designer
Fred Segal Jeans, 8100 Melrose Ave, Los Angeles CA 90046, USA

Segal, George — Actor
A Mgmt, 12001 Ventura Place, #340, Studio City CA 91604 USA

Segal, Michael — Actor
27 Cyprus Ave, Finchley, London N3 1SS, England

Segal, Peter — Director, Producer, Writer
Creative Artists Agency, 2000 Ave of Stars, #100, Los Angeles CA 90067 USA

Segal, Uri — Conductor
M A Artists Mgmt, 28 Sheffield Terrace, London W8 7NA, England

Segan, Noah — Actor, Producer
United Talent Agency, 9336 Civic Center Dr, Beverly Hills CA 90210 USA

Segel, Jason — Actor
W M E Entertainment, 9601 Wilshire Blvd, #300, Beverly Hills CA 90210 USA

Segelke, Herman N — Baseball Player
PO Box 2513, Antioch CA 94531, USA

Seger, Bob — Singer, Songwriter
3841 LaPlaya Lane, Orchard Lake MI 48324, USA

Seger, Shea — Singer
Helter Skelter, 347-353 Chiswick High Road, London W4 4HS, England

Segerstam, Leif S — Composer, Conductor
Garvey & Ivor, 59 Lansdowne Place, Hove BN3 1FL, England

Segui, David V — Baseball Player
13421 Leavenworth Road, Kansas City KS 66109, USA

Segui, Diego P — Baseball Player
7520 King St, #J, Overland Park KS 66214, USA

Segura, Francisco (Pancho) — Tennis Player
Rancho La Costa Hotel & Spa, 7690 Camino Real, Carlsbad CA 92009, USA

Seguso, Robert — Tennis Player
3405 54th Dr W, Bradenton FL 34210, USA

Sehorn, Jason H — Football Player, Sportscaster
1901 Wild Holly Lane, Charlotte NC 28226, USA

Seibel, Anne — Production Designer, Art Director
Sheldon Prosnit Agency, 800 S Robertson Blvd, #6, Los Angeles CA 90035, USA

Seibert, Kurt E — Baseball Player
95 Amberwood Circle, Irmo SC 29063, USA

Seidel, Guenter — Equestrian
2108 Oxford Ave, Cardiff-by-the-Sea CA 92007, USA

Seidel, Martie — Singer (Dixie Chicks)
Strategic Artists Mgmt, 1100 Glendon Ave, #1100, Los Angeles CA 90024, USA

Seidelman, Susan — Director
Michael Shedler, 350 5th Ave, New York NY 10118, USA

Seidenberg, Dennis — Ice Hockey Player
20073 N 85th Place, Scottsdale AZ 85255, USA

Seidenberg, Ivan G — Businessman
Verizon Communications, 1095 Ave of Americas, New York NY 10036, USA

Seidler, David — Writer
Independent Talent Group, Oxford House, 76 Oxford St, London W1D 1BS, England

Seidler, Helga — Track Athlete
Bersarinstr 42, 09130 Chemnitz, Germany

Seifert, George G — Football Coach, Sportscaster
1276 Estate Dr, Los Altos Hills CA 94024, USA

Seiffert, Lisa — Model
Elite Model Mgmt, 404 Park Ave S, #900, New York NY 10016 USA

Seigner, Emmanuelle — Actress
3 Quai Malaquais, 75006 Paris, France

Seigner, Mathilde — Actress
Artmedia, 20 Ave Rapp, 75007 Paris, France

Seignoret, Clarence H A — President, Dominica
24 Cork St, Roseau, Dominica

Seikaly, Ronald F (Rony) — Basketball Player
2060 N Bay Road, Miami Beach FL 33140, USA

Seilacher, Adolf — Geologist, Geophysicist
Yale University, Geology/Geophysics Laboratory, New Haven CT 06520, USA

Seilheimer, Ricky A (Rick) — Baseball Player
401 Hickory Hollow Lane, Brenham TX 77833, USA

Seiling, Richard J (Ric) — Ice Hockey Player
71 Christina Dr, North Chili NY 14514, USA

Seiling, Rodney A (Rod) — Ice Hockey Player
Toronto Hotel Assn, 590-207 Queens Quay W, Toronto ON M5J 1A7, Canada

Seimetz, Amy — Actress
One Entertainment, 12 W 57th St, #PH 1, New York NY 10019 USA

Seinfeld, Jerry — Actor, Comedian
Shapiro/West Assoc, 141 El Camino, #205, Beverly Hills CA 90212, USA

Seinfeld, John H — Chemical Engineer
363 Patrician Way, Pasadena CA 91105, USA

Seiple, Larry R — Football Player
1361 W Golfview Dr, Pembroke Pines FL 33026, USA

Seipp, Michelle — Actress
Chateau/Billings Talent Agency, 8489 W 3rd St, #1032, Los Angeles CA 90048, USA

Seitzer, Kevin L — Baseball Player
2845 W 137th Terrace, Overland Park KS 66224, USA

Seiwald, Robert J — Inventor (Fluorescent Dye)
59 Burnside Ave, San Francisco CA 94131, USA

Seixas, E Victor (Vic), Jr — Tennis Player
8 Harbor Point Dr, #207, Mill Valley CA 94941, USA

Seizinger, Katja — Alpine Skier
Rudolf-Epp-Str 48, 69412 Eberbach, Germany

Sejima, Kazuyo — Pritzker Architect Laureate
Sanaa Ltd, 2-2-35-6B Higashi-Shinagawa, 140 0002 Tokyo, Japan

Sekler, Eduard F — Educator, Architect
Harvard University, Graduate Design School, Gund Hall, Cambridge MA 02138, USA

Sela, Michael — Immunologist, Chemist
Weizmann Science Institute, Immunology Dept, Rehovot 76100, Israel

Selander, Robert K — Biologist
Pennsylvania State University, Biology Dept, University Park PA 16802, USA

Selanne, Teemu I — Ice Hockey Player
31731 Madre Selva Lane, Trabuco Canyon CA 92679, USA

Selby, David — Actor
S M S Talent, 8383 Wilshire Blvd, #230, Beverly Hills CA 90211 USA

Selby, Hubert, Jr — Writer
Bloomsbury Publishing, 36 Soho Square, London W1D 3Q4, England

Selby, R Briton (Brit) — Ice Hockey Player
174 Divadale Dr, East York ON M4G 2P6, Canada

Selby, Tony — Actor
Associated International Mgmt, Fairfax House, Fulwood Place, London WC1V 6HU, England

Selby, William F (Bill) — Baseball Player
4468 Misty Oaks Lane, Nesbit MS 38651, USA

Seldes, Marian — Actress
Paradigm Agency, 360 Park Ave S, #1600, New York NY 10010 USA

Seldin, Donald W — Physician
Texas Southwestern Medical Center, 5323 Harry Hines Blvd, Dallas TX 75390, USA

Seldon, Bruce — Boxer
Rocco DePersia, 35 Kings Highway E, #102, Haddonfield NJ 08033, USA

Sele, Aaron H — Baseball Player
4 Oak Tree Dr, Newport Beach CA 92660, USA

Seles, Monica — Tennis Player
2895 Dick Wilson Dr, Sarasota FL 34240, USA

Self, Bill — Basketball Coach
University of Kansas, Athletic Dept, Allen Fieldhouse, Lawrence KS 66045, USA

Self, Clarence E — Football Player
43W689 Willow Creek Court, Elburn IL 60119, USA

Self, Todd — Baseball Player
10238 Cardiff Dr, Keithville LA 71047, USA

Selfridge, Andrew P (Andy) — Football Player
3400 Dunscroft Court, Keswick VA 22947, USA

Selick, Henry — Director
Laika Entertainment, 1400 NW 22nd Ave, Portland OR 97210, USA

Selig, Allan H (Bud) — Baseball Executive
Commissioner's Office, 777 E Wisconsin Ave, #3060, Milwaukee WI 53202, USA

Selig, Franz-Josef — Opera Singer
I M G Artists, Hogarth Business Park, Chiswick, London W4 2TH, England

Selim, Ali — Director, Writer
I C M Partners, 10250 Constellation Blvd, #900, Los Angeles CA 90067 USA

Selivanov, Alexander — Ice Hockey Player
1379 80th St S, Saint Petersburg FL 33707, USA

Sellars, Peter — Director
American National Theater, Kennedy Center, 2700 F St NW, Washington DC 20566, USA

Selldorf, Annabelle — Architect
Selldorf Architects, 860 Broadway, #200, New York NY 10003, USA

Selleca, Connie — Actress
Binder Assoc, 1465 Lindacrest Dr, Beverly Hills CA 90210, USA

Selleck, Tom — Actor
PO Box 1029, Penrose CO 81240, USA

Seller, Peg — Synchronized Swimmer, Coach
72 Monkswood Crescent, Newmarket ON L3Y 2K1, Canada

Sellers, Bradley D (Brad) — Basketball Player
682 Arbor Way, Aurora OH 44202, USA

Sellers, Franklin — Religious Leader
Reformed Episcopal Church, 2001 Frederick Road, Catonsville MD 21228, USA

Sellers, Jeffrey D (Jeff) — Baseball Player
266 Raines Road, Easley NC 29640, USA

Sellers, Piers J — Astronaut
16011 Craighurst Dr, Houston TX 77059, USA

Sellers, Ron F — Football Player
1111 Green Bayberry Dr, Palm Beach Gardens FL 33418, USA

Sells, David W (Dave) — Baseball Player
700 Blue Ridge Lane, Vacaville CA 95688, USA

Selmon, Dewey W — Football Player
2725 S Berry Road, Norman OK 73072, USA

Selten, Reinhard — Nobel Economics Laureate
Hardtweg 23, 53639 Konigswinter, Germany

Seltmann, Sally — Singer, Songwriter
Agency Group Ltd, 142 W 57th St, #600, New York NY 10019 USA

Seltz, Rolland A — Basketball Player
3328 Oswego Heights Road, Saint Paul MN 55126, USA

Seltzer, David — Director, Writer
I C M Partners, 10250 Constellation Blvd, #900, Los Angeles CA 90067 USA

Selverstone, Katy — Actress
Agency Group, 9348 Civic Center Dr, #200, Beverly Hills CA 90210 USA

Selvie, George — Football Player
Saint Louis Rams, 901 N Broadway, Saint Louis MO 63101, USA

Selvy, Franklin D (Frank) — Basketball Player
18 Oglethorpe Lane, Hilton Head SC 29926, USA
Selway, Philip J (Phil) — Drummer (Radiohead)
Courtyard, 21 Nursery, Sutton Courtenay, Abingdon, Oxon OX14 4UA, England
Selwood, Brad — Ice Hockey Player
77 Colonel Wayling Blvd, Sharon ON L0G 1V0, Canada
Selya, Bruce M — Judge
US Court of Appeals, US Courthouse, Pastore Building, Kennedy Plaza, Providence RI 02903, USA
Selznick, Brian — Writer, Illustrator
Scholastic Press, 555 Broadway, New York NY 10012 USA
Semak, Michael W — Photographer
1796 Spruce Hill Road, Pickering ON L1V 1S4, Canada
Sember, Michael D (Mike) — Baseball Player
285 S Country Club Blvd, Boca Raton FL 33487, USA
Semel, David — Director, Producer
W M E Entertainment, 9601 Wilshire Blvd, #300, Beverly Hills CA 90210 USA
Semel, Terry S — Businessman
Yahoo!, 701 1st Ave, Sunnyvale CA 94089, USA
Semenchuk, Ekaterina — Opera Singer
I M G Artists, Hogarth Business Park, Chiswick, London W4 2TH, England
Semenov, Anatoli A — Ice Hockey Player
4015 Royal Vista Circle, Corona CA 92881, USA
Semenova, Juliana — Basketball Player
Zalalela 4-35, Riga 1010, Latvia
Seminara, Frank P — Baseball Player
8029 Harbor View Terrace, Brooklyn NY 11209, USA
Semiz, Teata — Bowler
27 Burnside Place, Haskell NJ 07420, USA
Semizorova, Nina L — Ballerina
2 Zhukovskaya St, #8, Moscow, Russia
Semkow, Jerzy G — Conductor
Opus 3 Artists, 470 Park Ave S, #900N, New York NY 10016 USA
Semler, Dean — Cinematographer, Director
4260 Arcola Ave, Toluca Lake CA 91602, USA
Sempe, Jean-Jacques — Cartoonist
4 Rue du Moulin-Vert, 75014 Paris, France
Semple Thompson, Carol — Golfer
2045 Henry Road, Sewickley PA 15143, USA
Semple, Maria — Writer, Producer
Little Brown, 3 Center Plaza, #100, Boston MA 02108 USA
Semple, Robert B, Jr — Journalist
New York Times, Editorial Dept, 229 W 43rd St, New York NY 10036 USA
Semproch, Roman A (Ray) — Baseball Player
4220 Buechner Ave, Cleveland OH 44109, USA
Semyonov, Vladilen G — Ballet Dancer
15/17-504 Roubinshteina St, 191002 Saint Petersburg, Russia
Sen, Amartya K — Nobel Economics Laureate
Trinity College, Economics Dept, Cambridge CB2 1TQ, England
Sen, Mrinal — Director
C501 Talkatora Road, New Delhi 110 01, India
Sen, Nandana — Actress
Prinicipal Entertainment,130 W 42nd St, #614, New York NY 10036, USA
Sen, Riya — Actress, Model
62B Ruia Park, Huhu, Mumbai MS 400049, India
Sen, Sushmita — Beauty Queen, Actress
Beach Queen, #600 Rd, Versova Andheri (W), Mumbai MS 400061, India
Sena, Dominic — Director
W M E Entertainment, 9601 Wilshire Blvd, #300, Beverly Hills CA 90210 USA
Sendel, Peter — Biathlete
Zallaer Str 9, 98599 Oberhof, Germany
Senderens, Alain — Chef
Restaurant Lucas Carton, 9 Place de la Madeleine, 75008 Paris, France
Sendlein, Robin B — Football Player
5645 Friars Road, #379, San Diego CA 92110, USA
Senff, Dina (Nida) — Swimmer
D W Couturier-Senff, Praam 122, 1186 TL Amstelveen, Netherlands
Senior, Peter — Golfer
International Mgmt Group, 1 Erieview Plaza, 1360 E 9th St, Cleveland OH 44114 USA
Senna, Bruno — Auto Racing Driver
Williams F1, Grove, Wantage, Oxfordshire OX12 0DQ, England
Sennewald, Robert W — Army General
311 S Lee St, Alexandria VA 22314, USA
Sensabaugh, Gerald L — Football Player
12251 Heron Cove Court, Jacksonville FL 32218, USA
Sensibaugh, J Michael (Mike) — Football Player
18414 Woodlands Terrace Dr, Glencoe MO 63038, USA
Sentelle, David B — Judge
US Court of Appeals, 333 Constitution Ave NW, #4400, Washington DC 20001, USA
Seoane, Manuel M (Manny) — Baseball Player
4703 N Rome Ave, Tampa FL 33603, USA
Seon Hwa Lee — Golfer
Ladies Pro Golf Assn, 100 International Golf Dr, Daytona Beach FL 32124 USA
Sepe, Crescenzio Cardinal — Religious Leader
Villa Betania, Via Urbans VIII 16, 00165 Rome, Italy
Septimus, Jacob (Jake) — Producer, Director, Writer
Creative Artists Agency, 2000 Ave of Stars, #100, Los Angeles CA 90067 USA
Sepulveda, Charlie — Jazz Trumpeter
Ralph Mercado Mgmt, 568 Broadway, #608, New York NY 10012, USA
Sepulveda, Daniel W — Football Player
Pittsburgh Steelers, 3400 S Water St, Pittsburgh PA 15203 USA
Serafini, Daniel J (Dan) — Baseball Player
4380 Garratt Circle, Sparks NV 89436, USA
Serafinowicz, Peter — Actor, Comedian
Troika, 74 Clerkenwell Road, #300, London EC1M 5QA, England
Seraphine, Oliver J — Prime Minister, Dominica
44 Green's Lane, Goodwill, Dominica

Serbedzija, Rade — Actor
United Agents, 12-26 Lexington St, London W1F 0LE, England

Serebrier, Jose — Conductor, Composer
20 Queensgate Gardens, London SW7 5LZ, England

Serebrov, Alexander A — Cosmonaut
Cosmonaut Training Center, Star City, 141160 Zvezdny Gorodok, Moscow Oblast, Russia

Seredova, Alena — Model, Actress
Riccardo Gay Model Mgmt, Corso Vercelli 40, 20145 Milan, Italy

Sereno, Paul — Paleontologist
University of Chicago, Paleontology Dept, Chicago IL 60537, USA

Seres, Fiona — Writer, Actress
Independent Talent Group, Oxford House, 76 Oxford St, London W1D 1BS, England

Seresin, Michael — Cinematographer
59 North Wharf Road, London W2 1LA, England

Sereys, Jacques — Actor
84 Blvd Malesherbes, 75008 Paris, France

Sergeant, Peta — Actress
Sue Barnett & Associates, 1/96 Albion St, Surry Hills NSW 2010, Australia

Sergei, Ivan — Actor
A P A Talent/Literary Agency, 405 S Beverly Dr, #300, Beverly Hills CA 90212 USA

Serig, Jennifer — Fashion Designer
Perception Public Relations, 13333 Ventura Blvd, #203, Sherman Oaks CA 91423, USA

Serkin, Peter A — Concert Pianist
C M Artists, 127 W 96th St, #13B, New York NY 10025 USA

Serkis, Andy — Actor
Lou Coulson Assoc, 37 Berwick St, London W1V 8RS, England

Serlemitsos, Peter J — Astronomer
B B X R T Project, Goddard Space Flight Center, Greenbelt MD 20771, USA

Serlenga, Nikki — Soccer Player
1489 Hawthorne Ave NW, Atlanta GA 30309, USA

Sermet, Huseyin — Composer, Concert Pianist
Harrison/Parrott, 5-6 Albion Court, London W6 0QT, England

Sermon, Erick — Rap Artist (EPMD)
I C M Partners, 10250 Constellation Blvd, #900, Los Angeles CA 90067 USA

Serna, Assumpta — Actress
8306 Wilshire Blvd, #438, Beverly Hills CA 90211, USA

Serna, Pepe — Actor
Vox Inc, 6420 Wilshire Blvd, #1080, Los Angeles CA 90048 USA

Serniz, Teata — Bowler
Professional Bowlers Assn, 719 2nd Ave, #701, Seattle WA 98104 USA

Serota, Nicholas A — Museum Executive
Tate Britain, Millbank, London SW1P 4RG, England

Serowik, Jeff — Ice Hockey Player
371 Davisville Road, East Falmouth MA 02536, USA

Serpico, Terry — Actor
Don Buchwald/Fortitude, 6500 Wilshire Blvd, #2200, Los Angeles CA 90048 USA

Serra, Eduardo — Cinematographer
United Agents, 12-26 Lexington St, London W1F 0LE, England

Serra, Richard — Sculptor
173 Duane St, New York NY 10013, USA

Serralles, Jeanine — Actress
Don Buchwald/Fortitude, 6500 Wilshire Blvd, #2200, Los Angeles CA 90048 USA

Serrano, Jimmy — Baseball Player
2943 E Erika Court, Grand Junction CO 81504, USA

Serrano, Nestor — Actor
D2 Mgmt, 9255 Sunset Blvd, #600, West Hollywood CA 90069, USA

Serratos, Christian — Actress
W M E Entertainment, 9601 Wilshire Blvd, #300, Beverly Hills CA 90210 USA

Serre, Jean-Pierre — Abel Mathematics Laureate
6 Ave de Montespan, 75116 Paris, France

Serreau, Coline — Director
Artmedia, 20 Ave Rapp, 75007 Paris, France

Serres, Jacques — Actor
Artmedia, 20 Ave Rapp, 75007 Paris, France

Servais, Scott D — Baseball Player
4409 Triple Eagle Trail, Larkspur CO 80118, USA

Servan-Schreiber, Jean-Claude — Journalist
147 Bis Rue d'Alesia, 75014 Paris, France

Server, Josh — Actor
Amsel Eisenstadt Frazier, 5055 Wilshire Blvd, #865, Los Angeles CA 90036 USA

Service, Scott D — Baseball Player
9920 Prechtel Road, Cincinnati OH 45252, USA

Servis, John C — Thoroughbred Racing Trainer
2649 Woodsview Dr, Bensalem PA 19020, USA

Servitto, Matt — Actor
Abrams Artists, 275 7th Ave, #2600, New York NY 10001 USA

Sesselmann, Lauren — Soccer Player
Canadian Soccer, Place Soccer Canada, 237 Metcalfe St, Ottawa ON K2P 1R2, Canada

Sessions, John — Actor, Writer
Markham & Froggatt, Julian House, 4 Windmill St, London W1P 1HF, England

Sessions, Ramon — Basketball Player
Charlotte Bobcats, 333 E Trade St, #A, Charlotte NC 28202 USA

Sessions, Ronnie — Singer, Guitarist, Songwriter
PO Box 242, Horseshoe Bend AR 72536, USA

Sessions, William S — Law Enforcement Official, Judge
112 E Pecan St, #2900, San Antonio TX 78205, USA

Sessler, Gerhard M — Inventor (Telephone Microphone)
Fichtenstra 30B, 64285 Darmstadt, Germany

Seth, Vikram — Writer
Curtis Brown, 37 Queensferry St, Edinburgh EH2 4QS, Scotland

Settani, Sandra — Model
Playboy Promotions, 2706 Media Center Dr, Los Angeles CA 90065 USA

Settle, Matthew — Actor
United Talent Agency, 9336 Civic Center Dr, Beverly Hills CA 90210 USA

Setzer, Brian — Singer, Guitarist
W M E Entertainment, 9601 Wilshire Blvd, #300, Beverly Hills CA 90210 USA

Setzer, Dennis
Saint Paul's Church Road, #47A, Asheville NC 28803, USA — Auto, Truck Racing Driver

Setzer, Philip
I M G Artists, Burlington Lane, Chiswick, London W4 2TH, England — Violinist (Emerson String Quartet)

Setziol-Phillips, Monica
542 NE Hill St, Sheridan OR 97378, USA — Sculptor

Seubert, Richard A (Rich)
35 Oak Lane, Wayne NJ 07470, USA — Football Player

Sevcik, Jaroslav
Dalhousie Memorial Arena, 6185 South St, Halifax NS B3H 1T7, Canada — Ice Hockey Player

Sevcik, John J
10107 Shinnecock Hills Dr, Austin TX 78747, USA — Baseball Player

Sevele, Feleti V
Prime Minister's Office, PO Box 62, Taufa'ahau Road, Nuku'alofa, Tonga — Prime Minister, Tonga

Severance, Joan
PO Box 282, Carbondale CO 81623, USA — Model, Actress

Severin, G Timothy (Tim)
Inchybridge, Timoleague, County Cork, Ireland — Explorer

Severinsen, Carl H (Doc)
11812 San Vicente Blvd, #200, Los Angeles CA 90049, USA — Jazz Trumpeter, Conductor

Severinson, Albert H (Al)
133 Warren Ave, Mystic CT 06355, USA — Baseball Player

Severson, Jeffrey K (Jeff)
216 College Park Dr, Seal Beach CA 90740, USA — Football Player

Severson, John
PO Box 10699, Lahaina, Maui HI 96761, USA — Publisher

Severson, Kimberly (Kim)
631 Dobby Creek Road, Scottsville VA 24590, USA — Equestrian

Severson, Richard A (Rich)
1036 N 145th Circle, Omaha NE 68154, USA — Baseball Player

Severyn, Brent
4521 Avebury Dr, Plano TX 75024, USA — Ice Hockey Player

Sevier, Corey
Innovative Artists, 1505 10th St, Santa Monica CA 90401 USA — Actor

Sevigny, Chloe
W M E Entertainment, 9601 Wilshire Blvd, #300, Beverly Hills CA 90210 USA — Actress

Sevy, Jeffrey E (Jeff)
PO Box 2177, Loomis CA 95650, USA — Football Player

Seward, Adam H
8905 Coast Walk Circle, Las Vegas NV 89117, USA — Football Player

Seward, George C
48 Greenacres Ave, Scarsdale NY 10583, USA — Attorney

Sewell, Rufus
Julian Belfrage Assoc, 9 Argyll St, #300, London W1F 7TG, England — Actor

Sewell, Steven E (Steve)
15918 E Crestridge Place, Centennial CO 80015, USA — Football Player

Seweryn, Andrzej
Comedie Francaise, Place Colette, 75001 Paris, France — Actor

Sexsmith, Ron
S L Feldman Mgmt, 1505 W 2nd Ave, #200, Vancouver BC V6H 3Y4, Canada — Singer, Songwriter

Sexson, Richmond L (Richie)
24708 NW 4th Court, Ridgefield WA 98642, USA — Baseball Player

Sexton, Brendan, III
Innovative Artists, 1505 10th St, Santa Monica CA 90401 USA — Actor

Sexton, Brent
Greene Assoc, 1901 Ave of Stars, #130, Los Angeles CA 90067 USA — Actor

Sexton, Chad R
311 Hive, 8904 Florence Dr, Omaha NE 68147, USA — Drummer (311)

Sexton, Charlie
Don Buchwald/Fortitude, 6500 Wilshire Blvd, #2200, Los Angeles CA 90048 USA — Actor

Sexton, Christopher P (Chris)
7030 Baytowne Dr, Cincinnati OH 45247, USA — Baseball Player

Sexton, Jimmy D
2680 Baxter Road, Wilmer AL 36587, USA — Baseball Player

Sexton, John
New York University, President's Office, Washington Square, New York NY 10012, USA — Educator

Sexton, John W
2217 Miner St, Costa Mesa CA 92627, USA — Photographer

Sexton, Michael R (Mike)
World Poker Tour Enterprises, 1920 Main St, #1150, Irvine CA 92615, USA — Poker Player

Seydoux, Geraldine
Johns Hopkins University, Molecular Biology Dept, Baltimore MD 21218, USA — Molecular Biologist, Geneticist

Seydoux, Lea
Creative Artists Agency, 2000 Ave of Stars, #100, Los Angeles CA 90067 USA — Actress

Seyferth, Dietmar
Massachusetts Institute of Technology, Chemistry Dept, Cambridge MA 02139, USA — Chemist

Seyfried, Amanda
Innovative Artists, 1505 10th St, Santa Monica CA 90401 USA — Actress

Seyfried, Gordon C
56428 Lowe Ave, Yucca Valley CA 92284, USA — Baseball Player

Seymour, Cara
Innovative Artists, 1505 10th St, Santa Monica CA 90401 USA — Actress

Seymour, Jane
Catfish Productions, 22631 Pacific Coast Highway, #313, Malibu CA 90265, USA — Actress

Seymour, John
239 S Helix Ave, #26, Solana Beach CA 92075, USA — Senator, CA

Seymour, Lynn
Artistes in Action, 16 Balderton St, London W1Y 1TF, England — Ballerina

Seymour, Paul C
4188 Shoals Dr, Okemos MI 48864, USA — Football Player

Seymour, Richard V
862 Chattooga Trace, Suwanee GA 30024, USA — Football Player

Seymour, Stephanie
4180 Ruffin Road, #235, San Diego CA 92123, USA — Model

Seymour, Stephanie K
US Court of Appeals, US Courthouse, 333 W 4th St, #411, Tulsa OK 74103, USA — Judge

Sezer, Ahmet Necdet — President, Turkey
Milli Savunma Bakanligi, 06100 Ankara, Turkey

Sfeir, Nasrallah Pierre Cardinal — Religious Leader
Patriarcat Maronite, Bkerke, Lebanon

Sgouros, Dimitris — Concert Pianist
Tompazi 28 Str, Piraeus 18537, Greece

Shaara, Jeff — Writer
Ballatine Books, 1745 Broadway, New York NY 10019 USA

Shaback, Nicholas (Nick) — Basketball Player
3019 49th St, Astoria NY 11103, USA

Shabala, Adam — Baseball Player
2800 W North Ave, #303, Chicago IL 60647, USA

Shack, Edward S P (Eddie) — Ice Hockey Player
508 Fairlawn Ave, North York ON M5M 1V2, Canada

Shackelford, Ted — Actor
12305 Valley Heart Dr, Studio City CA 91604, USA

Shackleford, Charles E — Basketball Player
107 E Peyton Ave, Kinston NC 28501, USA

Shadyac, Tom — Director
W M E Entertainment, 9601 Wilshire Blvd, #300, Beverly Hills CA 90210 USA

Shafer, Martin — Producer, Writer
Castle Rock Entertainment, 335 N Maple Dr, #350, Beverly Hills CA 90210, USA

Shaffer, Atticus — Actor
Osbrink Talent Agency, 4343 Lankershim Blvd, #100, North Hollywood CA 91602 USA

Shaffer, James C (Munky) — Guitarist (Korn)
The Firm, 2049 Century Park E, #2550, Los Angeles CA 90067 USA

Shaffer, Kevin C — Football Player
5779 Legends Club Circle, Braselton GA 30517, USA

Shaffer, Lee P, II — Basketball Player
3822 Nottaway Road, Durham NC 27707, USA

Shaffer, Paul — Orchestra Leader, Keyboardist
Panacea Entertainment, 13587 Andalusia Dr E, Camarillo CA 93012, USA

Shaffer, Peter L — Writer
Lantz, 888 7th Ave, #2500, New York NY 10106, USA

Shagan, Steve — Writer
10375 Wilshire Blvd, #10E, Los Angeles CA 90024, USA

Shagari, A Shehu U A — President, Nigeria
22 Shehu Crescent, PO Box 162, Adarawa, Sokoto State, Nigeria

Shaggy — Singer
Paradigm Agency, 360 N Crescent Dr, North Building, Beverly Hills CA 90210 USA

Shagimuratova, Albina — Opera Singer
I M G Artists, Hogarth Business Park, Chiswick, London W4 2TH, England

Shaguch, Marina — Opera Singer
I M G Artists, Hogarth Business Park, Chiswick, London W4 2TH, England

Shah, Idries — Writer
A P Watt Ltd, 26/28 Bedford Row, London WC1R 4HL, England

Shah, Satish — Actor, Comedian
30A Anand Nagar, Forjeet St, Mumbai MS 400036, India

Shah, Sonal — Actress, Singer
Don Buchwald/Fortitude, 6500 Wilshire Blvd, #2200, Los Angeles CA 90048 USA

Shaham, Gil — Concert Violinist
Canary Classics, Knifedge Ltd, 4 Margaret St, London W1W 8RF, England

Shaham, Orli — Concert Pianist
Opus 3 Artists, 470 Park Ave S, #900N, New York NY 10016 USA

Shahi, Sarah — Actress, Model
McKeon-Myones Mgmt, 3500 W Olive Ave, #770, Burbank CA 91505, USA

Shaiman, Marc — Composer, Lyricist
8476 Brier Dr, Los Angeles CA 90046, USA

Shake, Christi — Model
Starr Entertainment, 2518 Lodge Forest Dr, Sparrows Point MD 21219, USA

Shakes, Paul — Ice Hockey Player
RR 4 PO, Slayner ON L0M 1S0, Canada

Shakespeare, Frank J, Jr — Businessman, Diplomat
303 Coast Blvd, La Jolla CA 92037, USA

Shakin' Stevens — Singer, Songwriter
Agency Group Ltd, 142 W 57th St, #600, New York NY 10019 USA

Shakira — Singer, Songwriter
Epic Records, 550 Madison Ave, #600, New York NY 10022 USA

Shakman, Matt — Actor, Director
W M E Entertainment, 9601 Wilshire Blvd, #300, Beverly Hills CA 90210 USA

Shakur, Mustafa — Basketball Player
Washington Wizards, M C I Centre, 601 F St NW, Washington DC 20004 USA

Shalala, Donna E — Secretary, Health & Human Services
University of Miami, President's Office, Coral Gables FL 33124, USA

Shales, Thomas W — Journalist
Washington Post, Editorial Dept, 1150 15th St NW, Washington DC 20071, USA

Shalhoub, Tony — Actor
I C M Partners, 10250 Constellation Blvd, #900, Los Angeles CA 90067 USA

Shalit, Gene — Film Critic
NBC-TV, News Dept, 30 Rockefeller Plaza, #270E, New York NY 10112 USA

Sham, Brad M — Sportscaster
Dallas Cowboys, 1 Cowboys Parkway, Irving TX 75063 USA

Shamblin, Allen — Songwriter
Built On Rock Music, PO Box 417, Franklin TN 37065, USA

Shamsky, Art — Baseball Player
PO Box 1400, New York NY 10163, USA

Shanahan, Brendan F — Ice Hockey Player
47 Saquatucket Bluffs Road, Harwich Port MA 02646, USA

Shanahan, Mike — Football Coach
20 Cherry Hills Farm Dr, Englewood CO 80113, USA

Shanahan, R Michael — Financier
Capital Research & Mgmt, 333 S Hope St, #5500, Los Angeles CA 90071, USA

Shand, David (Dave) — Ice Hockey Player
307 N Harris St, Saline MI 48176, USA

Shand, Remy — Singer, Songwriter
S L Feldman Mgmt, 1505 W 2nd Ave, #200, Vancouver BC V6H 3Y4, Canada

Shandling, Garry — Actor, Comedian
I C M Partners, 10250 Constellation Blvd, #900, Los Angeles CA 90067 USA
Shandrowsky, Alex — Labor Leader
Marine Engineer Beneficial Assn, 444 N Capitol St NW, Washington DC 20001, USA
Shane, Bob — Singer (Kingston Trio)
Fuji Productions, PO Box 34397, San Diego CA 92163, USA
Shange, Ntozake — Writer
Saint Martin's Press, 175 5th Ave, #400, New York NY 10010, USA
Shanice — Singer, Songwriter
Richard Walters, PO Box 2789, Toluca Lake CA 91610 USA
Shankar, Anoushka — Sitar Player, Singer, Composer
Opus 3 Artists, 470 Park Ave S, #900N, New York NY 10016 USA
Shankar, Naren — Producer, Writer
Rothman Brecher Agency, 9465 Wilshire Blvd, #840, Beverly Hills CA 90212, USA
Shankar, Ravi — Concert Sitar Player, Composer
17 Warden Court, Gowalia Tank Road, Mumbai 36, India
Shankle, Joel — Track Athlete
16181 Berryvale Lane, Culpepper VA 22701, USA
Shankman, Adam — Director
United Talent Agency, 9336 Civic Center Dr, Beverly Hills CA 90210 USA
Shanks, Michael — Actor, Writer, Director
Don Buchwald/Fortitude, 6500 Wilshire Blvd, #2200, Los Angeles CA 90048 USA
Shanle, Scott — Football Player
3736 Loyola Dr, #263, Kenner LA 70065, USA
Shanley, John Patrick — Writer
Creative Artists Agency, 2000 Ave of Stars, #100, Los Angeles CA 90067 USA
Shannon — Singer
Bad Boy Entertainment, 1440 Broadway, #16, New York NY 10018 USA
Shannon, Carver B — Football Player
6005 S La Cienega Blvd, Los Angeles CA 90056, USA
Shannon, Colleen — Model
Identity Talent Agency, 9107 Wilshire Blvd, #450, Beverly Hills CA 90210 USA
Shannon, Darrin A — Ice Hockey Player
Clarica, 23 Victoria St W, Alliston ON L9R 1S9, Canada
Shannon, Darryl — Ice Hockey Player
18 Landings Dr, Buffalo NY 14228, USA
Shannon, Howard P (Howie) — Basketball Player, Coach
4009 Valdez Court, Plano TX 75074, USA
Shannon, Karissa — Model
Playboy Promotions, 2706 Media Center Dr, Los Angeles CA 90065 USA
Shannon, Kristina — Model
Playboy Promotions, 2706 Media Center Dr, Los Angeles CA 90065 USA
Shannon, Mem — Singer, Guitarist, Songwriter
Miasma Mgmt, 1048 Hesper Ave, Metairie LA 70005, USA
Shannon, Michael — Actor
Creative Artists Agency, 2000 Ave of Stars, #100, Los Angeles CA 90067 USA
Shannon, Molly — Actress, Comedienne
Gersh Agency, 9465 Wilshire Blvd, #600, Beverly Hills CA 90212 USA
Shannon, Polly — Actress
Noble Caplan Abrams, 1260 Yonge St, #200, Toronto ON M4T 1W6, Canada
Shannon, Randy L — Football Player, Coach
7420 SW 107th Ave, #7-207, Miami FL 33173, USA
Shannon, T Michael (Mike) — Baseball Player
3104 Southwick Dr, Saint Charles MO 63301, USA
Shannon, Vicellous Reon — Actor
Don Buchwald/Fortitude, 6500 Wilshire Blvd, #2200, Los Angeles CA 90048 USA
Shanteau, Eric L — Swimmer
Premier Management Group, 1100 Crescent Green, #104, Cary, NC 27518 USA
Shantz, Robert C (Bobby) — Baseball Player
152 E Mount Pleasant Ave, Ambler PA 19002, USA
Shao, En — Conductor
I M G Artists, Hogarth Business Park, Chiswick, London W4 2TH, England
Shapiro, Alan — Director, Producer, Writer
Gersh Agency, 9465 Wilshire Blvd, #600, Beverly Hills CA 90212 USA
Shapiro, Anna D — Director
Abrams Artists, 9200 W Sunset Blvd, #1125, West Hollywood CA 90069 USA
Shapiro, Harold T — Educator
10 Campbelton Circle, Princeton NJ 08540, USA
Shapiro, Irwin I — Physicist
17 Lantern Lane, Lexington MA 02421, USA
Shapiro, Joel E — Sculptor
Pace Wildenstein Gallery, 32 E 57th St, #400, New York NY 10022, USA
Shapiro, Maurice M — Astrophysicist
5225 Pooks Hill Road, #1122S, Bethesda MD 20814, USA
Shapiro, Paul — Director, Producer, Writer
A P A Talent/Literary Agency, 405 S Beverly Dr, #300, Beverly Hills CA 90212 USA
Shapiro, Robert B — Businessman
Monsanto Co, 800 N Lindbergh Blvd, Saint Louis MO 63167, USA
Shapiro, Robert L — Attorney
2224 Century Hill, Los Angeles CA 90067, USA
Sharaf, Essam A — Prime Minister, Egypt
Prime Minister's Office, PO Box 191, 1 Majlis El-Shaab St, Cairo, Egypt
Sharapova, Maria Y — Tennis Player
International Mgmt Group, 1 Erieview Plaza, 1360 E 9th St, Cleveland OH 44114 USA
Sharbino, Saxon — Actress
W M E Entertainment, 9601 Wilshire Blvd, #300, Beverly Hills CA 90210 USA
Share, Charles E (Charlie) — Basketball Player
12922 Twin Meadows Court, Saint Louis MO 63146, USA
Sharer, Kevin W — Businessman
Amgen Inc, 1 Amgen Center Dr, Newbury Park CA 91320, USA
Shargin, Yuri G — Cosmonaut
Cosmonaut Training Center, Star City, 141160 Zvezdny Gorodok, Moscow Oblast, Russia
Sharian, John — Actor
Industry Entertainment, 955 Carillo Dr, #300, Los Angeles CA 90048 USA
Sharif, Omar — Actor
Steve Kenis Co, Royalty House, 72-74 Dean St, London WID 3SG, England

Shandling - Sharif

Sharipov, Salizhan S — Cosmonaut
Cosmonaut Training Center, Star City, 141160 Zvezdny Gorodok, Moscow Oblast, Russia
Sharissa — Singer
Virgin Records, 150 5th Ave, Front 3, New York NY 10011 USA
Sharkey, Edward J (Ed) — Football Player
3615 Russell Road, Centralia WA 98531, USA
Sharkey, Jack — Writer
39927 Chippewa Circle, Murrieta CA 92562, USA
Sharma, Barbara — Actress
PO Box 29125, Los Angeles CA 90029, USA
Sharma, Madhav — Actor
Ken McReddie Assoc, 11 Connaught Place, London W2 2ET, England
Sharma, Rakesh — Cosmonaut, India
Hindustan Aeronautics, Bangalore 560037, India
Sharman, Helen P — Cosmonaut, England
National Physical Laboratory, Hampton Road, Teddington, Middlesex TW11 0L, England
Sharman, Jim — Director
M&L, 49 Daringhurst St, Kings Cross NSW 2100, Australia
Sharman, William W (Bill) — Basketball Player, Coach, Executive
138 Paseo De Gracia, Redondo Beach CA 90277, USA
Sharockman, Edward C (Ed) — Football Player
8955 Thomas Lane, Saint Paul MN 55125, USA
Sharon, Richard L (Dick) — Baseball Player
PO Box 325, Dillon MT 59725, USA
Sharp, Dee Dee — Singer
Cape Entertainment, 8432 NW 31st Court, Sunrise FL 33351, USA
Sharp, Doug — Bobsled Athlete
US Bobsled/Skeleton Federation, 1631 Mesa Ave, #A, Colorado Springs CO 80906 USA
Sharp, Isadore — Businessman
Four Seasons Hotels, 1165 Leslie St, Toronto ON M3C 2K8, Canada
Sharp, Keesha — Actress, Director
Gartner/Green Entertainment, 5225 Wilshire Blvd, #1200, Los Angeles CA 90036, USA
Sharp, Kevin — Singer
Rising Star, 1415 River Landing Way, Woodstock GA 30188, USA
Sharp, Leslie — Actress
I C M Partners, 10250 Constellation Blvd, #900, Los Angeles CA 90067 USA
Sharp, Linda K — Basketball Coach
Phoenix Mercury, American West Arena, 201 E Jefferson St, Phoenix AZ 85004 USA
Sharp, Marsha — Basketball Coach
Texas Tech University, Athletic Dept, Lubbock TX 79409, USA
Sharp, Phillip A — Nobel Medicine Laureate
36 Fairmont Ave, Newton MA 02458, USA
Sharp, Scott — Auto Racing Driver
Extreme Speed Motorsports, 7782 Jack James Drive, Stuart FL 34997, USA
Sharp, Timm — Actor
United Talent Agency, 9336 Civic Center Dr, Beverly Hills CA 90210 USA
Sharp, Walter L — Army General
Commander, UN Command & US Forces Korea, Unit 15327, APO AP 96218, USA
Sharp, William H (Bill) — Baseball Player
2244 Thornwood Ave, Wilmette IL 60091, USA
Sharpe, Luis E, Jr — Football Player
19188 Beaverland St, Detroit MI 48219, USA
Sharpe, Rochelle P — Journalist
94 Dudley St, #2, Brookline MA 02445, USA
Sharpe, Shannon — Football Player, Sportscaster
867 Carlton Ridge NE, Atlanta GA 30342, USA
Sharpe, Sterling — Football Player, Sportscaster
81 Running Fox Road, Columbia SC 29223, USA
Sharpe, Thomas R (Tom) — Writer
38 Tunwells Lane, Great Shelford, Cambridge CB2 5LJ, England
Sharpe, William F — Nobel Economics Laureate
PO Box 610, Los Altos CA 94023, USA
Sharper, Darren M — Football Player
100 S Pointe Dr, #2808, Miami Beach FL 33139, USA
Sharper, H James (Jamie), Jr — Football Player
11613 Heverley Court, Glen Allen VA 23059, USA
Sharpless, Josh — Baseball Player
206 Mountain Dr, Carnegie PA 15106, USA
Sharpless, K Barry — Nobel Chemistry Laureate
Scripps Research Institute, 10550 Torrey Pines Road, La Jolla CA 92037, USA
Sharpley, Glen — Ice Hockey Player
Sharpley Sports, 536 Highland St, Haliburton ON K0M 1S0, Canada
Sharpton, Al — Social Activist, Religious Leader
104 W 145th St, New York NY 10039, USA
Sharqi, Sheikh Hamad ibn Muhammad Ash — Ruler, Fujairah
Royal Palace, Emiri Court, PO Box 1, Fujairah, United Arab Emirates
Shatalov, Valdimir A — Cosmonaut
Cosmonaut Training Center, Star City, 141160 Zvezdny Gorodok, Moscow Oblast, Russia
Shatkin, Aaron J — Molecular Biologist
1381 Rahway Road, Scotch Plains NJ 07076, USA
Shatner, William — Actor
Le Big Boss Productions, Paramount Studios, 5555 Melrose Ave, Hollywood CA 90038, USA
Shattuck, Kim — Singer, Guitarist (Muffs)
I C M Partners, 730 5th Ave, New York NY 10019 USA
Shaud, Grant — Actor
Innovative Artists, 1505 10th St, Santa Monica CA 90401 USA
Shaud, John A — Air Force General, Association Executive
Air Force Aid Society, 241 18th St S, #202, Arlington VA 22202, USA
Shaughnessy, Charles — Actor
Stone Manners Salners, 9911 W Pico Blvd, #1400, Los Angeles CA 90035 USA
Shaunessy, Scott — Ice Hockey Player
1 Treetop Lane, Duxbury MA 02332, USA
Shave, Jonathan T (Jon) — Baseball Player
1801 Park Way Dr, Fernandina Beach FL 32034, USA
Shaver, Billy Joe — Singer, Songwriter
435 N Martell Ave, Los Angeles CA 90036, USA

Shaver, Helen
Forward Entertainment, 9255 Sunset Blvd, #805, Los Angeles CA 90069, USA — Actress, Director

Shaver, Jeffrey T (Jeff)
9651 E Clinton St, Scottsdale AZ 85260, USA — Baseball Player

Shavers, China
Innovative Artists, 1505 10th St, Santa Monica CA 90401 USA — Actress

Shavers, Ernie
2275 Linley Court, Denver CO 80219, USA — Boxer

Shaw, Amanda
Poorman Mayfield Music Group, 5500 Prytania St, #625, New Orleans LA 70115, USA — Singer, Fiddle Player

Shaw, Bernard
5801 Nicholson Lane, #1516, Rockville MD 20852, USA — Commentator

Shaw, Bernard L
14 Monkbridge Road, Leeds, West Yorks LS6 4DX, England — Chemist

Shaw, Brad
1866 Braumton Court, Chesterfield MO 63017, USA — Hockey Player, Coach

Shaw, Brewster H, Jr
3519 Rice Blvd, Houston TX 77005, USA — Astronaut

Shaw, Brian K
540 Brickell Key Dr, #1513, Miami FL 33131, USA — Basketball Player

Shaw, Bryony
Lynx Sports Mgmt, Lymington Road, Lymington, Hampshire SO41 5S5, England — Yachtswoman

Shaw, David
6920 Plainfield Road, Columbia SC 29206, USA — Ice Hockey Player

Shaw, David
Stanford University, Stanford CA 94305 USA — Football Coach

Shaw, Dennis W
14844 Priscilla St, San Diego CA 92129, USA — Football Player

Shaw, Donald W (Don)
857 Waterford Villas Dr, Lake Saint Louis MO 63367, USA — Baseball Player

Shaw, Fiona
I C M Partners, 10250 Constellation Blvd, #900, Los Angeles CA 90067 USA — Actress

Shaw, Hannah
Why Not Model Agency, Via Zenale 9, 20123 Milan, Italy — Model

Shaw, Ivan
Innovative Artists, 1505 10th St, Santa Monica CA 90401 USA — Actor

Shaw, Jane
Intel Corp, 2200 Mission College Blvd, Santa Clara CA 95054, USA — Businesswoman

Shaw, Jason
Innovative Artists, 1505 10th St, Santa Monica CA 90401 USA — Actor, Model

Shaw, Jeffrey L (Jeff)
1215 Storybrook Dr, Washington Court House OH 43160, USA — Baseball Player

Shaw, Joe
Ken McReddie Assoc, 11 Connaught Place, London W2 2ET, England — Actor

Shaw, John H
Harvard University, Geophysics Dept, Cambridge MA 02138, USA — Geophysicist

Shaw, Kenneth E (Pete)
699 14th St, #356, San Diego CA 92101, USA — Football Player

Shaw, Lindsey
Paradigm Agency, 360 N Crescent Dr, North Building, Beverly Hills CA 90210 USA — Actress

Shaw, Marlena
100 Redstone St, Las Vegas NV 89145, USA — Singer

Shaw, Martin
Ken McReddie Assoc, 11 Connaught Place, London W2 2ET, England — Actor

Shaw, Run Run
Shaw House, Lot 220 Clear Water Bay Road, Kowloon, Hong Kong, China — Producer

Shaw, Ryan
Monterey International, 200 W Superior St, #202, Chicago IL 60654 USA — Singer

Shaw, Scott
20771 Lake Road, Rocky River OH 44116, USA — Photojournalist

Shaw, Stan
Metropolitan Talent Agency, 7020 La Presa Dr, Los Angeles CA 90068 USA — Actor

Shaw, Terrance B (Terry)
PO Box 701645, Dallas TX 75370, USA — Football Player

Shaw, Thomas R (Tommy)
Alliance Artists, 1825 Lockeway Dr, #204, Alpharetta GA 30004, USA — Singer, Guitarist (Styx); Songwriter

Shaw, Timothy A (Tim)
5315 River Ave, Newport Beach CA 92663, USA — Swimmer, Water Polo Player

Shaw, Victoria
V L S Mgmt, PO Box 58175, Nashville TN 37205, USA — Singer, Songwriter

Shaw, Vinessa
I C M Partners, 10250 Constellation Blvd, #900, Los Angeles CA 90067 USA — Actress, Model

Shaw, William L (Billy)
573 Old Rothell Road, Toccoa GA 30577, USA — Football Player

Shawkat, Alia
Basra Entertainment, 8-444 Perez Road, #O, Cathedral City CA 92234, USA — Actress

Shawn Jay
Geffen Records, 10900 Wilshire Blvd, #1000, Los Angeles CA 90024 USA — Rap Artist (Field Mob)

Shawn, Wallace
Stone Manners Salners, 9911 W Pico Blvd, #1400, Los Angeles CA 90035 USA — Actor, Writer

Shay, Jerome P (Jerry)
81 E Shasta St, Chula Vista CA 91910, USA — Football Player

Shaye, Lin
Don Buchwald/Fortitude, 6500 Wilshire Blvd, #2200, Los Angeles CA 90048 USA — Actress

Shaye, Robert K
New Line Cinema, 116 N Robertson Blvd, #400, Los Angeles CA 90048, USA — Businessman

Shaye, Skyler
Artists Only Mgmt, 10203 Santa Monica Blvd, Los Angeles CA 90067, USA — Actress

Shayk, Irina
I M G Models, 304 Park Ave S, #PH-North, New York NY 10010 USA — Model

Shaykh, Hanan al-
Rogers Coleridge White, 20 Powis Mews, London W11 1JN, England — Writer

Shchedrin, Rodion K
25/9 Tverskaya St, #31, 103050 Moscow, Russia — Composer

Shea, Aaron T
2992 Waterfall Way, Westlake OH 44145, USA — Football Player

Shea, Charity B/W/R, 9100 Wilshire Blvd, #500W, Beverly Hills CA 90212 USA	Actress
Shea, Eric 27710 Jubilee Run Road, Pearblossom CA 93553, USA	Actor
Shea, George Beverly 1300 Harmon Place, Minneapolis MN 55403, USA	Singer
Shea, John Don Buchwald/Fortitude, 6500 Wilshire Blvd, #2200, Los Angeles CA 90048 USA	Actor
Shea, Judith 124 Chambers St, New York NY 10007, USA	Artist, Sculptor
Shea, Katt I C M Partners, 10250 Constellation Blvd, #900, Los Angeles CA 90067 USA	Actress
Shea, Pat P B S Records, PO Box 991, Orchard Park NY 14127, USA	Singer, Songwriter
Shea, Robert M Director, Command Control Communications, HqUSMC, Washington DC 20380, USA	Marine Corps General
Shea, Terry Miami Dolphins, 7500 SW 30th St, Davie FL 33314 USA	Football Coach
Sheaffer, Danny T 165 Savannah Lane, Mount Airy NC 27030, USA	Baseball Player
Shealy, Ryan N 2168 NE 63rd Court, Fort Lauderdale FL 33308, USA	Baseball Player
Shear, Jules Concerted Efforts, PO Box 440326, Somerville MA 02144 USA	Singer, Songwriter
Shear, Rhonda J Cast Productions, 2550 Greenvalley Road, Los Angeles CA 90046, USA	Actress, Comedienne, Model
Sheard, Kierra (Kiki) E M I Gospel, PO Box 5085, Brentwood TN 37024, USA	Singer
Shearer, Al Safran Co, 8748 Holloway Dr, West Hollywood CA 90069, USA	Actor
Shearer, Alan Newcastle United F C, Saint James Park, Newcastle-Tyne NE1 4ST, England	Soccer Player
Shearer, Bob Int'l Management Group, 281 Clarence St, Sydney NSW 2000, Australia	Golfer
Shearer, Harry J Affirmative Entertainment, 425 N Robertson Blvd, Los Angeles CA 90048, USA	Actor, Comedian
Shearer, Peter M Scripps Oceanography Institute, Geophysics Dept, La Jolla CA 92093, USA	Geophysicist
Shearer, S Bradford (Brad) 1909 Lakeshore Dr, #B, Austin TX 78746, USA	Football Player
Shearn, Tom 20429 Rita Blanca Circle, Pflugerville TX 78660, USA	Baseball Player
Shears, Jake Girlie Action, 59 W 19th St, #4B, New York NY 10011 USA	Singer (Scissors Sisters)
Shearsmith, Reece Independent Talent Group, Oxford House, 76 Oxford St, London W1D 1BS, England	Actor
Sheckler, Ryan A 927 Calle Negocio, #K, San Clemente CA 92673, USA	Skateboarder, Actor
Shectman, Stephen A Carniegie Observatories, 813 Santa Barbara St, Pasadena CA 91101, USA	Astronomer
Shedd, Kendrick D (Kenny) 1928 Tioga Pass Way, Antioch CA 94531, USA	Football Player
Sheedy, Ally Innovative Artists, 1505 10th St, Santa Monica CA 90401 USA	Actress
Sheehan, Doug Judy Schoen, 606 N Larchmont Blvd, #309, Los Angeles CA 90004 USA	Actor
Sheehan, Neil 4505 Klingle St NW, Washington DC 20016, USA	Journalist
Sheehan, Patricia A (Patty) 8395 Panorama Dr, Reno NV 89511, USA	Golfer
Sheehan, Patrick 2913 Ashton Terrace, Oviedo FL 32765, USA	Golfer
Sheehan, Susan 4505 Klingle St NW, Washington DC 20016, USA	Writer
Sheehy, Gail H 300 E 57th St, #18D, New York NY 10022, USA	Writer
Sheehy, Neil K Sheehy Hockey, 900 2nd Ave S, #1650, Minneapolis MN 55402, USA	Ice Hockey Player
Sheehy, Timothy K (Tim) Sheehy Hockey, 4 Boswell Lane, Southborough MA 01772, USA	Ice Hockey Player
Sheeler, Jim Rocky Mountain News, Editorial Dept, 101 W Colfax Ave, #500, Denver CO 80202, USA	Journalist
Sheen, Charles (Charlie) Evolution Entertainment, 901 N Highland Ave, Los Angeles CA 90038 USA	Actor
Sheen, Jacqueline Playboy Promotions, 2706 Media Center Dr, Los Angeles CA 90065 USA	Actress, Model
Sheen, Martin 29351 Bluewater Road, Malibu CA 90265, USA	Actor
Sheen, Michael Roxanne Vacca Mgmt, 73 Bleak St, London W1R 3LF, England	Actor
Sheeran, Josette UN World Food Program, Cesare Giulio Viola 68/70, 00148 Rome, Italy	Government Official, Journalist
Sheets, Andrew M (Andy) 104 Villaggio Dr, Lafayette LA 70508, USA	Baseball Player
Sheets, Ben M 105 E Shore Road, Monroe LA 71203, USA	Baseball Player
Sheets, Larry K 1411 Chippendale Road, Luther Timonium MD 21093, USA	Baseball Player
Sheffer, Craig Innovative Artists, 1505 10th St, Santa Monica CA 90401 USA	Actor
Sheffield, Frederick J (Fred) 11664 McDougall, Tustin CA 92782, USA	Basketball Player
Sheffield, Gary A 6752 Ralston Beach Circle, Tampa FL 33614, USA	Baseball Player
Sheffield, William J (Bill) PO Box 91476, Anchorage AK 99509, USA	Governor, AK

Sheik, Duncan	Singer, Songwriter
Sweet180, 141 W 28th St, #300, New York NY 10001, USA	
Sheil, Kate Lyn	Actress
One Entertainment, 12 W 57th St, #PH 1, New York NY 10019 USA	
Sheila E	Singer, Drummer
Universal Attractions, 135 W 26th St, #1200, New York NY 10001 USA	
Sheindlin, Judy (Judge)	Entertainer, Judge
Big Ticket Television, 5842 W Sunset Blvd, #303, Los Angeles CA 90028, USA	
Sheiner, David S	Actor
Commercials Unlimited, 190 N Canon Dr, #202, Beverly Hills, CA 90210 USA	
Sheinkin, Rachel	Writer, Lyricist
New York University, New York NY 10012 USA	
Shelby, John T	Baseball Player
2232 Broadhead Lane, Lexington KY 40515, USA	
Shelby, Mark	Jazz Bassist, Composer
Thomas Cassidy, 11761 E Speedway Blvd, Tucson AZ 85748 USA	
Sheldon, Roland F (Rollie)	Baseball Player
614 NE Coronado St, Lees Summit MO 64063, USA	
Sheldon, Scott P	Baseball Player
5202 Blue Cypress Lane, League City TX 77573, USA	
Shell, Arthur (Art)	Football Player, Coach
419 Rilea Way, Oakland CA 94605, USA	
Shell, Donnie	Football Player
2945 Shandon Road, Rock Hill SC 29730, USA	
Shellenback, James P (Jim)	Baseball Player
10627 Dreamy Lane, Parker AZ 85344, USA	
Shelley, Barbara	Actress
Ken McReddie Assoc, 11 Connaught Place, London W2 2ET, England	
Shelley, Carole	Actress, Singer
CornerStone Talent Agency, 37 W 20th St, #1107, New York NY 10011, USA	
Shelley, Howard G	Concert Pianist, Conductor
Caroline Baird Artists, Farmoor Eynsham, Oxon OX29 4DA, England	
Shelley, Jody	Ice Hockey Player
211 Chestnut St, Haddonfield NJ 08033, USA	
Shelley, Pete	Singer, Guitarist (Buzzcocks)
Free Trade Agency, Chapel Place, Rivington St, London EC2A 3DQ, England	
Shelley, Rachel	Actress
Independent Talent Group, Oxford House, 76 Oxford St, London W1D 1BS, England	
Shelley, Steve	Drummer (Sonic Youth)
Silva Artist Mgmt, 722 Seward St, Los Angeles CA 90038, USA	
Shelmerdine, Kirk	Auto Racing Engineer
Kirk Shelmerdine Racing, PO Box 1133, Welcome NC 27374, USA	
Shelton, Abigail	Actress
Dale Garrick, 1017 N La Cienega Blvd, #109, West Hollywood CA 90069 USA	
Shelton, Blake T	Singer, Songwriter
W M E Entertainment, 1600 Division St, #300, Nashville TN 37203 USA	
Shelton, Chris	Baseball Player
6382 Shady Grove Circle, Salt Lake City UT 84121, USA	
Shelton, Daimon	Football Player
9069 Quail Feather Way, Elk Grove CA 95624, USA	
Shelton, Deborah	Actress, Beauty Queen
2265 Westwood Blvd, #251, Los Angeles CA 90064, USA	
Shelton, Lonnie J	Basketball Player
3883 Union Ave, #5, Bakersfield CA 93305, USA	
Shelton, Lonnie J (L J)	Football Player
6034 W Trovita Place, Chandler AZ 85226, USA	
Shelton, Lynn	Director
United Talent Agency, 9336 Civic Center Dr, Beverly Hills CA 90210 USA	
Shelton, Marley C	Actress
Untitled Entertainment, 350 S Beverly Dr, #200, Beverly Hills CA 90212 USA	
Shelton, Richard E	Football Player
6367 Raw Hyde Trail N, Jacksonville FL 32210, USA	
Shelton, Ricky Van	Singer, Guitarist, Songwriter
PO Box 111, Woodlawn VA 24381, USA	
Shelton, Robert N	Educator
University of Arizona, President's Office, Tucson AZ 85721, USA	
Shelton, Ronald W (Ron)	Director
W M E Entertainment, 9601 Wilshire Blvd, #300, Beverly Hills CA 90210 USA	
Shelton, Samantha	Actress
Untitled Entertainment, 350 S Beverly Dr, #200, Beverly Hills CA 90212 USA	
Shelton, Uriah	Actor
Coast to Coast Talent, 3350 Barham Blvd, Los Angeles CA 90068 USA	
Shemi, Calman	Artist
Jacques Soussana Graphics, 37 Pierre Koenig St, Jerusalem 91401, Israel	
Shen Wei	Choreographer
Shen Wei Dance Arts, 520 8th Ave, #303, New York NY 10018, USA	
Shen Xue	Figure Skater
Skating Assn, 56 Zhongguancun South St, Haidian, Beijing 100044, China	
Shen, Parry	Actor
Stone Manners Salners, 9911 W Pico Blvd, #1400, Los Angeles CA 90035 USA	
Shenandoah, Joanne	Singer, Songwriter
Oneida Nation Territory, PO Box 450, Oneida NY 13421, USA	
Shengelaia, Eldar N	Director, Writer
Ioseliani St 37, #58, 380091 Tbilisi, Georgia	
Shengelaia, Georgy N	Director
Kekelidze St 16, #12, 380091 Tbilisi, Georgia	
Shenk, Thomas E	Molecular Biologist
Princeton University, Molecular Biology Dept, Princeton NJ 08544, USA	
Shenkman, Ben	Actor
Suskin Mgmt, 2 Charlton St, #5K, New York NY 10014, USA	
Shenton, Ann	Synthesizer Player (Add N to X)
Kork Agency, 1880 Century Park E, #711, Los Angeles CA 90067 USA	
Shepard, Dax	Actor
Creative Artists Agency, 2000 Ave of Stars, #100, Los Angeles CA 90067 USA	
Shepard, Devon	Writer, Producer
I C M Partners, 10250 Constellation Blvd, #900, Los Angeles CA 90067 USA	

Shepard, Jean — Singer
Billy Deaton Talent, 1214 16th Ave S, Nashville TN 37212 USA

Shepard, Jewel — Actress, Model
A P A Talent/Literary Agency, 405 S Beverly Dr, #300, Beverly Hills CA 90212 USA

Shepard, Jules — Social Activist
7120 Minstrel Way, #206, Columbia MD 21045, USA

Shepard, Richard — Director, Writer
W M E Entertainment, 9601 Wilshire Blvd, #300, Beverly Hills CA 90210 USA

Shepard, Roger N — Psychologist
6041 Fair Oaks Blvd, Carmichael CA 95608, USA

Shepard, Samuel K (Sam) — Writer, Actor
I C M Partners, 730 5th Ave, New York NY 10019 USA

Shepard, Vonda — Singer, Songwriter
Marleah Leslie Assoc, 1645 Vine St, #712, Los Angeles CA 90028, USA

Shepherd, Ben — Bassist (Soundgarden)
Susan Silver Mgmt, 6523 California Ave SW, #348, Seattle WA 98136, USA

Shepherd, Cybill — Actress, Model
Hofflund/Polone, 9465 Wilshire Blvd, #420, Beverly Hills CA 90212 USA

Shepherd, Elizabeth — Actress
London Mgmt, 2-4 Noel St, London W1V 3RB, England

Shepherd, Kenny Wayne — Guitarist
PO Box 1355, Benton LA 71006, USA

Shepherd, Morgan — Auto, Truck Racing Driver
Shepherd Racing Ventures, 4905 Jeffrey Lane, Conover NC 28613, USA

Shepherd, Neferteri — Model
Amsel Eisenstadt Frazier, 5055 Wilshire Blvd, #865, Los Angeles CA 90036 USA

Shepherd, Ronald W (Ron) — Baseball Player
5821 FM 349, Kilgore TX 75662, USA

Shepherd, Sherri — Actress
Creative Artists Agency, 2000 Ave of Stars, #100, Los Angeles CA 90067 USA

Shepherd, Sherrie — Cartoonist (Francie)
United Feature Syndicate, PO Box 5610, Cincinnati OH 45201 USA

Shepherd, William M — Astronaut
18623 Prince William Lane, Houston TX 77058, USA

Sheppard, Anna — Costume Designer
I C M Partners, 10250 Constellation Blvd, #900, Los Angeles CA 90067 USA

Sheppard, Delia — Actress, Model
Kazarian/Spencer/Ruskin, 11969 Ventura Blvd, #300, Studio City CA 91604 USA

Sheppard, Gregg — Ice Hockey Player
2521 Blue Jay Crescent, North Battleford SK S9A 3Z3, Canada

Sheppard, Henry F, Jr — Football Player
313 Waterstone, Victoria TX 77901, USA

Sheppard, Jonathan E — Steeplechase Racing Trainer
287 Lamborn Town Road, West Grove PA 19390, USA

Sheppard, Lito D — Football Player
18960 SW 39th Court, Miramar FL 33029, USA

Sheppard, Mark — Actor
Ken McReddie Assoc, 11 Connaught Place, London W2 2ET, England

Sheppard, Ray — Ice Hockey Player
19110 Fox Landing Dr, Boca Raton FL 33434, USA

Sheppard, T G — Singer, Guitarist
R J Kaltenbach Mgmt, PO Box 550, Harvard IL 60033, USA

Sher, Antony — Actor
I C M Partners, Marlborough House, 10 Earlham St, #300, London WC2H 9LNP, England

Sher, Bartlett — Director
Creative Artists Agency, 2000 Ave of Stars, #100, Los Angeles CA 90067 USA

Sher, Eden — Actress
Innovative Artists, 1505 10th St, Santa Monica CA 90401 USA

Shera, Mark — Actor
PO Box 15717, Beverly Hills CA 90209, USA

Sherbedgia, Rade — Actor
United Agents, 12-26 Lexington St, London W1F 0LE, England

Sherffius, John — Editorial Cartoonist
Saint Louis Post Dispatch, Editorial Dept, 900 N Tucker, Saint Louis MO 63101, USA

Sheridan, Bonnie Bramlett — Singer (Delaney & Bonnie), Actress
18011 Martha St, Encino CA 91316, USA

Sheridan, Dave — Actor
Media Artists Group, 8255 Sunset Blvd, Los Angeles CA 90046, USA

Sheridan, Dinah — Actress
Infinite Partners, Pinewood Studios, Iver Heath, Buckinghamshire SLO ONH, England

Sheridan, Howard M — Radiologist, Businessman
4020 Sheridan St, #B, Hollywood FL 33021, USA

Sheridan, James P (Jamey) — Actor
Brillstein Entertainment Partners, 9150 Wilshire Blvd, #350, Beverly Hills CA 90212 USA

Sheridan, Jim — Director, Producer
Hell's Kitchen International, 21 Mespil Road, Dublin 4, Ireland

Sheridan, Lisa — Actress
TalentWorks, 3500 W Olive Ave, #1400, Burbank CA 91505 USA

Sheridan, Liz — Actress
11333 Moorpark, #427, North Hollywood CA 91602, USA

Sheridan, Neil R — Baseball Player
150 Chaucer Court, Pleasant Hill CA 94523, USA

Sheridan, Nicolette — Actress
B/W/R, 9100 Wilshire Blvd, #500W, Beverly Hills CA 90212 USA

Sheridan, Patrick A (Pat) — Baseball Player
31654 Taft St, Wayne MI 48184, USA

Sheridan, Tayler — Actress
Evolution Entertainment, 901 N Highland Ave, Los Angeles CA 90038 USA

Sheridan, Tony — Singer
Gems, PO Box 1031, Montrose CA 91021, USA

Sheridan, Tye — Actor
Mosiac Media Group, 9200 W Sunset Blvd, #1000, Los Angeles CA 90069 USA

Sherk, Jerry M — Football Player
1819 Bel Air Terrace, Encinitas CA 92024, USA

Sherk, Kathy — Golfer
1333 Dorval Dr, Oakville ON L6M 4G2, Canada

Sherlock, Nancy J N A S A, Johnson Space Center, 2101 NASA Road, Houston TX 77058 USA	Astronaut
Sherman, Alex (Allie) 136 E 55th St, #12H, New York NY 10022, USA	Football Player, Coach
Sherman, Bobby 1870 Sunset Plaza Dr, Los Angeles CA 90069, USA	Singer, Actor
Sherman, Cindy M 9 Debrosses St, #520A, New York NY 10032, USA	Photographer
Sherman, Darrell E 12622 Memorial Way , #1144, Moreno Valley CA 92553, USA	Baseball Player
Sherman, Heath B PO Box 54, Glen Flora TX 77443, USA	Football Player
Sherman, Michael (Mickey) Sherman & Richichi, 27 5th St, Stamford CT 06905, USA	Attorney
Sherman, Michael F (Mike) 3337 Arapaho Ridge Dr, College Station TX 77845, USA	Football Coach
Sherman, Patsy O 1451 Highview Ave, Saint Paul MN 55121, USA	Chemist, Inventor (Scotchgard)
Sherman, Richard M Cowans DeBaets Abrahams, 41 Madison Ave, 3400, New York NY 10010, USA	Composer, Lyricist
Sherman, Rodney J (Rod) PO Box 4551, Incline Village NV 89450, USA	Football Player
Sherman-Palladino, Amy Creative Artists Agency, 2000 Ave of Stars, #100, Los Angeles CA 90067 USA	Producer, Director, Writer
Sherod, Edmund (Ed) 519 Montvale Ave, Richmond VA 23222, USA	Basketball Player
Sherrard, Michael W (Mike) PO Box 992, Agoura Hills CA 91376, USA	Football Player
Sherrill, Betty McMillen Inc, 155 E 56th St, #500, New York NY 10022, USA	Interior Designer
Sherrill, George F 2092 Lee Place, Memphis TN 38104, USA	Baseball Player
Sherrington, Georgina J G M, 15 Lexham Mews, London W8 6JW, England	Actress
Sherry, Fionnuala Thranesgate 2B, Oslo 473, Norway	Violinist (Secret Garden)
Sherry, Norman B (Norm) 4383 Nobel Dr, #89, San Diego CA 92122, USA	Baseball Player, Manager
Sherven, Gord 184 Hampshire Grove NW, Calgary AB T3A 5B3, Canada	Ice Hockey Player
Sherwin, Timothy T (Tim) 6 Mill Road, Latham NY 12110, USA	Football Player
Sherwood, Alison Milwaukee Journal Sentinel, Editorial Dept, PO Box 371, Milwaukee WI 53201 USA	Journalist
Sherwood, Brad C E S D, 10635 Santa Monica Blvd, #130, Los Angeles CA 90025 USA	Actor, Comedian
Shesol, Jeff Creators Syndicate, 737 3rd St, Hermosa Beach CA 90254 USA	Cartoonist (Thatch)
Sheth, Sheetal Defining Artists Agency, 10 Universal City Plaza, #2000, Universal City CA 91608, USA	Actress
Shetty, Reshma Station 3 Entertainment, 300 W 55th St, #5L, New York NY 10019, USA	Actress
Shetty, Shilpa 12 Dev Darshan, 262 Saint Anthony Road, Chembur, Mumbai 400071, India	Actress
Shetty, Sunil 18/B Prithvi Apartments, Altamont Road, Mumbai MS 400026, India	Actor
Shevchenki, Andriy F C Milan, Via Filippo Turati 3, 20121 Milan, Italy	Soccer Player
Shi, David E Furman University, President's Office, Greenville SC 29613, USA	Educator
Shiancoe, Visanthe 2316 City Place, Edgewater NJ 07020, USA	Football Player
Shicoff, Neil Opera et Concert, 37 Rue de la Chaussee d'Antin, 75009 Paris, France	Opera Singer
Shields, Ashley Atlanta Dream, 83 Walton St NW, #400, Atlanta, GA 30303 USA	Basketball Player
Shields, Ben Abrams Artists, 9200 W Sunset Blvd, #1125, West Hollywood CA 90069 USA	Actor
Shields, Blake Kass & Stokes Mgmt, 9229 W Sunset Blvd, #504, Los Angeles CA 90069 USA	Actor
Shields, Brooke Christa Inc, 9200 Sunset Blvd, #600, Los Angeles CA 90069, USA	Model, Actress
Shields, Perry US Tax Court, 400 2nd St NW, Washington DC 20217, USA	Judge
Shields, R Scot 16139 Pine Valley Dr, Northville MI 48168, USA	Baseball Player
Shields, Robert Robert Shields Designs, PO Box 3161, Cottonwood AZ 86326, USA	Mime (Shields & Yarnell), Artist
Shields, Stephen C (Steve) 123 E Balboa Blvd, Newport Beach CA 92661, USA	Ice Hockey Player
Shields, Stephen M (Steve) 4969 Leonard Dr, Gadsden AL 35903, USA	Baseball Player
Shields, Will H 13125 W 127th Place, Overland Park KS 66213, USA	Football Player
Shields, William D (Billy) 12701 Treeridge Terrace, Poway CA 92064, USA	Football Player
Shifflett, Steven E (Steve) 24004 E 172nd St, Pleasant Hill MO 64080, USA	Baseball Player
Shifrin, David C M Artists, 127 W 96th St, #13B, New York NY 10025 USA	Concert Clarinetist
Shifty Shellshock Q Prime, 729 7th Ave, #1600, New York NY 10019, USA	Rap Artist, Lyricist (Crazy Town)
Shigeta, James C E S D, 10635 Santa Monica Blvd, #130, Los Angeles CA 90025, USA	Actor
Shikler, Aaron Meredith Long Co, 2323 San Felipe St, Houston TX 77019, USA	Artist

Shiley Newhouse, Jean — Track Athlete
11000 Sunnybrae Ave, Chatsworth CA 91311, USA
Shiller, Robert J — Economist
Yale University, Cowles Foundation, PO Box 208281, New Haven CT 06520, USA
Shima, Masatoshi — Electronics Engineer
Shima Co, 260 Tsurumaki, Omika Haramachishi, Fukushima 975-0049, Japan
Shimell, William — Opera Singer
I M G Artists, Hogarth Business Park, Chiswick, London W4 2TH, England
Shimer, Brian — Bobsled Athlete
2613 Lakeview Dr, Naples FL 34112, USA
Shimerman, Armin — Actor
Stone Manners Salners, 9911 W Pico Blvd, #1400, Los Angeles CA 90035 USA
Shimizu, Jenny — Model, Actress
Elite Model Mgmt, 404 Park Ave S, #900, New York NY 10016 USA
Shimizu, Takashi — Director
Media Complex, 7-6-52-408 Akasaka, Minatoku, Tokyo 107-0052, Japan
Shimkus, Joanna — Actress
Creative Artists Agency, 2000 Ave of Stars, #100, Los Angeles CA 90067 USA
Shimomura, Osamu — Nobel Chemistry Laureate
324 Sippewissett Road, Falmouth MA 02540, USA
Shimono, Sab — Actor
12711 Ventura Blvd, #440, Studio City CA 91604, USA
Shimony, Abner E — Physicist
16 Claflin Road, #2, Brookline MA 02445, USA
Shin Sang Ho — Sculptor
Hong-ik University, Sangsu Dong, Ma Po Gu, Seoul 121-791, South Korea
Shin Yong Moon — Geneticist
National University, Sillimdong, Gwanakgu, Seoul 151-742, South Korea
Shin, Jiyai — Golfer
Ladies Pro Golf Assn, 100 International Golf Dr, Daytona Beach FL 32124 USA
Shinabarger, Tim — Sculptor
Legacy Gallery, 75 N Cache Ave, Box 4977, Jackson WY 83001, USA
Shinall, Zakary S (Zak) — Baseball Player
16605 Sell Circle, Huntington Beach CA 92649, USA
Shindle, Katherine (Kate) — Beauty Queen, Actress
Gage Group, 14724 Ventura Blvd, #505, Sherman Oaks CA 91403 USA
Shine, Michael (Mike) — Track Athlete
508 Royal Road, State College PA 16801, USA
Shiner, Richard E (Dick), Jr — Football Player
19 Fox Trail, Gettysburg PA 17325, USA
Shinners, J John T — Football Player
N120W14985 Freistadt Road, Germantown WI 53022, USA
Shinoda, Mike — Singer (Linkin Park)
The Firm, 2049 Century Park E, #2550, Los Angeles CA 90067 USA
Shinseki, Eric K (Ric) — Secretary, Veterans Affairs; General
Veteran Affairs Department, 810 Vermont Ave NW, Washington DC 20420 USA
Shinya, Hiromi — Gastroenterologist
Beth Israel Medical Center, Endoscopy Unit, 1st Ave & 16th St, New York NY 10461, USA
Shipka, Kiernan — Actress
42 West, 11400 W Olympic Blvd, #1100, Los Angeles CA 90064 USA
Shipler, David K — Journalist
4005 Thornapple St, Chevy Chase MD 20815, USA
Shipley, Craig B — Baseball Player
Boston Red Sox, Fenway Park, 4 Yawkey Way, Boston MA 02215 USA
Shipley, Jennifer M — Prime Minister, New Zealand
Club de Madrid, C/Goya 5-7, Pasaje 2, 28001 Madrid, Spain
Shipley, Walter V — Financier
Chase Manhattan Corp, 270 Park Ave, New York NY 10017, USA
Shipman, Claire — Commentator
ABC-TV, News Dept, 77 W 66th St, New York NY 10023 USA
Shipp, E R — Columnist
New York Daily News, Editorial Dept, 220 E 42nd St, New York NY 10017, USA
Shipp, Jerry — Basketball Player
PO Box 370, Kingston OK 73439, USA
Shipp, John Wesley — Actor
Stewart Talent, 318 W 53rd St, #201, New York NY 10019, USA
Shirakawa, Hideki — Nobel Chemistry Laureate
University of Tsukuba, Chemistry Dept, Sakura-Mura, Ibaraki 000 305, Japan
Shiraki, Ryan — Director, Writer, Actor
A P A Talent/Literary Agency, 405 S Beverly Dr, #300, Beverly Hills CA 90212 USA
Shire, David L — Composer
250 Piermont Ave, Piermont NY 10968, USA
Shire, Talia — Actress, Director
10730 Bellagio Road, Los Angeles CA 90077, USA
Shirk, Gary L — Football Player
PO Box 287, Laporte PA 18626, USA
Shirley, Andrew P (Drew) — Guitarist (Switchfoot)
The Firm, 2049 Century Park E, #2550, Los Angeles CA 90067 USA
Shirley, Barton A (Bart) — Baseball Player
6538 Orangetip Dr, Corpus Christi TX 78414, USA
Shirley, Danny — Singer (Confederate Railroad)
Bobby Roberts, 3050 Business Park Circle, #303, Goodlettsville TN 37221 USA
Shirley, George I — Opera Singer
University of Michigan, Music School, Ann Arbor MI 48109, USA
Shirley, John — Writer
Tarcher/Penguin Press, 375 Hudson St, Basement 3, New York NY 10014, USA
Shirley, Robert C (Bob) — Baseball Player
761 W 13th St, Tulsa OK 74127, USA
Shirley-Quirk, John S — Opera Singer
511 N Chapel Gate Lane, Baltimore MD 21229, USA
Shirreffs, John A — Thoroughbred Racing Trainer
Hollywood Park Race Track, Barn 55 S, PO Box 369, Inglewood CA 90306, USA
Shiver, Sanders T — Football Player
16507 Ariel Court, Bowie MD 20716, USA
Shivers, Chris — Rodeo Bull Rider
192 Shivers Road, Jonesville LA 71343, USA

V.I.P. Address Book

Shivers, Roy L — Football Player
2067 Hidden Hollow Lane, Henderson NV 89012, USA

Shkaplerov, Anton N — Cosmonaut
Cosmonaut Training Center, Star City, 141160 Zvezdny Gorodok, Moscow Oblast, Russia

Shoals, Roger R — Football Player
365 Righters Mill Road, Gladwyne PA 19035, USA

Shobert, Don W (Bubba) — Motorcycle Racing Rider
8905 153rd St, Wolfforth TX 79382, USA

Shocked, Michelle — Singer, Guitarist, Songwriter
Siddons Assoc, 584 N Larchmont Blvd, Los Angeles CA 90004, USA

Shockley, J Costen — Baseball Player
493 Wilson St, Georgetown DE 19947, USA

Shockley, Jeremy C — Football Player
1330 West Ave, #3601, Miami Beach FL 33139, USA

Shockley, William — Actor
JKA Talent Agency, 12725 Ventura Blvd, #H, Studio City CA 91604, USA

Shoebottom, Bruce — Ice Hockey Player
40 Woodfield Dr, Scarborough ME 04074, USA

Shoecraft, John A — Balloonist
Shoecraft Contracting Co, 7430 E Stetson Dr, Scottsdale AZ 85251, USA

Shoemaker, Carolyn S — Geologist, Astronomer
US Geological Survey, 2255 N Gemini Dr, Flagstaff AZ 86001, USA

Shoemaker, Craig — Actor, Comedian
Levity Entertainment Group, 6701 Center Drive W, #1111, Los Angeles CA 90045, USA

Shoemaker, Robert M — Army General
PO Box 768, Belton TX 76513, USA

Shofner, Delbert M (Del) — Football Player
1665 Del Mar Ave, San Marino CA 91108, USA

Shofner, James (Jim) — Football Player, Coach
9620 Champions Dr, Granbury TX 76049, USA

Shoji, Dave — Volleyball Coach
University of Hawaii, Athletic Dept, Hilo HI 96720, USA

Shoji, Tadashi — Fashion Designer
Tadashi Shoji Assoc, 3016 E 44th St, Vernon CA 90058, USA

Shonekan, Ernest A O — President, Nigeria
12 Alexander Ave, Ikoyi, Lagos, Nigeria

Shonin, Georgi S — Cosmonaut, Air Force General
Cosmonaut Training Center, Star City, 141160 Zvezdny Gorodok, Moscow Oblast, Russia

Shonta, Charles J (Chuck) — Football Player
17435 Ava Court, New Boston MI 48164, USA

Shooter, Eric M — Neurobiologist
370 Golden Oak Dr, Portola Valley CA 94028, USA

Shopay, Thomas M (Tom) — Baseball Player
10145 NW 19th St, Doral FL 33172, USA

Shope, Allan — Architect
Shope Reno Wharton, 18 Marshall St, #114, Norwalk CT 06854, USA

Shoppach, Kelly B — Baseball Player
6117 Forest River Dr, Fort Worth TX 76112, USA

Shor, Miriam — Actress
Impression Entertainment, 9229 W Sunset Blvd, #700, Los Angeles CA 90069, USA

Shor, Peter W — Applied Mathematician
47 Manor Ave, Wellesley MA 02482, USA

Shore, David — Writer, Producer
Shore Z Productions, 9100 Wilshire Blvd, #400W, Beverly Hills CA 90212, USA

Shore, Gary — Director, Producer
Anonymous Content, 3532 Hayden Ave, Culver City CA 90232 USA

Shore, Howard — Composer
Columbia Artists Mgmt Inc, 1790 Broadway, #702, New York NY 10019 USA

Shore, Pauly — Actor, Comedian
Innovative Artists, 1505 10th St, Santa Monica CA 90401 USA

Shore, Roberta — Actress
PO Box 71639, Salt Lake City UT 84171, USA

Shore, Stephen — Photographer
Bard College, Photography Dept, Annandale-on-Hudson NY 12504, USA

Shores, Del — Producer, Writer
Del Shores Productions, 8581 Santa Monica Blvd, #560, West Hollywood CA 90069, USA

Short, Brandon D — Football Player
6700 Fairview Road, #430, Charlotte NC 28210, USA

Short, Columbus — Actor
Brillstein Entertainment Partners, 9150 Wilshire Blvd, #350, Beverly Hills CA 90212 USA

Short, Eugene — Basketball Player
8111 Fondren Lake Dr, Houston TX 77071, USA

Short, Margaret E — Artist
105 Garibaldi St, Lake Oswego OR 97035, USA

Short, Martin — Actor, Comedian, Singer
Brillstein Entertainment Partners, 9150 Wilshire Blvd, #350, Beverly Hills CA 90212 USA

Short, Purvis — Basketball Player
8111 Fondren Lake Dr, Houston TX 77071, USA

Short, Rick — Baseball Player
3021 Forsythe Court, Peoria IL 61614, USA

Short, Roger V — Biologist
18 Gwingana Crescent, Glen Waverley VIC 3150, Australia

Short, Wes — Golfer
11128 Sea Hero Lane, Austin TX 78748, USA

Short, William R (Bill) — Baseball Player
2975 57th St, Sarasota FL 34243, USA

Shorter, Frank — Track Athlete
558 Utica Court, Boulder CO 80304, USA

Shorter, Wayne — Jazz Saxophonist, Composer
Universal Attractions, 135 W 26th St, #1200, New York NY 10001 USA

Shorthill, Richard W — Engineer
University of Utah, Mechanical Engineering Dept, Salt Lake City UT 84112, USA

Shortland, Cate — Director, Writer
Industry Entertainment, 955 Carillo Dr, #300, Los Angeles CA 90048 USA

Shortridge, George — Golfer
13896 Ironstone Trail NW, Anoka MN 55303, USA

S

Shivers - Shortridge

Shortridge, Kennedy F — Microbiologist
University of Auckland, Medical Dept, PB 92019, Auckland, New Zealand
Shortridge, Stephen C — Actor, Artist
223 E Sherman Ave, Coeur D'Alene ID 83814, USA
Shortz, Will — Columnist
New York Times, Editorial Dept, 229 W 43rd St, New York NY 10036 USA
Shostakovich, Maxim D — Conductor, Concert Pianist
Columbia Artists Mgmt Inc, 1790 Broadway, #702, New York NY 10019 USA
Shouse, Brian D — Baseball Player
3121 W Summerbend Court, Peoria IL 61615, USA
Shouse, Dexter — Basketball Player
4523 E Rhonda Dr, Phoenix AZ 85018, USA
Show, Grant — Actor
Innovative Artists, 1505 10th St, Santa Monica CA 90401 USA
Showalter, Michael — Actor, Producer, Writer
United Talent Agency, 9336 Civic Center Dr, Beverly Hills CA 90210 USA
Showalter, William N (Buck), III — Baseball Manager
9736 Hathaway St, Dallas TX 75220, USA
Shower, Kathy — Model, Actress
Playboy Promotions, 2706 Media Center Dr, Los Angeles CA 90065 USA
Shreve, Anita — Writer
Little Brown, 3 Center Plaza, #100, Boston MA 02108 USA
Shreve, Susan R — Writer
3506 35th St NW, Washington DC 20016, USA
Shribman, David M — Journalist, Cartoonist
Boston Globe, Editorial Dept, 1130 Connecticut NW, #520, Washington DC 20036, USA
Shrider, Richard G (Dick) — Basketball Player
6666 Morning Sun Road, Oxford OH 45056, USA
Shrimpton, Jean — Model, Actress
Abbey Hotel, Penzance, Cornwall TR18 4AR, England
Shriner, Kin — Actor
63 Cavalry Road, Weston CT 06883, USA
Shriner, Wil — Entertainer, Director
5313 Quakertown Ave, Woodland Hills CA 91364, USA
Shriver, Loren J — Astronaut
2513 Nimbus Dr, Estes Park CO 80517, USA
Shriver, Maria O — Commentator
Hyperion Books, 114 5th Ave, New York NY 10011 USA
Shriver, Pamela H (Pam) — Tennis Player
8743 Mylander Lane, #R, Towson MD 21286, USA
Shroff, Jackie — Actor
1302 Le Pepeyon, Mount Mary Road, Bandra, Mumbai MS 400050, India
Shrontz, Frank A — Businessman
2949 81st Place, #P, Mercer Island WA 98040, USA
Shtalenkov, Mikhail A — Ice Hockey Player
7 Faenza, Newport Coast CA 92657, USA
Shtokolov, Boris T — Opera Singer
Kirov Ballet Theater, 1 Pl Iskusstr, 190000 Saint Petersburg, Russia
Shu Qi — Actress, Model
I M G Models, 8 Rue Danielle Casanova, 75002 Paris, France
Shu, Yiqian — Artist
30 SW 167th Ave, Beaverton OR 97006, USA
Shuba, George T — Baseball Player
3421 Bentwillow Lane, Youngstown OH 44511, USA
Shuchuk, Gary — Ice Hockey Player
5713 Lancashier Court, Fitchburg WI 53711, USA
Shue, Andrew — Actor
Creative Artists Agency, 2000 Ave of Stars, #100, Los Angeles CA 90067 USA
Shue, Elisabeth — Actress
Management 360, 9111 Wilshire Blvd, Beverly Hills CA 90210 USA
Shue, Eugene W (Gene) — Basketball Coach, Executive
4338 Redwood Ave, #303, Marina del Rey CA 90292, USA
Shuey, Paul K — Baseball Player
5252 Mill Dam Road, Wake Forest NC 27587, USA
Shuffield, Joey — Drummer (Fastball)
Russell Carter Artists, 567 Ralph Mcgill Blvd NE, Atlanta GA 30312, USA
Shui, Lan — Conductor
Singapore Symphony, 4 Battery Road #20-01, 049908 Singapore
Shukor, Sheikh Muszaphar — Cosmonaut
Cosmonaut Training Center, Star City, 141160 Zvezdny Gorodok, Moscow Oblast, Russia
Shula, David D (Dave) — Football Coach
10805 Indian Trail, Cooper City FL 33328, USA
Shula, Donald F (Don) — Football Player, Coach
16 Indian Creek Island Road, Indian Creek Village FL 33154, USA
Shula, Mike — Football Player, Coach
19140 Peninsula Club Dr, Cornelius NC 28031, USA
Shuler, Ellie G (Buck), Jr — Air Force General
32 Willow Way W, Alexander City AL 35010, USA
Shuler, Mickey C, Sr — Football Player
332 Belle Vista Dr, Marysville PA 17053, USA
Shulgin, Alexander — Chemist
1483 Shulgin Road, Lafayette CA 94549, USA
Shulman, Douglas H — Government Official
Internal Revenue Service, 1111 Constitution Ave NW, Washington DC 20224, USA
Shulman, Julius — Interior Designer
314 E Arrellaga St, Santa Barbara CA 93101, USA
Shultz, George P — Secretary, State, Treasury & Labor
776 Dolores St, Stanford CA 94305, USA
Shum, Harry, Jr — Actor, Dancer
Innovative Artists, 1505 10th St, Santa Monica CA 90401 USA
Shumate, John H — Basketball Player, Coach
16406 S 12th Place, Phoenix AZ 85048, USA
Shumeyko Hegre, Luba — Model
Ocinum, Rua das Hortas, 9050-024 Funchal Madeira, Portugal
Shumpert, Terrance D (Terry) — Baseball Player
8432 Fairview Court, Lone Tree CO 80124, USA

Shure, Aaron   Writer, Producer
Katz Golden Sullivan Rosenman, 2001 Wilshire Blvd, #400, Santa Monica CA 90403, USA

Shurmur, Pat   Football Coach
Cleveland Browns, 76 Lou Groza Blvd, Berea OH 44017 USA

Shuster, John   Curling Athlete
Curling Assn, 5525 Clem's Way, Stevens Point WI 54482 USA

Shutler, Philip D   Marine Corps General
8917 Braeburn Dr, Annandale VA 22003, USA

Shutt, Steve   Ice Hockey Player
137 Easton Circle, Fairhope AL 36532, USA

Shuttleworth, Mark   Tourist Cosmonaut
H B D Venture Capital, PO Box 1159, Durbanville 7551, South Africa

Shvachka, Anzhelina   Opera Singer
I M G Artists, Hogarth Business Park, Chiswick, London W4 2TH, England

Shved, Alexey V   Basketball Player
Minnesota Timberwolves, Target Center, 600 1st Ave N, Minneapolis MN 55403 USA

Shy, Leslie F (Les)   Football Player
512 N McClurg Court, #3611, Chicago IL 60611, USA

Shyamalan, M Night   Director, Writer
W M E Entertainment, 9601 Wilshire Blvd, #300, Beverly Hills CA 90210 USA

Shyer, Charles R   Director, Writer
W M E Entertainment, 9601 Wilshire Blvd, #300, Beverly Hills CA 90210 USA

Shyne   Rap Artist
Entertainment Artists, PO Box 120824, Nashville TN 37212 USA

Sia, Beau   Actor
Creative Artists Agency, 2000 Ave of Stars, #100, Los Angeles CA 90067 USA

Siana   Model
2113 Cocoa Circle, Virginia Beach VA 23454, USA

Siani, Michael J (Mike)   Football Player
3601 W Broadway, #25-102, Columbia MO 65203, USA

Siaosi Tupov V   King, Tonga
Royal Palace, PO Box 6, Nuku'alofa, Tonga

Sibbett, Jane   Actress
John Carrabino Mgmt, 5900 Wilshire Blvd, #406, Los Angeles CA 90036 USA

Siberry, Jane   Singer, Songwriter
Sheeba, 238 Davenport Road, #291, Toronto ON M5R 1J6, Canada

Sibley, Antoinette   Ballerina
Royal Dancing Academy, 36 Battersea Square, London SW11 3LT, England

Sichting, Jerry L   Basketball Player, Executive
3190 Country Club Road, Martinsville IN 46151, USA

Siddall, Joseph C (Joe)   Baseball Player
2785 Sierra Dr, Windsor ON N9E 2Y9, Canada

Siddig, Alexander   Actor
Markham & Froggatt, Julian House, 4 Windmill St, London W1P 1HF, England

Siddons, Anne R   Writer
767 Vermont Road, Atlanta GA 30319, USA

Sidibe, Gabourey   Actress
Principal Entertainment, 130 W 42nd St, New York NY 10036, USA

Sidibe, Modibo   Prime Minister, Mali
Prime Minister's Office, BP 97, Bamako, Mali

Sidlin, Murray   Conductor
Catholic University, Music School, Washington DC 20064, USA

Sidney, Dainon T   Football Player
605 Lakemeade Point, Old Hickory TN 37138, USA

Sidora, Drew   Actress
I C M Partners, 10250 Constellation Blvd, #900, Los Angeles CA 90067 USA

Sidorenko, Wladimir   Boxer
Universum Boxing Promotion, Am Stadtrand 27, 22047 Hamburg, Germany

Sidorkiewicz, Peter   Ice Hockey Player
1056 Swiss Heights, Oshawa ON L1K 3B4, Canada

Sidorski, Sergei S   Prime Minister, Belarus
Prime Minister's Office, Pl Nezavisimosti, 220010 Minsk, Belarus

Sidran, Ben   Jazz Entertainer, Composer
Blue Moon/Go Jazz Records, PO Box 2023, Madison WI 53701, USA

Siebel Newsom, Jennifer   Actress
Don Buchwald/Fortitude, 6500 Wilshire Blvd, #2200, Los Angeles CA 90048 USA

Siebels, Jonathan L (Jon)   Guitarist (Eve 6)
Agency Group Ltd, 1880 Century Park E, #711, Los Angeles CA 90067 USA

Siebern, Norman L (Norm)   Baseball Player
4181 5th Ave NW, Naples FL 34119, USA

Siebert, Paul E   Baseball Player
1711 Acker St, Orlando FL 32837, USA

Siebert, Wilfred C (Sonny)   Baseball Player
2583 Brush Creek Road, Saint Louis MO 63129, USA

Siebler, Dwight L   Baseball Player
11565 S 204th St, Gretna NE 68028, USA

Sieg, Derek   Director, Writer
United Agents, 12-26 Lexington St, London W1F 0LE, England

Siega, Marcos   Director
Creative Artists Agency, 2000 Ave of Stars, #100, Los Angeles CA 90067 USA

Siegal, John W (Johnny)   Football Player
PO Box 47, Harvey's Lake PA 18618, USA

Siegal, Barnard S (Bernie)   Surgeon, Writer
61 Oxbow Lane, Woodbridge CT 06525, USA

Siegel, Barry   Journalist
Los Angeles Times, Editorial Dept, 202 W 1st St, Los Angeles CA 90012 USA

Siegel, David   Director, Producer, Writer
W M E Entertainment, 9601 Wilshire Blvd, #300, Beverly Hills CA 90210 USA

Siegel, Eric   Actor
I C M Partners, 10250 Constellation Blvd, #900, Los Angeles CA 90067 USA

Siegel, Herbert J   Businessman
Chris-Craft Industries, 55 E 59th St, #22B, New York NY 10022, USA

Siegel, Janis   Singer (Manhattan Transfer)
I C M Partners, 730 5th Ave, New York NY 10019 USA

Siegel, Jay   Singer, Guitarist (Tokens)
Brothers Mgmt, 141 Dunbar Ave, Fords NJ 08863 USA

Siegel, Mike — Actor, Comedian
Parallel Entertainment, 9420 Wilshire Blvd, #250, Beverly Hills CA 90212 USA

Siegel, Randolph — Publisher
Parade, Publisher's Office, 711 3rd Ave, New York NY 10017, USA

Siegel, Robert — Architect
Gwathmey-Siegel Architects, 475 10th Ave, #300, New York NY 10018, USA

Siegel, Robert C — Commentator
National Public Radio, 635 Massachusetts Ave NW, #1, Washington DC 20001, USA

Siegfried — Animal Illusionist (Siegfried & Roy)
Kirvin Doak Communications, 7935 W Sahara Ave, #201, Las Vegas NV 89117, USA

Siekevitz, Philip — Cell Biologist
290 W End Ave, New York NY 10023, USA

Siemaszko, Casey — Actor
Abrams Artists, 9200 W Sunset Blvd, #1125, West Hollywood CA 90069 USA

Siemaszko, Nina — Actress
Vanguard Management Group, 8060 Melrose Ave, #400, Los Angeles CA 90046, USA

Sieminski, Charles L (Chuck) — Football Player
5000 Village Way, #406, Marcus Hook PA 19061, USA

Siemionow, Maria — Reconstructive Surgeon
Cleveland Clinic, 9500 Euclid Ave, Cleveland OH 44195 USA

Siemon, Jeffrey G (Jeff) — Football Player
5401 Londonderry Road, Minneapolis MN 55436, USA

Siena, James — Artist
83 Canal St, #508, New York NY 10002, USA

Siering, Lauri — Swimmer
PO Box 1031, Mammoth Lakes CA 93546, USA

Sierra, Gregory — Actor
3374 Punta Alta, #C, Laguna Woods CA 92637, USA

Sierra, Ruben A — Baseball Player
12355 SW 51st St, Miami Fl 33175, USA

Siers, Kevin — Editorial Cartoonist
Charlotte Observer, Editorial Dept, 600 S Tryon St, Charlotte NC 28202, USA

Sieuwright, Ebe — Actor
Associated International Mgmt, Fairfax House, Fulwood Place, London WC1V 6HU, England

Sievers, Eric — Football Player
11550 Great Falls Way, Great Falls VA 22066, USA

Sievers, Roy E — Baseball Player
11505 Bellefontaine Road, Saint Louis MO 63138, USA

Siew, Vincent C — Prime Minister, Taiwan
Kuomintang, #232-234, Sec 2, BaDe Road, Zhongshan District, Taipei, Taiwan

Siff, Maggie — Actress
Abrams Artists, 9200 W Sunset Blvd, #1125, West Hollywood CA 90069 USA

Sifford, Charlie — Golfer
7540 Sanctuary Circle, Brecksville OH 44141, USA

Sigel, Beanie — Rap Artist
I C M Partners, 10250 Constellation Blvd, #900, Los Angeles CA 90067 USA

Sigel, Jay — Golfer
1284 Farm Road, Berwyn PA 19312, USA

Sigel, N Thomas (Tom) — Cinematographer
I C M Partners, 10250 Constellation Blvd, #900, Los Angeles CA 90067 USA

Sights, Shay — Actress
15030 Ventura Blvd, #556, Sherman Oaks CA 91403, USA

Siglar, Ricky A — Football Player
13901 Newton St, #406, Overland Park KS 66223, USA

Sigler, Jamie-Lynn — Actress, Singer
Paradigm Agency, 360 N Crescent Dr, North Building, Beverly Hills CA 90210 USA

Sigler, John C — Association Executive
National Rifle Association, 11250 Waples Mill Road, Fairfax VA 22030, USA

Sigman, Stan — Businessman
Cingular Wireless, 5565 Glenridge Connector, Atlanta GA 30342, USA

Siguroardottir, Johanna — Prime Minister, Iceland
Premier's Office, Stornarroshusino v/Laekjartou, 150 Reykjavik, Iceland

Sigwart, Ulrich — Heart Surgeon
Centre Hospitalier Universitaire Vaudois, 1011 Lausanne, Switzerland

Sihol, Caroline — Actress
Artmedia, 20 Ave Rapp, 75007 Paris, France

Siilasvuo, Ensio — Army General, Finland
Castrenikatu 6A17, 00530 Helsinki 53, Finland

Siimann, Mart — Prime Minister, Estonia
Riigikugu, Lossi Plats 1A, Tallinn 0100, Estonia

Sikahema, Vai — Football Player
28 Abington Road, Mount Laurel NJ 08054, USA

Sikander, Shahzia — Artist
Deitch Projs, 76 Grand St, New York NY 10013, USA

Sikes, Cynthia — Actress
250 Delfern Dr, Los Angeles CA 90077, USA

Sikharulidze, Anton T — Figure Skater
Skating Federation, Luznetskaya Nab 8, 119871 Moscow, Russia

Sikking, James B — Actor
258 S Carmelina Ave, Los Angeles CA 90049, USA

Sikma, Jack W — Basketball Player
9125 NE 21st Place, Clyde Hill WA 98004, USA

Sikorski, Brian — Baseball Player
17930 Wexford St, Roseville MI 48066, USA

Sikovetsky, Dimitry — Conductor, Concert Violinist
I M G Artists, Hogarth Business Park, Chiswick, London W4 2TH, England

Silajdzic, Haris — Co-Prime Minister, Bosnia & Herzegovina
President's Office, Marsala Titz 7, 71000 Sarajevo, Bosnia & Herzegovina

Silas, James E — Basketball Player
6800 Thistle Hill Way, Austin TX 78754, USA

Silas, Paul T — Basketball Player, Coach
2463 Peninsula Shores Court, Denver NC 28037, USA

Silas, Samuel L (Sam) — Football Player
PO Box 308, Hawthorne NJ 07507, USA

Silatolu, Ratu Timoci — Prime Minister, Fiji
Prime Minister's Office, New Government Buildings, 6 Berkeley Crescent, Suva, Viti Levu, Fiji

Silberling, Bradley (Brad) — Director, Writer
United Talent Agency, 9336 Civic Center Dr, Beverly Hills CA 90210 USA
Silberman, Laurence H — Judge, Diplomat
US Court of Appeals, 333 Constitution Ave NW, #4400, Washington DC 20001, USA
Silberstein, Diane Wichard — Publisher
Playboy, Publisher's Office, 680 N Lake Shore Dr, Chicago IL 60611, USA
Silbey, Robert J — Chemist
Massachusetts Institute of Technology, Chemistry Dept, Cambridge MA 02139, USA
Siler, Eugene E, Jr — Judge
403 Sycamore St, #1, Williamsburg KY 40769, USA
Silja, Anja — Opera Singer
Artists Mgmt, Rutistr 52, 8044 Zurich, Switzerland
Silk, Alexandria — Exotic Dancer, Model
396 Bethany St, Thousand Oaks CA 91360, USA
Silk, Anna — Actress
K G Talent, 55-1/2 Sumach St, Toronto, ON M5A 3J6, Canada
Silk, David M (Dave) — Ice Hockey Player
PO Box 130, Minot MA 02055, USA
Sill, Aleta — Bowler
Professional Bowlers Assn, 719 2nd Ave, #701, Seattle WA 98104 USA
Silla, Felix — Actor
5313 Magenta Court, Las Vegas NV 89108, USA
Sillas, Karen — Actress
PO Box 725, Wading River NY 11792, USA
Silliman, Ron — Writer
262 Orchard Road, Paoli PA 19301, USA
Sillinger, Mike — Ice Hockey Player, Executive
Edmonton Oilers, 11230 110th St, Edmonton AB T5G 3H7, Canada
Sillman, Amy — Artist
705 Driggs Ave, Brooklyn NY 11211, USA
Sills, Douglas (Doug) — Actor, Singer
TalentWorks, 3500 W Olive Ave, #1400, Burbank CA 91505 USA
Sills, Stephen — Architect, Interior Designer
Sills Huniford Assoc, 30 E 67th St, #300, New York NY 10065, USA
Silpa, Mitch — Actor, Comedian
OmniPop Talent Group, 4605 Lankershim Blvd, #201, Toluca Lake CA 91602 USA
Siltala, Michael (Mike) — Ice Hockey Player
1693 Ruscombe Close, Mississauga ON L5J 1Y4, Canada
Silva, Alan Jones — Circus Tightrope Walker
Cirque du Soleil, 8400 2nd Ave, Montreal QC H1Z 4M6, Canada
Silva, Anibal Antonio Cavaco — President, Portugal
President's Office, Palacio de Belem, Calcada da Ajuda 11, 1349 022 Lisbon, Portugal
Silva, Carlos — Baseball Player
280 Bergamot Dr, Hamel MN 55340, USA
Silva, Daniel — Writer
3512 Winfield Lane NW, Washington DC 20007, USA
Silva, Henry — Actor
8747 Clifton Way, #305, Beverly Hills CA 90211, USA
Silva, Jose L — Baseball Player
401 Pappan Dr, Imperial PA 15126, USA
Silva, Thiago E — Soccer Player
Confederacion de Futebol, Rua Victor Civita 66, #1, Rio de Janeiro 22775 044, Brazil
Silver, Horace — Jazz Pianist, Composer
Impulse/Verve Records, Worldwide Plaza, 825 8th Ave, New York NY 10019, USA
Silver, Jeffrey — Producer
United Talent Agency, 9336 Civic Center Dr, Beverly Hills CA 90210 USA
Silver, Joan Micklin — Director, Producer, Writer
Silverfilm Productions, 510 Park Ave, #9B, New York NY 10022, USA
Silver, Joel — Producer
Silver Pictures, 4000 Warner Blvd, Burbank CA 91522, USA
Silver, Joshua D — Inventor (Adjustable Corrective Glasses)
Clarendon Laboratory, Parks Road, Oxford OX1 3PU, England
Silver, Nathaniel A (Nate) — Statistician
New York Times, FiveThirtyEight, Editorial Dept, 229 W 43rd St, New York NY 10036, USA
Silver, Nicky — Writer
W M E Entertainment, 9601 Wilshire Blvd, #300, Beverly Hills CA 90210 USA
Silver, Scott — Director, Writer
Creative Artists Agency, 2000 Ave of Stars, #100, Los Angeles CA 90067 USA
Silvera, Charles A R (Charlie) — Baseball Player
1240 Manzanita Dr, Millbrae CA 94030, USA
Silverberg, Robert — Writer
PO Box 13160, Station E, Oakland CA 94661, USA
Silveri, Scott — Producer, Writer
W M E Entertainment, 9601 Wilshire Blvd, #300, Beverly Hills CA 90210 USA
Silverio, Luis P — Baseball Player
9600 NW 58th Court, Parkland FL 33076, USA
Silverman, Barry G — Judge
US Court of Appeals, 230 N 1st St, Phoenix AZ 85004, USA
Silverman, Henry R — Businessman
Cendant Corp, 9 W 57th St, New York NY 10019, USA
Silverman, Jonathan — Actor
Untitled Entertainment, 350 S Beverly Dr, #200, Beverly Hills CA 90212 USA
Silverman, Kenneth E — Writer, Educator
New York University, English Dept, 19 University Place, New York NY 10003, USA
Silverman, Peter — Writer
Paradigm Agency, 360 N Crescent Dr, North Building, Beverly Hills CA 90210 USA
Silverman, Sarah — Actress, Comedienne, Producer
Creative Artists Agency, 2000 Ave of Stars, #100, Los Angeles CA 90067 USA
Silvers, Robert — Artist
Henry Holt, 175 5th Ave, #400, New York NY 10010 USA
Silverstein, Craig — Producer, Writer
W M E Entertainment, 9601 Wilshire Blvd, #300, Beverly Hills CA 90210 USA
Silverstein, Joseph H — Conductor, Concert Violinist
Utah Symphony Orchestra, 123 W South Temple, Salt Lake City UT 84101, USA
Silverstone, Alicia — Actress
United Talent Agency, 9336 Civic Center Dr, Beverly Hills CA 90210 USA

Silvestri, Alan A — Composer
Gorfaine/Schwartz, 4111 W Alameda Ave, #509, Burbank CA 91505 USA
Silvestri, David J (Dave) — Baseball Player
15511 Country Mill Court, Chesterfield MO 63017, USA
Silvestrini, Achille Cardinal — Religious Leader
Oriental Churches Congregation, Via Conciliazione 34, 00193 Rome, Italy
Silvetti, Jorge — Architect
Machado & Silvetti, 500 Harrison Ave, Boston MA 02118, USA
Silvia — Queen Consort, Sweden
Kungliga Slottet, Stottsbacken, 111 30 Stockholm, Sweden
Silvstedt, Victoria — Model, Actress
Abrams Artists, 9200 W Sunset Blvd, #1125, West Hollywood CA 90069 USA
Sim, Jonathan (Jon) — Ice Hockey Player
104 Willow Ave, New Glasgow NS B2H 1Z5, Canada
Sim, Keong — Actor
Omnipop Talent Group, 4605 Lankershim Blvd, #201, Toluca Lake CA 91602 91602, USA
Sima, Raymond Ndong — Prime Minister, Gabon
Prime Minister's Office, BP 91, Immeuble du 2 Decembre, Libreville, Gabon
Simanek, Robert E — Korean War Marine Corps Hero (CMH)
25194 Westmoreland Dr, Farmington Hills MI 48336, USA
Simas, William A (Bill) — Baseball Player
6084 Millerton Road, Friant CA 93626, USA
Simbomana, Adrien — Prime Minister, Burundi
PO Box 2251, Vugizo, Bujumbura, Burundi
Sime, David W (Dave) — Track Athlete, Physician
9140 Bay Dr, Surfside FL 33154, USA
Simeone, Diane M — Oncologist
University of Michigan Comprehensive Cancer Center, 1500 E Medical Center Dr, Ann Arbor MI 48109, USA
Simeoni, Sara — Track Athlete
Via di Castello, Veronese 32, 37010 Rivoli Verona, Italy
Simes, John W (Jack), II — Cyclist
7753 Probst Hill Road, New Tripoli PA 18066, USA
Simic, Charles — Writer
PO Box 192, Strafford NH 03884, USA
Simien, Tracy A — Football Player
409 N Martin Luther King St, Sweeny TX 77480, USA
Simitis, Konstantinos (Kostas) — Prime Minister, Greece
Maximus Mansion, Herodou Atticou 19, 10674 Athens, Greece
Simmer, Charlie — Ice Hockey Player
70 Coulee View SW, Calgary AB T3H 5J6, Canada
Simmonds, Kennedy A — Prime Minister, Saint Kitts & Nevis
PO Box 167, Earle Morne Development, Basseterre, Saint Kitts & Nevis
Simmons, Adele S — Foundation Executive, Educator
Catherine T MacArthur Foundation, 140 S Dearborn St, #1000, Chicago IL 60603, USA
Simmons, Bill — Sportscaster
ESPN-TV, ESPN Plaza, 935 Middle St, Bristol CT 06010 USA
Simmons, Brian E — Football Player
6417 Lake Burden View Dr, Windermere FL 34786, USA
Simmons, Brian L — Baseball Player
226 Village Dr, Canonsburg PA 15317, USA
Simmons, Chelan — Actress
Intellectual Artists Mgmt, 10585 Santa Monica Blvd, #135, Los Angeles CA 90025, USA
Simmons, Clyde, Jr — Football Player
3948 3rd St S, #344, Jacksonville Beach FL 32250, USA
Simmons, Curtis T (Curt) — Baseball Player
200 Park Road, Ambler PA 19002, USA
Simmons, Dan — Writer
Little Brown, 3 Center Plaza, #100, Boston MA 02108 USA
Simmons, Don — Ice Hockey Player
4998 Skerkston Road, RR 1, Ridgway ON L0S 1N9, Canada
Simmons, Gene — Singer, Bassist (Kiss)
Gene Simmons Co, PO Box 16075, Beverly Hills CA 90209, USA
Simmons, H A Kendall — Football Player
1725 Altamont Court, Auburn AL 36830, USA
Simmons, Harris H — Financier
Zions Bancorp, 1 S Main St, Salt Lake City UT 84133, USA
Simmons, Henry — Actor
Principato-Young, 9465 Wilshire Blvd, #880, Beverly Hills CA 90212 USA
Simmons, J K — Actor
Gersh Agency, 41 Madison Ave, #3301, New York NY 10010 USA
Simmons, Jaason — Actor
Gilbertson Entertainment, 1334 3rd Street Promenade, #201, Santa Monica CA 90401 USA
Simmons, Jason L — Football Player
2307 Cezanne Circle, Missouri City TX 77459, USA
Simmons, Jerry B — Football Player
30227 Avenida Selecta, Rancho Palos Verdes CA 90275, USA
Simmons, Johnny — Actor
W M E Entertainment, 9601 Wilshire Blvd, #300, Beverly Hills CA 90210 USA
Simmons, Joseph — Rap Artist (Run-DMC)
Richard Walters, PO Box 2789, Toluca Lake CA 91610 USA
Simmons, Kimora Lee — Model, Fashion Designer
Phat Fashions, 512 Fashion Ave, #4300, New York NY 10018, USA
Simmons, Lionel J — Basketball Player
108 Wellesley Court, Mount Laurel NJ 08054, USA
Simmons, Nelson B — Baseball Player
4445 Rosebud Lane, #B, La Mesa CA 91941, USA
Simmons, Richard — Physical Fitness Instructor
Richard Simmons Inc, 8899 Beverly Blvd, #811, Los Angeles CA 90048, USA
Simmons, Robert G (Bob) — Football Player
16040 Chalfont Circle, Dallas TX 75248, USA
Simmons, Rudd — Producer
Claire Best Assoc, 736 Seward St, Los Angeles CA 90038, USA
Simmons, Russell — Music Producer, Fashion Designer
Simmons-Lathan Media Group, 6100 Wilshire Blvd, #1111, Los Angeles CA 90048, USA
Simmons, Ruth J — Educator
Brown University, President's Office, Providence RI 02912, USA

Simmons, Tabitha — Stylist, Shoe Designer
Tabitha Simmons Accessories, 601 West 26th St, #309, New York, NY 10001, USA

Simmons, Ted L — Baseball Player
PO Box 26, Chesterfield MO 63006, USA

Simms, Christopher D (Chris) — Football Player
811 Lynnbrook Road, Nashville TN 37215, USA

Simms, Larry — Actor
3441 Lewis Ave, Long Beach CA 90807, USA

Simms, Michael E (Mike) — Baseball Player
PO Box 96011, Southlake TX 76092, USA

Simms, Philip (Phil) — Football Player, Sportscaster
930 Old Mill Road, Franklin Lakes NJ 07417, USA

Simms, Travis — Boxer
28 Martin Luther King, #43, South Norwalk CT 06854, USA

Simollardes, Drew — Singer (Reveille)
David Levin Mgmt, 200 W 57th St, #308, New York NY 10019, USA

Simon, Bob — Commentator
CBS-TV, News Dept, 2020 M St NW, Washington DC 20036 USA

Simon, Carly — Singer, Songwriter
Ciancia Mgmt, 1 William Morris Place, Beverly Hills CA 90212, USA

Simon, Chris — Ice Hockey Player
PO Box 1, Wawa ON P0S 1K0, Canada

Simon, Corey J — Football Player
6089 Leigh Read Road, Tallahassee FL 32309, USA

Simon, David — Producer, Writer, Actor
Creative Artists Agency, 2000 Ave of Stars, #100, Los Angeles CA 90067 USA

Simon, Dick — Auto Racing Executive
24896 SeaCrest Dr, Dana Point CA 92829, USA

Simon, George W — Astronaut
PO Box 62, Sunspot NM 88349, USA

Simon, Hugh — Actor
Ken McReddie Assoc, 11 Connaught Place, London W2 2ET, England

Simon, James E (Jim) — Football Player
8501 SW 103rd Ave, Gainesville FL 32608, USA

Simon, John I — Film, Drama Critic
New York Magazine, Editorial Dept, 444 Madison Ave, #1400, New York NY 10022, USA

Simon, Josette — Actress
Conway Van Gelder Grant, 8-12 Broadwick St, #300, London W1F 8HW, England

Simon, Leon M — Mathematician
Stanford University, Mathematics Dept, Stanford CA 94305, USA

Simon, Lou Anna — Educator
Michigan State University, President's Office, East Lansing MI 48824, USA

Simon, Melvin I — Biologist
California Institute of Technology, Biology Dept, Pasadena CA 91125, USA

Simon, Neil — Writer
350 Park Ave, #1600, New York NY 10022, USA

Simon, Paul — Singer, Guitarist, Songwriter
Paul Simon Music, 1619 Broadway, #500, New York NY 10019, USA

Simon, Sam — Producer, Writer, Animator
Paradigm Agency, 360 N Crescent Dr, North Building, Beverly Hills CA 90210 USA

Simon, Scott — Commentator, Writer
NBC-TV, News Dept, 30 Rockefeller Plaza, #270E, New York NY 10112 USA

Simonds, Charles F — Sculptor, Architect
26 E 22nd St, New York NY 10010, USA

Simone, Hannah — Actress
Gersh Agency, 9465 Wilshire Blvd, #600, Beverly Hills CA 90212 USA

Simoneau, Mark L — Football Player
1018 Park Ave, Rose Hill KS 67133, USA

Simoneau, Yves — Director
W M E Entertainment, 9601 Wilshire Blvd, #300, Beverly Hills CA 90210 USA

Simonini, Edward C (Ed) — Football Player
3825 E 66th St, Tulsa OK 74136, USA

Simonis, Adrianus J Cardinal — Religious Leader
Aartsbisdom, BP 14019, Maliebaan, 3508 SB Utrecht, Netherlands

Simonov, Yuriy I — Conductor
Moscow Symphony Orchestra, Gorky Park, 9 Krymsky Val, 119049 Moscow, Russia

Simons, Douglas E (Doug) — Baseball Player
1988 Mount Olive Road, Lookout Mountain GA 30750, USA

Simons, Ed — Singer, Musician (Chemical Brothers)
9PR, 65-69 White Lion St, London N1 9PR, England

Simons, Elwyn L — Anthropologist
Duke University, Primate Center, 3705 Erwin Road, Durham NC 27705, USA

Simons, Raf — Fashion Designer
House of Dior, 30 Ave Montaigne 75008 Paris, France

Simons, Timothy (Tim) — Actor
United Talent Agency, 9336 Civic Center Dr, Beverly Hills CA 90210 USA

Simontacchi, Jason — Baseball Player
6924 Birdie Lane, Saint Louis MO 63129, USA

Simonyan, Mikhail — Concert Violinist
I M G Artists, 152 W 57th St, #500, New York NY 10019 USA

Simonyi, Charles — Tourist Cosmonaut
International Software Corp, 2821 Northup Way, #250, Bellevue WA 98004, USA

Simpkins, L Dixon (Dickey) — Basketball Player
6104 Saint Andrews Way, Hixson TN 37343, USA

Simpson, Alan — Educator
Yellow Gate Farm, Little Compton RI 02837, USA

Simpson, Alan K — Senator, WY
1201 Sunshine Ave, PO Box 270, Cody WY 82414, USA

Simpson, Ashlee — Singer, Songwriter, Actress
Creative Artists Agency, 2000 Ave of Stars, #100, Los Angeles CA 90067 USA

Simpson, Bill — Auto Racing Executive
Simpson Performance Products, 328 FM 306, New Braunfels TX 78130, USA

Simpson, Bobby — Ice Hockey Player
4779 Limestone Lane NW, Acworth GA 30102, USA

Simpson, Carl W — Football Player
2507 Brentwood Road, Decatur GA 30032, USA

Simpson, Carole — Commentator
ABC-TV, News Dept, 77 W 66th St, New York NY 10023 USA

Simpson, Charles R — Judge
US Tax Court, 400 2nd St NW, Washington DC 20217, USA

Simpson, Claire — Film Editor
Independent Talent Group, Oxford House, 76 Oxford St, London W1D 1BS, England

Simpson, Cody — Singer, Songwriter
PO Box 1766, Studio City CA 91614, USA

Simpson, Craig — Ice Hockey Player
CBC-TV, PO Box 500, Station A, Toronto ON M5W 1E6, Canada

Simpson, Daryl — Singer (Celtic Tenors)
PO Box 32, Kells, County Meath, Ireland

Simpson, Derrick (Duckie) — Singer (Black Uhuru)
Agency Group, 9348 Civic Center Dr, #200, Beverly Hills CA 90210 USA

Simpson, Geoffrey — Cinematographer
PO Box 3194, Bellevue Hills NSW 2023, Australia

Simpson, J F Webb — Golfer
Professional Golfer's Assn, PO Box 109601, Palm Beach Gardens FL 33410 USA

Simpson, Jessica — Singer, Songwriter, Actress, Model
Sony Pictures Entertainment, 10202 W Washington Blvd, Culver City CA 90232, USA

Simpson, Jimmi — Actor
W M E Entertainment, 9601 Wilshire Blvd, #300, Beverly Hills CA 90210 USA

Simpson, Joe A — Baseball Player
4681 Jefferson Township Lane, Marietta GA 30066, USA

Simpson, Josh — Artist
Frank Williams Road, Shelburne Falls MA 01370, USA

Simpson, Juliene Brazinski — Basketball Player
PO Box 1267, Stroudsburg PA 18360, USA

Simpson, Martin — Guitarist
Adastra-Moneypenny, 2 Star Row, Driffield, E Yorkshire YO25 9Xa, England

Simpson, Orenthal James (O J) — Football Player, Actor, Sportscaster
Lovelock Correctional Center, #1027820, 1200 Prison Road, Lovelock NV 89419, USA

Simpson, Ralph D — Basketball Player
7578 S Duquesne Way, Aurora CO 80016, USA

Simpson, Richard C (Dick) — Baseball Player
PO Box 3593, Culver City CA 90231, USA

Simpson, Scott — Golfer
15778 Paseo Hermosa, Poway CA 92064, USA

Simpson, Suzi — Model, Actress
24338 El Toro Road, #E315, Laguna Woods CA 92637, USA

Simpson, Tim — Golfer
1061 Spy Glass Hill, Greensboro GA 30642, USA

Simpson, Tom — Keyboardist (Snow Patrol)
Big Life Mgmt, 67-69 Charlton St, London NW1 1HY, England

Simpson, Valerie — Singer (Ashford & Simpson), Songwriter
Spirit Media, PO Box 43591, Phoenix AZ 85080, USA

Simpson, Wayne K — Baseball Player
330 E Collamer Dr, Carson CA 90746, USA

Simpson, William T (Bill) — Football Player
5732 Huntley Ave, Garden Grove CA 92845, USA

Simpson-Miller, Portia L — Prime Minister, Jamaica
Prime Minister's Office, 1 Devon Road, PO Box 272, Kingston 6, Jamaica

Sims, Allan E (Al) — Ice Hockey Player
4215 Winding Way Dr, Fort Wayne IN 46835, USA

Sims, Barry A — Football Player
369 Golden Grass Dr, Alamo CA 94507, USA

Sims, Billy R — Football Player
PO Box 3147, Coppell TX 75019, USA

Sims, Christopher A (Chris) — Economist
Princeton University, Economics Dept, Princeton NJ 08544, USA

Sims, Duane B (Duke) — Baseball Player
10509 Shoalhaven Dr, Las Vegas NV 89134, USA

Sims, Ernie, III — Football Player
Indianapolis Colts, 7001 W 56th St, Indianapolis IN 46254 USA

Sims, Jocko — Actor
Benedetti Management, 13101 W Washington Blvd, #234, Culver City CA 90066, USA

Sims, Keith A — Football Player
1522 SW 37th St, Fort Lauderdale FL 33312, USA

Sims, Kenneth W (Ken) — Football Player
PO Box 236, Kosse TX 76653, USA

Sims, Molly — Model, Actress
W M E Entertainment, 9601 Wilshire Blvd, #300, Beverly Hills CA 90210 USA

Sims, Neil — Drummer (Catherine Wheel)
Paradigm Agency, 360 Park Ave, #1600, New York NY 10022 USA

Sims, Robert A (Bob) — Basketball Player
915 Highland Ave, #3, Duarte CA 91010, USA

Sims, Ryan O — Football Player
311 Yellow Poplar Terrace, Spartanburg SC 29306, USA

Sinatra, Christina (Tina) — Actress, Writer
30966 Broach Beach Road, Malibu CA 90265, USA

Sinatra, Nancy — Singer, Actress
Boots Enterprises, PO Box 10236, Beverly Hills CA 90213, USA

Sinatro, Matthew S (Matt) — Baseball Player
2619 239th Ave SE, Sammamish WA 98075, USA

Sinbad — Actor, Comedian
A P A Talent/Literary Agency, 405 S Beverly Dr, #300, Beverly Hills CA 90212 USA

Sinclair, Christine M — Soccer Player
Western New York Flash, Sahlen Sports Park, 7070 Seneca St, Elma NY 14059, USA

Sinclair, Claire — Model, Actress
Playboy Promotions, 2706 Media Center Dr, Los Angeles CA 90065 USA

Sinclair, Clive M — Inventor (Pocket Calculator)
Sinclair Research, 7 York Central, 70 York Way, London N1 9AG, England

Sinclair, Michael G (Mike) — Football Player
1914 Pannell St, Houston TX 77020, USA

Sinclair, Nancy — Actress
Studio Talent Group, 1328 12th St, Santa Monica CA 90401, USA

Sinclair, Reggie — Ice Hockey Player
10 Golf Club Court, Rothesay NB E2H 2P1, Canada

Sindelar, Joey — Golfer
18 Prospect Ridge, Horseheads NY 14845, USA

Sinden, Donald A — Actor
Rats Castle, Isle of Oxney, Kent TN30 7HX, England

Sinden, Harold J (Harry) — Ice Hockey Player, Coach, Executive
9 Olde Village Dr, Winchester MA 01890, USA

Sinegal, James — Businessman
Costco Wholesale Corp, 999 Lake Dr, #200, Issaquah WA 98027, USA

Singer, Bryan — Director, Producer
Bad Hat Productions, 10201 W Pico Blvd, Building 50, Los Angeles CA 90064, USA

Singer, Eric W — Drummer (Kiss, Alice Cooper)
E D M Productions, 11684 Ventura Blvd, #408, Studio City CA 91604, USA

Singer, Isadore M — Abel Mathematics Laureate
Massachusetts Institute of Technology, Mathematics Dept, Cambridge MA 02139, USA

Singer, Jerome L — Psychologist
Yale University, Zigler Center, New Haven CT 06520, USA

Singer, Lori — Actress
Jackoway Tyerman Wertheimer, 1925 Century Park E, #2200, Los Angeles CA 90067 USA

Singer, Marc — Actor
David Shapira Assoc, 193 N Robertson Blvd, Beverly Hills CA 90211 USA

Singer, Maxine F — Educator, Molecular Biochemist
5410 39th St NW, Washington DC 20015, USA

Singer, Peter A D — Philosopher, Ethicist
Princeton University, Human Values Center, Princeton NJ 08544, USA

Singer, Rachel — Actress
Bauman Assoc, 250 W 57th St, #2223, New York NY 10107 USA

Singer, William R (Bill) — Baseball Player
1119 Mallard Marsh Dr, Osprey FL 34229, USA

Singh, Amrita — Actress
Lokhandwala Complex, #5, Andheri Link Road, Mumbai MS 400058, India

Singh, Bipin — Dancer, Choreographer
Manipuri Nartanalaya, 15A Bipin Pal Road, Kolkata 700026, India

Singh, Tjinder — Singer (Cornershop)
Zzonked Public Relations, Burford Road, London E15 2SP, England

Singh, Vijay — Golfer
210 N Serenata Dr, #532, Ponte Vedra Beach FL 32082, USA

Singler, Kyle E — Basketball Player
Detroit Pistons, Palace, 4 Championship Dr, Auburn Hills MI 48326 USA

Singletary, Daryle — Singer
Bobby Roberts, 3050 Business Park Circle, #303, Goodlettsville TN 37221 USA

Singletary, Michael (Mike) — Football Player, Coach
18411 Nicklaus Way, Eden Prairie MN 55347, USA

Singletary, Tony — Director
A P A Talent/Literary Agency, 405 S Beverly Dr, #300, Beverly Hills CA 90212 USA

Singleton, Alshermond G (Al) — Football Player
8 Cromwell Dr, Chester NJ 07930, USA

Singleton, Chris — Football Player
4700 S Fulton Ranch Blvd, #63, Chandler AZ 85248, USA

Singleton, Christopher V (Chris) — Baseball Player
2038 Town Manor Court, Dacula GA, Belgium 30019, USA

Singleton, Isaac — Actor
Coolwaters Productions, 10061 Riverside Dr, Box 531, Toluca Lake CA 91602 USA

Singleton, Kenneth W (Kenny) — Baseball Player
10 Sparks Farm Road, Sparks MD 21152, USA

Singleton, Margie — Singer
Country Music Spectacular, PO Box 567, Hendersonville TN 37077, USA

Singleton, William D — Publisher
MediaNews Group, 101 W Colfax Ave, Denver CO 80202, USA

Sinha, Mala — Actress
8 Turner Road, Bandra, Mumbai MS 400050, India

Sinha, Shatrughan — Actor
104 Green Star Apts, Sherly Rajan Road, Bandra, Mumbai MS 400050, India

Sinisalo, Ikka — Ice Hockey Player
6221 Main St, Voorhees NJ 08043, USA

Sinise, Gary — Actor
Creative Artists Agency, 2000 Ave of Stars, #100, Los Angeles CA 90067 USA

Sinise, Moira — Actress
Creative Artists Agency, 2000 Ave of Stars, #100, Los Angeles CA 90067 USA

Sinkford, William — Religious Leader
Unitarian Universalist Assn, President's Office, 25 Beacon St, Boston MA 02108, USA

Sinn, Pearl — Golfer
132 21st Place, Manhattan Beach CA 90266, USA

Sinner, George A — Governor, ND
101 3rd St N, Moorhead MN 56560, USA

Sinsheimer, Robert L — Biologist, Educator
4606 Via Cavente, Santa Barbara CA 93110, USA

Sinyavskaya, Tamara I — Opera Singer
Kunstleragentur Raab & Bohm, Plankengasse 7, 1010 Vienna, Austria

Siorpaes, Gildo — Bobsled Athlete
Olympic Committee, Foro Italico, Largo Lauro de Bosis 15, 00135 Rome, Italy

Siouxsie Sioux — Singer (Siouxsie & the Banshees)
Helter Skelter, 347-353 Chiswick High Road, London W4 4HS, England

Sipchen, Bob — Journalist
Los Angeles Times, Editorial Dept, 202 W 1st St, Los Angeles CA 90012 USA

Sipe, Brian W — Football Player
1630 Luneta Dr, Del Mar CA 92014, USA

Sipinen, Arto K — Architect
Munkkiniemenranta 39, 00330 Helsinki, Finland

Sipos, Shaun — Actor
Innovative Artists, 1505 10th St, Santa Monica CA 90401 USA

Sir Mix-A-Lot — Rap Artist
Richard Walters, PO Box 2789, Toluca Lake CA 91610 USA

Siraguso, Tony — Football Player, Sportscaster
15 Annabelle Lane, Florham Park NJ 07932, USA

Sircar, Tiya — Actress
John Carrabino Mgmt, 5900 Wilshire Blvd, #406, Los Angeles CA 90036, USA

Siren, Heikki — Architect
Tiirasaarentie 35, 00200 Helsinki, Finland

Siren, Katri A H — Architect
Tiirasaarentie 35, 00200 Helsinki, Finland

Siren, Ville — Ice Hockey Player
Saint Louis Blues, Scott Trade Center, 1401 Clark Ave, Saint Louis MO 63103 USA

Sirgo, Otto — Actor, Director
Televisa, Blvd A Lopez Mateos 232, Colonia San Angel, DF CP 01060, Mexico

Siri Singh Sahib — Religious Leader
Sikh, PO Box 351149, Los Angeles CA 90035, USA

Sirico, Tony — Actor
McGowan Mgmt, 8733 W Sunset Blvd, #103, West Hollywood CA 90069 USA

Sirikit — Queen, Thailand
Royal Residence, Chitralada Villa, 9 Rama VI Road, Soi 30, Bangkok 10400, Thailand

Sirindhorn — Princess, Thailand
Royal Residence, Chitralada Villa, 9 Rama VI Road, Soi 30, Bangkok 10400, Thailand

Sirleaf, Ellen Johnson — President, Liberia; Nobel Peace Laureate
President's Office, Executive Mansion, Capitol Hill, Monrovia, Liberia

Sirmon, Peter A — Football Player
5729 Sterling Oaks Dr, Brentwood TN 37027, USA

Sirola, Joseph A — Actor
T G M D Talent, 6767 Forest Lawn Dr, #101, Los Angeles CA 90068, USA

Sirtis, Marina — Actress
Polaris Entertainment, 8048 W 3rd St, #300, Los Angeles CA 90048 USA

Sisemore, Jerald G (Jerry) — Football Player
17301 Whippoorwill Trail, Leander TX 78645, USA

Sisk, Douglas R (Doug) — Baseball Player
3610 42nd Ave NE, Tacoma WA 98422, USA

Sisk, Tommie W — Baseball Player
164 E 4635 N, Provo UT 84604, USA

Siska, Adam T — Bassist (Academy Is)
Decaydance Records, 9229 W Sunset Blvd, #900, West Hollywood CA 90069, USA

Siskin, Paul — Interior Designer
Siskin Valls Inc, 21 W 58th St, #2B, New York NY 10019, USA

Sislen, Myrna — Concert Guitarist
Lindy Martin Mgmt, 1007 Lakewater Dr, Henrico VA 23229, USA

Sisqo — Singer (Dru Hill)
I C M Partners, 10250 Constellation Blvd, #900, Los Angeles CA 90067 USA

Sissel — Singer
Stageway Impressario, Skuteviksboder 11, 5035 Bergen, Norway

Sister Bliss — Musician (Faithless)
Helter Skelter, 347-353 Chiswick High Road, London W4 4HS, England

Sister Max — Fashion Designer
Mount Everest Centre for Buddhist Studies, Katmandu, Nepal

Sisto, Jeremy — Actor
United Talent Agency, 9336 Civic Center Dr, Beverly Hills CA 90210 USA

Sistrunk, Manuel (Manny) — Football Player
3856 Williams Road, Montgomery AL 36110, USA

Sistrunk, Otis — Football Player
PO Box 372, Dupont WA 98327, USA

Sitbon, Martine — Fashion Designer
6 Rue de Braque, 75003 Paris, France

Sites, Brian — Actor
Innovative Artists, 1505 10th St, Santa Monica CA 90401 USA

Sitkovetsky, Dmitry — Concert Violinist, Conductor
Kunstleragentur Raab & Bohm, Plankengasse 7, 1010 Vienna, Austria

Sittenfeld, Curtis — Writer
Random House, 1745 Broadway, #1800, New York NY 10019 USA

Sittler, Darryl G — Ice Hockey Player
18 Jedburgh Road, Toronto ON M5M 3J6, Canada

Sittler, Walter — Actor
Strossackerstr 81A, 70563 Stuttgart, Germany

Sitton, Charles E (Charlie) — Basketball Player
3035 SW Homesteader Road, West Linn OR 97068, USA

Sivad, Darryl — Actor
Commercial Talent, 9255 Sunset Blvd, #505, Los Angeles CA 90069, USA

Siwy, James G (Jim) — Baseball Player
6919 April Wind Ave, Las Vegas NV 89131, USA

Sixx, Nikki — Singer, Bassist, Drummer (Motley Crue)
936 Vista Ridge Lane, Westlake Village CA 91362, USA

Siza, Alvaro — Pritzker Architectural Laureate
Oporto University, Architecture School, 4150 755 Oporto, Portugal

Sizemore, Grady, III — Baseball Player
1951 W 26th St, #512, Cleveland OH 44113, USA

Sizemore, Ted C — Baseball Player
14030 Conway Road, Chesterfield MO 63017, USA

Sizemore, Tom — Actor
Global Artists Agency, 6253 Hollywood Blvd, #508, Los Angeles CA 90028 USA

Sizova, Alla I — Ballerina
Universal Ballet School, 4301 Harewood Road NE, Washington DC 20017, USA

Sjoberg, Patrik — Track Athlete
Hokegatan 17, 416 66 Goteberg, Sweden

Sjoland, Patrik — Golfer
PGA European Tour, Wentworth Drive, Virginia Water Surrey GU25 4LX, England

Sjooblom, Lenna — Model
Playboy Promotions, 2706 Media Center Dr, Los Angeles CA 90065 USA

Sjostrom, Fredrik — Ice Hockey Player
18362 N 94th Place, Scottsdale AZ 85255, USA

Skabo, Paul — Test Pilot
260 Calle Aragon, #D, Laguna Woods CA 92637, USA

Skaggs, David L (Dave) — Baseball Player
11131 Arlington Ave, Riverside CA 92505, USA

Skaggs, James L (Jimmie) — Football Player
421 Falcon Ridge Road, Ellensburg WA 98926, USA

Skaggs, Ricky — Singer, Guitarist
380 Forest Retreat, Hendersonville TN 37075, USA
Skah, Khalid — Track Athlete
Boite Postale 2577, Fez, Morocco
Skalde, Jarrod — Ice Hockey Player
305 1/2 E Front St, Bloomington IL 61701, USA
Skalski, Joseph D (Joe) — Baseball Player
15546 Drexel Ave, Dolton IL 60419, USA
Skansi, Paul A — Football Player
23795 Brixton Place, Poulsbo WA 98370, USA
Skarda, Randy — Ice Hockey Player
26885 Noble Road, Excelsior MN 55331, USA
Skaricic, Marija — Actress
Croatian Audiovisual Center, Nova Ves 18, 10 000 Zacreb, Croatia
Skarmeta, Antonio — Writer
Mohrenstr 42, 10117 Berlin, Germany
Skarsgard, Alexander J H — Actor
Principal Entertainment, 1964 Westwood Blvd, #400, Los Angeles CA 90025 USA
Skarsgard, Bill — Actor
Agentfirman Planthaber/Kildén, Drottninggatan 55, 111 21 Stockholm, Sweden
Skarsten, Rachel — Actress
Creative Drive Artists, 66 King St E, #400, Toronto ON M5A 1J3, Canada
Skaugstad, David W (Dave) — Baseball Player
16222 Monterey Lane, #274, Huntington Beach CA 92649, USA
Skeggs, Leonard T, Jr — Biochemist
10212 Blair Lane, Willoughby OH 44094, USA
Skelly, James — Singer (Coral)
S J M Mgmt, St Matthews, Liverpool Road, Manchester M3 4NQ, England
Skelton, Byron G — Judge
US Court of Appeals, 717 Madison Ave NW, Washington DC 20439, USA
Skelton, Richard K (Rich), Jr — Rodeo Rider
1139 County Road 312, Llano TX 78643, USA
Skelton, Stuart — Opera Singer
I M G Artists, Hogarth Business Park, Chiswick, London W4 2TH, England
Skerrit, Roosevelt — Prime Minister, Dominica
Premier's Office, Government Headquarters, Kennedy Ave, Roseau, Dominica
Skerritt, Tom — Actor
Pitt Group, 9465 Wilshire Blvd, #420, Beverly Hills CA 90212, USA
Skiba, Matthew T (Matt) — Singer, Guitarist (Alkaline Trio)
X-Ray Touring, 77-79 Great Eastern St, London EC2A 3HU, England
Skibbie, Lawrence F — Army General
2309 S Queen St, Arlington VA 22202, USA
Skidmore, R Roe — Baseball Player
964 E Martin Dr, Decature IL 62521, USA
Skiles, Scott A — Basketball Player, Coach
3975 S Inverness Farm Road, Bloomington IN 47401, USA
Skillings, Muzz — Bassist (Living Colour)
Entertainment Artists, PO Box 120824, Nashville TN 37212 USA
Skin — Singer (Skunk Anansie)
13 Artists, 11-14 Kensington St, Brighton BN1 4AJ, England
Skinner, Albert L (Al) — Basketball Player, Coach
145 Great Plain Ave, Wellesley MA 02482, USA
Skinner, Claire — Actress
Markham & Froggatt, Julian House, 4 Windmill St, London W1P 1HF, England
Skinner, Joel P — Baseball Player
275 Pamilla Circle, Avon Lake OH 44012, USA
Skinner, John A (Jonty) — Swimmer, Coach
University of Alabama, Athletic Dept, Tuscaloosa AL 35487, USA
Skinner, Julie — Curling Athlete
Curling Assn, 1660 Vimont Court, Cumberland ON K4A 4J4, Canada
Skinner, Mike — Auto, Truck Racing Driver
Mike Skinner Enterprises, 201 Cessna Blvd, #4, Port Orange FL 32128, USA
Skinner, Robert R (Bob) — Baseball Player, Manager
1576 Diamond St, San Diego CA 92109, USA
Skinner, Samuel K — Secretary, Transportation; Businessman
Commonwealth Edison, 1 First National Plaza, PO Box 767, Chicago IL 60690, USA
Skinner, Sonny — Golfer
114 Northlake Dr, Sylvester GA 31791, USA
Skinner, Val — Golfer
44 Bridge Ave, Bay Head NJ 08742, USA
Skizas, Louis P (Lou) — Baseball Player
2101 W White St, #118, Champaign IL 61821, USA
Skjelbreid, Ann-Elen — Biathlete
5640 Eikelandsosen, Norway
Skjvorecky, Josef — Writer
Erindale College, English Dept, Toronto ON M5S 1A5, Canada
Skladany, Thomas E (Tom) — Football Player
6666 Highland Lakes Place, Westerville OH 43082, USA
Skloff, Michael — Composer
Gorfaine/Schwartz, 4111 W Alameda Ave, #509, Burbank CA 91505 USA
Skoglund, Sandy — Photographer, Sculptor
Janet Borden, 560 Broadway, #601, New York NY 10012, USA
Skok, Craig R — Baseball Player
981 Slash Pine Way, Lawrenceville GA 30043, USA
Skolimowski, Jerzy — Director, Actor
Film Polski, Ul Mazowiecka 6/8, 00-048 Warsaw, Poland
Skolnick, Mark H — Geneticist
University of Utah Medical Center, Genetics Dept, Salt Lake City UT 84112, USA
Skolnikoff, Eugene B — Political Scientist
1010 Waltham St, #542, Lexington MA 2421, USA
Skoog, Meyer U (Whitey) — Basketball Player, Coach
1302 W Traverse Road, #203, Saint Peter MN 56082, USA
Skorodenski, Warren — Ice Hockey Player
161 MacEwan Ridge Circle NW, Calgary AB T3K 3W3, Canada
Skoronski, Robert F (Bob) — Football Player
3807 Signature Dr, Middletown WI 53562, USA

Skorton, David J — Educator
Cornell University, President's Office, Ithaca NY 14853, USA
Skorupan, John P — Football Player
142 Crossing Ridge Trail, Cranberry Township PA 16066, USA
Skotheim, Robert A — Museum Executive
2120 Place Road, Port Angeles WA 98363, USA
Skou, Jens C — Nobel Chemistry Laureate
Rislundvej 9, Risskov 8240, Denmark
Skoula, Martin — Ice Hockey Player
2441 Sheridan Ave S, Minneapolis MN 55405, USA
Skouras, Thanos — Economist
8 Chlois St, 145 62 Athens, Greece
Skov, Glen — Ice Hockey Player
3898 Timber Ridge Court, Palm Harbor FL 34685, USA
Skovhus, Bo — Opera Singer
Balmer & Dixon Mgmt, Granitweg 2, 8006 Zurich, Switzerland
Skow, James J (Jim) — Football Player
748 Knollview Blvd, Ormond Beach FL 32174, USA
Skream — Electronic Musician (Magnetic Man)
Columbia Records, 9 Derry St, London W8 5HY, England
Skrebneski, Victor — Photographer
1350 N LaSalle Dr, Chicago IL 60610, USA
Skrepenak, Gregory A (Greg) — Football Player
Hyders Total Fitness Center, 400 Middle Road, Nanticoke PA 18634, USA
Skride, Baiba — Concert Violinist
Konzertdirektion Schmid, Konigstra 36, 30175 Hannover, Germany
Skriko, Petri — Ice Hockey Player
Kirjatyontekijankatu 4 A 3, Helsinki 00170, Finland
Skripochka, Oleg I — Cosmonaut
Cosmonaut Training Center, Star City, 141160 Zvezdny Gorodok, Moscow Oblast, Russia
Skrmetta, Matt — Baseball Player
827 Poinsetta Dr, Indian Harbour Beach FL 32937, USA
Skrovan, Steve — Actor, Comedian, Producer
W M E Entertainment, 9601 Wilshire Blvd, #300, Beverly Hills CA 90210 USA
Skrowaczewski, Stanislaw — Conductor, Composer
Minnesota Symphony, 1111 Nicollet Mall, Minneapolis MN 55403, USA
Skrudland, Brian — Ice Hockey Player
Argo Sales, 717 7th Ave SW, #1300, Calgary AB T2P 0Z3, Canada
Skube, Robert J (Bob) — Baseball Player
4153 W Charlotte Dr, Glendale AZ 85310, USA
Skvortsov, Alexander A — Cosmonaut
Cosmonaut Training Center, Star City, 141160 Zvezdny Gorodok, Moscow Oblast, Russia
Sky, Alison — Environmental Artist
60 Greene St, New York NY 10012, USA
Sky, Amy — Singer, Songwriter
Agency Group Ltd, 142 W 57th St, #600, New York NY 10019 USA
Sky, Jennifer — Actress
Dunham Literary, 110 William St, #2202, New York NY 10038 10038, USA
Skye, Azura — Actress
B/W/R, 9100 Wilshire Blvd, #500W, Beverly Hills CA 90212 USA
Skye, Ione — Actress
Sager Mgmt, 260 S Beverly Dr, #205, Beverly Hills CA 90212, USA
Skyrms, Brian — Philosopher
University of California, Philosophy Dept, Irvine CA 92697, USA
Slack, Reggie — Football Player
5973 Queen St, Milton FL 32570, USA
Slade, Bernard N — Writer
345 N Saltair Ave, Los Angeles CA 90049, USA
Slade, Chris — Drummer (AC/DC)
11 Leominster Road, Morden, Surrey SA4 6HN, England
Slade, Christopher C (Chris) — Football Player
4163 Onslow Place SE, Smyrna GA 30080, USA
Slade, David — Actor, Comedian, Director
Anonymous Content, 3532 Hayden Ave, Culver City CA 90232 USA
Slade, Isaac — Singer, Pianist (Fray)
A2 Mgmt, 624 Davis St, #200, Evanston IL 60201, USA
Slade, Jeff — Basketball Player
5354 Farmington Road, Toledo OH 43623, USA
Slade, Mark — Actor
38 Joppa Road, Worcester MA 01602, USA
Slade, Roy — Artist, Museum Executive
31 Island Way, #801, Clearwater FL 33767, USA
Slagle, James R — Computer Scientist
Massachusetts Institute of Technology, Mathematics Dept, Cambridge MA 02139, USA
Slagle, Roger L — Baseball Player
536 W 3rd St, Larned KS 67550, USA
Slaney, John — Ice Hockey Player
96 Mullen Dr, Sicklerville NJ 08081, USA
Slaney, Mary Decker — Track Athlete
87141 Kellmore St, Eugene OR 97402, USA
Slash — Singer, Guitarist (Guns N' Roses)
Collective, 8383 Wilshire Blvd, #1050, Beverly Hills CA 90211 USA
Slate, Jenny — Actress, Comedianne
W M E Entertainment, 9601 Wilshire Blvd, #300, Beverly Hills CA 90210 USA
Slaten, Douglas (Doug) — Baseball Player
233 Rennie Ave, Venice CA 90291, USA
Slater, Christian — Actor
United Talent Agency, 9336 Civic Center Dr, Beverly Hills CA 90210 USA
Slater, Helen — Actress
DeSante Frank Co, 10061 Riverside Dr, #377, Toluca Lake CA 91602, USA
Slater, Jackie R — Football Player
PO Box 6411, Orange CA 92863, USA
Slater, Kelly — Surfer, Actor
Quicksilver, 15202 Graham St, Huntington Beach CA 92649, USA
Slater, Mark W — Football Player
10545 Rome Ave, Young America MN 55397, USA

Slater, Reggie — Basketball Player
8 Saint Christopher Court, Sugar Land TX 77479, USA
Slater, Rodney E — Secretary, Transportation
Paton Boggs, 2050 M St NW, Washington DC 20036, USA
Slatkin, Leonard E — Conductor
Detroit Symphony, 3711 Woodward Ave, Detroit MI 48201, USA
Slaton, Anthony T (Tony) — Football Player
122 E Childs Ave, Merced CA 95341, USA
Slaton, James M (Jim) — Baseball Player
4082 N Arbor Lane, Buckeye AZ 85396, USA
Slattery, Anthony D J (Tony) — Actor
Belfield & Ward, 80-81 Saint Martin's Lane, London WC2N 4AA, England
Slattery, John M, Jr — Actor
Gersh Agency, 9465 Wilshire Blvd, #600, Beverly Hills CA 90212 USA
Slattvik, Simon — Nordic Combined Athlete
Bankgata 22, 2600 Lillehammer, Norway
Slaught, Donald M (Don) — Baseball Player
27 Middleridge Lane S, Rolling Hills CA 90274, USA
Slaughter, Karin — Writer
Delacorte Press, 1540 Broadway, New York NY 10036 USA
Slaughter, Tavaris J (T J) — Football Player
2035 Pinehurst Dr, Gardendale AL 35071, USA
Slaughter, Webster M — Football Player
3706 Rory Court, Missouri City TX 77459, USA
Slavin, Jonathan — Actor
Coronel Group, 1100 Glendon Ave, #1700, Los Angeles CA 90046, USA
Slavin, Neal — Photographer
62 Green St, New York NY 10012, USA
Slavitt, David R — Writer
35 West St, #5, Cambridge MA 02139, USA
Slay, Brandon — Freestyle Wrestler
6155 Lehman Dr, Colorado Springs CO 80918, USA
Slayback, William G (Bill) — Baseball Player
25710 Armstrong Circle, #E, Stevenson Ranch CA 91381, USA
Slayton, Maurice W — Financier
Conning Corp, City Place II, 185 Asylum St, #1500, Hartford CT 06103, USA
Slean, Sarah — Singer, Songwriter
Agency Group Ltd, 142 W 57th St, #600, New York NY 10019 USA
Sleater, Louis M (Lou) — Baseball Player
12 Bandon Court, #102, Lutherville Timonium MD 21093, USA
Sledge, Joni — Singer (Sister Sledge)
Nationwide Entertainment, 2756 N Green Valley Parkway, Henderson NV 89014 USA
Sledge, Kathy — Singer (Sister Sledge)
491 York Road, Jenkintown PA 19046, USA
Sledge, Percy — Singer
PO Box 220082, Great Neck NY 11022, USA
Sledge, Termel — Baseball Player
30041 Medford Place, Castaic CA 91384, USA
Sleiman, Haaz — Actor
Gersh Agency, 9465 Wilshire Blvd, #600, Beverly Hills CA 90212 USA
Slezak, Erika — Actress
I C M Partners, 730 5th Ave, New York NY 10019 USA
Slichter, Charles P — Physicist
61 Chestnut Court, Champaign IL 61822, USA
Slick, Grace — Singer (Jefferson Airplane), Songwriter
Mission Control, 15030 Ventura Blvd, #541, Sherman Oaks, CA, Bangladesh 91403, USA
Slim Helu, Carlos — Businessman
Telmex, Porque Via 198, Cuauhtemoc CP, 06599 Mexico City DF, Mexico
Sliwinska, Edyta — Dancer
Bloc Talent Agency, 5651 Wilshire Blvd, #C, Los Angeles CA 90036, USA
Sloan, Bridget — Gymnast
USA Gymnastics, 201 S Capital Ave, #300, Indianapolis IN 46275 USA
Sloan, David L — Football Player
2711 Nottingham St, Houston TX 77005, USA
Sloan, Edward J (Ed) — Singer, Guitarist (Crossfade)
216 Lincoln St, West Columbia SC 29170, USA
Sloan, Gerald E (Jerry) — Basketball Player, Coach
5583 W 13680 S, Herriman UT 84096, USA
Sloan, John — Actor
Innovative Artists, 1505 10th St, Santa Monica CA 90401 USA
Sloan, P F — Singer, Songwriter
All the Best, PO Box 164, Cedarhurst NY 11516, USA
Sloan, Stephen C (Steve) — Football Player, Coach, Administrator
6312 Masters Blvd, Orlando FL 32819, USA
Sloan, Tod — Ice Hockey Player
11 Hedge Road, RR 2, Sutton West ON L0E 1R0, Canada
Sloane, Lindsay — Actress
Gersh Agency, 9465 Wilshire Blvd, #600, Beverly Hills CA 90212 USA
Slocombe, Douglas — Cinematographer
London Mgmt, 2-4 Noel St, London W1V 3RB, England
Slocum, Heath — Golfer
5640 Keystone Road, Pensacola FL 32504, USA
Slocum, Matt — Instrumentalist (Sixpence), Songwriter
Nettwerk Mgmt, 1201 Villa Place, #206, Nashville TN 37212 USA
Slocumb, Heathcliff (Heath) — Baseball Player
1045 Arthur St, Uniondale NY 11553, USA
Slon, Steven — Editor
Saturday Evening Post, 1100 Waterway Blvd, Indianapolis IN 46202, USA
Slonimski, Piotr — Biologist
Le Haut Chantemesle, 72150 Courdemanche, France
Slonimsky, Sergey M — Composer
9 Kanal Griboedova, #97, 191186 Saint Petersburg, Russia
Slotnick, Joey — Actor
Gersh Agency, 9465 Wilshire Blvd, #600, Beverly Hills CA 90212 USA
Slotnick, Mortimer H — Artist
43 Amherst Dr, New Rochelle NY 10804, USA

Sloves, Marvin — Businessman
31 San Juan Ranch Road, Santa Fe NM 87506, USA
Sloviter, Dolores K — Judge
US Court of Appeals, Courthouse, 601 Market St, #18614, Philadelphia PA 19106, USA
Slowery, Kevin M — Baseball Player
1478 Quigg Dr, Pittsburgh PA 15241, USA
Sloyan, James — Actor
920 Kagawa St, Pacific Palisades CA 90272, USA
Sluby, Tom — Basketball Player
39 Poplar St, Ramsey NJ 07446, USA
Slug — Drummer (Marvelous 3)
Progressive Global Agency, 103 W Tyne Dr, Nashville TN 37205, USA
Sluman, Jeffrey G (Jeff) — Golfer
939 Cleveland Road, Hinsdale IL 60521, USA
Slusarski, Joseph A (Joe) — Baseball Player
11 Rodelle Woods Dr, Weldon Spring MO 63304, USA
Slutskaya, Irina E — Figure Skater
Skating Federation, Luznetskaya Nabererhnya 8, 11987 Moscow, Russia
Smail, Doug — Ice Hockey Player
Box 573, Blum TX 76627, USA
Smajstria, Craig L — Baseball Player
4606 Honey Creek Court, Pearland TX 77584, USA
Smale, Stephen — Mathematician
68 Highgate Road, Kensington CA 94707, USA
Small, Aaron J — Baseball Player
775 Loudon Road, Loudon TN 37774, USA
Small, Mary — Writer, Illustrator
PO Box 765, Rozelle NSW 2039, Australia
Small, Marya — Actress
CLInc, 843 N Sycamore Ave, Los Angeles CA 90038 USA
Small, Torrance R — Football Player
66 Chateau Mouton Dr, Kenner LA 70065, USA
Small, William N — Navy Admiral
1605 Bluecher Court, Virginia Beach VA 23454, USA
Smalley, Roy F, III — Baseball Player
6319 Timber Trail, Minneapolis MN 55439, USA
Smallwood, Dwana — Dancer
Alvin Ailey American Dance Foundation, 405 W 55th St, New York NY 10019, USA
Smallwood, Richard — Singer
Lone Oak Entertainment, 116 Huntington Place, Hendersonville TN 37075, USA
Smart, Amy — Actress
Gersh Agency, 9465 Wilshire Blvd, #600, Beverly Hills CA 90212 USA
Smart, Erinn — Fencer
201 S 18th St, #301, Philadelphia PA 19103, USA
Smart, J Keith — Basketball Player, Coach
5306 Asterwood Dr, Dublin CA 94568, USA
Smart, Jean — Actress
17351 Rancho St, Encino CA 91316, USA
Smart, Keeth — Fencer
15 Washington Place, #1F, New York NY 10003, USA
Smart, Shaka — Basketball Coach
Virginia Commonwealth, Athletic Dept, Richmond VA 23284, USA
Smatresek, Neal J — Educator
University of Nevada, President's Office, 4505 S Maryland Parkway, Las Vegas NV 89154, USA
Smeal, Eleanor C — Women's Activist
Feminist Majority Foundation, 1600 Wilson Blvd, #8014, Arlington VA 22209, USA
Smedile, Anthony — Drummer (Dig)
Overland Productions, 156 W 56th St, #500, New York NY 10019, USA
Smedsmo, Dale — Ice Hockey Player
609 3rd St NE, Roseau MN 56751, USA
Smedvig, Rolf — Concert Trumpeter
Columbia Artists Mgmt Inc, 1790 Broadway, #702, New York NY 10019 USA
Smee, Sebastian — Journalist
Boston Globe, Editorial Dept, 135 William Morrissey Blvd, Dorchester MA 02125 USA
Smehlik, Richard — Ice Hockey Player
8824 Hearthstone Dr, East Amherst NY 14051, USA
Smerek, Donald F (Don) — Football Player
1298 Valhalla Dr, Denver NC 28037, USA
Smerlas, Frederick C (Fred) — Football Player
23 Farwell St, Newtonville MA 02460, USA
Smigel, Robert — Actor, Comedian
Creative Artists Agency, 2000 Ave of Stars, #100, Los Angeles CA 90067 USA
Smigelsky, David W (Dave) — Football Player
4332 Nesting Place, Oakwood GA 30566, USA
Smiley, Jane G — Writer
235 El Caminto Road, Carmel Valley CA 93924, USA
Smiley, John P — Baseball Player
208 W 3rd Ave, Collegeville PA 19426, USA
Smiley, Justin — Football Player
721 Baldwin Palm Ave, Plantation FL 33324, USA
Smiley, Tava — Actress
P M K-B N C, 8687 Melrose Ave, #800, Los Angeles CA 90069 USA
Smiley, Tavis — Entertainer
Smiley Group, 4434 Crenshaw Blvd, Los Angeles CA 90043, USA
Smirnoff, Karina — Dancer
Continuum Entertainment, 303 Park Ave S, #1220, New York NY 10010, USA
Smirnoff, Yakov — Actor, Comedian
Comrade Entertainment, 3750 W 76 Country Blvd, Branson MO 65616, USA
Smirnov, Igor N — President, Transnistria
President's Office, 25 October Str, Tiraspol, Transnistria, Moldova
Smisek, Jeff — Businessman
United-Continental Airlines, 77 W Wacker Dr, Mezzanine, Chicago IL 60601, USA
Smit, Johannes H M (Jantje) — Singer
Postbus 100, 1130 AC Vollendamm, Netherlands
Smith Court, Margaret — Tennis Player
21 Lowanna Way, City Beach, Perth WA 6010, Australia

Smith, Aaron D — Football Player
4900 S Ulster St, #8-106, Denver CO 80237, USA
Smith, Adrian D — Architect
1100 W Summerfield Dr, Lake Forest IL 60045, USA
Smith, Adrian F — Guitarist (Iron Maiden)
Chipster, 800 Village Square Crossing, Palm Beach Gardens FL 33410 USA
Smith, Adrian H — Basketball Player
2829 Saddleback Dr, Cincinnati OH 45244, USA
Smith, Al F — Football Player
15 Pembroke St, Sugar Land TX 77479, USA
Smith, Alan E — Molecular Biologist
Genzyme Corp, 500 Kendall St, Cambridge MA 02142, USA
Smith, Alexander D (Alex) — Football Player
4665 Gaviota Court, Bonita CA 91902, USA
Smith, Alexander McCall — Writer
Pantheon Books, 1745 Broadway, New York NY 10019 USA
Smith, Alexis — Artist
1625 Shell Ave, Venice CA 90291, USA
Smith, Allison — Actress
Barry Freed, 2040 Ave of Stars, #400, Los Angeles CA 90067 USA
Smith, Amber — Model, Actress
I D Model Mgmt, 110 Green St, #702, New York NY 10012, USA
Smith, Andre D, Jr — Football Player
Cincinnati Bengals, 1 Paul Brown Stadium, Cincinnati OH 45202 USA
Smith, Andrea B — Artist
1590 Lokia St, Lahaina HI 96761, USA
Smith, Anna Deavere — Actress
Creative Artists Agency, 2000 Ave of Stars, #100, Los Angeles CA 90067 USA
Smith, Anne — Tennis Player
Bew Ravs, 3737 Cole Ave, #110, Dallas TX 75204, USA
Smith, Anthony B — Football Player
2724 Hunters Point Dr, Wexford PA 15090, USA
Smith, Anthony W — Football Player
PO Box 573, Fontana CA 92334, USA
Smith, Antonio D — Football Player
2015 Grand River Dr, Richmond TX 77406, USA
Smith, Antonique — Actress, Singer
P M K-B N C, 8687 Melrose Ave, #800, Los Angeles CA 90069 USA
Smith, Antowain D — Football Player
2121 Hepburn St, #917, Houston TX 77054, USA
Smith, April — Writer
427 7th St, Santa Monica CA 90402, USA
Smith, Arlene — Singer (Chantels)
Veta Gardner, 1661 SE Goucho Ave, Port Saint Lucie FL 34952, USA
Smith, Arthur — Guitarist, Songwriter
PO Box 11715, Charlotte NC 28220, USA
Smith, Arthur K, Jr — Educator
45 Wexford Club Dr, Hilton Head SC 29928, USA
Smith, Artie E — Football Player
3809 W 68th St, Stillwater OK 74074, USA
Smith, B — Model, Publisher, Restauranteur
B Smith with Style, 168 Park Ave, Harrison NY 10528, USA
Smith, Barbara Herrnstein — Educator
Duke University, Science & Cultural Theory Center, Durham NC 27708, USA
Smith, Barry — Synthesizer Player (Add N to X)
Kork Agency, 1880 Century Park E, #711, Los Angeles CA 90067 USA
Smith, Barton E (Barty) — Football Player
2290 Dabney Road, Richmond VA 23230, USA
Smith, Beau — Cartoonist
Flying Fist Ranch, PO Box 706, Ceredo WV 25507, USA
Smith, Ben — Cartoonist (Ratz)
King Features Syndicate, 300 W 57th St, #1500, New York NY 10019 USA
Smith, Ben — Ice Hockey Coach
47 Norwood Heights, Gloucester MA 01930, USA
Smith, Benjamin J (Ben) — Football Player
211 Cobblestone Trail, Avondale Estates GA 30002, USA
Smith, Billy E — Baseball Player
9246 Mare Country, San Antonio TX 78254, USA
Smith, Billy Ray, Jr — Football Player
14755 Caminito Porta Delgada, Del Mar CA 92014, USA
Smith, Blake — Guitarist (Fig Dish)
Metropolitan Entertainment Group, 2 Penn Plaza, #1500, New York NY 10121, USA
Smith, Bob — Golfer
PO Box 6511, Ventura CA 93006, USA
Smith, Bobby — Ice Hockey Player
10800 E Cactus Road, #46, Scottsdale AZ 85259, USA
Smith, Bobby Gene — Baseball Player
1267 Tucker Road, #15, Hood River OR 97031, USA
Smith, Brad — Astronomer
Jet Propulsion Laboratory, 4800 Oak Grove Dr, Pasadena CA 91109 USA
Smith, Brad — Ice Hockey Player
Colorado Avalanche, Pepsi Center, 1000 Chopper Circle, Denver CO 80204 USA
Smith, Brady — Actor
Schachter Entertainment, 1157 S Beverly Dr, #200, Los Angeles CA 90035 USA
Smith, Brady M — Football Player
3555 Moye Trail, Duluth GA 30097, USA
Smith, Brent M — Football Player
258 Ridgewood Dr, Pontotoc MS 38863, USA
Smith, Brick D — Baseball Player
4743 Amity Place, Charlotte NC 28212, USA
Smith, Bruce A — Businessman
Tesoro Petroleum Corp, 300 Concord Plaza Dr, San Antonio TX 78216, USA
Smith, Bruce B — Football Player
1640 Spring House Trail, Virginia Beach VA 23455, USA
Smith, C Douglas (Doug) — Football Player
25661 Pacific Crest Dr, Mission Viejo CA 92692, USA

Smith, C Reginald (Reggie) — Baseball Player
Reggie Smith Baseball Center, 16161 Ventura Blvd, #775, Encino CA 91436, USA
Smith, Calvin — Track Athlete
16703 Sheffield Park Dr, Lutz FL 33549, USA
Smith, Carl R — Air Force General
2345 S Queen St, Arlington VA 22202, USA
Smith, Carter — Director
Cinetic Mgmt, 555 W 25th St, #400, New York NY 10001 USA
Smith, Cedric D — Football Player
14808 Benson St, Overland Park KS 66221, USA
Smith, Chadwick G (Chad) — Drummer (Red Hot Chili Peppers)
Q Prime, 729 7th Ave, #1600, New York NY 10019 USA
Smith, Charles D — Basketball Player
PO Box 433, Cedar Grove NJ 07009, USA
Smith, Charles E (Charlie) — Football Player
1906 Crescent Dr, Monroe LA 71202, USA
Smith, Charles H (Charlie) — Football Player
14074 Skyline Blvd, Oakland CA 94619, USA
Smith, Charles H (Chuck) — Football Player
8819 Steeplechase Dr, Knoxville TN 37922, USA
Smith, Charles Martin — Actor, Director
A P A Talent/Literary Agency, 405 S Beverly Dr, #300, Beverly Hills CA 90212 USA
Smith, Chelsi — Beauty Queen, Singer, Actress
335 E San Augustine St, Deer Park TX 77536, USA
Smith, Chris — Golfer
208 S Bellerive Dr, Peru IN 46970, USA
Smith, Christina — Model
Playboy Promotions, 2706 Media Center Dr, Los Angeles CA 90065 USA
Smith, Christine — Model
Playboy Promotions, 2706 Media Center Dr, Los Angeles CA 90065 USA
Smith, Christoper W (Chris) — Baseball Player
4206 Dawn Lane, Oceanside CA 92056, USA
Smith, Christopher — Director, Writer
United Agents, 12-26 Lexington St, London W1F 0LE, England
Smith, Christopher — Physiologist, Pharmacologist
King's College, Strand, London WC2R 2LS, England
Smith, Chuck — Baseball Player
1300 Saint Charles Place, #810, Pembroke Pines FL 33026, USA
Smith, Clifford V, Jr — Educator, Foundation Executive
1205 NW Kline Place, Corvallis OR 97330, USA
Smith, Colin — Rowing Athlete
Leander Club, Henley on Thames, Leander RG9 2LP, England
Smith, Connie — Singer
PO Box 428, Portland TN 37148, USA
Smith, Cotter — Actor
Innovative Artists, 1505 10th St, Santa Monica CA 90401 USA
Smith, D Brooks — Judge
US Court of Appeals, Allegheny Center, Old Route 22 W, Duncansville PA 16635, USA
Smith, Dallas — Ice Hockey Player
4390 SW 107th Ave, #4, Beaverton OR 97005, USA
Smith, Dan F — Businessman
Lyondell Petrochemical Co, 1221 McKinney St, #700, Houston TX 77010, USA
Smith, Daniel C (Dan), Jr — Baseball Player
4411 Adonis Dr, Salt Lake City UT 84124, USA
Smith, Danny — Actor, Producer, Writer
Roger A Pliakas, 9720 Wilshire Blvd, #700, Beverly Hills CA 90212, USA
Smith, Darden — Singer, Guitarist, Songwriter
A G F Entertainment, 30 W 21st St, #700, New York NY 10010, USA
Smith, Darrin A — Football Player
7274 NW 19th Court, Pembroke Pines FL 33024, USA
Smith, Daryl C — Baseball Player
3 Sunny Hills Court, Randallstown MD 21133, USA
Smith, David Lee — Actor
Chaotic Mgmt, 4221 Wilshire Blvd, #395, Los Angeles CA 90010, USA
Smith, David R — Electrical Engineer
Duke University, Electrical Engineering Dept, Durham NC 27708, USA
Smith, David W (Dave) — Football Player
3709 E Meadowview Dr, Gilbert AZ 85298, USA
Smith, Dean E — Basketball Coach
University of North Carolina, Athletic Dept, PO Box 2126, Chapel Hill NC 27515, USA
Smith, Dennis — Football Player
2450 Achilles Dr, Los Angeles CA 90046, USA
Smith, Derek — Ice Hockey Player
201 Bramblewood Lane, East Amherst NY 14051, USA
Smith, Derek M — Football Player
3352 Adams Run, Encinitas CA 92024, USA
Smith, Derrick — Ice Hockey Player
Durham Fury, 595 Wentworth St E, Oshawa ON L1H 3V8, Canada
Smith, Detron N — Football Player
1209 Collinwood West Dr, Austin TX 78753, USA
Smith, Dick — Diving Coach
PO Box 1831, Dewey AZ 86327, USA
Smith, Donald L (Don) — Football Player
3338 Pineview Dr, Holiday FL 34691, USA
Smith, Donna — Model, Actress
Playboy Promotions, 2706 Media Center Dr, Los Angeles CA 90065 USA
Smith, Doug — Football Player, Coach
25661 Pacifc Crest Dr, Mission Viejo CA 92692, USA
Smith, Douglas (Doug) — Basketball Player
25482 Pennsylvania Ave, Novi MI 48375, USA
Smith, Douglas (Doug) — Actor
Medavoy Mgmt, 10203 Santa Monica Blvd, #400, Los Angeles CA 90067 USA
Smith, Dylan — Actor
TalentWorks, 3500 W Olive Ave, #1400, Burbank CA 91505 USA
Smith, E Alexander (Alex) — Football Player
9604 Gretna Green Dr, Tampa FL 33626, USA

Smith, E Perry
14251 E Wyoming Place, Aurora CO 80012, USA — Football Player

Smith, E Z
2036 N Farris Ave, Fresno CA 93704, USA — Photographer

Smith, Earl C
2764 N Leonard Ave, Fresno CA 93737, USA — Baseball Player

Smith, Earl J (J R), III
New York Knicks, Madison Square Garden, 2 Penn Plaza, New York, NY 10121 USA — Basketball Player

Smith, Elliott A
850 N Jefferson St, #A205, Jackson MS 39202, USA — Football Player

Smith, Elmore
PO Box 241475, Cleveland OH 44124, USA — Basketball Player

Smith, Emmitt J, III
15001 Winnwood Road, Dallas TX 75254, USA — Football Player, Sportscaster

Smith, Erik Scott
Leverage Mgmt, 3030 Pennsylvania Ave, Santa Monica CA 90404 USA — Actor, Singer

Smith, Ethel
McMillen Inc, 155 E 56th St, #500, New York NY 10022, USA — Interior Designer

Smith, F Dean
PO Box 71, Breckenridge TX 76424, USA — Track Athlete

Smith, Faryl
Agency Group Ltd, 361-373 City Road, London EC1V 2QA, England — Singer

Smith, Floyd
138 Stonehenge Dr, Orchard Park NY 14127, USA — Ice Hockey Player

Smith, Frankie L
620 N Grayson St, Groesbeck TX 76642, USA — Football Player

Smith, Frederick W
F D X Corp, 942 S Shady Grove Road, Memphis TN 38120, USA — Businessman

Smith, G Seth
76 Sunline Dr, Brandon MS 39042, USA — Baseball Player

Smith, Gary
Colorado Rapids, 1000 Chopper Circle, Denver CO 80204 USA — Soccer Coach

Smith, Geoff
42-1525 Westside Road S, Kelowna BC V1Z 3Y3, Canada — Ice Hockey Player

Smith, George
Universal Press Syndicate, 4520 Main St, #700, Kansas City MO 64111 USA — Cartoonist (Smith Family)

Smith, George E
Bell Laboratories, 600 Mountain Ave, Murray Hill NJ 07974, USA — Nobel Physics Laureate

Smith, Gerard
World Tennis Assn, 133 1st St NE, Saint Petersburg FL 33701, USA — Publisher, Tennis Executive

Smith, Gordon C
14227 Kellywood Lane, Houston TX 77079, USA — Football Player

Smith, Gordon H
116 S Main St, #3, Pendleton OR 97801, USA — Senator, OR

Smith, Gordon J (Gord)
6 Carriage Dr, West Haven CT 06516, USA — Ice Hockey Player

Smith, Gregory
Paradigm Agency, 360 N Crescent Dr, North Building, Beverly Hills CA 90210 USA — Actor

Smith, Gregory D (Greg)
9930 SW Lumbee Lane, Tualatin OR 97062, USA — Basketball Player

Smith, Gregory White
129 1st Ave SW, Aiken SC 29801, USA — Writer

Smith, Hamilton O
13607 Hanover Pike, Reisterstown MD 21136, USA — Nobel Medicine Laureate

Smith, Harold R (Hal)
9514 Londonderry Court, Fort Smith AR 72908, USA — Baseball Player

Smith, Harold W (Hal)
637 Houston St, Columbus TX 78934, USA — Baseball Player

Smith, Harrison
Minnesota Vikings, 9520 Viking Dr, Eden Prairie MN 55344 USA — Football Player

Smith, Harry
580 E Cuyahoga Falls Ave, Akron OH 44310, USA — Bowler

Smith, Harry
CBS-TV, News Dept, 51 W 52nd St, New York NY 10019 USA — Commentator

Smith, Harry E (Blackjack)
805 Leawood Terrace, Columbia MO 65203, USA — Football Player, Coach

Smith, Hedrick L
6935 Wisconsin Ave, #208, Chevy Chase MD 20815, USA — Journalist

Smith, Hunter D
9601 E 300 S, Zionesville IN 46077, USA — Football Player

Smith, Ian Michael
C E S D, 10635 Santa Monica Blvd, #130, Los Angeles CA 90025 USA — Actor

Smith, Irvin M (Irv)
11552 W Green Dr, Youngtown AZ 85363, USA — Football Player

Smith, J D, Jr
3332 Florida St, Oakland CA 94602, USA — Football Player

Smith, J Dwight
PO Box 98, Varnville SC 29944, USA — Baseball Player

Smith, Jackie L
1566 Walpole Dr, Chesterfield MO 63017, USA — Football Player

Smith, Jaclyn
10398 Sunset Blvd, #1200, Los Angeles CA 90077, USA — Actress

Smith, Jaden
W M E Entertainment, 9601 Wilshire Blvd, #300, Beverly Hills CA 90210 USA — Actor

Smith, James (Bonecrusher)
6850 Blue Heron Blvd, #302, Myrtle Beach SC 29588, USA — Boxer

Smith, James A (Jim)
3805 Chimney Rock Dr, Flower Mound TX 75022, USA — Football Player

Smith, James L (Jimmy)
1730 S Arroyo Lane, Gilbert AZ 85295, USA — Baseball Player

Smith, James Ray (Jim Ray)
7049 Cliffbrook Dr, Dallas TX 75254, USA — Football Player

Smith, Jason M
Pro-Rep Entertainment, 113-276 Midpark Way SE, Calgary AB T2X 1J6, Canada — Ice Hockey Player

Smith, Jason Matthew
Greene Assoc, 1901 Ave of Stars, #130, Los Angeles CA 90067 USA — Actor

Smith, Jason V — Basketball Player
New Orleans Hornets, 1250 Poydras St, #101, New Orleans LA 70113 USA
Smith, Jason W — Baseball Player
6350 Golden Acres Dr, Cottondale AL 35453, USA
Smith, Jean Kennedy — Diplomat, Foundation Executive
4 Sutton Place, New York NY 10022, USA
Smith, Jerry E — Judge
US Court of Appeals, 515 Rusk Ave, #12015, Houston TX 77002, USA
Smith, Jimmy Lee, Jr — Football Player
105 Long Leaf Place, Madison MS 39110, USA
Smith, John F (Jack), Jr — Businessman
767 5th Ave, New York NY 10153, USA
Smith, John M — Football Player
184 Centre St, Dover MA 02030, USA
Smith, John Thomas (J T) — Football Player
1904 Chasewood Circle, Arlington TX 76011, USA
Smith, John W — Freestyle Wrestler, Coach
5315 S Sangre Road, Stillwater OK 74074, USA
Smith, Jonathan Z — Historian, Religion Educator
University of Chicago, History of Religion Dept, Chicago IL 60637, USA
Smith, Joseph L (Joe) — Basketball Player
7639 Leafwood Dr, Norfolk VA 23518, USA
Smith, Joshua (Josh) — Basketball Player
Atlanta Hawks, Centennial Tower, 101 Marietta St NW, #1900, Atlanta GA 30303 USA
Smith, Justin — Football Player
2222 Terra Nova Lane, San Jose CA 95121, USA
Smith, K Akili M — Football Player
PO Box 95, Jamul CA 91935, USA
Smith, Kathy — Physical Fitness Instructor
42080 State St, Palm Desert CA 92211, USA
Smith, Katie — Basketball Player
2494 Farleigh Road, Columbus OH 43221, USA
Smith, Keely Shaye — Entertainer, Writer
W M E Entertainment, 9601 Wilshire Blvd, #300, Beverly Hills CA 90210 USA
Smith, Keith L — Baseball Player
5823 13th St E, Bradenton FL 34203, USA
Smith, Kellita — Actress
Stone Manners Salners, 9911 W Pico Blvd, #1400, Los Angeles CA 90035 USA
Smith, Ken — Landscape Architect
80 Warren St, #28, New York NY 10007, USA
Smith, Kenneth (Kenny) — Basketball Player, Sportscaster
Octagon Worldwide, 1751 Pinnacle Dr, #1500, McLean VA 22102 USA
Smith, Kenneth E (Ken) — Baseball Player
100 Lansdowne Blvd, Youngstown OH 44506, USA
Smith, Kerr — Actor
Gersh Agency, 9465 Wilshire Blvd, #600, Beverly Hills CA 90212 USA
Smith, Kevin — Director, Writer
View Askew Productions, PO Box 93339, Los Angeles CA 90093, USA
Smith, Kevin Max — Singer (DC Talk), Songwriter
True Artist Mgmt, 227 3rd Ave N, Franklin TN 37064, USA
Smith, Kurtwood L — Actor
Progressive Artists Agency, 1041 N Formosa Ave, West Hollywood CA 90046 USA
Smith, Lacey B — Historian
Northwestern University, History Dept, Evanston IL 60208, USA
Smith, Lance — Football Player
4600 Nobility Court, Charlotte NC 28269, USA
Smith, Lanty L — Financier
Wachovia Corp, 301 S College St, #4000, Charlotte NC 28202, USA
Smith, Larry — Basketball Player
1767 Lakeside Dr, Vicksburg MS 39180, USA
Smith, Lauren Lee — Actress
Gersh Agency, 9465 Wilshire Blvd, #600, Beverly Hills CA 90212 USA
Smith, Lavenski R — Judge
11 Twin Pine Place, Little Rock AR 72210, USA
Smith, Lee — Writer
219 N Churton St, Hillsborough NC 27278, USA
Smith, Lee — Editor
Gersh Agency, 9465 Wilshire Blvd, #600, Beverly Hills CA 90212 USA
Smith, Lee A — Baseball Player
PO Box 399, Castor LA 71016, USA
Smith, Leroy P (Roy) — Baseball Player
472 Gramatan Ave, #G2, Mount Vernon NY 10552, USA
Smith, Leslie C — WW II Army Air Corps Hero
1700 Tice Valley Blvd, #221, Walnut Creek CA 94595, USA
Smith, Lois — Actress
Abrams Artists, 420 Madison Ave, #1400, New York NY 10017, USA
Smith, Lonnie — Baseball Player
145 Wesley Forest Dr, Fayetteville GA 30214, USA
Smith, Lonnie Liston, Jr — Jazz Keyboardist
Associated Booking Corp, 501 Madison Ave, #603, New York NY 10022 USA
Smith, Louis — Gymnast
Huntingdon Gymnastic Club, Claytons Way, Huntingdon PE29 1UT, England
Smith, Lovie L — Football Player, Coach
Chicago Bears, 1000 Football Dr, Lake Forest IL 60045 USA
Smith, M Elizabeth (Liz) — Columnist
160 E 38th St, #33C, New York NY 10016, USA
Smith, Madeline — Actress
Joan Gray, Sunbury Island, Sunbury on Thames, Middlesex, England
Smith, Maggie — Actress
Independent Talent Group, Oxford House, 76 Oxford St, London W1D 1BS, England
Smith, Margo — Singer, Songwriter
Tri-Star Enterprises, PO Box 3367 Brentwood, TN 37024
Smith, Marilynn — Golfer
3784 N 162nd Lane, Goodyear AZ 85395, USA
Smith, Mark E — Baseball Player
1312 Elmhurst Lane, Flower Mound TX 75028, USA

Smith, Marquis T 843 51st St, San Diego CA 92114, USA	Football Player
Smith, Martha Dedicated Agency, 7417 Van Nuys Blvd, #102, Van Nuys CA 91405, USA	Actress, Model
Smith, Marvel A 30 Waterfront Dr, Pittsburgh PA 15222, USA	Football Player
Smith, Marvin (Smitty) Joel Chriss, 60 E 8th St, #34N, New York NY 10003 USA	Jazz Drummer
Smith, Matt Troika, 74 Clerkenwell Road, #300, London EC1M 5QA, England	Actor
Smith, Matt 213 Chaingate Circle, Landenberg PA 19350, USA	Baseball Player
Smith, Mel Rights House, 34-43 Russell St, London WC2B 5HA, England	Actor, Comedian
Smith, Michael A (Mike) 3226 Livingston Road, Jackson MS 39213, USA	Baseball Player
Smith, Michael W Blanton Harrell Cooke, 5250 Virginia Way, #110, Brentwood TN 37027, USA	Singer, Keyboardist, Songwriter
Smith, Michael W (Mike) 619 Feamster Dr, Houston TX 77022, USA	Football Player, Coach
Smith, Mike Las Vegas Sun, Editorial Dept, 2275 Corporate Circle, #300, Henderson NV 89074, USA	Editorial Cartoonist
Smith, Mike Atlanta Falcons, 4400 Falcon Parkway, Flowery Branch GA 30542 USA	Football Player, Coach
Smith, Mike 3445 NE 210th St, Miami FL 33180, USA	Thoroughbred Racing Jockey
Smith, Mindy Main Road Mgmt, 195 Chrystie St, #901F, New York NY 10002, USA	Singer, Songwriter
Smith, Nathaniel B (Nate) 6365 Tahoe Dr, Atlanta GA 30349, USA	Baseball Player
Smith, Neil 9423 Nall Ave, Overland Park KS 66207, USA	Football Player
Smith, Nicholas Michelle Braidman, 10/11 Lower John St, London W1R 3PE, England	Actor
Smith, Nolan D Portland Trail Blazers, Rose Garden, 1 N Center Court St, Portland OR 97227 USA	Basketball Player
Smith, O Guinn 2 Hawthorne Place, #3P, Boston MA 02114, USA	Track Athlete
Smith, Onterrio P PO Box 38252, Sacramento CA 95838, USA	Football Player
Smith, Orlando (Tubby) University of Minnesota, Athletic Dept, Minneapolis MN 55455, USA	Basketball Coach
Smith, Osborne E (Ozzie) 201 Kendall Bluff Court, Chesterfield MO 63017, USA	Baseball Player, Sportscaster
Smith, Otis F 607 Applewood Ave, Altamonte Springs Fl 32714, USA	Basketball Player
Smith, Parrish I C M Partners, 10250 Constellation Blvd, #900, Los Angeles CA 90067 USA	Rap Artist (EPMD)
Smith, Patti Feinstein Mgmt, 8560 W Sunset Blvd, West Hollywood CA 90069, USA	Singer, Songwriter
Smith, Paul L 711 Trevino Lane, Conroe TX 77302, USA	Baseball Player
Smith, Peter J (Pete) 10030 Halstead Dr, Suwanee GA 30024, USA	Baseball Player
Smith, Peter L (Pete) 3512 Dixon Lane, The Villages FL 32162, USA	Baseball Player
Smith, R Jackson 122 Palmers Hill Road, #3101, Stamford CT 06902, USA	Diver
Smith, R Jeffrey Washington Post, Editorial Dept, 1150 15th St NW, Washington DC 20071 USA	Journalist
Smith, Ralph A PO Box 1406, McComb MS 39649, USA	Football Player
Smith, Raonall A 1609 119th Street Court NW, Gig Harbor WA 98332, USA	Football Player
Smith, Raymond E (Ray) 17183 Poblado Court, San Diego CA 92127, USA	Baseball Player
Smith, Regan Furniture Row Racing, 5641 Broadway Denver CO 80216, USA	Auto Racing Driver
Smith, Renee Felice Don Buchwald/Fortitude, 6500 Wilshire Blvd, #2200, Los Angeles CA 90048 USA	Actress
Smith, Rex Re/Max Realtors, 6695 E Pacific Coast Highway, #150, Long Beach CA 90803, USA	Actor
Smith, Richard H (Dick) 1926 Norwood Lane, State College PA 16803, USA	Baseball Player
Smith, Rick RR 1, Perth Road Village ON K0H 2L0, Canada	Ice Hockey Player
Smith, Riley Innovative Artists, 1505 10th St, Santa Monica CA 90401 USA	Actor
Smith, Robaire F 4002 Silver Ridge Blvd, Missouri City TX 77459, USA	Football Player
Smith, Robert Primary Talent International, 10-11 Jockey's Fields, London WC1R 4BN, England	Singer, Guitarist (Cure)
Smith, Robert C (Bob) 9012 Rocky Lake Court, Sarasota FL 34238, USA	Senator, NH
Smith, Robert E (Bobby) 2822 60th Ave, Oakland CA 94605, USA	Baseball Player
Smith, Robert Gray (Graysmith) San Francisco Chronicle, 901 Mission St, San Francisco CA 94103, USA	Editorial Cartoonist
Smith, Robert H 1277 Parkview Ave, Pasadena CA 91103, USA	Financier
Smith, Robert Lee Speer Entertainment Services, PO Box 2620, McDonough GA 30253, USA	Singer (Tams)
Smith, Robert S 25601 Thistle Valley Court, Porter TX 77365, USA	Football Player
Smith, Robyn 1155 San Ysidro Dr, Beverly Hills CA 90210, USA	Thoroughbred Racing Jockey

Smith, Roderick (Rod) — Football Player
6304 Charrington Dr, Englewood CO 80111, USA

Smith, Roger — Actor
2707 Benedict Canyon Dr, Beverly Hills CA 90210, USA

Smith, Roger Guenveur — Actor
Don Buchwald/Fortitude, 6500 Wilshire Blvd, #2200, Los Angeles CA 90048 USA

Smith, Rolland — Commentator
CBS-TV, News Dept, 524 W 57th St, New York NY 10019, USA

Smith, Ron — Drag Racing Driver
14933 165th Place SE, Renton WA 98059, USA

Smith, Ronald (Ron) — Football Player
1822 Ura Lane, Northglenn CO 80234, USA

Smith, Ronnie Ray — Track Athlete
752 W Athens Blvd, Los Angeles CA 90044, USA

Smith, Russell — Singer (Amazing Rhythm Aces), Songwriter
Gen-X Entertainment, PO Box 128164, Nashville TN 37212, USA

Smith, Sam — Basketball Player
246 Calvary Colony Road, Memphis TN 38127, USA

Smith, Scott B — Writer
Lynne Pleshette Agency, 2700 N Beachwood Dr, Los Angeles CA 90068, USA

Smith, Shawnee — Actress
Kritzer Levine Wilkins Griffin, 11872 La Grange Ave, #100, Los Angeles CA 90025 USA

Smith, Shelley — Actress, Model
4184 Colfax Ave, Studio City CA 91604, USA

Smith, Sheridan — Actress
Independent Talent Group, Oxford House, 76 Oxford St, London W1D 1BS, England

Smith, Sherman L — Football Player
1032 N 41st Place, Renton WA 98056, USA

Smith, Sinjin — Volleyball Player, Model
Beach Volleyball Camps, PO Box 1714, Pacific Palisades CA 90272, USA

Smith, Stanley R (Stan) — Tennis Player
2 Widewater Road, Hilton Head SC 29926, USA

Smith, Stephanie — Singer
Gotee Records, 1746 General George Patton Dr, Brentwood TN 37027, USA

Smith, Stephen C (Steve) — Football Player
1104 Lake Shore Dr, Barrington IL 60010, USA

Smith, Steve — Basketball Coach
Oak Hill Academy, Atheltic Dept, 2635 Oak Hill Road, Mouth of Wilson VA 24363, USA

Smith, Steve (T J Tatters) — Clown
Big Apple Circus, 505 8th Ave, #1900, New York NY 10018 USA

Smith, Steven — Labor Leader
National Rural Letter Carriers Assn, 1630 Duke St, #200, Alexandria VA 22314, USA

Smith, Steven (Steve) — Football Player
Philadelphia Eagles, 1 Novacare Way, Philadelphia PA 19145 USA

Smith, Steven A (Steve) — Football Player
2717 Millwood Dr, Richardson TX 75082, USA

Smith, Steven D (Steve) — Basketball Player
755 Heards Ferry Road NW, Atlanta GA 30328, USA

Smith, Steven L — Astronaut
N A S A, Johnson Space Center, 2101 NASA Road, Houston TX 77058 USA

Smith, Stevronne L (Steve) — Football Player
Carolina Panthers, Ericsson Stadium, 800 S Mint St, Charlotte NC 28202 USA

Smith, Susan M — Model
Playboy Promotions, 2706 Media Center Dr, Los Angeles CA 90065 USA

Smith, Tangela N — Basketball Player
San Antonio Silver Stars, 1 AT&T Center, San Antonio TX 78219 USA

Smith, Taran Noah — Actor
Full Circle Mgmt, 12665 Kling St, Studio City CA 91604, USA

Smith, Tasha — Actress
A P A Talent/Literary Agency, 405 S Beverly Dr, #300, Beverly Hills CA 90212 USA

Smith, Taylor — Golfer
1157 Sandlake Road, Saint Augustine FL 32092, USA

Smith, Thomas L, Jr — Football Player
360 N C Highway 37 N, Gates NC 27937, USA

Smith, Tommie — Track Athlete, Football Player
1800 Lilburn Stone Mountain Road, Stone Mountain GA 30087, USA

Smith, Tony — Basketball Player
2645 N 40th St, Milwaukee WI 53210, USA

Smith, Travian D — Football Player
13841 County Road 2167D, Tatum TX 75691, USA

Smith, Travis W — Baseball Player
1865 Cherry St, Clarkston WA 99403, USA

Smith, Troy — Football Player
Baltimore Ravens, Ravens Stadium, 1 Winning Dr, Baltimore MD 21230 USA

Smith, Vernice C — Football Player
4347 Arajo Court, Orlando FL 32812, USA

Smith, Vernon L — Nobel Economics Laureate
336 N Lemon St, Orange CA 92866, USA

Smith, Vince — Singer, Songwriter
Process Talent Mgmt, 439 Wiley Ave, Franklin PA 16323, USA

Smith, Vinson R — Football Player
807 Alexander St, #807, Statesville NC 28677, USA

Smith, Walter — Computer Software Designer
Microsoft Corp, 1 Microsoft Way, Redmond WA 98052, USA

Smith, Walter H F — Oceanographer, Cartologist
National Oceanic/Atmospheric Admin, 14th St & Constitution Ave, Washington DC 20230, USA

Smith, Wayne L — Football Player
7730 S Bishop St, Chicago IL 60620, USA

Smith, Wendy — Singer, Guitarist (Prefab Sprout)
Paradigm Agency, 360 N Crescent Dr, North Building, Beverly Hills CA 90210 USA

Smith, Wilbur A — Writer
Charles Pick Consultancy, 21 Dagmar Terrace, London N1 2BN, England

Smith, Will — Actor, Singer, Rap Artist
Creative Artists Agency, 2000 Ave of Stars, #100, Los Angeles CA 90067 USA

Smith, William — Actor
Spotlight, 7 Leicester Place, London WC2H 7RJ, England

Smith, William (Bill), Jr 45-090 Namoku St, #E2, Kaneohe HI 96744, USA	Swimmer
Smith, William (Billy) NY Islanders Alumni Assn, 1535 Old Country Road, #1, Plainview NY 11803, USA	Ice Hockey Player
Smith, William D 7025 Fairway Oaks, Fayetteville PA 17222, USA	Navy Admiral
Smith, William J (Billy) 8356 Quail Meadow Way, West Palm Beach FL 33412, USA	Ice Hockey Player
Smith, William Jay 62 Luther Shaw Road, RR 1 Box 151, Cummington MA 01026, USA	Writer
Smith, William Y 6541 Brooks Place, Falls Church VA 22044, USA	Army General
Smith, Willie E 1330 E 68th St, Savannah GA 31404, USA	Baseball Player
Smith, Willow Overbrook Entertainment, 450 N Roxbury Dr, #400, Beverly Hills CA 90210, USA	Actress, Singer
Smith, Wyatt Coast to Coast Talent, 3350 Barham Blvd, Los Angeles CA 90068 USA	Actor
Smith, Yeardley A P A Talent/Literary Agency, 405 S Beverly Dr, #300, Beverly Hills CA 90212 USA	Actress
Smith, Zadie A P Watt, 20 John St, London WC1N 2DR, England	Writer
Smith, Zane W 420 Windship Place NW, Atlanta GA 30327, USA	Baseball Player
Smith-Cameron, J Gersh Agency, 9465 Wilshire Blvd, #600, Beverly Hills CA 90212 USA	Actress
Smither, Chris Mark Pucci Media, 5000 Oak Bluff Court, Atlanta GA 30350, USA	Singer, Guitarist, Songwriter
Smitherman, Stephen PO Box 1890, McAlester OK 74502, USA	Baseball Player
Smithers, William 2202 Anacapa St, Santa Barbara CA 93105, USA	Actor
Smithies, Oliver 318 Umstead Dr, Chapel Hill NC 27516, USA	Nobel Medicine Laureate
Smithson, B Mike 25405 Swan Creek Road, Centerville TN 37033, USA	Baseball Player
Smit-McPhee, Kodi I C M Partners, 10250 Constellation Blvd, #900, Los Angeles CA 90067 USA	Actor
Smit-McPhee, Sianoa I C M Partners, 10250 Constellation Blvd, #900, Los Angeles CA 90067 USA	Actress
Smitrovich, Bill 3512 Crownridge Dr, Sherman Oaks CA 91403, USA	Actor
Smits, Jimmy United Talent Agency, 9336 Civic Center Dr, Beverly Hills CA 90210 USA	Actor
Smits, Rik 8346 E 550 S, Zionsville IN 46077, USA	Basketball Player
Smiun, Dick 2073 Donegal Circle, Salt Lake City UT 84109, USA	Basketball Player
Smoke Geffen Records, 10900 Wilshire Blvd, #1000, Los Angeles CA 90024, USA	Rap Artist (Field Mob)
Smolan, Rick Workman Publishers, 225 Varick St, #900, New York NY 10014, USA	Photographer
Smolinski, Bryan A 4869 Stoneleigh Road, Bloomfield Hills MI 48302, USA	Ice Hockey Player
Smolinski, Mark W 3300 Country Club Road, Petoskey MI 49770, USA	Football Player
Smolka, James W PO Box 2123, Lancaster CA 93539, USA	Test Pilot
Smolla, Rodney A Furman University, President's Office, 3300 Poinsetta Highway, Greenville SC 29613, USA	Educator
Smollett, Jurnee I C M Partners, 10250 Constellation Blvd, #900, Los Angeles CA 90067 USA	Actress
Smoltz, John A 700 Foxhollow Run, Alpharetta GA 30004, USA	Baseball Player
Smoot, George F, III Lawrence Berkeley Laboratory, 1 Cyclotron Road, Berkeley CA 94720, USA	Nobel Physics Laureate
Smoove, J B W M E Entertainment, 9601 Wilshire Blvd, #300, Beverly Hills CA 90210 USA	Actor, Comedian, Writer
Smothers, Dick Smothers Winery, PO Box 219, Kenwood CA 95452, USA	Actor, Comedian (Smothers Brothers)
Smothers, Tom Smothers Winery, PO Box 219, Kenwood CA 95452, USA	Actor, Comedian (Smothers Brothers)
Smulders, Cobie United Talent Agency, 9336 Civic Center Dr, Beverly Hills CA 90210 USA	Actress
Smurfit, Victoria Arts Rights Group, 4 Great Portland St, London W1W 8PA, England	Actress
Smyl, Stanley P (Stan) Vancouver Canucks, 800 Griffiths Way, Vancouver BC V6B 6G1, Canada	Ice Hockey Player
Smyth, Greg 62 Carrick Dr, Saint John's NF A1A 4N7, Canada	Ice Hockey Player
Smyth, Joe O-Seven Artist Mgmt, PO Box 210586, Nashville TN 37221, USA	Singer, Drummer (Sawyer Brown)
Smyth, Patty 23712 Malibu Colony Road, Malibu CA 90265, USA	Singer, Songwriter
Smyth, Randy 17136 Bluewater Lane, Huntington Beach CA 92649, USA	Yachtsman
Smyth, Ryan A G Chance Restaurant, 2550-10155 102nd St NW, Edmonton ON T5J 4G8, Canada	Ice Hockey Player
Smyth, Steve 44005 Northgate Ave, Temecula CA 92592, USA	Baseball Player
Smythe, Danny Horizon Mgmt, PO Box 8770, Endwell NY 13762, USA	Singer, Drummer (Box Tops)
Snead, Esix 1332 42nd St, Orlando FL 32839, USA	Baseball Player
Snead, Jesse Caryle (J C) 11815 SE Plandome Dr, Hobe Sound FL 33455, USA	Golfer

S

Snead, Norman B (Norm)	Football Player
6311 Courthouse Road, Providence Forge VA 23140, USA	
Snead, W T, Sr	Religious Leader
Baptist Convention Missionary, PO Box 1602, Los Angeles CA 90001, USA	
Snedden, Stephen	Actor
Marshak/Zachary Co, 8840 Wilshire Blvd, #100, Beverly Hills CA 90211 USA	
Snedeker, Brandt	Golfer
4307 Glen Eden Dr, Nashville TN 37205, USA	
Snee, Christopher (Chris)	Football Player
1049 Clark Road, Franklin Lake NJ 07417, USA	
Sneed, Ed	Golfer
4155 Nottinghill Gate Road, Columbus OH 43220, USA	
Sneed, Floyd	Drummer (Three Dog Night)
Creative Artists Agency, 2000 Ave of Stars, #100, Los Angeles CA 90067 USA	
Snegur, Mircea Ion	President, Moldova
62A Puschin Str, Chsinev, Moldova	
Snell, Esmond E	Biochemist
819 Tempted Ways Dr, Longmont CO 80504, USA	
Snell, Ian D	Baseball Player
15612 Lemon Fish Dr, Bradenton FL 34202, USA	
Snell, Matthews (Matt)	Football Player
Snell Construction, 175 Clendenny Ave, Jersey City NJ 07304, USA	
Snell, Nathaniel (Nate)	Baseball Player
272 Hampton Dr, Orangeburg SC 29118, USA	
Snell, Peter	Track Athlete
6452 Dunston Lane, Dallas TX 75214, USA	
Snell, Ray M	Football Player
1411 W Linebaugh Ave, Tampa FL 33612, USA	
Snelling, Chris	Baseball Player
PO Box 184, Sumner WA 98390, USA	
Snelson, Kenneth D	Sculptor, Artist
37 W 12th St, New York NY 10011, USA	
Snepsts, Harold	Ice Hockey Player
5623 Highfield Dr, Burnaby BC V5B 1E4, Canada	
Sneva, Tom	Auto Racing Driver
3301 E Valley Vista Lane, Paradise Valley AZ 85253, USA	
Sniadecki, James B (Jim)	Football Player
3267 Congressional Circle, Fairfield CA 94534, USA	
Snicket, Lemony	Writer
Harper Collins Publishers, 10 E 53rd St, Cellar 1, New York NY 10022 USA	
Snider, David D (Dee)	Singer (Twisted Sister)
Rebellion Entertainment, 2440 Broadway, #111, New York NY 10024, USA	
Snider, Edward M (Ed)	Ice Hockey Executive
PO Box 25088, Philadelphia PA 19147, USA	
Snider, Malcolm P	Football Player
3997 Orchard Heights Road NW, Salem OR 97304, USA	
Snider, Mike	Banjo Player, Comedian
PO Box 610, Gleason TN 38229, USA	
Snider, R Michael	Medical Researcher
Pfizer Pharmaceuticals, Eastern Point Road, Groton CT 06340, USA	
Snider, Todd	Singer, Songwriter
Gold Mountain, 3940 Laurel Canyon Blvd, #444, Studio City CA 91604 USA	
Snider, Van V	Baseball Player
1615 Windsor Dr, Cleveland OH 44124, USA	
Snipes, Wesley	Actor
Snell & Wilmer, 600 Anton Ave, #1400, Costa Mesa CA 92626, USA	
Snitzler, Larry	Concert Guitarist
Lindy Martin Mgmt, 1007 Lakewater Dr, Henrico VA 23229, USA	
Snook, Frank W	Baseball Player
2580 Elysium Ave, Eugene OR 97401, USA	
Snook, Sarah	Actress
United Talent Agency, 9336 Civic Center Dr, Beverly Hills CA 90210 USA	
Snoop Dogg-Lion	Rap Artist
Paradigm Agency, 360 N Crescent Dr, North Building, Beverly Hills CA 90210 USA	
Snopek, Christopher S (Chris)	Baseball Player
101 Ashton Park Blvd, Madison WS 39110, USA	
Snow	Singer, Songwriter
Richard Walters, PO Box 2789, Toluca Lake CA 91610 USA	
Snow, Brittany	Actress
I C M Partners, 10250 Constellation Blvd, #900, Los Angeles CA 90067 USA	
Snow, D J (Michelle)	Basketball Player
Washington Mystics, Verizon Center, 401 9th St NW, #750, Washington DC 20004 USA	
Snow, Eric	Basketball Player
3115 Manor Bridge Dr, Alpharetta GA 30004, USA	
Snow, Garth	Ice Hockey Player
4 Weeping Willow Court, Glen Head NY 11545, USA	
Snow, Gene	Drag Racing Driver
Snowman Racing, 5719 Airport Freeway, Haltom City TX 76117, USA	
Snow, Jack T (J T)	Baseball Player
15 Bridle Court, Hillsborough CA 94010, USA	
Snow, John W	Secretary, Treasury; Businessman
Cerberus Capital Mgmt, 299 Park Ave, #2300, New York NY 10171, USA	
Snow, Justin W	Football Player
1826 Milford St, Carmel IN 46032, USA	
Snow, Mark	Composer
Robert Urband Assoc, 8981 W Sunset Blvd, #311, West Hollywood CA 90069, USA	
Snowden, James J (Jim)	Football Player
8647 Point of Woods Dr, Manassas VA 20110, USA	
Snowden, M L	Sculptor
Masterpiece Publishing, 5 Watson, Irvine CA 92618, USA	
Snowdon, Earl of (A C R Armstrong-Jones)	Photographer
22 Launceston Place, London W8 5RL, England	
Snowdon, Lisa	Model, Actress
Money Mgmt, 42A Berwick St, London W1F 8RZ, England	
Snuggerud, Dave	Ice Hockey Player
4529 Saddlewood Dr, Minnetonka MN 55345, USA	

Snyder, Allan W — Optical Scientist
National University, Optical Science Center, Canberra ACT 2601, Australia

Snyder, Barbara — Educator
Case Western University, President's Office, Aldebert Hall, Cleveland OH 44106, USA

Snyder, Bill — Football Coach
Kansas State University, Athletic Dept, Manhattan KS 66506, USA

Snyder, Christoper R (Chris) — Baseball Player
4921 W Electra Lane, Glendale AZ 85310, USA

Snyder, Evan — Neurologist
Harvard Medical School, 25 Shattuck St, Boston MA 02115, USA

Snyder, Gary S — Writer
18442 MacNab Cypress Road, Nevada City CA 95959, USA

Snyder, Gerald G (Jerry) — Baseball Player
2553 Wild Oak Forest Lane, Seabrook TX 77586, USA

Snyder, J Cory — Baseball Player
468 N Loafer Dr, Payson UT 84651, USA

Snyder, James R (Jimmy) — Baseball Player, Manager
7516 Dunbridge Dr, Odessa FL 33556, USA

Snyder, Joey, III — Golfer
8811 E Riviera Dr, Scottsdale AZ 85260, USA

Snyder, Kirk P — Basketball Player
Minnesota Timberwolves, Target Center, 600 1st Ave N, Minneapolis MN 55403 USA

Snyder, Kyle E — Baseball Player
1869 Upper Cove Terrace, Sarasota FL 34231, USA

Snyder, Liza — Actress
Susan Smith, 1344 N Wetherly Dr, Los Angeles CA 90069 USA

Snyder, Richard J (Dick) — Basketball Player
4621 E Mockingbird Lane, Paradise Valley AZ 85253, USA

Snyder, Russell H (Russ) — Baseball Player
PO Box 264, Nelson NE 68961, USA

Snyder, Solomon H — Psychiatrist, Pharmacologist
3801 Canterbury Road, #1001, Baltimore MD 21218, USA

Snyder, Suzanne — Actress
Premiere Artists Agency, 1875 Century Park E, #2250, Los Angeles CA 90067 USA

Snyder, William D — Photojournalist
Rochester Institute of Technology, Photojournalism Dept, Rochester NY 14623, USA

Snyder, Zack — Director, Writer
Cruel & Unusual Films, 4000 Warner Blvd, Building 90, Burbank CA 91522, USA

Snyderman, Nancy — Surgeon, Entertainer
ABC-TV, News Dept, 77 W 66th St, New York NY 10023 USA

So Ywon Ryu — Golfer
Ladies Pro Golf Assn, 100 International Golf Dr, Daytona Beach FL 32124 USA

So, Perry — Conductor
Harrison/Parrott, 5-6 Albion Court, London W6 0QT, England

Soares, Mario A N L — President, Portugal
Rua Dr Joao Soares #2-3, 1600 Lisbon, Portugal

Sobchuk, Dennis J — Ice Hockey Player
PO Box 2541, Carefree AZ 85377, USA

Sobel, Dava — Writer
Walker Co, 435 Hudson St, New York NY 10014, USA

Sobers, Ricky B — Basketball Player
6530 Annie Oakley Dr, #1414, Henderson NV 89014, USA

Sobieski, Leelee — Actress
Mosiac Media Group, 9200 W Sunset Blvd, #1000, Los Angeles CA 90069 USA

Sobrero Markgraf, Kate — Soccer Player
5055 N Cumberland Blvd, Milwaukee WI 53217, USA

Sobule, Jill — Singer, Songwriter
Podell Talent Agency, 22 W 21st St, #900, New York NY 10010, USA

Sochor, James (Jim) — Football Coach
1018 Kent Dr, Davis CA 95616, USA

Sodano, Angelo Cardinal — Religious Leader
Office of Secretary of State, Plaza Apostolico, 00120 Vatican City

Soderbergh, Steven A — Director
Anonymous Content, 3532 Hayden Ave, Culver City CA 90232 USA

Soderholm, Eric T — Baseball Player
10S360 Hampshire Lane W, Willowbrook IL 60527, USA

Soderqvist, Johan — Composer
First Artists, 1631 N Bristol St, #B20, Santa Ana CA 92706 USA

Sodowski, Clint R — Baseball Player
351 Whippoorwill Road, Ponca City OK 74604, USA

Soedergren, Anders — Cross Country Skier
Hinderstigen 4, 831 32 Ostersund, Sweden

Soell, Stefan — Photographer
Fotodesign Stefan Soell, Gewerbepark, Fallenbrunner 17, 88045 Friedrichshafen, Germany

Soetaert, Douglas H (Doug) — Ice Hockey Player
13006 66th Ave SE, Snohomish WA 98296, USA

Sofaer, Abraham D — Attorney
1200 Bryant St, Palo Alto CA 94301, USA

Sofer, Rena — Actress
Framework Entertainment, 9057 Nemo St, #C, West Hollywood CA 90069 USA

Soffer, Jesse Lee — Actor
Innovative Artists, 1505 10th St, Santa Monica CA 90401 USA

Sofield, William — Interior Designer, Artist
Studio Sofield, 380 Lafayette St, #300, New York NY 10003, USA

Softley, Iain — Director
32A Carnaby St, London W1V 1PA, England

Sogliuzzo, Andre — Actor
W M E Entertainment, 9601 Wilshire Blvd, #300, Beverly Hills CA 90210 USA

Sohn, Kurt F — Football Player
6 Paine Commons, Yaphank NY 11980, USA

Sohn, Sonja — Actress
A P A Talent/Literary Agency, 405 S Beverly Dr, #300, Beverly Hills CA 90212 USA

Sojo, Luis B — Baseball Player
6002 Palm Shadow Way, #1210, Tampa FL 33647, USA

Soklosky, Bing — Cinematographer
4654 Cartwright Ave, North Hollywood CA 91602, USA

Soko — Singer, Actress
Agence Artiste Adequet, 80 Rue d'Amsterdam, 75009 Paris, France

Sokoloff, Marla — Actress
A P A Talent/Literary Agency, 405 S Beverly Dr, #300, Beverly Hills CA 90212 USA

Sokolov, Grigory L — Concert Pianist
Konzertdirektion Schmid, Konigstra 36, 30175 Hannover, Germany

Sokolov, Valeriy — Concert Violinist
Harrison/Parrott, 5-6 Albion Court, London W6 0QT, England

Sokomanu, A George — President, Vanuatu
Mele Village, PO Box 1319, Port Vila, Vanuatu

Sokurov, Alexander N — Director
Smolenskaya Nab 4, #222, 199048 Saint Petersburg, Russia

Solana Madariaga, Javier — Government Official, Spain
European Union Foreign Office, Rue de la Loi, 1048 Brussels, Belgium

Solberg, Magnar — Biathlete
Stabellvn 60, 7000 Trondheim, Norway

Soleil, Stella — Singer
Kurfirst/Blackwell, 601 W 26th St, #11, New York NY 10001, USA

Soleri, Paolo — Architect, Sculptor
Cosanti Foundation, 6433 Doubletree Road, Paradise Valley AZ 85253, USA

Soles, P J — Actress
Paradigm Agency, 360 N Crescent Dr, North Building, Beverly Hills CA 90210 USA

Solh, Rashid el- — Prime Minister, Lebanon
Chambre de Deputes, Place de l'Etoile, Beirut, Lebanon

Solich, Frank — Football Coach
Ohio University, Athletic Dept, Athens OH 45701, USA

Solinger, Bob — Ice Hockey Player
65-101 Grove Dr, Spruce Grove AB T7X 3H7, Canada

Solis, Alex — Thoroughbred Racing Jockey
2241 Redwood Dr, Glendora CA 91741, USA

Solis, Hilda I — Secretary of Labor; Representative, CA
Labor Department, 200 Constitution Ave NW, Washington DC 20210 USA

Soljacic, Marin — Physicist
Massachusetts Institute of Technology, Physics Dept, Cambridge MA 02139, USA

Sollett, Peter — Director
W M E Entertainment, 9601 Wilshire Blvd, #300, Beverly Hills CA 90210 USA

Sollscher, Goran — Concert Guitarist
Herbert Barrett, 266 W 37th St, #2000, New York NY 10018 USA

Solo, Ksenia — Actress
Abrams Artists, 9200 W Sunset Blvd, #1125, West Hollywood CA 90069 USA

Soloff, Lew — Trumpeter (Blood Sweat & Tears)
Abby Hoffer, 223 1/2 E 48th St, New York NY 10017 USA

Soloman, Sean C — Space Scientist
Carnegie Institution, Terrestrial Magnetism Dept, Washington DC 20015, USA

Solomon, Ariel E — Football Player
5045 51st St, Boulder CO 80301, USA

Solomon, Bruce — Actor
Hollander, 14011 Ventura Blvd, #202W, Sherman Oaks CA 91423, USA

Solomon, Jesse W — Football Player
401 SW Bunker St, Madison FL 32340, USA

Solomon, Robert — Economist
8502 W Howell Road, Bethesda MD 20817, USA

Solomon, Susan — Atmospheric Chemist
National Oceanic/Atmospheric Admin, 325 Broadway, Boulder CO 80305, USA

Solondz, Todd — Director, Writer
W M E Entertainment, 9601 Wilshire Blvd, #300, Beverly Hills CA 90210 USA

Solovay, Robert M — Mathematician
University of California, Mathematics Dept, Berkeley CA 94720, USA

Soloviyev, Vladimir A — Cosmonaut
Khovanskaya Ul D 3, Kv 28, 129515 Moscow, Russia

Solovyev, Anatoly Y — Cosmonaut
Cosmonaut Training Center, Star City, 141160 Zvezdny Gorodok, Moscow Oblast, Russia

Solovyev, Sergei A — Director, Writer
Akademika Pilyugina Str 8, Korp 1, #330, 117393 Moscow, Russia

Solow, Robert M — Nobel Economics Laureate
1010 Waltham St, #328, Lexington MA 02421, USA

Solt, Ronald M (Ron) — Football Player
1200 Thornhurst Road, Bear Creek Township PA 18702, USA

Soltan, Jerzy — Architect
148 Boylston St, Watertown MA 02472, USA

Soltau, Gordon L (Gordy) — Football Player
1290 Sharon Park Dr, #50, Menlo Park CA 94025, USA

Solvay, Jacques E — Businessman
Solvay & Cie SA, Rue du Prince Albert 33, 1050 Brussels, Belgium

Solzhenitsyn, Ignat — Concert Pianist
Columbia Artists Mgmt Inc, 1790 Broadway, #702, New York NY 10019 USA

Som, Peter — Fashion Designer
Peter Som Inc, 215 W 40th St, New York NY 10018, USA

Somare, Michael T — Prime Minister, Papua New Guinea
Prime Minister's Office, Parliament House, Waigani 131 N D, Papua New Guinea

Somerhalder, Ian — Actor
I C M Partners, 10250 Constellation Blvd, #900, Los Angeles CA 90067 USA

Somers, Gwen — Actress, Model
Alice Fries Agency, 1927 Vista Del Mar Ave, Los Angeles CA 90068, USA

Somers, Suzanne — Actress
Port Carling Productions, 23961 Craftsman Road, Calabasas CA 91302, USA

Somerset, Williard F (Willie) — Basketball Player
6441 Oak View Dr, Harrisburg PA 17112, USA

Somerville, Bonnie — Actress, Singer
McKeon-Myrones Mgmt, 3500 Olive Ave, #770, Burbank CA 91505 USA

Somerville, David (Dave) — Singer (Diamonds)
10061 Riverside Dr, #114, Toluca Lake CA 91602, USA

Somerville, Robert E — Religion Educator
Columbia University, Religion Dept, Claremont Hall, New York NY 10027, USA

Sommaruga, Cornelio — Association Executive
16 Chemin des Crets-de-Champel, 1206 Geneva, Switzerland

Sommer, Alfred — Epidemiologist
Johns Hopkins University, Hygiene/Public Health School, Baltimore MD 21218, USA
Sommer, Elke — Actress, Model
Literature Unlimited, 1850 N Whitley Ave, #1020, Los Angeles CA 90028, USA
Sommer, Josef — Actor
Don Buchwald/Fortitude, 6500 Wilshire Blvd, #2200, Los Angeles CA 90048 USA
Sommer, Richard O (Rich), II — Actor
A P A Talent/Literary Agency, 405 S Beverly Dr, #300, Beverly Hills CA 90212 USA
Sommer, Ron — Businessman
Deutsche Telekom, Friedrich-Ebert-Allee 140, 53113 Bonn, Germany
Sommer, Roy — Ice Hockey Player
65 Roman Dr, Shrewsbury MA 01545, USA
Sommer-Bodenbu, Angela — Writer, Artist
PO Box 834, Silver City NM 88062, USA
Sommers, Joanie — Singer
Xentel, 101 NE 3rd Ave, #203, Fort Lauderdale FL 33301, USA
Sommers, Stephen — Director
Sommers Co, 204 Santa Monica Blvd, #A, Santa Monica CA 90401, USA
Sommore, Laura Rambough — Actress, Comedienne
Paradigm Agency, 360 N Crescent Dr, North Building, Beverly Hills CA 90210 USA
Somorjai, Gabor A — Chemist
665 San Luis Road, Berkeley CA 94707, USA
Son, Masayoshi — Inventor (Pocket Electronic Translator)
24-1 Nihonbash, Hakozakicho, Chuuku, Tokyo 103-8501, Japan
Sondeckis, Saulis — Conductor
Saint Petersburg Hermitage Orchestra, Mikhailovskaya Str 2, 191186 Saint Petersburg, Russia
Sondheim, Stephen J — Composer, Lyricist
265 Wollaton Vale, Wollato, Nottingham NG8 2PX, England
Sonefeld, Jim — Drummer (Hootie & the Blowfish)
FishCo Mgmt, 2519 Devine Street Columbia SC 29205, USA
Song, Brenda — Actress
United Talent Agency, 9336 Civic Center Dr, Beverly Hills CA 90210 USA
Songaila, Antoinette — Astronomer
University of Hawaii, Astronomy Dept, Honolulu HI 96822, USA
Songaila, Darius — Basketball Player
141 S Longfellow Lane, Mooresville NC 28117, USA
Soni, Karan — Actor
Michael Zanuck's Agency, 28035 Dorothy Dr, #120, Agoura Hills CA 91301, USA
Soni, Rebecca — Swimmer
University of Southern California, Trojan Swim Club, Athletic Dept, Los Angeles CA 90089, USA
Sonja — Queen, Norway
Det Kongelige Slott, Drammensveien 1, 0010 Oslo, Norway
Sonnanstine, Andrews M (Andy) — Baseball Player
526 Reimer Road, Wadsworth OH 44281, USA
Sonnenfeld, Barry — Director
W M E Entertainment, 9601 Wilshire Blvd, #300, Beverly Hills CA 90210 USA
Sonnenfeldt, Helmut — Businessman, Educator
5600 Wisconsin Ave, #1505, Chevy Chase MD 20815, USA
Sonnenschein, Hugo F — Educator, Economist
1126 E 59th St, Chicago IL 60637, USA
Sonnichsen, Matt — Volleyball Player
Newberry College, Athletic Dept, Newberry SC 29108, USA
Sonnier, Jo-El — Singer, Guitarist
Fat City Artists, 1906 Chet Atkins Place, #502, Nashville TN 37212 USA
Sonzero, Jim — Director, Writer
United Talent Agency, 9336 Civic Center Dr, Beverly Hills CA 90210 USA
Soo Yun Kang — Golfer
Ladies Pro Golf Assn, 100 International Golf Dr, Daytona Beach FL 32124 USA
Soomekh, Bahar — Actress
McClure Assoc, 5225 Wilshire Blvd, #909, Los Angeles CA 90036, USA
Sope Mautamata, Barak T — Prime Minister, Vanuatu
Melanesian Progressive Pati (MPP), PO Box 39, Port Vila, Vanuatu
Sophia — Queen Consort, Spain
Palacio de la Zarzuela, 28071 Madrid, Spain
Sophie — Hereditary Princess, Liechtenstein
Heriditary Princess's Residence, Schloss Vaduz, 9490 Vaduz, Liechtenstein
Sorbo, Kevin — Actor
914 Westwood Blvd, #584, Los Angeles CA 90024, USA
Sorel, Edward — Artist, Illustrator
156 Franklin St, New York NY 10013, USA
Sorel, Jean — Actor
Agents Associes, 201 Rue du Faubourg Saint Honore, 75008 Paris, France
Sorel, Louise — Actress
20 E 74th St, #3F, New York NY 10021, USA
Sorensen, Andrew A — Educator
Greenville Hospital System, 701 Grove Road, Greenville SC 29605, USA
Sorensen, Holly B — Producer, Writer, Actress
United Talent Agency, 9336 Civic Center Dr, Beverly Hills CA 90210 USA
Sorensen, Jacki F — Physical Fitness Expert
Jacki's Inc, 129 1/2 N Woodland Blvd, #5, Deland FL 32720, USA
Sorensen, Lary A — Baseball Player
42515 Northville Place Dr, #406, Northville MI 48167, USA
Sorensen, Nicholas C (Nick) — Football Player
305 Grandview Dr, Blacksburg VA 24060, USA
Sorenson, B Reed — Auto Racing Driver
4623 Rivers Edge Village, #6508, Ponce Inlet FL 32127, USA
Sorenson, Garrett — Opera Singer
I M G Artists, Hogarth Business Park, Chiswick, London W4 2TH, England
Sorenson, Heidi — Model, Actress
Shelly & Pierce, 13775A Mono Way, #220, Sonora CA 95370 USA
Sorenstam, Annika — Golfer
International Mgmt Group, 1 Erieview Plaza, 1360 E 9th St, Cleveland OH 44114 USA
Sorenstam, Charlotta — Golfer
1411 W Whitman Court, Anthem AZ 85086, USA
Sorey, Revie C, II — Football Player
10 E Delaware Place, #31C, Chicago IL 60611, USA

Sorgi, James (Jim)
1316 Greenstone Dr, Danville IN 46122, USA — Football Player

Soriano, Alfonso G
21 E Huron St, #3301, Chicago IL 60611, USA — Baseball Player

Soriano, Edward
Northrop Grumman, 1840 Century Park E, Los Angeles CA 90067, USA — Army General

Soriano, Rafael
15001 35th Ave W, #5-202, Lynnwood WA 98087, USA — Baseball Player

Sorkin, Aaron B
W M E Entertainment, 9601 Wilshire Blvd, #300, Beverly Hills CA 90210 USA — Producer, Writer

Sorkin, Andrew Ross
Creative Artists Agency, 2000 Ave of Stars, #100, Los Angeles CA 90067 USA — Actor

Sorkin, Arleen
Creative Artists Agency, 2000 Ave of Stars, #100, Los Angeles CA 90067 USA — Actress

Sorlie, Donald M
6947 Wagner Way NW, #A, Gig Harbor WA 98335, USA — Test Pilot

Sorokin, Peter P
5 Ashwood Road, South Salem NY 10590, USA — Physicist

Soros, George
Soros Fund Mgmt, 888 7th Ave, #2900, New York NY 10106, USA — Financier

Sorrell, Henry T
404 Oak St, Talladega AL 35160, USA — Football Player

Sorrell, John W
Lawns, 16 South Grove, London N6 6BJ, England — Fashion Designer

Sorrell, Martin
Ogilvy & Mather Worldwide, 1 Soldiers Field Park, #413, Boston MA 02163, USA — Businessman

Sorrento, Paul A
5918 Mont Blance Place NW, Issaquah WA 98027, USA — Baseball Player

Sortun, Henrik M (Rick)
6708 16th Ave NW, Seattle WA 98117, USA — Football Player

Sorum, Matt
Sanctuary Mgmt, 15301 Ventura Blvd, Building B, Sherman Oaks CA 91403, USA — Drummer (Velvet Revolver)

Sorvino, Mira K
Untitled Entertainment, 350 S Beverly Dr, #200, Beverly Hills CA 90212 USA — Actress

Sorvino, Paul
Innovative Artists, 1505 10th St, Santa Monica CA 90401 USA — Actor

Sosa, Elias M
3126 Summerfield Ridge Lane, Matthews NC 28105, USA — Baseball Player

Sosa, Ernest
Brown University, Philosophy Dept, Providence RI 02912, USA — Philosopher

Sosa, Samuel (Sammy)
505 N Lake Shore Dr, #5500, Chicago IL 60611, USA — Baseball Player

Sosnovska, Olga
Innovative Artists, 1505 10th St, Santa Monica CA 90401 USA — Actress

Sossamon, Shannyn
Management Production Entertainment, 9229 Sunset Blvd, #301, West Hollywood CA 90069, USA — Actress

Sostorics, Colleen
Team Canada, 2424 University Dr NW, Calgary AB T2N 3Y9, Canada — Ice Hockey Player

Sotillo, Nolan A
United Talent Agency, 9336 Civic Center Dr, Beverly Hills CA 90210 USA — Actor

Sotin, Hans
Schulheide 10, 21227 Bendestorf, Germany — Opera Singer

Sotkilava, Zurab L
Bolshoi Theater, Teatralnaya Pl 1, 103009 Moscow, Russia — Opera Singer

Soto, Blanca
Latin World Entertainment, 3470 NW 82nd Ave, #670, Miami FL 33122, USA — Actress

Soto, Geovany
6319 Perch Creek Dr, Houston TX 77049, USA — Baseball Player

Soto, Jock
New York City Ballet, Lincoln Center Plaza, New York NY 10023 USA — Ballet Dancer

Soto, Mario M
Cincinnati Reds, Great American Ball Park, 100 Main St, Cincinnati OH 45202 USA — Baseball Player

Soto, Talisa
Paradigm Agency, 360 N Crescent Dr, North Building, Beverly Hills CA 90210 USA — Actress, Model

Sotomayor Sanabria, Javier
International Mgmt Group, 1 Erieview Plaza, 1360 E 9th St, Cleveland OH 44114 USA — Track Athlete

Sotomayor, Antonio
3 LeRoy Place, San Francisco CA 94109, USA — Artist

Sotomayor, Sonia M
US Supreme Court, 1 1st St NE, Washington DC 20543 USA — Supreme Court Justice

Soualem, Zinedine
Voyez Mon Agent, 20 Ave Rapp, 75007 Paris, France — Actor

Souare, Ahmed Tidiane
Prime Minister's Office, PO Box 5141, Cite des Nations, Conakry, Guinea — Prime Minister, Guinea

Souchon, Alain
Voyez Mon Agent, 20 Ave Rapp, 75007 Paris, France — Singer

Soukupova, Hana
Mega Model Agency, Kaiser-Wilhelm-Stra 93, 20355 Hamburg, Germany — Model

Soul, David
Diamond Mgmt, 31 Percy St, London W1T 2DD, England — Actor, Singer

Soulja Boy
Soulja Boy Music, 113 Shadow Lane, Batesville MS 38606, USA — Rap Artist

Soumare, Cheikh Hadjibou
Prime Minister's Office, Ave Leopold Sedar Senghor, Dakar, Senegal — Prime Minister, Senegal

Soumyanath, Amala
Oregon Health Science University, 3181 SW Jackson Park Dr, Portland OR 97239 USA — Neurologist

Souray, Sheldon S
4124 Madella Ave, Sherman Oaks CA 91403, USA — Ice Hockey Player

Sourouzian, Hourig
31 Abu El Reda, 11211 Cairo-Zamalek, Egypt — Archaeologist

Soutar, Dave
6910 Chickasaw Bayou Road, Bradenton FL 34203, USA — Bowler

Soutar, Judy
6910 Chickasaw Bayou Road, Bradenton FL 34203, USA — Bowler

Soutendijk, Renee
Marion Rosenberg, PO Box 69826, West Hollywood CA 90069 USA — Actress

Souter, David H — Supreme Court Justice
214 Hopkins Green Road, Contoocook NH 03229, USA
Southam, James — Cross Counry Skier
18230 Norway Dr, Anchorage AK 99516, USA
Souther, J D — Singer, Guitarist, Songwriter
Paul Hanan Mgmt, 7775 Sunset Blvd, #118, Los Angeles CA 90046, USA
Southern, Edwin M — Biochemist
Oxford University, Wellington Square, Oxford OX1 2JD, England
Southern, Silas (Eddie) — Track Athlete
2006 Custer Parkway, Richardson TX 75080, USA
Southern, Taryn — Actress, Singer
I C M Partners, 10250 Constellation Blvd, #900, Los Angeles CA 90067 USA
Southwick, Leslie H — Judge
US Court of Appeals, Eastland Courthouse, 245 E Capitol St, Jackson MS 39201, USA
Southworth, William F (Bill) — Baseball Player
320 Dobbins Road, Saint Louis MO 63119, USA
Souto de Moura, Eduardo — Pritzker Architectual Laureate
University of Oporto, Architecture Faculty, Praca Gomes Teixeira, 4099 002 Porto, Portugal
Souza, K Mark — Baseball Player
1120 Dumas Way, Roseville CA 95747, USA
Sova, Peter M — Cinematographer
1492 Roses Brook Road, South Kortright NY 13842, USA
Sovern, Michael I — Educator, Attorney
Columbia University, Law School, 435 W 116th St, New York NY 10027, USA
Sovran, Gino — Basketball Player
2669 Cheswick Dr, Troy MI 48084, USA
Sowell, Arnold (Arnie) — Track Athlete
1647 Waterstone Lane, #1, Charlotte NC 28262, USA
Sowell, Jerald M — Football Player
201 Stockton Dr, Southlake TX 76092, USA
Sowell, Thomas — Economist
Stanford University, Hoover Institution, Stanford CA 94305, USA
Sowells, Richard A (Rich) — Football Player
16718 Chewton Glen St, Tomball TX 77377, USA
Sowers, Jeremy — Baseball Player
43793 Apache Wells Terrace, Leesburg VA 20176, USA
Soyer, Ferdi Sabit — Prime Minister, Turkish Northern Cypress
Prime Minister's Office, Via Mersin 10, Lefkosa, Turkish Northern Cypress
Soyinka, Wole — Nobel Literature Laureate
University of Nevada, Creative Writing Dept, Las Vegas NV 89154, USA
Soyster, Harry E — Army General
56 Lakeview Ave, #14, New Canaan CT 06840, USA
Sozzi, Sebastian — Actor
Harvest Talent Mgmt, PO Box 279, Jefferson Valley NY 10535, USA
Spaak, Ruth — Artist
20 Sandfield Road, Stratford upon Avon, Warwickshire CV37 9AG, England
Spacek, Jaroslav — Ice Hockey Player
5944 Corinne Lane, Clarence Center NY 14032, USA
Spacek, Sissy — Actress
PO Box 22, #640, Cobham VA 22947, USA
Spacey, Kevin — Actor
Joanne Horowitz Mgmt, 9350 Wilshire Blvd, #224, Beverly Hills CA 90212, USA
Spacks, Patricia M — Educator
249 E Jefferson St, Charlottesville VA 22902, USA
Spade, David — Actor, Comedian
W M E Entertainment, 9601 Wilshire Blvd, #300, Beverly Hills CA 90210 USA
Spade, Kate — Fashion Designer
48 W 25th St, #400, New York NY 10010, USA
Spader, James — Actor
I C M Partners, 10250 Constellation Blvd, #900, Los Angeles CA 90067 USA
Spaelty, Valeria — Curling Athlete
Curling Assn, PO Box 606, 3000 Bern, Switzerland
Spagnola, John S — Football Player
414 Hillbrook Road, Bryn Mawr PA 19010, USA
Spagnuolo, Steve J — Football Coach
New Orleans Saints, 5800 Airline Highway, Metairie LA 70003 USA
Spain, Douglas — Actor
Kritzer Levine Wilkins Griffin, 11872 La Grange Ave, #100, Los Angeles CA 90025 USA
Spalding, Esperanza — Singer, Bassist, Composer
Montuno Producciones, Calle Rosello 246, #5-2, 08008 Barcelona, Spain
Spalding, Leslie — Golfer
1055 O'Malley Dr, Billings MT 59102, USA
Spall, Rafe — Actor
Troika, 74 Clerkenwell Road, #300, London EC1M 5QA, England
Spall, Timothy — Actor
Markham & Froggatt, Julian House, 4 Windmill St, London W1P 1HF, England
Spampinato, Joey — Bassist (NRBQ)
Skyline Music, 2270 Maiden Lane SW, Roanoke VA 24015, USA
Spampinato, Johnny — Guitarist (NRBQ)
Skyline Music, 2270 Maiden Lane SW, Roanoke VA 24015, USA
Span, K Denard — Baseball Player
Minnesota Twins, Metrodome, 34 Kirby Puckett Place, Minneapolis MN 55415 USA
Spanbauer, Tom — Writer
Houghton Mifflin Harcourt, 215 Park Ave S, #1200, New York NY 10003 USA
Spander, Art — Sportswriter
San Francisco Examiner, Editorial Dept, 110 5th Ave, San Francisco CA 94118, USA
Spangler, Albert D (Al) — Baseball Player
27202 Afton Way, Huffman TX 77336, USA
Spani, Gary L — Football Player
3920 NE Sequoia St, Lees Summit MO 64064, USA
Spano, Joe — Actor
Sutton-Barth Vennari, 145 S Fairfax Ave, #310, Los Angeles CA 90036 USA
Spano, Robert — Conductor
Opus 3 Artists, 470 Park Ave S, #900N, New York NY 10016 USA
Spano, Vincent — Actor
Glick Agency, 1321 7th St, #203, Santa Monica CA 90401 USA

Spanswick, Willaim H (Bill)	Baseball Player
1200 Commonwealth Circle, #202, Naples FL 34116, USA	
Sparks, Dana	Actress
Vox Inc, 6420 Wilshire Blvd, #1080, Los Angeles CA 90048 USA	
Sparks, Daniel	Basketball Player
2396 N Bruceville Road, Vincennes IN 47591, USA	
Sparks, Hal	Actor, Singer, Comedian
Innovative Artists, 1505 10th St, Santa Monica CA 90401 USA	
Sparks, J Jeffrey (Jeff)	Baseball Player
714 W 42nd St, Houston TX 77018, USA	
Sparks, Jordin	Singer, Actress
Varela Media, 14 E 77th St, #3F, New York NY 10075, USA	
Sparks, Nicholas C	Writer
United Talent Agency, 9336 Civic Center Dr, Beverly Hills CA 90210 USA	
Sparks, Paul	Actor
Gersh Agency, 41 Madison Ave, #3301, New York NY 10010 USA	
Sparks, Phillippi D	Football Player
4812 W Avenida del Rey, Phoenix AZ 85083, USA	
Sparks, Stephanie	Golfer
48 Redwood Lane, Wheeling WV 26003, USA	
Sparks, Steven W (Steve)	Baseball Player
4019 Colony Oaks Dr, Sugar Land TX 77479, USA	
Sparrow, Rory D	Basketball Player
111 Valley Road, Montclair NJ 07042, USA	
Sparv, Camilla	Actress
Tisherman Agency, 6767 Forest Lawn Dr, #101, Los Angeles CA 90068 USA	
Sparxxx, Bubba	Rap Artist
Media Artists Group, 333 E 43rd St, #115, New York NY 10017, USA	
Speake, Robert C (Bob)	Baseball Player
4742 SW Urish Road, Topeka KS 66610, USA	
Speakes, Stephen M	Army General
Deputy CofStaff, Resourcing/Programs, HqUSA, Pentagon, Washington DC 20310, USA	
Speakman-Pitt, William	Korean War South African Army Hero (VC)
Victoria Cross Assn, Old Admiralty Building, London SW1A 2BL, England	
Spear, Laurinda H	Architect
Arquitectonica International, 801 Brickell Ave, #1100, Miami FL 33131, USA	
Spearin, Charles	Musician
Agency Group Ltd, 142 W 57th St, #600, New York NY 10019 USA	
Spearritt, Hannah	Actress, Singer, Model
United Agents, 12-26 Lexington St, London W1F 0LE, England	
Spears, Aries	Actor, Comedian
Brillstein Entertainment Partners, 9150 Wilshire Blvd, #350, Beverly Hills CA 90212 USA	
Spears, Britney	Singer, Actress, Model
Tri-Star Sports & Entertainment, 215 Ward Circle, #200, Brentwood TN 37027, USA	
Spears, Glen F	Air Force General
Commander, 12th Air Force, Davis-Monthan Air Force Base AZ 85707 USA	
Spears, Jamie Lynn	Actress
Tri Star Sports & Entertainment, 450 N Roxbury Dr, #602, Beverly Hills CA 90210, USA	
Spears, Marcus D	Football Player
18634 Cypress Lake Village Dr, Cypress TX 77429, USA	
Spears, Marcus R	Football Player
3876 Shady Creek Court, Frisco TX 75033, USA	
Spears, Stephen	Sculptor
2021 County Road 33, Fair Hope AL 36532, USA	
Speck, Christa	Model
Marty Krofft, 7710 Woodrow Wilson Dr, Los Angeles CA 90046, USA	
Speck, Fred	Ice Hockey Player
2165 Country Club Dr, #23, Burlington ON L7M 4H4, Canada	
Speck, R Clifford (Cliff)	Baseball Player
823 S Nueva Vista Dr, Palm Springs CA 92264, USA	
Speck, Will	Director
Management 360, 9111 Wilshire Blvd, Beverly Hills CA 90210 USA	
Specter, Rachel	Actress
Innovative Artists, 1505 10th St, Santa Monica CA 90401 USA	
Speech	Rap Artist (Arrested Development)
Agency Group Ltd, 142 W 57th St, #600, New York NY 10019 USA	
Speeckaert, Glynn	Cinematographer
Dattner Disposto, 10635 Santa Monica Blvd, #165, Los Angeles CA 90025, USA	
Speed, Horace A	Baseball Player
6821 State Boulevard Extension, Meridian MS 39305, USA	
Speed, Lake C	Auto Racing Driver
Bud Moore Engineering, 400 N Fairview St, Spartanburg SC 29303, USA	
Speed, Scott A	Auto, Truck Racing Driver
Red Bull Racing, 136 Knob Hill Road, Mooresville NC 28117, USA	
Speed, U Grant	Sculptor
139 S 400 E, Lindon UT 84042, USA	
Speedman, Scott	Actor
Gary Goddard Agency, 10 Sainte Mary St, #305, Toronto, ON M4Y 1P9, Canada	
Speer, Hugo	Actor
Independent Talent Group, Oxford House, 76 Oxford St, London W1D 1BS, England	
Speers, Ted	Ice Hockey Player
61515 Brookway Dr, South Lyon MI 48178, USA	
Spehr, Timothy J (Tim)	Baseball Player
8524 Briargrove Dr, Woodway TX 76712, USA	
Speier, Chris E	Baseball Player
3614 El Encarto Dr, Calabasas CA 91302, USA	
Speight, Lester (Rasta)	Actor, Producer
T C A/Jed Root, 9220 Sunset Blvd, #315, Los Angeles CA 90069, USA	
Speights, Marresse	Basketball Player
Memphis Grizzlies, 191 Beale St, Memphis TN 38103 USA	
Speigner, Levale	Baseball Player
1041 Bond St, Thomasville GA 31757, USA	
Speir, Dona	Model, Actress
Playboy Promotions, 2706 Media Center Dr, Los Angeles CA 90065 USA	
Speiser, Jerry	Drummer (Men at Work)
T P A, PO Box 124, Round Corner NSW, Australia	

Spektor, Regina Big Hassle, 44 Wall St, #2200, New York NY 10005, USA	Singer, Pianist, Songwriter
Spelke, Elizabeth S Harvard University, Psychology Dept, Cambridge MA 02138, USA	Psychologist
Spelling, Randy United Talent Agency, 9336 Civic Center Dr, Beverly Hills CA 90210 USA	Actor
Spelling, Tori 594 S Mapleton Dr, Los Angeles CA 90024, USA	Actress
Spellman, Alonzo R 1201 W Queen St, Tulsa OK 74127, USA	Football Player
Spellman, John D 7048 51st Ave NE, Seattle WA 98115, USA	Governor, WA
Spence, A Michael 768 Mayfield Dr, Stanford CA 94305, USA	Nobel Economics Laureate
Spence, Bruce Johnson & Laird Management, PO Box 78340, Grey Lynn Auckland 1245, New Zealand	Actor
Spence, Gerry 3325 N University Ave, #200B, Provo UT 84604, USA	Attorney
Spence, J Robert (Bob) 3081 Bonita Woods Dr, Bonita CA 91902, USA	Baseball Player
Spence, Nicky I M G Artists, 152 W 57th St, #500, New York NY 10019 USA	Opera Singer
Spence, Sebastian Kirk Talent Agencies, 70 E 2nd Ave, #301, Vancouver BC V5T 1B1, Canada	Actor
Spencer, Abigail I C M Partners, 10250 Constellation Blvd, #900, Los Angeles CA 90067 USA	Actress
Spencer, Andre 1315 W Gage Ave, Los Angeles CA 90044, USA	Basketball Player
Spencer, Baldwin Prime Minister's Office, Factory Road, Saint John's, Antigua & Barbuda	Prime Minister, Antigua & Barbuda
Spencer, Bud Smile Productions, Via Cortina d'Ampezzo 156, 00135 Rome, Italy	Actor
Spencer, Chaske Josselyne Herman Assoc, 345 E 56th St, #3B, New York NY 10022, USA	Actor
Spencer, Chris Parallel Entertainment, 9420 Wilshire Blvd, #250, Beverly Hills CA 90212 USA	Actor, Comedian
Spencer, Daryl D 2740 S Larkin St, Wichita KS 67216, USA	Baseball Player
Spencer, Des Sheraton Mirage, Davidson St, Port Douglas 4871 QLD, Australia	Artist
Spencer, Elizabeth 402 Longleaf Dr, Chapel Hill NC 27517, USA	Writer
Spencer, Elmore 2770 Foxlair Trail, Atlanta GA 30349, USA	Basketball Player
Spencer, Felton L 4102 Nicholas Roy Court, Prospect KY 40059, USA	Basketball Player
Spencer, Freddie 7055 Speedway Blvd, #E106, Las Vegas NV 89115, USA	Motorcycle Racing Rider
Spencer, George E 8160 Hickory Ave, Galena OH 43021, USA	Baseball Player
Spencer, J Robert Polaris Entertainment, 8048 W 3rd St, #300, Los Angeles CA 90048, USA	Actor, Singer
Spencer, James A (Jimmy), Jr 5331 Talavero Place, Parker CO 80134, USA	Football Player, Coach
Spencer, Jesse Management 360, 9111 Wilshire Blvd, Beverly Hills CA 90210 USA	Actor, Musician
Spencer, Jimmy 597 Kenway Loop, Mooresville NC 28117, USA	Auto Racing Driver
Spencer, Lara W M E Entertainment, 9601 Wilshire Blvd, #300, Beverly Hills CA 90210 USA	Actress
Spencer, LaVryle Berkley Publishing Group, 375 Hudson St, Basement 1, New York NY 10014 USA	Writer
Spencer, M Shane 2858 Manzanita View Road, Alpine CA 91901, USA	Baseball Player
Spencer, Octavia W M E Entertainment, 9601 Wilshire Blvd, #300, Beverly Hills CA 90210 USA	Actress
Spencer, Scott Harper Collins Publishers, 10 E 53rd St, Cellar 1, New York NY 10022 USA	Writer
Spencer, Sean 3584 E Calistoga Court, Port Orchard WA 98366, USA	Baseball Player
Spencer, Shawntae 3714 Henley Dr, Pittsburgh PA 15235, USA	Football Player
Spencer, Sidney New York Liberty, Madison Square Garden, 2 Penn Plaza, New York NY 10121 USA	Basketball Player
Spencer, Stanley R (Stan) 3100 NE 188th St, Ridgefield WA 98642, USA	Baseball Player
Spencer, Timothy A (Tim) 1675 N Pebble Beach Way, Vernon Hills IL 60061, USA	Football Player
Spencer-Devlin, Muffin 1278 Glenneyre St, #155, Laguna Beach CA 92651, USA	Golfer
Spenn, Frederick C (Fred) 105 Heather Lane, Parrish FL 34219, USA	Baseball Umpire
Sperber Carter, Paula 10331 SW 102nd Ave, Miami FL 33176, USA	Bowler
Sperl, Natalie Denise C E S D, 10635 Santa Monica Blvd, #130, Los Angeles CA 90025 USA	Actress
Sperring, Robert W (Rob) 13302 Chriswood Dr, Cypress TX 77429, USA	Baseball Player
Speth, James G 986 Forest Road, New Haven CT 06515, USA	Government Official
Spezialy, Tom Jackoway Tyerman Wertheimer, 1925 Century Park E, #2200, Los Angeles CA 90067 USA	Producer, Writer
Spheeris, Penelope Spheeris Films, 3940 Laurel Canyon Blvd, #18, Studio City CA 91604, USA	Director
Spice 1 Richard Walters, PO Box 2789, Toluca Lake CA 91610 USA	Rap Artist

S

Spektor - Spice 1

Spicer, Kimberly — Model
Playboy Promotions, 2706 Media Center Dr, Los Angeles CA 90065 USA

Spicer, Paul — Football Player
136 Greenbriar Estates Dr, Saint Johns FL 32259, USA

Spicer, Robert O (Bob) — Baseball Player
423 McPhee Dr, Fayetteville NC 28305, USA

Spicer, William E, III — Physicist
620 Sand Hill Road, #305E, Palo Alto CA 94304, USA

Spiegel, Scott — Director
A P A Talent/Literary Agency, 405 S Beverly Dr, #300, Beverly Hills CA 90212 USA

Spiegelman, Art — Illustrator, Writer
Raw Books & Graphics, 27 Greene St, New York NY 10013, USA

Spielberg, David — Actor
10537 Cushdon Ave, Los Angeles CA 90064, USA

Spielberg, Steven — Director
Dreamworks SKG, 1000 Flower St, Glendale CA 91201, USA

Spielman, C Christopher (Chris) — Football Player, Sportscaster
2094 Edgemont Road, Columbus OH 43212, USA

Spielmann, Gotz — Director, Writer
I C M Partners, 10250 Constellation Blvd, #900, Los Angeles CA 90067 USA

Spierig, Michael — Director
W M E Entertainment, 9601 Wilshire Blvd, #300, Beverly Hills CA 90210 USA

Spierig, Peter — Director
W M E Entertainment, 9601 Wilshire Blvd, #300, Beverly Hills CA 90210 USA

Spiers, Ronald I — Diplomat
1329 Middletown Road, South Londonderry VT 05155, USA

Spiers, William J (Bill) — Baseball Player
9233 Old State Road, Cameron SC 29030, USA

Spiezio, Edward W (Ed) — Baseball Player
2027 Taller Road, Morris IL 60450, USA

Spiezio, Scott E — Baseball Player
7615 Saratoga Road, Morris IL 60450, USA

Spikes, Cameron W — Football Player
35 Raven Dr, Bryan TX 77808, USA

Spikes, Jack E — Football Player
9537 Highland View Dr, Dallas TX 75238, USA

Spikes, L Charles (Charlie) — Baseball Player
531 N Border Dr, Bogalusa LA 70427, USA

Spikes, Takeo G — Football Player
5005 Heatherwood Court, Roswell GA 30075, USA

Spilborghs, Ryan A — Baseball Player
1204 Suncast Lane, #2, El Dorado Hills CA 95762, USA

Spiller, Michael A — Cinematographer
2418 Roscomare Road, Los Angeles CA 90077, USA

Spillner, Daniel R (Dan) — Baseball Player
18505 SE Newport Way, #C113, Issaquah WA 98027, USA

Spilman, W Harry — Baseball Player
4423 S Saint Phillips Road, Mount Vernon IN 47620, USA

Spindler, Marc R — Football Player
6993 Bond Trail, Clarkston MI 48348, USA

Spindt, Capp — Inventor (Field Emission Display Screen)
S R I International, 333 Ravenswood Ave, Menlo Park CA 94025, USA

Spinella, Stephen — Actor
Innovative Artists, 1505 10th St, Santa Monica CA 90401 USA

Spinelli, Jerry — Writer
331 Melvin Road, Phoenixville PA 19460, USA

Spiner, Brent — Actor
Innovative Artists, 1505 10th St, Santa Monica CA 90401 USA

Spinetta, Jean-Cyril — Businessman
Groupe Air France, 45 Rue de Paris, 95747 Roissy CDG Cedex, France

Spinks, Cory — Boxer
6167 Tennessee St, Saint Louis MO 63111, USA

Spinks, Leon — Boxer
209 Jones St, Hollister MO 65672, USA

Spinks, Michael — Boxer
925 Centre Road, Wilmington DE 19807, USA

Spinks, Scipio R — Baseball Player
11422 Rock Bridge Lane, Sugar Land TX 77498, USA

Spinotti, Dante — Cinematographer
334 14th St, Santa Monica CA 90402, USA

Spires, Gregory T (Greg) — Football Player
26202 Ridgefield Park Lane, Cypress TX 77433, USA

Spiric, Nikola — Chairman, Bosnia & Herzegovina
Prime Minister's Office, Alipasina 1, 71000 Sarajevo, Bosnia & Herzegovina

Spiridakos, Tracy — Actress
Gersh Agency, 9465 Wilshire Blvd, #600, Beverly Hills CA 90212 USA

Spiro, Jordana — Actress
I C M Partners, 10250 Constellation Blvd, #900, Los Angeles CA 90067 USA

Spirtas, Kevin — Actor
Stone Manners Salners, 9911 W Pico Blvd, #1400, Los Angeles CA 90035 USA

Spitz, Mark A — Swimmer
Premier Management Group, 1100 Crescent Green, #104, Cary, NC 27518 USA

Spitz, Sabine — Cyclist
Sabine Spitz Sport Pro, Ralf Schaeuble, Diegeringerstr 17, 79730 Murg, Germany

Spitzer, Eliot L — Governor, NY
Current TV, Viewpoint Show, 435 Hudson St, #400, New York NY 10014, USA

Spitzer, Robert — Psychiatrist
Columbia University, Psychiatry School, New York NY 10027, USA

Spitzer, Toby — Religious Leader, Rabbi
Congregation Dorshei Tzedek, 60 Highland St, West Newton MA 02465, USA

Spivakov, Vladimir T — Conductor, Concert Violinist
Kosmodamianskaya Embankment 52, #301, 115054 Moscow, Russia

Spivey, Ernest L (Junior), Jr — Baseball Player
4140 S Ambrosia Dr, Chandler AZ 85248, USA

Spizzirri, Angelo — Actor
Don Buchwald/Fortitude, 6500 Wilshire Blvd, #2200, Los Angeles CA 90048 USA

Splatt, Rachelle — Drag Racing Driver
Rachelle Splatt Racing, 37 MacQuarie Drive, Thomastown VIC 3074, Australia
Spoelstra, Erik — Basketball Coach
Miami Heat, American Airlines Arena, 601 Biscayne Blvd, Miami FL 33132 USA
Spoljaric, Paul N — Baseball Player
545 Gramiak Road, Kelowna BC V1X 1K4, Canada
Sponenburgh, Mark — Sculptor
5562 NW Pacific Coast Highway, Seal Rock OR 97376, USA
Spong, John S — Religious Leader
24 Puddingstone Road, Morris Plains NJ 07950, USA
Spooneybarger, Tim — Baseball Player
7815 Eight Mile Creek Road, Pensacola FL 32526, USA
Spork, Shirley — Golfer
73010 Somera Road, Palm Desert CA 92260, USA
Sporkin, Stanley — Government Official, Judge
US District Court, Courthouse, 3rd St & Constitution Ave NW, Washington DC 20001, USA
Sporleder, Gregory — Actor
Brian Wilkins Mgmt, 10585 Santa Monica Blvd, #120, Los Angeles CA 90025, USA
Sposa, Mike — Golfer
11678 Sunrise View Lane, Wellington FL 33449, USA
Spose — Rap Artist
Agency Group Ltd, 142 W 57th St, #600, New York NY 10019 USA
Spotakova, Barbora — Track Athlete
A S C Dukla Prague, Oddil Aletiky, PS 59, 16044 Prague 6, Czech Republic
Spottiswoode, Roger — Director
9696 Culver Blvd, #203, Culver City CA 90232, USA
Spound, Michael — Actor
Kazarian/Spencer/Ruskin, 11969 Ventura Blvd, #300, Studio City CA 91604 USA
Spradlin, Danny R — Football Player
1011 Laurie St, Maryville TN 37803, USA
Spradlin, Jerry C — Baseball Player
25208 Pennsylvania Ave, Lomita CA 90717, USA
Spragan, Donald (Donnie), Jr — Football Player
312 Riviera Dr, Union City CA 94587, USA
Sprague, Edward N (Ed), Jr — Baseball Player
4677 Pine Valley Circle, Stockton CA 95219, USA
Sprague, Edward N (Ed), Sr — Baseball Player
19015 N Davis Road, Lodi CA 95242, USA
Sprague, Jack — Truck Racing Driver
X-Press Motorsports, 610 Performance Road, Mooresville NC 28117, USA
Spratlan, Lewis — Composer
Amherst College, Music Dept, Amherst MA 01002, USA
Sprayberry, Dylan — Actor
United Talent Agency, 9336 Civic Center Dr, Beverly Hills CA 90210 USA
Sprayberry, James M — Vietnam War Army Hero
426 Holiday Dr, Titus AL 36080, USA
Sprecher, Jill — Director, Producer, Writer
Paradigm Agency, 360 N Crescent Dr, North Building, Beverly Hills CA 90210 USA
Sprecher, Karen — Director, Producer, Writer
Paradigm Agency, 360 N Crescent Dr, North Building, Beverly Hills CA 90210 USA
Spreitler, Taylor — Actress
Coast to Coast Talent, 3350 Barham Blvd, Los Angeles CA 90068 USA
Sprewell, Latrell F — Basketball Player
850 W Dean Road, Milwaukee WI 53217, USA
Spriggs, George H — Baseball Player
77A W Bay Front Road, Lothian MD 20711, USA
Spriggs, Larry M — Basketball Player
23900 Cancuna Court, Huson MT 59846, USA
Spring, Frank — Ice Hockey Player
638 Upper Ottawa St, Hamilton ON L8T 3T5, Canada
Spring, Jack R — Baseball Player
PO Box 118, Colbert WA 99005, USA
Spring, Justin E — Gymnast
University of Illinois, Athletic Dept, Champaign IL 61820, USA
Spring, Sherwood C — Astronaut
2116 McDonough Lane, San Diego CA 92106, USA
Springer, Dennis L — Baseball Player
1060 W Windsor Court, Hanford CA 93230, USA
Springer, Jerry — Entertainer; Mayor, Cincinnati
Coast to Coast Talent, 3350 Barham Blvd, Los Angeles CA 90068 USA
Springer, Michael (Mike) — Golfer
1482 E Forest Oaks Dr, Fresno CA 93730, USA
Springer, Robert C — Astronaut
202 Village Circle, Sheffield AL 35660, USA
Springer, Russell P (Russ) — Baseball Player
PO Box 185, 4357 Highway 8, Pollock LA 71467, USA
Springer, Steven M (Steve) — Baseball Player
6962 Carla Circle, Huntington Beach CA 92647, USA
Springfield, Rick — Singer, Actor
Ron Weisner, 515 Ocean Ave, Santa Monica CA 90402, USA
Springs, Alice — Photographer
Residence Saint-Roman, 7 Ave Saint-Ramon, #T1008, Monte Carlo, Monaco
Springs, Kirk E — Football Player
10091 Thoroughbred Lane, Cincinnati OH 45231, USA
Springs, Shawn — Football Player
11090 Whitstone Place, Reston VA 20194, USA
Springsteen, Bruce — Singer, Songwriter
3561 Ambassador Dr, Wellington FL 33414, USA
Springsteen, Jay R — Motorcycle Racing Rider
3774 S Shore Dr, Lapeer MI 48446, USA
Sprinkle, Edward A (Ed) — Football Player
13340 Edinburgh Dr, Palos Heights IL 60463, USA
Sproles, Darren L — Football Player
New Orleans Saints, 5800 Airline Highway, Metairie LA 70003 USA
Sprouse, Cole — Actor
I/D Public Relations, 7060 Hollywood Blvd, #800, Los Angeles CA 90028 USA

Sprouse, Dylan — Actor
I/D Public Relations, 7060 Hollywood Blvd, #800, Los Angeles CA 90028 USA

Sprout, Robert S (Bob) — Baseball Player
1609 Cypress Point, Lady Lake FL 32159, USA

Sprowl, Robert J (Bobby) — Baseball Player
4711 Leeward Ave, Northport AL 35473, USA

Spruce, Andrew (Andy) — Ice Hockey Player
1223 Kantora Road, Lively ON P3Y 1H8, Canada

Spurgeon, Jay — Baseball Player
212 Hartsdale Road, Rochester NY 14622, USA

Spurlock, Morgan — Actor, Director
Arlook Group, 205 S Beverly Dr, #209, Beverly Hills CA 90212, USA

Spurrier, Stephen O (Steve) — Football Player, Coach
126 Beaver Ridge Dr, Elgin SC 29045, USA

Spuzich, Sandra — Golfer
Ladies Pro Golf Assn, 100 International Golf Dr, Daytona Beach FL 32124 USA

Squibb, June — Actress
Gage Group, 14724 Ventura Blvd, #505, Sherman Oaks CA 91403 USA

Squier, Billy — Singer, Guitarist, Songwriter
Paradise Artists, PO Box 1821, Ojai CA 93024 USA

Squier, Ken — Sportscaster
Ken Squier Productions, 9 Stowe St, Waterbury VT 05676, USA

Squire, Chris — Bassist (Yes)
Sun Artists, 9 Hillgate St, London W8 7SP, England

Squirek, Jack S — Football Player
4051 Vezbar Dr, Seven Hills OH 44131, USA

Squires, Michael L (Mike) — Baseball Player
9548 Autumnwood Circle, Kalamazoo MI 49009, USA

Squyres, Steven W — Space Scientist
Cornell University, Planetary Science Dept, Ithaca NY 14853, USA

Srinivasan, Rangaswamy — Inventor (Excimer Laser)
UVTech Assoc, 98 Cedar Lane, Ossining NY 10562, USA

St Clair, Jessica — Actress, Comedienne
Creative Artists Agency, 2000 Ave of Stars, #100, Los Angeles CA 90067 USA

St Clair, R Michael (Mike) — Football Player
1606 Birchwood Ave, Cincinnati OH 45224, USA

St Clair, Robert B (Bob) — Football Player
3312 Parker Hill Road, Santa Rosa CA 95404, USA

St Croix, Rick — Ice Hockey Player
27 Brigantine Bay, Winnipeg MB R3P 1R1, Canada

St George, William R — Navy Admiral
862 San Antonio Place, San Diego CA 92106, USA

St James, Lyn — Auto Racing Driver
L S J Racing, 57 Gasoline Alley, #D, Indianapolis IN 46222, USA

St James, Rebecca — Singer
Smallbone Mgmt, 709 W Main St, #1, Franklin TN 37064, USA

St Jean, Leonard W (Len). — Football Player
32 Ledgebrook Ave, Stoughton MA 02072, USA

St John, Jill — Actress
Borinstein Oreck Bogart, 3172 Dona Susana Dr, Studio City CA 91604 USA

St John, Kristoff — Actor
8743 Hanna Ave, Canoga Park NY 91304, USA

St John, Lara — Concert Violinist
Ancalgaon Records, 459 Columbus Ave, #300, New York NY 10024, USA

St John, Paige — Journalist
Sarasota Herald-Tribune, Editorial Dept, 1741 Main St, Sarasota FL 34236, USA

St John, Scott — Concert Violinist, Viola Player
Frank Salomon, 121 W 27th St, #703, New York NY 10001 USA

St John, Trevor — Actor
Innovative Artists, 1505 10th St, Santa Monica CA 90401 USA

St Laurent, Andre — Ice Hockey Player
947 Rue Riverview, Otterburn Park QC J3H 1Z1, Canada

St Laurent, Dollard H — Ice Hockey Player
Les Tour Angrignons, 1500 Angrignon Blvd, LaSalle QC H8N 3H8, Canada

St Louis, Frantz — Actor
Artists Agency, 1180 S Beverly Dr, #301, Los Angeles CA 90035 USA

St Louis, Martin — Ice Hockey Player
18145 Longwater Run Dr, Tampa FL 33647, USA

St Marseille, Francis L (Frank) — Ice Hockey Player
RR 4, Ashton ON 0A 1B0, Canada

St Patrick, Mathew — Actor
Ace Media, 9200 W Sunset Blvd, #1000, Los Angeles CA 90069, USA

St Pier, Natasha — Singer
Guy Cloutier, 446 Blvd Saint Lautenbur 900, Montreal QC H2W 1Z5, Canada

St Pierre, Brian — Football Player
Carolina Panthers, Ericsson Stadium, 800 S Mint St, Charlotte NC 28202 USA

St Pierre, Monique — Model, Actress
Playboy Promotions, 2706 Media Center Dr, Los Angeles CA 90065 USA

Staab, Rebecca — Actress
Stone Manners Salners, 9911 W Pico Blvd, #1400, Los Angeles CA 90035 USA

Staal, Eric C — Ice Hockey Player
6009 Over Hadden Court, Raleigh NC 27614, USA

Staal, Jordan — Ice Hockey Player
Candy Mountain Road, RR 6, Thunder Bay ON P7C 5N5, Canada

Stabile, Nick — Actor
Raw Talent Mgmt, 9615 Brighton Way, #300, Beverly Hills CA 90210 USA

Stabiner, Karen — Writer
Voice/Hyperion Books, 77 W 66th St, #1100, New York NY 10023, USA

Stablein, Brian P — Football Player
899 John Michael Way, Columbus OH 43235, USA

Stablein, George C — Baseball Player
2903 Penman, Tustin CA 92782, USA

Stabler, Ken M (Kenny) — Football Player
7311 Bay Road, #A, Mobile AL 36605, USA

Stacey Q — Singer, Actress, Songwriter
641 S Palm St, #D, La Habra CA 90631, USA

Stacey, John — Actor
Gavin Barker Assoc, 2D Wimpole St, London W1G 0EB, England
Stackhouse, Jerry D — Basketball Player
5266 Settles Bridge Road, Suwanee GA 30024, USA
Stackhouse, Ron — Ice Hockey Player
RR 2, Haliburton ON K0M 1S0, Canada
Stackpole, H C (Hank) — Marine Corps General
Asia-Pacific Security Studies Center, 2058 Maluhia Road, Honolulu HI 96815, USA
Stackpole, Michael A — Writer
PO Box 60333, Phoenix AZ 85082, USA
Stacomb, Kevin M — Basketball Player
14 Florida Ave, Jamestown RI 02835, USA
Stacy, Billy M — Football Player
400 Colonial Circle, Starkville MS 39759, USA
Stacy, Hollis — Golfer
9400 W 10th Ave, Lakewood CO 80215, USA
Stacy, Peter (Spider) — Singer (Pogues)
Agency Group Ltd, 361-373 City Road, London EC1V 2QA, England
Stadlen, Lewis J — Actor
Gage Group, 315 W 57th St, #4H, New York NY 10019 USA
Stadler, Craig R — Golfer
113 Elk Crossing, Evergreen CO 80439, USA
Stadler, Sergei V — Concert Violinist, Conductor
Kaiserstr 43, 80801 Munich, Germany
Stadtman, Thressa C — Biochemist
16907 Redland Road, Derwood MD 20855, USA
Staehle, Marvin G (Marv) — Baseball Player
19421 Cromwell Court, #208, Fort Myers FL 33912, USA
Stafford, J Matthew — Football Player
Detroit Lions, 222 Republic Dr, Allen Park MI 48101 USA
Stafford, James Francis Cardinal — Religious Leader
Pontifical Council for the Laity, Piazza S Calisto 16, 00153 Rome, Italy
Stafford, James W (Jim) — Singer, Songwriter
Dick Hall Productions, 1767 Lakewood Ranch Blvd, Bradenton FL 34211, USA
Stafford, Jimmy — Guitarist (Train)
Jon Landau, 150 Rowayton Ave, Norwalk CT 06853, USA
Stafford, Michelle — Actress
Glick Agency, 1250 6th St, #100, Santa Monica CA 90401, USA
Stafford, Nancy — Actress
PO Box 11807, Marina del Rey CA 90295, USA
Stafford, Thomas P — Astronaut, Air Force General
A V D, PO Box 604, Glenn Dale MD 20769, USA
Stafford-Clark, Max — Director, Actor
Royal Court Theatre, Sloane Square, London SW1 8AS, England
Stager, Gus — Swimming Coach
University of Michigan, Athletic Dept, Ann Arbor MI 48104, USA
Staggers, Jonathan L (Jon), Jr — Football Player
3835 Oakes Dr, Hayward CA 94542, USA
Staggs, Jeffrey H (Jeff) — Football Player
4641 Jeri Way, El Cajon CA 92020, USA
Stahl, Larry F — Baseball Player
1506 E Main St, #A, Belleville IL 62221, USA
Stahl, Lesley R — Commentator
CBS-TV, News Dept, 51 W 52nd St, New York NY 10019 USA
Stahl, Lisa — Actress
Shelly & Pierce, 13775A Mono Way, #220, Sonora CA 95370 USA
Stahl, Nick — Actor
I C M Partners, 10250 Constellation Blvd, #900, Los Angeles CA 90067 USA
Stahl, Norman H — Judge
US Court of Appeals, 1 Courthouse Way, Boston MA 02110, USA
Stahl-David, Michael — Actor
B/W/R, 9100 Wilshire Blvd, #500W, Beverly Hills CA 90212 USA
Stahle, Louise — Golfer
Gaylord Sports Mgmt, 13845 N Northsight Blvd, #200, Scottsdale AZ 85260 USA
Stahler, Jeff — Editorial Cartoonist
United Feature Syndicate, PO Box 5610, Cincinnati OH 45201 USA
Stahoviak, Scott E — Baseball Player
507 Balmoral Court, Grayslake IL 60030, USA
Stai, Brenden M — Football Player
5333 New Castle Road, Lincoln NE 68516, USA
Staiano-Coico, Lisa — Educator
City College of New York, President's Office, 160 Convent Ave, New York NY 10031, USA
Staiger, Roy J — Baseball Player
1233 Tyler Dr, Lebanon MO 65536, USA
Staios, Steve — Ice Hockey Player
1213 Newbridge Trace NE, Atlanta GA 30319, USA
Stairs, Matthew W (Matt) — Baseball Player
79 Skyline Road, Bangor ME 04401, USA
Staite, Jewel — Actress
Elements Entertainment, 1635 N Cahuenga Blvd, #500, Los Angeles CA 90028, USA
Stajan, Matthew (Matt) — Ice Hockey Player
1369 Victor Ave, Mississauga ON L5G 3A2, Canada
Stalder, Keith J — Marine Corps General
Commanding General, 2nd Marine Expeditionary Force, Camp Lejeune NC 28542 USA
Staley, Dawn M — Basketball Player, Coach
Dawn Staley Foundation, 1224 Glenwood Road, Columbia SC 29204, USA
Staley, Duce — Football Player
150 N 9th St, West Columbia SC 29169, USA
Staley, Joan — Actress, Model
24516 Windsor Dr, #B, Valencia CA 91355, USA
Staley, William P (Bill) — Football Player
9210 Todd Road, Potter Valley CA 95469, USA
Stallard, E Tracy — Baseball Player
PO Box 905, Wise VA 24293, USA
Stallard, Tom — Rowing Athlete
Leander Club, Henley on Thames, Leander RG9 2LP, England

Stallings, Eugene C (Gene), Jr — Football Coach
6508 County Road 43200, Powderly TX 75473, USA
Stallings, George — Religious Leader
African American Catholic Congregation, 1015 I St NE, Washington DC 20002, USA
Stallings, Larry J — Football Player
555 Town Hall Court, Saint Louis MO 63141, USA
Stallone, Frank — Actor, Singer, Songwriter
Rogers & Cowan, 8687 Melrose Ave, #G700, West Hollywood CA 90069 USA
Stallone, Sylvester — Actor, Director, Writer
W M E Entertainment, 9601 Wilshire Blvd, #300, Beverly Hills CA 90210 USA
Stalls, David M — Football Player
2800 Forest St, Denver CO 80207, USA
Stallworth, David A (Dave) — Basketball Player
4400 N Rushwood St, Wichita KS 67226, USA
Stallworth, Donte' L — Football Player
6 Arvis Court, Sacramento CA 95835, USA
Stallworth, Issac (Bud) — Basketball Player
14 Westwood Road, Lawrence KS 66044, USA
Stallworth, Johnny L (John) — Football Player
302 Osman Dr, Madison AL 35756, USA
Stam, Jessica — Model
International Model Mgmt, 25 Dunlop St E, Barrie ON L4M 1A2, Canada
Stam, Katie — Beauty Queen
Miss America Organization, 1370 Ave of Americas, #1600, New York NY 10019 USA
Stamberg, Josh — Actor
Abrams Artists, 9200 W Sunset Blvd, #1125, West Hollywood CA 90069 USA
Stamberg, Peter — Interior Designer
Stamberg Aferiat Architecture, 126 5th Ave, #13A, New York NY 10011, USA
Stamer, Joshua L (Josh) — Football Player
202 Oxford Creek Road, Cary NC 27519, USA
Stamile, Lauren — Actress
Schumacher Mgmt, 10323 Santa Monica Blvd, #101, Los Angeles CA 90024, USA
Stamkos, Steven — Ice Hockey Player
Tampa Bay Lightning, 401 Channelside Dr, Tampa FL 33602 USA
Stamler, Lorne — Ice Hockey Player
2806 Marie Court, Clearwater FL 33761, USA
Stamm, Daniel — Director, Writer
Creative Artists Agency, 2000 Ave of Stars, #100, Los Angeles CA 90067 USA
Stamm, Michael E (Mike) — Swimmer
3929 Everett Ave, Oakland CA 94602, USA
Stamos, John — Actor
Brillstein Entertainment Partners, 9150 Wilshire Blvd, #350, Beverly Hills CA 90212 USA
Stamp, Terence — Actor
Untitled Entertainment, 350 S Beverly Dr, #200, Beverly Hills CA 90212 USA
Stamps, Sylvester — Football Player
1831 Eisenhower Dr, Vicksburg MS 39180, USA
Stams, Frank M — Football Player
2870 Marcia Blvd, Cuyahoga Falls OH 44223, USA
Stan, Sebastian — Actor
W M E Entertainment, 9601 Wilshire Blvd, #300, Beverly Hills CA 90210 USA
Stanat, Dug — Sculptor, Animator
46828 Bradley St, Fremont CA 94539, USA
Stanback, Haskell L — Football Player
173 Buckingham Court, Roanoke VA 24019, USA
Stanbury, John B — Pharmacologist
10 Longwood Dr, #106, Westwood MA 02090, USA
Standhardt, Kenneth — Artist
4875 Garnet St, Eugene OR 97405, USA
Standiford, Les — Writer
Harper/Collins, 10 E 53rd St, Cellar 1, New York NY 10022, USA
Standing, George — Ice Hockey Player
34 Cliff Ave, Huntsville ON P1H 1G1, Canada
Standing, John — Actor
United Agents, 12-26 Lexington St, London W1F 0LE, England
Standridge, Jason — Baseball Player
6228 Cardinal Dr, Pinson AL 35126, USA
Stanek, Al — Baseball Player
96 Allyn St, Holyoke MA 01040, USA
Stanfel, Richard (Dick) — Football Player, Coach
1104 Juniper Parkway, Libertyville IL 60048, USA
Stanfield, Frederic W (Fred) — Ice Hockey Player
59 Cheshire Lane, East Amherst NY 14051, USA
Stanfield, Kevin B — Baseball Player
7565 Newcomb St, San Bernardino CA 92410, USA
Stanfill, William T (Bill) — Football Player
3117 Wisteria Court, Albany GA 31721, USA
Stanford, Aaron — Actor
Management 360, 9111 Wilshire Blvd, Beverly Hills CA 90210 USA
Stanford, Angela — Golfer
6225 Pecan Orchard Court, Fort Worth TX 76179, USA
Stanford, Jason — Baseball Player
4505 W Mesquital del Oro, Tucson AZ 85742, USA
Stang, Peter J — Organic Chemist
University of Utah, Chemistry Dept, Salt Lake City UT 84112, USA
Stangassinger, Thomas — Alpine Skier
Hofgasse 19, 5422 Durenberg-Hallein, Austria
Stange, A Lee — Baseball Player
436 Dolphin St, Melbourne Beach FL 32951, USA
Stange, Maya — Actress
L M C M, 99 Spring St, #100, Bondi Junction NSW 2022, Australia
Stanhope, Doug — Actor, Comedian
Hype Entertainment, 8350 Wilshire Blvd, #200, Beverly Hills CA 90211, USA
Stanhouse, Donald J (Don) — Baseball Player
4 Creekmere Dr, Roanoke TX 76262, USA
Stanich, George — Track Athlete, Basketball Player
15816 Marigold Ave, Gardena CA 90249, USA

Stanifer, Rob — Baseball Player
13547 Las Palmas Dr, Largo FL 33774, USA
Stanishev, Sergei — Prime Minister, Bulgaria
Prime Minister's Office, 1 Dondukov Blvd, 1000 Sofia, Bulgaria
Stanka, Joe D — Baseball Player
32718 Weymouth Court, Fulshear TX 77441, USA
Stankalla, Stefan — Alpine Skier
Furstenstr 14, 82467 Garmisch-Partenkirchen, Germany
Stankiewicz, Andrew N (Andy) — Baseball Player
9729 Wren Bluff Dr, San Diego CA 92127, USA
Stankiewicz, Myron — Ice Hockey Player
53 Tynedale Ave, London ON N6H 5P6, Canada
Stankovic, Borislav (Boris) — Basketball Executive
PO Box 7005, 81479 Munich, Germany
Stankowski, Paul — Golfer
4713 Rangewood Dr, Flower Mound TX 75028, USA
Stanley, Allan H — Ice Hockey Player
RR 3, Fennelon Falls ON K0M 1S0, Canada
Stanley, B Chadwick (Chad) — Football Player
21451 Merlot Lane, Tyler TX 75703, USA
Stanley, Christopher — Actor
A P A Talent/Literary Agency, 405 S Beverly Dr, #300, Beverly Hills CA 90212 USA
Stanley, Daryl — Ice Hockey Player
Boc 164, Balmoral MB R0C 0H0, Canada
Stanley, Frederick B (Fred) — Baseball Player
2109 Winthrop Hill Road, Argyle TX 76226, USA
Stanley, James C (Jim) — Producer, Writer
Paradigm Agency, 360 N Crescent Dr, North Building, Beverly Hills CA 90210 USA
Stanley, Marianne Crawford — Basketball Coach
Los Angeles Sparks, 888 S Figueroa St, #2010, Los Angeles CA 90017 USA
Stanley, Mitchell J (Mickey) — Baseball Player
6370 Cunningham Lake Road, Brighton MI 48116, USA
Stanley, P Stephen — Navy Admiral
Director, Force Structure Resources, Joint Staff, Pentagon, Washington DC 20318 USA
Stanley, Paul — Singer, Guitarist (Kiss)
McGhee Entertainment, 8730 W Sunset Blvd, #200, West Hollywood CA 90069, USA
Stanley, R Michael (Mike) — Baseball Player
1108 NE 10th Ave, Fort Lauderdale FL 33304, USA
Stanley, Ralph — Guitarist, Singer
7455 Dr Ralph Stanley Highway, Coeburn WA 24230, USA
Stanley, Robert W (Bob) — Baseball Player
30 Tansy Ave, Stratham NH 03885, USA
Stanley, Samuel L, Jr — Educator
State University of New York, President's Office, Stony Brook NY 11784, USA
Stanley, Steven M — Paleobiologist
4308 Folly Quarter Road, Ellicott City MD 21042, USA
Stanley, Walter — Football Player
23977 E Alamo Place, Aurora CO 80016, USA
Stanowski, Wally — Ice Hockey Player
227 Mill Road, Toronto ON M9C 1Y3, Canada
Stansbury, Terence — Basketball Player
901 N Franklin St, #2, Wilmington DE 19806, USA
Stansfield Smith, Colin — Architect
Three Ministers House, 76 High St, Winchester, Hants SO23 8UL, England
Stansfield, Lisa — Singer, Songwriter
PO Box 59, Ashwell, Herts SG7 5NG, England
Stansky, Peter D L — Historian
375 Pinehill Road, Hillsborough CA 94010, USA
Stantis, Scott — Editorial Cartoonist (Buckets)
Birmingham News, Editorial Dept, 2200 4th Ave N, Birmingham AL 35203, USA
Stanton, Andrew — Animator, Director, Writer
Pixar Animation, 1200 Park Ave, Emeryville CA 94608, USA
Stanton, Doug — Writer
Charles Scribner's Sons, 866 3rd Ave, New York NY 10022 USA
Stanton, Harry Dean — Actor
14527 Mulholland Dr, Los Angeles CA 90077, USA
Stanton, Jeff — Motorcycle Racing Rider
1137 Athens Road, Sherwood MI 49089, USA
Stanton, Leroy B — Baseball Player
1751 N Norwood Lane, Florence SC 29506, USA
Stanton, Michael T (Mike) — Baseball Player
PO Box 1154, Woodinville WA 98072, USA
Stanton, Molly — Actress
Gersh Agency, 9465 Wilshire Blvd, #600, Beverly Hills CA 90212 USA
Stanton, Paul — Ice Hockey Player
2150 Sheepshead Dr, Naples FL 34102, USA
Stanton, Phil — Entertainer (Blue Man Group)
Blue Man Group Productions, 411 Lafayette St, #300, New York NY 10003, USA
Stanton, W Michael (Mike) — Baseball Player
19602 Indigo Lake Dr, Magnolia TX 77355, USA
Stanton-Ogulnick, Alysa — Religious Leader, Rabbi
Congregation Bayt Shalom, 4351 E 10th St, Greenville NC 27858, USA
Stanzler, Wendey — Director, Producer
Verve Talent/Literary Agency, 9696 Culver Blvd, #301, Culver City CA 90232 USA
Stapinski, Helene — Writer
Saint Martin's Press, 175 5th Ave, #400, New York NY 10010 USA
Staples, Mavis — Singer (Staple Singers)
PO Box 498360, Chicago IL 60649, USA
Stapleton, David L — Baseball Player
51 N Bayview Ave, Fairhope AL 36532, USA
Stapleton, Jean — Actress
155 W 68th St, #29C, New York NY 10023, USA
Stapleton, Kevin — Actor
Roth Assoc, 250 W 85th St, New York NY 10024, USA
Stapleton, Mike — Ice Hockey Player
PO Box 1896, Sault Sainte Marie MI 49783, USA

S

Stapleton, Oliver — Cinematographer
Independent Talent Group, Oxford House, 76 Oxford St, London W1D 1BS, England

Stapleton, Pat — Ice Hockey Player
623 Saulsberry St, Strathroy ON N7G 3R4, Canada

Stapleton, Sullivan — Actor
W M E Entertainment, 9601 Wilshire Blvd, #300, Beverly Hills CA 90210 USA

Stapleton, Walter K — Judge
US Court of Appeals, Federal Building, 844 N King St, Wilmington DE 19801, USA

Stapp, Scott — Singer (Creed), Lyricist
Agency Group Ltd, 142 W 57th St, #600, New York NY 10019 USA

Star, Darren W — Director, Producer
Darren Star Productions, 9200 Sunset Blvd, #430, Los Angeles CA 90069, USA

Star, Ryan — Singer, Songwriter
Creative Artists Agency, 2000 Ave of Stars, #100, Los Angeles CA 90067 USA

Starbird, Kate — Basketball Player
Indiana Fever, Conseco Fieldhouse, 125 S Pennsylvania, Indianapolis IN 46204 USA

Starbuck, Jo Jo — Figure Skater
33 Pomeroy Road, Madison NJ 07940, USA

Starck, Philippe — Architect, Industrial Designer
Starck-Ubix, 27 Rue Pierre Poli, 92130 Issey-le-Mooulineaux, France

Starfield, Barbara H — Physician
Johns Hopkins University, Hygiene School, 624 N Broadway, Baltimore MD 21205, USA

Stargell, Tony L — Football Player
131 Jenny Road, Grantville GA 30220, USA

Starikov, Sergei V — Ice Hockey Player
209 Greenbrook Road, Green Brook NJ 08812, USA

Stark, Dennis J (Denny) — Baseball Player
213 N Elm St, Edgerton OH 43517, USA

Stark, Don — Actor
Premier Talent Group, 4370 Tujunda Ave, #110, Studio City CA 91604, USA

Stark, Graham — Actor
31 Temple Ave, London N20 9EJ, England

Stark, Jonathan — Tennis Player
10559 NW Tudor Lane, Portland OR 97229, USA

Stark, Koo — Actress
Rebecca Blond, 69A King's Road, London SW3 4NX, England

Stark, Matthew S (Matt) — Baseball Player
3203 E Birchwood Place, Chandler AZ 85249, USA

Stark, Melissa — Sportscaster, Commentator
NBC-TV, News Dept, 30 Rockefeller Plaza, #270E, New York NY 10112 USA

Stark, Nathan J — Attorney
4000 Cathedral Ave NW, #132, Washington DC 20016, USA

Stark, Rohn T — Football Player
PO Box 10067, Lahaina HI 96761, USA

Starke, Anthony — Actor
Geddes Agency, 8430 Santa Monica Blvd, #201, West Hollywood CA 90069 USA

Starke, George L — Football Player
1406 Corcoran St NW, #A, Washington DC 20009, USA

Starker, Janos — Concert Cellist
1241 Winfield Road, Bloomington IN 47401, USA

Starks, Duane L — Football Player
12495 Stoneway Court, Davie FL 33330, USA

Starks, John L — Basketball Player
PO Box 8146, Stamford CT 06905, USA

Starks, Maximillian W (Max), IV — Football Player
11247 San Jose Blvd, #108, Jacksonville FL 32223, USA

Starks, Randolph (Randy), Jr — Football Player
2535 SW 105th Terrace, Davie FL 33324, USA

Starks, Scott D — Football Player
12774 Oxford Crossing Dr, Jacksonville FL 32224, USA

Starkweather, Gary K — Optical Engineer
10274 Parkwood Dr, #7, Cupertino CA 95014, USA

Starling, H Denby — Navy Admiral
Commander, Naval Cyber Command, 2465 Guadalcanal, Little Creek VA 23521, USA

Starling, James D — Army General
3581 Joshua Road, Shingle Springs CA 95682, USA

Starling, Marlon — Boxer
235 Main St, #9C1, West Hartford CT 06106, USA

Starn, Douglas — Photographer
Stux Gallery, 163 Mercer St, #1, New York NY 10012, USA

Starn, Mike — Photographer
Stux Gallery, 163 Mercer St, #1, New York NY 10012, USA

Starner, Shelby — Singer
Morebarn Music, 30 Hillcrest Ave, Morristown NJ 07960, USA

Starnes, James R — WW II Army Air Corps Hero
16001 Lakeshore Villa Dr, #330, Tampa FL 33613, USA

Starnes, Vaughn A — Cardiac, Lung Surgeon
Stanford University Medical Center, Heart/Lung Transplant Dept, Stanford CA 94305, USA

Starr, Albert — Cardiac Surgeon
1792 SW Montgomery Dr, Portland OR 97201, USA

Starr, B Bartlett (Bart) — Football Player, Coach
2065 Royal Fern Lane, Birmingham AL 35244, USA

Starr, Blaze — Exotic Dancer
HC 70, Box 1477, Wilsonville WV 25699, USA

Starr, Brenda K — Singer
Brothers Mgmt, 141 Dunbar Ave, Fords NJ 08863 USA

Starr, David — Auto, Truck Racing Driver
Boys Will Be Boys Racing, 610 Performance Road, Mooresville NC 28115, USA

Starr, Kay — Singer
Ira Okun Entertainment, 1459 Lauren Court, Encinitas CA 92024, USA

Starr, Kenneth W — Government Official, Judge
Baylor University, President's Office, Waco TX 76798, USA

Starr, Martin — Actor
United Talent Agency, 9336 Civic Center Dr, Beverly Hills CA 90210 USA

Starr, Paul E — Sociologist
Princeton University, Sociology Dept, Green Hall, Princeton NJ 08544, USA

Stapleton - Starr

Starr, Randy   Singer (Insiders), Songwriter
D D S, 230 Park Ave, New York NY 10169, USA

Starr, Richard E (Dick)   Baseball Player
613 N Crescent Dr, Kittanning PA 16201, USA

Starr, Ringo   Singer, Drummer (Beatles)
Rocca Bella, 90 Jermyn St, #100, London SW1Y 6JD, England

Starrette, Herman P (Herm)   Baseball Player
103 Howard Pond Loop, Statesville NC 28625, USA

Starring, Stephen D   Football Player
9035 S Tenaya Way, Las Vegas NV 89113, USA

Starzewski, Tomasz   Fashion Designer
House of Tomasz Starzewski, 15-17 Pont St, London SW1X 9EH, England

Starzl, Thomas E   Surgeon
University of Pittsburgh Medical School, Surgery Dept, Pittsburgh PA 15261, USA

Stashower, Daniel   Writer
E P Dutton, 375 Hudson St, New York NY 10014 USA

Stashwick, Todd   Actor
A P A Talent/Literary Agency, 405 S Beverly Dr, #300, Beverly Hills CA 90212 USA

Stasiuk, Victor J (Vic)   Ice Hockey Player
7 Canyon Gardens W, Leftbridge AB T1K 6V1, Canada

Stassforth, Bowen   Swimmer
26203 Birchfield Ave, Rancho Palos Verdes CA 90275, USA

Stastny, Anton   Ice Hockey Player
Route de Broye 45, 1008 Prilli, Swtizerland

Stastny, Paul   Ice Hockey Player
Colorado Avalanche, Pepsi Center, 1000 Chopper Circle, Denver CO 80204 USA

Stastny, Peter   Ice Hockey Player
465 S Mason Road, Saint Louis MO 63141, USA

Staszak, Ray   Ice Hockey Player
8273 96th Court S, Boynton Beach FL 33472, USA

Staten, Vince   Writer
9323 Loch Lea Lane, Louisville KY 40291, USA

Statham, Harry   Basketball Coach
McKendree College, Athletic Dept, Lebanon IL 62254, USA

Statham, Jason   Actor
Current Entertainment, 9378 Wilshire Blvd, #210, Beverly Hills CA 90212, USA

Static, Wayne   Vocalist, Guitarist (Static-X), Actor
United Talent Agency, 9336 Civic Center Dr, Beverly Hills CA 90210 USA

Station, Larry W, Jr   Football Player
PO Box 471, Seale AL 36875, USA

Staton, Aaron   Actor
I C M Partners, 10250 Constellation Blvd, #900, Los Angeles CA 90067 USA

Staton, Candi   Singer
Capital Entertainment, 1201 N St NW, #A5, Washington DC 20005, USA

Staub, Daniel J (Rusty)   Baseball Player
403 S Sapodilla Ave, #214, West Palm Beach FL 33401, USA

Staubach, Roger T   Football Player
5242 Ravine Dr, Dallas TX 75220, USA

Stauber, Liz   Actress
Blue Ridge, 535 W 23rd St, #S10A, New York NY 10011, USA

Stauber, Robb   Ice Hockey Player
Stauber's Goal Crease, 7401A Washington Ave S, Minneapolis MN 55439, USA

Stauffer, Timothy J(Tim)   Baseball Player
1464 Summit Ave, Cardiff CA 92007, USA

Stauffer, William A (Bill)   Basketball Player
13808 Sheridan Ave, Urbandale IA 50323, USA

Staunton, Imelda   Actress
Conway Van Gelder Grant, 8-12 Broadwick St, #300, London W1F 8HW, England

Staurovsky, Jason C   Football Player
4822 E 87th Place, Tulsa OK 74137, USA

Staveley, William D M   Navy Admiral, England
Thames Health Authority, 40 Eastbourne Terrace, London W2 3QR, England

Stavridis, James G   Navy Admiral
Commander, US European Command, Stuttgart, Unit 30400, APO AE 09128 USA

Stayskal, Wayne   Editorial Cartoonist
Tampa Tribune, Editorial Dept, 200 S Parker St, Tampa FL 33606, USA

Staysniak, Joseph A (Joe)   Football Player
4094 Forest Dr, Brownsburg IN 46112, USA

Stead, Erin E   Illustrator
MacMillan, 1177 Ave of Americas, #1965, New York NY 10036 USA

Stead, Philip   Writer
MacMillan, 1177 Ave of Americas, #1965, New York NY 10036 USA

Steadman, Alison   Actress
Artist Rights Group, 4 Great Portland Place, London W1W 8PA, England

Steadman, J Richard   Sports Orthopedic Surgeon
Steadman Hawkins Clinic, 181 W Meadows Dr, #400, Vail CO 81657, USA

Steadman, Mark   Writer
450 Pin-du-Lac Dr, Central SC 29630, USA

Steadman, Ralph I   Cartoonist, Illustrator
Old Loose Court, Loose Valley, Maidstone, Kent ME15 9SE, England

Steadman, Robert L   Cinematographer
15925 Temecula St, Pacific Palisades CA 90272, USA

Stearns, Cheryl   Skydiver
613 Saddlebred Lane, Raeford NC 28376, USA

Stearns, Jeff   Actor
Abrams Artists, 9200 W Sunset Blvd, #1125, West Hollywood CA 90069 USA

Stearns, John H   Baseball Player
2251 Shell Beach Road, #36, Pismo Beach CA 93449, USA

Stebbins, Richard V   Track Athlete
10675 Gramercy Place, #317, Columbia MD 21044, USA

Stebbins, Theodore Ellis, Jr   Art Historian
Harvard University, Fogg Art Museum, Cambridge MA 02138, USA

Steber, Christopher L   Actor
Gavin Barker Assoc, 2D Wimpole St, London W1G 0EB, England

Stecher, Mario   Nordic Combined Skier
Leins 103, 6471 Arzi im Pitztal, Austria

Stecher, Renate Meissner- — Track Athlete
Haydnstr 11, #526/38, 07749 Jena, Germany
Stecher, Theodore P — Astronomer
U I T Project, Goddard Space Flight Center, Greenbelt MD 20771, USA
Stechschulte, Gene — Baseball Player
206 Wellington Place, Findlay OH 45840, USA
Steckel, Les — Football Player, Coach
195 Blew Court, East Brunswick NJ 08816, USA
Stecker, Aaron — Football Player
3235 Saracen Way, Verona WI 53593, USA
Ste-Croix, Gilles — Circus Executive
Cirque du Soleil, 8400 2nd Ave, Montreal QC H1Z 4M6, Canada
Steding, Katy — Basketball Player, Coach
21625 SW 100th Dr, Tualatin OR 97062, USA
Steed, Joel E — Football Player
12607 Blanco Terrace Lane, Houston TX 77041, USA
Steel of Aikwood, David M S — Government Official, England
Aikwood Tower, Ettrick Bridge, Selkirkshire Sel TD7 5HJ, Scotland
Steel, Amy — Actress
Imperium 7 Artists, 5455 Wilshire Blvd, #1706, Los Angeles CA 90036 USA
Steel, Danielle F — Writer
PO Box 470130, San Francisco CA 94147, USA
Steel, John — Drummer (Animals)
Lustig Talent, PO Box 770850, Orlando FL 32877 USA
Steele, Allan M, Jr — Writer
1640 S Sepulveda Blvd, #218, Los Angeles CA 90025, USA
Steele, Barbara — Actress
2460 Benedict Canyon Dr, Beverly Hills CA 90210, USA
Steele, Dan — Bobsled Athlete
US Bobsled/Skeleton Federation, 1631 Mesa Ave, #A, Colorado Springs CO 80906 USA
Steele, George (Animal) — Professional Wrestler, Actor
PO Box 321343, Cocoa Beach FL 32932, USA
Steele, J Lendale (Glen), Jr — Football Player
188 Marshdale Ave SW, Concord NC 28025, USA
Steele, Jeffrey — Singer, Songwriter
Lofton Creek Records, 13751 Lebanon Road, Old Hickory TN 37138, USA
Steele, Larry N — Basketball Player
PO Box 372, Vernonia OR 97064, USA
Steele, Michael — Singer, Bassist (Bangles)
Bangles Mall, PO Box 180, 1341 W Fullerton Ave, Chicago IL 60614, USA
Steele, Richard — Boxing Referee
2438 Antler Point Dr, Henderson NV 89074, USA
Steele, Sarah — Actress
Gersh Agency, 41 Madison Ave, #3301, New York NY 10010 USA
Steele, Shelby — Writer
San Jose State University, English Dept, San Jose CA 95192, USA
Steele, Tim — Auto Racing Driver
11433 24th Ave, Marne MI 49435, USA
Steele, Tommy — Singer, Actor
International Management Group, 3 Burlington Lane, London W4 2TH, England
Steele-Perkins, Christopher H — Photographer
49 Saint Francis Road, London SE22 8DE, England
Steels, James E (Jim) — Baseball Player
1654 Via Rico, Santa Maria CA 93454, USA
Steen, Anders — Ice Hockey Player
Farjestadsvagen 85, Karlstad 85 465, Sweden
Steen, Jessica — Actress
Open Entertainment, 6612 Waring Ave, Los Angeles CA 90038, USA
Steen, Paprika — Actress
Paradigm Agency, 360 N Crescent Dr, North Building, Beverly Hills CA 90210 USA
Steenburgen, Mary — Actress
Management 360, 9111 Wilshire Blvd, Beverly Hills CA 90210 USA
Steenland, Douglas — Businessman
Northwest Airlines, 2700 Lone Oak Parkway, Saint Paul MN 55121, USA
Steenstra, Kenneth G (Ken) — Baseball Player
1228 Pheasant Court, Liberty MO 64068, USA
Steeples, Eddie — Actor
Innovative Artists, 1505 10th St, Santa Monica CA 90401 USA
Steers, Burr — Director
Creative Artists Agency, 2000 Ave of Stars, #100, Los Angeles CA 90067 USA
Steevens, Morris D (Morrie) — Baseball Player
14465 Cadillac Dr, San Antonio TX 78248, USA
Stefan, Gregory S — Ice Hockey Player
37648 Baywood Dr, #33, Farmington Hills MI 48335, USA
Stefan, Patrik — Ice Hockey Player
1450 Bluebird Canyon Dr, Laguna Beach CA 92651, USA
Stefani, Gwen — Singer (No Doubt), Songwriter
Schiff Co, 8440 Warner Dr, #B1, Culver City CA 90232 USA
Stefanich, Jim — Bowler
1444 Coral Bell Dr, Joliet IL 60435, USA
Stefanik, Mike — Auto Racing Driver
106 Pierremount Ave, New Britain CT-6-53
Stefaniuk, Robert — Actor, Director
Loeb & Loeb, 10100 Santa Monica Blvd, #2200, Los Angeles CA 90067 USA
Stefaniw, Morris — Ice Hockey Player
801-100 4th Ave SW, Calgary AB T2P 3N2, Canada
Stefanovich, Tamara — Concert Pianist
Harrison/Parrott, 5-6 Albion Court, London W6 0QT, England
Stefanski, Bud — Ice Hockey Player
RR 1, Buckhorn ON K0L 1J0, Canada
Stefanson, Leslie — Actress
I C M Partners, 10250 Constellation Blvd, #900, Los Angeles CA 90067 USA
Stefanyshyn-Piper, Heidemarie M — Astronaut
3722 W Pine Brook Way, Houston TX 77059, USA
Stefecekova, Zuzana — Markswoman
Jurkovicova 1, 94911 Nitra, Slovakia

Stefero, John R 6239 Chestnut Oak Lane, Linthicum Heights MD 21090, USA	Baseball Player
Steffen, Britta Regine Eichhorn, Bizestr 1, 13088 Berlin, Germany	Swimmer
Steffen, James W (Jim) 1440 Westway, Arnold MD 21012, USA	Football Player
Steffes, Kent 14675 Titus St, Panorama City CA 91402, USA	Volleyball Player
Steger, Charles W Virginia Polytechnic Institute, President's Office, Blacksburg VA 24061, USA	Educator
Steger, Michael Stone Manners Salners, 9911 W Pico Blvd, #1400, Los Angeles CA 90035 USA	Actor
Stegman, David W (Dave) 3234 Simmons Dr, Grove City OH 43123, USA	Baseball Player
Steiger, Ueli 2222 Kenilworth Ave, Los Angeles CA 90039, USA	Cinematographer
Steigerwalt, Gary Pro Musicus Foundation, 1351 Ocean Front Walk, #203, Santa Monica CA 90401, USA	Concert Pianist
Steilen, Mark I C M Partners, 10250 Constellation Blvd, #900, Los Angeles CA 90067 USA	Director, Writer
Stein, Ben Innovative Artists, 1505 10th St, Santa Monica CA 90401 USA	Actor, Comedian
Stein, Chris Agency Group Ltd, 142 W 57th St, #600, New York NY 10019 USA	Guitarist (Blondie)
Stein, Ed Rocky Mountain News, Editorial Dept, 101 W Colfax Ave, #500, Denver CO 80202, USA	Editorial Cartoonist
Stein, Elias M 132 Dodds Lane, Princeton NJ 08540, USA	Mathematician
Stein, Gilbert (Gil) National Hockey League, 650 5th Ave, #3300, New York NY 10019, USA	Ice Hockey Executive
Stein, Jeremy C Federal Reserve System, 20th St & Constitution Ave NW, Washington DC 20551, USA	Government Leader, Economist
Stein, Mark Future Vision, 280 Riverside Dr, #12L, New York NY 10025, USA	Singer, Organist (Vanilla Fudge)
Stein, Robert McCall's, Editor's Office, 375 Lexington Ave, New York NY 10017, USA	Editor
Stein, W Blake 115 Bonne Vie Dr, Brandon MS 39047, USA	Baseball Player
Stein, William A (Bill) 10421 Grayhawk Lane, Fort Worth TX 76244, USA	Baseball Player
Steinbach, Alice Baltimore Sun, Editorial Dept, 501 N Calvert St, Baltimore MD 21278, USA	Journalist
Steinbach, Eric 2043 W Fletcher St, Chicago IL 60618, USA	Football Player
Steinbach, Terry L Terry Steinbach Scholarship Fund, PO Box 181, Hamel MN 55340, USA	Baseball Player
Steinbacher, Arabella I M G Artists, Bandelstrasse 35, 30171 Hannover, Germany	Concert Violinist
Steinbauer, Ben United Talent Agency, 9336 Civic Center Dr, Beverly Hills CA 90210 USA	Director, Producer
Steinberg, Daniel University of California Medical School, 9500 Gilman Dr, La Jolla CA 92093, USA	Physician
Steinberg, David Coolwaters Productions, 10061 Riverside Dr, Box 531, Toluca Lake CA 91602 USA	Actor, Comedian, Director
Steinberg, Jon W M E Entertainment, 9601 Wilshire Blvd, #300, Beverly Hills CA 90210 USA	Producer, Writer
Steinberg, Mark Mannes College of Music, 150 W 85th St, New York NY 10024, USA	Concert Violinist
Steinberg, Paul New Yorker, Editorial Dept, 4 Times Square, Basement C1B, New York NY 10036 USA	Cartoonist
Steinberg, Saul P Reliance Group Holdings, 5 Hanover Square, #1401, New York NY 10004, USA	Businessman
Steinberg, William (Billy) McDaniel Entertainment, 1311 Broadway, Santa Monica CA 90404, USA	Lyricist
Steinberger, Jack 25 Chemin des Merles, 1213 Onex, Geneva, Switzerland	Nobel Physics Laureate
Steindorff, Scott Stone Village, 1036 Carol Dr, West Hollywood CA 90069, USA	Producer, Writer
Steinem, Gloria 118 E 73rd St, New York NY 10021, USA	Women's Activist, Editor
Steiner, F George 32 Barrow Road, Cambridge, England	Writer
Steiner, Melvin J (Mel) 27217 White Alder Court, Murrieta CA 92562, USA	Baseball Umpire
Steiner, Michael 704 Broadway, New York NY 10003, USA	Sculptor, Artist
Steiner, Paul Washington Times, Editorial Dept, 3600 New York Ave NE, Washington DC 20002, USA	Editorial Cartoonist
Steiner, Peter New Yorker, Editorial Dept, 4 Times Square, Basement C1B, New York NY 10036 USA	Cartoonist
Steiner, Tommy Shane Collinsworth, 50 Music Square W, #702, Nashville TN 37203, USA	Singer
Steinfeld, Hailee I C M Partners, 10250 Constellation Blvd, #900, Los Angeles CA 90067 USA	Actress
Steinfeld, Jake 622 Toyopa Dr, Pacific Palisades CA 90272, USA	Actor, Body Builder
Steinfort, Frederick W (Fred) PO Box 24981, Denver CO 80224, USA	Football Player
Steinhafel, Gregg W Target Corp, 1000 Nicollet Mall, Minneapolis MN 55403, USA	Businessman
Steinhardt, Arnold Herbert Barrett, 266 W 37th St, #2000, New York NY 10018 USA	Violinist (Guarneri String Quartet)
Steinhardt, Paul J 1000 Cedargrove Road, Wynnewood PA 19096, USA	Physicist
Steinhardt, Richard University of California, Biology Dept, Berkeley CA 94720, USA	Biologist

Steinhauer, Sherri — Golfer
5010 Hammersley Road, Madison WI 53711, USA
Steinkraus, William (Bill) — Equestrian
40 Great Island, Darien CT 06820, USA
Steinkuhler, Dean E — Football Player
8041 S 37th St, Lincoln NE 68516, USA
Steinman, James R (Jim) — Composer, Songwriter
D A S Communications, 83 Riverside Dr, New York NY 10024, USA
Steinmetz, Richard — Actor
Melanie Greene Mgmt, 425 N Robertson Blvd, West Hollywood CA 90048 USA
Steinseifer Bates, Carolyn L (Carrie) — Swimmer
9309 Benzon Dr, Pleasanton CA 94588, USA
Steinwedell, Nicole — Actress
I C M Partners, 10250 Constellation Blvd, #900, Los Angeles CA 90067 USA
Steir, Pat — Artist
601 W 26th St, #1207, New York NY 10001, USA
Steirer, Ricky F — Baseball Player
1015 Haverhill Road, Baltimore MD 21229, USA
Steitz, Joan A — Biochemist
45 Prospect Hill Road, Branford CT 06405, USA
Steitz, Thomas A — Nobel Chemistry Laureate
Yale University, Molecular Biophysics Dept, New Haven CT 06520, USA
Stelfox, Shirley — Actress
Associated International Mgmt, Fairfax House, Fulwood Place, London WC1V 6HU, England
Stella, Frank P — Artist, Sculptor
17 Jones St, New York NY 10014, USA
Stelle, Kellogg S — Physicist
Imperial College, Prince Consort Road, London SW7 2BZ, England
Stemkowski, Peter D (Pete) — Ice Hockey Player
146 Albany Blvd, #21C, Atlantic Beach NY 11509, USA
Stemle, Steve — Baseball Player
4011 Weatherby Way, New Albany IN 47150, USA
Stempniak, Lee — Ice Hockey Player
4469 Clinton St, Buffalo NY 14224, USA
Stemrick, Gregory E (Greg), Sr — Football Player
1012 Matthews Dr, Cincinnati OH 45215, USA
Sten, Sanna — Rowing Athlete
Helsingin Soutuklubi Ry, Kousatie 17 E 10, 00430 Helsinki, Finland
Stenerud, Jan — Football Player
3180 Shieks Place, Colorado Springs CO 80904, USA
Stengade, Stine — Actress
Sten Hassing, Carit Etlars Vej 3, 1814 Frederiksberg C, Denmark
Stenger, Brian F — Football Player
7921 Kellogg Creek Dr, Mentor OH 44060, USA
Stenhouse, Michael S (Mike) — Baseball Player
70 Woodbury Road, Cranston RI 02905, USA
Stenlund, Vern — Ice Hockey Player
1220 Cabana Road W, Windsor ON N9G 1B7, Canada
Stenmark, Ingemar — Alpine Skier
Residence l'Annonciade, 17 Ave de l'Anncenciade, 98000 Monte Carlo, Monaco
Stenner, Charles E, Jr — Air Force General
Chief, Air Force Reserve, HqUSAF, Pentagon, Washington DC 20310 USA
Stennett, Renaldo A (Rennie) — Baseball Player
6519 Boticelli Dr, Lake Worth FL 33467, USA
Stensrud, Michael I (Mike) — Football Player
304 S Winnebago St, Lake Mills IA 50450, USA
Stepanek, Ondrej — Canoeing Athlete
S K Neumanna 386, 25001 Brandy's Nad Labem, Tschenchien, Czech Republic
Stepanova, Maria — Basketball Player
Phoenix Mercury, American West Arena, 201 E Jefferson St, Phoenix AZ 85004 USA
Stepanovich, Aleksandar (Alex) — Football Player
939 W 29th St, Lorain OH 44052, USA
Stepashin, Sergei V — Prime Minister, Russia; Army General
Accounts Chamber, Zubovskaya Pl 2, 119992 Moscow, Russia
Stephanie — Princess, Monaco
Palais Grimaldi, 2 Blvd du Moulins, 98015 Monte Carlo, Monaco
Stephanopoulos, George R — Journalist, Government Official
ABC-TV, News Dept, 5010 Creston St, Hyattsville MD 20781 USA
Stephanson, Ken — Ice Hockey Player
6 Heron Road, Box 1491, Siglavik MB R0C 1B0, Canada
Stephen, Louis R (Buzz) — Baseball Player
15512 Sycamore St, Porterville CA 93257, USA
Stephen, Marcus — President, Nauru
President's Office, Government Offices, Yaren, Nauru
Stephen, Scott D — Football Player
4132 Palm Tree Court, La Mesa CA 91941, USA
Stephens, Aaron — Actor
Michael Bruno Group, 13576 Cheltenham Dr, Sherman Oaks CA 91423, USA
Stephens, G Eugene (Gene) — Baseball Player
602 Erin Ave, Monroe LA 71201, USA
Stephens, Jamain — Football Player
105 W 6th St, Tabor City NC 28463, USA
Stephens, John M — Baseball Player
1325 Oak Point Court, Venice FL 34292, USA
Stephens, Louanne — Actress
Mary Collins Agency, 2909 Cole Ave, #250, Dallas TX 75204, USA
Stephens, Stanley G (Stan) — Governor, MT
4 Capitol Court, Helena MT 59601, USA
Stephens, Thomas G (Tom) — Football Player
69 Orchard Road, Swampscott MA 01907, USA
Stephens, Toby — Actor
United Agents, 12-26 Lexington St, London W1F 0LE, England
Stephenson, Bob — Ice Hockey Player
8 Tufts Crescent, Outlook SK S0L 2N0, Canada
Stephenson, C Earl — Baseball Player
4043 Zacks Mill Road, Angier NC 27501, USA

Stephenson, Debra — Actress, Comedienne
Independent Talent Group, Oxford House, 76 Oxford St, London W1D 1BS, England
Stephenson, Dwight E — Football Player
6241 N Dixie Highway, Fort Lauderdale FL 33334, USA
Stephenson, Garrett C — Baseball Player
947 W State St, Eagle ID 83616, USA
Stephenson, Gordon — Architect
55/14 Albert St, Claremont WA 6010, Australia
Stephenson, Jan L — Golfer
3522 Shallot Dr, #107, Orlando FL 32835, USA
Stephenson, John H (Johnny) — Baseball Player
7 Mauroner Dr, Hammond LA 70401, USA
Stephenson, Neal T — Writer
Avon Books, 1350 Ave of Americas, New York NY 10019 USA
Stephenson, Phillip R (Phil) — Baseball Player
1307 Hancock St, Dodge City KS 67801, USA
Stephenson, Randall — Businessman
A T & T Inc, 175 E Houston St, San Antonio TX 78205, USA
Stephenson, Robert L (Bobby) — Baseball Player
1518 Brookhaven Blvd, Norman OK 73072, USA
Stephens-Tysland, Kelly — Ice Hockey Player
Experience Momentum, 4720 200th St SW, Lynnwood WA 98036, USA
Stepnoski, Mark M — Football Player
1131 Meadow Creek Dr, #C1108, Irving TX 75038, USA
Steppe, M Holbrook (Brook) — Basketball Player
3486 Clare Cottage Terrace, Palm Desert CA 92211, USA
Steranka, Joe — Golf Executive
Professional Golfer's Assn, PO Box 109601, Palm Beach Gardens FL 33410 USA
Steranko, Jim — Cartoonist
PO Box 974, Reading PA 19603, USA
Sterban, Richard A — Singer (Oak Ridge Boys)
329 Rockland Road, Hendersonville TN 37075, USA
Sterkel, Jill — Swimmer
2206 Heritage Well Lane, Pflugerville TX 78660, USA
Sterling, Annette — Singer (Martha & Vandellas)
Soundedge Personal Mgmt, 332 Southdown Road, Huntington NY 11743, USA
Sterling, Maury — Actor
Innovative Artists, 1505 10th St, Santa Monica CA 90401 USA
Sterling, Mindy — Actress
Groundlings, 7307 Melrose Ave, Los Angeles CA 90046, USA
Sterling, Randall W (Randy) — Baseball Player
2516 Linda Ave, Key West FL 33040, USA
Sterling, Tisha — Actress
PO Box 235, Ketchum ID 83340, USA
Stern, Bert — Photographer
330 E 39th St, New York NY 10016, USA
Stern, Daniel — Actor
C E S D, 10635 Santa Monica Blvd, #130, Los Angeles CA 90025 USA
Stern, David — Religious Leader, Rabbi
8500 Hillcrest Ave, Dallas TX 75225, USA
Stern, David J — Basketball Executive
National Basketball Assn, 645 5th Ave, #1800, New York NY 10022 USA
Stern, David J — Conductor
I M G Artists, Hogarth Business Park, Chiswick, London W4 2TH, England
Stern, Fritz R — Historian
15 Claremont Ave, New York NY 10027, USA
Stern, Gardner — Writer, Producer
Paradigm Agency, 360 N Crescent Dr, North Building, Beverly Hills CA 90210 USA
Stern, Gary H — Government Official, Financier
Federal Reserve Bank, PO Box 291, Minneapolis MN 55480, USA
Stern, Gerald — Writer
W W Norton, 500 5th Ave, #600, New York NY 10110 USA
Stern, Howard A — Entertainer
Don Buchwald/Fortitude, 10 E 44th St, New York NY 10017 USA
Stern, Joseph — Actor, Producer
Creative Artists Agency, 2000 Ave of Stars, #100, Los Angeles CA 90067 USA
Stern, Marcus — Journalist
San Diego Union-Tribune, Editorial Dept, 350 Camino Reina, San Diego CA 92108 USA
Stern, Melvin E — Oceanographer
Florida State University, Oceanography Dept, Tallahassee FL 32306, USA
Stern, Michael (Mike) — Jazz Guitarist
Universal Attractions, 135 W 26th St, #1200, New York NY 10001 USA
Stern, Richard G — Writer
University of Chicago, English Dept, Chicago IL 60637, USA
Stern, Robert A M — Architect
Robert A M Stern Architects, 460 W 34th St, #1800, New York NY 10001, USA
Stern, Ronnie — Ice Hockey Player
224 Oakwood Blvd, Hustisford WI 53034, USA
Stern, Shoshannah — Actress
C E S D, 257 Park Ave S, #950, New York NY 10010 USA
Stern, Thomas E (Tom) — Cinematographer
I C M Partners, 10250 Constellation Blvd, #900, Los Angeles CA 90067 USA
Sternberg, Robert J — Psychologist
4321 S Western Road, Stillwater OK 74074, USA
Sternberg, Sigmund — Religous Leader, Templeton Laureate
80 East End Road, London N3 2SY, England
Sternberg, Thomas — Businessman
Staples Inc, PO Box 9265, Framingham MA 01701, USA
Sternecky, Neal — Cartoonist (Pogo)
52 Bluebird Lane, Naperville IL 60565, USA
Sternhagen, Frances — Actress
152 Sutton Manor Road, New Rochelle NY 10801, USA
Sternin, Joshua — Producer, Writer
Morris Yorn Barnes, 2000 Ave of Stars, #300N, Los Angeles CA 90067 USA
Sternlicht, Barry — Interior Designer
Starwood Capital Group, 591 W Putnam Ave, Greenwich CT 06830, USA

Sterrett, Samuel B — Judge
US Tax Court, 400 2nd St NW, Washington DC 20217, USA

Stetter, Karl O — Microbiologist
Universtat Regensburg, Universitats Str 31, 93053 Regensburg, Germany

Stetter, Mitch B — Baseball Player
3120 N Marigold Dr, Phoenix AZ 85018, USA

Stettner, Louis — Photographer
172 W 79th St, #6G, New York NY 10024, USA

Stettner, Patrick — Director
United Talent Agency, 9336 Civic Center Dr, Beverly Hills CA 90210 USA

Steuer, Ingo — Figure Skater
Liebigstr 9, 0911 Chemnitz, Germany

Steussie, Todd E — Football Player
59 Clermont Lane, Saint Louis MO 63124, USA

Stevenin, Robinson — Actor
Artmedia, 20 Ave Rapp, 75007 Paris, France

Stevens, Amber — Actress
I C M Partners, 10250 Constellation Blvd, #900, Los Angeles CA 90067 USA

Stevens, Andrew — Actor
CineTel Films, 8255 Sunset Blvd, Los Angeles CA 90046, USA

Stevens, April — Singer
19530 Superior St, Northridge CA 91324, USA

Stevens, Brad — Basketball Coach
Butler University, Athletic Dept, Indianapolis IN 46208, USA

Stevens, Brinke — Actress
PO Box 7112, Van Nuys CA 91409, USA

Stevens, Carrie — Model, Actress
C A Talent, 25 Palatine, #437, Irvine CA 92612, USA

Stevens, Charles A (Chuck) — Baseball Player
12591 George Reyburn Road, Garden Grove CA 92845, USA

Stevens, Chuck — Photographer
PO Box 422782, San Francisco CA 94142, USA

Stevens, Connie — Singer, Actress
Forever Spring, 426 S Robertson Blvd, Los Angeles CA 90048, USA

Stevens, D Lee — Baseball Player
9157 Buck Hill Dr, Littleton CO 80126, USA

Stevens, Dan — Actor
Julian Belfrage Assoc, 9 Argyll St, #300, London W1F 7TG, England

Stevens, Dana — Director, Writer, Actress
United Talent Agency, 9336 Civic Center Dr, Beverly Hills CA 90210 USA

Stevens, David J (Dave) — Baseball Player
2630 Candlewood Way, La Habra CA 90631, USA

Stevens, Dorit — Actress, Model
22425 Ventura Blvd, #118, Woodland Hills CA 91364, USA

Stevens, Eileen — Social Activist
126 Marion St, Sayville NY 11782, USA

Stevens, Eric Sheffer — Actor
A P A Talent/Literary Agency, 405 S Beverly Dr, #300, Beverly Hills CA 90212 USA

Stevens, Fisher — Actor
Paradigm Agency, 360 N Crescent Dr, North Building, Beverly Hills CA 90210 USA

Stevens, Gary — Thoroughbred Racing Jockey
136 W Carter Ave, Sierra Madre CA 91024, USA

Stevens, George, Jr — Producer
C E S D, 10635 Santa Monica Blvd, #130, Los Angeles CA 90025 USA

Stevens, Howard M, Jr — Football Player
235 Cedarhurst Lane, Franklinton NC 27525, USA

Stevens, Jan — Composer
Gorfaine/Schwartz, 4111 W Alameda Ave, #509, Burbank CA 91505 USA

Stevens, Jeffrey A (Jeff) — Baseball Player
Chicago Cubs, Wrigley Field, 1060 W Addison St, Chicago IL 60613 USA

Stevens, Jerramy — Football Player
10047 Main St, #515, Bellevue WA 98004, USA

Stevens, John A — Ice Hockey Player, Coach
Los Angeles Kings, Staples Center, 1111 S Figueroa St, Los Angeles CA 90015 USA

Stevens, John Paul — Supreme Court Justice
US Supreme Court, 1 1st St NE, Washington DC 20543 USA

Stevens, Kenneth N — Electrical Engineer
15298 SE Oregon Trail Dr, Clackamas OR 97015, USA

Stevens, Kevin M — Ice Hockey Player
37 Hawkins Place, Duxbury MA 02332, USA

Stevens, Louis D — Inventor (Disk Storage Device)
421 Coates Dr, Aptos CA 95003, USA

Stevens, Mark — Writer
New York Times, Editorial Dept, 229 W 43rd St, New York NY 10036 USA

Stevens, Mick — Cartoonist
New Yorker, Editorial Dept, 4 Times Square, Basement C1B, New York NY 10036 USA

Stevens, Rachel L — Actress, Singer (S Club 7), Model
Artist Rights Group, 4 Great Portland Place, London W1W 8PA, England

Stevens, Ray — Singer, Songwriter
Bobby Roberts Co, PO Box 1547, Goodlettsville TN 37070, USA

Stevens, Richard G (Dick) — Football Player
4100 Cimmaron Trail, Granbury TX 76049, USA

Stevens, Rise — Opera Singer
930 5th Ave, New York NY 10021, USA

Stevens, Robert J — Businessman
Lockheed Martin Corp, 6801 Rockledge Dr, Bethesda MD 20817, USA

Stevens, Robert M — Cinematographer
1920 S Beverly Glen Blvd, #106, Los Angeles CA 90025, USA

Stevens, Rogers — Guitarist (Blind Melon)
Shapiro Co, 9229 W Sunset Blvd, #607, West Hollywood CA 90069 USA

Stevens, Scott — Ice Hockey Player
280 Spook Hollow Road, Far Hills NJ 07931, USA

Stevens, Shadoe — Actor, Entertainer
James Kellem Assoc, 8033 Sunset Blvd, #115, Los Angeles CA 90046, USA

Stevens, Shakin' — Singer, Songwriter
Mgmt Gerd Kehren, Postfach 1455, 41804 Erkelenz, Germany

Stevens, Stella Actress, Model
2180 Coldwater Canyon Dr, Beverly Hills CA 90210, USA
Stevens, Steven Actor
Stevens Group, 3518 Cahuenga Blvd W, Los Angeles CA 90068, USA
Stevens, Taylor Writer
Crown Publishing Group, 1745 Broadway, New York NY 10019 USA
Stevens, Tony Bassist (Foghat)
Lustig Talent, PO Box 770850, Orlando FL 32877 USA
Stevenson, Adlai E, III Senator, IL
20 N Clark St, #750, Chicago IL 60602, USA
Stevenson, DeShawn Basketball Player
1348 Lake Whitney Dr, Windermere FL 34786, USA
Stevenson, G Raymond (Ray) Actor
Conway Van Gelder Grant, 8-12 Broadwick St, #300, London W1F 8HW, England
Stevenson, Jeremy Ice Hockey Player
7899 W 6 Mile Road, Brimley MI 49715, USA
Stevenson, John Animator
I/D Public Relations, 7060 Hollywood Blvd, #800, Los Angeles CA 90028 USA
Stevenson, Juliet Actress
68 Pall Mall, London SW1Y 5ES, England
Stevenson, Miriam J Beauty Queen
Miss Universe Organization, 1370 Ave of Americas, #1600, New York NY 10019 USA
Stevenson, Parker Actor
A K A Talent, 6310 San Vicente Blvd, #200, Los Angeles CA 90048 USA
Stevenson, Turner Ice Hockey Player
4530 251st Way NE, Redmond WA 98053, USA
Stevenson, Venetia Actress
4827 Riverton Ave, North Hollywood CA 91601, USA
Steverson, Todd A Baseball Player
109 W Glenhaven Dr, Phoenix AZ 85045, USA
Stevie B Singer, Songwriter
Paramount Entertainment, 12 Kosakowski Dr, Morris Plains NJ 07590 USA
Steward, John Drummer (Fishbone)
Silverback Mgmt, 9469 Jefferson Blvd, #101, Culver City CA 90232, USA
Stewart, Al Singer, Guitarist, Songwriter
Chapman & Co, 14011 Ventura Blvd, #405, Sherman Oaks CA 91423, USA
Stewart, Alana Actress
Boulevard Mgmt, 21731 Ventura Blvd, #300, Woodland Hills CA 91364, USA
Stewart, Alec Cricketer
Surrey County Cricket Club, Kennington Oval, London SE11 5SS, England
Stewart, Amy Actress
Amsel Eisenstadt Frazier, 5055 Wilshire Blvd, #865, Los Angeles CA 90036 USA
Stewart, Andrew D (Andy) Baseball Player
641 Geddes St, Wilmington DE 19805, USA
Stewart, Anthony W (Tony) Auto Racing Driver
Stewart-Haas Racing, 6001 Haas Way, Kannapolis NC 28081, USA
Stewart, Bill Jazz Drummer
Blue Note Records, 6920 W Sunset Blvd, Los Angeles CA 90028 USA
Stewart, Blair J Ice Hockey Player
1604 Cottenham Lane, Virginia Beach VA 23454, USA
Stewart, Cameron G (Cam) Ice Hockey Player
2929 Buffalo Speedway, #218, Houston TX 77098, USA
Stewart, Carl E Judge
US Court of Appeals, 300 Fannin St, Shreveport LA 71101, USA
Stewart, Catherine Mary Actress
Don Buchwald/Fortitude, 6500 Wilshire Blvd, #2200, Los Angeles CA 90048 USA
Stewart, Charlotte Actress
E J C Mgmt, 6562 Hollywood Blvd, Los Angeles CA 90028, USA
Stewart, Chelsea Soccer Player
Canadian Soccer, Place Soccer Canada, 237 Metcalfe St, Ottawa ON K2P 1R2, Canada
Stewart, David A (Dave) Keyboardist, Guitarist (Eurythmics)
I C M Partners, 10250 Constellation Blvd, #900, Los Angeles CA 90067 USA
Stewart, David A (Dave) Composer
Gorfaine/Schwartz, 4111 W Alameda Ave, #509, Burbank CA 91505 USA
Stewart, David K (Dave) Baseball Player
17762 Vineyard Lane, Poway CA 92064, USA
Stewart, Donald L (Don) Televangelist
Don Stewart Ministries, PO Box 2960, Phoenix AZ 85062, USA
Stewart, Eve Art Director
Dattner Dispoto, 10635 Santa Monica Blvd, #165, Los Angeles CA 90025, USA
Stewart, French Actor
Innovative Artists, 1505 10th St, Santa Monica CA 90401 USA
Stewart, Garry Dancer
Australian Dance Theatre, 126 Belair Road, Hawthorn SA 5062 Australia
Stewart, Ian Government Official, England
House of Commons, Westminster, London SW1A 0AA, England
Stewart, Ian K Baseball Player
125 Rainbow Lane, Candler NC 28715, USA
Stewart, James B Journalist
Wall Street Journal, Editorial Dept, 1 World Financial Center, New York NY 10281, USA
Stewart, James F (Jimmy) Baseball Player
15644 Eastbourn Dr, Odessa FL 33556, USA
Stewart, James O Football Player
4610 34th Ave, Vero Beach FL 32967, USA
Stewart, Jason Actor
Brillstein Eniertainment Partners, 9150 Wilshire Blvd, #350, Beverly Hills CA 90212 USA
Stewart, Jermaine Singer
Richard Walters, PO Box 2789, Toluca Lake CA 91610 USA
Stewart, Jim Ice Hockey Player
57 Lincoln St, Spencer MA 01562, USA
Stewart, John Y (Jackie) Auto Racing Driver
Clayton House, Butler Cross, Ellesborough, Bucks HP17 0UR, England
Stewart, Jon Actor, Comedian, Writer
I C M Partners, 10250 Constellation Blvd, #900, Los Angeles CA 90067 USA
Stewart, Kimberly Actress, Model, Producer
Amsel Eisenstadt Frazier, 5055 Wilshire Blvd, #865, Los Angeles CA 90036 USA

Stewart, Kordell — Football Player
Robinson Griege Theole, 5950 Sherry Lane, #700, Dallas TX 75225, USA

Stewart, Kristen — Actress
Gersh Agency, 9465 Wilshire Blvd, #600, Beverly Hills CA 90212 USA

Stewart, Larry — Singer, Guitarist
Fitzgerald-Hartley, 1908 Wedgewood Ave, Nashville TN 37212, USA

Stewart, Lisa — Singer
Friedman & LaRosa, 1344 Lexington Ave, New York NY 10128, USA

Stewart, Martha H — Businesswoman, Entertainer, Publisher
Martha Stewart Living Omnimedia, 11 W 42nd St, #2500, New York NY 10036, USA

Stewart, Mary — Writer
House of Letterawe, Lock Awe, Argyll PA33 1AH, Scotland

Stewart, Matt — Football Player
4389 Village Club Dr, Powell OH 43065, USA

Stewart, Melvin, Jr — Swimmer
7308 Seneca Falls Loop, Austin TX 78739, USA

Stewart, Michael A — Football Player
103 Los Padres Dr, Thousand Oaks CA 91361, USA

Stewart, Natalie — Singer (Floetry), Songwriter
DreamWorks Records, 1000 Flower St, Glendale CA 91201 USA

Stewart, Patrick — Actor
Independent Talent Group, Oxford House, 76 Oxford St, London W1D 1BS, England

Stewart, Paul — Ice Hockey Player
16 Bridgeview Circle, Walpole MA 02081, USA

Stewart, Pete — Singer, Guitarist (Tait)
True Artist Mgmt, 227 3rd Ave N, Franklin TN 37064, USA

Stewart, Philip J — Ecologist
Oxford University, Plant Sciences Dept, Oxford OX1 2JD, England

Stewart, Potter — Judge
US Court of Appeals, US Courthouse, 100 E 5th St, #317, Cincinnati OH 45202, USA

Stewart, R J — Writer, Producer
A P A Talent/Literary Agency, 405 S Beverly Dr, #300, Beverly Hills CA 90212 USA

Stewart, Ralph — Ice Hockey Player
175 Sherwood Dr, Thunder Bay ON P7B 6L1, Canada

Stewart, Ray — Golfer
2777 DeHavilland Place, Abbotsford BC V2T 5E2, Canada

Stewart, Robert H (Bob) — Ice Hockey Player
16756 Kehrs Mill Estates Dr, Chesterfield MO 63005, USA

Stewart, Robert L — Astronaut, Army General
815 Sun Valley Dr, Woodland Park CO 80863, USA

Stewart, Roderick D (Rod) — Singer, Songwriter
Artists Group International, 150 E 58th, New York NY 10155, USA

Stewart, Ryan E — Football Player
2715 Owens Ave SW, Marietta GA 30064, USA

Stewart, Scott — Baseball Player
5243 Hickory Knoll Lane, Mount Holly NC 28120, USA

Stewart, Shannon H — Baseball Player
14348 SW 156th Ave, Miami FL 33196, USA

Stewart, Tommy — Drummer (Godsmack)
Front Line Mgmt, 1100 Glendon Ave, #2000, Los Angeles CA 90024 USA

Stewart, Tonea — Actress
Alabama State University, Theater Arts Dept, Montgomery AL 36101, USA

Stewart, Tyler — Drummer (Barenaked Ladies)
Nettwerk Mgmt, 6525 W Sunset Blvd, #800, Los Angeles CA 90028 USA

Stewart, Will Foster — Actor
8730 Santa Monica Blvd, #1, West Hollywood CA 90069, USA

Stewart, William W (Bill) — Baseball Player
44842 Aspen Ridge Dr, Northville MI 48168, USA

Stezer, Philip — Violinist (Emerson String Quartet)
I M G Artists, Burlington Lane, Chiswick, London W4 2TH, England

Stice, Eric — Psychologist
Oregon Research Institute, 1715 Franklin Blvd, Eugene OR 97403, USA

Stich, Michael — Tennis Player
Ernst-Barlach-Str 44, 25336 Elmshorn, Germany

Stich, Stephen P — Philosopher
55 Liberty St, #8A, New York NY 10005, USA

Sticht, J Paul — Businessman
11732 Lake House Court, North Palm Beach FL 33408, USA

Stickel, Fred A — Publisher
Portland Oregonian, 1320 SW Broadway, Portland OR 97201, USA

Stickles, Edward (Ted) — Swimmer
1142 Sharynwood Dr, Baton Rouge LA 70808, USA

Stickney, Timothy D — Actor
TalentWorks, 3500 W Olive Ave, #1400, Burbank CA 91505 USA

Sticky Fingaz — Rap Artist (Onyx), Actor
I C M Partners, 10250 Constellation Blvd, #900, Los Angeles CA 90067 USA

Stieb, David A (Dave) — Baseball Player
3375 Cory Dr, Reno NV 89509, USA

Stieber, Tamar — Journalist
Albuquerque Journal, Editorial Dept, 7777 Jefferson NE, Albuquerque NM 87109, USA

Stiefel, Ethan — Ballet Dancer
American Ballet Theatre, 890 Broadway, #300, New York NY 10003 USA

Stiegler, Josef (Pepi) — Alpine Skier
PO Box 290, Teton Village WY 83025, USA

Stielike, Ulrich (Uli) — Soccer Player, Manager
Casa Postale 78, 2000 Neuchatel, Switzerland

Stienburg, Trevor — Ice Hockey Player
2376 Connaught Ave, Halifax NS B3L 2Z4, Canada

Stienke, James L (Jim) — Football Player
4707 Interlachen Lane, Austin TX 78747, USA

Stiers, David Ogden — Actor
Mitchell K Stubbs Assoc, 8695 W Washington Blvd, #204, Culver City CA 90232 USA

Stieve, Terry A — Football Player
1407 Vail Place, Saint Louis MO 63104, USA

Stigers, Curtis — Singer, Saxophonist
C Winston Simone Mgmt, 1790 Broadway, #1000, New York NY 10019, USA

Stiglitz, Joseph E	Nobel Economics Laureate
Columbia University, Economics Dept, New York NY 10027, USA	
Stigman, Richard L (Dick)	Baseball Player
12914 5th Ave S, Burnsville MN 55337, USA	
Stigwood, Robert C	Producer
Barton Manor, Whippingham, East Cowes, PO32 6LB, Isle of Wight, England	
Stiles, Darron	Golfer
130 Wild Turkey Run, Pinehurst NC 28374, USA	
Stiles, Jackie	Basketball Player
Patrick J Stiles, 115 E Hamilton, Claflin KS 67525, USA	
Stiles, Julia	Actress
Untitled Entertainment, 350 S Beverly Dr, #200, Beverly Hills CA 90212 USA	
Stiles, Neil	Businessman
Daily Variety, President's Office, 5900 Wilshire Blvd, #3100, Los Angeles CA 90036, USA	
Stiles, Ryan	Actor, Comedian
A P A Talent/Literary Agency, 405 S Beverly Dr, #300, Beverly Hills CA 90212 USA	
Stilgoe, Richard	Lyricist
Noel Gray Artists, 24 Denmark St, London WC2H 8NJ, England	
Still, Arthur B (Art)	Football Player
9813 Betsy Ross Court, Liberty MO 64068, USA	
Still, Ken	Golfer
1210 Princeton St, Fircrest WA 98466, USA	
Still, Ray	Concert Oboist, Conductor
41 W McKinsey Road, #206, Severna Park MD 21146, USA	
Still, Susan L	Astronaut
N A S A, Johnson Space Center, 2101 NASA Road, Houston TX 77058 USA	
Still, Valerie	Basketball Player
Valerie Still Foundation, PO Box 452, Powell OH 43065, USA	
Still, William C, Jr	Chemist
Columbia University, Chemistry Dept, New York NY 10027, USA	
Stiller, Ben	Actor, Comedian, Director
Red Hour Films, 629 N La Brea Ave, Los Angeles CA 90036, USA	
Stiller, Jerry	Actor, Comedian
118 Riverside Dr, #5A, New York NY 10024, USA	
Stillman, Cory	Ice Hockey Player
397 Sweet Bay Ave, Plantation FL 33324, USA	
Stillman, Royle E	Baseball Player
580 J B Court, Glenwood Springs CO 81601, USA	
Stillman, Whit	Director
Mosiac Media Group, 9200 W Sunset Blvd, #1000, Los Angeles CA 90069 USA	
Stills, Kenneth L (Ken)	Football Player
647 Michael St, Oceanside CA 92057, USA	
Stills, Stephen	Singer, Guitarist (Crosby Stills Nash)
I C M Partners, 10250 Constellation Blvd, #900, Los Angeles CA 90067 USA	
Stillwagon, Jim R	Football Player
3999 Parkway Lane, Hilliard OH 43026, USA	
Stillwell, Kurt A	Baseball Player
1105 Lassen View Dr, Westwood CA 96137, USA	
Stilwell, Richard D	Opera Singer
Columbia Artists Mgmt Inc, 1790 Broadway, #702, New York NY 10019 USA	
Stilwell, Victoria	Actress
W M E Entertainment, 103 New Oxford St, London WC1A 1DD, England	
Stinchcomb, Jonathan (Jon)	Football Player
1010 Chateau Lafitte Dr W, Kenner LA 70065, USA	
Stinchcomb, Matthew D (Matt)	Football Player
301 Anderson Road, Alameda CA 94502, USA	
Stine, Richard	Editorial Cartoonist
PO Box 348, Hansville WA 98340, USA	
Stine, Robert L (R L)	Writer
225 W 71st St, New York NY 10023, USA	
Stiner, Carl W	Army General
Special Operations Warrior Foundation, PO Box 13483, Tampa FL 33681, USA	
Sting	Singer, Actor, Bassist, Songwriter
Markham & Froggatt, Julian House, 4 Windmill St, London W1P 1HF, England	
Stinnett, Kelly L	Baseball Player
845 N Harris Dr, Mesa AZ 85203, USA	
Stinson, G Robert (Bob)	Baseball Player
1309 Bando Lane, The Villages FL 32162, USA	
Stinson, Lemuel D	Football Player
7629 Grassland Dr, Fort Worth TX 76133, USA	
Stipanovich, Stephen E (Steve)	Basketball Player
14 Ridgecreek, Saint Louis MO 63141, USA	
Stipe, J Michael	Singer (REM), Songwriter
REM/Athens Ltd, 170 College Ave, Athens GA 30601, USA	
Stirling, Rachel	Actress
United Agents, 12-26 Lexington St, London W1F 0LE, England	
Stirratt, John	Bassist (Uncle Tupelo, Wilco)
Tom Margherita Mgmt, 2200 W Foster Ave, #2, Chicago IL 60625, USA	
Stitch, Stephen P	Philosopher
Rutgers University, Philosophy Dept, New Brunswick NJ 08901, USA	
Stith, Bryant L	Basketball Player
20697 Governor Harrison Parkway, Freeman VA 23856, USA	
Stits, William D (Bill)	Football Player
1177 Eolus Ave, Encinitas CA 92024, USA	
Stivrins, Alex F	Basketball Player
11330 Sundown Dr, Scottsdale AZ 85260, USA	
Stix-Brunell, Beatriz	Ballerina
Morphoses/Wheeldon Co, 800 5th Ave, #18F, New York NY 10065, USA	
Stock, Barbara	Actress
22532 Margarita Dr, Woodland Hills CA 91364, USA	
Stock, Mark A	Football Player
16549 Levade Dr, Leesburg VA 20176, USA	
Stock, P J	Ice Hockey Player
Team 990, 1310 Greene Ave, #300, Montreal QC H3Z 2B5, Canada	
Stock, Wesley G (Wes)	Baseball Player
PO Box 1309, Allyn WA 98524, USA	

Stockard, Aaron — Writer
W M E Entertainment, 9601 Wilshire Blvd, #300, Beverly Hills CA 90210 USA

Stockdale, Andrew — Singer, Guitarist (Wolfmother)
John Watson Mgmt, PO Box 281, Surry Hills NSW 2010, Australia

Stockdale, Gretchen — Actress
Don Buchwald/Fortitude, 6500 Wilshire Blvd, #2200, Los Angeles CA 90048 USA

Stocker, Kevin D — Baseball Player
1204 N Murray Lane, Liberty Lake WA 99019, USA

Stockett, Kathryn — Writer
G P Putnam's Sons, 375 Hudson St, New York NY 10014 USA

Stockman, Phil — Baseball Player
3519 Beachhill Dr, Atlanta GA 30340, USA

Stockman, Shawn — Singer (Boyz II Men)
Creative Talent Management Group, 433 N Camden Dr, #600, Beverly Hills CA 90210, USA

Stockmayer, Walter H — Physical Chemist
Willey Hill, Norwich VT 05055, USA

Stockton, Dave K — Golfer
30378 Copper Hill Court, Redlands CA 92373, USA

Stockton, David — Cinematographer
Dattner Dispoto, 10635 Santa Monica Blvd, #165, Los Angeles CA 90025, USA

Stockton, David, Jr — Golfer
10 Carrera Dr, Redlands CA 92373, USA

Stockton, Dick — Sportscaster
5781 NW 24th Ave, #901, Boca Raton FL 33496, USA

Stockton, John H — Basketball Player
538 W Sumner Ave, Spokane WA 99204, USA

Stockton, Richard L (Dick) — Tennis Player
715 Stadium Dr, San Antonio TX 78212, USA

Stockwell, Dean — Actor
Abrams Artists, 9200 W Sunset Blvd, #1125, West Hollywood CA 90069 USA

Stockwell, Jeff — Writer, Producer
United Talent Agency, 9336 Civic Center Dr, Beverly Hills CA 90210 USA

Stockwell, John — Actor, Director
I C M Partners, 10250 Constellation Blvd, #900, Los Angeles CA 90067 USA

Stoddard, Jack — Ice Hockey Player
27-4275 Millcroft Park Dr, Burlington ON L7M 4L9, Canada

Stoddard, Robert L (Bob) — Baseball Player
15760 Sunnyside Ave, Morgan Hill CA 95037, USA

Stoddard, Timothy P (Tim) — Baseball Player
4545 Gettysburg Dr, Rolling Meadows IL 60008, USA

Stoermer, Mark — Bassist (Killers)
W M E Entertainment, 9601 Wilshire Blvd, #300, Beverly Hills CA 90210 USA

Stofa, John C — Football Player
7344 Jefferson Meadows Dr, Blacklick OH 43004, USA

Stogner, Patrick — Actor
C E S D, 10635 Santa Monica Blvd, #130, Los Angeles CA 90025 USA

Stoicheff, Boris P — Physicist
66 Collier St, #6B, Toronto ON M4W 1L9, Canada

Stojakovic, Predrag (Peja) — Basketball Player
501 Gibson Dr, #424, Roseville CA 95678, USA

Stojko, Elvis — Figure Skater
Mentor Marketing, 2 Saint Clair Ave E, Toronto ON M4T 2T, Canada

Stok, Barbara — Cartoonist (Barbaraal)
PO Box 1012, 9701 BA Groningen, Netherlands

Stoker, Michael G P — Virologist
3 Barrington House, Southacre Dr, Cambridge CB2 2TY, England

Stoker, Richard — Composer
Ricordi Co, 210 New King's Road, London SW6 4NZ, England

Stokes, Brian — Baseball Player
12140 66th Ave, Seminole FL 33772, USA

Stokes, Gregory L (Greg) — Basketball Player
2505 Plymouth St, Marion IA 52302, USA

Stokes, John — WW II Navy Air Force Hero
351 Windermere Blvd, #411, Alexandria LA 71303, USA

Stokes, L Fred — Football Player
4673 Anson Lane, Orlando FL 32814, USA

Stokes, Patrick T — Businessman
Anheuser-Busch Co, 1 Busch Place, Saint Louis MO 63118, USA

Stokkan, Bill — Auto Racing Executive
Championship Auto Racing, 5350 Lakeview Parkway S Dr, Indianapolis IN 46268 USA

Stokley, Brandon — Football Player
1029 Anaconda Dr, Castle Rock CO 80108, USA

Stoklos, Randy — Volleyball Player
Beach Volleyball Camps, PO Box 1714, Pacific Palisades CA 90272, USA

Stole, Mink — Actress
635 Colorado Ave, #3B, Baltimore MD 21210, USA

Stolhanske, Eric — Actor, Comedian, Writer, Producer
United Talent Agency, 9336 Civic Center Dr, Beverly Hills CA 90210 USA

Stoll, Corey — Actor
Suskin Mgmt, 2 Charlton St, #5K, New York NY 10014, USA

Stolle, Frederick S — Tennis Player
Turnberry Isle Yacht & Racquet Club, 19735 Turnberry Way, Miami FL 33180, USA

Stoller, Fred — Actor
Amsel Eisenstadt Frazier, 5055 Wilshire Blvd, #865, Los Angeles CA 90036 USA

Stoller, Mike — Composer
Leiber/Stoller Entertainment, 9000 W Sunset Blvd, #720, West Hollywood CA 90069, USA

Stolley, Paul D — Epidemiologist, Pharmacologist
10205 Wincopin Circle, #312, Columbia MD 21044, USA

Stolojan, Theodor — Prime Minister, Romania
Aurel Vlaicu 42-44, #3, Sector 2, Bucharest, Romania

Stolper, Pinchas — Religious Leader
Orthodox Jewish Congregations Union, 11 Broadway, New York NY 10004, USA

Stoltenberg, Brian D — Football Player
3207 W Farmington Lane, Sugar Land TX 77479, USA

Stoltenberg, Jens — Prime Minister, Norway
Prime Minister's Office, Akersgaten 42, Ploensgt 8, 0030 Oslo, Norway

Stoltz, Eric	Actor, Director, Producer
Creative Artists Agency, 2000 Ave of Stars, #100, Los Angeles CA 90067 USA	
Stoltz, Kelley	Singer, Songwriter
Agency Group Ltd, 142 W 57th St, #600, New York NY 10019 USA	
Stoltz, Roland	Ice Hockey Player
Lilgatan 16, Skelleftea 93 154, Sweden	
Stoltzman, Richard L	Concert Clarinetist
Frank Salomon, 121 W 27th St, #703, New York NY 10001 USA	
Stolze, Lena	Actress
Agentur Carola Studlar, Neuroeder Str 1C, 82152 Planegg, Germany	
Stone, Angie	Singer, Songwriter
Universal Attractions, 135 W 26th St, #1200, New York NY 10001 USA	
Stone, Charles, III	Director, Actor
United Talent Agency, 9336 Civic Center Dr, Beverly Hills CA 90210 USA	
Stone, Curtis	Chef
W M E Entertainment, 9601 Wilshire Blvd, #300, Beverly Hills CA 90210 USA	
Stone, D Dean	Baseball Player
213 13th St, Silvis IL 61282, USA	
Stone, Doug	Singer, Songwriter
PO Box 943, Springfield TN 37172, USA	
Stone, Dwight	Football Player
1128 Deep Hollow Court, Waxhaw NC 28173, USA	
Stone, E Donald (Donnie)	Football Player
101 W H St, Jenks OK 74037, USA	
Stone, Edward C, Jr	Space Scientist, Physicist
PO Box 40747, Pasadena CA 91114, USA	
Stone, Emma	Actress
Anonymous Content, 3532 Hayden Ave, Culver City CA 90232 USA	
Stone, Eugene D (Gene)	Baseball Player
6897 Highway 262 SE, Othello WA 99344, USA	
Stone, Fred	Artist
Equinart Inc, 5911 Colodny Dr, Agoura Hills CA 91301, USA	
Stone, George H	Baseball Player
1206 Eastland Ave, Ruston LA 71270, USA	
Stone, H Ronald (Ron)	Baseball Player
11720 NW Lovejoy St, Portland OR 97229, USA	
Stone, Isaac (Biz)	Businessman
Twitter Inc, 795 Folsom St, #600, San Francisco CA 94107, USA	
Stone, Jeffrey G (Jeff)	Baseball Player
RR 1 Box 392, Portageville MO 63873, USA	
Stone, Jennifer	Actress
United Talent Agency, 9336 Civic Center Dr, Beverly Hills CA 90210 USA	
Stone, Jessica	Actress
Paradigm Agency, 360 N Crescent Dr, North Building, Beverly Hills CA 90210 USA	
Stone, Joss	Singer, Songwriter, Actress
Conway Van Gelder Grant, 8-12 Broadwick St, #300, London W1F 8HW, England	
Stone, Kenneth B (Ken), Jr	Football Player
16 W Riverside Dr, Jupiter FL 33469, USA	
Stone, Lara C	Model
I M G Models, 304 Park Ave S, #PH-North, New York NY 10010 USA	
Stone, Matt	Animator, Writer
Morris Yorn Barnes, 2000 Ave of Stars, #300N, Los Angeles CA 90067 USA	
Stone, Michael A	Football Player
23162 Coventry Woods Lane, Southfield MI 48034, USA	
Stone, Nicole L (Nikki)	Freestyle Aerials Skier
5272 Heather Lane, Park City UT 84098, USA	
Stone, Oliver W	Director, Writer
Ixtlan Corp, 12233 W Olympic Blvd, #322, Los Angeles CA 90064, USA	
Stone, Ricky	Baseball Player
6494 Lakeview Court, Hamilton OH 45011, USA	
Stone, Robert A	Writer
PO Box 967, Block Island RI 02807, USA	
Stone, Sharon	Actress, Model
Chuck Binder Mgmt, 1465 Lindacrest Dr, Beverly Hills CA 90210 USA	
Stone, Skyler	Actor, Comedian
Justice & Ponder, PO Box 480033, Los Angeles CA 90048 90048, USA	
Stone, Sly	Singer, Keyboardist, Songwriter
Richard Walters, PO Box 2789, Toluca Lake CA 91610 USA	
Stone, Steven M (Steve)	Baseball Player, Sportscaster
9261 N 128th Way, Scottsdale AZ 85259, USA	
Stonebarger, Suzanne	Volleyball Player, Model
Association of Volleyball Professionals, 960 Knox St, #A, Torrance CA 90502 USA	
Stoneman, William H (Bill)	Baseball Player, Executive
2519 N San Miguel Dr, Orange CA 92867, USA	
Stoner, Alyson R	Actress, Dancer
Paradigm Agency, 360 N Crescent Dr, North Building, Beverly Hills CA 90210 USA	
Stoner, Casey	Motorcycle Racing Rider
Ducati Moto G P, Via C Ducati 3, 40132 Bologna, Italy	
Stones, Dwight E	Track Athlete
4790 Irvine Blvd, #105, Irvine CA 92620, USA	
Stonesipher, Donald H (Don)	Football Player
1502 Canberry Court, Wheeling IL 60090, USA	
Stonestreet, Eric	Actor
I C M Partners, 10250 Constellation Blvd, #900, Los Angeles CA 90067 USA	
Stookey, Paul	Singer (Peter Paul & Mary), Songwriter
Fritz/Byers Mgmt, 1455 N Doheny Dr, Los Angeles CA 90069, USA	
Stoops, Robert A (Bob)	Football Coach
University of Oklahoma, Athletic Dept, 108 E Brooks St, Norman OK 73069, USA	
Stoppard, Tom S	Writer
United Agents, 12-26 Lexington St, London W1F 0LE, England	
Storaro, Vittorio	Cinematographer
Via Divino Amore 2, 00040 Frattocchie Merino, Italy	
Storch, Larry	Actor, Comedian
330 W End Ave, #17F, New York NY 10023, USA	
Storey, Awvee	Basketball Player
Edge Sports Int'l, 3649 W Chase St, #100, Skokie IL 60076, USA	

Storey, David M — Writer
2 Lyndhurst Gardens, London NW3, England
Stork, Jeffrey (Jeff) — Volleyball Player
Pepperdine University, Athletic Dept, 24255 Pacific Coast Highway, Malibu CA 90263, USA
Storke, Adam — Actor
Don Buchwald/Fortitude, 6500 Wilshire Blvd, #2200, Los Angeles CA 90048 USA
Storm, Gregory — Actor
Paradigm Agency, 360 N Crescent Dr, North Building, Beverly Hills CA 90210 USA
Storm, Hannah — Commentator, Sportscaster
CBS-TV, News Dept, 51 W 52nd St, New York NY 10019 USA
Storm, Jim — Ice Hockey Player
2609 Harvest Hills Dr, Brighton MI 48114, USA
Storm, Tempest — Exotic Dancer
3905 Cambridge St, #3, Las Vegas NV 89119, USA
Stormare, Peter — Actor
Collective, 8383 Wilshire Blvd, #1050, Beverly Hills CA 90211 USA
Stormer, Horst L — Nobel Physics Laureate
20 E 9th St, #14P, New York NY 10003, USA
Storms, Kirsten — Actress
Paradigm Agency, 360 N Crescent Dr, North Building, Beverly Hills CA 90210 USA
Storr, Jamie — Ice Hockey Player
Jamie Storr Goalie School, 650 N Sepulveda Blvd, Los Angeles CA 90049, USA
Story, Karl — Illustrator (Nightwing)
D C Comics, 1700 Broadway, #400, New York NY 10019 USA
Story, Liz — Pianist, Songwriter
S R O Artists, PO Box 9532, Madison WI 53715, USA
Story, Tim — Director, Producer
United Talent Agency, 9336 Civic Center Dr, Beverly Hills CA 90210 USA
Stossel, John — Commentator
Beresford Apartments, 211 Central Park West, #15K, New York NY 10024, USA
Stosur, Samatha J (Sam) — Tennis Player
Tennis Australia, Melbourne Park, Batman Avenue, Melbourne VIC 3121, Australia
Stothers, Mike — Ice Hockey Player
Grand Rapids Griffins, 130 Fulton St W, #111, Grand Rapids MI 49503, USA
Stott, Kathryn L — Concert Pianist
Jane Ward, 38 Townfield, Rickmansworth, Herts WD3 2DD, England
Stott, Ken — Actor
Rights House, 34-43 Russell St, London WC2B 5HA, England
Stott, Nicole M P — Astronaut
N A S A, Johnson Space Center, 2101 NASA Road, Houston TX 77058 USA
Stottlemyre, Melvin L (Mel) — Baseball Player
26004 SE 27th St, Sammamish WA 98075, USA
Stottlemyre, Todd V — Baseball Player
6918 E Bronco Dr, Paradise Valley AZ 85253, USA
Stotts, Terry — Basketball Coach
Portland Trail Blazers, Rose Garden, 1 N Center Court St, Portland OR 97227 USA
Stoudamire, Damon L — Basketball Player
8325 Broadway St, #202, Pearland TX 77581, USA
Stoudemire, Amar'e — Basketball Player
346 E Tuckey Lane, Phoenix AZ 85012, USA
Stouder, Sharon M — Swimmer
144 Loucks Ave, Los Altos CA 94022, USA
Stoudt, Bud — Bowler
431 Lehman St, Lebanon PA 17046, USA
Stoudt, Clifford L (Cliff) — Football Player
5348 Drumcally Lane, Dublin OH 43017, USA
Stouffer, Kelly W — Football Player
7430 370th Trail, Rushville NE 69360, USA
Stoughton, Blaine — Ice Hockey Player
267th Ave SW, Dauphin MB R7N 1W5, Canada
Stoutmire, Omar A — Football Player
980 S Coit Road, #1433, Prosper TX 75078, USA
Stovall, Dale E — Vietnam War Air Force Hero
7440 Arroyo Lane, Missoula MT 59808, USA
Stovall, DaRond — Baseball Player
1107 Goelz Dr, East Saint Louis IL 62203, USA
Stovall, Jerry L — Football Player
7948 Wrenwood Blvd, #C, Baton Rouge LA 70809, USA
Stovall, Maurice A, Jr — Football Player
4406 Kendal Court, Valrico FL 33596, USA
Stover Irwin Russ, Juno — Diver
512 Lanai Circle, Union City CA 94587, USA
Stover, George — Actor
PO Box 10005, Baltimore MD 21285, USA
Stover, J Matthew (Matt) — Football Player
15 Ivy Reach Court, Cockeysville MD 21030, USA
Stover, Jeffrey O (Jeff) — Football Player
260 Cohasset Road, #190, Chico CA 95926, USA
Stover, Stewart L (Smokey) — Football Player
140 Ridgela Circle, Duson LA 70529, USA
Stowe, David H, Jr — Businessman
435 L'Ambiance Dr, #308 Longboat Key FL 34228, USA
Stowe, Harold R (Hal) — Baseball Player
1361 Union New Hope Road, Gastonia NC 28056, USA
Stowe, Madeleine — Actress
Brillstein Entertainment Partners, 9150 Wilshire Blvd, #350, Beverly Hills CA 90212 USA
Stowe, Tyronne K — Football Player
PO Box 164, Chandler AZ 85244, USA
Stowell, Austin — Actor
Creative Artists Agency, 2000 Ave of Stars, #100, Los Angeles CA 90067 USA
Stowers, Christopher J (Chris) — Baseball Player
3773 Wakefield Hall Square SE, Smyrna GA 30080, USA
Stowers, Saleisha — Model
Elite Model Mgmt, 404 Park Ave S, #900, New York NY 10016 USA
Stoyanov, Krasimir M — Cosmonaut, Bulgaria
Cosmonaut Training Center, Star City, 141160 Zvezdny Gorodok, Moscow Oblast, Russia

Stoyanovich, Peter (Pete)	Football Player
18185 Parkshore Dr, Northville MI 48168, USA	
St-Pierre, Kim	Ice Hockey Player
Team Canada, 2424 University Dr NW, Calgary AB T2N 3Y9, Canada	
Stracey, John H	Boxer
8 Serpentine Road, Wallasey CH44 0AX, England	
Strachan, Michael D (Mike)	Football Player
105 Yellowstone St, Kenner LA 70065, USA	
Strachan, Rodney (Rod)	Swimmer
3250 Cabrillo Highway, Harmony CA 93435, USA	
Strachan, Stephen M (Steve)	Football Player
161 Old Post Road, Mooresville NC 28117, USA	
Strader, Cam	Auto Racing Driver
J R Motorsports, 349 Cayuga Dr, Mooresville NC 28117, USA	
Stradford, Troy E	Football Player
James Crystal Radio Group, 6600 N Andrews Ave, #160, Fort Lauderdale FL 33309, USA	
Stradlin, Izzy	Guitarist (Guns N' Roses)
Front Line Mgmt, 1100 Glendon Ave, #2000, Los Angeles CA 90024 USA	
Stradling, Harry A, Jr	Cinematographer
3664 Avenida Callada, Calabasas CA 91302, USA	
Strahan, Michael A	Football Player, Actor, Sportscaster
23679 Calabasas Road, Calabasas CA 91302, USA	
Strahler, Michael W (Mike)	Baseball Player
8 Canyon Draw, Alamogordo NM 88310, USA	
Strahovski, Yvonne	Actress
McKeon-Myrones Mgmt, 3500 Olive Ave, #770, Burbank CA 91505 USA	
Straight, Susan	Writer
Hyperion Books, 114 5th Ave, New York NY 10011 USA	
Strain, Joseph A (Joe)	Baseball Player
8668 E Otero Circle, Centennial CO 80112, USA	
Strain, Julie	Actress, Model
J S Inc, 8491 Sunset Blvd, #1850, West Hollywood CA 90069, USA	
Strain, Sammy	Singer (O'Jays)
Associated Booking Corp, 501 Madison Ave, #603, New York NY 10022 USA	
Strait, Donald	WW II Army Air Corps Hero
6 Burning Tree Place, Jackson Springs NC 27281, USA	
Strait, George	Singer, Guitarist
Erv Woolsey Co, 1000 18th Ave S, Nashville TN 37212, USA	
Strait, Steven	Actor, Singer
3 Arts Entertainment, 9460 Wilshire Blvd, #700, Beverly Hills CA 90212 USA	
Straka, Martin	Ice Hockey Player
HC Pizen Stefanikovo, Namesti 1, 30133 Pizen, Czech Republic	
Strampe, Bob	Bowler
31029 Louise Court, Warren MI 48088, USA	
Strampe, Robert E (Bob)	Baseball Player
19210 W Lance Hill Road, Cheney WA 99004, USA	
Stranahan, Frank	Golfer
8400 Heritage Club Dr, West Palm Beach FL 33412, USA	
Strand, Mark	Writer
5825 S Dorchester Ave, #9W, Chicago IL 60637, USA	
Strand, Robin	Actor
4500 Morella Ave, Valley Village CA 91607, USA	
Strane, John	WW II Navy Air Force Hero
18230 Mirasol Dr, San Diego CA 92128, USA	
Strang, Deborah	Actress
McCabe Group, 3211 Cahuenga Blvd W, #104, Los Angeles CA 90068, USA	
Strang, William G	Mathematician
7 Southgate Road, Wellesley MA 02482, USA	
Strange, Curtis N	Golfer, Sportscaster
147 S Spooners St, Morehead City NC 28557, USA	
Strange, J Douglas (Doug)	Baseball Player
435 Heights Dr, Gibsonia PA 15044, USA	
Strange, Pat	Baseball Player
156 Mill St, Springfield MA 01108, USA	
Strange, Sarah	Actress
Elizabeth Hodgson Mgmt. 1536 W 12th Ave, #5, Vancouver BC V6J 2E1, Canada	
Strassen, Volker	Mathematician
Oskar-Pletsch-Str 12, 01324 Dresden, Germany	
Strasser, Robin	Actress
Innovative Artists, 235 Park Ave S, #1000, New York NY 10003 USA	
Strasser, Teresa	Actress, Comedienne
Renaissance Mgmt, P O Box 17379, Beverly Hills CA 90209, USA	
Strasser, Todd	Writer
PO Box 859, Larchmont NY 10538, USA	
Strassman, Marcia	Actress
Geddes Agency, 8430 Santa Monica Blvd, #201, West Hollywood CA 90069 USA	
Stratas, Teresa	Opera Singer
Vincent Farrell Assoc, 481 8th Ave, #340, New York NY 10001, USA	
Strathairn, David	Actor
I C M Partners, 10250 Constellation Blvd, #900, Los Angeles CA 90067 USA	
Stratham, Jason	Actor
Creative Artists Agency, 2000 Ave of Stars, #100, Los Angeles CA 90067 USA	
Stratton, Arthur (Art)	Ice Hockey Player
General Delivery, Succ Main, Saint Adolphie MB R5A 1A3, Canada	
Stratton, Charlie	Actor
Judi Farkas Mgmt, 116 N Mansfield Ave, Los Angeles CA 90036, USA	
Stratton, D Michael (Mike)	Football Player
2611 Shore Lane Dr, Knoxville TN 37932, USA	
Stratton, Dennis	Guitarist (Iron Maiden)
Sanctuary Music Mgmt, 82 Bishop's Bridge Road, London W2 6BB, England	
Straub, Chester J	Judge
US Court of Appeals, Moynihan Courthouse, 500 Pearl St, New York NY 10007, USA	
Straub, Peter F	Writer
53 W 85th St, New York NY 10024, USA	
Straughan, Peter	Writer
Casorotto Ramsay, Waverley House, 7-12 Noel St, London W1F 8GQ, England	

S

Strause, Colin — Visual Effects Producer, Director
Hydraulx, 1447 2nd St, #200, Santa Monica CA 90401, USA
Strause, Greg — Visual Effects Producer, Director
Hydraulx, 1447 2nd St, #200, Santa Monica CA 90401, USA
Strauss, Neil — Writer
Anderson Group Public Relations, 8060 Melrose Ave, #400, Los Angeles CA 90046, USA
Strauss, Peter — Actor
Stone Manners Salners, 9911 W Pico Blvd, #1400, Los Angeles CA 90035 USA
Strauss, Robert S — Political Executive, Diplomat
Akin Gump Strauss, 1333 New Hampshire Ave NW, #400, Washington DC 20036, USA
Straw, John W (Jack) — Government Official, England
House of Commons, Westminster, London SW1A 0AA, England
Strawberry, Darryl E — Baseball Player
1802 Sterling Oaks Dr, Saint Peters MO 63376, USA
Strawbridge, George W, Jr — Throughbred, Steeplechase Racing Owner
Augustin Stables, Greenlawn Road, Cochranville PA 19330, USA
Strawder, Joe — Basketball Player
3037 SW Taylors Ferry Road, Portland OR 97219, USA
Streck, Ron — Golfer
7527 S 84th East Ave, Tulsa OK 74133, USA
Streck, Ronald J — Association Executive
Healthcare Distribution Mgmt Assn, 1821 Michael Faraday Dr, Reston VA 20190, USA
Streep, Meryl — Actress
Creative Artists Agency, 2000 Ave of Stars, #100, Los Angeles CA 90067 USA
Street, Elliott — Actor
Atlanta Models & Talent, 309 Maple Dr, #201, Atlanta GA 30354, USA
Street, Huston L — Baseball Player
8300 Big View Dr, Austin TX 78730, USA
Street, Picabo — Alpine Skier
PO Box 321, Hailey ID 83333, USA
Street, Rebecca — Actress
255 Cabrini Blvd, #7G, New York NY 10040, USA
Streets, Tai — Football Player
16134 Hillcrest Circle, Orland Park IL 60467, USA
Streets, The — Rap Artist
Coalition Mgmt, 12 Barley Mow Passage, London W4 4PH, England
Streisand, Barbra — Singer, Actress, Director
160 W 96th St, New York NY 10025, USA
Streit, Kurt — Opera Singer
I M G Artists, Hogarth Business Park, Chiswick, London W4 2TH, England
Streitenfeld, Marc — Composer
First Artists, 1631 N Bristol St, #B20, Santa Ana CA 92706 USA
Strekalov, Gennady M — Cosmonaut
Federation Peace Committee, 36 Mira Prospekt, 129090 Moscow, Russia
Strel, Martin — Swimmer
Marathon Swim Mgmt Group, 227 H St, #207, Salt Lake City UT 84103, USA
Strenger, Richard G (Rich) — Football Player
1064 Arborak Way, Lake Orion MI 48362, USA
Stresi, Alexia — Actress
Artmedia, 20 Ave Rapp, 75007 Paris, France
Streuli, Walter H (Walt) — Baseball Player
1107 Westminster Dr, Greensboro NC 27410, USA
Strianese, Michael — Businessman
L-3 Communications, 600 3rd Ave, New York NY 10016, USA
Stricker, Steven C (Steve) — Golfer
5804 N Sherman Ave, Madison WI 53704, USA
Stricker, Williams L (Bill) — Basketball Player
2930 Driftwood Place, #70, Stockton CA 95219, USA
Strickland, Donald D — Football Player
1110 Gilman Ave, San Francisco CA 94124, USA
Strickland, Gail — Actress
14732 Oracle Place, Pacific Palisades CA 90272, USA
Strickland, James M (Jim) — Baseball Player
2139 Equestrian Road, Paso Robles CA 93446, USA
Strickland, KaDee — Actress
Anonymous Content, 3532 Hayden Ave, Culver City CA 90232 USA
Strickland, Keith — Drummer (B-52's)
Direct Management Group, 947 N La Cienega Blvd, #G, West Hollywood CA 90069, USA
Strickland, Rodney (Rod) — Basketball Player
3120 Hemingway Lane, Lexington KY 40513, USA
Strickland, Scott M — Baseball Player
415 Enchanted River Dr, Spring TX 77388, USA
Strickson, Mark — Actor
Evans & Reiss, 100 Fawe Park Road, London SW15 2EA, England
Strider, Marjorie V — Artist, Sculptor
170 Clint Finger Lane, Saugerties NY 12477, USA
Strieber, Whitney — Writer, Producer, Actor
Gersh Agency, 9465 Wilshire Blvd, #600, Beverly Hills CA 90212 USA
Strief, Zachary D (Zach) — Football Player
5480 Carterway Dr, Milford OH 45150, USA
Strigl, Dennis F (Denny) — Businessman
Verizon Communications, 140 West St, New York NY 10007, USA
Strik, Reshad — Actor
B/W/R, 9100 Wilshire Blvd, #500W, Beverly Hills CA 90212 USA
Striker, Gisela — Philosopher
Harvard University, Philosophy Dept, Cambridge MA 02138, USA
Stringer, Arthur (Art) — Football Player
12680 Royal Shores Dr, Conroe TX 77303, USA
Stringer, C Vivian — Basketball Coach
Rutgers University, Athletic Dept, New Brunswick NJ 08903, USA
Stringer, Howard — Businessman
186 Riverside Dr, New York NY 10024, USA
Stringert, Harold L (Hal) — Football Player
1711 Dole St, #603, Honolulu HI 96822, USA
Stringfellow, Ken — Musician (Posies), Songwriter
Bright Touring Artists, 1 Irving Place, V18C, New York NY 10003, USA

Strause - Stringfellow

934 · V.I.P. Address Book

Stringfield, Sherry — Actress
John Carrabino Mgmt, 5900 Wilshire Blvd, #406, Los Angeles CA 90036 USA
Stritch, Elaine — Singer, Actress
Carlyle Hotel, 35 E 76th St, New York NY 10021, USA
Strittmatter, Mark A — Baseball Player
6533 Dutch Creek St, Littleton CO 80130, USA
Strobel, Eric M — Ice Hockey Player
6617 129th St W, Saint Paul MN 55124, USA
Strobel, Heidi — Illusionist, Model
RR 1 Box 274A, Long Lane MO 65590, USA
Stroble, Bobby — Golfer
526 W 2nd Ave, Albany GA 31701, USA
Strock, Donald J (Don) — Football Player, Coach
1512 Passion Vine Circle, Weston FL 33326, USA
Strode, Haley — Actress
Paradigm Agency, 360 N Crescent Dr, North Building, Beverly Hills CA 90210 USA
Strohmayer, John E — Baseball Player
1825 Crosby Lane, Redding CA 96003, USA
Strohmayer, Tod — Astronomer
Goddard Space Flight Center, NASA/GSFC, Greenbelt MD 20771, USA
Strollsteimer, Jason E — Singer, Guitarist (VonBondies)
Tsunami Entertainment, 2525 Hyperion Ave, Los Angeles CA 90027, USA
Strolz, Hubert — Alpine Skier
6767 Warth 19, Austria
Strom, Brent T — Baseball Player
2202 N Catalina Vista Loop, Tucson AZ 85749, USA
Strom, Brock T — Football Player
4301 W 110th St, Leawood KS 66211, USA
Strom, Richard J (Rick) — Football Player
8905 Moor Park Run, Duluth GA 30097, USA
Strom, Sally — Artist
2388 SW Vermont St, #36, Portland OR 97219, USA
Stroman, Susan — Choreographer, Director
42 West, 220 W 42nd St, #1200, New York NY 10036 USA
Stromberg, Robert — Art Director, Production Designer
United Talent Agency, 9336 Civic Center Dr, Beverly Hills CA 90210 USA
Strominger, Jack L — Biochemist
Dana Faber Cancer Institute, Biochemistry Dept, 44 Binney St, Boston MA 02115, USA
Strong, Barrett — Singer, Songwriter
Motown Records, 6255 W Sunset Blvd, Los Angeles CA 90028 USA
Strong, Brenda — Actress
Liberman/Zerman Mgmt, 252 N Larchmont Blvd, #200, Los Angeles CA 90004 USA
Strong, Daniel W (Danny) — Actor, Writer
Sweeney Entertainment, 6253 Hollywood Blvd, #201, Los Angeles CA 90028, USA
Strong, Joe — Baseball Player
1340 Corcoran Ave, Vallejo CA 94589, USA
Strong, Ken — Ice Hockey Player
1773 Grosvenor Place, Mississauga ON L5L 3V8, Canada
Strong, Mack C — Football Player
14343 SE 92nd St, Newcastle WA 98059, USA
Strong, Mark — Actor
Markham & Froggatt, Julian House, 4 Windmill St, London W1P 1HF, England
Strong, Mary — Sportscaster
N F L Network, 10950 Washington Blvd, #100, Culver City CA 90232 USA
Strong, Maurice F — Government Official, Canada
S3 Holdings, 150 Isabella St, #100, Ottawa ON K1S 1V7, Canada
Strong, Rider — Actor
United Talent Agency, 9336 Civic Center Dr, Beverly Hills CA 90210 USA
Stroock, Daniel W — Mathematician
55 Frost St, Cambridge MA 02140, USA
Strossen, Nadine — Attorney, Association Executive
450 Riverside Dr, #51, New York NY 10027, USA
Stroucken, Albert — Businessman
Owens-Illinois Inc, 1 Michael Owens Way, Perrysburg OH 43551, USA
Stroud, Don — Actor
500 Lunalilo Home Road, #16A, Honolulu HI 96825, USA
Stroud, Edwin M (Ed) — Baseball Player
1696 Oak St SW, Warren OH 44485, USA
Stroud, Marcus L — Football Player
964 Detroit St, Jacksonville FL 32254, USA
Stroughter, Stephen L (Steve) — Baseball Player
323 NE 2nd Ave, Visalia CA 93291, USA
Stroup, Jessica — Actress
I C M Partners, 10250 Constellation Blvd, #900, Los Angeles CA 90067 USA
Stroup, Theodore G (Ted), Jr — Army General
2085 Hopewood Dr, Falls Church VA 22043, USA
Strouse, Charles — Composer
171 W 57th St, New York NY 10019, USA
Strout, Elizabeth — Writer
Random House, 1745 Broadway, #1800, New York NY 10019 USA
Strube, Juergen F — Businessman
B A S F Corp, Aktiengesellschaft, 67056 Ludwigshafen, Germany
Strudwick, Suzanne — Golfer
5525 Crestwood Dr, Knoxville TN 37914, USA
Struever, Stuart M — Anthropologist
2000 Sheridan Road, Evanston IL 60208, USA
Strug, Kerri — Gymnast
2611 N Santa Lucia Dr, Tucson AZ 85715, USA
Struth, Thomas — Photographer
Achenbachstr 74, 40237 Dusseldorf, Germany
Struthers, Sally — Actress
Vincent Cirrincione Assoc, 1516 N Fairfax Ave, Los Angeles CA 90046 USA
Struve, Nicolas — Actor
Artmedia, 20 Ave Rapp, 75007 Paris, France
Struycken, Carel — Actor
PO Box 1365, Avalon CA 90704, USA

Strykert, Ron — Guitarist (Men at Work)
T P A, PO Box 124, Round Corner NSW 2158, Australia

Stuart, Bradley (Brad) — Ice Hockey Player
131 Pinta Court, Los Gatos CA 95030, USA

Stuart, Freundel J — Prime Minister, Barbados
Prime Minister's Office, Bay St, Saint Michael, Bridgetown, Barbados

Stuart, James Patrick — Actor
Brillstein Entertainment Partners, 9150 Wilshire Blvd, #350, Beverly Hills CA 90212 USA

Stuart, Jason — Actor, Comedian
Ideal Talent Agency, 10806 Ventura Blvd, #2, Studio City CA 91604, USA

Stuart, Jill — Fashion Designer
550 Fashion Ave, #2400, New York NY 10018, USA

Stuart, Katie — Actress
Pacific Artists Mgmt, 1285 W Broadway, #685, Vancouver BC V6H 3X8, Canada

Stuart, Marty — Singer, Mandolin Player, Songwriter
Shore Fire Media, 32 Court St, #1600, Brooklyn NY 11201 USA

Stuart, Maxine — Actress
S D B Partners, 1801 Ave of Stars, #902, Los Angeles CA 90067 USA

Stubblefield, Dana W — Football Player
5226 Pisa Court, San Jose CA 95138, USA

Stubblefield, Mickey — Baseball Player
4870 Seldon Way SE, Smyrna GA 30080, USA

Stubbs, Franklin L — Baseball Player
PO Box 325, Goshen KY 40026, USA

Stubbs, Imogen M — Actress
Nick Hern Books, Glasshouse, 49A Goldhawk Road, London W12 8QP, England

Stubing, Lawrence G (Moose) — Baseball Player, Manager
10821 Laconia Dr, Villa Park CA 92861, USA

Stuck, Hans-Joachim — Auto Racing Driver
Harmstatt 3, 6352 Ellmau/Tirol, Austria

Stuckey, Henry L — Football Player
3615 Winchester Ave, Atlantic City NJ 08401, USA

Stuckey, James D (Jim) — Football Player
1314 Headquarters Plantation Dr, Johns Island SC 29455, USA

Stuckey, Rodney N — Basketball Player
14215 SE 255th Place, Kent WA 98042, USA

Studdard, David D (Dave) — Football Player
4490 S Clarkson St, Englewood CO 80113, USA

Studdard, Ruben — Singer
Favor Public Relations, 5900 Wilshire Blvd, #2600, Los Angeles CA 90036, USA

Studer, Cheryl — Opera Singer
International Performing Artists, 125 Crowfield Dr, Knoxville TN 37922, USA

Studin, Jan — Publisher
Better Homes & Gardens, Publisher's Office, 1716 Locust, Des Moines IA 50309, USA

Studney, Dan — Actor
Paradigm Agency, 360 N Crescent Dr, North Building, Beverly Hills CA 90210 USA

Studstill, Patrick L (Pat) — Football Player
2235 Linda Flora Dr, Los Angeles CA 90077, USA

Studt, Amy — Singer, Pianist
19 Music & Mgmt, 35-37 Parkgate Road, London SW11 4NP, England

Studwell, J Scott — Football Player
10415 Brown Farm Circle, Eden Prairie MN 55347, USA

Stuffel, Paul H — Baseball Player
25786 Buttercup Court, Bonita Springs FL 34135, USA

Stufflebeem, John — Navy Admiral
Director, Navy Staff, HqUSN, Pentagon, Washington DC 20350 USA

Stuhlbarg, Michael — Actor
Viking Entertainment, 445 W 23rd St, #1A, New York NY 10011, USA

Stuhr, Jerzy — Actor, Director
Graffiti Ltd, Ul SW Gertrudy 5, 31 107 Cracow, Poland

Stukes, Charles (Charlie) — Football Player
4020 Cedar Grove Crest, Chesapeake VA 23321, USA

Stulce, Michael D (Mike) — Track Athlete
5711 Hunters Chase Court, Lithonia GA 30038, USA

Stults, Eric W — Baseball Player
13810 Ranier Dr, Middlebury, IN 46540, USA

Stults, George S — Actor, Model
Bleu Entertainment, 5225 Wilshire Blvd, #401, Los Angeles CA 90036, USA

Stultz, Geoffrey S (Geoff) — Actor
United Talent Agency, 9336 Civic Center Dr, Beverly Hills CA 90210 USA

Stultz, Jack C — Army General
Chief, Army Reserve, HqUSA, Pentagon, Washington DC 20310, USA

Stump, David — Cinematographer
H F W D Creative Representation, 394 E Glaucus St, Encinitas CA 92024, USA

Stump, James G (Jim) — Baseball Player
7432 Creekside Dr, Lansing MI 48917, USA

Stump, Patrick — Singer, Guitarist (Fall Out Boy)
PO Box 219, 1187 Wilmette Ave, Wilmette IL 60091, USA

Stumpel, Jozef — Ice Hockey Player
6301 Osprey Terrace, Coconut Creek FL 33073, USA

Stumpf, John — Financier
Wells Fargo, 420 Montgomery St, San Francisco CA 94104, USA

Stumpf, Kenneth E — Vietnam War Army Hero (CMH)
16528 State Highway 131, Tomah WI 54660, USA

Stumpf, Paul K — Biochemist
1515 Shasta Dr, #2219, Davis CA 95616, USA

Stunyo-Korpak, Jeanne G — Diver
1435 Almagre Peak Dr, Colorado Springs CO 80921, USA

Stuper, John A — Baseball Player
38 Lake St, Hamden CT 06517, USA

Stupnitsky, Gene — Actor, Comedian, Writer
W M E Entertainment, 9601 Wilshire Blvd, #300, Beverly Hills CA 90210 USA

Stupp, Samuel I — Engineer
Northwestern University, Engineering Dept, Evanston IL 60208, USA

Stupples, Karen L — Golfer
9736 Covent Garden Dr, Orlando FL 32827, USA

Sturckow, Frederick W (Rick) — Astronaut
RR 2 Box 14, Dickinson TX 77539, USA
Sturgeon, Peter — Ice Hockey Player
23 Millwood Road, Erin ON N0B 1T0, Canada
Sturges, Shannon — Actress
Precision Entertainment, 6338 Wilshire Blvd, Los Angeles CA 90048, USA
Sturgess, Jim — Actor
Garricks, Angel House, 76 Mallinson Road, London SW11 1BN, England
Sturm, Felix — Boxer
Universum Boxing Promotion, Am Stadtrand 27, 22047 Hamburg, Germany
Sturm, Jerry G — Football Player
3 Niblick Lane, Littleton CO 80123, USA
Sturm, Marco J — Ice Hockey Player
500 Atlantic Ave, #14P, Boston MA 02210, USA
Sturm, Yfke — Model
I M G Models, 304 Park Ave S, #PH-North, New York NY 10010 USA
Sturman, Eugene — Sculptor, Artist
190 Loma Metisse St, Malibu CA 90265, USA
Sturr, Jimmy — Orchestra Leader
United Polka Artists, PO Box 1, Florida NY 10921, USA
Sturridge, Charles — Director
United Agents, 12-26 Lexington St, London W1F 0LE, England
Sturt, Frederick N (Fred) — Football Player
120 N Berkey Southern Road, Swanton OH 43558, USA
Sturtze, Tanyon J — Baseball Player
501 Knights Run Ave, #2316, Tampa FL 33602, USA
Sturzaker, David — Actor
Ken McReddie Assoc, 11 Connaught Place, London W2 2ET, England
Styler, Trudie — Actress, Producer
Maven Pictures, 380 Lafayette St, #202, New York NY 10003, USA
Styles P — Rap Artist (Lox)
I C M Partners, 10250 Constellation Blvd, #900, Los Angeles CA 90067 USA
Styles, Lorenzo C — Football Player
10276 Oxford Dr, Lewiston ID 83501, USA
Stynes, Christopher D (Chris) — Baseball Player
1980 NE 7th St, #106, Deerfield Beach FL 33441, USA
Styron, Alexandra — Writer
Little Brown, 3 Center Plaza, #100, Boston MA 02108 USA
Suarez Gonzalez, Adolfo — Prime Minister, Spain
Antonio Maura 4, 28014 Madrid, Spain
Suarez, Anne — Actress
U B B A, 6 Rue de Braque, 75003 Paris, France
Suarez, Jeremy — Actor
Innovative Artists, 1505 10th St, Santa Monica CA 90401 USA
Suarez, Kenneth R (Ken) — Baseball Player
6000 Forest Lane, Fort Worth TX 76112, USA
Suau, Anthony — Photojournalist
Denver Post, Editorial Dept, PO Box 1709, Denver CO 80201, USA
Subkoff, Tara — Actress
I C M Partners, 10250 Constellation Blvd, #900, Los Angeles CA 90067 USA
Subotnick, Morton L — Composer
25 Minetta Lane, #4B, New York NY 10012, USA
Substance, Markee — Keyboardist (Kosheen)
Moksha Mgmt, PO Box 102, London E15 2HH, England
Such, Richard S (Dick) — Baseball Player
7614 Divot Dr, Sanford NC 27332, USA
Sucharetza, Marla — Actress
Abrams Artists, 9200 W Sunset Blvd, #1125, West Hollywood CA 90069 USA
Suchecka, Rysia — Interior Designer
N B B J Architecture/Design, 111 S Jackson St, Seattle WA 98104, USA
Suchet, David — Actor
Ken McReddie Assoc, 11 Connaught Place, London W2 2ET, England
Suchocka, Hanna — Prime Minister, Poland
Urzad Rady Ministrow, Al Ujazdowskie 1/3, 00-567 Warsaw, Poland
Suchy, Radoslav — Ice Hockey Player
7801 N 54th St, Paradise Valley AZ 85253, USA
Sud, Veena — Producer
Creative Artists Agency, 2000 Ave of Stars, #100, Los Angeles CA 90067 USA
Sudakis, William P (Bill) — Baseball Player
44054 Elkhorn Trail, Indian Wells CA 92210, USA
Sudan, Madhu — Computer Scientist
81 Benton Road, Somerville MA 02143, USA
Sudano, Brooklyn — Actress, Singer
A P A Talent/Literary Agency, 405 S Beverly Dr, #300, Beverly Hills CA 90212 USA
Sudduth, Skipp — Actor, Director
One Entertainment, 12 W 57th St, #PH 1, New York NY 10019 USA
Sudduth-Smith, Jill — Synchronized Swimmer
9917 Calabasas Ave, Las Vegas NV 89117, USA
Sudeikis, Jason — Actor, Comedian
Creative Artists Agency, 2000 Ave of Stars, #100, Los Angeles CA 90067 USA
Sugar, Leo T — Football Player
7161 Golden Eagle Court, #1012, Fort Myers FL 33912, USA
Sugar, Steve — DJ Musician (Mike & Sugar)
Future Music, Bayerstr 77A, 80335 Munich, Germany
Sugarman, Burt — Producer
Giant Group, 9440 Santa Monica Blvd, #407, Beverly Hills CA 90210, USA
Sugg, B Alan — Educator
University of Arkansas, President's Office, Fayetteville AR 72701, USA
Sugg, Diana K — Journalist
Baltimore Sun, Editorial Dept, 501 N Calvert St, Baltimore MD 21278, USA
Suggs, M Louise — Golfer
424 Royal Crescent Court, Saint Augustine FL 32092, USA
Suggs, Shafer L — Football Player
12849 Barrow Lane, Plainfield IL 60585, USA
Suggs, Terrell R — Football Player
281 N Brookside St, Chandler AZ 85225, USA

Suggs, W Walter (Walt), Jr — Football Player
11105 Bradyville Pike, Readyville TN 37149, USA

Suh, Yeree — Opera Singer
I M G Artists, Hogarth Business Park, Chiswick, London W4 2TH, England

Suhey, Matthew J (Matt) — Football Player
550 Carriage Way, Deerfield IL 60015, USA

Suhl, Harry — Physicist
University of California, Physics Dept, 9500 Gilman Dr, La Jolla CA 92093, USA

Suhonen, Alpo — Ice Hockey Coach
Chicago Blackhawks, United Center, 1901 W Madison St, Chicago IL 60612 USA

Suhr, Jennifer Stuczynski (Jenn) — Track Athlete
730 Jenkins Road, Churchville NY 14428, USA

Suhrheinrich, Richard F — Judge
US Court of Appeals, 315 W Allegan St, #210, Lansing MI 48933, USA

Suhrstedt, Timothy (Tim) — Cinematographer
Innovative Artists, 1505 10th St, Santa Monica CA 90401 USA

Sui, Anna — Fashion Designer
113 Greene St, Front A, New York NY 10012, USA

Suits, Julia — Editorial Cartoonist
Creators Syndicate, 737 3rd St, Hermosa Beach CA 90254 USA

Sukarnoputri, D F Megawati — President, Indonesia
Dewan Perwakilan Rakyat, Jalan Gatot Subroto 16, Jakarta, Indonesia

Sukla, Edward A (Ed) — Baseball Player
16 Perch, Irvine CA 92604, USA

Sukova, Helena — Tennis Player
1 Ave Grande Bretagne, Monte Carlo, Monaco

Sukowa, Barbara — Actress
Artmedia, 20 Ave Rapp, 75007 Paris, France

Sularz, Guy P — Baseball Player
10818 N 83rd St, Scottsdale AZ 85260, USA

Suleiman, Michel — President, Lebanon; General
President's Office, Palais de Baebda, Beirut, Lebanon

Sulfsted, Alex F — Football Player
8140 Shawnee Run Road, Cincinnati OH 45243, USA

Suliman, Ali — Actor
Paradigm Agency, 360 N Crescent Dr, North Building, Beverly Hills CA 90210 USA

Sulkin, Gregg — Actor
D2 Mgmt, 9255 Sunset Blvd, #600, West Hollywood CA 90069, USA

Sullanmaa, Jani — Curling Athlete
Curling Assn, Kalatorppa 2A62, 02230 Espoo, Finland

Sullenberger, Chesley B (Sully) — Airline Pilot Hero
General Delivery, Danville CA 94526, USA

Sulliman, S Douglas (Doug) — Ice Hockey Player
PO Box 28964, Scottsdale AZ 85255, USA

Sullinger, Jared — Basketball Player
Boston Celtics, 226 Causeway St, #4, Boston MA 02114 USA

Sullivan, Brian — Ice Hockey Player
392 E Beach Road, Charlestown RI 02813, USA

Sullivan, Camille — Actress
Red Mgmt, Box 3, 415 W Esplanade, North Vancouver BC V7M 1A6, Canada

Sullivan, Chip — Golfer
49 Homestead Circle, Troutville VA 24175, USA

Sullivan, Christopher P (Chris) — Football Player
64 Wagon Wheel Road, North Attleboro MA 02760, USA

Sullivan, Cory — Baseball Player
405 Overlook Court, Evanston WY 82930, USA

Sullivan, Daniel J (Dan) — Football Player
25 Algonquin Ave, Andover MA 01810, USA

Sullivan, Danny — Auto Racing Driver
PO Box 34290, Louisville KY 40232, USA

Sullivan, David — Actor
Intellectual Artists Mgmt, 10585 Santa Monica Blvd, #135, Los Angeles CA 90025, USA

Sullivan, Erik Per — Actor
Suzanne Smith, 451 Greenwich St, #500, New York NY 10103, USA

Sullivan, Franklin L (Frank) — Baseball Player
2715 Apapane St, Lihue HI 96766, USA

Sullivan, George (Red) — Ice Hockey Player
RR 2, Indian River ON K0L 2B0, Canada

Sullivan, Gordon R — Army General
Strategic Studies Institute, War College, 122 Forbes Ave, Carlisle PA 17013, USA

Sullivan, Jazmine — Singer, Songwriter
Creative Artists Agency, 2000 Ave of Stars, #100, Los Angeles CA 90067 USA

Sullivan, Kathryn D — Astronaut
795 Old Oak Trace, Columbus OH 43235, USA

Sullivan, Kevin — Journalist
Washington Post, Editorial Dept, 1150 15th St NW, Washington DC 20071 USA

Sullivan, Kevin J — Air Force General
Deputy CofS, Logistics/Installations, HqUSAF, Pentagon, Washington DC 20330 USA

Sullivan, Kyle R — Actor
Abrams Artists, 9200 W Sunset Blvd, #1125, West Hollywood CA 90069 USA

Sullivan, Liam K — Actor, Comedian
Kazarian/Spencer/Ruskin, 11969 Ventura Blvd, #300, Studio City CA 91604 USA

Sullivan, Louis W — Secretary, Health & Human Services
223 Chestnut St, Atlanta GA 30314, USA

Sullivan, Marc C — Baseball Player
2038 W 1st S, #100, Fort Myers FL 33901, USA

Sullivan, Michael — Labor Leader
Sheet Metal Workers Union, 1750 New York Ave NW, #600, Washington DC 20006, USA

Sullivan, Michael J (Mike) — Governor, WY; Diplomat
1124 S Durbin St, Casper WY 82601, USA

Sullivan, Michael J (Mike) — Golfer
Mike Sullivan Golf School, 5715 Fayetteville Road, Raleigh NC 27603, USA

Sullivan, Mike — Ice Hockey Player, Coach
256 Washington St, Duxbury MA 02332, USA

Sullivan, Nicole — Actress
Innovative Artists, 1505 10th St, Santa Monica CA 90401, USA

Sullivan, Patrick J (Pat) — Football Player, Coach
1717 Indian Creek Dr, Birmingham AL 35243, USA
Sullivan, Paul E — Navy Admiral
Commander, Naval Sea Systems, 1333 Isaac Hull Ave SE, Washington Navy Yard DC 20376 USA
Sullivan, Peter — Ice Hockey Player
316 Fairway Road, Regina SK S4Y 1J5, Canada
Sullivan, Russell G M (Russ) — Baseball Player
1701 Hill 'n' Dale St, Fredericksburg VA 22405, USA
Sullivan, Sean — Actor
Caldwell Jeffrey, 943 Queen St E, #200, Toronto ON M4M 1J6, Canada
Sullivan, Stacy — Actress
Cassell Levy Talent Agency, 843 N Sycamore Ave, Los Angeles CA 90038, USA
Sullivan, Steve — Ice Hockey Player
5536 Iron Gate Dr, Franklin TN 37069, USA
Sullivan, Susan — Actress
15355 Mulholland Dr, Los Angeles CA 90077, USA
Sullivan, Tom — Actor
Paradigm Agency, 360 N Crescent Dr, North Building, Beverly Hills CA 90210 USA
Sullivan, W Scott — Baseball Player
1649 Mayfair Court, Auburn AL 36830, USA
Sullivan, William D — Navy Admiral
US Representative, NATO Military Committee, PSC 80, Box 300, APO AE 09724 USA
Sulston, John E — Nobel Medicine Laureate
39 Mingle Lane, Stapleford, Cambridge CB2 5BG, England
Sultan Salman Abdulaziz Al-Saud — Astronaut, Saudi Arabia
Tourism/Antiquities Commission, PO Box 66680, Riyadh 11586, Saudi Arabia
Sultan, Altoon — Artist
PO Box 2, Groton VT 05046, USA
Sultan, Donald K — Artist
19 E 70th St, New York NY 10021, USA
Sulzberger, Arthur O, Jr — Publisher, Businessman
New York Times Co, Publisher's Office, 229 W 43rd St, New York NY 10036, USA
Sumika, Aya — Actress
I C M Partners, 10250 Constellation Blvd, #900, Los Angeles CA 90067 USA
Sumino, Naoko — Astronaut
NASDA, Tsukuba Space Center, 2-1-1 Sengen, Tukubashi, Ibaraka 305, Japan
Sumlin, Kevin — Football Coach
Texas A&M University, Athletic Dept, College Station TX 77843, USA
Summar, Trent — Singer (New Row Mob)
Grassroots Media, 1005 S Orlando Ave, Los Angeles CA 90035, USA
Summe, Gregory L — Businessman
PerkinElmer Inc, 45 William St, Wellesley MA 02481, USA
Summer, Cree — Actress, Singer
W M E Entertainment, 9601 Wilshire Blvd, #300, Beverly Hills CA 90210 USA
Summerall, George A (Pat) — Football Player, Sportscaster
710 S White Chapel Blvd, Southlake TX 76092, USA
Summerhays, Bruce P — Golfer
2 Condie Circle, Farmington UT 84025, USA
Summers, Andrew (Andy) — Singer, Guitarist (Police)
21A Noel St, London W1V 3PD, England
Summers, Carol — Artist
2817 Smith Grade, Santa Cruz CA 95060, USA
Summers, Dana — Cartoonist (Lug Nuts, Bound & Gagged)
Orlando Sentinel, Editorial Dept, 633 N Orange Ave, Lobby, Orlando FL 32801, USA
Summers, Jerry — Singer (Dovells)
American Promotions, 2011 Ferry Ave, #U19, Camden NJ 08104, USA
Summers, Lawrence H (Larry) — Educator; Secretary, Treasury
National Economic Council, 1600 Pennsylvania Ave NW, Washington DC 20502, USA
Summers, Linda — Model
Playboy Promotions, 2706 Media Center Dr, Los Angeles CA 90065 USA
Summers, Marc — Entertainer
Rebel Entertainment Partners, 5700 Wilshire Blvd, #456, Los Angeles CA 90036, USA
Summers, Tara — Actress
I C M Partners, 10250 Constellation Blvd, #900, Los Angeles CA 90067 USA
Summerville, Trish — Costume Designer
Costume Designers Guild, 11969 Ventura Blvd, #100, Studio City CA 91604, USA
Summitt, Pat S Head — Basketball Player, Coach
3720 River Trace Lane, Knoxville TN 37920, USA
Sumner, Charles (Charlie) — Football Player, Coach
PO Box 11621, Lahaina HI 96761, USA
Sumner, Mickey — Actress
I C M Partners, 10250 Constellation Blvd, #900, Los Angeles CA 90067 USA
Sumner, Peter — Actor
Morrissey Mgmt, 77 Glebe Point Road, Glebe NSW 2037, Australia
Sumner, Walter H (Walt) — Football Player
PO Box 112, Ocilla GA 31774, USA
Sumners, Rosalyn D — Figure Skater
13314 NE 86th Place, Redmond WA 98052, USA
Sumpter, Jeremy — Actor
Innovative Artists, 1505 10th St, Santa Monica CA 90401 USA
Sun Dandan — Speed Skater
Skating Assn, 56 Zhongguancun South St, Haidian, Beijing 100044, China
Sundaresh, S (Sundi) — Businessman
Adeptec Inc, 691 S Milpitas Blvd, Milpitas CA 95035, USA
Sunday, Gabriel — Actor
Abrams Artists, 9200 W Sunset Blvd, #1125, West Hollywood CA 90069 USA
Sundberg, James H (Jim) — Baseball Player
2308 Newforest Court, Arlington TX 76017, USA
Sunde, Milton J (Milt) — Football Player
6008 W 104th St, Minneapolis MN 55438, USA
Sundhage, Pia — Soccer Player, Coach
US Women's Soccer, 1801 S Prairie Ave, Chicago IL 60616, USA
Sundin, Gordon V (Gordie) — Baseball Player
15600 Old 41 N, Naples FL 34110, USA
Sundin, Mats J — Ice Hockey Player
International Management Group, 801 6th St SW, Calgary AB T2P 3V8, Canada

S

Sundvold, Jon T — Basketball Player
2700 Westbrook Way, Columbia MO 65203, USA
Sung Kang — Actor
I C M Partners, 10250 Constellation Blvd, #900, Los Angeles CA 90067 USA
Sung, Elizabeth — Actress
G V A Talent, 9229 W Sunset Blvd, #320, West Hollywood CA 90069, USA
Sung, Shi Yeon — Conductor
I M G Artists, Hogarth Business Park, Chiswick, London W4 2TH, England
Sunjata, Daniel — Actor
United Talent Agency, 9336 Civic Center Dr, Beverly Hills CA 90210 USA
Sunohara, Vicky — Ice Hockey Player
Team Canada, 2424 University Dr NW, Calgary AB T2N 3Y9, Canada
Sununu, John H — Governor, NH; Government Official
49 Linden Road, Hampton Falls NH 03844, USA
Sunyayev, Rashid A — Astronomer
Space Studies Institute, Profsoyuznaya Str 84/32, 117910 Moscow, Russia
Supernaw, Douglas A (Doug) — Singer, Songwriter
PO Box 2921, Bandera TX 78003, USA
Suplee, Ethan — Actor
Don Buchwald/Fortitude, 6500 Wilshire Blvd, #2200, Los Angeles CA 90048 USA
Suppan, Jeffrey S (Jeff) — Baseball Player
17836 Sidwell St, Granada Hills CA 91344, USA
Suraev, Maxim V — Cosmonaut
Cosmonaut Training Center, Star City, 141160 Zvezdny Gorodok, Moscow Oblast, Russia
Sure!, Al B — Singer, Songwriter
I C M Partners, 10250 Constellation Blvd, #900, Los Angeles CA 90067 USA
Surhoff, William J (B J) — Baseball Player
5 Fenton St, Rye NY 10580, USA
Surin, Bruny — Track Athlete
PO Box 2, Succ Saint Michel, Montreal QC H2A 3L8, Canada
Surmelis, Angelo — Actor
Paradise Group, PO Box 69451, West Hollywood CA 90069, USA
Surnow, Joel — Producer
Paradigm Agency, 360 N Crescent Dr, North Building, Beverly Hills CA 90210 USA
Surovy, Nicolas — Actor
Hartig-Hilepo Agency, 54 W 21st St, #610, New York NY 10010 USA
Surtain, Patrick F — Football Player
2704 Boot Lane, Weston FL 33331, USA
Surtees, John — Auto Racing Driver
Team Surtees, Fircroft Way, Edenbridge, Kent TN8 6EJ, England
Susa, Conrad — Composer
433 Eureka St, San Francisco CA 94114, USA
Suschitzky, J Peter — Cinematographer
13 Priory Road, London NW6 4NN, England
Suschitzky, Wolfgang — Cinematographer
Douglas House, 6 Maida Ave, #11, London W2 1TG, England
Susi, Carol Ann — Actress
846 N Sweetzer Ave, West Hollywood CA 90069, USA
Susi, Lolly — Actress
Actual Management, 7 Great Russell St, London WC1B 3NH, England
Suskind, Patrick — Writer
Diogenes Verlag AG, Sprecherstr 8, 8032 Zurich, Switzerland
Suslick, Kenneth S — Chemist
University of Illinois, Chemistry Dept, Champaign IL 61820, USA
Susman, Todd — Actor
Sutton-Barth Vennari, 145 S Fairfax Ave, #310, Los Angeles CA 90036 USA
Susser, Craig — Actor
I C M Partners, 10250 Constellation Blvd, #900, Los Angeles CA 90067 USA
Sussman, Adam — Writer, Producer
Brian Lutz Mgmt, 6464 Sunset Blvd, #860, Los Angeles CA 90028, USA
Sussman, Kevin — Actor
C E S D, 257 Park Ave S, #950, New York NY 10010 USA
Sussman, Susan — Writer
A P A Talent/Literary Agency, 405 S Beverly Dr, #300, Beverly Hills CA 90212 USA
Sutcliffe, David — Actor
Noble-Caplan Agency, 1260 Yonge St, #200, Toronto ON M4T 1W6, Canada
Sutcliffe, Richard L (Rick) — Baseball Player
616 NE Seabrook Court, Lees Summit MO 64064, USA
Suter, Gary — Ice Hockey Player
2128 County Road D, Lac du Flambu WI 54538, USA
Suter, Robert A (Rob) — Ice Hockey Player
4332 McConnell St, Fitchburg WI 53711, USA
Suter, Ryan — Ice Hockey Player
1554 Shining Ore Dr, Brentwood TN 37027, USA
Sutherland, Darrell W — Baseball Player
1011 NW Jeffrey Place, Beaverton OR 97006, USA
Sutherland, David — Golfer
5431 Tree Side Dr, Carmichael CA 95608, USA
Sutherland, Donald — Actor
Creative Artists Agency, 2000 Ave of Stars, #100, Los Angeles CA 90067 USA
Sutherland, Douglas A (Doug) — Football Player
511 Kenilworth Ave, Duluth MN 55803, USA
Sutherland, Gary L — Baseball Player
338 Oakcliff Road, Monrovia CA 91016, USA
Sutherland, Ivan E — Computer Scientist
California Institute of Technology, Computer Science Dept, Pasadena CA 91125, USA
Sutherland, Kevin — Golfer
1230 Carter Road, Sacramento CA 95864, USA
Sutherland, Kiefer — Actor
Management 360, 9111 Wilshire Blvd, Beverly Hills CA 90210 USA
Sutherland, Kristine — Actress
S M S Talent, 8383 Wilshire Blvd, #230, Beverly Hills CA 90211 USA
Sutherland, Leonardo C (Leo) — Baseball Player
12082 Nieta Dr, Garden Grove CA 92840, USA
Sutherland, Peter D — Government Official, Ireland
68 Eglinton Road, Dublin 4, Ireland

S

Sutherland - Svoboda

Svoboda, Petr — Ice Hockey Player
Sportrust Assoc, 818 18th St, #F, Santa Monica CA 90403, USA
Swaby, Donn — Actor
C E S D, 10635 Santa Monica Blvd, #130, Los Angeles CA 90025 USA
Swados, Elizabeth A — Writer, Composer
360 Central Park West, #16G, New York NY 10025, USA
Swagerty, Jane — Swimmer
9128 N 70th St, Paradise Valley AZ 85253, USA
Swagerty, Keith M — Basketball Player
22232 17th Ave SE, #205, Bothell WA 98021, USA
Swaggart, Jimmy L — Evangelist
PO Box 262550, Baton Rouge LA 70826, USA
Swaggerty, William D (Bill) — Baseball Player
116 S Forney Ave, Hanover PA 17331, USA
Swail, Julie — Water Polo Player, Coach
University of California, Athletic Dept, Irvine CA 92697, USA
Swain, Chelse E A — Actress
inMomemtum Mgmt, 14622 Ventura Blvd, #778, Sherman Oaks CA 91403, USA
Swain, Dominique — Actress
Don Buchwald/Fortitude, 6500 Wilshire Blvd, #2200, Los Angeles CA 90048 USA
Swain, Garry — Ice Hockey Player
PO Box 729, West Simsbury CT 06092, USA
Swain, John W — Football Player
409 E 135th St, Burnsville MN 55337, USA
Swain, Michael L (Mike) — Judo Athlete
128 W Campbell Ave, Campbell CA 95008, USA
Swallow, Jerod — Ice Dancer, Coach
Detroit Skating Club, 888 Denison Court, Bloomfield Hills MI 48302, USA
Swaminathan, Monkombu S — Geneticist
M S Swaminathan Foundation, 3 Cross St, Taramani, Madras 600113, India
Swan, Billy — Singer, Songwriter
Muirhead Mgmt, 202 Fulham Road, Chelsea, London SW10 9PJ, England
Swan, Craig S — Baseball Player
296 Sound Beach Ave, Old Greenwich CT 06870, USA
Swan, John W D — Prime Minister, Bermuda
11 Grape Bay Dr, Paget PG 06, Bermuda
Swan, Michael — Actor
13576 Cheltenham Dr, Sherman Oaks CA 91423, USA
Swan, Richard G — Mathematician
700 Melrose Ave, #M3, Winter Park FL 32789, USA
Swan, Robert — Explorer
2041, 561 Keystone Ave, PM Box 640, Reno NV 89503, USA
Swan, Serinda — Actress
United Talent Agency, 9336 Civic Center Dr, Beverly Hills CA 90210 USA
Swanepoel, Candice — Model
I M G Models, 304 Park Ave S, #PH-North, New York NY 10010 USA
Swank, Hilary — Actress
2 S Films, 10390 Santa Monica Blvd, #210, Los Angeles CA 90025, USA
Swanke, Karl V — Football Player
4 Butternut Court, Essex Junction VT 05452, USA
Swann, Charles D — Football Player
5815 Vinings Retreat Court SW, Mableton GA 30126, USA
Swann, Eric J — Football Player
2321 Carex Court, Elk Grove CA 95757, USA
Swann, Lynn C — Football Player, Sportscaster
506 Hegner Way, #2, Sewickley PA 15143, USA
Swanson, Arthur L (Red) — Baseball Player
1139 Chippenham Dr, Baton Rouge LA 70808, USA
Swanson, August G — Physician
3146 Portage Bay Place E, #H, Seattle WA 98102, USA
Swanson, Jackie — Actress
15155 Albright St, Pacific Palisades CA 90272, USA
Swanson, Judith — Actress
Persona Mgmt, 40 E 9th St, New York NY 10003, USA
Swanson, Kristy — Actress, Model
Inphenate, 9701 Wilshire Blvd, #1000, Beverly Hills CA 90212 USA
Swanson, Stanley L (Stan) — Baseball Player
1705 E Whaley St, Longview TX 75601, USA
Swanson, Steven R — Astronaut
1414 Blueberry Lane, Friendswood TX 77546, USA
Swanson, William H — Businessman
Raytheon Co, 870 Winter St, Waltham MA 02451, USA
Swaray, Estelle — Singer, Rap Artist
Atlantic Records, 1290 Ave of Americas, Concourse 4, New York NY 10104, USA
Sward, Anne — Actress
Talent Management Group, 339 E 3900 S, #210, Salt Lake City UT 84107, USA
Swardson, Nick — Actor, Comedian, Writer
Brillstein Entertainment Partners, 9150 Wilshire Blvd, #350, Beverly Hills CA 90212 USA
Swartzbaugh, David T (Dave) — Baseball Player
113 Orchard St, Middletown OH 45044, USA
Swatek, Barret — Actress
Imperium 7 Artists, 5455 Wilshire Blvd, #1706, Los Angeles CA 90036 USA
Sway — Entertainer
Bloom Effect, 112 S Portland Ave, #3A, Brooklyn NY 11217, USA
Swayne, Harry V — Football Player
2702 Baubitz Road, Reistertown MD 21136, USA
Swayze, Don — Actor
Baron Entertainment, 13848 Ventura Blvd, #A, Sherman Oaks CA 91423, USA
Swead, Stephen — Government Official
Fannie Mae, 3900 Wisconsin Ave NW, Washington DC 20016, USA
Sweat, Keith — Singer, Songwriter
PO Box 1002, Bronx NY 10466, USA
Sweat, Lynn — Artist
17 Good Hill Road, Weston CT 06883, USA
Swedberg, Heidi — Actress
Frontline Mgmt, 8265 Sunset Blvd, #209, West Hollywood CA 90046, USA

Swedberg, Jaclyn — Model, Actress
Playboy Promotions, 2706 Media Center Dr, Los Angeles CA 90065 USA
Swedlin, Rosalie — Producer
Anonymous Content, 3532 Hayden Ave, Culver City CA 90232 USA
Sweeney, Alison — Actress
United Talent Agency, 9336 Civic Center Dr, Beverly Hills CA 90210 USA
Sweeney, Bob — Ice Hockey Player
110 Brookview Dr, North Andover MA 01845, USA
Sweeney, Brian E — Baseball Player
199 Morsemere Ave, Yonkers NY 10703, USA
Sweeney, Calvin E — Football Player
4120 Olympiad Dr, Los Angeles CA 90043, USA
Sweeney, D B — Actor
Rain Management Group, 1631 21st St, Santa Monica CA 90404, USA
Sweeney, Donald C (Don) — Ice Hockey Player, Executive
5 Shady Nook Lane, Lynnfield MA 01940, USA
Sweeney, I Anne — Businesswoman
Disney Media Network, 3800 W Alameda Ave, #B, Burbank CA 91505, USA
Sweeney, James J (Jim) — Football Player
119 Justabout Road, Venetia PA 15367, USA
Sweeney, John E — Representative, NY
5 Plantation Crescent, Clifton Park NY 12065, USA
Sweeney, John J — Labor Leader
AFL-CIO, 1750 New York Ave NW, Lobby 1, Washington DC 20006, USA
Sweeney, Julia — Actress, Comedienne
W M E Entertainment, 9601 Wilshire Blvd, #300, Beverly Hills CA 90210 USA
Sweeney, Mark P — Baseball Player
6394 W Dublin Lane, Chandler AZ 85226, USA
Sweeney, Michael J (Mike) — Baseball Player
PO Box 1193, Rancho Santa Fe CA 92067, USA
Sweeney, Pepper — Actor
Gage Group, 14724 Ventura Blvd, #505, Sherman Oaks CA 91403 USA
Sweeney, Ryan J — Baseball Player
6941 Waterview Dr SW, Cedar Rapids IA 52404, USA
Sweeney, Sunny M — Singer, Songwriter, Guitarist
Republic Nashville Records, 1219 16th Ave S, Nashville TN 37212, USA
Sweeney, Terry — Actress, Comedienne
Creative Artists Agency, 2000 Ave of Stars, #100, Los Angeles CA 90067 USA
Sweeney, Tim — Ice Hockey Player
47 Ledgewood Dr, Hanover MA 02339, USA
Sweeney, Walter F (Walt) — Football Player
6048 Gullstrand St, San Diego CA 92122, USA
Sweet, Joseph L (Joe) — Football Player
1530 NE 89th Court, Vancouver WA 98664, USA
Sweet, Matthew — Singer, Songwriter
Russell Carter Artists Mgmt, 567 Ralph Mcgill Blvd NE, Atlanta GA 30312, USA
Sweet, Richard J (Rick) — Baseball Player
1503 NE 89th Court, Vancouver WA 98664, USA
Sweet, Sharon — Opera Singer
Kunstleragentur Raab & Bohm, Plankengasse 7, 1010 Vienna, Austria
Sweeten, Madylin — Actress
Innovative Artists, 1505 10th St, Santa Monica CA 90401 USA
Sweetland, Brad — Animator
Pixar Animation, 1200 Park Ave, Emeryville CA 94608, USA
Sweetnam, Skye — Singer, Songwriter
Creative Artists Agency, 3310 W End Ave, #500, Nashville TN 37203 USA
Swensen, Joseph A — Conductor, Composer
Malmo Opera, Ronneholmsv 20, 200 10 Malmo, Sweden
Swenson, Inga — Actress, Singer
3351 Halderman St, Los Angeles CA 90066, USA
Swenson, Jesse — Actor
Innovative Artists, 1505 10th St, Santa Monica CA 90401 USA
Swenson, Rick — Dog Sled Racer
PO Box 16205, Two Rivers AK 99716, USA
Swenson, Robert C (Bob) — Football Player
PO Box 403, Erie CO 80516, USA
Swenson, Ruth Ann — Opera Singer
Metropolitan Opera Assn, Lincoln Center Plaza, New York NY 10023 USA
Swensson, Earl S — Architect
Earl Swensson Assoc, 2100 W End Ave, #1200, Nashville TN 37203, USA
Swiczinsky, Helmut — Architect
Coop Himmelblau, Seilerstatte 16/11A, 81010 Vienna, Austria
Swienton, Gregory T — Businessman
Ryder System Inc, 11690 NW 105th St, Medley FL 33178, USA
Swift — Rap Artist (D-12)
Coast to Coast Talent, 3350 Barham Blvd, Los Angeles CA 90068 USA
Swift, Clive — Actor
Roxane Vacca Mgmt, 8 Silver Place, London W1R 3LJ, England
Swift, Douglas A (Doug) — Football Player
265 S 25th St, Philadelphia PA 19103, USA
Swift, Graham C — Writer
A P Watt, 20 John St, London WC1N 2DR, England
Swift, Harley E (Skeeter) — Basketball Player
4987 Highway 11 W, Kingsport TN 37660, USA
Swift, Hewson H — Biologist
University of Chicago, Cell Biology Dept, Chicago IL 60637, USA
Swift, Jeremy — Actor
Independent Talent Group, Oxford House, 76 Oxford St, London W1D 1BS, England
Swift, Scott H — Navy Admiral
Commander, 7th Fleet Yokosuka Japan, FPO AP 96601 USA
Swift, Stephen J — Judge
US Tax Court, 400 2nd St NW, Washington DC 20217, USA
Swift, Stromile — Basketball Player
3256 S Silverwind Cove, Memphis TN 38125, USA
Swift, Taylor — Singer, Guitarist, Songwriter
Taylor Swift Enterprises, 242 W Main St, PM Box 412, Hendersonville TN 37075, USA

Swift - Sylvester

Swift, William C (Bill) — Baseball Player
5880 E Sapphire Lane, Paradise Valley AZ 85253, USA
Swilley, Dennis N — Football Player
1020 Gruene River Dr, New Braunfels TX 78132, USA
Swilling, Patrick T (Pat) — Football Player
4425 Plum Orchard Ave, New Orleans LA 70126, USA
Swinburne, Clare — Actress
Associated International Mgmt, Fairfax House, Fulwood Place, London WC1V 6HU, England
Swindells, William, Jr — Businessman
Willamette Industries, 1300 SW 5th Ave, #500, Portland OR 97201, USA
Swindle, Orson — Government Official
500 University Ave, #309, Honolulu HI 96826, USA
Swindoll, Charles R — Evangelist, Writer
Insight for Living, 211 Imperial Highway, Fullerton CA 92835, USA
Swingle, Paul C — Baseball Player
6844 S Whetstone Place, Chandler AZ 85249, USA
Swingley, Douglas L (Doug) — Dog Sled Racer
Po Box 672, Lincoln MT 59639, USA
Swink, James E (Jim) — Football Player
723 Euclid Ave, Rusk TX 75785, USA
Swinny, Wayne — Guitarist (Saliva)
Helter Skelter, 347-353 Chiswick High Road, London W4 4HS, England
Swinson, Aaron — Basketball Player
1004 Longley Cove, Heathrow FL 32746, USA
Swinton, Reginald T (Reggie) — Football Player
14200 Wimbledon Loop, Little Rock AR 72210, USA
Swinton, Tilda — Actress
Hamilton Hodell, 66-68 Margaret St, London W1W 8SR, England
Swisher, Carl C — Anthropologist
Institute of Human Origins, 1288 9th St, Berkeley CA 94710, USA
Swisher, Nicholas T (Nick) — Baseball Player
6803 E Main St, #6601, Scottsdale AZ 85251, USA
Swisher, Steven E (Steve) — Baseball Player
432 60th St, Vienna WV 26105, USA
Swisten, Amanda — Actress
Xposure Public Relations, 8271 Melrose Ave, #110, Los Angeles CA 90046, USA
Swit, Loretta — Actress
Malibu Business/Shipping Center, 23852 Pacific Coast Highway, Malibu CA 90265, USA
Switzer, Barry — Football Player, Coach
700 W Timberdell Road, Norman OK 73072, USA
Switzer, Jon M — Baseball Player
1109 Elder Circle, Austin TX 78733, USA
Switzer, Louis — Interior Designer
Switzer Group, 535 5th Ave, #1100, New York NY 10017, USA
Swizz Beatz — Rap Artist, Music Producer
5W Public Relations, 888 7th Ave, #1200, New York NY 10106, USA
Swoboda, Ronald A (Ron) — Baseball Player
315 Alonzo St, New Orleans LA 70115, USA
Swoopes, Sheryl — Basketball Player
2020 Eldridge Parkway, #4605, Houston TX 77077, USA
Sy, Omar — Actor
Agence Artiste Adequet, 80 Rue d'Amsterdam, 75009 Paris, France
Syal, Meera — Actress, Comedienne, Writer
United Agents, 12-26 Lexington St, London W1F 0LE, England
Syberberg, Hans-Jurgen — Director
Genter Str 15A, 80805 Munich, Germany
Sybil — Singer
Mission Control, City Business Center, Lower Road, London SE16 2XB, England
Sydney, Harry F — Football Player
1558 Cardinal Lane, Green Bay WI 54313, USA
Sydnor, Charles W, Jr — Businessman, Educator
Commonwealth Public Broadcasting Corp, 23 Sesame St, Richmond VA 23235, USA
Sydor, Darryl — Ice Hockey Player
3358 Windmill Curve, Saint Paul MN 55129, USA
Syed Sirajuddin Syed Putra Jamallullail — Head of State, Malaysia
Sultan's Palace, Istana Bukit Serene, 50502 Kuala Lumpur, Malaysia
Sykes, Eugene C (Gene) — Football Player
15809 Council Ave, Baton Rouge LA 70817, USA
Sykes, Jesse — Singer, Songwriter
Barsuk Records, PO Box 22546, Seattle WA 98122, USA
Sykes, Lynn R — Geologist
100 Washington Spring Road, RR 1 Box 248, Palisades NY 10964, USA
Sykes, Nathan J — Singer (Wanted)
Industry Music Group, 128 Regent Road, Hanley Stoke, Trent ST1 3AY, England
Sykes, Peter — Director
International Talent Booking, Ariel House, 74A Charlotte St, #100 London W1T 4QJ, England
Sykes, Phil — Ice Hockey Player
1486 Brooke Court, Hastings MN 55033, USA
Sykes, Richard B — Businessman, Microbiologist
Imperial College, Exhibition Road, London SW7 2AZ, England
Sykes, Robert J (Bob) — Baseball
1451 County Road 900 E, Carmi IL 62821, USA
Sykes, Wanda — Actress, Comedienne
W M E Entertainment, 9601 Wilshire Blvd, #300, Beverly Hills CA 90210 USA
Sykora, Petr — Ice Hockey Player
2548 Appletree Dr, Pittsburgh PA 15241, USA
Sylbert, Anthea — Costume Designer
13949 Ventura Blvd, #309, Sherman Oaks CA 91423, USA
Sylvester, Charles (Chuck) — Harness Racing Trainer
PO Box 1066, Williamstown NJ 08094, USA
Sylvester, Dean — Ice Hockey Player
51 Upland Road, Plympton MA 02367, USA
Sylvester, George H — Air Force General
4571 Conicville Road, Mount Jackson VA 22842, USA
Sylvester, Harold — Actor
Gage Group, 14724 Ventura Blvd, #505, Sherman Oaks CA 91403 USA

Sylvester, Michael — Opera Singer
Columbia Artists Mgmt Inc, 1790 Broadway, #702, New York NY 10019 USA
Sylvester, Steven P (Steve) — Football Player
10425 Londonderry Court, Cincinnati OH 45242, USA
Sylvestri, Don — Ice Hockey Player
1610 Redfern St, Sudbury ON P3A 3S9, Canada
Sylvian, David — Singer, Guitarist (Japan)
Agency Group Ltd, 142 W 57th St, #600, New York NY 10019 USA
Symington, J Fife, III — Governor, AZ
1700 W Washington St, Phoenix AZ 85007, USA
Symms, Steven D — Senator, ID
127 S Fairfax St, #137, Alexandria VA 22314, USA
Symon, Michael — Chef, Restauranteur
Lola Restaurant, 2058 E 4th St, Cleveland OH 44115, USA
Symone, Raven — Actress, Singer
United Talent Agency, 9336 Civic Center Dr, Beverly Hills CA 90210 USA
Syms, Sylvia — Actress
Barry Brown, 47 West Square, London SE11 4SP, England
Synek, Ondrej — Rowing Athlete
A S C Dukla Prague, Oddil Aletiky, PS 59, 16044 Prague 6, Czech Republic
Sypek, Richard — Actor
Paradigm Agency, 360 N Crescent Dr, North Building, Beverly Hills CA 90210 USA
Syracuse, Joe — Writer, Actor, Director
United Talent Agency, 9336 Civic Center Dr, Beverly Hills CA 90210 USA
Syron, Richard F — Financier, Government Official
Federal Home Loan Mortgage, 8200 Jones Branch Dr, McLean VA 22102, USA
Szabados, Shannon — Ice Hockey Player
Team Canada, 2424 University Dr NW, Calgary AB T2N 3Y9, Canada
Szabo, Istvan — Director
Vaci 6, 1132 Budapest, Hungary
Szaro, Richard J (Rich) — Football Player
171 Metropolitan Ave, Brooklyn NY 11211, USA
Szczerbiak, Walter R (Wally) — Basketball Player, Sportscaster
26 Peabody Road, Cold Spring Harbor NY 11724, USA
Szekely, Eva — Swimmer
Szepvolgyi Utca 4/B, 1025 Budapest, Hungary
Szekessy, Karen — Photographer
Haynstr 2, 20249 Hamburg, Germany
Szemborski, Stanley R — Navy Admiral
Director, Program Analysis/Evaluation, HqUSN, Pentagon, Washington DC 20350, USA
Szep, Paul M — Editorial Cartoonist
10610 Andrew Lane, Seminole FL 33777, USA
Szewczenko, Tanja — Figure Skater, Model, Actress
D E U, Betzenweg 34, 81247 Munich, Germany
Szigmond, Vilmos — Cinematographer
PO Box 2230, Los Angeles CA 90078, USA
Szmanda, Eric — Actor
A P A Talent/Literary Agency, 405 S Beverly Dr, #300, Beverly Hills CA 90212 USA
Szohr, Jessica — Actress
I C M Partners, 10250 Constellation Blvd, #900, Los Angeles CA 90067 USA
Szoka, Edmund C Cardinal — Religious Leader
Prefecture for Economic Affairs, 00120 Vatican City
Szolkowy, Robin — Figure Skater
Eisstadion Ingo Steuer, Wittgensdorfner Str 2A, 09114 Chemnitz, Germany
Szostak, Jack W — Nobel Medicine Laureate
Harvard Medical School, 25 Shattuck St, Boston MA 02115 USA
Szot, Paulo — Actor, Singer
Opera et Concert, 37 Rue de la Chaussee d'Antin, 75009 Paris, France
Szott, David A (Dave) — Football Player
11 Manor Dr, Morristown NJ 07960, USA
Szulc, Radoslaw — Conductor
Harrison/Parrott, 5-6 Albion Court, London W6 0QT, England
Szuminski, Jason E — Baseball Player
680 Serra St, #W402, Stanford CA 94305, USA
Szymanski, James P (Jim) — Football Player
541 Riverwalk Dr, Mason MI 48854, USA
Szymanski, Richard F (Dick) — Football Player
5270 Forest Edge Court, Sanford FL 32771, USA

T Hooft, Gerardus — Nobel Physics Laureate
Leuvenlaan 4, Postbus 80.195, 3508 Utrecht TD, Netherlands

T, Mr — Actor
15203 La Maida St, Sherman Oaks CA 91403, USA

Tabachnik, Michel — Composer, Conductor
Garvey & Ivor, 59 Lansdowne Place, Hove BN3 1FL, England

Tabackin, Lewis B (Lew) — Jazz Flutist, Saxophonist
38 W 94th St, New York NY 10025, USA

Tabai, Ieremia T — President, Kiribati
Foreign Affairs Ministry, PO Box 68, Bairiki, Tarawa, Kiribati

Tabak, Zan — Basketball Player
230 W Superior St, #510, Chicago IL 60654, USA

Tabaka, Jeffrey J (Jeff) — Baseball Player
1481 Norview Dr, Clinton OH 44216, USA

Tabaksblat, Morris — Businessman
Reed Elsevier, Sara Burgerhartstr 25, 1055 KV Amsterdam, Netherlands

Tabaracci, Rick — Ice Hockey Player
7771 Westhills Trail, Park City UT 84098, USA

Tabata, Maki — Speed Skater
Skating Federation, 1-1-1 Jinnan, #414, Shibuyaku, Tokyo 150-8050, Japan

Tabin, Clifford S — Geneticist, Molecular Biologist
Harvard Medical School, 240 Longwood Ave, Boston MA 02115, USA

Tabitha 'Masentle — Princess, Lesotho
Royal Palace, PO Box 524, Maseru, Lesotho

Tabler, Patrick S (Pat) — Baseball Player
8715 Blome Road, Cincinnati OH 45243, USA

Tabor, Philip M (Phil) — Football Player
519 E Harrison Ave, Wheaton IL 60187, USA

Tabora, Roy Gonzalez — Artist
Tabora Gallery, 2005 Kalia Road, Honolulu HI 96815, USA

Tabori, Kristoffer — Actor
International Artistes, 235 Regent St, London W1R 8AX, England

Tabori, Laszlo — Track Athlete
2221 W Olive Ave, Burbank CA 91506, USA

Tacha, Deanell R — Judge
US Court of Appeals, 4830 W 15th St, Lawrence KS 66049, USA

Tadic, Boris — President, Serbia
President's Office, Nemanjina 11, 11000 Belgrade, Serbia

Taff, Russ — Singer
Glickman Entertainment Group, PO Box 570815, Tarzana CA 91357, USA

Taffe, Jeff — Ice Hockey Player
1455 Truax Circle, Hastings MN 55033, USA

Taffoni, Joseph A (Joe) — Football Player
605 Golf Links Court, Chapin SC 29036, USA

Tafoya, Joseph P (Joe) — Football Player
14341 189th Way NE, Woodinville WA 98072, USA

Tafoya, Michele — Sportscaster
ESPN-TV, ESPN Plaza, 935 Middle St, Bristol CT 06010 USA

Taft, John — Ice Hockey Player
5224 Oaklawn Ave, Minneapolis MN 55424, USA

Taft, William H, IV — Diplomat
Fried Frank Assoc, 1001 Pennsylvania Ave NW, #800, Washington DC 20004, USA

Tagawa, Cary-Hiroyuki — Actor
Abrams Artists, 9200 W Sunset Blvd, #1125, West Hollywood CA 90069 USA

Tagg, Barclay — Thoroughbred Racing Trainer
86 Geranium Ave, Floral Park NY 11001, USA

Taghmaoui, Said — Actor
Innovative Artists, 1505 10th St, Santa Monica CA 90401 USA

Tagle, Luis Antonio G — Religious Leader
Archdiocese, 121 Arzobispo St, Intramuros, PO Box 132, 1099 Manila, Philippines

Tagliabue, Paul J — Football Executive
4149 Parkglen Court NW, Washington DC 20007, USA

Taglianetti, Peter A — Ice Hockey Player
67 Bayhill Dr, Bridgeville PA 15017, USA

Taglioni, Alice — Actress
Artmedia, 20 Ave Rapp, 75007 Paris, France

Taguchi, So — Baseball Player
12931 Twin Meadows Court, Saint Louis MO 63146, USA

Tahir, Faran — Actor
Greene Assoc, 1901 Ave of Stars, #130, Los Angeles CA 90067 USA

Taillibert, Roger R — Architect
163 Rue de la Pompe, 75116 Paris, France

Tait, John B — Football Player
1235 Ashbury Lane, Libertyville IL 60048, USA

Tait, Michael D — Singer (DC Talk, Tait, Newsboys)
True Artist Mgmt, 227 3rd Ave N, Franklin TN 37064, USA

Taittinger, Claude — Businessman
9 Place Saint-Nicaise, BP 2741, 51061 Reims Cedex, France

Tajbert, Vitali — Boxer
Spotlight Boxing, Am Stadtrand 27, 22047 Hamburg, Germany

Takac, Robby — Bassist (Goo Goo Dolls)
Atlas/Third Rail Entertainment, 9200 W Sunset Blvd, West Hollywood CA 90069, USA

Takacs, Tibor — Director
A P A Talent/Literary Agency, 405 S Beverly Dr, #300, Beverly Hills CA 90212 USA

Takacs-Nagy, Gabor — Concert Violinist
Case Postale 186, 1245 Collonge-Bellerive, Switzerland

Takagi, Toranosuke — Auto Racing Driver
Nakajima Planning, 1-3-10 Higushi, Shivuyaku, Tokyo 150-0011, Japan

Takahashi, Daisuke — Figure Skater
Kansai University Skate Club, 3-3-35 Yamatecho, Suitashi, Osaka 564 8680 Japan

Takahashi, Joseph S — Neuroscientist
Northwestern University, Neurobiology Dept, 2153 Campus Dr, Evanston IL 60208, USA

Takahashi, Michiaki — Immunologist
Osaka University, Microbe Diseases Institute, Osaka 565-0871, Japan

Takahashi, Naoko — Track Athlete
Sekisui Chemical Co, 4-4-2 Nishitenma, Kitaku, Osaka 530-8565, Japan

Takase, Megumi — Soccer Player
Football Assn, 3-10-15 Hongo, Bunkyoku, Tokyo 113 0033 Japan
Takei, George — Actor
Hosato Enterprises, 419 N Larchmont Blvd, #41, Los Angeles CA 90004, USA
Takezawa, Kyoko — Concert Violinist
Opus 3 Artists, 470 Park Ave S, #900N, New York NY 10016 USA
Takko, Kari — Ice Hockey Player
Dallas Stars, 2601 Ave of Stars, #100, Frisco TX 75034 USA
Tal, Alona — Actress
Innovative Artists, 1505 10th St, Santa Monica CA 90401 USA
Tal, Shiraz — Model
Women Mgmt, 199 Lafayette St, New York NY 10012, USA
Talaba, Marian — Opera Singer
I M G Artists, Hogarth Business Park, Chiswick, London W4 2TH, England
Talafous, Dean — Ice Hockey Player
2418 Foxglove Circle, Hudson WI 54016, USA
Talagi, Toke T — Premier, Niue
Premier's Office, PO Box 40, Alofi, Niue Island
Talalay, Paul — Pharmacologist
5512 Boxhill Lane, Baltimore MD 21210, USA
Talalay, Rachel — Director
A P A Talent/Literary Agency, 405 S Beverly Dr, #300, Beverly Hills CA 90212 USA
Talamini, Robert G (Bob) — Football Player
3577 Cave Creek Manor, Las Cruces NM 88011, USA
Talancon, Ana Claudia — Actress
Gold Levin, 8424-A Santa Monica Blvd, #706, Los Angeles CA 90069, USA
Talat, Mehmet Ali — President, Turkish Northern Cyprus
President's Office, Turkish North Cypress, Via Mersin 10, Lefkosa, Turkey
Talavera, Tracee — Gymnast
106 Mandala Court, Walnut Creek CA 94596, USA
Talbert, David E — Director, Producer, Writer
Brillstein Entertainment Partners, 9150 Wilshire Blvd, #350, Beverly Hills CA 90212 USA
Talbert, Diron V — Football Player
PO Box 388, Rosenberg TX 77471, USA
Talbert, Don L — Football Player
PO Box 261, 3027 Highway 123, Richmond TX 77406, USA
Talbot, Don — Swimming Coach
Sports Federation, 333 River Road, Vanier, Ottawa ON K1L 8B9, Canada
Talbot, Frederick L (Fred) — Baseball Player
7701 Lunceford Lane, Falls Church VA 22043, USA
Talbot, Jena-Guy — Ice Hockey Player
4248 Notre Dame Quest St, Trois-Rivieres QC G9A 4Z5, Canada
Talbot, Maxime — Ice Hockey Player
111 Bellevue Ave, Pittsburgh PA 15229, USA
Talbot, Nita — Actress
3420 Merrimac Road, Los Angeles CA 90049, USA
Talbot, Robert D (Bob) — Baseball Player
608 W Kaweah Ave, Visalia CA 93277, USA
Talbot, Stephen H — Actor, Producer
University of California, Graduate Journalism School, Berkeley CA 94720, USA
Talbot, Susan — Actress
Media Artists Group, 8222 Melrose Ave, #203, Los Angeles CA 90048 USA
Talbott, Michael — Actor
2011 Euclid Ave, Waverly IA 50677, USA
Talbott, N Strobridge (Strobe), III — Journalist, Association Executive
Brookings Institution, 1775 Massachusetts Ave NW, Washington DC 20036, USA
Talese, Gay — Writer
154 E Atlantic Blvd, Ocean City NJ 08226, USA
Tali, Anu — Conductor
Tali Management, Kohtu 3, 10130 Tallinn, Estonia
Taliaferro, George — Football Player
2708 Olcott Blvd, Bloomington IN 47401, USA
Taliaferro, Myron E (Mike) — Football Player
7332 Oakbluff Dr, Dallas TX 75254, USA
Tallas, Rob — Ice Hockey Player
1884 Classic Dr, Coral Springs FL 33071, USA
Tallchief, Maria — Ballerina
Chicago Lyric Opera, 20 N Wacker Dr, #400, Chicago IL 60606, USA
Tallet, Brian C — Baseball Player
3167 McClendon Court, Baton Rouge LA 70810, USA
Talley, Darryl V — Football Player
8713 Lake Tibet Court, Orlando FL 32836, USA
Talley, Gary — Singer, Guitarist (Box Tops)
Horizon Mgmt, PO Box 8770, Endwell NJ 13762, USA
Talley, Joel E — Vietnam War Air Force Hero
20 Lakeshore Dr, Shalimar FL 32579, USA
Tallman, Bob — Rodeo Sportscaster
3401 Lone Star Road, Poolville TX 76487, USA
Tallman, Patricia — Actress
Innovative Artists, 1505 10th St, Santa Monica CA 90401 USA
Tallman, Richard C — Judge
US Court of Appeals, US Courthouse, 1010 5th Ave, Seattle WA 98104, USA
Tallon, Dale — Ice Hockey Player
1533 W Everett Road, Lake Forest IL 60045, USA
Tally, Ted — Writer
Creative Artists Agency, 2000 Ave of Stars, #100, Los Angeles CA 90067 USA
Talon, Amelia — Model
Playboy Promotions, 2706 Media Center Dr, Los Angeles CA 90065 USA
Talton, Marion L (Tim) — Baseball Player
130 Hardy Talton Road, Pikeville NC 27863, USA
Talwalkar, Abhijit Y — Businessman
L S I Logic Corp, 1621 Barber Lane, Milpitas CA 95035, USA
Tam, Jeffrey E (Jeff) — Baseball Player
5255 Pina Vista Dr, Melbourne FL 32934, USA
Tam, Vivienne — Fashion Designer
550 Fashion Ave, #2000, New York NY 10018, USA

Tamahori, Lee — Director
W M E Entertainment, 9601 Wilshire Blvd, #300, Beverly Hills CA 90210 USA

Tamaian, Ion — Artist
Sibiu, Str Stadionului, 557260 Selimbar, Romania

Tamargo, John F — Baseball Player
19018 Fern Meadow Loop, Lutz FL 33558, USA

Tamaro, Janet — Producer, Writer
Creative Artists Agency, 2000 Ave of Stars, #100, Los Angeles CA 90067 USA

Tamaryn — Singer
Agency Group Ltd, 142 W 57th St, #600, New York NY 10019 USA

Tamasy, Paul — Writer
Gotham Group, 7250 Melrose Ave, Los Angeles CA 90046, USA

Tamayo Mendez, Arnaldo — Cosmonaut, Cuba
Calle 16, #504, C/5A y 7MA, Miramar, Ciudad Havana 11300, Cuba

Tambellini, Roger — Golfer
32513 N Scottsdale Road, #105, Scottsdale AZ 85266, USA

Tambellini, Steve — Ice Hockey Player
9 Laurel Place, Port Moody BC 33H 4N1, Canada

Tambiah, Stanley J — Anthropologist
Harvard University, Anthropology Dept, Cambridge MA 02138, USA

Tamblyn, Amber — Actress
United Talent Agency, 9336 Civic Center Dr, Beverly Hills CA 90210 USA

Tamblyn, Russell I (Russ) — Actor, Dancer
Hyler Mgmt, 20 Ocean Park Blvd, #25, Santa Monica CA 90405 USA

Tambor, Jeffrey — Actor
Burstein Co, 15304 W Sunset Blvd, #208, Pacific Palisades CA 90272 USA

Tamburello, Benjamin A (Ben), Jr — Football Player
4385 Milner Road W, Birmingham AL 35242, USA

Tamer, Chris — Ice Hockey Player
4215 Cornwell Lane, Whitmore Lake MI 48189, USA

Tamia — Singer, Songwriter, Actress
Universal Attractions, 135 W 26th St, #1200, New York NY 10001 USA

Tamm, Ralph E — Football Player
942 Lake Gulch Road, Castle Rock CO 80104, USA

Tamme, Jacob — Football Player
Denver Broncos, 13655 E Broncos Parkway, Englewood CO 80112 USA

Tan Dun — Composer
Columbia Artists Mgmt Inc, 1790 Broadway, #702, New York NY 10019 USA

Tan, Amy R — Writer
I C M Partners, 10250 Constellation Blvd, #900, Los Angeles CA 90067 USA

Tan, Melvyn — Concert Pianist
Valerie Barber Mgmt, 4 Winsley St, #305, London W1N 7AR, England

Tanabe, David — Ice Hockey Player
2321 Fieldstone Curve, Saint Paul MN 55129, USA

Tanaka, Asuna — Soccer Player
Football Assn, 3-10-15 Hongo, Bunkyoku, Tokyo 113 0033 Japan

Tanaka, Koichi — Nobel Chemistry Laureate
Shimadzu Corp, 1 Nishinokyo-Kuwabaracho, Nakagoku, Kyoto 604 8511, Japan

Tanaka, Shoji — Physicist
Superconductivity Laboratory, 1-10-13 Shinonome, Kotoku, Tokyo 135 0062, Japan

Tanana, Frank D — Baseball Player
28492 S Harwich Dr, Farmington Hills MI 48334, USA

Tancill, Chris — Ice Hockey Player
14 Kingswood Circle, Verona WI 53593, USA

Tancredi, Melissa P J — Soccer Player
Canadian Soccer, Place Soccer Canada, 237 Metcalfe St, Ottawa ON K2P 1R2, Canada

Tandja, Mamadou — President, Niger
President's Office, State House, Aso Villa, Abuja, Niger

Tanen, Sloane — Writer
Bloomsbury Publishing, 36 Soho Square, London W1D 3Q4, England

Tanenbaum, Robert K — Writer
Robert K Tanenbaum Law Offices, 708 N Roxbury Dr, Beverly Hills CA 90210, USA

Tang Fei — Prime Minister, Taiwan
Kuomintang, 11 Chang Shan South Road, Taipei 100, Taiwan

Tang, David — Fashion Designer
Shanghai Tang, 148 Connaught Road Central, #2300, Hong Kong, China

Tang, Muhai — Conductor
I M G Artists, Hogarth Business Park, Chiswick, London W4 2TH, England

Tanguay, Alex — Ice Hockey Player
78 Jackson St, #1, Denver CO 80206, USA

Tani, Daniel M — Astronaut
14827 Sparkling Bay Lane, Houston TX 77062, USA

Taniguchi, Tadatsugu — Molecular Biologist
University of Tokyo Medical Center, 7-3-1, Hongo, Bunkyoku, Tokyo 113 0033 Japan

Tank — Singer, Songwriter
J L Entertainment, 511 Ave of Americas, #230, New York NY 10011, USA

Tankersley, Taylor M — Baseball Player
853 Chartier Court, Asheboro NC 27205, USA

Tankian, Serj — Singer, Musician (System of a Down)
Velvet Hammer Music, 9014 Melrose Ave, West Hollywood CA 90069, USA

Tanksley, Rick — Singer
Teerajay Music, PO Box 183, White House TN 37188, USA

Tanksley, Steven D — Plant Geneticist
Cornell University, Plant Genetics Dept, Emerson Hall, Ithaca NY 14853, USA

Tannahill, Don — Ice Hockey Player
10113 Lakeview Dr, Rancho Mirage CA 92270, USA

Tannehill, Ryan T — Football Player
Miami Dolphins, 7500 SW 30th St, Davie FL 33314 USA

Tannen, Deborah F — Writer
Georgetown University, Linguistics Dept, Washington DC 20057, USA

Tannen, Steven O (Steve) — Football Player
735 N Niagara St, Burbank CA 91505, USA

Tannenwald, Theodore, Jr — Judge
US Tax Court, 400 2nd St NW, Washington DC 20217, USA

Tanner, Alain — Director
Chemin Point-du-Jour 12, 1202 Geneva, Switzerland

Tanner, Antwon — Actor
TalentWorks, 3500 W Olive Ave, #1400, Burbank CA 91505 USA
Tanner, Barron K — Football Player
7556 W Oregon Ave, Glendale AZ 85303, USA
Tanner, Bruce M — Baseball Player
324 Hearthstone Dr, New Castle PA 16105, USA
Tanner, John P — Ice Hockey Player
Hewlett Packard, 5150 Spectrum Way, Mississauga ON L4W 5G1, Canada
Tanner, John S — Representative, TN
Prime Policy Group LLP, 1110 Vermont Ave NW, #1000, Washington DC 20005, USA
Tanner, Joseph R (Joe) — Astronaut
800 Nelson Park Lane, Longmont CO 80503, USA
Tanner, Roscoe — Tennis Player
1109 Gnome Trail, Lookout Mountain TN 37350, USA
Tannous, Afif I — Government Official
6912 Oak Court, Annandale VA 22003, USA
Tanon Ortiz, Olga T — Singer, Composer
Universal Attractions, 135 W 26th St, #1200, New York NY 10001 USA
Tantawi, Mohammed Hussein — Army Field Marshal
Sharia 23 July, Kobri-el-Kobra, Cairo, Egypt
Tanti, Tony — Ice Hockey Player
Tanti Interiors, 121-2323 Boundray Road, Vancouver BC V5M 4V8, Canada
Tanuja — Actress
14 Usha Kiran 15, M L Dhahanukar Marg, Mumbai MS 400026, India
Tanuvasa, Maa J — Football Player
PO Box 893309, Mililani HI 96789, USA
Tanzi, Vito — Economist
5912 Walhondine Road, Bethesda MD 20816, USA
Tao, Conrad — Concert Pianist
I M G Artists, Hogarth Business Park, Chiswick, London W4 2TH, England
Tao, Terence — Mathematician
University of California, Mathematics Dept, Los Angeles CA 90024, USA
Taormina, Sheila — Swimmer, Triathlete
172 Nautica Mile Dr, Clermont FL 34711, USA
Tapani, Kevin R — Baseball Player
781 Ferndale Road N, Wayzata MN 55391, USA
Tape, Gerald F — Physicist
90 Camino Espejo, Santa Fe NM 87507, USA
Tapert, Robert G — Producer, Director, Writer
Senator International, 8750 Wilshire Blvd, Beverly Hills CA 90211, USA
Taplitz, Daniel — Director
United Talent Agency, 9336 Civic Center Dr, Beverly Hills CA 90210 USA
Tapp, Darryl A — Football Player
862 Independence Court, Philadelphia PA 19147, USA
Tapper, Zoe — Actress
Independent Talent Group, Oxford House, 76 Oxford St, London W1D 1BS, England
Tapping, Amanda — Actress
Characters Talent Agency, 1505 W 2nd Ave, #200, Vancouver BC V6H 3Y4, Canada
Tarabay, Nick E — Actor
Domain Talent, 9229 W Sunset Blvd, #710, West Hollywood CA 90069 USA
Tarand, Andres — Prime Minister
Riigikogu, Lossi Plats 1A, Tallinn 10130, Estonia
Tarantino, Quentin — Director
W M E Entertainment, 9601 Wilshire Blvd, #300, Beverly Hills CA 90210 USA
Taranu, Cornel — Composer, Conductor
Gh Dima Music Academy, IIC Bratianu Str 25, 3400 Cluj, Romania
Tarasco, Anthony G (Tony) — Baseball Player
3528 Maplewood Ave, Los Angeles CA 90066, USA
Tarasova, Tatiana — Figure Skating Coach
Connecticut Skating Center, 300 Alumni Road, Newington CT 06111, USA
Tarasovic, George K — Football Player
1503 Michael Dr, Pittsburgh PA 15227, USA
Tarbuck, Jimmy (Tarby) — Actor, Comedian
118 Beaufort St, London SW3 6BU, England
Tardif, Marc — Ice Hockey Player
Charlesbourg Toyota, 16070 H-Bourassa, Charlesbourg PQ G1G 3Z8, Canada
Tardio, Chris — Actor
Framework Entertainment, 9057 Nemo St, #C, West Hollywood CA 90069 USA
Tarelkin, Yevgeny I — Cosmonaut
Cosmonaut Training Center, Star City, 141160 Zvezdny Gorodok, Moscow Oblast, Russia
Tarjan, Robert E — Mathematician
4 Constitution Hill E, Princeton NJ 08540, USA
Tarkanian, Jerry — Basketball Coach
4767 Ocean Blvd, #1005, San Diego CA 92109, USA
Tarkenton, Francis A (Fran) — Football Player, Businessman
Tarkenton Co, 3340 Peachtree Road NE, #2570, Atlanta GA 30326, USA
Tarpley, Roy J — Basketball Player
819 Foxridge Dr, Arlington TX 76017, USA
Tarr, Curtis W — Government Official, Businessman
Intermet Corp, 900 Wilshire Dr, #270, Troy MI 48084, USA
Tarr, Juraj — Canoeing Athlete
Topolova 7, 94501 Komarno, Slovakia
Tarses, Jamie — Producer
W M E Entertainment, 9601 Wilshire Blvd, #300, Beverly Hills CA 90210 USA
Tarses, Matt — Producer, Writer
W M E Entertainment, 9601 Wilshire Blvd, #300, Beverly Hills CA 90210 USA
Tartabull Guzman, Jose M — Baseball Player
1658 W 72nd St, Hialeah FL 33014, USA
Tartabull Mora, Danilio (Danny) — Baseball Player
27337 Garza Dr, Santa Clarita CA 91350, USA
Tartaglia, Antonio — Bobsled Athlete
Olympic Committee, Foro Italico, Largo Lauro de Bosis 15, 00135 Rome, Italy
Tartakovsky, Genndy — Producer, Director
W M E Entertainment, 9601 Wilshire Blvd, #300, Beverly Hills CA 90210 USA
Tarter, Jill — Astrophysicist
Seti Institute Research Center, 2035 Mountain View, Mountain View CA 94043, USA

Tartt, Donna — Writer
Rogers Coleridge White, 20 Powis Mews, London W11 1JN, England

Tarver, Antonio D — Boxer
4701 Rue Bordeaux, Lutz FL 33558, USA

Tarzier, Carol — Sculptor
1217 32nd St, Emeryville CA 94608, USA

Tasby, Willie, Jr — Baseball Player
1210 E Renfro St, Plant City FL 33563, USA

Taschner, Jack G — Baseball Player
2170 Hidden Creek Road, Neenah WI 54956, USA

Tashima, A Wallace — Judge
US Court of Appeals, 125 S Grand Ave, Pasadena CA 91105, USA

Tasker, Steven J (Steve) — Football Player, Sportscaster
16 Gypsy Lane, East Aurora NY 14052, USA

Tata, Sam B — Photographer
Chemin Millette Wentworth, Nord QC J0T 1Y0, Canada

Tatarek, Robert F (Bob) — Football Player
5829 Southhall Road, Birmingham AL 35213, USA

Tataryn, Dave — Ice Hockey Player
27 Fairway Court, Horseshoe Valley ON L0K 1N0, Canada

Tataurangi, Phillip M (Phil) — Golfer
PO Box 15325, Irvine CA 92623, USA

Tate, Bruce — Singer (Penguins)
David Harris Enterprises, 24210 E Fork Road, #9, Azusa CA 91702, USA

Tate, Catherine — Actress
United Talent Agency, 9336 Civic Center Dr, Beverly Hills CA 90210 USA

Tate, David F — Football Player
3481 S Blackhawk Way, Aurora CO 80014, USA

Tate, Frank — Boxer
9560 Deering Dr, #18, Houston TX 77036, USA

Tate, Geoffrey W (Geoff) — Singer (Queensryche), Songwriter
Monterey International, 200 W Superior St, #202, Chicago IL 60654 USA

Tate, Grady — Jazz Drummer, Singer
Abby Hoffer, 223 1/2 E 48th St, New York NY 10017 USA

Tate, James V — Writer
PO Box 9668, North Amherst MA 01059, USA

Tate, Jeffrey P — Conductor
Columbia Artists Mgmt Inc, 1790 Broadway, #702, New York NY 10019 USA

Tate, Larenz — Actor
A P A Talent/Literary Agency, 405 S Beverly Dr, #300, Beverly Hills CA 90212 USA

Tate, Randy — Religious Leader, Representative, WA
Christian Coalition, 100 Centerville Turnpike, Virginia Beach VA 23463, USA

Tate, Stuart D (Stu) — Baseball Player
695 Liberty Hill Road, Toney AL 35773, USA

Tatel, David S — Judge
US Court of Appeals, 333 Constitution Ave NW, #4400, Washington DC 20001, USA

Tatham, Chuck — Actor, Writer
Collective, 8383 Wilshire Blvd, #1050, Beverly Hills CA 90211 USA

Tatopolous, Patrick — Special Effects Director
I C M Partners, 10250 Constellation Blvd, #900, Los Angeles CA 90067 USA

Tattersall, David — Cinematographer
Lucasfilm, PO Box 2459, San Rafael CA 94912, USA

Tatulli, Mark — Cartoonist (Heart of the City)
Universal Press Syndicate, 4520 Main St, #700, Kansas City MO 64111 USA

Tatum, Bradford — Actor
Brad Warshaw Mgmt, 8228 Sunset Blvd, Los Angeles CA 90046, USA

Tatum, Channing — Actor, Model
Management 360, 9111 Wilshire Blvd, Beverly Hills CA 90210 USA

Tatum, Kenneth R (Ken) — Baseball Player
19 Oakdale Dr, Montevallo AL 35115, USA

Tatum, W Earl — Basketball Player
2300 W Skyline Road, Milwaukee WI 53209, USA

Tatupu, M Mea'alofa (Lofa) — Football Player
PO Box 1053, Bellevue WA 98009, USA

Taubensee, Edward K (Eddie) — Baseball Player
2582 S Maguire Road, #287, Ocoee FL 34761, USA

Taubman, A Alfred — Businessman
Taubman Co, 200 E Long Lake Road, #300, Bloomfield Hills MI 48304, USA

Taubman, Anatole — Actor
United Agents, 12-26 Lexington St, London W1F 0LE, England

Taubman, William — Writer
Amherst College, Political Science Dept, Amherst MA 01002, USA

Taupin, Bernie — Singer, Songwriter
2905 Roundup Road, Santa Ynez CA 93460, USA

Tauran, Jean-Louis Cardinal — Religious Leader
Palazzo Apostolico, 00120 Vatican City

Taurasi, Diana — Basketball Player
Phoenix Mercury, American West Arena, 201 E Jefferson St, Phoenix AZ 85004 USA

Tauriello, Dena — Drummer (Antigone Rising)
W Mgmt, 266 Elizabeth St, #1A, New York NY 10012, USA

Tausch, Terry W — Football Player
2804 Ryder Court, Plano TX 75093, USA

Tauscher, Hansjorg — Alpine Skier
Schwand 7, 87561 Oberstdorf, Germany

Tauscher, Mark G — Football Player
2964 Nessie Lane, Sun Prairie WI 53590, USA

Taussig, Donald F (Don) — Baseball Player
1111 Ocean Dunes Circle, Jupiter FL 33477, USA

Tautolo, Terry L — Football Player
5713 E Huntdale St, Long Beach CA 90808, USA

Tautou, Audrey — Actress
Artmedia, 20 Ave Rapp, 75007 Paris, France

Tauziat, Nathalie — Tennis Player
Federation de Tennis, 1 Ave Gordon Bennett, 75016 Paris, France

Tauzin, Wilbert J (Billy) — Association Official; Representative, LA
Pharmaceutical Research, 1100 15th St NW, #900, Washington DC 20005, USA

Tavare, Jay — Actor
Paul Greenstone, 3008 Sorrelwood Dr, San Ramon CA 94582, USA

Tavares, John — Lacrosse Player
Buffalo Bandits, H S B C Arena, 1 Knox Place, Buffalo NY 14216, USA

Tavares, Sara — Singer, Songwriter
Columbia Artists Mgmt Inc, 1790 Broadway, #702, New York NY 10019 USA

Tavarez Carmen, Julian — Baseball Player
1108 Fireside Trail, Broadview Heights OH 44147, USA

Tavener, John K — Composer
Chester Music, 8-9 Firth St, London W1V 5TZ, England

Taveras Fabian, Franklin C (Frank) — Baseball Player
Calle 31, #16 Los Colinos, Santiago, Dominican Republic

Taveras, Willy — Baseball Player
5535 Memorial Dr, #F, Houston TX 77007, USA

Taverner, Sonia — Ballerina
PO Box 2039, Stony Plain AB T7Z 1X6, Canada

Tavernier, Bertrand R M — Director
I C M Partners, Marlborough House, 10 Earlham St, #300, London WC2H 9LNP, England

Tawan, Serria — Model
Playboy Promotions, 2706 Media Center Dr, Los Angeles CA 90065 USA

Taye, John — Sculptor
1412 E Jefferson St, Boise ID 83712, USA

Taylor, Aaron M — Football Player
278 Black Amber Way, Brentwood CA 94513, USA

Taylor, Andy — Guitarist (Duran Duran)
D D Productions, 93A Westbourne Park Villas, London W2 5ED, England

Taylor, Angel — Singer, Songwriter
A2 Mgmt, 2336 W Belmont Ave, Chicago IL 60618, USA

Taylor, Angelo F — Track Athlete
Vector Sports Mgmt, 417 Keller Parkway, Keller TX 76248, USA

Taylor, Anna Diggs — Judge
US District Court, US Courthouse, 231 W Lafayette Blvd, #827, Detroit MI 48226, USA

Taylor, Anthony P — Basketball Player
5300 Parkview Dr, #1093, Lake Oswego OR 97035, USA

Taylor, Antonio (Tony) — Baseball Player
8415 NW 165th Terrace, Hialeah FL 33016, USA

Taylor, Ben — Singer, Songwriter
Force of Nature Enterprises, 171 Pier Ave, #425, Santa Monica CA 90405, USA

Taylor, Benedict — Actor
Rhubarb, 1a Devonshire Road, Chiswick, London W4 2EU, England

Taylor, Bobby (Chief) — Ice Hockey Player
3912 Americana Dr, Tampa FL 33634, USA

Taylor, Brian — Director, Writer
United Talent Agency, 9336 Civic Center Dr, Beverly Hills CA 90210 USA

Taylor, Brian D — Basketball Player
3622 Green Vista Dr, Encino CA 91436, USA

Taylor, Bruce B — Baseball Player
8 Highland Park Road, Rutland MA 01543, USA

Taylor, Bruce L — Football Player
10324 Pontofino Circle, Trinity FL 34655, USA

Taylor, Buck — Actor
Linda McAlister Talent, 100 Oak Lane, Waxahachie TX 75167, USA

Taylor, Cecil P — Jazz Pianist, Composer
Abby Hoffer, 223 1/2 E 48th St, New York NY 10017 USA

Taylor, Charles — Philosopher, Templeton Religion Laureate
6603 Jeanne Mance, Montreal PQ H2V 4LI, Canada

Taylor, Charles G (Chuck) — Baseball Player
1535 Georgetown Lane, Murfreesboro TN 37129, USA

Taylor, Charles R (Charley) — Football Player, Executive
12032 Canter Lane, Reston VA 20191, USA

Taylor, Chester L — Football Player
29006 Burning Tree Lane, Romulus MI 48174, USA

Taylor, Christian M — Producer, Director, Writer
Creative Artists Agency, 2000 Ave of Stars, #100, Los Angeles CA 90067 USA

Taylor, Christine — Actress
United Talent Agency, 9336 Civic Center Dr, Beverly Hills CA 90210 USA

Taylor, Christy — Actress
10990 Massachusetts Ave, #3, Los Angeles CA 90024, USA

Taylor, Daren — Drummer (Airborne Toxic Event)
Island Def Jam Records, 8920 W Sunset Blvd, #200, West Hollywood CA 90069 USA

Taylor, Dave — Ice Hockey Player, Executive
Dallas Stars, 2601 Ave of Stars, #100, Frisco TX 75034 USA

Taylor, David M — Football Player
82 Manchester St, Glen Rock PA 17327, USA

Taylor, Doris A — Cardiovascular Repair Researcher
University of Minnesota Medical School, Stem Cell Dept, Minneapolis MN 55455, USA

Taylor, Dwight B — Baseball Player
5163 Queen Mary Lane, Jackson MS 39209, USA

Taylor, Dylan — Actor
Thruline Entertainment, 9250 Wilshire Blvd, #100, Beverly Hills CA 90212 USA

Taylor, Edwin W — Biophysicist, Molecular Geneticist
University of Chicago, Biophysics Dept, 920 E 58th St, Chicago IL 60637, USA

Taylor, Eric — Bassist (Saving Abel)
Virgin Records, 338 N Foothill Road, Beverly Hills CA 90210 USA

Taylor, Everett E (Ed) — Football Player
2901 Clarke Road, Memphis TN 38115, USA

Taylor, Femi — Actress, Dancer
Coolwaters Productions, 10061 Riverside Dr, Box 531, Toluca Lake CA 91602 USA

Taylor, Finn — Director, Writer, Actor
Creative Artists Agency, 2000 Ave of Stars, #100, Los Angeles CA 90067 USA

Taylor, Frederick — Writer
Jane Turnbull Agency, 58 Elgin Crescent, London W11 2JJ, England

Taylor, Gilbert — Cinematographer
Cinematography Society, 11 Croft, Gerrards Cross, Bucks SL9 9AE, England

Taylor, Gwendoline — Actress
Auckland Actors, P O Box 56460, Dominion Road, Auckland 1446, New Zealand , USA

Taylor, Harry E — Baseball Player
2125 Cooks Lane, Fort Worth TX 76120, USA

Taylor, Henry S — Writer
1120 Aqua Vista Dr NW, Gig Harbor WA 98335, USA

Taylor, Holland — Actress
Gersh Agency, 9465 Wilshire Blvd, #600, Beverly Hills CA 90212 USA

Taylor, Ivan (Ike) — Football Player
4206 Lenox Oval, Pittsburgh PA 15237, USA

Taylor, J Herbert — Botanist
110 Wood Road, #H210, Los Gatos CA 95030, USA

Taylor, James — Opera Singer
Kunstler Sekretariat am Gasteig, Rosenheimer Str 52, 81669 Munich, Germany

Taylor, James — Singer, Songwriter
2238 Dundas St W, PO Box 59039, Toronto ON, M6R 3B5, Canada

Taylor, James (J T) — Singer (Kool & the Gang)
Brothers Mgmt, 141 Dunbar Ave, Fords NJ 08863 USA

Taylor, James A — Vietnam War Army Hero (CMH)
PO Box 284, Trinity Center CA 96091, USA

Taylor, James Arnold — Actor
19360 Rinaldi St, #501, Porter Ranch CA 91326, USA

Taylor, James C (Jim) — Football Player
7840 Walden Road, Baton Rouge LA 70808, USA

Taylor, Jason P — Football Player
2980 Paddock Road, Weston FL 33331, USA

Taylor, Jennifer B — Model, Actress
Stewart Talent, 58 W Huron, Chicago IL 60654, USA

Taylor, Jermaine — Boxer
PO Box 3456, Little Rock AR 72203, USA

Taylor, Jill — Model
Playboy Promotions, 2706 Media Center Dr, Los Angeles CA 90065 USA

Taylor, Jill Bolte — Neuroanatomist
University of Indiana Medical School, Neuroanatomy Dept, Bloomington IN 47405, USA

Taylor, Jim — Producer
Ad Hominem Enterprises, 506 Santa Monica Blvd, #400, Santa Monica CA 90401, USA

Taylor, John — Bassist (Duran Duran)
D D Productions, 93A Westbourne Park Villas, London W2 5ED, England

Taylor, John G — Football Player
PO Box 326, Fresno CA 93708, USA

Taylor, Jonathan — Producer, Director
I C M Partners, 10250 Constellation Blvd, #900, Los Angeles CA 90067 USA

Taylor, Joseph H, Jr — Nobel Physics Laureate
272 Hartley St, Princeton NJ 08540, USA

Taylor, Kathleen — Businesswoman
Four Seasons Hotels, 1165 Leslie St, Toronto ON M3C 2K8, Canada

Taylor, Keith G — Football Player
PO Box 12324, Chandler AZ 85248, USA

Taylor, Kitrick L — Football Player
14892 Stephenson St, Moreno Valley CA 92555, USA

Taylor, Lawrence J — Football Player
5796 Devon St, Port Orange FL 32127, USA

Taylor, Lili — Actress
I C M Partners, 10250 Constellation Blvd, #900, Los Angeles CA 90067 USA

Taylor, Lionel — Football Player, Coach
201 Pinnacle Dr SE, #3614, Rio Rancho NM 87124, USA

Taylor, Mark C — Ice Hockey Player
Cyclone Taylor Hockey, 10386 Nordel Court, Delta BC V4G 1J7, Canada

Taylor, Meldrick — Boxer
2917 N 4th St, Philadelphia PA 19133, USA

Taylor, Meshach — Actor
Gilbertson Entertainment, 1334 3rd Street Promenade, #201, Santa Monica CA 90401 USA

Taylor, Mick — Guitarist (Rolling Stones)
Jacobson & Colin, 60 Madison Ave, #1026, New York NY 10010, USA

Taylor, Nicole R (Niki) — Model
Tri Star Sports/Entertainment Group, 215 Ward Circle, #200, Brentwood TN 37027, USA

Taylor, Noah — Actor
Linsten Morris Mgmt, 3 Gladstone St, #301, Newtown NSW 2042, Australia

Taylor, Otis, Jr — Football Player
6608 Woodson Road, Raytown MO 64133, USA

Taylor, Paul B — Dancer, Choreographer
Paul Taylor Dance Co, 551 Grand St, Lobby A, New York NY 10002, USA

Taylor, Penny — Basketball Player
Phoenix Mercury, American West Arena, 201 E Jefferson St, Phoenix AZ 85004 USA

Taylor, R Scott — Baseball Player
925 Indian Bridge Lane, Defiance OH 43512, USA

Taylor, Rachael — Actress
Marquee Mgmt, Gate House, 188 Oxford St, Paddington NSW 2021, Australia

Taylor, Reggie — Baseball Player
828 Havird St, Newberry SC 29108, USA

Taylor, Regina — Actress
Innovative Artists, 1505 10th St, Santa Monica CA 90401 USA

Taylor, Renee — Actress
C E S D, 10635 Santa Monica Blvd, #130, Los Angeles CA 90025 USA

Taylor, Richard C (Dick) — Guitarist (Pretty Things)
Talent Consultants International, 105 Shad Row, #B, Piermont NY 10968 USA

Taylor, Richard E — Nobel Physics Laureate
757 Mayfield Ave, Stanford CA 94305, USA

Taylor, Richard L — Costume & Special Effects Designer
Weta Workshop, PO Box 15208, Miramar, Wellington, New Zealand

Taylor, Rip — Actor, Comedian
1133 N Clark Dr, Los Angeles CA 90035, USA

Taylor, Robert — Actor
Marquee Mgmt, The Gatehouse, 188 Oxford St, #B, Paddington NSW 2021, Australia

Taylor, Robert D (Hawk) — Baseball Player
136 Skyway Dr, Murray KY 42071, USA

Taylor, Robert E (Rob) — Football Player
1820 Rebecca Road, Lutz FL 33548, USA

Taylor, Robert L (Bob) — Baseball Player
27 Sunnybrook Road, Springfield MA 01119, USA
Taylor, Rod — Actor
Contemporary Artists, 610 Santa Monica Blvd, #202, Santa Monica CA 90401 USA
Taylor, Roger — Tennis Player
Salterswell Farm, Moreton-in-the-Marsh, Gloucester GL53 7HN, England
Taylor, Roger A — Drummer (Duran Duran)
D D Productions, 93A Westbourne Park Villas, London W2 5ED, England
Taylor, Roger M — Drummer (Queen)
Neal Levin, 15260 Ventura Blvd, #1700, Sherman Oaks CA 91403, USA
Taylor, Roland M (Fatty) — Basketball Player
3812 Homewood Ave, Ashtabula OH 44004, USA
Taylor, Ronald W (Ron) — Baseball Player
19 Alvin Ave, Toronto ON M4T 2A7, Canada
Taylor, Roosevelt (Rosey) — Football Player
7331 Ebbtide Dr, New Orleans LA 70126, USA
Taylor, Samuel D (Sammy) — Baseball Player
PO Box 152, Woodruff SC 29388, USA
Taylor, Sandra — Actress, Model
I P A Network, 231 E Alessandro Blvd, #A355, Riverside CA 92508, USA
Taylor, Shane — Actor
Emptage Hallett, 14 Rathbone Place, London W1T 1HT, England
Taylor, Tamara — Actress
Greene Assoc, 1901 Ave of Stars, #130, Los Angeles CA 90067 USA
Taylor, Tate — Actor, Director
W M E Entertainment, 9601 Wilshire Blvd, #300, Beverly Hills CA 90210 USA
Taylor, Ted — Ice Hockey Player
PO Box 244, Oak Lake MB R0M 1P0, Canada
Taylor, Teresa — Drummer (Butthole Surfers)
Kork Agency, 1880 Century Park E, #711, Los Angeles CA 90067, USA
Taylor, Terry D — Baseball Player
743 W Walnut Ave, Crestview FL 32536, USA
Taylor, Teyana — Rap Artist
Star Trak/Interscope Records, 2220 Colorado Ave, Santa Monica CA 90404, USA
Taylor, Tiffany — Model, Actress
PO Box 4511, West Hills CA 91308, USA
Taylor, Tim — Ice Hockey Player
9119 Woodridge Run Dr, Tampa FL 33647, USA
Taylor, Travis L — Football Player
120 Jacob Court, Fayetteville GA 30214, USA
Taylor, Vanessa — Actress, Model
Management 360, 9111 Wilshire Blvd, Beverly Hills CA 90210 USA
Taylor, Vaughn — Golfer
2536 Queens Court, Grovetown GA 30813, USA
Taylor, William H (Billy) — Baseball Player
201 Washington Place, Thomasville GA 31792, USA
Taylor, William M (Bill) — Baseball Player
PO Box 146, Acton CA 93510, USA
Taylor, William T (Billy) — Football Player
3 Greenwich Dr, #86, Jersey City NJ 07305, USA
Taylor-Capps, Nancy — Golfer
3205 Tallia Court, Charlotte NC 28269, USA
Taylor-Compton, Scout — Actress
Gersh Agency, 9465 Wilshire Blvd, #600, Beverly Hills CA 90212 USA
Taylor-Gordon, Hannah — Actress
Independent Talent Group, Oxford House, 76 Oxford St, London W1D 1BS, England
Taylor-Taylor, Courtney — Singer, Guitarist (Dandy Warhols)
Monqui Records, PO Box 5908, Portland OR 97228, USA
Taylor-Young, Leigh — Actress
11300 W Olympic Blvd, #610, Los Angeles CA 90064, USA
Taymor, Julie — Director, Lyricist
Cinetic Mgmt, 555 W 25th St, #400, New York NY 10001 USA
TaZEL, Erica — Actress
Peter Strain, 5455 Wilshire Blvd, #1812, Los Angeles CA 90036 USA
Tazoi, Jim Y — WW II Army Hero
13360 N 600 W, Garland UT 84312, USA
Tcherezov, Ivan Y — Biathlete
Biathlon Union, Luzhnetskaja Nab 8, 119270 Moscow, Russia
Tchongo Domingos, Salvador — Government Official, Guinea-Bissau
Assembleia Nacional Popular, Bisseau, Guinea-Bissau
Tchoudov, Maxim A — Biathlete
Biathlon Union, Luzhnetskaja Nab 8, 119270 Moscow, Russia
Te Kanawa, Kiri — Opera Singer
Nick Grace Mgmt, 69 Sheen Road, Richmond, Surrey TW9 1YJ, England
Teacher, Brian D — Tennis Player
Tennis Academy, Arroyo Seca Racquet Club, 920 Lohman Lane, South Pasadena CA 91030, USA
Teachout, John — Body Builder
1410 Stetson Green, San Antonio TX 78258, USA
Teaff, Grant G — Football Coach, Executive
8265 Forest Ridge Dr, Waco TX 76712, USA
Teagarden, Taylor H — Baseball Player
2007 Blestem Lane, Carrollton TX 75007, USA
Teagle, Terry M — Basketball Player
2111 Heatherwood Dr, Missouri City TX 77489, USA
Teague, Fred E (Trey), III — Football Player
862 Ashport Road, Jackson TN 38305, USA
Teague, George T — Football Player
6561 Meadow Lark Dr, Montgomery AL 36116, USA
Teague, Jeffrey D (Jeff) — Basketball Player
Atlanta Hawks, Centennial Tower, 101 Marietta St NW, #1900, Atlanta GA 30303 USA
Teague, Lewis — Director
Gersh Agency, 9465 Wilshire Blvd, #600, Beverly Hills CA 90212 USA
Teague, Marquis — Basketball Player
Chicago Bulls, United Center, 1901 W Madison St, Chicago IL 60612 USA
Teague, Marshall — Actor
Geddes Agency, 8430 Santa Monica Blvd, #201, West Hollywood CA 90069 USA

Teahen, Mark T — Baseball Player
8610 E Via Del Sol Dr, Scottsdale AZ 85255, USA

Teal, Clare — Singer
Agency Group Ltd, 142 W 57th St, #600, New York NY 10019 USA

Teal, Willie, Jr — Football Player
1322 Westchester Dr, Baton Rouge LA 70810, USA

Teale, Owen — Actor
Markham & Froggatt, Julian House, 4 Windmill St, London W1P 1HF, England

Teasdale, Joseph P — Governor, MO
Commerce Tower, 911 Main St, #1210, Kansas City MO 64105, USA

Teasley, Nikki — Basketball Player
Tulsa Shock, B O K Center, 200 S Denver, Tulsa OK 74103 USA

Teasley, Ronald (Ron) — Baseball Player
19317 Coyle St, Detroit MI 48235, USA

Tebbit of Chingford, Norman B — Government Official, England
House of Lords, Westminster, London SW1A 0PW, England

Tebow, Timothy R (Tim) — Football Player
New York Jets, 1 Jets Dr, Florham Park NJ 07932 USA

Tedeschi, David — Editor
Innovative Artists, 1505 10th St, Santa Monica CA 90401 USA

Tedeschi, Susan — Singer
S L Feldman Mgmt, 1505 W 2nd Ave, #200, Vancouver BC V6H 3Y4, Canada

Tedford, Travis — Actor
Acme Agency, 4727 Wilshire Blvd, #333, Los Angeles CA 90010, USA

Tee, Brian — Actor
TalentWorks, 3500 W Olive Ave, #1400, Burbank CA 91505 USA

Tee, Hayden — Actor, Singer
Lambert House Enterprises, PO Box 226, Collaroy Beach NSW 2097, Australia

Teegarden, Aimee — Actress
Innovative Artists, 1505 10th St, Santa Monica CA 90401 USA

Teevens, Eugene F (Buddy) — Football Coach
Dartmouth College, Athletic Dept, Hanover NH 03755, USA

Tefkin, Blair — Actress, Singer, Songwriter
Bossyroots Records, 8033 W Sunset Blvd, #850, Los Angeles CA 90046, USA

Teich, Malvin C — Electrical Engineer
Boston University, Electrical/Computer Engineering Dept, Boston MA 02215, USA

Teichman, Axel — Cross Country Skier
Neue Str 8, 98559 Oberhof, Germany

Teitel, Robert — Actor, Producer
Creative Artists Agency, 2000 Ave of Stars, #100, Los Angeles CA 90067 USA

Teitelbaum, Bill — Cartoonist (Bottom Liners)
Tribune Media Services, 435 N Michigan Ave, #1500, Chicago IL 60611 USA

Teitelbaum, Eric — Cartoonist (Bottom Liners)
Tribune Media Services, 435 N Michigan Ave, #1500, Chicago IL 60611 USA

Teitelbaum, Zalman — Religious Leader, Rabbi
Satmar Hasidic, 87 Morton St, Brooklyn NY 11211, USA

Teitell, Conrad L — Attorney
Cummings & Lockwood, 6 Landmark Square, Stamford CT 06901, USA

Teixeira, Mark C (Tex) — Baseball Player
2220 King Fisher Dr, Westlake TX 76262, USA

Tejada, Miguel O M — Baseball Player
3013 NE 20th Court, Fort Lauderdale FL 33305, USA

Tejeda, Robinson G — Baseball Player
45 Appletree Lane, #D, Old Bridge NJ 08857, USA

Tejera, Michael — Baseball Player
14271 SW 18th St, Miami FL 33175, USA

Tekulve, Kenton C (Kent) — Baseball Player
1531 Sequoia Dr, Pittsburgh PA 15241, USA

Tela — Rap Artist
American Talent Agency, 26 Finney Farm Road, Croton on Hudson NY 10520, USA

Telavi, Willy — Prime Minister, Tuvalu
Prime Minister's Office, Vaiaku, Funafuti, Tuvalu

Telfair, Sebastian — Basketball Player
Phoenix Suns, 201 E Jefferson St, Phoenix AZ 85004 USA

Telfer, Paul — Actor
Don Buchwald/Fortitude, 6500 Wilshire Blvd, #2200, Los Angeles CA 90048 USA

Telford, Anthony C — Baseball Player
9109 Cypress Keep Lane, Odessa FL 33556, USA

Telgheder, David W — Baseball Player
50 Orchard Crest Dr, Westtown NY 10998, USA

Telito, Filoimea — Governor General, Tuvalu
Governor General's Office, Government House, Vaiaku, Funafuti, Tuvalu

Tellefsen, Christopher — Editor
Claire Best Assoc, 736 Seward St, Los Angeles CA 90038, USA

Teller — Comedian, Illusionist (Penn & Teller)
A P A Talent/Literary Agency, 405 S Beverly Dr, #300, Beverly Hills CA 90212 USA

Teller, Juergen — Photographer
1 Telford Road, London W10 5SH, England

Teller, Miles — Actor
Creative Artists Agency, 2000 Ave of Stars, #100, Los Angeles CA 90067 USA

Tellmann, Thomas J (Tom) — Baseball Player
1021 Yankee Bush Road, Warren PA 16365, USA

Tellqvist, K Mikael — Ice Hockey Player
7932 E Feathersong Lane, Scottsdale AZ 85255, USA

Telnaes, Ann C — Editorial Cartoonist
Tribune Media Services, 435 N Michigan Ave, #1500, Chicago IL 60611 USA

Teltscher, Eliot — Tennis Player, Coach
Pepperdine University, Athletic Dept, Malibu CA 90265, USA

Teltscher, Kate — Historian
Bloomsbury Publishing, 36 Soho Square, London W1D 3Q4, England

Telushkin, Joseph — Religious Leader, Rabbi, Writer
Center for Learning & Leadership, 440 Park Ave S, #400, New York NY 10016, USA

Temchen, Sybil — Actress
Untitled Entertainment, 350 S Beverly Dr, #200, Beverly Hills CA 90212 USA

Temerlin, J Liener — Businessman
201 E John Carpenter Freeway, Irving TX 75062, USA

Temesvari, Andrea ProServe, 1101 Woodrow Wilson Blvd, #1800, Arlington VA 22209 USA	Tennis Player
Temirkanov, Yuri K State Philharmonia, Mikhailovskaya 2, 191186 Saint Petersburg, Russia	Conductor
Temple, Collis 2614 Dalrymple Dr, Baton Rouge LA 70808, USA	Basketball Player
Temple, Juno V United Talent Agency, 9336 Civic Center Dr, Beverly Hills CA 90210 USA	Actress
Templeman, Simon A P A Talent/Literary Agency, 405 S Beverly Dr, #300, Beverly Hills CA 90212 USA	Actor
Templeton, Ben Tribune Media Services, 2 Perry St, Cortlandt Manor NY 10567, USA	Cartoonist (Motley's Crew)
Templeton, Garry L 13552 Del Poniente Road, Poway CA 92064, USA	Baseball Player
Tena, Natalia Curtis Brown Group, 28-29 Haymarket, #500, London SW1Y 4SP, England , USA	Actress
Tenace, F Gene 2650 Cliff Hawk Court, Redmond OR 97756, USA	Baseball Player, Manager
Tenet, George J Allen & Co, 711 5th Ave, New York NY 10022, USA	Government Official
Teng, Vienna Rounder Records, 1 Rounder Way, Burlington MA 01803 USA	Singer, Pianist, Songwriter
TenHolt, Friso Keizergracht 614, Amsterdam, Netherlands	Artist
Tenison, Renee Tenison Group, 171 Pier Ave, #403, Santa Monica CA 90405, USA	Model, Actress
Tennant, Andy Creative Artists Agency, 2000 Ave of Stars, #100, Los Angeles CA 90067 USA	Director, Writer
Tennant, David Independent Talent Group, Oxford House, 76 Oxford St, London W1D 1BS, England	Actor, Director
Tennant, Neil F W M E Entertainment, 9601 Wilshire Blvd, #300, Beverly Hills CA 90210 USA	Singer (Pet Shop Boys)
Tennant, Scott University of Southern California, Thornton Music School, Los Angeles CA 90089, USA	Guitarist (LAGQ)
Tennant, Stella Select Model Mgmt, 17 Ferdinand St, London NW1 8EU, England	Model
Tennant, Veronica National Ballet of Canada, 157 King St E, Toronto ON M5C 1G9, Canada	Ballerina
Tennant, Victoria Glick Agency, 1321 7th St, #203, Santa Monica CA 90401 USA	Actress
Tennant, Victoria C E S D, 10635 Santa Monica Blvd, #130, Los Angeles CA 90025 USA	Actress
Tenneson, Joyce PO Box 228, Rockport ME 04856, USA	Photographer
Tenney, Jon Kritzer Levine Wilkins Griffin, 11872 La Grange Ave, #100, Los Angeles CA 90025 USA	Actor
Tennille, Toni 1040 Sun Wood Dr, Las Vegas NV 89145, USA	Singer (Captain & Tennille)
Tennison, Chalee Buddy Lee Attractions, 38 Music Square E, #300, Nashville TN 37203 USA	Singer
Tensi, Stephen M (Steve) 300 Flannery Fork Road, Blowing Rock NC 28605, USA	Football Player
Tent, Kevin Eastern Talent Agency, 849 S Broadway, #811, Los Angeles CA 90014, USA	Editor
Tenuta, Judy 13504 Contour Dr, Sherman Oaks CA 91423, USA	Actress, Comedienne
Tepedino, Frank R 2 Pear Court, Saint James NY 11780, USA	Baseball Player
Tequila, Tila 8033 Sunset Blvd, #1029, West Hollywood CA 90046, USA	Singer, Model
Teraoka, Masami 41-048 Kaulu St, Waimanalo HI 96795, USA	Artist
Terbenche, Paul F 238 Victoria St N, Port Hope ON L1A 3N4, Canada	Ice Hockey Player
Terborgh, John W Duke University, Tropical Conservation Center, PO Box 90381, Durham NC 27708, USA	Ecologist, Environmentalist
Terebey, Susan California State University, Physics & Astronomy Dept, Los Angeles CA 90032, USA	Astronomer
Terentieva, Nina N Bolshoi Theater, Teatralnaya Pl 1, 103009 Moscow, Russia	Opera Singer
Tereshchenko, Sergei A 121-18 Kounaev Str, 480100 Almaty, Kazakhstan	Prime Minister, Kazakhstan
Tereshinski, Joseph P (Joe), Sr 6508 Millwood Road, Bethesda MD 20817, USA	Football Player
Tereshkova, Valentina V Int'l Co-operation Assn, Vozdvizhenka Str 14-18, 103885 Moscow, Russia	Cosmonaut
Terfel Jones, Bryn Harlequin Agency, 203 Fidlas Road, Cardiff CF4 5NA, Wales	Opera Singer
Tergesen, Lee Industry Entertainment, 955 Carillo Dr, #300, Los Angeles CA 90048 USA	Actor
Terminator X Brookes Co, 8223 Gulana Ave, Playa del Rey CA 90293, USA	Rap Artist (Public Enemy)
Ter-Petrossian, Levon A Marshal Baghramian Prospect 19, 375016 Yerevan, Armenia	President, Armenia
Terra, Scott Abrams Artists, 9200 W Sunset Blvd, #1125, West Hollywood CA 90069 USA	Actor
Terracciano, Anthony P S L M Corp, 12061 Bluemont Way, Reston VA 20190, USA	Financier
Terrace, Herbert S 17 Campfire Road, Chappaqua NY 10514, USA	Anthropologist, Primatologist
Terranova, Joe Joe Taylor Artist Agency, PO Box 279, Williamstown NJ 37068 USA	Singer (Danny and the Juniors)
Terrazas Sandoval, Julio Cardinal Arzobispado, Casilla 25, Calle Ingavi 49, Santa Cruz de la Sierra, Bolivia	Religious Leader
Terrell, C Walter (Walt) 1304 Oxley Court, Union KY 41091, USA	Baseball Player

Terrell, David W (Dave) — Football Player
43628 Cather Court, Ashburn VA 20147, USA

Terrell, Ernie — Boxer
11136 S Parnell, Chicago IL 60628, USA

Terrell, Patrick C (Pat) — Football Player
2490 Madrid Way S, Saint Petersburg FL 33712, USA

Terreri, Christopher A (Chris) — Ice Hockey Player
120 Lake Dr, Mountain Lakes NJ 07046, USA

Terrile, Richard — Astronomer
2121 E Woodlyn Road, Pasadena CA 91104, USA

Terrion, Greg — Ice Hockey Player
Terrion Esso Service, PO Box 428, Marmoro ON K0K 2M0, Canada

Terris, Malcolm — Actor
14 England's Lane, London NW3, England

Terry, Adam S — Football Player
507 Adams Road, Webster NY 14580, USA

Terry, Christopher A (Chris) — Football Player
8209 Marshall Brae Dr, Raleigh NC 27616, USA

Terry, Clark — Jazz Trumpeter, Singer
4720 S Beech St, Pine Bluff AR 71603, USA

Terry, Claude L — Basketball Player
14815 E Sandstone Court, Fountain Hills AZ 85268, USA

Terry, Jason E — Basketball Player
105 Kingston Minor NE, Atlanta GA 30342, USA

Terry, John — Soccer Player
Chelsea F C, Stamford Bridge, Fulham Road, London SW6 1HS, England

Terry, John — Actor
1 Mgmt, 9000 W Sunset Blvd, #1550, Los Angeles CA 90069 USA

Terry, John Q — Architect
Old Exchange, Dedham, Colchester, Essex CO7 6HA, England

Terry, Megan D — Writer
2309 Hanscom Blvd, Omaha NE 68105, USA

Terry, Nigel — Actor
PO Box 1116, Belfast BT2 7AJ, Northern Ireland

Terry, Ralph W — Baseball Player
801 Park St, Larned KS 67550, USA

Terry, Randall A — Social Activist
Operation Rescue National, PO Box 360221, Melbourne FL 32936, USA

Terry, Ruth — Singer, Actress
622 Hospitality Dr, Rancho Mirage CA 92270, USA

Terry, Scott R — Baseball Player
4943 Montford Dr, Saint Louis MO 63128, USA

Terry, Tony — Singer
Green Light Talent Agency, PO Box 3172, Beverly Hills CA 90212 USA

Terwilliger, W Wayne — Baseball Player
1909 Clear Creek Dr, Weatherford TX 76087, USA

Terzic, Adnan — Prime Minister, Bosnia & Herzegovina
Prime Minister's Office, Alipasina 1, 71000 Sarajevo, Bosnia & Herzegovina

Terzopoulos, Dmitri — Computer Scientist
University of California, Computer Science Dept, Los Angeles CA 90024, USA

Tesh, John — Composer, Pianist, Entertainer
TeshMedia Group, 13245 Riverside Dr, #305, Sherman Oaks CA 91423, USA

Teske, Rachel — Golfer
Gaylord Sports Mgmt, 13845 N Northsight Blvd, #200, Scottsdale AZ 85260 USA

Tesori, Jeanine — Composer
W M E Entertainment, 9601 Wilshire Blvd, #300, Beverly Hills CA 90210 USA

Tessaro, Kathleen — Writer
William Morrow, 1350 Ave of Americas, New York NY 10019, USA

Tessier, John — Opera Singer
I M G Artists, Hogarth Business Park, Chiswick, London W4 2TH, England

Tessier, Orval — Ice Hockey Player
411 McDonell Crescent, Cornwall ON K6H 5N7, Canada

Tessier-Lavigne, Marc — Neurobiologist
255 Selby Lane, Atherton CA 94027, USA

Tessmer, Jay W — Baseball Player
5312 NW Akbar Court, Port Saint Lucie FL 34986, USA

Testa, Franco — Cyclist
Via Calvi 15, 32021 Mogliano, Italy

Testa, Mary — Actress, Singer
Gage Group, 315 W 57th St, #4H, New York NY 10019 USA

Testa, Sylvio — Photographer
Les Jardines du Golf, 06210 Mandelieu, Alpes Maritimes, France

Testaverde, Vincent F (Vinny) — Football Player
17122 Gunn Highway, Odessa FL 33556, USA

Testi, Fabio — Actor
Via Siacci 38, 00197 Rome, Italy

Testino, Mario — Photographer
National Portrait Gallery, Saint Martins Place, London WC2H 0HE, England

Teteak, Deral D — Football Player
8067 Palomino Dr, Naples FL 34113, USA

Teter, Hannah — Snowboard Athlete, Model
1554 Plumas Circle, South Lake Tahoe CA 96150, USA

Teton, John — Social Activist
Earthlight Pictures, 791 4th St, Lake Oswego OR 97034, USA

Tetriani, Lina — Opera Singer
I M G Artists, Hogarth Business Park, Chiswick, London W4 2TH, England

Tettamanzi, Dionigi Cardinal — Religious Leader
Arcivescovado, Piazza Matteotti 4, 16123 Genoa, Italy

Tettleton, Mickey L — Baseball Player
PO Box 721860, Norman OK 73070, USA

Tetzlaff, Christian — Concert Violinist
Konzertdirektion Schmid, Konigstra 36, 30175 Hannover, Germany

Teufel, Timothy S (Tim) — Baseball Player, Manager
PO Box 3517, Jupiter FL 33469, USA

Teukolsky, Saul A — Astrophysicist
Cornell University, Physics/Astronomy Dept, Ithaca NY 14853, USA

Teut, Nate	Baseball Player
2010 Sugar Creek Dr, Waukee IA 50263, USA	
Tewell, Doug	Golfer
15216 Fairview Farm Road, Edmond OK 73013, USA	
Tewes, Lauren	Actress
Actor's Group Agency, 3400 Beacon Ave S, Seattle WA 98144, USA	
Tewkesbury, Joan F	Director, Writer
Creative Artists Agency, 2000 Ave of Stars, #100, Los Angeles CA 90067 USA	
Tewksbury, Robert A (Bob)	Baseball Player
63 Ridge Road, Concord NH 03301, USA	
Tews, Andreas	Boxer
Pflaumenbaum, Brunnenstr 32, 19053 Schwerin, Germany	
Texada, Tia	Actress
Power & Twersky Business Mgmt, 13801 Ventura Blvd, Sherman Oaks CA 91423, USA	
Thabeet, Hasheem	Basketball Player
Oklahoma City Thunder, 211 N Robinson Ave, #300, Oklahoma City OK 73102 USA	
Thaborik, Marian	Ice Hockey Player
301 Kenwood Parkway, #401, Minneapolis MN 55403, USA	
Thaci, Hashim	Prime Minister, Kosovo
Prime Minister's Office, Assembly, Mother Theresa St, 10000 Pristina, Kosovo	
Thacker, Brian M	Vietnam War Army Hero (CMH)
11413 Monterey Dr, Silver Spring MD 20902, USA	
Thacker, Charles P	Computer Engineer
543 Tennyson Ave, Palo Alto CA 94301, USA	
Thacker, Thomas P (Tom)	Basketball Player
3655 Dogwood Lane, Cincinnati OH 45213, USA	
Thackery, Jimmy	Singer, Guitarist (Nighthawks)
Mongrel Music, 743 Center Blvd, Fairfax CA 94930, USA	
Thagard, Norman E	Astronaut, Physician
502 N Ride, Tallahassee FL 32303, USA	
Thain, John A	Financier
C I T Group, 505 5th Ave, New York NY 10017, USA	
Thaler, Richard H	Economist
University of Chicago, Booth Business School, Chicago IL 60637, USA	
Thalia	Singer, Actress
Sunshine Sachs & Assoc, 149 5th Ave, #700, New York NY 10010, USA	
Thalmann, Melchior	Gymnast
Kreuzbuhlstr 43, 8600 Dubendorf, Switzerland	
Thames, Marcus M	Baseball Player
101 Mount Moriah Circle, Louisville MS 39339, USA	
Than Shwe	Head of State, Myanmar; General
Head of State Office, Theinbyu Road, Yangon, Myanmar	
Thani, Sheikh Hamad ibn Khalifa al-	Emir, Qatar
Royal Palace, PO Box 923, Doha, Qatar	
Thani, Tamim Bin Hamad al-	Emir Designate, Qatar
Royal Palace, PO Box 923, Doha, Qatar	
Thapa, Surya Bahadur	Prime Minister, Nepal
Tangal, Kathmandu, Bagmati 44601, Nepal	
Tharp, Twyla	Dancer, Choreographer
Twyla Tharp Productions, 336 Central Park West, #17B, New York NY 10025, USA	
Tharpe, Larry J	Football Player
3665 Greenbriar Road E, Macon GA 31204, USA	
Thatcher of Lincolnshire, Margaret H	Prime Minister, England
11 Dulwich Gate, Dulwich, London SE12, England	
Thatcher, David J	WW II Army Air Corps Hero
440 Dearborn Ave, Missoula MT 59801, USA	
Thatcher, Joseph (Joe)	Baseball Player
310 Ruddell Dr, Kokomo IN 46901, USA	
Thatcher, Karen	Ice Hockey Player
USA Hockey, 1775 Bob Johnson Dr, Colorado Springs CO 80906 USA	
Thatcher, Roland C, IV	Golfer
18 Floweruff Court, Spring TX 77380, USA	
Thaxton, James I (Jim)	Football Player
4319 Deergrove Road, Memphis TN 38141, USA	
Thayer, Bill	Explorer
PO Box 233, Snohomish WA 98291, USA	
Thayer, Brynn	Actress
PO Box 15006, Beverly Hills CA 90209, USA	
Thayer, Gregory A (Greg)	Baseball Player
1000 3rd St N, Sauk Rapids MN 56379, USA	
Thayer, Helen	Explorer, Skier
PO Box 233, Snohomish WA 98291, USA	
Thayer, Maria	Actress
A P A Talent/Literary Agency, 405 S Beverly Dr, #300, Beverly Hills CA 90212 USA	
Thayer, Thomas A (Tom)	Football Player
50 Nohea Kai Dr, #I303, Lahaina HI 96761, USA	
Thayer, W Paul	Government Official, Businessman
10200 Hollow Way, Dallas TX 75229, USA	
Theberge, Greg	Ice Hockey Player
31 Edgar, Sundridge ON P0A 1Z0, Canada	
Theile, David	Swimmer
84 Woodville St, Hendea, Brisbane QLD 4011, Australia	
Thein Sein	President, Myanmar; General
President's Office, Zaw Gyi St, Mayangon Tsp, Yangon, Myanmar	
Theismann, Joseph R (Joe)	Football Player, Sportscaster
PO Box 186, Leesburg VA 20178, USA	
Theiss, Brooke	Actress
Characters Talent Agency, 8 Elm St, Toronto ON M5G 1G7, Canada	
Theiss, Duane C	Baseball Player
66 Juniper Ave, Westerville OH 43081, USA	
Thelan, Jodi	Actress
8428 Melrose Place, #C, West Hollywood CA 90069, USA	
Theler, Derek	Actor
Paradigm Agency, 360 N Crescent Dr, North Building, Beverly Hills CA 90210 USA	
Theobald, Ronald M (Ron)	Baseball Player
319 Jacaranda Place, Fullerton CA 92832, USA	

T

Theodorakis, Mikis — Composer
Epifanous 1, Akropolis, Athens, Greece

Theodore, George B — Baseball Player
1388 Princeton Ave, Salt Lake City UT 84105, USA

Theodore, Jose — Ice Hockey Player
238 S Maya Palm Dr, Boca Raton FL 33432, USA

Theodorescu, Monica — Equestrian
Gestit Lindenhof, 48336 Sassenberg, Germany

Theodosakis, Jason — Physician, Writer
Saint Martin's Press, 175 5th Ave, #400, New York NY 10010 USA

Theodosius, Primate Metropolitan — Religious Leader
Orthodox Church in America, PO Box 675 RR 25A, Syosset NY 11791, USA

Therien, Christopher B (Chris) — Ice Hockey Player
15 Milford Dr, Marlton NJ 08053, USA

Theriot, Ryan S — Baseball Player
241 Granville Court, Baton Rouge LA 70810, USA

Theron, Charlize — Actress, Model
W M E Entertainment, 9601 Wilshire Blvd, #300, Beverly Hills CA 90210 USA

Theroux, Justin — Actor, Director
Creative Artists Agency, 2000 Ave of Stars, #100, Los Angeles CA 90067 USA

Theroux, Paul E — Writer
35 Elsynge Road, London SW18 2NR, England

Therrien, Michel — Ice Hockey Player, Coach
118 Carriage Dr, McKnight PA 15237, USA

Theus, Reggie W — Basketball Player, Coach
4259 Enoro Dr, Los Angeles CA 90008, USA

Theusner, Ulrike — Model
Take 2 Model Mgmt, 6 Willow St, London EC2 4BH, England

Thewlis, David — Actor
Ken McReddie Assoc, 11 Connaught Place, London W2 2ET, England

Theys, Didier — Auto Racing Driver
5773 N 78th Place, Scottsdale AZ 85259, USA

Thibaudet, Jean-Yves — Concert Pianist
M L Falcone, 55 W 68th St, #1114, New York NY 10023, USA

Thibault, Charles — Physiologist
4 Place Jussieu, 75005 Paris, France

Thibault, Jocelyn — Ice Hockey Player
550 Ch du Domaine, RR 5, Saint-Denis-de-Brompton QC J0B 2P0, Canada

Thibault, Mike F — Basketball Coach
Connecticut Sun, 1 Mohegan Sun Blvd, Uncasville CT 06382 USA

Thibiant, Aida — Fashion Consultant
Institut de Beaute, 449 N Canon Dr, Beverly Hills CA 90210, USA

Thich Quang Do — Religious Activist
Thanh Zinh Zen Monastery, Ho Chi Minh City, Vietnam

Thicke, Alan — Actor
7110 Gobernador Canyon Road, Carpinteria CA 93013, USA

Thicke, Chris — Mandolin Player
Nonesuch Records, 75 Rockefeller Plaza, #800, New York NY 10019 USA

Thicke, Robin A — Singer
W M E Entertainment, 9601 Wilshire Blvd, #300, Beverly Hills CA 90210 USA

Thiedemann, Fritz — Equestrian
Ostreherweg 28, 25746 Heide, Germany

Thiele, Gerhard P J — Astronaut, Germany
European Space Center, Linder Hohe, Box 906096, 51127 Cologne, Germany

Thielemann, Ray C (R C) — Football Player
210 Rose Meadow Lane, Alpharetta GA 30005, USA

Thielemans, Jean B (Toots) — Jazz Harmonica Player, Guitarist
Peter Levinson Communications, 2575 Palisade Ave, #11H, Bronx NY 10463, USA

Thielen, Gunter — Businessman
Bertelsmann AG, Carl-Bertelsmann-Str 270, 33311 Guetersloh, Germany

Thiemens, Mark H — Chemist
University of California, Chemistry Dept, 9500 Gilman Dr, La Jolla CA 92093, USA

Thieriot, Max — Actor
Gersh Agency, 9465 Wilshire Blvd, #600, Beverly Hills CA 90212 USA

Thierry, John F — Football Player
6884 Arias Way, Painesville OH 44077, USA

Thiessen, Tiffani — Actress
Paradigm Agency, 360 N Crescent Dr, North Building, Beverly Hills CA 90210 USA

Thiffault, Leo — Ice Hockey Player
1340 Marble Dr, Columbus OH 43227, USA

Thigpen, Curtis B — Baseball Player
1405 W 51st St, Austin TX 78756, USA

Thigpen, Robert T (Bobby) — Baseball Player
1857 Brightwaters Blvd NE, Saint Petersburg FL 33704, USA

Thigpen, Yancey D — Football Player
7210 Yellowhorn Trail, Waxhaw NC 28173, USA

Thile, Christopher S (Chris) — Mandolinist, Guitarist (Nickel Creek)
Creative Artists Agency, 2000 Ave of Stars, #100, Los Angeles CA 90067 USA

Thinnes, Roy — Actor
163 Amsterdam Ave, #307, New York NY 10023, USA

Thirlby, Olivia — Actress
Management 360, 9111 Wilshire Blvd, Beverly Hills CA 90210 USA

Thirlwell, J G — Singer, Songwriter
Agency Group Ltd, 142 W 57th St, #600, New York NY 10019 USA

Thirsk, Robert B (Bob) — Astronaut, Canada
N A S A, Johnson Space Center, 2101 NASA Road, Houston TX 77058 USA

Thistlethwaite, Anthony — Musician (Waterboys)
Agency Group Ltd, 142 W 57th St, #600, New York NY 10019 USA

Thobele, Dingaan B — Boxer
1202 Chiwelo, PO Chiwelo, Soweto 1818, South Africa

Thoen, Skip — Basketball Player
330 Buckland Trace, Louisville KY 40245, USA

Thoenen, Richard C (Dick) — Baseball Player
862 Smith St, Harrisburg OR 97446, USA

Thoeni, Gustav — Alpine Skier, Coach
39026 Prato Allo Stelvio-Prao BZ, Italy

Thom, Bing W
1430 Burrard St, Vancouver BC V6Z 2A3, Canada — Architect
Thoma, Georg
Bisten 6, 79856 Hinterzarten, Germany — Nordic Combined Athlete
Thomas, Aaron N
3793 NW Sparrow Place, Corvallis OR 97330, USA — Football Player
Thomas, Adalius D
195 Highway 9, Kellyton AL 35089, USA — Football Player
Thomas, Andrew S W (Andy)
N A S A, Johnson Space Center, 2101 NASA Road, Houston TX 77058 USA — Astronaut
Thomas, Aurelius
PO Box 91157, Columbus OH 43209, USA — Football Player
Thomas, B Clendon
7508 Rumsey Road, Oklahoma City OK 73132, USA — Football Player
Thomas, B J
Honeymoon Music, PO Box 120003, Arlington TX 76012, USA — Singer, Songwriter
Thomas, Barbara S
News International, 1 Virginia St, London E1 9XY, England — Government Official
Thomas, Benjamin (Ben), Jr
2155 Herndon St, Auburn AL 36830, USA — Football Player
Thomas, Betty
Dominant Pictures, 1438 N Gower St, Building 35, Los Angeles CA 90028, USA — Actress, Director
Thomas, Billy M
626 Sweetbrush, San Antonio TX 78258, USA — Army General
Thomas, Blair L
401 Gulph Ridge Dr, King of Prussia PA 19406, USA — Football Player
Thomas, Broderick L
12004 Opal Creek Dr, Pearland TX 77584, USA — Football Player
Thomas, Cal
Creative Artists Agency, 2000 Ave of Stars, #100, Los Angeles CA 90067 USA — Actor
Thomas, Calvin L
908 Manchester Ave, Westchester IL 60154, USA — Football Player
Thomas, Carla
Rodgers Redding, PO Box 4603, Macon GA 31208 USA — Singer
Thomas, Charles
137 Black Oak Dr, Asheville NC 28804, USA — Baseball Player
Thomas, Charles G (Chuck)
2201 Purple Majesty Court, Las Vegas NV 89117, USA — Football Player
Thomas, Clarence
US Supreme Court, 1 1st St NE, Washington DC 20543 USA — Supreme Court Justice
Thomas, Craig
United Talent Agency, 9336 Civic Center Dr, Beverly Hills CA 90210 USA — Actor, Producer
Thomas, D Etan
2147 Vittoria Court, Bowie MD 20721, USA — Basketball Player
Thomas, Damien
Curtis Brown Group, 28-29 Haymarket St, #500, London SW1Y 4SP, England — Actor
Thomas, Dave G
2115 Salt Myrtle Lane, Orange Park FL 32003, USA — Football Player
Thomas, David
Allied Artists, 42 Montpelier Square, London SE10 8HP, England — Concert Singer
Thomas, David (Dave)
M B S T Entertainment, 345 N Maple Dr, #200, Beverly Hills CA 90210 USA — Actor, Comedian
Thomas, David Clayton
Music Avenue Inc, 43 Washington St, Groveland MA 01834, USA — Singer (Blood Sweat & Tears)
Thomas, David L
Billions Corp, 3522 W Armitage Ave, Chicago IL 60647 USA — Singer (Pere Ubu)
Thomas, Debra J (Debi)
2601 Windward Blvd, Champaign IL 61821, USA — Figure Skater
Thomas, Dennis (Dee Tee)
Spirit Media, PO Box 43591, Phoenix AZ 85080 USA — Saxophonist (Kool & the Gang)
Thomas, Derrel O
112 Juniperhill Lane, Riverside CA 92506, USA — Baseball Player
Thomas, Donald A
1029 Hart Road, Towson MD 21286, USA — Astronaut
Thomas, Donald Michael (D M)
Coach House, Rashleigh Vale, Tregolls Road, Truro, Cornwall TR1 1TJ, England — Writer
Thomas, Dontarrious D
9132 Creek Way, Savage MN 55378, USA — Football Player
Thomas, Earl L
4202 Clearwater City, Missouri City TX 77459, USA — Football Player
Thomas, Earlie B
PO Box 1445, Laporte CO 80535, USA — Football Player
Thomas, Eddie Kaye
Gersh Agency, 9465 Wilshire Blvd, #600, Beverly Hills CA 90212 USA — Actor
Thomas, Elizabeth Marshall
80 E Mountain Road, Peterborough NH 03458, USA — Anthropologist, Environmentalist, Writer
Thomas, Emma
Bloom Hergott Diemer, 150 S Rodeo Dr, #300, Beverly Hills CA 90212 USA — Producer
Thomas, Emmitt E
4603 NE Dick Howser Circle, Lees Summit MO 64064, USA — Football Player, Coach
Thomas, Frank E
1540 Villa Rica Dr, Henderson NV 89052, USA — Baseball Player
Thomas, Frank J
118 Doray Dr, Pittsburgh PA 15237, USA — Baseball Player
Thomas, Gareth
Emptage Hall, 14 Rathbone Place, London W1T 1HT, England — Actor
Thomas, Gareth
University of California, Materials Science Dept, Berkeley CA 94720, USA — Engineer
Thomas, George E, Jr
5804 Ivrea Dr, Sarasota FL 34238, USA — Baseball Player
Thomas, Geraint
Team Barolworld, Trav Via Provinciale 1/C, 25030 Adro (BS), Italy — Cyclist
Thomas, Heather
Innovative Artists, 1505 10th St, Santa Monica CA 90401 USA — Actress
Thomas, Heidi
Lichtman/Salners, 15865 Royal Haven Place, Sherman Oaks CA 91403 USA — Actress

Thomas, Helen A — Journalist
2501 Calvert St NW, #404, Washington DC 20008, USA

Thomas, Henry — Actor
Brillstein Entertainment Partners, 9150 Wilshire Blvd, #350, Beverly Hills CA 90212 USA

Thomas, Henry L, Jr — Football Player
16811 Southern Oaks Dr, Houston TX 77068, USA

Thomas, Henry W — Writer
3214 Warder St NW, Washington DC 20010, USA

Thomas, Hollis — Baseball Player
9163 SE 48th Court Road, Ocala FL 34480, USA

Thomas, Hollis, Jr — Football Player
5957 McLeod Rd, Las Vegas NV 89120, USA

Thomas, Ian — Singer, Songwriter
Anthem Entertainment, 189 Carlton St, Toronto ON M5A 2K7, Canada

Thomas, Irma — Singer
Universal Attractions, 135 W 26th St, #1200, New York NY 10001 USA

Thomas, Irving — Basketball Player
5117 Lakosee Court, Orlando FL 32818, USA

Thomas, Isiah L, III — Basketball Player, Executive, Coach
Florida International University, Athletic Dept, Miami FL 33199, USA

Thomas, J Gorman — Baseball Player
5 Reef Club, Hilton Head Island SC 29926, USA

Thomas, J Leroy (Lee) — Baseball Player
14260 Manderleigh Woods Dr, Chesterfield MO 63017, USA

Thomas, Jake — Actor
Stan Rogow Productions, 3000 Olympic Blvd, Santa Monica CA 90404, USA

Thomas, James (J T) — Football Player
408 Arden Dr, Monroeville PA 15146, USA

Thomas, James E (Jim), Jr — Basketball Player
4499 Willow Hill Road, Portal GA 30450, USA

Thomas, Jay — Actor
Don Buchwald/Fortitude, 6500 Wilshire Blvd, #2200, Los Angeles CA 90048 USA

Thomas, Joe — Football Player
2276 Stones Throw, Westlake OH 44145, USA

Thomas, John C — Track Athlete
51 Mulberry St, Brockton MA 02302, USA

Thomas, John M — Chemist
Royal Institution, 21 Albemarle St, London W1X 4BS, England

Thomas, John T (Bud) — Baseball Player
2475 Woodland Dr, Sedalia MO 65301, USA

Thomas, Johnny, Jr — Football Player
1818 Darby Lane, Fresno TX 77545, USA

Thomas, Jonathan Taylor — Actor
Innovative Artists, 1505 10th St, Santa Monica CA 90401 USA

Thomas, Julian — Archaeologist
Manchester University, Archaeology Dept, Manchester M13 9PL, England

Thomas, Keith V — Historian
Broad Gate, Broad St, Ludlow, Shropshire SY8 1NJ, England

Thomas, Khleo — Actor
Luber Rocklin Entertainment, 8530 Wilshire Blvd, #555, Beverly Hills CA 90211 USA

Thomas, Kiwaukee S — Football Player
9329 Mangrove Court, Tampa FL 33647, USA

Thomas, Kurt — Gymnast
4421 Hidden Hill Road, Norman OK 73072, USA

Thomas, Kurt V — Basketball Player
1826 Brook Terrace Trail, Dallas TX 75232, USA

Thomas, Lamar N — Football Player
10524 NW 13th Lane, Gainesville FL 32606, USA

Thomas, Larry W — Baseball Player
3825 Graham Lane, Eight Mile AL 36613, USA

Thomas, Lavale A — Football Player
7602 Antlers Lane, Charlotte NC 28210, USA

Thomas, Linn — Model, Actress
80 5th Avenue, #908, Box 21, New York NY 10011, USA

Thomas, Mark A — Football Player
556 Hillsboro St, Monticello GA 31064, USA

Thomas, Marlo — Actress
420 E 54th St, #28G, New York NY 10022, USA

Thomas, Mary — Singer (Crystals)
American Mgmt, 19948 Mayall St, Chatsworth CA 91311, USA

Thomas, Michael Tilson — Conductor, Concert Pianist
San Francisco Symphony, Davies Symphony Hall, San Francisco CA 94102, USA

Thomas, Norris L — Football Player
3202 Boston Ave, Pascagoula MS 39581, USA

Thomas, Orlando P — Football Player
330 Mill Pond Dr, Youngsville LA 70592, USA

Thomas, Patrick S (Pat) — Football Player
612 Middle Cove Dr, Plano TX 75023, USA

Thomas, Patrick W (Pat) — Football Player
PO Box 17622, Jacksonville FL 32245, USA

Thomas, Peter — Composer
Via Riviera 28, 6976 Castagnola/Lugano, Switzerland

Thomas, Philip Michael — Actor
PO Box 23714, Brooklyn NY 11202, USA

Thomas, Pinklon — Boxer
2045 Wild Tamarind Blvd, Orlando FL 32828, USA

Thomas, Randy — Football Player
2254 Nelms Dr SW, Atlanta GA 30315, USA

Thomas, Ray — Flutist, Singer (Moody Blues)
Insight Mgmt, 1222 16th Ave S, #300, Nashville TN 37212, USA

Thomas, Reg — Ice Hockey Player
7245 Colonel Talbot Road, London ON N6L 1H9, Canada

Thomas, Richard — Actor
2027 Kentucky Route 825, Hagerhill KY 41222, USA

Thomas, Rob — Singer (Matchbox 20), Songwriter
United Talent Agency, 9336 Civic Center Dr, Beverly Hills CA 90210 USA

Thomas, Robb W 179 NW Outlook Vista Dr, Bend OR 97701, USA	Football Player
Thomas, Robert D 223 Mariomi Road, New Canaan, CT 06840	Publisher
Thomas, Robert R (Bob) 259 Linden St, Glen Ellyn IL 60137, USA	Football Player
Thomas, Robin Marshak/Zachary Co, 8840 Wilshire Blvd, #100, Beverly Hills CA 90211 USA	Actor
Thomas, Rodney D PO Box 664, Groveton TX 75845, USA	Football Player
Thomas, Roy J 6881 SW 167th Place, Beaverton OR 97007, USA	Baseball Player
Thomas, Rozonda (Chilli) Diggit Entertainment, 6 W 18th St, #800, New York NY 10011, USA	Rap Artist (TLC), Actress
Thomas, Scott 49 Redspire Way, East Amherst NY 14051, USA	Ice Hockey Player
Thomas, Sean Bloomsbury Publishing, 36 Soho Square, London W1D 3Q4, England	Writer
Thomas, Sean Patrick Innovative Artists, 1505 10th St, Santa Monica CA 90401 USA	Actor
Thomas, Serena Scott S M S Talent, 8383 Wilshire Blvd, #230, Beverly Hills CA 90211 USA	Actress
Thomas, Sidney R US Court of Appeals, 316 N 26th St, #5405, Billings MT 59101, USA	Judge
Thomas, Stanley B (Stan) 10827 159th Court NE, Redmond WA 98052, USA	Baseball Player
Thomas, Steve Plain & Simple, 289 Bering Ave, Toronto ON M8Z 3A5, Canada	Ice Hockey Player
Thomas, Steve 'This Old House' Show, PO Box 2284, South Burlington VT 05407, USA	Entertainer
Thomas, Tamara Craig Independent Artists Agency, 9601 Wilshire Blvd, #750, Beverly Hills CA 90210, USA	Actress
Thomas, Thurman L 7562 Eddy Road, Colden NY 14033, USA	Football Player
Thomas, Tillman J Prime Minister's Office, Botanical Gardens, Tanteen, Saint George's, Grenada	Prime Minister, Grenada
Thomas, Timothy J (Tim), Jr 29 James Ave, Middleton MA 01949, USA	Ice Hockey Player
Thomas, Timothy M (Tim) Dallas Mavericks, Pavilion, 2909 Taylor St, Dallas TX 75226 USA	Basketball Player
Thomas, Tommy Ivett Stone Agency, W292N6910 Dorn Road, Hartland WI 53029, USA	Singer
Thomas, Tony Creative Artists Agency, 2000 Ave of Stars, #100, Los Angeles CA 90067 USA	Producer, Writer, Actor
Thomas, Tyrus W Charlotte Bobcats, 333 E Trade St, #A, Charlotte NC 28202 USA	Basketball Player
Thomas, Wayne San Jose Sharks, San Jose Arena, 525 W Santa Clara St, San Jose CA 95113 USA	Ice Hockey Player
Thomas, William (Tra), III 17 Elderberry Dr, Medford NJ 08055, USA	Football Player
Thomas, William H, Jr 2401 Echo Dr, Amarillo TX 79107, USA	Football Player
Thomas, Zachary M (Zach) PO Box 491631, Charlotte NC 28269, USA	Football Player
Thomas-Graham, Pamela Liz Claiborne Inc, 1441 Broadway, New York NY 10018, USA	Businesswoman
Thomason, C J Peter Strain, 5455 Wilshire Blvd, #1812, Los Angeles CA 90036 USA	Actor
Thomason, Harry Z 10732 Riverside Dr, North Hollywood CA 91602, USA	Producer
Thomason, M Erskine 932 Dial Place, Laurens SC 29360, USA	Baseball Player
Thomason, Marsha Domain Talent, 9229 W Sunset Blvd, #710, West Hollywood CA 90069 USA	Actress
Thomason, Robert L (Bobby) 2645 Bucknell Ave, Charlotte NC 28207, USA	Football Player
Thomassin, Gerald Artmedia, 20 Ave Rapp, 75007 Paris, France	Actor
Thomasson, Gary L 8300 N 53rd St, Paradise Valley AZ 85253, USA	Baseball Player
Thome, James H (Jim) 125 E 8th St, Hinsdale IL 60521, USA	Baseball Player
Thomerson, Tim Innovative Artists, 1505 10th St, Santa Monica CA 90401 USA	Actor
Thomese, P F Bloomsbury Publishing, 36 Soho Square, London W1D 3Q4, England	Writer
Thomopoulos, Anthony D 5357 Long Shadow Court, Westlake Village CA 91362, USA	Businessman
Thompson, Alexis (Lexi) Ladies Pro Golf Assn, 100 International Golf Dr, Daytona Beach FL 32124 USA	Golfer
Thompson, Andrea Sovereign Talent Group, 8421 Wilshire Blvd, #200, Beverly Hills CA 90211 USA	Actress
Thompson, Andrew J (Andy) 1405 Bayshore Blvd, Tampa FL 33606, USA	Baseball Player
Thompson, Anthony 5035 E DeAnn Dr, Bloomington IN 47404, USA	Football Player, Coach
Thompson, April Yvette SimonSez Entertainment, 12 Desbrosses St, New York NY 10013, USA	Actress
Thompson, Arland L 6692 S Routt St, Littleton CO 80127, USA	Football Player
Thompson, Aundra 12060 Galva Dr, Dallas TX 75243, USA	Football Player
Thompson, Barbara 1721 Edgebrook Dr, Rockford IL 61107, USA	Baseball Player
Thompson, Bennie 10157 Placid Lake Court, Columbia MD 21044, USA	Football Player

Thompson, Bobb'e J — Rap Artist, Actor
I C M Partners, 10250 Constellation Blvd, #900, Los Angeles CA 90067 USA

Thompson, Bobby L — Baseball Player
7006 Hunters Glen Dr, Charlotte NC 28214, USA

Thompson, Brent K — Ice Hockey Player
New York Islanders, 1255 Hempstead Turnpike, Uniondale NY 11553 USA

Thompson, Brian — Actor, Director, Writer
David Shapira Assoc, 193 N Robertson Blvd, Beverly Hills CA 90211 USA

Thompson, Brooke — Actress
10515 Mersham Hill Dr, Bakersfield CA 93311, USA

Thompson, Brooks J — Basketball Player
29222 Oakview Ridge, Boerne TX 78015, USA

Thompson, Caroline W — Writer, Director
I C M Partners, 10250 Constellation Blvd, #900, Los Angeles CA 90067 USA

Thompson, Charles L (Tim) — Baseball Player
536 Summit Dr, Lewistown PA 17044, USA

Thompson, Chaun T — Football Player
10514 Huffines Dr, Rowlett TX 75089, USA

Thompson, Chris — Producer, Writer
Rothman Brecher Agency, 9465 Wilshire Blvd, #840, Beverly Hills CA 90212 USA

Thompson, Christopher — Actor
Artmedia, 20 Ave Rapp, 75007 Paris, France

Thompson, Christopher — Astrophysicist
University of North Carolina, Astrophysics Dept, Chapel Hill NC 27599, USA

Thompson, Cornelius A (Corny) — Basketball Player
207 Lamentation Dr, Berlin CT 06037, USA

Thompson, Darrell A — Football Player
4220 Oakview Lane N, Minneapolis MN 55442, USA

Thompson, David O — Basketball Player, Executive
5114 Berkeley Creek Lane, Charlotte NC 28277, USA

Thompson, David W — Space Scientist, Businessman
Orbital Science Corp, 21839 Atlantic Blvd, Dulles VA 20166, USA

Thompson, Derek — Baseball Player
3212 Pine Shadow Dr, Land O'Lakes FL 34639, USA

Thompson, Derrius D — Football Player
3820 Vitruvian Way, #118, Addison TX 75001, USA

Thompson, Don — Businessman
McDonald's Corp, McDonald's Plaza, 1 Kroc Dr, Oak Brook IL 60523, USA

Thompson, Edward K — Editor
300 Riverside Dr, #10E, New York NY 10025, USA

Thompson, Edward T — Editor
11 Cotswold Dr, North Salem NY 10560, USA

Thompson, Emma — Actress
Hamilton Hodell, 66-68 Margaret St, London W1W 8SR, England

Thompson, Ernest — Writer
RR 1 Box 3240, Ashland NH 03217, USA

Thompson, Errol — Ice Hockey Player
PO Box 58, Station Main, Summerside PE C1N 4P6, Canada

Thompson, F M (Daley) — Track Athlete
Olympic Assn, 1 Wadsworth Plain, London SW18 1EH, England

Thompson, Fred Dalton — Senator, TN; Actor
Paradigm Agency, 360 Park Ave S, #1600, New York NY 10010 USA

Thompson, G Ralph — Religious Leader
Seventh-Day Adventists, 12501 Old Columbia Pike, Silver Spring MD 20904, USA

Thompson, Gary — Basketball Player
2531 Park Vista Circle, Ames IA 50014, USA

Thompson, Gary Scott — Writer, Producer
W M E Entertainment, 9601 Wilshire Blvd, #300, Beverly Hills CA 90210 USA

Thompson, Gerald — Opera Singer
I M G Artists, Hogarth Business Park, Chiswick, London W4 2TH, England

Thompson, Gina — Singer
Richard Walters, PO Box 2789, Toluca Lake CA 91610 USA

Thompson, Hilary — Actress
13202 Weddington St, Sherman Oaks CA 91401, USA

Thompson, Hugh D (Rocky) — Golfer
2608 Chamberlain Dr, Plano TX 75023, USA

Thompson, Hugh L — Educator
752 Bayside Dr, #402, Cape Canaveral FL 32920, USA

Thompson, Ian — Landscape Architect
Bloomsbury Publishing, 36 Soho Square, London W1D 3Q4, England

Thompson, Jack — Actor
June Cann Mgmt, 118 Oxford St, Woollahra NSW 2025, Australia

Thompson, Jack B — Football Player
10439 7th Ave SW, Seattle WA 98146, USA

Thompson, James — Writer
G P Putnam's Sons, 375 Hudson St, New York NY 10014 USA

Thompson, James B, Jr — Geologist
1010 Waltham St, #1, Lexington MA 02421, USA

Thompson, James R (Jim), Jr — Governor, IL
Winston & Strawn, 35 W Wacker Dr, #2800, Chicago IL 60601, USA

Thompson, James R, Jr — Space Administrator
5046 Somerby Dr SE, Huntsville AL 35802, USA

Thompson, Jason — Basketball Player
Sacramento Kings, Arco Arena, 1 Sports Parkway, Sacramento CA 95834 USA

Thompson, Jason C — Actor
Innovative Artists, 1505 10th St, Santa Monica CA 90401 USA

Thompson, Jason D — Baseball Player
4056 Summerfield Dr, Troy MI 48085, USA

Thompson, Jason M — Baseball Player
10359 Trillium Dr, Las Vegas NV 89135, USA

Thompson, Jennifer (Jenny) — Swimmer
6 Evans Dr, Dover NH 03820, USA

Thompson, Jill — Cartoonist
D C Comics, 1700 Broadway, #400, New York NY 10019 USA

Thompson, Jody — Actress
Characters Talent, 200-1505 W 2nd Ave, Vancouver BC V6H 3Y4, Canada

Thompson, John Griggs
University of Florida, Mathematics Dept, PO Box 118105, Gainesville FL 32611, USA — Abel Mathematics Laureate

Thompson, John R
3636 16th St NW, #B1161, Washington DC 20010, USA — Basketball Player, Coach, Sportscaster

Thompson, Justin W
37111 Edgewater Dr, Pinehurst TX 77362, USA — Baseball Player

Thompson, Kenan
United Talent Agency, 9336 Civic Center Dr, Beverly Hills CA 90210 USA — Actor

Thompson, Kenneth L
A T & T Bell Lucent Laboratory, 600 Mountain Ave, New Providence NJ 07974 USA — Computer Scientist

Thompson, Klay A
Golden State Warriors, 1011 Broadway, Oakland CA 94605 USA — Basketball Player

Thompson, L Donnell
7503 Kepley Road, Chapel Hill NC 27517, USA — Football Player

Thompson, Lamont D
1320 Wildwing Lane, Vallejo CA 94591, USA — Football Player

Thompson, Larry D
PepsiCo, 700 Anderson Hill Road, Purchase NY 10577, USA — Government Official

Thompson, LaSalle
3805 Northcliff Lane, Roseville CA 95747, USA — Basketball Player

Thompson, Lea
Innovative Artists, 1505 10th St, Santa Monica CA 90401 USA — Actress

Thompson, Lee (Kix)
I T F, Ariel House, 74A Charlotte St, London W1T 4QJ, England — Singer, Saxophonist (Madness)

Thompson, Leonard I
5534 W Glenrosa Ave, Phoenix AZ 85031, USA — Football Player

Thompson, Leonard S
9010 Marsh View Court, Ponte Vedra FL 32082, USA — Golfer

Thompson, Linda
Shore Fire Media, 32 Court St, #1600, Brooklyn NY 11201 USA — Singer

Thompson, Linda
6342 Sycamore Meadows Dr, Malibu CA 90265, USA — Actress, Songwriter

Thompson, Lonnie
Ohio State University, Geology Dept, Columbus OH 43210, USA — Glaciologist

Thompson, Mark R
2600 Chandler Dr, #1311, Bowling Green KY 42104, USA — Baseball Player

Thompson, Mike
Detroit Free Press, Editorial Dept, 600 W Fort St, Detroit MI 48226 USA — Editorial Cartoonist

Thompson, Milton B (Milt)
PO Box 663, Williamstown NJ 08094, USA — Baseball Player

Thompson, Mychal G
11 Paverstone Lane, Laderna Ranch CA 92694, USA — Basketball Player

Thompson, Norman J (Norm)
PO Box 4552, Hayward CA 94540, USA — Football Player

Thompson, Obadele
Amateur Athletics Assn, PO Box 46, Bridgetown, Barbados — Track Athlete

Thompson, Paul R J N
M A M A Group, 57-65 Worship Ave, London EC2A 2DU, England — Drummer (Franz Ferdinand)

Thompson, Paul S
3422 N 40th St, Milwaukee WI 53216, USA — Basketball Player

Thompson, Reece
Play Mgmt, 807 Powell St, #220, Vancouver BC V6A 1H7, Canada — Actor

Thompson, Reyna O
1502 NW 183rd Terrace, Pembroke Pines FL 33029, USA — Football Player

Thompson, Richard
Rosebud Agency, PO Box 170429, San Francisco CA 94117 USA — Singer, Songwriter, Guitarist

Thompson, Richard
Universal Press Syndicate, 4520 Main St, #700, Kansas City MO 64111 USA — Cartoonist (Cul de Sac)

Thompson, Richard G
Oakland Athletics, McAfee Coliseum, 7000 Coliseum Way, #3, Oakland CA 94621 USA — Baseball Player

Thompson, Richard N (Rich)
7 Chambers Court, Huntington Station NY 11746, USA — Baseball Player

Thompson, Ricky D
1277 Brazos Bluff Dr, China Spring TX 76633, USA — Football Player

Thompson, Robert L (Bobby)
10712 S 7th Ave, Inglewood CA 90303, USA — Football Player

Thompson, Robert R (Robby)
4438 Gun Club Road, West Palm Beach FL 33406, USA — Baseball Player

Thompson, Rocky L
Oklahoma City Barons, 501 N Walker, #140, Oklahoma City OK 73102, USA — Ice Hockey Player

Thompson, Ryan O
2153 Fullerton Dr, Indianapolis IN 46214, USA — Baseball Player

Thompson, Sarah
Brillstein Entertainment Partners, 9150 Wilshire Blvd, #350, Beverly Hills CA 90212 USA — Actress

Thompson, Scott
Sovereign Talent Group, 8421 Wilshire Blvd, #200, Beverly Hills CA 90211 USA — Actor, Singer

Thompson, Scott
ShopRunner, 225 Washington St, #300, Conshohocken PA 19428, USA — Businessman

Thompson, Scottie
M P G Mgmt, 1136 Roxbury Drive, Los Angeles CA 90035, USA — Actress

Thompson, Sophie
Saint James Mgmt, 22 Groom Place, London SW1, England — Actress

Thompson, Steve M
Victory Foursquare Gospel Church, 11911 State Ave, Marysville WA 98271, USA — Football Player

Thompson, Sue
Curb Entertainment, 3907 W Alameda Ave, #200, Burbank CA 91505, USA — Singer, Guitarist

Thompson, Susanna
Paradigm Agency, 360 N Crescent Dr, North Building, Beverly Hills CA 90210 USA — Actress

Thompson, Taylor Ann
A P A Talent/Literary Agency, 405 S Beverly Dr, #300, Beverly Hills CA 90212 USA — Actress

Thompson, Ted C
222 Nicolet Place, De Pere WI 54115, USA — Football Player

Thompson, Teddy
Gold Village Entertainment, 72 Madison Ave, #800, New York NY 10016, USA — Singer, Songwriter

Thompson, Teri
Red Talent, 9595 Wilshire Blvd, #900, Beverly Hills CA 90212, USA — Actress

Thompson, Tessa
Greene Assoc, 1901 Ave of Stars, #130, Los Angeles CA 90067 USA — *Actress*

Thompson, Tina M
Los Angeles Sparks, 888 S Figueroa St, #2010, Los Angeles CA 90017 USA — *Basketball Player*

Thompson, Tommy G
1313 Manassas Trail, Madison WI 53718, USA — *Secretary, Health & Human Services*

Thompson, Tristan T J
Cleveland Cavaliers, Gund Arena, 1 Center Court, Cleveland OH 44115 USA — *Basketball Player*

Thompson, U Leroy
5005 Princess Anne Court, Knoxville TN 37918, USA — *Football Player*

Thompson, V Scot
330 Dodds Road, Butler PA 16002, USA — *Baseball Player*

Thompson, Verlon
V N S Records, 9 Music Square S, #148, Nashville TN 37203, USA — *Singer, Guitarist, Songwriter*

Thompson, Wilbur (Moose)
1111 Stevely Ave, Long Beach CA 90815, USA — *Track Athlete*

Thompson, William A (Billy)
6522 Jackson Court, Littleton CO 80130, USA — *Football Player*

Thompson, William T (Billy)
19678 Palm Spring Dr, Boca Raton FL 33428, USA — *Basketball Player*

Thompson, Willis H (Weegie)
14501 Felbridge Way, Midlothian VA 23113, USA — *Football Player*

Thoms, Arthur W (Art), Jr
90 Goodfellow Dr, Moraga CA 94556, USA — *Football Player*

Thoms, Tracie
Gersh Agency, 41 Madison Ave, #3301, New York NY 10010 USA — *Actress*

Thomsen, Cecile
Art Mgmt, Kronprinsensgade 9A, Copenhagen K, CPH 1114, Denmark — *Actress*

Thomsen, Martha E
Playboy Promotions, 2706 Media Center Dr, Los Angeles CA 90065 USA — *Actress, Model*

Thomsen, Ulrich
Greene Assoc, 1901 Ave of Stars, #130, Los Angeles CA 90067 USA — *Actor*

Thomson of Fleet, David
Thomson Newspapers, 65 Queen St W, Toronto ON M5H 2M8, Canada — *Businessman*

Thomson, Brian E
5 Little Dowling St, Paddington NSW 2021, Australia — *Designer*

Thomson, Cyndi
The Firm, 2049 Century Park E, #2550, Los Angeles CA 90067 USA — *Singer*

Thomson, Erik
R G M Associates, 64-76 Kippax St, #202, Surry Hills NSW 2010, Australia — *Actor*

Thomson, Floyd
General Delivery, Dunchurch ON P0A 1G0, Canada — *Ice Hockey Player*

Thomson, Gordon
Gage Group, 14724 Ventura Blvd, #505, Sherman Oaks CA 91403 USA — *Actor*

Thomson, H C (Hank)
PO Box 38, Mullett Lake MI 49761, USA — *Harness Racing Official*

Thomson, James A
University of Wisconsin, Morgridge Research Institute, Madison WI 53706, USA — *Biologist*

Thomson, John C
1414 E Kent St, Sulphur LA 70663, USA — *Baseball Player*

Thomson, Judith J
Massachusetts Institute of Technology, Philosophy Dept, Cambridge MA 02139, USA — *Philosopher, Metaphysician*

Thomson, June
KNBC-TV, News Dept, 3000 W Alameda Ave, Burbank CA 91523, USA — *Commentator*

Thomson, Kim
Caroline Dawson, 125 Gloucester Road, London SW7 4TE, England — *Actress*

Thomson, Kristen
LaFeaver Talent Mgmt, 162 John St, #300, Toronto ON M5V 2E5, Canada — *Actress*

Thomson, Peter W
Carmel House, 44 Mathoura Road, Toorak VIC 3142, Australia — *Golfer*

Thomson, Rupert
Bloomsbury Publishing, 36 Soho Square, London W1D 3Q4, England — *Writer*

Thon, Olaf
Rosenthaler Str 40-41, Hackesche Hofe, 10178 Berlin, Germany — *Soccer Player*

Thon, Richard W (Dickie)
C17 Calle Lirio del Mar, Urb Dorado del Mar, Dorado PR 00646, USA — *Baseball Player*

Thone, Charles
Erickson & Sederstrom, 301 S 13th St, #400, Lincoln NE 68508, USA — *Governor, NE*

Thor, Brad
Pocket Books, 1230 Ave of Americas, New York NY 10020 USA — *Writer*

Thora
C E S D, 10635 Santa Monica Blvd, #130, Los Angeles CA 90025 USA — *Actress*

Thorburn, Clifford C D (Cliff)
31 West Side Dr, Markham ON L3P 7J5, Canada — *Snooker Player*

Thorell, Clarke
Paradigm Agency, 360 N Crescent Dr, North Building, Beverly Hills CA 90210 USA — *Actor*

Thoresen, Jan
Curling Assn, Sognsveien 75, Serviceboks 1, 0840 Oslo, Norway — *Curling Athlete*

Thorin, Donald E, Sr
15260 Ventura Blvd, #1040, Sherman Oaks CA 91403, USA — *Cinematographer*

Thormodsgard, Paul G
7752 E Rose Lane, Scottsdale AZ 85250, USA — *Baseball Player*

Thorn, Christopher
Shapiro Co, 9229 W Sunset Blvd, #607, West Hollywood CA 90069 USA — *Guitarist (Blind Melon)*

Thorn, Erin
New York Liberty, Madison Square Garden, 2 Penn Plaza, New York NY 10121 USA — *Basketball Player*

Thorn, Paul
Paradigm Agency, 360 N Crescent Dr, North Building, Beverly Hills CA 90210 USA — *Singer, Songwriter*

Thorn, Rodney K (Rod)
17008 Treviso Way, Naples FL 34110, USA — *Basketball Player, Executive*

Thorn, Tracey
J F D Mgmt, Acklam Workshops, 10 Acklam Road, London W10 5QZ, England — *Singer (Everything But the Girl)*

Thornburgh, Richard L (Dick)
Kirkpatrick & Lockhart, 210 6th Ave, #1100, Pittsburgh PA 15222, USA — *Attorney General; Governor, PA*

Thorne, Bella
Kritzer Levine, 11872 La Grange Ave, #100, Los Angeles CA 90025, USA — *Actress*

Thorne, Callie Gersh Agency, 41 Madison Ave, #3301, New York NY 10010 USA	Actress
Thorne, Frank 1967 Grenville Road, Scotch Plains NJ 07076, USA	Cartoonist (Moonshine McJuggs)
Thorne, Gary 55 W Chops Point Road, Bath ME 04530, USA	Commentator
Thorne, Kip S California Institute of Technology, Physics Dept, Pasadena CA 91125, USA	Physicist
Thornell, Jack R 3421 Tennessee Ave, Kenner LA 70065, USA	Photojournalist
Thorne-Smith, Courtney W M E Entertainment, 9601 Wilshire Blvd, #300, Beverly Hills CA 90210 USA	Actress, Model
Thornhill, Lisa 208-11 Anin St, Bedford Nova Scotia B4A 4E3, Canada	Actress
Thorning-Schmidt, Helle Christiansborg Palace, Prins Jorgens Gard 11, 1218 Copenhagen K, Denmark	Prime Minister, Denmark
Thornton, Al Golden State Warriors, 1011 Broadway, Oakland CA 94605 USA	Basketball Player
Thornton, Billy Bob Media Talent Group, 9200 W Sunset Blvd, #550, West Hollywood CA 90069 USA	Actor, Director
Thornton, Frank David Daly, 586A King Road, London SW6 2DX, England	Actor
Thornton, James M 1010 Fuller Road, Gurnee IL 60031, USA	Football Player
Thornton, Joseph E (Joe) 20121 Hill Ave, Saratoga CA 95070, USA	Ice Hockey Player
Thornton, Kathryn C 100 Bedford Place, Charlottesville VA 22903, USA	Astronaut
Thornton, Kevin J-Bird Entertainment, 4905 S Atlantic Ave, Ponce Inlet FL 32127 USA	Singer (Color Me Badd)
Thornton, Louis (Lou) 725 Henderson Road, Hope Hull AL 36043, USA	Baseball Player
Thornton, Matthew J (Matt) 9820 W Eagle Talon Trail, Peoria AZ 85383, USA	Baseball Player
Thornton, Melody J H Mgmt, 420 Lexington Ave, #331, New York NY 10170 USA	Singer (Pussycat Dolls), Actress
Thornton, Michael E 17040 W FM 1097 Road, #6101, Montgomery TX 77356, USA	Vietnam War Navy Air Hero (CMH)
Thornton, Otis B 4312 Ave L, Birmingham AL 35208, USA	Baseball Player
Thornton, Robert G (Bob) 27865 Espinoza, Mission Viejo CA 92692, USA	Basketball Player
Thornton, Scott C 624 30th St, Manhattan Beach CA 90266, USA	Ice Hockey Player
Thornton, Shawn 12 Sackville St, #2, Charlestown MA 02129, USA	Ice Hockey Player
Thornton, Sidney 8537 Parkdale Dr, Shreveport LA 71108, USA	Football Player
Thornton, Sigrid Australian Film Institute, 236 Dorcas St, South Melbourne VIC 3205, Australia	Actress
Thornton, Tiffany C E S D, 10635 Santa Monica Blvd, #130, Los Angeles CA 90025 USA	Actress
Thornton, William E 7640 Pimilco Lane, Boerne TX 78015, USA	Astronaut
Thornton, Zach Club Deportivo Chivas, 18400 Avalon Blvd, #500, Carson CA 90746 USA	Soccer Player
Thorogood, George Monterey International, 200 W Superior St, #202, Chicago IL 60654 USA	Singer, Guitarist
Thorp, H Holden University of North Carolina, Chancellor's Office, South Building, Chapel Hill NC 27599, USA	Educator
Thorpe, Harriet Gavin Barker Assoc, 2D Wimpole St, London W1G 0EB, England	Actress
Thorpe, Ian Grand Slam International, PO Box 402, Manly NSW 1655, Australia	Swimmer
Thorpe, J Jeremy 2 Orme Square, Bayswater, London W2 4RS, England	Government Official, England
Thorpe, Jason	Actor
Thorpe, Jimmy L (Jim) 1612 Kersley Circle, Lake Mary FL 32746, USA	Golfer
Thorpe, Otis H PO Box 400, Canfield OH 44406, USA	Basketball Player
Thorsness, Leo K 239 Watterson Way, Madison AL 35756, USA	Vietnam Air Force Hero (CMH)
Thorson, Linda Noble Caplan Abrams, 1260 Yonge St, #200, Toronto ON M4T 1W6, Canada	Actress
Thost, Nicola German Competitors Assn, Kuppenheimstr 15, 75179 Pforzheim, Germany	Snowboard Skier
Thouless, David James University of Washington, Physics Dept, Seattle WA 98195, USA	Physicist
Thrash, James 16005 Hampton Road, Hamilton VA 20158, USA	Football Player
Thrash, William G 8 Hadley Lane, Hilton Head Island SC 29926, USA	Marine Corps General
Threadgill, Henry L Joel Chriss, 60 E 8th St, #34N, New York NY 10003 USA	Jazz Saxophonist, Composer
Threatt, Sedale E PO Box 1085, Alabaster AL 35007, USA	Basketball Player
Threets, Erick 2080 Vintage Lane, Livermore CA 94550, USA	Baseball Player
Threlfall, David James Sharkey, 34 Kingly Court, London W1R 5LE, England	Actor
Thrift, Clifford R (Cliff) 705 Trisha Lane, Norman OK 73072, USA	Football Player
Thorne, Malachi Classic Tank, 650 N Bronson Ave, Los Angeles CA 90004, USA	Actor

Throop, George L
239 Windwood Lane, Sierra Madre CA 91024, USA — Baseball Player

Thrower, James M (Jim)
17421 Pontchartrain Blvd, Detroit MI 48203, USA — Football Player

Thuillier, Luc
Artmedia, 20 Ave Rapp, 75007 Paris, France — Actor

Thumann, Chad
United Talent Agency, 9336 Civic Center Dr, Beverly Hills CA 90210 USA — Writer, Actor

Thun, Matteo
9 Via Appiani, 20121 Milan, Italy — Interior Designer

Thune, Nick
3 Arts Entertainment, 9460 Wilshire Blvd, #700, Beverly Hills CA 90212 USA — Actor, Comedian

Thunman, Nils R
1516 S Willemore Ave, Springfield IL 62704, USA — Navy Admiral

Thuot, Pierre J
22897 Thornbury Dr, Hollywood MD 20636, USA — Astronaut

Thurber, Rawson Marshall
Creative Artists Agency, 2000 Ave of Stars, #100, Los Angeles CA 90067 USA — Director, Writer, Actor

Thurier, Blaine
Skrzyniarz & Mallean, 9229 Sunset Blvd, #525, Los Angeles CA 90069, USA — Singer, Director

Thurlow, Stephen C (Steve)
198 Shore Road, Old Greenwich CT 06870, USA — Football Player

Thurman, Dennis L
1 Jets Dr, Florham Park NJ 07932, USA — Football Player

Thurman, Gary M
225 W 32nd St, Indianapolis IN 46208, USA — Baseball Player

Thurman, James D
Commanding General, Army Forces Command, Atlanta GA 30330 USA — Army General

Thurman, Michael R (Mike)
1360 7th St, West Linn OR 97068, USA — Baseball Player

Thurman, Uma
Untitled Entertainment, 350 S Beverly Dr, #200, Beverly Hills CA 90212 USA — Actress, Model

Thurman, William E
10 Firestone Dr, Pinehurst NC 28374, USA — Air Force General

Thurmond, Mark A
1614 Kings Castle Dr, Katy TX 77450, USA — Baseball Player

Thurmond, Nathaniel (Nate)
5094 Diamond Heights Blvd, #B, San Francisco CA 94131, USA — Basketball Player, Executive

Thurow, Lester C
Massachusetts Institute of Technology, Economics Dept, Cambridge MA 02139, USA — Economist

Thurston, Frederick C (Fuzzy)
E1462 Grandview Road, Waupaca WI 54981, USA — Football Player

Thurston, Joseph W (Joe)
9024 Paso Robles Way, Elk Grove CA 95758, USA — Baseball Player

Thyer, Mario
170 Silver Road, Bangor ME 04401, USA — Ice Hockey Player

Thyne, T J
Greene Assoc, 1901 Ave of Stars, #130, Los Angeles CA 90067 USA — Actor

Thyssen, Greta
444 E 82nd St, New York NY 10028, USA — Actress

TI
J L Entertainment, 18653 Ventura Blvd, #340, Tarzana CA 91356 USA — Rap Artist, Actor

Tian, Valerie
Greene Assoc, 1901 Ave of Stars, #130, Los Angeles CA 90067 USA — Actress

Tiant, Luis C
24 Southwood Dr, Southborough MA 01772, USA — Baseball Player

Tiao, Luc-Adolphe
Prime Minister's Office, 03 BP 7027, Ouagadougou 03, Burkina Faso — Prime Minister, Burkina Faso

Tibbetts, Billy
79 Jericho Road, Scituate MA 02066, USA — Ice Hockey Player

Tibbs, Jay L
905 Smith Road, Oneonta AL 35121, USA — Baseball Player

Ticci, Stefano
Olympic Committee, Foro Italico, Largo Lauro de Bosis 15, 00135 Rome, Italy — Bobsled Athlete

Tice, George A
581 Kings Highway E, Atlantic Hills NJ 07716, USA — Photographer

Tice, John K
1004 Bartlett Loop, West Point NY 10996, USA — Football Player

Tice, Michael P (Mike)
1213 Ashbury Lane, Libertyville IL 60048, USA — Football Player, Coach

Tich
Gerd Kehren Mgmt, Postfach 1408, 41804 Erkelenz, Germany — Musician (Dave Dee Dozy Beaky Mick Tich)

Tichy, Milan
2413 NW 7th St, Boynton Beach FL 33426, USA — Ice Hockey Player

Tickner, Charles (Charlie)
5410 Sunset Dr, Littleton CO 80123, USA — Figure Skater

Ticotin, Rachel
Stone Manners Salners, 9911 W Pico Blvd, #1400, Los Angeles CA 90035 USA — Actress

Tidrow, Richard W (Dick)
324 NE Warrington Court, Lees Summit MO 64064, USA — Baseball Player

Tidwell, Moody R, III
US Claims Court, 717 Madison Place NW, Washington DC 20439, USA — Judge

Tiefenthaler, Verle M
1852 Quint Ave, Carroll IA 51401, USA — Baseball Player

Tiegs, Cheryl
809 Nimes, Los Angeles CA 90077, USA — Model

Tierney, Garrett
Stunt Company Media, 20 Jay St, #208, Brooklyn NY 11201, USA — Bassist (Brand New)

Tierney, Maura
Creative Artists Agency, 2000 Ave of Stars, #100, Los Angeles CA 90067 USA — Actress

Tierney, William (Bill)
Denver University, Athletic Dept, Peter Barton Stadium, Denver CO 80210, USA — Lacrosse Coach

Tiffany
Sharp & Assoc, 1516 N Fairfax Ave, Los Angeles CA 90046, USA — Singer, Model

Tiffany, John
Casorotto Ramsay, Waverley House, 7-12 Noel St, London W1F 8GQ, England — Director

Tiffee, Terry R — Baseball Player
2620 Calico Creek Dr, North Little Rock AR 72116, USA
Tiffin, Pamela — Actress
15 W 67th St, New York NY 10023, USA
Tigah — Rap Artist
Columbia Records, 9830 Wilshire Blvd, Beverly Hills CA 90212 USA
Tigar, Kenneth — Actor
Gage Group, 14724 Ventura Blvd, #505, Sherman Oaks CA 91403 USA
Tigelaar, Liz — Producer, Writer
W M E Entertainment, 9601 Wilshire Blvd, #300, Beverly Hills CA 90210 USA
Tiger, Lionel — Anthropologist, Social Scientist
248 W 23rd St, #400, New York NY 10011, USA
Tigerman, Stanley — Architect
910 N Lakeshore Dr, #2916, Chicago IL 60611, USA
Tighe, Kevin — Actor
Domain Talent, 9229 W Sunset Blvd, #710, West Hollywood CA 90069 USA
Tijan, Robert — Biochemist, Molecular Biologist
Howard Hughes Medical Institution, 4000 Jones Bridge Road, Chevy Chase MD 20815, USA
Tilbrook, Glenn — Singer, Guitarist (Squeeze)
Agency Group Ltd, 361-373 City Road, London EC1V 2QA, England
Tilelli, John H, Jr — Army General
Stanford University, International Studies Dept, Stanford CA 94305, USA
Tilghman, Kelly — Sportscaster
Golf Channel, 7580 Commerce Center Dr, Orlando FL 32819, USA
Tilghman, Shirley M C — Educator, Molecular Biologist
Princeton University, President's Office, Princeton NJ 08544, USA
Tiliakos, Dimitris — Opera Singer
I M G Artists, Hogarth Business Park, Chiswick, London W4 2TH, England
Till, James E — Biophysicist, Cell Biologist
182 Briar Hill Ave, Toronto ON M4R 1H9, Canada
Tilleman, Michael J (Mike) — Football Player
180 Country Road 800 NW, Havre MT 59501, USA
Tiller, Nadja — Actress
Via Tamporiva 26, 6976 Castagnola, Switzerland
Tillerson, Rex W — Businessman
ExxonMobil Corp, 5959 Las Colinas Blvd, Irving TX 75039, USA
Tilley, Patrick L (Pat) — Football Player, Coach
PO Box 4523, Shreveport LA 71134, USA
Tilley, Tom — Ice Hockey Player
14724 Maple St, Overland Park KS 66223, USA
Tilling, Camilla — Opera, Concert Singer
Harrison/Parrott, 5-6 Albion Court, London W6 0QT, England
Tillis, Mel — Singer, Guitarist, Songwriter
Mel Tillis Enterprises, PO Box 305, Silver Springs FL 34489, USA
Tillis, Pam — Singer, Songwriter
PO Box 128575, Nashville TN 37212, USA
Tillman, Charles — Football Player
31227 Sage Court, Libertyville IL 60048, USA
Tillman, George, Jr — Director, Producer, Writer
State Street Pictures, 9255 W Sunset Blvd, #528, Los Angeles CA 90069, USA
Tillman, Kerry J (Rusty) — Baseball Player
8711 Newton Road, #61, Jacksonville FL 32216, USA
Tillman, Lewis D — Football Player
PO Box 166, Madison MS 39130, USA
Tillman, Robert L — Businessman
Lowe's Companies, 1605 Curtis Bridge Road, Wilkesboro NC 28697, USA
Tillman, Spencer A — Football Player
19 Lake Mist Court, Sugar Land TX 77479, USA
Tillman, Travares A — Football Player
3720 Tanglewood Dr SE, Atlanta GA 30339, USA
Tillmans, Wolfgang — Artist, Photographer
Maureen Paley Interim Art, 21 Herald St, London E 6JT, England
Tillotson, Johnny — Singer
American Mgmt, 19948 Mayall St, Chatsworth CA 91311, USA
Tilly, Jennifer — Actress
Innovative Artists, 1505 10th St, Santa Monica CA 90401 USA
Tilly, Meg — Actress
I F A Talent Agency, 8730 W Sunset Blvd, #490, West Hollywood CA 90069 USA
Tilson, Joseph (Joe) — Artist
2 Brook Street Mansions, 41 Davies St, London W1Y 1FJ, England
Tilton, Charlene — Actress
Mike Pingel, 1155 Hacienda Place, #309, West Hollywood CA 90069, USA
Tilton, Robert — Evangelist
Robert Tilton Ministries, PO Box 819000, Dallas TX 75381, USA
Timbaland — Rap Artist, Music Producer
W M E Entertainment, 9601 Wilshire Blvd, #300, Beverly Hills CA 90210 USA
Timberlake, Gary D — Baseball Player
14016 Waters Edge Dr, Louisville KY 40245, USA
Timberlake, Justin — Singer ('N Sync), Actor
W M E Entertainment, 9601 Wilshire Blvd, #300, Beverly Hills CA 90210 USA
Timchal, Cindy — Lacrosse Coach
University of Maryland, Athletic Dept, College Park MD 20742, USA
Timken, William R, Jr — Businessman, Diplomat
State Department, 2201 C St NW, Washington DC 20520 USA
Timko, Brittany — Soccer Player
Canadian Soccer, Place Soccer Canada, 237 Metcalfe St, Ottawa ON K2P 1R2, Canada
Timlin, Addison — Actress
Gersh Agency, 9465 Wilshire Blvd, #600, Beverly Hills CA 90212 USA
Timlin, Michael A (Mike) — Baseball Player
355 High Ridge Way, Castle Rock CO 80108, USA
Timmer, Marianne — Speed Skater
K N S B, Postbus 1120, 3800 BC Amersfoort, Netherlands
Timmerman, Adam L — Football Player
1635 585th St, Cherokee IA 51012, USA
Timmermann, Thomas H (Tom) — Baseball Player
197 Coyote Court, Pinckney MI 48169, USA

Timmermann, Ulf — Track Athlete
Conrad Blenkle Str 34, 13055 Berlin, Germany

Timmins, Margo — Singer (Cowboy Junkies)
S L Feldman Mgmt, 1505 W 2nd Ave, #200, Vancouver BC V6H 3Y4, Canada

Timmins, Michael — Guitarist (Cowboy Junkies), Songwriter
S L Feldman Mgmt, 1505 W 2nd Ave, #200, Vancouver BC V6H 3Y4, Canada

Timmins, Peter — Drummer (Cowboy Junkies)
S L Feldman Mgmt, 1505 W 2nd Ave, #200, Vancouver BC V6H 3Y4, Canada

Timmons, Jeffrey B (Jeff) — Singer (98 Degrees)
Rudolph & Beer, 432 Park Ave S, New York NY 10016, USA

Timmons, Osborne L (Ozzie) — Baseball Player
4901 S 83rd St, Tampa FL 33619, USA

Timms, Michele — Basketball Player
Phoenix Mercury, American West Arena, 201 E Jefferson St, Phoenix AZ 85004 USA

Timofeyeva, Nina V — Ballerina
Bolshoi Theater, Teatralnaya Pl 1, 103009 Moscow, Russia

Timofti, Nicolae — President, Moldova
Presidential Palace, 23 Nicolae Iorge Str, 227033 Chishinev, Moldova

Timonen, Kimmo S (Kime) — Ice Hockey Player
125 Upland Way, Haddonfield NJ 08033, USA

Timoney, John F — Law Enforcement Official
Miami Police Department, 400 NW 2nd Ave, Miami FL 33128, USA

Timpson, Michael D — Football Player
3020 Crested Circle, Orlando FL 32837, USA

Timsit, Patrick — Actor
Artmedia, 20 Ave Rapp, 75007 Paris, France

Tindemans, Leonard C (Leo) — Prime Minister, Belgium
Jan Verbertlei 24, 2650 Edegem, Belgium

Tindle, David — Artist
Via Giovanni Pacchini 118B, S Maria del Giudice, 55058 Lucca, Italy

Ting, Alice — Chemist
Massachusetts Institute of Technology, Chemistry Dept, Cambridge MA 02139, USA

Ting, Samuel C C — Nobel Physics Laureate
2 Eliot Place, Jamaica Plain MA 02130, USA

Tinglehoff, H Michael (Mick) — Football Player
20517 Kalmeadow Court, Lakeview MN 55044, USA

Tingley, Ronald I (Ron) — Baseball Player
349 Omni Dr, Sparks NV 89441, USA

Tinker, Grant A — Businessman
541 Perugia Way, Los Angeles CA 90077, USA

Tinkham, Michael — Physicist
6126 SE Grant St, Portland OR 97215, USA

Tinoisamoa, Pisa D — Football Player
4384 Austin Pass Dr, Saint Charles MO 63304, USA

Tinordi, Mark — Ice Hockey Player
545 Devonshire Court, Severna Park MD 21146, USA

Tinsley, Bruce — Editorial Cartoonist
King Features Syndicate, 300 W 57th St, #1500, New York NY 10019 USA

Tinsley, Jackson B (Jack) — Editor
Fort Worth Star-Telegram, Editorial Dept, 808 Throckmorton St, Fort Worth TX 76102 USA

Tinsley, Jamaal L — Basketball Player
12122 Ellingwood Dr, Auburndale FL 33823, USA

Tinsley, Jeremy — Poker Player
World Poker Tour, 1041 N Formosa Blvd, #PH 2, West Hollywood CA 90046, USA

Tinsley, Lee O — Baseball Player
237 Tenor St, Shelbyville KY 40065, USA

Tippett, Andre B — Football Player
17 Knob Hill St, Sharon MA 02067, USA

Tippett, David (Dave) — Ice Hockey Player, Coach, Executive
10287 E Diamond Rim Dr, Scottsdale AZ 85255, USA

Tippett, Phil — Animator
Tippett Studio, 2741 10th St, Berkeley CA 94710, USA

Tippin, Aaron — Singer, Songwriter
Webster Assoc, PO Box 23015, Nashville TN 37202, USA

Tippins, Kenny (Ken) — Football Player
524 Renaissance Way, Conyers GA 30012, USA

Tipton, Analeigh — Actress
Thirdhill Entertainment, 195 S Beverly Dr, #400, Beverly Hills CA 90212, USA

Tipton, Dave L — Football Player, Coach
915 Bonneville Ave, Sunnyvale CA 94087, USA

Tipton, Glenn R — Guitarist (Judist Priest)
Trinfold Mgmt, 12 Oval Road, #300, Camden, London NW1 7D4, England

Tiriac, Ion — Tennis Player, Coach
Ion Tiriac/T V Enterprises, 251 E 49th St, New York NY 10017, USA

Tirico, Michael J (Mike) — Sportscaster
ESPN-TV, ESPN Plaza, 935 Middle St, Bristol CT 06010 USA

Tirimo, Martino — Concert Pianist, Conductor
1 Romeyn Road, London SW16 2NU, England

Tirio, Dave — Guitarist (Plain White T's)
One Moment Mgmt, PO Box 55156, Sherman Oaks CA 91413 USA

Tisby, Dexter — Singer (Penguins)
David Harris Enterprises, 24210 E Fork Road, #9, Azusa CA 91702, USA

Tisch, James S — Businessman
Loews Corp, 667 Madison Ave, #700, New York NY 10065, USA

Tisch, Steve — Writer
1162 Tower Road, Beverly Hills CA 90210, USA

Tischinski, Thomas A (Tom) — Baseball Player
9905 N Donnelly Ave, Kansas City MO 64157, USA

Tisdale, Ashley — Actress, Singer, Songwriter
Blondie Girl Productions, 1040 N Las Palmas, Building 40, Los Angeles CA 90038, USA

Tishby, Noa — Actress
Burstein Co, 15304 W Sunset Blvd, #208, Pacific Palisades CA 90272 USA

Titanic, Morris — Ice Hockey Player
146 Delta Road, Buffalo NY 14226, USA

Titensor, Glen W — Football Player
729 Montrose Court, Flower Mound TX 75022, USA

Title, Stacy — Director
I C M Partners, 10250 Constellation Blvd, #900, Los Angeles CA 90067 USA
Titmuss, Abi — Model, Entertainer
Money Mgmt, 42A Berwick St, London W1F 8RE, England
Tito, Dennis A — Tourist Cosmonaut
1800 Alta Mura Road, Pacific Palisades CA 90272, USA
Titov, German M — Ice Hockey Player
9 Aspen Ridge Gate SW, Calgary AB T3H 5V4, Canada
Titov, Vladimir G — Cosmonaut
3 Hovanskaya Str 8, 129515 Moscow, Russia
Titov, Yuri E — Gymnast
Kolokolnikov Per 6, #19, 103045 Moscow, Russia
Tits, Jacques L — Abel Mathematics Laureate
12 Rue du Moulin des Pres, 75013 Paris, France
Tittle, Yelberton A (Y A) — Football Player
168 Elana Ave, Atherton CA 94027, USA
Titus, Christopher — Actor, Comedian, Writer
Gersh Agency, 9465 Wilshire Blvd, #600, Beverly Hills CA 90212 USA
Tizard, Catherine A — Governor General, New Zealand
1/12A Wallace St, Herne Bay, Auckland 1011, New Zealand
Tizon, Albert — Journalist
Seattle Times, Editorial Dept, 1120 John St, Seattle WA 98109 USA
Tjarnqvist, C Daniel — Ice Hockey Player
Colorado Avalanche, Pepsi Center, 1000 Chopper Circle, Denver CO 80204 USA
Tjeknavorian, Loris-Zare — Composer, Conductor
State Philharmonia, Mashtots Prospekt 46, 0002 Yerevan, Armenia
Tjoflat, Gerald B — Judge
US Court of Appeals, 311 W Monroe St, Jacksonville FL 32202, USA
Tkachuk, Keith — Ice Hockey Player
11243 Hunters Pond Road, Saint Louis MO 63141, USA
Tkaczuk, Walter R (Walt) — Ice Hockey Player
River Valley Golf & Country Club, RR 3, Saint Mary's ON N0M 2G0, Canada
To, Johnnie — Director
Milky Way Image, Milky Way Building, #1F, 77 Hung To Road, Kwun Tong, Hong Kong, China
Toback, James — Director, Writer
I C M Partners, 10250 Constellation Blvd, #900, Los Angeles CA 90067 USA
Tobeck, Robert L (Robbie) — Football Player
6620 320th St E, Eatonville WA 98328, USA
Tober, Barbara D — Editor
620 Park Ave, New York NY 10065, USA
Tobey, James — Actor
Paradigm Agency, 360 N Crescent Dr, North Building, Beverly Hills CA 90210 USA
Tobian, Gary M — Diver
9171 Belted Kingfisher Road, Blaine WA 98230, USA
Tobias, Andrew — Writer
787 NE 71st St, Miami FL 33138, USA
Tobias, Oliver — Actor
Agentur Lentz, Barestr 48, 80799 Munich, Germany
Tobias, Randall L — Businessman, Diplomat
State Department, 2201 C St NW, Washington DC 20520 USA
Tobias, Robert M — Labor Leader
American University, Public Affairs School, Washington DC 20057, USA
Tobik, David V (Dave) — Baseball Player
848 Chancellor Heights Dr, Ballwin MO 63011, USA
Tobin, Don — Cartoonist (Little Woman)
12312 Ranchwood Road, Santa Ana CA 92705, USA
Tobin, James R — Businessman
Baxter Scientific, 1 Boston Scientific Place, Natick MA 01760, USA
Tobin, Robert G — Businessman
Ahold USA, 1385 Hancock St, Quincy MA 02169, USA
Tobin, Vince — Football Coach
15997 W Monterey Way, Goodyear AZ 85395, USA
Tobolowsky, Stephen — Actor
Innovative Artists, 1505 10th St, Santa Monica CA 90401 USA
TobyMac — Singer, Rap Artist (DC Talk)
True Artist Mgmt, 227 3rd Ave B, Franklin TN 37064, USA
Toca, Jorge L — Baseball Player
7940 NW 167th Terrace, Hialeah FL 33016, USA
Tocchet, Rick — Ice Hockey Player, Coach
PO Box 13563, Pittsburgh PA 15243, USA
Tochi, Brian — Actor
247 S Beverly Dr, #102, Beverly Hills CA 90212, USA
Toczyska, Stefania — Opera Singer
Stafford Law, 6 Barham Close, Weybridge, Surrey KT13 9PR, England
Todd, Ann E — Actress
2419 Oregon St, Berkeley CA 94705, USA
Todd, C Richard — Football Player
PO Box 478, Florence AL 35631, USA
Todd, Hallie — Actress
In-House Media, 13636 Ventura Blvd, #298, Sherman Oaks CA 91423, USA
Todd, Harry W — Businessman
Carlisle Enterprises, 777 Fay Ave, La Jolla CA 92037, USA
Todd, James R (Jim), Jr — Baseball Player
21639 Hill Gail Way, Parker CO 80138, USA
Todd, Josh — Singer (Buckcherry)
Tenth Street Entertainment, 270 Lafayette St, #706, New York NY 10012, USA
Todd, Kevin — Ice Hockey Player
15 Narla Lane, Utica NY 13501, USA
Todd, Lani — Model
Playboy Promotions, 2706 Media Center Dr, Los Angeles CA 90065 USA
Todd, Lee — Educator
University of Kentucky, President's Office, Lexington KY 40506, USA
Todd, Mark J — Equestrian Rider
PO Box 507, Cambridge, New Zealand
Todd, Mia Doi — Singer, Guitarist, Songwriter
Fanatic Promotion, 135 W 29th St, #1101, New York NY 10001, USA

Todd, Tony — Actor
Innovative Artists, 1505 10th St, Santa Monica CA 90401 USA
Todd, Virgil H — Religious Leader, Educator
3095 E Glengarry Road, Memphis TN 38128, USA
Todorovsky, Piotr Y — Director
Vernadskogo Prospect 70A, #23, 117454 Moscow, Russia
Toennies, Jan Peter — Physicist
Ewaldstr 7, 37075 Gottingen, Germany
Toews, Jeffrey M (Jeff) — Football Player
11924 Silver Oak Dr, Davie FL 33330, USA
Toews, Jonathan B — Ice Hockey Player
Chicago Blackhawks, United Center, 1901 W Madison St, Chicago IL 60612 USA
Toews, Loren J — Football Player
165 Hawthorne Ave, Los Altos Hills CA 94022, USA
Tofani, Loretta A — Journalist
Philadelphia Inquirer, Editorial Dept, 400 N Broad St, Philadelphia PA 19130, USA
Toffler, Alvin — Writer, Futurist
Random House, 1745 Broadway, #1800, New York NY 10019 USA
Toft, Rod — Bowler
11350 12th St N, Lake Elmo MN 55042, USA
Tognini, Michel — Cosmonaut, France; Air Force General
European Space Center, Linder Hohe, Box 906096, 51127 Cologne, Germany
Tognoni, Gina — Actress
Innovative Artists, 1505 10th St, Santa Monica CA 90401 USA
Togo, Jonathan — Actor
C E S D, 10635 Santa Monica Blvd, #130, Los Angeles CA 90025 USA
Togunde, Victor — Actor
Greater Visions Artists Talent Agency, 8981 W Sunset Blvd, #101, West Hollywood CA 90069 USA
Toibin, Colm — Writer
23 Carnew St, Arbour Hill, Dublin 7, County Dublin, Ireland
Tokarev, Valery I — Cosmonaut
Cosmonaut Training Center, Star City, 141160 Zvezdny Gorodok, Moscow Oblast, Russia
Tokes, Laszlo — Religious Leader, Political Activist
Craivei Str 1, 3700 Oradea, Romania
Tokody, Ilona — Opera Singer
Hungarian State Opera, Andrassy Utca 22, 1062 Budapest, Hungary
Tokombayeva, Aysulu A — Ballerina
Usenbaev Str 37, #33, 720021 Bishkek, Kyrgystan
Tolan, Peter — Actor, Director, Producer
Fedora Entertainment, 15300 Ventura Blvd, Sherman Oaks CA 91403, USA
Tolan, Robert (Bobby) — Baseball Player
804 Woodstock St, Bellaire TX 77401, USA
Tolbert, B Thomas (Tom) — Basketball Player
368 Creedon Circle, Alameda CA 94502, USA
Tolbert, Berlinda — Actress
Pallas Mgmt, 12535 Chandler Blvd, #1, Valley Village CA 91607, USA
Tolbert, L James (Jim) — Football Player
2435 Corinna Court, San Diego CA 92105, USA
Tolbert, Mike — Football Player
Carolina Panthers, Ericsson Stadium, 800 S Mint St, Charlotte NC 28202 USA
Tolbert, Raymond L (Ray) — Basketball Player
2205 Crestwood Dr, Anderson IN 46016, USA
Tolbert, Tony L — Football Player
475 S White Chapel Blvd, Southlake TX 76092, USA
Tolcher, Michael — Singer, Guitarist, Songwriter
Elevation Group, 1408 Encinal Ave, #A, Alameda CA 94501, USA
Toledano, Eric — Director
Creative Artists Agency, 2000 Ave of Stars, #100, Los Angeles CA 90067 USA
Toledo, Esteban — Golfer
61 Rockport, Irvine CA 92602, USA
Toledo, Francisco — Artist
Vorpal Gallery, 1 Front St, #1550, San Francisco CA 94111, USA
Toledo, Isabel — Fashion Designer
277 5th Ave, New York NY 10016, USA
Toledo, Rafael — Actor
Culbertson Group, 8430 Santa Monica Blvd, #210, West Hollywood CA 90069, USA
Tolentino, Jose F — Baseball Player
26711 Caceres Circle, Mission Viejo CA 92691, USA
Toles, Thomas G (Tom) — Editorial Cartoonist
4625 46th St NW, Washington DC 20016, USA
Tolhurst, Lol — Drummer (Cure)
Primary Talent Int'l, 10-11 Jockey's Fields, London WC1R 4BN, England
Toliver, Freddie L (Fred) — Baseball Player
674 Medical Center Dr, San Bernardino CA 92411, USA
Toliver, Kristi — Basketball Player
Chicago Sky, 20 W Kinzie St, #1010, Chicago IL 60654 USA
Tolkan, James — Actor
Paradigm Agency, 360 N Crescent Dr, North Building, Beverly Hills CA 90210 USA
Toll, Joanne — Producer
W M E Entertainment, 9601 Wilshire Blvd, #300, Beverly Hills CA 90210 USA
Toll, Robert I — Businessman
Toll Brothers, 250 Gibraltar Road, Horsham PA 19044, USA
Tollberg, Brian — Baseball Player
2104 39th St W, Bradenton FL 34205, USA
Tollefson, Dave — Football Player
Oakland Raiders, 1220 Harbor Bay Parkway, Alameda CA 94502 USA
Tolles, Tommy — Golfer
233 Park Dr, Hendersonville NC 28739, USA
Tolleson, J Wayne — Baseball Player
313 Mossycup Oak Court, Spartanburg SC 29306, USA
Tolliver, Billy Joe — Football Player
9837 Neesonwood Dr, Shreveport LA 71106, USA
Tolman, Timothy L (Tim) — Baseball Player
11425 N Ingot Loop, Tucson AZ 85737, USA
Tolsky, Susan — Actress
10815 Acama St, North Hollywood CA 91602, USA

Tom, Heather — Actress
Smart Public Relations, 8033 W Sunset Blvd, #1033, West Hollywood CA 90046, USA
Tom, Kiana — Physical Fitness Expert, Model
PO Box 1111, Sunset Beach CA 90742, USA
Tom, Lauren — Actress
Pop Art Mgmt, PO Box 55363, Sherman Oaks CA 91413, USA
Tom, Logan M L — Volleyball Player
2001 E 21st St, #136, Signal Hill CA 90755, USA
Tom, Nicholle — Actress
TalentWorks, 3500 W Olive Ave, #1400, Burbank CA 91505 USA
Toma, David — Writer
PO Box 854, Rahway NJ 07065, USA
Tomalty, Glenn — Ice Hockey Player
5423 Boomerang Way, RR 6, Fernie BC V0B 1M6, Canada
Tomanek, Richard C (Dick) — Baseball Player
165 Duff Dr, Avon Lake OH 44012, USA
Tomasevicz, Curtis (Curt) — Bobsled Athlete
Team Holcomb, PO Box 118, Oakley UT 84055, USA
Tomasson, Helgi — Ballet Dancer, Director
San Francisco Ballet, 455 Franklin St, San Francisco CA 94102, USA
Tomba, Alberto — Alpine Skier
Castel dei Britti, 40100 Bologna, Italy
Tomberlin, Andy L — Baseball Player
7411 Crooked Creek Church Road, Monroe NC 28110, USA
Tombs, Tina — Golfer
5919 N 45th St, Phoenix AZ 85018, USA
Tomczak, Michael J (Mike) — Football Player
139 Witherow Road, Sewickley PA 15143, USA
Tomei, Concetta — Actress
Innovative Artists, 1505 10th St, Santa Monica CA 90401 USA
Tomei, Marisa — Actress
Creative Artists Agency, 2000 Ave of Stars, #100, Los Angeles CA 90067 USA
Tomi, Vicente Ehate — Prime Minister, Equatorial Guinea
Prime Minister's Office, Malabo, Equatorial Guinea
Tomich, Jared J — Football Player
2222 Red River Dr, Schererville IN 46375, USA
Tomita, Stan — Photographer
2439 Saint Louis Dr, Honolulu HI 96816, USA
Tomita, Tamlyn — Actress
Geddes Agency, 8430 Santa Monica Blvd, #201, West Hollywood CA 90069 USA
Tomjanovich, Rudolph (Rudy) — Basketball Player, Coach
19 West Lane, Houston TX 77019, USA
Tomko, Brett D — Baseball Player
14008 Lake Poway Road, Poway CA 92064, USA
Tomko, Jozef Cardinal — Religious Leader
Villa Betania, Via Urbano VIII-16, 00165 Rome, Italy
Tomlak, Mike — Ice Hockey Player
2200 Bordeaux Crescent, Thunder Bay ON P7K 1C2, Canada
Tomlin, David A (Dave) — Baseball Player
2020 Clayton Pike, Manchester OH 45144, USA
Tomlin, Lily — Actress, Comedienne
W M E Entertainment, 9601 Wilshire Blvd, #300, Beverly Hills CA 90210 USA
Tomlin, Mike — Football Coach
1224 Shady Ave, Pittsburgh PA 15232, USA
Tomlin, Randy L — Baseball Player
153 Ridgeview Lane, Madison Heights VA 24572, USA
Tomlinson, Charles — Writer
Bristol University, English Dept, Bristol BS8 1TH, England
Tomlinson, Derek J (Ray) — Computer Scientist, Inventor
B B & N Technologies, 10 Moulton St, Cambridge MA 02138, USA
Tomlinson, Eleanor — Actress
Conway Van Gelder Grant, 8-12 Broadwick St, #300, London W1F 8HW, England
Tomlinson, John — Opera Singer
Music International, 13 Ardilaun Road, Highbury, London N5 2QR, England
Tomlinson, LaDainian — Football Player
18755 Heritage Dr, Poway CA 92064, USA
Tomlinson, Mel A — Ballet Dancer
790 Riverside Dr, #6B, New York NY 10032, USA
Tompkins, Paul F — Actor
Avalon Mgmt, 4a Exmoor St, London W10 6BD, England
Tompkins, Ronald E (Ron) — Baseball Player
25072 Leucadia St, #G, Laguna Niguel CA 92677, USA
Tompkins, Susie — Fashion Designer
2500 Steiner St, #PH, San Francisco CA 94115, USA
Toms, David — Golfer
6606 Gilbert Dr, Shreveport LA 71106, USA
Toms, Thomas H (Tommy) — Baseball Player
126 Leadbetter Road, Wayne ME 04284, USA
Tomsco, George — Musician (Fireballs)
Fireballs Entertainment, 1224 Cottonwood, Raton NM 87740, USA
Tomsic, Dubravka — Concert Pianist
Hazard Chase, Richmond House, 16-20 Regent St, Cambridge BB2 1DB, England
Tomsic, Ronald (Ron) — Basketball Player
22 Twilight Bluff, Newport Beach CA 92657, USA
Tomson, Shaun — Surfer
Solitude Clothing, 1206 Coast Village Circle, Santa Barbara CA 93108, USA
Tonchi, Stefano — Editor
W, Editorial Dept, 1166 Ave of Americas, #1500, New York NY 10036, USA
Toneff, Robert (Bob) — Football Player
18 Dutch Valley Lane, San Anselmo CA 94960, USA
Tonegawa, Susumu — Nobel Medicine Laureate
101 Chestnut Hill Road, Chestnut Hill MA 02467, USA
Tonelli, John — Ice Hockey Player
4 Vincent Lane, Armonk NY 10504, USA
Toner, Mike — Journalist
Atlanta Journal-Constitution, Editorial Dept, 223 Perimeter Center Parkway, Atlanta GA 30346, USA

Toney, Andrew — Basketball Player
1613 14th Ave N, Birmingham AL 35204, USA
Toney, Anthony — Football Player
632 Donner Way, Salinas CA 93906, USA
Toney, Sedric A — Basketball Player
3831 Sweetwater Dr, Brecksville OH 44141, USA
Tong Jian — Figure Skater
Skating Assn, 56 Zhongguancun South St, Haidian, Beijing 100044, China
Tong, Anote — President, Kiribati
President's Office, PO Box 68, Bairiki, Tarawa Atoll, Kiribati
Tong, Matthew C H (Matt) — Drummer (Bloc Party)
Coalition Mgmt, 12 Barley Mow Passage, London W4 4PH, England
Tong, Stanley — Director
Innovative Artists, 1505 10th St, Santa Monica CA 90401 USA
Tongue, Reginal C (Reggie) — Football Player
1353 Saint Albans Dr, Baton Rouge LA 70810, USA
Tonini, Ersilio Cardinal — Religious Leader
Via Santa Teresa 8, 48100 Ravenna, Italy
Tonioli, Bruno — Dance Judge
Independent Talent Group, Oxford House, 76 Oxford St, London W1D 1BS, England
Tonis, Mike — Baseball Player
9231 Bella Vista Place, Elk Grove CA 95624, USA
Tonkin, Peter F — Architect
Tonkin Zulaikha Greer, 2 Liverpool Lane, East Sydney NSW 2010, Australia
Tonkin, Phoebe — Actress
I C M Partners, 10250 Constellation Blvd, #900, Los Angeles CA 90067 USA
Tonnesen, Bill — Landscape Architect
105 E 15th St, Tempe AZ 85281, USA
Tookey, Tim — Ice Hockey Player
21008 W Ridge Road, Buckeye AZ 85396, USA
Toolson, Andrew K (Andy) — Basketball Player
722 Ranch Circle, Alpine UT 84004, USA
Toom, Tanel — Director
W M E Entertainment, 9601 Wilshire Blvd, #300, Beverly Hills CA 90210 USA
Toomay, Patrick J (Pat) — Football Player
221 Tornasol Lane NE, Albuquerque NM 87113, USA
Toomer, Amani A — Football Player
25 Regency Place, Weehawken NJ 07086, USA
Toomey, Sean — Ice Hockey Player
1741 Saunders Ave, Saint Paul MN 55116, USA
Toomey, William A (Bill) — Track Athlete
4360 Park Terrace Dr, #160, Westlake Village CA 91361, USA
Toomin, Amy — Writer, Producer
United Talent Agency, 9336 Civic Center Dr, Beverly Hills CA 90210 USA
Toon, Al L, Jr — Football Player
PO Box 620770, Middleton WI 53562, USA
Tootoo, Jordin J K — Ice Hockey Player
2600 Hillsboro Pike, #359, Nashville TN 37212, USA
Toparovsky, Simon — Sculptor
5760 W Adams Blvd, Los Angeles CA 90016, USA
Topol, Chaim — Actor
22 Vale Court, Maidville, London W9 1RT, England
Topolanek, Mirek — Prime Minister, Czech Republic
Premier's Office, Nabrezi Edvarda Benese 4, 118 01 Prague 1, Czech Republic
Topolsky, Ken — Director
A P A Talent/Literary Agency, 405 S Beverly Dr, #300, Beverly Hills CA 90212 USA
Topper, John — Singer (Blues Traveler)
Monterey Peninsula Artists, 404 W Franklin St, Monterey CA 93940 USA
Toppin, Ruperto (Rupe) — Baseball Player
PO Box 25724, Miami FL 33102, USA
Toppo, Telesphore P Cardinal — Religious Leader
Archdiocese, PO Box 5, Purulia Road, Ranchi 834001 Jharkland, India
Toradze, Alexander — Concert Pianist
Columbia Artists Mgmt Inc, 1790 Broadway, #702, New York NY 10019 USA
Torbert, Stephanie — Photographer
3824 Harriet Ave, Minneapolis MN 55409, USA
Torborg, Jeffrey A (Jeff) — Baseball Player, Manager
47 Railroad Ave, Manahawkin NJ 08050, USA
Torcato, Anthony D (Tony) — Baseball Player
1547 SW Clay St, Dallas OR 97338, USA
Torchetti, John — Ice Hockey Coach
14 Crows Nest Lane, Marshfield MA 2050, USA
Torczon, Laverne J — Football Player
6472 Country Club Dr, Columbus NE 68601, USA
Torenstra, Waldemar — Actor
Mover Shaker, De Lairessestraat 141, Amsterdam 1075 HJ, Netherlands
Torgeson, LaVern E — Football Player
17672 Gainsford Lane, Huntington Beach CA 92649, USA
Torii, Keiko U — Biologist
Washington University, Torii Lab, Biology Dept, Box 355325, Seattle WA 98195, USA
Tork, Peter — Singer, Bassist (Monkees)
524 Anselmo Ave, #102, San Anselmo CA 94960, USA
Torke, Michael — Composer
Columbia Artists Mgmt Inc, 1790 Broadway, #702, New York NY 10019 USA
Torkelson, Eric G — Football Player
1196 Pleasant Valley Dr, Oneida WI 54155, USA
Tormis, Veljo — Composer
Estonian Academy of Music, Ravala Pst 16, Tallinn 10143, Estonia
Tormohlen, Gene — Basketball Player
2248 Walker Dr, Lawrenceville GA 30043, USA
Torn, Rip — Actor
Sovereign Talent Group, 8421 Wilshire Blvd, #200, Beverly Hills CA 90211 USA
Torng, Hwa C — Inventor (Computer Processor)
Cornell University, Electrical Engineering Dept, Ithaca NY 14853, USA
Torok, Mitchell — Singer, Guitarist, Songwriter
5100 Weaver Road, #702, Lake Charles LA 70605, USA

Torp, Niels A — Architect
Industrigaten 59, PO Box 5387, 0304 Oslo, Norway
Torrance, Ingrid — Actress
Lucas Talent, 100 W Pender St, #700, Vancouver BC V6B 1RB, Canada
Torrance, Sam — Golfer
Parallel Murray Mgmt, 56 Ennismore Gardens, London SW7 1AJ, England
Torre, Frank J — Baseball Player
13901 Palm Grove Place, West Palm Beach FL 33418, USA
Torre, Joseph P (Joe) — Baseball Player, Manager
20 Lawrence Lane, Harrison NY 10528, USA
Torrealba, Yorvit — Baseball Player
3801 S Ocean Dr, #15F, Hollywood FL 33019, USA
Torrence, Dean — Singer (Jan & Dean), Songwriter
18932 Gregory Lane, Huntington Beach CA 92646, USA
Torrence, Gwendolyn (Gwen) — Track Athlete
Gold Medal Mgmt, 1750 14th St, Boulder CO 80302, USA
Torrence, Nate — Actor
Messina Baker Entertainment, 955 Carrillo Dr, #100, Los Angeles CA 90048 USA
Torres Delgado, Dayanara — Beauty Queen, Actress
Univision, 605 3rd Ave, #1200, New York NY 10158 USA
Torres, Dara — Swimmer, Model
9840 Bay Leaf Court, Parkland FL 33076, USA
Torres, Diego — Singer
Felix Productions, Av Figueroa Alcorta 3221, Buenos Aires 1215, Argentina
Torres, Eve — Dancer, Model, Wrestler
World Wrestling Entertainment, Titan Towers, 1241 E Main St, Stamford CT 06902 USA
Torres, Felix — Baseball Player
HC 1 Box 6424, Santa Isabel PR 00757, USA
Torres, Fina — Director
I C M Partners, 10250 Constellation Blvd, #900, Los Angeles CA 90067 USA
Torres, Gina — Actress
Framework Entertainment, 9057 Nemo St, #C, West Hollywood CA 90069 USA
Torres, Harold — Singer (Crests)
PO Box 5357, Spring Hill FL 34611, USA
Torres, Hector E — Baseball Player
662 Lexington St, Dunedin FL 34698, USA
Torres, Hector S J (Tico) — Drummer (Bon Jovi)
Bon Jovi Mgmt, 809 Elder Circle, Austin TX 78733, USA
Torres, Oscar Orlando — Actor, Writer, Producer
Caliber Media, 9229 W Sunset Blvd, #705, West Hollywood CA 90069, USA
Torres, Raffi — Ice Hockey Player
118 Church St, Markham ON L3P 2M4, Canada
Torres, Rosendo (Rusty) — Baseball Player
250 N Cedar St, Massapequa NY 11758, USA
Torres, Salomon R — Baseball Player
101 Crimson Dr, Pittsburgh PA 15237, USA
Torres, Tommy — Singer, Songwriter
Sony Music Miami, 605 Lincoln Road Road, #700, Miami Beach FL 33139 USA
Torressani, Alessandra — Actress
United Talent Agency, 9336 Civic Center Dr, Beverly Hills CA 90210 USA
Torreton, Philippe — Actor
Artmedia, 20 Ave Rapp, 75007 Paris, France
Torretta, Gino L — Football Player
7830 SW 48th Court, Miami FL 33143, USA
Torrey, Bill — Ice Hockey Player, Executive
2740 Clubhouse Pointe, West Palm Beach FL 33409, USA
Torrey, Rich — Cartoonist (Hartland)
King Features Syndicate, 300 W 57th St, #1500, New York NY 10019 USA
Torrez, Michael A (Mike) — Baseball Player
1015 Frances Court, Naperville IL 60563, USA
Torriero, Talan — Actor
I C M Partners, 10250 Constellation Blvd, #900, Los Angeles CA 90067 USA
Torrijos Espino, Martin E — President, Panama
Palacio Presidencial, Valija 50, Panama City 1, Panama
Torrini, Emiliana — Singer, Songwriter
One Little Indian Records, 34 Trinity Crescent, London SW17 7AE, England
Torrissen, Birger — Nordic Skier
PO Box 216, Lakeville CT 06039, USA
Torruella, Juan R — Judge
US Court of Appeals, 150 Ave Carlos Chardon, #119, San Juan PR 00918, USA
Torry, Guy — Actor, Comedian
New Wave Entertainment, 2660 W Olive Ave, Burbank CA 91505, USA
Torry, Joe — Actor, Comedian
Proclaim Talent Agency, PO Box 23158, New Orleans LA 70183, USA
Tortelier, Yan Pascal — Conductor, Concert Violinist
M A de Valmalete, Building Gaceau, 11 Ave Delcasse, 75635 Paris, France
Torti, Robert — Actor
Big House Studios, 4420 Lankershim Blvd, North Hollywood CA 91602, USA
Tortorella, John — Ice Hockey Coach
108 3rd Ave, Saint Pete Beach FL 33706, USA
Tortorella, Nico — Actor
Gersh Agency, 9465 Wilshire Blvd, #600, Beverly Hills CA 90212 USA
Torv, Anna — Actress
United Mgmt, Marlborough House, 61 Marlborough St, #400-45, Surry Hills NSW 2010, Australia
Torvalds, Linus — Computer Software Designer
Open Source Development Laboratories, 12725 SW Millikan Way, Beaverton OR 97005, USA
Torvbraaten, Tore — Curling Athlete
Curling Assn, Sognsveien 75, Serviceboks 1, 0840 Oslo, Norway
Torve, Kelvin C — Baseball Player
18701 Hammock Lane, Davidson NC 28036, USA
Torvill, Jayne — Ice Dancer
Sue Young, PO Box 32, Heathfield, East Sussex TN21 0BW, England
Tory, Anna — Actress
Conway Van Gelder Grant, 8-12 Broadwick St, #300, London W1F 8HW, England
Tosca, Carlos — Baseball Manager
PO Box 3623, Brandon FL 33509, USA

Toscano, Harry — Golfer
231 Rose Hill Dr, New Castle PA 16105, USA

Tosh, Daniel — Actor, Comedian
W M E Entertainment, 9601 Wilshire Blvd, #300, Beverly Hills CA 90210 USA

Toskala, Vesa — Ice Hockey Player
Calgary Flames, PO Box 1540, Station M, Calgary AB T2P 3B9, Canada

Toski, Bob — Golfer
20914 Hamaca Court, Boca Raton FL 33433, USA

Totenberg, Nina — Commentator
National Public Radio, 635 Massachusetts Ave NW, #1, Washington DC 20001, USA

Toth, Melissa — Costume Designer
Gersh Agency, 9465 Wilshire Blvd, #600, Beverly Hills CA 90212 USA

Toth, Thomas J (Tom) — Football Player
13723 Lindsay Dr, Orland Park IL 60462, USA

Totmianina, Tatiana — Figure Skater
Skating Federation, Luznetskaya Nabererhnya 8, 119871 Moscow, Russia

Totten, Robert — Director
PO Box 7180, Big Bear Lake CA 92315, USA

Totter, Audrey — Actress
Motion Picture Country Home, 23388 Mulholland Dr, Woodland Hills CA 91364, USA

Totushek, John B — Navy Admiral
Military Officers Assn, 201 N Washington St, Alexandria VA 22314, USA

Touadera, Faustin-Archange — Prime Minister, Central African Republic
Prime Minister's Office, Primature, Bangui, Central African Republic

Tough, Kelly — Model, Actress
Playboy Promotions, 2706 Media Center Dr, Los Angeles CA 90065 USA

Toulouse, Gerard — Physicist
Laboratoire de Physique d'E N S, 24 Rue Lhomond, 75231 Paris, France

Tountas, Pete — Bowler
10100 N Calle del Carnero, Tucson AZ 85737, USA

Toups, Fontaine — Bassist, Guitarist, Singer (Versus)
Ground Control Touring, 20 Jay St, #838, Brooklyn NY 11201, USA

Touraine, Jean-Louis — Immunologist
Edouard-Herriot Hopital, Place d'Arsonval, 69437 Lyons Cedex 03, France

Toure, Daby — Singer, Songwriter
Rosebud Agency, PO Box 170429, San Francisco CA 94117 USA

Toure, Younoussi — Prime Minister, Mali
Union Economique/Monetaire, 01 BP 543, Ouagadougou 01, Burkina Faso

Tournet, Scott — Guitarist (Grace Potter & Nocturnals)
Paradigm Agency, 404 W Franklin St, Monterey CA 93940 USA

Tournier, Michel — Writer
Le Presbytere, Choisel, 78460 Chevreuse, France

Toussaint, Allen — Jazz Singer, Pianist, Composer
272 Abalon Court, New Orleans LA 70114, USA

Toussaint, Beth — Actress
Innovative Artists, 1505 10th St, Santa Monica CA 90401 USA

Toussaint, Lorraine — Actress
Innovative Artists, 1505 10th St, Santa Monica CA 90401 USA

Tovar, Steven E (Steve) — Football Player
5607 Wagstaff Dr, Lawrence KS 66049, USA

Tovey, Bramwell — Conductor
I M G Artists, Hogarth Business Park, Chiswick, London W4 2TH, England

Tovey, Russell — Actor
Sue Terry Voices, 18 Broadwick St, #300, London W1F 8HS, England

Tovoli, Luciano — Cinematographer
United Talent Agency, 9336 Civic Center Dr, Beverly Hills CA 90210 USA

Towe, Monte C — Basketball Player, Coach
2125 Gold Valley Dr, Murfreesboro TN 37130, USA

Tower, Joan P — Composer
Bard College, Music Dept, Annandale on Hudson NY 12504, USA

Tower, Keith R — Basketball Player
12530 Aldershot Lane, Windermere FL 34786, USA

Towers, Constance — Actress
Cassell-Levy, 843 N Sycamore Ave, Los Angeles CA 90038, USA

Towers, Joshua E (Josh) — Baseball Player
1033 Crescent Falls St, Henderson NV 89011, USA

Towery, William C (Blackie) — Basketball Player
314 W Carlisle St, Marion KY 42064, USA

Towle, Stephen R (Steve) — Football Player
609 NE Lake Pointe Dr, Lees Summit MO 64064, USA

Towles, Justin R (J R) — Baseball Player
13806 Lowell Ave, Tomball TX 77377, USA

Towne, Robert — Director, Writer
1417 San Remo Dr, Pacific Palisades CA 90272, USA

Townend, Peter — Surfer, Publisher
820 Geneva Ave, #A, Huntington Beach CA 92648, USA

Towner, Ralph N — Jazz Guitarist, Pianist
Ted Kurland, 173 Brighton Ave, Allston MA 02134 USA

Townes, Charles H — Nobel Physics, Templeton Prize Laureate
1850 Alice St, #713, Oakland CA 94612, USA

Townes, Linton R — Basketball Player
PO Box 254, Luray VA 22835, USA

Towns, Lester, III — Football Player
2225 Hawkins St, #131, Charlotte NC 28203, USA

Towns, Morris M — Football Player
7102 Rusting Oaks Dr, Richmond TX 77469, USA

Townsell, Joseph R (Jo Jo) — Football Player
PO Box 606, Gardnerville NV 89410, USA

Townsend, Andre — Football Player
6206 Providence Club Dr, Mableton GA 30126, USA

Townsend, Colleen — Actress
National Presbyterian Church, 4101 Nebraska Ave NW, Washington DC 20016, USA

Townsend, Heath — Model
I M G Models, 304 Park Ave S, #PH-North, New York NY 10010 USA

Townsend, Jill Perry — Artist, Sculptor
Skob Knob Studios, 1936 NE 63rd St, Lincoln City OR 97367, USA

Townsend, John W, Jr — Space Scientist
6532 79th St, Cabin John MD 20818, USA
Townsend, Milon — Artist
Blue Moon Press, 262 Moul Road, Hilton NY 14468, USA
Townsend, Raymond — Basketball Player
5160 Cribari Knolls, San Jose CA 95135, USA
Townsend, Robert — Actor, Director
A P A Talent/Literary Agency, 405 S Beverly Dr, #300, Beverly Hills CA 90212 USA
Townsend, T Deshea — Football Player
3208 Lenox Oval, Pittsburgh PA 15237, USA
Townsend, Tammy — Actress, Singer
Abrams Artists, 275 7th Ave, #2600, New York NY 10001 USA
Townshend, Graeme S — Ice Hockey Player
PO Box 1231, Saco ME 04072, USA
Townshend, Peter D B — Singer, Guitarist (Who), Songwriter
4 Friars Lane, Richmond, Surrey TW9 1NL, England
Toy, Camden — Actor
Coolwaters Productions, 10061 Riverside Dr, Box 531, Toluca Lake CA 91602 USA
Toynton, Ian — Director, Producer
Creative Artists Agency, 2000 Ave of Stars, #100, Los Angeles CA 90067 USA
Toyoda, Akio — Businessman
Toyota Motor Corp, 1 Toyotacho, Toyota City, Aichi Pref 471-8701, Japan
Toyoda, Shoichiro — Businessman
Keidanren Kaikan Building, 1-9-4 Ohtemachi, Chuyodaku, Tokyo 100 8188, Japan
Tozer, Faye L — Singer, Actress
Concorde International Artistes, 101 Shepherds Bush Road, London W6 7LP, England
Tozzi, Umberto — Singer, Songwriter
Momy Records, Le Vallespir, 25 Blvd Du, 98000 Monaco, Monaco
T-Pain — Singer, Rap Artist, Songwriter, Actor
American Talent Agency, 248 W 35th St, # 501 New York NY 10001, USA
Traa — Bassist (POD)
Atlantic Records, 9229 W Sunset Blvd, #900, West Hollywood CA 90069 USA
Traber, William H (Billy), Jr — Baseball Player
836 Lomita St, El Segundo CA 90245, USA
Trabert, M Anthony (Tony) — Tennis Player
115 Knotty Pine Trail, Ponte Vedra Beach FL 32082, USA
Tracewski, Richard J (Dick) — Baseball Player, Manager
5 Flora Dr, Peckville PA 18452, USA
Trachsel, Stephen P (Steve) — Baseball Player
18750 Heritage Dr, Poway CA 92064, USA
Trachta, Jeff — Actor
590 S Indian Trail, Palm Springs CA 92264, USA
Trachtenberg, Michelle — Actress
United Talent Agency, 9336 Civic Center Dr, Beverly Hills CA 90210 USA
Tracy, Andrew M (Andy) — Baseball Player
2226 Park Circle, Lewis Center OH 43035, USA
Tracy, Chad A — Baseball Player
9422 Sir Huon Lane, Waxhaw NC 28173, USA
Tracy, James E (Jim) — Baseball Player, Manager
7112 Woodhall Court, Presto PA 15142, USA
Tracy, Keegan Connor — Actress
S M S Talent, 8383 Wilshire Blvd, #230, Beverly Hills CA 90211 USA
Tracy, Paul — Auto Racing Driver
10524 Allthorn Ave, Las Vegas NV 89144, USA
Trager, Milton — Physical Therapist
Trager Institute, 3800 Park East Dr, #100, Beachwood OH 44122, USA
Trahan, Donald R (D J), Jr — Golfer
32 Eastlake Road, Mount Pleasant SC 29464, USA
Train, Harry D, II — Navy Admiral
401 College Place, #10, Norfolk VA 23510, USA
Train, Kristina — Singer, Songwriter
Blue Note Records, 6920 W Sunset Blvd, Los Angeles CA 90028 USA
Trainor, Bernard E — Marine Corps General
46874 Grissom St, Sterling VA 20165, USA
Trainor, Jerry — Actor
I C M Partners, 10250 Constellation Blvd, #900, Los Angeles CA 90067 USA
Trainor, Kevin — Actor
Ken McReddie Assoc, 11 Connaught Place, London W2 2ET, England
Trainor, Saxon — Actress
Sager Mgmt, 260 S Beverly Dr, #205, Beverly Hills CA 90212, USA
Trammell, Alan S — Baseball Player, Manager
191 22nd St, Del Mar CA 92014, USA
Trammell, Sam — Actor
Innovative Artists, 1505 10th St, Santa Monica CA 90401 USA
Trammell, Terry — Sports Orthopedic Surgeon
Orthopedics-Indianapolis, 1801 N Senate Blvd, #200, Indianapolis IN 46202, USA
Trammell, Thomas J (Bubba) — Baseball Player
4672 NW 114th St, #310, Doral FL 33178, USA
Transtromer, Tomas G — Nobel Literature Laureate
Stadahuset, 421 87 Vasteras, Sweden
Traore, Diouncounda — Acting President, Mali
President's Office, BP 1463, Bamako, Mali
Trapp, John Q — Basketball Player
4785 Primavera St, Las Vegas NV 89122, USA
Traub, Charles H — Photographer
39 E 10th St, New York NY 10003, USA
Traub, Sophie — Actress
Characters Talent Mgmt, 8 Elm St, Toronto ON M5G 1G7, Canada
Traub, Yaron — Conductor
Opus 3 Artists, 470 Park Ave S, #900N, New York NY 10016 USA
Traue, Antje — Actress
United Talent Agency, 9336 Civic Center Dr, Beverly Hills CA 90210 USA
Trautmann, Richard — Judo Athlete
Horemansstr 29, 80636 Munich, Germany
Trautwig, Al — Sportscaster
NBC-TV, Sports Dept, 30 Rockefeller Plaza, #270E, New York NY 10112 USA

Travanti, Daniel J — Actor
1077 Melody Road, Lake Forest IL 60045, USA
Travers, Pat — Singer, Guitarist
A R M, 1257 Arcade St, Saint Paul MN 55106, USA
Travers, William E (Bill) — Baseball Player
10 Shoreline Dr, Foxboro MA 02035, USA
Travis, Dale — Opera Singer
Columbia Artists Mgmt Inc, 1790 Broadway, #702, New York NY 10019 USA
Travis, Kylie — Model, Actress
Hartig-Hilepo Agency, 54 W 21st St, #610, New York NY 10010 USA
Travis, Nancy — Actress
A P A Talent/Literary Agency, 405 S Beverly Dr, #300, Beverly Hills CA 90212 USA
Travis, Pete — Director
W M E Entertainment, 9601 Wilshire Blvd, #300, Beverly Hills CA 90210 USA
Travis, Randy — Singer, Guitarist, Songwriter
Pure Fix Entertainment, 15333 N Pima Road, #145, Scottsdale AZ 85258, USA
Travis, Scott — Drummer (Judas Priest)
Trinifold Mgmt, 12 Oval Road, #300, Camden, London NW1 7DH, England
Travis, Stacey — Actress
Essential Talent Mgmt, 6399 Wilshire Blvd, #400, Los Angeles CA 90048, USA
Traviss, Karen — Writer
Scovil Chichak Galen, 276 5th Ave, #708, New York NY 10001, USA
Travolta, Ellen — Actress
6470 E Sunnyside Road, Coeur D'Alene ID 83814, USA
Travolta, Joey — Singer, Director
23634 Tiara St, Woodland Hills CA 91367, USA
Travolta, John — Actor
1504 Live Oak Lane, Santa Barbara CA 93105, USA
Traxler, William B, Jr — Judge
US Court of Appeals, Powell Courthouse, 1100 E Main St, Richmond VA 23219, USA
Traya, Misti — Actress
Abrams Artists, 9200 W Sunset Blvd, #1125, West Hollywood CA 90069 USA
Traylor, B Keith — Football Player
508 E Shreveport St, Broken Arrow OK 74011, USA
Traylor, Susan — Actress
Abrams Artists, 275 7th Ave, #2600, New York NY 10001 USA
Traynor, J Michael — Attorney
3131 Eton Ave, Berkeley CA 94705, USA
Traynor, John (Jay) — Singer (Jay & the Americans)
Jet Music, 17 Pauline Court, Rensselaer NY 12144, USA
Traynowicz, Mark J — Football Player
1668 Sioux St, Lincoln NE 68502, USA
Trcic, Michael — Sculptor
175 Goodrow Lane, Sedona AZ 86336, USA
Treach — Rap Artist (Naughty By Nature)
Don Buchwald/Fortitude, 6500 Wilshire Blvd, #2200, Los Angeles CA 90048 USA
Treacy, Philip — Fashion Designer
Philip Treacy Ltd, 69 Elizabeth St, London SW1W 9PJ, England
Treadaway, Harry — Actor
United Agents, 12-26 Lexington St, London W1F 0LE, England
Treadaway, Luke — Actor
Hamilton Hodell, 66-68 Margaret St, London W1W 8SR, England
Treadell, Victoria M (Vicki) — High Commissioner, New Zealand
High Commissioner's Office, 44 Hill St, Wellington 6011, New Zealand
Treadway, H Jeffrey (Jeff) — Baseball Player
8812 Estes Road, Macon GA 31220, USA
Treadway, James C, Jr — Government Official
Laurel Ledge Farm, Croton Lake Road, RR 4, Mount Kisco NY 10549, USA
Treadwell, David M — Football Player
9141 E Star Hill Place, Lone Tree CO 80124, USA
Treanor, Matthew A (Matt) — Baseball Player
460 NW 115th Way, Coral Springs FL 33071, USA
Trebek, Alex — Entertainer
3405 Fryman Road, Studio City CA 91604, USA
Trebelhorn, Thomas L (Tom) — Baseball Player, Manager
7753 E Montebello Ave, Scottsdale AZ 85250, USA
Trebil, Dan — Ice Hockey Player
8551 Big Woods Lane, Eden Prairie MN 55347, USA
Trebunskaya, Anna — Dancer
Abrams Artists, 9200 W Sunset Blvd, #1125, West Hollywood CA 90069 USA
Tree, Michael — Violist (Guarneri String Quartet)
45 E 89th St, New York NY 10128, USA
Tregear, Lucy — Actress
Gavin Barker Assoc, 2D Wimpole St, London W1G 0EB, England
Treisman, Anne M — Psychologist
Princeton University, Psychology Dept, Princeton NJ 08544, USA
Treitler, Leo — Musicologist
City University of New York, Graduate Center, 365 5th Ave, #8204, New York NY 10016, USA
Trejo, Danny — Actor
Amsel Eisenstadt Frazier, 5055 Wilshire Blvd, #865, Los Angeles CA 90036 USA
Trelford, Donald G — Editor
15 Fowler Road, London N1 2EA, England
Tremblay, Francois-Louis — Speed Skater
C P V Quebec, Arena Duberger, Duberger Park, 3050 Boul Central, Quebec QC G1P3N9, Canada
Tremblay, Gilles — Ice Hockey Player
104-218 Rue Notre-Dame, Repentigny QC P1B 7R5, Canada
Tremblay, Mario — Ice Hockey Player, Coach
743 Passaic Ave, #412, Clifton NJ 07012, USA
Tremblay, Michel — Writer
294 Carre Saint Louis, #5E, Montreal QC H2X 1A4, Canada
Tremblay, Yannick — Ice Hockey Player
9911 Carrington Lane, Alpharetta GA 30022, USA
Tremel, William L (Bill) — Baseball Player
315 E 23rd Ace, Altoona PA 16601, USA
Tremie, Christopher J (Chris) — Baseball Player
484 Marion Lane, New Waverly TX 77358, USA

Tremonti, Mark T — Guitarist (Creed, Alter Bridge)
Agency Group, 1776 Broadway, #430, New York NY 10019, USA

Trenary, Jill — Figure Skater
4445 Governors Point, Colorado Springs CO 80906, USA

Trent, Gary D — Basketball Player
1150 Northwood Circle, New Albany OH 43054, USA

Trentini, Caroline — Model
Why Not Model Mgmt, Via Zenale 9, 20123 Milan, Italy

Trento, Joseph — Writer
Public Education Center, 1830 Connecticut Ave NW, #3, Washington DC 20009, USA

Trepagnier, Jeffrey (Jeff) — Basketball Player
1414 N McDivitt Ave, Compton CA 90221, USA

Treschev, Sergei Y — Cosmonaut
Cosmonaut Training Center, Star City, 141160 Zvezdny Gorodok, Moscow Oblast, Russia

Tress, Arthur — Photographer
2705 Marlborough Lane, Cambria CA 93428, USA

Tressel, James P (Jim) — Football Coach
Indianapolis Colts, 7001 W 56th St, Indianapolis IN 46254 USA

Tresvant, John B — Basketball Player
14814 61st Dr SE, Snohomish WA 98296, USA

Trethewey, Natasha — Writer
Houghton Mifflin Harcourt, 215 Park Ave S, #1200, New York NY 10003 USA

Tretiak, Vladislav — Ice Hockey Player
Hockey Federation, Luzhnetskaia Naberezhnaia 8, 119992 Moscow, Russia

Tretiakov, Alexander V — Skeleton Athlete
Ski Assn, Luzhnetskaya Nab 8, 119270 Moscow, Russia

Tretyakov, Victor V — Concert Violinist
Berlin Konzeragentur Monika Ott, Dramburger Str 46, 12683 Berlin, Germany

Treu, Adam R — Football Player
3176 NW Shevlin Meadows Dr, Bend OR 97701, USA

Trever, John — Editorial Cartoonist
Albuquerque Journal, Editorial Dept, 717 Silver Ave SW, Albuquerque NM 87102, USA

Trevi, Gloria — Singer, Songwriter
I C M Partners, 10250 Constellation Blvd, #900, Los Angeles CA 90067 USA

Trevino, Alejandro (Alex) — Baseball Player
PO Box 288, Houston TX 77001, USA

Trevino, Lee B — Golfer
4906 Park Lane, Dallas TX 75220, USA

Trevino, Michael — Actor
Greene Assoc, 1901 Ave of Stars, #130, Los Angeles CA 90067 USA

Trevino, Rick — Singer
Warner Bros Records, 20 Music Square East, Nashville TN 37203 USA

Trevor, William — Writer
Viking Press, 375 Hudson St, New York NY 10014, USA

Trevorrow, Colin — Director, Writer
3 Arts Entertainment, 9460 Wilshire Blvd, #700, Beverly Hills CA 90212 USA

Trey Songz — Singer, Songwriter
Atlantic Records, 1290 Ave of Americas, Concourse 3, New York NY 10104 USA

Trezeguet, David N — Soccer Player
F C Juventus, Corso Galilo Ferraris 32, 10128 Turin, Italy

Triandos, C Gus — Baseball Player
PO Box 5642, San Jose CA 95150, USA

Triano, Jay — Basketball Coach
Toronto Raptors, Air Canada Center, 20 Bay St, Toronto ON M5J 2N8, Canada

Trias, Jasmine S — Singer
Universal Records, 70 Universal City Plaza, Universal City CA 91608 USA

Tribbett, Greg (Gurgg) — Guitarist (Mudvayne)
Agency Group Ltd, 142 W 57th St, #600, New York NY 10019 USA

Tribe, Laurence H — Attorney, Educator
Harvard University, Law School, Griswold Hall, Cambridge MA 02138, USA

Trible, Paul S, Jr — Senator, VA; Educator
Christopher Newport University, President's Office, 50 University Place, Newport News VA 23606, USA

Trichet, Jean-Claude — Financier
5 Rue de Beaujolais, 75001 Paris, France

Trick Daddy — Rap Artist
Slip-N-Slide/Warlock Records, 919 4th St, Miami Beach FL 33139, USA

Trickett, Lisbeth (Libby) C — Swimmer
Swimming Australia, 12/7 Beissel St, Bekonnen ACT 2617, Australia

Trickle, Richard (Dick) — Auto Racing Driver
PO Box 645, Skyland NC 28776, USA

Tricky — Rap Artist, Songwriter
Little Big Man, 155 Ave of Americas, #700, New York NY 10013, USA

Triffle, Carol — Director
Imago Theater, PO Box 15182, Portland OR 97293, USA

Trigger, Sarah — Actress
Forward Entertainment, 9255 Sunset Blvd, #805, Los Angeles CA 90069, USA

Triggs Hodge, Andrew — Rowing Athlete
Molesey Boat Club, Barge Walk, East Molesey, Surrey KT8 9AJ, England

Trillin, Calvin M — Writer
New Yorker, Editorial Dept, 4 Times Square, Basement C1B, New York NY 10036 USA

Trillo, J Manuel (Manny) — Baseball Player
7309 W Coyle Ave, Chicago IL 60631, USA

Trimble, David W — Nobel Peace Laureate
2 Queen St, Lurgan, County Armagh BT66 8BQ, Northern Ireland

Trimble, Vance H — Editor
25 Oakhurst St, Wewoka OK 74884, USA

Trimble, Vivian — Keyboardist (Luscious Jackson)
Metropolitan Entertainment, 2 Penn Plaza, #2600, New York NY 10121, USA

Trimmer, H William — Macrobiotics Engineer
1345 McLaurin Road, Siler City NC 27344, USA

Trimper, Tim — Ice Hockey Player
1028 Broughton Lane, Newmarket ON L3X 2L7, Canada

Trina — Rap Artist
Pyramid Entertainment, 377 Rector Place, #21A, New York NY 10280 USA

Trinh, Eugene — Astronaut
N A S A Headquarters, 300 E St SW, Washington DC 20546, USA

Trinidad, Felix (Tito) — Boxer
RR 6 Box 11479, San Juan PR 00926, USA

Trinkaus, Erik — Paleontologist
Washington University, Paleontolgy Dept, PO Box 1214, Saint Louis MO 63188, USA

Trinneer, Connor — Actor
Abrams Artists, 9200 W Sunset Blvd, #1125, West Hollywood CA 90069 USA

Trintignant, Jean-Louis — Actor
Les Visiteurs du Soir, 40 Rue de la Folie Regnault, 75011 Paris, France

Triplett, Kirk — Golfer
4527 N 61st Place, Scottsdale AZ 85251, USA

Triplett, William C (Bill) — Football Player
222 Beechwood Dr, Youngstown OH 44506, USA

Trippe, Thomas G — Physicist
Lawrence Livermore Laboratory, 7000 East Ave, Livermore CA 94550 USA

Trippi, Charles L (Charlie) — Football Player
125 Riverhill Court, Athens GA 30606, USA

Tripplehorn, Jeanne — Actress
Gersh Agency, 9465 Wilshire Blvd, #600, Beverly Hills CA 90212 USA

Tripplett, Larry C J — Football Player
4065 Ambergate Place, Dublin CA 94568, USA

Tripucka, Francis J (Frank) — Football Player
39 Schindler Way, Fairfield NJ 07004, USA

Tripucka, P Kelly — Basketball Player
14 Devon Road, Boonton NJ 07005, USA

Tristan, Dorothy — Actress
Film Acres, 2622 E 850 N, La Porte IN 46350, USA

Trlicek, Richard A (Ricky) — Baseball Player
PO Box 1109, La Grange TX 78945, USA

Troccoli, Kathleen C (Kathy) — Singer, Songwriter
K T Designs, 5543 Edmondson Pike, #7A, Nashville TN 37211, USA

Troche, Celeste — Golfer
560 Perry St, #108, Auburn AL 36830, USA

Troche, Rose — Actress, Writer, Director, Producer
Gersh Agency, 9465 Wilshire Blvd, #600, Beverly Hills CA 90212 USA

Trocheck, Kathy H — Writer
Harper Collins Publishers, 10 E 53rd St, Cellar 1, New York NY 10022 USA

Troe, Jurgen — Chemist
Universitat Gottingen, Tammannstr 6, 37077 Gottingen, Germany

Troedson, Richard L (Rich) — Baseball Player
899 Bowen Ave, San Jose CA 95123, USA

Troger, Christian-Alexander — Swimmer
I Muncher Swim Club, Josefstr 26, 82941 Deisenhofen, Germany

Trohman, Joe — Guitarist (Fall Out Boy)
PO Box 219, 1187 Wilmette Ave, Wilmette IL 60091, USA

Troisgros, Pierre E R — Chef, Restauranteur
20 Route de Commelle, 42120 Le Coteau, France

Trollope, Joanna — Writer
Crossworld Publishing, 61-63 Uxbridge Road, London W5 5SA, England

Trombetta, Monica — Actress
I C M Partners, 730 5th Ave, New York NY 10019 USA

Trombley, Michael S (Mike) — Baseball Player
2 Hilltop Park, Wilbraham MA 01095, USA

Trombone Shorty — Jazz Trombonist, Band Leader
Rosebud Agency, PO Box 170429, San Francisco CA 94117 USA

Tronnier, Ellen — Baseball Player
PO Box 255, Palmyra WI 53156, USA

Troost, Ernest — Singer, Songwriter
First Artists Mgmt, 4764 Park Granada, #210, Calabasas CA 91302 USA

Troska, Zdenek — Director
Hostice u Volyne 77, 387 01 Volyne, Czech Republic

Trosper, Jennifer Harris — Space Scientist
Jet Propulsion Laboratory, 4800 Oak Grove Dr, Pasadena CA 91109 USA

Trost, Barry M — Chemist
24510 Amigos Court, Los Altos Hills CA 94024, USA

Trost, Carlisle A H — Navy Admiral
11 Compromise St, Annapolis MD 21401, USA

Trott, Stephen S — Judge, Singer (Highwaymen)
US Court of Appeals, US Courthouse, 550 W Fort St, Boise ID 83724, USA

Trotter, De'Hashia T (Deedee) — Track Athlete
9900 Brannigan Circle, Knoxville TN 37923, USA

Trotter, Jeremiah — Football Player
6863 F M 1398, Parkton MD 21120, USA

Trottier, Bryan J — Ice Hockey Player, Coach
504 Bluegrass Dr, Canonsburg PA 15317, USA

Trottier, Guy — Ice Hockey Player
1003 Hazel Ave, Englewood OH 45322, USA

Trotz, Barry — Ice Hockey Coach
9001 Demery Court, Brentwood TN 37027, USA

Trouble Valli — Guitarist (Crazy Town)
Q Prime, 729 7th Ave, #1600, New York NY 10019, USA

Troughton, Sam — Actor
Markham & Froggatt, Julian House, 4 Windmill St, London W1P 1HF, England

Trounson, Alan — Biologist
Monash University, Immunology/Stem Cell Laboratory, Monash VIC 3800, Australia

Troup, P William (Bill), III — Football Player
4 Quail Wood Court, Parkton MD 21120, USA

Troupe, Benjamin L (Ben) — Football Player
1105 Rannoch Place, Nashville TN 37220, USA

Troupe, Tom — Actor, Writer
8829 Ashcroft Ave, West Hollywood CA 90048, USA

Trout, Michael N (Mike) — Baseball Player
Los Angeles Angels, Angel Stadium, 2000 E Gene Autry Way, Anaheim CA 92806 USA

Trout, Steven R (Steve) — Baseball Player
PO Box 1155, Tinley Park IL 60477, USA

Trout, Walter — Singer, Guitarist, Songwriter
Fish-Net Productions, 5840 W Craig Road, #120-228, Las Vegas NV 89130, USA

Trower, Robin — Singer, Guitarist (Procol Harum)
Stardust Enterprises, 4600 Franklin Ave, Los Angeles CA 90027, USA

Troxel, Gary — Singer (Fleetwoods)
11471 Earle Dr, Mount Vernon WA 98273, USA

Troxel, Melanie — Auto Racing Driver
PO Box 637, Brownsburg IN 46112, USA

Troy, Michael F (Mike) — Swimmer
21187 E Alyssa Road, Queen Creek AZ 85142, USA

Troyer, Verne — Actor
12400 Ventura Blvd, #630, Studio City CA 91604, USA

Trpceski, Simon — Concert Pianist
Kirshbaum Demler Assoc, 711 W End Avenue, #5KN, New York, NY 10025, USA

Truax, William F (Billy) — Football Player
735 Ruth Ave, Gulfport MS 39501, USA

Truby, Chris — Baseball Player
12244 Silverado Dr, Fishers IN 46037, USA

Trucco, Michael — Actor, Director
McKeon-Myrones Mgmt, 3500 Olive Ave, #770, Burbank CA 91505 USA

Trucks, Derek — Orchestra Leader, Guitarist
Monterey International, 200 W Superior St, #202, Chicago IL 60654 USA

Trucks, Toni — Actress
Greene Assoc, 1901 Ave of Stars, #130, Los Angeles CA 90067 USA

Trucks, Virgil O (Fire) — Baseball Player
1016 Waterford Trail, Calera AL 35040, USA

Trudeau, Garry B — Cartoonist (Doonesbury)
459 Columbus Ave, #200, New York NY 10024, USA

Trudeau, Jack F — Football Player
9150 Timberwolf Lane, Zionsville IN 46077, USA

True, Rachel — Actress
Kritzer Levine Wilkins Griffin, 11872 La Grange Ave, #100, Los Angeles CA 90025 USA

Trueba, Fernando — Animator, Producer, Writer
Creative Artists Agency, 2000 Ave of Stars, #100, Los Angeles CA 90067 USA

Trueblood, Jeremy T — Football Player
10603 Keswick Place, Tampa FL 33626, USA

Truesdale, Yanic — Actor
Nancy Iannios Public Relations, PO Box 430, Signal Mountain TN 37377 USA

Truex, Lambertson — Fashion Designer
I C Insight Communications, Piazzale Baiamonti 4, 20154 Milan, Italy

Truex, Martin L, Jr — Auto Racing Driver
172 Tennessee Circle, Mooresville NC 28117, USA

Trufant, Marcus L — Football Player
15504 SE 79th Place, Newcastle WA 98059, USA

Truhill, Geraldine Sloan (Jerri) — Astronaut Candidate
1431 Lamp Post Lane, Richardson TX 75080, USA

Truitt, Olanda R — Football Player
1901 16th Way N, Bessemer AL 35020, USA

Trujillo, Chadwick — Astronomer
California Institute of Technology, Astronomy Dept, Pasadena CA 91125, USA

Trujillo, Michael A (Mike) — Baseball Player
16373 6475 Road, Montrose CO 81403, USA

Trujillo, Robert — Bassist (Ozzy Osborne, Metallica)
Q Prime, 729 7th Ave, #1600, New York NY 10019 USA

Trujillo, Solomon D — Businessman
Qwest Communications, 700 Qwest Tower, 1801 California St, Denver CO 80202, USA

Trull, Donald D (Don) — Football Player
8706 Bloomfield Turn, Missouri City TX 77459, USA

Trulli, Jarno — Auto Racing Driver
Casa del Muschna, 7513 Silvaplana, Switzerland

Trulsen, Paal — Curling Athlete
Curling Assn, Sognsveien 75, Serviceboks 1, 0840 Oslo, Norway

Truluck, R-Kal K — Football Player
418 McDonough St, Saint Charles MO 63301, USA

Truly, Richard H — Astronaut, Space Administrator, Admiral
2340 Juniper Court, Golden CO 80401, USA

Truman, Dan — Pianist, Keyboardist (Diamond Rio)
Modern Mgmt, 1625 Broadway, #600, Nashville TN 37203, USA

Truman, James — Editor
Conde Nast Publications, Editorial Office, 4 Times Square, New York NY 10036, USA

Trumka, Richard L — Labor Leader
AFL-CIO, 1750 New York Ave NW, Lobby 1, Washington DC 20006, USA

Trump, Donald J — Businessman, Actor
Trump Organization, 725 5th Ave, Basement, New York NY 10022, USA

Trump, Ivana — Businesswoman, Model
10 E 64th St, New York NY 10065, USA

Trump, Ivanka — Model
W M E Entertainment, 9601 Wilshire Blvd, #300, Beverly Hills CA 90210 USA

Trumpy, Robert T (Bob), Jr — Football Player, Sportscaster
75 Oak St, Cincinnati OH 45246, USA

Trundy, Natalie — Actress
2109 S Wilbur Ave, Walla Walla WA 99362, USA

Truscott, Lucian K, IV — Writer
Avon/William Morrow, 1350 Ave of Americas, #200, New York NY 10019 USA

Trusnik, Jason — Football Player
Cleveland Browns, 76 Lou Groza Blvd, Berea OH 44017 USA

Truth Hurts — Singer, Songwriter, Actress
Aftermath/Interscope Records, 2220 Colorado Ave, Santa Monica CA 90404, USA

Tryba, Ted — Golfer
6321 Cheryl St, Orlando FL 32819, USA

Tryggvason, Bjarni V — Astronaut, Canada
Space Agency, 6767 Route de Aeroport, Saint Hubert QC J3Y 8Y9, Canada

Trynin, Jennifer — Singer, Songwriter, Guitarist
Vector Mgmt, PO Box 120479, Nashville TN 37212 USA

Tryon, W Augustus (Ty), IV — Golfer
8713 Esplanade, #1, Orlando FL 32836, USA

Tsakalidis, Iakovos (Jake) — Basketball Player
6940 E Doubletree Ranch Road, Paradise Valley AZ 85253, USA

Tsallagova, Elena — Opera Singer
I M G Artists, Hogarth Business Park, Chiswick, London W4 2TH, England

Tsamis, George A — Baseball Player
12 Sweetbriar Court, Colchester CT 06415, USA

Tsantiris, Len — Soccer Coach
University of Connecticut, Athletic Dept, Storrs CT 06239, USA

Tsao, I Fu — Chemical Engineer
University of Michigan, Chemical Engineering Dept, Ann Arbor MI 48109, USA

Tscharnke, Tim — Cross Country Skier
Ulf Tscharnke, Simmersbergstra 55, 98666 Masserberg Ortsteil Schnett, Germany

Tschetter, Kris — Golfer
13 Culpepper St, Warrenton VA 20186, USA

Tschogi, John M — Basketball Player
295 Shirley St, Chula Vista CA 91910, USA

Tschumi, Bernard — Architect
7 Rue Pecquay, 75004 Paris, France

Tschutscher, Klaus — Prime Minister, Liechtenstein
Prime Minister's Office, Peter-Kaiser-Platz 1, 9490 Vaduz, Liechtenstein

Tsereteli, Zurab K — Sculptor
21 Prechistenka St, 119034 Moscow, Russia

Tsia, Ming — Chef
Blue Ginger, 583 Washington St, Wellesley MA 02482, USA

Tsibliyev, Vasili V — Cosmonaut
Cosmonaut Training Center, Star City, 141160 Zvezdny Gorodok, Moscow Oblast, Russia

Tsien, Billie — Interior Designer
Tod Williams Billie Tsien Architects, 222 Central Park S, New York NY 10019, USA

Tsien, Richard W — Neurobiologist
29 Washington Square W, #15A, New York NY 10011, USA

Tsien, Roger Y — Nobel Chemistry Laureate
University of California, Chemistry Dept, 9500 Gilman Dr, La Jolla CA 92093, USA

Tsitouris, John P — Baseball Player
5207 Austin Road, Monroe NC 28112, USA

Tsonga, Jo-Wilfried — Tennis Player
Association of Tennis Professionals, 200 Tournament Road, Ponte Vedra Beach FL 32082 USA

Tsopei, Kiriaki (Corinna) — Beauty Queen, Actress
Miss Universe Organization, 1370 Ave of Americas, #1600, New York NY 10019, USA

Tsou, Cece — Actress, Producer, Writer
C E S D, 10635 Santa Monica Blvd, #130, Los Angeles CA 90025 USA

Tsoucalas, Nicholas — Judge
US Court of International Trade, 1 Federal Plaza, New York NY 10278, USA

Tsu, Irene — Actress
House of Representatives, 1434 6th St, #1, Santa Monica CA 90401 USA

Tsui, Daniel C — Nobel Physics Laureate
53 College Road W, Princeton NJ 08540, USA

Tsui, Lap-Chee — Molecular Geneticist, Educator
Hong Kong University, Vice Chancellor's Office, Pokfulam Road, Hong Kong, China

Tsujii, Nobuyuki — Concert Pianist
I M G Artists, Hogarth Business Park, Chiswick, London W4 2TH, England

Tsuno, Yoshikazu — Prime Minister, Japan
Imperial Palace, 1-1 Chiyoda, Chiyodaku, Tokyo 100 0001, Japan

Tsvangirai, Morgan R — Prime Minister, Zimbabwe
Prime Minister's Office, Private Bag 7700, Causeway, Harare, Zimbabwe

Tua, David — Boxer
Gotham Boxing, 1414 Ave of Americas, #404, New York NY 10019, USA

Tuan, Nguyan — Sculptor
Masterpiece Publishing, 5 Watson, Irvine CA 92618, USA

Tuan, Yi-Fu — Humanistic Geographer
University of Wisconsin, Geography Dept, Madison WI 53706, USA

Tubbs, Gregory A (Greg) — Baseball Player
833 Clay Ave, Cookeville TN 38501, USA

Tubbs, Tony — Boxer
913 Alcorn Lane, Muscatine IA 52761, USA

Tubbs, Winfred O — Football Player
4212 Debbie Dr, Grand Prairie TX 75052, USA

Tuberville, Thomas H (Tommy) — Football Coach
Texas Tech University, Athletic Dept, Lubbock TX 79409, USA

Tucci, Michael — Actor
1425 Irving Ave, Glendale CA 91201, USA

Tucci, Roberto Cardinal — Religious Leader
Palazzo Pio, Piazza Pia 3, 00193 Rome, Italy

Tucci, Stanley — Actor, Director
Olive Productions, 161 Ave of Americas, #1100, New York NY 10013, USA

Tuccillo, Liz — Writer, Producer
United Talent Agency, 9336 Civic Center Dr, Beverly Hills CA 90210 USA

Tuchman, Maurice — Museum Curator
150 E 57th St, #PH 1A, New York NY 10022, USA

Tuck, Jessica — Actress
Greene Assoc, 1901 Ave of Stars, #130, Los Angeles CA 90067 USA

Tuck, Justin L — Football Player
New York Giants, Meadowlands Stadium, 102 Route 120, East Rutherford NJ 07073 USA

Tucker, Anand — Director
United Talent Agency, 9336 Civic Center Dr, Beverly Hills CA 90210 USA

Tucker, Barbara — Singer
Nene Musik Productions, 1460 SW Santiago Ave, Port Saint Lucie FL 34953 USA

Tucker, Bill — Bowler
26126 Meadowcrest Blvd, Huntington Woods MI 48070, USA

Tucker, Chris — Actor, Comedian
W M E Entertainment, 9601 Wilshire Blvd, #300, Beverly Hills CA 90210 USA

Tucker, Darcy — Ice Hockey Player
8754 Crooked Stick Court, Lone Tree CO 80124, USA

Tucker, Duncan — Director, Writer
Brillstein Entertainment Partners, 9150 Wilshire Blvd, #350, Beverly Hills CA 90212 USA

Tucker, John — Ice Hockey Player
19833 Michigan Ave, Odessa FL 33556, USA

Tucker, Jonathan — Actor
United Talent Agency, 9336 Civic Center Dr, Beverly Hills CA 90210 USA

Tucker, Lisa — Actress, Singer
Creative Artists Agency, 2000 Ave of Stars, #100, Los Angeles CA 90067 USA
Tucker, Michael — Fertility Biologist
Reproductive Biology, 5505 Peachtree Dunwoody Road NE, Atlanta GA 30342, USA
Tucker, Michael — Actor
Stone Manners Salners, 9911 W Pico Blvd, #1400, Los Angeles CA 90035 USA
Tucker, Michael A — Baseball Player
407 Maple Ave N, Lehigh Acres FL 33972, USA
Tucker, Rex T — Football Player
2300 Culpepper Dr, Midland TX 79705, USA
Tucker, Robert L (Bob), Jr — Football Player
8 Hunter Road, Hazleton PA 18201, USA
Tucker, Ryan H — Football Player
24752 Eagle Pointe, Columbia Station OH 44028, USA
Tucker, Tanya — Singer
Webster Assoc, PO Box 23015, Nashville TN 37202, USA
Tucker, Thomas J (T J) — Baseball Player
6616 Ridge Top Dr, New Port Richey FL 34655, USA
Tucker, Tony — Boxer
Club Prana, 1619 7th Ave, Ybor City, Tampa FL 33605, USA
Tucker, Trent — Basketball Player
433 River St, Minneapolis MN 55401, USA
Tucker, Y Arnold — Football Player
PO Box 514, Hilbert WI 54129, USA
Tuckwell, Barry E — Concert French Horn Player, Conductor
Gallo & Giordano, 76 W 86th St, New York NY 10024, USA
Tudor, John T — Baseball Player
5 Nathan Lane, Middleton MA 01949, USA
Tudor, Rob A — Ice Hockey Player
69 Cimarron Meadows Way, Okotoks AB T1S 1V9, Canada
Tudyk, Alan — Actor
Gersh Agency, 9465 Wilshire Blvd, #600, Beverly Hills CA 90212 USA
Tuer, Al — Ice Hockey Player
Calgary Flames, PO Box 1540, Station M, Calgary AB T2P 3B9, Canada
Tueting, Sarah — Ice Hockey Player
488 Ash St, Winnetka IL 60093, USA
Tufts, Robert M (Bob) — Baseball Player
6738 108th St, #A27, Forest Hills NY 11375, USA
Tufuga Efi, Tupuola Taisi — Head of State, Samoa
Head of State's Office, Government House, Vailima, Apia, Samoa
Tuggle, Anthony I — Football Player
12345 Plymouth Dr, Baton Rouge LA 70807, USA
Tuggle, Jessie L — Football Player
540 Avala Court, Alpharetta GA 30022, USA
Tugnutt, Ronald F B (Ron) — Ice Hockey Player
10 Beech Grove Gardens, Stittsville ON K2S 1W5, Canada
Tuiasosopo, Manu A — Football Player
14616 NE 184th Place, Woodinville WA 98072, USA
Tuilaepa Sailele Maljelegaio — Prime Minister, Samoa
Prime Minister's Office, PO Box 193, Apia, Samoa
Tuitert, Mark — Speed Skater
Skating Federation, Postbus 1120, 3800 BC Amersfoort, Netherlands
Tu'ivakano, Lord — Prime Minister, Tonga
Prime Minister's Office, PO Box 62, Taufa'ahau Road, Nuku'alofa, Tonga
Tuke, Blair — Yachtsman
Kerikeri Cruising Club, 346 Opito Bay Road, R D 1, Kerikeri 0294, Bay of Islands, New Zealand
Tukur, Ulrich — Actor
Anne Alvares Correa, 34 Rue Jouffroy d'Abbans, 75017 Paris, France
Tulafono, Togiola T A — Governor, AS
Governor's Office, Executive Office Building, #300, Pago Pago AS 96799 USA
Tullis, William J (Willie) — Football Player
10018 Knoboak Dr, #4, Houston TX 77080, USA
Tulloch, Elizabeth (Bitsie) — Actress
W M E Entertainment, 9601 Wilshire Blvd, #300, Beverly Hills CA 90210 USA
Tulloch, Stephen M — Football Player
629 Palisades Court, Brentwood TN 37027, USA
Tully, Caitlin — Concert Violinist
I M G Artists, Hogarth Business Park, Chiswick, London W4 2TH, England
Tulowitzki, Troy T — Baseball Player
Colorado Rockies Foundation, 2001 Blake St, Denver CO 80205, USA
Tulving, Endel — Psychologist
45 Baby Point Crescent, York ON M6S 2B7, Canada
Tuman, Jerame D — Football Player
1303 Hidden Canyon Court, Sewickley PA 15143, USA
Tumi, Christian W Cardinal — Religious Leader
Archveche, BP 179, Douala, Cameroon
Tune, Thomas J (Tommy) — Dancer, Actor, Choreographer
I C M Partners, 10250 Constellation Blvd, #900, Los Angeles CA 90067 USA
Tung Chee Hwa — Chief Executive, Hong Kong
Emeritus Chief Executive's Office, 28 Kennedy Road, Hong Kong, China
Tunie, Tamara — Actress
Paradigm Agency, 360 N Crescent Dr, North Building, Beverly Hills CA 90210 USA
Tunnell, B Lee — Baseball Player
6000 Kingsbridge Dr, Oklahoma City OK 73162, USA
Tunney, Jim — Football Referee
PO Box 1440, Pebble Beach CA 93953, USA
Tunney, John V — Senator, CA
304 Chautauqua Blvd, Pacific Palisades CA 90272, USA
Tunney, Robin — Actress
Creative Artists Agency, 2000 Ave of Stars, #100, Los Angeles CA 90067 USA
Tunnicliffe, Anna — Yachtswoman
New York Yacht Club, 37 W 44th St, New York NY 10036, USA
Tunstall, Kate V (K T) — Singer, Guitarist, Songwriter
Creative Artists Agency, 2000 Ave of Stars, #100, Los Angeles CA 90067 USA
Tuohy, Kat — Actress, Comedienne
OmniPop Talent Group, 4605 Lankershim Blvd, #201, Toluca Lake CA 91602 USA

Tupa, Thomas J (Tom) 6761 Rivercrest Dr, Brecksville OH 44141, USA	Football Player
Tupman, Matt 3 Lincoln St, Concord NH 03301, USA	Baseball Player
Tupov VI Royal Palace, PO Box 6, Nuku'alofa, Tonga	King, Tonga
Tupper, James I C M Partners, 10250 Constellation Blvd, #900, Los Angeles CA 90067 USA	Actor
Tur, Arlene Gersh Agency, 9465 Wilshire Blvd, #600, Beverly Hills CA 90212 USA	Actress, Comedienne
Turang, Brian C 3014 McNab Ave, Long Beach CA 90808, USA	Baseball Player
Turco, Marty 3616 N Wayne Ave, Chicago IL 60613, USA	Ice Hockey Player
Turco, Paige Gersh Agency, 9465 Wilshire Blvd, #600, Beverly Hills CA 90212 USA	Actress
Turcotte, Alfie 816 Hawk Dr, Wolverine Lake MI 48390, USA	Ice Hockey Player
Turcotte, Darren North Bay Skyhawks, 100 Chippewa W, North Bay ON P1B 6G2, Canada	Ice Hockey Player
Turcotte, Donald L (Don) 27104 Middle Golf Dr, El Macero CA 95618, USA	Geophysicist
Turcotte, Jean-Claude Cardinal 1071 Rue de la Cathedrale, Montreal QC H2B 2V4, Canada	Religious Leader
Turcotte, Mathieu Speed Skating Canada, 2781 Lancaster Road, #402, Ottawa ON K1B 1A7, Canada	Speed Skater
Turcotte, Ron J M 82 Seattle Slew Dr, Howell NJ 07731, USA	Thoroughbred Racing Jockey
Turek, Roman Sports Corp, 10088 102nd Ave, Edmonton AB T5J 2Z1, Canada	Ice Hockey Player
Turgeon, Mark University of Maryland, College Park MD 20742 USA	Basketball Coach
Turgeon, Pierre 1075 E Oxford Lane, Englewood CO 80113, USA	Ice Hockey Player
Turgoose, Thomas Troika, 74 Clerkenwell Road, #300, London EC1M 5QA, England	Actor
Turk, Danilo President's Office, Erjavceva 17, 61000 Ljublijana, Slovenia	President, Slovenia
Turk, Matt E 5114 Evergreen St, Bellaire TX 77401, USA	Football Player
Turkel, Ann 10701 Wilshire Blvd, #2001, Los Angeles CA 90024, USA	Actress, Model
Turkoglu, Hidayet (Hedo) 322 E Central Blvd, #1203, Orlando FL 32801, USA	Basketball Player
Turkson, Peter K A Cardinal Archdiocese, PO Box 112, Cape Coast, Ghana	Religious Leader
Turley, Kyle D 1715 Championship Blvd, Franklin TN 37064, USA	Football Player
Turley, Robert L (Bob) 3284 Chipping Wood Court, Alpharetta GA 30004, USA	Baseball Player
Turlington, Christy United Talent Agency, 9336 Civic Center Dr, Beverly Hills CA 90210 USA	Model, Director
Turman, Glynn R Elkins Mgmt, 8306 Wilshire Blvd, #3643, Beverly Hills CA 90211, USA	Actor
Turnage, Mark-Anthony Cathy Nelson, Court House, Dorstone, Herefordshire HR3 6AW, England	Composer
Turnball, Ian 23930 Ocean Ave, #154, Torrance CA 90505, USA	Ice Hockey Player
Turnbloom, Lucas Southern Cross, Editorial Dept, 3888 Paducah Dr, San Diego CA 92117, USA	Editorial Cartoonist
Turnbow, T Derrick 2224 Brienz Valley Dr, Franklin TN 37064, USA	Baseball Player
Turnbull, Perry 2186 Cedar Forest Court, Chesterfield MO 63017, USA	Ice Hockey Player
Turnbull, Renaldo A 9507 Chanson Place, Matthews NC 28105, USA	Football Player
Turnbull, Wendy 822 Boylston Dt, #203, Chestnut Hill MA 02467, USA	Tennis Player
Turnbull, William Waddington Galleries, 11 Cork St, London W1S 3LT, England	Artist
Turner, Aidan Creative Artists Agency, 2000 Ave of Stars, #100, Los Angeles CA 90067 USA	Actor
Turner, Alexander D (Alex) Wildlife Entertainment, 21 Heathman's Road, London SW6 4TJ, England	Singer, Guitarist (Arctic Monkeys)
Turner, Andy Windish Agency, 1658 N Milwaukee Ave, #211, Chicago IL 60647, USA	Musician (Plaid)
Turner, Bree Brillstein Entertainment Partners, 9150 Wilshire Blvd, #350, Beverly Hills CA 90212 USA	Actress
Turner, Cathy 251 East Ave, Hilton NY 14468, USA	Speed Skater
Turner, Cecil A 2717 Dog Leg Trail, McKinney TX 75069, USA	Football Player
Turner, Christopher W (Chris) 28553 N Quarry Dr, Elberta AL 36530, USA	Baseball Player
Turner, Craig Hardin-Simmons University, President's Office, Abilene TX 79698, USA	Educator
Turner, Dean 26900 Captains Lane, Franklin MI 48025, USA	Ice Hockey Player
Turner, Dylan Associated International Mgmt, Fairfax House, Fulwood Place, London WC1V 6HU, England	Actor
Turner, Edwin L Princeton University, Astrophysical Sciences Dept, Princeton NJ 08544, USA	Astrophysicist
Turner, Elston H 23 Commanders Cove, Missouri City TX 77459, USA	Basketball Player
Turner, Floyd, Jr 9626 Garden Row Dr, Sugar Land TX 77498, USA	Football Player

Turner, Fred L — Businessman
McDonald's Corp, McDonald's Plaza, 1 Kroc Dr, Oak Brook IL 60523, USA
Turner, Gideon — Actor
Ken McReddie Assoc, 11 Connaught Place, London W2 2ET, England
Turner, Guinevere — Actress
Jaret Entertainment, 6973 Birdview Ave, Malibu CA 90265, USA
Turner, James A (Jim) — Football Player
14155 W 59th Place, Arvada CO 80004, USA
Turner, James T — Judge
US Claims Court, 717 Madison Place NW, Washington DC 20439, USA
Turner, James, Jr — Businessman
General Dynamics, 2941 Fairview Park Dr, #100, Falls Church VA 22042, USA
Turner, Janine — Actress, Model
Linda McAlister Talent, 530 S Lake Ave, #435, Pasadena CA 91101, USA
Turner, Jeffrey S (Jeff) — Basketball Player
1590 Woodland Ave, Winter Park FL 32789, USA
Turner, John N W — Prime Minister, Canada
59 Oriole Road, Toronto ON M4V 2E9, Canada
Turner, John W (Jerry) — Baseball Player
1935 18th St, #B, Santa Monica CA 90404, USA
Turner, John, Jr — Football Player
3217 Cedar Ave S, Minneapolis MN 55407, USA
Turner, Josh — Singer, Guitarist
Modern Mgmt, 1625 Broadway, #600, Nashville TN 37203, USA
Turner, Karri — Actress
Premiere Artists Agency, 1875 Century Park E, #2250, Los Angeles CA 90067 USA
Turner, Kathleen — Actress
Don Buchwald/Fortitude, 6500 Wilshire Blvd, #2200, Los Angeles CA 90048 USA
Turner, Keena — Football Player, Coach
8200 W Erb Way, Tracy CA 95304, USA
Turner, Kenneth C (Ken) — Baseball Player
PO Box 252, San Marcus. CA 92079, USA
Turner, Kevin — Businessman
Microsoft Corp, 1 Microsoft Way, Redmond WA 98052, USA
Turner, Marcus J — Football Player
5032 Meadow Wood Ave, Lakewood CA 90712, USA
Turner, Michael — Football Player
912 Chattanooga Trace, Suwanee GA 30024, USA
Turner, Morgan — Actress
I C M Partners, 10250 Constellation Blvd, #900, Los Angeles CA 90067 USA
Turner, Morris (Morrie) — Cartoonist (Wee Pals)
PO Box 3004, Berkeley CA 94703, USA
Turner, Norv — Football Coach
PO Box 400, Del Mar CA 92014, USA
Turner, Odessa — Football Player
177 Cortland Terrace, Teaneck NJ 07666, USA
Turner, P Kevin — Football Player
215 Liberty Lake Dr, Vestavia AL 35242, USA
Turner, R E (Ted), III — Sports Executive, Yachtsman, Businessman
Turner Foundation, 133 Luckie St NW, #200, Atlanta GA 30303, USA
Turner, R Gerald — Educator
Southern Methodist University, President's Office, Dallas TX 75275, USA
Turner, Robert H (Bake) — Football Player
PO Box 277, Alpine TX 79831, USA
Turner, Ronald L — Businessman
Ceridian Corp, 3311 E Old Shakopee Road, Minneapolis MN 55425, USA
Turner, Shane L — Baseball Player
3032 Van Reed Road, Reading PA 19608, USA
Turner, Sherri — Golfer
5 Alpine St, Carbondale CO 81623, USA
Turner, Sophie — Actress
Independent Talent Group, Oxford House, 76 Oxford St, London W1D 1BS, England
Turner, Stansfield — Navy Admiral, Government Official
600 New Hampshire Ave NW, #800, Washington DC 20037, USA
Turner, Steve — Guitarist (Green River, Mudhoney)
Legends of 21st Century, 7 Trinity Row, Florence MA 01062, USA
Turner, Tina — Singer, Actress
R D W M Services, 37 Limerston St, London SW10 0BQ, England
Turner, Tyrin — Actor
Williams Talent Agency, 1438 N Gower St, Building 35, Los Angeles CA 90028, USA
Turner, Vernon M — Football Player
86 Crosshill St, Staten Island NY 10301, USA
Turner, W Matthew (Matt) — Baseball Player
829 Della Dr, Lexington KY 40504, USA
Turner, William (Bill) — Basketball Player
3271 Wisteria Tree St, Las Vegas NV 89135, USA
Turner, William H (Billy), Jr — Thoroughbred Racing Trainer
230 Nassau Blvd, Garden City NY 11530, USA
Turnesa, Marc — Golfer
Professional Golfer's Assn, PO Box 109601, Palm Beach Gardens FL 33410 USA
Turnley, David C — Photojournalist
34 Rue des Frances Bourgeois, 75003 Paris, France
Turnovsky, Martin — Conductor
Gerhild Baron, Dornbacher Str 41/III/2, 1170 Vienna, Austria
Turow, Scott F — Writer
233 S Wacker Dr, #8000, Chicago IL 60606, USA
Turre, Steve — Jazz Trombonist
Brad Simon Organization, 155 W 46th St, #500, New York NY 10036 USA
Turrell, James A — Artist
Skystone Foundation, PO Box 220, Flagstaff AZ 86002, USA
Turteltaub, Jon — Director
Junction Entertainment, 500 S Buena Vista St, Animation Building, Burbank CA 91521, USA
Turturro, Aida — Actress
Framework Entertainment, 9057 Nemo St, #C, West Hollywood CA 90069 USA
Turturro, John — Actor, Director
987 Terracina St, Santa Paula CA 93060, USA

Turturro, Nicholas — Actor, Director
Kritzer Levine Wilkins Griffin, 11872 La Grange Ave, #100, Los Angeles CA 90025 USA
Turunen, Tarja — Singer, Songwriter
N E M S Enterprises, Av Rivadavia 4686, 14 Capital Federal, Argentina
Tushingham, Rita — Actress
Lip Service, 4 Kingly St, London W1R 5LF, England
Tusk, Donald F — Prime Minister, Poland
Ul Ursad Rady Ministrow, Ul Wiejska 4/8, 00 583 Warsaw, Poland
Tuten, Melvin E, Jr — Football Player
13779 Mottlestone Dr, Pickerington OH 43147, USA
Tuten, Richard L (Rick) — Football Player
1146 SE 15th St, Ocala FL 34471, USA
Tutone, Tommy — Singer, Dancer
Edge Mgmt, 10850 Wilshire Blvd, #380, Los Angeles CA 90024, USA
Tutor, Ronald N — Producer, Businessman
Tutor Perini Corp, 15901 Olden St, Sylmar CA 91342, USA
Tuttle, Jerry O — Navy Admiral
J O T Enterprises, 5875 Trinity Parkway, #130, Centreville VA 20120, USA
Tuttle, Steve — Ice Hockey Player
928 Belfair Road, Bellevue WA 98004, USA
Tuttle, William G T, Jr — Army General
9707 Ceralene Dr, Fairfax VA 22032, USA
Tutu, Desmond M — Nobel Peace Laureate, Religious Leader
PO Box 1092, Milnerton 744, Cape Town, South Africa
Tuur, Regilio — Boxer
New York Boxing Club, 1616 Whitestone Expressway, Whitestone NY 11357, USA
Tuzzolino, Tony — Ice Hockey Player
75 Chasewood Lane, East Amherst NY 14051, USA
Tveit, Aaron — Actor
Innovative Artists, 1505 10th St, Santa Monica CA 90401 USA
Tverdovsky, Oleg I — Ice Hockey Player
8850 E Garden View Dr, Anaheim CA 92808, USA
Twaalfhoven, Merlijn — Composer
La Vie Sur Terre, Palamedesstr 9-1, 1054 HS Amsterdam, Netherlands
Twain, Shania — Singer, Songwriter, Model
Special Artists Agency, 9465 Wilshire Blvd, #820, Beverly Hills CA 90212 USA
Twardzik, Dave J — Basketball Player, Executive
1670 Balmy Beach Dr, Apopka FL 32703, USA
Tway, Bob — Golfer
6300 Oak Heritage Trail, Edmond OK 73025, USA
Tweed, Shannon — Actress, Model
Characters Talent Mgmt, 8 Elm St, Toronto ON M5G 1G7, Canada
Tweedy, Cheryl — Singer (Girls Aloud)
Polydor Records, 364-366 Kensington High St, London W14 8NS, England
Tweedy, Jeff — Singer, Guitarist (Uncle Tupelo, Wilco)
Tom Margherita Mgmt, 2200 W Foster Ave, #2, Chicago IL 60625, USA
Tweet — Singer, Songwriter
Violator Mgmt, 36 W 25th St, New York NY 10010, USA
Twellman, Taylor — Soccer Player, Sportscaster
ESPN-TV, ESPN Plaza, 935 Middle St, Bristol CT 06010 USA
Twigg, Rebecca — Cyclist
7001 Old Redmond Road, #E318, Redmond WA 98052, USA
Twiggs, Greg — Golfer
31421 N 69th St, Scottsdale AZ 85266, USA
Twiggy — Model, Actress
4 Saint Georges House, Hanover Square, London W1R 9AJ, England
Twilley, Dwight — Singer, Keyboardist, Songwriter
Paradise Artists, PO Box 1821, Ojai CA 93024 USA
Twilley, Howard J, Jr — Football Player
7040 Hill Forest Dr, Dallas TX 75230, USA
Twist, Tony — Ice Hockey Player
63 Nordic Lane, Defiance MO 63341, USA
Twista — Rap Artist
Courtney Barnes Group, 1680 N Vine St, #1119, Los Angeles CA 90028, USA
Twitty, Howard — Golfer
8007 E Mercer Lane, Scottsdale AZ 85260, USA
Twitty, Jeffrey D (Jeff) — Baseball Player
812 Willow Cove Road, Chapin SC 29036, USA
Twohy, David — Director
603 Ocean Ave, #3, Santa Monica CA 90402, USA
Twohy, Mike — Cartoonist
605 Beloit Ave, Kensington CA 94708, USA
Twohy, Robert — Cartoonist
New Yorker, Editorial Dept, 4 Times Square, Basement C1B, New York NY 10036 USA
Twomey, Steve — Journalist
City University of New York, Graduate Journalism School, 219 W 40th St, New York NY 10018, USA
Tydings, Joseph D — Senator, MD
2705 Pocock Road, Monkton MD 21111, USA
Tye, Larry — Writer
Random House, 1745 Broadway, #1800, New York NY 10019 USA
Tyers, Kathy — Writer
Martha Millard Agency, 204 Park Ave, Madison NJ 07940, USA
Tykwer, Tom — Director, Writer, Actor
Herbstfilm Produktion, Hufelandstr 33, 10407 Berlin, Germany
Tyler, Aisha — Actress, Comedienne
United Talent Agency, 9336 Civic Center Dr, Beverly Hills CA 90210 USA
Tyler, Anne — Writer
8 Roland Gardens, Baltimore MD 21210, USA
Tyler, Bonnie — Singer, Songwriter
Darmstadter Landstr 7-9, 60594 Frankfurt, Germany
Tyler, Brian — Composer
Kaufman & Bernstein, 1925 Century Park E, #800, Los Angeles CA 90067, USA
Tyler, James Michael — Actor
A K A Talent, 6310 San Vicente Blvd, #200, Los Angeles CA 90048, USA
Tyler, Judy — Model
Playboy Promotions, 2706 Media Center Dr, Los Angeles CA 90065 USA

Tyler, Liv — Actress, Model
Untitled Entertainment, 350 S Beverly Dr, #200, Beverly Hills CA 90212 USA

Tyler, Maurice M — Football Player
7066 Whitfield Dr, Riverdale GA 30296, USA

Tyler, Richard — Fashion Designer
Richard Tyler Couture, 727 Washington St, New York NY 10014, USA

Tyler, Robert — Actor
Don Buchwald/Fortitude, 10 E 44th St, New York NY 10017 USA

Tyler, Steven V — Singer (Aerosmith), Songwriter
Front Line Mgmt, 1100 Glendon Ave, #2000, Los Angeles CA 90024 USA

Tyler, Terry C — Basketball Player
6500 Tauton Road NW, Albuquerque NM 87120, USA

Tyler, Wendell A — Football Player
44143 20th St W, Lancaster CA 93534, USA

Tylo, Hunter — Actress, Model
11684 Ventura Blvd, #910, Studio City CA 91604, USA

Tylo, Michael — Actor
11684 Ventura Blvd, #910, Studio City CA 91604, USA

Tylor, Jud — Director
TalentWorks, 3500 W Olive Ave, #1400, Burbank CA 91505 USA

Tylski, Richard L (Rich) — Football Player
5456 Tierra Verde Lane, Jacksonville FL 32258, USA

Tyminski, Dan — Singer, Guitarist (Union Station)
Doobie Shea Records, 2008 Sadie Lane, Goodlettsville TN 37072, USA

Tyner, Jason R — Baseball Player
5535 Sul Ross, Beaumont TX 77706, USA

Tyner, McCoy — Jazz Pianist, Composer
Abby Hoffer, 223 1/2 E 48th St, New York NY 10017 USA

Tyner, Tray — Golfer
208 Plantation Path, Boerne TX 78006, USA

Tynes, Lawrence J — Football Player
5 Ponds Way, Oakland NJ 07436, USA

Tyree, David M — Football Player
15 Fox Hill Dr, Wayne NJ 07470, USA

Tyrell, Steve — Singer
Soundtrack Music Assoc, 1460 4th St, #308, Santa Monica CA 90401, USA

Tyrrell, Timothy G (Tim) — Football Player
17 Fallstone Dr, Streamwood IL 60107, USA

Tyson, Cicely — Actress
315 W 70th St, New York NY 10023, USA

Tyson, Ian — Singer, Songwriter
Richard Flohil Assoc, 60 McGill St, Toronto ON M5B 1H2, Canada

Tyson, John H — Businessman
Tyson Foods Inc, 2200 W Don Tyson Parkway, Springdale AR 72762, USA

Tyson, Laura D — Government Official, Economist
London Business School Sussex Place, Regent Park, London NW1 4SA, England

Tyson, Michael G (Mike) — Boxer
Williams Talent Agency, 1438 N Gower St, Building 25, Los Angeles CA 90028, USA

Tyson, Michael R (Mike) — Baseball Player
479 Thunderhead Canyon Dr, Ballwin MO 63011, USA

Tyson, Neil de Grasse — Astrophysicist
Hayden Planetarium, 81 Central Park W, New York NY 10024, USA

Tyson, Richard — Actor
C E S D, 10635 Santa Monica Blvd, #130, Los Angeles CA 90025 USA

Tyurin, Mikhail — Cosmonaut
Cosmonaut Training Center, Star City, 141160 Zvezdny Gorodok, Moscow Oblast, Russia

Ubach, Alanna — Actress
Margrit Polak Mgmt, 1920 Hillhurst, #405, Los Angeles CA 90027 90027, USA
Uchida, Irene A — Geneticist
20 North Shore Blvd W, Burlington ON L7T 1A1, Canada
Uchida, Mitsuko — Concert Pianist
Konzertdirektion Schmid, Konigstra 36, 30175 Hannover, Germany
Udenio, Fabiana — Actress
House of Representatives, 1434 6th St, #1, Santa Monica CA 90401 USA
Uderzo, Albert — Cartoonist
Les Editions Albert Rene, 26 Ave Victor Hugo, 75016 Paris, France
Udoka, Ime S — Basketball Player
PO Box 40802, Portland OR 97240, USA
Udovenko, Hennadiy Y — Government Official, Ukraine
Desyatynna Str 10, #2, 01025 Kiev, Ukraine
Udrih, Beno — Basketball Player
46 Arnold Palmer, San Antonio TX 78257, USA
Udvar-Hazy, Steven F — Businessman, Philanthropist
67 Beverly Park, Beverly Hills CA 90210, USA
Udvari, Frank — Ice Hockey Referee
6 Willow St, Waterloo ON N2J 2S3, Canada
Udy, Helene — Actress
Society Entertainment, 15303 Ventura Blvd, Building C, Sherman Oaks CA 91403, USA
Ueberroth, Peter V — Baseball, Olympics Executive
184 Emerald Bay, Laguna Beach CA 92651, USA
Uecker, Gunther — Artist
Kaiserstr 10, 40221 Dusseldorf, Germany
Uecker, R Keith — Football Player
169 Dorchester Road, Akron OH 44313, USA
Uecker, Robert G (Bob) — Actor, Baseball Player, Sportscaster
W131N7867 N Country Club Court, Menomonee Falls WI 53051, USA
Uelses, John — Track Athlete
30660 Rolling Hills Dr, Valley Center CA 92082, USA
Uelsmann, Jerry N — Photographer
5701 SW 17th Dr, Gainesville FL 32608, USA
Ufland, Len — Actor, Director
16900 NE 19th Ave, North Miami Beach FL 33162, USA
Uggams, Leslie — Singer, Actress
Gage Group, 315 W 57th St, #4H, New York NY 10019 USA
Uggla, Dan — Baseball Player
2004 Lincoln Road, Spring Hill TN 37174, USA
Ughi, Uto — Concert Violinist
Cannareggio 4990/E, 30121 Venice, Italy
U-God — Rap Artist (Wu-Tang Clan)
A&M Entertainment, 13280 NE Freeway, #F328, Houston TX 77040, USA
Ugueto, Luis E — Baseball Player
6009 188th Lane NE, #201, Redmond WA 98052, USA
Uhalt, Alfred H — Astronaut
2533 Shalmar Dr, Colorado Springs CO 80915, USA
Uhl, George R — Geneticist
Johns Hopkins University Medical Center, Genetics Dept, Baltimore MD 21218, USA
Uhl, Petr — Human Rights Activist
Pravo, Slezska 13, 121 50 Prague, Czech Republic
Uhlenbeck, Karen K — Mathematician
University of Texas, Mathematics Dept, Austin TX 78712, USA
Uhlenhake, Jeffrey A (Jeff) — Football Player
1304 Normandy Dr, Newark OH 43055, USA
Uhrmann, Michael — Ski Jumper
Harslemstr 2, 94139 Breitenberg, Germany
Uhry, Alfred F — Writer
Marshall Purdy, 226 W 47th St, #900, New York NY 10036, USA
Ulbrich, Jeffrey W (Jeff) — Football Player
2316 88th Place NE, Clyde Hill WA 98004, USA
Ulene, Arthur L — Physician, Entertainer
6511 Moore Dr, Los Angeles CA 90048, USA
Ulevich, Neal H — Photojournalist
11954 Glencoe Dr, Denver CO 80233, USA
Uliger, Scott M — Baseball Player
4149 W Russell Ave, Visalia CA 93277, USA
Ulion-Silverman, Gretchen — Ice Hockey Player
640 Pleasant St, Framingham MA 01701, USA
Ullman, Norman V A (Norm) — Ice Hockey Player
819-25 Austin Dr, Markham ON L3R 8H4, Canada
Ullman, Ricky — Actor
Gersh Agency, 41 Madison Ave, #3301, New York NY 10010 USA
Ullman, Tracey — Actress, Comedienne, Singer
Special Artists Agency, 9465 Wilshire Blvd, #820, Beverly Hills CA 90212 USA
Ullmann, Liv I — Actress
101 W 79th St, #8F, New York NY 10024, USA
Ullrich, Jan — Cyclist
Burgunderweg 10, 79291 Merdingen, Germany
Ulmer, C Arthur (Artie) — Football Player
2200 Enclave Mill Dr, Dacula GA 30019, USA
Ulmer, Frances (Fran) — Educator
University of Alaska, Chancellor's Office, 3211 Providence Dr, Anchorage AK 99508, USA
Ulmer, Kristen — Extreme Athlete
3734 Thousand Oaks Circle, Salt Lake City UT 84124, USA
Ulrich, Lars — Drummer (Metallica)
Q Prime, 729 7th Ave, #1600, New York NY 10019 USA
Ulrich, Skeet — Actor
Brillstein Entertainment Partners, 9150 Wilshire Blvd, #350, Beverly Hills CA 90212 USA
Ulrich, Thomas — Boxer
Brunsbutteler Damm 29, 13581 Berlin, Germany
Ultra Nate — Singer
Peach Bisquit, 963 Kent Ave, Brooklyn NY 11205, USA
Ulusu, Bulent — Prime Minister, Turkey; Navy Admiral
Ciftehavuzlar Yesilbahar 50K 8/27, Kadikoy/Istanbul, Turkey

Ulvaeus, Bjorn — Singer (ABBA), Composer
Mono Music, Sodra Brobanken 41A, Skeppsjolmen, 111 49 Stockholm, Sweden

Ulvang, Vegard — Cross Country Skier
Fjellveien 53, 9900 Kirkenes, Norway

Umbarger, James H (Jim) — Baseball Player
3909 W Harmont Dr, Phoenix AZ 85051, USA

Umberger, R J — Ice Hockey Player
835 Rose Mary Hill Dr, Pittsburgh PA 15239, USA

Umbers, Mark — Actor
Ken McReddie Assoc, 11 Connaught Place, London W2 2ET, England

Umemoto, Nanako — Architect
118 E 59th St, #402, New York NY 10022, USA

Umhoefer, David — Journalist
Journal Sentinal, Editorial Dept, 6525 W Bluemound Road, Milwaukee WI 53213, USA

Umphlett, Thomas M (Tommy) — Baseball Player
104 Berkley Road, Ahoskie NC 27910, USA

Unanue, Emil R — Immunopathologist
Washington University Medical School, Pathology Dept, Saint Louis MO 63110, USA

Underwood, Blair — Actor
I C M Partners, 10250 Constellation Blvd, #900, Los Angeles CA 90067 USA

Underwood, Carrie — Singer, Songwriter
8 Wentworth Place, Brentwood TN 37027, USA

Underwood, Jacob — Singer (O-Town)
Trans Continental Records, 127 W Church St, #350, Orlando FL 32801, USA

Underwood, Jay — Actor
6100 Wilshire Blvd, #1170, Los Angeles CA 90048, USA

Underwood, Olen U — Football Player
PO Box 2514, Conroe TX 77305, USA

Underwood, Patrick J (Pat) — Baseball Player
708 Riverview Dr, Kokomo IN 46901, USA

Underwood, Sara Jean — Model, Actress
I A G Entertainment, 5189 Argonne Court, San Diego CA 92117, USA

Underwood, Scott — Drummer (Train)
Jon Landau, 150 Rowayton Ave, Norwalk CT 06853, USA

Unel, Birol — Actor
Agentur Drews, Schumannstr 16, 10117 Berlin, Germany

Uner, Idil — Actress
Neue Schonhauser Str 16, 10178 Berlin, Germany

Ungaro, Emanuel M — Fashion Designer
2 Ave Montaigne, 75008 Paris, France

Unger, Brian — Entertainer
A P A Talent/Literary Agency, 405 S Beverly Dr, #300, Beverly Hills CA 90212 USA

Unger, Deborah Kara — Actress
Seven Summits Mgmt, 8906 W Olympic Blvd, Beverly Hills CA 90211 USA

Unger, Garry D — Ice Hockey Player
Banff Hockey Academy, Box 2422, Banff AB T1L 1B9, Canada

Unger, Joe — Actor
718 N Kings, #30, West Hollywood CA 90069, USA

Unger, Kay — Fashion Designer
Saint Gillian Sportswear, 498 Fashion Ave, New York NY 10018, USA

Unger, Roger H — Internist
Texas Southwestern Medical Center, 5323 Harry Hines Blvd, Dallas TX 75390, USA

Union, Gabrielle — Actress
Intellectual Artists Mgmt, 10585 Santa Monica Blvd, #135, Los Angeles CA 90025, USA

Unroe, Timothy Brian (Tim) — Baseball Player
2719 S Joplin, Mesa AZ 85209, USA

Unruh, James A — Businessman
5426 E Morrison Lane, Paradise Valley AZ 85253, USA

Unseld, Westley S (Wes) — Basketball Player, Coach, Executive
2210 Cedar Circle Dr, Catonsville MD 21228, USA

Unser, Alfred (Al), Jr — Auto Racing Driver
PO Box 56696, Albuquerque NM 87187, USA

Unser, Alfred (Al), Sr — Auto Racing Driver
7625 Central Ave NW, Albuquerque NM 87121, USA

Unser, Delbert E (Del) — Baseball Player
33516 N 79th Way, Scottsdale AZ 85266, USA

Unser, Robbie — Auto Racing Driver
806 Laguayra Dr NE, Albuquerque NM 87108, USA

Unser, Robert W (Bobby) — Auto Racing Driver
7617 Frederick Lane SW, Albuquerque NM 87121, USA

Unutoa, Morris T — Football Player
829 S Jordan Way, Lehi UT 84043, USA

Upatnieks, Juris — Optical Engineer
Applied Optics, 2662 Valley Dr, Ann Arbor MI 48103, USA

Upchurch, Richard (Rick) — Football Player
4104 SE 20th Place, #B2, Cape Coral FL 33904, USA

Upham, John L — Baseball Player
1502 Pierre Ave, Windsor ON N9C 2K7, Canada

Upham, Misty A — Actress
Innovative Artists, 1505 10th St, Santa Monica CA 90401 USA

Uphoff-Becker, Nicole — Equestrian
Freiherr-von-Lanen-Str 15, 48231 Warendorf, Germany

Upshaw, Dawn — Opera Singer
Nonesuch Records, 75 Rockefeller Plaza, #800, New York NY 10019 USA

Upshaw, Marvin A (Marv) — Football Player
3851 Madrone Ave, Oakland CA 94619, USA

Upshaw, Regan C — Football Player
746 Walker Road, #16, Great Falls VA 22066, USA

Upshaw, Willie C — Baseball Player
74 James St, Fairfield CT 06824, USA

Upton, Kate — Model
I M G Models, 304 Park Ave S, #PH-North, New York NY 10010 USA

Upton, Melvin E (B J) — Baseball Player
1428 Harbour Walk Road, Tampa FL 33602, USA

Urango, Juan — Boxer
Groupe Yvon Michel, 10172 Saint-Laurent, Montreal QC H3L 2N8, Canada

Urb, Johann — Actor
A P A Talent/Literary Agency, 405 S Beverly Dr, #300, Beverly Hills CA 90212 USA

Urban, Jerheme W — Football Player
217 Fleetwood Dr, San Antonio TX 78232, USA

Urban, Karl L — Actor
Principato-Young, 9465 Wilshire Blvd, #880, Beverly Hills CA 90212 USA

Urban, Keith — Singer
PO Box 40725, Nashville TN 37204, USA

Urbano, Michael (Mike) — Drummer (Smash Mouth)
Creative Artists Agency, 2000 Ave of Stars, #100, Los Angeles CA 90067 USA

Urbanski, Douglas — Producer, Writer
Douglas Management Group, PO Box 691763, West Hollywood CA 90069, USA

Urbanski, Krzystof — Conductor
Indianapolis Symphony, 32 E. Washington St., #600, Indianapolis, IN 46204, USA

Urdang, Leslie — Producer
United Talent Agency, 9336 Civic Center Dr, Beverly Hills CA 90210 USA

Ure, Midge — Singer, Guitarist
115A Glenthorne, Hammersmith, London W6 0LJ, England

Uresti, Omar — Golfer
2503 Pebble Beach Dr, Austin TX 78747, USA

Uribe, Juan C — Baseball Player
425 Shoreline Road, Lake Barrington IL 60010, USA

Urich, Justin — Actor
Talent Group, 5670 Wilshire Blvd, #820, Los Angeles CA 90036, USA

Urie, Brendon B — Singer, Guitarist (Panic at the Disco)
Crush Music Mgmt, 60-62 E 11th St, #700, New York NY 10002, USA

Urie, Michael — Actor
Gersh Agency, 9465 Wilshire Blvd, #600, Beverly Hills CA 90212 USA

Urkal, Oktay — Boxer
Frank Bleydorn, Goethestr 25, 12207 Berlin, Germany

Urlacher, Brian K — Football Player
15044 W Little Saint Marys Road, Libertyville IL 60048, USA

Urmanov, Aleksei — Figure Skater
Union of Skaters, Luzhnetskaya Nab 8, 119871 Moscow, Russia

Urosa Savino, Jorge L Cardinal — Religious Leader
Archdiocese of Caracas, Plaza Bolivar, Apt 954, Caracas 1010A, Venezuela

Urquhart, Brian E — Diplomat
Howard Farms, Jerusalem Road, Tyringham MA 01264, USA

Urseth, Bonnie — Actress
Gage Group, 14724 Ventura Blvd, #505, Sherman Oaks CA 91403 USA

Urzi, Daniela — Model
Rebel Mgmt, Concepcion Arenal 3425, #2-45, Buenos Aires, Argentina

Usachyov, Yury V — Cosmonaut
Cosmonaut Training Center, Star City, 141160 Zvezdny Gorodok, Moscow Oblast, Russia

Usery, Willie J, Jr — Secretary, Labor
1101 S Arlington Ridge Road, Arlington VA 22202, USA

Usher — Rap Artist, Actor
W M E Entertainment, 9601 Wilshire Blvd, #300, Beverly Hills CA 90210 USA

Usher, Robert R (Bob) — Baseball Player
1022 N 5th St, San Jose CA 95112, USA

Usher, Thomas J — Businessman
U S X Corp, 600 Grant St, #450, Pittsburgh PA 15219, USA

Usova, Maya — Ice Dancer
Igloo Skating Rink, 3033 Fostertown, Mount Laurel NJ 08054, USA

Ut, Nick — Photographer
Associated Press, Photo Dept, 221 S Figueroa St, #300, Los Angeles CA 90012, USA

Utay, William — Actor
Arlene Thornton, 12711 Ventura Blvd, #490, Studio City CA 91604, USA

Utkina, Sveta — Model
I M G Models, 304 Park Ave S, #PH-North, New York NY 10010 USA

Utley, Garrick — Commentator
ABC-TV, News Dept, 8 Carburton St, London W1P 7DT, England

Utley, Michel G (Mike) — Football Player
PO Box 349, Orondo WA 98843, USA

Utt, Benjamin M (Ben) — Football Player
143 Blackland Road NW, Atlanta GA 30342, USA

Uvarov, Andrei I — Ballet Dancer
Bolshoi Theater, Teatralnaya Pl 1, 103009 Moscow, Russia

Uvini, Bruno — Soccer Player
Confederacion de Futebol, Rua Victor Civita 66, #1, Rio de Janeiro 22775 044, Brazil

Uzawa, Hirofumi — Economist
Kamiyamacho 20-23, Shibuyaku, Tokyo, Japan

Vacano, Jost — Cinematographer
Leoprechtingstr 18, 81739 Munich, Germany
Vacanti, Charles A — Surgeon
Massachusetts University Medical Center, Anesthesiology Dept, Worcester MA 02139, USA
Vacariou, Nicolae — President, Romania
Romanian Senate, Piata Revolutiei, 71243 Bucharest, Romania
Vaccaro, Brenda — Actress
C E S D, 10635 Santa Monica Blvd, #130, Los Angeles CA 90025 USA
Vacendak, Stephen T (Steve) — Basketball Player
608 Gaston St, #100, Raleigh NC 27603, USA
Vachon, Rogatien R (Rogie) — Ice Hockey Player
648 Oxford Ave, Venice CA 90291, USA
Vachss, Andrew H — Writer
106-23 Metro Ave, Forest Hills NY 11375, USA
Vactor, Theodore F (Ted) — Football Player
11504 Channing Dr, Silver Spring MD 20902, USA
Vadim, Christian — Actor
Voyez Mon Agent, 20 Ave Rapp, 75007 Paris, France
Vadnais, Carol — Ice Hockey Player
Prouix Vadnais, 955 Rue Bergar, Laval QC H7L 4Z6, Canada
Vaduva, Leontina — Opera Singer
Stafford Law, 6 Barham Close, Weybridge, Surrey KT13 9PR, England
Vagelos, P Roy — Businessman, Biochemist
82 Mosle Road, Far Hills NJ 07931, USA
Vagnorius, Gediminas — Prime Minister, Lithuania
Parliament, Prospekt Gedimino 53, 2002 Vilnius, Lithuania
Vago, Constant — Pathologist
Chemin Serre de Laurian, 30100 Ales, France
Vagt, Robert F — Foundation Executive, Educator
Heinz Endowments, 30 Dominion Tower, 625 Liberty Ave, Pittsburgh PA 15222, USA
Vahala, Elina — Concert Violinist
Sublime Music Agency, Ruusulankatu 14, 00250 Helsinki, Finland
Vahi, Tiit — Prime Minister, Estonia
Coalition Eesti Koonderakond, Raekoja Plats 16, 10146 Tallinn, Estonia
Vai, Steve — Guitarist (Alcatrazz, Whitesnake)
Creative Artists Agency, 2000 Ave of Stars, #100, Los Angeles CA 90067 USA
Vail Evans, Justina — Actress
651 N Kilkea Dr, Los Angeles CA 90048, USA
Vail, Eric — Ice Hockey Player
10055 Piney Ridge Walk, Alpharetta GA 30022, USA
Vail, Michael L (Mike) — Baseball Player
7946 San Jose Road, El Paso TX 79915, USA
Vail, Thomas — Editor
29225 Chagrin Blvd, #200, Beachwood OH 44122, USA
Vaillancourt, Sarah M — Ice Hockey Player
Team Canada, 2424 University Dr NW, Calgary AB T2N 3Y9, Canada
Vaive, Rick — Ice Hockey Player
Toronto Maple Leafs, AirCanada Center, 40 Bay St, Toronto ON M5J 2K2, Canada
Vajiralongkorn — Crown Prince, Thailand
Royal Residence, Chitralada Villa, 9 Rama VI Road, Soi 30, Bangkok 10400, Thailand
Vajna, Andrew G — Producer
Cinergi Productions, 2308 Broadway, Santa Monica CA 90404, USA
Vajpayee, Atal Behari — Prime Minister, India
7 Race Course Road, New Delhi 110011, India
Valabik, Boris — Ice Hockey Player
Boston Bruins, 100 Legends Way, #250, Boston MA 02114 USA
Valance, Holly — Singer, Actress
Jon Fowler Mgmt, 60A Highgate High St, London N6 5HX, England
Valanciunas, Jonas — Basketball Player
Toronto Raptors, Air Canada Center, 20 Bay St, Toronto ON M5J 2N8, Canada
Valandrey, Charlotte — Actress
Artmedia, 20 Ave Rapp, 75007 Paris, France
Valar, Paul — Skier
34 Hubertus Ring, Franconia NH 03580, USA
Valbusa, Fulvio — Cross Country Skier
Biancaneve 7, 37021 Bosco Chiesanuova, Italy
Valderrama, Carlos — Soccer Player
Colorado Rapids, 1000 Chopper Circle, Denver CO 80204 USA
Valderrama, Wilmer — Actor
United Talent Agency, 9336 Civic Center Dr, Beverly Hills CA 90210 USA
Valdes, Ismael — Baseball Player
4001 26th St, Vero Beach FL 32960, USA
Valdes, Jesus (Chucho) — Jazz Pianist
D L Media, 124 N Highland Ave, Bala Cynwyd PA 19004 USA
Valdes, Marc C — Baseball Player
7519 Paula Dr, Tampa FL 33615, USA
Valdes, Maximiano — Conductor
C M Artists, 127 W 96th St, #13B, New York NY 10025 USA
Valdespino, Hilario (Sandy) — Baseball Player
3937 Lilac Haze St, Las Vegas NV 89147, USA
Valdez, Luis — Writer
El Teatro Capesino, 705 4th St, San Juan Bautista CA 95045, USA
Valdivielso Lopez, Jose L — Baseball Player
14 Rita Dr, Mount Sinai NY 11766, USA
Valdivieso Sarmiento, Alfonso — Government Official, Colombia
Foreign Affairs Ministry, Palacio San Carlos, Santa Fe, Bogota, Colombia
Vale, Jerry — Singer
40960 Glenmore Dr, Palm Desert CA 92260, USA
Valek, Vladimir — Conductor
Cesky Rozhlas, Vinohradska 12, 120 00 Prague 2, Czech Republic
Valen, Nancy — Actress
Michael Bruno Group, 13576 Cheltenham Dr, Sherman Oaks CA 91423, USA
Valensi, Nick — Guitarist (Strokes)
M V O Ltd, 370 7th Ave, #807, New York NY 10001, USA
Valente, Benita — Opera Singer
Maurice Mayer, 201 W 54th St, #1C, New York NY 10019, USA

Vacano - Valente

Valente, Catarina — Singer, Guitarist, Actress
Villa Corallo, Via ai Ronci 12, 6816 Bissone, Switzerland

Valenti, James — Opera Singer
I M G Artists, Hogarth Business Park, Chiswick, London W4 2TH, England

Valentin Rosario, J Javier R — Baseball Player
Cincinnati Reds, Great American Ball Park, 100 Main St, Cincinnati OH 45202 USA

Valentin Rosario, Jose A — Baseball Player
3714 E Park Ave, Phoenix AZ 85044, USA

Valentin, Dave — Jazz Flutist
Abby Hoffer, 223 1/2 E 48th St, New York NY 10017 USA

Valentin, John W — Baseball Player
37 Golden Lane, Hazlet NJ 07730, USA

Valentin, Jose A — Baseball Player
3714 E Park Ave, Stamford CT 06903, USA

Valentine, Amber — Singer, Guitarist (Jucifer)
Vamp Music Source, 902 W Franklin Ave, #15, Minneapolis MN 55405, USA

Valentine, Brooke — Singer
Virgin Records, 338 N Foothill Road, Beverly Hills CA 90210 USA

Valentine, Christopher W (Chris) — Ice Hockey Player
Bell Sensplex, 1565 Maple Grove Road, Kanata ON K2V 1A3, Canada

Valentine, Dan — Businessman
C-Cube Microsystems, 1551 McCarthy Blvd, Milpitas CA 95035, USA

Valentine, Darnell T — Basketball Player
7546 SW Ashford St, Portland OR 97224, USA

Valentine, Dean — Businessman
First Family Entertainment, 9595 Wilshire Blvd, #407, Beverly Hills CA 90212, USA

Valentine, DeWain — Artist
17921 S Western Ave, Gardena CA 90248, USA

Valentine, Ellis C — Baseball Player
2708 Bridgemarker Dr, Grand Prairie TX 75054, USA

Valentine, Fred L — Baseball Player
4838 Blagden Ave NW, Washington DC 20011, USA

Valentine, Gary — Actor, Comedian
Innovative Artists, 1505 10th St, Santa Monica CA 90401 USA

Valentine, Greg — Professional Wrestler
13045 Farmington Trail, Seminole FL 33776, USA

Valentine, Hilton — Guitarist (Animals)
Lustig Talent, PO Box 770850, Orlando FL 32877 USA

Valentine, Jacqui — Singer, Bassist (Civet)
Kirky Organization, 9200 Sunset Blvd, #600, Los Angeles CA 90069, USA

Valentine, James — Guitarist (Maroon 5)
J Records, 745 5th Ave, #600, New York NY 10151 USA

Valentine, James W — Paleobiologist
1351 Glendale Ave, Berkeley CA 94708, USA

Valentine, Joseph J (Joe) — Baseball Player
4168 Chiffon Lane, North Port FL 34287, USA

Valentine, Karen — Actress
PO Box 4531, Valley Village CA 91617, USA

Valentine, Kathy — Singer, Guitarist, Bassist (Go-Go's)
Direct Management Group, 947 N La Cienega Blvd, #G, West Hollywood CA 90069, USA

Valentine, Raymond C — Agronomist
University of California, Plant Growth Laboratory, Davis CA 95616, USA

Valentine, Robert J (Bobby) — Baseball Player, Manager, Sportscaster
71 Wynnewood Lane, Stamford CT 06903, USA

Valentine, Scott — Actor
Diverse Talent Group, 9911 Pico Blvd, #350W, Los Angeles CA 90035 USA

Valentine, Steve — Actor
Greater Visions Artists Talent Agency, 8981 W Sunset Blvd, #101, West Hollywood CA 90069 USA

Valentine, William N — Physician
2128 Quail Point Circle, Medford OR 97504, USA

Valentine, Zachary B (Zack) — Football Player
162 Harvest Road, Swedesboro NJ 08085, USA

Valentinetti, Vito J — Baseball Player
271 Summit Ave, Mount Vernon NY 10552, USA

Valentino — Fashion Designer
Palazzo Mignanelli, Piazza Mignanelli 22, 00187 Rome, Italy

Valentino, Bobby — Singer
Agency for Artists, 244 5th Ave, #H230, New York NY 10001, USA

Valentino, Jim — Cartoonist
Image Comics, 1071 N Batavia St, #A, Orange CA 92867, USA

Valentino, Victoria — Model
Playboy Promotions, 2706 Media Center Dr, Los Angeles CA 90065 USA

Valenza, Tasia — Actress
Danis Panaro Nist, 9201 W Olympic Blvd, Beverly Hills CA 90212, USA

Valenzuela, Fernando — Baseball Player
2123 N Beachwood Dr, Los Angeles CA 90068, USA

Valeriani, Richard G — Commentator
23 Island View Dr, Sherman CT 06784, USA

Valiant, Leslie G — Computer Scientist
50 Tyler Road, Belmont MA 02478, USA

Valiquette, John J (Jack) — Ice Hockey Player
28 Peacock Lane, Barrie ON L4N 3R8, Canada

Valk, Garry — Ice Hockey Player
681 Baycrest Dr, North Vancouver BC V7G 1N7, Canada

Vall, Ély Ould Mohamed — President, Mauritania; Army Officer
President's Office, Cabinet Building, PO Box 2, Majuro, Marshall Islands

Valle, David (Dave) — Baseball Player
2260 95th Ave NE, Clyde Hill WA 98004, USA

Vallee, Roy — Businessman
Avnet Inc, 2211 S 47th St, Phoenix AZ 85034, USA

Vallely, James (Jim) — Writer
Brillstein Entertainment Partners, 9150 Wilshire Blvd, #350, Beverly Hills CA 90212 USA

Vallely, John S — Basketball Player
2042 Commodore Road, Newport Beach CA 92660, USA

Valletta, Amber E — Model, Actress
Creative Artists Agency, 2000 Ave of Stars, #100, Los Angeles CA 90067 USA

Valley, Mark — Actor
Vox Inc, 6420 Wilshire Blvd, #1080, Los Angeles CA 90048 USA
Valli, Frankie — Singer, Guitarist
I C M Partners, 10250 Constellation Blvd, #900, Los Angeles CA 90067 USA
Vallien, Bertil — Artist
Roleks Vall, 621 93 Visby, Sweden
Vallini, Agostino Cardinal — Religious Leader
Apolstolic Signatura, Palazzo della Cancelleria, 00186 Rome, Italy
Valmon, Andrew — Track Athlete
16403 Danforth Circle, Rockville MD 20853, USA
Valory, Ross L — Bassist (Journey)
Front Line Mgmt, 1100 Glendon Ave, #2000, Los Angeles CA 90024 USA
Valuev, Nikolai — Boxer
Box-Way, Zaharyevskaya Ul 12, 191123 Saint Petersburg, Russia
Valverde, Jose R — Baseball Player
Detroit Tigers, Comerica Park, 2100 Woodward Ave, Detroit MI 48201 USA
Valverde, Maria — Actress
Tavistock Wood Mgmt, 45 Conduit St, London W1S 2YN, England
VanAcker, Drew — Actor
Greene Assoc, 1901 Ave of Stars, #130, Los Angeles CA 90067 USA
VanAllsburg, Chris — Artist, Writer
Scholastic Press, 555 Broadway, New York NY 10012 USA
VanAlmsick, Franziska (Franzi) — Swimmer
Eichhorn, Bizetstr 1, 13088 Berlin, Germany
VanAmerongen, Jerry — Cartoonist (Neighborhood)
10926 Owensmouth Ave, Chatsworth CA 91311, USA
VanAmstel, Louis — Dancer, Choreographer
Jay D Schwartz Assoc, 3151 Cahuenga Blvd, #220, Los Angeles CA 90068, USA
VanArk, Joan — Actress
Don Buchwald/Fortitude, 6500 Wilshire Blvd, #2200, Los Angeles CA 90048 USA
VanArsdale, Richard A (Dick) — Basketball Player, Executive
5434 E Lincoln Dr, Paradise Valley AZ 85253, USA
VanArsdale, Thomas A (Tom) — Basketball Player
7510 N Eucalyptus Dr, Paradise Valley AZ 85253, USA
Vanasse, Karine — Actress
W M E Entertainment, 9601 Wilshire Blvd, #300, Beverly Hills CA 90210 USA
VanBenschoten, John — Baseball Player
5918 Milburne Dr, Milford OH 45150, USA
VanBerg, John C (Jack) — Thoroughbred Racing Trainer
420 Fair Hill Dr, #1, Elkton MD 21921, USA
VanBerkel, Bernard F (Ben) — Architect
U N Studio, Stradhouderskade 113, 1073 AX Amsterdam NH, Netherlands
Vanbiesbrouck, John — Ice Hockey Player
67960 Campground Road, Washington MI 48095, USA
VanBoxmeer, John M — Ice Hockey Player
8033 E Santa Cruz Ave, Orange CA 92869, USA
VanBrabant, C Oscar (Ozzie) — Baseball Player
5389 William Dr, Lexington MI 48450, USA
VanBreda Kolff, Jan M — Basketball Player, Coach
1102 French Town Lane, Franklin TN 37067, USA
VanBuren, Abigail — Columnist (Dear Abby)
Phillips-Van Buren Inc, 1880 Century Park E, #1400, Los Angeles CA 90067, USA
VanBuren, Jermaine — Baseball Player
557 Acree Lane, Columbus OH 43228, USA
VanCamp, Emily — Actress
Thruline Entertainment, 9250 Wilshire Blvd, #100, Beverly Hills CA 90212 USA
Vance, Courtney B — Actor
Lighthouse Entertainment, 9220 Sunset Blvd, #200, West Hollywood CA 90069, USA
Vance, Eric D — Football Player
17613 Archland Pass Road, Lutz FL 33558, USA
Vance, G Christopher (Chris) — Actor
Paradigm Agency, 360 N Crescent Dr, North Building, Beverly Hills CA 90210 USA
Vance, Gene C (Sandy) — Baseball Player
5863 Chelton Dr, Oakland CA 94611, USA
Vance, John H (Jack) — Writer
119 Oppenheimer Lane, Princeton NJ 08540, USA
Vance, Kenny — Singer (Jay & the Americans)
PO Box 950116, Far Rockaway NY 11695, USA
VanCitters, Robert L — Physiologist, Biophysicist
University of Washington Medical School, Physiology Dept, Seattle WA 98815, USA
VanClief, D G — Thoroughbred Racing Executive
Breeders' Cup Ltd, 2525 Harrodsburg Road, #500, Lexington KY 40504, USA
Van-Culin, Samuel — Religious Leader
16A Burgate, Canterbury CT1 2HG, England
VanDam, Jose — Opera Singer
Zurich Artists, Rutistr 52, 8044 Zurich-Gockhausen, Switzerland
VandeBerg, Edward J (Ed) — Baseball Player
4903 S Meadows Place, Chandler AZ 85248, USA
VandenBerg, Lodewijk — Astronaut
Constellation Technology Corp, 7887 Bryan Dairy Road, #100, Seminole FL 33777, USA
VandenBergh, Maarten A — Businessman
Lloyds T S B Group, 71 Lombard St, London EC3P 3BS, England
VandenBosch, Kyle D — Football Player
2331 E Cedar Place, Chandler AZ 85249, USA
Vandenbussche, Ryan — Ice Hockey Player
RE/Max Erie Shores Realty, 103 Queensway East, Simco ON N3Y 4M5, Canada
VanDenHoogenband, Pieter — Swimmer
PO Box 302, 6800 AH, Arnhem, Netherlands
Vander, Musetta — Actress
David Shapira Assoc, 193 N Robertson Blvd, Beverly Hills CA 90211 USA
VanderArk, Brad — Bassist (Verve Pipe)
Artist in Mind, 14100 Dickens St, #2, Sherman Oaks CA 91423, USA
VanderArk, Brian — Singer, Guitarist (Verve Pipe)
Artist in Mind, 14100 Dickens St, #2, Sherman Oaks CA 91423, USA
VanDerBeek, James — Actor
Paradigm Agency, 360 N Crescent Dr, North Building, Beverly Hills CA 90210 USA

Vanderbeek, Matthew J (Matt) — Football Player
54 Endless Vista, Aliso Viejo CA 92656, USA

Vanderberg Shaw, Helen — Synchronized Swimming Coach
Heaven's Fitness, 301 14th St NW, Calgary AB T2N 2A1, Canada

VanderBerge, Camille — Sculptor
Solomon Dubnick Gallery, 1017 25th St, Sacramento CA 95816, USA

Vanderbundt, William G (Skip) — Football Player
4225 Los Coches Way, Sacramento CA 95864, USA

Vanderham, Joanna — Actress
W M E Entertainment, 9601 Wilshire Blvd, #300, Beverly Hills CA 90210 USA

VanDerham, Katarina — Model
PO Box 64666, Los Angeles CA 90064, USA

Vanderhoef, Larry N — Educator
615 Francisco Place, Davis CA 95616, USA

Vanderjagt, Michael J (Mike) — Football Player
631 Lewis Court, Marco Island FL 34145, USA

Vanderkaay, Peter — Swimmer
5787 Bewster Road, Rochester MI 48306, USA

Vanderkelen, Ronald (Ron) — Football Player
5300 Vernon Ave S, #307, Minneapolis MN 55436, USA

Vanderloo, Mark — Model
Wilhelmina Models, 300 Park Ave S, #200, New York NY 10010 USA

Vandermeersch, Bernard — Anthropologist
University of Bordeaux, Anthropology Dept, Bordeaux, France

VanderPoel, J Mark — Football Player
14760 Ave 208, Tulare CA 93274, USA

VanDerPol, Anneliese — Actress
Gage Group, 14724 Ventura Blvd, #505, Sherman Oaks CA 91403 USA

Vanderpool, Clare — Writer
Random House, 1745 Broadway, #1800, New York NY 10019 USA

VanDerRym, Sim — Architect, Designer
Ecological Design Institute, PO Box 858, Inverness CA 94937, USA

Vanderveen, Loet — Sculptor
Lime Creek 5, Big Sur CA 93920, USA

VanDerveer, Tara — Basketball Coach
1036 Cascade Dr, Menlo Park CA 94025, USA

VanDerWal, Frederique — Model
Innovative Artists, 1505 10th St, Santa Monica CA 90401 USA

VanderWal, John H — Baseball Player
5142 Abbeydale Dr SW, Grand Rapids MI 49546, USA

VanDerWee, Herman F A — Historian
Ettingestraat 10, 9170 Saint-Pauwels, Belgium

Vanderzalm, Bas — Association Executive
Medical Teams International, 14150 SW Milton Court, Portland OR 97224, USA

VandeSande, Theo A — Cinematographer
Innovative Artists, 1505 10th St, Santa Monica CA 90401 USA

VandeVen, Monique — Actress, Director
Features Creative Mgmt, Entrepotdok 76A, 101 AD Amsterdam, Netherlands

VandeWeghe, Albert — Swimmer
7712 W Skyline Dr, Tulsa OK 74107, USA

Vandeweghe, Ernest E (Ernie) — Basketball Player, Physician
PO Box 3006, Englewood CO 80155, USA

Vandeweghe, Ernest M (Kiki) — Basketball Player, Coach, Executive
PO Box 3006, Englewood CO 80155, USA

VandeWetering, John E — Educator
29 Brickstone Circle, Rochester NY 14620, USA

VanDien, Casper — Actor
A P A Talent/Literary Agency, 405 S Beverly Dr, #300, Beverly Hills CA 90212 USA

VanDoren, Mamie — Actress, Dancer, Model
3419 Via Lido, #184, Newport Beach CA 92663, USA

VanDorp, Wayne — Ice Hockey Player
380 Laurentian Crescent, Coquitlam BC V3K 1Y5, Canada

VanDusen, Frederick W (Fred) — Baseball Player
331 Gillette Dr, Franklin TN 37069, USA

VanDusen, Granville — Actor
10974 Alta View Dr, Studio City CA 91604, USA

VanDuyne, Robert S (Bob) — Football Player
1810 Douglas Ave, Clearwater FL 33755, USA

VanDyke, Barry — Actor
27800 Blythdale Road, Agoura CA 91301, USA

VanDyke, Bruce R — Football Player
143 Lakeview Dr, Canonsburg PA 15317, USA

VanDyke, Dick — Actor
23215 Mariposa de Oro, Malibu CA 90265, USA

VanDyke, F Alexander (Alex) — Football Player
8338 Sea Island Court, Elk Grove CA 95758, USA

VanDyke, Jerry — Actor, Comedian
J Cast Productions, 2550 Greenvalley Road, Los Angeles CA 90046, USA

VanDyke, Leroy — Singer
Leroy Van Dyke Enterprises, 29000 Highway V, Smithton MO 65350, USA

VanDyke, Milton D — Aeronautical Engineer
Stanford University, Applied Mechanics Dept, Stanford CA 94305, USA

VanDyke, Philip — Actor
1464 Madera Road, #108N, Simi Valley CA 93065, USA

VanDyke, William G — Businessman
Donaldson Co, 1400 W 94th St, Minneapolis MN 55431, USA

VanDyken Rouen, Amy — Swimmer, Sportscaster
20343 N Hayden Road, #105, Scottsdale AZ 85255, USA

VanEeghen, Mark K — Football Player
90 Woodstock Lane, Cranston RI 02920, USA

VanEgmond, Timothy L (Tim) — Baseball Player
8839 Callaway Road, Gay GA 30218, USA

Vanek, John — Basketball Referee
9th St, RD 1, Nesquehoning PA 18240, USA

Vanek, Thomas — Ice Hockey Player
9131 Curry Lane, Clarence Center NY 14032, USA

Vaness, Carol
I C M Artists, 40 W 57th St, #1800, New York NY 10019 USA — Opera Singer

Vanessa-Mae
Mel Bush, Stratford Saye, 20 Wellington, Bournemouth BH8 8JN, England — Concert, Rock Violinist

Vanessa-Mae
PO Box 363, Bournemouth, Dorset BH7 6LA, England — Singer, Violinist

VanEvery, John
555 Dixon Dr, Brandon MS 39047, USA — Baseball Player

VanExcel, Nicky M (Nick)
3102 Noble Lakes Lane, Houston TX 77082, USA — Basketball Player

VanFraasen, Bastiaan C
1347 Curtis St, Berkeley CA 94702, USA — Philosopher

VanGaalen, Chad
Agency Group Ltd, 142 W 57th St, #600, New York NY 10019 USA — Musician

Vangelis
Robert Urband Assoc, 8981 W Sunset Blvd, #311, West Hollywood CA 90069, USA — Composer

Vangen, Scott D
N A S A, Johnson Space Center, 2101 NASA Road, Houston TX 77058 USA — Astronaut

Vangorder, David T (Dave)
212 Black Eagle Ave, Henderson NV 89002, USA — Baseball Player

VanGorp, Michele
Minnesota Lynx, Target Center, 600 1st Ave N, Minneapolis MN 55403 USA — Basketball Player

VanGrunsven, Theodora E G (Anky)
Bonengang 1, 5421 BZ Gemert, Netherlands — Equestrian

Vangsness, Kirsten
Abrams Artists, 9200 W Sunset Blvd, #1125, West Hollywood CA 90069 USA — Actress

VanGundy, Jeff
W M E Entertainment, 9601 Wilshire Blvd, #300, Beverly Hills CA 90210 USA — Basketball Coach, Sportscaster

VanGundy, Stan
Orlando Magic, 8701 Maitland Summit Blvd, Orlando FL 32810 USA — Basketball Coach

VanHalen, Alex
12024 Summit Circle, Beverly Hills CA 90210, USA — Drummer (Van Halen)

VanHalen, Eddie
20411 Chapter Dr, Woodland Hills CA 91364, USA — Singer, Guitarist (Van Halen)

VanHalen, Wolfgang
Jackoway Tyerman Wertheimer, 1925 Century Park E, #2200, Los Angeles CA 90067 USA — Singer, Guitarist

VanHamel, Martine
290 Riverside Dr, New York NY 10025, USA — Ballerina

VanHeek, Margaret
Schering-Plough Research, 2000 Galloping Hill Road, Kenilworth NJ 07033, USA — Chemist

VanHekken, Andy
4742 64th St, Holland MI 49423, USA — Baseball Player

VanHelden, Armand
Ministry of Sound, 103 Grant St, London SE1 6DP, England — Music Producer

VanHellmond, Andy
71 Hyde Road, Stratford ON N5A 7Z3, Canada — Ice Hockey Referee

VanHeusen, William P (Billy)
835 Hudson St, Denver CO 80220, USA — Football Player

VanHoften, James C D A
Bechtel National Inc, 50 Beale St, San Francisco CA 94105, USA — Astronaut

VanHolde, Kensal E
229 NW 32nd St, Corvallis OR 97330, USA — Biochemist

VanHolt, Brian
Paradigm Agency, 360 N Crescent Dr, North Building, Beverly Hills CA 90210 USA — Actor

VanHorn, Buddy
4409 Ponca Ave, Toluca Lake CA 91602, USA — Director

VanHorn, Christian
Opus 3 Artists, 470 Park Ave S, #900N, New York NY 10016 USA — Opera Singer

VanHorn, Douglas C (Doug)
149 Feronia Way, Rutherford NJ 07070, USA — Football Player

VanHorn, Patrick
Brillstein Entertainment Partners, 9150 Wilshire Blvd, #350, Beverly Hills CA 90212 USA — Actor

VanHorne, Keith
680 Thornmeadow Road, Riverwoods IL 60015, USA — Football Player

VanHouten, Carice
Troika, 74 Clerkenwell Road, #300, London EC1M 5QA, England — Actress

VanHoy, Jay
Parts & Labor, 177 N 10th St, #F, Brooklyn NY 11211, USA — Producer

Vanhoye, Albert Cardinal
Biblical Commission, Borgo S Spirito 4, CP 6139, 00195 Roma-Prati, Italy — Religious Leader

Vanian, David (Dave)
Leave Home Booking, 10 W Broadway, #608, Salt Lake City UT 84101, USA — Singer (Damned)

Vanilla Ice
Media Artists Group, 333 E 43rd St, #115, New York NY 10017, USA — Rap Artist, Actor

VanImpe, Ed C
849 Streams Dr, West Chester PA 19382, USA — Ice Hockey Player

Vanity
39279 Paseo Padre Parkway, #214, Fremont CA 94538, USA — Singer, Actress, Model

VanKooten, Katie
I M G Artists, Hogarth Business Park, Chiswick, London W4 2TH, England — Opera Singer

VanLandingham, William J
3023 Old Hillsboro Road, Franklin TN 37064, USA — Baseball Player

VanLeeuwen, Troy D
The Firm, 2049 Century Park E, #2550, Los Angeles CA 90067 USA — Guitarist (Perfect Circle)

VanLiere, Donna
Saint Martin's Press, 175 5th Ave, #400, New York NY 10010 USA — Writer

VanLyck, Henry
Z B F Agentur, Friedrichstr 39, 10969 Berlin, Germany — Actor

Vannelli, Gino
McLachlan Scruggs, 2821 Bransford Ave, Nashville TN 37204, USA — Singer, Songwriter

VanNistelrooy, Ruud
F C Real Madrid, Avda Concha Espana 1, 28036 Madrid, Spain — Soccer Player

Vannoni, Dina Marue
PO Box 473, Chino CA 91708, USA — Model

VanNote, Jeffrey A (Jeff)
345 Hollyberry Dr, Roswell GA 30076, USA — Football Player

Vannucci, Ronnie, Jr — Drummer (Killers)
W M E Entertainment, 9601 Wilshire Blvd, #300, Beverly Hills CA 90210 USA

Vanocur, Sander — Commentator
C E S D, 10635 Santa Monica Blvd, #130, Los Angeles CA 90025 USA

Vanous, Lucky — Model, Actor
28345 La Calenta, Mission Viejo CA 92692, USA

VanOuten, Denise — Actress
Artist Rights Group, 4 Great Portland Place, London W1W 8PA, England

Vanover, Larry W — Baseball Umpire
3037 Sterling Court, Owensboro KY 42303, USA

Vanover, Tamarick T — Football Player
703 NW Wilson St, Lake City FL 32055, USA

VanPatten, Dick — Actor
13920 Magnolia Blvd, Sherman Oaks CA 91423, USA

VanPatten, Joyce — Actress
Robert Levy Assoc, 9220 W Sunset Blvd, #206, West Hollywood CA 90069, USA

VanPatten, Nels — Actor
12439 Magnolia Blvd, #197, Valley Village CA 91607, USA

VanPatten, Timothy — Actor, Director
Creative Artists Agency, 2000 Ave of Stars, #100, Los Angeles CA 90067 USA

VanPatten, Vincent — Actor
Michael Slessinger, 8730 W Sunset Blvd, #220W, West Hollywood CA 90069 USA

VanPeebles, Mario — Actor, Director
Don Buchwald/Fortitude, 6500 Wilshire Blvd, #2200, Los Angeles CA 90048 USA

VanPeebles, Melvin — Director, Writer
353 W 56th St, #10F, New York NY 10019, USA

VanPelt, Bo — Golfer
3025 Backmeyer Road, Richmond IN 47374, USA

VanPelt, G Alexander (Alex) — Football Player
2080 Shady Lane, Green Bay WI 54313, USA

VanPoppel, Todd M — Baseball Player
340 Springfield Bend, Argyle TX 76226, USA

VanPraagh, James — Actor, Producer
Special Artists Agency, 9465 Wilshire Blvd, #820, Beverly Hills CA 90212 USA

VanRensselaer, Miles — Artist
1352-54 River Road, Lopatcong NJ 08865, USA

VanRiper, Paul K — Marine Corps General
Marine Corps Heritage Foundation, PO Box 998, 307 5th Ave, Quantico VA 22134, USA

VanRompuy, Herman A — Prime Minister, Belgium
European Council, Rue de la Loi 175, 1048 Brussels, Belgium

VanRyn, Benjamin A (Ben) — Baseball Player
8911 Saddle Trail, San Antonio TX 78255, USA

VanRyn, Mike — Ice Hockey Player
17681 SW 54th St, Southwest Ranches FL 33331, USA

VanSant, Gus G, Jr — Director
W M E Entertainment, 9601 Wilshire Blvd, #300, Beverly Hills CA 90210 USA

VanSanten, Shantel — Actress, Model
Leverage Mgmt, 3030 Pennsylvania Ave, Santa Monica CA 90404 USA

VanScott, Eugene J — Dermatologist
3 Hidden Lane, Abington PA 19001, USA

VanSickle, Craig W — Writer, Producer, Director
Paradigm Agency, 360 N Crescent Dr, North Building, Beverly Hills CA 90210 USA

Vanska, Osmo — Conductor
Minnesota Symphony, Orchestra Hall, 1111 Nicollet Mall, Minneapolis MN 55403, USA

VanSlyke, Andrew J (Andy) — Baseball Player
710 S Price Road, Saint Louis MO 63124, USA

Vanstone, Ellen — Producer
Alpern Group, 15645 Royal Oak Road, Encino CA 91436, USA

VanSusteren, Greta — Commentator
Fox-TV, News Dept, 5151 Wisconsin Ave NW, #100, Washington DC 20016 USA

VanUmmerson, Claire A — Educator
Cleveland State University, President's Office, Cleveland OH 44115, USA

VanValkenburgh, Deborah — Actress
Beth Stein Assoc, 920 Abbot Kinney Blvd, Venice CA 90291, USA

VanVooren, Monique — Actress
165 E 66th St, New York NY 10065, USA

VanWachem, Loedwijk C — Businessman
Royal Dutch Petroleum, 30 Van Bylandtaan, 2596 HR Hague, Netherlands

VanWageningen, Yorick — Actor
Conway Van Gelder Grant, 8-12 Broadwick St, #300, London W1F 8HW, England

VanWagner, James P (Jimmy) — Football Player
5246 N Royal Dr, Traverse City MI 49684, USA

VanWinkle, Travis — Actor
I C M Partners, 10250 Constellation Blvd, #900, Los Angeles CA 90067 USA

VanWormer, Steve — Actor
Vox Inc, 6420 Wilshire Blvd, #1080, Los Angeles CA 90048 USA

VanWyngarden, Andrew — Singer, Guitarist, Pianist (MGMT)
Paradigm Agency, 404 W Franklin St, Monterey CA 93940 USA

VanZandt, Steven — Guitarist, Actor
Renegade Nation Holdings, 434 Ave of Americas, #6R, New York NY 10011, USA

VanZant, Johnny — Singer (Lynyrd Skynyrd), Songwriter
Vector Mgmt, PO Box 120479, Nashville TN 37212 USA

VanZweden, Jaap — Conductor
I M G Artists, Hogarth Business Park, Chiswick, London W4 2TH, England

Varad'a, Vaclav — Ice Hockey Player
9042 Stonebriar Dr, Clarence Center NY 14032, USA

Varadhan, Srinivasa S R — Abel Mathematics Laureate
New York University, Courant Institute, 251 Mercer St, New York NY 10012, USA

Varady, Julia — Opera Singer
Hanns Eisler Musik Hochschule, Charlottenstra 55, 10117 Berlin, Germany

Varda, Agnes — Director
Cine-Tamaris, 86-88 Rue Daguerre, 75014 Paris, France

Vardalos, Nia — Actress, Writer
Untitled Entertainment, 350 S Beverly Dr, #200, Beverly Hills CA 90212 USA

Vardell, Thomas A (Tommy) — Football Player
2424 E Ruby Hill Dr, Pleasanton CA 94566, USA

Varejao, Anderson F — Basketball Player
Cleveland Cavaliers, Gund Arena, 1 Center Court, Cleveland OH 44115 USA
Varekova, Veronica — Model
Next Model Mgmt, 9 Boul de la Madeleine, 75001 Paris, France
Varela, Fernando — Singer
Agency Group Ltd, 142 W 57th St, #600, New York NY 10019 USA
Varela, Leonor — Actress
Kritzer Levine Wilkins Griffin, 11872 La Grange Ave, #100, Los Angeles CA 90025 USA
Varga, Imre — Sculptor
Bartha Utca 1, 1126 Budapest XII, Hungary
Vargas Llosa, Mario — Nobel Literature Laureate
Las Magnolias 295, 6 Piso, Barranco, Lima 4, Peru
Vargas, Devin — Boxer
Star Boxing, 991 Morris Park Ave, Bronx NY 10462, USA
Vargas, Elizabeth — Commentator
ABC-TV, News Dept, 77 W 66th St, New York NY 10023 USA
Vargas, Fernando — Boxer
1695 Mesa Verde Ave, #220, Ventura CA 93003, USA
Vargas, Ieda Maria — Beauty Queen
Miss Universe Organization, 1370 Ave of Americas, #1600, New York NY 10019 USA
Vargas, Jacob — Actor
Paradigm Agency, 360 N Crescent Dr, North Building, Beverly Hills CA 90210 USA
Vargas, Jason M — Baseball Player
14775 Keota Lane, Apple Valley CA 92307, USA
Vargas, Jay R — Vietnam War Marine Corps Hero (CMH)
12466 Thornbush Court, San Diego CA 92131, USA
Vargo, Tim — Businessman
AutoZone Inc, 123 S Front St, Memphis TN 38103, USA
Varitek, Jason A — Baseball Player
PO Box 669, Suwanee GA 30024, USA
Varlamarv, Sergei — Ice Hockey Player
213 Germain St, Saint John NB E2L 2G5, Canada
Varma, Indira — Actress
I C M Partners, 10250 Constellation Blvd, #900, Los Angeles CA 90067 USA
Varmus, Harold E — Nobel Medicine Laureate
1 Gracie Square, #1E, New York NY 10028, USA
Varney, Carleton B, Jr — Interior Designer
Dorothy Draper Co, 60 E 56th St, #1000, New York NY 10022, USA
Varney, Richard F (Pete) — Baseball Player
14 Juniper Ridge Road, Acton MA 01720, USA
Varon, Lisa Marie — Model
131 Promenade Court, Louisville KY 40223, USA
Varrela, Leonor — Actress
Kritzer Levine Wilkins Griffin, 11872 La Grange Ave, #100, Los Angeles CA 90025 USA
Varrichone, Frank J — Football Player
26 Coffin Brook Road, Alton NH 03809, USA
Varshavsky, Alexander — Cell Biologist
California Institute of Technology, Cell Biology Dept, Pasadena CA 91125, USA
Varsho, Gary A — Baseball Player, Manager
11921 Starr Road, Chili WI 54420, USA
Vartan, Michael — Actor
Thruline Entertainment, 9250 Wilshire Blvd, #100, Beverly Hills CA 90212 USA
Vartan, Sylvie — Singer
Artmedia, 20 Ave Rapp, 75007 Paris, France
Varty, Keith — Fashion Designer
Bosco di San Francesco #6, 60020 Sirolo, Italy
Varvatos, John — Fashion Designer
Soho New York, 149 Mercer St, New York NY 10012, USA
Varvel, Gary — Editorial Cartoonist
PO Box 1121, Brownsburg IN 46112, USA
Vasary, Tamas — Concert Pianist, Conductor
Magyar Radio Zenekari Iroda, Brody Sandor Utica 5, 1800 Budapest, Hungary
Vasconcellos Ferreira, Gabriel — Soccer Player
F C Milan, Via Filippo Turati 3, 20121 Milan, Italy
Vasconcellos, Martha M C — Beauty Queen
2 Oak Terrace, #4, Somerville MA 02143, USA
Vasgersian, Matt — Sportscaster
7211 Eads Ave, La Jolla CA 92037, USA
Vasher, Nathaniel D (Nathan) — Football Player
1850 N Sawgrass St, Vernon Hills IL 60061, USA
Vasilyev, Vladimir V — Ballet Dancer, Executive
Smolenskaya Naberezhnaya 5/13 62, 121099 Moscow, Russia
Vaske, Dennis J — Ice Hockey Player
16141 S Codo Dr, Homer Glen IL 60491, USA
Vasquez Rana, Mario — Publisher
El Sol de Mexico, Guillermo Prieto 7, Cuauhtemoc DF 06470, Mexico
Vasquez, Jacinto — Thoroughbred Racing Jockey
4449 18th Terrace, Ocala FL 34479, USA
Vasquez, Wilfredo — Boxer
Call 1 D-3, Urb San Fernando, Bayamon PR 00957, USA
Vasser, Jimmy — Auto Racing Driver
8605 Robinson Ridge Dr, Las Vegas NV 89117, USA
Vassilieva, Sofia — Actress
Brillstein Entertainment Partners, 9150 Wilshire Blvd, #350, Beverly Hills CA 90212 USA
Vassiliou, George V — President, Cyprus
PO Box 874, 21 Academiou Ave, Aglandjia, Nicosia, Cyprus
Vasyuchenko, Yuri — Ballet Dancer
Bolshoi Theater, Teatralnaya Pl 1, 103009 Moscow, Russia
Vasyutin, Vladimir V — Cosmonaut
Cosmonaut Training Center, Star City, 141160 Zvezdny Gorodok, Moscow Oblast, Russia
Vataha, Randel E (Randy) — Football Player
36 Longmeadow Road, Lincoln MA 01773, USA
Vatcher, James E (Jim) — Baseball Player
16039 Northfield St, Pacific Palisades CA 90272, USA
Vatchkov, Deyan — Opera Singer
I M G Artists, Hogarth Business Park, Chiswick, London W4 2TH, England

Vaughan, Greg — Actor
Abrams Artists, 9200 W Sunset Blvd, #1125, West Hollywood CA 90069 USA

Vaughan, Jimmie — Guitarist (Fabulous Thunderbirds)
2300 S 3rd St, Austin TX 78704, USA

Vaughan, Martha — Biochemist
11608 W Hill Dr, Rockville MD 20852, USA

Vaughan, Peter — Actor
Independent Talent Group, Oxford House, 76 Oxford St, London W1D 1BS, England

Vaughan, Tom — Director, Writer
United Agents, 12-26 Lexington St, London W1F 0LE, England

Vaughn, Ben — Singer, Songwriter, Guitarist
Creative Artists Agency, 2000 Ave of Stars, #100, Los Angeles CA 90067 USA

Vaughn, Bruce — Golfer
5615 N Monroe St, Hutchinson KS 67502, USA

Vaughn, Charles (Chico) — Basketball Player
21358 State Highway 127, Tamms IL 62988, USA

Vaughn, Clyde — Army General
Director, Army National Guard, HqUSA, Pentagon, Washington DC 20310, USA

Vaughn, Dewayne M — Baseball Player
5501 NW 37th St, Warr Acres OK 73122, USA

Vaughn, Gregory L (Greg) — Baseball Player
10830 Sheldon Woods Way, Elk Grove CA 95624, USA

Vaughn, Jacque — Basketball Player, Coach
715 Coving Court, Lawrence KS 66049, USA

Vaughn, Jimmie — Guitarist
Artemis Records, 130 5th Ave, #7, New York NY 10011, USA

Vaughn, Matthew — Director, Producer, Actor
Independent Talent Group, Oxford House, 76 Oxford St, London W1D 1BS, England

Vaughn, Maurice S (Mo) — Baseball Player
5455 Rings Road, #100, Dublin OH 43017, USA

Vaughn, Ned — Actor
James/Levy Mgmt, 3500 W Olive Ave, #1470, Burbank CA 91505 USA

Vaughn, Robert — Actor
68 Salem View Dr, Ridgefield CT 06877, USA

Vaughn, Thomas R (Tom) — Football Player
860 E Linda Lane, Gilbert AZ 85234, USA

Vaughn, Tichina — Opera Singer
I M G Artists, Hogarth Business Park, Chiswick, London W4 2TH, England

Vaughn, Vince — Actor
Wild West Picture Show Productions, 1210 N La Brea Ave, West Hollywood CA 90038, USA

Vaught, Loy S — Basketball Player
838 Andover Court SE, Grand Rapids MI 49508, USA

Vaugier, Emmanuelle — Actress
A P A Talent/Literary Agency, 405 S Beverly Dr, #300, Beverly Hills CA 90212 USA

Vaupen, Drew — Producer, Writer
I C M Partners, 10250 Constellation Blvd, #900, Los Angeles CA 90067 USA

Vavakin, Leonid V — Architect
Academy of Architecture, Dmitrova Str 24, 103874 Moscow, Russia

Vavasseur, Sophie — Actress
Troika, 74 Clerkenwell Road, #300, London EC1M 5QA, England

Vayda, Brandon Michael — Actor
Stone Manners Salners, 9911 W Pico Blvd, #1400, Los Angeles CA 90035 USA

Vaydik, Greg — Ice Hockey Player
3211 Wessex Circle, Richardson TX 75082, USA

Vazquez Rosas, Tabare R — President, Uruguay
Chacra El Paso de la Arena, Montevideo, Uruguay

Vazquez, Javier C — Baseball Player
1441 S Prairie Ave, Chicago IL 60605, USA

Veal, Orville I (Coot) — Baseball Player
238 Stone Gables Dr, Gray GA 31032, USA

Veale, Robert A (Bob) — Baseball Player
2833 Bush Blvd, Birmingham AL 35208, USA

Veals, Elton A — Football Player
2981 Joyce Dr, Baton Rouge LA 70814, USA

Veasey, Josephine — Opera Singer
5 Meadow View, Whitechurch, Hantsforshire RG28 7BL, England

Veber, Francis P — Director
Artmedia, 20 Ave Rapp, 75007 Paris, France

Vecchione, Mike — Marine Scientist
National Oceanic/Atmospheric Admin, 14th St & Constitution Ave, Washington DC 20230, USA

Vecsei, Eva H — Architect
4417 Circle Road, Montreal QC H3W 1Y6, Canada

Vecsey, George S — Sportswriter
New York Times, Editorial Dept, 229 W 43rd St, New York NY 10036, USA

Vedder, Ed (Eddie) — Singer (Pearl Jam), Songwriter
Curtis Mgmt, 1900 S Corgiat Dr, Seattle WA 98108, USA

Vedernikov, Alexander — Conductor
Askonas Holt, Lincoln House, 300 High Holborn, London WC1V 7JH, England

Vee, Bobby — Singer, Songwriter
Jimmy Dean Entertainment, 1160 Riverbend Road, Richmond VA 23231, USA

Vega Polanco, Amelia — Beauty Queen, Actress
Trump Model Agency, 91 5th Ave, #300, New York NY 10003 USA

Vega, Alexa — Actress
John Carrabino Mgmt, 5900 Wilshire Blvd, #406, Los Angeles CA 90036 USA

Vega, Paz — Actress
Mangement Production Entertainment, 9229 Sunset Blvd, #301, West Hollywood CA 90069, USA

Vega, Suzanne N — Singer, Songwriter
Michael Hausman Artists Mgmt, 511 Ave of Americas, #197, New York NY 10011, USA

Vega, Tata — Singer
Universal Attractions, 135 W 26th St, #1200, New York NY 10001 USA

Vegas, Jhonattan — Golfer
Professional Golfer's Assn, PO Box 109601, Palm Beach Gardens FL 33410 USA

Veglio, Antonio M Cardinal — Religious Leader
Pastorial Care of Migrants & Itinerant People, Piazza S Calisto 16, 00120 Vatican City

Veiga, Carlos A Wahnon de C — Prime Minister, Cape Verde
W V Consultants, CP43A Praia, Santiago, Cape Verde

Veigel, Allen F (Al) — Baseball Player
1907 Dover Ave, Dover OH 44622, USA
Veihmeyer, John B — Businessman
K P M G, 345 Park Ave, New York NY 10154, USA
Veil, Simone — Government Official, France
11 Place Vauban, 75007 Paris, France
Veingard, Allen S — Football Player
1940 NW 180th Way, Pembroke Pines FL 33029, USA
Veirs, Laura — Singer, Songwriter
Billions Corp, 3522 W Armitage Ave, Chicago IL 60647, USA
Veisor, Michael D (Mike) — Ice Hockey Player
16091 W Lakepoint Court, Prairieville LA 70769, USA
Veitch, Darren W — Ice Hockey Player
3410 Maricopa Highway, Ojai CA 93023, USA
Veitch, John M — Thoroughbred Racing Trainer
Kentucky Horse Racing Authority, 4063 Ironwood Turnpike, Lexington KY 40511, USA
Veitch, Tom — Writer
PO Box 479, Lincoln City OR 97367, USA
Vejar, Chico — Boxer
9531 State Highway 151, #8102, San Antonio TX 78251, USA
Vejtasa, Stanley W (Swede) — WW II Navy Air Force Hero
1649 Summit Lane, Escondido CA 92025, USA
Velan, Chris — Singer, Songwriter
Agency Group Ltd, 142 W 57th St, #600, New York NY 10019 USA
Velard, Julian — Singer, Songwriter, Pianist
Agency Group Ltd, 142 W 57th St, #600, New York NY 10019 USA
Velarde, Randy L — Baseball Player
4902 Thames Court, Midland TX 79705, USA
Velasquez, Jacquelyn D (Jaci) — Singer
Front Line Mgmt, 1100 Glendon Ave, #2000, Los Angeles CA 90024 USA
Velasquez, Jorge L, Jr — Thoroughbred Racing Jockey
2701 Valentine Ave, #407, Bronx NY 14058, USA
Velasquez, Patricia — Model, Actress
A P A Talent/Literary Agency, 405 S Beverly Dr, #300, Beverly Hills CA 90212 USA
Velazquez, Frederico A (Freddie) — Baseball Player
Jose Amado Solier #70, Santo Domingo, Dominican Republic
Velazquez, Nadine — Actress
Kritzer Levine Wilkins Griffin, 11872 La Grange Ave, #100, Los Angeles CA 90025 USA
Veldhuis, Magdalena J M (Marleen) — Swimmer
Eiffel Swimming PSV, Het Lover 40, 5501 CR Veldhoven, Netherlands
Velez, Eddie — Actor
Stone Manners Salners, 9911 W Pico Blvd, #1400, Los Angeles CA 90035 USA
Velez, Lauren — Actress
T M T Entertainment Group, 648 Broadway, #1002, New York NY 10012, USA
Velez, Natalia — Model
Mega Models Miami, 420 Lincoln Road, Miami Beach FL 33139, USA
Velgos, Alicia — Actress
Advance L A, 77904 Santa Monica Blvd, #200, Los Angeles CA 90046, USA
Velikhov, Yevgeni P — Physicist
Kurchatovskiy Institute, Kurchatova Pl 1, 123182 Moscow, Russia
Velischek, Randy — Ice Hockey Player
22 Hemlock Lane, Kinnelon NJ 07405, USA
Veljohnson, Reginald — Actor, Writer
22309 Haynes St, Woodland Hills CA 91303, USA
Vella, John A — Football Player
1890 Saint George Road, Danville CA 94526, USA
Vellucci, Mike — Ice Hockey Player
17302 Cameron Dr, Northville MI 48168, USA
Veloso, Caetano — Singer, Guitarist, Songwriter
International Music Network, 278 Main St, #400, Gloucester MA 01930 USA
Veloso, Moreno — Singer, Songwriter
Luaka Bop, 195 Chrystie St, #901, New York NY 10002, USA
Veloz, David — Director, Producer, Writer
Creative Artists Agency, 2000 Ave of Stars, #100, Los Angeles CA 90067 USA
Velten, Andreas — Optical Physicist
Morgridge Research Institute, PO Box 7667, Madison WI 53707, USA
Veltman, Jim (Scoop) — Lacrosse Player
Agincort Collegiate Institute, Athletic Dept, Toronto ON M1S 1R6, Canada
Veltman, Martinus J G — Nobel Physics Laureate
University of Michigan, Randall Laboratory, Ann Arbor MI 48109, USA
Veltri, Rachel — Actress, Model
Luber Rocklin Entertainment, 8530 Wilshire Blvd, #555, Beverly Hills CA 90211 USA
Venable, W McKinley (Mac) — Baseball Player
107 Clark St, San Rafael CA 94901, USA
Venables, Terry F — Soccer Coach
Terry Venables Holdings, 213 Putney Bridge Road, London SW15 2NY, England
Venafro, Michael R (Mike) — Baseball Player
15151 Whimbrel Court, Fort Myers FL 33908, USA
Venasky, Vic — Ice Hockey Player
4307 W 234th Place, Torrance CA 90505, USA
Vendela — Model
I M G Models, 304 Park Ave S, #PH-North, New York NY 10010 USA
Vendler, Helen H — Educator, Writer
54 Trowbridge St, #2, Cambridge MA 02138, USA
Vendt, Erik — Swimmer
22 Anchorage Road, North Falmouth MA 02556, USA
Veneruzzo, Gary — Ice Hockey Player
185 Fanshaw St, Thunder Bay ON P7C 5T7, Canada
Venet, Bernar — Sculptor, Artist
145 Ave of Americas, #5C, New York NY 10013, USA
Venetiaan, R Ronald — President, Suriname
Presidential Palace, Onafhankelikheidsplein 1, Paramaribo, Suriname
Vengerov, Maxim — Concert Violinist
Columbia Artists Mgmt Inc, 1790 Broadway, #702, New York NY 10019 USA
Venito, Lenny — Actor
Paradigm Agency, 360 N Crescent Dr, North Building, Beverly Hills CA 90210 USA

V.I.P. Address Book

Veigel - Venito

Venlet, David J — Navy Admiral
Commander, Naval Air Systems Command, Patuxent River MD 20670 USA

Venora, Diane — Actress
Don Buchwald/Fortitude, 6500 Wilshire Blvd, #2200, Los Angeles CA 90048 USA

Venter, J Craig — Molecular Biologist
11210 S Glen Road, Potomac MD 20854, USA

Venters, Jonathan W (Jonny) — Baseball Player
Atlanta Braves, Turner Field, 755 Hank Aaron Dr, Atlanta GA 30315 USA

Ventimiglia, John — Actor
Paul Kohner, 9300 Wilshire Blvd, #555, Beverly Hills CA 90212 USA

Ventimiglia, Milo — Actor
Creative Artists Agency, 2000 Ave of Stars, #100, Los Angeles CA 90067 USA

Ventresca, Vincent — Actor
Thruline Entertainment, 9250 Wilshire Blvd, #100, Beverly Hills CA 90212 USA

Ventura, Robin M — Baseball Player
1088 Newsom Springs Road, Arroyo Grande CA 93420, USA

Ventura-Merkel, Catherine — Publisher
A A R P Magazine, Publisher's Office, 601 E St NW, Washington DC 20049, USA

Venturella, Michelle — Softball Player
Iowa University, 219 Carver Hawkeye Arena, Iowa City IA 52242, USA

Venturi, Ken — Golfer
161 Waterford Circle, Rancho Mirage CA 92270, USA

Venturi, Rick — Football Coach
1935 Sumter Ridge Court, Chesterfield MO 63017, USA

Venturi, Robert — Pritzker Architectural Laureate
Venturi Scott Brown Assoc, 4236 Main St, Philadelphia PA 19127, USA

Venturini, Tisha — Soccer Player
7101 Del Rio Ave, Modesto CA 95356, USA

Venzago, Mario — Conductor
Indianapolis Symphony, 32 E Washington St, #600, Indianapolis IN 46204, USA

Vera, Billy — Singer, Songwriter, Actor
Sutton-Barth Vennari, 145 S Fairfax Ave, #310, Los Angeles CA 90036 USA

Veras, Jose E — Baseball Player
New York Mets, Shea Stadium, 12301 Roosevelt Ave, Corona NY 11368 USA

Veras, Quilvio A P — Baseball Player
4244 Vineyard Circle, Weston FL 33332, USA

Verba, Ross R — Football Player
3066 Arden Place, Saint Paul MN 55129, USA

Verbeek, Lotte — Actress
Innovative Artists, 1505 10th St, Santa Monica CA 90401 USA

Verbeek, Pat — Ice Hockey Player
Verbeek Farm, RR 1, Wyoming ON N0N 1T0, Canada

Verbinski, Gregor (Gore) — Director, Writer, Animator
Anonymous Content, 3532 Hayden Ave, Culver City CA 90232 USA

Verchota, Philip J (Phil) — Ice Hockey Player
PO Box 1181, Bemidji MN 56619, USA

Verdi, Bob — Sportswriter
Chicago Tribune, Editorial Dept, 435 N Michigan Ave, #1, Chicago IL 60611, USA

Verdi, Maria — Actress
Artmedia, 20 Ave Rapp, 75007 Paris, France

Verdin, Clarence — Football Player
6221 Eastover Dr, New Orleans LA 70128, USA

Verdu, Maribel — Actress
Paola Bonelli,Viale Parioli 50, 00187 Rome, Italy

Verdugo, Elena — Actress
PO Box 2048, Chula Vista CA 91912, USA

Verdy, Violette — Ballerina
2000 Broadway, #2B, New York NY 10023, USA

Vereen, Ben — Actor, Dancer, Singer
Innovative Artists, 1505 10th St, Santa Monica CA 90401 USA

Veres, David S (Dave) — Baseball Player
871 Diamond Ridge Circle, Castle Rock CO 80108, USA

Veres, Randolph R (Randy) — Baseball Player
9213 W Frank Ave, Peoria AZ 85382, USA

Vergara, Sofia — Singer, Actress, Model
Creative Artists Agency, 2000 Ave of Stars, #100, Los Angeles CA 90067 USA

Verghese, Abraham — Writer
United Talent Agency, 9336 Civic Center Dr, Beverly Hills CA 90210 USA

Verhagen, Eduard — Pediatrician
Groningen University Medical Center, Pediatrics Dept, Hanzeplein 1, 9700 RB Groningen, Netherlands

Verheiden, Mark — Producer, Writer
Creative Artists Agency, 2000 Ave of Stars, #100, Los Angeles CA 90067 USA

Verhoeven, Lis — Actress
Agentur Doris Mattes, 14 Merzstr, 81679 Munich, Germany

Verhoeven, Paul — Director
I C M Partners, 10250 Constellation Blvd, #900, Los Angeles CA 90067 USA

Verhoeven, Peter G (Pete) — Basketball Player
12722 Fargo Ave, Hanford CA 93230, USA

Verica, Tom — Actor
20 Ironsides St, #18, Marina del Rey CA 90292, USA

Veris, Garin L — Football Player
2 Christine Dr, Atkinson NH 03811, USA

Verkaik, Petra — Actress, Model
Playboy Promotions, 2706 Media Center Dr, Los Angeles CA 90065 USA

Verlaine, Tom — Singer, Bassist (Television)
Primary Talent International, 10-11 Jockey's Fields, London WC1R 4BN, England

Verlander, Justin B — Baseball Player
3928 Fairfax Dr, Troy MI 48083, USA

Verma, Inder M — Molecular Biologist
Salk Institute, 10100 N Torrey Pines Road, La Jolla CA 92037, USA

Vermeij, Geerat J — Evolutionary Biologist, Paleontologist
University of California, Geology Dept, Davis CA 95616, USA

Vermeil, Richard A (Dick) — Football Coach, Sportscaster
775 Fairview Road, Coatesville PA 19320, USA

Vermes, Peter — Soccer Player, Manager
Sporting Kansas City, 210 W 19th Terrace, #200, Kansas City MO 64108 USA

Vermilyea, Jamie — Baseball Player
7051 E Calle Arandas, Tucson AZ 85750, USA
Vernarsky, Kris — Ice Hockey Player
13192 Hunt Road, Riley MI 48041, USA
Vernes, Edith — Actress
Voyez Mon Agent, 20 Ave Rapp, 75007 Paris, France
Vernet, Claire — Actress
Agence France Degrand, 25 Rue du General Foy, 75008 Paris, France
Vernon, Annie — Rowing Athlete
Marlow Rowing Club, 17 Elizabeth Road, Marlow SL7 1RH, England
Vernon, Conrad — Director, Writer, Actor
United Talent Agency, 9336 Civic Center Dr, Beverly Hills CA 90210 USA
Vernon, Kate — Actress
Shelter Entertainment, 9454 Wilshire Blvd, #715, Beverly Hills CA 90212 USA
Vernon, Mike — Ice Hockey Player
Bear Mountain, 208-2800 Bryn Mawr Road, Victoria BC V9B 3T4, Canada
Vernonesi, Alberto — Conductor
I M G Artists, Hogarth Business Park, Chiswick, London W4 2TH, England
Veroni, Craig — Actor
Muse Artists, 401-207 W Hastings St, Vancouver BC V6B 1H7, Canada
Veronica — Singer, Actress
Cheryl K Warner Productions, PO Box 179, Hermitage TN 37076, USA
Veronica, Mayra — Model, Beauty Queen
Parallel Entertainment, 9420 Wilshire Blvd, #250, Beverly Hills CA 90212 USA
Veronis, John J, Jr — Publisher
Veronis Suhler Stevenson, 350 Park Ave, New York NY 10022, USA
Verplank, Scott — Golfer
1850 W Waterloo Road, Edmond OK 73025, USA
Verraros, James C (Jim) — Singer, Actor
Stiletto Entertainment, 8295 S La Cienega Blvd, Inglewood CA 90301, USA
Verrell, Cec — Actress
Michael Slessinger, 8730 W Sunset Blvd, #220W, West Hollywood CA 90069 USA
Versace, Dick — Basketball Coach
Memphis Grizzlies, 191 Beale St, Memphis TN 38103 USA
Versace, Donatella — Fashion Designer
Gianni Versace SpA, Via Manzoni 38, 20121 Milan, Italy
Versaldi, Giuseppe Cardinal — Religious Leader
Palazzo della Congregazioni, Largo del Colonnato 3, 00193 Rome, Italy
Verser, David — Football Player
21 Bellemonte Ave, Lakeside Park KY 41017, USA
Versini, Marie — Actress
23 Residence Elysses, 78170 La Celle-Saint Cloud, France
Verveen, Arie — Actor
Global Artists Agency, 6253 Hollywood Blvd, #508, Los Angeles CA 90028, USA
Ververgaert, Dennis A — Ice Hockey Player
34484 Stoneleigh Ave, Abbotsford BC V2S 8N5, Canada
Verwaayen, Ben — Businessman
Alcatel-Lucent, 54 Rue le Boetie, 75006 Paris, France
Verwey, Bob — Golfer
International Mgmt Group, 1 Erieview Plaza, 1360 E 9th St, Cleveland OH 44114 USA
Very, Charlotte — Actress
Cineart, 36 Rue de Ponthieu, 75008 Paris, France
Veryzer, Thomas M (Tom) — Baseball Player
41 Union Ave, Islip NY 11751, USA
Vesely, Jan — Baskeball Player
Washington Wizards, M C I Centre, 601 F St NW, Washington DC 20004 USA
Vesey, Jim — Ice Hockey Player
11 Ellwood St, Charlestown MA 02129, USA
Vesser, Dale A — Army General
1313 Merchant Lane, McLean VA 22101, USA
Vessey, John W, Jr — Army General
27650 Little Whitefish Road, Garrison MN 56450, USA
Vessey, Tricia — Actress, Director, Producer
Jackoway Tyerman Wertheimer, 1925 Century Park E, #2200, Los Angeles CA 90067 USA
Vest, Jake — Cartoonist (That's Jake)
PO Box 350757, Grand Island FL 32735, USA
Vesterbacka, Peter — Video Game Designer
Rovio Mobile Ltd, Keilaranta 17, 02150 Espoo, Finland
Vestiel, Franck — Director, Writer
Paradigm Agency, 360 N Crescent Dr, North Building, Beverly Hills CA 90210 USA
Vetri, Victoria — Actress
610 N Van Ness Ave, Los Angeles CA 90004, USA
Vetrov, Aleksandr — Ballet Dancer
Bolshoi Theater, Teatralnaya Pl 1, 103009 Moscow, Russia
Vettel, Sebastian — Auto Racing Driver
Red Bull Racing, Bradbourne Drive, Tilbrook, Milton Keynes, MK7 8BJ, England
Vettori, Ernst — Ski Jumper
Fohrenweg 1, 6060 Absam-Eichat, Austria
Vevers, Stuart — Fashion Designer
Mulberry Ltd, Kilver Court, Shepton Mallet, Somerset BA4 5NF, England
Veysey, Sid — Ice Hockey Player
178 Ridgevale Dr, Bedford NS B4A 3S7, Canada
Viator, John A — Biological Engineer
University of Missouri, Life Sciences Center, Columbia MO 65211, USA
Vicent, Tania — Speed Skater
Speed Skating Canada, 2781 Lancaster Road, #402, Ottawa ON K1B 1A7, Canada
Vicius, Nicole — Actress
Innovative Artists, 1505 10th St, Santa Monica CA 90401 USA
Vick, Michael D — Football Player
21 Haywagon Trail, Hampton VA 23669, USA
Vickaryous, Jake — Chemist
University of Oregon, Chemistry Dept, Eugene OR 97403, USA
Vickers, Brian L — Auto Racing Driver
27 High Tech Blvd, Thomasville NC 27360, USA
Vickers, Jonathan S (Jon) — Opera Singer
Collingtree, 18 Riddells Bay Road, Warwick WK 04, Bermuda

V

Vickers, Kipp E — Football Player
PO Box 78365, Indianapolis IN 46278, USA
Vickers, Mike — Guitarist (Manfred Mann)
E M I Records, 43 Brook Green, London W6 7EF, England
Vickers, Steve — Ice Hockey Player
238 Zokol Dr, Aurora ON L4G 0C2, Canada
Vickrey, Dan — Singer, Guitarist (Counting Crowes)
Creative Artists Agency, 2000 Ave of Stars, #100, Los Angeles CA 90067 USA
Victor, James — Actor
H David Moss, 733 Seward St, #PH, Los Angeles CA 90038 USA
Victor, Renee — Actress
Independent Artists, 9601 Wilshire Blvd, #750, Beverly Hills CA 90210, USA
Victoria — Crown Princess, Sweden
Royal Palace, Kung Slottet, Stottsbacken, 111 30 Stockholm, Sweden
Victorino, Shane P — Baseball Player
1997 Alcova Ridge Dr, Las Vegas NV 89135, USA
Vidal, Cesar — Singer, Guitarist (Caesars)
Paradigm Agency, 360 Park Ave, #1600, New York NY 10022 USA
Vidal, Christina — Actress
McGowan Mgmt, 8733 W Sunset Blvd, #103, West Hollywood CA 90069 USA
Vidal, Deborah — Golfer
2033 Paramount Dr, Los Angeles CA 90068, USA
Vidal, Jean-Pierre — Alpine Skier
Ski Federation, 50 Rue de Marquisats, BP 51, 74011 Annecy Cedex, France
Vidal, Lisa — Actress
Paul Kohner, 9300 Wilshire Blvd, #555, Beverly Hills CA 90212 USA
Vidal, Ricardo J Cardinal — Religious Leader
Chancery, D Jakoselam Str, PO Box 52, Cebu City 6000, Philippines
Vidal, Tanya — Actress
McGowan Mgmt, 8733 W Sunset Blvd, #103, West Hollywood CA 90069 USA
Vidmar, Peter — Gymnast
18 Downfield Way, Trabuco Canyon CA 92679, USA
Vidrio Serrano, Nestor V — Soccer Player
Federacion de Futbol, Colima 373 Colonia Roma, Delegacion Cuauhtemoc Mexico DF 06700, Mexico
Vidro, Jose A C — Baseball Player
159 Wentworth Ave, Brockton MA 02301, USA
Viehboeck, Franz A — Cosmonaut, Austria
Hauptstr 102/Top 3, 1140 Vienna, Austria
Vieillard, Roger — Artist
7 Rue de l'Estrapade, 75005 Paris, France
Vieira, Jelon — Choreographer
Pentocle/Danceworks, 246 W 38th St, #800, New York NY 10018, USA
Vieira, Marcelo — Soccer Player
F C Real Madrid, Avda Concha Espana 1, 28036 Madrid, Spain
Vieira, Meredith — Commentator
Meredith Vieira Productions, 888 7th Ave, #503, New York NY 10106, USA
Vieira, Patrick — Soccer Player
F C Juventus, Corso Galilo Ferraris 32, 10128 Turin, Italy
Viellard, Eric — Actor
Artmedia, 20 Ave Rapp, 75007 Paris, France
Vieluf, Vince — Actor, Writer, Director
Station3, 1051 N Cole Ave, Ste B, Los Angeles CA 90038, USA
Viener, John — Actor, Writer
United Talent Agency, 9336 Civic Center Dr, Beverly Hills CA 90210 USA
Viesturs, Ed — Mountaineer
4462 NE Mill Heights Circle, Bainbridge Island WA 98110, USA
Vieth, Michelle — Actress, Model
Televisa, Blvd A Lopez Mateos 232, Colonia San Angel, DF CP 01060, Mexico
Vig, Butch — Drummer (Garbage), Record Producer
Creative Artists Agency, 2000 Ave of Stars, #100, Los Angeles CA 90067 USA
Vigil, Frederico — Artist
National Hispanic Cultural Center, 1701 4th St SW, Albuquerque NM 87102, USA
Vigman, Gillian — Actress, Comedienne
Brillstein Entertainment Partners, 9150 Wilshire Blvd, #350, Beverly Hills CA 90212 USA
Vigna, Marino — Cyclist
Via Bruno Buozzi 130, 20089 Rozzano, Italy
Vigneault, Alain — Ice Hockey Player, Coach
Vancouver Canucks, 800 Griffiths Way, Vancouver BC V6B 6G1, Canada
Vignelli, Lella — Interior Designer
Vignelli Assoc, 130 E 67th St, New York NY 10065, USA
Vignelli, Massimo — Interior Designer
Vignelli Assoc, 130 E 67th St, New York NY 10065, USA
Vigneron, Thierry — Track Athlete
Adidas USA, 685 Cedar Crest Road, Spartanburg SC 29301, USA
Vigoda, Abe — Actor
190 E 72nd St, #15B, New York NY 10021, USA
Vigoda, Valerie — Singer, Violinist (GrooveLily)
GrooveLily, PO Box 11570, Glendale CA 91226, USA
Vikander, Alicia — Actress
Actors in Scandanavia, Jaakarinkatu 10, 00150 Helsinki, Finland
Viktorenko, Aleksandr S — Cosmonaut
Cosmonaut Training Center, Star City, 141160 Zvezdny Gorodok, Moscow Oblast, Russia
Vila, Bob — Entertainer, Writer
115 Kingston St, #300, Boston MA 02111, USA
Vilanch, Bruce — Actor, Comedian, Writer
Paradigm Agency, 360 N Crescent Dr, North Building, Beverly Hills CA 90210 USA
Vilar, Tracy — Actress
Raw Talent Mgmt, 9615 Brighton Way, #300, Beverly Hills CA 90210 USA
Vilaro, Eduardo — Dancer, Choreographer
Ballet Hispanico, 167 W 89th St, New York NY 10024, USA
Vilas, Guillermo — Tennis Player
Ave Foch 86, 75016 Paris, France
Vilasuso, Jordi — Actor
Artistry Mgmt, 340 N Camden Dr, #302, Beverly Hills CA 90210, USA
Vilenkin, Alex — Physicist, Astronomer
Tufts University, Physics & Astronomy Dept, Medford MA 02155, USA

Villa, Carlos	Artist
San Francisco Art Institute, 800 Chestnut St, San Francisco CA 94133, USA	
Villafuerte, Brandon	Baseball Player
PO Box 188, North Bridgton ME 04057, USA	
Villanueva, Charlie	Basketball Player
Detroit Pistons, Palace, 4 Championship Dr, Auburn Hills MI 48326 USA	
Villanueva, Daniel D (Danny)	Football Player
PO Box 258, Somis CA 93066, USA	
Villapiano, Philip J (Phil)	Football Player
21 Riverside Dr, Rumson NJ 07760, USA	
Villaraigosa, Antonio	Mayor, Los Angeles
Mayor's Office, City Hall, 200 N Spring St, Los Angeles CA 90012, USA	
Villari, Guy	Singer (Regents)
293 Airport Road, Liberty NY 12754, USA	
Villarrial, Christopher H (Chris)	Football Player
7234 Bibbs Road, Little Valley NY 14755, USA	
Villarroel, Vernoica	Opera Singer
Columbia Artists Mgmt Inc, 1790 Broadway, #702, New York NY 10019 USA	
Villasenor, Diego	Architect
Gob Tiburcio Montiel 96, Col S M Chapultepec, Mexico City DF 11850, Mexico	
Villazon, Rolando	Opera Singer
Zemsky/Green Mgmt, 104 W 73rd St, #1, New York NY 10023, USA	
Villegas, Camilo	Golfer
318 W Riverside Dr, Tequesta FL 33469, USA	
Villella, Edward J	Ballet Dancer, Choreographer
Miami City Ballet, Roca Center, 2200 Liberty Ave, Miami Beach FL 33139, USA	
Villeneuve, Denis	Director, Writer
Claude Girard, 5230 Boul Saint-Laurent, Montreal QC H2T 1S1, Canada	
Villeneuve, Gilles	Ice Hockey Player
38 Grey Lane, Levittown NY 11756, USA	
Villeneuve, Jacques	Auto Racing Driver
B A R Team, PO Box 5014, Brackley, Northamptonshire NN13 7YY, England	
Villiers, Christopher	Actor
Hillman Trelfall, 33 Brookfield, Highgate W Hill, London N6 6AT, England	
Villone, Ronald T (Ron), Jr	Baseball Player
855 NE Mulberry Dr, Boca Raton FL 33487, USA	
Vilma, Jonathan P	Football Player
1331 Brickell Bay Dr, #2709, Miami FL 33131, USA	
Viloria, Brian	Boxer
Gary Gittlesohn, 14372 Mulholland Dr, Los Angeles CA 90077, USA	
Vilsack, Thomas (Tom)	Secretary, Agriculture; Governor, IA
Agriculture Department, 14th St & Independence Ave SW, Washington DC 20250 USA	
Vimond, Paul M	Architect
91 Ave Niel, 75017 Paris, France	
Vin Rock	Rap Artist (Naughty By Nature)
Evolution Talent Agency, 1501 Broadway, #1301, New York NY 10036 USA	
Vina, Fernando	Baseball Player
9464 Clementine Way, Elk Grove CA 95758, USA	
Vinatieri, Adam M	Football Player
12850 Horseferry Road, Carmel IN 46032, USA	
Vince, Pruitt Taylor	Actor
Burstein Co, 15304 Sunset Blvd, #208, Pacific Palisades CA 90272, USA	
Vincelette, Dan	Ice Hockey Player
1345 Rue Bernier, RR 3, Acton Vale QC J0H 1A0, Canada	
Vincent, Amy	Cinematographer
5932 Graciosa Dr, Los Angeles CA 90068, USA	
Vincent, Brian	Actor
Imperium 7, 5455 Wilshire Blvd, #1706, Los Angeles CA 90036, USA	
Vincent, Cerina	Actress
Brillstein Entertainment Partners, 9150 Wilshire Blvd, #350, Beverly Hills CA 90212 USA	
Vincent, Francis T (Fay), Jr	Baseball Executive
290 Harbor Dr, Stamford CT 06902, USA	
Vincent, J Samuel (Sam)	Basketball Player, Coach
PO Box 27459, Lansing MI 48909, USA	
Vincent, James F (Jim), Jr	Choreographer, Dance Executive
Netherlands Dance Theater, Schedeldoekshaven 60 , 2501 CH Den Haag, Netherlands	
Vincent, Jan-Michael	Actor
Freeman & Sutton, 8961 W Sunset Blvd, #200, West Hollywood CA 90069, USA	
Vincent, Jay F	Basketball Player
PO Box 27459, Lansing MI 48909, USA	
Vincent, Keydrick T	Football Player
1769 Derby Glen Dr, Orlando FL 32837, USA	
Vincent, Rhonda	Singer
Upper Mgmt, 21750 Potter Road, Kirksville MO 63501, USA	
Vincent, Richard F	Army Field Marshal, England
House of Lords, Westminster, London SW1A 0PW, England	
Vincent, Rick	Singer, Songwriter
Carter Career Mgmt, 1028 18th Ave S, #B, Nashville TN 37212 USA	
Vincent, Troy D	Football Player
18900 Longhouse Place, Leesburg VA 20176, USA	
Vincent, Virginia	Actress
4738 Works Place, San Diego CA 92116, USA	
Vincentelli, Francois	Actor
Artmedia, 20 Ave Rapp, 75007 Paris, France	
Vincenzi, Penny	Writer
Overlook Press, 141 Wooster St, #4B, New York NY 10012, USA	
Vincz, Melanie	Actress
2212 Earle Court, Redondo Beach CA 90278, USA	
Vineyard, David K (Dave)	Baseball Player
1850 Tariff Road, Left Hand WV 25251, USA	
Vingt-Trois, Andre A Cardinal	Religious Leader
Ordinary of France, 7 Rue Saint Vincent, 75018 Paris Cedex 08, France	
Vining, David	Gastroenterologist
2210 Bellefontaine St, #D, Houston TX 77030, USA	
Vinogradov, Pavel V	Cosmonaut
Cosmonaut Training Center, Star City, 141160 Zvezdny Gorodok, Moscow Oblast, Russia	

V

Villa - Vinogradov

Vinoly, Rafael — Architect
50 Vandam St, New York NY 10013, USA

Vinson, Charles A (Charlie) — Baseball Player
3821 Walters Lane, District Heights MD 20747, USA

Vinson, Sharni — Actress, Model, Dancer
Flutie Entertainment, 9320 Wilshire Blvd, #202, Beverly Hills CA 90212 USA

Vint, Jesse Lee, III — Actor
Film Artists, 13563 1/2 Ventura Blvd, #200, Sherman Oaks CA 91423 USA

Vinterberg, Thomas — Director
Nimbus Film Productions, Hauchsvej 17, Frederiksberg 1825, Denmark

Vinton, Bobby — Singer
M P I Talent Agency, 9255 W Sunset Blvd, #804, West Hollywood CA 90069, USA

Vinton, Will — Animator, Director, Producer
Creative Artists Agency, 2000 Ave of Stars, #100, Los Angeles CA 90067 USA

Viola, Bill — Sculptor, Video Artist
282 Granada Ave, Long Beach CA 90803, USA

Viola, Frank J, Jr — Baseball Player
9868 Kilgore Road, Orlando FL 32836, USA

Viola, Lisa — Dancer
Paul Taylor Dance Co, 551 Grand St, Lobby A, New York NY 10002, USA

Virata, Cesar E — Prime Minister, Philippines
63 E Maya Dr, Quezon City, Philippines

Virden, Claude — Basketball Player
337 Fernwood Dr, Akron OH 44320, USA

Virdon, William C (Bill) — Baseball Player, Manager
1311 E River Road, Springfield MO 65804, USA

Viren, Lasse — Track Athlete
Suomen Urheilulitto Ry, Box 25202, 00250 Helsinki 25, Finland

Virgil, Osvaldo J (Ozzie), Jr — Baseball Player
5444 W Credance Blvd, Glendale AZ 85310, USA

Virgil, Osvaldo J (Ozzie), Sr — Baseball Player
4316 W Mescal St, Glendale AZ 85304, USA

Virsaladze, Eliso K — Concert Pianist
Moscow Conservatory, Bolshaya Nikitskaya Str 13/6, 125009 Moscow, Russia

Virts, Terry W, Jr — Astronaut
1904 Edgewater Court, Friendswood TX 77546, USA

Virtue, Tom — Actor
C E S D, 10635 Santa Monica Blvd, #130, Los Angeles CA 90025 USA

Visconti, Tony — Music Producer
Star Mangement Group, 1311 Mamaroneck Ave, #220, White Plains NY 10605, USA

Viscuso, Sal — Actor
Imperium 7 Talent, 5455 Wilshire Blvd, #1706, Los Angeles CA 90036, USA

Vise, David A — Journalist
Washington Post, Editorial Dept, 1150 15th St NW, Washington DC 20071, USA

Vishnevskaya, Galina P — Opera Singer
Gazetny Per 13, #79, 103009 Moscow, Russia

Vishnevski, Vitaly — Ice Hockey Player
Internatioanl Sports Advisors, 878 Ridge View Way, Franklin Lakes NJ 07417, USA

Vishnyova, Diana V — Ballerina
Mariinsky Theater, Teatralnaya Square 1, 190000 Saint Petersburg, Russia

Visitor, Nana — Actress
Pantheon Talent, 1801 Century Park E, #1910, Los Angeles CA 90067, USA

Visnjic, Goran — Actor
Management 360, 9111 Wilshire Blvd, Beverly Hills CA 90210 USA

Visnovsky, Lubomir — Ice Hockey Player
1531 9th St, Manhattan Beach CA 90266, USA

Viso, Michel — Spatinaut, France
7 Domaine Chateau-Gaillard, 94700 Maisons-d'Alfort, France

Visser, Angela — Beauty Queen, Actress
4127 Crisp Canyon Road, Sherman Oaks CA 91403, USA

Visser, Douwe — Religious Leader
World Reformed Churches, 150 Rt de Ferney, 1211 Geneva 2, Switzerland

Visser, Lesley — Sportscaster
CBS-TV, Sports Dept, 51 W 52nd St, New York NY 10019 USA

Vissi, Anna — Singer
Confidential Talent Agency, 745 5th Ave, #800, New York NY 10151, USA

Vitale, Dick — Sportscaster, Basketball Coach
7810 Mathern Court, Bradenton FL 34202, USA

Vitali, Massimo — Photographer
Bonni Benrubi Gallery, 41 E 57th St, #1300, New York NY 10022, USA

Vitamin C — Singer, Actress
I C M Partners, 10250 Constellation Blvd, #900, Los Angeles CA 90067 USA

Vitez, Michael — Journalist
Philadelphia Inquirer, Editorial Dept, 400 N Broad St, Philadelphia PA 19130, USA

Vitiello, Joseph D (Joe) — Baseball Player
13615 Old El Camino Real, San Diego CA 92130, USA

Vitko, Joseph J (Joe) — Baseball Player
1853 Frankstown Road, #1, Johnstown PA 15902, USA

Vito, Robert D — Actor
Strong Management, 9350 Wilshire Blvd, #224, Beverly Hills CA 90212, USA

Vitolo, Dennis — Auto Racing Driver
2130 Intracoastal Dr, Fort Lauderdale FL 33305, USA

Vitorgan, Emmanuil — Actor; Director
Maly Kislovsky Per 7, #26, 103009 Moscow, Russia

Vitousek, Peter M — Botanist, Ecologist
Stanford University, Biological Science Dept, Stanford CT 94305, USA

Vittadini, Adrienne — Fashion Designer
Adrienne Vittadini Inc, 575 Fashion Ave, New York NY 10018, USA

Vitti, Monica — Actress
I P C, Via Francesco Siacci 38, 00197 Rome, Italy

Vittori, Roberto — Astronaut
European Space Center, Linder Hohe, Box 906096, 51127 Cologne, Germany

Vitukhnovskaya, Alina A — Writer
Leningradskoye Shosse 80, #89, 125565 Moscow, Russia

Vivas, Miguel A — Director, Writer, Actor
United Talent Agency, 9336 Civic Center Dr, Beverly Hills CA 90210 USA

Vivek — Actor, Comedian
9 Subhiksha Apts, 5 Tank St, U I Colony, Chennai TN 600024, India

Viviani, Gabriele — Opera Singer
I M G Artists, Hogarth Business Park, Chiswick, London W4 2TH, England

Vizcaino Arias, J Luis — Baseball Player
5876 Germaine Lane, La Jolla CA 92037, USA

Vizquel Gonzalez, Omar E — Baseball Player
2704 212th Ave SE, Sammamish WA 98075, USA

Vlady, Marina — Actress
10 Ave de Marivaux, 78800 Mission Lafitte, France

Vlasic, Blanka — Track Athlete
Hrvatski Atletski Savez, Krizaniceva 5, 10000 Zagreb, Croatia

Vlk, Miloslav Cardinal — Religious Leader
Arcibiskupstvi, Hradcanske Nam 16/56, 119 02 Prague 1, Czech Republic

Vo Nguyen Giap — Army General, Vietnam
Dang Cong San Vietnam, 1C Blvd Hoang Van Thu, Hanoi, Vietnam

Voda, Jan K — Surgeon
608 NW 9th St, Oklahoma City OK 73102, USA

Vodianova, Natalia — Model
D N A Model Mgmt, 555 W 25th St, #600, New York NY 10001 USA

Vodopyanova, Natalia — Basketball Player
Seattle Storm, Key Arena, 351 Elliott Ave W, #500, Seattle WA 98119 USA

Voegele, Kate — Singer, Songwriter, Actress
Wilspro Mgmt, 1335 Barton Ave, Point Pleasant NJ 08742, USA

Voelker, Sabine — Speed Skater
Rube Marketing, Maximilian-Welsch Str 7, 99084 Erfurt, Germany

Voevodsky, Vladimir — Mathematician
22 Earle Lane, Princeton NJ 08540, USA

Vogel, Darlene — Actress
Michael Slessinger, 8730 W Sunset Blvd, #220W, West Hollywood CA 90069 USA

Vogel, Frank — Basketball Coach
Indiana Pacers, Conseco Fieldhouse, 125 S Pennsylvania, Indianapolis IN 46204 USA

Vogel, Mike — Actor
W M E Entertainment, 9601 Wilshire Blvd, #300, Beverly Hills CA 90210 USA

Vogel, Mitch — Actor
3335 Honeysuckle Ave, Palmdale CA 93550, USA

Vogel, Paula — Writer
Gersh Agency, 9465 Wilshire Blvd, #600, Beverly Hills CA 90212 USA

Vogel, Robert L (Bob) — Football Player
2065 N Galena Road, Sunbury OH 43074, USA

Vogelsong, Ryan A — Baseball Player
637 W Jardin Dr, Casa Grande AZ 85122, USA

Vogelstein, Bert — Geneticist, Oncologist
Johns Hopkins University, Medical School, Oncology Center, Baltimore MD 21218, USA

Vogler, Jan — Concert Cellist
Moira Johnson Consulting, 180 Metcalfe St, #404, Ottawa ON K2P 1P5, Canada

Vogler, Timothy (Tim) — Football Player
6710 Woodland Dr, Hamburg NY 14075, USA

Vogt, Peter K — Virologist
Scripps Institute, Oncovirology Dept, 10550 N Torrey Pines, La Jolla CA 92037, USA

Vogts, Hans-Hubert (Berti) — Soccer Player
Football Assoc, 2208 Nobel Ave, 1025 Baku, Azerbaijan

Vohor, Serge — Prime Minister, Vanuatu
Moderate Parties Union, PO Box 698, Port Via, Vanuatu

Voie, Angelica — Opera Singer
Harrison/Parrott, 5-6 Albion Court, London W6 0QT, England

Voight, Deborah — Opera Singer
21C Media Group, 162 W 56th St, #506, New York NY 10019, USA

Voight, Jon — Actor
9660 Oak Pass Road, Beverly Hills CA 90210, USA

Voight, Karen — Physical Fitness Expert
Entertaining Fitness, 827 Chautauqua Blvd, Pacific Palisades CA 90272, USA

Voight, Stuart A (Stu) — Football Player
8832 Hunters Way, Saint Paul MN 55124, USA

Voigt, Deborah — Opera Singer
I M G Artists, 152 W 57th St, #500, New York NY 10019 USA

Voigt, John D (Jack) — Baseball Player
1759 Bayshore Road, Nokomis FL 34275, USA

Voisine, Roch — Singer, Songwriter
Don Jones Productions, 550 Wellington St, London ON N6A 3P9, Canada

Vokoun, Tomas — Ice Hockey Player
6685 NW 122nd Ave, Parkland FL 33076, USA

Volberding, Paul A — Oncologist
General Hospital, AIDS Activities Dept, 995 Protrero, San Francisco CA 94110, USA

Volchenkov, Anton — Ice Hockey Player
New Jersey Devils, Arena, 50 State Route 120, East Rutherford NJ 07073 USA

Volcker, Paul A — Government Official, Financier
151 E 79th St, New York NY 10075, USA

Volek, David — Ice Hockey Player
5 Blue Sky Court, Huntington NY 11743, USA

Volek, J William (Billy) — Football Player
12487 Valley Vista Lane, Fresno CA 93730, USA

Volf, Jaroslav — Canoeing Athlete
S K Neumanna 386, 25001 Brandys Nad Labem, Czech Republic

Volibracht, Michaele — Fashion Designer, Artist
Bill Blass Ltd, 236 5th Ave, #800, New York NY 10001, USA

Volk, Igor P — Cosmonaut
G N C-R F L II, Zhukovskiy 2, 140160 Moscow, Russia

Volk, Patricia — Writer
Gloria Loomis, 133 E 35th St, New York NY 10016, USA

Volk, Richard R (Rick) — Football Player
15860 Irish Ave, Monkton MD 21111, USA

Volkert, Stephan — Rowing Athlete
Semmelweisstr 42, 51061 Cologne, Germany

Volkmann, Elisabeth — Opera Singer
Sonnenstr 20, 80331 Munich, Germany

Volkov, Aleksandr A — Cosmonaut
Cosmonaut Training Center, Star City, 141160 Zvezdny Gorodok, Moscow Oblast, Russia

Volkov, Alexander — Basketball Player
1413 Waterford Green Dr, Mariette GA 30068, USA

Volkov, Sergei A — Cosmonaut
Cosmonaut Training Center, Star City, 141160 Zvezdny Gorodok, Moscow Oblast, Russia

Volkow, Nora D — Physician
National Drug Abuse Institute, 6001 Executive Blvd, Bethesda MD 20892, USA

Vollbracht, Michaele — Fashion Designer, Artist
General Delivery, Safety Harbor FL 34695, USA

Volle, Michael — Opera Singer
I M G Artists, Hogarth Business Park, Chiswick, London W4 2TH, England

Vollenweider, Andreas — Concert Harpist
Sempacher Str 16, 8032 Zurich, Switzerland

Vollman, William T — Writer
2090 8th Ave, Sacramento CA 95818, USA

Vollmer, Dana W — Swimmer
4002 Laramie Dr, Granbury TX 76049, USA

Volmar, Douglas (Doug) — Ice Hockey Player
120 Royal Oak Dr, #L, Bel Air MD 21015, USA

Volmer, Arvo — Conductor
Estonia National Opera, Estonia Ave 4, 10148 Tallinn, Estonia

Volodos, Arcadi — Concert Pianist
Columbia Artists Mgmt Inc, 1790 Broadway, #702, New York NY 10019 USA

Voloshin, Valeri — Cosmonaut
Cosmonaut Training Center, Star City, 141160 Zvezdny Gorodok, Moscow Oblast, Russia

Volstad, Christopher K (Chris) — Baseball Player
11774 Hemlock St, Palm Beach Gardens FL 33410, USA

Volynov, Boris V — Cosmonaut
Cosmonaut Training Center, Star City, 141160 Zvezdny Gorodok, Moscow Oblast, Russia

VonAroldingen, Karin — Ballerina
New York City Ballet, Lincoln Center Plaza, New York NY 10023 USA

VonD, Kat — Entertainer, Tattoo Artist
Creative Artists Agency, 2000 Ave of Stars, #100, Los Angeles CA 90067 USA

VonDaniken, Erich — Writer
Postfach, 3803 Beatenberg, Switzerland

VonDetten, Erik T — Actor
Innovative Artists, 1505 10th St, Santa Monica CA 90401 USA

VonDohnanyi, Christoph — Conductor
Cleveland Orchestra, Severance Hall, Cleveland OH 44106, USA

VonDonnersmarck, Florian H — Director
United Talent Agency, 9336 Civic Center Dr, Beverly Hills CA 90210 USA

Vondracek, Lukas — Concert Pianist
Harrison/Parrott, Lucile-Grahn-Str 37, 81675 Munich, Germany

VonEschenbach, Andrew — Surgeon, Government Official
US Food & Drug Administration, 5600 Fishers Lane, Rockville MD 20857, USA

VonEsmarch, Nick — Actor
TalentWorks, 3500 W Olive Ave, #1400, Burbank CA 91505 USA

VonFurstenberg, Betsy — Actress
230 Central Park West, #16A, New York NY 10024, USA

VonFurstenberg, Diane — Fashion Designer
444 W 14th St, New York NY 10014, USA

VonGarnier, Katja — Director, Writer
Above the Line, Wielandstr 5, 10625 Berlin, Germany

Vongerichten, Jean-Georges — Chef
Jean-Georges Restaurant, 19 Greene St, New York NY 10013, USA

VonGerkan, Manon — Model
Trump Model Mgmt, 91 5th Ave, #300, New York NY 10003, USA

VonGrunigen, Michael — Alpine Skier
Chalet Sunneblick, 3778 Schonried, Switzerland

VonHagens, Gunther — Anatomist
Institute for Plastination, Rathausstr 11, 69126 Heidelberg, Germany

VonHippel, Peter H — Chemist
1900 Crest Dr, Eugene OR 97405, USA

VonHoff, Bruce F — Baseball Player
423 S River Hills Dr, Tampa FL 33617, USA

VonHohenzollern, Furst — Heir, House of Hohenzollern-Sigmaringen
Landhaus Josefslust, 72488 Sigmaringen, Germany

VonKlitzing, Klaus — Nobel Physics Laureate
Max Planck Institute, Heisenbergstr 1, 70506 Stuttgart, Germany

Vonn, Lindsey K — Alpine Skier
1740 Stewart St, Santa Monica CA 90404, USA

VonOelhoffen, Kimo K — Football Player
402 Adams St, Richland WA 99352, USA

VonOhlen, David (Dave) — Baseball Player
653 Windmill Ave, West Babylon NY 11704, USA

VonOtter, Anne Sofie — Opera Singer
Opus 3 Artists, 470 Park Ave S, #900N, New York NY 10016 USA

VonQuast, Veronika — Actress
Z B F Agentur, Friedrichstr 39, 10969 Berlin, Germany

VonRingelheim, Paul H — Sculptor
9 Great Jones St, New York NY 10012, USA

VonRydingsvard, Ursula — Sculptor
78 Ingraham St, Brooklyn NY 11237, USA

VonSaltza Olmstead, S Christine (Chris) — Swimmer
520 Crocker Road, Sacramento CA 95864, USA

VonSchamann, Uwe D W — Football Player
1236 Loma Dr, Norman OK 73072, USA

VonStade, Frederica — Opera Singer
333 Kennedy St, Oakland CA 94606, USA

VonSydow, Max — Actor
Diamond Mgmt, 31 Percy St, London W1T 2DD, England

VonTeese, Dita — Model, Actress, Dancer
Dishell Multimedia Group, 8306 Wilshire Blvd, #833, Beverly Hills CA 90211, USA

VonTrier, Lars — Director
Zentropa Entertainments, Filmbyen 22, 2650 Hvidovre, Denmark

VonTrotta, Margarethe — Director
Above The Line, Wielandstr 5, 10625 Berlin, Germany
VonWeizsacker, Richard — President, Germany
Am Kupfergraben 7, 10117 Berlin, Germany
Voog, Ana — Singer, Songwriter
M C A Records, 1755 Broadway, New York NY 10019 USA
Voorhees, John J — Dermatologist
3965 Waldenwood Dr, Ann Arbor MI 48105, USA
Voorhies, Lark — Actress
Cyrus & Cyrus, 9935 S Santa Monica Blvd, Beverly Hills CA 90212, USA
Voorman, Klaus — Artist
K & K Galleries, Grindelalla 182, 20144 Hamburg, Germany
Vorgan, Gigi — Actress
3637 Stone Canyon, Sherman Oaks CA 91403, USA
Voris, Cyrus — Writer, Producer, Actor
United Talent Agency, 9336 Civic Center Dr, Beverly Hills CA 90210 USA
Voronin, Vladimir N — President, Moldova
Presidential Palace, 23 Nicolae Iorge Str, 227033 Chishinev, Moldova
Vorontsov, Nikolai N — Geneticist, Zoologist
Koltsov Biology Institute, Vavilova Str 26, 117334 Moscow, Russia
Voroshilo, Aleksander S — Opera Singer
Bolshoi Theater, Teatralnaya Pl 1, 103009 Moscow, Russia
Vosberg, Edward J (Ed) — Baseball Player
7839 E Marquise Dr, Tucson AZ 85715, USA
Vosloo, Arnold — Actor
A P A Talent/Literary Agency, 405 S Beverly Dr, #300, Beverly Hills CA 90212 USA
Voss, Brian — Bowler
6115 Abbotts Bridge Road, #111, Duluth GA 30097, USA
Voss, James S — Astronaut
4207 Indian Sunrise Court, Houston TX 77059, USA
Voss, John — Biochemist
University of California, Biochemistry Dept, Davis CA 95616, USA
Voss, Torsten — Track Athlete
Dunkirchener Str 74, 47839 Krefeld, Germany
Voss, William E (Bill) — Baseball Player
10625 E Oak Creek Trail, Cornville AZ 86325, USA
VosSavant, Marilyn — Writer
Parade Publications, 711 3rd Ave, New York NY 10017, USA
Vostell, Wolf — Video Artist
Giesebrechstr 12, 10629 Berlin, Germany
Votaw, Ty — Golf Executive
Ladies Pro Golf Assn, 100 International Golf Dr, Daytona Beach FL 32124 USA
Votsis, Gloria — Actress
T M T Entertainment Group, 648 Broadway, #912, New York, NY 10012, USA
Votto, Joseph D (Joey) — Baseball Player
4 Nantucket Crescent, Brampton ON L6S 3X5, Canada
Voyagis, Yorgo — Actor
Anne Alvares Correa, 34 Rue Jouffroy d'Abbans, 75017 Paris, France
Voyles, Brad — Baseball Player
314 East Ave, Casco WI 54205, USA
Vraa, Sanna — Model, Actress
Irv Schechter, 9460 Wilshire Blvd, #300, Beverly Hills CA 90212 USA
Vrabel, Michael G (Mike) — Football Player
777 W Orange Road, Delaware OH 43015, USA
Vraciu, Alexander (Alex) — WW II Navy Air Force Hero
309 Merrilee Place, Danville CA 94526, USA
Vranes, Daniel L (Danny) — Basketball Player
6480 Canyon Ranch Road, Salt Lake City UT 84121, USA
Vratogna, Marco — Opera Singer
I M G Artists, Hogarth Business Park, Chiswick, London W4 2TH, England
Vuarnet, Jean — Alpine Skier
Chalet Squaw Peak, 74110 Auoriaz, France
Vucevic, Nikola — Basketball Player
Orlando Magic, 8701 Maitland Summit Blvd, Orlando FL 32810 USA
Vuckovich, Peter D (Pete) — Baseball Player
86 Leonard St, Johnstown PA 15902, USA
Vuitton, Henri-Louis — Fashion Designer
30 Rue la Boetie 8th Ave, Paris, France
Vujanovic, Filip — President, Montenegro
Presidential Palace, Cetinje, Montenegro
Vukoto, Mick — Ice Hockey Player
PO Box 3213, 7 Peases Point Road, Edgartown MA 02539, USA
Vukovich, George S — Baseball Player
305 W Calle Gota, Sahuarita AZ 85629, USA
Vuolo, Lindsey — Model
Playboy Promotions, 2706 Media Center Dr, Los Angeles CA 90065 USA
Vuono, Carl E — Army General
5796 Westchester St, Alexandria VA 22310, USA
Vyborny, David — Ice Hockey Player
4075 Blendon Grove Way, Columbus OH 43230, USA
Vyent, Louise — Model
Pauline's Talent Corp, 379 W Broadway, #502, New York NY 10012 USA

Waakataar-Savoy, Paul — Singer, Guitarist (A-Ha), Songwriter
Agency Group Ltd, 361-373 City Road, London EC1V 2QA, England
Waalkes, Otto — Actor, Comedian
Papenhuder Str 61, 22087 Hamburg, Germany
Wachowski, Andy — Director
Circle of Confusion, 107-23 71st Road, #300, Forest Hills NY 11375, USA
Wachowski, Laurence (Lana) — Director
Circle of Confusion, 107-23 71st Road, #300, Forest Hills NY 11375, USA
Wachs, Caitlin — Actress
I C M Partners, 10250 Constellation Blvd, #900, Los Angeles CA 90067 USA
Wachtel, Christine — Track Athlete
Rostock Sports Club, Rostock, 17033 Mecklenburg-Vorpommoern, Germany
Wachter, Anita — Alpine Skier
Gantschierstr 579, 6780 Schruns, Austria
Wackerman, Brooks — Drummer (Bad Religion)
Goldstar Mgmt, PO Box 130, Ross on Wye HR9 6WY, England
Wada, Tsuyoshi — Baseball Player
Baltimore Orioles, Oriole Park, 333 W Camden St, Baltimore MD 21201 USA
Waddell, Chris — Model, Skier
Athletes for Hope, 3 Bethesda Metro Center, #450, Bethesda MD 20814, USA
Waddell, Don — Ice Hockey Player
2554 Thurleston Lane, Duluth GA 30097, USA
Waddell, Ernest — Actor
Stone Manners Salners, 9911 W Pico Blvd, #1400, Los Angeles CA 90035 USA
Waddell, John Henry — Artist
10050 E Waddell Road, Cornville AZ 86325, USA
Waddell, Justine — Actress
United Agents, 12-26 Lexington St, London W1F 0LE, England
Waddell, Thomas D (Tom) — Baseball Player
10171 E Achi St, Tucson AZ 85748, USA
Waddington of Read, David — Governor General, Bermuda
39 Chester Way, #4, London SE11 4UR, England
Waddington, Steven — Actor
Julian Belfrage Assoc, 9 Argyll St, #300, London W1F 7TG, England
Waddle, Thomas (Tom) — Football Player, Sportscaster
8190 Tollbridge Dr, West Chester OH 45069, USA
Waddy, William D (Billy) — Football Player
2838 Highway 88, Minneapolis MN 55418, USA
Wade, Abdoulaye — President, Senegal
President's Office, Ave Roume, BP 168, Dakar, Senegal
Wade, Adam — Singer
C E S D, 257 Park Ave S, #950, New York NY 10010 USA
Wade, Chrissie — Musician (Alien Sex Fiend)
Mission Control, City Business Center, Lower Road, London SE16 2XB, England
Wade, Dwyane T — Basketball Player
9330 SW 59th Place, Miami FL 33156, USA
Wade, Jason M — Singer, Guitarist (Lifehouse)
Universal/Geffen Records, 2220 Colorado Ave, Santa Monica CA 90404, USA
Wade, Justin — Actor
TalentWorks, 3500 W Olive Ave, #1400, Burbank CA 91505 USA
Wade, Nik — Musician (Alien Sex Fiend)
Mission Control, City Business Center, Lower Road, London SE16 2XB, England
Wade, R John — Football Player
3540 Traveler Road, Harrisonburg VA 22801, USA
Wade, S Virginia — Tennis Player
International Mgmt Group, Pier House, Chiswick, London W4M 3NN, England
Wade, Todd M — Football Player
705 Nottingham Dr, Oxford MS 38655, USA
Wade, William J (Bill), Jr — Football Player
PO Box 210124, Nashville TN 37221, USA
Wadham, Julian — Actor
Ken McReddie Assoc, 11 Connaught Place, London W2 2ET, England
Wadhams, Wayne — Singer, Keyboardist (Fifth Estate)
73 Hemenway, Boston MA 02115, USA
Wadkins, Bobby — Golfer
204 Kinloch Road, Manakin Sabot VA 23103, USA
Wadkins, Lanny — Golfer, Sportscaster
6002 Kettering Court, Dallas TX 75248, USA
Wadlow, Jeff — Director, Writer
Tower of Babbel Entertainment, 854 N Spaulding Ave, Los Angeles CA 90046, USA
Wadsworth, Charles W — Concert Pianist
PO Box 157, Charleston SC 29402, USA
Wadsworth, Fred — Golfer
823 Bryon Road, Columbia SC 29205, USA
Waechter, Douglas M (Doug) — Baseball Player
4590 13th Way NE, Saint Petersburg FL 33703, USA
Waena, Nathaniel — Governor General, Solomon Islands
Governor General's House, Box 252, Honiara, Guadacanal, Solomon Islands
Wafer, Vakeaton Q (Von) — Basketball Player
2503 Dallas St, Houston TX 77003, USA
Wages, Harmon L — Football Player
1846 Margaret St, #3C, Jacksonville FL 32204, USA
Wages, William — Cinematographer
Innovative Artists, 1505 10th St, Santa Monica CA 90401 USA
Waggoner, Brooke — Singer, Songwriter
Agency Group Ltd, 142 W 57th St, #600, New York NY 10019 USA
Waggoner, Lyle — Actor
1124 Oak Mirage Place, Westlake Village CA 91362, USA
Waggoner, Paul E — Agronomist
314 Vineyard Point Road, Guilford CT 06437, USA
Wagner, Allison — Swimmer
912 NW 45th Terrace, Gainesville FL 32605, USA
Wagner, Amber — Opera Singer
I M G Artists, Hogarth Business Park, Chiswick, London W4 2TH, England
Wagner, Barbara A — Figure Skater
Alpharetta Family Skate Center, 10800 Davis Dr, Alpharetta GA 30009, USA

Wagner, Bruce — Writer, Producer, Actor
United Talent Agency, 9336 Civic Center Dr, Beverly Hills CA 90210 USA
Wagner, Bryan J — Football Player
6020 Arlyne Lane, Medina OH 44256, USA
Wagner, Catherine — Photographer
308 Precita Ave, San Francisco CA 94110, USA
Wagner, Chuck — Actor, Singer
1200 Maldonado Dr, Pensacola Beach FL 32561, USA
Wagner, Dajuan M — Basketball Player
Golden State Warriors, 1011 Broadway, Oakland CA 94605 USA
Wagner, Fred — Cartoonist (Grin & Bear It)
King Features Syndicate, 300 W 57th St, #1500, New York NY 10019 USA
Wagner, Gary E — Baseball Player
1707 Northbrook Court, Seymour IN 47274, USA
Wagner, Harold A — Businessman
4031 Savannah Trail, Santa Rosa CA 95404, USA
Wagner, Jill — Model, Actress
Collective, 8383 Wilshire Blvd, #1050, Beverly Hills CA 90211 USA
Wagner, Johnson — Golfer
Professional Golfer's Assn, PO Box 109601, Palm Beach Gardens FL 33410 USA
Wagner, Kathy — Actress
Integrated Films, 1154 N Wetherly Dr, Los Angeles CA 90069, USA
Wagner, Katie — Actress
Creative Managment Entertainment, 2050 S Bundy Dr, #280, Los Angeles CA 90025, USA
Wagner, Kristina — Actress
PO Box 491035, Los Angeles CA 90049, USA
Wagner, Kurt — Singer (Lambchop)
High Road Touring, 751 Bridgeway, #200, Sausalito CA 94965 USA
Wagner, Lindsay — Actress
22817 Ventura Blvd, #888, Woodland Hills CA 91364, USA
Wagner, Lindsay — Model
Playboy Promotions, 2706 Media Center Dr, Los Angeles CA 90065 USA
Wagner, Lisa — Bowler
Professional Bowlers Assn, 719 2nd Ave, #701, Seattle WA 98104 USA
Wagner, Lou — Actor
Amsel Eisenstadt Frazier, 5055 Wilshire Blvd, #865, Los Angeles CA 90036 USA
Wagner, Louis C, Jr — Army General
6336 Manchester Way, Alexandria VA 22304, USA
Wagner, Mark D — Baseball Player
1838 Willow Arms Dr, Ashtabula OH 44004, USA
Wagner, Matthew (Matt) — Cartoonist
4340 Horton Road, West Linn OR 97068, USA
Wagner, Melinda — Composer
Theodore Presser, 588 N Gulph Road, #B, King of Prussia PA 19406, USA
Wagner, Michael R (Mike) — Football Player
203 E Wild Cherry Dr, Mars PA 16046, USA
Wagner, Paul A — Baseball Player
32 Ambito Place, Hot Springs AR 71909, USA
Wagner, Philip M — Columnist
32 Montgomery St, Boston MA 02116, USA
Wagner, Robert — Actor
Chuck Binder Mgmt, 1465 Lindacrest Dr, Beverly Hills CA 90210 USA
Wagner, Robert W — Army General
Commander, Joint Forces Command, Norfolk VA 23551, USA
Wagner, Robin S A — Stage, Set Designer
Robin Wagner Studio, 890 Broadway, New York NY 10003, USA
Wagner, Ryan S — Baseball Player
59 County Road 311, Yoakum TX 77995, USA
Wagner, Sune Rose — Singer, Guitarist (Ravenonettes)
Orchard, 100 Park Ave, #200, New York NY 10017, USA
Wagner, William E (Billy) — Baseball Player
5066 Jones Mill Road, Crozet VA 22932, USA
Wagner-Augustin, Katrin — Canoeing Athlete
Kaastaienallee 35, 14471 Potsdam, Germany
Wagoner, Dan — Dancer, Choreographer
Contemporary Dance Theater, 17 Duke's Road, London WC1H 9AB, England
Wagoner, David R — Writer
5416 154th Place SW, Edmonds WA 98026, USA
Wagoner, Harold E — Architect
331 Lindsey Dr, Berwyn PA 19312, USA
Wahl, Ken — Actor
9654 W 131st St, #206, Palos Park IL 60464, USA
Wahlberg, Donnie — Singer, Actor
16815 Bircher St, Granada Hills CA 91344, USA
Wahlberg, Mark — Actor, Singer, Model
W M E Entertainment, 9601 Wilshire Blvd, #300, Beverly Hills CA 90210 USA
Wahle, Michael J (Mike) — Football Player
6210 Avenida Cresta, La Jolla CA 92037, USA
Wahlgren, Olof G C — Editor
Nicoloviusgatan 5B, 217 57 Malmo, Sweden
Wahlstrom, Jarl H — Religious Leader
Borgstrominkuja 1A10, 00840 Helsinki 84, Finland
Waigel, Theodor — Government Official, Germany
Oberrohr, 86513 Ursberg, Germany
Waihee, John D, III — Governor, HI
745 Fort Street Mall, #600, Honolulu HI 96813, USA
Wain, Bea — Singer
Society of Singers, 15846 Ventura Blvd, #304, Sherman Oaks CA 91403, USA
Wain, David B — Director
Principato-Young, 9465 Wilshire Blvd, #880, Beverly Hills CA 90212 USA
Wainhouse, David P (Dave) — Baseball Player
6101 85th Place SE, Mercer Island WA 98040, USA
Wainwright, Adam P — Baseball Player
2100 Brook Hill Court, Chesterfield MO 63017, USA
Wainwright, Angel M — Actress
Amatruda Benson Assoc, 9107 Wilshire Blvd, #500, Beverly Hills CA 90210, USA

Wainwright, Loudon, III — Singer, Songwriter
Rosebud Agency, PO Box 170429, San Francisco CA 94117 USA
Wainwright, Martha — Singer, Songwriter
Billions Corp, 3522 W Armitage Ave, Chicago IL 60647 USA
Wainwright, Rufus M — Singer, Songwriter
M C T Mgmt, 520 8th Ave, #2001, New York NY 10018, USA
Wainwright, Rupert — Director, Actor, Writer
Luber Rocklin Entertainment, 8530 Wilshire Blvd, #555, Beverly Hills CA 90211 USA
Waite, Alison — Model
Playboy Promotions, 2706 Media Center Dr, Los Angeles CA 90065 USA
Waite, Grant — Golfer
1615 SE 73rd Place, Ocala FL 34480, USA
Waite, John — Singer (Babys, Bad English), Songwriter
Rounder Records, 1 Rounder Way, Burlington MA 01803 USA
Waite, Liam — Actor
Wyckoff Assoc, 11350 Ventura Blvd, #100, Studio City CA 91604, USA
Waite, Ralph — Actor
PO Box 810, Palm Desert CA 92261, USA
Waite, Terence H (Terry) — Religious Leader
Wheelrights, Green Harvest, Bury Saint Edmunds, Suffolk IP29 4DH, England
Waiters, Granville S — Basketball Player
3740 Moor Ridge Lane, Canal Winchester OH 43110, USA
Waiters, Van A — Football Player
6021 NW 201st Lane, Hialeah FL 33015, USA
Waits, M Richard (Rick) — Baseball Player
PO Box 1001, Patagonia AZ 85624, USA
Waits, Tom — Singer, Pianist, Songwriter
W M E Entertainment, 9601 Wilshire Blvd, #300, Beverly Hills CA 90210 USA
Waitt, Theodore W (Ted) — Businessman
Gateway Inc, 7565 Irvine Center Dr, Irvine CA 92618, USA
Waitz, Richard H — Cinematographer
405 Zenith Ave, Lafayette CO 80026, USA
Wajda, Andrzej — Director
Japanese/Technology Center, Ul Konopnickiej 26, 30 302 Cracow, Poland
Wakamatsu, W Donald (Don) — Baseball Player, Manager
8740 Ramblewood Court, Keller TX 76248, USA
Wakata, Koichi — Astronaut, Japan
Japanese Aerospace Exploration Agency, 2-1-1 Sengen, Tsukuba-shi, Ibaraki 305 8505, Japan
Waked, Amr — Actor
Ken McReddie Assoc, 11 Connaught Place, London W2 2ET, England
Wakefield, Rhys — Actor
R G M Associates, 64-76 Kippax St, #202, Surry Hills NSW 2010, Australia
Wakefield, Timothy S (Tim) — Baseball Player
241 Lansing Island Dr, Indian Harbour Beach FL 32937, USA
Wakeham of Maldon, John — Government Official, England
House of Lords, Westminster, London SW1A 0PW, England
Wakeland, Chris — Baseball Player
60997 Luttrell Lane, Saint Helens OR 97051, USA
Wakeley, Amanda — Fashion Designer
7 Old Park Lane, London W1K 1QR, England
Wakelin, Cara — Model, Actress
Playboy Promotions, 2706 Media Center Dr, Los Angeles CA 90065 USA
Wakeling, Dave — Singer (General Public, English Beat)
Arcadia Group Mgmt, 11400 W Olympic Blvd, #200, Los Angeles CA 90064, USA
Wakely, Ernie — Ice Hockey Player
11052 E Roundup Dr, Dewey AZ 86327, USA
Wakeman, Rick — Keyboardist, Songwriter
I C M Partners, Marlborough House, 10 Earlham St, #300, London WC2H 9LNP, England
Wakoski, Diane — Writer
607 Division St, East Lansing MI 48823, USA
Walbeck, Matthew L (Matt) — Baseball Player
8216 Olive Ave, Fair Oaks CA 95628, USA
Walchuk, Don — Curling Athlete
Curling Assn, 1660 Vimont Court, Cumberland ON K4A 4J4, Canada
Walcott, Derek A — Nobel Literature Laureate
PO Box GM 926, Castries, Saint Lucia, West Indies
Walcott, Gregory — Actor
22246 Saticoy St, Canoga Park CA 91303, USA
Walcott, Jennifer — Model, Actress
O'Grady Entertainment Group, 4550 Via Marina, #305, Marina del Rey CA 90292, USA
Walcutt, John — Actor
Defining Artists Agency, 10 Universal City Plaza, #2000, Universal City CA 91608, USA
Wald, Patricia M — Judge
US Court of Appeals, 3rd & Constitution NW, Washington DC 20001, USA
Waldau, Nicolaj Coster — Actor
Lindberg Mgmt, Lavendelstre De 5-7, Baghuset 4 Sal, 1462 Copenhagen K, Denmark
Waldegrave of North Hill, William — Government Official, England
66 Palace Gardens Terrace, London W8 4RR, England
Waldemore, Stanley A (Stan) — Football Player
PO Box 611, New Vernon NJ 07976, USA
Walden, Jordan C — Baseball Player
Los Angeles Angels, Angel Stadium, 2000 E Gene Autry Way, Anaheim CA 92806 USA
Walden, Lynette — Actress
Metropolitan Talent Agency, 7020 La Presa Dr, Los Angeles CA 90068 USA
Walden, Robert — Actor, Director, Writer
Bret Adams Agency, 448 W 44th St, New York NY 10036, USA
Walden, Robert E (Bobby) — Football Player
107 Springfield Dr, Bainbridge GA 39819, USA
Walden, W G (Snuffy) — Composer
Gorfaine/Schwartz, 4111 W Alameda Ave, #509, Burbank CA 91505 USA
Waldhauser, Thomas D — Marine Corps General
Commander, Central Command, 7115 S Boundary, MacDill Air Force Base FL 33621 USA
Waldie, Marc R — Volleyball Player
14020 E Ayesbury Circle, Wichita KS 67228, USA
Waldner, Jan-Ove — Table Tennis Player
Banda, Skjulstagatan 10, 632 29 Eskilstuna, Sweden

Wainwright - Waldner

Waldo, Janet — Actress
C E S D, 10635 Santa Monica Blvd, #130, Los Angeles CA 90025 USA
Waldorf, Duffy — Golfer
17100 Halsted St, Northridge CA 91325, USA
Waldron, Jeffrey — Cinematographer
United Talent Agency, 9336 Civic Center Dr, Beverly Hills CA 90210 USA
Waldron, Jeremy J — Educator, Attorney
1061 Keith Ave, Berkeley CA 94708, USA
Waldrop, Alex — Thoroughbred Racing Executive
National Thoroughbred Racing, 2525 Harrodsburg Road, #500, Lexington KY 40504, USA
Wales, Jimmy D (Jimbo) — Internet Encyclopedia Designer
Wikipedia Foundation, 200 2nd Ave S, #358, Saint Petersburg FL 33701, USA
Wales, Ross — Swimmer
2233 Eastern Ave, #1B, Cincinnati OH 45202, USA
Walesa, Lech — Nobel Peace Laureate; President, Poland
Ul Dlugi Targ 24, 80828 Gdansk, Poland
Walewander, James (Jim) — Baseball Player
5023 Albridal Way, San Ramon CA 94582, USA
Walger, Sonya — Actress
Gersh Agency, 9465 Wilshire Blvd, #600, Beverly Hills CA 90212 USA
Walheim, Rex J — Astronaut
142 Hidden Lake Dr, League City TX 77573, USA
Walia, Sonu — Actress
20 Anchorage, Juhu-Versova Link Road, Andheri (W), Mumbai MS 400058, India
Walk, Neal — Basketball Player
6030 N 11th Ave, Phoenix AZ 85013, USA
Walk, Robert V (Bob) — Baseball Player
2494 Shadowbrook Dr, Wexford PA 15090, USA
Walken, Christopher — Actor
I C M Partners, 10250 Constellation Blvd, #900, Los Angeles CA 90067 USA
Walker, Adam C — Football Player
923 Bucknell Ave, Johnstown PA 15905, USA
Walker, Alan C — Anthropologist
Pennsylvania State University, Anthropology Dept, Pittsburgh PA 16802, USA
Walker, Alice M — Writer, Social Activist
PO Box 378, Philo CA 95466, USA
Walker, Ally — Actress
Luber Rocklin Entertainment, 8530 Wilshire Blvd, #555, Beverly Hills CA 90211 USA
Walker, Andrew Kevin — Actor, Writer
Kennedy/Miller Productions, 30 Orwell St, Sydney NSW 2011, Australia
Walker, Andrew W — Actor
Amanda Rosenthal Talent, 1255 University St, #502, Montreal QC H3B 3V8, Canada
Walker, Anthony B (Tony) — Baseball Player
2724 Morgan Dr, San Ramon CA 94583, USA
Walker, Antoine D — Basketball Player
450 W Huron St, Chicago IL 60654, USA
Walker, Arnetia — Actress
1040 4th St, #406, Santa Monica CA 90403, USA
Walker, Benjamin — Actor
Inspire Entertainment, 2332 Cotner Ave, #302. Los Angeles CA 90064, USA
Walker, Bill — Basketball Player
New York Knicks, Madison Square Garden, 2 Penn Plaza, New York, NY 10121 USA
Walker, Bracy W — Football Player
5683 Notting Hill Road, Gurnee IL 60031, USA
Walker, Bradley G (Butch) — Singer, Guitarist (Marvelous 3)
Crush Music Mgmt, 60-62 E 11th St, #700, New York NY 10003, USA
Walker, Brian — Cartoonist (Hi & Lois)
King Features Syndicate, 300 W 57th St, #1500, New York NY 10019 USA
Walker, Bruce R — Football Player
279 Eastlawn St, Detroit MI 48215, USA
Walker, Charles D — Astronaut
Boeing Co, 1200 Wilson Blvd, MC RS00, Arlington VA 22209, USA
Walker, Charles D (Chuck) — Football Player
1613 Tradd Court, Chesterfield MO 63017, USA
Walker, Charls E — Economist
19207 Racine Court, Montgomery Village MD 20886, USA
Walker, Chester (Chet) — Basketball Player
124 Fleet St, Marina del Rey CA 90292, USA
Walker, Chris — Actor
Rolf Kruger, 121 Gloucester Place, London W1H 3PJ, England
Walker, Clay — Singer
W M E Entertainment, 1600 Division St, #300, Nashville TN 37203 USA
Walker, Cleotha (Chico) — Baseball Player
450 W Huron St, Chicago IL 60654, USA
Walker, Clint — Actor
101 W McKnight Way, #B303, Grass Valley CA 95949, USA
Walker, Colleen — Golfer
3612 Sugar Loaf Lane, Valrico FL 33596, USA
Walker, Darnell R — Football Player
715 N Terrace Blvd, Muskogee OK 74401, USA
Walker, Darrell — Basketball Player, Coach
16122 Patriot Dr, Little Rock AR 72212, USA
Walker, David M — Government Official
Comeback America Initiative, 211 State St, #401, Bridgeport CT 06604, USA
Walker, Denard A — Football Player
17214 Lechlade Lane, Dallas TX 75252, USA
Walker, Derek — Architect
2 General Sage Dr, Santa Fe NM 87505, USA
Walker, Derrick — Auto Racing Executive
Walker Racing, 4035 Championship Dr, Indianapolis IN 46268, USA
Walker, DeWayne — Football Coach
New Mexico State University, Athletic Dept, Box 30001, Las Cruces NM 88003, USA
Walker, Dreama — Actress
Gersh Agency, 9465 Wilshire Blvd, #600, Beverly Hills CA 90212 USA
Walker, Duane A — Baseball Player
2509 Georgia Ave, Deer Park TX 77536, USA

Walker, Eamonn — Actor
Joseph, 2 Tunstall Road, #1, London SW9 8BN, England

Walker, Fiona — Actress
13 Despard Road, London N19 5NP, England

Walker, G Mickey — Football Player
22828 S Maple Point Road, Pickford MI 49774, USA

Walker, Gary L — Football Player
PO Box 138, Lavonia GA 30553, USA

Walker, George T, Jr — Composer
323 Grove St, Montclair NJ 07042, USA

Walker, Greg — Cartoonist (Hi & Lois)
King Features Syndicate, 300 W 57th St, #1500, New York NY 10019 USA

Walker, Greg T — Singer, Bassist (Blackfoot)
Artists International Mgmt, 9850 Sandalfoot Blvd, #458, Boca Raton FL 33428 USA

Walker, Gregory L (Greg) — Baseball Player
530 N Lake Shore Dr, #1009, Chicago IL 60611, USA

Walker, Herschel J — Football Player
2210 King Fisher Dr, Westlake TX 76262, USA

Walker, Hezekiah X, Jr — Singer, Choir Director, Religious Leader
Love Fellowship Tabernacle, 464 Liberty Ave, Brooklyn NY 11207, USA

Walker, I Kenyatta — Football Player
14813 Tudor Chase Dr, Tampa FL 33626, USA

Walker, James T (Jamie) — Baseball Player
11450 W 187th St, Spring Hill KS 66083, USA

Walker, Javon L — Football Player
7375 Talon Trail, Parker CO 80138, USA

Walker, Jerry A — Baseball Player
2015 Collins Blvd, Ada OK 74820, USA

Walker, Jerry Jeff — Singer, Guitarist, Songwriter
Goodknight Music, PO Box 39, Austin TX 78767, USA

Walker, Jimmie (J J) — Actor, Comedian
Roger Paul, 1650 Broadway, New York NY 10019, USA

Walker, Joe Louis — Singer, Guitarist
Oceanside Talent, 124 Virginia Place, #3, Costa Mesa CA 92627, USA

Walker, John — Track Athlete
Jeffs Road, RD Papatoetoe, New Zealand

Walker, John E — Nobel Chemistry Laureate
M R C Molecular Biology Lab, Hills Road, Cambridge CB2 2QH, England

Walker, John M, Jr — Judge
US Court of Appeals, Moynihan Courthouse, 500 Pearl St, New York NY 10007, USA

Walker, Jon Patrick — Actor
Paradigm Agency, 360 N Crescent Dr, North Building, Beverly Hills CA 90210 USA

Walker, Kemba H — Basketball Player
Charlotte Bobcats, 333 E Trade St, #A, Charlotte NC 28202 USA

Walker, Kenneth (Kenny) — Basketball Player
2252 Terrace Woods Park, Lexington KY 40513, USA

Walker, Kenneth H — Interior Designer
Future Brand, 300 Park Ave S, #700, New York NY 10010, USA

Walker, Kevin — Baseball Player
759 Chestnut Ave, Holtville CA 92250, USA

Walker, Kevin (Geordie) — Guitarist (Killing Joke)
Agency Group, 9348 Civic Center Dr, #200, Beverly Hills CA 90210 USA

Walker, Kurt — Ice Hockey Player
1951 N Wesley Chapel Road, Eatonton GA 31024, USA

Walker, Langston B — Football Player
1281 Alder Creek Circle, San Leandro CA 94577, USA

Walker, Larry K R — Baseball Player
1667 Flagler Parkway, West Palm Beach FL 33411, USA

Walker, Leonore — Psychologist
Nova Southeastern University, Psychology Dept, Fort Lauderdale FL 33308, USA

Walker, Little Toby — Singer
PO Box 219, Wantagh NY 11793, USA

Walker, Liza — Actress
Jonathan Altaras Assoc, 11 Garrick St, London WC2E 9AR, England

Walker, Lucy — Director, Producer, Actress
Circle of Confusion, 8548 Washington Blvd, Culver City CA 90232, USA

Walker, Mack — Historian
Johns Hopkins University, History Dept, Baltimore MD 21218, USA

Walker, Malcolm E, Jr — Football Player
7140 Winterwood Lane, Dallas TX 75248, USA

Walker, Marcy — Actress
Leslie Bader, 2686 Lakewood Place, Westlake Village CA 91361, USA

Walker, Marquis R — Football Player
11576 Cherrylawn St, Detroit MI 48221, USA

Walker, Michael C (Mike) — Baseball Player
23195 Tankerley Road, Brooksville FL 34601, USA

Walker, Michael Patrick — Composer, Lyricist
W M E Entertainment, 1325 Ave of Americas, New York NY 10019 USA

Walker, Mort — Cartoonist (Beetle Bailey, Sarge)
61 Studio Road, Stamford CT 06903, USA

Walker, Paul — Actor
United Talent Agency, 9336 Civic Center Dr, Beverly Hills CA 90210 USA

Walker, Peter — Director
23 Bentick St, London W1, England

Walker, Peter — Landscape Architect
Peter Walker Partners, 739 Allston Way, Berkeley CA 94710, USA

Walker, Peter B (Pete) — Baseball Player
2 White Oak Lane, Quaker Hill CT 06375, USA

Walker, Phillip (Phil) B — Basketball Player
720 E Phil Ellena St, Philadelphia PA 19119, USA

Walker, Polly — Actress
Hamilton Hodell, 66-68 Margaret St, London W1W 8SR, England

Walker, R Thomas (Tom) — Baseball Player
817 Whippoorwill Hill Road, Gibsonia PA 15044, USA

Walker, Rebecca — Writer
W M E Entertainment, 9601 Wilshire Blvd, #300, Beverly Hills CA 90210 USA

Walker, Rick Football Player
906 Winstead St, Great Falls VA 22066, USA
Walker, Sandra Opera Singer
Columbia Artists Mgmt Inc, 1790 Broadway, #702, New York NY 10019 USA
Walker, Sarah E B Opera Singer
152 Inchmery Road, London SE6 1DF, England
Walker, Scott Ice Hockey Player
301 Bailey Ridge Dr, Morrisville NC 27560, USA
Walker, Scott Singer
Negus-Fancy Co, 78 Portland Road, London W11 1HE, England
Walker, Tonja Actress
Tonja Walker Productions, 404 E 76th St, #15C, New York NY 10021, USA
Walker, Tyler L Baseball Player
45 Via del Sol, Nicasio CA 94946, USA
Walker, Val J Football Player
3857 S Versailles Ave, Dallas TX 75209, USA
Walker, Walter F (Wally) Basketball Player
154 Lombard St, #58, San Francisco CA 94111, USA
Walker, Wayne H Football Player
2033 S White Pine Lane, Boise ID 83706, USA
Walker, Wesley D Football Player
5841 Edmond Ave, Huntington Station NY 11746, USA
Wall, Angus Editor
Creative Artists Agency, 2000 Ave of Stars, #100, Los Angeles CA 90067 USA
Wall, Brian A Sculptor
306 Lombard St, San Francisco CA 94133, USA
Wall, David Ballet Dancer
Royal Ballet, Covent Garden, Bow St, London WC2E 9DD, England
Wall, Donnell L (Donne) Baseball Player
116 River Breeze Way, Saint Louis MO 63129, USA
Wall, Erin Opera Singer
Columbia Artists Mgmt Inc, 1790 Broadway, #702, New York NY 10019 USA
Wall, Frederick T Physical Chemist
2044 Kerwood Ave, Los Angeles CA 90025, USA
Wall, John F Army General
507 Hanover St, Fredericksburg VA 22401, USA
Wall, Lyndsay Ice Hockey Player
USA Hockey, 1775 Bob Johnson Dr, Colorado Springs CO 80906 USA
Wall, M Danny Financier
1031 Chartwell Court, Salt Lake City UT 84103, USA
Wall, Stanley A (Stan) Baseball Player
9907 E 80th St, Raytown MO 64138, USA
Walla, Christopher (Chris) Singer, Guitarist (Death Cab for Cutie)
Zeitgeist Artist Mgmt, 660 York St, #216, San Francisco CA 94110, USA
Wallace, Aaron J Football Player
9327 Edinburgh Lane, Frisco TX 75035, USA
Wallace, Andy Auto Racing Driver
Childress-Howard Motorsports, PO Box 889, Denver NC 28037, USA
Wallace, Anthony F C Anthropologist
University of Pennsylvania, Anthropology Dept, Philadelphia PA 19014, USA
Wallace, B Michael (Mike) Football Player
Pittsburgh Steelers, 3400 S Water St, Pittsburgh PA 15203 USA
Wallace, B Steven (Steve) Football Player
305 Heards Ferry Road NW, Atlanta GA 30328, USA
Wallace, Ben Basketball Player
Phoenix Suns, 201 E Jefferson St, Phoenix AZ 85004 USA
Wallace, Bruce Geneticist
940 McBryde Dr, Blacksburg VA 24060, USA
Wallace, Christopher (Chris) Commentator
Fox-TV, News Dept, 205 E 67th St, New York NY 10065 USA
Wallace, Craig K Physician
National Institutes of Health, 9000 Rockville Pike, Bethesda MD 20892, USA
Wallace, Dee Actress
Amsel Eisenstadt Frazier, 5055 Wilshire Blvd, #865, Los Angeles CA 90036 USA
Wallace, Don Actor
S M S Talent, 8383 Wilshire Blvd, #230, Beverly Hills CA 90211 USA
Wallace, Gerald J Basketball Player
8381 Providence Road, Charlotte NC 28277, USA
Wallace, J Clifford Judge
US Court of Appeals, 940 Front St, #5140, San Diego CA 92101, USA
Wallace, Jane Entertainer
Cosgrove-Meurer Productions, 4303 W Verdugo Ave, Burbank CA 91505, USA
Wallace, Jeffrey A (Jeff) Baseball Player
2904 Federal Ave, Alliance OH 44601, USA
Wallace, Julie T Actress
Annette Stone, 9 Newburgh St, London W1V 1LH, England
Wallace, Kenny Auto Racing Driver
8995 Harris Road, Concord NC 28027, USA
Wallace, Marcia Actress
Avo Talent Agency, 8500 Melrose Ave, #212, West Hollywood CA 90069, USA
Wallace, Marilyn Writer
Random House, 1745 Broadway, #1800, New York NY 10019 USA
Wallace, Michael S (Mike) Baseball Player
12483 Elk Run Road, Midland VA 22728, USA
Wallace, Mike Auto Racing Driver
Morgan-McClure Racing, 26502 Newbanks Road, Abington VA 24210, USA
Wallace, Randall Director
Media Talent Group, 9200 Sunset Blvd, #550, West Hollywood CA 90069, USA
Wallace, Rasheed A Basketball Player
1979 Arthurs Way, Rochester Hills MI 48306, USA
Wallace, Rheagan Actress
Creative Management Group, 8522 National Blvd, #108, Culver City CA 90232 USA
Wallace, Robert C (Bob) Football Player
44111 N 43rd Dr, New River AZ 85087, USA
Wallace, Robert Glenn Businessman
PO Box 10003, College Station TX 77842, USA

W

Walker - Wallace

Wallace, Russell W (Rusty), Jr — Auto Racing Driver
16229 Jettson Road, Cornelius NC 28031, USA
Wallach, Eli — Actor
90 Riverside Dr, #6B, New York NY 10024, USA
Wallach, Evan J — Judge
US International Trade Court, 1 Federal Plaza, New York NY 10278, USA
Wallach, Timothy C (Tim) — Baseball Player
21750 Deveron Cove, Yorba Linda CA 92887, USA
Wallack, Melissa — Writer
I C M Partners, 10250 Constellation Blvd, #900, Los Angeles CA 90067 USA
Wallberg, Heinz — Conductor
Stocksiepen, 45133 Essen, Germany
Wallem, Linda — Producer
Jackoway Tyerman Wertheimer, 1925 Century Park E, #2200, Los Angeles CA 90067 USA
Wallenda, Delilah — Circus Tightrope Walker
3650 Henrietta Place, Sarasota FL 34234, USA
Wallenda, Nikolas (Nik) — Circus Tightrope Walker
Wallenda Enterprises, PO Box 52551, Sarasota FL 34232, USA
Wallenda, Tino — Circus Tightrope Walker
3650 Henrietta Place, Sarasota FL 34234, USA
Waller, Anthony — Director
Seven Arts Pictures, 6121 W Sunset Blvd, #512, Los Angeles CA 90028, USA
Waller, Robert James — Writer
12 Old Harper Road, Harper TX 78631, USA
Waller, Ronald B (Ron) — Football Player
8773 Concord Road, Seaford DE 19973, USA
Wallerstein, Ralph G — Hematologist
3447 Clay St, San Francisco CA 94118, USA
Wallfisch, Raphael — Concert Cellist
Ikon Artists Mgmt, 52 Upper St, #111B, London N1 0QH, England
Williams, David — Actor
Troika, 74 Clekrenwell St, London EC1M 5QA, England
Wallin, Niclas — Ice Hockey Player
244 Johnson Ave, Los Gatos CA 95030, USA
Walling, Camryn — Actor
Abrams Artists, 9200 W Sunset Blvd, #1125, West Hollywood CA 90069 USA
Walling, Dennis (Denny) — Baseball Player
PO Box 1312, Waynesboro VA 22980, USA
Wallinger, Karl — Keyboardist, Songwriter
Agency Group Ltd, 142 W 57th St, #600, New York NY 10019 USA
Wallis, Annabelle — Actress
I C M Partners, 10250 Constellation Blvd, #900, Los Angeles CA 90067 USA
Wallis, H Joseph (Joe) — Baseball Player
PO Box 659, Chesterfield MO 63006, USA
Wallis, Michael — Writer
Perfect Impressions, 154 Seminole Dr, Springfield IL 62704, USA
Wallis, Shani — Actress, Singer
15460 Vista Haven, Sherman Oaks CA 91403, USA
Walliser, Maria — Alpine Skier
Selfwingert, 7208 Malans, Switzerland
Walls, C Wesley — Football Player
8711 Lake Challis Lane, Charlotte NC 28226, USA
Walls, Denise (Nee-C) — Singer (Annointed), Songwriter
2113 South Ave, Youngstown OH 44502, USA
Walls, Everson C — Football Player
4812 Portrait Lane, Plano TX 75024, USA
Walls, Jeannette — Writer
Charles Scribner's Sons, 866 3rd Ave, New York NY 10022 USA
Walls, Lenny B — Football Player
2800 Bush St, San Francisco CA 94115, USA
Walmsley, Jon — Actor
Howard Talent West, 10657 Riverside Dr, Toluca Lake CA 91602, USA
Walsch, Neale Donald — Writer
Trident Media Group, 41 Madison Ave, #3600, New York NY 10010 USA
Walser, Derrick — Ice Hockey Player
592 Lorne St, New Glasgow NS B2H 4L3, Canada
Walser, Martin — Writer
Zum Hecht 36, 88662 Uberlingen-Nussdorf, Germany
Walsh Jennings, Kerri L — Volleyball Player
PO Box 33053, Los Gatos CA 95031, USA
Walsh, Amanda — Actress
I C M Partners, 10250 Constellation Blvd, #900, Los Angeles CA 90067 USA
Walsh, Baillie — Director
Independent Talent Group, Oxford House, 76 Oxford St, London W1D 1BS, England
Walsh, David M — Cinematographer
Gersh Agency, 9465 Wilshire Blvd, #600, Beverly Hills CA 90212 USA
Walsh, David P (Dave) — Baseball Player
500 Concord Lane, Edmond OK 73003, USA
Walsh, Diana Chapman — Educator
Wellesley College, President's Office, Wellesley MA 02181, USA
Walsh, Don — Underwater Explorer
International Maritime Inc, 14758 Sitkum Lane, Myrtle Point OR 97458, USA
Walsh, Donnie — Basketball Coach, Executive
Indiana Pacers, Conseco Fieldhouse, 125 S Pennsylvania, Indianapolis IN 46204 USA
Walsh, Dylan — Actor
Gersh Agency, 9465 Wilshire Blvd, #600, Beverly Hills CA 90212 USA
Walsh, Gwynyth — Actress
Allman/Rea Mgmt, 141 Barrington Ave, Los Angeles CA 90049, USA
Walsh, Joe — Singer, Guitarist (Eagles); Songwriter
Front Line Mgmt, 1100 Glendon Ave, #2000, Los Angeles CA 90024 USA
Walsh, John — Producer, Director, Actor
3111 S Dixie Highway, #244, West Palm Beach FL 33405, USA
Walsh, John, Jr — Museum Executive
J Paul Getty Museum, Getty Center, 1200 Getty Center Dr, Los Angeles CA 90049, USA
Walsh, Kate — Actress
Creative Artists Agency, 2000 Ave of Stars, #100, Los Angeles CA 90067 USA

Walsh, Kimberly J
Concorde International, 101 Shepherds Bush Road, London W6 7LP, England — Singer (Girls Aloud)
Walsh, Lawrence E
1902 Bedford St, Nichols Hills OK 73116, USA — Government Official, Attorney
Walsh, M Emmet
S L J Mgmt, 833 N Edinburgh Ave, PH 11, Los Angeles CA 90046, USA — Actor
Walsh, Maiara
A P A Talent/Literary Agency, 405 S Beverly Dr, #300, Beverly Hills CA 90212 USA — Actress
Walsh, Martin
Independent Talent Group, Oxford House, 76 Oxford St, London W1D 1BS, England — Editor
Walsh, Martin
National Organization on Disability, 910 16th NW, #400, Washington DC 20006, USA — Association Executive
Walsh, Matt
Principato-Young, 9465 Wilshire Blvd, #880, Beverly Hills CA 90212 USA — Actor, Comedian, Producer
Walsh, Patrick C
Johns Hopkins University, Brady Urological Institute, Baltimore MD 21205, USA — Urologist
Walsh, Peter
Paradigm Agency, 360 N Crescent Dr, North Building, Beverly Hills CA 90210 USA — Actor
Walsh, Stephen J (Steve)
8801 Wellington View Dr, West Palm Beach FL 33411, USA — Football Player
Walsh, Sydney
Connor Ankrum Assoc, 1680 Vine St, #1016, Los Angeles CA 90028, USA — Actress
Walsh, Tom
PO Box 133, Philomath OR 97370, USA — Sculptor
Walsh, Willie
British Airways, Waterside, PO Box 365, Harmondsworth UB7 0GB, England — Businessman
Walsman, Leanna
I C M Partners, 10250 Constellation Blvd, #900, Los Angeles CA 90067 USA — Actress
Walter, Gene W
1901 Fairway Dr, LaGrange KY 40031, USA — Baseball Player
Walter, Harriet
Conway Van Gelder Grant, 8-12 Broadwick St, #300, London W1F 8HW, England — Actress
Walter, Jessica
Anonymous Content, 3532 Hayden Ave, Culver City CA 90232 USA — Actress
Walter, Joseph F (Joe), Jr
4136 Binley Dr, Richardson TX 75082, USA — Football Player
Walter, Lisa Ann
Abrams Artists, 9200 W Sunset Blvd, #1125, West Hollywood CA 90069 USA — Actress, Comedienne, Writer, Producer
Walter, Michael D (Mike)
6900 SW Knollwood St, Tualatin OR 97062, USA — Football Player
Walter, Robert D
Cardinal Health, 7000 Cardinal Place, Dublin OH 43017, USA — Businessman
Walter, Ryan
Vancouver Canucks, 800 Griffiths Way, Vancouver BC V6B 6G1, Canada — Ice Hockey Player
Walter, Tracey
Stone Manners Salners, 9911 W Pico Blvd, #1400, Los Angeles CA 90035 USA — Actress
Walter, Ulrich
I B M Germany, Schonaicherstr 220, 71032 Boblingen, Germany — Astronaut, Germany
Walters, Barbara
944 5th Ave, #6, New York NY 10021, USA — Commentator
Walters, Charles L (Charlie)
1717 Sutton Lane, Saint Paul MN 55118, USA — Baseball Player
Walters, Dale
Ringside Fitness, 4 Bentall Centre, #49271, Vancouver BC V5Y 1C7, Canada — Boxer
Walters, David
Premier Management Group, 1100 Crescent Green, #104, Cary, NC 27518 USA — Swimmer
Walters, David L
RR 2, Watts OK 74964, USA — Governor, OK
Walters, Harry N
D H C Holdings Corp, 125 Thomas Dale, Williamsburg VA 23185, USA — Government Official
Walters, Jamie
Atlantic Records, 9229 W Sunset Blvd, #900, West Hollywood CA 90069 USA — Actor, Singer
Walters, Julie
I C M Partners, 10250 Constellation Blvd, #900, Los Angeles CA 90067 USA — Actress
Walters, Kirk
Toledo Blade, Editorial Dept, 541 N Superior St, Toledo OH 43660, USA — Editorial Cartoonist
Walters, Lisa
211 S Westland Ave, #2, Tampa FL 33606, USA — Golfer
Walters, Melora
Medavoy Mgmt, 10203 Santa Monica Blvd, #400, Los Angeles CA 90067 USA — Actress
Walters, Michael C (Mike)
79070 Desert Stream Dr, La Quinta CA 92253, USA — Baseball Player
Walters, Minette
Panmacmillan, 20 New Wharf Road, London N1 9RR, England — Writer
Walters, Peter I
22 Hill St, London W1X 7FU, England — Businessman
Walters, Rex A
690 45th Ave, San Francisco CA 94121, USA — Basketball Player
Walters, Ron
8 Garrison Crescent, Sherwood Park AB T8A 2S8, Canada — Ice Hockey Player
Walters, Stanley P (Stan)
2021 W Wesley Road NW, Atlanta GA 30327, USA — Football Player
Walters, Susan
Allman/Rea Mgmt, 9255 Sunset Blvd, #600, Los Angeles CA 90069, USA — Actress
Walters, Troy M
2843 Prado, Grand Prairie TX 75054, USA — Football Player
Walterscheid, Leonard W (Len)
2312 I Road, Grand Junction CO 81505, USA — Football Player
Walthall, Romy
Defining Artists, 10 Universal City Plaza, #2000, Universal City CA 91608 USA — Actress
Walthan, John
1354 NE Todd George Road, Lees Summit MO 64086, USA — Baseball Manager
Walther, Herbert
Egenhoferstr 7A, 81243 Munich, Germany — Physicist
Walther, Paul G
6555 Riverside Dr NW, Atlanta GA 30328, USA — Basketball Player

W

Walther - Wanner

Walther, Philip — Physicist
University of Vienna, Physics Dept, Boltzmanngasse 5, 1090 Vienna, Austria

Walton, Anthony J (Tony) — Costume, Set Designer
Costume Design Guild, 11969 Ventura Blvd, #100, Studio City CA 91604, USA

Walton, Anthony J (Tony) — Scenic Designer, Illustrator
I C M Partners, 730 5th Ave, New York NY 10019 USA

Walton, Bruce K — Baseball Player
10704 Sunset Canyon Dr, Bakersfield CA 93311, USA

Walton, Cedar A, Jr — Jazz Pianist
Bridge Agency, 35 Clark St, #A5, Brooklyn Heights NY 11201, USA

Walton, Christy R — Businesswoman
Wal-Mart Stores, 702 SW 8th St, Bentonville AR 72712, USA

Walton, Daniel J (Danny) — Baseball Player
PO Box 296, Huntsville UT 84317, USA

Walton, David — Actor
One Set One Rep Productions, 839 N Gardner St, Los Angeles CA 90046, USA

Walton, Jim C — Businessman
CNN-TV, 190 Marietta Ave SW, Atlanta GA 30303 USA

Walton, Joseph (Joe) — Football Player, Coach
8 Windycrest Dr, Beaver Falls PA 15010, USA

Walton, Kendall L — Philosopher
University of Michigan, Philosophy Dept, Ann Arbor MI 48109, USA

Walton, Lawrence J (Larry) — Football Player
PO Box 32204, Phoenix AZ 85064, USA

Walton, Luke T — Basketball Player
1613 Gates Ave, Manhattan Beach CA 90266, USA

Walton, Mike — Ice Hockey Player
Re/Max Professionals, 200-270 Kingsway, Etobicoke ON M9A 3T7, Canada

Walton, S Robson (Rob) — Businessman
Wal-Mart Stores, 702 SW 8th St, Bentonville AR 72716, USA

Walton, William T (Bill), III — Basketball Player, Sportscaster
1010 Myrtle Way, San Diego CA 92103, USA

Waltrip, Darrell L — Auto, Truck Racing Driver
Michael Waltrip Racing, 20310 Chartwell Center Dr, Cornelius NC 28031, USA

Waltrip, Michael C (Mike) — Auto Racing Driver
Michael Waltrip Racing, 20310 Chartwell Center Dr, Cornelius NC 28031, USA

Waltz, Christoph — Actor
Players Agentur Mgmt, Sophienstra 21, 10178 Berlin-Mitte, Germany

Waltz, Lisa — Actress
Stone Manners Salners, 9911 W Pico Blvd, #1400, Los Angeles CA 90035 USA

Waluska, Nick — Guitarist (Wondermints)
Paradise Artists, PO Box 1821, Ojai CA 93024 USA

Walz, Carl E — Astronaut
15506 Eagle Tavern Lane, Centreville VA 20120, USA

Walz, Wesley (Wes) — Ice Hockey Player
10435 Raleigh Road, Saint Paul MN 55129, USA

Wamala, Emmanuel Cardinal — Religious Leader
PO Box 14125, Mengo, Kampala, Uganda

Wambach, M Abigail (Abby) — Soccer Player
Powerplay Consultants, 1600 Parkwood Circle SE, #600, Atlanta GA 30339, USA

Wambaugh, Joseph — Writer
3520 Kellogg Way, San Diego CA 92106, USA

Wamsley, Rick — Ice Hockey Player
Saint Louis Blues, Scott Trade Center, 1401 Clark Ave, Saint Louis MO 63103 USA

Wan Li — Government Official, China
State Council, People's Congress, Tian An Men Square, Beijing, China

Wanamaker, Zoe — Actress
Conway Van Gelder Grant, 8-12 Broadwick St, #300, London W1F 8HW, England

Wand, Seth P — Football Player
5515 NW 93rd St, Kansas City MO 64154, USA

Wang Chunlu — Speed Skater
Skating Assn, 56 Zhongguancun South St, Haidian, Beijing 100044, China

Wang Jida — Sculptor
7612 35th Ave, #3E, Jackson Heights NY 11372, USA

Wang Junxia — Track Athlete
Athletic Assn, 9 Tiyuguan Road, Chongwen District, Beijing 100061, China

Wang Meng — Speed Skater
Skating Assn, 56 Zhongguancun South St, Haidian, Beijing 100044, China

Wang Tian Ren — Sculptor
Shaanxi Sculpture Institute, Longshoucun, Xi'am, Shaanxi 710016, China

Wang Zhi Zhi — Basketball Player
Miami Heat, American Airlines Arena, 601 Biscayne Blvd, Miami FL 33132 USA

Wang, Chien-Ming — Baseball Player
New York Yankees, Yankee Stadium, E 161st St & River Ave, Bronx NY 10451 USA

Wang, Garrett — Actor
501 E Del Mar Blvd, #310, Pasadena CA 91101, USA

Wang, Henry Y — Chemical Engineer
University of Michigan, Chemical Engineering Dept, Ann Arbor MI 48109, USA

Wang, Peggy — Singer (Pains of Being Pure at Heart)
Slumberland Records, PO Box 19029, Oakland CA 94619, USA

Wang, Taylor G — Astronaut, Physicist
1224 Arno Dr, Sierra Madre CA 91024, USA

Wang, Vera — Fashion Designer
Vera Wang Bridal House, 225 W 39th St, #900, New York NY 10018, USA

Wang, Wayne — Director
I C M Partners, 10250 Constellation Blvd, #900, Los Angeles CA 90067 USA

Wang, Zhong L — Nanotechnologist
Georgia Institute of Technology, Nanostructure Center, Atlanta GA 30332, USA

Wangchuck, Jigme Khesar Namgyal — King, Bhutan
Royal Palace, Tashichhodzong, Thimphu, Bhutan

Wangchuck, Lyonpo Khandu — Prime Minister, Bhutan
Jangsa, Shari Geog, Paro, Bhutan

Wangchuk, Jigme Singye — King, Bhutan
Royal Palace, Tashichhodzong, Thimphu, Bhutan

Wanner, H Eric — Foundation Executive
Russell Sage Foundation, 112 E 64th St, New York NY 10065, USA

Wannstedt, David R (Dave)	Football Coach
151 Rock Haven Lane, Pittsburgh PA 15228, USA	
Wanzer, Robert F (Bobby)	Basketball Player
28 Greenwood Park, Pittsford NY 14534, USA	
Waples, Keith	Harness Racing Driver
PO Box 632, Durham ON N0G 1R0, Canada	
Waples, Ronald (Ron)	Harness Racing Driver, Trainer
7 Mill Run W, Hightstown NJ 08520, USA	
Wapner, Joseph A	Entertainer, Judge
C E S D, 10635 Santa Monica Blvd, #130, Los Angeles CA 90025 USA	
Wapnick, Steven L (Steve)	Baseball Player
5934 Woodcliffe Dr, Windsor CO 80550, USA	
Wappel, Gord	Ice Hockey Player
5544 Kartusch Place, Regina SK S4X 4K1, Canada	
Warbeck, Stephen	Composer
United Agents, 12-26 Lexington St, London W1F 0LE, England	
Warburton, Patrick	Actor
Sutton-Barth Vennari, 145 S Fairfax Ave, #310, Los Angeles CA 90036 USA	
Warby, Kenneth P (Ken)	Boat Racing Driver
7432 State Route 128, Miamitown OH 45041, USA	
Warchus, Matthew	Director
Hamilton Hodell, 66-68 Margaret St, London W1W 8SR, England	
Ward, Aaron	Ice Hockey Player
112 Ronsard Lane, Cary NC 27511, USA	
Ward, Andre	Boxer
Prince Boxing Gym, 3030 Jensen Dr, Houston TX 77026, USA	
Ward, Anita	Singer
Richard Walters, PO Box 2789, Toluca Lake CA 91610 USA	
Ward, Bryan A	Baseball Player
140 Bannock Court, East Dundee IL 60118, USA	
Ward, Burt	Actor
Gentle Giants & Adoptions, PO Box 6005, Norco CA 92860, USA	
Ward, Burton	Auto Racing Driver
Bill Davis Racing, 301 Old Thomasville Road, Winston Salem NC 27107, USA	
Ward, Cameron (Cam)	Ice Hockey Player
1608 Shambrook Court, Raleigh NC 27614, USA	
Ward, Carlos N	Jazz Saxophonist (B T Express)
Star-Vest Mgmt, 102 Ryders Lane, East Brunswick NJ 08816, USA	
Ward, Charlie	Football, Basketball Player
3717 Drake St, Houston TX 77005, USA	
Ward, Christopher L J (Chris)	Football Player
PO Box 1365, Inglewood CA 90308, USA	
Ward, Colin N	Baseball Player
PO Box 21413, Mesa AZ 85277, USA	
Ward, Dale	Singer (Crescendo)
A Crosse the World, PO Box 23066, London W11 3FR, England	
Ward, David	Opera Singer
1 Kennedy Crescent, Lake Wanaka, New Zealand	
Ward, David S	Director, Writer
I C M Partners, 10250 Constellation Blvd, #900, Los Angeles CA 90067 USA	
Ward, Dedric L	Football Player
3435 N 45th St, Phoenix AZ 85018, USA	
Ward, Dixon	Ice Hockey Player
Okanagan Hockey School, 201-851 Eckhardt W, Penticton BC V2A 9C4, Canada	
Ward, Douglas Turner	Actor, Writer
Negro Ensemble Co, 303 W 42nd St, #501, New York NY 10036, USA	
Ward, Edward J (Ed)	Ice Hockey Player
9150 Weathervane Trail, Galesburg MI 49053, USA	
Ward, Fred	Actor
A P A Talent/Literary Agency, 405 S Beverly Dr, #300, Beverly Hills CA 90212 USA	
Ward, Gemma	Model
Creative Artists Agency, 2000 Ave of Stars, #100, Los Angeles CA 90067 USA	
Ward, Hines E, Jr	Football Player
155 Fairfax Road, Pittsburgh PA 15221, USA	
Ward, Jacky	Singer
821 19th Ave S, Nashville TN 37203, USA	
Ward, Jeff	Motorcycle Racing Rider
Speed Technologies, 9716 S Virginia St, Reno NV 89511, USA	
Ward, JoAnn	Actress, Producer
Creative Artists Agency, 2000 Ave of Stars, #100, Los Angeles CA 90067 USA	
Ward, John H	Football Player
9501 Silver Lake Dr, Oklahoma City OK 73162, USA	
Ward, John T, Jr	Thoroughbred Racing Trainer
573 Clay Kiser Road, Paris KY 40361, USA	
Ward, Jonathan	Actor
Auckland Actors, PO Box 56460, Dominion Road, Auckland 1030, New Zealand	
Ward, Kevin M	Baseball Player
160 F Ave, Coronado CA 92118, USA	
Ward, Lauren	Actress
Gavin Barker Assoc, 2D Wimpole St, London W1G 0EB, England	
Ward, M	Singer (She & Him), Songwriter
Ground Control Touring, 420 W Main St, Carrboro NC 27510, USA	
Ward, Maitland	Actress
Shelter Entertainment, 9454 Wilshire Blvd, #715, Beverly Hills CA 90212 USA	
Ward, Mary B	Actress
Innovative Artists, 1505 10th St, Santa Monica CA 90401 USA	
Ward, Mickey (Irish)	Boxer
132 Upham St, Lowell MA 01851, USA	
Ward, Pam	Sportscaster
ESPN-TV, ESPN Plaza, 935 Middle St, Bristol CT 06010 USA	
Ward, Preston M	Baseball Player
4371 De Silva Place, Las Vegas NV 89121, USA	
Ward, R Duane	Baseball Player
1723 Letsche St, #90, Pittsburgh PA 15212, USA	
Ward, Rachel	Actress, Director
Himber Entertainment, PO Box 950, South Orange NJ 07079 USA	

Ward, Rebecca — Fencer
Oregon Fencing Alliance, 4840 SW Western Ave, #80, Beaverton OR 97005, USA
Ward, Robert — Composer
2701 Pickett Road, #4022, Durham NC 27705, USA
Ward, Robert R (Bob) — Football Player
515 N Academy St, Greensboro MD 21639, USA
Ward, Ronald (Scooter) — Singer (Cold)
Front Line Mgmt, 1100 Glendon Ave, #2000, Los Angeles CA 90024 USA
Ward, Ronald L (Ron) — Ice Hockey Player
3178 W 140th St, Cleveland OH 44111, USA
Ward, Sela — Actress
Management 360, 9111 Wilshire Blvd, Beverly Hills CA 90210 USA
Ward, Susan — Actress, Model
Pakula/King, 9229 W Sunset Blvd, #315, West Hollywood CA 90069 USA
Ward, Tom — Actor
Independent Talent Group, Oxford House, 76 Oxford St, London W1D 1BS, England
Ward, Turner M — Baseball Player
232 Autumn Dr, Saraland AL 36571, USA
Ward, Vincent — Director, Writer, Actor
United Talent Agency, 9336 Civic Center Dr, Beverly Hills CA 90210 USA
Ward, Wendy — Golfer
12850 Sassin Station Road N, Edwall WA 99008, USA
Ward, William E (Kip) — Army General
Commander, US Africa Command, APO AE 09751, USA
Ward, William T (Bill) — Singer, Drummer (Black Sabbath)
Sharon Osborne Mgmt, 8899 Beverly Blvd, #905, West Hollywood CA 90048, USA
Ward, Zach — Actor
Diverse Talent Group, 9911 W Pico Blvd, #350W, Los Angeles CA 90035, USA
Warden, John — Attorney
Sullivan & Cromwell 125 Broad St, New York NY 10004, USA
Warden, Jonathan E (Jon) — Baseball Player
6575 Oasis Dr, Loveland OH 45140, USA
Warden, Rick — Actor
Independent Talent Group, Oxford House, 76 Oxford St, London W1D 1BS, England
Wardlaw, Kim McLane — Judge
US Court of Appeals, 125 S Grand Ave, Pasadena CA 91105, USA
Wardle, Curtis J (Curt) — Baseball Player
13900 Pheasant Knoll Lane, Moreno Valley CA 92553, USA
Ware, Andre — Football Player, Sportscaster
3910 Wood Park, Sugar Land TX 77479, USA
Ware, Billy — Percussionist (BeauSoleil)
Rosebud Agency, PO Box 170429, San Francisco CA 94117 USA
Ware, Chris — Cartoonist
Fantagraphics Books, 7563 Lake City Way NE, Seattle WA 98115, USA
Ware, DeMarcus — Football Player
690 Rockingham Court, Colleyville TX 76034, USA
Ware, Derek G — Football Player
2315 W Shannon St, Chandler AZ 85224, USA
Ware, Jeffrey A (Jeff) — Baseball Player
2560 Mulberry Loop, Virginia Beach VA 23456, USA
Ware, Justin — Writer, Actor
Gersh Agency, 9465 Wilshire Blvd, #600, Beverly Hills CA 90212 USA
Warfield, Eric A — Football Player
705 NE Seabrook Circle, Lees Summit MO 64064, USA
Warfield, Paul D — Football Player
16 Normandy Way, Rancho Mirage CA 92270, USA
Warfield, Sonja — Writer
Creative Artists Agency, 2000 Ave of Stars, #100, Los Angeles CA 90067 USA
Wargo, Tom — Golfer
2801 Putter Dr, Centralia IL 62801, USA
Warhola, James — Writer, Illustrator
56 Walkers Hill, Tivoli NY 12583, USA
Wariner, Steve — Singer, Guitarist, Songwriter
Steve Wariner Productions, PO Box 1647, Franklin TN 37065, USA
Waring, Todd — Actor
145 W 45th St, #1204, New York NY 10036, USA
Warkentin, Thomas (Tom) — Cartoonist (Flash Gordon)
King Features Syndicate, 300 W 57th St, #1500, New York NY 10019 USA
Warlock, Billy — Actor
Abrams Artists, 9200 W Sunset Blvd, #1125, West Hollywood CA 90069 USA
Warmenhoven, Daniel J — Businessman
Network Appliance Inc, 495 E Java Dr, Sunnyvale CA 94089, USA
Warnecke, Mark — Swimmer
Am Schichtmeister 100, 58453 Witten, Germany
Warner, Amelia — Actress
Authentic Talent Mgmt, 45 Main St, #1004, Brooklyn NY 11201 USA
Warner, Chris — Cartoonist (Black Cross)
Dark Horse Publishing, 10956 SE Main St, Portland OR 97222 USA
Warner, Cornell — Basketball Player
2479 Glen Meadow Lane, Escondido CA 92027, USA
Warner, Curtis E (Curt) — Football Player
Curt Warner Chevrolet, 10811 SE Mill Plain Blvd, Vancouver WA 98664, USA
Warner, David — Actor
Julian Belfrage Assoc, 9 Argyll St, #300, London W1F 7TG, England
Warner, Douglas A, III — Financier
J P Morgan Chase, 270 Park Ave, #1200, New York NY 10017, USA
Warner, Jack D — Baseball Player
5938 W Calle Lejos, Glendale AZ 85310, USA
Warner, Jack Lionel — Architect
Warner Group Architects, 1250 Coast Village Road, #J, Santa Barbara CA 93108, USA
Warner, Jane — Model
166 Ditching Road, Brighton Essex BN1 6JA, England
Warner, Jim — Ice Hockey Player
2011 Upper Saint Dennis Road, Saint Paul MN 55116, USA
Warner, John J (Jackie) — Baseball Player
19136 Highway 18 N, Apple Valley CA 92307, USA

Warner, John W	Senator, VA
Atoka Farm, PO Box 1320, Middleburg VA 20118, USA	
Warner, Julie	Actress
Innovative Artists, 1505 10th St, Santa Monica CA 90401 USA	
Warner, Kirk	Football Player
110 S 5th St, Cochran GA 31014, USA	
Warner, Kurtis E (Kurt)	Football Player
6712 E Cheney Dr, Paradise Valley AZ 85253, USA	
Warner, Malcolm-Jamal	Actor
Abrams Artists, 9200 W Sunset Blvd, #1125, West Hollywood CA 90069 USA	
Warner, Margaret	Commentator
News Hour Show, 2700 S Quincy St, #250, Arlington VA 22206, USA	
Warner, T C	Actress
S D B Partners, 1801 Ave of Stars, #902, Los Angeles CA 90067 USA	
Warner, Todd	Sculptor
155 NW 11th St, Boca Raton FL 33432, USA	
Warner, Tom	Producer
Carsey-Warner Productions, 4024 Radford Ave, Building 3, Studio City CA 91604, USA	
Warner, Ty	Toy Designer
Ty Inc, PO Box 5377, Hinsdale IL 60522, USA	
Warnes, Jennifer	Singer, Songwriter
Donald Miller, 12746 Kling St, Studio City CA 91604, USA	
Warnock, John E	Businessman
Adobe Systems, 375 Park Ave, San Jose CA 95110, USA	
Warren G	Rap Artist
Green Light Talent Agency, PO Box 3172, Beverly Hills CA 90212 USA	
Warren, Christoper (Chris), Jr	Actor
Innovative Artists, 1505 10th St, Santa Monica CA 90401 USA	
Warren, Christopher C (Chris), Jr	Football Player
13707 Black Spruce Way, Chantilly VA 20151, USA	
Warren, Cicero	Baseball Player
119 Brookwood St, East Orange NJ 07018, USA	
Warren, Diane	Songwriter
1896 Rising Glen Road, Los Angeles CA 90069, USA	
Warren, Donald J (Don)	Football Player
13507 Wilder Court, Clifton VA 20124, USA	
Warren, Estella	Model, Actress
Don Buchwald/Fortitude, 6500 Wilshire Blvd, #2200, Los Angeles CA 90048 USA	
Warren, Fran	Singer
Richard Barz, 21 Cobble Creek Dr, Tannersville PA 18372 USA	
Warren, Frederick M	Architect
65 Cambridge Terrace, Christchurch 1, New Zealand	
Warren, Gerard T	Football Player
13786 NE 222nd Place, Raiford FL 32083, USA	
Warren, Gloria	Singer, Actress
16872 Bosque Dr, Encino CA 91436, USA	
Warren, Gregory R (Greg)	Football Player
14 S 18th St, Pittsburgh PA 15203, USA	
Warren, J Robin	Nobel Medicine Laureate
178 Lake St, Perth WA 6000, Australia	
Warren, Jennifer	Actress
1675 Old Oak Road, Los Angeles CA 90049, USA	
Warren, Kenneth S	Immunologist
Picower Medical Research Institute, 350 Community Dr, Manhasset NY 11030, USA	
Warren, Kiersten	Actress
Mitchell K Stubbs Assoc, 8695 W Washington Blvd, #204, Culver City CA 90232 USA	
Warren, Lamont A	Football Player
17735 Sorrel Ridge Dr, Spring TX 77388, USA	
Warren, Lesley Ann	Actress
Innovative Artists, 1505 10th St, Santa Monica CA 90401 USA	
Warren, Marc	Actor
Ken McReddie Assoc, 11 Connaught Place, London W2 2ET, England	
Warren, Michael (Mike)	Actor, Basketball Player
21216 Escondido St, Woodland Hills CA 91364, USA	
Warren, Richard D (Rick)	Evangelist, Writer
Saddleback Church, 1 Saddleback Parkway, Lake Forest CA 92630, USA	
Warren, Robert G (Bobby)	Basketball Player
989 Hardin Wadesboro Road, Hardin KY 42048, USA	
Warren, Ron	Baseball Player
4025 Paddock Road, #401, Cincinnati OH 45229, USA	
Warren, Rosanna	Writer
11 Robinwood Ave, Needham MA 02492, USA	
Warren, Thomas L	Association Executive
National Wildlife Federation, 11100 Wildlife Center Dr, Reston VA 20190, USA	
Warren, Tom	Triathlete
2393 La Marque St, San Diego CA 92109, USA	
Warren, Ty'ron M (Ty)	Football Player
22 Ronald C Meyer Dr, North Attleboro MA 02760, USA	
Warren, William M, Jr	Businessman
Energen Corp, 605 Richard Arrington Jr Blvd N, Birmingham AL 35203, USA	
Warrener, Rhett	Ice Hockey Player
761 W Ferry St, Buffalo NY 14222, USA	
Warren-Green, Christopher	Conductor, Concert Violinist
Charlotte Symphony Orchestra, 301 S Tryon St, #1700, Charlotte, NC 28282, USA	
Warrick, Hakim H	Basketball Player
Phoenix Suns, 201 E Jefferson St, Phoenix AZ 85004 USA	
Warrick, Peter	Football Player
4305 17th St E, Ellenton FL 34222, USA	
Warwick, Carl W	Baseball Player
14102 Bonney Brier Circle, Houston TX 77069, USA	
Warwick, Dionne	Singer
Red Entertainment, 16 Penn Plaza, #824, New York NY 10001, USA	
Warwick, Lonnie P	Football Player
828 Main St, Mount Hope WV 25880, USA	
Wasdin, John T	Baseball Player
2676 Riverport Dr S, Jacksonville FL 32223, USA	

Washburn, Abigail — Banjo Player
Paradigm Agency, 360 N Crescent Dr, North Building, Beverly Hills CA 90210 USA
Washburn, Barbara — Cartographer
1010 Waltham St, #D327, Lexington MA 02421, USA
Washburn, Beverly — Actress
2561 Olivia Heights Ave, Henderson NV 89052, USA
Washburn, Jarrod M — Baseball Player
10003 Olinger Road, Webster WI 54893, USA
Washburn, Ray C — Baseball Player
1103 N 49th St, Seattle WA 98103, USA
Washington, Alonzo — Cartoonist (Omega Man)
Omega 7, PO Box 171046, Kansas City KS 66117, USA
Washington, Christopher (Chris) — Football Player
PO Box 17823, San Diego CA 92177, USA
Washington, Claudell — Baseball Player
4081 Clayton Road, #227, Concord CA 94521, USA
Washington, Denzel — Actor
Rogers & Cowan, 8687 Melrose Ave, #G700, West Hollywood CA 90069 USA
Washington, DeWayne N — Football Player
6205 Rocky Creek Way, Wake Forest NC 27587, USA
Washington, Eugene (Gene) — Football Player
2725 N Jewell Lane, Minneapolis MN 55447, USA
Washington, Gene A — Football Player
10521 Bellagio Road, Los Angeles CA 90077, USA
Washington, Hayma — Producer
A P A Talent/Literary Agency, 405 S Beverly Dr, #300, Beverly Hills CA 90212 USA
Washington, Herbert (Herb) L — Baseball Player
640 Saddlebrook Dr, Youngstown OH 44512, USA
Washington, Isaiah — Actor
Vincent Cirrincione Assoc, 1516 N Fairfax Ave, Los Angeles CA 90046 USA
Washington, James H (Jim) — Basketball Player
1108 Cardinal Way SW, Atlanta GA 30311, USA
Washington, Joe D — Football Player
Meadow Lark, 4 Treadwell Court, Lutherville Timonium MD 21093, USA
Washington, Joseph W (Joe) — Football Player
434 E 42nd Place, Chicago IL 60653, USA
Washington, Justin (Baby) — Singer, Pianist
Headline Talent, PO Box 131518, Staten Island NY 10313 USA
Washington, Keith L — Football Player
548 Parkview Dr, Grand Prairie TX 75052, USA
Washington, Kermit A — Basketball Player
7208 NE Hazel Dell Ave, Vancouver WA 98665, USA
Washington, Kerry — Actress
Creative Artists Agency, 2000 Ave of Stars, #100, Los Angeles CA 90067 USA
Washington, Larue — Baseball Player
6323 Reseda Blvd, #16, Tarzana CA 91335, USA
Washington, Leon (Neon) — Football Player
Seattle Seahawks, 12 Seahawks Way, Renton WA 98056 USA
Washington, Lionel — Football Player
5 Gleneagles Dr, La Place LA 70068, USA
Washington, MaliVai — Tennis Player
5 S Roscoe Blvd, Ponte Vedra Beach FL 32082, USA
Washington, Marcus C — Football Player
18263 Mullfield Village Terrace, Leesburg VA 20176, USA
Washington, Marvin A — Football Player
3616 Cripple Creek Dr, Dallas TX 75224, USA
Washington, Mickey L — Football Player
12115 Ashley Circle Dr E, Houston TX 77071, USA
Washington, Mike L — Football Player
366 Ridge Water Dr, Pike Road AL 36064, USA
Washington, Richard L — Basketball Player
4606 SE Logus Road, Portland OR 97222, USA
Washington, Rico — Baseball Player
2050 Old Clinton Road, Macon GA 31211, USA
Washington, Ronald (Ron) — Baseball Player, Manager
1400 S Clearview Parkway, New Orleans LA 70123, USA
Washington, Russell E (Russ) — Football Player
4375 Florida St, #4, San Diego CA 92104, USA
Washington, Theodore (Ted), Jr — Football Player
2715 Joust St, North Las Vegas NV 89030, USA
Washington, Todd P — Football Player
211 Glyndon Meadow Road, Reisterstown MD 21136, USA
Washington, U L — Baseball Player
PO Box 164, Stringtown OK 74569, USA
Washington, Wilson — Basketball Player
2625 Mapleton Ave, Norfolk VA 23504, USA
Wasif, Imaad — Singer, Songwriter
Agency Group Ltd, 142 W 57th St, #600, New York NY 10019 USA
Wasikowska, Mia — Actress
W M E Entertainment, 9601 Wilshire Blvd, #300, Beverly Hills CA 90210 USA
Waslewski, Gary L — Baseball Player
1799 E Terrestrial Place, Tucson AZ 85737, USA
Wasmeier, Markus — Alpine Skier
Breitensteinstr 14D, 83727 Schliersee-Neuhaus, Germany
Wasmuth, Conny — Canoing Athlete
S C Magdeburg, Friedrich-Ebert-Str 68, 39114 Magdeburg, Germany
Wass, Ted — Actor, Director, Producer
I C M Partners, 10250 Constellation Blvd, #900, Los Angeles CA 90067 USA
Wasserburg, Gerald J — Geophysicist
PO Box 2959, Florence OR 97439, USA
Wasserman, Dan — Editorial Cartoonist
Boston Globe, Editorial Dept, 135 William Morrissey Blvd, Dorchester MA 02125, USA
Wasserman, Robert H — Physiologist, Veterinarian
358 Savage Farm Dr, Ithaca NY 14850, USA
Wasson, Erin — Model
I M G Models, 304 Park Ave S, #PH-North, New York NY 10010 USA

Watanabe, Gedde — Actor
TalentWorks, 3500 W Olive Ave, #1400, Burbank CA 91505 USA
Watanabe, Katsuaki — Businessman
Toyota Motor Corp, 1 Toyotacho, Toyota City, Aichi Pref 471-8701, Japan
Watanabe, Kazuhide — Businessman
Mazda Motor Co, 3-1 Shinchi, Fuchucho, Akigun, Hiroshima 730-8670, Japan
Watanabe, Ken — Actor, Producer, Director
K-Dash (I), 2-7-10-5F Higashi, Shibuya, Tokyo 150-0011, Japan
Watanabe, Milio — Computer Scientist
Nippon Electric Co, Computer Labs, 5-33-1 Shiba, Tokyo, Japan
Watanabe, Sadao — Jazz Saxophonist
International Music Network, 278 Main St, #400, Gloucester MA 01930 USA
Watanabe, Shigeo — Businessman
Bridgestone Corp, 10-1-1 Kyobashi, Chuoku, Tokyo 104-8340, Japan
Waterbury, Steven C (Steve) — Baseball Player
710 N Garfield St, Marion IL 62959, USA
Waterhouse, Gabriel M (Gai) — Thoroughbred Racing Trainer
Gai Waterhouse Racing, PO Box 834, Kensington NSW 1465, Australia
Waterman, Dennis — Actor
Associated International Mgmt, Fairfax House, Fulwood Place, London WC1V 6HU, England
Waterman, Felicity — Actress
PO Box 234, Elk CA 95432, USA
Waterman, Hannah — Actress
C A M, 55-59 Shaftesbury Ave, London W1D 6LD, England
Waterman, Michael S — Mathematician
University of Southern California, Mathematics Dept, Los Angeles CA 90089, USA
Waterman, Pete — Actor
Fremantle Media, 2700 Colorado Ave, #450, Santa Monica CA 90404 USA
Waterman, Robert H — Writer
Enterprise Media, 91 Harvey St, Cambridge MA 02140, USA
Waters, Alice — Chef
Chez Panisse, 1517 Shattuck Ave, Berkeley CA 94709, USA
Waters, Brian D — Football Player
6911 W 138th Terrace, Overland Park KS 66223, USA
Waters, Charles T (Charlie) — Football Player, Coach
9305 Moss Trail, Dallas TX 75231, USA
Waters, Crystal — Singer
Borg Warner, 1849 Breward Road, Arden NC 28704, USA
Waters, Derek — Actor
United Talent Agency, 9336 Civic Center Dr, Beverly Hills CA 90210 USA
Waters, Dina — Actress
Gersh Agency, 9465 Wilshire Blvd, #600, Beverly Hills CA 90212 USA
Waters, Drew — Actor, Model
A P A Talent/Literary Agency, 405 S Beverly Dr, #300, Beverly Hills CA 90212 USA
Waters, John — Director, Writer, Actor
United Talent Agency, 9336 Civic Center Dr, Beverly Hills CA 90210 USA
Waters, John B — Government Official
405 Burridge Waters Edge, Sevierville TN 37862, USA
Waters, Lou — Commentator
CNN-TV, 190 Marietta Ave SW, Atlanta GA 30303 USA
Waters, Mark — Director, Producer, Writer
Creative Artists Agency, 2000 Ave of Stars, #100, Los Angeles CA 90067 USA
Waters, Richard — Publisher
13919 Woods Run Court, Centreville VA 20121, USA
Waters, Roger — Singer, Bassist (Pink Floyd)
One Fifteen, Globe House, Middle Lane Mews, London N8 8PN, England
Waterston, Katherine — Actress
United Talent Agency, 9336 Civic Center Dr, Beverly Hills CA 90210 USA
Waterston, Sam — Actor
Gersh Agency, 9465 Wilshire Blvd, #600, Beverly Hills CA 90212 USA
Wathan, John D — Baseball Player, Manager
1354 NE Todd George Road, Lees Summit MO 64086, USA
Watkins, Calvert W — Educator
University of California, Classics Dept, Los Angeles CA 90024, USA
Watkins, Carlene — Actress
Bresler Kelly Assoc, 11500 W Olympic Blvd, #400, Los Angeles CA 90064 USA
Watkins, David R (Dave) — Baseball Player
506 Ridgewood Road, Louisville KY 40207, USA
Watkins, Dean A — Inventor (Electron Tubes), Businessman
Watkins-Johnson Co, 401 River Oaks Parkway, San Jose CA 95134, USA
Watkins, Hays T, Jr — Businessman
2111 Cedarfield Lane, Henrico VA 23233, USA
Watkins, Michael W — Director, Producer
Creative Artists Agency, 2000 Ave of Stars, #100, Los Angeles CA 90067 USA
Watkins, Michaela — Actress, Comedienne
I C M Partners, 10250 Constellation Blvd, #900, Los Angeles CA 90067 USA
Watkins, Michelle — Actress
Capital Artists, 6404 Wilshire Blvd, #950, Los Angeles CA 90048, USA
Watkins, Robert C (Bob) — Baseball Player
4417 W 58th Place, Los Angeles CA 90043, USA
Watkins, Robert L (Bobby) — Football Player
1112 Devonshire Dr, DeSoto TX 75115, USA
Watkins, Sara U — Singer, Fiddler (Nickel Creek)
Nonesuch Records, 75 Rockefeller Plaza, #800, New York NY 10019 USA
Watkins, Scott A — Baseball Player
14660 W 18th St, Sand Springs OK 74063, USA
Watkins, Sean C — Guitarist (Nickel Creek)
Q-Prime South, 131 S 11th St, Nashville TN 37206 USA
Watkins, Simon C — Immunologist
University of Pittsburgh Medical School, Immunology Dept, Pittsburgh PA 15260, USA
Watkins, Steve — Baseball Player
3408 Evanston Ave, Lubbock TX 79407, USA
Watkins, Tionne (T-Boz) — Rap Artist (TLC)
Venture I A B, 3211 Cahuenga Blvd W, #104, Los Angeles CA 90068, USA
Watkins, Tuc — Actor
Stone Manners Salners, 9911 W Pico Blvd, #1400, Los Angeles CA 90035 USA

W

Watanabe - Watkins

Watley, Jody — Singer
T C I, 1560 Broadway, #1308, New York NY 10036, USA
Watling, Leonor — Actress
Alsiro Garcia-Maroto Talent Agency, Calle De Los Invencibles 8, Bajo, 28019 Madrid, Spain
Watlington, J Neal — Baseball Player
PO Box 418, Yanceyville NC 27379, USA
Watney, Nicholas A (Nick) — Golfer
816 Veramar Court, Henderson NV 89052, USA
Watrous, Cynthia — Actress
Principal Entertainment, 1964 Westwood Blvd, #400, Los Angeles CA 90025 USA
Watrous, William R (Bill), Jr — Jazz Trombonist
G N P/Crescendo Records, 8271 Melrose Ave, #104, Los Angeles CA 90046, USA
Watson Richardson, Lillian (Pokey) — Swimmer
4960 Maunalani Circle, Honolulu HI 96816, USA
Watson, A J — Auto Racing Engineer
5420 Crawfordsville Road, Indianapolis IN 46224, USA
Watson, Adrienne — Actress, Comedienne
OmniPop Talent Group, 4605 Lankershim Blvd, #201, Toluca Lake CA 91602 USA
Watson, Albert M — Photographer
44 Laight St, #1A, New York NY 10013, USA
Watson, Alberta — Actress
Gary Goddard Assoc, 10 Saint Mary St, #305, Toronto ON M4Y 1P9, Canada
Watson, Alexander F — Diplomat
Nature Conservancy International, 4245 Fairfax Dr, #100, Arlington VA 22203, USA
Watson, Allen K — Baseball Player
6144 65th St, Middle Village NY 11379, USA
Watson, Barry — Actor
Innovative Artists, 1505 10th St, Santa Monica CA 90401 USA
Watson, Benjamin S (Ben) — Football Player
12397 Steeplechase Lane, Strongsville OH 44149, USA
Watson, Bryan J — Ice Hockey Player
400 Madison St, Alexandria VA 22314, USA
Watson, Cecil J — Physician
Abbott Northwestern Hospital, 2727 Chicago Ave, Minneapolis MN 55407, USA
Watson, Dale — Singer
Crowley Artist Mgmt, 602 Wayside Dr, Wimberley TX 78676, USA
Watson, Debbie — Singer
PO Box 1570, Goodlettsville TN 37070, USA
Watson, E Bruce — Environmentalist
Rensselaer Polytechnic Institute, Earth & Environmental Dept, Troy NY 12180, USA
Watson, Earl J — Basketball Player
4310 N Holly Court, Kansas City MO 64116, USA
Watson, Elizabeth M — Law Enforcement Official
Houston Police Department, Chief's Office, 1200 Travis St, Houston TX 77002, USA
Watson, Emily — Actress
Independent Talent Group, Oxford House, 76 Oxford St, London W1D 1BS, England
Watson, Emma — Actress, Model
Markham & Froggatt, Julian House, 4 Windmill St, London W1P 1HF, England
Watson, Gene — Singer, Guitarist
Brokaw Co, 2603 Westwood, Nashville TN 37203, USA
Watson, George L (Bubba), Jr — Golfer
Professional Golfer's Assn, PO Box 109601, Palm Beach Gardens FL 33410 USA
Watson, Jack H, Jr — Government Official
Long Aldridge Norman, 1900 K St NW, Washington DC 20006, USA
Watson, James A (Jim) — Ice Hockey Player
1702 Coventry Lane, Glen Mills PA 19342, USA
Watson, James D — Nobel Medicine Laureate
Bungtown Road, Cold Spring Harbor NY 11724, USA
Watson, Jamie L — Basketball Player
PO Box 761, Elm City NC 27822, USA
Watson, Jill — Figure Skater
Desert Schools Coyote Center, 15829 N 83rd Ave, Peoria AZ 85382, USA
Watson, Kenneth M — Physicist, Oceanographer
8515 Costa Verde Blvd, #2008, San Diego CA 92122, USA
Watson, Lillian — Opera Singer
I M G Artists, Hogarth Business Park, Chiswick, London W4 2TH, England
Watson, Mark — Baseball Player
555 Spender Trace, Atlanta GA 30350, USA
Watson, Martha — Track Athlete
5509 Royal Vista Lane, Las Vegas NV 89149, USA
Watson, Mills — Actor
PO Box 600, Talent OR 97540, USA
Watson, Patrick — Singer, Songwriter
Agency Group Ltd, 142 W 57th St, #600, New York NY 10019 USA
Watson, Patty Jo — Anthropologist
Washington University, Anthropology Dept, PO Box 1114, Saint Louis MO 63188, USA
Watson, Paul — Photojournalist
Toronto Star, Editorial Dept, 1 Yonge St, Toronto ON M5E 1E6, Canada
Watson, Paul — Environmental Activist
Sea Shepherd Conservation Society, PO Box 2670, Malibu CA 90265, USA
Watson, Richard Jesse — Illustrator
2305 Ivy St, Port Townsend WA 98368, USA
Watson, Robert E (Bobby) — Basketball Player
1625 Sherwood Dr, Owensboro KY 42301, USA
Watson, Robert J (Bob) — Baseball Player
18103 Darling Point Court, Cypress TX 77429, USA
Watson, Robert M (Bobby), Jr — Jazz Saxophonist
Hot Jazz Mgmt, 328 W 43rd St, #4FW, New York NY 10036, USA
Watson, Russell — Singer
PO Box 806, Manchester M60 2XS, England
Watson, Stephen E — Businessman
Dayton Hudson, 1000 Nicollet Mall, Minneapolis MN 55403, USA
Watson, Stephen R (Steve) — Football Player
4675 S Vine Way, Englewood CO 80113, USA
Watson, Thomas S (Tom) — Golfer
16104 Riggs Road, Stilwell KS 66085, USA

Watson, Wayne — Singer
T B A Artist Mgmt, 300 10th Ave S, Nashville TN 37203, USA

Watson, William C (Bill) — Ice Hockey Player
1725 Vermillon Road, Duluth MN 55803, USA

Watson-Johnson, Vernee — Actress
C E S D, 10635 Santa Monica Blvd, #130, Los Angeles CA 90025 USA

Watt, Ben — Guitarist, Singer, Songwriter
J F D Mgmt, Acklam Workshops, 10 Acklam Road, London W10 5QZ, England

Watt, Edward D (Eddie) — Baseball Player
940 Locust St, North Bend NE 68649, USA

Watt, James G — Secretary, Interior
PO Box 3705, Jackson Hole WY 83001, USA

Watt, Michael D (Mike) — Singer, Bassist (Porno for Pyros)
Agency Group Ltd, 142 W 57th St, #600, New York NY 10019 USA

Watt, Tom — Ice Hockey Coach
Calgary Flames, PO Box 1540, Station M, Calgary AB T2P 3B9, Canada

Watt-Cloutier, Sheila — Social Activist
Inuit Circumpolar, 170 Laurier Ave, #504, Ottawa ON K1P 5V5, Canada

Wattelet, Frank L — Football Player
4 Deer Run Dr, Joplin MO 64804, USA

Wattenberg, Ben J — Demographer
American Enterprise Institute, 1150 17th St NW, Washington DC 20036, USA

Watters, Mark — Composer, Conductor
Air Edel, 8687 Melrose Ave, #900, Los Angeles CA 90069 USA

Watters, Richard J (Rickie) — Football Player
6263 Cypress Chase Dr, Windermere FL 34786, USA

Watters, Sam — Singer (Color Me Badd)
J-Bird Entertainment, 4905 S Atlantic Ave, Ponce Inlet FL 32127 USA

Watters, Tim — Ice Hockey Player
2390 E Camelback Road, #100, Phoenix AZ 85016, USA

Wattleton, A Faye — Association Executive
Center for Advancement of Women, 165 W 46th St, #512, New York NY 10036, USA

Watts, Andre — Concert Pianist
C M Artists, 127 W 96th St, #13B, New York NY 10025 USA

Watts, Charles R (Charlie) — Drummer (Rolling Stones)
Munro Sounds, 5 Wandsworth Plain, London SW18 1ES, England

Watts, Daniele — Actress
Anonymous Content, 3532 Hayden Ave, Culver City CA 90232 USA

Watts, Donald E (Slick) — Basketball Player
5015 256th Ave NE, Redmond WA 98053, USA

Watts, Elizabeth — Opera Singer
Ingpen & Williams, 131 Putney Bridge Road, London SW15 2PA, England

Watts, Ernest J (Ernie) — Jazz Saxophonist
De Leon Artists, PO Box 21329, Piedmont CA 94620 USA

Watts, Ernie — Art Director, Stage Designer
I C M Partners, 730 5th Ave, New York NY 10019 USA

Watts, Heather — Ballerina
New York City Ballet, Lincoln Center Plaza, New York NY 10023 USA

Watts, Julius Caesar (J C), Jr — Representative, OK; Football Player
J C Watts Companies, 600 13th St NW, #790, Washington DC 20005, USA

Watts, Lou — Singer (Chumbawamba)
Doug Smith Assoc, PO Box 1151, London W3 8ZJ, England

Watts, Naomi — Actress
Untitled Entertainment, 350 S Beverly Dr, #200, Beverly Hills CA 90212 USA

Watts, Quincy — Track Athlete
H S International Sports Mgmt, 9871 Irvine Center Dr, Irvine CA 92618, USA

Watts, Ronald M (Ron) — Basketball Player
875 Grace St, #101, Herndon VA 20170, USA

Waugh, John S — Chemist
60 Conant Road, Lincoln MA 01773, USA

Waugh, Scott — Director
I C M Partners, 10250 Constellation Blvd, #900, Los Angeles CA 90067 USA

Waugh, Stephen R (Steve) — Cricketer
Team-Duet, 3 Winnie St, Cremone NSW 2090, Australia

Wauters, Ann H W — Basketball Player
Seattle Storm, Key Arena, 351 Elliott Ave W, #500, Seattle WA 98119 USA

Wax, Ruby — Actress, Comedienne
United Agents, 12-26 Lexington St, London W1F 0LE, England

Waxman, Seth P — Government Official, Attorney
Wilmer Hale, 1875 Pennsylvania Ave NW, Washington DC 20006, USA

Wayans, Damon — Actor, Comedian
I C M Partners, 10250 Constellation Blvd, #900, Los Angeles CA 90067 USA

Wayans, Damon, Jr — Actor
Mosiac Media Group, 9200 W Sunset Blvd, #1000, Los Angeles CA 90069 USA

Wayans, Dwayne — Actor
16405 Mulholland Dr, Los Angeles CA 90049, USA

Wayans, Keenen Ivory — Actor, Director
Wayans Brothers Entertainment, 8730 W Sunset Blvd, #290, Los Angeles CA 90069, USA

Wayans, Kim — Actress, Writer, Director
A P A Talent/Literary Agency, 405 S Beverly Dr, #300, Beverly Hills CA 90212 USA

Wayans, Marlon — Actor, Comedian
Wayans Brothers Entertainment, 8730 W Sunset Blvd, #290, Los Angeles CA 90069, USA

Wayans, Shawn — Actor
Modus Entertainment, 8730 W Sunset Blvd, #290, West Hollywood CA 90069, USA

Wayda, Stephen — Photographer
Celebrity Pictures, 5757 Wilshire Blvd, Beverly Hills CA 90210, USA

Wayne, Gary A — Baseball Player
5762 W Ashbury Place, Lakewood CO 80227, USA

Wayne, John Ethan — Actor
Wayne Enterprises, 210 62nd St, Newport Beach CA 92663, USA

Wayne, Justin — Baseball Player
302 Muirfield Court, Jupiter FL 33458, USA

Wayne, Nathaniel (Nate), Jr — Football Player
2878 Grey Moss Pass, Duluth GA 30097, USA

Wayne, Patrick J — Actor
10502 Whipple St, Toluca Lake CA 91602, USA

Wayne, Reggie — Football Player
17000 Berkshire Court, Southwest Ranches FL 33331, USA

Wearing, Gillian — Artist
Maureen Paley Interim Art, 21 Herald St, London E2 6JT, England

Weary, J Fredrick (Fred) — Football Player
11315 Sailwing Creek Court, Pearland TX 77584, USA

Weatherall, David J — Hematologist
8 Cumnor Rise Road, Cumnor Hill, Oxford OX2 9HD, England

Weatherly, Michael — Actor
Anonymous Content, 3532 Hayden Ave, Culver City CA 90232 USA

Weatherly, Shawn N — Actress, Beauty Queen
Connor Ankrum Assoc, 1680 Vine St, #1016, Los Angeles CA 90028, USA

Weatherman, Woodroe (Woody) — Guitarist (Corrosion of Conformity)
Chipster, 800 Village Square Crossing, Palm Beach Gardens FL 33410 USA

Weathers, Carl — Actor, Football Player
2228 Walnut Ave, Venice CA 90291, USA

Weathers, J David (Dave) — Baseball Player
979 Lexington Highway, Loretto TN 38469, USA

Weatherspoon, Clarence — Basketball Player
PO Box 117, Crawford MS 39743, USA

Weatherspoon, Teresa G — Basketball Player
Los Angeles Sparks, 888 S Figueroa St, #2010, Los Angeles CA 90017 USA

Weatherston, Katie — Ice Hockey Player
Team Canada, 2424 University Dr NW, Calgary AB T2N 3Y9, Canada

Weaver, Al — Actor
Julian Belfrage Assoc, 9 Argyll St, #300, London W1F 7TG, England

Weaver, Anthony L — Football Player
801 Anderson St, Bellaire TX 77401, USA

Weaver, Charles E (Charlie) — Football Player
309 W Muncie Ave, Fresno CA 93711, USA

Weaver, DeWitt — Golfer
Weaver Golf Solutions, 5640 Golf Club Dr, Braselton GA 30517, USA

Weaver, Earl S — Baseball Player, Manager
3000 SW 62nd Ave, Miami FL 33155, USA

Weaver, Fritz — Actor
161 W 75th St, #15A, New York NY 10023, USA

Weaver, Gary L — Football Player
3496 Arden Road, Hayward CA 94545, USA

Weaver, J Eric — Baseball Player
2641 Weaver Road, Illiopolis IL 62539, USA

Weaver, James — Cartoonist
3438 Admiralty Lane, Indianapolis IN 46240, USA

Weaver, Jason — Actor
Luber Rocklin Entertainment, 8530 Wilshire Blvd, #555, Beverly Hills CA 90211 USA

Weaver, Jeffrey C (Jeff) — Baseball Player
1740 Classic Rose Court, Westlake Village CA 91362, USA

Weaver, Jered D — Baseball Player
3321 Billie Court, Simi Valley CA 93063, USA

Weaver, Leonard — Football Player
Philadelphia Eagles, 1 Novacare Way, Philadelphia PA 19145 USA

Weaver, Michael — Actor
Brillstein Entertainment Partners, 9150 Wilshire Blvd, #350, Beverly Hills CA 90212 USA

Weaver, Reg — Labor Leader
National Education Assn, 1201 16th St NW, Washington DC 20036, USA

Weaver, Roger E — Baseball Player
65 Moyer St, Canajoharie NY 13317, USA

Weaver, Sigourney — Actress
Arcieri Assoc, 305 Madison Ave, #2315, New York NY 10165 USA

Weaver, T Jed — Football Player
3012 SW Timber Ave, Redmond OR 97756, USA

Weaver, W Herman — Football Player
8105 Hamilton Mill Dr, Chattanooga TN 37421, USA

Weaver, Warren E — Chemist
7607 Horsepen Road, Richmond VA 23229, USA

Weaving, Hugo — Actor
Shanahan Mgmt, 91 Campbell St, #300, Surry Hills NSW 2010, Australia

Webb, Alexander D (Alex) — Photographer
151 W 25th St, New York NY 10001, USA

Webb, Anthony J (Spud) — Basketball Player
1453 Mosslake Dr, DeSoto TX 75115, USA

Webb, Brandon T — Baseball Player
8814 E Ann Way, Scottsdale AZ 85260, USA

Webb, Chloe — Actress
PO Box 2824, Venice CA 90294, USA

Webb, Christiaan — Singer, Musician, Songwriter
SuperVision Mgmt, 109B Regents Park Road, London NW1 8UR, England

Webb, Derek W — Singer, Guitarist (Caedmon's Call)
Third Coast Artists, 2021 21st Ave S, #220, Nashville TN 37212, USA

Webb, Donald W (Don) — Football Player
906 Roland Court, Jefferson City MO 65101, USA

Webb, Henry G (Hank) — Baseball Player
4527 Lake Valencia Blvd W, Palm Harbor FL 34684, USA

Webb, James R (Jimmy) — Football Player
1319 S Prairie Flower Road, Turlock CA 95380, USA

Webb, Jimmy — Singer, Songwriter
1560 N Laurel Ave, #109, Los Angeles CA 90046, USA

Webb, Justin — Singer, Musician, Songwriter
SuperVision Mgmt, 109B Regents Park Road, London NW1 8UR, England

Webb, Karrie — Golfer
725 Presidential Dr, Boynton Beach FL 33435, USA

Webb, Lardarius — Football Playeer
Baltimore Ravens, Ravens Stadium, 1 Winning Dr, Baltimore MD 21230 USA

Webb, Lee — Evangelist, Commentator
700 Club, 977 Centerville Turnpike, Virginia Beach VA 23463, USA

Webb, Richmond J — Football Player
4120 Humphrey Dr, Dallas TX 75216, USA

Webb, Russell (Russ) — Water Polo Player
611 Knob Hill Ave, Redondo Beach CA 90277, USA
Webb, Sarah K — Yachtswoman
Lynx Sports Mgmt, Lymington Road, Lymington, Hampshire SO41 5S5, England
Webb, Steve — Ice Hockey Player
27 Barberry Lane, Center Moriches NY 11934, USA
Webb, Tamilee — Physical Fitness Instructor
12920 Carmel Creek Road, #31, San Diego CA 92130, USA
Webb, Veronica — Model, Actress
Don Buchwald/Fortitude, 10 E 44th St, New York NY 10017 USA
Webb, Watt W — Applied Physicist
Cornell University, BioPhysics Program, Ithaca NY 14853, USA
Webb, Wayne — Bowler
5850 Freeport Blvd, Sacramento CA 95822, USA
Webber, Julian Lloyd — Concert Cellist
I M G Artists, Hogarth Business Park, Chiswick, London W4 2TH, England
Webber, Mark — Actor
Innovative Artists, 1505 10th St, Santa Monica CA 90401 USA
Webber, Mark A — Auto Racing Driver
Octagon, 166 William Dr, Woolloomooloo NSW 2011, Australia
Webber, Peter — Director
United Agents, 12-26 Lexington St, London W1F 0LE, England
Webber, Tristan — Fashion Designer
Brower Lewis Public Relations, 74 Gloucester Place, London W1H 3HN, England
Weber, Arnold R — Educator
Northwestern University, Chancellor's Office, Evanston IL 60208, USA
Weber, Ben — Baseball Player
5550 Baird St, Groves TX 77619, USA
Weber, Ben, Jr — Cartoonist
King Features Syndicate, 300 W 57th St, #1500, New York NY 10019 USA
Weber, Bernard — Explorer, Filmmaker
New7Wonders Foundation, PO Box 1212, 8034 Zurich, Switzerland
Weber, Bruce — Basketball Coach
University of Illinois, Athletic Dept, Assembly Hall, Champaign IL 61820, USA
Weber, Bruce — Photographer
Little Bear, 135 Watts St, #5, New York NY 10013, USA
Weber, Charles F (Chuck), Jr — Football Player
12740 Cobblestone Creek Road, Poway CA 92064, USA
Weber, Charlie — Actor
Warren Cowan Assoc, 8899 Beverly Blvd, #918, Los Angeles CA 90048, USA
Weber, Eberhard — Jazz Bassist, Cellist, Composer
Ted Kurland, 173 Brighton Ave, Allston MA 02134 USA
Weber, Emmanuelle — Actress
Artmedia, 20 Ave Rapp, 75007 Paris, France
Weber, George B — Association Executive
Chemin Moise-Duboule 19, 1209 Geneva, Switzerland
Weber, J Vincent (Vin) — Representative, MN
Clark & Weinstock, 601 13th St NW, #410S, Washington DC 20005, USA
Weber, Jack — Actor
C E S D, 10635 Santa Monica Blvd, #130, Los Angeles CA 90025 USA
Weber, Jacques — Actor
U B B A, 6 Rue de Braque, 75003 Paris, France
Weber, Jake — Actor
Paradigm Agency, 360 N Crescent Dr, North Building, Beverly Hills CA 90210 USA
Weber, Joseph F — Marine Corps General
Commanding General, 3rd Marine Expeditionary Force Okinawa, FPO AP 96602 USA
Weber, Mary E — Astronaut
14 Hawkview St, Portola Valley CA 94028, USA
Weber, Neil A — Baseball Player
1 Morning View, Irvine CA 92603, USA
Weber, Peter D (Pete) — Bowler
10500 Saint Xavier Lane, Saint Ann MO 63074, USA
Weber, Robert M (Bob) — Cartoonist
New Yorker, Editorial Dept, 4 Times Square, Basement C1B, New York NY 10036 USA
Weber, Shea M — Ice Hockey Player
4527 Yancey Dr, Nashville TN 37215, USA
Weber, Stephen L — Educator
San Diego State University, President's Office, San Diego CA 92182, USA
Weber, Steven — Actor
Brillstein Entertainment Partners, 9150 Wilshire Blvd, #350, Beverly Hills CA 90212 USA
Webre, Septime — Choreographer
Washington Ballet, 3515 Wisconsin Ave NW, Washington DC 20016, USA
Webster, Corey J — Football Player
66 Mallard Place, Secaucus NJ 07094, USA
Webster, James — Musicologist
Cornell University, Music Dept, Ithaca NY 14853, USA
Webster, Jeffrey T (Jeff) — Basketball Player
10405 SE 15th St, Oklahoma City OK 73130, USA
Webster, Larry M, Jr — Football Player
12 Oakridge Court, Elkton MD 21921, USA
Webster, Leonard N (Lenny) — Baseball Player
6211 Bridgeport Dr, Charlotte NC 28215, USA
Webster, Martell — Basketball Player
Washington Wizards, M C I Centre, 601 F St NW, Washington DC 20004 USA
Webster, Mitchell D (Mitch) — Baseball Player
3120 NE 91st Terrace, Kansas City MO 64156, USA
Webster, Raymond G (Ray) — Baseball Player
311 5th St, Marysville CA 95901, USA
Webster, Robert D (Bob) — Diver
269 Hacienda Carmel, Carmel CA 93923, USA
Webster, Tom — Ice Hockey Player
1750 Longfellow Dr, Canton MI 48187, USA
Webster, Victor — Actor
Innovative Artists, 1505 10th St, Santa Monica CA 90401 USA
Webster, William G — Army General
Commander, Army Central, Camp Arifjan Kuwait, APO AE 09306, USA

Webster, William H — Law Enforcement Official
4777 Dexter St NW, Washington DC 20007, USA

Wecker, Andreas — Gymnast
Am Dorfplatz 1, 16766 Klein-Ziethen, Germany

Wecker, Kendra — Basketball Player
San Antonio Silver Stars, 1 AT&T Center, San Antonio TX 78219 USA

Weddington, Michael W (Mike) — Football Player
237 Sycamore Grove St, Simi Valley CA 93065, USA

Weddington, Sarah R — Attorney
Weddington Center, 709 W 14th St, Austin TX 78701, USA

Wedel, Dieter — Director
Nibelungenfestspiele, Von-Steuben-Str 5, 67549 Worms, Germany

Weder, Gustav — Bobsled Athlete
Haltenstr 2, Stachen/TG, Switzerland

Wedge, Chris — Animator, Director, Producer
Blue Sky Studios, 1 American Lane, Greenwich CT 06831, USA

Wedge, Eric M — Baseball Player, Manager
8285 SE 82nd St, Mercer Island WA 98040, USA

Wedgeworth, Ann — Actress
70 Riverside Dr, New York NY 10024, USA

Wedman, Scott D — Basketball Player
7912 NW Scenic Dr, Kansas City MO 64152, USA

Weed, Maurice James — Composer
308 Overlook Road, #55, Asheville NC 28803, USA

Weeden, Brandon K — Football Player
Cleveland Browns, 76 Lou Groza Blvd, Berea OH 44017 USA

Weege, Reinhold — Producer
2035 Via Don Benito, La Jolla CA 92037, USA

Weekes, Kevin — Ice Hockey Player
9251 Yonge St, #8-887, Richmond Hill ON L4C 9T3, Canada

Weekes, Stephen K (Steve) — Ice Hockey Player
2883 Thurleston Lane, Duluth GA 30097, USA

Weekley, Thomas B (Boo) — Golfer
2555 New York St, Jay FL 32565, USA

Weeks, Jared — Singer (Saving Abel), Songwriter
Virgin Records, 338 N Foothill Road, Beverly Hills CA 90210 USA

Weeks, John D — Chemist
15301 Watergate Road, Silver Spring MD 20905, USA

Weeks, John R — Architect
39 Jackson's Lane, Highgate, London N6 5SR, England

Weeks, Kent R — Archaeologist
American University, 113 Kar El Aini St, Cairo 11511, Egypt

Weeks, Perdita — Actress
Troika, 74 Clerkenwell Road, #300, London EC1M 5QA, England

Weeks, Rickie D — Baseball Player
7473 Park Springs Circle, Orlando FL 32835, USA

Weeks, Wendell — Businessman
Corning Inc, Houghton Park, Corning NY 14931, USA

Weese, Miranda — Ballerina
New York City Ballet, Lincoln Center Plaza, New York NY 10023 USA

Weger, Michael R (Mike) — Football Player
825 Markwood Dr, Oxford MS 38655, USA

Wegman, William E (Bill) — Baseball Player
20521 Heather Court, Lawrenceburg IN 47025, USA

Wegman, William G — Artist, Photographer
239 W 18th St, New York NY 10011, USA

Wegner, Paul D — Sculptor
PO Box 603, Prather CA 93651, USA

Wegryn Gross, Halley — Actress
Innovative Artists, 1505 10th St, Santa Monica CA 90401 USA

Wehling, Ulrich — Nordic Combined Athlete
Skiverband, Hubertusstr 1, 81477 Munich, Germany

Wehner, John P — Baseball Player
105 Avery's Way, Cranberry Township PA 16066, USA

Wehrli, Roger R — Football Player
204 Fox Haven Court, O'Fallon MO 63368, USA

Wehrmeister, David T (Dave) — Baseball Player
115 Sharene Lane, #20, Walnut Creek CA 94596, USA

Wei Hui — Writer
Pocket Books, 1230 Ave of Americas, New York NY 10020 USA

Wei, James — Chemical Engineer
571 Lake St, Princeton NJ 08540, USA

Weibel, Ewald R — Biologist
University of Berne, Biology Dept, Hochshulstr 4, 3012 Berne, Switzerland

Weibel, Robert — Pediatrician
University of Pennsylvania Medical School, Pediatrics Dept, Philadelphia PA 19104, USA

Weibring, D A — Golfer
5865 Versailles Ave, Frisco TX 75034, USA

Weicker, Lowell P, Jr — Governor, Senator, CT
PO Box 877, Old Lyme CT 06371, USA

Weida, Johnny A — Air Force General, Educator
Deputy Chief of Staff, Operations Plans, HqUSA, Pentagon, Washington DC 20310 USA

Weide, Robert B — Director, Writer
Whyaduck Productions, 4804 Laurel Canyon Blvd, PMB 502, North Hollywood CA 91607, USA

Weidenbaum, Murray L — Government Official, Economist
6231 Rosebury Ave, Saint Louis MO 63105, USA

Weider, Josef E (Joe) — Publisher, Body Building Executive
Weider Health & Fitness, 21100 Erwin St, Woodland Hills CA 91367, USA

Weidinger, Christine — Opera Singer
Robert Lombardo Assoc, Harkness Plaza, 61 W 62nd St, #6F, New York NY 10023 USA

Weidlinger, Paul — Civil Engineer
Weidlinger Assoc, 375 Hudson Ave, #1200, New York NY 10014, USA

Weidner, Bert J — Football Player
517 NW 106th Ave, Plantation FL 33324, USA

Weidner, Brant — Basketball Player
1111 Colfax St, Evanston IL 60201, USA

Weigand, Cary Lathan — Artist
1666 China Gulch Road, Jacksonville OR 97530, USA
Weigel, Teri — Actress, Model
6433 Topanga Canyon Blvd, #103, Woodland Hills CA 91303, USA
Weigert, Robin — Actress
Innovative Artists, 1505 10th St, Santa Monica CA 90401 USA
Weight, Douglas D (Doug) — Ice Hockey Player
72 Feeks Lane, Locust Valley NY 11560, USA
Weihenmayer, Erik — Mountaineer
682 Partridge Circle, Golden CO 80403, USA
Weikl, Bernd — Opera Singer
Opera et Concert, 37 Rue de la Chaussee d'Antin, 75009 Paris, France
Weil, Andrew — Physician
1670 N Kolb Road, #240, Tucson AZ 85715, USA
Weil, Bruno — Conductor, Composer
Ingpen & Williams, 131 Putney Bridge Road, London SW15 2PA, England
Weil, Cynthia — Songwriter
Gorfaine/Schwartz, 4111 W Alameda Ave, #509, Burbank CA 91505 USA
Weil, Frank A — Association Executive
Smithsonian Institution, 900 Jefferson Dr SW, Washington DC 20560, USA
Weil, Liza — Actress
Principal Entertainment, 1964 Westwood Blvd, #400, Los Angeles CA 90025 USA
Weiland, John H — Businessman
C F Bard Co, 730 Central Ave, Murray Hill NJ 07974, USA
Weiland, Paul — Director
I C M Partners, 10250 Constellation Blvd, #900, Los Angeles CA 90067 USA
Weiland, Scott — Singer (Stone Temple Pilots), Songwriter
Brillstein Entertainment Partners, 9150 Wilshire Blvd, #350, Beverly Hills CA 90212 USA
Weilerstein, Alisa — Concert Cellist
Opus 3 Artists, 470 Park Ave S, #900N, New York NY 10016 USA
Weill, David (Dave) — Track Athlete
120 Mountain Spring Ave, San Francisco CA 94114, USA
Weill, Sanford I (Sandy) — Businessman
Citigroup Inc, 55 E 52nd St, New York NY 10055, USA
Wein, George — Musical Producer
Festival Productions, 30 Irving Place, #600, New York NY 10003, USA
Weinbach, Lawrence A — Businessman
Unisys Corp, Unisys Way, Blue Bell PA 19424, USA
Weinberg, Gerhard L — Historian
1416 Mount Willing Road, Efland NC 27243, USA
Weinberg, Max — Drummer (E-Street Band)
633 Cooper Road, Atlantic Highlands NJ 07716, USA
Weinberg, Mike — Actor
Innovative Artists, 1505 10th St, Santa Monica CA 90401 USA
Weinberg, Robert A — Cancer Researcher, Biochemist
Whitehead Institute, 9 Cambridge Center, Cambridge MA 02142, USA
Weinberg, Steven — Nobel Physics Laureate
University of Texas, Physics Dept, 2613 Wichita St, Austin TX 78712, USA
Weinbrecht, Donna — Freestyle Moguls Skier
177 High Crest Dr, West Milford NJ 07480, USA
Weiner, Art E — Football Player
404 Kimberly Dr, Greensboro NC 27408, USA
Weiner, Erik — Writer, Producer, Commentator
Bleeker Street Entertainment, 853 Broadway, #1214, New York NY 10003, USA
Weiner, Gerald (Gerry) — Government Official, Canada
40 Fredmir St, Dollard-des-Ormeaux PQ H9A 2R3, Canada
Weiner, Jennifer — Writer
Engelman Co, 55 E 9th St, New York NY 10003, USA
Weiner, Jessica — Writer
Hay House, 250 Park Ave S, #201, New York NY 10003, USA
Weiner, Matthew — Producer, Writer
Creative Artists Agency, 2000 Ave of Stars, #100, Los Angeles CA 90067 USA
Weiner, Mel — Artist
Silverlake Mosaics, 1809 San Jacinto St, Los Angeles CA 90026, USA
Weiner, Michael — Baseball Executive, Labor Leader
Major League Baseball Players Assn, 803 3rd Ave, New York NY 10022, USA
Weiner, Timothy E (Tim) — Journalist
New York Times, Editorial Dept, 1627 I St NW, #700, Washington DC 20006, USA
Weingarten, David M — Architect
Ace Architects, 330 2nd St, Oakland CA 94607, USA
Weingarten, Gene — Journalist
Washington Post, Editorial Dept, 1150 15th St NW, Washington DC 20071 USA
Weingarten, Randi — Labor Leader, Educator
American Federation of Teachers, 555 New Jersey Ave NW, Washington DC 20001, USA
Weingarten, Reid H — Attorney
Steptoe & Johnson, 1330 Connecticut Ave NW, Washington DC 20036, USA
Weinger, Scott — Actor, Producer, Writer
W M E Entertainment, 9601 Wilshire Blvd, #300, Beverly Hills CA 90210 USA
Weinhold, Matt — Actor, Comedian
OmniPop Talent Group, 4605 Lankershim Blvd, #201, Toluca Lake CA 91602 USA
Weinke, Christopher J (Chris) — Football Player
12504 Portmarnock Court, Charlotte NC 28277, USA
Weinman, Rosalyn (Roz) — Producer, Writer
United Talent Agency, 9336 Civic Center Dr, Beverly Hills CA 90210 USA
Weinrich, Eric J — Ice Hockey Player
337 Sea Meadows Lane, Yarmouth ME 04096, USA
Weinstein, Diane Gilbert — Judge
US Court of Claims, 717 Madison Place NW, Washington DC 20439, USA
Weinstein, Harvey — Producer
Weinstein Company, 345 Hudson St, #1300, New York NY 10014, USA
Weinstein, Jack B — Judge
US District Court, US Courthouse, 225 Cadman Plaza E, Brooklyn NY 11201, USA
Weinstein, Paula — Producer
Creative Artists Agency, 2000 Ave of Stars, #100, Los Angeles CA 90067 USA
Weintraub, Jerry — Producer
Jerry Weintraub Productions, 4000 Warner Blvd, #1, Burbank CA 91522, USA

Weir, Alex — Guitarist (Brothers Johnson)
Green Light Talent Agency, PO Box 3172, Beverly Hills CA 90212 USA

Weir, Gillian C — Concert Organist, Harpsichordist
Denny Lyster Artists, PO Box 155, Stanmore HA1 3WF, England

Weir, John G (Johnny) — Figure Skater
Ice Vault Arena, 10 Nevins Road, Wayne NJ 07470, USA

Weir, Judith — Composer
Chester Music, 14-15 Berners St, London W1T 3LJ, England

Weir, Mike — Golfer
2960 Oberland Road, Sandy UT 84092, USA

Weir, Peter L — Director, Writer
Australian Director's Guild, PO Box 211, Rozelle, Sydney NSW 2039, Australia

Weir, Stephnie C — Actress, Comedienne
A P A Talent/Literary Agency, 405 S Beverly Dr, #300, Beverly Hills CA 90212 USA

Weir, Wally — Ice Hockey Player
448 Lakeshore Road, Beaconsfield QC H9W 4J5, Canada

Weir, William F (Bill) — Commentator
ABC-TV, News Dept, 77 W 66th St, New York NY 10023 USA

Weis, Albert J (Al) — Baseball Player
902 S Poplar Ave, Elmhurst IL 60126, USA

Weis, Charles J (Charlie) — Football Coach
University of Kansas, Athletic Dept, Lawrence KS 66045, USA

Weis, Joseph F, Jr — Judge
US Court of Appeals, US Courthouse, 700 Grant St, #2270, Pittsburgh PA 15219, USA

Weisacosky, Edward L (Ed) — Football Player
3291 2nd Ave SE, Naples FL 34117, USA

Weisberg, Ruth E — Artist
11452 W Washington Blvd, Los Angeles CA 90066, USA

Weisberger, Lauren — Writer, Actress
Simon & Schuster, 1230 Ave of Americas, Concourse 1, New York NY 10020 USA

Weisel, Heidi — Fashion Designer
Heidi Weisel Inc, 420 W 14th St, #4SE, New York NY 10014, USA

Weishoff, Paula — Volleyball Player
20021 Colgate Circle, Huntington Beach CA 92646, USA

Weishuhn, Clayton C (Clay) — Football Player
4521 Kropala Road, San Angelo TX 76905, USA

Weiskopf, Tom — Golfer
Weiskopf Designs, 20875 N Pima Road, #C4-173, Scottsdale AZ 85255, USA

Weiskrantz, Lawrence — Psychologist
Oxford University, Experimental Psychology Dept, Oxford OX1 3UD, England

Weisman, Annie — Actress, Producer, Writer
Gersh Agency, 9465 Wilshire Blvd, #600, Beverly Hills CA 90212 USA

Weisman, Sam — Actor, Director, Producer
United Talent Agency, 9336 Civic Center Dr, Beverly Hills CA 90210 USA

Weiss, Avi — Religious Leader, Rabbi
Hebrew Institute of Riverdale, 3700 Henry Hudson Parkway, Bronx NY 10463, USA

Weiss, Brian L — Psychotherapist, Writer
Weiss Institute, PO Box 560788, Miami FL 33256, USA

Weiss, Cole Evan — Actor
Greene Assoc, 1901 Ave of Stars, #130, Los Angeles CA 90067 USA

Weiss, Daniel B (D B) — Producer, Writer
Creative Artists Agency, 2000 Ave of Stars, #100, Los Angeles CA 90067 USA

Weiss, David (David Was) — Musician (Was Not Was), Songwriter
United Talent Agency, 9336 Civic Center Dr, Beverly Hills CA 90210 USA

Weiss, Gary L — Baseball Player
1700 Weiss Lane, Brenham TX 77833, USA

Weiss, Janet — Singer, Drummer (Sleater-Kinney)
High Road Touring, 751 Bridgeway, #200, Sausalito CA 94965 USA

Weiss, Julie — Costume Designer
I C M Partners, 10250 Constellation Blvd, #900, Los Angeles CA 90067 USA

Weiss, Kenneth R — Journalist
Los Angeles Times, Editorial Dept, 202 W 1st St, Los Angeles CA 90012 USA

Weiss, Margaret — Writer
T S R, PO Box 707, Renton WA 98057, USA

Weiss, Marion — Architect, Sculptor
Weiss/Manfredi, 130 W 29th St, #1200, New York NY 10001, USA

Weiss, Mary — Singer (Shangri-Las)
Norton Records, PO Box 646, Cooper Station, New York NY 10276, USA

Weiss, Michael — Figure Skater
5301 Wisconsin Ave NW, #425, Washington DC 20015, USA

Weiss, Michael T — Actor, Director
Robert Stein Mgmt, 1180 S Beverly Drive, #304, Los Angeles CA 90035, USA

Weiss, Mitch — Journalist
Toledo Blade, 541 N Superior St, Toledo OH 43660 USA

Weiss, Orion — Concert Pianist
I M G Artists, Hogarth Business Park, Chiswick, London W4 2TH, England

Weiss, Robert W (Bob) — Basketball Player, Coach
3309 E Saint Andrews Way, Seattle WA 98112, USA

Weiss, Stephen — Ice Hockey Player
899 NW 123rd Dr, Coral Springs FL 33071, USA

Weiss, Walter W — Baseball Player
1275 Castle Point Dr, Castle Rock CO 80104, USA

Weissenbach, Jean — Geneticist
Genoscope, 2 Rue Gaston Cremieur, 91006 Evry Cedex, France

Weissensteiner, Gerda — Luge, Bobsled Athlete
Olympic Committee, Foro Italico, Largo Lauro de Bosis 15, 00135 Rome, Italy

Weissflog, Jens — Ski Jumper
Markt 2, 09484 Kurort Oberwiesenthal, Germany

Weissman, Irving L — Cancer Biologist, Pathologist
Stanford University, Pathology Dept, Beckman Center, Stanford CA 94305, USA

Weissman, Robert — Businessman
I M S Health Inc, 1499 Post Road, #12, Fairfield CT 06824, USA

Weisz, Rachel — Actress
Independent Talent Group, Oxford House, 76 Oxford St, London W1D 1BS, England

Weithaas, Antje — Concert Violinist
C L B Mgmt, 28 Earlswood Road, London NW10 5QB, England

Weithorn, Michael J — Director, Writer
I C M Partners, 10250 Constellation Blvd, #900, Los Angeles CA 90067 USA

Weitz, Bruce — Actor
18826 Erwin St, Tarzana CA 91335, USA

Weitz, Patricia — Writer
Riverhead/Penguin Books, 375 Hudson St, Basement 1, New York NY 10014, USA

Weitz, Paul — Director, Producer, Actor
Depth of Field, 1724 Whitley Ave, Los Angeles CA

Weitz, Paul J — Astronaut
3086 N Tam O'Shanter Dr, Flagstaff AZ 86004, USA

Weitzman, Howard L — Attorney
2049 Central Park East, #1400, Los Angeles CA 90067, USA

Weitzman, Matt — Producer, Writer, Actor
Creative Artists Agency, 2000 Ave of Stars, #100, Los Angeles CA 90067 USA

Weitzman, Richard L (Rick) — Basketball Player
76 Birch St, Peabody MA 01960, USA

Weixler, Jess — Actress, Writer
Gersh Agency, 9465 Wilshire Blvd, #600, Beverly Hills CA 90212 USA

Weizenbaum, Zoe — Actress
Innovative Artists, 1505 10th St, Santa Monica CA 90401 USA

Wejbe, Jolean — Actress
Abrams Artists, 9200 W Sunset Blvd, #1125, West Hollywood CA 90069 USA

Welbourn, John R — Football Player
3301 Palos Verdes Dr N, Palos Verdes Estates CA 90274, USA

Welch, Florence — Singer (Florence & the Machine)
Universal-Island Records, 22 Saint Peters Square, London W6 9NW, England

Welch, Gillian — Singer
Almo Sounds Records, 360 N La Cienega Blvd, West Hollywood CA 90048 USA

Welch, Herbert D (Herb), Jr — Football Player
999 La Senda, Santa Barbara CA 93105, USA

Welch, Jack — Astronomer
University of California, Electrical Engineering Dept, Berkeley CA 94720, USA

Welch, John F, Jr — Businessman
3135 Easton Turnpike, Fairfield CT 06828, USA

Welch, Justin — Drummer (Elastica)
C M O Mgmt, Ransomes Dock, 35-37 Parkgate Road, London SW11 4NP, England

Welch, Kevin — Singer, Songwriter
Keith Case Assoc, 1025 17th Ave S, #200, Nashville TN 37212 USA

Welch, Larry D — Air Force General
Henry L Stimson Center, 1111 19th St NW, #1200, Washington DC 20036, USA

Welch, Lenny — Singer
Lustig Talent, PO Box 770850, Orlando FL 32877 USA

Welch, Lisa — Model
Playboy Promotions, 2706 Media Center Dr, Los Angeles CA 90065 USA

Welch, Michael — Actor
Innovative Artists, 1505 10th St, Santa Monica CA 90401 USA

Welch, Raquel — Actress
Innovative Artists, 1505 10th St, Santa Monica CA 90401 USA

Welch, Robert L (Bob) — Baseball Player
11055 E Gold Dust Ave, Scottsdale AZ 85259, USA

Welch, Robert W (Bo), III — Production Designer, Director
United Talent Agency, 9336 Civic Center Dr, Beverly Hills CA 90210 USA

Welch, Tahnee — Actress, Model
John Doherity Mgmt, 125 Christopher St, #6C, New York NY 10014, USA

Weld, Tuesday K — Actress
711 W End Ave, #5KN, New York NY 10025, USA

Weld, William F — Governor, MA
Hale & Dorr, 60 State St, #25, Boston MA 02109, USA

Weldon, Fay — Writer
Casorotto Ramsay, Waverley House, 7-12 Noel St, London W1F 8GQ, England

Weldon, Joan — Actress
67 E 78th St, New York NY 10075, USA

Weldon, W Casey — Football Player
380 Castleton Ave, #5, Tallahassee FL 32312, USA

Weldon, William C — Businessman
Johnson & Johnson, 1 Johnson & Johnson Plaza, New Bruswick NJ 08933, USA

Welker, Frank — Actor
C E S D, 10635 Santa Monica Blvd, #130, Los Angeles CA 90025 USA

Welker, Wesley C (Wes) — Football Player
42 Commonwealth Ave, #5, Boston MA 02116, USA

Welland, Colin — Actor, Writer
United Agents, 12-26 Lexington St, London W1F 0LE, England

Wellber, Omer Meir — Conductor
I M G Artists, Hogarth Business Park, Chiswick, London W4 2TH, England

Wellemeyer, Todd A — Baseball Player
8402 Westover Dr, Prospect KY 40059, USA

Weller, Freddie — Singer, Songwriter
Ace Productions, PO Box 428, Portland TN 37148, USA

Weller, Frederick (Fred) — Actor
Baumgarten Mgmt, 11925 Wilshire Blvd, #310, Los Angeles CA 90025, USA

Weller, Josh — Singer, Songwriter
Agency Group Ltd, 142 W 57th St, #600, New York NY 10019 USA

Weller, Michael — Writer
Gersh Agency, 9465 Wilshire Blvd, #600, Beverly Hills CA 90212 USA

Weller, Paul — Singer, Musician (Jam), Songwriter
Go Discs Ltd, 72 Black Lion Lane, Hammersmith, London W6 9BE, England

Weller, Peter — Actor
A P A Talent/Literary Agency, 405 S Beverly Dr, #300, Beverly Hills CA 90212 USA

Weller, Walter — Conductor, Concert Violinist
Harrison/Parrott, 5-6 Albion Court, London W6 0QT, England

Welles, Terri — Model, Actress
PO Box 2549, Del Mar CA 92014, USA

Wellford, Harry W — Judge
US Court of Appeals, Federal Building, 167 N Main St, Memphis TN 38103, USA

Welling, Tom — Actor, Model
Tom Welling Productions, 9350 Wilshire Blvd, #250, Beverly Hills CA 90212, USA

Welliver, Titus	Actor
Leverage Mgmt, 3030 Pennsylvania Ave, Santa Monica CA 90404, USA	
Wellman, Brad E	Baseball Player
733 Graham Court, Danville CA 94526, USA	
Wellman, Gary J	Football Player
1638 Wellington Place, Westlake Village CA 91361, USA	
Wellman, Mac	Writer
Brooklyn College, Play Writing Dept, Brooklyn NY 11210, USA	
Wellman, William, Jr	Actor
15935 Meadowcrest Road, Sherman Oaks CA 91403, USA	
Wellner, Jon	Actor
Greater Vision Artists Talent Agency, 8981 Sunset Blvd, #101, Los Angeles CA 90069, USA	
Wells, Albert P	WW II Marine Corps Air Force Hero
903 Park Lane, Santa Barbara CA 93108, USA	
Wells, Annie	Photojournalist
Press Democrat, Editorial Dept, 427 Mendocino Ave, Santa Rosa CA 95401, USA	
Wells, Audrey	Writer, Director, Producer
Creative Artists Agency, 2000 Ave of Stars, #100, Los Angeles CA 90067 USA	
Wells, Chris	Ice Hockey Player
7228 Ridge Way, Park City UT 84098, USA	
Wells, Colin	Actor
Associated International Mgmt, Fairfax House, Fulwood Place, London WC1V 6HU, England	
Wells, Cory	Singer (Three Dog Night)
PO Box 96597, Las Vegas NV 89193, USA	
Wells, D Dean	Football Player
1146 Copperfield Dr, Georgetown IN 47122, USA	
Wells, David L (Dave)	Baseball Player
PO Box 8107, Rancho Santa Fe CA 92067, USA	
Wells, Dawn	Actress
Scott Stander Assoc, 4533 Van Nuys Blvd, #401, Sherman Oaks CA 91403 USA	
Wells, Gawen D (Bonzi)	Basketball Player
6416 N Bobtail Dr, Muncie IN 47304, USA	
Wells, Jay	Ice Hockey Player
Hockey School, 990 Keg Lane, RR 22, Paris ON N3L 3E2, Canada	
Wells, Joel W	Football Player
11 Flicker Point, Greenville SC 29609, USA	
Wells, John	Producer, Director
John Wells Productions, 4000 Warner Blvd, Building 1, Burbank CA 91522, USA	
Wells, Kerry Anne	Beauty Queen
Miss Universe Organization, 1370 Ave of Americas, #1600, New York NY 10019 USA	
Wells, Llewellyn	Producer, Director
United Talent Agency, 9336 Civic Center Dr, Beverly Hills CA 90210 USA	
Wells, Mark R	Ice Hockey Player
2341 Union Road, #132, West Seneca NY 14224, USA	
Wells, Matthew	Rowing Athlete
Leander Club, Henley on Thames, Leander RG9 2LP, England	
Wells, Patricia	Journalist
Harper Collins Publishers, 10 E 53rd St, Cellar 1, New York NY 10022 USA	
Wells, R Kip	Baseball Player
12891 Westbrook Dr, Tyler TX 75704, USA	
Wells, Reggie A	Football Player
2569 E Cherrywood Place, Chandler AZ 85249, USA	
Wells, Robert L (Bob)	Baseball Player
154 Wilcox Road, Cowiche WA 98923, USA	
Wells, Simon	Director
Todd Smith Assoc, 11835 W Olympic Blvd, #640, Los Angeles CA 90064, USA	
Wells, Stephen G	Educator
University of Nevada Reno, President's Office, Reno NV 89511, USA	
Wells, Theodore V, Jr	Attorney
Paul Weiss Rifkind Warton Garrison, 1285 Ave of Americas, New York NY 10019, USA	
Wells, Thomas B	Judge
US Tax Court, 400 2nd St NW, Washington DC 20217, USA	
Wells, Vernon, III	Baseball Player
2251 King Fisher Dr, Westlake TX 76262, USA	
Wells, Warren	Football Player
1399 Pipkin St, Beaumont TX 77705, USA	
Wells, Wayne A	Freestyle Wrestler
2010 S Broadway, Edmond OK 73013, USA	
Welp, Christian (Chris)	Basketball Player
20618 38th Dr SE, Bothell WA 98021, USA	
Welser-Most, Franz	Conductor
Cleveland Symphony, Severance Hall, 11001 Euclid Ave, Cleveland OH 44106, USA	
Welsh, Christopher C (Chris)	Baseball Player
12640 Huey Lane, Walton KY 41094, USA	
Welsh, Darrell G	Hero
102 El Rancho Way, San Antonio TX 78209, USA	
Welsh, David (Dave)	Guitarist (Fray)
A2 Mgmt, 624 Davis St, #200, Evanston IL 60201, USA	
Welsh, Irvine	Writer
Independent Talent Group, Oxford House, 76 Oxford St, London W1D 1BS, England	
Welsh, Moray M	Concert Cellist
28 Somerfield Ave, Queens Park, London NW6 6JY, England	
Welsh, Stephanie	Photojournalist
PO Box 277, Wayne ME 04284, USA	
Welsman, Carol	Singer, Pianist
Agency Group Ltd, 142 W 57th St, #600, New York NY 10019 USA	
Welsome-Martin, Eileen	Journalist
2040 Locust St, Denver CO 80207, USA	
Welteroth, Richard J (Dick)	Baseball Player
122 Eldred St, Williamsport PA 17701, USA	
Wen Jiabao	Premier, China
Premier's Office, Zhonganahai, Beijing 100017, China	
Wen, Ming-Na	Actress
9903 Santa Monica Blvd, #575, Beverly Hills CA 90212, USA	
Wendell, Krissy	Ice Hockey Player
325 9th St SE, Minneapolis MN 55414, USA	

Wendell, Steven J (Turk) — Baseball Player
227 Hidden Valley Lane, Castle Rock,CO 80108, USA
Wendelstedt, H Hunter, III — Baseball Umpire
3044 SW 98th Way, Gainesville FL 32608, USA
Wenden, Michael — Swimmer
Palm Beach Currumbin Center, Thrower Dr, Palm Beach Queens, Australia
Wenders, E Wilhelm (Wim) — Director
Neue Road Movies, Ackerstr 14/15, #4HH, 10115 Berlin, Germany
Wendkos, Gina — Writer
Industry Entertainment, 955 Carillo Dr, #300, Los Angeles CA 90048 USA
Wendl, Ingrid Turkovic- — Figure Skater
Parliament, Innere Stadt, Dr Karl-Renner Ring 3, 2004 Vienna, Austria
Wendt, George — Actor
Gage Group, 14724 Ventura Blvd, #505, Sherman Oaks CA 91403 USA
Wendt, Henry, III — Businessman
560 Warbass Way, Friday Harbor WA 98250, USA
Wengert, Donald P (Don) — Baseball Player
13100 Cedarwood Ave, Clive IA 50325, USA
Wengren, Mike — Drummer (Disturbed)
Mitch Schneider Organization, 14724 Ventura Blvd, #500, Sherman Oaks CA 91403 USA
Wenham, David — Actor
Markham & Froggatt, Julian House, 4 Windmill St, London W1P 1HF, England
Wenner, Jann S — Publisher, Producer
37 W 70th St, New York NY 10023, USA
Wennington, William P (Bill) — Basketball Player
1985 Oak Grove Lane, Lake Forest IL 60045, USA
Wensink, John — Ice Hockey Player
29311 Bidwell Creek Road, Fredericktown MO 63645, USA
Wenstrom, Matt — Basketball Player
15714 Blanco Trails Lane, Cypress TX 77429, USA
Went, Joseph J — Marine Corps General
9204 Kristin Lane, Fairfax VA 22032, USA
Wentworth, Alexandra — Actress, Comedienne, Writer
Gersh Agency, 9465 Wilshire Blvd, #600, Beverly Hills CA 90212 USA
Wentz, Pete — Bassist (Fall Out Boy), Lyricist
PO Box 219, 1187 Wilmette Ave, Wilmette IL 60091, USA
Wenz, Otto — Cycling Executive
14230 W Armour Ave, New Berlin WI 53151, USA
Wenzel, Andreas — Alpine Skier
9494 Planken 56, Liechtenstein
Wenzel, Hanni Weirather- — Alpine Skier
Fanalwegle 4, 9494 Schaan, Liechtenstein
Wenzel, Kurt — Writer
Random House, 1745 Broadway, #1800, New York NY 10019 USA
Wepner, Chuck — Boxer
153 Ave E, Bayonne NJ 07002, USA
Wepper, Fritz — Actor
N D F, Joseph-Dollinger-Bogen 26, 80807 Munich, Germany
Werbach, Adam — Environmentalist
Sierra Club, 85 2nd St, #200, San Francisco CA 94105, USA
Werbowy, Daria — Model
I M G Models, 304 Park Ave S, #PH-North, New York NY 10010 USA
Werdann, Robert — Basketball Player
4739 40th St, #5F, Sunnyside NY 11104, USA
Werenka, Bradley J (Brad) — Ice Hockey Player
PO Box 92030, Edgemont RPO, Calgary AB T3A 6L9, Canada
Werkheiser, Devon — Actor
Coast to Coast Talent, 3350 Barham Blvd, Los Angeles CA 90068, USA
Werley, George W — Baseball Player
15415 Elk Ridge Lane, Chesterfield MO 63017, USA
Werner, Anna — Commentator
KHOU-TV, News Department, 1945 Allan Parkway, Houston TX 77019, USA
Werner, Carla — Singer, Songwriter
PO Box 3241, Tamarama NSW 2026, Australia
Werner, Clyde L — Football Player
3009 Islandview Court, Gig Harbor WA 98335, USA
Werner, Donald P (Don) — Baseball Player
2204 Briarwood Blvd, Arlington TX 76013, USA
Werner, Marianne — Track Athlete
Gauseland 2A, 44227 Dortmund, Germany
Werner, Peter — Director
Paradigm Agency, 360 N Crescent Dr, North Building, Beverly Hills CA 90210 USA
Werner, Roger L, Jr — Businessman
Prime Sports Ventures, 10000 Santa Monica Blvd, Los Angeles CA 90067, USA
Werner, Tom — Producer
Good Humor Television, 9255 W Sunset Blvd, #1040, West Hollywood CA 90069, USA
Wersching, Annie — Actress
S M S Talent, 8383 Wilshire Blvd, #230, Beverly Hills CA 90211 USA
Wersching, Raimund (Ray) — Football Player
18 Buttercup Lane, San Carlos CA 94070, USA
Wert, Donald R (Don) — Baseball Player
341 Smithville Road, New Providence PA 17560, USA
Werth, Isabell — Equestrian
Winterswicker Feld 4, 47495 Rheinberg, Germany
Werth, Jayson R — Baseball Player
PO Box 13457, Springfield IL 62791, USA
Wertheim, Jorge — Association Executive
UNESCO, Director's Office, UN Plaza, New York NY 10017, USA
Wertheimer, Fredric M — Public Policy Activist
3502 Macomb St NW, Washington DC 20016, USA
Wertheimer, Linda — Commentator
National Public Radio, 635 Massachusetts Ave NW, #1, Washington DC 20001, USA
Wertimer, Ned — Actor
Acme Talent, 4727 Wilshire Blvd, #333, Los Angeles CA 90010, USA
Wertmuller, Lina — Director
Piazza Clotilde, 00196 Rome, Italy

Wertmuller, Massimo — Actor
Carol Levi Mgmt, Via G Pisanelli 2, 00196 Rome, Italy

Wertz, Matt — Singer, Songwriter
Creative Artists Agency, 2000 Ave of Stars, #100, Los Angeles CA 90067 USA

Wertz, William C (Bill) — Baseball Player
26514 Mingo Dr, Perrysburg OH 43551, USA

Wescott, Seth B — Snowboarding Athlete
Octagon Worldwide, 2 Union St, #300, Portland ME 04101 USA

Wesker, Arnold — Writer
Hay on Wye, Hereford HR3 5RJ, England

Wesley, Dante J — Football Player
104 Fawn Cove, White Hall AR 71602, USA

Wesley, David B — Basketball Player
2506 Baywater Canyon Dr, Pearland TX 77584, USA

Wesley, Glen E — Ice Hockey Player
5305 Newstead Manor Lane, Raleigh NC 27606, USA

Wesley, Gregory L (Greg) — Football Player
9752 Sunset Circle, Lenexa KS 66220, USA

Wesley, Norman H — Businessman
Fortune Brands Inc, 520 Lake Cook Road, Deerfield IL 60015, USA

Wesley, Paul — Actor, Producer
I C M Partners, 10250 Constellation Blvd, #900, Los Angeles CA 90067 USA

Wesley, Rutina — Actress
Inspire Entertainment, 2332 Cotner Ave, #302, Los Angeles CA 90064, USA

Wesley, Trevor (Blake) — Ice Hockey Player
Okanagan Hockey School, 101-697 Wade W, Penticton BC V2A 1V6, Canada

Wesley, Walter (Walt) — Basketball Player
6417 Scott Lane, Fort Myers FL 33966, USA

Wessel, Henry, Jr — Photographer
PO Box 475, Richmond CA 94807, USA

Wesson, Barry — Baseball Player
36 Shore Dr NE, Brookhaven MS 39601, USA

West, Adam — Actor
PO Box 3477, Ketchum ID 83340, USA

West, Billy — Actor
Danis Panaro Nist, 9201 W. Olympic Blvd, Beverly Hills CA 90212, USA

West, Chandra — Actress
Characters Talent Mgmt, 8 Elm St, Toronto ON M5G 1G7, Canada

West, Charles (Charlie) — Football Player
184 Laurel Ridge, South Salem NY 10590, USA

West, Cornel — Theologian, Sociologist
Princeton University, Afro American Studies Program, Princeton NJ 08544, USA

West, David J — Businessman
Hershey Co, 100 Crystal A Dr, PO Box 810, Hershey PA 17033, USA

West, David L — Baseball Player
1242 SW Seahawk Way, Palm City FL 34990, USA

West, Delonte — Basketball Player
8805 Charm Court, Brandywine MD 20613, USA

West, Dominic — Actor
W M E Entertainment, 9601 Wilshire Blvd, #300, Beverly Hills CA 90210 USA

West, Edward L (Ed), Jr — Football Player
1930 Ma Lee Dr, Moody AL 35004, USA

West, Ernest E — Korean War Army Hero (CMH)
912 Adams Ave, Greenup KY 41144, USA

West, Geoffrey — Theoretical Physicist
Santa Fe Institute, 1399 Hyde Park Road, Santa Fe NM 87501, USA

West, J Douglas (Doug) — Basketball Player
1131 Meridian Dr, Presto PA 15142, USA

West, Jacqueline — Costume Designer
Gersh Agency, 9465 Wilshire Blvd, #600, Beverly Hills CA 90212 USA

West, James E — Inventor (Telephone Microphone)
724 Berkeley Ave, Plainfield NJ 07062, USA

West, Jason — Video Games Developer
Respawn Entertainment, 5990 Sepulveda Blvd, Van Nuys CA 91411, USA

West, Jeffrey H (Jeff) — Football Player
12376 Adair Creek Way NE, Redmond WA 98053, USA

West, Jerome A (Jerry) — Basketball Player, Coach, Executive
Golden State Warriors, 1011 Broadway, Oakland CA 94605 USA

West, Joel — Model, Actor
Don Carroll Mgmt, 14211 Hatteras St, Sherman Oaks CA 91401, USA

West, Joseph H (Joe) — Baseball Umpire
17531 Cobblestone Lane, Clermont FL 34711, USA

West, Josh — Rowing Athlete
22 Cherwell St, Oxford OX 41BG, England

West, Kanye — Rap Artist, Music Producer
3200 Cherry Creek South Dr, #620, Denver CO 80209, USA

West, Keith — Bassist, Singer (Heartland)
Country Thunder Records, 1016 17th Ave S, Nashville TN 37212, USA

West, Leslie — Singer, Guitarist (Mountain)
James Faith Entertainment, 318 Wynne Lane, #14, Port Jefferson NY 11777, USA

West, Lizzie — Singer
Warner Bros Records, 3300 Warner Blvd, Burbank CA 91505 USA

West, Mario M — Basketball Player
390 Vine Mountain Way, Mableton GA 30126, USA

West, Mark A — Basketball Player
644 Old Wagner Road, Petersburg VA 23805, USA

West, Martin — Actor
427 N Canon Dr, Beverly Hills CA 90210, USA

West, Maura — Actress
Innovative Artists, 1505 10th St, Santa Monica CA 90401 USA

West, Nathan — Actor
United Talent Agency, 9336 Civic Center Dr, Beverly Hills CA 90210 USA

West, Paul — Writer
Elaine Markson Agency, 44 Greenwich Ave, #300, New York NY 10011, USA

West, Roland D — Basketball Player
7464 Shaker Run Lane, West Chester OH 45069, USA

West, Samuel — Actor
United Agents, 12-26 Lexington St, London W1F 0LE, England
West, Shane — Actor
Luber Rocklin Entertainment, 8530 Wilshire Blvd, #555, Beverly Hills CA 90211 USA
West, Shelly — Singer
Acts Nashville Talent, 1103 Bell Grimes Lane, Nashville TN 37207, USA
West, Simon — Director, Producer, Writer
Simon West Productions, 3450 Cahuenga Blvd W, Building 510, Los Angeles CA 90068, USA
West, Stu — Bassist (Damned)
Leave Home Booking, 10 W Broadway, #608, Salt Lake City UT 84101, USA
West, Timothy L — Actor
Gavin Barker Assoc, 2D Wimpole St, London W1G 0EB, England
West, Togo D, Jr — Secretary, Veterans Affairs
922 N Cameron Ave, Winston Salem NC 27101, USA
West, Willie T — Football Player
PO Box 50430, Eugene OR 97405, USA
Westbrook, Brian C — Football Player
6204 Blue Sage Lane, Upper Marlboro MD 20772, USA
Westbrook, Bryant A — Football Player
28017 N 17th Dr, Phoenix AZ 85085, USA
Westbrook, Dexter — Basketball Player
200 E Church Lane, #405, Philadelphia PA 19144, USA
Westbrook, Jacob C (Jake) — Baseball Player
PO Box 574, Danielsville GA 30633, USA
Westbrook, Michael D — Football Player
2797 E Teakwood Place, Chandler AZ 85249, USA
Westbrook, Peter — Fencer
15 Washington Place, #1F, New York NY 10003, USA
Westbrook, Russell — Basketball Player
Oklahoma City Thunder, 211 N Robinson Ave, #300, Oklahoma City OK 73102 USA
Westbrooks, Gregory M (Greg) — Football Player
3832 10th Avenue Place, Moline IL 61265, USA
Westenhiser, Jamie — Model
Playboy Promotions, 2706 Media Center Dr, Los Angeles CA 90065 USA
Westenra, Hayley — Singer
Decca Music Group, 347-353 Chiswick High Road, London W4 4HS, England
Westerberg, Paul — Singer, Guitarist, Songwriter
Mitch Schneider Organization, 14724 Ventura Blvd, #500, Sherman Oaks CA 91403 USA
Westfall, V Edward (Ed) — Ice Hockey Player
699 Hillside Ave, New Hyde Park NY 11040, USA
Westfeldt, Jennifer — Actress
Innovative Artists, 1505 10th St, Santa Monica CA 90401 USA
Westhead, Paul W — Basketball Coach
University of Oregon, Athletic Dept, Eugene OR 97403, USA
Westheimer, Gerald — Optometrist
582 Santa Barbara Road, Berkeley CA 94707, USA
Westheimer, Ruth S — Sex Therapist, Psychologist
C E S D, 10635 Santa Monica Blvd, #130, Los Angeles CA 90025 USA
Westin, Av — Businessman, Journalist
King World Productions, 1700 Broadway, #3200, New York NY 10019, USA
Westlake, Waldon T (Wally) — Baseball Player
3800 61st St, Sacramento CA 95820, USA
Westling, Jon — Educator
285 Goddard Ave, Brookline MA 02445, USA
Westmore, McKenzie K — Actress, Singer
W M E Entertainment, 9601 Wilshire Blvd, #300, Beverly Hills CA 90210 USA
Westmoreland, James — Actor
8019 1/2 W Norton Ave, West Hollywood CA 90046, USA
Westmoreland, Richard C (Dick) — Football Player
5601 Sea Reef Place, San Diego CA 92154, USA
Weston, Celia — Actress
Innovative Artists, 235 Park Ave S, #1000, New York NY 10003 USA
Weston, Ken — Sound Mixer
I C M Partners, 10250 Constellation Blvd, #900, Los Angeles CA 90067 USA
Weston, Kim — Singer
Powerplay, PO Box 533, 5434 W Sample Road, Margate FL 33073, USA
Weston, Michael — Actor
Management 360, 9111 Wilshire Blvd, Beverly Hills CA 90210 USA
Weston, Michael L (Mickey) — Baseball Player
2702 Eisenhower Ave, Valparaiso IN 46383, USA
Weston, Randolph (Randy) — Jazz Pianist
PO Box 749, Maplewood NJ 07040, USA
Weston, Stan — Businessman
Leisure Concepts, 1414 Ave of Americas, New York NY 10019, USA
Weston-Jones, Tom — Actor
Markham & Froggatt, Julian House, 4 Windmill St, London W1P 1HF, England
Westphal, Paul D — Basketball Player, Coach
1424 Granvia Altamira, Palos Verdes Estates CA 90274, USA
Westwick, Edward G (Ed) — Actor, Singer
Emptage Hallett, 14 Rathbone Place, London W1T 1HT, England
Westwood, Joey — Bassist (Red Jumpsuit Apparatus)
Virgin Records, 338 N Foothill Road, Beverly Hills CA 90210 USA
Westwood, Vivienne — Fashion Designer
Lanterns #3, Old School House, Bridge Lane, London SW11 3AD, England
Wetherbee, James D — Astronaut
3818 Trailstone Lane, Katy TX 77494, USA
Wetherby, Jeffrey B (Jeff) — Baseball Player
28410 Great Bend Place, Fresno CA 93710, USA
Wethington, Charles T, Jr — Educator
2926 Four Pines Dr, Lexington KY 40502, USA
Wetnight, Ryan S — Football Player
95 W Prescott Ave, Clovis CA 93619, USA
Wetoska, Robert S (Bob) — Football Player
1295 Forest Glen Dr S, Winnetka IL 60093, USA
Wetteland, John K — Baseball Player
1229 Kentucky Derby Dr, Argyle TX 76226, USA

W

West - Wetteland

Wetter, Friedrich Cardinal Erziozese Munich, Postfach 100551, 80079 Munich, Germany	Religious Leader
Wetterich, Brett 149 Morning Dew Circle, Jupiter FL 33458, USA	Golfer
Wettig, Patricia Innovative Artists, 1505 10th St, Santa Monica CA 90401 USA	Actress
Wetton, John Siren Artist Mgmt, 4446 W 169th St, Lawndale CA 90260, USA	Singer, Bassist (Asia, UK)
Wetzel, Carl 9401 James Ave S, #11, Minneapolis MN 55431, USA	Ice Hockey Player
Wetzel, Donald C (Don) 5706 Trail Meadow Dr, Dallas TX 75230, USA	Inventor (Automated Teller Machine)
Wetzel, Gary G PO Box 84, Oak Creek WI 53154, USA	Vietnam War Army Hero (CMH)
Wetzel, John F 13011 N Sunrise Canyon Lane, Marana AZ 85658, USA	Basketball Player, Coach
Wetzel, Robert G 16 Dunbrook, Tuscaloosa AL 35406, USA	Botanist
Wetzel, Robert L 1425 Dartmouth Road, Columbus GA 31904, USA	Army General
Wever, Merritt Innovative Artists, 1505 10th St, Santa Monica CA 90401 USA	Actress
Wever, Stefan M 7 Corte Los Sombras, Greenbrae CA 94904, USA	Baseball Player
Wexler, Haskell 1247 Lincoln Blvd, #585, Santa Monica CA 90401, USA	Cinematographer
Wexler, Nancy S Hereditary Disease Foundation, 3960 Broadway, New York NY 10032, USA	Clinical Psychologist
Wexler, Robert Brandeis-Bardin, 1101 Peppertree, Brandeis CA 93064, USA	Religious Leader, Rabbi, Educator
Wexler, Robert F Middle East Peace Center, 633 Pennsylvania NW, #500, Washington DC 20004, USA	Representative, FL
Weyerhaeuser, George Weyerhaeuser Co, 33663 32nd Ave S, Federal Way WA 98023, USA	Businessman
Weymouth, Tina Premier Talent, 3 E 54th St, #1100, New York NY 10022 USA	Bassist (Talking Heads, Tom Tom Club)
Whalen, James F (Jim), Jr 9 Wauketa Road, Gloucester MA 01930, USA	Football Player
Whalen, Laurence J US Tax Court, 400 2nd St NW, Washington DC 20217, USA	Judge
Whalen, Lindsay M Minnesota Lynx, Target Center, 600 1st Ave N, Minneapolis MN 55403 USA	Basketball Player
Whalen, Sara 10 Francis Dr, Greenlawn NY 11740, USA	Soccer Player
Whaley, Frank A P A Talent/Literary Agency, 405 S Beverly Dr, #300, Beverly Hills CA 90212 USA	Actor
Whaley, Suzi 15 Whitehall Place, Farmington CT 06032, USA	Golfer
Whalin, Justin G Deborah Miller, 9454 Wilshire Blvd, #715, Beverly Hills CA 90212, USA	Actor
Whalley, Joanne Lou Coulson Assoc, 37 Berwick St, London W1V 8RS, England	Actress
Whalum, Kirk Cole Classic Mgmt, PO Box 231, Canoga Park CA 91305, USA	Jazz Saxophonist
Whang, Suzanne I C M Partners, 10250 Constellation Blvd, #900, Los Angeles CA 90067 USA	Actress
Whannell, Leigh Paradigm Agency, 360 N Crescent Dr, North Building, Beverly Hills CA 90210 USA	Actor
Wharram, Ken 382 Aubrey St W, North Bay ON P1B 6H9, Canada	Ice Hockey Player
Wharton, Bernard Shope Reno Wharton, 18 Marshall St, #114, Norwalk CT 06854, USA	Architect
Wharton, G Travelle 103 Havendale Dr, Fountain Inn SC 29644, USA	Football Player
Whatley, Ennis 42 Brinkwood Road, Brookeville MD 20833, USA	Basketball Player
Whatmore, Sarah L Fremantle Media, 2700 Colorado Ave, #450, Santa Monica CA 90404 USA	Singer
Wheatcroft, Georgina Curling Assn, 1660 Vimont Court, Cumberland ON K4A 4J4, Canada	Curling Athlete
Wheatley, Ben W M E Entertainment, 9601 Wilshire Blvd, #300, Beverly Hills CA 90210 USA	Director
Wheatley, Kevin Seven Summits Mgmt, 8906 W Olympic Blvd, Beverly Hills CA 90211 USA	Actor
Wheatley, Tyrone A 5500 Sandstone Way, Fayetteville NY 13066, USA	Football Player
Wheaton, David PO Box 401, Tonka Bay MN 55331, USA	Tennis Player
Wheaton, Wil Monolith Press, 713 W Duarte Road, #G, Arcadia CA 91007, USA	Actor
Whedon, Joseph H (Joss) Creative Artists Agency, 2000 Ave of Stars, #100, Los Angeles CA 90067 USA	Actor, Director, Producer
Wheeldon, Christopher Morphoses/Wheeldon Co, 800 5th Ave, #18F, New York NY 10065, USA	Choreographer, Ballet Dancer
Wheeler, Adam 4854 Jedediah Smith Road, Colorado Springs CO 80922, USA	Greco-Roman Wrestler
Wheeler, Cheryl Morningstar Mgmt, PO Box 1770, Hendersonville TN 37077, USA	Singer, Songwriter
Wheeler, Clinton 199 Scenic View Lane, Stone Mountain GA 30087, USA	Basketball Player
Wheeler, Daniel M (Dan) 215 Harrison Ave, Belleair Beach FL 33786, USA	Baseball Player
Wheeler, Dwight 2012 Sunnyslope Lane, Goodlettsville TN 37072, USA	Football Player
Wheeler, Gary Perkins & Will, 330 N Wabash Ave, #3600, Chicago IL 60611, USA	Interior Designer

Name / Address	Occupation
Wheeler, H Anthony South Inverleith Manor, 31/6 Kinnear Road, Edinburgh EH3 5PG, Scotland	Architect
Wheeler, Howard A (Humpy) Wheeler Co, PO Box 1327, Cornelius NC 28031, USA	Auto Racing Executive
Wheeler, John A 414 Troy Court, Claremont CA 91711, USA	Actor
Wheeler, Maggie Affirmative Entertainment, 425 N Robertson Blvd, Los Angeles CA 90048 USA	Actress
Wheeler, Mark A 101 Meadowridge Cove, San Marcos TX 78666, USA	Football Player
Wheeler, Nicholas D (Nick) Creative Artists Agency, 2000 Ave of Stars, #100, Los Angeles CA 90067 USA	Singer, Guitarist (All-American Rejects)
Wheeler-Nicholson, Dana Glick Agency, 1321 7th St, #203, Santa Monica CA 90401 USA	Actress
Wheelock, Douglas H PO Box 580408, Houston TX 77258, USA	Astronaut
Wheelock, Gary R 3354 N Park St, Buckeye AZ 85396, USA	Baseball Player
Whelan, Bill Sony Records, 2100 Colorado Ave, Santa Monica CA 90404 USA	Composer
Whelan, Gary Ken McReddie Assoc, 11 Connaught Place, London W2 2ET, England	Actor
Whelan, Jill Scott Stander Assoc, 4533 Van Nuys Blvd, #401, Sherman Oaks CA 91403 USA	Actress
Whelan, Julia M Innovative Artists, 1505 10th St, Santa Monica CA 90401 USA	Actress
Whelan, Nicky United Talent Agency, 9336 Civic Center Dr, Beverly Hills CA 90210 USA	Actress, Model
Whelan, Peter Lemon Unna Durbridge, Holland Park, 24 Pottery Lane, London W11 4LZ, England	Writer
Whelan, Wendy New York City Ballet, Lincoln Center Plaza, New York NY 10023 USA	Ballerina
Whelchel, Lisa Arcieri Assoc, 305 Madison Ave, #2315, New York NY 10165 USA	Actress
Wheless, Jamy 405 Fair St, Petaluma CA 94952, USA	Animator
Whicker, Alan D Trinity, Jersey JE3 5BA, Channel Islands, England	Commentator
Whigham, Larry J 33 Collins Road, Hattiesburg MS 39401, USA	Football Player
Whigham, Shea Principal Entertainment, 1964 Westwood Blvd, #400, Los Angeles CA 90025 USA	Actor
Whillock, Jack F 2118 River Ridge Road, Arlington TX 76017, USA	Baseball Player
Whimper, Guy 1010 Main St, New Bern NC 28560, USA	Football Player
Whinnery, Barbara Baier/Kleinman, 3575 Cahuenga Blvd, #500, Los Angeles CA 90068 USA	Actress
Whirry, Shannon Ford/Robert Black Agency, 4032 N Miller Road, #104, Scottsdale AZ 95251, USA	Actress
Whisenant, Matthew M (Matt) 1035 Fairview Dr, La Canada Flintridge CA 91011, USA	Baseball Player
Whisenhunt, Ken 6905 E Cheney Dr, Paradise Valley AZ 85253, USA	Football Player, Coach
Whishaw, Anthony 7A Albert Place, Victoria Road, London W8 5PD, England	Artist
Whishaw, Ben Hamilton Hodell, 66-68 Margaret St, London W1W 8SR, England	Actor
Whisler, J Steven Phelps Dodge Corp, 1 N Central Ave, #100, Phoenix AZ 85004, USA	Businessman
Whiston, Donald (Don) 2 Jeffreys Neck Road, Ipswich MA 01938, USA	Ice Hockey Player
Whitacre, Edward E, Jr General Motors Corp, 100 Renaissance Center, Detroit MI 48243, USA	Businessman
Whitaker, Denzel Luber Rocklin Entertainment, 8530 Wilshire Blvd, #555, Beverly Hills CA 90211 USA	Actor
Whitaker, Forest Spirit Dance Entertainment, 1023 N Orange Dr, Los Angeles CA 90038, USA	Actor, Director
Whitaker, Jack 500 Berwyn Baptist Road, Devon PA 19333, USA	Sportscaster
Whitaker, Jack International Golf Partners, 3300 PGA Blvd, #820, Palm Beach Gardens FL 33410, USA	Golfer
Whitaker, Louis R (Lou), Jr 17 Brownstone Lane, Greensboro NC 27410, USA	Baseball Player
Whitaker, Meade US Tax Court, 400 2nd St NW, Washington DC 20217, USA	Judge
Whitaker, Pernell 310 Nottawat Court, Chesapeake VA 23320, USA	Boxer
Whitaker, Steve E 900 SE 6th Court, Fort Lauderdale FL 33301, USA	Baseball Player
Whitbread, Fatima Javel-Inn, Mill Hill, Shenfield, Brentwood, Essex CM15 8EU, England	Track Athlete
Whitby, William E (Bill) 13926 Huntersville Concord Road, Huntersville NC 28078, USA	Baseball Player
Whitcomb, Bob Whitcomb Racing, 9201 Garrison Road, Charlotte NC 28278, USA	Auto Racing Executive
Whitcomb, Edgar D 15415 Rome Road, Rome IN 47574, USA	Governor, IN
Whitcomb, Ian PO Box 451, Altadena CA 91003, USA	Singer, Songwriter
White, Adrian D 688 Allen Lane, Orange Park FL 32073, USA	Football Player
White, Alan, III Ignition Mgmt, 54 Linhope St, London NW1 6HL, England	Drummer (Yes, Oasis)
White, Andrew N, III Vezco Productions, 163 Main St, Odessa ON K0H 2H0, Canada	Jazz Saxophonist

White, Andrew R (Whitey) — Guitarist (Kaiser Chiefs)
Red Light Mgmt, 8439 Sunset Blvd, West Hollywood CA 90069, USA
White, Betty M — Actress, Comedienne
PO Box 491965, Los Angeles CA 90049, USA
White, Brian — Ice Hockey Player
3 Gedick Road, Burlington MA 01803, USA
White, Brian J, Jr — Actor
United Talent Agency, 9336 Civic Center Dr, Beverly Hills CA 90210 USA
White, Brooke — Singer, Songwriter, Actress
Glick Agency, 1321 7th St, #203, Santa Monica CA 90401 USA
White, Bryan — Singer, Songwriter
Holly Co, 3415 W End Ave, #101G, Nashville TN 37203, USA
White, Charles R — Football Player, Administrator
31841 Via Faisan, Trabuco Canyon CA 92679, USA
White, Charlie — Ice Dancer
Arctic Edge Skating Club, 46615 Michigan Ave, Canton MI 48188, USA
White, Chris — Bassist (Zombies)
Lustig Talent, PO Box 770850, Orlando FL 32877 USA
White, Devon M — Baseball Player
6440 E Sierra Vista Dr, Paradise Valley AZ 85253, USA
White, Dewayne (D J), Jr — Basketball Player
Charlotte Bobcats, 333 E Trade St, #A, Charlotte NC 28202 USA
White, Donna — Golfer
200 Caribe Court, Greenacres FL 33413, USA
White, Dwayne A — Football Player
2117 Pinehurst Way, Coral Springs FL 33071, USA
White, Edmund V — Writer
I C M Partners, 10250 Constellation Blvd, #900, Los Angeles CA 90067 USA
White, Edward A (Ed) — Football Player
PO Box 1437, Julian CA 92036, USA
White, Eugene — Baseball Player
4166 Lockhart Dr N, Jacksonville FL 32209, USA
White, G Edward — Educator, Attorney
University of Virginia, Law School, Charlottesville VA 22903, USA
White, Gabriel A (Gabe) — Baseball Player
1571 Lakeview Dr, Sebring FL 33870, USA
White, Gary C — Biologist
Water.org, 920 Main St, #1800, Kansas City MO 64105, USA
White, Harvey D — Cardiologist
Green Lane Hospital, Cardioloy Dept, PB 92189, Auckland 1030, New Zealand
White, Hubert L (Hubie) — Basketball Player
101 E Gowen Ave, Philadelphia PA 19119, USA
White, J Colin — Ice Hockey Player
81 Western Ave, Morristown NJ 07960, USA
White, J Michael (Mike) — Baseball Player
26438 S Jardin Dr, Sun Lakes AZ 85248, USA
White, Jack — Singer, Guitarist (White Stripes)
Monotone Mgmt, 820 Seward St, Los Angeles CA 90038, USA
White, Jaleel — Actor
Pantheon Talent, 1801 Century Park E, #1910, Los Angeles CA 90067, USA
White, James C (Jim) — Football Player
14430 Andrea Way Lane, Houston TX 77083, USA
White, James L — Writer
I C M Partners, 10250 Constellation Blvd, #900, Los Angeles CA 90067 USA
White, James W, IV — Basketball Player
New York Knicks, Madison Square Garden, 2 Penn Plaza, New York, NY 10121 USA
White, Jason — Football Player
3203 Stone Dr, Tuttle OK 73089, USA
White, Jeordie O — Bassist (Marilyn Manson, Perfect Circle)
Coast II Coast Entertainment, 8671 Wilshire Blvd, Beverly Hills CA 90211, USA
White, Jeris J — Football Player
15 N Wisner St, Frederick MD 21701, USA
White, Jerome C (Jerry) — Baseball Player
343 N Wildwood, Hercules CA 94547, USA
White, Jessica — Model
Elite Model Mgmt, 345 N Maple Dr, #176, Beverly Hills CA 90210 USA
White, John H — Photojournalist
Chicago Sun-Times, Editorial Dept, 401 N Wabash Ave, Chicago IL 60611 USA
White, John Patrick — Actor
C E S D, 10635 Santa Monica Blvd, #130, Los Angeles CA 90025 USA
White, Joseph H (Jo Jo) — Basketball Player
2 Mansfield Road, Middleton MA 01949, USA
White, Josh, Jr — Singer
23625 Ripple Creek, Novi MI 48375, USA
White, Joy Lynn — Singer
Fat City Artists, 1906 Chet Atkins Place, #502, Nashville TN 37212 USA
White, Julie — Actress, Singer
Himber Entertainment, PO Box 950, South Orange NJ 07079 USA
White, Karyn — Singer
Cavaleri Assoc, 178 S Victory Blvd, #205, Burbank CA 91502, USA
White, Katie — Singer, Guitarist (Ting Tings)
Paradigm Agency, 404 W Franklin St, Monterey CA 93940 USA
White, Lari — Singer, Songwriter
R C A Records, 1400 18th Ave S, Nashville TN 37212 USA
White, Lee A — Football Player
600 Langtry Dr, Las Vegas NV 89107, USA
White, Lillias — Actress
TalentWorks, 3500 W Olive Ave, #1400, Burbank CA 91505 USA
White, Lorenzo M — Football Player
2860 Somerset Dr, #111, Lauderdale Lakes FL 33311, USA
White, Marco P — Chef
The Restaurant, 66 Knightsbridge, London SW1X 7LA, England
White, Marilyn — Track Athlete
9605 6th Ave, Inglewood CA 90305, USA
White, Mark — Musician (Spin Doctors)
D A S Communications, 83 Riverside Dr, New York NY 10024 USA

White, Mary Anne — Chemist
30 Burnt Log Crescent, Etobicoke ON M9C 2J8, Canada
White, Matthew J (Matt) — Baseball Player
1853 Old Route 9, Windsor MA 01270, USA
White, Maurice — Singer (Earth Wind & Fire), Songwriter
Spirit Media, PO Box 43591, Phoenix AZ 85080, USA
White, Meg — Singer, Drummer (White Stripes)
Monotone Mgmt, 820 Seward St, Los Angeles CA 90038, USA
White, Michael D — Businessman
DirecTV, 2230 E Imperial Hwy, El Segundo CA 90245, USA
White, Michael Jai — Actor, Director
Rip Cord Productions, 5555 Melrose Ave, #115, Los Angeles CA 90038, USA
White, Michael R — Mayor, Cleveland
11655 Blue Ridge Road, Newcomerstown OH 43832, USA
White, Michael S — Producer
48 Dean St, London W1V 5HL, England
White, Mike — Football Coach
115 Grand Canal, Newport Beach CA 92662, USA
White, Mike — Actor, Director, Writer
United Talent Agency, 9336 Civic Center Dr, Beverly Hills CA 90210 USA
White, Miles D — Businessman
Abbott Laboratories, 100 Abbott Park Road, North Chicago IL 60064, USA
White, Myron A — Baseball Player
3201 S Deegan Dr, Santa Ana CA 92704, USA
White, Nera D — Basketball Player
RR 3 Box 165, Lafayette TN 37083, USA
White, Persia — Singer, Songwriter, Actress
Stone Manners Salners, 9911 W Pico Blvd, #1400, Los Angeles CA 90035 USA
White, Peter — Actor
S M S Talent, 8383 Wilshire Blvd, #230, Beverly Hills CA 90211 USA
White, Randy L — Football Player
1360 E Frontier Parkway, Prosper TX 75078, USA
White, Raymond P, Jr — Oral Surgeon
1506 Velma Road, Chapel Hill NC 27514, USA
White, Rex — Auto Racing Driver
187 Rivers Road, #222, Fayetteville GA 30214, USA
White, Richard A (Rick) — Baseball Player
2860 Windy Ridge Dr, Springfield OH 45502, USA
White, Robert — Artist
380 Millwood Ave, Winchester VA 22601, USA
White, Robert M — Meteorologist
Somerset House II, 5610 Wisconsin Ave, #1506, Chevy Chase MD 20815, USA
White, Ron — Actor, Writer, Producer
A P A Talent/Literary Agency, 405 S Beverly Dr, #300, Beverly Hills CA 90212 USA
White, Rondell B — Baseball Player
407 Creekside Dr, Gray GA 31032, USA
White, Rory W — Basketball Player
5303 32nd St S, Fargo ND 58104, USA
White, Roy H — Baseball Player
534 Mill Pond Way, Eatontown NJ 07724, USA
White, Royce A — Basketball Player
Houston Rockets, 1730 Jefferson St, Houston TX 77003 USA
White, Samuel (Sammy) — Football Player
102 Margaret Dr, Monroe LA 71203, USA
White, Sharod L (Roddy) — Football Player
2540 Shumard Oak Dr, Braselton GA 30517, USA
White, Shaun — Snowboard, Skateboard Athlete
Burton Snowboards, 80 Industrial Parkway, Burlington VT 05401, USA
White, Sheldon D — Football Player
PO Box 622, Novi MI 48376, USA
White, Sherman E (Sherm) — Football Player
2710 Summerland Road, Aromas CA 95004, USA
White, Stanley R (Stan) — Football Player
10716 Pot Spring Road, Cockeysville MD 21030, USA
White, Stephen G (Steve) — Football Player
72 Morton Ave, West Hempstead NY 11552, USA
White, Steven A — Navy Admiral, Businessman
Stone & Webster Engineering, 4 Mount Royal Ave, #420, Marlboro MA 01752, USA
White, Susanna — Director
United Talent Agency, 9336 Civic Center Dr, Beverly Hills CA 90210 USA
White, Sylvain — Director
United Talent Agency, 9336 Civic Center Dr, Beverly Hills CA 90210 USA
White, Timothy D — Anthropologist
University of California, Human Evolutionary Studies Laboratory, Berkeley CA 94720, USA
White, Timothy P — Educator
University of California, Chancellor's Office, 900 University Ave, Riverside CA 92521, USA
White, Vanna — Entertainer, Actress, Model
'Wheel of Fortune' Show, 10202 W Washington Blvd, #2000, Culver City CA 90232, USA
White, Verdine — Bassist (Earth Wind & Fire), Songwriter
Spirit Media, PO Box 43591, Phoenix AZ 85080, USA
White, W Daniel (Danny) — Football Player
902 E San Angelo Ave, Gilbert AZ 85234, USA
White, Willard W — Opera Singer
10 Montague Ave, London SE4 1YP, England
White, William B (Bill) — Baseball Player, Executive
8517 Barn Owl, San Antonio TX 78255, USA
White, William E — Football Player
2323 Woodland Hall Dr, Powell OH 43065, USA
Whited, Edward M (Ed) — Baseball Player
PO Box 34, Carmel IN 46082, USA
Whitehead, Axle — Actor
United Talent Agency, 9336 Civic Center Dr, Beverly Hills CA 90210 USA
Whitehead, Barb — Golfer
9820 E Thompson Peak Parkway, #707, Scottsdale AZ 85255, USA
Whitehead, Colson — Writer
Doubleday Press, 1745 Broadway, New York NY 10019 USA

W

White - Whitehead

Whitehead, Geoffrey — Actor
Bryan Drew, Quadrant House, 80-82 Regent St, London W1B 5AU, England
Whitehead, Jerome C — Basketball Player
1543 Merritt Dr, El Cajon CA 92020, USA
Whitehead, John A — Physical Oceanographer
Woods Hole Oceanographic Institution, Physical Oceanography Dept, Woods Hole MA 02543, USA
Whitehead, John C — Foundation Executive, Financier
Goldman Sachs Foundation, 85 Broad St, Building 85, New York NY 10004, USA
Whitehead, Lorne A — Inventor (Prism Light Guide System)
T I R Systems, 77 Riverfront Gate, Burnaby BC V5J 5M4, Canada
Whitehead, Nicole — Model
Playboy Promotions, 2706 Media Center Dr, Los Angeles CA 90065 USA
Whitehead, Paxton — Actor
Gary Goddard Agency, 10 Saint Mary's St, Toronto ON M4Y 1P9, Canada
Whitehead, Rachel — Sculptor
Luhring Augustine Gallery, 531 W 24th St, New York NY 10011, USA
Whitehead, Richard F — Navy Admiral
American Cage & Machine Co, 135 S LaSalle St, Chicago IL 60603, USA
Whitehead, Ruben A (Bud) — Football Player
5438 N Brooks Ave, Fresno CA 93711, USA
Whitehurst, C David — Football Player
11010 Linbrook Lane, Duluth GA 30097, USA
Whitehurst, Walter R (Wally) — Baseball Player
102 Beverly Dr, Bay Saint Louis MS 39520, USA
Whitelaw, Billie — Actress
Rose Cottage, Plum St, Glensford, Suffolk C010 7PX, England
Whiteman, Andrew — Guitarist (Apostle of Hustle)
High Road Touring, 751 Bridgeway, #200, Sausalito CA 94965 USA
Whitemore, Hugh — Writer
Creative Artists Agency, 2000 Ave of Stars, #100, Los Angeles CA 90067 USA
Whitemore, Willet F, Jr — Cancer Researcher
2 Hawthorne Lane, Manhasset NY 11030, USA
Whiten, Mark A — Baseball Player
5810 Jefferson Park Dr, Tampa FL 33625, USA
Whiteread, Rachel — Sculptor
Anthony D'Offay, 22 Dering St, London W1R 9AA, England
Whitesell, Emily — Writer, Producer, Actress
Rain Management Group, 1631 21st St, Santa Monica CA 90404, USA
Whitesell, John P — Director
Collective, 8383 Wilshire Blvd, #1050, Beverly Hills CA 90211 USA
Whitesell, Sean — Actor, Producer, Writer
United Talent Agency, 9336 Civic Center Dr, Beverly Hills CA 90210 USA
Whiteside, Matthew C (Matt) — Baseball Player
255 Palisades Ridge Court, Eureka MO 63025, USA
Whitesides, George M — Chemist
124 Grasmere St, Newton MA 02458, USA
Whitfield, Charles Malik — Actor
Paradigm Agency, 360 N Crescent Dr, North Building, Beverly Hills CA 90210 USA
Whitfield, Dondre — Actor
Paul Kohner, 9300 Wilshire Blvd, #555, Beverly Hills CA 90212 USA
Whitfield, Fred — Rodeo Rider
17915 Becker Road, Hockley TX 77447, USA
Whitfield, Fred D — Baseball Player
2532 Fairview Road, Gadsden AL 35904, USA
Whitfield, Lynn — Actress
Allman/Rea Mgmt, 9355 Sunset Blvd, #600, Los Angeles CA 90069, USA
Whitfield, Malvin G (Mal) — Track Athlete
1322 28th St SE, Washington DC 20020, USA
Whitfield, Simon — Triathlete
Triathlon Canada, 4050 Wheelwright Crest, Mississauga ON L5L 2X5, Canada
Whitfield, Terry B — Baseball Player
849 Clearfield Dr, Millbrae CA 94030, USA
Whitfield, Trent — Ice Hockey Player
8781 Piney Orchard Parkway, Odenton MD 21113, USA
Whitford, Bradley E (Brad) — Guitarist (Aerosmith)
Front Line Mgmt, 1100 Glendon Ave, #2000, Los Angeles CA 90024 USA
Whitham, Gerald B — Mathematician
California Institute of Technology, Mathematics Dept, Pasadena CA 91125, USA
Whiting, Lynn S — Thoroughbred Racing Trainer
Lynn S Whiting Stable, 700 Central Ave, Louisville KY 40208, USA
Whitlam, E Gough — Prime Minister, Australia
Westfield Towers, 100 William St, Sydney NSW 2011, Australia
Whitley, Kym — Actress
Innovative Artists, 1505 10th St, Santa Monica CA 90401 USA
Whitlock, Isiah, Jr — Actor
Liebman Entertainment, 25 E 21st St, #PH, New York NY 10010 USA
Whitlow, Robert E (Bob) — Football Player
2005 S Rogers St, #41, Bloomington IN 47403, USA
Whitman, Kari — Actress, Model
House of Representatives, 1434 6th St, #1, Santa Monica CA 90401 USA
Whitman, Mae — Actress
I C M Partners, 10250 Constellation Blvd, #900, Los Angeles CA 90067 USA
Whitman, Margaret C (Meg) — Businesswoman
Hewlett Packard Co, 3000 Hanover St, Palo Alto CA 94304, USA
Whitman, Marina Von Neumann — Economist, Government Official
University of Michigan, Public Policy School, Ann Arbor MI 48109, USA
Whitman, Slim — Singer, Guitarist
3830 Old Jennings Road, Middleburg FL 32068, USA
Whitman, Stuart — Actor
749 San Ysidro Road, Santa Barbara CA 93108, USA
Whitmore, James, Jr — Actor
1284 La Brea St, Thousand Oaks CA 91362, USA
Whitmore, Jon — Educator
Texas Tech University, President's Office, Lubbock TX 79409, USA
Whitmore, Kay — Ice Hockey Player
National Hockey League, 50 Bay St, #1100, Toronto ON M5J 2X8, Canada

Whitmore, Tamika — Basketball Player
Connecticut Sun, 1 Mohegan Sun Blvd, Uncasville CT 06382 USA
Whitner, Donte — Football Player
San Francisco 49ers, 4949 Centennial Blvd, Santa Clara CA 95054 USA
Whitney, Ashley A — Swimmer
124 Hearthstone Manor Circle, Brentwood TN 37027, USA
Whitney, CeCe — Actress
16857 San Fernando Mission Blvd, #46, Granada Hills CA 91344, USA
Whitney, David — Basketball Coach, Baseball Player
2178 Popps Ferry Road, Biloxi MS 39532, USA
Whitney, Grace Lee — Actress
PO Box 1869, Coarsegold CA 93614, USA
Whitney, Ray — Ice Hockey Player
2908 Spaldwick Court, Raleigh NC 27613, USA
Whitney, Ryan — Ice Hockey Player
7 Stone Ave, Scituate MA 02066, USA
Whitson, Eddie L (Ed) — Baseball Player
10473 Mackenzie Way, Dublin OH 43017, USA
Whitson, Peggy A — Astronaut
306 Lakeview Circle, Seabrook TX 77586, USA
Whitt, Ernest L (Ernie) — Baseball Player
37370 Moravian Dr, Clinton Township MI 48036, USA
Whittaker, James (Jim) — Mountaineer
2023 E Sims Way, #277, Port Townsend WA 98368, USA
Whittaker, Jodie — Actress
Independent Talent Group, Oxford House, 76 Oxford St, London W1D 1BS, England
Whittaker, Roger — Singer, Songwriter
B M L Mgmt, 426 Marsh Point Circle, Saint Augustine FL 32080, USA
Whitted, Alvis J — Football Player
3 New Bedford Court, Durham NC 27704, USA
Whittenton, U Jesse — Football Player
1748 Boulders Dr, Las Cruces NM 88011, USA
Whittingham, Charles A — Publisher
1 E 66th St, #13D, New York NY 10065, USA
Whittington, Arthur L (Art) — Football Player
6709 La Tijera Blvd, #190, Los Angeles CA 90045, USA
Whittington, Bill — Auto Racing Driver
1881 W State Road 84, Fort Lauderdale FL 33315, USA
Whittington, Reginald (Don) — Auto Racing Driver
1881 W State Road 54, Fort Lauderdale FL 33315, USA
Whittle, Jason — Football Player
PO Box 1980, Osage Beach MO 65065, USA
Whitton, Margaret — Actress, Producer, Director
Tashtego Films, 11 W 10th St, New York NY
Whitwam, David R — Businessman
Whirlpool Corp, 2000 N State St, RR 63, Benton Harbor MI 49022, USA
Whitworth, Andrew J — Football Player
903 Adams Crossing, #110, Cincinnati OH 45202, USA
Whitworth, Johnny — Actor, Producer
Greene Assoc, 1901 Ave of Stars, #130, Los Angeles CA 90067 USA
Whitworth, Kathrynne A (Kathy) — Golfer
1735 Mistletoe Dr, Flower Mound TX 75022, USA
Whyte, Sandra — Ice Hockey Player
81 Golden Hills Road, Saugus MA 01906, USA
Whyte, Sean — Ice Hockey Player
14315 W Desert Hills Dr, Surprise AZ 85379, USA
Wi, Charlie — Golfer
9400 Burnet Ave, #109, North Hills CA 91343, USA
Wiberg, Kenneth B — Chemist
160 Carmalt Road, Hamden CT 06517, USA
Wiberg, Pernilla — Alpine Skier
Katterunsvagen 32, 60 210 Norrkopping, Sweden
Wickander, Kevin D — Baseball Player
4319 W Banff Lane, Glendale AZ 85306, USA
Wickenheiser, Hayley — Ice Hockey Player
Team Canada, 2424 University Dr NW, Calgary AB T2N 3Y9, Canada
Wicker, Floyd E — Baseball Player
1758 W Greensboro-Chapel Hill Road, Snow Camp NC 27349, USA
Wickersham, David C (Dave) — Baseball Player
9118 W 104th Terrace, Overland Park KS 66212, USA
Wickersham, Emily — Actress
W M E Entertainment, 9601 Wilshire Blvd, #300, Beverly Hills CA 90210 USA
Wickham, John A, Jr — Army General
13500 N Rancho Vistoso Blvd, #519, Tucson AZ 85755, USA
Wickham, Madeleine — Writer
Thomas Dunne/Saint Martin's Press, 175 5th Ave, #400, New York NY 10010, USA
Wicki-Fink, Agnes — Actress
Weisgerberstr 2, 80805 Munich, Germany
Wickman, Robert J (Bob) — Baseball Player
6568 Cheyenne Dr, Abrams WI 54101, USA
Wickner, Reed B — Geneticist
National Institutes of Health, 9000 Rockville Pike, Bethesda MD 20892, USA
Wickner, Sue H — Molecular Biolgist
N C I Molecular Biology Laboratory, 37 Convent Dr, Bethesda MN 20892, USA
Wicks, Ben — Editorial Cartoonist
38 Yorkville Ave, Toronto ON M4W 1L5, Canada
Wicks, Chuck — Singer, Songwriter
Sony/B M G Records, 9830 Wilshire Blvd, Beverly Hills CA 90212, USA
Wicks, Ron — Ice Hockey Player
4 McLaughlin Road S, Brampton ON L6Y 3B2, Canada
Wicks, Sidney — Basketball Player
8650 Cashio St, #5, Los Angeles CA 90035, USA
Wicks, Sue — Basketball Player
New York Liberty, Madison Square Garden, 2 Penn Plaza, New York NY 10121 USA
Wickwire, Jim — Mountaineer
1416 W Roy St, Seattle WA 98112, USA

Whitmore - Wickwire

Wickwire, Maria — Sculptor
PO Box 2911, Battle Creek WA 97604, USA

Wicoff, Erika — Golfer
7815 Four Leaf Dr, Greenville IN 47124, USA

Widby, G Ronald (Ron) — Football, Basketball Player
542 Mahler Road, Wichita Falls TX 76310, USA

Widdoes, Jamie — Director, Producer, Actor
United Talent Agency, 9336 Civic Center Dr, Beverly Hills CA 90210 USA

Widdoes, Kathleen — Actress
24 E 11th St, New York NY 10003, USA

Widdrington, Peter N T — Businessman
Laidlaw Inc, 3221 N Service Road, Burlington ON L7R 3Y8, Canada

Widell, David H (Dave) — Football Player
13050 Wexford Hollow Road N, Jacksonville FL 32224, USA

Widell, Douglas J (Doug) — Football Player
4638 Pebble Brook Dr, Jacksonville FL 32224, USA

Wideman, John Edgar — Writer
University of Massachusetts, English Dept, Amherst MA 01003, USA

Widger, Christopher J (Chris) — Baseball Player
95 Fort Mott Road, Pennsville NJ 08070, USA

Widman, Herbert (Herb) — Water Polo Player
844 Monarch Circle, San Jose CA 95138, USA

Widmann, Jorg — Concert Clarinetist, Composer
Schott Music, Weihergarten 5, 55116 Mainz, Germany

Widmer, Corey E — Football Player
PO Box 1201, Manhattan MT 59741, USA

Widmer-Schlumpf, Eveline — President, Switzerland
Federal Chancellery, Bundeshaus-W, Bundesgasse, 3033 Berne, Switzerland

Widom, Benjamin — Chemist
204 The Parkway, Ithaca NY 14850, USA

Wie, Michelle — Golfer
17217 Leal Ave, Cerritos CA 90703, USA

Wiebe, Susanne — Fashion Designer
Amalienstr 39, 80799 Munich, Germany

Wiegert, Zachary A (Zach) — Football Player
919 N 264th St, Waterloo NE 68069, USA

Wieghaus, Thomas R (Tom) — Baseball Player
9724 E 8000 Road, #N, Grant Park IL 60940, USA

Wiegmann, Casey P — Football Player
21010 W 60th Terrace, Shawnee KS 66218, USA

Wiehl, Christopher — Actor
A P A Talent/Literary Agency, 405 S Beverly Dr, #300, Beverly Hills CA 90212 USA

Wielicki, Krzysztof — Mountaineer
Ul A Frycza Modrzewskiego 21, 43 100 Tychy, Poland

Wieman, Carl E — Nobel Physics Laureate
University of Colorado, Physics Dept, Campus Box 440, Boulder CO 80309, USA

Wiemer, Jason — Ice Hockey Player
428-5201 Dalhousie Dr NW, Calgary AB T3A 5Y7, Canada

Wiener, Jacques L, Jr — Judge
US Court of Appeals, 600 Camp St, New Orleans LA 70130, USA

Wier, Murray N — Basketball Player, Coach
118 Goodwater St, Georgetown TX 78633, USA

Wiercinski, Francis — Army General
Deputy Commander in Chief, Army Pacific Command, Honolulu HI 96861 USA

Wieringa, Jeffrey A — Navy Admiral
Director, Defense Security Cooperation Agency, Pentagon, Washington DC 20301, USA

Wieschaus, Eric F — Nobel Medicine Laureate
11 Pelham St, Boston MA 02118, USA

Wiese, John P — Judge
US Claims Court, 717 Madison Place NW, Washington DC 20439, USA

Wiesel, Elie — Writer, Nobel Peace Laureate
10155 Collins Ave, #1502, Bal Harbor FL 33154, USA

Wiesenhahn, Robert B (Bob) — Basketball Player
3315 Hickorycreek Dr, Cincinnati OH 45244, USA

Wiesler, Robert G (Bob) — Baseball Player
2325 Indiancup Dr, Florissant MO 63033, USA

Wiesner, Kenneth (Ken) — Track Athlete
3601 Meta Lake Road, Eagle River WI 54521, USA

Wiest, Dianne — Actress
I C M Partners, 730 5th Ave, New York NY 10019 USA

Wiggin, Paul — Football Player, Coach
5013 Ridge Road, Minneapolis MN 55436, USA

Wiggin, Tom — Actor
Don Buchwald/Fortitude, 6500 Wilshire Blvd, #2200, Los Angeles CA 90048 USA

Wiggins, Audrey — Singer
PO Box 121196, Nashville TN 37212, USA

Wiggins, Bradley M — Cyclist
Team High Road, 425 O'Connor Way, San Luis Obispo CA 93405, USA

Wiggins, Jermaine — Football Player
111 Boston St, Topsfield MA 1983, USA

Wiggins, John — Singer
W M E Entertainment, 1600 Division St, #300, Nashville TN 37203 USA

Wiggins, Laura Slade — Actress
Osbrink Talent Agency, 4343 Lankershim Blvd, #100, North Hollywood CA 91602 USA

Wiggins, Mitchell L — Basketball Player
PO Box 5072, Kinston NC 28503, USA

Wiggins, Phil — Singer, Harmonica Player, Songwriter
Blue Mountain Artists, 810 Tyvola Road, #114, Charlotte NC 28217, USA

Wigginton, Ty A — Baseball Player
120 Manitoba Lane, Mooresville NC 28117, USA

Wigglesworth, Marian McKean — Alpine Skier
General Delivery, Wilson WY 83014, USA

Wigglesworth, Mark — Conductor
C M Artists, 127 W 96th St, #13B, New York NY 10025 USA

Wigglesworth, Ryan — Composer, Conductor
Konzertdirektion Schmid, Konigstra 36, 30175 Hannover, Germany

Wiggs, Susan — Writer
PO Box 4469, Rolling Bay WA 98061, USA

Wightman, Arthur S — Mathematician, Physicist
16 Balsam Lane, Princeton NJ 08540, USA

Wihtol, Alexander A (Sandy) — Baseball Player
1889 Anthony Court, Mountain View CA 94040, USA

Wiig, Kristen C — Actress, Comedienne, Writer
United Talent Agency, 9336 Civic Center Dr, Beverly Hills CA 90210 USA

Wiik, Sven — Skier
PO Box 774484, Steamboat Springs CO 80477, USA

Wiita, Carrie — Actress
OmniPop Talent Group, 4605 Lankershim Blvd, #201, Toluca Lake CA 91602 USA

Wilander, Mats — Tennis Player
104 Cove Creek Road, Hailey ID 83333, USA

Wilborn, Thaddeaus I (Ted) — Baseball Player
6671 Pocket Road, Sacramento CA 95831, USA

Wilbraham, John H G — Concert Cornetist, Trumpeter
9 Cuthbert St, Wells, Somerset BA5 2AW, England

Wilbur, Delbert Q (Del) — Baseball Player
4378 Autumn Lane, Lewiston NY 14092, USA

Wilbur, Richard C — Judge
US Tax Court, 400 2nd St NW, Washington DC 20217, USA

Wilbur, Richard P — Writer
87 Dodswell Road, Cummington MA 01026, USA

Wilbur, Richard S — Physician, Association Executive
985 Hawthorne Place, Lake Forest IL 60045, USA

Wilburn, Johnnie R (J R), Jr — Football Player
2211 Chalkwell Dr, Midlothian VA 23113, USA

Wilburn, Ken — Basketball Player
17 E Meyran Ave, Somers Point NJ 08244, USA

Wilby, James — Actor
Artist Rights Group, 4 Great Portland Place, London W1W 8PA, England

Wilcher, Mary — Actress
Levine Mgmt, 9028 W Sunset Blvd, #PH1, West Hollywood CA 90069, USA

Wilcher, Michael D (Mike) — Football Player
1501 Fairlakes Place, Bowie MD 20721, USA

Wilcox, Barry — Ice Hockey Player
18859 86th Ave, Surrey BC V4N 3G5, Canada

Wilcox, Chris R — Basketball Player
Boston Celtics, 226 Causeway St, #4, Boston MA 02114 USA

Wilcox, Daniel — Football Player
4119 Old Washington Blvd, Halethorpe MD 21227, USA

Wilcox, David — Singer, Songwriter
Elizabeth Rush Agency, 82 Cumberland Ave, Verona NJ 07044, USA

Wilcox, David (Dave) — Football Player
94471 Willamette Dr, Junction City OR 97448, USA

Wilcox, Larry — Actor
10 Appaloosa Lane, Bell Canyon CA 91307, USA

Wilcox, Lisa — Actress
Stone Manners Salners, 9911 W Pico Blvd, #1400, Los Angeles CA 90035 USA

Wilcox, Milton E (Milt) — Baseball Player
1630 Lakeview Dr, Wolverine Lake MI 48390, USA

Wilcox, Shannon — Actress
20518 Pacific Coast Highway, Malibu CA 90265, USA

Wilcutt, Terence W (Terry) — Astronaut
N A S A, Johnson Space Center, 2101 NASA Road, Houston TX 77058 USA

Wilczek, Frank A — Nobel Physics Laureate
4 Wyman Road, Cambridge MA 02138, USA

Wild, John P — Astronomer
1 Grant Crescent, #4, Griffith ACT 2603, Australia

Wilde, Claudine — Actress
Actors Connection Agentur, Kuckucksberg 9, 22952 La Tjensee, Germany

Wilde, Gabriella — Actress
I C M Partners, 10250 Constellation Blvd, #900, Los Angeles CA 90067 USA

Wilde, Kim — Singer, Songwriter
Marty Wilde, Thatched Rest, Queen Hoo Lane, Tewin, Hertfordshire AL6 0LT, England

Wilde, Olivia — Actress
Hamilton Hodell, 66-68 Margaret St, London W1W 8SR, England

Wilde, Patricia — Ballerina, Artistic Director
Pittsburgh Ballet Theater, 2900 Liberty Ave, Pittsburgh PA 15201, USA

Wilder, Alan C — Synthesizer Musician (Depeche Mode)
Creative Artists Agency, 2000 Ave of Stars, #100, Los Angeles CA 90067 USA

Wilder, Don — Cartoonist (Crock)
North American Syndicate, 235 E 45th St, New York NY 10017 USA

Wilder, Gene — Actor, Director
476 Scofieldtown Road, Stamford CT 06903, USA

Wilder, James — Actor
Chasen Agency, 8899 Beverly Blvd, #716, Los Angeles CA 90048 USA

Wilder, James C — Football Player
49 S Shirley St, Pontiac MI 48342, USA

Wilder, L Douglas — Governor, VA; Educator
Mayor's Office, City Hall, 900 E Broad St, Richmond VA 23219, USA

Wildes, Kevin W — Educator
Loyola University, President's Office, 6363 Saint Charles Ave, New Orleans LA 70118, USA

Wildman, George — Cartoonist (Popeye)
601 N Atlantic Ave, #603, New Smyrna FL 32169, USA

Wildman, Valerie — Actress
Scott Hart Mgmt, 14622 Ventura Blvd, #746, Sherman Oaks CA 91403, USA

Wildmon, Donald — Social Activist
National Federation of Decency, PO Box 1398, Tupelo MS 38802, USA

Wilds, Tristan — Actor
I C M Partners, 10250 Constellation Blvd, #900, Los Angeles CA 90067 USA

Wiles, Andrew J — Mathematician
Princeton University, Mathematics Dept, Princeton NJ 08544, USA

Wiles, Jason — Actor
Brillstein Entertainment Partners, 9150 Wilshire Blvd, #350, Beverly Hills CA 90212 USA

Wiles, Michael Shamus — Actor
Greene Assoc, 1901 Ave of Stars, #130, Los Angeles CA 90067 USA
Wiles, Randall E (Randy) — Baseball Player
3716 Lake Catherine Dr, Harvey LA 70058, USA
Wiley, John F (Jack) — Football Player
1330 India Hook Road, #306, Rock Hill SC 29732, USA
Wiley, Lee — Singer
Country Crossroads, 7787 Monterey St, Gilroy CA 95020, USA
Wiley, Marcellus V — Football Player
5132 S Garth Ave, Los Angeles CA 90056, USA
Wiley, Morlon D — Basketball Player
2521 Fallview Lane, Carrollton TX 75007, USA
Wiley, Richard E — Government Official
Wiley Rein, 1776 K St NW, #1100, Washington DC 20006, USA
Wiley, William T — Artist
PO Box 661, Forest Knolls CA 94933, USA
Wilfong, Robert D (Rob) — Baseball Player
126 Maverick Dr, San Dimas CA 91773, USA
Wilford, Ernest L, Jr — Football Player
1516 Chatham Court, Saint Augustine FL 32092, USA
Wilford, John Noble, Jr — Journalist
232 W 10th St, New York NY 10014, USA
Wilfork, Vince L — Football Player
11 White Dove Road, Franklin MA 02038, USA
Wilhelm, David C — WW II Army Air Corps Hero
3333 E Florida Ave, #113, Denver CO 80210, USA
Wilhelm, Erik B — Football Player
PO Box 1602, Clackamas OR 97015, USA
Wilhelm, James W (Jim) — Baseball Player
348 Laurel Way, Mill Valley CA 94941, USA
Wilhelm, John W — Labor Leader
Hotel & Restaurant Employees Union, 1219 28th St NW, Washington DC 20007, USA
Wilhelm, Kati — Biathlete
Sport Marketing, Schaumainkai 91, 60596 Frankfurt am Main, Germany
Wilhelm, Matthew (Matt) — Football Player
14944 Huntington Gate Dr, Poway CA 92064, USA
Wilhoite, Kathleen — Actress
Gersh Agency, 9465 Wilshire Blvd, #600, Beverly Hills CA 90212 USA
Wilk, Brad — Drummer (Rage Against the Machine)
The Firm, 2049 Century Park E, #2550, Los Angeles CA 90067 USA
Wilk, Vic — Golfer
1350 N Town Center Dr, #2082, Las Vegas NV 89144, USA
Wilkening, Laurel L — Educator
University of California, Chancellor's Office, Irvine CA 92717, USA
Wilkens, Leonard R (Lenny), Jr — Basketball Player, Coach, Executive
3429 Evergreen Point Road, Medina WA 98039, USA
Wilker, Greg — Photographer
3601 NW Adriatic Lane, Jensen Beach FL 34957, USA
Wilkerson, Bruce A — Football Player
2013 Breakers Point, Knoxville TN 37922, USA
Wilkerson, Curtis V — Baseball Player
PO Box 182993, Arlington TX 76096, USA
Wilkerson, Douglas (Doug) — Football Player
PO Box 7090, Rancho Santa Fe CA 92067, USA
Wilkerson, Isabel — Journalist
New York Times, Editorial Dept, 229 W 43rd St, New York NY 10036, USA
Wilkerson, Robert L (Bob) — Basketball Player
PO Box 7453, Upper Marlboro MD 20792, USA
Wilkerson, S Bradley (Brad) — Baseball Player
5640 Native Dancer Road S, Palm Beach Gardens FL 33418, USA
Wilkerson, Tim — Drag Racing Driver
Demand Flow Racing, 2901 Stevenson Dr, Springfield IL 62703, USA
Wilkes, Debbi — Figure Skater
Skate Canada, 865 Shefford Road, Ottawa ON K1J 1H9, Canada
Wilkes, Glenn — Basketball Coach
Stetson University, Athletic Dept, Campus Box 8359, DeLand FL 32720, USA
Wilkes, Jamaal A — Basketball Player
7846 W 81st St, Playa del Rey CA 90293, USA
Wilkes, Reggie W — Football Player
6912 Wissahickon Ave, Philadelphia PA 19119, USA
Wilkie, Bob — Ice Hockey Player
303 S Forge Road, Palmyra PA 17078, USA
Wilkie, Chris — Guitarist (Dubstar)
Primary Talent Int'l, 2-12 Petonville Road, London N1 9PL, England
Wilkie, David — Ice Hockey Player
15309 Tucker St, Bennington NE 68007, USA
Wilkie, David A — Swimmer
Oaklands, Queens Hill, Ascot, Berkshire, England
Wilkin, Richard E — Religious Leader
Winebrenner Theological Seminary, 950 N Main St, Findlay OH 45840, USA
Wilkins Perez, Laisha — Actress
Televisa, Blvd A Lopez Mateos 232, Colonia San Angel, DF CP 01060, Mexico
Wilkins, Barry — Ice Hockey Player
2230 W Monroe St, Chandler AZ 85224, USA
Wilkins, Donna — Golfer
3617 Bancroft Main NW, Kennesaw GA 30144, USA
Wilkins, Eric L — Baseball Player
1650 W Joshua Lane, Meridian ID 83642, USA
Wilkins, J Dominique — Basketball Player
4415 Felix Way SE, Smyrna GA 30082, USA
Wilkins, Jeffrey A (Jeff) — Football Player
8288 S Raccoon Road, Canfield OH 44406, USA
Wilkins, Marc A — Baseball Player
1636 State Route 314 N, Mansfield OH 44903, USA
Wilkins, Maurice (Mac) — Track Athlete
1915 NW Columbine Lane, Portland OR 97229, USA

Wilkins, Richard D (Rick) — Baseball Player
12766 Longview Dr W, Jacksonville FL 32223, USA
Wilkins, William W, Jr — Judge
US Court of Appeals, PO Box 10648, Greenville SC 29603, USA
Wilkinson, Adrienne — Actress
Greater Visions Artists Talent Agency, 8981 W Sunset Blvd, #101, West Hollywood CA 90069 USA
Wilkinson, Amanda — Singer (Wilkinsons)
Fitzgerald-Hartley, 1908 Wedgewood Ave, Nashville TN 37212, USA
Wilkinson, Clive — Interior Designer, Architect
Clive Wilkinson Architect, 6116 Washington Blvd, Culver City CA 90232, USA
Wilkinson, Dale W — Basketball Player
3045 Goldfield Dr, Pocatello ID 83201, USA
Wilkinson, Daniel R (Dan) — Football Player
222 Republic Dr, Allen Park MI 48101, USA
Wilkinson, J Harvie, III — Judge
US Court of Appeals, 255 W Main St, Charlottesville VA 22902, USA
Wilkinson, Joseph B, Jr — Navy Admiral
340 Chesapeake Dr, Great Falls VA 22066, USA
Wilkinson, June — Model, Actress
4060 E Grenora Way, Long Beach CA 90815, USA
Wilkinson, Kendra — Actress, Model
A P A Talent/Literary Agency, 405 S Beverly Dr, #300, Beverly Hills CA 90212 USA
Wilkinson, Laura — Diver
PO Box 131961, Spring TX 77393, USA
Wilkinson, Leon — Bassist (Lynyrd Skynyrd)
Alliance Artists, 6025 Comers Parkway, #202, Norcross GA 30092, USA
Wilkinson, Neil — Ice Hockey Player
PO Box 57, Sherwood OR 97140, USA
Wilkinson, Rhian — Soccer Player
Canadian Soccer, Place Soccer Canada, 237 Metcalfe St, Ottawa ON K2P 1R2, Canada
Wilkinson, Signe — Editorial Cartoonist
Philadelphia Daily News, Editorial Dept, 400 N Broad, Philadelphia PA 19130, USA
Wilkinson, Steve — Singer (Wilkinsons)
Fitzgerald Hartley, 1908 Wedgewood Ave, Nashville TN 37212, USA
Wilkinson, Tom — Actor
Lou Coulson Assoc, 37 Berwick St, London W1V 8RS, England
Wilkinson, Tyler — Singer (Wilkinsons)
Fitzgerald Hartley, 1908 Wedgewood Ave, Nashville TN 37212, USA
Wilks, Carol — Director
Associated International Mgmt, Fairfax House, Fulwood Place, London WC1V 6HU, England
Wilks, Jimmy R (Jim) — Football Player
4314 Leaflock Lane, Katy TX 77450, USA
Will, George F — Columnist
9 Grafton St, Chevy Chase MD 20815, USA
Will, Robert L (Bob) — Baseball Player
3417 S Country Club Road, Woodstock IL 60098, USA
Will.I.Am — Rap Artist (Elephunk, Black Eyed Peas)
Susan Blond Inc, 50 W 57th St, #1400, New York NY 10019 USA
Willard, Fred C — Actor, Comedian
Amsel Eisenstadt Frazier, 5055 Wilshire Blvd, #865, Los Angeles CA 90036 USA
Willard, Gerald D (Jerry) — Baseball Player
1421 Kumquat Place, Oxnard CA 93036, USA
Willard, Kenneth H (Ken) — Football Player
3071 Vistapoint Road, Midlothian VA 23113, USA
Willard, Rod — Ice Hockey Player
18 Overlook Dr, Wilbraham MA 01095, USA
Willcocks, David V — Concert Organist, Conductor
13 Grange Road, Cambridge CB3 9AS, England
Willcuts, Lori — Singer
Willcutts, 1102 N Springbrook Road, Newberg OR 97132, USA
Willem-Alexander — Crown Prince, Netherlands
Binnenhof 19, 2513 AA The Hague, Netherlands
Willet, E Crosby — Glass Artist
Willet Stained Glass Studios, 811 E Cayuga St, Philadelphia PA 19124, USA
Willett, Chad — Actor
Storylab Productions, 440 W 17th Ave, Vancouver BC V5Y2A2, Canada
Willett, Malcolm — Cartoonist (Tight Corner)
Universal Press Syndicate, 4520 Main St, #700, Kansas City MO 64111 USA
Willette, JoAnn — Actress
I C M Partners, 10250 Constellation Blvd, #900, Los Angeles CA 90067 USA
Will-Halpin, Maggie — Golfer
12423 Camoustie Lane, Richmond VA 23236, USA
Willhite, Gerald W — Football Player
10464 Iliff Court, Rancho Cordova CA 95670, USA
William — Prince, England
Clarence House, Stable Yard Gate, London SW1A 1BA, England
Williams of Crosby, Shirley V T B — Government Official, England
House of Lords, Westminster, London SW1A 0PW, England
Williams, Aeneas D — Football Player
PO Box 16291, Saint Louis MO 63105, USA
Williams, Alfred H — Football Player
Sports Radio 104.3, 7800 E Orchard Road, Greenwood Village CO 80111, USA
Williams, Allison — Actress
Paradigm Agency, 360 N Crescent Dr, North Building, Beverly Hills CA 90210 USA
Williams, Alvin L — Basketball Player
Toronto Raptors, Air Canada Center, 20 Bay St, Toronto ON M5J 2N8, Canada
Williams, Andy — Drummer (Doves)
C E S D, 10635 Santa Monica Blvd, #130, Los Angeles CA 90025 USA
Williams, Ann Claire — Judge
US Court of Appeals, 219 S Dearborn St, Chicago IL 60604, USA
Williams, Anson — Actor
24612 Skyline View Dr, Malibu CA 90265, USA
Williams, Anthony D (Tony) — Football Player
1918 Bridgewater Dr, Lake Mary FL 32746, USA
Williams, Ashley — Actress
Gersh Agency, 9465 Wilshire Blvd, #600, Beverly Hills CA 90212 USA

W

Wilkins - Williams

Williams, Ashley C — Actress
Mind the Art Entertainment, 346 Gates Ave, #2D, New York NY 11216, USA

Williams, Austin — Actor
Gersh Agency, 9465 Wilshire Blvd, #600, Beverly Hills CA 90212 USA

Williams, Barbara — Actress
S M S Talent, 8383 Wilshire Blvd, #230, Beverly Hills CA 90211 USA

Williams, Barry — Actor, Singer
Amsel Eisenstadt Frazier, 5055 Wilshire Blvd, #865, Los Angeles CA 90036 USA

Williams, Bernabe F (Bernie) — Baseball Player, Guitarist, Composer
5 Hallock Place, Armonk NY 10504, USA

Williams, Bernard (Bernie) — Baseball Player
1801 14th St, #210, Oakland CA 94607, USA

Williams, Beth — Model
Playboy Promotions, 2706 Media Center Dr, Los Angeles CA 90065 USA

Williams, Betty — Nobel Peace Laureate
Knock Inverin, County Galway, Ireland

Williams, Billy — Cinematographer
Coach House, Hawkshill Place, Esher, Surrey KT10 9HY, England

Williams, Billy Dee — Actor
Coolwaters Productions, 10061 Riverside Dr, Box 531, Toluca Lake CA 91602 USA

Williams, Billy L — Baseball Player
586 Prince Edward Road, Glen Ellyn IL 60137, USA

Williams, Brian — Football Player
8704 Shady Hill Court, Colfax NC 27235, USA

Williams, Brian — Commentator
NBC-TV, News Dept, 30 Rockefeller Plaza, #270E, New York NY 10112 USA

Williams, Brian M — Football Player
1133 Ashington Place, DeSoto TX 75115, USA

Williams, Brian O — Baseball Player
2409 Colt Lane, Crowley TX 76036, USA

Williams, Brian S — Football Player
1725 Charleston Lane, Waconia MN 55387, USA

Williams, Bunny — Interior Designer
306 E 61st St, #500, New York NY 10065, USA

Williams, C K — Writer
Princeton University, English Dept, Princeton NJ 08544, USA

Williams, Calvin J, Jr — Football Player
5032 Yellowood Ave, Baltimore MD 21209, USA

Williams, Cara — Actress
9903 Santa Monica Blvd, #606, Beverly Hills CA 90212, USA

Williams, Carnell L (Cadillac) — Football Player
6127 Parkside Meadow Dr, Tampa FL 33625, USA

Williams, Caroline — Actress
International Talent Agency, 10 NBC Universal Studios Plaza, #2000, Universal City CA 91608, USA

Williams, Cecil — Religious Leader, Social Activist
Glide Memorial United Methodist Church, 330 Ellis St, San Francisco CA 94102, USA

Williams, Charles E (Charlie) — Basketball Player
18675 Parkland Dr, #409, Shaker Heights OH 44122, USA

Williams, Charles L (Buck) — Basketball Player
9219 Fox Meadow Lane, Potomac MD 20854, USA

Williams, Charles P (Charlie) — Baseball Player
44 Frederick Ave, Port Orange FL 32127, USA

Williams, Charlie U — Football Player
3052 England Parkway, Grand Prairie TX 75054, USA

Williams, Christine — Model
Playboy Promotions, 2706 Media Center Dr, Los Angeles CA 90065 USA

Williams, Christopher J (Chris) — Actor
Artist Mgmt, 1118 15th St, #1, Santa Monica CA 90403, USA

Williams, Christy — Artist
2745 NE 89th St, Seattle WA 98115, USA

Williams, Cindy — Actress
Cindy Williams Productions, 499 Canon Dr, #216, Beverly Hills CA 90210, USA

Williams, Clarence — Photojournalist
Los Angeles Times, Editorial Dept, 145 S Spring St, Los Angeles CA 90012, USA

Williams, Clarence, III — Actor
Flick East-West, 9057 Nemo St, #A, West Hollywood, CA 90069 USA

Williams, Clevan (Tank) — Football Player
4053 Alexis Dr, Antioch TN 37013, USA

Williams, Clifford (Cliff) — Bassist (AC/DC)
Alberts Music, 9 Rangers Road, Neutral Bay, Sydney NSW 2089, Australia

Williams, Clyde A — Football Player
9754 Highway 79, Bethany LA 71007, USA

Williams, Colleen — Commentator
KNBC-TV, News Dept, 3000 W Alameda Ave, Burbank CA 91523, USA

Williams, Cress — Actor
Abrams Artists, 275 7th Ave, #2600, New York NY 10001 USA

Williams, Curtis — Singer (Penguins)
David Harris Enterprises, 24210 E Fork Road, #9, Azusa CA 91702, USA

Williams, Cynda — Actress
Innovative Artists, 1505 10th St, Santa Monica CA 90401 USA

Williams, D Keith — Baseball Player
1756 N Avignon Lane, Clovis CA 93619, USA

Williams, Dafydd R (David) — Astronaut
N A S A, Johnson Space Center, 2101 NASA Road, Houston TX 77058 USA

Williams, Dallas M — Baseball Player
7638 Allenwood Circle, Indianapolis IN 46268, USA

Williams, Dan, II — Football Player
4731 Corina Place NE, Roswell GA 30075, USA

Williams, Dana — Bassist, Drummer (Diamond Rio)
Modern Mgmt, 1625 Broadway, #600, Nashville TN 37203, USA

Williams, Dana L — Baseball Player
121 Arlene Dr, North Versailles PA 15137, USA

Williams, Dar — Singer, Songwriter
Agency Group Ltd, 142 W 57th St, #600, New York NY 10019 USA

Williams, Darryl E — Football Player
7351 Peppertree Circle S, Davie FL 33314, USA

Williams, Dave (Tiger) — Ice Hockey Player
Pacific Rodera Energy, 1100-550 6th Ave SW, Calgary AB T2P 0S2, Canada
Williams, David — Actor
Independent Talent Group, Oxford House, 76 Oxford St, London W1D 1BS, England
Williams, David L — Football Player
15816 Crest Lane, Gardena CA 90249, USA
Williams, David L (Dave) — Football Player
76752 Chrysanthemum Way, Palm Desert CA 92211, USA
Williams, David W — Football Player
650 Flying Hawk Trail, Waynesville NC 28786, USA
Williams, Dean E — Businessman
309 Carlyle Lake Dr, Saint Louis MO 63141, USA
Williams, DeAngelo — Football Player
6942 Curlee Court, Charlotte NC 28277, USA
Williams, Delvin, Jr — Football Player
173 Sierra Vista Ave, #11, Mountain View CA 94043, USA
Williams, Demorrio D — Football Player
San Diego Chargers, 4020 Murphy Canyon Road, San Diego CA 92123 USA
Williams, Deniece Niecy — Singer
Scott Stander Assoc, 4533 Van Nuys Blvd, #401, Sherman Oaks CA 91403 USA
Williams, Deron M — Basketball Player
6190 Murdoch Woods Place, Salt Lake City UT 84121, USA
Williams, Derrick — Basketball Player
Minnesota Timberwolves, Target Center, 600 1st Ave N, Minneapolis MN 55403 USA
Williams, Don — Basketball Player
6109 Rosedale Dr, Hyattsville MD 20782, USA
Williams, Don — Singer, Guitarist, Songwriter
Bobby Roberts, 3050 Business Park Circle, #303, Goodlettsville TN 37221 USA
Williams, Donald E — Astronaut
Science Applications Int'l, 2200 Space Park Dr, #200, Houston TX 77058, USA
Williams, Doug — Actor, Comedian
J K A Talent Agency, 8033 W Sunset Blvd, #115, West Hollywood CA 90046, USA
Williams, Douglas L (Doug) — Football Player, Coach
10546 Greensprings Dr, Tampa FL 33626, USA
Williams, Dudley — Dancer
Alvin Ailey American Dance Foundation, 405 W 55th St, New York NY 10019, USA
Williams, E Virginia — Artistic Director, Choreographer
Boston Ballet, 19 Clarendon St, Boston MA 02116, USA
Williams, Earl C — Baseball Player
61 Winston Dr, Somerset NJ 08873, USA
Williams, Easy — Actor
Judy Schoen, 606 N Larchmont Blvd, #309, Los Angeles CA 90004 USA
Williams, Edward L (Eddie) — Baseball Player
6229 Meadowgrass Lane, Las Vegas NV 89103, USA
Williams, Edy — Actress, Model
PO Box 6325, Woodland Hills CA 91365, USA
Williams, Elmo — Director, Producer
1249 Iris St, Brookings OR 97415, USA
Williams, Eric D — Football Player
4529 Dakota Trail, Saint Charles MO 63304, USA
Williams, Eric M — Football Player
11147 Corsicana Dr, Frisco TX 75035, USA
Williams, Eric T — Football Player
215 Haywood St, Garner NC 27529, USA
Williams, Erik G — Football Player
1 Wortham Court, Bear DE 19701, USA
Williams, Errick L (Ricky), Jr — Football Player
2307 Castilla Isle, Fort Lauderdale FL 33301, USA
Williams, Esther — Swimmer, Actress
9377 Readcrest Dr, Beverly Hills CA 90210, USA
Williams, Evan — Businessman
Twitter Inc, 795 Folsom St, #600, San Francisco CA 94107, USA
Williams, Frederick B (Freedom) — Rap Artist (C & C Music Factory)
Richard Walters, PO Box 2789, Toluca Lake CA 91610 USA
Williams, Freeman — Basketball Player
450 W 41st Place, Los Angeles CA 90037, USA
Williams, Gary Anthony — Actor
Coast to Coast Talent, 3350 Barham Blvd, Los Angeles CA 90068 USA
Williams, Gary B — Basketball Player, Coach
University of Maryland, Athletic Dept, College Park MD 20742, USA
Williams, George E — Baseball Player
N5250 County Road M, West Salem WI 54669, USA
Williams, Gerald — Football Player
9613 Callis Court, Harrisburg NC 28075, USA
Williams, Gerald F — Baseball Player
17011 Candeleda de Avila, Tampa FL 33613, USA
Williams, Greg Alan — Actor
Burns Agency, 3800 Bretton Woods Road , Decatur GA 30032, USA
Williams, Gregory — Educator
University of Cincinnati, President's Office, 2600 Clifton Ave, Cincinnati OH 45221, USA
Williams, Gregory S (Woody) — Baseball Player
5110 Newpoint Dr, Fresno TX 77545, USA
Williams, Gus — Basketball Player
290 Collins Ave, #9H, Mount Vernon NY 10552, USA
Williams, Hal — Actor
Halmarter Enterprise, PO Box 14405, Palm Desert CA 92255, USA
Williams, Hank, III — Singer, Songwriter
Azar Entertainment, 103 Roseleigh Cove, Batesville MS 38606, USA
Williams, Hank, Jr — Singer, Guitarist, Songwriter
W M E Entertainment, 1600 Division St, #300, Nashville TN 37203 USA
Williams, Harland — Actor, Comedian
Gersh Agency, 9465 Wilshire Blvd, #600, Beverly Hills CA 90212 USA
Williams, Harold M — Museum Executive
J Paul Getty Museum, Getty Center, 1200 Getty Center Dr, Los Angeles CA 90049, USA
Williams, Harvey L — Football Player
16815 Southern Oaks Dr, Houston TX 77068, USA

Williams, Hayley N	Singer, Keyboardist (Paramore)
Big Hassle, 44 Wall St, #2200, New York NY 10005, USA	
Williams, Herbert L (Herb)	Basketball Player, Coach
New York Knicks, Madison Square Garden, 2 Penn Plaza, New York, NY 10121 USA	
Williams, Hershel W	WW II Marine Corps Hero (CMH)
3450 Wire Branch Road, Ona WV 25545, USA	
Williams, Holly	Singer, Guitarist, Songwriter
Sandbox Mgmt, 54 Music Square E, #200, Nashville TN 37203, USA	
Williams, Howard E (Howie)	Basketball Player
1940 Hamilton Lane, Carmel CA 46032, USA	
Williams, Howard L (Howie)	Football Player
4731 Proctor Ave, Oakland CA 94618, USA	
Williams, Hype	Director, Producer, Writer
Creative Artists Agency, 2000 Ave of Stars, #100, Los Angeles CA 90067 USA	
Williams, Ivy	Writer
Mediachase, 834 N Harper Ave, Los Angeles CA 90046, USA	
Williams, J D	Actor
Don Buchwald/Fortitude, 6500 Wilshire Blvd, #2200, Los Angeles CA 90048 USA	
Williams, Jack K	Medical Administrator
Texas Medical Center, 2450 Holcombe Blvd, #1, Houston TX 77021, USA	
Williams, Jaimie	Actress
1019 Kane Concourse, #202, Bay Harbour Islands FL 33154, USA	
Williams, Jamal	Football Player
7710 Hazard Center Dr, #E, San Diego CA 92108, USA	
Williams, James (Fly)	Basketball Player
682 Ralph Ave, #2E, Brooklyn NY 11212, USA	
Williams, James A	Army General
8928 Maurice Lane, Annandale VA 22003, USA	
Williams, James A	Labor Leader
Painters & Allied Trades, 1750 New York Ave NW, #501, Washington DC 20006, USA	
Williams, James A (Froggy)	Football Player
296 Sugarberry Circle, Houston TX 77024, USA	
Williams, James D	Navy Admiral
20 Johnson Lane, Westport Island ME 04578, USA	
Williams, James F (Jimy)	Baseball Player, Manager
1401 Olde Post Road, Palm Harbor FL 34683, USA	
Williams, James H (Jimmy)	Football Player
54 Pennington Court, Buffalo NY 14228, USA	
Williams, James O	Football Player
330 S Western Ave, Lake Forest IL 60045, USA	
Williams, Jason C	Basketball Player
6103 Louise Cove Dr, Windermere FL 34786, USA	
Williams, Jay	Football Player
1306 Roxanna Road NW, Washington DC 20012, USA	
Williams, Jayson	Basketball Player, Sportscaster
NBC-TV, Sports Dept, 30 Rockefeller Plaza, #270E, New York NY 10112 USA	
Williams, Jeffrey N	Astronaut
4918 Cross Creek Lane, League City TX 77573, USA	
Williams, Jerrol L	Football Player
2562 Mizzoni Circle, Henderson NV 89052, USA	
Williams, Jesse	Actor
W M E Entertainment, 9601 Wilshire Blvd, #300, Beverly Hills CA 90210 USA	
Williams, Jessica	Jazz Pianist
T-Best Talent Agency, 508 Honey Lake Court, Danville CA 94506 USA	
Williams, JoBeth	Actress
Innovative Artists, 1505 10th St, Santa Monica CA 90401 USA	
Williams, Jody	Nobel Peace Laureate
663 Lancaster St, Fredericksburg VA 22405, USA	
Williams, John	Concert Guitarist
Arts Management Group, 1133 Broadway, #1025, New York NY 10010, USA	
Williams, John A	Writer
693 Forest Ave, Teaneck NJ 07666, USA	
Williams, John C	Archery Athlete
833 Cordova Ave, Ormond Beach FL 32174, USA	
Williams, John L	Football Player
1709 Husson Ave, Palatka FL 32177, USA	
Williams, John T	Conductor, Composer
333 Loring Ave, Los Angeles CA 90024, USA	
Williams, Johnny	Football Player
31921 Camino Capistrano, #13, San Juan Capistrano CA 92675, USA	
Williams, Joseph	Composer
Gorfaine/Schwartz, 4111 W Alameda Ave, #509, Burbank CA 91505 USA	
Williams, Juan	Writer
Fox-TV, News Dept, 205 E 67th St, New York NY 10065 USA	
Williams, Kameelah	Rap Artist (702)
Richard Walters, PO Box 2789, Toluca Lake CA 91610 USA	
Williams, Karl D	Football Player
2153 McKenzie Road, Mesquite TX 75181, USA	
Williams, Kate	Actress
I C M Partners, 10250 Constellation Blvd, #900, Los Angeles CA 90067 USA	
Williams, Keller	Singer, Songwriter, Guitarist
Keller's Cellar, PO Box 1777, Fredericksburg VA 22402, USA	
Williams, Kelli	Actress, Singer
I C M Partners, 10250 Constellation Blvd, #900, Los Angeles CA 90067 USA	
Williams, Kenneth R (Ken)	Baseball Player
6430 E Sierra Vista Dr, Paradise Valley AZ 85253, USA	
Williams, Kevin E	Basketball Player
1102 Blake Ave, #2, Brooklyn NY 11208, USA	
Williams, Kiely A	Actress, Singer (Cheetah Girls)
W M E Entertainment, 9601 Wilshire Blvd, #300, Beverly Hills CA 90210 USA	
Williams, Lee E	Football Player
11651 NW 4th St, Plantation FL 33325, USA	
Williams, Lenae T	Basketball Player
A A I Sports, 16000 Dallas Parkway, #300, Dallas TX 75248, USA	
Williams, Lorenzo	Basketball Player
6001 Palm Trace Landings Dr, #318, Davie FL 33314, USA	

Williams, Lucinda — Singer, Songwriter
High Road Touring, 751 Bridgeway, #300, Sausalito CA 94965, USA
Williams, Lynn R — Labor Leader
Harvard University, Politics Institute, 79 Kennedy St, Cambridge MA 02138, USA
Williams, Madieu M — Football Player
PO Box 96503, Washington DC 20090, USA
Williams, Maisie — Actress
Louise Johnson Mgmt, Arle Court, Cheltenham, Gloucestershire GL51 6PN, England
Williams, Maiya — Producer, Writer
A P A Talent/Literary Agency, 405 S Beverly Dr, #300, Beverly Hills CA 90212 USA
Williams, Maizie U — Singer (Boney M)
International Artists, PO Box 10034, 47563 Goch, Germany
Williams, Malinda — Actress
Inspire Entertainment, 9800 Wilshire Blvd, Beverly Hills CA 90212, USA
Williams, Mario J — Football Player
701 W Friar Tuck Lane, Houston TX 77024, USA
Williams, Mark — Bowler
Professional Bowlers Assn, 719 2nd Ave, #701, Seattle WA 98104 USA
Williams, Mark W — Baseball Player
1453 Trumansburg Road, Ithaca NY 14850, USA
Williams, Marvin G — Basketball Player
Utah Jazz, Energy Solutions Arena, 301 W South Temple, Salt Lake City UT 84101 USA
Williams, Mary Alice — Commentator
'Daily Rounds', Discovery Channel, 7700 Wisconsin Ave, Bethesda MD 20814, USA
Williams, Mason — Singer, Guitarist, Composer
PO Box 5105, Eugene OR 97405, USA
Williams, Matt — Writer, Director, Producer
Wind Dancer Productions, 200 W 57th St, #601, New York NY 10019, USA
Williams, Matthew D (Matt) — Baseball Player
4400 N Scottsdale Road, #381, Scottsdale AZ 85251, USA
Williams, Maurice — Singer, Songwriter
Willis Blume Agency, PO Box 509, Spartanburg SC 29304, USA
Williams, Maurice (Mo) — Basketball Player
Los Angeles Clippers, Staples Center, 1111 S Figueroa St, Los Angeles CA 90015 USA
Williams, Maurice C — Football Player
3653 Eastbury Dr, Jacksonville FL 32224, USA
Williams, Maurice J — Association Executive
Overseas Development Council, 1875 Connecticut Ave NW, Washington DC 20009, USA
Williams, Maurice J (Moe) — Football Player
10801 SW Fox Brown Road, Indiantown FL 34956, USA
Williams, Meadow — Actress, Producer, Writer
GruntWorks Entertainment, 548 Broadhollow Road, Melville NY 11747, USA
Williams, Melvin G (Mel), Jr — Navy Admiral
Commander, 2nd Fleet, FPO AE 09506 USA
Williams, Merriwether — Writer, Producer
Collective, 8383 Wilshire Blvd, #1050, Beverly Hills CA 90211 USA
Williams, Michael D (Mike) — Football Player
Jacksonville Jaguars, 1 AllTel Stadium Place, Jacksonville FL 32202 USA
Williams, Michael D (Mike) — Baseball Player
240 Horseshoe Farm Road, Pembroke VA 24136, USA
Williams, Michael J (Mike) — Football Player
2152 NW 74th Ave, Hollywood FL 33024, USA
Williams, Michael Kenneth — Actor
Collective, 8383 Wilshire Blvd, #1050, Beverly Hills CA 90211 USA
Williams, Micheal D — Basketball Player
1005 Lakeridge Court, Colleyville TX 76034, USA
Williams, Michelle — Actress
Creative Artists Agency, 2000 Ave of Stars, #100, Los Angeles CA 90067 USA
Williams, Michelle — Singer (Destiny's Child)
I C M Partners, 10250 Constellation Blvd, #900, Los Angeles CA 90067 USA
Williams, Mitchell S (Mitch) — Baseball Player
67 Highbridge Blvd, Medford NJ 08055, USA
Williams, Montel — Entertainer, Talk Show Host
Mountain Movers, 433 W 53rd St, New York NY 10019, USA
Williams, Nathaniel R (Nate) — Basketball Player
132 Stanmore Circle, Vallejo CA 94591, USA
Williams, Nigel — Writer, Producer
Judy Daish Assoc, 2 Saint Charles Place, London W10 6EG, England
Williams, Olivia — Actress
Independent Talent Group, Oxford House, 76 Oxford St, London W1D 1BS, England
Williams, Otis — Singer (Temptations)
Barry Pollock Assoc, 9255 Sunset Blvd, #404, West Hollywood CA 90069, USA
Williams, Patrick (Pat) — Football Player
2839 Wilds Lane NW, Prior Lake MN 55372, USA
Williams, Patrick M — Composer
3156 Mandeville Canyon Road, Los Angeles CA 90049, USA
Williams, Paul (Punisher) — Boxer
Goossen Tutor Promotions, 15300 Ventura Blvd, #400, Sherman Oaks CA 91403 USA
Williams, Paul Andrew — Actor, Director, Writer
United Agents, 12-26 Lexington St, London W1F 0LE, England
Williams, Paul H — Songwriter, Actor
8491 W Sunset Blvd, #1150, West Hollywood CA 90069, USA
Williams, Perry A — Football Player
480 Canyon Oaks Dr, #A, Oakland CA 94605, USA
Williams, Perry L — Football Player
273 Old Laurinberg Road, Hamlet NC 28345, USA
Williams, Pharrell — Singer, Rap Artist (NERD), Songwriter
42 West, 220 W 42nd St, #1200, New York NY 10036 USA
Williams, Phillip L — Publisher
Los Angeles Times, Publisher's Office, 202 W 1st St, Los Angeles CA 90012, USA
Williams, Rachel — Model, Actress
Berzon Talent Agency, 23 Seton Road, Irvine CA 92612, USA
Williams, Randall D (Randy) — Baseball Player
11410 F M 586 S, Brookesmith TX 76827, USA
Williams, Randy — Track Athlete
5655 N Marty Ave, #204, Fresno CA 93711, USA

Williams, Redford B, Jr — Internist
Duke University Medical School, Box 3708, Durham NC 27706, USA

Williams, Reggie — Basketball Player
2016 Calloway St, Temple Hills MD 20748, USA

Williams, Reginald (Reggie) — Football Player
10 N Summerlin Ave, #53, Orlando FL 32801, USA

Williams, Reginald (Reggie), Jr — Football Player
7635 Wexford Club Dr E, Jacksonville FL 32256, USA

Williams, Richard E — Animator, Cartoonist (Pink Panther)
138 Royal College St, London NW1 OTA, England

Williams, Robbie — Singer
I E Management, 111 Frithville Gardens, London W12 7JQ, England

Williams, Robert A (Bobby) — Football Player
602 Stone Barn Road, Towson MD 21286, USA

Williams, Robert C — Football Player
347 Walnut Grove Lane, Coppell TX 75019, USA

Williams, Robert J (Ben) — Football Player
5961 Huntview Dr, Jackson MS 39206, USA

Williams, Robert Walter — Physicist
University of Washington, Physics Dept, Seattle WA 98195, USA

Williams, Robin — Actor, Comedian
1 Blackfield Dr, #409, Belvedere-Tiburon CA 94920, USA

Williams, Roderick — Opera Singer
Ingpen & Williams, 131 Putney Bridge Road, London SW15 2PA, England

Williams, Roland L — Football Player
5671 Wrenwyck Place, Weldon Spring MO 63304, USA

Williams, Ronald A — Businessman
Aetna Inc, 151 Farmington Ave, Hartford CT 06156, USA

Williams, Roshumba — Model, Actress
Innovative Artists, 1505 10th St, Santa Monica CA 90401 USA

Williams, Rowan D — Religious Leader
Lambert Palace, London SE1 9JU, England

Williams, Roy — Basketball Coach
University of North Carolina, PO Box 2126, Chapel Hill NC 27515, USA

Williams, Roy E, Jr — Football Player
Chicago Bears, 1000 Football Dr, Lake Forest IL 60045 USA

Williams, Roy L — Football Player
4100 Buckingham Place, Colleyville TX 76034, USA

Williams, Roydell — Football Player
641 Old Hickory Blvd, #416, Brentwood TN 37027, USA

Williams, Ryan Piers — Director, Producer, Writer
Rugolo Entertainment, 195 S Beverly Drive, #400, Beverly Hills CA 90212, USA

Williams, Samuel F (Sam) — Football Player
28960 Westfield St, Livonia MI 48150, USA

Williams, Saul — Rap Artist
Agency Group Ltd, 1880 Century Park E, #711, Los Angeles CA 90067 USA

Williams, Serena J — Tennis Player
Women's Tennis Assn, 1 Progress Plaza, #1500, Saint Petersburg FL 33701 USA

Williams, Shad C — Baseball Player
4682 E Cornell Ave, Fresno CA 93703, USA

Williams, Shaun L — Football Player
11738 Gruen St, Sylmar CA 91342, USA

Williams, Shelden — Basketball Player
Brooklyn Nets, 15 Metro Tech Center, #1100, Brooklyn NY 11201 USA

Williams, Sherman C — Football Player
119 Patricia Ave, Mobile AL 36610, USA

Williams, Sidney (Sid) — Football Player
1044 W 82nd St, Los Angeles CA 90044, USA

Williams, Simon — Actor
Dalzell & Beresford, 26 Astwood Mews, London SW7 4DE, England

Williams, Speed — Rodeo Rider
9550 Tradewind St, Amarillo TX 79118, USA

Williams, Stanley W (Stan) — Baseball Player
4702 Hayter Ave, Lakewood CA 90712, USA

Williams, Stephanie E — Actress
S M S Talent, 8383 Wilshire Blvd, #230, Beverly Hills CA 90211 USA

Williams, Stephen — Anthropologist
1017 Foothills Trail, Santa Fe NM 87505, USA

Williams, Stephen F — Judge
US Court of Appeals, 333 Constitution Ave NW, #4400, Washington DC 20001, USA

Williams, Steve — Rowing Athlete
Leander Club, Henley on Thames, Leander RG9 2LP, England

Williams, Steven — Actor
Stone Manners Salners, 9911 W Pico Blvd, #1400, Los Angeles CA 90035 USA

Williams, Sunita L — Astronaut
1522 Festival Dr, Houston TX 77062, USA

Williams, Tamika — Basketball Player
Minnesota Lynx, Target Center, 600 1st Ave N, Minneapolis MN 55403 USA

Williams, Tavares (Monty) — Basketball Player, Coach
316 Dorrington Blvd, Metairie LA 70005, USA

Williams, Terrence — Basketball Player
Sacramento Kings, Arco Arena, 1 Sports Parkway, Sacramento CA 95834 USA

Williams, Terrie — Biologist
University of California, Biology Dept, Santa Cruz CA 95064, USA

Williams, Terry — Drummer (Dire Straits)
Damage Mgmt, 16 Lambton Place, London W11 2SH, England

Williams, Thomas S Cardinal — Religious Leader
Viard, 21 Eccleston Hill, PO Box 1937, Wellington 6015, New Zealand

Williams, Tod — Architect
Tod Williams Billie Tsien Architects, 222 Central Park S, New York NY 10019, USA

Williams, Tod — Director, Producer, Writer
United Talent Agency, 9336 Civic Center Dr, Beverly Hills CA 90210 USA

Williams, Todd — Actor
Sanders/Armstrong/Caserta Mgmt, 2120 Colorado Ave, #120, Santa Monica CA 90404 USA

Williams, Todd M — Baseball Player
16707 Whispering Glen Dr, Lutz FL 33558, USA

Williams, Tom — Ice Hockey Player
2411 Princess Ave, Windsor ON N8T 1V2, Canada
Williams, Tonya Lee — Actress
Artists Agency, 1180 S Beverly Dr, #301, Los Angeles CA 90035 USA
Williams, Treat — Actor
A P A Talent/Literary Agency, 405 S Beverly Dr, #300, Beverly Hills CA 90212 USA
Williams, Tyler James — Actor
Osbrink Talent Agency, 4343 Lankershim Blvd, #100, North Hollywood CA 91602 USA
Williams, U Tyrone — Football Player
6939 Westchester Circle, Bradenton FL 34202, USA
Williams, Ulis — Track Athlete
2511 29th St, Santa Monica CA 90405, USA
Williams, Van — Actor
Shelly & Pierce, 13775A Mono Way, #220, Sonora CA 95370 USA
Williams, Vanessa A — Actress
Shadow, 10 Universal City Plaza, #2000, Universal City CA 91608, USA
Williams, Vanessa L — Actress, Singer, Beauty Queen
United Talent Agency, 9336 Civic Center Dr, Beverly Hills CA 90210 USA
Williams, Venus E S — Tennis Player
Women's Tennis Assn, 1 Progress Plaza, #1500, Saint Petersburg FL 33701 USA
Williams, Victor — Actor
Imperium 7, 5455 Wilshire Blvd, #1706, Los Angeles CA 90036, USA
Williams, Victoria — Singer, Guitarist, Songwriter
High Road Touring, 751 Bridgeway, #200, Sausalito CA 94965 USA
Williams, Virginia — Actress
Collective, 8383 Wilshire Blvd, #1050, Beverly Hills CA 90211 USA
Williams, Wade — Actor
S M S Talent, 8383 Wilshire Blvd, #230, Beverly Hills CA 90211 USA
Williams, Walter (Buddy) — Baseball Player
15700 Good Hope Road, Silver Spring MD 20905, USA
Williams, Walter A (Walt) — Baseball Player
2417 Monterey St, Brownwood TX 76801, USA
Williams, Walter A (Walt) — Basketball Player
3240 Beaumont St, Temple Hills MD 20748, USA
Williams, Walter F — Businessman
RR 4, Saucon Valley Road, Bethlehem PA 18015, USA
Williams, Walter Ray, Jr — Bowler
7903 SE 12th Circle, Ocala FL 34480, USA
Williams, Walter, Sr — Singer (O'Jays)
Associated Booking Corp, 501 Madison Ave, #603, New York NY 10022 USA
Williams, Warren, Jr — Football Player
1203 Gerald Ave, West Hempstead NY 11552, USA
Williams, Wendy — Actress
I C M Partners, 10250 Constellation Blvd, #900, Los Angeles CA 90067 USA
Williams, William (Curly) — Baseball Player
2729 20th St, Sarasota FL 34234, USA
Williams, William A — Astronaut
Environmental Protection Agency, 200 SW 35th St, Corvallis OR 97333, USA
Williams, William G (Billy) — Baseball Umpire
RR 2 Box 822, Coconut Creek FL 33073, USA
Williams, Willie — Baseball Player
2729 20th St, Sarasota FL 34234, USA
Williams, Willie A — Football Player
PO Box 871445, Mesquite TX 75187, USA
Williams, Willie J, Jr — Football Player
5410 Handscrabble Road, Blythewood SC 29016, USA
Williamson, Carlton — Football Player
300 White Springs Lane, Peachtree City GA 30269, USA
Williamson, Corliss M — Basketball Player
Arkansas Baptist College, Athletic Dept, 1621 King Dr, Little Rock AR 72202, USA
Williamson, Frederick R (Fred) — Actor, Football Player
H David Moss, 733 Seward St, #PH, Los Angeles CA 90038, USA
Williamson, Jama — Actress
TalentWorks, 3500 W Olive Ave, #1400, Burbank CA 91505 USA
Williamson, Jay — Golfer
24 Clemont Lane, Saint Louis MO 63124, USA
Williamson, Kevin — Director, Producer, Writer
W M E Entertainment, 9601 Wilshire Blvd, #300, Beverly Hills CA 90210 USA
Williamson, Marianne — Psychotherapist
Los Angeles Center for Living, 8265 W Sunset Blvd, West Hollywood CA 90046, USA
Williamson, Mark A — Baseball Player
1260 Hidden Mountain Dr, El Cajon CA 92019, USA
Williamson, Matthew — Fashion Designer
37 Percy St, London W1P 2DJ, England
Williamson, Michael — Writer
10400 Hutting Place, Silver Spring MD 20902, USA
Williamson, Michael — Photojournalist
Washington Post, Editorial Dept, 1150 15th St NW, Washington DC 20071 USA
Williamson, Mykelti T — Actor
Innovative Artists, 1505 10th St, Santa Monica CA 90401 USA
Williamson, Oliver E — Nobel Economics Laureate
University of California, Economics Dept, Berkeley CA 94720, USA
Williamson, Richard — Football Coach
5137 Morrowick Road, Charlotte NC 28226, USA
Williamson, Samuel R, Jr — Educator
University of the South, President's Office, Sewanee TN 37375, USA
Williamson, Scott — Baseball Player
21563 Fox Road, Guilford IN 47022, USA
Williamson, Troy — Football Player
Jacksonville Jaguars, 1 AllTel Stadium Place, Jacksonville FL 32202 USA
Williams-Paisley, Kimberly — Actress
Kritzer Levine Wilkins Griffin, 11872 La Grange Ave, #100, Los Angeles CA 90025 USA
Willie D — Rap Artist (Geto Boys)
Entertainment Artists, PO Box 120824, Nashville TN 37212 USA
Williford, D Vann — Basketball Player
4455 Fair Oaks Lane, High Point NC 27265, USA

Willig, Matthew J (Matt) — Football Player
4241 Prado de los Pajaros, Calabasas CA 91302, USA
Willimon, Beau — Writer
Creative Artists Agency, 2000 Ave of Stars, #100, Los Angeles CA 90067 USA
Willing, Nick — Director
Independent Talent Group, Oxford House, 76 Oxford St, London W1D 1BS, England
Willingham, Joshua D (Josh) — Baseball Player
108 Cascade Dr, Florence AL 35633, USA
Willingham, Tyrone — Football Coach
Octagon Worldwide, 1751 Pinnacle Dr, #1500, McLean VA 22102 USA
Willis, Alicia Leigh — Actress
Innovative Artists, 1505 10th St, Santa Monica CA 90401 USA
Willis, Brian Davis — Drummer (Quarterflash)
Pacific Talent Agency, PO Box 19145, Portland OR 97280, USA
Willis, Bruce W — Actor
Creative Artists Agency, 2000 Ave of Stars, #100, Los Angeles CA 90067 USA
Willis, Carl B — Baseball Player
6811 Lipscomb Dr, Durham NC 27712, USA
Willis, Dave — Writer, Producer, Actor
Brillstein Entertainment Partners, 9150 Wilshire Blvd, #350, Beverly Hills CA 90212 USA
Willis, Dinah — Model
Playboy Promotions, 2706 Media Center Dr, Los Angeles CA 90065 USA
Willis, Dontrelle — Baseball Player
9820 E Thompson Peak Parkway, #726, Scottsdale AZ 85255, USA
Willis, Frederick F (Fred), III — Football Player
PO Box 558, Swampscott MA 01907, USA
Willis, Garrett — Golfer
528 Mountain Pass Lane, Knoxville TN 37923, USA
Willis, Gordon — Cinematographer
I C M Partners, 10250 Constellation Blvd, #900, Los Angeles CA 90067 USA
Willis, James G (Jim) — Baseball Player
PO Box 35, Boyce LA 71409, USA
Willis, Keith — Football Player
116 Coffeeberry Court, Garner NC 27529, USA
Willis, Kelly — Singer, Songwriter
4007 Lullwood Road, Austin TX 78722, USA
Willis, Kevin A — Basketball Player
1481 Jones Road, Roswell GA 30075, USA
Willis, Michael H (Mike) — Baseball Player
6234 Taggart St, Houston TX 77007, USA
Willis, O Mitchell (Mitch) — Football Player
1398 Fairhaven Dr, Mansfield TX 76063, USA
Willis, Patrick L — Football Player
San Francisco 49ers, 4949 Centennial Blvd, Santa Clara CA 95054 USA
Willis, Ray — Football Player
8200 Poole Road, Knightdale NC 27545, USA
Willis, Rumer — Actress
Untitled Entertainment, 350 S Beverly Dr, #200, Beverly Hills CA 90212 USA
Willison, Mike — Bassist (Fig Dish)
Metropolitan Entertainment Group, 2 Penn Plaza, #1500, New York NY 10121, USA
Willits, Reggie G — Baseball Player
Los Angeles Angels, Angel Stadium, 2000 E Gene Autry Way, Anaheim CA 92806 USA
Willman, David — Journalist
Los Angeles Times, Editorial Dept, 202 W 1st St, Los Angeles CA 90012 USA
Willms, Andre — Rowing Athlete
Rennebogen 94, 39130 Magdeburg, Germany
Willoch, Kare I — Prime Minister, Norway
Blokkaveien 6B, 0282 Oslo, Norway
Willoughby, James A (Jim) — Baseball Player
PO Box 707, Eufaula OK 74432, USA
Willoughby, William W (Bill) — Basketball Player
350 W Englewood Ave, Englewood NJ 07631, USA
Wills, Elliott T (Bump) — Baseball Player
1802 Briar Meadow Dr, Arlington TX 76014, USA
Wills, Garry — Historian
Northwestern University, History Dept, Evanston IL 60201, USA
Wills, Mark — Singer, Songwriter
Scott Welch Mgmt, 1515 Harding Place, Nashville TN 37215, USA
Wills, Maurice M (Maury) — Baseball Player, Manager
M & R Sports, 5 Dalton Valley Dr, Saint Peters MO 63376, USA
Wills, Rick — Bassist (Foreigner)
Hard to Handle Mgmt, 16501 Ventura Blvd, #602, Encino CA 91436, USA
Wills, Theodore C (Ted) — Baseball Player
10585 E Duckpoint Way, Clovis CA 93619, USA
Willsie, Brian — Ice Hockey Player
45 Meadowbrook Road, Randolph NJ 07869, USA
Willson-Piper, Marty — Guitarist (Church)
Globeshine, 101 Chamberlayne Road, London NW10 5ND, England
Wilmarth, Christopher — Artist, Sculptor
Betty Cunningham, 541 W 25th St, Front 2, New York NY 10001, USA
Wilmarth, Dick — Dog Sled Racer
1111 F St, Anchorage AK 99501, USA
Wilmer, Douglas — Actor
Julian Belfrage Assoc, 9 Argyll St, #300, London W1F 7TG, England
Wilmer, Harry A — Psychiatrist
Texas Health Science Center, Psychiatric Dept, San Antonio TX 78284, USA
Wilmet, Paul R — Baseball Player
PO Box 330074, Nashville TN 37203, USA
Wilmore, Barry E (Butch) — Astronaut
3002 Bryant Lane, Webster TX 77598, USA
Wilmore, Larry — Actor, Comedian, Writer
United Talent Agency, 9336 Civic Center Dr, Beverly Hills CA 90210 USA
Wilmot, David — Actor
Macfarlane Chard, 7 Adelaide St, Dun Laoghaire, Dublin, Ireland
Wilms, Andre — Actor
Voyez Mon Agent, 20 Ave Rapp, 75007 Paris, France

Wilmsmeyer, Klaus, Jr 8209 Paddington Dr, Louisville KY 40222, USA	Football Player
Wilmut, Ian Roslin Institute, Roslin Bio Centre, Midlothian EH25 9PS, Scotland	Geneticist, Embryologist
Wilpon, Fred 100 Sheep Lane, Locust Valley NY 11560, USA	Baseball Executive
Wilson of Tillyorn, David C House of Lords, Westminster, London SW1A 0PW, England	Government Official, England; Diplomat
Wilson, Adrian L 10104 E Shangri La Road, Scottsdale AZ 85260, USA	Football Player
Wilson, Aldra K (Al) 11561 Warrington Court, Parker CO 80138, USA	Football Player
Wilson, Alexander G (Sandy) 2 Southwell Gardens, #4, London SW7 4SB, England	Composer, Writer
Wilson, Alexandra Greater Visions Artists Talent Agency, 8981 W Sunset Blvd, #101, West Hollywood CA 90069 USA	Actress
Wilson, Allan B University of California, Molecular Biology Dept, Berkeley CA 94724, USA	Molecular Biologist
Wilson, Andrew United Talent Agency, 9336 Civic Center Dr, Beverly Hills CA 90210 USA	Actor
Wilson, Andrew N (A N) 21 Arlington Road, London NW1 7ER, England	Writer
Wilson, Ann D H K Mgmt, 9200 W Sunset Blvd, #530, West Hollywood CA 90069 USA	Singer (Heart)
Wilson, Ben C3 Presents, 98 San Jacinto Blvd, #400, Austin TX 78701, USA	Keyboardist (Blues Traveler)
Wilson, Blaine 7441 Murrayfield Dr, Columbus OH 43085, USA	Gymnast
Wilson, Blenda J California State University, President's Office, Northridge CA 91330, USA	Educator
Wilson, Brenard K 1246 Dalemere Dr, Nashville TN 37207, USA	Football Player
Wilson, Brian D Agency Group Ltd, 1880 Century Park E, #711, Los Angeles CA 90067 USA	Singer (Beach Boys), Songwriter
Wilson, Brian P 741 S Banning Circle, Mesa AZ 85206, USA	Baseball Player
Wilson, C A S John John Wilson Assoc, 27 Horsell Road, London N5 1XL, England	Architect
Wilson, C Richard (Ricky) Red Light Mgmt, 8439 Sunset Blvd, West Hollywood CA	Singer (Kaiser Chiefs)
Wilson, C Wade 6126 Mimosa Lane, Dallas TX 75230, USA	Football Player
Wilson, Carey 85 Jean Louis Road, Winnipeg MB R2N 4A9, Canada	Ice Hockey Player
Wilson, Carnie 19528 Ventura Blvd, #624, Tarzana CA 91356, USA	Singer (Wilson Phillips, Wilsons)
Wilson, Casey R United Talent Agency, 9336 Civic Center Dr, Beverly Hills CA 90210 USA	Actress, Writer
Wilson, Cassandra Front Row Productions, 215 S 4th St, Forest City IA 50436, USA	Singer
Wilson, Cedrick 380 N Island Dr, #312, Memphis TN 38103, USA	Football Player
Wilson, Chandra Abrams Artists, 275 7th Ave, #2600, New York NY 10001 USA	Actress
Wilson, Charles J 5444 Calder Dr, Tallahassee FL 32317, USA	Football Player
Wilson, Charles K (Charlie) Universal Attractions, 135 W 26th St, #1200, New York NY 10001 USA	Singer (Gap Band), Songwriter
Wilson, Charles R US Court of Appeals, 801 N Florida Ave, #200, Tampa FL 33602, USA	Judge
Wilson, Chris Washington Redskins, 21300 Redskin Park Dr, Ashburn VA 20147 USA	Football Player
Wilson, Christopher J (C J) Los Angeles Angels, Angel Stadium, 2000 E Gene Autry Way, Anaheim CA 92806 USA	Baseball Player
Wilson, Cindy Direct Management Group, 947 N La Cienega Blvd, #G, West Hollywood CA 90069, USA	Singer, Guitarist (B-52's)
Wilson, Colin H Tetherdown, Trewallock Lane, Gorran Haven, Cornwall PL26 6NT, England	Writer
Wilson, Craig 1423 Lake Blvd, Davis CA 95616, USA	Water Polo Player
Wilson, Craig 8241 Drybank Dr, Huntington Beach CA 92646, USA	Baseball Player
Wilson, Craig F 3427 E Tere St, Phoenix AZ 85044, USA	Baseball Player
Wilson, Dan Monterey Peninsula Artists, 404 W Franklin St, Monterey CA 93940 USA	Singer, Guitarist, Songwriter
Wilson, Dan OmniPop Talent Group, 4605 Lankershim Blvd, #201, Toluca Lake CA 91602 USA	Actor, Comedian
Wilson, Daniel A (Dan) 2161 E Interlaken Blvd, Seattle WA 98112, USA	Baseball Player
Wilson, Darnell 1917 E Foxmoor Lane, Lafayette IN 47905, USA	Boxer
Wilson, David Morgan State University, President's Office, Baltimore MD 21239, USA	Educator
Wilson, David C (Dave) 2247 Farolito Ave, Long Beach CA 90815, USA	Football Player
Wilson, David E New York Giants, Meadowlands Stadium, 102 Route 120, East Rutherford NJ 07073 USA	Football Player
Wilson, David Mackenzie Lifeboat House, Castletown IM9 1LD, Isle of Man, England	Museum Executive
Wilson, Dean 10914 Iris Canyon Lane, Las Vegas NV 89135, USA	Golfer
Wilson, Desi B 8 Janet Lane, Glen Cove NY 11542, USA	Baseball Player
Wilson, Desire 4197 Serenade Road, Castle Rock CO 80104, USA	Auto Racing Driver

Wilson, Doug Ice Hockey Player
5620 Country Club Parkway, San Jose CA 95138, USA
Wilson, Duncan S (Dunc) Ice Hockey Player
Box 28, Rossland BC V0G 1Y0, Canada
Wilson, Edward O Writer, Zoologist
1010 Waltham St, #A208, Lexington MA 02421, USA
Wilson, Elizabeth Actress
Paradigm Agency, 360 N Crescent Dr, North Building, Beverly Hills CA 90210 USA
Wilson, Eugene Skier
2775 Ranchview Lane N, #1, Minneapolis MN 55447, USA
Wilson, F Paul Writer
1933 State Route 35, #337, Wall Township NJ 07719, USA
Wilson, F Perry Chemical Engineer
225 N 56th St, #217, Lincoln NE 68504, USA
Wilson, Frank Auto Racing Executive
North Carolina Motor Speedway, PO Box 2801, Daytona Beach FL 32120, USA
Wilson, Gahan Cartoonist, Writer
New Yorker, Editorial Dept, 4 Times Square, Basement C1B, New York NY 10036 USA
Wilson, George (Jiff) Basketball Player
151 Twin Lakes Dr, Fairfield OH 45014, USA
Wilson, Gerald S Jazz Trumpeter, Composer
4625 Brynhurst Ave, Los Angeles CA 90043, USA
Wilson, Gibril D Football Player
20 10th St NW, #2302, Atlanta GA 30309, USA
Wilson, Glenn D Baseball Player
300 Tara Park, Conroe TX 77302, USA
Wilson, Gretchen Singer, Guitarist
Club 27, PO Box 708, Lebanon TN 37088, USA
Wilson, Hugh Director
I C M Partners, 10250 Constellation Blvd, #900, Los Angeles CA 90067 USA
Wilson, Jack E Baseball Player
12467 San Sebastian Court, Santa Rosa Valley CA 93012, USA
Wilson, Jack M Educator
University of Massachusetts, President's Office, 225 Franklin St, #3300, Boston MA 02110, USA
Wilson, Jacquelyn Writer
Transworld Publishers, 61-63 Uxbridge Road, London W5 5SA, England
Wilson, James (J C) Football Player
4785 Young Road, Waldorf MD 20601, USA
Wilson, James G (Jim) Baseball Player
8112 NW Bacon Road, Vancouver WA 98665, USA
Wilson, James M Geneticist
University of Pennsylvania Medical Center, Genetics Dept, Philadelphia PA 19104, USA
Wilson, Jane Artist
317 W 83rd St, #2E, New York NY 10024, USA
Wilson, Jean D Endocrinologist
Texas Southwestern Medical Center, 5323 Harry Hines Blvd, Dallas TX 75390, USA
Wilson, Jeannie Actress
4330 Talofa Ave, Toluca Lake CA 91602, USA
Wilson, Jennifer Opera, Concert Singer
I M G Artists, The Light Box, 111 Power Road, London W4 5PY, England
Wilson, Jerry L Football Player
19814 Moss Bark Trail, Richmond TX 77407, USA
Wilson, Jessica Actress, Comedienne
OmniPop Talent Group, 4605 Lankershim Blvd, #201, Toluca Lake CA 91602 USA
Wilson, John (Johnny), Sr Baseball Player
8 Hillcrest Dr, Lock Haven PA 17745, USA
Wilson, Johnnie E Army General
Dimensions International, 2800 Eisenhower Ave, #300, Alexandria VA 22314, USA
Wilson, Josh Baseball Player
2304 Cramden Road, Pittsburgh, PA MI 15241, USA
Wilson, Joshua (Josh) Football Player
515 Quincy Ave NE, Renton WA 98059, USA
Wilson, Julie Singer, Actress
Scott Stander Assoc, 4533 Van Nuys Blvd, #401, Sherman Oaks CA 91403 USA
Wilson, Justin Drummer (Reveille)
David Levin Mgmt, 200 W 57th St, #308, New York NY 10019, USA
Wilson, Kenneth G Nobel Physics Laureate
Ohio State University, Physics Dept, 174 W 18th Ave, Columbus OH 43210, USA
Wilson, Keri-Lynn Conductor
I M G Artists, Hogarth Business Park, Chiswick, London W4 2TH, England
Wilson, Kim Singer, Musician (Fabulous Thunderbird)
Ricci Assoc, 28205 Agoura Road, Agoura Hills CA 91301, USA
Wilson, Kris Baseball Player
PO Box 15, Chillicothe MO 64601, USA
Wilson, Kristen Actress
Silverstone Entertainment, 10 Universal City Plaza, #2400, Universal City CA 91608, USA
Wilson, Lambert Actor
Rights House, 34-43 Russell St, London WC2B 5HA, England
Wilson, Landon Ice Hockey Player
127 Tennyson Place, Coppell TX 75019, USA
Wilson, Lawrence F (Larry) Football Player, Executive
11834 N Blackheath Road, Scottsdale AZ 85254, USA
Wilson, Linda S Educator
26 Honey Locust Dr, Topsham ME 04086, USA
Wilson, Luke Actor
I/D Public Relations, 7060 Hollywood Blvd, #800, Los Angeles CA 90028 USA
Wilson, Mara Actress
Harry Gold Assoc, 3500 W Olive Ave, #1400, Burbank CA 91505, USA
Wilson, Marc D Football Player
10820 157th Ave NE, Woodinville WA 98072, USA
Wilson, Marie Actress
Michael Bruno Group, 13576 Cheltenham Dr, Sherman Oaks CA 91423, USA
Wilson, Mark J Golfer
N41W27751 Ishnala Trail, Pewaukee WI 53072, USA
Wilson, Mary Singer (Supremes)
2654 W Horizon Ridge Parkway, #B5, Henderson NV 89052, USA

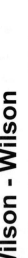

Wilson, Melanie Irv Schechter, 9460 Wilshire Blvd, #300, Beverly Hills CA 90212 USA	Actress
Wilson, Michael (Tack) 1623 Schnell Dr, Arabi LA 70032, USA	Baseball Player
Wilson, Mike 4647 Lake Charles Dr, Independence OH 44131, USA	Ice Hockey Player
Wilson, Mike R 2908 N Poinsettia Ave, Manhattan Beach CA 90266, USA	Football Player
Wilson, Murray Wilson Consulting, 432-410 Bank St, Ottawa ON K2P 1Y8, Canada	Ice Hockey Player
Wilson, Nancy M P I Talent Agency, 1801 Ave of Stars, #1420, Los Angeles CA 90067, USA	Singer
Wilson, Nancy L Peters Mgmt, PO Box 1710, Topanga CA 90290, USA	Singer (Heart)
Wilson, Nemiah 11000 E Idaho Place, Aurora CO 80012, USA	Football Player
Wilson, Nigel E 35 Sabbe Crescent, Ajax ON L1T 4E3, Canada	Baseball Player
Wilson, Olin C 1508 Circa del Lago, B110, San Marcos CA 92078, USA	Astronomer
Wilson, Otis R 426 W Shadow Creek Dr, Vernon Hills IL 60061, USA	Football Player
Wilson, Owen C United Talent Agency, 9336 Civic Center Dr, Beverly Hills CA 90210 USA	Actor
Wilson, Patrick Anonymous Content, 3532 Hayden Ave, Culver City CA 90232 USA	Singer, Actor
Wilson, Patrick Oklahoma Medical Research Foundation, 825 NE 13th St, Oklahoma City OK 73104, USA	Immunologist
Wilson, Paul Big Life Mgmt, 67-69 Charlton St, London NW1 1HY, England	Bassist, Pianist (Snow Patrol)
Wilson, Paul A 949 Lenmore Court, Orlando FL 32812, USA	Baseball Player
Wilson, Peta I C M Partners, 10250 Constellation Blvd, #900, Los Angeles CA 90067 USA	Actress, Model
Wilson, Peter L Architekturburo Bolles & Wilson, Alter Steinweg 17, 48143 Munster, Germany	Architect
Wilson, Philippa C (Pippa) Lynx Sports Mgmt, Lymington Road, Lymington, Hampshire SO41 5S5, England	Yachtswoman
Wilson, Preston J R 136 Paloma Dr, Coral Gables FL 33143, USA	Baseball Player
Wilson, Rainn W M E Entertainment, 9601 Wilshire Blvd, #300, Beverly Hills CA 90210 USA	Actor, Comedian
Wilson, Ralph C, Jr 99 Kercheval Ave, Grosse Pointe Farms MI 48236, USA	Football Executive
Wilson, Rebel W M E Entertainment, 9601 Wilshire Blvd, #300, Beverly Hills CA 90210 USA	Actress
Wilson, Reno Vanguard Mangement Group, 8060 Melrose Ave, #400, Los Angeles CA 90046, USA	Actor
Wilson, Richard (Rick) 535 E Ormsby Ave, Louisville KY 40203, USA	Basketball Player
Wilson, Richard G (Rick) 1624 Reno Run, Lewisville TX 75077, USA	Ice Hockey Player
Wilson, Richard K Genome Sequencing Center, 4444 Forest Park Ave, Saint Louis MO 63108, USA	Geneticist
Wilson, Ricky 8007 Oak Ridge Court, Bowie MD 20715, USA	Basketball Player
Wilson, Rik 12076 Manchester Road, Saint Louis MO 63131, USA	Ice Hockey Player
Wilson, Rita Creative Artists Agency, 2000 Ave of Stars, #100, Los Angeles CA 90067 USA	Actress, Singer
Wilson, Robert Charles Bantam Books, 1745 Broadway, New York NY 10019 USA	Writer
Wilson, Robert J (Red) 806 Cabot Lane, Madison WI 53711, USA	Baseball Player
Wilson, Robert M R W Work Ltd, 55 Washington St, #216, Brooklyn NY 11201, USA	Actor
Wilson, Robert W 38 Cole Court, Dumont NJ 07628, USA	Nobel Physics Laureate
Wilson, Robin Stone Manners Salners, 9911 W Pico Blvd, #1400, Los Angeles CA 90035 USA	Singer (Gin Blossoms, Pharaohs)
Wilson, Ronald L (Ron) Hamilton Bulldogs, 101 York Blvd, Hamilton ON L8R 3L4, Canada	Ice Hockey Player
Wilson, Ronald L (Ron) 17 Middleton Gardens Place, Bluffton SC 29910, USA	Ice Hockey Player, Coach
Wilson, Roy University of Colorado, President's Office, Denver CO 80217, USA	Educator
Wilson, Ruth Markham & Froggatt, Julian House, 4 Windmill St, London W1P 1HF, England	Actress
Wilson, S O'Neil (Neil) 4300 Highway 412 W, Lexington TN 38351, USA	Baseball Player
Wilson, Samuel W Hampden-Sydney College, President's Office, Hampden-Sydney VA 23943, USA	Army General, Educator
Wilson, Scott Andrew Freedman Personal Mgmt, 20 Ironsides Street, #18, Marina del Rey CA 90292, USA	Actor
Wilson, Sheree J Metropolitan Talent Agency, 7020 La Presa Dr, Los Angeles CA 90068 USA	Actress
Wilson, Stacy E Bowdoin College, Athletic Dept, Brunswick ME 04011, USA	Ice Hockey Player
Wilson, Stanley W (Stan) 4701 Hayter St, Lakewood CA 90712, USA	Baseball Player
Wilson, Stephanie D N A S A, Johnson Space Center, 2101 NASA Road, Houston TX 77058 USA	Astronaut
Wilson, Stephen D (Steve) 23-1041 Comox St, Vancouver BC V6E 1K1, Canada	Baseball Player
Wilson, Stephen E (Steve) West Jefferson Middle School, 9449 Barnes Ave, Conifer CO 80433, USA	Basketball Player

Wilson, Steve A 3706 Village Estates Place, Tampa FL 33618, USA	Football Player
Wilson, Steven A (Steve) 8516 Doughton Dr, Bahama NC 27503, USA	Football Player
Wilson, Steven J Agency Group Ltd, 361-373 City Road, London EC1V 2QA, England	Singer, Guitarist (Porcupine Tree)
Wilson, Stuart I C A Talent Mgmt, 818 12th St, #9, Santa Monica CA 90403, USA	Actor
Wilson, Thomas F A P A Talent/Literary Agency, 405 S Beverly Dr, #300, Beverly Hills CA 90212 USA	Actor
Wilson, Tom 2679 Tanglewood Court, Lake Havasu City AZ 86403, USA	Baseball Player
Wilson, Torrie Diverse Talent Group, 9911 Pico Blvd, #350W, Los Angeles CA 90035 USA	Professional Wrestler, Model
Wilson, Tracy CTV-TV, PO Box 9, Station O, Scarborough ON M4A 2M9, Canada	Ice Dancer, Sportscaster
Wilson, Trevor 824 15th St, Hermosa Beach CA 90254, USA	Basketball Player
Wilson, Trevor K 11857 White Lane, Oregon City OR 97045, USA	Baseball Player
Wilson, Trisha Wilson Assoc, 3811 Turtle Creek Dr, #1500, Dallas TX 75219, USA	Interior Designer
Wilson, Vance A 6368 Elizabeth Ave, Springdale AR 72762, USA	Baseball Player
Wilson, Wayne M 183 Willowdale Dr, Shepherdstown WV 25443, USA	Football Player
Wilson, William 130 Belmont St, Englewood NJ 07631, USA	Basketball Player
Wilson, William H (Mookie) 1111 Heyward Wilson Road, Eastover SC 29044, USA	Baseball Player
Wilson, William J Harvard University, Kennedy School of Government, Cambridge MA 02138, USA	Sociologist
Wilson, Willie J 18 Vianney Ave, Scarborough ON M1L 4V4, Canada	Baseball Player
Wilson, Woody King Features Syndicate, 300 W 57th St, #1500, New York NY 10019 USA	Cartoonist (Rex Morgan MD)
Wilson-Johnson, David R 28 Englefield Road, London N1 4ET, England	Opera Singer
Wilson-Sampras, Bridgette L Abrams Artists, 9200 W Sunset Blvd, #1125, West Hollywood CA 90069 USA	Actress, Singer
Wilton, Penelope I C M Partners, 10250 Constellation Blvd, #900, Los Angeles CA 90067 USA	Actress
Wiltsie, Jennifer Gavin Barker Assoc, 2D Wimpole St, London W1G 0EB, England	Actress
Wimbley, Kamerion 17400 Sawgrass Circle, North Royalton OH 44133, USA	Football Player
Wimmer, Brian Integrated Mgmt, 1041 N Formosa Ave, West Hollywood CA 90046, USA	Actor
Wimmer, Kurt Creative Artists Agency, 2000 Ave of Stars, #100, Los Angeles CA 90067 USA	Director
Wimmer, Scott Richard Childress Racing, 425 Industrial Dr, Welcome NC 27374, USA	Auto Racing Driver
Winans, BeBe Strategic Artists Mgmt, 1100 Glendon Ave, #1100, Los Angeles CA 90024, USA	Singer
Winans, CeCe Shore Fire Media, 32 Court St, #1600, Brooklyn NY 11201 USA	Singer
Winans, Jeff D 610 La Siesta Court, Turlock CA 95380, USA	Football Player
Winans, Mario Bad Boy Entertainment, 1440 Broadway, #16, New York NY 10018 USA	Singer
Winans, Matthew 21 Saint George Place, Sandy Hook CT 06482, USA	Baseball Umpire
Winans, Vicki Covenant Agency, 123 California Ave, #116, Santa Monica CA 90403 USA	Singer
Winant, Scott Hansen Jacobson Teller, 450 N Roxbury Dr, #800, Beverly Hills CA 90210 USA	Producer, Director
Winborne, Hughes I C M Partners, 10250 Constellation Blvd, #900, Los Angeles CA 90067 USA	Editor
Winborne, Jamie L 195 Roscoe Lee Circle, Wetumpka AL 36092, USA	Football Player
Winbush, Angela Joyce Agency, 370 Harrison Ave, Harrison NY 10528, USA	Singer, Songwriter
Winbush, Camille Stone Manners Salners, 9911 W Pico Blvd, #1400, Los Angeles CA 90035 USA	Actress
Winbush, Troy A P A Talent/Literary Agency, 405 S Beverly Dr, #300, Beverly Hills CA 90212 USA	Actor
Winceniak, Edward J (Ed) 10828 S Ave O, Chicago IL 60617, USA	Baseball Player
Wincer, Simon G Creative Artists Agency, 2000 Ave of Stars, #100, Los Angeles CA 90067 USA	Director
Winchester, Jesse Keith Case Assoc, 1025 17th Ave S, #200, Nashville TN 37212 USA	Singer, Pianist, Songwriter
Winchester, Philip Independent Talent Group, Oxford House, 76 Oxford St, London W1D 1BS, England	Actor
Winchester, Scott J 4705 Oakridge Dr, Midland MI 48640, USA	Baseball Player
Winchester, Simon Harper Collins Publishers, 10 E 53rd St, Cellar 1, New York NY 10022 USA	Writer
Wincott, Michael Edith Grove Inc, 5900 Wilshire Blvd, #2250, Los Angeles CA 90036, USA	Actor
Winder, Sammy Winder Construction Co, 4823 Green Crossing Road, Jackson MS 39213, USA	Football Player
Windhorn, Gordon R (Gordie) 145 Bent Creek Road, Danville VA 24540, USA	Baseball Player
Windis, Tony J 404 1st St, Rawlins WY 82301, USA	Basketball Player

Windon, Stephen F — Cinematographer
PO Box 659, Northbridge, Sydney NSW 2063, Australia
Windsor, Barbara — Actress, Comedienne
104 Crouch Hill, London NB 9EA, England
Windsor, David — Baseball Player
23972 Dublin St, Lake Forest CA 92630, USA
Windsor, Robert E (Bob) — Football Player
2625 Legends Way, Ellicott City MD 21042, USA
Wine, Robert P (Bobbie), Sr — Baseball Player, Manager
2614 Woodland Ave, Eagleville PA 19403, USA
Winegardner, Mark — Writer
Florida State University, English Dept, Tallahassee FL 32306, USA
Wineland, David J — Nobel Physics Laureate
National Institute of Standards & Technology, 325 Broadway, Boulder CO 80305, USA
Winfield, Antoine D — Football Player
10451 White Tail Crossing, Eden Prairie MN 55347, USA
Winfield, David M (Dave) — Baseball Player
2235 Stratford Circle, Los Angeles CA 90077, USA
Winfield, Leroy (Lee) — Basketball Player
7638 Forest View Dr, Saint Louis MO 63121, USA
Winfield, Rodney M — Artist
3483 Ocean Ave, Carmel CA 93923, USA
Winfrey, Oprah — Entertainer, Actress
Harpo Productions, 345 N Maple Dr, #315, Beverly Hills CA 90210, USA
Winfrey, Roy — Baseball Player
2903 Renfro Dr NW, Atlanta GA 30318, USA
Wing, Andrea — Photographer
Crown Bay Marina, #310, PM Box 10, Saint Thomas VI 00802, USA
Wing, Sean — Actor
Innovative Artists, 1505 10th St, Santa Monica CA 90401 USA
Wingate, David G S — Basketball Player
11404 Glaetzer Lane, Charlotte NC 28270, USA
Winger, Debra — Actress
I C M Partners, 10250 Constellation Blvd, #900, Los Angeles CA 90067 USA
Wingti, Paias — Prime Minister, Papua New Guinea
Marea Haus, Waigani, PO Box 6605, Port Moresby, Boroko, Papua New Guinea
Wink, Chris — Entertainer (Blue Man Group)
Blue Man Productions, 411 Lafayette St, #300, New York NY 10003, USA
Winkelried, Jon — Financier
Goldman Sachs Co, 85 Broad St, Building 85, New York NY 10004, USA
Winkler, Angela — Actress
Erna Baumbauer Mgmt, Kaplerstr 2, 81679 Munich, Germany
Winkler, Hans-Gunter — Equestrian
Dr Rau Allee 48, 48231 Warendorf, Germany
Winkler, Henry — Actor, Producer
PO Box 49914, Los Angeles CA 90049, USA
Winkler, Irwin — Director, Producer
Irwin Winkler Productions, 211 S Beverly Dr, #220, Beverly Hills CA 90212, USA
Winkler, Max — Actor, Writer, Producer
Creative Artists Agency, 2000 Ave of Stars, #100, Los Angeles CA 90067 USA
Winkles, Bobby B — Baseball Manager
78452 Calle Huerta, La Quinta CA 92253, USA
Winn, D Randolph (Randy) — Baseball Player
59 Leeds Court E, Danville CA 94526, USA
Winn, James F (Jim) — Baseball Player
3440 S Delaware Ave, #123, Springfield MO 65804, USA
Winnefeld, James A (Sandy), Jr — Navy Admiral
Vice Chairman, Joint Chiefs of Staff, Pentagon, Washington DC 20318 USA
Winner, Michael R — Director, Producer
219 Kensington High St, London W8 6BD, England
Winnick, Katheryn — Actress
Gersh Agency, 9465 Wilshire Blvd, #600, Beverly Hills CA 90212 USA
Winningham, Herman S (Herm) — Baseball Player
1542 Belleville Road, Orangeburg SC 29115, USA
Winningham, Mare — Actress
I F A Talent Agency, 8730 W Sunset Blvd, #490, West Hollywood CA 90069 USA
Winship, Anna — Actress
Marian Berzon Talent Agency, 23 Seton Road, Irvine CA 92612, USA
Winslet, Kate — Actress
United Agents, 12-26 Lexington St, London W1F 0LE, England
Winslow, Dan — Singer, Guitarist (Trashmen)
H T M/Headline Talent Mgmt, 39398 Moonlight Bay Trail, Pelican Rapids MN 56572 USA
Winslow, Kellen B, II — Football Player
2431 Cornerstone, Westlake OH 44145, USA
Winslow, Kellen B, Sr — Football Player, Administrator
Central State University, Athletic Dept, PO Box 1004, Wilberforce OH 45384, USA
Winslow, Michael — Actor, Comedian
Venture I A B, 3211 Cahuenga Blvd W, #104, Los Angeles CA 90068, USA
Winstead, Mary Elizabeth — Actress
Creative Artists Agency, 2000 Ave of Stars, #100, Los Angeles CA 90067 USA
Winston, Charlie — Singer, Songwriter
Agency Group Ltd, 142 W 57th St, #600, New York NY 10019 USA
Winston, Eric J — Football Player
4811 Palmetto St, Bellaire, TX 77401, USA
Winston, George — Pianist, Composer
Dancing Cat Productions, PO Box 4287, Santa Cruz CA 95063, USA
Winston, Roy C — Football Player
708 Highway 401, Napoleonville LA 70390, USA
Winstone, Ray — Actor
C A M, 111 Shoreditch High St, #400, London E1 6JN, England
Winter, Alex — Actor
A P A Talent/Literary Agency, 405 S Beverly Dr, #300, Beverly Hills CA 90212 USA
Winter, Blaise — Football Player
W5837 Royaltroon Dr, Menasha WI 54952, USA
Winter, Donald — Government Official
Navy Department, Secretary's Office, Pentagon, Washington DC 20350, USA

W	**Winter, Edgar** Edge Mgmt, 10850 Wilshire Blvd, #380, Los Angeles CA 90024, USA	Singer, Guitarist, Keyboardist
	Winter, Edward D 32070 Waterside Lane, Westlake Village CA 91361, USA	Actor
	Winter, Eric United Talent Agency, 9336 Civic Center Dr, Beverly Hills CA 90210 USA	Actor
	Winter, Fred (Tex) Los Angeles Lakers, Staples Center, 1111 S Figueroa St, Los Angeles CA 90015 USA	Basketball Coach
	Winter, Johnny Bullseye Mgmt, PO Box 3207, Stamford CT 06905, USA	Singer, Guitarist
	Winter, Olaf An der Pirschheide 28, 14471 Potsdam, Germany	Canoeing Athlete
	Winter, Paul T Earth Music Productions, PO Box 72, Litchfield CT 06759, USA	Jazz, New Age Musician
	Winter, Ralph K, Jr US Court of Appeals, 141 Church St, New Haven CT 06510, USA	Judge
	Winter, Terence P Creative Artists Agency, 2000 Ave of Stars, #100, Los Angeles CA 90067 USA	Writer, Producer
	Winter, William F 633 N State St, Jackson MS 39202, USA	Governor, MS
	Winterbottom, Michael Independent Talent Group, Oxford House, 76 Oxford St, London W1D 1BS, England	Director, Producer
	Winterhart, Paul Little Big Man, 39A Grammercy Park N, #1C, New York NY 10010, USA	Drummer (Kula Shaker)
	Winters, Abby PO Box 343, Fitzroy VIC 3065, Australia	Photographer
	Winters, Brian J 6144 S Moline Way, Englewood CO 80111, USA	Basketball Player, Coach
	Winters, Dean United Talent Agency, 9336 Civic Center Dr, Beverly Hills CA 90210 USA	Actor
	Winters, Edward G, III Commander, Special Warfare Command, 2000 Trident Way, Coronado CA 92155 USA	Navy Admiral
	Winters, Frank M 820 17th St, Union City NJ 07087, USA	Football Player
	Winters, Jonathan Locations Plus, 755 Romero Canyon Road, Santa Barbara CA 93108, USA	Actor, Comedian
	Winters, Lisa Playboy Promotions, 2706 Media Center Dr, Los Angeles CA 90065 USA	Model
	Winters, Michael Mitchell K Stubbs Assoc, 8695 W Washington Blvd, #204, Culver City CA 90232 USA	Actor
	Winters, Michael J (Mike) 13644 Boquita Dr, Del Mar CA 92014, USA	Baseball Umpire
	Winters, Mickey Playboy Promotions, 2706 Media Center Dr, Los Angeles CA 90065 USA	Model
	Winther, Peter Gersh Agency, 9465 Wilshire Blvd, #600, Beverly Hills CA 90212 USA	Director, Producer, Writer
	Wintour, Anna Vogue, Editor's Office, 4 Times Square, #1200, New York NY 10036, USA	Editor
	Winwood, Stephen L (Steve) Trinley Cottage, Trinley, Gloucester GL19 4EU, England	Singer, Musician (Traffic); Songwriter
	Wire, Coy M 586 Park Dr NE, Atlanta GA 30306, USA	Football Player
	Wire, William S, II 706 Overton Park, Nashville TN 37215, USA	Businessman
	Wirth, Billy Creative Management Group, 8522 National Blvd, #108, Culver City CA 90232 USA	Actor, Director
	Wirth, Timothy E United Nations Foundation, 1225 Connecticut Ave NW, Washington DC 20036, USA	Senator, CO
	Wise, L DeWayne 709 Old Lexington Highway, Chapin SC 29036, USA	Baseball Player
	Wise, Matthew J (Matt) 11627 E Twilight Court, Chandler AZ 85249, USA	Baseball Player
	Wise, Phillip V (Phil) 11511 Poppy St NW, Minneapolis MN 55433, USA	Football Player
	Wise, Phyllis M University of Washington, President's Office, Gerberding Hall, Seattle WA 98195, USA	Neurobiologist, Educator
	Wise, Ray Abrams Artists, 9200 W Sunset Blvd, #1125, West Hollywood CA 90069 USA	Actor
	Wise, Richard C (Rick) 15160 NW Oakhills Dr, Beaverton OR 97006, USA	Baseball Player
	Wise, Willie M 2320 185th Place NE, Redmond WA 98052, USA	Basketball Player
	Wiseman, Brian 5917 Delores St, #B, Houston TX 77057, USA	Ice Hockey Player
	Wiseman, Frederick Zipporah Films, 1 Richdale Ave, #4, Cambridge MA 02140, USA	Producer
	Wiseman, Len R Creative Artists Agency, 2000 Ave of Stars, #100, Los Angeles CA 90067 USA	Director, Producer, Writer
	Wiseman, Mac PO Box 17028, Nashville TN 37217, USA	Singer
	Wish Bone Life Entertainment, 15441 Red Hill Ave, #G, Tustin CA 92780, USA	Rap Artist (Bone Thugs-N-Harmony)
	Wishart, Leonard P, III 19360 Magnolia Grove Square, #315, Leesburg VA 20176, USA	Army General
	Wisniewski, Andreas Gregory David Mayo, Reinhardtstra 35, 10117 Berlin, Germany	Actor
	Wisniewski, Stephen A (Steve) 36 El Alamo Court, Danville CA 94526, USA	Football Player
	Wisniewski, Tom W M E Entertainment, 9601 Wilshire Blvd, #300, Beverly Hills CA 90210 USA	Guitarist (MxPx)
	Wisocky, Rebecca Connor Ankrum Assoc, 1680 Vine St, #1016, Los Angeles CA 90028, USA	Actress
	Wisoff, Peter J K (Jeff) 4268 Brindisi Place, Pleasanton CA 94566, USA	Astronaut
	Wissman, David A (Dave) PO Box 38, Derby VT 05829, USA	Baseball Player

Winter - Wissman

Wiste, Jim	Ice Hockey Player
701 S University Blvd, Denver CO 80209, USA	
Wistert, Albert A (Ox)	Football Player
1411 NE Olson Dr, Grants Pass OR 97526, USA	
Wistrom, Grant A	Football Player
1625 E Delmar St, Springfield MO 65804, USA	
Witasick, Gerald A (Jay)	Baseball Player
200 Wellington Court, Bel Air MD 21014, USA	
Witcher, Richard V (Dick)	Football Player
2031 E Taxidea Way, Phoenix AZ 85048, USA	
Withem, Shannon B	Baseball Player
39668 Dorchester Circle, Canton MI 48188, USA	
Withers, Bill	Singer, Songwriter
Mattie Music Group, PO Box 16698, Beverly Hills CA 90209, USA	
Withers, Jane	Actress
Keller & Vanderneth Business Mgmt, 1133 Broadway, #911, New York NY 10010, USA	
Withers, Pick	Drummer (Dire Straits)
Damage Mgmt, 16 Lambton Place, London W11 2SH, England	
Witherspoon, John	Actor, Comedian
Levity Entertainment, 6701 Center Drive W, #1111, Los Angeles CA 90045 USA	
Witherspoon, Reese	Actress
Management 360, 9111 Wilshire Blvd, Beverly Hills CA 90210 USA	
Witherspoon, Tim	Boxer
Shuler Memorial Boxing Gym, 750 N Brooklyn St, Philadelphia PA 19104, USA	
Witherspoon, William C (Will)	Football Player
4535 Wayland Dr, Nashville TN 37215, USA	
Witiuk, Doris	Baseball Player
11821 N Hemlock St, Spokane WA 99218, USA	
Witiuk, Steve	Ice Hockey Player
6 Leacock Ave, Winnipeg MB R3K 0G2, Canada	
Witkin, Jerome	Artist
201 Whitestone Dr, Syracuse NY 13215, USA	
Witkin, Joel-Peter	Photographer
1707 Five Points Road SW, Albuquerque NM 87105, USA	
Witkop, Bernhard	Chemist
3807 Montrose Driveway, Chevy Chase MD 20815, USA	
Witman, Jon D	Football Player
568 Woodsview Lane, Hellam PA 17406, USA	
Witmer, Tamara	Model
Playboy Promotions, 2706 Media Center Dr, Los Angeles CA 90065 USA	
Witmeyer, Ronald H (Ron)	Baseball Player
PO Box 763, Rancho Santa Fe CA 92067, USA	
Witt, Alicia	Actress
Brillstein Entertainment Partners, 9150 Wilshire Blvd, #350, Beverly Hills CA 90212 USA	
Witt, Brendan	Ice Hockey Player
691 Park Ave, Huntington NY 11743, USA	
Witt, George A	Baseball Player
2209 Catalina St, Laguna Beach CA 92651, USA	
Witt, Howard	Actor
Gage Group, 315 W 57th St, #4H, New York NY 10019 USA	
Witt, Kevin J	Baseball Player
6350 Concho Bay Dr, Houston TX 77041, USA	
Witt, Michael A (Mike)	Baseball Player
37 Poppy Hills Road, Laguna Nigel CA 92677, USA	
Witt, Paul Junger	Writer, Producer, Director
16032 Valley Vista Blvd, Encino CA 91436, USA	
Witt, Robert A (Bobby)	Baseball Player
4601 Winewood Court, Colleyville TX 76034, USA	
Witt, Robert E	Educator
University of Alabama, President's Office, PO Box 870100, Tuscaloosa AL 35487, USA	
Witt, Vicki	Model
Playboy Promotions, 2706 Media Center Dr, Los Angeles CA 90065 USA	
Witte, Luke	Basketball Player
3223 Arbor Pointe Dr, Charlotte NC 28210, USA	
Witten, C Jason	Football Player
501 King Ranch Road, Southlake TX 76092, USA	
Witten, Edward	Theoretical Physicist, Mathematician
Institute for Advanced Study, Einstein Lane, Princeton NJ 08540 USA	
Witter, Cherie	Model, Actress
Playboy Promotions, 2706 Media Center Dr, Los Angeles CA 90065 USA	
Witter, Junior	Boxer
Cybersportsbox, 23 Minna Road, Sheffield, South York S3 9AZ, England	
Witter, Karen	Actress, Model
H/H/M, 247 S Beverly Dr, #102, Beverly Hills CA 90212, USA	
Witting, Steve	Actor
Paradigm Agency, 360 N Crescent Dr, North Building, Beverly Hills CA 90210 USA	
Wittman, Randy S	Basketball Player, Coach
8646 French Curve, Eden Prairie MN 55347, USA	
Witty, Chris	Speed Skater
2644 E 2940 S, Salt Lake City UT 84109, USA	
Witucki, Casimir L (Cas)	Football Player
3909 Spring Terrace, #248, Temple Hills MD 20748, USA	
Wlaschiha, Tom	Actor
Agentur Hubchen, Pariser Str 20, 10707 Berlin, Germany	
Wockel-Eckert, Barbel	Track Athlete
Im Bangert 61, 64750 Lutzelbach, Germany	
Wockenfuss, John B	Baseball Player
26 Wallamsey Lane, Chesapeake City MD 21915, USA	
Woelki, Rainer M Cardinal	Religious Leader
Archdiocese, Niederwallstr 8-9, 10017 Berlin, Germany	
Woerner, Scott A	Football Player
11268 Turner Road, Hampton GA 30228, USA	
Woerth, Douglas	Labor Leader
Airline Pilots Union, 535 Herndon Parkway, Herndon VA 20170, USA	
Woertz, Patricia	Businesswoman
Archer Daniels Midland Co, 4666 Faries Parkway, #1, Decatur IL 62526, USA	

Wiste - Woertz

Woese, Carl R — Microbiologist
806 W Delaware Ave, Urbana IL 61801, USA
Wofford, Harris L — Senator, PA
955 26th St NW, #501, Washington DC 20037, USA
Woggon, Bill — Cartoonist (Katy Keene)
2724 Cabot Court, Thousand Oaks CA 91360, USA
Wohl, Bess — Actress, Writer
Untitled Entertainment, 350 S Beverly Dr, #200, Beverly Hills CA 90212 USA
Wohl, David B (Dave) — Basketball Player, Coach, Executive
137 Morley Circle, Melville NY 11747, USA
Wohlberg, Jeffrey — Religious Leader, Rabbi
Adas Israel Congregation, 565 Broadway, Passaic NJ 07055, USA
Wohlers, Mark E — Baseball Player
135 Old Cedar Lane, Alpharetta GA 30004, USA
Wohlford, James E (Jim) — Baseball Player
24186 Lomitas Dr, Woodlake CA 93286, USA
Wohlhuter, Richard C (Rick) — Track Athlete
175 Dickinson Dr, Wheaton IL 60189, USA
Wohlwender-Fricker, Marian — Baseball Player
15210 Portside Dr, #401, Fort Myers FL 33908, USA
Woit, Benedict F (Benny) — Ice Hockey Player
607-20 Harding Blvd W, Richmond Hill ON L4C 9S4, Canada
Woiwode, Larry — Writer
State University of New York, English Dept, Binghamton NY 13901, USA
Wojciechowski, John S — Football Player
13317 Clyde Road, Holly MI 48442, USA
Wojtowicz, R P — Labor Leader
Railway Carmen Union, 3 Research Place, Rockville MD 20850, USA
Wolanin, Craig — Ice Hockey Player
4891 Gallagher Road, Rochester MI 48306, USA
Wolcott, Gregory — Actor
PO Box 622, Canoga Park CA 91305, USA
Wolcott, Robert W (Bob) — Baseball Player
3323 Bryson Way, Medford OR 97504, USA
Wolczanski, Peter T — Chemist
Cornell University, Chemistry Dept, Ithaca NY 14853, USA
Wolde-Giorgis Lucha, Girma — President, Ethiopia
President's Office, Presidential Palace, PO Box 1362, Addis Ababa, Ethiopia
Wolf, Dale E — Governor, DE
4830 Kennett Pike, #3221, Wilmington DE 19807, USA
Wolf, David A — Astronaut
1714 Neptune Lane, Houston TX 77062, USA
Wolf, Dick — Producer
W M E Entertainment, 9601 Wilshire Blvd, #300, Beverly Hills CA 90210 USA
Wolf, James (Jim) — Baseball Umpire
1507 E Glenhaven Dr, Phoenix AZ 85048, USA
Wolf, Joseph F (Joe) — Football Player
2324 Lehigh Parkway N, Allentown PA 18103, USA
Wolf, Josh — Actor, Comedian, Writer
Parallel Entertainment, 9420 Wilshire Blvd, #250, Beverly Hills CA 90212 USA
Wolf, Naomi — Writer
Royce Carlton Inc, 866 United Nations Plaza, #587, New York NY 10017, USA
Wolf, Peter — Singer (J Geils Band)
Nick Ben-Meir, 652 N Doheny Dr, West Hollywood CA 90069, USA
Wolf, Randall C (Randy) — Baseball Player
8054 Royer Ave, Canoga Park CA 91304, USA
Wolf, Sally — Opera Singer
Columbia Artists Mgmt Inc, 1790 Broadway, #702, New York NY 10019 USA
Wolf, Scott — Actor
United Talent Agency, 9336 Civic Center Dr, Beverly Hills CA 90210 USA
Wolf, Sigrid — Alpine Skier
6652 Elbigenalp 45A, Austria
Wolf, Vicente — Interior Designer
Vicente Wolf Assoc, 333 W 39th St, New York NY 10018, USA
Wolf, Walter B (Wally) — Baseball Player
18580 Corte Fresco, Rancho Santa Fe CA 92091, USA
Wolfe, Art — Photographer
520 1st Ave S, Seattle WA 98104, USA
Wolfe, Bernard (Bernie) — Ice Hockey Player
8012 Glenbrook Road, Bethesda MD 20814, USA
Wolfe, Brian — Baseball Player
32524 Sprucewood Way, Lake Elsinore CA 92532, USA
Wolfe, Collette — Actress
Gersh Agency, 9465 Wilshire Blvd, #600, Beverly Hills CA 90212 USA
Wolfe, George C — Director
Loeb & Loeb, 10100 Santa Monica Blvd, #2200, Los Angeles CA 90067 USA
Wolfe, James — Sculptor
1945 Cerro Gordo St, Los Angeles CA 90039, USA
Wolfe, Laurence A (Larry) — Baseball Player
5200 Blossomwood Court, Fair Oaks CA 95628, USA
Wolfe, Nathan D — Virologist
Global Viral Forcasting Initiative, 1 Sutter, #600, San Francisco CA 94104, USA
Wolfe, Ralph S — Microbiologist
University of Illinois, Microbiology Dept, Burrill Hall, Urbana IL 61801, USA
Wolfe, Robert H — Producer, Writer
I C M Partners, 10250 Constellation Blvd, #900, Los Angeles CA 90067 USA
Wolfe, Sterling — Actor
2609 Wyoming Ave, #A, Burbank CA 91505, USA
Wolfe, Thad A — Air Force General
4790 Longwood Point, Colorado Springs CO 80906, USA
Wolfe, Thomas K (Tom), Jr — Writer
Felker Toczak Gellman, 10880 Wilshire Blvd, #2070, Los Angeles CA 90024 USA
Wolfenden of Westcott, John F — Educator
White House, Guildford Road, Westcott near Dorking, Surrey, England
Wolfensohn, James D — Financier
James D Wolfensohn Co, 599 Lexington Ave, New York NY 10022, USA

Wolfenstein, Lincoln — Physicist
Carnegie-Mellon University, Physics Dept, 5000 Forbes, Pittsburgh PA 15213, USA

Wolfermann, Klaus — Track Athlete
Puma Sportschu, Postfach 1420, 91074 Herzogenraurach, Germany

Wolfe-Simon, Felisa — Biogeochemist
N A S A Astrobiology, Harvard University, 20 Oxford St Cambridge MA 02138, USA

Wolff, Alexander D (Alex) — Actor, Singer (Naked Brothers Band)
Creative Artists Agency, 2000 Ave of Stars, #100, Los Angeles CA 90067 USA

Wolff, Bob — Sportscaster
3 Salisbury Point, #2E, Nyack NY 10960, USA

Wolff, Christian — Composer
Zinnkopfstr 6, 83229 Aschau/Chiemsee, Germany

Wolff, Christoph J — Educator
182 Washington St, Belmont MA 02478, USA

Wolff, Hugh — Conductor
Van Walsum Mgmt, Tower Building, 11 York Road, London SE1 7NX, England

Wolff, Nathaniel M (Nat) — Singer (Naked Brothers Band), Songwriter
Creative Artists Agency, 2000 Ave of Stars, #100, Los Angeles CA 90067 USA

Wolff, Sanford I — Labor Leader
8141 Broadway, New York NY 10023, USA

Wolff, Tobias J A — Writer
Stanford University, English Dept, Stanford CA 94305, USA

Wolff, Torben — Biologist, Zoologist
Hesseltoften 12, 2900 Hellerup, Denmark

Wolfley, Craig A — Football Player
331 Station St, Bridgeville PA 15017, USA

Wolfley, Ronald P (Ron) — Football Player
17612 N 41st Place, Phoenix AZ 85032, USA

Wolford, William C (Will) — Football Player
205 Waterleaf Way, Louisville KY 40207, USA

Wolfowitz, Paul D — Financier, Government Official
American Express Institute, 1150 17th St NW, Washington DC 20036, USA

Wolk, James — Actor
W M E Entertainment, 9601 Wilshire Blvd, #300, Beverly Hills CA 90210 USA

Wolkowitch, Bruno — Actor
Artmedia, 20 Ave Rapp, 75007 Paris, France

Woll, Cynthia — Actress
2050 High Tower Road, #2, Los Angeles CA 90068, USA

Woll, Deborah Ann — Actress
Paradigm Agency, 360 N Crescent Dr, North Building, Beverly Hills CA 90210 USA

Wollack, Brad — Actor, Writer, Producer
Creative Artists Agency, 2000 Ave of Stars, #100, Los Angeles CA 90067 USA

Wollman, Harvey L — Governor, SD
RR 1 Box 43, Hitchcock SD 57348, USA

Wollman, Roger L — Judge
US Court of Appeals, Federal Building, 400 S Phillips, Sioux Falls SD 57104, USA

Wolodarsky, Wallace (Wally) — Producer, Writer
I C M Partners, 10250 Constellation Blvd, #900, Los Angeles CA 90067 USA

Wolpe, David — Religious Leader, Rabbi
Sinai Temple, 10400 Wilshire Blvd, Los Angeles CA 90024, USA

Wolpe, Lenny — Actor
Gage Group, 315 W 57th St, #4H, New York NY 10019 USA

Wolski, Wojciech (Wojtek) — Ice Hockey Player
Washington Capitals, 627 N Glebe Road, #850, Arlington VA 22203 USA

Wolstenholme, Christopher T (Chris) — Bassist (Muse)
Hall or Nothing P R, 35-37 Parkgate Road, London SW11 4NP, England

Wolters, Kara — Basketball Player
137 Westfield Dr, Holliston MA 01746, USA

Woltman, Rhea A — Astronaut
17 Polo Circle, Colorado Springs CO 80906, USA

Womack, Anthony D (Tony) — Baseball Player
8301 Marcliffe Court, Waxhaw NC 28173, USA

Womack, Floyd S — Football Player
105 Grandview Circle, Brandon MS 39047, USA

Womack, Horace G (Dooley) — Baseball Player
209 Weeping Cherry Lane, Columbia SC 29212, USA

Womack, James E — Biologist, Agricultural Researcher
2105 Farley, College Station TX 77845, USA

Womack, Lee Ann — Singer
W M E Entertainment, 1600 Division St, #300, Nashville TN 37203 USA

Womack, Robert D (Bobby) — Singer, Guitarist, Songwriter
Columbia Records, 9830 Wilshire Blvd, Beverly Hills CA 90212 USA

Womble, Royce C — Football Player
6350 Newt Patterson Road, Mansfield TX 76063, USA

Won Hye Kyung — Speed Skater
Skating Union, 88 Bangyee-Dong, Songpaku, Seoul 138 749, South Korea

Wonder, Stevie — Singer, Songwriter
Steveland Morris Music, 4616 W Magnolia Blvd, Burbank CA 91505, USA

Wonder, Wayne — Singer, Songwriter
Headline Entertainment, 8 Haughton Ave, Kingston 10, Jamaica

Wonders, Rich — Bowler
720 Augusta St, Racine WI 53402, USA

Wondolowski, Christopher E (Chris) — Soccer Player
San Jose Earthquakes, 451 El Camino Real, #220, Santa Clara CA 95050 USA

Wong Kar Wai — Director
Creative Artists Agency, 2000 Ave of Stars, #100, Los Angeles CA 90067 USA

Wong, Bradley D (B D) — Actor
Gersh Agency, 9465 Wilshire Blvd, #600, Beverly Hills CA 90212 USA

Wong, James — Director, Producer, Writer
W M E Entertainment, 9601 Wilshire Blvd, #300, Beverly Hills CA 90210 USA

Wong, Kailee W — Football Player
5410 Valerie St, Bellaire TX 77401, USA

Wong, Kirk — Actor, Director
Global Artists Agency, 6253 Hollywood Blvd, #508, Los Angeles CA 90028, USA

Wong, Russell — Actor
Innovative Artists, 1505 10th St, Santa Monica CA 90401 USA

Wong, Sue — Fashion Designer
3030 W 6th St, Los Angeles CA 90020, USA
Wong-Staal, Flossie — Molecular Biologist
University of California, Molecular Biology Dept, La Jolla CA 92093, USA
Wonsley, George I — Football Player
2875 Spring Meadow Court, Indianapolis IN 46268, USA
Woo Suk Hwang — Geneticist
National University, Sillimdong, Gwanakgu, Seoul 151-742, South Korea
Woo, John — Director, Producer
Lion Rock Productions, 5100 Goldleaf Circle, #230, Los Angeles CA 90056, USA
Wood — Drummer (British Sea Power)
Agency Group Ltd, 361-373 City Road, London EC1V 2QA, England
Wood, Adam K C — Lieutenant Governor, Isle of Man
Lieutenant Governor's Office, Government House, Onchan, Isle of Man
Wood, Annie — Actress
Amsel Eisenstadt Frazier, 5055 Wilshire Blvd, #865, Los Angeles CA 90036 USA
Wood, Anthony — Businessman
Roku Co, 12980 Saratoga Ave, #D, Saratoga CA 95070, USA
Wood, Barbara — Writer
1201 University Dr, #106-177, Riverside CA 92507, USA
Wood, Brenton — Singer
Groove Entertainment, 1005 N Alfred St, #2, West Hollywood CA 90069, USA
Wood, C Norman — Air Force General
214 Lower Field Road, Dunnsville VA 22454, USA
Wood, Carolyn — Swimmer
4380 SW 86th Ave, Portland OR 97225, USA
Wood, Carri — Golfer
2001 Sabal Ridge Court, #H, Palm Beach Gardens FL 33418, USA
Wood, Charles G — Writer
Gordon Dickinson, 2 Crescent Grove, London SW4 7AH, England
Wood, David L — Basketball Player
5915 Crescent Moon Court, Reno NV 89511, USA
Wood, Diane P — Judge
US Court of Appeals, 219 S Dearborn St, Chicago IL 60604, USA
Wood, Duane S — Football Player
407 W Caddo Ave, Wilburton OK 74578, USA
Wood, Elijah — Actor
W M E Entertainment, 9601 Wilshire Blvd, #300, Beverly Hills CA 90210 USA
Wood, Evan Rachel — Actress
Creative Artists Agency, 2000 Ave of Stars, #100, Los Angeles CA 90067 USA
Wood, Glen — Auto Racing Executive
57 Rhody Creek Loop, Stuart VA 24171, USA
Wood, Gordon S — Historian
77 Keene St, Providence RI 02906, USA
Wood, Jacob (Jake), Jr — Baseball Player
9129 Daytona Dr, Pensacola FL 32506, USA
Wood, Janet — Actress
Acme Talent, 4727 Wilshire Blvd, #333, Los Angeles CA 90010, USA
Wood, Jason W — Baseball Player
9899 N Cascade Dr, Fresno CA 93730, USA
Wood, John A — Astrophysicist, Geologist
1716 Cambridge St, #16, Cambridge MA 02138, USA
Wood, Kerry L — Baseball Player
6838 E Chey Dr, Paradise Valley AZ 85253, USA
Wood, Kimba M — Judge
US District Court House, 40 Foley Square, #104, New York NY 10007, USA
Wood, Lana — Actress
1131 Oriole Circle, Fillmore CA 93015, USA
Wood, Laurie J — Model, Actress
Playboy Promotions, 2706 Media Center Dr, Los Angeles CA 90065 USA
Wood, Leonard — Auto Racing Driver
Wood Brothers Racing, 21 Performance Dr, Stuart VA 24171, USA
Wood, M Richard (Dick) — Football Player
41 Audubon Place, Newnan GA 30265, USA
Wood, Maurice — Physician
RR 2 Box 543B, Hot Springs VA 24445, USA
Wood, Michael B (Mike) — Baseball Player
1199 Cherlynn Terrace, West Palm Beach FL 33406, USA
Wood, Michael S (Mike) — Football Player
630 N Geyer Road, Saint Louis MO 63122, USA
Wood, Nigel K — Astronaut, England
Boscome Down Royal Air Force Base, Amesbury, Wiltshire SP4 0JF, England
Wood, O Leon — Basketball Player
4217 Faculty Ave, Long Beach CA 90808, USA
Wood, Oliver — Cinematographer
1549 N Gardner St, Los Angeles CA 90046, USA
Wood, R Brandon — Baseball Player
19550 N Grayhawk Dr, #1110, Scottsdale AZ 85255, USA
Wood, Rachel Hurd — Actress
Troika, 74 Clerkenwell Road, #300, London EC1M 5QA, England
Wood, Randolph B (Randy) — Ice Hockey Player
2 Bridge St, Manchester MA 01944, USA
Wood, Richard M — Football Player, Coach
5413 Windbrush Dr, Tampa FL 33625, USA
Wood, Robert J — Astronaut
McDonnell Douglas Corp, PO Box 516, Saint Louis MO 63166, USA
Wood, Ronald (Ron) — Guitarist (Rolling Stones)
Monroe Sounds, 5 Church Row, Wandsworth Plain, London SW18 1ES, England
Wood, Wilbur F, Jr — Baseball Player
3 Elmbrook Road, Bedford MA 01730, USA
Wood, William V (Willie) — Football Player
Willie Wood Mechanical Systems, 7941 16th St NW, Washington DC 20012, USA
Woodall, D Bradley (Brad) — Baseball Player
3539 John Muir Dr, Middleton WI 53562, USA
Woodall, F Alley (Al) — Football Player
131 Field Crest Road, New Canaan CT 06840, USA

Woodall, Jerry M — Electrical Engineer, Inventor
Yale University, Microelectronic Center, 105 Wall St, New Haven CT 06511, USA
Woodall, Lee A — Football Player
63 Sleepy Hollow Dr, Detroit MI 48227, USA
Woodall, Trinny — Actress
Artist Rights Group, 4 Great Portland Place, London W1W 8PA, England
Woodard, Alfre — Actress
I C M Partners, 10250 Constellation Blvd, #900, Los Angeles CA 90067 USA
Woodard, Charlayne — Actress, Writer
Sovereign Talent Group, 8421 Wilshire Blvd, #200, Beverly Hills CA 90211, USA
Woodard, Kenneth E (Ken) — Football Player
15389 Steel St, #201, Detroit MI 48227, USA
Woodard, Lynette — Basketball Player
4807 Pin Oak Park, #3210, Houston TX 77081, USA
Woodard, Michael C (Mike) — Baseball Player
PO Box 35, Maywood IL 60153, USA
Woodard, Rickey — Jazz Saxophonist
J V C Music, 3800 Barham Blvd, #409, Los Angeles CA 90068, USA
Woodard, Ronald B — Businessman
MagnaDrive Inc, 600 108th Ave NE, #1014, Bellevue WA 98004, USA
Woodard, Shannon — Actress
Untitled Entertainment, 350 S Beverly Dr, #200, Beverly Hills CA 90212 USA
Woodard, Steven L (Steve) — Baseball Player
800 Frost Court SW, Hartselle AL 35640, USA
Woodbine, Bokeem — Actor
Gersh Agency, 9465 Wilshire Blvd, #600, Beverly Hills CA 90212 USA
Woodbridge, Todd — Tennis Player
Advantage International, PO Box 3297, North Burnley, VIC 3121, Australia
Woodburn, Danny — Actor
Artists Group, 3345 Wilshire Blvd, #915, Los Angeles CA 90010, USA
Woodcock, John M — Football Player
1040 Tioga Court, Lincoln CA 95648, USA
Wooden, Shawn A — Football Player
17741 SW 12th St, Pembroke Pines FL 33029, USA
Woodeshick, Thomas (Tom) — Football Player
PO Box 716, Blakeslee PA 18610, USA
Woodforde, Mark — Tennis Player
Octagon Worldwide, 1751 Pinnacle Dr, #1500, McLean VA 22102 USA
Woodgate, Daniel (Woody) — Drummer (Madness)
I T F, Ariel House, 74A Charlotte St, London W1T 4QJ, England
Woodgette, Wanita D — Singer (Danity Kane)
Bad Boy Entertainment, 1440 Broadway, #16, New York NY 10018 USA
Woodhall, Richard (Richie) — Boxer
Tony Clayman, 58/60 Kensington Church St, London W8 4DB, England
Woodhead, Cynthia — Swimmer
PO Box 1193, Riverside CA 92502, USA
Woodhead, Danny — Football Player
New England Patriots, 1 Patriot Place, Foxboro MA 02035 USA
Woodland, Gary — Golfer
Professional Golfer's Assn, PO Box 109601, Palm Beach Gardens FL 33410 USA
Woodland, Lauren — Actress
Michael Bruno Group, 13576 Cheltenham Dr, Sherman Oaks CA 91423, USA
Woodley, Arthur — Singer
Opus 3 Artists, 470 Park Ave S, #900N, New York NY 10016 USA
Woodley, Dan — Ice Hockey Player
6347 S Yukon Court, Littleton CO 80123, USA
Woodley, LaMarr D — Football Player
1635 Heritage Dr, Pittsburgh PA 15237, USA
Woodley, Shailene — Actress
Savage Agency, 6212 Banner Ave, Los Angeles CA 90038 USA
Woodlief, Douglas E (Doug) — Football Player
4953 Santa Evinita Dr, Fort Mohave AZ 86426, USA
Woodmansee, John W, Jr — Army General
23 Cattail Pond Dr, Frisco TX 75034, USA
Woodruff, Blake — Actor
Amsel Eisenstadt Frazier, 5055 Wilshire Blvd, #865, Los Angeles CA 90036 USA
Woodruff, Bob — Commentator
ABC-TV, News Dept, 77 W 66th St, New York NY 10023 USA
Woodruff, Bob — Singer, Songwriter
Jim Della Croce Mgmt, 1229 17th Ave S, Nashville TN 37212, USA
Woodruff, Dwayne D — Football Player
10382 Grubbs Road, Wexford PA 15090, USA
Woodruff, Judy C — Commentator
CNN-TV, News Dept, 820 1st St NE, #1000, Washington DC 20002 USA
Woods, Alvis (Al) — Baseball Player
2600 San Leandro Blvd, #1004, San Leandro CA 94578, USA
Woods, Aubrey — Actress
Bryan Drew, Quadrant House, 80-82 Regent St, London W1B 5AU, England
Woods, Barbara Alyn — Actress
Stone Manners Salners, 9911 W Pico Blvd, #1400, Los Angeles CA 90035 USA
Woods, Christine — Actress
Gersh Agency, 9465 Wilshire Blvd, #600, Beverly Hills CA 90212 USA
Woods, Donald R (Don) — Football Player
6340 Calle Tesoro NW, Albuquerque NM 87114, USA
Woods, Elbert (Ickey) — Football Player
505 E Sharon Road, #A, Cincinnati OH 45246, USA
Woods, Eldrick T (Tiger) — Golfer
501 N Highway A1A, Jupiter FL 33477, USA
Woods, Gary L — Baseball Player
PO Box 151, Solvang CA 93464, USA
Woods, George — Track Athlete
7631 Green Hedge Road, Edwardsville IL 62025, USA
Woods, James — Actor
Gersh Agency, 9465 Wilshire Blvd, #600, Beverly Hills CA 90212 USA
Woods, James J (Jim) — Baseball Player
4509 Gardenia Ave, Keyes CA 95328, USA

Woods, Larry D — Football Player
8906 Covent Garden St, Houston TX 77031, USA

Woods, LeVar — Football Player
570 Auburn Hills Dr, Coralville IA 52241, USA

Woods, Michael — Actor
Mavrick Artists, 6100 Wilshire Blvd, #550, Los Angeles CA 90048, USA

Woods, Nan — Actress
Geddes Agency, 8430 Santa Monica Blvd, #201, West Hollywood CA 90069 USA

Woods, Paul — Ice Hockey Player
4276 S Shore St, Waterford MA 48328, USA

Woods, Philip W (Phil) — Jazz Clarinetist, Saxophonist, Composer
PO Box 278, Delaware Water Gap PA 18327, USA

Woods, Rick L — Football Player
1567 76th Ave N, Saint Petersburg FL 33702, USA

Woods, Robert E — Football Player
4922 Devonshire Ave, Memphis TN 38117, USA

Woods, Robert S — Actor
PO Box 492, Kinderhook NY 12106, USA

Woods, Ronald L (Ron) — Baseball Player
5209 Desert Star Dr, Las Vegas NV 89130, USA

Woods, S Anthony (Tony) — Football Player
69 Stengel Ave, Newark NJ 07112, USA

Woods, Simon — Actor
Independent Talent Group, Oxford House, 76 Oxford St, London W1D 1BS, England

Woods, Skip — Director, Producer, Writer
Creative Artists Agency, 2000 Ave of Stars, #100, Los Angeles CA 90067 USA

Woods, Stuart — Writer
G P Putnam's Sons, 375 Hudson St, New York NY 10014 USA

Woods, Susan — Actress
28164 Sloan Canyon Road, #A, Castaic CA 91384, USA

Woods, Zach — Actor
Innovative Artists, 1505 10th St, Santa Monica CA 90401 USA

Woodside, D B — Actor
Don Buchwald/Fortitude, 6500 Wilshire Blvd, #2200, Los Angeles CA 90048 USA

Woodson, Abraham B (Abe) — Football Player
3680 Waynesvill St, Las Vegas NV 89122, USA

Woodson, Charles — Football Player
10010 Tavistock Road, Orlando FL 32827, USA

Woodson, Herbert H — Electrical Engineer
1034 Liberty Park Dr, Austin TX 78746, USA

Woodson, Jacqueline — Writer
Bantam Books, 1745 Broadway, New York NY 10019 USA

Woodson, Marvin L (Marv) — Football Player
3050 Redmond Dr, #2207, Dallas TX 75211, USA

Woodson, Michael D (Mike) — Basketball Player, Coach
New York Knicks, Madison Square Garden, 2 Penn Plaza, New York, NY 10121 USA

Woodson, Richard L (Dick) — Baseball Player
27879 Panorama Hills Dr, Menifee CA 92584, USA

Woodson, Robert L, Sr — Urban Activist
National Neighborhood Enterprise Center, 1424 16th St NW, Washington DC 20036, USA

Woodson, Roderick K (Rod) — Football Player, Sportscaster
3304 Medallion Court, Pleasanton CA 94588, USA

Woodson, Tracy M — Baseball Player
1559 Byfield Parkway, Valparaiso IN 46385, USA

Woodson, Warren V — Football Coach
12680 Hillcrest Road, #1106, Dallas TX 75230, USA

Woodson, William R — Educator
North Carolina State University, Chancellor's Office, Peele Hall, Raleigh NC 27695, USA

Woodville, Kate — Actress
20141 S Sweetbriar Road, West Linn OR 97068, USA

Woodward, Christopher M (Chris) — Baseball Player
15049 Howelhurst Dr, Baldwin Park CA 91706, USA

Woodward, Joanne G — Actress
Warren Cowan, 8899 Beverly Blvd, #918, Los Angeles CA 90048 USA

Woodward, John F — Navy Admiral, England
Navy Secretary, Naval Base, Portsmouth, Hants PO1 3LS, England

Woodward, Kirsten — Fashion Designer
Kirsten Woodward Hats, 26 Portobello Green Arcade, London W10, England

Woodward, Margaret H (Maggie) — Air Force General
Commander 17th Air Force, Ramstein Air Force Base, Unit 3300, APO AE 09094 , USA

Woodward, Morgan — Actor
2111 Rockledge Road, Los Angeles CA 90068, USA

Woodward, Neil W, III — Astronaut
1935 Edgemont Place W, Seattle WA 98199, USA

Woodward, Robert J (Rob) — Baseball Player
58 Eastman Hill Road, Lebanon NH 03766, USA

Woodward, Robert U (Bob) — Journalist
3305 Old Point Road, Edgewater MD 21037, USA

Woodward, Roger R — Concert Pianist, Conductor, Composer
L H Productions, 2/37 Hendy Ave, Coogee NSW 2034, Australia

Woodward, William F (Woody) — Baseball Player
10 San Marco Court, Palm Coast FL 32137, USA

Woody — Singer (Dru Hill)
Mercury Records, 11150 Santa Monica Blvd, #1000, Los Angeles CA 90025 USA

Woody, Damien M — Football Player
3 Roconan Dr, Mendham NJ 7945, USA

Wool, Christopher — Artist
Luhring Augustine Gallery, 531 W 24th St, New York NY 10011, USA

Wooldridge, Floyd L — Baseball Player
214 Barber St, Greenfield MO 65661, USA

Woolery, Chuck — Entertainer
26135 Plymouth Road, Redford MI 48239, USA

Woolfolk, Harold E (Butch) — Football Player
4519 Magnolia Lane, Sugar Lane TX 77478, USA

Woolford, Donnell — Football Player
725 Lumber Lane, Charlotte NC 28214, USA

Woolgar, Fenella Independent Talent Group, Oxford House, 76 Oxford St, London W1D 1BS, England	Actress
Woollard, Robert G (Bob) RR 1 Box 456, Hamptonville NC 27020, USA	Basketball Player
Woolley, Bennie L (Chip), Jr 135 Road 5018, Bloomfield NM 87413, USA	Thoroughbred Racing Trainer
Woolley, Jason D 4019 Quarton Road, Bloomfield MI 48302, USA	Ice Hockey Player
Woolley, Kenneth F 790 George St, #500, Sydney NSW 2000, Australia	Architect
Woolsey, Elizabeth D Trail Creek Ranch, 7100 West Trail Creek Road, Wilson WY 83014, USA	Alpine Skier, Executive
Woolsey, R James Shea & Gardner, 901 New York Ave NW, Washington DC 20001, USA	Government Official
Woolsey, Ralph A 23388 Mulholland Dr, #109, Woodland Hills CA 91364, USA	Cinematographer
Woolsey, William T 1032 Seascape Circle, Rodeo CA 94572, USA	Swimmer
Woolstenhulme, Rick, Jr Untitled Entertainment, 350 S Beverly Dr, #200, Beverly Hills CA 90212 USA	Drummer (Lifehouse)
Woolvett, Jaimz Noble Caplan Abrams, 1260 Yonge St, #200, Toronto ON M4T 1W6, Canada	Actor
Woomble, Roddy Agency Group Ltd, 361-373 City Road, London EC1V 2QA, England	Singer (Idlewild)
Woosnam, Ian H Dyffryn, Morda Road, Oswestry, Shropshire SY11 2AY, Wales	Golfer
Woosnam, Phil 2211 Mainsail Dr, Marietta GA 30062, USA	Soccer Executive
Wooten, Hubert (Daddy), Jr 120 Sandy Dr, Goldsboro NC 27534, USA	Baseball Player
Wooten, Jim ABC-TV, News Dept, 5010 Creston St, Hyattsville MD 20781 USA	Commentator
Wooten, John B 3760 Paradise Hills Dr, #2601, Euless TX 76040, USA	Football Player
Wooten, Nicholas W M E Entertainment, 9601 Wilshire Blvd, #300, Beverly Hills CA 90210 USA	Producer, Writer
Wooten, Ronald J (Ron) 2401 Lewis Grove Lane, Raleigh NC 27608, USA	Football Player
Wooten, Victor Skyline Music, 2270 Maiden Lane SW, Roanoke VA 24015, USA	Jazz Bassist, Composer
Wooten, W Shawn 765 Ali Lane, Santa Monica CA 90402, USA	Baseball Player
Wootten, Morgan 6912 Wells Parkway, University Park MD 20782, USA	Basketball Coach
Wopat, Tom Innovative Artists, 1505 10th St, Santa Monica CA 90401 USA	Actor, Singer
Word, Barry Q 5746 Janneys Mill Circle, Haymarket VA 20169, USA	Football Player
Word, Weldon R 626 Hurst Dr, Tyler TX 75703, USA	Engineer (Paveway Smart Bomb)
Worden, Alfred M PO Box 8065, Vero Beach FL 32963, USA	Astronaut
Wordsworth, Barry I M G Artists, Hogarth Business Park, Chiswick, London W4 2TH, England	Conductor
Workman, A K (Hank) 307 19th St, Santa Monica CA 90402, USA	Baseball Player
Workman, Haywoode W 13711 Inoma St, #104, Tampa FL 33613, USA	Basketball Player
Workman, Vincent I (Vince), Jr 98 Southfield Ave, #605, Stamford CT 06902, USA	Football Player
Worley, Brian PO Box 1471, Brentwood TN 37024, USA	Singer (Stamps Quartet)
Worley, Darryl International Artist Mgmt, 311 Robinhood Road, Brentwood TN 37027, USA	Singer
Worley, Jo Anne Terry M Hill, 41910 Boardwalk, #A2, Palm Desert CA 92211 USA	Actress, Comedienne
Worley, Timothy A (Tim) Worley Global Enterprises, PO Box 14477, Huntsville AL 35815, USA	Football Player
Worndl, Frank Burgsiedlung 19C, 87527 Sonthofen, Germany	Alpine Skier
Woronov, Mary Studio Talent Group, 1328 12th St, Santa Monica CA 90401, USA	Actress
Worrell, Cameron J 2829 E Christopher Dr, Fresno CA 93720, USA	Football Player
Worrell, Peter 3707 Coral Tree Circle, Coconut Creek FL 33073, USA	Ice Hockey Player
Worrell, Timothy H (Tim) 4719 W El Cortez Place, Phoenix AZ 85083, USA	Baseball Player
Worrell, Todd R 810 Simmons Ave, Saint Louis MO 63122, USA	Baseball Player
Worsham, Del PO Box 1329, Chino Hills CA 91709, USA	Drag Racing Driver
Worth, Maurice Delta Air Lines, Hartsfield International Airport, Atlanta GA 30320, USA	Businessman
Wortham, Barron W 8608 Busch Gardens Dr, Fort Worth TX 76123, USA	Football Player
Wortham, Richard C (Rich) 1708 Mira Vista, Leander TX 78641, USA	Baseball Player
Worthington, Allan F (Al) 12070 Highway 55, Sterrett AL 35147, USA	Baseball Player
Worthington, Craig R 10019 Mattock Ave, Downey CA 90240, USA	Baseball Player
Worthington, Sam Anonymous Content, 3532 Hayden Ave, Culver City CA 90232 USA	Actor
Worthy, James A 5750 Corbett St, Los Angeles CA 90016, USA	Basketball Player, Sportscaster

Woolgar - Worthy

Worthy, Richard (Rick) — Actor
S M S Talent, 8383 Wilshire Blvd, #230, Beverly Hills CA 90211 USA

Wortman, Keith D — Football Player
240 Big Sky Dr, Saint Charles MO 63304, USA

Wortman, Kevin — Ice Hockey Player
42 David Dr, Saugus MA 01906, USA

Wosner, Shai — Concert Pianist
Opus 3 Artists, 470 Park Ave S, #900N, New York NY 10016 USA

Wottle, David J (Dave) — Track Athlete
9245 Forest Hill Lane, Germantown TN 38139, USA

Wotton, Mark — Ice Hockey Player
Pro-Rep Entertainment, 113-276 Midpark Way SE, Calgary AB T2X 1J6, Canada

Wotus, Ronald A (Ron) — Baseball Player
6 Monteria Lane, Martinez CA 94553, USA

Wotzel, Mandy — Figure Skater
Olympic Ice Rink, 1080 Centre Road, Melbourne VIC 3167, Australia

Wouk, Herman — Writer
303 W Crestview Dr, Palm Springs CA 92264, USA

Woytowicz-Rudnicka, Stefania — Concert Singer
Al Przyjaciol 3 m 13, 00 565 Warsaw, Poland

Woywitka, Jeff — Ice Hockey Player
RR 1, Mannville AB T0B 2W0, Canada

Wozniacki, Caroline — Tennis Player
Lagardere Unlimited, 4 Rue de Presbourg, 75016 Paris, France

Wozniak, Steve — Computer Designer, Inventor
16400 Blackberry Hill Road, Los Gatos CA 95030, USA

Wozniewski, Andrew (Andy) — Ice Hockey Player
322 Lakeview Dr, Buffalo Grove IL 60089, USA

Wragg, John — Sculptor
6 Castle Lane, Devizes, Wiltshire SN10 1HJ, England

Wray, Gordon R — Engineer, Designer
Stonestack, Rempstone, Loughborough, Leics LE12 6RH, England

Wray, Margaret Jane — Opera Singer
Columbia Artists Mgmt Inc, 1790 Broadway, #702, New York NY 10019 USA

Wregget, Ken — Ice Hockey Player
176 Fieldgate Dr, Pittsburgh PA 15241, USA

Wrenn, Peter — Harness Racing Driver
5215 Wren Court, Carmel IN 46033, USA

Wrenn, Robert (Bob) — Golfer
8908 Watlington Road, Henrico VA 23229, USA

Wrighster, George F, III — Football Player
3014 Summit Place, Birmingham AL 35243, USA

Wright Shapiro, Elizabeth — Actress
United Talent Agency, 9336 Civic Center Dr, Beverly Hills CA 90210 USA

Wright, Adam — Singer, Guitarist (Wrights)
Third Coast Artists Mgmt, 2021 21st Ave S, #220, Nashville TN 37212, USA

Wright, Alex — Actress
A P A Talent/Literary Agency, 405 S Beverly Dr, #300, Beverly Hills CA 90212 USA

Wright, Alexander — Football Player
501 S Mississippi St, Amarillo TX 79106, USA

Wright, Angela — Actress
Commercial Talent, 9255 Sunset Blvd, #505, Los Angeles CA 90069, USA

Wright, Ben — Sportscaster
CBS-TV, Sports Dept, 51 W 52nd St, New York NY 10019 USA

Wright, Betty — Singer
Rodgers Redding, PO Box 4603, Macon GA 31208 USA

Wright, Beverly — Environmental Activist, Sociologist
Deep South Environment Justice Center, 2601 Gentilly Blvd, New Orleans LA 70122, USA

Wright, Bonnie — Actress
United Agents, 12-26 Lexington St, London W1F 0LE, England

Wright, Bradford N (Brad) — Basketball Player
1050 S Cloverdale Ave, Los Angeles CA 90019, USA

Wright, Bryant — Religious Leader
Johnson Ferry Baptist Church, 955 Johnson Ferry Road, Marietta GA 30068, USA

Wright, Charles J — Football Player
2698 Wakefield Lane, Westlake OH 44145, USA

Wright, Charles P, Jr — Writer
940 Locust Ave, Charlottesville VA 22901, USA

Wright, Chely — Singer, Actress
Creative Artists Agency, 2000 Ave of Stars, #100, Los Angeles CA 90067 USA

Wright, Clyde — Baseball Player
528 S Jeanine St, Anaheim CA 92806, USA

Wright, Craig M — Architect
C M Wright Inc, 722 N La Cienega Blvd, West Hollywood CA 90069, USA

Wright, David A — Baseball Player
1105 Hillston Court, Chesapeake VA 23322, USA

Wright, Dick — Editorial Cartoonist
Columbus Dispatch, Editorial Dept, 34 S 3rd St, Columbus OH 43215, USA

Wright, Donald C (Don) — Editorial Cartoonist
PO Box 1176, Palm Beach FL 33480, USA

Wright, Dorell L — Basketball Player
158 Twin Peaks Dr, Walnut Creek CA 94595, USA

Wright, Doug — Writer
I C M Partners, 730 5th Ave, New York NY 10019 USA

Wright, Edgar — Director, Writer
Independent Talent Group, Oxford House, 76 Oxford St, London W1D 1BS, England

Wright, Elmo — Football Player
11419 Olympia Dr, Houston TX 77077, USA

Wright, Eric A — Football Player
Tampa Bay Buccaneers, 1 W Buccaneer Place, Tampa FL 33607 USA

Wright, Felix C — Football Player
2698 Wakefield Lane, Westlake OH 44145, USA

Wright, Gary — Singer, Songwriter
Air Tight Mgmt, 115 West Road, Winsted CT 06098, USA

Wright, George D — Baseball Player
4228 NE 18th St, Oklahoma City OK 73121, USA

Wright, Heather — Actress
1 Sunnyside, Wimbledon, London SW19, England
Wright, J Richard (Ricky) — Baseball Player
2502 Clark Lane, Paris TX 75460, USA
Wright, James C (Jim), Jr — Representative, TX; Speaker
Texas Christian University, Political Science Dept, Fort Worth TX 76129, USA
Wright, James E — Historian
7 Quail Dr, Etna NH 03750, USA
Wright, Jamey A — Baseball Player
4325 Fairfax Ave, Dallas TX 75205, USA
Wright, Jaret — Baseball Player
23 Calle Viviana, San Clemente CA 92673, USA
Wright, Jay — Writer
General Delivery, Piermont NH 03779, USA
Wright, Jay — Basketball Coach
Villanova University, Athletic Dept, Villanova PA 19085, USA
Wright, Jeff D — Football Player
23426 N 21st Place, Phoenix AZ 85024, USA
Wright, Jeffrey — Actor
Creative Artists Agency, 2000 Ave of Stars, #100, Los Angeles CA 90067 USA
Wright, Jeffrey R (Jeff) — Football Player
420 W Bluejay Dr, Chandler AZ 85286, USA
Wright, Joe — Director, Producer, Actor
Shoebox Films, 82 Berwick St, London W1F 8TP, England
Wright, John — Ice Hockey Player
116 Hillsdale Ave, Toronto ON M5P 1G5, Canada
Wright, John M, Jr — Army General
5195 Cottingham Place, Alexandria VA 22304, USA
Wright, Judith A — Writer
17 Devonport St, #1, Lyons ACT 2060, Australia
Wright, Julian — Basketball Player
212 Forest Oaks Dr, New Orleans LA 70131, USA
Wright, Kendall — Football Player
Tennessee Titans, 460 Great Circle Road, Nashville TN 37228 USA
Wright, Kenneth W (Ken) — Baseball Player
1651 Ora Dr, Pensacola FL 32506, USA
Wright, L Rayfield — Football Player
PO Box 2833, Weatherford TX 76086, USA
Wright, Larry — Ice Hockey Player
Regina Fire Dept, PO Box 1790, Regina SK S4P 3C8, Canada
Wright, Lawrence — Writer
Wylie Agency, 250 W 57th St, #2114, New York NY 10107 USA
Wright, Lawrence A — Judge
US Tax Court, 400 2nd St NW, Washington DC 20217, USA
Wright, Lizz — Singer
Verve Forecast Records, Worldwide Plaza, 825 8th Ave, New York NY 10019, USA
Wright, Louis D — Football Player
2263 S Quentin Way, #F301, Aurora CO 80014, USA
Wright, Mary K (Mickey) — Golfer
2972 SE Treasure Island Road, Port Saint Lucie FL 34952, USA
Wright, Max — Actor
Bresler Kelly Assoc, 11500 W Olympic Blvd, #400, Los Angeles CA 90064 USA
Wright, Michael — Actor
Don Buchwald/Fortitude, 6500 Wilshire Blvd, #2200, Los Angeles CA 90048 USA
Wright, Michelle — Singer
Savannah Music, 205 Powell Place, #214, Brentwood TN 37027, USA
Wright, Nathaniel (Nate) — Football Player
11247 Zorita Court, San Diego CA 92124, USA
Wright, Pat — Singer (Crystals)
Lustig Talent, PO Box 770850, Orlando FL 32877 USA
Wright, Peter — WW II Army Air Corps Hero
29 Devon Ave, Croton on Hudson NY 10520, USA
Wright, Peter R — Ballet Dancer, Choreographer
10 Chiswick Wharf, London W4 2SR, England
Wright, Randall S (Randy) — Football Player
2890 Commerce Park Dr, Fitchburg WI 53719, USA
Wright, Robin — Actress, Model
Creative Artists Agency, 2000 Ave of Stars, #100, Los Angeles CA 90067 USA
Wright, Ronald L (Winky) — Boxer
2800 52nd St N, Saint Petersburg, FL 33710, USA
Wright, Ronald W (Ron) — Baseball Player
310 S 2100 E, Saint George UT 84790, USA
Wright, Sarah — Actress
I C M Partners, 10250 Constellation Blvd, #900, Los Angeles CA 90067 USA
Wright, Shannon — Singer (Wrights), Songwriter
Third Coast Artists Mgmt, 2021 21st Ave S, #220, Nashville TN 37212, USA
Wright, Sharone A — Basketball Player
6080 Lakeview Road, #3504, Warner Robins GA 31088, USA
Wright, Stephen — Writer
Knopf Publishers, 1745 Broadway, New York NY 10019 USA
Wright, Stephen (Steve) — Actor
Conway Van Gelder Grant, 8-12 Broadwick St, #300, London W1F 8HW, England
Wright, Stephen H (Steve) — Football Player
14 Conifer Square, Augusta GA 30909, USA
Wright, Steve T — Football Player
14 Conifer Square, Augusta GA 30909, USA
Wright, Steven — Actor, Comedian
Brillstein Entertainment Partners, 9150 Wilshire Blvd, #350, Beverly Hills CA 90212 USA
Wright, Tanisha L — Basketball Player
Seattle Storm, Key Arena, 351 Elliott Ave W, #500, Seattle WA 98119 USA
Wright, Thomas — Actor
W M E Entertainment, 9601 Wilshire Blvd, #300, Beverly Hills CA 90210 USA
Wright, Thomas S (Tom) — Baseball Player
1116 Poplar Springs Church Road, Shelby NC 28152, USA
Wright, Toby L — Football Player
1602 E Winston Dr, Phoenix AZ 85042, USA

Name & Address	Profession
Wright, Trevor Evolution Entertainment, 901 N Highland Ave, Los Angeles CA 90038 USA	Actor
Wright, Tyler 1982 Chatfield Road, Columbus OH 43221, USA	Ice Hockey Player
Wright, Will Stupid Fun Club, 721 Channing Way, Berkeley CA 94720, USA	Video Game Designer, Producer, Writer
Wrightman, Timothy J (Tim) 612 Unity Lane, Weiser ID 83672, USA	Football Player
Wrightson, Bernard (Bernie) 924 Birch Ave, Escondido CA 92027, USA	Diver
Wrigley, William, Jr William Wrigley Jr Co, 410 N Michigan Ave, Lower Level, Chicago IL 60611, USA	Businessman
Wroblewski, David Ecco/Harper Collins Publishers, 10 E 53rd St, Cellar 1, New York NY 10022, USA	Writer
Wrona, Richard J (Rick) 2946 E 57th St, Tulsa OK 74105, USA	Baseball Player
Wrubel, Bill Creative Artists Agency, 2000 Ave of Stars, #100, Los Angeles CA 90067 USA	Writer, Producer
Wryn, Rhiannon Leigh B/W/R, 9100 Wilshire Blvd, #500W, Beverly Hills CA 90212 USA	Actress
Wu Man Opus 3 Artists, 470 Park Ave S, #900N, New York NY 10016 USA	Pipa Player
Wu, Alice Creative Artists Agency, 2000 Ave of Stars, #100, Los Angeles CA 90067 USA	Director, Writer
Wu, Daniel Creative Artists Agency, 2000 Ave of Stars, #100, Los Angeles CA 90067 USA	Actor, Director, Writer
Wu, Jason 240 W 35th St, #1100, New York NY 10001, USA	Fashion Designer
Wu, Sau Lan 29 Oxford St, Cambridge MA 02138, USA	Physicist
Wu, Tai Tsun 29 Oxford St, Cambridge MA 02138, USA	Physicist
Wu, Vivian S M S Talent, 8383 Wilshire Blvd, #230, Beverly Hills CA 90211 USA	Actress
WuDunn, Sheryl New York Times, Editorial Dept, 229 W 43rd St, New York NY 10036, USA	Journalist
Wuerffel, Daniel C (Danny) 424 Mimosa Dr, Decatur GA 30030, USA	Football Player
Wuerl, Donald W Cardinal 5001 Eastern Ave, Hyattsville MD 20782, USA	Religious Leader
Wuertz, Michael J 15209 N Thompson Peak Parkway, #B111, Scottsdale AZ 85260, USA	Baseball Player
Wuethrich, Kurt Federal Technology Institute, E T H Hvnggerberg, Zurich 8093, Switzerland	Nobel Chemistry Laureate
Wuhl, Robert C E S D, 10635 Santa Monica Blvd, #130, Los Angeles CA 90025 USA	Actor
Wuhrer, Kari Innovative Artists, 1505 10th St, Santa Monica CA 90401 USA	Actress
Wullbrandt, John PO Box 246, Carpinteria CA 93014, USA	Artist
Wunder, Ingolf I M G Artists, Hogarth Business Park, Chiswick, London W4 2TH, England	Concert Pianist
Wunderlich, Claudia Dt Handballbund, Strobelallee 56, Dortmund, Germany	Handball Player
Wunderlich, Paul Haynstr 2, 20249 Hamburg, Germany	Artist
Wunsch, Carl I 78 Washington Ave, Cambridge MA 02140, USA	Oceanographer
Wunsch, Gerald (Jerry) 2601 Red Maple Road, Wausau WI 54401, USA	Football Player
Wunsch, Kelly 11613 Hunters Green Trail, Austin TX 78732, USA	Baseball Player
Wuorinen, Charles P Howard Stokar Mgmt, 870 W End Ave, New York NY 10025, USA	Composer
Wurlitzer, Rudolph Two Dollar Radio Publishing, 141 E Town St, #200, Columbus OH 43215, USA	Writer
Wurster, Charles D Commander, US Coast Guard Pacific, Coast Guard Island, Alameda CA 94501 USA	Coast Guard Admiral
Wurster, Donald C Commander, Special Operations Command, Hurlburt Field FL 32544 USA	Air Force General
Wurz, Alexander Benetton-Mecachrome, Enstone, Chipping Norton, Oxon OX7 4EE, England	Auto Racing Driver
Wust, Ireen Referee Sportsmarketing, Postbus 15, 9851 Lieserbrucke, Austria	Speed Skater
Wuycik, Dennis M 31 Rogerson Dr, Chapel Hill NC 27517, USA	Basketball Player
Wyatt, Greg A 320 W 86th St, PH South, New York NY 10024, USA	Sculptor
Wyatt, Harry M, III Director, Air National Guard, HqUSAF, Pentagon, Washington DC 20330 USA	Air Force General
Wyatt, Helen 7714 Deerfield Road, Loves Park IL 61111, USA	Baseball Player
Wyatt, J Douglas (Doug) 4055 Hogan Dr, #301, Tyler TX 75709, USA	Football Player
Wyatt, Jennifer Carolina Group, 2321 Devine St, #A, Columbia SC 29205, USA	Golfer
Wyatt, Kimberly Creative Artists Agency, 2000 Ave of Stars, #100, Los Angeles CA 90067 USA	Singer (Pussycat Dolls)
Wyatt, Leslie Arkansas State University, President's Office, State University AR 72467, USA	Educator
Wyatt, Shannon 8949 Falling Creek Court, Annandale VA 22003, USA	Actress
Wyatt, Sharon 16830 Ventura Blvd, #300, Encino CA 91436, USA	Actress
Wyche, Samuel D (Sam) 1138 Walhalla Highway, Pickens SC 29671, USA	Football Coach, Sportscaster

Wyeth, James Browning — Artist
Lookout Farm, 701 Smiths Bridge Road, Wilmington DE 19807, USA
Wyland — Artist
Wyland Studios, 5 Columbia, Aliso Viejo CA 92656, USA
Wylde, Chris — Actor
Stone Manners Salners, 9911 W Pico Blvd, #1400, Los Angeles CA 90035 USA
Wylde, Peter — Equestrian
247 Wood Dale Dr, Wellington FL 33414, USA
Wylde, Zakk — Singer, Guitarist, Songwriter
Survival Mgmt, 30765 Pacific Coast Highway, #325, Malibu CA 90265, USA
Wyle, Noah — Actor
Brillstein Entertainment Partners, 9150 Wilshire Blvd, #350, Beverly Hills CA 90212 USA
Wylenzek, Thomasz — Canoeing Athlete
Alfred Krupp Str 47, 45131 Essen, Germany
Wylie, Adam — Actor
Management 101, 5527 1/2 Cahuenga Blvd, North Hollywood CA 91601 USA
Wylie, Paul — Figure Skater
9819 Deer Brook Lane, Charlotte NC 28210, USA
Wyludda, Ilke — Track Athlete
Liebigstr 9, 0911 Chemnitz, Germany
Wyman, David M — Football Player
20918 NE Redmond Fall City Road, Redmond WA 98053, USA
Wyman, James T — Businessman
1185 Ferndale Road W, Wayzata MN 55391, USA
Wyman, William G (Bill) — Bassist (Rolling Stones)
Ripple Productions, 344 Kings Road, London SW3 5UR, England
Wymore, Patrice — Actress
Port Antonio, Jamaica, British West Indies
Wyms, Ellis R — Football Player
15706 Tremout Hollow Lane, Houston TX 77044, USA
Wynalda, Eric — Soccer Player
2313 Stormcroft Court, Westlake Village CA 91361, USA
Wyn-Davies, Geraint — Actor
Innovative Artists, 1505 10th St, Santa Monica CA 90401 USA
Wynder, A J — Basketball Player
1 Cardenti Court, Newark DE 19702, USA
Wyndham, Alex — Actor
Finch & Partners, 29-37 Heddon St, London W1B 4BR, England
Wyndham, Victoria — Actress
Don Buchwald/Fortitude, 6500 Wilshire Blvd, #2200, Los Angeles CA 90048 USA
Wynegar, Harold D (Butch) — Baseball Player
PO Box 915811, Longwood FL 32791, USA
Wyner, George — Actor
3450 Laurie Place, Studio City CA 91604, USA
Wyner, Yehudi — Composer
Brandeis University, Music Dept, Waltham MA 02454, USA
Wyngarde, Peter — Actor
4 Acre Lane, Clock Face, Saint Helen's, Lancashire WA9 4DZ, England
Wynn, Bob — Golfer
78455 Calle Orense, La Quinta CA 92253, USA
Wynn, James S (Jimmy) — Baseball Player
5507 Sandy Field Court, Rosharon TX 77583, USA
Wynn, Renaldo L — Football Player
9504 Empire Rock St, Las Vegas NV 89143, USA
Wynn, Stephen A — Businessman
Desert Inn Hotel, 3245 Las Vegas Blvd S, Las Vegas NV 89109, USA
Wynne, Billy V — Baseball Player
7722 Greenwich Court W, Jacksonville FL 32277, USA
Wynne, Marvell — Baseball Player
39640 Del Val Dr, Murrieta CA 92562, USA
Wynott, Ryan — Actor
Savage Agency, 6212 Banner Ave, Los Angeles CA 90038 USA
Wynter, Sarah — Actress
Paradigm Agency, 360 N Crescent Dr, North Building, Beverly Hills CA 90210 USA
Wyrozub, Randy — Ice Hockey Player
6717 Westminster Dr, East Amherst NY 14051, USA
Wysocki, Benjamin J (Ben) — Drummer (Fray)
A2 Mgmt, 624 Davis St, #200, Evanston IL 60201, USA
Wysocki, Jacob — Actor
Osbrink Talent Agency, 4343 Lankershim Blvd, #100, North Hollywood CA 91602 USA
Wysocki, Jon — Drummer (Staind)
The Firm, 2049 Century Park E, #2550, Los Angeles CA 90067 USA

Xhelilaj, Nik — Actor
Cinematography National Center, Blvd Aleksander Mojsiu 77, 1012 Tirana, Albania
Xiahui Fan — Cosmologist
University of Arizona, Astronomy Dept, Tucson AZ 85721, USA
Xiang Liu — Track Athlete
Global Athletes & Marketing, 437 Boylston St, Boston MA 02116, USA
Xiao, Xiangming — Biologist
University of New Hampshire, Earth Oceans Space Institute, Durham NH 03824, USA
Xie Bingxin — Writer
Central Nationalities Institute, Residential Qtrs, Beijing 100081, China
Xie Tieli — Director
Beijing Film Studio, 19 Beihuan Xilu Road, Beijing 100088, China
Xu Bing — Artist
540 Metropolitan Ave, #A, Brooklyn NY 11211, USA
Xu Xing — Geologist
Academy of Sciences, 52 Sanlihe Road, Beijing 100864, China
Xue Wei — Concert Violinist
134 Sheaveshill Ave, London NW9, England
Xuereb, Emmanuel — Actor
Acme Talent Agency, 4727 Wilshire Blvd, #333, Los Angeles CA 90010 USA
Xuereb, Salvator — Actor
Martin Berneman Mgmt, 5820 Wilshire Blvd, #200, Los Angeles CA 90036 USA
Xzibit — Rap Artist, Actor
Management 360, 9111 Wilshire Blvd, Beverly Hills CA 90210 USA
Ya'alon, Moshe — Army General, Israel
Chief of Staff, Israeli Defense Forces, Kaplan St, Tel Aviv 67659, Israel
Yablans, Frank — Producer
88 Bull Path, East Hampton NY 11937, USA
Yachmenev, Vitali A — Ice Hockey Player
182 Silver Lady Lane, North Bay ON P1B 8G4, Canada
Yacoub, Magdi H — Surgeon
National Heart & Lung Institute, Dovehouse St, London SW3 6LY, England
Yager, Faye — Social Activist
Children of the Underground, 902 Curlew Court NW, Atlanta GA 30327, USA
Yager, Rick — Cartoonist (Buck Rogers)
King Features Syndicate, 300 W 57th St, #1500, New York NY 10019 USA
Yagudin, Alexei — Figure Skater
Connecticut Skating Center, 300 Alumni Road, Newington CT 06111, USA
Yaitanes, Gregory C (Greg) — Director, Producer
Creative Artists Agency, 2000 Ave of Stars, #100, Los Angeles CA 90067 USA
Yake, Terry — Ice Hockey Player
26 Mockingbird Lane, Tiverton RI 02878, USA
Yakin, Boaz — Director, Producer, Writer
Cinetic Mgmt, 555 W 25th St, #400, New York NY 10001 USA
Yakupov, Nail R — Ice Hockey Player
Edmonton Oilers, 11230 110th St, Edmonton AB T5G 3H7, Canada
Yamagata, Hiro — Artist
1050 Ave D, Redondo Beach CA 90277, USA
Yamagata, Rachael — Singer, Pianist, Songwriter
Paradigm Agency, 360 Park Ave, #1600, New York NY 10022 USA
Yamaguchi, Kristi T — Figure Skater
290 Las Quebradas Lane, Alamo CA 94507, USA
Yamaguchi, Roy — Restauranteur
Roy's Restaurant, Kai Plaza, 6600 Kalaniaole Highway, Honolulu HI 96825, USA
Yamame, Marlene Mitsuko — Actress
Herb Tannen, 10801 National Blvd, #101, Los Angeles CA 90064 USA
Yamamoto, Kansai — Fashion Designer
103 Grand St, New York NY 10013, USA
Yamamoto, Yohji — Fashion Designer
Yamamoto Europe, 155 Rue Saint-Martin, 75003 Paris, France
Yamanaka, Shinya — Nobel Medicine Laureate
Kyoto University, 53 Kawaharacho, Shogoin Yoshida, Sakyoku, Kyoto 606-8507, Japan
Yamanaka, Tsuyoshi — Swimmer
6-10-33-212 Akasaka, Minatoku, Tokyo, Japan
Yamani, Sheikh Ahmed Zaki — Government Official, Saudi Arabia
PO Box 14850, Jeddah 21434, Saudi Arabia
Yamano, Hiroshi — Artist
Galleria Silecchia, 20 S Palm Ave, Sarasota FL 34236, USA
Yamasaki, Taro M — Photojournalist
People, Editorial Dept, Time-Life Building, New York NY 10020, USA
Yamashita, Iris — Writer
Circle of Confusion, 8548 Washington Blvd, Culver City CA 90232, USA
Yamashita, Yasuhiro — Judo Athlete, Coach
1117 Kitakaname, Hitatsuka Kanagawa 259-1207, Japan
Yamassoum, Negoum — Prime Minister, Chad
PO Box 43121, N'Djamena, Moursal, Chad
Yamazaki, Naoko — Astronaut, Japan
Japanese Aerospace Exploration Agency, 2-1-1 Sengen, Tsukuba-shi, Ibaraki 305 8505, Japan
Yan — Singer, Guitarist (British Sea Power)
Agency Group Ltd, 361-373 City Road, London EC1V 2QA, England
Yan, Liangkun — Conductor
Central Philharmonic Society, 11-1 Hepingjie, Beijing 100013, China
Yanagimachi, Ryuzo — Biologist
University of Hawaii, Biology Dept, 1960 East-West Road, Honolulu HI 96822, USA
Yancy, Emily — Actress
Geddes Agency, 8430 Santa Monica Blvd, #201, West Hollywood CA 90069 USA
Yanez, Eduardo — Actor
Independent Group, 8444 Wilshire Blvd, #500, Beverly Hills CA 90211, USA
Yang di-Pertuan Agong XIII — Sultan, Malaysia
Sultan's Palace, Istana Bukit Serene, 50502 Kuala Lumpur, Malaysia
Yang Liwei — Taikonaut, China
Satellite Launch Center, Jiuquan, Guangzhou Province, China
Yang, Chen Ning — Nobel Physics Laureate
8 Dorfer Lane, Nesconset NY 11767, USA
Yang, Jerry — Businessman, Computer Programmer
Asian Pacific Fund, 225 Bush St, #590, San Francisco CA 94104, USA

Xhelilaj - Yang

Yang, Philemon Y   Prime Minister, Cameroon
Prime Minister's Office, BP 1057, Yaounde, Cameroon
Yang, Shang-Fa   Biochemist
118 Villanova Dr, Davis CA 95616, USA
Yang, Xao (Jerry)   Poker Player
30380 River Estate Dr, Madera CA 93636, USA
Yang, Young Eun (Y E)   Golfer
Professional Golfer's Assn, PO Box 109601, Palm Beach Gardens FL 33410 USA
Yang, Zhiguang   Artist
Guangzhou Fine Art Institute, 257 Chang Hang Dong Lu St, Guangzhou, China
Yani Tseng   Golfer
9713 Chiltern Garden Dr, Orlando FL 32827, USA
Yankelovich, Daniel   Social Scientist
Public Agenda Foundation, 6 E 39th St, #900, New York NY 10016, USA
Yankovic, Al (Weird Al)   Actor, Comedian, Singer, Songwriter
14 E Mountain Road, Katonah NY 10536, USA
Yankowski, Ronald W (Ron)   Football Player
1318 Wulfert Road, Sanibel FL 33957, USA
Yannas, I V   Polymer Scientist, Mechanical Engineer
Massachusetts Institute of Technology, Engineering School, Cambridge MA 02139, USA
Yanni   Keyboardist, Songwriter
10563 Arcole Court, Wellington FL 33449, USA
Yano, Kyoko   Soccer Player
Football Assn, 3-10-15 Hongo, Bunkyoku, Tokyo 113 0033 Japan
Yanofsky, Charles   Biologist
725 Mayfield Ave, Stanford CA 94305, USA
Yanofsky, Nicole (Nikki)   Singer, Songwriter
A440 Entertainment, 3500 de Maisonneuve W, #800, Montreal QC H3Z 3C1, Canada
Yanukovych, Viktor F   Prime Minister, Ukraine
President's Office, Bankova Str 11, 01220 Kiev, Ukraine
Yao Ming   Basketball Player
18923 Crescent Bay Dr, Houston TX 77094, USA
Yao, Andrew C C   Mathematician
Princeton University, Mathematics Dept, Princeton NJ 08544, USA
Yapo, Mennan   Director
Spielkind, Zimmerstr 11, 10969 Berlin, Germany
Yarborough, W Caleb (Cale)   Auto Racing Driver
Yarborough Racing, 2723 W Palmetto St, #8, Florence SC 29501, USA
Yarbrough, Glenn   Singer, Songwriter (Limeliters)
PO Box 331368, Nashville TN 37203, USA
Yardley, Jim   Journalist
New York Times, Editorial Dept, 229 W 43rd St, New York NY 10036 USA
Yardley, Jonathan   Journalist, Critic
223 Hawthorne Road, Baltimore MD 21210, USA
Yared, Gabriel   Composer
V2 Scandinavia, Bondegatan 64C, 116 33 Stockholm, Sweden
Yarnall, Celeste   Actress
2899 Agoura Road, #315, Westlake CA 91361, USA
Yarno, George A   Football Player
1081 White Pine Flats Road, Troy ID 83871, USA
Yarno, John R   Football Player
10535 158th Ave NE, Redmond WA 98052, USA
Yaro, Boris   Photojournalist
17042 Calahan St, Northridge CA 91325, USA
Yarrow, Noel Peter   Singer (Peter Paul & Mary), Songwriter
27 W 67th St, #5E, New York NY 10023, USA
Yary, A Ronald (Ron)   Football Player
38886 Calle de Companero, Murrieta CA 92562, USA
Yasbeck, Amy   Actress
Innovative Artists, 1505 10th St, Santa Monica CA 90401 USA
Yashin, Aleksei   Ice Hockey Player
6 Polo Dr, Old Westbury NY 11568, USA
Yastrzemski, Carl M   Baseball Player
22 Lakeshore Road, Boxford MA 01921, USA
Yasutake, Patti   Actress
145 S Fairfax Ave, #310, Los Angeles CA 90036, USA
Yates, Angie   Rodeo Rider
5711 N State Highway 18, Stephenville TX
Yates, Bill   Cartoonist (Redeye)
King Features Syndicate, 300 W 57th St, #1500, New York NY 10019 USA
Yates, David   Director
Casorotto Ramsay, Waverley House, 7-12 Noel St, London W1F 8GQ, England
Yates, Dorian A M   Body Builder
Mr Olympia Corner, 21100 Erwin St, Woodland Hills CA 91367, USA
Yates, Erica Lyndzey   Actress, Comedienne
OmniPop Talent Group, 4605 Lankershim Blvd, #201, Toluca Lake CA 91602 USA
Yates, J D   Rodeo Rider
1235 Lane 30 1/4, Pueblo CO 81006, USA
Yates, Jim   Drag Racing Driver
Jim Yates Racing, 2725B Old Washington Road, Waldorf MD 20601, USA
Yates, Robert   Auto Racing Executive
18923 Cove Side Lane, Cornelius NC 28031, USA
Yates, Robert E (Bob)   Football Player
391 Bentwood Dr, Spring Branch TX 78070, USA
Yates, Ronald W (Ron)   Air Force General
525 Silhouette Way, Monument CO 80132, USA
Yates, Tyler K   Baseball Player
3718 Omao Road, Koloa HI 96756, USA
Yau, Alan   Restauranteur, Chef
Wagamama Ltd, Waverley House, 7-12 Noel St, London W1F 8GQ, England
Yau, Horng-Tzer   Mathematician
New York University, Mathematics Dept, New York NY 10012, USA
Yau, Shing-Tung   Mathematician
Harvard University, Mathematics Dept, 1 Oxford St, Cambridge MA 02138, USA
Yawer, Sheik Ghazi Mashal Ajil al-   President, Iraq
Al-Sijound Majalis, Karradat Mariam, Baghdad, Iraq

Y

Yang - Yawer

Name / Address	Profession
Yawney, Trent 215 Belleplaine Ave, Park Ridge IL 60068, USA	Ice Hockey Player, Coach
Ybarra y Churruca, Emilio de Banco Bilbao-Vizcaya, Paseo de la Castellana 81, 28046 Madrid, Spain	Financier
Ye, Xiaogang Central Music Conversatory, 43 Baojia St, Xicheng District, Beijing 100031 P R, China	Composer
Yeager, Andrea PO Box 11720, 155 Nighthawk Dr, Aspen CO 81612, USA	Tennis Player
Yeager, Bunny 585 NE 92nd St, Miami Shores FL 33138, USA	Photographer, Model
Yeager, Charles E (Chuck) PO Box 1507, Penn Valley CA 95946, USA	Test Pilot, Air Force General
Yeager, Jeana 302 Chaparral Dr, Sunnyvale TX 75182, USA	Experimental Airplane Pilot
Yeager, Stephen W (Steve) PO Box 34184, Granada Hills CA 91394, USA	Baseball Player
Yeagley, Jerry 1418 S Sare Road, Bloomington IN 47401, USA	Soccer Coach
Yeakel, G Scott 14224 E Kalil Dr, Scottsdale AZ 85259, USA	Astronaut
Yearwood, Trisha Trisha Yearwood Inc, 3310 W End Ave , #400, Nashville TN 37203, USA	Singer
Yeates, Jeffrey L (Jeff) 3793 Club Dr NE, Atlanta GA 30319, USA	Football Player
Yelchin, Anton Creative Artists Agency, 2000 Ave of Stars, #100, Los Angeles CA 90067 USA	Actor
Yelding, Eric G PO Box 325, Montrose AL 36559, USA	Baseball Player
Yeley, Christopher B H (J J) Mayfield Motorsports, 2220 Highway 49 N, Harrisburg NC 28075, USA	Auto, Truck Racing Driver
Yeliseyev, Aleksei S Bauman Higher Technical School, Baumanskaya UI 5, 107005 Moscow, Russia	Cosmonaut
Yelle E M I Records, 150 5th Ave, #700, New York NY 10011 USA	Singer, Songwriter
Yelle, Staphane 212 Maplehurst Point, Littleton CO 80126, USA	Ice Hockey Player
Yellen, Janet L 3933 Highwood Court NW, Washington DC 20007, USA	Government Official, Financier
Yellen, Linda B Keckins Projects, 3 Sheridan Square, New York NY 10014, USA	Producer, Director
Yellowbird, Shane Agency Group Ltd, 142 W 57th St, #600, New York NY 10019 USA	Singer, Songwriter
Yelvington, Richard J (Dick), Jr 2105 Barbe St, Lake Charles LA 70601, USA	Football Player
Yen, Donnie Paradigm Agency, 360 N Crescent Dr, North Building, Beverly Hills CA 90210 USA	Actor
Yeo, Mike Minnesota Wild, XCel Energy Arena, 1275 Saint Antoine W, Saint Paul MN 55104 USA	Hockey Coach
Yeoh, Michelle Gotham Group, 9255 Sunset Blvd, #515, Los Angeles CA 90069, USA	Actress
Yeohlee Yeohlee Designs, 225 W 35th St, #1600, New York NY 10001, USA	Fashion Designer
Yeoman, Owain Safran Co, 2000 Ave of Stars, #600N Los Angeles CA 90067, USA	Actor
Yeoman, Robert D 2847 Delaware Ave, Santa Monica CA 90404, USA	Cinematographer
Yeoman, William F (Bill) 3030 Country Club Blvd, Sugar Land TX 77478, USA	Football Player, Coach
Yepremian, Garabed S (Garo) 200 W Harmony Road, West Grove PA 19390, USA	Football Player
Yergin, Daniel H Cambridge Energy Research Assoc, 55 Cambridge Parkway, Cambridge MA 02142, USA	Writer
Yerman, Jack 753 Camellia Dr, Paradise CA 95969, USA	Track Athlete
Yershov, Valery Rima Fine Art, 7130 E Main St, Scottsdale AZ 85251, USA	Artist
Yes, Phyllis A 23 SW Boundary St, Portland OR 97239, USA	Artist, Sculptor
Yespica, Aida Lela Mora Mgmt, Viale Monza 9, 20125 Milan, Italy	Model, Actress
Yester, Jim Variety Artists, 793 Higuera St, #6, San Luis Obispo CA 93401 USA	Singer, Guitarist (Association)
Yeston, Maury Yale University, Music Dept, New Haven CT 06520, USA	Composer
Yett, Richard M (Rich) 5840 E Fairbrook Circle, Mesa AZ 85205, USA	Baseball Player
Yeun, Steven S D B Partners, 1801 Ave of Stars, #902, Los Angeles CA 90067 USA	Actor
Yeutter, Clayton K 10955 Martingale Court, Potomac MD 20854, USA	Secretary, Agriculture
Yevtushenko, Yevgeny A Kutuzovski Prospekt 2/1, #101, 121248 Moscow, Russia	Writer
Yewcic, Thomas J (Tom) 31 Cherokee Road, Arlington MA 02474, USA	Football, Baseball Player
Yi Jianlian Dallas Mavericks, Pavilion, 2909 Taylor St, Dallas TX 75226 USA	Basketball Player
Yi Mun Yol Wylie Agency, 250 W 57th St, #2114, New York NY 10107 USA	Writer
Yi So Yeon Advanced Science/Technology Institute, Yuseong, Daejeon, South Korea	Cosmonaut, South Korea
Yi, Charlyne Mosiac Media Group, 9200 W Sunset Blvd, #1000, Los Angeles CA 90069 USA	Actress, Comedienne
Yilmaz, A Mesut Basbakanlik, Bakanliklar, Ankara, Turkey	Prime Minister, Turkey
Ying Huang Columbia Artists Mgmt Inc, 1790 Broadway, #702, New York NY 10019 USA	Actress, Opera Singer

Yingluck Shinawatra — Prime Minister, Thailand
Prime Minister's Office, Thanon Nakhon Patnom, Bangkok 10300, Thailand

Yoakam, Dwight — Singer, Guitarist, Songwriter
Bluebird House, 10153 1/2 Riverside Drive, #419, Universal City CA 91602, USA

Yoav — Singer, Songwriter
Creative Artists Agency, 2000 Ave of Stars, #100, Los Angeles CA 90067 USA

Yoba, Malik — Actor
Innovative Artists, 1505 10th St, Santa Monica CA 90401 USA

Yoccoz, Jean-Christophe — Mathematician
University of Paris-Sud (Orsey), 91405 Orsay-Cedex-Bait 425, France

Yock, Robert J — Judge
US Claims Court, 717 Madison Place NW, Washington DC 20439, USA

Yocum, Matt — Sportscaster
9910 Devonshire Dr, Huntsville NC 28078, USA

Yoffie, Eric — Religious Leader, Rabbi
Union for Reform Judaism, 633 3rd Ave, #700, New York NY 10017, USA

Yoken, Mel B — Writer
261 Carroll St, New Bedford MA 02740, USA

Yonath, Ada — Nobel Chemistry Laureate
Weizmann Science Institute, PO Box 26, Rehovot 76100, Israel

Yong, Cao — Artist
Pierside Hunt Gallery, 300 Pacific Coast Highway, Huntington Beach CA 92648, USA

Yoo, Aaron — Actor
Blue Ridge Entertainment, 535 W 23rd St, #S10A, New York NY 10011, USA

Yoon, Bora — Composer
I M G Artists, Hogarth Business Park, Chiswick, London W4 2TH, England

Yorio, Kimberly — Writer
Y C Media, 145 W 28th St, #1200, New York NY 10001, USA

York, Francine — Actress
PO Box 55008, Sherman Oaks CA 91413, USA

York, Glen P — Vietnam War Air Force Hero
1620 E Driftwood Dr, Tempe AZ 85283, USA

York, James H (Jim) — Baseball Player
31262 Via del Verde, San Juan Capistrano CA 92675, USA

York, John J — Actor
Stone Manners Salners, 9911 W Pico Blvd, #1400, Los Angeles CA 90035 USA

York, Kathleen (Bird) — Actress, Singer, Songwriter
Bauman Redanty Shaul Agency, 5757 Wilshire Blvd, #473, Los Angeles CA 90036 USA

York, Lila — Choreographer
Paul Taylor Dancer Co, 551 Grand St, Lobby A, New York NY 10002, USA

York, Marty — Actor
PO Box 55183, Valencia CA 91385, USA

York, Michael — Actor
Peter Strain, 5455 Wilshire Blvd, #1812, Los Angeles CA 90036 USA

York, Michael (Mike) — Ice Hockey Player
6105 W Longview Dr, East Lansing MI 48823, USA

York, Michael M — Journalist
Lexington Herald-Leader, Editorial Dept, Main & Midland, Lexington KY 40507, USA

York, Rachel — Actress
Stone Manners Salners, 9911 W Pico Blvd, #1400, Los Angeles CA 90035 USA

York, Raymond — Thoroughbred Racing Jockey
27918 Taft Highway, Taft CA 93268, USA

York, Taylor — Guitarist (Paramore), Songwriter
Big Hassle, 44 Wall St, #2200, New York NY 10005, USA

Yorke, Thom — Singer (Radiohead)
Courtyard, 21 Nursery, Sutton Courteney, Abingdon, Oxon OX14 4UA, England

Yorkin, Alan (Bud) — Producer, Director
Bud Yorkin Productions, 250 Delfern Dr, Los Angeles CA 90077, USA

Yorkin, Peg — Women's Activist
Fund for Feminist Majority, 1600 Wilson Blvd, #704, Arlington VA 22209, USA

Yorn, Peter (Pete) — Singer, Songwriter
Trampoline Records, 8581 Santa Monica Blvd, #511, West Hollywood CA 90069, USA

Yorzyk, William A (Bill) — Swimmer
162 W Sturbridge Road, #7, East Brookfield MA 01515, USA

Yost, E Frederick (Ned), III — Baseball Player, Manager
108 Victoria Dr, La Grange GA 30240, USA

Yost, Graham J — Actor, Producer, Writer
Creative Artists Agency, 2000 Ave of Stars, #100, Los Angeles CA 90067 USA

Yost, Paul A, Jr — Coast Guard Admiral
James Madison Memorial Foundation, 200 K St NW, Washington DC 20001, USA

Yothers, Tina — Actress, Singer
12368 Apple Dr, Chino CA 91710, USA

Youk Chhang — Social Activist
Documentation Center, 66 Preah Sihanouok Blvd, Phnom Penh, Cambodia

Youkilis, Kevin E — Baseball Player
19475 N Grayhawk Dr, #1083, Scottsdale AZ 85255, USA

Youmans, Floyd E — Baseball Player
1915 E Noel St, Tampa FL 33610, USA

Youmans, Maurice E (Maury) — Football Player
300 Beach Dr NE, #2104, Saint Petersburg FL 33701, USA

Young Buck — Rap Artist (G-Unit)
Paradigm Agency, 360 N Crescent Dr, North Building, Beverly Hills CA 90210 USA

Young Jeezy — Rap Artist
I C M Partners, 10250 Constellation Blvd, #900, Los Angeles CA 90067 USA

Young MC — Rap Artist
Entertainment Artists, PO Box 120824, Nashville TN 37212 USA

Young, Adam — Singer/Songwriter/Musician (Owl City)
Foundations Artist Mgmt, 628 Broadway, #503, New York NY 10012, USA

Young, Aden — Actor
Artist Representation Co, 1147 S Big Island Road, RR 1, Demoresville ON K0K 1W0, Canada

Young, Adrian — Drummer (No Doubt)
Rebel Waltz, 31652 2nd Ave, Laguna Beach CA 92651, USA

Young, Alan — Actor
T G M D Talent Agency, 6767 Forest Lawn Dr, #101, Los Angeles CA 90068, USA

Young, Andrew — Diplomat; Mayor, Atlanta
National Council of Churches, 523 Spring Oaks Blvd, Altamonte Springs FL 32714, USA

Young, Angus M
Alberts Music, 9 Rangers Road, Neutral Bay, Sydney NSW 2089, Australia — Guitarist (AC/DC), Songwriter

Young, Anthony W
13107 Ellsmere Dr, Houston TX 77015, USA — Baseball Player

Young, Archie (Dropo)
1804 Ethel Ave SW, Birmingham AL 35211, USA — Baseball Player

Young, B Asa (Ace)
Creative Artists Agency, 2000 Ave of Stars, #100, Los Angeles CA 90067 USA — Singer, Songwriter, Actor

Young, Barbara
5078 Edinboro Lane, Wilmington NC 28409, USA — Baseball Player

Young, Bellamy
Framework Entertainment, 9057 Nemo St, #C, West Hollywood CA 90069 USA — Actress

Young, Bob
King Features Syndicate, 300 W 57th St, #1500, New York NY 10019 USA — Cartoonist (Tim Tyler's Luck)

Young, Bob
I C M Partners, 10250 Constellation Blvd, #900, Los Angeles CA 90067 USA — Producer

Young, Brian
Big Hassle, 157 Chambers St, #1200, New York NY 10007, USA — Singer, Drummer (Fountains of Wayne)

Young, Bryant C
8454 NW 64th Lane, Gainesville FL 32653, USA — Football Player

Young, Burt
Higgins Harte Int'l, 11 Pioneer Blvd, #F, Mequite NV 89027, USA — Actor

Young, C Duane
3704 Olney Road, Kalamazoo MI 49006, USA — Football Player

Young, Charle E
PO Box 1276, Woodinville WA 98072, USA — Football Player

Young, Christopher
Costa Communications, 8265 Sunset Blvd, #101, Los Angeles CA 90046, USA — Composer

Young, Christopher A (Chris)
Ron Shapiro Mgmt, 56 W 22nd St, #601, New York NY 10010, USA — Singer

Young, Christopher B (Chris)
Arizona Diamondbacks, Chase Field, 401 E Jefferson, Phoenix AZ 85003 USA — Baseball Player

Young, Christopher R (Chris)
966 Muirlands Vista Way, La Jolla CA 92037, USA — Baseball Player

Young, Cliff
Breen Agency, 25 Music Square W, Nashville TN 37203, USA — Singer, Guitarist (Caedmon's Call)

Young, Colville N
Governor General's Office, Belize House, Belnopan, Belize — Governor General, Belize

Young, Curtis A (Curt)
10800 E Cactus Road, #2, Scottsdale AZ 85259, USA — Baseball Player

Young, Cyrus (Cy)
518 Grimes Ave, Modesto CA 95358, USA — Track Athlete

Young, Danielle
Breen Agency, 25 Music Square W, Nashville TN 37203, USA — Singer, Guitarist (Caedmon's Call)

Young, Dean
King Features Syndicate, 300 W 57th St, #1500, New York NY 10019 USA — Cartoonist (Blondie)

Young, Delmon D
3922 E Northridge Circle, Mesa AZ 85215, USA — Baseball Player

Young, Delwyn R
2212 Radcourt Dr, Hacienda Heights CA 91745, USA — Baseball Player

Young, Dmitri D
Washington Nationals, 1500 S Capitol St SE, Washington DC 20003 USA — Baseball Player

Young, Earl
Atlantic/Buddah Records, 1290 Ave of Americas, Concourse 3, New York NY 10104, USA — Singer (Trammps)

Young, Earl V
4344 Livingston Ave, Dallas TX 75205, USA — Track Athlete

Young, Eric O
120 Brewster Ave, Piscataway NJ 08854, USA — Baseball Player

Young, Ernest W (Ernie)
8995 E Palm Ridge Dr, Scottsdale AZ 85260, USA — Baseball Player

Young, Fred
Webster & Assoc PR, PO Box 23015, Nashville TN 37202, USA — Singer, Drummer (Kentucky Headhunters)

Young, Frederick K (Fredd)
4200 Real del Sur, Las Cruces NM 88011, USA — Football Player

Young, George L
8926 N Cox Road, Casa Grande AZ 85194, USA — Track Athlete

Young, Gerald A
10014 Rain Cloud Dr, Houston TX 77095, USA — Baseball Player

Young, Guard
4000 Worthington Dr, Norman OK 73072, USA — Gymnast

Young, Heather Rae
Playboy Promotions, 2706 Media Center Dr, Los Angeles CA 90065 USA — Model

Young, Howard (Howie)
5527 N 22nd Dr, Phoenix AZ 85015, USA — Ice Hockey Player

Young, J Steven (Steve)
Forever Young Foundation, 21952 S Brandon St, Farmington Hills MI 48336, USA — Football Player, Sportscaster

Young, Jacob
Community Entertainment, 12100 Wilshire Blvd, #1135, Los Angeles CA 90025, USA — Actor

Young, Jesse Colin
Skyline Music, 2270 Maiden Lane SW, Roanoke VA 24015, USA — Singer, Guitarist, Bassist, Songwriter

Young, Jim
US Military Academy, Athletic Dept, West Point NY 10966, USA — Football Coach

Young, John Lloyd
I C M Partners, 10250 Constellation Blvd, #900, Los Angeles CA 90067 USA — Actor, Singer

Young, John T
124 W 57th St, Los Angeles CA 90037, USA — Baseball Player

Young, John W
N A S A, Johnson Space Center, 2101 NASA Road, Houston TX 77058 USA — Astronaut

Young, John Zachary
1 Crossroads, Brill, Bucks HP18 9TL, England — Zoologist

Young, Kathryn
323 Date Ave, Imperial Beach CA 91932, USA — Golfer

Young, Kathy
Cape Entertainment, 8432 NW 31st Court, Sunrise FL 33351, USA — Singer

Young, Keone
Gage Group, 14724 Ventura Blvd, #505, Sherman Oaks CA 91403 USA — Actor

Young, Kevin   Track Athlete
H S International Sports Mgmt, 9871 Irvine Center Dr, Irvine CA 92618, USA
Young, Kevin S   Baseball Player
832 E Taurus Place, Chandler AZ 85249, USA
Young, Larry E   Baseball Umpire
PO Box 255, Roscoe IL 61073, USA
Young, Laurence Retman   Astronaut
217 Thorndike St, #108, Cambridge MA 02141, USA
Young, Lee Thompson   Actor
Rain Management Group, 1631 21st St, Santa Monica CA 90404, USA
Young, Lonnie R   Football Player
16699 W Papago St, Goodyear AZ 85338, USA
Young, M Adrian   Football Player
10300 4th St, #100, Rancho Cucamonga CA 91730, USA
Young, Malcolm M   Guitarist (AC/DC), Songwriter
Alberts Music, 9 Rangers Road, Neutral Bay, Sydney NSW 2089, Australia
Young, Matthew J (Matt)   Baseball Player
471 Maylin St, Pasadena CA 91105, USA
Young, Michael B   Baseball Player
3508 Bryn Mawr Dr, Dallas TX 75225, USA
Young, Michael D (Mike)   Football Player
275 S Arroyo Parkway, #717, Pasadena CA 91105, USA
Young, Michael D (Mike)   Baseball Player
1166 Rockspring Way, Antioch CA 94531, USA
Young, Michael K   Educator
808 36th Ave E, Seattle WA 98112, USA
Young, Mighty Joe   Singer, Guitarist
Jay Reil, 3430 Bayberry Dr, Northbrook IL 60062, USA
Young, Neil   Singer, Songwriter
I C M Partners, 10250 Constellation Blvd, #900, Los Angeles CA 90067 USA
Young, Nick   Basketball Player
Philadelphia 76ers, 1st Union Center, 3601 S Broad St, Philadelphia PA 19148 USA
Young, Paul A   Singer
Mission Control, 44 Alexander, Meole Brace, Shrewsbury SY3 9HS, England
Young, R Gilchrist I (Chris)   Composer
First Artists Mgmt, 4764 Park Granada, #210, Calabasas CA 91302 USA
Young, Richard   Singer, Guitarist (Kentucky Headhunters)
Webster & Assoc PR, PO Box 23015, Nashville TN 37202, USA
Young, Richard S   Space Scientist
137 Saint Croix Ave, Cocoa Beach FL 32931, USA
Young, Richard S   Photographer
110 Highlever Road, London W10 6PL, England
Young, Rickey D   Football Player
2438 Grenadier Ave N, Saint Paul MN 55128, USA
Young, Robert (Nat)   Surfer
8 Bay St, Angourie NSW 2464, Australia
Young, Robert E   Football Player
159 Boyd Lane, Carthage MS 39051, USA
Young, Roger   Director
Freedman Broder & Company, 10100 Santa Monica Blvd, Los Angeles CA 90067, USA
Young, Roynell   Football Player
11823 Beinhorn Dr, Houston TX 77065, USA
Young, Rusty   Pedal Steel Musician (Poco)
Rick Alter Mgmt, 1018 17th Ave S, #12, Nashville TN 37212, USA
Young, S Ulysses   Baseball Player
4023 W 60th St, Los Angeles CA 90043, USA
Young, Samuel D (Sam)   Basketball Player
Philadelphia 76ers, 1st Union Center, 3601 S Broad St, Philadelphia PA 19148 USA
Young, Scott A   Ice Hockey Player
17 Sandy Ridge Road, Sterling MA 01564, USA
Young, Sean   Actress
Gregg Edwards Mgmt, 6072 Franklin Ave, #304, Los Angeles CA 90028, USA
Young, Shelby   Actress
United Talent Agency, 9336 Civic Center Dr, Beverly Hills CA 90210 USA
Young, Simone   Conductor
Hamburgische Staatsoper, Grosse Theaterstr 25, 20354 Hamburg, Germany
Young, Sophie   Basketball Player
San Antonio Silver Stars, 1 AT&T Center, San Antonio TX 78219 USA
Young, Steve   Singer, Guitarist, Songwriter
I C M Partners, 10250 Constellation Blvd, #900, Los Angeles CA 90067 USA
Young, Thaddeus C   Basketball Player
Philadelphia 76ers, 1st Union Center, 3601 S Broad St, Philadelphia PA 19148 USA
Young, Tim   Ice Hockey Player
15808 Park Terrace Dr, Eden Prairie MN 55346, USA
Young, Timothy R (Tim)   Baseball Player
20730 SE Sherry Ave, Blountstown FL 32424, USA
Young, Tom   Basketball Coach
Washington Wizards, M C I Centre, 601 F St NW, Washington DC 20004 USA
Young, Valerie D   Actress
Bobby Ball Agency, 4116 W Magnolia Blvd, #205, Burbank CA 91505, USA
Young, Vince P, Jr   Football Player
12006 Legend Manor Dr, Houston TX 77082, USA
Young, Vincent   Actor
Bohemia Group, 8170 Beverly Blvd, #102, Los Angeles CA 90048, USA
Young, Warren H   Ice Hockey Player
5960 Murray Ave, Bethel Park PA 15102, USA
Young, Wendell E   Ice Hockey Player
1616 E Campbell St, Arlington Heights IL 60004, USA
Young, Wilbur E, Jr   Football Player
119 Hartford Court, Charlottesville VA 22902, USA
Young, William   Labor Leader
National Assn of Letter Carriers, 100 Indiana NW, #709, Washington DC 20001, USA
Young, William Allen   Actor
5519 S Holt Ave, Los Angeles CA 90056, USA
Young, William J L (Willie)   Football Player
PO Box 426, Grambling LA 71245, USA

Young - Young

Young, William R (Will) — Singer, Actor
19 Music & Mgmt, 35-37 Parkgate Road, London SW11 4NP, England
Young, Wise — Neuroscientist
Rutgers University, Collaborative Neuroscience Center, New Brunswick NJ 08901, USA
Youngberg, Renae — Baseball Player
2001 Gasparilla Road, #A25, Placida FL 33946, USA
Youngblood, H Jackson (Jack) — Football Player, Sportscaster
4377 Steed Terrace, Winter Park FL 32792, USA
Youngblood, Jimmy L (Jim) — Football Player
1000 Kilgore Bridge Road, Woodruff SC 29388, USA
Youngblood, Joel R — Baseball Player
4446 E Camelback Road, #113, Phoenix AZ 85018, USA
Youngen, Lois J — Baseball Player
45 Prall Lane, Eugene OR 97405, USA
Younger, Ben — Director, Producer, Writer
Brillstein Entertainment Partners, 9150 Wilshire Blvd, #350, Beverly Hills CA 90212 USA
Youngerman, Jack — Artist, Sculptor
PO Box 508, Bridgehampton NY 11932, USA
Younghans, Tom — Ice Hockey Player
52 Douglas St, # 3, Saint Paul MN 55102, USA
Young-Ochowicz, Sheila G — Speed Skater, Cyclist
945 Hutchinson Ave, Palo Alto CA 94301, USA
Youngs, Elaine — Volleyball Player
Q Sports Marketing, 534 W Evergreen St, Wheaton IL 60187 USA
Younis, Waqar — Cricketer
Surrey County Cricket Club, Kennington Oval, London SE11 5SS, England
Yount, Robin R — Baseball Player
5040 E Shea Blvd, #254, Scottsdale AZ 85254, USA
Youso, Frank M — Football Player
PO Box 1046, International Falls MN 56649, USA
Yowarsky, Walter (Walt) — Football Player
395 Dogwood Place NW, Cleveland TN 37312, USA
Yo-Yo — Singer, Actress
Bridge & Tunnel Communications, 9157 Sunset Blvd, #205, West Hollywood CA 90069, USA
Ysebaert, Paul R — Ice Hockey Player
10 Harbor Blvd, #W528, Destin FL 32541, USA
Yu Panglin — Businessman, Philanthropist
Super 8 Hotel, 4 Shang Meilin Kaifeng Road, Shenzhen 518001, China
Yu, Jessica — Director, Producer, Writer
Anonymous Content, 3532 Hayden Ave, Culver City CA 90232 USA
Yu, Ronny — Director, Producer, Writer
Gersh Agency, 9465 Wilshire Blvd, #600, Beverly Hills CA 90212 USA
Yuan Enfeng — Singer
Provincial Broadcasting/TV Station, Xian, Shaanxi, China
Yuan, Ron — Actor
I C M Partners, 10250 Constellation Blvd, #900, Los Angeles CA 90067 USA
Yuasa, Joji — Composer
1517 Shields Ave, Encinitas CA 92024, USA
Yudashkin, Valentin A — Fashion Designer
Valentin Yudashkin Fashion House, Kutuzovsky Pr 19, 121151 Moscow, Russia
Yudhoyono, Susilo Bambang — President, Indonesia; Army General
President's Office, 15 Jalam Merdeka Utara, Jarkata, Indonesia
Yudof, Mark G — Educator
University of California, President's Office, 1111 Franklin, Oakland CA 94607, USA
Yue Jingyu — Swimmer
Physical Culture/Sports Bureau, 9 Tiyuguan Road, Beijing, China
Yulin, Harris — Actor
Parseghian Planco, 322 8th Ave, #601, New York NY 10001, USA
Yun Suk-Young — Soccer Player
Football Assn, 1-131 Sinmunno, 2-Ga Jongno-Gu, Seoul 110 062, South Korea
Yune, Karl — Actor
Framework Entertainment, 9057 Nemo St, #C, West Hollywood CA 90069 USA
Yune, Rick — Actor
I C M Partners, 10250 Constellation Blvd, #900, Los Angeles CA 90067 USA
Yung Joc — Rap Artist
Brass Artists, 9025 Wilshire Blvd, #400, Beverly Hills CA 90211, USA
Yunis, Jorge J — Geneticist, Pathologist
Thomas Jefferson University, Jefferson Medical College, Philadelphia PA 19107, USA
Yunus, Muhammad — Nobel Peace Laureate
Grameen Bank Bhavan, Mirpur 1, Dhaka 1216, Bangladesh
Yurchikhin, Fyodor N — Cosmonaut
N A S A, Johnson Space Center, 2101 NASA Road, Houston TX 77058 USA
Yushkevich, Dmitri S — Ice Hockey Player
International Sports Advisors, 878 Ridge View Way, Franklin Lakes NJ 07417, USA
Yuspa, Cathy — Producer
I C M Partners, 10250 Constellation Blvd, #900, Los Angeles CA 90067 USA
Yustman, Odette — Actress, Model
Evolution Entertainment, 901 N Highland Ave, Los Angeles CA 90038 USA
Yusuf — Singer, Songwriter
Creative Artists Agency, 2000 Ave of Stars, #100, Los Angeles CA 90067 USA
Yusupova, Lidia — Social Activist
Memorial Library, Malyy Karetnyy Pereulok 12, 127051 Moscow, Russia
Yzaguirre, Raul — Social Activist
National Council of La Raza, 1111 19th St NW, #1000, Washington DC 20036, USA
Yzerman, Stephen G (Steve) — Ice Hockey Player, Executive
PO Box 488, Bloomfield Hills MI 48303, USA

Zabaleta, Nicanor — Concert Harpist
Villa Izar, Aldapeta, 20009 San Sebasatian, Spain
Zabel, Bryce — Writer, Producer, Director
Morse Taylor Esq, 14724 Ventura Boulevard, Sherman Oaks CA 91403, USA
Zabel, David — Writer, Producer
W M E Entertainment, 9601 Wilshire Blvd, #300, Beverly Hills CA 90210 USA
Zabel, Mark — Canoeing Athlete
Grosse Fischerei 18A, 39240 Calbe/Saale, Germany
Zabel, Steven G (Steve) — Football Player
6000 Oak Tree Road, Edmond OK 73025, USA
Zabransky, Libor — Ice Hockey Player
Rybarska Specialka Zabransky Koliste 59, Brno 60200, Czech Republic
Zabriski, Bruce — Golfer
6228 Winding Lake Dr, Jupiter FL 33458, USA
Zabriskie, Grace — Actress
Innovative Artists, 1505 10th St, Santa Monica CA 90401 USA
Zachara, Jan — Boxer
Sladkovicova 13, 018 51 Nova Dubnica, Czech Republic
Zacharias, Christian — Concert Pianist, Conductor
I M G Artists, Hogarth Business Park, Chiswick, London W4 2TH, England
Zachry, Patrick P (Pat) — Baseball Player
7611 Bosque Blvd, Woodway TX 76712, USA
Zackham, Justin — Producer, Director, Writer
Two Tons Films, 375 Greenwich St, New York NY 10013, USA
Zadan, Craig — Producer
Creative Artists Agency, 2000 Ave of Stars, #100, Los Angeles CA 90067 USA
Zadeh, Lofti A — Computer Scientist (Fuzzy Logic)
904 Mendocino Ave, Berkeley CA 94707, USA
Zadel, C William — Businessman
Millipore Corp, 75 Wiggins Ave, Bedford MA 01730, USA
Zadora, Pia — Actress, Singer, Model
Levine Communications, 9100 Wilshire Blvd, 540 E Tower, Beverly Hills CA 90212, USA
Zaentz, Saul — Producer
Saul Zaentz Co, 2600 10th St, Berkeley CA 94710, USA
Zaffaroni, Alejandro C — Biochemist
Alza Corp, 6500 Paseo Padre Parkway, Fremont CA 94555, USA
Zagorin, Perez — Historian
1015 33rd St NW, #606, Washington DC 20007, USA
Zagrosek, Lothar — Conductor
Kunstler Sekretariat am Gasteig, Rosenheimer Str 52, 81669 Munich, Germany
Zagunis, Mariel — Fencer
Robert F Zagunis, 20235 SW Gassner Road, Beaverton OR 97007, USA
Zahn, Geoffrey C (Geof) — Baseball Player
6536 Walsh Road, Dexter MI 48130, USA
Zahn, Paula A — Commentator
188 E 76th St, New York NY 10021, USA
Zahn, Steve — Actor
Innovative Artists, 1505 10th St, Santa Monica CA 90401 USA
Zahn, Timothy — Writer
PO Box 1755, Coos Bay OR 97420, USA
Zahn, Wayne — Bowler
5018 S Barley Court, Gilbert AZ 85298, USA
Zaillian, Steven — Director, Writer
Film Rights, 159 S Beverly Dr, Beverly Hills CA 90212, USA
Zaine, Rod — Ice Hockey Player
64 Drouin St, Ottawa ON K1K 2A7, Canada
Zakarin, Mark — Writer, Producer
Gersh Agency, 9465 Wilshire Blvd, #600, Beverly Hills CA 90212 USA
Zaks, Jerry — Director
Helen Merrill, 825 8th Ave, #2600, New York NY 10019, USA
Zal, Roxana — Actress
8265 W Sunset Blvd, #101, West Hollywood CA 90046, USA
Zalapski, Zarley B — Ice Hockey Player
Eishockey Club Olten, Postfach 523, 4601 Olten, Switzerland
Zalesky, Jim — Freestyle Wrestler, Coach
University of Iowa, Athletic Dept, Iowa City IA 52242, USA
Zaletin, Sergei — Cosmonaut
Cosmonaut Training Center, Star City, 141160 Zvezdny Gorodok, Moscow Oblast, Russia
Zalyotin, Sergei V — Cosmonaut
Cosmonaut Training Center, Star City, 141160 Zvezdny Gorodok, Moscow Oblast, Russia
Zamba, Frieda — Surfer
2706 S Central Ave, Flagler Beach FL 32136, USA
Zambarloukos, Haris — Cinematographer
United Agents, 12-26 Lexington St, London W1F 0LE, England
Zambello, Francesca — Director
Opus 3 Artists, 470 Park Ave S, #900N, New York NY 10016 USA
Zambrano, Eduardo Jose — Baseball Player
166 N 44-157 Coromoto, Maracaibo, Venezuela
Zametkin, Alan J — Psychiatrist
National Mental Health Institute, 9000 Rockville Pike, Bethesda MD 20892, USA
Zamfir, Gheorghe — Concert Pan-Pipes Player, Conductor
Lenhartzstr 15, 20249 Hamberg, Germany
Zamka, George D — Astronaut
1936 Mandy Lane, League City TX 77573, USA
Zampella, Vince — Video Games Developer
Respawn Entertainment, 5990 Sepulveda Blvd, Van Nuys CA 91411, USA
Zamuner, Robert F (Rob) — Ice Hockey Player
4317 Beau Rivage Circle, Lutz FL 33558, USA
Zanardi, Alessandro (Alex) — Auto Racing Driver
Via B Bordone 12, 35134 Padova, Italy
Zander, Carl A — Football Player
2536 W Palomino Dr, Chandler AZ 85224, USA
Zander, Robin — Singer, Guitarist (Cheap Trick)
Oakie Dokie Mgmt, 6090 Central Ave, Saint Petersburg FL 33707, USA
Zander, Thomas — Greco-Roman Wrestler
Grundfeldstr 23, 73432 Aalen, Germany

Zanders, Emmanuel	Football Player
11015 Goodwood Blvd, Baton Rouge LA 70815, USA	
Zandonella, Roberto	Bobsled Athlete
Olympic Committee, Foro Italico, Largo Lauro de Bosis 15, 00135 Rome, Italy	
Zane, Billy	Actor
Paradigm Agency, 360 N Crescent Dr, North Building, Beverly Hills CA 90210 USA	
Zane, Frank	Body Builder
PO Box 1090, La Mesa CA 91944, USA	
Zane, Lisa	Actress
505 N Lake Shore Dr, #5407, Chicago IL 60611, USA	
Zanes, Dan	Singer, Songwriter
Harriet Sternberg Mgmt, 4530 Gloria Ave, Encino CA 91436, USA	
Zanetti, Eugenio	Actor, Director, Production Designer
Sandra Marsh Assoc, 9150 Wilshire Blvd, #220, Beverly Hills CA 90212 USA	
Zanetti, Massimo	Conductor
I M G Artists, Hogarth Business Park, Chiswick, London W4 2TH, England	
Zanier, Michael (Mike)	Ice Hockey Player
306 Rossland Ave, Trail BC V1R 3M8, Canada	
Zanni, Dominick T (Dom)	Baseball Player
7 Sussex Ave, Massapequa NY 11758, USA	
Zano, Nick	Actor
I C M Partners, 10250 Constellation Blvd, #900, Los Angeles CA 90067 USA	
Zanotto, Kendra	Synchronized Swimmer
18834 Lakeview Court, Los Gatos CA 95033, USA	
Zanova Steindler, Alena (Aja)	Figure Skater
Wollman Skating Rink, 830 5th Ave, New York NY 10065, USA	
Zanuck, Lili Fini	Producer, Director
Zanuck Co, 16 Beverly Park, Beverly Hills CA 90210, USA	
Zanussi, Krzysztof	Director
Ul Kaniowska 114, 01 529, Warsaw, Poland	
Zanussi, Ronald K (Ron)	Ice Hockey Player
PO Box 11326, Saint Paul MN 55111, USA	
Zapata, Carmen	Actress
C E S D, 10635 Santa Monica Blvd, #130, Los Angeles CA 90025 USA	
Zapf, Hermann	Book, Type Designer
2 Hammarskjold Plaza, New York NY 10017, USA	
Zapiro	Editorial Cartoonist
Double Storey Books, PO Box 24299, Lansdowne 7779, South Africa	
Zapp, James (Jim)	Baseball Player
820 Youngs Lane, Nashville TN 37207, USA	
Zappa, Ahmet	Actor, Writer, Producer
I C M Partners, 10250 Constellation Blvd, #900, Los Angeles CA 90067 USA	
Zappa, Diva	Actress
J K A Talent Agency, 12725 Ventura Blvd, #H, Studio City CA 91604, USA	
Zappa, Dweezil	Singer, Guitarist, Actor
7885 Woodrow Wilson Dr, Los Angeles CA 90046, USA	
Zappa, Moon Unit	Singer, Actress
J K A Talent Agency, 12725 Ventura Blvd, #H, Studio City CA 91604, USA	
Zarate Serna, Carlos	Boxer
Gene Aguilera, PO Box 113, Montebello CA 90640, USA	
Zardari, Asif Ali	President, Pakistan
President's Office, Aiwan-e-Sadr, Mall & Mayo Roads, Islamabad, Pakistan	
Zasada, Sobieslaw	Auto Racing Driver
Zasada S A, Ul Omulewska 27, 04 128 Warsaw, Poland	
Zaslav, David M	Businessman
Discovery Communications Inc, One Discovery Place, Silver Spring MD 20910, USA	
Zatkoff, Roger	Football Player
882 Hidden Ravines Court, Birmingham MI 48009, USA	
Zatopkova, Dana	Track Athlete
Nad Kazankov 3, 171 00 Prague 7, Czech Republic	
Zaun, Gregory O (Gregg)	Baseball Player
26 E 6th St, #701, Cincinnati OH 45202, USA	
Zaveri, Anjala	Actress
604 Jupiter Apts, Yari Road, Andheri, Mumbai MS 400058, India	
Zavisha, Brad	Ice Hockey Player
General Delivery, Hines Creek AB T0H 2A0, Canada	
Zavos, Panos M	Biologist
181 Collins Lane, Lexington KY 40503, USA	
Zayas, David	Actor
Gersh Agency, 9465 Wilshire Blvd, #600, Beverly Hills CA 90212 USA	
Zayas, Victor Hugo	Artist
Brewery Art Complex, 2100 N Main St, #A10, Los Angeles CA 90031, USA	
Zaz	Singer
Sony Music, Neumarkter Str 28, 81673 Munich, Germany	
Zazzo, Lawrence	Opera Singer
Harrison/Parrott, 5-6 Albion Court, London W6 0QT, England	
Zdrok, Victoria N	Model, Actress, Dancer
PO Box 332, Pompton Lakes NJ 07442, USA	
Zea, Natalie	Actress
True Mgmt, 8964 W 25th St, Los Angeles CA 90034, USA	
Zech, Lando W, Jr	Navy Admiral, Government Official
1 White Flint N, 11555 Rockville Pike, Rockville MD 20852, USA	
Zeckendorf, William, Jr	Businessman
502 Park Ave, New York NY 10022, USA	
Zeckhauser, Richard J	Economist
138 Irving St, Cambridge MA 02138, USA	
Zedda, Alberto	Conductor, Composer
Academia Rossiniana, Via Rossini 1, 61100 Pesaro, Italy	
Zedillo Ponce de Leon, Ernesto	President, Mexico
Institutional Revolutionary, Insurges N 61, 06350 Mexico City DF, Mexico	
Zedlitz, Jean	Golfer
4587 Gatetree Circle, Pleasanton CA 94566, USA	
Zednik, Richard	Ice Hockey Player
4401 N Federal Highway, Boca Raton FL 33431, USA	
Zeffirelli, G Franco	Director
Via Lucio Volumnio 37, 00178 Rome, Italy	

Zegen, Michael (Mike) — Actor
United Talent Agency, 9336 Civic Center Dr, Beverly Hills CA 90210 USA
Zegers, Kevin — Actor
I C M Partners, 10250 Constellation Blvd, #900, Los Angeles CA 90067 USA
Zeglis, John D — Businessman
A T & T Wireless Group, 7277 164th Ave NE, Redmond WA 98052, USA
Zehetner, Nora — Actress
A P A Talent/Literary Agency, 405 S Beverly Dr, #300, Beverly Hills CA 90212 USA
Zehr, Joey — Actor, Drummer (Click Five)
Creative Artists Agency, 2000 Ave of Stars, #100, Los Angeles CA 90067 USA
Zehringer, Rick — Singer, Guitarist (McCoys)
Brothers Mgmt, 141 Dunbar Ave, Fords NJ 08863 USA
Zehrt, Monika Landgraf- — Track Athlete
Stormstr 42, 15827 Blankenfelde, Germany
Zeidel, Lazarus (Larry) — Ice Hockey Player
6663 Erdrick St, Philadelphia PA 19135, USA
Zeidler, Eberard H — Architect, Designer
Zeidler Grinnell Partnership, 315 Queen St W, Toronto ON M5V 2X2, Canada
Zeier, Eric R — Football Player
PO Box 327, Nashville GA 31639, USA
Zeifman, Jerome — Attorney
57 North St, #105, Danbury CT 06810, USA
Zeigler, C Dustin (Dusty) — Football Player
440 Hodgeville Road, Guyton GA 31312, USA
Zeigler, Marie — Baseball Player
2502 N 22nd Ave, Phoenix AZ 85009, USA
Zeile, Todd E — Baseball Player
2324 Crombie Court, Thousand Oaks CA 91361, USA
Zeitler, Kevin — Football Player
Cincinnati Bengals, 1 Paul Brown Stadium, Cincinnati OH 45202 USA
Zeitlin, Benh — Director
Lichter Grossman Nichols, 9200 Sunset Blvd, #1200, West Hollywood CA 90069, USA
Zelenka, Joseph J (Joe) — Football Player
12572 Highview Dr, Jacksonville FL 32225, USA
Zelenskaya, Yelena E — Opera Singer
Bolshoi Theater, Teatralnaya Pl 1, 103009 Moscow, Russia
Zelepukin, Valeri M — Ice Hockey Player
9595 Collins Ave Apt 610, Surfside FL 33154, USA
Zelezny, Jan — Track Athlete
Rue Armady 683, 29301 Boleslav, Czech Republic
Zeliaeva, Valentina — Model
Women Model Mgmt, 199 Lafayette St, #700, New York NY 10012 USA
Zellner, Hunndens G (Peppi) — Football Player
31 Dew Place, Forsyth GA 31029, USA
Zellweger, Renee — Actress
John Carrabino Mgmt, 5900 Wilshire Blvd, #406, Los Angeles CA 90036 USA
Zelman, Aaron — Writer, Producer
3 Arts Entertainment, 9460 Wilshire Blvd, #700, Beverly Hills CA 90212 USA
Zelman, Daniel — Producer, Writer, Actor
Stone Meyer Genow, 9665 Wilshire Blvd, #510, Beverly Hills CA 90212 USA
Zelmani, Sophie — Singer
United Stage Artists, PO Box 11029, 100 61 Stockholm, Sweden
Zem, Roschdy — Actor, Director
Artmedia, 20 Ave Rapp, 75007 Paris, France
Zeman, E Robert (Bob) — Football Player
4427 Maple Dr, Eagle River WI 54521, USA
Zeman, Jacklyn — Actress
Cynthia Snyder Public Relations, 5139 Colfax Ave, North Hollywood CA 91601, USA
Zeman, Milos — Prime Minister, Czech Republic
Urad Vlady CR, Nabr E Benese 4, Prague 1, Czech Republic
Zembriski, Walter — Golfer
6507 Doubletrace Lane, Orlando FL 32819, USA
Zemeckis, Robert L — Director
ImageMovers, 100 Universal City, Bungalow 5170, Los Angeles CA 91608, USA
Zen Ze Kiun, Joseph Cardinal — Religious Leader
Diocese of Hong Kong, 16 Caine Road, #12F, Hong Kong, China
Zendaya — Actress
Monster Talent Mgmt, 6333 W 3rd St, #912, Los Angeles CA 90036, USA
Zendejas, Anthony G (Tony) — Football Player
24430 Avendia de Marcia, Yorba Linda CA 92887, USA
Zender Meier, Gladys — Beauty Queen
Miss Universe Organization, 1370 Ave of Americas, #1600, New York NY 10019 USA
Zender, J W Hans — Conductor, Composer
Horbener Str 28, 79100 Freiburg, Germany
Zender, Stuart P J — Bassist (Jamiroquai)
Nettwerk Mgmt, 6525 W Sunset Blvd, #800, Los Angeles CA 90028 USA
Zent, Jason — Ice Hockey Player
271 Dartmouth St, #4G, Boston MA 02116, USA
Zentilli, Patricia — Actress
Characters Talent Agency, 8 Elm St, Toronto ON M5G 1G7, Canada
Zentmyer, George A, Jr — Plant Pathologist
955 S El Camino Real, #216, San Mateo CA 94402, USA
Zerbe, Anthony — Actor
1175 High Road, Santa Barbara CA 93108, USA
Zereoue, Amos L — Football Player
226 Westside Ave, #B, Freeport NY 11520, USA
Zerhouni, Elias A — Government Official, Physician
National Institutes of Health, 9000 Rockville Pike, Bethesda MD 20892, USA
Zero, Mark — Singer (Randy & the Rainbows)
PO Box 656507, Fresh Meadows NY 11365, USA
Zervas, Nicholas T — Neurosurgeon
100 Canton Ave, Milton MA 02186, USA
Zeta-Jones, Catherine — Actress, Model
Independent Talent Group, Oxford House, 76 Oxford St, London W1D 1BS, England
Zetsche, Dieter — Businessman
Daimler-Chrysler AG, Plieningerstr, 70546 Stuttgart, Germany

Zetterberg, C Henrik — Ice Hockey Player
1780 Hammond Court, Bloomfield Hills MI 48304, USA
Zetterlund Bush, Yoko — Volleyball Player
4055 Crystal Dawn Lane, #205, San Diego CA 92122, USA
Zetumer, Joshua (Josh) — Writer, Producer
United Talent Agency, 9336 Civic Center Dr, Beverly Hills CA 90210 USA
Zewail, Ahmed H — Nobel Chemist Laureate
871 Winston Ave, San Marino CA 91108, USA
Zezelj, Danijel — Cartoonist, Writer
D C Comics, 1700 Broadway, #400, New York NY 10019, USA
Zgonina, Jeffrey M (Jeff) — Football Player
5418 Lampasas St, Houston TX 77056, USA
Zhai Zhigang — Taikonaut, China
Satellite Launch Center, Jiuquan, Guangzhou Province, China
Zhamnov, Alexei Y — Ice Hockey Player
1950 N Orchard St, Chicago IL 60614, USA
Zhang Dan — Figure Skater
Skating Assn, 56 Zhonguachun South St, Beijing 100044, China
Zhang Hao — Figure Skater
Skating Assn, 56 Zhonguachun South St, Beijing 100044, China
Zhang Jie — Writer
501 Qian-Men Xi Da Jie, #97, Beijing 100031, China
Zhang Xianliang — Writer
Ningxia Writers' Assn, Yinchuan City, China
Zhang Yimou — Director
Edko Films, 1212 Tiwer 2, Admiralty Centre, Hong Kong, China
Zhang Ziyi — Actress
Flying Box Co, 1-4-20 Nishi Azabu, Minato, Tokyo 106 0031, Japan
Zhang, Haochen — Concert Pianist
I M G Artists, Hogarth Business Park, Chiswick, London W4 2TH, England
Zhang, Liping — Opera Singer
I C M Artists, 40 W 57th St, #1800, New York NY 10019 USA
Zhang, Xian — Conductor
Coro Sinfonico di Milano Giuseppe Verdi, Via Clerici 3, 20121 Milan, Italy
Zhao Hongbo — Figure Skater
Skating Assn, 56 Zhonguanchun South St, Beijing 100044, China
Zhao Yanxia — Opera Singer
24 Xusubai 2nd Lane, Beijing 100034, China
Zhe Xi Lo — Anthropologist
Carnegie Natural History Museum, 4400 Forbes Ave, Pittsburgh PA 15213, USA
Zhen Haixia — Basketball Player
Physical Culture Bureau, 9 Tiyuguan Lu, Beijing 100061, China
Zhenan Bao — Chemist, Inventor (Molecule Transistor)
A T & T Bell Lucent Laboratory, 600 Mountain Ave, New Providence NJ 07974 USA
Zheng, Wei — Astronomer
Johns Hopkins University, Astronomy Dept, Baltimore MD 21218, USA
Zhirinovsky, Vladimir V — Government Leader, Russia
State Duma, Okhotny Ryad 1, 103009 Moscow, Russia
Zhislin, Grigory Y — Concert Violinist
25 Whitehall Gardens, London W3 9RD, England
Zhitnik, Alexei N — Ice Hockey Player
8 Boxwood Way, Manhasset NY 11030, USA
Zholobov, Vitali M — Cosmonaut
Ul Yanvarskovo Vostaniya D 12, 252010 Kiev, Ukraine
Zhou Long — Composer
University of Missouri, Music Dept, Kansas City MO 64110, USA
Zhudov, Vyacheslav D — Cosmonaut
Cosmonaut Training Center, Star City, 141160 Zvezdny Gorodok, Moscow Oblast, Russia
Zhulin, Alexsander V (Sasha) — Ice Dancer
Skating Federation, Luchnesksaia Nab 8, 119871 Moscow, Russia
Zhvanetsky, Mikhail M — Writer, Actor
Lesnaya Str 4, #63, 125047 Moscow, Russia
Zia, Begum Khaleda — Prime Minister, Bangladesh
Bangladesh National Party, 29 Minto Road, Dhaka, Bangladesh
Ziblijew, Wassili — Cosmonaut
Cosmonaut Training Center, Star City, 141160 Zvezdny Gorodok, Moscow Oblast, Russia
Zich, Denise — Actress
Fitz & Skoglund, Linienstr 130, 10115 Berlin, Germany
Zicherman, Stu — Producer, Writer
W M E Entertainment, 9601 Wilshire Blvd, #300, Beverly Hills CA 90210 USA
Zick, Robert G (Bob) — Baseball Player
12028 S 45th St, Phoenix AZ 85044, USA
Zidan, Ali — Prime Minister, Libya
Prime Minister's Office, Monrovia, Liberia
Zidane, Zinedine — Soccer Player
F C Real Madrid, Avda Concha Espana 1, 28036 Madrid, Spain
Zidek, Jiri (George) — Basketball Player
551 Landfair Ave, Los Angeles CA 90024, USA
Zidi, Malik — Actor
Agence Artiste Adequet, 80 Rue d'Amsterdam, 75009 Paris, France
Zidlicky, Marek — Ice Hockey Player
2006 Sweetbriar Ave, Nashville TN 37212, USA
Ziegelmeyer, Nicole (Nikki) — Speed Skater
5912 Mastodon Pines Dr, Imperial MO 63052, USA
Ziegler, Alma — Baseball Player
403 Gold St, Auburn CA 95603, USA
Ziegler, Bill — Cartoonist
King Features Syndicate, 300 W 57th St, #1500, New York NY 10019 USA
Ziegler, Dolores — Opera Singer
Lynda Kay, 2702 Crestworth Lane, Buford GA 30519, USA
Ziegler, Jack — Cartoonist
New Yorker, Editorial Dept, 4 Times Square, Basement C1B, New York NY 10036 USA
Ziegler, John A, Jr — Ice Hockey Player
3 Club Dr, Jupiter FL 33469, USA
Ziegler, John L — Oncologist
University of California Cancer Center, 2340 Sutter St, San Francisco CA 94115, USA

Ziegler, Kate — Swimmer
George Mason University, Athletic Dept, Fairfax VA 22030, USA
Ziegler, Larry — Golfer
10315 Luton Court, Orlando FL 32836, USA
Ziegler, Marie — Baseball Player
6739 W Polk St, Phoenix AZ 85043, USA
Zielenbach, Jen — Bassist (Antigone Rising)
W Mgmt, 266 Elizabeth St, #1A, New York NY 10012, USA
Ziem, Steven G (Steve) — Baseball Player
1309 Avalon Ave, Beaumont CA 92223, USA
Ziemann, Sonja — Actress
Via del Alp Dorf, 7500 Saint Moritz, Switzerland
Ziemba, Karen — Singer, Actress, Dancer
TalentWorks, 3500 W Olive Ave, #1400, Burbank CA 91505 USA
Zien, Chip — Actor
Innovative Artists, 1505 10th St, Santa Monica CA 90401 USA
Zien, Sam (Cooking Guy) — Chef
Discovery Channel, 7700 Wisconsin Ave, Bethesda MD 20814 USA
Zierden, Don — Basketball Coach
Washington Wizards, M C I Centre, 601 F St NW, Washington DC 20004 USA
Ziering, Ian — Actor
Ellis Talent Group, 4705 Laurel Canyon Blvd, #300, Valley Village CA 91607, USA
Ziesak, Ruth — Opera Singer
Kunstler Sekretariat am Gasteig, Rosenheimer Str 52, 81669 Munich, Germany
Ziffren, Kenneth — Attorney
Ziffren Brittenham Branca, 1801 Century Park W, #700, Los Angeles CA 90067, USA
Ziglar, Zig — Businessman
Zig Ziglar Corp, 15303 Dallas Parkway, #550, Addison TX 75001, USA
Zigler, Edward F — Psychologist, Educator
Yale University, Bush Child Development Center, New Haven CT 06520, USA
Zikes, Les — Bowler
424 S Stuart Lane, Palatine IL 60067, USA
Zilinskas, Annette — Bassist (Bangles, Ringling Sisters)
Creative Artists Agency, 2000 Ave of Stars, #100, Los Angeles CA 90067 USA
Zillmer, Ruth — Baseball Player
PO Box 709, Walworth WI 53184, USA
Zils, John — Structural Engineer
N1513 Shore Haven Dr, Fontana WI 53125, USA
Zim Zum — Guitarist (Marilyn Manson); Songwriter
Mitch Schneider Organization, 14724 Ventura Blvd, #500, Sherman Oaks CA 91403 USA
Zima, Madeline — Actress
United Talent Agency, 9336 Civic Center Dr, Beverly Hills CA 90210 USA
Zimbalist, Efrem, Jr — Actor
1448 Holsted Dr, Solvang CA 93463, USA
Zimbalist, Stephanie — Actress
Franchot Mgmt, PO Box 48890A, Los Angeles CA 90048, USA
Zimerman, Krystian — Concert Pianist
Kernmatterstr 8B, 4102 Binningen, Switzerland
Zimm, Bruno H — Chemist
3762 Dupont St, San Diego CA 92106, USA
Zimmer, Constance — Actress
United Talent Agency, 9336 Civic Center Dr, Beverly Hills CA 90210 USA
Zimmer, Donald W (Don) — Baseball Player, Manager
7069 Key Haven Road, #201, Seminole FL 33777, USA
Zimmer, Hans F — Composer
Remote Control Productions, 1547 14th St, Santa Monica CA 90404, USA
Zimmer, Kim — Actress
Innovative Artists, 1505 10th St, Santa Monica CA 90401 USA
Zimmer, Robert — Educator
University of Chicago, President's Office, Chicago IL 60637, USA
Zimmerer, Wolfgang — Bobsled Athlete
Schwaigangerstr 22, 82418 Murnau, Germany
Zimmerman, Daniel H E (Dan) — Drummer (Gamma Ray)
United Talent Agency, 9336 Civic Center Dr, Beverly Hills CA 90210 USA
Zimmerman, Gary W — Football Player
17450 Skylines Road, Bend OR 97701, USA
Zimmerman, Howard E — Chemist
7813 Westchester Dr, Middleton WI 53562, USA
Zimmerman, Jeffrey R (Jeff) — Baseball Player
2416 Chippendale Road, West Vancouver BC V7S 3J2, Canada
Zimmerman, Joey — Actor
PO Box 450802, Kissimmee FL 34745, USA
Zimmerman, Mary Beth — Golfer
6452 Century Park Place SE, Mableton GA 30126, USA
Zimmerman, Philip (Phil) — Computer Software Designer
Network Assoc, 4677 Old Ironside Dr, Santa Clara CA 95054, USA
Zimmerman, Ryan W — Baseball Player
3301 Washington Blvd, Arlington VA 22201, USA
Zimmermann, Egon — Alpine Skier
Hotel Crystal Mountain, 6764 Lech Am Arlberg, Austria
Zimmermann, Frank Peter — Concert Violinist
Kunstler Sekretariat am Gasteig, Rosenheimer Str 52, 81669 Munich, Germany
Zimmermann, Jordan — Baseball Player
Washington Nationals, 1500 S Capitol St SE, Washington DC 20003 USA
Zimmermann, Markus — Bobsled Athlete
Waldhauserstr 51-53, 83471 Schonau am Konigsee, Germany
Zimmermann, Raquel — Model
D N A Model Mgmt, 555 W 25th St, #600, New York NY 10001 USA
Zimmermann, Serge — Concert Violinist
Kunstler Sekretariat am Gasteig, Rosenheimer Str 52, 81669 Munich, Germany
Zimmermann, Udo — Composer
Operhaus Leipzig, Augustusplatz, 04109 Leipzig, Germany
Zimpher, Nancy — Educator
Cincinnati University, President's Office, Cincinnati OH 45221, USA
Zingaretti, Luca — Actor
Carol Levi Mgmt, Via G Pisanelli 2, 00196 Rome, Italy

Z

Ziegler - Zingaretti

Zinke, Olaf — Speed Skater
Johannes Bobrowski Str 22, 12627 Berlin, Germany
Zinkernagel, Rolf M — Nobel Medicine Laureate
Rebhusstr 47, 8126 Zumikon, Switzerland
Zinman, David J — Conductor
Aspen Music Festival, 2 Music School Road, Aspen CO 81611, USA
Zinner, Nicholas J (Nick) — Guitarist, Songwriter (Yeah Yeah Yeahs)
Yeah Yeah Yeahs, 249 Metropolitan Ave, Brooklyn NY 11211, USA
Zinni, Anthony C (Tony) — Marine Corps General
139 Shady Creek Lane, Fredericksburg VA 22406, USA
Zinszer, Pamela — Actress, Model
Playboy Promotions, 2706 Media Center Dr, Los Angeles CA 90065 USA
Zinta, Preity — Actress
C10/A Ranwar Wadora Road, Off Hill Road, Bandra (W), Mumbai MS 400050, India
Zipp, Debbie — Actress
Commerical Talent, 9255 Sunset Blvd, #505, Los Angeles CA 90069, USA
Zippel, David — Lyricist
Kraft-Engel Mgmt, 15233 Ventura Blvd, #200, Sherman Oaks CA 91403 USA
Zischler, Hanns — Actor
Anne Alvares Correa, 34 Rue Jouffroy d'Abbans, 75017 Paris, France
Zisk, Craig — Director, Producer
United Talent Agency, 9336 Civic Center Dr, Beverly Hills CA 90210 USA
Zisk, Randall (Randy) — Director
Creative Artists Agency, 2000 Ave of Stars, #100, Los Angeles CA 90067 USA
Zisk, Richard W (Richie) — Baseball Player
4231 NE 26th Terrace, Lighthouse Point FL 33064, USA
Zito, Barry W — Baseball Player
16627 Gilmore St, Van Nuys CA 91406, USA
Zito, Chuck — Actor, Model
Prince Marketing Group, 18 Carillon Circle, Livingston NJ 07039 USA
Zittel, Harry — Actor
Innovative Artists, 1505 10th St, Santa Monica CA 90401 USA
Zlatoper, Ronald J (Zap) — Navy Admiral
1001 Kamokila Blvd, Kapolei HI 96707, USA
Zlokovic, Berislav V — Neurologist
University of Rochester, Medical Center, 601 Elmwood Ave, Rochester NY 14642, USA
Zmed, Adrian — Actor
Vincent Cirrincione Assoc, 1516 N Fairfax Ave, Los Angeles CA 90046 USA
Zmievskaya Petrenko, Galina Y (Nina) — Figure Skating Coach
Ice Vault Arena, 10 Nevins Road, Wayne NJ 07470, USA
Zmolek, Doug — Ice Hockey Player
537 Frederichs Dr SW, Rochester MN 55901, USA
Znaider, Nikolaj — Conductor, Concert Violinist
I M G Artists, Hogarth Business Park, Chiswick, London W4 2TH, England
Zobrist, Benjamin T (Ben) — Baseball Player
545 Overview Lane, Franklin TN 37064, USA
Zoch, Jacqueline — Rowing Athlete
3421 Charing Wood Lane, Birmingham AL 35242, USA
Zoe, Rachel — Fashion Designer, Stylist
Bravo-TV, 3000 N Alameda Ave, #250, Burbank CA 91523 USA
Zoeller, Frank (Fuzzy) — Golfer
418 Deer Run Trace, Floyds Knobs IN 47119, USA
Zoellick, Robert B — Government Official, Financier
Peterson Institute, 1750 Massachusetts Ave NW, Washington DC 20036, USA
Zoff, Dino — Soccer Player
F C Juventus, Corso Galilo Ferraris 32, 10128 Turin, Italy
Zokol, Richard F (Dick) — Golfer
Contemporary Communications, 1663 7th Ave W, Vancouver BC V6J 1S4, Canada
Zolak, Scott D — Football Player
40 Comstock Dr, Wrentham MA 02093, USA
Zoli, Winter Eve — Actress
Melanie Greene Mgmt, 425 N Robertson Blvd, West Hollywood CA 90048 USA
Zollar, Jawole Willa Jo — Dancer, Dance Executive
Urban Bush Women, 138 S Oxford St, 4B, Brooklyn, NY 11217, USA
Zoloth, Laurie — Educator
Northwestern University, Medical School, Bioethics Center, Evanston IL 60208, USA
Zombie, Rob — Singer (White Zombie), Director
Zombie HQ, 8491 Sunset Blvd, #215, West Hollywood CA 90069, USA
Zombo, Rick — Ice Hockey Player
2918 Ossenfort Road, Glencoe MO 63038, USA
Zonderland, Epke — Gymnast
PO Box 197, 8 530 AD Lemmer, Netherlands
Zook, John E — Football Player
4302 N Spyglass Circle, Wichita KS 67226, USA
Zoran — Fashion Designer
67 Hudson St, New York NY 10013, USA
Zordich, Michael E (Mike) — Football Player
373 S Hazelwood Ave, Youngstown OH 44509, USA
Zore, Edward — Businessman
Northwestern Mutual Financial Network, 720 E Wisconsin, Milwaukee WI 53202, USA
Zorich, Christopher R (Chris) — Football Player
1231 W 33rd Place, Chicago IL 60608, USA
Zorich, Louis — Actor
Don Buchwald/Fortitude, 6500 Wilshire Blvd, #2200, Los Angeles CA 90048 USA
Zorn, James A (Jim) — Football Player, Coach
2006 W Mercer Way, Mercer Island WA 98040, USA
Zsigmond, Vilmos — Cinematographer
Skouras Agency, 1149 3rd St, #300, Santa Monica CA 90403 USA
Zubak, Kresimir — Co-President, Bosnia-Herzegovina
Presidency, Marsala Titz 7A, 71000 Sarajevo, Bosnia-Herzegovina
Zubeir Wako, Gabriel Cardinal — Religious Leader
Archdiocese, PO Box 49, Khartoum, Sudan
Zuber, Maria T — Geophysicist
Massachusetts Institute of Technology, Geophysics Dept, Cambridge MA 02139, USA
Zubov, Sergei M — Ice Hockey Player
3916 Marquette St, Dallas TX 75225, USA

Zubrus, Dainius G — Ice Hockey Player
92 Union St, Montclair NJ 07042, USA

Zucker, Arianne — Actress, Model
Kritzer Levine Wilkins Griffin, 11872 La Grange Ave, #100, Los Angeles CA 90025 USA

Zucker, David — Director, Producer
Scott Free Productions, 42-44 Beak St, London W1F 9RH, England

Zucker, Jerry — Director, Producer
Zucker Productions, 1250 6th St, #201, Santa Monica CA 90401, USA

Zuckerberg, Mark — Businessman
Facebook, 156 University Ave, #200, Palo Alto CA 94301, USA

Zuckerman, Harriet A — Sociologist, Foundation Executive
Andrew W Mellon Foundation, 140 E 62nd St, New York NY 10065, USA

Zuckerman, Joshua R (Josh) — Actor
Gersh Agency, 9465 Wilshire Blvd, #600, Beverly Hills CA 90212 USA

Zuckerman, Mortimer B — Publisher
Boston Properties, 599 Lexington Ave, #1800, New York NY 10022, USA

Zuckermann, Ariel — Conductor, Concert Flutist
Georgian Chamber Orchestra, Hohe-Schul-Stra 4, 85049 Ingolstadt, Germany

Zuhdi, Nazih — Surgeon
3300 NW Expressway, Oklahoma City OK 73112, USA

Zuiker, Anthony E — Producer, Writer, Actor
Brillstein Entertainment Partners, 9150 Wilshire Blvd, #350, Beverly Hills CA 90212 USA

Zuke, Michael (Mike) — Ice Hockey Player
430 Norman Gate Dr, Ballwin MO 63011, USA

Zuker, Danny — Producer, Writer
Creative Artists Agency, 2000 Ave of Stars, #100, Los Angeles CA 90067 USA

Zukerman, Eugenia — Concert Flutist
Brooklyn College of Music, Bedford & H Aves, Brooklyn NY 11210, USA

Zukerman, Pinchas — Concert Violinist, Conductor
Kirshbaum Demler Assoc, 711 W End Ave, #5KN, New York NY 10025, USA

Zullo, Alan — Cartoonist (Hall of Shame)
Tribune Media Services, 435 N Michigan Ave, #1500, Chicago IL 60611 USA

Zuluaga, Luz Marina — Beauty Queen
Miss Universe Organization, 1370 Ave of Americas, #1600, New York NY 10019 USA

Zuma, Jacob G — President, South Africa
President's Office, Union Buildings, Pretoria 0001, South Africa

Zumthor, Peter — Architect
Suesswinggel 20, 7023 Haldenstein, Switzerland

Zuniga, Daphne — Actress
Bauman Redanty Shaul Agency, 5757 Wilshire Blvd, #473, Los Angeles CA 90036 USA

Zuniga, Jose — Actor
A P A Talent/Literary Agency, 405 S Beverly Dr, #300, Beverly Hills CA 90212 USA

Zuniga, Miles — Singer, Guitarist (Fastball)
Russell Carter Artists, 567 Ralph Mcgill Blvd NE, Atlanta GA 30312, USA

Zupko, Ramon — Composer
Western Michigan University, Music Dept, Kalamazoo MI 49008, USA

Zurbriggen, Pirmin — Alpine Skier
Hotel Larchenhof, 3905 Saas-Almagell, Switzerland

Zurer, Ayelet Z — Actress
Independent Artists, 9601 Wilshire Blvd, #750, Beverly Hills CA 90210 USA

ZurHausen, Harald — Nobel Medicine Laureate
Tumorvirus-C A T, Im Neuenheimer Feld 242, 69120 Heidelberg, Germany

Zurkowski-Holmes, Agnes — Baseball Player
206-2339 Lorne St, Regina SK S4P 2N2, Canada

Zurrer, Emily — Soccer Player
Canadian Soccer, Place Soccer Canada, 237 Metcalfe St, Ottawa ON K2P 1R2, Canada

Zuvella, Paul — Baseball Player
2040 Canyon Crest Ave, San Ramon CA 94582, USA

Zuverink, George — Baseball Player
1027 E McNair Dr, Tempe AZ 85283, USA

Zvereva, Natalia — Tennis Player
Women's Tennis Assn, 1 Progress Plaza, #1500, Saint Petersburg FL 33701 USA

Zvonareva, Vera I — Tennis Player
S F X Sports, 846 Lincoln Road, #500, Miami Beach Fl 33139 USA

Zwanzig, Robert W — Chemical Physicist
8300 Burdette Road, #423, Bethesda MD 20817, USA

Zweig, George — Theoretical Physicist
Los Alamos National Laboratory, PO Box 1663, Los Alamos NM 87544, USA

Zweig, Stefanie — Writer
Rothschldallee 9, 60389 Frankfurt/Main, Germany

Zwerling, Darrell — Actor
CLInc Talent, 843 N Sycamore Ave, Los Angeles CA 90038, USA

Zwick, Alyse Jean — Actress, Comedienne, Model
OmniPop Talent Group, 4605 Lankershim Blvd, #201, Toluca Lake CA 91602 USA

Zwick, Edward M (Ed) — Director, Producer
Creative Artists Agency, 2000 Ave of Stars, #100, Los Angeles CA 90067 USA

Zwick, Joel — Director
Irv Schechter, 9460 Wilshire Blvd, #300, Beverly Hills CA 90212 USA

Zwigoff, Terry — Director
W M E Entertainment, 9601 Wilshire Blvd, #300, Beverly Hills CA 90210 USA

Zwilich, Ellen Taaffe — Composer
Music Associates of America, 224 King St, Englewood NJ 07631, USA

Zwonitzer, Mark — Producer, Director, Writer
Simon & Schuster, 1230 Ave of Americas, Concourse 1, New York NY 10020 USA

Zylberstein, Elsa — Actress
Agence Artiste Adequet, 80 Rue d'Amsterdam, 75009 Paris, France

Zylis-Gara, Teresa — Opera Singer
16A Blvd de Belgique, Monaco-Ville, Monaco

Zylka, Chris — Actor
W M E Entertainment, 9601 Wilshire Blvd, #300, Beverly Hills CA 90210 USA

NECROLOGY

Listees of previous editions of the V.I.P. Address Book and the V.I.P. Address Book Update whose deaths have been reported prior to close of the compilation are listed below.

Aas, Roald E	Speed Skater
Abdnor, James	Senator, SD
Abercrombie, Ian	Actor
Abrahamian, Mark	Guitarist (Starship)
Abune Paulos	Religious Leader
Ader, Robert	Psychologist
Adler, Richard	Composer, Lyricist
Ahmed, Abdullah Yusuf	President, Somalia
Akerfelds, Darrel W	Baseball Player
Alden, Norman	Actor
Alekseyev, Vassily	Weightlifter
Alexander, Haim	Composer
Allais, Emile	Alpine Skier
Allen, J Presson	Writer, Producer
Allen, Phillip Richard	Actor
Allilueyeva, Svetlana I	Daughter of Josef Stalin
Amaral, Francisco Xavier do	President, Timor-Leste
Anand, Dev	Actor
Andre, Maurice	Concert Trumpeter
Angelopoulos, Theo	Director
Anhalt, Istvan	Composer
Antwine, Houston J	Football Player
Aponte Martinez, Luis Cardinal	Religious Leader
Appleton, Steven R	Businessman
Aptsiauri, Vladimir	Fencer
Aramony, William	Association Executive
Arden, John	Writer
Ardolino, Tom	Drummer (NRBQ)
Arliss, Dimitra	Actress
Armendariz, Pedro, Jr	Actor
Arms, Russell	Actor, Singer
Armstrong, Neil A	Astronaut
Armstrong, R G	Actor
Arnold, Eve	Photographer
Arnold, James R	Chemist
Arutiunian, Alexander G	Composer
Ash, Roy L	Businessman, Government Official
Asher, William	Director, Screenwriter
Askew, Luke	Actor
Aslin, Peter	Hockey Player
Astapovsky, Vladimir A	Soccer Player
Aulenti, Gae	Architect
Avedon, Doe	Actress, Model
Avery, Mary Ellen	Physician, Pediatrician
Babbitt, Bob	Bassist (Funk Brothers)
Babin, Rex	Editorial Cartoonist
Bada, Sunday	Track Athlete
Baker, John F, Jr	Vietnam War Army Hero (CMH)
Baldelli, Fortunato Cardinal	Religious Leader
Baldrige, Letitia	Businesswoman, Writer
Barfoot, Van T	WW II Army Hero (CMH)
Barnes, Harry G, Jr	Diplomat
Bartholomew, Kenneth E	Speed Skater
Bartholomew, Reginald	Diplomat
Bartow, B Gene	Basketball Coach
Barzun, Jacques M	Educator
Basilio, Carmen	Boxer
Bassett, Johnnie	Guitarist
Bassman, Lillian	Photographer
Bastien, Rolland (Red)	Professional Wrestler
Bate, Anthony	Actor
Beard, C Theodore (Ted)	Baseball Player
Beasley, R Palmer	Epidemiologist
Beezer, Robert R	Judge
Behenna, Richard K (Rick)	Baseball Player
Bell, Tommy	Astronaut Candidate
Bella, Ahmed Ben	President, Algeria
Bellugi, Piero	Conductor
Bendjedid, Chadli	President, Algeria
Benjamin, Karl S	Artist
Bennett, Dennis J	Baseball Player
Bennett, Emmett L	Educator
Benson, Sidney W	Organic Chemist
Berenstain, Jan	Writer, Illustrator
Berglund, Paavo A E	Conductor
Berkutov, Aleksandr	Rowing Athlete
Bethune, Zina	Actress
Bevilacqua, Anthony J Cardinal	Religious Leader
Bey, Turhan	Actor
Biggers, Dan	Actor

Biggs, Barton M	Financier
Binchy, Maeve	Writer
Bisher, J Furman	Sportswriter
Blvins, James L (Jimmy)	Boxer
Bjork, Anita	Actress
Blackfoot, J	Singer
Blatnick, Jeffrey C (Jeff)	Greco-Roman Wrestler
Bliss, Lucille	Actress
Bogart, Paul	Director
Bohovich, G Reed	Football Player
Bonniwell, Sean	Singer, Musician (Music Machine)
Boone, J R	Football Player
Boozer, Robert L (Bob)	Basketball Player
Borbon, Pedro	Baseball Player
Borgnine, Ernest	Actor
Boswell, David W (Dave)	Baseball Player
Bouchard, Emile J (Butch)	Ice Hockey Player
Boyer, Paul S	Historian
Brabham, Daniel E (Danny)	Football Player
Bradbury, Ray D	Writer
Brallier, Max B	Air Force General, Surgeon
Bramhall, Doyle, II	Singer, Guitarist, Songwriter
Brancato, Albert (Al)	Baseball Player
Breck, Peter	Actor
Breitbart, Andrew	Publisher, Commentator
Brennan, Peter J (Pete)	Basketball Player
Brenner, Allen R (Al)	Football Player
Breslow, Lester	Physician
Brevett, Lloyd	Bassist (Skatalites)
Brewer, John L (Johnny)	Football Player
Brimmer, Andrew F	Government Official, Economist
Britten, Roy J	Geneticist
Brookmeyer, Robert E (Bob)	Jazz Trombonist, Pianist
Brooks, John E	Educator
Brown, Chuck	Singer, Guitarist
Brown, Helen Gurley	Editor, Writer
Brown, James (Jim)	Actor
Brown, Lesley	Mother of 1st Test Tube Baby
Browne, Malcolm W	Journalist
Browning, James R	Judge
Buksar, George B	Football Player
Burke, James E	Businessman
Burke, Sarah	Freestyle Skier
Burnett, Bob	Singer (Highwaymen)
Burns, Phil	Actor
Bush, Lewis F	Football Player
Butcher, Donnis (Donnie)	Basketball Player
Butcher, Willard C	Financier
Byerly, Eldred W (Bud)	Baseball Player
Bygraves, Max	Singer, Songwriter
Cady, Frank	Actor
Cahill, Barry	Actor
Cahill, George F, Jr	Physician
Callahan, Robert F (Bob)	Football Player
Camacho, Hector (Macho)	Boxer
Camm, Frank A, Jr	Army General
Campbell, Keith H S	Biologist, Geneticist
Campbell, Milton G (Milt)	Track Athlete, Football Player
Canale, Justin D	Football Player
Cantamessa, Gene	Sound Editor
Carey, Andrew A (Andy)	Baseball Player
Carey, Hugh L	Governor, NY
Carlen, James A (Jim)	Football Coach
Carpaneda, Luigi	Fencer
Carpenter, Kenneth L (Ken)	Football Player
Carr of Hadley, L Robert	Government Official, England
Carr, James H (Jimmy)	Football Player
Carroll, Janet	Actress
Carsten, Peter	Actor
Carter, Donald J (Don)	Bowler
Carter, Elliott C, Jr	Composer
Carter, Gary E	Baseball Player
Carter, LaVerne	Bowler
Carter, Leslie	Singer, Actor
Cashman, John A, Jr	Harness Racing Executive
Catlett, Elizabeth	Sculptor
Catto, Henry E, Jr	Diplomat
Celardo, John	Cartoonist
Challis, Christopher	Cinematographer
Chamberlain, John A	Sculptor

NECROLOGY

Chappuis, Robert R (Bob)	Football Player
Charette, William R (Doc)	Korean War Navy Hero (CMH)
Charles, Teddy	Jazz Vibist, Composer
Charlip, A Remy	Choreographer, Dancer, Writer
Charnley, David F (Dave)	Boxer
Cheadle, David B (Dave)	Baseball Player
Chen Din Hwa	Businessman
Chertok, Boirs	Rocket Engineer
Chinaglia, Giorgio	Soccer Player
Chopra, Yash	Director, Producer, Writer
Chopra, Yash	Director, Producer
Christian, Roger A (Rog)	Ice Hockey Player
Cimino, Leonardo	Actor
Clark, Alfred A (Allie)	Baseball Player
Clark, Richard A (Dick)	Entertainer, Producer
Clive, John	Writer, Actor
Clyburn, Danny	Baseball Player
Coates, John	Animator
Coffin, Tristam P	Writer
Colalillo, Mike	WW II Army Hero (CMH)
Cole, Dennis	Actor
Collins, Gary	Actor
Collins, Sean	Surfing Executive
Colson, Charles W	Religious Leader, Watergate Figure
Commoner, Barry	Plant Physiologist, Ecologist
Compton, Lynn	WW II Army Hero
Connell, Elizabeth	Opera Singer
Cook, Carroll (Beano)	Sportscaster
Cook, Gregory L (Greg)	Football Player
Cooper, Emmanuel	Artist
Cornelius, Don	Producer
Corson, Dale R	Physicist, Educator
Cottrell, Alan H	Metallurgical Engineer
Courtland, Jerome	Actor
Covey, Stephen R	Writer
Cowan, George A	Chemist
Cowen, Zelman	Governor General, Australia
Cowles, John, Jr	Publisher
Cox, Glenn M	Baseball Player
Cragun, Richard	Ballet Dancer
Crain, Kurt	Football Player
Crandall, Paul H	Neurosurgeon
Crews, Harry E	Writer
Crist, Judith	Journalist
Crow, James F	Geneticist
Crumling, Eugene L (Gene)	Baseball Player
Cummings, Patrick M (Pat)	Basketball Player
Current, Michael W (Mike)	Football Player
Curson, Theodore (Ted)	Jazz Trumpeter, Flugelhorn Player
Curtis Cuneo, Ann E	Swimmer
Cyr, Paul	Ice Hockey Player
Dando, Shigemitsu	Judge
Daniel, Robert W, Jr	Representative, VA
Daniel, Simeon	Premier, Nevis
Danoff, Bettye	Golfer
Daoud, Ignace Moussa I Cardinal	Religious Leader
Darcel, Denise	Actress
D'Arcy, Barbara	Interior Designer
Darling, Clifford	Governor General, Bahamas
David, Hal	Lyricist
David, Tissa	Animator
Davidson, Benjamin E (Ben)	Football Player
Davies, Richard A (Dick)	Basketball Player
Davis, Carl	Composer, Conductor
Davis, Douglas S (Doug)	Football Player
Davis, Jack	Track Athlete
Davis, Michael	Bassist (MC5)
Davis, Tom	Actor, Comedian
Dawson, Richard	Actor, Comedian
DeLaMadrid Hurtado, Miguel	President, Mexico
Delaney, Shelagh	Writer
Denker, Henry	Writer
Denktas, Rauf R	President, Turkish Northern Cyprus
Derwinski, Edward J	Secretary, Veterans Affairs
Devesi, Baddekey	Governor General, Solomon Islands
DeZuniga, Tony	Cartoonist (Jonah Hex, Black Orchid)
Dial, Terri	Financier
Dichaussoy, Michel	Actor
Dickey, Robert Lee	Singer (James & Bobby Purify)
Dilip	Actor, Producer
Dillard, Doug	Singer, Actor
Diller, Phyllis	Actress, Comedienne
Dipietro, Robert L P (Bob)	Baseball Player
Dixon, John C (Sonny)	Baseball Player
Dokes, Michael	Boxer
Dorfman, Dan	Columnist, Commentator
Doty, Paul M	Biochemist
Drake, Jim	Sailplane Designer, Aeronautics Engineer
Drogosz, Leszek	Boxer
Dualde Santos de Lamadrid, Joaquin	Field Hockey Player
Dulbecco, Renato	Nobel Medicine Laureate
Dummett, Michael A E	Philosopher
Duncan, Cleveland (Cleve)	Singer (Penguins)
Duncan, Michael Clark	Actor
Dundee, Angelo	Boxing Manager
Dunham, Stephen	Actor
Dunn, Donald (Duck)	Bassist (Book T & the MG's)
Dunn, Patricia C	Businesswoman
Duong, Don	Actor
Durkin, John A	Senator, NH
Dye, William (Tippy)	Basketball Player, Coach
Dymally, Mervyn M	Representative, CA
Early, Joseph D	Representative, MA
Easterling, C Ray	Football Player
Easton, Robert	Actor
Eberts, Jake	Producer
Economaki, Christopher C (Chris)	Sportscaster
Edwards, Robert J	Editor
Ellis, Jimmy	Singer (Trammps)
Ellis, LeRoy	Basketball Player, Coach
Endler, James	Construction Engineer
Ephron, Nora	Writer, Director
Epper, Tony	Actor
Erhardt, Ronald P (Ron)	Football Coach
Erickson, Don L	Baseball Player
Everett, Chad	Actor
Everett, Marje	Thoroughbred Racing Executive
Evora, Cesaria	Singer
Ezinicki, William (Bill)	Ice Hockey Player
Faas, Horst	Photographer
Fairfax, John	Rowing Athlete
Fang Lizhi	Astrophysicist, Political Activist
Farentino, James	Actor
Farulli, Piero	Concert Violist
Fass, Horst	Photojournalist
Feasel, Grant E	Football Player
Fedoruk, Sylvia O	Physicist
Fekete, Eugene H (Gene)	Football Player
Felton, Norman F	Producer, Director, Writer
Felton, Ralph D	Football Player
Fetchick, Mike	Golfer
Figes, Eva	Writer
Finley, William	Actor
Finnegan, John	Actor
Fischer, Clare	Jazz Keyboardist, Composer
Fischer-Dieskau, Dietrich	Opera, Concert Singer; Conductor
Fisher, Roger D	Attorney, Educator
Fitch, John C	Auto Racing Driver
Fitzgerald, James F (Jim)	Basketball Executive
Flaman, Ferdinand C (Fernie)	Ice Hockey Player
Fleischmann, Martin	Electrochemist
Fletcher, Betty Binns	Judge
Fogle, James	Writer
Foley, John P Cardinal	Religious Leader
Forstmann, Theodore J (Ted)	Businessman, Sports Executive
Fournet, Sidney F (Sid)	Football Player
Francois-Poncet, Jean A	Government Official, France; Financier
Frankenthaler, Helen	Artist
Frankfurt, Stephen O	Businessman
Franzen, Ulrich J	Architect
Frazer, Dan	Actor
Frazier, W Wayne	Football Player
Freeman, Al, Jr	Actor
Fretwell, Elbert K, Jr	Educator
Frid, Jonathan	Actor
Friday, William C	Educator
Frink, Patrick E (Pat)	Basketball Player
Fuentes, Carlos	Writer
Fuest, Robert	Director
Fuller, Peter D	Thoroughbred Racing Owner
Fullmer, Don	Boxer
Funderburk, Hanley	Educator
Fussell, Paul	Writer, Educator
Gainsbourg, Charlotte	Actress
Galhia, Habib	Boxer
Galligan, Walter T	Air Force General

NECROLOGY

Galligan, Walter T — Air Force General
Gallup, George H, II — Statistician, Pollster
Galushka Doulounova, Vera — Volleyball Player
Ganao, Charles David — Prime Minister, Congo
Gantt, L Gregory (Greg) — Football Player
Garcia, Russell — Composer
Gardner, Keith — Track Athlete
Garrahy, J Joseph — Governor, RI
Gazzara, Ben — Actor
Genovese, Eugene D — Historian
George, Jean Craighead — Writer
Ghanem, Shukri — General Secretary, Libya
Gibb, Robin — Singer (Bee Gees), Songwriter
Gibbons, Samuel M (Sam) — Representative, FL
Giller, Walter — Actor
Gilman, Dorothy — Writer
Ginsberg, Myron N (Joe) — Baseball Player
Gits, Dean R — Attorney
Glaser, Robert — Psychologist
Glenamara of Glenridding — Government Official, England
Gligorov, Kiro — President, Macedonia
Glowna, Vladim — Actor, Director
Godwin, Thomas C (Tommy) — Cyclist
Goodman, Julian — Businessman
Goodway, Beverley — Photographer
Gordon, Al — Writer
Gordon, Cecil — Auto Racing Driver, Mechanic
Gorr, Rita — Opera Singer
Gourdine, Simon P — Labor Leader, Basketball Executive
Grachev, Pavel S — Army Marshal, Russia
Grady, Don — Actor, Songwriter
Gray, Dobie — Singer
Gray, Dulcie — Actress
Gray, Robert E (Bob) — Army General
Griffin, Oscar, Jr — Journalist
Griffith, Andrew S (Andy) — Actor, Singer
Grosbard, Ulu — Director
Grout, James — Actor
Haar, Charles M — Attorney, Educator
Hadley, Albert — Interior Designer
Hagman, Larry — Actor
Haines, Ralph E, Jr — Army General
Hall, Floyd D — Businessman
Hall, Katie — Representative, IN
Haller, Helmut — Soccer Player
Halman, Gregory A (Greg) — Baseball Player
Ham, Gregory N (Greg) — Musician (Men at Work)
Hamilton, Dennis E — Basketball Player
Hamilton, James A — Aeronautical Engineer
Hamilton, Leigh — Actress
Hamlisch, Marvin — Composer, Conductor
Han Suyin — Writer
Handler, Evelyn E — Educator
Hardy, Jonathan — Actor, Writer
Harris, Eric W — Football Player
Harrison, Harry — Writer
Harter, Dick — Basketball Coach
Hassard, Jerry — Track Coach
Hauptman, Herbert A — Nobel Chemistry Laureate
Havel, Vaclav — President, Czechoslovakia; Writer
Hazzard, Walter R (Walt), Jr — Basketball Player, Coach
Heafner, Vance — Golfer
Heap, Joseph L (Joe) — Football Player
Hearst, George R, Jr — Publisher
Heesters, Johannes — Singer, Actor
Hegyes, Robert — Actor
Heim, Michael H — Writer, Educator
Heineman, Ben W — Businessman
Helm, Levon — Singer, Drummer (Band); Actor
Helpern, David M — Businessman
Hemsley, Sherman — Actor
Hennessey, Tom — Football Player
Henry, Geoffrey A — Prime Minister, Cook Islands
Henze, Hans Werner — Composer, Conductor
Hershberger, N Michael (Mike) — Baseball Player
Heyman, Arthur B (Art) — Basketball Player
Heyman, I Michael — Association Executive, Educator
Hick, John H — Theologian
Hickey, Kevin J — Baseball Player
Hill, Frank A — WW II Army Air Corps Hero
Hill, S King — Football Player
Hinzman, Bill — Actor
Hirzebruch, Friedrich E P — Mathematician

Hitch, Lewis R (Lew) — Basketball Player
Hittle, Lloyd E — Baseball Player
Hoag, Charles — Basketball Player
Hoban, Russell C — Writer
Hobsbawm, Eric J H — Historian
Hoffman, Wayne M — Businessman
Holland, Heinrich D (Dick) — Geologist
Holloway, James W (Red) — Jazz Saxophonist
Holm, Celeste — Actress
Hossack, Michael — Musician (Doobie Brothers)
Houston, Whitney — Singer
Hrechkosy, Dave J — Ice Hockey Player
Hughes, Robert S F — Art Critic
Hussing, Peter — Boxer
Huth, Gerald B (Jerry) — Football Player
Huxley, Andrew F — Nobel Medicine Laureate
Hveger, Ragnhild — Swimmer
Illueca Sibauste, Jorge E — President, Panama
Ingle, John — Actor
Ionov, Vyacheslav — Canoeing Athlete
Isaac, James — Director
Ishara, Babu R (B R) — Director, Writer
Ishimoto, Yashuiro — Photographer
Ishioka, Eiko — Costume Designer
Ivanov, Eduard G — Ice Hockey Player
Ivanov, Nikolai P — Rowing Athlete
Ivanov, Valentin K — Soccer Player, Coach
Iverson, Christopher A (Duke) — Football Player
Iwasaki, Fukuzo — Businessman
Jabali, Warren — Basketball Player
Jackson, Gregory (Greg) — Basketball Player
James, Etta — Singer
Janklow, William J (Bill) — Governor, SD
Jansson, Gustav — Track Athlete
Jauss, Bill — Sportswriter
Jenkins, Edgar L (Ed) — Representative, GA
Jenkins, Jackie (Butch) — Actor
Jenkins, Paul — Artist
Jenkins, William T (Grumpy) — Drag Racing Driver
Jensen, Arthur R — Educational Psychologist
Jernberg, Sixten — Cross Country Skier
Johansen, John M — Architect
John, Carolyn — Actress
Johnson, Evelyn B — Aviatrix
Johnson, William L (Tiger), Sr — Football Player, Coach
Jones, David (Davy) — Singer, Guitarist (Monkees)
Jones, Eddie J — Football Executive
Jones, Jimmy — Singer, Songwriter
Joosten, Kathryn — Actress
Josephson, Erland — Actor
Joyce, Donald G (Don) — Football Player
Juneau, Pierre — Government Official, Canada
Jurinac, Sena — Opera Singer
Kallmann, Gerhard M — Architect
Kanwar, Raj — Director, Producer
Karlsson, Nils — Cross Country Skier
Karras, Alexander G (Alex) — Football Player, Actor
Katzenbach, Nicholas deB — Attorney General, Businessman
Keegan, John — Historian
Kelleher, Robert J — Tennis Executive, Judge
Keller, Harold K (Hal) — Baseball Player
Kelley, Mike — Artist, Musician
Kelly, David — Actor
Kelly, Leontine T C — Religious Leader
Kent, Glenn A — Air Force General
Keough, Harry J — Soccer Player, Coach
Keynan, Alexander — Microbiologist
Khanna, Rajesh — Actor
Khorana, Har Gobind — Nobel Medicine Laureate
Kiel, Blair A — Football Player
Kikutake, Kiyonori — Architect
Kim Jong Il — Supreme Commander, North Korea
King, Rodney G — Police Victim
King, Zalman — Director
Kinkade, Thomas — Artist
Kinmont Boothe, Jill — Alpine Skier
Klatt, William G (Bill) — Ice Hockey Player
Knowles, William S — Nobel Chemistry Laureate
Knox, Elyse — Actress
Koshkin, Aleksandr — Boxer
Kosichkin, Viktor — Speed Skater
Kovatch, John G (Johnny) — Football Player
Koyama, Tsutomu — Volleyball Player

NECROLOGY

Kriegsman, Alan M	Journalist
Kristel, Sylvia	Actress
Krutov, Vladimir Y	Ice Hockey Player
Kubert, Joe	Cartoonist (Tales of the Green Beret)
Kulej, Jerzy	Boxer
Kyros, Peter N	Representative, ME
Lakes, Roland H	Football Player
Lakshmi, S N	Actress
Langdon, David	Cartoonist
Lauder, Evelyn H	Social Activist
Lea, Barbara	Singer
Lea, Charles W (Charlie)	Baseball Player
Lear, Evelyn	Opera Singer
LeBrocquy, Louis	Artist
Ledley, Robert S	Inventor (Diagnostic X-Ray Systems)
LeGault, Lance	Actor
Legorreta Vilchis, Ricardo	Architect
Leitao, Antonio	Track Athlete
Leka Zog	King, Albania
Lent, Norman F	Representative, NY
Lenzi, Mark	Diver
Leonhardt, Gustave M	Concert Harpsichordist, Organist
Lerman, Leonard S	Molecular Biologist
Lewis, Johnny	Actor
Lewis, Judy	Actress
Light, James E, Jr	Air Force General
Lilly, Everett	Singer (Lilly Brothers)
Lindsey, George (Goober)	Actor, Singer
Lindsey, Mort	Orchestra Leader, Composer
Llewellyn, Barry	Singer (Heptones)
Lom, Herbert	Actor
Lopez, Lillian	Singer (Odyssey)
Lord, Jon D	Keyboardist (Deep Purple)
Lougheed, E Peter	Attorney
Louisiana Red	Singer, Guitarist, Harmonica Player
Lovelace, Jon B, Jr	Financier
Lovell, A C Bernard	Astronomer
Luce, R Duncan	Psychologist
Luckenbill, Theodore (Ted)	Basketball Player
Luhn, Nolan H	Football Player
Lyles, Leonard E (Lenny)	Football Player
Lyman, Richard W	Foundation Executive, Educator
Lynch, Gerald T (Jerry)	Baseball Player
Lynch, Richard	Actor
Lynn, Michael E (Mike), III	Football Executive
Macionis, John	Swimmer
MacPhail, Leland S (Lee), Jr	Baseball Executive
Madoc, Philip	Actor
Magnone, Guido	Mountaineer
Malone, Arthur L (Art)	Football Player
Mangiarotti, Edouardo	Fencer
Manoogian, Torkom	Religious Leader
Maoate, Terepai T	Prime Minister, Cook Islands
Marcus, Ruth B	Philosopher
Margulis, Lynn	Biologist, Botanist
Marin, Christian	Actor
Markovic, Ante	President, Croatia
Marre, Albert	Theatre Director
Marshall of Knightsbridge, Colin M	Businessman
Martin, Frank (Pancho)	Thoroughbred Racing Trainer
Martin, Slater N	Basketball Player
Martin, Tony	Singer, Actor
Martini, Carlo Maria Cardinal	Religious Leader
Mathews, Terry A	Baseball Player
Mathieu, Georges V A	Artist
Matsushita, Masaharu	Businessman
Mattioli, Joseph	Auto Racing Executive
May, Willie	Track Athlete
McCaffrey, Anne	Writer
McCain, Jerry	Singer, Harmonica Player, Guitarist
McCarthy, Paul F, Jr	Navy Admiral
McCartney, Forrest S	Air Force General
McCracken, Paul W	Government Official, Economist
McDonnell, Sanford N	Businessman
McGeady, Sister Mary Rose	Social Activist
McGlockton, Chester	Football Player
McGovern, George S	Senator, SD
McGuire, Dorothy	Singer (McGuire Sisters)
McKenna, Bernard N (Barney)	Banjoist (Dubliners)
McKenzie, Scott	Singer, Songwriter
McKinney, Bill	Actor
McMorris, Jerry	Baseball Executive
McPhee, Frank M	Football Player

McPherson, Harry C, Jr	Government Official
McQuarrie, Ralph	Illustrator
Means, Russell	Indian Activist
Medina, Hazel J	Actress
Medina, Patricia	Actress
Medlin, John G, Jr	Financier
Meles Zenawi Asres	President & Prime Minister, Ethiopia
Menczel, Ivan	Soccer Player
Mercado Jarrin, Luis Edgardo	Prime Minister, Peru
Michel, Smarck	Prime Minister, Haiti
Midler, Mark	Fencer
Miki, Minouri	Composer
Milano, Fred	Singer (Dion & the Belmonts)
Miller, Claude	Director, Writer
Miller, George A	Psychologist
Miller, Joyce D	Labor Leader
Miller, Nolan	Fashion Designer
Millman, Irving	Inventor (Hepatitis B Tests, Vaccine)
Mills, John Atta	President, Ghana
Mincher, Donald R (Don)	Baseball Player
Miner, Roger J	Judge
Mintoff, Dominic	Prime Minister, Malta
Misago, Augustin	Religious Leader
Modell, Arthur B (Art)	Football Executive
Moffatt, John	Actor
Moggridge, William (Bill)	Industrial Designer
Mohieddin, Zakaria	Prime Minister, Egypt
Mojtabavi, Abdollah	Freestyle Wrestler
Molden, Frederick K (Freddie)	Football Player
Moldoff, Sheldon	Cartoonist
Mondy, Pierre	Actor
Montrose, Ronnie	Guitarist (Edgar Winter Group, Montrose)
Moon, Sun Myung	Religious Leader
Moorhead, Carlos J	Representative, CA
Morant, Richard	Actor
Morehead, James B	WW II Army Air Corps Hero
Moretti, Gianpiero	Auto Racing Driver
Morgan, Harry	Actor
Mori, Minoru	Businessman
Mori, Wataru	Pathologist
Moriarty, Phillip E (Phil)	Swimming Coach
Moritzen, Henning	Actor
Morvillo, Robert G	Attorney
Motian, S Paul	Jazz Drummer, Percussionist, Composer
Mueller, Donald F (Don)	Baseball Player
Mueller, Leslie C (Les)	Baseball Player
Murdock, George	Actor
Murdock, O J	Football Player
Mussa, Michael L	Economist
Mutharika, Bingu Wa	President, Malawi
Myrick, Robert H (Bob)	Baseball Player
Nayef bin Abdul-Aziz al Saud	Crown Prince, Saudi Arabia
Neighbors, William W (Billy)	Football Player
Neiman, LeRoy	Artist
Neisser, Ulric	Psychologist
Neville, John	Actor, Director
Noble, Nick	Singer
Norodom Kantol, Prince	Prime Minister, Cambodia
Norodom Sihanouk, Samdech Preah	King, Cambodia
Nunn, Howard R (Howie)	Baseball Player
O'Bradovich, James T (Jim)	Baseball Player
O'Donnell, Guillermo A	Political Scientist
O'Donnell, Mark	Writer
Oen, Alexander Dale	Swimmer
O'Hare, Michael	Actor
Ojukwu, Chukwuemeka O	President, Biafra; Army General
Old, Lloyd J	Cancer Biologist
O'Neil, John F	Baseball Player
O'Neill, Michael J	Editor
Ontiveros, Lupe	Actress
Osborne DuPont, Margaret	Tennis Player
Osborne, Burl	Editor, Publisher
Oshchehpkov, Stepan M	Canoist
Ostrom, Elinor	Nobel Economics Laureate
Otis, Johnny	Singer, Drummer, Pianist, Songwriter
Ovshinsky, Stanford R	Ovionics Engineer, Inventor
Owen, Henry	Diplomat
Owens, Everett (Cotton)	Auto Racing Driver
Owens, Rawleigh C (R C)	Football Player
Pakledinaz, Martin (Marty)	Costume Designer
Palillo, Ron	Actor
Panelli, John R	Football Player
Paratore, James (Jim)	Producer

NECROLOGY

Name	Occupation
Parnell, Melvin L (Mel)	Baseball Player
Parrott, H Ian	Composer
Paterno, Joseph V (Joe)	Football Coach
Paternoster, George	Football Player
Pauls, Edward A (Ed)	Inventor (NordicTrack)
Payne, Donald M	Representative, NJ
Pearson, Lindell E (Lindy)	Football Player
Perez, Johnny	Drummer (Sir Douglas Quintet)
Perez, Pascual G	Baseball Player
Perkins, Eddie	Boxer
Perry, Mary	Volleyball Player
Persons, Fern	Actress
Pesky, John M (Johnny)	Baseball Player
Peterson, Michael	Surfer
Phelan, John J, Jr	Financier
Philley, David E (Dave)	Baseball Player
Piazza, Marguerite	Opera Singer
Pierre, M Jamison (Jamie)	Extreme Free Skier
Pierson, Frank R	Director, Writer
Pininfarina, Sergio	Automobile Designer
Piraino, Marty	Bowler
Piszcz, Rafal	Canoeing Athlete
Pitakaka, Moses	Governor General, Solomon Islands
Pitts, Charles (Skip)	Guitarist (Bo-Keys)
Plank, Scott	Actor
Platt, Joseph B	Educator
Pockriss, Lee J	Songwriter
Poindexter, Alan G	Astronaut
Poling, Harold A	Businessman
Poll, Martin H	Producer
Pollak, Louis H	Judge
Polley, Eugene J	Inventor (Flash-Matic Remote Control)
Popa, Eli C	Football Player
Porokhovshchikov, Aleksander S	Actor, Director
Porsche, Ferdinand A (F A), III	Automobile Designer
Potter, E J	Motorcycle Racing Rider, Drag Driver
Powell, Jesse L	Football Player
Preston, Frances W	Businesswoman
Preston, Thomas A (Amarillo Slim), Jr	Poker Player
Previn, Dory	Singer, Songwriter
Price, Charles H, II	Diplomat, Financier
Price, Kenneth	Artist, Sculptor
Prochazka, Frantisek	Ice Hockey Player
Prudden, Bonnie	Physical Fitness Expert
Quigley, James M	Representative, PA
Rafferty, Bill	Actor
Raleigh, Don	Ice Hockey Player
Rambaldi, Carlo	Special Effects Artist
Ramsey, Norman F, Jr	Nobel Physics Laureate
Raska, Jiri	Ski Jumper
Raspberry, William J	Journalist
Rathmann, George B	Businessman
Rathmann, Jim	Auto Racing Driver
Ravi	Director, Composer
Raymond, Paula	Actress
Redman, Joyce	Actress
Reed, Herb	Singer (Platters)
Reed, John H	Governor, ME; Diplomat
Rees, Angharad	Actress
Reinhardt, Larry (Rhino)	Guitarist (Captain Beyond)
Restic, Joseph W (Joe)	Football Player, Coach
Ricci, Ruggiero	Concert Violinist
Rich, Adrienne	Writer
Rich, Elaine	Writer, Producer
Rich, Lee	Producer, Businessman
Richard, Jean-Louis	Actor, Director, Writer
Ride, Sally K	Astronaut
Risen, Arnold D (Arnie)	Basketball Player
Risk, Thomas N	Financier
Rizzi, James	Artist
Roberts, Joan	Actress
Robie, Carl	Swimmer
Robinson, Stacy L	Football Player
Rodriguez, Douglas	Boxer
Rojas, Raul	Boxer
Rokka, Olavi	Modern Pentathlete
Rollins, Kenneth H (Kenny)	Basketball Player
Rose, Charles G, III	Representative, NC
Rose, Murray	Swimmer
Rosoman, Leonard H	Artist
Ross, Al	Cartoonist
Ross, Jimmy D	Army General
Rosset, Barnet L, Jr	Publisher, Editor
Roundfield, Danny T (Dan)	Basketball Player
Rovick, John	Actor
Rowland, F Sherwood	Nobel Chemistry Laureate
Royal, Darrell K	Football Player, Coach
Rozsavolgyi, Istvan	Track Athlete
Rudakov, Yevhen V	Soccer Player
Rusoran, Peter	Water Polo Player
Russell, Bing	Actor
Russell, H Kenneth A (Ken)	Director
Russell, Joseph J (Sweet Joe)	Singer (Persuasions)
Rutherford, Ann	Actress
Ryan, John R (Rocky)	Football Player
Sabol, Stephen D (Steve)	Businessman
Sachs, Gloria	Fashion Designer
Sakurai, Takaeo	Boxer
Sales, Eugenio de Araujo Cardinal	Religious Leader
Sammet, George, Jr	Army General
Sams, Doris J	Baseball Player
Sanchez, Jose T Cardinal	Religious Leader
Sanders, Corrie	Boxer
Sandler, Marion O	Financier
Sanha, Malam Bacai	President, Guinea-Bissau
Sargent, John T	Publisher
Sargent, Wallace L W (Wal)	Astronomer
Sassoon, Vidal	Hair Stylist
Saul, Richard R (Rich)	Football Player
Savides, Harris	Cinematographer
Savitsky, George M	Football Player
Scaglietti, Sergio	Automobile Designer
Scalapino, Robert A	Political Scientist
Scalfaro, Oscar Luigi	President, Italy
Scarry, Michael J (Mike)	Football Player
Schintzius, Dwayne K	Basketball Player
Schlumpf, Leon	President, Switzerland
Schmidtmer, Christiane	Model, Actress
Schroder, Gerhard	Businessman
Scitovsky, Anne A	Economist
Scott, Barbara Ann	Figure Skater
Scott, Tony	Director
Scruggs, Earl	Singer, Banjoist, Songwriter
Searle, Ronald	Cartoonist, Animator
Seau, Tiana B (Junior), Jr	Football Player
Selznick, Eugene (Gene)	Volleyball Player
Sendak, Maurice B	Illustrator, Writer
Sewell, Harley E	Football Player
Shadid, Anthony	Journalist
Shamir, Yitzhak	Prime Minister, Israel
Sharp, Don	Director
Shebarshin, Leonid	Government Official, Russia
Shelby, Carroll	Auto Racing Driver, Executive
Shelton, Peter L	Architect
Shenouda III	Religious Leader
Sherman, Robert B	Songwriter, Writer
Shindo, Kaneto	Director
Silber, John R	Educator
Simon, Joe	Cartoonist (Captain America)
Simpson, Louis A M	Writer
Sims, Tom	Snowboard, Skateboard Athlete
Singh, Dara	Actor, Wrestler, Director, Producer
Singleton, Doris	Actress
Skon, Warren A (Andy)	Hero
Skopil, Otto R, Jr	Judge
Skowron, William J (Moose)	Baseball Player
Skvorecky, Josef V	Writer
Slatyer, Ralph O	Biologist, Ecologist
Slover, Karl	Actor
Smale, John G	Businessman
Smith, Hulett C	Governor, WV
Socrates	Soccer Player
Solomon, Fred (Freddie)	Football Player
South, Joe	Singer, Songwriter, Guitarist
Spears, Billie Jo	Singer
Specter, Arlen	Senator, PA
Spencer, Edson W	Businessman
Spinetti, Victor	Actor
Spinks, Terence (Terry)	Boxer
Spoonhour, Charles (Charlie)	Basketball Coach
Springstead, Martin J (Marty)	Baseball Umpire
St John of Fawsley, Norman A F	Government Official, England
Stad-de-Jong, Xenia	Track Athlete
Stallone, Sage	Actor
Stanley, Jimmy L	Football Player, Coach
Starr, Steve	Photojournalist

NECROLOGY

Statuto, Arthur G (Art)	Football Player
Staub, William	Inventor (Home Treadmill), Engineer
Stevens, Edward L (Ed)	Baseball Player
Stevens, Kaye	Singer, Actress
Stevens, Warren	Actor
Stevenson Lorenzo, Teofilo	Boxer
Stevenson, Larry	Skateboard Athlete
Steward, Emanuel	Boxing Trainer, Manager
Stewart, Bill (Stew)	Football Coach
Stewart, Martha	Actress, Singer
Stewart, Ronald G (Ron)	Ice Hockey Player
Stone, James L	Korean War Army Hero (CMH)
Stone, Ruth	Writer
Strincevich, Nicholas M (Nick)	Baseball Player
Stuart, Mel	Director, Producer, Writer
Sues, Alan	Actor
Sugar, Bert R	Writer, Editor
Suleiman, Omar	Vice President, Egypt
Sulzberger, Arthur Ochs, Sr	Publisher
Sumlin, Hubert	Singer, Guitarist
Summer, Donna	Singer, Songwriter
Summers, John J (Champ), Jr	Baseball Player
Summers, Yale	Actor
Surtees, Bruce	Cinematographer
Sutton, Joseph (Joe)	Football Player
Sykes, Eric	Actor, Comedian, Writer
Szasz, Thomas S	Psychiatrist
Szente, Andras	Canoeing Athlete
Szymborska, Wislawa	Nobel Literature Laureate
Tabone, Vincent (Censu)	President, Malta
Taittinger, Jean	Businessman
Talib, Naji	Prime Minister, Iraq; Army General
Tamm, Mary	Actress
Tanning, Dorothea	Artist
Tapia, John L (Johnny)	Boxer
Tapies, Antoni	Artist
Tarrant, Colin	Actor
Tasker, Roland (Rolly)	Yachtsman
Tate, Howard	Singer, Songwriter
Taylor, Joan	Actress
Termo, Leonard	Actor
Thaxter, Phyllis	Actress
Thomas, E Donnall	Nobel Medicine Laureate
Threlkeld, Richard D	Commentator
Thurston, William P	Mathematician
Tieman, Daniel T (Dan)	Basketball Player
Tiemann, Norbert T	Governor, NE
Tillotson, Thaddeus A (Thad)	Baseball Player
Tobias, Phillip V	Anatomist, Palaeoanthropologist
Tomasin, Jenny	Actress
Tonomura, Akira	Physicist
Tonry, Richard A	Representative, LA
Toppazzini, Jerome J (Jerry)	Ice Hockey Player
Tornade, Pierre	Actor
Train, Russell E	Government Official, Environmentalist
Tramiel, Jack	Businessman
Traub, Marvin S	Businessman
Travis, Neil	Editor
Treves, Frederick W	Actor
Trevor, Ranking	DJ Musician
Trimble, Joseph G (Joe)	Baseball Player
Trimble, Steven G (Steve)	Football Player
Tryon, Amy	Equestrian
Tubbs, Gerald J (Jerry)	Football Player
Tufeld, Richard N (Dick)	Actor
Tupov V, George	King, Tonga
Twyman, John K (Jack)	Basketball Player, Businessman
Tyrrell, Susan	Actress
Udvardi, Istvan	Water Polo Player
Ueltschi, Albert L	Businessman
Unger, Jim	Cartoonist (Herman)
Unsworth, Barry	Writer
Vale, Wylie W	Biochemist
VanBuren, Steve W	Football Player
Vance, E Eugene (Gene)	Basketball Player
VanDantzig, Rudi	Choreographer
VanRysel, Willy	Swimmer
Varte, Rosy	Actress
Vasiliev, Valery I	Ice Hockey Player
Vernon, Glen	Actor
Vidal, Gore	Writer
Vorotnikov, Vitaly	Chairman Council of Ministers, Russia
Voss, Janice E	Astronaut

Vyrupayev, Konstantin	Greco-Roman Wrestler
Waite, Richard H (Ric)	Cinematographer
Waksman, Byron H	Neuroimmunologist, Pathologist
Walker, LeRoy T	Track Coach, Executive, Educator
Wallace, Mike	Commentator
Waller, William L	Governor, MS
Walsh, William H (Bill)	Football Player
Wampler, William C	Representative, VA
Ward, Simon	Actor
Ward, Willa	Singer
Ware, David S	Jazz Musician
Watkins, James D	Secretary, Energy; Navy Admiral
Watson, Arthel L (Doc)	Singer, Guitarist, Banjoist
Watson, Raymond L	Businessman
Webster, Alexander (Alex)	Football Player, Coach
Weiss, David	Artist
Weissenberg, Alexis	Concert Pianist
Welch, Bob	Guitarist (Fleetwood Mac), Songwriter
Wells, Kitty	Singer
Wendell, Martin P (Marty)	Football Player
Wendelstedt, Harry H, Jr	Baseball Umpire
Wenzel, Ralph R	Football Player
Werder, Felix	Composer
Wexler, Jacqueline G	Educator
White, Kevin H	Mayor, Boston
White, Robert W (Bobby)	Football Player
Wicker, Thomas G (Tom)	Writer, Journalist
Williams, Andy	Singer
Williams, Dick Anthony	Actor
Williams, John M	Football Player
Williams, T Franklin	Physician
Williamson, Nicol	Actor
Wills, Frank L	Baseball Player
Wilson, James Q	Educator
Wilson, John (Johnny)	Ice Hockey Player
Wilson, Yvette	Actress, Comedienne
Windom, William	Actor
Withrow, J Calvin (Cal)	Football Player
Wohrman, Bill	Writer
Wolf, Christa	Writer
Woolridge, Orlando V	Basketball Player, Coach
Wright, Lawrence (Lonnie)	Football, Basketball Player
Yamashita, Toshihiko	Businessman
Yauch, Adam (MCA)	Rap Artist (Beastie Boys)
Yeosock, John J	Army General
Yost, Edward F J (Eddie)	Baseball Player, Manager
Yuricich, Matthew J	Special Effects Artist
Zable, Walter J	Businessman
Zador, Ervin	Water Polo Player
Zald, Mayer N	Sociologist
Zanuck, Richard D	Producer
Zaslow, Jeffrey L (Jeff)	Columnist
Zeisel, Eva	Industrial Designer
Zeitlin, Zvi	Concert Violinist
Zimble, James A	Navy Admiral, Physician
Zinder, Norton D	Geneticist

UNITED STATES SENATE

The men and women below are current members of the US Senate. They can be reached by writing them in care of **US Senate, Washington, DC 20510**.

Letters should be addressed:

The Honorable Jane/John Doe
US Senator from _____

Salutations in letters should be:

Dear Mr/Ms Senator

State	Name	State	Name
Alabama	Sessions, Jeferson B (Jeff), III	North Dakota	Hoeven, John H, III
Alabama	Shelby, Richard C	Ohio	Brown, Sherrod C
Alaska	Begich, Mark P	Ohio	Portman, Robert J (Rob)
Alaska	Murkowski, Lisa	Oklahoma	Coburn, Thomas A (Tom)
Arizona	Flake, Jeffry L (Jeff)	Oklahoma	Inhofe, James M (Jim)
Arizona	McCain, John S, III	Oregon	Merkley, Jeffrey A (Jeff)
Arkansas	Boozman, John N	Oregon	Wyden, Ronald L (Ron)
Arkansas	Pryor, Mark L	Pennsylvania	Casey, Robert P (Bob), Jr
California	Boxer, Barbara L	Pennsylvania	Toomey, Patrick J (Pat)
California	Feinstein, Dianne G B	Rhode Island	Reed, John F (Jack)
Colorado	Bennet, Michael	Rhode Island	Whitehouse, Sheldon
Colorado	Udall, Mark E	South Carolina	DeMint, James W (Jim)
Connecticut	Bloomenthal, Richard M	South Carolina	Graham, Lindsey O
Connecticut	Murphy, Christopher S (Chris)	South Dakota	Johnson, Timothy P (Tim)
Delaware	Carper, Thomas R. (Tom)	South Dakota	Thune, John, III
Delaware	Coons, Christopher A (Chris)	Tennessee	Alexander, A Lamar
Florida	Nelson, William (Bill)	Tennessee	Corker, Robert P (Bob), Jr
Florida	Rubio, Marco	Texas	Cornyn, John, III
Georgia	Chambliss, C Saxby	Texas	Cruz, R Edward (Ted)
Georgia	Isakson, John H (Johnny)	Utah	Hatch, Orrin G
Hawaii	Hirono, Mazie K	Utah	Lee, Michael S (Mike)
Hawaii	Inouye, Daniel K	Vermont	Leahy, Patrick J
Idaho	Crapo, Michael D	Vermont	Sanders, Bernard (Bernie)
Idaho	Risch, James E (Jim)	Virginia	Kaine, Timothy M (Tim)
Illinois	Durbin, Richard J (Dick)	Virginia	Warner, Mark R
Illinois	Kirk, Mark S	Washington	Cantwell, Maria E
Indiana	Coats, Daniel R (Dan)	Washington	Murray, Patricia L (Patty)
Indiana	Donnelly, Joseph S (Joe), Sr	West Virginia	Manchin, Joseph (Joe), III
Iowa	Grassley, Charles E (Chuck)	West Virginia	Rockefeller, John D, IV
Iowa	Harkin, Thomas R (Tom)	Wisconsin	Baldwin, Tammy S G
Kansas	Moran, Gerald W (Jerry)	Wisconsin	Johnson, Ron
Kansas	Roberts, C Patrick (Pat)	Wyoming	Barrasso, John A
Kentucky	McConnell, A Mitchell (Mitch), Jr	Wyoming	Enzi, Michael B (Mike)
Kentucky	Paul, Randall H (Rand)		
Louisiana	Landrieu, Mary L		
Louisiana	Vitter, David B		
Maine	Collins, Susan M		
Maine	King, Angus S, Jr		
Maryland	Cardin, Benjamin L (Ben)		
Maryland	Mikulski, Barbara A		
Massachusetts	Kerry, John F		
Massachusetts	Warren, Elizabeth		
Michigan	Levin, Carl M		
Michigan	Stabenow, Deborah A (Debbie)		
Minnesota	Franken, Al		
Minnesota	Klobuchar, Amy J		
Mississippi	Cochran, W Thad		
Mississippi	Wicker, Roger F		
Missouri	Blunt, Roy D		
Missouri	McCaskill, Claire		
Montana	Baucus, Max S		
Montana	Tester, Jon		
Nebraska	Fischer, Debra S (Deb)		
Nebraska	Johanns, Michael O (Mike)		
Nevada	Heller, Dean		
Nevada	Reid, Harry M		
New Hampshire	Ayotte, Kelly A		
New Hampshire	Shaheen, Jeanne		
New Jersey	Lautenberg, Frank R		
New Jersey	Menendez, Robert (Bob)		
New Mexico	Heinrich, Martin T		
New Mexico	Udall, Thomas S (Tom)		
New York	Gillibrand, Kirsten E R		
New York	Schumer, Charles E (Chuck)		
North Carolina	Burr, Richard M		
North Carolina	Hagan, Kay		
North Dakota	Heitkamp, Mary K (Heidi)		

UNITED STATES HOUSE OF REPRESENTATIVES

The men and women below are current members of the US House of Representatives. They can be reached by writing them in care of **US House of Representatives, Washington, DC 20515**.

Letters should be addressed: The Honorable Jane/John Doe
US Representative from _____

Salutations in letters should be: Dear Mr/Ms Representative

State	Name	State	Name
Alabama	Aderholt, Robert B	California	Speier, Karen L (Jackie)
Alabama	Bachus, Spencer T, III	California	Swalwell, Eric, Jr
Alabama	Bonner, Josiah R, (Jo), Jr	California	Takano, Mark A
Alabama	Brooks, Morris J (Mo)	California	Thompson, Michael C (Mike)
Alabama	Roby, Martha	California	Valadao, David
Alabama	Rogers, Michael D (Mike)	California	Vargas, Juan C
Alabama	Sewell, Terri	California	Waters, Maxine C
Alaska	Young, Donald E (Don)	California	Waxman, Henry A
American Samoa	Faleomavaega, Eni F H	Colorado	Coffman, Michael
Arkansas	Cotton, Thomas (Tom)	Colorado	DeGette, Diana L
Arkansas	Crawford, Rick	Colorado	Gardener, Cory
Arkansas	Griffin, J Timothy (Tim)	Colorado	Lamborn, Doug
Arkansas	Womack, Stephen A (Steve)	Colorado	Perlmutter, Edwin G (Ed)
Arizona	Barber, Ron	Colorado	Polis, Jared S (Jare)
Arizona	Franks, Trent	Colorado	Tipton, Scott R
Arizona	Gosar, Paul	Connecticut	Courtney, Joseph (Joe)
Arizona	Grijalva, Raul M	Connecticut	DeLauro, Rosa L
Arizona	Kirkpatrick, Ann	Connecticut	Himes, James A (Jim)
Arizona	Pastor, Edward L (Ed)	Connecticut	Larson, John B
Arizona	Salmon, Matthew J (Matt)	Connecticut	Esty, Elizabeth H
Arizona	Schweikert, David	Delaware	Carney, John C, Jr
Arizona	Sinema, Kyrsten	District/Columbia	Norton, Eleanor Holmes
California	Bass, Karen	Florida	Bilirakis, Gus M
California	Becerra, Xavier	Florida	Brown, Corrine
California	Bera, Ami	Florida	Buchanan, Vernon G (Vern)
California	Brownley, Julia	Florida	Castor, Kathlerine A (Kathy)
California	Calvert, Kenneth S (Ken)	Florida	Crenshaw, Ander
California	Campbell, John B T, Jr.	Florida	DeSantis, Ron
California	Capps, Lois G	Florida	Deutch, Theodore (Ted)
California	Cardenas, Tony	Florida	Diaz-Balart, Mario R
California	Chu, Judy	Florida	Frankel, Lois J
California	Cook, Paul	Florida	Garcia, Jose A (Joe)
California	Costa, James M (Jim)	Florida	Grayson, Alan M
California	Davis, Susan A	Florida	Hastings, Alcee L
California	Denham, Jeffrey (Jeff)	Florida	Mica, John L
California	Eshoo, Anna G	Florida	Miller, Jefferson B (Jeff)
California	Farr, Samuel S (Sam)	Florida	Murphy, Patrick E
California	Garamendi, John	Florida	Nugent, Richard B
California	Hahn, Janice	Florida	Posey, William (Bill)
California	Honda, Michael M (Mike)	Florida	Radel, Henry J (Trey)
California	Huffman, Jared	Florida	Rooney, Thomas J (Tom)
California	Hunter, Duncan D	Florida	Ros-Lehtinen, Ileana
California	Issa, Darrell E	Florida	Ross, Dennis B
California	LaMalfa, Doug	Florida	Southerland, Stephen E (Steve)
California	Lee, Barbara J	Florida	Wasserman Schultz, Debbie
California	Lofgren, Sue (Zoe)	Florida	Webster, Daniel
California	Lowenthal, Alan S	Florida	Wilson, Frederica
California	Matsui, Doris O	Florida	Yoho, Theodore S (Ted)
California	McCarthy, Kevin	Florida	Young, C W (Bill)
California	McClintock, Thomas M (Tom)	Georgia	Barrow, John J
California	McKeon, Howard P (Buck)	Georgia	Bishop, Sanford D, Jr
California	McNearey, Jerry	Georgia	Broun, Paul C, Jr
California	Miller, Gary G	Georgia	Collins, Doug
California	Miller, George, III	Georgia	Gingrey, J Phillip (Phil)
California	Napolitano, Grace F	Georgia	Graves, J Thomas (Tom)
California	Negrete McLeod, Gloria	Georgia	Johnson, Henry (Hank), Jr
California	Nunes, Devin	Georgia	Kingston, John H (Jack)
California	Pelosi, Nancy P D	Georgia	Lewis, John R
California	Peters, Scott H	Georgia	Price, Thomas E (Tom)
California	Rohrabacher, Dana	Georgia	Scott, J Austin
California	Roybal-Allard, Lucille	Georgia	Scott, David A
California	Royce, Edward R (Ed)	Georgia	Westmoreland, Lynn A
California	Ruiz, Raul	Georgia	Woodall, Robert (Rob)
California	Sanchez, Linda T	Guam	Bordallo, Madeleine
California	Sanchez, Loretta	Hawaii	Gabbard, Tulsi
California	Schiff, Adam B	Hawaii	Hanabusa, Colleen
California	Sherman, Bradley J (Brad)	Idaho	Labrador, Raul R

Idaho	Simpson, Michael K (Mike)	Michigan	Huizenga, William P (Bill)
Illinois	Callahan-Bustos, Cheryl L (Cheri)	Michigan	Kildee, Daniel T (Dan)
Illinois	Davis, Daniel K (Danny)	Michigan	Levin, Sander M
Illinois	Davis, Rodney L	Michigan	Miller, Candice S
Illinois	Duckworth, L Tammy	Michigan	Peters, Gray
Illinois	Enyart, William L (Bill), Jr	Michigan	Rogers, Michael J (Mike)
Illinois	Foster, G William (Bill)	Michigan	Upton, Frederick S (Fred)
Illinois	Gutierrez, Luis V	Michigan	Walberg, Timothy L (Tim)
Illinois	Hultgren, Randall M (Randy)	Minnesota	Bachmann, Michele M
Illinois	Jackson, Jesse L, Jr	Minnesota	Nolan, Richard M (Rick)
Illinois	Kinzinger, Adam A	Minnesota	Ellison, Keith M
Illinois	Lipinski, Daniel W (Dan)	Minnesota	Kline, John P
Illinois	Quigley, Michael (Mike)	Minnesota	McCollum, Betty L
Illinois	Roskam, Peter J	Minnesota	Paulsen, Erik
Illinois	Rush, Bobby L	Minnesota	Peterson, Collin C
Illinois	Schakowsky, Janice D (Jan)	Minnesota	Walz, Timothy J (Tim)
Illinois	Schneider, Bradley S (Brad)	Mississippi	Harper, Gregg
Illinois	Schock, Aaron	Mississippi	Nunnelee, P Alan
Illinois	Shimkus, John M	Mississippi	Palazzo, Steven M
Indiana	Brooks, Susan W	Mississippi	Thompson, Bennie G
Indiana	Bucshon, Larry D	Missouri	Clay, William L (Lacy), Jr
Indiana	Carson, Andre D	Missouri	Cleaver, Emanuel, II
Indiana	Messer, A Lucas (Luke)	Missouri	Emerson, Jo Ann
Indiana	Rokita, Theodore E (Todd)	Missouri	Graves, Samuel B (Sam)
Indiana	Stutzman, Marlin A	Missouri	Hartzler, Vicky J
Indiana	Visclosky, Peter J	Missouri	Long, William H (Billy)
Indiana	Walorski, Jackie	Missouri	Luetkemeyer, Blaine
Indiana	Young, Todd C	Missouri	Wagner, Ann
Iowa	Braley, Bruce	Montana	Daines, Steven (Steve)
Iowa	King, Steven A (Steve)	Nebraska	Fortenberry, Jeffrey L (Jeff)
Iowa	Latham, Thomas (Tom)	Nebraska	Smith, Adrian M
Iowa	Loebsack, David	Nebraska	Terry, Lee R
Kansas	Huelskamp, Timothy A (Tim)	Nevada	Amodei, Mark E
Kansas	Jenkins, Lynn	Nevada	Heck, Joseph J (Joe)
Kansas	Pompeo, Michael R (Mike)	Nevada	Horsford, Steven
Kansas	Yoder, Kevin	Nevada	Titus, Alice C (Dina)
Kentucky	Barr, Garland H (Andy)	New Hampshire	McLane Kuster, Ann (Annie)
Kentucky	Guthrie, Steven B (Brett)	New Hampshire	Shea-Porter, Carol
Kentucky	Massie, Thomas H	New Jersey	Andrews, Robert E (Rob)
Kentucky	Rogers, Harold D (Hal)	New Jersey	Frelinghuysen, Rodney P
Kentucky	Whitfield, Edward (Ed)	New Jersey	Garrett, E Scott
Kentucky	Yarmuth, John	New Jersey	Holt, Rush D, Jr
Louisiana	Alexander, Rodney M	New Jersey	Lance, Leonard
Louisiana	Cassidy, William (Bill)	New Jersey	LoBiondo, Frank A
Louisiana	Fleming, John	New Jersey	Pallone, Frank, Jr
Louisiana	Richmond, Cedric L	New Jersey	Pascrell, William J (Bill), Jr
Louisiana	Scalise, Stephen J (Steve)	New Jersey	Payne, Donald M
Maine	Michaud, Michael H (Mike)	New Jersey	Runyon, Jon D
Maine	Pingree, Chellie M	New Jersey	Sires, Albio
Maryland	Delaney, John K	New Jersey	Smith, Christopher H (Chris)
Maryland	Cummings, Elijah E	New Mexico	Lujan, Ben R, Jr
Maryland	Edwards, Donna F	New Mexico	Grisham, Michelle L
Maryland	Harris, Andrew P (Andy)	New Mexico	Pearce, Stevan E (Steve)
Maryland	Hoyer, Steny H	New York	Bishop, Timothy H (Tim)
Maryland	Ruppersberger, C A (Dutch)	New York	Clarke, Yvette D
Maryland	Sarbanes, John P S	New York	Crowley, Joseph
Maryland	Van Hollen, Chris	New York	Engel, Eliot L
Massachusetts	Capuano, Michael E (Mike)	New York	Gibson, Christopher P (Chris)
Massachusetts	Keating, William R (Bill)	New York	Grimm, Michael (Mike)
Massachusetts	Kennedy, Joseph P (Joe), III	New York	Hanna, Richard
Massachusetts	Lynch, Stephen F	New York	Higgins, Brian
Massachusetts	Markey, Edward J	New York	Hochul, Kathleen C (Kathy)
Massachusetts	McGovern, James P (Jim)	New York	Israel, Steve
Massachusetts	Neal, Richard E	New York	Jeffries, Hakeem S
Massachusetts	Tierney, John F	New York	King, Peter T
Massachusetts	Tsongas, Nicola S (Niki)	New York	Lowey, Nita M
Michigan	Amash, Justin	New York	Maffei, Daniel B (Dan)
Michigan	Benishek, Daniel J (Dan)	New York	Maloney, Carolyn B
Michigan	Bentivolio, Kerry	New York	Maloney, Sean P
Michigan	Camp, David L (Dave)	New York	McCarthy, Carolyn
Michigan	Conyers, John, Jr	New York	Meeks, Gregory W
Michigan	Dingell, John D, Jr	New York	Meng, Grace

UNITED STATES HOUSE OF REPRESENTATIVES

New York	Nadler, Jerrold L (Jerry)	South Carolina	Duncan, Jeffrey D (Jeff)
New York	Owens, William (Bill)	South Carolina	Gowdy, Howard W (Trey), III
New York	Rangel, Charles B	South Carolina	Mulvaney, John M (Mick)
New York	Reed, Thomas	South Carolina	Rice, Hugh T (Tom)
New York	Serrano, José E	South Carolina	Scott, Timothy E (Tim)
New York	Slaughter, Louise M	South Carolina	Wilson, Addison G (Joe), Sr
New York	Tonko, Paul D	South Dakota	Noem, Kristi L A
New York	Velazquez, Nydia M	Tennessee	Black, Diane L
North Carolina	Butterfield, George K (G K), Jr	Tennessee	Blackburn, Marsha
North Carolina	Coble, J Howard	Tennessee	Cohen, Stephen J (Steve)
North Carolina	Ellmers, Renee J	Tennessee	Cooper, James H S (Jim)
North Carolina	Foxx, Virginia A	Tennessee	DesJarlais, Scott E
North Carolina	Holding, George E B	Tennessee	Duncan, John J (Jimmy), Jr
North Carolina	Hudson, Richard	Tennessee	Fincher, Stephen
North Carolina	Jones, Walter B, Jr	Tennessee	Fleischmann, Charles J (Chuck)
North Carolina	Kissell, Larry	Tennessee	Roe, David P (Phil)
North Carolina	McHenry, Patrick T	Texas	Barton, Joseph L (Joe)
North Carolina	McIntyre, Douglas C (Mike), II	Texas	Brady, Kevin P
North Carolina	Pittenger, Robert	Texas	Burgess, Michael C
North Carolina	Price, David E	Texas	Carter, John R
North Carolina	Watt, Melvin L (Mel)	Texas	Castro, Joaquin
North Dakota	Cramer, Kevin	Texas	Conaway, Michael K (Mike)
North Mariana Islands	Sablan, Gregorio K C	Texas	Cuellar, Henry R
Ohio	Boehner, John A	Texas	Culberson, John A
Ohio	Chabot, Steven J (Steve)	Texas	Doggett, Lloyd A, II
Ohio	Fudge, Marcia L	Texas	Farenthold, R Blake
Ohio	Gibbs, Robert B (Bob)	Texas	Flores, William H (Bill)
Ohio	Johnson, William L (Bill)	Texas	Gallego, Pete P
Ohio	Jordan, James D (Jim)	Texas	Gohmert, Louis B (Louie), Jr
Ohio	Joyce, David P	Texas	Granger, Kay
Ohio	Kaptur, Marcia C (Marcy)	Texas	Green, Alexander N (Al)
Ohio	LaTourette, Steven C (Steve)	Texas	Green, R Eugene (Gene)
Ohio	Latta, Robert E (Bob)	Texas	Hall, Ralph M
Ohio	Renacci, James B (Jim)	Texas	Hensarling, Jeb
Ohio	Ryan, Timothy J (Tim)	Texas	Hinojosa, Ruben E
Ohio	Stivers, Stephen E (Steve)	Texas	Jackson-Lee, Sheila
Ohio	Tiberi, Patrick J (Pat)	Texas	Johnson, Eddie Bernice
Ohio	Turner, Michael R (Mike)	Texas	Johnson, Samuel R (Sam)
Ohio	Wenstrup, Brad	Texas	Marchant, Kenneth (Kenny)
Oklahoma	Bridenstine, James F (Jim)	Texas	McCaul, Michael T (Mike)
Oklahoma	Cole, Thomas J (Tom)	Texas	Neugebauer, R Randolph (Randy)
Oklahoma	Lankford, James	Texas	O'Rourke, Robert F (Beto)
Oklahoma	Lucas, Frank D	Texas	Olson, Peter G (Pete)
Oklahoma	Mullin, Markwayne	Texas	Poe, Lloyd (Ted)
Oregon	Blumenauer, Earl	Texas	Sessions, Peter A (Pete)
Oregon	Bonamici, Suzanne	Texas	Smith, Lamar S
Oregon	DeFazio, Peter A (Pete)	Texas	Stockman, Stephen E (Steve)
Oregon	Schrader, Kurt	Texas	Thornberry, William M (Mac)
Oregon	Walden, Gregory (Greg)	Texas	Veasey, Marc
Pennsylvania	Barletta, Louis J (Lou)	Texas	Vela, Filemon B, Jr
Pennsylvania	Brady, Robert A (Bob)	Texas	Weber, Randy
Pennsylvania	Cartwright, Matthew A (Matt)	Texas	Williams, JRoger
Pennsylvania	Dent, Charles W (Charlie)	Utah	Bishop, Robert W (Rob)
Pennsylvania	Doyle, Michael F (Mike)	Utah	Chaffetz, Jason
Pennsylvania	Fattah, Chaka	Utah	Matheson, James D (Jim)
Pennsylvania	Fitzpatrick, Michael G (Mike)	Utah	Stewart, Christopher D (Chris)
Pennsylvania	Gerlach, James (Jim)	Vermont	Welch, Peter F
Pennsylvania	Kelly, Michael (Mike)	Virgin Islands	Christian-Christensen, Donna M
Pennsylvania	Marino, A Thomas (Tom)	Virginia	Cantor, Eric I
Pennsylvania	Meehan, Patrick L (Pat)	Virginia	Connolly, Gerald E
Pennsylvania	Murphy, Timothy F (Tim)	Virginia	Forbes, J Randy
Pennsylvania	Perry, Scott G	Virginia	Goodlatte, Robert W (Bob)
Pennsylvania	Pitts, Joseph R (Joe)	Virginia	Griffith, H Morgan
Pennsylvania	Platts, Todd R	Virginia	Hurt, Robert
Pennsylvania	Rothfus, Keith J	Virginia	Moran, James P (Jim), Jr
Pennsylvania	Schwartz, Allyson Y	Viriginia	Rigell, E Scott
Pennsylvania	Shuster, William (Bill)	Virginia	Scott, Robert C (Bobby)
Pennsylvania	Thompson, Glenn	Virginia	Wittman, Robert J (Rob)
Puerto Rico	Pierluisi, Pedro	Virginia	Wolf, Frank R
Rhode Island	Cicilline, David N	Washington	DelBene, Suzan K
Rhode Island	Langevin, James R	Washington	Hastings, Richard N (Doc)
South Carolina	Clyburn, James E (Jim)	Washington	Heck, Dennis (Denny)

Washington	Herrera Beutler, Jaime	Wisconsin	Duffy, Sean P
Washington	Kilmer, Derek	Wisconsin	Kind, Ronald J (Ron)
Washington	Larsen, Richard R (Rick)	Wisconsin	Moore, Gwendolynne S (Gwen)
Washington	McDermott, James A (Jim)	Wisconsin	Petri, Thomas E (Tom)
Washington	McMorris Rogers, Cathy	Wisconsin	Pocan, Mark
Washington	Reichert, David G (Dave)	Wisconsin	Ribble, Reid J
Washington	Smith, D Adam	Wisconsin	Ryan, Paul D, Jr
West Virginia	Capito, Shelly Moore	Wisconsin	Sensenbrenner, F James, Jr (Jim)
West Virginia	McKinley, David	Wyoming	Lummis, Cynthia
West Virginia	Rahall, Nick Joe, II		

UNITED STATES GOVERNORS

The men and women below are current US Governors. They can be reached by writing them in care of **Governor's Office** at the addresses listed below.

Letters should be addressed: The Honorable Jane/John Doe
Governor from _____

Salutations in letters should be: Dear Mr/Ms Governor _____

Alabama	Bentley, Robert J	State Capitol, 600 Dexter Ave, Montgomery AL 36130, USA
Alaska	Parnell, Sean R	State Capitol Building, PO Box 110001, Juneau AK 99811, USA
American Samoa	Tulafono, Tugiola T A	Executive Office Building, #300, Utulei, Pago Pago, AS 96799
Arizona	Brewer, Janice K (Jan)	State Capitol, 1700 W Washington St, Phoenix AZ 85007, USA
Arkansas	Beebe, Michael D	State Capitol, #250, Little Rock AR 72201, USA
California	Brown, Edmund G (Jerry)	State Capital, #100, Sacramento CA 95814, USA
Colorado	Hickenlooper, John W	136 State Capitol, Denver CO 80203, USA
Connecticut	Malloy, Dan	State Capitol, 210 Capitol Ave, Hartford CT 06106, USA
Delaware	Markell, Jack A	Legislative Hall, Dover DE 19902, USA
Florida	Scott, Richard L (Rick)	PL 05 The Capitol, 400 S Monroe St, Tallahassee FL 32399, USA
Georgia	Deal, John N (Nathan)	State Capitol, #203, Atlanta GA 30334, USA
Guam	Calvo, Eddie Baza	Executive Chamber, PO Box 2950, Agana, GU 96932
Hawaii	Abercrombie, Neil	Executive Chambers, #500, Honolulu HI 96813, USA
Idaho	Otter, C L (Butch)	State Capitol, 700 W Jefferson, #200, Boise ID 83702, USA
Illinois	Quinn, Patrick J	State House, 207 Statehouse, Springfield IL 62706, USA
Indiana	Pence, Michael R (Mike)	State House, #206, Indianapolis IN 46204, USA
Iowa	Brandstad, Terry E	State Capitol, Des Moines IA 50319, USA
Kansas	Brownback, Samuel D (Sam)	Capitol, 300 SW 10th Ave, #212S, Topeka KS 66612, USA
Kentucky	Beshear, Steven L (Steve)	State Capitol, 700 Capitol Ave, #100, Frankfort KY 40601, USA
Louisiana	Jindal, Piyosh (Bobby)	State Capitol, PO Box 94004, Baton Rouge LA 70804, USA
Maine	LePage, Paul R	Blaine House, 1 State House Station, Augusta ME 04333, USA
Maryland	O'Malley, Martin J	State House, 100 State Circle, Annapolis MD 21401, USA
Massachusetts	Patrick, Deval L	State House, #360, Boston MA 02133, USA
Michigan	Snyder, Richard D (Rick)	State Capitol, PO Box 30013, Lansing MI 48909, USA
Minnesota	Dayton, Mark B	130 State Capitol, 75 Rev Dr MLK Jr Blvd, Saint Paul MN 55155, USA
Mississippi	Bryant, D Phillip (Phil)	State Capitol, PO Box 139, Jackson MS 39205, USA
Missouri	Nixon, Jeremiah W (Jay)	State Capitol, #218, PO Box 720, Jefferson City MO 65102, USA
Montana	Bullock, Steve	State Capitol, PO Box 0801, Helena MT 59620, USA
Nebraska	Heineman, David E (Dave)	State Capitol, PO Box 94848, Lincoln NE 68509, USA
Nevada	Sandoval, Brian E	State Capitol, 101 N Carson St, Carson City NV 89701, USA
New Hampshire	Hassan, Maggie	25 Capitol St, #212, Concord NH 03301, USA
New Jersey	Christie, Chris	State House, 125 W State St, PO Box 001, Trenton NJ 08625, USA
New Mexico	Martinez, Susana	State Capitol, #400, Santa Fe NM 87300, USA
New York	Cuomo, Andrew	State Capitol, Albany NY 12224, USA
North Carolina	McCruly, Patrick L (Pat)	State Capitol, 20301 Mail Service Center, Raleigh NC 27699, USA
North Dakota	Dalrymple, John (Jack)	State Capitol, 600 E Boulevard Ave, #101, Bismarck ND 58505, USA
Northern Marianas	Fitial, Benigno	Governor's Office, Caller Box 10007, Saipan, MP 96950
Ohio	Kasich, John R	State House, 77 S High St, #3000, Columbus OH 43215, USA
Oklahoma	Fallin, Mary	State Capitol, 2300 N Lincoln Blvd, #212, Oklahoma City OK 73105, USA
Oregon	Kitzhaber, John A	State Capitol, 900 Court St, #160, Salem OR 97301, USA
Pennsylvania	Corbett, Thomas (Tom)	Main Capitol, #225, Harrisburg PA 17120, USA
Puerto Rico	Fortuno, Luis G	La Fortaleza, PO Box 9020082, San Juan, PR 00902
Rhode Island	Chafee, Lincoln D	State House, Providence RI 02903, USA
South Carolina	Haley, Nimrata R (Nikki)	State Capitol, PO Box 11829, Columbia SC 29211, USA
South Dakota	Daugaard, Dennis M	State Capitol, 500 E Capitol Ave Pierre, SD 57501, USA
Tennessee	Haslam, William E (Bill)	State Capitol, Nashville TN 37243, USA
Texas	Perry, James R (Rick)	State Capitol, PO Box 12428, Austin TX 78711, USA
Utah	Herbert, Gary R	State Capitol, #200, Salt Lake City UT 84114, USA
Vermont	Shumlin, Peter S	Pavilion Building, 109 State St, Montpelier VT 05609, USA
Virginia	McDonnell, Robert F (Bob)	State Capitol, #300, Richmond VA 23219, USA

Virgin Islands	deJongh, John, Jr	Gov't House, 21-22 Kongens Gade, Charlotte Amalie, St. Thomas, VI 00802
Washington	Inselee, Jay R	State Capitol, PO Box 40002, Olympia WA 98504, USA
West Virginia	Tomblin, Earl R	1900 Kanawha St, Charleston WV 25305, USA
Wisconsin	Walker, Scott K	115 E State Capitol, Madison WI 53707, USA
Wyoming	Mead, Matthew H (Matt)	State Capitol, #124, Cheyenne WY 82002, USA

AGENCY ADDRESSES

42 West	11400 W Olympic Blvd, #1100	Los Angeles CA 90064, USA
Abrams Artists & Associates	9200 Sunset Blvd, #1125	West Hollywood CA 90069, USA
Abrams-Rubaloff & Lawrence	8075 W 3rd St	Los Angeles CA 90048, USA
A P A	405 S Beverly Dr, #405	Beverly Hills CA 90212, USA
A P A	250 W 57th St, #1701	New York NY 10107 USA
Agency Group	9348 Civic Center Dr, #200	Beverly Hills CA 90210, USA
Agency Group	142 W 57th St, #600	New York NY 10019, USA
Agency, The	3711 Ocean Front Walk, #1	Marina del Rey CA 90292, USA
Agents Associes Beaume	201 rue du Faubourg Saint Honore	75008 Paris, France
Agentur Killer	54 Harthauser Str	81545 Munich, Germany
Agentur DorisMattes	14 Merzstr	81679 Munich, Germany
Air Edel	8687 Melrose Ave, #900	West Hollywood CA 90069, USA
Altaras, Jonathan	11 Garrick St	London WC1V 2QA, England
Ambrosio/Mortimer & Associates	165 W 45th St	New York NY USA
Amsel Eisenstadt & Frazier	5055 Wilshire Blvd, #865	Los Angeles CA 90036, USA
Artists Agency	9171 Wilshire Blvd, #380	Los Angeles CA 90210, USA
Artmedia	20 Av Rapp	75007 Paris, France
Askonas Holt	Lincoln House, 300 High Holborn	London WC1V 7JH England
Associated Booking Agency	PO Box 2055	New York NY 10021, USA
Associated Talent International	1320 Armacost Ave, #2	Beverly Hills, CA 90212, USA
B/W/R Public Relations	9100 Wilshire Blvd, #500W	Los Angeles CA 90036, USA
Bauman Redanty & Shaul	5757 Wilshire Blvd, #473	Los Angeles CA 90036, USA
Belfrage, Julian	14 New Burlington St	London W1S 3DQ, England
Blake Agency	23441 Malibu Canyon Road	Malibu CA 90265, USA
Blanchard, Enterprises Nina	8826 Burton Way	Beverly Hills CA 90211, USA
Borinstein Oreck Bogart Agency	3172 Dona Susana Dr	Studio City CA 91604, USA
Boss Models	80 8th Ave	New York NY 10011, USA
Bragman, Nyman & Cafarelli	8687 Melrose Ave, #800	West Hollywood CA 90069, USA
Bresler Kelly & Associates	11500 W Olympic Blvd, #352	Los Angeles CA 90064, USA
Breslin, Herbert	333 E 57th St	New York NY 10022, USA
Brillstein Entertainment Partners	9150 Wilshire Blvd, #350	Beverly Hills CA 90212, USA
Buchwald, Don/Fortitude	6500 Wilshire Blvd, #2200	Los Angeles CA 90048, USA
Burton Agency, Iris	10100 Santa Monica Blvd, #1300	Los Angeles CA 90067, USA
Camden ITG Talent Agency	1501 Main St, #204	Venice CA 90291, USA
Carroll Agency, William	12811 Garden Grove Blvd, #209	Garden Grove CA 92843, USA
Cassidy Inc, Thomas	P O 1311	Tucson AZ 85702, USA
Cavaleri & Associates	178 S Victory Blvd, #205	Burbank CA 91502, USA
Century Artists	PO Box 59747	Santa Barbara CA 93150, USA
CESD	10635 Santa Monica Blvd, #130	Los Angeles CA 90025, USA
Chasin Agency	8899 Beverly Blvd, #716	Los Angeles CA 90048, USA
Chatto & Linnit	123A King's Road	London SW3 4PL, England
Circle Talent Associates	433 N Camden Dr, #400	Beverly Hills CA 90210, USA
Click Model Management	881 7th Ave	New York NY 10019, USA
CLInc Talent Agency	843 N Sycamore Ave	Los Angeles CA 90038, USA
C N A & Associates	1875 Century Park E, #2250	Los Angeles CA 90067, USA
Coast to Coast Talent Group	3350 Barham Blvd	Los Angeles CA 90068, USA
Columbia Artists Management	1790 Broadway, #702	New York NY 10019, USA
Commercials Unlimited	190 N Canon Drive, #202	Beverly Hills CA 90210, USA
Conner Agency, Hall	9169 Sunset Blvd	West Hollywood CA 90069, USA
Contemporary Artists	610 Santa Monica Blvd, #202	Santa Monica CA 90401, USA
Cosden Agency, Robert	3518 Cahuenga Blvd W, #200	Los Angeles CA 90068, USA
Cramer/Marder Artists	127 W 96th St, #13B	New York NY 10025, USA
Creative Artists Agency	2000 Avenue of Stars	Los Angeles CA 90067, USA
Creative Entertainment Associates	1950 Old Cuthbert Road, #J	Cherry Hill NJ, 08034, USA
Daish Associates, Judy	2 Saint Charles Place	London M10 6EG, England
D H Talent Agency	1800 N Highland Ave, #300	Los Angeles CA 90028, USA
Domain Talent	9229 Sunset Blvd, #710	Los Angeles CA 90069, USA
Elite Model Management	404 Park Ave S, #900	New York NY 10016, USA
Entertainment Talent Agency	9225 W Sunset Blvd, #805	West Hollywood CA 90069, USA
Epstein-Wyckoff & Associates	280 S Beverly Dr, #400	Beverly Hills CA 90212, USA
Famous Artists Agency	250 W 57th St	New York NY 10107, USA
Film Artists Associates	13563 1/2 Ventura Blvd, #200	Sherman Oaks CA 91423, USA

Firm, The	2049 Century Park E, #2550	Los Angeles CA 90067, USA
First Artists Agency	1631 N Bristol St, #B20	Santa Ana CA 92706, USA
Flick East-West Talents	9057 Nemo St, #A	West Hollywood CA 90069, USA
Ford Model Agency	111 5th Ave, #900	New York NY 10003, USA
Front Line Management	1100 Glendon Ave	Los Angeles CA 90024, USA
Gage Group	14724 Ventura Blvd, #505	Sherman Oaks CA 91403, USA
Geddes Agency	8430 Santa Monica Blvd, #201	West Hollywood CA 90069, USA
Gersh Agency	9465 Wilshire Blvd, #600	Beverly Hills CA 90212, USA
Gordon & Associates, Michelle	260 S Beverly Dr, #308	Beverly Hills CA 90212, USA
Gorfaine/Schwarz	4111 W Alameda Ave #509	Burbank CA 91505, USA
Grady Agency, Mary	269 S Beverly Dr, #1088	Beverly Hills CA 91212, USA
Greene & Associates	190 N Canon Dr, #200	Beverly Hills CA 90210, USA
Halliday & Associates, Buzz	8899 Beverly Blvd, #715	Los Angeles CA 90048, USA
Hallmark Entertainment	8033 Sunset Blvd, #1000	Los Angeles CA 90046, USA
Halpern & Associates	PO Box 5597	Santa Monica, CA 90409, USA
Handprint Entertainment	450 N Roxbury Dr, #602	Beverly Hills CA 90210, USA
HarrisonParrott	5-6 Albion Place	London W6 0QT, England
Henderson/Hogan Agency	9255 W Sunset Blvd, #803	West Hollywood CA 90069, USA
Hervey/Grimes Talent Agency	10561 Missouri, #2	Los Angeles CA 90025, USA
House of Representatives	1434 6th St, #1	Santa Monica CA 90401, USA
H T M/Headliner Talent Mgmt	39398 Moonlight Bay Trail	Pelican Rapids MN 56572, USA
Hyler Mgmt	3000 W Olympic Blvd, Bldg 5	Santa Monica CA 90404, USA
Hyphenate	1180 S Beverly Dr, #601	Beverly Hills CA 90212, USA
I/D Public Relations	7060 Hollywood Blvd	Los Angeles CA 90028, USA
I F A Talent Agency	8730 Sunset Blvd, #490	West Hollywood CA 90069, USA
Imagine Entertainment	9465 Wilshire Blvd, #700	Beverly Hills CA 90212, USA
I M G Models	304 Park Ave S, #1200	New York NY 10010, USA
Innovative Artists	1505 10th Street	Santa Monica CA 91401, USA
ICM Partners	10250 Constellation Blvd, #700	Los Angeles CA 90067, USA
ICM Partners	730 5th Ave	New York NY 10019, USA
ICM Partners	Marlborough House, 10 Earlham St, #300	London WC2H 9LN, England
International Management Group	1360 E 9th St, #1300	Cleveland OH 44114, USA
International Talent Group	304 Park Ave S, #100	New York NY 10153, USA
Joyce Agency	370 Harrison Ave	Harrison NY 10528, USA
Karg/Weissenbach Associates	9255 Sunset Blvd, #1115	Los Angeles CA 90065, USA
Katz Enterprises, Raymond	345 N Maple Dr, #205	Beverly Hills CA 90210, USA
Kazarian/Spencer/Ruskin & Assoc	11969 Ventura Blvd, #3	Studio City CA 91604, USA
Kohner Inc, Paul	9300 Wilshire Blvd, #555	Beverly Hills CA 90212, USA
Kosden Agency, Robert	7135 Hollywood Blvd, #PH2	Los Angeles CA 90046, USA
Kraft-Benjamin-Engel	9200 Sunset Blvd, #321	Los Angeles CA 90069, USA
Kritzer Levine Wilkins	11872 LaGrange Ave, #100	Los Angeles CA 90025, USA
Kurland Associates, Ted	173 Brighton Ave	Allston MA 02134, USA
L A Talent	7700 Sunset Blvd, #200	Los Angeles CA 90069, USA
Lee Attractions, Buddy	38 Music Square E, #200	Nashville TN 37203, USA
Light, Robert	6404 Wilshire Blvd	Los Angeles CA 90048, USA
Lighthouse Entertainment	9220 W Sunset Blvd, #200	West Hollywood CA 90069, USA
London Management	2-4 Noel St	London W1V 3RB, England
Lovell Associates	7095 Hollywood Blvd, #1006	Los Angeles CA 90028, USA
Luber Rocklin Entertainment	8530 Wilshire Blvd, #555	Beverly Hills CA 90211, USA
Main Title Entertainment	8383 Wilshire Blvd, #408	Beverly Hills CA 90211, USA
Management Javonovic	24 Kathi-Kobus-Str	80797 Munich, Germany
Markham & Froggatt	Julian House, 4 Windmill St	London W1P 1HF, England
Marshak Wycoff Associates	280 S Beverly Dr, #400	Beverly Hills CA 90212, USA
Marsh-Best Associates	9150 Wilshire Blvd, #220	Beverly Hills CA 90212, USA
M A X Agency	166 N Canon Dr	Beverly Hills CA 90210, USA
M C A Concerts	100 Universal City Plaza	Universal City CA 91608, USA
McKeon-Myrones Mgmt	3500 Olive Ave, #770	Burbank CA 91505, USA
Media Artists Group	8255 W Sunset Blvd	Los Angeles CA 90046, USA
Metropolitan Talent Agency	7020 La Presa Dr	Los Angeles CA 90048, USA
M E W Inc	8489 W 3rd St, #1100	Los Angeles CA 90048, USA
Miskin Agency	2355 Benedict Canyon	Beverly Hills CA 90210, USA
Monterey Peninsula Artists	404 W Franklin St	Monterey CA 93940, USA
Morris Yorn Barnes	2000 Avenue of Stars, #300N	Los Angeles CA 90067, USA
Moss Agency, Burton	8827 Beverly Blvd, #L	Los Angeles CA 90048, USA
Nathe & Associates, Susan	8281 Melrose Ave, #200	Los Angeles CA 90046, USA
Nationwide Entertainment	2756 N Green Valley Pkwy, #449	Henderson NV 89014, USA
Next Model Management	23 Watts St	New York NY 10013, USA
Octagon	1751 Pinnacle Dr, #1500	McLean VA 22102, USA

Opera et Concert	37 Rue de la Chaussee d'Autin	75009 Paris, France
Pakula/King & Associates	9229 Sunset Blvd, #315	West Hollywood CA 90069, USA
Paradigm Agency	360 N Crescent Dr, North Building	Beverly Hills CA 90210, USA
Parseghian Planco	388 2nd Ave, #506	New York NY 10010, USA
Pauline's Talent Corp	379 W Broadway, #502	New York NY 10012, USA
Peters Fraser Dunlop	Drury House, 34-43 Russell St	London WC2B 5HA, England
P M K-B N C	8687 Melrose Ave, #8	Los Angeles CA 90069, USA
Premier Artists Agency	1611 S Robertson Blvd	Los Angeles CA 90035, USA
Premier Talent Agency	3 E 54th St, #1100	New York NY 10022, USA
Progressive Artists Agency	1041 N Formosa Ave	West Hollywood CA 90046, USA
Rascoff/Zysblat Organization	2500 57th St	New York NY 10107, USA
Redway Associates, John	5 Denmark St	London WC2H 8LP, England
Reid Entertainment, John	Singes House, 32 Galena Road	London W6 0LT, England
Rich Management, Elaine	2400 Whitman Place	Los Angeles CA 90068, USA
Rogers & Cowan Agency	8687 Melrose Ave, #G700	West Hollywood CA 90069, USA
Rollins Joffe Morra Brezner	10201 Pico Blvd, #58	Los Angeles CA 90064, USA
Rosenberg Office, Marion	P O Box 9826	West Hollywood CA 90069, USA
Rothberg, Arlyne	349 S Linden Dr, #C	Beverly Hills CA 90212, USA
Rozon Mercer Mgmt	201 N Robertson Blvd, #F	Beverly Hills CA 90211, USA
Ruffalo Management, Joseph	9655 Wilshire Blvd, #850	Beverly Hills CA 90212, USA
Rush Artists Management	1600 Varick St	New York NY 10013, USA
Russo, Lynne	3624 Mound View Ave	Studio City CA 91604, USA
Sanford-Beckett-Skouras	1015 Gayley Ave, #300	Los Angeles CA 90024, USA
Savage Agency	6212 Banner Ave	Los Angeles CA 90038, USA
Schechter Co, Irv	9460 Wilshire Blvd, #300	Beverly Hills CA 90212, USA
Schiowitz/Clay	1680 Vine St, #614	Los Angeles CA 90028, USA
Schoen & Associates, Judy	606 N Larchmont Blvd, #309	Los Angeles CA 90004, USA
Schultz Agency, Kathleen	6442 Coldwater Canyon Ave, #206	Valley Glen CA 91606, USA
Schwartz Associates, Don	PO Box 3628	Los Angeles CA 90078, USA
S D B Partners, Inc	1801 Ave of Stars, #902	Los Angeles CA 90067, USA
Sekura/A Talent Agency	PO Box 931779	Los Angeles CA 90093, USA
Selected Artists Agency	3900 W Alameda Ave, #345	Burbank CA 91505, USA
Shapira & Associates, David	193 N Robertson Blvd	Beverly Hills CA 90211, USA
Shapiro-Lichtman Agency	8827 Beverly Blvd	Los Angeles CA 90048, USA
Sharkey Associates, James	34 Kingly Court	London W1R 4LE, England
Shelly & Pierce	612 Lighthouse Ave	Pacific Grove CA 93950, USA
Shelter Entertainment	9454 Wilshire Blvd, #715	Beverly Hills CA 90212, USA
Sherrell Agency, Lew	937 N Sinova	Mesa AZ 85205, USA
Shriver Public Relations, Evelyn	830 E Hillview Dr	Brentwood TN 37027, USA
Silver Massetti & Szatmary	8730 Sunset Blvd, #440	West Hollywood CA 90069, USA
Sindell & Associates, Richard	1910 Holmby Ave, #1	Los Angele, CA 90025, USA
Slessinger & Associates, Michael	8730 Sunset Blvd, #270	West Hollywood CA 90069, USA
Smith & Associates, Susan	1344 N Wetherly Dr	Los Angeles CA 90069, USA
Smith/Gosnell/Nicholson	PO Box 1156	Studio City CA 91614, USA
Somers Teitelbaum David	8840 Wilshire Blvd, #200	Beverly Hills CA 90211, USA
Special Artists Agency	9465 Wilshire Blvd, #470	Beverly Hills CA 90212, USA
Starwil Talent	433 N Camden Dr, #400	Beverly Hills CA 90210, USA
Sterling/Winters	2029 Century Park E, #1400	Los Angeles CA 90067, USA
Stone Manners Salners Agency	9911 W Pico Blvd #1400	Los Angeles CA 90035, USA
Strain & Associates, Peter	5455 Wilshire Blvd, #1812	Los Angeles CA 90036, USA
Talent Entertainment Group	9111 Wilshire Blvd	Beverly Hills CA 90210, USA
TalentWorks	3500 W Olive Ave, #1400	Burbank, CA 91505, USA
Tannen & Associates, Herb	10801 National Blvd, #101	Los Angeles CA 90064, USA
Thomas Agency, Robert	42350 Niagra Dr	Sterling Heights MI 48313, USA
Tisherman Agency	6767 Forest Lawn Dr, #101	Los Angeles CA 90068, USA
Twentieth Century Artists	19528 Ventura Blvd	Tarzana CA 91356, USA
United Agents	12-26 Lexington St	London W1F 0L#, England
United Talent Agency	9336 Civic Center Dr	Beverly Hills CA 90210, USA
Untitled Entertainment	1801 Century Park E, #700	Los Angeles CA 90067, USA
Variety Artists International	793 Higuera St, #600	San Luis Obispo CA 93401, USA
Webb Enterprises, Ruth	7095 Hollywood Blvd	Los Angeles CA 90028, USA
Wilder Agency	3151 Cahuenga Blvd W, #310	Los Angeles CA 90068, USA
Wilhelmina Artists	8383 Wilshire Blvd, #650	Beverly Hills CA 90211, USA
W K T Public Relations	335 N Maple Dr, #351	Beverly Hills CA 90210, USA
W M E Entertainment	9601 Wilshire Blvd	Beverly Hills CA 90210, USA
Wolfman Jack Entertainment	105 Rivershore Dr	Hertford NC 27944, USA
Z B F Agentur	Friedrichstr 39	10969 Berlin, Germany
Vox Inc	5670 Wilshire Blvd, #820	Los Angeles CA 90036, USA

SYNDICATE ADDRESSES

Associated Press	450 W 33rd St, #1500	New York NY 10001, USA
Creators Syndicate	5777 W Century Blvd, #700	Los Angeles CA 90045, USA
King Features Syndicate	300 W 57th St, #1500	New York NY 10019, USA
North American Syndicate	235 E 45th St	New York NY 10017, USA
Times-Mirror Syndicate	Times-Mirror Square	Los Angeles CA 90053, USA
Tribune Media Services	435 N Michigan Ave, #1500	Chicago IL 60611, USA
United Feature Syndicate	200 Madison Ave	New York NY 10016, USA
United Media Syndicate	200 Park Ave, #400	New York NY 10016, USA
United Press International	2 Pennsylvania Plaza, #1800	New York NY 10121, USA
Universal Press Syndicate	4520 Main St, #700	Kansas City MO 64111, USA

MAJOR TELEVISION STATION ADDRESSES

American Broadcasting Company

ABC-LA	500 S Buena Vista St	Burbank CA 91521, USA
ABC-NY	77 W 66th St	New York NY 10023, USA
KABC-TV	4151 Prospect Ave	Los Angeles CA 90027, USA
KGO-TV	900 Front St	San Francisco CA 94111, USA
KTRK-TV	3310 Bissonnet Dr	Houston TX 77005, USA
WABC-TV	7 Lincoln Square	New York NY 10023, USA
WCVB-TV (Boston)	5 TV Place	Needham MA 02194, USA
WFAA-TV	606 Young St	Dallas TX 75202, USA
WJLA-TV	3007 Tilden St NW	Washington DC 20008, USA
WLS-TV	190 N State St	Chicago IL 60601, USA
WPIV-TV	4100 City Line Ave	Philadelphia PA 19131, USA
WPLG-TV	3900 Biscayne Blvd	Miami FL 33137, USA
WSB-TV	1801 W Peachtree St NE	Atlanta GA 30309, USA
WVUE-TV	1025 S Jefferson Davis Parkway	New Orleans LA 70125, USA
WXYZ-TV (Detroit)	20777 W Ten-Mile Road	Southfield MI 48037, USA

Columbia Broadcasting System

CBS-LA	7800 Beverly Blvd	Los Angeles CA 90036, USA
CBS-NY	51 W 52nd St	New York NY 10019, USA
KCBS-TV	6121 Sunset Blvd	Los Angeles CA 90028, USA
KHOU-TV	1945 Allen Parkway	Houston TX 77019, USA
KPIX-TV	855 Battery St	San Francisco CA 94111, USA
KYW-TV	101 S Independence Mall E	Philadelphia PA 19106, USA
WBBM-TV	630 N McClurg Court	Chicago IL 60611, USA
WBZ-TV	1170 Soldiers Field Road	Boston MA 02134, USA
WCBS-TV	524 W 57th St	New York NY 10019, USA
WCIX-TV	8900 NW 18th Terrace	Miami FL 33172, USA
WUSA-TV	4100 Wisconsin Ave NW	Washington DC 20016, USA
WWL-TV	1024 N Rampart St	New Orleans LA 70116, USA

Fox Television

Fox-TV	10201 W Pico Blvd	Los Angeles CA 90035, USA
KDFW-TV	400 N Griffin St	Dallas TX 75202, USA
KRIV-TV	3935 Westheimer Road	Houston TX 77027, USA
KTTV-TV	5746 W Sunset Blvd	Los Angeles CA 90028, USA
KTVU-TV (San Francisco)	PO Box 22222	Oakland CA 94623, USA
WAGA-TV	1551 Briarcliff Road NE	Atlanta GA 30306, USA
WFLD-TV	205 N Michigan Ave	Chicago IL 60601, USA
WFXT-TV (Boston)	1000 Providence Highway	Dedham MA 02026, USA
WJBK-TV (Detroit)	16550 W Nine-Mile Road	Southfield MI 48075, USA
WNOL-TV	1661 Canal St	New Orleans LA 70112, USA
WNYW-TV	205 E 67th St	New York NY 10021, USA
WSVN-TV	1401 79th St Causeway	Miami FL 33141, USA
WTTG-TV	5151 Wisconsin Ave NW, #100	Washington DC 20016, USA
WTXF-TV	330 Market St	Philadelphia PA 19106, USA

MAJOR TELEVISION STATION ADDRESSES
National Broadcasting Company

KNBC-TV (Los Angeles)	3000 W Alameda Ave	Burbank CA 91523, USA
KPRC-TV	8181 Southwest Freeway	Houston TX 77074, USA
KRON-TV	1001 Van Ness Ave	San Francisco CA 94109, USA
KXAS-TV	3900 Barnett St	Fort Worth TX 76103, USA
WDIV-TV	550 W Lafayette Blvd	Detroit MI 48231, USA
WDSU-TV	520 Royal St	New Orleans LA 70130, USA
WMAG-TV	454 N Columbus Dr	Chicago IL 60611, USA
WMGM-TV (Philadelphia)	1601 New Road	Linwood NJ 08221, USA
WNBC-TV	30 Rockefeller Plaza, #207E	New York NY 10112, USA
WRC-TV	4001 Nebraska Ave NW	Washington DC 20016, USA
WTVJ-TV	316 N Miami Ave	Miami FL 33128, USA
WXIA-TV	1611 W Peachtree St NE	Atlanta GA 30309, USA

CABLE TELEVISION CHANNEL ADDRESSES

American Christian Television	6350 West Freeway	Fort Worth TX 76150, USA
American Movie Classics	150 Crossways Park W	Woodbury NY 11797, USA
Arts & Entertainment	235 E 45th St, #9	New York NY 10017, USA
Black Entertainment Network	One BET Plaza, 1900 W Place NE	Washington DC 20018, USA
British Broadcasting Company	Wood Lane	London W12 8Q, England
Cable News Network (CNN)	820 1st St NE, #1000	Washington DC 20002, USA
Canadian Broadcasting Company	1500 Bronson Ave	Ottawa ON K1G 3J5, Canada
Canadian Television Network	42 Charles St E	Toronto ON M4Y 1T5, Canada
Capital Cities/ABC	77 W 66th St	New York NY 10023, USA
Cartoon Network	1050 Techwood Dr NW	Atlanta GA 30318, USA
Christian Broadcasting Network	1000 Centerville Turnpike	Virginia Beach VA 23463, USA
Cinemax	1100 6th Ave	New York NY 10036, USA
Columbia Broadcasting System	51 W 52nd St	New York NY 10019, USA
Comedy Central	345 Hudson St, #300	New York NY 10014, USA
Consumer News & Business	2200 Fletcher Ave	Fort Lee NJ 07024, USA
Country Music Television	2806 Opryland Dr	Nashville TN 37214, USA
Court TV	600 Third Ave	New York NY 10016, USA
C-SPAN	400 N Capitol St NW, #650	Washington DC 20001, USA
CW Television Network	4000 Warner Blvd	Burbank CA 91522, USA
Discovery Channel	7700 Wisconsin Ave	Bethesda MD 20814, USA
Disney Channel	3800 W Alameda Ave	Burbank CA 91505, USA
E! (Entertainment Television)	5750 Wilshire Blvd	Los Angeles CA 90036, USA
ESPN (Entertainment & Sports)	ESPN Plaza, 935 Middle St	Bristol CT 06010, USA
Family Channel	PO Box 64549	Virginia Beach VA 23467, USA
Food Network	1180 Ave of Americas, #1200	New York NY 10036, USA
FX (Fox Net)	PO Box 900	Beverly Hills CA 90213, USA
Game Show Network	10202 W Washington Blvd	Culver City CA 90232, USA
Granada Television	36 Golden Square	London W1R 2AX, England
HGTV (Home & Garden TV)	PO Box 50970	Knoxville TN 37950, USA
History Channel	235 E 45th St, #9	New York NY 10017, USA
Home Box Office (HBO)	1100 Ave of Americas	New York NY 10036, USA
Home Shopping Network	PO Box 9090	Clearwater FL 34618, USA
Independent Film Channel	150 Crossways Park W	Woodbury NY 11797, USA
Learning Channel	7700 Wisconsin Ave	Bethesda MD 20814, USA
Lifetime	111 8th St	New York NY 10011, USA
Madison Square Garden Network	2 Pennsylvania Plaza	New York NY 10001, USA
Movie Channel (TMC)	1633 Broadway	New York NY 10019, USA
MTV (Music Television)	1515 Broadway	New York NY 10036, USA
National Broadcasting Company	30 Rockefeller Plaza	New York NY 10112, USA
Nickelodeon	1515 Broadway	New York NY 10036, USA
Oxygen	75 9th Avenue	New York NY 10011, USA
PBS (Public Broadcasting System)	1320 Braddock Place	Alexandria VA 22314, USA
Playboy Channel	9242 Beverly Blvd	Beverly Hills CA 90210, USA
Prime Ticket Network	10000 Santa Monica Blvd	Los Angeles CA 90067, USA
QVC Inc	1365 Enterprise Dr	West Chester PA 19380, USA
Sci-Fi Channel	1230 Ave of Americas	New York NY 10020, USA
Showtime Network	1633 Broadway	New York NY 10019, USA
TBN (Trinity Broadcast Network)	PO Box A	Tustin CA 92711, USA
TBS (Turner Broadcasting System)	1 CNN Center, PO Box 105366	Atlanta GA 30348, USA
Telemundo Group	1740 Broadway	New York NY 10019, USA
TNN (The Nashville Network)	2806 Opryland Dr	Nashville TN 37214, USA
TNT (Turner Network Television)	1050 Techwood Dr NW	Atlanta GA 30318, USA
TVA	1600 de Maisonneuve Blvd E	Montreal QC H2L 4P2, Canada

Univision Network	605 3rd Ave, #1200	New York NY 10158, USA
USA Cable Network	1230 Ave of Americas	New York NY 10020, USA
VH-1 (Video Hits One)	1515 Broadway	New York NY 10036, USA
Viewer's Choice	909 3rd Ave	New York NY 10022, USA
Warner Bros	4000 Warner Blvd	Burbank CA 91522, USA
Weather Channel	2600 Cumberland Parkway NW	Atlanta GA 30339, USA

RECORD COMPANY ADDRESSES

A&M Records	70 University City Plaza	Universal City CA 91608, USA
Angel Records	1750 N Vine St	Los Angeles CA 90028, USA
Angel Records	150 5th Ave	New York NY 10011, USA
Arista Records	8750 Wilshire Blvd, #300	Beverly Hills CA 90211, USA
Arista Records	745 5th Ave, #600	New York NY 10151, USA
Asylum Records	9229 Sunset Blvd, #718	West Hollywood CA 90069, USA
Asylum Records	75 Rockefeller Plaza	New York NY 10019, USA
Atlantic Records	9229 Sunset Blvd, #900	West Hollywood CA 90069, USA
Atlantic Records	1290 Ave of Americas, Concourse 3	New York NY 10104, USA
Blue Note Records	6920 Sunset Blvd	Los Angeles CA 90028, USA
Capitol Records	1750 N Vine St	Los Angeles CA 90028, USA
Capitol Records	810 7th Ave	New York NY 10019, USA
Chrysalis Records	8730 Sunset Blvd	West Hollywood CA 90069, USA
Chrysalis Records	810 7th Ave, #4	New York NY 10019, USA
Deutsche Grammaphon Records	810 7th Ave	New York NY 10019, USA
Dreamwork Records	1000 Flower St	Glendale CA 91201, USA
Elektra Records	75 Rockefeller Plaza	New York NY 10019, USA
E M I America Records	6920 Sunset Blvd	Los Angeles CA 90028, USA
E M I America Records	150 5th Ave, #700	New York NY 10011, USA
Epic Records	1211 S Highland Ave	Los Angeles CA 90019, USA
Epic Records	350 Madison Ave, #600	New York NY 10022, USA
Geffen Records	10900 Wilshire Blvd, #1000	Los Angeles CA 90024, USA
Geffen Records	1755 Broadway, #600	New York NY 10019, USA
Island Def Jam Records	8920 Sunset Blvd, #200	West Hollywood CA 90069, USA
Island Def Jam Records	925 8th St	New York NY 10019, USA
LaFace Records	3350 Peach Tree Road	Atlanta GA 30319, USA
London Records	810 7th Ave	New York NY 10019, USA
M C A Records	70 Universal City Plaza	Universal City CA 91608, USA
M C A Records	1755 Broadway	New York NY 10019, USA
Mercury Records	54 Music Square E, #300	Nashville TN 37203, USA
Motown Records	6255 Sunset Blvd	Los Angeles CA 90028, USA
Nonesuch Records	75 Rockefeller Plaza	New York NY 10019, USA
Phillips Records	810 7th Ave	New York NY 10019, USA
Polydor Records	70 Universal City Plaza	Universal City CA 91608, USA
Polydor Records	810 7th Ave	New York NY 10019, USA
Polygram Records	3800 W Alameda Ave, #1500	Burbank CA 91505, USA
Polygram Records	Worldwide Plaza, 825 8th Ave	New York NY 10019, USA
R C A Records	6363 Sunset Blvd, #429	Los Angeles CA 90028, USA
R C A Records	1540 Broadway, #3500	New York NY 10036, USA
Reprise Records	3300 Warner Blvd	Burbank CA 91505, USA
Reprise Records	75 Rockefeller Plaza	New York NY 10019, USA
Rhino Records	10635 Santa Monica Blvd	Los Angeles CA 90025, USA
Sire Records	3300 Warner Blvd	Burbank CA 91505, USA
Sire Records	75 Rockefeller Plaza	New York NY 10019, USA
Sony/Columbia/CBS Records	2100 Colorado Ave	Santa Monica CA 90404, USA
Sony/Columbia/CBS Records	550 Madison Ave, #600	New York NY 10022, USA
Verve Records	1755 Broadway, #600	New York NY 10019, USA
Virgin Records	338 N Foothill Road	Beverly Hills CA 90210, USA
Virgin Records	150 5th Ave, #700	New York NY 10011, USA
Warner Bros Records	3300 Warner Blvd	Burbank CA 91505, USA
Warner Bros Records	75 Rockefeller Plaza	New York NY 10019, USA
Windham Hill Records	PO Box 5501	Beverly Hills CA 90209, USA

PUBLISHER ADDRESSES

Atheneum Publishers	866 3rd Ave	New York NY10022, USA
Avon Books	1350 Ave of Americas	New York NY 10019, USA
Berkley Publishing	375 Hudson St, Basement 1	New York NY 10014, USA
Chronicle Books	680 2nd St	San Francisco CA 94107, USA
Crown Publishers	201 E. 50th St	New York NY 10022, USA
Delacorte/Bantam/Dell/Doubleday	1745 Broadway	New York NY 10019, USA

PUBLISHER ADDRESSES

Dodd Mead	6 Ram Ridge Road	Spring Valley NY 10977, USA
Dutton, EP/Penguin	375 Hudson St, Basement 1	New York NY 10014, USA
Farrar Straus Giroux	18 W 18th St, #700	New York NY 10011, USA
Grove Press	841 Broadway	New York NY 10003, USA
Harcourt Brace	525 B St	San Diego CA 92101, USA
Harper Collins	10 E 53rd St, Cellar 1	New York NY 10022, USA
Henry Holt	175 5th Ave, #400	New York NY 10010, USA
Houghton Mifflin	215 Park Ave S, #1200	New York NY 10003, USA
Hyperion Books	114 5th Ave	New York NY 10011, USA
Knopf/Ballatine/Fawcett	201 E 50th St	New York NY 10022, USA
Little Brown	1271 Ave of Americas	New York NY 10020, USA
Little Brown	3 Center Plaza, #100	Boston MA 02108, USA
McGraw Hill	1221 Ave of Americas, #C3A	New York NY 10020, USA
MacMillan	1177 Ave of Americas, #1965	New York NY 10036, USA
Morrow, William	1350 Ave of Americas, #200	New York NY 10019, USA
Mysterious Press/Warner Books	1271 6th Ave	New York NY 10020, USA
New American Library	1633 Broadway	New York NY 10019, USA
Norton, WW	500 5th Ave, #600	New York NY 10110, USA
Oxford University Press	198 Madison Ave, #800	New York NY 10016, USA
Pocket Books	1230 Ave of Americas	New York NY 10020, USA
Prentice-Hall	RR 9W	Englewood Cliffs NJ 07632, USA
Putnam's Sons, GP	375 Hudson St, Basement	New York NY 10014, USA
Random House	1745 Broadway, #B1	New York NY 10019, USA
Scholastic Press	555 Broadway	New York NY 10012, USA
Scribner's Sons, Charles	866 3rd Ave	New York NY 10022, USA
Simon & Schuster	1230 Ave of Americas, Concourse 1	New York NY 10020, USA
Saint Martin's Press	175 5th Ave, #400	New York NY 10010, USA
Viking Press	375 Hudson St, Basement 1	New York NY 10014, USA

PROFESSIONAL SPORTS TEAMS ADDRESSES

Baseball

Arizona Diamondbacks	Chase Field, 401 E Jefferson	Phoenix AZ 85003, USA
Atlanta Braves	Turner Field, 755 Hank Aaron Drive	Atlanta GA 30315, USA
Baltimore Orioles	Oriole Park, 333 W Camden St	Baltimore MD 21201, USA
Boston Red Sox	Fenway Park, 4 Yawkey Way	Boston MA 02215, USA
Chicago Cubs	Wrigley Field, 1060 W Addison St	Chicago IL 60613, USA
Chicago White Sox	US Cellular Field, 333 W 35th St	Chicago IL 60616, USA
Cincinnati Reds	Great American Ball Park, 100 Main St	Cincinnati OH 45202, USA
Cleveland Indians	Jacobs Field, 2401 Ontario St	Cleveland OH 44115, USA
Colorado Rockies	Coors Field, 2001 Blake St	Denver CO 80205, USA
Detroit Tigers	Comerica Park, 2100 Woodward Ave	Detroit MI 48201, USA
Houston Astros	Minute Maid Field, 501 Crawford St	Houston TX 77002, USA
Kansas City Royals	Kauffman Stadium, 1 Royal Way	Kansas City MO 64129, USA
Los Angeles Angels of Anaheim	Angel Stadium, 2000 Gene Autry Way	Anaheim CA 92806, USA
Los Angeles Dodgers	Dodger Stadium, 1000 Elysian Park Ave	Los Angeles CA 90090, USA
Miami Marlins	501 Marlins Way	Miami FL 33125, USA
Milwaukee Brewers	Miller Park, 1 Brewers Way	Milwaukee WI 53214, USA
Minnesota Twins	Metrodome, 34 Kirby Punkett Place	Minneapolis MN 55415, USA
New York Mets	Shea Stadium, 12301 Roosevelt Ave	Flushing NY 11368, USA
New York Yankees	Yankee Stadium, E 161st & River Ave	Bronx NY 10451, USA
Oakland Athletics	McAfee Coliseum, 7000 Coliseum Way, #3	Oakland CA 94621, USA
Philadelphia Phillies	Citizens Bank Park, 1 Citizens Bank Way	Philadelphia PA 19148, USA
Pittsburgh Pirates	PNC Park, 115 Federal St, #115B	Pittsburgh PA 15212, USA
San Diego Padres	Petco Park, 100 Park Blvd	San Diego CA 92101, USA
San Francisco Giants	AT&T Park, 24 Willie Mays Plaza	San Francisco CA 94107, USA
Seattle Mariners	Safeco Field, PO Box 4100	Seattle WA 98194, USA
Saint Louis Cardinals	Busch Stadium, 250 Stadium Plaza	Saint Louis MO 63102, USA
Tampa Bay Rays	Tropicana Field, 1 Tropicana Dr	Saint Petersburg FL 33705, USA
Texas Rangers	Ameriquest Field, 1000 Ballpark Way, #306	Arlington TX 76011, USA
Toronto Blue Jays	Skydome, 1 Blue Jay Way, #3200	Toronto ON M5V 1J1, Canada
Washington Nationals	1500 S Capital St SE	Washington DC 20003, USA

Men's Basketball

Atlanta Hawks	101 Marietta St NW, #1900	Atlanta GA 30303, USA
Boston Celtics	226 Causeway St, #400	Boston MA 02114, USA
Brooklyn Nets	15 MetroTech Center, #1100	Brooklyn NY 11201, USA
Charlotte Bobcats	333 E Trade St. #A	Charlotte NC 28202, USA
Chicago Bulls	United Center, 1901 W Madison St	Chicago IL 60612, USA

PROFESSIONAL SPORTS TEAMS ADDRESSES

Cleveland Cavaliers	Gund Arena, 1 Center Court	Cleveland OH 44115, USA
Dallas Mavericks	2500 Victory Ave	Dallas TX 75219, USA
Denver Nuggets	Pepsi Center, 1000 Chopper Circle	Denver CO 80204, USA
Detroit Pistons	Palace, 4 Championship Dr	Auburn Hills MI 48326, USA
Golden State Warriors	1011 Broadway	Oakland CA 94605, USA
Houston Rockets	1510 Polk St	Houston TX 77002, USA
Indiana Pacers	125 S Pennsylvania St	Indianapolis IN 46204, USA
Los Angeles Clippers	Staples Center, 1111 S Figueroa St	Los Angeles CA 90015, USA
Los Angeles Lakers	Staples Center, 1111 S Figueroa St	Los Angeles CA 90015, USA
Memphis Grizzlies	191 Beale St	Memphis TN 38103, USA
Miami Heat	601 Biscayne Blvd	Miami FL 33132, USA
Milwaukee Bucks	1001 N 4th St, #200	Milwaukee WI 53203, USA
Minnesota Timberwolves	Target Center, 600 1st Ave N	Minneapolis MN 55403, USA
New Orleans Hornets	1250 Poydras St, #101	New Orleans LA 70113, USA
New York Knicks	Madison Square Garden, 4 Penn Plaza	New York NY 10121, USA
Oklahoma City Thunder	211 N Robinson Ave, #300	Oklahoma City OK 73102, USA
Orlando Magic	8701 Maitland Summit Blvd	Orlando FL 32810, USA
Philadelphia 76ers	3601 S Broad St, #400	Philadelphia PA 19148, USA
Phoenix Suns	201 E Jefferson St	Phoenix AZ 85004, USA
Portland Trail Blazers	1 N Center Court St, #200, Rose Garden	Portland OR 97227, USA
Sacramento Kings	Arco, Arena, 1 Sports Parkway	Sacramento CA 95834, USA
San Antonio Spurs	Key Arena, 1 AT&T Center	San Antonio TX 78219, USA
Seattle Supersonics	1201 3rd Ave, #1000	Seattle WA 98101, USA
Toronto Raptors	20 Bay St, #1702	Toronto ON M5J 2N8, Canada
Utah Jazz	301 W South Temple	Salt Lake City UT 84101, USA
Washington Wizards	601 F St NW	Washington DC 20004, USA

Women's Basketball (WNBA)

Atlanta Dream	83 Walton St NW, #400	Atlanta GA 30303, USA
Chicago Sky	20 W Kinzie St, #1010	Chicago IL 60654, USA
Connecticut Sun	1 Mohegan Sun Blvd	Uncasville CT 06382, USA
Indiana Fever	125 S Pennsylvania St	Indianapolis IN 46204, USA
Los Angeles Sparks	888 S Figueroa St, #2010	Los Angeles CA 90017, USA
Minnesota Lynx	600 1st Ave N	Minneapolis MN 55403, USA
New York Liberty	2 Penn Plaza, #1400	New York NY 10121, USA
Phoenix Mercury	201 E Jefferson St	Phoenix AZ 85004, USA
Sacramento Monarchs	Arco Arena, 1 Sports Parkway	Sacramento CA 95834, USA
San Antonio Silver Stars	1 AT&T Center	San Antonio TX 78219, USA
Seattle Storm	351 Elliott Ave W, #500	Seattle WA 98119, USA
Tulsa Shock	BOK Center, 200 S Denver	Tulsa OK 74103, USA
Washington Mystics	Verizon Center, 401 9th St NW, #750	Washington DC 20004, USA

Football

Arizona Cardinals	PO Box 888	Phoenix AZ 85001, USA
Atlanta Falcons	4400 Falcon Parkway	Flowery Branch GA 30542, USA
Baltimore Ravens	Ravens Stadium, 1 Winning Dr	Owings Mills MD 21117, USA
Buffalo Bills	1 Bills Dr	Orchard Park NY 14127, USA
Carolina Panthers	Ericsson Stadium, 800 S Mint St	Charlotte NC 28202, USA
Chicago Bears	1000 Football Dr	Lake Forest IL 60045, USA
Cincinnati Bengals	1 Paul Brown Stadium	Cincinnati OH 45202, USA
Cleveland Browns	76 Lou Groza Blvd	Berea OH 44017, USA
Dallas Cowboys	1 Cowboys Parkway	Irving TX 75063, USA
Denver Broncos	13655 Broncos Parkway	Englewood, CO 80112, USA
Detroit Lions	222 Republic Drive	Allen Park MI 48101, USA
Green Bay Packers	1265 Lombardi Ave	Green Bay WI 54304, USA
Houston Texans	2 Reliant Park	Houston TX 77054, USA
Indianapolis Colts	7001 W 56th St	Indianapolis IN 46254, USA
Jacksonville Jaguars	1 AllTel Stadium Place	Jacksonville FL 32202, USA
Kansas City Chiefs	1 Arrowhead Dr	Kansas City KS 64129, USA
Miami Dolphins	7500 SW 30th St	Davie FL 33314, USA
Minnesota Vikings	9520 Viking Dr	Eden Prairie MN 55344, USA
New England Patriots	1 Patriot Place	Foxboro, MA 02035, USA
New Orleans Saints	5800 Airline Highway	Metairie LA 70003, USA
New York Giants	Meadowlands Stadium, 102 Route 120	East Rutherford NJ 07073, USA
New York Jets	1 Jets Dr	Florham Park NJ 07932, USA
Oakland Raiders	1220 Harbor Bay Parkway	Alameda CA 94502, USA
Philadelphia Eagles	1 NovaCare Way	Philadelphia PA 19145, USA
Pittsburgh Steelers	3400 S Water St	Pittsburgh PA 15203, USA

Saint Louis Rams	901 N Broadway	Saint Louis MO 63101, USA
San Diego Chargers	4020 Murphy Canyon Rd	San Diego CA 92123, USA
San Francisco 49ers	4949 Centennial Blvd	Santa Clara CA 95054, USA
Seattle Seahawks	12 Seahawks Way	Renton WA 98056, USA
Tampa Bay Buccaneers	1 W Buccaneer Place	Tampa FL 33607, USA
Tennessee Titans	460 Great Circle Road	Nashville TN 37228, USA
Washington Redskins	21300 Redskin Park Dr	Ashburn VA 20147, USA

Ice Hockey

Anaheim Ducks	2695 E Katella Ave	Anaheim CA 92806, USA
Boston Bruins	100 Legends Way, #250	Boston MA 02114, USA
Buffalo Sabres	1 Seymour Knox Plaza	Buffalo NY 14203, USA
Calgary Flames	PO Box 1540, Station M	Calgary AB T2P 3B9, Canada
Carolina Hurricanes	RBC Center, 1400 Edwards Mill Road	Raleigh NC 27607, USA
Chicago Blackhawks	United Center, 1901 W Madison St	Chicago IL 60612, USA
Colorado Avalanche	Pepsi Center, 1000 Chopper Circle	Denver CO 80204, USA
Columbus Blue Jackets	200 W Nationwide Blvd, Unit 1	Columbus OH 43215, USA
Dallas Stars	2601 Avenue of Stars	Frisco TX 75034, USA
Detroit Red Wings	Joe Louis Arena, 600 Civic Center Dr	Detroit MI 48226, USA
Edmonton Oilers	Edmonton Coliseum, 11230 110 St	Edmonton AB T5G 3G8, Canada
Florida Panthers	1 Panthers Parkway	Sunrise FL 33323, USA
Hartford Whalers	Coliseum, 242 Trumbull St, #800	Hartford CT 06103, USA
Los Angeles Kings	Staples Center, 1111 S Figueroa St	Los Angeles CA 90015, USA
Minnesota Wild	Xcel Energy Center, 1275 W Kellogg Blvd	Saint Paul MN 55104, USA
Montreal Canadiens	1275 Saint Antoine St W	Montreal QC H3C 5L2, Canada
Nashville Predators	501 Broadway	Nashville TN 37203, USA
New Jersey Devils	165 Mulberry St	Newark NJ 07102, USA
New York Islanders	1255 Hempstead Turnpike	Uniondale NY 11553, USA
New York Rangers	Madison Square Garden, 2 Penn Plaza	New York NY 10121, USA
Ottawa Senators	ScotiaBank Place, 1000 Palladium Dr	Kanata ON K2V 1A5, Canada
Philadelphia Flyers	1st Union Center, 3601 S Broad St	Philadelphia PA 19148, USA
Phoenix Coyotes	6751 N Sunset Blvd, #200	Glendale AZ 85305, USA
Pittsburgh Penguins	Consol Energy Center, 1001 5th Ave	Pittsburgh PA 15219, USA
Saint Louis Blues	ScottTrade Center, 1401 Clark Ave	Saint Louis MO 63103, USA
San Jose Sharks	525 W Santa Clara St	San Jose CA 95113, USA
Tampa Bay Lightning	401 Channelside Dr	Tampa FL 33602, USA
Toronto Maple Leafs	AirCanada Center, 40 Bay St, #400	Toronto ON M5J 2X2, Canada
Vancouver Canucks	800 Griffiths Way	Vancouver BC V6B 6G1, Canada
Washington Capitals	627 N Glebe Road	Arlington VA 22203, USA
Winnipeg Jets	260 Hargrave St	Winnipeg MB R3C 5S5, Canada

Men's Soccer

A S Rome Spa	Piazzale Dino Viola	00128 Rome, Italy
Chicago Fire	7000 S Harlem Ave	Bridgeview IL 60455, USA
Club Deportivo Chivas	Home Depot Center, 18400 Avalon Blvd	Carson CA 90746, USA
Colorado Rapids	1000 Chopper Circle	Denver CO 80204, USA
Columbus Crew	1 Black & Gold Blvd	Columbus OH 43211, USA
D C United	RFK Stadium, 2400 E Capitol St SE	Washington DC 20003 USA
F C Dallas	9200 World Cup Way, #202	Frisco TX 75034, USA
Houston Dynamo	1415 Louisiana, #3400	Houston TX 77002, USA
Kansas City Wizards	8900 State Line Road	Leawood MO 66206, USA
Los Angeles Galaxy	Home Depot Center, 18400 Avalon Blvd	Carson CA 90746, USA
New England Revolution	1 Patriot Place	Foxboro MA 02035, USA
Portland Timbers	1844 SW Morrison	Portland OR 97205, USA
Real Salt Lake	9256 S State St	Sandy UT 84070, USA
Red Bull New York	600 Cape May St	Harrison NJ 07029, USA
San Jose Earthquakes	451 El Camino Real, #220	Santa Clara CA 95050, USA
Seattle Sounders	12 Seahawks Way	Renton WA 98056, USA
Toronto F C	Maple Leaf Sports, 40 Bay St, #400	Toronto ON M5J 2X2, Canada
Vancouver Whitecaps	375 Water St, #550	Vancouver BC V6B 5C6, Canada
Montreal Impact	4750 Sherbrooke Est	Montreal QB H1V 3S8, Canada

Women's Soccer

Atlanta Beat	1955 Vaughn Road, #209	Kennesaw GA 30144, USA
Boston Breakers	400 Blue Hill Dr, #302	Westwood MA 02090, USA
Philadelphia Independence	Union Field, Seaport Dr	Chester, PA 19013, USA
Sky Blue F C	80 Cottontail Lane, #400	Somerset NJ 08873, USA
Western New York Flash	Sahlen Sports Park, 7070 Seneca St	Elma NY 14059 USA

Organization	Address	City/State/Country
Amateur Athletic Union	PO Box 10000	Lake Buena Vista FL 32830, USA
Amateur Softball Association	2801 NE 50th St	Oklahoma City OK 73111, USA
American Bicycle Association	1645 W Sunrise Blvd	Gilbert AZ 85233, USA
American Bowling Congress	5301 S 76th St	Greendale WI 53129, USA
American Horse Show Association	220 E 42nd St	New York NY 10017, USA
American Kennel Club	260 Madison Ave	New York NY 10016, USA
American League Baseball	350 Park Ave, #1800	New York NY 10022, USA
American Motorcycle Association	13515 Yarmouth Dr	Pickerington OH 43147, USA
American Power Boat Association	17640 E Nine Mile Road	East Detroit MI 48021, USA
American Professional Soccer League	122 C St, NW	Washington DC 20001, USA
American Water Ski Association	799 Overlook Dr	Winter Haven FL 33884, USA
Association of Int'l Amateur Boxing	Postamt Volkrdstr, Postlagernd	10319 Berlin, Germany
Association/Int'l Marathon/Road Races	20 Trongate	Glasgow G1 5ES, England
Association of Ski Racing Professionals	148 Porters Point Road	Colchester VT 05446, USA
Association of Surfing Professionals	16691 Gothard St	Huntington Beach CA 92648, USA
Association of Tennis Professionals	200 Tournament Road	Ponte Vedra Beach FL 32082, USA
Association of Volleyball Professionals	6100 Center Dr, #900	Los Angeles CA 90045, USA
Canadian Football League	110 Eglinton Ave	Toronto, ON M4R 1A3, Canada
Canadian National Sports/Recreation Ctr	1600 James Naismith Dr	Gloucestor ON KJB 5N4, Canada
Federation de International Hockey	Avenue des Arts 1 (bte 5)	1040 Brussels, Belgium
Federation de International Ski	Worbstr 210, 3073 Gumligen B	Berne, Switzerland
Federation International de Canoe	G Massaia 59	50134 Florence, Italy
Federation Int'l de Football Association	PO Box 85, Hitzigweg 11	8030 Zurich, Switzerland
Federation International de Gymnastics	Juraweg 12	8250 Lyss, Switzerland
Federation Int'l I de Tir a l'Arc (Archery)	Via Cerva 30	20122 Milan, Italy
Federation of International Volleyball	Ave de la Gare 12	1001 Lausanne, Switzerland
Federation of Int'l Amateur Cycling	Via Cassia N 490	00198 Rome, Italy
Federation of International Basketball	PO Box 700607, Kistlerhofstr 168	81379 Munich, Germany
Federation of Int'l Bobsleigh/Toboggan	Via Piranesi 44/b	20137 Milan, Italy
Federation of Int'l du Sport Automobiles	8 Place de la Concorde	75008 Paris, France
Federation of International Equestrian	PO Box 3000, Bolligenstr 54	32 Berne, Switzerland
FIFA Women's Football Association	37 Sussex Road, Ickenham	Middx UB10 8PN, England
Formula One Driver's Association	2 Rue Jean Jaures	1836 Luxembourg
Indy Racing League	4565 W 16th St	Indianapolis IN 46222, USA
International Badminton Federation	24 Winchcombe House	Cheltenham, Glos GL52 2NA, England
International Baseball Association	201 S Capitol Ave, #490	Indianapolis IN 46225, USA
International Boxing Federation	134 Evergreen Place	East Orange NJ 07018, USA
International Cricket Council	Lord's Cricket Ground	London NW8 8QN, England
International Curling Federation	2 Coates Crescent	Edinburgh EH3 7AN, England
International Game Fish Association	1301 E Atlantic Blvd	Pompano Beach FL 33060, USA
International Hot Rod Association	Highway 11E	Bristol TN 37620, USA
International Ice Hockey Federation	Bellevuestr 8	1190 Vienna, Austria
International Jai Alai Association	5 Calle Aldamar	San Sebastian 3, Spain
International Judo Federation	Avenida del Trabajo 2666	CP 1406, Buenos Aires, Argentina
International Luge Federation	Olympiadestr 168	8786 Rottenmann, Austria
International Motor Sports Assoc	1394 Broadway Ave	Braselton GA 30517, USA
International Olympic Committee	Chateau de Vidy	1007 Lausanne, Switzerland
International Roller Skating Federation	1500 S 70th St	Lincoln NE 68506, USA
International Rugby Football Board	PO Box 902	Auckland, New Zealand
International Skating Union	Promenade 73	7270 Davos-Platz, Switzerland
Int'l Sled Dog Racing Association	PO Box 446	Nordman ID 83848, USA
International Softball Federation	2801 NE 59th St	Oklahoma City OK 73111, USA
International Sport Automobile Fed	8 Rue de la Concorde	70008-E Paris, France
International Surfing Association	5580 La Jolla Blvd. #145	La Jolla CA 92037, USA
International Table Tennis Federation	53 London Rd, St Leonards-on-Sea	East Sussex TN37 6AY, England
International Tennis Federation	Palliser Road, Barons Court	London W14 9EN, England
International Volleyball Federation	Ave de la Gare 12	1003 Lausanne, Switzerland
International Weightlifting Federation	Rosemberg Hp U1	1374 Budapest PF 614, Hungary
International Yacht Racing Union	60 Knightsbridge, Westminster	London SWEX 7JX, England
Ladies Professional Bowlers Tour	7171 Cherryvales Blvd	Rockford IL 61112, USA
Ladies Professional Golf Association	100 International Golf Dr	Daytona Beach FL 32124, USA
Little League Baseball	PO Box 3485	Williamsport PA 17701, USA
Major Indoor Lacrosse League	2310 W 75th St	Shawnee Mission KS 66208, USA
Major League Baseball	350 Park Ave	New York NY 10022, USA
National Archery Association	1 Olympic Plaza	Colorado Springs CO 80909, USA
National Association of Stock Car Racing	1801 Speedway Blvd	Daytona Beach FL 32015, USA
National Assn/Intercollegiate Athletics	1221 Baltimore Ave	Kansas City MO 64105, USA
National Basketball Association	645 5th Ave, Fl 19	New York NY 10022, USA

OTHER SPORTS ORGANIZATION ADDRESSES

Organization	Address	City/State/Zip
National Collegiate Athletic Association	70 W Washington St	Indianapolis IN 46204, USA
National Football League	280 Park Ave, Fl 12W	New York NY 10017, USA
National Hockey League	1251 Ave of Americas	New York NY 10020, USA
National Hot Rod Association	2023 Financial Way	Glendora CA 91741, USA
National League Baseball	350 Park Ave, #1800	New York NY 10022, USA
National Professional Soccer League	229 3rd St NW	Canton OH 44702, USA
National Rifle Association	11250 Waples Mill Road	Fairfax VA 22030, USA
National Tractor Pullers Association	6155 Huntley Road, #B	Columbus OH 43229, USA
P G A Seniors Tour	112 PGA Tour Blvd	Ponte Vedra Beach FL 32082, USA
Professional Bowlers Association	1720 Merriman Road	Akron OH 44313, USA
Professional Golfers Association	100 Ave of Champions	Palm Beach Gardens FL 33410, USA
Professional Rodeo Cowboys	101 Pro Rodeo Dr	Colorado Springs CA 80919, USA
Professional Sports Car Racing	1394 Broadway Ave	Braselton GA 30517, USA
Special Olympics	1325 G St NW, #500	Washington DC 20005, USA
Thoroughbred Racing Association	420 Fair Hill Dr, #1	Elkton MD 21921, USA
Union International de Tir (Rifle)	Bavariaring 21	80336 Munich, Germany
United Systems of Independent Soccer	14497 N Dale Mabry Hwy, #2011	Tampa FL 33618, USA
US Auto Club	1720 Ruskin St	South Bend IN 46604, USA
US Bobsled Federation	421 Old Military Road	Lake Placid NY 12946, USA
US Cycling Federation	1 Olympic Plaza, Bldg 4	Colorado Springs CO 80909, USA
US Figure Skating Association	20 1st St	Colorado Springs CO 80906, USA
US Luge Association	35 Church St	Lake Placid NY 12946, USA
US Olympic Committee	1 Olympic Plaza, Bldg 6	Colorado Springs CO 80909, USA
US Polo Association	4059 Iron Works Pike	Lexington KY 40511, USA
US Skiing Association	1500 Kearns Blvd, #F100	Park City UT 84060, USA
US Soccer Federation	1801 S Prairie Ave, #11	Chicago IL 60616, USA
US Tennis Association	Flushing Meadow	Flushing NY 11368, USA
US Trotting Association	750 Michigan Ave	Columbus OH 43215, USA
US Youth Soccer Association	PO Box 18404	Memphis TN 38181, USA
USA Rugby	3595 E Fountain Blvd, #M2	Colorado Springs CO 80910, USA
USA Track & Field	4341 Starlight Dr	Indianapolis IN 46239, USA
Virginia Slims Women's Tennis	3135 Texas Commerce Tower	Houston TX 77002, USA
Women's Basketball Association	4011 N Bennington	Kansas City MO 64117, USA
Women's International Bowling Congress	5301 S 76th St	Greendale WI 53129, USA
Women's Int'l Surfing Association	PO Box 512	San Juan Capistrano CA 92675, USA
Women's Professional Volleyball Assn	840 Apollo St, #204	El Segundo CA 90245, USA
Women's Tennis Association	1 Progress Plaza, #1500	Saint Petersburg FL 33701, USA
World Boardsailing Association	Feldafinger Platz 2	81477 Munich, Germany
World Boxing Association	Rodrigo Sazagy, Apartado	4070 Panama City, Panama
World Boxing Council	Genova 33, Colonia Juarez	Cuahtemoc 0660, Mexico
World Taekwondo Federation	San 76 Yuksam-Dong	Kangnam-Ku, Seoul, Korea
World Team Tennis	445 N Wells St	Chicago IL 60610, USA
World Union of Karate Orgs	1-15-16 Toranomon, Minato-ku	Tokyo 105, Japan
World Wrestling Entertainment	1241 E Main St, Titan Towers	Stamford CT 06902, USA

HALLS OF FAME ADDRESSES

Hall of Fame	Address	City/State/Zip
Academy of Sports	4 Rue de Teheran	75008 Paris, France
Amateur Athletic Foundation of LA	2141 W Adams Blvd	Los Angeles CA 90018, USA
American Water Ski	799 Overlook Dr SE	Winter Park FL 33884, USA
Auto Racing	4790 W 16th St	Speedway IN 46224, USA
Classical Music	4 E 4th St	Cincinnati OH 45202, USA
College Football	1111 S Saint Joseph	South Bend IN 46601, USA
Hockey	30 Yonge St	Toronto ON M5E 1X8, Canada
International Boxing	PO Box 425	Canastota NY 13032, USA
International Gymnastics	227 Brooks St	Oceanside CA 92054, USA
International Motor Sports	PO Box 1018	Talladega AL 35160, USA
International Surfing	5580 La Jolla Blvd, #373	La Jolla CA 92037, USA
International Swimming	1 Hall of Fame Dr	Fort Lauderdale FL 33316, USA
International Tennis	194 Bellevue Ave	Newport RI 02840, USA
International Volleyball	PO Box 1895, 444 Dwight St	Hyoke MA 01040, USA
International Women's Sports	342 Madison Ave, #728	New York NY 10173, USA
Lacrosse Foundation	White Athletic Center, Homewood	Baltimore MD 21218, USA
Lawn Tennis Museum	All England Lawn Tennis Club	Wimbledon England
Ladies Professional Golf Assoc	2570 Volusia Ave	Daytona Beach FL 32114, USA
Naismith Basketball	1150 W Columbus Ave	Springfield MA 01105, USA
National Baseball	PO Box 590	Cooperstown NY 13326, USA
National Bowling Museum	111 Stadium Plaza	Saint Louis MO 63102, USA
National Cowboy	Heritage Center, 1700 NE 63rd St	Oklahoma City OK 73111, USA
National Cowgirl	111 W 4th St, #300	Fort Worth TX 76102, USA

BIBLIOGRAPHY

Academy Players Directory, Academy of Motion Picture Arts/Sciences, 8949 Wilshire Blvd, Beverly Hills CA 90211, USA
African Who's Who, African Journal Ltd, 54-A Tottenham Court Rd, London W1P 08T, England
Biographical Dictionary of Governors of the US, Meckler Publishing, Ferry Lane W, Westport CT 06880, USA
Biographical Dictionary of US Executive Branch, Greenwood Press, 51 Riverside Ave, Westport CT 06880, USA
Congressional Directory, Superintendent of Documents, US Government Printing Office, Washington DC 20402, USA
Contemporary Architects, St Martin's Press, 175 5th Ave, New York NY 10010, USA
Contemporary Designers, Gale Research Co, Book Tower, Detroit MI 48226, USA
Contemporary Theatre, Film & Television, Gale Research Co, Book Tower, Detroit MI 48226, USA
Corporate 1000, Washington Monitor, 1301 Pennsylvania Ave NW, Washington DC 20004, USA
Editor & Publisher International Yearbook, 575 Lexington Ave, New York NY 10022, USA
International Directory of Films & Filmmakers, St James Press, 175 5th Ave, New York NY 10010, USA
International Who's Who, Europa Publications Ltd, 18 Bedford Square, London WC1B 3JN, England
International Who's Who in Music, Biddles Ltd, Walnut Tree House, Guildford, Surrey GU1 1DA, England
Kraks BlaBog, Nytorv 17, 1450 Copenhagen K, Denmark
Major Companies of the Far East, Graham & Trotman Ltd, 66 Wilton Road, London SW1V 1DE, England
Major Companies of Europe, Graham & Trotman Ltd, 66 Wilton Road, London SW1V 1DE, England
Martindale-Hubbell Law Directory, Reed Publishing, Summit NJ 07902, USA
Moody's International Manual, Moody's Investors Service, 99 Church St, New York NY 10007, USA
Notable Australians, Paul Hamlyn Pty Ltd, 31 176 S Creek Road, Dee Why, WA 2099, Australia
Notable New Zealanders, Paul Hamlyn Pty Ltd, 31 Airedale St, Auckland, New Zealand
Prominent Personalities in USSR, Scarecrow Press, Metuchen NJ 08840, USA
US Court Directory, Government Printing Office, Washington DC 20401, USA
US Government Manual, National Archives & Records Service, General Services Administration, Washington DC 20408, USA
Who's Who, A & C Black Ltd, St Martin's Press, 175 5th Ave, New York NY 10010, USA
Who's Who in America, Marquis Who's Who, 200 E Ohio St, Chicago IL 60611, USA
Who's Who in American Art, R R Bowker Co, 1180 Ave of Americas, New York NY 1003, USA
Who's Who in American Politics, R R Bowker Co, 1180 Ave of Americas, New York NY 10036, USA
Who's Who in Canada, Global Press, 164 Commanden Blvd, Agincourt ON M1S 3C7, Canada
Who's Who in France, Editions Jacques Lafitte SA, 75008 Paris, France
Who's Who in Germany, Verlag AG Zurich, Germany
Who's Who in Israel, Bronfman Publishers Ltd, 82 Levinsky St, Tel Aviv 61010, Israel
Who's Who in Poland, Graphica Comense Srl, 22038 Taverreiro, Italy
Who's Who in Scandinavia, A Sutter Druckerei GmbH, 4300 Essen, Germany
Who's Who in Switzerland, Nagel Publishers, 5-5 bis de l'Orangeris, Geneva, Switzerland
Who's Who in the Theatre, Pitman Press, 39 Parker St, London WC2B 5PB, England
Who's Who in Washington, Tiber Reference Press, 4340 East-West Highway, Bethesda MD 20814, USA
Writer's Directory, St James Press, 213 W Institute Place, Chicago IL 60610, USA

Book design by Lee Ann Nelson.
Cover logo is Corvinus Skyline, Body type is Arial Narrow.
Production by Nelson Design, 9 Ridgeview Court, San Ramon, California 94583, USA

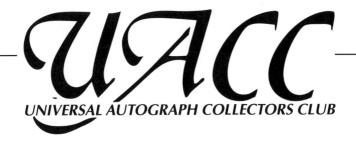

Here's what people are saying...

"Celebrity hounds may find much to peruse in this directory..."

—*Chronicle of Philanthropy*

"Best list of addresses available. Top percentage of replies at minimum cost per name."

—*Jack Hilton, Collector*

"Absolutely indispensable for enterprising professional journalists."

—*Larry Meyer, Author, Editor, Educator*

"Not only is it an invaluable source for business inquiries, political and charitable activities, it's fun to leaf through."

—*Mike Wagner, Private Investor*

"The book is the writer-researcher's best friend. This is a resource tool I can't afford to be without."

—*Hank Nuwer, Author, Reporter, Educator*

"The book ranks high for accuracy especially compared to other reference works. Ideally suited for organizations and media."

—*Pam Keyes, Miami News-Record*

"By far and away the most complete, comprehensive and definitive book for anybody who has ever wanted to contact anybody of notoriety."

—*Christopher Snowden, Collector*

"The best source I've ever seen in my 30 years of writing!!"

—*Henry Jake Bommer, Collector*

"A valuable reference for anyone desirous of reaching people who daily appear on the national or international scene. An excellent addition to any library."

—*Anne Thompson, Rocky Ford Daily Gazette*

"The Benjamin Franklin Award winner as Directory of the Year!"

—*Independent Book Publishers Association*

Have you visited our web page?

It's a great place to learn more about how the V.I.P. Address Book is compiled, read more about what people think of the book and even place your order conveniently online.

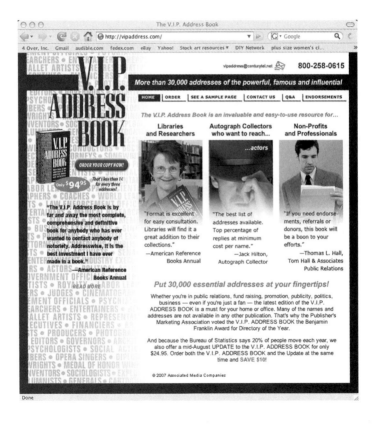

www.VIPaddress.com